Beth, this one is for you

About the Author

Wayne Weiten is a graduate of Bradley University and received his Ph.D. in social psychology from the University of Illinois, Chicago in 1981. He has taught at the College of DuPage and Santa Clara University and currently teaches at the University of Nevada, Las Vegas. He has received distinguished teaching awards from Division Two of the American Psychological Association (APA) and from the College of DuPage. He is a Fellow of Divisions 1 and 2 of the American Psychological Association and a Fellow of the Midwestern Psychological Association. In 1991 he helped chair the APA National Conference on Enhancing the Quality of Undergraduate Education in Psychology, and in 1996–1997 he served as president of the Society for the Teaching of Psychology. In 2006, one of the five national teaching awards given annually by the Society for the Teaching of Psychology was named in his honor. He currently is serving as president-elect of the Rocky Mountain Psychological Association. Weiten has conducted research on a wide range of topics, including educational measurement, jury decision making, attribution theory, pressure as a form of stress, cerebral specialization, and the technology of textbooks. He is also the author of *Psychology: Themes & Variations, Briefer Version* (2011, 8th ed.) and a co-author of *Psychology Applied to Modern Life: Adjustment in the Twenty-First Century* (with Dana S. Dunn and Elizabeth Yost Hammer, 2012, 10th ed.). Weiten has also created an educational CD-ROM titled *PsykTrek: A Multimedia Introduction to Psychology*.

To the Instructor

If I had to sum up in a single sentence what I hope will distinguish this text, that sentence would be this: I have set out to create a *paradox* instead of a *compromise.*

Let me elaborate. An introductory psychology text must satisfy two disparate audiences: professors and students. Because of the tension between the divergent needs and preferences of these audiences, textbook authors usually indicate that they have attempted to strike a compromise between being theoretical versus practical, comprehensive versus comprehensible, research oriented versus applied, rigorous versus accessible, and so forth. However, I believe that many of these dichotomies are false. As Kurt Lewin once remarked, "What could be more practical than a good theory?" Similarly, is rigorous really the opposite of accessible? Not in my dictionary. I maintain that many of the antagonistic goals that we strive for in our textbooks only *seem* incompatible and that we may not need to make compromises as often as we assume.

In my estimation, a good introductory textbook is a paradox in that it integrates characteristics and goals that appear contradictory. With this in mind, I have endeavored to write a text that is paradoxical in three ways. First, in surveying psychology's broad range of content, I have tried to show that its interests are characterized by both diversity *and* unity. Second, I have emphasized both research *and* application and how they work in harmony. Finally, I have aspired to write a book that is challenging to think about *and* easy to learn from. Let's take a closer look at these goals.

Goals

1. *To show both the unity and the diversity of psychology's subject matter.* Students entering an introductory psychology course are often unaware of the immense diversity of subjects studied by psychologists. I find this diversity to be part of psychology's charm, and throughout the book I highlight the enormous range of questions and issues addressed by psychology. Of course, psychology's diversity proves disconcerting for some students who see little continuity between such disparate areas of research as physiology, motivation, cognition, and abnormal behavior. Indeed, in this era of specialization, even some psychologists express concern about the fragmentation of the field.

However, I believe that the subfields of psychology overlap considerably and that we should emphasize their common core by accenting their connections and similarities. Consequently, I portray psychology as an integrated whole rather than as a mosaic of loosely related parts. A principal goal of this text, then, is to highlight the unity in psychology's intellectual heritage (the themes), as well as the diversity of psychology's interests and uses (the variations).

2. *To illuminate the process of research and its intimate link to application.* For me, a research-oriented book is not one that bulges with summaries of many studies but one that enhances students' appreciation of the logic and excitement of empirical inquiry. I want students to appreciate the strengths of the empirical approach and to see scientific psychology as a creative effort to solve intriguing behavioral puzzles. For this reason, the text emphasizes not only *what* psychologists know (and don't know) but *how* they attempt to find out. The book examines methods in some detail and encourages students to adopt the skeptical attitude of a scientist and to think critically about claims regarding behavior.

Learning the virtues of research should not mean that students cannot also satisfy their desire for concrete, personally useful information about the challenges of everyday life. Most researchers believe that psychology has a great deal to offer those outside the field and that we should share the practical implications of our work. In this text, practical insights are carefully qualified and closely tied to data, so that students can see the interdependence of research and application. I find that students come to appreciate the science of psychology more when they see that worthwhile practical applications are derived from careful research and sound theory.

3. *To make the text challenging to think about and easy to learn from.* Perhaps most of all, I have sought to create a *book of ideas* rather than a compendium of studies. I consistently emphasize concepts and theories over facts, and I focus on major issues and tough questions that cut across the subfields of psychology (for example, the extent to which behavior is governed by nature, nurture, and their interaction), as opposed to parochial debates (such as the merits of averaging versus adding in impression formation). Challenging students to think also means urging them to confront the complexity and ambiguity of psychological knowledge. Hence, the text doesn't skirt around gray areas, unresolved questions, and theoretical controversies. Instead, it encourages readers to contemplate open-ended questions, to examine their assumptions about behavior, and to apply psychological concepts to their own

lives. My goal is not simply to describe psychology but to stimulate students' intellectual growth.

However, students can grapple with "the big issues and tough questions" only if first master the basic concepts and principles of psychology—ideally, with as little struggle as possible. I never let myself forget that a textbook is a teaching tool. Accordingly, great care has been taken to ensure that the book's content, organization, writing, illustrations, and pedagogical aids work in harmony to facilitate instruction and learning.

Admittedly, these goals are ambitious. If you're skeptical, you have every right to be. Let me explain how I have tried to realize the objectives I have outlined.

Special Features

A variety of unusual features contribute, each in its own way, to the book's paradoxical nature. These special elements include unifying themes, Featured Studies, Personal Application sections, Critical Thinking Application sections, Reality Checks, a didactic illustration program, an integrated running glossary, Concept Checks, Key Learning Goals, interim Reviews of Key Learning Goals, and Practice Tests.

Unifying Themes

Chapter 1 introduces seven key ideas that serve as unifying themes throughout the text. The themes serve several purposes. First, they provide threads of continuity across chapters that help students see the connections among various areas of research in psychology. Second, as the themes evolve over the course of the book, they provide a forum for a relatively sophisticated discussion of enduring issues in psychology, thus helping to make this a "book of ideas." Third, the themes focus a spotlight on a number of basic insights about psychology and its subject matter that should leave lasting impressions on your students. In selecting the themes, the question I asked myself (and other professors) was "What do I really want students to remember five years from now?" The resulting themes are grouped into two sets.

THEMES RELATED TO PSYCHOLOGY AS A FIELD OF STUDY

Theme 1: Psychology is empirical. This theme is used to enhance the student's appreciation of psychology's scientific nature and to demonstrate the advantages of empiricism over uncritical common sense and speculation. I also use this theme to encourage the reader to adopt a scientist's skeptical attitude and to engage in more critical thinking about information of all kinds.

Theme 2: Psychology is theoretically diverse. Students are often confused by psychology's theoretical pluralism and view it as a weakness. I don't downplay or apologize for the field's theoretical diversity, because I honestly believe that it is one of psychology's greatest strengths. Throughout the book, I provide concrete examples of how clashing theories have stimulated productive research, how converging on a question from several perspectives can yield increased understanding, and how competing theories are sometimes reconciled in the end.

Theme 3: Psychology evolves in a sociohistorical context. This theme emphasizes that psychology is embedded in the ebb and flow of everyday life. The text shows how the spirit of the times has often shaped psychology's evolution and how progress in psychology leaves its mark on our society.

THEMES RELATED TO PSYCHOLOGY'S SUBJECT MATTER

Theme 4: Behavior is determined by multiple causes. Throughout the book, I emphasize, and repeatedly illustrate, that behavioral processes are complex and that multifactorial causation is the rule. This theme is used to discourage simplistic, single-cause thinking and to encourage more critical reasoning.

Theme 5: Behavior is shaped by cultural heritage. This theme is intended to enhance students' appreciation of how cultural factors moderate psychological processes and how the viewpoint of one's own culture can distort one's interpretation of the behavior of people from other cultures. The discussions that elaborate on this theme do not simply celebrate diversity. They strike a careful balance—that accurately reflects the research in this area—highlighting both cultural variations *and* similarities in behavior.

Theme 6: Heredity and environment jointly influence behavior. Repeatedly discussing this theme permits me to air out the nature versus nurture issue in all its complexity. Over a series of chapters, students gradually learn how biology shapes behavior, how experience shapes behavior, and how scientists estimate the relative importance of each. Along the way, students will gain an in-depth appreciation of what we mean when we say that heredity and environment interact.

Theme 7: People's experience of the world is highly subjective. All of us tend to forget the extent to which people view the world through their own personal lenses. This theme is used to explain the principles that underlie the subjectivity of human experience, to clarify its implications, and to repeatedly remind the readers that their view of the world is not the only legitimate one.

After introducing all seven themes in Chapter 1, I discuss different sets of themes in each chapter as they are relevant to the subject matter. The connections between a chapter's content and the unifying themes are highlighted in a standard section near the end of the chapter, in which I reflect on the "lessons to be learned" from the chapter. The discussions of the unifying themes are largely confined to these sections, titled "Reflecting on the Chapter's Themes." I have not tried to make every chapter illustrate a certain number of themes. Rather, the themes were allowed to emerge naturally, and I found that two to five surfaced in any given chapter. The chart below shows which themes are highlighted in each chapter. Color-coded icons near the beginning of each "Reflecting on the Chapter's Themes" section indicate the specific themes featured in the particular chapter.

Unifying Themes Highlighted in Each Chapter

	THEME						
Chapter	**1 Empiricism**	**2 Theoretical Diversity**	**3 Sociohistorical Context**	**4 Multifactorial Causation**	**5 Cultural Heritage**	**6 Heredity and Environment**	**7 Subjectivity of Experience**
1. The Evolution of Psychology	✓	✓	✓	✓	✓	✓	✓
2. The Research Enterprise in Psychology	✓						✓
3. The Biological Bases of Behavior	✓			✓		✓	
4. Sensation and Perception		✓			✓		✓
5. Variations in Consciousness		✓	✓	✓	✓		✓
6. Learning			✓			✓	
7. Human Memory		✓		✓			✓
8. Language and Thought	✓				✓	✓	✓
9. Intelligence and Psychological Testing			✓		✓	✓	
10. Motivation and Emotion		✓	✓	✓	✓	✓	
11. Human Development Across the Life Span		✓	✓	✓	✓	✓	
12. Personality		✓	✓		✓		
13. Social Behavior	✓				✓		✓
14. Stress, Coping, and Health				✓			✓
15. Psychological Disorders			✓	✓	✓	✓	
16. Treatment of Psychological Disorders		✓			✓		

Featured Studies

Each chapter except the first includes a Featured Study that provides a relatively detailed but succinct summary of a particular piece of research. Each Featured Study is presented in the conventional purpose-method-results-discussion format seen in journal articles, followed by a comment in which I discuss why the study is featured (to illustrate a specific method, raise ethical issues, and so forth). By showing research methods in action, I hope to improve students' understanding of how research is done while also giving them a painless introduction to the basic format of journal articles. Additionally, the Featured Studies show how complicated research can be, so students can better appreciate why scientists may disagree about the meaning of a study. The Featured Studies are fully incorporated into the flow of discourse in the text and are *not* presented as optional boxes.

In selecting the Featured Studies, I assembled a mixture of classic and recent studies that illustrate a wide variety of methods. To make them enticing, I tilted my selections in favor of those that students find interesting. Thus, readers will encounter explorations of the effects of sleep deprivation, the neuroanatomy of sexual arousal, and Milgram's legendary study of obedience.

Personal Applications

To reinforce the pragmatic implications of theory and research stressed throughout the text, each chapter closes with a Personal Application section that highlights the practical side of psychology. Each Personal Application devotes two to five *pages* of text (rather than the usual box) to a single issue that should be of special interest to many of your students. Although most of the Personal Application sections have a "how to" character, they continue to review studies and summarize data in much the same way as the main body of each chapter. Thus, they portray research and application not as incompatible polarities but as two sides of the same coin. Many of the Personal Applications—such as those on finding and reading journal articles, understanding art and illusion, and improving stress management—provide topical coverage unusual for an introductory text.

Critical Thinking Applications

A great deal of unusual coverage can also be found in the Critical Thinking Applications that follow the Personal Applications. Conceived by Diane Halpern (Claremont McKenna College), a leading authority on critical thinking, these applications are based on the assumption that critical thinking skills can be taught. They do not simply review research critically, as is typically the case in other introductory texts. Instead, these Applications introduce and model a host of critical thinking *skills*, such as looking for contradictory evidence or alternative explanations; recognizing anecdotal evidence, circular reasoning, hindsight bias, reification, weak analogies, and false dichotomies; evaluating arguments systematically; and working with cumulative and conjunctive probabilities.

The specific skills discussed in the Critical Thinking Applications are listed in the table on page ix, where they are organized into five categories using a taxonomy developed by Halpern (1994). In each chapter, some of these skills are applied to topics and issues related to the chapter's content. For instance, in the chapter that covers drug abuse (Chapter 5), the concept of alcoholism is used to highlight the immense power of definitions and to illustrate how circular reasoning can seem so seductive. Skills that are particularly important may surface in more than one chapter, so students see them applied in a variety of contexts. For example, in Chapter 7 students learn how hindsight bias can contaminate memory, while in Chapter 12 they see how hindsight can distort analyses of personality. Repeated practice across chapters should help students spontaneously recognize the relevance of specific critical thinking skills when they encounter certain types of information.

Reality Checks

Each chapter includes three or four Reality Checks, which address common misconceptions related to psychology and provide direct refutations of the misinformation. These Reality Checks are sprinkled throughout the chapters, appearing adjacent to the relevant material. Examples of misconceptions that are dispelled include the myth that B. F. Skinner raised his daughter in a Skinner box, leading to her becoming severely disturbed (Chapter 1); the notion that people only use 10% of their brains (Chapter 3); the assumption that people who are color blind see the world in black and white (Chapter 4); and the idea that it is dangerous to awaken someone who is sleepwalking (Chapter 5). Most of the misconceptions covered in these Reality Checks were addressed in previous editions, but not with direct refutations. In other words, accurate information was provided on the issues, but usually without explicitly stating the misconception and providing a rebuttal. Why the change in strategy? Around the time I was getting ready to start the revision for this edition, I ran across a fascinating article in *Teaching of Psychology* by Patricia Kowalski and Annette Taylor (2009). It summarized evidence that students typically come into introductory psychology with a variety of misconceptions and that, for the most part, they tend to

Taxonomy of Skills Covered in the Critical Thinking Applications	
Verbal Reasoning Skills	
Understanding the way definitions shape how people think about issues	Chapter 5
Identifying the source of definitions	Chapter 5
Avoiding the nominal fallacy in working with definitions and labels	Chapter 5
Understanding the way language can influence thought	Chapter 8
Recognizing semantic slanting	Chapter 8
Recognizing name calling and anticipatory name calling	Chapter 8
Recognizing and avoiding reification	Chapter 9
Argument/Persuasion Analysis Skills	
Understanding the elements of an argument	Chapter 10
Recognizing and avoiding common fallacies, such as irrelevant reasons, circular reasoning, slippery slope reasoning, weak analogies, and false dichotomies	Chapters 10 and 11
Evaluating arguments systematically	Chapter 10
Recognizing and avoiding appeals to ignorance	Chapter 9
Understanding how Pavlovian conditioning can be used to manipulate emotions	Chapter 6
Developing the ability to detect conditioning procedures used in the media	Chapter 6
Recognizing social influence strategies	Chapter 13
Judging the credibility of an information source	Chapter 13
Skills in Thinking as Hypothesis Testing	
Looking for alternative explanations for findings and events	Chapters 1, 9, and 11
Looking for contradictory evidence	Chapters 1, 3, and 9
Recognizing the limitations of anecdotal evidence	Chapters 2 and 16
Understanding the need to seek disconfirming evidence	Chapter 7
Understanding the limitations of correlational evidence	Chapters 11 and 14
Understanding the limitations of statistical significance	Chapter 14
Recognizing situations in which placebo effects might occur	Chapter 16
Skills in Working with Likelihood and Uncertainty	
Utilizing base rates in making predictions and evaluating probabilities	Chapter 14
Understanding cumulative probabilities	Chapter 15
Understanding conjunctive probabilities	Chapter 15
Understanding the limitations of the representativeness heuristic	Chapter 15
Understanding the limitations of the availability heuristic	Chapter 15
Recognizing situations in which regression toward the mean may occur	Chapter 16
Understanding the limits of extrapolation	Chapter 3
Decision-Making and Problem-Solving Skills	
Using evidence-based decision making	Chapter 2
Recognizing the bias in hindsight analysis	Chapters 7 and 12
Seeking information to reduce uncertainty	Chapter 14
Making risk-benefit assessments	Chapter 14
Generating and evaluating alternative courses of action	Chapter 14
Recognizing overconfidence in human cognition	Chapter 7
Understanding the limitations and fallibility of human memory	Chapter 7
Understanding how contrast effects can influence judgments and decisions	Chapter 4
Recognizing when extreme comparitors are being used	Chapter 4

leave the course with their misconceptions intact. To see whether this problem could be ameliorated, they tested the impact of direct refutations on students' misconceptions in the introductory course. Their data suggested that explicit repudiations of erroneous ideas reduce students' misconceptions more effectively than the simple provision of correct information. With that evidence in mind, I decided to craft this new feature that explicitly confronts and disputes common fallacies that range from oversimplified to profoundly inaccurate. Because the Reality Checks mostly supplement the normal coverage in the text, I chose to keep them very concise. They can usually be found in the margins of the pages.

A Didactic Illustration Program

When I first outlined my plans for this text, I indicated that I wanted the illustration program to have a genuine didactic purpose and that I wanted to be deeply involved in its development. In retrospect, I had no idea what I was getting myself into, but it has been a rewarding learning experience. In any event, I have been intimately involved in planning every detail of the illustration program. I have endeavored to create a program of figures, diagrams, photos, and tables that work hand in hand with the prose to strengthen and clarify the main points in the text.

The most obvious results of this didactic approach to illustration are the seven Illustrated Overviews that combine tabular information, photos, diagrams, and sketches to provide well-organized reviews of key ideas in the areas of history, research methods, sensation and perception, learning, personality theory, psychopathology, and psychotherapy. But I hope you will also notice the subtleties of the illustration program. For instance, diagrams of important concepts (conditioning, synaptic transmission, experimental design, and so forth) are often repeated in several chapters (with variations) to highlight connections among research areas and to enhance students' mastery of key ideas. Numerous easy-to-understand graphs of research results underscore psychology's foundation in research, and photos and diagrams often bolster each other (for example, see the treatment of classical conditioning in Chapter 6). Color is used carefully as an organizational device, and visual schematics are used to simplify hard-to-visualize concepts (for example, see the figure explaining reaction range for intelligence in Chapter 9). And we have strived to enhance the realism and pedagogical value of our drawings of the brain and other physiology. All of these efforts have gone toward the service of one master: the desire to make this an inviting book that is easy to learn from.

Integrated Running Glossary

An introductory text should place great emphasis on acquainting students with psychology's technical language—not for the sake of jargon, but because a great many of the key terms are also cornerstone concepts (for example, *independent variable, reliability,* and *cognitive dissonance*). This text handles terminology with a running glossary embedded in the prose itself. The terms are set off in ***blue boldface italics,*** and the definitions follow in **blue boldface roman** type. This approach retains the two advantages of a conventional running glossary: vocabulary items are made salient, and their definitions are readily accessible. However, the approach does so without interrupting the flow of discourse, while eliminating redundancy between text matter and marginal entries.

Concept Checks

To help students assess their mastery of important ideas, Concept Checks are sprinkled throughout the book (three to five per chapter). In keeping with my goal of making this a book of ideas, the Concept Checks challenge students to apply ideas instead of testing rote memory. For example, in Chapter 6 the reader is asked to analyze realistic examples of conditioning and identify conditioned stimuli and responses, reinforcers, and schedules of reinforcement. Many of the Concept Checks require the reader to put together ideas introduced in different sections of the chapter. For instance, in Chapter 2 students are asked to look for various types of deficiencies in hypothetical studies, and in Chapter 4 students are asked to identify parallels between vision and hearing. Some of the Concept Checks are quite challenging, but students find them engaging, and they report that the answers (available in Appendix A) are often illuminating. This edition includes 16 new Concept Checks, which fall near the end of each of the 16 chapters, that focus on the contributions of major theorists and researchers in the field.

Key Learning Goals and Reviews of Key Learning Goals

To help students organize, assimilate, and remember important ideas, each major section of every chapter begins with a succinct, numbered set of Key Learning Goals and ends with a detailed, numbered Review of Key Learning Goals. The Key Learning Goals are found adjacent to the level-one headings that begin each major section; the Reviews of Key Learning Goals are found at the end of each major section, just before the next level-one heading. The Key Learning Goals are thought-provoking learning objectives that should help students focus on the key issues in each section. Each Review of Key Learning Goals is an interim summary that addresses the issues posed in the preceding Learning Goals. Interspersing these reviews throughout the chapters permits students to check their understanding of each section's main ideas immediately after finishing the section instead of waiting until the end of the chapter. This approach also allows students to work with more modest-sized chunks of information.

Practice Tests

Each chapter ends with a 15-item multiple-choice Practice Test that should give students a realistic assessment of their mastery of that chapter and valuable practice in taking the type of test that many of them will face in the classroom (if the instructor uses the Test Bank). This feature grew out of some research that I conducted on students' use of textbook pedagogical devices (see Weiten, Guadagno, & Beck, 1996). This research indicated that students pay scant attention to some standard pedagogical devices. When I grilled my students to gain a better undertstanding of this finding, it quickly became apparent that students are very pragmatic about pedagogy. Essentially, their refrain was "We want study aids that will help us pass the next test." With this mandate in mind, I devised the Practice Tests. They should be very realistic, as I took most of the items from previous editions of the Test Bank (these items do not appear in the Test Bank for this edition).

In addition to the special features just described, the text includes a variety of more conventional, "tried and true" features. The back of the book contains a standard *alphabetical glossary.* Opening *outlines* preview each chapter, I make frequent use of *italics for emphasis,* and I depend on *frequent headings* to maximize organizational clarity. The preface for students describes these pedagogical devices in more detail.

Writing Style

I strive for a down-to-earth, conversational writing style; effective communication is always the paramount goal. My intent is to talk *with* the reader rather than throw information *at* the reader. To clarify concepts and maintain students' interest, I frequently provide concrete examples that students can relate to. As much as possible, I avoid using technical jargon when ordinary language serves just as well.

Making learning easier depends, above all else, on clear, well-organized writing. For this reason, I've worked hard to ensure that chapters, sections, and paragraphs are organized in a logical manner, so that key ideas stand out in sharp relief against supportive information.

Content

The text is divided into 16 chapters. The chapters are not grouped into sections or parts, primarily because such groupings can limit your options if you want to reorganize the order of topics. The chapters are written in a way that facilitates organizational flexibility, as I always assumed that some chapters might be omitted or presented in a different order.

The topical coverage in the text is relatively conventional, but there are some subtle departures from the norm. For instance, Chapter 1 presents a relatively "meaty" discussion of the evolution of ideas in psychology. This coverage of history lays the foundation for many of the crucial ideas emphasized in subsequent chapters. The historical perspective is also my way of reaching out to the students who find that psychology isn't what they expected it to be. If we want students to contemplate the mysteries of behavior, we must begin by clearing up the biggest mysteries of them all: "Where did these rats, statistics, synapses, and JNDs come from, what could they possibly have in common, and why doesn't this course bear any resemblance to what I anticipated?" I use history as a vehicle to explain how psychology evolved into its modern form and why misconceptions about its nature are so common.

I also devote an entire chapter (Chapter 2) to the scientific enterprise—not just the mechanics of research methods but the logic behind them. I believe that an appreciation of the nature of empirical evidence can contribute greatly to improving students' critical thinking skills. Ten years from now, many of the "facts" reported in this book will have changed, but an understanding of the methods of science will remain invaluable. An introductory psychology course, by itself, isn't going to make a student think like a scientist, but I can't imagine a better place to start the process. Essential statistical concepts are introduced in Chapter 2, but no effort is made to teach actual calculations. For those who emphasize statistics, Appendix B expands on statistical concepts.

Changes in the Ninth Edition

A good textbook must evolve with the field of inquiry it covers. Although the professors and students who used the first eight editions of this book did not clamor for alterations, there are some changes. I have already described the Reality Checks, which are new to this edition. Another new element is that each chapter-opening spread includes a puzzling paradox related to the upcoming content of the chapter. These paradoxes are brief brain teasers that I hope will provoke some thought and create a little intrigue as students embark on their reading of each chapter.

You may also notice that for the first time in nine editions, I have altered the order of the chapters. It is not a major reorganization. I have simply moved the chapter on social behavior up from Chapter 16 to Chapter 13. Why? Although some instructors juggle chapter order, most seem to assign the chapters in sequence. Many of us often fall behind our planned schedule and struggle to get through all the chapters we intended to cover. This reality means that the chapter on social psychology probably gets dropped more than other chapters because it comes at the end of the book. I think that this is an unfortunate situation in that the chapter on social psychology includes some of the most inherently interesting and important material in the course. So, after mulling it over for years, I decided it should no longer suffer the fate of being last. Of course, that means that another chapter has to become the precarious, final chapter. As you will see, that fate now falls to the chapter on the treatment of psychological disorders. Admittedly, this material is also important. But the text includes two chapters on clinical psychology—the chapter on disorders (15) and the one on treatment (16)—so even if the chapter on treatment gets dropped, students can have a healthy exposure to clinical psychology. This shift also means that the chapters on personality (12) and social psychology (13) fall together, which seems appropriate given the enormous overlap and historical kinship between these subfields.

A more subtle, and infinitely more challenging change in this edition is that I have reduced the length of the chapters. It was not easy, given the constant accumulation of interesting new findings in our field, but on average the chapters have been reduced by about 6%. That may not sound like much, but it is roughly equivalent to deleting an entire chapter. I have also made a systematic effort in this edition to reduce the reading level of the text. The Flesch-Kincaid readability estimates have been lowered for all sixteen chapters. In terms of grade level, I managed to reduce five of the chapters by about 3/4 of a grade and seven chapters by about 1/2 of a grade. These revisions should help make the book easier for your students to digest.

You will also find a variety of other changes in this edition, including four new chapter-opening vignettes (in Chapters 2, 11, 13, and 15) and five new Featured Studies (in Chapters 2, 4, 7, 11, and 12). Another major change is the addition of sixteen new Concept Checks that focus on the chief contributions and ideas of major theorists and researchers in the field. These Concept Checks, which appear near the end of the main body of each chapter, challenge students to match major theorists' names with their key innovations or accomplishments. They essentially replace the list of "key people" formerly found in the chapter-ending reviews. This feature will enable students to quickly and conveniently review "who did what" in a way that should be far superior to the old list of names.

The graphic design of the text has been refreshed and improved in a variety of ways. For instance, the beginning of each chapter features more dramatic illustrations that span two pages. In the line art, we have increased the use of color-coded text, and wherever possible we have replaced drawings of humans with actual photos that are integrated into our graphics and diagrams. We have also strived to make the photo program more engaging by adding a host of silhouetted images that are woven into the text columns, creating more a modern, magazine-like look.

Another new addition is an appendix that focuses on the timely issue of sustainability (Appendix D). It explains how sustainability depends on changes in individuals' behavior more than any other single factor. It focuses on the cognitive and behavioral processes that tend to impede environmentally responsible behavior, as well as the alterations in behavior that will be necessary to sustain the world's natural resources for future generations.

Of course, the book has been thoroughly updated to reflect recent advances in the field. One of the exciting things about psychology is that it is not a stagnant discipline. It continues to move forward at what seems a faster and faster pace. This progress has necessitated a number of specific content changes that you'll find sprinkled throughout the chapters. Finally, you will find over 1350 new references in this edition. Following is a list of specific content changes in each chapter of the ninth edition.

Chapter 1: The Evolution of Psychology

- Introduction of new text feature called Reality Checks, which will be sprinkled throughout the book
- New table highlighting ten popular myths about psychology
- New coverage discussing Watson's expulsion from academia and his successful application of psychology to advertising
- New Reality Check on the rumor that Skinner's daughter was raised in a Skinner box and grew up to be highly dysfunctional

- New data on the rise of the cognitive and neuroscience perspectives since the 1950s
- New Reality Check on the notion that psychology has always been part of mental health system
- Expanded Illustrated Overview of psychology's history (five new entries)
- New Reality Check on the oversimplification that psychology = the study of the mind
- New Reality Check on the belief that psychology and psychiatry are largely the same
- New research on the importance of study habits to college success
- Streamlined coverage of improving reading in the Personal Application

Chapter 2: The Research Enterprise in Psychology

- New Reality Check on how often social scientists use random sampling
- New Featured Study on how motives skew perception, reinforcing the theme that our experience of the world is highly subjective
- New example of naturalistic observation research focusing on how drivers make decisions at yellow lights
- An additional example illustrating an innovative, new way to conduct naturalistic observation
- Added example of case study research focusing on assessing the effectiveness of a specific therapy
- Interesting new example of survey research showing how the amount of time people watch TV relates to social class and health
- New Reality Check on correlation and causation
- New Reality Check on the meaning of statistical significance
- New discussion of the importance and value of meta-analysis
- New coverage of Arnett's (2008) critique of American psychology for its excessive reliance on American participants, thus ignoring 95% of the world's population
- Expanded analysis of placebo effects
- New Reality Check on the belief that placebo effects are weak effects
- New discussion of halo effects in making ratings in questionnaire research
- Critical Thinking Application profiles new research on the powerful influence of anecdotal evidence

Chapter 3: The Biological Bases of Behavior

- New Reality Check on the idea that neurons do all the information processing in the nervous system
- Streamlined discussion of neural transmission
- New research on endorphins and the "runner's high"
- New Reality Check on the myth that people use only 10% of their brains
- Compressed critique of the reliability and precision of functional-brain imaging technology
- Revised take on the role of the cerebellum
- New discussion of the possible evolutionary significance of hemispheric specialization in the brain
- New research relating weak cerebral lateralization to lower IQ and vulnerability to schizophrenia
- New coverage of the role of oxytocin in pair bonding
- New research on oxytocin's influence on empathy and trust
- New coverage of recent findings in epigenetics
- Streamlined Personal Application on the significance of hemispheric specialization
- New research showing that musicians have more bilateral hemispheric organization than others
- New research suggesting that music training may be related to enhanced cognitive performance
- New Reality Check on the belief that people are either right-brained or left-brained
- New Reality Check explaining that playing classical music for children will not enhance their brain development

Chapter 4: Sensation and Perception

- New research on how subliminal stimuli can sway behavior
- New Reality Check on the myth that reading in the dark or sitting close to the TV will damage one's vision
- Expanded discussion of the evolutionary significance of face-detecting cells in the brain
- New coverage of visual agnosia and prosopagnosia
- New Reality Check on the notion that people who are color blind see the world in black and white
- New research on how exposure to colors can influence psychological functioning
- New Featured Study on how the color red enhances men's attraction to women
- New research on how depth perception can be skewed by people's motivational states
- New discussion of how portable music players can cause hearing loss
- Revised coverage of pitch perception
- New Reality Check on the classic tongue map
- New discussion of the possibility that umami should be viewed as fifth basic taste
- New research on humans' ability to track faint scents
- New research on how contextual factors modulate the experience of pain

- New Reality Check on the belief that humans have just five senses
- New discussion in the Personal Application of *trompe l'oeil* art

Chapter 5: Variations in Consciousness

- New research reporting the counterintuitive finding that older adults may need less sleep than younger adults
- New data on whether growing older, by itself, leads to poor sleep in the elderly
- New research on ethnicity and sleep complaints
- New data linking REM sleep to neurogenesis
- New findings suggesting that REM sleep may enhance creativity
- New Reality Check on the notion that the effects of sleep deprivation are insignificant
- New discussion of hyperarousal as an explanation for insomnia
- New coverage of REM sleep behavior disorder
- New Reality Check on the belief that it is dangerous to awaken sleepwalkers
- New Reality Check dispelling the idea that a shocking dream could be fatal
- Added distinction between focused-attention and open-monitoring approaches to meditation
- New findings suggest that meditation can increase one's tolerance of pain
- New research suggesting that meditation has the potential to modify brain structure
- New Reality Check dispelling the myth that hypnotized individuals can perform feats that they could never perform otherwise
- New discussion of the combined impact of cannabis and alcohol on driving
- New research on napping and performance

Chapter 6: Learning

- New Reality Check on the notion that Pavlov's demonstration of classical conditioning relied on a bell
- New section on evaluative conditioning as a form of classical conditioning
- Streamlined coverage of classical conditioning in everyday life
- New discussion of what happened to Little Albert in the aftermath of Watson and Rayner's landmark study, including new evidence on Little Albert's identity
- New discussion of how overgeneralization may contribute to the emergence of panic disorder
- New discussion of the effects of delayed reinforcement
- New Reality Check explaining that rewarding a behavior every time is not the best way to ensure that it will last
- New Reality Check explaining that negative reinforcement and punishment are not the same thing
- New findings on the negative effects of corporal punishment in children
- Condensed discussion of biological constraints on conditioning
- New discussion of B. F. Skinner's theory of noncontingent reinforcement as an explanation for superstitious behavior
- New coverage of how superstitious behavior can be analyzed in terms of normal cognitive biases and errors that promote irrational reasoning
- New research showing that superstitious beliefs can actually influence people's performance
- Added discussion of how exposure to media violence may desensitize people to the effects of aggression in the real world
- New research on how desensitization to aggression may undermine helping behavior

Chapter 7: Human Memory

- New research on why cell phone conversations sap attention and impair driving
- New research on how the motivation to remember affects encoding
- New Reality Check questioning the conventional wisdom on the capacity of short-term memory
- New findings on the nature and significance of working memory capacity
- Expanded discussion of hypnosis and memory
- New Reality Check disputing the idea that hypnosis can enhance memory retrieval
- New research on the power of the misinformation effect
- New Reality Check explaining that memory is not like a mental videotape
- New Featured Study on destination memory—remembering to whom one has told what
- New Reality Check on the notion that forgetting is due to the decay of memory traces
- Streamlined coverage of the repressed memories controversy
- New work distinguishing two groups that report recovered memories of abuse that differ in the likelihood of corroboration
- Condensed coverage of the neuroscience of memory
- Expanded discussion of how H.M.'s case contributed to the understanding of memory
- Increased coverage of the testing effect on memory

Chapter 8: Language and Thought

- Expanded explanation of overregularizations in language development

- New research on how learning a second language can subsequently facilitate acquisition of a third language
- New discussion of how one's first language and second language are simultaneously active in bilingual individuals (i.e., there is no way to turn off L2 when using L1, and vice versa)
- New discussion of how bilingualism is associated with reduced language processing speed but with enhanced attentional control, working memory capacity, metalinguistic awareness, and problem solving
- New Reality Check on the notion that bilingualism undermines cognitive development
- New research on how bilingualism may protect against age-related cognitive decline
- Expanded description of Kanzi's comprehension of spoken English
- New Reality Check on whether language is unique to humans
- New research on the incubation effect in problem solving
- Expanded coverage of cultural disparities in cognitive style
- Updated research on choice overload and its roots
- New Reality Check on the assumption that the more choices people have, the better
- New research on the uncertainty effect—the finding that people value a known outcome over an unknown outcome even when the worst scenario for the unknown outcome is equal to the known outcome and the best scenario is clearly superior
- New Reality Check disputing the idea that effective decision making depends on thoughtful deliberation
- New evidence on the relationship between intelligence and vulnerability to cognitive bias and error, showing that even very bright people are not immune to irrational thinking
- New research on the myside bias—the tendency to evaluate evidence in a manner slanted in favor of one's opinions

Chapter 9: Intelligence and Psychological Testing

- New inclusion of the distinction between fluid and crystallized intelligence
- New take on the debate about the structure of intelligence
- New data on how students' self-perceptions of their abilities influence their academic performance
- Inclusion of Stanovich's (2009) criticism of how IQ tests do not assess rational thinking
- New Reality Check on the notion that IQ tests measure mental ability in a truly general sense
- New coverage of the degree to which IQ scores are stable over time
- New Reality Check on the idea that intelligence is a fixed, immutable trait
- Updated material on the definition of intellectual disability
- New Reality Check on the belief that most people with intellectual disability are severely retarded
- New Reality Check disputing the notion that gifted children tend to be frail introverts with emotional problems
- New research on stereotype threat and test performance
- New research on the correlation between IQ and the size of specific areas in the brain
- New research on the association between IQ and the volume of gray and white matter in the brain
- Compressed discussion of Sternberg's theory of intelligence
- New research on how people with higher intelligence tend to live longer
- New discussion of the possible mechanisms underlying the relationship between intelligence and mortality
- New research on how living abroad appears to enhance creativity

Chapter 10: Motivation and Emotion

- Additional data on how the quantity of food available influences the amount eaten
- New findings on the effects of the presence of others on eating behavior
- New material on how food advertisements influence eating behavior
- New data on the prevalence of obesity, and correlations between ethnicity and obesity
- New Reality Check on whether eating at night fosters weight gain
- Revived coverage of Schachter's externality hypothesis of obesity
- New material on Rodin's critique of the externality hypothesis
- Contemporary evaluation of the externality hypothesis
- New findings on gender disparities in orgasmic consistency and interest in sex
- Revised coverage of the effects of pornography
- New Reality Check on the misconception that most rapes are committed by strangers
- New research on the developmental roots of sexual orientation
- New coverage on the inaccuracy of affective forecasting
- Added coverage of a classic study of affective forecasting (Dunn, Wilson, & Gilbert, 2003)

- New discussion of the role of mirror neurons in the emotion of empathy
- New Reality Check on the accuracy of lie detectors
- New research on whether emotional facial expressions are innate
- Revised discussion of the relationship between income and subjective well-being, including a recent study by Kahneman and Deaton (2010)

Chapter 11: Human Development Across the Life Span

- Revised statistics and terminology on the threshold of viability
- New Reality Check on the wisdom of social drinking during pregnancy
- Added coverage of the effects of maternal emotions during prenatal development
- Added coverage of the effects of environmental toxins during prenatal development
- New section on fetal origins of adult diseases, such as diabetes and heart disease
- New material on cultural differences in temperament
- New Reality Check on bonding at birth and later attachment
- Added discussion of the strange situation procedure in coverage of attachment
- New section on how children's theory of mind progresses
- New findings on how adolescents and young adults progress through Marcia's identity statuses
- New Featured Study on the effects of peer influence on adolescents' risk taking
- New data on how self-esteem changes over the course of adulthood
- New Reality Check on the prevalence of the midlife crisis
- New data suggesting that cohabitation may no longer be a risk factor for marital dissolution
- New research on the transistion to parenthood
- New findings on the transition to the empty nest
- New Reality Check on the arrival of children and marital satisfaction
- New data on how older adults tend to feel an average of 13 years younger than they are
- Revised coverage of protective factors for Alzheimer's disease
- New discussion of whether cognitive training programs can slow cognitive decline in the elderly
- New data on gender differences in math achievement
- Added discussion of gender differences in the Big Five personality traits
- New findings on how fetal testosterone levels relate to subsequent gender-typing
- New research on the developmental significance of father absence

Chapter 12: Personality

- Expanded description of the Big Five traits
- New data on the relationship between the Big Five traits and socioeconomic class
- New Reality Check on the influence of the unconscious
- Sublimation added to the roster of defense mechanisms covered
- Condensed coverage of Adler's theory
- Expanded critique of Freudian theory
- New Reality Check on the power of situational forces
- New discussion of a proposed revision of Maslow's hierarchy of needs
- New Reality Check questioning the assumption that parents exert great influence over their children's personality
- Recent genetic mapping studies of specific genes and personality
- New findings on the neuroscience of personality
- Revised critique of biological models of personality
- Revised Illustrated Overview of personality theory, now including information on the assumptions of each approach
- New discussion of the history of narcissism as a personality trait
- New findings on the nature, correlates, and social consequences of narcissism
- New research on how levels of narcissism have increased in recent decades
- Streamlined coverage of terror management theory
- Individualism versus collectivism now included in discussion of culture and personality
- Added discussion of how cultural factors influence self-enhancement tendencies
- New Featured Study on whether collectivists know themselves better than individualists know themselves

Chapter 13 (formerly 16): The Social Behavior

- New research on the effects of brains versus beauty as related to income
- New data on the accuracy of inferences about personality based on "thin slices of behavior"
- Compressed coverage of attribution processes
- New evidence on the matching hypothesis based on real-world behavior at HOTorNOT.com website
- New findings on how physical attractiveness and similarity affect friendship formation
- New Reality Check on whether opposites attract in romantic relationships

- New coverage of the use of a "scientific approach" to matching people based on compatibility at eHarmony.com and similar websites
- New Reality Check on how well attitudes predict behavior
- Distinction between implicit and explicit attitudes introduced
- New coverage of how the Implicit Association Test (IAT) measures implicit attitudes
- New discussion of the correlates of implicit prejudice
- New coverage of the mere exposure effect
- New Reality Check on the notion that familiarity breeds contempt
- New discussion of normative and informational influence as motives for conformity
- Expanded coverage of Milgram's variations on his study of obedience
- New coverage of Burger's (2009) recent partial replication of Milgram's study
- New discussion of the effects of modern technology on the evolving nature of groups

Chapter 14 (formerly 13): Stress, Coping, and Health

- Now highlights the distinction between primary and secondary appraisal of stress, with new graphic
- New data on pressure and heart disease
- New Reality Check on the idea that stress is always imposed by outside forces
- New research on how positive emotions predict greater longevity
- New graphic illustrating Selye's general adaptation syndrome
- New coverage of sex differences in stress reactions
- New research on how stress affects attention
- New Reality Check on the belief that stress is always harmful
- New meta-analysis of the surprisingly strong association between social support and longevity
- New findings on cultural disparities in the type of social support people prefer
- Added coverage of the effects of second-hand smoke
- New Reality Check on the significance of failing in efforts to quit smoking
- Streamlined coverage of behavioral factors and AIDS
- New discussion of the importance of good sleep habits for minimizing physiological vulnerability to stress
- New discussion of the importance of considering base rates when evaluating claims about the value of medications and other treatments

Chapter 15 (formerly 14): Psychological Disorders

- New introductory vignette focuses on contemporary celebrities with obsessive-compulsive disorder
- New discussion of the influence of stigmatizing labels on the mentally ill
- New Reality Check on the belief that people with psychological disorders typically exhibit extremely bizarre behavior
- Added coverage of the debate about categorical versus dimensional approaches to describing disorders
- New data on the most common types of phobic fears
- New graphic on the most common types of compulsions seen in OCD patients
- Added discussion of how phobias can be acquired through observation or exposure to fear-inducing information
- Concept of anhedonia introduced in discussion of major depression
- New coverage of chronic depression
- Updated data on age-of-onset patterns for bipolar disorder
- New discussion of hormonal factors that contribute to depressive disorders
- New Reality Check on notion that schizophrenia refers to a split personality
- Updated coverage of neurochemical factors in the etiology of schizophrenia
- New research on whether cannabis use may help precipitate schizophrenia in young people who are vulnerable to the disorder
- New discussion of how schizophrenia may be caused by a disruption of neural connectivity
- New Reality Check on the belief that people with psychological disorders are often dangerous and violent

Chapter 16 (formerly 15): Treatment of Psychological Disorders

- New findings on the extent to which drug therapy has become the dominant mode of treatment for psychological disorders
- New research on the proportion of individuals seeking therapy who do not meet the criteria for a mental disorder
- New data on the demographics of who seeks treatment
- New Reality Check on the notion that seeking therapy is a sign of weakness
- New data on how psychiatrists are largely abandoning talk therapy
- Now includes marriage and family therapists in coverage of professions providing mental health services

- New table comparing the various mental health professions
- New Reality Check on the belief that the typical therapy patient lies on a couch and talks about the past
- New summary of the core features of modern psychodynamic therapies
- New section on couples/marital therapy
- New section on family therapy
- New discussion of exposure therapies for anxiety disorders
- Coverage of one-session treatment (OST) of phobias
- New research on the value of antidepressants in relation to the severity of patients' depression
- New Reality Check on the belief that psychological disorders are chronic and incurable
- New findings on how often psychiatrists prescribe multiple medications to patients
- New evidence on ethnic disparities in mental health care
- New data on declining expenditures on mental health care and emerging shortages of psychiatric beds

PsykTrek: A Multimedia Introduction to Psychology

PsykTrek is a multimedia supplement that provides students with new opportunities for active learning and reaches out to "visual learners" with greatly increased efficacy. *PsykTrek* is intended to give students a second pathway to learning much of the content of introductory psychology. Although it does not cover all of the content of the introductory course, I think you will see that a great many key concepts and principles can be explicated *more effectively* in an interactive audiovisual medium than in a textbook.

To get access, visit CengageBrain.com <http://CengageBrain.com>

PsykTrek consists of four components. The main component is a set of 65 *Interactive Learning Modules* that present the core content of psychology in a whole new way. These tutorials include thousands of graphics, hundred of photos, hundreds of animations, approximately four hours of narration, 40 carefully selected videos, and about 160 uniquely visual concept checks and quizzes. The 10 *Simulations* allow students to explore complex psychological phenomena in depth. They are highly interactive, experiential demonstrations that will enhance students' appreciation of research methods. The *Multimedia Glossary* allows students to look up over 800 psychological terms, access hundreds of pronunciations of obscure words, and pull up hundreds of related diagrams, photos, and videos. The *Video Selector* permits students (or faculty) to directly access the video segments that are otherwise embedded in the Interactive Learning Modules.

The key strength of *PsykTrek* is its ability to give students new opportunities for active learning outside of the classroom. For example, students can run through re-creations of classic experiments to see the complexities of data collection in action. Or they can play with visual illusions onscreen in ways that will make them doubt their own eyes. Or they can stack color filters on screen to demonstrate the nature of subtractive color mixing. *PsykTrek* is intended to supplement and complement *Psychology: Themes & Variations*. For instance, after reading about operant conditioning in the text, a student could work through three interactive tutorials on operant principles, watch four videos (including historic footage of B. F. Skinner shaping a rat), and then try to shape Morphy, the virtual rat, in one of the simulations.

For the first time *PsykTrek* is available in an online format that can make student access easier than ever. *PsykTrek* 3.0 includes three new Interactive Learning Modules: Attachment, Forgetting, and Conformity and Obedience. All of the modules now include a multiple-choice test, as well as an interactive quiz. We have also incorporated unit-level multiple-choice exams to permit students to better assess their mastery of content. And each unit includes a critical thinking exercise, written by Jeffry Ricker (Scottsdale Community College). Finally, the new version of *PsykTrek* contains additional videos, including historically noteworthy segments showing B. F. Skinner's shaping of pigeons to play Ping-Pong, Albert Bandura's Bobo doll study, and Stanley Milgram's legendary study of obedience.

Other Supplementary Materials

The teaching/learning package that has been developed to supplement *Psychology: Themes & Variations* includes many other useful tools. The development of all its parts was carefully coordinated so that they are mutually supportive. Moreover, the materials have been created and written by highly experienced, top-flight professors I have worked hard to recruit. Supplements are available to qualified adopters. Please consult your local sales representative for details.

Instructor's Resource Manual (coordinated by Randolph Smith and Benjamin Smith)

A talented roster of professors have contributed to the *Instructor's Resource Manual (IRM)* in their respective areas of expertise. The *IRM* was developed under the guidance of Randolph Smith, the former editor of the journal *Teaching of Psychology,* and Benjamin Smith. It contains a diverse array of materials designed to facilitate efforts to teach the introductory course and includes the following sections:

- The *Instructor's Manual,* by Randolph Smith (Lamar University) and Benjamin Smith (Lamar University), contains a wealth of detailed suggestions for lecture topics, class demonstrations, exercises, discussion questions, and suggested readings, organized around the content of each chapter in the text. It also highlights the connections between the text coverage and *PsykTrek* content and features an expanded collection of masters for class handouts.
- *Strategies for Effective Teaching,* by Joseph Lowman (University of North Carolina), discusses practical issues such as what to put in a course syllabus, how to handle the first class meeting, how to cope with large classes, and how to train and organize teaching assistants.
- *AV Media for Introductory Psychology,* by Russ Watson (College of DuPage), provides a comprehensive, up-to-date, critical overview of educational films relevant to the introductory course.
- *The Use of Computers in Teaching Introductory Psychology,* by Susan J. Shapiro (Indiana University–East), offers a thorough listing of computer materials germane to the introductory course and analyzes their strengths and weaknesses.
- *Introducing Writing in Introductory Psychology,* by Dana Dunn (Moravian College), discusses how to work toward enhancing students' writing skills in the context of the introductory course and provides suggestions and materials for specific writing assignments chapter by chapter.
- *Crossing Borders/Contrasting Behaviors: Using Cross-Cultural Comparisons to Enrich the Introductory Psychology Course,* by Ginny Zahn, Bill Hill, and Michael Reiner (Kennesaw State University), discusses the movement toward "internationalizing" the curriculum and provides suggestions for lectures, exercises, and assignments that can add a cross-cultural flavor to the introductory course.
- *Teaching Introductory Psychology with the World Wide Web,* by Michael R. Snyder (University of Alberta), discusses how to work Internet assignments into the introductory course and provides a guide to many psychology-related sites on the World Wide Web.

Test Bank (by Jeff Holmes)

A large, diversified, and carefully constructed *Test Bank* accompanies this text. The questions are closely tied to each chapter's Key Learning Goals. The items are categorized as (a) factual, (b) conceptual/applied, (c) integrative, or (d) critical thinking questions. The *Test Bank* also includes a separate section that contains about 600 multiple-choice questions based on the content of *PsykTrek's* Interactive Learning Modules. Data on item difficulty are included for many questions. For this edition, Jeff Holmes of Ithaca College carefully scrutinized every item for quality before he even began the update to accommodate the revised content of the text. And to keep item quality high, we decided to reduce the number of items per chapter to a more manageable number (maximum 250). I maintain that it is quicker, easier, and more efficient to select test questions from a reasonable number of items than to have to work through 400 items that inevitably include superficial variations on the same questions.

PowerLecture™

The fastest, easiest way to build powerful, customized media-rich lectures, PowerLecture provides a collection of book-specific PowerPoint lectures and class tools to enhance the educational experience. For classroom presentations, the CD-ROM includes PowerPoint lecture outlines with key images from the text integrated into it, and a complete library of graphics and photos from the book. An electronic version of the entire Instructor's Resource Manual is also found on the CD, which makes it easy to print or distribute handouts or exercises from the manual. The CD also includes an electronic version of the Test Bank. The *ExamView* software is user-friendly and allows teachers to insert their own questions and to edit those provided.

Psychology CourseMate

Psychology CourseMate is an online learning resource for your students. It includes:

- an interactive eBook
- interactive teaching and learning tools including:
  - Quizzes
  - Flashcards
  - Videos
  - and more
- Engagement Tracker, a first-of-its-kind tool that monitors student engagement in the course

CengageNOW™

CengageNOW offers all of your teaching and learning resources in one intuitive program organized around the essential activities you perform for class—lecturing, creating assignments, grading, quizzing (with Pre- and Post-Tests created by Billa Reiss of St. John's University), and tracking student progress and performance. CengageNOW's intuitive "tabbed" design allows you to navigate to all key functions with a single click, and a unique homepage tells you just what needs to be done and when. CengageNOW provides students access to an integrated eBook, interactive tutorials, videos, and animations that help them get the most out of your course.

WebTutor on Blackboard and WebCT

Jumpstart your course with customizable, rich, text-specific content within your Course Management System.

- Jumpstart – Simply load a WebTutor cartridge into your Course Management System.
- Customizable – Easily blend, add, edit, reorganize, or delete content.
- Content – Rich, text-specific content, media assets, quizzing, weblinks, discussion topics, interactive games and exercises, and more.

Whether you want to web-enable your class or put an entire course online, WebTutor delivers. Visit webtutor.cengage.com to learn more.

Video Resources

A wealth of video materials relevant to teaching the introductory psychology course are available from Cengage Learning, including the following.

ABC Videos: Introductory Psychology. These videos from the ABC television network feature short, high-interest clips about current studies and research in psychology. They are perfect for starting discussions or enriching lectures. Topics include brain damage, IQ measurement, sleep patterns, obsessive-compulsive disorder, obedience to authority, rules of attraction, and much more.

Volume I ISBN: 0-495-50306-1
Volume II ISBN: 0-495-59637-X
Volume III ISBN: 0-495-60490-9

Introductory Psychology, BBC Motion Gallery Video. *Introductory Psychology,* Vol. 1 drives home the relevance of course topics through short, provocative clips of current and historical events. Perfect for enriching lectures and engaging students in discussion, many of the segments on this volume have been gathered from BBC Motion Gallery. The 14 short (1–6 minutes) videos include topics such as emotional intelligence, attachment disorder, women and stress, and teen depression. Ask your Cengage Learning representative for a complete list of contents.

Vol. 1 ISBN: 9781111352608

Wadsworth Psychology: Research in Action. The Research in Action videos feature the work of research psychologists to give students an opportunity to learn about cutting-edge research—not just who is doing it, but also how it is done, and how and where the results are being used. By taking students into the laboratories of both established and up-and-coming researchers, and by showing research results being applied outside of the laboratory, these videos offer insight into both the research process and the many ways in which real people's lives are affected by research in the fields of psychology and neuroscience. The 46 videos in this series include interviews with many of the field's most prominent researchers including David Barlow, Roy Baumeister, Sheldon Cohen, Larry Squire, Claude Steele, Elizabeth Loftus, and Mark Snyder.

Vol. 1 DVD ISBN: 0495595209
Vol. 2 DVD ISBN: 0495598135

Revealing Psychology. The *Revealing Psychology* video (available on DVD) is ideal for both classroom presentation and online study. The clips include a refreshed and innovative Candid Camera-like segments depicting people in socially challenging situations, with a focus on applications of concepts and experimental variations; classic experiments in real-world context with a new look and feel; and personal profiles with interviews of real people talking about their lives in ways that illustrate social psychological concepts, such as conformity, personal space, and group polarization.

ISBN: 0547014538

Guest Lecture Series. The Guest Lecture Series features many talented teachers sharing their teaching tips and best practices on a wide range of topics, including: rational emotive behavior theory, blogging as an effective tool, demonstrations on taste, dramatizing perspectives in psychology, how to teach writing in psychology, and more. This series focuses on the teaching-learning process and is intended to help faculty in their course preparation and planning.

ISBN: 054700401X

Acknowledgments

Creating an introductory psychology text is a complicated challenge, and a small army of people have contributed to the evolution of this book. Foremost among them are the psychology editors I have worked with—Claire Verduin, C. Deborah Laughton, Phil Curson, Eileen Murphy, Edith Beard Brady, Michele Sordi, and Jon-David Hague—and the developmental editor for the first edition of this book, John Bergez. They have helped me immeasurably, and each has become a treasured friend along the way. I am especially indebted to Claire, who educated me in the intricacies of textbook publishing, and to John, who has left an enduring imprint on my writing.

The challenge of meeting a difficult schedule in producing this book was undertaken by a talented team of people coordinated by Joan Keyes, who did a superb job of pulling it all together. Credit for coordination of the text design goes to Vernon Boes, who was very creative in building on the previous design. Terri Wright handled photo research with enthusiasm and extraordinary efficiency, and Jackie Estrada did an outstanding job once again in copyediting the manuscript. Fred Harwin and Carol Zuber-Mallison made stellar contributions to the artwork.

A number of psychologists deserve thanks for the contributions they made to this book. I am grateful to Diane Halpern for her work on the Critical Thinking Applications; to Vinny Hevern for contributing the Web Links that can be found online; to Marky Lloyd for writing the online appendix on careers in psychology; to Kathy Hanisch for writing the appendix on I/O psychology; to Rick Stalling and Ron Wasden for their work on previous editions of the *Study Guide;* to Jeff Holmes for his revision of the *Test Bank;* to Randy Smith, Benjamin Smith, Joseph Lowman, Russ Watson, Dana Dunn, Ginny Zahn, Bill Hill, Michael Reiner, Susan Shapiro, and Michael Snyder for their contributions to the *Instructor's Resource Manual;* to Jeffry Ricker for devising *PsykTrek's* critical thinking exercises; to Susan Koger, Britain Scott, and Laurie Hollis-Walker for contributing the appendix on sustainability; to Randy Smith, David Matsumoto, and Jeremy Houska for contributing ancillary books; to Jim Calhoun for providing item analysis data for the test items; to Harry Upshaw, Larry Wrightsman, Shari Diamond, Rick Stalling, and Claire Etaugh for their help and guidance over the years; and to the chapter consultants listed on page xxii and the reviewers listed on pages xxiii and xxiv, who provided insightful and constructive critiques of various portions of the manuscript.

Many other people have also contributed to this project, and I am grateful to all of them for their efforts. Bill Roberts, Craig Barth, Nancy Sjoberg, John Odam, Fiorella Ljunggren, Jim Brace-Thompson, Susan Badger, Sean Wakely, Eve Howard, Tom Dorsaneo, Linda Rill, Joanne Terhaar, Marjorie Sanders, Kathryn Stewart, Lori Grebe, Dory Schaeffer, Margaret Parks, Kim Russell, and Jennie Redwitz helped with varied aspects of previous editions. Linda Schreiber, Pat Waldo, Kristin Makarewycz, Trina Tom, Liz Rhoden, Kelly Miller, and Lauren Keyes made valuable contributions to the current edition. At the College of DuPage, where I taught until 1991, all of my colleagues in psychology provided support and information at one time or another, but I am especially indebted to Barb Lemme, Alan Lanning, Pat Puccio, and Don Green. I also want to thank my former colleagues at Santa Clara University (especially Tracey Kahan, Tom Plante, and Jerry Burger) and my current colleagues at UNLV who have been fertile sources of new ideas. And I am indebted to the many graduate students that I have worked with at UNLV for their insightful questions and feedback in my seminar on teaching, and to Kerri Schafer and Erica Noles, who helped complete the reference entries.

My greatest debt is to my wife, Beth Traylor, who has been a steady source of emotional sustenance while enduring the rigors of her medical career, and to my son T. J., for making dad laugh all the time.

Wayne Weiten

Chapter Consultants

Chapter 1
David Baker
University of Akron
Charles L. Brewer
Furman University
C. James Goodwin
Wheeling Jesuit University
David Hothersall
Ohio State University
E. R. Hilgard
Stanford University
Michael G. Livingston
St. John's University

Chapter 2
Larry Christensen
Texas A & M University
Francis Durso
University of Oklahoma
Donald H. McBurney
University of Pittsburgh
Wendy Schweigert
Bradley University

Chapter 3
Nelson Freedman
Queen's University at Kingston
Michael W. Levine
University of Illinois, Chicago
Corinne L. McNamara
Kennesaw State University
James M. Murphy
Indiana University–Purdue University Indianapolis
Paul Wellman
Texas A & M University

Chapter 4
Nelson Freedman
Queen's University at Kingston
Kevin Jordan
San Jose State University
Michael W. Levine
University of Illinois, Chicago
John Pittenger
University of Arkansas, Little Rock
Lawrence Ward
University of British Columbia
Chrislyn E. Randell
Metropolitan State College of Denver

Chapter 5
Frank Etscorn
New Mexico Institute of Mining and Technology
Tracey L. Kahan
Santa Clara University
Charles F. Levinthal
Hofstra University
Wilse Webb
University of Florida

Chapter 6
A. Charles Catania
University of Maryland
Michael Domjan
University of Texas, Austin
William C. Gordon
University of New Mexico
Russell A. Powell
Grant MacEwan College
Barry Schwartz
Swarthmore College
Deborah L. Stote
University of Texas, Austin

Chapter 7
Tracey L. Kahan
Santa Clara University
Ian Neath
Purdue University
Tom Pusateri
Loras College
Stephen K. Reed
San Diego State University
Patricia Tenpenny
Loyola University, Chicago

Chapter 8
John Best
Eastern Illinois University
David Carroll
University of Wisconsin, Superior
Tom Pusateri
Loras College
Stephen K. Reed
San Diego State University

Chapter 9
Charles Davidshofer
Colorado State University
Shalynn Ford
Teikyo Marycrest University
Richrd J. Haier
University of California, Irvine
Timothy Rogers
University of Calgary
Dennis Saccuzzo
San Diego State University

Chapter 10
Robert Franken
University of Calgary
Russell G. Geen
University of Missouri
Douglas Mook
University of Virginia
D. Louis Wood
University of Arkansas, Little Rock

Chapter 11
Ruth L. Ault
Davidson College
John C. Cavanaugh
University of Delaware
Claire Etaugh
Bradley University
Doug Friedrich
University of West Florida
Barbara Hansen Lemme
College of DuPage

Chapter 12
Susan Cloninger
Russel Sage College
Caroline Collins
University of Victoria
Howard S. Friedman
University of California, Riverside
Christopher F. Monte
Manhattanville College
Ken Olson
Fort Hays State University

Chapter 13
Jerry M. Burger
Santa Clara University
Stephen L. Franzoi
Marquette University
Donelson R. Forsyth
Virginia Commonwealth University
Cheryl Kaiser
Michigan State University

Chapter 14
Robin M. DiMatteo
University of California, Riverside
Jess Feist
McNeese State University
Regan A. R. Gurung
University of Wisconsin, Green Bay
Chris Kleinke
University of Alaska, Anchorage

Chapter 15
David A. F. Haaga
American University
Richard Halgin
University of Massachusetts, Amherst
Chris L. Kleinke
University of Alaska, Anchorage
Elliot A. Weiner
Pacific University

Chapter 16
Gerald Corey
California State University, Fullerton
Herbert Goldenberg
California State University, Los Angeles
Jane S. Halonen
Alverno College
Thomas G. Plante
Santa Clara University

Reviewers

Lyn Y. Abramson
University of Wisconsin
Bill Adler
Collin County Community College
James R. M. Alexander
University of Tasmania
Gordon A. Allen
Miami University of Ohio
Elise L. Amel
University of St. Thomas
Ruth L. Ault
Davidson College
Jeff D. Baker
Southeastern Louisiana University
Mark Basham
Regis University
Gina J. Bates
Southern Arkansas University
Scott C. Bates
Utah State University
Derryl K. Beale
Cerritos Community College
Holly Beard
Midlands Technical College
Ashleah Bectal
U.S. Military Academy
Robert P. Beitz
Pima County Community College
Daniel R. Bellack
Trident Technical College
Stephen Blessing
University of Tampa
Robert Bornstein
Miami University
Bette L. Bottoms
University of Illinois, Chicago
Lyn Boulter
Catawba College
Amy Badura Brack
Creighton University
Nicole Bragg
Mount Hood Community College
Allen Branum
South Dakota State University
Robert G. Bringle
Indiana University–Purdue University Indianapolis
Michael Brislawn
Bellevue Community College
David R. Brodbeck
Sir Wilfred Grenfall College, Memorial University of Newfoundland
Dan W. Brunworth
Kishwaukee College
David M. Buss
University of Texas, Austin
James Butler
James Madison University
Mary M. Cail
University of Virginia
James F. Calhoun
University of Georgia
William Calhoun
University of Tennessee
Cari B. Cannon
Santiago Canyon College
Janet L. Chapman
U.S. Military Academy
Kevin Chun
University of San Francisco
Michael Clayton
Youngstown State University
Francis B. Colavita
University of Pittsburgh
Thomas B. Collins
Mankato State University
Stan Coren
University of British Columbia
Verne C. Cox
University of Texas at Arlington
Kenneth Cramer
University of Windsor
Dianne Crisp
Kwantlen University College
Norman Culbertson
Yakima Valley College
Betty M. Davenport
Campbell University
Stephen F. Davis
Emporia State University
Kenneth Deffenbacher
University of Nebraska
Kathy Denton
Douglas College
Marcus Dickson
Wayne State University
Deanna L. Dodson
Lebanon Valley College
Roger Dominowski
University of Illinois, Chicago
Dale V. Doty
Monroe Community College
Robert J. Douglas
University of Washington
Jim Duffy
Sir Wilfred Grenfall College, Memorial University of Newfoundland
James Eison
Southeast Missouri State University
Pamela G. Ely
St. Andrews Presbyterian College
M. Jeffrey Farrar
University of Florida
Donald Fields
University of New Brunswick
Alison Finstad
University of North Dakota
Thomas P. Fitzpatrick
Rockland Community College
Karen E. Ford
Mesa State College
Donelson R. Forsyth
Virginia Commonwealth University
Leslie D. Frazier
Florida International University
William J. Froming
University of Florida
Mary Ellen Fromuth
Middle Tennessee State University
Dean E. Frost
Portland State University
Nancy Frye
Long Island University
Judy Gentry
Columbus State Community College
Doba Goodman
York University
Jeffrey D. Green
Soka University
Richard Griggs
University of Florida
Arthur Gutman
Florida Institute of Technology
Jane S. Halonen
Alverno College
Roger Harnish
Rochester Institute of Technology
Philip L. Hartley
Chaffey College
Brad M. Hastings
Mount Aloysius College
Glenn R. Hawkes
Virginia Commonwealth University
Myra D. Heinrich
Mesa State College
George Hertl
Northwest Mississippi Community College
Lyllian B. Hix
Houston Community College
Mark A. Hopper
Loras College
John P. Hostetler
Albion College
Bruce Hunsberger
Wilfrid Laurier University
Mir Rabiul Islam
Charles Sturt University
Heide Island
University of Montana
Robert A. Johnston
College of William and Mary
Robert Kaleta
University of Wisconsin, Milwaukee
Jagdeep Kaur-Bala
University of Oregon
Alan R. King
University of North Dakota
Melvyn B. King
State University of New York, Cortland
James Knight
Humboldt State University
Mike Knight
Central State University
Ronald Kopcho
Mercer Community College
Barry J. Krikstone
Saint Michael's College

Jerry N. Lackey
Stephen F. Austin State University
Robin L. Lashley
Kent State University, Tuscarawas
Peter Leppman
University of Guelph
Charles F. Levinthal
Hofstra University
Wolfgang Linden
University of British Columbia
John Lindsay
Georgia College & State University
Evan Loehle-Conger
Madison Area Technical College
Diane Martichuski
University of Colorado, Boulder
Donald McBurney
University of Pittsburgh
Siobhan McEnaney-Hayes
Chestnut Hill College
Kathleen McCormick
Ocean County College
David G. McDonald
University of Missouri
Ronald K. McLaughlin
Juniata College
Sean P. Meegan
University of Utah
Steven E. Meier
University of Idaho
Sheryll Mennicke
University of Minnesota
Mitchell Metzger
Pennsylvania State University, Shenango

Richard Miller
Western Kentucky University
Mary Morris
Northern Territory University
Dan Mossler
Hampden-Sydney College
Darwin Muir
Queen's University at Kingston
Eric S. Murphy
University of Alaska, Anchorage
James M. Murphy
Indiana University–Purdue University Indianapolis
Michael Murphy
Henderson State University
Carnot E. Nelson
University of South Florida
John Nezlek
College of William and Mary
Rachel Nitzberg
University of California, Davis
David L. Novak
Lansing Community College
Richard Page
Wright State University
Joseph J. Palladino
University of Southern Indiana
John N. Park
Mankato State University
Phil Pegg
Western Kentucky University
Gayle Pitman
Sacramento City College
Bobby J. Poe
Belleville Area College
Gary Poole
Simon Fraser University

Michael Poulin
State University of New York–Buffalo
Russell Powell
Grant MacEwan College
Tracy Powell
Western Oregon University
Maureen K. Powers
Vanderbilt University
Janet Proctor
Purdue University
Frank. J. Provenzano
Greenville Technical College
Robin Raygor
Anoka-Ramsey Community College
Celia Reaves
Monroe Community College
Gary T. Reker
Trent University
Daniel W. Richards
Houston Community College
Kenneth M. Rosenberg
State University of New York, Oswego
Patricia Ross
Laurentian University
Angela Sadowski
Chaffey College
Sabato D. Sagaria
Capital University
Roger Sambrook
University of Colorado, Colorado Springs
Fred Shima
California State University Dominguez Hills

Susan A. Shodahl
San Bernardino Valley College
Steven M. Smith
Texas A & M University
Paul Stager
York University
Susan Snycerski
San Jose State University
Steven St. John
Rollins College
Marjorie Taylor
University of Oregon
Frank R. Terrant, Jr.
Appalachian State University
Donald Tyrrell
Franklin and Marshall College
Robin Valeri
St. Bonaventure University
Frank J. Vattano
Colorado State University
Wayne Viney
Colorado State University
Paul Wellman
Texas A & M University
Keith D. White
University of Florida
Randall D. Wight
Ouachita Baptist University
Daniel E. Wivagg
Baylor University
D. Louis Wood
University of Arkansas, Little Rock
John W. Wright
Washington State University
Cecilia Yoder
Oklahoma City Community College

Brief Contents

1

© Richard Bryant/Arcaid/Corbis

The Evolution of Psychology

2

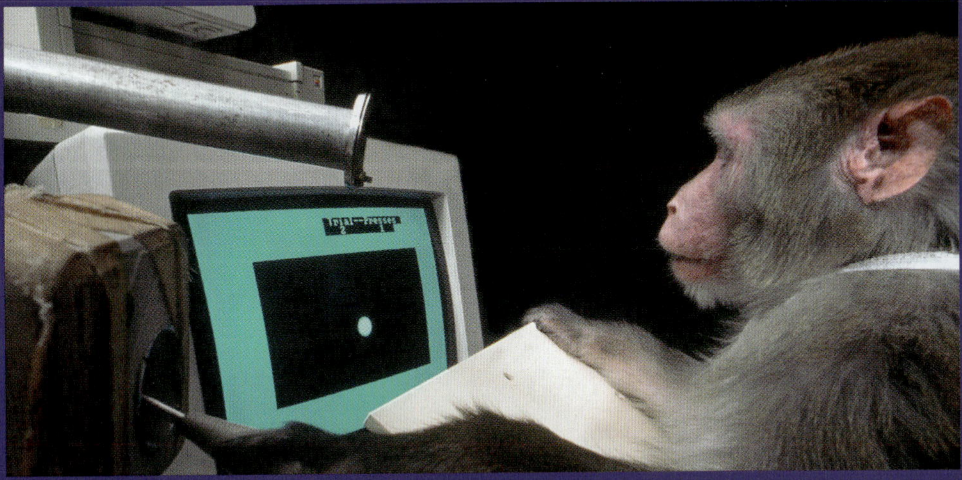

© Explorer / PhotoResearchers, Inc.

The Research Enterprise in Psychology

3

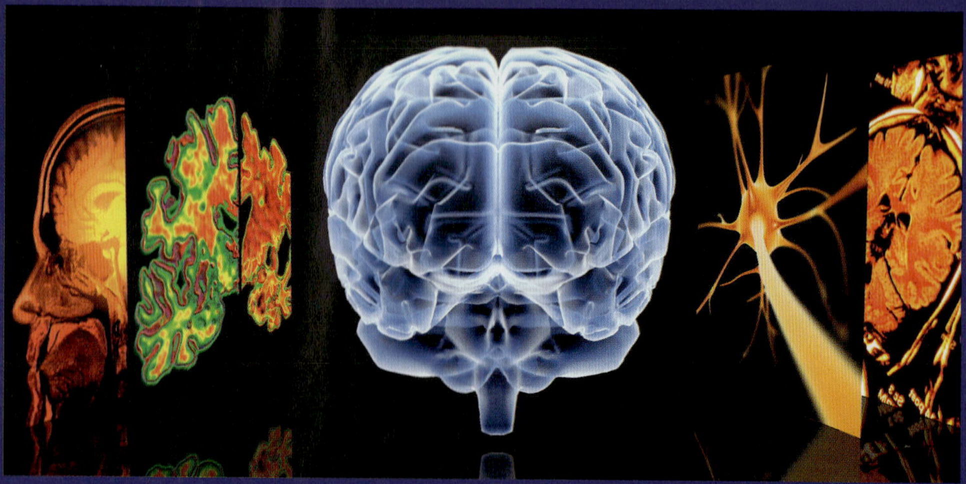
© Pasieka/SPL/Photo Researchers, Inc. PRinc_E07819 special number

The Biological Bases of Behavior

4

© Ocean/Corbis

Sensation and Perception

7

© Frank Chmura/Alamy

Human Memory

8

© Corbis/Age fotostock

Language and Thought

9

© Curtis Johnson/Getty Images

Intelligence and Psychological Testing

10

© Buzz Pictures/Alamy

Motivation and Emotion

11

© Masterfile RF

Human Development Across the Life Span

12

© Blue Jean Images/Alamy RF

Personality

13

© LUKE MACGREGOR/Reuters/Landov

Social Behavior

14

Stress, Coping, and Health

1

The Evolution of Psychology

© Richard Bryant/Arcaid/Corbis

What is psychology, and why is it worth your time to study? Let me approach these questions by sharing a couple of stories with you.

In 2005, Greg Hogan, a college sophomore, briefly achieved national notoriety when he was arrested for a crime. Greg wasn't anybody's idea of a likely criminal. He was the son of a Baptist minister and the president of his class. He played the cello in the university orchestra. He even worked part-time in the chaplain's office. So it shocked everybody who knew Greg when police arrested him at his fraternity house for bank robbery.

Earlier that day, Greg had faked having a gun and made away with over $2800 from a local bank. His reason? Over a period of months he had lost $5000 playing poker on the Internet. His lawyer said Greg's gambling habit had become "an addiction" (Dissell, 2005; McLoughlin & Paquet, 2005).

Greg eventually entered a clinic for treatment of his gambling problem. In a way, he was lucky—at least he got help. Moshe Pergament, a 19-year-old community college student in Long Island, New York, wasn't so fortunate. Moshe was shot to death after brandishing a gun at a police officer. The gun turned out to be plastic. On the front seat of his car was a note that began, "Officer, it was a plan. I'm sorry to get you involved. I just needed to die." Moshe had just lost $6000 betting on the World Series. His death was what people in law enforcement call "suicide by cop" (Lindsay & Lester, 2004).

These stories are at the extreme edge of a trend that concerns many public officials and mental health professionals: The popularity of gambling—from lotteries to sports betting to online poker—is booming, especially among the young (Jacobs, 2004). College students seem to be leading the way. To some observers, gambling on college campuses has become an "epidemic." Student bookies on some campuses make tens of thousands of dollars a year taking sports bets from other students. Television shows like *The World Series of Poker* are marketed squarely at college-student audiences. Poker sites on

***Paradox:** Psychology has a long past, but a short history.*

the web invite students to win their tuition by gambling online.

For most people, gambling is a relatively harmless—if sometimes expensive—pastime. However, estimates suggest that 5%–6% of teens and young adults develop serious problems with gambling—two to four times the rate for older adults (Jacobs, 2004; Petry, 2005; Winters et al., 2004). The enormous growth of pathological gambling among young people raises a host of questions. Is gambling dangerous? Can it really be addictive? What is an addiction, anyway? If pathological gamblers abuse drugs or commit crimes, is gambling the cause of their troubles, or is it a symptom of a deeper problem? Perhaps most critically of all, why do some people become pathological gamblers while the great majority do not? Every day millions of people in the United States play the lottery, bet on sports, or visit casinos without apparent harm. Yet others can't seem to stop gambling until they have lost everything—their savings, their jobs, their homes, and their self-respect. Why? What causes such perplexing, self-destructive behavior?

© Sashkin/Shutterstock

Psychology is about questions like these. More generally, psychology is about understanding *all* the things we do. All of us wonder sometimes about the reasons underlying people's behavior—why it's hard to diet, why we procrastinate about studying, why we fall in love with one person rather than another. We wonder why some people are outgoing while others are shy. We wonder why we sometimes do things that we know will bring us pain and anguish, whether it's clinging to a destructive relationship or losing our tuition money in a game of Texas Hold 'Em. The study of psychology is about all these things, and infinitely more.

Many of psychology's questions have implications for our everyday lives. For me, this is one of the field's major attractions—*psychology is practical.* Consider the case of gambling. Pathological gamblers suffer all kinds of misery, yet they can't seem to stop. Listen to the anguish of a gambler named Steve: "Over the past 2 years I have lost literally thousands . . . I have attempted to give up time after time, but failed every time. . . . I have debts around my neck which are destroying mine and my family's life. . . . I just want a massive light to be turned on with a message saying, 'This way to your old life, Steve'" (SJB, 2006).

What is the best way to help someone like Steve? Should he join a group like Gamblers Anonymous? Does counseling work? Are there drugs that can help? By probing the why's and how's of human behavior, psychology can help us find answers to pressing questions like these, as well as issues that affect each of us every day. You will see the practical side of psychology throughout this book, especially in the Personal Applications at the ends of chapters. These Applications focus on everyday problems, such as coping more effectively with stress, improving self-control, and dealing with sleep difficulties.

Beyond its practical value, psychology is worth studying because it provides a powerful *way of thinking.* All of us make judgments every day about why people do the things they do. For example, we might think that pathological gamblers are weak willed, or irrational, or just too dumb to understand that the odds are stacked against them. Or we might believe they are in the grip of an addiction that simply overpowers them. How do we decide which of these judgments—if any—are right?

Psychologists are committed to investigating questions about human behavior in a scientific way. This means that they seek to formulate precise questions about behavior and then test possible answers through systematic observation. This commitment to testing ideas means that psychology provides a means of building knowledge that is relatively accurate and dependable. It also provides a basis for assessing the assertions we hear every day about behavior, from friends and family, as well as in the popular media. Although most people probably don't think about it much, psychology is in the news all the time—in newspapers and magazines, on TV, radio, and the Internet. Unfortunately, this coverage is often distorted or grossly oversimplified, so that misinformation is commonplace. Thus, many "truisms" about behavior come to be widely believed when they really are misconceptions or myths. A small sampling of some popular myths related to psychology are shown in **Table 1.1**. This list of common misconceptions comes from an excellent book titled *50 Great Myths of Popular Psychology* (Lilienfeld et al., 2010). In the pages to come we'll touch on a number of misconceptions about psychology and provide more accurate, science-based information on these matters. For example, in Chapter 3 you will learn that the idea that people use only 10% of their brains is utter nonsense. Recent research suggests that the best way to dispel students' misconceptions is to confront them head on and provide a direct refutation (Kowalski & Taylor, 2009). Hence, throughout this book you will find a feature called Reality Checks that will highlight common fallacies and counter them with

Table 1.1 Popular Myths Related to Psychology

Myth	Relevant Chapter
Most people use only 10% of their brain power.	Chapter 3
Playing Mozart's music to infants boosts their intelligence.	Chapter 3
Subliminal messages can persuade people to purchase products.	Chapter 4
Hypnosis is a unique "trance" state that differs in kind from wakefulness.	Chapter 5
Hypnosis is useful for retrieving memories of forgotten events.	Chapter 7
The polygraph ("lie detector") test is an accurate means of detecting dishonesty.	Chapter 10
Opposites attract: We are most romantically attracted to people who differ from us.	Chapter 13
People with schizophrenia have multiple personalities.	Chapter 15
A large portion of criminals successfully use the insanity defense.	Chapter 15

SOURCE: Based on Lilienfeld, S. O., Lynn, S. J., Ruscio, J., & Beyerstein, B. L. (2010). *50 great myths of popular psychology: Shattering widespread misconceptions about human behavior.* Malden, MA: Wiley-Blackwell.

more accurate, realistic information. The Reality Check features will be found adjacent to relevant material.

As you go through this course, I hope you'll come to share my enthusiasm for psychology as a fascinating and immensely practical field of study. Let's begin our exploration by seeing how psychology has evolved from early speculations about behavior to a modern science. By looking at this evolution, you'll better understand psychology as it is today, a sprawling, multifaceted science and profession. We'll conclude our introduction with a look at seven unifying themes that will serve as connecting threads in the chapters to come. The chapter's Personal Application will review research that provides insights into how to be an effective student. Finally, the Critical Thinking Application will discuss how critical thinking skills can be enhanced.

Psychology's Early History

KEY LEARNING GOALS

1.1 Summarize Wundt's and Hall's accomplishments and contributions to psychology.

1.2 Describe the chief tenets of structuralism and functionalism and their impact on the development of psychology.

1.3 Articulate Freud's principal ideas and why they inspired controversy.

1.4 Trace the development of behaviorism and assess Watson's impact on the evolution of psychology.

1.5 Summarize Skinner's key insights and explain the emergence of humanism and its philosophy.

Psychology's story is one of people groping toward a better understanding of themselves. As psychology has evolved, its focus, methods, and explanatory models have changed. In this section we'll look at psychology's early years, as the discipline developed from philosophical speculations about the mind into a research-based science.

The term *psychology* comes from two Greek words, *psyche*, meaning the soul, and *logos*, referring to the study of a subject. These two Greek roots were first put together to define a topic of study in the 16th century, when *psyche* was used to refer to the soul, spirit, or mind, as distinguished from the body (Boring, 1966). Not until the early 18th century did the term *psychology* gain more than rare usage among scholars. By that time it had acquired its literal meaning, "the study of the mind."

Of course, psychology has a long past in that people have always wondered about the mysteries of the mind. In a way, psychology is as old as the human race. But it has a relatively short history, as psychology started to emerge as a scientific discipline only about 140 years ago.

A New Science Is Born: The Contributions of Wundt and Hall

PSYKTREK 1a

Psychology's intellectual parents were the disciplines of *philosophy* and *physiology*. By the 1870s a small number of scholars in both fields were actively exploring questions about the mind. How are bodily sensations turned into a mental awareness of the outside world? Are people's perceptions of the world accurate reflections of reality? How do mind and body interact? The philosophers and physiologists who were interested in the mind viewed such

© Cengage Learning 2013

Wilhelm Wundt
1832–1920

"Physiology informs us about those life phenomena that we perceive by our external senses. In psychology, the person looks upon himself as from within and tries to explain the interrelations of those processes that this internal observation discloses."

questions as fascinating issues *within* their respective fields. It was a German professor, Wilhelm Wundt (1832–1920), who eventually changed this view. Wundt mounted a campaign to make psychology an independent discipline rather than a stepchild of philosophy or physiology.

The time and place were right for Wundt's appeal. German universities were in a healthy period of expansion. Resources were available for new disciplines. Furthermore, the intellectual climate favored the scientific approach that Wundt advocated. Hence, his proposals were well received by the academic community. In 1879 Wundt succeeded in establishing the first formal laboratory for research in psychology at the University of Leipzig. In deference to this landmark event, historians have christened 1879 as psychology's "date of birth." Soon afterward, in 1881, Wundt established the first journal devoted to publishing research on psychology. All in all, Wundt's campaign was so successful that today he is widely characterized as the founder of psychology.

Wundt's conception of psychology was influential for decades. Borrowing from his training in physiology, Wundt (1874) declared that the new psychology should be a *science* modeled after fields such as physics and chemistry. What was the subject matter of the new science? According to Wundt, psychology's primary focus was *consciousness*—the awareness of immediate experience. *Thus, psychology became the scientific study of conscious experience.* This orientation kept psychology focused on the mind and mental processes. But it demanded that the methods psychologists used to investigate the mind be as scientific as those of chemists or physicists.

Wundt was a tireless, dedicated scholar who generated an estimated 54,000 pages of books and articles in his career (Bringmann & Balk, 1992). Studies in his lab focused on attention, memory, sensory processes, and reaction-time experiments that provided estimates of the duration of various mental processes (Fuchs & Milar, 2003). Outstanding young scholars, including many Americans, came to Leipzig to study under Wundt. Many of his students then fanned out across Germany and America, establishing the research laboratories that formed the basis for the new, independent science of psychology. Indeed, it was in North America that Wundt's new science grew by leaps and bounds. Between 1883 and 1893, some 23 new psychological research labs sprang up in the United States and Canada, at the schools shown in **Figure 1.1** (Benjamin, 2000). Many of the labs were started by Wundt's students, or by his students' students.

G. Stanley Hall (1846–1924), who studied briefly with Wundt, was a particularly important contributor to the rapid growth of psychology in America. Toward the end of the 19th century, Hall reeled off a series of "firsts" for American psychology. To begin with, he established America's first research laboratory in psychology at Johns Hopkins University in 1883. Four years later he launched America's first psychology journal. Furthermore, in 1892 he was

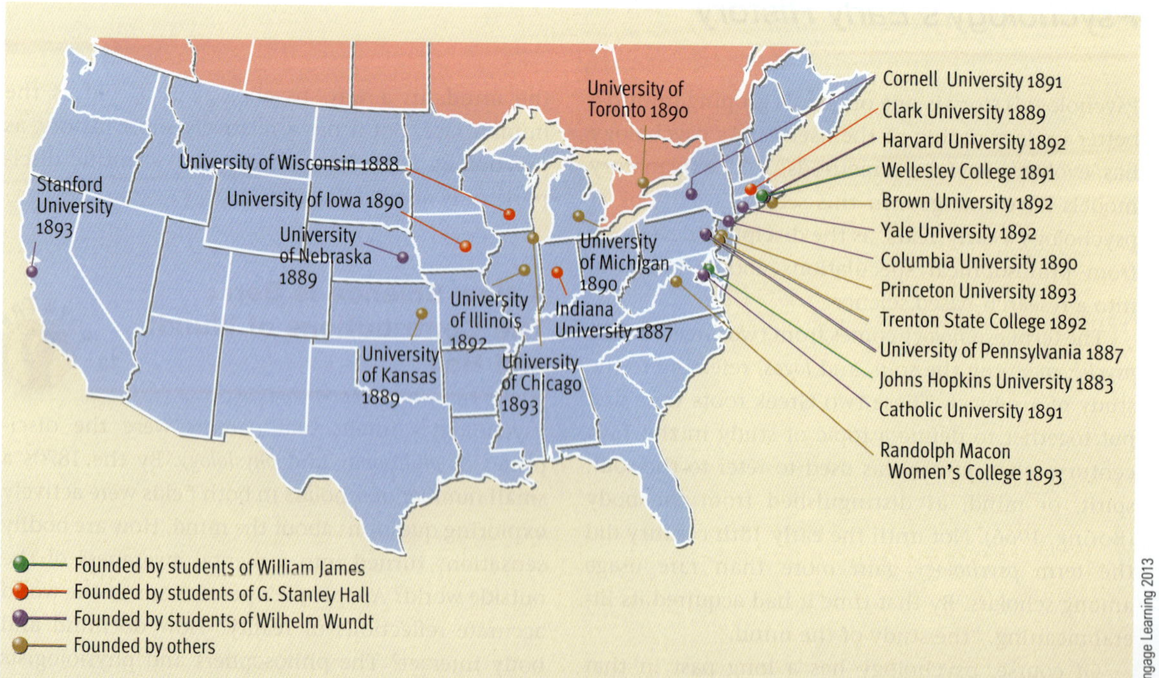

© Cengage Learning 2013

Figure 1.1
Early research laboratories in North America. This map highlights the location and year of founding for the first 23 psychological research labs established in North American colleges and universities. As the color coding shows, a great many of these labs were founded by the students of Wilhelm Wundt, G. Stanley Hall, and William James. (Based on Benjamin, 2000)

the driving force behind the establishment of the American Psychological Association (APA) and was elected its first president. Today the APA is the world's largest organization devoted to the advancement of psychology. It has over 150,000 members and affiliates. Hall never envisioned such a vast membership when he and 26 others set up their new organization.

The Battle of the "Schools" Begins: Structuralism Versus Functionalism

PSYKTREK 1a

While reading about how psychology became a science, you might have imagined that psychologists became a unified group of scholars who busily added new discoveries to an uncontested store of "facts." In reality, no science works that way. Competing schools of thought exist in most scientific disciplines. Sometimes the disagreements among these schools are sharp. Such diversity in thought is natural and often stimulates enlightening debate. In psychology, the first two major schools of thought, *structuralism* and *functionalism,* were entangled in the field's first great intellectual battle.

Structuralism emerged through the leadership of Edward Titchener, an Englishman who emigrated to the United States in 1892. He taught for decades at Cornell University. Titchener earned his degree in Wundt's Leipzig laboratory and expressed great admiration for Wundt's work. However, he brought his own version of Wundt's psychology to America (Hilgard, 1987; Thorne & Henley, 1997). ***Structuralism*** **was based on the notion that the task of psychology is to analyze consciousness into its basic elements and investigate how these elements are related.** Just as physicists were studying how matter is made up of basic particles, the structuralists wanted to identify and examine the fundamental components of conscious experience, such as sensations, feelings, and images.

Although the structuralists explored many questions, most of their work concerned sensation and perception in vision, hearing, and touch. To examine the contents of consciousness, the structuralists depended on the method of ***introspection,*** **or the careful, systematic self-observation of one's own conscious experience.** As practiced by the structuralists, introspection required training to make the *subject*—the person being studied—more objective and more aware. Once trained, participants were typically exposed to auditory tones, optical illusions, and visual stimuli under carefully controlled and systematically varied conditions and were asked to analyze what they experienced.

Archives of the History of American Psychology, University of Akron, Akron, Ohio.

The establishment of the first research laboratory in psychology by Wilhelm Wundt (far right) marked the birth of psychology as a modern science.

The functionalists took a different view of psychology's task. ***Functionalism*** **was based on the belief that psychology should investigate the function or purpose of consciousness, rather than its structure.** The chief impetus for the emergence of functionalism was the work of William James (1842–1910), a brilliant American scholar (and brother of novelist Henry James). James's formal training was in medicine. However, he did not find medicine to be intellectually challenging. He also felt he was too sickly to pursue a medical practice (Ross, 1991). So, when an opportunity arose in 1872, he joined the faculty of Harvard University to pursue a less arduous career in academia. Medicine's loss proved to be psychology's gain, as James quickly became an intellectual giant in the field. James's landmark book, *Principles of Psychology* (1890), became standard reading for generations of psychologists. It is perhaps the most influential text in the history of psychology (Weiten & Wight, 1992).

James's thinking illustrates how psychology, like any field, is deeply embedded in a network of cultural and intellectual influences. James had been impressed with Charles Darwin's (1859, 1871) concept of *natural selection*. According to the principle of ***natural selection,*** **heritable characteristics that provide a survival or reproductive advantage are more likely than alternative characteristics to be passed on to subsequent generations and thus come to be "selected" over time.** This cornerstone notion of Darwin's evolutionary theory suggested that the typical characteristics of a species must

© Cengage Learning 2013

William James 1842–1910

"It is just this free water of consciousness that psychologists resolutely overlook."

serve some purpose. Applying this idea to humans, James (1890) noted that consciousness obviously is an important characteristic of our species. Hence, he contended that psychology should investigate the *functions* rather than the *structure* of consciousness.

James also argued that the structuralists' approach missed the real nature of conscious experience. Consciousness, he argued, consists of a continuous *flow* of thoughts. In analyzing consciousness into its *elements,* the structuralists were looking at static points in that flow. James wanted to understand the flow itself, which he called the *stream of consciousness*. Today, people take this metaphorical description of mental life for granted, but at the time it was a revolutionary insight. As Leary (2003) put it, "No longer was consciousness depicted as some kind of encompassing mental container more or less full of such 'contents' as sensations, images, ideas, thoughts, feelings, and the like; rather it was now portrayed as a continually ongoing, wholistic experience or process" (p. 25). James went on to provide enormously influential analyses of many crucial issues in the emerging field of psychology. Among other things, his discussions of how people acquired *habits* laid the groundwork for progress in the study of learning, and his conception of the *self* provided the foundation for subsequent theories of personality (Leary, 2003).

Whereas structuralists naturally gravitated to the research lab, functionalists were more interested in how people adapt their behavior to the demands of the real world around them. This practical slant led them to introduce new subjects into psychology. Instead of focusing on sensation and perception, functionalists such as James McKeen Cattell and John Dewey began to investigate mental testing, patterns of development in children, the effectiveness of educational practices, and behavioral differences between the sexes. These new topics may have played a role in attracting the first women into the field of psychology (see **Figure 1.2**).

The impassioned advocates of structuralism and functionalism saw themselves as fighting for high stakes: the definition and future direction of the

Figure 1.2

Women pioneers in the history of psychology. Women have long made major contributions to the development of psychology (Milar, 2000; Russo & Denmark, 1987), and today nearly half of all psychologists are female. As in other fields, however, women have often been overlooked in histories of psychology (Furumoto & Scarborough, 1986). The three psychologists profiled here demonstrate that women have been making significant contributions to psychology almost from its beginning—despite formidable barriers to pursuing their academic careers.

Photos courtesy of the Archives of the History of American Psychology, University of Akron, Akron, Ohio.

Mary Whiton Calkins (1863–1930)

Mary Calkins, who studied under William James, founded one of the first dozen psychology laboratories in America at Wellesley College in 1891, invented a widely used technique for studying memory, and became the first woman to serve as president of the American Psychological Association in 1905. Ironically, however, she never received her Ph.D. in psychology. Because she was a woman, Harvard University only reluctantly allowed her to take graduate classes as a "guest student." When she completed the requirements for her Ph.D., Harvard would only offer her a doctorate from its undergraduate sister school, Radcliffe. Calkins felt that this decision perpetuated unequal treatment of the sexes, so she refused the Radcliffe degree.

Margaret Floy Washburn (1871–1939)

Margaret Washburn was the first woman to receive a Ph.D. in psychology. She wrote an influential book, *The Animal Mind* (1908), which served as an impetus to the subsequent emergence of behaviorism and was standard reading for several generations of psychologists. In 1921 she became the second woman to serve as president of the American Psychological Association. Washburn studied under James McKeen Cattell at Columbia University, but like Mary Calkins, she was only permitted to take graduate classes unofficially, as a "hearer." Hence, she transferred to Cornell University, which was more hospitable toward women, and completed her doctorate in 1894. Like Calkins, Washburn spent most of her career at a college for women (Vassar).

Leta Stetter Hollingworth (1886–1939)

Leta Hollingworth did pioneering work on adolescent development, mental retardation, and gifted children. Indeed, she was the first person to use the term *gifted* to refer to youngsters who scored exceptionally high on intelligence tests. Hollingworth (1914, 1916) also played a major role in debunking popular theories of her era that purported to explain why women were "inferior" to men. For instance, she conducted a study refuting the myth that phases of the menstrual cycle are reliably associated with performance decrements in women. Her careful collection of objective data on gender differences forced other scientists to subject popular, untested beliefs about the sexes to skeptical, empirical inquiry.

new science of psychology. Their war of ideas continued energetically for many years. Who won? Most historians give the edge to functionalism. Both schools of thought gradually faded away. However, functionalism fostered the development of two important descendants: behaviorism and applied psychology (Green, 2009). We will discuss both momentarily.

Freud Brings the Unconscious into the Picture

PSYKTREK 1a, 10a

Sigmund Freud (1856–1939) was an Austrian physician. Early in his career he dreamed of achieving fame by making an important discovery. His determination was such that in medical school he dissected 400 male eels to prove for the first time that they had testes. His work with eels did not make him famous, but his subsequent work with people did. Indeed, his theories made him one of the most controversial intellectual figures of modern times.

Freud's (1900, 1924, 1933) approach to psychology grew out of his efforts to treat mental disorders. In his medical practice, Freud treated people troubled by psychological problems such as irrational fears, obsessions, and anxieties with an innovative procedure he called *psychoanalysis* (described in detail in Chapter 16). Decades of experience probing into his patients' lives provided much of the inspiration for Freud's theory. He also gathered material by looking inward and examining his own anxieties, conflicts, and desires.

His work with patients and his own self-exploration persuaded Freud of the existence of what he called the unconscious. According to Freud, **the *unconscious* contains thoughts, memories, and desires that are well below the surface of conscious awareness but that nonetheless exert great influence on behavior.** Freud based his concept of the unconscious on a variety of observations. For instance, he noticed that seemingly meaningless slips of the tongue (such as "I decided to take a summer school *curse*") often appeared to reveal a person's true feelings. He also noted that his patients' dreams often seemed to express important feelings they were unaware of. Knitting these and other observations together, Freud eventually concluded that psychological disturbances are largely caused by personal conflicts existing at an unconscious level. More generally, his ***psychoanalytic theory*** **attempts to explain personality, motivation, and mental disorders by focusing on unconscious determinants of behavior.**

Freud's concept of the unconscious was not entirely new, but he put it on the map for the general population and elaborated on it like never before (Lothane, 2006). It is important to emphasize that the concept of the unconscious was a major departure from the prevailing belief that people are fully aware of the forces affecting their behavior. In arguing that behavior is governed by unconscious forces, Freud made the disconcerting suggestion that people are not masters of their own minds. Other aspects of Freud's theory also stirred up debate. For instance, he proposed that behavior is greatly influenced by how people cope with their sexual urges. At a time when people were far less comfortable discussing sexual issues than they are today, even scientists were offended and scandalized by Freud's emphasis on sex. Small wonder, then, that Freud was soon engulfed in controversy.

In part because of its controversial nature, Freud's theory was slow to gain influence. However, he was a superb and prolific writer who campaigned vigorously for his psychoanalytic movement (Messer & McWilliams, 2003). As a result, his approach gradually won acceptance within medicine, attracting prominent followers such as Carl Jung and Alfred Adler. Important public recognition from psychology came in 1909, when G. Stanley Hall invited Freud to give a series of lectures at Clark University in Massachusetts (see the photo below).

By 1920 psychoanalytic theory was widely known around the world. However, it continued to meet with considerable resistance in psychology (Fancher, 2000). Most psychologists contemptuously viewed psychoanalytic theory as unscientific speculation that would eventually fade away (Hornstein, 1992). They turned out to be wrong. Psychoanalytic ideas steadily gained credence in the culture at large, influencing thought in medicine, the arts, and literature (Rieber, 1998). According to Hornstein (1992), by the 1940s, "Psychoanalysis was becoming so popular that it threatened

© Cengage Learning 2013

Sigmund Freud 1856–1939

"The unconscious is the true psychical reality; in its innermost nature it is as much unknown to us as the reality of the external world."

Courtesy of the Clark University Archives.

A portrait taken at the famous Clark University psychology conference, September 1909. Pictured are Freud, G. Stanley Hall, and four of Freud's students and associates. Seated, left to right: Freud, Hall, and Carl Jung; standing: Abraham Brill, Ernest Jones, and Sandor Ferenczi.

CONCEPT CHECK 1.1

Understanding the Implications of Major Theories: Wundt, James, and Freud

Check your understanding of the implications of some of the major theories reviewed in this chapter by indicating who is likely to have made each of the statements quoted below. Choose from the following theorists: (a) Wilhelm Wundt, (b) William James, and (c) Sigmund Freud. You'll find the answers in Appendix A in the back of the book.

_______ 1. "He that has eyes to see and ears to hear may convince himself that no mortal can keep a secret. If the lips are silent, he chatters with his fingertips; betrayal oozes out of him at every pore. And thus the task of making conscious the most hidden recesses of the mind is one which it is quite possible to accomplish."

_______ 2. "The book which I present to the public is an attempt to mark out a new domain of science. . . . The new discipline rests upon anatomical and physiological foundations. . . . The experimental treatment of psychological problems must be pronounced from every point of view to be in its first beginnings."

_______ 3. "Consciousness, then, does not appear to itself chopped up in bits. Such words as 'chain' or 'train' do not describe it fitly. . . . It is nothing jointed; it flows. A 'river' or 'stream' are the metaphors by which it is most naturally described."

to eclipse psychology entirely" (p. 258). Thus, the widespread popular acceptance of psychoanalytic theory essentially forced psychologists to apply their scientific methods to the topics Freud had studied: personality, motivation, and abnormal behavior. As they turned to these topics, many of them saw merit in some of Freud's notions (Rosenzweig, 1985). Psychoanalytic theory continued to generate heated debate, but it survived to become an influential theoretical perspective. Today, many psychoanalytic concepts have filtered into the mainstream of psychology (Luborsky & Barrett, 2006; Pincus, 2006; Westen, Gabbard, & Ortigo, 2008).

© Cengage Learning 2013

John B. Watson 1878–1958

"The time seems to have come when psychology must discard all references to consciousness."

Watson Alters Psychology's Course: Behaviorism Makes Its Debut

PSYKTREK 1a, 5b

One reason psychoanalysis struggled to gain acceptance within psychology was that it conflicted in many basic ways with the tenets of *behaviorism,* a new school of thought that gradually became dominant within psychology between 1913 and the late 1920s. Founded by John B. Watson (1878–1958), ***behaviorism* is a theoretical orientation based on the premise that scientific psychology should study only observable behavior.** It is important to understand what a radical change this definition represented. Watson (1913, 1919) proposed that psychologists *abandon the study of consciousness altogether* and focus exclusively on behaviors that they could observe directly. In essence, he was trying to redefine what scientific psychology should be about.

Why did Watson argue for such a fundamental shift in direction? Because to him, the power of the scientific method rested on the idea of *verifiability.* In principle, scientific claims can always be verified (or disproved) by anyone who is able and willing to make the required observations. However, this power depends on studying things that can be observed objectively. Otherwise, the advantage of using the scientific approach—replacing vague speculation and personal opinion with reliable, exact knowledge—is lost. In Watson's view, mental processes are not a proper subject for scientific study because they are ultimately private events. After all, no one can see or touch another's thoughts. Consequently, if psychology was to be a science, it would have to give up consciousness as its subject matter and become instead the *science of behavior.*

***Behavior* refers to any overt (observable) response or activity by an organism.** Watson asserted that psychologists could study anything that people do or say—shopping, playing chess, eating, complimenting a friend. However, according to Watson, they could *not* study scientifically the thoughts, wishes, and feelings that might accompany these observable behaviors. Obviously, psychology's shift away from the study of consciousness was incompatible with psychoanalytic theory. By the 1920s Watson had become an outspoken critic of Freud's views (Rilling, 2000). Proponents of behaviorism and psychoanalysis engaged in many heated theoretical debates in the ensuing decades.

Watson's radical reorientation of psychology did not end with his redefinition of its subject matter. He also staked out a rather extreme position on one of psychology's oldest and most fundamental questions: the issue of *nature versus nurture.* This age-old debate is concerned with whether behavior is determined mainly by genetic inheritance ("nature") or by environment and experience ("nurture"). To oversimplify, the question is this: Is a great concert pianist or a master criminal born, or made? Watson argued that each is made, not born. In other words, he downplayed the importance of heredity. He maintained that behavior is governed primarily by the environment. Indeed, he boldly claimed:

Give me a dozen healthy infants, well-formed, and my own special world to bring them up in and I'll guarantee to take any one at random and train him to become any type of specialist I might select—doctor, lawyer, artist, merchant-chief, and yes, even beggar-man and thief, regardless of his talents, penchants, tendencies, abilities, vocations and race of his ancestors. I am going beyond my facts and I admit it, but so have the advocates of the contrary and they have been doing it for many thousands of years. (1924, p. 82)

For obvious reasons, Watson's tongue-in-cheek challenge was never put to a test. Admittedly, this widely cited quote oversimplified Watson's views on the nature-nurture issue (Todd & Morris, 1992). Yet his writings contributed greatly to the strong environmental slant that became associated with behaviorism (Horowitz, 1992).

Influenced by Ivan Pavlov's discovery of the conditioned reflex (see Chapter 6), the behaviorists eventually came to view psychology's mission as an attempt to relate overt behaviors ("responses") to observable events in the environment ("stimuli"). Because the behaviorists investigated stimulus-response relationships, the behavioral approach is often referred to as *stimulus-response (S-R) psychology*.

Behaviorism's stimulus-response approach contributed to the rise of animal research in psychology. Having deleted consciousness from their scope of concern, behaviorists no longer needed to study human participants who could report on their mental processes. Many psychologists thought that animals would make better research subjects anyway. One key reason was that experimental research is often more productive if experimenters can exert considerable *control* over their subjects. Otherwise, too many complicating factors enter into the picture and contaminate the experiment. Obviously, a researcher can have much more control over a lab rat or pigeon than over a human participant. Thus, the discipline that had begun its life a few decades earlier as the study of the mind now found itself heavily involved in the study of simple responses made by laboratory animals.

Although Watson's views shaped the evolution of psychology for many decades, he ended up watching the field's progress from the sidelines. Because of a heavily publicized divorce scandal in 1920, Watson was forced to resign from Johns Hopkins University (Buckley, 1994). Bitterly disappointed, he left academia at the age of 42, never to return. Psychology's loss proved to be the business world's gain, as Watson went on to become an innovative, successful advertising executive (Brewer, 1991; Coon, 1994). The advertising industry was just emerging as a national force in the 1920s, and Watson quickly became one of its most prominent practitioners at the J. Walter Thompson agency. He pioneered fear appeals, testimonials, selling the "prestige" of products, and promotion of style over substance, all of which remain basic principles in modern marketing (Buckley, 1982). Moreover, "through an enormous output of books, magazine articles, and radio broadcasts he was able to establish himself as the public spokesman for the profession of psychology and an expert on subjects ranging from childrearing to economics. In effect, Watson became the first 'pop' psychologist" (Buckley, 1982, p. 217). So, ironically, Watson became the public face of the discipline that had banished him from its mainstream.

© Cengage Learning 2013

Skinner Questions Free Will as Behaviorism Flourishes

PSYKTREK 1a, 10b

The advocates of behaviorism and psychoanalysis tangled frequently during the 1920s, 1930s, and 1940s. As psychoanalytic thought slowly gained a foothold within psychology, many psychologists softened their stance on the acceptability of studying internal mental events. However, this movement toward the consideration of internal states was vigorously opposed by B. F. Skinner (1904–1990), an American psychologist whose thinking was influenced by the work of Ivan Pavlov and John B. Watson (Dinsmoor, 2004; Moore, 2005).

Skinner (1953) championed a return to Watson's strict focus on observable behavior. Skinner did not deny the existence of internal mental events. However, he insisted that they could not be studied scientifically. Moreover, there was no need to study them. According to Skinner, if the stimulus of food is followed by the response of eating, we can fully describe what is happening without making any guesses about whether the animal is experiencing hunger. Like Watson, Skinner also emphasized how environmental factors mold behavior.

The fundamental principle of behavior documented by Skinner is deceptively simple: *Organisms tend to repeat responses that lead to positive outcomes, and they tend not to repeat responses that lead to neutral or negative outcomes*. Despite its simplicity, this principle turns out to be quite powerful. Working primarily with lab rats and pigeons trained in operant conditioning devices that came to be known as Skinner boxes, he showed that

© Cengage Learning 2013

B. F. Skinner
1904–1990

"I submit that what we call the behavior of the human organism is no more free than its digestion."

© Bruno Passigatti/Shutterstock

CONCEPT CHECK 1.2

Understanding the Implications of Major Theories: Watson, Skinner, and Rogers

Check your understanding of the implications of some of the major theories reviewed in this chapter by indicating who is likely to have made each of the statements quoted below. Choose from the following: (a) John B. Watson, (b) B. F. Skinner, and (c) Carl Rogers. You'll find the answers in Appendix A at the back of the book.

_______ **1.** "In the traditional view, a person is free. . . . He can therefore be held responsible for what he does and justly punished if he offends. That view, together with its associated practices, must be reexamined when a scientific analysis reveals unsuspected controlling relations between behavior and environment."

_______ **2.** "I do not have a Pollyanna view of human nature. . . . Yet one of the most refreshing and invigorating parts of my experience is to work with [my clients] and to discover the strongly positive directional tendencies which exist in them, as in all of us, at the deepest levels."

_______ **3.** "Our conclusion is that we have no real evidence of the inheritance of traits. I would feel perfectly confident in the ultimately favorable outcome of careful upbringing of a healthy, well-formed baby born of a long line of crooks, murderers and thieves, and prostitutes."

© Cengage Learning 2013

Carl Rogers 1902–1987

"It seems to me that at bottom each person is asking, 'Who am I, really? How can I get in touch with this real self, underlying all my surface behavior? How can I become myself?'"

(Davidson, 2000). The most prominent architects of the humanistic movement have been Carl Rogers (1902–1987) and Abraham Maslow (1908–1970). Rogers (1951) argued that human behavior is governed primarily by each individual's sense of self, or "self-concept"—which animals presumably lack. Both he and Maslow (1954) maintained that to fully understand people's behavior, psychologists must take into account the fundamental human drive toward personal growth. They asserted that people have a basic need to continue to evolve as human beings and to fulfill their potentials. In fact, the humanists argued that many psychological disturbances are the result of thwarting these uniquely human needs.

Fragmentation and dissent have reduced the influence of humanism in recent decades. Some advocates, though, have predicted a renaissance for the humanistic movement (Taylor, 1999). To date, the humanists' greatest contribution to psychology has probably been their innovative treatments for psychological problems and disorders. For example, Carl Rogers pioneered a new approach to psychotherapy—called *person-centered therapy*—that remains extremely influential today (Kirschenbaum & Jourdan, 2005).

REVIEW OF KEY LEARNING GOALS

1.1 Psychology became an independent discipline when Wilhelm Wundt established the first psychological research laboratory in 1879 at Leipzig, Germany. Wundt, who is widely characterized as the founder of psychology, viewed psychology as the scientific study of consciousness. The new discipline grew rapidly in North America in the late 19th century, as illustrated by G. Stanley Hall's career. Hall established America's first research lab in psychology and founded the American Psychological Association.

1.2 The structuralists, led by Edward Titchener, believed that psychology should use introspection to analyze consciousness into its basic elements. The functionalists, inspired by the ideas of William James, believed that psychology should focus on the purpose and adaptive functions of consciousness. Functionalism paved the way for behaviorism and applied psychology and had more of a lasting impact than structuralism.

1.3 Sigmund Freud was an Austrian physician who invented psychoanalysis. His psychoanalytic theory emphasized the unconscious determinants of behavior and the importance of sexuality. Freud's ideas were controversial, and they met with resistance in academic psychology. However, as more psychologists developed an interest in personality, motivation, and abnormal behavior, psychoanalytic concepts were incorporated into mainstream psychology.

1.4 Behaviorists, led by John B. Watson, argued that psychology should study only observable behavior. Thus, they campaigned to redefine psychology as the science of behavior. Emphasizing the importance of the environment over heredity, the behaviorists began to explore stimulus-response relationships, often using laboratory animals as subjects.

1.5 Working with laboratory rats and pigeons, American behaviorist B. F. Skinner demonstrated that organisms tend to repeat responses that lead to positive consequences and not to repeat responses that lead to neutral or negative consequences. Based on the belief that all behavior is fully governed by external stimuli, Skinner argued that free will is an illusion. Finding both behaviorism and psychoanalysis unsatisfactory, advocates of a new theoretical orientation called humanism became influential in the 1950s. Humanism, led by Abraham Maslow and Carl Rogers, emphasized the unique qualities of human behavior and humans' freedom and potential for personal growth.

Psychology's Modern History

KEY LEARNING GOALS

1.6 Discuss how historical events contributed to the emergence of psychology as a profession.

1.7 Describe two trends emerging in the 1950s–1960s that represented a return to psychology's intellectual roots.

1.8 Explain why Western psychology has shown an increased interest in cultural variables in recent decades.

1.9 Discuss the emergence and basic ideas of evolutionary psychology.

1.10 Explain the development and principal tenets of the positive psychology movement.

The principal storyline of psychology's early history was its gradual maturation into a research-based science. The seminal work of Wundt, Hall, James, Watson, Skinner, and a host of other pioneers served to establish psychology as a respected scientific discipline in the halls of academia. As you will learn momentarily, the principal storyline of psychology's modern history has been its remarkable growth into a multifaceted scientific and professional enterprise. In more recent decades psychology's story has been marked by expanding boundaries and broader interests.

Psychology Comes of Age as a Profession

PSYKTREK 1a

As you probably know, psychology is not all pure science. It has a highly practical side. Many psychologists provide a variety of professional services to the public. Their work falls within the domain of ***applied psychology*, the branch of psychology concerned with everyday, practical problems.** This branch of psychology, so prominent today, was actually slow to develop. A small number of early psychologists dabbled in various areas of applied psychology. However, it remained on the fringes of mainstream psychology until World War II (Benjamin et al., 2003). Not until the 1950s did psychology really start to come of age as a profession.

The first applied arm of psychology to achieve any prominence was *clinical psychology*. As practiced today, ***clinical psychology* is the branch of psychology concerned with the diagnosis and treatment of psychological problems and disorders.** In the early days, however, the emphasis was almost exclusively on psychological testing and adjustment problems in schoolchildren. Although the first psychological clinic was established as early as 1896, by 1937 only about one in five members of the American Psychological Association reported an interest in clinical psychology (Goldenberg, 1983). Clinicians were a small minority in a field devoted primarily to research.

That picture was about to change with dramatic swiftness. During World War II (1939–1945), many academic psychologists were pressed into service as clinicians. They were needed to screen military recruits and to treat soldiers suffering from trauma. Many of these psychologists (often to their surprise) found the clinical work to be challenging and rewarding, and a substantial portion continued to do clinical work after the war. More significant, some 40,000 American veterans returned to seek postwar treatment in Veterans Administration (VA) hospitals for their psychological scars. With the demand for clinicians far greater than the supply, the VA stepped in to finance many new training programs in clinical psychology. These programs, emphasizing training in the treatment of psychological disorders as well as psychological testing, proved attractive. Within a few years, about half the new Ph.D.'s in psychology were specializing in clinical psychology. Most went on to offer professional services to the public (Goldenberg, 1983). Assessing the impact of World War II, Routh and Reisman (2003) characterize it as "a watershed in the history of clinical psychology. In its aftermath, clinical psychology received something it had not received before: enormous institutional support" (p. 345). Thus, during the 1940s and 1950s the prewar orphan of applied/professional psychology started to mature into a robust, powerful adult.

In the academic world, many traditional research psychologists were alarmed by the professionalization of the field. They argued that the energy and resources previously devoted to research would be diluted. Because of conflicting priorities, tensions between the research and professional arms of psychology continued to grow. The American Psychological Association has worked diligently to represent both the scientific and professional branches of psychology. However, many researchers complained that the APA had come to be dominated by clinicians. In 1988 this rift stimulated some research psychologists to form a new organization, now called the Association for Psychological Science (APS). APS serves exclusively as an advocate for the science of psychology.

Despite the conflicts, the professionalization of psychology has continued at a steady pace. In fact, the trend has spread into additional areas of psychology. Today the broad umbrella of applied psychology covers a variety of professional specialties, including school psychology, industrial/organizational psychology, counseling psychology, and emerging new areas, such as forensic psychology (Benjamin & Baker, 2004). Whereas psychologists were once almost exclusively academics, the vast majority of today's psychologists devote some of their time to providing professional services.

Reality CHECK

Misconception

Psychologists have always been involved in the treatment of mental illness.

Reality

In the first six decades of its existence as an independent discipline, psychology had virtually no role in the diagnosis and treatment of mental illness, which was thoroughly dominated by psychiatry. Psychologists were mostly academics and researchers. It was only during World War II and its aftermath that psychology was drawn into the field of mental health.

Psychology Returns to Its Roots: Renewed Interest in Cognition and Physiology

PsykTrek 1a

While applied psychology started to blossom in the 1950s, research in psychology continued to evolve. Ironically, two trends that emerged in the 1950s and picked up momentum in 1960s represented a return to psychology's roots in the 19th century, when psychologists were principally interested in consciousness and physiology. Since the 1950s and 1960s, psychologists have shown a renewed interest in consciousness (now called "cognition") and the physiological bases of behavior.

***Cognition* refers to the mental processes involved in acquiring knowledge.** In other words, cognition involves thinking or conscious experience. For many decades, the dominance of behaviorism discouraged the investigation of "unobservable" mental processes (Mandler, 2002). During the 1950s and 1960s, however, research on cognition slowly began to emerge (Miller, 2003). The research of Swiss psychologist Jean Piaget (1954) focused increased attention on the study of children's cognitive development, while the work of Noam Chomsky (1957) elicited new interest in the psychological underpinnings of language. Around the same time, Herbert Simon and his colleagues (Newell, Shaw, & Simon, 1958) began influential, groundbreaking research on problem solving that eventually led to a Nobel prize for Simon (in 1978). These advances sparked a surge of interest in cognitive processes.

Since then, cognitive theorists have argued that psychology must include the study of internal mental events to fully understand behavior (Gardner, 1985; Neisser, 1967). Advocates of the *cognitive perspective* point out that the ways people think about events surely influence how they behave. Consequently, focusing exclusively on overt behavior yields an incomplete picture of why individuals behave as they do. Equally important, psychologists investigating decision making, reasoning, and problem solving have shown that methods *can* be devised to study cognitive processes scientifically. The methods are different from those used in psychology's early days. Yet, modern research on the inner workings of the mind has put the *psyche* back in psychology. In fact, many observers maintain that the cognitive perspective has become the dominant one in contemporary psychology. Some interesting data support this assertion, as shown in **Figure 1.4**, which plots estimates of the research productivity of four theoretical perspectives since 1950. As you can see, since 1975 the cognitive perspective has generated more published articles than any other (Spear, 2007).

The 1950s and 1960s also saw many important discoveries that highlighted the interrelations among mind, body, and behavior (Thompson & Zola, 2003). For example, James Olds (1956) showed that electrical stimulation of the brain could evoke emotional responses such as pleasure and rage in animals. Other work, which eventually earned a Nobel prize for Roger Sperry (in 1981), showed that the right and left halves of the brain are specialized to handle different types of mental tasks (Gazzaniga, Bogen, & Sperry, 1965). The 1960s also brought the publication of David Hubel and Torsten Wiesel's (1962, 1963) Nobel prize–winning work on how visual signals are processed in the brain.

These and many other findings stimulated an increase in research on the biological, and especially the neurobiological, bases of behavior. Advocates of the *biological or neuroscience perspective* maintain that much of human and animal behavior can be explained in terms of the brain structures and biochemical processes that allow organisms to behave. As you can see in **Figure 1.4**, the prominence of the

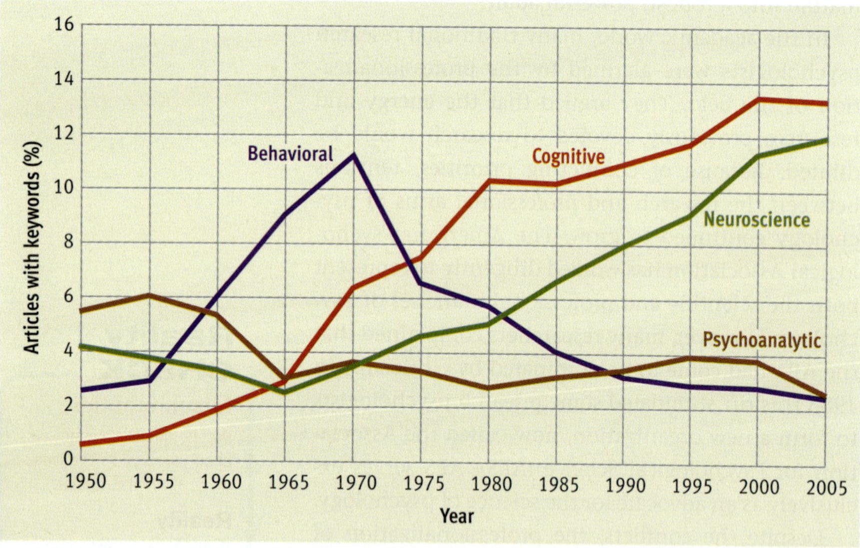

© Cengage Learning 2013

Figure 1.4

The relative prominence of four major schools of thought in psychology. To estimate the relative productivity and influence of various theoretical orientations in recent decades, Joseph Spear (2007) conducted a keyword search of the psychological research literature indexed in PsycINFO to estimate the percentage of articles relevant to each school of thought. Obviously, his approach is just one of many ways one might gauge the prominence of various theoretical orientations in psychology. Nonetheless, the data are thought provoking. His findings suggest that the cognitive perspective surpassed the behavioral perspective in its influence on research sometime around 1975 and that it has continued as the leading perspective since then. As you can see, his data also demonstrate that the neuroscience perspective has grown steadliy in influence since the 1950s.

SOURCE: Adapted from Spear, J. H. (2007). Prominent schools or other active specialties? A fresh look as some trends in psychology. *Review of General Psychology, 11,* 363–380. Copyright © 2007 by the American Psychological Association.

neuroscience perspective has grown steadily since the 1950s (Spear, 2007). In the 19th century the young science of psychology had a heavy physiological emphasis. Thus, increased interest in the biological bases of behavior represents another return to psychology's heritage. The cognitive and neuroscience perspectives are compared with other contemporary theoretical perspectives in **Table 1.2**.

Psychology Broadens Its Horizons: Increased Interest in Cultural Diversity

PsykTrek 1a

Throughout psychology's history, most researchers have worked under the assumption that they were seeking to identify general principles of behavior that would be applicable to all of humanity (Smith, Spillane, & Annus, 2006). In reality, however, psychology has largely been a Western (North American and European) enterprise (Gergen et al. 1996; Norenzayan & Heine, 2005). The vast majority of research has been conducted in the United States by middle- and upper-class white psychologists who have used mostly middle- and upper-class white males as participants (Hall, 1997; Norenzayan & Heine, 2005). Traditionally, Western psychologists have paid scant attention to how well their theories and research might apply to non-Western cultures, to ethnic minorities in Western societies, or even to women as opposed to men.

In recent decades, though, Western psychologists have begun to recognize that their neglect of cultural variables has diminished the value of their work. They are now devoting increased attention to culture as a determinant of behavior. What brought about this shift? The new interest in culture appears mainly attributable to two recent trends: (1) advances in communication, travel, and international trade have "shrunk" the world and increased global interdependence, bringing more and more Americans and Europeans into contact with people from non-Western cultures; and (2) the ethnic makeup of the Western world has become an increasingly diverse multicultural mosaic (Brislin, 2000; Hermans & Kempen, 1998; Mays et al., 1996).

These trends have prompted more and more Western psychologists to broaden their horizons and incorporate cultural factors into their theories and research (Lonner, 2009; Markus & Hamedani, 2007; Matsumoto & Yoo, 2006). These psychologists are striving to study previously underrepresented groups of subjects to test the generality of earlier findings and to catalog both the differences and similarities among cultural groups. They are working to increase knowledge of how culture is transmitted through socialization practices and how culture colors one's view of the world. They are seeking to learn how people cope with cultural change and to find ways to reduce misunderstandings and conflicts in intercultural interactions. In addition, they are trying to enhance understanding of how cultural groups are affected by prejudice, discrimination, and racism. In all these efforts, they are striving to understand the unique experiences of culturally diverse people *from the point of view of those people.* These efforts to ask new questions, study new groups, and apply new perspectives promise to enrich the discipline of psychology (Fowers & Davidov, 2006; Lehman, Chiu, & Schaller, 2004; Matsumoto, 2003; Sue, 2003).

Psychology Adapts: The Emergence of Evolutionary Psychology

PsykTrek 1a

Another relatively recent development in psychology has been the emergence of *evolutionary psychology* as an influential theoretical perspective. Evolutionary psychologists assert that the patterns of behavior seen in a species are products of evolution in the same way that anatomical characteristics are. ***Evolutionary psychology* examines behavioral processes in terms of their adaptive value for members of a species over the course of many generations.** The basic premise of evolutionary psychology is that natural selection favors behaviors that enhance organisms' reproductive success—that is, passing on genes to the next generation. Thus, if a species is highly aggressive,

Illustrated Overview of Psychology's History

1870 1880 1890 1900 1910 1920 1930

1875

First demonstration laboratories are set up independently by **William James** (at Harvard) and Wilhelm Wundt (at the University of Leipzig).

1879

Wilhelm Wundt establishes first research laboratory in psychology at Leipzig, Germany.

1881

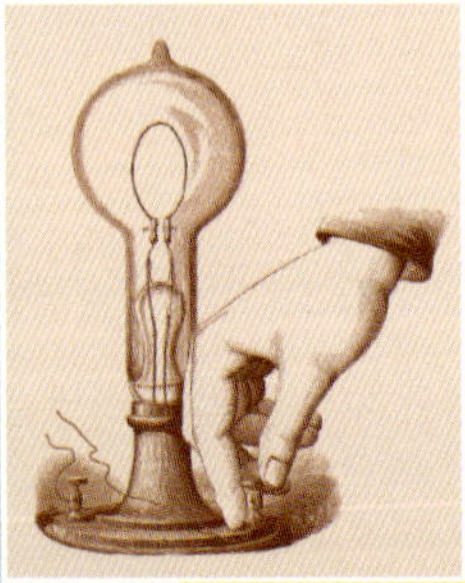

Wilhelm Wundt establishes first journal devoted to research in psychology.

1883

G. Stanley Hall establishes America's first research laboratory in psychology at Johns Hopkins University.

1888

Sir Francis Galton develops the concept of correlation which will allow generations of scientists to quantify associations between variables.

1890

William James publishes his seminal work, *The Principles of Psychology*.

1892

G. Stanley Hall founds American Psychological Association.

1904

Ivan Pavlov shows how conditioned responses are created, paving the way for stimulus-response psychology.

1905

Alfred Binet develops first successful intelligence test in France.

1908

Margaret Washburn publishes *The Animal Mind*, which serves as an impetus for behaviorism.

1909

Sigmund Freud's increasing influence receives formal recognition as G. S. Hall invites Freud to give lectures at Clark University.

1913

John B. Watson writes classic behaviorism manifesto, arguing that psychology should study only observable behavior.

1914

Leta Hollingworth publishes pioneering work on the psychology of women.

1914–1918

Widespread intelligence testing is begun by military during World War I.

1916

Lewis Terman publishes Stanford-Binet Intelligence Scale, which becomes the world's foremost intelligence test.

1920s

Gestalt psychology nears its peak influence.

1933

Sigmund Freud's influence continues to build as he publishes *New Introductory Lectures on Psychoanalysis*.

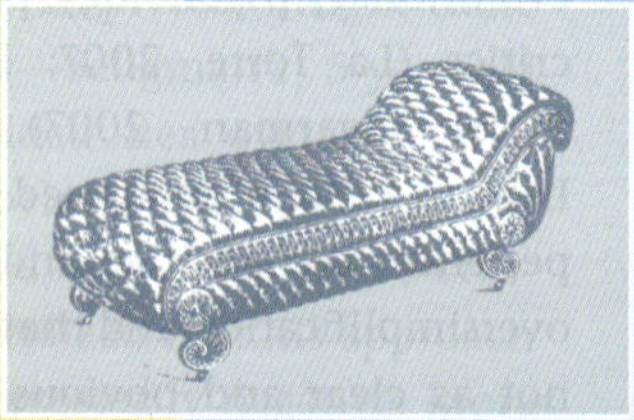

1936

Hans Selye launc
the study of psyc
logical stress.

SOURCES: Wright brothers/Kitty Ha
© Stock Montage, Inc.; administeri
intelligence text: © Bettmann Corb
on phone: Antman Archives/The Im
Works; Washburn: Archives of the
of American Psychology, University
of Akron, Akron, Ohio; Edison's lam
Adapted from *The Scientific Americ*
New York, 10 January 1880; 1909:
University: Courtesy of Clark Univer
Archives; Hollingworth: Archives of
History of American Psychology, Un
of Akron, Akron, Ohio; Pavlov and d
© Bettmann Corbis; Kahneman: Co
of Daniel Kahneman; atomic bomb:
Photo12/The Image Works; shuttle
NASA; Loftus: Courtesy of Elizabeth
Clark: © Bettmann Corbis; Maccoby
© Chuck Painter/Stanford News Se
Seligman: Courtesy of Martin E. P.
Seligman; Erikson: © AP Images; V
soldiers: © AP/Images; All other im
© Cengage Learning 2013

1940 1950 1960 1970 1980 1990 2000

1941–1945

Rapid growth in clinical psychology begins in response to huge demand for clinical services created by World War II and its aftermath.

1947

Kenneth and Mamie **Clark** publish work on prejudice that is cited in landmark 1954 Supreme Court decision outlawing segregation.

1950

Erik Erikson writes *Childhood and Society* in which he extends Freud's theory of development across the life span.

Early 1950s

John Bowlby begins influential research on the nature of the attachment bond between mothers and infants.

1951

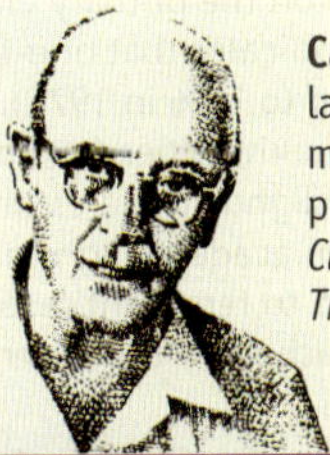

Carl Rogers helps launch humanistic movement with publication of *Client-Centered Therapy*.

1953

B. F. Skinner publishes his influential *Science and Human Behavior*, advocating radical behaviorism similar to Watson's.

1954

Abraham Maslow's *Motivation and Personality* helps fuel humanistic movement.

1956

The cognitive revolution is launched at watershed conference where Herbert Simon, George Miller, and Noam Chomsky report three major advances in just one day.

1963

Stanley Milgram conducts controversial study of obedience to authority, which may be the most famous single study in psychology's history.

1958

Joseph Wolpe launches behavior therapy with his description of systematic desensitization treatment for phobias.

1963

Albert Bandura publishes landmark research on media violence and aggression as his social learning theory adds a cognitive slant to behaviorism.

1961–1964

Roger Sperry's split-brain research and work by David Hubel and Torsten Wiesel on how cortical cells respond to light help rejuvenate the biological perspective in psychology.

1980s

Increased global interdependence and cultural diversity in Western societies spark surge of interest in how cultural factors mold behavior.

1981

Roger Sperry wins Nobel prize (in physiology and medicine) for split-brain studies.

1974

Eleanor Maccoby and Carol Jacklin publish their landmark review of research on gender differences, which galvanizes research in this area.

1971

B. F. Skinner creates furor over radical behaviorism with his controversial book *Beyond Freedom and Dignity*.

1978

Herbert Simon wins Nobel prize (in economics) for research on cognition.

Early 1990s

Evolutionary psychology emerges as a major new theoretical perspective.

1990s

The repressed memories controversy stimulates influential research by **Elizabeth Loftus** and others on the malleability and fallibility of human memory.

Late 1990s

Martin Seligman launches the positive psychology movement.

2000

Eric Kandel wins Nobel Prize (in physiology and medicine) for his research on the biochemistry of memory.

1988

Research psychologists form American Psychological Society (APS) to serve as an advocate for the science of psychology.

2002

Daniel Kahneman wins Nobel Prize (in economics) for his research on decision making.

KEY LEARNING GOALS

1.11 Discuss the growth of psychology, and identify the most common work settings for contemporary psychologists.

1.12 List and describe nine major research areas in psychology.

1.13 List and describe six professional specialties in psychology, and distinguish between clinical psychology and psychiatry.

Psychology Today: Vigorous and Diversified

We began this chapter with an informal description of what psychology is about. Now that you have a feel for how psychology has developed, you can better appreciate a definition that does justice to the field's modern diversity: ***Psychology* is the science that studies behavior and the physiological and cognitive processes that underlie it, and it is the profession that applies the accumulated knowledge of this science to practical problems.**

Contemporary psychology is a thriving science and profession. Its growth has been remarkable. One simple index of this growth is the dramatic rise in membership in the American Psychological Association. **Figure 1.5** shows that APA membership has increased ninefold since 1950. In the United States, psychology is the second most popular undergraduate major. The field accounts for almost 10% of all doctoral degrees awarded in the sciences and humanities. The comparable figure in 1945 was only 4% (Howard et al., 1986). Of course, psychology is an international enterprise. Today, over 2100 technical journals from all over the world publish research articles on psychology. Thus, by any standard of measurement—the number of people involved, the number of degrees granted, the number of journals published—psychology is a healthy, growing field.

Psychology's vigorous presence in modern society is also demonstrated by the great variety of settings in which psychologists work. They were once found almost exclusively in academia. Today, however, colleges and universities are the primary work setting for fewer than 30% of American psychologists. The remaining 70% work in hospitals, clinics, police departments, research institutes, government agencies, business and industry, schools, nursing homes, counseling centers, and private practice. **Figure 1.6** shows the distribution of psychologists employed in various categories of settings.

Clearly, contemporary psychology is a multifaceted field. This is especially apparent when we consider the many areas of specialization in both the science and the profession of psychology.

Reality CHECK

Misconception

Psychology is the study of the mind.

Reality

When the term was coined in the 16th century, *psychology* did refer to the study of the mind, but the term's original meaning is much too narrow today. Since the 19th century, scientific psychology has focused heavily on physiological processes, and the 20th century brought a new focus on overt behavior. Modern psychology encompasses the study of behavior and the mental and physiological processes that regulate behavior.

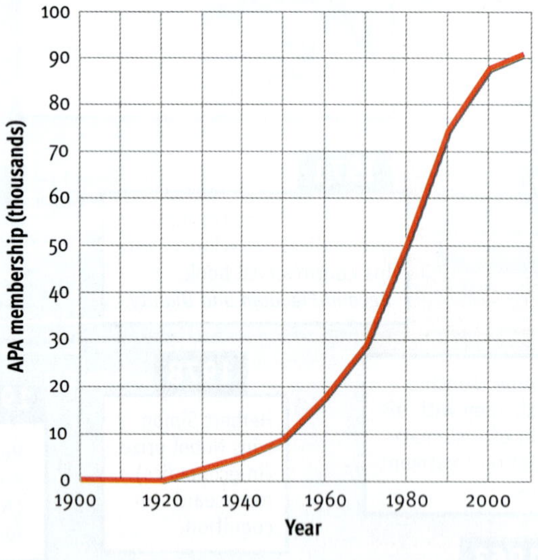

Figure 1.5

Membership in the American Psychological Association, 1900–2007. The steep rise in the number of psychologists in the APA since 1950 testifies to psychology's remarkable growth as a science and a profession. If graduate student members are also counted, the APA has about 150,000 members. (Based on data published by the American Psychological Association)

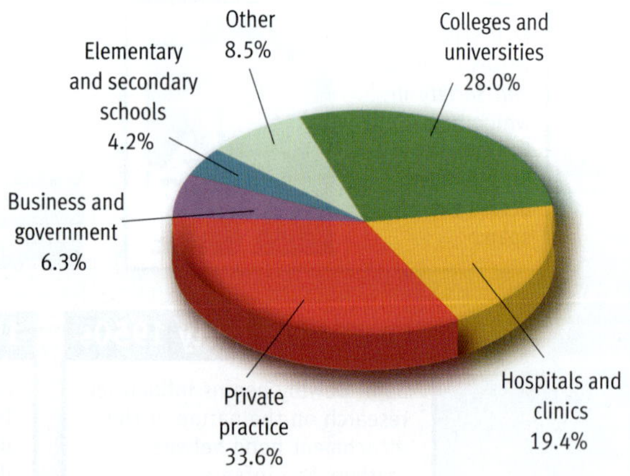

Figure 1.6

Employment of psychologists by setting. The work settings in which psychologists are employed have become quite diverse. Survey data on the primary employment setting of APA members indicates that one-third are in private practice (compared to 12% in 1976), while only 28% work in colleges and universities (compared to 47% in 1976). These data may slightly underestimate the percentage of psychologists in academia, given the competition between APA and APS to represent research psychologists. (Based on data published by the American Psychological Association)

Research Areas in Psychology

Most psychologists receive broad training that provides them with knowledge about many areas of psychology. However, they usually specialize when it comes to doing research. Such specialization is necessary because the subject matter of psychology has become so vast over the years. Today it is virtually impossible for anyone to stay abreast of the new research in all specialties. Specialization is also necessary because specific skills and training are required to do research in some areas.

The nine major research areas in modern psychology are (1) developmental psychology, (2) social psychology, (3) experimental psychology, (4) physiological psychology, (5) cognitive psychology, (6) personality, (7) psychometrics, (8) educational psychology, and (9) health psychology. **Figure 1.7** describes these areas briefly and shows the percentage of research psychologists in the APA who identify each area as their primary interest. As you can see, social psychology and developmental psychology have become especially active areas of research.

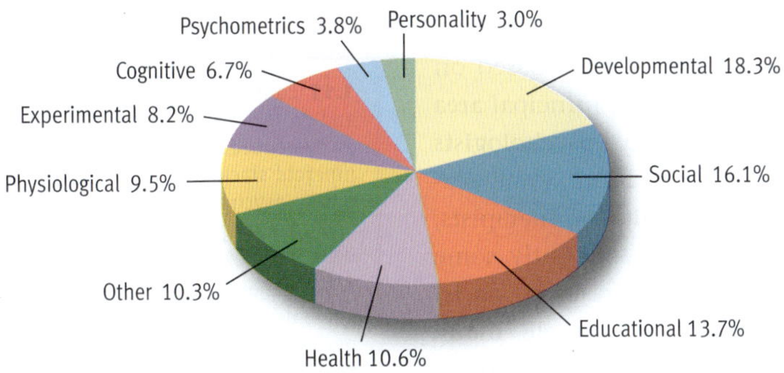

Area	Focus of research
Developmental psychology	Looks at human development across the life span. Developmental psychology once focused primarily on child development, but today devotes a great deal of research to adolescence, adulthood, and old age.
Social psychology	Focuses on interpersonal behavior and the role of social forces in governing behavior. Typical topics include attitude formation, attitude change, prejudice, conformity, attraction, aggression, intimate relationships, and behavior in groups.
Educational psychology	Studies how people learn and the best ways to teach them. Examines curriculum design, teacher training, achievement testing, student motivation, classroom diversity, and other aspects of the educational process.
Health psychology	Focuses on how psychological factors relate to the promotion and maintenance of physical health and the causation, prevention, and treatment of illness.
Physiological psychology	Examines the influence of genetic factors on behavior and the role of the brain, nervous system, endocrine system, and bodily chemicals in the regulation of behavior.
Experimental psychology	Encompasses the traditional core of topics that psychology focused on heavily in its first half-century as a science: sensation, perception, learning, conditioning, motivation, and emotion. The name experimental psychology is somewhat misleading, as this is not the only area in which experiments are done. Psychologists working in all the areas listed here conduct experiments.
Cognitive psychology	Focuses on "higher" mental processes, such as memory, reasoning, information processing, language, problem solving, decision making, and creativity.
Psychometrics	Is concerned with the measurement of behavior and capacities, usually through the development of psychological tests. Psychometrics is involved with the design of tests to assess personality, intelligence, and a wide range of abilities. It is also concerned with the development of new techniques for statistical analysis.
Personality	Is interested in describing and understanding individuals' consistency in behavior, which represents their personality. This area of interest is also concerned with the factors that shape personality and with personality assessment.

© Cengage Learning 2013

Figure 1.7
Major research areas in contemporary psychology. Most research psychologists specialize in one of the nine broad areas described here. The figures in the pie chart reflect the percentage of academic and research psychologists belonging to the APA who identify each area as their primary interest. (Based on data published by the American Psychological Association)

Reality CHECK

Misconception

Psychology and psychiatry are largely the same.

Reality

Psychiatry is a branch of medicine that has always focused almost exclusively on the treatment of mental disorders. Psychology is an academic field that is vastly broader in scope, focusing on learning, perception, human development, memory, intelligence, and social behavior, although it does have a clinical arm concerned with mental disorders. Psychologists and psychiatrists get very different kinds of training, earn different degrees, and tend to have different approaches to the treatment of mental illness (see Chapter 16).

Professional Specialties in Psychology

Applied psychology consists of four well-established areas of specialization and a couple of new, emerging specialties. The four established professional specialties are (1) clinical psychology, (2) counseling psychology, (3) school psychology, and (4) industrial/organizational psychology. The two emerging specialties are clinical neuropsychology and forensic psychology. Descriptions of all six of these specialties can be found in **Figure 1.8**, along with the percentage of professional psychologists in the APA who cite each area as their chief interest. As the graphic indicates, clinical psychology is the most prominent and widely practiced professional specialty in the field.

The data in **Figures 1.7** and **1.8** are based on APA members' reports of their single, principal area of specialization. However, many psychologists work on both research and application. Some academic psychologists work as consultants, therapists, and counselors on a part-time basis. Similarly, some applied psychologists conduct basic research on issues related to their specialty. For example, many clinical psychologists are involved in research on the nature and causes of abnormal behavior.

Some people are confused about the difference between clinical psychology and psychiatry. The confusion is understandable, as both clinical psychologists and psychiatrists are involved in analyzing and treating psychological disorders. Although some overlap exists between the two professions, the training and educational requirements for the two are quite different. Clinical psychologists go to graduate school to earn one of several doctoral degrees (Ph.D., Ed.D., or Psy.D.) in order to enjoy full status in their profession. Psychiatrists go to medical school for their postgraduate education, where they receive general training in medicine and earn an M.D. degree. They then specialize by completing residency training in psychiatry at a hospital. Clinical psychologists and psychiatrists also differ in the way they tend to approach the treatment of mental disorders, as we will see in Chapter 16. To summarize, ***psychiatry* is a branch of medicine concerned with the diagnosis and treatment of psychological problems and disorders.** In contrast, clinical psychology takes a nonmedical approach to such problems.

REVIEW OF KEY LEARNING GOALS

1.11 Contemporary psychology is a diversified science and profession that has grown rapidly in recent decades, as evidenced by the fact that APA membership has grown ninefold since 1950. The main work settings for contemporary psychologists are (1) private practice, (2) colleges and universities, (3) hospitals and clinics, and (4) business and government.

1.12 Major areas of research in modern psychology include developmental psychology, social psychology, experimental psychology, physiological psychology, cognitive psychology, personality, psychometrics, educational psychology, and health psychology.

1.13 Applied psychology encompasses six professional specialties: clinical psychology, counseling psychology, school psychology, industrial/organizational psychology, clinical neuropsychology, and forensic psychology. Although clinical psychology and psychiatry share some of the same interests, they are different professions with different types of training. Psychiatrists are physicians who specialize in the diagnosis and treatment of mental disorders, whereas clinical psychologists take a nonmedical approach to psychological problems.

KEY LEARNING GOALS

1.14 Clarify the text's three unifying themes relating to psychology as a field of study.

1.15 Clarify the text's four unifying themes relating to psychology's subject matter.

Seven Unifying Themes

The enormous breadth and diversity of psychology make it a challenging subject for the beginning student. In the pages ahead you will be introduced to many areas of research and a multitude of ideas, concepts, and principles. Fortunately, ideas are not all created equal. Some are far more important than others. In this section, I will highlight seven fundamental themes that will reappear in a number of variations as we move from one area of psychology to another in this text. You have already met some of these key ideas in our review of psychology's past and present. Now we will isolate them and highlight their significance. In the remainder of the book these ideas serve as organizing themes to provide threads of continuity across chapters. They will also help you see the connections among the various areas of research in psychology.

In studying psychology, you are learning about both behavior and the scientific discipline that investigates it. Accordingly, our seven themes come in two sets. The first set consists of statements highlighting crucial aspects of psychology as a way of thinking and as a field of study. The second set consists of broad generalizations about psychology's

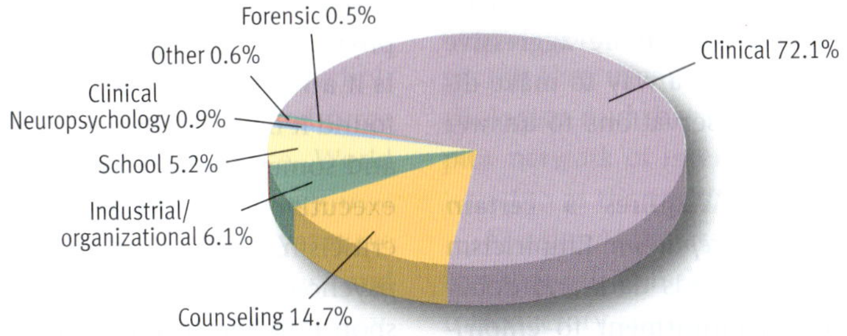

Specialty	Focus of professional practice
Clinical psychology	Clinical psychologists are concerned with the evaluation, diagnosis, and treatment of individuals with psychological disorders, as well as treatment of less severe behavioral and emotional problems. Principal activities include interviewing clients, psychological testing, and providing group or individual psychotherapy.
Counseling psychology	Counseling psychology overlaps with clinical psychology in that specialists in both areas engage in similar activities—interviewing, testing, and providing therapy. However, counseling psychologists usually work with a somewhat different clientele, providing assistance to people struggling with everyday problems of moderate severity. Thus, they often specialize in family, marital, or career counseling.
Industrial and organizational psychology	Psychologists in this area perform a wide variety of tasks in the world of business and industry. These tasks include running human resources departments, working to improve staff morale and attitudes, striving to increase job satisfaction and productivity, examining organizational structures and procedures, and making recommendations for improvements.
School psychology	School psychologists strive to promote the cognitive, emotional, and social development of children in schools. They usually work in elementary or secondary schools, where they test and counsel children having difficulties in school and aid parents and teachers in solving school-related problems.
Clinical neuropsychology	Clinical neuropsychologists are involved in the assessment and treatment of people who suffer from central nervous system dysfunctions due to head trauma, dementia, stroke, seizure disorders, and so forth.
Forensic psychology	Forensic psychologists apply psychological principles to issues arising in the legal system, such as child custody decisions, hearings on competency to stand trial, violence risk assessments, involuntary commitment proceedings, and so forth.

© Cengage Learning 2013

Figure 1.8
Principal professional specialties in contemporary psychology. Most psychologists who deliver professional services to the public specialize in one of the six areas described here. The figures in the pie chart reflect the percentage of APA members delivering professional services who identify each area as their chief specialty. (Based on data published by the American Psychological Association)

subject matter: behavior and the cognitive and physiological processes that underlie it.

Themes Related to Psychology as a Field of Study

Looking at psychology as a field of study, we see three crucial ideas: (1) psychology is empirical, (2) psychology is theoretically diverse, and (3) psychology evolves in a sociohistorical context. Let's look at each of these ideas in more detail.

Theme 1: Psychology Is Empirical

Everyone tries to understand behavior. Most of us have our own personal answers to questions such as why some people are hard workers, why some are overweight, and why others stay in demeaning relationships. If all of us are amateur psychologists, what makes scientific psychology different? The critical difference is that psychology is *empirical*. This aspect of psychology is fundamental, and virtually every page of this book reflects it.

What do we mean by empirical? ***Empiricism* is the premise that knowledge should be acquired through observation.** This premise is crucial to the scientific method that psychology embraced in the late 19th century. To say that psychology is empirical means that its conclusions are based on direct observation rather than on reasoning, speculation, traditional beliefs, or common sense. Psychologists are not content with having ideas that simply *sound* plausible. They conduct research to *test* their ideas.

© Steve Raymer/Corbis

Cultural background has an enormous influence on people's behavior, shaping everything from modes of dress to sexual values and norms. Increased global interdependence brings more and more people into contact with cultures other than their own. This increased exposure to diverse cultures only serves to underscore the importance of cultural factors.

groups within societies—which it does—but the concept can also be applied to small groups (a tiny Aboriginal tribe in Australia, for example) and to nonethnic groups (gay culture, for instance).

Triandis (2007) emphasizes that culture has a dual nature, existing both outside and inside people. Culture lies outside of people in that one can identify various customs, practices, and institutions that mold people's behavior. Culture lies inside people in that everything that happens to them is viewed through a cultural lens—a way of thinking—that cannot be set aside. Moreover, because a cultural background is widely shared, members feel little need to discuss it with others and often take it for granted. For example, you probably don't spend much time thinking about the importance of living in rectangular rooms, trying to minimize body odor, limiting yourself to one spouse at a time, or using credit cards to obtain material goods and services.

Even though we generally fail to appreciate its influence, our cultural heritage has a pervasive impact on our thoughts, feelings, and behavior (Matsumoto & Juang, 2008; Triandis, 2007). For example, in North America, when people are invited to dinner in someone's home, they generally show their appreciation of their host's cooking efforts by eating all of the food they are served. In India, this behavior would be insulting to the host, as guests are expected to leave some food on their plates. The leftover food acknowledges the generosity of the host, implying that he or she provided so much food the guest could not eat it all (Moghaddam, Taylor, & Wright, 1993).

The influence of culture is everywhere. However, generalizations about cultural groups must always be tempered by the realization that great diversity also exists within any society or ethnic group (Markus & Hamedani, 2007). Researchers may be able to pinpoint genuinely useful insights about Ethiopian, Korean American, or Ukrainian culture, for example. But it would be foolish to assume that all Ethiopians, Korean Americans, or Ukrainians exhibit identical behavior. It is also important to realize that both differences and similarities in behavior occur across cultures. As we will see repeatedly, psychological processes are characterized by both cultural variance and invariance. Caveats aside, if we hope to achieve a sound understanding of human behavior, we need to consider cultural determinants.

Theme 6: Heredity and Environment Jointly Influence Behavior

Are individuals who they are—athletic or artistic, quick tempered or calm, shy or outgoing, energetic or laid back—because of their genetic inheritance or because of their upbringing? This question about the importance of nature versus nurture, or heredity versus environment, has been asked in one form or another since ancient times. Historically, the nature-versus-nurture question was framed as an all-or-none proposition. In other words, theorists argued that personal traits and abilities are governed either entirely by heredity or entirely by environment. John B. Watson, for instance, asserted that personality and ability depend almost exclusively on an individual's environment. In contrast, Sir Francis Galton, a 19th-century pioneer in mental testing (see Chapter 9), maintained that personality and ability depend almost entirely on genetic inheritance.

Today, most psychologists agree that heredity and environment are both important. A century of research has shown that genetics and experience jointly influence an individual's intelligence, temperament, personality, and susceptibility to many psychological disorders (Grigerenko & Sternberg, 2003; Plomin, 2004; Rutter, 2006). If we ask whether individuals are born or made, psychology's answer is "Both." This does not mean that nature versus nurture is a dead issue. Lively debate about the *rela-*

Nature or nurture? As a young actress, Lindsay Lohan appeared to have a wonderful career ahead of her. But then it began unraveling, as she battled alcohol and drug problems, started exhibiting erratic behavior, and became embroiled in a host of legal problems. What might account for this deterioration? Heredity? Environment? Or some combination of the two? One could point to experience, as she came from a broken home that was apparently riddled with parental conflict. But one could also speculate about the role of genetics, as her father has had his own issues with alcohol, and he has indicated that his father was an alcoholic. It is often very difficult to tease apart the intertwined contributions of heredity and environment. In any event, the nature versus nurture question comes up endlessly in efforts to understand behavior.

tive influence of genetics and experience continues unabated. Furthermore, psychologists are actively seeking to understand the complex ways in which genetic inheritance and experience interact to mold behavior.

Theme 7: People's Experience of the World Is Highly Subjective

Even elementary perception—for example, of sights and sounds—is not a passive process. People actively process incoming stimulation, selectively focusing on some aspects of that stimulation while ignoring others. Moreover, they impose organization on the stimuli that they pay attention to. These tendencies combine to make perception personalized and subjective.

The subjectivity of perception was demonstrated nicely in a classic study by Hastorf and Cantril (1954). They showed students at Princeton and Dartmouth universities a film of a recent football game between the two schools. The students were told to watch for rules infractions. Both groups saw the same film, but the Princeton students "saw" the Dartmouth players engage in twice as many infractions as the Dartmouth students "saw." The investigators concluded that the game "actually was many different games and that each version of the events that transpired was just as 'real' to a particular person as other versions were to other people" (Hastorf & Cantril, 1954). In this study, the subjects' perceptions were swayed by their motives. It shows how people sometimes see what they *want* to see.

Other studies reveal that people also tend to see what they *expect* to see. For example, Harold Kelley (1950) showed how perceptions of people are influenced by their reputation. Kelley told students that their class would be taken over by a new lecturer, whom they would be asked to evaluate later. Before the class, the students were given a short description of the incoming instructor, with one important variation. Half the students were led to expect a "warm" person, while the other half were led to expect a "cold" one (see **Figure 1.9**). All the subjects were exposed to the same 20 minutes of lecture and interaction with the new instructor. However, the group of subjects who *expected* a warm person rated the instructor as more considerate, sociable, humorous, good natured, informal, and humane

Figure 1.9
Manipulating person perception. Read the accompanying description of Mr. Blank carefully. If you were about to hear him give a lecture, would this description bias your perceptions of him? You probably think not, but when Kelley (1950) altered one adjective in this description (replacing the word *warm* with *cold*), the change had a dramatic impact on subjects' ratings of the guest lecturer.

SOURCE: Description from Kelley, H. H. (1950). The warm-cold variable in first impressions of persons. *Journal of Personality, 8*, 431–439. Copyright © 1950, John Wiley and Sons.

CONCEPT CHECK 1.3

Identifying the Contributions of Major Theorists and Researchers

Check your recall of the principal ideas of important theorists and researchers covered in this chapter by matching the people listed on the left with the appropriate contributions described on the right. If you need help, the crucial pages describing each person's ideas are listed in parentheses. Fill in the letters for your choices in the spaces provided on the left. You'll find the answers in Appendix A.

Major Theorists and Researchers

_______ 1. John B. Watson (pp. 8–9)

_______ 2. Sigmund Freud (pp. 7–8)

_______ 3. Wilhelm Wundt (p. 4)

_______ 4. William James (pp. 5–6)

_______ 5. Margaret Floy Washburn (p. 6)

_______ 6. B. F. Skinner (pp. 9–10)

_______ 7. Carl Rogers (pp. 10–12)

Key Ideas and Contributions

a. This theorist was the founder of behaviorism. He proposed that psychologists should abandon the study of consciousness altogether.

b. This individual, who authored *The Animal Mind* (1908), was the first woman to receive a Ph.D. in psychology.

c. This influential American researcher showed that organisms tend to repeat responses that lead to positive outcomes. He also argued that free will is an illusion.

d. Widely viewed as the founder of psychology, this person established the first laboratory for research in psychology in 1879.

e. This theorist focused on the unconscious and sexuality, causing considerable controversy. He also invented psychoanalytic theory.

f. This Harvard scholar was the chief architect of functionalism, arguing that psychology should investigate the *functions* rather than the *structure* of consciousness.

g. This advocate of humanism took an optimistic view of human nature and was a major critic of psychoanalytic and behavioral theories.

than the subjects in the group who had expected a cold person.

Thus, it is clear that motives and expectations color people's experiences. To some extent, individuals see what they want to see or what they expect to see. This subjective bias in perception turns out to explain a variety of behavioral tendencies that would otherwise be perplexing (Pronin, Gilovich, & Ross, 2004; Pronin, Lin, & Ross, 2002).

Human subjectivity is precisely what the scientific method is designed to counteract. In using the scientific approach, psychologists strive to make their observations as objective as possible. In some respects, overcoming subjectivity is what science is all about. Left to their own subjective experience, people might still believe that the earth is flat and that the sun revolves around it. Thus, psychologists are committed to the scientific approach because they believe it is the most reliable route to accurate knowledge.

Now that you have been introduced to the text's organizing themes, let's turn to an example of how psychological research can be applied to the challenges of everyday life. In our first Personal Application, we'll focus on a subject that should be highly relevant to you: how to be a successful student. In the Critical Thinking Application that follows it, we discuss the nature and importance of critical thinking skills.

REVIEW OF KEY LEARNING GOALS

1.14 Psychology is empirical because psychologists base their conclusions on observation through research rather than reasoning or common sense. Psychology is theoretically diverse, as there are many competing schools of thought in the field. This diversity has fueled progress and is a strength rather than a weakness. Psychology also evolves in a sociohistorical context, as trends, issues, and values in society influence what goes on in psychology, and vice versa.

1.15 Behavior is determined by multiple causes, as most aspects of behavior are influenced by complex networks of interacting factors. Although cultural heritage is often taken for granted, it has a pervasive impact on people's thoughts, feelings, and behavior. Lively debate about the relative importance of nature versus nurture continues, but it is clear that heredity and environment jointly influence behavior. People's experience of the world is highly subjective, as they sometimes see what they want to see or what they expect to see.

Improving Academic Performance

> **KEY LEARNING GOALS**
>
> **1.16** Review three important considerations in designing a program to promote adequate studying.
>
> **1.17** Discuss some strategies for enhancing reading comprehension and for getting more out of lectures.
>
> **1.18** Summarize advice provided on improving test-taking strategies.

Answer the following "true" or "false."

___ **1** If you have a professor who delivers chaotic, hard-to-follow lectures, there is little point in attending class.

___ **2** Cramming the night before an exam is an effective method of study.

___ **3** In taking lecture notes, you should try to be a "human tape recorder" (that is, write down everything your professor says).

___ **4** You should never change your answers to multiple-choice questions because your first hunch is your best hunch.

All of the above statements are false. If you answered them all correctly, you may have already acquired the kinds of skills and habits that facilitate academic success. If so, however, you are *not* typical. Today, many students enter college with poor study skills and habits—and it's not entirely their fault. The American educational system generally provides minimal instruction on good study techniques. In this first Application, we will try to remedy this situation to some extent by reviewing some insights that psychology offers on how to improve academic performance. We will discuss how to promote better study habits, how to enhance reading efforts, how to get more out of lectures, and how to improve test-taking strategies. You may also want to jump ahead and read the Personal Application for Chapter 7, which focuses on how to improve everyday memory.

Developing Sound Study Habits

People tend to assume that academic performance in college is largely determined by students' intelligence or general mental ability. This belief is supported by the fact that college admissions tests (the SAT and ACT), which basically assess general cognitive ability, predict college grades fairly well (Berry & Sackett, 2009; Kobrin et al., 2008). What is far less well known, however, is that measures of study skills, habits, and attitudes also predict college grades pretty well. In a recent, large-scale review of 344 independent samples consisting of over 72,000 students, Crede and Kuncel (2008) reported that aggregate measures of study skills and habits predicted college grades almost as well as admissions tests did and that they accounted for variability in performance that the admissions tests could not account for. In other words, this massive review of evidence found that study habits are almost as influential as ability in determining college success. The practical meaning of this finding is that most students probably underestimate the importance of their study skills. And bear in mind, whereas most adults probably cannot increase their mental ability much, they can usually enhance their study habits considerably.

In any event, the first step toward effective study habits is to face up to the reality that studying usually involves hard work. You don't have to feel guilty if you don't look forward to studying. Most students don't. Once you accept the premise that studying doesn't come naturally, it should be apparent that you need to set up an organized program to promote adequate study. According to Siebert and Karr (2003), such a program should include the following considerations:

1. *Set up a schedule for studying.* If you wait until the urge to study strikes you, you may still be waiting when the exam rolls around. Thus, it is important to allocate definite times to studying. Review your various time obligations (work, chores, and so on) and figure out in advance when you can study. When allotting certain times to studying, keep in mind that you need to be wide awake and alert. Be realistic about how long you can study at one time before you wear down from fatigue. Allow time for study breaks—they can revive sagging concentration.

It's important to write down your study schedule. A written schedule serves as a reminder and increases your commitment to following it. You should begin by setting up a general schedule for the quarter or semester, like the one in **Figure 1.10** on the next page. Then, at the beginning of each week, plan the specific assignments that you intend to work on during each study session. This approach to scheduling should help you avoid cramming for exams at the last minute. Cramming is not an effective study strategy for most students (Underwood, 1961; Wong, 2006; Zechmeister & Nyberg, 1982). It will strain your memorization capabilities, can tax your energy level, and may stoke the fires of test anxiety.

In planning your weekly schedule, try to avoid the tendency to put off working on major tasks such as term papers and reports. Time-management experts such as Alan Lakein (1996) point out that many people tend to tackle simple, routine tasks first, saving larger tasks for later when they supposedly will have more time. This common tendency leads many individuals to repeatedly delay working on major assignments until it's too late to do a good job. A good way to avoid this trap is to break major assignments down into smaller tasks that can be scheduled individually.

2. *Find a place to study where you can concentrate.* Where you study is also important. The key is to find a place where distractions are likely to be minimal. Most people cannot study effectively while TV shows or music are on or while other people are talking. Don't depend on willpower to carry you through such distractions. It's much easier to plan ahead and avoid the distractions altogether. In fact, you would be wise to set up one or two specific places to use solely for study (Hettich, 1998).

Figure 1.10

One student's general activity schedule for a semester. Each week the student fills in the specific assignments to work on during each study period.

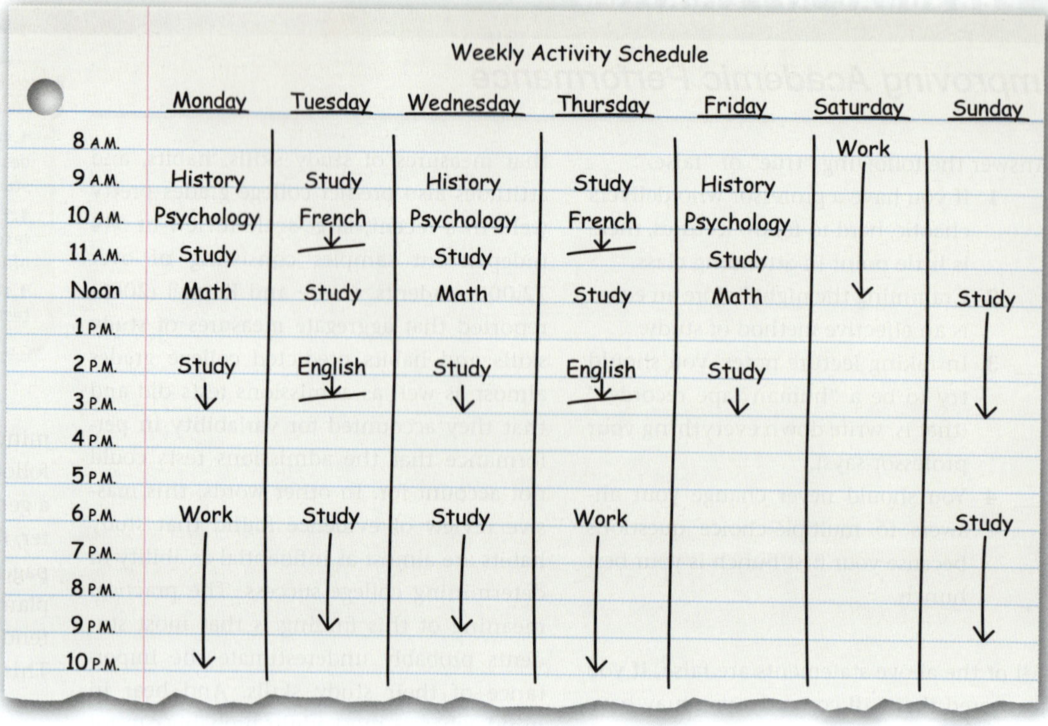

© Cengage Learning 2013

3. *Reward your studying.* One reason that it is so difficult to be motivated to study regularly is that the payoffs often lie in the distant future. The ultimate reward, a degree, may be years away. Even short-term rewards, such as an A in the course, may be weeks or months away. To combat this problem, it helps to give yourself immediate, tangible rewards for studying, such as a snack, TV show, or phone call to a friend. Thus, you should set realistic study goals for yourself, then reward yourself when you meet them. The systematic manipulation of rewards involves harnessing the principles of *behavior modification* described by B. F. Skinner and other behavioral psychologists. These principles are covered in the Chapter 6 Personal Application.

© Paul Cox/arabianEye/Corbis

Improving Your Reading

Much of your study time is spent reading and absorbing information. The keys to improving reading comprehension are to preview reading assignments section by section, work hard to actively process the meaning of the information, strive to identify the key ideas of each paragraph, and carefully review these key ideas after each section. Modern textbooks often contain a variety of learning aids that you can use to improve your reading. If a book provides a chapter outline, chapter summary, or learning objectives, don't ignore them. They can help you recognize the important points in the chapter. Graphic organizers (such as the Concept Charts available online for this text) can also enhance understanding of text material (Nist & Holschuh, 2000). A lot of effort and thought go into formulating these and other textbook learning aids. It is wise to take advantage of them.

Another important issue related to textbook reading is whether and how to mark up reading assignments. Many students deceive themselves into thinking that they are studying by running a marker through a few sentences here and there in their text. If they do so without thoughtful selectivity, they are simply turning a textbook into a coloring book. This situation probably explains why some professors are skeptical about the value of highlighting in textbooks. Nonetheless, research suggests that highlighting textbook material *is* a useful strategy—if students are reasonably effective in focusing on the main ideas in the material and if they subsequently review what they have highlighted (Caverly, Orlando, & Mullen, 2000). When executed effectively, highlighting can foster active reading, improve reading comprehension, and reduce the amount of material that must be reviewed later (Van Blerkom, 2006). The key to effective text marking is to identify (and highlight) only the main ideas, key supporting details, and technical terms (Daiek & Anter, 2004). Most textbooks are carefully crafted such that every paragraph has a purpose for being there. Try to find the sentence or two that best captures the purpose of each paragraph. Text marking is a delicate balancing act. If you highlight too little of the content, you are not identifying enough of the key ideas. But if you highlight too much of the content, you are not going to succeed in condensing what you have to review to a manageable size.

Getting More Out of Lectures

Lectures are sometimes boring and tedious. But it is a simple fact that poor class attendance is associated with poor grades. For example, in one study, Lindgren (1969) found that absences from class were much more common among "unsuccessful" students (grade average C– or below) than among "successful" students (grade average B or above), as shown in **Figure 1.11**. Even when you have an instructor who delivers hard-to-follow lectures, it is still important to go to class. If nothing else, you can get a feel for how the instructor thinks, which can help you anticipate the content of exams and respond in the manner expected by your professor.

Fortunately, most lectures are reasonably coherent. Studies indicate that attentive, accurate note taking *is* associated with enhanced learning and performance in college classes (Titsworth & Kiewra, 2004; Williams & Eggert, 2002). However, research also shows that many students' lecture notes are surprisingly incomplete, with the average student often recording less than 40% of the crucial ideas in a lecture (Armbruster, 2000). Thus, the key to getting more out of lectures is to stay motivated, stay attentive, and expend the effort to make your notes as complete as possible. Books on study skills (Longman & Atkinson, 2005; McWhorter,

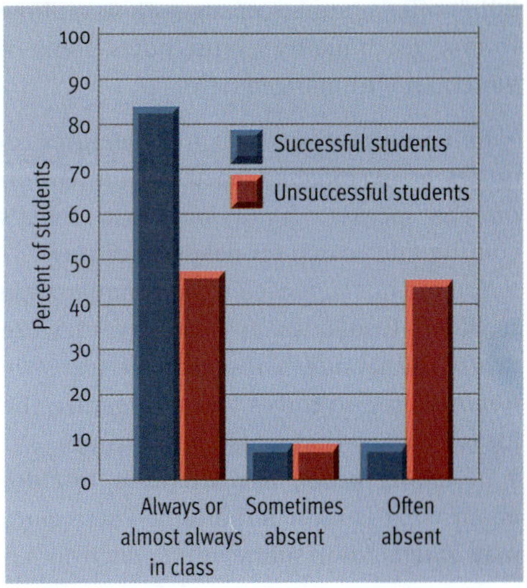

© Cengage Learning 2013

Figure 1.11

Attendance and grades. When Lindgren (1969) compared the class attendance of successful students (B average or above) and unsuccessful students (C– average or below), he found a clear association between poor attendance and poor grades.

DOONESBURY © 2007 by G. B. Trudeau. Dist. by UNIVERSAL PRESS SYNDICATE. Reprinted with permission. All rights reserved.

2007) offer a number of suggestions on how to take good-quality lecture notes, some of which are summarized here:

- Extracting information from lectures requires *active listening.* Focus full attention on the speaker. Try to anticipate what's coming and search for deeper meanings.
- You are not supposed to be a human tape recorder. Insofar as possible, try to write down the lecturer's thoughts *in your own words.* Doing so forces you to organize the ideas in a way that makes sense to you.
- In taking notes, pay attention to clues about what is most important. These clues may range from subtle hints, such as an instructor repeating a point, to not-so-subtle hints, such as an instructor saying "You'll run into this again."
- In delivering their lectures most professors follow an organized outline, which they may or may not share with the class (on the blackboard or via a presentation tool, such as PowerPoint). Insofar as you can decipher the outline of a lecture, try to organize your notes accordingly.
- *Asking questions* during lectures can be helpful. Doing so keeps you actively involved in the lecture and allows you to clarify points that you may have misunderstood. Many students are more bashful about asking questions than they should be. They don't realize that most professors welcome questions.

Improving Test-Taking Strategies

Let's face it—some students are better than others at taking tests. ***Testwiseness* is the ability to use the characteristics and format of a cognitive test to maximize one's score.** Students clearly vary in testwiseness, and such variations are reflected in performance on exams (Geiger, 1997; Rogers & Yang, 1996). Testwiseness is *not* a substitute for knowledge of the subject matter. However, skill in taking tests can help you show what you know when it is critical to do so (Flippo, Becker & Wark, 2000).

A number of myths exist about the best way to take tests. For instance, it is widely believed that students shouldn't go back and change their answers to multiple-choice questions. Benjamin, Cavell, and Shallenberger (1984) found this to be the dominant belief among college *faculty* as well as students (see **Figure 1.12**). However, the old adage that "your first hunch is your best hunch" on tests has been shown to be wrong. Empirical studies clearly and consistently indicate that, over the long run, changing answers pays off. Benjamin and his colleagues reviewed 20 studies on this issue. Their findings are presented in **Figure 1.13**. As you can see, answer changes that go from a wrong answer to a right answer outnumber changes that go from a right answer to a wrong one by a sizable margin. The popular belief that answer changing is harmful is probably attributable to painful memories of right-to-wrong changes. In any case, you can see how it pays to be familiar with sound test-taking strategies.

General Tips

The principles of testwiseness were first described by Millman, Bishop, and Ebel (1965). Here are a few of their general ideas:

- If efficient time use appears crucial, set up a mental schedule for progressing through the test. Make a mental note to check whether you're one-third finished when a third of your time is gone.
- Don't waste time pondering difficult-to-answer questions excessively. If you have no idea at all, just guess and go on. If you need to devote a good deal of time to the question, skip it and mark it so you can return to it later if time permits.
- Adopt the appropriate level of sophistication for the test. Don't read things into questions. Sometimes students make things

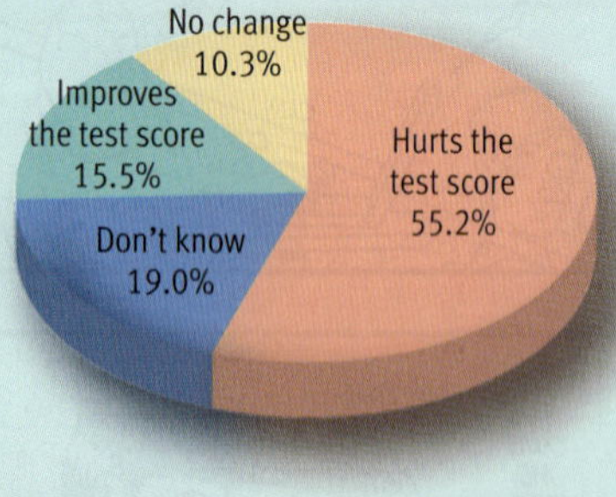

Figure 1.12

Beliefs about the effects of answer changing on tests. Ludy Benjamin and his colleagues (1984) asked 58 college faculty whether changing answers on tests is a good idea. Like most students, the majority of the faculty felt that answer changing usually hurts a student's test score, even though the research evidence contradicts this belief (see **Figure 1.13**).

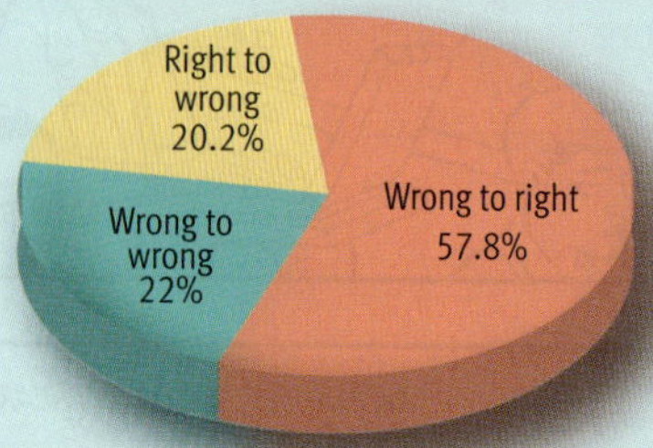

Figure 1.13

Actual effects of changing answers on multiple-choice tests. When the data from all the relevant studies were combined by Benjamin et al. (1984), they indicated that answer changing on tests generally *increased* rather than *reduced* students' test scores. It is interesting to note the contrast between beliefs about answer changing (see **Figure 1.12**) and the actual results of this practice.

Figures 1.12 & 1.13: © Cengage Learning 2013

more complex than they were intended. Often, simple-looking questions are just what they appear to be.

- If you complete all of the questions and still have some time remaining, review the test. Make sure that you have recorded your answers correctly. If you were unsure of some answers, go back and reconsider them.

Tips for Multiple-Choice Exams

Sound test-taking strategies are especially important with multiple-choice (and true-false) questions. These types of questions often include clues that may help you converge on the correct answer (Mentzer, 1982; Weiten, 1984). You may be able to improve your performance on such tests by considering the following points (Flippo, 2000; Millman et al., 1965; Smith, 2005; Van Blerkom, 2006):

- Always read each question completely. Continue reading even if you find your anticipated answer among the options. A more complete option may be farther down the list.
- Learn how to quickly eliminate options that are highly implausible. Many questions have only two plausible options, accompanied by "throwaway" options for filler. You should work at spotting these implausible options so that you can quickly discard them and narrow your task.
- Be alert to the fact that information relevant to one question is sometimes given away in another test item.
- On items that have "all of the above" as an option, if you know that just two of the options are correct, you should choose "all of the above." If you are confident that one of the options is incorrect, you should eliminate this option and "all of the above" and choose from the remaining options.
- Options that represent broad, sweeping generalizations tend to be incorrect. You should be vigilant for words such as *always, never, necessarily, only, must, completely, totally,* and so forth that create these improbable assertions.
- In contrast, options that represent carefully qualified statements tend to be correct. Words such as *often, sometimes, perhaps, may,* and *generally* tend to show up in these well-qualified statements.

Tips for Essay Exams

Little research has been done on testwiseness as it applies to essay exams. That's because relatively few clues are available in the essay format. Nonetheless, various books (Flippo, 2000; Pauk, 1990; Wong, 2006) offer tips based on expert advice. Performance on essay tests can be enhanced by (1) looking over the questions first and making judicious time allocations, (2) taking some time on the front end to plan the organization of your answer instead of plunging in without planning, and (3) making liberal use of the technical terminology that you have learned in the course.

In summary, sound study skills and habits are crucial to academic success. Intelligence alone won't do the job (although it certainly helps). Good academic skills do not develop overnight. They are acquired gradually, so be patient with yourself. Fortunately, tasks such as reading textbooks, writing papers, and taking tests get easier with practice. Ultimately, I think you'll find that the rewards—knowledge, a sense of accomplishment, and progress toward a degree—are worth the effort.

REVIEW OF KEY LEARNING GOALS

1.16 To foster sound study habits, you should devise a written study schedule and reward yourself for following it. Try to avoid the tendency to put off working on major tasks. You should also try to find one or two specific places for studying that are relatively free of distractions.

1.17 You should use active reading techniques to select the most important ideas from the material you read. Highlighting textbook material *is* a useful strategy—if you are reasonably effective in focusing on the main ideas in the material and if you subsequently review what you have highlighted. The key to good note taking is to strive to make lecture notes as complete as possible. It's important to use active listening techniques and to record lecturers' ideas in your own words.

1.18 In taking tests, it's a good idea to devise a schedule for progressing through an exam, to adopt the appropriate level of sophistication, to avoid wasting time on troublesome questions, and to review your answers. On multiple-choice tests it is wise to read questions completely, to quickly eliminate implausible options, and to be wary of sweeping generalizations. On essay tests, it helps to allocate time wisely, to emphasize good organization, and to use technical vocabulary when appropriate.

KEY LEARNING GOALS

1.19 Explain the nature of critical thinking skills.
1.20 Evaluate some weaknesses in evolutionary explanations for gender differences in spatial abilities.

Developing Critical Thinking Skills: An Introduction

If you ask any group of professors, parents, employers, or politicians, "What is the most important outcome of an education?" The most popular answer is likely to be "the development of the ability to think critically." ***Critical thinking* is purposeful, reasoned, goal-directed thinking that involves solving problems, formulating inferences, working with probabilities, and making carefully thought-out decisions.** Critical thinking is the use of cognitive skills and strategies that increase the probability of a desirable outcome. Such outcomes would include good career choices, effective decisions in the workplace, wise investments, and so forth. In the long run, critical thinkers should have more desirable outcomes than people who are not skilled in critical thinking (Halpern, 1998, 2003). Here are some of the skills exhibited by critical thinkers:

- They understand and use the principles of scientific investigation. (How can the effectiveness of punishment as a disciplinary procedure be determined?)
- They apply the rules of formal and informal logic. (If most people disapprove of sex sites on the Internet, why are these sites so popular?)
- They carefully evaluate the quality of information. (Can I trust the claims made by this politician?)
- They analyze arguments for the soundness of the conclusions. (Does the rise in drug use mean that a stricter drug policy is needed?)

The topic of thinking has a long history in psychology. It dates back to Wilhelm Wundt in the 19th century. Modern cognitive psychologists have found that a useful model of critical thinking has at least two components: (1) knowledge of the skills of critical thinking—the *cognitive component,* and (2) the attitude or disposition of a critical thinker—the *emotional or affective component.* Both are needed for effective critical thinking.

Instruction in critical thinking is based on two assumptions: (1) a set of skills or strategies exists that students can learn to recognize and apply in appropriate contexts; (2) if the skills are applied appropriately, students will become more effective thinkers (Halpern, 2007). Critical thinking skills that would be useful in any context might include understanding how reasons and evidence support or refute conclusions; distinguishing among facts, opinions, and reasoned judgments; using principles of likelihood and uncertainty when thinking about probabilistic events; generating multiple solutions to problems and working systematically toward a desired goal; and understanding how causation is determined. This list provides some typical examples of what is meant by the term *critical thinking skills.* Because these skills are useful in a wide variety of contexts, they are sometimes called *transcontextual skills.*

It is of little use to know the skills of critical thinking if you are unwilling to exert the hard mental work to use them or if you have a sloppy or careless attitude toward thinking. A critical thinker is willing to plan, flexible in thinking, persistent, able to admit mistakes and make corrections, and mindful of the thinking process. The use of the word *critical* represents the notion of a critique or evaluation of thinking processes and outcomes. It is not meant to be negative (as in a "critical person") but rather to convey that critical thinkers are vigilant about their thinking (Riggio & Halpern, 2006).

The Need to Teach Critical Thinking

Decades of research on instruction in critical thinking have shown that the skills and attitudes of critical thinking need to be deliberately and consciously taught, because they often do not develop by themselves with standard instruction in a content area (Nisbett, 1993). For this reason, each chapter in this text ends with a Critical Thinking Application. The material presented in each of these Critical Thinking Applications relates to the chapter topics. However, the focus is on how to think about a particular issue, line of research, or controversy. Because the emphasis is on the thinking process, you may be asked to consider conflicting interpretations of data, judge the credibility of information sources, or generate your own testable hypotheses. The specific critical thinking skills highlighted in each lesson are summarized in a table so that they are easily identified. Some of the skills will show up in multiple chapters. The goal is to help you spontaneously select the appropriate critical thinking skills when you encounter new information. Repeated practice with selected skills across chapters should help you develop this ability.

An Example

As explained in the main body of the chapter, *evolutionary psychology* is emerging as an influential school of thought. To show you how critical thinking skills can be applied to psychological issues, let's examine the evolutionary explanation of gender differences in spa-

NON SEQUITUR © 2004 by Wiley Miller. Distributed by UNIVERSAL PRESS SYNDICATE. Reprinted with permission. All rights reserved.

tial talents and then use some critical thinking strategies to evaluate this explanation.

On the average, males tend to perform slightly better than females on most visual-spatial tasks, especially tasks involving mental rotation of images and navigation in space (Halpern, 2000; Silverman & Choi, 2005; see **Figure 1.14**). Irwin Silverman and his colleagues maintain that these gender differences originated in human evolution as a result of the gender-based division of labor in ancient hunting-and-gathering societies (Silverman & Phillips, 1998; Silverman et al., 2000). According to this analysis, males' superiority in mental rotation and navigation developed because the chore of *hunting* was largely assigned to men over the course of human history. These skills would have facilitated success on hunting trips (by helping men to traverse long distances, aim projectiles at prey, and so forth) and thus would have been favored by natural selection. In contrast, women in ancient societies generally had responsibility for *gathering* food rather than hunting it. This was an efficient division of labor because women spent much of their adult lives pregnant, nursing, or caring for the young. Therefore, they could not travel long distances. Silverman and Eals (1992) thus hypothesized that females ought to be superior to males on spatial skills that would have facilitated gathering, such as memory for locations. This is exactly what they found in a series of four studies. Thus, evolutionary psychologists explain gender differences in spatial ability—like other aspects of human behavior—in terms of how such abilities evolved to meet the adaptive pressures faced by our ancestors.

How can you critically evaluate these claims? If your first thought was that you need more information, good for you, because you are already showing an aptitude for critical thinking. Some additional information about gender differences in cognitive abilities is presented in Chapter 11 of this text. You also need to develop the habit of asking good questions, such as, "Are there alternative explanations for these results? Are there contradictory data?" Let's briefly consider each of these questions.

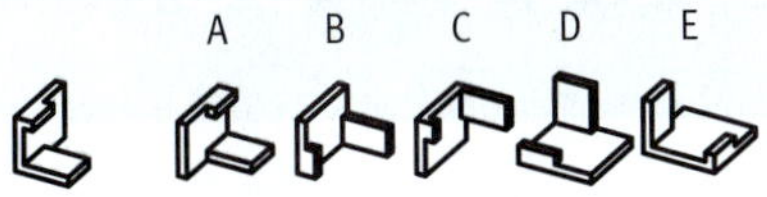

Figure 1.14
An example of a spatial task involving mental rotation. Spatial reasoning tasks can be divided into a variety of subtypes. Studies indicate that males perform slightly better than females on most, but not all, spatial tasks. The tasks on which males are superior often involve mentally rotating objects, such as in the problem shown here. In this problem, the person has to figure out which object on the right (A through E) could be a rotation of the object at the left. The answer is B.

SOURCE: Based on Stafford, R. E., & Gullikson, H. (1962). *Identical Blocks*, Form AA.

Are there alternative explanations for gender differences in spatial skills? Well, there certainly are other explanations for males' superiority on most spatial tasks. For example, one could attribute this finding to the gender-typed activities that males are encouraged to engage in more than females, such as playing with building blocks, Lego sets, Lincoln Logs, and various types of construction sets, as well as a variety of spatially oriented video games. These gender-typed activities appear to provide boys with more practice than girls on most types of spatial tasks (Voyer, Nolan, & Voyer, 2000), and experience with spatial activities appears to enhance spatial skills (Lizarraga & Ganuza, 2003). For example, one study found that just 10 hours of playing an action video game could produce substantial gains in spatial ability (Feng, Spence, & Pratt, 2007). If we can explain gender differences in spatial abilities in terms of disparities in the everyday activities of contemporary males and females, we may have no need to appeal to natural selection.

Are there data that run counter to the evolutionary explanation for modern gender differences in spatial skills? Again, the answer is yes. Some scholars who have studied hunting-and-gathering societies suggest that women often traveled long distances to gather food and that women were often involved in hunting (Adler, 1993). In addition, women wove baskets and clothing and worked on other tasks that required spatial thinking (Halpern, 1997). Moreover—think about it—men on long hunting trips obviously needed to develop a good memory for locations or they might never have returned home. So, there is room for some argument about exactly what kinds of adaptive pressures males and females faced in ancient hunting-and-gathering societies.

Thus, you can see how considering alternative explanations and contradictory evidence weakens the evolutionary explanation of gender differences in spatial abilities. The questions we raised about alternative explanations and contradictory data are two generic critical thinking questions that can be asked in a wide variety of contexts. The answers to these questions do *not* prove that evolutionary psychologists are wrong in their explanation of gender differences in visual-spatial skills. They do, however, *weaken* the evolutionary explanation. In thinking critically about psychological issues, you will see that it makes more sense to talk about the *relative strength of an argument* as opposed to whether an argument is right or wrong, because we will be dealing with complex issues that rarely lend themselves to being correct or incorrect.

REVIEW OF KEY LEARNING GOALS

1.19 Critical thinking is the use of cognitive skills and strategies that increase the probability of a desirable outcome. A critical thinker is flexible, vigilant, able to admit mistakes, and mindful of the thinking process.

1.20 Evolutionary psychologists attribute gender differences in spatial abilities to the gender-based division of labor in hunting-and-gathering societies. However, alternative explanations have been offered for these differences, focusing on the gender-typed activities that modern males and females engage in. There also are contradictory data regarding the adaptive pressures faced by females and males in hunting-and-gathering societies.

Table 1.3 Critical Thinking Skills Discussed in This Application

Skill	Description
Looking for alternative explanations for findings and events	In evaluating explanations, the critical thinker explores whether there are other explanations that could also account for the findings or events under scrutiny.
Looking for contradictory evidence	In evaluating the evidence presented on an issue, the critical thinker attempts to look for contradictory evidence that may have been left out of the debate.

© Cengage Learning 2013

Chapter 1 Practice Test

1. For which of the following is Wilhelm Wundt primarily known?
   A. the establishment of the first formal laboratory for research in psychology
   B. the distinction between mind and body as two separate entities
   C. the discovery of how signals are conducted along nerves in the body
   D. the development of the first formal program for training in psychotherapy
2. G. Stanley Hall is noteworthy in the history of psychology because he:
   A. established the first American research laboratory in psychology.
   B. launched America's first psychological journal.
   C. was the driving force behind the establishment of the American Psychological Association.
   D. did all of the above.
3. Which of the following approaches might William James criticize for examining a movie frame by frame instead of seeing the motion in the motion picture?
   A. structuralism
   B. functionalism
   C. dualism
   D. humanism
4. Which of the following approaches might suggest that forgetting to pick his mother up at the airport was Henry's unconscious way of saying that he did not welcome her visit?
   A. psychoanalytic
   B. behavioral
   C. humanistic
   D. cognitive
5. Fred, a tennis coach, insists that he can make any reasonably healthy individual into an internationally competitive tennis player. Fred is echoing the thoughts of:
   A. Sigmund Freud.
   B. John B. Watson.
   C. Abraham Maslow.
   D. William James.
6. Which of the following is a statement with which Skinner's followers would agree?
   A. Most behavior is controlled by unconscious forces.
   B. The goal of behavior is self-actualization.
   C. Nature is more influential than nurture.
   D. Free will is an illusion.
7. Which of the following approaches has the most optimistic view of human nature?
   A. humanism
   B. behaviorism
   C. psychoanalysis
   D. structuralism
8. Which of the following historical events created a demand for clinicians that was far greater than the supply?
   A. World War I
   B. the Depression
   C. World War II
   D. the Korean War
9. Which of the following is *not* an important interest of the positive psychology movement?
   A. positive institutions and communities
   B. positive symptoms in mental disorders
   C. positive subjective experiences
   D. positive individual traits
10. The study of the endocrine system and genetic mechanisms would most likely be undertaken by a:
    A. clinical psychologist.
    B. physiological psychologist.
    C. social psychologist.
    D. educational psychologist.
11. The fact that psychologists do not all agree about the nature and development of personality demonstrates:
    A. that there are many ways of looking at the same phenomenon.
    B. the fundamental inability of psychologists to work together in developing a single theory.
    C. the failure of psychologists to communicate with one another.
    D. the possibility that personality may simply be incomprehensible.
12. A multifactorial causation approach to behavior suggests that:
    A. most behaviors can be explained best by single-cause explanations.
    B. most behavior is governed by a complex network of interrelated factors.
    C. data must be subjected to rigorous statistical analysis in order to make sense.
    D. explanations of behavior tend to build up from the simple to the complex in a hierarchical manner.
13. Psychology's answer to the question of whether we are born or made tends to be:
    A. we are born.
    B. we are made.
    C. we are both born and made.
    D. neither.
14. In regard to changing answers on multiple-choice tests, research indicates that ______________ changes tend to be more common than other types of changes.
    A. wrong to right
    B. right to wrong
    C. wrong to wrong
15. Critical thinking skills:
    A. are abstract abilities that cannot be identified.
    B. usually develop spontaneously through normal content instruction.
    C. usually develop spontaneously without any instruction.
    D. need to be deliberately taught, because they often do not develop by themselves with standard content instruction.

Answers

1 A p. 4
2 D pp. 4–5
3 A p. 6
4 A p. 7
5 B pp. 8–9
6 D p. 10
7 A p. 11
8 C p. 13
9 B p. 17
10 B p. 21
11 A p. 24
12 B p. 25
13 C pp. 26–27
14 A p. 32
15 D p. 34

Media Resources

PsykTrek

To view a demo: **www.cengage.com/psychology/psyktrek**
To order: **www.cengage.com/psychology/weiten**

Go to the PsykTrek website or CD-ROM for further study of the concepts in this chapter. Both online and on the CD-ROM, PsykTrek includes dozens of learning modules with videos, animations, and quizzes, as well as simulations of psychological phenomena and a multimedia glossary that includes word pronunciations.

© Cengage Learning 2008

Visit Module 1a (*Psychology's Timeline*) to see a multimedia overview of psychology's evolution as a discipline.

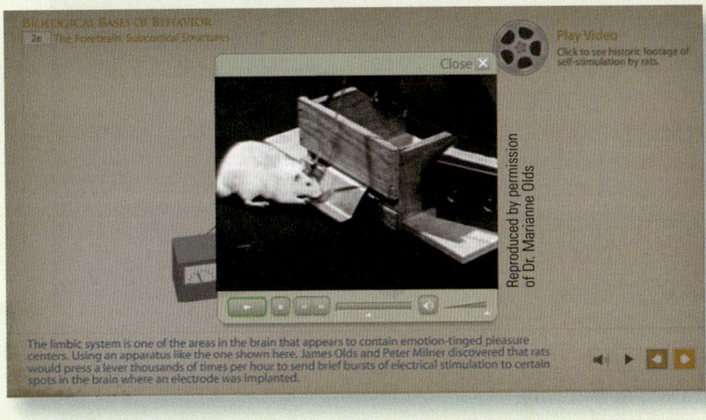

© Cengage Learning 2008

Go to the Video Selector or Module 2e (*The Forebrain: Subcortical Structures*) to see historic footage of James Olds's discovery of "pleasure centers" in the brain (mentioned on page 14).

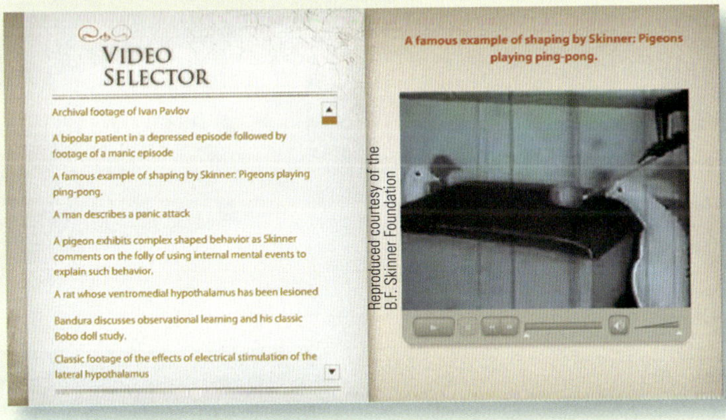

© Cengage Learning 2008

Go to the Video Selector or Module 5c (*Overview of Operant Conditioning*) to see pigeons playing Ping-Pong—the famous example of behavioral control by B.F. Skinner mentioned on page 10.

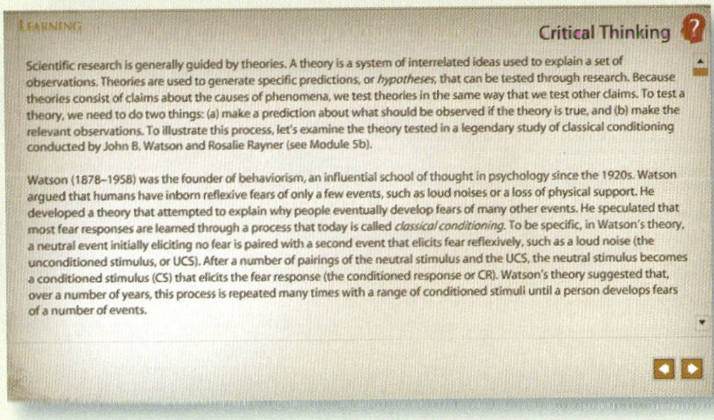

© Cengage Learning 2008

Check out the Critical Thinking Exercise for Unit 5 (*Theory Development and the Testing of Theories*) for an enlightening discussion of how one can evaluate the plausibility of competing theories, such as those introduced in this chapter.

Online Study Tools

Log in to **CengageBrain** to access the resources your instructor requires. For this book, you can access:

CourseMate brings course concepts to life with interactive learning, study, and exam preparation tools that support the printed textbook. A textbook-specific website, Psychology CourseMate includes an integrated interactive eBook and other interactive learning tools such as quizzes, flashcards, videos, and more.

CengageNow is an easy-to-use online resource that helps you study in less time to get the grade you want—NOW. Take a pre-test for this chapter and receive a personalized study plan based on your results that will identify the topics you need to review and direct you to online resources to help you master those topics. Then take a post-test to help you determine the concepts you have mastered and what you will need to work on. If your textbook does not include an access code card, go to CengageBrain.com to gain access.

WebTutor is more than just an interactive study guide. WebTutor is an anytime, anywhere customized learning solution with an eBook, keeping you connected to your textbook, instructor, and classmates.

Aplia. If your professor has assigned Aplia homework:

1. Sign in to your account
2. Complete the corresponding homework exercises as required by your professor.
3. When finished, click "Grade It Now" to see which areas you have mastered, which need more work, and detailed explanations of every answer.

Visit **www.cengagebrain.com** to access your account and purchase materials.

2

The Research Enterprise in Psychology

© Explorer / PhotoResearchers, Inc.

- Does sleeping less than seven hours a day reduce how long you will live?
- Do violent video games make people more aggressive?
- Can you make better decisions by not deliberating about them?
- Can women judge men's testosterone levels in just one glance?
- Do IQ scores predict how long people will live?

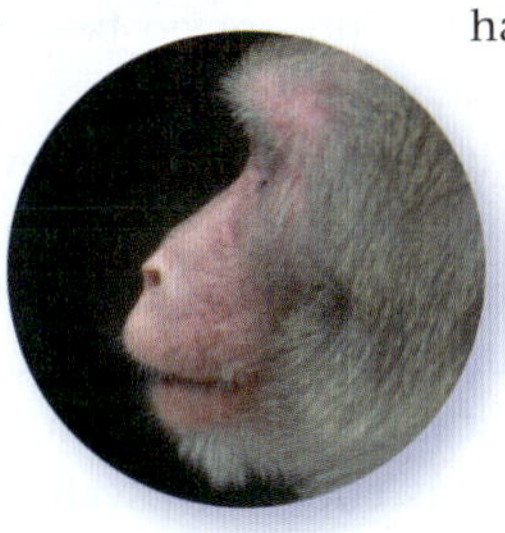

Questions, questions, questions—everyone has questions about behavior. Investigating these questions is what psychology is all about.

Some of these questions pop up in everyday life. Many a parent, for example, has wondered whether violent video games might be having a harmful effect on their children's behavior. Other questions explored by psychologists might not occur to most people. For example, you may never have wondered about what effects your IQ or sleeping habits could have on your life expectancy, or whether women can judge men's testosterone levels. Of course, now that you've been exposed to these questions, you may be curious about the answers!

In the course of this book, you'll find out what psychologists have learned about the five questions asked above. Right now I want to call your attention to the most basic question of all—namely, how should we go about investigating questions like these? How do we find answers to our questions about behavior that are accurate and trustworthy?

As noted in Chapter 1, *psychology is empirical*. Psychologists are committed to addressing questions about behavior through formal, systematic observation. This commitment to the empirical method is what makes psychology a scientific endeavor. Many people may have beliefs about the effects of playing violent video games based on personal opinion, a feeling of aversion toward violence, a generally permissive attitude toward children's games, anecdotal reports from parents, or other

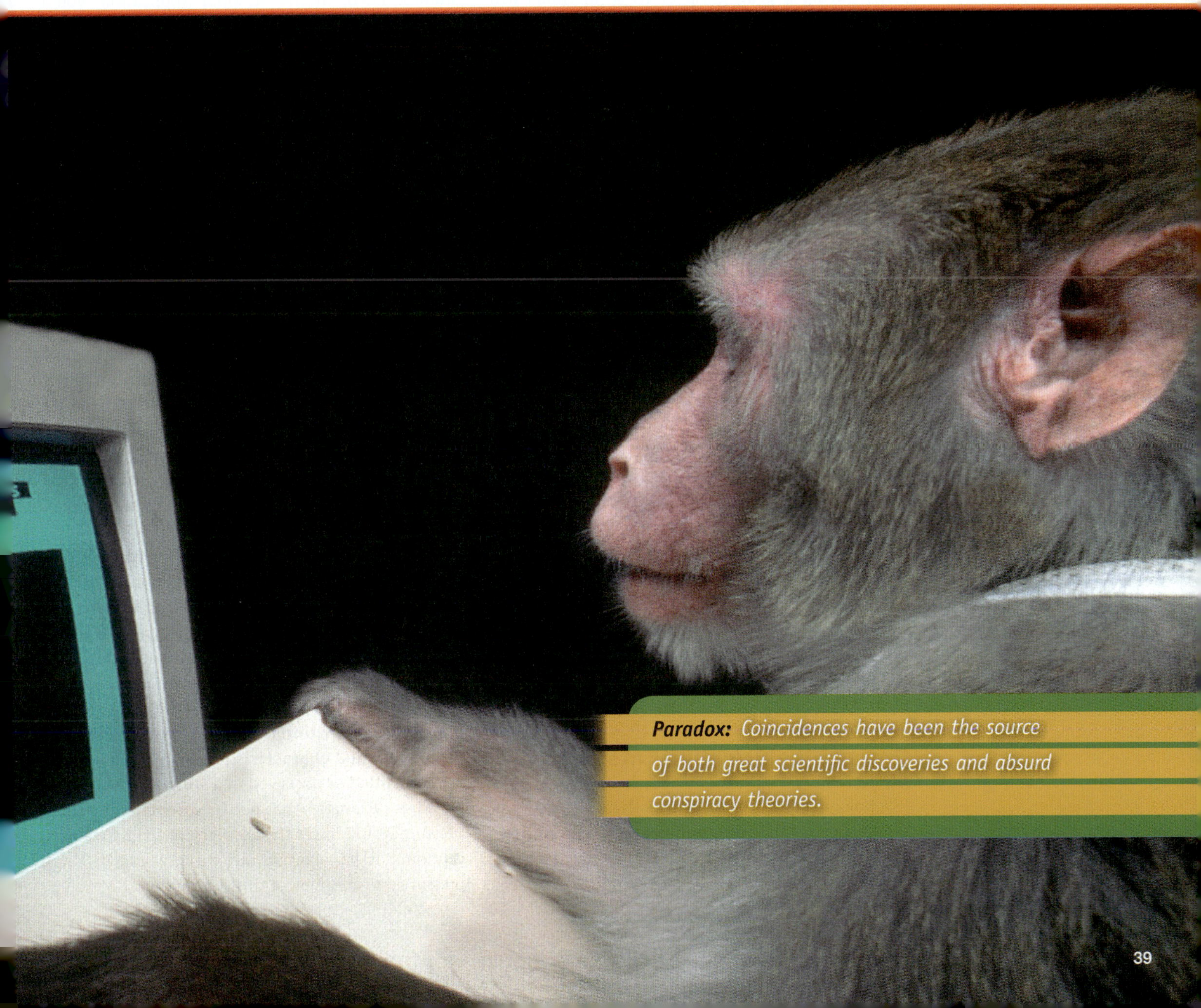

sources. As scientists, however, psychologists withhold judgment on questions like these until they have objective evidence based on valid, reproducible studies. Even then, their judgments are likely to be carefully qualified so that they do not go beyond what the evidence actually shows.

Gathering and evaluating that empirical evidence is an exercise in creative problem solving. As scientists, psychologists have to figure out how to make observations that will shed light on the puzzles they want to solve—and stand up to the critical scrutiny of their peers. In this endeavor psychologists rely on a large toolkit of research methods, because different kinds of questions call for different strategies of investigation. In this chapter, you'll learn about some of the principal methods used by psychologists in their research.

Why should you care about psychologists' research methods? There are at least two good reasons. First, having a good grasp of these methods will enhance your ability to understand the information you will be reading in the rest of this book, all of which is based on research. Second, becoming familiar with the logic of the empirical approach will improve your ability to think critically about claims concerning behavior. This ability is important because you are exposed to such claims—in conversations with friends, in advertising, in the news media—nearly every day. Learning how to evaluate the basis of these claims can make you a more skilled consumer of psychological information.

We'll begin our introduction to the research process in psychology by examining the scientific approach to the study of behavior. From there we'll move to the specific research methods that psychologists use most frequently. We'll also see how and why psychologists use statistics in their research.

Scientific methods have stood the test of time, but individual scientists are human and fallible. For this reason we'll conclude our discussion with a look at some common flaws in research. This section alone can make you a more skilled evaluator of claims that are said to be based on psychological studies. Then, in the Personal Application, you'll learn how to find and read journal articles that report on research. Finally, in the Critical Thinking Application, we'll examine the perils of a type of evidence people are exposed to all the time—anecdotal evidence.

KEY LEARNING GOALS

2.1 Explain science's main assumption, and describe the goals of the scientific enterprise.

2.2 Clarify the relations among theory, hypotheses, and research.

2.3 Outline the steps in a scientific investigation.

2.4 Identify the advantages of the scientific approach.

Looking for Laws: The Scientific Approach to Behavior

Whether the object of study is gravitational forces or people's behavior under stress, *the scientific approach assumes that events are governed by some lawful order.* As scientists, psychologists assume that behavior is governed by discernible laws or principles, just as the movement of the earth around the sun is governed by the laws of gravity. The behavior of living creatures may not seem as lawful and predictable as the "behavior" of planets. However, the scientific enterprise is based on the belief that there *are* consistencies or laws that can be uncovered. Fortunately, the plausibility of applying this fundamental assumption to psychology has been supported by the discovery of a great many such consistencies in behavior, some of which provide the subject matter for this text.

Goals of the Scientific Enterprise

Psychologists and other scientists share three sets of interrelated goals: measurement and description, understanding and prediction, and application and control.

1. *Measurement and description.* Science's commitment to observation requires that an investigator figure out a way to measure the phenomenon under study. For example, a psychologist could not investigate whether men are more or less sociable than women without first developing some means of measuring sociability. Thus, the first goal of psychology is to develop measurement techniques that make it possible to describe behavior clearly and precisely.

2. *Understanding and prediction.* A higher-level goal of science is understanding. Scientists believe that they understand events when they can explain the reasons for the occurrence of the events. To evaluate their understanding, scientists make and test predictions called hypotheses. A ***hypothesis* is a tentative statement about the relationship between two or more variables. *Variables* are any measurable conditions, events, characteristics, or behaviors that are controlled or observed in a study.** If we hypothesized, for example, that putting people under time pressure would lower the accuracy of their time perception, the variables in our study would be time pressure and accuracy of time perception.

3. *Application and control.* Ultimately, many scientists hope that the information they gather will be of some practical value in helping to solve everyday problems. Once people understand a phenomenon, they often can exert more control over it. Today, the profession of psychology attempts to apply research findings to practical problems in schools, businesses, factories, and mental hospitals. For example, a school psychologist might use findings about the causes of math anxiety to devise a program to help students control their math phobias.

How do theories help scientists achieve their goals? As noted in Chapter 1, psychologists do not set out just to collect isolated facts about relationships between variables. To build toward a better understanding of behavior, they construct theories. **A *theory* is a system of interrelated ideas used to explain a set of observations.** For example, using a handful of concepts, such as natural selection and reproductive fitness, evolutionary theorists in psychology attempt to explain a diverse array of known facts about mating preferences, jealousy, aggression, sexual behavior, and so forth (see Chapter 1). Thus, by integrating apparently unrelated facts and principles into a coherent whole, theories permit psychologists to make the leap from the *description* of behavior to the *understanding* of behavior. Moreover, the enhanced understanding afforded by theories guides future research by generating new predictions and suggesting new lines of inquiry (Fiske, 2004; Higgins, 2004).

A scientific theory must be testable. The cornerstone of science is its commitment to putting ideas to an empirical test. Most theories are too complex to be tested all at once. For example, it would be impossible to devise a single study that could test all the many facets of evolutionary theory. Rather, in a typical study, investigators test one or two specific hypotheses derived from a theory. If their findings support the hypotheses, confidence in the theory that the hypotheses were derived from grows. If their findings fail to support the hypotheses, confidence in the theory diminishes. The theory may then be revised or discarded (see **Figure 2.1**). Thus, theory construction is a gradual, iterative process that is always subject to revision.

Steps in a Scientific Investigation

Curiosity about a question provides the point of departure for any kind of investigation, scientific or otherwise. Scientific investigations, however, are *systematic.* They follow an orderly pattern, which is outlined in **Figure 2.2** on the next page. Let's look at how this standard series of steps was followed in a study of *naive realism* conducted by David Sherman, Leif Nelson, and Lee Ross (2003). Sherman and his colleagues wanted to investigate whether adversaries in political debates overestimate the gap between their views.

Step 1: Formulate a Testable Hypothesis

The first step in a scientific investigation is to translate a theory or an intuitive idea into a testable hypothesis. Sherman et al. (2003) noted that in heated

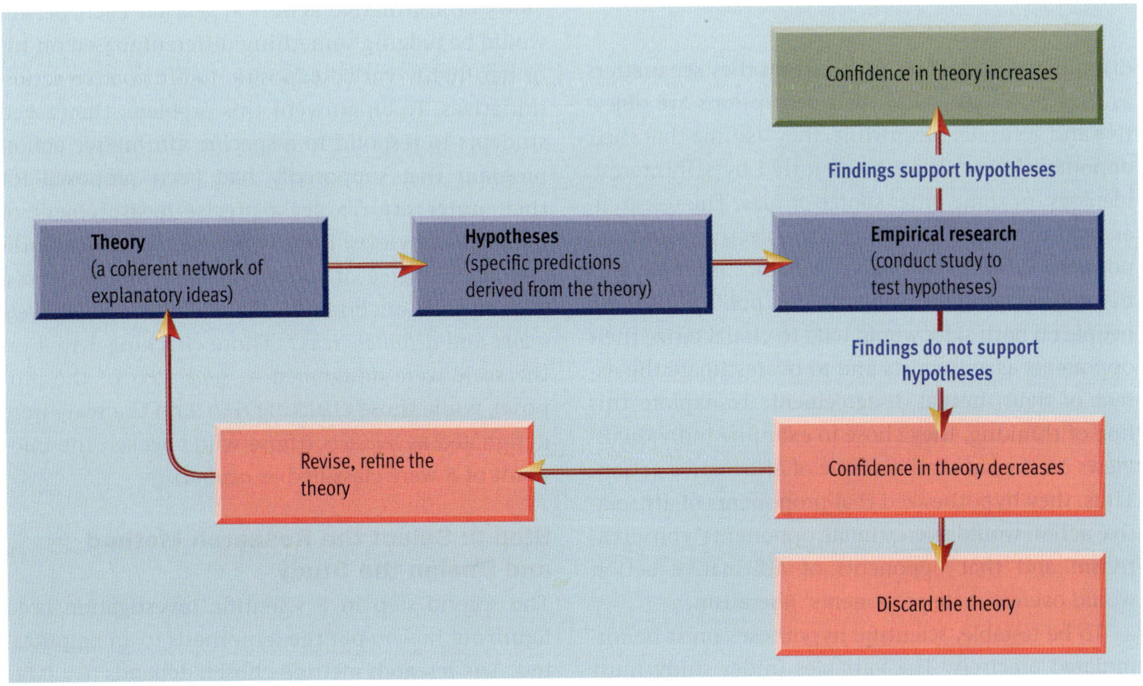

© Cengage Learning 2013

Figure 2.1
Theory construction.
A good theory will generate a number of testable hypotheses. In a typical study, only one or a few of these hypotheses can be evaluated. If the evidence supports the hypotheses, confidence in the theory they were derived from generally grows. If the hypotheses are not supported, confidence in the theory decreases, and revisions to the theory may be made to accommodate the new findings. If the hypotheses generated by a theory consistently fail to garner empirical support, the theory may be discarded altogether. Thus, theory construction and testing is a gradual process.

Figure 2.2

Flowchart of steps in a scientific investigation. As illustrated in the study by Sherman, Nelson, and Ross (2003), a scientific investigation consists of a sequence of carefully planned steps, beginning with the formulation of a testable hypothesis and ending with the publication of the study, if its results are worthy of examination by other researchers.

© Cengage Learning 2013

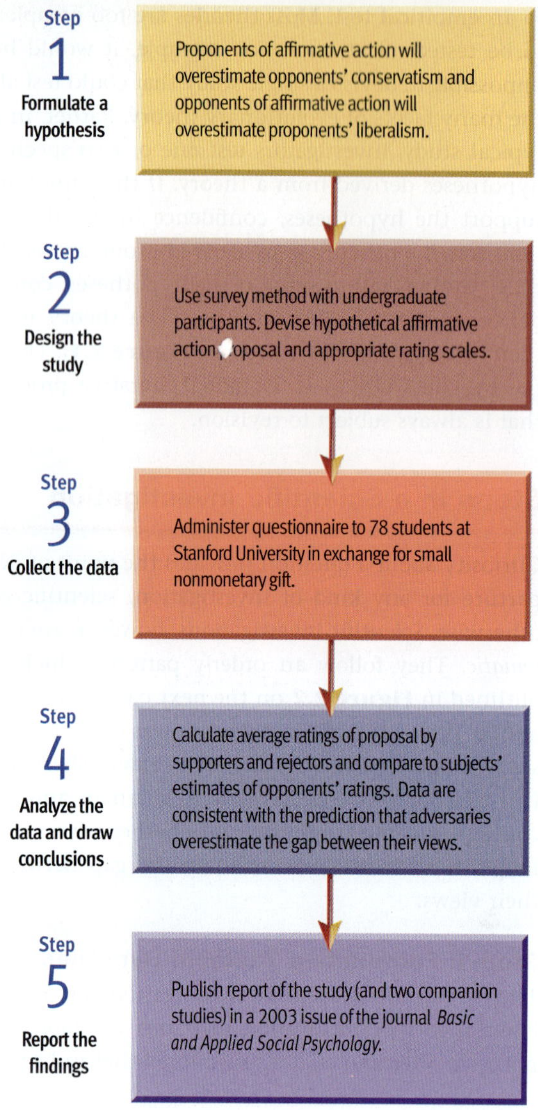

© 2004 by Sidney Harris/Science Cartoons Plus.com

disputes people seem to assume that they see matters as they really are—that their perceptions are objective and accurate. Meanwhile, they assume that their opponents' views must be distorted by self-interest, ideology, or some other source of bias. The researchers call this belief in one's own objectivity and opponents' subjectivity "naive realism." Sherman and his colleagues speculated that in political debates people on both sides would tend to characterize their opponents as extremists and to overestimate the extent of their mutual disagreement. To explore this line of thinking, they chose to examine individuals' views on the contentious issue of affirmative action. Thus, they hypothesized that proponents of affirmative action would overestimate opponents' conservativism and that opponents of affirmative action would overestimate proponents' liberalism.

To be testable, scientific hypotheses must be formulated precisely. The variables under study must be clearly defined. Researchers achieve these clear formulations by providing operational definitions of the relevant variables. **An *operational definition* describes the actions or operations that will be used to measure or control a variable.** Operational definitions establish precisely what is meant by each variable in the context of a study.

To illustrate, let's see how Sherman and his colleagues operationalized their variables. They decided that the issue of affirmative action is too complex and multifaceted to ask people about their views of affirmative action *in general*. Each person would be judging something different, based on his or her highly varied exposure to affirmative action initiatives. To circumvent this problem, they asked students to respond to a specific affirmative action program that supposedly had been proposed for their university. To get a precise measurement of participants' views, they asked the students to indicate their degree of support for the proposal on a 9-point scale anchored by the descriptions *definitely adopt* and *definitely reject*. Those checking 1 to 4 on the scale were designated as *supporters* of the proposal, while those checking 6 to 9 on the scale were designated as *rejecters* (those who checked the midpoint of 5 were classified as *neutral*).

Step 2: Select the Research Method and Design the Study

The second step in a scientific investigation is to figure out how to put the hypothesis to an empirical test. The research method chosen depends to a large degree on the nature of the question under study. The various methods—experiments, case studies, surveys, naturalistic observation, and so forth—each have advantages and disadvantages. The researcher has to ponder the pros and cons, then select the strategy that appears to be the most appropriate and practical. In this case, Sherman and colleagues decided that their question called for *survey* research. This method involves administering questionnaires or interviews to people.

Once researchers have chosen a general method, they must make detailed plans for executing their study. Thus, Sherman and associates had to decide how many people they needed to survey and where they would get their participants. ***Participants,* or *subjects,* are the persons or animals whose behavior is systematically observed in a study.** For their first study, the researchers chose to use 78 undergraduates (45 women and 29 men) at Stanford University. They also had to devise a plausible-sounding affirmative action proposal that students could evaluate, and they had to craft rating scales that would permit the assessment of subjects' political ideology and their perceptions of their opponents' political ideology.

Table 2.1 Key Data Collection Techniques in Psychology

Technique	Description
Direct observation	Observers are trained to watch and record behavior as objectively and precisely as possible. They may use some instrumentation, such as a stopwatch or video recorder.
Questionnaire	Subjects are administered a series of written questions designed to obtain information about attitudes, opinions, and specific aspects of their behavior.
Interview	A face-to-face dialogue is conducted to obtain information about specific aspects of a subject's behavior.
Psychological test	Participants are administered a standardized measure to obtain a sample of their behavior. Tests are usually used to assess mental abilities or personality traits.
Physiological recording	An instrument is used to monitor and record a specific physiological process in a subject. Examples include measures of blood pressure, heart rate, muscle tension, and brain activity.
Examination of archival records	The researcher analyzes existing institutional records (the archives), such as census, economic, medical, legal, educational, and business records.

© Cengage Learning 2013

Step 3: Collect the Data

The third step in a research endeavor is to collect the data. Researchers use a variety of ***data collection techniques,* which are procedures for making empirical observations and measurements.** Commonly used techniques include direct observation, questionnaires, interviews, psychological tests, physiological recordings, and examination of archival records (see **Table 2.1**). The data collection techniques used in a study depend largely on what is being investigated. For example, questionnaires are well suited for studying attitudes, psychological tests for studying personality, and physiological recordings for studying the biological bases of behavior. Depending on the nature and complexity of the study, data collection can often take months. It sometimes even requires years of work. One advantage of the survey method, however, is that data can often be collected quickly and easily, which was true in this case. Sherman and his colleagues simply had their subjects complete a carefully designed questionnaire in exchange for a small nonmonetary gift.

Step 4: Analyze the Data and Draw Conclusions

The observations made in a study are usually converted into numbers, which constitute the raw data of the study. Researchers use *statistics* to analyze their data and to decide whether their hypotheses have been supported. Thus, statistics play an essential role in the scientific enterprise. Based on their statistical analyses, Sherman et al. (2003) concluded that their data supported their hypothesis. As predicted, they found that supporters of the affirmative action proposal greatly overestimated the conservativism of the rejectors of affirmative action. And the rejectors of the affirmativve action proposal greatly overestimated the liberalism of the supporters (see **Figure 2.3**). The data indicated that the actual (average) attitudes of the two groups were not all that far apart, but each group *assumed* that their opponents held very dissimilar views. Obviously, insofar as this finding may be true of political debates in general, it sheds light on (1) why it is often so difficult for opposing sides to bridge the (perceived) gap between them, and (2) why people often have such pervasively negative views of their adversaries.

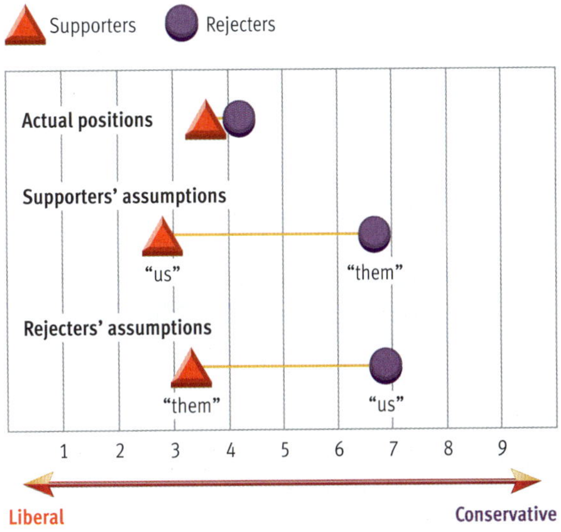

Figure 2.3
Results of the Sherman et al. (2003) study. As you can see, the actual liberal-conservative positions of the supporters and rejectors of the affirmative action proposal were not all that far apart (top row). However, when supporters of the proposal were asked to estimate the average rating given by other supporters as well as those who rejected the proposal, they assumed that a huge gap existed between the two groups (middle row). Similarly, when those who were against the proposal were asked to make the same estimates (bottom row), they also overestimated the disparity between the two groups.

SOURCE: Sherman, D. K., Nelson, L. D., & Ross, L. D. (2003). Naive realism and affirmative action: Adversaries are more similar than they think. *Basic and Applied Social Psychology, 25,* 275–289. Copyright © 2003; used with permission of Taylor & Francis; permission conveyed by Copyright Clearance Center, Inc.

Step 5: Report the Findings

The publication of research results is a fundamental aspect of the scientific enterprise (Roberts, Brown, & Smith-Boydston, 2003). Scientific progress can be achieved only if researchers share their findings with one another and with the general public. Therefore, the final step in a scientific investigation is to write up a concise summary of the study and its findings. Typically, researchers prepare a report that is delivered at a scientific meeting and submitted to a journal for publication. **A *journal* is a periodical that publishes technical and scholarly material, usually in a narrowly defined area of inquiry.** The study by Sherman and his colleagues was published, along with two companion studies, in a journal called *Basic and Applied Social Psychology.*

Figure 2.4

The peer review process for journal submissions. Scientists use an elaborate peer review process to determine whether studies merit publication in a technical journal. The goal of this process is to maximize the quality and reliability of published scientific findings.

The process of publishing scientific studies allows other experts to evaluate and critique new research findings. When articles are submitted to scientific journals, they go through a demanding *peer review process* that is summarized in **Figure 2.4**. Experts thoroughly scrutinize each submission. They carefully evaluate each study's methods, statistical analyses, and conclusions, as well as its contribution to knowledge and theory. The peer review process is so demanding, many top journals reject over 90% of submitted articles! The purpose of the peer review process is to ensure that journals publish reliable findings based on high-quality research. The peer review process is a major strength of the scientific approach because it greatly reduces the likelihood of publishing erroneous findings.

Advantages of the Scientific Approach

Science is certainly not the only method that can be used to draw conclusions about behavior. Everyone uses logic, casual observation, and good old-fashioned common sense. Because the scientific method often requires painstaking effort, it seems reasonable to ask what advantages make it worth the trouble.

Basically, the scientific approach offers two major advantages. The first is its clarity and precision. Commonsense notions about behavior tend to be vague and ambiguous. Consider the old adage "Spare the rod and spoil the child." What exactly does this generalization about childrearing amount to? How severely should children be punished if parents are not to "spare the rod"? How do we assess whether a child qualifies as "spoiled"? A fundamental problem is that such statements have different meanings, depending on the person. When people disagree about this assertion, it may be because they are talking about entirely different things. In contrast, the scientific approach requires that researchers use operational definitions to specify *exactly* what they are talking about when they formulate hypotheses. This clarity and precision enhance communication about important ideas.

The second and perhaps greatest advantage offered by the scientific approach is its relative intolerance of error. Scientists are trained to be skeptical. They subject their ideas to empirical tests. They also scrutinize one another's findings with a critical eye. They demand objective data and thorough documentation before they accept ideas. When the findings of two studies conflict, the scientist tries to figure out why, usually by conducting additional research. In contrast, common sense and casual observation often tolerate contradictory generalizations, such as "Opposites attract" and "Birds of a feather flock together." Furthermore, commonsense analyses involve little effort to verify ideas or detect errors. Thus, many "truisms" about behavior that come to be widely believed are simply myths.

All this is not to say that science has an exclusive copyright on truth. However, the scientific approach does tend to yield more accurate and dependable information than casual analyses and armchair speculation. Knowledge of scientific data can thus provide a useful benchmark against which to judge claims and information from other kinds of sources.

Now that we have had an overview of how the scientific enterprise works, we can focus on how specific research methods are used. ***Research methods* consist of various approaches to the observation, measurement, manipulation, and control of variables in empirical studies.** In other words, they are general strategies for conducting studies. No single research method is ideal for all purposes and situations. Much of the ingenuity in research involves selecting and tailoring the method to the question at hand. The next two sections of this chapter discuss the two basic types of methods used in psychology: *experimental research methods* and *descriptive/correlational research methods.*

REVIEW OF KEY LEARNING GOALS

2.1 The scientific approach assumes that there are laws of behavior that can be discovered through empirical research. The goals of the science of psychology include (1) the measurement and description of behavior, (2) the understanding and prediction of behavior, and (3) the application of this knowledge to the task of controlling behavior.

2.2 By integrating apparently unrelated facts into a coherent whole, theories permit psychologists to make the leap from the description of behavior to the understanding of behavior. Confidence in a theory increases when hypotheses derived from it are supported by research.

2.3 A scientific investigation follows a systematic pattern that includes five steps: (1) formulate a testable hypothesis, (2) select the research method and design the study, (3) collect the data, (4) analyze the data and draw conclusions, and (5) report the findings.

2.4 One major advantage of the scientific approach is its clarity in communication, which is promoted by its use of operational definitions. Another key advantage is its relative intolerance of error, which is promoted by scientists' constant testing of hypotheses and skeptical scrutiny of research findings.

Looking for Causes: Experimental Research

KEY LEARNING GOALS

2.5 Describe the experimental method, independent and dependent variables, and experimental and control groups.

2.6 Explain how experiments can vary in format and design.

2.7 Describe the Featured Study on how motives can influence visual perception.

2.8 Evaluate the major advantages and disadvantages of the experimental method.

Does misery love company? This question intrigued social psychologist Stanley Schachter. When people feel anxious, he wondered, do they want to be left alone, or do they prefer to have others around? Schachter's review of relevant theories suggested that in times of anxiety people would want others around to help them sort out their feelings. Thus, his hypothesis was that increases in anxiety would cause increases in the desire to be with others, which psychologists call the *need for affiliation.* To test this hypothesis, Schachter (1959) designed a clever experiment.

The *experiment* is a research method in which the investigator manipulates a variable under carefully controlled conditions and observes whether any changes occur in a second variable as a result. The experiment is a relatively powerful procedure that allows researchers to detect cause-and-effect relationships. Psychologists depend on this method more than any other.

Although its basic strategy is straightforward, in practice the experiment is a fairly complicated technique. A well-designed experiment must take into account a number of factors that could affect the clarity of the results. To see how an experiment is designed, let's use Schachter's study as an example.

Independent and Dependent Variables

PSYKTREK SIM1,1b

The purpose of an experiment is to find out whether changes in one variable (let's call it *X*) cause changes in another variable (let's call it *Y*). To put it more concisely, we want to find out *how X affects Y.* In this formulation, we refer to *X* as the *independent variable* and to *Y* as the *dependent variable.*

An *independent variable* is a condition or event that an experimenter varies in order to see its impact on another variable. The independent variable is the variable that the experimenter controls or manipulates. It is hypothesized to have some effect on the dependent variable, and the experiment is conducted to verify this effect. **The *dependent variable* is the variable that is thought to be affected by manipulation of the independent variable.** In psychology studies, the dependent variable is usually a measurement of some aspect of the participants' behavior. The independent variable is called *independent* because it is *free* to be varied by the experimenter. The dependent variable is called *dependent* because it is thought to *depend* (at least in part) on manipulations of the independent variable.

In Schachter's experiment, *the independent variable was the subjects' anxiety level.* He manipulated anxiety level in a clever way. Participants assembled in his lab were told by a "Dr. Zilstein" that they would be participating in a study on the physiological effects of electric shock. They were further informed that during the experiment they would receive a series of electric shocks while their pulse and blood pressure were being monitored. Half of the subjects were warned that the shocks would be very painful. They made up the *high-anxiety* group. The other half of the participants (the *low-anxiety* group) were told that the shocks would be mild and painless. In reality, there was no plan to shock anyone at any time. These orientation procedures were simply intended to evoke different levels of anxiety. After the orientation, the experimenter indicated that there would be a delay while he prepared the shock apparatus for use. The participants were asked whether they would prefer to wait alone or in the company of others. *The participants' desire to affiliate with others was the dependent variable.*

Experimental and Control Groups

SIM1, 1b

In an experiment the investigator typically assembles two groups of subjects who are treated differently with regard to the independent variable. These two groups are referred to as the experimental group and the control group. **The *experimental group* consists of the subjects who receive some special treatment in regard to the independent variable. The *control group* consists of similar subjects who do *not* receive the special treatment given to the experimental group.**

In the Schachter study, the participants in the high-anxiety condition constituted the experimental group. They received a special treatment designed to create an unusually high level of anxiety. The participants in the low-anxiety condition served as the control group. They were not exposed to the special anxiety-arousing procedure.

It is crucial that the experimental and control groups in a study be alike, except for the different treatment that they receive in regard to the independent variable. This stipulation brings us to the logic that underlies the experimental method. If the two groups are alike in all respects *except for the variation created by the manipulation of the independent variable,* any differences between the two groups on the dependent variable *must be due to the manipulation of the independent variable.* In this way researchers isolate the effect of the independent variable on the dependent variable. Schachter, for example, isolated the impact of anxiety on the need for affiliation. As predicted, he found that increased anxiety led to increased affiliation. As **Figure 2.5** indicates, the percentage of participants in the high-anxiety group who wanted to wait with others was nearly twice that of the low-anxiety group.

CONCEPT CHECK 2.1

Recognizing Independent and Dependent Variables

Check your understanding of the experimental method by identifying the independent variable (IV) and dependent variable (DV) in the following investigations. Note that one study has two IVs and another has two DVs. You'll find the answers in Appendix A in the back of the book.

1. A researcher is interested in how heart rate and blood pressure are affected by viewing a violent film sequence as opposed to a nonviolent film sequence.
   IV ____________________
   DV ____________________
2. An organizational psychologist develops a new training program to improve clerks' courtesy to customers in a large chain of retail stores. She conducts an experiment to see whether the training program leads to a reduction in the number of customer complaints.
   IV ____________________
   DV ____________________
3. A researcher wants to find out how stimulus complexity and stimulus contrast (light/dark variation) affect infants' attention to stimuli. He manipulates stimulus complexity and stimulus contrast and measures how long infants stare at various stimuli.
   IV ____________________
   DV ____________________
4. A social psychologist investigates the impact of group size on subjects' conformity in response to group pressure.
   IV ____________________
   DV ____________________

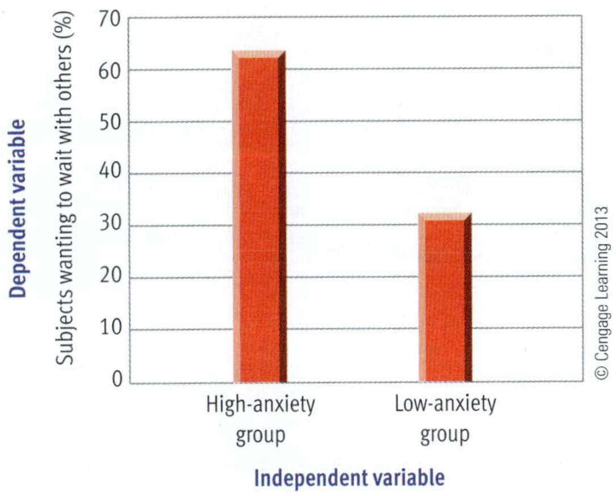

Figure 2.5
Results of Schachter's study of affiliation. The percentage of people wanting to wait with others was higher in the high-anxiety (experimental) group than in the low-anxiety (control) group, consistent with Schachter's (1959) hypothesis that anxiety would increase the desire for affiliation. The graphic portrayal of these results allows us to see at a glance the effects of the experimental manipulation on the dependent variable.

Extraneous Variables

SIM1,1b

As we have seen, the logic of the experimental method rests on the assumption that the experimental and control groups are alike except for their treatment in regard to the independent variable. Any other differences between the two groups can cloud the situation and make it impossible to draw conclusions about how the independent variable affects the dependent variable.

In practical terms, of course, it is impossible to ensure that two groups of participants are exactly alike in *every* respect. In reality, the experimental and control groups have to be alike only on dimensions relevant to the dependent variable. Thus, Schachter did not need to worry about whether his two groups were similar in hair color, height, or interest in ballet. These variables were unlikely to influence the dependent variable of affiliation behavior.

Instead, experimenters concentrate on ensuring that the experimental and control groups are alike on a limited number of variables that could have a bearing on the results of the study. These variables are called extraneous, secondary, or nuisance variables. ***Extraneous variables*** **are any variables other than the independent variable that seem likely to influence the dependent variable in a specific study.**

In Schachter's study, one extraneous variable would have been the subjects' tendency to be sociable. Why? Because participants' sociability could affect their desire to be with others (the dependent variable). If the participants in one group had happened to be more sociable (on the average) than those in the other group, the variables of anxiety and sociability would have been confounded. **A *confounding of variables* occurs when two variables are linked together in a way that makes it difficult to sort out their specific effects.** When an extraneous variable is confounded with an independent variable, a researcher cannot tell which is having what effect on the dependent variable.

Unanticipated confoundings of variables have wrecked innumerable experiments. That is why so much care, planning, and forethought must go into designing an experiment. One of the key qualities that separates a talented experimenter from a mediocre one is the ability to foresee troublesome extraneous variables and control them to avoid confoundings.

Experimenters use a variety of safeguards to control for extraneous variables. For instance, subjects are usually assigned to the experimental and control groups randomly. ***Random assignment*** **of subjects occurs when all subjects have an equal chance of being assigned to any group or condition in the study.** When experimenters distribute subjects into groups through some random procedure, they can be reasonably confident that the groups will be similar in most ways. **Figure 2.6** on the next page provides an overview of the elements in an experiment, using Schachter's study as an example.

Variations in Designing Experiments

SIM1,1b

We have discussed the experiment in only its simplest format, with just one independent variable and one dependent variable. Actually, many variations are possible in conducting experiments. Because you'll be learning about experiments with more complicated designs, these variations merit a brief mention.

First, it is sometimes advantageous to use only one group of subjects who serve as their own control group. The effects of the independent variable are evaluated by exposing this single group to two different conditions—an *experimental condition* and a *control condition.* For example, imagine that you wanted to study the effects of loud music on typing performance. You could have a group of participants work on a typing task while loud music was played (experimental condition) and in the absence of music (control condition). This approach would ensure that the participants in the experimental and control conditions would be alike on any extraneous

Reality CHECK

Misconception

Psychological research depends on random sampling.

Reality

It is *random assignment* (in experiments) that is a routine procedure in psychological research. *Random sampling* is relatively infrequent. A random sample is one chosen solely by chance. Random digit dialing *can* be used to administer short questionnaires, but the vast majority of psychological studies use samples of convenience. Working with limited resources, scientists strive to obtain representative samples, but random sampling is not practical (imagine the cost if researchers in Topeka had to bring 200 randomly selected people from all over the U.S. to their lab).

Figure 2.6

The basic elements of an experiment. As illustrated by the Schachter (1959) study, the logic of experimental design rests on treating the experimental and control groups exactly alike (to control for extraneous variables) except for the manipulation of the independent variable. In this way, the experimenter attempts to isolate the effects of the independent variable on the dependent variable.

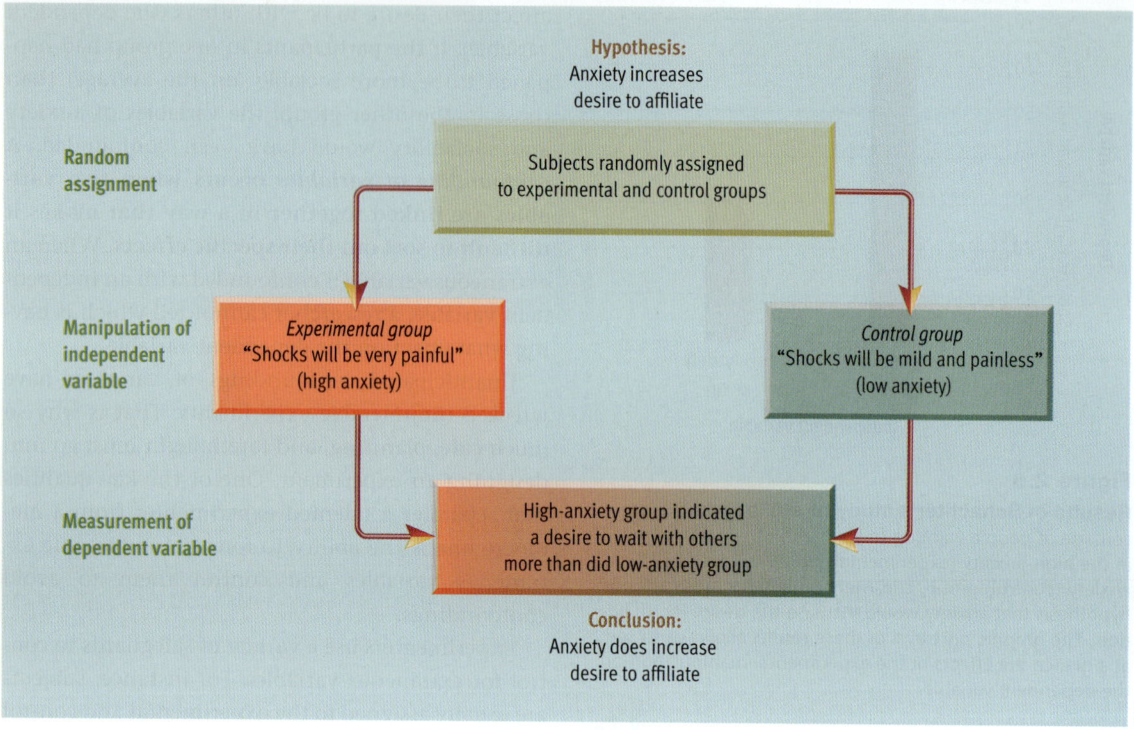

variables involving their personal characteristics, such as motivation or typing skill. After all, the same people would be studied in both conditions. When subjects serve as their own control group, the experiment is said to use a *within-subjects design* because comparisons are made within the same group of participants. In contrast, when two or more independent groups of subjects are exposed to a manipulation of an independent variable, the experiment is said to use a *between-subjects design* because comparisons are made between two different groups of participants. Although within-subjects designs are not used as frequently as between-subjects designs, they are advantageous for certain types of investigations. They also require fewer participants, and they ensure that the experimental and control groups are equivalent (Davis & Bremner, 2006).

Second, it is possible to manipulate more than one independent variable in a single experiment. Researchers often manipulate two or three independent variables to examine their joint effects on the dependent variable. For example, in another study of typing performance, you could vary both room temperature and the presence of distracting music (see **Figure 2.7**). The main advantage of this ap-

Figure 2.7

Manipulation of two independent variables in an experiment. As this example shows, when two independent variables are manipulated in a single experiment, the researcher has to compare four groups of subjects (or conditions) instead of the usual two. The main advantage of this procedure is that it allows an experimenter to see whether two variables interact.

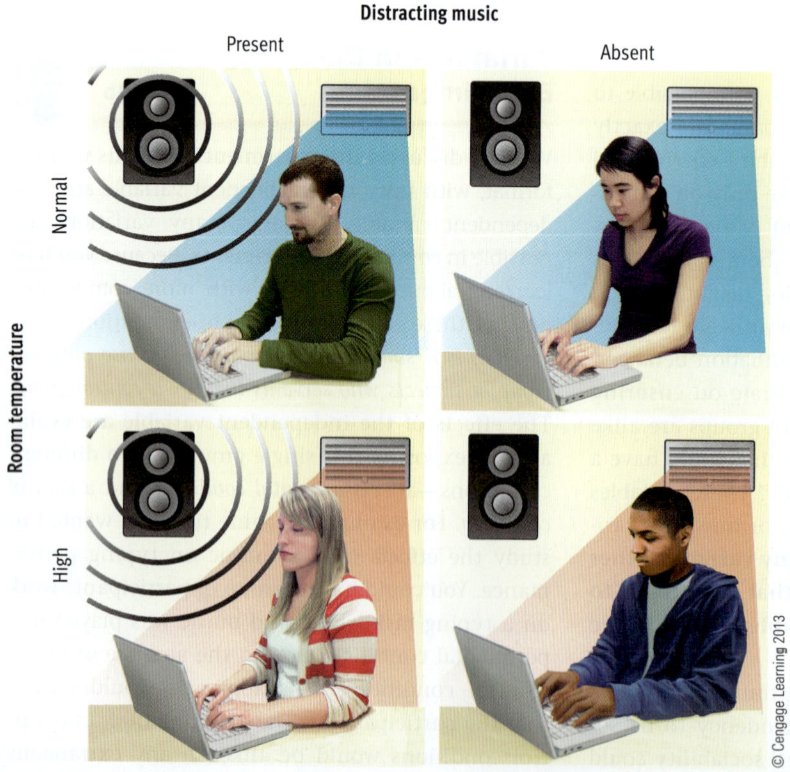

proach is that it permits the experimenter to see whether two variables interact. An *interaction* means that the effect of one variable depends on the effect of another. For instance, if we found that distracting music impaired typing performance only when room temperature was high, we would be detecting an interaction.

Third, it is also possible to use more than one dependent variable in a single study. Researchers frequently use a number of dependent variables to get a more complete picture of how experimental manipulations affect subjects' behavior. For example, in your studies of typing performance, you would probably measure two dependent variables: speed (words per minute) and accuracy (number of errors).

Now that you're familiar with the logic of the experiment, let's turn to our Featured Study for Chapter 2. You will find a Featured Study in each chapter from this point onward. These studies are provided to give you in-depth examples of how psychologists conduct empirical research. Each is described in a way that resembles a journal article, thereby acquainting you with the format of scientific reports (see the Personal Application at the end of the chapter for more information on this format). The Featured Study for this chapter gives you another example of an experiment in action.

FEATURED STUDY

Subjectivity in Perception: Seeing What We Want to See

SOURCE: Balcetis, E., & Dunning, D. (2006). See what you want to see: Motivational influences on visual perception. *Journal of Personality and Social Psychology, 91,* 612–625.

We noted in Chapter 1 that our experience of the world tends to be highly subjective. In interpreting events, we tend to see what we expect to see, and what we want to see. Of course, complex events, such as a passionate political speech, a complicated negotiation, or an evaluation of several job candidates, invite a certain amount of interpretation. In this research, Emily Balcetis and David Dunning set out to determine whether the tendency to see what we want to see applies even to simple instances of basic visual perception. In a series of experiments they briefly exposed participants to ambiguous visual stimuli that could have positive or negative repercussions for the participants. They wanted to determine whether these motivational factors would influence what the subjects saw. They hypothesized that participants' motives would shape their perceptual experiences. We'll look at their first experiment (in a series of five) in some detail, and then briefly describe the followup experiments.

Method

Participants. A total of 88 undergraduate students at Cornell University served as subjects. They earned extra credit in their psychology courses for their participation in the research. Each subject was run individually.

Procedure. Participants arriving at a lab for a supposed taste-testing study were told that they would be assigned to one of two tasks. One of the tasks appeared benign (drinking fresh orange juice). The other task appeared potentially very unpleasant (consuming a noxious-smelling, vile-looking health food drink). Subjects were told to sit at a computer that would randomly assign their task (beverage) by presenting either a number or a letter. About half were told that a letter would mean they were assigned to the desirable task and the other half were led to hope for a number. All of the participants were exposed to an extremely brief (400 milliseconds) presentation of the same, ambiguous stimulus. This stimulus could be interpreted as either the number 13 or the letter B (see **Figure 2.8**). Then, the computer appeared to crash. When informed of the crash, the experimenter acted surprised and asked each subject if the computer displayed anything before the crash. After the participant responded, the experimenter asked the individual to fill out a short questionnaire (which probed for suspicion about the purpose of the study) and left the room to supposedly prepare the beverage.

Results

Participants who recognized that the stimulus was ambiguous or who guessed the purpose of the experiment were excluded from the analyses. The data for the remaining subjects are summarized in **Figure 2.9** on the next page. Among people hoping for a letter, 72% saw the letter B and none saw a number. Among those hoping for a number, 60.5% reported seeing the number 13 and 23.7% saw the letter B (in both conditions, some people failed to see anything). Collapsing across both conditions and looking only at those who reported seeing something, 82% of the participants indicated that they saw the stimulus that they would be motivated to see. Obviously, the results provided initial support for the hypothesis that people's motives influence their perceptions. However, the authors acknowledged that the participants might have lied about what they saw to avoid having to consume the unpleasant drink. So, they conducted some additional studies to rule out this explanation.

Additional Experiments

To gain insight about whether participants were lying, the study was repeated with unambiguous displays of the letter B and the number 13. All of the subjects

Figure 2.8
Ambiguous stimulus used by Balcetis and Dunning (2006). Participants saw brief presentations of this stimulus, which could be viewed as a letter (B) or as a number (13). The study explored whether motivational factors would influence what people tend to see. © Cengage Learning 2013

Figure 2.9

Effects of motivation on visual perception. In their experiment, Balcetis and Dunning (2006) manipulated subjects' motivation to hope to see a letter or number flashed on a computer screen. As you can see, participants who were hoping for a letter either saw a letter or nothing, and those who hoped to see a number were far more likely to see a number than a letter.

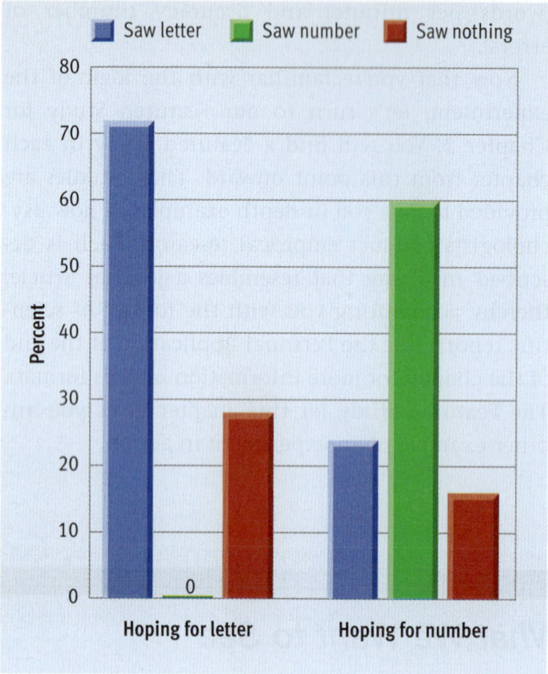

© Cengage Learning 2013

exposed to an undesirable stimulus that would result in consumption of the noxious drink made accurate reports, indicating that deception was probably not a problem in the original study. Two other studies, using complicated, unobtrusive measures, yielded results suggesting that participants were making sincere reports about what they thought they saw. And the findings were replicated with a different type of ambiguous stimulus.

Discussion

The authors concluded, "Our results suggest that people's desires for a particular outcome bias their perceptual set, such that they are more prepared to see what they hope for rather than what they fear" (p. 622). And they assert that this interesting form of wishful thinking seems to occur outside of people's conscious awareness.

Comment

This study was featured because it addresses an interesting question using a reasonably straightforward experimental design. It also provides a dramatic demonstration of one of this text's unifying themes—that people's experience of the world is highly subjective.

Advantages and Disadvantages of Experimental Research

The experiment is a powerful research method. Its principal advantage is that it permits conclusions about cause-and-effect relationships between variables. Researchers are able to draw these conclusions about causation because the precise control available in the experiment allows them to isolate the relationship between the independent variable and the dependent variable while neutralizing the effects of extraneous variables. No other research method can duplicate this strength of the experiment. This advantage is why psychologists usually prefer to use the experimental method whenever possible.

For all its power, however, the experiment has limitations. One problem is that experiments are often artificial. Because experiments require great control over proceedings, researchers must often construct simple, contrived situations to test their hypotheses experimentally. For example, to investigate decision making in juries, psychologists have conducted many experiments in which subjects read a brief summary of a trial and then record their individual "verdicts" of innocence or guilt. This approach allows the experimenter to manipulate a variable, such as the race of the defendant, to see whether it affects the participants' verdicts. However, critics have pointed out that having a participant read a short case summary and make an individual decision cannot really compare to the complexities of real trials (Weiten & Diamond, 1979). In actual court cases, jurors may spend weeks listening to confusing testimony while making subtle judgments about the credibility of witnesses. They then retire for hours of debate to arrive at a group verdict, which is quite different from rendering an individual decision. Many researchers have failed to do justice to this complex process in their laboratory experiments. When experiments are highly artificial, doubts arise about the applicability of findings to everyday behavior outside the experimental laboratory.

Another disadvantage is that the experimental method can't be used to explore some research questions. Psychologists are frequently interested in the effects of factors that cannot be manipulated as independent variables because of ethical concerns or practical realities. For instance, you might be interested in whether a nutritionally poor diet during pregnancy increases the likelihood of birth defects. This clearly is a significant issue. However, you obviously cannot select 100 pregnant women and assign 50 of them to a condition in which they consume an inadequate diet. The potential risk to the health of the women and their unborn children would make this research strategy unethical.

© Hannah Mentz/Corbis

In other cases, manipulations of variables are difficult or impossible. For example, you might want to know whether being brought up in an urban as opposed to a rural area affects people's values. An experiment would require you to randomly assign similar families to live in urban and rural areas, which obviously is impossible to do. To explore this question, you would have to use descriptive/correlational research methods, which we turn to next.

REVIEW OF KEY LEARNING GOALS

2.5 Experimental research involves the manipulation of an independent variable to determine its effect on a dependent variable. This research is usually done by comparing experimental and control groups, which must be alike in regard to important extraneous variables. Any differences between the groups in the dependent variable ought to be due to manipulation of the independent variable, as long as there are no confounds.

2.6 Experimental designs may vary. For example, sometimes an experimental group serves as its own control group. And many experiments have more than one independent variable or more than one dependent variable.

2.7 In our first Featured Study, Balcetis and Dunning (2006) used the experimental method to demonstrate that people's motives can shape their perceptions, such that they tend to see what they want to see.

2.8 The experiment is a powerful research method that permits conclusions about cause-and-effect relationships between variables. However, the experimental method is often not usable for a specific problem, and many experiments tend to be artificial.

Looking for Links: Descriptive/Correlational Research

KEY LEARNING GOALS

2.9 Explain the role of naturalistic observation, case studies, and surveys in psychological research.

2.10 Evaluate the major advantages and disadvantages of descriptive/correlational research.

As we just noted, in some situations psychologists cannot exert experimental control over the variables they want to study. In these cases, investigators must rely on *descriptive/correlational research methods,* which include naturalistic observation, case studies, and surveys. What distinguishes these methods is that the researcher cannot manipulate the variables under study. This lack of control means that these methods cannot be used to demonstrate cause-and-effect relationships between variables. *Descriptive/correlational methods only permit investigators to describe patterns of behavior and discover links or associations between variables.* That is not to suggest that associations are unimportant. You'll see in this section that information on associations between variables can be extremely valuable in our efforts to understand behavior.

Naturalistic Observation

What determines whether drivers stop or continue when they see a yellow light? Are there ethnic differences in sociability? These are just a couple examples of the kinds of questions that have been explored through naturalistic observation in recent studies. **In *naturalistic observation* a researcher engages in careful observation of behavior without intervening directly with the subjects.** This type of research is called *naturalistic* because behavior is allowed to unfold naturally (without interference) in its natural environment—that is, the setting in which it would normally occur. Of course, researchers have to make careful plans to ensure systematic, consistent observations (Angrosino, 2007). Let's look at two examples. One recent study concerned with accident prevention used a system of three video cameras to record drivers' reactions to yellow lights at an intersection (Elmitiny et al., 2010). The cameras and other equipment allowed the researchers to gather information on each vehicle's place in the flow of traffic, speed, and distance from the light. They were then able relate these data to the drivers' on-the-fly decisions when the traffic light changed from green to yellow. The study provided some useful insights into the factors that lead people to inadvertently run red lights.

© Robert F. Balazik/Shutterstock

Another recent study (Ramirez-Esparza et al., 2007) examined ethnic differences in sociability using an innovative device called an electronically activated recorder (EAR). The EAR is an unobtrusive, portable audio recorder carried by participants that periodically records their conversations and other ambient sounds as they go about their normal daily activities (Mehl, 2007). Using this clever device, the researchers investigated an interesting paradox: Although

© Tim Mantoani/Masterfile

A creative use of naturalistic observation allowed researchers to gain new insights into ethnic differences in sociability.

stereotypes suggest that Mexicans are outgoing and sociable, when asked they rate themselves as less sociable than Americans. The study supported this paradox, finding that Mexican participants rated themselves as less extraverted than American participants rated themselves. But the EAR data on actual daily behavior showed that Mexicans were *more* sociable than their American counterparts.

The major strength of naturalistic observation is that it allows researchers to study behavior under conditions that are less artificial than in experiments. Another plus is that engaging in naturalistic observation can represent a good starting point when little is known about the behavior under study. And, unlike case studies and surveys, naturalistic observation can be used to study animal behavior. Many landmark studies of animal behavior, such as Jane Goodall's (1986, 1990) work on the social and family life of chimpanzees, have depended on naturalistic observation. More recent examples of naturalistic observation with animals include studies of communication in Australian sea lions (Charrier, Pitcher, & Harcourt, 2009), mating preferences in Eastern bluebirds (Liu et al., 2009), and tool use in wild spider monkeys (Lindshield & Rodrigues, 2009).

A major problem with this method is that researchers often have trouble making their observations unobtrusively so that they don't affect their participants' behavior. ***Reactivity* occurs when a subject's behavior is altered by the presence of an observer.** Even animals may exhibit reactivity if observational efforts are readily apparent (Iredale, Nevill, & Lutz, 2010). Another disadvantage is that it often is difficult to translate naturalistic observations into numerical data that permit precise statistical analyses.

Case Studies

What portion of people who commit suicide suffer from psychological disorders? Which disorders are most common among victims of suicide? In health care visits during the final month of their lives, do people who commit suicide communicate their intent to do so? A research team in Finland wanted to investigate the psychological characteristics of people who take their own lives (Henriksson et al., 1993; Isometsa et al., 1995). Other researchers had explored these questions, but the Finnish team planned a comprehensive, national study of unprecedented scope. Their initial sample consisted of all the known suicides in Finland for an entire year.

The research team decided that their question called for a case study approach. **A *case study* is an in-depth investigation of an individual subject.** When this method is applied to victims of suicide, the case studies are called *psychological autopsies*. A variety of data collection techniques can be used in case studies. In normal circumstances, when the participants are not deceased, typical techniques include interviewing the subjects, interviewing people who are close to the subjects, direct observation of the participants, examination of records, and psychological testing. In this study, the investigators conducted thorough interviews with the families of the suicide victims and with the health care professionals who had treated them. The researchers also

© Michael Nichols/National Geographic Stock

The method of naturalistic observation can be particularly useful in studying animals in their natural habitats. For example, Jane Goodall conducted groundbreaking research on the social lives of chimpanzees through years of painstaking naturalistic observation.

examined the suicide victims' medical, psychiatric, and social agency records, as well as relevant police investigations and forensic reports. Comprehensive case reports were then assembled for each person who committed suicide.

These case studies revealed that in 93% of the suicides the victim suffered from a significant psychological disorder (Henriksson et al., 1993). The most common diagnoses, by a large margin, were depression and alcohol dependence. In 571 cases, victims had a health care appointment during the last four weeks of their lives, but only 22% of these people discussed the possibility of suicide during their final visit (Isometsa et al., 1995). Even more surprising, the sample included 100 people who saw a health professional on the same day they killed themselves, yet only 21% of these individuals raised the issue of suicide. The investigators concluded that mental illness is a contributing factor in virtually all completed suicides and that the vast majority of suicidal people do not spontaneously reveal their intentions to health care professionals.

Clinical psychologists, who diagnose and treat psychological problems, routinely do case studies of their clients (see **Figure 2.10**). When clinicians assemble a case study for diagnostic purposes, they generally are *not* conducting empirical research. Case study *research* typically involves investigators analyzing a collection or consecutive series of case studies to look for patterns that permit general conclusions. For example, one recent study (Arcelus et al., 2009) evaluated the efficacy of a treatment called interpersonal psychotherapy (IPT) for people suffering from bulimia (an eating disorder marked by out-of-control overeating followed by self-induced vomiting, fasting, and excessive exercise). Careful case assessments were made of 59 bulimic patients before, during, and after the sixteen-session course of IPT treatment. The results demonstrated that interpersonal therapy can be an effective treatment for bulimic disorders.

Case studies are particularly well suited for investigating certain phenomena, especially the roots of psychological disorders and the efficacy of selected therapeutic practices (Fishman, 2007). They can also provide compelling, real-life illustrations that bolster a hypothesis or theory. However, the main problem with case studies is that they are highly subjective. Information from several sources must be knit together to capture an impression of the subject. In this process, clinicians and researchers often focus selectively on information that fits with their expectations, which usually reflect their theoretical slant. Thus, it is relatively easy for investigators to see what they expect to see in case study research. Another worrisome issue is that the clinical samples typically used in case study research are often unrepresentative of the general population.

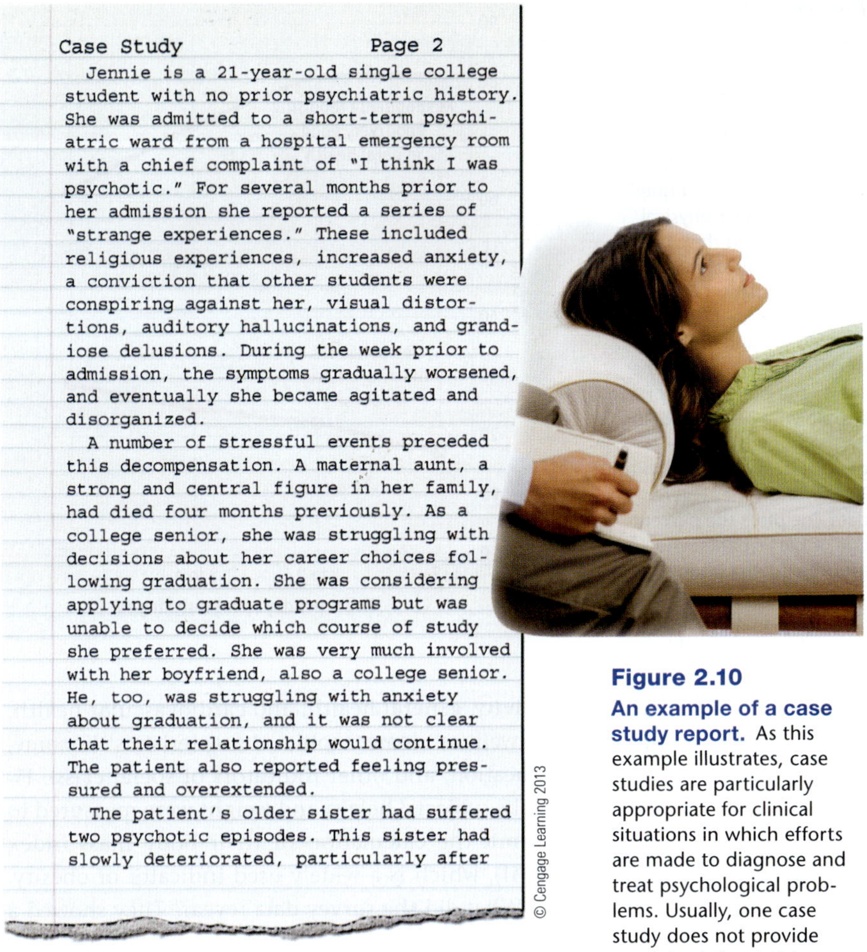

Case Study Page 2

Jennie is a 21-year-old single college student with no prior psychiatric history. She was admitted to a short-term psychiatric ward from a hospital emergency room with a chief complaint of "I think I was psychotic." For several months prior to her admission she reported a series of "strange experiences." These included religious experiences, increased anxiety, a conviction that other students were conspiring against her, visual distortions, auditory hallucinations, and grandiose delusions. During the week prior to admission, the symptoms gradually worsened, and eventually she became agitated and disorganized.

A number of stressful events preceded this decompensation. A maternal aunt, a strong and central figure in her family, had died four months previously. As a college senior, she was struggling with decisions about her career choices following graduation. She was considering applying to graduate programs but was unable to decide which course of study she preferred. She was very much involved with her boyfriend, also a college senior. He, too, was struggling with anxiety about graduation, and it was not clear that their relationship would continue. The patient also reported feeling pressured and overextended.

The patient's older sister had suffered two psychotic episodes. This sister had slowly deteriorated, particularly after

© Cengage Learning 2013
© Alain SHRODER/Getty Images

Figure 2.10
An example of a case study report. As this example illustrates, case studies are particularly appropriate for clinical situations in which efforts are made to diagnose and treat psychological problems. Usually, one case study does not provide much basis for deriving general laws of behavior. However, if you examine a series of case studies involving similar problems, you can look for threads of consistency that may yield general conclusions.

SOURCE: Greenfeld, D. (1985). *The psychotic patient: Medication and psychotherapy.* New York: The Free Press. Copyright © 1985 by David Greenfeld. Reprinted by permission of the author.

Surveys

Does the amount of time that people spend watching TV predict their physical health? Is social class related to people's TV viewing habits? These were the intriguing questions explored by a British research team that was interested in the health ramifications of sedentary behavior. Their study depended on survey data. **In a *survey* researchers use questionnaires or interviews to gather information about specific aspects of participants' background, attitudes, beliefs, or behavior.** In this case, Stamatakis and colleagues (2009) conducted household interviews with a representative sample of the adult population of Scotland. Almost 8000 participants were interviewed about how many hours per day they devote to television or other screen-based entertainment (including video games and material on computers). The participants were also questioned about their physical

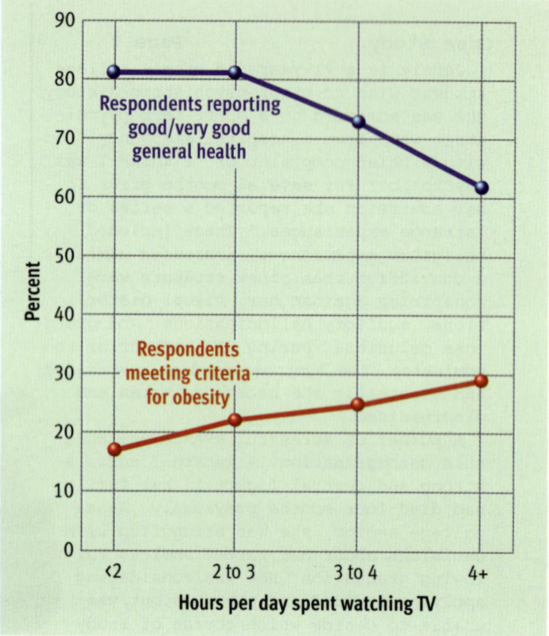

© Cengage Learning 2013

Figure 2.11

TV viewing in relation to health indicators. In the survey by Stamatakis and colleagues (2009), participants provided information about their daily TV viewing habits, answered questions about their physical health, and had their height and weight measured to permit calculation of their body mass index (BMI), which is a standard index of obesity. The blue data line shows the percentage of people who reported being in good or very good general health in relation to TV viewing time. The red data line plots the percentage of participants who met the criteria of obesity in relation to TV watching. Clearly, as TV time increased, general health tended to decline and obesity tended to increase.

activity, general health, and cardiovascular health, as well as demographic characteristics (income, education, and other indicators of social class). Finally, subjects' height and weight were measured to permit the calculation of their body mass index (BMI), which is a widely used indicator of obesity.

What did the survey data reveal? They showed a clear association between the amount of time allocated to screen-based entertainment and impaired health. The more people watched TV, the more likely they were to be obese or to report doctor-diagnosed diabetes or cardiovascular disease, and the less likely they were to report good general health (see **Figure 2.11**). The data also uncovered a rather strong link between social class and time devoted to screen-based entertainment. The people from lower socioeconomic strata spent considerably more time in front of TVs and other screens (see **Figure 2.12**). The results of the study underscored the health ramifications of sedentary behavior. And it demonstrated that lower social class is a key risk factor for elevated sedentary behavior.

Surveys are often used to obtain information on aspects of behavior that are difficult to observe directly. Surveys also make it relatively easy to collect data on attitudes and opinions from large samples of participants. As Fife-Schaw (2006b) notes, "The humble questionnaire is probably the single most common research tool in the social sciences" (p. 212). However, potential participants' tendency to cooperate with surveys appears to have declined noticeably in recent decades (Tourangeau, 2004). The growing resentment of intrusive telemarketing and heightened concerns about privacy and identity theft seem to be the culprits underlying the reduced response rates for research surveys. This problem may be partially offset by new technology, as survey studies are increasingly being conducted over the Internet (Skitka & Sargis, 2006). The major weakness of surveys is that they depend on *self-report data.* As we'll discuss later, intentional deception, wishful thinking, memory lapses, and poorly worded questions can distort participants' verbal reports about their behavior (Krosnick, 1999).

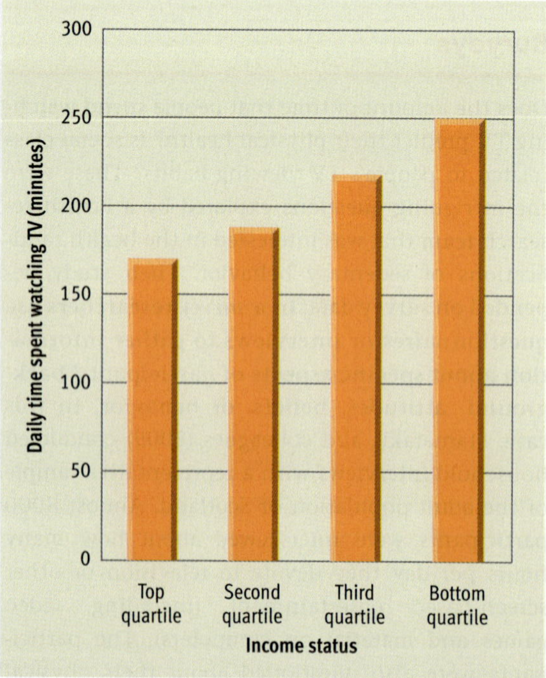

© Cengage Learning 2013

Figure 2.12

Socioeconomic class and time devoted to TV viewing. In the Stamatakis et al. (2009) survey study, data were gathered on participants' income, education, and occupation to investigate the relationship between social class and TV viewing habits. The data relating income to TV viewing are graphed here. The data show a substantial association between income and TV viewing time. As income declines, sedentary activity in front of TVs and other screens clearly increases. The data for the other two indicators of socioeconomic class (education and occupation) uncovered a similar relationship between social class and TV viewing.

Advantages and Disadvantages of Descriptive/Correlational Research

Descriptive/correlational research methods have advantages and disadvantages, which are compared with the strengths and weaknesses of experimental research in an Illustrated Overview of research methods that appears on pages 64–65. As a whole, the foremost advantage of these methods is that they give researchers a way to explore questions that could not be examined with experimental procedures. For example, after-the-fact analyses would be the only ethical way to investigate the possible link between poor maternal nutrition and birth defects in humans. In a similar vein, if researchers hope to learn how urban and rural upbringing relate to people's values, they have to depend on descriptive methods, since they can't control where subjects grow up. Thus, *descriptive/correlational research broadens the scope of phenomena that psychologists are able to study.*

CONCEPT CHECK 2.2

Matching Research Methods to Questions

Check your understanding of the uses and strengths of various research methods by figuring out which method would be optimal for investigating the following questions about behavioral processes. Choose from the following methods: (a) experiment, (b) naturalistic observation, (c) case study, and (d) survey. Indicate your choice (by letter) next to each question. You'll find the answers in Appendix A in the back of the book.

_______ 1. Are people's attitudes about nuclear disarmament related to their social class or education?

_______ 2. Do people who suffer from anxiety disorders share similar early childhood experiences?

_______ 3. Do troops of baboons display territoriality—that is, do they mark off an area as their own and defend it from intrusion by other baboons?

_______ 4. Can the presence of food-related cues (delicious-looking desserts in advertisements, for example) cause an increase in the amount of food that people eat?

Unfortunately, descriptive methods have one significant disadvantage: Investigators cannot control events to isolate cause and effect. *Consequently, correlational research cannot demonstrate conclusively that two variables are causally related.* Consider for instance, the correlation between time spent watching TV and poor health uncovered by Stamatakis and colleagues (2009). Their data do not permit us to conclude that sedentary behavior has a *causal* impact on health. Other factors might play a role in this association. For example, sedentary behavior could co-vary with some other factor, such as social class (which it did), that could be responsible for the observed differences in health.

"CONTRARY TO THE POPULAR VIEW, OUR STUDIES SHOW THAT IT IS REAL LIFE THAT CONTRIBUTES TO VIOLENCE ON TELEVISION."

© 2004 by Sidney Harris/ScienceCartoons Plus.com

REVIEW OF KEY LEARNING GOALS

2.9 Naturalistic observation involves careful, prolonged observation of behavior in its natural setting without any intervention. Clinical research depends heavily on case studies, which involve in-depth investigations of individuals. In a survey, researchers interview participants or administer questionnaires to gather information on specific aspects of attitudes or behavior. Each approach has its unique strengths and weaknesses.

2.10 Descriptive/correlational research methods allow psychologists to explore issues that might not be open to experimental investigation because the variables of interest cannot be manipulated. However, these research methods cannot demonstrate cause-effect relationships.

Looking for Conclusions: Statistics and Research

KEY LEARNING GOALS

2.11 Describe three measures of central tendency and one measure of variability.

2.12 Distinguish between positive and negative correlations.

2.13 Discuss correlation in relation to prediction and causation.

2.14 Clarify the meaning of statistical significance.

Whether researchers use experimental or correlational methods, they need some way to make sense of their data. ***Statistics* is the use of mathematics to organize, summarize, and interpret numerical data.** Statistical analyses permit researchers to draw conclusions based on their observations. Many students find statistics intimidating. Yet statistics are an integral part of modern life. Although you may not realize it, you are bombarded with statistics nearly every day. When you read about economists' projections for inflation, when you check a baseball player's batting average, when you see the popularity ratings of television shows, you are dealing with statistics. In this section, we will examine a few basic statistical concepts that will help you understand the research discussed throughout this book.

For the most part, we won't concern ourselves with the details of statistical *computations*. These details and some additional statistical concepts are discussed in Appendix B at the back of the book. At this juncture, we will discuss only the purpose, logic, and value of the two basic types of statistics: descriptive statistics and inferential statistics.

Descriptive Statistics 1c, 1d

***Descriptive statistics* are used to organize and summarize data.** They provide an overview of numerical data. Key descriptive statistics include measures of central tendency, measures of variability, and the coefficient of correlation. Let's take a brief look at each of these.

Central Tendency 1c

In summarizing numerical data, researchers often want to know what constitutes a typical or average score. To answer this question, they use three measures of central tendency: the median, the mean, and the mode. **The *median* is the score that falls exactly in the center of a distribution of scores.** Half of the scores fall above the median and half fall below it. **The *mean* is the arithmetic average of the scores in a distribution.** It is obtained by adding up all the scores and dividing by the total number of scores. Finally, **the *mode* is the most frequent score in a distribution.**

In general, the mean is the most useful measure of central tendency because additional statistical manipulations can be performed on it that are not possible with the median or mode. However, the mean is sensitive to extreme scores in a distribution, which can sometimes make the mean misleading. To illustrate, imagine that you're interviewing for a sales position at a company. Unbeknownst to you, the company's five salespeople earned the following incomes in the previous year: $20,000, $20,000, $25,000, $35,000, and $200,000. You ask how much the typical salesperson earns in a year. The sales director proudly announces that her five salespeople earned a *mean* income of $60,000 last year (the calculations are shown in **Figure 2.13**). However, before you order that new sports car, you had better inquire about the *median* and *modal* income for the sales staff. In this case, one extreme score ($200,000) has inflated the mean, making it unrepresentative of the sales staff's earnings. Here, the median ($25,000) and the mode ($20,000) both provide better estimates of what you are likely to earn.

Variability 1c

In describing a set of data, it is often useful to have some estimate of the variability among the scores. ***Variability* refers to how much the scores in a data set vary from each other and from the mean. The *standard deviation* is an index of the amount of variability in a set of data.** When variability is great, the standard deviation will be relatively large. When variability is low, the standard deviation will be smaller. This relationship is apparent if you examine the two sets of data in **Figure 2.14**. The mean is the same for both sets of scores. But variability clearly is greater in set B than in set A. This greater variability yields a higher standard deviation for set B than for set A. Estimates of variability play a crucial role when researchers use statistics to decide whether the results of their studies support their hypotheses.

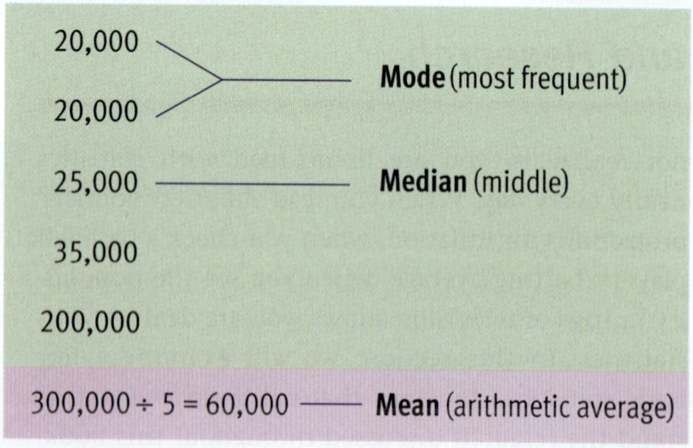

© Cengage Learning 2013

Figure 2.13
Measures of central tendency. The three measures of central tendency usually converge, but that is not always the case, as these data illustrate. Which measure is most useful depends on the nature of the data. Generally, the mean is the best index of central tendency, but in this instance the median is more informative.

Speed (miles per hour)

Set A Perfection Boulevard		Set B Wild Street
35		21
34		37
33		50
37		28
38		42
40		37
36		39
33		25
34		23
30		48
35	Mean	35
2.87	Standard deviation	10.39

© Cengage Learning 2013

Figure 2.14
Variability and the standard deviation. Although these two sets of data produce the same mean, or average, an observer on Wild Street would see much more variability in the speeds of individual cars than an observer on Perfection Boulevard. As you can see, the standard deviation for set B is higher than that for set A because of the greater variability in set B.

Correlation

1d

A *correlation* exists when two variables are related to each other. Researchers often want to quantify the strength of an association between two variables, such as between class attendance and course grades, or between cigarette smoking and physical disease. In this effort, they depend extensively on a useful descriptive statistic: the correlation coefficient. **The *correlation coefficient* is a numerical index of the degree of relationship between two variables.** A correlation coefficient indicates (1) the direction (positive or negative) of the relationship and (2) how strongly the two variables are related.

Positive Versus Negative Correlation A *positive correlation* indicates that two variables co-vary in the *same* direction. This means that high scores on variable *X* are associated with high scores on variable *Y* and that low scores on variable *X* are associated with low scores on variable *Y*. For example, a positive correlation exists between high school grade point average (GPA) and subsequent college GPA. That is, people who do well in high school tend to do well in college. Likewise, those who perform poorly in high school tend to perform poorly in college (see **Figure 2.15**).

In contrast, a *negative* correlation indicates that two variables co-vary in the *opposite* direction. This means that people who score high on variable *X* tend to score low on variable *Y*, whereas those who score low on *X* tend to score high on *Y*. For example, in most college courses a negative correlation exists between how frequently students are absent and how well they perform on exams. Students who have a high number of absences tend to get low exam scores, while students who have a low number of absences tend to earn higher exam scores (see **Figure 2.15**).

If a correlation is negative, a minus sign (−) is always placed in front of the coefficient. If a correlation is positive, a plus sign (+) may be placed in front of the coefficient, or the coefficient may be shown with no sign. Thus, if there's no sign, the correlation is positive.

Strength of the Correlation Whereas the positive or negative sign indicates the direction of an association, the *size of the coefficient* indicates the *strength* of an association between two variables. The coefficient can vary between 0 and +1.00 (if positive) or between 0 and −1.00 (if negative). A coefficient near 0 indicates no relationship between the variables; that is, high or low scores on variable *X* show no consistent relationship to high or low scores on variable *Y*. A coefficient of +1.00 or −1.00 indicates a perfect, one-to-one correspondence between the two variables. Most correlations fall between these extremes.

The closer the correlation is to either −1.00 or +1.00, the stronger the relationship (see **Figure 2.16** on the next page). Thus, a correlation of .90 represents a stronger tendency for variables to be associated than a correlation of .40 does. Likewise, a correlation of −.75 represents a stronger relationship than a correlation of −.45. Keep in mind that the

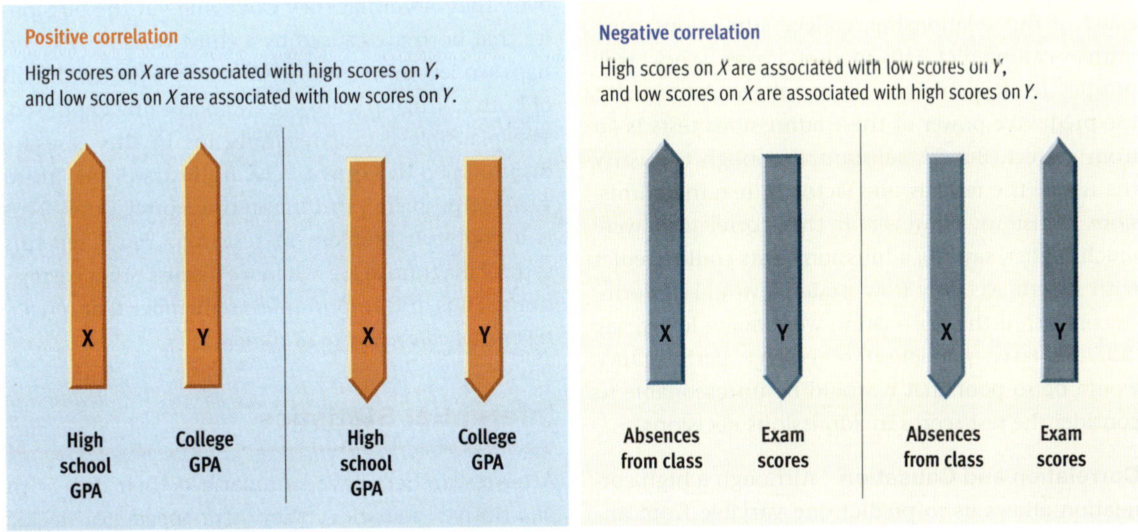

© Cengage Learning 2013

Figure 2.15
Positive and negative correlation. Notice that the terms *positive* and *negative* refer to the direction of the relationship between two variables, not to its strength. Variables are positively correlated if they tend to increase and decrease together; they are negatively correlated if one tends to increase when the other decreases.

Figure 2.16

Interpreting correlation coefficients. The magnitude of a correlation coefficient indicates the strength of the relationship between two variables. The sign (plus or minus) indicates whether the correlation is positive or negative. The closer the coefficient comes to +1.00 or −1.00, the stronger the relationship between the variables.

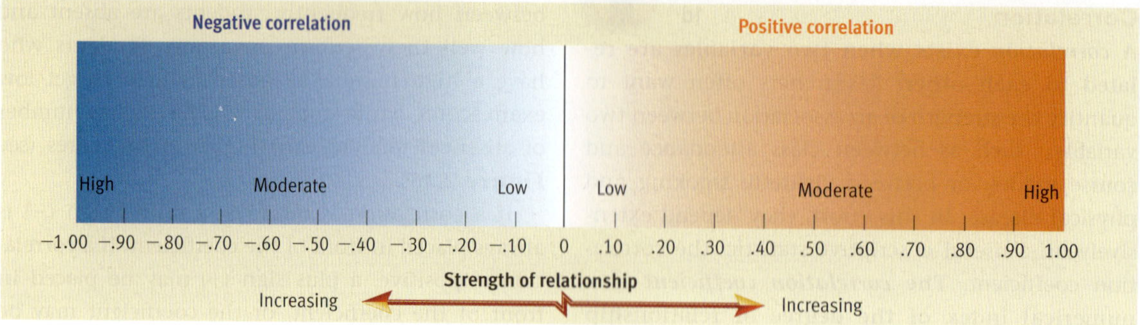

© Cengage Learning 2013

strength of a correlation depends only on the *size* of the coefficient. The positive or negative sign simply indicates the *direction* of the relationship. Therefore, a correlation of −.60 reflects a stronger relationship than a correlation of +.30. The computation of correlation coefficients permits researchers to precisely quantify the strength of the associations between variables.

Correlation and Prediction You may recall that one of the key goals of scientific research is accurate *prediction*. A close link exists between the magnitude of a correlation and the power it gives scientists to make predictions. *As a correlation increases in strength (gets closer to either −1.00 or +1.00), the ability to predict one variable based on knowledge of the other variable increases.*

To illustrate, consider how college admissions tests (such as the SAT or ACT) are used to predict college performance. When students' admissions test scores and first-year college GPA are correlated, researchers generally find moderate positive correlations in the .40s and .50s (Kobrin et al., 2008). Because of this relationship, college admissions committees can predict with modest accuracy how well prospective students will do in college. Admittedly, the predictive power of these admissions tests is *far* from perfect. But it's substantial enough to justify the use of the tests as one factor in making admissions decisions. However, if this correlation were much higher, say .90, admissions tests could predict with superb accuracy how students would perform. In contrast, if this correlation were much lower, say .20, the tests' prediction of college performance would be so poor that it would be unreasonable to consider the test scores in admissions decisions.

Correlation and Causation Although a high correlation allows us to predict one variable from another, it does not tell us whether a cause-effect relationship exists between the two variables. The problem is that variables can be highly correlated even though they are not causally related. For example, there is a substantial positive correlation between the size of young children's feet and the size of their vocabulary. That is, larger feet are associated with a larger vocabulary. Obviously, increases in foot size do not *cause* increases in vocabulary size. Nor do increases in vocabulary size cause increases in foot size. Instead, both are caused by a third variable: an increase in the children's age.

When we find that variables *X* and *Y* are correlated, we can safely conclude only that *X* and *Y* are related. We do not know *how X* and *Y* are related. We do not know whether *X* causes *Y* or *Y* causes *X* or whether both are caused by a third variable. For example, survey studies have found a positive correlation between smoking and the risk of experiencing a major depressive disorder (Johnson & Breslau, 2006; Kinnunen et al., 2006). It's clear that an association exists between smoking and depression. But it's hard to tell what's causing what. The researchers acknowledge that they don't know whether smoking makes people more vulnerable to depression or whether depression increases the tendency to smoke. Moreover, they note that they can't rule out the possibility that both are caused by a third variable (*Z*). Perhaps anxiety and neuroticism increase the likelihood of both taking up smoking and becoming depressed. The plausible causal relationships in this case are diagrammed in **Figure 2.17**. It illustrates the "third variable problem" in interpreting correlations. This is a common problem in research. You'll see this type of diagram again when we discuss other correlations. Thus, it is important to remember that *correlation is not equivalent to causation.*

Inferential Statistics

After researchers have summarized their data with descriptive statistics, they still need to decide whether their data support their hypotheses. ***Inferential statistics* are used to interpret data and draw conclusions.** Working with the laws of probability, researchers use inferential statistics to evalu-

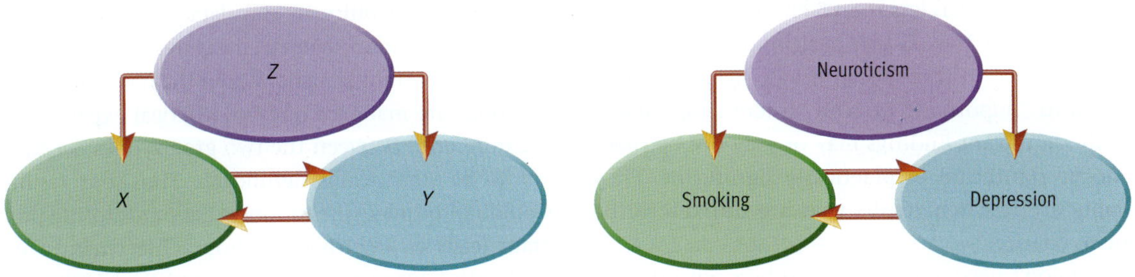

Figure 2.17

Three possible causal relations between correlated variables. If variables *X* and *Y* are correlated, does *X* cause *Y*, does *Y* cause *X*, or does some hidden third variable, *Z*, account for the changes in both *X* and *Y*? As the relationship between smoking and depression illustrates, a correlation alone does not provide the answer. We will encounter this problem of interpreting the meaning of correlations frequently in our discussions of behavioral research. © Cengage Learning 2013

Reality CHECK

Misconception

A strong correlation between variables suggests that one of those variables causes the other.

Reality

The magnitude of a correlation is not a useful guide to the likelihood of causation. Two variables could be highly correlated, but both could be caused by a third variable. In contrast, a relatively low correlation might reflect a genuine, but weak causal effect.

ate the possibility that their results might be due to the fluctuations of chance.

To illustrate this process, envision a hypothetical experiment. A computerized tutoring program (the independent variable) is designed to increase sixth-graders' reading achievement (the dependent variable). Our hypothesis is that program participants (the experimental group) will score higher than nonparticipants (the control group) on a standardized reading test given near the end of the school year. Let's assume that we compare 60 subjects in each group. We obtain the following results, reported in terms of participants' grade-level scores for reading:

Control group		*Experimental group*
6.3	Mean	6.8
1.4	Standard deviation	2.4

We hypothesized that the training program would produce higher reading scores in the experimental group than in the control group. Sure enough, that is indeed the case. However, we have to ask ourselves a critical question: Is this observed difference between the two groups large enough to support our hypothesis? That is, do the higher scores in the experimental group reflect the effect of the training program? Or could a difference of this size have occurred by chance? If our results could easily have occurred by chance, they don't provide meaningful support for our hypothesis.

When statistical calculations indicate that research results are not likely to be due to chance, the results are said to be *statistically significant.* You will probably hear your psychology professor use this phrase quite frequently. In discussing research, it is routine to note that "statistically significant differences were found." In statistics, the word *significant* has a precise and special meaning. ***Statistical significance*** **is said to exist when the probability that the observed findings are due to chance is very low.** "Very low"

CONCEPT CHECK 2.3

Understanding Correlation

Check your understanding of correlation by interpreting the meaning of the correlation in item 1 and by guessing the direction (positive or negative) of the correlations in item 2. You'll find the answers in Appendix A.

1. Researchers have found a substantial positive correlation between youngsters' self-esteem and their academic achievement (measured by grades in school). Check any acceptable conclusions based on this correlation.
   ______ a. Low grades cause low self-esteem.
   ______ b. There is an association between self-esteem and academic achievement.
   ______ c. High self-esteem causes high academic achievement.
   ______ d. High ability causes both high self-esteem and high academic achievement.
   ______ e. Youngsters who score low in self-esteem tend to get low grades, and those who score high in self-esteem tend to get high grades.
2. Indicate whether you would expect the following correlations to be positive or negative.
   ______ a. The correlation between age and visual acuity (among adults).
   ______ b. The correlation between years of education and income.
   ______ c. The correlation between shyness and the number of friends one has.

Reality CHECK

Misconception

Statistically significant findings are sure to yield accurate conclusions.

Reality

Statistically significant findings are *likely* to yield accurate conclusions, but they are never a sure thing. Although statistical significance indicates that the likelihood of spurious findings is very low, it is never zero. When findings are significant at the .05 level, there is a 5% chance that the conclusion about the hypothesis is wrong.

is usually defined as less than 5 chances in 100. This is referred to as the *.05 level of significance.*

Notice that in this special usage, *significant* does not mean "important" or even "interesting." Statistically significant findings may or may not be theoretically significant or practically significant. They simply are research results that are unlikely to be due to chance.

You don't need to be concerned here with the details of how statistical significance is calculated. However, it is worth noting that a key consideration is the amount of variability in the data. That is why the standard deviation, which measures variability, is such an important statistic. When the necessary computations are made for our hypothetical experiment, the difference between the two groups does *not* turn out to be statistically significant. Thus, our results would not be adequate to show that our tutoring program leads to improved reading achievement. Psychologists have to do this kind of statistical analysis as part of virtually every study. Thus, inferential statistics are an integral element in the research enterprise.

REVIEW OF KEY LEARNING GOALS

2.11 Psychologists use descriptive statistics to organize and summarize their numerical data. The mean, median, and mode are widely used measures of central tendency. The mean tends to be the most useful of these indexes, but it can be distorted by extreme scores. Variability is usually measured with the standard deviation, which increases as the variability in a data set grows.

2.12 Correlations may be either positive (when two variables co-vary in the same direction) or negative (when two variables co-vary in the opposite direction). The closer a correlation is to either +1.00 or −1.00, the stronger the association is.

2.13 As a correlation increases in strength, the ability to predict one variable based on knowledge of the other variable increases. However, a correlation is no assurance of causation. When variables are correlated, we do not know whether *X* causes *Y*, or *Y* causes *X*, or a third variable causes both.

2.14 Hypothesis testing involves deciding whether observed findings support the researcher's hypothesis. Findings are statistically significant only when they are extremely unlikely to be due to chance.

KEY LEARNING GOALS

2.15 Articulate the importance of replication in research.

2.16 Recognize sampling bias and placebo effects in research.

2.17 Recognize problems with self-report data and experimenter bias in research.

Looking for Flaws: Evaluating Research

Scientific research is a more reliable source of information than casual observation or popular belief. However, it would be wrong to conclude that all published research is free of errors. We need to recognize that scientists are fallible human beings who do not conduct flawless research. Their personal biases in designing and interpreting studies can sometimes distort research results.

For these reasons, researchers are reluctant to settle scientific questions on the basis of just one empirical study. Instead, important questions usually generate a flurry of studies to see whether key findings will stand the test of replication. ***Replication*** **is the repetition of a study to see whether the earlier results are duplicated.** The replication process helps science identify and purge erroneous findings. Of course, the replication process sometimes leads to contradictory results. You'll see some examples in later chapters. Inconsistent findings on a research question can be frustrating and confusing for students. However, some inconsistency in results is to be expected, given science's commitment to replication.

Fortunately, one of the strengths of the empirical approach is that scientists work to reconcile or explain conflicting results. In their efforts to make sense of inconsistent research results, psychologists are increasingly depending on a technique called *meta-analysis,* which came into vogue in the 1980s (Cooper, 1990, 2010). ***Meta-analysis*** **combines the statistical results of many studies of the same question, yielding an estimate of the size and consistency of a variable's effects.** For example, Gentile and colleagues (2009) combined the results of 115 studies of gender differences in specific aspects of self-esteem. Among other things, they found that males tend to have somewhat higher self-esteem related to physical appearance and athletic ability; females score higher in self-esteem related to moral-ethical attributes; and gender differences in academic self-esteem are negligible. Meta-analysis allows researchers to test the generalizability of findings and the strength of a variable's effects across people, places, times, and variations in procedure in a relatively precise and objective way (Durlak, 2003; O'Sullivan, 2006).

As you will see in upcoming chapters, scientific advances often emerge out of efforts to double-check perplexing findings or to explain contradictory research results. Thus, like all sources of information, scientific studies need to be examined with a critical eye. This section describes a number of common methodological problems that often spoil studies. Being aware of these pitfalls will make you more skilled in evaluating research.

Sampling Bias

A *sample* is the collection of subjects selected for observation in an empirical study. In contrast, **the *population* is the much larger collection of animals or people (from which the sample is drawn) that researchers want to generalize about** (see **Figure 2.18**). For example, when political pollsters attempt to predict elections, all the voters in a jurisdiction represent the population, and the voters who are actually surveyed constitute the sample. If a researcher was interested in the ability of 6-year-old children to form concepts, those 6-year-olds actually studied would be the sample, and all similar 6-year-old children (perhaps those in modern, Western cultures) would be the population.

Empirical research always involves making statistical inferences about a population based on a sample (Sturgis, 2006). The strategy of observing a limited sample in order to generalize about a much larger population rests on the assumption that the sample is reasonably *representative* of the population. A sample is representative if its composition is similar to the composition of the population. ***Sampling bias* exists when a sample is not representative of the population from which it was drawn.** When a sample is not representative, generalizations about the population may be inaccurate. For instance, if a political pollster were to survey only people in posh shopping areas frequented by the wealthy, the pollster's generalizations about the voting public as a whole would be off the mark.

As we discussed in Chapter 1, American psychologists have historically tended to undersample ethnic minorities and people from non-Western cultures. In a recent analysis of this problem, Jeffrey Arnett (2008) reviewed the sample composition of studies published in six major APA-owned journals in recent years. He found that 68% of the samples came from the United States and another 27% from Europe or English-speaking countries, with only 5% coming from the remainder of the world. He asserts that the focus on American subjects is extremely disproportionate, given that the United States accounts for less than 5% of the world's population. Moreover, although the United States has become more culturally diverse, Arnett notes that the vast majority of American samples have been predominantly European American and have depended much too heavily on white middle- and upper-class college students. He argues that this excessive reliance on American samples and college students seems likely to distort findings in many research areas. In general, then, when you have concerns or doubts about the results of a study, the first thing to examine is the composition of the sample.

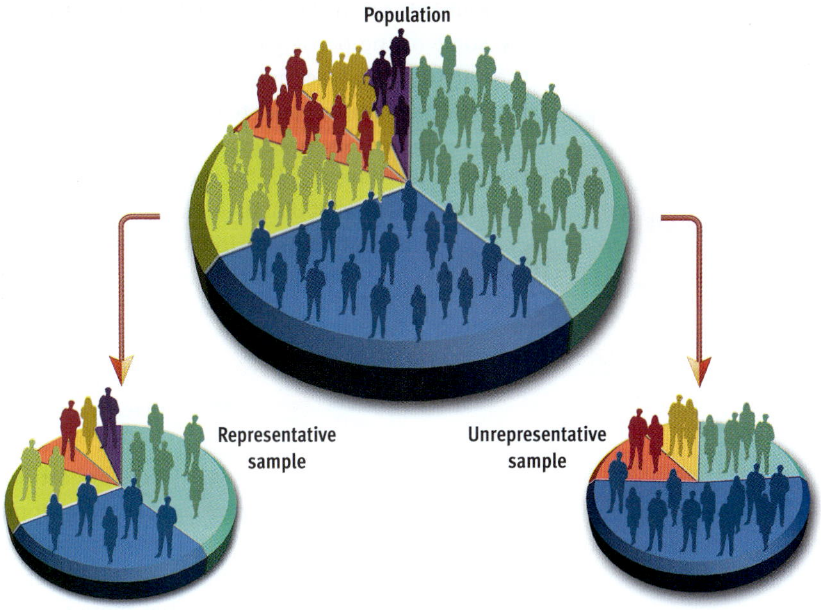

Figure 2.18
The relationship between the population and the sample. The process of drawing inferences about a population based on a sample works only if the sample is reasonably representative of the population. A sample is representative if its demographic makeup is similar to that of the population, as shown on the left. If some groups in the population are overrepresented or underrepresented in the sample, as shown on the right, inferences about the population may be skewed or inaccurate. © Cengage Learning 2013

Placebo Effects

In pharmacology, a *placebo* is a substance that resembles a drug but has no actual pharmacological effect. In studies that assess the effectiveness of medications, placebos are given to some subjects to control for the effects of a treacherous extraneous variable: participants' expectations. Placebos are used because researchers know that participants' expectations can influence their feelings, reactions, and behavior (Stewart-Williams, 2004). **Thus, *placebo effects* occur when participants' expectations lead them to experience some change even though they receive empty, fake, or ineffectual treatment.** In medicine, placebo effects are well documented (Benedetti, 2009). Many physicians tell of patients being "cured" by prescriptions of sugar pills. Placebo effects have also been seen in lab

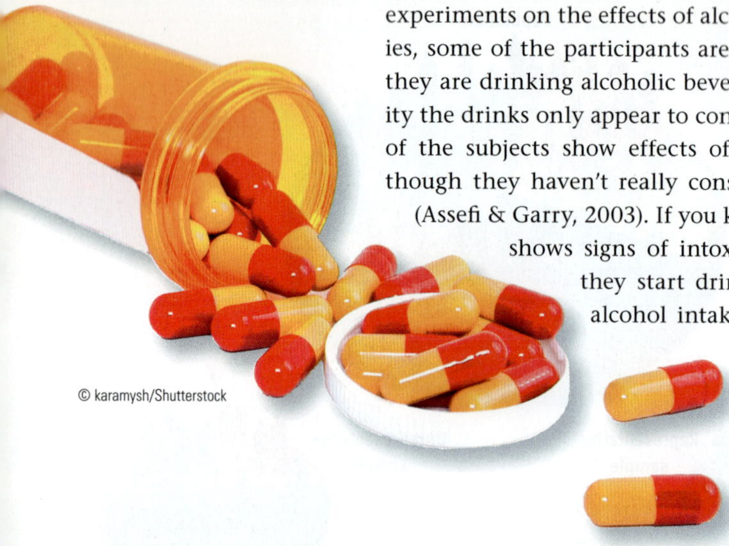

© karamysh/Shutterstock

experiments on the effects of alcohol. In these studies, some of the participants are led to believe that they are drinking alcoholic beverages when in reality the drinks only appear to contain alcohol. Many of the subjects show effects of intoxication even though they haven't really consumed any alcohol (Assefi & Garry, 2003). If you know someone who shows signs of intoxication as soon as they start drinking, before their alcohol intake could take effect physiologically, you have seen placebo effects in action. Placebo effects are attributable to people's expectations (Colagiuri & Boakes, 2010; Oken, 2008). However, recent studies have demonstrated that mere expectations can have important physiological effects. For example, studies of placebos given to subjects to reduce pain suggest that the placebos actually alter activity in brain circuits that are known to suppress pain (Wager, Scott, & Zubieta, 2007; Zubieta et al., 2005).

In the realm of research, participants' expectations can be powerful determinants of their perceptions and behavior when they are under the microscope in an empirical study. For example, a number of studies have found that meditation can improve people's energy level, mental and physical health, and happiness (Alexander et al., 1990; Reibel et al., 2001; Walton et al., 2004). However, in many of the early studies of meditation, researchers assembled their experimental groups with volunteer subjects who were eager to learn meditation. Most of these subjects *wanted* and *expected* meditation to have beneficial effects. Their positive expectations may have colored their subsequent ratings of their energy level, happiness, and so on. Better-designed studies have shown that meditation can be beneficial (see Chapter 5). However, placebo effects have probably exaggerated these benefits in some studies (Canter, 2003; Caspi & Burleson, 2005; Shapiro, 1987).

Researchers should guard against placebo effects whenever subjects are likely to have expectations that a treatment will affect them in a certain way. The possible role of placebo effects can be assessed by including a fake version of the experimental treatment (a placebo condition) in a study.

Distortions in Self-Report Data

Research psychologists often work with *self-report data,* consisting of subjects' verbal accounts of their behavior. This is the case whenever questionnaires, interviews, or personality inventories are used to measure variables. Self-report methods can be quite useful. They take advantage of the fact that people have a unique opportunity to observe themselves full-time (Baldwin, 2000). However, self-reports can be plagued by several kinds of distortion.

One of the most problematic of these distortions is **the *social desirability bias,* which is a tendency to give socially approved answers to questions about oneself.** Participants who are influenced by this bias try hard to create a favorable impression, especially when they are asked about sensitive issues (Tourangeau & Yan, 2007). For example, many survey respondents will report that they voted in an election, gave to a charity, or attend church regularly when in fact it is possible to determine that these assertions are untrue (Granberg & Holmberg, 1991; Hadaway, Marler, & Chaves, 1993). Respondents influenced by social desirability bias also tend to report that they are healthier, happier, and less prejudiced than other types of evidence would suggest. People who answer questions in socially desirable ways take slightly longer to respond to the questions. This suggests that they are carefully "editing" their responses (Holtgraves, 2004).

Other problems can also produce distortions in self-report data (Krosnick, 1999; Schuman & Kalton, 1985). Respondents misunderstand questionnaire items surprisingly often, and the way questions are worded can shape subjects' responses (Schwarz, 1999). Memory errors can undermine the accuracy of verbal reports. Response sets are yet another problem. **A *response set* is a tendency to respond to questions in a particular way that is unrelated to the content of the questions.** For example, some people tend to agree with nearly everything on a questionnaire (Krosnick & Fabrigar, 1998). Yet another source of concern is the ***halo effect,* which occurs when one's overall evaluation of a person, object, or institution spills over to influence more specific ratings.** For example, a supervisor's global assessment of an employee's merit might sway specific ratings of the employee's dependability, initiative, communication, knowledge, and so forth. The crux of the problem is that a rater is unable to judge specific evaluative dimensions independently. Obviously, distortions like these can produce inaccurate results. Although researchers have devised ways to neutralize these problems—such as carefully pretesting survey instruments—we should be cautious in drawing conclusions from self-report data (Schaeffer, 2000).

Reality CHECK

Misconception

Placebo effects tend to be weak effects.

Reality

Not necessarily. In recent years scientists have developed new respect for the power of the placebo. The strength of placebo effects can vary considerably, depending on the condition treated, the plausibility of the placebo, and a variety of other factors. However, a careful review of the evidence concluded that placebo effects often are powerful effects, frequently approaching the strength of the treatment effects to which they are compared (Wampold et al., 2005; Wampold, Imel, & Minami, 2007).

Experimenter Bias

As scientists, psychologists try to conduct their studies in an objective, unbiased way so that their own views will not influence the results. But scientists are human beings whose preconceptions, preferences, and expectations may occasionally influence their work. It is understandable, then, that *experimenter bias* is a possible source of error in research.

***Experimenter bias* occurs when a researcher's expectations or preferences about the outcome of a study influence the results obtained.** Experimenter bias can slip through to influence studies in many subtle ways. One problem is that researchers, like others, sometimes *see what they want to see.* For instance, when experimenters make apparently honest mistakes in recording subjects' responses, the mistakes tend to be heavily slanted in favor of supporting the hypothesis (O'Leary, Kent, & Kanowitz, 1975).

Research by Robert Rosenthal (1976) suggests that experimenter bias may lead researchers to unintentionally influence the behavior of their subjects. In a classic study, Rosenthal and Fode (1963) recruited undergraduate psychology students to serve as the "experimenters." The students were told that they would be collecting data for a study of how participants rated the success of people portrayed in photographs. In a pilot study, photos were selected that generated (on the average) neutral ratings on a scale extending from –10 (extreme failure) to +10 (extreme success). Rosenthal and Fode then manipulated the expectancies of their experimenters. Half of them were told that, based on pilot data, they would probably obtain average ratings of –5. The other half were led to expect average ratings of +5. The experimenters were forbidden from conversing with their subjects except for reading some standardized instructions. Even though the photographs were exactly the same for both groups, the experimenters who *expected* positive ratings *obtained* significantly higher ratings than those who expected negative ratings.

How could the experimenters have swayed the participants' ratings? According to Rosenthal, the experimenters may have unintentionally influenced their subjects by sending subtle nonverbal signals as the experiment progressed. Without realizing it, they may have smiled, nodded, or sent other positive cues when participants made ratings that were in line with the experimenters' expectations. Thus, experimenter bias may influence both researchers' observations and their subjects' behavior (Rosenthal, 1994, 2002).

The problems associated with experimenter bias can be neutralized by using a double-blind procedure. **The *double-blind procedure* is a research strategy in which neither participants nor experimenters know which subjects are in the experimental or control groups.** It's not particularly unusual for participants to be "blind" about their treatment condition. However, the double-blind procedure keeps the experimenter in the dark as well. Of course, a member of the research team who isn't directly involved with subjects keeps track of who is in which group.

CONCEPT CHECK 2.4

Detecting Flaws in Research

Check your understanding of how to conduct sound research by looking for methodological flaws in the following studies. You'll find the answers in Appendix A.

Study 1. A researcher announces that he will be conducting an experiment to investigate the detrimental effects of sensory deprivation on perceptual-motor coordination. The first 40 students who sign up for the study are assigned to the experimental group, and the next 40 who sign up serve in the control group. The researcher supervises all aspects of the study's execution. Experimental subjects spend two hours in a sensory deprivation chamber, where sensory stimulation is minimal. Control subjects spend two hours in a waiting room that contains magazines and a TV. All subjects then perform ten 1-minute trials on a pursuit-rotor task that requires them to try to keep a stylus on a tiny rotating target. The dependent variable is their average score on the pursuit-rotor task.

Study 2. A researcher wants to know whether there is a relationship between age and racial prejudice. She designs a survey in which respondents are asked to rate their prejudice against six different ethnic groups. She distributes the survey to over 500 people of various ages who are approached at a shopping mall in a low-income, inner-city neighborhood.

Check the flaws that are apparent in each study.

Methodological flaw	Study 1	Study 2
Sampling bias	__________	__________
Placebo effects	__________	__________
Distortions in self-reports	__________	__________
Confounding of variables	__________	__________
Experimenter bias	__________	__________

Courtesy of Robert Rosenthal

Robert Rosenthal

"Quite unconsciously, a psychologist interacts in subtle ways with the people he is studying so that he may get the response he expects to get."

REVIEW OF KEY LEARNING GOALS

2.15 Scientists often try to replicate research findings to double-check their validity. Although this process leads to some contradictory findings, science works toward reconciling and explaining inconsistent results. Meta-analysis is a useful tool for sorting out conflicting research results.

2.16 Sampling bias occurs when a sample is not representative of the population of interest. Placebo effects occur when participants' expectations cause them to change their behavior in response to a fake treatment.

2.17 Distortions in self-reports, such as response sets and the social desirability bias, are a source of concern whenever questionnaires and personality inventories are used to collect data. Experimenter bias occurs when researchers' expectations and desires distort their observations or unintentionally influence their subjects' behavior.

Illustrated Overview of Key Research Methods in Psychology

RESEARCH METHOD	DESCRIPTION	EXAMPLE APPLIED TO RESEARCH ON AGGRESSION

EXPERIMENT

Description: Manipulation of an independent variable under carefully controlled conditions to see whether any changes occur in a dependent variable.

Example: Schachter's (1959) study of whether increased anxiety leads to increased affiliation.

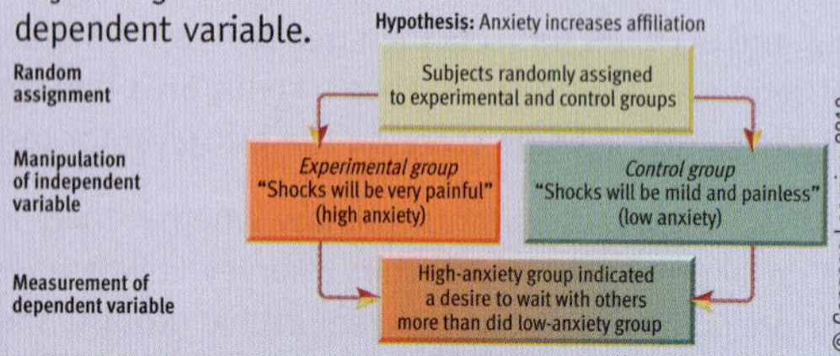

© Cengage Learning 2013

Example applied to research on aggression: Youngsters are randomly assigned to watch a violent or nonviolent film (manipulation of the independent variable), and some aspect of aggression (the dependent variable) is measured in a laboratory situation.

© T.M.O.Pictures/Alamy; (TV screen) © Andre Blais/Shutterstock

NATURALISTIC OBSERVATION

Description: Careful, usually prolonged observation of behavior in its natural setting, without direct intervention.

Example: The Ramirez-Esparza et al. (2007) study comparing sociability in Mexican and American samples, using an electronically activated recorder (EAR).

© Tim Mantoani/Masterfile

Example applied to research on aggression: Youngsters' spontaneous acts of aggression during recreational activities on their playgound are recorded unobtrusively by a team of carefully trained observers.

© Laurence Mouton/Getty Images

CASE STUDIES

© Alain SHRODER/Getty Images

Description: In-depth investigation of a single individual using direct interview, direct observation, review of records, interviews of those close to the person, and other data sources.

Example: The Isometsa et al. (1995) study of all known suicide cases in Finland for an entire year.

Example applied to research on aggression: Detailed case histories are worked up for youngsters referred to counseling because of excessive aggressive behavior in school. The children are interviewed, as are their parents and teachers.

© Will & Deni McIntyre/CORBIS

SURVEYS

Description: Use of questionnaires or interviews to gather information about specific aspects of participants' behavior, attitudes, and beliefs.

Example: The Stamatakis et al. (2009) study of sedentary behavior, which related hours per day devoted to TV viewing to social class and physical health.

© Gabe Palmer/Alamy

Example applied to research on aggression: A large sample of youngsters are given a questionnaire describing hypothetical scenarios that might be expected to trigger aggressive behavior and are asked about how they think they would respond in the situations.

© David Grossman/Alamy

ADVANTAGES

DISADVANTAGES

Precise control over variables can eliminate alternative explanations for findings.

Researchers are able to draw conclusions about cause-and-effect relationships between variables.

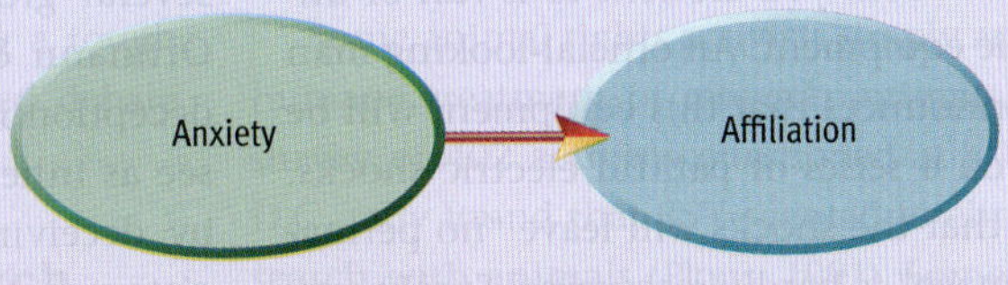

Confounding of variables must be avoided.

Contrived laboratory situations are often artificial, making it risky to generalize findings to the real world.

Ethical concerns and practical realities preclude experiments on many important questions.

© Cengage Learning 2013

Artificiality that can be a problem in laboratory studies is minimized.

It can be good place to start when little is known about the phenomena under study.

Unlike other descriptive/correlational methods, it can be used to study animal as well as human behavior.

© Michael Nichols/National Geographic Stock

It can be difficult to remain unobtrusive; even animal behavior may be altererd by the observation process.

Researchers are unable to draw causal conclusions.

Observational data are often difficult to quantify for statistical analyses.

Case studies are well suited for study of psychological disorders and therapeutic practices.

Individual cases can provide compelling illustrations to support or undermine a theory.

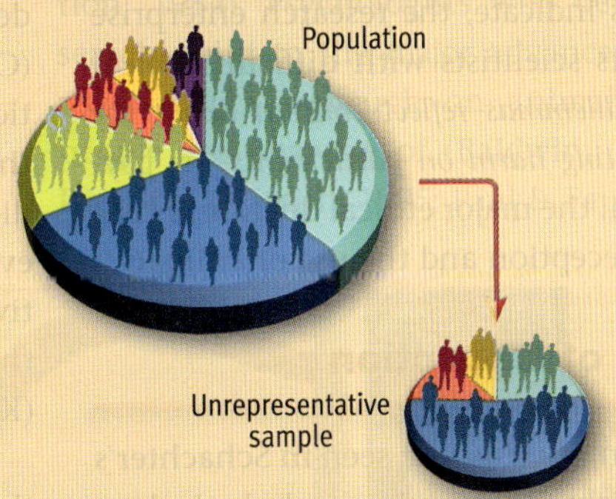

Subjectivity makes it easy to see what one expects to see based on one's theoretical slant.

Researchers are unable to draw causal conclusions.

Clinical samples are often unrepresentative and suffer from sampling bias.

© Cengage Learning 2013

Data collection can be relatively easy, saving time and money.

Researchers can gather data on difficult-to-observe aspects of behavior.

Questionnaires are well suited for gathering data on attitudes, values, and beliefs from large samples.

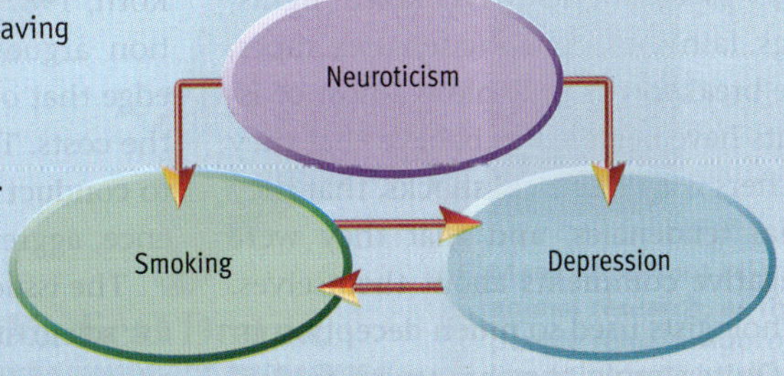

Self-report data are often unreliable, due to intentional deception, social desirability bias, response sets, memory lapses, and poor wording of questions.

Researchers are unable to draw causal conclusions.

© Cengage Learning 2013

Courtesy of Neal Miller

Neal Miller

"Who are the cruel and inhumane ones, the behavioral scientists whose research on animals led to the cures of the anorexic girl and the vomiting child, or those leaders of the radical animal activists who are making an exciting career of trying to stop all such research and are misinforming people by repeatedly asserting that it is without any value?"

them are advances in the treatment of mental disorders, neuromuscular disorders, strokes, brain injuries, visual defects, headaches, memory defects, high blood pressure, and problems with pain (Carroll & Overmier, 2001; Domjan & Purdy, 1995). To put the problem in context, Neal Miller (1985), a prominent psychologist who has done pioneering work in several areas, noted the following:

At least 20 million dogs and cats are abandoned each year in the United States; half of them are killed in pounds and shelters, and the rest are hit by cars or die of neglect. Less than 1/10,000 as many dogs and cats were used in psychological laboratories. . . . Is it worth sacrificing the lives of our children in order to stop experiments, most of which involve no pain, on a vastly smaller number of mice, rats, dogs, and cats? (p. 427)

Far more compelling than Miller are the advocates for disabled people who have entered the fray to campaign against the animal rights movement in recent years. For example, Dennis Feeney (1987), a psychologist disabled by paraplegia, quotes a newsletter from an organization called The Incurably Ill for Animal Research:

No one has stopped to think about those of us who are incurably ill and are desperately waiting for new research results that can only be obtained through the use of animals. We have seen successful advances toward other diseases, such as polio, diphtheria, mumps, measles, and hepatitis through animal research. We want the same chance for a cure, but animal rights groups would deny us this chance. (p. 595)

As you can see, the manner in which animals can ethically be used for research is a highly charged controversy. Psychologists are becoming increasingly sensitive to this issue. Although animals continue to be used in research, strict regulations have been imposed that govern nearly every detail of how laboratory animals can be used for research purposes (Ator, 2005; Garnett, 2005).

Ethical Principles in Research

The ethics issues that we have discussed in this section have led the APA to develop a set of ethical standards for researchers (American Psychological Association, 2002; see **Figure 2.19**). Although most psychological studies are fairly benign, these ethical principles are intended to ensure that both human and animal subjects are treated with dignity. Some of the most important guidelines for research with human participants include the following: (1) participation in research should always be voluntary, and people should be allowed to withdraw from a study at any time; (2) participants should not be subjected to harmful or dangerous treatments; (3) if a study requires deception, participants should be debriefed (informed of the true nature and purpose of the research) as soon as possible; and (4) participants' right to privacy should never be compromised. Crucial guidelines for research with animals include (1) harmful or painful procedures cannot be justified unless the potential benefits of the research are substantial, and (2) research animals are entitled to decent living conditions.

Figure 2.19

Ethics in research. Key ethical principles in psychological research, as set forth by the American Psychological Association (2002), are summarized here. These principles are meant to ensure the welfare of both human and animal subjects.

APA Ethical Guidelines for Research

1. A subject's participation in research should be voluntary and based on informed consent. Subjects should never be coerced into participating in research. They should be informed in advance about any aspects of the study that might be expected to influence their willingness to cooperate. Furthermore, they should be permitted to withdraw from a study at any time if they so desire.

2. Participants should not be exposed to harmful or dangerous research procedures. This guideline is intended to protect subjects from psychological as well as physical harm. Thus, even stressful procedures that might cause emotional discomfort are largely prohibited. However, procedures that carry a modest risk of moderate mental discomfort may be acceptable.

3. If an investigation requires some deception of participants (about matters that do not involve risks), the researcher is required to explain and correct any misunderstandings as soon as possible. The deception must be disclosed to subjects in "debriefing" sessions as soon as it is practical to do so without compromising the goals of the study.

4. Subjects' rights to privacy should never be violated. Information about a subject that might be acquired during a study must be treated as highly confidential and should never be made available to others without the consent of the participant.

5. Harmful or painful procedures imposed upon animals must be thoroughly justified in terms of the knowledge to be gained from the study. Furthermore, laboratory animals are entitled to decent living conditions that are spelled out in detailed rules that relate to their housing, cleaning, feeding, and so forth.

6. Prior to conducting studies, approval should be obtained from host institutions and their research review committees. Research results should be reported fully and accurately, and raw data should be promptly shared with other professionals who seek to verify substantive claims. Retractions should be made if significant errors are found in a study subsequent to its publication.

REVIEW OF KEY LEARNING GOALS

2.18 Critics argue that deception in research is unethical because it is inherently immoral, may undermine participants' trust in others, and may expose them to high levels of stress. Those who defend deception in research argue that many important issues could not be investigated without misleading subjects and that the negative effects of deception on participants have been overestimated.

2.19 Critics of animal research argue that it violates animals' rights and that the findings of animal studies may not generalize to humans. Psychologists who defend animal research argue that it has brought major advances that are worth the costs.

2.20 The APA has formulated ethical principles to serve as guidelines for researchers. Human subjects' participation should be voluntary, they should not be exposed to harmful treatments, they should be debriefed about deception, and their privacy should be respected. Animal subjects are entitled to decent living conditions and should not be exposed to dangerous procedures unless the potential benefits of the research are substantial.

CONCEPT CHECK 2.5

Identifying the Contributions of Major Theorists and Researchers

Check your recall of the principal ideas of important theorists and researchers covered in this chapter by matching the people listed on the left with the appropriate contributions described on the right. If you need help, the crucial pages describing each person's ideas are listed in parentheses. Fill in the letters for your choices in the spaces provided on the left. You'll find the answers in Appendix A.

Major Theorists and Researchers	Key Ideas and Contributions
_______ 1. Neal Miller (p. 68)	a. This individual conducted an influential study which demonstrated that experimenter bias can lead researchers to unintentionally influence the behavior of their subjects.
_______ 2. Robert Rosenthal (p. 63)	b. This researcher conducted a classic experiment on whether anxiety increases the desire to be with others.
_______ 3. Stanley Schachter (pp. 45–48)	c. This person has been a prominent defender of the value of animal research in psychology.

Reflecting on the Chapter's Themes

KEY LEARNING GOALS

2.21 Identify the two unifying themes highlighted in this chapter.

Empiricism

Subjectivity of Experience

Two of our seven unifying themes emerged strongly in this chapter. First, the entire chapter is a testimonial to the idea that psychology is empirical. Second, we saw numerous examples of how people's experience of the world can be highly subjective. Let's examine each of these points in more detail.

As explained in Chapter 1, the empirical approach entails testing ideas, basing conclusions on systematic observation, and relying on a healthy brand of skepticism. All those features of the empirical approach have been apparent in our review of the research enterprise in psychology.

As you have seen, psychologists test their ideas by formulating clear hypotheses that involve predictions about relations between variables. They then use a variety of research methods to collect data so they can see whether their predictions are supported. The data collection methods are designed to make researchers' observations systematic and precise. The entire venture is saturated with skepticism. Psychologists are impressed only by research results that are highly unlikely to have occurred by chance. In planning and executing their research, they are constantly on the lookout for methodological flaws. They submit their articles to a demanding peer review process so that other experts can subject their methods and conclusions to critical scrutiny. Collectively, these procedures represent the essence of the empirical approach.

The subjectivity of personal experience was apparent in our discussion of how adversaries overestimate the gap between their views. It also showed up in our Featured Study, which showed that two people experiencing the same event can have different feelings about it because of differing expectations. Subjective perception was also prominent in our coverage of methodological problems, especially placebo effects and experimenter bias. When subjects report beneficial effects from a fake treatment (the placebo), it's because they expected to see these effects. As pointed out in Chapter 1, psychologists and other scientists are not immune to the effects of subjective experience. Although they are trained to be objective, even scientists may see what they expect to see or what they want to see. This is one reason that the empirical approach emphasizes precise measurement and a skeptical attitude. The highly subjective nature of experience is exactly what the empirical approach attempts to neutralize.

The publication of empirical studies allows us to apply a critical eye to the research enterprise. However, you cannot critically analyze studies unless you know where and how to find them. In the upcoming Personal Application, we will discuss where studies are published, how to find studies on specific topics, and how to read research reports. In the subsequent Critical Thinking Application, we'll analyze the shortcomings of anecdotal evidence, which should help you to appreciate the value of empirical evidence.

REVIEW OF KEY LEARNING GOALS

2.21 The empirical nature of psychology was elucidated throughout this chapter. Empiricism involves testing hypotheses, basing conclusions on systematic observation, and taking a skeptical approach. The chapter also showed repeatedly that our experience of the world is highly subjective.

PERSONAL APPLICATION

Finding and Reading Journal Articles

KEY LEARNING GOALS

2.22 Characterize the nature of technical journals.
2.23 Explain how to use PsycINFO to search for research literature in psychology.
2.24 Describe the standard organization of journal articles reporting on empirical research.

Answer the following "yes" or "no."

___ **1** I have read about scientific studies in newspapers and magazines and sometimes wondered, "How did they come to those conclusions?"

___ **2** When I go to the library, I often have difficulty figuring out how to find information based on research.

___ **3** I have tried to read scientific reports and found them to be too technical and difficult to understand.

If you responded "yes" to any of the above statements, you have struggled with the information explosion in the sciences. We live in a research-oriented society. The number of studies conducted in most sciences is growing at a dizzying pace. This expansion has been particularly spectacular in psychology. Moreover, psychological research increasingly commands attention from the popular press because it is often relevant to people's personal concerns.

This Personal Application is intended to help you cope with the information explosion in psychology. It assumes that there may come a time when you need to examine original psychological research. Perhaps it will be in your role as a student (working on a term paper, for instance), in another role (parent, teacher, nurse, administrator), or merely out of curiosity. In any case, this Application explains the nature of technical journals and discusses how to find and read articles in them. You can learn more about how to use library resources in psychology from an excellent little book titled *Library Use: A Handbook for Psychology* (Reed & Baxter, 2003).

The Nature of Technical Journals

PsykTrek 1e

As you will recall from earlier in the chapter, a *journal* is a periodical that publishes technical and scholarly material, usually in a narrowly defined area of inquiry. Scholars in most fields—whether economics, chemistry, education, or psychology—publish the bulk of their work in these journals. Journal articles represent the core of intellectual activity in any academic discipline. Although they are periodicals, you generally will not find technical journals at your local newsstand. Even public libraries carry relatively few professional journals. Academic libraries and professors account for the vast majority of subscriptions to technical journals. Individual professors typically subscribe to five to ten journals that publish articles in their area of expertise, whereas large college libraries subscribe to thousands of professional journals.

In general, journal articles are written for other professionals in the field. Hence, authors assume that their readers are other interested economists or chemists or psychologists. Because journal articles are written in the special language unique to a particular discipline, they are often difficult for nonprofessionals to understand. You will be learning a great deal of psychology's special language in this course, which will improve your ability to understand articles in psychology journals.

In psychology, most journal articles are reports that describe original empirical studies. These reports permit researchers to disseminate their findings to the scientific com-

© Wayne Weiten 2000

munity. Another common type of article is the review article. *Review articles* summarize and reconcile the findings of a large number of studies on a specific issue. Some psychology journals also publish comments or critiques of previously published research, book reviews, theoretical treatises, and descriptions of methodological innovations.

Finding Journal Articles

1e

Reports of psychological research are commonly mentioned in newspapers and popular magazines. These summaries can be helpful to readers, but they often embrace the most sensational conclusions that might be drawn from the research. They also tend to include many oversimplifications and factual errors. Thus, if a study mentioned in the press is of interest to you, you may want to track down the original article to ensure that you get accurate information.

Most discussions of research in the popular press do not mention where you can find the original technical article. However, there is a way to find out. A computerized database called PsycINFO makes it possible to locate journal articles by specific researchers or scholarly work on specific topics. This huge online database, which is updated constantly, contains brief summaries, or *abstracts,* of journal articles, books, and chapters in edited books, reporting, reviewing, or theorizing about psychological research. Over 2400 journals are checked regularly to select items for inclusion. The abstracts are concise—about 75 to 175 words. They briefly describe the hypotheses, methods, results, and conclusions of the studies. Each abstract should allow you to determine whether an article is relevant to your interests. If it is, you should be able to find the article in your library (or to order it) because a complete bibliographic reference is provided.

Although news accounts of research rarely mention where a study was published, they often mention the name of the researcher. If you have this information, the easiest way to find a specific article is to search PsycINFO for materials published by that researcher. For example, let's say you read a news report that summarized the research on motives influencing perception that was described earlier in the chapter (the Featured Study). Let's assume that the news report mentioned that David Dunning of Cornell University was one of the authors and that the article was published in 2006. To track down the original article, you would search for publications by David Dunning in 2006. If you conducted this search, you would turn up a list of five items (four journal articles and one chapter in a book). The information for these publications is shown in **Figure 2.20**. The first item in the list appears to be the article you

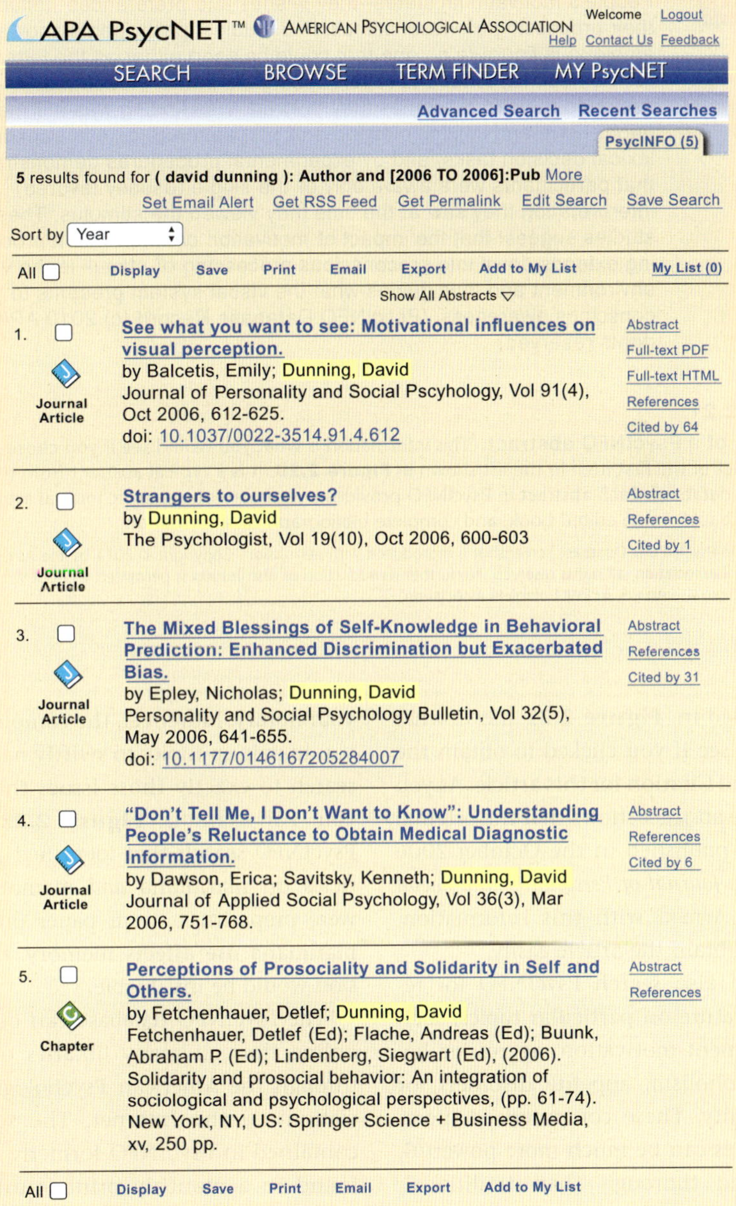

© Cengage Learning 2013

Figure 2.20

Searching PsycINFO. If you searched PsycINFO for publications by David Dunning in 2006, the database would return the 5 listings shown here. The first four are journal articles and the last item is a chapter in an edited book. The first item in the list appears to be the article of interest. For each item, you can choose to see its abstract or its full PsycINFO record (the abstract plus subject descriptors and other details). In some cases (depending on the version of PsycINFO that your library has ordered) you can click to see the full PsycINFO record plus references, or the *full text* of some articles.

SOURCE: The PsycINFO® Database screenshot is reproduced with permission. Copyright © 2011 by the American Psychological Association, all rights reserved. No further reproduction or distribution is permitted without written permission from the American Psychological Association.

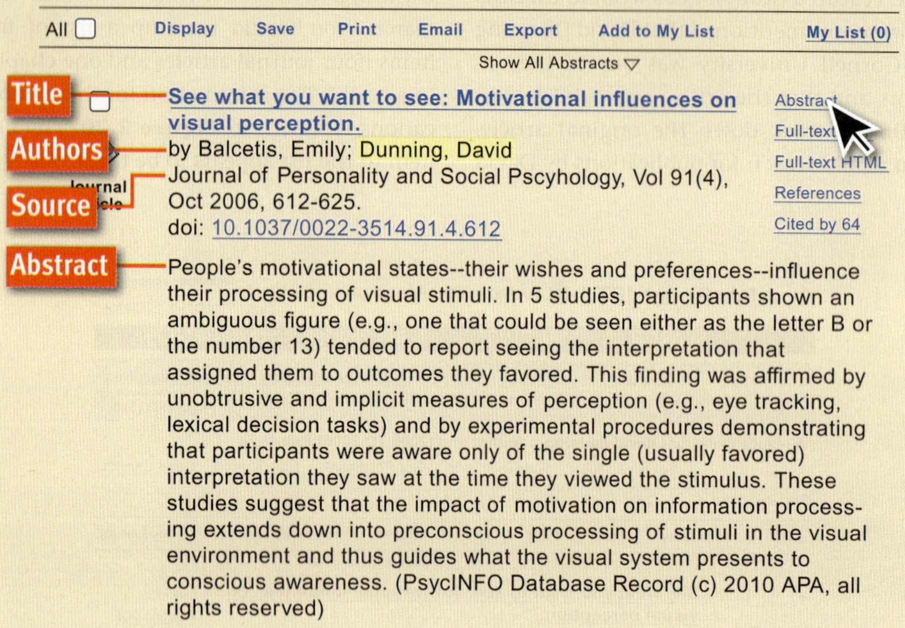

© Cengage Learning 2013

Figure 2.21

Example of a PsycINFO abstract. This information is what you would see if you chose to view the abstract of the first item in the list shown in **Figure 2.20**. It is a typical abstract from the online PsycINFO database. Each abstract in PsycINFO provides a summary of a specific journal article, book, or chapter in an edited book, and complete bibliographical information.

SOURCE: The PsycINFO® Database screenshot is reproduced with permission. Copyright © 2011 by the American Psychological Association, all rights reserved. No further reproduction or distribution is permitted without written permission from the American Psychological Association.

are interested in. **Figure 2.21** shows what you would see if you clicked to obtain the Abstract and Citation for this article. As you can see, the abstract shows that the original report was published in the October 2006 issue of the *Journal of Personality and Social Psychology*. Armed with this information, you could obtain the article easily.

You can also search PsycINFO for research literature on particular topics, such as achievement motivation, aggressive behavior, alcoholism, appetite disorders, or artistic ability. These computerized literature searches can be much more powerful, precise, and thorough than traditional, manual searches in a library. PsycINFO can sift through several million articles in a matter of seconds to identify *all* the articles on a subject, such as alcoholism. Obviously, there is no way you can match this efficiency stumbling around in the stacks at your library. Moreover, the computer allows you to pair up topics to swiftly narrow your search to exactly those issues that interest you. For example, **Figure 2.22** shows a PsycINFO search that identified all the articles on marijuana *and* memory. If you were preparing a term paper on whether marijuana use affects memory, this precision would be invaluable.

The PsycINFO database can be accessed online through many libraries or directly through the American Psychological Association via the Internet. The summaries contained in PsycINFO formerly were also found in a monthly print journal called *Psychological Abstracts*. However, the publication of this journal was discontinued in 2006 after 80 years of service as it became an antiquated source of information in comparison to the PsycINFO database (Benjamin & VandenBos, 2006).

Reading Journal Articles

Once you find the journal articles you want to examine, you need to know how to decipher them. You can process the information in such articles more efficiently if you understand how they are organized. Depending on your needs and purpose, you may want to simply skim through some of the sections. Journal articles follow a fairly standard organization, which includes the following sections and features.

Abstract

Most journals print a concise summary at the beginning of each article. This abstract allows readers scanning the journal to quickly decide whether articles are relevant to their interests.

Introduction

The introduction presents an overview of the problem studied in the research. It mentions relevant theories and quickly reviews previous research that bears on the problem, usually citing shortcomings in previous research that necessitate the present study. This review of the current state of knowledge on the topic usually progresses to a specific and precise statement regarding the hypotheses under investigation.

Method

The method section provides a thorough description of the research methods used in the study. Information is provided on the subjects used, the procedures followed, and the data collection techniques employed. This description is made detailed enough to permit another researcher to attempt to replicate the study.

Results

The data obtained in the study are reported in the results section. This section often creates problems for novice readers because it includes complex statistical analyses, figures, tables, and graphs. This section does *not* include any inferences based on the data. Such conclusions are supposed to follow in the next section. Instead, it simply

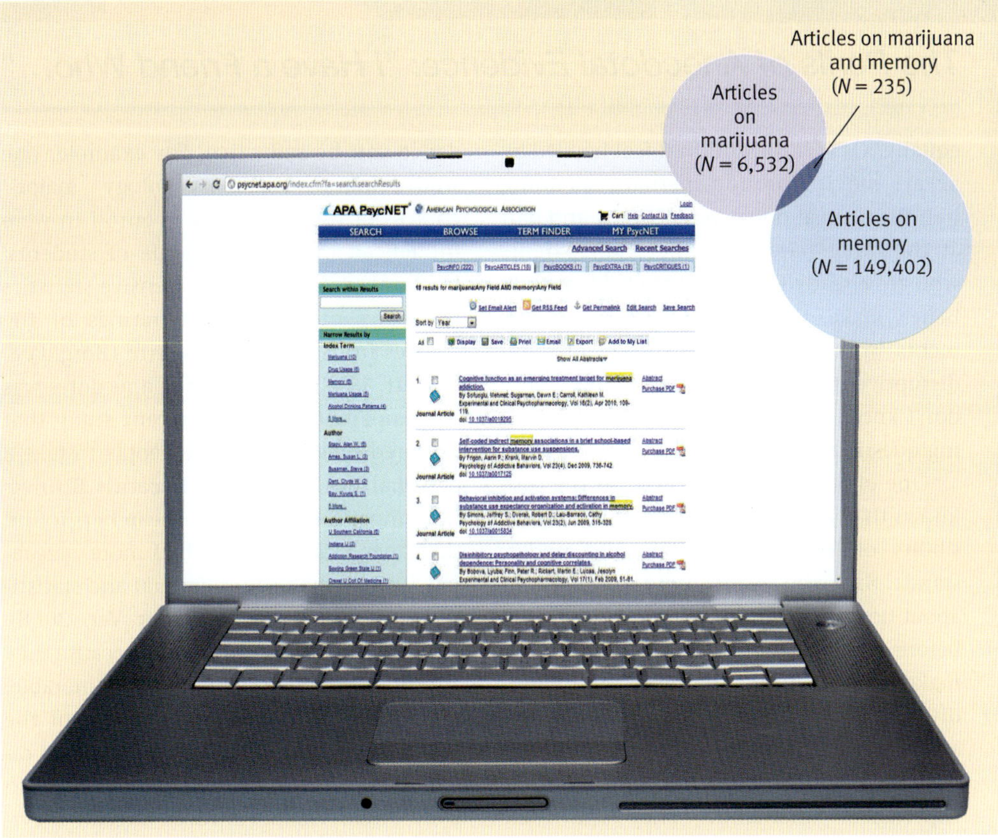

Figure 2.22

Combining topics in a PsycINFO search. A computerized literature search can be a highly efficient way to locate the specific research that you need. For example, if you had set out in June 2010 to find all the psychological literature on marijuana and memory using PsycINFO, you would have obtained the results summarized here. At that time, the database contained 149,402 articles related to memory and 6,532 articles related to marijuana. The search depicted here yielded 235 abstracts that relate to both marijuana and memory. Thus, in a matter of moments, the computer can sift through over 2 million abstracts to find those that are most germane to a specific question, such as: Does marijuana use affect memory?

SOURCE: The PsycINFO® Database screenshot is reproduced with permission. Copyright © 2011 by the American Psychological Association, all rights reserved. No further reproduction or distribution is permitted without written permission from the American Psychological Association.

Jeffrey Coolidge/RF Getty Images; inset: © Cengage Learning 2003

contains a concise summary of the raw data and the statistical analyses.

Discussion

In the discussion section you will find the conclusions drawn by the author(s). In contrast to the results section, which is a straightforward summary of empirical observations, the discussion section allows for interpretation and evaluation of the data. Implications for theory and factual knowledge in the discipline are discussed. Conclusions are usually qualified carefully. Any limitations in the study may be acknowledged. This section may also include suggestions for future research on the issue.

References

At the end of each article you will find a list of bibliographic references for any studies cited. This list permits you to examine firsthand other relevant studies mentioned in the article. The references list is often a rich source of leads about other articles that are germane to the topic that you are looking into.

REVIEW OF KEY LEARNING GOALS

2.22 Journals publish technical and scholarly material. Usually they are written for other professionals in a narrow area of inquiry. In psychology, most journal articles are reports of original research. Subscriptions to journals are mostly held at academic libraries.

2.23 PsycINFO is a computerized database that contains brief summaries of newly published journal articles, books, and chapters in edited books. Works on specific topics and publications by specific authors can be found by using the search mechanisms built into the database. Computerized literature searches can be much more powerful and precise than manual searches.

2.24 Journal articles are easier to understand if one is familiar with the standard format. Most articles include six elements: abstract, introduction, method, results, discussion, and references.

KEY LEARNING GOALS

2.25 Recognize anecdotal evidence and understand why it is unreliable.

The Perils of Anecdotal Evidence: "I Have a Friend Who..."

Here's a tough problem. Suppose you are the judge in a family law court. As you look over the cases that will come before you today, you see that one divorcing couple have managed to settle almost all of the important decisions with minimal conflict—such as who gets the house, who gets the car and the dog, and who pays which bills. However, there is one crucial issue left: Each parent wants custody of the children. Because they could not reach an agreement on their own, the case is now in your court. How can you determine what is in the best interests of the children?

Child custody decisions have major consequences for all of the parties involved. As you review the case records, you see that both parents are loving and competent. There are no obvious reasons for selecting one parent over the other as the primary caretaker. In considering various alternatives, you mull over the possibility of awarding *joint custody*. This is an arrangement in which the children spend half their time with each parent, instead of the more usual arrangement where one parent has primary custody and the other has visitation rights. Joint custody seems to have some obvious benefits. But you are not sure how well these arrangements actually work. Will the children feel more attached to both parents if the parents share custody equally? Or will the children feel hassled by always moving around, perhaps spending half the week at one parent's home and half at the other parent's home? Can parents who are already feuding over child custody issues make these complicated arrangements work? Or is joint custody just too disruptive to everyone's life? You really don't know the answer to any of these vexing questions.

One of the lawyers involved in the case knows that you are thinking about the possibility of joint custody. She also understands that you want more information about how well joint custody tends to work before you make a decision. To help you make up your mind, she tells you about a divorced couple that has had a joint custody arrangement for many years. She offers to have them appear in court to describe their experiences "firsthand." They and their children can answer any questions you might have about the pros and cons of joint custody. They should be in the best position to know how well joint custody works because they are living it. Sounds like a reasonable plan. What do you think?

I hope you said, "No, no, no!" What's wrong with asking someone who's been there how well joint custody works? The crux of the problem is that the evidence a single family brings to the question of joint custody is ***anecdotal evidence*, which consists of personal stories about specific incidents and experiences.** Anecdotal evidence can be seductive. For example, one study found that psychology majors' choices of future courses to enroll in were influenced more by a couple of students' brief anecdotes than by extensive statistics on many other students' ratings of the courses from the previous term (Borgida & Nisbett, 1977). The power of anecdotes was also apparent in a more recent study that explored how to persuade people to take a personal health risk (for hepatitis B infection) more seriously. The researchers found that anecdotal accounts had more persuasive impact than sound factual and statistical evidence (de Wit, Das, & Vet, 2008). Anecdotes readily sway people because they are often concrete, vivid, and memorable. Many politicians are keenly aware of the power of anecdotes and frequently rely on a single vivid story rather than solid data to sway voters' views. However, anecdotal evidence is fundamentally flawed (Ruscio, 2006; Stanovich, 2004).

What, exactly, is wrong with anecdotal evidence? Let's use some of the concepts introduced in the main body of the chapter to analyze its shortcomings. First, in the language of research designs, the anecdotal experiences of one family resemble a single *case study*. The story they tell about their experiences with joint custody may be quite interesting, but their experiences—good or bad—cannot be used to generalize to other couples. Why not? Because they are only one family. They may be unusual in some

DILBERT © 2002 Scott Adams. Used By permission of UNIVERSAL UCLICK. All rights reserved.

© Jacob Taposchaner/Photographer's Choice/Getty Images

An abundance of anecdotal reports suggest that an association exists between the full moon and strange, erratic behavior. These reports often sound compelling, but as the text explains, anecdotal evidence is flawed in many ways. When researchers have examined the issue systematically, they have consistently found no association between lunar phases and the incidence of psychiatric emergencies, domestic violence, suicide, and so forth (Biermann et al., 2005; Chudler, 2007; Dowling, 2005; Kung & Mrazek, 2005; Lilienfeld & Arkowitz, 2009; McLay, Daylo, & Hammer, 2006).

way that affects how well they manage joint custody. To draw general conclusions based on the case study approach, you need a systematic series of case studies. Then you can look for threads of consistency. A single family is a sample size of one, which surely is not large enough to derive broad principles that would apply to other families.

Second, anecdotal evidence is similar to *self-report data,* which can be distorted for a variety of reasons, such as people's tendency to give socially approved information about themselves (the *social desirability bias*). When researchers use tests and surveys to gather self-report data, they can take steps to reduce or assess the impact of distortions in their data. But there are no comparable safeguards with anecdotal evidence. Thus, the family that appears in your courtroom may be eager to make a good impression and unknowingly slant their story accordingly.

Anecdotes are often inaccurate and riddled with embellishments. We will see in Chapter 7 that memories of personal experiences are far more malleable and far less reliable than widely assumed (Loftus, 2004; Schacter, 2001). And, although it would not be an issue in this case, in other situations *anecdotal evidence often consists of stories that people have heard about others' experiences.* Hearsay evidence is not accepted in courtrooms for good reason. As stories are passed on from one person to another, they often become increasingly distorted and inaccurate.

Can you think of any other reasons for being wary of anecdotal evidence? After reading the chapter, perhaps you thought about the possibility of *sampling bias.* Do you think that the lawyer will pick a couple at random from all those who have been awarded joint custody? It seems highly unlikely. If she wants you to award joint custody, she will find a couple for whom this arrangement worked very well. If she wants you to award sole custody to her client, she will find a couple whose inability to make joint custody work had dire consequences for their children. One reason people love to work with anecdotal evidence is that it is so readily manipulated. They can usually find an anecdote or two to support their position, whether or not these anecdotes are representative of most people's experiences.

If the testimony of one family cannot be used in making this critical custody decision, what sort of evidence should you be looking for? One goal of effective critical thinking is to make decisions based on solid evidence. This process is called *evidence-based decision making.* In this case, you would need to consider the overall experiences of a large sample of families who have tried joint custody arrangements. In general, across many different families, did the children in joint custody develop well? Was there a disproportionately high rate of emotional problems or other signs of stress for the children or the parents? Was the percentage of families who returned to court at a later date to change their joint custody arrangements higher than for other types of custody arrangements? You can probably think of additional information that you would want to collect regarding the outcomes of various custody arrangements.

In examining research reports, many people recognize the need to evaluate the evidence by looking for the types of flaws described in the main body of the chapter (sampling bias, experimenter bias, and so forth). Curiously, though, many of the same people then fail to apply the same principles of good evidence to their personal decisions in everyday life. The tendency to rely on the anecdotal experiences of a small number of people is sometimes called the *"I have a friend who . . ." syndrome,* because no matter what the topic is, it seems that someone will provide a personal story about a friend as evidence for his or her particular point of view. In short, when you hear people support their assertions with personal stories, a little skepticism is in order.

Table 2.2 Critical Thinking Skills Discussed in This Application

Skill	Description
Recognizing the limitations of anecdotal evidence	The critical thinker is wary of anecdotal evidence, which consists of personal stories used to support one's assertions. Anecdotal evidence tends to be unrepresentative, inaccurate, and unreliable.
Using evidence-based decision making	The critical thinker understands the need to seek sound evidence to guide decisions in everyday life.

© Cengage Learning 2013

REVIEW OF KEY LEARNING GOALS

2.25 Anecdotal evidence consists of personal stories about specific incidents and experiences. However, anecdotal evidence is usually based on the equivalent of a single case study, which is not an adequate sample, and there are no safeguards to reduce the distortions often found in self-report data. Many anecdotes are inaccurate, secondhand reports of others' experiences.

Chapter 2 Practice Test

1. A tentative prediction about the relationship between two variables is:
   A. a confounding of variables.
   B. an operational definition.
   C. a theory.
   D. a hypothesis.

2. Researchers must describe the actions that will be taken to measure or control each variable in their studies. In other words, they must:
   A. provide operational definitions of their variables.
   B. decide if their studies will be experimental or correlational.
   C. use statistics to summarize their findings.
   D. decide how many subjects should participate in their studies.

3. A researcher found that clients who were randomly assigned to same-sex groups participated more in group therapy sessions than clients who were randomly assigned to coed groups. In this experiment, the independent variable was:
   A. the amount of participation in the group therapy sessions.
   B. whether or not the group was coed.
   C. the clients' attitudes toward group therapy.
   D. how much the clients' mental health improved.

4. A researcher wants to see whether a protein-enriched diet will enhance the maze-running performance of rats. One group of rats are fed the high-protein diet for the duration of the study; the other group continues to receive ordinary rat chow. In this experiment, the diet fed to the two groups of rats is the _________ variable.
   A. correlated
   B. control
   C. dependent
   D. independent

5. In a study of the effect of a new teaching technique on students' achievement test scores, an important extraneous variable would be the students':
   A. hair color.
   B. athletic skills.
   C. IQ scores.
   D. sociability.

6. Whenever you have a cold, you rest in bed, take aspirin, and drink plenty of fluids. You can't determine which remedy is most effective because of which of the following problems?
   A. sampling bias
   B. distorted self-report data
   C. confounding of variables
   D. experimenter bias

7. A psychologist monitors a group of nursery-school children, recording each instance of helping behavior as it occurs. The psychologist is using:
   A. the experimental method.
   B. naturalistic observation.
   C. case studies.
   D. the survey method.

8. Among the advantages of descriptive/correlational research is (are):
   A. it allows investigators to isolate cause and effect.
   B. it permits researchers to study variables that would be impossible to manipulate.
   C. it can demonstrate conclusively that two variables are causally related.
   D. both a and b.

9. Which of the following correlation coefficients would indicate the strongest relationship between two variables?
   A. .58
   B. .19
   C. −.97
   D. −.05

10. When psychologists say that their results are statistically significant, they mean that the results:
    A. have important practical applications.
    B. have important implications for scientific theory.
    C. are unlikely to be due to the fluctuations of chance.
    D. are all of the above.

11. Sampling bias exists when:
    A. the sample is representative of the population.
    B. the sample is not representative of the population.
    C. two variables are confounded.
    D. the effect of the independent variable can't be isolated.

12. The problem of experimenter bias can be avoided by:
    A. not informing participants of the hypothesis of the experiment.
    B. telling the subjects that there are no "right" or "wrong" answers.
    C. using a research strategy in which neither subjects nor experimenter know which participants are in the experimental and control groups.
    D. having the experimenter use only nonverbal signals when communicating with the participants.

13. Critics of deception in research have assumed that deceptive studies are harmful to participants. The empirical data on this issue suggest that:
    A. many deceptive studies do produce significant distress for subjects who were not forewarned about the possibility of deception.
    B. most participants in deceptive studies report that they enjoyed the experience and didn't mind being misled.
    C. deceptive research seriously undermines subjects' trust in others.
    D. both a and c are the case.

14. PsycINFO is:
    A. a new journal that recently replaced *Psychological Abstracts.*
    B. a computerized database containing abstracts of articles, chapters, and books reporting psychological research.
    C. a reference book that explains the format and techniques for writing journal articles.
    D. a computerized database containing information about studies that have not yet been published.

15. Anecdotal evidence:
    A. is often concrete, vivid, and memorable.
    B. tends to influence people.
    C. is fundamentally flawed and unreliable.
    D. is all of the above.

Answers

1 D p. 40
2 A p. 42
3 B p. 46
4 D p. 46
5 C p. 47
6 C p. 47
7 B p. 51
8 B pp. 54–55
9 C pp. 57–58
10 C pp. 59–60
11 B p. 61
12 C p. 63
13 B p. 66
14 B p. 71
15 D pp. 74–75

PsykTrek

To view a demo: **www.cengage.com/psychology/psyktrek**
To order: **www.cengage.com/psychology/weiten**

Go to the PsykTrek website or CD-ROM for further study of the concepts in this chapter. Both online and on the CD-ROM, PsykTrek includes dozens of learning modules with videos, animations, and quizzes, as well as simulations of psychological phenomena and a multimedia glossary that includes word pronunciations.

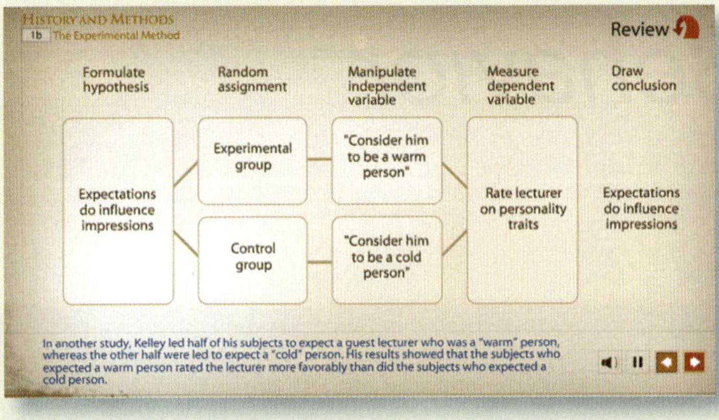

© Cengage Learning 2008

Work through Module 1b (*The Experimental Method*) to enhance your appreciation of how experiments are conducted.

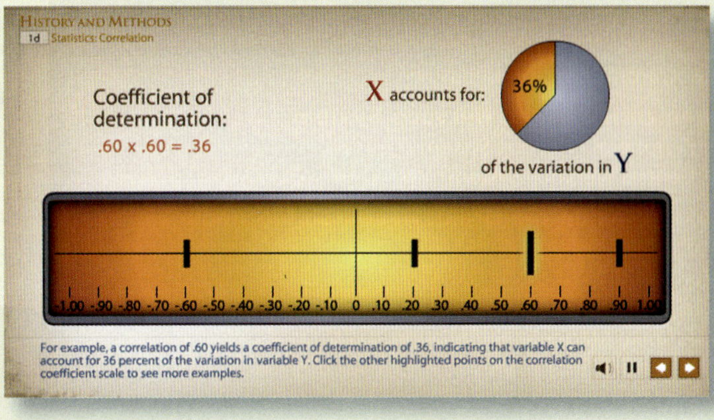

© Cengage Learning 2008

Increase your understanding of correlation by working through Module 1d (*Statistics: Correlation*) which will allow you to plot a scatter diagram and explore numerous examples.

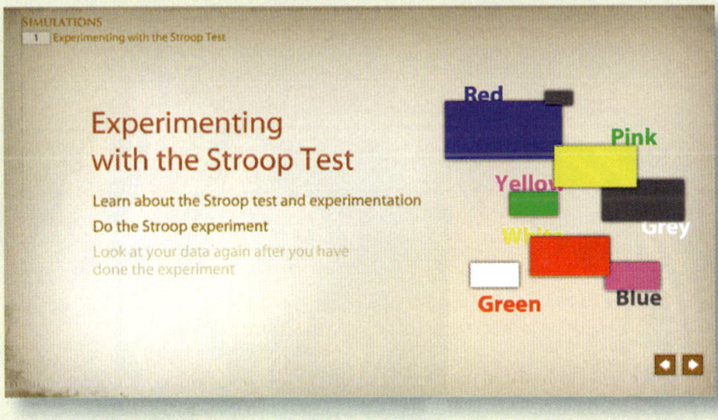

© Cengage Learning 2008

Go to Simulation 1 (*Experimenting with the Stroop Test*) to participate in an experiment in which you can collect data on yourself and see concrete examples of independent and dependent variables and experimental and control conditions in action.

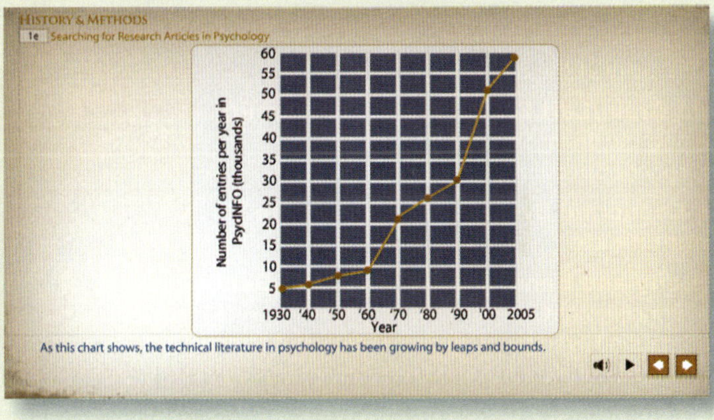

© Cengage Learning 2008

Explore Module 1e (*Searching for Research Articles in Psychology*) to learn how to use PsycINFO to find studies on specific topics in psychology.

Online Study Tools

Log in to **CengageBrain** to access the resources your instructor requires. For this book, you can access:

CourseMate brings course concepts to life with interactive learning, study, and exam preparation tools that support the printed textbook. A textbook-specific website, Psychology CourseMate includes an integrated interactive eBook and other interactive learning tools such as quizzes, flashcards, videos, and more.

CengageNow is an easy-to-use online resource that helps you study in less time to get the grade you want—NOW. Take a pre-test for this chapter and receive a personalized study plan based on your results that will identify the topics you need to review and direct you to online resources to help you master those topics. Then take a post-test to help you determine the concepts you have mastered and what you will need to work on. If your textbook does not include an access code card, go to CengageBrain.com to gain access.

WebTutor is more than just an interactive study guide. WebTutor is an anytime, anywhere customized learning solution with an eBook, keeping you connected to your textbook, instructor, and classmates.

Aplia. If your professor has assigned Aplia homework:

1. Sign in to your account
2. Complete the corresponding homework exercises as required by your professor.
3. When finished, click "Grade It Now" to see which areas you have mastered, which need more work, and detailed explanations of every answer.

Visit **www.cengagebrain.com** to access your account and purchase materials.

3

The Biological Bases of Behavior

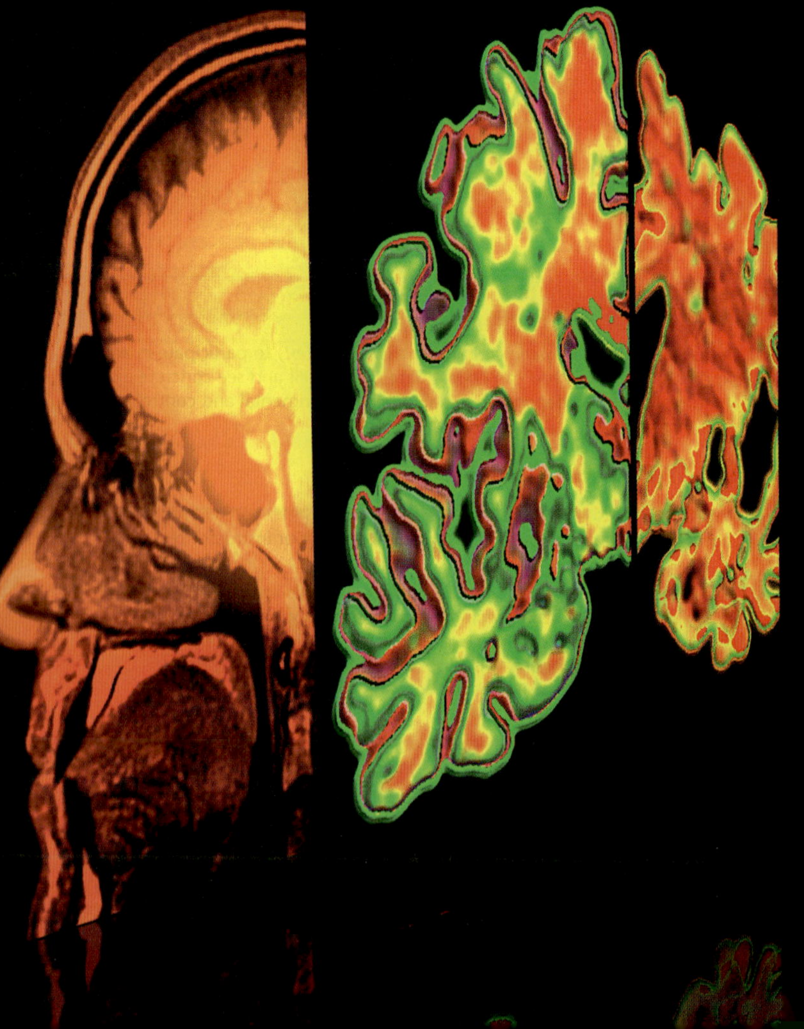

© Pasieka/SPL/Photo Researchers, Inc. PRinc_E07819 special number

An ordinary-looking, 30-year-old mother of three is walking down the street in a seedy neighborhood around 10 p.m. when she encounters a drugged-out man who presses a knife to her throat and threatens to kill her. Remarkably, the woman shows no signs of fear. Her heart rate doesn't quicken, her breathing doesn't change, she doesn't get nervous. Her completely calm, unruffled response to her attacker so unnerves *him* that he lets her go! Meet the woman who knows no fear.

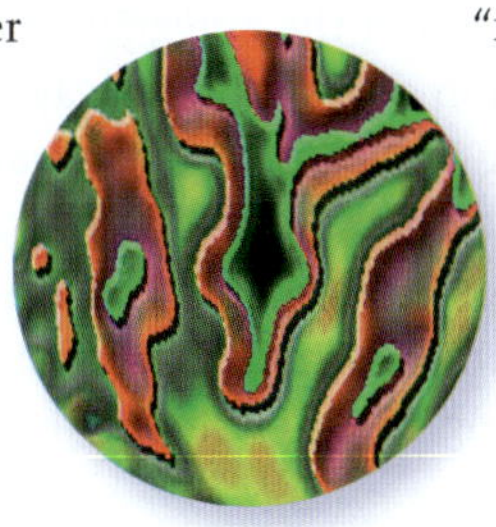

The woman in this story, known by her initials, SM, has attracted interest from scientists who are intrigued by her apparent inability to experience fear. In a recent study designed to investigate SM's fearlessness, researchers exposed her to a variety of situations that would trigger fear in most people (Feinstein et al., 2011). For ethical reasons they chose fear-inducing stimuli that posed relatively little risk of actual harm. For example, they took her to an exotic pet store where they exposed her to snakes and spiders. What was her reaction? Instead of being scared, SM was fascinated and repeatedly asked to touch large snakes and a tarantula that were not safe to handle. Next, the scientists took SM to a famous haunted house. While others patrons screamed in fright, SM giggled and poked one of the "monsters" in the head—again scaring *him*. Taking yet another tack, the researchers showed SM clips from scary movies, such as *The Ring*. She found the clips entertaining, but she experienced no fear. Finally, the researchers used a variety of methods to determine whether SM experiences other emotions. Their results revealed that SM exhibits all the other basic emotions—anger, sadness, disgust, happiness, surprise—much like anyone else. Other tests demonstrated that SM scores normally on measures of intelligence, language, and memory.

Why is SM absolutely fearless, while she experiences other emotions? What could cause such a bizarre, exquisitely specific emotional deficit? It turns out that in childhood SM suffered an extremely rare disease that destroyed a small structure called the

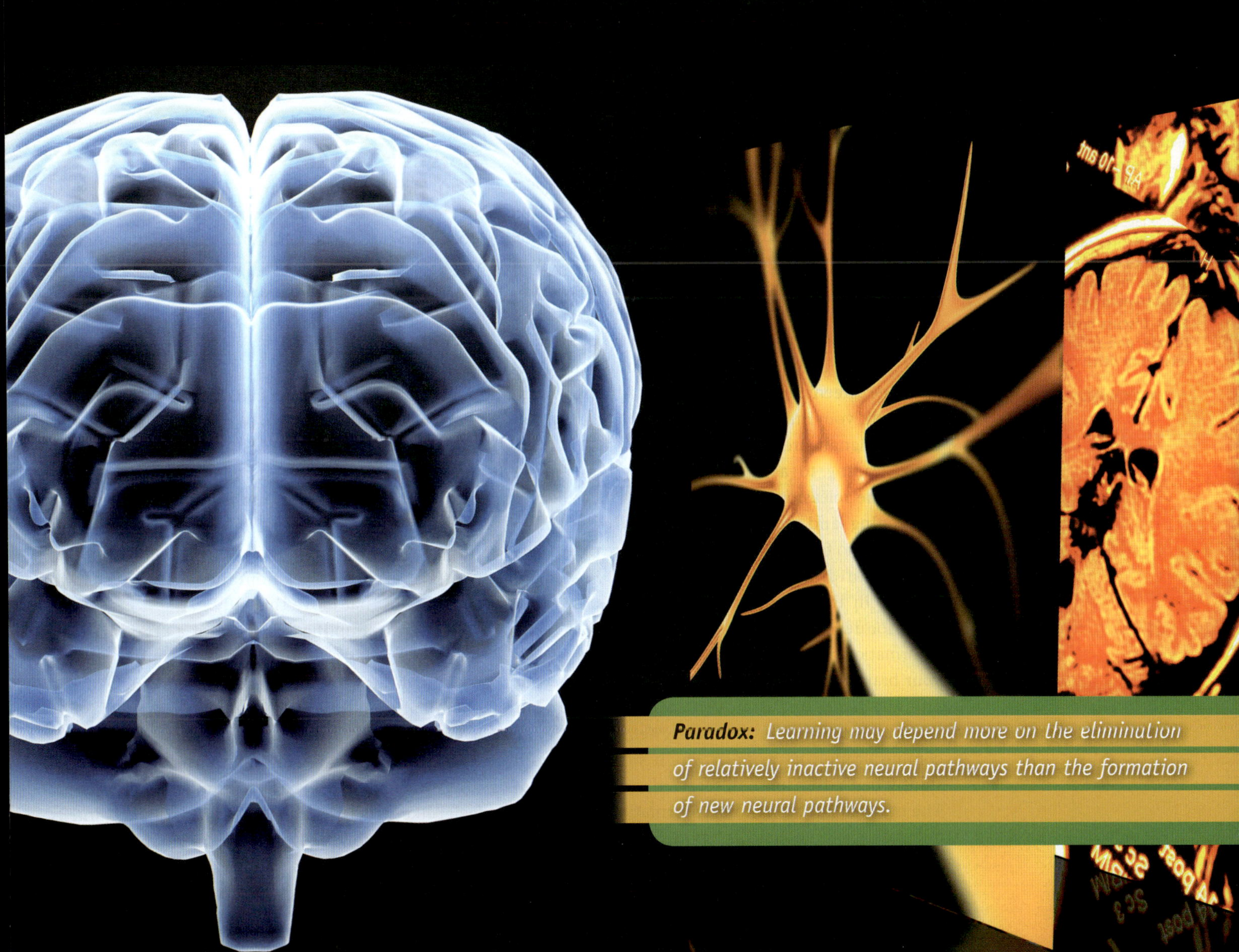

Paradox: *Learning may depend more on the elimination of relatively inactive neural pathways than the formation of new neural pathways.*

amygdala in both the right and left halves of her brain. Many studies, mostly with animals, have suggested that the amygdala is a crucial control center for the experience of fear. SM's case provides compelling, new *human* evidence that the amygdala has a unique role in the regulation of fear. By the way, if you are thinking that being fearless sounds appealing, think again. The research on SM has shown that she is fundamentally deficient when it comes to detecting when she's in danger, which is why she has a long history of getting herself into perilous situations.

SM's unusual case provides a dramatic demonstration that people's behavioral functioning is ultimately controlled by the brain. The fact that SM feels all the other emotions except fear shows just how precise the biological bases of behavior can be. The human brain is so complex, no computer has ever come remotely close to duplicating it. Your nervous system contains as many cells busily integrating and relaying information as there are stars in our galaxy. Whether you are scratching your nose or composing an essay, the activity of those cells underlies what you do. It is little wonder, then, that many psychologists have dedicated themselves to exploring the biological bases of behavior.

How do mood-altering drugs work? Are the two halves of the brain specialized to perform different functions? Are some mental illnesses the result of chemical imbalances in the brain? To what extent is intelligence determined by biological inheritance? As you will see in this chapter, these questions only begin to suggest the countless ways in which biology is fundamental to the study of behavior.

KEY LEARNING GOALS

3.1 Identify the various parts of the neuron and the main functions of glial cells.

3.2 Describe the neural impulse, and explain how neurons communicate at chemical synapses.

3.3 Discuss some of the functions of acetylcholine and the monoamine neurotransmitters.

3.4 Discuss how GABA, glutamate, and endorphins are related to behavior.

Communication in the Nervous System

Imagine that you're watching an action-packed movie. As the tension mounts, your palms sweat and your heart beats faster. You begin shoveling popcorn into your mouth, carelessly spilling some in your lap. If someone were to ask you what you were doing at this moment, you would probably say, "Nothing—just watching the movie." Yet some highly complex processes are occurring without your thinking about them. A stimulus (the light from the screen) is striking your eye. Almost instantaneously, your brain is interpreting the light stimulus and signals are flashing to other parts of your body, leading to a flurry of activity. Your sweat glands are releasing perspiration, your heartbeat is quickening, and muscular movements are enabling your hand to find the popcorn and, more or less successfully, lift it to your mouth.

Even in this simple example, you can see that behavior depends on rapid information processing. Information travels immediately from your eye to your brain, from your brain to the muscles of your arm and hand, and from your palms back to your brain. In essence, your nervous system is a complex communication network in which signals are constantly being transmitted, received, and integrated. The nervous system handles information, just as the circulatory system handles blood. In this section, we take a look at how communication occurs in the nervous system.

Nervous Tissue: The Basic Hardware

PsykTrek 2a

Your nervous system is living tissue composed of cells. The cells in the nervous system fall into two major categories: *neurons* and *glia*.

Neurons

PsykTrek 2a

***Neurons* are individual cells in the nervous system that receive, integrate, and transmit information.** They are the basic links that permit communication within the nervous system. The vast majority of them communicate only with other neurons. However, a small minority receive signals from outside the nervous system (from sensory organs) or carry messages from the nervous system to the muscles that move the body.

A highly simplified drawing of a "typical" neuron is shown in **Figure 3.1**. **The *soma,* or cell body, contains the cell nucleus and much of the chemical machinery common to most cells** (*soma* is Greek for "body"). The rest of the neuron is devoted exclusively to handling information. The neurons in **Figure 3.1** have a number of branched, feeler-like structures called *dendritic trees* (*dendrite* is a Greek word for "tree"). Each individual branch is a *dendrite*. ***Dendrites* are the parts of a neuron that are specialized to receive information.** Most neu-

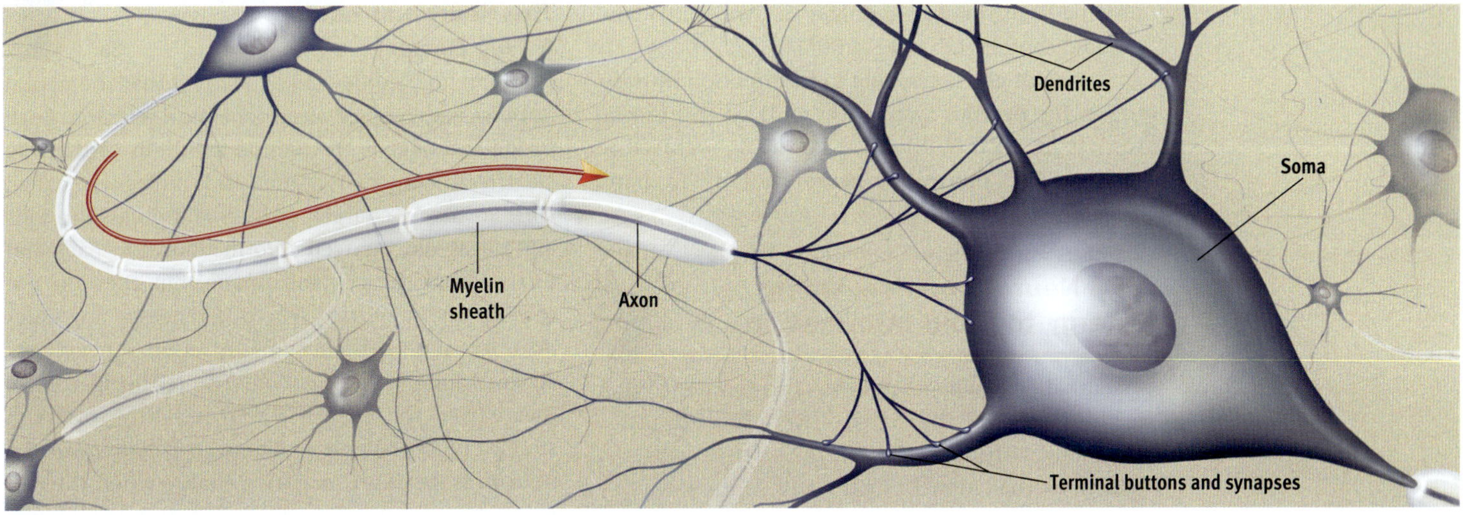

© Cengage Learning 2013

Figure 3.1

Structure of the neuron. Neurons are the communication links of the nervous system. This diagram highlights the key parts of a neuron, including specialized receptor areas (dendrites), the cell body (soma), the axon fiber along which impulses are transmitted, and the terminal buttons, which release chemical messengers that carry signals to other neurons. Neurons vary considerably in size and shape and are usually densely interconnected.

rons receive information from many other cells—sometimes thousands of others—and so have extensive dendritic trees.

From the many dendrites, information flows into the cell body and then travels away from the soma along the *axon* (from the Greek for "axle"). **The *axon* is a long, thin fiber that transmits signals away from the soma to other neurons or to muscles or glands.** Axons may be quite long (sometimes several feet), and they may branch off to communicate with a number of other cells.

In humans, many axons are wrapped in cells with a high concentration of a white, fatty substance called *myelin*. The *myelin sheath* is insulating material that encases some axons and that acts to speed up the transmission of signals that move along axons (Zorumski, Isenberg, & Mennerick, 2009). If an axon's myelin sheath deteriorates, its signals may not be transmitted effectively. The loss of muscle control seen with the disease *multiple sclerosis* is due to a degeneration of myelin sheaths (Joffe, 2009).

The axon ends in a cluster of ***terminal buttons*, which are small knobs that secrete chemicals called neurotransmitters.** These chemicals serve as messengers that may activate nearby neurons. The points at which neurons interconnect are called *synapses*. **A *synapse* is a junction where information is transmitted from one neuron to another** (*synapse* is from the Greek for "junction"). To summarize, information is received at the dendrites, is passed through the soma and along the axon, and is transmitted to the dendrites of other cells at meeting points called synapses.

Glia

2a

***Glia* are cells found throughout the nervous system that provide various types of support for neurons.** Glia (literally "glue") tend to be much smaller than neurons, but they outnumber neurons by about 10 to 1. Glial cells appear to account for over 50% of the brain's volume. Glial cells serve many functions. For example, they supply nourishment to neurons, help remove neurons' waste products, and provide insulation around many axons. The myelin sheaths that encase some axons are derived from special types of glial cells. Glia also play a complicated role in the development of the nervous system in the human embryo.

These functions, which have been known for many years, made glial cells the unsung heroes of the nervous system. However, recent research indicates that glia may also send and receive chemical signals (Deitmer & Rose, 2010; Fields, 2004). Some types of glia can detect neural impulses and send signals to other glial cells. Neuroscientists are now trying to figure out how this signaling system works with the neural communication system. Some of the early findings and theorizing have proven very interesting. For example, recent research suggests that glial cells may play an important role in memory formation (Bains & Oliet, 2007) and that gradual deterioration of glial tissue might contribute to Alzheimer's disease (Streit, 2005). Other research suggests that glial cells play a crucial role in the experience of chronic pain (Milligan & Watkins, 2009). Impaired neural-glial communication may also contribute to psychological disorders, such as schizo-

Reality CHECK

Misconception

Neurons are responsible for all the information processing in the nervous system.

Reality

Until recently, it *was* thought that the transmission and integration of informational signals was the exclusive role of the neurons. However, newer research has demonstrated that glial cells also play an important role in information processing.

phrenia (Hashimoto, Shimizu, & Iyo, 2005) and mood disorders (Lee et al., 2007).

Although glia contribute to information processing in the nervous system, the bulk of this crucial work is handled by the neurons. Thus, we need to examine the process of neural activity in more detail.

The Neural Impulse: Using Energy to Send Information 2a

What happens when a neuron is stimulated? What is the nature of the signal—the *neural impulse*—that moves through the neuron? These were the questions that Alan Hodgkin and Andrew Huxley set out to answer in their groundbreaking experiments with axons removed from squid. They chose squid because the squid has a pair of "giant" axons that are about a hundred times larger than those in humans (which still makes them only about as thick as a human hair). This large size permitted Hodgkin and Huxley to insert fine wires called *microelectrodes* into the axons. By using the microelectrodes to record the electrical activity in individual neurons, they unraveled the mystery of the neural impulse.

The Neuron at Rest: A Tiny Battery 2a

Hodgkin and Huxley (1952) learned that the neural impulse is a complex electrochemical reaction. Both inside and outside the neuron are fluids containing electrically charged atoms and molecules called *ions*. Positively charged sodium and potassium ions and negatively charged chloride ions flow back and forth across the cell membrane, but they do not cross at the same rate. The difference in flow rates leads to a slightly higher concentration of negatively charged ions inside the cell. The resulting voltage means that the neuron at rest is a tiny battery, a store of potential energy. **The *resting potential* of a neuron is its stable, negative charge when the cell is inactive.** As shown in **Figure 3.2(a)**, this charge is about −70 millivolts, roughly one-twentieth of the voltage of a flashlight battery.

The Action Potential 2a

As long as the voltage of a neuron remains constant, the cell is quiet, and no messages are being sent. When the neuron is stimulated, channels in its cell membrane open, briefly allowing positively charged sodium ions to rush in. For an instant, the neuron's charge is less negative, or even positive, creating an action potential (McCormick, 2008). **An *action potential* is a very brief shift in a neuron's electrical charge that travels along an axon.** The firing of an action potential is reflected in the voltage spike shown in **Figure 3.2(b)**. Like a spark traveling along a trail of gunpowder, the voltage change races down the axon.

After the firing of an action potential, the channels in the cell membrane that opened to let in sodium close up. Some time is needed before they are ready to open again, and the neuron cannot fire until then. **The *absolute refractory period* is the minimum length of time after an action poten-**

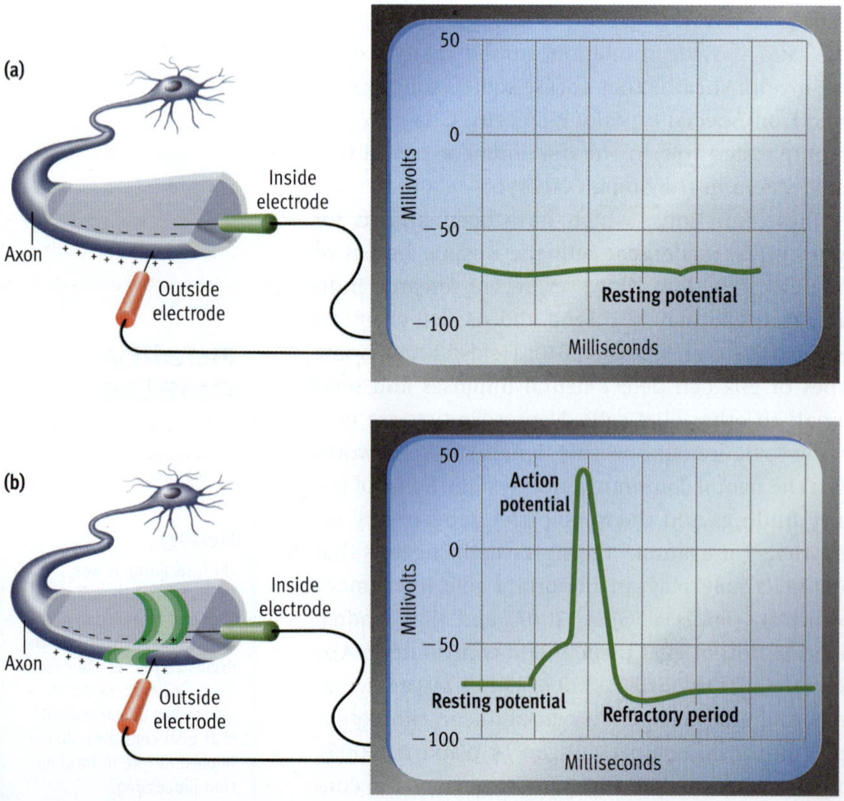

© Cengage Learning 2013

Figure 3.2

The neural impulse. The electrochemical properties of the neuron allow it to transmit signals. The electric charge of a neuron can be measured with a pair of electrodes connected to an oscilloscope, as Hodgkin and Huxley showed with a squid axon. Because of its exceptionally thick axons, the squid has frequently been used by scientists studying the neural impulse. **(a)** At rest, the neuron's voltage hovers around −70 millivolts. **(b)** When a neuron is stimulated, a brief jump occurs in its voltage, resulting in a spike on the oscilloscope recording of the neuron's electrical activity. This change in voltage, called an action potential, travels along the axon like a spark traveling along a trail of gunpowder.

tial during which another action potential cannot begin. This "down time" isn't very long, only 1 or 2 milliseconds. It is followed by a brief *relative refractory period,* during which the neuron can fire, but its threshold for firing is elevated, so more intense stimulation is required to start an action potential.

The All-or-None Law 2a

The neural impulse is an all-or-none proposition, like firing a gun. You can't half-fire a gun. The same is true of the neuron's firing of action potentials. Either the neuron fires or it doesn't, and its action potentials are all the same size (Kandel, 2000). That is, weaker stimuli do not produce smaller action potentials.

Even though the action potential is an all-or-nothing event, neurons *can* convey information about the strength of a stimulus. They do so by varying the *rate* at which they fire action potentials. In general, a stronger stimulus will cause a cell to fire a more rapid volley of neural impulses than a weaker stimulus will. For example, a dim light might trigger 5 action potentials per second in a visual cell, whereas brighter lights might trigger 100 or 200 impulses per second (Burkhardt, 2010).

Various neurons transmit neural impulses at different speeds. For example, thicker axons transmit neural impulses more rapidly than thinner ones do. Neural impulses travel very fast, moving at up to 100 meters per second, which is equivalent to more than 200 miles per hour. The entire, complicated process of neural transmission takes only a few thousandths of a second. In the time it has taken you to read this description of the neural impulse, billions of such impulses have been transmitted in your nervous system!

The Synapse: Where Neurons Meet 2b

In the nervous system, the neural impulse functions as a signal. For that signal to have any meaning for the system as a whole, it must be transmitted from the neuron to other cells. As noted earlier, this transmission takes place at special junctions called *synapses,* which depend on *chemical* messengers.

Sending Signals: Chemicals as Messengers 2b

A "typical" synapse is shown in **Figure 3.3** on the next page. The first thing that you should notice is that the two neurons don't actually touch. They are separated by the *synaptic cleft,* a microscopic gap between the terminal button of one neuron and the cell membrane of another neuron. Signals have to jump this gap to permit neurons to communicate. In this situation, the neuron that sends a signal across the gap is called the *presynaptic neuron.* The neuron that receives the signal is called the *postsynaptic neuron.*

How do messages travel across the gaps between neurons? The arrival of an action potential at an axon's terminal buttons triggers the release of ***neurotransmitters*—chemicals that transmit information from one neuron to another.** Within the buttons, most of these chemicals are stored in small sacs, called *synaptic vesicles.* The neurotransmitters are released when a vesicle fuses with the membrane of the presynaptic cell and its contents spill into the synaptic cleft (Schwarz, 2008). Neurotransmitters then spread across the synaptic cleft to the membrane of the receiving cell. There they may bind with special molecules in the postsynaptic cell membrane at various *receptor sites.* These sites are specifically "tuned" to recognize and respond to some neurotransmitters but not to others.

Receiving Signals: Postsynaptic Potentials 2b

When a neurotransmitter and a receptor molecule combine, reactions in the cell membrane cause a ***postsynaptic potential (PSP),* a voltage change at a receptor site on a postsynaptic cell membrane.**

CONCEPT CHECK 3.1

Understanding Nervous System Hardware Using Metaphors

A useful way to learn about the structures and functions of parts of the nervous system is through metaphors. Check your understanding of the basic components of the nervous system by matching the metaphorical descriptions below with the correct terms in the following list: (a) glia, (b) neuron, (c) soma, (d) dendrite, (e) axon, (f) myelin, (g) terminal button, (h) synapse. You'll find the answers in Appendix A.

_______ 1. Like a tree. Also, each branch is a telephone wire that carries incoming messages to you.

_______ 2. Like the insulation that covers electrical wires.

_______ 3. Like a silicon chip in a computer that receives and transmits information between input and output devices as well as between other chips.

_______ 4. Like an electrical cable that carries information.

_______ 5. Like the maintenance personnel who keep things clean and in working order so the operations of the enterprise can proceed.

_______ 6. Like the nozzle at the end of a hose, from which water is squirted.

_______ 7. Like a railroad junction, where two trains may meet.

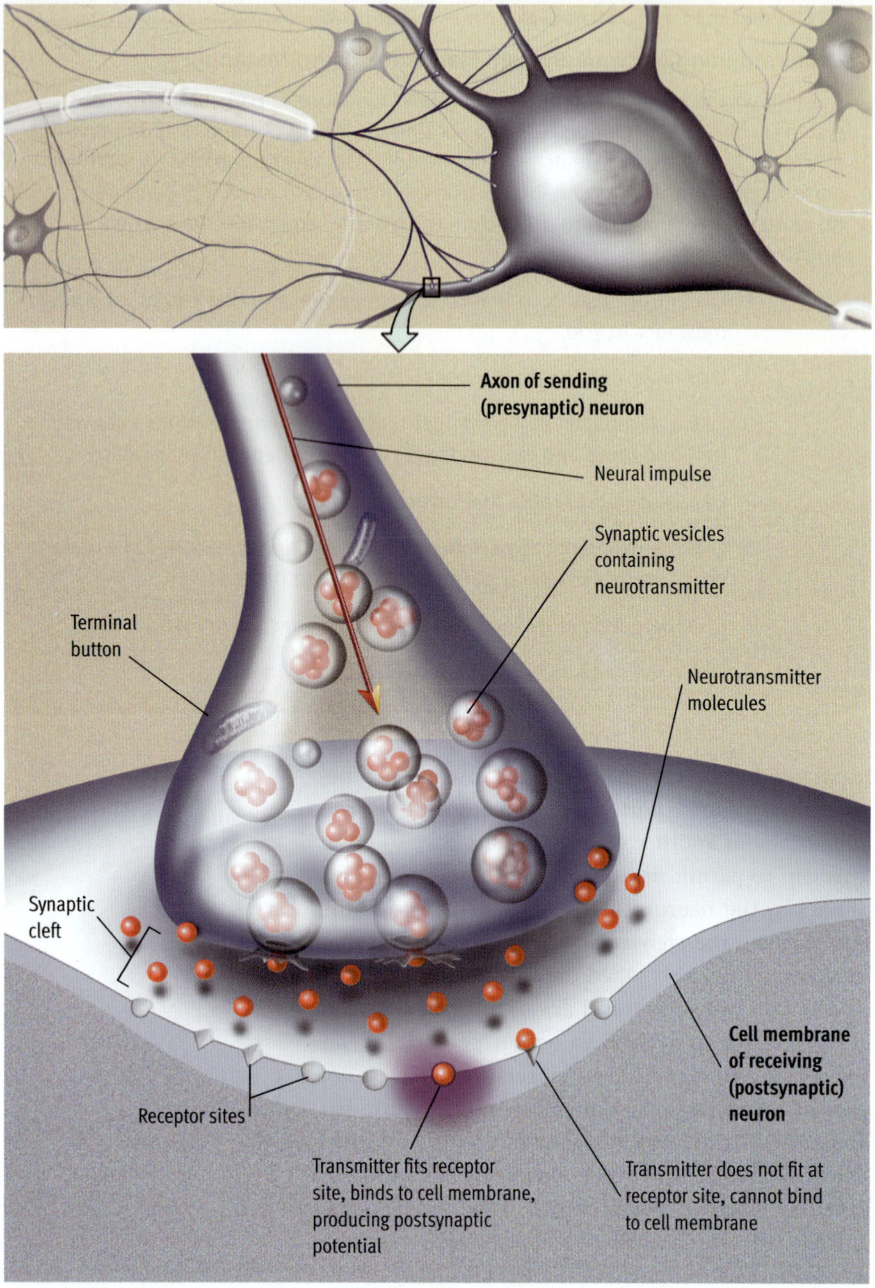

© Cengage Learning 2013

Figure 3.3

The synapse. When a neural impulse reaches an axon's terminal buttons, it triggers the release of chemical messengers called neurotransmitters. The neurotransmitter molecules diffuse across the synaptic cleft and bind to receptor sites on the postsynaptic neuron. A specific neurotransmitter can bind only to receptor sites that its molecular structure will fit into, much like a key must fit a lock.

Postsynaptic potentials do *not* follow the all-or-none law like action potentials do. Instead, postsynaptic potentials vary in size (the amount of voltage change). Moreover, they increase or decrease the *probability* of a neural impulse in the receiving cell in proportion to the amount of voltage change.

Two types of messages can be sent from cell to cell: excitatory and inhibitory. An *excitatory PSP* is a positive voltage shift that increases the likelihood that the postsynaptic neuron will fire action potentials. An *inhibitory PSP* is a negative voltage shift that decreases the likelihood that the postsynaptic neuron will fire action potentials. The direction of the voltage shift, and thus the nature of the PSP (excitatory or inhibitory), depends on which receptor sites are activated in the postsynaptic neuron (Kandel, 2000).

The excitatory or inhibitory effects produced at a synapse last only a fraction of a second. Then neurotransmitters drift away from receptor sites or are inactivated by enzymes that metabolize (convert) them into inactive forms. Most are reabsorbed into the presynaptic neuron through ***reuptake*, a process in which neurotransmitters are sponged up from the synaptic cleft by the presynaptic membrane.** Reuptake allows synapses to recycle their materials. Reuptake and the other key processes in synaptic transmission are summarized in **Figure 3.4**.

Integrating Signals: Neural Networks

PSYKTREK 2b

A neuron may receive a symphony of signals from *thousands* of other neurons. The same neuron may pass its messages along to thousands of neurons as well. Thus, a neuron must do a great deal more than simply relay messages it receives. It must *integrate* signals arriving at many synapses before it "decides" whether to fire a neural impulse. If enough excitatory PSPs occur in a neuron, the electrical currents can add up, causing the cell's voltage to reach the threshold at which an action potential will be fired. However, if many inhibitory PSPs also occur, they will tend to cancel the effects of excitatory PSPs. Thus, the state of the neuron is a weighted balance between excitatory and inhibitory influences (Byrne, 2008).

As Rita Carter (1998) has pointed out in *Mapping the Mind,* "The firing of a single neuron is not enough to create the twitch of an eyelid in sleep, let alone a conscious impression. . . . Millions of neurons must fire in unison to produce the most trifling thought" (p. 19). Most neurons are interlinked in complex chains, pathways, circuits, and networks. Our perceptions, thoughts, and actions depend on *patterns* of neural activity in elaborate neural net-

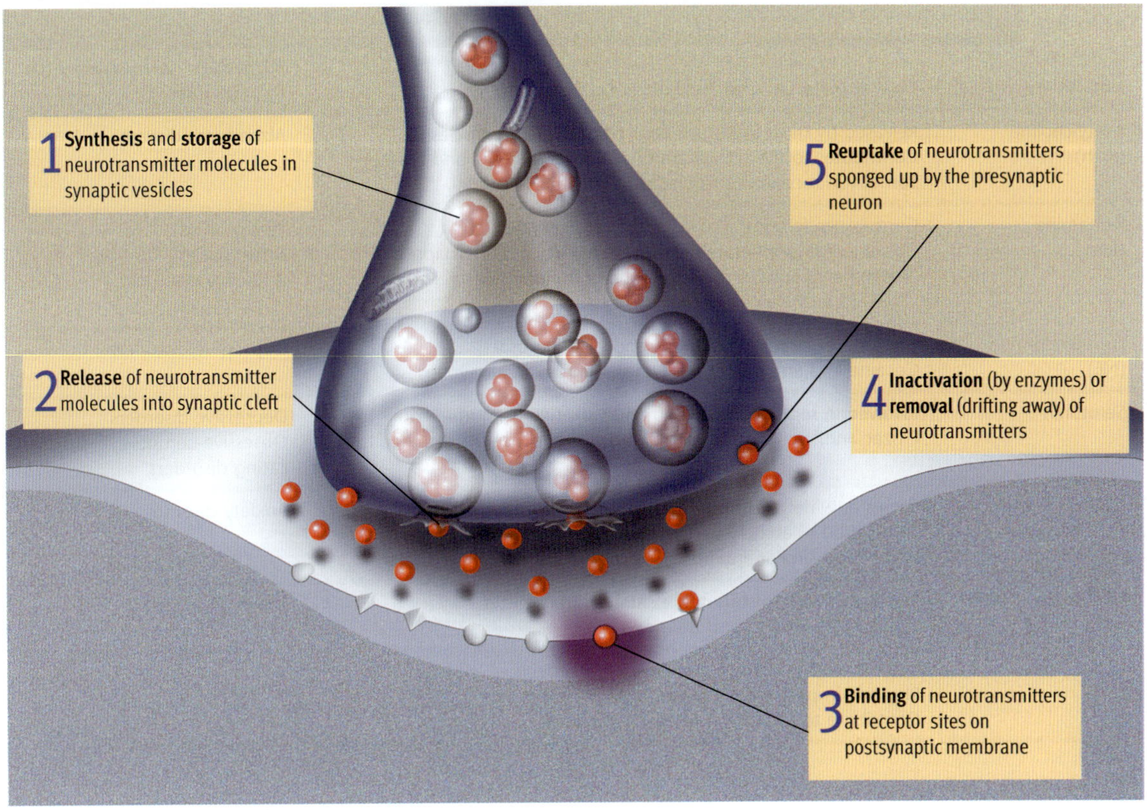

© Cengage Learning 2013

Figure 3.4

Overview of synaptic transmission. The main elements in synaptic transmission are summarized here, superimposed on a blowup of the synapse seen in **Figure 3.3**. The five key processes involved in communication at synapses are (1) synthesis and storage, (2) release, (3) binding, (4) inactivation or removal, and (5) reuptake of neurotransmitters. As you'll see in this chapter and the remainder of the book, the effects of many phenomena—such as pain, drug use, and some diseases—can be explained in terms of how they alter one or more of these processes (usually at synapses releasing a specific neurotransmitter).

works. These networks consist of interconnected neurons that frequently fire together or sequentially to perform certain functions (Song et al., 2005). The links in these networks are fluid, as new synaptic connections may be made while some old connections wither away (Hua & Smith, 2004).

Ironically, the *elimination of old synapses* appears to play a larger role in the sculpting of neural networks than the *creation of new synapses.* The nervous system normally forms more synapses than needed and then gradually eliminates the less-active ones. For example, the number of synapses in the human visual cortex peaks at around age 1 and then declines, as diagrammed in **Figure 3.5** (Huttenlocher, 1994). This elimination of old or less-active synapses is called *synaptic pruning,* and it is a key process in the formation of the neural networks that are crucial to communication in the nervous system (Tapia & Lichtman, 2008).

Neurotransmitters and Behavior

PSYKTREK 2b, 4d

As we have seen, the nervous system relies on chemical messengers, called neurotransmitters, to communicate information between neurons. These

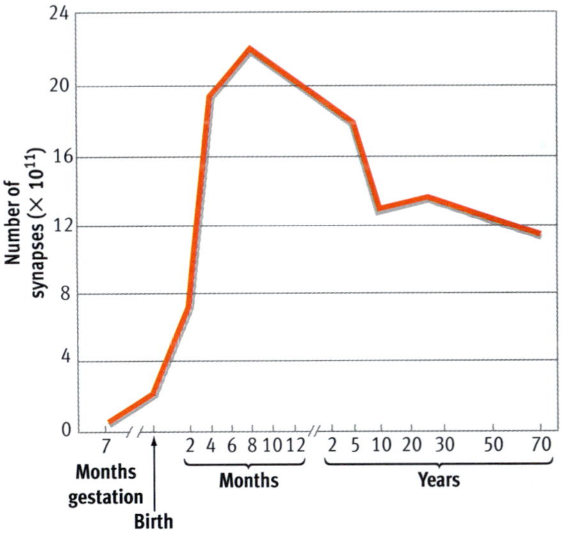

Figure 3.5

Synaptic pruning. This graph summarizes data on the estimated number of synapses in the human visual cortex as a function of age (Huttenlocher, 1994). As you can see, the number of synapses in this area peaks at around age 1 and then mostly declines over the course of the life span. This decline reflects the process of *synaptic pruning,* which involves the gradual elimination of less active synapses.

SOURCE: Data based on Huttenlocher, P. R. (1994). Synaptogenesis in human cerebral cortex. In G. Dawson & K. W. Fischer (Eds.), *Human behavior and the developing brain.* New York: Guilford Press. Graphic adapted from Kolb, B. & Whishaw, I. Q. (2001). *An introduction to brain and behavior.* New York: Worth Publishers.

Table 3.1 Common Neurotransmitters and Some of Their Relations to Behavior

Neurotransmitter	Characteristics and Relations to Behavior	Disorders Associated with Dysregulation
Acetylcholine (ACh)	Released by motor neurons controlling skeletal muscles Contributes to the regulation of attention, arousal, and memory Some ACh receptors stimulated by nicotine	Alzheimer's disease
Dopamine (DA)	Contributes to control of voluntary movement Cocaine and amphetamines elevate activity at DA synapses Dopamine circuits in medial forebrain bundle characterized as "reward pathway"	Parkinsonism Schizophrenic disorders Addictive disorders
Norepinephrine (NE)	Contributes to modulation of mood and arousal Cocaine and amphetamines elevate activity at NE synapses	Depressive disorders
Serotonin	Involved in regulation of sleep and wakefulness, aggression Prozac and similar antidepressant drugs affect serotonin circuits	Depressive disorders Obsessive-compulsive disorders Eating disorders
GABA	Serves as widely distributed inhibitory transmitter, contributing to regulation of anxiety and sleep/arousal Valium and similar antianxiety drugs work at GABA synapses	Anxiety disorders
Glutamate	Serves as widely distributed excitatory transmitter Involved in learning and memory	Schizophrenia
Endorphins	Resemble opiate drugs in structure and effects Play role in pain relief and response to stress Contribute to regulation of eating behavior	

© Cengage Learning 2013

neurotransmitters are fundamental to behavior, playing a key role in everything from muscle movements to moods and mental health.

So far we've discussed two neurotransmitters—one for excitatory potentials and one for inhibitory potentials. But there are many kinds of neurotransmitters. There are nine well-established, classic (small-molecule) transmitters, about 40 additional neuropeptide chemicals that function at least part-time as neurotransmitters, and a variety of recently recognized "novel" neurotransmitters (Snyder, 2002; Zorumski et al., 2009).

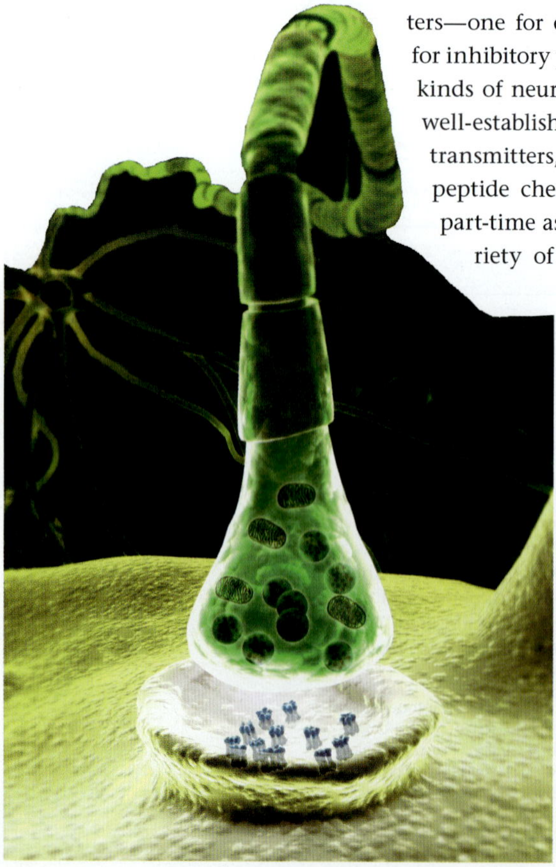

© 3D4Medical/Phototake

Specific neurotransmitters work at specific kinds of synapses. You may recall that transmitters deliver their messages by binding to receptor sites on the postsynaptic membrane. However, a transmitter cannot bind to just any site. The binding process operates much like a lock and key, as was shown in **Figure 3.3**. Just as a key has to fit a lock to work, a transmitter has to fit into a receptor site for binding to occur. As a result, specific transmitters can deliver signals at only certain locations on cell membranes. Such specialization reduces crosstalk between densely packed neurons, making the nervous system's communication more precise (Deutch & Roth, 2008).

Let's briefly review some of the most interesting findings about how specific neurotransmitters regulate behavior, as summarized in **Table 3.1**.

Acetylcholine

PSYKTREK 2b

The discovery that cells communicate by releasing chemicals was first made in connection with the transmitter *acetylcholine* (ACh). ACh has been found throughout the nervous system. It's the only transmitter between motor neurons and voluntary muscles. Every move you make—typing, walking, talking, breathing—depends on ACh released to your muscles by motor neurons (Kandel & Siegelbaum, 2000). ACh also appears to contribute to attention, arousal, and memory. An inadequate supply of ACh in certain areas of the brain is associated with the memory losses seen in Alzheimer's disease (Bourgeois, Seaman, & Servis, 2003). Although ACh depletion does *not* appear to be the crucial causal factor underlying Alzheimer's disease, the drug treatments currently available, which can slow the progress of the disease (slightly), work by amplifying ACh activity (Neugroschl et al., 2005).

The activity of ACh (and other neurotransmitters) may be influenced by other chemicals in the brain. Although synaptic receptor sites are sensitive to specific neurotransmitters, sometimes they can be "fooled" by other chemical substances. For example, if you smoke tobacco, some of your ACh synapses will be stimulated by the nicotine that arrives in your brain. At these synapses, the nicotine acts like ACh itself. It binds to receptor sites for ACh, causing postsynaptic potentials (PSPs). In technical language, nicotine is an ACh agonist. **An *agonist* is a chemical that mimics the action of a neurotransmitter.**

Not all chemicals that fool synaptic receptors are agonists. Some chemicals bind to receptors but fail to produce a PSP (the key slides into the lock, but it doesn't work). In effect, they temporarily *block* the action of the natural transmitter by occupying its receptor sites, rendering them unusable. Thus, they act as antagonists. **An *antagonist* is a chemical that opposes the action of a neurotransmitter.** For example, the drug *curare* is an ACh antagonist; it blocks action at the same ACh synapses that are fooled by nicotine. As a result, muscles are unable to move. Some South American natives put a form of curare on arrow tips; then if they wound an animal, the curare blocks the synapses from nerve to muscle, causing paralysis.

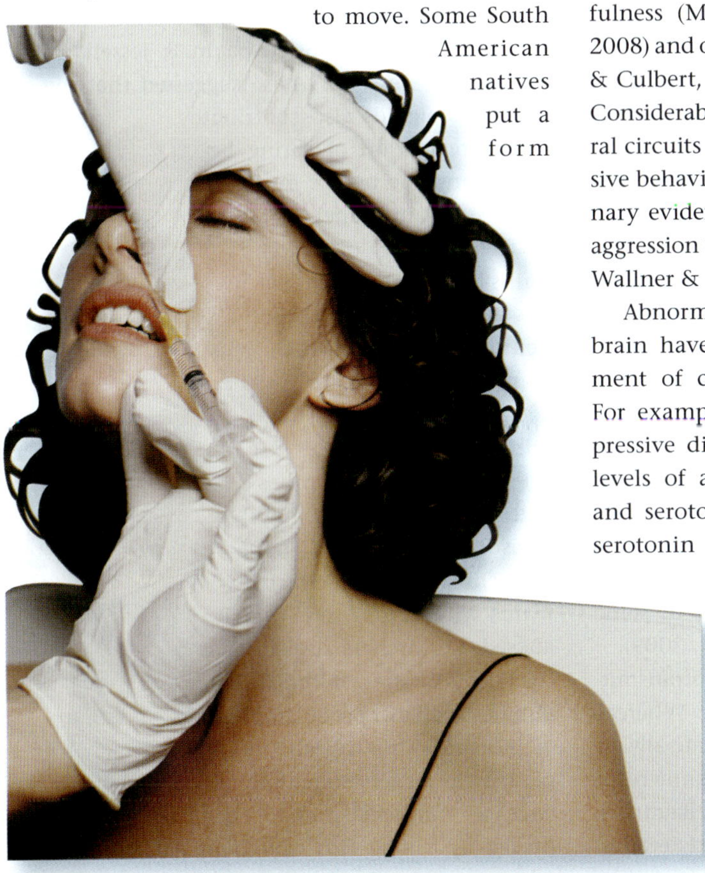

© Digital Vision/Getty Images

Cosmetic botox treatments temporarily reduce wrinkles by blocking ACh receptors at synapses between motor neurons and voluntary muscles (in the vicinity of the injection). This action basically paralyzes muscles to prevent wrinkles from forming. The cosmetic effects last only about three to five months, however, because the synapse adapts and new ACh receptors are gradually generated.

Monoamines

PSYKTREK 2b, 4d

The *monoamines* include three neurotransmitters: dopamine, norepinephrine, and serotonin. Neurons using these transmitters regulate many aspects of everyday behavior. Dopamine (DA), for example, is used by neurons that control voluntary movements. The degeneration of such neurons in a specific area of the brain causes *Parkinsonism*, a disease marked by tremors, muscular rigidity, and reduced control over voluntary movements (DeLong, 2000). The drug (L-dopa) that is used to treat Parkinsonism is converted to dopamine in the brain to partially make up for diminished dopamine activity.

© AP Images

Muhammed Ali is a well-known victim of Parkinson's disease. Roughly one million Americans suffer from this disease, which is caused by a decline in the synthesis of the neurotransmitter dopamine. The reduction in dopamine synthesis occurs because of the deterioration of a structure located in the midbrain.

Serotonin-releasing neurons appear to play a prominent role in the regulation of sleep and wakefulness (Monti, Jantos, & Monti, 2008) and of eating behavior (Klump & Culbert, 2007; Steiger et al., 2005). Considerable evidence also suggests that neural circuits using serotonin modulate aggressive behavior in animals, and some preliminary evidence relates serotonin activity to aggression in humans (Carrillo et al., 2009; Wallner & Machatschke, 2009).

Abnormal levels of monoamines in the brain have been related to the development of certain psychological disorders. For example, people who suffer from depressive disorders appear to have lowered levels of activation at norepinephrine (NE) and serotonin synapses. Abnormalities at NE and serotonin synapses are implicated because most antidepressant drugs exert their main effects at these synapses (Johnson et al., 2009; Thase, 2009). Abnormalities in serotonin circuits have also been implicated as a factor in eating disorders (Halmi, 2008), and in obsessive-compulsive disorders (Hollander & Simeon, 2008).

In a similar fashion, the *dopamine hypothesis* asserts that abnormal activity at dopamine synapses plays a crucial role in the development of *schizophrenia*. This severe mental illness is marked by irrational thought, hallucinations,

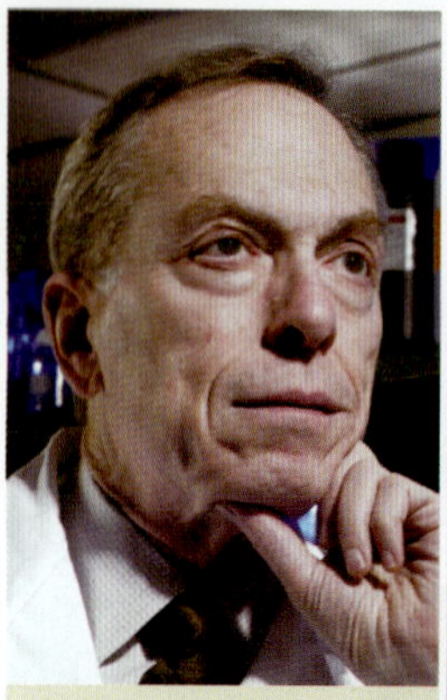

Courtesy of Solomon Snyder

Solomon Snyder

"Brain research of the past decade, especially the study of neurotransmitters, has proceeded at a furious pace, achieving progress equal in scope to all the accomplishments of the preceding 50 years—and the pace of discovery continues to accelerate."

poor contact with reality, and deterioration of routine adaptive behavior. Afflicting roughly 1% of the population, schizophrenia requires hospitalization more often than any other psychological disorder (see Chapter 15). Studies suggest that overactivity in dopamine circuits is part of the neurochemical basis for schizophrenia (Javitt & Laruelle, 2006). Why? Primarily because the therapeutic drugs that tame schizophrenic symptoms are known to be DA antagonists that reduce the neurotransmitter's activity (Minzenberg, Yoon, & Carter, 2008).

Temporary alterations at monoamine synapses also appear to account for the powerful effects of amphetamines and cocaine. These stimulants seem to exert most of their effects by creating a storm of increased activity at dopamine and norepinephrine synapses (King & Ellinwood, 2005; Repetto & Gold, 2005). Some theorists believe that the rewarding effects of most abused drugs depend on increased activity in a particular dopamine pathway (Koob, Everitt, & Robbins, 2008; see Chapter 5). Furthermore, dysregulation in this dopamine pathway appears to be the chief factor underlying drug craving and addiction (Nestler & Malenka, 2004).

GABA and Glutamate

PsykTrek 2b

Another group of transmitters consists of *amino acids*. One of these, *gamma-aminobutyric acid* (GABA) is notable in that it seems to produce only *inhibitory* postsynaptic potentials. Some transmitters, such as ACh and NE, are versatile. They can produce either excitatory or inhibitory PSPs, depending on the synaptic receptors they bind to. However, GABA appears to have inhibitory effects at virtually all synapses where it is present. GABA receptors are widely distributed in the brain and may be present at 40% of all synapses. GABA appears to be responsible for much of the inhibition in the central nervous system. Studies suggest that GABA is involved in the regulation of anxiety in humans and that disturbances in GABA circuits may contribute to some types of anxiety disorders (Garakani et al., 2009).

Glutamate is another amino acid neurotransmitter that's widely distributed in the brain. Whereas GABA has only inhibitory effects, glutamate always has excitatory effects. Glutamate is best known for its contribution to learning and memory (Baudry & Lynch, 2001; Lovinger, 2010). In recent decades, disturbances in glutamate circuits have been implicated as factors that might contribute to certain features of schizophrenic disorders (Javitt & Laruelle, 2006).

Endorphins

PsykTrek 2b, 4d

In 1970, after a horseback-riding accident, Candace Pert, a graduate student in neuroscience, lay in a hospital bed receiving frequent shots of *morphine*, a painkilling drug derived from the opium plant. This experience left her with a driving curiosity about how morphine works. A few years later, she and Solomon Snyder rocked the scientific world by showing that *morphine exerts its effects by binding to specialized receptors in the brain* (Pert & Snyder, 1973).

This discovery raised a perplexing question: Why would the brain be equipped with receptors for morphine, a powerful, addictive opioid drug not normally found in the body? It occurred to Snyder, Pert, and others that the nervous system must have its own, endogenous (internally produced) morphine-like substances. Investigators dubbed these as-yet undiscovered substances *endorphins*—internally produced chemicals that resemble opiates in structure and effects. A search for the body's natural opiate ensued. A number of endogenous opioids were soon identified (Hughes et al., 1975). Subsequent studies revealed that endorphins and their receptors are widely distributed in the human body and that they clearly contribute to the modulation of pain (Apkarian et al., 2005; Basbaum & Jessell, 2000). Subsequent research has suggested that the endogenous opioids also contribute to the regulation of eating behavior and the body's response to stress (Adam & Epel, 2007).

The discovery of endorphins has led to new theories and findings on the neurochemical bases of pain and pleasure. In addition to their painkilling effects, opiate drugs such as morphine and heroin produce highly pleasurable feelings of euphoria. This euphoric effect explains why heroin is so widely abused. Researchers suspect that the body's natural endorphins may also be capable of producing feelings of pleasure. This capacity might explain why joggers sometimes experience a "runner's high." The pain caused by a long run may trigger the release of endorphins, which neutralize some of the pain and create a feeling of exhilaration (Harte, Eifert, & Smith, 1995). The long-held suspicion that en-

© paul prescott/Shutterstock

dorphins might underlie the "runner's high" experience was supported in a recent study that used brain-imaging technology to track endorphin release in the brain (Boecker et al., 2008). Ten joggers were administered brain scans just before and just after a 2-hour endurance run. As hypothesized, the post-run brain scans showed a surge in the production of endorphins in selected areas of the participants' brains.

In this section we have highlighted just a few of the more interesting connections between neurotransmitters and behavior. But biochemical processes in the nervous system are incredibly complex. Although scientists have learned a great deal about neurotransmitters and behavior, much still remains to be discovered.

CONCEPT CHECK 3.2

Linking Brain Chemistry to Behavior

Check your understanding of relations between brain chemistry and behavior by indicating which neurotransmitters have been linked to the phenomena listed below. Choose your answers from the following list: (a) acetylcholine, (b) norepinephrine, (c) dopamine, (d) serotonin, (e) endorphins. Indicate your choice (by letter) in the spaces on the left. You'll find the answers in Appendix A.

_______ 1. A transmitter involved in the regulation of sleep and perhaps aggression.

_______ 2. The two monoamines that have been linked to depression.

_______ 3. Chemicals that resemble opiate drugs in structure and that are involved in pain relief.

_______ 4. A neurotransmitter for which abnormal levels have been implicated in schizophrenia.

_______ 5. The only neurotransmitter between motor neurons and voluntary muscles.

REVIEW OF KEY LEARNING GOALS

3.1 Neurons receive, integrate, and transmit signals. Information is received at the dendrites. It is then passed through the soma and along the axon. Finally, it is transmitted to the dendrites of other cells at meeting points called synapses, which is where neurotransmitters are released from terminal buttons. Glial cells provide various types of support for neurons and contribute to signal transmission in the nervous system.

3.2 The neural impulse is a brief change in a neuron's electrical charge that moves along an axon. An action potential is an all-or-none event. Neurons convey information about the strength of a stimulus by changes in their rate of firing. Action potentials trigger the release of chemicals called neurotransmitters that spread across a synapse to communicate with other neurons. Transmitters bind with receptors, causing excitatory or inhibitory PSPs. Whether the postsynaptic neuron fires a neural impulse depends on the balance of excitatory and inhibitory PSPs.

3.3 The transmitter ACh plays a key role in muscular movement. Serotonin circuits may contribute to the regulation of sleep, eating, and aggression. Depression is associated with reduced activation at norepinephrine and serotonin synapses. Schizophrenia has been linked to overactivity at dopamine synapses. Cocaine and amphetamines appear to exert their main effects by altering activity at DA and NE synapses.

3.4 GABA is an important amino acid transmitter whose inhibitory effects appear to regulate anxiety. Glutamate is another amino acid transmitter, best known for its role in memory. Endorphins, which resemble opiates, contribute to pain relief and may modulate eating and stress reactions.

Organization of the Nervous System

KEY LEARNING GOALS

3.5 Provide an overview of the peripheral nervous system, including its subdivisions.

3.6 Distinguish between the central nervous system and the peripheral nervous system.

Clearly, communication in the nervous system is fundamental to behavior. So far we have looked at how individual cells communicate with one another. In this section, we examine the organization of the nervous system as a whole.

Experts believe that there are an estimated *100 billion* neurons in the human brain (Kandel, 2000). If you counted them nonstop at the rate of one per second, you'd be counting for over 3000 years! And, remember, most neurons have synaptic connections to many other neurons, so there may be *100 trillion* synapses in a human brain!

The fact that neurons and synapses are so abundant as to be uncountable probably contributes to the widely held belief that people "use only 10% of their brains." But this curious tidbit of folk wisdom is utter nonsense (McBurney, 1996). If 90% of the human brain consisted of unused "excess baggage," localized brain damage would not be a problem much of the time. In reality, damage in even very tiny areas of brain usually has severe, disruptive effects (Zillmer, Spiers, & Culbertson, 2008). Furthermore, brain-imaging research shows that even simple mental operations depend on activity spread

Reality CHECK

Misconception

People use only about 10% of their brains.

Reality

There is no way to quantify the percentage of the brain that is "in use" at any specific time or over longer spans of time. The 10% myth appeals to people because it suggests that they have a huge reservoir of untapped potential. Hucksters selling self-improvement programs often talk about the 10% myth because it makes their claims and promises seem more realistic ("Unleash your potential!").

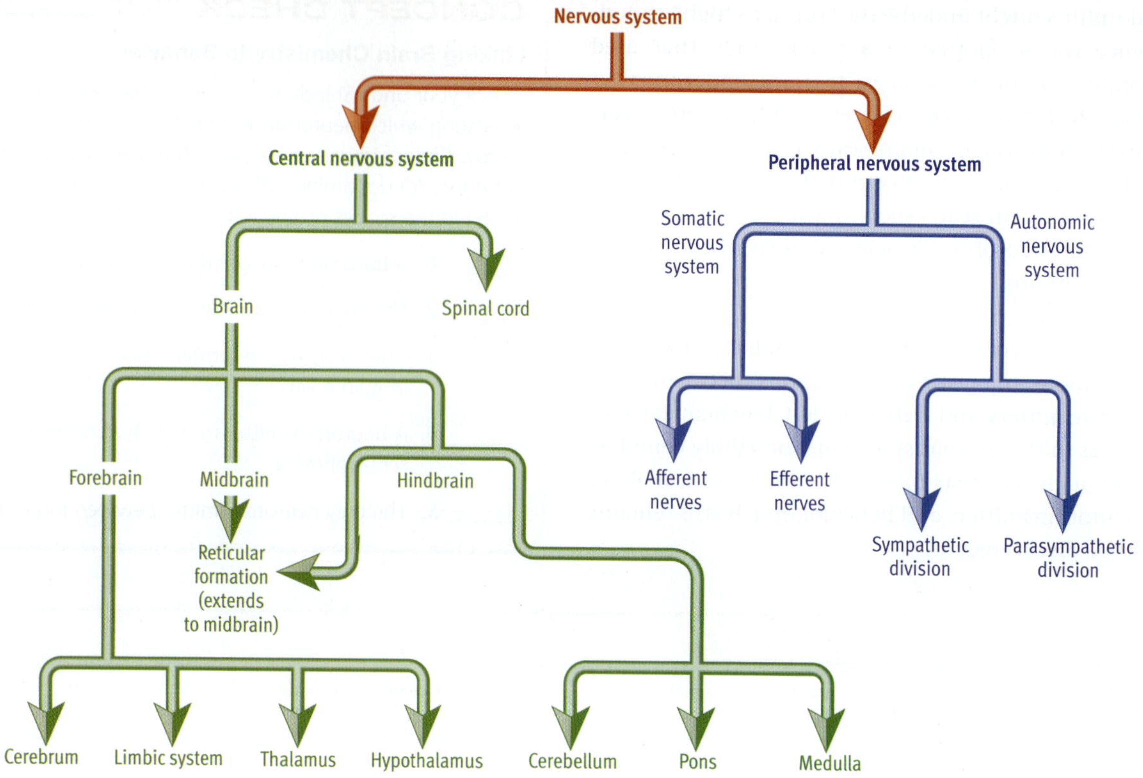

Figure 3.6

Organization of the human nervous system. This overview of the human nervous system shows the relationships of its various parts and systems. The brain is traditionally divided into three regions: the hindbrain, midbrain, and forebrain. The peripheral nervous system is made up of the somatic nervous system, which controls voluntary muscles and sensory receptors, and the autonomic nervous system, which controls the involuntary activities of smooth muscles, blood vessels, and glands.

© Cengage Learning 2013

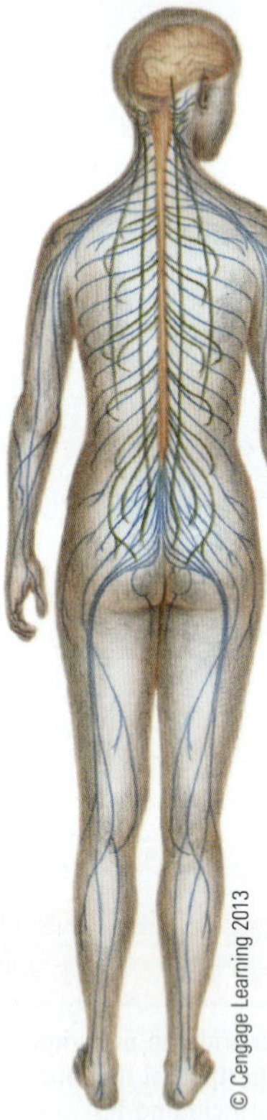

Figure 3.7

The central and peripheral nervous systems. The central nervous system (CNS) consists of the brain and the spinal cord. The peripheral nervous system consists of the remaining nerves that fan out throughout the body. The peripheral nervous system is further divided into the somatic nervous system, which is shown in blue, and the autonomic nervous system, which is shown in green.

across several or more areas in the brain. Even during sleep, the brain is highly active.

In any event, the multitudes of neurons in your nervous system have to work together to keep information flowing effectively. To see how the nervous system is organized to accomplish this end, we will divide it into two main parts: the peripheral nervous system and the central nervous system. **Figure 3.6** presents an organizational chart that shows all the relationships that flow from these two parts of the nervous system.

The Peripheral Nervous System 2a, 8c

The *peripheral nervous system* is made up of all those nerves that lie outside the brain and spinal cord. *Nerves* are bundles of neuron fibers (axons) that are routed together in the peripheral nervous system (see **Figure 3.7**). This portion of the nervous system is just what it sounds like: the part that extends outside the central nervous system. The peripheral nervous system is composed of two primary systems: the *somatic nervous system* and the *autonomic nervous system*.

The Somatic Nervous System 2a

The somatic nervous system lets you feel the world and move around in it. **The *somatic nervous system* is made up of nerves that connect to voluntary skeletal muscles and to sensory receptors.** These nerves are the cables that carry information from receptors in the skin, muscles, and joints to the central nervous system (CNS) and that carry commands from the CNS to the muscles. These functions require two kinds of nerve fibers. ***Afferent nerve fibers* are axons that carry information inward to the central nervous system from the periphery of the body. *Efferent nerve fibers* are axons that carry information outward from the central nervous system to the periphery of the body.** Each body nerve contains many axons of each type. Thus, somatic nerves are "two-way streets" with incoming (afferent) and outgoing (efferent) lanes.

The Autonomic Nervous System 2a, 8c

The autonomic nervous system controls automatic, involuntary, visceral functions that people don't normally think about, such as heart rate, digestion, and perspiration (Powley, 2008; see **Figure 3.8**). **Thus, the *autonomic nervous system (ANS)* is made up of nerves that connect to the heart, blood vessels, smooth muscles, and glands.** As its name hints, the autonomic system is a separate (autonomous) system, although it is ultimately governed by the central nervous system.

The autonomic nervous system controls much of the physiological arousal that occurs when people experience emotions. For example, imagine that you're arriving home alone one night when you notice that your front door is ajar and a window is broken. Suspecting that your home has been broken into, your heart rate and breathing will speed up. As you cautiously make your way inside, your blood pressure may surge, you may get goosebumps, and your palms may begin to sweat. These difficult-to-control reactions are aspects of autonomic arousal.

Walter Cannon (1932), one of the first psychologists to study this reaction, called it the *fight-or-flight response*. Cannon carefully monitored this response in cats—after confronting them with dogs. He concluded that organisms generally respond to threat by preparing physiologically for attacking (fight) or fleeing (flight) from the enemy.

The autonomic nervous system can be subdivided into two branches: the sympathetic division and the parasympathetic division (see **Figure 3.8**). **The *sympathetic division* is the branch of the autonomic nervous system that mobilizes the body's resources for emergencies.** It creates the fight-or-flight response. Activation of the sympathetic division inhibits digestive processes and drains blood from the periphery, lessening bleeding in the case of an injury. Key sympathetic nerves send signals to the adrenal glands, triggering the release of hormones that ready the body for exertion. In contrast, **the *parasympathetic division* is the branch of the autonomic nervous system that generally conserves bodily resources.** It activates processes that allow the body to save and store energy. For example, actions by parasympathetic nerves slow heart rate, reduce blood pressure, and promote digestion.

The Central Nervous System 2a

The *central nervous system (CNS)* consists of the brain and the spinal cord (see **Figure 3.7**). It is protected by the skull and by enclosing sheaths called the *meninges* (hence *meningitis*, the name for the disease in which the meninges become inflamed). In addition, the central nervous system is bathed in its own special nutritive "soup," the *cerebrospinal fluid (CSF)*. The cerebrospinal fluid nourishes the brain and provides a protective cushion for it. The hollow cavities in the brain that are filled with CSF are called *ventricles* (see **Figure 3.9** on the next page).

The Spinal Cord

The *spinal cord* is part of the central nervous system. Like the brain, it is enclosed by the meninges and bathed in CSF. In short, the spinal cord is an extension of the brain. The spinal cord connects the brain to the rest of the body through the peripheral nervous system.

The spinal cord runs from the base of the brain to just below the level of the waist. It houses bundles of axons that carry the brain's commands to peripheral nerves and that relay sensations from the periphery of the body to the brain. Many forms of paralysis result from spinal cord damage. This fact underscores the critical role the spinal cord plays in

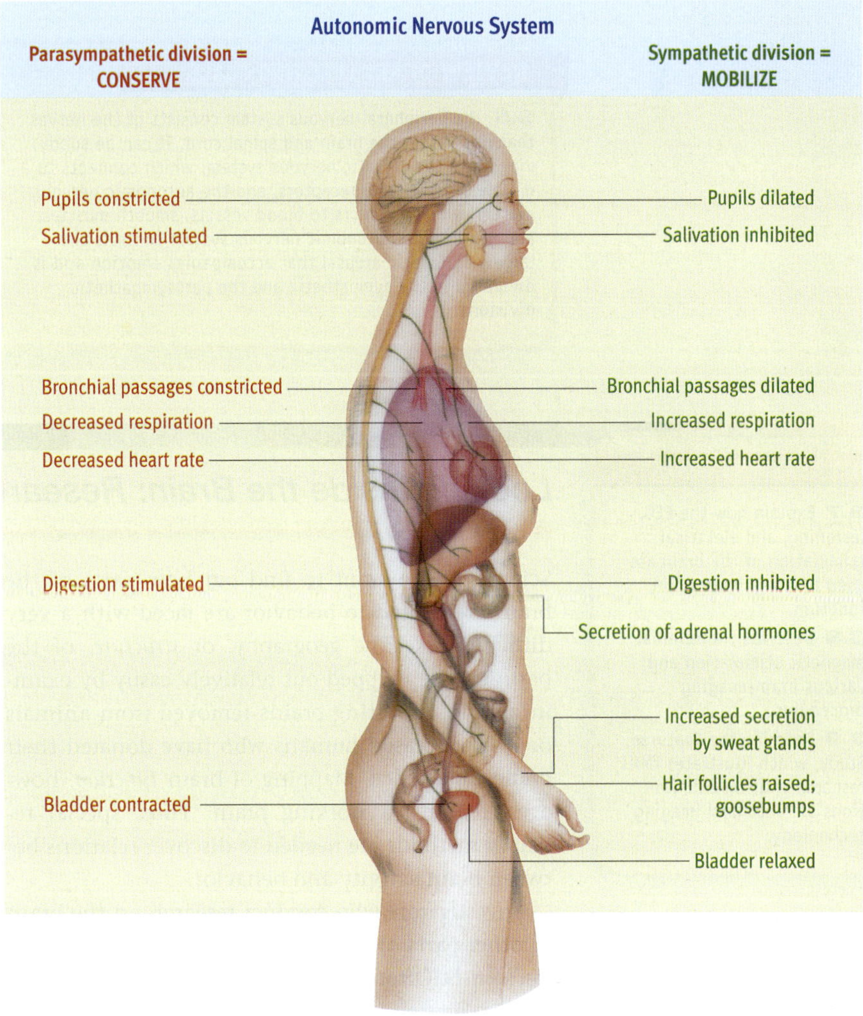

© Cengage Learning 2013

Figure 3.8
The autonomic nervous system (ANS). The ANS is composed of the nerves that connect to the heart, blood vessels, smooth muscles, and glands. The ANS is divided into the sympathetic division, which mobilizes bodily resources in times of need, and the parasympathetic division, which conserves bodily resources. Some of the key functions controlled by each division of the ANS are summarized in the diagram.

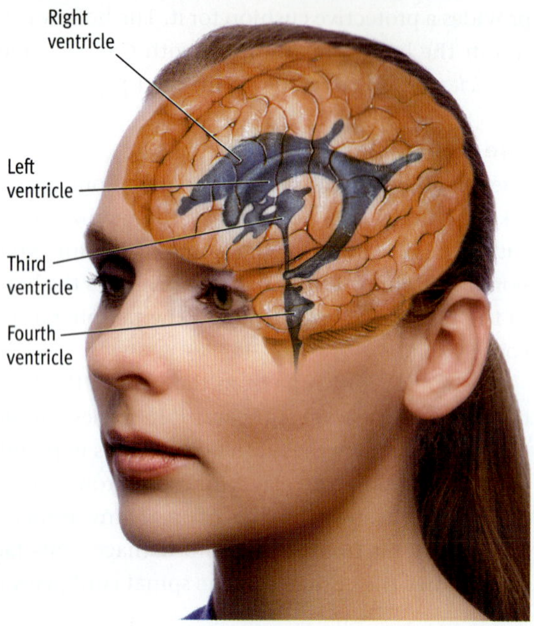

Figure 3.9

The ventricles of the brain. Cerebrospinal fluid (CSF) circulates around the brain and the spinal cord. The hollow cavities in the brain filled with CSF are called ventricles. The four ventricles in the human brain are depicted here.

© Cengage Learning 2013

transmitting signals from the brain to the motor neurons that move the body's muscles.

The Brain

The crowning glory of the central nervous system is, of course, the *brain.* Anatomically, the brain is the part of the central nervous system that fills the upper portion of the skull. Although it weighs only about 3 pounds and could be held in one hand, the brain contains billions of interacting cells. These cells integrate information from inside and outside the body, coordinate the body's actions, and enable human beings to talk, think, remember, plan, create, and dream.

Because of its central importance for behavior, the brain is the subject of the next three sections of the chapter. We begin by looking at the remarkable methods that have enabled researchers to unlock some of the brain's secrets.

REVIEW OF KEY LEARNING GOALS

3.5 The peripheral nervous system consists of the nerves that lie outside the brain and spinal cord. It can be subdivided into the somatic nervous system, which connects to muscles and sensory receptors, and the autonomic nervous system, which connects to blood vessels, smooth muscles, and glands. The autonomic nervous system controls the largely automatic arousal that accompanies emotion and is divided into the sympathetic and the parasympathetic divisions.

3.6 The central nervous system consists of the brain and spinal cord. Hollow cavities in the brain called ventricles contain cerebrospinal fluid. The spinal cord connects the brain to the rest of the body through the peripheral nervous system.

KEY LEARNING GOALS

3.7 Explain how the EEG, lesioning, and electrical stimulation of the brain are used to investigate brain function.

3.8 Describe transcranial magnetic stimulation and various brain-imaging procedures.

3.9 Describe the Featured Study, which illustrates fMRI research and some limitations of functional imaging technology.

Looking Inside the Brain: Research Methods

Scientists who want to find out how parts of the brain are related to behavior are faced with a very difficult task. The geography, or *structure,* of the brain can be mapped out relatively easily by examining and dissecting brains removed from animals or from deceased humans who have donated their bodies to science. Mapping of brain *function,* however, requires a working brain. Thus, special research methods are needed to discover relations between brain activity and behavior.

Investigators who conduct research on the brain or other parts of the nervous system are called *neuroscientists.* Often, brain research involves collaboration by neuroscientists from several disciplines, including anatomy, physiology, biology, neurology, neurosurgery, psychiatry, and psychology. Neuroscientists use many specialized techniques to investigate connections between the brain and behavior. They have relied most heavily on electrical recordings, lesioning, and electrical stimulation. More recently, transcranial magnetic stimulation and brain-imaging techniques, such as CT and MRI scans, have enhanced neuroscientists' ability to study brain structure and function.

Electrical Recordings

2c

The electrical activity of the brain can be recorded, much as Hodgkin and Huxley recorded the electrical activity of individual neurons. Recordings of single cells in the brain have proven valuable, but scientists also need ways to record the simultaneous activity of the billions of neurons in the brain. Fortunately, in 1929 a German psychiatrist named Hans Berger invented a machine that could record broad patterns of brain electrical activity. **The *electroencephalograph (EEG)* is a device that monitors the electrical activity of the brain over time by**

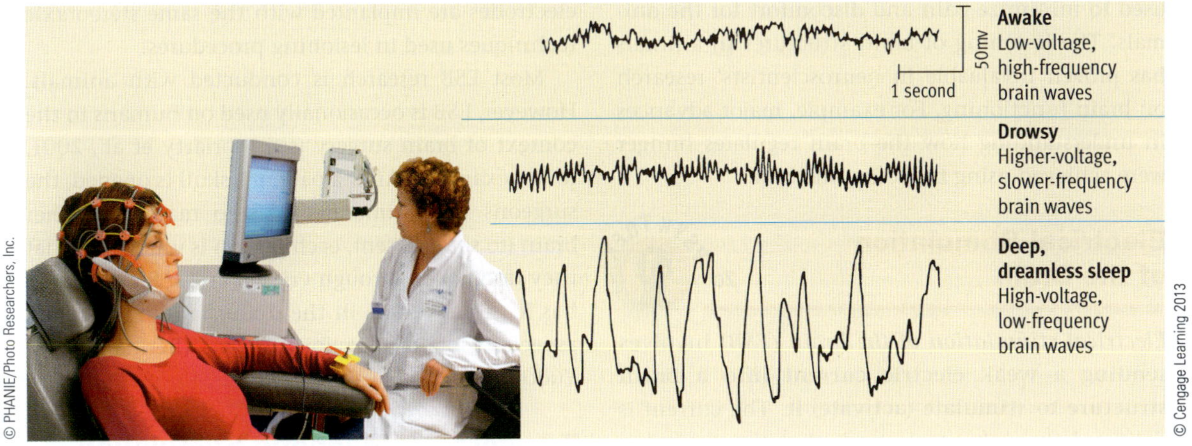

Figure 3.10

The electroencephalograph (EEG). Recording electrodes attached to the surface of the scalp permit the EEG to record electrical activity in the cortex over time. The EEG provides output in the form of line tracings called brain waves. Brain waves vary in frequency (cycles per second) and amplitude (measured in voltage). Various states of consciousness are associated with different brain waves. Characteristic EEG patterns for alert wakefulness, drowsiness, and deep, dreamless sleep are shown here. The use of the EEG in research is discussed in more detail in Chapter 5.

SOURCE: Brain wave graphic adapted from Hauri, P. (1982). *Current concepts: The sleep disorders.* Kalamazoo, MI: The Upjohn Company. Reprinted by permission.

means of recording electrodes attached to the surface of the scalp (see **Figure 3.10**). An EEG electrode sums and amplifies electric potentials occurring in many thousands of brain cells.

Usually, six to ten recording electrodes are attached (with paste) at various places on the skull. The resulting EEG recordings are translated into line tracings, commonly called *brain waves.* These brain-wave recordings provide a useful overview of the electrical activity in the brain. Different brain-wave patterns are associated with different states of mental activity (Martin, 1991; Westbrook, 2000), as shown in **Figure 3.10**. The EEG is often used in the clinical diagnosis of brain damage, epilepsy, and other neurological disorders. In research applications, the EEG can be used to identify patterns of brain activity that occur when participants engage in specific behaviors or experience specific emotions. For example, in one study, researchers used EEG recordings to investigate how meditation affects brain activity (Lagopoulos et al., 2009). Overall, EEG technology has contributed greatly to our understanding of brain-behavior relations (Eastman, 2004; Rosler, 2005). For example, you'll see in Chapter 5 that the EEG has been particularly valuable to researchers exploring the neural bases of sleep.

Lesioning

PSYKTREK 2c

Many major insights about brain-behavior relations have resulted from observations of behavioral changes in people who have suffered damage in specific brain areas (Rorden & Karnath, 2004). However, this type of research has its limitations. There are not a lot of subjects to examine, and it is often difficult to determine the exact location and the severity of subjects' brain damage. Furthermore, variations in the participants' histories create additional variables that make it difficult to isolate cause-and-effect relationships between brain damage and behavior.

To study more precisely the relations between brain and behavior, scientists sometimes observe what happens when specific brain structures in animals are purposely disabled. ***Lesioning*** **involves destroying a piece of the brain.** It is typically done by inserting an electrode into a brain structure and passing a high-frequency electric current through it to burn the tissue and disable the structure.

Lesioning requires researchers to get an electrode to a particular place buried deep inside the brain. They do so with a *stereotaxic instrument,* a device used to implant electrodes at precise brain locations. The use of this surgical device is described in **Figure 3.11**. Of course, appropriate anesthetics are

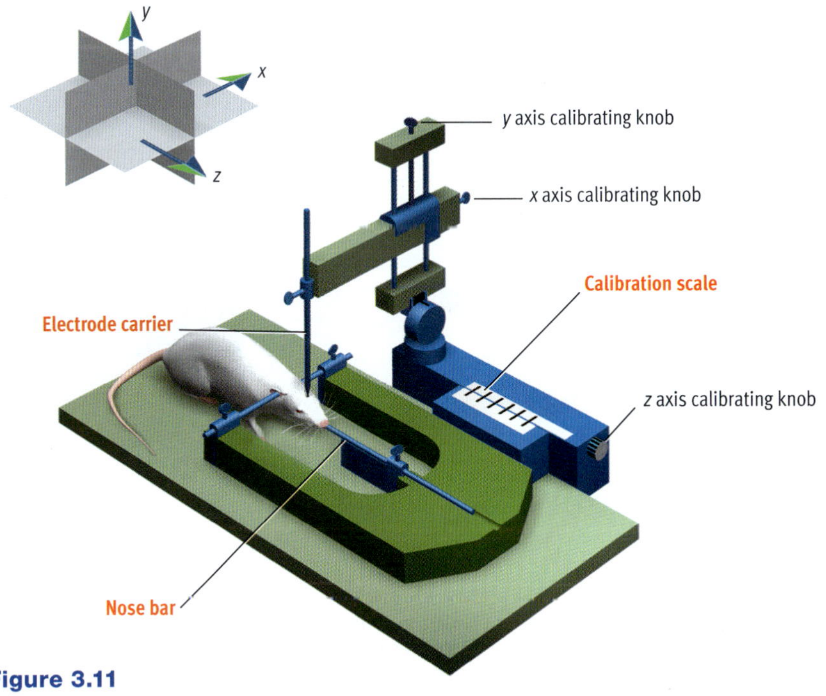

Figure 3.11

An anesthetized rat in a stereotaxic instrument. This rat is undergoing brain surgery. After consulting a detailed map of the rat brain, researchers use the control knobs on the apparatus to position an electrode along the three axes (*x, y,* and *z*) shown in the upper left corner. This precise positioning allows researchers to implant the electrode in an exact location in the rat's brain.

© Cengage Learning 2013

used to minimize pain and discomfort for the animals. The lesioning of brain structures in animals has proven invaluable in neuroscientists' research on brain functioning. For example, major advances in understanding how the brain regulates hunger were achieved using the lesion method.

Electrical Stimulation of the Brain

PSYKTREK 2c

***Electrical stimulation of the brain (ESB)* involves sending a weak electric current into a brain structure to stimulate (activate) it.** The current is delivered through an electrode, but the current is different from that used in lesioning. This sort of electrical stimulation does not exactly duplicate normal signals in the brain. However, it is usually a close enough approximation to activate the brain structures in which the electrodes are lodged. If areas deep within the brain are to be stimulated, the electrodes are implanted with the same stereotaxic techniques used in lesioning procedures.

Most ESB research is conducted with animals. However, ESB is occasionally used on humans in the context of brain surgery (see Moriarty et al., 2001, for an example). After a patient's skull is opened, the surgeons may stimulate areas to map his or her brain (to some extent, each person is unique) so that they don't slice through critical areas. ESB research has led to advances in the understanding of many aspects of brain-behavior relations (Berman, 1991; Yudofsky, 1999).

Transcranial Magnetic Stimulation

***Transcranial magnetic stimulation (TMS)* is a new technique that permits scientists to temporarily enhance or depress activity in a specific area of the brain.** In TMS, a magnetic coil mounted on a small paddle is held over a specific area of a subject's head (see **Figure 3.12**). The coil creates a magnetic field that penetrates to a depth of 2 centimeters (Sack & Linden, 2003). By varying the timing and duration of the magnetic pulses, a researcher can either increase or decrease the excitability of neurons in the targeted tissue (George et al., 2007; Sandrini & Manenti, 2009). Thus far, researchers have mostly been interested in temporarily deactivating specific areas of the brain to learn more about their functions. In essence, this technology allows scientists to create "virtual lesions" in human subjects for short periods of time, using a painless, noninvasive method (Siebner et al., 2009). Moreover, this approach avoids the numerous uncontrolled variables that plague the study of natural lesions in humans with brain damage (Rafal, 2001).

After suppressing activity in a specific area of the brain, scientists put subjects to work on a perceptual or cognitive task to see whether the virtual lesion interferes with performance. For example, this approach has been used to explore whether specific areas of the brain are involved in particular aspects of visual processing (McKeefry, Burton, & Morland, 2010), short-term memory (Silvanto & Cattaneo, 2010), and language (Manenti et al., 2010).

The chief limitation of TMS is that it cannot be used to study areas deep within the brain. Still, its potential as a research tool is enormous (Sparing, Hesse, & Fink, 2010). Moreover, scientists are studying whether it might have potential as a therapeutic treatment for eating disorders (Van den Eynde et al., 2010), anxiety disorders (Zwanzger et al., 2009), depression (Fitzgerald, 2009), and schizophrenia (Matheson et al., 2010).

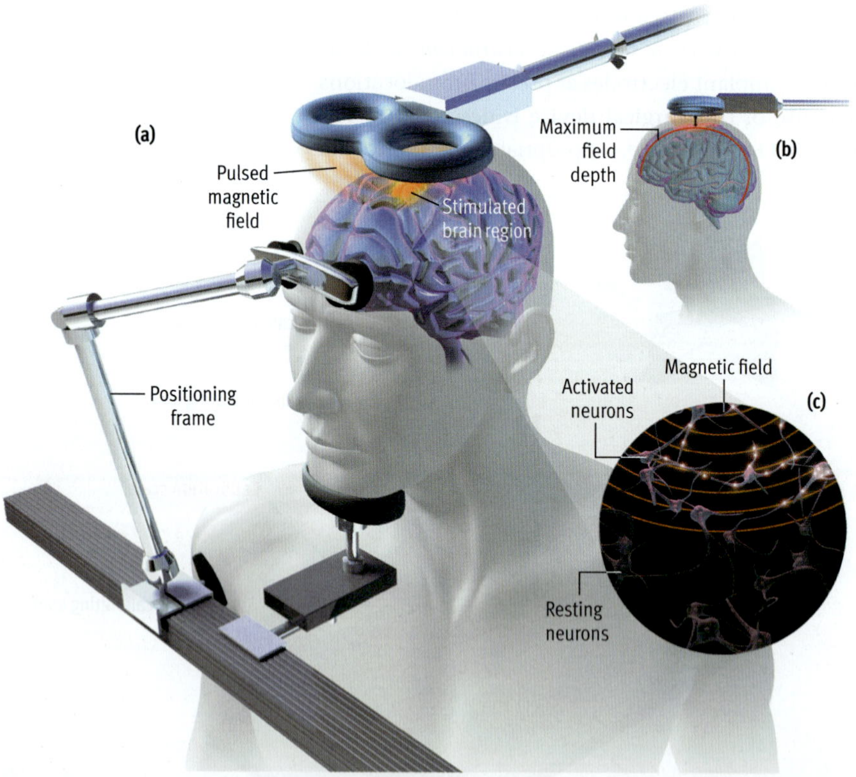

Figure 3.12

Transcranial magnetic stimulation (TMS). In TMS, magnetic pulses are delivered to a localized area of the brain from a magnet mounted on a small paddle **(a)**. The magnetic field penetrates to a depth of only 2 centimeters **(b)**. This technique can be used to either increase or decrease the excitability of the affected neurons. The inset at bottom right depicts neurons near the surface of the brain being temporarily activated by TMS **(c)**.

SOURCE: Adapted from Bremner, J. D. (2005). *Brain imaging handbook.* New York: W. W. Norton, p. 34. © Bryan Christie Design.

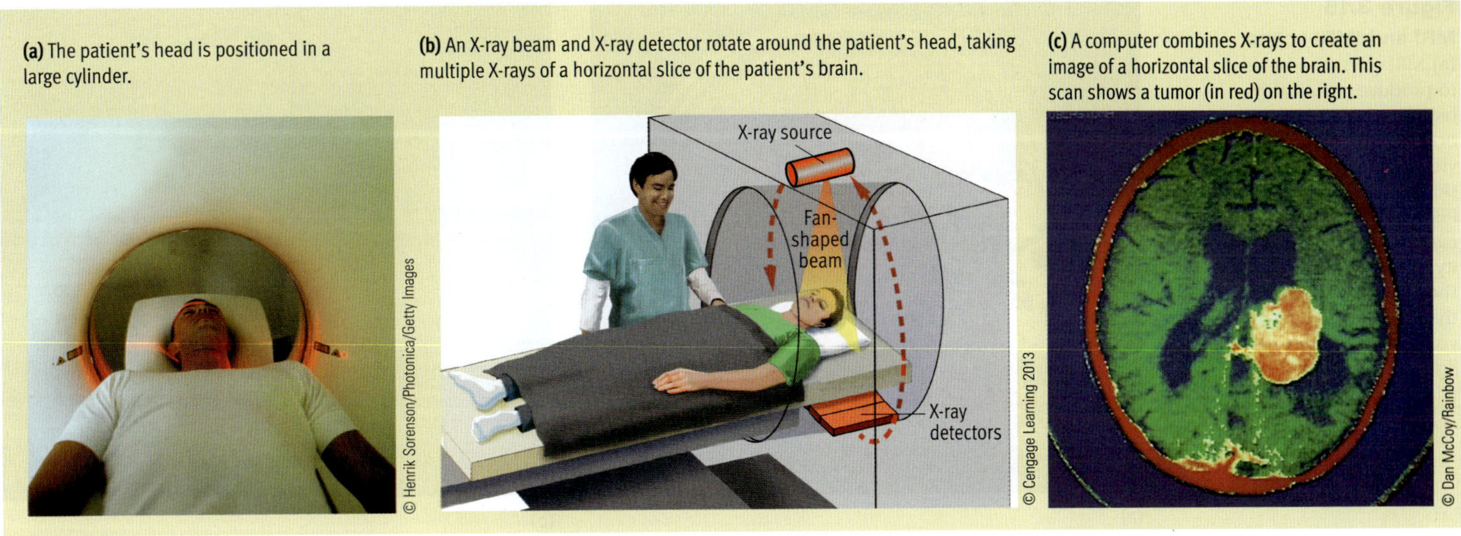

© Cengage Learning 2013

Figure 3.13

CT technology. CT scans can be used in research to examine aspects of brain structure. They provide computer-enhanced X-rays of horizontal slices of the brain. **(a)** The patient's head is positioned in a large cylinder, as shown here. **(b)** An X-ray beam and X-ray detector rotate around the patient's head, taking multiple X-rays of a horizontal slice of the patient's brain. **(c)** A computer combines X-rays to create an image of a horizontal slice of the brain. This scan shows a tumor (in red) on the right.

Brain-Imaging Procedures

PSYKTREK 2c

In recent decades, the invention of new brain-imaging devices has led to spectacular advances in science's ability to look into the brain (Raichle, 2006). These procedures include CT scans, PET scans, and MRI scans.

The *CT (computerized tomography) scan* is a computer-enhanced X-ray of brain structure. Multiple X-rays are shot from many angles, and the computer combines the readings to create a vivid image of a horizontal slice of the brain (see **Figure 3.13**). The entire brain can be visualized by assembling a series of images representing successive slices. Of the modern brain-imaging techniques, the CT scan is the least expensive and most widely used in research. For example, many researchers have used CT scans to look for abnormalities in brain structure among people suffering from specific types of mental illness, especially schizophrenia. This research has uncovered an interesting association between schizophrenic disturbance and enlargement of the brain's ventricles (Shenton & Kubicki, 2009). Scientists are currently trying to determine whether this ventricular enlargement is a cause or a consequence of schizophrenia (see Chapter 15).

In research on how brain and behavior are related, *PET (positron emission tomography) scanning* is proving especially valuable (Staley & Krystal, 2009). Whereas CT scans can portray only brain *structure,* PET scans can examine brain *function,* mapping actual *activity* in the brain over time. In PET scans, radioactively tagged chemicals are introduced into the brain. They serve as markers of blood flow or metabolic activity in the brain, which can be monitored with X-rays. Thus, a PET scan can provide a color-coded map indicating which areas of the brain become active when subjects clench their fist, sing, or contemplate the mysteries of the universe (see **Figure 3.14**). In this way, neuroscientists are using PET scans to better pinpoint the brain areas that handle various types of mental activities (Gronholm et al., 2005; Perrin et al., 2005). Because PET scans monitor chemical processes, they can also be used to study the activity of specific neurotransmitters.

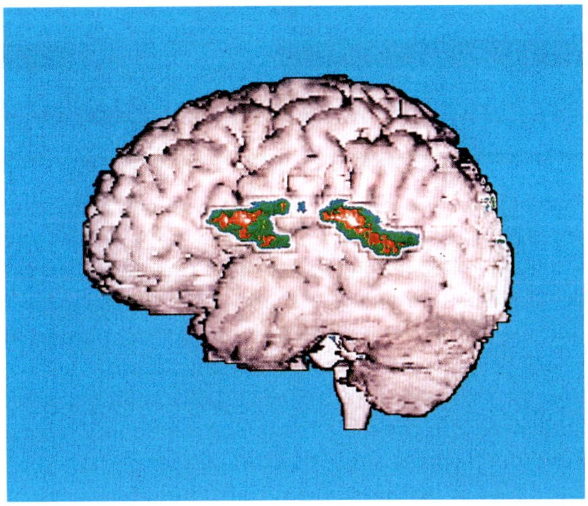

Figure 3.14

PET scans. PET scans are used to map brain activity rather than brain structure. They provide color-coded maps that show areas of high activity in the brain over time. The PET scan shown here pinpointed two areas of high activity (indicated by the red and green colors) when a research participant worked on a verbal short-term memory task.

Figure 3.15

MRI and fMRI scans.

(a) MRI scans can be used to produce remarkably high-resolution pictures of brain structure. A vertical view of a brain from the left side is shown here. **(b)** Like PET scans, functional MRIs can monitor chemical activity in the brain. This image shows regions of the brain that were activated by the visual stimulus of a flashing light.

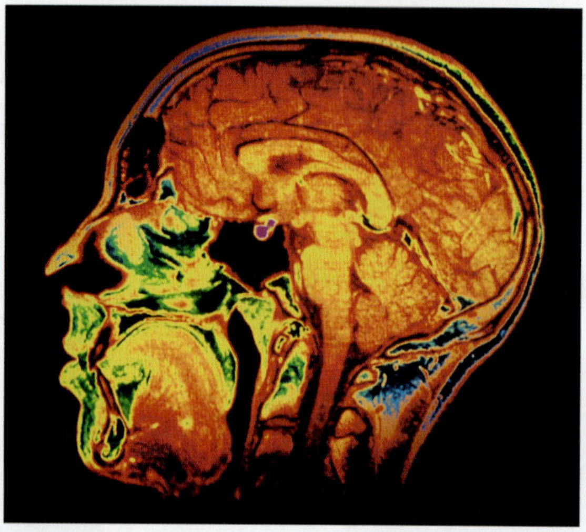

© ISM-Sovereign/PhotoTake

(a)

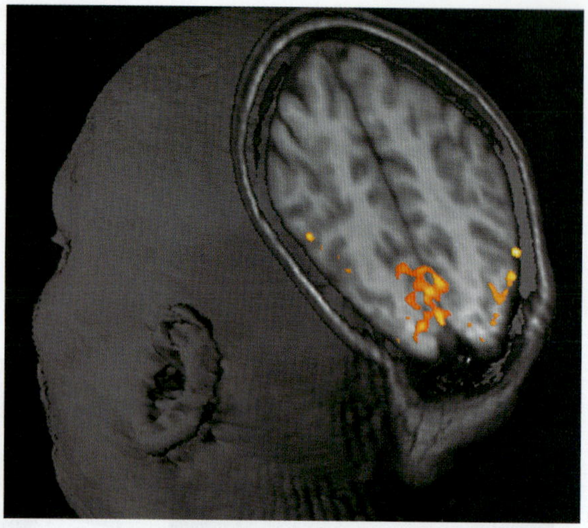

Courtesy and by permission of Dr. Jack Belliveau, Chief, NMR, MGH

(b)

For example, PET scans have helped researchers determine how amphetamines affect activity in dopamine circuits in the human brain (Oswald et al., 2005).

The *MRI (magnetic resonance imaging) scan* uses magnetic fields, radio waves, and computerized enhancement to map out brain structure. MRI scans provide much better images of brain structure than CT scans (Vythilingam et al., 2005), producing three-dimensional pictures of the brain that have remarkably high resolution (see **Figure 3.15a**). MRI scans have provided useful insights about depressive disorders. For example, they were critical in determining that depression is associated with shrinkage of the hippocampus (Drevets, Gadde, & Krishnan, 2009). *Functional magnetic resonance imaging (fMRI)* is a new variation on MRI technology that monitors blood flow and oxygen consumption in the brain to identify areas of high activity (Mason, Krystal, & Sanacora, 2009). This technology is exciting because, like PET scans, it can map actual *activity* in the brain over time, but with vastly greater precision (see **Figure 3.15b**). For example, using fMRI scans, researchers have identified patterns of brain activity associated with cocaine craving in cocaine addicts (Duncan et al., 2007), the contemplation of a loved one (Cheng et al., 2010), the visual recognition of shapes and textures (Stylianou-Korsnes et al., 2010), and the decision making required by risky gambles (Tom et al., 2007).

Research with fMRI scans has given neuroscientists a new appreciation of the complexity and interdependence of brain organization. The opportunity to look at ongoing brain function has revealed that even simple, routine mental operations depend on coordinated activation of several or more areas in the brain (Raichle, 2006). Both types of MRI technology have proven extremely valuable in behavioral research in the last decade. Our Featured Study for this chapter is a functional MRI study that investigated whether males' and females' brains may be wired somewhat differently.

FEATURED STUDY

Probing the Anatomy of Sexual Arousal

SOURCE: Hamann, S., Herman, R. A., Nolan, C. L., & Wallen, K. (2004). Men and women differ in amygdala response to visual sexual stimuli. *Nature Neuroscience, 7,* 411–416.

Many interesting differences exist between males and females in typical patterns of sexual behavior, as you will learn in upcoming chapters (see Chapter 10 in particular). One well-known disparity between the sexes is that men tend to be more interested than women in visually depicted sexual stimuli. Many theorists believe that men's fondness for visual sexual stimuli has been hardwired into the male brain by evolutionary forces. But other theorists argue that this gender gap could be a product of learning and socialization. The present study was a pioneering effort to harness fMRI technology to shed some new light on this complicated question. Stephan Hamann and his colleagues at Emory University set out to see if they could find a neuroanatomical basis for gender differences in responsiveness to visual sexual stimuli. Based on existing knowledge of brain function, they hypothesized that males might show greater activation than females in the *amygdala* and *hypothalamus,* areas of the brain thought to be implicated in the modulation of emotion and sexual motivation (look ahead to **Figure 3.16** on page 99 to see these areas).

Method

Participants. Potential subjects were prescreened to verify that they were heterosexual and that they found visual erotica sexually arousing. Obviously, people who found such material to be offensive would not make good subjects given the purpose of the study. The nature of the study was described to them in advance so they could provide informed consent. The final subject pool consisted of 14 females (mean age 25.0 years) and 14 males (mean age 25.9 years).

Materials. Four types of visual stimuli were presented: (1) pictures of heterosexual couples engaged in explicit sexual activity, (2) pictures of attractive, opposite-sex nudes in modeling poses, (3) pictures of clothed males and females in nonsexual interactions, and (4) a plain cross that subjects were asked to fixate on. The sexual stimuli were carefully screened in a pilot study to ensure that female subjects would find them arousing (pornographic images are generally geared toward men, which would have biased the results).

Procedure. Stimuli were presented on viewing screens inside special goggles to accommodate the fMRI recording equipment. Subjects were instructed to view each stimulus carefully. A brain scan was completed for each stimulus presentation, and subjects rated the stimuli on various dimensions.

Results

Males and females returned similar ratings of how attractive and how arousing both types of sexual stimuli were. For the most part, the sexual stimuli evoked similar patterns of brain activation in the male and female subjects. Both sexes showed roughly equal activation of areas associated with visual processing, attention, and reward. Against this backdrop of similarities, however, some important disparities were found. As predicted, in response to sexual stimuli, males exhibited greater activation than females in the hypothalamus and the right and left amygdala.

Discussion

The authors assert that "the current findings suggest a possible neural basis for the greater role of visual stimuli in human male sexual behavior" (p. 415). In other words, they conclude that their findings provide some preliminary support for the notion that males' and females' brains may be wired somewhat differently. However, they are quick to note that this gender difference could be attributable to either genetics (nature) or experience (nurture).

Comment

This study was featured because it is a particularly interesting example of how new brain-imaging techniques are being used to investigate brain-behavior relations. Science depends on observation. Improvements in scientists' ability to observe the brain have resulted in new opportunities to explore how brain structure and function are related to psychological phenomena. It is an exciting time for the neurosciences, and great advances in our understanding of the brain may be on the horizon.

That said, I hasten to add that brain-imaging techniques suffer from more technical and interpretive problems than is widely appreciated. The stunning images yielded by these incredibly sophisticated devices suggest that their measurements of brain structure and function are more precise, reliable, and unambiguous than they actually are (Shermer, 2008). In reality, brain-imaging procedures, especially those that map brain function, provide only a rough approximation of what is going on inside a subject's brain. PET and fMRI scans do not measure neural activity directly. They only show areas of increased metabolic activity in relation to some baseline condition (in this case, viewing the fixation cross). The areas that "light up" depend to some extent on what was chosen as a baseline for comparison (Uttal, 2001, 2002). More important, increased metabolic activity in an area does not prove that the area plays a crucial role in a particular psychological function (Sack et al., 2002).

Brain scans also require numerous arcane technical decisions that can influence the results obtained (Culham, 2006; Wager, Hernandez, & Lindquist, 2009). These problems and a number of other complications probably explain why the results of brain scan studies have turned out to be less consistent than scientists originally expected (Cabeza & Nyberg, 2000; Dobbs, 2005). Caveats aside, brain-imaging procedures have greatly enhanced our ability to look inside the brain. But the results of such studies should be scrutinized with a critical eye, just like any other research.

REVIEW OF KEY LEARNING GOALS

3.7 Neuroscientists use a variety of methods to investigate brain-behavior relations. The EEG can record broad patterns of electrical activity in the brain. Different EEG brain waves are associated with different states of consciousness. Lesioning involves destroying a piece of the brain to see the effect on behavior. Another technique is electrical stimulation of areas in the brain in order to activate them.

3.8 Transcranial magnetic stimulation is a new, noninvasive technique that permits scientists to create temporary virtual lesions in human subjects. In recent decades, new brain-imaging procedures have been developed. CT scans and MRI scans provide images of brain structure. PET scans and fMRI scans can track brain activity.

3.9 The Featured Study used fMRI technology to explore whether males' and females' brains may be wired differently. Brain-imaging techniques have enormous potential as research tools. However, brain scans are not as precise and unambiguous as they appear to be.

KEY LEARNING GOALS

3.10 Review the key functions of the medulla, pons, cerebellum, and midbrain.

3.11 Summarize the principal functions of the thalamus, hypothalamus, and key structures in the limbic system.

3.12 Locate the four lobes in the cerebral cortex, and state some of their key functions.

3.13 Summarize evidence on the brain's plasticity.

The Brain and Behavior

Now that we have examined selected techniques of brain research, let's look at what researchers have discovered about the functions of various parts of the brain.

The brain can be divided into three major regions: the hindbrain, the midbrain, and the forebrain. The principal structures found in each of these regions are listed in the organizational chart of the nervous system in **Figure 3.6**. You can see where these regions are located in the brain by looking at **Figure 3.16**. They can be found easily in relation to the *brainstem*. The brainstem looks like its name—it appears to be a stem from which the rest of the brain "flowers," like a head of cauliflower. At the brainstem's lower end, it looks like an extension of the spinal cord. At its higher end, it lies deep within the brain.

We'll begin at the brain's lower end, where the spinal cord joins the brainstem. Notice, as we proceed upward, how the functions of brain structures go from the regulation of basic bodily processes on the lower end to the control of "higher" mental processes toward the top of the brain.

The Hindbrain

PSYKTREK 2d

The *hindbrain* includes the cerebellum and two structures found in the lower part of the brainstem: the medulla and the pons. The *medulla*, which attaches to the spinal cord, controls largely unconscious but vital functions. These include circulating blood, breathing, maintaining muscle tone, and regulating reflexes such as sneezing, coughing, and salivating. The *pons* (literally "bridge") includes a bridge of fibers that connects the brainstem with the cerebellum. The pons also contains several clusters of cell bodies involved with sleep and arousal.

The *cerebellum* (literally "little brain") is a relatively large and deeply folded structure located next to the back surface of the brainstem. The cerebellum is critical to the coordination of movement and to the sense of equilibrium, or physical balance (Mauk & Thach, 2008). Although the actual commands for muscular movements come from higher brain centers, the cerebellum plays a key role in organizing the sensory information that guides these movements. It's your cerebellum that allows you to hold your hand out to the side and then smoothly bring your finger to a stop on your nose. This exercise is a useful roadside test for drunk driving because the cerebellum is one of the structures first depressed by alcohol. Damage to the cerebellum disrupts fine motor skills, such as those involved in writing, typing, or playing a musical instrument. Recent research has revealed that the cerebellum contributes to the control of other functions besides motor skills. Surprisingly, brain circuits running from the cerebellum to the prefrontal cortex appear to be involved in higher-order functions, including attention, planning, and visual perception (Dum & Strick, 2009).

The Midbrain

PSYKTREK 2d

The *midbrain* is the segment of the brainstem that lies between the hindbrain and the forebrain. The midbrain contains an area that's concerned with integrating sensory processes such as vision and hearing (Stein, Wallace, & Stanford, 2000). An important system of dopamine-releasing neurons that projects into various higher brain centers originates in the midbrain. Among other things, this dopamine system is involved in the performance of voluntary movements. The decline in dopamine synthesis that causes Parkinsonism is due to degeneration of a structure located in the midbrain (DeLong, 2000).

Running through both the hindbrain and the midbrain is the *reticular formation* (see **Figure 3.16**). Located at the central core of the brainstem, the reticular formation contributes to the modulation of muscle reflexes, breathing, and pain perception (Saper, 2000). It is best known, however, for its role in the regulation of sleep and arousal. Activity in the ascending fibers of the reticular formation contributes to arousal (Steriade, 2005).

The Forebrain

PSYKTREK 2e, 2f

The *forebrain* is the largest and most complex region of the brain, encompassing a variety of structures, including the thalamus, hypothalamus, limbic system, and cerebrum (consult **Figure 3.16** once again). The thalamus, hypothalamus, and limbic system form the core of the forebrain. All three structures are located near the top of the brainstem. Above them is the *cerebrum*—the center of complex thought. The wrinkled surface of the cerebrum is the *cerebral cortex*—the outer layer of the brain, which looks like a cauliflower.

Figure 3.16

Structures and areas in the human brain. (Top left) This photo of a human brain shows many of the structures discussed in this chapter. **(Top right)** The brain is divided into three major areas: the hindbrain, midbrain, and forebrain. These subdivisions actually make more sense for the brains of other animals than for the human brain. In humans, the forebrain has become so large it makes the other two divisions look trivial. However, the hindbrain and midbrain aren't trivial; they control such vital functions as breathing, waking, and maintaining balance. **(Bottom)** This cross section of the brain highlights key structures and some of their principal functions. As you read about the functions of a brain structure, such as the corpus callosum, you may find it helpful to visualize it. © Cengage Learning 2013

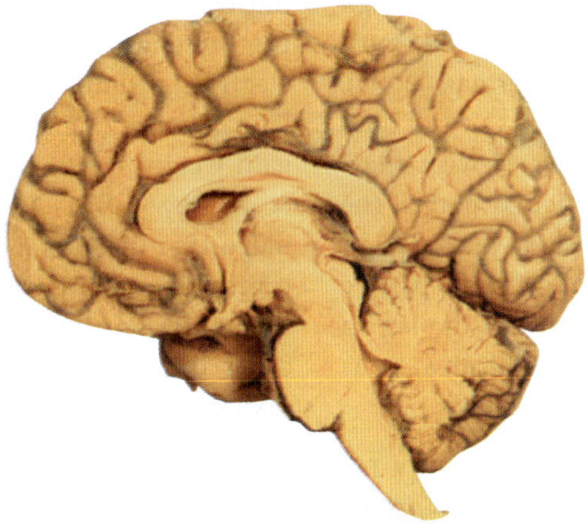
© Cengage Learning 2013

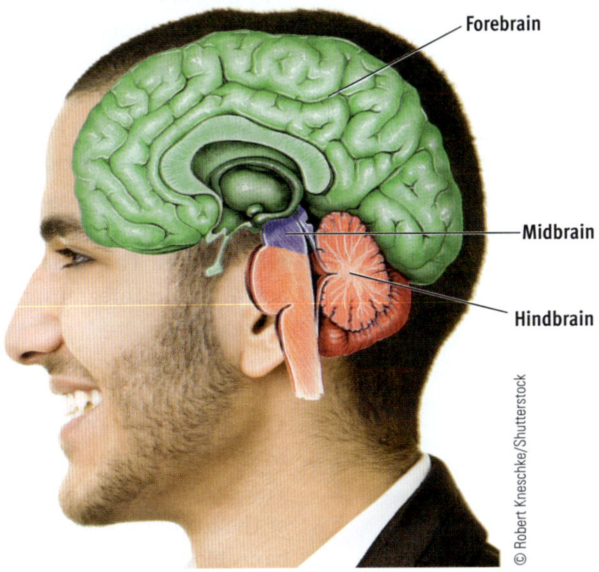

© Robert Kneschke/Shutterstock

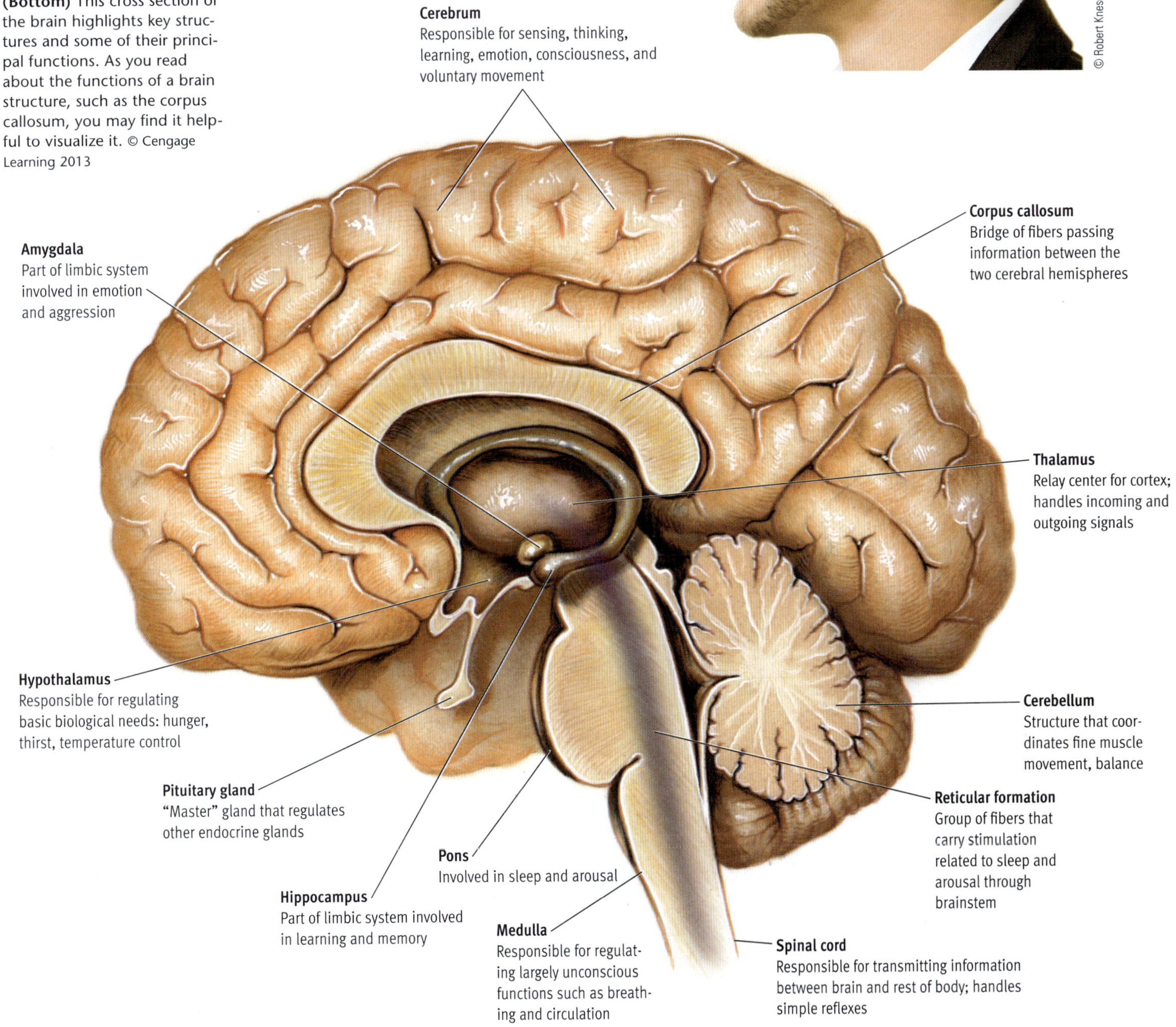

The Thalamus: A Relay Station 2e

The *thalamus* is a structure in the forebrain through which all sensory information (except smell) must pass to get to the cerebral cortex (Sherman, 2009). This way station is made up of clusters of cell bodies, or somas. Each cluster is concerned with relaying sensory information to a particular part of the cortex. However, it would be a mistake to characterize the thalamus as nothing more than a passive relay station. The thalamus also appears to play an active role in integrating information from various senses.

The Hypothalamus: A Regulator of Biological Needs 2e

The *hypothalamus* is a structure found near the base of the forebrain that's involved in the regulation of basic biological needs. The hypothalamus lies beneath the thalamus (*hypo* means "under," making the hypothalamus the area under the thalamus). Although no larger than a kidney bean, the hypothalamus contains various clusters of cells that have many key functions. One such function is to control the autonomic nervous system (Card, Swanson, & Moore, 2008). In addition, the hypothalamus serves as a vital link between the brain and the *endocrine system* (a network of hormone-producing glands, discussed later in this chapter).

The hypothalamus plays a major role in the regulation of basic biological drives related to survival, including the so-called "four F's": fighting, fleeing, feeding, and "mating." For example, when researchers lesion the lateral areas (the sides) of the hypothalamus, animals lose interest in eating. They must be fed intravenously or they starve, even in the presence of abundant food. In contrast, when electrical stimulation (ESB) is used to *activate* the lateral hypothalamus, animals eat constantly and gain weight rapidly (Grossman et al., 1978; Keesey & Powley, 1975). These results don't necessarily mean that the lateral hypothalamus is the "hunger center" in the brain. But it is clear that the hypothalamus contributes to the control of hunger and other basic biological processes, including thirst, sexual motivation, and temperature regulation (Card et al., 2008).

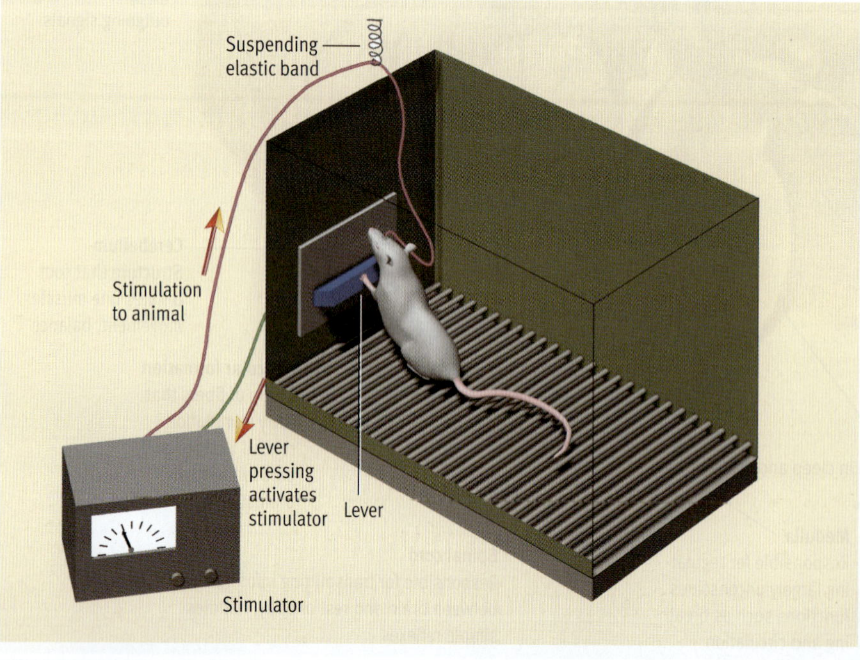

© Cengage Learning 2013

Figure 3.17
Electrical stimulation of the brain (ESB) in the rat. Olds and Milner (1954) were using an apparatus like that depicted here when they discovered self-stimulation centers, or "pleasure centers," in the brain of a rat. In this setup, the rat's lever pressing earns brief electrical stimulation that is sent to a specific spot in the rat's brain where an electrode has been implanted.

The Limbic System: The Center of Emotion 2e

The *limbic system* is a loosely connected network of structures located roughly along the border between the cerebral cortex and deeper subcortical areas (hence the term *limbic,* which means "border"). First described by Paul MacLean (1954), the limbic system is *not* a well-defined anatomical system with clear boundaries. Indeed, scientists disagree about which structures it includes (Van Hoesen, Morecraft, & Semendeferi, 1996). Broadly defined, the limbic system includes the hypothalamus, the hippocampus, the amygdala, the olfactory bulb, and the cingulate gyrus. The limbic system is involved in the regulation of emotion, memory, and motivation.

The *hippocampus* and adjacent structures clearly play a role in memory processes (Shrager & Squire, 2009). Some theorists believe that the hippocampal region is responsible for the *consolidation* of memories for factual information (Dudai, 2004). Consolidation involves the conversion of information into a durable memory code.

Similarly, there is ample evidence linking the limbic system to the experience of emotion, but the exact mechanisms of control are not yet well understood. Recent evidence suggests that the *amygdala* may play a central role in the learning of fear responses and the processing of other basic emotional responses (Phelps, 2006; LeDoux, Schiller, & Cain, 2009). The limbic system is also one of the areas in the brain that appears to be rich in emotion-tinged "pleasure centers." This intriguing possibility first surfaced, quite by chance, in brain stimulation research with rats. James Olds and Peter Milner (1954) discovered that a rat would press a lever repeatedly to send brief bursts of electrical stimulation to a specific spot in its brain where an electrode was accidentally implanted (see **Figure 3.17**). Much to their surprise, the rat kept coming back for more self-stimulation in this area. Subsequent studies showed that rats and monkeys would press a lever *thousands of times per hour,* until they sometimes collapsed from exhaustion, to stimulate certain brain sites. Although the experimenters obviously couldn't ask the animals about it, they *inferred* that the animals were experiencing some sort of pleasure.

The brain contains a number of self-stimulation centers, many of them in the limbic system (Olds & Fobes, 1981). The heaviest concentration appears to be where the *medial forebrain bundle* (a bundle of axons) passes through the hypothalamus. The medial forebrain bundle is rich in dopamine-releasing neurons. The rewarding effects of ESB at self-stimulation sites may be largely mediated by the activation of these dopamine circuits (Koob et al., 2008). The pleasurable effects of opiate and stimulant drugs (cocaine and amphetamines) also appear to depend in part on excitation of this dopamine system (Wise, 1999, 2002). Recent evidence suggests that the so-called "pleasure centers" in the brain may not be anatomical centers so much as neural circuits releasing dopamine.

The Cerebrum: The Center of Complex Thought

PsykTrek 2f

The *cerebrum* is the largest and most complex part of the human brain. It includes the brain areas that are responsible for the most complex mental activities, including learning, remembering, thinking, and consciousness itself. **The *cerebral cortex* is the intricately folded outer layer of the cerebrum.** The cortex has many wrinkles and bends, so that its large surface area—about 1.5 square feet—can be packed into the limited volume of the skull (Hubel & Wiesel, 1979).

The cerebrum is divided into two halves called hemispheres. Hence, **the *cerebral hemispheres* are the right and left halves of the cerebrum** (see **Figure 3.18** on the next page). The hemispheres are separated by a longitudinal fissure that runs from the front to the back of the brain. This fissure descends to a thick band of fibers called the *corpus callosum* (also shown in **Figure 3.18**). **The *corpus callosum* is the structure that connects the two cerebral hemispheres.** (We'll discuss the functional specialization of the cerebral hemispheres in the next section of this chapter.) Each cerebral hemisphere is divided into four parts called *lobes.* To some extent, each of these lobes is dedicated to specific purposes. The location of these lobes can be seen in **Figure 3.19** on the next page.

The *occipital lobe,* at the back of the head, includes the cortical area where most visual signals are sent and visual processing begins. This area is called the *primary visual cortex.* We'll discuss how it is organized in Chapter 4.

The *parietal lobe* is forward of the occipital lobe. It includes the area that registers the sense of touch, called the *primary somatosensory cortex.* Various sections of this area receive signals from different regions of the body. When ESB is delivered in these parietal lobe areas, people report physical sensations—as if someone actually touched them on the arm or cheek, for example. The parietal lobe is also involved in integrating visual input and in monitoring the body's position in space.

The *temporal lobe* (meaning "near the temples") lies below the parietal lobe. Near its top, the temporal lobe

© Apollofoto/Shutterstock

© photomak/Shutterstock

© Jason Stitt/Shutterstock

What areas of the brain are activated in these people?

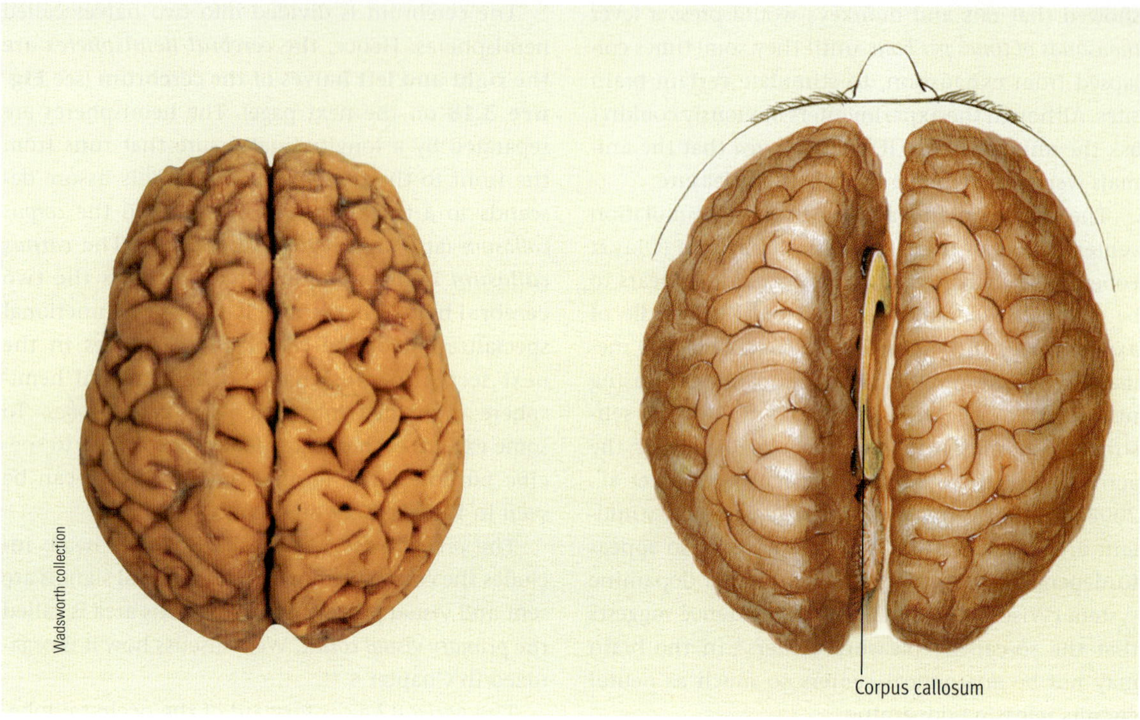

Figure 3.18

The cerebral hemispheres and the corpus callosum. (Left) As this photo shows, the longitudinal fissure running down the middle of the brain (viewed from above) separates the left and right halves of the cerebral cortex. **(Right)** In this drawing the cerebral hemispheres have been "pulled apart" to reveal the corpus callosum. This band of fibers is the communication bridge between the right and left halves of the human brain.

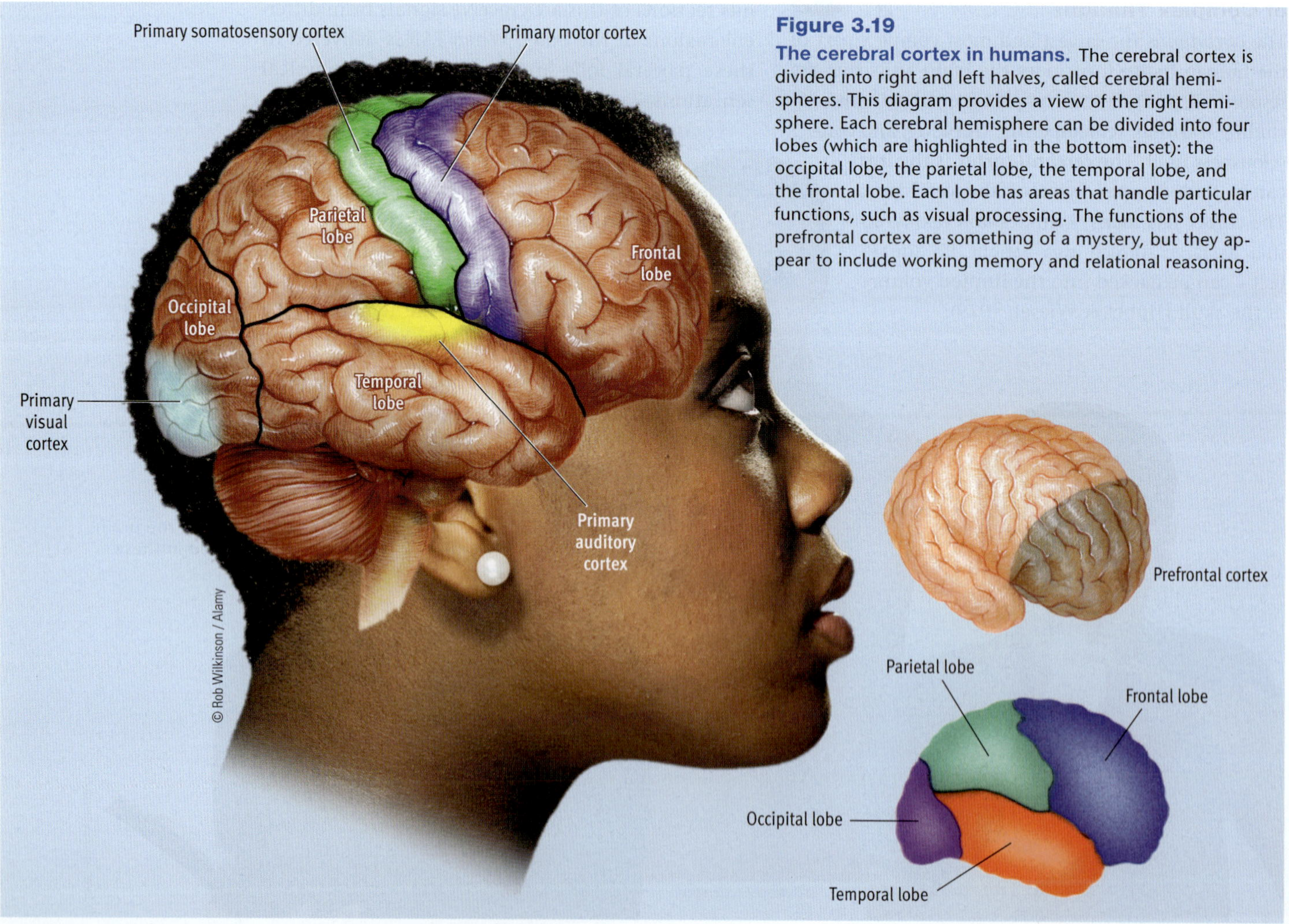

Figure 3.19

The cerebral cortex in humans. The cerebral cortex is divided into right and left halves, called cerebral hemispheres. This diagram provides a view of the right hemisphere. Each cerebral hemisphere can be divided into four lobes (which are highlighted in the bottom inset): the occipital lobe, the parietal lobe, the temporal lobe, and the frontal lobe. Each lobe has areas that handle particular functions, such as visual processing. The functions of the prefrontal cortex are something of a mystery, but they appear to include working memory and relational reasoning.

contains an area devoted to auditory processing, called the *primary auditory cortex*. As we'll see momentarily, damage to an area in the temporal lobe on the left side of the brain can impair the comprehension of speech and language.

Continuing forward, we find the *frontal lobe,* the largest lobe in the human brain. It contains the principal areas that control the movement of muscles, called the *primary motor cortex*. ESB applied in these areas can cause actual muscle contractions. The amount of motor cortex used to control a body part depends not on the part's size but on the diversity and precision of its movements. Thus, more of the cortex is given to parts we have fine control over, such as fingers, lips, and the tongue. Less of the cortex is devoted to larger parts that make crude movements, such as the thighs and shoulders (see **Figure 3.20**).

An area just in front of the primary motor cortex is where "mirror neurons" were first discovered accidentally in the mid-1990s. An Italian research team (Gallese et al., 1996) were recording activity in individual neurons as monkeys reached for various objects. A member of the research team happened to reach out and pick up one of the designated objects, and much to his amazement the monkey's neuron fired just as it had previously when the monkey picked up the object itself. The researchers went on to find many such neurons in the frontal lobe, which they christened mirror neurons. ***Mirror neurons* are neurons that are activated by performing an action or by seeing another monkey or person perform the same action.**

Researchers have used fMRI scans to demonstrate that humans also have mirror neuron circuits, which have been found in both the frontal and parietal lobes (Iacoboni & Dapretto, 2006; Rizzolatti & Craighero, 2004). It is hard to convey just how much excitement this discovery has generated among neuroscientists. Mirror neurons appear to provide a new model for understanding complex social cognition at a neural level. Recent research has suggested that mirror neurons may play a fundamental role in the acquisition of new motor skills (Buccino & Riggio, 2006) and the imitation of others, which is crucial to much of human development (Rizzolatti, 2005). They may also contribute to the understanding of others' intentions and the ability to feel empathy for others (Kaplan & Iacoboni, 2006). Thus, the accidental discovery of mirror neurons may have a dramatic impact on brain-behavior research in the years to come.

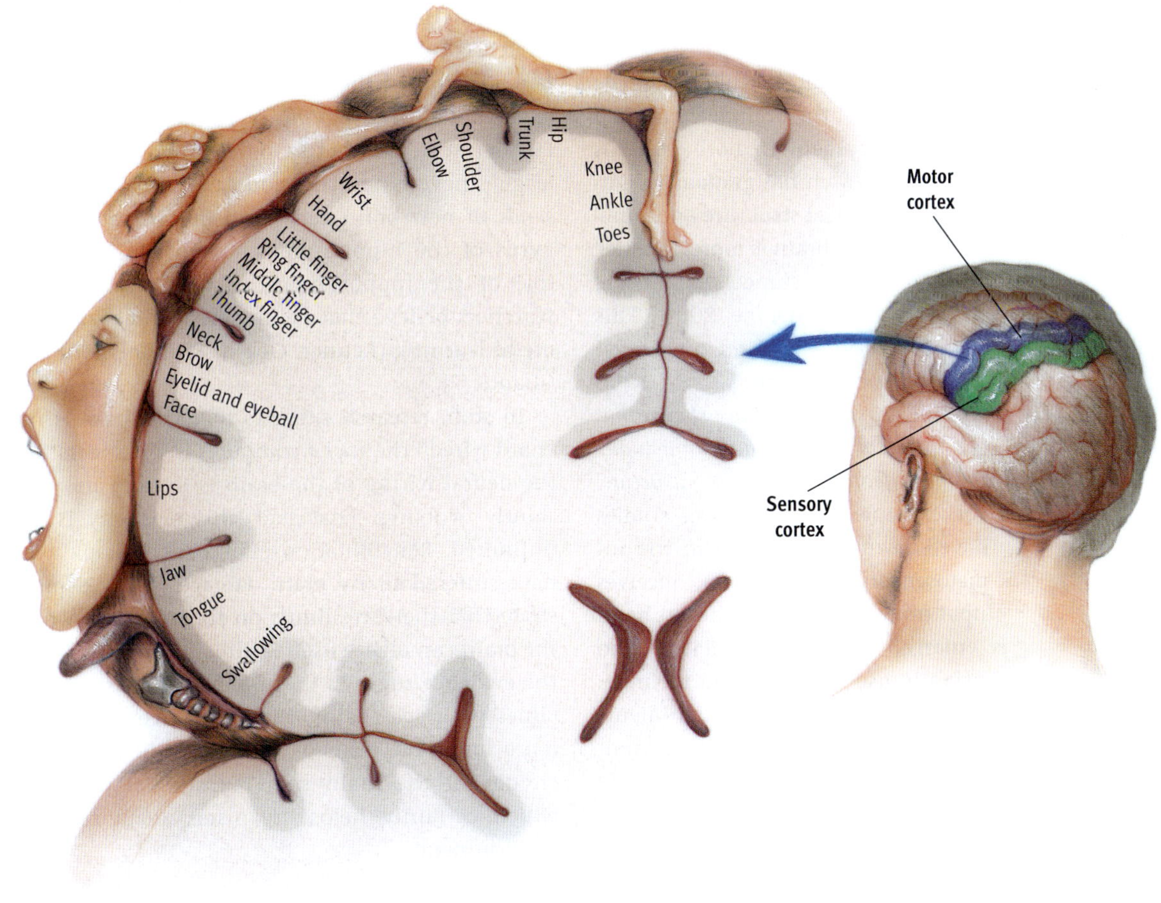

Figure 3.20

The primary motor cortex. This diagram shows the amount of motor cortex devoted to the control of various muscles and limbs. The anatomical features in the drawing are distorted because their size is proportional to the amount of cortex devoted to their control. As you can see, more of the cortex is allocated to controlling muscle groups that must make relatively precise movements.

© Cengage Learning 2013

The portion of the frontal lobe to the front of the motor cortex, which is called the *prefrontal cortex* (see the inset in **Figure 3.19**), is something of a mystery. This area is disproportionately large in humans, accounting for about one-third of the cerebral cortex (Huey, Krueger, & Grafman, 2006). In light of this fact, it was once assumed to house the highest, most abstract intellectual functions. However, this view was eventually dismissed as an oversimplification. Still, recent studies suggest that the prefrontal cortex *does* contribute to an impressive variety of higher-order functions. These include working memory, which is a temporary buffer that processes current information (Sala & Courtney, 2007); reasoning about relations between objects and events (Knowlton & Holyoak, 2009); and some types of decision making (Summerfield & Koechlin, 2009). Its contribution to working memory and reasoning about relations has led some theorists to suggest that the prefrontal cortex houses some sort of "executive control system." This system is thought to monitor, organize, integrate, and direct thought processes (Beer, Shimamura, & Knight, 2004; Kane & Engle, 2002). Much remains to be learned, however, as the prefrontal cortex constitutes a huge chunk of the brain with many subareas whose specific functions are still being worked out (Miller & Wallis, 2008).

The Plasticity of the Brain

It was once believed that significant changes in the anatomy and organization of the brain were limited to early periods of development in both humans and animals. However, research has gradually demonstrated that the anatomical structure and functional organization of the brain is more "plastic" or malleable than widely assumed (Kolb, Gibb, & Robinson, 2003; Pascual-Leone, 2009). This conclusion is based on several lines of research.

First, studies have shown that aspects of experience can actually shape features of brain structure. For example, brain-imaging studies have shown that an area in the somatosensory cortex that receives input from the fingers of the left hand is enlarged in string musicians who constantly use the left hand to finger the strings of their instruments (Elbert et al., 1995). Similarly, subjects given three months to practice and master a juggling routine show structural changes in brain areas known to handle the processing of visual and motor tasks (Draganski et al., 2004). Researchers have also found greater dendritic branching and synaptic density in the brains of rats raised in a stimulating, enriched environment, as opposed to a dull, barren environment (Van Praag, Zhao, & Gage, 2004; see the Critical Thinking Application for this chapter).

© D. Hurst/Alamy

Second, research has shown that damage to incoming sensory pathways or the destruction of brain tissue can lead to neural reorganization. For example, when scientists amputated the third finger in an owl monkey, the part of its cortex that formerly responded to the third finger gradually became responsive to the second and fourth fingers (Kaas, 2000). And in blind people, areas in the occipital lobe that are normally dedicated to visual processing are "recruited" to help with verbal processing (Amedi et al., 2004). Neural reorganization has also been seen in response to brain damage as healthy neurons attempt to compensate for the loss of nearby neurons (Cao et al., 1994; Lipert et al., 2000).

Third, studies indicate that the adult brain can generate new neurons. Until recently it was thought that the brain formed all its neurons by infancy at the latest. It was believed that ***neurogenesis*—the formation of new neurons**—did not occur in adult humans. However, research eventually demonstrated convincingly that adult humans can form new neurons in the olfactory bulb and the hippocampus (DiCicco-Bloom & Falluel-Morel, 2009). Furthermore, Elizabeth Gould (2004) and her colleagues have found that adult monkeys form *thousands* of new brain cells each day in the dentate gyrus of the hippocampus. Given the important role of the hippocampus in memory, some researchers believe that neurogenesis might contribute to learning (Leuner, Gould, & Shors, 2006; see Chapter 7).

In sum, research suggests that the brain is not "hard wired" the way a computer is. It appears that the neural wiring of the brain is flexible and constantly evolving. That said, this plasticity is not unlimited. Rehabilitation efforts with people who have suffered severe brain damage clearly demonstrate that there are limits on the extent to which the brain can rewire itself (Zillmer et al., 2008). And the evidence suggests that the brain's plasticity declines with age (Rains, 2002). Younger brains are more malleable than older ones. Still, the neural circuits of the brain show substantial plasticity, which certainly helps organisms adapt to their environments.

REVIEW OF KEY LEARNING GOALS

3.10 Structures in the hindbrain include the medulla, pons, and cerebellum. The medulla regulates functions such as breathing and circulation; the cerebellum is involved in motor coordination and balance; and the pons contributes to sleep and arousal. The midbrain plays a role in the coordination of sensory processes.

3.11 In the forebrain, the thalamus is a relay station through which all sensory information (except smell) must pass to get to the cortex. The hypothalamus is involved in the regulation of basic biological drives such as hunger and sex. The limbic system is a network of loosely connected structures located along the border between the cortex and deeper subcortical areas. It includes the hippocampus, which appears to play a role in memory; the amygdala, which is involved in the regulation of emotion; and areas rich in self-stimulation sites.

3.12 The cerebrum is the brain area implicated in the most complex mental activities. The cortex is the cerebrum's intricately folded outer layer, which is subdivided into four lobes. These lobes and their primary known functions are the occipital lobe (vision), the parietal lobe (touch), the temporal lobe (hearing), and the frontal lobe (movement of the body). Although the prefrontal cortex is something of a mystery, it is known to be involved in some memory, reasoning, and decision-making functions.

3.13 Studies show that experience can affect brain structure, that brain damage can lead to neural reorganization, and that neurogenesis (formation of new neurons) can occur in some areas of the adult brain. Thus, the structure and function of the brain appears to be more plastic than widely believed.

CONCEPT CHECK 3.3

Relating Disorders to the Nervous System

Imagine that you are working as a neuropsychologist at a clinic. You are involved in the diagnosis of the cases described below. You are asked to identify the probable cause(s) of the disorders in terms of nervous system malfunctions. Based on the information in this chapter, indicate the probable location of any brain damage or the probable disturbance of neurotransmitter activity. The answers can be found in the back of the book in Appendix A.

Case 1. Miriam is exhibiting language deficits. In particular, she does not seem to comprehend the meaning of words. ______

Case 2. Camille displays tremors and muscular rigidity and is diagnosed as having Parkinsonism. ______

Case 3. Ricardo, a 28-year-old computer executive, has gradually seen his strength and motor coordination deteriorate badly. He is diagnosed as having multiple sclerosis. ______

Case 4. Wendy is highly irrational, has poor contact with reality, and reports hallucinations. She is given a diagnosis of schizophrenic disorder. ______

Right Brain/Left Brain: Cerebral Laterality

KEY LEARNING GOALS

3.14 Explain how split-brain research changed our understanding of the brain's hemispheric organization.

3.15 Describe research on cerebral specialization in normal subjects and what this research has revealed.

As we saw in the previous section, the cerebrum—the center of complex thought—is divided into two separate hemispheres (see **Figure 3.18**). Recent decades have seen an exciting flurry of research on the specialized abilities of the right and left cerebral hemispheres. Some theorists have gone so far as to suggest that we really have two brains in one!

Hints of this hemispheric specialization have been available for many years, from cases in which one side of a person's brain has been damaged. The left hemisphere was implicated in the control of language as early as 1861, by Paul Broca, a French surgeon. Broca was treating a patient who had been unable to speak for 30 years. After the patient died, Broca showed that the probable cause of the speech deficit was a localized lesion on the left side of the frontal lobe. Since then, many similar cases have shown that this area of the brain—known as *Broca's area*—plays an important role in the *production* of speech (see **Figure 3.21**). Another major language

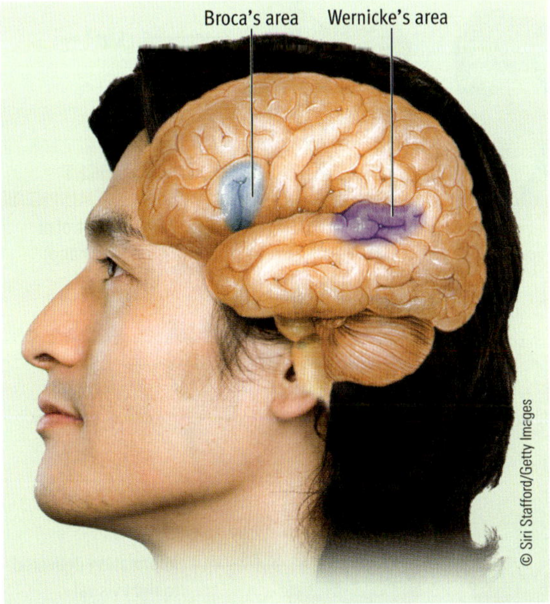

Figure 3.21
Language processing in the brain. This view of the left hemisphere highlights the location of two centers for language processing in the brain: *Broca's area,* which is involved in speech production, and *Wernicke's area,* which is involved in language comprehension.
© Cengage Learning 2013

© Photo by Paz/Cal Tech. Courtesy of Roger Sperry

Roger Sperry

"Both the left and right hemispheres of the brain have been found to have their own specialized forms of intellect."

center—*Wernicke's area*—was identified in the temporal lobe of the left hemisphere in 1874. Damage in Wernicke's area (see **Figure 3.21**) usually leads to problems with the *comprehension* of language.

Evidence that the left hemisphere usually processes language led scientists to characterize it as the "dominant" hemisphere. Because thoughts are usually coded in terms of language, the left hemisphere was given the lion's share of credit for handling the "higher" mental processes, such as reasoning, remembering, planning, and problem solving. Meanwhile, the right hemisphere came to be viewed as the "nondominant," or "dumb," hemisphere, lacking any special functions or abilities.

This characterization of the left and right hemispheres as major and minor partners in the brain's work began to change in the 1960s. It all started with landmark research by Roger Sperry, Michael Gazzaniga, and their colleagues who studied "split-brain" patients: individuals whose cerebral hemispheres had been surgically disconnected (Gazzaniga, 1970; Gazzaniga, Bogen, & Sperry, 1965; Sperry, 1982). In 1981 Sperry received a Nobel prize in physiology/medicine for this work.

Bisecting the Brain: Split-Brain Research

PSYKTREK 2f, SIM2

In *split-brain surgery* the bundle of fibers that connects the cerebral hemispheres (the corpus callosum) is cut to reduce the severity of epileptic seizures. It is a radical procedure that's chosen only as a last resort in exceptional cases that have not responded to other forms of treatment (Wolford, Miller, & Gazzaniga, 2004). But the surgery provides scientists with an unusual opportunity to study people who have had their brain literally split in two.

To appreciate the logic of split-brain research, you need to understand how sensory and motor information is routed to and from the two hemispheres. *Each hemisphere's primary connections are to the opposite side of the body.* Thus, the left hemisphere controls, and communicates with, the right hand, right arm, right leg, right eyebrow, and so on. In contrast, the right hemisphere controls, and communicates with, the left side of the body.

Vision and hearing are more complex. Both eyes deliver information to both hemispheres, but a separation of input still exists. Stimuli in the right half of the *visual field* are registered by receptors on the left side of each eye, which send signals to the left hemisphere. Stimuli in the left half of the visual field are transmitted by both eyes to the right hemisphere (see **Figure 3.22**). Auditory inputs to each ear also go to both hemispheres. However, connections to the opposite hemisphere are stronger or more immediate.

For the most part, people don't notice this asymmetric, "crisscrossed" organization because the two hemispheres are in close communication with each other. However, when the two hemispheres are surgically disconnected, the functional specialization of the brain becomes apparent.

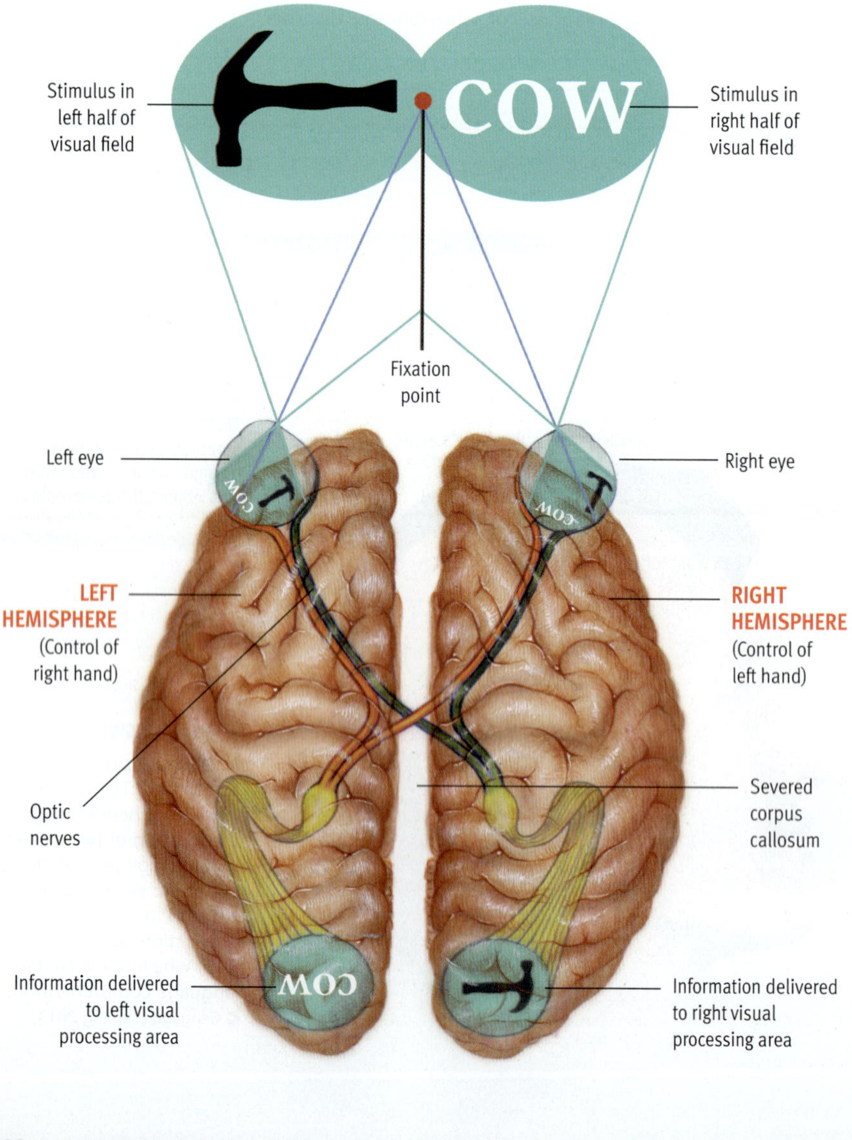

Figure 3.22

Visual input in the split brain. If a participant stares at a fixation point, the point divides the subject's visual field into right and left halves. Input from the right visual field (the word COW in this example) strikes the left side of each eye and is transmitted to the left hemisphere. Input from the left visual field (a picture of a hammer in this example) strikes the right side of each eye and is transmitted to the right hemisphere. Normally, the hemispheres share the information from the two halves of the visual field, but in split-brain patients, the corpus callosum is severed, and the two hemispheres cannot communicate. Hence, the experimenter can present a visual stimulus to just one hemisphere at a time.

© Cengage Learning 2013

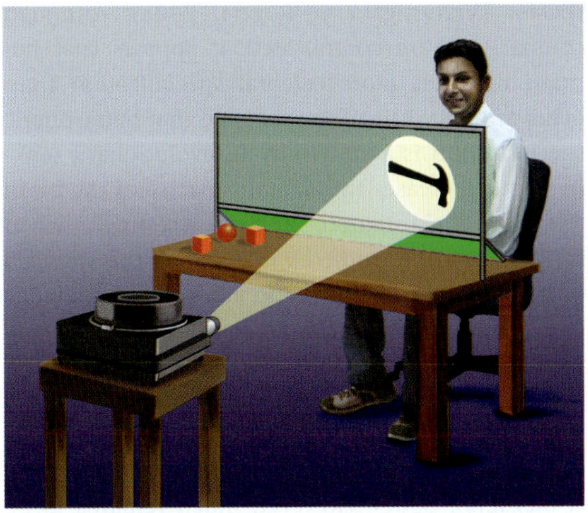

© Cengage Learning 2013

Figure 3.23

Experimental apparatus in split-brain research. On the left is a special slide projector that can present images very briefly, before the subject's eyes can move and thus change the visual field. Images are projected on one side of the screen to present stimuli to just one hemisphere. The portion of the apparatus beneath the screen is constructed to prevent participants from seeing objects that they may be asked to handle with their right or left hand, another procedure that can be used to send information to just one hemisphere.

In their classic study of split-brain patients, Gazzaniga, Bogen, and Sperry (1965) briefly presented visual stimuli such as pictures, symbols, and words in a single visual field (the left or the right) so that the stimuli would be sent to only one hemisphere. The stimuli were projected onto a screen in front of the participants, who stared at a fixation point (a spot) in the center of the screen (see **Figure 3.23**).

When pictures were flashed in the right visual field and thus sent to the left hemisphere, the split-brain subjects were able to name and describe the objects depicted (such as a cup or spoon). However, the subjects were *not* able to name and describe the same objects when they were flashed in the left visual field and sent to the right hemisphere. In a similar fashion, an object placed out of view in the right hand (communicating with the left hemisphere) could be named. However, the same object placed in the left hand (right hemisphere) could not be. These findings supported the notion that language is housed in the left hemisphere.

Although the split-brain subjects' right hemisphere was not able to speak up for itself, further tests revealed that it *was* processing the information presented. If subjects were given an opportunity to *point out a picture* of an object they had held in their left hand, they were able to do so. They were also able to point out pictures that had been flashed to the left visual field. Furthermore, the right hemisphere (left hand) turned out to be *superior* to the left hemisphere (right hand) in assembling little puzzles and copying drawings, even though the subjects were right-handed. These findings provided the first compelling demonstration that the right hemisphere has its own special talents. Subsequent studies of additional split-brain patients showed the right hemisphere to be better than the left on a variety of visual-spatial tasks, including discriminating colors, arranging blocks, and recognizing faces.

Courtesy of Michael S. Gazzaniga

Michael Gazzaniga

"Nothing can possibly replace a singular memory of mine: that of the moment when I discovered that case W.J. could no longer verbally describe (from his left hemisphere) stimuli presented to his freshly disconnected right hemisphere."

Hemispheric Specialization in the Intact Brain

2f, SIM2

The problem with the split-brain operation, of course, is that it creates an abnormal situation. The vast majority of us remain "neurologically intact." Moreover, the surgery is done only with people who suffer from prolonged, severe cases of epilepsy. These people may have had somewhat atypical brain organization even before the operation. Moreover, the number of split-brain patients has been quite small; only 10 split-brain patients have been studied intensively (Gazzaniga, 2008). Thus, theorists couldn't help wondering whether it was safe to generalize broadly from the split-brain studies. For this reason, researchers developed methods that allowed them to study cerebral specialization in the intact brain.

One method involves looking at ***perceptual asymmetries*—left-right imbalances between the**

© 1988. Used by permission of John L. Hart FLP, and Creators Syndicate, Inc.

cerebral hemispheres in the speed of visual or auditory processing. As just discussed, it is possible to present visual stimuli to just one visual field at a time. In normal individuals, the input sent to one hemisphere is quickly shared with the other. However, subtle differences in the "abilities" of the two hemispheres can be detected by precisely measuring how long it takes participants to recognize different types of stimuli.

For instance, when *verbal* stimuli are presented to the right visual field (and thus sent to the *left hemisphere* first), they are identified more quickly and more accurately than when they are presented to the left visual field (and sent to the right hemisphere first). The faster reactions in the left hemisphere presumably occur because it can recognize verbal stimuli on its own, while the right hemisphere has to take extra time to "consult" the left hemisphere. In contrast, the *right hemisphere* is faster than the left on *visual-spatial* tasks, such as locating a dot or recognizing a face (Bradshaw, 1989; Bryden, 1982).

Researchers have also used a variety of other approaches to explore hemispheric specialization in normal people. For the most part, their findings have converged nicely with the results of the split-brain studies (Reuter-Lorenz & Miller, 1998). Overall, the findings suggest that the two hemispheres are specialized, with each handling certain types of cognitive tasks better than the other (Corballis, 2003; Gazzaniga, 2005; Springer & Deutsch, 1998). *The left hemisphere usually is better on tasks involving verbal processing, such as language, speech, reading, and writing. The right hemisphere exhibits superiority on many tasks involving nonverbal processing, such as most visual-spatial and musical tasks, and tasks involving the perception of others' emotions.*

Hemispheric specialization is not unique to humans, as it has been observed in a variety of other species (Vallortigara & Rogers, 2005). Although comparisons are complicated, it appears that humans manifest more cerebral specialization than other animals. Theorists speculate that hemispheric specialization is adaptive in an evolutionary sense in that it increases the neural capacity of the brain (Hopkins & Cantalupo, 2008). Interestingly, when researchers have studied variations in the strength of hemispheric specialization among humans, they have found links between weak lateralization and certain negative outcomes. For instance, weak lateralization has been associated with lower IQ scores (Corballis, Hattie, & Fletcher, 2008) and elevated vulnerability to schizophrenia (Spironelli, Angrilli, & Stegagno, 2008). However, much remains to be learned about these intriguing correlations.

Hemispheric specialization is a fascinating area of research that has broad implications, which we'll discuss further in the Personal Application. For now, however, let's leave the brain and turn our attention to the endocrine system.

REVIEW OF KEY LEARNING GOALS

3.14 The cerebrum is divided into right and left hemispheres connected by the corpus callosum. Evidence that the left cerebral hemisphere usually processes language led scientists to view it as the dominant hemisphere. However, studies of split-brain patients revealed that the right and left halves of the brain each have unique talents, with the right hemisphere being specialized to handle visual-spatial functions.

3.15 Studies of perceptual asymmetries in normal subjects also showed that the left hemisphere is better equipped to handle verbal processing, whereas the right hemisphere is more adept at nonverbal processing, including visual-spatial tasks and musical tasks. Hemispheric specialization may be adaptive by virtue of increasing the brain's neural capacity.

KEY LEARNING GOALS

3.16 Describe the key elements of the endocrine system.

3.17 Discuss some ways in which hormones regulate behavior.

The Endocrine System: Another Way to Communicate

The major way the brain communicates with the rest of the body is through the nervous system. However, the body has a second communication system that is also important to behavior: the endocrine system. **The *endocrine system* consists of glands that secrete chemicals into the bloodstream that help control bodily functioning.** The messengers in this communication network are called hormones. ***Hormones* are the chemical substances released by the endocrine glands.** In a way, hormones are like the neurotransmitters of the nervous system. Hormones are stored for subsequent release as chemical messengers. Once released, they diffuse through the bloodstream and bind to special receptors on target cells. In fact, some chemical substances do double duty, functioning as hormones when they're released in the endocrine system and as neurotransmitters in the nervous system (norepinephrine, for example). However, there are some important differences between hormones and neurotransmitters. Neural messages generally are transmitted short distances with lightning speed (measured in millisec-

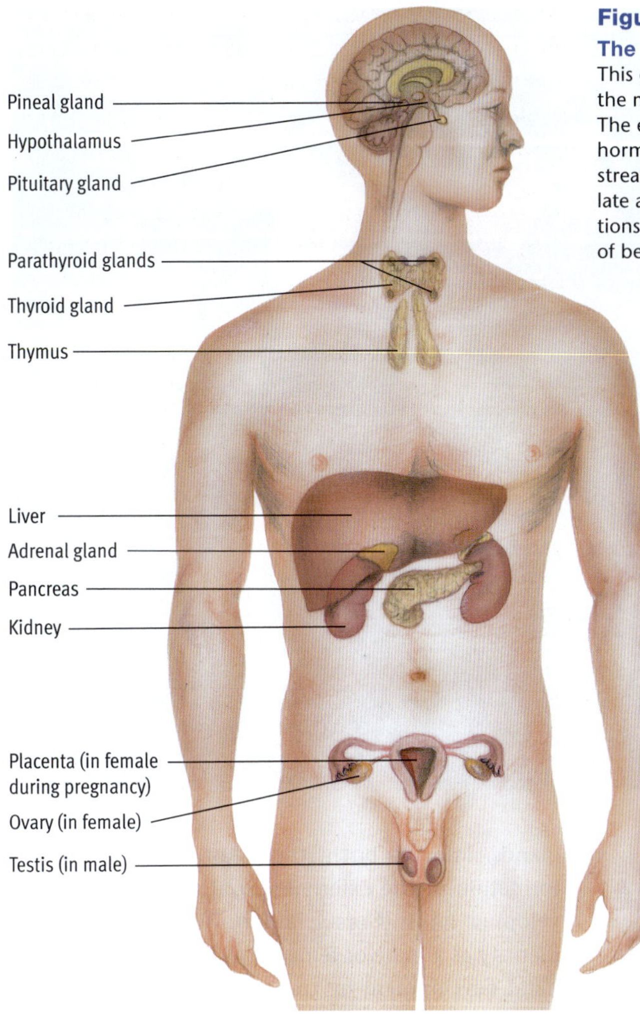

Figure 3.24

The endocrine system. This graphic depicts most of the major endocrine glands. The endocrine glands secrete hormones into the bloodstream. These chemicals regulate a variety of physical functions and affect many aspects of behavior.

© Cengage Learning 2013

onds) along very specific pathways. In contrast, hormonal messages often travel to distant cells at a much slower speed (measured in seconds and minutes) and tend to be less specific, as they can act on many target cells throughout the body.

The major endocrine glands are shown in **Figure 3.24**. Some hormones are released in response to changing conditions in the body and act to regulate those conditions. For example, hormones released by the stomach and intestines help control digestion. Kidney hormones play a part in regulating blood pressure. And pancreatic hormone (insulin) is essential for cells to use sugar from the blood. Hormone release tends to be *pulsatile.* That is, hormones tend to be released several times per day in brief bursts or pulses that last only a few minutes. The levels of many hormones increase and decrease in a rhythmic pattern throughout the day.

Much of the endocrine system is controlled by the nervous system through the *hypothalamus* (Gore, 2008). This structure at the base of the forebrain has intimate connections with the pea-sized *pituitary gland.* **The *pituitary gland* releases a great variety of hormones that fan out around the body, stimulating actions in the other endocrine glands.** In this sense, the pituitary is the "master gland" of the endocrine system, although the hypothalamus is the real power behind the throne.

The intermeshing of the nervous system and the endocrine system can be seen in the fight-or-flight response described earlier. In times of stress, the hypothalamus sends signals along two pathways—through the autonomic nervous system and through the pituitary gland—to the adrenal glands (Clow, 2001). In response, the adrenal glands secrete so-called "stress hormones" that radiate throughout the body, preparing it to cope with an emergency.

A topic of current research interest centers on the effects of ***oxytocin*—a hormone released by the pituitary gland, which regulates reproductive behaviors.** Oxytocin has long been known to trigger contractions when a woman gives birth and to stimulate the mammary glands to release milk for breastfeeding (Donaldson & Young, 2008). However, newer research suggests that this hormone has far-reaching effects on complex social behavior.

For example, an extensive body of research indicates that oxytocin fosters adult-adult pair bonding in many mammals (Lim & Young, 2006), and preliminary research suggests that similar effects may be found in humans (Bartz & Hollander, 2006; Donaldson & Young, 2008). In one study male participants worked on a task in which they tried to infer people's mental states from subtle social cues, thereby measuring their empathy. Performance was enhanced when subjects inhaled an oxytocin spray prior to working on this "mind-reading" task (Domes et al., 2007). Another study found that oxytocin increased males' empathy levels in response to photos of emotional situations (Hurlemann et al., 2010).

Recent research also suggests that oxytocin may foster trust in humans. In one fascinating study, male students participated in an investment-bargaining simulation in which the "investors" could send a portion of their financial stake to a "trustee," which tripled the money, but then they had to *hope* that the trustee would send a decent portion of the investment back to them (Kosfeld et al., 2005). Investors who inhaled an oxytocin spray before the simulation were far more trusting and sent more money to the trustees than control subjects. Other studies have also found a link between oxytocin and trusting behavior (Morhenn et al., 2008; Zak, Kurzban, & Matzner, 2005).

Hormones also help to modulate human physiological development. For example, among the more interesting hormones released by the pituitary are the *gonadotropins,* which affect the *gonads,* or sexual

© Mika/Corbis

Research suggests that oxytocin, a hormone released by the pituitary gland, may help to foster empathy and trust in humans.

glands. Prior to birth, these hormones direct the formation of the external sexual organs in the developing fetus (Gorski, 2000). Thus, your sexual identity as a male or female was shaped during prenatal development by the actions of hormones. At puberty, increased levels of sexual hormones are responsible for the emergence of secondary sexual characteristics, such as male facial hair and female breasts (Susman, Dorn, & Schiefelbein, 2003). The actions of other hormones are responsible for the spurt in physical growth that occurs around puberty (see Chapter 11).

These developmental effects of hormones illustrate how genetic programming has a hand in behavior. Obviously, the hormonal actions that shaped your sex were determined by your genetic makeup. Similarly, the hormonal changes in early adolescence that launched your growth spurt and aroused your interest in sexuality were preprogrammed over a decade earlier by your genetic inheritance. Which brings us to the role of heredity in shaping behavior.

REVIEW OF KEY LEARNING GOALS

3.16 The endocrine system consists of glands that secrete hormones, which are chemicals involved in the regulation of basic bodily processes. Hormone release tends to be pulsatile. The control centers for the endocrine system are the hypothalamus and the pituitary gland.

3.17 Hormones regulate many aspects of behavior, such as the fight-or-flight response, which occurs in response to stress. Recent research suggests that the hormone oxytocin fosters bonding, empathy, and trust. Hormones regulate many aspects of physiological development, such as sexual differentiation.

KEY LEARNING GOALS

3.18 Describe the structures and processes involved in genetic transmission.

3.19 Distinguish between genotype and phenotype, and explain polygenic inheritance.

3.20 Compare the special methods used to investigate the influence of heredity on behavior.

Heredity and Behavior: Is It All in the Genes?

As you have learned throughout this chapter, biological makeup is intimately related to an individual's behavior. That is why your genetic inheritance, which shapes your biological makeup, may have much to do with your behavior. Most people realize that physical characteristics such as height, hair color, blood type, and eye color are largely shaped by heredity. But what about psychological characteristics, such as intelligence, moodiness, impulsiveness, and shyness? To what extent are people's behavioral qualities molded by their genes? These questions are the central focus of *behavioral genetics*—an interdisciplinary field that studies the influence of genetic factors on behavioral traits.

As we saw in Chapter 1, questions about the relative importance of heredity versus environment are very old ones in psychology. However, research in behavioral genetics has grown by leaps and bounds since the 1970s, and this research has shed new light on the age-old nature versus nurture debate. Ironically, although behavioral geneticists have mainly sought to demonstrate the influence of heredity on behavior, their recent work has also highlighted the importance of the environment, as we shall see in this section.

Basic Principles of Genetics

Every cell in your body contains enduring messages from your mother and father. These messages are found on the *chromosomes* that lie within the nucleus of each cell.

Chromosomes and Genes

***Chromosomes* are strands of DNA (deoxyribonucleic acid) molecules that carry genetic informa-**

tion (see **Figure 3.25**). Every cell in humans, except the sex cells (sperm and eggs), contains 46 chromosomes. These chromosomes operate in 23 pairs, with one chromosome of each pair being contributed by each parent. Parents make this contribution when fertilization creates a ***zygote,* a single cell formed by the union of a sperm and an egg.** The sex cells that form a zygote each have 23 chromosomes. Together they contribute the 46 chromosomes that appear in the zygote and in all the body cells that develop from it. Each chromosome in turn contains thousands of biochemical messengers called genes. ***Genes* are DNA segments that serve as the key functional units in hereditary transmission.**

If all offspring are formed by a union of the parents' sex cells, why aren't family members identical clones? The reason is that a single pair of parents can produce an extraordinary variety of combinations of chromosomes. When sex cells form in each parent, it's a matter of chance as to which member of each chromosome pair ends up in the sperm or egg. Each parent's 23 chromosome pairs can be scrambled in over 8 million (2^{23}) different ways, yielding roughly 70 trillion possible configurations (2^{46}) when sperm and egg unite. Actually, this is a conservative estimate. It doesn't take into account complexities such as *mutations* (changes in the genetic code) or *crossing over* during sex-cell formation (an interchange of material between chromosomes). Thus, genetic transmission is a complicated process, and everything is a matter of probability. Except for identical twins, each person ends up with a unique genetic blueprint.

Like chromosomes, genes operate in pairs, with one gene of each pair coming from each parent. **In the *homozygous condition,* the two genes in a specific pair are the same. In the *heterozygous* condition, the two genes in a specific pair are different** (see **Figure 3.26**). In the simplest scenario, a single pair of genes determines a trait. Attached versus detached earlobes provide a nice example. When both parents contribute a gene for the same type of earlobe (the *homozygous* condition), the child will have an earlobe of that type. When the parents contribute genes for different types of earlobes (the *heterozygous* condition), one gene in the pair—called the *dominant gene*—overrides or masks the other,

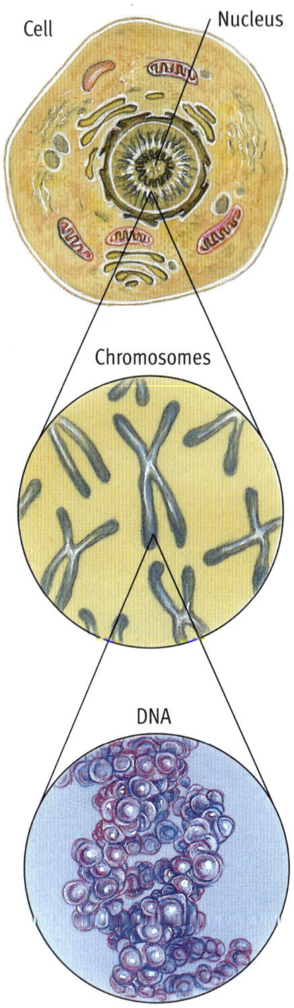

Figure 3.25

Genetic material. This series of enlargements shows the main components of genetic material. **(Top)** In the nucleus of every cell are chromosomes, which carry the information needed to construct new human beings. **(Center)** Chromosomes are threadlike strands of DNA that carry thousands of genes, the functional units of hereditary transmission. **(Bottom)** DNA is a spiraled double chain of molecules that can copy itself to reproduce. © Cengage Learning 2013

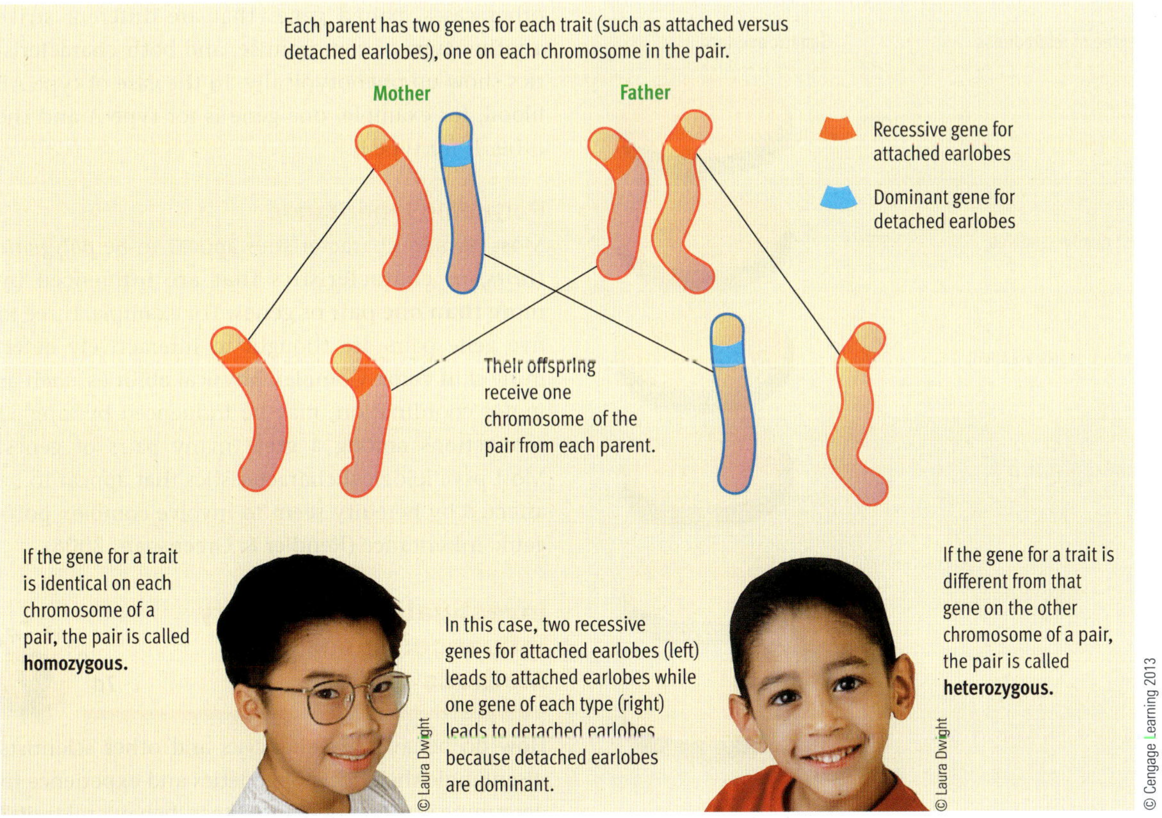

Figure 3.26

Homozygous and heterozygous genotypes. Like chromosomes, genes operate in pairs, with one gene in each pair coming from each parent. When paired genes are the same, they are said to be *homozygous.* When paired genes are different, they are said to be *heterozygous.* Whether people have attached or detached earlobes is determined by a single pair of genes. In the heterozygous condition, genes for detached earlobes are dominant over genes for attached earlobes.

called the *recessive gene*. Thus, **a *dominant gene* is one that is expressed when paired genes are different. A *recessive gene* is one that is masked when paired genes are different.** In the case of earlobes, genes for detached earlobes are dominant over genes for attached earlobes.

Because genes operate in pairs, a child has a 50% probability of inheriting a specific gene in a particular gene pair from each parent. Thus, the *genetic relatedness* of parents and children is said to be 50%. The genetic relatedness of other types of relatives can be calculated in the same way; the results are shown in **Figure 3.27**. As you can see, genetic relatedness ranges from 100% for identical twins down to 6.25% for second cousins. The numbers in **Figure 3.27** are purely theoretical. But the key to the concept of genetic relatedness is that members of a family share more of the same genes than nonmembers, and closer relatives share a larger proportion of genes than more-distant relatives. These realities explain why family members tend to resemble one another and why this resemblance tends to be greater among closer relatives.

Relationship	Degree of relatedness		Genetic overlap
Identical twins		100%	
Fraternal twins Brother or sister Parent or child	First-degree relatives	50%	
Grandparent or grandchild Uncle, aunt, nephew, or niece Half-bother or half-sister	Second-degree relatives	25%	
First cousin	Third-degree relatives	12.5%	
Second cousin	Fourth-degree relatives	6.25%	
Unrelated		0%	

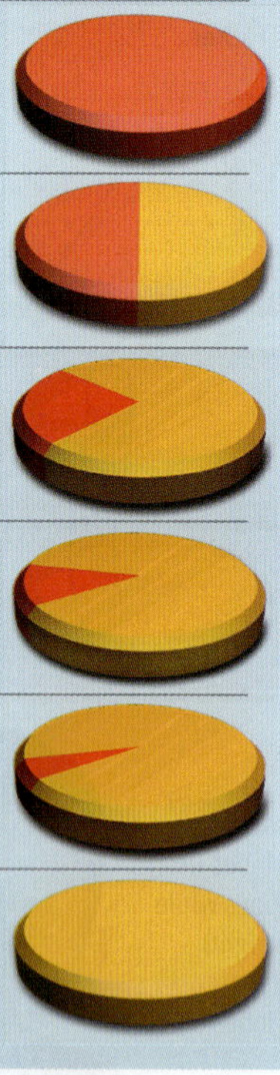

© Cengage Learning 2013

Figure 3.27

Genetic relatedness. Research on the genetic bases of behavior takes advantage of the different degrees of genetic relatedness between various types of relatives. If heredity influences a trait, relatives who share more genes should be more similar with regard to that trait than are more distant relatives, who share fewer genes. Comparisons involving various degrees of biological relationships will come up frequently in later chapters.

Genotype Versus Phenotype

It might seem that two parents with the same manifest trait, such as detached earlobes, should always produce offspring with that trait. However, that isn't always the case. For instance, two parents with detached earlobes can produce a child with attached earlobes. This happens because there are unexpressed recessive genes in the family's gene pool—in this case, genes for attached earlobes.

This point brings us to the distinction between genotype and phenotype. ***Genotype* refers to a person's genetic makeup. *Phenotype* refers to the ways in which a person's genotype is manifested in observable characteristics.** Different genotypes (such as two genes for detached earlobes as opposed to one gene for detached and one for attached) can yield the same phenotype (detached earlobes). Genotype is determined at conception and is fixed forever. In contrast, phenotypic characteristics (hair color, for instance) may change over time. They may also be modified by environmental factors.

Genotypes translate into phenotypic characteristics in a variety of ways. Not all gene pairs operate according to the principles of dominance. In some instances, when paired genes are different, they produce a blend, an "averaged out" phenotype. In other cases, paired genes that are different strike another type of compromise, and both characteristics show up phenotypically. In the case of type AB blood, for example, one gene is for type A and the other is for type B.

Polygenic Inheritance

Most human characteristics appear to be ***polygenic traits*, or characteristics that are influenced by more than one pair of genes.** For example, three to five gene pairs are thought to interactively determine skin color. Complex physical abilities, such as motor coordination, may be influenced by tangled interactions among a great many pairs of genes. Most psychological characteristics that appear to be affected by heredity seem to involve complex polygenic inheritance (Kendler & Greenspan, 2006).

Investigating Hereditary Influence: Research Methods

PSYKTREK 7d

How do behavioral geneticists and other scientists disentangle the effects of genetics and experience to determine whether heredity affects behavioral traits? Researchers have designed special types of studies to assess the impact of heredity. Of course, with humans they are limited to correlational rather than experimental methods, as they cannot manipulate genetic variables by assigning subjects to mate with each other (this approach, called *selective breeding,* is used in animal studies). The three most important methods in human research are family studies, twin studies, and adoption studies. After examining these classic methods of research, we'll discuss the impact of new developments in genetic mapping.

Family Studies

7d

In *family studies* researchers assess hereditary influence by examining blood relatives to see how much they resemble one another on a specific trait. If heredity affects the trait under scrutiny, researchers should find phenotypic similarity among relatives. Furthermore, they should find more similarity among relatives who share more genes. For instance, siblings should exhibit more similarity than cousins.

Numerous family studies have been conducted to assess the contribution of heredity to the development of schizophrenic disorders. These disorders strike approximately 1% of the population, yet as **Figure 3.28** reveals, 9% of the siblings of schizophrenic patients exhibit schizophrenia themselves (Gottesman, 1991). Thus, these first-degree relatives of schizophrenic patients show a risk for the disorder that's nine times higher than normal. This risk is greater than that observed for more distantly related, second-degree relatives, such as nieces and nephews (4%), who, in turn, are at greater risk than third-degree relatives, such as second cousins (2%). This pattern supports the claim that genetic inheritance influences the development of schizophrenic disorders (Kirov & Owen, 2009).

Such family studies can indicate whether a trait runs in families, but they do not provide conclusive evidence that the trait is influenced by heredity. Why not? Because family members generally share not only genes but also similar environments. Furthermore, closer relatives are more likely to live together than more distant relatives. Thus, genetic similarity and environmental similarity *both* tend to be greater for closer relatives. Either of these confounded variables could be responsible when greater phenotypic similarity is found in closer relatives. Family studies can offer useful insights about the possible impact of heredity, but they cannot provide definitive evidence.

Twin Studies

7d

Twin studies can yield better evidence about the possible role of genetic factors. **In *twin studies* researchers assess hereditary influence by comparing the resemblance of identical twins and fraternal twins with respect to a trait.** The logic of twin studies hinges on the genetic relatedness of identical and fraternal twins (see **Figure 3.29** on the next page). ***Identical (monozygotic) twins* emerge from one zygote that splits for unknown reasons.** Thus, they have exactly the same genotype; their genetic relatedness is 100%. ***Fraternal (dizygotic) twins* result when two eggs are fertilized simultaneously by different sperm cells, forming two separate zygotes.** Fraternal twins are no more alike in genetic makeup than any two siblings born to a pair of parents at different times. Their genetic relatedness is only 50%.

Fraternal twins provide a useful comparison to identical twins because in both cases the twins

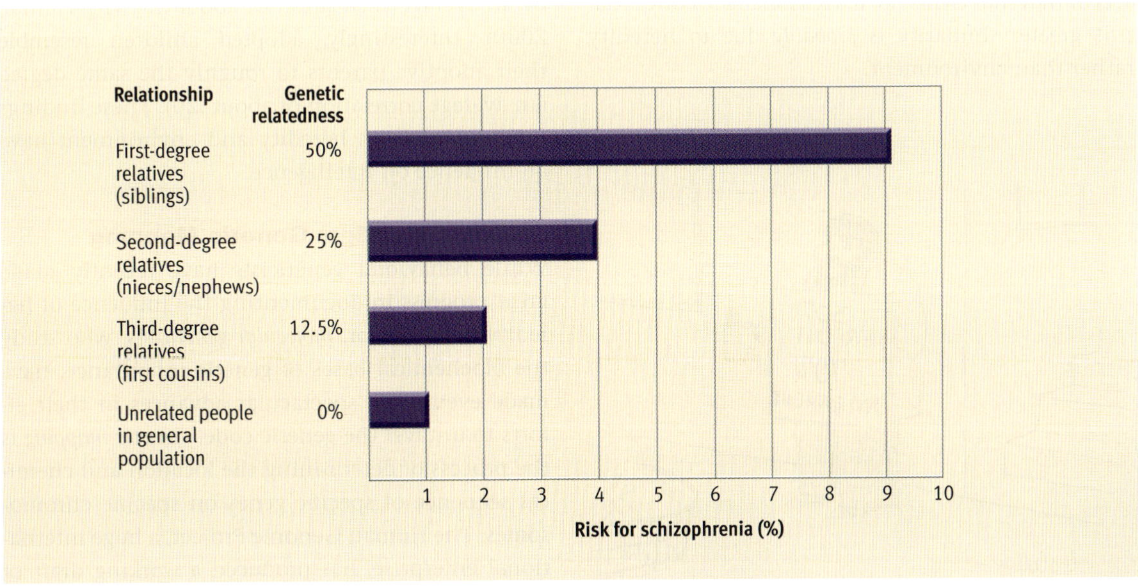

© Cengage Learning 2013

Figure 3.28

Family studies of risk for schizophrenic disorders. First-degree relatives of schizophrenic patients have an elevated risk of developing a schizophrenic disorder (Gottesman, 1991). For instance, the risk for siblings of schizophrenic patients is about 9% instead of the baseline 1% for unrelated people. Second- and third-degree relatives have progressively smaller elevations in risk for this disorder. Although these patterns of risk do not prove that schizophrenia is partly inherited, they are consistent with this hypothesis.

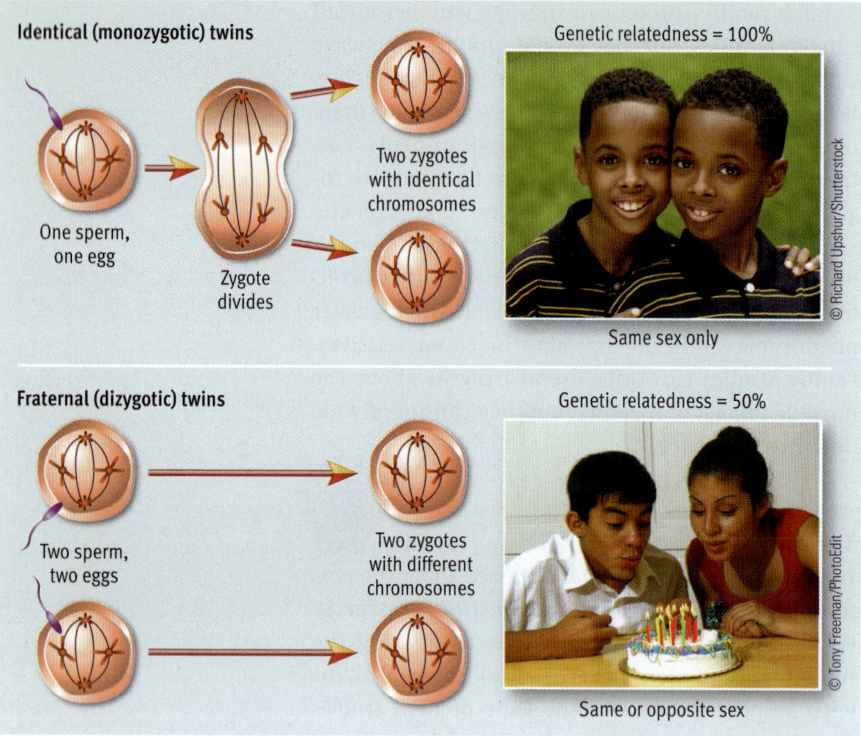

Figure 3.29

Identical versus fraternal twins. Identical (monozygotic) twins emerge from one zygote that splits, so their genetic relatedness is 100%. Fraternal (dizygotic) twins emerge from two separate zygotes, so their genetic relatedness is only 50%.

SOURCE: Adapted from Kalat, J. (2008). *Introduction to psychology* (8 ed.). Belmont, CA: Wadsworth. Wadsworth is a part of Cengage Learning, Inc. Reproduced by permission. www.cengage.com/permissions.

usually grow up in the same home, at the same time, exposed to the same configuration of relatives, neighbors, peers, teachers, events, and so forth. Thus, both kinds of twins normally develop under equally similar environmental conditions. However, identical twins share more genetic kinship than fraternal twins. Consequently, if sets of identical twins tend to exhibit more similarity on a trait than sets of fraternal twins do, it's reasonable to infer that this greater similarity is *probably* due to heredity rather than environment.

© Leo Cullum/The New Yorker Collection/www.cartoonbank.com

Twin studies have been conducted to assess the impact of heredity on a variety of traits. Some representative results are summarized in **Figure 3.30**. The higher correlations found for identical twins indicate that they tend to be more similar to each other than fraternal twins on measures of general intelligence and measures of specific personality traits, such as extraversion (Plomin et al., 2008). These results support the notion that intelligence and personality are influenced to some degree by genetic makeup. However, the fact that identical twins are far from identical in intelligence and personality also shows that environment influences these characteristics.

Adoption Studies

PsykTrek 7d

Adoption studies **assess hereditary influence by examining the resemblance between adopted children and both their biological and their adoptive parents.** Generally, adoptees are used as subjects in this type of study only if they were given up for adoption in early infancy and were raised without having contact with their biological parents. The logic underlying the adoption study approach is quite simple. If adopted children resemble their biological parents on a trait, even though they were not raised by them, genetic factors probably influence that trait. In contrast, if adopted children resemble their adoptive parents, even though they inherited no genes from them, environmental factors probably influence the trait.

In recent years, adoption studies have contributed to science's understanding of how genetics and the environment influence intelligence. The research shows modest similarity between adopted children and their biological parents, as indicated by an average correlation of about .22 (Grigerenko, 2000). Interestingly, adopted children resemble their adoptive parents to roughly the same degree (an average correlation of about .20). These findings suggest that both heredity and environment have an influence on intelligence.

The Cutting Edge: Genetic Mapping

While behavioral geneticists have recently made great progress in documenting the influence of heredity on behavior, *molecular geneticists,* who study the biochemical bases of genetic inheritance, have made even more spectacular advances in their efforts to unravel the genetic code. *Genetic mapping* is the process of determining the location and chemical sequence of specific genes on specific chromosomes. The Human Genome Project, a huge international enterprise, has produced a working draft of the sequence of all 3 billion letters of DNA in the human genome, and the chromosomal locations of almost all human genes have been identified (Collins et al., 2006; Kelsoe, 2004). Gene maps, by themselves, do not reveal which genes govern which traits. However, the compilation of a precise genetic map may fuel a quantum leap in the ability of scientists to pinpoint links between specific genes and specific traits and disorders. For example, medical researchers have already identified the genes responsible for cystic fibrosis, Huntington's chorea, and muscular dystrophy.

Will genetic mapping permit researchers to discover the genetic basis for intelligence, extraversion, schizophrenia, musical ability, and other *behavioral* traits? Perhaps someday, but progress is likely to be painstakingly slow (Caspi & Moffitt, 2006; Plomin & McGuffin, 2003). Thus far, the major medical breakthroughs from genetic mapping have involved dichotomous traits (you either do or do not have the trait, such as muscular dystrophy) governed by a single gene pair. However, most behavioral traits do not involve a dichotomy, as everyone has varying amounts of intelligence, musical ability, and so forth. Moreover, virtually all behavioral traits appear to be *polygenic* and are shaped by many genes rather than a single gene. Because of these and many other complexities, scientists are not likely to find a single gene that controls intelligence, extraversion, or musical talent (Plomin, Kennedy, & Craig, 2006). The challenge will be to identify specific networks of genes that each exert modest influence over particular aspects of behavior.

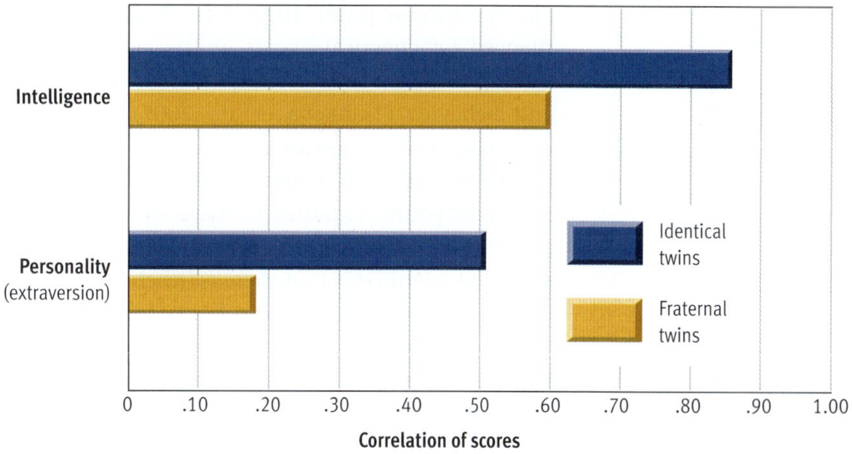

Figure 3.30

Twin studies of intelligence and personality. Identical twins tend to be more similar than fraternal twins (as reflected in higher correlations) with regard to intelligence and specific personality traits, such as extraversion. These findings suggest that intelligence and personality are influenced by heredity. (Data from Plomin et al., 2001) © Cengage Learning 2013

The Interplay of Heredity and Environment

What scientists find again and again is that heredity and experience jointly influence most aspects of behavior. Moreover, their effects are interactive—genetics and experience play off each other (Gottesman & Hanson, 2005; Rutter, 2006, 2007). For example, consider what researchers have learned about the development of schizophrenic disorders. Although the evidence indicates that genetic factors influence the development of schizophrenia, it does *not* appear that anyone directly inherits the disorder itself. Rather, what people appear to inherit is a certain degree of *vulnerability* to the disorder (McDonald & Murphy, 2003; Paris, 1999). Whether this vulnerability is ever converted into an actual disorder depends on each person's experiences in life. As we'll discuss in Chapter 15, certain types of stressful experience seem to evoke the disorder in people who are more vulnerable to it. Thus, as Danielle Dick and Richard Rose (2002) put it in a review of behavioral genetics research, "Genes confer dispositions, not destinies" (p 73).

In recent years, research in the emerging field of *epigenetics* has only served to further demonstrate that genetic and environmental factors are inextricably intertwined. ***Epigenetics* is the study of heritable changes in gene expression that do not involve modifications to the DNA sequence.** It turns

CONCEPT CHECK 3.4

Recognizing Hereditary Influence

Check your understanding of the methods scientists use to explore hereditary influences on specific behavioral traits by filling in the blanks in the descriptive statements below. The answers can be found in the back of the book in Appendix A.

1. The findings from family studies indicate that heredity may influence a trait if ______________ show more trait similarity than ______________.
2. The findings from twin studies suggest that heredity influences a trait if ______________ show more trait similarity than ______________.
3. The findings from adoption studies suggest that heredity influences a trait if children adopted at a young age share more trait similarity with their ______________ than their ______________.
4. The findings from family studies, twin studies, or adoption studies suggest that heredity does not influence a trait when ______________ is not related to ______________

out that specific genes' effects can be dampened or silenced by chemical events at the cellular level, leading to phenotypic alterations in traits, health, and behavior (Tsankova et al., 2007). Moreover, these chemical events can be stimulated by environmental events, such as poor nurturance when offspring are young, exposure to stress, or peculiarities in diet (McGowan, Meaney, & Szyf, 2008). What has surprised scientists is that these *epigenetic marks* that influence gene expression can be passed on to successive generations (Masterpasqua, 2009). Theorists suspect that epigenetic changes may contribute to a variety of psychological disorders, including schizophrenia (Zhang & Meaney, 2010). The finding that genes themselves are not exempt from environmental influence has a number of far-reaching implications. Among other things, it means that efforts to quantify the influence of heredity versus environment, informative though they may be, are ultimately artificial (Lickliter, 2009).

REVIEW OF KEY LEARNING GOALS

3.18 The basic units of genetic transmission are genes housed on chromosomes. Genes operate in pairs, which may be homozygous or heterozygous. When a pair of genes are heterozygous, one may be dominant and the other recessive. The key to the concept of genetic relatedness is that closer relatives share a larger proportion of genes than more-distant relatives.

3.19 Genotype refers to one's genetic makeup, whereas phenotype refers to one's observable characteristics. Genotypes are translated into phenotypes in many ways. Most behavioral qualities appear to involve polygenic inheritance, which means that many pairs of genes play a role in influencing the traits.

3.20 Researchers assess hereditary influence through a variety of methods, including family studies, twin studies, adoption studies, and genetic mapping. Family studies cannot provide conclusive evidence that a trait is influenced by heredity. Twin studies can provide much better evidence. Research indicates that most behavioral qualities are influenced jointly by heredity and environment, which play off of each other in complex interactions. New work in epigenetics has further demonstrated that genetic and environmental factors are deeply intertwined.

KEY LEARNING GOALS

3.21 Describe the four key insights that represent the essence of Darwin's theory of evolution.

3.22 Describe some refinements that have been made to evolutionary theory.

3.23 Provide some examples of animal behavior that represent adaptations.

The Evolutionary Bases of Behavior

To round out our look at the biological bases of behavior, we need to discuss how evolutionary forces have shaped many aspects of human and animal behavior. As you may recall from Chapter 1, *evolutionary psychology* is a major new theoretical perspective in the field that analyzes behavioral processes in terms of their adaptive significance. In this section, we'll outline some basic principles of evolutionary theory and relate them to animal behavior. These ideas will create a foundation for later chapters, where we'll see how evolutionary principles can enhance our understanding of many aspects of human behavior.

Darwin's Insights

Charles Darwin, the legendary British naturalist, was *not* the first person to describe the process of evolution. Well before Darwin's time, other biologists who had studied the earth's fossil record noted that various species appeared to have undergone gradual changes over the course of a great many generations. What Darwin (1859) contributed in his landmark book, *The Origin of Species,* was a creative, new explanation for *how and why* evolutionary changes unfold over time. He identified *natural selection* as the engine that fuels the process of evolution (Dewsbury, 2009).

The mystery that Darwin set out to solve was complicated. He wanted to explain how the characteristics of a species might have changed over generations and why these changes tended to be surprisingly adaptive. In other words, he wanted to shed light on why organisms tend to have characteristics that serve them well in the context of their environments. How did giraffes acquire their long necks that allow them to reach high into acacia trees to secure their main source of food? How did woodpeckers develop their sharp, chisel-shaped beaks that permit them to probe trees for insects so effectively? How did frogs develop their long and powerful hindlimbs that enable them to catapult through the air on land and move swiftly through water? Darwin's explanation for the seemingly purposive nature of evolution centered on four crucial insights.

First, he noted that organisms vary in endless ways, such as size, speed, strength, aspects of appearance, visual abilities, hearing capacities, digestive processes, cell structure, and so forth. Second, he noted that some of these characteristics are heritable—that is, they are passed down from one generation to the next. Although genes and chromosomes had not yet been discovered, the concept of heredity was well established. In Darwin's theory, variations in hereditary traits provide the raw materials for evolution. Third, borrowing from the work of Thomas Malthus, he noted that organisms tend to produce offspring at a pace that outstrips the local availability of food supplies, living space, and other crucial resources. As a population increases and resources dwindle, the competition for precious resources intensifies. Thus, it occurred to Darwin—and this was his grand insight—that variations in hereditary traits might affect organisms' ability to obtain the resources necessary for survival and reproduction. Fourth, building on this insight, Darwin argued that if a specific heritable trait contributes to an organism's survival or reproductive success, organisms with that trait should produce more offspring than those without the trait (or those with less of the trait). Hence, the prevalence of that trait should gradually increase over generations—resulting in evolutionary change.

Although evolution is widely characterized as a matter of "survival of the fittest," Darwin recognized from the beginning that survival is only important insofar as it relates to reproductive success. Indeed, in evolutionary theory, ***fitness* refers to the reproductive success (number of descendants) of an individual organism relative to the average reproductive success in the population.** *Variations in reproductive success within a species are what really fuels evolutionary change.* But survival is crucial because organisms typically need to mature and thrive before they can reproduce. So, Darwin theorized that there ought to be two ways in which traits might contribute to evolution: by providing either a survival advantage or a reproductive advantage. For example, a turtle's shell has great protective value that provides a survival advantage. In contrast, a firefly's emission of light is a courtship overture that provides a reproductive advantage.

© Eberhard Brunner/Photolibrary

To summarize, the principle of ***natural selection* claims that heritable characteristics that provide a survival or reproductive advantage are more likely than alternative characteristics to be passed on to subsequent generations and thus come to be "selected" over time.** Please note, the process of natural selection works on *populations* rather than *individual organisms.* Evolution occurs when the gene pool in a population changes gradually as a result of selection pressures. This process tends to be extremely gradual—it generally takes thousands to millions of generations for one trait to be selected over another.

Darwin's theory had at least two important, far-reaching implications (Buss, 2009). First, it suggested that the awe-inspiring diversity of life is the result of an unplanned, natural process rather than divine creation. Second, it implied that humans are not unique and that they share a common ancestry with other species. Although these implications would prove highly controversial, Darwin's theory eventually gained considerable acceptance because it provided a compelling explanation for how the characteristics of various species gradually changed over many generations and for the functional, adaptive direction of these changes.

Later Refinements to Evolutionary Theory

Although Darwin's evolutionary theory quickly gained many supporters, it also remained controversial for decades. One legitimate objection was that the theory did not provide an adequate explanation for the details of the inheritance process. This shortcoming was eventually rectified. Gregor Mendel's previously ignored work on patterns of inheritance started attracting attention around 1900. Research building on his insights led to major advances in the understanding of heredity over the next several decades. By 1937, these advances were enough to permit Theodore Dobzhansky to write a fairly comprehensive and convincing account of the evolutionary process in genetic terms. Dobzhansky's combining of Darwinian natural selection and Mendelian genetics was enormously influential, and by the 1950s the core tenets of evolutionary theory enjoyed widespread acceptance among scientists.

Contemporary models of evolution recognize that

© Bettmann/Corbis

Charles Darwin

"Can we doubt (remembering that many more individuals are born than can possibly survive) that individuals having any advantage, however slight, over others, would have the best chance of surviving and procreating their kind? . . . This preservation of favourable variations and the rejection of injurious variations, I call Natural Selection."

natural selection operates on the gene pool of a population. *Adaptations* are the key product of the process of evolution. **An *adaptation* is an inherited characteristic that increased in a population (through natural selection) because it helped solve a problem of survival or reproduction during the time it emerged.** Because of the gradual, incremental nature of evolution, adaptations sometimes linger in a population even though they no longer provide a survival or reproductive advantage. For example, humans show a taste preference for fatty substances that was adaptive in an era of hunting and gathering, when dietary fat was a scarce source of important calories. However, in our modern world, where dietary fat is typically available in abundance, this taste preference leads many people to consume too much fat, resulting in obesity, heart disease, and other health problems. Thus, the preference for fatty foods has become a liability for human survival. Organisms' environments often undergo changes so that adaptations that were once beneficial become obsolete. As you will see, evolutionary psychologists have found that many aspects of human nature reflect the adaptive demands faced by our ancient ancestors rather than modern demands.

Behaviors as Adaptive Traits

Scholarly analyses of evolution have focused primarily on the evolution of *physical characteristics* in the animal kingdom, but from the very beginning, Darwin recognized that natural selection was applicable to *behavioral traits* as well. Studying the evolutionary roots of behavior is more difficult than studying the evolutionary bases of physical traits because behavior is more transient. Although the fossil record *can* leave clues about past organisms' behavior (such as its prey or nesting habits), it leaves much more detailed information about organisms' physical characteristics. Nonetheless, it's clear that a species' typical patterns of behavior often reflect evolutionary solutions to adaptive problems.

Consider, for instance, the eating behavior of rats, who show remarkable caution when they encounter new foods. Rats are versatile animals that are found in an enormous range of habitats and can live off quite a variety of foods. But consuming such a variety of foods can present risks. Some foods can be toxic, so rats must be cautious. When they encounter unfamiliar foods, they consume only small amounts and won't eat two new foods together. If the consumption of a new food is followed by illness, they avoid that food in the future (Logue, 1991). These precautions allow rats to learn what makes them sick while reducing the likelihood of consuming a lethal amount of something poisonous. These patterns of eating behavior are highly adaptive solutions to the food selection problems faced by rats.

Let's look at some additional examples of how evolution has shaped organisms' behavior. Avoiding predators is a nearly universal problem for organisms. Because of natural selection, many species have developed physical characteristics, such as special coloration, that allow them to blend in with their environments, making detection by predators more difficult. Many organisms also engage in elaborate *behavioral maneuvers* to hide themselves. For example, the grasshopper pictured below has dug itself a small trench in which to hide and has used its midlegs to pull pebbles over its back (Alcock, 1998). This clever hiding behavior is just as much a product of evolution as the grasshopper's remarkable camouflage.

Many behavioral adaptations are designed to improve organisms' chances of reproductive success. Consider, for instance, the wide variety of species in which females actively choose which male to mate with. In many such species, females demand material goods and services from males in return for

© Courtesy of John Alcock

The behavior that helps this grasshopper hide from predators is a product of evolution, just like the physical characteristics that help it blend in with its surroundings.

copulation opportunities. For example, in one type of moth, males have to spend hours extracting sodium from mud puddles. They then give the sodium to possible mates, who use it to supply their larvae with an important nutritional element (Smedley & Eisner, 1996). In the black-tipped hangingfly, females insist on a nuptial gift of food before they mate. They reject suitors bringing unpalatable food, and they tie the length of subsequent copulation to the size of the nuptial gift (Thornhill, 1976).

The adaptive value of trading sex for material goods that can aid the survival of an organism and its offspring is obvious, but the evolutionary significance of other mating strategies is more perplexing. In some species characterized by female choice, the choices hinge on males' appearance and courtship behavior. Females usually prefer males sporting larger or more brightly colored ornaments, or those capable of more extreme acoustical displays. For example, female house finches are swayed by redder feathers, whereas female wild turkeys are enticed by larger beak ornaments (see **Table 3.2** for additional examples). What do females gain by selecting males with redder feathers, larger beaks, and other arbitrary characteristics? This is one of the more difficult questions in evolutionary biology, and addressing all the complexities that may be involved would take us far beyond the scope of this discussion. But, caveats aside, favored attributes generally seem to be indicators of males' relatively good genes, sound health, low parasite load, or superior ability to provide future services, such as protection or food gathering, all of which may serve to make their offspring more viable (Alcock, 2005).

Table 3.2 Female Mate Choices Based on Differences in Males' Morphological and Behavioral Attributes

Species	Favored attribute
Scorpionfly	More symmetrical wings
Barn swallow	More symmetrical and larger tail ornaments
Wild turkey	Larger beak ornaments
House finch	Redder feathers
Satin bowerbird	Bowers with more ornaments
Cichlid fish	Taller display "bower"
Field cricket	Longer calling bouts
Woodhouse's toad	More frequent calls

SOURCE: Adapted from Alcock, J. (1998). *Animal behavior* (p. 463). Sunderland, MA: Sinauer Associates. Copyright © 1998 John Alcock. Reprinted by permission of Sinauer Associates and the author.

© Cengage Learning 2013

CONCEPT CHECK 3.5

Identifying the Contributions of Major Theorists and Researchers

Check your recall of the principal ideas of important theorists and researchers covered in this chapter by matching the people listed on the left with the appropriate contributions described on the right. If you need help, the crucial pages describing each person's ideas are listed in parentheses. Fill in the letters for your choices in the spaces provided on the left. You'll find the answers in Appendix A.

Major Theorists and Researchers

_____ 1. Charles Darwin (pp. 116–117)

_____ 2. Alan Hodgkin and Andrew Huxley (p. 82)

_____ 3. James Olds and Peter Milner (pp. 100–101)

_____ 4. Solomon Snyder (p. 88)

_____ 5. Roger Sperry and Michael Gazzaniga (pp. 106–107)

Key Ideas and Contributions

a. This researcher showed that morphine exerts its effects by binding to specialized receptors in the brain, leading to the discovery of endorphins.

b. In the 1950s, this research team discovered self-stimulation sites in the rat brain, suggesting that the limbic system may include "pleasure centers."

c. This 19-century theorist, who invented the concepts of fitness and natural selection, was the original architect of evolutionary theory.

d. These researchers conducted the original split-brain studies, which demonstrated that the right and left hemispheres of the brain each have their own special abilities.

e. These researchers used axons taken from squid to conduct influential research on the biochemical bases of the neural impulse.

REVIEW OF KEY LEARNING GOALS

3.21 Darwin argued that if a heritable trait contributes to an organism's survival or reproductive success, organisms with that trait should produce more offspring than those without the trait and that the prevalence of that trait should gradually increase over generations—thanks to natural selection.

3.22 Dobzhansky's integration of Darwin's ideas and Mendelian genetics led to widespread acceptance of evolutionary theory among scientists. Because of the gradual, incremental nature of evolution, adaptations sometimes linger in a population even though they no longer provide a survival or reproductive advantage.

3.23 Theorists have focused primarily on the evolution of *physical characteristics* in the animal kingdom, but from the very beginning Darwin recognized that natural selection was applicable to *behavioral traits* as well. Examples of behaviors sculpted by evolution include eating behavior, the avoidance of predators, and mating strategies.

KEY LEARNING GOALS

3.24 Identify the three unifying themes that were highlighted in this chapter.

Heredity and Environment

Multifactorial Causation

Empiricism

Reflecting on the Chapter's Themes

Three of our seven themes stood out in this chapter: (1) heredity and environment jointly influence behavior, (2) behavior is determined by multiple causes, and (3) psychology is empirical. Let's look at each of these points.

In Chapter 1, when it was first emphasized that heredity and environment jointly shape behavior, you may have been a little perplexed about how your genes could be responsible for your sarcastic wit or your interest in art. In fact, there are no genes for behavior per se. Experts do not expect to find genes for sarcasm or artistic interest, for example. Insofar as your hereditary endowment plays a role in your behavior, it does so *indirectly,* by molding the physiological machine that you work with. Thus, your genes influence your physiological makeup, which in turn influences your personality, temperament, intelligence, interests, and other traits. Bear in mind, however, that genetic factors do not operate in a vacuum. Genes exert their effects in an environmental context. The impact of genetic makeup depends on environment, and the impact of environment depends on genetic makeup.

It was evident throughout the chapter that behavior is determined by multiple causes, but this fact was particularly apparent in the discussions of schizophrenia. At various points in the chapter, we saw that schizophrenia may be a function of (1) abnormalities in neurotransmitter activity, (2) structural defects in the brain (enlarged ventricles), and (3) genetic vulnerability to the illness. These findings do not contradict one another. Rather, they demonstrate that a complex array of biological factors are involved in the development of schizophrenia. In Chapter 15, we'll see that a variety of environmental factors also play a role in the multifactorial causation of schizophrenia.

The empirical nature of psychology was apparent in the numerous discussions of the specialized research methods used to study the physiological bases of behavior. As you know, the empirical approach depends on precise observation. Throughout this chapter, you've seen how investigators have come up with innovative methods to observe and measure elusive phenomena, such as electrical activity in the brain, neural impulses, brain function, cerebral specialization, and the impact of heredity on behavior. The point is that empirical methods are the lifeblood of the scientific enterprise. When researchers figure out how to better observe something, their new methods usually facilitate major advances in our scientific knowledge. That's why brain-imaging techniques and genetic mapping hold such exciting promise.

The importance of empiricism will also be apparent in the upcoming Personal Application and Critical Thinking Application. In both you'll see that it's important to learn to distinguish between scientific findings and conjecture based on those findings.

REVIEW OF KEY LEARNING GOALS

3.24 The interactive influence of heredity and environment was highlighted in this chapter, as was the multifactorial causation of behavior. The special research techniques used to study the biological bases of behavior show that empirical methods are the lifeblood of the scientific enterprise.

PERSONAL APPLICATION

Evaluating the Concept of "Two Minds in One"

KEY LEARNING GOALS

3.25 Describe four popular beliefs regarding the specialization of the cerebral hemispheres.

3.26 Critically evaluate popular ideas on cerebral specialization and cognitive processes.

Answer the following "true" or "false."

___ **1** The right and left brains give people two minds in one.

___ **2** Each half of the brain has its own special mode of thinking.

___ **3** Some people are left-brained while others are right-brained.

Do people have two minds in one that think differently? Do some people depend on one side of the brain more than the other? Is the right side of the brain neglected? These questions are too complex to resolve with a simple true or false, but in this Application we'll take a closer look at the issues involved in these proposed applications of the findings on cerebral specialization. You'll learn that some of these ideas are plausible, but in many cases the hype has outstripped the evidence.

Earlier, we described Roger Sperry's Nobel prize–winning research with split-brain patients, whose right and left hemispheres were disconnected (to reduce epileptic seizures). The split-brain studies showed that the previously underrated right hemisphere has some special talents of its own. This discovery detonated an explosion of research on cerebral laterality.

Cerebral Specialization and Cognitive Processes

PSYKTREK 2f, SIM2

Using a variety of methods, scientists have compiled mountains of data on the specialized abilities of the right and left hemispheres. These findings have led to extensive theorizing about how the right and left brains might be related to cognitive processes. Some of the more intriguing ideas include the following:

1. *The two hemispheres are specialized to process different types of cognitive tasks* (Corballis, 1991; Ornstein, 1977). The findings of many researchers have been widely interpreted as showing that the left hemisphere handles verbal tasks, including language, speech, writing, math, and logic, while the right hemisphere handles nonverbal tasks, including spatial problems, music, art, fantasy, and creativity. These conclusions have attracted a great deal of public interest and media attention. For example, **Figure 3.31** shows a *Newsweek* artist's depiction of how the brain divides its work.

2. *Each hemisphere has its own independent stream of consciousness* (Bogen, 1985, 2000; Pucetti, 1981). For instance, Joseph Bogen has asserted, "Pending further evidence, I believe that each of us has two minds in one person" (Hooper & Teresi, 1986, p. 221). Supposedly, this duality of consciousness goes largely unnoticed because of the considerable overlap between the experiences of each independent mind. Ultimately, though, according to Bogen, the apparent unity of consciousness is but an illusion.

3. *The two hemispheres have different modes of thinking* (Banich & Heller, 1998; Davis & Dean, 2005). According to this notion, the documented differences between the hemispheres in dealing with verbal and nonverbal materials are caused by more basic differences in *how* the hemispheres process information. The standard version of this theory holds that the reason the left hemisphere handles verbal material well is that it's analytic, abstract, rational, logical, and linear. In contrast, the right hemisphere is thought to be better equipped to handle spatial and musical material because it's synthetic, concrete, nonrational, intuitive, and holistic.

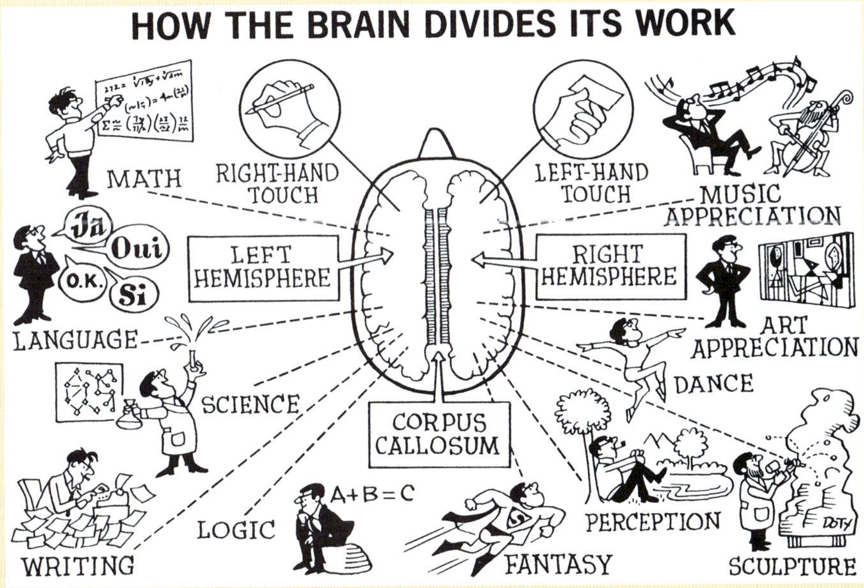

Figure 3.31
Popular conceptions of hemispheric specialization. As this *Newsweek* diagram illustrates, depictions of hemispheric specialization in the popular press have often been oversimplified.
SOURCE: Cartoon courtesy of Roy Doty.

© Cro Magnon/Alamy

Does artistic ability depend on being "right-brained?" The popular press has certainly suggested that this is the case, but as your text explains, there is no solid empirical evidence to support this assertion.

4. *People vary in their reliance on one hemisphere as opposed to the other* (Pink, 2005; Zenhausen, 1978). Allegedly, some people are "left-brained." Their greater dependence on their left hemisphere supposedly makes them analytic, rational, and logical. Other people are "right-brained." Their greater use of their right hemisphere supposedly makes them intuitive, holistic, and irrational. Being right-brained or left-brained is thought to explain many personal characteristics, such as whether an individual likes to read, is good with maps, or enjoys music. This notion of "brainedness" has even been used to explain occupational choice. Supposedly, right-brained people are more likely to become artists or musicians, while left-brained people are more likely to become writers or scientists.

Complexities and Qualifications

The ideas just outlined are the source of considerable debate among psychologists and neuroscientists. They are intriguing and have clearly captured the imagination of the general public. However, the research on cerebral specialization is complex, and doubts have been raised about many of these ideas (Efron, 1990; Springer & Deutsch, 1998). Let's examine each point.

1. There *is* ample evidence that the right and left hemispheres are specialized to handle different types of cognitive tasks, *but only to a degree* (Brown & Kosslyn, 1993; Corballis, 2003). Doreen Kimura (1973) compared the abilities of the right and left hemispheres to quickly recognize letters, words, faces, and melodies in a series of perceptual asymmetry studies, like those described earlier in the chapter. She found that the superiority of one hemisphere over the other was usually quite modest, as you can see in **Figure 3.32**, which shows superiority ratios for four cognitive tasks.

Furthermore, in normal individuals, the hemispheres don't work alone. As Hellige (1993a) notes, "In the intact brain, it is unlikely that either hemisphere is ever completely uninvolved in ongoing processing" (p. 23). Most tasks probably engage *both* hemispheres, albeit to different degrees (Beeman & Chiarello, 1998; Ornstein, 1997). Research suggests that as cognitive tasks become more complex and difficult, the more likely it is that *both* hemispheres will be involved (Weissman & Banich, 2000).

Furthermore, people differ in their patterns of cerebral specialization (Springer & Deutsch, 1998). Some people display little specialization—that is, their hemispheres seem to have equal abilities on various types of tasks. Others even reverse the usual specialization, so that verbal processing might be housed in the right hemisphere. These unusual patterns are especially common among left-handed people (Josse & Tzourio-Mazoyer, 2004). Accomplished musicians may be another exception to the rule. Two recent studies have found that experienced musicians exhibit more bilateral cerebral organization than comparable nonmusicians (Gibson, Folley, & Park, 2009; Patston et al., 2007). This bilaterality may develop because musicians often have to use both hands independently to play their instruments. If this explanation is accurate, it would provide another example of how experience can shape brain organization. In any event, it is clear that the functional specialization of the cerebral hemispheres is not set in concrete.

2. The evidence for the idea that people have a separate stream of consciousness in each hemisphere is weak. There *are* clear signs of such duality among *split-brain patients* (Bogen, 1990; Mark, 1996). But this duality is probably a unique by-product of the radical procedure that they have undergone—the surgical disconnection of their hemispheres (Bradshaw, 1981). In fact, many theorists have been impressed by the degree to which even split-brain patients mostly experience *unity* of consciousness (Gazzaniga, 2008; Wolford et al., 2004). There is little empirical basis for the idea that people have two independent streams of awareness neatly housed in the right and left halves of the brain.

3. Similarly, there is little direct evidence to support the notion that each hemisphere has its own mode of thinking, or *cognitive style* (Bradshaw, 1989; Corballis, 2007). This notion is plausible and there *is* some supportive evidence, but the evidence is inconsistent and more research is needed (Gordon, 1990; Reuter-Lorenz & Miller, 1998). One key problem with this idea is that aspects of cognitive style have proven difficult to define and measure. For instance, there is de-

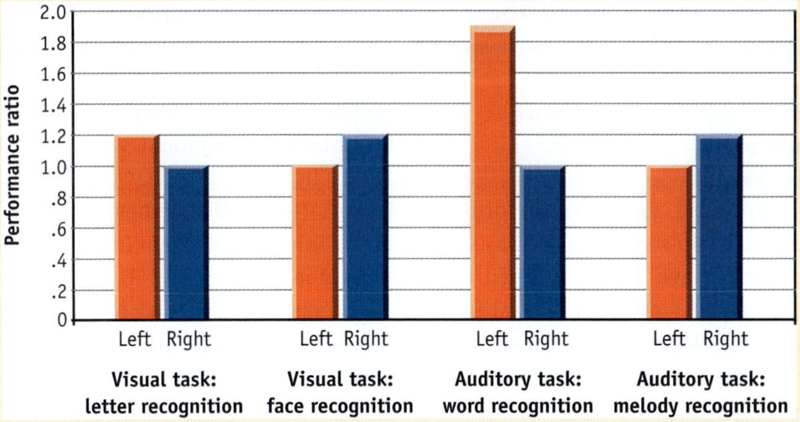

Figure 3.32

Relative superiority of one brain hemisphere over the other in studies of perceptual asymmetry. These performance ratios from a study by Doreen Kimura (1973) show the degree to which one hemisphere was "superior" to the other on each type of task in one study of normal participants. For example, the right hemisphere was 20% better than the left hemisphere in quickly recognizing melodic patterns (ratio 1.2 to 1). Most differences in the performance of the two hemispheres are quite small.

© Cengage Learning 2013

bate about the meaning of analytic versus synthetic thinking, or linear versus holistic thinking.

4. The evidence on the assertion that some people are left-brained while others are right-brained is inconclusive at best (Hellige, 1990). This notion has some plausibility—*if* it means only that some people consistently display more activation of one hemisphere than the other. However, researchers have yet to develop reliable measures of these possible "preferences" in cerebral activation. As a result, there are no empirical data linking brainedness to musical ability, occupational choice, or the like (Knecht et al., 2001; Springer & Deutsch, 1998).

In summary, the theories linking cerebral specialization to cognitive processes are highly speculative. There's nothing wrong with theoretical speculation. Unfortunately, the tentative, conjectural nature of these ideas about cerebral specialization has gotten lost in the popular book descriptions of research on the right and left hemispheres (Coren, 1992). Popular writers continue to churn out allegedly scientific books, applying brain lateralization concepts to a variety of new topics on which there often is little or no real evidence. Thus, one can find books on how to have right-brain sex (Wells, 1991), develop right-brain social skills (Snyder, 1989), become better organized by relying on the right hemisphere (Silber, 2004), and maximize one's leadership effectiveness by shifting between right- and left-brain modes of leadership (Décosterd, 2008). Cerebral specialization is an important and intriguing area of research. However, it is unrealistic to expect that the hemispheric divisions in the brain will provide a biological explanation for every dichotomy related to thinking.

Reality CHECK

Misconception

People are either left-brained or right-brained, and this disparity can predict their abilities and interests.

Reality

Pop psychology books with no scientific basis routinely discuss how being right-brained or left-brained ought to relate to personal talents and occupational choice. There is just one small problem. If you search the research literature, you'll find no studies that have addressed these issues.

REVIEW OF KEY LEARNING GOALS

3.25 It's widely believed that each cerebral hemisphere has its own stream of consciousness and mode of thinking, which are applied to specific types of cognitive tasks. It has also been suggested that people vary in their reliance on the right and left halves of the brain.

3.26 The cerebral hemispheres *are* specialized for handling different cognitive tasks, but only to a degree, as most tasks engage both hemispheres. Moreover, people vary in their patterns of hemispheric specialization. Evidence for duality in consciousness divided along hemispheric lines is weak. Evidence on whether people vary in brainedness and whether the two hemispheres vary in cognitive style is inconclusive. Popular ideas about the right and left brain have gone far beyond the actual research findings.

KEY LEARNING GOALS

3.27 Explain how neuroscience research has been overextrapolated to educational issues.

Building Better Brains: The Perils of Extrapolation

Summarizing the implications of research in neuroscience, science writer Ronald Kotulak (1996) concluded, "The first three years of a child's life are critically important to brain development" (pp. ix–x). Echoing this sentiment, the president of a U.S. educational commission asserted that "research in brain development suggests it is time to rethink many educational policies" (Bruer, 1999, p. 16). Based on findings in neuroscience, many states launched expensive programs in the 1990s intended to foster better neural development in infants. For example, the governor of Georgia at the time, Zell Miller, sought funding to distribute classical music tapes to the state's infants, saying, "No one doubts that listening to music, especially at a very early age, affects the spatial-temporal reasoning that underlies math, engineering, and chess" (Bruer, 1999, p. 62). Well-intended educational groups and Hollywood celebrities have argued for the creation of schools for infants on the grounds that enriched educational experiences during infancy will lead to enhanced neural development.

What are these practical, new discoveries about the brain that will permit parents and educators to optimize infants' brain development? Well, we'll discuss the pertinent research momentarily, but it's not as new or as practical as suggested in many quarters (Chance, 2001).

In recent years, many child-care advocates and educational reformers have used research in neuroscience as the rationale for the policies they have sought to promote. This strategy has led to the publication of numerous books on "brain-based learning" (see Jensen, 2000, 2006; Sousa, 2000; Sprenger, 2001; Zull, 2002) and the development of curricular programs that have been adopted at many schools (Goswami, 2006). The people advocating these ideas have good intentions, but the neuroscience rationale has been stretched to the breaking point. The result? An enlightening case study in overextending research findings.

The Key Findings on Neural Development

The education and child-care reformers who have used brain science as the basis for their campaigns have primarily cited two key findings: the discovery of critical periods in neural development and the demonstration that rats raised in "enriched environments" have more synapses than rats raised in "impoverished environments." Let's look at each of these findings.

A *critical period* is a limited time span in the development of an organism when it is optimal for certain capacities to emerge because the organism is especially responsive to certain experiences. The seminal research on critical periods in neural development was conducted by Torsten Wiesel and David Hubel (1963, 1965) in the 1960s. They showed that if an eye of a newborn kitten is sutured shut early in its development (typically the first 4 to 6 weeks), the kitten will become permanently blind in that eye. However, if the eye is covered for the same amount of time at later ages (after 4 months) blindness does not result. Such studies show that certain types of visual input are necessary during a critical period of development. Otherwise, neural pathways between the eye and brain will not form properly. Basically, what happens is that the inactive synapses from the closed eye are displaced by the active synapses from the open eye. Critical periods have been found for other aspects of neural development and in other species, but a great deal remains to be learned. Based on this type of research, some educational and child-care reformers have argued that the first three years of life are a critical period for human neural development.

The pioneering work on environment and brain development was begun in the 1960s by Mark Rosenzweig and his colleagues (1961, 1962). They raised some rats in an impoverished environment, (housed individually in small, barren cages) and other rats in an enriched environment (housed in groups of 10 to 12 in larger cages, with a variety of objects available for exploration), as shown in **Figure 3.33**. They found that the rats raised in the enriched environment performed better on problem-solving tasks than the impoverished rats and had slightly heavier brains and a thicker cerebral cortex in some areas of the brain. Subsequent research by William Greenough demonstrated that enriched environments resulted in heavier and thicker cortical areas by virtue of producing denser dendritic branching, more synaptic contacts, and richer neural networks (Greenough, 1975; Greenough & Volkmar, 1973). More recently, scientists have learned that enriched environments also promote the newly discovered process of *neurogenesis* in the brain (Nithianantharajah & Hannan, 2006). Based on this type of research, some child-care reformers have argued that human infants need to be brought up in enriched

Figure 3.33

Enriched environments in the study of rats' neural development. In the studies by Rosenzweig and colleagues (1961, 1962), rats housed in an impoverished environment were raised alone in small cages, whereas rats housed in enriched environments were raised in groups and were given playthings that were changed daily. Although the enriched conditions provided more stimulating environments than what laboratory rats normally experience, they may not be any more stimulating than rats' natural habitats. Thus, the "enriched" condition may reveal more about the importance of normal stimulation than about the benefits of extra stimulation (Gopnik, Meltzoff, & Kuhl, 1999).

© Cengage Learning 2013

environments during the critical period before age 3 to promote synapse formation and to optimize the development of their emerging neural circuits.

The findings on critical periods and the effects of enriched environments were genuine breakthroughs in neuroscience. However, except for the recent research on neurogenesis, they certainly aren't *new* findings, as suggested by various political action groups. Moreover, one can raise many doubts about whether this research can serve as a meaningful guide for decisions about day-care programs, educational policies, and welfare reform (Goswami, 2006; Thompson & Nelson, 2001).

The Tendency to Overextrapolate

Extrapolation occurs when an effect is estimated by extending beyond some known values or conditions. Extrapolation is a normal process, but some extrapolations are conservative, plausible projections drawn from directly relevant data, whereas others are wild leaps of speculation based on loosely related data. The extrapolations made regarding the educational implications of critical periods and environmental effects on synapse formation are highly conjectural *overextrapolations*. The studies that highlighted the possible importance of early experience in animals have all used extreme conditions to make their comparisons, such as depriving an animal of all visual input or raising it in stark isolation. Thus, so-called "enriched" environments probably resemble normal conditions in the real world, whereas the standard laboratory environment may reflect extreme environmental deprivation (Gould, 2004). In light of the findings, it seems plausible to speculate that children probably need normal stimulation to experience normal brain development. However, great difficulty arises when these findings are extended to conclude that adding *more* stimulation to a normal environment will be beneficial to brain development (Shatz, 1992).

The ease with which people fall into the trap of overextrapolating has been particularly apparent in recent recommendations that infants listen to classical music to enhance their brain development. These recommendations have been derived from a few studies that showed that college students' performance on spatial reasoning tasks was enhanced slightly for about 10–15 minutes after listening to a brief Mozart recording (Rauscher, Shaw, & Ky, 1993, 1995). This peculiar finding, dubbed the "Mozart effect," has proven difficult to replicate (Gray & Della Sala, 2007; Steele, 2003). But the pertinent point here is that there was no research on how classical music affects *infants,* no research relating classical music to *brain development,* and no research on anyone showing *lasting effects.* Nonetheless, many people (including the governor of Georgia) were quick to extrapolate the shaky findings on the Mozart effect to infants' brain development.

Ironically, there is much better evidence linking *musical training* to enhanced cognitive performance. Studies have found a thought-provoking association between measures of intelligence and the extent of individuals' exposure to music lessons (Schellenberg, 2004, 2005, 2006). Of course, if you think critically about this correlation, it might only mean that brighter youngsters are more likely to take music lessons (researchers are still working to sort it all out).

In any event, as noted in Chapter 1, thinking critically about issues often involves asking questions such as: What is missing from this debate? Is there any contradictory evidence? In the debate about brain-based learning, there is some contradictory evidence that's worthy of consideration. The basis for advocating infant educational programs is the belief that the brain is malleable during the hypothesized critical period of birth to age 3 but not at later ages. However, Greenough's work on synaptic formation and other lines of research suggest that the brain remains somewhat malleable throughout life, responding to stimulation into old age (Thompson & Nelson, 2001). Thus, advocates for the aged could just as readily argue for new educational initiatives for the elderly to help them maximize their intellectual potential.

Another problem is the implicit assumption that greater synaptic density is associated with greater intelligence. As noted in the main body of the chapter, there is evidence that infant animals and humans begin life with an overabundance of synaptic connections and that learning involves selective *pruning* of inactive synapses (Huttenlocher, 2003; Rakic, Bourgeois, & Goldman-Rakic, 1994). Thus, in the realm of synapses, more may *not* be better. In conclusion, there may be many valid reasons for increasing educational programs for infants, but research in neuroscience does not appear to provide a clear rationale for much in the way of specific infant-care policies (Bruer, 2002; Bruer & Greenough, 2001).

Reality CHECK

Misconception

Exposing infants and children to classical music can enhance their brain development and boost their intelligence.

Reality

If only it were that easy! The so-called Mozart effect has garnered a great deal of publicity, but the actual findings are utterly unimpressive. A recent meta-analysis of nearly 40 studies concluded that "there is little support for the Mozart effect" (Pietschnig, Voracek, & Formann, 2010). The typical dependent variable in these studies is a low-level spatial task (paper folding and cutting) that won't get anyone through college. When small, short-term positive effects are observed, they appear to be due to the fact that music can be arousing, not to any durable change in the architecture of the brain.

Table 3.3 Critical Thinking Skills Discussed in This Application

Skill	Description
Understanding the limits of extrapolation	The critical thinker appreciates that extrapolations are based on certain assumptions, vary in plausibility, and ultimately involve speculation.
Looking for contradictory evidence	In evaluating the evidence presented on an issue, the critical thinker attempts to look for contradictory evidence that may have been left out of the debate.

© Cengage Learning 2013

REVIEW OF KEY LEARNING GOALS

3.27 Some education and child-care reformers have used research in neuroscience as the basis for their campaigns. However, research has not demonstrated that birth to 3 is a critical period for human neural development or that specific enrichment programs can enhance brain development. These assertions are highly conjectural overextrapolations from existing data.

Chapter 3 Practice Test

1. A neural impulse is initiated when a neuron's charge momentarily becomes less negative, or even positive. This event is called:
   A. an action potential.
   B. a resting potential.
   C. impulse facilitation.
   D. inhibitory.

2. Neurons convey information about the strength of stimuli by varying:
   A. the size of their action potentials.
   B. the velocity of their action potentials.
   C. the rate at which they fire action potentials.
   D. all of the above.

3. Alterations in activity at dopamine synapses have been implicated in the development of:
   A. anxiety.
   B. schizophrenia.
   C. Alzheimer's disease.
   D. nicotine addiction.

4. Tania just barely avoided a head-on collision on a narrow road. With heart pounding, hands shaking, and body perspiring, Tania recognizes that these are signs of the body's fight-or-flight response, which is controlled by the:
   A. empathetic division of the peripheral nervous system.
   B. parasympathetic division of the autonomic nervous system.
   C. somatic division of the peripheral nervous system.
   D. sympathetic division of the autonomic nervous system.

5. The hindbrain consists of the:
   A. endocrine system and the limbic system.
   B. reticular formation.
   C. thalamus, hypothalamus, and cerebrum.
   D. cerebellum, medulla, and pons.

6. Juan is watching a basketball game. The neural impulses from his eyes will ultimately travel to his primary visual cortex, but first they must pass through the:
   A. amygdala.
   B. hypothalamus.
   C. thalamus.
   D. pons.

7. The _________ lobe is to hearing as the occipital lobe is to vision.
   A. frontal
   B. temporal
   C. parietal
   D. cerebellar

8. Paul has profound difficulty producing spoken language. If his problem is attributable to brain damage, the damage would probably be found in:
   A. the cerebellum.
   B. Sperry's area.
   C. Broca's area.
   D. Wernicke's area.

9. Sounds presented to the right ear are registered:
   A. only in the right hemisphere.
   B. only in the left hemisphere.
   C. more quickly in the right hemisphere.
   D. more quickly in the left hemisphere.

10. In people whose corpus callosums have not been severed, verbal stimuli are identified more quickly and more accurately:
    A. when sent to the right hemisphere first.
    B. when sent to the left hemisphere first.
    C. when presented to the left visual field.
    D. when presented auditorally rather than visually.

11. Hormones are to the endocrine system as _________________ are to the nervous system.
    A. nerves
    B. synapses
    C. neurotransmitters
    D. action potentials

12. Jenny has brown hair and blue eyes and is 5′8″ tall. What is being described is Jenny's:
    A. genotype.
    B. phenotype.
    C. somatotype.
    D. physique.

13. Adopted children's similarity to their biological parents is generally attributed to _____________; adopted children's similarity to their adoptive parents is generally attributed to _____________.
    A. heredity; the environment
    B. the environment; heredity
    C. the environment; the environment
    D. heredity; heredity

14. In evolutionary theory, ____________ refers to the reproductive success of an individual organism relative to the average reproductive success in the population.
    A. natural selection
    B. gene flow
    C. adaptation
    D. fitness

15. For which of the following assertions is the empirical evidence strongest?
    A. The two cerebral hemispheres are specialized to handle different types of cognitive tasks.
    B. People have a separate stream of consciousness in each hemisphere.
    C. Each hemisphere has its own cognitive style.
    D. Some people are right-brained, while others are left-brained.

Answers

1 A pp. 82–83	6 C p. 100	11 C pp. 108–109
2 C p. 83	7 B pp. 101–103	12 B p. 112
3 B pp. 87–88	8 C p. 105	13 A p. 114
4 D p. 91	9 D p. 106	14 D p. 117
5 D pp. 90, 98	10 B p. 108	15 A pp. 122–123

Chapter 3 Media Resources

PsykTrek

To view a demo: **www.cengage.com/psychology/psyktrek**
To order: **www.cengage.com/psychology/weiten**

Go to the PsykTrek website or CD-ROM for further study of the concepts in this chapter. Both online and on the CD-ROM, PsykTrek includes dozens of learning modules with videos, animations, and quizzes, as well as simulations of psychological phenomena and a multimedia glossary that includes word pronunciations.

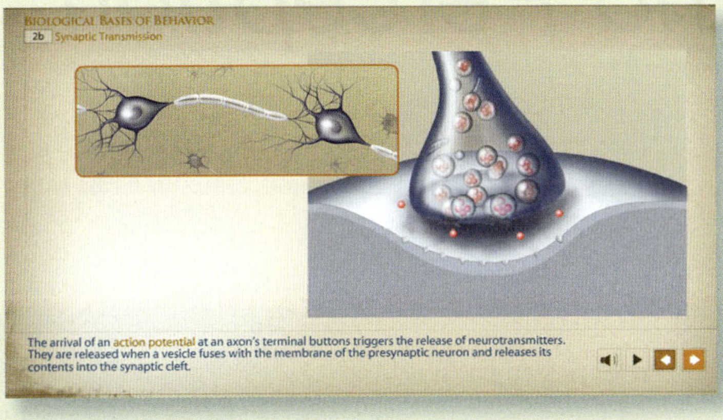

© Cengage Learning 2008

Visit Module 2b (*Synaptic Transmission*) to see animations of various aspects of the neural impulse.

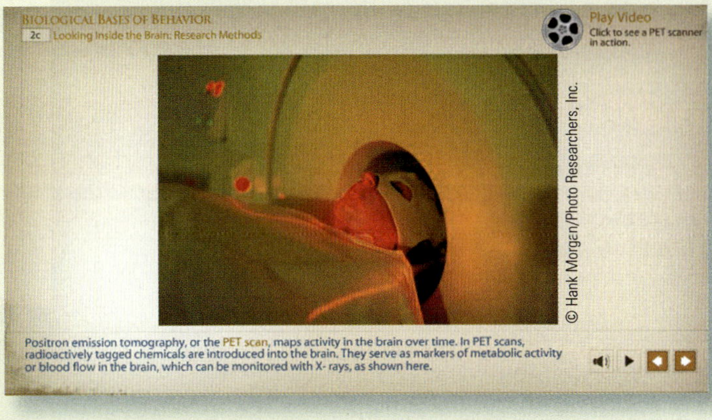

© Cengage Learning 2008

Go to Module 2c (*Looking Inside the Brain: Research Methods*) to learn how electrical stimulation, lesioning, CT scans, PET scans, and MRI scans are used to investigate brain function.

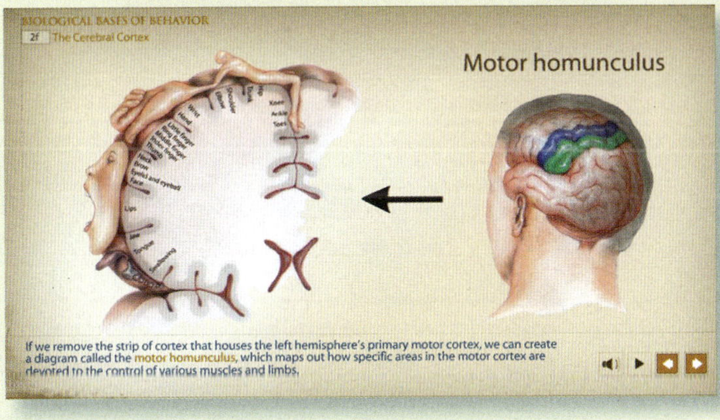

© Cengage Learning 2008

Explore Modules 2d (*The Hindbrain and Midbrain*), 2e (*The Forebrain: Subcortical Structures*), and 2f (*The Cerebral Cortex*) for detailed tours of how various areas of the brain are related to behavior.

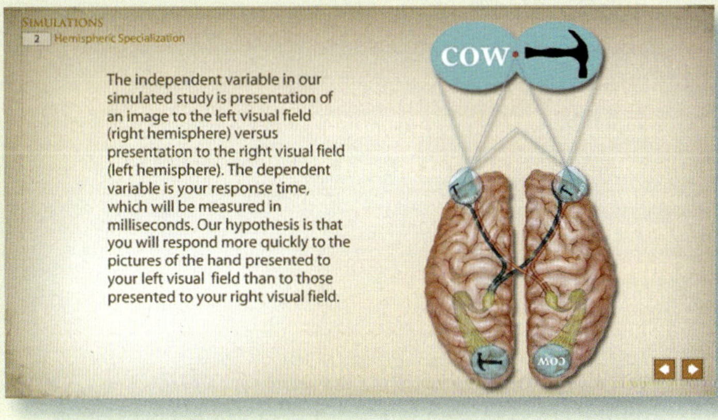

© Cengage Learning 2008

Go to Simulation 2 (*Hemispheric Specialization*) to participate in an experiment on the abilities of your right brain versus your left brain.

Online Study Tools

Log in to **CengageBrain** to access the resources your instructor requires. For this book, you can access:

CourseMate brings course concepts to life with interactive learning, study, and exam preparation tools that support the printed textbook. A textbook-specific website, Psychology CourseMate includes an integrated interactive eBook and other interactive learning tools such as quizzes, flashcards, videos, and more.

CengageNow is an easy-to-use online resource that helps you study in less time to get the grade you want—NOW. Take a pre-test for this chapter and receive a personalized study plan based on your results that will identify the topics you need to review and direct you to online resources to help you master those topics. Then take a post-test to help you determine the concepts you have mastered and what you will need to work on. If your textbook does not include an access code card, go to CengageBrain.com to gain access.

WebTutor is more than just an interactive study guide. WebTutor is an anytime, anywhere customized learning solution with an eBook, keeping you connected to your textbook, instructor, and classmates.

Aplia. If your professor has assigned Aplia homework:

1. Sign in to your account
2. Complete the corresponding homework exercises as required by your professor.
3. When finished, click "Grade It Now" to see which areas you have mastered, which need more work, and detailed explanations of every answer.

Visit **www.cengagebrain.com** to access your account and purchase materials.

4

Sensation and Perception

© Ocean/Corbis

Take a look at the adjacent photo. What do you see? You probably answered, "a rose" or "a flower." But is that what you really see? No, this isn't a trick question. Let's examine the odd case of "Dr. P." It shows that there's more to seeing than meets the eye.

Dr. P was an intelligent and distinguished music professor who began to exhibit some worrisome behaviors that seemed to be related to his vision. Sometimes he failed to recognize familiar students by sight, although he knew them instantly by the sound of their voices. Sometimes he acted as if he saw faces in inanimate objects, cordially greeting fire hydrants and parking meters as if they were children. On one occasion, reaching for what he thought was his hat, he took hold of his wife's head and tried to put it on! Except for these kinds of visual mistakes, Dr. P was a normal, talented man.

Ultimately Dr. P was referred to Oliver Sacks, a neurologist, for an examination. During one visit, Sacks handed Dr. P a fresh red rose to see whether he would recognize it. Dr. P took the rose as if he were being given a model of a geometric object rather than a flower. "About six inches in length," Dr. P observed, "a convoluted red form with a linear green attachment."

"Yes," Sacks persisted, "and what do you think it is, Dr. P?"

"Not easy to say," the patient replied. "It lacks the simple symmetry of the Platonic solids . . ."

"Smell it," the neurologist suggested. Dr. P looked perplexed, as if being asked to smell symmetry, but he complied and brought the flower to his nose. Suddenly, his confusion cleared up. "Beautiful. An early rose. What a heavenly smell" (Sacks, 1987, pp. 13–14).

What accounted for Dr. P's strange inability to recognize faces and familiar objects by sight? There was nothing wrong with his eyes. He could readily spot a pin on the floor. And it's not as if his

rather than the *constants* in their sensory input. It allows people to ignore the obvious. After all, you don't need constant confirmation that your clothes are still on. But, like most organisms, people are interested in changes in their environment that may signal threats to safety. Thus, as its name suggests, sensory adaptation probably is a behavioral adaptation that has been sculpted by natural selection (McBurney, 2010). Sensory adaptation also shows once again that there is no one-to-one correspondence between sensory input and sensory experience.

The psychophysics concepts covered so far show that there is a complex relationship between the world outside and people's perceived experience of it.

© Len Green/Shutterstock

Because of sensory adaptation, people who live near foul-smelling industrial plants tend to grow accustomed to the stench in the air, whereas visitors may initially be overwhelmed by the same odors.

As we review each of the principal sensory systems in detail, we'll see repeatedly that people's experience of the world depends on both the physical stimuli they encounter and their active processing of stimulus inputs. We begin our exploration of the senses with vision—the sense that most people think of as nearly synonymous with a direct perception of reality. The case is actually quite different, as you'll see.

REVIEW OF KEY LEARNING GOALS

4.1 Psychophysicists use a variety of methods to relate sensory inputs to subjective perception. They have found that absolute thresholds are not really absolute. The size of a just noticeable difference tends to be a constant proportion of the size of the initial stimulus.

4.2 According to signal-detection theory, the detection of sensory inputs is influenced by "noise" in the system and by decision-making strategies. Signal-detection theory replaces Fechner's sharp threshold with the concept of detectability and emphasizes that factors besides stimulus intensity influence detectability.

4.3 In recent years, a number of researchers have demonstrated that perception can occur without awareness. However, research indicates that the effects of subliminal perception are relatively weak and probably of little practical concern.

4.4 Prolonged stimulation may lead to sensory adaptation, which involves a reduction in sensitivity to constant stimulation. Sensory adaptation keeps people tuned in to the changes rather than the constants in their sensory input.

KEY LEARNING GOALS

4.5 List the three properties of light and the aspects of visual perception that they influence.

4.6 Describe the role of the lens and pupil in the functioning of the eye.

4.7 Explain how the retina contributes to visual information processing.

4.8 Trace the routing of signals from the eye to the brain, and explain the brain's role in visual information processing.

4.9 Distinguish two types of color mixing, compare the chief theories of color vision, and describe research on how color can influence psychological functioning.

The Visual System: Essentials of Sight

"Seeing is believing"; good ideas are "bright"; a good explanation is "illuminating." As these common expressions show, humans are visual animals. People rely heavily on their sense of sight, and they equate it with what is trustworthy (seeing is believing). Although it's taken for granted, you'll see (there it is again) that the human visual system is amazingly complex. Furthermore, as in all sensory domains, what people "sense" and what they "perceive" may be quite different. In this section, we'll focus on basic sensory processes in the visual system; in the following section, we'll look at higher-level perceptual processes in vision.

The Stimulus: Light

PSYKTREK 3a

For people to see, there must be light. *Light* is a form of electromagnetic radiation that travels as a wave, moving, naturally enough, at the speed of light. As **Figure 4.5(a)** shows, light waves vary in *amplitude* (height) and in *wavelength* (the distance between peaks). Amplitude affects mainly the perception of brightness, while wavelength affects mainly the perception of color. The lights humans normally see are mixtures of several wavelengths. Thus, light can also vary in its *purity* (how varied the mix is). Purity influences perception of the saturation, or richness, of colors. *Saturation* refers to the relative amount of whiteness in a color. The less whiteness seen in a color, the more saturated it is (see **Figure 4.6**). Of course, most objects do not emit light, they reflect it (the sun, lamps, and fireflies being some exceptions).

What most people call light includes only the wavelengths that humans can see. But as **Figure 4.5(c)** shows, the visible spectrum is only a slim portion of the total range of wavelengths. Vision is a filter that permits people to sense but a fraction of the real world. Other animals have different capabilities and so live in a quite different visual world. For

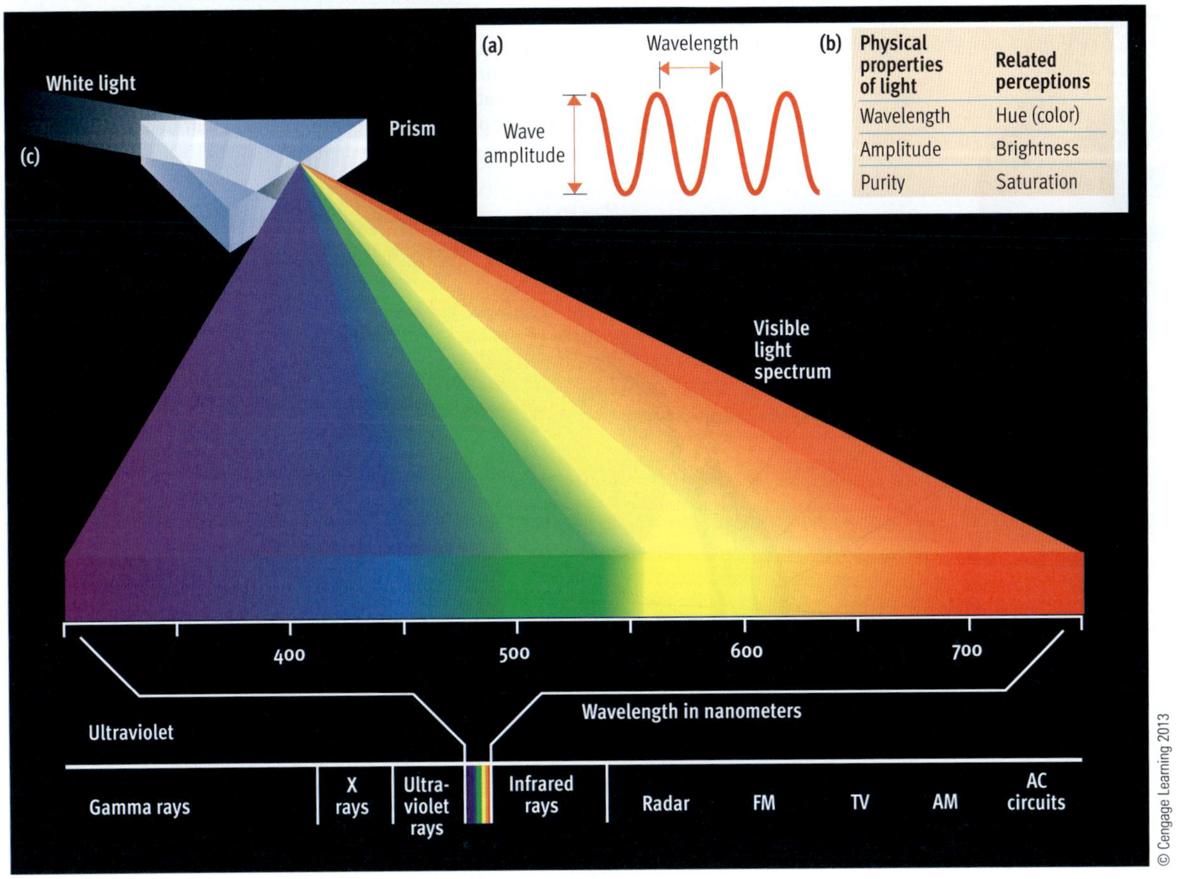

Figure 4.5

Light, the physical stimulus for vision. **(a)** Light waves vary in amplitude and wavelength. **(b)** Within the spectrum of visible light, amplitude (corresponding to physical intensity) affects mainly the experience of brightness. Wavelength affects mainly the experience of color, and purity is the key determinant of saturation. **(c)** If white light (such as sunlight) passes through a prism, the prism separates the light into its component wavelengths, creating a rainbow of colors. However, visible light is only the narrow band of wavelengths to which human eyes happen to be sensitive.

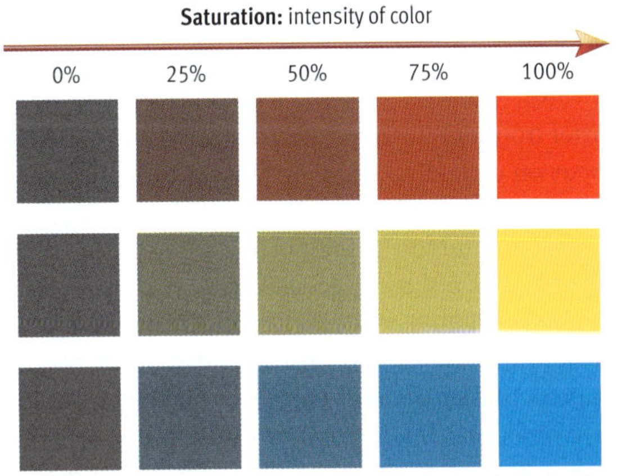

Figure 4.6

Saturation. Saturation refers to the amount of whiteness in a color. As you can see in these two examples, as the amount of whiteness declines (moving to the right), the saturation or richness of a color increases. © Cengage Learning 2013

example, many insects can see shorter wavelengths than humans, in the *ultraviolet* spectrum, whereas many fish and reptiles can see longer wavelengths, in the *infrared* spectrum. Although the sense of sight depends on light waves, for people to *see,* incoming visual input must be converted into neural impulses that are sent to the brain. Let's investigate how this transformation is accomplished.

The Eye: A Living Optical Instrument

PSYKTREK 3a

The eyes serve two main purposes: They channel light to the neural tissue that receives it, called the *retina,* and they house that tissue. The structure of the eye is shown in **Figure 4.7** on the next page. Each eye is a living optical instrument that creates an image of the visual world on the light-sensitive retina lining its inside back surface.

Light enters the eye through a transparent "window" at the front, the *cornea.* The cornea and the crystalline *lens,* located behind it, form an upside-down image of objects on the retina. The brain corrects the image, knowing the rule for relating positions on the retina to the corresponding positions in the world.

The *lens* is the transparent eye structure that focuses the light rays falling on the retina. The lens is made up of relatively soft tissue, capable of adjustments that facilitate a process called accommodation. *Accommodation* occurs when the curvature of the lens adjusts to alter visual focus. When you focus on a close object, the lens of your eye gets

Figure 4.7

The human eye. Light passes through the cornea, pupil, and lens and falls on the light-sensitive surface of the retina, where images of objects are reflected upside down. The lens adjusts its curvature to focus the images falling on the retina. The iris and pupil regulate the amount of light passing into the rear chamber of the eye. © Cengage Learning 2013

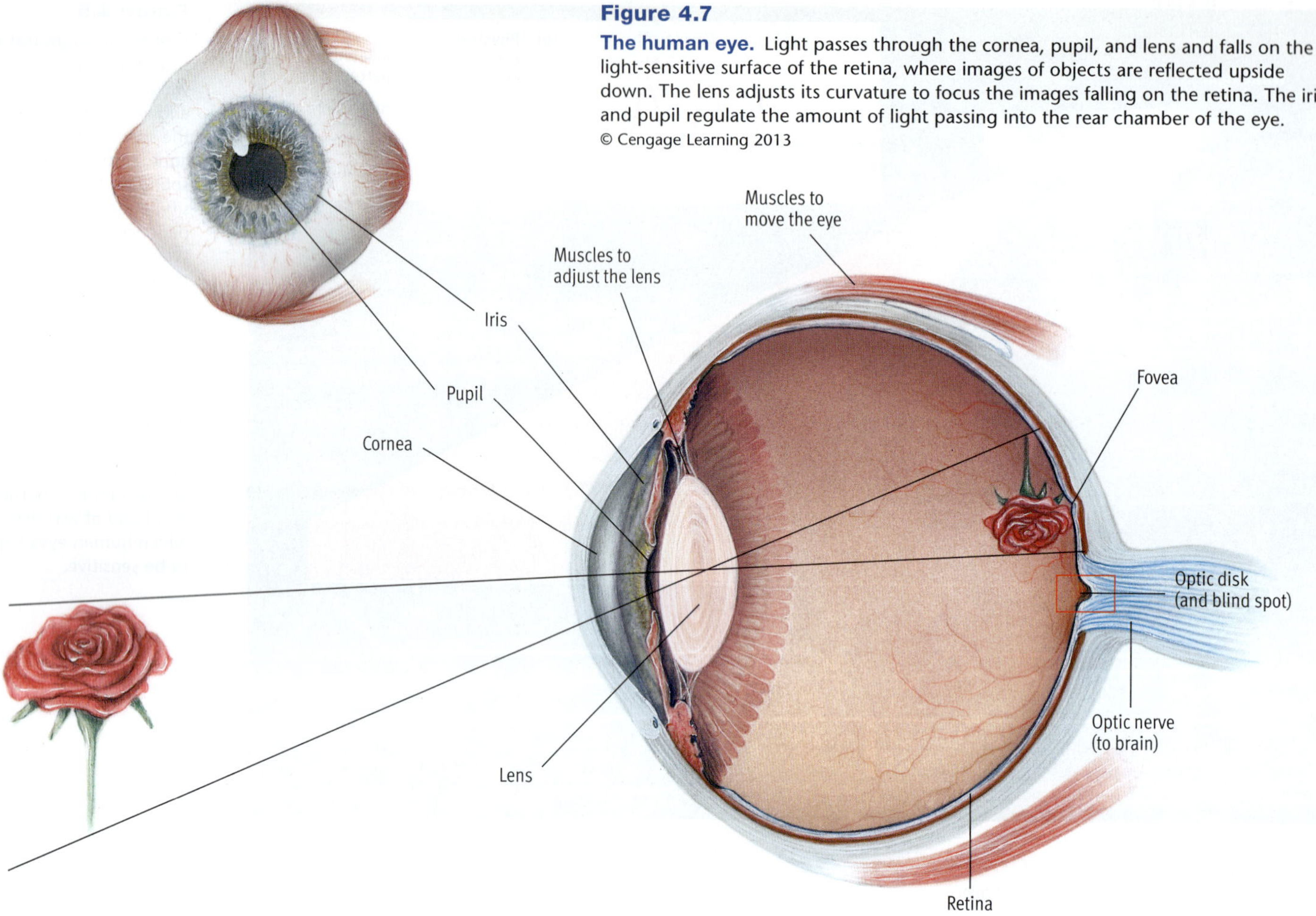

fatter (rounder) to give you a clear image. When you focus on distant objects, the lens flattens out to give you a better image.

Some common visual deficiencies are attributable to light not being focused clearly on the retina (Oyster, 1999). For example, **in *nearsightedness,* close objects are seen clearly but distant objects appear blurry** because the focus of light from distant objects falls a little short of the retina (see **Figure 4.8**). This problem occurs when the cornea or lens bends light too much, or when the eyeball is too long. **In *farsightedness,* distant objects are seen clearly but close objects appear blurry** because the focus of light from close objects falls behind the retina (see **Figure 4.8**). This problem typically occurs when the eyeball is too short.

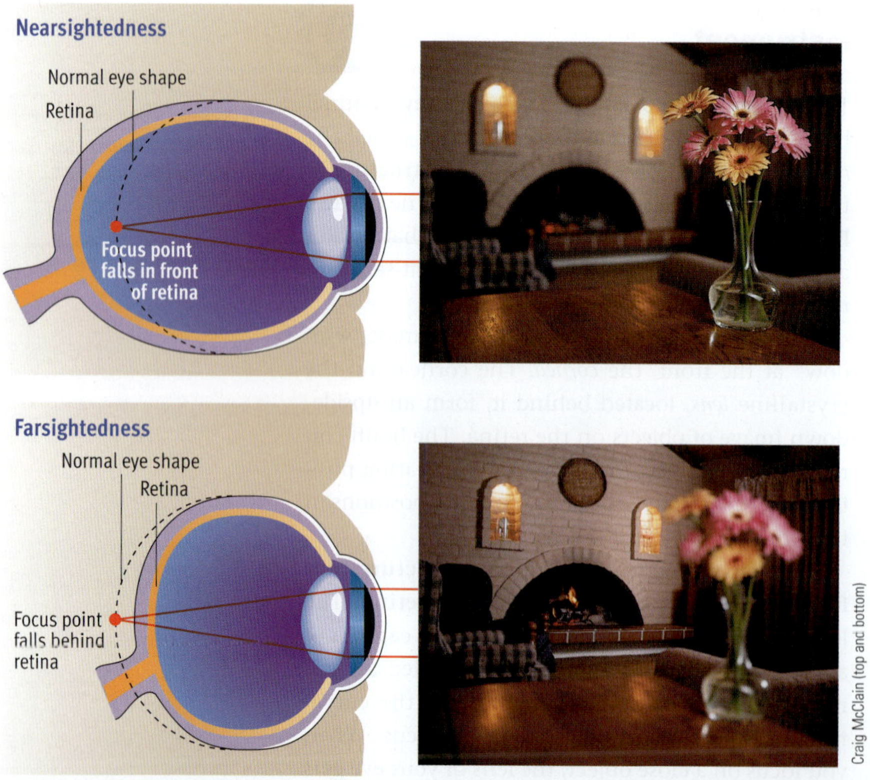

Figure 4.8

Nearsightedness and farsightedness. The pictures shown here simulate how a scene might look to nearsighted and farsighted people. Nearsightedness occurs because light from distant objects focuses in front of the retina. Farsightedness is due to the opposite situation—light from close objects focuses behind the retina. © Cengage Learning 2013

The eye can make adjustments to alter the amount of light reaching the retina. The *iris*—the colored ring of muscle surrounding the *pupil*—regulates the amount of light entering the eye because it controls the size of the pupil. **The *pupil* is the opening in the center of the iris that permits light to pass into the rear chamber of the eye.** When the pupils are constricted, they let less light into the eye, but they sharpen the image falling on the retina. When the pupils are dilated (opened more), they let more light in, but the image is less sharp. In bright light, the pupils constrict to take advantage of the sharpened image, but in dim light, the pupils dilate; image sharpness is sacrificed to allow more light to fall on the retina so that more remains visible.

The Retina: The Brain's Ambassador in the Eye

PSYKTREK 3b

The *retina* is the neural tissue lining the inside back surface of the eye; it absorbs light, processes images, and sends visual information to the brain. You may be surprised to learn that the retina *processes* images. But it's actually a piece of the central nervous system that happens to be located in the eyeball. Much as the spinal cord is a complicated extension of the brain, the retina is the brain's ambassador in the eye. About half as thick as a credit card, this thin sheet of neural tissue contains a complex network of specialized cells arranged in layers (Rodieck, 1998), as shown in **Figure 4.9**.

Reality CHECK

Misconception

Sitting too close to the TV/reading in the dark/spending too much time in front of a computer screen will damage your vision.

Reality

These activities may make your eyes feel tired or strained, but there is no evidence that they can damage your eyes or lead to any permanent changes in vision.

The axons that run from the retina to the brain converge at the ***optic disk*, a hole in the retina where the optic nerve fibers exit the eye.** Because the optic disk is a *hole* in the retina, you cannot see the part of an image that falls on it. It is therefore known as the *blind spot*. You may not be aware that you have a blind spot in each eye, as each normally compensates for the blind spot of the other.

Visual Receptors: Rods and Cones

PSYKTREK 3b

The retina contains millions of receptor cells that are sensitive to light. Surprisingly, these receptors are located in the innermost layer of the retina. Hence, light must pass through several layers of cells before it gets to the receptors that actually detect it. Interestingly, only about 10% of the light arriving at the cornea reaches these receptors (Leibovic, 1990). The retina contains two types of receptors, *rods* and *cones*. Their names are based on their shapes, as rods are elongated and cones are stubbier. Rods outnumber cones by a huge margin, as humans have

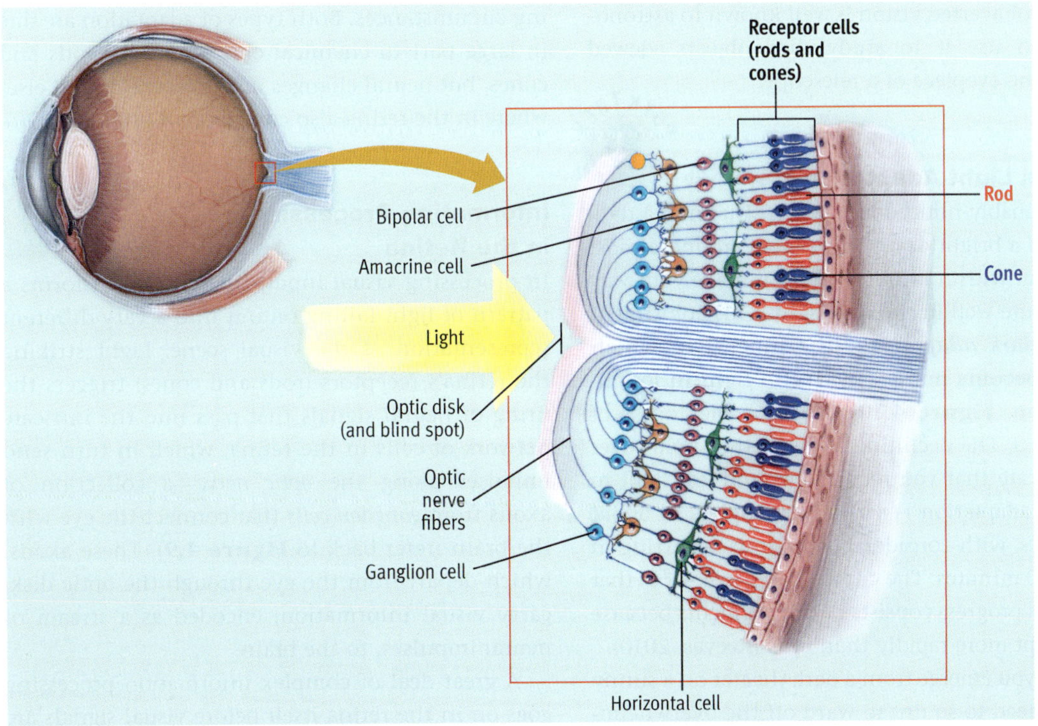

© Cengage Learning 2013

Figure 4.9

The retina. The close-up shows the several layers of cells in the retina. The cells closest to the back of the eye (the rods and cones) are the receptor cells that actually detect light. The intervening layers of cells receive signals from the rods and cones and form circuits that begin the process of analyzing incoming information. The visual signals eventually converge into *ganglion cells*, whose axons form the optic fibers that make up the optic nerve. These optic fibers all head toward the "hole" in the retina where the optic nerve leaves the eye—the point known as the optic disk (which corresponds to the blind spot).

100–125 million rods but only 5–6.4 million cones (Frishman, 2001).

***Cones* are specialized visual receptors that play a key role in daylight vision and color vision.** The cones handle most of people's daytime vision because bright lights dazzle the rods. The special sensitivities of cones also allow them to play a major role in the perception of color. However, cones do not respond well to dim light, which is why you don't see color very well in low illumination. Nonetheless, cones provide better *visual acuity*—that is, sharpness and precise detail—than rods. Cones are concentrated most heavily in the center of the retina and quickly fall off in density toward its periphery. **The *fovea* is a tiny spot in the center of the retina that contains only cones; visual acuity is greatest at this spot.** When you want to see something sharply, you usually move your eyes so the object is centered in the fovea.

***Rods* are specialized visual receptors that play a key role in night vision and peripheral vision.** Rods handle night vision because they are up to 100 times more sensitive than cones to dim light (Kefalov, 2010). They also handle the lion's share of peripheral vision, as they greatly outnumber cones in the periphery of the retina. The density of the rods is greatest just outside the fovea and gradually decreases toward the periphery of the retina. Because of the distribution of rods, when you want to see a faintly illuminated object in the dark, it's best to look slightly above or below the place it should be. Averting your gaze this way moves the image from the cone-filled fovea, which requires more light, to the rod-dominated area just outside the fovea, which requires less light. This trick of averted vision is well known to astronomers, who use it to study dim objects viewed through the eyepiece of a telescope.

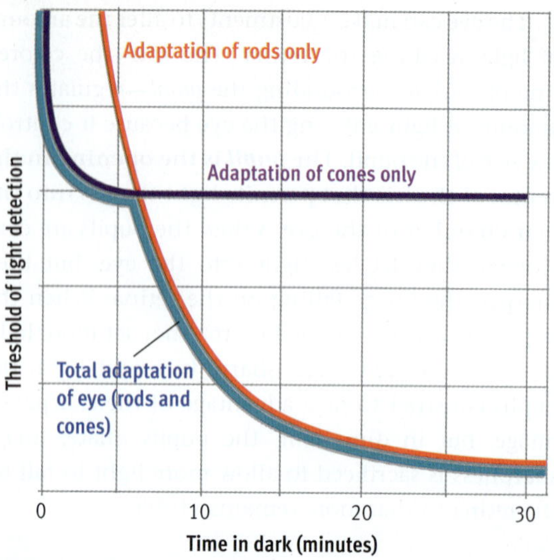

Figure 4.10

The process of dark adaptation. The declining thresholds over time indicate that your visual sensitivity is improving, as less and less light is required to see. Visual sensitivity improves markedly during the first 5 to 10 minutes after entering a dark room, as the eye's bright-light receptors (the cones) rapidly adapt to low light levels. However, the cones' adaptation, which is plotted in purple, soon reaches its limit, and further improvement comes from the rods' adaptation, which is plotted in red. The rods adapt more slowly than the cones, but they are capable of far greater visual sensitivity in low levels of light. © Cengage Learning 2013

Dark and Light Adaptation

PSYKTREK 3b

You've probably noticed that when you enter a dark theater on a bright day, you stumble around almost blindly. But within minutes you can make your way around quite well in the dim light. This adjustment is called ***dark adaptation*—the process in which the eyes become more sensitive to light in low illumination. Figure 4.10** maps out the course of this process. The declining absolute thresholds over time indicate that you require less and less light to see. Dark adaptation is virtually complete in about 30 minutes, with considerable progress occurring in the first 10 minutes. The curve (in **Figure 4.10**) that charts this progress consists of two segments because cones adapt more rapidly than rods (Reeves, 2010).

When you emerge from a dark theater on a sunny day, you need to squint to ward off the overwhelming brightness, and the reverse of dark adaptation occurs. ***Light adaptation* is the process whereby the eyes become less sensitive to light in high illumination.** As with dark adaptation, light adaptation improves your visual acuity under the prevailing circumstances. Both types of adaptation are due in large part to chemical changes in the rods and cones, but neural changes in the receptors and elsewhere in the retina also contribute (Frumkes, 1990).

Information Processing in the Retina

PSYKTREK 3b

In processing visual input, the retina transforms a pattern of light falling onto it into a very different representation of the visual scene. Light striking the retina's receptors (rods and cones) triggers the firing of neural signals that pass into the intricate network of cells in the retina, which in turn send impulses along the *optic nerve*—a collection of axons from *ganglion cells* that connect the eye with the brain (refer back to **Figure 4.9**). These axons, which depart from the eye through the optic disk, carry visual information, encoded as a stream of neural impulses, to the brain.

A great deal of complex information processing goes on in the retina itself before visual signals are sent to the brain. Ultimately, the information from over 100 million rods and cones converges to travel along 1 million axons in the optic nerve (Slaughter, 1990). Rod and cone receptors funnel signals to a particular visual cell in the retina that make up that cell's *receptive field*. Thus, **the *receptive field* of a visual cell is the retinal area that, when stimulated, affects the firing of that cell.**

Receptive fields in the retina come in a variety of shapes and sizes. Particularly common are circular fields with a center-surround arrangement (Levitt, 2010). In these receptive fields, light falling in the center has the opposite effect of light falling in the surrounding area (see **Figure 4.11**). For example, the rate of firing of a visual cell might be *increased* by light in the *center* of its receptive field and *decreased* by light in the *surrounding area,* as **Figure 4.11** shows. Other visual cells may work in just the opposite way. Either way, when receptive fields are stimulated, retinal cells send signals both toward the brain and *laterally* (sideways) toward nearby visual cells. These lateral signals allow visual cells in the retina to have interactive effects on each other.

Vision and the Brain

3c

Light falls on the eye, but you see with your brain. Although the retina does an unusual amount of information processing for a sensory organ, visual input is meaningless until it's processed in the brain.

CONCEPT CHECK 4.1

Understanding Sensory Processes in the Retina

Check your understanding of sensory receptors in the retina by completing the following exercises. Consult Appendix A for the answers.

The receptors for vision are rods and cones in the retina. These two types of receptors have many important differences, which are compared systematically in the chart below. Fill in the missing information to finish the chart.

Dimension	Rods	Cones
Physical shape	*Elongated*	
Number in the retina		*5–6.4 million*
Area of the retina in which they are dominant receptor	*Periphery*	
Critical to color vision		
Critical to peripheral vision		*No*
Sensitivity to dim light	*Strong*	
Speed of dark adaptation		*Rapid*

Visual Pathways to the Brain

3c

How does visual information get to the brain? Axons from ganglion cells leaving the back of each eye form the optic nerves, which travel to the ***optic chiasm*—the point at which the optic nerves from the inside half of each eye cross over and then project to the opposite half of the brain.** This arrangement ensures that signals from both eyes go to both hemispheres of

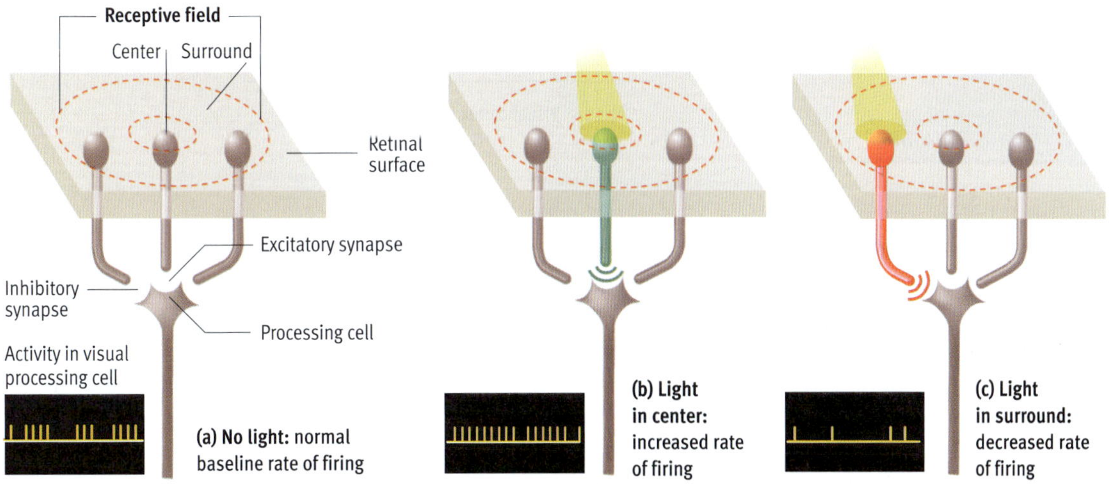

Figure 4.11

Receptive fields in the retina. Visual cells' receptive fields—made up of rods and cones in the retina—are often circular with a center-surround arrangement **(a)**, so that light striking the center of the field produces the opposite result of light striking the surround. In the receptive field depicted here, light in the center produces excitatory effects (symbolized by green at the synapse) and increased firing in the visual cell **(b)**, whereas light in the surround produces inhibitory effects (symbolized by red at the synapse) and decreased firing **(c)**. Interestingly, no light in the receptive field and light in both center and surround produce similar baseline rates of firing. This arrangement makes the visual cell particularly sensitive to *contrast,* which facilitates the extremely important task of recognizing the *edges* of objects. © Cengage Learning 2013

Figure 4.12

Visual pathways through the brain. **(a)** Input from the right half of the visual field strikes the left side of each retina and is transmitted to the left hemisphere (shown in blue). Input from the left half of the visual field strikes the right side of each retina and is transmitted to the right hemisphere (shown in red). The nerve fibers from each eye meet at the optic chiasm, where fibers from the inside half of each retina cross over to the opposite side of the brain. After reaching the optic chiasm, the major visual pathway projects through the lateral geniculate nucleus (LGN) in the thalamus and onto the primary visual cortex (shown with solid lines). A second pathway detours through the superior colliculus and then projects through the thalamus and onto the primary visual cortex (shown with dotted lines). **(b)** This inset shows a vertical view of how the optic pathways project through the thalamus and onto the visual cortex in the back of the brain [the two pathways mapped out in diagram **(a)** are virtually indistinguishable from this angle].

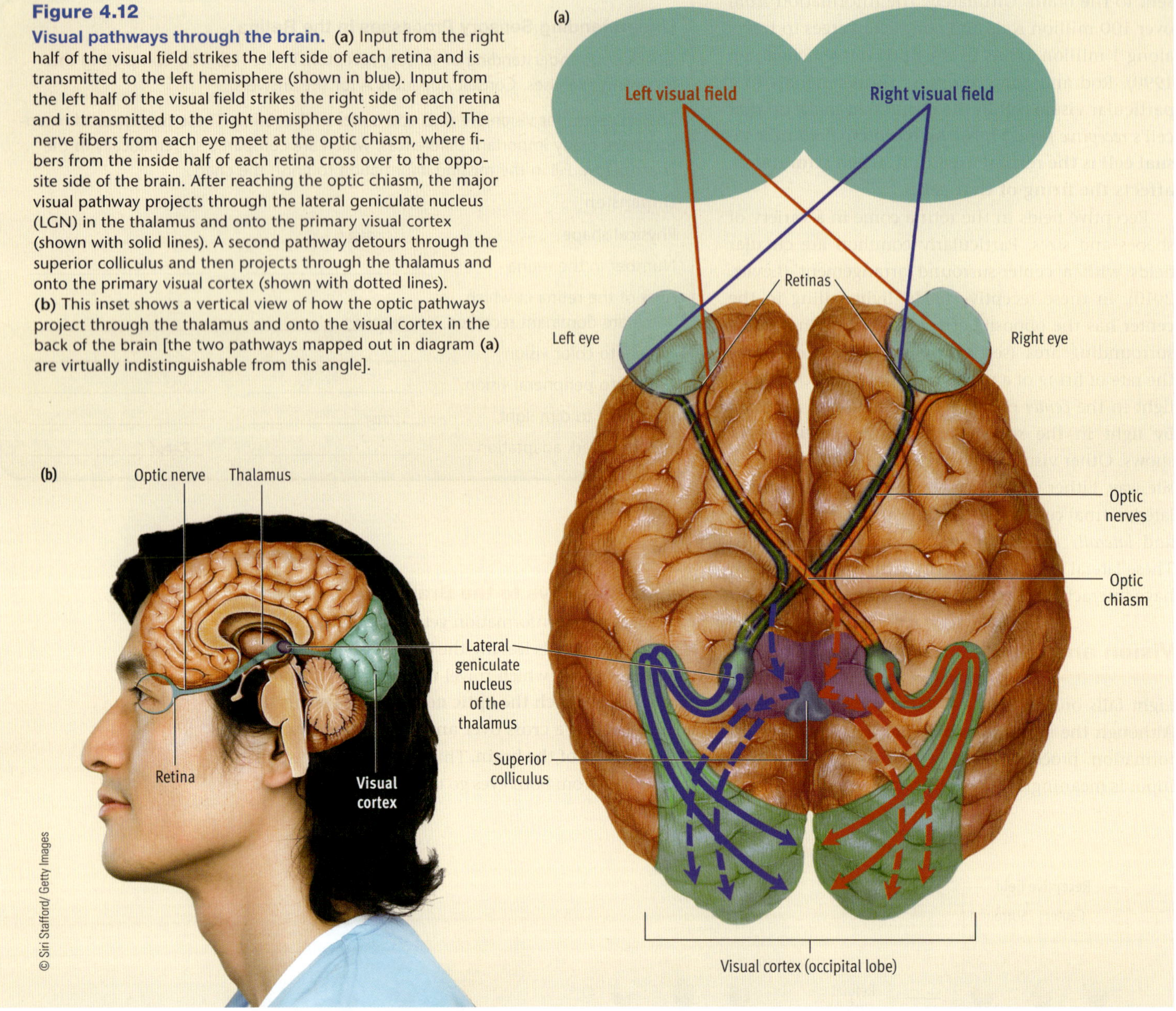

© Siri Stafford/ Getty Images

© Cengage Learning 2013

the brain. Thus, as **Figure 4.12** shows, axons from the left half of each retina carry signals to the left side of the brain, and axons from the right half of each retina carry information to the right side of the brain.

After reaching the optic chiasm, the optic nerve fibers diverge along two pathways. The main pathway, which handles the perception of color, form, contrast, and motion, projects into the thalamus, the brain's major relay station. Here, about 90% of the axons from the retinas connect to synapses in the *lateral geniculate nucleus* (LGN) (Pasternak, Bisley, & Calkins, 2003). Visual signals are processed in the LGN and then distributed to areas in the occipital lobe that make up the *primary visual cortex* (see **Figure 4.12**). The second visual pathway leaving the optic chiasm branches off to an area in the midbrain called the *superior colliculus* before traveling through the thalamus and on to the occipital lobe. The principal function of the second pathway appears to be the perception of motion and the coordination of visual input with other sensory input (Casanova et al., 2001; Stein & Meredith, 1993).

Information Processing in the Visual Cortex

PsykTrek 3c

Most visual input eventually arrives in the primary visual cortex in the occipital lobe. Explaining how the cortical cells in this area respond to light used to pose a perplexing problem. Researchers investigating the

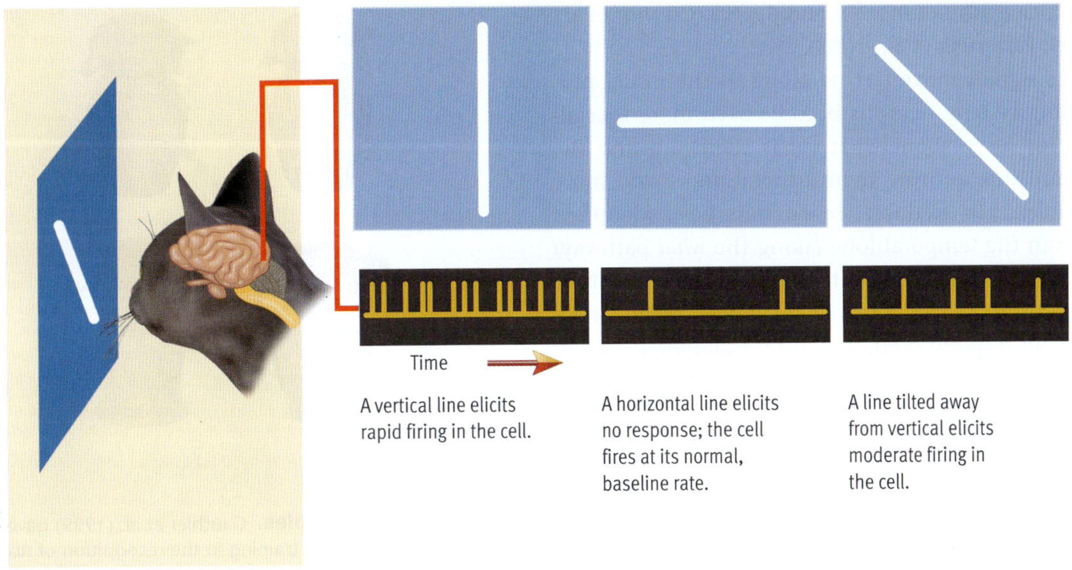

© Cengage Learning 2013

Courtesy of David Hubel

David Hubel

"One can now begin to grasp the significance of the great number of cells in the visual cortex. Each cell seems to have its own specific duties."

Figure 4.13

Hubel and Wiesel's procedure for studying the activity of neurons in the visual cortex. As the cat is shown various stimuli, a microelectrode records the firing of a neuron in the cat's visual cortex. The figure shows the electrical responses of a visual cell apparently "programmed" to respond to lines oriented vertically.

question placed microelectrodes in the primary visual cortex of animals to record action potentials from individual cells. They would flash spots of light in the retinal receptive fields that the cells were thought to monitor, but there was rarely any response.

According to David Hubel and Torsten Wiesel (1962, 1963), they discovered the solution to this mystery quite by accident. One of the projector slides they used to present a spot to a cat had a crack in it. The spot elicited no response, but when they removed the slide, the crack moved through the cell's receptive field, and the cell fired like crazy in response to the moving dark line. It turns out that individual cells in the primary visual cortex don't really respond much to little spots—they are much more sensitive to lines, edges, and other more complicated stimuli. Armed with new slides, Hubel and Wiesel embarked on years of painstaking study of the visual cortex (see **Figure 4.13**). Their work eventually earned them a Nobel prize in 1981.

Hubel and Wiesel (1979, 1998, 2005) identified various types of specialized cells in the primary visual cortex that respond to different stimuli. For example, *simple cells* respond best to a line of the correct width, oriented at the correct angle, and located in the correct position in its receptive field. *Complex cells* also care about width and orientation, but they respond to any position in their receptive fields. The key point of all this is that the cells in the visual cortex seem to be highly specialized. They have been characterized as ***feature detectors,* neurons that respond selectively to very specific features of more complex stimuli.** According to some theorists, most visual stimuli could ultimately be represented by combinations of lines such as those registered by these feature detectors (Maguire, Weisstein, & Klymenko, 1990).

After visual input is processed in the primary visual cortex, it's often routed to other cortical areas for additional processing. These signals travel through two streams that have sometimes been characterized as the *what* and *where pathways* (see **Figure 4.14**). The *ventral stream* processes the details of *what* objects are out there (the perception of form and color), while the *dorsal stream* processes *where* the objects are

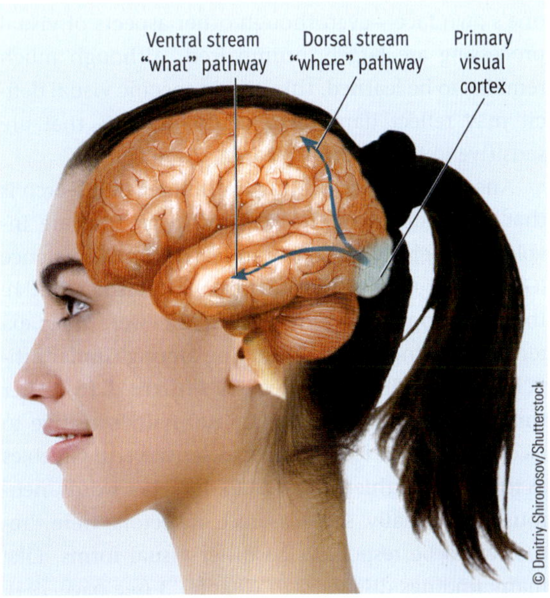

© Dmitriy Shironosov/Shutterstock

Figure 4.14

The *what* and *where* pathways from the primary visual cortex. Cortical processing of visual input is begun in the primary visual cortex. From there, signals are shuttled onward to a variety of other areas in the cortex along a number of pathways. Two prominent pathways are highlighted here. The *dorsal stream,* or *where pathway,* which processes information about motion and depth, moves on to areas of the parietal lobe. The *ventral stream,* or *what pathway,* which processes information about color and form, moves on to areas of the temporal lobe.

© Cengage Learning 2013

(the perception of motion and depth) (Connor et al., 2009; Pasternak et al., 2003).

As signals move farther along in the visual processing system, neurons become even more specialized or fussy about what turns them on, and the stimuli that activate them become more and more complex. For example, researchers have identified cells in the temporal lobe (along the *what* pathway) of monkeys and humans that are especially sensitive to pictures of faces (Kanwisher & Yovel, 2009). These neurons respond even to pictures that merely *suggest* the form of a face (Cox, Meyers, & Sinha, 2004).

The discovery of neurons that respond to facial stimuli raises an obvious question: Why does the cortex have face detectors? Theorists are far from sure, but one line of thinking is that the ability to quickly recognize faces—such as those of friends or foes—probably has had adaptive significance over the course of evolution (Sugita, 2009). Thus, natural selection *may* have wired the brains of some species to quickly respond to faces. Consistent with this hypothesis, recent research has demonstrated that basic aspects of face perception are apparent in infants (McKone, Crookes, & Kanwisher, 2009).

In any event, the discovery of the *what pathway* and the neurons inside it that respond specifically to faces have shed new light on visual disorders that have perplexed scientists for decades. For example, as we noted at the beginning of the chapter (in our discussion of Dr. P.), some people exhibit **visual agnosia—an inability to recognize objects**—even though their eyes function just fine (Behrmann, 2010). This perplexing condition now has a plausible explanation—it is probably a result of damage somewhere along the visual pathway that handles object recognition. Consider also the condition of ***prosopagnosia*, which is an inability to recognize familiar faces**—including one's own face—even though other aspects of visual processing are largely unimpaired. Although much remains to be learned, this highly specific visual deficit may reflect damage to neural circuits that are sensitive to facial stimuli (Farah, 2006).

Another dramatic finding in this area of research is that the neurons in the *what* pathway that are involved in perceiving faces can learn from experience (Gauthier & Curby, 2005; Palmeri & Gauthier, 2004). In one eye-opening study, participants were given extensive training in discriminating among similar artificial objects called Greebles (see **Figure 4.15**). After this training, neurons that are normally sensitive to faces were found to be almost as sensitive to Greebles as to faces (Gauthier et al., 1999). In other words, neurons that usually serve as face detectors were "retooled" to be responsive to other visual forms. Like many findings discussed in Chapter 3 (see page 104), these results demonstrate that the functional organization of the brain is somewhat "plastic" and that the brain can be rewired by experience.

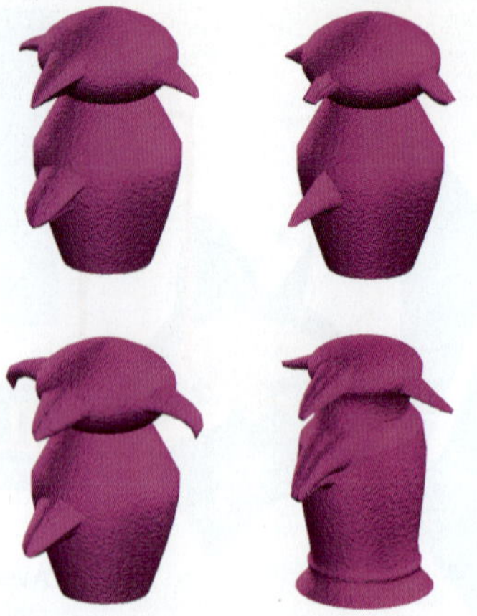

Figure 4.15

Distinguishing Greebles. Gauthier et al. (1999) gave subjects seven hours of training in the recognition of novel stimuli called Greebles, four of which are shown here. This training was conducted to explore whether neurons that normally respond to faces could be retuned by experience.

SOURCE: Gauthier, I., Tarr, M. J., Anderson, A. W., Skudlarksi, P. L., & Gore, J. C. (1999). Activation of the middle fusiform "face area" increases with experience in recognizing novel objects. *Nature Neuroscience, 2,* 568–573. (Figure 1a, p. 569). Reprinted by permission from Macmillan Publishers Ltd.

Viewing the World in Color 3d

So far, we've considered only how the visual system deals with light and dark. Let's journey now into the world of color. On the one hand, you can see perfectly well without seeing in color. Many animals get by with little or no color vision, and no one seemed to suffer back when all photographs, movies, or TV shows were in black and white. On the other hand, color clearly adds rich information to our perception of the world. The ability to identify objects is enhanced by the addition of color (Tanaka, Weiskopf, & Williams, 2001). Thus, some theorists have suggested that color vision evolved in humans and monkeys because it improved their abilities to find food through foraging, to spot prey, and to quickly recognize predators (Spence et al., 2006). Although the purpose of color vision remains elusive, scientists have learned a great deal about the mechanisms underlying the perception of color.

The Stimulus for Color 3d

As noted earlier, the lights people see are mixtures of various wavelengths. Perceived color is primarily a function of the dominant wavelength in these mixtures. In the visible spectrum, lights with the

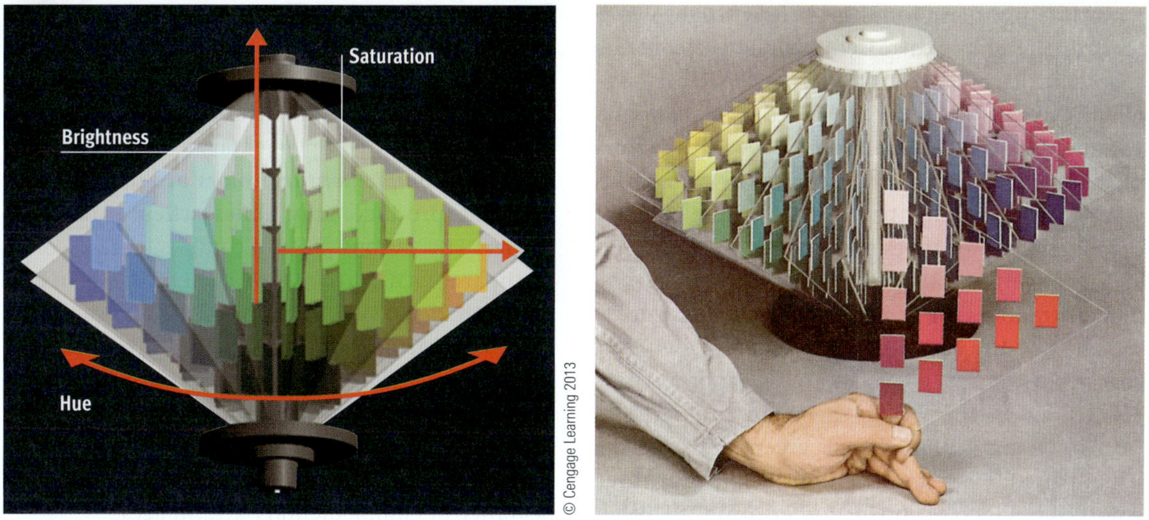

© Cengage Learning 2013

Courtesy of BASF

Figure 4.16

The color solid. The color solid shows how color varies along three perceptual dimensions: brightness (increasing from the bottom to the top of the solid), hue (changing around the solid's perimeter), and saturation (increasing toward the periphery of the solid).

longest wavelengths appear red, whereas those with the shortest appear violet. Take note of the word *appear;* color is a psychological interpretation—it's not a physical property of light itself.

Although wavelength wields the greatest influence, perception of color depends on complex blends of all three properties of light. *Wavelength* is most closely related to hue, *amplitude* to brightness, and *purity* to saturation. These three dimensions of color are illustrated in the *color solid* shown in **Figure 4.16**.

As a color solid demonstrates, people can perceive many different colors. In fact, experts estimate that humans can discriminate among millions of colors (Webster, 2010). Most of these diverse variations are the result of mixing a few basic colors. There are two kinds of color mixture: subtractive and additive. ***Subtractive color mixing*** **works by removing some wavelengths of light, leaving less light than was originally there.** Subtractive color mixing can be demonstrated by stacking color filters. If you look through a sandwich of yellow and blue cellophane filters, they will block out certain wavelengths. The middle wavelengths that are left will look green. Mixtures of different colors of paints also involve subtractive mixing.

Additive color mixing **works by superimposing lights, putting more light in the mixture than exists in any one light by itself.** If you shine red, green, and blue spotlights on a white surface, you'll have an additive mixture. As **Figure 4.17** shows, additive and subtractive mixtures of the same colors produce different results. Human processes of color perception parallel additive mixing much more closely than subtractive mixing, as you'll see in the following discussion of theories of color vision.

Trichromatic Theory of Color Vision

PSYKTREK 3d

The *trichromatic theory* of color vision (*tri* for "three," *chroma* for "color") was first stated by Thomas Young and modified later by Hermann von Helmholtz (1852). The *trichromatic theory of color vision* holds that the human eye has three types of receptors

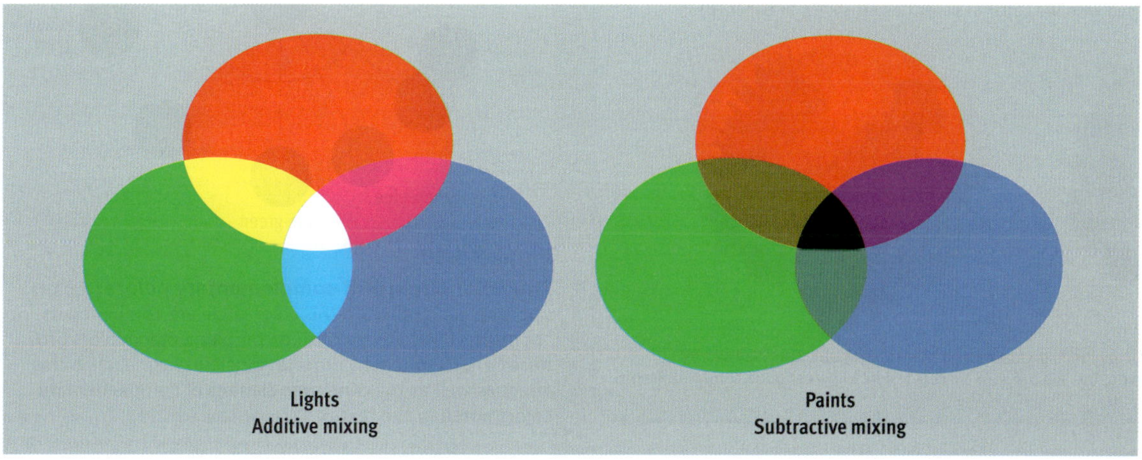

© Cengage Learning 2013

Figure 4.17

Additive versus subtractive color mixing. Lights mix additively because all the wavelengths contained in each light reach the eye. If red, blue, and green lights are projected onto a white screen, they produce the colors shown on the left, with white at the intersection of all three lights. If paints of the same three colors were combined in the same way, the subtractive mixture would produce the colors shown on the right, with black at the intersection of all three colors. As you can see, additive and subtractive color mixing produce different results.

with differing sensitivities to different light wavelengths. Helmholtz theorized that the eye contains specialized receptors sensitive to the specific wavelengths associated with red, green, and blue. According to this model, people can see all the colors of the rainbow because the eye does its own "color mixing" by varying the ratio of neural activity among these three types of receptors.

The impetus for the trichromatic theory was the demonstration that a light of any color can be matched by the additive mixture of three *primary colors*. Any three colors that are appropriately spaced out in the visible spectrum can serve as primary colors, although red, green, and blue are usually used. Does it sound implausible that three colors should be adequate for creating all other colors? If so, consider that this is exactly what happens on your color TV screen or computer monitor (Stockman, 2010).

Most of the known facts about color blindness also meshed well with trichromatic theory. ***Color blindness*** **encompasses a variety of deficiencies in the ability to distinguish among colors.** Color blindness occurs much more frequently in males than in females (Tait & Carroll, 2010). Most people who are color blind are *dichromats;* that is, they make do with only two types of color receptors. There are three types of dichromats, and each type is insensitive to one of the primary colors: red, green, or blue, although the latter is rare (Reid & Usrey, 2008). The three deficiencies, then, support the notion that there are three sets of receptors for color vision, as proposed by trichromatic theory.

Opponent Process Theory of Color Vision

PsykTrek 3d

Although trichromatic theory explained some facets of color vision well, it ran aground in other areas. Consider complementary afterimages, for instance. ***Complementary colors*** **are pairs of colors that produce gray tones when mixed together.** The various pairs of complementary colors can be arranged in a *color circle,* such as the one in **Figure 4.18**. If you stare at a strong color and then look at a white background, you'll see an ***afterimage*—a visual image that persists after a stimulus is removed.** The color of the afterimage will be the *complement* of the color you originally stared at. Trichromatic theory cannot account for the appearance of complementary afterimages.

Here's another peculiarity to consider. If you ask people to describe colors but restrict them to using three names, they run into difficulty. For example, using only red, green, and blue, they simply don't feel comfortable describing yellow as "reddish green." However, if you let them have just one more name, they usually choose yellow; they can then describe any color quite well (Gordon & Abramov, 2001). If colors can be reduced to three primaries, why are four color names required to describe the full range of possible colors?

In an effort to answer questions such as these, Ewald Hering proposed the *opponent process theory* in 1878. The *opponent process theory of color vision* holds that color perception depends on receptors that make opposite responses to three pairs of colors. The three pairs he proposed were red versus green, yel-

Reality CHECK

Misconception

People who are colorblind see the world in black and white.

Reality

The term color *blindness* is somewhat misleading, since only a tiny minority of those who are characterized as colorblind are monochromats who see the world in black and white. The vast majority of color blind people are dichromats who cannot see certain colors. Panel **(a)** shows what the most common type of dichromat would see if presented with the batch of paper flowers shown in panel **(b)**.

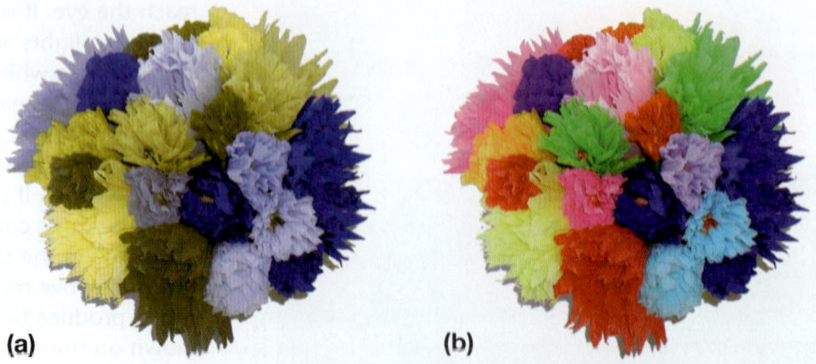

(a) (b)

SOURCE: From Goldstein, E. B. (2007). *Sensation and perception* (7 ed.). Belmont, CA: Wadsworth. Wadsworth is a part of Cengage Learning, Inc. Reproduced by permission. www.cengage.com/permissions

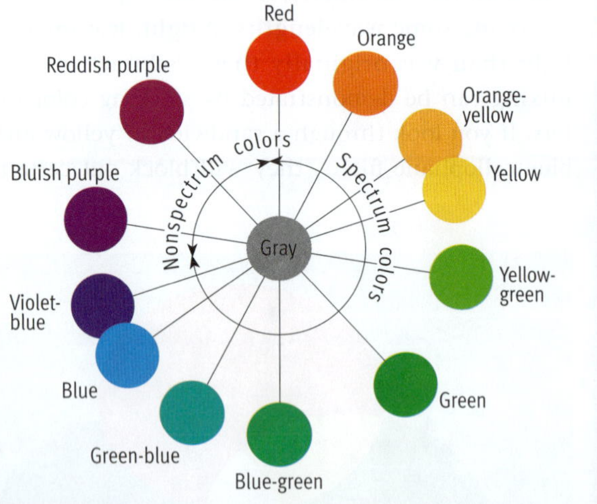

© Cengage Learning 2013

Figure 4.18

The color circle and complementary colors. Colors opposite each other on this color circle are complements, or "opposites." Additively mixing complementary colors produces gray. Opponent process principles help explain this effect as well as the other peculiarities of complementary colors noted in the text. © Cengage Learning 2013 low versus blue, and black versus white. The antagonistic processes in this theory provide plausible explanations for complementary afterimages and the need for four names (red, green, blue, and yellow) to describe colors. Opponent process theory also explains some aspects of color blindness. For instance, it can explain why dichromats typically find it hard to distinguish either green from red or yellow from blue.

Reconciling Theories of Color Vision

PSYKTREK 3d

Advocates of trichromatic theory and opponent process theory argued about the relative merits of their models for almost a century. Most researchers assumed that one theory must be wrong and the other must be right. In recent decades, however, it has become clear that *it takes both theories to explain color vision.* Eventually, a physiological basis for both theories was found. Research that earned George Wald a Nobel prize demonstrated that *the eye has three types of cones,* with each type being most sensitive to a different band of wavelengths, as shown in **Figure 4.19** (Gegenfurtner, 2010; Wald, 1964). The three types of cones represent the three different color receptors predicted by trichromatic theory.

Researchers also discovered a biological basis for opponent processes. They found cells in the retina, LGN, and visual cortex *that respond in opposite ways to red versus green and blue versus yellow* (Purves, 2009; Zrenner et al., 1990). For example, specific ganglion cells in the retina are excited by green and inhibited by red. Other retinal ganglion cells work in just the opposite way, as predicted in opponent process theory.

In summary, the perception of color appears to involve sequential stages of information processing (Gegenfurtner, 2010; Hurvich, 1981). The receptors that do the first stage of processing (the cones) seem to follow the principles outlined in trichromatic theory. In later stages of processing, at least some cells in the retina, the LGN, and the visual cortex seem to follow the principles outlined in opponent process theory. As you can see, vigorous theoretical debate about color vision produced a solution that went beyond the contributions of either theory alone.

Effects of Color on Behavior

A newly emerging area of research concerns the effects that specific colors have on psychological functioning. Although there has long been an extensive popular literature on how colors affect behavior, this literature has mostly been based on speculation rather than sound empirical research. Recently, however, Andrew Elliot and his colleagues (Elliot & Maier, 2007; Moller, Elliot, & Maier, 2009) have formulated a theory of how color might influence behavior and have begun a series of carefully controlled experiments to test specific hypotheses. According to Elliot et al. (2007), colors can have automatic, unconscious effects on behavior. They assert that these effects are probably rooted in two basic sources. First, people learn associations based on certain colors being paired repeatedly with certain experiences. For instance, red ink is usually used to mark students' errors and red lights and red signs are often used to warn of danger. Second, over the course of human evolution certain colors may have had adaptive significance for survival or reproduction. For example, blood and fire, which often appear red, both can signal danger.

In their first study of the behavioral effects of color, Elliot et al. (2007) theorized that red is associated with the danger of failure in achievement settings. Hence, they tested the hypothesis that exposure to the color red has a negative effect on performance in achievement situations. In one study, participants taking a subtest of an IQ test were exposed to a white, red, or green test booklet cover prior to taking the subtest. As hypothesized, subjects exposed to the red cover scored significantly lower on the test than those exposed to the green or white covers. Subsequent studies showed that the color red undermines performance in achievement contexts by evoking avoidance tendencies that disrupt attention (Elliot et al., 2009; Maier, Elliot, & Lichtenfeld, 2008). Our Featured Study for this chapter profiles another intriguing investigation of the effects of color.

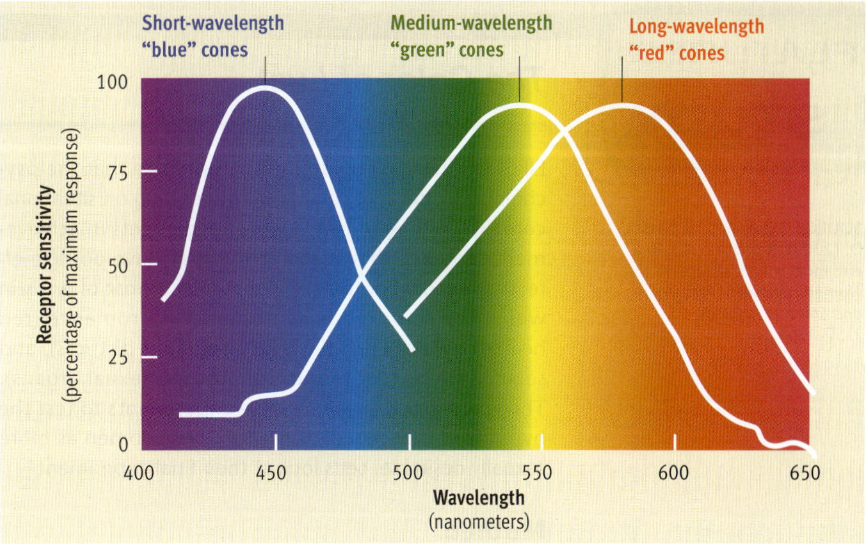

© Cengage Learning 2013

Figure 4.19
Three types of cones. Research has identified three types of cones that show varied sensitivity to different wavelengths of light. As the graph shows, these three types of cones correspond only roughly to the red, green, and blue receptors predicted by trichromatic theory, so it is more accurate to refer to them as cones sensitive to short, medium, and long wavelengths.

SOURCE: Wald, G., & Brown, P. K. (1965). Human color vision and color blindness. *Symposium Cold Spring Harbor Laboratory of Quantitative Biology, 30,* 345–359 (p. 351). Copyright © 1965. Reprinted by permission of the author.

FEATURED STUDY

SOURCE: Elliot, A. J., & Niesta, D. (2008). Romantic red: Red enhances men's attraction to women. *Journal of Personality and Social Psychology, 95,* 1150–1164.

The Color of Lust

Elliot and his colleagues (2007) emphasize that the psychological effects of colors vary depending on situational contexts. Although red has negative effects in achievement contexts, they assert that it may have positive effects in sexual contexts. They review a host of ways in which the color red is associated with romance (red hearts on Valentine's day), lust (red light districts), and sexual liaisons (the redness of aroused sexual organs). They conducted a series of five experiments to test the hypothesis that red leads men to view women as more sexually desirable. Let's look at their final experiment.

Method

Participants. Twenty-three male undergraduates served as subjects. Participation was restricted to heterosexuals who were not colorblind.

Procedure. Participants were told that the experiment was on first impressions of the opposite sex. They were asked to look briefly at a photo of a moderately attractive young woman (her attractiveness was rated at 6.80 on a 9-point scale in a pilot study) wearing a form-fitting blouse. The independent variable was the color of the blouse, which was manipulated to be either red or blue while controlling for equivalent brightness and saturation.

Measures. The dependent variables were the participants' ratings of the woman's perceived attractiveness, her sexual desirability, and their interest in dating her. The subjects were also asked how much money they would be willing to spend on a date with the woman.

© Valentin Mosich'ev/Shutterstock

Results

The red blouse led to significantly higher attractiveness ratings than the blue blouse. The data for sexual desirability and dating interest are shown in **Figure 4.20**. As you can see, the red blouse produced higher ratings on both variables. Participants in the red condition also reported that they would be willing to spend more money on a date with the woman than those in the blue condition did.

Discussion

The findings of this experiment were consistent with the results of the other experiments in the series. In two of the other studies, red was found to generate greater attraction than white or green. In another study the effects of red were shown to be limited to sexual attraction, as the subjects' ratings of the target woman's overall likeability were not swayed by color. Interestingly, the data from the studies also suggested that the men were unaware of how they were swayed by the color red. The authors concluded, "that red is an aphrodiasiac for men is not only valuable information for both men and women in the mating game, but also should prove of considerable interest to fashion and image consultants, product designers, and marketers and advertisers, among (many) others" (p. 1161).

Comment

The study of sensation and perception is one of the oldest areas of scientific research in psychology. Yet this study shows that there are still fascinating areas of inquiry that remain unexplored. It just takes some creativity and insight to recognize them. The influence of color on psychological functioning should be a fertile area of research in the future. Indeed, in a more recent follow-up study, Elliot and his colleagues (2010) found that the color red also fosters greater attraction when women evaluate men, although for somewhat different reasons.

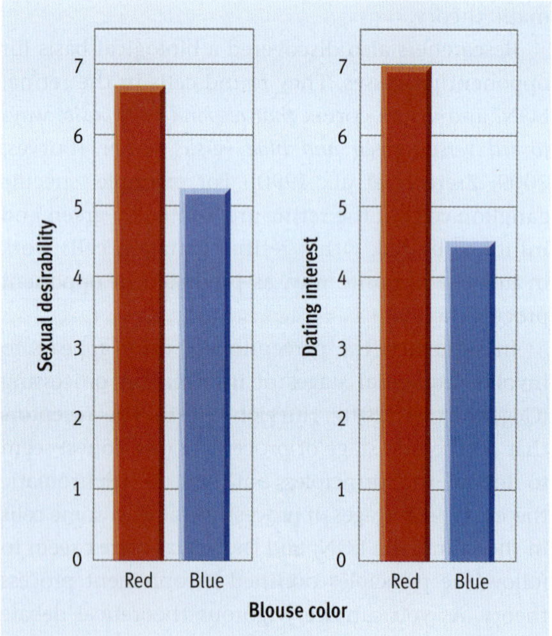

© Cengage Learning 2013

Figure 4.20
Color and sexual attraction. As you can see, in the study by Elliot and Niesta (2008), the color of the woman's blouse had a substantial impact on participants' attraction to her. When her blouse was red males rated her as being more sexually desirable (left) and indicated that they had a greater interest in dating her (right).

SOURCE: Elliot, A. J., & Niesta, D. (2008). Romantic red: Red enhances men's attraction to women. *Journal of Personality and Social Psychology, 95,* 1150–1164. Figure 5b and 5d. © American Psychological Association, reprinted by permission.

REVIEW OF KEY LEARNING GOALS

4.5 Light varies in terms of wavelength, amplitude, and purity. Perceptions of color (hue) are primarily a function of light wavelength. Amplitude mainly affects brightness, and purity mainly affects saturation.

4.6 Light enters the eye through the cornea and pupil and is focused upside down on the retina by the lens. Distant objects appear blurry to nearsighted people, while close objects appear blurry to farsighted people. The pupils control the amount of light entering the eye.

4.7 The retina is the neural tissue in the eye that absorbs light, processes images, and sends visual signals to the brain. Cones, which are concentrated in the fovea, play a key role in daylight vision and color perception. Rods, which have their greatest density just outside the fovea, are critical to night vision and peripheral vision. Dark adaptation and light adaptation both involve changes in the retina's sensitivity to light. Receptive fields are areas in the retina that affect the firing of visual cells.

4.8 The optic nerves from the inside half of each eye cross at the optic chiasm and then project to the opposite half of the brain. Two visual pathways send signals to different areas of the primary visual cortex. The main pathway is routed through the LGN in the thalamus. After processing in the primary visual cortex, visual information is shuttled along the *what* and *where* pathways to other cortical areas. Research suggests that the visual cortex contains cells that function as feature detectors. The *what pathway* contains neurons that are especially sensitive to faces.

4.9 There are two types of color mixing: additive and subtractive. Human color perception depends on processes that resemble additive color mixing. The trichromatic theory holds that people have three types of receptors that are sensitive to wavelengths associated with red, green, and blue. The opponent process theory holds that color perception depends on receptors that make antagonistic responses to red-green, blue-yellow, and black-white. The evidence now suggests that both theories are necessary to account for color vision. A new line of research is exploring how various colors influence behavior. The evidence suggests that the color red undermines achievement strivings, but enhances sexual attraction.

The Visual System: Perceptual Processes

KEY LEARNING GOALS

4.10 Discuss the subjectivity of form perception and the phenomenon of inattentional blindness.

4.11 Explain feature analysis, and distinguish between bottom-up and top-down processing.

4.12 Describe Gestalt principles of visual perception, and clarify the nature of perceptual hypotheses.

4.13 Describe the monocular and binocular cues used in depth perception, and discuss cultural variations in depth perception.

4.14 Describe perceptual constancies and illusions in vision, and discuss cultural variations in susceptibility to certain illusions.

We have seen how sensory receptors in the eye transform light into neural impulses that are sent to the brain. We focus next on how the brain makes sense of it all—how does it convert streams of neural impulses into perceptions of chairs, doors, friends, automobiles, and buildings? In this section we explore *perceptual processes* in vision, such as the perception of forms, objects, depth, and so forth.

Perceiving Forms, Patterns, and Objects

PSYKTREK 3c, 3e

The drawing in **Figure 4.21** is a poster for a circus act involving a trained seal. Take a good look at it. What do you see?

No doubt you see a seal balancing a ball on its nose and a trainer holding a fish and a whip. But suppose you had been told that the drawing is actually a poster for a costume ball. Would you have perceived it differently?

If you focus on the idea of a costume ball (stay with it a minute if you still see the seal and trainer), you will probably see a costumed man and woman in **Figure 4.21**. She's handing him a hat, and he has a sword in his right hand. This tricky little sketch was made ambiguous quite intentionally. It's a ***reversible figure*, a drawing that is compatible with two interpretations that can shift back and forth.** Another classic reversible figure is shown in **Figure 4.22** on the next page. What do you see? A rabbit or a duck? It all depends on how you look at the drawing.

The key point is simply this: *The same visual input can result in radically different perceptions.* No one-to-one

Figure 4.21
A poster for a trained seal act. Or is it? The picture is an ambiguous figure, which can be interpreted as either of two scenes, as explained in the text.

Figure 4.22

Another ambiguous figure. What animal do you see here? As the text explains, two very different perceptions are possible. This ambiguous figure was devised around 1900 by Joseph Jastrow, a prominent psychologist at the turn of the 20th century (Block & Yuker, 1992).

correspondence exists between sensory input and what you perceive. *This is a principal reason that people's experience of the world is subjective.* Perception involves much more than passively receiving signals from the outside world. It involves the *interpretation* of sensory input. To some extent, this interpretive process can be influenced by manipulating people's *expectations*. For example, information given to you about the drawing of the "circus act involving a trained seal" created a ***perceptual set*—a readiness to perceive a stimulus in a particular way.** A perceptual set creates a certain bias in how someone interprets sensory input.

Form perception also depends on the *selection* of sensory input—that is, what people focus their attention on (Chun & Wolfe, 2001). A visual scene may include many objects and forms. Some of them may capture viewers' attention, while others may not. This fact has been demonstrated in dramatic fashion in studies of ***inattentional blindness,* which involves the failure to see visible objects or events because one's attention is focused elsewhere.** In one such study (Simons & Chabris, 1999), participants watched a video of a group of people in white shirts passing a basketball that was laid over another video of people in black shirts passing a basketball (the two videos were partially transparent). The observers were instructed to focus on one of the two teams and press a key whenever that team passed the ball. Thirty seconds into the task, a woman carrying an umbrella clearly walked through the scene for four seconds. You might guess that this bizarre development would be noticed by virtually all the observers, but 44% of the participants failed to see the woman. Moreover, when someone in a gorilla suit strolled through the same scene, even more subjects (73%) missed the unexpected event!

Additional studies using other types of stimulus materials have demonstrated that people routinely overlook obvious forms that are unexpected (Most et al., 2005). Inattentional blindness may account for many automobile accidents, as accident reports frequently include the statement "I looked right there, but I never saw them" (Shermer, 2004). Although this phenomenon can happen to an attentive and unimpaired driver, research shows that inattentional blindness increases when people talk on a cell phone or are even just *slightly* intoxicated (Clifasefi, Takarangi, & Bergman, 2006; Strayer & Drews, 2007).

The idea that we see much less of the world than we think we do surprises many people, but an auditory parallel exists that people take for granted (Mack, 2003). Think of how often you have had someone clearly say something to you, but you did not hear a word of what was said because you were "not listening." Inattentional blindness is essentially the same thing in the visual domain.

An understanding of how people perceive forms and objects also requires knowledge of how people *organize* their visual inputs. Several influential approaches to this issue emphasize *feature analysis.*

Feature Analysis: Assembling Forms

PsykTrek 3c

The information received by your eyes would do you little good if you couldn't recognize objects and forms—ranging from words on a page to mice in your cellar and friends in the distance. According to some theories, perceptions of form and pattern entail *feature analysis* (Lindsay & Norman, 1977; Maguire et al., 1990). ***Feature analysis* is the process of detecting specific elements in visual input and assembling them into a more complex form.** In other words, you start with the components of a form, such as lines, edges, and corners, and build them into perceptions of squares, triangles, stop signs, bicycles, ice cream cones, and telephones. An application of this model of form perception is diagrammed in **Figure 4.23**.

Feature analysis assumes that form perception involves ***bottom-up processing,* a progression from individual elements to the whole** (see **Figure 4.24**). The plausibility of this model was bolstered greatly when Hubel and Wiesel showed that cells in the visual cortex operate as highly specialized feature detectors. Indeed, their findings strongly suggested that at least some aspects of form perception involve feature analysis.

Can feature analysis provide a complete account of how people perceive forms? Clearly not. A crucial problem for the theory is that form perception often does not involve bottom-up processing. In fact, there is ample evidence that perceptions of form frequently involve ***top-down processing,* a progression from the whole to the elements** (see **Figure 4.24**).

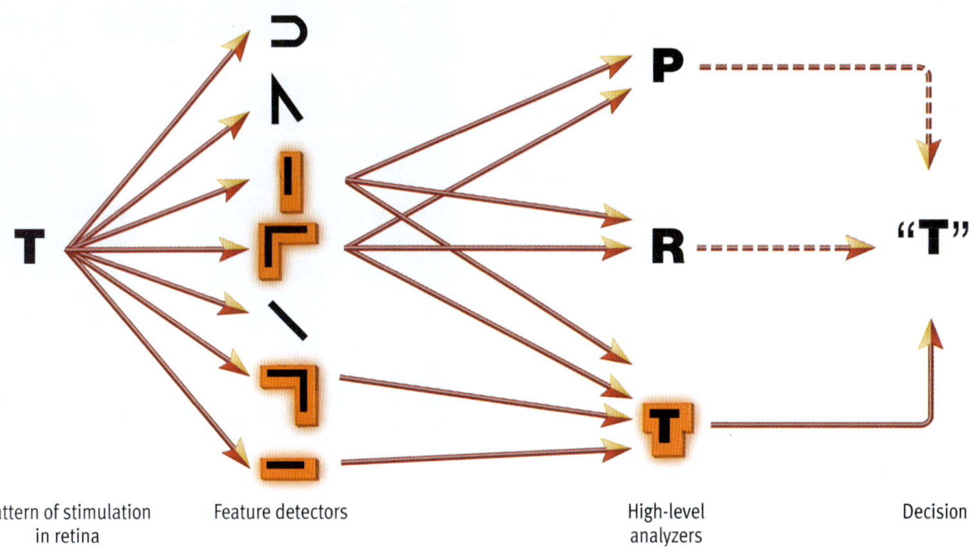

Figure 4.23
Feature analysis in form perception. One vigorously debated theory of form perception is that the brain has cells that respond to specific aspects or features of stimuli, such as lines and angles. Neurons functioning as higher-level analyzers then respond to input from these "feature detectors." The more input each analyzer receives, the more active it becomes. Finally, other neurons weigh signals from these analyzers and make a "decision" about the stimulus. In this way perception of a form is arrived at by assembling elements from the bottom up. © Cengage Learning 2013

For example, there is evidence that people can perceive a word before its individual letters, a phenomenon that has to reflect top-down processing (Johnston & McClelland, 1974). If readers depended exclusively on bottom-up processing, they would have to analyze the features of letters in words to recognize them and then assemble the letters into words. This task would be terribly time-consuming and would slow down reading speed to a snail's pace.

Subjective contours is another phenomenon traditionally attributed to top-down processing, although that view is changing (Gunn et al., 2000; Murray et al., 2004). ***Subjective contours*** **involves the perception of contours where none actually exist.** Consider, for instance, the triangle shown in **Figure 4.25**. We see the contours of the triangle easily, even though no physical edges or lines are present. It's hard to envision how feature detectors could detect edges that are not really there, so most theorists have argued that bottom-up models of form perception are unlikely to account for subjective contours. In any event, it appears that both top-down and bottom-up processing have their place in form perception.

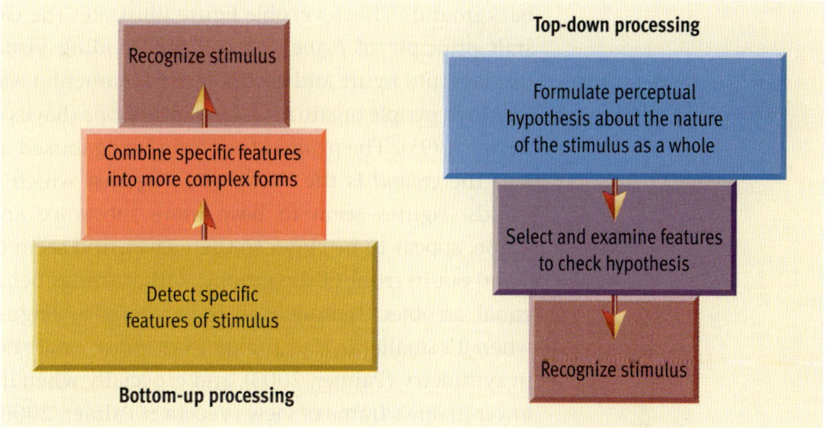

© Cengage Learning 2013

Figure 4.24
Bottom-up versus top-down processing. As explained in these diagrams, bottom-up processing progresses from individual elements to whole elements, whereas top-down processing progresses from the whole to the individual elements.

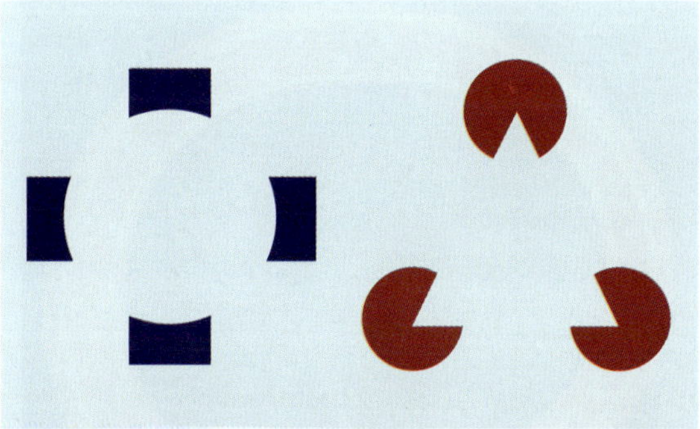

© Cengage Learning 2013

Figure 4.25
Subjective contours. Your perception of the triangle on the right and the circle on the left results from subjective contours that are not really there. The effect is so powerful, the triangle and circle appear lighter than the background, which they are not. To demonstrate the illusory nature of these contours for yourself, cover the red circles that mark off the triangle. You'll see that the triangle disappears.

Looking at the Whole Picture: Gestalt Principles

PSYKTREK 3e

Top-down processing is clearly at work in the principles of form perception described by the Gestalt psychologists. *Gestalt psychology* was an influential school of thought that emerged out of Germany during the first half of the 20th century. (*Gestalt* is a German word for "form" or "shape.") Gestalt psychologists repeatedly demonstrated that *the whole can be greater than the sum of its parts.*

Archives of the History of American Psychology, University of Akron, Akron, Ohio

Max Wertheimer

"The fundamental 'formula' of Gestalt theory might be expressed in this way: There are wholes, the behaviour of which is not determined by that of their individual elements."

A simple example of this principle is the *phi phenomenon,* first described by Max Wertheimer in 1912. **The *phi phenomenon* is the illusion of movement created by presenting visual stimuli in rapid succession.** You encounter examples of the phi phenomenon nearly every day. For example, movies and TV consist of separate still pictures projected rapidly one after the other. You see smooth motion, but in reality the "moving" objects merely take slightly different positions in successive frames. Viewed as a whole, a movie has a property (motion) that isn't evident in any of its parts (the individual frames). The Gestalt psychologists formulated a series of principles that describe how the visual system organizes a scene into discrete forms (Schirillo, 2010). Let's examine some of these principles.

Figure and Ground Take a look at **Figure 4.26.** Do you see the figure as two silhouetted faces against a white background, or as a white vase against a black background? This reversible figure illustrates the Gestalt principle of *figure and ground.* Dividing visual displays into figure and ground is a fundamental way in which people organize visual perceptions (Baylis & Driver, 1995). The *figure* is the thing being looked at, and the *ground* is the background against which it stands. Figures seem to have more substance and shape, appear to be closer to the viewer, and seem to stand out in front of the ground. Other things being equal, an object is more likely to be viewed as a figure when it's smaller in size, higher in contrast, or greater in symmetry (Palmer, 2003), and especially when it's lower in one's frame of view (Vecera & Palmer, 2006). More often than not, your visual field may contain many figures sharing a background. The following Gestalt principles relate to how these elements are grouped into higher-order figures (Palmer, 2003).

Figure 4.26

The principle of figure and ground. Whether you see two faces or a vase depends on which part of this drawing you see as figure and which as background. Although this reversible drawing allows you to switch back and forth between two ways of organizing your perception, you can't perceive the drawing both ways at once.

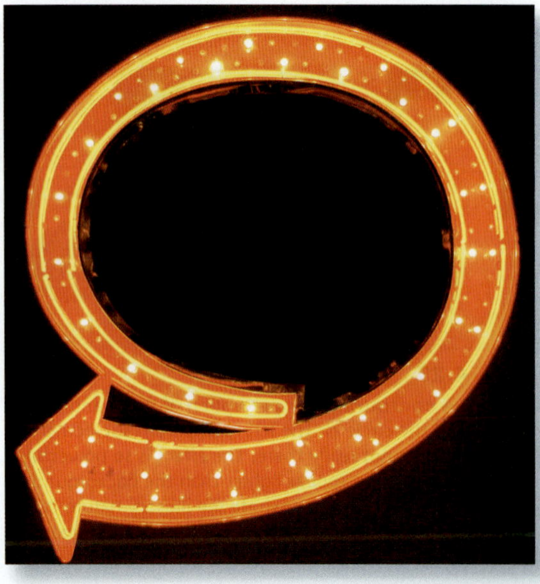

© Brandon Jennings/Shutterstock

The illusion of movement created by this neon sign is an instance of the phi phenomenon, which is also at work in movies and television. The phi phenomenon illustrates the Gestalt principle that the whole can have properties that are not found in any of its parts.

Proximity Things that are near one another seem to belong together. The black dots in the upper left panel of **Figure 4.27(a)** could be grouped into vertical columns or horizontal rows. However, people tend to perceive rows because of the effect of proximity (the dots are closer together horizontally).

Closure People often group elements to create a sense of *closure,* or completeness. Thus, you may "complete" figures that actually have gaps in them. This principle is demonstrated in the upper right panel of **Figure 4.27(b)**.

Similarity People also tend to group stimuli that are similar. This principle is apparent in **Figure 4.27(c)**, in which viewers group elements of similar lightness into the number two.

Simplicity The Gestaltists' most general principle was the law of *Pragnanz,* which translates from German as "good form." The idea is that people tend to group elements that combine to form a good figure. This principle is somewhat vague in that it's often difficult to spell out what makes a figure "good" (Biederman, Hilton, & Hummel, 1991). Some theorists maintain that goodness is largely a matter of simplicity, asserting that people tend to organize forms in the simplest way possible (see **Figure 4.27d**). But the concept of simplicity is also plagued by ambiguity (Donderi, 2006).

Continuity The principle of continuity reflects people's tendency to follow in whatever direction they've been led. Thus, people tend to connect

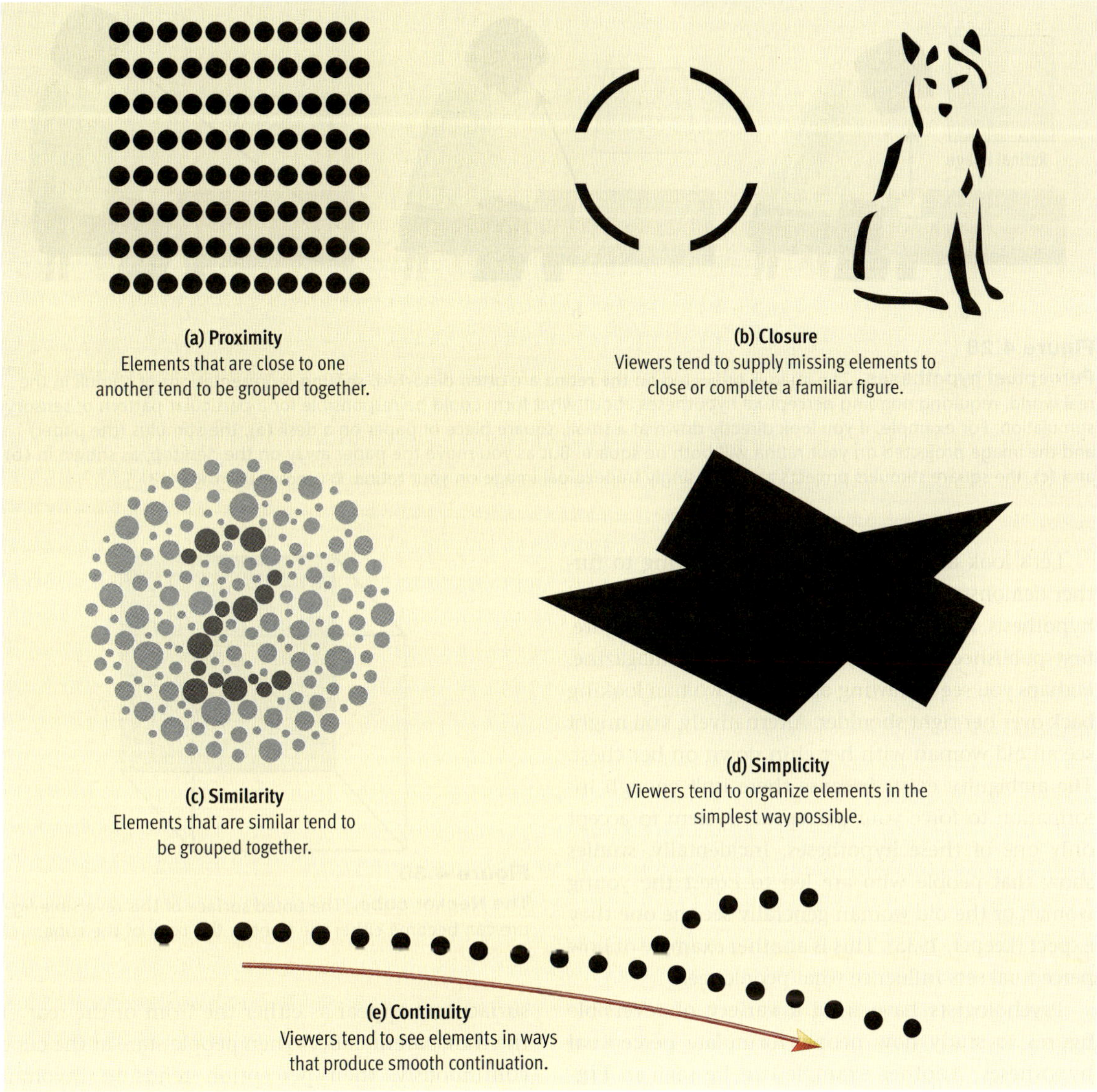

© Cengage Learning 2013

Figure 4.27

Gestalt principles of perceptual organization. Gestalt principles help explain some of the factors that influence form perception. **(a) Proximity:** These dots might well be organized in vertical columns rather than horizontal rows, but because of proximity (the dots are closer together horizontally), they tend to be perceived in rows. **(b) Closure:** Even though the figures are incomplete, you fill in the blanks and see a circle and a dog. **(c) Similarity:** Because of similarity of color, you see dots organized into the number 2 instead of a random array. If you did not group similar elements, you wouldn't see the number 2 here. **(d) Simplicity:** You could view this as a complicated 11-sided figure, but given the preference for simplicity, you are more likely to see it as an overlapping rectangle and triangle. **(e) Continuity:** You tend to group these dots in a way that produces a smooth path rather than an abrupt shift in direction.

points that result in straight or gently curved lines that create "smooth" paths, as shown in the bottom panel of **Figure 4.27(e)**.

Although Gestalt psychology is no longer an active theoretical orientation in modern psychology, its influence is still felt in the study of perception (Banks & Krajicek, 1991). The Gestalt psychologists raised many important questions that still occupy researchers, and they left a legacy of many useful insights about form perception that have stood the test of time (Sharps & Wertheimer, 2000).

Formulating Perceptual Hypotheses

The Gestalt principles provide some indications of how people organize visual input. However, scientists are still one step away from understanding how these organized perceptions result in a representation of the real world. In visual perception, the images projected on the retina are distorted, two-dimensional versions of their actual, three-dimensional counterparts. For example, consider the stimulus of a square such as the one in **Figure 4.28** on the next page. If the square is lying on a desk in front of you, it is actually projecting a trapezoid on your retinas, because the top of the square is farther from your eyes than the bottom. Obviously, the trapezoid is a distorted representation of the square. If what people have to work with is so distorted, how do they get an accurate view of the world out there?

One explanation is that people are constantly making and testing *hypotheses* about what's out there in the real world (Gregory, 1973). Thus, **a *perceptual hypothesis* is an inference about what form could be responsible for a pattern of sensory stimulation.** The square in **Figure 4.28** may project a trapezoidal image on your retinas, but your perceptual system "guesses" correctly that it's a square—and that's what you see.

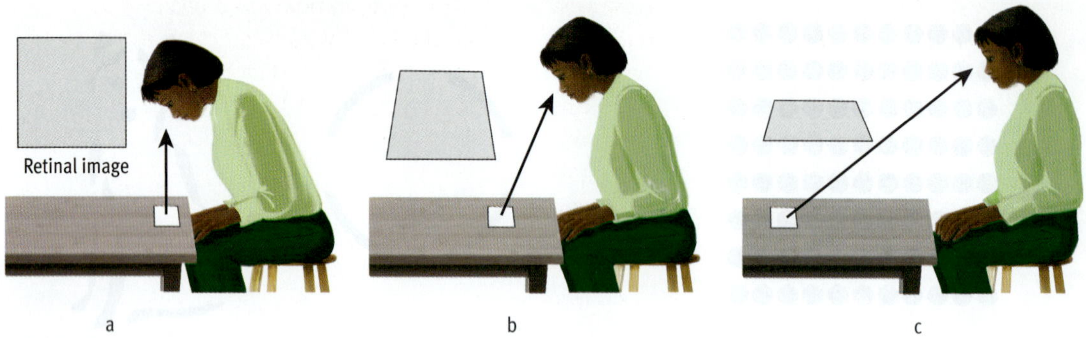

Figure 4.28

Perceptual hypotheses. The images projected on the retina are often distorted, shifting representations of stimuli in the real world, requiring ongoing perceptual hypotheses about what form could be responsible for a particular pattern of sensory stimulation. For example, if you look directly down at a small, square piece of paper on a desk **(a)**, the stimulus (the paper) and the image projected on your retina will both be square. But as you move the paper away on the desktop, as shown in **(b)** and **(c)**, the square stimulus projects an increasingly trapezoidal image on your retina. © Cengage Learning 2013

Let's look at another ambiguous drawing to further demonstrate the process of making a perceptual hypothesis. **Figure 4.29** is a famous reversible figure, first published as a cartoon in a humor magazine. Perhaps you see a drawing of a young woman looking back over her right shoulder. Alternatively, you might see an old woman with her chin down on her chest. The ambiguity exists because there isn't enough information to force your perceptual system to accept only one of these hypotheses. Incidentally, studies show that people who are led to *expect* the young woman or the old woman generally see the one they expect (Leeper, 1935). This is another example of how perceptual sets influence what people see.

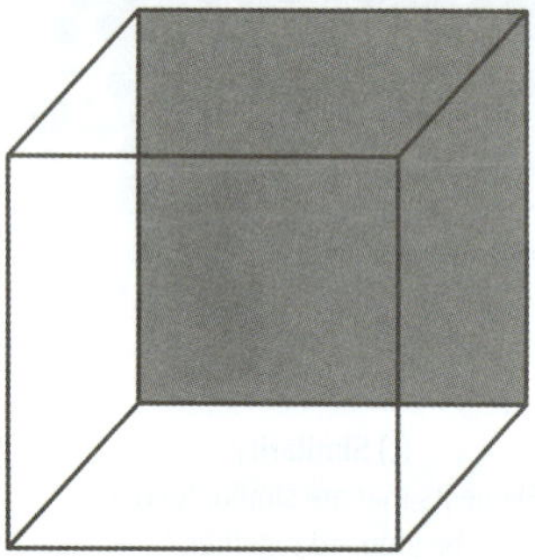

Figure 4.30

The Necker cube. The tinted surface of this reversible figure can become either the front or the back of the cube.

Psychologists have used a variety of reversible figures to study how people formulate perceptual hypotheses. Another example can be seen in **Figure 4.30**, which shows the *Necker cube*. The shaded surface can appear as either the front or the rear of the transparent cube. When people stare at the cube continuously, their perception tends to involuntarily alternate between these possibilities (Leopold et al., 2002).

Figure 4.29

A famous reversible figure. What do you see? Consult the text to learn what the two possible interpretations of this figure are.

The *context* in which something appears often guides people's perceptual hypotheses (Bravo, 2010). To illustrate, take a look at **Figure 4.31**. What do you see? You probably saw the words "THE CAT."

Figure 4.31

Context effects. You probably read these letters as "THE CAT" even though the middle letter of each word is the same. This simple demonstration shows that the context in which a stimulus is seen can affect your perceptual hypotheses.

But look again; the middle characters in both words are identical. You identified an "H" in the first word and an "A" in the second because of the surrounding letters, which created an expectation—another example of top-down processing in visual perception. The power of expectations explains why typographocal errors like those in this sentance often pass unoberved (Lachman, 1996).

Perceiving Depth or Distance

3f

More often than not, forms and figures are objects in space. Spatial considerations add a third dimension to visual perception. ***Depth perception* involves interpretation of visual cues that indicate how near or far away objects are.** To make judgments of distance, people rely on a variety of cues, which can be classified into two types: binocular and monocular (Hochberg, 1988; Proffitt & Caudek, 2003).

Binocular Cues

3f

Because they are set apart, the eyes each have a slightly different view of the world. ***Binocular depth cues* are clues about distance based on the differing views of the two eyes.** Today's 3D movies take advantage of this fact. Two cameras are used to record slightly different images of the same scene. The special polarized glasses that viewers wear separate the images for each eye. The brain then supplies the "depth," and you perceive a three-dimensional scene.

The principal binocular depth cue is ***retinal disparity,* which refers to the fact that objects within 25 feet project images to slightly different locations on the right and left retinas, so the right and left eyes see slightly different views of the object.** The closer an object gets, the greater the disparity between the images seen by each eye. Thus, retinal disparity increases as objects come closer, providing information about distance. Another binocular cue is ***convergence,* which involves sensing the eyes converging toward each other as they focus on closer objects.**

© ImageSource/Getty Images

Monocular Cues

3f

***Monocular depth cues* are clues about distance based on the image in either eye alone.** There are two kinds of monocular cues to depth. One kind is the result of active use of the eye in viewing the world. For example, if you cover one eye and move your head from side to side, closer objects appear to move more than distant objects.

The other kind of monocular cues are ***pictorial depth cues*—clues about distance that can be given in a flat picture.** There are many pictorial cues to depth, which is why some paintings and photographs seem so realistic that you feel you can climb right into them. Six prominent pictorial depth cues are described and illustrated in **Figure 4.32** on the next page. *Linear perspective* is a depth cue reflecting the fact that lines converge in the distance. Because details are too small to see when they are far away, *texture gradients* can provide information about depth. If an object comes between you and another object, it must be closer to you, a cue called *interposition. Relative size* is a cue because closer objects appear larger. *Height in plane* reflects the fact that distant objects appear higher in a picture. Finally, the familiar effects of shadowing make *light and shadow* useful in judging distance.

There appear to be some cultural differences in the ability to take advantage of pictorial depth cues in two-dimensional drawings. These differences were first investigated by Hudson (1960, 1967), who presented pictures like that shown in **Figure 4.33** on page 155 to various cultural groups in South Africa. Hudson's approach was based on the assumption that subjects who indicate that the hunter is trying to spear the elephant instead of the antelope don't understand the depth cues (interposition, relative size, height in plane) in the picture, which place the elephant in the distance. Hudson found that subjects from a rural South African tribe (the Bantu), who had little exposure at that time to pictures and photos, frequently misinterpreted the depth cues in his pictures. Similar difficulties with depth cues in pictures have been documented for other cultural groups who have little experience with two-dimensional representations of three-dimensional space (Berry et al., 1992). Thus, the application of pictorial

© Royalty Free/Corbis

Linear perspective Parallel lines that run away from the viewer seem to get closer together.

© Jean-Marc Truchet/Getty Images

Texture gradient As distance increases, a texture gradually becomes denser and less distinct.

© Ron Fehling/Masterfile

Interposition The shapes of near objects overlap or mask those of more distant ones.

© Jose Fuste Raga/zefa/Corbis

Relative size If separate objects are expected to be of the same size, the larger ones are seen as closer.

© Chris George/Alamy

Height in plane Near objects are low in the visual field; more distant ones are higher up.

U. S. Department of Energy

Light and shadow Patterns of light and dark suggest shadows that can create an impression of three-dimensional forms.

Figure 4.32

Pictorial cues to depth. Six pictorial depth cues are explained and illustrated here. Although one cue stands out in each photo, in most visual scenes several pictorial cues are present. Try looking at the light-and-shadow picture upside down. The change in shadowing reverses what you see.

CONCEPT CHECK 4.2

Recognizing Pictorial Depth Cues

Painters routinely attempt to create the perception of depth on a flat canvas by using pictorial depth cues. **Figure 4.32** describes and illustrates six pictorial depth cues, most of which are apparent in van Gogh's colorful piece *Corridor in the Asylum* (1889). Check your understanding of depth perception by trying to spot the depth cues in the painting.

In the list below, check off the depth cues used by van Gogh. The answers can be found in the back of the book in Appendix A. You can learn more about how artists use the principles of visual perception in the Personal Application at the end of this chapter.

_______ 1. Interposition

_______ 2. Height in plane

_______ 3. Texture gradient

_______ 4. Relative size

_______ 5. Light and shadow

_______ 6. Linear perspective

van Gogh, Vincent, *Corridor in the Asylum* (1889), gouache and watercolor, 24 3/8 x 18 1/2 inches (61.5 x 47 cm). Metropolitan Museum of Art. Bequest of Abby Aldrich Rockefeller, 1948. (48.190.2) Photograph © 1998 The Metropolitan Museum of Art.

Figure 4.33

Testing understanding of pictorial depth cues. In his cross-cultural research, Hudson (1960) asked subjects to indicate whether the hunter is trying to spear the antelope or the elephant. He found cultural disparities in subjects' ability to make effective use of the pictorial depth cues, which place the elephant in the distance and make it an unlikely target.

SOURCE: Adapted by permission from an illustration by Ilil Arbel, in Deregowski, J. B. (1972, November). Pictorial perception and culture. *Scientific American, 227* (5), p. 83. Reproduced with permission. Copyright © 2011 by Scientific American, Inc. All rights reserved.

BIZARRO

Bizarro © 1991 Dan Piraro King Features Syndicate

depth cues to images varies to some degree across cultures.

Recent research has shown that estimates of distance can be skewed by people's motivational states. Studies suggest that people see desirable objects as closer to them than less desirable objects. For example, Balcetis and Dunning (2010) found that participants who are very thirsty estimate that a bottle of water sitting across a room is closer to them than participants who are not thirsty. In another study, subjects were asked to estimate the distance between them and a $100 bill that they had a chance to win or a $100 bill that they knew belonged to the experimenter. Once again, the more desirable object (the $100 bill that could be won) was perceived to be closer than the less desirable one. Thus, like other perceptual experiences, judgments of distance can be highly subjective.

Perceptual Constancies in Vision

When a person approaches you from a distance, his or her image on your retinas gradually changes in size. Do you perceive that the person is growing right before your eyes? Of course not. Your perceptual system constantly makes allowances for this variation in sensory input. In doing so, it relies in part on perceptual constancies. **A *perceptual constancy* is a tendency to experience a stable perception in the face of continually changing sensory input.** Among other things, people tend to view objects as having a stable size, shape, brightness, hue, and texture (Goldstein, 2010).

The Power of Misleading Cues: Visual Illusions

PSYKTREK SIM3, 3g

In general, perceptual constancies, depth cues, and principles of visual organization (such as the Gestalt laws) help people perceive the world accurately. Sometimes, however, perceptions are based on inappropriate assumptions, and *visual illusions* can result. **A *visual illusion* involves an apparently inexplicable discrepancy between the appearance of a visual stimulus and its physical reality.**

One famous visual illusion is the *Muller-Lyer illusion,* shown in **Figure 4.34**. The two vertical lines in this figure are equally long, but they certainly

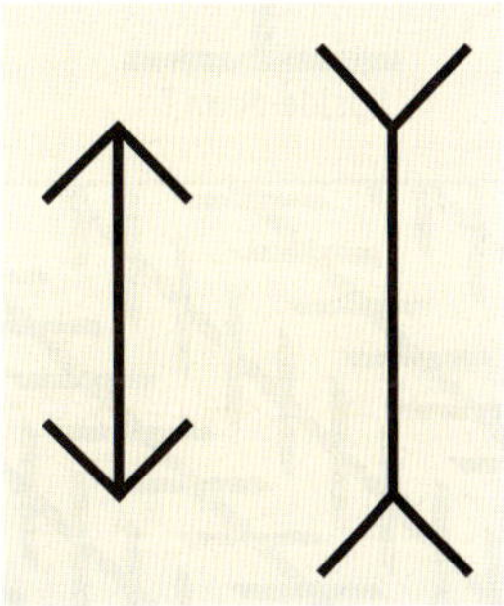

Figure 4.34

The Müller-Lyer illusion. The vertical lines in this classic illusion are very deceptive. Although they do not appear to be the same length, they are. Go ahead, measure them.

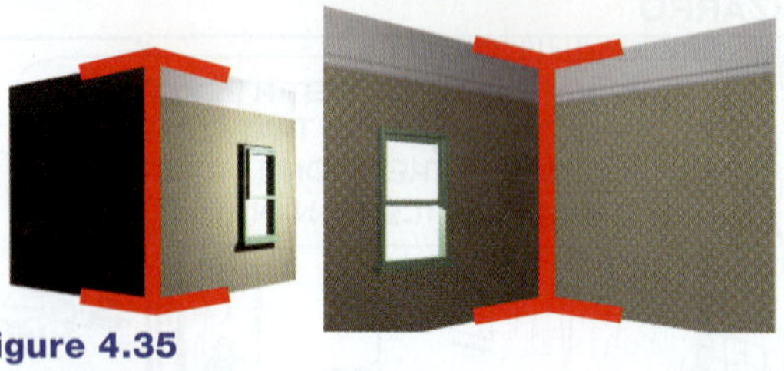

Figure 4.35

Explaining the Müller-Lyer illusion. The figure on the left seems to be closer, since it looks like an outside corner thrust toward you, whereas the figure on the right looks like an inside corner thrust away from you. Given retinal images of the same length, you assume that the "closer" line is shorter.
© Cengage Learning 2013

don't look that way. Why not? Several mechanisms probably play a role (Day, 1965; Gregory, 1978). The figure on the left looks like the outside of a building, thrust toward the viewer, while the one on the right looks like an inside corner, thrust away (see **Figure 4.35**). The vertical line in the left figure therefore seems closer. If two lines cast equally long retinal images but one seems closer, the closer one is assumed to be shorter. Thus, the Müller-Lyer illusion may result from a combination of size constancy processes and misperception of depth.

The geometric illusions shown in **Figure 4.36** also demonstrate that visual stimuli can be highly deceptive. The *Ponzo illusion,* which is shown at the top left of **Figure 4.36**, appears to result from the same factors at work in the Müller-Lyer illusion (Coren & Girgus, 1978). The upper and lower horizontal lines are the same length, but the upper one appears longer. This illusion probably occurs because the converging lines convey linear perspective, a key depth cue suggesting that the upper line lies farther away. **Figure 4.37** shows a drawing by Stanford University psychologist Roger Shepard (1990) that creates a similar illusion. The second monster appears much larger than the first, even though they are really identical in size.

In the 1930s, Adelbert Ames designed a striking illusion that makes use of misperception of distance (Behrens, 2010). It's called, appropriately enough, the *Ames room.* This specially created room is built with a trapezoidal rear wall and a sloping floor and ceiling. When viewed from the correct point, as in the picture, it looks like an ordinary rectangular room (see **Figure 4.38**). But in reality, the left corner is much taller and much farther from the viewer than the right corner. Hence, bizarre illusions unfold in the Ames room. People standing in the right corner appear to be giants, while those standing in the left corner appear to be midgets. Even more disconcerting, a person who walks across the room

Figure 4.36

Four geometric illusions. **Ponzo:** The horizontal lines are the same length. **Poggendorff:** The two diagonal segments lie on the same straight line. **Upside-down T:** The vertical and horizontal lines are the same length. **Zollner:** The long diagonals are all parallel (try covering up some of the short diagonal lines if you don't believe it).

Figure 4.37

A monster of an illusion. The principles underlying the Ponzo illusion also explain the striking illusion seen here, in which two identical monsters appear to be quite different in size, although they really are equal in size.

SOURCE: Shepard, R. N. (1990). *Mind sights.* New York: W. H. Freeman. Copyright © 1990 by Roger N. Shepard. Reprinted by permission of Henry Holt & Company.

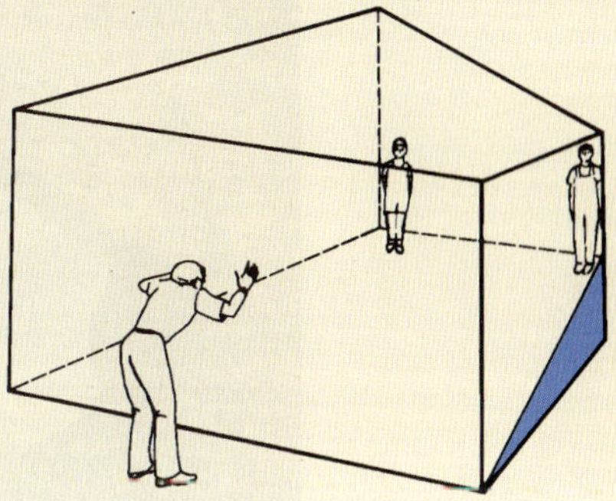

Figure 4.38

The Ames room. The diagram on the right shows the room as it is actually constructed. However, the viewer assumes that the room is rectangular, and the image cast on the retina is consistent with this hypothesis. Because of this reasonable perceptual hypothesis, the normal perceptual adjustments made to preserve size constancy lead to the illusions described in the text. For example, naive viewers "conclude" that the boy on the right is much larger than the other, when in fact he is merely closer.

© Wayne Weiten 1997

© Cengage Learning 2013

from right to left appears to shrink before your eyes! The Ames room creates these misperceptions by toying with the perfectly reasonable assumption that the room is vertically and horizontally rectangular.

Impossible figures create another form of illusion. ***Impossible figures*** **are objects that can be represented in two-dimensional pictures but cannot exist in three-dimensional space.** These figures may look fine at first glance, but a closer look reveals that they are geometrically inconsistent or impossible. Three widely studied impossible figures are shown in **Figure 4.39**, and a more recent impossible figure created by Roger Shepard (1990) can be seen in **Figure 4.40**. Notice that specific portions of these figures are reasonable, but they don't add up to a sensible whole (Macpherson, 2010). The parts don't interface properly. The initial illusion that the figures make sense is probably a result of bottom-up processing. You perceive specific features of the figure as acceptable but are baffled as they're built into a whole.

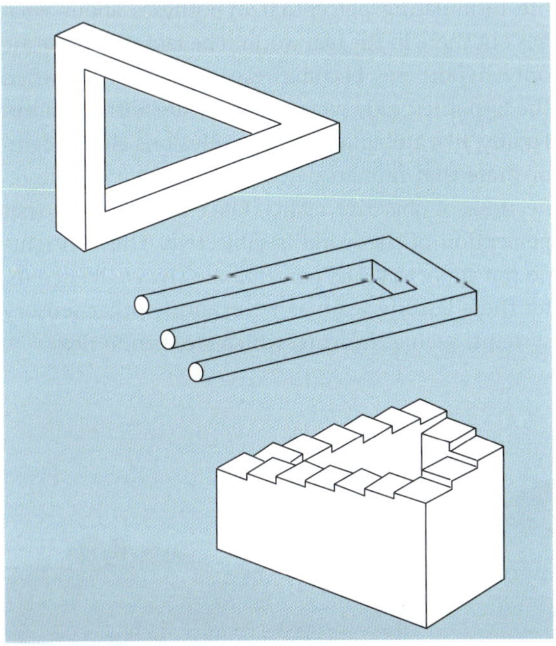

Figure 4.39

Three classic impossible figures. These figures are impossible, yet they clearly exist—on the page. What makes them impossible is that they appear to be three-dimensional representations yet are drawn in a way that frustrates mental attempts to "assemble" their features into possible objects. It's difficult to see the drawings simply as lines lying in a plane—even though this perceptual hypothesis is the only one that resolves the contradiction.

Figure 4.40

Another impossible figure. This impossible figure, drawn by Stanford University psychologist Roger Shepard (1990), seems even more perplexing than the classic impossible figure that it is based on (the one seen in the middle of **Figure 4.39**).

SOURCE: Shepard, R. N. (1990). *Mind sights.* New York: W. H. Freeman. Copyright © 1990 by Roger N. Shepard. Reprinted by permission of Henry Holt & Company.

A puzzling perceptual illusion common in everyday life is the moon illusion: the moon looks larger when at the horizon than when overhead.

© N. R. Rowan/The Image Works

Obviously, illusions such as impossible figures and their real-life relative, the Ames room, involve a conspiracy of cues intended to deceive the viewer. Many visual illusions, however, occur quite naturally. A well-known example is the *moon illusion* (see the photo above). The full moon appears to be as much as 50% smaller when overhead than when looming on the horizon (Ross & Plug, 2002). As with many of the other illusions we have discussed, the moon illusion appears to be due mainly to size constancy effects coupled with the misperception of distance (Coren & Aks, 1990; Kaufman et al., 2007), although other factors may also play a role (Suzuki, 2007). The moon illusion shows that optical illusions are part of everyday life. Indeed, many people are virtually addicted to an optical illusion called television (an illusion of movement created by a series of still images presented in quick succession).

Cross-cultural studies have uncovered some interesting differences among cultural groups in their propensity to see certain illusions (Masuda, 2010). For example, Segall, Campbell, and Herskovits (1966) found that people from a variety of non-Western cultures are less susceptible to the Müller-Lyer illusion than Western samples. What could account for this difference? The most plausible explanation is that in the West, we live in a "carpentered world" dominated by straight lines, right angles, and rectangular rooms, buildings, and furniture. Thus, our experience prepares us to readily view the Müller-Lyer figures as inside and outside corners of buildings—inferences that help foster the illusion (Segall et al., 1990). In contrast, people in many non-Western cultures, such as the Zulu (see the photo below) who were tested by Segall and associates (1966), live in a less carpentered world, making them less prone to see the Müller-Lyer figures as building corners.

What do illusions reveal about visual perception? They drive home the point that people go through life formulating perceptual hypotheses about what lies out there in the real world. The fact that these are only hypotheses becomes especially striking when the hypotheses are wrong, as they are with illusions. Finally, like ambiguous figures, illusions clearly demonstrate that human perceptions are not simple reflections of objective reality. Once again, we see that perception of the world is subjective. These insights do not apply to visual perception only. We'll encounter these lessons again as we examine other sensory systems, such as hearing, which we turn to next.

Unlike people in Western nations, the Zulus live in a culture where straight lines and right angles are scarce. Thus, they are not affected by such phenomena as the Müller-Lyer illusion nearly as much as people raised in environments that abound with rectangular structures.

© Alan Evrard/Robert Harding/Getty Images

REVIEW OF KEY LEARNING GOALS

4.10 Reversible figures and perceptual sets demonstrate that the same visual input can result in very different perceptions. Form perception depends on both the selection and interpretation of sensory inputs. Inattentional blindness involves the failure to see readily visible objects.

4.11 According to feature analysis theories, people detect specific features in stimuli and build them into recognizable forms through bottom-up processing, which involves a progression from elements to the whole. However, form perception also involves top-down processing, which involves a progression from the whole to the elements.

4.12 Gestalt psychology emphasized that the whole may be greater than the sum of its parts (features). Objects are more likely to be viewed as figure rather than ground when they are smaller, higher in contrast or symmetry, and lower in one's frame of view. Gestalt principles of form perception include proximity, similarity, continuity, closure, and simplicity. Other approaches to form perception emphasize that people develop perceptual hypotheses about the external stimuli that could be responsible for various patterns of sensory stimulation.

4.13 Binocular cues such as retinal disparity and convergence can contribute to depth perception. Depth perception depends primarily on monocular cues, including pictorial cues such as texture gradient, linear perspective, light and shadow, interposition, relative size, and height in plane. People from pictureless societies have some difficulty in applying pictorial depth cues to two-dimensional pictures.

4.14 Perceptual constancies in vision help viewers deal with the ever-shifting nature of sensory input. Visual illusions demonstrate that perceptual hypotheses can be inaccurate and that perceptions are not simple reflections of objective reality. Researchers have found some interesting cultural differences in susceptibility to the Müller-Lyer and Ponzo illusions.

The Auditory System: Hearing

KEY LEARNING GOALS

4.15 List the three properties of sound and the aspects of auditory perception that they influence.

4.16 Summarize information on human hearing capacities and the potential effects of loud noise on hearing loss.

4.17 Describe how sensory processing occurs in the ear.

4.18 Compare the place and frequency theories of pitch perception, and discuss the resolution of the debate.

Stop reading for a moment, close your eyes, and listen carefully. What do you hear?

Chances are, you'll discover that you're immersed in sounds: street noises, a high-pitched laugh from the next room, the buzzing of a fluorescent lamp, perhaps some background music you put on a while ago but forgot about. As this little demonstration shows, physical stimuli producing sound are present almost constantly, but you're not necessarily aware of these sounds.

Like vision, the auditory (hearing) system provides input about the world "out there," but not until incoming information is processed by the brain. An auditory stimulus—a screech of tires, someone laughing, the hum of the refrigerator—produces a sensory input in the form of sound waves reaching the ears. The perceptual system must somehow transform this stimulation into the psychological experience of hearing. We'll begin our discussion of hearing by looking at the stimulus for auditory experience: sound.

The Stimulus: Sound

PSYKTREK 3h

Sound waves are vibrations of molecules, which means that they must travel through some physical medium, such as air. They move at a fraction of the speed of light. Sound waves are usually generated by vibrating objects, such as a guitar string, a loudspeaker cone, or your vocal cords. However, sound waves can also be generated by forcing air past a chamber (as in a pipe organ), or by suddenly releasing a burst of air (as when you clap).

Like light waves, sound waves are characterized by their *amplitude,* their *wavelength,* and their *purity* (see **Figure 4.41**). The physical properties of amplitude, wavelength, and purity affect mainly the perceived (psychological) qualities of *loudness, pitch,* and *timbre,* respectively. However, the physical properties of sound interact in complex ways to produce perceptions of these sound qualities (Hirsh & Watson, 1996).

Human Hearing Capacities

PSYKTREK 3h

Wavelengths of sound are described in terms of their *frequency,* which is measured in cycles per second, or *hertz (Hz).* For the most part, higher frequencies are perceived as having higher pitch. That is, if you strike the key for high C on a piano, it will produce higher-frequency sound waves than the key for low C. Although the perception of pitch depends

(a)

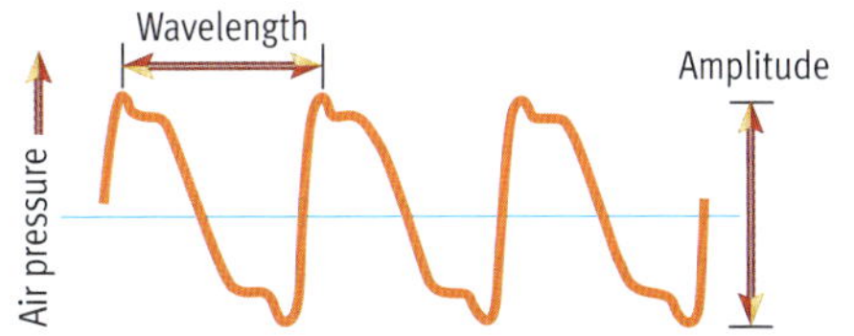

(b)

Physical properties of sound	Related perceptions
Amplitude	Loudness
Frequency	Pitch
Purity	Timbre

Figure 4.41

Sound, the physical stimulus for hearing. **(a)** Like light, sound travels in waves—in this case, waves of air pressure. A smooth curve would represent a pure tone, such as that produced by a tuning fork. Most sounds, however, are complex. For example, the wave shown here is for middle C played on a piano. The sound wave for the same note played on a violin would have the same wavelength (or frequency) as this one, but the "wrinkles" in the wave would be different, corresponding to the differences in timbre between the two sounds. **(b)** The table shows the main relations between objective aspects of sound and subjective perceptions. © Cengage Learning 2013

Figure 4.42

Sound pressure and auditory experience. The threshold for human hearing (graphed in green) is a function of both sound pressure (decibel level) and frequency. Human hearing is keenest for sounds at a frequency of about 2000 Hz; at other frequencies, higher decibel levels are needed to produce sounds people can detect. On the other hand, the human threshold for pain (graphed in red) is almost purely a function of decibel level.

© Cengage Learning 2013

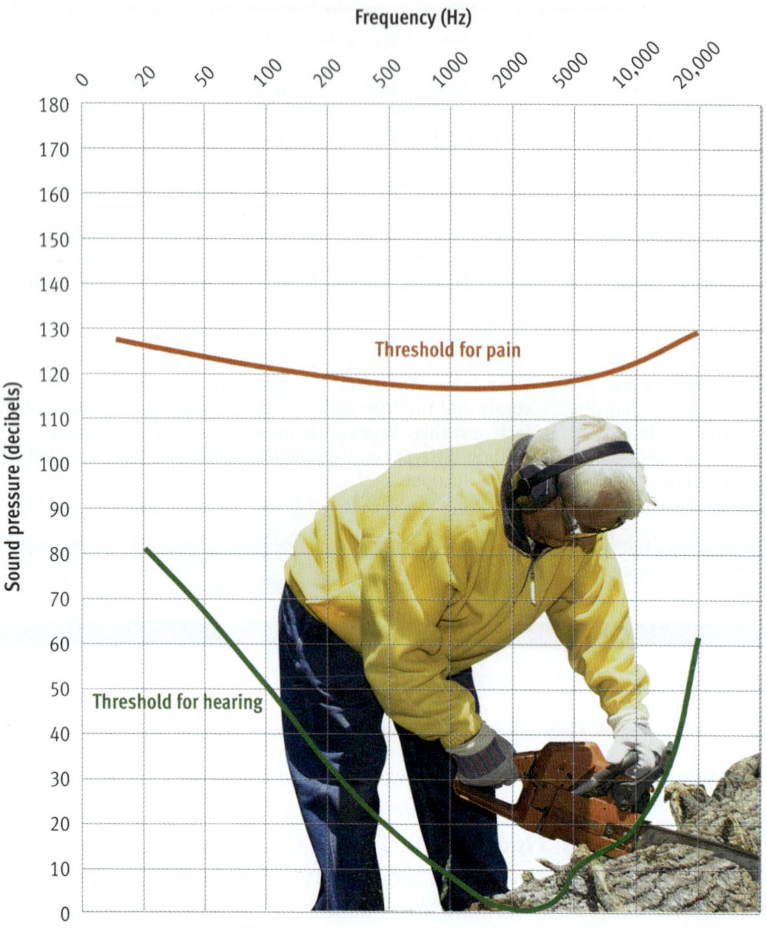

© Betts Anderson Loman/PhotoEdit

mainly on frequency, the amplitude of the sound waves also influences it.

Just as the visible spectrum is only a portion of the total spectrum of light, so, too, what people can hear is only a portion of the available range of sounds. Humans can hear sounds ranging from a low of 20 Hz up to a high of about 20,000 Hz. Sounds at either end of this range are harder to hear, and sensitivity to high-frequency tones declines as adults grow older (Dubno, 2010). Other organisms have different capabilities. Low-frequency sounds under 10 Hz are audible to homing pigeons, for example. At the other extreme, bats and porpoises can hear frequencies well above 20,000 Hz.

In general, the greater the amplitude of sound waves, the louder the sound perceived. Whereas frequency is measured in hertz, amplitude is measured in *decibels (dB)*. The relationship between decibels (which measure a physical property of sound) and loudness (a psychological quality) is complex. A rough rule of thumb is that perceived loudness doubles about every 6–10 decibels (Florentine & Heinz, 2010). Very loud sounds can jeopardize the quality of your hearing. In work settings, chronic exposure to more than 85 decibels is considered risky and is strictly regulated (Eggermont, 2010). Even brief exposure to sounds over 120 decibels can be painful and can cause damage to your auditory system (Daniel, 2007).

In recent years there has been great concern about hearing loss in young people using personal listening devices who play their music too loudly (Morata, 2007). Portable music players can easily deliver over 100 decibels through headphones. One study found significant hearing impairment in 14% of the young people sampled (Peng, Tao, Huang, 2009). Unfortunately, adolescents tend to not take the risk of hearing loss very seriously (Vogel et al., 2008). However, it is a problem that is likely to lead to a great deal of preventable hearing loss, given the increased popularity of portable music players (Daniel, 2007; Vogel et al., 2007).

As shown in **Figure 4.42**, the absolute thresholds for the weakest sounds people can hear differ for sounds of various frequencies. The human ear is most sensitive to sounds at frequencies near 2000 Hz. That is, these frequencies yield the lowest absolute thresholds. To summarize, amplitude is the principal determinant of loudness, but loudness ultimately depends on an interaction between amplitude and frequency.

People are also sensitive to variations in the purity of sounds. The purest sound is one that has only a single frequency of vibration, such as that produced by a tuning fork. But most everyday sounds are complex mixtures of many frequencies. The purity or complexity of a sound influences how *timbre* is perceived. To understand timbre, think of a note with precisely the same loudness and pitch played on a French horn and then on a violin. The difference you perceive in the sounds is a difference in timbre.

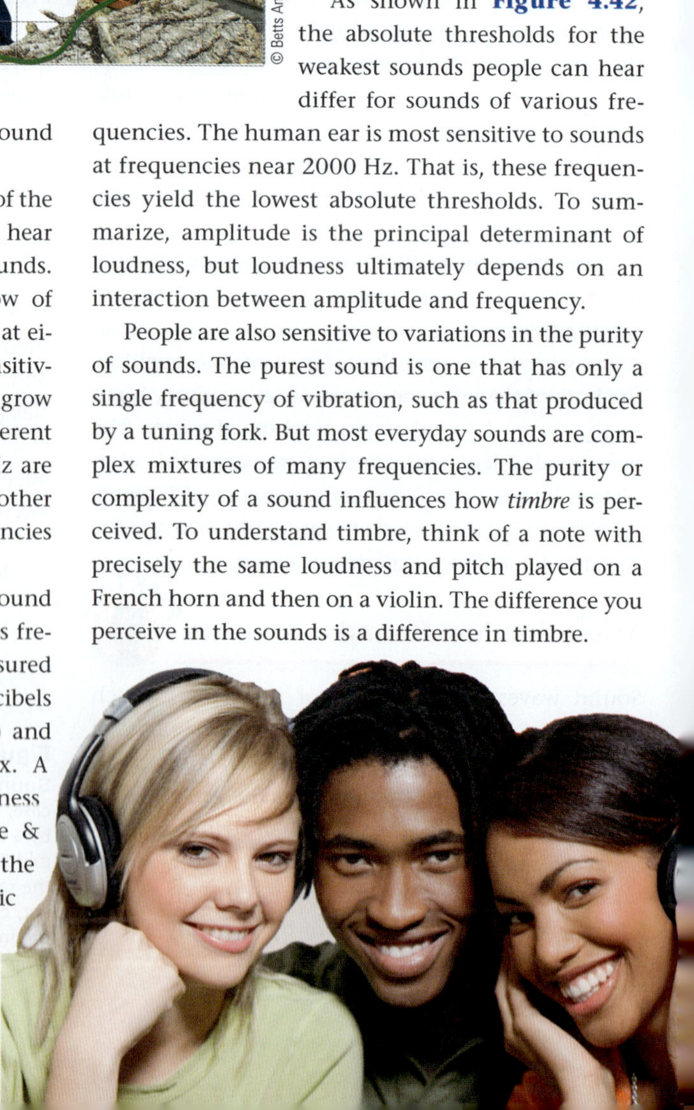

© 1999-2011 Masterfile Corporation

Sensory Processing in the Ear

PSYKTREK 3h

Like your eyes, your ears channel energy to the neural tissue that receives it. **Figure 4.43** shows that the human ear can be divided into three sections: the external ear, the middle ear, and the inner ear. Sound is conducted differently in each section. The external ear depends on the *vibration of air molecules*. The middle ear depends on the *vibration of movable bones*. And the inner ear depends on *waves in a fluid*, which are finally converted into a stream of neural signals sent to the brain (Hackney, 2010).

The *external ear* consists mainly of the *pinna*, a sound-collecting cone. When you cup your hand behind your ear to try to hear better, you're enlarging that cone. Many animals have large external ears that they can aim directly toward a sound source. However, humans can adjust their aim only crudely, by turning their heads. Sound waves collected by the pinna are funneled along the auditory canal toward the *eardrum*, a taut membrane that vibrates in response.

In the *middle ear*, the vibrations of the eardrum are transmitted inward by a mechanical chain made up of the three tiniest bones in your body (the hammer, anvil, and stirrup), known collectively as the *ossicles*. The ossicles form a three-stage lever system that converts relatively large movements with little force into smaller motions with greater force. The ossicles serve to amplify tiny changes in air pressure.

The *inner ear* consists largely of the ***cochlea*, a fluid-filled, coiled tunnel that contains the receptors for hearing.** The term *cochlea* comes from the Greek word for a spiral-shelled snail, which this chamber resembles (see **Figure 4.44** on the next page). Sound enters the cochlea through the *oval window*, which is vibrated by the ossicles. The ear's neural tissue, analogous to the retina in the eye, lies within the cochlea. This tissue sits on the *basilar membrane* that divides the cochlea into upper and lower chambers. The basilar membrane, which runs the length of the spiraled cochlea, holds the auditory receptors. The auditory receptors are called *hair cells* because of the tiny bundles of hairs that protrude from them. Waves in the fluid of the inner ear stimulate the hair cells. Like the rods and cones in the eye, the hair cells convert this physical stimulation into neural impulses that are sent to the brain (Hackett & Kaas, 2009).

These signals are routed through the thalamus to the auditory cortex, which is located mostly in the temporal lobes of the brain. Studies demonstrate

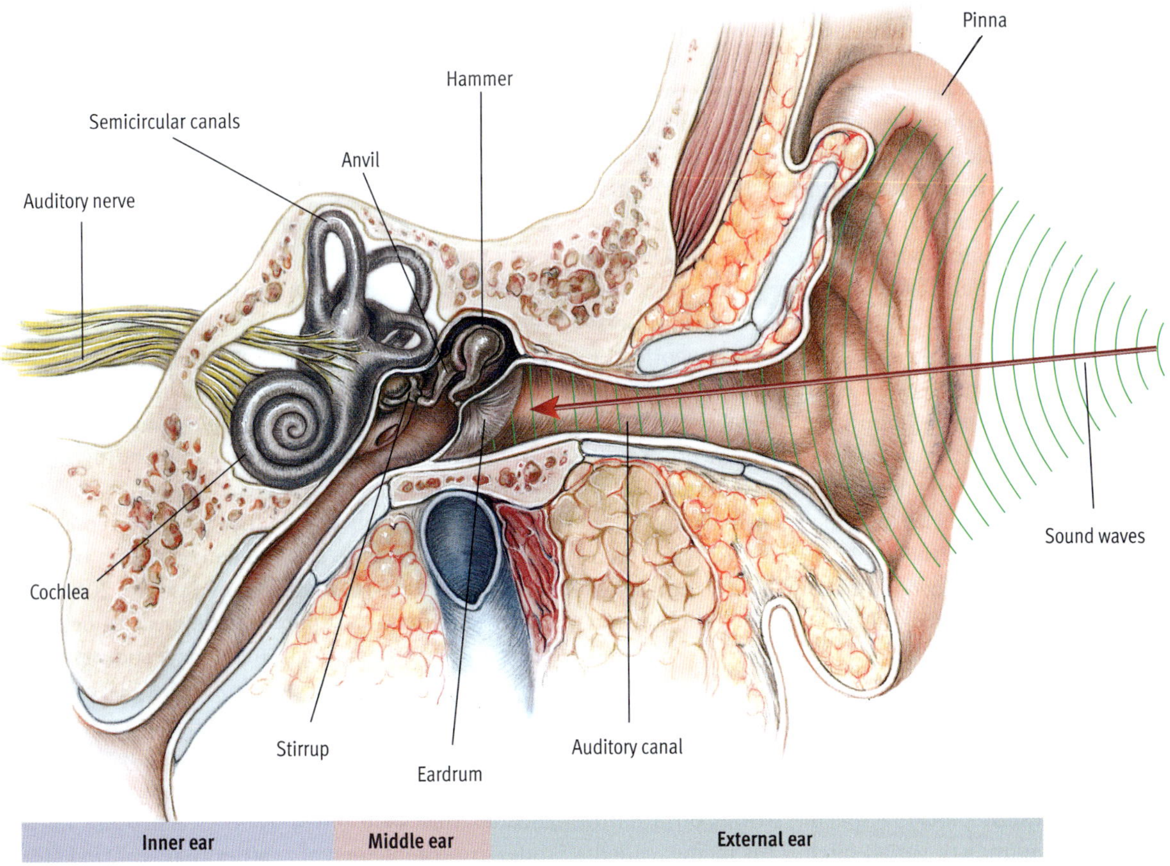

Figure 4.43

The human ear. Converting sound pressure to information processed by the nervous system involves a complex relay of stimuli. Waves of air pressure create vibrations in the eardrum, which in turn cause oscillations in the tiny bones in the inner ear (the hammer, anvil, and stirrup). As they are relayed from one bone to the next, the oscillations are magnified and then transformed into pressure waves moving through a liquid medium in the cochlea. These waves cause the basilar membrane to oscillate, stimulating the hair cells that are the actual auditory receptors (see **Figure 4.44**). © Cengage Learning 2013

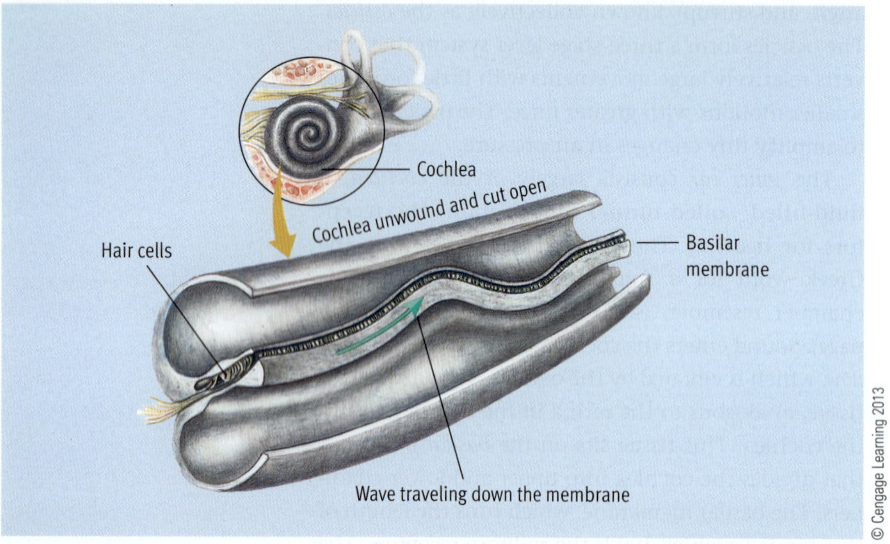

Figure 4.44

The basilar membrane. This graphic shows how the cochlea might look if it were unwound and cut open to reveal the basilar membrane, which is covered with thousands of hair cells (the auditory receptors). Pressure waves in the fluid filling the cochlea cause oscillations to travel in waves down the basilar membrane, stimulating the hair cells to fire. Although the entire membrane vibrates, as predicted by frequency theory, the point along the membrane where the wave peaks depends on the frequency of the sound stimulus, as suggested by place theory.

that the auditory cortex has specialized cells—similar to the feature detectors found in the visual cortex—that have special sensitivity to certain features of sound (Pickles, 1988).

Auditory Perception: Theories of Hearing

Theories of hearing need to account for how sound waves are physiologically translated into the perceptions of pitch, loudness, and timbre. To date, most of the theorizing about hearing has focused on the perception of pitch, which is reasonably well understood. Researchers' understanding of loudness and timbre perception is primitive by comparison. Consequently, we'll limit our coverage to theories of pitch perception.

Two theories have dominated the debate on pitch perception: *place theory* and *frequency theory.* You'll be able to follow the development of these theories more easily if you can imagine the spiraled cochlea unraveled, so that the basilar membrane becomes a long, thin sheet, lined with about 16,000 individual hair cells (see **Figure 4.44**).

Hermann von Helmholtz

"The psychic activities, by which we arrive at the judgment that a certain object of a certain character exists before us at a certain place, are generally not conscious activities but unconscious ones. . . . It may be permissible to designate the psychic acts of ordinary perception as unconscious inferences."

Place Theory

Long ago, Hermann von Helmholtz (1863) proposed that specific sound frequencies vibrate specific portions of the basilar membrane, producing distinct pitches, just as plucking specific strings on a harp produces sounds of varied pitch. This model, called *place theory,* holds that perception of pitch corresponds to the vibration of different portions, or places, along the basilar membrane. Place theory assumes that hair cells at various locations respond independently and that different sets of hair cells are vibrated by different sound frequencies. The brain then detects the frequency of a tone according to which area along the basilar membrane is most active.

Frequency Theory

Other theorists in the 19th century proposed an alternative theory of pitch perception, called frequency theory (Rutherford, 1886). *Frequency theory* holds that perception of pitch corresponds to the rate, or frequency, at which the entire basilar membrane vibrates. This theory views the basilar membrane as more like a drumhead than a harp. According to frequency theory, the whole membrane vibrates in unison in response to sounds. However, a particular sound frequency, say 3000 Hz, causes the basilar membrane to vibrate at a corresponding rate of 3000 times per second. The brain detects the frequency of a tone by the rate at which the auditory nerve fibers fire.

Reconciling Place and Frequency Theories

The competition between these two theories is like the dispute between the trichromatic and opponent process theories of color vision. As with that argument, the debate between place and frequency theories generated roughly a century of research. Although both theories proved to have some flaws, *both turned out to be valid in part.*

Helmholtz's place theory was basically on the mark except for one detail: the hair cells along the basilar membrane are not independent. They vibrate together, as suggested by frequency theory. The actual pattern of vibration, described in Nobel prize–winning research by Georg von Békésy (1947), is a traveling wave that moves along the basilar membrane. Place theory is correct, however, in that the wave peaks at a particular place, depending on the frequency of the sound wave.

The current thinking is that pitch perception depends on both place and frequency coding of vibrations along the basilar membrane (Moore, 2010, Yost, 2010). Low-frequency pure tones appear to be translated into pitch through frequency coding. High-frequency pure tones appear to rely on place coding. And complex tones seem to depend on complex combinations of frequency and place coding. Although much remains to be learned, once again we find that theories that were pitted against each other for decades are complementary rather than contradictory.

REVIEW OF KEY LEARNING GOALS

4.15 Sound varies in terms of wavelength (frequency), amplitude, and purity. Wavelength mainly affects perceptions of pitch, amplitude mainly influences perceptions of loudness, and purity is the key determinant of timbre.

4.16 The human ear can detect sounds between 20 and 20,000 Hz, but it is most sensitive to sounds around 2000 Hz. In general, higher-amplitude sound waves are perceived as louder. Even brief exposure to sounds over 120 decibels can be painful and damaging.

4.17 Sound is transmitted through the external ear via air conduction to the middle ear. In the middle ear, sound waves are translated into the vibration of tiny bones called ossicles. In the inner ear, fluid conduction vibrates hair cells along the basilar membrane in the cochlea. These hair cells are the receptors for hearing.

4.18 Place theory proposed that pitch perception depends on where vibrations occur along the basilar membrane. Frequency theory countered with the idea that pitch perception depends on the rate at which the basilar membrane vibrates. Modern evidence suggests that both theories work together to explain pitch perception.

CONCEPT CHECK 4.3

Comparing Vision and Hearing

Check your understanding of both vision and hearing by comparing key aspects of sensation and perception in these senses. The dimensions of comparison are listed in the first column below. The second column lists the answers for the sense of vision. Fill in the answers for the sense of hearing in the third column. The answers can be found in Appendix A in the back of the book.

Dimension	Vision	Hearing
1. Stimulus	*Light waves*	______
2. Elements of stimulus and related perceptions	*Wavelength/hue*	______
	Amplitude/brightness	______
	Purity/saturation	______
3. Receptors	*Rods and cones*	______
4. Location of receptors	*Retina*	______
5. Main location of processing in brain	*Occipital lobe*	______
	Visual cortex	______

The Chemical Senses: Taste and Smell

KEY LEARNING GOALS

4.19 Describe the stimulus and receptors for taste, and discuss some determinants of taste preferences.

4.20 Review research on individual differences in taste sensitivity, and explain what is meant by the perception of flavor.

4.21 Describe the stimulus and receptors for smell and discuss humans' olfactory abilities.

Psychologists have devoted most of their attention to the visual and auditory systems. Although less is known about the chemical senses of taste and smell, both play a critical role in people's experience of the world. Let's take a brief look at what psychologists have learned about **the *gustatory system*—the sensory system for taste**—and its close cousin, **the *olfactory system*—the sensory system for smell.**

The Gustatory System: Taste

True wine lovers go through an elaborate series of steps when they are served a good bottle of wine. Typically, they begin by drinking a little water to cleanse their palate. Then they sniff the cork from the wine bottle, swirl a small amount of the wine around in a glass, and sniff the odor emerging from the glass. Finally, they take a sip of the wine, rolling it around in their mouth for a short time before swallowing it. At last they are ready to judge it. Is such an elaborate process really necessary? Or is it just a harmless ritual passed on through tradition? You'll find out in this section.

The physical stimuli for the sense of taste are chemical substances that are soluble (dissolvable in water). The gustatory receptors are clusters of taste cells found in the *taste buds* that line the trenches around tiny bumps on the tongue (see **Figure 4.45** on the next page). When these cells absorb chemicals dissolved in saliva, they trigger neural impulses that are routed through the thalamus to the cortex. Interestingly, taste cells have a short life. They last only about ten days and are constantly being replaced (Cowart, 2005).

Are the elaborate wine-tasting rituals of wine lovers just a pretentious tradition, or do they make sense in light of what science has revealed about the gustatory system? Your text answers this question in this section.

© Andersen Ross/Getty Images

Figure 4.45

The tongue and taste. Taste buds are clustered around tiny bumps on the tongue called papillae. The three types of papillae are distributed on the tongue as shown here. The taste buds found in each type of papillae show slightly different sensitivities to the four basic tastes, as mapped out in the graph at the top. Thus, sensitivity to the primary tastes varies across the tongue, but these variations are small, and all four primary tastes can be detected wherever there are taste receptors. © Cengage Learning 2013

SOURCE: Adapted from Bartoshuk, L. M. (1993). Genetic and pathological taste variation: What can we learn from animal models and human disease? In D. Chadwick, J. Marsh, & J. Goode (Eds.), *The molecular basis of smell and taste transduction* (pp. 251–267). New York: Wiley.

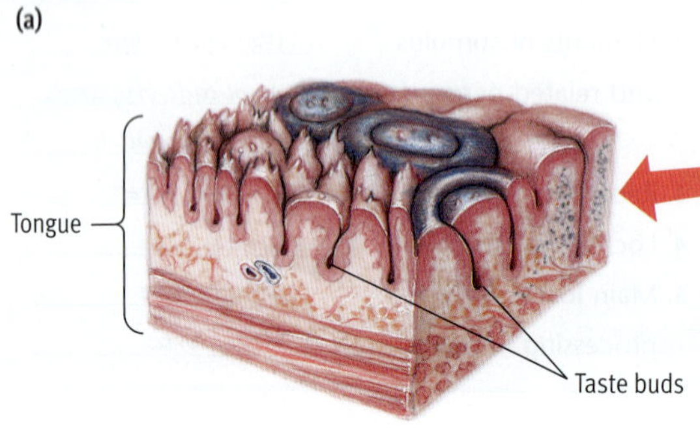

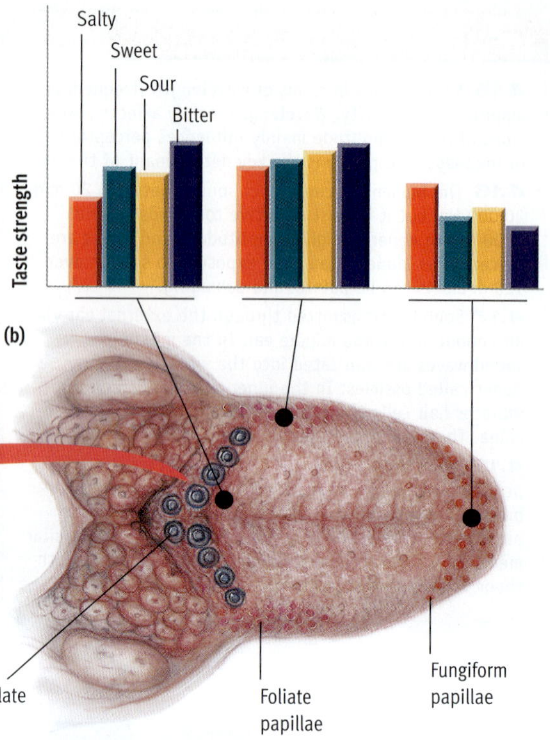

Reality CHECK

Misconception

Sensitivity to the four primary tastes varies greatly across the tongue, as depicted in the tongue map shown below.

Reality

For decades it was reported that taste buds sensitive to the four primary tastes are distributed unevenly across the tongue in the manner shown here. However, these classic tongue maps were based on a misinterpretation of early research data. Although there are some small variations in sensitivity to specific tastes on the tongue, all four primary tastes can be detected wherever there are taste receptors.

© Cengage Learning 20`3

It's generally agreed that there are four *primary tastes:* sweet, sour, bitter, and salty (Buck, 2000). However, scientists are increasingly recognizing a fifth primary taste called *umami,* which is a Japanese word for the *savory* taste of glutamate found in foods like meats and cheeses (DuBois, 2010). The case for umami as a fifth basic taste has been strengthened by recent evidence that umami substances activate specific receptors on the tongue (Di Lorenzo & Rosen, 2010). Sensitivity to the primary tastes is distributed somewhat unevenly across the tongue, but the variations in sensitivity are quite small and highly complicated (Bartoshuk, 1993b; see **Figure 4.45**). Perceptions of taste quality appear to depend on complex *patterns* of neural activity initiated by taste receptors (Erickson, DiLorenzo, & Woodbury, 1994). Taste signals are routed through the thalamus and onto the *insular cortex* in the frontal lobe, where the initial cortical processing takes place (Di Lorenzo & Rosen, 2010).

Some basic taste preferences appear to be inborn and to be automatically regulated by physiological mechanisms. In humans, for instance, newborn infants react positively to sweet tastes and negatively to strong concentrations of bitter or sour tastes (Cowart, 2005). To some extent, these innate taste preferences are flexible, changing to accommodate the body's nutritional needs (Scott, 1990).

Although some basic aspects of taste perception may be innate, taste preferences are largely learned and heavily influenced by social processes (Rozin, 1990). Most parents are aware of this fact and intentionally try—with varied success—to mold their children's taste preferences early in life (Patrick et al., 2005). This extensive social influence contributes greatly to the striking ethnic and cultural disparities found in taste preferences (Kittler & Sucher, 2008). Foods that are a source of disgust in Western

© Nayashkova Olga/Shutterstock

© Malcolm S. Kirk

Guy Mary-Rousseliere/Catholic Mission, Northwest, Canada

© Danielle Pelligrini/Science Source/Photo Researchers, Inc.

Grubs. For most North Americans, the thought of eating a worm would be totally unthinkable. For the Asmat of New Guinea, however, a favorite delicacy is the plump, white, 2-inch larva or beetle grub.

Fish eyes. For some Eskimo children, raw fish eyes are like candy. Here you see a young girl using the Eskimo's all-purpose knife to gouge out the eye of an already-filleted Artic fish.

Blood. Several tribes in East Africa supplement their diet with fresh blood that is sometimes mixed with milk. They obtain the blood by puncturing a cow's jugular vein with a sharp arrow. The blood-milk drink provides a rich source of protein and iron.

© Cengage Learning 2013

Figure 4.46
Culture and taste preferences. Taste preferences are heavily influenced by learning and vary dramatically from one society to the next, as these examples demonstrate.

cultures—such as worms, fish eyes, and blood—may be delicacies in other cultures (see **Figure 4.46**). To a large degree, variations in taste preferences depend on what one has been exposed to (Capaldi & VandenBos, 1991; Zellner, 1991). Exposure to particular foods varies along ethnic lines because different cultures have different traditions in food preparation, different agricultural resources, different climates to work with, and so forth.

Research by Linda Bartoshuk and others reveals that people vary considerably in their sensitivity to certain tastes. These individual differences depend in part on the density of taste buds on the tongue, which appears to be a matter of genetic inheritance (Bartoshuk, 1993a). People characterized as *nontasters,* as determined by their insensitivity to PTC (phenythiocarbamide), or its close relative, PROP (propylthiouracil), tend to have about one-fourth as many taste buds per square centimeter as people at the other end of the spectrum, who are called *supertasters* (Miller & Reedy, 1990). Supertasters also have specialized taste receptors that are not found in nontasters (Bufe et al., 2005). In the United States, roughly 25% of people are nontasters, another 25% are supertasters, and the remaining 50% fall between these extremes and are characterized as *medium tasters* (Di Lorenzo & Youngentob, 2003). Supertasters and nontasters respond similarly to many foods, but supertasters are much more sensitive to certain sweet and bitter substances (Prescott, 2010). These variations in sensitivity mean that when two people taste the same food they will not necessarily have the same sensory experience. Thus, in regard to taste, different people live in somewhat different sensory worlds (Breslin, 2010).

These differences in taste sensitivity influence people's eating habits in ways that can have important repercussions for their physical health. For example, supertasters tend to consume fewer high-fat foods, which is likely to reduce their risk for cardiovascular disease (Duffy, Lucchina, & Bartoshuk, 2004). Supertasters also tend to react more negatively to alcohol and smoking, thereby reducing their likelihood of developing drinking problems or nicotine addiction (Duffy, Peterson, & Bartoshuk, 2004; Snedecor et al., 2006). The main health disadvantage identified for supertasters is that they respond more negatively to many vegetables, which seems to hold down their vegetable intake (Basson et al., 2005; Dinehart et al., 2006). Overall, however, supertasters tend to have better health habits than nontasters, thanks to their strong reactions to certain tastes (Duffy, 2004).

Women are somewhat more likely to be supertasters than men (Bartoshuk, Duffy, & Miller, 1994). Some psychologists speculate that the gender gap in this trait may have evolutionary significance. Over the course of evolution, women have generally been more involved than men in feeding children. Increased reactivity to sweet and bitter tastes would have been adaptive in that it would have made women more sensitive to the relatively scarce high-caloric foods (which often taste sweet) needed for survival and to the toxic substances (which often taste bitter) that hunters and gatherers needed to avoid.

So far, we've been discussing taste, but what we're really interested in is the *perception of flavor.* Flavor is

Courtesy of Linda Bartoshuk

Linda Bartoshuk

"Good and bad are so intimately associated with taste and smell that we have special words for the experiences (e.g., repugnant, foul). The immediacy of the pleasure makes it seem absolute and thus inborn. This turns out to be true for taste but not for smell."

a combination of taste, smell, and the tactile sensation of food in one's mouth (Smith & Margolskee, 2006). Odors make a surprisingly great contribution to the perception of flavor (Lawless, 2001). The ability to identify flavors declines noticeably when odor cues are absent. You might have noticed this interaction when you ate a favorite meal while enduring a severe head cold. The food probably tasted bland because your stuffy nose impaired your sense of smell.

Now that we've explored the dynamics of taste, we can return to our question about the value of the wine-tasting ritual. This elaborate ritual is in fact an authentic way to put wine to a sensitive test. The aftereffects associated with sensory adaptation make it wise to cleanse one's palate before tasting the wine. Sniffing the cork, and the wine in the glass, is important because odor is a major determinant of flavor. Swirling the wine in the glass helps release the wine's odor. And rolling the wine around in your mouth is especially critical, because it distributes the wine over the full diversity of taste cells. It also forces the wine's odor up into the nasal passages. Thus, each action in this age-old ritual makes a meaningful contribution to the tasting.

The Olfactory System: Smell

Humans are usually characterized as being relatively insensitive to smell. In this regard they are often compared unfavorably to dogs, which are renowned for their ability to track a faint odor over long distances. Are humans really inferior in the sensory domain of smell? Let's examine the facts.

In many ways, the sense of smell is much like the sense of taste. The physical stimuli are chemical substances—volatile ones that can evaporate and be carried in the air. These chemical stimuli are dissolved in fluid—specifically, the mucus in the nose. The receptors for smell are *olfactory cilia,* hairlike structures in the upper portion of the nasal passages (see **Figure 4.47**). They resemble taste cells in that they have a short life (30–60 days) and are constantly being replaced (Buck, 2000). Olfactory receptors have axons that synapse with cells in the *olfactory bulb* and then are routed directly to the olfactory cortex in the temporal lobe and other areas in the cortex (Scott, 2008). This arrangement is unique. *Smell is the only sensory system in which incoming information is not routed through the thalamus before it projects to the cortex.*

Odors cannot be classified as neatly as tastes, since efforts to identify primary odors have proven unsatisfactory (Doty, 1991). Humans have about 350 different types of olfactory receptors (Buck, 2004). Most olfactory receptors respond to a wide range of odors. Specific odors trigger responses in different

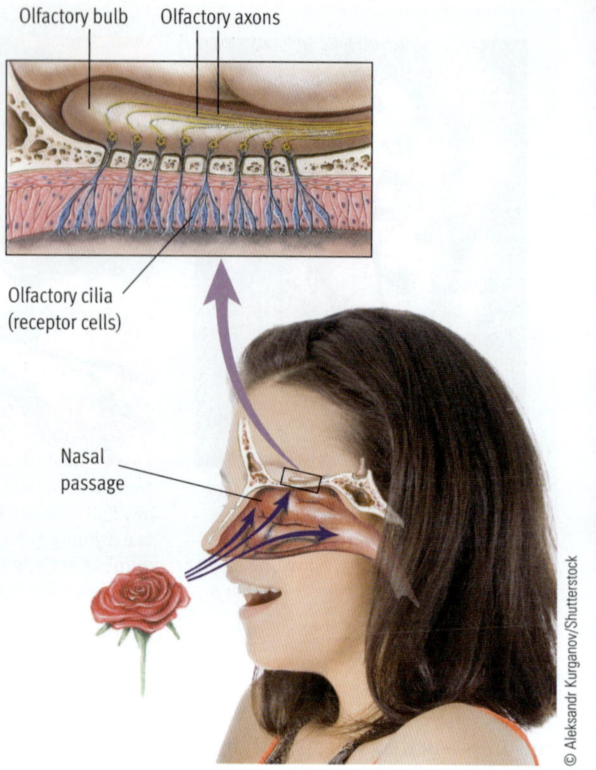

Figure 4.47

The olfactory system. Odor molecules travel through the nasal passages and stimulate olfactory cilia. An enlargement of these hairlike olfactory receptors is shown in the inset. The olfactory nerves transmit neural impulses through the olfactory bulb to the brain. © Cengage Learning 2013

combinations of receptors (Doty, 2010). Like the other senses, the sense of smell shows sensory adaptation. The perceived strength of an odor usually fades to less than half its original strength within about 4 minutes (Cain, 1988).

Humans can distinguish a great many odors, with estimates of the number of distinct odors ranging from 10,000 (Axel, 1995) to 100,000 (Firestein, 2001). However, when people are asked to identify the sources of specific odors (such as smoke or soap), their performance is rather mediocre. For some unknown reason, people have a hard time attaching names to odors (Cowart & Rawson, 2001).

How do human olfactory capacities compare to those of other species? We do have notably fewer olfactory receptors than many other animals (Wolfe et al., 2006). Our relative paucity of such receptors probably reflects evolutionary trends that gradually allocated more and more of the brain to color vision (Gilad et al., 2004). However, recent studies have found that humans and monkeys, when compared to other mammals, have a better sense of smell than previously thought (Laska, Seibt, & Weber, 2000; Sheperd, 2004). For example, one innovative study (Porter et al., 2007) that asked humans to get on their hands and knees to track the scent of chocolate oil that had been dribbled through a field found that the subjects performed quite well and that their patterns of tracking mimicked those of dogs (see **Figure 4.48**). Gordon Sheperd (2004, p. 0574) offers several possible explanations for our surprising olfactory capabilities, including the fact that "humans smell with bigger and better brains."

Figure 4.48

Scent tracking in humans. Porter and colleagues (2007) compared scent tracking in humans and dogs and concluded that they are more similar than one might expect. One experiment demonstrated that most subjects could track the scent of chocolate oil through a field. And when humans' tracking patterns were compared to that of dogs tracking the scent of a pheasant dragged through a field, the spatial patterns were similar. The time-lapse photo on the left shows an example of a dog's tracking trail (in red) on one trial (yellow shows the trail of the pheasant). The photo on the right shows a similar example of a human subject's tracking trail.

SOURCE: Porter, J., Craven, B., Khan, R. M., Chang, S-J., Kang, I., Judkewitz, B., Volpe, J., Settles, G., & Sobel, N. (2007). Mechanisms of scent-tracking in humans. *Nature Neuroscience,* 10(1), 27–29. Figure 1. Reprinted by permission from Macmillan Publishers Ltd.

REVIEW OF KEY LEARNING GOALS

4.19 The taste buds are sensitive to four basic tastes: sweet, sour, bitter, and salty. Umami (savory) may represent a fifth basic taste. Sensitivity to these tastes is distributed unevenly across the tongue, but the variations are small. Some basic taste preferences appear to be innate, but taste preferences are largely learned as a function of what one is exposed to. Taste preferences are also heavily influenced by cultural background.

4.20 Supertasters are much more sensitive to some tastes than nontasters, with medium tasters falling in between these extremes. Nontasters tend to be more susceptible to the lure of sweets, high-fat foods, alcohol, and smoking, which means their consumption habits tend to be less healthy than those of supertasters. The perception of flavor involves a mixture of taste, smell, and the tactile sensation of food in one's mouth.

4.21 Like taste, smell is a chemical sense. Chemical stimuli activate receptors, called olfactory cilia, that line the nasal passages and are constantly replaced. Smell is the only sense that's not routed through the thalamus. Humans can distinguish a huge number of odors, but their performance on odor identification tasks tends to be mediocre. Nonetheless, humans have greater olfactory capacities than widely believed.

The Sense of Touch

KEY LEARNING GOALS

4.22 Describe the processes involved in the perception of pressure on the skin.

4.23 Trace the two pathways along which pain signals travel, and discuss evidence that the perception of pain is subjective.

4.24 Explain the gate-control theory of pain perception and recent findings related to it.

If there is any sense that people trust almost as much as sight, it's the sense of touch. Yet, like all the senses, touch involves converting the sensation of physical stimuli into a psychological experience—and it can be fooled.

The physical stimuli for touch are mechanical, thermal, and chemical energies that impinge on the skin. These stimuli can produce perceptions of tactile stimulation (the pressure of touch against the skin), warmth, cold, and pain. The human skin is saturated with at least six types of sensory receptors, four of which are depicted in **Figure 4.49** on the next page. To some degree, these different types of receptors are specialized for different functions, such as for registering pressure, heat, cold, and so forth. However, these distinctions are not as clear as researchers had originally expected (Sinclair, 1981).

Feeling Pressure

If you've ever been on a mosquito-infested picnic, you can appreciate the need to quickly locate tactile stimulation. The sense of touch meets this need for tactile localization very efficiently. Cells in the nervous system that respond to touch are sensitive to specific patches of skin. These skin patches, which vary considerably in size, are the functional equivalents of *receptive fields* in vision. Like visual receptive fields, they often involve a center-surround arrangement. Thus, stimuli falling in the center produce the opposite effect of stimuli falling in the surrounding area (Kandel & Jessell, 1991).

The nerve fibers that carry incoming information about tactile stimulation are routed through the spinal cord to the brainstem. There, the fibers from

Figure 4.49

Receptors in the skin. Human skin houses quite a variety of receptors in a series of layers. The four types of receptors shown in this diagram all respond to various aspects of pressure, stretching, and vibration. In addition to these receptors, free nerve endings in the skin respond to pain, warmth, and cold, and hair-follicle receptors register the movement of hairs.

SOURCE: Goldstein, E. B. (2007). *Sensation and perception.* Belmont, CA: Wadsworth. Wadsworth is a part of Cengage Learning, Inc. Reproduced by permission. www.cengage.com/permissions.

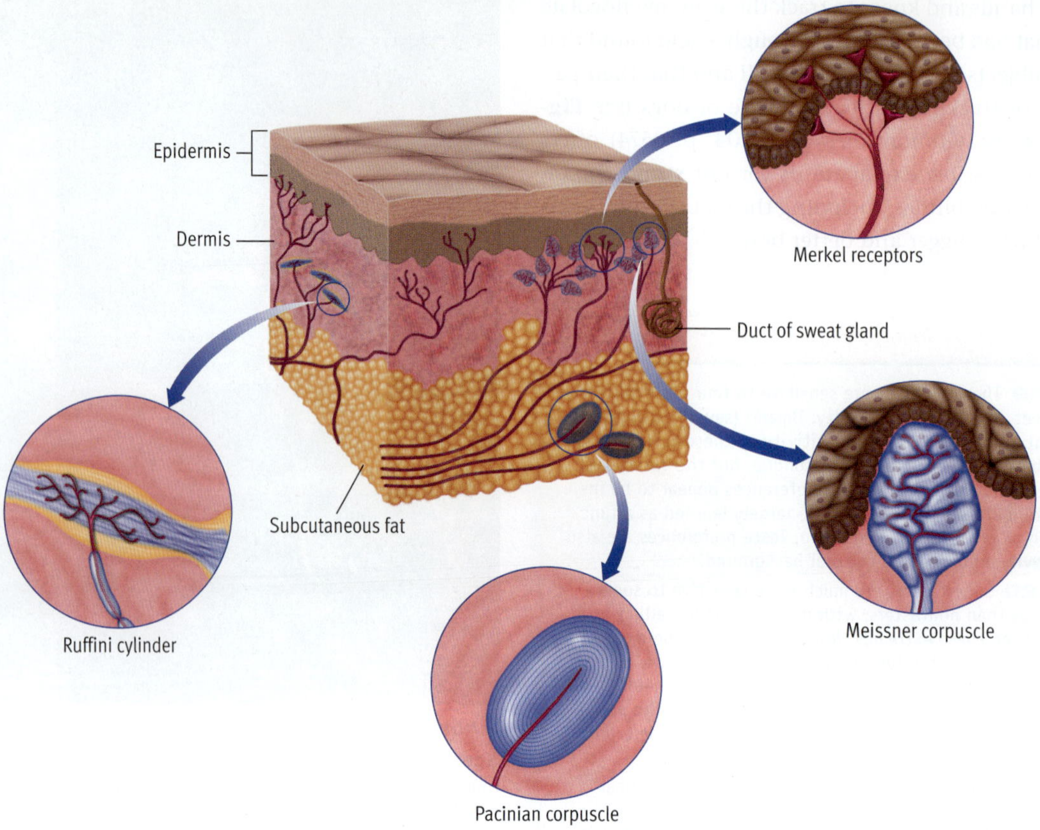

each side of the body cross over mostly to the opposite side of the brain. The tactile pathway then projects through the thalamus and onto the *somatosensory cortex* in the brain's parietal lobe. Some cells in the somatosensory cortex function like the *feature detectors* discovered in vision (Gardner & Kandel, 2000). They respond to specific features of touch, such as a movement across the skin in a particular direction.

Feeling Pain

As unpleasant as it is, the sensation of pain is crucial to survival. Pain is a marvelous warning system. It tells people when they should stop shoveling snow or remove their hand from a hot oven. Although a life without pain may sound appealing, people born with a rare, congenital insensitivity to pain would disagree, as they routinely harm themselves (Coderre, Mogil, & Bushnell, 2003). However, chronic pain is a frustrating, demoralizing affliction that affects roughly 75 million people in American society (Gallagher & Rosenthal, 2007). Although scientists have learned a great deal about the neural bases for the experience of pain, clinical treatment of pain remains only moderately effective (Scholz & Woolf, 2002). Thus, there are pressing practical reasons for psychologists' keen interest in the perception of pain.

Pathways to the Brain

The receptors for pain are mostly free nerve endings in the skin. Pain messages are transmitted to the brain via two types of pathways that pass through different areas in the thalamus (Cholewiak & Cholewiak, 2010). One is a *fast pathway* that registers localized pain and relays it to the cortex in a fraction of a second. This is the system that hits you with sharp pain when you first cut your finger. The second system uses a *slow pathway* that lags a second or two behind the fast system. This pathway (which also carries information about temperature) conveys the less localized, longer-lasting, aching or burning pain that comes after the initial injury. The slow pathway depends on thin neurons called *C fibers,* whereas the fast pathway is mediated by thicker neurons called *A-delta fibers* (see **Figure 4.50**). Pain signals may be sent to many areas in the cortex, as well as to subcortical centers associated with emotion (such as the hypothalamus and amygdala), depending in part on the nature of the pain (Hunt & Mantyh, 2001).

Puzzles in Pain Perception

Pain perception is inherently subjective. Some people with severe injuries report little pain, whereas other people with much more modest injuries report agonizing pain (Coderre et al., 2003). Hence, it is impossible to devise a genuinely objective index of pain

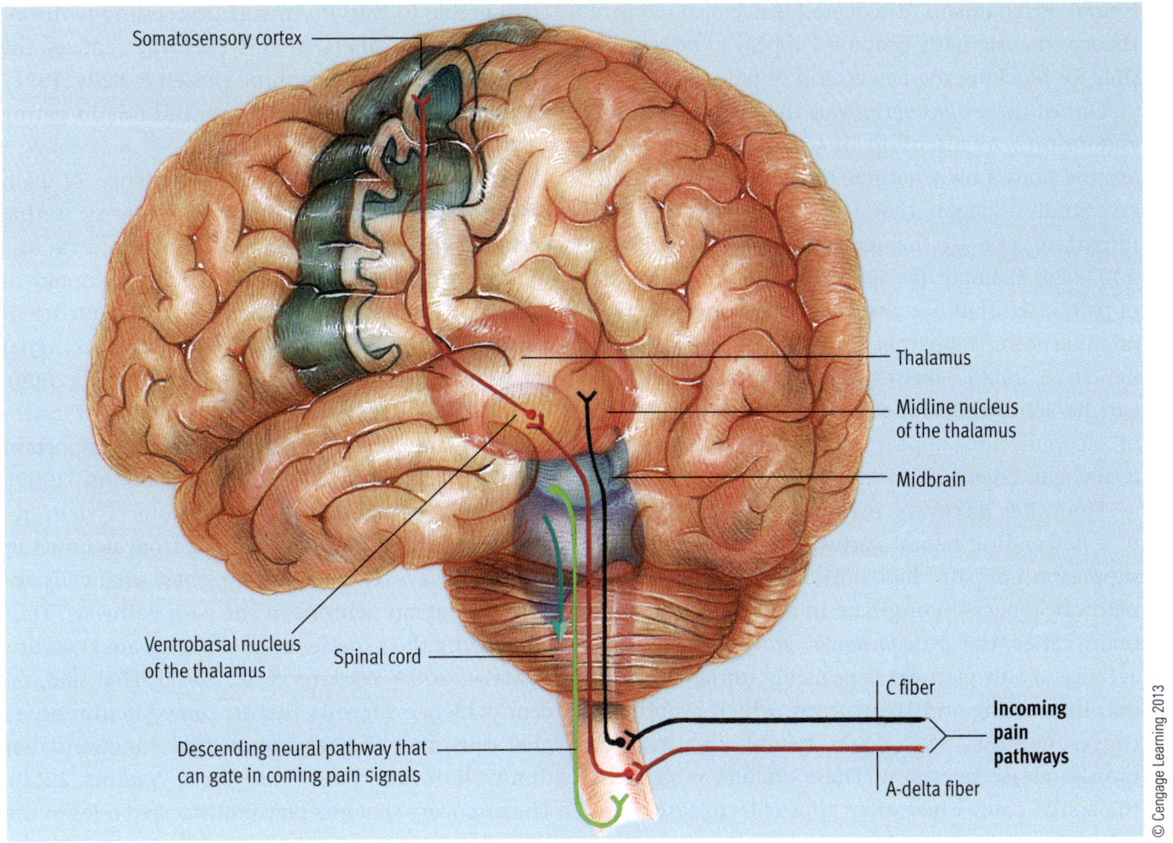

Figure 4.50

Pathways for pain signals. Pain signals are sent inward from receptors to the brain along the two ascending pathways depicted here in red and black. The fast pathway (red) and the slow pathway (black) depend on different types of nerve fibers and are routed through different parts of the thalamus. The gate-control mechanism hypothesized by Melzack and Wall (1965) apparently depends on signals in a descending pathway (shown in green) that originates in an area of the midbrain.

experience. As Rollman (2010, p. 717) puts it, there is no "pain thermometer." The subjective nature of pain is illustrated by placebo effects. As we saw in Chapter 2, many people suffering from pain report relief when given a placebo—such as an inactive "sugar pill" that's presented to them as if it were a painkilling drug (Benedetti, 2008; Stewart-Williams, 2004). Evidence regarding the subjective quality of pain has also come from studies that have found ethnic and cultural differences in pain tolerance (Ondeck, 2003). It appears that culture does not affect the process of pain perception so much as the willingness to tolerate certain types of pain (Zatzick & Dimsdale, 1990).

Several recent studies have also highlighted how contextual factors influence the experience of pain. For example, one recent study found that the experience of pain was reduced when female participants looked at a picture of their boyfriend or held their boyfriend's hand (Master et al., 2009). In a similar vein, another study found that looking at pleasant pictures reduced subjects' pain responses, whereas looking at unpleasant pictures led to stronger pain reactions (Roy et al., 2009). And a study by Gray and Wegner (2008) demonstrated that pain responses increase when participants believe that the pain was inflicted upon them intentionally, rather than accidentally.

The psychological element in pain perception becomes clear when something distracts your attention and the hurting temporarily disappears. For example, imagine that you've just hit your thumb with a hammer and it's throbbing with pain. Suddenly, your child cries out that there's a fire in the laundry room. As you race to deal with this emergency, you forget all about the pain in your thumb. As you can see, then, tissue damage that sends pain impulses on their way to the brain doesn't necessarily result in the experience of pain. Thus, any useful explanation of pain perception must be able to answer a critical question: How does the central nervous system block incoming pain signals?

In an influential effort to answer this question, Ronald Melzack and Patrick Wall (1965) devised the gate-control theory of pain. *Gate-control theory* holds that incoming pain sensations must pass through a "gate" in the spinal cord that can be closed, thus blocking ascending pain signals. The gate in this model is not an anatomical structure but a pattern of neural activity that inhibits incoming pain signals. Melzack and Wall suggested that this imaginary gate can be closed by signals from peripheral receptors or by signals from the brain. They theorized that the latter mechanism can help explain how factors such as attention and expectations can shut off pain signals. As a whole, research suggests that the concept of a gating mechanism for pain has merit (Craig & Rollman, 1999; Sufka & Price, 2002).

Neural mechanisms discovered since gate-control theory was originally proposed appear to be responsible for blocking the perception of pain.

One of these discoveries was the identification of endorphins. As discussed in Chapter 3, *endorphins* are the body's own natural morphinelike painkillers. Studies suggest that the endorphins play an important role in the modulation of pain (Pert, 2002). For example, placebo effects in the treatment of pain often (but not always) depend on the action of endorphins (Eippert et al., 2009; Price, Finniss, & Benedetti, 2008). Likewise, the analgesic effects that can be achieved through the ancient Chinese art of acupuncture appear to involve endorphins (Cabyoglu, Ergene, & Tan, 2006).

The other discovery involved the identification of a descending neural pathway that mediates the suppression of pain (Basbaum & Jessell, 2000). This pathway appears to originate in an area of the midbrain called the *periaqueductal gray (PAG).* Neural activity in this pathway is probably initiated by endorphins acting on PAG neurons, which eventually trigger impulses sent down neural circuits that mostly release serotonin. These circuits synapse in the spinal cord, where they appear to release more endorphins, thus inhibiting the activity of neurons that would normally transmit incoming pain impulses to the brain (see **Figure 4.50**). The painkilling effects of morphine appear to be at least partly attributable to activity in this descending pathway, as cutting the fibers in this pathway reduces the analgesic effects of morphine (Jessell & Kelly, 1991). Clearly, this pathway plays a central role in gating incoming pain signals.

Our understanding of the experience of pain continues to evolve. The newest discovery is that certain types of *glial cells* may contribute to the modulation of pain (Watkins, 2007). As noted in Chapter 3, only relatively recently have neuroscientists realized that glial cells contribute to signal transmission in the nervous system (Fields, 2004). At least two types of glia in the spinal cord (astrocytes and microglia) appear to play an important role in *chronic pain* (Milligan & Watkins, 2009). These glia are activated by immune system responses to infection or by signals from neurons in pain pathways. Once activated, these glial cells appear to "egg on neurons in the pain pathway," thus amplifying the experience of chronic pain (Watkins & Maier, 2003; Watkins et al., 2007). That said, recent evidence suggests that in some circumstances glial cells may also serve protective functions that diminish or limit pain (Milligan & Watkins, 2009). The discovery that glia play multifaceted roles in the human pain system may eventually lead to the development of new drugs for treating chronic pain.

One final point merits emphasis as we close our tour of the human sensory systems. Although we

CONCEPT CHECK 4.4

Identifying the Contributions of Major Theorists and Researchers

Check your recall of the principal ideas of important theorists and researchers covered in this chapter by matching the people listed on the left with the appropriate contributions described on the right. If you need help, the crucial pages describing each person's ideas are listed in parentheses. Fill in the letters for your choices in the spaces provided on the left. You'll find the answers in Appendix A.

Major Theorists and Researchers	Key Ideas and Contributions
______ 1. Linda Bartoshuk (p. 165)	a. This nineteenth-century theorist developed both the trichromatic theory of color vision and the place theory of pitch perception.
______ 2. Hermann von Helmholtz (pp. 143–144, 162)	b. In the 1960s, these theorists developed the gate-control theory of pain, which holds that incoming pain signals can be blocked by neural mechanisms.
______ 3. David Hubel and Torsten Wiesel (p. 141)	c. This person has conducted a great deal of influential research on the gustatory system, including pioneering work comparing supertasters and nontasters.
______ 4. Ronald Melzack and Patrick Wall (p. 169)	d. This advocate of Gestalt psychology, who was the first person to describe the phi phenomenon, asserted that in perception, the whole is often greater than the sum of its parts.
______ 5. Max Wertheimer (p. 150)	e. This research team won a Nobel prize for discovering three types of specialized visual cells in the occipital lobe, which have been characterized as feature detectors.

have discussed the various sensory domains separately, it's important to remember that all the senses send signals to the same brain, where the information is pooled. We have already encountered examples of sensory integration. For example, it's at work when the sight and smell of food influence taste. *Sensory integration is the norm in perceptual experience.* For instance, when you sit around a campfire, you *see* it blazing, you *hear* it crackling, you *smell* it burning, and you feel the *touch* of its warmth. If you cook something over it, you may even *taste* it. Thus, perception involves building a unified model of the world out of integrated input from all the senses (Kayser, 2007; Stein, Wallace, & Stanford, 2001).

REVIEW OF KEY LEARNING GOALS

4.22 The skin houses many types of sensory receptors. They respond to pressure, temperature, and pain. Tactile localization depends on receptive fields similar to those seen for vision. Some cells in the somatosensory cortex appear to function like feature detectors.

4.23 Pain signals are sent to the brain along two pathways that are characterized as fast and slow. The perception of pain is highly subjective. Placebo effects in pain treatment and cultural variations in pain tolerance highlight the subjective nature of pain perception.

4.24 Gate-control theory holds that incoming pain signals can be blocked in the spinal cord. Endorphins and a descending neural pathway appear responsible for the suppression of pain by the central nervous system. Recent studies indicate that glial cells contribute to the modulation of chronic pain.

Reflecting on the Chapter's Themes

KEY LEARNING GOALS

4.25 Identify the three unifying themes that were highlighted in this chapter.

In this chapter, three of our unifying themes stood out in sharp relief: theoretical diversity, human experience is highly subjective, and cultural factors can shape behavior. Let's discuss the value of theoretical diversity first. Contradictory theories about behavior can be disconcerting and frustrating for theorists, researchers, teachers, and students alike. Yet this chapter provided two dramatic demonstrations of how theoretical diversity can lead to progress in the long run. For decades, the trichromatic and opponent process theories of color vision and the place and frequency theories of pitch perception were viewed as fundamentally incompatible. As you know, in each case the evidence eventually revealed that both theories were needed to fully explain the sensory processes that each sought to explain individually. If it hadn't been for these theoretical debates, current understanding of color vision and pitch perception might be far more primitive.

Our coverage of sensation and perception should also have enhanced your appreciation of why human experience of the world is highly subjective. As ambiguous figures and visual illusions clearly show, there is no one-to-one correspondence between sensory input and perceived experience of the world. Perception is an active process in which people organize and interpret the information received by the senses. These interpretations are shaped by a number of factors, including the environmental context and perceptual sets. Small wonder, then, that people often perceive the same event in very different ways.

Finally, this chapter provided numerous examples of how cultural factors can shape behavior—even in an area of research where one might expect to find little cultural influence. Most people are not surprised to learn that there are cultural differences in attitudes, values, social behavior, and development. But perception is widely viewed as a basic, universal process that should be the same across cultures. In most respects it is, as the similarities among cultural groups in perception far outweigh the differences. Nonetheless, we saw cultural variations in depth perception, susceptibility to illusions, and taste preferences. Thus, even a fundamental, heavily physiological process such as perception can be modified to some degree by one's cultural background.

The following Personal Application demonstrates the subjectivity of perception once again. It focuses on how painters have learned to use the principles of visual perception to achieve a variety of artistic goals.

Theoretical Diversity

Subjectivity of Experience

Cultural Heritage

REVIEW OF KEY LEARNING GOALS

4.25 This chapter provided two dramatic demonstrations of the value of theoretical diversity. It also provided numerous examples of how and why people's experience of the world is highly subjective. Finally, it highlighted the importance of cultural background.

Reality CHECK

Misconception

Humans have five senses: sight, hearing, taste, smell, and touch.

Reality

Our coverage in this chapter would seem to support this assertion. But humans have other sensory systems that we were unable to cover due to space constraints. For example, the *kinesthetic system* monitors the positions of the various parts of the body through receptors in the muscles and joints. And the *vestibular system,* which relies on fluid movements in the semicircular canals in the inner ear, provides our sense of balance, or equilibrium.

Illustrated Overview of Five Major Senses

SENSE	STIMULUS	ELEMENTS OF THE STIMULUS

The Visual System: SIGHT

Stimulus: Light is electromagnetic radiation that travels in waves. Humans can register only a slim portion of the total range of wavelengths, from 400 to 700 nanometers.

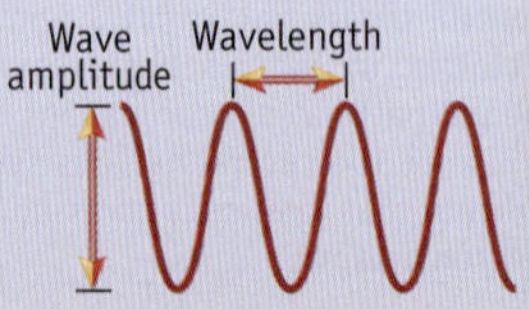

© John White Photos/Alamy

Elements of the stimulus: Light waves vary in *amplitude, wavelength,* and *purity,* which influence perceptions as shown below.

Physical properties	Related perceptions
Wavelength	Hue (color)
Amplitude	Brightness
Purity	Saturation

The Auditory System: HEARING

Stimulus: Sound waves are vibrations of molecules, which means that they must travel through some physical medium, such as air. Humans can hear wavelengths between 20 and 20,000 Hz.

© Photodisc/Getty Imagesz

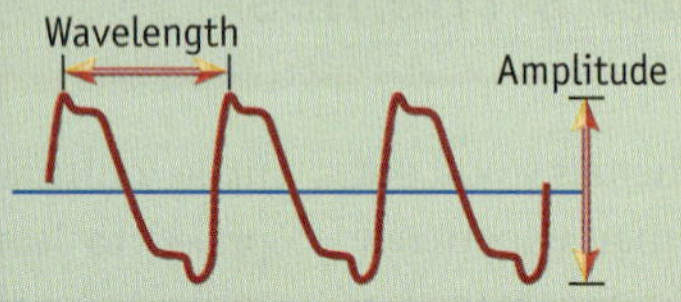

Elements of the stimulus: Sound waves vary in *amplitude, wavelength,* and *purity,* which influence perceptions, as shown below.

Physical properties	Related perceptions
Amplitude	Loudness
Wavelength	Pitch
Purity	Timbre

The Gustatory System: TASTE

Stimulus: The stimuli for taste generally are chemical substances that are soluble (dissolvable in water). These stimuli are dissolved in the mouth's saliva.

© Lisa Woollett/Photofusion Picture Library/Alamy

Elements of the stimulus: It is generally, but not universally, agreed that there are four primary tastes: *sweet, sour, bitter,* and *salty*.

The Olfactory System: SMELL

© Blend Images/Jamie Grill

Stimulus: The stimuli are volatile chemical substances that can evaporate and be carried in the air. These chemical stimuli are dissolved in the mucus of the nose.

Elements of the stimulus: Efforts to identify primary odors have proven unsatisfactory. If primary odors exist, there must be a great many of them.

The Tactile System: TOUCH

Stimulus: The stimuli are mechanical, thermal, and chemical energy that impinge on the skin.

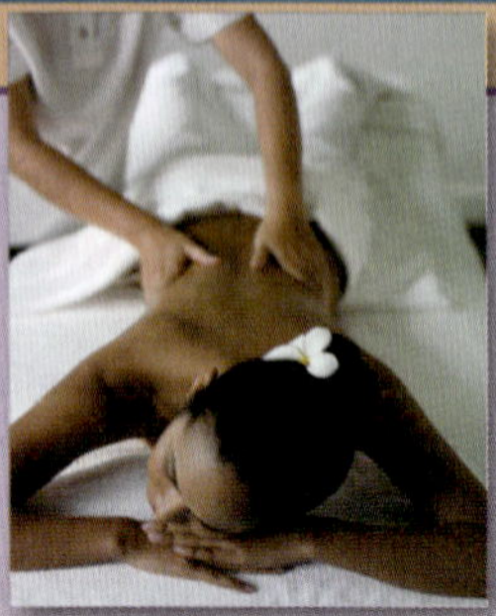
© IS713/ Image Source Pink/Alamy

Elements of the stimulus: Receptors in the skin can register *pressure, warmth, cold,* and *pain*.

All illustrations on this page © Cengage Learning 201

NATURE AND LOCATION OF RECEPTORS

BRAIN PATHWAYS IN INITIAL PROCESSING

The *retina*, which is neural tissue lining the inside back surface of the eye, contains millions of receptor cells called *rods* and *cones*. Rods play a key role in night and peripheral vision; cones play a key role in daylight and color vision.

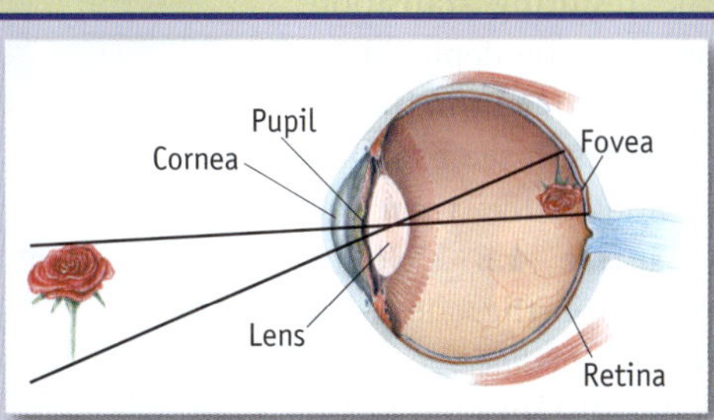

Neural impulses are routed through the *LGN* in the *thalamus* and then distributed to the *primary visual cortex* at the back of the *occipital lobe*.

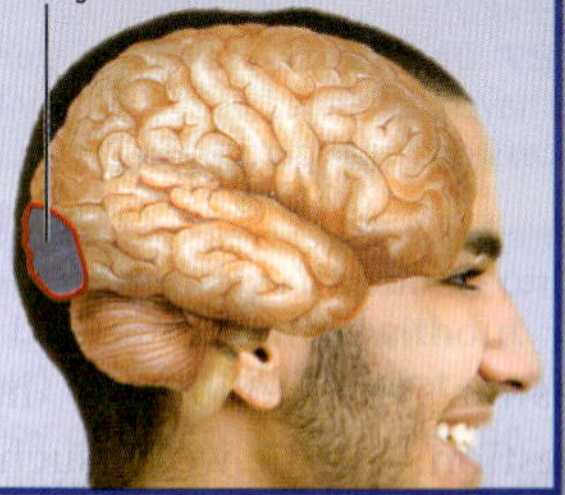

The receptors for hearing are tiny *hair cells* that line the *basilar membrane* that runs the length of the *cochlea*, a fluid-filled, coiled tunnel in the inner ear.

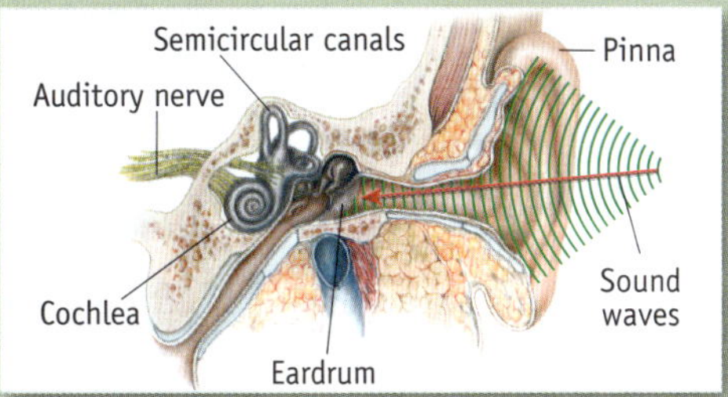

Neural impulses are routed through the *thalamus* and then sent to the *primary auditory cortex*, which is mostly located in the *temporal lobe*.

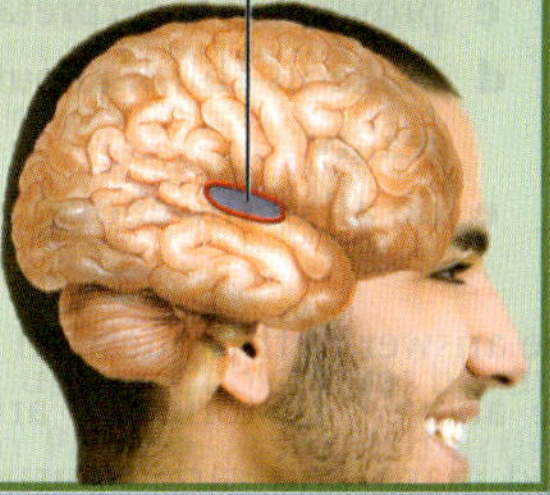

The gustatory receptors are clusters of *taste cells* found in the *taste buds* that line the trenches around tiny bumps in the tongue. Taste cells have a short life span (about 10 days) and are constantly being replaced.

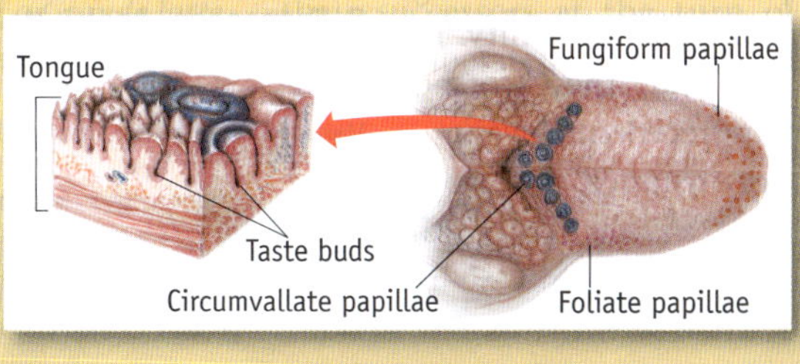

Neural impulses are routed through the *thalamus* and on to the *insular cortex* in the frontal lobe.

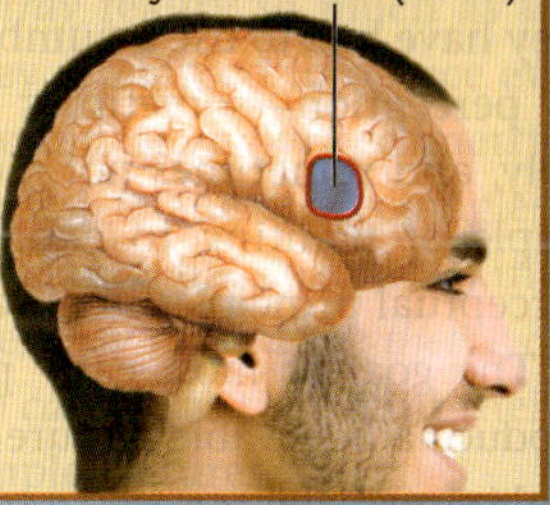

The receptors for smell are *olfactory cilia*, hairlike structures in the upper portion of the nasal passages. Like taste cells, they have a short lifespan (about 30–60 days) and are constantly being replaced.

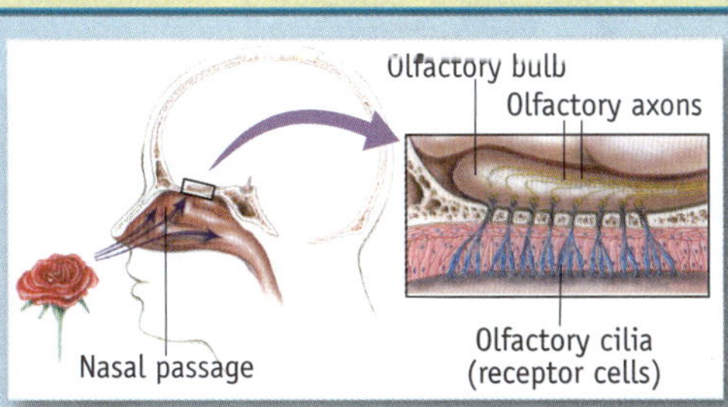

Neural impulses are routed through the *olfactory bulb* and then sent directly to the *olfactory cortex* in the *temporal lobe* and other cortical areas. Smell is the only sensory input not routed through the thalamus.

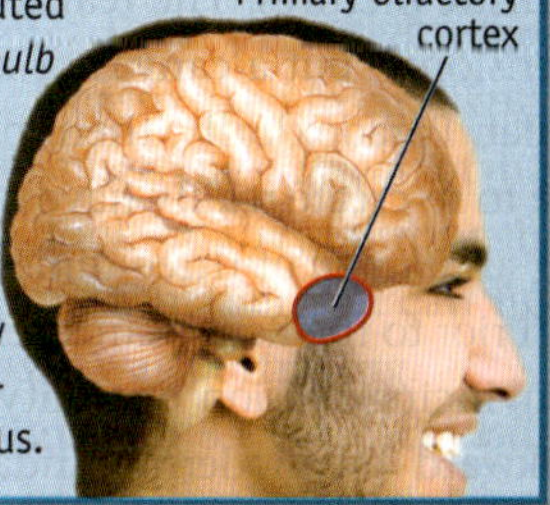

The human skin is saturated with at least six types of sensory receptors. The four types shown here respond to pressure, whereas *free nerve endings* in the skin respond to pain, warmth, and cold.

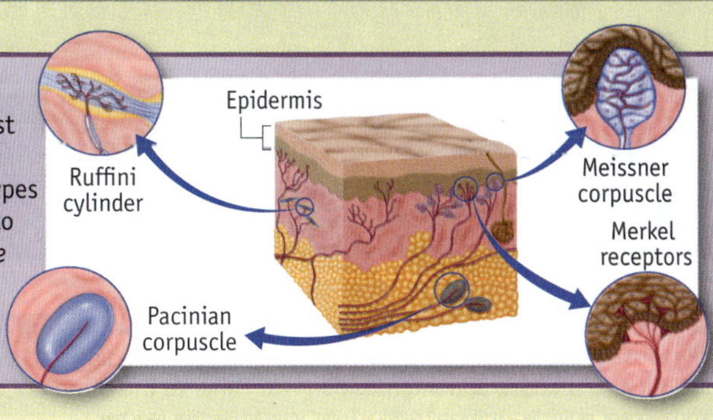

Neural impulses are routed through the *brainstem* and *thalamus* and on to the *somatosensory cortex* in the *parietal lobe*.

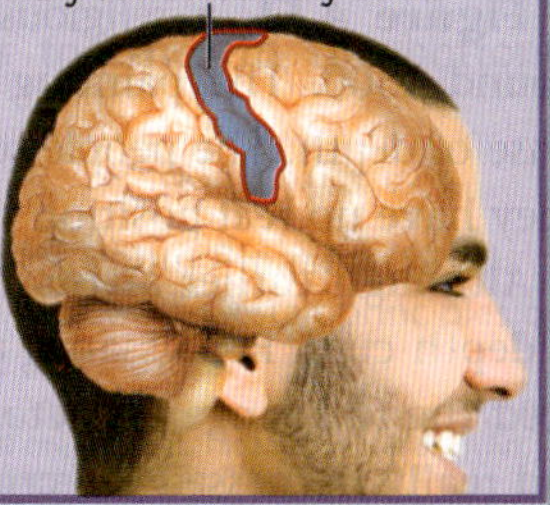

Head (all): © Robert Kneschke/Shutterstock

All illustrations on this page © Cengage Learning 2013

Chapter 4 Practice Test

1. In psychophysical research, the absolute threshold has been arbitrarily defined as:
   A. the stimulus intensity that can be detected 100% of the time.
   B. the stimulus intensity that can be detected 50% of the time.
   C. the minimum amount of difference in intensity needed to tell two stimuli apart.
   D. a constant proportion of the size of the initial stimulus.

2. A tone-deaf person would probably not be able to tell two musical notes apart unless they were very different. We could say that this person has a relatively large:
   A. just noticeable difference.
   B. relative threshold.
   C. absolute threshold.
   D. detection threshold.

3. In their study of the influence of subliminal perception, Karremans and his colleagues (2006) found:
   A. absolutely no evidence of such influence.
   B. evidence that subliminal stimuli influenced subjects' drink preferences.
   C. that subliminal stimuli do not really exist.
   D. that it is nearly impossible to measure subliminal effects.

4. In farsightedness:
   A. close objects are seen clearly but distant objects appear blurry.
   B. the focus of light from close objects falls behind the retina.
   C. the focus of light from distant objects falls a little short of the retina.
   D. a and b.
   E. a and c.

5. The collection of rod and cone receptors that funnel signals to a particular visual cell in the retina make up that cell's:
   A. blind spot.
   B. optic disk.
   C. opponent process field.
   D. receptive field.

6. The visual pathway that has been characterized as ______________ travels through the dorsal stream to the parietal lobes, whereas the pathway that has been labeled the ______________ travels through the ventral stream to the temporal lobes.
   A. the *what* pathway; the *where* pathway
   B. the *where* pathway; the *what* pathway
   C. the *opponent process* pathway; the *trichromatic* pathway
   D. the *trichromatic* pathway; the *opponent process* pathway

7. Which theory would predict that the American flag would have a green, black, and yellow afterimage?
   A. subtractive color mixing
   B. opponent process theory
   C. additive color mixing
   D. trichromatic theory

8. The illusion of movement created by presenting visual stimuli in rapid succession is called:
   A. convergence.
   B. retinal disparity.
   C. motion parallax.
   D. the phi phenomenon.

9. In a painting, train tracks may look as if they go off into the distance because the artist draws the tracks as converging lines, a pictorial cue to depth known as:
   A. interposition.
   B. texture gradient.
   C. convergence.
   D. linear perspective.

10. The fact that cultural groups with less exposure to carpentered buildings are less susceptible to the Müller-Lyer illusion suggests that:
    A. not all cultures test perceptual hypotheses.
    B. people in technologically advanced cultures are more gullible.
    C. illusions can be experienced only by cultures that have been exposed to the concept of illusions.
    D. perceptual inferences can be shaped by experience.

11. The hair cells that serve as auditory receptors are found:
    A. on the eardrum in the auditory canal.
    B. on the eardrum in the cochlea.
    C. on the basilar membrane in the auditory canal.
    D. on the basilar membrane in the cochlea.

12. Perception of pitch can best be explained by:
    A. place theory.
    B. frequency theory.
    C. both place theory and frequency theory.
    D. neither theory.

13. In what way(s) is the sense of taste like the sense of smell?
    A. There are four primary stimulus groups for both senses.
    B. Both systems are routed through the thalamus on the way to the cortex.
    C. The physical stimuli for both senses are chemical substances dissolved in fluid.
    D. All of the above.
    E. None of the above.

14. Which school of painting applied the theory of feature analysis to canvas by building figures out of simple features?
    A. Kineticism
    B. Impressionism
    C. Surrealism
    D. Cubism

15. In the study by Kenrick and Gutierres (1980), exposing male subjects to a TV show dominated by extremely beautiful women:
    A. had no effect on their ratings of the attractiveness of a prospective date.
    B. increased their ratings of the attractiveness of a prospective date.
    C. decreased their ratings of the attractiveness of a prospective date.
    D. increased their ratings of their own attractiveness.

Answers

1 B p. 131	6 B pp. 141–142	11 D pp. 161–162
2 A p. 131	7 B p. 144	12 C p. 162
3 B pp. 132–133	8 D p. 150	13 C p. 166
4 B p. 136	9 D pp. 153–154	14 D p. 175
5 D p. 139	10 D pp. 153, 155	15 C pp. 178–179

PsykTrek

To view a demo: **www.cengage.com/psychology/psyktrek**
To order: **www.cengage.com/psychology/weiten**

Go to the PsykTrek website or CD-ROM for further study of the concepts in this chapter. Both online and on the CD-ROM, PsykTrek includes dozens of learning modules with videos, animations, and quizzes, as well as simulations of psychological phenomena and a multimedia glossary that includes word pronunciations.

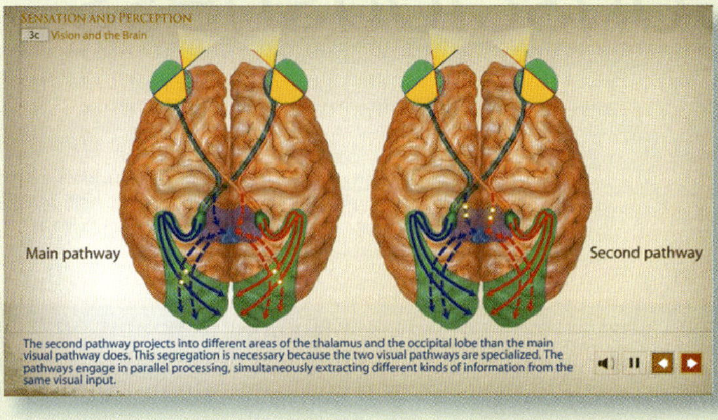

© Cengage Learning 2008

Visit Modules 3b (*The Retina*) and 3c (*Vision and the Brain*) to see animations of how visual signals are transmitted from the eye to the brain.

© Cengage Learning 2008

Play with color filters in Module 3d (*Perception of Color*) to see subtractive color mixing in action, or try manipulating an example of the phi phenomenon in Module 3e (*Gestalt Psychology*).

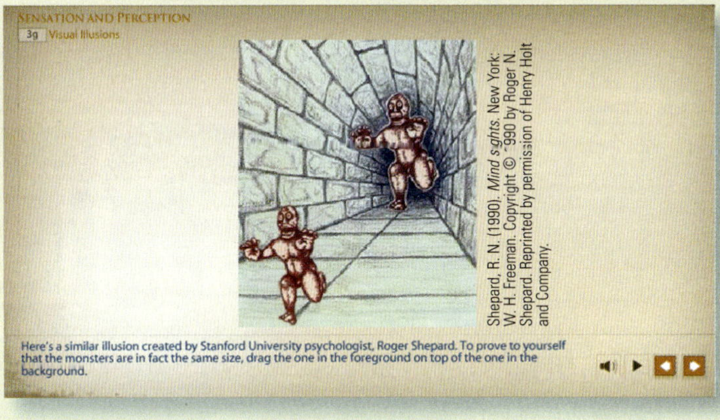

Shepard, R. N. (1990). *Mind sights*. New York: W. H. Freeman. Copyright © 1990 by Roger N. Shepard. Reprinted by permission of Henry Holt and Company.

© Cengage Learning 2008

Go to Module 3g (*Visual Illusions*) to play with stunning illusions and watch a video on the Ames room in which people appear to change size right before your eyes.

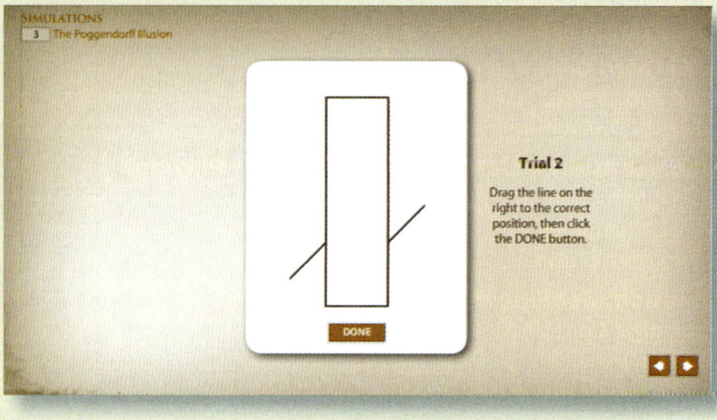

© Cengage Learning 2008

Try Simulation 3 (*The Poggendorff Illusion*) in which you get to tinker with a classic illusion to see how various factors enhance or diminish the illusion.

Online Study Tools

Log in to **CengageBrain** to access the resources your instructor requires. For this book, you can access:

CourseMate brings course concepts to life with interactive learning, study, and exam preparation tools that support the printed textbook. A textbook-specific website, Psychology CourseMate includes an integrated interactive eBook and other interactive learning tools such as quizzes, flashcards, videos, and more.

CengageNow is an easy-to-use online resource that helps you study in less time to get the grade you want—NOW. Take a pre-test for this chapter and receive a personalized study plan based on your results that will identify the topics you need to review and direct you to online resources to help you master those topics. Then take a post-test to help you determine the concepts you have mastered and what you will need to work on. If your textbook does not include an access code card, go to CengageBrain.com to gain access.

WebTutor is more than just an interactive study guide. WebTutor is an anytime, anywhere customized learning solution with an eBook, keeping you connected to your textbook, instructor, and classmates.

Aplia. If your professor has assigned Aplia homework:

1. Sign in to your account
2. Complete the corresponding homework exercises as required by your professor.
3. When finished, click "Grade It Now" to see which areas you have mastered, which need more work, and detailed explanations of every answer.

Visit **www.cengagebrain.com** to access your account and purchase materials.

5

Variations in Consciousness

© Warner Bros./Photofest

Nathaniel Kleitman and Eugene Aserinsky couldn't believe their eyes—or their subjects' eyes, either. It was the spring of 1952, and Kleitman, a physiologist and prominent sleep researcher, was investigating the slow, rolling eye movements displayed by subjects at the onset of sleep. Kleitman had begun to wonder whether these slow eye movements would show up during later phases of sleep. The trouble was that watching a subject's closed eyelids all night long was a surefire way to put the *researcher* to sleep. Smartly, Kleitman and Aserinsky, a graduate student, came up with a better way to document eye movements. Near the participants' eyes, they pasted electrodes that could pick up the small electrical signals generated by moving eyeballs and transmitted them to a machine. These signals then moved a pen on the machine's chart recorder, much like an electroencephalograph (EEG) traces brain waves (see Chapter 3). The result was an objective record of subjects' eye movements during sleep that could be studied at any time (Dement, 1992).

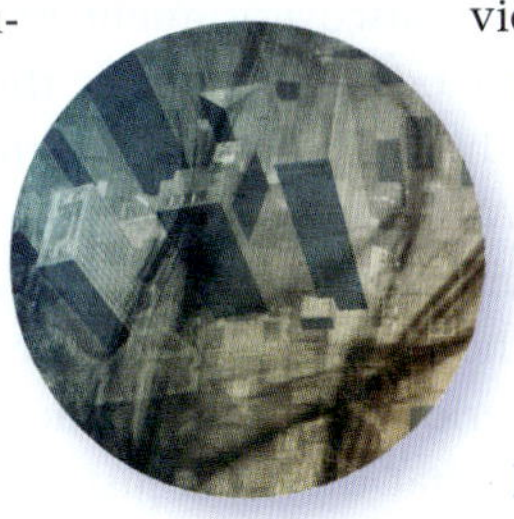

One night, while one of their participants was asleep, the researchers were astonished to see a tracing in the recording that suggested a different, much more rapid eye movement. This result was so unexpected that at first they thought the recording device was defective. "It was a rickety old thing, anyway," a technician in Kleitman's lab recalled (Coren, 1996, p. 21). Only when they decided to walk in and personally observe sleeping subjects were the researchers convinced that the eye movements were real. The subjects were deeply asleep, yet the bulges in their closed eyelids showed that their eyeballs were moving laterally in sharp jerks, first in one direction and then in the other. It was almost as if the sleeping subjects were watching an action movie. The researchers wondered—what in the world was going on?

In hindsight, it's amazing that no one had discovered these rapid eye movements before. It turns out that periods of rapid eye movement are a routine part of sleep in humans and many animals. In

fact, you can observe them for yourself in your pet dog or cat. The phenomenon had been there for everyone to see for eons, but those who noticed must not have attached any significance to it.

Kleitman and Aserinsky's discovery might have remained something of an oddity, but then they had a brainstorm. Could the rapid eye movements be related to dreaming? With the help of William Dement, a medical student who was interested in dreams, they soon found the answer. When Dement woke up subjects during periods of rapid eye movement, about 80% reported that they had just been having a vivid dream. By contrast, only a small minority of subjects awakened during other phases of sleep reported that they had been dreaming. Dement knew that he was onto something. "I was overwhelmed with excitement," he wrote later (Dement, 1992, pp. 24–25). Years later, EEG recordings showed that periods of rapid eye movement were also associated with marked changes in brain-wave patterns. What Kleitman and his graduate students had stumbled on was considerably more than an oddity: It was a window into the most private aspect of consciousness imaginable—the experience of dreaming (Gottesmann, 2009).

As you will learn in this chapter, the discovery of rapid eye movement (REM) sleep blossomed into a number of other fascinating insights about what goes on in the brain during sleep. This research is just one example of how contemporary psychologists have tried to come to grips with the slippery topic of consciousness. Over time, consciousness has represented something of a paradox for psychology. On the one hand, people's conscious experience—their awareness of themselves and the world around them, their thoughts, and even their dreams—would seem to be an obvious and central concern for psychologists. On the other hand, psychology is committed to the empirical approach, which requires having objective, replicable ways of studying a given phenomenon. And consciousness is the ultimate in subjective experience. No one can directly observe another person's consciousness. People have a hard enough time even describing their own conscious experience to someone else (Schooler & Fiore, 1997). Yet in recent decades, researchers have been finding inventive ways to shed some objective light on the mysteries of consciousness.

We'll begin our tour of variations in consciousness with a few general points about the nature of consciousness. After that, much of the chapter will be a "bedtime story," as we take a long look at sleep and dreaming. We'll continue our discussion of consciousness by examining hypnosis, meditation, and the effects of mind-altering drugs. The Personal Application addresses a number of practical questions about sleep and dreams. Finally, the Critical Thinking Application looks at the concept of alcoholism to highlight the power of definitions.

KEY LEARNING GOALS

5.1 Discuss the nature and evolution of consciousness.

5.2 Articulate the relationship between consciousness and EEG activity.

On the Nature of Consciousness

Consciousness is the awareness of internal and external stimuli. Your consciousness includes (1) your awareness of external events ("The professor just asked me a hard question about medieval history"), (2) your awareness of your internal sensations ("My heart is racing and I'm starting to sweat"), (3) your awareness of your self as the unique being having these experiences ("Why me?"), and (4) your awareness of your thoughts about these experiences ("I'm going to make a fool of myself!"). In short, consciousness is personal awareness.

The contents of your consciousness are continually changing. Rarely does consciousness come to a standstill. It moves, it flows, it fluctuates, it wanders (Wegner, 1997). Recognizing that consciousness is in constant flux, William James (1902) long ago named this flow the *stream of consciousness.* If you could tape-record your thoughts, you would find an endless flow of ideas that zigzag in all directions. As you will soon learn, even when you sleep your consciousness moves through a series of transitions. Constant shifting and changing seem to be part of the essential nature of consciousness.

Variations in Levels of Awareness

Whereas William James emphasized the stream of consciousness, Sigmund Freud (1900) wanted to examine what goes on *beneath* the surface of this stream. As explained in Chapter 1, Freud argued that people's feelings and behavior are influenced by *unconscious* needs, wishes, and conflicts that lie below the surface of conscious awareness. According to Freud, the stream of consciousness has depth. Conscious and unconscious processes are different *levels of awareness.* Thus, Freud was one of the first theorists to recognize that consciousness is not an all-or-none phenomenon.

Since Freud's time, research has shown that people continue to maintain some awareness during sleep and sometimes even when they are put under anesthesia for surgery. How do we know? Because some stimuli can still penetrate awareness. For example, people under surgical anesthesia occasionally hear comments made during their surgery, which they later repeat to their surprised surgeons (Merikle, 2007). Such incidents occur infrequently (in about 0.2% of surgeries), but they do happen (Kihlstrom & Cork, 2007). Other research indicates that while people are asleep they can register external events to some degree (K. B. Campbell, 2000; Dang-Vu, 2009). A good example is the new parent who can sleep through a loud thunderstorm or a buzzing alarm clock but who immediately hears the muffled sound of the baby crying down the hall. The parent's selective sensitivity to sounds means that some mental processing must be going on even during sleep.

The Evolutionary Roots of Consciousness

Why do humans experience consciousness? Like other aspects of human nature, consciousness must have evolved because it helped our ancient ancestors survive and reproduce (Ornstein & Dewan, 1991). That said, there is plenty of debate about exactly how consciousness proved adaptive (Güzeldere, Flanagan, & Hardcastle, 2000). One line of thinking is that consciousness allowed our ancestors to think through courses of action and their consequences. They could figure out the best course without having to actually perform actions that may have led to harmful consequences (Plotkin, 1998). In other words, a little forethought and planning may have proved valuable in efforts to obtain food, avoid predators, and find mates. A number of alternative explanations focus on other adaptive benefits of personal awareness, but relatively little empirical evidence exists to judge any of their merits (Polger, 2007). Thus, the evolutionary bases of consciousness remain elusive.

Consciousness and Brain Activity

PsykTrek 4b

Consciousness does not arise from any distinct structure in the brain but rather from activity in distributed networks of neural pathways (Kinsbourne, 1997; Singer, 2007). Scientists are increasingly using brain-imaging methods to explore the link between brain activity and consciousness (Wager, Hernandez, & Lindquist, 2009). However, historically the most commonly used indicator of variations in consciousness has been the EEG, which records activity from broad swaths of the cortex. **The *electroencephalograph (EEG)* is a device that monitors the electrical activity of the brain over time by means of recording electrodes attached to the surface of the scalp.** Ultimately, the EEG summarizes the rhythm of cortical activity in the brain in terms of line tracings called *brain waves*. These tracings vary in *amplitude* (height) and *frequency* (cycles per second, abbreviated *cps*). You can see what brain waves look like if you glance ahead to **Figure 5.4** on page 190. Human brain-wave activity is usually divided into four principal bands based on the frequency of the brain waves. These bands, named after letters in the Greek alphabet, are *beta* (13–24 cps), *alpha* (8–12 cps), *theta* (4–7 cps), and *delta* (under 4 cps).

Different patterns of EEG activity are associated with different states of consciousness, as summarized in **Table 5.1**. For instance, when you're alertly engaged in problem solving, beta waves tend to dominate. When you're relaxed and resting, alpha waves increase. When you slip into deep, dreamless sleep, delta waves become more prevalent. These correlations are far from perfect, but changes in EEG activity are closely related to variations in consciousness (Wallace & Fisher, 1999).

As is often the case with correlations, researchers are faced with a chicken-or-egg puzzle when it comes to the relationship between mental states and the brain's electrical activity. If you become drowsy while you are reading this passage, your brain-wave activity will probably change. But are these changes causing your drowsiness, or is your drowsiness causing the changes in brain-wave activity? Or are the drowsiness and the shifts in brain-wave activity both caused by a *third* factor—perhaps signals coming from a subcortical area in the brain? (See **Figure 5.1** on the next page.) Frankly, no one knows. All that is known for sure is that variations in consciousness are correlated with variations in brain activity.

EEG measures of brain-wave activity have provided investigators with a method for mapping out

Table 5.1 EEG Patterns Associated with States of Consciousness

EEG Pattern	Frequency (cps)	Typical States of Consciousness
Beta (β)	13–24	Normal waking thought, alert problem solving
Alpha (α)	8–12	Deep relaxation, blank mind, meditation
Theta (θ)	4–7	Light sleep
Delta (Δ)	less than 4	Deep sleep

© Cengage Learning 2013

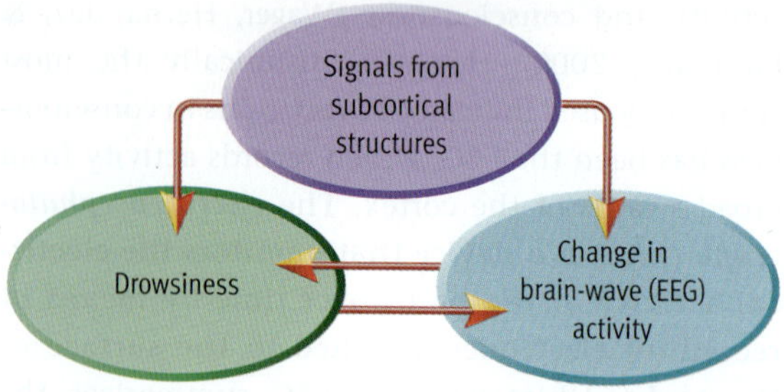

Figure 5.1

The correlation between mental states and cortical activity. As discussed in Chapter 2, because of the "third-variable problem," correlations alone do not establish causation. For example, strong correlations exist between drowsiness and a particular pattern of cortical activity, as reflected by EEG brain waves. But does drowsiness cause a change in cortical activity, or do changes in cortical activity cause drowsiness? Or does some third variable—such as signals from the brainstem or other subcortical structures—account for the changes in both brain waves and drowsiness?
© Cengage Learning 2013

the mysterious state of consciousness called sleep. As we will see in the next two sections of the chapter, this state turns out to be far more complex and varied than you might expect.

REVIEW OF KEY LEARNING GOALS

5.1 William James emphasized that consciousness is a continually changing stream of mental activity. Consciousness varies along a continuum of levels of awareness. Consciousness may have evolved because it allowed humans to think through the possible consequences of their actions and avoid some negative outcomes.

5.2 People maintain some degree of awareness during sleep and sometimes while under anesthesia. Brain waves vary in amplitude and frequency (cps) and are divided into four bands: beta, alpha, theta, and delta. Each type of brain wave is associated with different states of consciousness.

KEY LEARNING GOALS

5.3 Summarize what is known about human biological clocks and their relationship to sleep.

5.4 Explain how people get out of sync with their circadian rhythms and how these rhythms can be realigned.

Biological Rhythms and Sleep

Variations in consciousness are shaped in part by biological rhythms. Rhythms pervade the world around us. The daily alternation of light and darkness, the annual pattern of the seasons, and the phases of the moon all reflect this rhythmic quality of repeating cycles. Humans and apparently all other species display biological rhythms that are tied to these planetary rhythms (Foster, 2004; Kriegsfeld & Nelson, 2009). ***Biological rhythms* are periodic fluctuations in physiological functioning.** The existence of these rhythms means that organisms have internal "biological clocks" that somehow monitor the passage of time.

The Role of Circadian Rhythms

PSYKTREK 4a

***Circadian rhythms* are the 24-hour biological cycles found in humans and many other species.** In humans, circadian rhythms are particularly influential in the regulation of sleep (Moore, 2006). However, daily cycles also produce rhythmic variations in blood pressure, urine production, hormonal secretions, and other physical functions (see **Figure 5.2**). These cycles also affect alertness, short-term memory, and other aspects of cognitive performance (Refinetti, 2006; Van Dongen & Dinges, 2005). For instance, body temperature varies rhythmically in a daily cycle. It usually peaks in the afternoon and reaches its low point in the depths of the night.

Research indicates that people generally fall asleep as their body temperature begins to drop and awaken as it begins to rise once again (Szymusiak, 2009). Researchers have concluded that circadian rhythms can leave individuals physiologically primed to fall asleep most easily at a particular time of day (Richardson, 1993). This optimal time varies from person to person, depending on their schedules. Finding your ideal bedtime may help promote better-quality sleep during the night (Akerstedt et al., 1997). People often characterize themselves as a "night person" or a "morning person," preferences that reflect individual variations in circadian rhythms (Minkel & Dinges, 2009).

To study biological clocks, researchers have monitored physiological processes while subjects are cut off from exposure to the cycle of day and night and all other external time cues. These studies have demonstrated that circadian rhythms generally persist even when external time cues are eliminated. However, when people are isolated in this way, their cycles run a little longer than normal, about 24.2 hours on the average (Czeisler, Buxton, & Khalsa, 2005). Investigators aren't sure why this slight drift toward a longer cycle occurs, but it's not apparent under normal circumstances because daily exposure to light *readjusts* people's biological clocks.

In fact, researchers have worked out many of the details regarding how the day-night cycle resets biological clocks. When exposed to light, some receptors in the retina send direct inputs to a small structure in

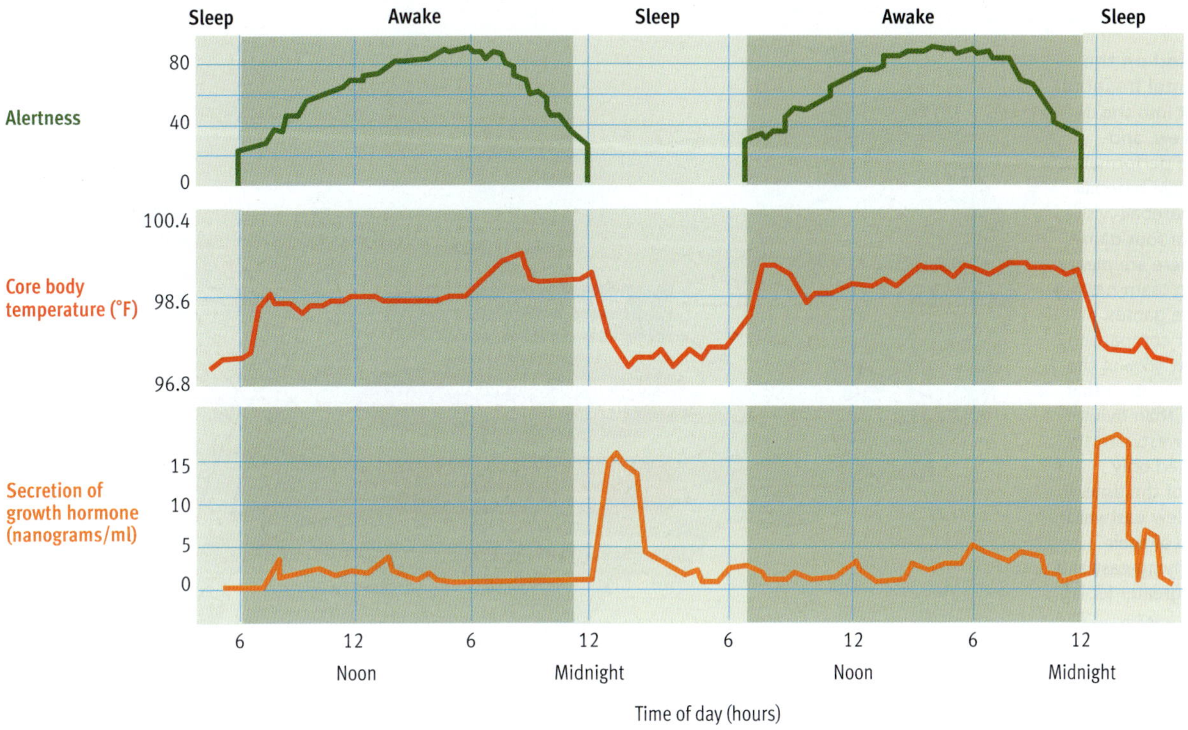

Figure 5.2

Examples of circadian rhythms. These graphs show how alertness, core body temperature, and the secretion of growth hormone typically fluctuate in a 24-hour rhythm. Note how body temperature declines when people fall asleep. © Cengage Learning 2013

SOURCE: Adapted from chart, "Circadian Rhythms" in the book by Coleman, R. (1986). *Wide awake at 3:00 A.M.* New York: W. H. Freeman. Copyright © 1986 by Richard M. Coleman. Reprinted by permission of Henry Holt & Co.

the hypothalamus called the *suprachiasmatic nucleus (SCN)* (Weaver & Reppert, 2008). The SCN then sends signals to the nearby *pineal gland,* whose secretion of the hormone *melatonin* plays a key role in adjusting biological clocks (Norman, 2009).

Ignoring Circadian Rhythms 4a

When you ignore your biological clock and go to sleep at unusual times, the quality of your sleep typically suffers. Getting out of sync with your circadian rhythms is also the cause of *jet lag.* When you fly across several time zones, your biological clock keeps time as usual, even though official clock time changes. You then go to sleep at the "wrong" time and are likely to experience difficulty falling asleep and poor quality sleep. This poor sleep can continue for several days and can make you feel fatigued, sluggish, and irritable (Arendt, Stone, & Skene, 2005).

People differ in how quickly they can reset their biological clocks to compensate for jet lag, and the speed of readjustment depends on the direction traveled. Generally, it's easier to fly westward and lengthen your day than it is to fly eastward and shorten it (Arendt et al., 2005). This east-west disparity in jet lag is sizable enough to have an impact on the performance of sports teams. Studies have found that teams flying westward perform significantly better than teams flying eastward in professional baseball (Recht, Lew, & Schwartz, 1995; see **Figure 5.3** on the next page) and college football (Worthen & Wade, 1999). A rough rule of thumb for jet lag is that the readjustment process takes about a day for each time zone crossed when you fly eastward, and about two-thirds of a day per time zone when you fly westward (Monk, 2006).

Rotating work shifts and late-night shifts that are endured by many nurses, firefighters, and industrial workers also play havoc with biological rhythms. About 17% of the United States workforce works nights or rotating shifts (Richardson, 2006). Shift rotation tends to have far more detrimental effects than jet lag (Monk, 2000). People suffering from jet lag get their circadian rhythms realigned within a matter of days, but workers on night or rotating shifts are constantly at odds with local time cues and normal rhythms. Studies show that such workers get less total sleep and poorer quality sleep. These work schedules can also have a negative impact on employees' productivity and accident proneness at work, the quality of their social relations at home, and their mental health (Cruz, della Rocco, & Hackworth, 2000; Waage et al., 2009). Studies have also linked rotating shifts to a higher incidence of many physical diseases, including cancer, diabetes, ulcers, high

© Alex Staroseltsev/Shutterstock

Figure 5.3

Effects of direction traveled on the performance of professional baseball teams. To gain some insight into the determinants of jet lag, Recht, Lew, and Schwartz (1995) analyzed the performance of visiting teams in major league baseball over a three-year period. In baseball, visiting teams usually play three or four games in each destination city, so there are plenty of games in which the visiting team has not traveled the day before. These games, which served as a baseline for comparison, were won by the visiting team 46% of the time. Consistent with the observation that flying west creates less jet lag than flying east, visiting teams that flew westward the day (or night) before performed only slightly worse, winning 44% of the time. In contrast, visiting teams that flew eastward the day before won only 37% of their games, presumably because flying east and shortening one's day creates greater jet lag.

SOURCE: Adapted from Kalat, J. W. (2007). *Biological Psychology* with CD and INFOTRAC (9 ed.). Belmont, CA: Wadsworth. Wadsworth is a part of Cengage Learning, Inc. Reproduced by permission. www.cengage.com/permissions.

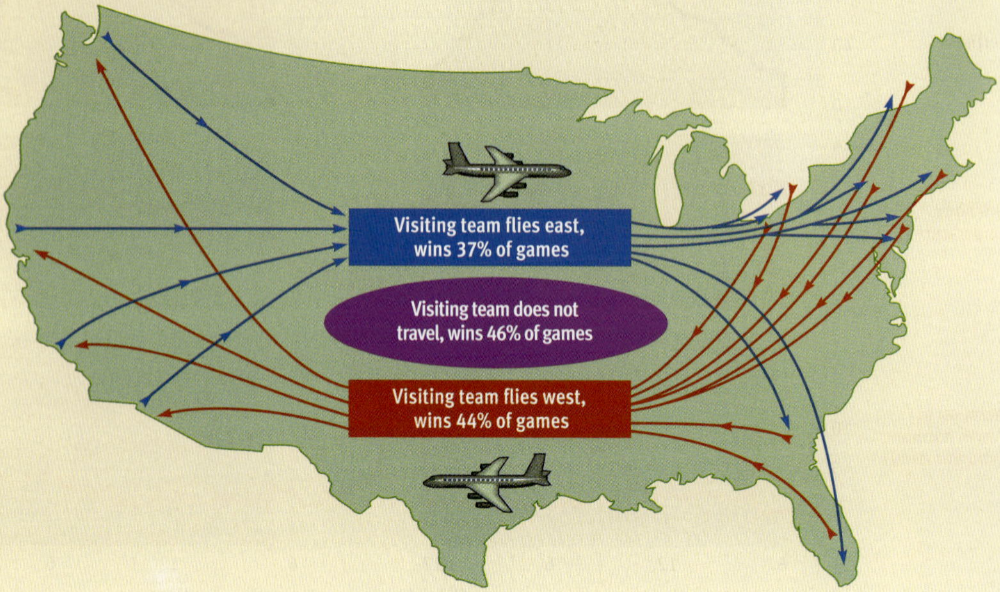

© Cengage Learning 2013

blood pressure, and heart disease (Kriegsfeld & Nelson, 2009).

Realigning Circadian Rhythms

Scientists have begun to look for new ways to help people realign their daily rhythms. One promising line of research has focused on giving people small doses of the hormone melatonin, which as we have noted appears to regulate the human biological clock. The evidence from a number of studies suggests that melatonin *can* reduce the effects of jet lag by helping travelers resynchronize their biological clocks. These research results are inconsistent, however (Arendt & Skene, 2005; Monk, 2006). One reason for the inconsistent findings is that the timing of the melatonin dose in combating jet lag is crucial. But because calculating the optimal timing is complicated, it's easy to get it wrong (Arendt, 2009).

Researchers have also tried carefully timed exposure to bright light as a treatment to realign circadian rhythms in rotating shift workers in industrial settings. Positive effects have been seen in some studies (Lowden, Akerstedt, & Wibom, 2004). This treatment can accelerate workers' adaptation to a new sleep-wake schedule, leading to improvements in sleep quality and alertness during work hours. However, the effects of bright-light administration have been modest and somewhat inconsistent (Rogers & Dinges, 2002). It isn't a realistic option in many work settings either. Another strategy to help rotating shift workers involves carefully planning their rotation schedules to reduce the severity of their circadian disruption (Smith, Fogg, & Eastman, 2009). Although enlightened scheduling practices and other interventions can help, the unfortunate reality is that most people find rotating shift work very difficult (Arendt, 2010).

REVIEW OF KEY LEARNING GOALS

5.3 Biological rhythms are periodic fluctuations in physiological functioning, which indicate that most organisms have internal biological clocks. The cycle of sleep and wakefulness is influenced considerably by circadian rhythms, even when people are cut off from the cycle of light and darkness. Exposure to light resets biological clocks by affecting the activity of the suprachiasmatic nucleus and the pineal gland, which secretes the hormone melatonin.

5.4 Ignoring your biological clock by going to sleep at an unusual time may have a negative effect on your sleep. Being out of sync with circadian rhythms is one reason for jet lag and for the unpleasant nature of rotating shift work. Melatonin may have value in efforts to alleviate the effects of jet lag. Bright light administration and circadian-friendly rotation schedules can sometimes reduce the negative effects of rotating shift work.

The Sleep and Waking Cycle

KEY LEARNING GOALS

5.5 Compare REM and NREM sleep, and describe the nightly sleep cycle.

5.6 Summarize age trends in patterns of sleep and cultural influences on sleep.

5.7 Discuss the neural and evolutionary bases of sleep.

5.8 Describe the effects of sleep deprivation and the health ramifications of sleep loss.

5.9 Identify the symptoms of insomnia, sleep apnea, night terrors, nightmares, somnambulism, and REM sleep behavior disorder.

Although it's a familiar state of consciousness, sleep is widely misunderstood. Historically, people have thought of sleep as a single, uniform state of physical and mental inactivity, during which the brain is "shut down" (Dement, 2003). In reality, sleepers experience quite a bit of physical and mental activity throughout the night. Scientists have learned a great deal about sleep since the landmark discovery of REM sleep in the 1950s.

The advances in psychology's understanding of sleep are the result of hard work by researchers who have spent countless nighttime hours watching other people sleep. This work is done in sleep laboratories, where volunteer subjects come to spend the night. Sleep labs have one or more "bedrooms" in which the subjects retire, usually after being hooked up to a variety of physiological recording devices. In addition to an EEG, the other two crucial devices are **an *electromyograph (EMG),* which records muscular activity and tension, and an *electrooculograph (EOG),* which records eye movements** (Carskadon & Rechtschaffen, 2005; Collop, 2006). Typically, other instruments are also used to monitor heart rate, breathing, pulse rate, and body temperature. The researchers observe the sleeping subject through a window (or with a video camera) from an adjacent room, where they also monitor the physiological recording equipment (see the adjacent photo). Most subjects adapt in just one night to the lab environment and return to their normal mode of sleeping (Carskadon & Dement, 2005).

Cycling Through the Stages of Sleep

PSYKTREK 4b

Not only does sleep occur in a context of daily rhythms, but subtler rhythms are evident within the experience of sleep itself. During sleep, people cycle through a series of five stages. Let's take a look at what researchers have learned about the changes that occur during each of these stages (Carskadon & Dement, 2005; Pace-Schott, 2009; Rosenthal, 2006).

Stages 1–4

PSYKTREK 4b

Although it may only take a few minutes, the onset of sleep is gradual, with no obvious transition point between wakefulness and sleep (Rechtschaffen, 1994). The length of time it takes people to fall asleep varies considerably, but the *average* in a recent study of over 35,000 people from ten countries was 25 minutes (Soldatos et al., 2005). Falling-asleep time depends on quite a range of factors, including how long it has been since the person has slept, where the person is in his or her circadian cycle, and the amount of noise or light in the sleep environment, as well as the person's age, desire to fall asleep, boredom level, recent caffeine or drug intake, and stress level, among other things (Broughton, 1994). In any event, stage 1 is a brief transitional stage of light sleep that usually lasts only 10–12 minutes (Rama, Cho, & Kushida, 2006). Breathing and heart rate slow as muscle tension and body temperature decline. The alpha waves that probably dominated EEG activity just before falling asleep give way to lower-frequency EEG activity in which theta waves are prominent (see **Figure 5.4** on the next page). *Hypnic jerks,* those brief muscular contractions that occur as people fall asleep, generally occur during stage 1 drowsiness (Broughton, 1994).

As the sleeper descends through stages 2, 3, and 4 of the cycle, respiration rate, heart rate, muscle tension, and body temperature continue to decline. During stage 2, which typically lasts about 10–25 minutes, brief bursts of higher-frequency brain waves, called *sleep spindles,* appear against a background of mixed EEG activity (refer to **Figure 5.4** once again). Gradually, brain waves become higher in amplitude and slower in frequency, as the body moves into a deeper form of sleep, called slow-wave sleep. ***Slow-wave***

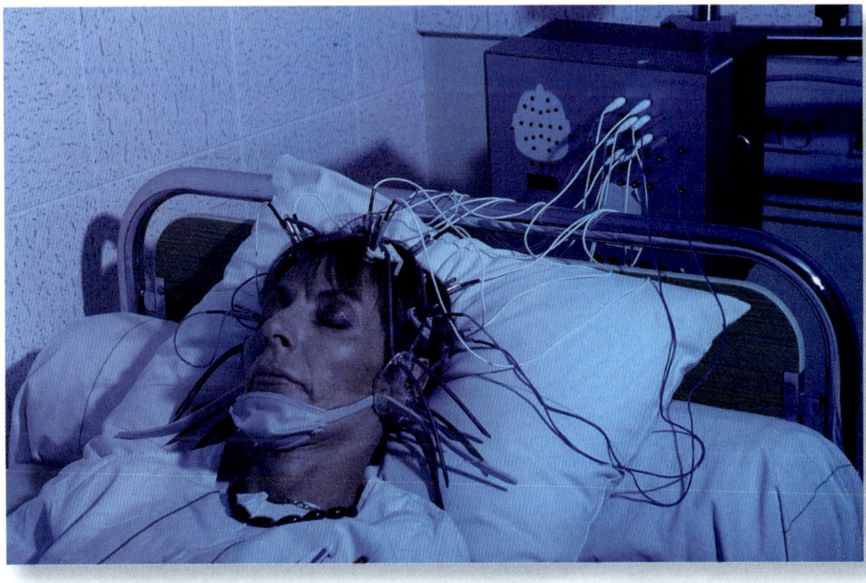

© Christian Voulgaropoulos/ISM/Phototake. All rights reserved.

Researchers in a sleep laboratory can observe subjects while using elaborate equipment to record physiological changes during sleep. This kind of research has disclosed that sleep is a complex series of physical and mental states.

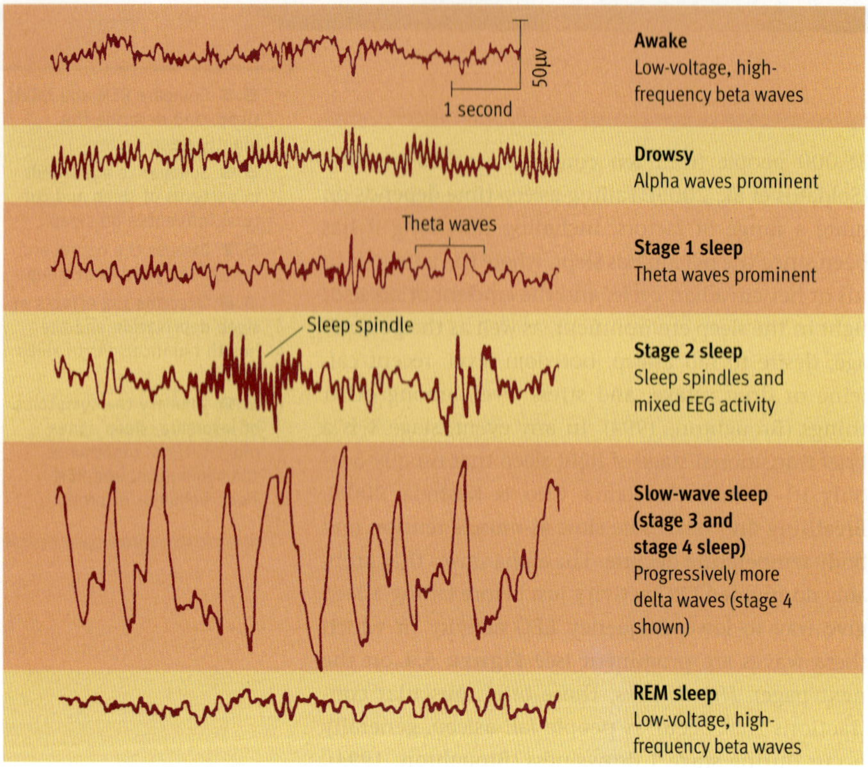

© Cengage Learning 2013

Figure 5.4

EEG patterns in sleep and wakefulness. Characteristic brain waves vary depending on one's state of consciousness. Generally, as people move from an awake state through deeper stages of sleep, their brain waves decrease in frequency (cycles per second) and increase in amplitude (height). However, brain waves during REM sleep resemble "wide-awake" brain waves.

SOURCE: Adapted from Hauri, P. (1982). *Current concepts: The sleep disorders.* Kalamazoo, MI: The Upjohn Company. Reprinted by permission.

***sleep (SWS)* consists of sleep stages 3 and 4, during which high-amplitude, low-frequency delta waves become prominent in EEG recordings.** Typically, individuals reach slow-wave sleep in about a half-hour and stay there for roughly 30 minutes. Then the cycle reverses itself and the sleeper gradually moves back upward through the lighter stages. That's when things start to get especially interesting.

© Ana Blazic/Shutterstock

REM Sleep 4b

When sleepers reach what should be stage 1 again, they usually go into the *fifth* stage of sleep. This is the stage most widely known as *REM sleep.* As we have seen, REM is an abbreviation for the *rapid eye movements* prominent during this stage. In a sleep lab, researchers use an electrooculograph to monitor these lateral (side-to-side) movements that occur beneath the sleeping person's closed eyelids. However, these movements can be seen with the naked eye if you closely watch someone in the REM stage of sleep (little ripples move back and forth across his or her closed eyelids). Decades of research have shown that virtually all mammals and birds exhibit REM sleep (see the photo on page 191 for a notable exception).

In humans, the REM stage tends to be a "deep" stage of sleep in the sense that people are relatively hard to awaken from it. The REM stage is also marked by irregular breathing and pulse rate. Muscle tone is extremely relaxed—so much so that bodily movements are minimal and the sleeper is virtually paralyzed. *Although REM is a relatively deep stage of sleep, EEG activity is dominated by high-frequency beta waves that resemble those observed when people are alert and awake* (see **Figure 5.4** again).

This paradox is probably related to the association between REM sleep and dreaming. As noted earlier, when subjects are awakened during various stages of sleep and asked whether they are dreaming, most dream reports come from the REM stage (Dement, 1978; McCarley, 1994). Although decades of research have revealed that some dreaming also occurs in the non-REM stages, dreaming is most frequent, vivid, and memorable during REM sleep (Pace-Schott, 2005).

To summarize, ***REM sleep* is a relatively deep stage of sleep marked by rapid eye movements, high-frequency, low-amplitude brain waves, and vivid dreaming.** It is such a special stage of sleep that the other four stages are often characterized simply as "non-REM sleep." ***Non-REM (NREM) sleep* consists of sleep stages 1 through 4, which are marked by an absence of rapid eye movements, relatively little dreaming, and varied EEG activity.**

Repeating the Cycle 4b

During the course of a night, people usually repeat the sleep cycle about four times. As the night wears on, the cycle changes gradually. The first REM period is relatively short, lasting only a few minutes. Subsequent REM periods get progressively longer, peaking at around 40–60 minutes. Additionally, NREM intervals tend to get shorter, and descents into NREM stages usually become more shallow. These trends can be seen in **Figure 5.5** on pages 192–193, which provides an overview of a typical night's sleep cycle. These trends mean that most slow-wave sleep occurs early in the sleep cycle and that REM sleep tends to pile up in the second half of the sleep cycle. Across the entire cycle, adults typically spend about 15%–20% of their sleep time in slow-wave sleep and another 20%–25% in REM sleep (Rama et al., 2006).

Age Trends in Sleep

PSYKTREK 4b

Age alters the sleep cycle. What we have described so far is the typical pattern for adults. Children, however, display different patterns. Newborns will sleep six to eight times in a 24-hour period, often exceeding a total of 16 hours of sleep. Fortunately for parents, during the first several months much of this sleep begins to get consolidated into one particularly long nighttime sleep period (Huber & Tononi, 2009). Interestingly, infants spend much more of their sleep time in the REM stage than adults do. In the first few months, REM accounts for about 50% of babies' sleep, as compared to 20% of adults' sleep. During the remainder of the first year, the REM portion of infants' sleep declines to roughly 30% (Ohayon et al., 2004). The REM portion of sleep continues to decrease gradually until it levels off at about 20% (see **Figure 5.6** on the next page).

During adulthood, gradual, age-related changes in sleep continue. The proportion of REM sleep remains fairly stable (Floyd et al., 2007), but the percentage of slow-wave sleep declines while the percentage of time spent in stage 1 increases slightly (Rissling & Ancoli-Israel, 2009). These shifts toward lighter sleep *may* contribute to the increased frequency of nighttime awakenings seen among the elderly (Klerman et al., 2004). As **Figure 5.6** shows, the average amount of total sleep time also declines with advancing age.

Until recently it was assumed that this decline in sleep time was because older people have more difficulty initiating sleep or remaining asleep. In other words, it was attributed to a decrease in their ability to sleep effectively. However, a recent, carefully controlled laboratory study that allowed for extended

© Steve Bloom Images/Alamy

REM sleep is not unique to humans. Nearly all mammals and birds exhibit REM sleep. The only known exceptions among warm-blooded vertebrates are dolphins and some whales (Morrison, 2003). Dolphins are particularly interesting, as they sleep while swimming, resting one hemisphere of the brain while the other hemisphere remains alert.

CONCEPT CHECK 5.1

Comparing REM and NREM Sleep

A table here could have provided you with a systematic comparison of REM sleep and NREM sleep, but that would have deprived you of the opportunity to check your understanding of these sleep phases by creating your own table. Fill in each of the blanks below with a word or phrase highlighting the differences between REM and NREM sleep with regard to the various characteristics specified. You can find the answers in the back of the book in Appendix A.

Characteristic	REM sleep	NREM sleep
1. Type of EEG activity	________	________
2. Eye movements	________	________
3. Dreaming	________	________
4. Depth (difficulty in awakening)	________	________
5. Percentage of total sleep (in adults)	________	________
6. Increases or decreases (as percentage of sleep) during childhood	________	________
7. Timing in sleep cycle (dominates early or late)	________	________

Figure 5.5

An overview of the cycle of sleep. The white line charts how a typical, healthy, young adult moves through the various stages of sleep during the course of a night. This diagram also shows how dreams and rapid eye movements tend to coincide with REM sleep, whereas posture changes occur between REM periods (because the body is nearly paralyzed during REM sleep). Notice how the person cycles into REM four times, as descents into NREM sleep get shallower and REM periods get longer. Thus, slow-wave sleep is prominent early in the night, while REM sleep dominates the second half of a night's sleep. Although these patterns are typical, keep in mind that sleep patterns vary from one person to another and that they change with age.

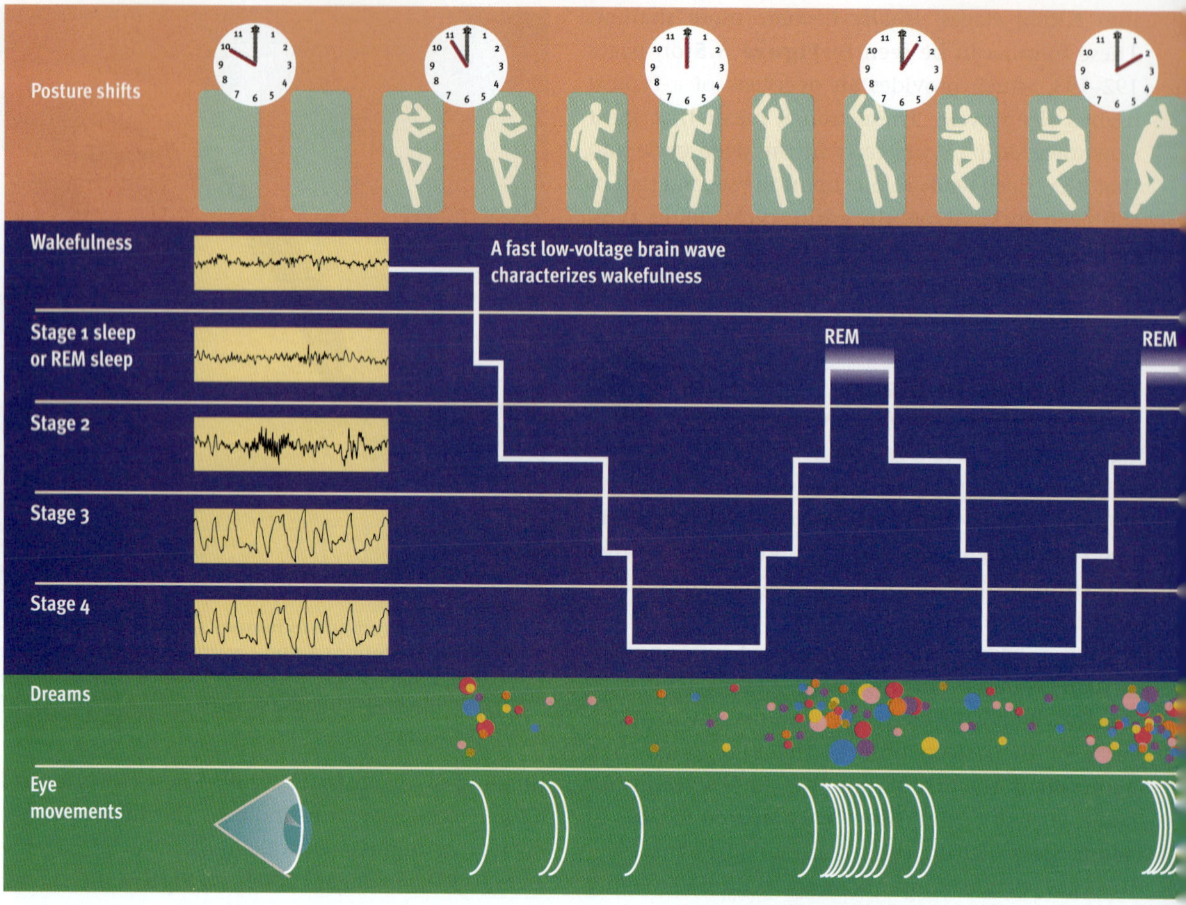

Figure 5.6

Changes in sleep patterns over the life span. Both the total amount of sleep per night and the portion of sleep that is REM sleep change with age. Sleep patterns change most dramatically during infancy, with total sleep time and amount of REM sleep declining sharply in the first two years of life. After a noticeable drop in the average amount of sleep in adolescence, sleep patterns remain relatively stable, although total sleep and slow-wave sleep continue to decline gradually with age.

© Cengage Learning 2013

SOURCE: Adapted from an updated revision of a figure in Roffwarg, H. P., Muzio, J. N., & Dement, W. C. (1966). Ontogenetic development of human sleep-dream cycle. *Science, 152,* 604–609. Copyright © 1966 by the American Association for the Advancement of Science. Reprinted with permission from AAAS.

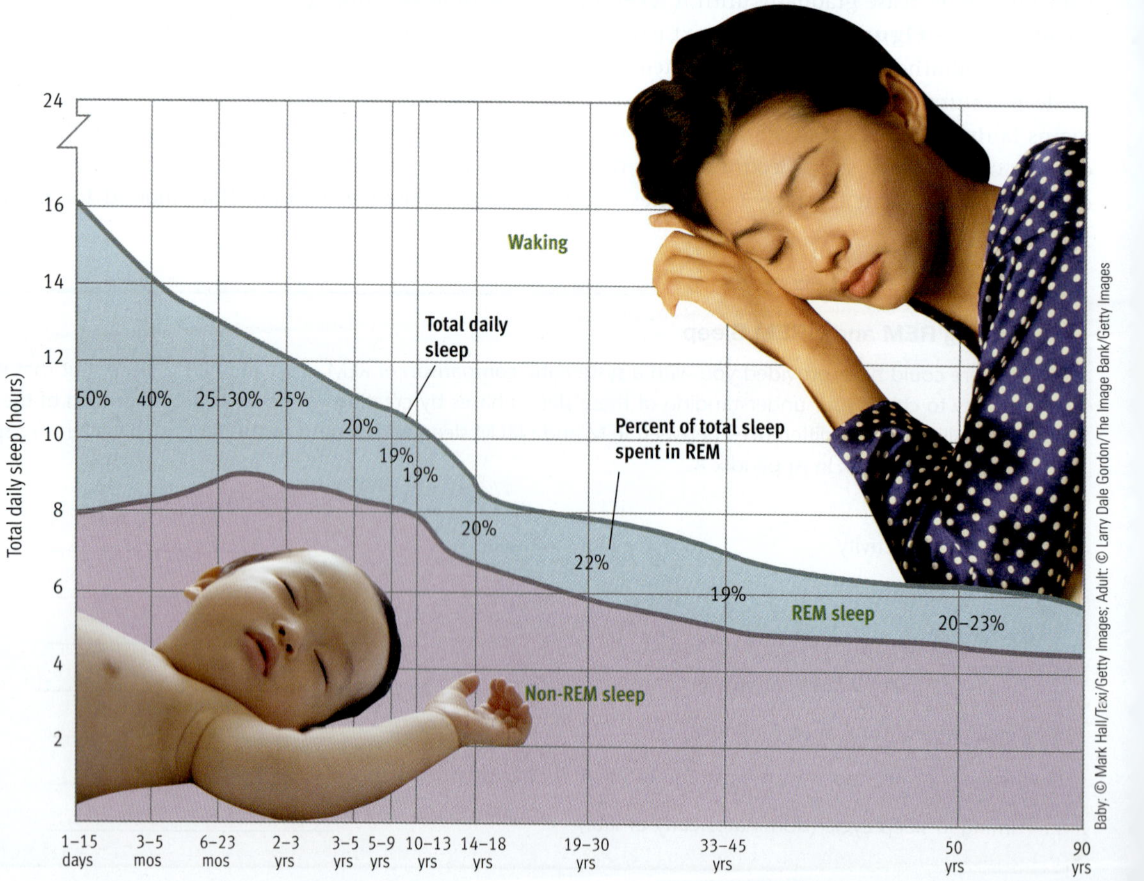

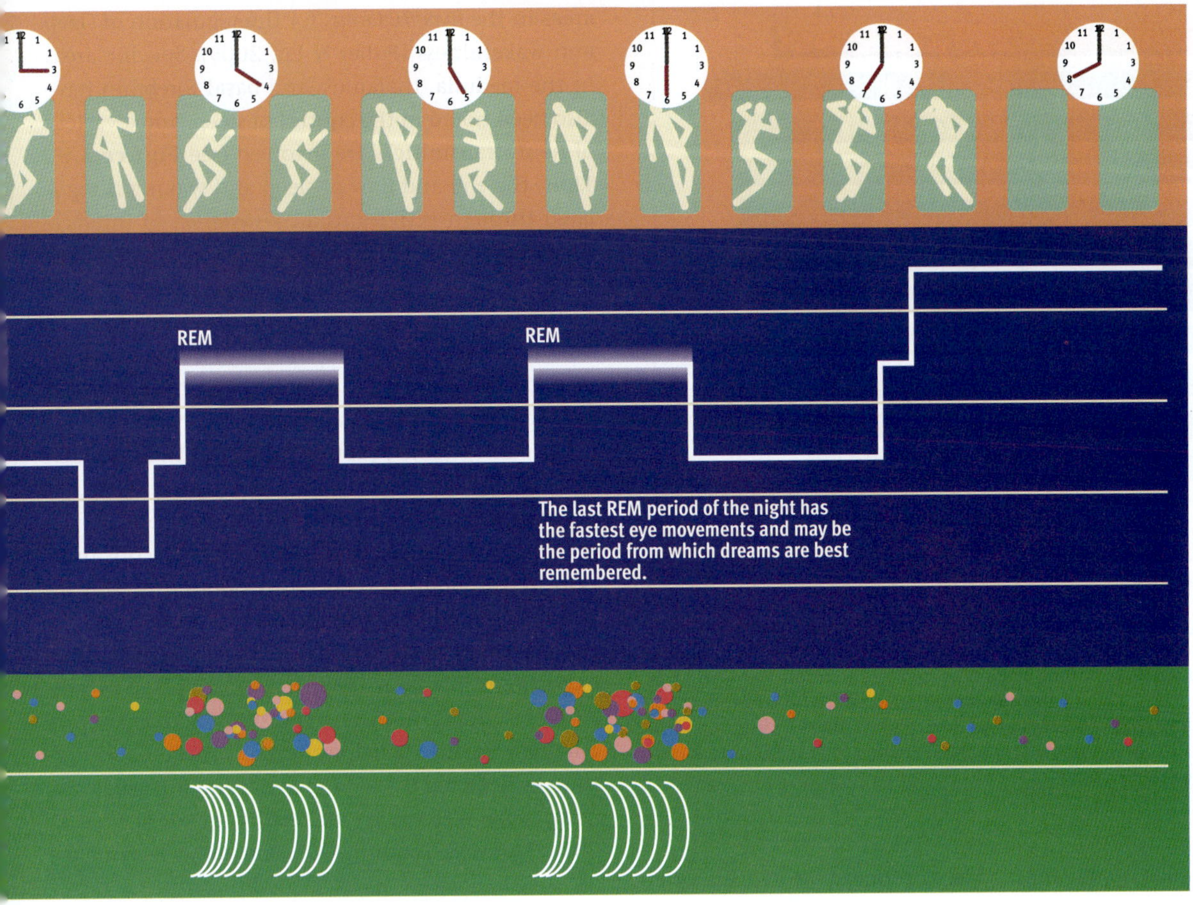

sleep opportunities found that older adults (ages 60–80) showed significantly less sleepiness during the day than younger adults (ages 18–30), even though the older group chose to sleep an average of 1.5 fewer hours per day (Klerman & Dijk, 2008). The authors conclude that the elderly *may* simply need less sleep than younger adults. Consistent with this line of thinking, another recent study yielded the surprising finding that older adults tolerate sleep deprivation with less impairment than younger adults (Duffy et al., 2009). Older people do have more difficulty adapting to circadian phase shifts, such as those produced by jet lag or rotating workshifts (Monk, 2005a), but excessive daytime sleepiness does not increase with age (Young, 2004). The bottom line is that growing older, by itself, does not appear to lead to poor sleep if elderly people remain healthy (Vitiello, 2009). Although sleep complaints escalate with age, much of this escalation is the result of increases in health problems that interfere with sleep.

Culture and Sleep

The psychological and physiological experience of sleep does not appear to vary much across cultures. For example, a cross-cultural survey (Soldatos et al., 2005) found relatively modest differences in the average amount of time that people sleep and in the time it takes for them to fall asleep (see **Figure 5.7** on the next page). That said, a recent poll of people in the United States found some ethnic disparities in subjective estimates of individuals' sleep quality (National Sleep Foundation, 2010). In this poll, whites (20%) and African Americans (18%) were more likely to report that they "rarely" or "never" enjoyed a good night's sleep than either Hispanics (14%) or Asians (9%). Another recent study also found that Asians reported fewer sleep complaints than other ethnic groups (Grandner, Patel, et al., 2010b). The same study also looked at the influence of social class on sleep and concluded that lower income and education was associated with more sleep complaints.

Napping practices do vary along cultural lines. In many societies, shops close and activities are curtailed in the afternoon to permit people to enjoy a 1- to 2-hour midday nap. These "siesta cultures" are found mostly in tropical regions of the world (Webb & Dinges, 1989). There, this practice is adaptive in that it allows people to avoid working during the hottest part of the day. As a rule, the siesta tradition is not found in industrialized societies, where it conflicts with the emphasis on productivity and the

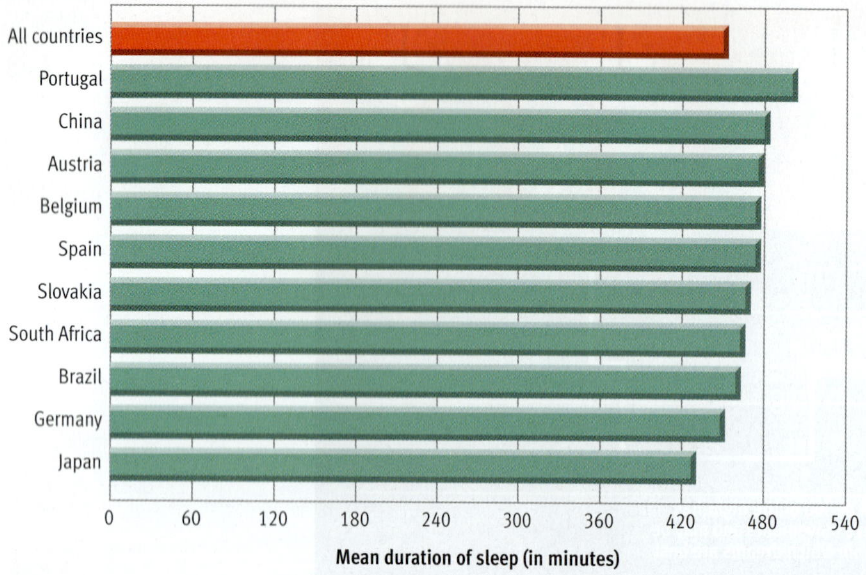

Figure 5.7

Cultural variations in how long people tend to sleep. A recent study (Soldatos et al., 2005) surveyed over 35,000 people in ten countries about various aspects of their sleep habits. This graph shows the average duration of nighttime sleep reported by the respondents in each country. Although Japan was a bit of an "outlier," the cultural differences are rather modest. Cultural variability in the average time required to fall asleep was also modest. Consistent with previous findings, the results of this study suggest that the basic architecture of sleep does not vary much across cultures. © Cengage Learning 2013

philosophy that "time is money." Moreover, when industrialization comes to a siesta culture, it undermines the practice. For instance, modernization in Spain has led to a decline in midday napping there (Kribbs, 1993).

The Neural and Evolutionary Bases of Sleep

The rhythm of sleep and waking appears to be regulated primarily by subcortical structures that lie deep within the brain. One brain structure that's important to sleep and wakefulness is the *reticular formation* in the core of the brainstem (Garcia-Rill, 2009; Steriade, 2005). ***The ascending reticular activating system (ARAS)* consists of the incoming nerve fibers running through the reticular formation that influence physiological arousal.** As you can see in **Figure 5.8**, the ARAS spreads into many areas of the cortex. When these ascending fibers are cut in the brainstem of a cat, the result is continuous sleep (Moruzzi, 1964). Electrical stimulation along the same pathways produces arousal and alertness.

Many other brain structures are also involved in the regulation of sleeping and waking (Marks, 2006). For example, activity in the *pons* and adjacent areas in the *midbrain* seems to be critical to the generation of REM sleep (Siegel, 2005). Recent research has focused on the importance of various areas in the *hypothalamus* for the regulation of sleep and wakefulness (Fuller & Lu, 2009). Specific areas in the medulla, thalamus, and basal forebrain have also been noted in the control of sleep, and a variety of neurotransmitters are involved (see **Figure 5.8**). Thus, the ebb and flow of sleep and waking is regulated through activity in a *constellation* of interacting brain centers (Pace-Schott, Hobson, & Stickgold, 2008).

What is the evolutionary significance of sleep? The fact that sleep is seen in a highly diverse range of organisms and that it appears to have evolved independently in birds and mammals suggests that it has considerable adaptive value. But theorists disagree about *how* exactly sleep is adaptive. One hypothesis is that sleep evolved to conserve organisms' energy. For example, in humans energy consumption by the brain is reduced by about 30% during sleep (Siegel, 2009). An alternative hypothesis is that the inactivity of sleep is adaptive because it reduces exposure to predators and the consumption of precious resources. A third hypothesis is that sleep is adaptive because it helps animals restore bodily resources depleted by waking activities. But what, exactly, sleep restores is not readily apparent (Frank, 2006; Huber & Tononi, 2009). Overall, the evidence

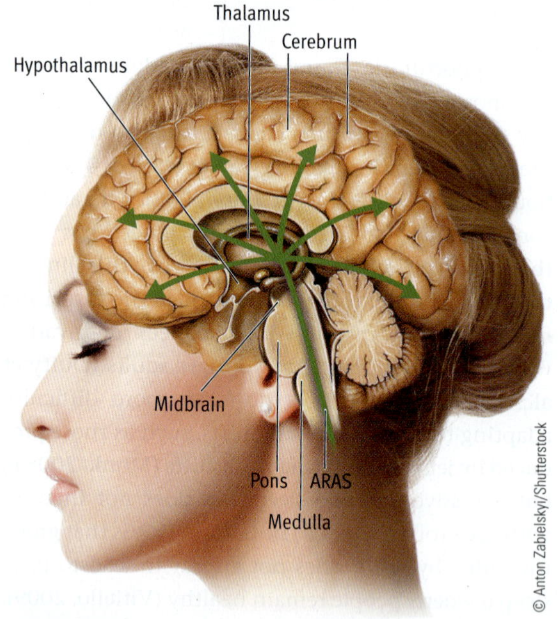

Figure 5.8

The ascending reticular activating system (ARAS) and other areas involved in sleep. A number of brain areas and structures interact to regulate sleep and waking, including all those highlighted in this graphic. Particularly important are the pons and the ARAS (represented by the green arrows), which conveys neural stimulation to many areas of the cortex. Recent research has focused on the role of the hypothalamus. But the bottom line is that sleep depends on an interacting constellation of brain structures. © Cengage Learning 2013 seems strongest for the energy conservation and inactivity hypotheses, but there is room for extensive debate about the evolutionary bases of sleep (Siegel, 2009; Zepelin, Siegel, & Tobler, 2005).

Doing Without: Sleep Deprivation

Do people really need eight hours of sleep per night? A great many people, including countless college students, try to get by on less sleep than that. Many sleep experts believe that much of American society suffers from chronic sleep deprivation (Walsh, Dement, & Dinges, 2005). It appears that more and more people are trying to squeeze additional waking hours out of their days as they attempt to juggle work, family, household, and school responsibilities. Let's look at the research on the effects of sleep deprivation.

Sleep Restriction

Research has mostly focused on *partial sleep deprivation,* or *sleep restriction,* which occurs when people make do with substantially less sleep than normal over a period of time. Research findings and expert opinions on this matter have varied over recent decades. One reason for these differences is that the effects of sleep restriction vary depending on the amount of sleep lost, on where subjects are in their circadian cycles when tested, and on the nature of the task (Bonnet, 2000; Dorrian & Dinges, 2006). Moreover, recent research has also found differences among individuals in how sensitive they are to sleep restriction (Minkel, Banks, & Dinges, 2009). The emerging consensus, however, is that sleep restriction has far more negative effects than most people assume, as will be apparent in our Featured Study for this chapter.

Courtesy of William Dement

William Dement

"Sleep deprivation is a major epidemic in our society. . . . Americans spend so much time and energy chasing the American dream, that they don't have much time left for actual dreaming."

FEATURED STUDY

The Surprising Costs of Sleep Deprivation

SOURCE: Van Dongen, H. P. A., Maislin, G., Mullington, J. M., & Dinges, D. F. (2003). The cumulative cost of additional wakefulness: Dose-response effects on neurobehavioral functions and sleep physiology from chronic sleep restriction and total sleep deprivation. *Sleep, 26,* 117–126.

Numerous studies of sleep deprivation have been conducted in recent decades, but given the inherent challenges in conducting research in this area, most of them have suffered from methodological weaknesses. For example, many studies have failed to keep participants under supervision to make sure they do not consume stimulants or get more sleep than they are supposed to. Even carefully controlled studies have generally been too brief (typically a few days) to effectively assess the cumulative impact of sleep deprivation. The present study attempted to correct these shortcomings in a highly controlled and exceptionally precise effort to compare and quantify the effects of sleep restriction and total sleep deprivation.

Method

Participants and design. The subjects were 48 healthy, young adults (ages 21–38) who were carefully screened to ensure that they were drug-free and had no medical, psychological, or sleep-related disorders. They agreed to not use any alcohol, tobacco, or caffeine for two weeks prior to the study. The participants were randomly assigned to one of four groups: a control group that slept 8 hours per night, a sleep-restriction group who were allowed 6 hours of sleep per night, a sleep-restriction group who were allowed 4 hours of sleep per night, and a total-deprivation group who were not permitted any sleep. The total-deprivation group went without any sleep for 3 days; the other three groups followed their sleep schedules for 14 days.

Procedure. The volunteers reported to the lab for one day of adaptation (to sleep with recording devices hooked up) and 2 days of baseline recordings before the sleep manipulations were begun. Participants stayed in the laboratory throughout the study. When scheduled to be awake, they were given batteries of cognitive tests every 2 hours. Between test sessions they were allowed to read, watch movies, and interact. During scheduled sleep times, they were hooked up to standard sleep lab recording devices and retired with the lights off.

Measures. The repeated tests of participants' mental functioning included (a) a series of psychomotor vigilance tasks that assessed alertness, (b) a series of digit-symbol matching tasks that assessed short-term memory, and (c) a series of arithmetic tasks that assessed complex problem solving. In each testing session, subjects also responded to a self-report scale that assessed their subjective feelings of sleepiness.

Results

As anticipated, the control group who were not deprived of sleep showed no cognitive deficits over the course of 14 days, while the total-deprivation group showed rapid and steep deterioration on all measures. These baselines provided useful comparisons to assess the impact of the two sleep-restriction conditions. Participants restricted to 4 or 6 hours of sleep showed a gradual decline in performance on the cognitive measures over the course of the 14 days. These declines in performance were substantial. By the end of the study, the group limited to 6 hours sleep showed cognitive impairments that were equivalent to those seen after 1 day of total sleep deprivation, and the group limited to 4 hours of sleep showed declines comparable to those caused by 2 days of total sleep deprivation. Participants' ratings of their sleepiness soared rapidly in the total-deprivation group but grew gradually and moderately in the sleep-restriction groups.

Discussion

The authors conclude that "even relatively moderate sleep restriction—if sustained night after night—can seriously impair waking neurobehavioral functions in healthy young adults" (p. 124). They assert that their findings contradict the claim made in some quarters that humans gradually adapt to sleep restriction so that impairments become relatively modest after a while. And they note that participants' cognitive deficits were consistent over many repeated tests, thus undermining the notion that deprivation effects might be limited to a few points in the day because of waxing and waning performance. Finally, they point out that participants' ratings of their own sleepiness were minor compared to the steep decline in their performance. This finding suggests that people may not appreciate the extent to which sleep restriction undermines their mental functioning.

Comment

This study was selected because it shows how carefully crafted controls can enhance the quality of empirical research and thus yield more compelling findings. Many previous studies of sleep restriction had observed less severe deterioration in participants' performance, but the exceptional control of extraneous variables in the present study lends greater credence to its findings. The disconnect between participants' ratings of their sleepiness and the size of the cognitive deficits observed also provides yet another demonstration that human experience is highly subjective.

Our Featured Study is representative of a great deal of recent research suggesting that the effects of sleep deprivation are not as benign as widely believed. Studies indicate that sleep restriction can impair individuals' attention, reaction time, cognitive speed and accuracy, motor coordination, and decision making (Dinges, Rogers, & Baynard, 2005). Sleep deprivation has also been blamed for a large proportion of transportation accidents and mishaps in the workplace (Walsh et al., 2005). For example, sleep restriction appears to be a contributing factor in many motor vehicle accidents (Abe et al., 2010). Unfortunately, research shows that sleep-deprived individuals are not particularly good at predicting if and when they will fall asleep (Kaplan, Itoi, & Dement, 2007). Thus, tired drivers often fail to pull off the road when they should.

Studies also suggest that nighttime workers in many industries often fall asleep on the job (Roehrs et al., 2005). The recent reports of air traffic controllers falling asleep in situations where a momentary lapse in attention could be incredibly costly show how serious this problem is. Experts have *estimated* that accidents attributed to drowsiness induced by sleep deprivation cost the U.S. economy as much as $56 billion annually (Durmer & Dinges, 2005).

A large number of traffic accidents occur because drivers get drowsy or fall asleep at the wheel. Although the effects of sleep deprivation seem innocuous, sleep loss can be deadly.

© AP Images/Gerry Broome

Selective Deprivation

The unique quality of REM sleep led researchers to look into the effects of a special type of sleep deprivation: *selective deprivation*. In a number of laboratory studies, subjects were awakened over a period of nights whenever they began to go into the REM stage. These subjects usually got a decent amount of sleep in NREM stages, but they were selectively deprived of REM sleep.

What are the effects of REM deprivation? The evidence suggests that it has little noticeable impact on daytime functioning, but it *does* have some interesting effects on subjects' patterns of sleeping (Bonnet, 2005). As the nights go by in REM-deprivation studies, it becomes necessary to awaken the subjects more and more often to deprive them of their REM sleep, because they shift into REM more and more frequently (as opposed to the usual four times a night). In one study, researchers had to awaken a subject 64 times by the third night of REM deprivation, as shown in **Figure 5.9** (Borbely, 1986). Furthermore, when a REM-deprivation experiment comes to an end and participants are allowed to sleep without interruption, they experience a "rebound effect." That is, they spend extra time in REM periods for one to three nights to make up for their REM deprivation (Bonnet, 2005).

Similar results have been observed when subjects have been selectively deprived of slow-wave sleep (Bonnet, 2005). As the nights go by, more awaken-

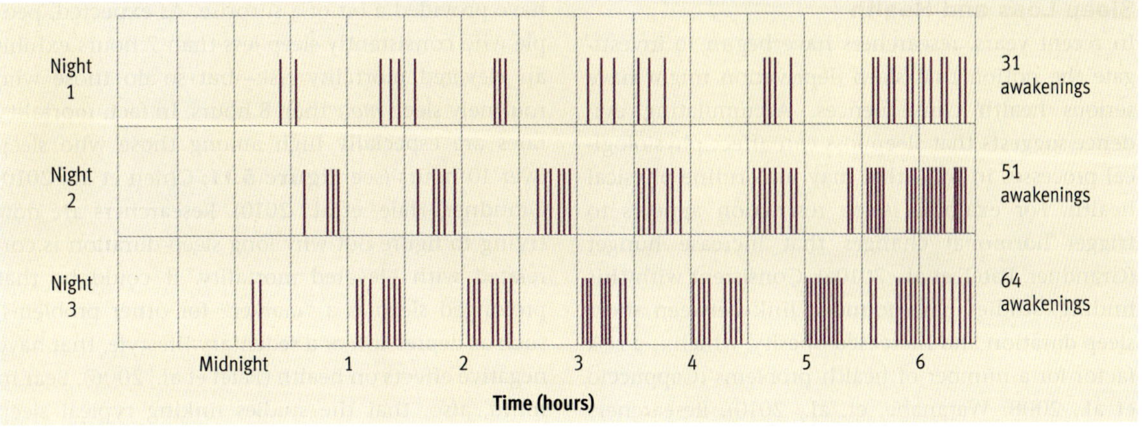

Figure 5.9

The effects of REM deprivation on sleep. This graph plots how often researchers had to awaken a subject over the course of three nights of REM deprivation. Notice how the awakenings rapidly became more frequent during the course of each night and from night to night. This pattern of awakenings illustrates how a REM-deprived subject tends to compensate by repeatedly slipping back into REM sleep.

SOURCE: Adapted from Borbléy, A. (1986). *Secrets of sleep* (English translation). New York: Basic Books. © 1988 Alexander Borbléy. Reprinted by permission of Basic Books, a member of the Perseus Books Group. Alexander Borbléy, Das Geheimnis des Schlafes: Neue Wege und Erkenntnisse der Forschung © 1984 Duetsche Verlags-Anstalt, Munich, a member of Verlagssgruppe Random House GmbH.

ings are required to prevent SWS, and after deprivation of SWS people experience a rebound effect (Borbely & Achermann, 2005). What do theorists make of these spontaneous pursuits of REM and slow-wave sleep? They conclude that people must have specific *needs* for REM and slow-wave sleep—and rather strong needs, at that.

Why do we need REM and slow-wave sleep? Some recent studies suggest that REM and slow-wave sleep contribute to firming up learning that takes place during the day—a process called *memory consolidation* (Gais & Born, 2004; Stickgold, 2001). Efforts to explore this hypothesis have led to some interesting findings in recent years. For example, in one study participants were given training on a perceptual-motor task and then retested 12 hours later. Subjects who slept during the 12-hour interval showed substantial *improvement* in performance that was not apparent in subjects who did not sleep (Walker et al., 2002). A number of similar studies have shown that sleep seems to enhance subjects' memory of specific learning activities that occurred during the day and that depriving subjects of either REM sleep or slow-wave sleep reduces these increments in memory (Walker, 2009; Walker & Stickgold, 2004). Studies also find that the length of time spent in REM and SWS correlates with the degree to which subjects' memory performance is enhanced (Walker & Stickgold, 2006). The theoretical meaning of these findings is still being debated, but the most widely accepted explanations center on how time spent in specific stages of sleep may stabilize or solidify memories formed during the day (Rasch & Born, 2008; Stickgold, 2005).

In related research, investigators have found that REM sleep appears to foster the recently discovered process of *neurogenesis* (Guzman-Marin et al., 2008; Meerlo et al., 2009). As noted in Chapter 3, ***neurogenesis* refers to the formation of new neurons.** This finding meshes with the data linking REM sleep to memory consolidation because other, independent lines of research suggest that neurogenesis contributes to learning (Leuner, Gould, & Shors, 2006; see Chapter 7).

Further underscoring the importance of REM sleep, some studies even suggest that REM may promote creative insights related to previous learning (Stickgold & Walker, 2004). In one study, participants worked on a challenging task requiring creativity before and after an opportunity to take a nap or enjoy quiet rest (Cai et al., 2009). The naps were monitored physiologically and subjects were divided into those who experienced REM during their nap and those who did not. The REM sleep group showed dramatic increases in creative performance after the nap that were not seen in the group that did not experience REM or the group that engaged in quiet rest (see **Figure 5.10**).

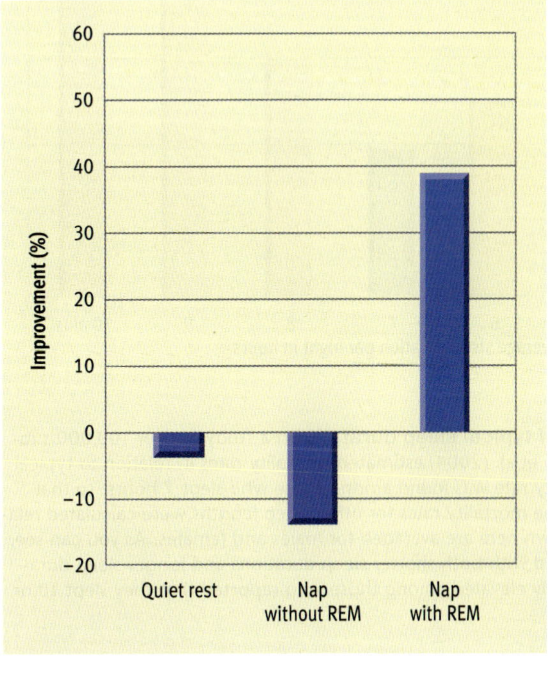

Figure 5.10

Enhanced creativity after a nap with REM sleep. Participants in the Cai et al. (2009) study worked on a difficult measure of creativity and then were instructed to take a nap or engage in quiet rest. Napping subjects were divided into those who went into REM during their nap and those who did not. After their naps or quiet rest, participants worked on the creativity test again. Although the REM nappers only logged an average of 14 minutes in REM, their performance on the creativity test improved by almost 40%, whereas the other groups showed no improvement.

SOURCE: Adapted from Cai, D. J., Mednick, S. A., Harrison, E. M., Kanady, J. C., & Mednick, S. C. (2009). REM, not incubation, improves creativity by priming associative networks. *Proceedings of the National Academy of Sciences, 106,* 10130–10134. ESPOND.

Reality CHECK

Misconception

The effects of partial sleep deprivation generally are modest and insignificant.

Reality

The basis for this belief is that the most obvious effect of sleep deprivation is increased sleepiness, which sounds pretty harmless. However, sleep deprivation impairs attention, motor coordination, decision making, and memory and increases the likelihood of many kinds of accidents. Moreover, sleep loss is associated with increased vulnerability to a variety of serious diseases and elevated mortality.

Sleep Loss and Health

In recent years, researchers have begun to investigate the notion that sleep deprivation might have serious health consequences. Accumulating evidence suggests that sleep loss can affect physiological processes in ways that may undermine physical health. For example, sleep restriction appears to trigger hormonal changes that increase hunger (Grandner, Patel, et al., 2010a). Consistent with this finding, studies have found a link between short sleep duration and increased obesity, which is a risk factor for a number of health problems (Cappuccio et al., 2008; Watanabe, et. al., 2010). Researchers have also found that sleep loss leads to impaired immune system functioning (Motivala & Irwin, 2007) and increased inflammatory responses (Patel et al., 2009), which are likely to heighten vulnerability to a variety of diseases. Hence, it's not surprising that studies have uncovered links between short sleep duration and an increased risk for diabetes (Knutson & Van Cauter, 2008), hypertension (Gangwisch et al., 2006), and cardiovascular disease (King et al., 2008; Sabanayagam & Shankar, 2010).

These findings have motivated researchers to explore the correlation between habitual sleep time and overall mortality. The results of this research have provided a bit of a surprise. As expected, people who consistently sleep less than 7 hours exhibit an elevated mortality risk—but so do those who routinely sleep *more* than 8 hours. In fact, mortality rates are especially high among those who sleep over 10 hours (see **Figure 5.11**; Chien et al., 2010; Grandner, Hale, et al., 2010). Researchers are now trying to figure out why long sleep duration is correlated with elevated mortality. It could be that prolonged sleep is a "marker" for other problems, such as depression or a sedentary lifestyle, that have negative effects on health (Patel et al., 2006). Bear in mind, also, that the studies linking typical sleep duration to mortality have depended on participants' *self-report estimates* of how long they normally sleep, which could be inaccurate. In any event, the relationship between sleep and health is an emerging area of research that probably will yield some very interesting findings in the years to come.

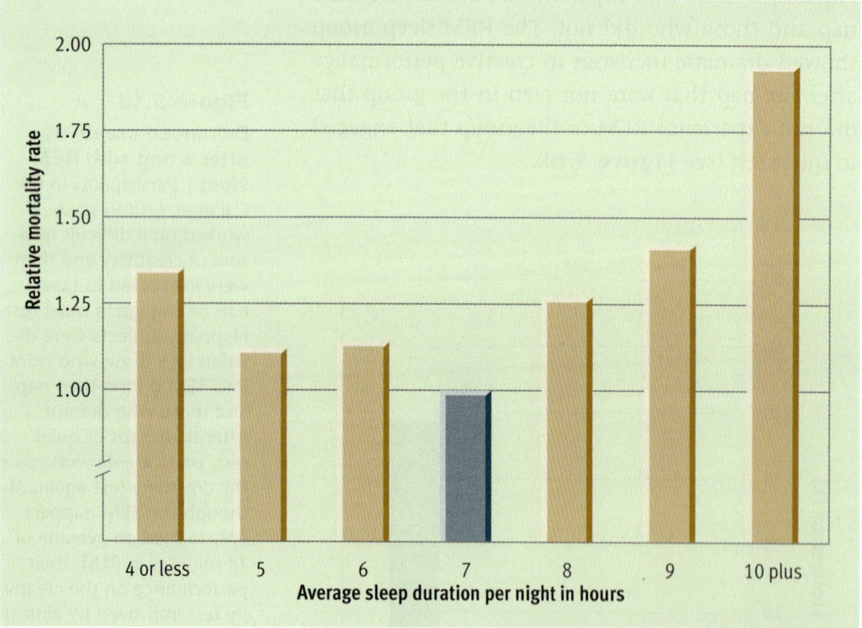

Figure 5.11

Mortality rates as a function of typical sleep duration. In a study of over 100,000 subjects followed ten years, Tamakoshi et al. (2004) estimated mortality rates in relation to typical sleep duration. The lowest mortality rate was found among those who slept 7 hours, so that figure was arbitrarily set to 1.00; the mortality rates for other sleep lengths were calculated relative to that baseline. The rates shown here are averaged for males and females. As you can see, higher mortality rates are associated with both shorter sleep durations and longer sleep durations. Mortality rates were especially elevated among those who reported that they slept 10 or more hours per night.

Problems in the Night: Sleep Disorders

Not everyone is able to consistently enjoy the luxury of a good night's sleep. In this section we will briefly discuss what is currently known about a variety of sleep disorders.

Insomnia

Insomnia is the most common sleep disorder. ***Insomnia* refers to chronic problems in getting adequate sleep.** It occurs in three basic patterns: (1) difficulty in falling asleep initially, (2) difficulty in remaining asleep, and (3) persistent early-morning awakening. Difficulty falling asleep is the most common problem among young people, whereas trouble staying asleep and early-morning awakenings are the most common syndromes among middle-aged and elderly people (Hublin & Partinen, 2002). Insomnia may sound like a minor problem to those who haven't struggled with it, but it can be a very unpleasant ailment. Insomniacs have to endure the pain of watching their precious sleep time tick away as they toss and turn in restless frustration. Moreover, insomnia is associated with daytime fatigue, impaired cognitive functioning, an elevated risk for accidents, reduced productivity, depression, anxiety, substance abuse, hypertension, and increased health problems (see **Figure 5.12**; Edinger & Means, 2005; Kyle, Morgan, & Espie, 2010; Vgontzas et al., 2008).

Prevalence Estimates of the prevalence of insomnia vary considerably because surveys have to depend on respondents' highly subjective judgments of whether their sleep is adequate. Results vary depending on how survey questions are posed (Ohayon & Guilleminault, 2006). Another complicating consideration is that nearly everyone suffers *occasional* sleep difficulties because of stress, disruptions of biological rhythms, or other temporary conditions. Fortunately, these problems clear up for most people. But research *estimates* suggest that about 30%–35% of adults contend with insomnia, and about half to two-thirds of these people suffer from severe or frequent insomnia (Brown, 2006; Zorick & Walsh, 2000). The prevalence of insomnia increases with age and is about 50% more common in women than in men (Partinen & Hublin, 2005).

Causes Insomnia can have a variety of causes (Hauri, 2002; Roehrs, Zorick, & Roth, 2000; Roth & Drake, 2004). In some cases, excessive anxiety and tension prevent relaxation and keep people awake. Insomnia is frequently a side effect of emotional problems, such as depression, or of significant stress, such as pressures at work. Understandably, health problems such as back pain, ulcers, and asthma can lead to difficulties falling or staying asleep. And it's clear that the use of certain recreational drugs (especially stimulants) and a variety of prescription medications may lead to problems as well (Welsh & Fugit, 2006). All that said, recent research has suggested that the primary cause of insomnia may be that some people are predisposed to insomnia because they have a higher level of physiological arousal than the average person (Stepanski, 2006). According to this *hyperarousal model* of insomnia, some people tend to exhibit elevated heart rate, high metabolic activation, increased body temperature, hormonal patterns that fuel arousal, and EEG patterns associated with arousal (Bonnet & Arand, 2010). This chronic, heightened physiological activation presumably makes these people especially vulnerable to insomnia (Riemann et al., 2010).

Treatment A huge portion of people suffering from insomnia do not pursue professional treatment (Sivertsen et al., 2006). Many of them probably depend on over-the-counter sleep aids, which have questionable value (Mahowald & Schenck, 2005a). The most common approach in the medical treatment of insomnia is the prescription of two classes of drugs: *benzodiazepine sedatives* (such as Dalmane, Halcion, and Restoril), which were originally developed to relieve anxiety, and newer *nonbenzodiazepine sedatives* (such as Ambien, Sonata, and Lunesta), which were designed primarily for sleep problems

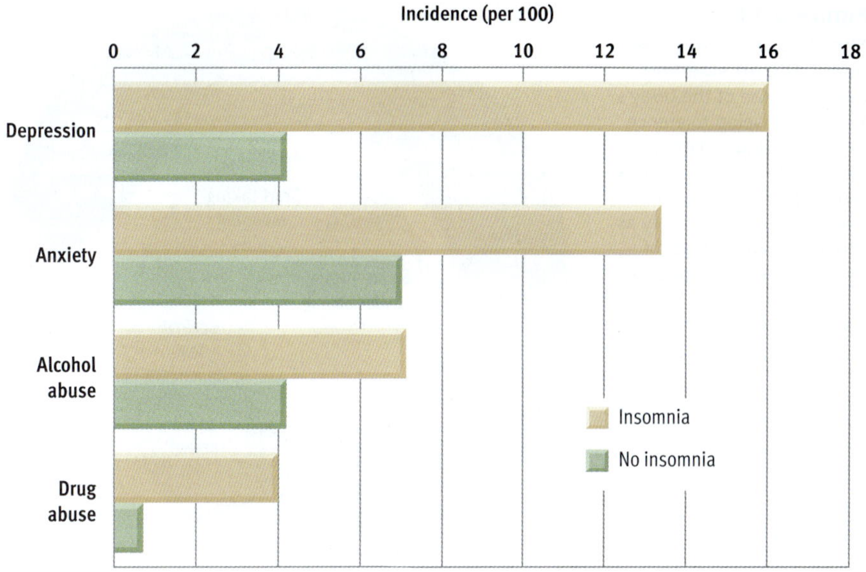

Figure 5.12

Psychiatric conditions associated with insomnia. Insomnia may sound like a trivial problem, but as the text notes, it is associated with an elevated vulnerability to a variety of problems. Data on the magnitude of this elevation are shown here for depression, anxiety, alcohol abuse, and drug abuse, based on research by Breslau et al. (1996). Of course, causation is probably bidirectional in these relationships. Depression, for instance, probably contributes to the causation of insomnia and is caused by insomnia. In any event, the elevations in the incidence of these psychiatric maladies are sizable. © Cengage Learning 2013

SOURCE: Adapted from Breslau, N., Roth, T., Rosenthal, L., & Andreski, P. (1996). Sleep disturbance and psychiatric disorders: A longitudinal epidemiological study of young adults. *Biological Psychiatry, 39*(6), 411–418. Copyright © 1996, with permission from Elsevier.

(Mendelson, 2005). Both types of sedative medications are fairly effective in helping people fall asleep more quickly. They reduce nighttime awakenings and increase total sleep (Lee-Chiong & Sateia, 2006; Mendelson, 2005). Nonetheless, sedative drugs may be used to combat insomnia *too* frequently. Although sleep experts argue that in the past physicians prescribed sleeping pills far too readily, about 5%–15% of adults still use sleep medication with some regularity (Hublin & Partinen, 2002).

Sedatives can be a poor long-term solution for insomnia, for a number of reasons (Roehrs & Roth, 2000; Wesson et al., 2005). One problem is that sedatives have carryover effects that can make people drowsy and sluggish the next day and impair their functioning (Vermeeren, 2004). They can also cause an overdose in combination with alcohol or opiate drugs. Moreover, with continued use most sedatives gradually become less effective, so some people increase their dose to higher levels, creating a vicious circle of escalating dependency and daytime sluggishness (Lader, 2002; see **Figure 5.13** on the next page). Another problem is that when people abruptly discontinue their sleep medication, they can experience unpleasant withdrawal symptoms and increased insomnia (Lee-Chiong & Sateia, 2006). Fortunately, the newer generation of nonbenzodiazepine

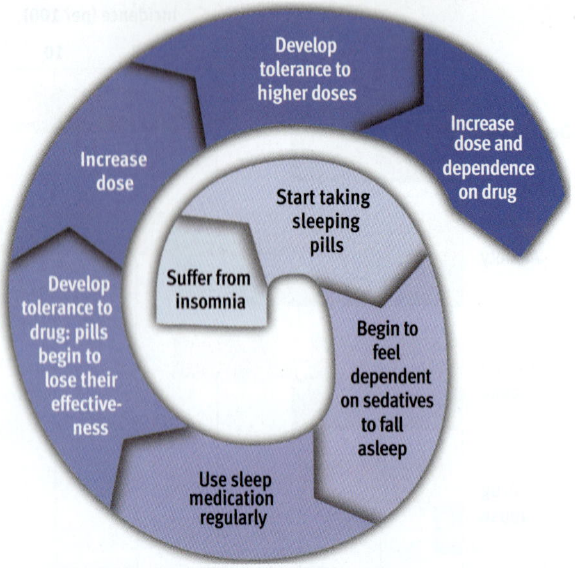

Figure 5.13

The vicious circle of dependence on sleeping pills. Because of the body's ability to develop tolerance to drugs, using sedatives routinely to "cure" insomnia can lead to a vicious circle of escalating dependency as larger and larger doses of the sedative are needed to produce the same effect.
© Cengage Learning 2013

sedatives have reduced (but not eliminated) many of the problems associated with previous generations of sleeping pills (Sanger, 2004). In conclusion, sedatives need to be used cautiously and conservatively.

Aside from medications, it is difficult to generalize about how insomnia should be treated, because the many causes call for different solutions. Relaxation procedures and behavioral interventions can be helpful for many individuals (Morin, 2002, 2005). Recent studies suggest that cognitive-behavioral treatments are just as effective as medication in the short term and that these interventions produce more long-lasting benefits than drug therapies (Sivertsen et al., 2006; Smith et al., 2002). Some additional insights about how to combat insomnia are presented in the Personal Application at the end of this chapter.

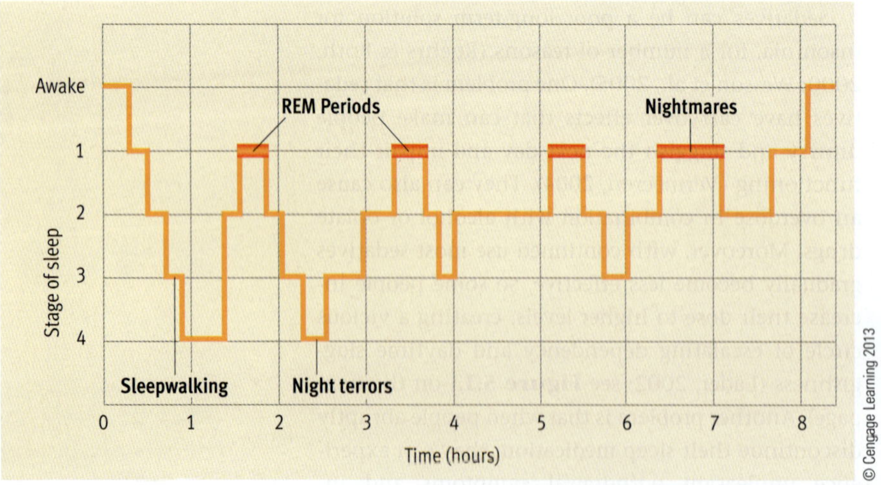

Figure 5.14

Sleep problems and the cycle of sleep. Different sleep problems tend to occur at different points in the sleep cycle. Whereas sleepwalking and night terrors are associated with slow-wave sleep, nightmares are associated with the heightened dream activity of REM sleep.

Other Sleep Problems

Insomnia is the most common difficulty associated with sleep, but people are plagued by many other types of sleep problems as well. Here we'll look at the symptoms, causes, and prevalence of five additional sleep problems, as described by Kryger, Roth, and Dement (2005) and Hirshkowitz, Seplowitz-Hafkin, & Sharafkhaneh (2009).

Sleep apnea **involves frequent, reflexive gasping for air that awakens a person and disrupts sleep.** Some victims are awakened from their sleep hundreds of times a night. Apnea occurs when a person literally stops breathing for a minimum of 10 seconds. This disorder, which is usually accompanied by loud snoring, is seen in about 2% of women and about 4% of men. There's a higher incidence among older adults, postmenopausal women, and those who are obese (Sanders & Givelber, 2006). As you might expect, sleep apnea can have a disruptive effect on sleep, leading to excessive daytime sleepiness. Sleep apnea is a more serious disorder than widely appreciated because it increases vulnerability to hypertension, coronary disease, and stroke (Hahn, Olson, & Somers, 2006). In fact, one study found that severe apnea tripled individuals' mortality risk (Young et al., 2008). Apnea may be treated via lifestyle modifications (weight loss, reduced alcohol intake, improved sleep hygiene), drug therapy, special masks and oral devices that improve airflow, and upper airway and craniofacial surgery (Phillips & Kryger, 2005; Veasey, 2009).

Nightmares **are anxiety-arousing dreams that lead to awakening, usually from REM sleep** (see **Figure 5.14**). Typically, a person who awakens from a nightmare recalls a vivid dream and may have difficulty getting back to sleep. Significant stress in one's life is associated with increased frequency and intensity of nightmares (Nielsen & Levin, 2009). Although about 5% of adults have occasional troubles with nightmares, these frightening episodes are mainly a problem among children (Schredl, 2009). Most youngsters have sporadic nightmares, but *persistent* nightmares may reflect an emotional disturbance. If a child's nightmares are frequent and unpleasant, counseling may prove helpful. But most children outgrow the problem on their own.

Night terrors **(also called sleep terrors) are abrupt awakenings from NREM sleep accompanied by intense autonomic arousal and feelings of panic.** Night terrors can produce drastic inceases in heart rate. They usually occur during stage 4 sleep early in the night, as shown in **Figure 5.14** (Nielsen & Zadra, 2000). Victims typically let out a piercing cry, bolt upright, and then stare into space. They do not usually recall a coherent dream, although they may remember a simple, frightening image. The panic normally fades quickly, and a return to sleep is fairly easy. Night terrors occur in adults, but they are especially common in children ages 3 to 8. Night terrors are *not* indicative of an emotional disturbance. Night terrors are often a temporary problem that do not require treatment.

***Somnambulism*, or sleepwalking, occurs when a person arises and wanders about while remaining asleep.** About 15% of children and 3% of adults exhibit repetitive sleepwalking (Cartwright, 2006). Sleepwalking tends to occur during the first 3 hours of sleep, when individuals are in slow-wave sleep (see **Figure 5.14**). Episodes may last from 15 seconds to 30 minutes (Aldrich, 2000). Sleepwalkers may awaken during their journey, or they may return to bed without any recollection of their trip. The causes of this unusual disorder are unknown, although it appears to have a genetic predisposition (Keefauver & Guilleminault, 1994). Also, episodes may be more likely in people who use nonbenzodiazepine sedatives, especially Ambien (Gunn & Gunn, 2006). Sleepwalking does not appear to be a manifestation of underlying emotional or psychological problems (Mahowald, 1993). However, while sleepwalking, some people have engaged in inappropriate aggressive or sexual behavior (Cartwright, 2006). Sleepwalkers *are* prone to accidents, including life-threatening ones (Gunn & Gunn, 2006).

***REM sleep behavior disorder (RBD)* is marked by potentially troublesome dream enactments during REM periods.** People who exhibit this syndrome may talk, yell, gesture, flail about, or leap out of bed during their REM dreams. When questioned, many report that they were being chased or attacked in their dreams. Their dream enactments can get surprisingly violent, and they often hurt themselves or their bed partners (Mahowald & Schenck, 2005b). RBD occurs mostly in men, who typically begin experiencing this problem in their fifties or sixties. As noted earlier, people in REM sleep normally are virtually paralyzed, which prevents dream enactments. The cause of RBD appears to be some sort of deterioration in the brainstem structures that are normally responsible for this immobilization during REM periods (Tippmann-Peikert et al., 2006).

Reality CHECK

Misconception

Sleepwalkers are acting out their dreams and it is dangerous to awaken them.

Reality

Sleepwalking does not occur in conjunction with dreams. It is not rare for sleepwalkers to hurt themselves. Hence, it's best to waken people (gently) from a sleepwalking episode. Waking them is much safer than letting them wander about.

"Wait! Don't! It can be dangerous to wake them!"

© Joe Dator/The New Yorker Collection/www.cartoonbank.com.

REVIEW OF KEY LEARNING GOALS

5.5 When people fall asleep, they pass through a series of stages in cycles of approximately 90 minutes. Slow-wave sleep consists of stages 3 and 4, during which delta waves are prominent. During the REM stage, sleepers experience rapid eye movements, brain waves that are characteristic of waking thought, and vivid dreaming. The sleep cycle tends to be repeated about four times a night. REM sleep gradually becomes more predominant and NREM sleep dwindles.

5.6 The REM portion of sleep declines during childhood, leveling off at around 20%. During adulthood, slow-wave sleep tends to decline. Total sleep time decreases for most elderly people, perhaps because older people need less sleep. Culture appears to have relatively little impact on the physiological experience of sleep, but it does influence napping patterns.

5.7 The neural bases of sleep are complex. Arousal depends on activity in the ascending reticular activating system, but a constellation of brain structures and neurotransmitters contribute to the regulation of the sleep and waking cycle. Hypotheses about the evolutionary bases of sleep focus on energy conservation, reduced exposure to predators, and restoration of resources depleted by waking activity.

5.8 The Featured Study showed that sleep restriction produces a gradual decline in cognitive performance that is substantial. Increased sleepiness can be a significant problem that appears to contribute to many transportation accidents and mishaps at work. Research on selective sleep deprivation suggests that people need REM sleep and slow-wave sleep. These stages of sleep may contribute to memory consolidation. Short sleep duration is associated with a variety of health problems. People who sleep 7–8 hours per day have lower mortality rates than individuals who are long or short sleepers.

5.9 There are three patterns of insomnia, which involves difficulty getting adequate sleep. Sleeping pills generally are a poor solution for insomnia, although they can be helpful in the short term. Sleep apnea involves frequent gasping for air, which occurs when people stop breathing. Night terrors are abrupt awakenings from NREM sleep accompanied by panic, whereas nightmares are anxiety-arousing dreams that typically awaken one from REM sleep. Somnambulism (sleepwalking) typically occurs during slow-wave sleep. REM sleep behavior disorder (RBD) is marked by potentially troublesome dream enactments during REM periods.

KEY LEARNING GOALS

5.10 Discuss the nature of dreams and findings on dream content.

5.11 Describe cultural variations in beliefs about the nature and importance of dreams.

5.12 Explain three theories of dreaming.

The World of Dreams

For the most part, dreams are not taken very seriously in Western societies. But Robert Van de Castle (1994) points out that dreams have sometimes changed the world. For example, Van de Castle describes how René Descartes's philosophy of dualism, Frederick Banting's discovery of insulin, Elias Howe's refinement of the sewing machine, and Mohandas Gandhi's strategy of nonviolent protest were all inspired by dreams. In his wide-ranging discussion, Van de Castle also relates how the Surrealist painter Salvador Dali characterized his works as "dream photographs" and how legendary filmmakers Ingmar Bergman, Orson Welles, and Federico Fellini all drew on their dreams in making their films. Thus, Van de Castle concludes that "dreams have had a dramatic influence on almost every important aspect of our culture and history" (p. 10).

What exactly is a dream? This question is more complex and controversial than you might guess (Pagel et al., 2001). The conventional view is that dreams are mental experiences during REM sleep that have a storylike quality, include vivid visual imagery, are often bizarre, and are regarded as perceptually real by the dreamer (Antrobus, 1993). However, theorists have begun to question virtually every aspect of this characterization. Decades of research on the contents of dreams has shown that dreams are not as bizarre as widely assumed (Domhoff, 2007). Recent findings have shown that dreams are in fact *not* the exclusive property of REM sleep (Nir & Tononi, 2009). Studies that have focused on dream reports from non-REM stages of sleep have found that these dreams appear to be less vivid, visual, emotional, and storylike than REM dreams (Antrobus & Wamsley, 2009; McNamara et al., 2007). And research suggests that dreamers realize they are dreaming more often than previously thought and that mental processes during sleep are more similar to waking thought processes than is widely assumed (Kahan, 2001; Kahan & LaBerge, 1994, 1996). Thus, the concept of dreaming is undergoing some revision in scientific circles.

Reality CHECK

Misconception

If you fall from a height in a dream, you'd better wake up on the plunge downward, because if you hit the bottom, the shock to your system could so great that you could die in your sleep.

Reality

Think about this one for a moment. *If* it were a genuine problem, who would have reported it? You can be sure that no one has ever testified to experiencing a fatal dream. This myth presumably exists because many people do awaken during the downward plunge, thinking that they've averted a close call. In reality, people do have dreams about their own death—and live to tell about them.

The Contents of Dreams

What do people dream about? Overall, dreams are not as exciting as advertised. Perhaps dreams are seen as exotic because people are more likely to remember their more bizarre nighttime dramas (De Koninck, 2000). After analyzing the contents of more than 10,000 dreams, Calvin Hall (1966) concluded that most dreams are relatively mundane. They tend to unfold in familiar settings with a cast of characters dominated by family, friends, and colleagues. We are more tolerant of logical discrepancies and implausible scenarios in our dreams than in our waking thought (Kahn, 2007), but in dreams we generally move through sensible, realistic virtual worlds (Nielsen & Stenstrom, 2005). The one nearly universal element of dreams is a coherent sense of self—we almost always experience dreams from a first-person perspective (Valli & Revonsuo, 2009).

Certain themes tend to be more common than others in dreams. **Figure 5.15** lists the most common dream themes reported by 1,181 college students in a study of typical dream content (Nielsen et al., 2003). It shows that people dream quite a bit about sex, aggression, and misfortune. As you can see, people often dream about negative and potentially traumatic events, including being killed. However, the notion that a traumatic dream could be fatal is nonsense. According to Hall, dreams tend to center on classic sources of internal conflict, such as the conflict between taking chances and playing it safe. Hall was struck by how rarely people dream about public affairs and current events. Typically, dreams are self-centered; people dream mostly about themselves.

Links Between Dreams and Waking Life

Though dreams seem to belong in a world of their own, what people dream about is affected by what is going on in their lives (Wamsley & Stickgold, 2009). If you're struggling with financial problems, worried about an upcoming exam, or sexually attracted to a classmate, these themes may very well show up in your dreams. As Domhoff (2001) put it, "Dream content in general is continuous with waking conceptions and emotional preoccupations" (p. 13). Freud noticed long ago that the contents of waking life tend to spill into dreams; he labeled this spillover the *day residue.*

On occasion, the content of dreams can also be affected by stimuli experienced while one is dreaming (De Koninck, 2000). For example, William Dement sprayed water on one hand of sleeping subjects while they were in the REM stage (Dement & Wolpert, 1958). Subjects who weren't awakened by the water were awakened by the experimenter a

Rank	Dream content	Total prevalence
1	Chased or pursued, not physically injured	81.5
2	Sexual experiences	76.5
3	Falling	73.8
4	School, teachers, studying	67.1
5	Arriving too late, e.g., missing a train	59.5
6	Being on the verge of falling	57.7
7	A person now alive as dead	54.1
8	Trying again and again to do something	53.5
9	Flying or soaring through the air	48.3
10	Vividly sensing . . . a presence in the room	48.3
11	Failing an examination	45.0
12	Physically attacked (beaten, stabbed, raped)	42.4
13	Being frozen with fright	40.7
14	A person now dead as alive	38.4
15	Being a child again	36.7
16	Being killed	34.5
17	Swimming	34.3
18	Insects or spiders	33.8
19	Being nude	32.6
20	Being inappropriately dressed	32.5
21	Discovering a new room at home	32.3
22	Losing control of a vehicle	32.0
23	Eating delicious foods	30.7
24	Being half awake and paralyzed in bed	27.2
25	Finding money	25.7

© Image Source/Alamy

© Ray Grover/Alamy

Figure 5.15

Common themes in dreams. Studies of dream content find that certain themes are particularly common. The data shown here are from a study of 1181 college students in Canada (Nielsen et al., 2003). This list shows the 25 dreams most frequently reported by the students. Total prevalence refers to the percentage of students reporting each dream.

© Cengage Learning 2013

SOURCE: Nielsen, T. A., Zadra, A. L., Simard, V., Saucier, S., Stenstrom, P., Smith, C., & Kuiken, D. (2003). The typical dreams of Canadian university students. *Dreaming, 13,* 211–235. Copyright © 2003 Association for the Study of Dreams. [from Table 1, p. 217]

short time later and asked what they had been dreaming about. Dement found that 42% of the subjects had incorporated the water into their dreams. They said that they had dreamt that they were in rainfalls, floods, baths, swimming pools, and the like. Some people report that they sometimes experience the same sort of phenomenon at home when the sound of their alarm clock fails to awaken them. The alarm is incorporated into their dream as a loud engine or a siren, for instance. As with day residue, the incorporation of external stimuli into dreams shows that people's dream world is not entirely separate from their real world.

Culture and Dreams

Striking cross-cultural variations occur in beliefs about the nature of dreams and the importance attributed to them (Lohmann, 2007). In modern Western society, people typically distinguish between the "real" world they experience while awake and the "imaginary" world they experience while dreaming. Some people realize that events in the

© 2004 by Sidney Harris. ScienceCartoonPlus.com

real world can affect their dreams, but relatively few believe that events in their dreams hold any significance for their waking life.

In many non-Western cultures, however, dreams are viewed as important sources of information about oneself, about the future, or about the spiritual world (Kracke, 1991). Although no culture confuses dreams with waking reality, many view events in dreams as another type of reality that may be just as important as events experienced while awake. In some instances, people are even held responsible for their dream actions. Among the New Guinea Arapesh, for example, an erotic dream about someone may be viewed as the equivalent of an adulterous act. People in some cultures believe that dreams provide information about the future—good or bad omens about upcoming battles, hunts, births, and so forth (Tedlock, 1992).

© Courtesy of Rosalind Cartwright

Rosalind Cartwright

"One function of dreams may be to restore our sense of competence. . . . It is also probable that in times of stress, dreams have more work to do in resolving our problems and are thus more salient and memorable."

In regard to dream content, both similarities and differences occur across cultures in the types of dreams that people report (Domhoff, 2005b; Hunt, 1989). Some basic dream themes appear to be nearly universal (falling, being pursued, having sex). However, the contents of dreams vary some from one culture to another because people in different societies deal with different worlds while awake. Take, for example, the Siriono, a hunting-and-gathering people of the Amazon who were almost always hungry and spent most of their time in a grim search for food. *Half* of their reported dreams focused on hunting, gathering, and eating food (D'Andrade, 1961).

Theories of Dreaming

© National Library of Medicine

Sigmund Freud

"[Dreams are] the royal road to the unconscious."

Many theories have been proposed to explain why people dream. Sigmund Freud (1900) believed that the principal purpose of dreams is *wish fulfillment.* He thought that people fulfill unconscious urges and unmet needs through wishful thinking in dreams. For example, if you were feeling unconscious guilt about being rude to a friend, you might dream about the incident in a way that renders you blameless. Freud asserted that the wish-fulfilling quality of many dreams may not be obvious because the unconscious attempts to censor and disguise the true meaning of dreams. Freud distinguished between the *manifest content* and the *latent content* of a dream. **The *manifest content* consists of the plot of a dream at a surface level. The *latent content* refers to the hidden or disguised meaning of the events in the plot.** Freud felt that deciphering the latent content of a dream is a complex matter that requires intimate knowledge of the dreamer's current issues and childhood conflicts. Freud's influential theory sounded plausible when it was proposed over 100 years ago, but research has not provided much support for Freud's conception of dreaming (Fisher & Greenberg, 1996). Nonetheless, Freud's view remains popular among people. A recent study found that a substantial majority of people from three very different cultures endorsed the Freudian notion that dreams contain hidden truths (Morewedge & Norton, 2009).

Other theorists, such as Rosalind Cartwright (1977; Cartwright & Lamberg, 1992), have proposed that dreams provide an opportunity to work through everyday problems and emotional issues in one's life. According to her *cognitive, problem-solving view,* considerable continuity exists between waking and sleeping thought. Proponents of this view believe that dreams allow people to engage in creative thinking about pressing personal issues because dreams are not restrained by logic or realism. Consistent with this view, Cartwright (1991) found that women going through divorce frequently dreamt about divorce-related problems. Cartwright's analysis is thought provoking, but critics point out that just because people dream about problems from their waking life doesn't mean they're dreaming up solutions (Blagrove, 1992, 1996). Nonetheless, recent research showing that sleep can enhance learning (Walker & Stickgold, 2004) adds new credibility to the problem-solving view of dreams (Cartwright, 2004).

J. Allan Hobson and colleagues argue that dreams are simply the by-product of bursts of activity from subcortical areas in the brain. Their *activation-synthesis model* (Hobson & McCarley, 1977; McCarley, 1994) and its more recent revisions (Hobson, 2007; Hobson, Pace-Schott, & Stickgold, 2000) propose that dreams are *side effects* of the neural activation that produces the beta brain waves during REM sleep that are associated with wakefulness. According to this model, neurons firing periodically in lower brain centers (especially the pons) send random signals to the cortex (the seat of complex thought). The cortex supposedly synthesizes (constructs) a dream to make sense out of these signals. The activation-synthesis model does *not* assume that dreams are meaningless. As Hobson (1988) put it, "Dreams are as meaningful as they can be under the adverse working conditions of the brain in REM sleep" (p. 214). In contrast to the theories of Freud and Cartwright, this theory obviously downplays the role of emotional factors as determinants of dreams. Like other theories of dreams, the activation-synthesis model has its share of critics. They point out that the model has a hard time explaining the fact that dreaming occurs outside of REM sleep, that damage to the pons does not eliminate dreaming, and that the contents of dreams are considerably more meaningful than the model would predict (Domhoff, 2005a; Foulkes, 1996; Solms, 2000).

These approaches, summarized in **Figure 5.16**, are only three out of many theories about the functions of dreams. All theories of dreaming include a great deal of conjecture and some liberal inferences from research. In the final analysis, the purpose of dreaming remains a mystery.

We'll encounter more unsolved mysteries in the next two sections of this chapter as we discuss hypnosis and meditation. Whereas sleep and dreams are familiar to everyone, most people have little familiarity with hypnosis and meditation. Both involve deliberate efforts to temporarily alter consciousness.

REVIEW OF KEY LEARNING GOALS

5.10 The conventional view is that dreams are mental experiences during REM sleep that have a storylike quality, include vivid imagery, are often bizarre, and are regarded as perceptually real by the dreamer, but theorists have begun to question many aspects of this view. Dreams are not as bizarre as widely assumed. The content of one's dreams may be affected by what is going on in one's life and by external stimuli that are experienced during the dream.

5.11 In many non-Western cultures, dreams are viewed as important sources of information. Cultures vary in beliefs about the nature of dreams, dream recall, dream content, and dream interpretation.

5.12 Freud argued that the principal purpose of dreams is wish fulfillment. He distinguished between the manifest and latent content of dreams. Cartwright has articulated a problem-solving view. Hobson and colleagues assert that dreams are side effects of the neural activation seen during REM sleep.

J. Allan Hobson

"Activation-synthesis ascribes dreaming to brain activation in sleep. The principal engine of this activation is the reticular formation of the brainstem."

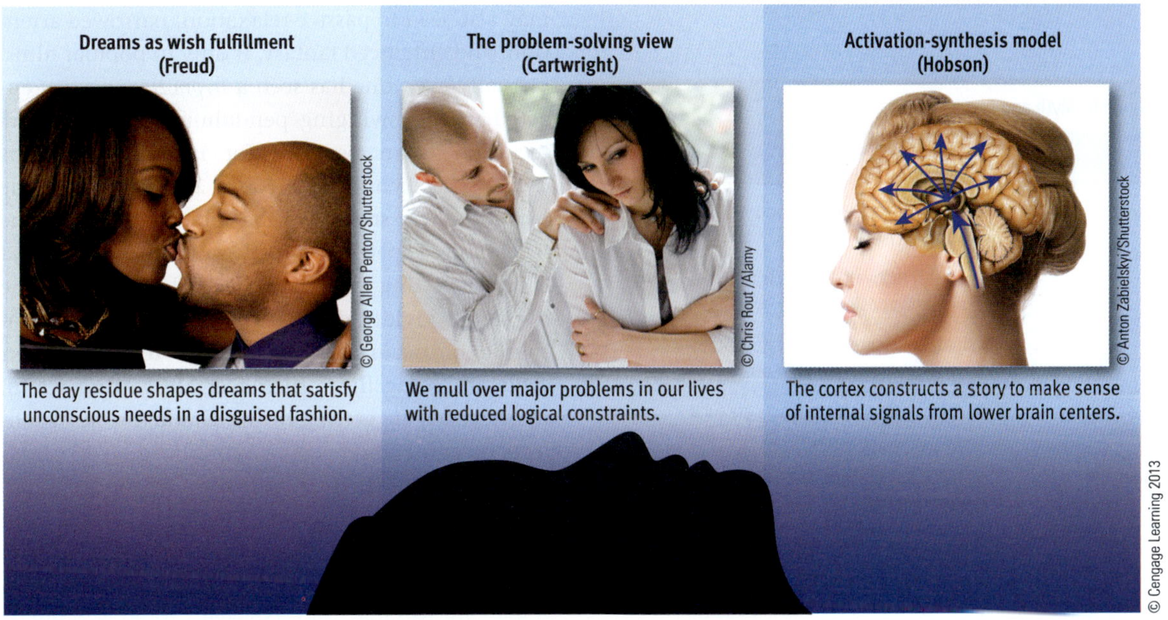

Figure 5.16

Three theories of dreaming. Dreams can be explained in a variety of ways. Freud stressed the wish-fulfilling function of dreams. Cartwright emphasizes the problem-solving function of dreams. Hobson asserts that dreams are merely a by-product of periodic neural activation. All three theories are speculative and have their critics.

Hypnosis: Altered Consciousness or Role Playing?

KEY LEARNING GOALS

5.13 Discuss hypnotic susceptibility, and list some prominent effects of hypnosis.

5.14 Compare the role-playing and altered-state theories of hypnosis.

Hypnosis has a long and checkered history. It all began with a flamboyant 18th-century Austrian physician by the name of Franz Anton Mesmer (Pintar, 2010). Working in Paris, Mesmer claimed to cure people of illnesses through an elaborate routine involving a "laying on of hands." Mesmer had some complicated theories about how he had harnessed "animal magnetism." However, we know today that he had simply stumbled onto the power of suggestion. It was rumored that the French government offered him a princely amount of money to disclose how he effected his cures. He refused, probably because he didn't really know. Eventually he was dismissed as a charlatan and run out of town by the local authorities. Although officially discredited, Mesmer inspired followers—practitioners of "mesmerism"—who continued to ply their trade. To this day, our language preserves the memory of Franz Mesmer: When we are under the spell of an event or a story, we are "mesmerized."

Eventually, a Scottish physician, James Braid, became interested in the trancelike state that could be induced by the mesmerists. It was Braid who popularized the term *hypnotism* in 1843, borrowing it from the Greek word for sleep (Pintar, 2010). Braid thought that hypnotism could be used to produce anesthesia for surgeries. However, just as hypnosis was catching on as a general anesthetic, more powerful and reliable chemical anesthetics were discovered. Interest in hypnotism then dwindled.

Hypnotism has since led a curious dual existence. On the one hand, it's been the subject of numerous scientific studies. Furthermore, it's enjoyed considerable use as a clinical tool by physicians, dentists, and psychologists for over a century and has empirically supported value in the treatment of a variety of psychological and physical ailments (Covino & Pinnell, 2010; Nash et al., 2009; Spiegel & Maldonado, 2009). On the other hand, however, an assortment of entertainers and quacks have continued in the less respectable tradition of mesmerism, using hypnotism for parlor tricks and gimmickry. It's little wonder, then, that many myths about hypnosis have come to be widely accepted (see **Figure 5.17**). In this section, we'll work on clearing up some of the confusion surrounding hypnosis.

Hypnosis: Myth and Reality

If you think . . .	The reality is . . .
Relaxation is an important feature of hypnosis.	It's not. Hypnosis has been induced during vigorous exercise.
It's mostly just compliance.	Many highly motivated subjects fail to experience hypnosis.
It's a matter of willful faking.	Physiological responses indicate that hypnotized subjects generally are not lying.
It has something to do with a sleeplike state.	It does not. Hypnotized subjects are fully awake.
Responding to hypnosis is like responding to a placebo.	Placebo responsiveness and hypnotizability are not correlated.
People who are hypnotized lose control of themselves.	Subjects are perfectly capable of saying no or terminating hypnosis.
Hypnosis can enable people to "relive" the past.	Age-regressed adults behave like adults play-acting as children.
When hypnotized, people can remember more accurately.	Hypnosis may actually muddle the distinction between memory and fantasy and may artificially inflate confidence.
Hypnotized people do not remember what happened during the session.	Posthypnotic amnesia does not occur spontaneously.
Hypnosis can enable people to perform otherwise impossible feats of strength, endurance, learning, and sensory acuity.	Performance following hypnotic suggestions for increased muscle strength, learning and sensory acuity does not exceed what can be accomplished by motivated subjects outside hypnosis.

© Cengage Learning 2013

Figure 5.17

Misconceptions regarding hypnosis. Mistaken ideas about the nature of hypnosis are common. Some widely believed myths about hypnosis are summarized here, along with more accurate information on each point, based on an article by Michael Nash (2001), a prominent hypnosis researcher. Many of these myths and realities are discussed in more detail in the text.

SOURCE: Adapted from Nash, M. R. (2001, July). The truth and the hype of hypnosis. *Scientific American, 285,* 36–43. Reproduced with permission. Copyright © 2001 by Scientific American, Inc. All rights reserved.

Hypnotic Induction and Susceptibility

***Hypnosis* is a systematic procedure that typically produces a heightened state of suggestibility.** It may also lead to passive relaxation, narrowed attention, and enhanced fantasy. If only in popular films, virtually everyone has seen a *hypnotic induction* enacted with a swinging pendulum. Actually many techniques can be used for inducing hypnosis (Gibbons & Lynn, 2010; Nash, 2008). Usually, the hypnotist will suggest to the subject that he or she is relaxing. Repetitively, softly, subjects are told that they are getting tired, drowsy, or sleepy. Often, the hypnotist vividly describes bodily sensations that should be occurring. Subjects are told that their arms are going limp, their feet are getting warm, their eyelids are getting heavy. Gradually, most subjects succumb and become hypnotized.

People differ in how well they respond to hypnotic induction. Ernest and Josephine Hilgard have done extensive research on this variability in *hypnotic susceptibility.* Responsiveness to hypnosis is a stable, measurable trait (Spiegel, 2008; Woody & Barnier, 2008). It can be estimated with the Stanford Hypnotic Susceptibility Scale (SHSS) or its derivative, the Harvard Group Scale of Hypnotic Susceptibility. The distribution of scores on the SHSS is graphed in **Figure 5.18**. Not everyone can be hypnotized. About 10%–20% of the population do not respond well at all. At the other end of the continuum, about 10%–15% of people are exceptionally good hypnotic subjects (Hilgard, 1965). As Kihlstrom (2007) notes, "the most dramatic phenomena of hypnosis—the ones that really count as reflecting alterations in consciousness—are generally observed in those 'hypnotic virtuosos' who comprise the upper 10%–15% of the distribution of hypnotizability" (p. 446). People who are highly hypnotizable may even slip in and out of hypnotic-like states spontaneously without being aware of it (Spiegel, 2007).

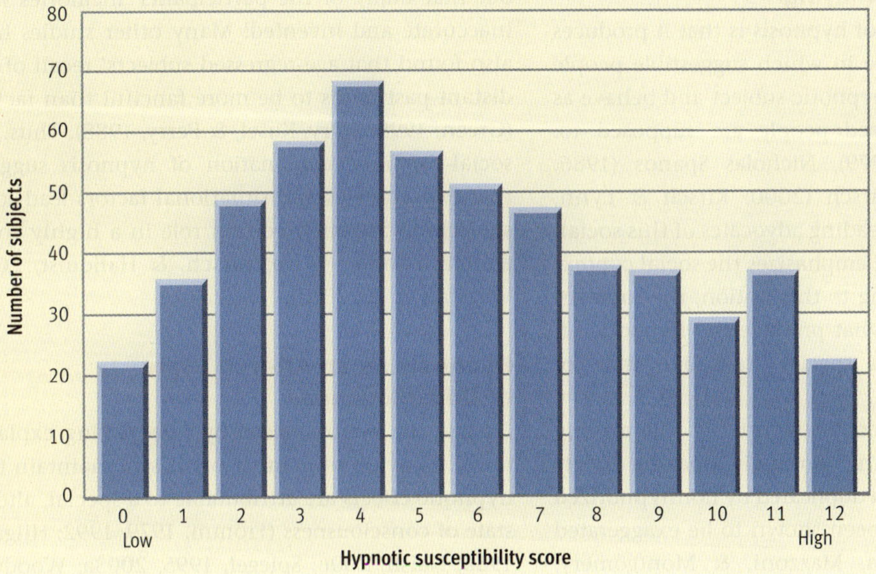

Figure 5.18

Variation in hypnotic susceptibility. This graph shows the distribution of scores of more than 500 subjects on the Stanford Hypnotic Susceptibility Scale. As you can see, responsiveness to hypnotism varies widely, and many people are not very susceptible to hypnotic induction.

SOURCE: Adapted from Hilgard, E. (1965). *Hypnotic susceptibility.* San Diego: Harcourt Brace Jovanovich. Copyright © 1965 by Ernest R. Hilgard. Reprinted by permission of Ernest R. Hilgard.

© Cengage Learning 2013

Hypnotic Phenomena

Many interesting effects can be produced through hypnosis. Some of the more prominent include:

1. *Analgesia.* While hypnotized, some participants can withstand treatments that would normally cause pain (Patterson, 2004). Some physicians and dentists have even used hypnosis as a substitute for anesthetic drugs. Hypnosis can be surprisingly effective in the treatment of both acute and chronic pain (Boly et al., 2007; Jensen & Patterson, 2008). Hypnotic analgesia exceeds placebo effects, does not appear to be mediated by simple relaxation, and does not appear to depend on the action of endorphins (Kihlstrom, 2007).

2. *Sensory distortions and hallucinations.* Hypnotized participants may be led to experience auditory or visual hallucinations (Spiegel, 2003b). They may hear sounds or see things that are not there, or fail to hear or see stimuli that are present. In one study, for instance, hypnotized participants were induced to "see" a cardboard box that blocked their view of a television (Spiegel et al., 1985). Subjects may also have their sensations distorted so that something sweet tastes sour or an unpleasant odor smells fragrant.

3. *Disinhibition.* Generally, it's difficult to get hypnotized participants to do things that they would normally consider unacceptable. But hypnosis *can* sometimes reduce inhibitions that would normally prevent subjects from acting in ways that they would see as socially undesirable. Hypnotized subjects have been induced to throw what they believed to be a toxic substance into the face of a research assistant. Similarly, stage hypnotists are sometimes successful in getting people to disrobe in public. One lay hypnotist even coaxed a man into robbing a bank (Deyoub, 1984). This disinhibition effect may occur simply because hypnotized people feel that they cannot be held responsible for their actions while they are hypnotized.

4. *Posthypnotic suggestions and amnesia.* Suggestions made during hypnosis may influence a subject's later behavior (Cox & Bryant, 2008). The most common posthypnotic suggestion is the creation of posthypnotic amnesia. That is, participants are told that they will remember nothing that happened while they were hypnotized. Such subjects usually claim to remember nothing, as ordered. However, when pressed, many of these subjects acknowledge that they have not really forgotten the information (Kirsch & Lynn, 1998).

Theories of Hypnosis

Although a number of theories have been developed to explain hypnosis, it's still not well understood. One popular view is that hypnotic effects occur because participants are put into a special, altered state of consciousness, called a *hypnotic trance* (Christensen, 2005). Although hypnotized subjects may feel as though they're in an altered state, they do not seem to show reliable alterations in brain activity that are unique to hypnosis (Burgess, 2007; Lynn et al., 2007). The failure to find special changes in brain activity consistently associated with hypnosis has led some theorists to conclude that hypnosis is a normal state of consciousness that is characterized by dramatic role playing.

© Courtesy of X. Ted Barber

Theodore Barber

"Thousands of books, movies, and professional articles have woven the concept of 'hypnotic trance' into the common knowledge. And yet there is almost no scientific support for it."

Hypnosis as Role Playing

One influential view of hypnosis is that it produces a normal mental state in which suggestible people act out the role of a hypnotic subject and behave as they think hypnotized people are supposed to. Theodore Barber (1979), Nicholas Spanos (1986, 1991), and Irving Kirsch (2000; Kirsch & Lynn, 1998) have been the leading advocates of this social-cognitive view, which emphasizes the social context of hypnosis. According to this notion, the subjects' *role expectations* are what produce the hypnotic effects, rather than a special trancelike state of consciousness.

Two lines of evidence support the role-playing view. First, many of the seemingly amazing effects of hypnosis have been duplicated by nonhypnotized participants or have been shown to be exaggerated (Kirsch, 1997; Kirsch, Mazzoni, & Montgomery, 2007). For example, anecdotal reports that hypnosis can enhance memory have not stood up well to empirical testing. Although hypnosis may sometimes foster recall in some people, studies have tended to find that hypnotized participants make more memory errors than nonhypnotized participants, even though they often feel more confident about their recollections (McConkey, 1992; Scoboria et al., 2002). These findings suggest that no special state of consciousness is required to explain hypnotic feats.

The second line of evidence involves demonstrations that hypnotized participants are often acting out a role. For example, Martin Orne (1951) regressed hypnotized subjects back to their sixth birthday and asked them to describe it. They responded with detailed descriptions that appeared to represent great feats of hypnosis-enhanced memory. However, instead of accepting this information at face value, Orne compared it with information that he had obtained from the subjects' parents. It turned out that many of the participants' memories were inaccurate and invented! Many other studies have also found that age-regressed subjects' recall of the distant past tends to be more fanciful than factual (Green, 1999; Perry, Kusel, & Perry, 1988). Thus, the social-cognitive explanation of hypnosis suggests that expectancies and situational factors lead some subjects to act out a certain role in a highly cooperative manner (Lynn, Kirsch, & Hallquist, 2008; Wagstaff et al., 2010).

Hypnosis as an Altered State of Consciousness

Despite the doubts raised by role-playing explanations, many prominent theorists still maintain that hypnotic effects are attributable to a special, altered state of consciousness (Fromm, 1979, 1992; Hilgard, 1986; Naish, 2006; Spiegel, 1995, 2003a; Woody & Sadler, 2008). These theorists argue that it's doubtful that role playing can explain all hypnotic phenomena. For instance, they assert that even the most cooperative subjects are unlikely to endure surgery without a drug anesthetic just to please their physician and live up to their expected role. They also cite studies in which hypnotized participants have continued to display hypnotic responses when they thought they were alone and not being observed (Perugini et al., 1998). If hypnotized participants were merely acting, they would drop the act when alone.

The most influential explanation of hypnosis as an altered state of awareness has been offered by Ernest Hilgard (1986, 1992). According to Hilgard, hypnosis creates a *dissociation* in consciousness. ***Dissociation* is a splitting off of mental processes into two separate, simultaneous streams of awareness.** In other words, Hilgard theorizes that hypnosis splits consciousness into two streams. One stream is in communication with the hypno-

Reality CHECK

Misconception

Under hypnosis, people can perform feats that they could never perform otherwise.

Reality

Stage hypnotists make their living by getting people to do things that appear out of the ordinary. For example, much has been made of the fact that hypnotized subjects can be used as "human planks" (see the adjacent photo). However, it turns out that nonhypnotized subjects can match this feat. Research suggests that all the phenomena produced in hypnosis can also be produced by suggestion without hypnosis.

© AP Images/BOOKSTAVER

"The Amazing Kreskin" demonstrates that proper positioning is the only requirement for the famous human plank feat.

tist and the external world, while the other is a difficult-to-detect "hidden observer." Hilgard believes that many hypnotic effects are a product of this divided consciousness. For instance, he suggests that a hypnotized person might appear unresponsive to pain because the pain isn't registered in the portion of consciousness that communicates with other people.

One appealing aspect of Hilgard's theory is that *divided consciousness* is a common, normal experience. For example, people will often drive a car a great distance, responding to traffic signals and other cars, with no recollection of having consciously done so. In such cases, consciousness is clearly divided between driving and the person's thoughts about other matters. This common experience has long been known as *highway hypnosis.* In this condition, there's even an "amnesia" for the component of consciousness that drove the car, similar to posthypnotic amnesia. In summary, Hilgard presents hypnosis as a plausible variation in consciousness that has ties to everyday experience.

© Chuck Painter/Stanford News Service

Ernest Hilgard

"Many psychologists argue that the hypnotic trance is a mirage. It would be unfortunate if this skeptical view were to gain such popularity that the benefits of hypnosis are denied to the numbers of those who could be helped."

REVIEW OF KEY LEARNING GOALS

5.13 Hypnosis has had a long and curious history since the era of Mesmerism in the 18th century. Hypnotic susceptibility is a stable trait. Hypnosis can produce anesthesia, sensory distortions, disinhibition, and posthypnotic amnesia.

5.14 One approach to hypnosis is to view it as a normal state of consciousness in which subjects play the role of being hypnotized. Another approach asserts that hypnosis leads to an altered state in which consciousness is split into two streams of awareness.

Meditation: Seeking Higher Consciousness

KEY LEARNING GOALS

5.15 Explain the nature of meditation, and describe its physiological correlates.

5.16 Assess the evidence on the long-term benefits of meditation.

Recent years have seen growing interest in the ancient discipline of meditation. ***Meditation* refers to a family of practices that train attention to heighten awareness and bring mental processes under greater voluntary control.** There are many approaches to meditation. In North America, the most widely practiced approaches are rooted in Eastern religions (Hinduism, Buddhism, and Taoism). However, meditation has been practiced throughout history as an element of all religious and spiritual traditions, including Judaism and Christianity (Walsh & Shapiro, 2006). Moreover, the practice of meditation can be largely divorced from religious beliefs. In fact, most Americans who meditate have only vague ideas regarding its religious significance. Of interest to psychology is the fact that meditation involves a deliberate effort to alter consciousness.

Approaches to meditation can be classified into two main styles that reflect how attention is directed: *focused attention* or *open monitoring* (Cahn & Polich, 2006; Manna et al., 2010). In focused-attention approaches, attention is concentrated on a specific object, image, sound, or bodily sensation (such as breathing). The intent in narrowing attention is to clear the mind of its clutter. In open-monitoring approaches, attention is directed to the contents of one's moment-to-moment experience in a nonjudgmental and nonreactive way. The intent in expanding attention is to become a detached observer of the flow of one's own sensations, thoughts, and feelings. Both approaches seek to achieve a "higher" form of consciousness than what people normally experience. The meditative disciplines that have received the most research attention are Transcendental Meditation (TM) and mindfulness meditation. Mindfulness meditation is an open-monitoring approach with roots in Zen Buddhism, whereas TM is primarily a focused-attention approach with roots in Hinduism.

Physiological Correlates

What happens when an experienced meditator goes into the meditative state? One intriguing finding is that alpha waves and theta waves become more prominent in EEG recordings (Cahn & Polich, 2006; Lagopoulos et al., 2009). Many studies also find that subjects' heart rate, skin conductance, respiration rate, oxygen consumption, and carbon dioxide elimination decline (see **Figure 5.19** on the next page; Dillbeck & Orme-Johnson, 1987; Fenwick, 1987; Travis, 2001). Taken together, these changes suggest that meditation leads to a potentially beneficial physiological state characterized by suppression of bodily arousal. However, some researchers have argued that

© Dean Mitchell/Shutterstock

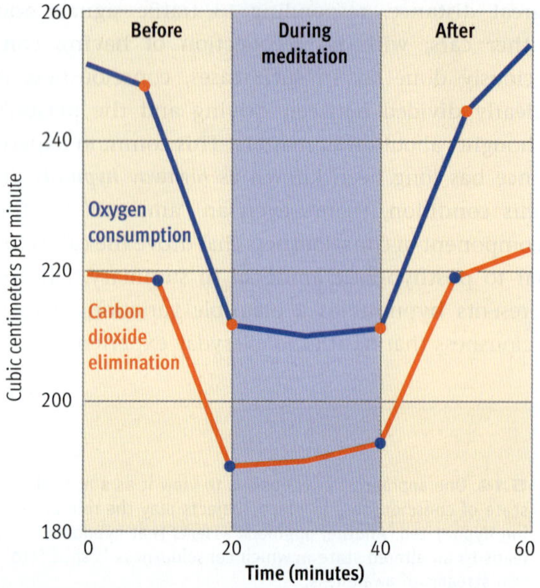

Figure 5.19

The suppression of physiological arousal during transcendental meditation. The physiological changes shown in the graph are evidence of physical relaxation during the meditative state. However, critics argue that similar changes may also be produced by systematic relaxation procedures. © Cengage Learning 2013

SOURCE: Adapted from Wallace, R. K., & Benson, H. (1972, February). The physiology of meditation. *Scientific American, 226*, 85–90. Graphic redrawn from illustration on p. 86 by Lorelle A. Raboni. Copyright © 1972 by Scientific American, Inc.

a variety of systematic relaxation training procedures can produce similar results (Holmes, 1987; Shapiro, 1984). But mere relaxation hardly seems like an adequate explanation for the transcendent experiences reported by many meditators.

Long-Term Benefits

Research suggests that meditation may have some long-term value in reducing the effects of stress (Grossman et al., 2004; Salmon et al., 2004). In particular, regular meditation is associated with lower levels of some "stress hormones" (Infante et al., 2001) and enhanced immune response (Davidson et al., 2003a). Research also suggests that meditation can improve mental health while reducing anxiety and drug abuse (Alexander et al., 1994). Other studies report that meditation may have beneficial effects on self-esteem (Emavardhana & Tori, 1997), mood and one's sense of control (Easterlin & Cardena, 1999), depression (Kabat-Zinn, 2003), eating disorders (Kristeller, Baer, & Quillian-Wolever, 2006), and overall well-being (Reibel et al., 2001). In the physiological domain, research has suggested that meditation may help to control blood pressure (Barnes, Treiber, & Davis, 2001), improve cardiovascular health (Walton et al., 2004), and enhance patterns of sleep (Pattanashetty et al., 2010). Finally, although more difficult to measure, some theorists assert that meditation can enhance human potential by improving focus, heightening awareness, building emotional resilience, and fostering moral maturity (Walsh & Shapiro, 2006).

These reports on the favorable effects of meditation need to be viewed with some caution. At least *some* of these effects may be just as attainable through systematic relaxation or other mental focusing procedures (Shapiro, 1984; Smith, 1975). Critics also wonder whether placebo effects, sampling bias, inability to use double-blind procedures, and other methodological problems may affect some of the reported benefits of meditation (Baer, 2003; Bishop, 2002; Canter, 2003; Caspi & Burleson, 2005). That said, the quality of meditation research appears to be improving, and recent years have brought some eye-opening findings.

For example, a number of recent experiments have demonstrated that meditation can increase the tolerance of pain, which could have important implications for the management of a variety of health problems (Grant & Rainville, 2009; Grant et al., 2010; Zeidan et al., 2010). Grant and Rainville (2009) compared the pain sensitivity of thirteen experienced Zen meditators and thirteen comparable nonmeditators. Carefully controlled pain was administered by applying a heating plate to participants' calves. The meditators were able to handle considerably more pain than the nonmeditators. Moreoever, a follow-up study suggested that the meditators' greater pain tolerance was associated with increased thickness in brain regions that register pain (Grant et al., 2010). In other words, it appeared that meditation experience had produced enduring alterations in brain structure that were responsible for meditators' increased pain tolerance. Other recent studies have also reported evi-

CONCEPT CHECK 5.2

Relating EEG Activity to Variations in Consciousness

Early in the chapter we emphasized the intimate relationship between brain activity and variations in consciousness. Check your understanding of this relationship by indicating the kind of EEG activity (alpha, beta, theta, or delta) that would probably be dominant in each of the following situations. The answers are in Appendix A.

_______ 1. You are playing a video game.

_______ 2. You are deep in meditation.

_______ 3. You have just fallen asleep.

_______ 4. You are sleepwalking across the lawn.

_______ 5. You are in the midst of a terrible nightmare.

dence suggesting that meditation may have the potential to modify brain structure. For instance, Luders et al. (2009) examined experienced meditators and found that they had significantly more gray matter (than control subjects) in several regions of the brain. Clearly, a great deal of additional research is needed, but these are impressive, thought-provoking findings that would seem to undermine the idea that meditation is nothing more than relaxation.

REVIEW OF KEY LEARNING GOALS

5.15 Meditation refers to a family of practices that train attention to heighten awareness and bring mental processes under greater voluntary control. Approaches to meditation can be classified into two main styles that reflect how attention is directed: focused attention and open monitoring. Studies suggest that meditation leads to a potentially beneficial physiological state characterized by suppression of bodily arousal.

5.16 Evidence suggests that meditation may reduce stress hormones, enhance self-esteem and well-being, and reduce vulnerability to a variety of diseases. However, some critics argue that the benefits of meditation can be gained through any effective relaxation procedure. Recent research suggests that meditation can alter brain structure.

Altering Consciousness with Drugs

KEY LEARNING GOALS

5.17 Identify the major types of abused drugs, and explain why their effects vary.

5.18 Understand how psychoactive drugs exert their effects in the brain, and distinguish between psychological and physical dependence.

5.19 Summarize evidence on the major health risks associated with drug abuse.

5.20 Evaluate controversies related to the risks of marijuana and ecstasy (MDMA).

Like hypnosis and meditation, drugs are commonly used in deliberate efforts to alter consciousness. In this section, we focus on the use of drugs for nonmedical purposes, commonly referred to as "drug abuse" or "recreational drug use." Drug abuse reaches into every corner of modern society. Although small declines occurred in the overall abuse of drugs in the 1980s, survey data show that illicit drug use has mostly been increasing since the 1960s (Compton et al., 2005). Despite extraordinary efforts to reduce drug abuse, it seems reasonable to conclude that widespread recreational drug use is here to stay for the foreseeable future (Winick & Norman, 2005).

Recreational drug use often inspires more rhetoric than reason. For instance, a former president of the American Medical Association made headlines when he declared that marijuana "makes a man of 35 sexually like a man of 70." In reality, the research findings don't support this assertion. This physician later retracted his statement, admitting that he had made it up simply to campaign against marijuana use (Leavitt, 1995). Such scare tactics can backfire by undermining the credibility of drug education efforts.

Recreational drug use involves personal, moral, political, and legal issues that are not matters for science to resolve. Bottom line, the more knowledgeable you are about drugs, the more informed your decisions and opinions about them will be. Accordingly, this section describes the types of drugs that are most commonly used for recreational purposes and summarizes their effects on consciousness, behavior, and health.

Principal Abused Drugs and Their Effects

PSYKTREK 4c

The drugs that people use recreationally are *psychoactive*. ***Psychoactive drugs* are chemical substances that modify mental, emotional, or behavioral functioning.** Not all psychoactive drugs produce effects that lead to recreational use. Generally, people prefer drugs that elevate their mood or produce other pleasurable changes in consciousness.

The principal types of recreational drugs are described in **Table 5.2** on the next page. The table lists representative drugs in each of six categories. It also summarizes how the drugs are taken, their medical uses, their effects on consciousness, and their common side effects (based on Julien, Advokat, & Comaty, 2008; Levinthal, 2008; Lowinson et al., 2005). The six categories of psychoactive drugs that we will focus on are narcotics, sedatives, stimulants, hallucinogens, cannabis, and alcohol. We'll also discuss one specific drug that has grown in popularity but is not listed in the table (because it doesn't fit into traditional drug categories): MDMA, better known as "ecstasy."

***Narcotics,* or *opiates,* are drugs derived from opium that are capable of relieving pain.** The main drugs in this category are heroin and morphine, although less potent opiates such as codeine, Demerol, and methadone are also abused. The emerging problem in this category is a new drug called oxycodone (trade name: OxyContin). Its time-release format was supposed to make it an effective analgesic with less potential for abuse than

Table 5.2 Psychoactive Drugs: Methods of Ingestion, Medical Uses, and Effects

Drugs	Methods of Ingestion	Principal Medical Uses	Desired Effects	Potential Short-Term Side Effects
Narcotics (opiates) Morphine Heroin Oxycodone	Injected, smoked, oral	Pain relief	Euphoria, relaxation, anxiety reduction, pain relief	Lethargy, drowsiness, nausea, impaired coordination, impaired mental functioning, constipation
Sedatives Barbiturates (e.g., Seconal) Nonbarbiturates (e.g., Quaalude)	Oral, injected	Sleeping pill, anticonvulsant	Euphoria, relaxation, anxiety reduction, reduced inhibitions	Lethargy, drowsiness, severely impaired coordination, impaired mental functioning, emotional swings, dejection
Stimulants Amphetamines Cocaine	Oral, sniffed, injected, freebased, smoked	Treatment of hyperactivity and narcolepsy, local anesthetic (cocaine only)	Elation, excitement, increased alertness, increased energy, reduced fatigue	Increased blood pressure and heart rate, increased talkativeness, restlessness, irritability, insomnia, reduced appetite, increased sweating and urination, anxiety, paranoia, increased aggressiveness, panic
Hallucinogens LSD Mescaline Psilocybin	Oral	None	Increased sensory awareness, euphoria, altered perceptions, hallucinations, insightful experiences	Dilated pupils, nausea, emotional swings, paranoia, jumbled thought processes, impaired judgment, anxiety, panic reaction
Cannabis Marijuana Hashish THC	Smoked, oral	Treatment of glaucoma and chemotherapy—induced nausea and vomiting; other uses under study	Mild euphoria, relaxation, altered perceptions, enhanced awareness	Elevated heart rate, bloodshot eyes, dry mouth, reduced short-term memory, sluggish motor coordination, sluggish mental functioning, anxiety
Alcohol	Drinking	None	Mild euphoria, relaxation, anxiety reduction, reduced inhibitions	Severely impaired coordination, impaired mental functioning, increased urination, emotional swings, depression, quarrelsomeness, hangover

© Cengage Learning 2013

the other opiates (Cicero, Inciardi, & Munoz, 2005). But people quickly learned that they could grind it up and gain a powerful high, leading to a new epidemic of serious drug abuse, especially in rural areas of the United States (Tunnell, 2005). The opiate drugs can produce an overwhelming sense of euphoria or well-being. This euphoric effect has a relaxing, "Who cares?" quality that makes the high an attractive escape from reality. Common side effects include lethargy, nausea, and impaired mental and motor functioning.

***Sedatives* are sleep-inducing drugs that tend to decrease central nervous system (CNS) activation and behavioral activity.** People abusing sedatives, or "downers," generally consume larger doses than are prescribed for medical purposes. The desired effect is a euphoria similar to that produced by drinking large amounts of alcohol. Feelings of tension or dejection are replaced by a relaxed, pleasant state of intoxication, accompanied by loosened inhibitions. Side effects include drowsiness, unpredictable emotional swings, and severe impairments in motor coordination and mental functioning.

***Stimulants* are drugs that tend to increase CNS activation and behavioral activity.** Stimulants range from mild, widely available drugs, such as caffeine and nicotine, to stronger, carefully regulated ones, such as cocaine. Our focus here is on cocaine and amphetamines. Cocaine is a natural substance that comes from the coca shrub. In contrast, amphetamines are synthesized in a pharmaceutical lab. Cocaine and amphetamines have fairly similar effects, except that cocaine produces a briefer high. Stimulants produce a euphoria very different from that created by narcotics or sedatives. They produce an elated, energetic "I can conquer the world!" feeling as well as increased alertness. In recent years, cocaine and amphetamines have become available in much more potent (and dangerous) forms than before. "Freebasing" is a chemical treatment used to extract nearly pure cocaine from ordinary street cocaine. "Crack" is the most widely distributed byproduct of this process, consisting of chips of pure cocaine that are usually smoked. Amphetamines are increasingly sold as a crystalline powder, called "crank" or "crystal meth" (short for "methamphetamine"), that may be snorted or injected intravenously. Side effects of stimulants may include restlessness, anxiety, paranoia, and insomnia.

***Hallucinogens* are a diverse group of drugs that have powerful effects on mental and emotional functioning, marked most notably by distortions in sensory and perceptual experience.** The main hallucinogens are LSD, mescaline, and psilocybin. These drugs have similar effects, although they vary in potency. Hallucinogens produce euphoria, in-

"JUST TELL ME WHERE YOU KIDS GET THE IDEA TO TAKE SO MANY DRUGS."

© 2004 by Sidney Harris. ScienceCartoonPlus.com

creased sensory awareness, and a distorted sense of time. They can lead to profound, dreamlike, "mystical" feelings that are difficult to describe. This effect is why they have been used in religious ceremonies in some cultures for centuries. Unfortunately, at the other end of the emotional spectrum, hallucinogens can also produce nightmarish feelings of anxiety and paranoia, commonly called a "bad trip." Other side effects include impaired judgment and jumbled thought processes.

***Cannabis* is the hemp plant from which marijuana, hashish, and THC are derived.** Marijuana is a mixture of dried leaves, flowers, stems, and seeds taken from the plant. Hashish comes from the plant's resin. Smoking is the usual route of ingestion for both marijuana and hashish. THC is the active chemical ingredient in cannabis, which can be synthesized for research purposes (for example, to give to animals, who can't very well smoke marijuana). When smoked, cannabis has an immediate impact that may last several hours. The desired effects of the drug are a mild, relaxed euphoria and enhanced sensory awareness. Unintended effects may include increased heart rate, anxiety, sluggish mental functioning, and impaired memory.

***Alcohol* encompasses a variety of beverages containing ethyl alcohol,** such as beers, wines, and distilled liquors (whiskey, vodka, rum, and so forth). The concentration of ethyl alcohol varies from about 4% in most beers to 40% in 80-proof liquor—and even more in higher-proof liquors. When people drink, the central effect is a relaxed euphoria that temporarily boosts self-esteem, as problems seem to melt away and inhibitions fade. Common side effects include severe impairments in mental and motor functioning, mood swings, and quarrelsomeness. Alcohol is the most widely used recreational drug in our society.

***MDMA* is a compound drug related to both amphetamines and hallucinogens, especially mescaline.** MDMA was originally formulated in 1912 but was not widely used in the United States until the 1990s when as "ecstasy" it became popular in the rave and club scene. MDMA produces a high that typically lasts a few hours or more. Users report that they feel warm, friendly, euphoric, sensual, insightful, and empathetic, but alert and energetic. Problematic side effects include increased blood pressure, muscle tension, sweating, blurred vision, insomnia, and transient anxiety.

Factors Influencing Drug Effects

The drug effects summarized in **Table 5.2** are the *typical* ones. Drug effects can vary from person to person and even for the same person in different situations. The impact of any drug depends in part on the user's age, mood, motivation, personality, previous experience with the drug, body weight, and physiology. The dose and potency of a drug, the method of intake, and the setting in which a drug is taken also influence its effects (Leavitt, 1995). Our theme of *multifactorial causation* clearly applies to the effects of drugs.

So, too, does our theme emphasizing the *subjectivity of experience*. Expectations are potentially powerful factors that can influence the user's perceptions of a drug's effects. You may recall from the discussion of placebo effects in Chapter 2 that some people who are misled to *think* that they are drinking alcohol show signs of intoxication (Assefi & Garry, 2003). If people *expect* a drug to make them feel giddy, serene, or profound, their expectation may contribute to the feelings they experience.

A drug's effects can also change as the person's body develops a tolerance for the chemical as a result of continued use. ***Tolerance* refers to a progressive decrease in a person's responsiveness to a drug.** Tolerance usually leads people to consume larger and larger doses of a drug to attain the effects they desire. Most drugs produce tolerance effects, but some do so more rapidly than others. For example, tolerance to alcohol usually builds slowly, while tolerance to heroin increases much more quickly. **Table 5.3** on the next page indicates whether various categories of drugs tend to produce tolerance rapidly or gradually.

Table 5.3 Psychoactive Drugs: Tolerance, Dependence, Potential for Fatal Overdose, and Health Risks

Drugs	Tolerance	Risk of Physical Dependence	Risk of Psychological Dependence	Fatal Overdose Potential	Health Risks
Narcotics (opiates)	Rapid	High	High	High	Infectious diseases, accidents, immune suppression
Sedatives	Rapid	High	High	High	Accidents
Stimulants	Rapid	Moderate	High	Moderate to high	Sleep problems, malnutrition, nasal damage, hypertension, respiratory disease, stroke, liver disease, heart attack
Hallucinogens	Gradual	None	Very low	Very low	Accidents, acute panic
Cannabis	Gradual	None	Low to moderate	Very low	Accidents, lung cancer, respiratory disease, pulmonary disease, increased vulnerability to psychosis
Alcohol	Gradual	Moderate	Moderate	Low to high	Accidents, liver disease, malnutrition, brain damage, neurological disorders, heart disease, stroke, hypertension, ulcers, cancer, birth defects

© Cengage Learning 2013

Mechanisms of Drug Action

PSYKTREK 4d

Most drugs have effects that reverberate throughout the body. However, psychoactive drugs work mainly by altering neurotransmitter activity in the brain. As discussed in Chapter 3, neurotransmitters are chemicals that transmit information between neurons at junctions called *synapses*.

The actions of amphetamines and cocaine illustrate how drugs have selective, multiple effects on neurotransmitter activity (see **Figure 5.20**). Amphetamines exert their main effects on two of the monoamine neurotransmitters: norepinephrine (NE) and dopamine (DA). Indeed, the name *amphetamines* reflects the kinship between these drugs and the *monoamines*. Amphetamines mainly increase the release of DA and NE by presynaptic neurons. They also interfere with the reuptake of DA and NE from synaptic clefts (Koob & Le Moal, 2006). These actions serve to increase the levels of dopamine and norepinephrine at the affected synapses. Cocaine shares some of these actions, which is why cocaine

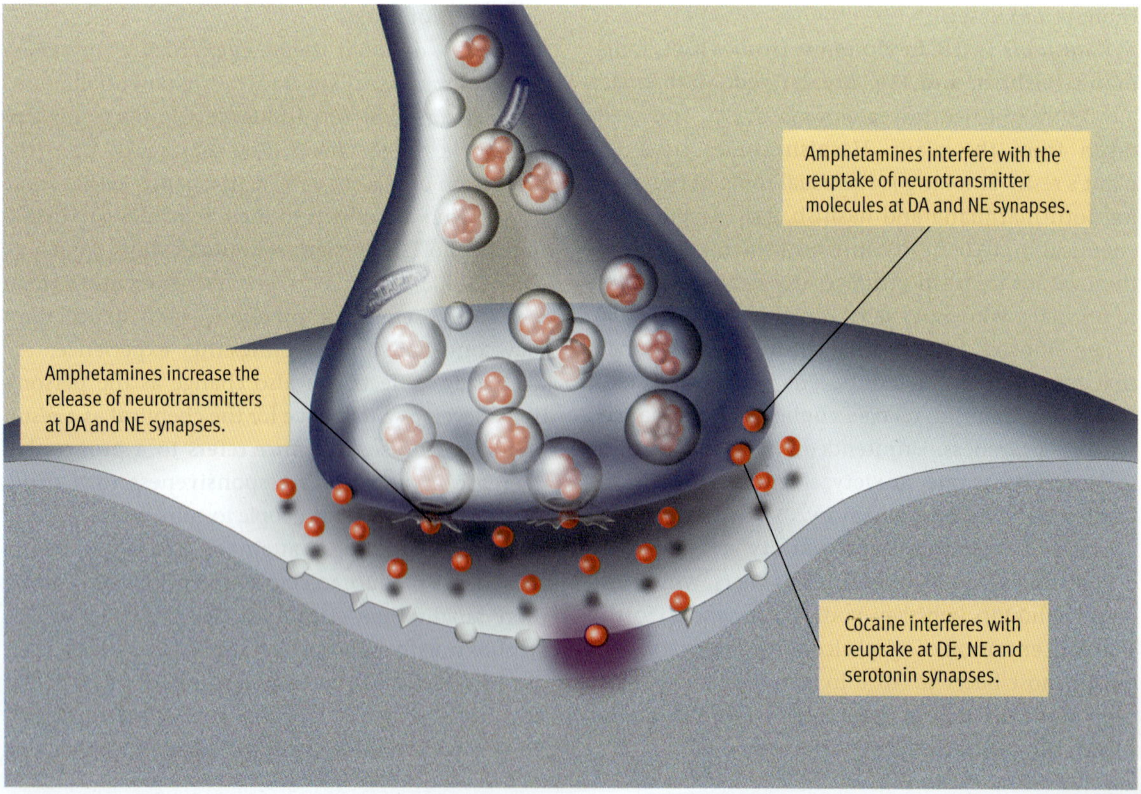

© Cengage Learning 2013

Figure 5.20
Stimulant drugs and neurotransmitter activity. Like other psychoactive drugs, amphetamines and cocaine alter neurotransmitter activity at specific synapses. Amphetamines primarily increase the release of dopamine (DA) and norepinephrine (NE) and secondarily inhibit the reuptake of these neurotransmitters. Cocaine slows the reuptake process at DA, NE, and serotonin synapses. The psychological and behavioral effects of the drugs have largely been attributed to their impact on dopamine circuits.

and amphetamines produce similar stimulant effects. Cocaine mainly blocks reuptake at DA, NE, and serotonin synapses. For both amphetamines and cocaine, elevated activity in certain *dopamine circuits* is believed to be crucial to the drugs' pleasurable, rewarding effects (Volkow, Fowler, & Wang, 2004).

Although specific drugs exert their initial effects in the brain on a wide variety of neurotransmitter systems, many theorists believe that virtually all abused drugs eventually increase activity in a particular neural pathway, called the *mesolimbic dopamine pathway* (Nestler & Malenka, 2004). This neural circuit (see **Figure 5.21**) has been described as a "reward pathway" (Pierce & Kumaresan, 2006). Large and rapid increases in the release of dopamine along this pathway are thought to be the crucial neural basis of the reinforcing effects of most abused drugs (Knapp & Kornetsky, 2009; Volkow et al., 2004).

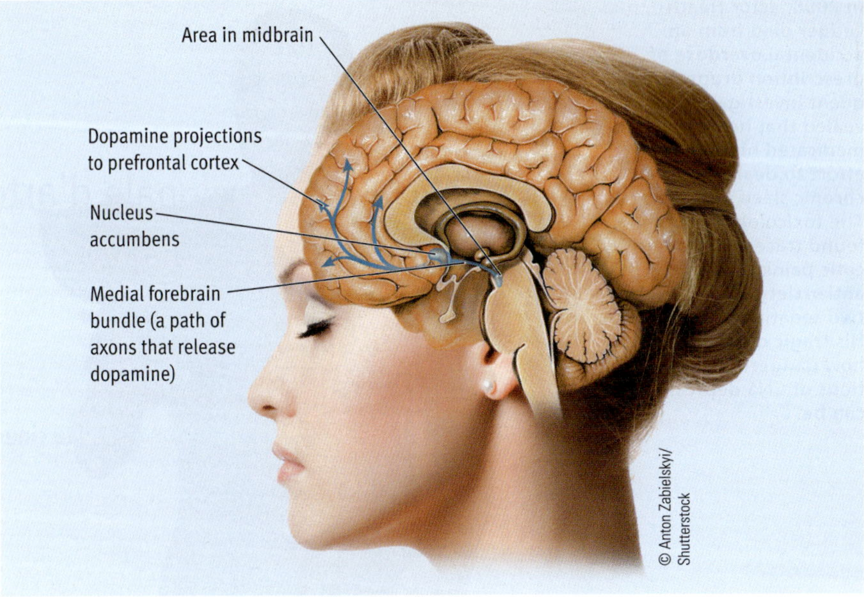

Figure 5.21
The "reward pathway" in the brain. The neural circuits shown here in blue make up the *mesolimbic dopamine pathway.* Axons in this pathway run from an area in the midbrain through the medial forebrain bundle to the *nucleus accumbens* and on to the prefrontal cortex. Recreational drugs affect a variety of neurotransmitter systems, but theorists believe that heightened dopamine activity in this pathway—especially the portion running from the midbrain to the nucleus accumbens—is responsible for the reinforcing effects of most abused drugs.

Drug Dependence

PSYKTREK 4c

People can become either physically or psychologically dependent on a drug. Physical dependence is a common problem with narcotics, sedatives, alcohol, and stimulants. ***Physical dependence*** **exists when a person must continue to take a drug to avoid withdrawal illness.** The symptoms of withdrawal illness depend on the specific drug. Withdrawal from heroin, barbiturates, and alcohol can produce fever, chills, tremors, convulsions, vomiting, cramps, diarrhea, and severe aches and pains. Withdrawal from stimulants can lead to a more subtle syndrome, marked by fatigue, apathy, irritability, and disorientation. Withdrawal also triggers a cascade of negative emotions and powerful urges for drug pursuit, which often lead people to relapse and reinstate their drug use (Baker et al., 2006).

Psychological dependence **exists when a person must continue to take a drug to satisfy intense mental and emotional craving for the drug.** Psychological dependence is more subtle than physical dependence, but the need it creates can be powerful. Cocaine, for instance, can produce an overwhelming psychological need for continued use. Psychological dependence is possible with all recreational drugs, although it seems rare for hallucinogens.

Both types of dependence are established gradually with repeated use of a drug. It was originally assumed that only physical dependence has a physiological basis. But theorists now believe that both types of dependence reflect alterations in synaptic transmission (Di Chara, 1999; Self, 1997). Dysregulation in the mesolimbic dopamine pathway appears to be a major factor underlying addiction (Nestler & Malenka, 2004), but long-term changes in other neural circuits running through the amygdala and prefrontal cortex may also contribute to drug craving (Kalivas & Volkow, 2005). Drugs vary in their potential for creating either physical or psychological dependence. **Table 5.3** provides estimates of the risk of each kind of dependence for the six categories of recreational drugs covered in our discussion.

Drugs and Health

PSYKTREK 4c

Recreational drug use can affect health in a variety of ways. The three principal ways are by triggering an overdose, by producing various types of physiological damage (direct effects), and by causing health-impairing behavior (indirect effects).

Overdose

PSYKTREK 4c

Any drug can be fatal if a person takes enough of it, but some drugs are much more dangerous than others. **Table 5.3** shows estimates of the risk of accidentally consuming a lethal overdose of each listed drug. Drugs that are CNS depressants—sedatives, narcotics, and alcohol—carry the greatest risk of overdose. It's important to note that these drugs are additive with each other, so many overdoses involve lethal *combinations* of CNS depressants. What happens when a person overdoses on these drugs? The respiratory

© AP Images/Domenico Stinellis

In 2008, actor Heath Ledger died from an accidental overdose of prescription drugs. Subsequent investigation revealed that he had overmedicated himself in an effort to deal with chronic sleep problems. The toxicology report found traces of two narcotic painkillers, two antianxiety agents, and two sedative medications. His tragic death illustrates how dangerous combinations of CNS depressants can be.

system grinds to a halt, producing coma, brain damage, and death within a brief period. Fatal overdoses with CNS stimulants usually involve a heart attack, stroke, or cortical seizure. Deaths caused by overdoses of stimulant drugs used to be *relatively* infrequent, but overdoses have increased sharply as more people have experimented with freebasing, smoking crack, and using other, more dangerous modes of ingestion (Repetto & Gold, 2005).

Direct Effects

PSYKTREK 4c

In some cases, drugs cause tissue damage directly. For example, chronic snorting of cocaine can damage nasal membranes. Cocaine use can also foster cardiovascular disease, and crack smoking is associated with several respiratory problems (Gold & Jacobs, 2005; Gourevitch & Arnsten, 2005). Long-term, excessive alcohol consumption is associated with an elevated risk for a wide range of serious health problems, including liver damage, ulcers, hypertension, stroke, heart disease, neurological disorders, and some types of cancer (Johnson & Ait-Daoud, 2005; Mack, Franklin, & Frances, 2003).

Indirect Effects

PSYKTREK 4c

The negative effects of drugs on physical health are often indirect results of the drugs' impact on behavior. For instance, people using stimulants tend not to eat or sleep properly. Sedatives increase the risk of accidental injuries because they severely impair motor coordination. People who abuse downers often trip down stairs, fall off stools, and suffer other mishaps. Many drugs impair driving ability, increasing the risk of automobile accidents. Alcohol, for instance, may contribute to roughly 40% of all automobile deaths (Hingson & Sleet, 2006). Intravenous drug users risk contracting infectious diseases that can be spread by unsterilized needles. In recent years, acquired immune deficiency syndrome (AIDS) has been transmitted at an alarming rate through the population of intravenous drug users (Des Jarlais, Hagan, & Friedman, 2005).

The major health risks (other than overdose) of various recreational drugs are listed in the sixth column of **Table 5.3**. As you can see, alcohol appears to have the most diverse negative effects on physical health. The irony, of course, is that alcohol is the only recreational drug listed that is legal.

Controversies Concerning Marijuana

The possible health risks related to marijuana use have generated much debate in recent years. The evidence suggests that chronic marijuana use increases the risk for respiratory and pulmonary disease (Aldington et al., 2007; Tashkin et al., 2002). Some studies have also found a link between long-term marijuana use and the risk for lung cancer, although the data are surprisingly sparse and inconsistent (Aldington et al., 2008; Hall & Degenhardt, 2009a). Although cannabis impairs driving less than alcohol does, there's convincing evidence that smoking marijuana increases the risk of automobile accidents if users drive while high (Richer & Bergeron, 2009). The combination of cannabis and alcohol may be particularly dangerous (Sewell, Poling, & Sofuoglu, 2009). People under the influence of marijuana alone tend to appreciate their impairment and try to compensate for being high (by driving more slowly, for instance), but alcohol suppresses these compensatory strategies and increases risk taking (Hall & Degenhardt, 2009b). Finally, a rash of recent studies have reported an unexpected link between cannabis use and severe psychotic disorders, including schizophrenia (Barrigon et al., 2010; DiForti et al., 2007). Obviously, the vast majority of marijuana users do not develop psychoses, but it appears that cannabis may trigger psychotic illness in individuals who have a genetic vulnerability to such disorders (Degenhardt et al., 2009; D'Souza, 2007). These dangers are listed in **Table 5.3**. Some other widely publicized dangers are omitted because the findings on these other risks have been exaggerated or remain debatable. Here is a brief overview of the evidence on some of these debates:

- *Does marijuana reduce one's immune response?* Research with animals clearly shows that cannabis can suppress various aspects of immune system responding (Cabral & Pettit, 1998). However, infectious diseases do not appear to be more common among marijuana smokers than among nonsmokers. Thus, it appears unlikely that marijuana increases susceptibility to infectious diseases in humans (Bredt et al., 2002; Hall & Degenhardt, 2009b).
- *Does marijuana lead to impotence and sterility in men?* In animal research, cannabis temporarily decreases testosterone levels and sperm production (Brown & Dobs, 2002). Citing these findings, the popular media have frequently implied that marijuana is likely to make men sterile and impotent. However, research with humans has yielded weak, inconsistent, and reversible effects on testosterone and sperm levels (Brown & Dobs, 2002). At present, the evidence suggests that marijuana has little lasting impact on male smokers' fertility or sexual functioning (Grinspoon, Bakalar, & Russo, 2005).
- *Does marijuana have negative effects on cognitive functioning?* Until relatively recently, studies had failed to find any durable cognitive deficits attributable to cannabis use. However, a flood of studies in the last decade using more elaborate and precise assessments of cognitive functioning *have* found an association between chronic, heavy marijuana use and measurable impairments in attention, learning, and memory (see **Figure 5.22**) that show up when users are not high (Hanson et al., 2010; Medina et al., 2007; Solowij et al., 2002). That said, the cognitive deficits that have been observed are modest and certainly not disabling. And some research suggests that the deficits may disappear after 3 to 4 weeks of marijuana abstinence (Hanson et al., 2010; Pope et al., 2001). Although more research is needed, the recent studies in this area provide some cause for concern.

© Yellowj/Shtterstock

New Findings Regarding Ecstasy

Like marijuana, ecstasy is viewed as a harmless drug in some quarters. But accumulating empirical evidence is beginning to alter that perception. Research on MDMA is in its infancy, so conclusions about its risks must be cautious. MDMA does not appear to be especially addictive, but psychological dependence clearly can become a problem for some people. MDMA has been implicated in cases of stroke, heart attack, seizures, heat stroke, and liver damage. Its exact contribution, however, is hard to gauge because MDMA users typically consume quite a variety of drugs, and ecstasy often contains contaminants (Grob & Poland, 2005; Scholey et al., 2004). Chronic, heavy use of ecstasy appears to be

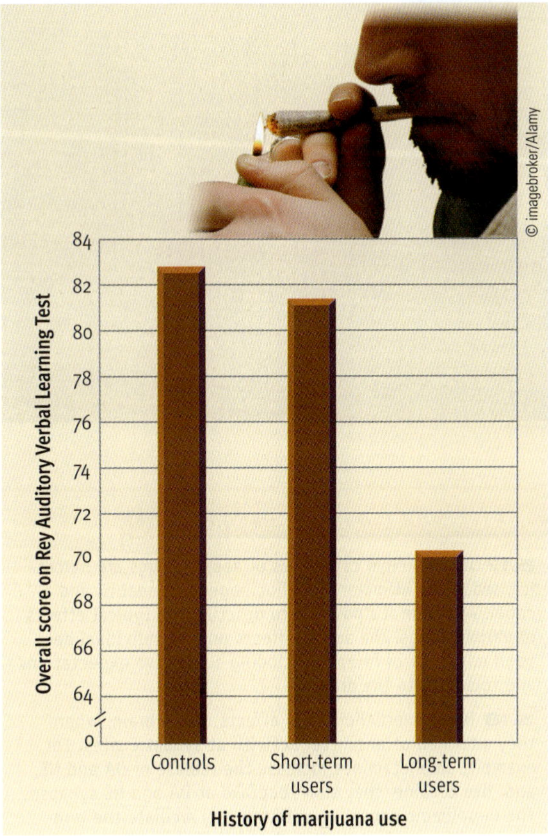

Figure 5.22
Chronic cannabis use and cognitive performance. Solowij and associates (2002) administered a battery of neuropsychological tests to fifty-one long-term cannabis users who had smoked marijuana regularly for an average of 24 years, fifty-one short-term cannabis users who had smoked marijuana regularly for an average of 10 years, and thirty-three control subjects who had little or no history of cannabis use. The cannabis users were required to abstain from smoking marijuana for a minimum of 12 hours prior to their testing. The study found evidence suggestive of subtle cognitive impairments among the long-term cannabis users on many of the tests. The graph depicts the results observed for overall performance on the Rey Auditory Verbal Learning Test, which measures several aspects of memory functioning.

CONCEPT CHECK 5.3

Recognizing the Unique Characteristics of Commonly Abused Drugs

From our discussion of the principal psychoactive drugs, it is clear that considerable overlap exists among the categories of drugs in terms of their methods of ingestion, medical uses, desired effects, and short-term side effects. Each type of drug, however, has at least one or two characteristics that make it different from the other types. Check your understanding of the unique characteristics of each type of drug by indicating which of them has the characteristics listed below. Choose from the following: (a) narcotics/opiates, (b) sedatives, (c) stimulants, (d) hallucinogens, (e) cannabis, and (f) alcohol. You'll find the answers in Appendix A.

_______ 1. Creates increased alertness and energy, buoyant elation, reduced fatigue.

_______ 2. No recognized medical use. May lead to insightful or "mystical" experiences.

_______ 3. Used as a "sleeping pill" because it reduces CNS activity.

_______ 4. Contributes to 40% of all traffic fatalities.

_______ 5. Derived from opium; used for pain relief.

_______ 6. Health risks of concern include respiratory and pulmonary disease and lung cancer.

© Laurence Manning/Corbis

MDMA, better known as "ecstasy," surged in popularity in the 1990s in the context of "raves" and dance clubs. Although many people view MDMA as a relatively harmless drug, recent research suggests otherwise.

associated with sleep disorders, depression, and elevated anxiety and hostility (Fisk, Montgomery, & Murphy, 2009; Morgan, 2000). Moreover, studies of former MDMA users suggest that ecstasy may have subtle, long-term effects on cognitive functioning. Quite a few studies have found memory deficits in former users (Hadjiefthyvoulou et al., 2010; Laws & Kokkalis, 2007). Other studies have found decreased performance on laboratory tasks requiring attention and learning (Murphy et al., 2009). In short, the preliminary evidence suggests that MDMA may be more harmful than widely assumed.

REVIEW OF KEY LEARNING GOALS

5.17 The principal categories of abused drugs are narcotics, sedatives, stimulants, hallucinogens, cannabis, and alcohol. Although it's possible to describe the typical effects of various drugs, the actual effects on any individual depend on a host of factors, including subjective expectations and tolerance to the drug.

5.18 Drugs exert their main effects in the brain, where they alter neurotransmitter activity at synaptic sites. For example, amphetamines increase the release of DA and NE, and, like cocaine, they slow reuptake at DA and NE synapses. The mesolimbic dopamine pathway may mediate the reinforcing effects of most abused drugs. Physical dependence exists when people must continue drug use to avoid withdrawal. Psychological dependence involves intense mental and emotional craving for a drug. Both types of dependence reflect changes in synaptic transmission.

5.19 Recreational drug use can prove harmful to health by producing an overdose, by causing tissue damage, or by increasing health-impairing behavior. The chances of accidentally consuming a lethal overdose are greatest for the CNS depressants and cocaine. Direct tissue damage occurs most frequently with alcohol and cocaine.

5.20 Cannabis may increase risk for respiratory disease, lung cancer, accidents, psychotic disorders, and subtle cognitive impairments. Concerns about immune response and reproductive health appear to be exaggerated. Preliminary evidence suggests that MDMA may be more dangerous than widely assumed.

KEY LEARNING GOALS

5.21 Identify the five unifying themes highlighted in this chapter.

Reflecting on the Chapter's Themes

Sociohistorical Context

Subjectivity of Experience

Cultural Heritage

Multifactorial Causation

Theoretical Diversity

This chapter highlights five of our unifying themes. First, we saw how psychology evolves in a sociohistorical context. Psychology began as the science of consciousness in the 19th century, but consciousness proved difficult to study empirically. Research on consciousness dwindled after John B. Watson and others redefined psychology as the science of behavior. However, in the 1960s people began to turn inward, showing a new interest in altering consciousness through drug use, meditation, hypnosis, and biofeedback. Psychologists responded to these social trends by beginning to study variations in consciousness in earnest. This renewed interest in consciousness shows how social forces can have an impact on psychology's evolution.

A second theme that predominates in this chapter is the idea that people's experience of the world is highly subjective. We encountered this theme when we learned that people often misjudge the quality and quantity of their sleep and that the changes of consciousness produced by drugs depend significantly on personal expectations.

Third, we saw once again how culture molds some aspects of behavior. Although the basic physiological process of sleep appears largely the same from one society to another, culture influences certain aspects of sleep habits. It can also have much impact on whether people remember their dreams and how they interpret and feel about their dreams.

Fourth, we learned once again that behavior is governed by multifactorial causation. For example, we discussed how the effects of jet lag, sleep deprivation, and psychoactive drugs depend on a number

CONCEPT CHECK 5.4

Identifying the Contributions of Major Theorists and Researchers

Check your recall of the principal ideas of important theorists and researchers covered in this chapter by matching the people listed on the left with the appropriate contributions described on the right. If you need help, the crucial pages describing each person's ideas are listed in parentheses. Fill in the letters for your choices in the spaces provided on the left. You'll find the answers in Appendix A.

Major Theorists and Researchers

______ 1. Rosalind Cartwright (pp. 204–205)

______ 2. William Dement (pp. 184, 195)

______ 3. Sigmund Freud (pp. 204–205)

______ 4. Ernest Hilgard (pp. 208–209)

______ 5. J. Alan Hobson (pp. 204–205)

______ 6. William James (p. 184)

Key Ideas and Contributions

a. According to this theorist's view, the principal purpose of dreams is wish fulfillment. He also distinguished between the manifest content and latent content of dreams.

b. According to this theorist's activation-synthesis model, dreams are side effects of the neural activation that produces beta waves during REM sleep.

c. This theorist emphasized that the contents of consciousness are always changing. He referred to this continuous flow of thought as the stream of consciousness.

d. According to this theorist's cognitive, problem-solving view, dreams provide an opportunity to work through everyday problems unrestrained by logic.

e. This person contributed to the discovery of REM sleep. He has also argued that chronic sleep deprivation is a major problem in modern society.

f. This theorist uses the concept of dissociation to explain many of the effects of hypnosis.

of interacting factors. Likewise, we saw that insomnia is rooted in a constellation of causal factors.

Finally, the chapter illustrated psychology's theoretical diversity. We discussed conflicting theories about dreams, hypnosis, and meditation. For the most part, we did not see these opposing theories converging toward resolution as we did in the areas of sensation and perception. However, it's important to emphasize that rival theories don't always merge neatly into tidy models of behavior. Many theoretical controversies go on indefinitely. This fact does not negate the value of theoretical diversity. While it's always nice to resolve a theoretical debate, the debate itself can advance knowledge by stimulating and guiding empirical research.

Indeed, our upcoming Personal Application demonstrates that theoretical debates need not be resolved in order to advance knowledge. Many theoretical controversies and enduring mysteries remain in the study of sleep and dreams. Nonetheless, researchers have accumulated a great deal of practical information on these topics, which we'll discuss in the next few pages.

REVIEW OF KEY LEARNING GOALS

5.21 Five of our unifying themes were highlighted in this chapter. We saw that psychology evolves in a sociohistorical context, that experience is highly subjective, that culture influences many aspects of behavior, that behavior is determined by multiple causes, and that psychology is characterized by theoretical diversity.

KEY LEARNING GOALS

5.22 Summarize the evidence on various practical questions about sleep.

5.23 Summarize the evidence on various practical questions about dreams.

Addressing Practical Questions About Sleep and Dreams

Indicate whether the following statements are "true" or "false."

___ **1** Naps rarely have a refreshing effect.

___ **2** Some people never dream.

___ **3** When people cannot recall their dreams, it's because they are trying to repress them.

___ **4** Only an expert in symbolism, such as a psychoanalytic therapist, can interpret the real meaning of dreams.

These assertions were all drawn from the Sleep and Dreams Information Questionnaire (Palladino & Carducci, 1984), which measures practical knowledge about sleep and dreams. Are they true or false? You'll see in this Application.

Common Questions About Sleep

How much sleep do people need? The average amount of daily sleep for young adults is 7.5 hours. However, there's quite a bit of variation in how long people sleep. Based on a synthesis of data from many studies, Webb (1992) estimates that sleep time is normally distributed as shown in **Figure 5.23**. Sleep needs vary some from person to person. That said, many sleep experts believe that most people would function more effectively if they increased their amount of sleep (Banks & Dinges, 2007). Bear in mind, too, that research suggests that people who sleep 7–8 hours per night have the lowest mortality rates (Patel et al., 2004; Tamakoshi et al., 2004).

Can short naps be refreshing? Some naps are beneficial and some aren't. The effectiveness of napping varies from person to person. Also, the benefits of any specific nap depend on the time of day and the amount of sleep one has had recently (Dinges, 1993). On the negative side, naps are not very *efficient* ways to sleep because you're often just getting into the deeper stages of sleep when your nap time is up. Naps tend to be more beneficial when they are rich in slow-wave sleep or REM sleep (Mednick & Drummond, 2009). Another potential problem is that overly long naps or naps that occur too close to bedtime can disrupt nighttime sleep (Thorpy & Yager, 2001).

Nonetheless, many highly productive people (including Thomas Edison, Winston Churchill, and John F. Kennedy) have made effective use of naps. Naps can enhance subsequent alertness and task performance and reduce sleepiness (Ficca et al., 2010). Evidence also suggests that naps can improve learning and memory—even more so than loading up on caffeine (Mednick et al., 2008). In conclusion, naps can be refreshing for most people (so the first statement opening this Application is false), and they can pay off in the long run if they don't interfere with nighttime sleep.

What is the significance of yawning and snoring? Yawning is a universal phenomenon seen in all cultural groups—not to mention other mammals, birds, fish, and reptiles (Baenninger, 1997). Contrary to popular belief, yawning is not a response to a buildup of carbon dioxide or a shortage of oxygen (Provine, 2005). However, as reputed, yawning *is* correlated with sleepiness and boredom (Provine, 2005). According to one theory, the principal function of yawning is to cool the brain down (Gallup & Gallup, 2007). The most fascinating and perplexing facet of yawning is that it's

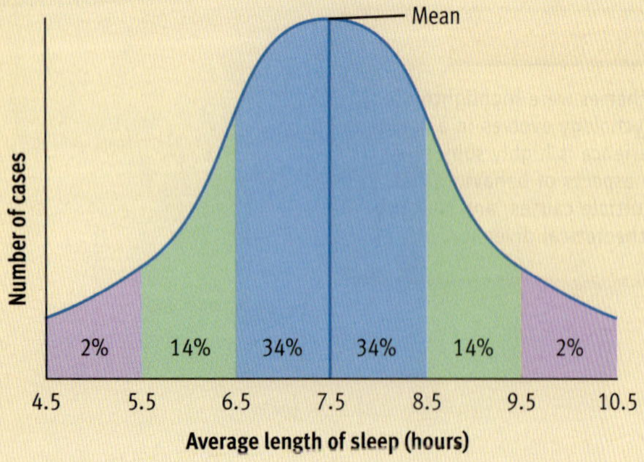

Figure 5.23

Variation in sleep length. Based on data from a variety of sources, Webb (1992) estimates that average sleep length among young adults is distributed normally, as shown here. Although most young adults sleep an average of 6.5 to 8.5 hours per night, some people sleep less and some sleep more.

SOURCE: Adapted from Webb, W. B. (1992). *Sleep, the gentle tyrant* (2nd ed.). Bolton, MA: Anker Publishing Co. Copyright © 1992 by Anker Publishing Co. Adapted by permission.

© Cengage Learning 2013

contagious—seeing others yawn creates a powerful urge to follow suit (Platek, Mohamed, & Gallup, 2005).

Snoring is a common phenomenon seen in roughly 30%–40% of adults (Hoffstein, 2005). Snoring increases after age 35, occurs in men more than women, and is more common among people who are overweight (Kryger, 1993; Stoohs et al., 1998). Many factors, including colds, allergies, smoking, and some drugs, can contribute to snoring, mainly by forcing people to breathe through their mouths while sleeping. Some people who snore loudly disrupt their own sleep as well as that of their bed partners. It can be difficult to prevent snoring in some people, whereas others are able to reduce their snoring by simply losing weight or by sleeping on their side instead of their back (Lugaresi et al., 1994). Snoring may seem like a trivial problem, but it's associated with sleep apnea and cardiovascular disease, and it may have considerably more medical significance than most people realize (Dement & Vaughn, 1999; Olson & Park, 2006).

What can be done to avoid sleep problems? There are many ways to improve your chances of getting satisfactory sleep (see **Figure 5.24**). Most of them involve developing sensible daytime habits that won't interfere with sleep (see Foldvary-Schaefer, 2006; Maas, 1998; Stepanski & Wyatt, 2003; Thorpy & Yager, 2001; Zarcone, 2000). For example, if you've been having trouble sleeping at night, it's wise to avoid daytime naps so that you will be *tired* when bedtime arrives. Some people find that daytime exercise helps them fall asleep more readily at bedtime (King et al., 1997). Of course, the exercise should be part of a regular regimen that doesn't leave one sore or aching.

It's also a good idea to minimize consumption of stimulants such as caffeine or nicotine. Because coffee and cigarettes aren't prescription drugs, people don't appreciate how much the stimulants they contain can heighten physical arousal. Many foods (such as chocolate) and beverages (such as cola drinks) contain more caffeine than people realize. Also, bear in mind that ill-advised eating habits can interfere with sleep. Try to avoid going to bed hungry, uncomfortably stuffed, or soon after eating foods that disagree with you.

In addition to these prudent habits, two other preventive measures are worth mentioning. First, try to establish a reasonably regular bedtime. This habit will allow you to take advantage of your circadian rhythm, so you'll be trying to fall asleep when your body is primed to cooperate. Second, create a favorable environment for sleep. This advice belabors what should be obvious, but many people fail to heed it. Make sure you have a good bed that is comfortable for you. Take steps to ensure that your bedroom is quiet enough and that the humidity and temperature are to your liking.

What can be done about insomnia? First, don't panic if you run into a little trouble sleeping. An overreaction to sleep problems can begin a vicious circle of escalating problems, like that depicted in **Figure 5.25** on the next page. If you jump to the conclusion that you're becoming an insomniac, you may approach sleep with anxiety that will aggravate the problem. The harder you work at falling asleep, the less success you're likely to have. As noted earlier, temporary

Suggestions for Better Sleep

1. Reduce stress as much as possible.
2. Exercise to stay fit.
3. Keep mentally stimulated during the day.
4. Eat a proper diet.
5. Stop smoking.
6. Reduce caffeine intake.
7. Avoid alcohol near bedtime.
8. Take a warm bath before bed.
9. Maintain a relaxing atmosphere in the bedroom.
10. Establish a bedtime ritual.
11. Have pleasurable sexual activity.
12. Clear your mind at bedtime.
13. Try some bedtime relaxation techniques.
14. Avoid trying too hard to get to sleep.
15. Learn to value sleep.

© Cengage Learning 2013

Figure 5.24

Improving the quality of one's sleep. In his book *Power Sleep,* James Maas (1998) offers this advice for people concerned about enhancing their sleep. Maas argues convincingly that good daytime habits can make all the difference in the world to the quality of one's sleep.

SOURCE: Adapted from Maas, J. B. (1998). *Power sleep.* New York: Random House. Copyright © 1998 by James B. Mass, Ph. D. Reprinted by permission of Villard Books, a division of Random House, Inc.

© Topham/The Image Works

People typically get very upset when they have difficulty falling asleep. Unfortunately, the emotional distress tends to make it even harder for people to get to sleep.

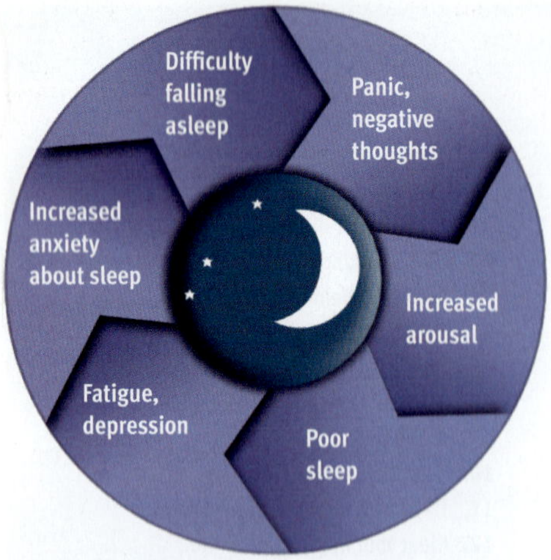

Figure 5.25
The vicious circle of anxiety and sleep difficulty. Anxiety about sleep difficulties leads to poorer sleep, which increases anxiety further, which in turn leads to even greater difficulties in sleeping. © Cengage Learning 2013

sleep problems are common and generally clear up on their own.

One sleep expert, Dianne Hales (1987), lists 101 suggestions for combating insomnia in her book *How to Sleep Like a Baby.* Many involve "boring yourself to sleep" by playing alphabet games, reciting poems, or listening to your clock. Another recommended strategy is to engage in some not-so-engaging activity. For instance, you might try reading your dullest textbook. It could turn out to be a superb sedative. Whatever you think about, try to avoid ruminating about the current stresses and problems in your life. Research has shown that the tendency to ruminate is one of the key factors contributing to insomnia (Kales et al., 1984).

Anything that relaxes you—whether it's music, meditation, prayer, or a warm bath—can aid you in falling asleep. Experts have also devised systematic relaxation procedures that can make these efforts more effective. You may want to learn about techniques such as *progressive relaxation* (Jacobson, 1938), *autogenic training* (Schultz & Luthe, 1959), or the *relaxation response* (Benson & Klipper, 1988). If you have to consult a professional for help, the good news is that there are a variety of nondrug interventions that have proven effective in the treatment of insomnia (Kierlin, 2008).

Common Questions About Dreams

Does everyone dream? Yes. Some people just don't *remember* their dreams. However, when these people are brought into a sleep lab and awakened from REM sleep, they report having been dreaming—much to their surprise (statement 2 at the start of this Application is false). Scientists have studied a small number of people who have sustained brain damage in the area of the *pons* that has wiped out their REM sleep, but even these people report dreams (Klosch & Kraft, 2005).

Why don't some people remember their dreams? The evaporation of dreams appears to be quite normal. Most dreams are lost forever unless unless people wake up during or just after a dream. Even then, dream recall fades quickly (Nir & Tononi, 2009). Most of the time, people who recall dreams are remembering their *last* dream from their final REM period. Hobson's (1989) educated guess is that people probably forget 95%–99% of their dreams. This forgetting is natural and not due to repression, so statement 3 is also false. People who never remember their dreams probably have a sleep pattern that puts too much time between their last REM/dream period and awakening, so even their last dream is forgotten.

Are dreams instantaneous? No. It has long been speculated that dreams flash through consciousness almost instantaneously. According to this notion, complicated plots that would require 20 minutes to think through in waking life could bolt through the dreaming mind in a second or two. However, modern research suggests that this isn't the case (LaBerge, 2007; Weinstein, Schwartz, & Arkin, 1991).

Do dreams require interpretation? Most theorists would say yes, but interpretation may not be as difficult as generally assumed. People have long believed that dreams are symbolic and that it's necessary to interpret the symbols to understand the meaning of dreams. We saw earlier in the chapter that Freud, for instance, believed

FRANK AND ERNEST

FRANK & ERNEST © 2006 Thaves. Reprinted by permission of UNIVERSAL UCLICK for UFS. All rights reserved.

Photofest/Warner Bros. Pictures © Warner Bros. Pictures

The plot of the hit movie *Inception,* which revolves around the notion that one could steal someone's dreams, or implant dreams without their knowledge, is pure science fiction. But the inspiration for the movie apparently was the real phenomenon of lucid dreaming. Reports indicate that director Christopher Nolan has long been fascinated by the puzzling concept of lucid dreams.

that dreams have a hidden ("latent") content that represented their true meaning. Thus, a Freudian therapist might equate such dream events as walking into a tunnel or riding a horse with sexual intercourse.

Freudian theorists assert that dream interpretation is a complicated task requiring considerable knowledge of symbolism. However, many dream theorists argue that symbolism in dreams is less deceptive and mysterious than Freud thought (Faraday, 1974; Foulkes, 1985; Hall, 1979). Calvin Hall makes the point that dreams require some interpretation simply because they are more visual than verbal. That is, pictures need to be translated into ideas. According to Hall, dream symbolism is highly personal, and the dreamer may be the person best equipped to decipher a dream (statement 4 is also false). Thus, it is not unreasonable for you to try to interpret your own dreams. Unfortunately, you'll never know whether you're "correct," because there is no definitive way to judge the validity of different dream interpretations.

What is lucid dreaming? Generally, when people dream, they aren't aware that they're dreaming. Occasionally, however, some people experience "lucid" dreams in which they recognize that they're dreaming (LaBerge, 2007). Typically, normal dreams become lucid when people question something strange in a dream and recognize that they must be dreaming. **In *lucid dreams* people can think clearly about the circumstances of waking life and the fact that they are dreaming, yet they remain asleep in the midst of a vivid dream.** Perhaps the most intriguing aspect of this dual consciousness is that people can often exert some control over the events unfolding in their lucid dreams (LaBerge, 1990).

REVIEW OF KEY LEARNING GOALS

5.22 Naps can prove helpful, although they may not be a very efficient way to sleep. Yawning appears to be associated with boredom and sleepiness but is not well understood. Snoring may have more health significance than most people realize. People can do many things to avoid or reduce sleep problems. Individuals troubled by transient insomnia should avoid panic, pursue effective relaxation, and try distracting themselves so they don't work too hard at falling asleep.

5.23 Everyone dreams, but some people don't remember their dreams. Freud asserted that dreams require interpretation, but modern theorists assert that this process may not be as complicated as Freud assumed. In lucid dreams, people consciously recognize that they're dreaming and exert some control over the events in their dreams.

KEY LEARNING GOALS

5.24 Recognize the influence of definitions, and understand the nominal fallacy.

Is Alcoholism a Disease? The Power of Definitions

Alcoholism is a major problem in most, if not all, societies. As we saw in the chapter, alcohol is a dangerous drug. Alcoholism destroys countless lives, tears families apart, and is associated with an elevated risk for a variety of physical ailments (Johnson & Ait-Daoud, 2005). With roughly 15 million problem drinkers in the United States (Mack et al., 2003), it seems likely that alcoholism has touched the lives of a majority of Americans.

In almost every discussion about alcoholism, someone will ask, "Is alcoholism a disease?" If alcoholism is a disease, it's a strange one, because the alcoholic is the most direct cause of his or her own sickness. If alcoholism is *not* a disease, then what else might it be? Over the course of history, alcoholism has been categorized under many labels, from a personal weakness to a crime, a sin, a mental disorder, and a physical illness (Meyer, 1996). Each of these definitions carries important personal, social, political, and economic implications.

Consider, for instance, the consequences of characterizing alcoholism as a disease. If that is the case, alcoholics should be treated like diabetics, heart patients, or victims of other physical illnesses. That is, they should be viewed with sympathy and should be given appropriate medical and therapeutic interventions to foster recovery from their illness. These treatments should be covered by medical insurance and delivered by health care professionals. Just as important, if alcoholism is defined as a disease, it should lose much of its stigma. After all, we don't blame people with diabetes or heart disease for their illnesses. Yes, alcoholics admittedly contribute to their own disease (by drinking too much), but so do many victims of diabetes and heart disease, who eat the wrong foods, fail to control their weight, and so forth (McLellan et al., 2000). And, as is the case with many physical illnesses, one can inherit a genetic vulnerability to alcoholism (Lin & Anthenelli, 2005). So it's difficult to argue that alcoholism is caused solely by one's behavior.

Conversely, if alcoholism is defined as a personal failure or a moral weakness, alcoholics are less likely to be viewed with sympathy and compassion. They might be admonished to quit drinking, be put in prison, or be punished in some other way. These responses to their alcoholism would be run primarily by the legal system rather than the health care system since medical help is not designed to fix moral failings. Obviously, the interventions that would be available would not be covered by health insurance, which would have enormous financial repercussions (for both health care providers and alcoholics).

The key point here is that definitions lie at the center of many complex debates. They can have profound and far-reaching implications. People tend to think of definitions as insignificant, arbitrary sets of words found buried in thick dictionaries compiled by elitists. But definitions are *not* insignificant. They wield enormous power to shape how people think about important issues. An endless array of issues boil down to matters of definition. For example, the next time you hear people arguing over whether a particular movie is pornographic, whether the death penalty is cruel and unusual punishment, or whether spanking is child abuse, you'll find it helps to focus the debate on clarifying the definitions of the crucial concepts.

So, how can we resolve the debate about whether alcoholism is a disease? Scientists generally try to resolve their debates by conducting research to achieve a better understanding of the phenomena under study. You may have noticed already that the assertion "We need more research on this issue . . ." is a frequent refrain in this text. Is more research the answer in this case? For once, the answer is "no." There is no conclusive way to determine whether alcoholism is a disease. It's not as though there is a "right" answer to this question that we can discover through more and better research.

The question of whether alcoholism is a disease is a *matter of definition:* Does alcoholism fit the currently accepted definition of a disease? If you consult medical texts or dictionaries, you'll find that *disease is typically defined as an impairment in the normal functioning of an organism that alters its vital functions.* Given that alcoholism clearly impairs people's normal functioning and disrupts a variety of vital functions (see **Figure 5.26**), it seems reasonable to characterize it as a disease. This has been the dominant view in the United States since the middle of the 20th century (Maltzman, 1994; Meyer, 1996). This view has only been strengthened by recent evidence that addiction to alcohol (and other drugs) is the result of dysregulation in key neural circuits in the brain (Cami & Farre, 2003).

Still, many critics express strong doubts about the wisdom of defining alcoholism as a disease (Peele, 1989, 2000). They often raise a question that comes up frequently in arguments about definitions: Who should have the power to make the definition? In this case, the power lies in the hands of the medical community, which seems sensible, given that disease is a medical concept. But some critics argue that the medical community has a strong bias in favor of defining conditions as diseases because doing so creates new markets and fuels economic growth for the health industry (Nikelly, 1994). Thus, debate about whether alcoholism is a disease seems likely to continue for the indefinite future.

To summarize, definitions generally do not emerge out of research. They're typically crafted by experts or authorities in a specific field who try to reach a consensus about how to best define a particular concept. Thus, in analyzing the validity of a definition, you need to look not only at the definition itself but at where it came from. Who decided what the definition should be? Does the source of the definition seem legitimate and appropriate? Did the authorities who formulated the definition have any biases that should be considered?

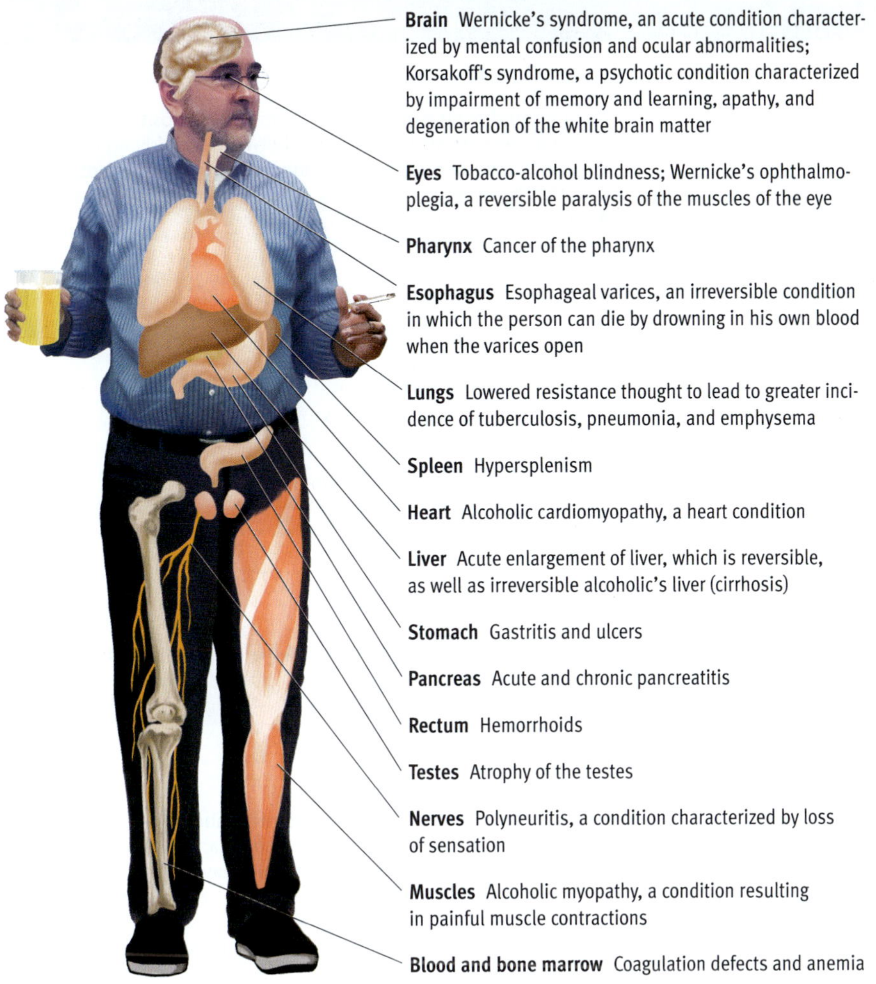

Figure 5.26

Physiological malfunctions associated with alcoholism. This chart amply demonstrates that alcoholism is associated with a diverse array of physiological maladies. In and of itself, however, this information does not settle the argument about whether alcoholism should be regarded as a disease. It all depends on one's definition of what constitutes a disease.

SOURCE: Edlin, G., & Golanty, E. (1992). *Health and wellness: A holistic approach.* Boston: Jones & Bartlett. Copyright © 1992 by Jones & Bartlett Publishers, Inc. www.jbpub.com. Reprinted by permission.

© Cengage Learning 2013

One additional point about definitions is worth discussing. Perhaps because definitions are imbued with so much power, people have an interesting tendency to incorrectly use them as *explanations* for the phenomena they describe. This logical error, which equates *naming* something with *explaining* it, is sometimes called the *nominal fallacy.* Names and labels that are used as explanations may sound reasonable at first glance, but definitions do not really have any explanatory value; they simply specify what certain terms mean. Consider an example. Let's say your friend Frank has a severe drinking problem. You're sitting around with some other friends discussing why Frank drinks so much. Rest assured, at least one of these friends will assert that "Frank drinks too much because he's an alcoholic." This is circular reasoning, which is just as useless as explaining that Frank is an alcoholic because he drinks too much. It tells us nothing about *why* Frank has a drinking problem.

The diagnostic labels that are used in the classification of mental disorders—labels such as schizophrenia, depression, autism, and obsessive-compulsive disorder—seem to invite this type of circular reasoning. For example, people often say things like "That person is delusional because she's schizophrenic," or "He's afraid of small, enclosed places because he's claustrophobic." These statements are just as logical as saying "She is a redhead because she has red hair." The logical fallacy of mistaking a label for an explanation will get us as far in our understanding as a dog gets in chasing its own tail.

Table 5.4 **Critical Thinking Skills Discussed in This Application**

Skill	Description
Understanding the way definitions shape how people think about issues	The critical thinker appreciates the enormous power of definitions and the need to clarify definitions in efforts to resolve disagreements.
Identifying the source of definitions	The critical thinker recognizes the need to determine who has the power to make specific definitions and to evaluate their credibility
Avoiding the nominal fallacy in working with definitions and labels	The critical thinker understands that labels do not have explanatory value.

© Cengage Learning 2013

REVIEW OF KEY LEARNING GOALS

5.24 Like many questions, the issue of whether alcoholism should be regarded as a disease is a matter of definition. In evaluating the validity of a definition, one should look not only at the definition but also at where it came from. People have a tendency to use definitions as explanations for the phenomena they describe; this nominal fallacy involves circular reasoning.

Chapter 5 Practice Test

1. An EEG would indicate primarily _____ activity while you take this test.
   A. alpha
   B. beta
   C. delta
   D. theta

2. Other things being equal, which of the following flights would lead to the greatest difficulty with jet lag?
   A. northward
   B. southward
   C. eastward
   D. westward

3. Slow-wave sleep consists of stages ________ of sleep and is dominated by ________ waves.
   A. 1 and 2; beta
   B. 2 and 3; alpha
   C. 3 and 4; delta
   D. 1 and 2; delta

4. As the sleep cycle evolves through the night, people tend to:
   A. spend more time in REM sleep and less time in NREM sleep.
   B. spend more time in NREM sleep and less time in REM sleep.
   C. spend a more or less equal amount of time in REM sleep and NREM sleep.
   D. spend more time in stage 4 sleep and less time in REM sleep.

5. Newborn infants spend about _____% of their sleep time in REM, while adults spend about _____% of their sleep time in REM.
   A. 20; 50
   B. 50; 20
   C. 20; 20
   D. 50; 50

6. Tamara has taken part in a three-day study in which she was awakened every time she went into REM sleep. Now that she is home sleeping without interference, it is likely that she will:
   A. exhibit psychotic symptoms for a few nights.
   B. experience severe insomnia for about a week.
   C. spend extra time in REM sleep for a few nights.
   D. spend less time in REM sleep for a few nights.

7. Which of the following is associated with REM sleep?
   A. sleep apnea
   B. somnambulism
   C. night terrors
   D. nightmares

8. Which of the following is *not* true of cultural influences on dream experiences?
   A. The ability to recall dreams is fairly consistent across cultures.
   B. In some cultures, people are held responsible for their dream actions.
   C. In Western cultures, dreams are not taken very seriously.
   D. People in some cultures believe that dreams provide information about the future.

9. The activation-synthesis theory of dreaming contends that:
   A. dreams are simply the by-product of bursts of activity in the brain.
   B. dreams provide an outlet for energy invested in socially undesirable impulses.
   C. dreams represent the person's attempt to fulfill unconscious wishes.
   D. dreams are an attempt to restore a neurotransmitter balance within the brain.

10. A common driving experience is "highway hypnosis," in which one's consciousness seems to be divided between the driving itself and one's conscious train of thought. This phenomenon is consistent with the idea that hypnosis is:
    A. an exercise in role playing.
    B. a dissociated state of consciousness.
    C. a goal-directed fantasy.
    D. not an altered state of consciousness.

11. Stimulant is to depressant as:
    A. cocaine is to alcohol.
    B. mescaline is to barbiturates.
    C. caffeine is to amphetamines.
    D. alcohol is to barbiturates.

12. Amphetamines work by increasing the levels of __________________ in a variety of ways.
    A. GABA and glycine
    B. melatonin
    C. acetylcholine
    D. norepinephrine and dopamine

13. Which of the following drugs would be most likely to result in a fatal overdose?
    A. LSD
    B. mescaline
    C. marijuana
    D. sedatives

14. Which of the following is a true statement about naps?
    A. Daytime naps invariably lead to insomnia.
    B. Daytime naps are invariably refreshing and an efficient way to rest.
    C. Daytime naps are not very efficient ways to sleep, but their effects are sometimes beneficial.
    D. Taking many naps during the day can substitute for a full night's sleep.

15. Definitions:
    A. generally emerge out of research.
    B. often have great explanatory value.
    C. generally exert little influence over how people think.
    D. are usually constructed by experts or authorities in a specific field.

Answers

1 B p. 185	6 C p. 196	11 A pp. 211–213
2 C pp. 187–188	7 D p. 200	12 D p. 214
3 C pp. 189–190	8 A pp. 203–204	13 D pp. 214–216
4 A pp. 190, 192–193	9 A pp. 204–205	14 C p. 220
5 B pp. 191–192	10 B p. 209	15 D pp. 224–225

Chapter 5 Media Resources

PsykTrek

To view a demo: **www.cengage.com/psychology/psyktrek**
To order: **www.cengage.com/psychology/weiten**
Go to the PsykTrek website or CD-ROM for further study of the concepts in this chapter. Both online and on the CD-ROM, PsykTrek includes dozens of learning modules with videos, animations, and quizzes, as well as simulations of psychological phenomena and a multimedia glossary that includes word pronunciations.

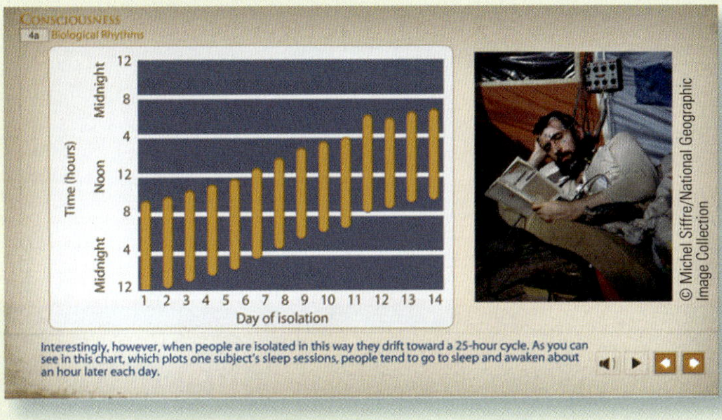

© Michel Siffre/National Geographic Image Collection
© Cengage Learning 2008

Check out Module 4a (*Biological Rhythms*) to learn more about how biological rhythms influence sleep and performance.

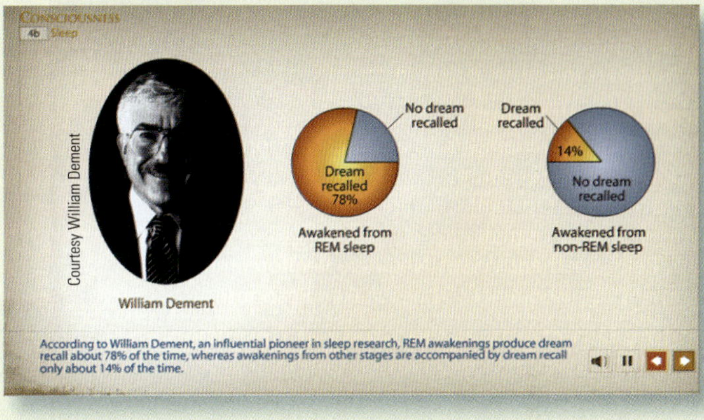

Courtesy William Dement
© Cengage Learning 2008

Explore Module 4b (*Sleep*) for more details on how people cycle through the stages of sleep.

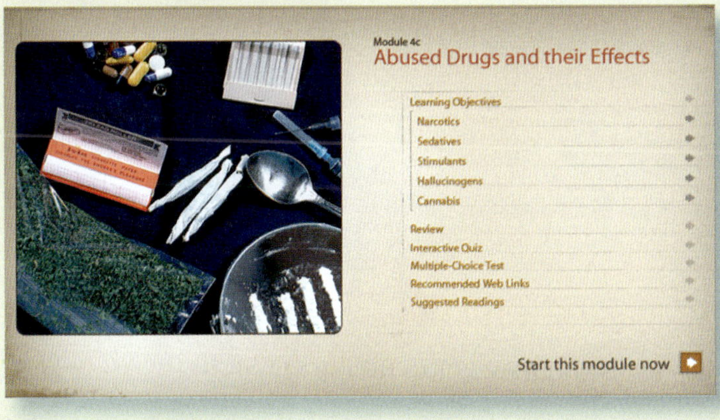

© Cengage Learning 2008

Go to Module 4c (*Abused Drugs and Their Effects*) to get more information about the effects and risks of five categories of widely abused drugs.

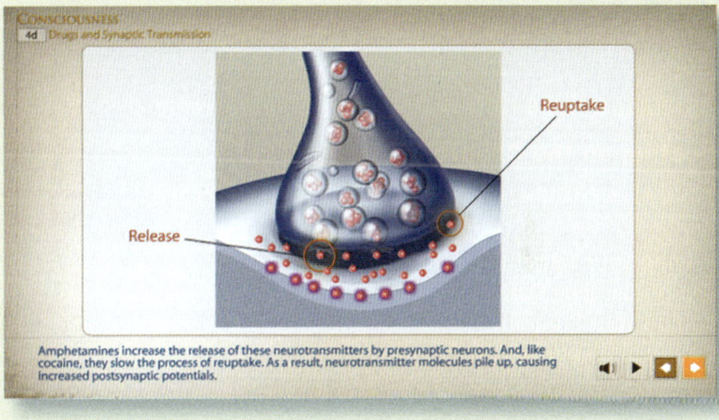

© Cengage Learning 2008

Access Module 4d (*Drugs and Synaptic Transmission*) to view animations of how various drugs exert their effects by altering neurotransmitter activity at specific synapses.

Online Study Tools

Log in to **CengageBrain** to access the resources your instructor requires. For this book, you can access:

CourseMate brings course concepts to life with interactive learning, study, and exam preparation tools that support the printed textbook. A textbook-specific website, Psychology CourseMate includes an integrated interactive eBook and other interactive learning tools such as quizzes, flashcards, videos, and more.

CengageNow is an easy-to-use online resource that helps you study in less time to get the grade you want—NOW. Take a pre-test for this chapter and receive a personalized study plan based on your results that will identify the topics you need to review and direct you to online resources to help you master those topics. Then take a post-test to help you determine the concepts you have mastered and what you will need to work on. If your textbook does not include an access code card, go to CengageBrain.com to gain access.

WebTutor is more than just an interactive study guide. WebTutor is an anytime, anywhere customized learning solution with an eBook, keeping you connected to your textbook, instructor, and classmates.

Aplia. If your professor has assigned Aplia homework:

1. Sign in to your account
2. Complete the corresponding homework exercises as required by your professor.
3. When finished, click "Grade It Now" to see which areas you have mastered, which need more work, and detailed explanations of every answer.

Visit **www.cengagebrain.com** to access your account and purchase materials.

6

Learning

© AP Photo/Phelan M. Ebenhack

Let's see if you can guess the answer to a riddle. What do the following scenarios have in common?

- In 1953 a Japanese researcher observed a young macaque (a type of monkey) on the island of Koshima washing a sweet potato in a stream before eating it. No one had ever seen a macaque do this before. Soon, other members of the monkey's troop were behaving the same way. Several generations later, macaques on Koshima still wash their potatoes before eating them (De Waal, 2001).
- In 2005 Wade Boggs was elected to baseball's Hall of Fame. Boggs was as renowned for his superstitions as he was for his great hitting. For 20 years, Boggs ate chicken every day of the year. Before games, he followed a strict set of rituals that included stepping on the bases in reverse order, running wind sprints at precisely 17 minutes past the hour, and tossing exactly three pebbles off the field. Every time he stepped up to hit during a game, he drew the Hebrew letter *chai* in the dirt with his bat. For Boggs, the slightest change in this routine was very upsetting (Gaddis, 1999; Vyse, 2000).

- Barn swallows in Minnesota built nests inside a Home Depot warehouse store, safe from the weather and from predators. So how do they get in and out to bring food to their chicks when the doors are closed? They flutter near the motion sensors that operate the doors until they open.
- A firefighter in Georgia routinely braves life-threatening situations to rescue people in distress. Yet the firefighter is paralyzed with fear whenever he sees someone dressed as a clown. He has been terrified of clowns ever since the third grade (Ryckeley, 2005).

What common thread runs through these diverse situations? What connects a superstitious ballplayer or a clown-phobic firefighter to potato-washing monkeys and door-opening swallows?

***Paradox:** The more parents try to suppress aggressive behavior with physical punishment, the more aggressive their children tend to be.*

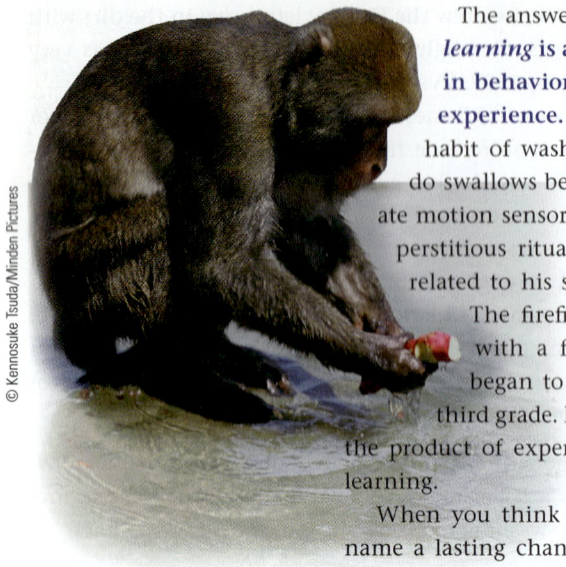

© Kennosuke Tsuda/Minden Pictures

The answer is *learning*. To a psychologist, ***learning* is any relatively durable change in behavior or knowledge that is due to experience.** Macaques aren't born with the habit of washing their sweet potatoes, nor do swallows begin life knowing how to operate motion sensors. Wade Boggs adopted his superstitious rituals because they seemed to be related to his successfully hitting a baseball. The firefighter in Georgia wasn't born with a fear of clowns, since he only began to be frightened of them in the third grade. In short, all these behaviors are the product of experience—that is, they represent learning.

When you think about it, it would be hard to name a lasting change in behavior that *is not* the result of experience. That's why learning is one of the most fundamental concepts in all of psychology. Learning shapes personal habits, such as nailbiting; personality traits, such as shyness; personal preferences, such as a distaste for formal clothes; and emotional responses, such as reactions to favorite songs. If all your learned responses could somehow be stripped away, little of your behavior would be left. You wouldn't be able to talk, read a book, or cook yourself a hamburger. You'd be about as complex and interesting as a turnip.

As the examples at the start of this chapter show, learning is not an exclusively human process. Learning is pervasive in the animal world as well, a fact that won't amaze anyone who's ever owned a dog or seen a trained seal in action. Another insight, however, is even more startling: *The principles that explain learned responses in animals explain much of human learning, too.* Thus, the same mechanisms that explain how barn swallows learn to operate an automated door can account for a professional athlete's bizarre superstitions. In fact, many of the most fascinating discoveries in the study of learning originated in studies of animals.

In this chapter, you'll see how fruitful the research into learning has been and how wide ranging its applications are. We'll focus most of our attention on a specific kind of learning: conditioning. *Conditioning* involves learning connections between events that occur in an organism's environment (eating chicken and having success hitting a baseball is one example). In researching conditioning, psychologists study learning at a fundamental level. This strategy has paid off with insights that have laid the foundation for the study of more complex forms of learning, such as learning by observation (the kind of learning that may account for the Koshima macaques picking up one monkey's habit of washing her sweet potatoes). In the Personal Application, you'll see how you can harness the principles of conditioning to improve your self-control. The Critical Thinking Application shows how conditioning procedures can be used to manipulate emotions.

KEY LEARNING GOALS

6.1 Describe Pavlov's demonstration of classical conditioning and the key elements in this form of learning.

6.2 Clarify how classical conditioning may shape emotions, physiological processes, and attitudes.

6.3 Describe acquisition, extinction, and spontaneous recovery in classical conditioning.

6.4 Compare the processes of generalization and discrimination, and review the classic study of Little Albert.

6.5 Explain what happens in higher-order conditioning.

Classical Conditioning

Do you go weak in the knees at the thought of standing on the roof of a tall building? Does your heart race when you imagine encountering a harmless garter snake? If so, you can understand, at least to some degree, what it's like to have a phobia. ***Phobias* are irrational fears of specific objects or situations.** Mild phobias are common. Over the years, students in my classes have described their phobic responses to a diverse array of stimuli, including bridges, elevators, tunnels, heights, dogs, cats, bugs, snakes, professors, doctors, strangers, thunderstorms, and germs. If you have a phobia, you may have wondered how you managed to acquire such a perplexing fear. Chances are, it was through classical conditioning (Antony & McCabe, 2003).

Classical conditioning* is a type of learning in which a stimulus acquires the capacity to evoke a response that was originally evoked by another stimulus.** The process was first described around 1900 by Ivan Pavlov, and it's sometimes called ***Pavlovian conditioning in tribute to him. The term *conditioning* came from Pavlov's determination to discover the "conditions" that produce this kind of learning. The learning process described by Pavlov was characterized as "classical" conditioning decades later (starting in the 1940s) to distinguish it from other types of conditioning that attracted research interest around then (Clark, 2004).

Pavlov's Demonstration: "Psychic Reflexes"

PSYKTREK 5a

Ivan Pavlov was a prominent Russian physiologist who did Nobel prize–winning research on digestion. He was an absentminded but brilliant professor obsessed with his research. Legend has it that Pavlov once reprimanded an assistant who was late for an experiment because of people fighting in the streets during the Russian Revolution. The assistant defended himself, saying, "But Professor, there's a revolution going on with shooting in the streets!" Pavlov supposedly replied, "What the hell difference does a revolution make when you've work to do in the laboratory? Next time there's a revolution, get up earlier!" Apparently, dodging bullets was no excuse for delaying the march of scientific progress (Fancher, 1979; Gantt, 1975).

Pavlov was studying the role of saliva in the digestive processes of dogs when he stumbled onto what he called "psychic reflexes" (Pavlov, 1906). Like many

© Bettmann/Corbis

Surrounded by his research staff, the great Russian physiologist Ivan Pavlov (center, white beard) demonstrates his famous classical conditioning experiment with dogs.

great discoveries, Pavlov's was partly accidental, although he had the insight to recognize its significance. His subjects were dogs restrained by harness in a chamber (see **Figure 6.1**). Their saliva was collected by a surgically implanted tube in the salivary gland. Pavlov would present meat powder to a dog and then collect the resulting saliva. As his research progressed, he noticed that dogs accustomed to the procedure would start salivating *before* the meat powder was presented. For instance, they would salivate in response to a clicking sound made by the device that was used to present the meat powder.

Intrigued by this unexpected finding, Pavlov decided to investigate further. He paired the presentation of the meat powder with various stimuli. In some experiments, he used a simple auditory stimulus—the presentation of a tone. After the tone and the meat powder had been presented together a number of times, the tone was presented alone. What happened? The dogs responded by salivating to the sound of the tone alone.

What was so significant about a dog salivating when a tone was presented? The key is that the tone had started out as a *neutral* stimulus. That is, it did not originally produce the response of salivation. However, Pavlov managed to change that by pairing the tone with a stimulus (meat powder) that *did*

© Bettmann/Corbis

Ivan Pavlov

"Next time there's a revolution, get up earlier!"

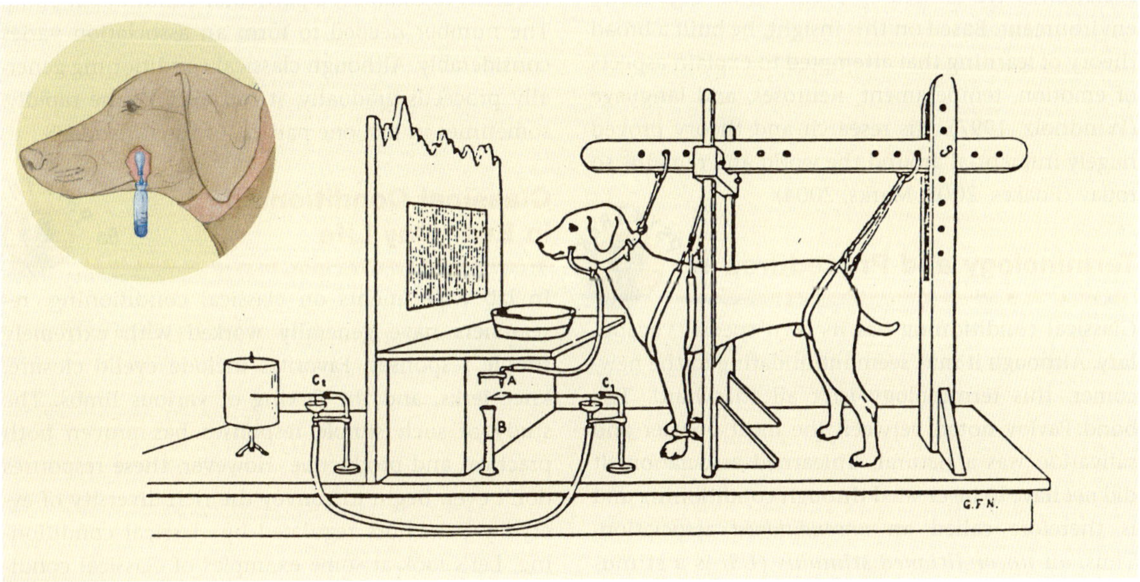

© Cengage Learning 2013

Figure 6.1

Classical conditioning apparatus. An experimental arrangement similar to the one depicted here (taken from Yerkes & Morgulis, 1909) has typically been used in demonstrations of classical conditioning, although Pavlov's original setup (see inset) was quite a bit simpler. The dog is restrained in a harness. A tone is used as the conditioned stimulus (CS), and the presentation of meat powder is used as the unconditioned stimulus (US). The tube inserted into the dog's salivary gland allows precise measurement of its salivation response. The pen and rotating drum of paper on the left are used to maintain a continuous record of salivary flow. **(Inset)** The less elaborate setup that Pavlov originally used to collect saliva on each trial is shown here (Goodwin, 1991).

SOURCE: Adapted from Yerkes, R. M., & Morgulis, S. (1909). The method of Pavlov in animal psychology. *Psychological Bulletin, 6,* 257–273. American Psychological Association. INSET SOURCE: From Goodwin, C. J. (1991). Misportraying Pavlov's apparatus. *American Journal of Psychology 104(1),* 135–141. © 1991 by the Board of Trustees of the University of Illinois.

Reality CHECK

Misconception

In Pavlov's demonstration of the conditioned reflex, the conditioned stimulus was the ringing of a bell.

Reality

The details of Pavlov's studies have been distorted over the years as the adjacent cartoon demonstrates. Pavlov did try using a bell as a CS, but in his classic 1906 article he reported that a bell was not a very effective stimulus because it tended to startle the dogs and disrupt their behavior (Goodwin, 1991). Pavlov used a variety of conditioned stimuli; the sound of a tone was the preferred auditory stimulus.

Drawing by John Chase, www.chasetoons.com

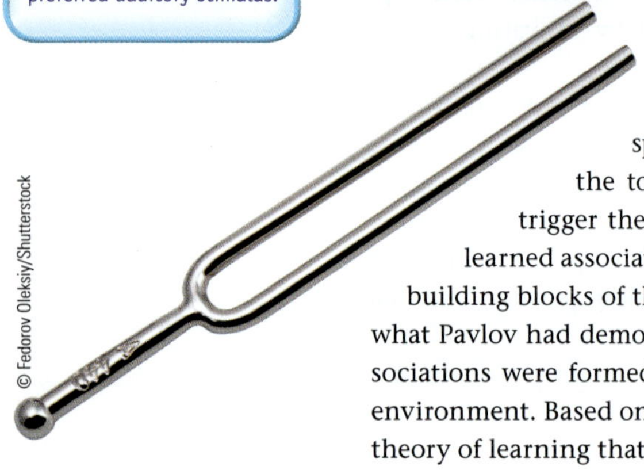

© Fedorov Oleksiy/Shutterstock

produce the salivation response. Through this process, the tone acquired the capacity to trigger the response of salivation. Such learned associations were viewed as the basic building blocks of the entire learning process. So what Pavlov had demonstrated was how learned associations were formed by events in an organism's environment. Based on this insight, he built a broad theory of learning that attempted to explain aspects of emotion, temperament, neuroses, and language (Windholz, 1997). His research and theory proved hugely influential around the world and remains so today (Boakes, 2003; Marks, 2004).

Terminology and Procedures 5a

Classical conditioning has its own special vocabulary. Although it may seem intimidating to the newcomer, this terminology isn't all that hard. The bond Pavlov noted between the meat powder and salivation was a natural, unlearned association. It did *not* have to be created through conditioning and is therefore called an *unconditioned* association. Thus, **an *unconditioned stimulus (US)* is a stimulus that evokes an unconditioned response without previous conditioning. An *unconditioned response (UR)* is an unlearned reaction to an unconditioned stimulus that occurs without previous conditioning.**

In contrast, the link between the tone and salivation was established through conditioning. It is therefore called a *conditioned* association. Thus, **a *conditioned stimulus (CS)* is a previously neutral stimulus that has, through conditioning, acquired the capacity to evoke a conditioned response. A *conditioned response (CR)* is a learned reaction to a conditioned stimulus that occurs because of previous conditioning.** In Pavlov's initial demonstration, the UR and CR were both salivation. When evoked by the US (meat powder), salivation was an unconditioned response. When evoked by the CS (the tone), salivation was a conditioned response. Although the unconditioned response and conditioned response sometimes consist of the same behavior, there usually are subtle differences between them. Conditioned responses often are weaker or less intense, and in some cases the UR and CR may be quite different, albeit closely related. For example, if an animal is given a brief shock as a US, the unconditioned response is *pain*, whereas the conditioned response is *fear* of imminent pain. In any event, the procedures involved in classical conditioning are outlined in **Figure 6.2**.

Pavlov's "psychic reflex" came to be called the *conditioned reflex*. Classically conditioned responses have traditionally been described as reflexes and are said to be ***elicited* (drawn forth)** because most of them are relatively automatic or involuntary. Finally, **a *trial* in classical conditioning consists of any presentation of a stimulus or pair of stimuli.** Psychologists are interested in how many trials are required to establish a particular conditioned bond. The number needed to form an association varies considerably. Although classical conditioning generally proceeds gradually, it *can* occur quite rapidly, sometimes in just one pairing of the CS and US.

Classical Conditioning in Everyday Life 5a

In lab experiments on classical conditioning, researchers have generally worked with extremely simple responses. Favorites include eyelid closure, knee jerks, and the flexing of various limbs. The study of such simple responses has proven both practical and productive. However, these responses don't even begin to convey the rich diversity of everyday behaviors regulated by classical conditioning. Let's look at some examples of classical conditioning taken from everyday life.

Conditioned Fear and Anxiety 5a

Classical conditioning often plays a key role in shaping emotional responses such as fears. Phobias are a good example of such responses. Case studies of patients suffering from phobias suggest that many irrational fears can be traced back to experiences that involve classical conditioning (Antony & McCabe, 2003; Muris & Mercklebach, 2001). It's easy to imagine how such conditioning can occur outside of the lab. For example, a student of mine troubled by a severe bridge phobia was able to pinpoint childhood conditioning experiences as the source of her phobia (see **Figure 6.3**). Whenever her family drove to visit her grandmother, they had to cross a rickety, old bridge in the countryside. Her father, in a misguided attempt at humor, would stop short of the bridge and carry on about the great danger. The young girl was terrified by her father's joke. Hence, the bridge became a conditioned stimulus eliciting great fear. The fear then spilled over to *all* bridges and 40 years later she was still troubled by this phobia.

Everyday fear responses that are less severe than phobias may also be products of classical conditioning. For instance, if you cringe when you hear the sound of a dentist's drill, this response is a result of classical conditioning. In this case, pain has been paired with the sound of the drill, which became a CS eliciting your cringe. That is *not* to say that traumatic experiences associated with stimuli *automatically* lead to conditioned fears or phobias. Whether fear conditioning takes place depends on many factors. Some people acquire conditioned fears less readily than others, probably because of differences in their genetic makeup (Hettema et al., 2003).

Other Conditioned Emotional Responses

PSYKTREK 5a

Classical conditioning is not limited to producing unpleasant emotions such as fear. Many pleasant emotional responses are also acquired through classical conditioning. Consider the following example, described by a woman who wrote a letter to a newspaper columnist about the news that a company was bringing back a discontinued product—Beemans gum. She wrote:

That was the year I met Charlie. I guess first love is always the same. . . . Charlie and I went out a lot. He chewed Beemans gum and he smoked. . . . We would go to all the passion pits—the drive-in movies and the places to park. We did a lot of necking. . . [but] Charlie and I drifted apart. We both ended up getting married to different people.

And the funny thing is . . . for years the combined smell of cigarette smoke and Beemans gum made my knees weak. Those two smells were Charlie to me. When I would smell the Beemans and the cigarette smoke, I could feel the butterflies dancing all over my stomach.

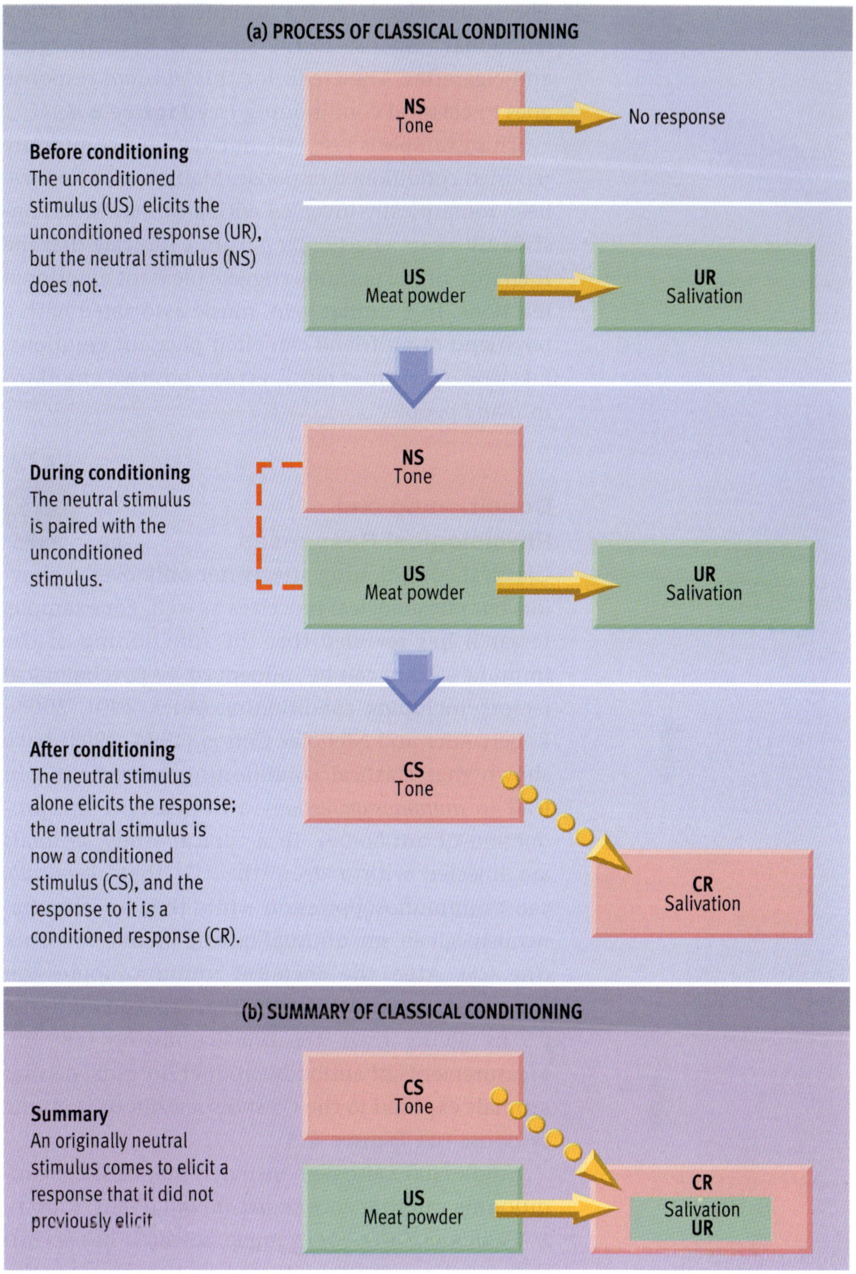

© Cengage Learning 2013

Figure 6.2

The sequence of events in classical conditioning. **(a)** Moving downward, this series of three panels outlines the sequence of events in classical conditioning, using Pavlov's original demonstration as an example. **(b)** As you encounter other examples of classical conditioning throughout the book, you will see many diagrams like the one in this panel, each providing snapshots of specific instances of classical conditioning.

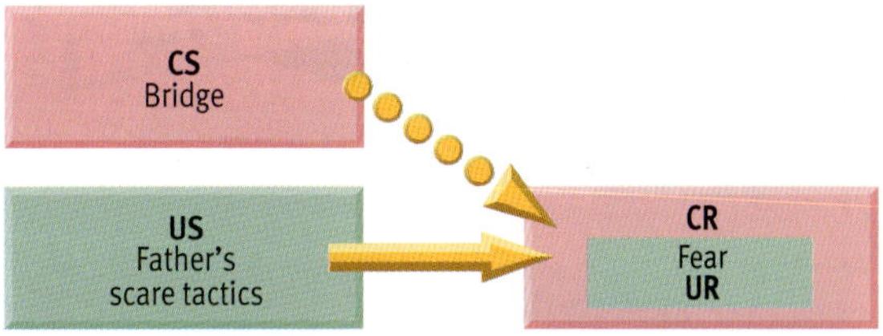

Figure 6.3

Classical conditioning of a fear response. Many emotional responses that would otherwise be puzzling can be explained by classical conditioning. In the case of one woman's bridge phobia, the fear originally elicited by her father's scare tactics became a conditioned response to the stimulus of bridges. © Cengage Learning 2013

The writer clearly had a unique and long-lasting emotional response to the smell of Beemans gum and cigarettes. The credit for this *pleasant* response goes to classical conditioning (see **Figure 6.4**).

This example is just a slight twist on a commonly reported conditioned response. Many men who have been romantically involved with a woman who consistently wears a particular perfume indicate that the fragrance of the perfume triggers pleasant emotional reactions. In a similar vein, music associated with a boyfriend or girlfriend can elicit pleasant emotions. Likewise, Christmas music evokes positive emotions in many people.

Conditioning and Physiological Responses

PSYKTREK 5a

Classical conditioning affects not only overt behaviors but physiological processes as well. For example, research has revealed that the functioning of the immune system can be influenced by psychological factors, including conditioning (Ader, 2001, 2003). Robert Ader and Nicholas Cohen (1984, 1993) have shown that classical conditioning procedures can lead to *immunosuppression*—a decrease in the production of antibodies. In a typical study, animals are injected with a drug (the US) that *chemically* causes immunosuppression while they are simultaneously given an unusual-tasting liquid to drink (the CS). After the chemical immunosuppression has ended, some of the animals are reexposed to the CS by giving them the unusual-tasting solution. Measurements of antibody production indicate that animals exposed to the CS show a reduced immune response (see **Figure 6.5**).

Studies have also demonstrated that classical conditioning can influence *sexual arousal* (Pfaus, Kippin, & Centeno, 2001). For example, research has shown that quail can be conditioned to become sexually aroused by a neutral, nonsexual stimulus—such as a

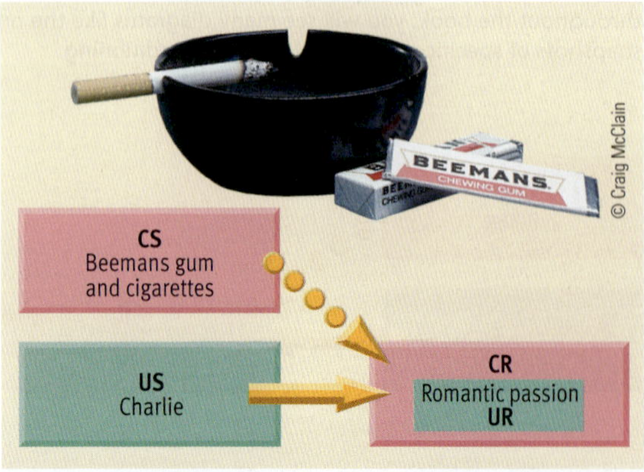

© Cengage Learning 2013

Figure 6.4
Classical conditioning and romance. Pleasant emotional responses can be acquired through classical conditioning, as illustrated by one person's unusual conditioned response to the aroma of Beemans gum and cigarette smoke.

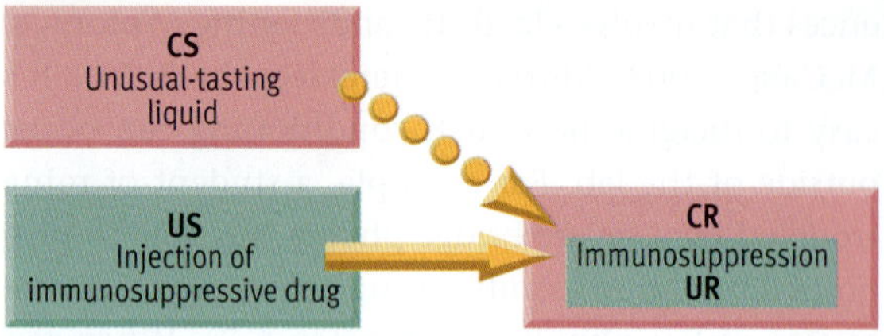

Figure 6.5
Classical conditioning of immunosuppression. When a neutral stimulus is paired with a drug that chemically causes immunosuppression, it can become a CS that elicits immunosuppression on its own. Thus, even the immune response can be influenced by classical conditioning.
© Cengage Learning 2013

red light—that has been paired with opportunities to copulate (Domjan, 1992, 1994). Conditioned stimuli can even elicit *increased sperm release* in male quail—a conditioned response that would convey an obvious evolutionary advantage (Domjan, Blesbois, & Williams, 1998). Researchers have also conditioned quail to develop sexual fetishes for inanimate objects (Cetinkaya & Domjan, 2006; Koksal et al., 2004). This line of animal research may shed light on aspects of human sexual interactions. Seductive lingerie, mood music, lit candles, and the like that are often paired with sexual relations probably become conditioned stimuli that elicit arousal (as you might guess, this hypothesis has been difficult to investigate with human subjects). Classical conditioning may also underlie the development of sexual fetishes in humans. If quail can be conditioned to find a red light arousing, it seems likely that humans may be conditioned to be aroused by objects such as shoes, boots, leather, and undergarments that may be paired with sexual relations.

Evaluative Conditioning of Attitudes

Pavlovian conditioning can also influence people's attitudes. In recent decades, researchers have shown great interest in a subtype of classical conditioning called *evaluative conditioning*. ***Evaluative conditioning* refers to changes in the liking of a stimulus that result from pairing that stimulus with other positive or negative stimuli.** In other words, evaluative conditioning involves the acquisition of likes and dislikes, or preferences, through classical conditioning. Typically, a neutral stimulus is paired with unconditioned stimuli that trigger positive reactions so that the neutral stimulus becomes a conditioned stimulus that elicits similar positive reactions. For example, in one recent study pleasant music paired with two unknown brands of root beer had significant effects on participants' liking for the root beers (Redker & Gibson, 2009). Another study showed that pairing an attractive face gazing directly at the viewer with various peppermint brands swayed subjects' brand preferences (Strick, Holland, & van Knippenberg, 2008). In another investigation, funny cartoons paired with two types of energy drinks increased participants' liking of the drinks (Strick et al., 2009; see **Figure 6.6**).

Obviously, advertising campaigns routinely try to take advantage of evaluative conditioning (see the Critical Thinking Application for this chapter). Advertisers often pair their products with US's that elicit pleasant emotions (Till & Priluck, 2000). The most common strategy is to present a product in association with an attractive person or enjoyable surroundings. Advertisers hope that these pairings will make their products conditioned stimuli that evoke good feelings. For example, automobile manufacturers like to show their sport utility vehicles in beautiful outdoor scenes that evoke pleasant feelings and nostalgic thoughts of past vacations.

A current source of debate is whether evaluative conditioning is a special (i.e., somewhat different) form of classical conditioning. Some studies suggest that attitudes can be shaped through evaluative conditioning without participants' conscious awareness (Olson & Fazio, 2001) and that evaluative conditioning is remarkably durable (Walther, Nagengast, & Trasselli, 2005). Other studies suggest that awareness is crucial to evaluative conditioning (Stahl, Unkelbach, & Corneille, 2009) and that it does not display exceptional durability (Lipp, Oughton, & LeLievre, 2003). Consensus on these issues does not appear to be on the horizon. Nonetheless, a great deal of empirical evidence attests to the fact that evaluative conditioning can shape people's attitudes (Hofmann et al., 2010).

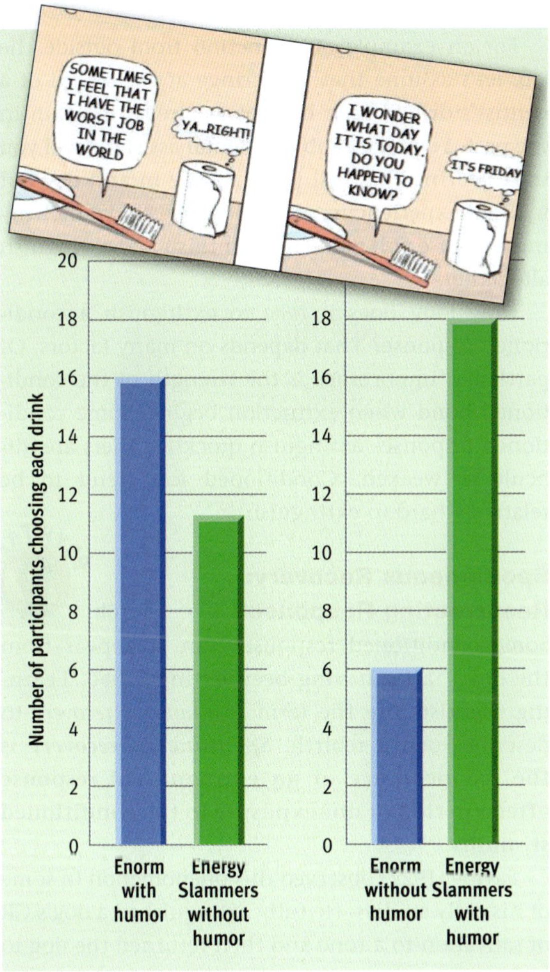

© Cengage Learning 2013

Figure 6.6

Evaluative conditioning with humor. In a study of evaluative conditioning, Strick et al. (2009) paired 10 humorous or nonhumorous cartoons with two energy drinks. The nonhumorous control cartoons were created by taking an amusing cartoon and changing the text so it was no longer funny (see example at top). Pairing the energy drinks with humor had a positive effect on participants' attitudes about the drinks. Moreoever, these positive attitudes influenced subjects' actual behavior when they later had a chance to consume one of the drinks. When the drink *Enorm* had been paired with humor, participants tended to prefer it, and when the drink *Energy Slammers* had been paired with humor, it was chosen far more often.

SOURCE: Adapted from Strick, M., van Baaren, R. B., Holland, R. W., & van Knippenberg, A. (2009). Humor in advertisements enhances product liking by mere association. *Journal of Experimental Psychology: Applied, 15*, 35–45. Figures 1 and 4. Copyright © 2009 American Psychological Association.

Basic Processes in Classical Conditioning

PSYKTREK 5b

Classical conditioning is often portrayed as a mechanical process that inevitably leads to a certain result. This view reflects the fact that most conditioned responses are reflexive and difficult to control—Pavlov's dogs would've been hard pressed to withhold their salivation. Similarly, most people with phobias have great difficulty suppressing their fear. However, this vision of classical conditioning as an "irresistible force" is misleading because it fails to consider the many factors involved in classical conditioning (Kehoe & Macrae, 1998). In this section, we'll look at basic processes in classical conditioning to expand on the rich complexity of this form of learning.

Acquisition: Forming New Responses

PSYKTREK 5b

We've already discussed *acquisition* without attaching a name to the process. ***Acquisition* refers to the initial stage of learning something.** Pavlov theorized that the acquisition of a conditioned response depends on *stimulus contiguity*, or the occurrence of stimuli together in time and space.

Stimulus contiguity is important, but learning theorists now realize that contiguity alone doesn't automatically produce conditioning (Miller & Grace, 2003). People are bombarded daily by countless stimuli that could be perceived as being paired, yet only some of these pairings produce classical conditioning. Consider the woman who developed a conditioned emotional reaction to the smell of Beemans gum and cigarettes. There were no doubt other stimuli that shared contiguity with her boyfriend, Charlie. He smoked, so ashtrays were probably present, but she doesn't get weak in the knees at the sight of an ashtray.

If conditioning does not occur to all the stimuli present in a situation, what determines its occurrence? Evidence suggests that stimuli that are new, unusual, or especially intense have more potential to become CSs than routine stimuli, probably because they are more likely to stand out among other stimuli (Hearst, 1988).

Extinction: Weakening Conditioned Responses

5b

Fortunately, a newly formed stimulus-response bond does not necessarily last indefinitely. If it did, learning would be inflexible, and organisms would have difficulty adapting to new situations. Instead, the right circumstances produce ***extinction*, the gradual weakening and disappearance of a conditioned response tendency.**

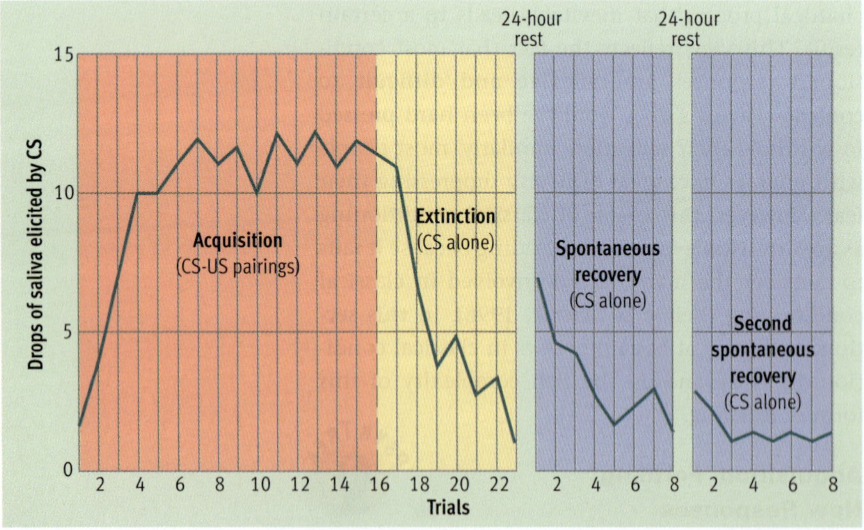

© Cengage Learning 2013

Figure 6.7

Acquisition, extinction, and spontaneous recovery. During acquisition, the strength of the dog's conditioned response (measured by the amount of salivation) increases rapidly, then levels off near its maximum. During extinction, the CR declines erratically until it's extinguished. After a "rest" period in which the dog is not exposed to the CS, a spontaneous recovery occurs, and the CS once again elicits a (weakened) CR. Repeated presentations of the CS alone reextinguish the CR, but after another "rest" interval, a weaker spontaneous recovery occurs.

Extinction occurs in classical conditioning when the conditioned stimulus is consistently presented *alone,* without the unconditioned stimulus. For example, when Pavlov consistently presented *only* the tone to a previously conditioned dog, the tone gradually lost its capacity to elicit the response of salivation. Such a sequence of events is depicted in the tan portion of **Figure 6.7**, which graphs the amount of salivation by a dog over a series of conditioning trials. Note how the salivation response declines during extinction.

For an example of extinction from outside the lab, let's assume that you cringe at the sound of a dentist's drill, which has been paired with pain in the past. You take a job as a dental assistant and you start hearing the drill (the CS) day in and day out without experiencing any pain (the US). Your cringing response will gradually diminish and extinguish altogether.

How long does it take to extinguish a conditioned response? That depends on many factors. Of particular importance is the strength of the conditioned bond when extinction begins. Some conditioned responses extinguish quickly; others are difficult to weaken. Conditioned *fears* tend to be relatively hard to extinguish.

Spontaneous Recovery: Resurrecting Responses

5b

Some conditioned responses can "reappear from the dead" after having been extinguished. Learning theorists use the term *spontaneous recovery* to describe such a rebirth. ***Spontaneous recovery* is the reappearance of an extinguished response after a period of nonexposure to the conditioned stimulus.**

Pavlov (1927) observed this phenomenon in some of his early studies. He fully extinguished a dog's CR of salivation to a tone and then returned the dog to its home cage for a "rest interval" (a period of nonexposure to the CS). At a later date, when the dog was brought back to the chamber for retesting, the tone was sounded and the salivation response reappeared. Although the response had returned, the amount of salivation was less than it had been at its peak strength. If Pavlov consistently presented the CS by itself again, the response reextinguished quickly. However, in some of the dogs, the response made still another spontaneous recovery (typically even weaker than the first) after they had spent another period in their cages (see **Figure 6.7** once again).

More recent studies have uncovered a related phenomenon called the ***renewal effect*—if a response is extinguished in a different environment than**

where it was acquired, the extinguished response will reappear if the animal is returned to the original environment where acquisition took place. This phenomenon, along with the evidence on spontaneous recovery, suggests that extinction somehow *suppresses* a conditioned response rather than *erasing* a learned association. In other words, *extinction does not appear to lead to unlearning* (Bouton & Woods, 2009). The theoretical meaning of spontaneous recovery and the renewal effect is complex and the subject of some debate. However, their practical meaning is quite simple. Even if you manage to rid yourself of an unwanted conditioned response (such as cringing when you hear a dental drill), there is an excellent chance that it may make a surprise reappearance later. This reality may also help explain why people who manage to give up cigarettes, drugs, or poor eating habits for a while often relapse and return to their unhealthy habits (Bouton, 2000, 2002). The renewal effect is also one of the reasons that conditioned fears and phobias are difficult to extinguish permanently (Hermans et al., 2006).

Stimulus Generalization and the Case of Little Albert

PSYKTREK 5b

After conditioning has occurred, organisms often show a tendency to respond not only to the exact CS used but also to other, similar stimuli. For example, Pavlov's dogs might have salivated in response to a different-sounding tone, or you might cringe at the sound of a jeweler's as well as a dentist's drill. These are examples of stimulus generalization. ***Stimulus generalization*** **occurs when an organism that has learned a response to a specific stimulus responds in the same way to new stimuli that are similar to the original stimulus.** Generalization is adaptive given that organisms rarely encounter the exact same stimulus more than once (Thomas, 1992). Stimulus generalization is also commonplace. We have already discussed a real-life example: the woman who acquired a bridge phobia during her childhood because her father scared her whenever they went over a particular old bridge. The original CS for her fear was that specific bridge, but her fear was ultimately *generalized* to all bridges.

John B. Watson, the founder of behaviorism (see Chapter 1), conducted an influential early study of generalization. Watson and a colleague, Rosalie Rayner, examined the generalization of conditioned fear in an 11-month-old boy, known in the annals of psychology as "Little Albert." Like many babies, Albert was initially unafraid of a live white rat. Then Watson and Rayner (1920) paired the presentation of the rat with a loud, startling sound (made by striking a steel gong with a hammer). Albert *did* show fear in response to the loud noise. After seven pairings of the rat and the gong, the rat was established as a CS eliciting a fear response (see **Figure 6.8**). Five days later, Watson and Rayner

CONCEPT CHECK 6.1

Identifying Elements in Classical Conditioning

Check your understanding of classical conditioning by trying to identify the unconditioned stimulus (US), unconditioned response (UR), conditioned stimulus (CS), and conditioned response (CR) in each of the examples below. Fill in the diagram next to each example. You'll find the answers in Appendix A in the back of the book.

1. Sam is 3 years old. One night his parents build a roaring fire in the family room fireplace. The fire spits out a large ember that hits Sam in the arm, giving him a nasty burn that hurts a great deal for several hours. A week later, when Sam's parents light another fire in the fireplace, Sam becomes upset and fearful, crying and running from the room.

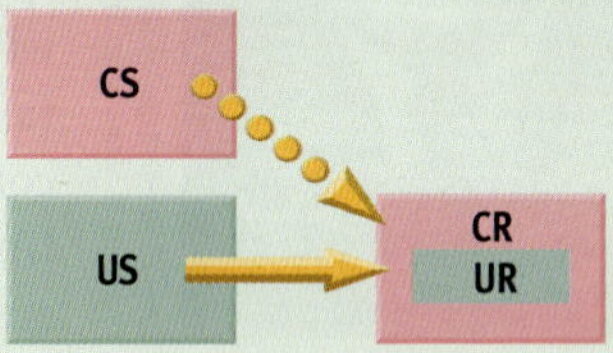

2. Melanie is driving to work on a rainy highway when she notices that the brake lights of all the cars just ahead of her have come on. She hits her brakes but watches in horror as her car glides into a four-car pileup. She's badly shaken up in the accident. A month later she's driving in the rain again and notices that she tenses up every time she sees brake lights come on ahead of her.

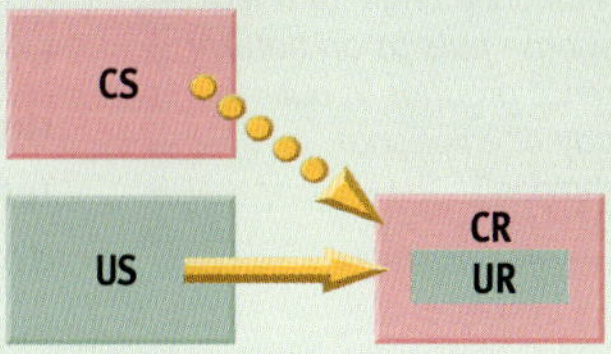

3. At the age of 24, Tyrone has recently developed an allergy to cats. When he's in the same room with a cat for more than 30 minutes, he starts wheezing. After a few such allergic reactions, he starts wheezing as soon as he sees a cat in a room.

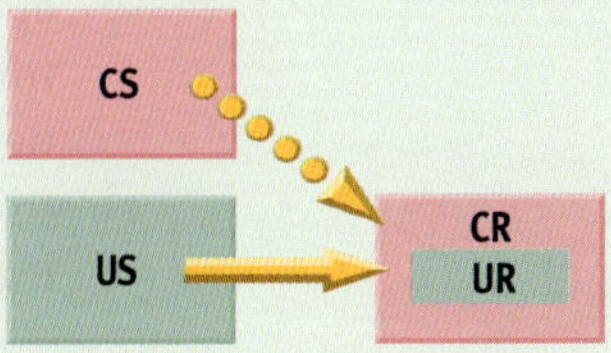

© Cengage Learning 2013

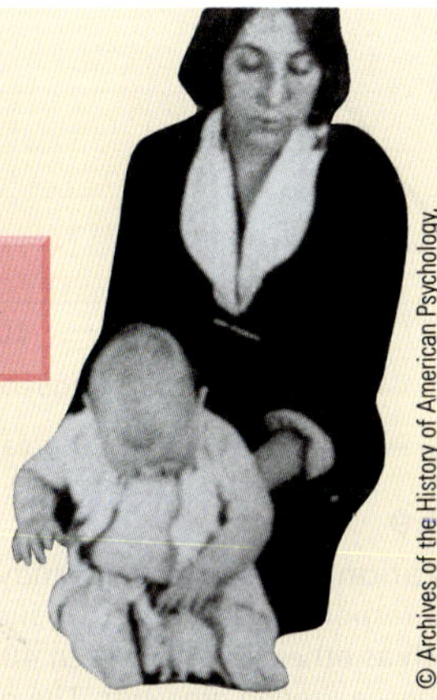

Figure 6.8

The conditioning of Little Albert. The diagram shows how Little Albert's fear response to a white rat was established. Albert's fear response to other white, furry objects illustrates generalization. In the photo, made from a 1919 film, John B. Watson's collaborator, Rosalie Rayner, is shown with Little Albert before he was conditioned to fear the rat.

© Archives of the History of American Psychology, University of Akron, Akron, Ohio

© Cengage Learning 2013

Archives of the History of American Psychology, University of Akron, Akron, Ohio

John B. Watson

"Surely this proof of the conditioned origin of a fear response puts us on natural science grounds in our study of emotional behavior."

exposed the youngster to other stimuli that resembled the rat in being white and furry. They found that Albert's fear response generalized to a variety of stimuli, including a rabbit, a dog, a fur coat, a Santa Claus mask, and Watson's hair.

What happened to Little Albert? Did he grow up with a phobia of Santa Claus? There was endless speculation for decades because no one had any idea who Albert was or what happened to him. He was taken from the hospital where Watson and Rayner conducted their study before they got around to extinguishing the conditioned fears that they had created, and he was never heard of again. Watson and Rayner were roundly criticized in later years for failing to ensure that Albert experienced no lasting ill effects. Their failure to do so clearly was remiss by today's much stricter code of research ethics, but normal for the time. Recently, after 90 years of mystery, a team of history sleuths managed to track down Little Albert's identity and explain why he vanished into thin air (Beck, Levinson, & Irons, 2009). It appears that his real name was Douglas Merritte, the son of a wet nurse who worked near Watson's lab. Sadly, he had a very brief life, perishing at the age of 6 from acquired hydrocephalus. Little information is available on his short life, so we will never know whether he experienced any ill effects from his participation in one of psychology's most legendary studies.

The likelihood and amount of generalization to a new stimulus depend on the similarity between the new stimulus and the original CS (Balsam, 1988). The basic law governing generalization is this: *The more similar new stimuli are to the original CS, the greater the generalization.* This principle can be quantified in graphs called *generalization gradients,* such as those shown in **Figure 6.9**. These generalization gradients map out how a dog conditioned to salivate to a tone of 1200 hertz might respond to other tones. As you can see, the strength of the generalization response declines as the similarity between the new stimuli and the original CS decreases.

The process of generalization can have important implications. For example, it appears to contribute to the development of *panic disorder,* which involves recurrent, overwhelming anxiety attacks that occur suddenly and unexpectedly (see Chapter 15). Recent research suggests that panic patients have a tendency to overgeneralize—that is, to have broader generalization gradients than control subjects—when exposed to stimuli that trigger anxiety (Lissek et al., 2010). Thus, conditioned fear to a stimulus environment where panic occurs (say, a specific shopping mall) readily generalizes to similar stimulus situations (all shopping malls), fueling the growth of patients' panic disorder.

Stimulus Discrimination

PsykTrek 5b

Stimulus discrimination is just the opposite of stimulus generalization. ***Stimulus discrimination* occurs when an organism that has learned a response to a specific stimulus does *not* respond in the same way to new stimuli that are similar to the original stimulus.** Like generalization, discrimination is adaptive in that an animal's survival may hinge on its being able to distinguish friend from foe, or edible from poisonous food (Thomas, 1992). Organisms can gradually learn to discriminate between an original CS and similar stimuli if they have adequate experience with both. For instance, let's say your pet dog runs around, excitedly wagging its tail, whenever it hears your car pull up in the driveway. Initially it will probably respond to *all* cars that pull into the driveway (stimulus generalization). However, if there is anything distinctive about the sound of your car, your dog may gradually respond with excitement to only your car and not to other cars (stimulus discrimination).

The development of stimulus discrimination usually requires that the original CS (your car) continue to be paired with the US (your arrival) and that similar stimuli (the other cars) not be paired with the US. As with generalization, a basic law gov-

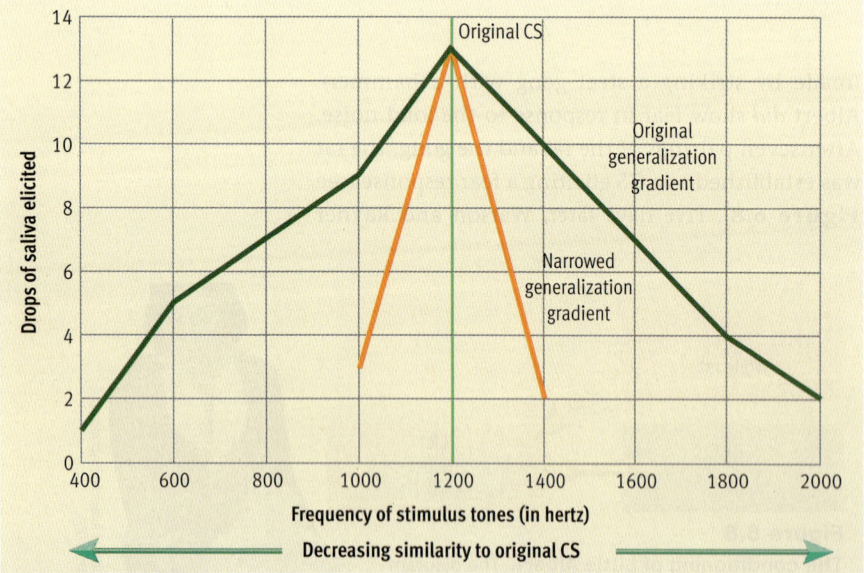

© Cengage Learning 2013

Figure 6.9

Generalization gradients. In a study of stimulus generalization, an organism is typically conditioned to respond to a specific CS, such as a 1200-hertz tone, and then is tested with similar stimuli, such as other tones between 400 and 2000 hertz. Graphs of the organism's responding are called *generalization gradients.* The graphs normally show, as depicted here, that generalization declines as the similarity between the original CS and the new stimuli decreases. When an organism gradually learns to *discriminate* between a CS and similar stimuli, the generalization gradient tends to narrow around the original CS (as shown in orange).

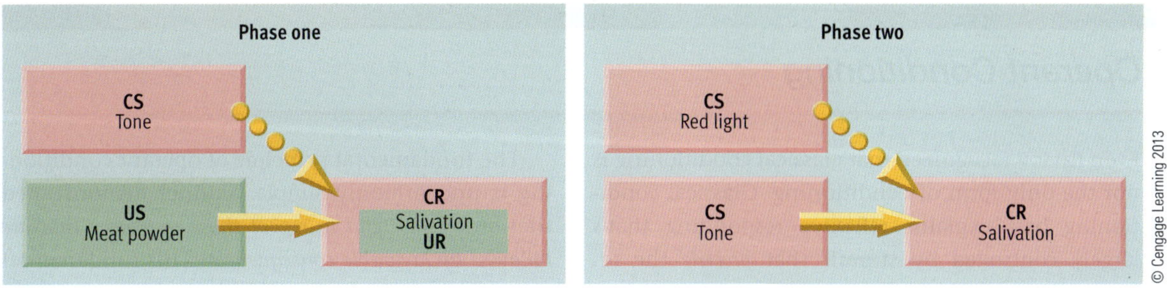

Figure 6.10

Higher-order conditioning. Higher-order conditioning involves a two-phase process. In the first phase, a neutral stimulus (such as a tone) is paired with an unconditioned stimulus (such as meat powder) until it becomes a conditioned stimulus that elicits the response originally evoked by the US (such as salivation). In the second phase, another neutral stimulus (such as a red light) is paired with the previously established CS, so that it also acquires the capacity to elicit the response originally evoked by the US.

erns discrimination: *The less similar new stimuli are to the original CS, the greater the likelihood (and ease) of discrimination.* Conversely, if a new stimulus is quite similar to the original CS, discrimination will be relatively hard to learn. What happens to a generalization gradient when an organism learns a discrimination? It gradually narrows around the original CS, which means that the organism is generalizing to a smaller and smaller range of similar stimuli (consult **Figure 6.9** again).

Higher-Order Conditioning

PSYKTREK 5b

Imagine that you were to conduct the following experiment. First, you condition a dog to salivate in response to the sound of a tone by pairing the tone with meat powder. Once the tone is firmly established as a CS, you pair the tone with a new stimulus, let's say a red light, for 15 trials. You then present the red light alone, without the tone. Will the dog salivate in response to the red light?

The answer is "yes." Even though the red light has never been paired with the meat powder, the light will acquire the capacity to elicit salivation by virtue of being paired with the tone (see **Figure 6.10**). This is a demonstration of ***higher-order conditioning,* in which a conditioned stimulus functions as if it were an unconditioned stimulus.** Higher-order conditioning shows that classical conditioning does not depend on the presence of a genuine, natural US. An already established CS can do just fine. In higher-order conditioning, new conditioned responses are built on the foundation of already established conditioned responses. Many human conditioned responses are the product of higher-order conditioning (Rescorla, 1980). For example, many drivers react to the sight of a police car with a surge of anxiety, even if they are going under the speed limit. This reflexive response is an example of higher-order conditioning. The visual stimulus of a police car has probably been paired with a traffic ticket in the past. The traffic ticket is a previously established CS.

REVIEW OF KEY LEARNING GOALS

6.1 Classical conditioning explains how a neutral stimulus can acquire the capacity to elicit a response originally elicited by another stimulus. This kind of conditioning was originally described by Ivan Pavlov, who conditioned dogs to salivate in response to the sound of a tone. The key elements in classical conditioning are the unconditioned stimulus (US), the unconditioned response (UR), the conditioned stimulus (CS), and the conditioned response (CR). Classically conditioned responses are said to be elicited.

6.2 Many kinds of everyday responses are regulated through classical conditioning, including phobias, mild fears, and pleasant emotional responses. Even physiological responses such as immune system functioning and sexual arousal respond to classical conditioning. Evaluative conditioning is a type of Pavlovian conditioning that can influence attitudes.

6.3 Stimulus contiguity plays a key role in the acquisition of new conditioned responses, but it does not produce conditioning automatically. A conditioned response may be weakened and extinguished when the CS is no longer paired with the US. In some cases, spontaneous recovery or the renewal effect occurs and an extinguished response reappears.

6.4 Conditioning may generalize to additional stimuli that are similar to the original CS. Watson and Rayner conducted an influential early study of generalization with a subject known as Little Albert, whose fear response to a rat generalized to a variety of other white, furry objects. The opposite of generalization is discrimination, which involves not responding to stimuli that resemble the original CS.

6.5 Classical conditioning does not require a genuine unconditioned stimulus, as an already established CS can serve the same role. Higher-order conditioning occurs when a CS functions as if it were a US.

KEY LEARNING GOALS

6.6 Explain Skinner's principle of reinforcement, and describe the terminology and procedures in operant research.

6.7 Describe shaping, extinction, generalization, and discrimination in operant conditioning.

6.8 Identify various types of schedules of reinforcement, and discuss their typical effects.

6.9 Distinguish between positive and negative reinforcement, and differentiate escape learning from avoidance learning.

6.10 Describe punishment, and assess issues related to punishment as a disciplinary procedure.

Operant Conditioning

Even Pavlov recognized that classical conditioning is not the only form of conditioning. Classical conditioning best explains reflexive responding that's largely controlled by stimuli that *precede* the response. However, humans and other animals make a great many responses that don't fit this description. Consider the response that you are engaging in right now: studying. It's definitely not a reflex (life might be easier if it were). The stimuli that govern it (exams and grades) do not precede it. Instead, your studying is mainly influenced by stimulus events that *follow* the response—specifically, its *consequences*.

In the 1930s, this kind of learning was named *operant conditioning* by B. F. Skinner. The term was derived from his belief that in this type of responding, an organism "operates" on the environment instead of simply reacting to stimuli. Learning occurs because responses come to be influenced by the outcomes that follow them. Thus, ***operant conditioning* is a form of learning in which responses come to be controlled by their consequences.** Learning theorists originally distinguished between classical and operant conditioning as two separate forms of learning on the grounds that *classical conditioning regulated reflexive, involuntary responses, whereas operant conditioning governed voluntary responses*. This distinction holds up much of the time, but it's not absolute (Allan, 1998; Turkkan, 1989). Some theorists argue that classical and operant conditioning should be viewed as two different aspects of a single learning process (Donahoe & Vegas, 2004).

Skinner's Demonstration: It's All a Matter of Consequences

PSYKTREK 5c

B. F. Skinner had great admiration for Pavlov's work (Catania & Laties, 1999) and used it as the foundation for his own theory, even borrowing some of Pavlov's terminology (Dinsmoor, 2004). And, like Pavlov, Skinner (1953, 1969, 1984) conducted some deceptively simple research that became very influential (Lattal, 1992). He got off to a rough start, however. His first book, *The Behavior of Organisms* (1938), sold only 80 copies in its first four years in print. But he went on to become, in the words of historian Albert Gilgen (1982), "without question the most famous American psychologist in the world" (p. 97).

© AP Images

B. F. Skinner

"Operant conditioning shapes behavior as a sculptor shapes a lump of clay."

The fundamental principle of operant conditioning is uncommonly simple. Skinner demonstrated that *organisms tend to repeat those responses that are followed by favorable consequences*. This fundamental principle is embodied in Skinner's concept of reinforcement. ***Reinforcement* occurs when an event following a response increases an organism's tendency to make that response.** In other words, a response is strengthened because it leads to rewarding consequences (see **Figure 6.11**).

The principle of reinforcement may be simple, but it's immensely powerful. Skinner and his followers have shown that much of everyday behavior is regulated by reinforcement. For example, you put money in a soda vending machine and get a soft drink back as a result. You go to work because this behavior leads to your receiving paychecks. You tell jokes, and your friends laugh—so you tell some more. The principle of reinforcement clearly governs complex aspects of human behavior.

Please note, reinforcement is defined *after the fact,* in terms of its *effect* on behavior (strengthening a response). Something that is clearly reinforcing for an organism at one time may not function as a reinforcer later (Catania, 1992). For example, food may not be reinforcing if an organism is not hungry. Similarly, something that serves as a reinforcer for one person may not function as a reinforcer for another person. For instance, parental approval is a potent reinforcer for most children, but not all. To know whether an event is reinforcing, researchers must make it contingent on a response and observe whether the rate of this response increases.

"Mommy, we keep saying 'go home, kitty-cat' -- but she just keeps hanging around here!"

Family Circus © 1971 Bill Keane, Inc. King Features Syndicate.

Terminology and Procedures

PsykTrek 5c

Like Pavlov, Skinner created a prototype experimental procedure that has been repeated (with variations) thousands of times. In this procedure, an animal, typically a rat or a pigeon, is placed in an *operant chamber* that has come to be better known as a "Skinner box" (much to Skinner's chagrin). **An *operant chamber,* or *Skinner box,* is a small enclosure in which an animal can make a specific response that is recorded while the consequences of the response are systematically controlled.** In the boxes designed for rats, the main response made available is pressing a small lever mounted on one side wall (see **Figure 6.12**). In the boxes made for pigeons, the designated response is pecking a small disk mounted on a side wall. Because operant responses tend to be voluntary, they are said to be *emitted* rather than *elicited.* **To *emit* means to send forth.**

The Skinner box permits the experimenter to control the reinforcement contingencies that are in effect for the animal. ***Reinforcement contingencies***

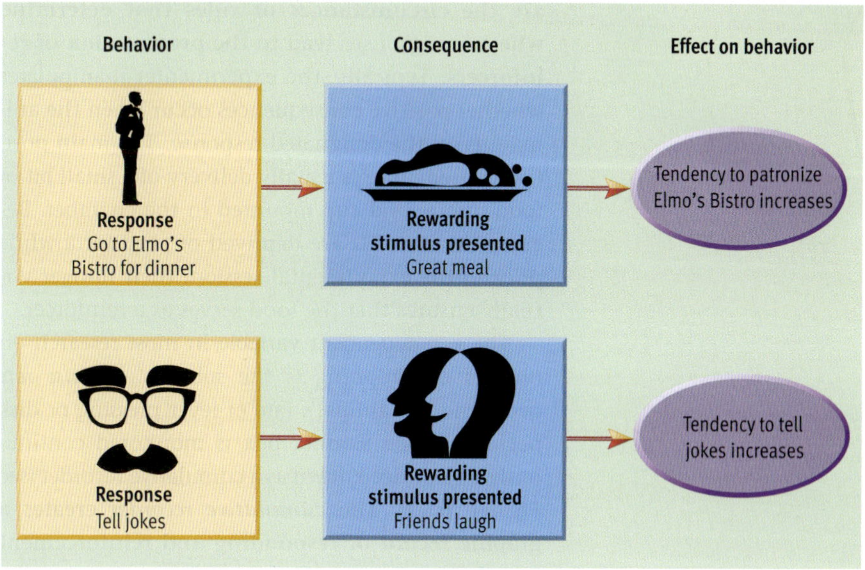

© Cengage Learning 2013

Figure 6.11

Reinforcement in operant conditioning. According to Skinner, reinforcement occurs when a response is followed by rewarding consequences and the organism's tendency to make the response increases. The two examples diagrammed here illustrate the basic premise of operant conditioning—that voluntary behavior is controlled by its consequences. These examples involve positive reinforcement (for a comparison of positive and negative reinforcement, see **Figure 6.18**).

Figure 6.12

Skinner box and cumulative recorder. **(a)** This diagram highlights some of the key features of an operant chamber, or Skinner box. In this apparatus designed for rats, the response under study is lever pressing. Food pellets, which may serve as reinforcers, are delivered into the food cup on the right. The speaker and light permit manipulations of auditory and visual stimuli, and the electric grid gives the experimenter control over aversive consequences (shock) in the box. **(b)** A cumulative recorder connected to the box keeps a continuous record of responses and reinforcements. A small segment of a cumulative record is shown here. The entire process is automatic as the paper moves with the passage of time; each lever press moves the pen up a step, and each reinforcement is marked with a slash. **(c)** This photo shows the real thing—a rat being conditioned in a Skinner box. Note the food dispenser on the right, which was omitted from the diagram.

© Cengage Learning 2013

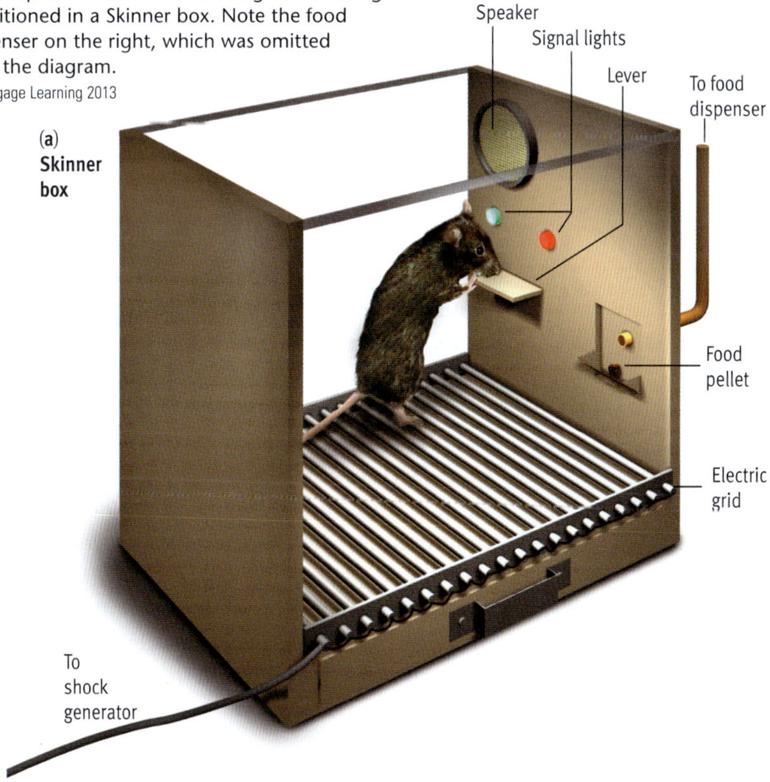

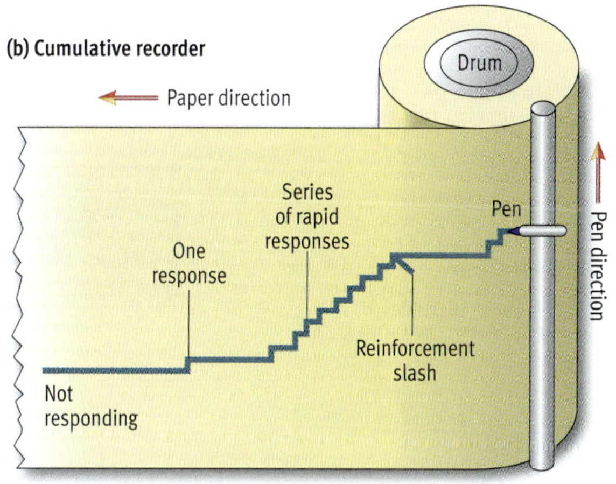

(c)

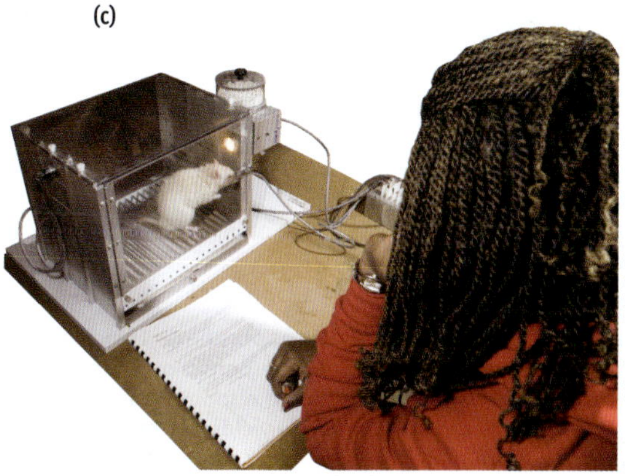

Courtesy of Professor Rick Stalling and Bradley University. Photo by Duane Zehr.

are the circumstances or rules that determine whether responses lead to the presentation of reinforcers. Typically, the experimenter manipulates whether positive consequences occur when the animal makes the designated response. The main positive consequence is usually delivery of a small bit of food into a food cup mounted in the chamber. Because the animals are deprived of food for a while prior to the experimental session, their hunger virtually ensures that the food serves as a reinforcer.

The key dependent variable in most research on operant conditioning is the subjects' *response rate* over time. An animal's rate of lever pressing or disk pecking in the Skinner box is monitored continuously by a device known as a cumulative recorder (see **Figure 6.12**). **The *cumulative recorder* creates a graphic record of responding and reinforcement in a Skinner box as a function of time.** The recorder works by means of a roll of paper that moves at a steady rate underneath a movable pen. When there is no responding, the pen stays still and draws a straight horizontal line, reflecting the passage of time. Whenever the designated response occurs, however, the pen moves upward a notch. The pen's movements produce a graphic summary of the animal's responding over time. The pen also makes slash marks to record the delivery of each reinforcer.

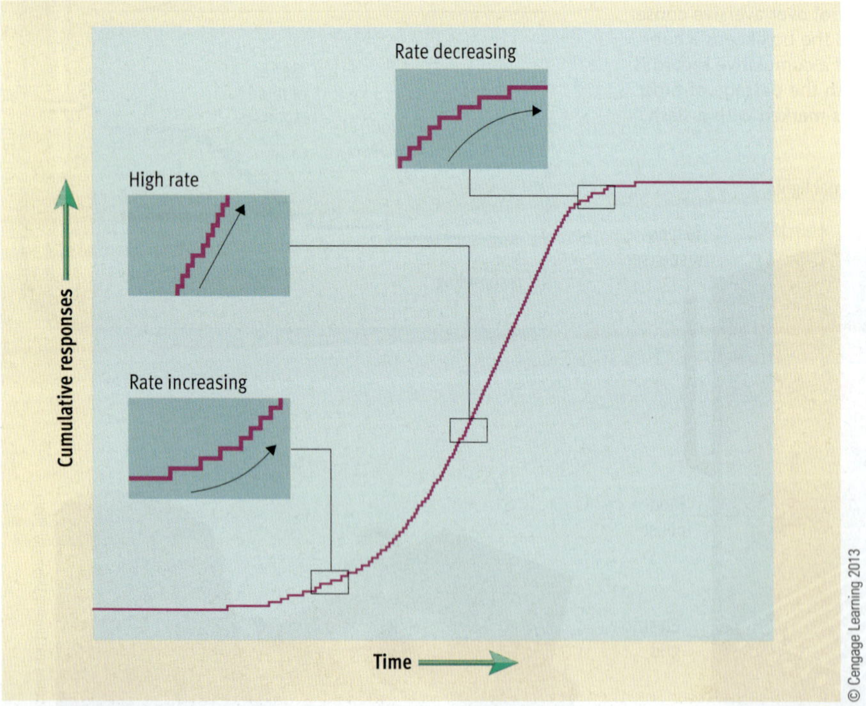

Figure 6.13
A graphic portrayal of operant responding. The results of operant conditioning are often summarized in a graph of cumulative responses over time. The insets magnify small segments of the curve to show how an increasing response rate yields a progressively steeper slope (bottom); a high, steady response rate yields a steep, stable slope (middle); and a decreasing response rate yields a progressively flatter slope (top).

The results of operant-conditioning studies are usually portrayed in graphs. In these graphs, the horizontal axis is used to mark the passage of time, while the vertical axis is used to plot the accumulation of responses, as shown in **Figure 6.13**. In interpreting these graphs, the key consideration is the *slope* of the line that represents the record of responding. *A rapid response rate produces a steep slope, whereas a slow response rate produces a shallow slope.* Because the response record is cumulative, the line never goes down. It can only go up as more responses are made or flatten out if the response rate slows to zero. The magnifications shown in **Figure 6.13** show how slope and response rate are related.

Operant theorists make a distinction between unlearned, or primary, reinforcers as opposed to conditioned, or secondary, reinforcers. ***Primary reinforcers* are events that are inherently reinforcing because they satisfy biological needs.** A given species has a limited number of primary reinforcers because they are closely tied to physiological needs. In humans, primary reinforcers include food, water, warmth, sex, and perhaps affection expressed through hugging and close bodily contact. ***Secondary, or conditioned, reinforcers* are events that acquire reinforcing qualities by being associated with primary reinforcers.** The events that function as secondary reinforcers vary among members of a species because they depend on learning. Examples of common secondary reinforcers in humans include money, good grades, attention, flattery, praise, and applause. Similarly, people *learn* to find stylish clothes, sports cars, fine jewelry, and exotic vacations reinforcing.

Basic Processes in Operant Conditioning SIM4, 5c

Although the principle of reinforcement is strikingly simple, many other processes involved in operant conditioning make this form of learning just as complex as classical conditioning. In fact, some of the *same* processes are involved in both types of conditioning. In this section, we'll discuss how the processes of acquisition, extinction, generalization, and discrimination occur in operant conditioning.

Acquisition and Shaping SIM4, 5c

As in classical conditioning, *acquisition* in operant conditioning refers to the initial stage of learning some new pattern of responding. However, the procedures used to create an operant response are different from those used to create the typical conditioned response. Operant responses are usually established through a gradual process called

***shaping,* which consists of repeatedly reinforcing closer and closer approximations of a desired response until the desired response is achieved.**

Shaping is necessary when an organism does not, on its own, emit the desired response. For example, when a rat is first placed in a Skinner box, it may not press the lever at all. In this case, an experimenter begins shaping by releasing food pellets whenever the rat moves toward the lever. As this response becomes more frequent, the experimenter starts requiring a closer approximation of the desired response, possibly releasing food only when the rat actually touches the lever. As reinforcement increases the rat's tendency to touch the lever, the rat will spontaneously press the lever on occasion, finally providing the experimenter with an opportunity to reinforce the designated response. These reinforcements will gradually increase the rate of lever pressing.

The mechanism of shaping is the key to training animals to perform impressive tricks. When you go to a zoo, circus, or marine park and see bears riding bicycles, monkeys playing the piano, and whales leaping through hoops, you are witnessing the results of shaping. To demonstrate the power of shaping techniques, Skinner once trained some pigeons so that they appeared to play a crude version of Ping-Pong. They would run about at opposite ends of a tiny Ping-Pong table and peck the ball back and forth. Keller and Marian Breland, a couple of psychologists influenced by Skinner, went into the business of training animals for advertising and entertainment purposes. One of their better known feats was shaping "Priscilla, the Fastidious Pig" to turn on a radio, eat at a kitchen table, put dirty clothes in a hamper, run a vacuum, and then "go shopping" with a shopping cart. Of course, Priscilla picked the sponsor's product off the shelf in her shopping expedition (Breland & Breland, 1961).

Extinction

PSYKTREK SIM4, 5c

In operant conditioning, *extinction* refers to the gradual weakening and disappearance of a response tendency because the response is no longer followed by reinforcers. Extinction begins in operant conditioning whenever previously available reinforcement is stopped. In lab studies with rats, this usually means that the experimenter stops delivering food when the rat presses the lever. When the extinction process is begun, a brief surge often occurs in the rat's responding, followed by a gradual decline in response rate until it approaches zero. The same effects are generally seen in the extinction of human behaviors.

A key issue in operant conditioning is how much *resistance to extinction* an organism will display when reinforcement is stopped. ***Resistance to extinction* occurs when an organism continues to make a response after delivery of the reinforcer has been terminated.** The greater the resistance to extinction, the longer the responding will continue. People often want to strengthen a response in such a way that it will be relatively resistant to extinction. For instance, most parents want to see their child's studying response survive even if the child hits a rocky stretch when studying doesn't lead to reinforcement (good grades). In a similar fashion, a casino wants to see patrons continue to gamble, even if they encounter a lengthy losing streak. Thus, a high degree of resistance

© Karen Moskowitz/Getty Images

© Courtesy of Animal Behavior Enterprises, Inc.

© Gary Crabbe/Alamy

Shaping—an operant technique in which an organism is rewarded for closer and closer approximations of the desired response—is used in teaching both animals and humans. It is the main means of training animals to perform unnatural tricks. Breland and Breland's (1961) famous subject, "Priscilla, the Fastidious Pig," is shown in the center.

to extinction can be desirable in many situations. Resistance to extinction depends on a variety of factors. Chief among them is the *schedule of reinforcement* used during acquisition, a matter that we will discuss a little later in this chapter.

Stimulus Control: Generalization and Discrimination

Operant responding is ultimately controlled by its consequences, as organisms learn response-outcome (R-O) associations (Colwill, 1993). However, stimuli that *precede* a response can also exert considerable influence over operant behavior. When a response is consistently followed by a reinforcer *in the presence of a particular stimulus,* that stimulus comes to serve as a "signal" indicating that the response is likely to lead to a reinforcer. Once an organism learns the signal, it tends to respond accordingly (Honig & Alsop, 1992). For example, a pigeon's disk pecking may be reinforced only when a small light behind the disk is lit. When the light is out, pecking does not lead to the reward. Pigeons quickly learn to peck the disk only when it's lit. The light that signals the availability of reinforcement is called a *discriminative stimulus*. ***Discriminative stimuli* are cues that influence operant behavior by indicating the probable consequences (reinforcement or nonreinforcement) of a response.**

© David Cantrille/Alamy

Discriminative stimuli play a key role in the regulation of operant behavior. For example, birds learn that hunting for worms is likely to be reinforced after a rain. Children learn to ask for sweets when their parents are in a good mood. Drivers learn to slow down when the highway is wet. Human social behavior is also regulated extensively by discriminative stimuli. Consider the behavior of asking someone out for a date. Many people emit this response only cautiously, after receiving many signals (such as eye contact, smiles, encouraging conversational exchanges) that reinforcement (a favorable answer) is fairly likely. The potential power of discriminative stimuli to govern behavior has recently been demonstrated in dramatic fashion (Talwar et al., 2002). Research has shown it's possible to use operant procedures to train what *Time* magazine called "roborats," radio-controlled rodents that can be precisely directed through complex environments (see **Figure 6.14**).

Reactions to a discriminative stimulus are governed by the processes of *stimulus generalization* and *stimulus discrimination,* just like reactions to a CS in classical conditioning. For instance, envision a cat that comes running into the kitchen whenever it hears the sound of a can opener because that sound has become a discriminative stimulus signaling a good chance of getting fed. If the cat also responded to the sound of a new kitchen appliance (say a blender), this response would represent *generalization*—responding to a new stimulus as if it were the original. *Discrimination* would occur if the cat learned to respond only to the can opener and not to the blender.

As you have learned in this section, the processes of acquisition, extinction, generalization, and discrimination in operant conditioning parallel these same processes in classical conditioning. **Table 6.1** compares these processes in the two kinds of conditioning.

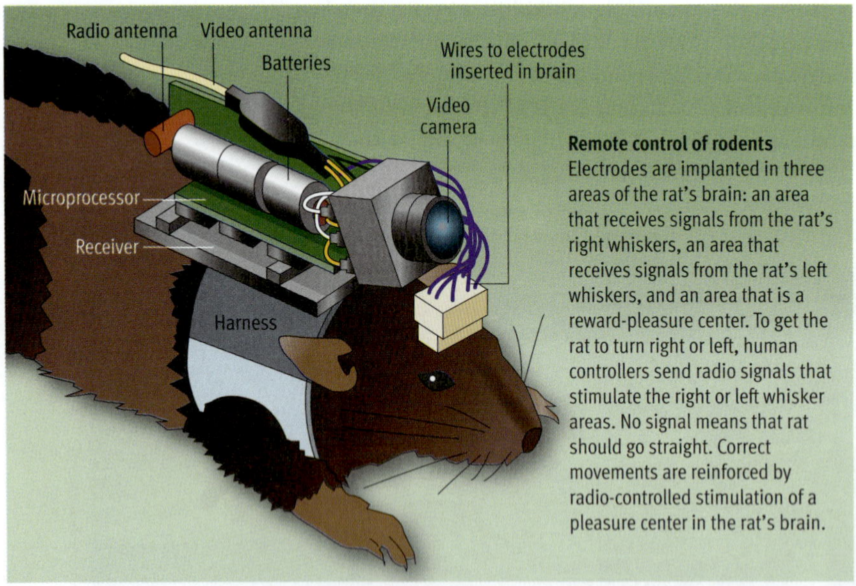

© Cengage Learning 2013

Figure 6.14

Remote-controlled rodents: An example of operant conditioning in action. In a study that almost reads like science fiction, Sanjiv Talwar and colleagues (2002) used operant conditioning procedures to train radio-controlled "roborats" that could have a variety of valuable applications, such as searching for survivors in a collapsed building. As this graphic shows, radio signals can be used to direct the rat to go forward or turn right or left, while a video feed is sent back to a control center. The *reinforcer* in this setup is brief electrical stimulation of a pleasure center in the rat's brain (see Chapter 3), which can be delivered by remote control. The brief shocks sent to the right or left whiskers are *discriminative stimuli* that indicate which types of responses will be reinforced. The entire procedure depended on extensive *shaping.*

Table 6.1 Comparison of Basic Processes in Classical and Operant Conditioning

Process and Definition	Description in Classical Conditioning	Description in Operant Conditioning
Acquisition: The initial stage of learning	CS and US are paired, gradually resulting in CR.	Responding gradually increases because of reinforcement, possibly through shaping.
Extinction: The gradual weakening and disappearance of a conditioned response tendency	CS is presented alone until it no longer elicits CR.	Responding gradually slows and stops after reinforcement is terminated.
Stimulus generalization: An organism's responding to stimuli other than the original stimulus used in conditioning	CR is elicited by new stimulus that resembles original CS.	Responding increases in the presence of new stimulus that resembles original discriminative stimulus.
Stimulus discrimination: An organism's lack of response to stimuli that are similar to the original stimulus used in conditioning	CR is not elicited by new stimulus that resembles original CS	Responding does not increase in the presence of new stimulus that resembles original discriminative stimulus.

© Cengage Learning 2013

Patterns of Reinforcement

PSYKTREK 5d

In operant conditioning, a favorable outcome is much more likely to strengthen a response if the outcome follows *immediately*. If a delay occurs between a response and the positive outcome, the response may not be strengthened. Furthermore, studies show that the longer the delay between the designated response and the delivery of the reinforcer, the more slowly conditioning proceeds (Mazur, 1993; McDevitt & Williams, 2001). For example, in one study rats were reinforced for pressing a lever immediately or after a delay of 4 seconds or 10 seconds (Schlinger & Blakely, 1994). As you can see in **Figure 6.15**, the 4-second delay slowed learning, and the 10-second delay prevented acquisition of the lever-pressing response. Although humans can handle longer delays than animals, delayed reinforcers are also less effective with human subjects.

Obviously, organisms make innumerable responses that do not lead to favorable consequences. It would be nice if people were reinforced every time they took an exam, watched a movie, hit a golf shot, asked for a date, or made a sales call. However, in the real world most responses are reinforced only some of the time. How does this fact affect the potency of reinforcers? To find out, operant psychologists have devoted an enormous amount of attention to how *schedules of reinforcement* influence operant behavior (Ferster & Skinner, 1957; Skinner, 1938, 1953).

A *schedule of reinforcement* determines which occurrences of a specific response result in the presentation of a reinforcer. The simplest pattern is continuous reinforcement. ***Continuous reinforcement* occurs when every instance of a designated response is reinforced.** In the lab, experimenters often use continuous reinforcement to shape and establish a new response before moving on to more realistic schedules involving intermittent reinforcement. ***Intermittent,* or *partial, reinforcement* occurs when a designated response is reinforced only some of the time.**

Which do you suppose leads to longer-lasting effects—being reinforced every time you emit a response or being reinforced only some of the time? Studies show that, given an equal number of reinforcements, *intermittent* reinforcement makes a response more resistant to extinction than continuous reinforcement does (Falls, 1998). In other words, organisms continue responding longer after removal of reinforcers when a response has been reinforced only

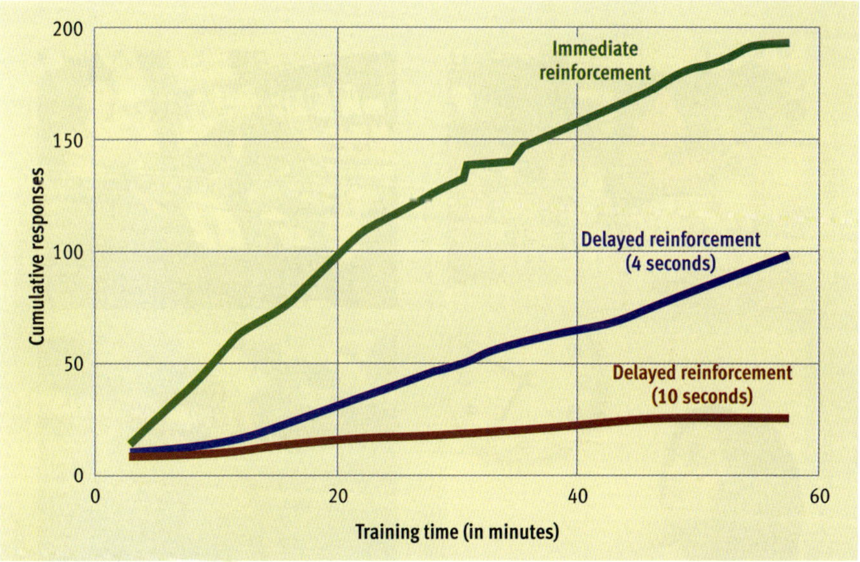

© Cengage Learning 2013

Figure 6.15

Effects of delayed reinforcement. In a study by Schlinger and Blakely (1994) rats were trained to press a lever. Reinforcement was immediate for one group and was delayed by 4 seconds or 10 seconds in two other groups. As you can see, immediate reinforcement led to quick acquisition of the lever-pressing response, whereas a 4-second delay slowed learning dramatically, and a 10-second delay did not result in any meaningful learning.

SOURCE: Adapted from Schlinger, H., & Blakely, E. (1994). The effects of delayed reinforcement and a response-produced auditory stimulus on the acquisition of operant behavior in rats. *Psychological Record, 44,* 391–410.

Reality CHECK

Misconception

The best way to ensure that a desired behavior will persist is to reward the behavior every time it occurs.

Reality

This statement certainly sounds logical, but research clearly shows that continuous reinforcement generates less resistance to extinction than intermittent reinforcement. If you want a response to remain strong in the absence of reinforcement, you should reinforce the response intermittently so that the organism becomes accustomed to some degree of nonreinforcement.

some of the time. In fact, schedules of reinforcement that provide only sporadic delivery of reinforcers can yield great resistance to extinction. This finding explains why behaviors that are reinforced only occasionally—such as youngsters' temper tantrums—can be very durable and difficult to eliminate.

Reinforcement schedules come in many varieties, but four particular types of intermittent schedules have attracted the most interest. These schedules are described here along with examples drawn from the lab and everyday life (see **Figure 6.16** for additional examples).

Ratio schedules require the organism to make the designated response a certain number of times to gain reinforcement. **With a *fixed-ratio (FR) schedule,* the reinforcer is given after a fixed number of nonreinforced responses.** *Examples:* (1) A rat is reinforced for every tenth lever press. (2) A salesperson receives a bonus for every fourth gym membership sold. **With a *variable-ratio (VR) schedule,* the reinforcer is given after a variable number of nonreinforced responses.** The number of nonreinforced responses varies around a predetermined average. *Examples:* (1) A rat is reinforced for every tenth lever press on the average. The exact number of responses required for reinforcement varies from one time to the next. (2) A slot machine in a casino pays off once every six tries on the average. The number of nonwinning responses between payoffs varies greatly from one time to the next.

Figure 6.16

Reinforcement schedules in everyday life. Complex human behaviors are regulated by schedules of reinforcement. Piecework in factories is reinforced on a fixed-ratio schedule. Playing slot machines is based on variable-ratio reinforcement. Watching the clock at work is rewarded on a fixed-interval basis (the arrival of quitting time is the reinforcer). Surfers waiting for a big wave are rewarded on a variable-interval basis.

© Cengage Learning 2013

Interval schedules require a time period to pass between the presentation of reinforcers. **With a *fixed-interval (FI) schedule,* the reinforcer is given for the first response that occurs after a fixed time interval has elapsed.** *Examples:* (1) A rat is reinforced for the first lever press after a 2-minute interval has elapsed and then must wait 2 minutes before being able to earn the next reinforcement. (2) A man washing his clothes periodically checks to see whether each load is finished. The reward (clean clothes) is available only after a fixed time interval (corresponding to how long the washer takes to complete a cycle) has elapsed, and checking responses during the interval are not reinforced. **With a *variable-interval (VI) schedule,* the reinforcer is given for the first response after a variable time interval has elapsed.** The interval length varies around a predetermined average. *Examples:* (1) A rat is reinforced for the first lever press after a 1-minute interval has elapsed, but the following intervals are 3 minutes, 2 minutes, 4 minutes, and so on—with an average length of 2 minutes. (2) A person repeatedly dials a busy phone number (getting through is the reinforcer).

More than 50 years of research has yielded an enormous volume of data on how these schedules of reinforcement are related to patterns of responding (Williams, 1988; Zeiler, 1977). Some of the more prominent findings are summarized in **Figure 6.17**, which depicts typical response patterns generated by each schedule. For example, with fixed-interval schedules, a pause in responding usually occurs after each reinforcer is delivered. Responding then gradually increases to a rapid rate at the end of the interval. This pattern of behavior yields a "scalloped" response curve. In general, ratio schedules tend to produce more rapid responding than interval schedules. Why? Because faster responding leads to reinforcement sooner when a ratio schedule is in effect. Variable schedules tend to generate steadier response rates and greater resistance to extinction than their fixed counterparts.

Most of the research on reinforcement schedules was conducted on rats and pigeons in Skinner boxes. However, the available evidence suggests that humans react to schedules of reinforcement in much the same way as animals (De Villiers, 1977; Perone, Galizio, & Baron, 1988). For example, when animals are placed on ratio schedules, shifting to a higher ratio (that is, requiring more responses per reinforcement) tends to generate faster responding. Managers of factories that pay on a piecework basis (a fixed-ratio schedule) have seen the same reaction in humans. Shifting to a higher ratio (more pieces for the same pay) usually stimulates harder work

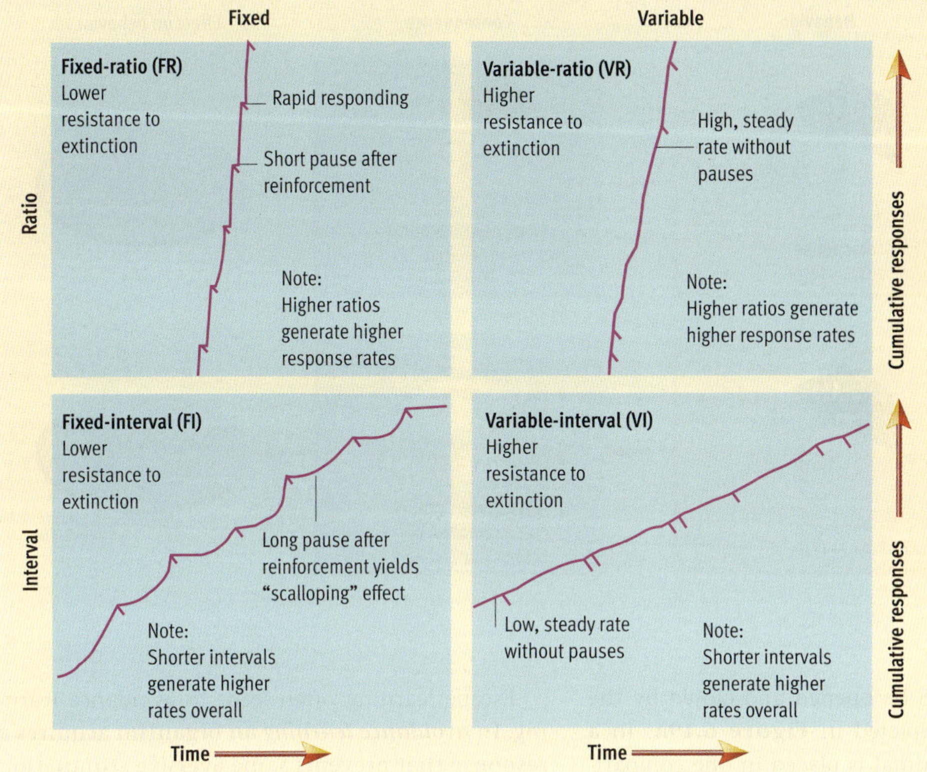

Figure 6.17

Schedules of reinforcement and patterns of response. In graphs of operant responding, such as these, a steeper slope indicates a faster rate of response and the slash marks reflect the delivery of reinforcers. Each type of reinforcement schedule tends to generate a characteristic pattern of responding. In general, ratio schedules tend to produce more rapid responding than interval schedules (note the steep slopes of the FR and VR curves). In comparison to fixed schedules, variable schedules tend to yield steadier responding (note the smoother lines for the VR and VI schedules on the right) and greater resistance to extinction. © Cengage Learning 2013

and greater productivity (although workers often complain). There are many other parallels between animals' and humans' reactions to various schedules of reinforcement. For instance, with rats and pigeons, variable-ratio schedules yield steady responding and great resistance to extinction. Similar effects are routinely observed among people who gamble. Most gambling is reinforced according to variable-ratio schedules, which tend to produce rapid, steady responding and great resistance to extinction—exactly what casino operators want.

Positive Reinforcement Versus Negative Reinforcement

PSYKTREK 5e, 5f

According to Skinner, reinforcement can take two forms, which he called *positive reinforcement* and *negative reinforcement* (see **Figure 6.18** on the next page). ***Positive reinforcement* occurs when a response is strengthened because it is followed by the presentation of a rewarding stimulus.** Thus far, our examples of reinforcement have involved positive reinforcement. Good grades, tasty meals, paychecks, scholarships, promotions, nice clothes, attention, and flattery are all positive reinforcers.

In contrast, ***negative reinforcement* occurs when a response is strengthened because it is followed by the removal of an aversive (unpleasant) stimulus.** Don't let the word "negative" confuse you. Negative reinforcement *is* reinforcement. Like all reinforcement it involves a favorable outcome that *strengthens* a response tendency. However, this strengthening takes place because a response leads to the *removal of an unpleasant stimulus* rather than the arrival of a pleasant stimulus (see **Figure 6.18**).

In lab studies, negative reinforcement is usually accomplished as follows: While a rat is in a Skinner box, a moderate electric shock is delivered to the animal through the floor of the box. When the rat presses the lever, the shock is turned off for a period of time. Thus, lever pressing leads to removal of an aversive stimulus (shock), which reliably strengthens the rat's lever-pressing response. Everyday human behavior appears to be regulated extensively by negative reinforcement. Consider a handful of examples: You rush home in the winter to get out of the cold. You clean house to get rid of a mess. You give in to a roommate or spouse to bring an unpleasant argument to an end.

Negative reinforcement plays a key role in both escape learning and avoidance learning. **In *escape learning*, an organism acquires a response that decreases or ends some aversive stimulation.** Psychologists often study escape learning in the lab with rats that are conditioned in a *shuttle box*. The shuttle box has two compartments connected by a

Figure 6.18
Positive reinforcement versus negative reinforcement. In positive reinforcement, a response leads to the presentation of a rewarding stimulus. In negative reinforcement, a response leads to the removal of an aversive stimulus. Both types of reinforcement involve favorable consequences and both have the same effect on behavior: The organism's tendency to emit the reinforced response is strengthened.

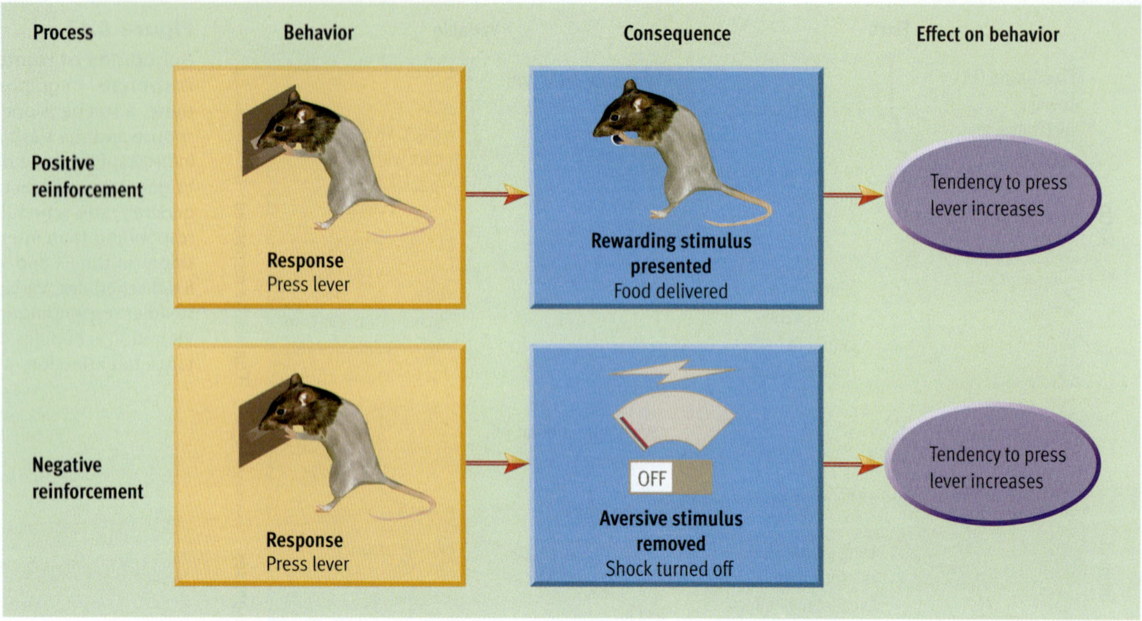

© Cengage Learning 2013

doorway, which can be opened and closed by the experimenter, as depicted in **Figure 6.19a**. In a typical study, an animal is placed in one compartment. The shock in the floor of that compartment is turned on, with the doorway open. The animal learns to escape the shock by running out the door. This escape response leads to the removal of an aversive stimulus (shock), so it's seen as being strengthened through negative reinforcement. If you were to leave a party where you were getting picked on by peers, you would be engaging in an escape response.

Escape learning often leads to avoidance learning. **In *avoidance learning* an organism acquires a response that prevents some aversive stimulation from occurring.** In shuttle box studies of avoidance learning, the experimenter simply gives the animal a signal that shock is forthcoming. The typical signal is a light that goes on a few seconds prior to the shock. At first, the rat runs only when shocked (escape learning). Gradually, however, the animal learns to run to the safe compartment as soon as the light comes on, showing avoidance learning. Similarly, if you were to quit going to parties because of your concern about being picked on, you would be demonstrating avoidance learning.

Avoidance learning presents an interesting example of how classical conditioning and operant conditioning can work together to regulate behavior (Levis, 1989; Mowrer, 1947). In avoidance learning, the warning light that goes on before the shock becomes a CS (through classical conditioning) eliciting reflexive, conditioned fear in the animal. However, the response of fleeing to the other side of the box is operant behavior. This response is presumably strengthened through *negative reinforcement* because it reduces the animal's conditioned fear (see **Figure 6.19b**). Thus in avoidance learning, a fear response is acquired through classical conditioning and an avoidance response is maintained by operant conditioning.

The principles of avoidance learning shed some light on why phobias are so resistant to extinction (Levis, 1989; Levis & Brewer, 2001). Suppose you have a phobia of elevators. Chances are, you acquired your phobia through classical conditioning. At some point in your past, elevators became paired

CONCEPT CHECK 6.2

Recognizing Schedules of Reinforcement

Check your understanding of schedules of reinforcement in operant conditioning by indicating the type of schedule that would be in effect in each of the examples below. In the spaces on the left, fill in CR for continuous reinforcement, FR for fixed-ratio, VR for variable-ratio, FI for fixed-interval, and VI for variable-interval. The answers can be found in Appendix A in the back of the book.

_______ **1.** Sarah is paid on a commission basis for selling computer systems. She gets a bonus for every third sale.

_______ **2.** Juan's parents let him earn some pocket money by doing yard work approximately (on average) once a week.

_______ **3.** Martha is fly-fishing. Think of each time that she casts her line as the response that may be rewarded.

_______ **4.** Jamal, who is in the fourth grade, gets a gold star from his teacher for every book he reads.

_______ **5.** Skip, a professional baseball player, signs an agreement that his salary increases will be renegotiated every third year.

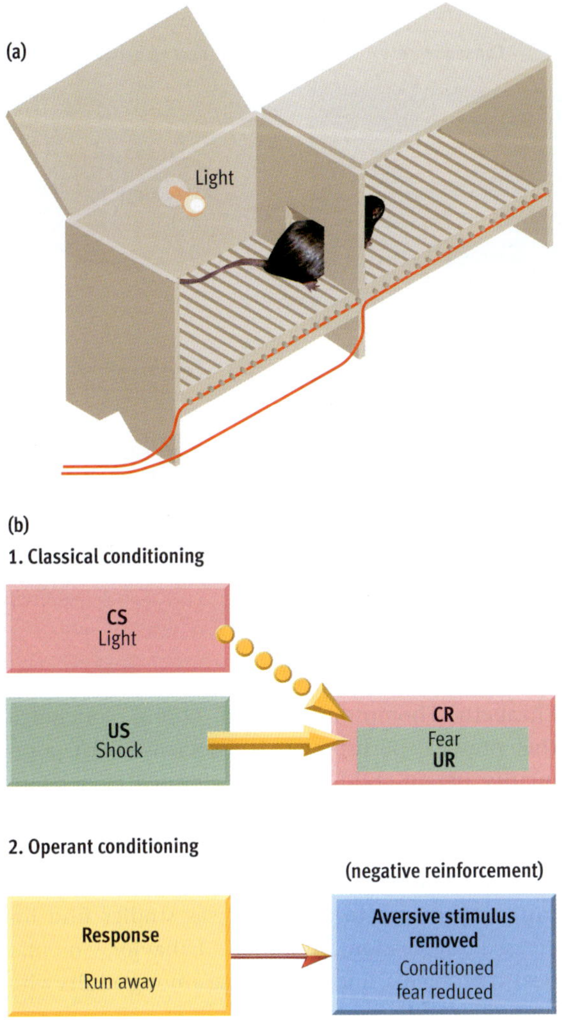

Figure 6.19

Escape and avoidance learning. **(a)** Escape and avoidance learning are often studied with a shuttle box like that shown here. Warning signals, shock, and the animal's ability to flee from one compartment to another can be controlled by the experimenter. **(b)** Avoidance begins because classical conditioning creates a conditioned fear that is elicited by the warning signal **(panel 1)**. Avoidance continues because it is maintained by operant conditioning **(panel 2)**. Specifically, the avoidance response is strengthened through negative reinforcement, since it leads to removal of the conditioned fear.

© Cengage Learning 2013

with a frightening event. Now whenever you need to use an elevator, you experience conditioned fear. If your phobia is severe, you probably take the stairs instead. Taking the stairs is an avoidance response that should lead to consistent reinforcement by relieving your conditioned fear. Thus, it's hard to get rid of phobias for two reasons. First, responses that allow you to avoid a phobic stimulus earn reinforcement each time they are made—so the avoidance behavior is strengthened and continues. Second, these avoidance responses prevent any opportunities to extinguish the phobic conditioned response because you're never exposed to the conditioned stimulus (in this case, riding in an elevator).

Punishment: Consequences That Weaken Responses

PsykTrek 5e

Reinforcement is defined in terms of its consequences: It *increases* an organism's tendency to make a certain response. There are also consequences that *decrease* an organism's tendency to make a particular response. In Skinner's model of operant behavior, such consequences are called *punishment.*

***Punishment* occurs when an event following a response weakens the tendency to make that response.** In a Skinner box, the use of punishment is very simple. When a rat presses the lever or a pigeon pecks the disk, it receives a brief shock. This outcome usually leads to a rapid decline in the animal's response rate (Dinsmoor, 1998). Punishment typically involves presentation of an aversive stimulus (for instance, spanking a child). However, it may also involve the removal of a rewarding stimulus (for instance, taking away a child's TV-watching privileges).

The concept of punishment in operant conditioning is confusing to many students on two counts. First, they often equate it with negative reinforcement, which is entirely different. By definition, negative reinforcement *strengthens* a response, whereas punishment *weakens* a response. As you can see in **Figure 6.20** on the next page, punishment and negative reinforcement are opposite sequences of events that produce opposite effects on behavior.

The second source of confusion involves the tendency to equate punishment with *disciplinary procedures* used by parents, teachers, and other authority figures. In the operant model, punishment occurs any time undesirable consequences weaken a response tendency. Defined in this way, the concept of punishment goes far beyond things like parents spanking children and teachers handing out detentions. For example, if you wear a new outfit and your classmates make fun of it, your behavior will have been punished and your tendency to emit this response (wear the same clothing) will probably decline. Similarly, if you go to a restaurant and have a horrible meal, your response will have been punished, and you will be less likely to go to that restaurant again.

Although punishment in operant conditioning encompasses far more than disciplinary acts, it *is* used frequently for disciplinary purposes. In light of this situation, it's worth looking at the research on punishment as a disciplinary measure. About three-quarters of parents report that they sometimes spank their children (Straus & Stewart, 1999). But quite a bit of controversy exists about the wisdom of using spanking or other physical punishment. Opponents of corporal punishment argue that it produces many unintended and undesirable side effects

Reality CHECK

Misconception

Negative reinforcement is essentially the same thing as punishment.

Reality

Negative reinforcement and punishment both involve aversive stimuli, but the similarity ends there. Negative reinforcement involves the *removal* of an unpleasant stimulus, thereby *strengthening* a response. Punishment involves the *presentation* of an unpleasant stimulus, thereby *weakening* a response. Thus, they are opposite procedures that yield opposite effects on behavior.

Figure 6.20

Comparison of negative reinforcement and punishment. Although punishment can occur when a response leads to the removal of a rewarding stimulus, it more typically involves the presentation of an aversive stimulus. Students often confuse punishment with negative reinforcement because they associate both with aversive stimuli. However, as this diagram shows, punishment and negative reinforcement represent opposite procedures that have opposite effects on behavior.

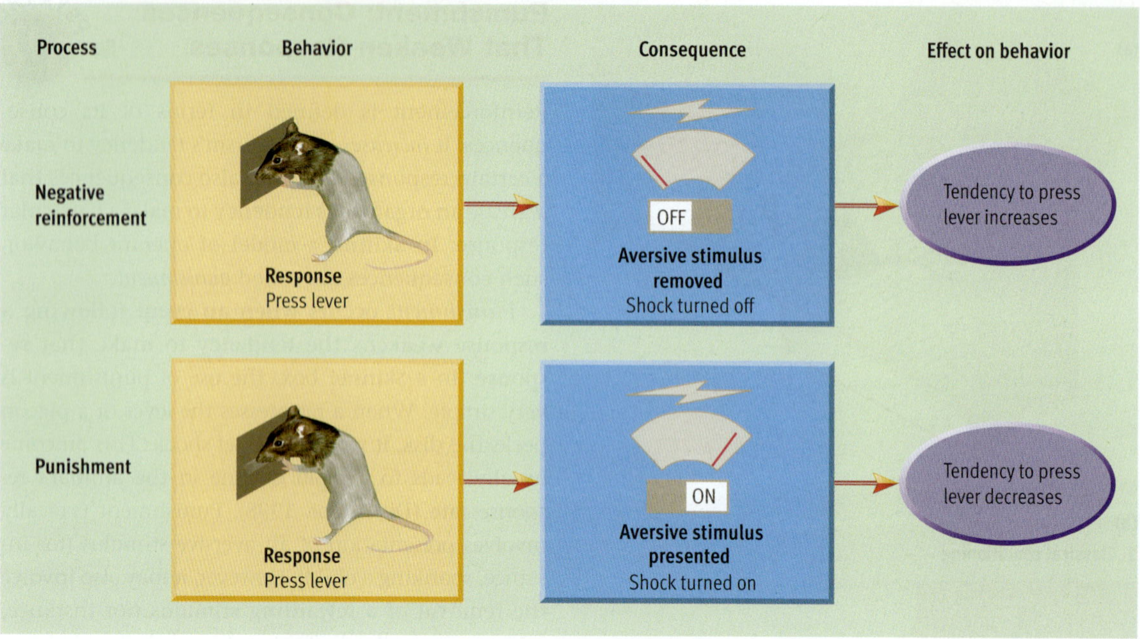

© Cengage Learning 2013

(Lytton, 1997; McCord, 2005; Straus, 2000). For example, they worry that physical punishment may trigger strong emotional responses, including anxiety, anger, and resentment, and that it can generate hostility toward the source of the punishment, such as a parent. Some theorists also argue that children who are subjected to a lot of physical punishment tend to become more aggressive than average. These views were bolstered by a comprehensive review of the empirical research on physical punishment with children. Summarizing the results of 88 studies, Elizabeth Thompson Gershoff (2002) concluded that physical punishment is associated with poor-quality parent-child relations; elevated aggression, delinquency, and behavioral problems in youngsters; and an increased likelihood of children being abused. Moreover, she concluded that these effects can carry over into adulthood, as studies find increased aggression, criminal behavior, mental health problems, and child abuse among adults who were physically punished as children.

Some experts disagreed with Gershoff's stinging indictment of punishment. They pointed out that the evidence linking spanking to negative effects is correlational, and correlation is no assurance of causation (Kazdin & Benjet, 2003). Perhaps spanking causes children to be more aggressive, but it's also plausible that aggressive children cause their parents to rely more on physical punishment (see **Figure 6.21**). Based on objections such as these, Baumrind, Larzelere, & Cowan (2002) asserted that the empirical evidence "does not justify a blanket injunction against mild to moderate disciplinary spanking" (p. 586).

Since then, however, evidence on the negative effects of corporal punishment has continued to pile up (Lynch et al., 2006; Mulvaney & Mebert, 2007). Many of these newer studies have statistically controlled for children's initial level of aggression and other confounding variables, which strengthens the case for a causal link between spanking and negative outcomes. For example, Straus and Paschall (2009) assessed how often children were spanked and their cognitive ability in a group ages 2–4 and another group ages 5–9. When they retested the children's cognitive ability four years later, they

CONCEPT CHECK 6.3

Recognizing Outcomes in Operant Conditioning

Check your understanding of the various types of consequences that can occur in operant conditioning by indicating whether the examples below involve positive reinforcement (PR), negative reinforcement (NR), punishment (P), or extinction (E) (assume that each of these procedures is effective in changing the frequency of the behavior in the expected direction). The answers can be found in Appendix A.

_______ 1. Antonio gets a speeding ticket.

_______ 2. Diane's supervisor compliments her on her hard work.

_______ 3. Leon goes to the health club for a rare workout and pushes himself so hard that his entire body aches and he throws up.

_______ 4. Audrey lets her dog out so she won't have to listen to its whimpering.

_______ 5. Richard shoots up heroin to ward off tremors and chills associated with heroin withdrawal.

_______ 6. Sharma constantly complains about minor aches and pains to obtain sympathy from colleagues at work. Three co-workers who share an office with her decide to ignore her complaints instead of responding with sympathy.

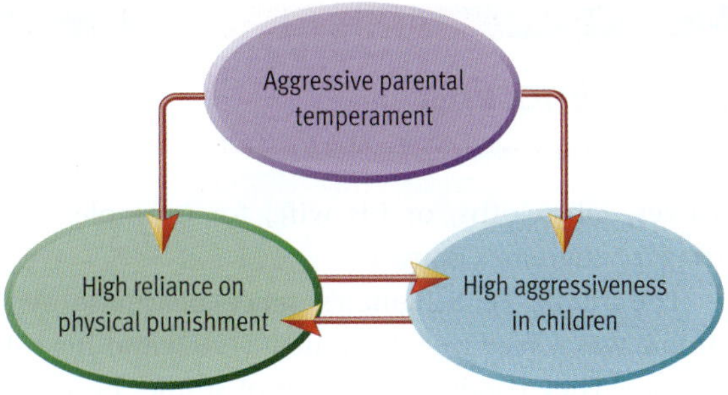

Figure 6.21

The correlation between physical punishment and aggressiveness. As we have discussed in other chapters, a correlation does not establish causation. It seems plausible that extensive reliance on physical punishment causes children to be more aggressive, as many experts suspect. However, it is also possible that highly aggressive children cause their parents to depend heavily on physical punishment. Or, perhaps parents with an aggressive, hostile temperament pass on genes for aggressiveness to their children, rely on heavy use of physical punishment, and model aggressive behavior.

© Cengage Learning 2013

found that those who were spanked showed a disadvantage in IQ scores (see **Figure 6.22**). Another study found that spanking at age 1 predicted increased aggressive behavior at age 2 and lower cognitive ability scores at age 3 (Berlin et al., 2009). Yet another carefully controlled, large-scale study found that heavy use of physical punishment when children were age 3 was associated with higher levels of aggression at age 5 (Taylor et al., 2010). In light of findings such as these, an American Psychological Association task force recently concluded that parents should not use corporal punishment (Graham-Bermann, 2009).

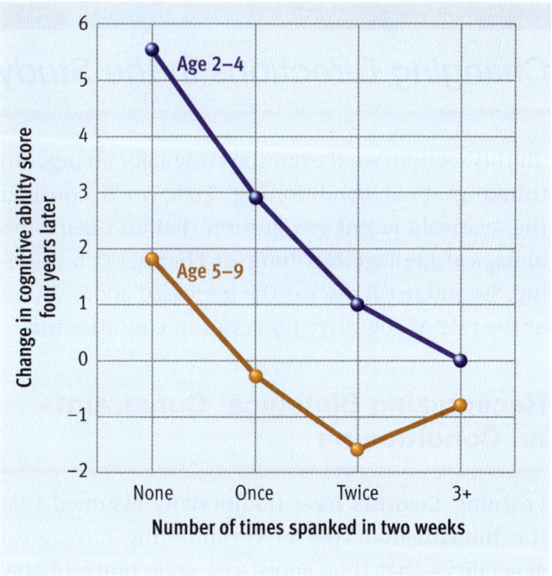

© Cengage Learning 2013

Figure 6.22

Corporal punishment and cognitive development. Straus and Paschall (2009) studied 806 children who were age 2–4 at the beginning of the study and another group of 704 children who were age 5–9 when the study commenced. They gathered data from the youngsters' mothers on how often the children were spanked in two recent weeks and administered age-appropriate assessments of cognitive ability. The children's cognitive ability was retested four years later. In both groups the children who were not spanked showed an advantage in cognitive development in comparison to those who had experienced corporal punishment. In the age 2–4 group, for example, the IQ gap between those who were not spanked and those who were spanked 3+ times in the baseline assessment was over five points.

SOURCE: Adapted from Straus, M. A., & Paschall, M. J. (2009). Corporal punishment by mothers and development of children's cognitive ability: A longitudinal study of two nationally representative age cohorts. *Journal of Aggression, Maltreatment, and Trauma, 18,* 459–483. Figure 1. Copyright © Taylor & Francis Group. Reprinted by permission of the publisher (Taylor & Francis Group, http://informaworld.com).

REVIEW OF KEY LEARNING GOALS

6.6 Skinner pioneered the study of operant conditioning, working mainly with rats and pigeons in Skinner boxes. Reinforcement occurs when an event following a response increases an organism's tendency to emit that response. The key dependent variable in operant conditioning is the rate of response over time, which is tracked by a cumulative recorder. Primary reinforcers are unlearned; secondary reinforcers acquire their reinforcing quality through conditioning.

6.7 Shaping involves gradually reinforcing closer and closer approximations of the desired response. Shaping is the key to training animals to perform impressive tricks. In operant conditioning, extinction occurs when reinforcement for a response is terminated and the rate of that response declines. Operant responses are regulated by discriminative stimuli, which are cues that signal whether reinforcement is likely. These stimuli are subject to the same processes of generalization and discrimination that occur in classical conditioning.

6.8 Delayed reinforcement undermines learning. Schedules of reinforcement influence patterns of operant responding. Intermittent schedules of reinforcement include fixed-ratio, variable-ratio, fixed-interval, and variable-interval schedules. Intermittent schedules produce greater resistance to extinction than similar continuous schedules. Ratio schedules tend to yield higher rates of response than interval schedules. Shorter intervals and higher ratios are associated with faster responding.

6.9 Positive reinforcement occurs when a response is strengthened because it's followed by the presentation of a rewarding stimulus. Negative reinforcement occurs when a response is strengthened because it's followed by the removal of an aversive stimulus. In escape learning, an organism acquires a response that decreases or ends aversive stimulation, whereas in avoidance learning an organism acquires a response that prevents aversive stimulation. The process of avoidance learning may shed light on why phobias are so difficult to eliminate.

6.10 Punishment involves aversive consequences that lead to a decline in response strength. Issues associated with the application of physical punishment as a disciplinary procedure include emotional side effects, increased aggressive behavior, and behavioral problems. Recent research suggests that corporal punishment may inhibit cognitive development in children.

KEY LEARNING GOALS

6.11 Articulate the theoretical significance of conditioned taste aversion.

6.12 Explain the concept of preparedness, and discuss whether the laws of learning are universal.

6.13 Describe Tolman's research on latent learning and its theoretical importance.

6.14 Understand the theoretical implications of research on signal relations and response-outcome relations.

Changing Directions in the Study of Conditioning

In this section, we'll examine two major changes in thinking about conditioning. First, we'll consider the relatively recent recognition that an organism's biological heritage can limit or channel conditioning. Second, we'll discuss the increased appreciation of the role of cognitive processes in conditioning.

Recognizing Biological Constraints on Conditioning

Learning theorists have traditionally assumed that the fundamental laws of conditioning have great generality—that they apply to a wide range of species. Although no one ever suggested that hamsters could learn physics, until the 1960s most psychologists assumed that associations could be conditioned between any stimulus an organism could register and any response it could make. However, findings in recent decades have demonstrated that there are limits to the generality of conditioning principles imposed by an organism's biological heritage.

© Courtesy of John Garcia

John Garcia

"Taste aversions do not fit comfortably within the present framework of classical or instrumental conditioning: These aversions selectively seek flavors to the exclusion of other stimuli. Interstimulus intervals are a thousandfold too long."

Conditioned Taste Aversion

A number of years ago, a prominent psychologist, Martin Seligman, dined out with his wife and enjoyed a steak with sauce béarnaise. About 6 hours afterward, he developed a wicked case of stomach flu and endured severe nausea. Subsequently, when he ordered sauce béarnaise, he was chagrined to discover that its aroma alone nearly made him throw up.

Seligman's experience was not unique. Many people develop aversions to food that has been followed by nausea from illness, alcohol intoxication, or food poisoning (Rosenblum, 2009). However, Seligman was puzzled by his aversion to béarnaise sauce (Seligman & Hager, 1972). On the one hand, it appeared to be the straightforward result of classical conditioning, as diagrammed in **Figure 6.23**. On the other hand, Seligman recognized that his aversion to béarnaise sauce seemed to violate certain basic principles of conditioning. First, the lengthy delay of 6 hours between the CS (the sauce) and the US (the flu) should have prevented conditioning from occurring. Second, why was it that *only* the béarnaise sauce became a CS eliciting nausea? Why not other stimuli that were present in the restaurant? Shouldn't plates, knives, tablecloths, or his wife, for example, also trigger Seligman's nausea?

© Robyn Mackenzie/Shutterstock

The riddle of Seligman's sauce béarnaise syndrome was solved by John Garcia (1989) and his colleagues. They conducted a series of studies on *conditioned taste aversion* (Garcia, Clarke, & Hankins, 1973; Garcia & Koelling, 1966; Garcia & Rusiniak, 1980). They manipulated the kinds of stimuli preceding the onset of nausea and other noxious experiences in rats, using radiation to artificially induce the nausea. They found that when taste cues were followed by nausea, rats quickly acquired conditioned taste aversions. However, when taste cues were followed by other types of noxious stimuli (such as shock), rats did *not* develop conditioned taste aversions. Furthermore, visual and auditory stimuli followed by nausea also failed to produce conditioned aversions. In short, Garcia and his co-workers found that it was almost impossible to create certain associations, whereas taste-nausea associations (and odor-nausea associations) were almost impossible to prevent.

What is the theoretical significance of this unique readiness to make connections between taste and nausea? Garcia argues that it's a by-product of the evolutionary history of mammals. Animals that consume poisonous foods and survive must learn not to repeat their mistakes. Natural selection will favor organisms that quickly learn what *not* to eat. Thus, evolution may have biologically programmed some organisms to learn certain types of associations more easily than others.

Preparedness and Phobias

According to Martin Seligman (1971) and other theorists (Öhman, 1979; Öhman, Dimberg, & Öst, 1985), evolution has also programmed organisms to

Figure 6.23

Conditioned taste aversion. Martin Seligman's aversion to sauce béarnaise was clearly the product of classical conditioning. However, as the text explains, his acquisition of this response *appeared* to violate basic principles of classical conditioning. This paradox was resolved by John Garcia's work on conditioned taste aversions (see the text). © Cengage Learning 2013 acquire certain fears more readily than others because of a phenomenon called *preparedness*. ***Preparedness* involves species-specific predispositions to be conditioned in certain ways and not others.** Seligman believes that preparedness can explain why certain phobias are vastly more common than others. People tend to develop phobias to snakes, spiders, heights, and darkness relatively easily. However, even after painful experiences with hammers, knives, hot stoves, and electrical outlets, phobic fears of these objects are rare. What characteristics do common phobic objects, such as heights and darkness, share? Most were once genuine threats to our ancient ancestors. Consequently, a fear response to such objects may have survival value for our species. According to Seligman, evolutionary forces gradually wired the human brain to acquire conditioned fears of these objects easily and rapidly.

Lab simulations of phobic conditioning have provided some support for the concept of preparedness (Mineka & Öhman, 2002). For example, slides of phobic stimuli (snakes, spiders) for which we seem to show a preparedness and slides of neutral stimuli (flowers, mushrooms) or modern fear-relevant stimuli (guns, knives) have been paired with shock. Consistent with the concept of preparedness, physiological monitoring of the participants indicates that the prepared phobic stimuli tend to produce more rapid conditioning, stronger fear responses, and greater resistance to extinction. Arne Öhman and Susan Mineka (2001) have elaborated on the theory of preparedness, outlining the key elements of what they call an *evolved module for fear learning*. They assert that this evolved module is (1) preferentially activated by stimuli related to survival threats in evolutionary history, (2) automatically activated by these stimuli, (3) relatively resistant to conscious efforts to suppress the resulting fears, and (4) dependent on neural circuitry running through the amygdala.

People tend to develop phobias to snakes very easily but to hot stoves rarely, even though the latter can be just as painful. Preparedness theory can explain this paradox.

Left: © Don Farrall/Digital Vision/Getty Images; right: © Inspirestock Inc./Alamy

Evolutionary Perspectives on Learning

Clearly, several lines of research suggest that there are species-specific biological constraints on learning. So, what is the current thinking on the idea that the laws of learning are *universal* across various species? The predominant view among learning theorists seems to be that the basic mechanisms of learning are *similar* across species but that these mechanisms have sometimes been modified in the course of evolution as species have adapted to the specialized demands of their environments (Shettleworth, 1998). According to this view, learning is a very general process because the biological bases of learning and the basic problems confronted by various organisms are much the same across species. For example, developing the ability to recognize stimuli that signal important events (such as lurking predators) is probably adaptive for virtually any organism. However, given that different organisms confront different adaptive problems to survive and reproduce, it makes sense that learning has evolved along somewhat different paths in different species (Hollis, 1997; Sherry, 1992).

Recognizing Cognitive Processes in Conditioning

Pavlov, Watson, and their followers traditionally viewed conditioning as a mechanical process in which stimulus-response associations are "stamped in" by experience. Learning theorists asserted that because creatures such as flatworms and sea slugs can be conditioned, conditioning can't depend on higher mental processes. Most mainstream theories of conditioning at the time did not allocate any role to cognitive processes. In recent decades, however, research findings have led theorists to shift toward more cognitive explanations of conditioning. Let's review how this transition gradually occurred.

Latent Learning and Cognitive Maps

The first major psychologist to chip away at the conventional view of learning was an American psychologist named Edward C. Tolman (1932, 1938).

Archives of the History of American Psychology, University of Akron, Akron, Ohio

Edward C. Tolman

"Learning consists not in stimulus-response connections but in the building up in the nervous system of sets which function like cognitive maps."

Tolman and his colleagues conducted a series of studies that posed some difficult questions for the prevailing views of conditioning. In one landmark study (Tolman & Honzik, 1930), three groups of food-deprived rats learned to run a complex maze over a series of once-a-day trials (see **Figure 6.24a**). The rats in Group A received a food reward when they got to the end of the maze each day. Because of this reinforcement, their performance in running the maze gradually improved over the course of 17 days (see **Figure 6.24b**). The rats in Group B did not receive any food reward. Lacking reinforcement, this group showed only modest improvement in performance. Group C was the critical group; they did not get any reward for their first 10 trials in the maze, but they were rewarded from the 11th trial onward. The rats in this group showed little improvement in performance over the first 10 trials (just like Group B). But once reinforcement began on the 11th trial, they showed sharp improvement on subsequent trials. In fact, their performance was even a little better than that of the Group A rats who had been rewarded after every trial (see **Figure 6.24b**).

Tolman concluded that the rats in Group C had been learning about the maze all along, just as much as the rats in group A, but they had no motivation to demonstrate this learning until a reward was introduced. Tolman called this phenomenon ***latent learning*—learning that is not apparent from behavior when it first occurs.** *Why did these findings present a challenge for the prevailing view of learning?* First, they suggested that learning can take place in the absence of reinforcement—at a time when learned responses were thought to be stamped in by reinforcement. Second, they suggested that the rats who displayed latent learning had formed a *cognitive map* of the maze (a mental representation of the spatial layout) at a time when cognitive processes were thought to be irrelevant to understanding conditioning even in humans.

Tolman (1948) went on to conduct other studies that suggested cognitive processes play a role in conditioning. But his ideas mostly attracted rebuttals and criticism from the influential learning theorists of his era (Hilgard, 1987). In the long run, however, Tolman's ideas prevailed, as models of conditioning eventually started to incorporate cognitive factors.

Signal Relations

One theorist who has been especially influential in highlighting the potential importance of cognitive factors in conditioning is Robert Rescorla (1978, 1980; Rescorla & Wagner, 1972). Rescorla asserts that environmental stimuli serve as signals and that some stimuli are better, or more dependable, signals than others. Hence, he has manipulated *signal relations* in classical conditioning—that is, CS-US rela-

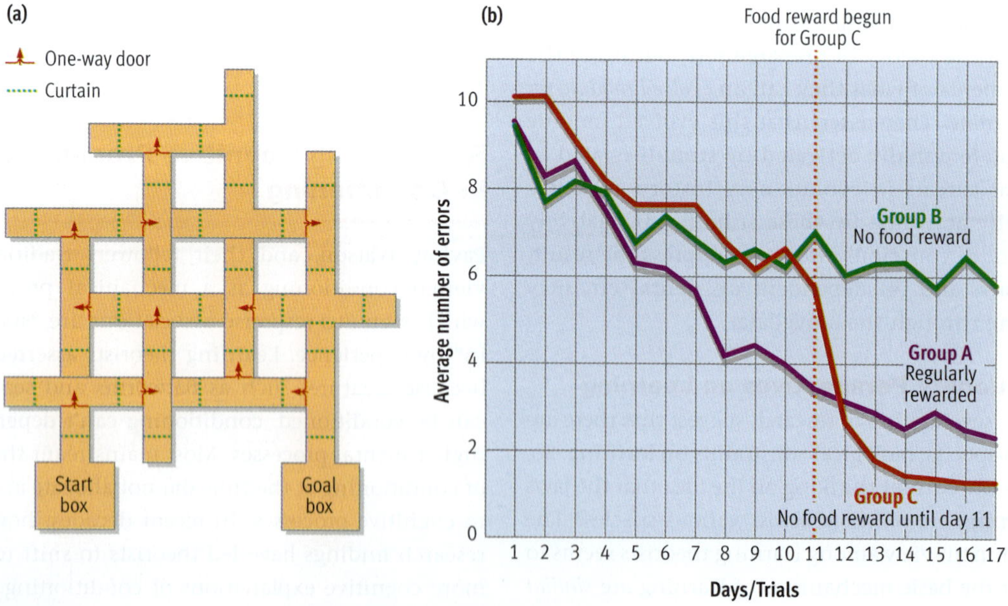

Figure 6.24

Latent learning. (*a*) In the study by Tolman and Honzik (1930), rats learned to run the complicated maze shown here. (**b**) The results they obtained are summarized in this graph. The rats in Group C showed a sudden improvement in performance when a food reward was introduced on Trial 11. Tolman concluded that the rats in this group were learning about the maze all along but that their learning remained "latent" until reinforcement was made available. © Cengage Learning 2013

SOURCE: Adapted from Tolman, E. C., & Honzik, C. H. (1930). Introduction and removal of reward and maze performance in rats. *University of California Publications in Psychology, 4*, 257–275.

tions that influence whether a CS is a good signal. A "good" signal is one that allows accurate prediction of the US.

In essence, Rescorla manipulates the *predictive value* of a conditioned stimulus by varying the proportion of trials in which the CS and US are paired. Consider the following example. A tone and shock are paired 20 times for one group of rats; otherwise, these rats are never shocked. For these rats the CS (tone) and US (shock) are paired in 100% of the experimental trials. Another group of rats also receive 20 pairings of the tone and shock. However, the rats in this group are also exposed to the shock on 20 other trials when the tone does *not* precede it. For this group, the CS and US are paired in only 50% of the trials. Thus, the two groups of rats have had an equal number of CS-US pairings, but the CS is a better signal or predictor of shock for the 100% CS-US group than for the 50% CS-US group.

Rescorla found that the CS elicits a much stronger response in the 100% CS-US group than in the 50% CS-US group. The two groups have received an equal number of CS-US pairings, so this difference must be due to the greater predictive power of the CS for the 100% group. Numerous studies of signal relations have shown that the predictive value of a CS is an influential factor governing classical conditioning (Rescorla, 1978).

Response-Outcome Relations and Reinforcement

Studies of response-outcome relations and reinforcement also highlight the role of cognitive processes in conditioning. Imagine that on the night before an important exam you study hard while repeatedly playing a Coldplay song. The next morning you earn an A on your exam. Does this result strengthen your tendency to play Coldplay's music before exams? Probably not. Chances are, you will recognize the logical relation between the response of studying hard and the reinforcement of a good grade, and only the response of studying will be strengthened (Killeen, 1981).

However, it's not out of the realm of possibility that you might develop a habit of playing Coldplay before big exams. Many years ago, B. F. Skinner argued that "superstitious behavior" could be established through *noncontingent reinforcement*, which occurs when a response is accidentally strengthened by a reinforcer that follows it, even though delivery of the reinforcer was not a result of the response. In a classic study, Skinner (1948) put eight pigeons in operant chambers that were set up to deliver reinforcement every 15 seconds, regardless of what responses the pigeons were making. In Skinner's judgment, six of the eight pigeons started displaying quirky, superstitious responses, such as head-bobbing or turning counter-clockwise. Skinner's theory that noncontingent reinforcement is the basis for superstitious behavior held sway for many years, but researchers eventually failed to replicate his findings (Staddon & Simmelhag, 1971). Thus, noncontingent reinforcement clearly is not as powerful or influential as Skinner originally believed.

That said, superstitious behavior is extremely common, and accidental reinforcements *may* sometimes contribute to these superstitions, along with various types of erroneous reasoning (Ono, 1987; Vyse, 1997). There are extensive anecdotal reports of athletes exhibiting superstitious responses, such as those displayed by baseball legend Wade Boggs, discussed at the beginning of the chapter. Numerous other athletes have reported wearing a special pair of socks, eating the same lunch, going through special rituals, and so on to enhance their chances of success (Bleak & Frederick, 1998; Ciborowski, 1997; Gmelch, 1978). And these quirks are certainly not limited to athletes (Wargo, 2008). For example, most people compulsively need to "knock on wood" after mentioning their good fortune in some area. One recent study (Risen & Gilovich, 2008) showed that many people subscribe to the belief that it is bad luck to "tempt fate." In one part of the study participants read about a student named Jon who had applied to prestigious Stanford University for graduate school. Jon's mother sent him a Stanford T-shirt before he had learned whether he had been accepted by Stanford. The subjects generally believed that Jon's prospects of acceptance would be higher if he did not tempt fate by wearing the T-shirt before getting accepted.

Contemporary research on superstitious behavior tends to ascribe it to normal cognitive biases and errors that promote irrational reasoning (discussed in Chapter 8) rather than to the unpredictable vagaries of operant conditioning (Pronin et al., 2006; Wegner & Wheatley, 1999). Interestingly, a recent study found that superstitious beliefs can actually enhance performance (Damisch, Stoberock, & Mussweiler, 2010). Participants who were given a "lucky ball" sank more putts on a putting green than control subjects. And subjects who were allowed to hang onto a lucky charm performed better on memory and reasoning tasks than those who had to surrender their lucky charm. So, silly though they may seem, superstitions may actually influence people's outcomes.

In any case, it is clear that reinforcement is *not* automatic when favorable consequences follow a response. People actively reason out the relations

© Courtesy of Robert Rescorla

Robert Rescorla

"Pavlovian conditioning is a sophisticated and sensible mechanism by which organisms represent the world. . . . I encourage students to think of animals as behaving like little statisticians. . . . They really are very finely attuned to small changes in the likelihood of events."

Senator John McCain is famous for his superstitions. He won't accept salt shakers that are handed to him, he won't comment on his electoral prospects without knocking on wood, he won't toss his hat on a bed, and an aide always carries his lucky pen (Wargo, 2008). Noncontingent reinforcement may contribute to superstitions such as these, but cognitive biases and irrational reasoning also play a role.

© AP Images/John Raoux

between responses and the outcomes that follow. When a response is followed by a desirable outcome, the response is more likely to be strengthened if the person thinks that the response *caused* the outcome. In sum, modern, reformulated models of conditioning view it as a matter of detecting the *contingencies* among environmental events (Beckers et al., 2006; Penn & Povinelli, 2007). The new, cognitively oriented theories of conditioning are quite a departure from older theories that depicted conditioning as a mindless, mechanical process. We can also see this new emphasis on cognitive processes in our next topic, observational learning.

REVIEW OF KEY LEARNING GOALS

6.11 Conditioned taste aversions can be readily acquired even when a lengthy delay occurs between the CS and US. The findings on conditioned taste aversion suggest that evolution may have programmed some organisms to learn certain types of associations more easily than others.

6.12 Preparedness appears to explain why people acquire phobias of ancient sources of threat much more readily than modern sources of threat. Evolutionary psychologists argue that learning processes vary somewhat across species because different species have to grapple with very different adaptive problems.

6.13 Tolman's studies suggested that learning can take place in the absence of reinforcement, which he called latent learning. His findings suggested that cognitive processes contribute to conditioning, but his work was not influential at the time.

6.14 Rescorla's work on signal relations showed that the predictive value of a CS is an influential factor governing classical conditioning. When a response is followed by a desirable outcome, the response is more likely to be strengthened if the response appears to have *caused* the outcome. Noncontingent reinforcement, cognitive biases, and irrational reasoning appear to contribute to superstitious behavior. Studies of signal relations and response-outcome relations suggest that cognitive processes play a larger role in conditioning than originally believed.

CONCEPT CHECK 6.4

Distinguishing Between Classical Conditioning and Operant Conditioning

Check your understanding of the usual differences between classical conditioning and operant conditioning by indicating the type of conditioning process involved in each of the following examples. In the space on the left, place a C if the example involves classical conditioning, an O if it involves operant conditioning, or a B if it involves both. The answers can be found in Appendix A.

______ 1. Whenever Midori takes her dog out for a walk, she wears the same old blue windbreaker. Eventually, she notices that her dog becomes excited whenever she puts on this windbreaker.

______ 2. The Creatures are a successful rock band with three hit albums to their credit. They begin their U.S. tour featuring many new, unreleased songs, all of which draw silence from their concert fans. The same fans cheer wildly when the Creatures play any of their old hits. Gradually, the band reduces the number of new songs it plays and starts playing more of the old standbys.

______ 3. When Cindy and Mel first fell in love, they listened constantly to the Creatures' hit song "Transatlantic Obsession." Although several years have passed, whenever they hear this song they experience a warm, romantic feeling.

______ 4. For nearly 20 years Ralph has worked as a machinist in the same factory. His new foreman is never satisfied with Ralph's work and criticizes him constantly. After a few weeks of heavy criticism, Ralph experiences anxiety whenever he arrives at work. He starts calling in sick more and more often to evade this anxiety.

Observational Learning

KEY LEARNING GOALS

6.15 Explain the nature and importance of observational learning.

6.16 List the basic processes in observational learning.

6.17 Describe the Featured Study profiling Bandura's classic research on TV models and aggression.

6.18 Discuss modern research on the effects of media violence.

Can classical and operant conditioning account for all learning? Absolutely not. Consider how people learn a fairly basic skill such as driving a car. They don't hop naively into an automobile and start trying random things until one leads to a favorable result. On the contrary, most people learning to drive know exactly where to place the key and how to get started. How are these responses acquired? Through *observation*. Most new drivers have years of experience observing others drive, and they put those observations to work. Learning through observation accounts for a great deal of learning.

***Observational learning* occurs when an organism's responding is influenced by the observation of others, who are called models.** This process has been investigated extensively by Albert Bandura (1977, 1986). Bandura does not see observational learning as entirely separate from classical and operant conditioning. Instead, he asserts that it greatly extends the reach of these conditioning processes. Whereas previous conditioning theorists emphasized the organism's direct experience, Bandura has demonstrated that both classical and operant conditioning can take place "vicariously" through observational learning.

Essentially, observational learning involves being conditioned indirectly by virtue of observing another's conditioning (see **Figure 6.25**). To illustrate, suppose you observe a friend behaving assertively with a car salesperson. You see your friend's assertive behavior reinforced by the exceptionally good buy she gets on the car. Your own tendency to behave assertively with salespeople might well be strengthened as a result. Notice that the reinforcement is experienced by your friend, not you. The good buy should strengthen your friend's tendency to bargain assertively, but your tendency to do so may also be strengthened indirectly.

Bandura's theory of observational learning can help explain why physical punishment tends to increase aggressive behavior in children, even when it's intended to do just the opposite. Parents who depend on physical punishment unwittingly serve as *models* for aggressive behavior. In this situation, actions speak louder than words—because of observational learning.

Basic Processes

Bandura has identified four key processes that are crucial in observational learning. The first two—attention and retention—highlight the importance of cognition in this type of learning.

- *Attention.* To learn through observation, you must pay attention to another person's behavior and its consequences.
- *Retention.* You may not have occasion to use an observed response for weeks, months, or even years. Thus, you must store a mental representation of what you have witnessed in your memory.
- *Reproduction.* Enacting a modeled response depends on your ability to reproduce the response by converting your stored mental images into overt behavior. This step may not be easy for some responses. For example, most people cannot execute a breathtaking windmill dunk after watching Derrick Rose do it in a basketball game.
- *Motivation.* Finally, you are unlikely to reproduce an observed response unless you are motivated to do so. Your motivation depends on whether you encounter a situation in which you believe that the response is likely to pay off for you.

© Photo by Keeble, courtesy of Albert Bandura

Albert Bandura

"Most human behavior is learned by observation through modeling."

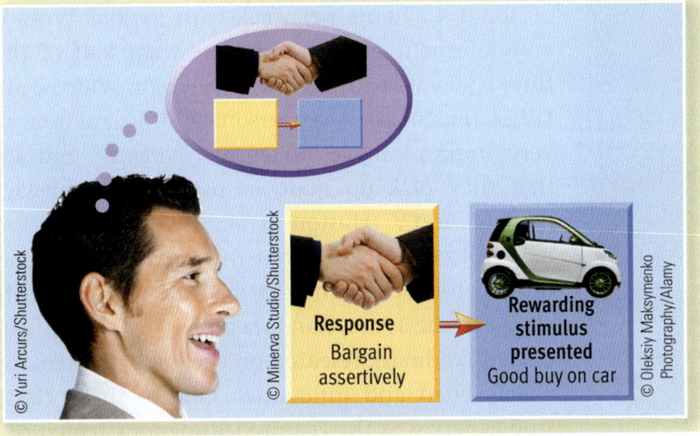

Figure 6.25

Observational learning. In observational learning, an observer attends to and stores a mental representation of a model's behavior (example: assertive bargaining) and its consequences (example: a good buy on a car). If the observer sees the modeled response lead to a favorable outcome, the observer's tendency to emit the modeled response will be strengthened.

© Cengage Learning 2013

Observational learning occurs in both humans and animals. For example, no one trained this dog to "pray" with its owner; the chihuahua just picked up the response through observation. In a similar vein, children acquire a diverse array of responses from role models through observational learning.

Animals can also learn through observation (Öhman & Mineka, 2001; Zentall, 2003). A simple example is the thieving behavior of the English titmouse, a small bird renowned for its early-morning raids on its human neighbors. The titmouse has learned how to open aluminum caps on bottles of milk delivered to the porches of many homes in England. The titmouse then skims the cream from the top of the milk. This clever learned behavior has been passed down from one generation of titmouse to the next through observational learning.

The English titmouse has learned how to break into milk bottles to swipe cream from its human neighbors. This behavior has been passed across generations through observational learning.

Observational Learning and the Media Violence Controversy

The power of observational learning has been at the center of a long-running controversy about the effects of media violence. Children spend an average of about 40 hours per week with various types of entertainment media, and more than half of that time is devoted to watching television, videos, and DVDs (Bushman & Anderson, 2001). Children are very impressionable. Extensive evidence indicates that they pick up many responses from viewing models on TV (Huston et al., 1992). Social critics have voiced concern about the amount of violence on television ever since TV became popular in the 1950s. In the 1960s, Bandura and his colleagues conducted landmark research on the issue that remains widely cited and influential. One of those classic studies serves as the Featured Study for Chapter 6.

FEATURED STUDY

The Power of Modeling: What They See Is What You Get

SOURCE: Bandura, A., Ross, D. & Ross, S. (1963b). Vicarious reinforcement and imitative learning. *Journal of Abnormal & Social Psychology, 67*, 601–607.

This study was designed to explore the influence of observing the consequences of another's behavior on the learning of aggressive behavior in children. In a previous study, the same researchers had shown that children exposed to an aggressive adult model displayed more aggression than children exposed to a similar but nonaggressive model (Bandura, Ross, & Ross, 1961). The first study used live (in-person) adult models who did or did not play very roughly with a 5-foot-tall inflatable clown (known as a "Bobo doll") while in the same room with the children. A second study by the same research team investigated whether filmed models were as influential as in-person models (Bandura, Ross, & Ross, 1963a). The researchers found that a TV depiction of an adult model roughing up the Bobo doll led to increased aggression just as exposure to a live model had. In this third study of the series, the investigators used filmed models and manipulated the consequences experienced by the aggressive models. The hypothesis was that children who saw the models reinforced for their aggression would become more aggressive than children who saw the models punished for their aggression.

Method

Subjects. The subjects were 40 girls and 40 boys drawn from a nursery school. The average age for the 80 children was 4 years, 3 months.

Procedure. While at the nursery school, each child was invited to play in a toy room. On the way to the toy room, an adult escort indicated that she needed to stop in her office for a few minutes. The child was told to watch a TV in the office during this brief delay. On the TV, the child was exposed to one of three 5-minute film sequences. In the *aggressive-model-rewarded* condition, Rocky and Johnny are playing and Rocky attacks Johnny, striking him with a baton, throwing a ball at him repeatedly, and dragging him off to a far corner of the room. The final scene shows Rocky having a great time with the toys while helping himself to soda and cookies. In the *aggressive-model-punished* condition, Rocky engages in the same pattern of aggression, but the outcome is different. Johnny rises to the challenge and thrashes Rocky, who is shown cowering in a corner in the final scene. In the *nonaggressive-model-control* condition, Rocky and Johnny are simply shown engaged in vigorous play without any aggression. In a fourth condition, the *no-model-control* condition, the child did not watch TV while in the office.

After the brief stop in the adult's office, the child was taken to the toy room, as promised, where he or she was allowed to play alone with a diverse array of toys that allowed for either aggressive or nonaggressive play. Among the toys were two Bobo dolls that served as convenient targets for aggressive responses. The child's play was observed through a one-way mirror from an adjoining room. The key dependent variable was the number of aggressive acts displayed by the child during the 20-minute play period.

Results

Children in the *aggressive-model-rewarded* condition displayed significantly more total aggression and imitative aggression (specific aggressive acts similar to Rocky's) than children in the *aggressive-model-punished* condition. The amount of imitative aggression exhibited by children in each of the four conditions is summarized in **Figure 6.26**. A clear elevation of imitative aggression was observed only among the children who saw aggression pay off with reinforcement for the model.

Discussion

The results supported a basic premise of Bandura's theory—that observers are more likely to imitate another's behavior when that behavior leads to positive consequences than when it leads to negative consequences. Of particular interest was the fact that filmed models were shown to influence the likelihood of aggressive behavior in children.

Comment

This classic series of studies by Bandura, Ross, and Ross played a prominent role in the early stages of the vigorous debate about the impact of televised violence. People concerned about media violence noted that aggression on TV shows usually leads to rewards and admiration for heroic TV characters. The findings of this study suggested that youngsters watching aggressive models on TV are likely to learn that aggressive behavior pays off. Critics argued that Bandura's Bobo doll studies were too artificial to be conclusive. This criticism led to hundreds of more realistic experiments and correlational studies on the possible link between TV violence and aggressiveness.

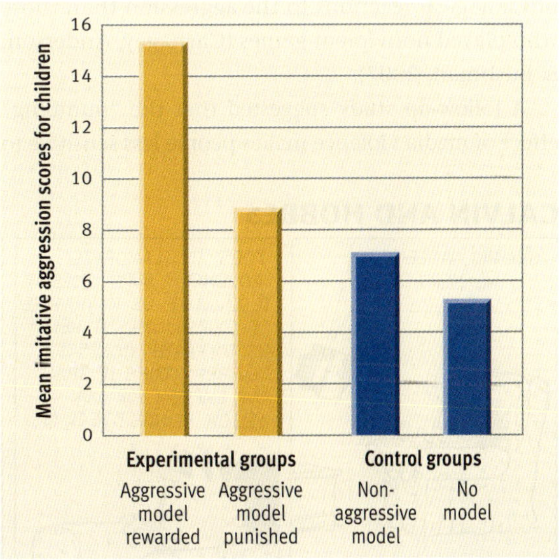

© Cengage Learning 2013

Figure 6.26
Filmed models and aggression. Bandura, Ross, and Ross (1963b) found that acts of imitative aggression were most frequent among children exposed to an aggressive role model on TV whose aggression was rewarded, as predicted by Bandura's theory of observational learning.

Subsequent research demonstrated that youngsters are exposed to an astonishing amount of violence when they watch TV. The National Television Violence Study, a large-scale review of the content of network and cable television shows, revealed that 61% of programs contained violence, 44% of violent actors were enticing role models (i.e., the "good guys"), 75% of violent actions occurred without punishment or condemnation, and 51% of violent actions were "sanitized," as they did not show any apparent pain (Anderson et al., 2003).

Does this steady diet of media violence foster increased aggression? Decades of research since Bandura's pioneering work indicate that the answer is "yes" (Bushman & Huesmann, 2001). The short-term effects of media violence have been investigated in hundreds of experimental studies. These studies consistently demonstrate that exposure to TV and movie violence increases the likelihood of physical aggression, verbal aggression, aggressive thoughts, and aggressive emotions in both children and adults (Anderson et al., 2003).

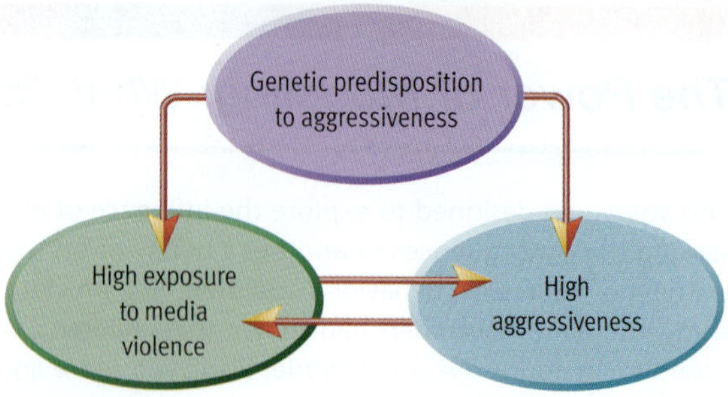

Figure 6.27

The correlation between exposure to media violence and aggression. The more violence children watch on TV, the more aggressive they tend to be, but this correlation could reflect a variety of underlying causal relationships. Although watching violent shows probably causes increased aggressiveness, it is also possible that aggressive children are drawn to violent shows. Or perhaps a third variable (such as a genetic predisposition to aggressiveness) leads to both a preference for violent shows and high aggressiveness.

© Cengage Learning 2013

© Art Directors & TRIP/Alamy

A particular source of concern in recent research has been the finding that exposure to media violence appears to desensitize people to the effects of aggression in the real world. Desensitization means that people show muted reactions to real violence. For example, in one study participants were randomly assigned to play violent or nonviolent video games for 20 minutes. Then their physiological reactions to video recordings of real-life aggression (prison fights, police confrontations, and such) were monitored. The subjects who had played violent video games for a mere 20 minutes showed smaller physiological reactions to the aggression than those who played nonviolent games (Carnagey, Anderson, & Bushman, 2007).

A follow-up study suggested that the "numbing" effect of media violence makes people less sensitive to the suffering of others and less likely to help others in need (Bushman & Anderson, 2009). In this study, participants who had just played a violent or nonviolent video game overheard a staged fight (just outside the door of the lab) in which one person was injured. The aggressive actor clearly had left the scene, so there was no perceived danger to the participants. Researchers monitored how long it took subjects to come out into the hall to offer help to the groaning victim. Participants who had just played a violent video game took much longer to help (average 73 seconds) than those who had just played a nonviolent game (16 seconds). Thus, it appears that media violence can desensitize individuals to acts of aggression.

The real-world and long-term effects of media violence have been investigated through correlational research. The findings of these studies show that the more violence children watch on TV, the more aggressive they tend to be at home and at school (Huesmann & Miller, 1994). Of course, critics point out that this correlation could reflect a variety of causal relationships (see **Figure 6.27**). Perhaps high aggressiveness in children causes an increased interest in

CALVIN AND HOBBES

CALVIN AND HOBBES © 1995 by Bill Wasserman. Distributed by Universal Press Syndicate. Reprinted with permission. All rights reserved.

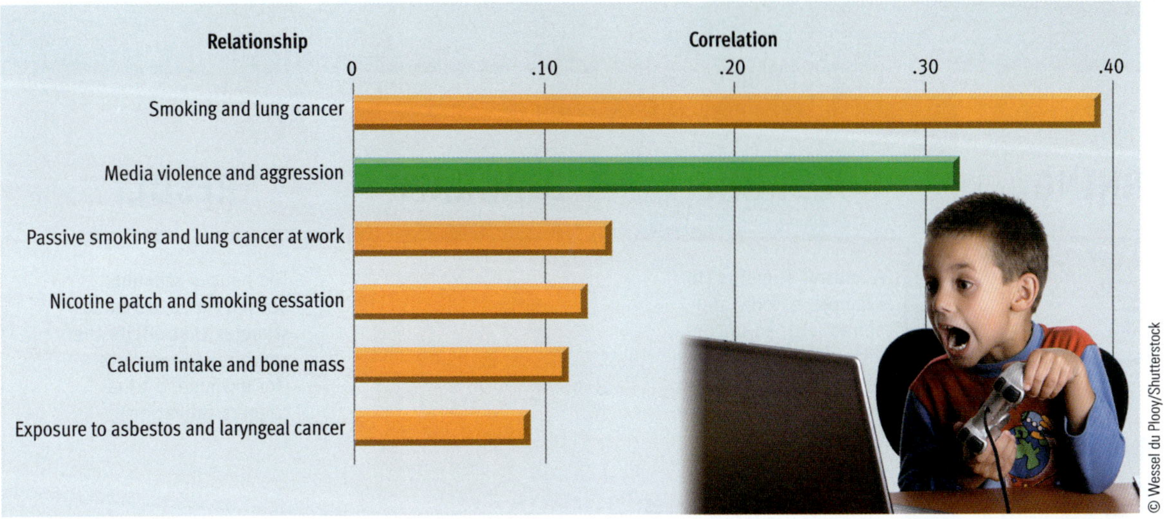

Figure 6.28

Comparison of the relationship between media violence and aggression to other correlations. Many studies have found a correlation between exposure to media violence and aggression. However, some critics have argued that the correlation is too weak to worry about. In a rebuttal of this assertion, Bushman and Anderson (2001) note that the average correlation in studies of media violence and aggression is .31. They point out that this association is almost as strong as the correlation between smoking and the probability of developing lung cancer, which is viewed as very relevant to real-world issues. © Cengage Learning 2013

SOURCE: Adapted from Bushman, B. J., & Anderson, C. A. (2001). Media violence and the American public. *American Psychologist, 56*(6–7), 477–489. Figure 2. Copyright © 2001 American Psychological Association. Reprinted by permission of the publisher and author.

violent television shows. However, a handful of long-term studies that have followed the same subjects since the 1960s and 1970s have clarified the causal relations underlying the link between media violence and elevated aggression. These studies show that the extent of youngsters' exposure to media violence in childhood predicts their aggressiveness in adolescence and early adulthood, but not vice versa (Huesmann, 1986; Huesmann et al., 2003). In other words, high exposure to media violence precedes, and presumably causes, high aggressiveness.

The empirical evidence linking media violence to aggression is clear, convincing, and unequivocal. In fact, the strength of the association between media violence and aggression is nearly as great as the correlation between smoking and cancer (Bushman & Anderson, 2001; see **Figure 6.28**). Nonetheless, the general public remains uncertain, perhaps even skeptical. One reason is that everyone knows individuals (perhaps themselves) who were raised on a robust diet of media violence but who do not appear to be particularly aggressive. If media violence is so horrible, why aren't we all axe murderers? The answer is that aggressive behavior is influenced by a number of factors besides media violence, which has only a "modest" effect on people's aggressiveness. The problem, experts say, is that TV and movies reach millions upon millions of people, so even a small effect can have big repercussions (Bushman & Anderson, 2001). Suppose that 25 million people watch an extremely violent program. Even if only 1 in 100 viewers become a little more prone to aggression, that is 250,000 people who are a bit more likely to wreak havoc in someone's life.

In any event, the heated debate about media violence shows that observational learning plays an important role in regulating behavior. It represents a third major type of learning that builds on the first two types—classical conditioning and operant conditioning. These three basic types of learning are summarized and compared in an Illustrated Overview on pages 262–263.

REVIEW OF KEY LEARNING GOALS

6.15 In observational learning, an organism is conditioned vicariously by watching a model's conditioning. Both classical and operant conditioning can occur through observational learning, which extends their influence. The principles of observational learning have been used to explain why physical punishment increases aggressive behavior.

6.16 Observational learning depends on the processes of attention, retention, reproduction, and motivation. Even animals can learn through observation.

6.17 In a landmark study, Bandura and colleagues demonstrated that exposure to aggressive TV models led to increased aggression in children, especially when the TV models were reinforced for their aggression.

6.18 Research on observational learning has played a central role in the debate about the effects of media violence for many decades. Both experimental and correlational studies suggest that violent TV shows, movies, and video games contribute to increased aggression among children and adults and desensitization to the effects of aggression.

Illustrated Overview of Three Types of Learning

TYPE OF LEARNING	PROCEDURE	RESULT
CLASSICAL CONDITIONING (Ivan Pavlov)	A neutral stimulus (for example, a tone) is paired with an unconditioned stimulus (such as food) that elicits an unconditioned response (salivation).	The neutral stimulus becomes a conditioned stimulus that elicits the conditioned response (for example, a tone triggers salivation).
OPERANT CONDITIONING (B. F. Skinner)	In a stimulus situation, a response is followed by favorable consequences (reinforcement) or unfavorable consequences (punishment).	If reinforced, the response is strengthened (emitted more frequently); if punished, the response is weakened (emitted less frequently).
OBSERVATIONAL LEARNING (Albert Bandura)	An observer attends to a model's behavior (for example, aggressive bargaining) and its consequences (for example, a good buy on a car).	The observer stores a mental representation of the modeled response; the observer's tendency to emit the response may be strengthened or weakened, depending on the consequences observed.

CLASSICAL CONDITIONING

Ivan Pavlov

DIAGRAM:

© Cengage Learning 2013

OPERANT CONDITIONING

B. F. Skinner

DIAGRAM:

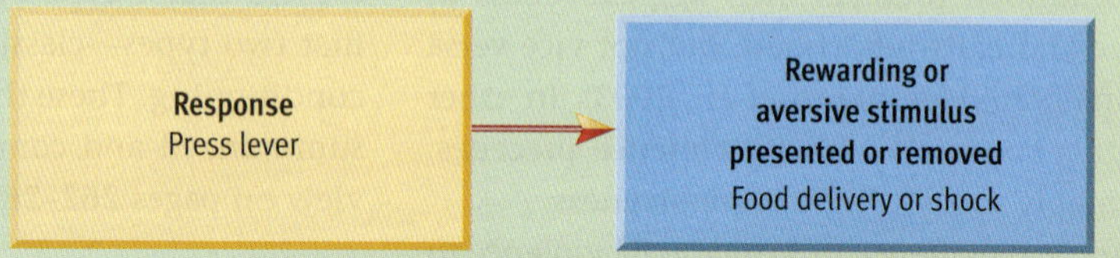

© Cengage Learning 2013

OBSERVATIONAL LEARNING

Albert Bandura

DIAGRAM:

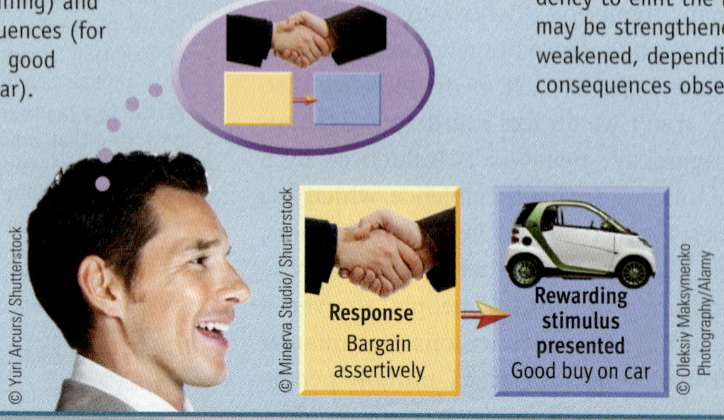

© Yuri Arcurs/ Shutterstock
© Minerva Studio/ Shutterstock
© Oleksiy Maksymenko Photography/Alamy
Illustrations of Pavlov, Skinner, and Bandura: © Cengage Learning 2013

TYPICAL KINDS OF RESPONSES	EXAMPLES IN ANIMALS	EXAMPLES IN HUMANS
Mostly (but not always) involuntary reflexes and visceral responses	Dogs learn to salivate to the sound of a tone that has been paired with meat powder.  © Bettmann/Corbis	Little Albert learns to fear a white rat and other white, furry objects through classical conditioning. 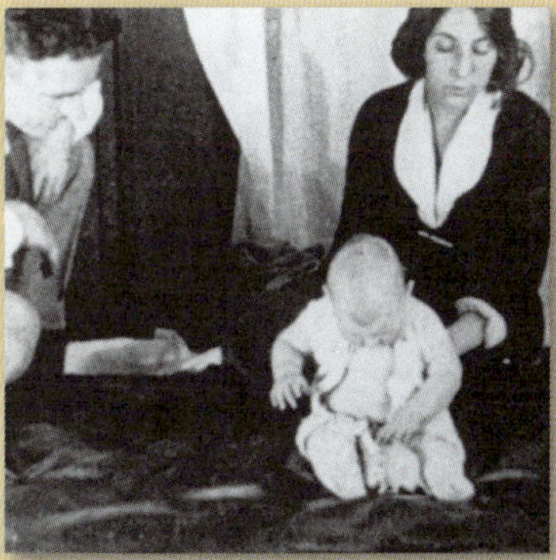 Archives of the History of American Psychology, University of Akron
Mostly (but not always) voluntary, spontaneous responses	Trained animals perform remarkable feats because they have been reinforced for gradually learning closer and closer approximations of responses they do not normally emit.  Courtesy of Animal Behavior Enterprises, Inc.	Casino patrons tend to exhibit high, steady rates of gambling, as most games of chance involve complex variable-ratio schedules of reinforcement.  © Masterfile/Royalty Free
Mostly voluntary responses, often consisting of novel and complex sequences	A dog spontaneously learns to mimic a human ritual.  © AP Images/Itsuo Inouye	A young girl performs a response that she has acquired through observation.  © Tom Morrison/Stone/Getty Images

CONCEPT CHECK 6.5

Identifying the Contributions of Major Theorists and Researchers

Check your recall of the principal ideas of important theorists and researchers covered in this chapter by matching the people listed on the left with the appropriate contributions described on the right. If you need help, the crucial pages describing each person's ideas are listed in parentheses. Fill in the letters for your choices in the spaces provided on the left. You'll find the answers in Appendix A.

Major Theorists and Researchers	Key Ideas and Contributions
_____ 1. Albert Bandura (pp. 257–259)	a. Known as the founder of behaviorism, this theorist conducted an influential early study of stimulus generalization with a young boy known as Little Albert.
_____ 2. John Garcia (p. 252)	b. This researcher showed that conditioned taste aversions are acquired quickly and easily because of mammals' evolutionary history.
_____ 3. Ivan Pavlov (pp. 230–237)	c. This influential American researcher described the process of operant conditioning, in which responses come to be controlled by their consequences.
_____ 4. Robert Rescorla (pp. 254–255)	d. This theorist conducted pioneering research on latent learning and cognitive maps. He was an early advocate of the view that conditioning involves cognitive processes.
_____ 5. Martin Seligman (pp. 252–253)	e. This person described the process of classical conditioning, including extinction and spontaneous recovery.
_____ 6. B. F. Skinner (pp. 240–247)	f. This person described the process of observational learning and conducted influential research on the effects of TV violence.
_____ 7. Edward C. Tolman (pp. 253–254)	g. This contemporary researcher showed that the predictive value of a conditioned stimulus influences the strength of conditioning, thus highlighting the importance of cognitive processes in classical conditioning.
_____ 8. John B. Watson (pp. 237–238)	h. This theorist used the concept of preparedness to explain why some phobias are acquired more readily than others, thus highlighting biological constraints on conditioning.

KEY LEARNING GOALS

6.19 Identify the two unifying themes highlighted in this chapter.

Reflecting on the Chapter's Themes

Heredity & Environment

Sociohistorical Context

Two of our seven unifying themes stood out in this chapter. First, you can see how nature and nurture interactively govern behavior. Second, looking at psychology in its sociohistorical context, you can see how progress in psychology spills over to affect trends and values in society at large. Let's examine each of these points in more detail.

In regard to nature versus nurture, research on learning clearly demonstrates the enormous power of the environment in shaping behavior. Pavlov's model of classical conditioning shows how experiences can account for everyday fears and other emotional responses. Skinner's model of operant conditioning shows how reinforcement and punishment can mold everything from a child's bedtime whimpering to an adult's restaurant preferences. Indeed, many learning theorists once believed that *all* aspects of behavior could be explained in terms of environmental determinants. In recent decades, however, studies of conditioned taste aversion and preparedness have shown that there are biological constraints on conditioning. Thus, even in explanations of learning—an area once dominated by nurture theories—we see once again that biology and experience jointly influence behavior.

The history of research on conditioning also shows how progress in psychology can seep into every corner of society. For example, the behaviorists' ideas about reinforcement and punishment have influenced patterns of discipline in our society. Research on operant conditioning has also affected management styles in the business world, leading to an increased emphasis on positive reinforcement. In the educational arena, the concept of individualized, programmed learning is a spinoff from behavioral research. The fact that the principles of conditioning are routinely applied in homes, businesses, schools, and factories clearly shows that psychology is not an ivory tower endeavor.

In the upcoming Personal Application, you will see how you can apply the principles of conditioning to improve your self-control, as we discuss the technology of behavior modification.

REVIEW OF KEY LEARNING GOALS

6.19 Two of our key themes were especially apparent in our coverage of learning and conditioning. One theme involves the interaction of heredity and environment in learning. The other involves the way progress in psychology affects society at large.

PERSONAL APPLICATION

Achieving Self-Control Through Behavior Modification

KEY LEARNING GOALS

6.20 Describe how to specify your target behavior and gather baseline data for a self-modification program.

6.21 Discuss how to design, execute, and evaluate a self-modification program.

Answer the following "yes" or "no."

___ **1** Do you have a hard time passing up food, even when you're not hungry?

___ **2** Do you wish you studied more often?

___ **3** Would you like to cut down on your smoking or drinking?

___ **4** Do you experience difficulty in getting yourself to exercise regularly?

If you answered "yes" to any of these questions, you have struggled with the challenge of self-control. This Application discusses how you can use the principles and techniques of behavior modification to improve your self-control. ***Behavior modification*** **is a systematic approach to changing behavior through the application of the principles of conditioning.** Advocates of behavior modification assume that behavior is mainly a product of learning, conditioning, and environmental control. They further assume that *what is learned can be unlearned.* Thus, they set out to "recondition" people to produce more desirable and effective patterns of behavior.

© Exactostock/Superstock

Overeating is just one of the many types of maladaptive habits that can be reduced or eliminated through self-modification techniques.

The technology of behavior modification has been applied with great success in schools, businesses, hospitals, factories, child-care facilities, prisons, and mental health centers (Kazdin, 2001; O'Donohue, 1998; Rachman, 1992). Moreover, behavior modification techniques have proven particularly valuable in efforts to improve self-control. Our discussion will borrow liberally from an excellent book on self-modification by David Watson and Roland Tharp (2007). We will discuss five steps in the process of self-modification, which are outlined in **Figure 6.29** on the next page.

Specifying Your Target Behavior

The first step in a self-modification program is to specify the target behavior(s) that you want to change. Behavior modification can only be applied to a clearly defined, overt response. Yet many people have difficulty pinpointing the behavior they hope to alter. They tend to describe their problems in terms of unobservable personality *traits* rather than overt *behaviors*. For example, asked what behavior he would like to change, a man might say, "I'm too irritable." That may be true, but it's of little help in designing a self-modification program. To use a behavioral approach, vague statements about traits need to be translated into precise descriptions of specific target behaviors.

To identify target responses, you need to ponder past behavior or closely observe future behavior and list specific *examples* of responses that lead to the trait description. For instance, the man who regards himself as "too irritable" might identify two overly frequent responses, such as arguing with his wife and snapping at his children. These are specific behaviors for which he could design a self-modification program.

Gathering Baseline Data

The second step in behavior modification is to gather baseline data. You need to systematically observe your target behavior for a period of time (usually a week or two) before you work out the details of your program. In gathering your baseline data, you need to monitor three things.

First, you need to determine the initial response level of your target behavior. You can't tell whether your program is working effectively unless you have a baseline for comparison. In most cases, you would simply keep track of how often the target response occurs in a certain time interval. Thus, you might count the daily frequency of snapping at your children, smoking cigarettes, or biting your fingernails. *It's crucial to gather accurate data.* You should record the behavior as soon as possible after it occurs. It's usually best to portray these records graphically (see **Figure 6.30** on the next page).

Second, you need to monitor the *antecedents* of your target behavior. Antecedents are events that typically precede the target

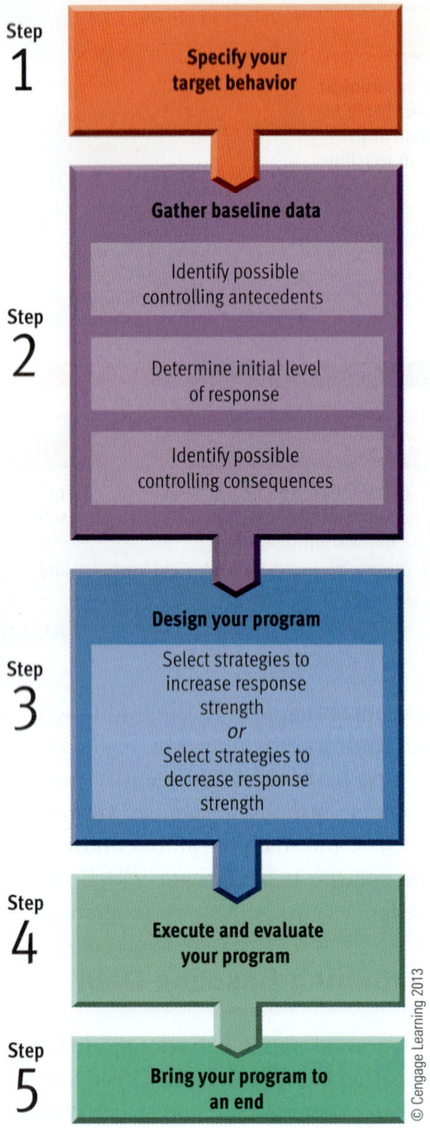

Figure 6.29

Steps in a self-modification program. This flowchart provides an overview of the five steps necessary to execute a self-modification program. Many people are tempted to plunge into their program and skip the first two steps, but these steps are critical to success.

response. Often these events play a major role in evoking your target behavior. For example, if your target is overeating, you might discover that the bulk of your overeating occurs late in the evening while you watch TV. If you can pinpoint this kind of antecedent-response connection, you may be able to design your program to circumvent or break the link.

Third, you need to monitor the typical consequences of your target behavior. Try to identify the reinforcers that are maintaining an undesirable target behavior, or the unfavorable outcomes that are suppressing a desirable target behavior. In trying to identify reinforcers, remember that avoidance behavior is usually maintained by negative reinforcement. That is, the payoff for avoidance is usually the removal of something aversive, such as anxiety or a threat to self-esteem. You should also take into account the fact that a response may not be reinforced every time, as most behavior is maintained by intermittent reinforcement.

Designing Your Program

Once you have selected a target behavior and gathered adequate baseline data, it's time to plan your intervention program. Generally speaking, your program will be designed to either increase or decrease the frequency of a target response.

Increasing Response Strength

Efforts to increase the frequency of a target response depend largely on the use of positive reinforcement. In other words, you reward yourself for behaving properly. Although the basic strategy is quite simple, doing it well involves a number of considerations.

Selecting a Reinforcer To use positive reinforcement, you need to find a reward that will be effective for you. Reinforcement is subjective. What is reinforcing for one person may not be reinforcing for another. To determine your personal reinforcers you need to ask yourself questions such as: What do I like to do for fun? What makes me feel good? What would be a nice present? What would I hate to lose? (See **Figure 6.31**.)

You don't have to come up with spectacular new reinforcers that you've never experienced before. *You can use reinforcers that you're already getting.* However, you have to restructure the contingencies so that you get them only if you behave appropriately. For example, if you normally buy ten iTunes songs per week, you might make these purchases contingent on studying a certain number of hours during the week.

Arranging the Contingencies Once you have chosen your reinforcer, you have to set up reinforcement contingencies. These contingencies will describe the exact behavioral goals that must be met and the reinforcement that may then be awarded. For example, in a program to increase exercise, you might

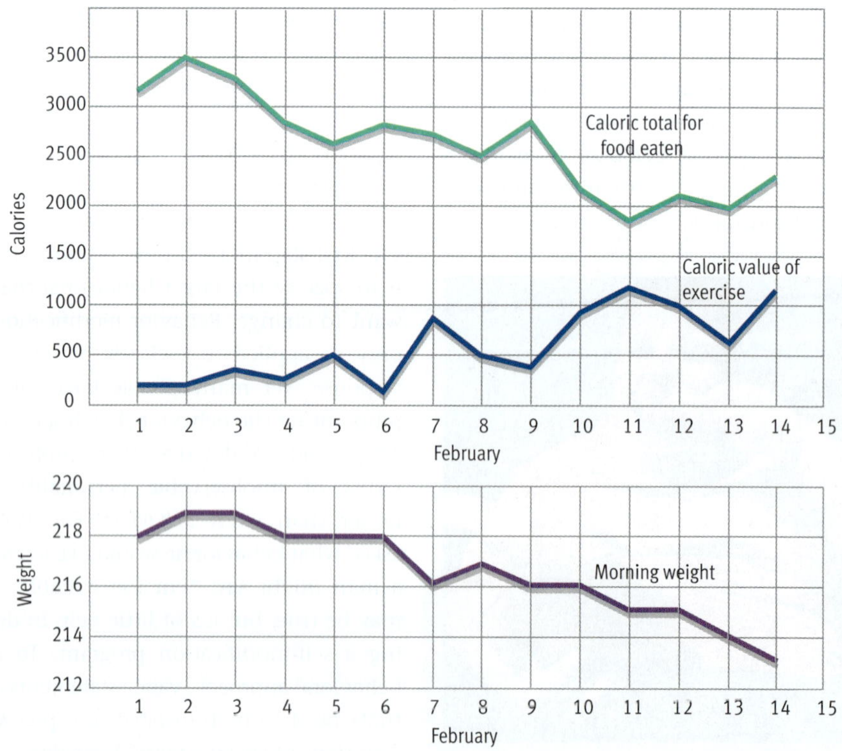

Figure 6.30

Example of recordkeeping in a self-modification program. Graphic records are ideal for tracking progress in behavior modification efforts. The records shown here illustrate what people would be likely to track in a behavior modification program for weight loss. © Cengage Learning 2013

Selecting a Reinforcer

1. What will be the rewards of achieving your goal?
2. What kind of praise do you like to receive, from yourself and others?
3. What kinds of things do you like to have?
4. What are your major interests?
5. What are your hobbies?
6. What people do you like to be with?
7. What do you like to do with those people?
8. What do you do for fun?
9. What do you do to relax?
10. What do you do to get away from it all?
11. What makes you feel good?
12. What would be a nice present to receive?
13. What kinds of things are important to you?
14. What would you buy if you had an extra $20? $50? $100?
15. On what do you spend your money each week?
16. What behaviors do you perform every day? (Don't overlook the obvious or commonplace.)
17. Are there any behaviors you usually perform instead of the target behavior?
18. What would you hate to lose?
19. Of the things you do every day, which would you hate to give up?
20. What are your favorite daydreams and fantasies?
21. What are the most relaxing scenes you can imagine?

© Cengage Learning 2013

Figure 6.31

Choosing a reinforcer for a self-modification program. Finding a good reinforcer to use in a behavior modification program can require a lot of thought. The questions listed here can help people identify their personal reinforcers.

SOURCE: Adapted from Watson, D. L., & Tharp, R. G. (1997). *Self-directed behavior: Self-modification for personal adjustment.* Belmont, CA: Wadsworth. Wadsworth is a part of Cengage Learning, Inc. Reproduced by permission. www.cengage.com/permissions

make spending $40 on clothes (the reinforcer) contingent on having jogged 15 miles during the week (the target behavior).

Try to set behavioral goals that are both challenging and realistic. You want your goals to be challenging so that they lead to improvement in your behavior. However, setting unrealistically high goals—goals you likely won't be able to reach—often leads to discouragement. This is a common mistake in self-modification.

Decreasing Response Strength

Let's turn now to the challenge of reducing the frequency of an undesirable response. You can go about this task in a number of ways. Your principal options include reinforcement, control of antecedents, and punishment.

Reinforcement Reinforcers can be used in an indirect way to decrease the frequency of a response. This statement may sound paradoxical since you have learned that reinforcement strengthens a response. The trick lies in how you define the target behavior. For example, in the case of overeating, you might define your target behavior as eating more than 1600 calories a day (an excess response that you want to decrease) or eating less than 1600 calories a day (a deficit response that you want to increase). You can choose the latter definition and reinforce yourself whenever you eat less than 1600 calories in a day. Thus, you can reinforce yourself for not emitting a response, or for emitting it less, and thereby decrease a response through reinforcement.

Control of Antecedents A worthwhile strategy for decreasing the occurrence of an undesirable response may be to identify its antecedents and avoid exposure to them. This strategy is especially useful when you're trying to decrease the frequency of your consumption, such as drinking or eating. In the case of overeating, for instance, the easiest way to resist temptation is to avoid having to face it. Thus, you might stay away from favorite restaurants, minimize time spent in your kitchen, shop for groceries just after eating (when willpower is higher), and avoid purchasing favorite foods.

Punishment The strategy of decreasing unwanted behavior by punishing yourself for that behavior is an obvious option that people tend to overuse. The biggest problem with punishment in a self-modification effort is that it's difficult to follow through and punish yourself. But there may be situations in which your manipulations of reinforcers need to be bolstered by the threat of punishment.

If you're going to use punishment, keep two guidelines in mind. First, don't use punishment alone. Use it in conjunction with positive reinforcement. If you set up a program in which you can earn only negative consequences, you probably won't stick to it. Second, use a relatively mild punishment so that you'll actually be able to administer it to yourself.

Executing and Ending Your Program

The fourth step is to put your program to work by enforcing the contingencies that you have carefully planned. You need to continue to accurately record the frequency of your target behavior so you can evaluate your progress. The success of your program depends on your not "cheating." The most common form of cheating is to reward yourself when you have not actually earned it.

You can do two things to increase the likelihood that you will comply with your program. One is to make up a ***behavioral contract*—a written agreement outlining a promise to adhere to the contingencies of a behavior modification program.** Signing such a contract in front of friends or family seems to make many people take their program more seriously. You can further reduce the likelihood of cheating by having someone other than yourself dole out the reinforcers and punishments.

In the fifth and final step, you should spell out in your program the conditions under which you will bring it to an end. Doing so involves setting end goals such as reaching a certain weight, studying with a certain regularity, or going without cigarettes for a certain length of time. It's often a good idea to phase out your program by planning a gradual reduction in the frequency or potency of your reinforcement for appropriate behavior.

REVIEW OF KEY LEARNING GOALS

6.20 Behavior modification techniques can be used to increase one's self-control. The first step in self-modification involves explicitly specifying the overt, measurable target behavior to be increased or decreased. The second step involves gathering data about the initial rate of the target response and identifying any typical antecedents and consequences associated with the behavior.

6.21 If you are trying to increase the strength of a response, you'll depend on positive reinforcement contingencies that should be spelled out exactly. A number of strategies can be used to decrease the strength of a response, including reinforcement, control of antecedents, and punishment. In executing and evaluating your program you should use a behavioral contract, monitor your behavior carefully, and decide how and when you will phase out your program.

KEY LEARNING GOALS

6.22 Recognize how classical conditioning is used to manipulate emotions.

Manipulating Emotions: Pavlov and Persuasion

With all due respect to the great Ivan Pavlov, when we focus on his demonstration that dogs can be trained to slobber in response to a tone, it's easy to lose sight of the importance of classical conditioning. At first glance, most people don't see a relationship between Pavlov's slobbering dogs and anything that they're even remotely interested in. However, in the main body of the chapter, we saw that classical conditioning actually contributes to the regulation of many important aspects of behavior, including fears, phobias, and other emotional reactions; immune function and other physiological processes; food preferences; and even sexual arousal. In this Application, you'll learn that classical conditioning is routinely used to manipulate emotions in persuasive efforts. If you watch TV, you have been subjected to Pavlovian techniques. An understanding of these techniques can help you recognize when your emotions are being manipulated by advertisers, politicians, and the media.

Manipulation efforts using Pavlovian conditioning generally involve *evaluative conditioning.* As noted earlier in the main body of the chapter, evaluative conditioning consists of efforts to transfer the liking attached to a US to a new CS. The key to this process is simply to manipulate the automatic, subconscious associations that people make in response to various stimuli. Let's look at how this manipulation is done in advertising, business negotiations, and the world of politics.

Classical Conditioning in Advertising

The art of manipulating people's associations has been perfected by the advertising industry. Advertisers consistently endeavor to pair the products they are peddling with stimuli that seem likely to elicit positive emotional responses (see **Figure 6.32**). An extensive variety of stimuli are used for this purpose. Products are paired with well-liked celebrity spokespersons; depictions of warm, loving families; beautiful pastoral scenery; cute, cuddly pets; enchanting, rosy-cheeked children; upbeat, pleasant music; and settings that reek of wealth. Advertisers also like to pair their products with exciting events, such as the NBA Finals, and cherished symbols, such as flags and the Olympic rings insignia. But, above all else, advertisers like to link their products with sexual imagery and extremely attractive models—especially, attractive women (Reichert, 2003; Reichert & Lambiase, 2003).

Advertisers mostly seek to associate their products with stimuli that evoke pleasurable feelings of a general sort. But in some cases they try to create more specific associations. For example, cigarette brands sold mainly to men are frequently paired with tough-looking men in rugged settings to create an association between the cigarettes and masculinity. In contrast, cigarette brands that are mainly marketed to women are paired with images that evoke feelings of femininity. In a similar vein, manufacturers of designer jeans typically seek to forge associations between their products and things that are young, urban, and hip. Advertisers marketing expensive automobiles or platinum credit cards pair their products with symbols of affluence, luxury, and privilege, such as mansions, butlers, and dazzling jewelry.

Classical Conditioning in Business Negotiations

In the world of business interactions, two standard practices are designed to get customers to make an association between

Figure 6.32

Classical conditioning in advertising. Many advertisers attempt to make their products conditioned stimuli that elicit pleasant emotional responses by pairing their products with attractive or popular people or sexual imagery.

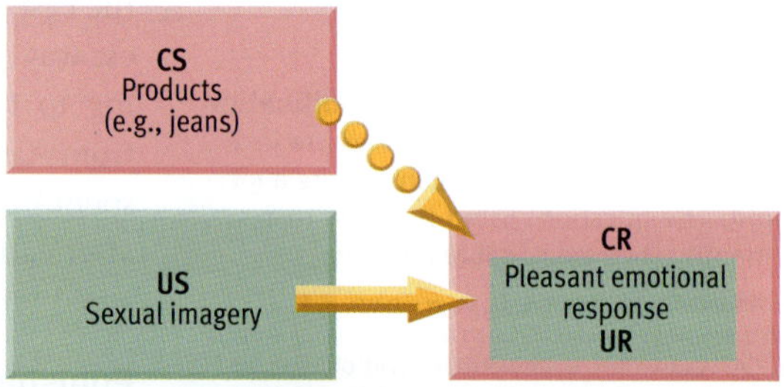

© Richard H. Cohen/Corbis

© Cengage Learning 2013

one's company and pleasurable feelings. The first is to take customers out to dinner at fine restaurants. Providing delicious food and fine wine in a luxurious environment is a powerful unconditioned stimulus that reliably elicits pleasant feelings likely to be associated with the host. The second practice is the strategy of entertaining customers at major events, such as concerts and football games. Over the last couple of decades, America's sports arenas have largely been rebuilt with vastly more "luxury skyboxes" to accommodate this business tactic. It reaches its zenith every year at the Super Bowl, where most of the seats go to the guests of Fortune 500 corporations. This practice pairs the host with both pleasant feelings and the excitement of a big event.

It's worth noting that these strategies take advantage of other processes besides classical conditioning. They also make use of the *reciprocity norm*—the social rule that one should pay back in kind what one receives from others (Cialdini, 2007). Thus, wining and dining clients creates a sense of obligation that they should reciprocate their host's generosity—presumably in their business dealings.

Classical Conditioning in the World of Politics

Like advertisers, candidates running for election need to influence the attitudes of many people quickly, subtly, and effectively. Evaluative conditioning helps them do so. For example, have you noticed how politicians show up at an endless variety of pleasant public events (such as the opening of a new mall) that often have nothing to do with their public service? When a sports team wins some sort of championship, local politicians are drawn like flies to the subsequent celebrations. They want to pair themselves with these positive events so that they are associated with pleasant emotions.

Election campaign ads use most of the same techniques as commercial ads. Candidates are paired with popular celebrities, wholesome families, pleasant music, and symbols of patriotism. Cognizant of the power of classical conditioning, politicians also exercise great care to ensure that they're not paired with people or events that might trigger negative feelings. For example, in 1999, when the U.S. government finally turned control of the Panama Canal over to Panama, President Bill Clinton and Vice-President Al Gore chose to not attend the ceremonies because this event was viewed negatively in some quarters.

The ultimate political perversion of the principles of classical conditioning probably occurred in Nazi Germany. The Nazis used many propaganda techniques to create prejudice toward Jews and members of other targeted groups (such as Gypsies). One such strategy was the repeated pairing of disgusting, repulsive images with stereotypical pictures of Jews. For example, the Nazis would show alternating pictures of rats or roaches crawling over filthy garbage and stereotypical Jewish faces so that the two images would become associated in the minds of the viewers. Thus, the German population was conditioned to have negative emotional reactions to Jews and to associate them with vermin to be exterminated.

Becoming More Aware of Classical Conditioning Processes

How effective are the efforts to manipulate people's emotions through classical conditioning? It's hard to say. In the real world, these strategies are always used in combination with other persuasive tactics, creating multiple confounds that make it difficult to assess the impact of the Pavlovian techniques (Walther et al., 2005). Lab research can eliminate these confounds, but surprisingly little research on these strategies has been published. Virtually all of it has dealt with advertising. The advertising studies suggest that classical conditioning can be effective and leave enduring imprints on consumers' attitudes (Grossman & Till, 1998; Shimp, Stuart, & Engle, 1991; Walther & Grigoriadis, 2003). And research indicates that sexual appeals in advertising are attention getting, likable, and persuasive (Reichert, Heckler, & Jackson, 2001). But a great deal of additional research is needed.

What can you do to reduce the extent to which your emotions are manipulated through Pavlovian procedures? Well, you could turn off your radio and TV, cancel your magazine subscriptions, stop your newspaper, disconnect from the Internet, and withdraw into a media-shielded shell. That hardly seems realistic for most people, though. Realistically, the best defense is to make a conscious effort to become more aware of the pervasive attempts to condition your emotions and attitudes. Some research on persuasion suggests that *to be forewarned is to be forearmed* (Pfau et al., 1990). In other words, if you know how media sources try to manipulate you, you should be more resistant to their strategies.

REVIEW OF KEY LEARNING GOALS

6.22 Advertisers routinely pair their products with stimuli that seem likely to elicit positive emotions or other specific feelings. The business practice of taking customers out to dinner or to major events also takes advantage of Pavlovian conditioning. Politicians also work to pair themselves with positive events. The best defense against these tactics is to become more aware of efforts to manipulate your emotions.

Table 6.2 Critical Thinking Skills Discussed in This Application

Skill	Description
Understanding how Pavlovian conditioning can be used to manipulate emotions	The critical thinker understands how stimuli can be paired together to create automatic associations that people may not be aware of.
Developing the ability to detect conditioning procedures used in the media	The critical thinker can recognize Pavlovian conditioning tactics in commercial and political advertisements.

© Cengage Learning 2013

Chapter 6 Practice Test

1. After repeatedly pairing a tone with meat powder, Pavlov found that a dog will salivate when the tone is presented. Salivation to the tone is a(n):
A. unconditioned stimulus.
B. unconditioned response.
C. conditioned stimulus.
D. conditioned response.

2. Sam's wife always wears the same black nightgown whenever she is "in the mood" for sexual relations. Sam becomes sexually aroused as soon as he sees his wife in the nightgown. For Sam, the nightgown is a(n):
A. unconditioned stimulus.
B. unconditioned response.
C. conditioned stimulus.
D. conditioned response.

3. Watson and Rayner (1920) conditioned "Little Albert" to fear white rats by banging a hammer on a steel bar as the child played with a white rat. Later, it was discovered that Albert feared not only white rats but white stuffed toys and Santa's beard as well. Albert's fear of these other objects can be attributed to:
A. negative reinforcement.
B. stimulus generalization.
C. stimulus discrimination.
D. an overactive imagination.

4. The phenomenon of higher-order conditioning shows that:
A. only a genuine, natural US can be used to establish a CR.
B. auditory stimuli are easier to condition than visual stimuli.
C. visual stimuli are easier to condition than auditory stimuli.
D. an already established CS can be used in the place of a natural US.

5. Which of the following statements is (are) true?
A. Classical conditioning regulates reflexive, involuntary responses exclusively.
B. Operant conditioning regulates voluntary responses exclusively.
C. The distinction between the two types of conditioning is not absolute.
D. Both a and b.

6. A pigeon in a Skinner box is pecking the disk at a high, steady rate. The graph portraying this pigeon's responding will have:
A. a steep, unchanging slope.
B. a shallow, unchanging slope.
C. a progressively steeper slope
D. a progressively shallower slope.

7. A primary reinforcer has ________ reinforcing properties; a secondary reinforcer has ________ reinforcing properties.
A. biological; acquired
B. conditioned; unconditioned
C. weak; potent
D. immediate; delayed

8. The steady, rapid responding of a person playing a slot machine is an example of the pattern of responding typically generated on a ________ schedule.
A. fixed-ratio
B. variable-ratio
C. fixed-interval
D. variable-interval

9. Positive reinforcement ________ the rate of responding; negative reinforcement ________ the rate of responding.
A. increases; decreases
B. decreases; increases
C. increases; increases
D. decreases; decreases

10. Research on avoidance learning suggests that a fear response is acquired through ________ conditioning; the avoidance response is maintained as a result of ________ conditioning.
A. classical; operant
B. operant; classical
C. classical; classical
D. operant; operant

11. Nolan used to love tequila. However, a few weeks ago he drank way too much tequila and became very, very sick. His tendency to drink tequila has since declined dramatically. In operant terms, this sequence of events represents:
A. generalization
B. negative reinforcement.
C. higher-order conditioning.
D. punishment.

12. According to Rescorla, the strength of a conditioned response depends on:
A. the number of trials in which the CS and US are paired.
B. the number of trials in which the CS is presented alone.
C. the percentage of trials in which the CS and US are paired.
D. resistance to extinction.

13. The link between media violence and subsequent aggressive behavior may be explained by:
A. observational learning.
B. noncontingent reinforcement.
C. resistance to extinction.
D. classical conditioning.

14. The *second* step in a self-modification program is to:
A. specify the target behavior.
B. design your program.
C. gather baseline data.
D. set up a behavioral contact.

15. When advertisers pair their products with likable celebrities, pleasant music, and beautiful scenery, they are attempting to make their products:
A. unconditioned stimuli.
B. conditioned stimuli.
C. conditioned responses.
D. primary reinforcers.

Answers

1 D pp. 232–233
2 C pp. 232–233
3 B pp. 237–238
4 D p. 239
5 C p. 240
6 A p. 242
7 A p. 242
8 B pp. 246–247
9 C pp. 247–248
10 A pp. 248–249
11 D pp. 249–250
12 C pp. 254–255
13 A pp. 258–261
14 C pp. 265–266
15 B p. 268

Chapter 6 Media Resources

PsykTrek

To view a demo: **www.cengage.com/psychology/psyktrek**
To order: **www.cengage.com/psychology/weiten**

Go to the PsykTrek website or CD-ROM for further study of the concepts in this chapter. Both online and on the CD-ROM, PsykTrek includes dozens of learning modules with videos, animations, and quizzes, as well as simulations of psychological phenomena and a multimedia glossary that includes word pronunciations.

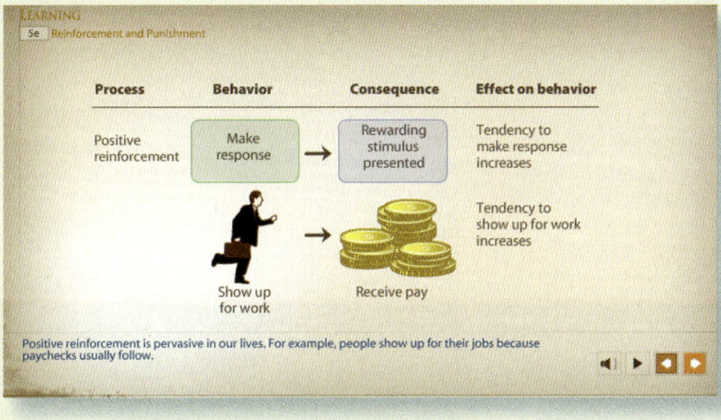

© Cengage Learning 2008

Explore the Unit 5 modules (5a through 5f) to improve your understanding of the principles of classical conditioning and operant conditioning.

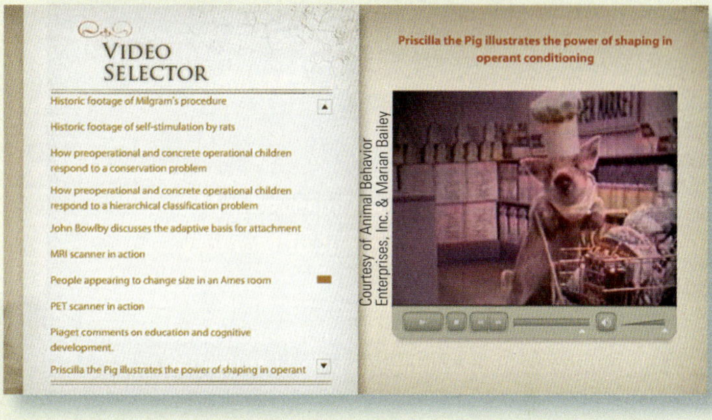

Courtesy of Animal Behavior Enterprises, Inc. & Marian Bailey
© Cengage Learning 2008

Go to the Video Selector to view famous subjects of behavioral research, including Priscilla the Pig, Little Albert, and Skinner's Ping-Pong-playing pigeons.

Reprinted by permission of Research Press
© Cengage Learning 2008

Go to the Video Selector to watch historic footage of influential behavior theorists, including Ivan Pavlov, B. F. Skinner, and Albert Bandura.

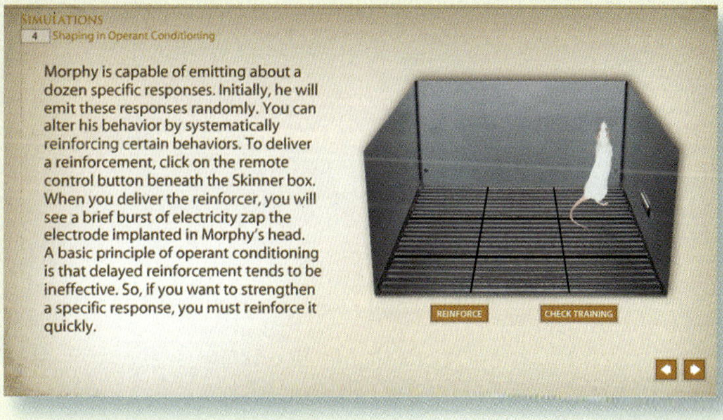

© Cengage Learning 2008

Discover the power of shaping by trying Simulation 4 (*Shaping in Operant Conditioning*), which allows you to shape Morphy, the virtual rat, to press a lever or run around in his box in whatever ways you dictate.

Online Study Tools

Log in to **CengageBrain** to access the resources your instructor requires. For this book, you can access:

CourseMate brings course concepts to life with interactive learning, study, and exam preparation tools that support the printed textbook. A textbook-specific website, Psychology CourseMate includes an integrated interactive eBook and other interactive learning tools such as quizzes, flashcards, videos, and more.

CengageNow is an easy-to-use online resource that helps you study in less time to get the grade you want—NOW. Take a pre-test for this chapter and receive a personalized study plan based on your results that will identify the topics you need to review and direct you to online resources to help you master those topics. Then take a post-test to help you determine the concepts you have mastered and what you will need to work on. If your textbook does not include an access code card, go to CengageBrain.com to gain access.

WebTutor is more than just an interactive study guide. WebTutor is an anytime, anywhere customized learning solution with an eBook, keeping you connected to your textbook, instructor, and classmates.

Aplia. If your professor has assigned Aplia homework:

1. Sign in to your account
2. Complete the corresponding homework exercises as required by your professor.
3. When finished, click "Grade It Now" to see which areas you have mastered, which need more work, and detailed explanations of every answer.

Visit **www.cengagebrain.com** to access your account and purchase materials.

7

Human Memory

© Frank Chmura/Alamy

If you live in the United States, you've undoubtedly handled thousands of American pennies. Surely, then, you remember what a penny looks like—or do you? Take a look at **Figure 7.1** on the next page. Which drawing corresponds to a real penny? Did you have a hard time selecting the real one? If so, you're not alone. Nickerson and Adams (1979) found that most people can't recognize the real penny in this collection of drawings. And their surprising finding was not a fluke. Undergraduates in England showed even worse memory for British coins (Jones, 1990). How can that be? Why do most of us have so poor a memory for an object we see every day?

Let's try another exercise. A definition of a word follows. It's not a particularly common word, but there's a good chance that you're familiar with it. Try to think of the word.

Definition: Favoritism shown or patronage granted by persons in high office to relatives or close friends.

If you can't think of the word, perhaps you can remember the letter of the alphabet it begins with, or what it sounds like. If so, you're experiencing the *tip-of-the-tongue phenomenon,* in which forgotten information feels like it's just out of reach. In this case, the word you may be reaching for is *nepotism.*

You've probably endured the tip-of-the-tongue phenomenon while taking exams. You blank out on a term that you're sure you know. You may feel as if you're on the verge of remembering the term, but you can't quite come up with it. Later, perhaps while you're driving home, the term suddenly comes to you. "Of course," you may say to yourself, "how could I forget that?" That's an interesting question. Clearly, the term was stored in your memory.

As these examples suggest, memory involves more than taking information in and storing it in some mental compartment. In fact, psychologists probing the workings of memory have had to grapple with three enduring questions: (1) How does information

Paradox: *Forgetting (of information that is no longer relevant) can enhance memory (for more important information).*

Figure 7.1

A simple memory test. Nickerson and Adams (1979) presented these 15 versions of an object most people have seen hundreds or thousands of times and asked, "Which one is correct?" Can you identify the real penny shown here?

SOURCE: Reprinted from Nickerson, R. S., & Adams, M. J. (1979). Long-term memory for a common object. *Cognitive Psychology, 11,* 287–307. Copyright © 1979 Elsevier Science with permission from Elsevier.

get *into* memory? (2) How is information *maintained* in memory? and (3) How is information pulled *back out* of memory? These three questions correspond to the three key processes involved in memory (see **Figure 7.2**): *encoding* (getting information in), *storage* (maintaining it), and *retrieval* (getting it out).

***Encoding* involves forming a memory code.** For example, when you form a memory code for a word, you might emphasize how it looks, how it sounds, or what it means. Encoding usually requires attention, which is why you may not be able to recall exactly what a penny looks like—most people don't pay much attention to the appearance of a penny. ***Storage* involves maintaining encoded information in memory over time.** Psychologists have focused much of their memory research on trying to identify just what factors help or hinder memory storage. But, as the tip-of-the-tongue phenomenon shows, information storage isn't enough to guarantee that you'll remember something. You need to be able to get information out of storage. ***Retrieval* involves recovering information from memory stores.** Research issues concerned with retrieval include the study of how people search memory and why some retrieval strategies are more effective than others.

Most of this chapter is devoted to an examination of memory encoding, storage, and retrieval. These basic processes help explain the ultimate puzzle in the study of memory: why people forget. Just as memory involves more than storage, forgetting involves more than "losing" something from the memory store. Forgetting may be due to deficiencies in any of the three key processes in memory—encoding, storage, or retrieval. After our discussion of forgetting, we will take a brief look at the physiological bases of memory. Finally, we will describe distinctions between various types of memory. The chapter's Personal Application provides some practical advice on how to improve your memory. The Critical Thinking Application discusses some reasons why memory is less reliable than people assume it to be.

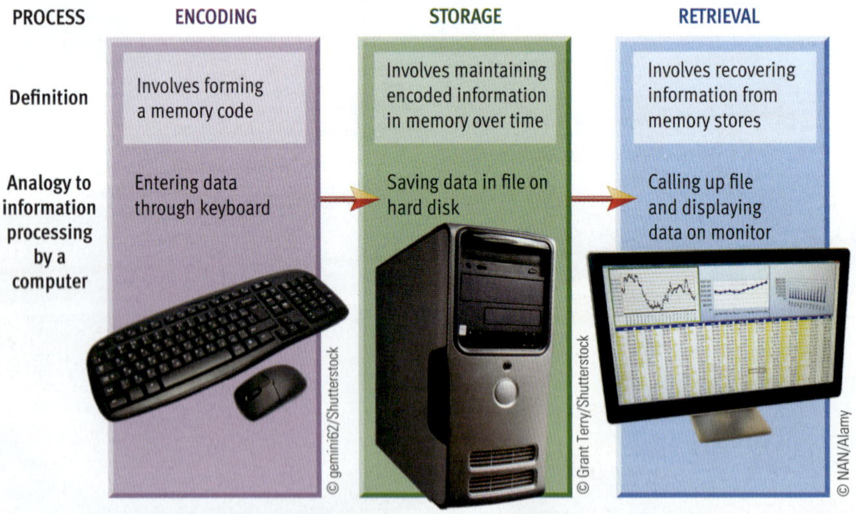

Figure 7.2

Three key processes in memory. Memory depends on three sequential processes: encoding, storage, and retrieval. Some theorists have drawn an analogy between these processes and elements of information processing by computers, as depicted here. The analogies for encoding and retrieval work pretty well, but the storage analogy is somewhat misleading. When information is stored on a hard drive, it remains unchanged indefinitely and you can retrieve an exact copy. As you will learn in this chapter, memory storage is a much more dynamic process. People's memories change over time and are rough reconstructions rather than exact copies of past events. © Cengage Learning 2013

Encoding: Getting Information into Memory

KEY LEARNING GOALS

7.1 Clarify the role of attention in memory, and discuss the effects of divided attention.

7.2 Describe the three types of encoding discussed by Craik and Lockhart, and explain how depth of processing relates to memory.

7.3 Identify four factors that can enrich encoding.

Have you ever been introduced to someone and then realized after only 30 seconds that you had already "forgotten" his or her name? This familiar kind of forgetting often results from a failure to form a memory code for the name. When you're introduced to people, you're usually busy sizing them up and thinking about what you're going to say. With your attention diverted, names go in one ear and out the other. You don't remember them because they aren't encoded for storage into memory. This common problem illustrates that active encoding is a crucial process in memory. In this section, we discuss the role of attention in encoding, various types of encoding, and ways to enrich the encoding process.

The Role of Attention

You generally need to pay attention to information if you intend to remember it (Lachter, Forster, & Ruthruff, 2004; Mulligan, 1998). For example, if you sit through a class lecture but pay little attention to it, you're unlikely to remember much of what the professor had to say. ***Attention* involves focusing awareness on a narrowed range of stimuli or events.** Selective attention is critical to everyday functioning. If your attention were distributed equally among all stimulus inputs, life would be utter chaos. You need to screen out most of the potential stimulation around you in order to read a book, converse with a friend, or even carry on a coherent train of thought.

Attention is often likened to a *filter* that screens out most potential stimuli while allowing a select few to pass through into conscious awareness. However, a great deal of debate has been devoted to *where* the filter is located in the information-processing system. The key issue in this debate is whether stimuli are screened out *early,* during sensory input, or *late,* after the brain has processed the meaning or significance of the input (see **Figure 7.3**).

Evidence on the "cocktail party phenomenon" suggests the latter. For example, imagine a young woman named Kate at a crowded party where many conversations are taking place. Kate is paying attention to her conversation with a friend and filtering out the other conversations. However, if someone in another conversation mentions her name, Kate may notice it, even though she has been ignoring that conversation. In experimental simulations of this situation, about 35% of participants report hearing their own name (Wood & Cowan, 1995). If selection is early, how can these people register input they've been blocking out? The cocktail party phenomenon suggests that attention involves *late* selection, based on the *meaning* of input.

Which view is supported by the weight of scientific evidence—early selection or late selection? Studies have found ample evidence for *both* as well as for intermediate selection (Posner & DiGirolamo, 2000; Treisman, 2009). These findings have led some theorists to conclude that the location of the attention filter may be flexible rather than fixed. According to Lavie (2005, 2007), the location depends on the "cognitive load" of current information processing. When one is attending to complicated, high-load tasks that consume much of one's attentional capacity, selection tends to occur early. However, when

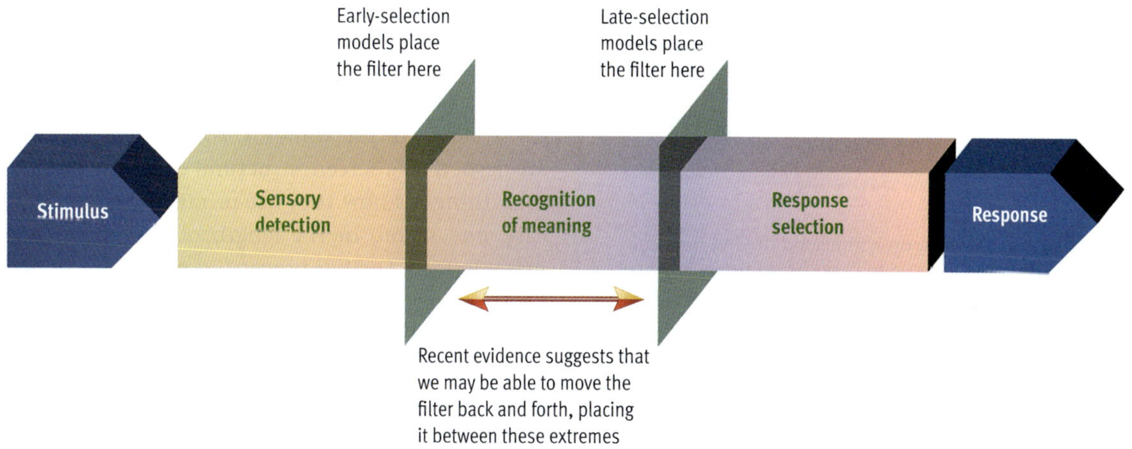

Figure 7.3
Models of selective attention. Early-selection models propose that input is filtered before meaning is processed. Late-selection models hold that filtering occurs after the processing of meaning. There is evidence to support early, late, and intermediate selection, suggesting that the location of the attentional filter may not be fixed. © Cengage Learning 2013

one is involved in simpler, low-load tasks, more attentional capacity is left over to process the meaning of distractions, allowing for later selection.

Wherever filtering occurs, it's clear that people have difficulty if they attempt to focus their attention on two or more inputs simultaneously. For example, if Kate tried to continue her original conversation while also monitoring the other conversation in which she was mentioned, she would struggle in her efforts to attend to both conversations and would remember less of her original conversation. Studies indicate that when participants are forced to divide their attention between memory encoding and some other task, large reductions in memory performance are seen (Craik, 2001; Craik & Kester, 2000).

Dr. Frank Ryan, "plastic surgeon to the stars," veered off a cliff on Pacific Coast Highway and died, apparently while texting.

Moreover, divided attention can have a negative impact on the performance of quite a variety of tasks, especially when the tasks are complex or unfamiliar (Pashler, Johnston, & Ruthruff, 2001). Although people tend to think that they can multitask with no deterioration in performance, research suggests that the human brain can effectively handle only one attention-consuming task at a time (Lien, Ruthruff, & Johnston, 2006). When people multitask, they really are switching their attention back and forth among tasks, rather than processing them simultaneously. That may be fine in some circumstances, but not in others.

Take, for example, the controversy about driving while talking on a cell phone. Carefully controlled research clearly demonstrates that cell phone conversations undermine people's driving performance, even when hands-free phones are used (Horrey & Wickens, 2006; Kass, Cole, & Stanny, 2007). One study of a simulated driving task found that cell phone conversations increased the chances of missing traffic signals and that they slowed down reactions to signals that were detected, as shown in **Figure 7.4** (Strayer & Johnston, 2001). Another study found that "the impairments associated with using a cell phone while driving can be as profound as those associated with driving while drunk" (Strayer, Drews, & Crouch, 2006).

A recent study shed some light on the finding that cell phone conversations are more distracting to drivers than conversations with passengers. The research showed that passengers adapt their conversation to the demands of the traffic and provide assistance to the driver (Drews, Pasupathi, & Strayer, 2008). In other words, when passengers see that traffic is heavy or that the driving task has become complicated, they reduce the rate and complexity of their communication and try to help the driver navigate through the situation. And as distracting as cell phone conversations are, research indicates that texting while driving is substantially more dangerous (Drews et al., 2009).

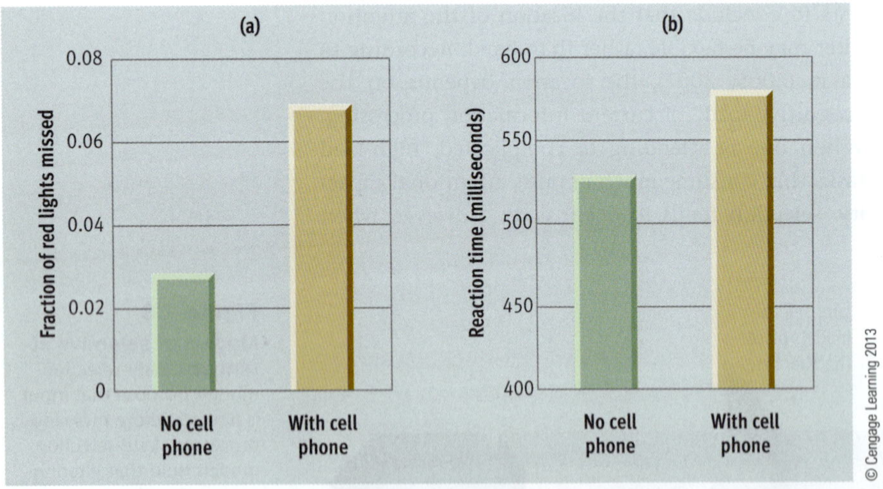

Figure 7.4

Divided attention and driving performance. Working on a simulated driving task, subjects in a study by Strayer and Johnston (2001) were supposed to brake as promptly as possible when they saw red lights while participating or not participating in a phone conversation. **(a)** The data on the left show that participants missed the red lights more than twice as often when engaged in a cell phone conversation. **(b)** The data on the right show that participants' reaction time to red lights was slower with the cell phone. (Data from Strayer & Johnston, 2001; graphic based on Goldstein, 2008)

SOURCE: Adapted from Strayer, D. L., & Johnston, W. A. (2001). Driven to distraction: Dual task studies of simulated driving and conversing on a cellular phone. *Psychological Science, 12,* 462–465. Copyright © 2001 Association for Psychological Science. Reprinted by permission of SAGE Publications.

Levels of Processing

PSYKTREK SIM5, 6a

Attention is critical to the encoding of memories. But not all attention is created equal. You can attend to things in different ways, focusing on different aspects of the stimulus input. According to some theorists, these qualitative differences in *how* people attend to information are important factors influencing how much they remember. Fergus Craik and Robert Lockhart (1972) proposed that incoming information can be processed at different levels. They maintained that in dealing with verbal information, people engage in three progressively deeper levels of processing: structural, phonemic, and semantic encoding (see **Figure 7.5**). *Structural encoding* is relatively shallow processing that emphasizes the physical structure of the stimulus. For example, if words are flashed on a screen, structural encoding registers such things as how they are printed (capital, lowercase, and so on) or the length of the words (how many letters). Further processing may result in *phonemic encoding,* which emphasizes what a word sounds like. Phonemic encoding involves naming or saying (perhaps silently) the words. Finally, *semantic encoding* emphasizes the meaning of verbal input. It involves thinking about the objects and actions the words represent. Craik and Lockhart's (1972) *levels-*

Level of processing	Type of encoding	Example of questions used to elicit appropriate encoding
Shallow processing	*Structural encoding:* emphasizes the physical structure of the stimulus	Is the word written in capital letters?
Intermediate processing	*Phonemic encoding:* emphasizes what a word sounds like	Does the word rhyme with weight?
Deep processing	*Semantic encoding:* emphasizes the meaning of verbal input	Would the word fit in the sentence: "He met a __________ on the street"?

Depth of processing

© Cengage Learning 2013

Figure 7.5

Levels-of-processing theory. According to Craik and Lockhart (1972), structural, phonemic, and semantic encoding—which can be elicited by questions such as those shown on the right—involve progressively deeper levels of processing, which should result in more durable memories.

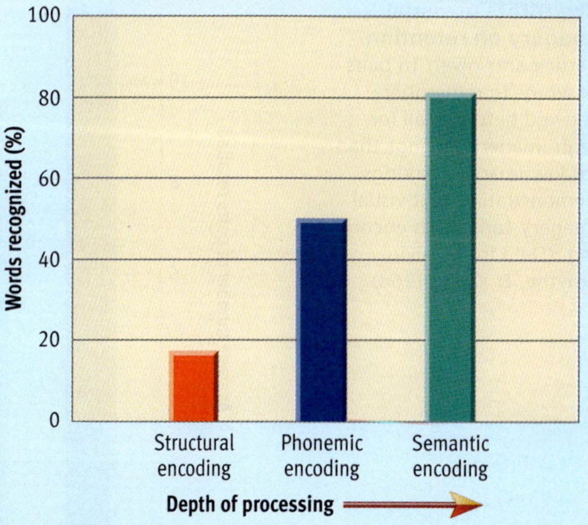

© Cengage Learning 2013

Figure 7.6

Retention at three levels of processing. In accordance with levels-of-processing theory, Craik and Tulving (1975) found that structural, phonemic, and semantic encoding, which involve progressively deeper levels of processing, led to progressively better retention.

of-processing theory proposes that deeper levels of processing result in longer-lasting memory codes.

In one experimental test of levels-of-processing theory, Craik and Tulving (1975) compared the memory effects of structural, phonemic, and semantic encoding. They directed participants' attention to particular aspects of briefly presented stimulus words by asking them questions about various characteristics of the words (see **Figure 7.5**). The questions were designed to engage the subjects in different levels of processing. After responding to 60 words, the participants received an unexpected test of their memory for the words. As predicted, the subjects' recall was low after structural encoding, notably better after phonemic encoding, and highest after semantic encoding (see **Figure 7.6**). The hypothesis that deeper processing leads to enhanced memory has been replicated in many studies (Craik, 2002; Lockhart & Craik, 1990).

Enriching Encoding

6a

Structural, phonemic, and semantic encoding do not exhaust the options when it comes to forming memory codes. There are other dimensions to encoding, dimensions that can enrich the encoding process and thereby improve memory.

Elaboration

Semantic encoding can often be enhanced through a process called elaboration. ***Elaboration* is linking a stimulus to other information at the time of encoding.** For example, let's say you read that phobias are often caused by classical conditioning, and you apply this idea to your own fear of spiders. In doing so, you are engaging in elaboration. The additional connections created by elaboration usually help people remember information. Differences in elaboration can help explain why different approaches to semantic processing result in varied amounts of retention (Toyota & Kikuchi, 2004, 2005; Willoughby, Motz, & Wood, 1997).

Visual Imagery

6a

Imagery, or the creation of visual images to represent words, can be used to enrich encoding. Some words are easier to create images for than others. If you were asked to remember the word *juggler,* you could readily form an image of someone juggling balls. However, if you were asked to remember the word *truth,* you would probably have more difficulty forming a suitable image. The difference is that *juggler* refers to a concrete object, whereas *truth* refers to an abstract concept. Allan Paivio (1969) has pointed out that it's easier to form images of concrete objects than of abstract concepts. He believes that this ease of image formation affects memory.

The beneficial effect of imagery on memory was demonstrated in a study by Paivio, Smythe, and Yuille (1968). They asked subjects to learn a list of 16 pairs of words. They manipulated whether the words were concrete, high-imagery words or abstract, low-imagery words. In terms of imagery potential, the list

Figure 7.7

The effect of visual imagery on retention. Participants given 16 pairs of words to remember showed better recall for high-imagery pairings than for low-imagery pairings, demonstrating that visual imagery can enrich encoding. (Data from Paivio, Smythe, & Yuille, 1968)

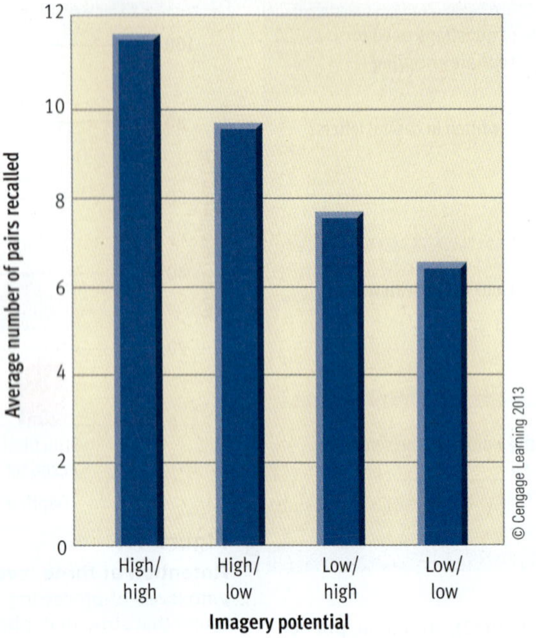

contained four types of pairings: high-high (*juggler-dress*), high-low (*letter-effort*), low-high (*duty-hotel*), and low-low (*quality-necessity*). The results showed that high-imagery words are easier to remember than low-imagery words (see **Figure 7.7**). Similar results were observed in a more recent study that controlled for additional factors (Paivio, Khan, & Begg, 2000).

According to Paivio (1986, 2007), imagery facilitates memory because it provides a second kind of memory code, and two codes are better than one. His *dual-coding theory* holds that memory is enhanced by forming semantic and visual codes, since either can lead to recall.

Self-Referent Encoding

Making material *personally* meaningful can also enrich encoding. People's recall of information tends to be slanted in favor of material that is relevant to them (Kahan & Johnson, 1992). ***Self-referent encoding*** **involves deciding how or whether information is personally relevant.** This approach to encoding was compared to structural, phonemic, and semantic encoding in a study by Rogers, Kuiper, and Kirker (1977). To induce self-referent encoding, they asked subjects to decide whether adjectives flashed on a screen applied to them personally. The results showed that self-referent encoding led to improved recall of the adjectives.

Motivation to Remember

Another factor that appears to influence encoding effectiveness is one's *motivation to remember (MTR)* at the time of encoding. When MTR is high at the time of encoding—typically because the information is perceived to be important—people are more likely to exert extra effort to attend to and organize information in ways that facilitate future recall. In a recent investigation, participants were asked to memorize facts about six people presented in photos (Kassam et al., 2009). Motivation to remember was manipulated, either at the time of encoding or at the time of retrieval, by offering participants a financial bonus for every fact they recalled about a specific target person. The results showed that increasing MTR at the time of encoding led to greater recall, whereas increasing MTR as the time of retrieval had little effect (see **Figure 7.8**). Thus, encoding processes can be enhanced by strong motivation.

Figure 7.8

The effect of motivation to remember (MTR) on subsequent recall. Participants' motivation to remember was increased either at the time of encoding, the time of retrieval, or not at all in a control condition. Raising MTR at the time of encoding increased recall, but raising MTR at the time of retrieval did not.

SOURCE: Adapted from Kassam, K. S., Gilbert, D. T., Swencionis, J. K., & Wilson, T. D. (2009). Misconceptions of memory: The Scooter Libby effect. *Psychological Science, 20,* 551–552. Copyright © 2009 SAGE Publications. Reprinted by permission of SAGE Publications.

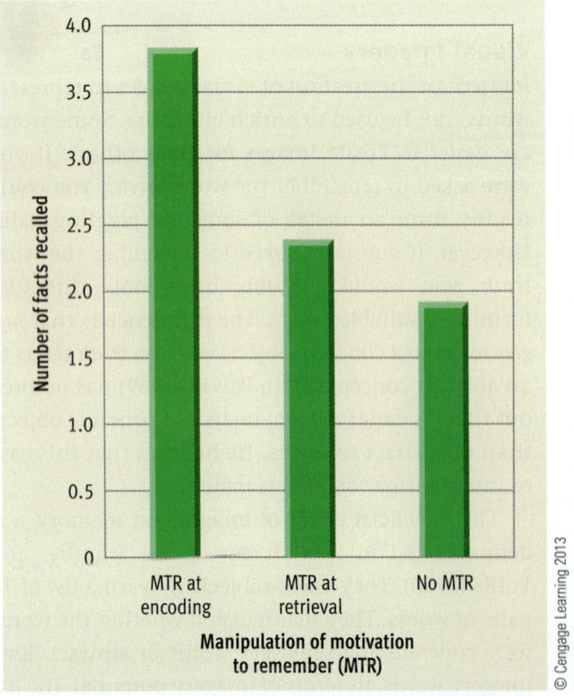

REVIEW OF KEY LEARNING GOALS

7.1 Attention, which fosters encoding, is inherently selective and has been compared to a filter. The cocktail party phenomenon suggests that input is screened late in mental processing. Evidence indicates that the location of the attention filter may be flexible, depending on the cognitive load of current processing. Divided attention undermines encoding and performance on other tasks, including driving.

7.2 According to levels-of-processing theory, structural, phonemic, and semantic encoding represent progressively deeper levels of processing. Deeper processing generally results in better recall of information.

7.3 Elaboration enriches encoding by linking a stimulus to other information. The creation of visual images to represent words can enrich encoding. Visual imagery may help by creating two memory codes rather than just one. Self-referent encoding that emphasizes personal relevance may be especially useful in facilitating retention. Increasing the motivation to remember at the time of encoding can enhance memory.

Storage: Maintaining Information in Memory

KEY LEARNING GOALS

7.4 Describe the sensory store in memory, and discuss the durability and capacity of short-term memory.

7.5 Describe Baddeley's model of working memory, and discuss the research on working memory capacity.

7.6 Review findings on the nature and durability of long-term memory.

7.7 Describe conceptual hierarchies and schemas, and their role in long-term memory.

7.8 Explain the role of semantic networks and connectionist networks in memory.

In their efforts to understand memory storage, theorists have historically related it to the technologies of their age (Roediger, 1980). One of the earliest models used to explain memory storage was the wax tablet. Both Aristotle and Plato compared memory to a block of wax that differed in size and hardness for various individuals. Remembering, according to this analogy, was like stamping an impression into the wax. As long as the image remained in the wax, the memory would remain intact.

Modern theories of memory reflect the technological advances of the 20th century. For example, many theories formulated at the dawn of the computer age drew an analogy between information storage by computers and information storage in human memory (Atkinson & Shiffrin, 1968, 1971; Broadbent, 1958; Waugh & Norman, 1965). The main contribution of these *information-processing theories* was to subdivide memory into three separate memory stores (Estes, 1999; Pashler & Carrier, 1996). The names for these stores and their exact characteristics varied some from one theory to the next. For purposes of simplicity, we'll organize our discussion around the model devised by Richard Atkinson and Richard Shiffrin, as it has proved to be the most influential of the information-processing theories. According to their model, incoming information passes through two temporary storage buffers—the sensory store and short-term store—before it's transferred into a long-term store (see **Figure 7.9**). Like the wax tablet before it, the information-processing model of memory serves as a metaphor. The three memory stores are not viewed as anatomical structures in the brain, but rather as functionally distinct types of memory.

Sensory Memory

PSYKTREK 6b

***Sensory memory* preserves information in its original sensory form for a brief time, usually only a fraction of a second.** Sensory memory allows the sensation of a visual pattern, sound, or touch to linger for a brief moment after the sensory stimulation is over. In the case of vision, people really perceive an *afterimage* rather than the actual stimulus. You can demonstrate the existence of afterimages for yourself by rapidly moving a lighted sparkler or flashlight in circles in the dark. If you move a sparkler fast enough, you should see a complete circle even though the light source is only a single point (see the adjacent photo). Sensory memory preserves the sensory image long enough for you to perceive a continuous circle rather than separate points of light.

The brief preservation of sensations in sensory memory is adaptive in that it gives you additional time to try to recognize stimuli. However,

© Wayne Weiten

Because the image of the sparkler persists briefly in sensory memory, when the sparkler is moved fast enough, the blending of afterimages causes people to see a continuous stream of light instead of a succession of individual points.

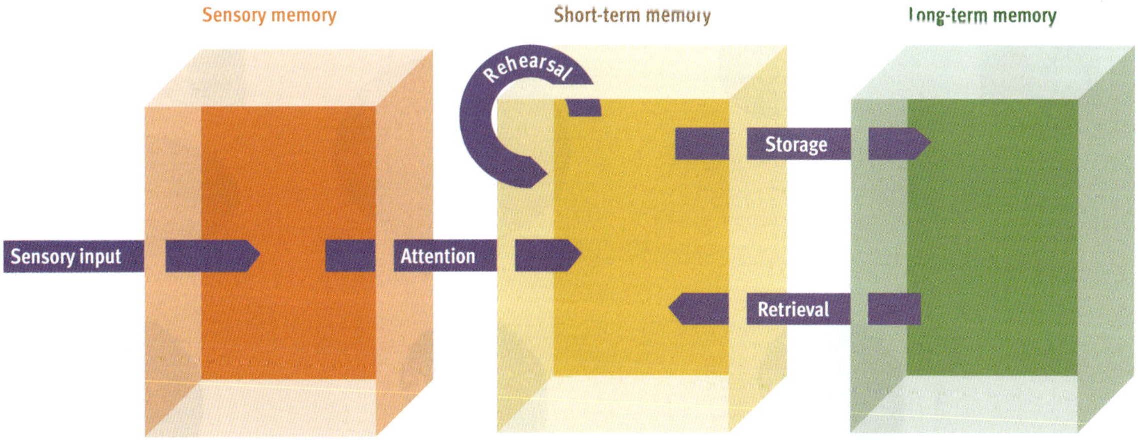

Figure 7.9

The Atkinson and Shiffrin model of memory storage. Atkinson and Shiffrin (1971) proposed that memory is made up of three information stores. *Sensory memory* can hold a large amount of information just long enough (a fraction of a second) for a small portion of it to be selected for longer storage. *Short-term memory* has a limited capacity, and unless aided by rehearsal, its storage duration is brief. *Long-term memory* can store an apparently unlimited amount of information for indeterminate periods. © Cengage Learning 2013 you'd better take advantage of this stimulus persistence immediately, because it doesn't last long. This brevity was demonstrated in a classic experiment by George Sperling (1960). His subjects saw three rows of letters flashed on a screen for just 1/20 of a second. A tone following the exposure signaled which row of letters the subject should report to the experimenter. Participants were fairly accurate when the signal occurred immediately. However, their accuracy steadily declined as the delay of the tone increased to one second. Why? Because memory traces in the sensory store decay in about 1/4 of a second (Massaro & Loftus, 1996). There is some debate about whether stimulus persistence really involves *memory storage* (Nairne, 2003). According to some theorists, the brief persistence of stimuli may be more like an echo than a memory.

Short-Term Memory 6b

***Short-term memory (STM)* is a limited-capacity store that can maintain unrehearsed information for about 10–20 seconds.** In contrast, information stored in long-term memory may last weeks, months, or years. However, there is a way that you can maintain information in your short-term store indefinitely. How? Primarily, by engaging in ***rehearsal*—the process of repetitively verbalizing or thinking about the information.** For instance, when you look up a phone number, you probably recite it over and over until you can dial it. Rehearsal keeps recycling the information through your short-term memory. This reliance on recitation illustrates why short-term memory has been thought to depend primarily on *phonemic encoding.*

Durability of Storage 6b

Without rehearsal, information in short-term memory is lost in 10 to 20 seconds (Nairne, 2003). This rapid loss was demonstrated in a study by Peterson and Peterson (1959). They measured how long undergraduates could remember three consonants if they couldn't rehearse them. To prevent rehearsal, the Petersons required the students to count backward by threes from the time the consonants were presented until they saw a light that signaled the recall test (see **Figure 7.10**). Their results showed that subjects' recall accuracy was pretty dismal (about 10%) after only 15 seconds. Theorists originally believed that the loss of information from short-term memory was due purely to time-related *decay* of memory traces. But follow-up research showed that *interference* from competing material also contributes (Lewandowsky, Duncan, & Brown, 2004; Nairne, 2002).

Capacity of Storage 6b

Short-term memory is also limited in the number of items it can hold. The small capacity of STM was pointed out by George Miller (1956) in a famous paper called "The Magical Number Seven, Plus or Minus Two: Some Limits on Our Capacity for Processing In-

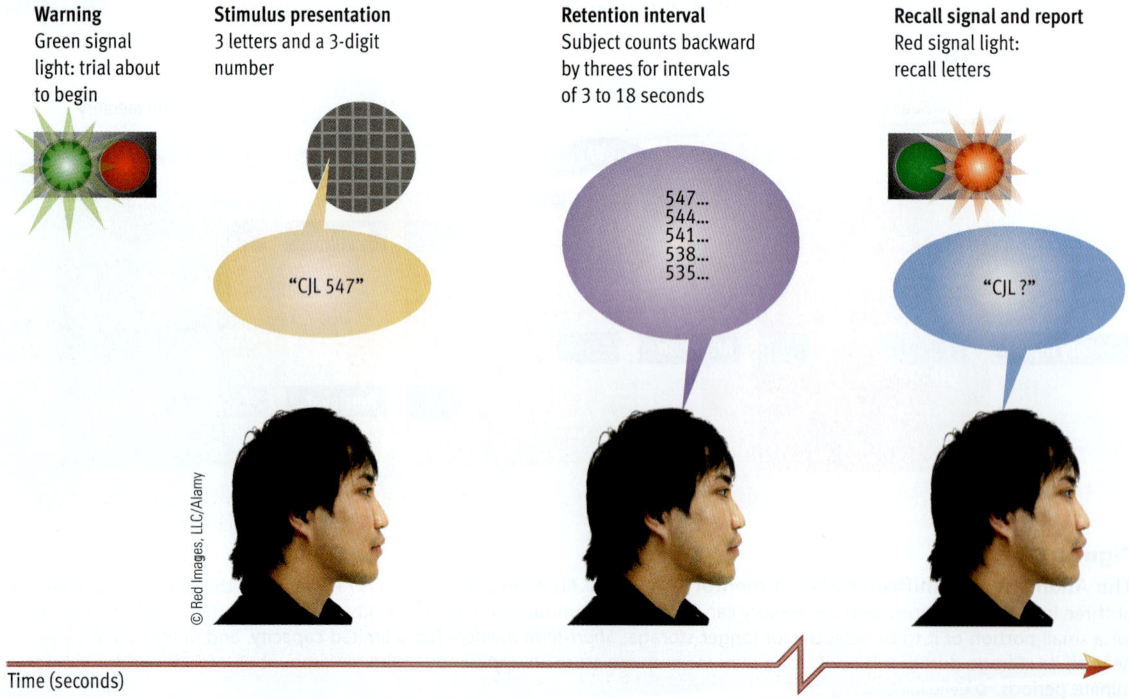

Figure 7.10
Peterson and Peterson's (1959) study of short-term memory. After a warning light was flashed, the participants were given three consonants to remember. The researchers prevented rehearsal by giving the subjects a three-digit number at the same time and telling them to count backward by threes from that number until given the signal to recall the letters. By varying the amount of time between stimulus presentation and recall, Peterson and Peterson (1959) were able to measure how quickly information was lost from short-term memory. © Cengage Learning 2013

formation." Miller noticed that people could recall only about seven items in tasks that required the use of STM. When short-term memory is filled to capacity, the insertion of new information "bumps out" some of the information currently in STM. The limited capacity of STM constrains people's ability to perform tasks in which they need to mentally juggle various pieces of information (Baddeley & Hitch, 1974).

The capacity of short-term memory may even be less than widely assumed. Nelson Cowan (2005, 2010) cites evidence indicating that the capacity of STM is *four* plus or minus *one*. The consensus on the capacity of STM seems to be moving toward this smaller estimate (Lustig et al., 2009). According to Cowan, the capacity of STM has historically been overestimated because researchers have often failed to take steps to prevent covert rehearsal or *chunking* by participants.

It has long been known that people can increase the capacity of their short-term memory by combining stimuli into larger, possibly higher-order units, called *chunks* (Simon, 1974). **A *chunk* is a group of familiar stimuli stored as a single unit.** You can demonstrate the effect of chunking by asking someone to recall a sequence of 12 letters grouped in the following way:

FB - INB - CC - IAIB - M

As you read the letters aloud, pause at the hyphens. Your subject will probably attempt to remember each letter separately because there are no obvious groups or chunks. But a string of 12 letters is too long for STM, so errors are likely. Now present the same string of letters to another person, but place the pauses in the following locations:

FBI - NBC - CIA - IBM

The letters now form four familiar chunks that should occupy only four slots in STM, resulting in successful recall (Bower & Springston, 1970).

To successfully chunk the letters I B M, a subject must first recognize these letters as a familiar unit. This familiarity has to be stored somewhere in long-term memory. Thus, in this case, information was transferred from long-term into short-term memory. This situation is not unusual. People routinely draw information out of their long-term memory banks to help them evaluate and understand information they're working with in short-term memory.

Short-Term Memory as "Working Memory"

PsykTrek 6b

Research eventually uncovered a number of problems with the original model of short-term memory (Bower, 2000). Among other things, studies showed that short-term memory is *not* limited to phonemic encoding and that decay is *not* the only process responsible for the loss of information from STM. These and other findings suggested that short-term memory involves more than a simple rehearsal buffer, as originally proposed. Alan Baddeley (1986, 1992, 2001, 2007) has developed a more complex, modular model of short-term memory that characterizes it as "working memory." Baddeley's model of working memory consists of the four components depicted in **Figure 7.11**.

The first component is the *phonological loop* that represented all of short-term memory in earlier models. This component is at work when you use recitation to temporarily hold on to a phone number. The second component in working memory is a *visuospatial sketchpad* that permits people to temporarily hold and manipulate visual images. This element is at work when you try to mentally rearrange the furniture in your bedroom or map out a route to travel somewhere. The third component is a *central executive* system. It controls the deployment of attention, switching the focus of attention and dividing attention as needed. The central executive also coordinates the actions of the other modules. The fourth component is the *episodic buffer*. It is a temporary, limited-capacity store that allows the various components of working memory to integrate information. It also serves as the interface between working memory and long-term memory.

The concept of working memory still includes the two key characteristics that originally defined short-term memory—limited capacity and storage

Reality CHECK

Misconception

The capacity of short-term memory (STM) is seven plus or minus two.

Reality

Calling this assertion a misconception is a little harsh, as it has been the conventional wisdom since the 1950s and there is room for argument on the matter. However, in the last decade or so researchers using more sophisticated methods have been chipping away at this maxim. The consensus among memory experts has shifted toward the belief that the capacity of STM is four plus or minus one.

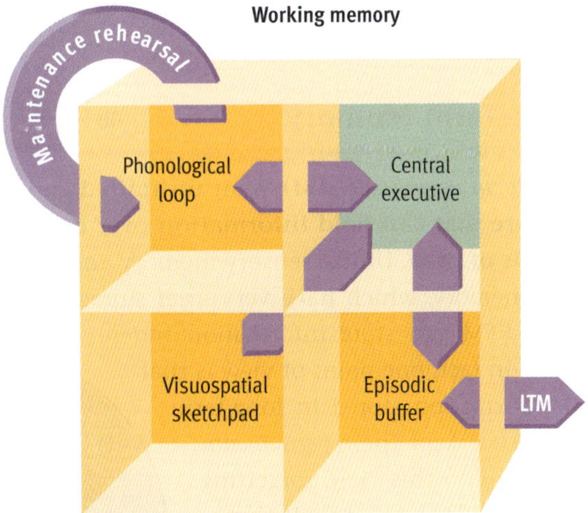

Figure 7.11

Baddeley's model of working memory. This diagram depicts the revised model of the short-term store proposed by Alan Baddeley. According to Baddeley (2001), working memory includes four components: a phonological loop, a visuospatial sketchpad, a central executive system, and an episodic buffer. The elements shown in yellow are memory stores, whereas the central executive is not. © Cengage Learning 2013

© Courtesy of Alan Baddeley

Alan Baddeley

"The concept of working memory proposes that a dedicated system maintains and stores information in the short term, and that this system underlies human thought processes."

duration. But Baddeley's model accounts for evidence that STM handles a greater variety of functions than previously thought.

Baddeley's model of working memory has generated an enormous volume of research. For example, studies have shown that people vary in how well they can juggle information in their working memory while fending off distractions (Engle, 2001). ***Working memory capacity (WMC)* refers to one's ability to hold and manipulate information in conscious attention.** WMC is a stable personal trait (Unsworth et al., 2005) that appears to be influenced to a considerable degree by heredity (Kremen et al., 2007). That said, WMC can be temporarily reduced by situational factors such as pressure to perform or excessive worry (Gimmig et al., 2006; Hayes, Hirsch, & Matthews, 2008).

Variations in working memory capacity correlate positively with measures of high-level cognitive abilities, such as reading comprehension, complex reasoning, and even intelligence (Conway, Kane, & Engle, 2003; Shelton et al., 2009, 2010). This finding has led some theorists to conclude that working memory capacity is critical to complex cognition and intelligence (Lepine, Barrouillet, & Camos, 2005). Variations in WMC also appear to influence musical ability, as reading music while playing an instrument taxes working memory capacity (Meinz & Hambrick, 2010). Some theorists argue that increases in WMC tens of thousands of years ago were crucial to the evolution of complex cognitive processes and creativity in humans (Coolidge & Wynn, 2009). These analyses are highly speculative, but they highlight the profound importance of working memory capacity (Balter, 2010).

Long-Term Memory

***Long-term memory (LTM)* is an unlimited capacity store that can hold information over lengthy periods of time.** Unlike sensory memory and short-term memory, which have very brief storage durations, LTM can store information indefinitely. In fact, one point of view is that all information stored in long-term memory is kept there *permanently*. According to this view, forgetting occurs only because people sometimes cannot *retrieve* needed information from LTM.

The notion that LTM storage may be permanent is certainly intriguing. Two interesting lines of research seemed to provide compelling evidence for permanent storage. However, each turned out to be less convincing than appeared at first glance. The first line of research consisted of some landmark studies conducted by Canadian neuroscientist Wilder Penfield in the 1960s. He reported triggering memories through electrical stimulation of the brain (ESB) during brain surgeries (Penfield & Perot, 1963). When Penfield used ESB (see Chapter 3) to map brain function in patients undergoing surgery for epilepsy, he found that stimulation of the temporal lobe sometimes elicited vivid descriptions of events long past. Patients would describe scenes that apparently came from their childhood—such as "being in a lumberyard" or "watching Mom make a phone call"—as if they were there once again. Penfield and others inferred that these descriptions were exact playbacks of long-lost memories unearthed by electrical stimulation of the brain.

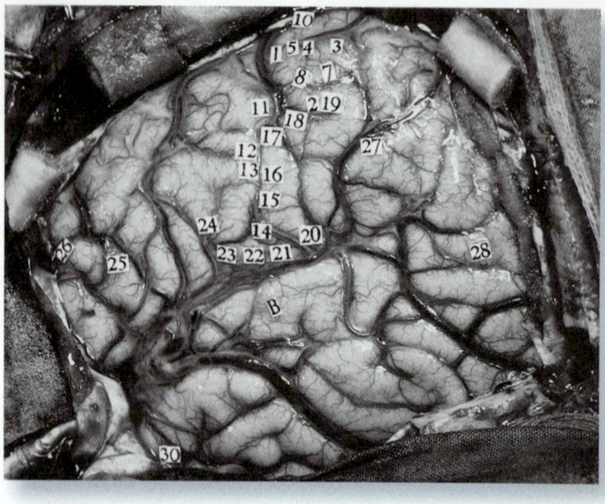

© Reproduced with the permission of the Literary Executors of the Wilder Penfield Estate, courtesy of William Feindel

Wilder Penfield and his associates conducted a series of studies with human subjects undergoing brain surgery for medical reasons. In these studies they used electrical stimulation of the brain to map out brain function in the cortex. In the course of these studies they thought they triggered long-lost memories when they stimulated areas in the temporal lobe (seen near the bottom of the photo). However, as your text explains, subsequent evidence led to a reinterpretation of their findings.

The second line of research has centered on the phenomenon of *flashbulb memories*. ***Flashbulb memories* are unusually vivid and detailed recollections of the circumstances in which people learned about momentous, newsworthy events.** For instance, many older adults in the United States can remember exactly where they were, what they were doing, and how they felt when they learned that President John F. Kennedy had been shot. Younger adults have a similar recollection related to the terrorist attacks that took place in New York and Washington, DC on September 11, 2001. The vivid detail of people's memories of how

© terekhov igor/Shutterstock

CONCEPT CHECK 7.1

Comparing the Memory Stores

Check your understanding of the three memory stores by filling in the blanks in the table below. The answers can be found in the back of the book in Appendix A.

Feature	Sensory memory	Short-term memory	Long-term memory
Main encoding format	*copy of input*		*largely semantic*
Storage capacity	*limited*		
Storage duration		*10–20 seconds*	

they learned about these events would seem to provide a striking example of permanent storage.

So, why don't these findings demonstrate that LTM storage is permanent? Let's look at each. Closer scrutiny eventually showed that the remarkable "memories" activated by ESB in Penfield's studies often included major distortions or factual impossibilities. For instance, the person who recalled being in a lumberyard had never actually been to one. The ESB-induced recollections of Penfield's subjects apparently were hallucinations, dreams, or loose reconstructions of events rather than exact replays of the past (Squire, 1987).

In a similar vein, subsequent research has undermined the notion that flashbulb memories represent an instance of permanent storage. Although flashbulb memories tend to be strong, vivid, and detailed, studies suggest they are neither as accurate nor as special as once believed (Hirst et al., 2009; Schmolck, Buffalo, & Squire, 2000). Like other memories, they become less detailed and complete with time and are often inaccurate (Cubelli & Della Sala, 2008; Talarico & Rubin, 2009). Recent research suggests that it is not extraordinary accuracy or longevity that distinguishes flashbulb memories. Rather, what makes them special is that people subjectively feel that these memories are exceptionally vivid, people have exceptional confidence (albeit misplaced) in their accuracy, and attach more emotional intensity to them (Talarico & Rubin, 2003, 2007). So, perhaps flashbulb memories are "special," but not in the way originally envisioned. In sum, although the possibility cannot be ruled out completely, there is no convincing evidence that memories are stored away permanently and that forgetting is all a matter of retrieval failure (Payne & Blackwell, 1998; Schacter, 1996).

© Sean Adair/Reuters

Flashbulb memories are vivid and detailed recollections of momentous events. For example, many people will long remember exactly where they were and how they felt when they learned about the terrorist attacks on the World Trade Center.

How Is Knowledge Represented and Organized in Memory?

PSYKTREK 6b

Over the years, memory researchers have wrestled endlessly with another major question relating to memory storage: How is knowledge represented and organized in memory? In other words, what forms do mental representations of information take? Most theorists seem to agree that they probably take a variety of forms, depending on the nature of the material that needs to be tucked away in memory. Most of the theorizing to date has focused on how factual knowledge may be represented in memory. In this section, we'll look at a small sample of the organizational structures that have been proposed for semantic information.

Figure 7.12

Conceptual hierarchies and long-term memory. Some types of information can be organized into a multilevel hierarchy of concepts, like the one shown here, which was studied by Bower and others (1969). They found that subjects remember more information when they organize it into a conceptual hierarchy.

SOURCE: Adapted from Bower, G. (1970). Organizational factors in memory. *Cognitive Psychology, 1*(1), 18–46. Copyright © 1970 Elsevier Science, with permission from Elsevier.

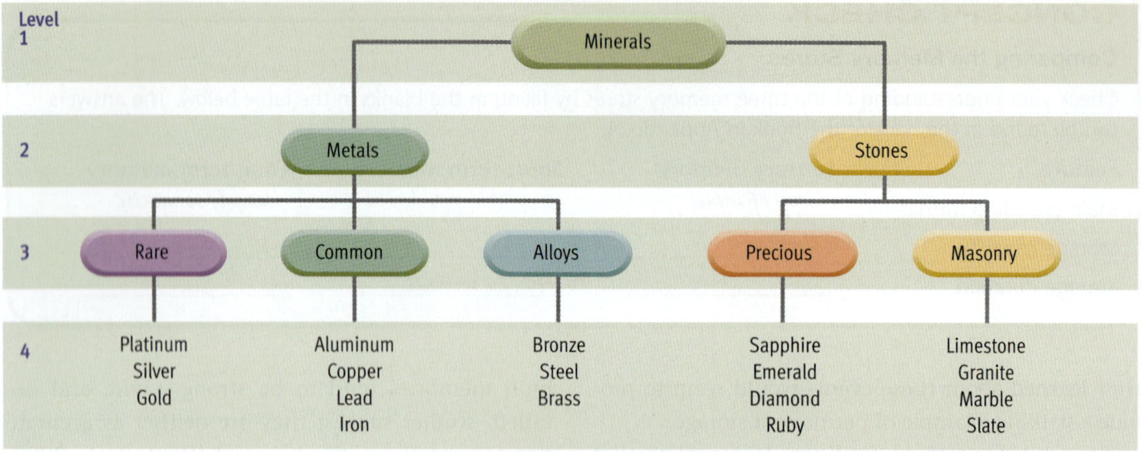

Clustering and Conceptual Hierarchies

PSYKTREK 6b

People spontaneously organize information into categories for storage in memory. This fact was apparent in a study by Bousfield (1953), who asked subjects to memorize a list of 60 words. Although presented in a scrambled order, each of the words in the list fit into one of four categories: animals, men's names, vegetables, or professions. Bousfield showed that subjects recalling this list engage in *clustering*—the tendency to remember similar or related items in groups. The words were not presented in organized groups, yet participants tended to remember them in bunches that belonged in the same category. Thus, when applicable, factual information is routinely organized into simple categories.

Similarly, when possible, factual information may be organized into conceptual hierarchies. **A *conceptual hierarchy* is a multilevel classification system based on common properties among items.** A conceptual hierarchy that a person might construct for minerals can be found in **Figure 7.12**. According to Gordon Bower (1970), organizing information into a conceptual hierarchy can improve recall dramatically.

Professor Smith's office is shown in this photo. Follow the instructions in the text to learn how Brewer and Treyens (1981) used it in a study of memory.

Schemas

PSYKTREK 6b

Imagine that you've just visited Professor Smith's office, which is shown in the adjacent photo. Take a brief look at the photo and then cover it up. Now pretend you must describe Professor Smith's office to a friend. Write down what you saw (in the picture).

Compare your description with the picture. Chances are your description will include elements—books or filing cabinets, for instance—that were *not* in the office. This common phenomenon demonstrates how *schemas* can influence memory.

A *schema* is an organized cluster of knowledge about a particular object or event abstracted from previous experience with the object or event. For example, college students have schemas for what professors' offices are like. When Brewer and Treyens (1981) tested the recall of 30 subjects who had briefly visited the office shown in the photo, most subjects recalled the desks and chairs. Few, though, recalled the wine bottle or the picnic basket, which aren't part of a typical office schema. Moreover, nine subjects in the Brewer and Treyens study falsely recalled that the office contained books.

These results and other studies (Tuckey & Brewer, 2003) suggest that *people are more likely to remember things that are consistent with their schemas than things that are not.* Although this principle seems applicable much of the time, the inverse is also true: *People sometimes exhibit better recall of things that violate their schema-based expectations* (Koriat, Goldsmith, & Pansky, 2000; Neuschatz et al., 2002). Information that really clashes with a schema may attract extra attention and deeper processing and thus become more memorable. For instance, if you saw a slot machine in a professor's office, you would probably remember it. In either case, it's apparent that information stored in memory is often organized around schemas (Brewer, 2000).

Semantic Networks

PSYKTREK 6b

Of course, not all information fits neatly into conceptual hierarchies or schemas. Much knowledge seems to be organized into less systematic frameworks, called semantic networks (Collins & Loftus, 1975). **A *semantic network* consists of nodes representing concepts, joined together by pathways that link related concepts.** A small semantic network is shown in **Figure 7.13**. The ovals are the nodes, and the words inside the ovals are the interlinked concepts. The lines connecting the nodes are the pathways. The length of each pathway represents the degree of association between two concepts. Shorter pathways imply stronger associations.

Semantic networks have proven useful in explaining why thinking about one word (such as *butter*) can make a closely related word (such as *bread*) easier to remember (Meyer & Schvaneveldt, 1976). According to Collins and Loftus (1975), when people think about a word, their thoughts naturally go to related words. These theorists call this process *spreading activation* within a semantic network. They assume that activation spreads out along the pathways of the semantic network surrounding the word. They also theorize that the strength of this activation decreases as it travels outward, much as ripples decrease in size as they radiate outward from a rock tossed into a pond. Consider again the semantic network shown in **Figure 7.13**. If subjects see the word *red,* words that are closely linked to it (such as *orange*) should be easier to recall than words that have longer links (such as *sunrises*).

Connectionist Networks and Parallel Distributed Processing (PDP) Models

Instead of taking their cue from how computers process information, *connectionist models* of memory take their inspiration from how neural networks appear to handle information. The human brain appears to depend extensively on *parallel distributed*

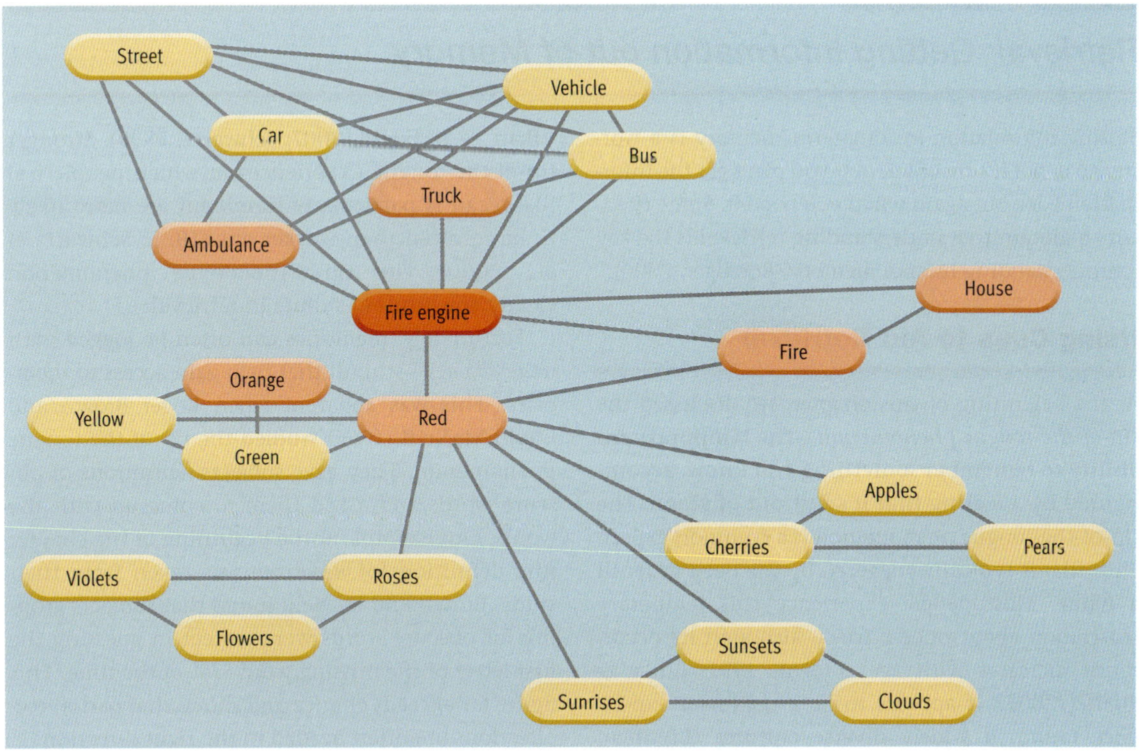

© Cengage Learning 2013

Figure 7.13

A semantic network. Much of the organization of long-term memory depends on networks of associations among concepts. In this highly simplified depiction of a fragment of a semantic network, the shorter the line linking any two concepts, the stronger the association between them. The coloration of the concept boxes represents activation of the concepts. This is how the network might look just after a person hears the words *fire engine.*

SOURCE: Adapted from Collins, A. M., & Loftus, E. F. (1975). A spreading activation theory of semantic processing. *Psychological Review, 82,* 407–428. Copyright © 1975 by the American Psychological Association.

processing—that is, simultaneous processing of the same information that is spread across networks of neurons. Based on this insight and basic findings about how neurons operate, ***connectionist* or *parallel distributed processing (PDP) models* assume that cognitive processes depend on patterns of activation in highly interconnected computational networks that resemble neural networks** (McClelland, 2000; McClelland & Rogers, 2003; McClelland & Rumelhart, 1985). A PDP system consists of a large network of interconnected computing units, or *nodes,* that operate much like neurons. These nodes may be inactive or they may send either excitatory or inhibitory signals to other units. Like an individual neuron, a specific node's level of activation reflects the weighted balance of excitatory and inhibitory inputs from many other units. Given this framework, *PDP models assert that specific memories correspond to particular patterns of activation in these networks* (McClelland, 1992). Connectionist networks bear some superficial resemblance to semantic networks, but there is a crucial difference. In semantic networks, specific nodes represent specific concepts or pieces of knowledge. In connectionist networks, a piece of knowledge is represented by a particular *pattern* of activation across an entire network. Thus, the information lies in the strengths of the *connections,* which is why the PDP approach is called "connectionism."

REVIEW OF KEY LEARNING GOALS

7.4 The sensory store preserves information in its original form, probably for only a fraction of a second. Some theorists view stimulus persistence as more like an echo than a memory. Short-term memory can maintain unrehearsed information for about 10–20 seconds. Short-term memory has a limited capacity that has long been believed to be about seven chunks of information. However, a more recent estimate suggesting that the capacity of STM is four items plus or minus one is becoming increasingly influential.

7.5 Short-term memory appears to involve more than a simple rehearsal loop and has been reconceptualized by Baddeley as working memory. Working memory includes the phonological loop, the visuospatial sketchpad, a central executive system, and an episodic buffer. Individual differences in working memory capacity correlate with measures of many cognitive abilities.

7.6 Long-term memory is an unlimited capacity store that may hold information indefinitely. Penfield's ESB research and the existence of flashbulb memories suggest that LTM storage may be permanent, but the evidence is not convincing.

7.7 Information in long-term memory can be organized in simple categories or multilevel classification systems called conceptual hierarchies. A schema is an organized cluster of knowledge about a particular object or event. Generally, people are more likely to remember things that are consistent with their schemas.

7.8 Semantic networks consist of concepts joined by pathways. Research suggests that activation spreads along the paths of semantic networks to activate closely associated words. Parallel distributed processing models of memory assert that specific memories correspond to particular patterns of activation in connectionist networks.

KEY LEARNING GOALS

7.9 Explain the tip-of-the-tongue phenomenon and how retrieval cues and context cues influence retrieval.

7.10 Understand the reconstructive nature of memory, and summarize research on the misinformation effect.

7.11 Apply the concepts of reality monitoring and source monitoring to everyday memory errors.

7.12 Explain the concept of destination memory and describe the Featured Study that investigated it.

Retrieval: Getting Information out of Memory

Storing information in long-term memory is a worthy goal, but it's insufficient if you can't get the information back out again when you need it. Some theorists maintain that understanding retrieval is the key to understanding human memory (Roediger, 2000).

Using Cues to Aid Retrieval

At the beginning of this chapter, we discussed the ***tip-of-the-tongue phenomenon*—the temporary inability to remember something you know, accompanied by a feeling that it's just out of reach.** The tip-of-the-tongue phenomenon is a common experience that is typically triggered by the need to recall a name. Most people experience this temporary frustration about once a week, although its occurrence increases with age (Brown, 1991; Burke & Shafto, 2004). It appears to be a universal experience found in widely diverse cultures (Brennen, Vikan, & Dybdahl, 2007; Schwartz, 1999). Stronger tip-of-the-tongue experiences in which people feel like recall is particularly imminent are more likely to be resolved than weaker ones (B. L. Schwartz et al., 2000) The tip-of-the-tongue phenomenon clearly constitutes a failure in retrieval.

Fortunately, memories can often be jogged with *retrieval cues*—stimuli that help gain access to memories. This was apparent when Roger Brown and David McNeill (1966) studied the tip-of-the-tongue phenomenon. They gave subjects definitions of obscure words and asked them to come up with the words. Our example at the beginning of the chapter (the definition for *nepotism*) was taken from their study. Brown and McNeill found that subjects groping for obscure words were correct in guessing the first letter of the missing word 57% of the time. This figure far exceeds chance and shows that partial recollections are often headed in the right direction.

Reinstating the Context of an Event

Let's test your memory: What did you have for breakfast two days ago? If you can't immediately answer, you might begin by imagining yourself sitting at the breakfast table. Trying to recall an event by putting yourself back in the context in which it occurred involves working with *context cues* to aid retrieval.

Context cues often facilitate the retrieval of information (Smith, 1988). Everyone experiences the effects of context cues. For instance, when you return after a number of years to a place you knew as a child, you are typically flooded with long-forgotten memories. Or consider how often you have gone from one room to another to get something (scissors, perhaps), only to discover that you can't remember what you were after. However, when you return to the first room (the original context), you suddenly recall what it was ("Of course, the scissors!"). These examples illustrate the potentially powerful effects of context cues on memory.

The technique of reinstating the context of an event has been used effectively in legal investigations to enhance eyewitness recall (Chandler & Fisher, 1996). The eyewitness may be encouraged to retrieve information about a crime by mentally replaying the sequence of events. The value of reinstating the context of an event may account for how hypnosis *occasionally* stimulates eyewitness recall (Meyer, 1992). The hypnotist usually attempts to reinstate the context of the event by telling the witness to imagine being at the scene of the crime once again.

Although it is widely believed by the general public that hypnosis can help people remember things that they would not normally recall (Green, 2003), extensive research has failed to demonstrate that hypnosis can enhance retrieval (Mazzoni, Heap, & Scoboria, 2010). The notion that hypnotists can use age regression to recover long-lost memories by instructing subjects to go back in time and relive past events has been discredited (Mazzoni, Heap, & Scoboria, 2010). Quite to the contrary, research suggests that hypnosis often increases individuals' tendency to report *incorrect* information (Lynn, Neuschatz, & Fite, 2002; Mazzoni & Lynn, 2007). Moreover, popular beliefs about the supposed beneficial effects of hypnosis on memory often lead hypnotized subjects to feel overconfident about the accuracy of their recall (Scoboria et al., 2002). Concerns about the accuracy of hypnosis-aided recall have led courts to be extremely cautious about allowing hypnosis-aided recollections as admissible testimony.

Reconstructing Memories and the Misinformation Effect

When you retrieve information from long-term memory, you're not able to pull up a "mental videotape" that provides an exact replay of the past. Your memories, to some extent, are sketchy *reconstructions* that may be distorted and may include details that didn't actually occur (Roediger, Wheeler, & Rajaram, 1993).

Research by Elizabeth Loftus (1979, 1992, 2005) and others on the *misinformation effect* has shown that reconstructive distortions show up frequently in eyewitness testimony. **The *misinformation effect* occurs when participants' recall of an event they witnessed is altered by introducing misleading postevent information.** For example, in one study Loftus and Palmer (1974) showed subjects a videotape of an automobile accident. Participants were then "grilled" as if they were providing eyewitness testimony, and biasing information was introduced. Some subjects were asked, "How fast were the cars going when they *hit* each other?" Other subjects were asked, "How fast were the cars going when they *smashed into* each other?" A week later, participants' recall of the accident was tested. They were asked whether they remembered seeing any broken glass in the accident (there was none). Subjects who had earlier been asked about the cars *smashing into* each other were more likely to "recall" broken glass. Why would they add this detail to their reconstructions of the accident? Probably because broken glass is consistent with their schema for cars *smashing* together (see **Figure 7.14**).

Reality CHECK

Misconception

Hypnosis can be used to retrieve memories of forgotten events.

Reality

Advocates of hypnosis have claimed that it can enhance recall for over a century, but the empirical evidence is quite clear. Hypnosis does not improve memory retrieval. Quite to the contrary, hypnotized subjects are more likely than others to get things wrong—and feel overconfident about their memories.

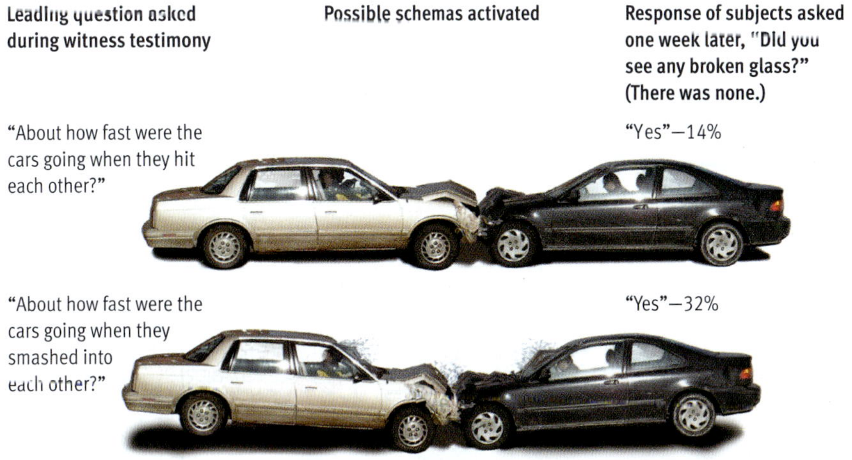

Figure 7.14

The misinformation effect. In an experiment by Loftus and Palmer (1974), participants who were asked leading questions in which cars were described as *hitting* or *smashing* each other were prone to recall the same accident differently one week later, demonstrating the reconstructive nature of memory. © Cengage Learning 2013

© Courtesy Elizabeth Loftus

Elizabeth Loftus

"One reason most of us, as jurors, place so much faith in eyewitness testimony is that we are unaware of how many factors influence its accuracy."

The misinformation effect, which has been replicated in countless studies, is a remarkably reliable phenomenon that has "challenged prevailing views about the validity of memory" (Zaragoza, Belli, & Payment, 2007, p. 37). The effect is difficult to escape, as even subjects who have been forewarned can be swayed by postevent misinformation (Loftus, 2005). Consider, for instance, a recent study by Chan, Thomas, and Bulevich (2009). The investigators noted that in real-life situations, eyewitnesses are often immediately asked to systematically recall an event before there is much opportunity to introduce misinformation. In contrast, the typical misinformation experiment does not include a recall effort prior to the exposure to misinformation. Chan and colleagues reasoned that "immediate recall should enhance retention of the witnessed event, thereby rendering an eyewitness less susceptible to misinformation" (p. 66). Surprisingly, however, immediate recall not only failed to reduce the misinformation effect, it actually increased the impact of misinformation! This finding provides yet another dramatic demonstration of the pervasive power of misinformation and the reconstructive nature of memory.

Similar distortions routinely occur without any crafty manipulations. Recent research has demonstrated that the simple act of retelling a story can introduce inaccuracies into memory (Marsh, 2007). When people retell stories, they tend to make a number of "adjustments" that depend on their goals, their audience, and the social context. Think about it: People tell stories to entertain others, to inform others, to impress others, to gain sympathy from their friends, and so forth. Depending on one's goals, one may streamline a story, embellish the facts, exaggerate one's role, omit important situational considerations, and so forth. Not surprisingly, when participants in one study were asked to evaluate the accuracy of recent retellings, they admitted that 42% were "inaccurate" and that another one-third contained "distortions" (Marsh & Tversky, 2004). People may be aware that they're being a little loose with the facts. However, what's interesting is that their intentional distortions can reshape their subsequent recollections of the same events. Somehow, the "real" story and the storyteller's "spin" on it probably begin to blend imperceptibly. So, even routine retellings of events can contribute to the malleability of memory.

Reality CHECK

Misconception

Memory is like a mental videotape that can provide faithful reproductions of past events.

Reality

Countless studies in recent decades have demonstrated that memories are incomplete, distorted, fuzzy reconstructions of past events. The adjectives that best describe memory are not *exact* or *accurate*, but rather *fragile, fallible,* and *malleable.*

Reality Monitoring, Source Monitoring, and Destination Memory

The misinformation effect and similar memory distortions may be due, *in part,* to the unreliability of a retrieval process called *reality monitoring,* which has been studied by Marcia Johnson and her colleagues. ***Reality monitoring* refers to the process of deciding whether memories are based on external sources (one's perceptions of actual events) or internal sources (one's thoughts and imaginations).** People engage in reality monitoring when they reflect on whether something actually happened or they only thought about it happening. This dilemma may sound like an odd problem that would arise only infrequently, but it isn't. People routinely ponder questions like "Did I pack the umbrella or only think about packing it?" "Did I take my morning pill or only intend to do so?" Studies indicate that people focus on several types of clues in making their reality-monitoring decisions (Johnson, 2006; Johnson, Kahan, & Raye, 1984; Kahan et al., 1999). When memories are rich in sensory information (you can recall the feel of shoving the umbrella into your suitcase) or contextual information (you can clearly see yourself in the hallway packing your umbrella), or when memories can be retrieved with little effort, one is more likely to infer that the event really happened. In contrast, one is more likely to infer that an event did *not* actually occur when memories of it lack sensory or contextual details or are difficult to retrieve. Age may influence reality monitoring, as older adults seem to be more vulnerable to reality monitoring errors than young adults (McDaniel et al., 2008).

BLONDIE

© 2008 by King Features Syndicate, Inc. World Rights reserved
www.Blondie.com
BLONDIE © King Features Syndicate

Research on reality monitoring eventually led Marcia Johnson to explore a related process, which she called *source monitoring*. ***Source monitoring* involves making attributions about the origins of memories.** Johnson maintains that source monitoring is a crucial facet of memory retrieval that contributes to many of the mistakes that people make in reconstructing their experiences (Johnson, 1996, 2006; Mitchell & Johnson, 2000). According to Johnson, memories are not tagged with labels that specify their sources. Thus, when people pull up specific memory records, they have to make decisions *at the time of retrieval* about where the memories came from (example: "Did I read that in the *New York Times* or *Rolling Stone*?"). Much of the time, these decisions are so easy and automatic, people make them without being consciously aware of the source-monitoring process. In other instances, however, they may consciously struggle to pinpoint the source of a memory. **A *source-monitoring error* occurs when a memory derived from one source is misattributed to another source.** For example, you might attribute your roommate's remark to your psychology professor, or something you heard on *Oprah* to your psychology textbook. Inaccurate memories that reflect source-monitoring errors may seem quite compelling. People often feel extremely confident about their authenticity even though the recollections really are inaccurate (Lampinen, Neuschatz, & Payne, 1999).

Source-monitoring errors appear to be commonplace and may shed light on many interesting memory phenomena. For instance, in studies of eyewitness suggestibility, some subjects have gone so far as to insist that they "remember" seeing something that was only verbally suggested to them. Most theories have a hard time explaining how people can have memories of events that they never actually saw or experienced. But this paradox doesn't seem all that perplexing when it's explained as a source-monitoring error (Lindsay et al., 2004).

Although the process of remembering the source of specific information has been the subject of a great deal of research, the opposite process—remembering who you have transmitted specific information to—has only recently become a focus of research. ***Destination memory* involves recalling to whom one has told what.** Gopie and MacLeod (2009) maintain that accurate destination memory is just as important as accurate source monitoring, although perhaps a bit more difficult, which brings us to our Featured Study for this chapter.

© Courtesy of Marcia K. Johnson

Marcia Johnson

"Our long-term goal is to develop ways of determining which aspects of mental experience create one's sense of a personal past and one's conviction (accurate or not) that memories, knowledge, beliefs, attitudes, and feelings are tied to reality in a veridical fashion."

FEATURED STUDY

Oops, I Forgot I Already Told You That!

SOURCE: Gopie, N., & MacLeod, C. M. (2009). Destination memory: Stop me if I've told you this before. *Psychological Science, 20*, 1492–1499.

You have probably had the embarrassing experience of telling someone a joke or story only to be informed that you had already told it to that person. These sorts of failures in destination memory are why people sometimes lead into a story with "Stop me if I told you this before." Gopie and MacLeod argue that destination memory is just as crucial as source memory. For example, supervisors need to remember to whom they delegated specific responsibilities, salespeople need to remember what they promised to which clients, teachers need to recall whether they have recounted an anecdote to a specific class, and liars need to recall which lies have been told to which people if they hope to avoid being caught in their web of lies. In this groundbreaking study, Gopie and MacLeod hypothesized that destination memory should be more fallible than source monitoring because people tend to be self-focused (on their message) when transmitting information to others. We'll look at the first of their three experiments in some detail and then briefly describe the follow-up studies.

Method

Participants. Sixty undergraduates at the University of Waterloo served as subjects. They received bonus credit in their courses for participating.

Procedure. Half of the participants were instructed to tell facts to pictures of famous people (assessing destination memory), whereas the other half were instructed to learn similar facts transmitted *from* pictures of famous people (source memory). They were not warned that their memory for the facts and faces would be tested later. The facts consisted of interesting general information (e.g., "The average person falls asleep in 12 minutes"). The famous people came from the world of sports, movies, music, and politics (e.g., Tom Cruise). The facts and famous people were presented on a computer monitor. In the destination memory condition, participants would read a fact on the monitor, press the space bar, and then repeat the fact to a famous person whose picture appeared on the monitor. In the source memory condition, participants would see a picture of a famous person, press the space bar, and then learn a fact from this person. In both conditions 50 facts were paired with 50 famous people.

Measures. Subjects took two memory tests. In the test of simple item memory, participants indicated whether or not they had been exposed to 20 facts and 20 faces (half the facts and faces had been presented and half had not). In the test of source and destination memory, participants indicated whether 40 facts had been transmitted to or received from 40 famous people (half were correct pairings and half were incorrect).

Results

The results of the study are summarized in **Figure 7.15**. There was no difference between the source and destination conditions in memory for facts, but the source condition produced better memory of the faces. The crucial data were those on the face-fact pairings. As you can see on the far right in **Figure 7.15**, these data showed that memory for sources of information was notably better than destination memory.

Discussion

The authors conclude that errors in destination memory tend to be more common than source monitoring errors, as they had hypothesized. In a second experiment they tested the idea that destination memory is more fragile because people are self-focused on the message they are transmitting, leaving less attention capacity to devote to encoding whom they are talking with. Their findings supported this explanation. A third experiment showed that reducing participants' self-focus improved destination memory, providing more support for their explanation.

Comment

This research was featured because it examined a common, everyday memory problem that is easy to relate to in a creative way. It also demonstrated that there are always new horizons to explore in psychology, as it opened up an entirely new domain of inquiry related to memory. The process of source monitoring has been an important area of inquiry for over two decades. It is perplexing that no one thought to explore the flipside of source monitoring for so many years, given that destination memory seems just as important to everyday functioning as source monitoring. In any event, research is under way to analyze the factors that influence destination memory. For instance, one recent study showed that age takes a toll on destination memory (Gopie, Craik, & Hasher, 2010). Older adults were found to be more likely to suffer from failures in destination memory than younger adults.

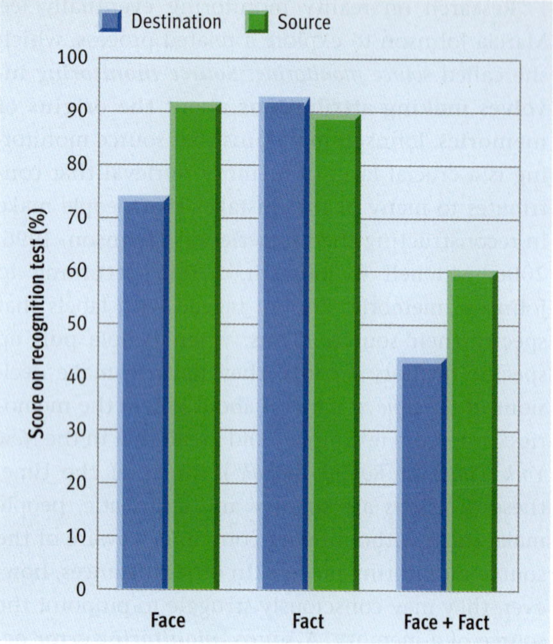

© Cengage Learning 2013

Figure 7.15

Comparing source and destination memory. Gopie and MacLeod (2009) found that memory for facts was excellent in both conditions, but memory for faces fell some in the destination memory condition. The critical comparison of source and destination memory was on the test in which participants had to recall which facts were transmitted to or from which famous people (face + fact). On this test, scores were significantly lower in the destination memory condition, suggesting that maintaining accurate destination memories is more challenging than source monitoring.

SOURCE: Adapted from Gopie, N., & MacLeod, C. M. (2009). Destination memory: Stop me if I've told you this before. *Psychological Science, 20*, 1492–1499. Copyright © 2009 SAGE Publications. Reprinted by permission of SAGE Publications.

REVIEW OF KEY LEARNING GOALS

7.9 The tip-of-the-tongue phenomenon is the temporary inability to remember something you know, which feels just out of reach. It clearly represents a failure in retrieval. Memories can be jogged by retrieval cues. Reinstating the context of an event can also facilitate recall. This factor may account for cases in which hypnosis appears to aid recall of previously forgotten information. However, hypnosis seems to increase people's tendency to report incorrect information.

7.10 Memories are not exact replicas of past experiences. Memory is partially reconstructive. Research by Loftus on the misinformation effect shows that information learned after an event can alter one's memory of the event. Even the simple act of retelling a story can introduce inaccuracies into memory.

7.11 Reality monitoring involves deciding whether memories are based on perceptions of actual events or on just thinking about the events. Source monitoring is the process of making attributions about the origins of memories. According to Johnson, source-monitoring errors appear to be common and may explain why people sometimes "recall" something that was only suggested to them.

7.12 Destination memory involves recalling to whom one has told what. The results of the Featured Study suggest that destination memory errors are more common than source-monitoring errors. Destination memory may be more fragile because people are self-focused on their message when talking to others.

Forgetting: When Memory Lapses

KEY LEARNING GOALS

7.13 Describe Ebbinghaus's forgetting curve, and discuss three measures of retention.

7.14 Assess ineffective encoding and decay as potential causes of forgetting.

7.15 Evaluate interference and factors in the retrieval process as potential causes of forgetting.

7.16 Summarize evidence on the controversy regarding recovered memories of childhood sexual abuse.

Forgetting gets "bad press" that it may not deserve. People tend to view forgetting as a failure, weakness, or deficiency in cognitive processing. But some memory theorists argue that forgetting is actually adaptive. How so? Imagine how cluttered your memory would be if you never forgot anything. According to Daniel Schacter (1999), you need to forget information that is no longer relevant, such as out-of-date phone numbers, discarded passwords, lines that were memorized for a tenth-grade play, and where you kept your important papers three apartments ago. Forgetting can reduce competition among memories that would otherwise cause confusion. In a recent study of this hypothesis, scientists used brain-imaging technology to track neural markers of cognitive effort in a series of tasks in which participants memorized pairs of words (Kuhl et al., 2007). They found that the forgetting of word pairs deemed "irrelevant" made it easier to remember the "relevant" word pairs and reduced the "demands" placed on crucial neural circuits. In short, they found that forgetting helped subjects remember the information they needed to remember.

Although forgetting may be adaptive in the long run, the fundamental question of memory research remains: Why do people forget information that they would like to remember? There isn't one simple answer to this question. Research has shown that forgetting can be caused by defects in encoding, storage, retrieval, or some combination of these processes.

How Quickly We Forget: Ebbinghaus's Forgetting Curve

PSYKTREK 6d

The first person to conduct scientific studies of forgetting was Hermann Ebbinghaus. He published a series of insightful memory studies way back in 1885. Ebbinghaus studied only one subject—himself. To give himself lots of new material to memorize, he invented ***nonsense syllables*—consonant-vowel-consonant arrangements that do not correspond to words** (such as BAF, XOF, VIR, and MEQ). He wanted to work with meaningless materials that would be uncontaminated by his previous learning.

Ebbinghaus was a remarkably dedicated researcher. In one study he went through over 14,000 practice repetitions, as he tirelessly memorized 420 lists of nonsense syllables (Slamecka, 1985). He tested his memory of these lists after various time intervals. **Figure 7.16** shows what he found. This diagram, called a ***forgetting curve*, graphs retention and forgetting over time.** Ebbinghaus's forgetting curve shows a precipitous drop in retention during the first few hours after the nonsense syllables were memorized. Thus, he concluded that most forgetting occurs very rapidly after learning something.

That's a depressing conclusion. What's the point of memorizing information if you're going to forget it all right away? Fortunately, subsequent research showed that Ebbinghaus's forgetting curve was unusually steep (Postman, 1985). Forgetting isn't usually quite as swift or as extensive as Ebbinghaus thought. One problem was that he was working with such meaningless material. When subjects memorize more meaningful material, such as prose or poetry, forgetting curves aren't nearly as steep. Studies of how well people recall their high school classmates suggest that forgetting curves for autobiographical information are even shallower (Bahrick, 2000). Also, different methods of measuring forgetting yield varied estimates of how quickly people forget. This variation underscores the importance of the methods used to measure forgetting, the matter we turn to next.

© Bettmann/Corbis

Hermann Ebbinghaus

"Left to itself every mental content gradually loses its capacity for being revived. . . . Facts crammed at examination time soon vanish."

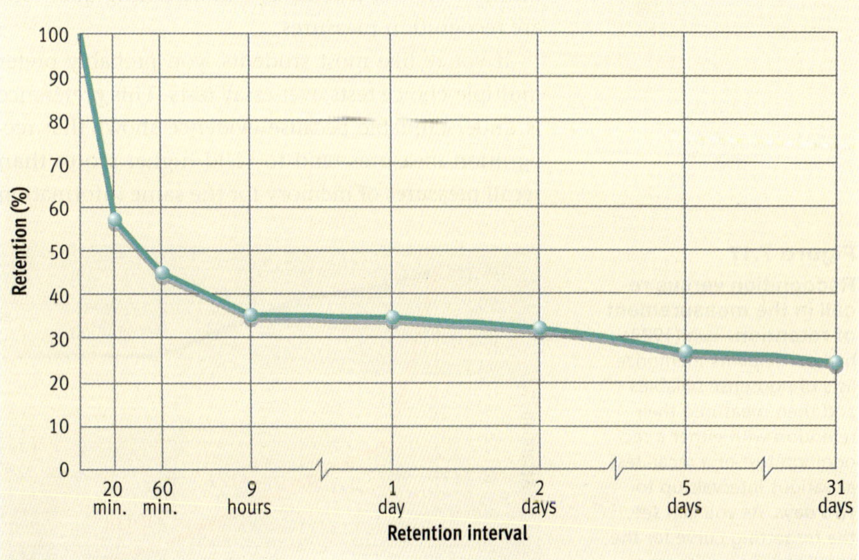

© Cengage Learning 2013

Figure 7.16

Ebbinghaus's forgetting curve for nonsense syllables. From his experiments on himself, Ebbinghaus (1885) concluded that forgetting is extremely rapid immediately after the original learning and then levels off. Although this generalization remains true, subsequent research has shown that forgetting curves for nonsense syllables are unusually steep.

Measures of Forgetting

SIM5, SIM6, 6d

To study forgetting empirically, psychologists need to be able to measure it precisely. Measures of forgetting inevitably measure retention as well. ***Retention*** **refers to the proportion of material retained (remembered).** In studies of forgetting, the results may be reported in terms of the amount forgotten or the amount retained. In these studies, the *retention interval* is the length of time between the presentation of materials to be remembered and the measurement of forgetting. The three principal methods used to measure forgetting are recall, recognition, and relearning (Lockhart, 1992).

Who is the current U.S. secretary of state? What movie won the Academy Award for best picture last year? These questions involve recall measures of retention. **A *recall* measure of retention requires subjects to reproduce information on their own without any cues.** If you were to take a recall test on a list of 25 words you had memorized, you would simply be told to write down as many of the words as you could remember.

In contrast, in a recognition test you might be shown a list of 100 words and asked to choose the 25 words that you had memorized. **A *recognition* measure of retention requires subjects to select previously learned information from an array of options.** Subjects not only have cues to work with, they have the answers right in front of them. In educational testing, essay questions and fill-in-the-blanks questions are recall measures of retention. Multiple-choice, true-false, and matching questions are recognition measures.

If you're like most students, you probably prefer multiple-choice tests over essay tests. This preference is understandable because evidence shows that recognition measures tend to yield higher scores than recall measures of memory for the same information (Lockhart, 2000). This situation was demonstrated many decades ago by Luh (1922), who measured subjects' retention of nonsense syllables with both a recognition test and a recall test. As **Figure 7.17** shows, subjects' performance on the recognition measure was far superior to their performance on the recall measure. There are two ways to look at this disparity between recall and recognition tests. One is to see recognition tests as especially *sensitive* measures of retention. The other is to see recognition tests as excessively *easy* measures of retention.

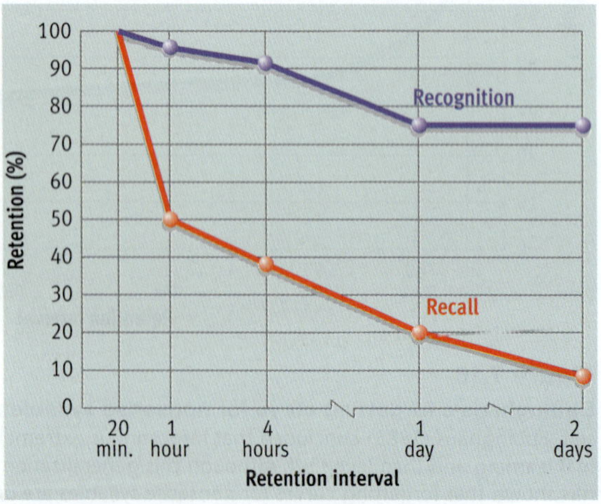

© Cengage Learning 2013

Figure 7.17
Recognition versus recall in the measurement of retention. Luh (1922) had participants memorize lists of nonsense syllables and then measured their retention with either a recognition test or a recall test at various intervals up to two days. As you can see, the forgetting curve for the recall test was quite steep, whereas the recognition test yielded much higher estimates of subjects' retention.

Actually, there is no guarantee that a recognition test will be easier than a recall test. Although this tends to be the case, the difficulty of a recognition test can vary greatly, depending on the number, similarity, and plausibility of the options provided as possible answers. To illustrate, see whether you know the answer to the following multiple-choice question:

The capital of Washington is:
a. Seattle
b. Spokane
c. Tacoma
d. Olympia

Most students who aren't from Washington find this a fairly difficult question. The answer is Olympia. Now take a look at the next question:

The capital of Washington is:
a. London
b. New York
c. Tokyo
d. Olympia

Most people can answer this question because the incorrect options are readily dismissed. Recognition measures of the same information can thus vary dramatically in difficulty.

The third method of measuring forgetting is relearning. **A *relearning* measure of retention requires a subject to memorize information a second time to determine how much time or how many practice trials are saved by having learned it before.** Subjects' *savings scores* provide an estimate of their retention. Relearning measures can detect retention that is overlooked by recognition tests (Crowder & Greene, 2000).

Why We Forget

6d

Measuring forgetting is only the first step in the long journey toward explaining why forgetting occurs. In this section, we explore the possible causes of forgetting, looking at factors that may affect encoding, storage, and retrieval processes.

Ineffective Encoding

6d

A great deal of forgetting may only *appear* to be forgetting. That's because the information in question may never have been inserted into memory in the first place. Since you can't really forget something you never learned, this phenomenon is sometimes called *pseudoforgetting.* We opened the chapter with an example of pseudoforgetting. People usually assume that they know what a penny looks like. Most people, however, have actually failed to encode this information. Pseudoforgetting is usually attributable to *lack of attention.*

Even when memory codes *are* formed for new information, subsequent forgetting may be the result of ineffective or inappropriate encoding (Brown & Craik, 2000). The research on levels of processing shows that some approaches to encoding lead to more forgetting than others (Craik & Tulving, 1975). For instance, if you're distracted while reading your textbooks, you may be doing little more than saying the words to yourself. This is *phonemic encoding,* which is inferior to *semantic encoding* for retention of verbal material. When you can't remember the information that you've read, your forgetting may be due to ineffective encoding.

Decay

6d

Instead of focusing on encoding, *decay theory* attributes forgetting to the impermanence of memory *storage.* Decay theory proposes that forgetting occurs because memory traces fade with time. The implicit assumption is that decay occurs in the physiological mechanisms responsible for memories. According to decay theory, the mere passage of time produces forgetting. This notion meshes nicely with commonsense views of forgetting.

As we noted earlier, evidence suggests that decay *does* contribute to the loss of information from the sensory and short-term memory stores. However, the critical task for theories of forgetting is to explain the loss of information from long-term memory. Researchers have *not* been able to reliably demonstrate that decay causes LTM forgetting (Slamecka, 1992).

If decay theory is correct, the principal cause of forgetting should be the passage of time. In studies of long-term memory, however, researchers have repeatedly found that time passage is not as influential as what happens during the time interval. Research has shown that forgetting depends not on the amount of time that has passed since learning but on the amount, complexity, and type of information that subjects have had to assimilate *during* the retention interval. The negative impact of competing information on retention is called *interference.*

Interference

6d

Interference theory proposes that people forget information because of competition from other material. Demonstrations of decay in long-term memory have remained elusive, but hundreds of studies have shown that interference influences forgetting (Anderson & Neely, 1996; Bower, 2000). In many of these studies, researchers have controlled interference by varying the *similarity* between the original material given to subjects (the test material) and the material studied in the intervening period. Interference is assumed to be greatest when intervening material is most similar to the test material. Decreasing the similarity should reduce interference and cause less forgetting.

This is exactly what McGeoch and McDonald (1931) found in an influential study. They had subjects memorize test material that consisted of a list of two-syllable adjectives. They varied the similarity of intervening learning by having subjects then memorize one of five lists. In order of decreasing similarity to the test material, the lists contained synonyms of the test words, antonyms of the test words, unrelated adjectives, nonsense syllables, and numbers. Later, subjects' recall of the test material was measured. **Figure 7.18** on the next page shows that as the similarity of the intervening material decreased, the amount of forgetting also decreased—because of reduced interference.

There are two kinds of interference: *retroactive* and *proactive* (Jacoby, Hessels, & Bopp, 2001). ***Retroactive interference* occurs when new information impairs the retention of previously learned information.** Retroactive interference occurs between the original learning and the retest on that learning, during the retention interval (see **Figure 7.19** on the next page). For example, the interference manipulated by McGeoch and McDonald (1931) was retroactive interference. In contrast, ***proactive interference* occurs when previously learned information interferes with the retention of new information.** Proactive interference is rooted in learning that comes *before* exposure to the test material (see **Figure 7.19**).

Retrieval Failure

6d

People often remember things that they were unable to recall at an earlier time. This phenomenon may be obvious only during struggles with the tip-of-the-tongue phenomenon, but it happens frequently. In fact, a great deal of forgetting may be due to breakdowns in the process of retrieval.

Why does an effort to retrieve something fail on one occasion and succeed on another? That's a tough question. One theory is that retrieval failures may be more likely when a mismatch occurs

Reality CHECK

Misconception

The principal cause of forgetting is the gradual decay of memory traces with time.

Reality

People subjectively feel like their memories gradually decay with the passage of time. But research has shown that the simple passage of time is not nearly as influential as other factors. Forgetting is mainly attributable to interference, ineffective encoding, reconstructive inaccuracy, and breakdowns in the retrieval process.

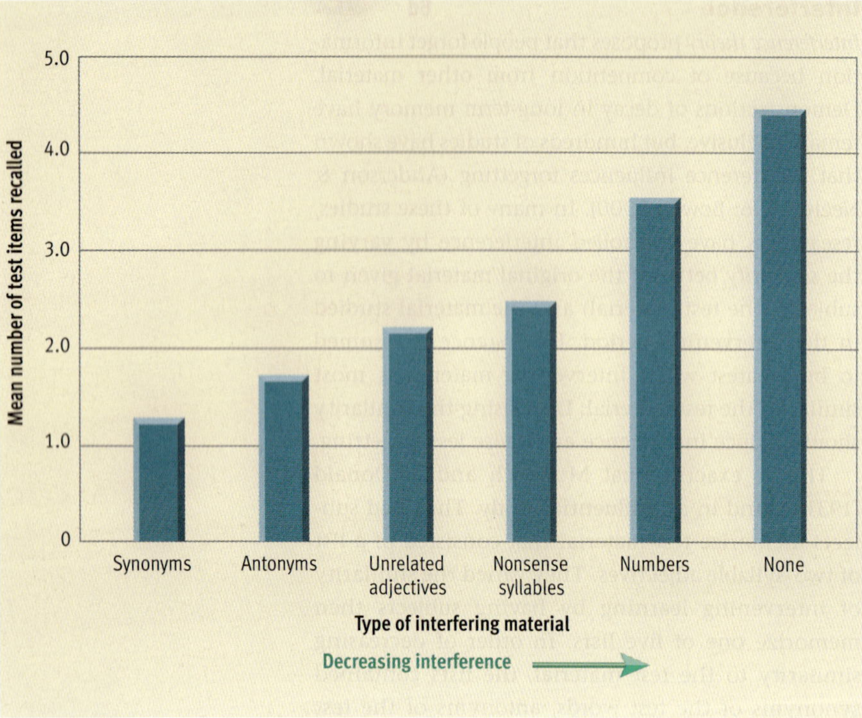

Figure 7.18

Effects of interference. According to interference theory, more interference from competing information should produce more forgetting. McGeoch and McDonald (1931) controlled the amount of interference with a learning task by varying the similarity of an intervening task. The results were consistent with interference theory. The amount of interference is greatest at the left of the graph, as is the amount of forgetting. As interference decreases (moving to the right on the graph), retention improves.

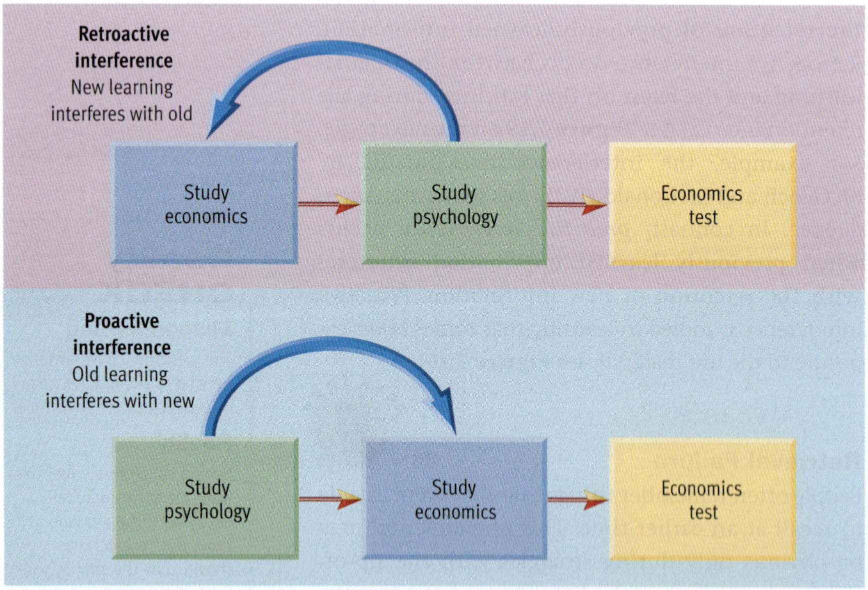

Figure 7.19

Retroactive and proactive interference. Retroactive interference occurs when learning produces a "backward" effect, reducing recall of previously learned material. Proactive interference occurs when learning produces a "forward" effect, reducing recall of subsequently learned material. For example, if you were to prepare for an economics test and then study psychology, the interference from the psychology study would be retroactive interference. However, if you studied psychology first and then economics, the interference from the psychology study would be proactive interference.

between retrieval cues and the encoding of the information you're searching for. According to the ***encoding specificity principle,*** **the value of a retrieval cue depends on how well it corresponds to the memory code.** This principle provides one explanation for the inconsistent success of retrieval efforts (Tulving & Thomson, 1973).

A related line of research indicates that memory is influenced by the "fit" between the processing during encoding and retrieval. ***Transfer-appropriate processing*** **occurs when the initial processing of information is similar to the type of processing required by the subsequent measure of retention.** For example, Morris, Bransford, and Franks (1977) gave subjects a list of words and a task that required either semantic or phonemic processing. Retention was measured with recognition tests that emphasized either the meaning or the sound of the words. Semantic processing yielded higher retention when the testing stressed semantic factors, while phonemic processing yielded higher retention when the testing stressed phonemic factors. Thus, retrieval failures are more likely when a poor fit occurs between the processing done during encoding and the processing invoked by the measure of retention (Lockhart, 2002; Roediger & Guynn, 1996).

Motivated Forgetting

PsykTrek 6d

Many years ago, Sigmund Freud (1901) came up with an entirely different explanation for retrieval failures. As we noted in Chapter 1, Freud asserted that people often keep embarrassing, unpleasant, or painful memories buried in their unconscious. For example, a person who was deeply wounded by perceived slights at a childhood birthday party might suppress all recollection of that party. In his therapeutic work with patients, Freud recovered many such buried memories. He theorized that the memories were there all along but that their retrieval was blocked by unconscious avoidance tendencies.

The tendency to forget things one doesn't want to think about is called *motivated forgetting,* or to use Freud's terminology, *repression.* In Freudian theory, ***repression*** **refers to keeping distressing thoughts and feelings buried in the unconscious** (see Chapter 12). Although it's difficult to demonstrate the operation of repression in lab studies (Holmes, 1995; Kihlstrom, 2002), a number of experiments suggest that people don't remember anxiety-laden material as quickly as emotionally neutral material, just as Freud proposed (Guenther, 1988; Reisner, 1998). Thus, when you forget unpleasant things, such as a dental appointment, a promise to help a friend move, or a term-paper deadline, motivated forgetting *may* be at work.

The Recovered Memories Controversy

SIM6

Interest in the phenomenon of repression has surged in recent years thanks to a rash of prominent reports involving the return of individuals' long-lost memories of sexual abuse and other traumas during childhood. The media have been flooded with reports of adults accusing their parents, teachers, and neighbors of horrific child abuse decades earlier, based on previously repressed memories. These parents, teachers, and neighbors have mostly denied the allegations. Many of them have seemed genuinely baffled by the accusations, and some previously happy families have been torn apart (Gudjonsson, 2001; McHugh et al., 2004). Some accused parents have argued that their children's recollections are false memories created inadvertently by well-intentioned therapists through the power of suggestion.

The controversy surrounding recovered memories of abuse is complex and difficult to sort out. The crux of the problem is that child abuse usually takes place behind closed doors. In the absence of corroborative evidence, there is no way to reliably distinguish genuine recovered memories from false ones. Some recovered memory incidents have been substantiated by independent witnesses or admissions of guilt from the accused (Brewin, 2003, 2007; Bull, 1999; Shobe & Schooler, 2001). But in the vast majority of cases, the allegations of abuse have been vehemently denied, and independent corroboration has not been available. What do psychologists and psychiatrists have to say about the authenticity of repressed memories? They are sharply divided on the issue.

Support for Recovered Memories

Many psychologists and psychiatrists, especially clinicians involved in the treatment of psychological disorders, largely accept recovered memories of abuse at face value (Banyard & Williams, 1999; Briere & Conte, 1993; Legault & Laurence, 2007; Skinner, 2001; Terr, 1994; Whitfield, 1995). For example, in a survey of British clinicians, 44% reported that they believed that recovered memories are always or usually genuine (Andrews, 2001). Clinicians who believe in recovered memories assert that sexual abuse in childhood is far more widespread than most people realize. One large-scale Canadian survey (MacMillan et al., 1997), using a random sample of 9953 residents of Ontario, found that 12.8% of the females and 4.3% of the males reported that they had been victims of sexual abuse during childhood (see **Figure 7.20**).

Supporters further assert that there's ample evidence that it's common for people to repress traumatic incidents in their unconscious (Del Monte, 2000; Wilsnack et al., 2002). In one widely cited study, L. M. Williams (1994) followed up on 129 female children who had been brought to a hospital emergency room for treatment of sexual abuse. When interviewed approximately 17 years later about a variety of things, including their history of sexual abuse, 38% of the women failed to report the original incident. Williams largely attributed this to amnesia for the incident. According to Freyd (1996, 2001; Freyd, DePrince, & Gleaves, 2007), sexual abuse by a parent

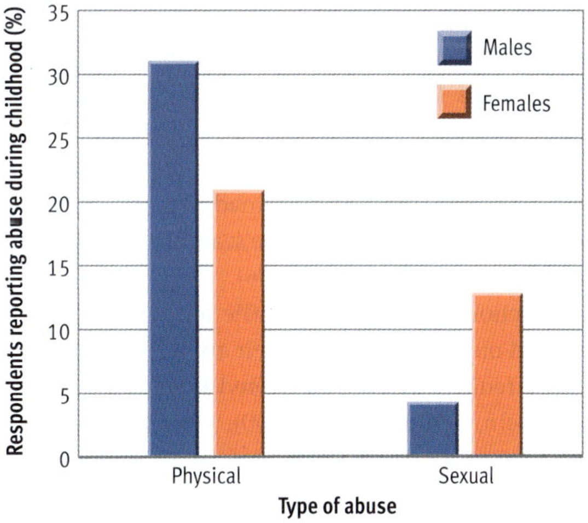

Figure 7.20

Estimates of the prevalence of childhood physical and sexual abuse. In one of the better efforts to estimate the prevalence of child abuse, MacMillan and her colleagues (1997) questioned a random sample of almost 10,000 adults living in the province of Ontario, Canada, about whether they were abused during childhood. As you can see, males were more likely to have experienced physical abuse and females were more likely to have suffered sexual abuse. The data support the assertion that millions of people have been victimized by childhood sexual abuse, which is far from rare.

© Cengage Learning 2013

CONCEPT CHECK 7.2

Figuring Out Forgetting

Check your understanding of why people forget by identifying the probable causes of forgetting in each of the following scenarios. Choose from (a) motivated forgetting (repression), (b) decay, (c) ineffective encoding, (d) proactive interference, (e) retroactive interference, or (f) retrieval failure. You will find the answers in Appendix A.

_______ 1. Ellen can't recall the reasons for the Webster-Ashburton Treaty because she was daydreaming when it was discussed in history class.

_______ 2. Rufus hates his job at Taco Heaven and is always forgetting when he is scheduled to work.

_______ 3. Ray's new assistant in the shipping department is named Jason Timberlake. Ray keeps calling him Justin, mixing him up with the singer Justin Timberlake.

_______ 4. Tania studied history on Sunday morning and sociology on Sunday evening. It's Monday, and she's struggling with her history test because she keeps mixing up prominent historians with influential sociologists.

evokes coping efforts that attempt to block awareness of the abuse because that awareness would interfere with normal attachment processes. The clinicians who accept the authenticity of recovered memories of abuse attribute the recent upsurge in recovered memories to therapists' and clients' increased sensitivity to an issue that people used to be reluctant to discuss.

Skepticism Regarding Recovered Memories

In contrast, many other psychologists, especially memory researchers, have expressed skepticism about the upsurge in the incidence of recovered memories that began in the 1990s (Kihlstrom, 2004; Laney & Loftus, 2005; Loftus, 1998, 2003; McNally, 2003, 2007; Takarangi et al., 2008). They point out that the women in the Williams (1994) study may have failed to report their earlier sexual abuse for a variety of reasons besides amnesia, including embarrassment, poor rapport with the interviewer, normal forgetfulness, or a conscious preference not to revisit painful experiences from the past (Loftus, Garry & Feldman, 1998; Pope & Hudson, 1998).

The skeptics do *not* say that people are lying about their previously repressed memories. Rather, they maintain that some suggestible people wrestling with emotional problems have been convinced by persuasive therapists that their emotional problems must be the result of abuse that occurred years before. Critics blame a minority of therapists who presumably have good intentions but who operate under the dubious assumption that virtually all psychological problems are attributable to childhood sexual abuse (Lindsay & Read, 1994; Loftus & Davis, 2006; Spanos, 1994). Using hypnosis, guided imagery, dream interpretation, and leading questions, they apparently prod and probe patients until they inadvertently create the memories of abuse that they're searching for (Lynn et al., 2003; Thayer & Lynn, 2006).

Psychologists who doubt the authenticity of repressed memories support their analysis by pointing to discredited cases of recovered memories (Brown, Goldstein, & Bjorklund, 2000). For instance, with the help of a church counselor, one woman recovered memories of how her minister father had repeatedly raped her, got her pregnant, and then aborted the pregnancy with a coat hanger. However, subsequent evidence revealed that the woman was still a virgin and that her father had had a vasectomy years before (Brainerd & Reyna, 2005). The skeptics also point to published case histories that clearly involved suggestive questioning and to cases in which patients have recanted recovered memories of sexual abuse after realizing that these memories were created by their therapists (Loftus, 1994; Shobe & Schooler, 2001). Indeed, quite a number of malpractice lawsuits have been filed against therapists for allegedly implanting false memories in patients (Brainerd & Reyna, 2005; Ost, 2006).

Those who question the accuracy of repressed memories also point to findings on the misinformation effect and the tendency to confuse real and imagined memories (reality-monitoring errors). They also point to other demonstrations of the relative ease of creating "memories" of events that never happened (Lindsay et al., 2004; Loftus & Cahill, 2007; Strange, Clifasefi, & Garry, 2007). For instance, working with college students, Ira Hyman and his colleagues have managed to implant recollections of fairly substantial events (such as spilling a punch bowl at a wedding, being in a grocery store when the fire sprinkler system went off, being hospitalized for an earache) in about 25% of their subjects, just by asking them to elaborate on events supposedly reported by their parents (Hyman, Husband, & Billings, 1995; Hyman & Kleinknecht, 1999). Other studies have succeeded in implanting false memories of nearly drowning (Heaps & Nash, 2001), of being attacked by a vicious animal (Porter, Yuille, & Lehman, 1999), and of becoming ill after eating a certain food (Bernstein & Loftus, 2009) in many participants. Moreover, subjects in these studies often feel very confident about their false memories, which frequently generate strong emotional reactions and richly detailed "recollections" (Loftus & Bernstein, 2005).

In a similar vein, building on much earlier work by James Deese (1959), Henry Roediger and Kathleen McDermott (1995, 2000) have devised a simple lab paradigm involving the learning of word lists that is remarkably reliable at producing memory illusions. In this procedure, now known as the *Deese-Roediger-McDermott (DRM) paradigm,* a series of lists of 15 words are presented to participants. They are asked to recall the words immediately after each list is presented and are given a recognition measure of their retention at the end of the session. The trick is that each list consists of a set of words (such as *bed, rest, awake, tired*) that are strongly associated with another target word that is not on the list (in this case, *sleep*). When subjects *recall* the words on each list, they remember the nonpresented target word over 50% of the time, and when they are given the final *recognition* test, they typically indicate that about 80% of the nonstudied target words were presented in the lists (see **Figure 7.21**). Using the DRM paradigm, false memories can be created reliably in normal, healthy participants in a matter of minutes, with no pressure or misleading information. Thus, this line of research provides a dramatic demonstration of how easy it is to get people to remember that they saw something they really didn't see (McDermott, 2007; Neuschatz et al., 2007).

Skepticism about the validity of recovered memories of abuse has also been fueled by the following observations and research findings:

- Many repressed memories of abuse have been recovered under the influence of hypnosis. However, an extensive body of research indicates that hypnosis tends to increase memory distortions while paradoxically making people feel more confident about their recollections (Mazzoni, Heap, & Scoboria, 2010; Mazzoni & Lynn, 2007).
- Many repressed memories of abuse have been recovered through therapists' dream interpretations. But as you learned in Chapter 5, dream interpretation depends on highly subjective guesswork that cannot be verified. Moreover, research shows that bogus dream interpretations can lead normal subjects to believe that they actually experienced the events suggested in the dream analyses (Loftus, 2000; Loftus & Mazzoni, 1998).
- Some recovered memories have involved incidents of abuse that occurred before the victim reached age 2 and even when the victim was still in the womb (Taylor, 2004). However, when adults are asked to recall their earliest memories, their oldest recollections typically don't go back to earlier than age 2 (Hayne, 2007; Morrison & Conway, 2010).

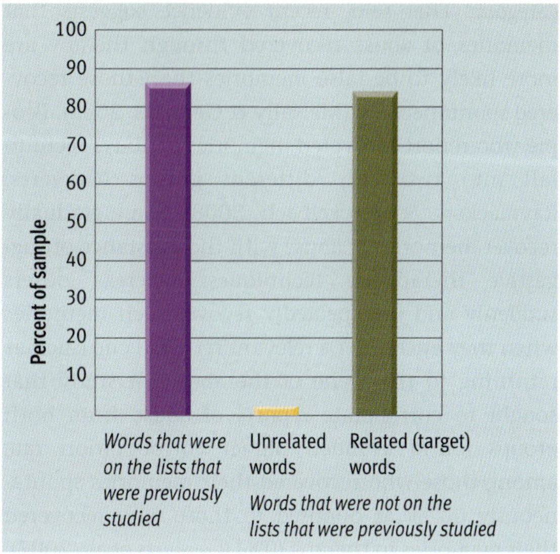

© Cengage Learning 2013

Figure 7.21
The prevalence of false memories observed by Roediger and McDermott (1995). This graph summarizes the recognition test results in Study 1 conducted by Roediger and McDermott (1995). Participants correctly identified words that had been on the lists that they had studied 86% of the time and only misidentified unrelated words that had not been on the lists 2% of the time, indicating that they were paying careful attention to the task. Nonetheless, they mistakenly reported that they "remembered" related target words that were *not* on the lists 84% of the time—a remarkably high prevalence of false memories.

Conclusions

So, what can we conclude about the emotionally charged recovered memories controversy? It seems pretty clear that therapists can unintentionally create false memories in their patients and that a significant portion of recovered memories of abuse are the product of suggestion (Follette & Davis, 2009; Ost, 2009) But it also seems likely that some cases of recovered memories are authentic (Brewin, 2007; Smith & Gleaves, 2007). It is difficult to estimate what proportion of recovered memories of abuse fall in each

DOONESBURY © 1994 by G. B. Trudeau. Distributed by Universal Press Syndicate. Reprinted with permission. All rights reserved.

category. That said, recent evidence suggests that memories of abuse recovered through therapy are more likely to be false memories than those recovered spontaneously (McNally & Geraerts, 2009). People who report recovered memories of abuse seem to fall into two very different groups (Geraerts, Raymaekers, & Merckelbach, 2008). Some gradually recover memories of abuse with the assistance of suggestive therapeutic techniques, whereas others suddenly and unexpectedly recover such memories when they encounter a relevant retrieval cue (such as returning to the scene of the abuse). A study that sought to corroborate reports of abuse from both groups found a much higher corroboration rate among those who recovered their memories spontaneously (37%) as opposed to those who recovered their memories in therapy (0%) (Geraerts et al., 2007).

Thus, the matter of recovered memories needs to be addressed with great caution. On the one hand, people should be extremely careful about accepting accounts of recovered memories of abuse in the absence of some corroboration. On the other hand, recovered memories of abuse cannot be summarily dismissed. It would be tragic if the repressed memories controversy made people overly skeptical about the all-too-real problem of childhood sexual abuse.

This controversy has helped inspire a great deal of research that has increased our understanding of just how fragile, fallible, malleable, and subjective human memory is. We are presumptuous to trust memory—whether recovered or not—to provide accurate recollections of the past. Moreover, the implicit dichotomy underlying the repressed memories debate—that some memories are true, whereas others are false—is misleading and oversimplified. Research demonstrates that all human memories are imperfect reconstructions of the past that are subject to many types of distortion.

REVIEW OF KEY LEARNING GOALS

7.13 Ebbinghaus's early studies of nonsense syllables suggested that people forget very rapidly. Subsequent research showed that Ebbinghaus's forgetting curve was exceptionally steep. Forgetting can be measured by asking people to recall, recognize, or relearn information. Different methods of measuring retention often produce different estimates of forgetting. Recognition measures tend to yield higher estimates of retention than recall measures.

7.14 Some forgetting, including pseudoforgetting, is caused by ineffective encoding of information, which is usually due to lack of attention. Decay theory proposes that forgetting occurs spontaneously with the passage of time. It has proven difficult to show that decay occurs in long-term memory.

7.15 Interference theory proposes that people forget information because of competition from other material. Proactive interference occurs when old learning interferes with new information. Retroactive interference occurs when new learning interferes with old information. Forgetting may also be a matter of retrieval failure. According to the encoding specificity principle, the effectiveness of a retrieval cue depends on how well it corresponds to the memory code that represents the stored item.

7.16 Those who tend to accept recovered memories of abuse note that child abuse is quite common and argue that repression is a normal response to it. Memory researchers who tend to be skeptical about recovered memories argue that a minority of therapists prod their patients until they inadvertently create the memories of abuse that they're searching for. They point out that countless studies have demonstrated that it is not all that difficult to create false memories and that memory is more malleable and less reliable than assumed. Memories recovered spontaneously appear more likely to be authentic than memories recovered in therapy.

KEY LEARNING GOALS

7.17 Describe evidence on the neural circuitry of memory, including work on long-term potentiation and neurogenesis.

7.18 Distinguish between two types of amnesia, and identify the anatomical structures implicated in memory.

In Search of the Memory Trace: The Physiology of Memory

For decades, neuroscientists have ventured forth in search of the physiological basis for memory, often referred to as the "memory trace." On several occasions, scientists have been excited by new leads, only to be led down blind alleys. For example, as we noted earlier, Wilder Penfield's work with electrical stimulation of the brain during surgery suggested that the cortex houses exact tape recordings of past experiences (Penfield & Perot, 1963). At the time, scientists believed that this was a major advance. Ultimately, it was not.

Similarly, James McConnell (1962) rocked the world of science when he reported that he had chemically transferred a specific memory of a conditioned reflex from one flatworm to another. McConnell boldly speculated that in the future chemists might be able to formulate pills containing the information for Physics 201 or History 101! Unfortunately, McConnell's studies proved difficult to replicate (Rilling, 1996). Today, decades after McConnell's "breakthrough," we are still a long way from breaking the chemical code for memory.

Investigators continue to explore a variety of leads about the physiological bases for memory. In light of past failures, these lines of research should probably be viewed with guarded optimism. But we'll look at some of the more promising approaches.

The Neural Circuitry of Memory

PsykTrek 6c

One line of research suggests that memory formation results in *alterations in synaptic transmission* at specific sites. According to this view, specific memories depend on biochemical changes that occur at specific synapses. Like McConnell, Eric Kandel (2001) and his colleagues have studied conditioned reflexes in a simple organism—a sea slug. In research that earned a Nobel prize for Kandel, they showed that reflex learning in the sea slug produces changes in the strength of specific synaptic connections by enhancing the availability and release of neurotransmitters at these synapses (Bailey & Kandel, 2009; Kennedy, Hawkins, & Kandel, 1992). Kandel believes that durable changes in synaptic transmission may be the neural building blocks of more complex memories as well.

Richard F. Thompson (1989, 1992, 2005) and his colleagues have shown that specific memories may depend on *localized neural circuits* in the brain. In other words, memories may create unique, reusable pathways in the brain along which signals flow. Thompson has traced the pathway that accounts for a rabbit's memory of a conditioned eyeblink response. The key link in this circuit is a microscopic spot in the *cerebellum,* a structure in the hindbrain (see **Figure 7.22**).

Evidence on *long-term potentiation* also supports the idea that memory traces consist of specific neural circuits. ***Long-term potentiation (LTP)* is a long-lasting increase in neural excitability at synapses along a specific neural pathway.** Researchers produce LTP artificially by sending a burst of high-frequency electrical stimulation along a neural pathway. But theorists suspect that natural events produce the same sort of potentiated neural circuit when a memory is formed (Lynch, 2004; Sweatt, 2009). LTP appears to involve changes in both presynaptic (sending) and postsynaptic (receiving) neurons in neural circuits in the hippocampus (refer to **Figure 7.22**) (Bi & Poo, 2001). The evidence on LTP has inspired promising work on the development of drugs that might enhance memory in humans (Lynch & Gall, 2006).

Recent research suggests that the process of *neurogenesis*—the formation of new neurons—may contribute to the sculpting of neural circuits that underlie memory. As we noted in Chapter 3, scientists have recently discovered that new brain cells are formed constantly in the *dentate gyrus* of the *hippocampus* (Gould, 2004; Leuner & Gould, 2010). Animal studies show that manipulations that suppress neurogenesis lead to memory impairments on many types of learning tasks and that conditions that increase neurogenesis are associated with enhanced learning on many tasks (Leuner, Gould, & Shors, 2006). According to Becker and Wojtowicz (2007), newly formed neurons are initially more excitable than mature neurons, so they may be more readily recruited into new neural circuits corresponding to memories. Moreover, neurogenesis provides the brain with a supply of neurons that vary in age. These variations may somehow allow the brain to "time stamp" some memories. The theorizing about how neurogenesis contributes to memory encoding is highly speculative (Jessberger, Aimone, & Gage, 2009). Despite this, research on neurogenesis is an exciting new line of investigation.

The Anatomy of Memory

PsykTrek 6c

Cases of *organic amnesia*—extensive memory loss due to head injury—are another source of clues about the physiological bases of memory. There are two basic types of amnesia: retrograde and anterograde (see **Figure 7.23** on the next page). ***Retrograde amnesia* involves the loss of memories for events that occurred prior to the onset of amnesia.** For example, a 25-year-old gymnast who sustains a head trauma might find the prior three years, or seven years, or her entire lifetime erased. ***Anterograde amnesia* involves the loss of memories for events that occur after the onset of amnesia.** For instance, after her accident, the injured gymnast might suffer impaired ability to remember people she meets, where she has parked her car, and so on.

The study of anterograde amnesia has proven to be an especially rich source of information about the

© Courtesy of Eric Kandel

Eric Kandel

"Learning results from changes in the strength of the synaptic connections between precisely interconnected cells."

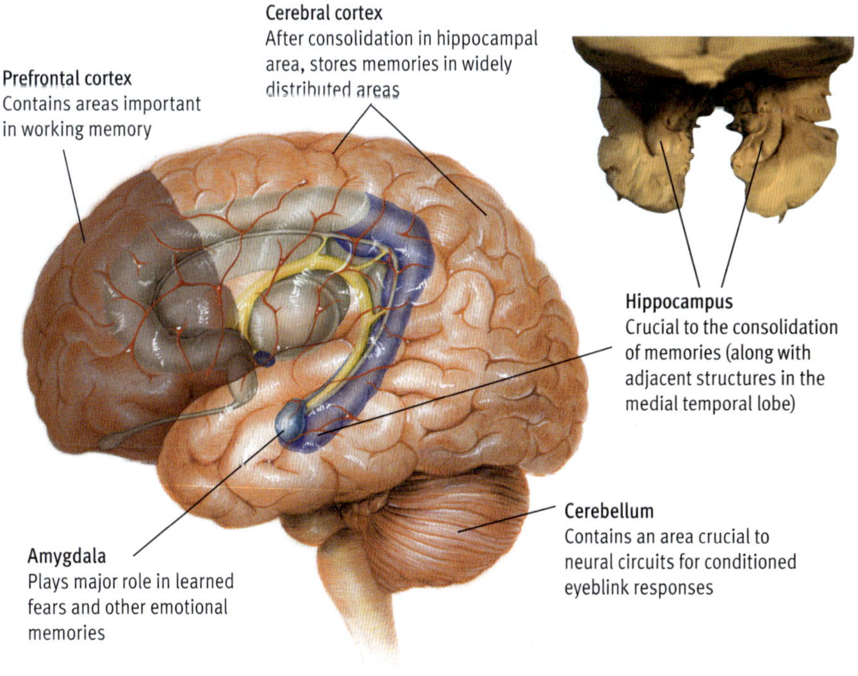

Figure 7.22

The anatomy of memory. All the brain structures identified here have been implicated in efforts to discover the anatomical structures involved in memory. The hippocampus is the hub of the medial temporal lobe memory system, which is thought to play a critical role in the consolidation of long-term memories. © Cengage Learning 2013

Figure 7.23
Retrograde versus anterograde amnesia. In retrograde amnesia, memory for events that occurred prior to the onset of amnesia is lost. In anterograde amnesia, memory for events that occur subsequent to the onset of amnesia suffers.
© Cengage Learning 2013

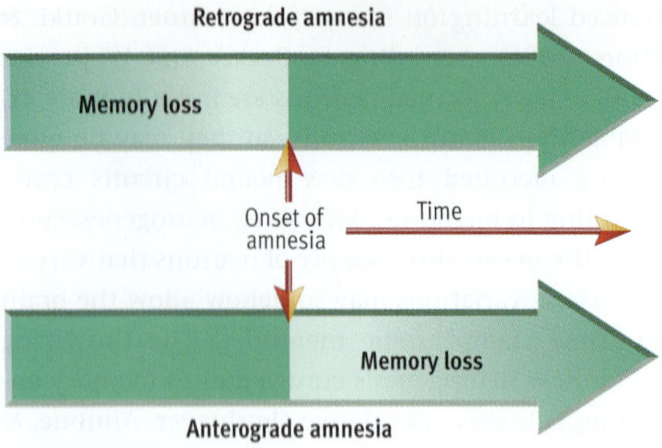

brain and memory. One well-known case, that of a man referred to as H.M., was followed from 1953 until his death in 2008 at the age of 82 (Corkin, 1984, 2002; Scoville & Milner, 1957). H.M. had surgery to relieve debilitating epileptic seizures that occurred up to 10 times a day. The surgery greatly reduced his seizures. Unfortunately, however, the surgery inadvertently wiped out most of his ability to form new long-term memories. H.M.'s short-term memory remained fine, and he could recall experiences prior to his surgery, but he had no recollection of anything that had happened since 1953 (other than about the most recent 20 seconds of his life). He did not recognize the doctors treating him, he couldn't remember routes to and from places, and he didn't know his own age. H.M. was unable to remember what he ate a few minutes ago, let alone what he had done in the years since his surgery. At age 66, after he had gray hair for years, he could not remember whether he had gray hair when asked, even though he looked in the mirror every day. Although he could not form new long-term memories, H.M.'s intelligence remained intact. He could care for himself (around his own home), carry on complicated conversations, and solve crossword puzzles. H.M.'s misfortune provided a golden opportunity for memory researchers.

In the decades after his surgery, over 100 researchers studied various aspects of his memory performance, leading to several major discoveries about the nature of memory (Maugh, 2008). As one scientist put it in commenting on H.M., "More was learned about memory by research with just one patient than was learned in the previous 100 years of research on memory" (Miller, 2009). More than 15 years prior to his death, Suzanne Corkin arranged for H.M.'s brain to be donated to Massachusetts General Hospital, where it was immediately subjected to extensive brain imaging after he passed away in 2008. His brain was subsequently moved to a lab at the University of California, San Diego, where one year after his death, it was cut into 2401 extremely thin slices for further study by scientists all over the world (Becker, 2009; Carey, 2009). The painstaking, methodical 53-hour dissection was broadcast live over the Web, where portions of the process were watched by over 400,000 people.

H.M.'s memory losses were originally attributed to the removal of his *hippocampus* (consult **Figure 7.22** again), although theorists eventually realized that other nearby structures that were removed also contributed to H.M.'s dramatic memory deficits (Delis & Lucas, 1996). Scientists now believe that the entire

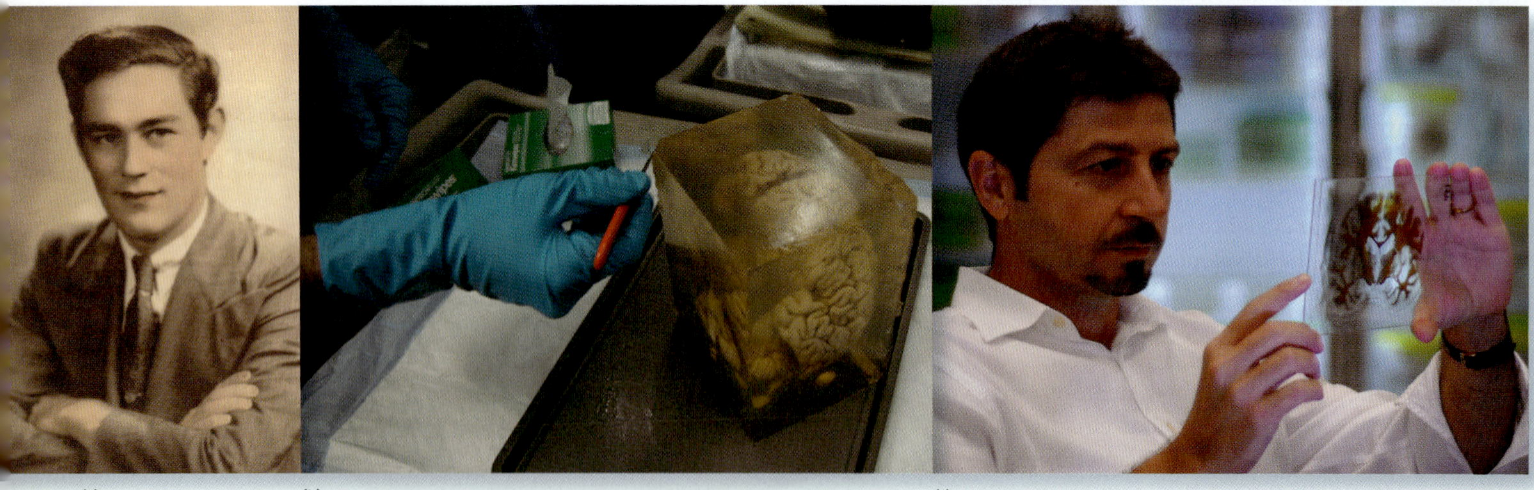
(a) (b) (c)

(a): Copyright © Suzanne Corkin, used with permission of The Wylie Agency LLC; (b & c) © The Brain Observatory, UC San Diego

To protect his privacy, H.M. was identified only by his initials for over 50 years. After his death it was revealed that his name was Henry Molaison. He is shown as a young man in (a). His death triggered a complex, multifaceted team effort, orchestrated by Suzanne Corkin of MIT, to preserve, image, and dissect the brain of the most important research subject in the history of neuroscience. His brain is shown in a mold of gelatin in (b). The challenge of slicing Molaison's brain into razor-thin sections for preservation and digital imaging was allocated to Jacob Annese of UCSD, who spent years preparing for the delicate task. Annese is shown looking at a mounted slide of a brain slice in (c). The digital atlas of Molaison's brain will reveal the exact boundaries of his surgical lesions. This information will permit scientists to analyze the precise relations between his brain damage and 50 years of data on his memory performance.

hippocampal region and adjacent areas in the cortex are critical for many types of long-term memory (Zola & Squire, 2000). Many scientists now refer to this broader memory complex as the *medial temporal lobe memory system* (Shrager & Squire, 2009). Given its apparent role in long-term memory, it's interesting to note that the hippocampal region is one of the first areas of the brain to sustain significant damage in the course of Alzheimer's disease, which produces severe memory impairment in many people, typically after age 65 (Albert & Moss, 2002; see Chapter 11).

Do these findings mean that memories are stored in the hippocampal region and adjacent areas? Probably not. Many theorists believe that the medial temporal lobe memory system plays a key role in the *consolidation* of memories (Dudai, 2004). ***Consolidation* is a hypothetical process involving the gradual conversion of information into durable memory codes stored in long-term memory.** According to this view, memories are consolidated in the hippocampal region and then stored in diverse and widely distributed areas of the cortex (Eichenbaum, 2004; Markowitsch, 2000). This setup allows new memories to become independent of the hippocampal region and to gradually be integrated with other memories already stored in various areas of the cortex (Frankland & Bontempi, 2005). Interestingly, recent research suggests that much of the consolidation process may unfold while people sleep (Stickgold & Walker, 2005).

As you can see, a variety of neural circuits and anatomical structures have been implicated as playing a role in memory. Looking for the physiological basis for memory is only slightly less daunting than looking for the physiological basis for thought itself.

REVIEW OF KEY LEARNING GOALS

7.17 According to Kandel, memory traces reflect alterations in neurotransmitter release at specific synapses. Thompson's research suggests that memory traces may consist of localized neural circuits. Memories may also depend on long-term potentiation, which is a durable increase in neural excitability at synapses along a specific neural pathway. Neurogenesis may contribute to the sculpting of neural circuits for memories.

7.18 In retrograde amnesia, a person loses memory for events prior to the amnesia. In anterograde amnesia, a person shows memory deficits for events subsequent to the onset of the amnesia. Studies of amnesia and other research suggest that the hippocampus and broader medial temporal lobe system play a major role in memory. These areas may be crucial to the consolidation of memories.

Systems and Types of Memory

KEY LEARNING GOALS

7.19 Compare and contrast declarative and nondeclarative (procedural) memory.

7.20 Distinguish between episodic and semantic memory.

7.21 Describe the nature and importance of prospective memory.

Some theorists believe that evidence on the physiology of memory is complicated and contradictory because investigators are probing into several distinct memory systems that may have different physiological bases. The various memory systems are distinguished primarily by the types of information they handle.

Declarative Versus Procedural Memory

6c

The most basic division of memory into distinct systems contrasts *declarative memory* with *nondeclarative* or *procedural memory* (Squire, 2004, 2009; see **Figure 7.24** on the next page). **The *declarative memory system* handles factual information.** It contains recollections of words, definitions, names, dates, faces, events, concepts, and ideas. **The *nondeclarative memory system* houses memory for actions, skills, conditioned responses, and emotional responses.** It contains *procedural memories* of how to execute perceptual-motor skills, such as riding a bike, typing, and tying one's shoes. To illustrate the distinction, if you know the rules of tennis (the number of games in a set, scoring, and such), this factual information is stored in declarative memory. If you remember how to hit a serve and swing through a backhand, these are procedural memories that are part of the nondeclarative system. The nondeclarative system also includes the memory base for conditioned reflexes and emotional reactions based on previous learning, such as a person's tensing up in response to the sound of a dental drill.

Support for the distinction between declarative and nondeclarative memory comes from evidence that the two systems seem to operate somewhat differently (Squire, Knowlton, & Musen, 1993). For instance, the recall of factual information (declarative memory) generally depends on conscious, effortful processes, whereas memory for conditioned reflexes (nondeclarative memory) is largely automatic and memories for skills often require little effort and attention (Johnson, 2003). People execute perceptual-motor tasks such as

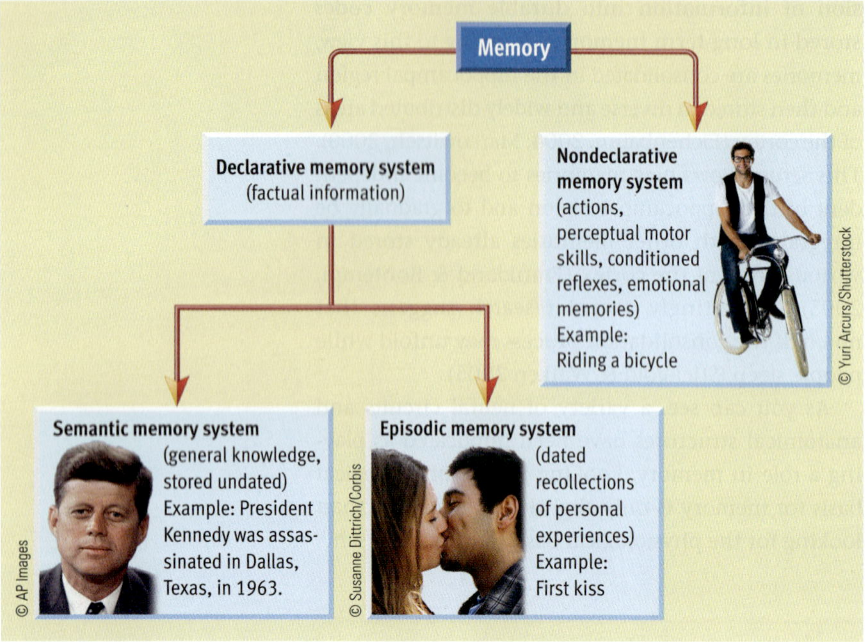

© Cengage Learning 2013

Figure 7.24

Theories of independent memory systems. Theorists have distinguished between declarative memory, which handles facts and information, and nondeclarative memory, which handles motor skills, conditioned responses, and emotional memories. Declarative memory is further subdivided into semantic memory (general knowledge) and episodic memory (dated recollections of personal experiences). The extent to which nondeclarative memory can be usefully subdivided remains the subject of debate, although many theorists view procedural memory, which handles actions and perceptual-motor skills, as an independent subsystem. (Adapted from Squire, 1987; Tulving, 1985, 1987)

Endel Tulving

"Memory systems constitute the major subdivisions of the overall organization of the memory complex. . . . An operating component of a system consists of a neural substrate and its behavioral or cognitive correlates."

playing the piano or typing with little conscious awareness of what they're doing. In fact, performance on such tasks sometimes deteriorates if people think too much about what they're doing. Another disparity is that the memory for skills (such as typing and bike riding) doesn't decline much over long retention intervals, whereas declarative memory appears more vulnerable to forgetting.

The notion that declarative and procedural memories are separate is supported by certain patterns of memory loss seen in amnesiacs. In many cases, declarative memory is severely impaired while procedural memory is left largely intact (Squire & Schrager, 2009). For example, H.M., the victim of amnesia discussed earlier, was able to learn and remember new motor skills, even though he couldn't remember what he looked like as he aged. The sparing of procedural memory in H.M. provided crucial evidence for the distinction between declarative and nondeclarative memory.

Researchers have made some progress toward identifying the neural bases of declarative versus nondeclarative memory. Declarative memory appears to be handled by the medial temporal lobe memory system and the far-flung areas of the cortex with which it communicates (Eichenbaum, 2003). Pinpointing the neural bases of nondeclarative memory has proven more difficult because it consists of more of a hodgepodge of memory functions. However, structures such as the cerebellum and amygdala appear to contribute (Delis & Lucas, 1996; Squire, 2004).

Semantic Versus Episodic Memory

Endel Tulving (1986, 1993, 2002) has further subdivided declarative memory into episodic and semantic memory (see **Figure 7.24**). Both contain factual information. However, episodic memory contains *personal facts* and semantic memory contains *general facts.* **The *episodic memory system* is made up of chronological, or temporally dated, recollections of personal experiences.** Episodic memory is a record of things you've done, seen, and heard. It includes information about *when* you did these things, saw them, or heard them. It contains recollections about being in a ninth-grade play, visiting the Grand Canyon, attending a Norah Jones concert, or going to a movie last weekend. Tulving (2001) emphasizes that the function of episodic memory is "time travel"—that is, to allow one to reexperience the past.

The *semantic memory system* contains general knowledge that is not tied to the time when the information was learned. Semantic memory contains information such as Christmas is December 25, dogs have four legs, and Phoenix is located in Arizona. You probably don't remember when you learned these facts. Such information is usually stored undated. The distinction between episodic and semantic memory can be better appreciated by drawing an analogy to books: Episodic memory is like an autobiography, while semantic memory is like an encyclopedia.

Some studies suggest that episodic and semantic memory may have distinct neural bases (Schacter, Wagner, & Buckner, 2000, Tulving, 2002). For instance, some amnesiacs forget mostly personal facts, while their recall of general facts is largely unaffected (Szpunar & McDermott, 2009). Brain-imaging studies suggest that the retrieval of episodic and semantic memories produces different—but overlapping—patterns of activation (Levine et al., 2004; Nyberg et al., 2002). However, debate continues about the neural substrates of episodic and semantic memory.

Prospective Versus Retrospective Memory

A 1984 paper with a clever title, "Remembering to Do Things: A Forgotten Topic" (Harris, 1984), introduced yet another distinction between types of memory: *prospective memory* versus *retrospective memory* (see **Figure 7.25**). This distinction does not refer

CONCEPT CHECK 7.3

Recognizing Various Types of Memory

Check your understanding of the various types of memory discussed in this chapter by matching the definitions below with the following: (a) sensory memory, (b) short-term memory, (c) long-term memory, (d) declarative memory, (e) nondeclarative memory, (f) episodic memory, and (g) semantic memory. The answers can be found in Appendix A.

_______ 1. Memory for factual information.

_______ 2. An unlimited capacity store that can hold information over lengthy periods of time.

_______ 3. The preservation of information in its original sensory form for a brief time, usually only a fraction of a second.

_______ 4. Chronological, or temporally dated, recollections of personal experiences.

_______ 5. The repository of memories for actions, skills, operations, and conditioned responses.

_______ 6. General knowledge that is not tied to the time when the information was learned.

_______ 7. A limited-capacity store that can maintain unrehearsed information for about 10–20 seconds.

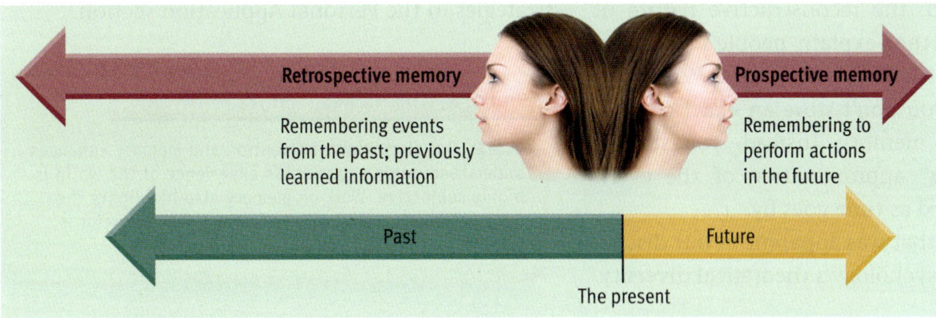

© Form Advertising/Alamy

Figure 7.25

Retrospective versus prospective memory. Most memory research has explored the dynamics of *retrospective memory,* which focuses on recollections from the past. However, *prospective memory,* which requires people to remember to perform actions in the future, also plays an important role in everyday life.

© Cengage Learning 2013

to independent *memory systems,* but rather to fundamentally different types of *memory tasks.* ***Prospective memory* involves remembering to perform actions in the future.** Examples of prospective memory tasks include remembering to grab your umbrella, to walk the dog, to call someone, and to grab the tickets for the big game. In contrast, ***retrospective memory* involves remembering events from the past or previously learned information.** Retrospective memory is at work when you try to recall who won the Super Bowl last year, when you reminisce about your high school days, or when you try to remember what your professor said in a lecture last week. Prospective memory has been a "forgotten" topic in that it has been the subject of relatively little study. But that has begun to change. Research on prospective memory has increased in recent years (McDaniel & Einstein, 2007).

Researchers interested in prospective memory argue that the topic merits far more study because it plays such a pervasive role in everyday life (Graf & Uttl, 2001). Think about it—a brief trip to attend class at school can be saturated with prospective memory tasks. You may need to remember to pack your notebook, take your cell phone, turn off the coffeemaker, and grab your umbrella before you even get out the door. Unfortunately, experiments demonstrate that it's easy to forget these kinds of intentions, especially when confronted by interruptions and distractions (Einstein et al., 2003). The recollection of intentions to undertake actions are often spontaneous—the intentions "pop" into people's minds unexpectedly (Einstein & McDaniel, 2005). People vary somewhat in their ability to successfully carry out prospective memory tasks (Searleman, 1996). Individuals who appear deficient in prospective memory are often characterized as "absent-minded."

REVIEW OF KEY LEARNING GOALS

7.19 Declarative memory is memory for facts, whereas nondeclarative memory is memory for actions, skills, and conditioned responses. Declarative memory depends more on conscious attention and is more vulnerable to forgetting.

7.20 Tulving subdivided declarative memory into episodic and semantic memory. Episodic memory is made up of temporally dated recollections of personal experiences, much like an autobiography. Semantic memory contains general facts, much like an encyclopedia.

7.21 Theorists have also distinguished between retrospective memory (remembering past events) and prospective memory (remembering to do things in the future). Prospective memory plays a pervasive role in everyday life.

KEY LEARNING GOALS

7.22 Identify the three unifying themes highlighted in this chapter.

Subjectivity of Experience

Theoretical Diversity

Multifactorial Causation

Reflecting on the Chapter's Themes

One of our integrative themes—the idea that people's experience of the world is subjective—stood head and shoulders above the rest in this chapter. Let's briefly review how the study of memory has illuminated this idea and then examine two other themes that are relevant.

First, our discussion of attention as inherently selective should have shed light on why people's experience of the world is subjective. To a great degree, what you see in the world around you depends on where you focus your attention. This is one of the main reasons that two people can be exposed to the "same" events and walk away with entirely different perceptions. Second, the reconstructive nature of memory should further explain people's tendency to view the world with a subjective slant. When you observe an event, you don't store an exact copy of the event in your memory. Instead, you store a rough, "bare bones" approximation of the event that may be reshaped as time goes by.

A second theme that was apparent in our discussion of memory is psychology's theoretical diversity. We saw illuminating theoretical debates about the nature of memory storage, the causes of forgetting, and the existence of multiple memory systems. Finally, the multifaceted nature of memory demonstrated once again that behavior is governed by multiple causes. For instance, your memory of a specific event may be influenced by your attention to it, your level of processing, your elaboration, your exposure to interference, how you search your memory store, how you reconstruct the event, and so forth. Given the multifaceted nature of memory, it should come as no surprise that there are many ways to improve memory. We discuss a variety of strategies in the Personal Application section.

REVIEW OF KEY LEARNING GOALS

7.22 Our discussion of attention and memory enhances understanding of why people's experience of the world is highly subjective. Work on memory also highlights the field's theoretical diversity and shows that behavior is governed by multiple causes.

CONCEPT CHECK 7.4

Identifying the Contributions of Major Theorists and Researchers

Check your recall of the principal ideas of important theorists and researchers covered in this chapter by matching the people listed on the left with the appropriate contributions described on the right. If you need help, the crucial pages describing each person's ideas are listed in parentheses. Fill in the letters for your choices in the spaces provided on the left. You'll find the answers in Appendix A.

Major Theorists and Researchers

_______ 1. Richard Atkinson and Richard Shiffrin (p. 279)

_______ 2. Alan Baddeley (pp. 281–282)

_______ 3. Fergus Craik and Robert Lockhart (pp. 276–277)

_______ 4. Hermann Ebbinghaus (p. 291)

_______ 5. Marcia Johnson (pp. 288–289)

_______ 6. Eric Kandel (p. 299)

_______ 7. Elizabeth Loftus (pp. 287–288, 296)

_______ 8. George Miller (pp. 280–281)

_______ 9. Endel Tulving (p. 302)

Key Ideas and Contributions

a. This nineteenth-century scholar invented nonsense syllables and showed that forgetting often occurs very rapidly.

b. This expert on short-term memory is famous for a paper titled "The Magical Number Seven, Plus or Minus Two."

c. These researchers developed an influential information-processing model of memory that described three memory stores: sensory memory, short-term memory, and long-term memory.

d. According to this theorist declarative memory should be subdivided into episodic memory and semantic memory.

e. This researcher developed a four-component model of working memory.

f. These researchers devised levels-of-processing theory, which proposes that deeper levels of processing result in longer-lasting memories.

g. This researcher described the misinformation effect and conducted extensive research on repressed memories.

h. This researcher described the process of source monitoring and the significance of source-monitoring errors.

i. Working with sea slugs, this researcher won a Nobel prize for demonstrating that alterations in synaptic transmission contribute to memory formation.

Improving Everyday Memory

KEY LEARNING GOALS

7.23 Discuss the importance of rehearsal, testing, distributed practice, and interference in efforts to improve everyday memory.

7.24 Discuss the value of deep processing, good organization, and mnemonic devices in efforts to improve everyday memory.

Answer the following "true" or "false."

____ **1** Memory strategies were recently invented by psychologists.

____ **2** Overlearning of information leads to poor retention.

____ **3** Outlining what you read is not likely to affect retention.

____ **4** Massing practice in one long study session is better than distributing practice across several shorter sessions.

Mnemonic devices **are strategies for enhancing memory.** They have a long and honorable history. In fact, one of the mnemonic devices covered in this Application—the method of loci—was described in Greece as early as 86–82 B.C. (Yates, 1966). Actually, mnemonic devices were even more crucial in ancient times than they are today. In ancient Greece and Rome, for instance, writing instruments were not readily available for people to jot down things they needed to remember, so they had to depend heavily on mnemonic devices.

Mnemonic devices can clearly be helpful in some situations (Wilding & Valentine, 1996). They are not a cure-all, however. They can be hard to apply to many everyday situations. Most books and training programs designed to improve memory probably overemphasize mnemonic techniques (Searleman & Herrmann, 1994). Although less exotic strategies, such as increasing rehearsal, engaging in deeper processing, and organizing material, are more crucial to everyday memory, we will discuss some popular mnemonics as we proceed through this Application. Along the way, you'll learn that all of our opening true-false statements are false. We will focus primarily on how to use memory principles to *enhance performance in academic pursuits*.

Engage in Adequate Rehearsal

PSYKTREK SIM5

Practice makes perfect, or so you've heard. In reality, practice is not likely to guarantee perfection. It usually leads to improved retention though. Studies show that retention improves with increased rehearsal (Greene, 1992). This improvement presumably occurs because rehearsal helps transfer information into long-term memory. Although rehearsal helps, people have a curious tendency to overestimate their knowledge of a topic and how well they will perform on a subsequent memory test of this knowledge (Koriat & Bjork, 2005). That's one reason it's a good idea to informally test yourself on information that you think you have mastered before confronting a real test.

In addition to checking your mastery, recent research suggests that testing actually enhances retention, a phenomenon dubbed the *testing effect* (Karpicke & Roediger, 2008; Roediger & Karpicke, 2006a). Studies have shown that taking a test on material increases performance on a subsequent test even more than studying for an equal amount of time (see **Figure 7.26**). Interestingly, the testing effect is observed on both closed-book and open-book exams (Agarwal et al., 2008). And the favorable effects of testing are enhanced if participants are provided feedback on their test performance (Butler & Roediger, 2008). Moreover, recent studies have demonstrated that the laboratory findings on the testing effect replicate in real-world educational settings (Larsen, Butler, & Roediger, 2009; McDaniel et al., 2007). Unfortunately, given the recent nature of this discovery, relatively few students are aware of the value of testing (Karpicke, Butler, & Roediger, 2009).

Why is testing so beneficial? The key appears to be that testing forces students to engage in effortful retrieval of information, which promotes future retention (Roediger et al., 2010). Indeed, even *unsuccessful* retrieval efforts can enhance retention (Kornell, Hays, & Bjork, 2009). In any event, self-testing appears to be an excellent memory tool, suggesting that it would be prudent to take the Practice Tests in this text or additional tests available on the website for the book.

Another way to enhance memory is to overlearn material (Driskell, Willis, & Copper, 1992). ***Overlearning*** **refers to continued rehearsal of material after you first appear to have mastered it.** In one study, after subjects had mastered a list of nouns (they recited the list without error), Krueger (1929) required them to continue rehearsing for 50% or 100% more trials. Measuring retention at intervals up to 28 days, Krueger found that greater overlearning was related to better recall of the list. Modern studies have also shown that overlearning can enhance performance on an exam that occurs

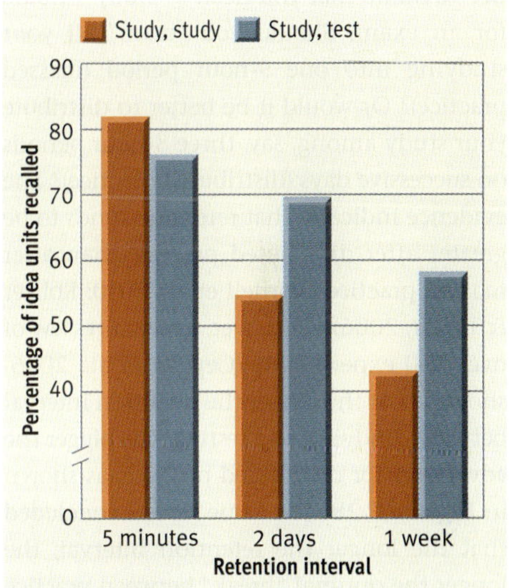

© Cengage Learning 2013

Figure 7.26

The testing effect. In one study by Roediger and Karpicke (2006b), participants studied a brief prose passage for 7 minutes. Then some of them studied it again for 7 minutes while others took a 7-minute test on the material. In the second phase of the study, subjects took another test on the material after either 5 minutes, 2 days, or 1 week. There wasn't much of a performance gap when subjects were tested over a 5-minute retention interval, but the testing group showed a significant advantage in recall when the retention interval was extended to 2 days or 1 week.

SOURCE: Roediger, H. L., III, & Karpicke, J. D. (2006). Test-enhanced learning: Taking memory tests improves long-term retention. *Psychological Science, 17*, 3, 249–255. Copyright © 2006 Blackwell Publishing. Reprinted by permission.

within a week, although the evidence on its long-term benefits (months later) is inconsistent (Peladeau, Forget, & Gagne, 2003; Rohrer et al., 2005).

One other point related to rehearsal is also worth mentioning. If you are memorizing some type of list, be aware of the serial-position effect, which is often observed when subjects are tested on their memory of lists (Murdock, 2001). **The *serial-position effect* occurs when subjects show better recall for items at the beginning and end of a list than for items in the middle** (see **Figure 7.27**). The reasons for the serial-position effect are complex and need not concern us. Its pragmatic implications are clear: If you need to memorize a list of, say, cranial nerves or past presidents, devote extra practice trials to items in the middle of the list and check your memorization of those items very carefully.

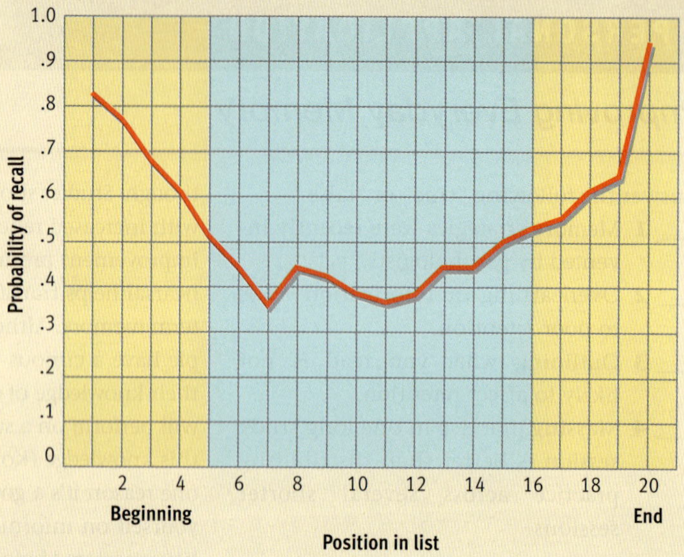

Figure 7.27

The serial-position effect. After learning a list of items to remember, people tend to recall more of the items from the beginning and the end of the list than from the middle, producing the characteristic U-shaped curve shown here. This phenomenon is called the serial-position effect.

SOURCE: Adapted from Rundus, D. (1971). Analysis of rehearsal processes in free recall. *Journal of Experimental Psychology, 89,* 63–77. Copyright © 1971 by the American Psychological Association.

© Cengage Learning 2013

Schedule Distributed Practice and Minimize Interference

Let's assume that you need to study 9 hours for an exam. Should you "cram" all your studying into one 9-hour period (massed practice)? Or would it be better to distribute your study among, say, three 3-hour periods on successive days (distributed practice)? The evidence indicates that retention tends to be greater after distributed practice than after massed practice (Kornell et al., 2010; Rohrer & Taylor, 2006). Moreover, a recent review of over 300 experiments (Cepeda et al., 2006) showed that the longer the retention interval between studying and testing, the bigger the advantage for distributed practice, as shown in **Figure 7.28**. The same review concluded that the longer the retention interval, the longer the optimal "break" between practice trials. When an upcoming test is more than two days away, the optimal interval between practice periods appears to be around 24 hours. The superiority of distributed practice over massed practice suggests that cramming is an ill-advised approach to studying for exams (Dempster, 1996).

Because interference is a major cause of forgetting, you'll probably want to think about how you can minimize it. This issue is especially important for students because memorizing information for one course can interfere with the retention of information for another course. Thus, the day before an exam in a course, you should study for that course only—if possible. If demands in other courses make that plan impossible, you should study the test material last.

Engage in Deep Processing and Organize Information

Research on levels of processing suggests that how *often* you go over material is less critical than the *depth* of processing that you engage in (Craik & Tulving, 1975). To remember what you read, you have to fully comprehend its meaning (Einstein & McDaniel, 2004). Many students could probably benefit if they spent less time on rote memorization and devoted more effort to actually paying attention to and analyzing the meaning of their reading assignments. In particular, it's useful to make material *personally* meaningful. When you read your textbooks, try to relate information to your own life and experience. For example, when you read about classical conditioning, try to think of your own responses that are attributable to classical conditioning.

It's also important to understand that retention tends to be greater when information is well organized (Einstein & McDaniel, 2004). Gordon Bower (1970) has shown that hierarchical organization is particularly helpful when it's applicable. Thus, it may be a good idea to *outline* reading assignments for school, since outlining forces you to organize material hierarchically. Consistent with this reasoning, there is some empirical evidence that outlining material from textbooks can enhance retention of the material (McDaniel, Waddill, & Shakesby, 1996).

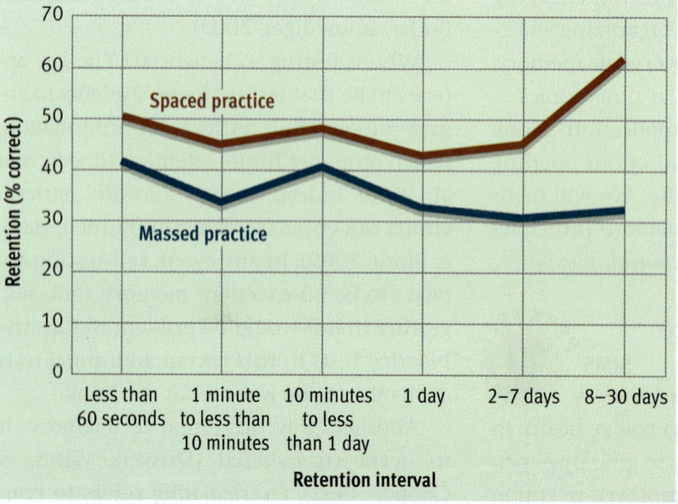

© Cengage Learning 2013

Figure 7.28

Effects of massed versus distributed practice on retention. In a review of over 300 experiments on massed versus distributed practice, Cepeda et al. (2006) examined the importance of the retention interval. As you can see, spaced practice was superior to massed practice at all retention intervals, but the gap widened at longer intervals. These findings suggest that distributed practice is especially advantageous when you need or want to remember material over the long haul.

Enrich Encoding with Mnemonic Devices

Many mnemonic devices—such as acrostics and acronyms—are designed to make abstract material more meaningful. Other mnemonic devices depend on visual imagery. As you may recall, Allan Paivio (1986, 2007) believes that visual images create a second memory code and that two codes are better than one.

Acrostics and Acronyms

Acrostics are phrases (or poems) in which the first letter of each word (or line) functions as a cue to help you recall information to be remembered. For instance, you may remember the order of musical notes with the saying "Every good boy does fine." A slight variation on acrostics is the *acronym*—a word formed out of the first letters of a series of words. Students memorizing the order of colors in the light spectrum often store the name "Roy G. Biv" to remember red, orange, yellow, green, blue, indigo, and violet. Notice that this acronym also takes advantage of the principle of chunking. Acrostics and acronyms that individuals create for themselves can be effective memory tools (Hermann, Raybeck, & Gruneberg, 2002).

Rhymes

Another verbal mnemonic that people often rely on is rhyming. You've probably repeated, "I before E except after C . . ." many times. Perhaps you also remember the number of days in each month with the old standby, "Thirty days hath September . . ." Rhyming something to remember it is an old and useful trick.

Link Method

The link method is a mnemonic that relies on the power of imagery. **The *link method* involves forming a mental image of items to be remembered in a way that links them together.** For instance, suppose that you need to remember some items to pick up at the drugstore: a news magazine, shaving cream, film, and pens. To remember these items, you might visualize a public figure on the magazine cover shaving with a pen while being photographed. The more bizarre you make your image, the more helpful it's likely to be (McDaniel & Einstein, 1986).

Method of Loci

Another visual mnemonic is the ***method of loci*, which involves taking an imaginary walk along a familiar path where images of items to be remembered are associated with certain locations.** The first step is to commit to memory a series of loci, or places along a path. Usually these loci are specific locations in your home or neighborhood. Then envision each thing you want to remember in one of these locations. Try to form distinctive, vivid images. When you need to remember the items, imagine yourself walking along the path. The various loci on your path should serve as cues for the retrieval of the images that you formed (see **Figure 7.29**). Evidence suggests that the method of loci can be effective in increasing retention (Moe & De Beni, 2004; Massen & Vterrodt-Plünnecke, 2006). Moreover, this method ensures that items are remembered in their *correct order* because the order is determined by the sequence of locations along the pathway. A recent study found that using loci along a pathway from home to work was more effective than a pathway through one's home (Massen et al., 2009).

Figure 7.29
The method of loci. In this example from Bower (1970), a person about to go shopping pairs items to remember with familiar places (loci) arranged in a natural sequence: (1) hot dogs/driveway; (2) cat food/garage interior; (3) tomatoes/front door; (4) bananas/coat closet shelf; (5) whiskey/kitchen sink. The shopper then uses imagery to associate the items on the shopping list with the loci, as shown in the drawing: (1) giant hot dog rolls down a driveway; (2) a cat noisily devours cat food in the garage; (3) ripe tomatoes are splattered on the front door; (4) bunches of bananas are hung from the closet shelf; (5) the contents of a bottle of whiskey gurgle down the kitchen sink. As the last panel shows, the shopper recalls the items by mentally touring the loci associated with them.

SOURCE: From Bower, G. H. (1970). Analysis of a mnemonic device. *American Scientist, 58,* 496–499. Copyright © 1970 by Scientific Research Society. Reprinted by permission.

REVIEW OF KEY LEARNING GOALS

7.23 Rehearsal, even when it involves overlearning, facilitates retention. Testing yourself on material also enhances retention. In memorizing lists, one should be wary of the serial-position effect. Distributed practice tends to be more efficient than massed practice. Study sessions should be scheduled in ways that minimize interference.

7.24 Deeper processing of material tends to result in greater retention. Evidence also suggests that organization enhances retention, so outlining texts may be valuable. Meaningfulness can be enhanced through the use of mnemonic devices such as acrostics and acronyms. The link method and the method of loci are mnemonic devices that depend on the value of visual imagery.

Understanding the Fallibility of Eyewitness Accounts

KEY LEARNING GOALS

7.25 Understand how hindsight bias and overconfidence contribute to the frequent inaccuracy of eyewitness memory.

A number of years ago, the Wilmington, Delaware, area was plagued by a series of armed robberies. The perpetrator was dubbed the "gentleman bandit" by the press because he was an unusually polite and well-groomed thief. The local media published a sketch of the gentleman bandit, and eventually an alert resident turned in a suspect who resembled the sketch. Much to everyone's surprise, the accused thief was a Catholic priest named Father Bernard Pagano—who vigorously denied the charges. Unfortunately for Father Pagano, his denials and alibis were unconvincing and he was charged with the crimes. At his trial, *seven* eyewitnesses confidently identified Father Pagano as the gentleman bandit. The prosecution was well on its way to a conviction when there was a stunning turn of events. Another man, Ronald Clouser, confessed to the police that he was the gentleman bandit. The authorities dropped the charges against Father Pagano, and the relieved priest was able to return to his normal life (Rodgers, 1982).

This bizarre tale of mistaken identity raises some interesting questions about memory. How could seven people "remember" seeing Father Pagnano commit armed robberies that he had nothing to do with? How could they mistake him for Ronald Clouser, when the two really didn't look very similar (see the adjacent photos)? How could they be so confident when they were so wrong? Perhaps you're thinking that this is just one case and it must be unrepresentative (which would be sound critical thinking). Well, yes, it *is* a rather extreme example, but researchers have compiled mountains of evidence that eyewitness testimony is not nearly as reliable or as accurate as widely assumed (Kassin et al., 2001; Wells, Memon, & Penrod, 2006). This finding is ironic in that people are most confident about their assertions when they can say, "I saw it with my own eyes." Television news shows use the title "Eyewitness News" to create the impression that they chronicle events with great clarity and accuracy. And our legal system accords special status to eyewitness testimony because it's considered much more dependable than hearsay or circumstantial evidence.

So, why are eyewitness accounts surprisingly inaccurate? Well, many factors and processes contribute. We'll begin by briefly reviewing some of the relevant processes that were introduced in the main body of the chapter. Then we'll focus on two common errors in thinking that also play a role.

Can you think of any memory phenomena described in the chapter that seem likely to undermine eyewitness accuracy? You could point to the fact that *memory is a reconstructive process,* and eyewitness recall is likely to be distorted by the schemas that people have for various events. A second consideration is that *witnesses sometimes make source-monitoring errors* and get confused about where they saw a face. For example, one rape victim mixed up her assailant with a guest on a TV show that she was watching when she was attacked. Fortunately, the falsely accused suspect had an airtight alibi, as he could demonstrate that he was on live television when the rape occurred (Schacter, 1996). Perhaps the most pervasive factor is the misinformation effect (Davis & Loftus, 2007). *Witnesses' recall of events is routinely distorted by information introduced after the event* by police officers, attorneys, news reports, and so forth. In addition to these factors, eyewitness inaccuracy is fueled by the *hindsight bias* and *overconfidence effects*.

The Contribution of Hindsight Bias

The *hindsight bias* is the tendency to mold one's interpretation of the past to fit how events actually turned out. When you know the outcome of an event, this knowledge slants your recall of how the event unfolded and what your thinking was at the time. With the luxury of hindsight, people have a curious tendency to say, "I knew it all along" when explaining events that objectively would have been difficult to foresee.

The tendency to exhibit the hindsight bias is normal, pervasive, and surprisingly strong (Guilbault et al., 2004). With regard to eyewitnesses, their recollections may often be distorted by knowing that a particular person has been arrested and accused of the crime in question. For example, Wells and Bradfield (1998) had simulated eyewitnesses select a perpetrator from a photo lineup. The eyewitnesses' confidence in

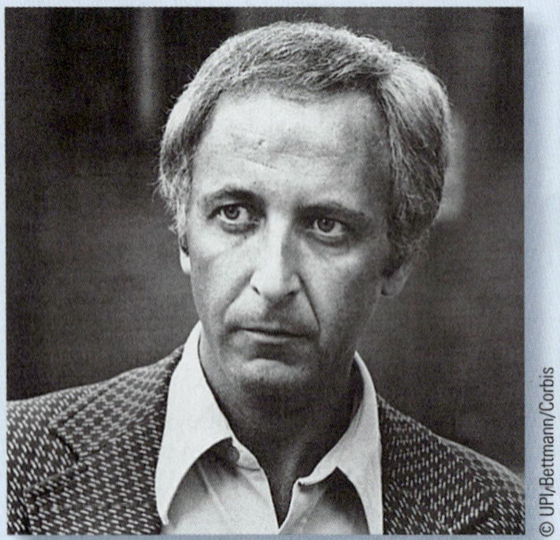

Although he doesn't look that much like the real "gentleman bandit," who is shown on the left, seven eyewitnesses identified Father Pagano (right) as the gentleman bandit, showing just how unreliable eyewitness accounts can be.

their identifications tended to be quite modest. This made sense given that the actual perpetrator was not even in the lineup. But when some subjects were told, "Good, you identified the actual suspect," they became highly confident about their identifications, which obviously were incorrect. In another study, participants read identical scenarios about a couple's first date that either had no ending or ended in a rape (described in one additional sentence). The subjects who received the rape ending reconstructed the story to be more consistent with their stereotypes of how rapes occur (Carli, 1999).

© Jim Arbogast/Digital Vision/Getty Images

Although courts give special credence to eyewitness testimony, scientific evidence indicates that eyewitness accounts are less reliable than widely assumed.

The Contribution of Overconfidence

Another flaw in thinking that contributes to inaccuracy in eyewitness accounts is people's tendency to be overconfident about the reliability of their memory. When tested for their memory of information, people tend to overestimate their accuracy (Koriat & Bjork, 2005; Lichtenstein, Fischhoff, & Phillips, 1982). In studies of eyewitness recall, participants also tend to be overconfident about their recollections. Although jurors are likely to be more convinced by eyewitnesses who appear confident, the evidence indicates that only a modest correlation is found between eyewitness confidence and eyewitness accuracy (Shaw, McClure, & Dykstra, 2007). Thus, many convictions of innocent people have been attributed to the impact of testimony from highly confident but mistaken eyewitnesses (Wells, Olson, & Charman, 2002).

Can you learn to make better judgments of the accuracy of your recall of everyday events? Yes, with effort you can get better at making accurate estimates of how likely you are to be correct in the recall of some fact or event. One reason that people tend to be overconfident is that if they can't think of any reasons that they might be wrong, they assume they must be right. Thus, overconfidence is fueled by yet another common error in thinking—*the failure to seek disconfirming evidence.* Even veteran scientists fall prey to this weakness, as most people don't seriously consider reasons that they might be wrong about something (Mynatt, Doherty, & Tweney, 1978).

Thus, to make more accurate assessments of what you know and don't know, it helps to engage in a deliberate process of considering why you might be wrong. Here is an example. Based on your reading of Chapter 1, write down the schools of thought associated with the following major theorists: William James, John B. Watson, and Carl Rogers. After you provide your answers, rate your confidence that the information you just provided is correct. Now, write three reasons that your answers might be wrong and three reasons they might be right.

Most people will balk at this exercise, arguing that they cannot think of any reasons why they might be wrong. But after some resistance, they can come up with several. Such reasons might include "I was half asleep when I read that part of the chapter" or "I might be confusing Watson and James." Reasons that you think you're right could include "I distinctly recall discussing this with my friend" or "I really worked on those names in Chapter 1." After listing reasons that you might be right and reasons that you might be wrong, rate your confidence in your accuracy once again. Guess what? Most people are less confident after going through such an exercise than they were.

The new confidence ratings tend to be more realistic than the original ratings (Koriat, Lichtenstein, & Fischhoff, 1980). Why? Because this exercise forces you to think more deeply about your answers and to search your memory for related information. Most people stop searching their memory as soon as they generate an answer they believe to be correct. Thus, the process of considering reasons that you might be wrong about something—a process that people rarely engage in—is a useful critical thinking skill that can reduce overconfidence effects. Better assessment of what you know and don't know can be an important determinant of the quality of the decisions you make and the way you solve problems and reason from evidence.

Table 7.1 Critical Thinking Skills Discussed in This Application

Skill	Description
Understanding the limitations and fallibility of human memory	The critical thinker appreciates that memory is reconstructive and that even eyewitness accounts may be distorted or inaccurate.
Recognizing the bias in hindsight analysis	The critical thinker understands that knowing the outcome of events biases our recall and interpretation of the events.
Recognizing overconfidence in human cognition	The critical thinker understands that people are frequently overconfident about the accuracy of their projections for the future and their recollections of the past.
Understanding the need to seek disconfirming evidence	The critical thinker understands the value of thinking about how or why one might be wrong about something.

© Cengage Learning 2013

REVIEW OF KEY LEARNING GOALS

7.25 Research indicates that eyewitness memory is not nearly as reliable or as accurate as widely believed. The hindsight bias, which is the tendency to reshape one's interpretation of the past to fit with known outcomes, often distorts eyewitness memory. People tend to be overconfident about their eyewitness recollections.

Chapter 7 Practice Test

1. Getting information into memory is called __________; getting information out of memory is called __________.
   A. storage; retrieval
   B. encoding; storage
   C. encoding; retrieval
   D. storage; encoding

2. The word *big* is flashed on a screen. A mental picture of the word *big* represents a __________ code; the definition "large in size" represents a __________ code; "sounds like pig" represents a __________ code.
   A. structural; phonemic; semantic
   B. phonemic; semantic; structural
   C. structural; semantic; phonemic
   D. phonemic; structural; semantic

3. Miles is listening as his mother rattles through a list of 15 or so things that he needs to remember to pack for an upcoming trip. According to George Miller, if Miles doesn't write the items down as he hears them, he will probably remember:
   A. fewer than 5 items from the list.
   B. about 10 to 12 items from the list.
   C. all the items from the list.
   D. 5 to 9 items from the list.

4. Which statement best represents current evidence on the durability of long-term storage?
   A. All forgetting involves breakdowns in retrieval.
   B. LTM is like a barrel of marbles in which none of the marbles ever leak out.
   C. There is no convincing evidence that all one's memories are stored away permanently.
   D. All long-term memories gradually decay at a constant rate.

5. An organized cluster of knowledge about a particular object or event is called a:
   A. semantic network.
   B. conceptual hierarchy.
   C. schema.
   D. retrieval cue.

6. The tip-of-the-tongue phenomenon:
   A. is a temporary inability to remember something you know, accompanied by a feeling that it's just out of reach.
   B. is clearly due to a failure in retrieval.
   C. reflects a permanent loss of information from LTM.
   D. is both a and b.

7. Roberto is telling Rachel about some juicy gossip when she stops him and informs him that she is the one who passed this gossip on to him about a week ago. In this example, Roberto has:
   A. been fooled by the misinformation effect.
   B. made a reality-monitoring error.
   C. made a source-monitoring error.
   D. made a destination memory error.

8. If decay theory is correct:
   A. information can never be permanently lost from long-term memory.
   B. forgetting is simply a case of retrieval failure.
   C. the principal cause of forgetting should be the passage of time.
   D. all of the above.

9. Bulldog McRae was recently traded to a new football team. He is struggling to remember the plays for his new team because he keeps mixing them up with the plays from his previous team. Bulldog's problem illustrates the operation of:
   A. retroactive interference.
   B. proactive interference.
   C. transfer-inappropriate processing.
   D. parallel distributed processing.

10. Research suggests that the *consolidation* of memories depends on activity in the:
    A. cerebellum.
    B. prefrontal cortex.
    C. medial temporal lobe.
    D. corpus callosum.

11. Your memory of how to ride a bicycle is contained in your __________ memory.
    A. declarative
    B. nondeclarative (procedural)
    C. structural
    D. episodic

12. Your knowledge that birds fly, that the sun rises in the east, and that $2 + 2 = 4$ is contained in your __________ memory.
    A. structural
    B. procedural
    C. episodic
    D. semantic

13. Dorothy memorized her shopping list. When she got to the store, however, she found she had forgotten many of the items from the middle of the list. This is an example of:
    A. inappropriate encoding.
    B. retrograde amnesia.
    C. proactive interference.
    D. the serial-position effect.

14. Overlearning:
    A. refers to continued rehearsal of material after the point of apparent mastery.
    B. promotes improved recall.
    C. should not be done, since it leads to increased interference.
    D. does both a and b.

15. The tendency to mold one's interpretation of the past to fit how events actually turned out is called:
    A. the overconfidence effect.
    B. selective amnesia.
    C. retroactive interference.
    D. the hindsight bias.

Answers

1 C p. 274	6 D p. 286	11 B pp. 301–302
2 C pp. 276–277	7 C p. 289	12 D p. 302
3 D pp. 280–281	8 C p. 293	13 D p. 306
4 C pp. 282–283	9 B pp. 293–294	14 D p. 305
5 C p. 284	10 C p. 301	15 D p. 308

PsykTrek

To view a demo: **www.cengage.com/psychology/psyktrek**
To order: **www.cengage.com/psychology/weiten**

Go to the PsykTrek website or CD-ROM for further study of the concepts in this chapter. Both online and on the CD-ROM, PsykTrek includes dozens of learning modules with videos, animations, and quizzes, as well as simulations of psychological phenomena and a multimedia glossary that includes word pronunciations.

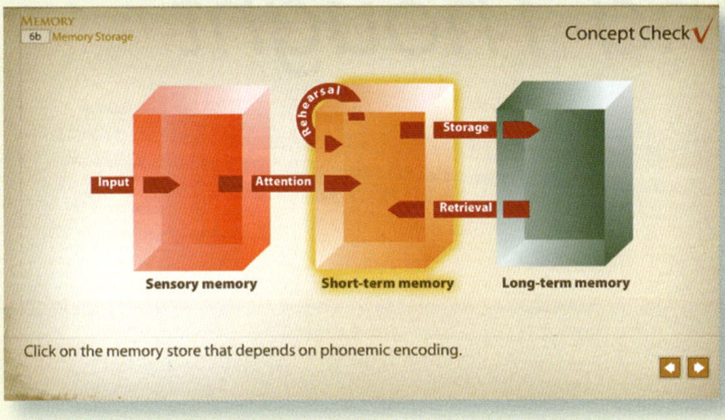

© Cengage Learning 2008

Visit Module 6a (*Memory Encoding*) and Module 6b (*Memory Storage*) to enhance your mastery of the essential principles of memory.

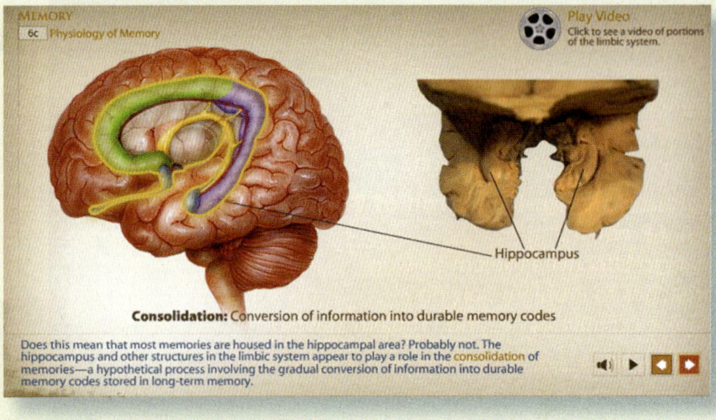

© Cengage Learning 2008

Explore Module 6c (*Physiology of Memory*) and Module 6d (*Forgetting*) to learn more about the neurological bases of memory and the reasons that we forget.

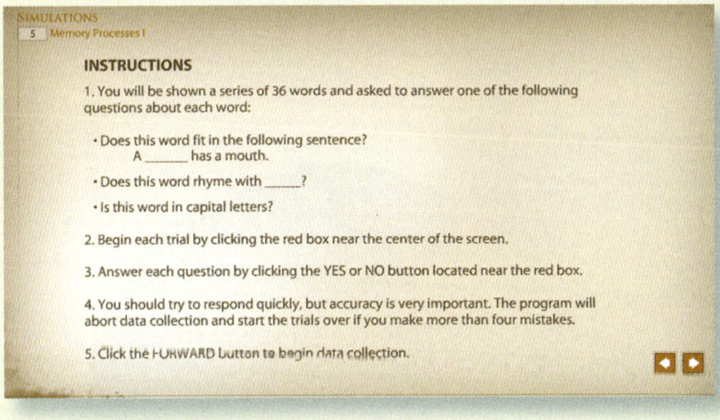

© Cengage Learning 2008

Go to Simulation 5 (*Memory Processes I*) to participate in a memory experiment that will demonstrate the influence of levels of processing.

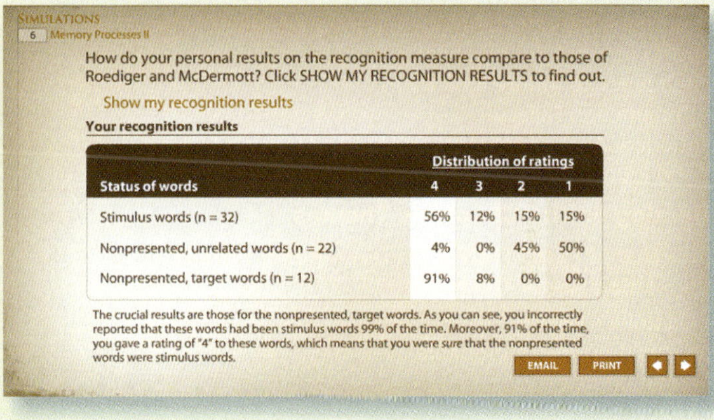

© Cengage Learning 2008

Discover how easy it is to develop false memories when you try Simulation 5 (*Memory Processes II*), which allows you to participate in a version of the Deese-Roediger-McDermott paradigm.

Online Study Tools

Log in to **CengageBrain** to access the resources your instructor requires. For this book, you can access:

CourseMate brings course concepts to life with interactive learning, study, and exam preparation tools that support the printed textbook. A textbook-specific website, Psychology CourseMate includes an integrated interactive eBook and other interactive learning tools such as quizzes, flashcards, videos, and more.

CengageNow is an easy-to-use online resource that helps you study in less time to get the grade you want—NOW. Take a pre-test for this chapter and receive a personalized study plan based on your results that will identify the topics you need to review and direct you to online resources to help you master those topics. Then take a post-test to help you determine the concepts you have mastered and what you will need to work on. If your textbook does not include an access code card, go to CengageBrain.com to gain access.

WebTutor is more than just an interactive study guide. WebTutor is an anytime, anywhere customized learning solution with an eBook, keeping you connected to your textbook, instructor, and classmates.

Aplia. If your professor has assigned Aplia homework:

1. Sign in to your account
2. Complete the corresponding homework exercises as required by your professor.
3. When finished, click "Grade It Now" to see which areas you have mastered, which need more work, and detailed explanations of every answer.

Visit **www.cengagebrain.com** to access your account and purchase materials.

8

Language and Thought

© Corbis/Age fotostock

"Mr. Watson—Mr. Sherlock Holmes," said Stamford, introducing us.

"How are you?" Holmes said, cordially, gripping my hand with a strength for which I should hardly have given him credit. "You have been in Afghanistan, I perceive."

"How on earth did you know that?" I asked, in astonishment.

(From A Study in Scarlet *by Arthur Conan Doyle)*

If you've ever read any Sherlock Holmes stories, you know that the great detective constantly astonished his stalwart companion, Dr. Watson, with his extraordinary deductions. Obviously, Holmes couldn't arrive at his conclusions without a chain of reasoning. Yet to him even an elaborate reasoning process was a simple, everyday act. Consider his feat of knowing at once, on first meeting Watson, that the doctor had been in Afghanistan. When asked, Holmes explained his reasoning as follows:

"I knew you came from Afghanistan. From long habit the train of thought ran so swiftly through my mind that I arrived at the conclusion without being conscious of the intermediate steps. There were such steps, however. The train of reasoning ran: 'Here is a gentleman of a medical type, but with the air of a military man. Clearly an army doctor, then. He has just come from the tropics, for his face is dark, and that is not the natural tint of his skin, for his wrists are fair. He has undergone hardship and sickness, as his haggard face says clearly. His left arm has been injured. He holds it in a stiff and unnatural manner. Where in the tropics could an English army doctor have seen much hardship and got his arm wounded? Clearly in Afghanistan.' The whole train of thought did not occupy a second."

© Nebojsa S/Shutterstock

Sherlock Holmes's deductive feats are fictional. But even to read and understand them—let alone imagine them, as Sir Arthur Conan Doyle did—is a remarkably complex mental act. Our everyday thought processes seem ordinary to us only

Paradox: *When faced with complex choices, quick, intuitive decisions often produce greater satisfaction than thoughtful deliberation.*

© Carnegie-Mellon University

Herbet Simon

"You couldn't use a word like mind *in a psychology journal—you'd get your mouth washed out with soap."*

because we take them for granted, just as Holmes saw nothing extraordinary in what to him was a simple deduction.

In reality, everyone is a Sherlock Holmes, continually performing impressive feats of thought. Even elementary perception—for instance, watching a football game or a ballet—involves elaborate cognitive processes. People must sort through distorted, constantly shifting perceptual inputs and deduce what they see out there in the real world. Imagine, then, the complexity of thought required to read a book, fix an automobile, or balance a checkbook. Of course, all this is not to say that human thought processes are flawless or unequaled. You probably own a $10 calculator that can run circles around you when it comes to computing square roots. As we'll see, some of the most interesting research in this chapter focuses on ways in which people's thinking can be limited, simplistic, or illogical.

In any event, as we have noted before, in psychology, ***cognition*** **refers broadly to mental processes or thinking.** When psychology first emerged as an independent science in the 19th century, it focused on the mind. Mental processes were explored through *introspection*—analysis of one's own conscious experience (see Chapter 1). Unfortunately, early psychologists' study of mental processes ran aground, as the method of introspection yielded unreliable results. Psychology's empirical approach depends on observation. Yet private mental events proved difficult to observe. Furthermore, during the first half of the 20th century, the study of cognition was actively discouraged by the theoretical dominance of behaviorism. Herbert Simon, a pioneer of cognitive psychology, recalls that "you couldn't use a word like *mind* in a psychology journal—you'd get your mouth washed out with soap" (Holden, 1986).

The 1950s brought a "cognitive revolution" in psychology (Baars, 1986). Renegade theorists, such as Herbert Simon, began to argue that behaviorists' exclusive focus on overt responses was doomed to yield an incomplete understanding of human functioning. More important, creative new approaches to research on cognitive processes led to exciting progress. In his book on the cognitive revolution, Howard Gardner (1985) noted that three major advances were reported at a watershed 1956 conference—in just one day! First, Herbert Simon and Allen Newell described the first computer program to successfully simulate human problem solving. Second, Noam Chomsky outlined a new model that changed the way psychologists studied language. Third, George Miller delivered the legendary paper that we discussed in Chapter 7, arguing that the capacity of short-term memory is seven (plus or minus two) items. Since then, cognitive science has grown into a robust, interdisciplinary enterprise (Simon, 1992). Besides memory (which we covered in Chapter 7), cognitive psychologists investigate the complexities of language, problem solving, decision making, and reasoning. We'll look at all these topics in this chapter, beginning with language.

KEY LEARNING GOALS

8.1 Define language and describe its structure.
8.2 Trace the development of human language during childhood.
8.3 Summarize the effects of bilingualism on language and cognitive development.
8.4 Evaluate language acquisition in animals and discuss the evolutionary bases of language.
8.5 Compare theoretical perspectives on language acquisition and assess the status of the linguistic relativity hypothesis.

Language: Turning Thoughts into Words

Language obviously plays a fundamental role in human behavior. If you were to ask people, "What characteristic most distinguishes humans from other living creatures?" a great many would reply, "Language." In this section, we'll discuss the structure and development of language and related topics, such as bilingualism and whether animals can learn language.

The Structure of Language

A *language* consists of symbols that convey meaning, plus rules for combining those symbols, that can be used to generate an infinite variety of messages. Human languages have a hierarchical structure (Ratner, Gleason, & Narasimhan, 1998). As **Figure 8.1** shows, basic sounds are combined into units with meaning, which are combined into words. Words are combined into phrases, which are combined into sentences.

Phonemes

At the base of the language hierarchy are ***phonemes*****, the smallest speech units in a language that can be distinguished perceptually.** Considering that an unabridged English dictionary contains more than 450,000 words, you might imagine that there must be a huge number of phonemes. In fact, linguists estimate that humans are capable of recognizing only about 100 such basic sounds. Moreover, no one language uses all of these phonemes. Different languages use different groups of about 20 to 80 phonemes. The English language is composed of about 40 phonemes, corresponding roughly to the 26 letters of the alpha-

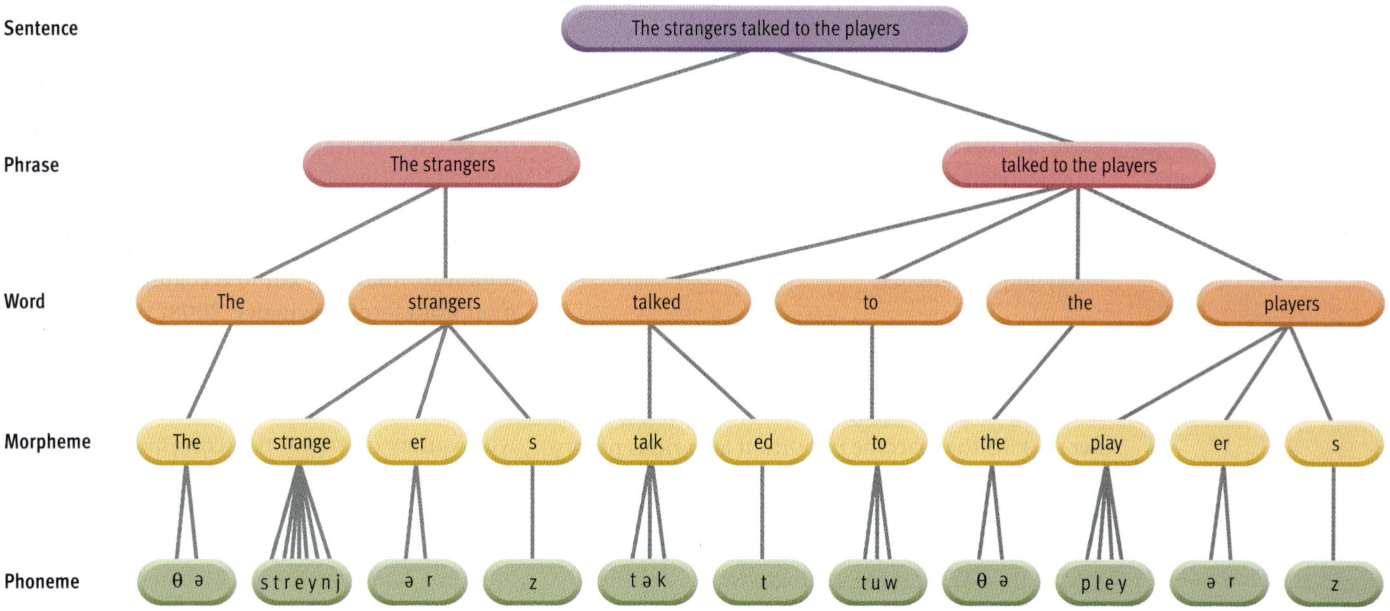

Figure 8.1

An analysis of a simple English sentence. As this example shows, verbal language has a hierarchical structure. At the base of the hierarchy are the *phonemes,* which are units of vocal sound that do not, in themselves, have meaning. The smallest units of meaning in a language are *morphemes,* which include not only root words but such meaning-carrying units as the past-tense suffix *ed* and the plural *s*. Complex rules of syntax govern how the words constructed from morphemes may be combined into phrases, and phrases into meaningful statements, or sentences. © Cengage Learning 2013

SOURCE: Clarke-Stewart, A., Friedman, S., & Koch, J. (1985). *Child development: A topical approach* (p. 417). New York: Wiley. Copyright © 1985 John Wiley & Sons, Inc. Reproduced with permission of John Wiley & Sons, Inc.

bet plus several variations (see **Table 8.1**). Working with this handful of basic sounds, people can understand and generate all the words in the English language—and invent new ones besides.

Table 8.1 Phonemic Symbols for the Sounds of American English

Consonants					
/p/	pill	/t/	toe	/g/	gill
/b/	bill	/d/	doe	/ŋ/	ring
/m/	mill	/n/	no	/h/	hot
/f/	fine	/s/	sink	/?/	uh-oh
/v/	vine	/z/	zinc	/l/	low
/θ/	thigh	/č/	choke	/r/	row
/ð/	thy	/ĵ/	joke	/y/	you
/š/	shoe	/k/	kill	/w/	win
/ž/	treasure				
Vowels					
/i/	beet	/ɪ/	bit	/e/	bait
/ɛ/	bet	/u/	boot	/ʊ/	foot
/o/	boat	/ɔ/	caught	/æ/	bat
/a/	pot	/^/	but	/ə/	sofa
/aɪ/	bite	/au/	out	/ɔɪ/	boy

© Cengage Learning 2013

SOURCE: From Hoff, E. (2005). *Language development*. Belmont, CA: Wadsworth. Wadsworth is a part of Cengage Learning, Inc. Reproduced by permission. www.cengage.com/permissions.

Morphemes and Semantics

***Morphemes* are the smallest units of meaning in a language.** There are approximately 50,000 English morphemes, which include root words as well as prefixes and suffixes. Many words, such as *fire, guard,* and *friend,* consist of a single morpheme. Many others represent combinations of morphemes. For example, the word *unfriendly* consists of three morphemes: the root word *friend,* the prefix *un,* and the suffix *ly*. Each of the morphemes contributes to the meaning of the entire word. ***Semantics* is the area of language concerned with understanding the meaning of words and word combinations.** Learning about semantics entails learning about the infinite variety of objects and actions that words refer to.

© Daisy Images/Alamy

Syntax

Of course, most utterances consist of more than a single word. People don't combine words randomly. ***Syntax* is a system of rules that specify how words can be arranged into sentences.** A simple rule of syntax is that a sentence must have both a *noun phrase* and a *verb phrase*. Thus, "The sound of cars is annoying" is a sentence. However, "The sound of cars" is not a sentence because it lacks a verb phrase.

Rules of syntax underlie all language use, even though you may not be aware of them. Thus, although they may not be able to verbalize the rule, virtually all English speakers know that an *article* (such as *the*) comes before the word it modifies. For example, you would never say *swimmer the* instead of *the swimmer.* How children learn the complicated rules of syntax is one of the major puzzles investigated by psychologists interested in language. Like other aspects of language development, children's acquisition of syntax seems to progress at an amazingly rapid pace. Let's look at how this remarkable development unfolds.

Milestones in Language Development

Learning to use language requires learning a number of skills that become important at various points in a child's development (Siegler & Alibali, 2005). We'll examine this developmental sequence by looking first at how children learn to pronounce words, then at their use of single words, and finally at their ability to combine words to form sentences (see **Table 8.2**).

Moving Toward Producing Words

Three-month-old infants display a surprising language-related talent: They can distinguish phonemes from all the world's languages, including phonemes that they do not hear in their environment. In contrast, adults cannot readily discriminate phonemes that aren't used in their native language. Actually, neither can 1-year-old children. This curious ability disappears by the time children reach 12 months of age (Kuhl et al., 2008; Werker & Tees, 1999). The exact mechanisms responsible for this transition are not understood. It's clear, though, that long before infants utter their first words, they are making amazing progress in learning the sound structure of their native language. Progress toward recognizing whole words also occurs during the first year. Although they don't know what the words mean yet, by around 8 months infants begin to recognize and store common word forms (Swingley, 2008).

During the first six months of life, a baby's vocalizations are dominated by crying, cooing, and laughter. Soon, infants are *babbling,* producing a wide variety of sounds that correspond to phonemes and, eventually, many repetitive consonant-vowel combinations, such as "lalalalalala." Babbling gradually becomes more complex, increasingly resembling the language spoken by parents and others in the child's environment (Hoff, 2005). Babbling lasts until around 18 months, continuing even after children utter their first words.

At around 10 to 13 months of age, most children begin to utter sounds that correspond to words. Most infants' first words are similar in phonetic form and meaning—even in different languages (Waxman, 2002). The initial words resemble the syllables that infants most often babble spontaneously. For example, words such as *dada, mama,* and *papa* are names for parents in many languages because they consist of sounds that are easy to produce.

Table 8.2 Overview of Typical Language Development

Age	General Characteristics
Months	
1–5	*Reflexive communication:* Vocalizes randomly, coos, laughs, cries, engages in vocal play, discriminates language from nonlanguage sounds
6–18	*Babbling:* Verbalizes in response to speech of others; responses increasingly approximate human speech patterns
10–13	*First words:* Uses words; typically to refer to objects
12–18	*One-word sentence stage:* Vocabulary grows slowly; uses nouns primarily; overextensions begin
18–24	*Vocabulary spurt:* Fast-mapping facilitates rapid acquisition of new words
Years	
2	*Two-word sentence stage:* Uses telegraphic speech; uses more pronouns and verbs
2.5	*Three-word sentence stage:* Modifies speech to take listener into account; overregularizations begin
3	Uses complete simple active sentence structure; uses sentences to tell stories that are understood by others; uses plurals
3.5	*Expanded grammatical forms:* Expresses concepts with words; uses four-word sentences
4	Uses private speech; uses five-word sentences
5	*Well-developed and complex syntax:* Uses more complex syntax; uses more complex forms to tell stories
6	Displays metalinguistic awareness

Note: Children often show individual differences in the exact ages at which they display the various developmental achievements outlined here.

© Cengage Learning 2013

Using Words

After children utter their first words, their vocabulary grows slowly for the next few months (Dapretto & Bjork, 2000). Toddlers typically can say between three and fifty words by 18 months. However, their *receptive vocabulary* is larger than their *productive vocabulary.* That is, they can comprehend more words spoken by others than they can produce to express themselves (Pan & Uccelli, 2009). Thus, toddlers can *understand* fifty words months before they can *say* fifty words. Toddlers' early words tend to refer most often to *objects* and secondarily to *social actions,* such as *hello* and *goodbye* (Camaioni, 2001). Children probably acquire nouns before verbs because the meanings of nouns, which often refer to distinct, concrete objects, tend to be easier to encode than the meanings of verbs, which often refer to more abstract relationships (Poulin-Dubois & Graham, 2007). However, this generalization may not apply to all languages (Bates, Devescovi, & Wulfeck, 2001).

Most youngsters' vocabularies soon begin to grow at a rapid pace, as a *vocabulary spurt* or *naming explosion* begins at around 18 months when toddlers realize that everything has a name (Camaioni, 2001) (see **Figure 8.2**). In building these impressive vocabularies, some 2-year-olds learn as many as twenty new words every week. *Fast mapping* appears to be one factor underlying this rapid growth of vocabulary (Carey, 2010; Gershkoff-Stowe & Hahn, 2007). ***Fast mapping* is the process by which children map a word onto an underlying concept after only one exposure.** Thus, children often add words like *tank, board,* and *tape* to their vocabularies after their first encounter with objects that illustrate these concepts. The vocabulary spurt may be attributable to children's improved articulation skills, improved understanding of syntax, underlying cognitive development, or some combination of these factors (MacWhinney, 1998). By the first grade, the average child has a vocabulary of approximately 10,000 words, which builds to an astonishing 40,000 words by the fifth grade (Anglin, 1993) (see **Figure 8.3**).

These efforts to learn new words are not flawless. Toddlers often make errors, such as overextensions and underextensions (Harley, 2008). **An *overextension* occurs when a child incorrectly uses a word to describe a wider set of objects or actions than it is meant to.** For example, a child might use the word *ball* for anything round—oranges, apples, even the moon. Overextensions usually appear in children's speech between ages 1 and 2½. Specific overextensions typically last up to several months. Toddlers are also prone to ***underextensions,* which occur when a child incorrectly uses a word to describe a narrower set of objects or actions than it is meant to.** For instance, a child might use the word *doll* to refer only to a single, favorite doll. Overextensions and underextensions show that toddlers are actively trying to learn the rules of language.

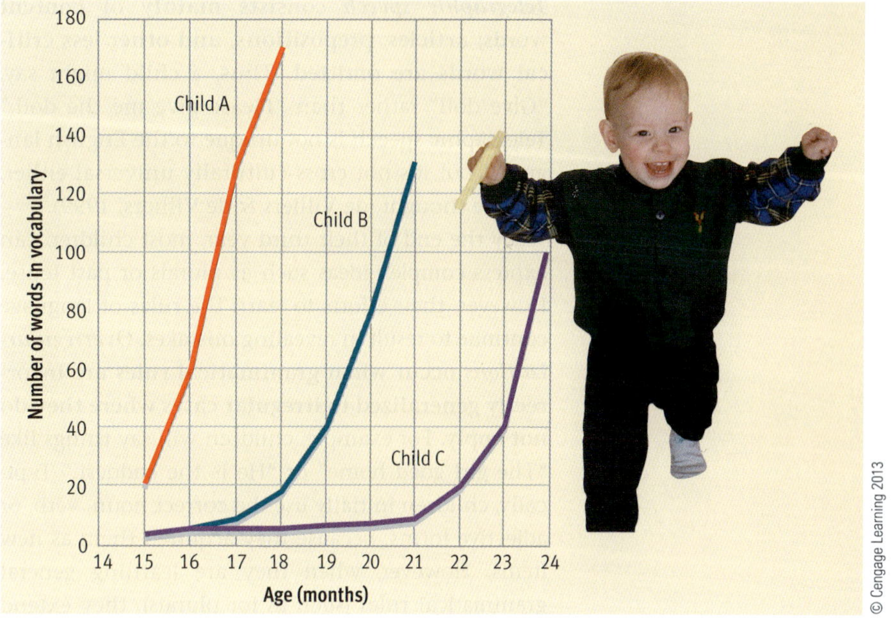

Figure 8.2

The vocabulary spurt. Children typically acquire their first 10–15 words very slowly, but they soon go through a *vocabulary spurt*—a period during which they rapidly acquire many new words. The vocabulary spurt usually begins at around 18 months, but children vary, as these graphs of three toddlers' vocabulary growth show.

SOURCE: Adapted from Goldfield, B. A., & Resnick, J. S. (1990). Early lexical acquisition: Rate, content, and the vocabulary spurt. *Journal of Child Language, 17,* 171–183. Copyright © 1990 by Cambridge University Press. Adapted by permission. Photo: Courtesy of Wayne Weiten

Combining Words

Children typically begin to combine words into sentences near the end of their second year. Early sentences are characterized as "telegraphic" because they resemble old-fashioned telegrams, which omitted nonessential words because senders were charged by the word (Bochner & Jones, 2003).

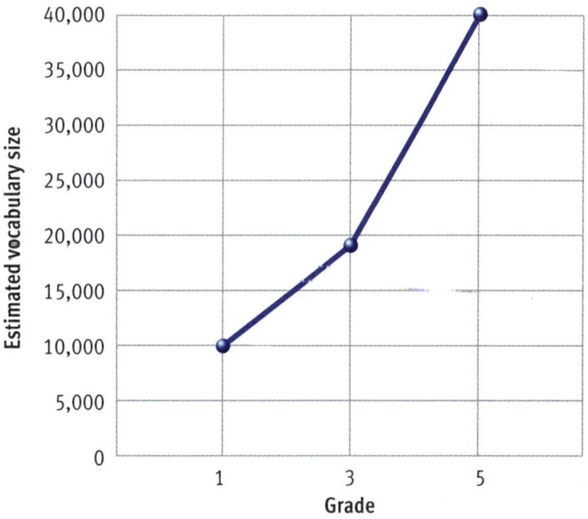

Figure 8.3

The growth of schoolchildren's vocabulary. Vocabulary growth is rapid during the early years of grade school. Youngsters' estimated vocabulary doubles about every two years between first grade and fifth grade. (Based on Anglin, 1993) © Cengage Learning 2013

***Telegraphic speech* consists mainly of content words; articles, prepositions, and other less critical words are omitted.** Thus, a child might say, "Give doll" rather than "Please give me the doll." Telegraphic speech is not unique to the English language, but it's not cross-culturally universal either, as once thought (de Villiers & de Villiers, 1999).

By the end of their third year, most children can express complex ideas such as plurals or past tense. However, their efforts to learn the rules of language continue to result in revealing mistakes. ***Overregularizations* occur when grammatical rules are incorrectly generalized to irregular cases where they do not apply.** For example, children will say things like "The girl goed home" or "He is the baddest." Typically, children initially use the correct noun, verb, or adjective forms, because they acquired them as new items. However, when they are learning general grammatical rules (such as for plurals), they extend the rules to nouns that are exceptions to the rule (such as "foots"). Overregularizations usually appear after children begin to learn grammatical rules. Thus, the progression goes from "feet" to "foots" and back to "feet" when children have further mastered grammatical rules. Cross-cultural research suggests that these overregularizations occur in all languages (Slobin, 1985). Overregularizations demonstrate that children are working actively to master the *rules* of language (Marcus, 1996). Children don't learn the fine points of grammar and usage in a single leap but gradually acquire them in small steps. Specific overregularizations often linger in a child's speech even though the child has heard the correct constructions many times (Maslen et al., 2004).

Refining Language Skills

Youngsters make their largest strides in language development in their first four to five years. However, they continue to refine their language skills during their school-age years. They generate longer and more complicated sentences as they receive formal training in written language.

As their language skills develop, school-age children begin to appreciate ambiguities in language. They can, for instance, recognize two possible meanings in sentences such as "Visiting relatives can be bothersome." This interest in ambiguities indicates that they're developing ***metalinguistic awareness*—the ability to reflect on the use of language.** As metalinguistic awareness grows, children begin to recognize that statements may have a *literal meaning* and an *implied meaning*. They begin to make more frequent and sophisticated use of metaphors, such as "We were packed in the room like sardines" (Gentner, 1988). Between the ages of 6 and 8, most children begin to appreciate irony and sarcasm (Creusere, 1999).

CONCEPT CHECK 8.1

Tracking Language Development

Check your understanding of how language skills progress in youngsters. Number the utterances below to indicate the developmental sequence in which they would probably occur. The answers can be found in Appendix A in the back of the book.

_______ 1. "Doggie," while pointing to a cow.

_______ 2. "The dogs runned away."

_______ 3. "Doggie run."

_______ 4. "The dogs ran away."

_______ 5. "Doggie," while pointing to a dog.

_______ 6. "Tommy thinks like his head is full of mashed potatoes."

Learning More Than One Language: Bilingualism

Given the complexities involved in acquiring one language, you may be wondering about the ramifications of being asked to learn *two* languages. ***Bilingualism* is the acquisition of two languages that use different speech sounds, vocabulary, and grammatical rules.** Bilingualism is quite common in Europe and many other regions. Nearly half of the world's population grows up bilingual (Hakuta, 1986; Snow, 1998). And bilingualism is far from rare even in the English-dominated United States, where roughly 6–7 million children speak a language other than English at home. Bilingualism has sparked considerable controversy in the United States. A number of new laws and court rulings have reduced the availability of bilingual educational programs in many school systems (Wiese & Garcia, 2007). These laws are based on the assumption that bilingualism hampers language development and has a negative impact on kids' educational progress. But does the empirical evidence support this assumption? Let's take a look at the research.

Does Learning Two Languages in Childhood Slow Down Language Development?

If kids are learning two languages simultaneously, does one language interfere with the other so that the acquisition of both is impeded? There is only a modest body of research on this question. Some studies *have* found that bilingual children have smaller vocabularies in each of their languages than *monolingual* children have in their one language (Umbel et al., 1992). But when their two overlapping vocabularies are added, their total vocabulary is similar or slightly superior to that of children learning a single language (Oller & Pearson, 2002). Taken as a whole, the available evidence suggests that bilingual and monolingual children are largely similar in the course and rate of their language development (de Houwer, 1995; Nicoladis & Genesee, 1997). Learning two languages simultaneously may not be as easy as learning just one. However, there's little empirical support for the belief that bilingualism has serious negative effects on language development (Hoff, 2005). Moreover, recent research suggests that learning two languages can subsequently facilitate the acquisition of a third language. Comparisons of bilingual and monolingual subjects suggest that bilinguals are better language learners—that the experience of becoming bilingual can enhance the learning of another language (Kaushanskaya & Marian, 2009).

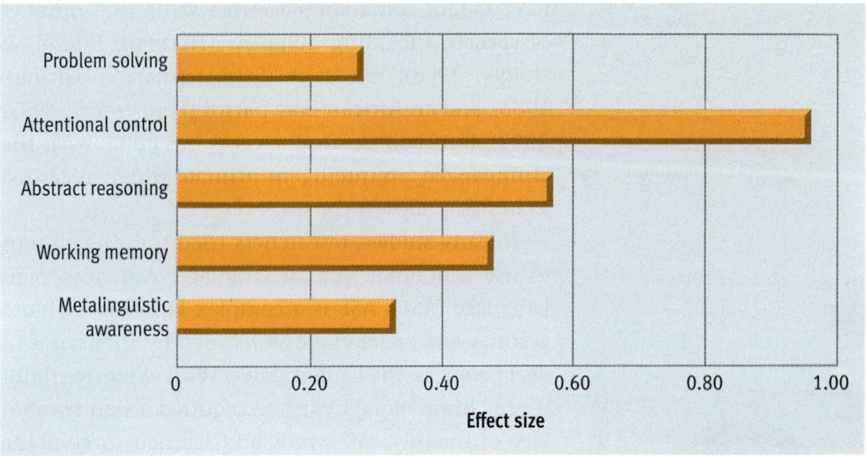

© Cengage Learning 2013

Figure 8.4

Cognitive benefits of bilingualism. A recent meta-analysis (Adesope et al., 2010) of research on the cognitive correlates of bilingualism uncovered some interesting benefits associated with bilingualism. The data shown here are mean *effect sizes* for five cognitive variables. An effect size is an estimate of the magnitude of one variable's effects on another. An effect size from .20 to .50 is considered meaningful but small; from .50 to .80 is characterized as moderate; and above .80 is regarded as large. Obviously, the effect sizes vary, but the data suggest that bilingualism enhances, rather than undermines, cognitive development.

Does Bilingualism Affect Cognitive Processes and Skills?

Does learning two languages slow down cognitive development or have a negative impact on intellectual skills? Some early studies suggested that the answer is "yes," but the studies suffered from fundamental flaws (Hakuta, 1986). Bilingual students tended to come from more impoverished backgrounds and were handicapped by having to take the IQ test in their second language (Hakuta, 2000). More recent, better-designed studies have found that bilingualism is associated with both advantages and disadvantages. The chief disadvantage is that bilinguals appear to have a slight handicap in terms of raw language *processing speed* and *verbal fluency* (the ease with which people can think of words). Evidence suggests that when bilingual people are reading, listening, or speaking in a specific language, to some extent both their first language (L1) and their second language (L2) are simultaneously active (Christoffels, De Groot, & Kroll, 2006; Hoshino & Kroll, 2008). In other words, there is no way to turn off L1 when using L2, or vice versa. This creates some cross-language interference that slows language processing and undermines verbal fluency (Michael & Gollan, 2005; Sandoval et al., 2010).

In contrast to this relatively minor disadvantage, the new research in this area suggests that bilingualism is associated with a surprising variety of potentially significant advantages. A recent meta-analysis of 63 studies found that bilingual individuals tend to score moderately higher than monolinguals on measures of attentional control, working memory capacity, metalinguistic awareness, abstract reasoning, and certain types of problem solving (Adesope et al., 2010; see **Figure 8.4**). How might bilingualism lead to these cognitive benefits? The current thinking focuses on the realization that L1 and L2 are simultaneously active in bilinguals. This competition forces bilinguals to learn to maximize their control of attention to resist intrusions and distractions and to increase the efficiency of their working memory. These increases in attentional control and working memory may, in turn, promote enhanced reasoning and problem solving.

Moreover, recent studies suggest that the cognitive benefits of bilingualism persist into adulthood and that they may even protect against age-related cognitive decline (Bialystok & Craik, 2010; Craik & Bialystok, 2010). For example, one influential study focused on people suffering from *dementia* (severe impairment of memory and cognitive functioning). It found that bilingual patients experienced the onset of dementia four years later, on average, than comparable monolingual patients (Bialystok, Craik, & Freedman, 2007). More research is needed, but recent studies suggest that bilingualism may be associated with unanticipated beneficial outcomes.

Reality CHECK

Misconception

Bilingualism undermines cognitive development.

Reality

It is widely believed that bilingualism interferes with cognitive development. But when researchers control for social class in their comparisons, they do not find cognitive deficits in bilingual youngsters. Moreover, recent research suggests that bilingualism may be associated with unexpected cognitive benefits.

Can Animals Develop Language?

Can other species besides humans develop language? Although this issue does not have the practical, sociopolitical repercussions of the bilingualism debate, it has intrigued researchers for many decades and has led to some fascinating research. Scientists have taught some language-like skills to a number of species, including dolphins (Herman, Kuczaj, & Holder, 1993), sea lions (Schusterman & Gisiner, 1988), and an African gray parrot (Pepperberg, 1993, 2002). But their greatest success has come with the chimpanzee, an intelligent primate widely regarded as humans' closest cousin.

In early studies, researchers tried training chimps to use a nonoral human language: American Sign Language (ASL). ASL is a complex language of hand gestures and facial expressions used by thousands of deaf people in the United States. With extensive training, a chimp named Washoe acquired a sign vocabulary of roughly 160 words and learned to combine these words into simple sentences, such as "Gimme flower" (Gardner & Gardner, 1969). These accomplishments were impressive. Critics, however, expressed doubts about whether Washoe and other chimps had really acquired *rules* of language. According to Terrace (1986), the chimps' sentences were the products of imitation and operant conditioning, rather than *generative* creations based on linguistic rules.

© Courtesy of Sue Savage-Rumbaugh, Georia State University Language Research Center

Sue Savage-Rumbaugh

"What Kanzi tells us is that humans are not the only species that can acquire language if exposed to it at an early age."

In more recent years, Sue Savage-Rumbaugh and her colleagues have reported some striking advances with *bonobo pygmy chimpanzees* that have fueled additional debate (Savage-Rumbaugh, 1991; Savage-Rumbaugh, Shanker, & Taylor, 1998; Savage-Rumbaugh, Rumbaugh, & Fields, 2006, 2009). In this line of research, the bonobos have learned to communicate with their caretakers by touching geometric symbols representing words on a computer-monitored keyboard. Savage-Rumbaugh's star pupil has been a chimp named Kanzi. Kanzi has acquired hundreds of words and used them in thousands of combinations. Many of these combinations have been spontaneous and seem to follow rules of language. For example, to specify whether he wanted to chase or be chased, Kanzi had to differentiate between symbol combinations in a way that appeared to involve the use of grammatical rules.

© PRNewsFoto/Great Ape Trust of Iowa

As the years went by, Kanzi's trainers noticed that he often seemed to understand the normal utterances that they exchanged with each other. They then began to systematically evaluate his comprehension of spoken English. At age 9, they tested his understanding of 660 sentences that directed Kanzi to execute simple actions, such as "Put the collar in the water." To make sure that he really *understood* the sentences, they included many novel constructions in which the actions were not obvious given the objects involved, such as "Put the raisins in the shoe," or "Go get the balloon that's in the microwave." Kanzi correctly carried out 72% of the 660 requests. Moreover, he demonstrated remarkable understanding of sentence structure, as he could reliably distinguish the actions requested by "Pour the Coke in the lemonade," as opposed to "Pour the lemonade in the Coke."

How have the linguistics experts reacted to Kanzi's surprising progress in language development? Some remain skeptical. Wynne (2004) has raised questions about the scoring system used to determine whether Kanzi "understood" oral requests. Wynne and other critics (Budiansky, 2004; Kako, 1999; Wallman, 1992) have also questioned whether Kanzi's communications show all the basic properties of a language. So, what can we conclude? Overall, the consensus seems to be that it is reasonable to assert that the ability to use language—in a basic, primitive way—may not be entirely unique to humans, as has been widely assumed.

However, make no mistake, there is no comparison between human linguistic abilities and those of apes or other animals. As remarkable as the language studies with apes are, they should make us marvel even more at the fluency, flexibility, and complexity of human language. A normal human toddler quickly surpasses even the most successfully trained chimps. In mastering language, children outstrip chimps the way jet airplanes outrace horse-drawn buggies. Why are humans so well suited for learning language? According to some theorists, this talent for language is a product of evolution.

FRANK & ERNEST

FRANK & ERNEST © 2007 Thaves. Reprinted by permission of UNIVERSAL UCLICK for UFS. All rights reserved.

Language in Evolutionary Context

All human societies depend on complex language systems. Even primitive cultures use languages that are just as complicated as those used in modern societies. The universal nature of language suggests that it's an innate human characteristic. Consistent with this view, Steven Pinker argues that humans' special talent for language is a species-specific trait that is the product of natural selection (Pinker, 1994, 2004; Pinker & Jackendoff, 2005). Pinker believes language is a valuable means of communication that has enormous adaptive value. As Pinker and Bloom (1992) point out, "There is an obvious advantage in being able to acquire information about the world secondhand . . . one can avoid having to duplicate the possibly time-consuming and dangerous trial-and-error process that won that knowledge" (p. 460). Dunbar (1996) argues that language evolved as a device to build and maintain social coalitions in increasingly larger groups. The evolution of language remains a matter of speculation and debate (Kirby, 2007). But it's easy to see how more-effective communication among our ancient ancestors could have aided hunting, gathering, fighting, and mating, and the avoidance of poisons, predators, and other dangers.

Although the adaptive value of language seems obvious, some scholars take issue with the assertion that human language is the product of evolution. For example, David Premack (1985) has expressed skepticism that small differences in language skill would influence reproductive fitness in primitive societies where all one had to communicate about was the location of the closest mastodon herd. In an effort to refute this argument, Pinker and Bloom (1992) point out that very small adaptive disparities are sufficient to fuel evolutionary change. For example, they assert that a trait variation that produces on average just 1% more offspring than its alternative genetic expression would increase in prevalence from 0.1% to 99.9% of the population in 4000 generations. That many generations may seem like an eternity. Yet, in the context of evolution, it's a modest amount of time.

Whether or not evolution gets the credit, language acquisition in humans seems remarkably rapid. This fact looms large in theories of language acquisition.

Theories of Language Acquisition

Since the 1950s, a great debate has raged about the key processes involved in language acquisition. As with arguments we have seen in other areas of psychology, this one centers on the *nature versus nurture* issue. The debate was started by the influential behaviorist B. F. Skinner (1957), who argued that environmental factors govern language development. His provocative analysis brought a rejoinder from Noam Chomsky (1959), who emphasized biological determinism. Let's examine their views and subsequent theories that stake out a middle ground.

Behaviorist Theories

The behaviorist approach to language was first outlined by Skinner in his book *Verbal Behavior* (1957). He argued that children learn language the same way they learn everything else: through imitation, reinforcement, and other established principles of conditioning. According to Skinner, vocalizations that are not reinforced gradually decline in frequency. The remaining vocalizations are shaped with reinforcers until they're correct. Behaviorists assert that by controlling reinforcement, parents encourage their children to learn the correct meaning and pronunciation of words (Staats & Staats, 1963). For example, as children grow older, parents may insist on closer and closer approximations of the word *water* before supplying the requested drink.

Reality CHECK

Misconception

Only humans can learn language.

Reality

It has long been assumed that language is unique to humans, but over the last 50 years researchers have helped quite a variety of animals to acquire some rudimentary language skills, including dolphins, sea lions, and a parrot, as well as apes and chimps. Admittedly, humans have a unique talent for language, but some other species are also capable of some language learning.

Behavioral theorists also use the principles of imitation and reinforcement to explain how children learn syntax. According to the behaviorists' view, children learn how to construct sentences by imitating the sentences of adults and older children. If children's imitative statements are understood, parents are able to answer their questions or respond to their requests, thus reinforcing their verbal behavior.

Noam Chomsky

"Even at low levels of intelligence, at pathological levels, we find a command of language that is totally unattainable by an ape."

Nativist Theories

Skinner's explanation of language acquisition soon inspired a critique and rival explanation from Noam Chomsky (1959, 1965). Chomsky pointed out that there are an infinite number of sentences in a language. It's therefore unreasonable to expect that children learn language by imitation. For example, in English, we add *ed* to the end of a verb to construct past tense. Children routinely overregularize this rule, producing incorrect verbs such as *goed, eated,* and *thinked.* Mistakes such as these are inconsistent with Skinner's emphasis on imitation because most adult speakers don't use ungrammatical words like *goed.* Children can't imitate things they don't hear. According to Chomsky, children learn *the rules of language,* not specific verbal responses, as Skinner proposed.

An alternative theory favored by Chomsky (1975, 1986, 2006) is that humans have an inborn or "native" propensity to develop language. (Here *native* is a variation on the word *nature* as it's used in the nature versus nurture debate.) *Nativist theory* proposes that humans are equipped with a ***language acquisition device (LAD)*—an innate mechanism or process that facilitates the learning of language.** According to this view, humans learn language for the same reason that birds learn to fly—because they're biologically equipped for it. The exact nature of the LAD has not been spelled out in nativist theories. It presumably consists of brain structures and neural wiring that leave humans well prepared to discriminate among phonemes, to fast-map words, to acquire rules of syntax, and so on.

Why does Chomsky believe that children have an innate capacity for learning language? One reason is that children seem to acquire language quickly and effortlessly. How could they develop so complex a skill in such a short time unless they have a built-in capacity for it? Another reason is that language development tends to unfold at roughly the same pace for most children, even though children obviously are reared in diverse home environments. This finding suggests that language development is determined by biological maturation more than personal experience. The nativists also cite evidence that the early course of language development is similar across very different cultures (Gleitman & Newport, 1996; Slobin, 1992). They interpret this to mean that children all over the world are guided by the same innate capabilities.

Interactionist Theories

Like Skinner, Chomsky has his critics (Bohannon & Bonvillian, 2009). They ask: What exactly is a language acquisition device? How does the LAD work? What are the neural mechanisms involved? They argue that the LAD concept is awfully vague. Other critics question whether the rapidity of early language development is as exceptional as nativists assume. They assert that it isn't fair to compare the rapid progress of toddlers, who are immersed in their native language, against the struggles of older students, who may devote only 10–15 hours per week to their foreign language course.

The problems apparent in Skinner's and Chomsky's explanations of language development have led some researchers to outline *interactionist theories* of language acquisition. These theories assert that biology and experience *both* make important contributions to the development of language. For example, *emergentist theories* argue that the neural circuits supporting language are not prewired but *emerge* gradually in response to language-learning experiences (Bates, 1999; MacWhinney, 2001, 2004). These theories tend to assume that incremental changes in connectionist networks (see Chapter 7) underlie children's gradual acquisition of various language skills (Elman, 1999).

Like the nativists, interactionists believe that the human organism is biologically well equipped for learning language. They also agree that much of this learning involves the acquisition of rules. However, like the behaviorists, they believe that social exchanges with parents and others play a critical role in molding language skills. Thus, interactionist theories maintain that a biological predisposition *and* a supportive environment both contribute to language development (see **Figure 8.5**).

Culture, Language, and Thought

Another long-running controversy in the study of language concerns the relations between culture, language, and thought. Obviously, people from different cultures generally speak different languages. But does your training in English lead you to think about certain things differently than someone who was raised to speak Chinese or French? In other words, does a cultural group's language determine their thought? Or does thought determine language?

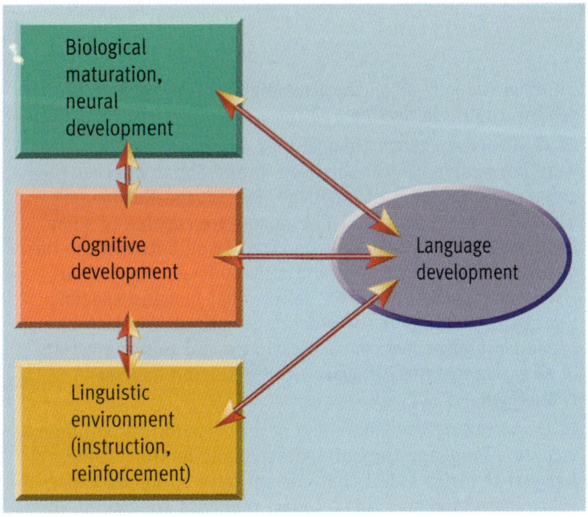

© Cengage Learning 2013

Figure 8.5

Interactionist theories of language acquisition. The interactionist view is that nature and nurture are both important to language acquisition. Maturation is thought to drive language development directly and to influence it indirectly by fostering cognitive development. Meanwhile, verbal exchanges with parents and others are also thought to play a critical role in molding language skills. The complex bidirectional relations depicted here shed some light on why there is room for extensive debate about the crucial factors in language acquisition.

Benjamin Lee Whorf (1956) has been the most prominent advocate of ***linguistic relativity,* the hypothesis that one's language determines the nature of one's thought.** Whorf speculated that different languages lead people to view the world differently. His classic example compared English and Eskimo views of snow. He asserted that the English language has just one word for snow, whereas the Eskimo language has many words that distinguish among falling snow, wet snow, and so on. Because of this language gap, Whorf argued that Eskimos perceive snow differently than English-speaking people do. However, Whorf's conclusion about these perceptual differences was based on casual observation rather than systematic cross-cultural comparisons of perceptual processes. Moreover, critics noted that advocates of the linguistic relativity hypothesis had carelessly overestimated the number of Eskimo words for snow while ignoring the variety of English words that refer to snow, such as slush and blizzard (Martin, 1986; Pullum, 1991).

Whorf's hypothesis has been the subject of considerable research and continues to generate spirited debate (Chiu, Leung, & Kwan, 2007; Gleitman & Papafragou, 2005). Many studies have focused on cross-cultural comparisons of how people perceive colors, because substantial variations exist among cultures in how colors are categorized with names. For example, some languages have a single color name that includes both blue and green, whereas other languages view light blue and dark blue as fundamentally different colors (Davies, 1998). If a language doesn't distinguish between blue and green, do people who speak that language think about colors differently than people in other cultures do?

Early efforts to answer this question suggested that the color categories in a language have relatively little influence on how people perceive and think about colors (Berlin & Kay, 1969; Rosch, 1973). However, recent studies have provided new evidence favoring the linguistic relativity hypothesis (Davidoff, 2001, 2004; Roberson et al., 2005). Studies of subjects who speak African languages that do not have a boundary between blue and green have found that language affects their color perception. They have more trouble making quick discriminations between blue and green colors than English-speaking subjects (Ozgen, 2004). Additional studies using a variety of methods have found that a culture's color categories shape subjects' similarity judgments and groupings of colors (Pilling & Davies, 2004; Roberson, Davies, & Davidoff, 2000). These findings have led Ozgen (2004) to conclude that "it is just possible that what you see when you look at the rainbow depends on the language you speak" (p. 98). Other studies have found that language also has some impact on how people think about motion (Gennari et al., 2002), time (Boroditsky, 2001), and shapes (Roberson, Davidoff, & Shapiro, 2002).

So, what is the status of the linguistic relativity hypothesis? At present, the debate seems to center on whether the new data are sufficient to support the original, "strong" version of the hypothesis (that a given language makes certain ways of thinking obligatory or impossible) or a "weaker" version of the hypothesis (that a language makes certain ways of thinking easier or more difficult). Either way, empirical support for the linguistic relativity hypothesis has increased dramatically in recent years.

Does the language you speak determine how you think? Yes, said Benjamin Lee Whorf, who argued that the Eskimo language, which has numerous words for snow, leads Eskimos to perceive snow differently than English speakers. Whorf's hypothesis has been the subject of spirited debate.

© Peter Arnold, Inc./Alamy

REVIEW OF KEY LEARNING GOALS

8.1 A language consists of symbols that convey meaning, plus rules for combining those symbols, that can be used to generate an infinite variety of messages. Human languages are structured hierarchically. At the bottom of the hierarchy are the basic sound units, called phonemes. At the next level are morphemes, the smallest units of meaning. Rules of syntax specify how words can be combined into sentences.

8.2 The initial vocalizations by infants are similar across languages. But their babbling gradually begins to resemble the sounds from their surrounding language. Children typically utter their first words around their first birthday. A vocabulary spurt often begins around 18 months. Most children begin to combine words by the end of their second year. Their early sentences are telegraphic. Over the next several years, children gradually learn the complexities of syntax and develop metalinguistic awareness.

8.3 Research does not support the assumption that bilingualism has a negative effect on language development. Evidence suggests that bilinguals have a slight handicap in language processing speed because there is no way to turn off L1 when using L2, or vice versa. However, bilingual individuals score higher than monolinguals on attentional control, working memory capacity, and other cognitive skills. Bilingualism may also afford some protection against age-related cognitive decline.

8.4 Efforts to teach chimpanzees American Sign Language were impressive. But doubts were raised about whether the chimps learned rules of language. Sue Savage-Rumbaugh's work with Kanzi suggests that chimps are capable of some basic language. But there is no comparison between the linguistic abilities of humans and other animals. Many theorists, such as Steven Pinker, believe that humans' special talent for language is the product of natural selection because more effective communication would confer a variety of adaptive benefits. However, this assertion has been challenged.

8.5 According to Skinner and other behaviorists, children acquire a language through imitation and reinforcement. Nativist theories assert that humans have an innate capacity to learn language rules. Today, theorists are moving toward interactionist perspectives, which emphasize the role of both biology and experience. The theory of linguistic relativity asserts that language determines thought, thus suggesting that people from different cultures may think about the world differently. Recent studies have provided new support for the linguistic relativity hypothesis.

KEY LEARNING GOALS

8.6 List the three types of problems proposed by Greeno.

8.7 Identify and describe four common barriers to effective problem solving.

8.8 Review a variety of general problem-solving strategies and heuristics.

8.9 Discuss cultural variations in cognitive style as they relate to problem solving.

Problem Solving: In Search of Solutions

Look at the two problems below. Can you solve them?

In the Thompson family there are five brothers, and each brother has one sister. If you count Mrs. Thompson, how many females are there in the Thompson family?

Fifteen percent of the people in Topeka have unlisted telephone numbers. You select 200 names at random from the Topeka phone book. How many of these people can be expected to have unlisted phone numbers?

These problems, borrowed from Sternberg (1986, p. 214), are exceptionally simple. Yet, many people fail to solve them. The answer to the first problem is *two:* The only females in the family are Mrs. Thompson and her one daughter, who is a sister to each of her brothers. The answer to the second problem is *none*—you won't find any people with *unlisted* phone numbers in the phone book.

Why do many people fail to solve these simple problems? You'll learn why in a moment when we discuss barriers to effective problem solving. But first, let's examine a scheme for classifying problems into a few basic types.

Types of Problems

PSYKTREK SIM7, 7e

***Problem solving* refers to active efforts to discover what must be done to achieve a goal that is not readily attainable.** Obviously, if a goal is readily attainable, there isn't a problem. But in problem-solving situations, one must go beyond the information given to overcome obstacles and reach a goal. Jim Greeno (1978) has proposed that problems can be categorized into three basic classes:

1. *Problems of inducing structure* require people to discover the relations among numbers, words, symbols, or ideas. The *series completion problems* and the *analogy problems* in **Figure 8.6** are examples of problems of inducing structure.

2. *Problems of arrangement* require people to arrange the parts of a problem in a way that satisfies some criterion. The parts can usually be arranged in many ways. However, only one or a few of the arrangements form a solution. The *string problem* and the *anagrams* in **Figure 8.6** fit in this category.

3. *Problems of transformation* require people to carry out a sequence of transformations in order to reach a specific goal. The *hobbits and orcs problem*

A. Analogy
What word completes the analogy?
Merchant : Sell : : Customer : _________
Lawyer : Client : : Doctor : _________

B. String problem
Two strings hang from the ceiling but are too far apart to allow a person to hold one and walk to the other. On the table are a book of matches, a screwdriver, and a few pieces of cotton. How could the strings be tied together?

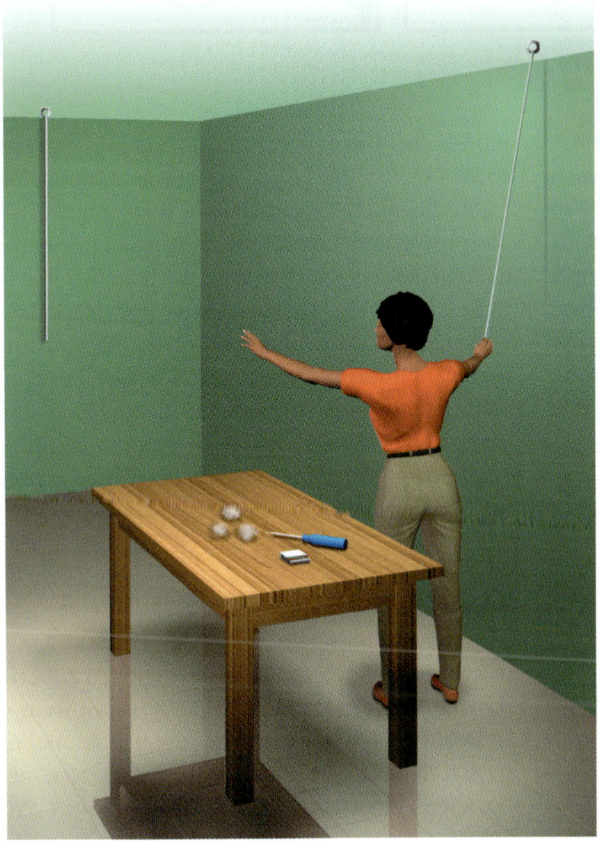

C. Hobbits and orcs problem
Three hobbits and three orcs arrive at a river bank, and they all wish to cross onto the other side. Fortunately, there is a boat, but unfortunately, the boat can hold only two creatures at one time. Also, there is another problem. Orcs are vicious creatures, and whenever there are more orcs than hobbits on one side of the river, the orcs will immediately attack the hobbits and eat them up. Consequently, you should be certain that you never leave more orcs than hobbits on either river bank. How should the problem be solved? It must be added that the orcs, though vicious, can be trusted to bring the boat back! (From Matlin, 1989, p. 319)

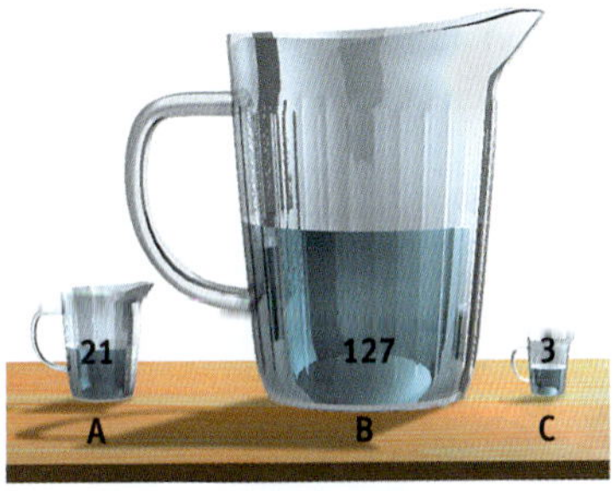

D. Water jar problem
Suppose that you have a 21-cup jar, a 127-cup jar, and a 3-cup jar. Drawing and discarding as much water as you like, you need to measure out exactly 100 cups of water. How can this be done?

E. Anagram
Rearrange the letters in each row to make an English word.
RWAET
KEROJ

F. Series completion
What number or letter completes each series?
1 2 8 3 4 6 5 6 ____
A B M C D M ____

Figure 8.6
Six standard problems used in studies of problem solving. Try solving the problems and identifying which class each belongs to before reading further. The problems can be classified as follows. The *analogy problems* and *series completion problems* are problems of inducing structure. The solutions for the analogy problems are *Buy* and *Patient*. The solutions for the series completion problems are *4* and *E*. The *string problem* and the *anagram problems* are problems of arrangement. To solve the string problem, attach the screwdriver to one string and set it swinging as a pendulum. Hold the other string and catch the swinging screwdriver. Then you need only untie the screwdriver and tie the strings together. The solutions for the anagram problems are *WATER* and *JOKER*. The *hobbits and orcs problem* and the *water jar problem* are problems of transformation. The solutions for these problems are outlined in **Figure 8.7** and **Figure 8.8**.
© Cengage Learning 2013

and the *water jar problem* in **Figure 8.6** are examples of transformation problems. Transformation problems can be challenging. Even though you know exactly what the goal is, seeing how the goal can be achieved is not usually obvious.

Greeno's list isn't an exhaustive scheme for classifying problems. But it provides a useful system for understanding some of the variety seen in problems.

Barriers to Effective Problem Solving

PSYKTREK 7e

On the basis of their studies of problem solving, psychologists have identified a number of barriers that can impede subjects' efforts to arrive at solutions. Common obstacles to effective problem solving include a focus on irrelevant information, functional fixedness, mental set, and the imposition of unnecessary constraints.

DILBERT © 2003 Scott Adams. Used By permission of UNIVERSAL UCLICK. All rights

Irrelevant Information 7e

We began our discussion of problem solving with two simple problems that people routinely fail to solve (see page 324). The catch is that these problems contain *irrelevant information* that leads people astray. In the first problem, the number of brothers is irrelevant in determining the number of females in the Thompson family. In the second problem, subjects tend to focus on the figures of 15% and 200 names. But this numerical information is irrelevant since all the names came out of the phone book.

Sternberg (1986) pointed out that people often incorrectly assume that all the numerical information in a problem is necessary to solve it. They therefore try to figure out how to use quantitative information before they even consider whether it's relevant. Focusing on irrelevant information can have adverse effects on reasoning and problem solving (Gaeth & Shanteau, 2000). Thus, effective problem solving requires that you attempt to figure out what information is relevant and what is irrelevant before proceeding.

Figure 8.7
Solution to the hobbits and orcs problem. This problem is difficult because it is necessary to temporarily work "away" from the goal.
© Cengage Learning 2013

Functional Fixedness 7e

Another common barrier to successful problem solving, identified by Gestalt psychologists, is ***functional fixedness*—the tendency to perceive an item only in terms of its most common use.** Functional fixedness has been seen in the difficulties that people have with the string problem in **Figure 8.6** (Maier, 1931b). Solving this problem requires finding a novel use for one of the objects: the screwdriver. Subjects tend to think of the screwdriver in terms of its usual functions—turning screws and perhaps prying things open. They have a hard time viewing the screwdriver as a weight. Their rigid way of thinking about the screwdriver illustrates functional fixedness (Dominowski & Bourne, 1994). Ironically, young children appear to be less vulnerable to functional fixedness than older children or adults because they have less knowledge about the conventional uses of various objects (Defeyter & German, 2003).

Mental Set 7e

Rigid thinking is also at work when a mental set interferes with effective problem solving. **A *mental set* exists when people persist in using problem-solving strategies that have worked in the past.** The effects of mental set were seen in a classic study

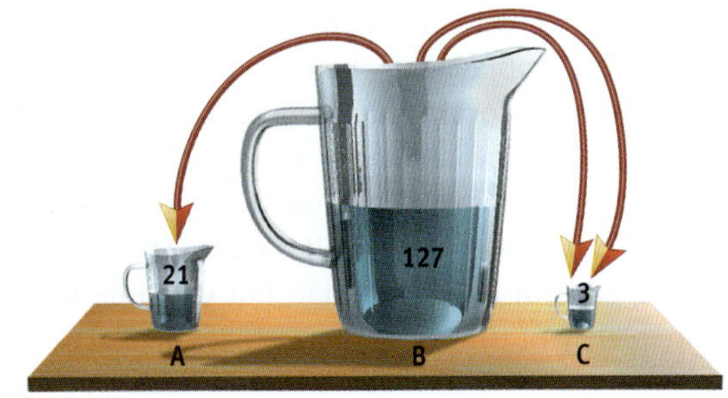

Figure 8.8

The method for solving the water jar problem. As explained in the text, the correct formula is B − A − 2C.

© Cengage Learning 2013

by Gestalt psychologist Abraham Luchins (1942). He asked subjects to work a series of water jar problems, like the one introduced earlier. Six such problems are outlined in **Figure 8.9**, which shows the capacities of the three jars and the amounts of water to be measured out. Try solving these problems.

Were you able to develop a formula for solving these problems? The first four all require the same strategy, which is described in **Figure 8.8**. You have to fill jar B, draw off once the amount that jar A holds, and draw off twice the amount that jar C holds. Thus, the formula for your solution is B − A − 2C. Although there is an obvious and much simpler solution (A − C) for the fifth problem (see **Figure 8.13** on page 330), Luchins found that most subjects stuck with the more cumbersome strategy that they had used in problems 1–4. Moreover, most subjects couldn't solve the sixth problem in the allotted time because they kept trying to use their proven strategy—but it does *not* work for this problem. The subjects' reliance on their "tried and true" strategy is an illustration of mental set in problem solving. This tendency to let one's thinking get into a rut is a common barrier to successful problem solving (Smith, 1995). Mental set may explain why having expertise in an area sometimes backfires and in fact hampers problem-solving efforts (Leighton & Sternberg, 2003).

Unnecessary Constraints

7e

Effective problem solving requires specifying all the constraints governing a problem *without assuming any constraints that don't exist.* An example of a problem in which people place an unnecessary constraint on the solution is the nine-dot problem shown in **Figure 8.10** (Maier, 1930). Without lifting your pencil from the paper, try to draw four straight lines that will cross through all nine dots. If you struggle with this one, don't feel bad. When a time limit of a few minutes is imposed on this problem, the typical solution rate is 0% (MacGregor, Ormerod, & Chronicle, 2001). The key factor that makes this a difficult problem is that most people will not draw lines outside the imaginary boundary that surrounds the dots. Notice that this constraint is not part of the problem statement. It's imposed only by the problem solver (Adams, 1980). Correct solutions, two of which are shown in **Figure 8.14** on page 330, extend outside the imaginary boundary. To solve this problem, you literally need to "think outside the box." This popular slogan, spawned by the nine-dot problem, reflects the fact that people often make assumptions that impose unnecessary constraints on problem-solving efforts.

The nine-dot problem is often solved with a burst of insight. ***Insight* occurs when people suddenly discover the correct solution to a problem after struggling with it for a while.** Problems requiring insight tend to be difficult for a variety of reasons.

	Capacity of empty jars			
Problem	*A*	*B*	*C*	*Desired amount of water*
1	14	163	25	99
2	18	43	10	5
3	9	42	6	21
4	20	59	4	31
5	23	49	3	20
6	28	76	3	25

© Cengage Learning 2013

Figure 8.9

Additional water jar problems. Using jars A, B, and C, with the capacities indicated in each row, figure out how to measure out the desired amount of water specified on the far right. The solutions are shown in **Figure 8.13**. (Based on Luchins, 1942)

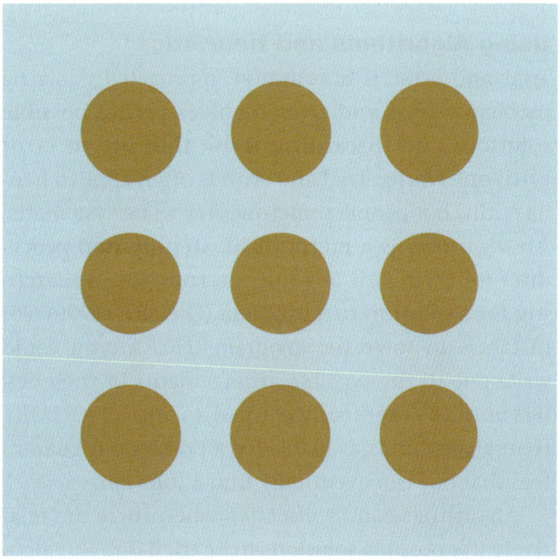

© Cengage Learning 2013

Figure 8.10

The nine-dot problem. Without lifting your pencil from the paper, draw no more than four lines that will cross through all nine dots. For possible solutions, see **Figure 8.14**.

SOURCE: Adams, J. L. (2001). *Conceptual blockbusting: A guide to better ideas.* Cambridge, MA: Basic Books. Copyright © 2001 by James L. Adams. Reprinted by permission of Basic Books, a member of the Perseus Books Group.

Difficulties may emerge from (1) how people structure the problem, (2) how they apply prior knowledge, or (3) how much they need to juggle information in working memory (Kershaw & Ohlsson, 2004). For example, in the nine-dot problem, the main barrier to a solution is that people tend to structure the problem poorly by imposing unnecessary boundaries. But people also struggle because their prior knowledge suggests that the "turns" in their lines should occur on the dots (rather than in the white space) and because envisioning all the options strains working memory. Although insight feels like a sudden "aha!" experience to problem solvers, some researchers have questioned whether insight solutions emerge full blown or are preceded by incremental movement toward a solution (Chronicle, MacGregor, & Ormerod, 2004). Recent studies suggest the latter—that insight breakthroughs are often preceded by gradual movement toward a solution that occurs outside of the problem solver's awareness (Novick & Bassok, 2005).

Approaches to Problem Solving

In their classic treatise on problem solving, Allen Newell and Herbert Simon (1972) used a spatial metaphor to describe the process of problem solving. They used the term ***problem space* to refer to the set of possible pathways to a solution considered by the problem solver.** They saw problem solving as a search in space. The problem solver's task is to find a solution path among the potential pathways that could lead from the problem's initial state to its goal state. The problem space metaphor highlights the fact that people must choose from among a variety of conceivable pathways or strategies in attempting to solve problems (Hunt, 1994). In this section, we'll examine some of these general strategies.

Using Algorithms and Heuristics

Trial and error is a common approach to solving problems. ***Trial and error* involves trying possible solutions and discarding those that are in error until one works.** Trial and error is often applied haphazardly, but people sometimes try to be systematic. **An *algorithm* is a methodical, step-by-step procedure for trying all possible alternatives in searching for a solution to a problem** (Dietrich, 1999). For instance, to solve the anagram IHCRA, you could write out all the possible arrangements of these letters until you eventually reached an answer (CHAIR). If an algorithm is available for a problem, it guarantees that one can eventually find a solution.

Algorithms can be effective when there are relatively few possible solutions to be tried out. But algorithms do not exist for many problems. They can also become impractical when the problem space is large. Consider, for instance, the problem shown in **Figure 8.11**. The challenge is to move just two matches to create a pattern containing four equal squares. Sure, you could follow an algorithm in moving pairs of matches about. But you'd better allocate plenty of time to this effort, as there are over 60,000 possible rearrangements to check out (see **Figure 8.15** on page 330 for the solution).

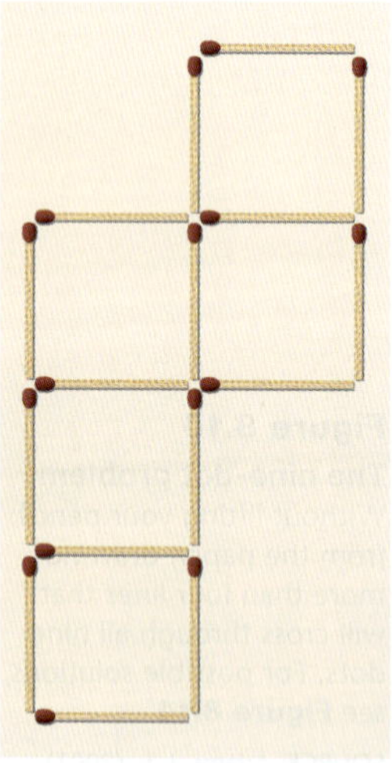

© Cengage Learning 2013

Figure 8.11

The matchstick problem. Move two matches to form four equal squares. A solution can be found in **Figure 8.15**.

SOURCE: Kendler, H. H. (1974). *Basic psychology.* Menlo Park, CA: Benjamin-Cummings. Copyright © 1974 The Benjamin-Cummings Publishing Co. Adapted by permission of Howard H. Kendler.

Because algorithms are inefficient, people often use shortcuts called *heuristics* in problem solving. **A *heuristic* is a guiding principle or "rule of thumb" used in solving problems or making decisions.** In solving problems, a heuristic allows you to discard some alternatives while pursuing selected alternatives that appear more likely to lead to a solution (Holyoak, 1995). Heuristics can be useful because they selectively narrow the problem space. They don't guarantee success though (Fischhoff, 1999; Hertwig & Todd, 2002). Helpful heuristics in problem solving include forming subgoals, working backward, searching for analogies, and changing the representation of a problem.

Forming Subgoals

A useful strategy for many problems is to formulate *subgoals,* intermediate steps toward a solution (Catrambone, 1998). When you reach a subgoal, you've solved part of the problem. Some problems have fairly obvious subgoals, and research has shown that people take advantage of them. For instance, in analogy problems, the first subgoal is usually to figure out the possible relations between the first two parts of the analogy. In a study by Simon and Reed (1976), subjects were asked to work on complex problems for which the subgoals weren't obvious. Providing the relevant subgoals helped the participants solve the problems much more quickly.

The wisdom of formulating subgoals can be seen in the *tower of Hanoi problem,* depicted in **Figure 8.12**. The terminal goal for this problem is to move all three rings on peg A to peg C, while abiding by two restrictions: only the top ring on a peg can be moved, and a ring must never be placed above a smaller ring. See whether you can solve the problem before continuing.

Dividing this problem into subgoals facilitates a solution (Kotovsky, Hayes, & Simon, 1985). If you think in terms of subgoals, your first task is to get ring 3 to the bottom of peg C. Breaking this task into sub-subgoals, you should figure out to move ring 1 to peg C, ring 2 to peg B, and ring 1 from peg C to peg B. These maneuvers allow you to place ring 3 at the bottom of peg C, thus meeting your first subgoal. Your next subgoal—getting ring 2 over to

CALVIN & HOBBES © by Bill Watterson. Distributed by Universal Press Syndicate. Reprinted with permission. All rights reserved.

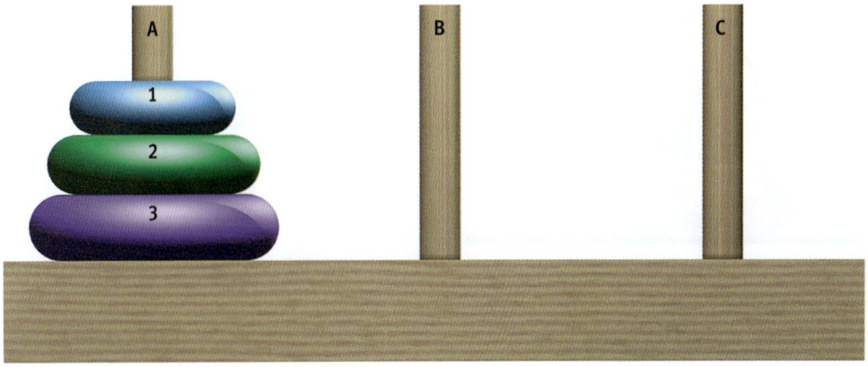

Figure 8.12
The tower of Hanoi problem. Your mission is to move the rings from peg A to peg C. You can move only the top ring on a peg and can't place a larger ring above a smaller one. The solution is explained in the text. © Cengage Learning 2013

peg C—can be accomplished in just two steps: move ring 1 to peg A and ring 2 to peg C. It should then be obvious how to achieve your final subgoal—getting ring 1 over to peg C.

Working Backward

Try to work the *lily pond problem* described below:

The water lilies on the surface of a small pond double in area every 24 hours. From the time the first water lily appears until the pond is completely covered takes 60 days. On what day is half of the pond covered with lilies?

If you're working on a problem that has a well-specified end point, you may find the solution more readily if you begin at the end and work backward. This strategy is the key to solving the lily pond problem (Davidson, 2003). If the entire pond is covered on the 60th day and the area covered doubles every day, how much is covered on the 59th day? One-half of the pond will be covered, and that happens to be the exact point you were trying to reach. The lily pond problem is remarkably simple when you work backward. In contrast, if you move forward from the starting point, you wrestle with questions about the area of the pond and the size of the lilies. You find the problem riddled with ambiguities.

© David Orcea/Shutterstock

Searching for Analogies

Searching for analogies is another of the major heuristics for solving problems (Holyoak, 2005). We reason by analogy constantly (Sternberg, 2009), and these efforts to identify analogies can facilitate innovative thinking (Gassmann & Zeschky, 2008). If you can spot an analogy between problems, you may be able to use the solution to a previous problem to solve a current one. Of course, using this strategy depends on recognizing the similarity between two problems, which itself can be a challenging problem. Nevertheless, recent studies of real-world problem-solving efforts show that we depend on analogies far more than most of us appreciate. For example, one study of design engineers recorded during their product development meetings found that they came up with an average of eleven analogies per hour of deliberation (Christensen & Schunn, 2007).

Analogies can be a powerful tool in efforts to solve problems. Unfortunately, people often are unable to recognize that two problems are similar and that an analogy might lead to a solution (Kurtz & Lowenstein, 2007). One reason that people have difficulty recognizing analogies is that they often focus on surface features of problems rather than their underlying structure (Bassok, 2003). Try to make use of analogies to solve the following two problems:

A teacher had 23 pupils in his class. All but 7 of them went on a museum trip and thus were away for the day. How many students remained in class that day?

Susan gets in her car in Boston and drives toward New York City, averaging 50 miles per hour. Twenty minutes

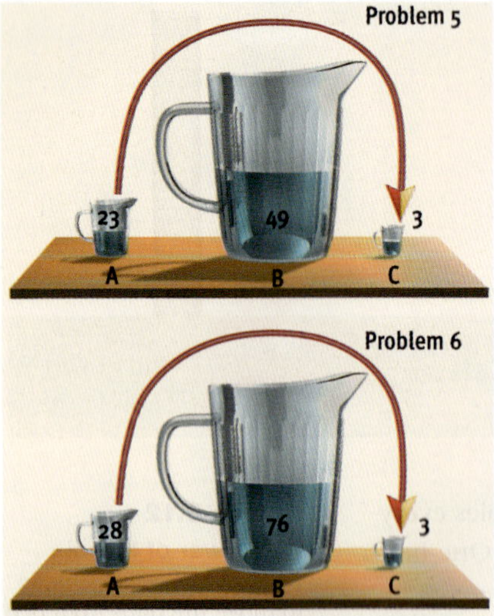

Figure 8.13

Solutions to the additional water jar problems. The solution for problems 1–4 is the same (B − A − 2C) as the solution shown in **Figure 8.8**. This method will work for problem 5, but there also is a simpler solution (A − C), which is the only solution for problem 6. Many subjects exhibit a mental set on these problems, as they fail to notice the simpler solution for problem 5.

© Cengage Learning 2013

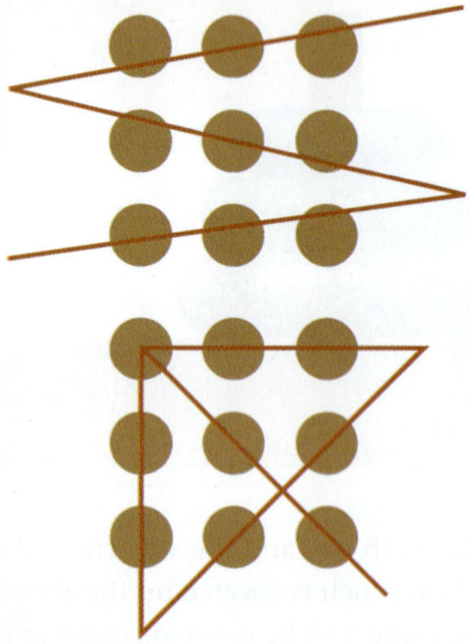

Figure 8.14

Two solutions to the nine-dot problem. The key to solving the problem is to recognize that nothing in the problem statement forbids going outside the imaginary boundary surrounding the dots.

© Cengage Learning 2013

SOURCE: Adams, J. L. (2001). *Conceptual blockbusting: A guide to better ideas.* Cambridge, MA: Basic Books. Copyright © 2001 by James L. Adams. Reprinted by permission of Basic Books, a member of the Perseus Books Group.

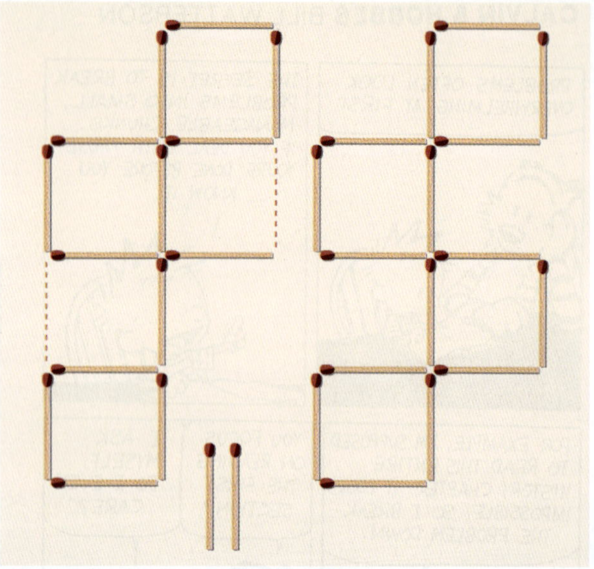

Figure 8.15

Solution to the matchstick problem. The key to solving this problem is to "open up" the figure, something many subjects are reluctant to do because they impose unnecessary constraints on the problem.

SOURCE: Kendler, H. H. (1974). *Basic psychology.* Menlo Park, CA: Benjamin-Cummings. Copyright © 1974 The Benjamin-Cummings Publishing Co. Adapted by permission of Howard H. Kendler.

© Cengage Learning 2013

later, Ellen gets in her car in New York City and starts driving toward Boston, averaging 60 miles per hour. Both women take the same route, which extends a total of 220 miles between the two cities. Which car is nearer to Boston when they meet?

These problems, taken from Sternberg (1986, pp. 213 and 215), resemble the ones that opened our discussion of problem solving. Each has an obvious solution that's hidden in irrelevant quantitative information. If you recognized this similarity, you probably solved the problems easily. If not, take another look now that you know what the analogy is. Neither problem requires any calculation whatsoever. The answer to the first problem is *7*. As for the second problem, when the two cars meet they're in the same place. Obviously, they have to be the same distance from Boston.

Changing the Representation of the Problem

Whether you solve a problem often hinges on how you envision it—your *representation of the problem.* Many problems can be represented in a variety of ways, such as verbally, mathematically, or spatially. You might represent a problem with a list, a table, an equation, a graph, a matrix of facts or numbers, a hierarchical tree diagram, or a sequential flowchart (Halpern, 2003). There isn't one ideal way to represent problems. However, when researchers compare experts and novices in a particular area of problem solving, they find that the experts strip away irrelevant details and represent problems much more efficiently (Pretz, Naples, & Sternberg, 2003). This finding highlights the importance of how problems are represented. Thus, when you fail to make progress on a problem with your initial representation, changing your representation is often a good strategy (Novick & Bassok, 2005). As an illustration, see whether you can solve the *bird and train problem* (from Bransford & Stein, 1993, p. 11):

Two train stations are 50 miles apart. At 1 P.M. on Sunday a train pulls out from each of the stations and the trains start toward each other. Just as the trains pull out from the stations, a hawk flies into the air in front of the first train and flies ahead to the front of the second train. When the hawk reaches the second train, it turns around and flies toward the first train. The hawk continues in this way until the trains meet. Assume that both trains travel at the speed of 25 miles per hour and the hawk flies at a constant speed of 100 miles per hour. How many miles will the hawk have flown when the trains meet?

This problem asks about the *distance* the bird will fly, so people tend to represent the problem spatially, as shown in **Figure 8.16**. Represented this way, the problem can be solved. The steps, though, are tedious and difficult. But consider another angle. The problem asks how far the bird will fly in the time it takes the trains to meet. Since we know how fast the bird flies, all we really need to know is how much *time* it takes for the trains to

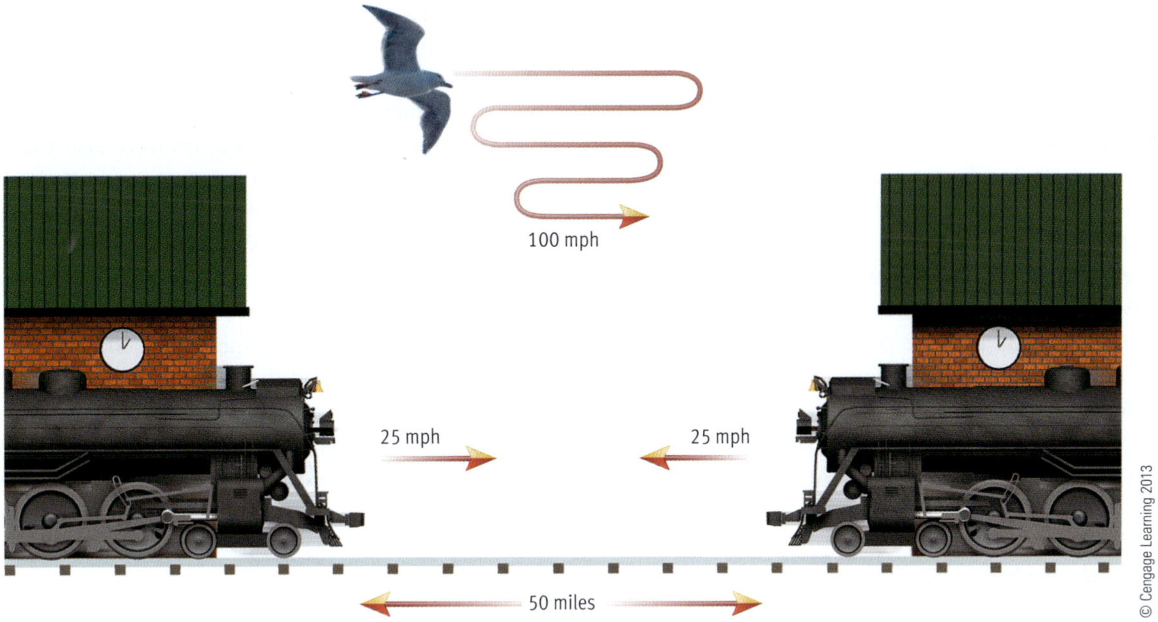

Figure 8.16
Representing the bird and train problem. The typical inclination is to envision this problem spatially, as shown here. However, as the text explains, this representation makes the problem much more difficult than it really is.

meet. Changing the representation of the problem from a question of *distance* to a question of *time* makes for an easier solution, as follows: The train stations are 50 miles apart. Since the trains are traveling toward each other at the same speed, they will meet midway and each will have traveled 25 miles. The trains are moving at 25 miles per hour. Hence, the time it takes them to meet 25 miles from each station is 1 hour. Since the bird flies at 100 miles per hour, it will fly 100 miles in the hour it takes the trains to meet.

Taking a Break: Incubation

When a problem is resistant to solution, there is much to be said for taking a break and not thinking about it for a while. After the break, you may find that you see the problem in a different light and new solutions may spring to mind. Obviously, there is no guarantee that a break will facilitate problem solving. But breaks pay off regularly enough that researchers have given the phenomenon a name: *incubation.* **An *incubation effect* occurs when new solutions surface for a previously unsolved problem after a**

CONCEPT CHECK 8.2

Thinking About Problem Solving

Check your understanding of problem solving by answering some questions about the following problem. Begin by trying to solve the problem.

The candle problem. Using the objects shown—candles, a box of matches, string, and some tacks—figure out how you could mount a candle on a wall so that it could be used as a light. Work on the problem for a while, then turn to page 332 to see the solution. After you've seen the solution, respond to the following questions. The answers are in Appendix A.

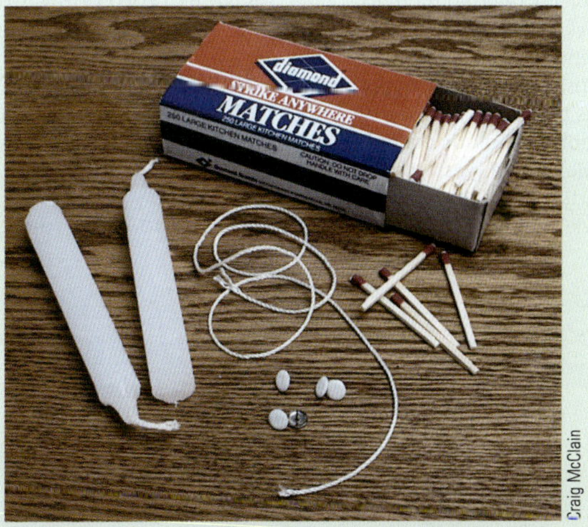

1. If it didn't occur to you that the matchbox could be converted from a container to a platform, this illustrates ________________ ________________.
2. While working on the problem, if you thought to yourself, "How can I create a platform attached to the wall?" you used the heuristic of ________________ ________________.
3. If it occurred to you suddenly that the matchbox could be used as a platform, this realization would be an example of ________________.
4. If you had a hunch that there might be some similarity between this problem and the string problem in **Figure 8.6** (the similarity is the novel use of an object), your hunch would illustrate the heuristic of ________________ ________ ________________.
5. In terms of Greeno's three types of problems, the candle problem is a(n) ________________ problem.

The solution to the candle problem in Concept Check 8.2.

period of not consciously thinking about the problem. Depending on the nature of the problem, incubation periods may be measured in minutes, hours, or days. The likelihood of an incubation effect depends on a number of task-related factors, but on the whole, incubation does tend to enhance problem solving (Dodds, Ward, & Smith, 2011; Sio & Ormerod, 2009). Research suggests that incubation effects can even occur during sleep (Cai et al., 2009; Stickgold & Walker, 2004). Some theorists believe that incubation effects occur because people continue to work on problems at an unconscious level after conscious effort has been suspended (Ellwood et al., 2009). However, several alternative explanations for incubation effects have also been proposed (Helie & Sun, 2010).

Culture, Cognitive Style, and Problem Solving

Do the varied experiences of people from different cultures lead to cross-cultural variations in problem solving? Yes, at least to some degree. Researchers have found cultural differences in the cognitive style that people exhibit in solving problems.

Richard Nisbett and his colleagues (Nisbett et al., 2001; Nisbett & Miyamoto, 2005) have argued that people from East Asian cultures (such as China, Japan, and Korea) display a *holistic cognitive style* that focuses on context and relationships among elements in a field, whereas people from Western cultures (America and Europe) exhibit an *analytic cognitive style* that focuses on objects and their properties rather than context. To put it simply, *Easterners see wholes where Westerners see parts.*

In one test of this hypothesis, Masuda and Nisbett (2001) presented computer-animated scenes of fish and other underwater objects to Japanese and American participants and asked them to report what they had seen. The initial comments of American subjects typically referred to the fish, whereas the initial comments of Japanese subjects usually referred to background elements (see **Figure 8.17**).

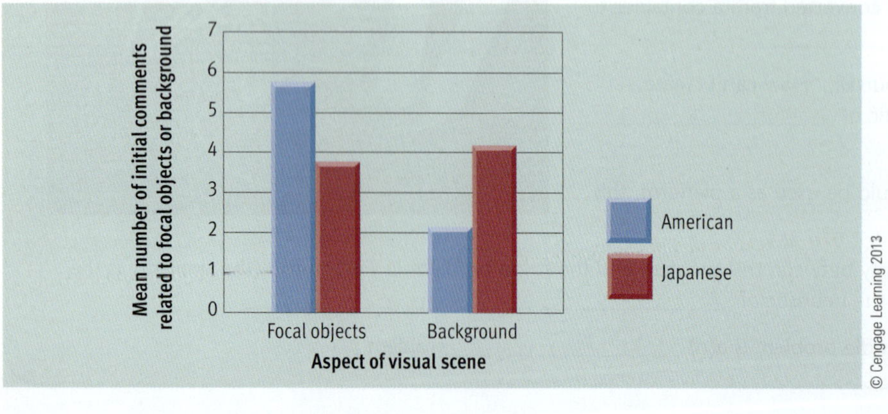

Figure 8.17
Cultural disparities in cognitive style. In one of the studies conducted by Masuda and Nisbett (2001), the participants were asked to describe computer-animated visual scenes. As you can see, the initial comments made by American subjects referred more to focal objects in the scenes, whereas the initial comments made by Japanese subjects referred more to background elements in the scenes. These findings are consistent with the hypothesis that Easterners see wholes (a holistic cognitive style) where Westerners see parts (an analytic cognitive style).

Furthermore, compared to the Americans, the Japanese participants made about 70% more statements about context or background and about twice as many statements about relationships between elements in the scenes. Other studies have also found that people from Asian cultures pay more attention to contextual information than people from North American cultures do (Kitayama et al., 2003).

Cultural variations in analytic versus holistic thinking appear to influence subjects' patterns of logical reasoning, their vulnerability to hindsight bias (see Chapter 7), and their tolerance of contradictions (Nisbett, 2003). Based on these and many other findings, Nisbett et al. (2001) conclude that "literally different cognitive processes are often invoked by East Asians and Westerners dealing with the same problem" (p. 305). These disparities in cognitive style seem to be rooted in variations in cultures' social orientation (Varnum et al., 2010). They appear to grow out of Western cultures' emphasis on the individual and independence as opposed to Eastern cultures' emphasis on the group and interdependence (see Chapters 12 and 13). Some theorists speculate that variations in cultural experiences may even lead to subtle cultural differences in neural structure, or how people's brains are "wired," but evidence on this hypothesis remains scant (Park & Huang, 2010).

Problems are not the only kind of cognitive challenge that people grapple with on a regular basis. Life also seems to constantly demand decisions. As you might expect, cognitive psychologists have shown great interest in the process of decision making, which is our next subject.

REVIEW OF KEY LEARNING GOALS

8.6 Greeno distinguished between three broad types of problems: problems of inducing structure, transformation problems, and arrangement problems.

8.7 Common barriers to problem solving include being distracted by irrelevant information, functional fixedness (only seeing an item's most common use), mental set (persisting with strategies that have worked in the past), and placing unnecessary constraints on one's solutions.

8.8 An algorithm is a procedure for trying all possible alternatives in searching for a solution to a problem. A heuristic is a rule of thumb. When people form subgoals, they break a problem into several parts. Sometimes it's useful to start at the goal state and work backward. Other general strategies include searching for analogies between new problems and old problems and changing the representation of problems. Research on incubation effects suggests that taking a break from a problem can sometimes enhance problem solving efforts.

8.9 Research indicates that cultural disparities exist in typical problem-solving strategies. Eastern cultures exhibit a more holistic cognitive style, while Western cultures display a more analytic cognitive style. In other words, Easterners see wholes where Westerners see parts.

Decision Making: Choices and Chances

KEY LEARNING GOALS

8.10 Articulate Simon's theory of bounded rationality and Schwartz's analysis of choice overload.

8.11 Distinguish the additive and elimination-by-aspects approaches to selecting an alternative.

8.12 Discuss research on factors that influence decisions about preferences, including the Featured Study.

8.13 Understand key heuristics used in risky decision making and how they can lead to flawed decisions.

8.14 Assess evolutionary theorists' evaluation of research on decision flaws, and describe fast and frugal heuristics.

Decisions, decisions. Life is full of them. You decided to read this book today. Earlier today you decided when to get up, whether to eat breakfast, and if so, what to eat. Usually you make routine decisions like these with little effort. But on occasion you need to make important decisions that require more thought. Big decisions—such as selecting a car, a home, or a job—tend to be difficult. The alternatives usually have a number of attributes that need to be weighed. For instance, in choosing among several cars, you may want to compare their costs, roominess, fuel economy, handling, acceleration, stylishness, reliability, safety features, and warranties.

Decision making **involves evaluating alternatives and making choices among them.** Most people try to be systematic and rational in their decision making. However, the work that earned Herbert Simon the 1978 Nobel prize in economics showed that people don't always live up to these goals. Before Simon's work, most traditional theories in economics assumed that people make rational choices to maximize their economic gains. Simon (1957) demonstrated that people have a limited ability to process and evaluate information on numerous facets of possible alternatives. Thus, Simon's ***theory of bounded rationality*** **asserts that people tend to use simple strategies in decision making that focus on only a few facets of available options and often result in "irrational" decisions that are less than optimal.** Spurred by Simon's analysis, psychologists have devoted several decades to the study of how cognitive biases distort people's decision making.

Making Choices: Basic Strategies

Many decisions involve choices about *preferences,* which can be made using a variety of strategies (Goldstein & Hogarth, 1997). In an influential book, Barry Schwartz (2004) has argued that people in modern societies are overwhelmed by an overabundance of such choices about preferences. For example, Schwartz describes how a simple visit to a local supermarket can require a consumer to choose from 285 varieties of cookies, 61 suntan lotions, 150 lipsticks, and 175 salad dressings. Increased choice is most tangible in the realm of consumer goods, but Schwartz argues that it also extends into more significant domains of life. Today, people tend to have unprecedented opportunities to make choices about how they will be educated, how and where they will work, how their intimate relationships will unfold, and even how they will look. Although enormous freedom of choice sounds attractive, Schwartz (2004) argues that the overabundance of choices in modern life has unexpected costs. He argues that people routinely make errors even when choosing among a handful of alternatives and that errors become much more likely when decisions become more complex. He further explains how having more alternatives increases the potential for postdecision regret. Ultimately, he argues, the malaise associated with *choice overload* undermines individuals' happiness and contributes to depression.

Consistent with this analysis, recent research has suggested that when consumers have too many choices (for a specific product), they are more likely to leave a store empty-handed (Jessup et al., 2009). Why? Studies suggest that when many choices are available, people are more likely to struggle in deciding which is the best option and so defer their decision (White & Hoffrage, 2009). Researchers have also found that having to make a lot of decisions depletes mental resources and undermines subsequent self-control (Vohs et al., 2008). How many choices are too many? That depends on many factors, but it appears that people prefer more choices up to a point, and then further increases in options lead to decreased satisfaction with the situation (Reutskaja & Hogarth, 2009). It's hard to say whether choice overload is as detrimental to well-being as some theorists believe. But it's clear that people wrestle with countless choices about preferences, and their reasoning about these decisions is often far from optimal. Among the strategies people use in making these types of decisions are giving scores to the alternatives to arrive at the best one and evaluating each alternative based on criteria in order to eliminate them one by one.

Imagine that your friend Brett has found two reasonably attractive apartments and is trying to decide between them. How should he go about selecting between his alternatives? If Brett wanted to use an *additive strategy,* he would list the attributes that influence his decision. Then he would rate the desirability of each apartment on each attribute. For example, let's say that Brett wants to consider four attributes: rent, noise level, distance to campus, and

Reality CHECK

Misconception

In making choices, people like to have lots of options; the more options the better.

Reality

Having choices is a good thing; people like to have a variety of options. But recent research on choice overload suggests that's true only up to a point. An overabundance of options can make decisions difficult and unpleasant, foster decision paralysis (an inability to decide), and lead to postdecision regret.

Table 8.3 Application of the Additive Model to Choosing an Apartment

Attribute	Apartment A	Apartment B
Rent	+1	+2
Noise level	−2	+3
Distance to campus	+3	−1
Cleanliness	+2	+2
Total	**+4**	**+6**

© Cengage Learning 2013

cleanliness. He might make ratings from −3 to +3, like those shown in **Table 8.3** on the next page, add up the ratings for each alternative, and select the one with the largest total. Given the ratings in **Table 8.3**, Brett should select apartment B. To make an additive strategy more useful, one can *weight* attributes differently, based on their importance (Shafir & LeBoeuf, 2004). For example, if Brett considers distance to campus to be twice as important as the other considerations, he could multiply his ratings of this attribute by 2. The distance rating would then be +6 for apartment A and −2 for apartment B. Apartment A would then become the preferred choice.

People also make choices by gradually eliminating less attractive alternatives (Slovic, 1990; Tversky, 1972). This strategy is called *elimination by aspects* because it assumes that alternatives are eliminated by evaluating them on each attribute or aspect in turn. Whenever any alternative fails to satisfy some minimum criterion for an attribute, it's eliminated from further consideration. To illustrate, suppose Juanita is looking for a new car. She may begin by eliminating all cars that cost over $24,000. Then she may eliminate cars that don't average at least 20 miles per gallon of gas. By continuing to reject choices that don't satisfy some minimum criterion on selected attributes, she can gradually eliminate alternatives until only a single car remains. The final choice in elimination by aspects depends on the order in which attributes are evaluated. For example, if cost was the last attribute Juanita evaluated, she could have previously eliminated all cars that cost under $24,000. If she has only $24,000 to spend, her decision-making strategy would not have brought her very far. Thus, when using elimination by aspects, it's best to evaluate attributes in the order of their importance.

Which decision strategies do people actually use? They adapt their approach to the demands of the task. When their choices are fairly simple, they use additive strategies. As choices become very complex, though, they shift toward simpler strategies, such as elimination by aspects (Payne & Bettman, 2004).

© Austin MacRae

Making Choices: Quirks and Complexities

Beyond the basics we've been discussing, research has turned up a number of quirks and complexities that people exhibit in making decisions about preferences. Some of the more interesting findings include the following:

- *Emotion influences decision making.* When people decide between various options (let's say two jobs), their evaluations of the options' specific attributes (such as salary, commute, and work hours) fluctuate more than most models of decision making anticipated (Shafir & LeBoeuf, 2004). Models of "rational" choice assumed that people know what they like and don't like and that these evaluations are stable. Research suggests otherwise, however. One reason is that people can be swayed by incidental emotional fluctuations (Lerner, Small, & Loewenstein, 2004).
- *If they can avoid it, people prefer to not have to grapple with uncertainty.* Consider the perplexing findings reported by Gneezy, List, and Wu (2006). They found that people were willing to pay more for a $50 gift certificate to a bookstore than for a 50/50 opportunity to get either a $50 or $100 gift certificate to the same store. It does not make sense to value a known outcome more than an unknown outcome when the worst scenario for the unknown outcome ($50) is equal to the known outcome ($50) and the best scenario is clearly superior ($100). A number of explanations have been proposed for this *uncertainty effect.* Recent research by Simonsohn (2009) suggests that the best explanation is a simple one: People do not like uncertainty, and this distaste can distort their decision making.
- *Judgments about the quality of various alternatives, such as consumer products, can be swayed by extraneous factors such as brand familiarity and price.* In one recent demonstration of this phenomenon, participants tasted wines and rated their quality (Plassmann et al., 2008). In some cases, they thought they were tasting two different wines. However, it was the same wine presented at two very different prices (such as $10 and $90). As you might guess, the more "expensive" wines garnered higher ratings. Moreover, brain imaging (fMRI scans) during the wine tasting showed higher activity in a brain region thought to register pleasure when subjects consumed the more "expensive" wine. These findings suggest that people really do get what they pay for in terms of subjective pleasure, and they indicate

that decisions about preferences can be distorted by considerations that should be irrelevant.

Another line of research has looked at whether decisions about preferences work out better when people engage in conscious deliberation or go with intuitive, unconscious feelings based on minimal deliberation. Ap Dijksterhuis and colleagues argue that the answer to this question depends on the complexity of the decision—probably not in the way you might guess, though, as you will see in our Featured Study.

FEATURED STUDY

Intuitive Decisions Versus Careful Deliberation: Which Leads to Better Decisions?

SOURCE: Dijksterhuis, A., Bos, M. W., Nordgren, L. F., & van Baaren, R. B. (2006). On making the right choice: The deliberation-without-attention effect. *Science, 311*(5763), 1005–1007.

"Look before you leap," we are told. Conventional wisdom suggests that important, complicated choices require thoughtful deliberation and that such thought is more likely to lead to decisions that prove satisfying. Scientific research on decision making has tended to echo conventional wisdom in touting the benefits of thorough deliberation. But Dijksterhuis and his colleagues (Dijksterhuis, 2004; Dijksterhuis & Nordgren, 2006; Dijksterhuis & van Olden, 2006) have argued that unconscious, intuitive thought processes sometimes lead to better decisions. Why? Primarily because of the limited capacity of conscious thought. As first noted by Herbert Simon and shown in countless studies, people have a surprisingly finite capacity for juggling information. Although one might guess that careful deliberation ought to be more valuable when choices are complicated, Dijksterhuis and his colleagues hypothesized just the opposite. They predicted that deliberate decisions would be superior to intuitive decisions when choices were simple but that intuitive, unconscious decisions would be superior when choices were complex. We'll examine two of the four studies they conducted to test this proposition.

Study A

Method. Eighty undergraduate participants read information about four hypothetical cars and were asked to choose their favorite. In the simple decision, only four attributes of each car were described, while in the complex version, subjects were given information on twelve attributes of the cars. The desirability of the cars was manipulated by making 75% of the attributes positive for one car, 50% positive for two cars, and 25% positive for one car. So, in both versions of the choice, one of the cars should have stood out as the optimal alternative. In the conscious-thought condition, participants were told to mull over their options for 4 minutes and report their choice. In the unconscious-thought condition, subjects were distracted from thinking about the decision for 4 minutes (they were kept busy solving anagrams) and were then asked for their choice of the best car.

Results. As shown in **Figure 8.18**, when the car choice was relatively simple, conscious thought was superior to unconscious thought in selecting the optimal auto. But when the choice was more complicated, unconscious thought was notably superior to conscious deliberation in selecting the best car.

Study B

Method. Sixty-one student participants indicated how many facets they would evaluate in deciding to purchase 40 consumer products, such as shampoos, shoes, and cameras, yielding a *decision complexity* score for each product. Subsequently, another group of 93 undergraduates picked a product from a list of items they had recently bought and were asked about how much conscious thought they put into the decision and how satisfied they were with their choice.

Results. **Figure 8.19** on the next page depicts participants' postchoice satisfaction for the six products that were chosen most frequently from the list, with the products listed in order of decision complexity (from left to right). As predicted, conscious deliberation promoted greater satisfaction when decisions were simple. Just the opposite occurred for complex decisions, however.

Discussion

The results of these two studies demonstrate what Dijksterhuis calls the *deliberation-without-attention effect.* When people are faced with complex choices, they tend to make better decisions if they don't devote careful attention to the matter. Dijksterhuis believes that deliberations are taking place—but outside of conscious

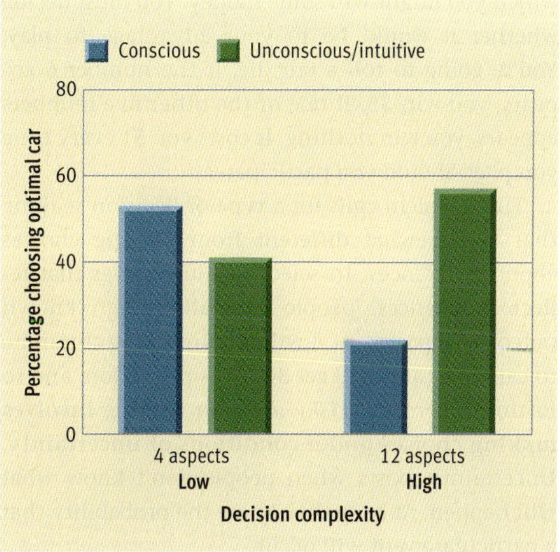

© Cengage Learning 2013

Figure 8.18
Conscious versus unconscious decision making in Study A. The percentage of participants who selected the optimal car in each condition is shown here. When the choice was simple (only four aspects of the car were described), conscious deliberation proved superior. However, when the choice was more complex (twelve aspects to consider), unconscious, intuitive thinking proved superior.

SOURCE: Dijksterhuis, A., Bos, M. W., Nordgren, L. F., & van Baaren, R. B. (2006). On making the right choice: The deliberation-without-attention effect. *Science, 311*(5763), 1005–1007. Copyright © 2006 the American Association for the Advancement of Science. Reprinted by permission from the AAAS.

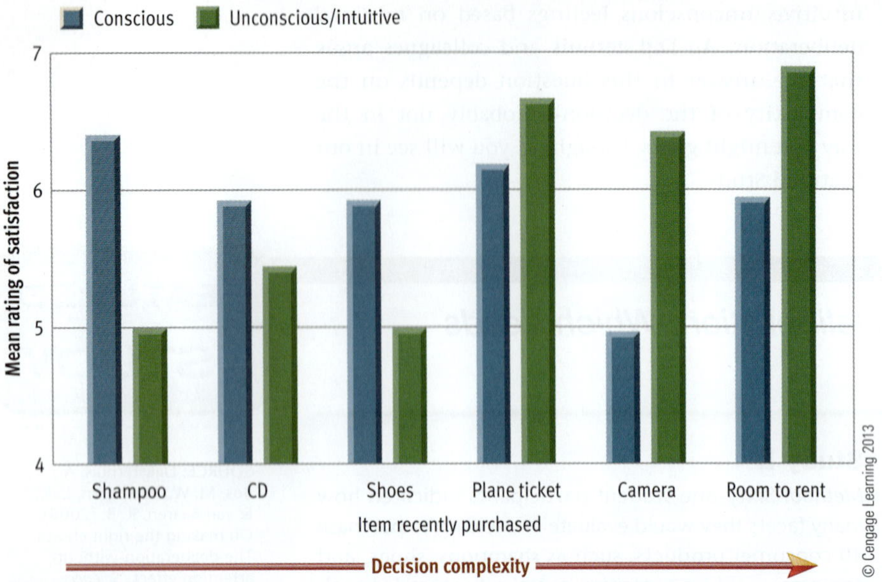

Figure 8.19

Postchoice satisfaction as a function of decision complexity in Study B. Mean ratings of postchoice satisfaction for the six products chosen most often are shown here. The products are arranged, from left to right, in order of increasing decision complexity. For each product, participants' ratings of how much they deliberated about their purchase were split at the median, dividing them into conscious versus unconscious decision makers. When decision complexity was low, conscious deliberation was associated with greater satisfaction, but when decision complexity was high, conscious deliberation was associated with less satisfaction.

SOURCE: Dijksterhuis, A., Bos, M. W., Nordgren, L. F., & van Baaren, R. B. (2006). On making the right choice: The deliberation-without-attention effect. *Science, 311*(5763), 1005–1007. Copyright © 2006 the American Association for the Advancement of Science. Reprinted by permission from the AAAS.

awareness. Thus, like studies of subliminal perception (see Chapter 4) and studies showing that sleep can enhance memory and problem solving (see Chapter 5), this study suggests that unconscious mental processes are more influential than widely assumed. The authors conclude that "there is no a priori reason to assume that the deliberation-without-attention effect does not generalize to other types of choices—political, managerial, or otherwise" (p. 1007).

Comment

This research was featured because it provided an elegant test of an interesting hypothesis that seems to defy common sense. It also illustrates the value of approaching an issue with different methodologies. Standing alone, the experimental study (A) on car choices might not be convincing. Four minutes of conscious thought is not much time for testing the efficacy of "careful deliberation," and one could quibble about whether the optimal car was really optimal for all subjects. But, when the carefully controlled experimental study is combined with the more realistic correlational study (B), the converging evidence provides impressive support for the authors' theory.

That said, critics note that it may be premature to broadly generalize these findings to diverse kinds of decision making in the real world (Haslam, 2007). In the studies thus far, even the "complex" choices have involved relatively simple decisions about product preferences. It's quite a leap to assume that physicians, corporate managers, and government leaders, who confront choices of profound complexity and importance, would make better decisions if they avoided careful deliberation. Although other lines of research also suggest that intuition can sometimes be superior to logic and reflection (Gladwell, 2005; Myers, 2002), the boundary conditions of this phenomenon need to be determined (Payne et al., 2008).

Taking Chances: Factors Weighed in Risky Decisions

Suppose you have the chance to play a dice game in which you might win some money. You must decide whether it would be to your advantage to play. You're going to roll a fair die. If the number 6 appears, you win \$5. If one of the other five numbers appears, you win nothing. It costs you \$1 every time you play. Should you participate?

This problem calls for a type of decision making that is somewhat different from making choices about preferences. In selecting alternatives that reflect preferences, people generally weigh known outcomes (apartment A will require a long commute to campus, car B will get 30 miles per gallon, and so forth). In contrast, ***risky decision making*** **involves making choices under conditions of uncertainty.** Uncertainty exists when people don't know what will happen. At best, they know the probability that a particular event will occur.

One way to decide whether to play the dice game would be to figure out the *expected value* of participation in the game. To do so, you would need to calculate the average amount of money you could expect to win or lose each time you play. The value of a win is \$4 (\$5 minus the \$1 entry fee). The value of a loss is −\$1. To calculate expected value, you also need to know the probability of a win or loss. Since a die has six faces, the probability of a win is 1 out of 6. The probability of a loss is then 5 out of 6. Thus, on five out of every six trials, you lose \$1. On one out of six, you win \$4. The game is beginning to sound unattractive, isn't it? We can figure out the precise expected value as follows:

$$\text{Expected value} = (\tfrac{1}{6} \times 4) + (\tfrac{5}{6} \times -1) = \tfrac{4}{6} + (-\tfrac{5}{6}) = -\tfrac{1}{6}$$

The expected value of this game is $-\frac{1}{6}$ of a dollar. This means that you lose an average of about 17 cents per turn. Now that you know the expected value, surely you won't agree to play. Or will you?

If we want to understand why people make the decisions they do, the concept of expected value is not enough. People often behave in ways that are inconsistent with expected value (Slovic, Lichtenstein, & Fischhoff, 1988). Anytime the expected value is negative, a gambler should expect to lose money. Yet a great many people gamble at racetracks and casinos and buy lottery tickets when they know the odds are against them.

To explain decisions that violate expected value, some theories replace the objective value of an outcome with its *subjective utility* (Fischhoff, 1988). Subjective utility represents what an outcome is personally worth to an individual. For example, buying a few lottery tickets may allow you to dream about becoming wealthy. Such subjective utilities vary from one person to another. Interestingly, however, studies show that people often make inaccurate predictions about how much subjective utility or enjoyment various experiences will yield (Loewenstein & Schkade, 1999).

Heuristics in Judging Probabilities

PsykTrek 7f

- What are your chances of passing your next psychology test if you study only 3 hours?
- How likely is a major downturn in the stock market during the upcoming year?
- What are the odds of your getting into graduate school in the field of your choice?

These questions ask you to make probability estimates. Amos Tversky and Daniel Kahneman (1974, 1982; Kahneman & Tversky, 2000) have conducted extensive research on the heuristics that people use in grappling with probabilities. This research earned Kahneman the Nobel prize in economics in 2002 (unfortunately, his collaborator, Amos Tversky, died in 1996).

Availability is one such heuristic. **The *availability heuristic* involves basing the estimated probability of an event on the ease with which relevant instances come to mind.** For example, you may estimate the divorce rate by recalling the number of divorces among your friends' parents. Recalling specific instances of an event is a reasonable strategy to use in estimating the event's probability. However, if instances occur often but you have difficulty retrieving them from memory, your estimate will be biased. For instance, it's easier to think of words that begin with a certain letter than words that contain that letter at some other position. Hence, people should tend to respond that there are more words starting with the letter *K* than words having a *K* in the third position. To test this hypothesis, Tversky and Kahneman (1973) selected five consonants (*K, L, N, R, V*) that occur more frequently in the third position of a word than in the first. Subjects were then asked whether each of the letters appears more often in the first or third position. Most of the subjects erroneously believed that all five letters were much more frequent in the first than in the third position, confirming the hypothesis.

Representativeness is another guide in estimating probabilities identified by Kahneman and Tversky (1982). **The *representativeness heuristic* involves basing the estimated probability of an event on how similar it is to the typical prototype of that event.** To illustrate, imagine that you flip a coin six times and keep track of how often the result is heads (H) or tails (T). Which of the following sequences is more likely?

1. T T T T T T
2. H T T H T H

People generally believe that the second sequence is more likely. After all, coin tossing is a random affair, and the second sequence looks much more representative of a random process than the first. In reality, the probability of each exact *sequence* is precisely the same ($1/2 \times 1/2 \times 1/2 \times 1/2 \times 1/2 \times 1/2 = 1/64$). Overdependence on the representativeness heuristic has been used to explain quite a variety of decision-making tendencies (Teigen, 2004), as you will see in the upcoming pages.

The Tendency to Ignore Base Rates

PsykTrek 7f

Steve is very shy and withdrawn, invariably helpful, but with little interest in people or in the world of reality. A meek and tidy soul, he has a need for order and structure and a passion for detail. Do you think Steve is a salesperson or a librarian? (Adapted from Tversky & Kahneman, 1974, p. 1124)

Using the *representativeness heuristic,* subjects tend to guess that Steve is a librarian because he resembles their prototype of a librarian (Tversky & Kahneman, 1982). In reality, this is not a wise guess, because it *ignores the base rates* of librarians and salespeople in the population. Salespeople outnumber librarians by a wide margin (roughly 75 to 1 in the United States). This fact makes it much more likely that Steve is in sales. But in estimating probabilities, people often ignore information on base rates.

Researchers are still debating how common it is for people to neglect base rate information (Birnbaum, 2004a; Koehler, 1996), but it does not appear to be a rare event. In fact, evidence indicates that people are particularly bad about applying base rates to themselves. For instance, Weinstein (1984; Weinstein & Klein, 1995) has found that people underestimate the

Courtesy of Daniel Kahneman

Daniel Kahneman

"The human mind suppresses uncertainty. We're not only convinced that we know more about our politics, our businesses, and our spouses than we really do, but also that what we don't know must be unimportant."

Courtesy of Barbara Tversky

Amos Tversky

"People treat their own cases as if they were unique, rather than part of a huge lottery. You hear this silly argument that 'The odds don't apply to me.' Why should God, or whoever runs this lottery, give you special treatment?"

CONCEPT CHECK 8.3

Recognizing Heuristics in Decision Making

Check your understanding of heuristics in decision making by trying to identify the heuristics used in the following examples. Each numbered element in the anecdote below illustrates a problem-solving heuristic. Write the relevant heuristic in the space on the left. You can find the answers in Appendix A.

______________ 1. Marsha can't decide on a college major. She evaluates all the majors available at her college on the attributes of how much she would enjoy them (likability), how challenging they are (difficulty), and how good the job opportunities are in the field (employability). She drops from consideration any major that she regards as "poor" on any of these three attributes.

______________ 2. When she considers history as a major, she thinks to herself, "Gee, I know four history graduates who are still looking for work" and concludes that the probability of getting a job using a history degree is very low.

______________ 3. She finds that every major gets a "poor" rating on at least one attribute, so she eliminates everything. Because this is unacceptable, she decides she has to switch to another strategy. Marsha finally focuses her consideration on five majors that received just one "poor" rating. She uses a 4-point scale to rate each of these majors on each of the three attributes she values. She adds up the ratings and selects the major with the highest total as her leading candidate.

risks of their own health-impairing habits while viewing others' risks much more accurately. Thus, smokers are realistic in estimating the degree to which smoking increases someone else's risk of heart attack but underestimate the risk for themselves. Similarly, people starting new companies ignore the high failure rate for new businesses, and burglars underestimate the likelihood that they will end up in jail.

The Conjunction Fallacy

PSYKTREK 7f

Imagine that you're going to meet a man who is an articulate, ambitious, power-hungry wheeler-dealer. Do you think it's more likely that he's a college teacher or a college teacher who's also a politician?

People tend to guess that the man is a "college teacher who's a politician" because the description fits with the typical prototype of politicians. But stop and think for a moment. The broader category of college teachers completely includes the smaller subcategory of college teachers who are politicians (see **Figure 8.20**). The probability of being in the subcategory cannot be higher than the probability of being in the broader category. It's a logical impossibility!

Tversky and Kahneman (1983) call this error the *conjunction fallacy*. **The *conjunction fallacy* occurs when people estimate that the odds of two uncertain events happening together are greater than the odds of either event happening alone.** The conjunction fallacy has been observed in a number of studies and has generally been attributed to the influence of the representativeness heuristic (Epstein, Donovan, & Denes-Raj, 1999), although some doubts have been raised about this interpretation (Fisk, 2004).

Evolutionary Analyses of Flaws in Human Decision Making

A central conclusion of the last 30 years of research on decision making has been that human decision-making strategies are riddled with errors and biases that yield surprisingly irrational results (Goldstein & Hogarth, 1997; Risen & Gilovich, 2007; Shafir & LeBoeuf, 2002). Theorists have discovered that people have "mental limitations" and have concluded that people are not as bright and rational as they think they are. This broad conclusion has led some evolutionary psychologists to reconsider the work on human decision making. Their take on the matter is quite interesting.

First, they argue that traditional decision research has imposed an invalid and unrealistic standard of rationality. The assumption is that people should be impeccable in applying the laws of deductive logic and statistical probability while objectively and precisely weighing multiple factors in arriving at decisions (Gigerenzer, 2000). Second, they argue that humans only *seem* irrational because cognitive psychologists

© 2005 Steve Kelley. *The Times-Picayune*. Reprinted with

have been asking the wrong questions and formulating problems in the wrong ways—ways that have nothing to do with the adaptive problems that the human mind has evolved to solve (Cosmides & Tooby, 1996).

According to Leda Cosmides and John Tooby (1994, 1996), the human mind consists of a large number of specialized cognitive mechanisms that have emerged over the course of evolution to solve specific adaptive problems, such as finding food, shelter, and mates, and dealing with allies and enemies. As a result, human decision and problem-solving strategies have been tailored to handle real-world adaptive problems. Participants perform poorly in cognitive research, say Cosmides and Tooby, because it confronts them with contrived, artificial problems that do not involve natural categories and have no adaptive significance.

Thus, evolutionary theorists assert that many errors in human reasoning, such as neglect of base rates and the conjunction fallacy, should vanish if classic lab problems are reformulated in terms of raw frequencies rather than probabilities and base rates. Consistent with this analysis, evolutionary psychologists have shown that some errors in reasoning that are seen in lab studies disappear or are decreased when problems are presented in ways that resemble the type of input humans would've processed in ancestral times (Brase, Cosmides & Tooby, 1998; Hertwig & Gigerenzer, 1999). The debate goes on (Shafir & LeBoeuf, 2002), but this evidence and other lines of research (Keys & Schwartz, 2007) are gradually reducing cognitive psychologists' tendency to characterize human reasoning as "irrational."

Figure 8.20

The conjunction fallacy. Subjects often fall victim to the conjunction fallacy, but as this diagram makes obvious, the probability of being in a subcategory (college teachers who are politicians) cannot be higher than the probability of being in the broader category (college teachers). As this case illustrates, it often helps to represent a problem in a diagram.

Fast and Frugal Heuristics

To further expand on the evolutionary point of view, Gerd Gigerenzer has argued that humans' reasoning largely depends on "fast and frugal heuristics" that are much simpler than the complicated mental processes studied in traditional cognitive research (Gigerenzer, 2000, 2004, 2008; Todd & Gigerenzer, 2000, 2007). According to Gigerenzer, organisms from toads to stockbrokers have to make fast decisions under demanding circumstances with limited information. In most instances organisms (including humans) don't have the time, resources, or cognitive capacities to gather all the relevant information, consider all the possible options, calculate all the probabilities and risks, and then make the statistically optimal decision. Instead, they use quick and dirty heuristics that are less than perfect but that work well enough most of the time to be adaptive in the real world.

Gigerenzer and his colleagues have shown that fast and frugal heuristics can be surprisingly effective. One heuristic that is often used in selecting between alternatives based on some quantitative dimension is the *recognition heuristic*. It works as follows: If one of two alternatives is recognized and the other is not, infer that the recognized alternative has the higher value. Consider the following questions—Which city has more inhabitants: San Diego or San Antonio? Hamburg or Munich? In choosing between U.S. cities, American college students weighed a lifetime of facts useful for inferring population and made the correct choice 71% of the time; in choosing between German cities about which they knew very little, the same students depended on the recognition heuristic and chose correctly 73% of the time (Goldstein & Gigerenzer, 2002). Thus, the recognition heuristic allowed students to perform just as well with very limited knowledge as they did with extensive knowledge.

Gigerenzer and his colleagues have found that other quick, one-reason decision-making strategies can yield inferences that are just as accurate as much more elaborate and time-consuming strategies that weigh many factors (Marewski, Gaissmaier, & Gigerenzer, 2010). And they have shown that people actually use these fast and frugal heuristics in diverse situations. Thus, the study of fast and frugal heuristics promises to be an

Reality CHECK

Misconception

Effective decision making requires careful analysis of the alternatives and thoughtful deliberation.

Reality

Research on fast and frugal heuristics and the deliberation-without-attention effect (see the Featured Study) demonstrate that good decision making does not necessarily *require* systematic, thorough deliberation. Although many decisions call for careful reflection, it appears that intuition has been underrated. Quick, simple, intuitive strategies can also yield good decisions. The challenge is to know when to go with intuition and when to rely on deliberation.

intriguing new line of research in the study of human decision making.

How have traditional decision-making theorists responded to the challenge presented by Gigerenzer and other evolutionary theorists? They acknowledge that people often rely on fast and frugal heuristics. But they argue that this finding doesn't make decades of research on carefully reasoned approaches to decision making meaningless. Rather, they propose *dual-process theories,* which posit that people depend on two very different modes or systems of thinking when making decisions (De Neys, 2006; Evans, 2007; Gilovich & Griffin, 2010; Kahneman, 2003). One system consists of quick, simple, effortless, automatic judgments, like Gigerenzer's fast and frugal heuristics, which traditional theorists characterize as "intuitive thinking." The second system consists of slower, more elaborate, effortful, controlled judgments, like those studied in traditional decision research. According to this view, the second system monitors and corrects the intuitive system as needed and takes over when complicated or important decisions loom. Thus, traditional theorists maintain that fast and frugal heuristics and reasoned, rule-governed decision strategies exist side-by-side and both need to be studied to fully understand decision making.

REVIEW OF KEY LEARNING GOALS

8.10 Simon's theory of bounded rationality suggests that human decision strategies are simplistic and often yield irrational results. Schwartz argues that in modern societies people suffer from choice overload, which leads to rumination, regret, and diminished well-being. Recent research suggests that people prefer more choices up to a point and then further increases in options lead to decreased satisfaction.

8.11 An additive decision model is used when people make decisions by rating the attributes of each alternative and selecting the alternative that has the highest sum of ratings. When elimination by aspects is used, people gradually eliminate alternatives whose attributes fail to satisfy some minimum criterion.

8.12 In making decisions, evaluations of options fluctuate more than expected. Research on the uncertainty effect suggests that people abhor uncertainty. Judgments of products may be influenced by their prices and other extraneous factors. Our Featured Study on the deliberation-without-awareness effect showed that intuitive, unconscious decisions may be more satisfying than those based on conscious deliberation, especially when choices are complex.

8.13 Models of how people make risky decisions focus on the expected value or subjective utility of various outcomes. The availability heuristic involves basing probability estimates on the ease with which relevant examples come to mind. The representativeness heuristic involves basing the estimated probability of an event on how similar it is to the prototype of that event. In estimating probabilities, people often ignore information on base rates due to the influence of the representativeness heuristic. The conjunction fallacy occurs when people estimate that the odds of two uncertain events happening together are greater than the odds of either event happening alone.

8.14 Evolutionary psychologists maintain that many errors and biases in human reasoning are greatly reduced when problems are presented in ways that resemble the type of input humans would have processed in ancestral times. They argue that human decision making is not as irrational as it seems in traditional cognitive research. Gigerenzer argues that people largely depend on fast and frugal decision heuristics that can be surprisingly effective. Dual-process theories propose that people depend on two modes of thinking in making decisions: fast and frugal heuristics and effortful, controlled deliberation.

CONCEPT CHECK 8.4

Identifying the Contributions of Major Theorists and Researchers

Check your recall of the principal ideas of important theorists and researchers covered in this chapter by matching the people listed on the left with the appropriate contributions described on the right. If you need help, the crucial pages describing each person's ideas are listed in parentheses. Fill in the letters for your choices in the spaces provided on the left. You'll find the answers in Appendix A.

Major Theorists and Researchers

_______ 1. Noam Chomsky (p. 322)

_______ 2. Gerd Gigerenzer (p. 339)

_______ 3. Daniel Kahneman and Amos Tversky (p. 337)

_______ 4. Steven Pinker (p. 321)

_______ 5. Herbert Simon (p. 333)

_______ 6. B. F. Skinner (p. 321)

Key Ideas and Contributions

a. These psychologists conducted pioneering research on the heuristics that people use in risky decision making, such as the availability and representativeness heuristics.

b. This Nobel prize–winning pioneer of cognitive psychology formulated the theory of bounded rationality.

c. This theorist argued that humans' special talent for language is a product of evolution.

d. This nativist theorist proposed that humans are equipped with an innate language acquistion device.

e. This famous behaviorist argued that language development depends on learning and conditioning.

f. This evolutionary-oriented theorist believes that humans' reasoning largely depends on fast and frugal hueristics.

Reflecting on the Chapter's Themes

KEY LEARNING GOALS

8.15 Identify the four unifying themes highlighted in this chapter.

Heredity & Environment

Empiricism

Cultural Heritage

Subjectivity of Experience

Four of our unifying themes have been especially prominent in this chapter. The first is the continuing question about the relative influence of heredity and environment. The controversy about how children acquire language skills replays the nature versus nurture debate. The behaviorist theory, that children learn language through imitation and reinforcement, emphasizes the importance of the environment. The nativist theory, that children come equipped with an innate language acquisition device, argues for the importance of biology. The debate is far from settled, but the accumulating evidence suggests that language development depends on both nature and nurture, as more recent interactionist theories have proposed.

The second pertinent theme is the empirical nature of psychology. For many decades, psychologists paid little attention to cognitive processes because most of them assumed that thinking is too private to be studied scientifically. During the 1950s and 1960s, however, psychologists began to devise creative new ways to measure mental processes. These innovations fueled the cognitive revolution that put the *psyche* (the mind) back in psychology. Thus, once again, we see how empirical methods are the lifeblood of the scientific enterprise.

Third, the study of cognitive processes shows how both similarities and differences occur across cultures in behavior. On the one hand, we saw that language development unfolds in much the same way in widely disparate cultures. On the other hand, we learned that there are interesting cultural variations in cognitive style.

The fourth theme is the subjective nature of human experience. We have seen that decision making is a highly subjective process. The subjectivity of decision processes will continue to be prominent in the upcoming Personal Application. It discusses some more common pitfalls in reasoning about decisions.

REVIEW OF KEY LEARNING GOALS

8.15 Our discussion of language acquisition showed once again that behavior is shaped by both nature and nurture. Recent progress in the study of cognitive processes showed how science depends on empirical methods. Research on decision making illustrated the importance of subjective perceptions. Cognitive processes are moderated—to a limited degree—by cultural factors.

PERSONAL APPLICATION

Understanding Pitfalls in Reasoning About Decisions

KEY LEARNING GOALS

8.16 Explain what is meant by the gambler's fallacy and the tendency to overestimate the improbable.

8.17 Describe the propensity to seek confirming information and myside bias.

8.18 Analyze the effects of framing on decisions, and describe loss aversion.

Consider the following scenario:

Laura is in a casino watching people play roulette. The 38 slots in the roulette wheel include 18 black numbers, 18 red numbers, and 2 green numbers. Hence, on any one spin, the probability of red or black is slightly less than 50-50 (.474 to be exact). Although Laura hasn't been betting, she has been following the pattern of results in the game very carefully. The ball has landed in red seven times in a row. Laura concludes that black is long overdue and she jumps into the game, betting heavily on black.

Has Laura made a good bet? Do you agree with Laura's reasoning? Or do you think that Laura misunderstands the laws of probability? You'll find out momentarily, as we discuss how people reason their way to decisions—and how their reasoning can go awry.

The pioneering work of Amos Tversky and Daniel Kahneman (1974, 1982) led to an explosion of research on risky decision making. In their efforts to identify the heuristics that people use in decision making, investigators stumbled onto quite a few misconceptions, oversights, and biases. It turns out that people deviate in predictable ways from optimal decision strategies—with surprising regularity (Dawes, 2001; Gilovich, Griffin, & Kahneman, 2002). Moreover, it appears that no one is immune to these errors in thinking. In recent research, Stanovich and West (2008) examined the relationship between intelligence (estimated by SAT scores) and the ability to avoid a number of cognitive biases and flaws. For the most part they found that cognitive ability did not correlate with the ability to avoid irrational errors in thinking. In other words, extremely bright people are just as vulnerable to irrational thinking as everyone else. Fortunately, however, some research suggests that increased awareness of common shortcomings in reasoning about decisions can lead to fewer errors in thinking and improved decision making (Milkman, Chugh, & Bazerman, 2009; Lilienfeld, Ammirati, & Landfield, 2009). With this goal in mind, let's look at some common pitfalls in decision making.

The Gambler's Fallacy 7f

Laura's reasoning in our opening scenario is flawed. Laura's behavior illustrates **the *gambler's fallacy*—the belief that the odds of a chance event increase if the event hasn't occurred recently.** People believe that the laws of probability should yield fair results. If they believe that a process is random, they expect the process to be self-correcting (Burns & Corpus, 2004). These aren't bad assumptions in the long run. However, they don't apply to individual, independent events.

The roulette wheel does not remember its recent results and make adjustments for them. Each spin of the wheel is an independent event. The probability of black on each spin remains at .474, even if red comes up 100 times in a row! The gambler's fallacy reflects the pervasive influence of the *representativeness heuristic*. In betting on black, Laura is predicting that future results will be more representative of a random process. This logic can be used to estimate the probability of black across a *string of spins*. But it doesn't apply to a *specific spin* of the roulette wheel.

Overestimating the Improbable 7f

Various causes of death are paired up below. In each pairing, which is the more likely cause of death?

Asthma or tornadoes?

Accidental falls or shooting accidents?

Tuberculosis or floods?

Suicide or murder?

Table 8.4 shows the actual mortality rates for each of these causes of death. As you can see, the first choice in each pair is the more common cause of death. If you guessed

© AP Images/The Cleaner, Mike Lawrence

The availability heuristic can be dramatized by juxtaposing the unrelated phenomena of floods and tuberculosis (TB). Many people are killed by floods, but far more die from tuberculosis (see **Table 8.4**). However, since the news media report flood fatalities frequently and prominently, but rarely focus on deaths from tuberculosis, people tend to assume that flood-related deaths are more common.

wrong for several of the pairings, don't feel bad. Like many other people, you may be a victim of the tendency to *overestimate the improbable*. People tend to greatly overestimate the likelihood of dramatic, vivid—but infrequent—events that receive heavy media coverage. As a result, the number of fatalities due to tornadoes, shooting accidents, floods, and murders is usually overestimated (Slovic, Fischhoff, & Lichtenstein, 1982). Fatalities caused by asthma and other common diseases that receive less media coverage tend to be underestimated. This tendency to exaggerate the improbable has generally been attributed to operation of the *availability heuristic* (Reber, 2004). Instances of floods, tornadoes, and such are readily available in memory because people are exposed to a great deal of media coverage of such events.

As a general rule, people's beliefs about what they should fear tend to be surprisingly inconsistent with actual probabilities (Glassner, 1999). This propensity was especially prominent in the aftermath of 9/11. Countless people were reluctant to fly because they were worried about the possibility of a terrorist attack (as the terrorists intended). To date, one's chances of being hurt in a terrorist attack on an airplane are utterly microscopic in comparison to one's chances of perishing in an automobile accident, yet people worry about the former and not the latter (Myers, 2001).

Table 8.4 Actual Mortality Rates for Selected Causes of Death

Cause of Death	Rate	Cause of Death	Rate
Asthma	2,000	Tornadoes	25
Accidental falls	6,021	Firearms accidents	320
Tuberculosis	400	Floods	44
Suicide	11,300	Homicide	6,800

Note: Mortality rates are per 100 million people and are based on the Statistical Abstract of the United States, 2001.

© Cengage Learning 2013

Confirmation Bias

Imagine a young physician examining a sick patient. The patient is complaining of a high fever and a sore throat. The physician must decide on a diagnosis from among a myriad possible diseases. The physician thinks that it may be the flu. She asks the patient if he feels "achey all over." The answer is "yes." The physician asks if the symptoms began a few days ago. Again, the response is "yes." The physician concludes that the patient has the flu. (Adapted from Halpern, 1984, pp. 215–216)

Do you see any flaws in the physician's reasoning? Has she probed into the causes of the patient's malady effectively? No, she has asked about symptoms that would be consistent with her preliminary diagnosis. She has not, however, inquired about symptoms that could rule it out. Her questioning of the patient illustrates ***confirmation bias*—the tendency to only seek information that is likely to support one's decisions and beliefs.** This bias is common in medical diagnosis and other forms of decision making (Nickerson, 1998). There's nothing wrong with searching for confirming evidence to support one's decisions. However, people should also seek disconfirming evidence—which they often neglect to do.

A closely related problem is *myside bias*—the tendency to evaluate evidence in a manner slanted in favor of one's own opinions (Stanovich & West, 2007). For example, in a recent study (Stanovich & West, 2008) subjects read that "Ford Explorers are eight times more likely than a typical family car to kill occupants of another car in a crash." They were informed that the German government was considering banning Ford Explorers and asked whether they agreed with the ban. In another condition, similar subjects read that a specific German car was eight times more likely to kill occupants of other cars. They were told that the U.S. government was considering banning the car and asked whether they agreed with the ban. Although the situations were identical, American subjects were significantly more likely to support the ban of the German car than the ban of the Ford Explorer. Myside bias may also explain why people tend to believe that the candidates they support will prevail in elections. For instance, a study of voters in the period leading up to the 2008 U.S. presidential election found that Democrats predicted that the Democratic candidate (Barack Obama) would win, whereas Republicans were much more likely to predict that the Republican candidate (John McCain) would win (Krizan, Miller, & Johar, 2010).

The Effects of Framing 7f

Another consideration in making decisions involving risks is the framing of questions (Tversky & Kahneman, 1988, 1991). ***Framing* refers to how decision issues are posed or how choices are structured.** People often allow a decision to be shaped by the language or context in which it's presented, rather than explore it from different perspectives. Consider the following scenario adapted from Kahneman and Tversky (1984, p. 343):

Imagine that the U.S. is preparing for the outbreak of a dangerous disease, which is expected to kill 600 people. Two alternative programs to combat the disease have been proposed. Assume that the exact scientific estimates of the consequences of the programs are as follows.

- *If Program A is adopted, 200 people will be saved.*
- *If Program B is adopted, there is a one-third probability that all 600 people will be saved and a two-thirds probability that no people will be saved.*

Kahneman and Tversky found that 72% of their subjects chose the "sure thing" (Program A) over the "risky gamble" (Program B). However, they obtained different results when the alternatives were reframed as follows:

- *If Program C is adopted, 400 people will die.*
- *If Program D is adopted, there is a one-third probability that nobody will die and a two-thirds probability that all 600 people will die.*

Although framed differently, Programs A and B represent the same probability situation as Programs C and D (see **Figure 8.21**). In spite of this, 78% of the subjects chose Program D. Thus, subjects chose the sure thing when the decision was framed in terms of lives saved. They went with the risky gamble, however, when the decision was framed in terms of lives lost. Obviously, sound decision making should yield consistent decisions that are not altered dramatically by superficial changes in how options are presented, so framing effects once again highlight the foibles of human decision making.

Loss Aversion

Another interesting phenomenon is *loss aversion*—in general, losses loom larger than gains of equal size (Kahneman & Tversky, 1979; Novemsky & Kahneman, 2005). Thus, most people expect that the negative impact of losing $1000 will be greater than the positive impact of wining $1000. Loss aversion can lead people to pass up excellent opportunities. For instance, subjects tend to decline a theoretical gamble in which they are given an 85% chance of doubling their life savings versus a 15% chance of losing their life savings, which mathematically is vastly more attractive than any bet one could place in a casino (Gilbert, 2006). Loss aversion can influence decisions in many areas of life, including choices of consumer goods, investments, business negotiations, and approaches to health care (Camerer, 2005; Klapper, Ebling, & Temme, 2005).

The problem with loss aversion, as Daniel Gilbert and his colleagues have shown, is that people generally overestimate the intensity and duration of the negative emotions they will experience after all sorts of losses, ranging from losing a job or romantic partner to botching an interview or watching one's team lose in a big game (Gilbert, Driver-Linn, & Wilson, 2002; Kermer et al., 2006) (see Chapter 10). Interestingly, people overestimate the emotional impact of losses because they do not appreciate how good most of us are at rationalizing, discounting, and distorting negative events in our lives.

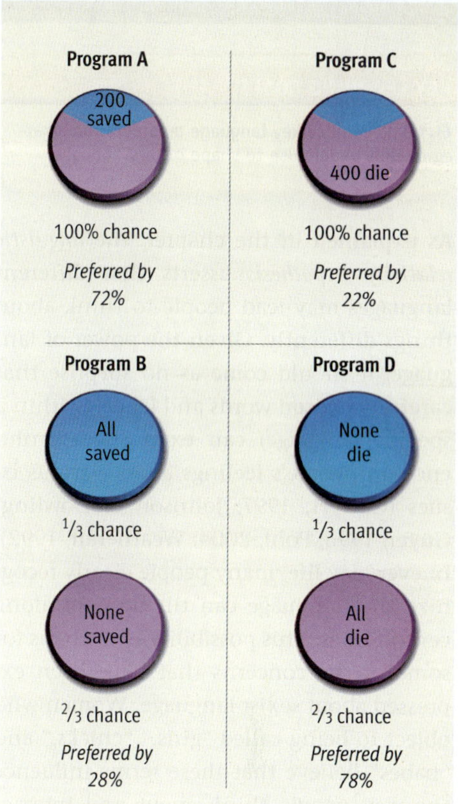

© Cengage Learning 2013

Figure 8.21
The framing of questions. This chart shows that Programs A and B are parallel in probability to Programs C and D, but these parallel pairs of alternatives lead subjects to make different choices. Studies show that when choices are framed in terms of possible gains, people prefer the safer plan. However, when choices are framed in terms of losses, people are more willing to take a gamble.

REVIEW OF KEY LEARNING GOALS

8.16 The gambler's fallacy is the belief that the odds of a chance event increase if the event hasn't occurred recently. People tend to inflate estimates of improbable events that garner heavy coverage in the media because of the availability heuristic.

8.17 People often exhibit confirmation bias—the tendency to only seek information that supports one's view. Myside bias is the tendency to evaluate evidence in a manner slanted in favor of one's own opinions.

8.18 Framing refers to how decision issues are posed or how choices are structured. Decisions can be influenced by the language in which they are framed. Most people expect that the negative impact of a loss will be greater than the positive impact of a similar gain. But research shows that people overestimate the impact of losses.

KEY LEARNING GOALS

8.19 Recognize key language manipulation strategies that people use to shape others' thought.

Shaping Thought with Language: "Only a Naive Moron Would Believe That"

As explained in the chapter, the *linguistic relativity hypothesis* asserts that different languages may lead people to think about things differently. Given the power of language, it should come as no surprise that carefully chosen words and labels (within a specific language) can exert subtle influence on people's feelings about various issues (Calvert, 1997; Johnson & Dowling-Guyer, 1996; Pohl, 2004; Weatherall, 1992). In everyday life, many people clearly recognize that language can tilt thought along certain lines. This possibility is the basis for some of the concerns that have been expressed about sexist language. Women who object to being called "girls," "chicks," and "babes" believe that these terms influence the way people think about and interact with women. In a similar vein, car dealerships that sell "preowned cars" and airlines that outline precautions for "water landings" are manipulating language to influence thought. Indeed, bureaucrats, politicians, advertisers, and big business have refined the art of shaping thought by tinkering with language, and to a lesser degree the same techniques are used by many people in everyday interactions. Let's look at two of these techniques: semantic slanting and name calling.

Semantic Slanting

Semantic slanting refers to deliberately choosing words to create specific emotional responses. For example, consider the crafty word choices made in the incendiary debate about abortion (Halpern, 1996). The anti-abortion movement recognized that it's better to be *for* something than to be *against* something and then decided to characterize its stance as "pro-life" rather than "anti-choice." Likewise, the faction that favored abortion did not like the connotation of an "anti-life" or "pro-abortion" campaign, so they characterized their position as "pro-choice." The position advocated is exactly the same either way. Yet the label clearly influences how people respond. Thinking along similar lines, some "pro-life" advocates have asserted that the best way to win the debate about abortion is to frequently use the words *kill* and *baby* in the same sentence (Kahane, 1992). Obviously, these are words that push people's buttons and trigger powerful emotional responses.

In his book *Doublespeak,* William Lutz (1989) provided an endless series of examples of how government, business, and advertisers manipulate language to bias people's thoughts and feelings. For example, in the language of the military, an invasion is a "preemptive counterattack," bombing the enemy is providing "air support," civilians accidentally killed or wounded by military strikes are "collateral damage," and troops killed by their own troops are "friendly casualties." In the world of business, layoffs and firings become "headcount reductions" or "workforce adjustments," whereas bad debts become "nonperforming assets." And in the language of bureaucrats, hospital deaths become "negative patient care outcomes" and tax increases become "revenue enhancement initiatives," leading Lutz to quip that "Nothing in life is certain except negative patient care outcome and revenue enhancement." You can't really appreciate how absurd this process can become until you go shopping for "genuine imitation leather" or "real counterfeit diamonds."

You don't have to be a bureaucrat or military spokesperson to use semantic slanting. If a friend of yours is annoyed at her 60-year-old professor for giving a tough exam and describes him as an "old geezer," she would be using semantic slanting. She would have communicated that the professor's age is a negative factor—one that is associated with a host of unflattering stereotypes about older people. And she would

© Joe Sohm/The Image Works

Semantic slanting, which consists of carefully choosing words to create specific emotional reactions, has been used extensively by both sides in the debate about abortion.

© AP Images/Cliff Owen

Briefings on the status of miliary actions are renowned for their creative but unintelligible manipulation of language, which is often necessary to obscure the unpleasant realities of war.

have implied that he gave a bad exam because of his outdated views or senility—all with a couple of well-chosen words. We are all the recipients of many such messages containing emotionally filled words and content. An important critical thinking skill is to recognize when semantic slanting is being used to influence how you think, so you can resist this subtle technique.

Take note of how the people around you and in the media refer to people from other racial and ethnic groups. You can probably determine a politician's attitude toward immigration, for example, by considering the words he or she uses when speaking about people from other countries. Are the students on your campus who come from outside the United States referred to as "international students" or "foreign students"? The term "international" seems to convey a more positive image, with associations of being cosmopolitan and worldly. On the other hand, the term "foreign" suggests someone who is strange. Clearly, it pays to be careful when selecting the words you use in your own communication.

Name Calling

Another way that word choice influences thinking is in the way people tend to label and categorize others through the strategy of *name calling.* People often attempt to neutralize or combat views they don't like by attributing such views to "radical feminists," "knee-jerk liberals," "right-wingers," "religious zealots," or "extremists." In everyday interactions, someone who inspires our wrath may be labeled as a "bitch," a "moron," or a "cheapskate." In these examples, the name calling is not subtle and is easy to recognize.

But name calling can also be used with more cunning and finesse. Sometimes, there is an *implied threat* that if you make an unpopular decision or arrive at a conclusion that isn't favored, a negative label will be applied to you. For instance, someone might say, "Only a naive moron would believe that" to influence your attitude on an issue. This strategy of *anticipatory name calling* makes it difficult for you to declare that you favor the negatively valued belief because it means that you make yourself look like a "naive moron." Anticipatory name calling can also invoke positive group memberships, such as asserting that "all true Americans will agree . . ." or "people in the know think that . . ." Anticipatory name calling is a shrewd tactic that can be effective in shaping people's thinking.

Regardless of your position on these issues, how would you respond to someone who says, "Only a knee-jerk liberal would support racial quotas or affirmative action programs that give unfair advantages to minorities." Or "Only a stupid bigot would oppose affirmative action programs that rectify the unfair discrimination that minorities face." Can you identify the anticipatory name calling and the attempts at semantic slanting in each of these examples? More important, can you resist attempts like these to influence how you think about complex social issues?

Table 8.5 Critical Thinking Skills Discussed in This Application

Skill	Description
Understanding the way language can influence thought	The critical thinker appreciates that when you want to influence how people think, you should choose your words carefully.
Recognizing semantic slanting	The critical thinker is vigilant about how people deliberately choose certain words to elicit specific emotional responses.
Recognizing name calling and anticipatory name calling	The critical thinker is on the lookout for name calling and the implied threats used in anticipatory name calling.

© Cengage Learning 2013

REVIEW OF KEY LEARNING GOALS

8.19 Language can exert subtle influence over how people feel about various issues. Semantic slanting refers to the deliberate choice of words to create specific emotional responses, as has been apparent in the debate about abortion. In anticipatory name calling, there's an implied threat that a negative label will apply to you if you express certain views.

Chapter 8 Practice Test

1. The 2-year-old child who refers to every four-legged animal as "doggie" is making which of the following errors?
   A. underextension
   B. overextension
   C. overregularization
   D. underregularization

2. Research suggests that bilingualism has a negative effect on:
   A. language development.
   B. cognitive development.
   C. metalinguistic awareness.
   D. none of the above.

3. Based on the work with Kanzi, which statement best summarizes the current status of the research on whether chimps can learn language?
   A. Chimps can acquire the use of symbols but cannot combine them into sentences or learn rules of language.
   B. Chimps are nearly as well suited for learning and using language as humans.
   C. Chimps are incapable even of learning the symbols of a language.
   D. Chimps can learn some basic language skills, but the linguistic capacities of humans are far superior.

4. Chomsky proposed that children learn language swiftly:
   A. because they possess an innate language acquisition device.
   B. through imitation, reinforcement, and shaping.
   C. as the quality of their thought improves with age.
   D. because they need to in order to get their increasingly complex needs met.

5. The linguistic relativity hypothesis is the notion that:
   A. one's language determines the nature of one's thought.
   B. one's thought determines the nature of one's language.
   C. language and thought are separate and independent processes.
   D. language and thought interact, with each influencing the other.

6. The nine-dot problem is:
   A. often solved suddenly with a burst of insight.
   B. difficult because people assume constraints that are not part of the problem.
   C. solved through fast mapping.
   D. both a and b.

7. Problems that require a common object to be used in an unusual way may be difficult to solve because of:
   A. mental set.
   B. irrelevant information.
   C. unnecessary constraints.
   D. functional fixedness.

8. A heuristic is:
   A. a flash of insight.
   B. a guiding principle or "rule of thumb" used in problem solving or decision making.
   C. a methodical procedure for trying all possible solutions to a problem.
   D. a way of making a compensatory decision.

9. Which of the following is *not* a heuristic used in solving problems?
   A. Working backward
   B. Fast mapping
   C. Forming subgoals
   D. Searching for analogies

10. According to Nisbett, Eastern cultures tend to favor a(n) _________ cognitive style, whereas Western cultures tend to display a(n) _________ cognitive style.
    A. analytic; holistic
    B. holistic; analytic
    C. heuristic; algorythmic
    D. algorythmic; heuristic

11. The theory of bounded rationality was originally developed by:
    A. Herbert Simon.
    B. Noam Chomsky.
    C. Steven Pinker.
    D. Gerd Gigerenzer.

12. When you estimate the probability of an event by judging the ease with which relevant instances come to mind, you are relying on:
    A. an additive decision-making model.
    B. the representativeness heuristic.
    C. the availability heuristic.
    D. a noncompensatory model.

13. The belief that the probability of heads is higher after a long string of tails:
    A. is rational and accurate.
    B. is an example of the "gambler's fallacy."
    C. reflects the influence of the representativeness heuristic.
    D. includes both b and c.

14. The tendency to overestimate the probability of events that get heavy media coverage reflects the operation of:
    A. framing effects.
    B. the representativeness heuristic.
    C. the availability heuristic.
    D. mental set.

15. If someone says, "Only a congenital pinhead would make that choice," this use of language would represent:
    A. confirmation bias.
    B. syntactic slanting.
    C. anticipatory name calling.
    D. telegraphic speech.

Answers

1 B p. 317	6 D p. 327	11 A p. 333
2 D pp. 318–319	7 D p. 326	12 C p. 337
3 D p. 320	8 B p. 328	13 D p. 342
4 A p. 322	9 B pp. 328–330	14 C p. 342
5 A p. 323	10 B p. 332	15 C p. 345

Chapter 8 Media Resources

PsykTrek

To view a demo: **www.cengage.com/psychology/psyktrek**
To order: **www.cengage.com/psychology/weiten**
Go to the PsykTrek website or CD-ROM for further study of the concepts in this chapter. Both online and on the CD-ROM, PsykTrek includes dozens of learning modules with videos, animations, and quizzes, as well as simulations of psychological phenomena and a multimedia glossary that includes word pronunciations.

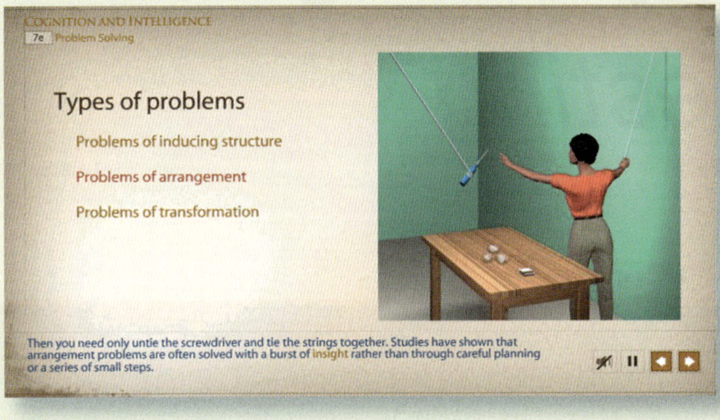

© Cengage Learning 2008

Go to Module 7e (*Problem Solving*) to learn about common barriers to effective problem solving.

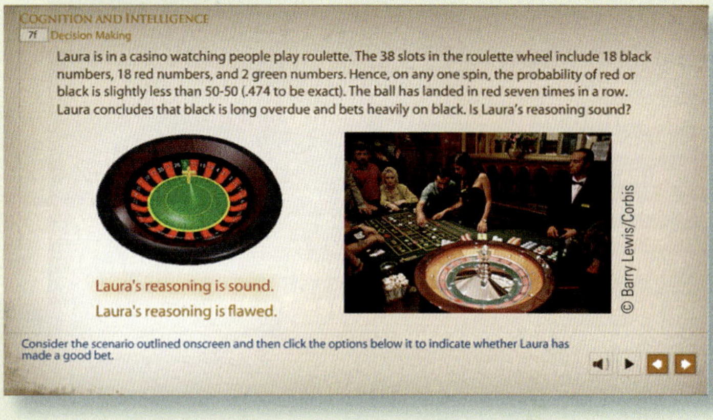

© Cengage Learning 2008

Visit Module 7f (*Decision Making*) to learn why people routinely make decisions that are riddled with errors and biases that yield surprisingly irrational results.

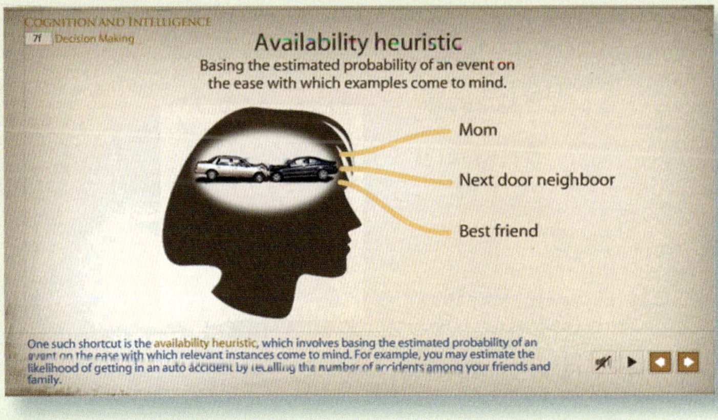

© Cengage Learning 2008

Access Module 7f (*Decision Making*) to enhance your understanding of the heuristics that people rely on in reasoning about decisions.

© Cengage Learning 2008

Try Simulation 7 (*Problem Solving*) to see if you can solve the classic hobbits and orcs problem that has been studied by generations of psychologists (it is not easy!).

Online Study Tools

Log in to **CengageBrain** to access the resources your instructor requires. For this book, you can access:

CourseMate brings course concepts to life with interactive learning, study, and exam preparation tools that support the printed textbook. A textbook-specific website, Psychology CourseMate includes an integrated interactive eBook and other interactive learning tools such as quizzes, flashcards, videos, and more.

CengageNow is an easy-to-use online resource that helps you study in less time to get the grade you want—NOW. Take a pre-test for this chapter and receive a personalized study plan based on your results that will identify the topics you need to review and direct you to online resources to help you master those topics. Then take a post-test to help you determine the concepts you have mastered and what you will need to work on. If your textbook does not include an access code card, go to CengageBrain.com to gain access.

WebTutor is more than just an interactive study guide. WebTutor is an anytime, anywhere customized learning solution with an eBook, keeping you connected to your textbook, instructor, and classmates.

Aplia. If your professor has assigned Aplia homework:

1. Sign in to your account
2. Complete the corresponding homework exercises as required by your professor.
3. When finished, click "Grade It Now" to see which areas you have mastered, which need more work, and detailed explanations of every answer.

Visit **www.cengagebrain.com** to access your account and purchase materials.

9

Intelligence and Psychological Testing

© Curtis Johnson/Getty Images

Have you ever thought about the role that psychological testing has played in your life? In all likelihood, your years in grade school and high school were filled with a variety of intelligence tests, achievement tests, aptitude tests, and occupational interest tests. In the lower grades, you were probably given standardized achievement tests once or twice a year. Perhaps you still have vivid memories of the serious atmosphere in the classroom, the very formal instructions ("Do not break the seal on this test until your examiner tells you to do so"), and the heavy pressure to work fast (I can still see Sister Dominic marching back and forth with her intense gaze riveted on her stopwatch).

Where you're sitting at this very moment may have been influenced by your performance on standardized tests. That is, the college you chose to attend may have hinged on your SAT or ACT scores. Moreover, your interactions with standardized tests may be far from finished. Even at this point in your life, you may be selecting your courses to gear up for the Graduate Record Exam (GRE) or the Medical College Admission Test (MCAT). After graduation, when you go job hunting, you may find that employers expect you to take still more psychological tests as they attempt to assess your personality, your motivation, and your talents.

The vast enterprise of modern testing evolved from psychologists' pioneering efforts to measure *general intelligence*. The first useful intelligence tests, which were created soon after the turn of the 20th century, left a great many "descendants." Today, over 2600 published psychological tests measure a diverse array of mental abilities and other behavioral traits. Indeed, psychological testing has become a big business that annually generates hundreds of millions of dollars in revenue (Koocher & Rey-Casserly, 2003).

© Chad McDermott/Shutterstock

Because your life is so strongly affected by how you perform on psychological tests, it pays to be aware of their strengths and limitations. In this chapter we'll explore many questions about testing, including the following:

- How did psychological testing become so prevalent in modern society?
- How do psychologists judge the validity of their tests?
- What exactly do intelligence tests measure?
- Is intelligence inherited? If so, to what extent?
- How do psychological tests measure creativity?

We'll begin by introducing some basic concepts in psychological testing. Then we'll explore the history of intelligence tests. Next we'll address practical questions about how intelligence tests work. After examining the nature versus nurture debate as it relates to intelligence, we'll explore some new directions in the study of intelligence. In the Personal Application, we'll discuss efforts to measure and understand another type of mental ability: creativity. In the Critical Thinking Application, we'll critique some of the reasoning used in the vigorous debate about the roots of intelligence.

KEY LEARNING GOALS

9.1 List and describe the principal categories of psychological tests.

9.2 Clarify the concepts of standardization and test norms.

9.3 Explain the meaning of test reliability and how it is estimated.

9.4 Distinguish among three types of validity.

Key Concepts in Psychological Testing

A ***psychological test*** **is a standardized measure of a sample of a person's behavior.** Psychological tests are measurement instruments. They're used to measure the *individual differences* among people in their abilities, aptitudes, interests, and aspects of personality.

Your responses to a psychological test represent a *sample* of your behavior. The word *sample* should alert you to one of the key limitations of psychological tests: A particular behavior sample may not be representative of your characteristic behavior. Everyone has bad days. A stomachache, a fight with a friend, a problem with your car—all might affect your responses to a particular test on a particular day.

This sampling problem is not unique to psychological testing. It's an unavoidable problem for any measurement technique that relies on sampling. For example, a physician taking your blood pressure might get an unrepresentative reading. Likewise, a football scout clocking a prospect's 40-yard sprint might get a misleading figure. Because of the limitations of the sampling process, test scores should always be interpreted *cautiously.*

© Bob Daemmrich/The ImagesWorks

Principal Types of Tests

PSYKTREK 7a

Psychological tests are used extensively in research. Most of them, though, were developed to serve a practical purpose outside of the lab. Most tests can be placed in one of two broad categories: mental ability tests and personality tests.

Mental Ability Tests

PSYKTREK 7a

Psychological testing originated with efforts to measure general mental ability. Today, tests of mental abilities remain the most common kind of psychological test. This broad class of tests includes three principal subcategories: intelligence tests, aptitude tests, and achievement tests.

Intelligence tests **measure general mental ability.** They're intended to assess intellectual potential rather than previous learning or accumulated knowledge. *Aptitude tests* are also designed to measure potential more than knowledge, but they break mental ability into separate components. Thus, ***aptitude tests*** **assess specific types of mental abilities.** For example, the Differential Aptitude Tests assess verbal reasoning, numerical ability, abstract reasoning, perceptual speed and accuracy, mechanical reasoning, space relations, spelling, and language usage. Like aptitude tests, *achievement tests* have a specific focus. However, they're supposed to measure previous learning instead of potential. Thus, ***achievement tests*** **gauge a person's mastery and knowledge of various subjects** (such as reading, English, or history).

Personality Tests

7a

If you had to describe yourself in a few words, what words would you use? Are you introverted? Independent? Ambitious? Enterprising? Conventional? Assertive? Domineering? Words such as these refer to personality traits. These *traits* can be assessed systematically with personality tests. There are more than 500 such tests. ***Personality tests* measure various aspects of personality, including motives, interests, values, and attitudes.** Many psychologists prefer to call these tests personality *scales* because, unlike tests of mental abilities, the questions do not have right or wrong answers. We'll look at the various types of personality scales in our upcoming chapter on personality (Chapter 12).

Standardization and Norms

SIM8, 7b

Both personality scales and tests of mental abilities are *standardized* measures of behavior. ***Standardization* refers to the uniform procedures used in the administration and scoring of a test.** All subjects get the same instructions, the same questions, and the same time limits so that their scores can be compared meaningfully. This means, for instance, that a person taking the Differential Aptitude Tests (DAT) in 1992 in San Diego, another taking the DAT in 2002 in Baltimore, and someone else taking it in 2012 in Peoria all confront the same test-taking task.

The standardization of a test's scoring system includes the development of test norms. ***Test norms* provide information about where a score on a psychological test ranks in relation to other scores on that test.** Test norms are important because in psychological testing everything is relative. Psychological tests tell you how you score *relative to other people*. They tell you, for instance, that you are average in creativity or slightly above average in clerical ability. These interpretations are derived from the test norms that help you understand what your test score means.

Usually, test norms allow you to convert your "raw score" on a test into a *percentile*. **A *percentile score* indicates the percentage of people who score at or below the score one has obtained.** Imagine that you take a 40-item assertiveness test and obtain a raw score of 26. In other words, you indicate a preference for the assertive option on 26 of the questions. Your score of 26 has little meaning until you consult the test norms and find out that it places you at the 82nd percentile. This normative information would indicate that you're as assertive as or more assertive than 82% of the sample of people who took the same test.

The sample of people the norms are based on is called a test's *standardization group* or *norm group*. Ideally, test norms are based on a large sample of people who were carefully selected to be representative of the broader population. For example, the norms for most intelligence tests are based on samples of 2000–6000 people whose demographic characteristics closely match the overall demographics of the United States (Woodcock, 1994). Norms for psychological tests need to be updated periodically with contemporary samples, as they may gradually grow old and out-of-date (Wasserman & Bracken, 2003). Intelligence tests have been standardized carefully, but the representativeness of standardization groups for other types of tests varies considerably.

Reliability

SIM8, 7b

Any kind of measuring device, whether it's a tire gauge, a bathroom scale, a stopwatch, or a psychological test, should be reasonably consistent. That is, repeated measurements should yield reasonably similar results. Psychologists call this quality *reliability*. To better appreciate the importance of reliability, think about how you would react if your bathroom scale were to give you several very different weights one morning. You would probably conclude that the scale was broken and think about replacing it. Consistency is essential to accuracy in measurement.

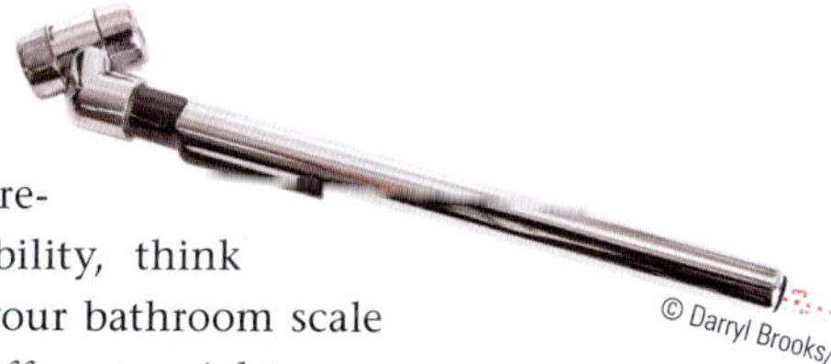
© Darryl Brooks/Shutterstock

***Reliability* refers to the measurement consistency of a test (or of other kinds of measurement techniques).** Psychological tests are not perfectly reliable. A test's reliability can be estimated in several ways (Hempel, 2005). One widely used approach is to check *test-retest reliability*, which is estimated by comparing subjects' scores on two administrations of a test. If we wanted to check the test-retest reliability of a newly developed test of assertiveness, we would ask a group of subjects to take the test on two occasions, probably a few weeks apart (see **Figure 9.1** on the next page). The idea is that assertiveness is a fairly stable aspect of personality that won't change in a matter of a few weeks. Thus, any changes in participants' scores across the two tests would likely reflect inconsistency in measurement.

Reliability estimates require the computation of correlation coefficients, which we introduced in

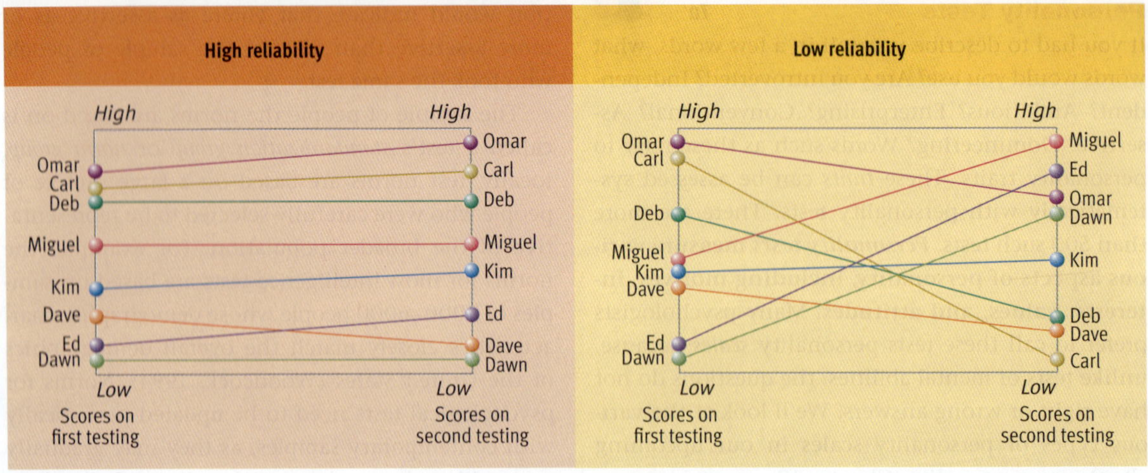

Figure 9.1

Test-retest reliability. In each panel, subjects' scores on the first administration of an assertiveness test are represented on the left, and their scores on a second administration of the same test a few weeks later are shown on the right. If participants obtain similar scores on both administrations, as in the left panel, the test measures assertiveness consistently and has high test-retest reliability. If they get very different scores on the second administration, as in the right panel, the test has low reliability.

Chapter 2 (see **Figure 9.2** for a brief review). **A *correlation coefficient* is a numerical index of the degree of relationship between two variables.** In estimating test-retest reliability, the two variables that must be correlated are the sets of scores from the two tests. If people get fairly similar scores on our two hypothetical assertiveness tests, this consistency yields a substantial positive correlation. The magnitude of the correlation gives us a precise indication of the test's consistency. The closer the correlation comes to +1.00, the more reliable the test is.

There are no absolute guidelines about acceptable levels of reliability. What's acceptable depends to some extent on the nature and purpose of the test (Fekken, 2000). The reliability estimates for most psychological tests range from the .70s through the .90s. The higher the reliability coefficient, the more consistent the test is. As reliability goes down, concern about measurement error increases. Tests that are used to make important decisions about people's lives should have reliability coefficients in the .90s (Nunnally & Bernstein, 1994).

Validity

PSYKTREK SIM8, 7b

Even if a test is quite reliable, we still need to be concerned about its validity. ***Validity* refers to the ability of a test to measure what it was designed to measure.** If we develop a new test of assertiveness, we have to provide some evidence that it really measures assertiveness. Increasingly, the term *validity* is also used to refer to the accuracy or usefulness of the *inferences* or *decisions* based on a test (Haladyna, 2006). This broader conception of validity highlights the fact that a specific test might be valid for one purpose, such as placing students in school, and invalid for another purpose, such as making employment decisions for a particular occupation. Va-

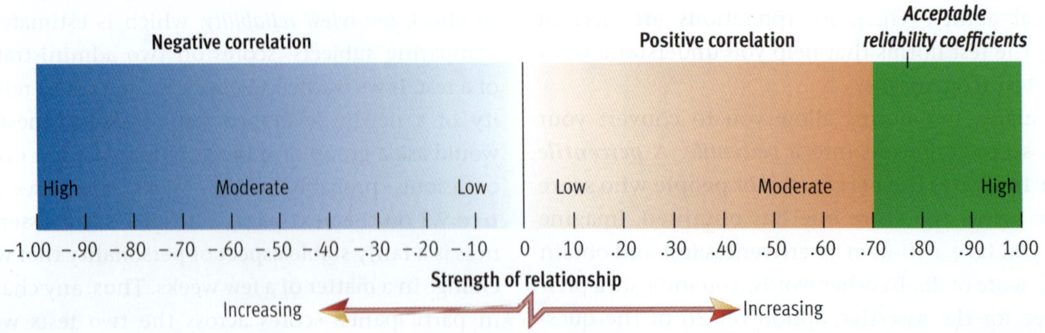

Figure 9.2

Correlation and reliability. As explained in Chapter 2, a positive correlation means that two variables co-vary in the *same* direction; a negative correlation means that two variables co-vary in the *opposite* direction. The closer the correlation coefficient gets to either −1.00 or +1.00, the stronger the relationship. At a minimum, reliability estimates for psychological tests must be fairly high positive correlations. Most reliability coefficients fall between .70 and .95. Tests used in "high stakes" testing should have reliability coefficients above .90. © Cengage Learning 2013 lidity can be estimated in several ways, depending on the nature and purpose of a test (Krueger & Kling, 2000; Wasserman & Bracken, 2003).

Content Validity 7b

Achievement tests and educational tests such as classroom exams should have adequate content validity. ***Content validity* refers to the degree to which the content of a test is representative of the domain it's supposed to cover.** Imagine a physics exam that includes questions on material that was not covered in class or in assigned reading. Such an exam would lack content validity. Achieving this type of validity depends on being able to clearly specify the content domain of interest (Kane, 2006).

Criterion-Related Validity 7b

Psychological tests are often used to make predictions about specific aspects of individuals' behavior, including performance in college, job capability, and suitability for training programs. Criterion-related validity is a central concern in such cases. ***Criterion-related validity* is estimated by correlating subjects' scores on a test with their scores on an independent criterion (another measure) of the trait assessed by the test.** For example, let's say you developed a test to measure aptitude for becoming an airplane pilot. You could check its validity by correlating subjects' scores on the aptitude test with subsequent ratings of their performance in their pilot training (see **Figure 9.3**). The performance ratings would be the independent criterion of pilot aptitude. If your test has reasonable validity, a fairly strong positive correlation should exist between your test and the pilot training ratings. Such a correlation would help validate your test's predictive ability.

Construct Validity 7b

Many psychological tests attempt to measure abstract personal qualities, such as creativity, intelligence, extraversion, or independence. No obvious criterion measures exist for these abstract qualities, which are called *hypothetical constructs*. In measuring abstract qualities, psychologists are concerned about ***construct validity*—the extent to which evidence shows that a test measures a particular hypothetical construct.**

The process of demonstrating construct validity can be complicated. It depends on starting with a clear idea of the hypothetical construct to be measured (Clark & Watson, 2003). Then it usually requires a series of studies that examine the correlations between the test and various measures *related* to the trait in question. A thorough demonstration of construct validity requires looking at the relations between a test and many other measures (Han, 2000). For example, some of the evidence on the construct validity of a measure of extraversion (the Expression scale from the Psychological Screening Inventory) is summarized in **Figure 9.4** on the next page. This network of correlation coefficients shows that the Expression scale correlates negatively, positively, or not at all with various measures, much as one would expect if the scale is really assessing extraversion. Ultimately, the overall pattern of correlations is what provides convincing (or unconvincing) evidence of a test's construct validity.

The complexities involved in showing construct validity will be apparent in our upcoming discussion of intelligence testing. The ongoing discussion about the construct validity of intelligence tests is one of the oldest debates in psychology. We'll look first at the origins of intelligence tests. This historical review will help you appreciate the current controversies about intelligence testing.

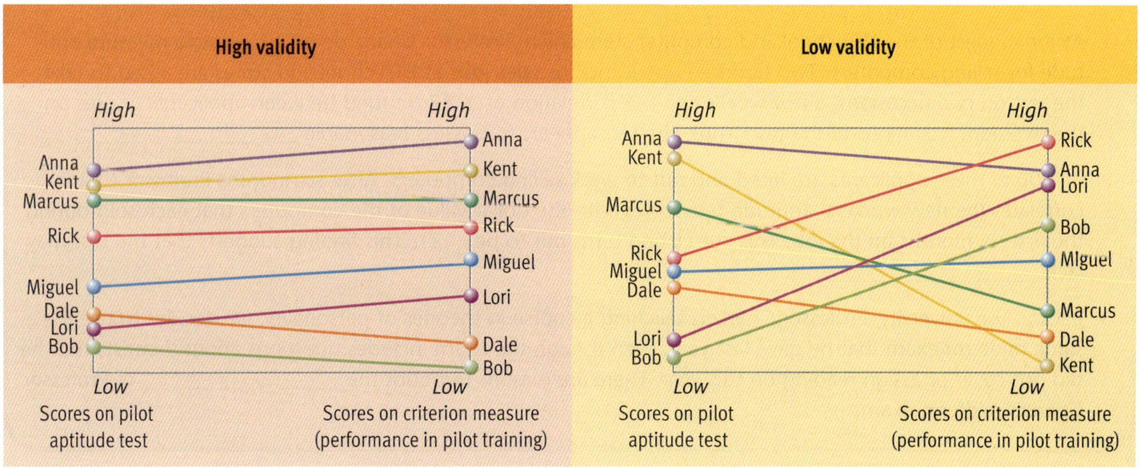

© Cengage Learning 2013

Figure 9.3
Criterion-related validity. To evaluate the criterion-related validity of a pilot aptitude test, a psychologist would correlate subjects' test scores with a criterion measure of their aptitude, such as ratings of their performance in a pilot training program. The validity of the test is supported if the people who score high on the test also score high on the criterion measure (as shown in the left panel), yielding a substantial correlation between the two measures. If little or no relationship exists between the two sets of scores (as shown in the right panel), the data do not provide support for the validity of the test.

Figure 9.4

Construct validity. Some of the evidence on the construct validity of the Expression Scale from the Psychological Screening Inventory is summarized here. This scale is supposed to measure the personality trait of *extraversion.* As you can see on the left side of this network of correlations, the scale correlates negatively with measures of social introversion, social discomfort, and neuroticism, just as one would expect if the scale is really tapping extraversion. On the right, you can see that the scale is correlated positively with measures of sociability and self-acceptance and another index of extraversion, as one would anticipate. At the bottom, you can see that the scale does not correlate either way with several traits that should be unrelated to extraversion. Thus, the network of correlations depicted here supports the idea that the Expression Scale measures the construct of extraversion. © Cengage Learning 2013

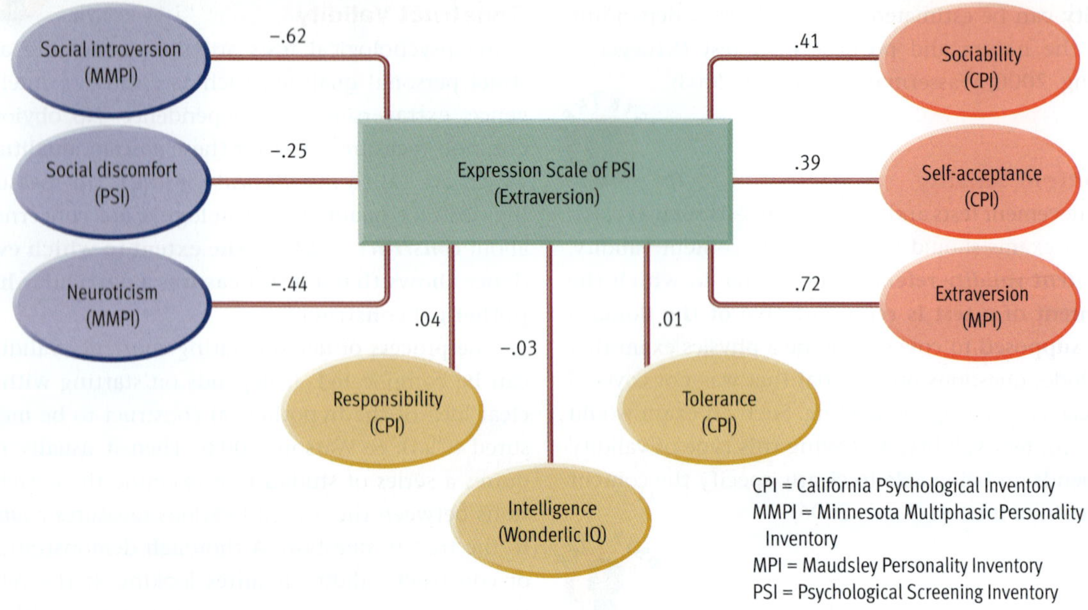

REVIEW OF KEY LEARNING GOALS

9.1 Psychological tests are standardized measures of behavior. Mental ability tests can be divided into intelligence tests, aptitude tests, and achievement tests. Personality tests measure behavioral traits, motives, and interests.

9.2 Standardization refers to the uniform procedures used in the administration and scoring of a test. Test scores are interpreted by consulting test norms to find out what represents a high or low score.

9.3 As measuring devices, psychological tests should produce consistent results, a quality called reliability. Test-retest reliability is estimated by comparing subjects' scores on two tests. Reliability estimates should yield fairly high positive correlations.

9.4 Validity refers to the degree to which there is evidence that a test measures what it was designed to measure. Content validity is crucial on classroom tests. Criterion-related validity is critical when tests are used to predict performance. Construct validity is critical when a test is designed to measure a hypothetical construct.

CONCEPT CHECK 9.1

Recognizing Basic Concepts in Testing

Check your understanding of basic concepts in psychological testing by answering the questions below. Select your responses from the following concepts. The answers are in Appendix A.

Test norms	Criterion-related validity
Test-retest reliability	Construct validity
Split-half reliability	Content validity

1. At the request of the HiTechnoLand computer store chain, Professor Charlz develops a test to measure aptitude for selling computers. Two hundred applicants for sales jobs at HiTechnoLand stores are asked to take the test on two occasions, a few weeks apart. A correlation of +.82 is found between applicants' scores on the two administrations of the test. Thus, the test appears to possess reasonable ________________.
2. All 200 of these applicants are hired and put to work selling computers. After six months Professor Charlz correlates the new workers' aptitude test scores with the dollar value of the computers that each sold during the first six months on the job. This correlation turns out to be −.21. This finding suggests that the test may lack ________________.
3. Back at the university, Professor Charlz is teaching a course in theories of personality. He decides to use the same midterm exam that he gave last year, even though the exam includes questions about theorists that he did not cover or assign reading on this year. There are reasons to doubt the ________________ of Professor Charlz's midterm exam.

The Evolution of Intelligence Testing

KEY LEARNING GOALS

9.5 Identify the contributions of Galton and Binet to the evolution of intelligence testing.

9.6 Summarize the contributions of Terman and Wechsler to the evolution of intelligence testing.

9.7 Outline the debate between Spearman and Thurstone about the structure of intelligence, and discuss the debate's current status.

Although the use of elaborate tests for selection purposes dates back to the Chinese Imperial examinations begun over 1400 years ago, the first modern psychological tests were invented only a little over a hundred years ago. Since then, reliance on psychological tests has grown gradually. In this section, we discuss the pioneers who launched psychological testing with their efforts to measure general intelligence.

Galton's Studies of Hereditary Genius

It all began with the work of a British scholar, Sir Francis Galton, in the later part of the 19th century. Galton, a cousin of Charles Darwin's, studied family trees and found that success and eminence appeared consistently in some families over generations. For the most part, these families were much like Galton's: well-bred, upper-class families with access to superior schooling. Yet Galton discounted the advantages of such an upbringing (Fancher, 2005). In his book *Hereditary Genius,* Galton (1869) concluded that success runs in families because great intelligence is passed from generation to generation through genetic inheritance.

To better demonstrate that intelligence is governed by heredity, Galton needed an objective measure of intelligence. He hypothesized that exceptionally bright people should exhibit exceptional sensory acuity. Working from this premise, he tried to assess innate mental ability by measuring simple sensory processes. Among other things, he measured sensitivity to high-pitched sounds, color perception, and reaction time (the speed of one's response to a stimulus). His efforts met with little success. Research eventually showed that the sensory processes he measured were largely unrelated to the criteria of mental ability that he was trying to predict, such as success in school or in professional life (Kaufman, 2000).

In pursuing this line of investigation, Galton coined the phrase *nature versus nurture* to refer to the heredity-environment issue (Fancher, 2009). He also pioneered the idea that the bell curve could be applied to psychological characteristics (Simonton, 2003). Along the way, he invented the concepts of *correlation* and *percentile test scores* as well (Roberts et al., 2005). Although Galton's mental tests were a failure, his work created an interest in the measurement of mental ability. This set the stage for a subsequent breakthrough by Alfred Binet, a prominent French psychologist.

Binet's Breakthrough

7c

In 1904 the Minister of Education in France asked Alfred Binet to devise a test to identify mentally subnormal children who could benefit from special education programs (Foschi & Ciciola, 2006). The commission was motivated by admirable goals. It wanted to avoid complete reliance on teachers' evaluations, which might often be subjective and biased.

In response to this need, Binet and a colleague, Theodore Simon, published the first useful test of general mental ability in 1905. They had the insight to load it with items that required abstract reasoning skills, rather than the sensory skills Galton had measured (Brody, 2000; Sternberg & Jarvin, 2003). Their scale was a success. It was inexpensive, easy to administer, objective, and capable of predicting children's performance in school fairly well (Siegler, 1992). Thanks to these qualities, its use spread across Europe and America.

The Binet-Simon scale expressed a child's score in terms of "mental level" or "mental age." A child's ***mental age* indicated that he or she displayed the mental performance typical of a child of that chronological (actual) age.** Thus, a child with a mental age of 6 performed like an average 6-year-old on the test at that point in time. Binet realized that his scale was a somewhat crude initial effort at measuring mental ability. He revised it in 1908 and again in 1911, the same year he died. Other psychologists then continued to build on Binet's work.

© Bettmann/Corbis

Alfred Binet

"The intelligence of anyone is susceptible of development. With practice, enthusiasm, and especially with method one can succeed in increasing one's attention, memory, judgment, and in becoming literally more intelligent than one was before."

Terman and the Stanford-Binet

7c

In America, Lewis Terman and his colleagues at Stanford University soon went to work on a major expansion and revision of Binet's test. Their work led to the 1916 publication of the Stanford-Binet Intelligence Scale (Terman, 1916). This revision was quite loyal to Binet's original conceptions. However, it incorporated a new scoring scheme based on William Stern's (1914) "intelligence quotient" (Minton, 2000). **An *intelligence quotient (IQ)* is a child's mental age divided by chronological age,**

Archives of the History of American Psychology, University of Akron, Akron, Ohio

Lewis Terman

"It is the method of tests that has brought psychology down from the clouds and made it useful to men; that has transformed the 'science of trivialities' into the 'science of human engineering.'"

multiplied by 100. As you can see, IQ scores originally involved actual quotients:

$$IQ = \frac{\text{Mental age}}{\text{Chronological age}} \times 100$$

The ratio of mental age to chronological age made it possible to compare children of different ages. In Binet's system, such comparisons had been awkward. Using the IQ ratio, all children (regardless of age) were placed on the same scale, which was centered at 100 if their mental age corresponded to their chronological age (see **Table 9.1** for examples of IQ calculations).

Terman made a strong case for the potential educational benefits of testing and became the key force behind American schools' widespread adoption of IQ tests (Chapman, 1988). As a result of his efforts, the Stanford-Binet quickly became the world's foremost intelligence test and the standard of comparison for virtually all intelligence tests that followed (White, 2000). Since its publication in 1916, the Stanford-Binet has been updated periodically, but the modern version remains true to the conception of intelligence originally put forth by Binet and Terman.

Wechsler's Innovations

PSYKTREK 7c

As chief psychologist at New York's massive Bellevue Hospital, David Wechsler was charged with overseeing the psychological assessment of thousands of adult patients. He found the Stanford-Binet somewhat unsatisfactory for this purpose. Thus, Wechsler set out to improve on the measurement of intelligence *in adults*. In 1939 he published the first high-quality IQ test designed specifically for adults, which came to be known as the Wechsler Adult Intelligence Scale (WAIS) (Wechsler, 1955, 1981, 1997). Ironically, Wechsler (1949, 1967, 1991, 2003) eventually devised downward extensions of his scale for children.

The Wechsler scales were characterized by at least two major innovations (Prifitera, 1994). First, Wechsler made his scales less dependent on subjects' verbal ability than the Stanford-Binet. He included many items that required nonverbal reasoning. Second, Wechsler discarded the intelligence

© 2004 by Sidney Harris/Science Cartoons Plus.com

quotient in favor of a new scoring scheme based on the *normal distribution*. This scoring system has since been adopted by most other IQ tests, including the Stanford-Binet. The term *intelligence quotient* lingers on in our vocabulary. But scores on intelligence tests are no longer based on an actual quotient. We'll take a close look at the modern scoring system for IQ tests a little later.

The Debate About the Structure of Intelligence

The first half of the 20th century also witnessed a long-running debate about the structure of intellect. The debate was launched by Charles Spearman, a British psychologist who invented a complicated statistical procedure called factor analysis. In ***factor analysis*, correlations among many variables are analyzed to identify closely related clusters of variables.** If a number of variables correlate highly with one another, the assumption is that a single factor is influencing all of them. Factor analysis attempts to identify these hidden factors.

Spearman (1904, 1927) used factor analysis to examine the correlations among tests of many specific mental abilities. He concluded that all cognitive abilities share an important core factor, which

Table 9.1 Calculating the Intelligence Quotient

Measure	Child 1	Child 2	Child 3	Child 4
Mental age (MA)	6 years	6 years	9 years	12 years
Chronological age (CA)	6 years	9 years	12 years	9 years
$IQ = \frac{MA}{CA} \times 100$	$\frac{6}{6} \times 100 = 100$	$\frac{6}{9} \times 100 = 67$	$\frac{9}{12} \times 100 = 75$	$\frac{12}{9} \times 100 = 133$

© Cengage Learning 2013

he labeled *g,* for *general* mental ability. Spearman recognized that people also have "special" abilities (such as numerical reasoning or spatial ability). However, he thought that individuals' ability in these specific areas is largely determined by their general mental ability (see **Figure 9.5**).

A very different view of the structure of intellect was soon proposed by L. L. Thurstone. He was an American psychologist who developed the test that evolved into the SAT (L. V. Jones, 2000). Using a somewhat different approach to factor analysis, Thurstone (1931b, 1938, 1955) concluded that intelligence involves multiple abilities. Thurstone argued that Spearman and his followers placed far too much emphasis on *g.* In contrast, Thurstone carved intelligence into seven independent factors called *primary mental abilities:* word fluency, verbal comprehension, spatial ability, perceptual speed, numerical ability, inductive reasoning, and memory.

The debate about the structure of intelligence continued for many decades, and in some respects the issue lingers in the background even today. Paradoxically, both views of the structure of intellect have remained influential. Armed with computers, modern researchers using enhanced approaches to factor analysis have shown again and again that batteries of cognitive tests are highly intercorrelated, as Spearman had suggested (Brody, 2005; Carroll, 1996; Gottfredson, 2009; Jensen, 1998). Researchers interested in the nature, determinants, and correlates of intelligence continue to focus heavily on the Holy Grail of *g* in their quest to understand mental ability.

However, in the 1980s, the developers of IQ tests began moving in the opposite direction. Their motivation was to give clinicians, educators, and school systems more information (than a single, global score) that could better aid them in the diagnosis of learning disabilities and the evaluation of children's potential. For theoretical guidance they turned to a model of intelligence that proposed that *g* should be divided into *fluid intelligence* and *crystallized intelligence* (Carroll, 1993; Cattell, 1963; Horn, 1985). ***Fluid intelligence* involves reasoning ability, memory capacity, and speed of information processing. *Crystallized intelligence* involves ability to apply acquired knowledge and skills in problem solving.** This distinction between fluid and crystallized intelligence led to further efforts to break *g* into basic components. These models have broadly guided the most recent revisions of the Stanford-Binet (Roid & Tippin, 2009), the Wechsler scales (O'Donnell, 2009), and many other IQ tests (Kaufman, 2009). Contemporary IQ tests are generally based on a hierarchical model of intelligence, which subdivides *g* into 10 to 15 specific abilities. The current version of the Stanford-Binet includes 10 subtests, and the most recent revision of a Wechsler scale has 15 subtests.

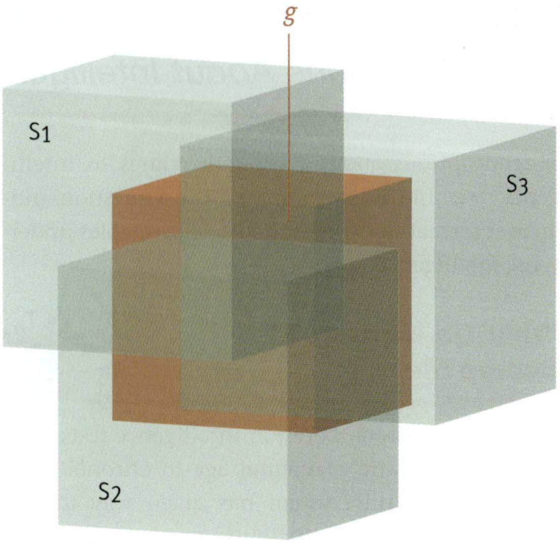

Figure 9.5

Spearman's *g.* In his analysis of the structure of intellect, Charles Spearman found that *specific* mental talents (S_1, S_2, S_3, and so on) were highly intercorrelated. Thus, he concluded that all cognitive abilities share a common core, which he labeled *g* for general mental ability. © Cengage Learning 2013

Thus, we have a curious paradox. Researchers and theorists tend to be obsessed with Spearman's *g.* However, clinicians and educators facing difficult diagnostic decisions, and the companies that develop tests for them, are more interested in the measurement of specific abilities in the tradition of Thurstone.

REVIEW OF KEY LEARNING GOALS

9.5 The first crude efforts to devise intelligence tests were made by Sir Francis Galton, who wanted to show that intelligence is inherited. Galton is also known for his pioneering work on correlation, percentiles, and the bell curve. Modern intelligence testing began with the work of Alfred Binet, a French psychologist who published the first useful intelligence test in 1905. Binet's scale measured a child's mental age.

9.6 Lewis Terman revised the original Binet scale to produce the Stanford-Binet in 1916. It introduced the intelligence quotient and became the standard of comparison for subsequent intelligence tests. David Wechsler devised an improved measure of intelligence for adults and a series of IQ tests that reduced the emphasis on verbal ability. He also introduced a new scoring system based on the normal distribution.

9.7 Spearman argued that all cognitive tests share a core, which he called *g,* whereas Thurstone asserted that intelligence is made up of many independent abilities. Both views remain influential today. Researchers are primarily interested in *g,* but contemporary IQ tests typically subdivide *g* into 10 to 15 specific abilities.

KEY LEARNING GOALS

9.8 Clarify the meaning of deviation IQ scores on modern intelligence tests.

9.9 Summarize evidence on the reliability and validity of modern IQ test scores.

9.10 Discuss the stability of IQ scores, and analyze how well they predict vocational success.

9.11 Discuss the use of IQ tests in non-Western cultures.

Basic Questions About Intelligence Testing

Misconceptions abound when it comes to intelligence tests. In this section, we'll use a question-and-answer format to explain the basic principles underlying intelligence testing.

What Do Modern IQ Scores Mean?

PsykTrek 7c

As we've discussed, scores on intelligence tests once represented a ratio of mental age to chronological age. However, this system has given way to one based on the normal distribution and the standard deviation (see Chapter 2). **The *normal distribution* is a symmetric, bell-shaped curve that represents the pattern in which many characteristics are dispersed in the population.** When a trait is normally distributed, most cases fall near the center of the distribution (an average score). The number of cases then gradually declines as one moves away from the center in either direction (see **Figure 9.6**).

The normal distribution was first discovered by 18th-century astronomers. They found that their measurement errors were distributed in a predictable way that resembled a bell-shaped curve. Since then, research has shown that many human traits, ranging from height to running speed to spatial ability, also follow a normal distribution. Psychologists eventually recognized that intelligence scores also fall into a normal distribution. This insight permitted David Wechsler to devise a more sophisticated scoring system for his tests that has been adopted by virtually all subsequent IQ tests. In this system, raw scores are translated into ***deviation IQ scores* that locate subjects precisely within the normal distribution, using the standard deviation as the unit of measurement.**

For most IQ tests, the mean of the distribution is set at 100 and the standard deviation (SD) is set at 15. These choices were made to provide continuity with the original IQ ratio (mental age to chronological age) that was centered at 100. In this system, which is shown in **Figure 9.6**, a score of 115 means that a person scored exactly one SD (15 points) above the mean. A score of 85 means that a person scored one SD below the mean. A score of 100 means that a person showed average performance. You don't really need to know how to work with standard deviations to understand this system (but if you're interested, consult Appendix B). *The key point is that modern IQ scores indicate exactly where you fall in the normal distribution of intelligence.* Thus, a score of 120 does not indicate that you answered 120 questions correctly. Nor does it mean that you have 120 "units" of intelligence. A deviation IQ score places you at a specific point in the normal distribution of intelligence.

Deviation IQ scores can be converted into percentile scores (see **Figure 9.6**). In fact, a major advantage of this scoring system is that a specific score on a specific test always translates into the same percentile score, regardless of the person's age group. The old system of IQ ratio scores lacked this consistency.

Do Intelligence Tests Have Adequate Reliability?

Do IQ tests produce consistent results when people are retested? Yes. Most IQ tests report commendable reliability estimates, with the correlations generally in the .90s (Kaufman, 2000). In comparison to most other types of psychological tests, IQ tests are exceptionally reliable. However, like other tests, they *sample* behavior, so a specific testing may yield an unrepresentative score.

Variations in examinees' motivation to take an IQ test or in their anxiety about the test can sometimes produce misleading scores (Hopko et al., 2005; Zimmerman & Woo-Sam, 1984). The most common problem is that low motivation or high anxiety may drag a person's score down on a particular occasion. For instance, a fourth-grader who is made to feel that the test is really important may get jittery and be unable to concentrate. The same child might score much higher on a subsequent testing by another examiner who creates a more comfortable atmosphere. Although the reliability of IQ tests is excellent, caution is always in order in interpreting test scores.

Do Intelligence Tests Have Adequate Validity?

Do intelligence tests measure what they're supposed to measure? Yes, but this answer has to be qualified very carefully. IQ tests are valid measures of the kind of intelligence that's necessary for one to do well in academic work. But if the purpose is to assess intelligence in a broader sense, the validity of IQ tests is debatable.

As you may recall, intelligence tests were originally designed with a relatively limited purpose in mind: to predict school performance. This has continued to be the principal purpose of IQ testing. As a result, efforts

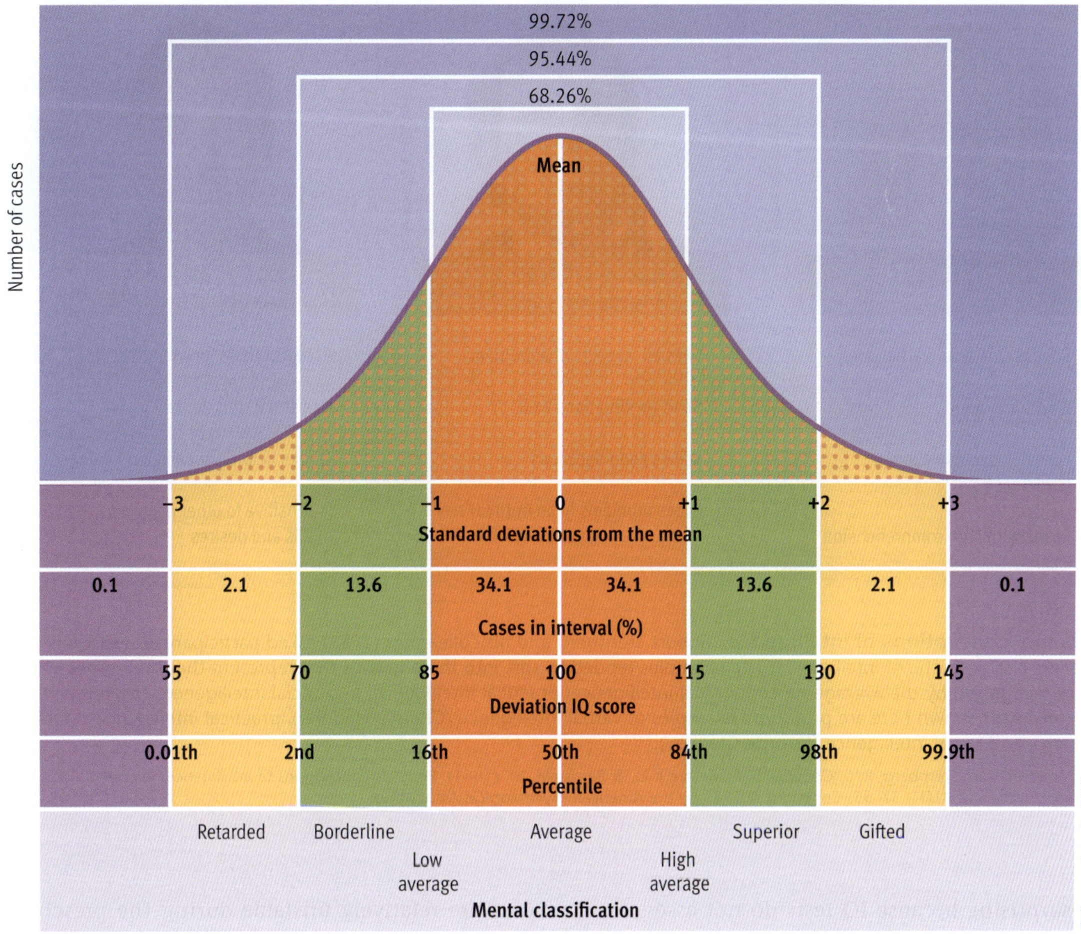

© Cengage Learning 2013

Figure 9.6

The normal distribution. Many characteristics are distributed in a pattern represented by this bell-shaped curve. The horizontal axis shows how far above or below the mean a score is (measured in plus or minus standard deviations). The vertical axis is used to graph the number of cases obtaining each score. In a normal distribution, the cases are distributed in a fixed pattern. For instance, 68.26% of the cases fall between +1 and −1 standard deviation. Modern IQ scores indicate where a person's measured intelligence falls in the normal distribution. On most IQ tests, the mean is set at an IQ of 100 and the standard deviation at 15. Any deviation IQ score can be converted into a percentile score. The mental classifications at the bottom of the figure are descriptive labels that roughly correspond to ranges of IQ scores.

to document the validity of IQ tests have usually concentrated on their relationship to grades in school. Typically, positive correlations in the .40s and .50s are found between IQ scores and school grades (Kline, 1991; Mackintosh, 1998). Moreover, a recent, huge study of over 70,000 children in England found an even stronger relationship between intelligence and educational achievement. Using composite measures of *g* and educational attainment, Deary and colleagues (2007) found correlations in the vicinity of .70.

These correlations are about as high as one could expect, given that many factors besides a person's intelligence are likely to affect grades and school progress. For example, school grades may be influenced by a student's motivation or personality, not to mention teachers' subjective biases. Indeed, a recent study reported that measures of students' *self-discipline* are surprisingly strong predictors of their school performance (Duckworth & Seligman, 2005). Other studies suggest that students' subjective perceptions of their abilities influence their academic performance, even after controlling for actual IQ (Greven et al., 2009; Spinath et al., 2006). In other words, holding actual IQ constant, students who *think* they are talented tend to perform somewhat better than those with more negative views of their ability. Thus, given all the other factors likely to influence performance in school, IQ tests appear to be reasonably valid indexes of school-related intellectual ability, or academic intelligence.

But the abilities assessed by IQ tests are not as broad or as general as widely assumed. When Robert Sternberg and his colleagues (1981) asked people to list examples of intelligence, they found that the examples fell into three categories: (1) *verbal intelligence,* (2) *practical intelligence,* and (3) *social intelligence* (see **Figure 9.7** on the next page). Thus, people generally recognize three basic components of intelligence. For the most part, IQ tests assess only the first of these three components, focusing somewhat narrowly on academic/verbal intelligence (Sternberg, 1998, 2003b).

Moreover, although the tests focus on *cognitive* abilities, Stanovich (2009) argues that they do not predict rational thinking and effective decision making in the real world nearly as well as we might expect. According to Stanovich, it is routine for people with high intelligence to make irrational, ill-advised decisions. He explains that this behavior

Reality CHECK

Misconception

IQ tests measure mental ability in a truly general sense.

Reality

IQ tests are characterized as measures of *general* mental ability, and the public has come to believe that IQ tests measure mental ability in a truly broad sense. In reality, however, IQ tests have always focused only on the abstract reasoning and verbal fluency that are essential to academic success. The tests do not tap social competence, practical problem solving, creativity, mechanical ingenuity, or artistic talent.

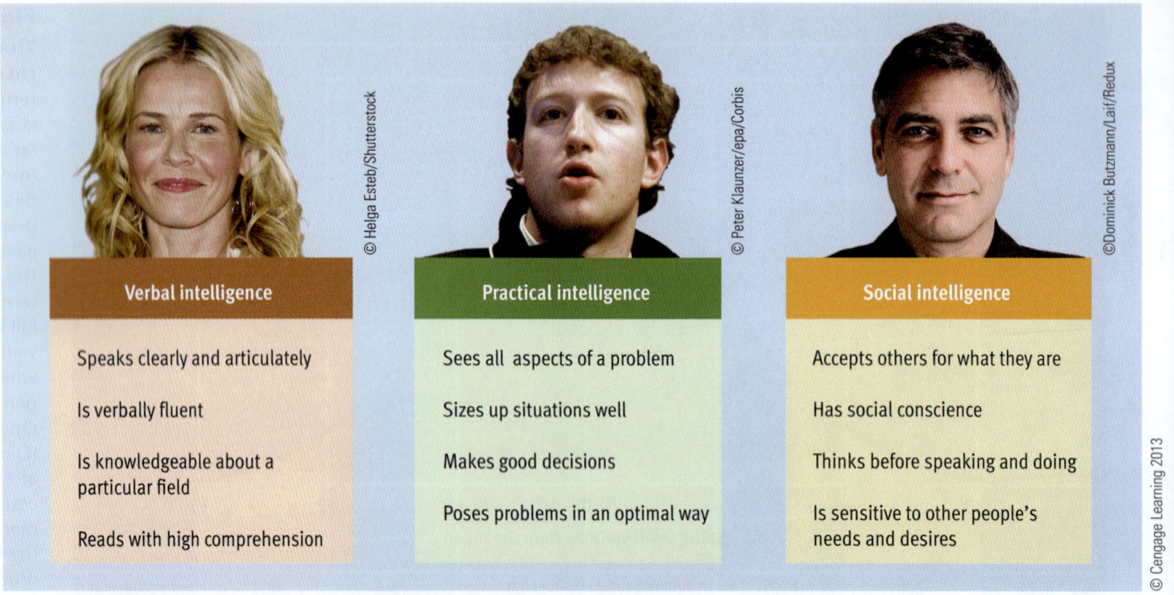

Figure 9.7

Laypersons' conceptions of intelligence. Robert Sternberg and his colleagues (1981) asked participants to list examples of behaviors characteristic of intelligence. The examples tended to sort into three groups that represent the three types of intelligence recognized by the average person: verbal intelligence, practical intelligence, and social intelligence. The three well-known individuals shown here are prototype examples of verbal intelligence (Chelsea Handler), practical intelligence (Mark Zuckerberg), and social intelligence (George Clooney).

SOURCE: Adapted from Sternberg, R. J., Conway, B. E., Keton, J. L., & Bernstein, M. (1981). People's conceptions of intelligence. *Journal of Personality and Social Psychology, 41*(1), 37–55. Copyright © 1981 by the American Psychological Association.

is not surprising because IQ tests do not assess the ability to think critically, weigh conflicting evidence, and engage in judicious reasoning.

Are Individuals' IQ Scores Stable Over Time?

You may have heard of hopeful parents who have their 2- or 3-year-old preschoolers tested to see whether they're exceptionally bright. These parents would have been better off saving their money, as IQ scores are relatively unstable during the preschool years and are not good predictors of scores in adolescence and adulthood. As children grow older, their IQ scores eventually stabilize (Brody, 1992; Hayslip, 1994). Note in **Figure 9.8** that at around the ages of 7 to 9, IQ tests become fairly accurate predictors of IQ at age 18. Studies that have followed participants into late adulthood have also found impressive stability. For instance, when Deary et al. (2000) tracked down subjects who had been tested at age 11 and retested them 66 years later at age 77, they found a correlation of .63 between the two testings. Although IQ scores tend to stabilize by age 9, substantial changes are seen in a sizable minority of people (Weinert & Hany, 2003). In conclusion, IQ scores tend to be stable, but they are not set in concrete.

Figure 9.8

The gradual stabilization of IQ scores. This graph plots the correlations between IQ scores obtained during childhood and subsequent adult IQ, measured at age 18. As you can see, preschool IQ scores are not very good predictors of adult IQ. However, IQ scores stabilize during the school years, and by age 9 the scores correlate in the .80s with adult IQ. (Adapted from Bayley, 1949)

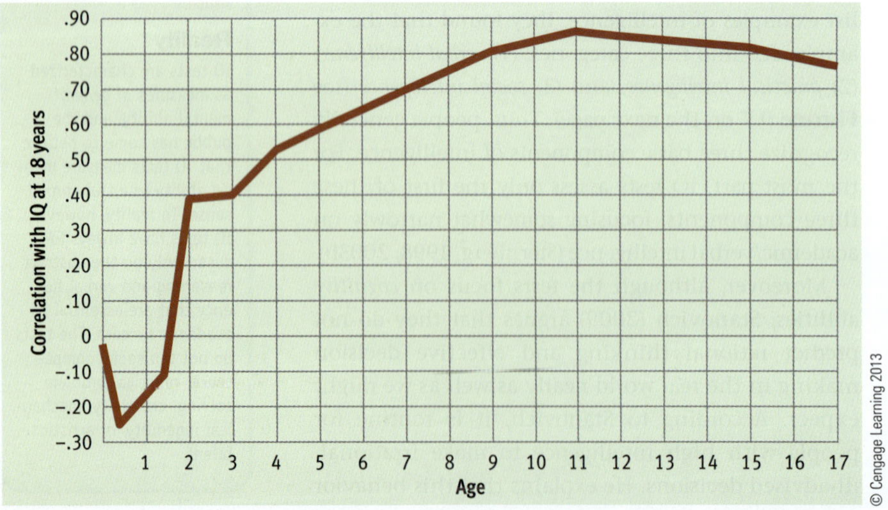

Reality CHECK

Misconception

Intelligence is a fixed, unchangeable trait, as IQ scores rarely change over time.

Reality

Intelligence is a fairly stable trait, but it definitely is not fixed. IQ scores merely indicate people's relative standing on a specific test at a specific age. This relative standing could improve or decline depending on people's circumstances. Some people experience significant changes in measured intelligence.

Do Intelligence Tests Predict Vocational Success?

Vocational success is a vague, value-laden concept that's difficult to quantify. Nonetheless, researchers have attacked this question by examining correlations between IQ scores and specific indicators of vocational success, such as income, the prestige of subjects' occupations, or ratings of subjects' job performance. The data relating IQ to occupational attainment are pretty clear. *People who score high on IQ tests are more likely than those who score low to end up in high-status jobs* (Gottfredson, 2003b; Herrnstein & Murray, 1994; Schmidt & Hunter, 2004). Because IQ tests measure school ability fairly well and because school performance is important in reaching certain occupations, this link between IQ scores and job status makes sense. Of course, the correlation between IQ and occupational attainment is moderate. For example, in a meta-analysis of many studies of the issue, Strenze (2007) found a correlation of .37 between IQ and occupational status. That figure means that there are plenty of exceptions to the general trend. Some people probably outperform brighter colleagues through bulldog determination and hard work. The relationship between IQ and income appears to be somewhat weaker. The meta-analysis by Strenze (2007) reported a correlation of .21 between IQ and income based on 31 studies. In one recent, large-scale study of American baby boomers, the correlation between intelligence and income was .30 (Zagorsky, 2007). These findings suggest that intelligence fosters vocational success but that the strength of the relationship is modest.

There is far more debate about whether IQ scores are effective predictors of performance *within* a particular occupation. On the one hand, research suggests that (a) there is a substantial correlation (about .50) between IQ scores and job performance; (b) this correlation varies somewhat depending on the complexity of a job's requirements but does not disappear even for low-level jobs (see **Figure 9.9**); (c) this association holds up even when workers have more experience at their jobs; and (d) measures of specific mental abilities and personality traits are much less predictive of job performance than measures of intelligence (Gottfredson, 2002; Ones, Viswesvaran, & Dilchert, 2005; Schmidt, 2002).

On the other hand, critics note that a correlation of .50 provides only modest accuracy in prediction (accounting for about 25% of the variation in job performance) (Goldstein, Zedeck, & Goldstein, 2002; Sternberg & Hedlund, 2002). Concerns have also been raised that when IQ tests are used for job selection, they can have an adverse impact on employment opportunities for many minority groups that tend to score somewhat lower (on average) on such tests (Murphy, 2002; Outtz, 2002).

In the final analysis, there is no question that intelligence is associated with vocational success. There is, however, room for argument about whether this association is strong enough to justify reliance on IQ testing in hiring employees.

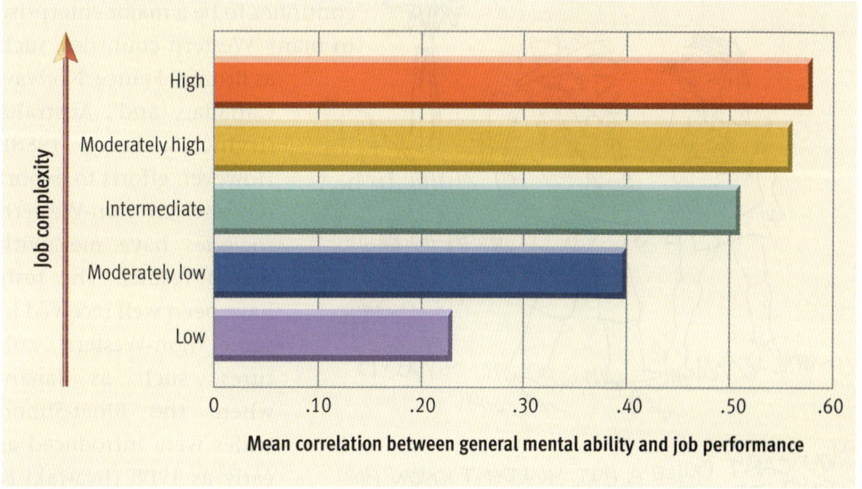

Figure 9.9

Intelligence as a predictor of job performance. Based on a review of 425 studies, Schmidt and Hunter (2004) report that the correlation between general mental ability and job performance depends on the complexity of the job. As jobs become more complicated, intelligence becomes a better predictor of performance. Schmidt and Hunter conclude that these correlations show that IQ tests can be valuable in hiring decisions. However, as the text explains, some other experts have reservations about using intelligence tests in employee selection.

Are IQ Tests Widely Used in Other Cultures?

In other Western cultures with European roots, IQ tests are widely used. In most non-Western cultures, they aren't. IQ testing has a long history and

The skills and knowledge that are crucial to success vary from one culture to the next. IQ tests were designed to assess the skills and knowledge valued in modern, Western cultures. They have proven useful in some non-Western cultures that value similar sets of skills, but they have also proven irrelevant in many cultures.

"YOU CAN'T BUILD A HUT, YOU DON'T KNOW HOW TO FIND EDIBLE ROOTS AND YOU KNOW NOTHING ABOUT PREDICTING THE WEATHER. IN OTHER WORDS, YOU DO TERRIBLY ON OUR I.Q. TEST."

© 2004 by Sidney Harris/Science Cartoons Plus.com

continues to be a major enterprise in many Western countries, such as Britain, France, Norway, Canada, and Australia (Irvine & Berry, 1988). However, efforts to export IQ tests to non-Western societies have met with mixed results. The tests have been well received in some non-Western cultures, such as Japan, where the Binet-Simon scales were introduced as early as 1908 (Iwawaki & Vernon, 1988). But they have been met with indifference or resistance in other cultures, such as China and India (Chan & Vernon, 1988; Sinha, 1983).

The bottom line is that Western IQ tests do not translate well into the language and cognitive frameworks of many non-Western cultures (Berry, 1994; Sternberg, 2004). Using an intelligence test with a cultural group other than the one for which it was originally designed can be problematic. The entire process of test administration, with its emphasis on rapid information processing, decisive responding, and the notion that ability can be quantified, is foreign to some cultures (Serpell, 2000). Moreover, different cultures have different conceptions of what intelligence is and value different mental skills (Baral & Das, 2004; Sato et al., 2004; Sternberg, 2007).

REVIEW OF KEY LEARNING GOALS

9.8 In the modern scoring system, deviation IQ scores indicate where people fall in the normal distribution of intelligence for their age group. On most tests, the mean is set at 100 and the standard deviation is set at 15.

9.9 IQ tests are exceptionally reliable. Reliability coefficients typically range into the .90s. IQ tests are reasonably valid measures of academic intelligence. They predict school grades and the number of years of school that people complete. However, they do not measure intelligence in a truly general sense.

9.10 IQ scores tend to stabilize around the ages of 7–9, but meaningful changes are possible. IQ scores are associated with occupational attainment and income, but the correlations are modest. There is active debate about whether IQ scores predict performance within an occupation well enough to be used in hiring decisions.

9.11 Intelligence testing is largely a Western enterprise. IQ tests are not widely used in most non-Western cultures. One reason is that different cultures have different conceptions of intelligence.

KEY LEARNING GOALS

9.12 Describe how intellectual disability is defined and divided into various levels.

9.13 Review what is known about the causes of intellectual disability.

9.14 Discuss the identification of gifted children and evidence on their personal qualities.

9.15 Articulate the drudge theory of exceptional achievement and alternative views.

Extremes of Intelligence

What are the cutoff scores for extremes in intelligence that lead children to be designated as mentally retarded or as gifted? On the low end, IQ scores roughly two standard deviations or more below the mean are regarded as subnormal. On the high end, children who score more than two or three standard deviations above the mean are regarded as gifted. However, designations of intellectual disability and giftedness should not be based exclusively on IQ test results. Let's look more closely at the evolving concepts of mental retardation and intellectual giftedness.

Intellectual Disability

The terminology used to refer to those who exhibit subnormal intelligence is undergoing a transition. For decades many authorities have expressed concerns about the term *retardation* because they see it as demeaning, stigmatizing, and powerful, in that people diagnosed with retardation seem to be totally defined by it (Bersani, 2007). These concerns finally led the American Association on Mental Retardation (AAMR) to change its name in 2006 to the American Association on Intellectual and Developmental Disabilities (AAIDD) (Schalock et al., 2007). The most recent edition of its classification manual, published in 2010, uses the term *intellectual disability* as a substitute for *mental retardation,* and U.S. federal laws are moving toward adopting the revised terminology. In this period of transition, I will use the two terms interchangeably here. One can only hope that the new terminology will eventually reduce the stigma associated with retardation. Unfortunately, such attitude change in the general public is far from a certainty. Since 1919 the official term for sub-

Table 9.2 Categories of Mental Retardation/Intellectual Disability

Category	IQ Range	Education Possible	Life Adaptation Possible
Mild	55–70	Typically, sixth grade by late teens; special education helpful; some graduate high school	Can be self-supporting in nearly normal fashion if environment is stable and supportive; may need help with stress
Moderate	40–55	Second to fourth grade by late teens; special education necessary	Can be semi-independent in sheltered environment; needs help with even mild stress
Severe	25–40	Limited speech, toilet habits, and so forth with systematic training	Can help contribute to self-support under total supervision
Profound	below 25	Little or no speech; not toilet-trained; relatively unresponsive to training	Requires total care

© Cengage Learning 2013

Note: As explained in the text, diagnoses of retardation should not be made on the basis of IQ scores alone.

normal intellectual functioning has been changed three times to make it less degrading (from feebleminded to mentally deficient to mentally retarded), but the stigma associated with intellectual disability remains strong (Detterman, 2010; King et al., 2009). In any event, ***mental retardation*** **or** ***intellectual disability*** **refers to subnormal general mental ability accompanied by deficiencies in adaptive skills, originating before age 18.** Adaptive skills consist of everyday living skills in three broad domains. These domains are *conceptual skills* (examples: managing money, writing a letter), *social skills* (making friends, coping with others' demands), and *practical skills* (preparing meals, using transportion, shopping).

There are two noteworthy aspects to this definition. First, the IQ criterion of subnormality is arbitrary. In the 1992 release of its classification manual, the AAMR (as it was then known) set a flexible cutoff line, which was an IQ score of 70 to 75 or below. This cutoff line could be drawn elsewhere. Indeed, the AAMR made the cutoff 70 (with caveats) in its 2002 edition and then returned to 70–75 in its 2010 edition. These periodic changes in the scoring norms for IQ tests have had erratic effects on the percentage of children falling below the cutoffs (Flynn, 2000; Kanaya, Scullin, & Ceci, 2003). Five IQ points may not sound like much. However, if the line is drawn exactly at 75 instead of 70, the number of people qualifying for special education programs doubles (King et al., 2009). Second, the requirement of deficits in everyday living skills is included because experts feel that high-stakes decisions should not be based on just a test score (Lichten & Simon, 2007). This requirement acknowledges that "school learning" is not the only important kind of learning. Unfortunately, the methods available for measuring everyday living skills have tended to be vague, imprecise, and subjective. Efforts to improve these assessments are under way (Detterman, Gabriel, & Ruthsatz, 2000; Lichten & Simon, 2007).

Levels

Historically, estimates of the prevalence of mental retardation in the population have varied between 1% and 3%. Recent evidence suggests that the prevalence of intellectual disability probably is around 1.5% (Ursano, Kartheiser, & Barnhill, 2008). Mental retardation has traditionally been classified into four levels characterized as mild, moderate, severe, or profound. **Table 9.2** lists the IQ range for each level and the typical behavioral and educational characteristics of individuals at each level.

As **Figure 9.10** shows, most of the people diagnosed with intellectual disability fall in the *mild* category (King et al., 2009). Only about 15% of those with intellectual disability exhibit obvious mental deficiencies. Many individuals with mild retardation are not all that easily distinguished from the rest of the population. The mental deficiency of children in the mild disability category often is not noticed until they have been in school a few years. Outside of school, many are considered normal. Furthermore, as many as two-thirds of these children manage to shed the label of retardation when they reach adulthood and leave the educational system (Popper et al., 2003). A significant portion of them become self-supporting and are integrated into the community. Some are even able to attend college (Getzel & Wehman, 2005).

Origins

Many organic conditions can cause mental retardation (Szymanski & Wilska, 2003). For example, *Down syndrome* is a condition marked by distinctive physical characteristics (such as slanted eyes, stubby limbs, and thin hair) that is associated with mild to severe retardation. Most children exhibiting this syndrome carry an extra chromosome. *Phenylketonuria* is a metabolic disorder (due to an inherited enzyme deficiency) that can lead to intellectual disability if it's not caught and treated in infancy. In *hydrocephaly,* an

Reality CHECK

Misconception

Most people who suffer from intellectual disability are severely retarded.

Reality

When people think about intellectual disability, their prototype for this condition is a severely retarded person who looks different and requires institutionalization. Working from this prototype, people assume that severe retardation is the most typical form of intellectual disability. In reality, it is the rarest form of intellectual disability. The vast majority (85%) of people with intellectual disability manifest mild retardation.

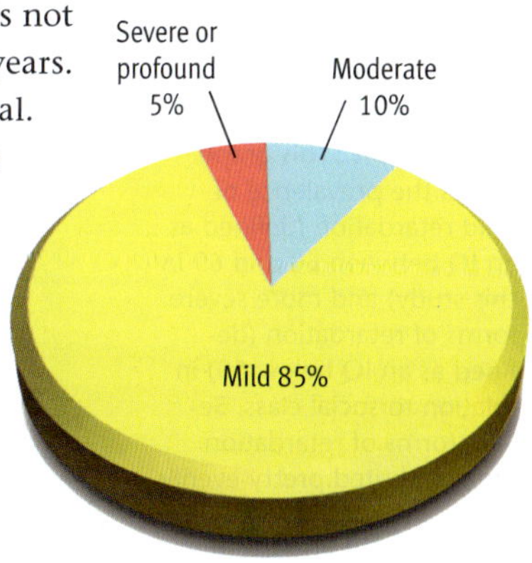

Figure 9.10

The prevalence of various levels of mental retardation. The vast majority (85%) of individuals diagnosed with retardation fall in the mild category (IQ: 55–70). Only about 15% of people with intellectual disability fall into the subcategories of moderate, severe, or profound retardation. © Cengage Learning 2013 excessive accumulation of cerebrospinal fluid in the skull destroys brain tissue and causes retardation. About 1000 such organic syndromes are known to cause retardation, with more being identified every year (Popper et al., 2003). But diagnosticians are unable to pin down an organic cause for as many as 30%–50% of cases (King et al., 2009).

The cases of unknown origin tend to involve milder forms of retardation. A number of theories have tried to identify the factors that underlie intellectual disability in the absence of a known organic pathology. Some theorists believe that subtle, difficult-to-detect physiological defects contribute to many of these cases. However, others believe the majority of cases are caused by a variety of unfavorable environmental factors. Consistent with this hypothesis, the vast majority of children with mild disability come from the lower socioeconomic classes (see **Figure 9.11**). Here a number of factors—such as greater marital instability and parental neglect, inadequate nutrition and medical care, and lower-quality schooling—may contribute to children's poor intellectual development (Popper et al., 2003).

Giftedness

Like intellectual disability, giftedness is widely misunderstood. This misunderstanding is a result, in part, of television and movies inaccurately portraying gifted children as social misfits and "nerds." But as we shall see, that stereotype is quite an exaggeration.

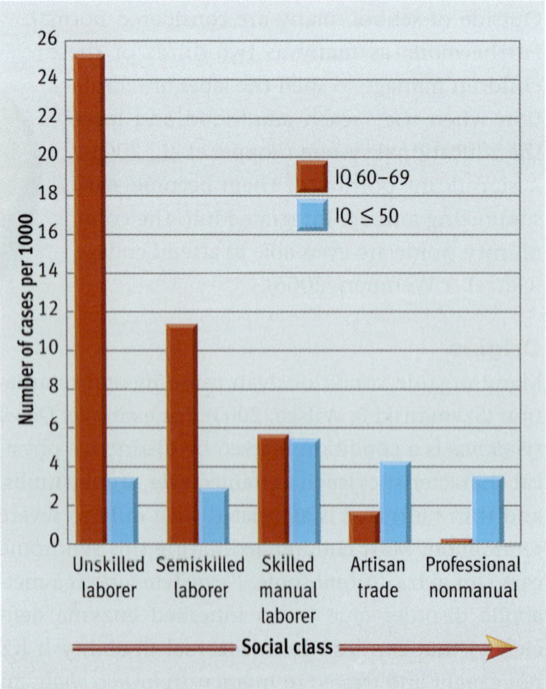

© Cengage Learning 2013

Figure 9.11
Social class and mental retardation. This graph charts the prevalence of mild retardation (defined as an IQ between 60 and 69 in this study) and more severe forms of retardation (defined as an IQ below 50) in relation to social class. Severe forms of retardation are distributed pretty evenly across the social classes, a finding that is consistent with the notion that they are the product of biological aberrations that are equally likely to strike anyone. In contrast, the prevalence of mild retardation is greatly elevated in the lower social classes, a finding that meshes with the notion that mild retardation is largely a product of unfavorable environmental factors. (Data from Popper and Steingard, 1994)

Identifying Gifted Children

Definitions of giftedness vary considerably (Kaufman & Sternberg, 2010). Some curious discrepancies exist between ideals and practice in how gifted children are identified. The experts consistently assert that giftedness should not be equated with high intelligence. They recommend that schools not rely too heavily on IQ tests to select gifted children (Sternberg, 2005c; von Karolyi & Winner, 2005). In practice, however, efforts to identify gifted children focus almost exclusively on IQ scores and rarely consider qualities such as creativity, leadership, or special talent in art or music (Newman, 2010). Most school districts consider children who fall in the upper 2%–3% of the IQ distribution to be gifted. Thus, the minimum IQ score for gifted programs usually falls somewhere around 130. The types of school programs and services available to gifted students vary enormously from one school district to the next (Olszewski-Kubilius, 2003).

Personal Qualities of the Gifted

Gifted children have long been stereotyped as weak, sickly, socially inept "bookworms" who are often emotionally troubled. The empirical evidence *largely* contradicts this view. The best evidence comes from a major longitudinal study of gifted children begun by Lewis Terman in 1921 (Terman, 1925; Terman & Oden, 1959). Other investigators have continued to study Terman's subjects through the present (Cronbach, 1992; Holahan & Sears, 1995; Lippa, Martin, & Friedman, 2000). This project represents psychology's longest-running study.

Terman's original subject pool consisted of around 1500 youngsters who had an average IQ of 150. In comparison to normal subjects, Terman's gifted children were found to be above average in height, weight, strength, physical health, emotional adjustment, mental health, and social maturity. As a group, Terman's subjects continued to exhibit better-than-average physical health, emotional stability, and social satisfaction throughout their adult years. A variety of other studies have also found that samples of high-IQ children are either average or above average in social and emotional development (Robinson, 2010).

However, some other lines of research raise some questions about this conclusion. For instance, Ellen Winner (1997, 1998) asserts that profoundly gifted children (those with an IQ above 180) are very different from moderately gifted children (those with an IQ of 130–150). She asserts that profoundly gifted children are often introverted and socially isolated. She also estimates that the incidence of interpersonal and emotional problems in this group is about twice as high as in other children. Another line of research, which is discussed in more detail in the Personal Application, has focused on samples of people who have displayed truly exceptional creative achievement. Contrary to the findings of the Terman study, investigators have found elevated rates of mental illness in these samples (Andreasen, 2005; Ludwig, 1998). Thus, the psychosocial adjustment of gifted individuals may depend in part on their level of giftedness.

Giftedness and Achievement in Life

Terman's gifted children grew up to be very successful by conventional standards. By midlife they had produced 92 books, 235 patents, and nearly 2200 scientific articles. Although Terman's gifted children accomplished a great deal, no one in the group achieved recognition for genius-level contributions. In retrospect, this finding may not be surprising. The concept of giftedness is applied to two very different groups. One consists of high-IQ children who are the cream of the crop in school. The other consists of eminent adults who make enduring contributions in their fields. According to Ellen Winner (2000), a sizable gap exists between these two groups. Joseph Renzulli (1986, 1999, 2005) theorizes that this rarer form of eminent giftedness depends on the intersection of three factors: high intelligence, high creativity, and high motivation (see **Figure 9.12**). He emphasizes that high intelligence alone does not usually foster genuine greatness. Thus, the vast majority of children selected for gifted school programs do not achieve eminence as adults or make genius-like contributions to society (Callahan, 2000; Richert, 1997; Winner, 2003).

Another hot issue in the study of giftedness concerns the degree to which extraordinary achievement depends on innate talent as opposed to intensive training and hard work. In recent years, the emphasis has been on what Simonton (2001) mockingly calls the "drudge theory" of exceptional achievement. According to this view, eminence primarily or entirely depends on dogged determination; endless, tedious practice; and outstanding mentoring and training (Bloom, 1985; Ericsson, Roring, & Nandagopal, 2007; Howe, 1999). This conclusion is based on studies of eminent scientists, artists, writers, musicians, and athletes, which show that they push themselves much harder and engage in far more deliberate practice than their less successful counterparts.

Although the evidence linking strenuous training and prodigious effort to world-class achievement is convincing, Winner (2000) points out that obsessive hard work and inborn ability may be confounded in retrospective analyses of eminent individuals. The youngsters who work the hardest may be those with the greatest innate talent, who are likely to find their efforts more rewarding than others. In other words, innate ability may be the key factor fostering the single-minded commitment that seems to be crucial to greatness. Simonton (1999b, 2005) has devised an elaborate theory of talent development that allocates a significant role to both innate ability and a variety of supportive environmental factors.

In sum, recent research has clearly demonstrated that quality training, monumental effort, and perseverance are crucial factors in greatness, but many experts on giftedness maintain that extraordinary achievement also requires rare, innate talent.

Reality CHECK

Misconception

Gifted children tend to be frail, socially unskilled introverts with emotional problems.

Reality

This belief may have some validity for a small subset of gifted children who are profoundly talented. But when studies focus on high-IQ children as a whole, they find above-average physical, social, and emotional development. For the most part, the stereotype of gifted children as frail and introverted is an *inaccurate* one.

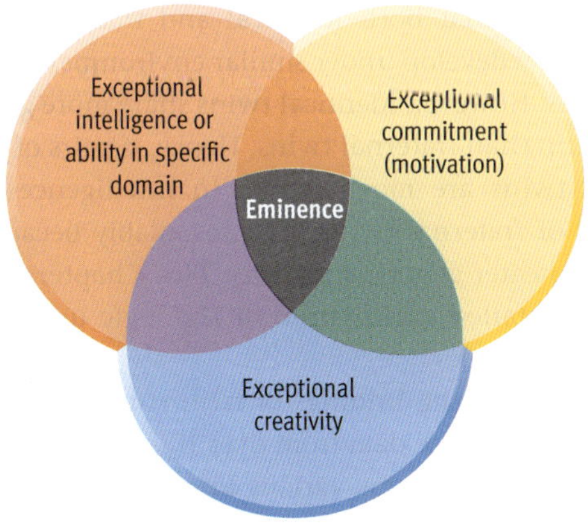

Figure 9.12

A three-ring conception of eminent giftedness. According to Renzulli (1986), high intelligence is only one of three requirements for achieving eminence. He proposes that a combination of exceptional ability, creativity, and motivation leads some people to make enduring contributions in their fields. © Cengage Learning 2013

SOURCE: Adapted from Renzulli, J. S. (1986). The three-ring conception of giftedness: A developmental model for creative productivity. In R. J. Sternberg and J. E. Davidson (Eds.), *Conceptions of giftedness*, pp. 53–92. Cambridge University Press.

Ten-year-old Moshe Kai Cavalin is a sophomore in college who has maintained an A+ average in his classes. Moshe clearly is a highly gifted child. Nonetheless, it is hard to say whether Moshe will go on to achieve eminence, which typically requires a combination of exceptional intelligence, extraordinary motivation, and high creativity.

© AP Images/Damian Dovarganes

REVIEW OF KEY LEARNING GOALS

9.12 Mental retardation, which has been reconceptualized as intellectual disability, refers to subnormal general mental ability accompanied by deficits in adaptive skills. IQ scores below 70 are usually diagnostic of mental retardation. Such diagnoses should not be based solely on test results. Four levels of retardation have been distinguished: mild, moderate, severe, and profound.

9.13 About 1000 organic conditions can cause retardation, but diagnosticians are unable to pinpoint a biological cause in 30%–50% of cases. Research suggests that cases of unknown origin are mostly caused by unfavorable environmental factors, such as poverty, neglect, and poor nutrition.

9.14 Children who obtain IQ scores above 130 may be viewed as gifted. But cutoffs for accelerated programs vary, and schools rely too much on IQ scores. Research by Terman showed that gifted children tend to be socially mature and well adjusted. However, Winner has expressed some concerns about the adjustment of profoundly gifted individuals.

9.15 Gifted youngsters typically become very successful. Most, however, do not make genius-level contributions because such achievements depend on a combination of high intelligence, creativity, and motivation. The drudge theory suggests that determination, hard work, and intensive training are the key to achieving eminence. But many theorists are reluctant to dismiss the importance of innate talent.

KEY LEARNING GOALS

9.16 Summarize evidence that heredity affects intelligence, and discuss the concept of heritability.

9.17 Describe various lines of research indicating that environment affects intelligence.

9.18 Explain the concept of reaction range, and discuss recent efforts to identify specific genes for intelligence.

9.19 Evaluate heredity, socioeconomic disadvantage, and stereotype threat as explanations for cultural differences in IQ.

Heredity and Environment as Determinants of Intelligence

Most early pioneers of intelligence testing maintained that intelligence is inherited (Cravens, 1992). Small wonder, then, that this view lingers among many people. Gradually, however, it has become clear that both heredity and environment influence intelligence (Bartels et al., 2002; Davis, Arden, & Plomin, 2008; Plomin, 2003). Does this mean that the nature versus nurture debate has been settled with respect to intelligence? Absolutely not. Theorists and researchers continue to argue *vigorously* about which of the two is more important, in part because the issue has such far-reaching sociopolitical implications.

Theorists who believe that intelligence is largely inherited downplay the value of special educational programs for underprivileged groups (Herrnstein & Murray, 1994; Kanazawa, 2006; Rushton & Jensen, 2005). They assert that a child's intelligence cannot be increased noticeably because genetic destiny cannot be altered. Other theorists take issue with this argument, pointing out that traits with a strong genetic component are not necessarily unchangeable (Flynn, 2007; Sternberg, Grigorenko, & Kidd, 2005). The people in this camp tend to maintain that even more funds should be allocated for remedial education programs, improved schooling in lower-class neighborhoods, and college financial aid for the underprivileged. Because the debate over the role of heredity in intelligence has direct relevance to important social issues and political decisions, we'll take a detailed look at this complex controversy.

Evidence for Hereditary Influence

PsykTrek 7d

Sir Francis Galton's observation in the late 19th century that intelligence runs in families was quite accurate. However, *family studies* can determine only whether genetic influence on a trait is *plausible,* not whether it's certain (see Chapter 3). Family members share not just genes, but similar environments. If high intelligence (or low intelligence) appears in a family over several generations, this consistency could reflect the influence of either shared genes *or* shared environment. Because of this problem, researchers must turn to *twin studies* and *adoption studies* to obtain more definitive evidence on whether heredity affects intelligence.

Twin Studies

PsykTrek 7d

The best evidence regarding the role of genetic factors in intelligence comes from studies that compare identical and fraternal twins. The rationale for twin studies is that both identical and fraternal twins normally develop under similar environmental conditions. However, identical twins share more genetic kinship than fraternal twins. Hence, if pairs of identical twins are more similar in intelligence than pairs of fraternal twins, it's presumably because of their greater genetic similarity. (See Chapter 3 for a more detailed explanation of the logic underlying twin studies.)

What are the findings of twin studies regarding intelligence? The data from over 100 studies of intellectual similarity for various kinds of kinship relations and childrearing arrangements are summarized in **Figure 9.13**. This figure plots the average correlation observed for various types of relationships. The average correlation for identical twins (.86) is very high. It indicates that identical twins tend to be quite similar in intelligence. The average correlation for fraternal twins (.60) is significantly lower. This correlation indicates that fraternal twins also tend to be similar in intelligence, but noticeably less so than

© Tom Wang/Shutterstock

identical twins. These results support the notion that IQ is inherited to a considerable degree (Bouchard, 1998; Plomin & Spinath, 2004).

Of course, critics have tried to poke holes in this line of reasoning. They argue that identical twins are more alike in IQ because parents and others treat them more similarly than they treat fraternal twins. This environmental explanation of the findings has some merit. After all, identical twins are always the same sex, and gender influences how a child is raised. However, this explanation seems unlikely in light of the evidence on identical twins who were reared apart because of family breakups or adoption (Bouchard, 1997; Bouchard et al., 1990). *Although reared in different environments, these identical twins still display greater similarity in IQ (average correlation: .72) than fraternal twins reared together (average correlation: .60).* Moreover, the gap in IQ similarity between identical twins and fraternal twins appears to widen in adulthood, suggesting paradoxically that the influence of heredity increases with age (Plomin & Spinath, 2004).

Adoption Studies

PsykTrek 7d

Research on adopted children also provides evidence about the effects of heredity (and of environment, as we shall see). If adopted children resemble their biological parents in intelligence even though they were not reared by these parents, this finding supports the genetic hypothesis. The relevant studies indicate that there is indeed more than chance similarity between adopted children and their biological parents (Plomin et al., 2008; refer again to **Figure 9.13**).

Heritability Estimates

PsykTrek 7d

Various experts have sifted through mountains of correlational evidence to estimate the *heritability* of intelligence. **A *heritability ratio* is an estimate of the proportion of trait variability in a population that is determined by variations in genetic inheritance.** Heritability can be estimated for any trait. For example, the heritability of height is estimated to be around 90% and the heritability of weight is estimated to be around 85% (Bouchard, 2004). Heritability can be estimated in a variety of

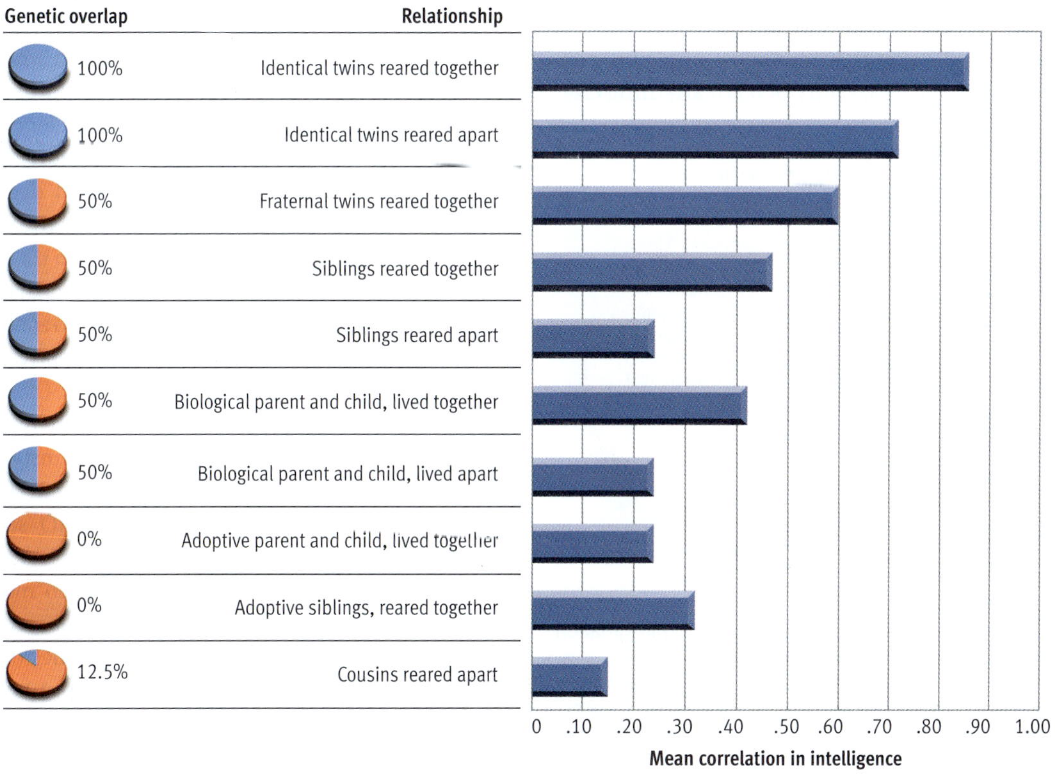

Figure 9.13

Studies of IQ similarity. The graph shows the mean correlations of IQ scores for people with various types of relationships, as obtained in studies of IQ similarity. Higher correlations indicate greater similarity. The results show that greater genetic similarity is associated with greater similarity in IQ, suggesting that intelligence is partly inherited (compare, for example, the correlations for identical and fraternal twins). However, the results also show that living together is associated with greater IQ similarity, suggesting that intelligence is partly governed by environment (compare, for example, the scores of siblings reared together and reared apart). (Data from McGue et al., 1993; Plomin & Spinath, 2004; Plomin et al., 2008) © Cengage Learning 2013 ways that appear logically and mathematically defensible (Grigerenko, 2000; Loehlin, 1994). Given the variety of methods available and the strong views that experts bring to the IQ debate, it should come as no surprise that heritability estimates for intelligence vary considerably (see **Figure 9.14**).

At the high end, some theorists estimate that the heritability of IQ ranges as high as 80% (Bouchard, 2004; Jensen, 1980, 1998). That is, they believe that only about 20% of the variation in intelligence is attributable to environmental factors. Estimates at the low end of the spectrum suggest that the heritability of intelligence is around 40% (Plomin, 2003), which means 60% would be attributable to environmental factors. *In recent years, the consensus estimates of the experts tend to hover around 50%* (Petrill, 2005; Plomin & Spinath, 2004).

However, it's important to understand that heritability estimates have certain limitations (Grigorenko, 2000; Johnson et al., 2009; Reeve & Hakel, 2002). First, a heritability estimate is a *group statistic* based on studies of trait variability within a specific group. A heritability estimate cannot be applied meaningfully to *individuals*. In other words, even if the heritability of intelligence were 70%, it would *not* mean that each individual's intelligence was 70% inherited. Second, a specific trait's *heritability may vary from one group to another* depending on a variety of factors. For instance, in a group with a given gene pool, heritability will decrease if a shift occurs toward rearing youngsters in more diverse circumstances. Why? Because environmental variability will be increased. Third, it is crucial to understand that "there really is no single fixed value that represents any true, constant value for the heritability of IQ or anything else" (Sternberg et al., 2005, p. 53). Heritability ratios are merely sample-specific estimates.

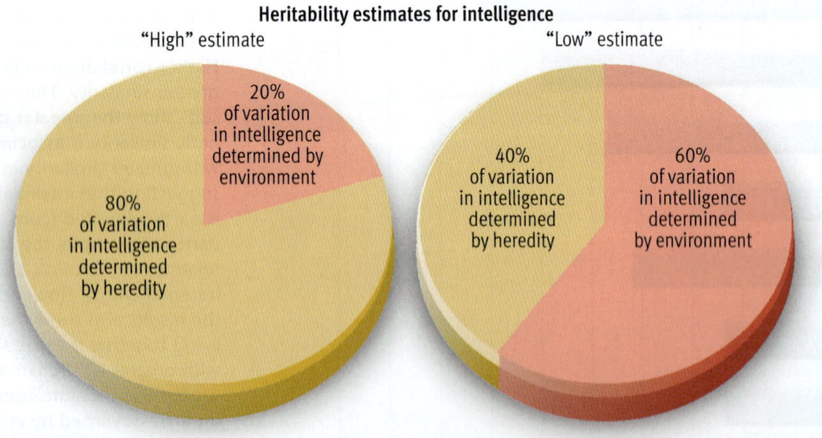

Figure 9.14

The concept of heritability. A heritability ratio is an estimate of the portion of trait variation in a population determined by heredity—with the remainder presumably determined by environment—as these pie charts illustrate. Typical heritability estimates for intelligence range between a high of 80% and a low of 40%. In recent years, the consensus of the experts seems to hover around 50%. Bear in mind that heritability ratios are *estimates* and have certain limitations that are discussed in the text. © Cengage Learning 2013

Evidence for Environmental Influence

7d

Heredity unquestionably influences intelligence. Yet a great deal of evidence indicates that upbringing also affects mental ability. In this section, we'll examine various approaches to research that show how life experiences shape intelligence.

Adoption Studies

7d

Research with adopted children provides useful evidence about the impact of experience as well as heredity (Dickens & Flynn, 2001; Locurto, 1990; Loehlin, Horn, & Willerman, 1997). Many of the correlations in **Figure 9.13** reflect the influence of the environment. For example, adopted children show some resemblance to their foster parents in IQ. This similarity is usually attributed to the fact that their foster parents shape their environment. Adoption studies also indicate that siblings reared together are more similar in IQ than siblings reared apart. This is true even for identical twins who have the same genetic endowment. Moreover, entirely unrelated children who are raised in the same home also show a significant resemblance in IQ. All of these findings indicate that environment influences intelligence.

Environmental Deprivation and Enrichment

If environment affects intelligence, children who are raised in substandard circumstances should experience a gradual decline in IQ as they grow older (since other children will be progressing more rapidly). This *cumulative deprivation hypothesis* was tested decades ago. Researchers studied children consigned to understaffed orphanages and children raised in the poverty and isolation of the back hills of Appalachia (Sherman & Key, 1932; Stoddard, 1943). Generally, investigators found that environmental deprivation led to the predicted erosion in IQ scores.

In contrast, children who are removed from a deprived environment and placed in circumstances more conducive to learning should benefit from their environmental enrichment. Their IQ scores should gradually increase. This hypothesis has been tested by studying children who have been moved from disadvantaged homes or institutional settings into middle- and upper-class adoptive homes (Scarr & Weinberg, 1977, 1983; Schiff & Lewontin, 1986). A recent meta-analysis of relevant studies found that adopted children scored notably higher on IQ tests that siblings or peers "left behind" in institutions or disadvantaged homes (van IJzendoorn & Juffer, 2005). These gains are sometimes reduced if children suffer from severe, lengthy deprivation prior to their adoptive placement. But the overall trends clearly show that improved environments lead to increased IQ scores for most adoptees. These findings show that IQ scores are not unchangeable and that they are sensitive to environmental influences.

Generational Changes: The Flynn Effect

The most interesting, albeit perplexing, evidence showcasing the importance of the environment is the finding that performance on IQ tests has steadily increased over generations. This trend was not widely appreciated until relatively recently, because the tests are renormed periodically with new standardization groups so that the mean IQ always remains at 100. However, in a study of the IQ tests used by the U.S. military, James Flynn noticed that the level of performance required to earn a score of 100 jumped upward every time the tests were renormed. Curious about this unexpected finding, he eventually gathered extensive data from 20 nations and demonstrated that IQ performance has been rising steadily all over the industrialized world since the 1930s (Flynn, 1987, 1999, 2003, 2007). Thus, the performance that today would earn you an average score of 100 would have earned you an IQ score of about 125 back in the 1930s (see **Figure 9.15**). Researchers who study intelligence are now scrambling to explain this trend, which has been dubbed the "Flynn effect." About the only thing they mostly agree on is that the Flynn effect has to be attributed to environmental factors. The modern world's gene pool could not have changed overnight (in evolutionary terms, 70 years is more like a fraction of a second) (Dickens & Flynn, 2001; Neisser, 1998; Sternberg et al., 2005).

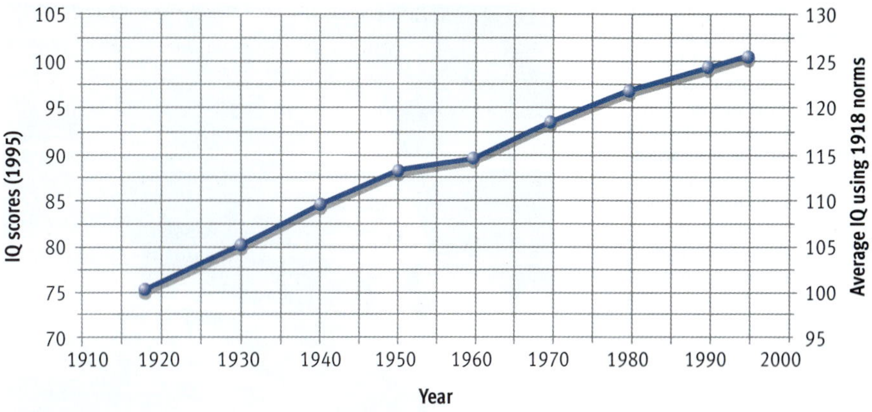

Figure 9.15

Generational increases in measured IQ. IQ tests are renormed periodically so that the mean score remains at 100. However, research by James Flynn has demonstrated that performance on IQ tests around the world was increasing throughout most of the twentieth century. This graph traces the estimated increases in IQ in the United States from 1918 to 1995. In relation to the axis on the right, the graph shows how average IQ would have increased if IQ tests continued to use 1918 norms. In relation to the axis on the left, the graph shows how much lower the average IQ score would have been in earlier years if 1995 norms were used. The causes of the "Flynn effect" are unknown, but they have to involve environmental factors.

© Cengage Learning 2013

SOURCE: Adapted from Flynn, J. R. (1998). IQ gains over time: Toward finding the causes. In U. Neisser (Ed.), *The rising curve: Long-term gains in IQ and related measures* (p. 37). Washington, DC: American Psychological Association. Copyright © by the American Psychological Association.

The Interaction of Heredity and Environment

PsykTrek 7d

Clearly, heredity and environment both influence intelligence to a significant degree. And their effects involve intricate, dynamic, reciprocal interactions (Grigerenko, 2000; Johnson, 2010; Petrill, 2005). Genetic endowments influence the experiences that people are exposed to, and environments influence the degree to which genetic predispositions are realized. In fact, many theorists now assert that the question of whether heredity or environment is more important ought to take a backseat to the question of *how they interact* to govern IQ.

One influential model of this interaction was championed most prominently by Sandra Scarr (1991). The model posits that heredity may set certain limits on intelligence and that environmental factors determine where individuals fall within these limits (Bouchard, 1997; Weinberg, 1989). According to this idea, genetic makeup places an upper limit on a person's IQ that can't be exceeded even when environment is ideal. Heredity is also thought to place a lower limit on an individual's IQ, although extreme circumstances (for example, being locked in an attic until age 10) could drag a person's IQ beneath this boundary. Theorists use the term ***reaction* range to refer to these genetically determined limits on IQ (or other traits).**

According to the reaction-range model, children reared in high-quality environments that promote the development of intelligence should score near the top of their potential IQ range (see **Figure 9.16** on the next page). Conversely, children reared under less ideal circumstances should score lower in their reaction range. The concept of a reaction range can explain why high-IQ children sometimes come from poor environments. It can also explain why low-IQ children sometimes come from very good environments. Moreover, it can explain these apparent paradoxes without discounting the role that environment undeniably plays.

Scientists hope to achieve a more precise understanding of how heredity and environment interactively govern intelligence by identifying the specific genes that influence general mental ability. Advances in molecular genetics, including the mapping of the

© Courtesy of Sandra Scarr

Sandra Scarr

"My research has been aimed at asking in what kind of environments genetic differences shine through and when do they remain hidden."

Carolyn Barnes grappled with an exceptionally difficult childhood that included bouts of homelessness and being abandoned by her mentally ill father. Yet she managed to graduate from Virginia Tech in just three years and was recognized as the top student in the College of Liberal Arts and Human Sciences. She has since enrolled in a doctoral program at the University of Michigan. The reaction range model can explain how high-IQ individuals can emerge from deprived, impoverished environments.

© AP Images/Don Petersen

human genome, are allowing researchers to search for individual genes that are associated with measures of intelligence (Posthuma et al., 2005). However, these studies have yielded minimal progress thus far (Johnson, 2010; Plomin, Kennedy, & Craig, 2006).

The problem with this new line of research is that intelligence may be influenced by hundreds of specific genes, and each gene may have a small effect that is extremely difficult to detect with current technologies (Petrill, 2005). In recent research, the *strongest* links found between genes and intelligence were each associated with less than half of 1% of the variation in intelligence (Plomin et al., 2006). Although researchers in this area hope to achieve breakthroughs as the technology of molecular genetics becomes more powerful, at this point the prospects for progress look rather bleak (Johnson, 2010).

CONCEPT CHECK 9.2

Understanding Correlational Evidence on the Heredity-Environment Question

Check your understanding of how correlational findings relate to the nature versus nurture issue by indicating how you would interpret the meaning of each "piece" of evidence described below. The numbers inside the parentheses are the mean IQ correlations observed for the relationships described, which are shown in **Figure 9.13**. In the spaces on the left, enter the letter H if the findings suggest that intelligence is shaped by heredity, enter the letter E if the findings suggest that intelligence is shaped by the environment, and enter the letter B if the findings suggest that intelligence is shaped by both (or either) heredity and environment. The answers can be found in Appendix A.

______ 1. Identical twins reared apart are more similar (.72) than fraternal twins reared together (.60).

______ 2. Identical twins reared together are more similar (.86) than identical twins reared apart (.72).

______ 3. Siblings reared together are more similar (.47) than siblings reared apart (.24).

______ 4. Biological parents and the children they rear are more similar (.42) than unrelated persons who are reared apart (no correlation if sampled randomly).

______ 5. Adopted children show similarity to their biological parents (.24) and to their adoptive parents (.24).

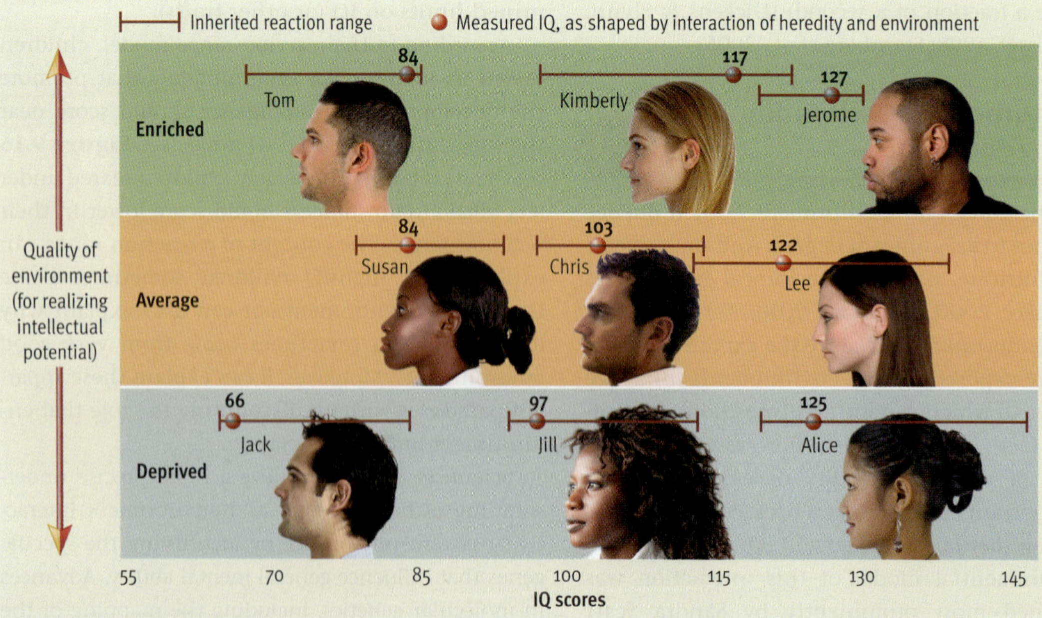

Top row (left to right): © Rui Vale de Sousa/Shutterstock; © WoodyStock/Alamy; © R. Gino Santa Maria/Shutterstock. Middle row: © Luba V Nel/Shutterstock; © Corbis Cusp/Alamy; © Image Source/Alamy. Bottom row: © photobank.ch/Shutterstock; © olly/Shutterstock; © swissmacky/Shutterstock.

© Cengage Learning 2013

Figure 9.16

Reaction range. The concept of reaction range posits that heredity sets limits on one's intellectual potential (represented by the horizontal bars), while the quality of one's environment influences where one scores within this range (represented by the dots on the bars). People raised in enriched environments should score near the top of their reaction range, whereas people raised in poor-quality environments should score near the bottom of their range. Genetic limits on IQ can be inferred only indirectly, so theorists aren't sure whether reaction ranges are narrow (like Jerome's) or wide (like Kimberly's). The concept of reaction range can explain how two people with similar genetic potential can be quite different in intelligence (compare Tom and Jack) and how two people reared in environments of similar quality can score quite differently (compare Alice and Jack).

Cultural Differences in IQ Scores

The age-old nature versus nurture debate lies at the core of the long-running controversy about ethnic differences in average IQ. The full range of IQ scores is seen in all ethnic groups. However, the average IQ for many of the larger minority groups in the United States (such as African Americans, Native Americans, and Hispanics) is somewhat lower than the average for whites. The typical disparity is around 10 to 15 points, depending on the group tested and the IQ scale used (Hunt & Carlson, 2007; Loehlin, 2000; Nisbett, 2005). Interestingly, data from the standardization samples for the Stanford-Binet and Wechsler scales suggests that the gap between blacks and whites has shrunk by about 4 to 7 points since the 1970s (Dickens & Flynn, 2006). There is relatively little argument about the existence of these group differences, variously referred to as racial, ethnic, or cultural differences in intelligence. The controversy concerns *why* the differences are found. A vigorous debate continues as to whether cultural differences in intelligence are attributable mainly to the influence of heredity or of environment.

Heritability as an Explanation

In 1969 Arthur Jensen sparked a heated war of words by arguing that racial differences in average IQ are largely the result of heredity. The cornerstone for Jensen's argument was his analysis suggesting that the heritability of intelligence is about 80%. Essentially, he asserted that (1) intelligence is largely genetic in origin, and (2) therefore, genetic factors are "strongly implicated" as the cause of ethnic differences in intelligence. Jensen's article triggered outrage and bitter criticism in many quarters, as well as a great deal of additional research on the determinants of intelligence. Twenty-five years later, Richard Herrnstein and Charles Murray (1994) reignited the same controversy with the publication of their widely discussed book *The Bell Curve*. They argued that ethnic differences in average intelligence are substantial, not easily reduced by educational programs for the disadvantaged, and at least partly genetic in origin. The implicit message throughout *The Bell Curve* was that disadvantaged groups cannot avoid their fate because it's their genetic destiny. And as recently as 2010, based on an extensive review of statistical evidence, J. Phillipe Rushton and Arthur Jensen (2010) argued that genetic factors account for the bulk of the gap between races in average IQ.

These analyses and conclusions have elicited many lengthy and elaborate rebuttals. Critics argue that heritability explanations for ethnic differences in IQ have a variety of flaws and weaknesses (Brody, 2003; Devlin et al., 2002; Horn, 2002; Nisbett, 2005, 2009; Sternberg, 2003b, 2005a). For example, recent research suggests that the heritability of intelligence may be notably lower in samples drawn from the lower socioeconomic classes as opposed to higher socioeconomic classes (Turkheimer et al., 2003). However, heritability estimates for intelligence have largely been based on samples drawn from white, middle-class, North American and European populations (Grigerenko, 2000). Hence, there is doubt about the validity of applying these heritability estimates to other cultural groups.

Moreover, even if one accepts the assumption that the heritability of IQ is very high, it does not follow logically that differences *between groups* must be due largely to heredity. Leon Kamin has presented a compelling analogy that highlights the logical fallacy in this reasoning (see **Figure 9.17**):

We fill a white sack and a black sack with a mixture of different genetic varieties of corn seed. We make certain that the proportions of each variety of seed are identical in each sack. We then plant the seed from the white sack in fertile Field A, while that from the black sack is planted in barren Field B. We will observe that within Field A, as within Field B, there is considerable variation in the height

© Courtesy of Arthur Jensen

Arthur Jensen

"Despite more than half a century of repeated efforts by psychologists to improve the intelligence of children, particularly those in the lower quarter of the IQ distribution relative to those in the upper half of the distribution, strong evidence is still lacking as to whether or not it can be done."

"I don't know anything about the bell curve, but I say heredity is everything."

© Charles Barsotti/The New Yorker Collection/www.cartoonbank.com

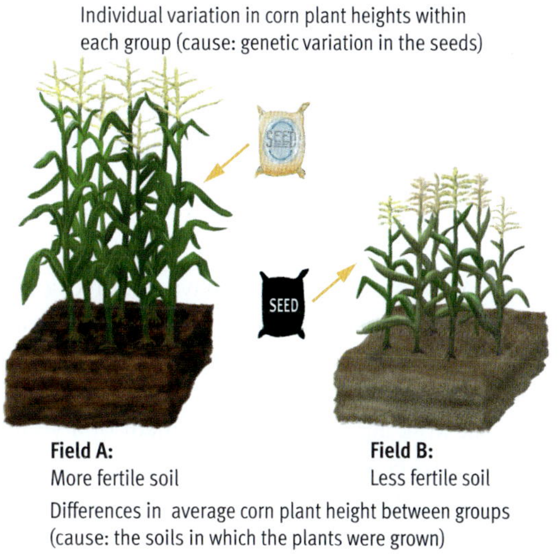

Figure 9.17

Genetics and between-group differences on a trait. Leon Kamin's analogy (see text) shows how between-group differences on a trait (the average height of corn plants) could be due to environment, even if the trait is largely inherited. The same reasoning can be applied to ethnic group differences in average intelligence.

© Cengage Learning 2013

of individual corn plants. This variation will be due largely to genetic factors (seed differences). We will also observe, however, that the average height of plants in Field A is greater than that in Field B. That difference will be entirely due to environmental factors (the soil). The same is true of IQs: differences in the average IQ of various human populations could be entirely due to environmental differences, even if within each population all variation were due to genetic differences! (Eysenck & Kamin, 1981, p. 97)

This analogy shows that even if *within-group differences* in IQ are highly heritable, *between-groups differences* in average IQ could still be caused *entirely* by environmental factors (Block, 2002). For decades, critics of Jensen's thesis have relied on this analogy rather than actual data to make the point that between-groups differences in IQ do not necessarily reflect genetic differences. They depended on the analogy because no relevant data were available. However, the recent discovery of the Flynn effect has provided compelling new data that are directly relevant (Dickens & Flynn, 2001; Flynn, 2003). Generational gains in IQ scores show that a between-groups disparity in average IQ (in this case the gap is between generations rather than ethnic groups) can be environmental in origin, even though intelligence is highly heritable.

The available evidence certainly does not allow us to rule out the possibility that ethnic and cultural disparities in average intelligence are partly genetic. And the hypothesis should not be dismissed without study simply because many people find it offensive or distasteful. However, there are several alternative explanations for the culture gap in intelligence that seem more plausible. Let's look at them.

Socioeconomic Disadvantage as an Explanation

Some theorists have approached the issue by trying to show that socioeconomic disadvantages are the main cause of ethnic differences in average IQ. Many social scientists argue that minority students' IQ scores are depressed because these children tend to grow up in deprived environments that create a disadvantage—both in school and on IQ tests. Obviously, living circumstances vary greatly within ethnic groups, but there is no question that, on the average, whites and minorities tend to be reared in different circumstances. Most minority groups have endured a long history of economic discrimination and are greatly overrepresented in the lower social classes. A lower-class upbringing tends to carry a number of disadvantages that work against the development of a youngster's full intellectual potential (Bigelow, 2006; Evans, 2004; Lott, 2002; McLoyd, 1998; Noble, McCandliss, & Farah, 2007; Seifer, 2001).

© Courtesy of Claude Steele

Claude Steele

"I believe that in significant part the crisis in black Americans' education stems from the power of this vulnerability to undercut identification with schooling."

In comparison to the middle and upper classes, lower-class children are more likely to come from large families and from single-parent homes. Such factors may often limit the parental attention they receive. Lower-class children also tend to be exposed to fewer books, to have fewer learning supplies, to have less privacy for concentrated study, and to get less parental assistance in learning. Typically, they also have poorer role models for language development, experience less encouragement to work hard on intellectual pursuits, and attend poorer-quality schools that are underfunded and understaffed. Many of these children grow up in crime-, drug-, and gang-infested neighborhoods where it is far more important to develop street intelligence than school intelligence. Some theorists also argue that children in the lower classes are more likely to suffer from malnutrition or to be exposed to environmental toxins (Brody, 1992). Any of these circumstances could interfere with youngsters' intellectual development (Bellinger & Adams, 2001; Grantham-McGregor, Ani, & Fernald, 2001).

In light of these disadvantages, it's not surprising that average IQ scores among children from lower social classes tend to run about 15 points below the average scores obtained by children from middle- and upper-class homes (Seifer, 2001; Williams & Ceci, 1997). This is the case even if race is factored out of the picture by studying whites exclusively. Given the effect that social class appears to have on test scores, many researchers argue that ethnic differences in intelligence are really social class differences in disguise.

Stereotype Threat as an Explanation

Socioeconomic disadvantages probably are a major factor in various minority groups' poor performance on IQ tests. Some theorists, however, maintain that other factors and processes are also at work. For example, Claude Steele (1992, 1997) has argued that negative stereotypes of stigmatized groups' intellectual abilities create feelings of vulnerability in the classroom. These feelings of *stereotype threat* can undermine group members' performance on tests, as well as other measures of academic achievement.

Steele points out that negative stereotypes of stigmatized groups are widely known. He further notes that members of minority groups are keenly aware of any negative stereotypes that exist regarding their intellect. Hence, when an African American or Hispanic American does poorly on a test, he or she must confront a disturbing possibility: *that others will attribute the failure to racial inferiority.* Similarly, females face stereotype threat when they venture into academic domains where stereotypes suggest that they are inferior to males, such as mathematics, engineering, and the physical sciences. That is, *they worry about people blaming their failures on their gender.*

Steele maintains that stereotype threat can contribute to academic underachievement in at least two ways. First, it can undermine students' emotional investment in academic work. Many students may "disidentify" with school and write off academic pursuits as a source of self-worth. Their academic motivation declines and their performance suffers as a result. Second, standardized tests such as IQ tests may be especially anxiety arousing for members of stigmatized groups because the importance attributed to the tests makes their stereotype vulnerability particularly salient. This anxiety may impair students' test performance by temporarily disrupting their cognitive functioning. How Steele tested his theory is the topic of our Featured Study.

FEATURED STUDY

Racial Stereotypes and Test Performance

SOURCE: Steele, C. M., & Aronson, J. (1995). Stereotype threat and the intellectual test performance of African Americans. *Journal of Personality and Social Psychology, 69,* 797–811.

In this article, Steele and Aronson report on a series of four studies that tested various aspects of Steele's theory about the ramifications of stereotype threat. We will examine their first study in some detail, and then discuss the remaining studies more briefly. The purpose of the first study was to test the hypothesis that raising the threat of stereotype vulnerability would have a negative impact on African American students' performance on a mental ability test.

Method

Participants. The participants were 114 black and white undergraduates attending Stanford University who were recruited through campus advertisements. As expected, given Stanford's highly selective admissions, both groups of students were well above average in academic ability, as evidenced by their mean scores on the verbal subtest of the SAT. The study compared black and white students with roughly equal ability and preparation (based on their SAT scores) to rule out cultural disadvantage as a factor.

Procedure. The participants were asked to take a challenging 30-minute test of verbal ability composed of items from the verbal subtest of the Graduate Record Exam (GRE). In one condition, the issue of stereotype threat was not made salient. The test was presented to subjects as a way for researchers to analyze problem-solving strategies (rather than as a measure of ability). In another condition, the specter of stereotype threat was raised. The test was presented as an index of a person's general verbal ability. The principal dependent variable was each subject's performance on the verbal test.

Results

When the African American students' stereotype vulnerability was not made obvious, the performance of the black and white students did not differ, as you can see in **Figure 9.18**. However, when the same test was presented in a way that increased blacks' stereotype threat, the African American students scored significantly lower than their white counterparts (see **Figure 9.18**).

Discussion

Based on their initial study, the authors inferred that stereotype threat appears to impair minority group members' test performance. They went on to replicate their finding in a second study of 40 black and white female students. In a third study, they demonstrated that their manipulations of stereotype threat were indeed activating thoughts about negative stereotypes, ability-related self-doubts, and performance apprehension in their African American participants. Their fourth study showed that stereotype vulnerability can be activated even when a test is not explicitly presented as an index of individual ability.

Comment

The concept of stereotype threat has the potential to clear up some of the confusion surrounding the controversial issue of racial disparities in IQ scores. It seems likely that socioeconomic disadvantage makes a substantial contribution to cultural differences in average IQ. However, various lines of evidence suggest that this factor cannot account for the culture gap by itself (Neisser et al., 1996). Thus, Steele's groundbreaking research has provided scientists with an entirely new explanatory tool for understanding the vexing cultural disparities in average IQ.

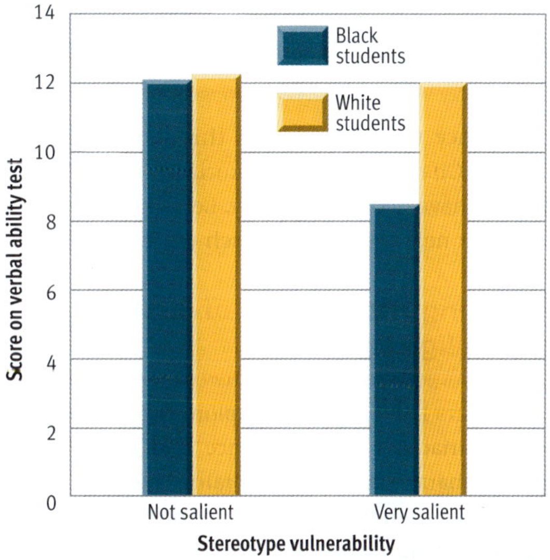

Figure 9.18
Stereotype vulnerability and test performance. Steele and Aronson (1995) compared the performance of African American and white students of equal ability on a 30-item verbal ability test constructed from difficult GRE questions. When the black students' stereotype vulnerability was not obvious, their performance did not differ from that of the white students; but when the specter of stereotype vulnerability was raised, the African American students performed significantly worse than the white students. © Cengage Learning 2013

SOURCE: Adapted from Steele, C. M., & Aronson, J. (1995). Stereotype threat and the intellectual test performance of African Americans. *Journal of Personality and Social Psychology, 69,* 797–811. Copyright © 1995 by the American Psychological Association.

The negative effects of stereotype threat have been replicated in numerous studies (Cadinu et al., 2005; Croizet et al., 2004; Shapiro & Neuberg, 2007). A recent meta-analysis of thirty-nine stereotype threat experiments concluded that cognitive tests tend to underestimate the ability of negatively stereotyped students in real-world settings (Walton & Spencer, 2009). Recent research has also provided new insight into *how* stereotype threat impairs test performance (Schmader, 2010). The evidence suggests that reminders of negative stereotypes lead people to expend precious mental resources suppressing negative thoughts and monitoring themselves for signs of failure. These distractions hijack the very cognitive resource—working memory—that is critical to success on complex cognitive tests. This reduction in working memory capacity undermines test performance.

Taken as a whole, the various alternative explanations for cultural and ethnic disparities in average IQ provide serious challenges to genetic explanations. Genetic explanations appear weak at best—and suspiciously racist at worst. Unfortunately, since the earliest days of IQ testing some people have used IQ tests to further elitist goals. The current controversy about ethnic differences in IQ is just another replay of a record that has been heard before. For instance, beginning in 1913, Henry Goddard tested a great many immigrants to the United States at Ellis Island in New York. He reported that the vast majority of Italian, Hungarian, and Jewish immigrants tested out as *feebleminded* (Kamin, 1974). As you can see, claims about ethnic deficits in intelligence are nothing new—only the victims have changed.

REVIEW OF KEY LEARNING GOALS

9.16 Twin studies show that identical twins, even when raised apart, are more similar in IQ than fraternal twins, suggesting that intelligence is inherited. Adoption studies reveal that people resemble their parents in intelligence even when not raised by them. Estimates of the heritability of intelligence range from 40% to 80%, with the consensus estimate hovering around 50%; however, heritability ratios have certain limitations.

9.17 Studies show that adopted children resemble their biological parents and adoptive siblings in intelligence. The effects of environmental deprivation and enrichment also indicate that IQ is shaped by experience. Generational changes in IQ (the Flynn effect) can only be the result of environmental factors.

9.18 The concept of reaction range posits that heredity places limits on one's intellectual potential while the environment determines where one falls within these limits. Scientists are striving to identify the specific genes that influence intelligence. Progress has been slow thus far, however. Intelligence may be shaped by hundreds of genes that each have tiny effects.

9.19 Arthur Jensen and the authors of *The Bell Curve* sparked controversy by arguing that cultural differences in average IQ are partly attributable to heredity. Even if the heritability of IQ is great, group differences in average intelligence may not be due to heredity. Many theorists note that ethnicity co-varies with social class, so socioeconomic disadvantage may contribute to low IQ scores among minority students. Claude Steele has suggested that stereotype threat contributes to the culture gap in average IQ. The Featured Study showed how the specter of negative stereotypes can impair test performance, perhaps by reducing working memory capacity.

KEY LEARNING GOALS

9.20 Summarize evidence on brain correlates of intelligence and the link between IQ and mortality.

9.21 Describe Sternberg's cognitive approach to intelligence and the three aspects of intelligence that he has identified.

9.22 Evaluate Gardner's theory of multiple intelligences.

New Directions in the Assessment and Study of Intelligence

Intelligence testing has been through a period of turmoil. Changes are on the horizon. In fact, many changes have occurred already. Let's look at some of the major new trends in research on intelligence.

Exploring Biological Correlates of Intelligence

Researchers have begun to explore the relations between variations in intelligence and variations in specific characteristics of the brain. The early studies in this area used various measures of head size as an indicator of brain size. These studies generally found positive, but very small correlations (average = .15) between head size and IQ (Vernon et al., 2000). This result led researchers to speculate that head size is probably a very crude index of brain size. This line of research might have languished, but the invention of sophisticated brain-imaging technologies revived it. Since the 1990s, quite a few studies have examined the correlation between IQ scores and measures of overall brain volume based on MRI scans (see Chapter 3), yielding an average correlation of about .35 (Anderson, 2003; McDaniel, 2005; Rushton & Ankney, 2007). Thus, it appears that larger brains are predictive of greater intelligence.

Many investigators suspect that the association between brain size and intelligence may reflect the enlargement of particular areas in the brain, or growth in certain types of brain tissue, rather than a global increase in brain size. Hence, these researchers are exploring whether IQ correlates with the size of specific regions in the brain. Based on their review of 37 brain-imaging studies, Jung and Haier (2007) theorize that intelligence depends on interactions among a constellation of key areas in the brain, including the prefrontal cortex, Broca's and Wernicke's areas, the somatosensory association cortex, the visual association cortex, and the anterior cingulate. The evidence is complex and more data are needed, but researchers have found some intriguing correlations between the volume of these specific areas in the brain and measures of intelligence (Colom et al., 2009; Haier, 2009).

Other researchers have approached this question by analyzing the relations between intelligence and measures of the amount of gray matter or white matter in individuals' brains. According to Luders et al. (2009a), the amount of gray matter should reflect the density of neurons and their dendrites, which may be predictive of information-processing capacity. In contrast, the amount of white matter should reflect the quantity of axons in the brain and their degree of myelin insulation, which may be predictive of the efficiency of neuronal communication. The findings thus far suggest that higher intelligence scores are correlated with increased volume of *both* gray matter and white matter, with the association being a little stronger for gray matter (Luders et al., 2009a; Narr et al., 2007).

One obvious implication of these findings, eagerly embraced by those who tout the influence of heredity on intelligence, is that genetic inheritance gives some people larger brains than others and that larger brain size promotes greater intelligence (Rushton, 2003). However, as always, we must be cautious about interpreting correlational data. As discussed in Chapter 3, research has demonstrated that an enriched environment can produce denser neural networks and heavier brains in laboratory rats (Rosenzweig & Bennett, 1996). Hence, it is also possible that causation runs in the opposite direction—that developing greater intelligence promotes larger brain size, much like weightlifting can promote larger muscles.

Research on the biological correlates of intelligence has turned up another interesting finding that seems likely to occupy researchers for some time to come. IQ scores measured in childhood correlate with longevity decades later. For example, one study has followed a large cohort of people in Scotland who were given IQ tests in 1932 when they were 11 years old (Deary et al., 2004; Deary, Whalley, & Starr, 2009). People who scored one standard deviation (15 points) below average on the IQ test in 1932 were only 79% as likely as those who scored average or above to be alive in 1997. Quite a number of studies have yielded the same conclusion: Smarter people live longer (Batty, Deary, & Gottfredson, 2007; Pearce et al., 2006; see **Figure 9.19**). The evidence suggests that higher intelligence reduces a broad variety of health risks. For example, higher IQ is associated with decreased mortality from cardiovascular diseases, cancers, and external causes (injuries, poisoning, violence, and so on) (Leon et al., 2009). And a study linking adolescent IQ to health problems at age 40 found that higher IQ was associated with a decreased risk for chronic lung disease, heart problems, hypertension, diabetes, and arthritis/rheumatism (Der, Batty, & Deary, 2009).

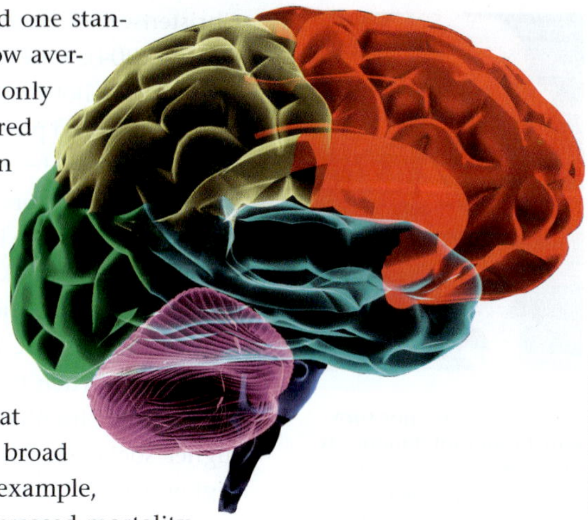

© YAKOBCHUK VASYL/Shutterstock

Why is higher IQ linked to increased longevity? Researchers have offered a variety of explanations (Arden, Gottfredson, & Miller, 2009; Batterham,

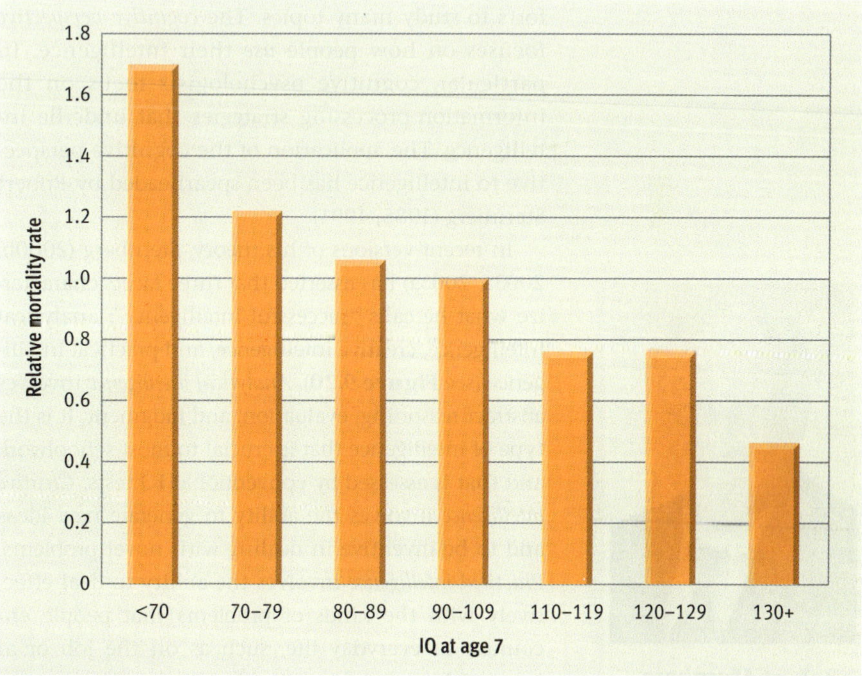

© Cengage Learning 2013

Figure 9.19

The relationship between childhood IQ and mortality. In a recent study, Leon et al. (2009) examined the association between IQ measured at age 7 and mortality through the age of 57 in a sample of over 11,000 people in the UK. The data in the graph are age-adjusted *relative* morality rates in comparison to the reference group of people scoring near average (90–109) in intelligence. Thus, in comparison to the reference group, people who scored 70–79 were 22% more likely to die by age 57, and people who scored over 130 were less than half as likely to die by age 57. As you can see, there is a clear trend. As IQ scores go up, mortality rates decline.

© AP Images/Nati Harnik

Researchers are not sure why higher intelligence is associated with greater longevity. Several processes may be at work. All we know at this point is that extremely bright people, such as Warren Buffett, have a better chance of living into their 80s and 90s than their less intelligent counterparts.

Christensen, & Mackinnon, 2009; Gottfredson & Deary, 2004). One possibility is that good genes could foster both higher intelligence and resilient health. A second possibility is that health self-care is a complicated lifelong mission for which brighter people are better prepared. In other words, smarter people may be more likely to avoid health-impairing habits (such as smoking and overeating), be proactive about health (such as exercising and taking vitamins), and use medical care more effectively (such as knowing when to seek treatment). A third possibility is that intelligence fosters career success, and higher social status decreases mortality. People in higher socioeconomic classes tend to have less-stressful jobs with lower accident risks, reduced exposure to toxins and pathogens, better health insurance, and greater access to medical care. Thus, affluence could be the key factor linking intelligence to longevity. These explanations are not mutually exclusive. They might all contribute to the association between IQ and longevity.

Investigating Cognitive Processes in Intelligent Behavior

As noted in Chapters 1 and 8, psychologists are increasingly taking a cognitive perspective in their efforts to study many topics. The *cognitive perspective* focuses on how people *use* their intelligence. In particular, cognitive psychologists focus on the information-processing strategies that underlie intelligence. The application of the cognitive perspective to intelligence has been spearheaded by Robert Sternberg (1985, 1991).

© Courtesy of Robert Sternberg

Robert Sternberg

"To understand intelligent behavior, we need to move beyond the fairly restrictive tasks that have been used both in experimental laboratories and in psychometric tests of intelligence."

In recent versions of his theory, Sternberg (2000b, 2003a, 2005a) has asserted that three facets characterize what he calls "successful intelligence": analytical intelligence, creative intelligence, and practical intelligence (see **Figure 9.20**). *Analytical intelligence* involves abstract reasoning, evaluation, and judgment. It is the type of intelligence that is crucial to most schoolwork and that is assessed by conventional IQ tests. *Creative intelligence* involves the ability to generate new ideas and to be inventive in dealing with novel problems. *Practical intelligence* involves the ability to deal effectively with the kinds of problems that people encounter in everyday life, such as on the job or at home. A big part of practical intelligence involves acquiring *tacit knowledge*—what one needs to know to work efficiently in an environment that is not explicitly taught and that often is not even verbalized.

Sternberg and his colleagues have gathered data suggesting that all three facets of intelligence can be measured reliably and that they are relatively independent (uncorrelated). They have also shown that the assessment of all three aspects of intelligence can improve the prediction of intelligent behavior in the real world (Grigorenko & Sternberg, 2001; Henry, Sternberg, & Grigorenko, 2005; Sternberg et al., 1999, 2001). Recent findings suggest that measurements based on Sternberg's model can be used as supplements to traditional tests (such as the SAT) to enhance the prediction of academic achievement (Stemler et al., 2006; Sternberg et al., 2006). Some critics doubt that Sternberg's measures will facilitate better prediction of meaningful outcomes than traditional IQ tests do (Gottfredson, 2003a). But that is an empirical question that should be resolved by future research. In any event, Sternberg certainly has been a strong voice arguing for a broader, expanded concept of intelligence, which is a theme that has been echoed by others.

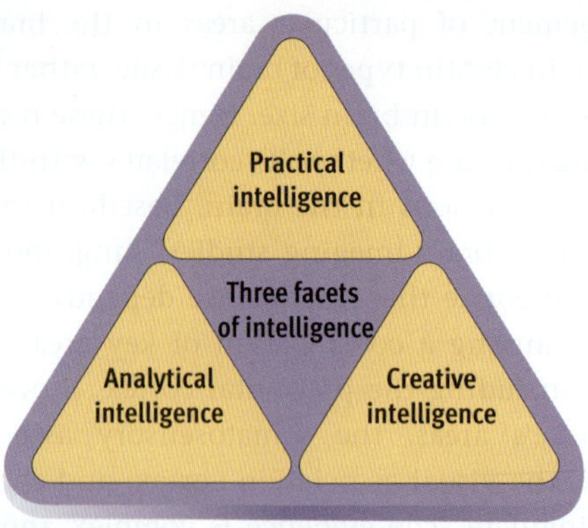

Figure 9.20

Sternberg's theory of intelligence. Sternberg's (2003a, 2005b) model of intelligence proposes that there are three aspects or types of intelligence: analytical intelligence, practical intelligence, and creative intelligence. According to Sternberg, traditional IQ tests focus almost exclusively on analytical intelligence. He believes that the prediction of real-world outcomes could be improved by broadening intelligence assessments to tap practical and creative intelligence. © Cengage Learning 2013

Expanding the Concept of Intelligence

In recent years, a number of theorists besides Sternberg have concluded that the focus of traditional IQ tests is too narrow. The most prominent proponent of this view has been Howard Gardner (1983, 1993, 1999, 2004, 2006). According to Gardner, IQ tests have generally emphasized verbal and mathematical skills to the exclusion of other important skills. He suggests the existence of a number of relatively autonomous human intelligences, which are listed in **Table 9.3**. To build his list of *multiple intelligences,* Gardner reviewed the evidence on cognitive capacities in normal individuals, people suf-

Table 9.3 Gardner's Eight Intelligences

Intelligence	End-States	Core Components
Logical-mathematical	Scientist Mathematician	Sensitivity to, and capacity to discern, logical or numerical patterns; ability to handle long chains of reasoning
Linguistic	Poet Journalist	Sensitivity to the sounds, rhythms, and meanings of words; sensitivity to the different functions of language
Musical	Composer Violinist	Abilities to produce and appreciate rhythm, pitch, and timbre; appreciation of the forms of musical expressiveness
Spatial	Navigator Sculptor	Capacities to perceive the visual-spatial world accurately and to perform transformations on one's initial perceptions
Bodily-kinesthetic	Dancer Athlete	Abilities to control one's body movements and to handle objects skillfully
Interpersonal	Therapist Salesperson	Capacities to discern and respond appropriately to the moods, temperaments, motivations, and desires of other people
Intrapersonal	Person with detailed, accurate self-knowledge	Access to one's own feelings and the ability to discriminate among them and draw upon them to guide behavior; knowledge of one's own strengths, weaknesses, desires, and intelligences
Naturalist	Biologist Naturalist	Abilities to recognize and categorize objects and processes in nature

© Cengage Learning 2013

SOURCE: Adapted from Gardner, H., & Hatch, T. (1989). Multiple intelligences go to school: Educational implications of the theory of multiple intelligences. *Educational Researcher*, 18 (8), 4–10. American Educational Research Association. Additional information from Gardner (1998).

fering from brain damage, and special populations, such as prodigies and idiot savants. He concluded that humans exhibit eight intelligences: logical-mathematical, linguistic, musical, spatial, bodily-kinesthetic, interpersonal, intrapersonal, and naturalist. These intelligences obviously include quite a variety of talents that are not assessed by conventional IQ tests. Gardner is investigating the extent to which these intelligences are largely independent, as his theory asserts. For the most part, he has found that people tend to display a mixture of strong, intermediate, and weak abilities, which is consistent with the idea that the various types of intelligence are independent.

Gardner's books have been popular, and his theory clearly resonates with many people (Shearer, 2004). His ideas have had an enormous impact on educators' attitudes and beliefs around the world (Cuban, 2004; Kornhaber, 2004). He has done a superb job of synthesizing research from neuropsychology, developmental psychology, cognitive psychology, and other areas to arrive at fascinating speculations about the structure of human abilities. In addition, he has raised thought-provoking questions about what abilities should be included under the rubric of intelligence (Eisner, 2004). However, he has his critics (Hunt, 2001; Klein, 1997; Morgan, 1996; Waterhouse, 2006). Some argue that his use of the term *intelligence* is so broad, encompassing virtually any valued human ability, as to make the term almost meaningless. These critics wonder whether there is any advantage to relabeling talents such as musical ability and motor coordination as forms of intelligence. Critics also note that Gardner's theory has not generated much research on the predictive value of measuring individual differences in the eight intelligences he has described. This research would require the development of tests to measure the eight intelligences, but Gardner loathes conventional testing. This situation makes it difficult to predict where Gardner's theory will lead, as research is crucial to the evolution of a theory.

Courtesy of Howard Gardner, photo © Jay Gardner

Howard Gardner

"It is high time that the view of intelligence be widened to incorporate a range of human computational capacities. . . . But where is it written that intelligence needs to be determined on the basis of tests?"

REVIEW OF KEY LEARNING GOALS

9.20 Recent research has uncovered a moderate positive correlation between IQ and overall brain volume estimated from MRI scans. Studies also suggest that IQ correlates with the size of specific areas in the brain and with the volume of gray and white matter. Researchers have also found that IQ measured in childhood correlates with longevity decades later. A variety of mechanisms may contribute to this surprising relationship.

9.21 Robert Sternberg's theory uses a cognitive perspective, which emphasizes the need to understand how people use their intelligence. According to Sternberg, the three facets of successful intelligence are analytical, creative, and practical intelligence.

9.22 Howard Gardner maintains that the concept of intelligence should be expanded to encompass a diverse set of eight types of abilities. Gardner's ideas have been influential, but some critics argue characterizing any valued human ability as an intelligence, makes the concept meaningless.

CONCEPT CHECK 9.3

Identifying the Contributions of Major Theorists and Researchers

Check your recall of the principal ideas of important theorists and researchers covered in this chapter by matching the people listed on the left with the appropriate contributions described on the right. If you need help, the crucial pages describing each person's ideas are listed in parentheses. Fill in the letters for your choices in the spaces provided on the left. You'll find the answers in Appendix A.

Major Theorists and Researchers

_______ 1. Alfred Binet (p. 355)

_______ 2. Francis Galton (p. 355)

_______ 3. Howard Gardner (pp. 376–377)

_______ 4. Arthur Jensen (p. 371)

_______ 5. Sandra Scarr (p. 369)

_______ 6. Charles Spearman (pp. 356–357)

_______ 7. Robert Sternberg (p. 376)

_______ 8. Lewis Terman (pp. 355–356)

_______ 9. David Wechsler (p. 356)

Key Ideas and Contributions

a. On the basis of a study of eminence and success in families, this theorist concluded that intelligence is inherited. He also invented the concept of correlation and coined the phrase *nature versus nurture*.

b. This person's theory takes a cognitive approach to intelligence. He argues that there are three key facets of human intelligence: analytical, creative, and practical intelligence.

c. This psychologist developed the Stanford-Binet Intelligence Scale, which originally described children's scores in terms of an intelligence quotient.

d. This French psychologist devised the first successful intelligence test, which expressed a child's score in terms of mental age.

e. This theorist argued that the heritability of intelligence is about 80% and that cultural differences in average IQ scores are primarily a product of heredity.

f. This person developed the first influential intelligence test designed specifically for adults. He also discarded the intelligence quotient in favor of a scoring scheme based on the normal distribution.

g. This theorist argued that there are eight types of human intelligence.

h. This person uses the concept of reaction range to explain the interaction of heredity and environment.

i. This theorist concluded that all cognitive abilities share an important core factor. He labeled this factor *g* for *general* mental ability.

KEY LEARNING GOALS

9.23 Identify the three unifying themes highlighted in this chapter.

Cultural Heritage

Heredity & Environment

Sociohistorical Context

Reflecting on the Chapter's Themes

Three of our integrative themes surfaced in this chapter. Our discussions illustrated that cultural factors shape behavior, that psychology evolves in a sociohistorical context, and that heredity and environment jointly influence behavior.

Pervasive psychological testing is largely a Western phenomenon. The concept of general intelligence also has a special, Western flavor to it. Many non-Western cultures have very different ideas about the nature of intelligence. Within Western societies, the observed ethnic differences in average intelligence also illustrate the importance of cultural factors. These disparities appear to be due in large part to cultural disadvantage and other culture-related considerations. Thus, we see once again that if we hope to achieve a sound understanding of behavior, we need to appreciate the cultural contexts in which behavior unfolds.

Human intelligence is shaped by a complex interaction of hereditary and environmental factors. We've drawn similar conclusions in previous chapters when looking at other aspects of behavior. However, this chapter should have enhanced your appreciation of this idea in at least two ways. First, we examined more of the details of how scientists arrive at the conclusion that heredity and environment jointly shape behavior. Second, we encountered dramatic illustrations of the immense importance attached to the nature versus nurture debate. For example, Arthur Jensen has been the target of savage criticism. After his controversial 1969 article, he was widely characterized as a racist. When he gave speeches, he was often greeted by protestors carrying signs, such as "Kill Jensen" and "Jensen Must Perish." Obviously, the debate about the inheritance of intelligence inspires passionate feelings in many people. In part, this is because the debate has far-reaching social and political implications, which brings us to another prominent theme in the chapter.

There may be no other area in psychology where the connections between psychology and society at large are so obvious. Prevailing social attitudes have always exerted some influence on testing practices and the interpretation of test results. In the first half of the 20th century, a strong current of racial and class prejudice was apparent in the United States and Britain. This prejudice supported the idea that IQ tests measured innate ability and that "undesirable" groups scored poorly because of their genetic inferiority. These beliefs did not go unchallenged within psychology, but their widespread acceptance in the field reflected the social values of the time. It's ironic that IQ tests have sometimes been associated with social prejudice since, when used properly, they provide relatively objective measures of mental ability that are less prone to bias than the subjective judgments of teachers or employers.

Today, psychological tests serve many diverse purposes. In the upcoming Personal Application, we focus on creativity tests and on the nature of creative thinking and creative people.

REVIEW OF KEY LEARNING GOALS

9.23 Our discussions of intelligence showed how heredity and environment interact to shape behavior, how psychology evolves in a sociohistorical context, and how one has to consider cultural contexts to fully understand behavior.

PERSONAL APPLICATION

Understanding Creativity

KEY LEARNING GOALS

9.24 Assess the role of insight and divergent thinking in creativity, and discuss the measurement of creativity.

9.25 Clarify the relations between creativity and personality, intelligence, and mental illness.

Answer the following "true" or "false."

___ **1** Creative ideas often come out of nowhere.

___ **2** Creativity usually occurs in a burst of insight.

___ **3** Creativity depends on divergent thinking.

People tend to view creativity as an essential trait for artists, musicians, and writers. However, it's important in *many* walks of life. In this Application, we'll discuss psychologists' efforts to measure and understand creativity. As we progress, you'll learn that all of the above statements are false.

The Nature of Creativity

***Creativity* involves the generation of ideas that are original and useful.** Creative thinking is fresh and inventive. But originality by itself is not enough. In addition to being different, creative thinking must be adaptive. It must be appropriate to the situation and problem.

Does Creativity Occur in a Burst of Insight?

It's widely believed that creativity usually involves sudden flashes of insight and great leaps of imagination. Robert Weisberg (1986) calls this belief the "aha! myth." Undeniably, creative bursts of insight do occur (Feldman, 1988). However, the evidence suggests that major creative achievements generally are logical extensions of existing ideas. Formulation of such ideas involves long, hard work and many small, faltering steps forward (Weisberg, 1993). Creative ideas don't come out of nowhere. They come from a deep well of experience and training in a specific area, whether it's music, painting, business, or science (Weisberg, 1999, 2006). As Snow (1986) put it, "Creativity is not a light bulb in the mind, as most cartoons depict it. It is an accomplishment born of intensive study, long reflection, persistence, and interest" (p. 1033).

Does Creativity Depend on Divergent Thinking?

According to many theorists, the key to creativity lies in *divergent thinking*—thinking "that goes off in different directions," as J. P. Guilford (1959) put it. Guilford distinguished between convergent thinking and divergent thinking. **In *convergent thinking* one tries to narrow down a list of alternatives to converge on a single correct answer.** For example, when you take a multiple-choice exam, you try to eliminate incorrect options until you hit on the correct response. Most training in school encourages convergent thinking. **In *divergent thinking* one tries to expand the range of alternatives by generating many possible solutions.** Imagine that you work for an advertising agency. To come up with as many slogans as possible for a client's product, you must use divergent thinking. Some of your slogans may be clear losers, and eventually you will have to engage in convergent thinking to pick the best. But coming up with the range of new possibilities depends on divergent thinking.

Thirty years of research on divergent thinking has yielded mixed results. As a whole, the evidence suggests that divergent thinking can contribute to creativity (Runco, 2004). However, it clearly does not represent the essence of creativity, as originally proposed (Brown, 1989; Plucker &

Renzulli, 1999; Weisberg, 2006). In retrospect, it was probably unrealistic to expect creativity to depend on a single cognitive skill.

Measuring Creativity SIM8

Although its nature may be elusive, creativity clearly is important in today's world. Creative masterpieces in the arts and literature enrich human existence. Creative insights in the sciences illuminate people's understanding of the world. Creative inventions fuel technological progress. Thus, it's understandable that psychologists have been interested in measuring creativity with psychological tests.

How Do Psychological Tests Measure Creativity? SIM8

A diverse array of psychological tests have been devised to measure individuals' creativity (Plucker & Makel, 2010). Usually, the items on creativity tests assess divergent thinking by giving respondents a specific starting point. They are then required to generate as many possibilities as they can in a short period of time. Typical items on a creativity test might include the following: (1) List as many uses as you can for a newspaper. (2) Think of as many fluids that burn as you can. (3) Imagine that people no longer need sleep and think of as many consequences as you can. Subjects' scores on these tests depend on the *number* of alternatives they generate and on the *originality* and *usefulness* of the alternatives.

How Well Do Tests Predict Creative Productivity?

In general, studies indicate that creativity tests are mediocre predictors of creative achievement in the real world (Hocevar & Bachelor, 1989; Plucker & Renzulli, 1999). Why? One reason is that these tests measure creativity in the abstract, as a *general trait*. However, the accumulation of evidence suggests that *creativity is specific to particular domains* (Amabile, 1996; Feist, 2004; Kaufman & Baer, 2002, 2004). Despite some rare exceptions, creative people usually excel in a single field, in which they typically have considerable training and expertise (Policastro & Gardner, 1999). A remarkably innovative physicist might have no potential to be a creative poet or an inventive advertising executive. Measuring this person's creativity outside of physics may be meaningless. Thus, creativity tests may have limited value because they measure creativity out of context.

Even if better tests of creativity were devised, predicting creative achievement would probably still prove difficult. Why? Because creative achievement depends on many factors besides creativity (Cropley, 2000). Creative productivity over the course of an individual's career will depend on his or her motivation, personality, and intelligence, as well as situational factors, including training, mentoring, and good fortune (Amabile, 2001; Feldman, 1999; Simonton, 1999a, 2004).

Correlates of Creativity

What are creative people like? Are they brighter, or more open minded, or less well adjusted than average? A great deal of research has been conducted on the correlates of creativity.

Is There a Creative Personality?

There is no single personality profile that accounts for creativity (Weisberg, 2006). However, investigators have found modest correlations between certain personality characteristics and creativity. Research suggests that highly creative people tend to be more independent, nonconforming, introverted, open to new experiences, self-confident, persistent, ambitious, dominant, and impulsive than less-creative folks (Feist, 1998, 2010). At the core of this set of personality characteristics are the related traits of nonconformity and openness to new experiences. Creative people tend to think for themselves and are less easily influenced by the opinions of others than the average person is. The importance of openness to new experiences can be seen in a new line of research suggesting that living abroad enhances creativity.

Although living abroad has long been viewed as a rite of passage for creative artists and writers, no one thought to take an empirical look at its impact until recently. In a series of studies, Maddux and Galinsky (2009) found that the amount of time spent living abroad correlated positively with measures of creativity. Interestingly, time spent in tourist travel abroad did *not* predict creativity. The contrasting effects of living and traveling abroad seems to depend on *acculturation*. Maddux and Galinsky found that the degree to which people adapted to foreign cultures was responsible for the association between living abroad and creativity. A subsequent study found that multicultural learning experiences appear to foster flexibility in thinking, which could enhance creativity (Maddux, Adam, & Galinsky, 2010).

Are Creativity and Intelligence Related?

Are creative people exceptionally smart? Conceptually, creativity and intelligence represent different types of mental ability. Thus, it's not surprising that correlations between measures of creativity and measures of intelligence are generally weak (Sternberg & O'Hara, 1999). For example, a recent meta-analysis of many studies reported a correlation of only .17 (Kim, 2005). However, some findings suggest that the association between creativity and intelligence is somewhat stronger than that. When Silvia (2008) administered several intelligence scales and calculated estimates of *g* for subjects, this higher-order measure of intelligence correlated over .40 with creativity.

One widely cited model of the relationship between creativity and intelligence is the *threshold hypothesis* proposed decades ago by pioneering creativity researchers (Barron, 1963; Torrance, 1962). According to this theory, creative achievements require a minimum level of intelligence. Thus, most highly creative people are probably well above average in intelligence. An IQ of 120 has been proposed as the minimum threshold for creative achievement (Lubart, 2003). One assumption of this model is that the correlation between IQ and creativity should be weaker among people above this IQ threshold than for those below it. Recent research, however, has failed to support this assumption (Kim, Cramond, & VanTassel-Baska, 2010). At this point, all we can conclude is that there appears to be a weak to modest association between IQ and creativity.

Is There a Connection Between Creativity and Mental Illness?

Some connection may exist between truly exceptional creativity and mental illness. The list of creative geniuses who suffered from psychological disorders is endless (Prentky, 1989). Kafka, Hemingway, Rembrandt, Van Gogh, Chopin, Tchaikovsky, Descartes, and Newton are but a few examples.

Of course, a statistical association cannot be demonstrated by citing a handful of examples. In this case, however, some statistical data are available, and these data *do* suggest a correlation between creative genius and maladjustment—in particular, mood disorders such as depression. When Nancy Andreasen studied 30 accomplished writers who had been invited as visiting faculty to the prestigious Iowa Writers Workshop, she found that 80% of her sample had suffered a mood disorder at some point in their lives (Andreasen, 1987, 2005). In a similar study of 59 female writers from another writers' conference, Ludwig (1994) found that 56% had experienced depression. These figures are far above the base rate (roughly 15%) for mood disorders in the general population. Other studies have also found an association between creativity and mood disorders, as well as other kinds of psychological disorders (Nettle, 2001; Silvia & Kaufman, 2010). Perhaps the most ambitious examination of the issue has been Arnold Ludwig's (1995) analyses of the biographies of 1004 people who achieved eminence in eighteen fields. He found greatly elevated rates of depression and other disorders among eminent writers, artists, and composers (see **Figure 9.21**). Recent studies suggest that mental illness may be especially elevated among poets (Kaufman, 2001, 2005).

Thus, accumulating empirical data tentatively suggest that a correlation may exist between major creative achievement and vulnerability to mood disorders. According to Andreasen (1996, 2005), creativity and maladjustment probably are *not* causally related. Instead, she speculates that certain personality traits and cognitive styles may both foster creativity and predispose people to psychological disorders. Another, more mundane possibility is that creative individuals' elevated pathology may simply reflect all the difficulty and frustration they experience as they struggle to get their ideas or works accepted in artistic fields that enjoy relatively little public support (Csikszentmihalyi, 1994, 1999b).

© Grant Perigo/age fotostock

Recent studies have discovered an interesting and unexpected correlation between creativity and the experience of living abroad. Theorists speculate that the process of adapting to new cultures may enhance flexible thinking.

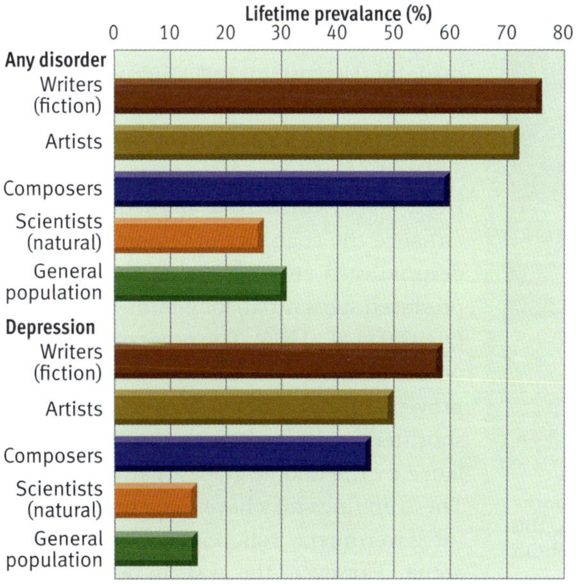

Figure 9.21

Estimated prevalence of psychological disorders among people who achieved creative eminence. Ludwig (1995) studied biographies of 1004 people who had clearly achieved eminence in one of eighteen fields and tried to determine whether each person suffered from any specific mental disorders in his or her lifetime. The data summarized here show the prevalence rates for depression and for a mental disorder of any kind for four fields where creativity is often the key to achieving eminence. As you can see, the estimated prevalence of mental illness was extremely elevated among eminent writers, artists, and composers (but not natural scientists) in comparison to the general population, with depression accounting for much of this elevation. © Cengage Learning 2013

REVIEW OF KEY LEARNING GOALS

9.24 Creativity involves the generation of original and useful ideas. Creativity does not usually involve sudden insight. Divergent thinking contributes to creativity but does not represent its essence. Creativity tests typically assess divergent thinking. Such tests are mediocre predictors of creative productivity in the real world. One problem is that creativity is specific to particular domains of expertise.

9.25 Creative people are more likely than others to exhibit certain personality traits, but the correlations between creativity and personality are weak. The association between creativity and intelligence is also weak to modest. Recent evidence suggests that creative geniuses may exhibit heightened vulnerability to mood disorders.

KEY LEARNING GOALS

9.26 Understand how appeals to ignorance and reification have cropped up in debates about intelligence.

The Intelligence Debate, Appeals to Ignorance, and Reification

A *fallacy* is a mistake or error in the process of reasoning. Cognitive scientists who study how people think have developed long lists of common errors that people make in their reasoning processes. One of these fallacies has a curious name, which is the *appeal to ignorance.* It involves misusing the general lack of knowledge or information on an issue (a lack of knowledge is a kind of ignorance) to support an argument. This fallacy often surfaces in the debate about the relative influence of heredity and environment on intelligence. But before we tackle the more difficult issue of how this fallacy shows up in the debate about intelligence, let's start with a simpler example.

Appeal to Ignorance

Do ghosts exist? This is probably not the kind of question you expected to find in your psychology textbook, but it can clarify the appeal to ignorance. Those who assert that ghosts *do* exist will often support their conclusion by arguing that no one can prove that ghosts do *not* exist; therefore, ghosts must exist. The lack of evidence or inability to show that ghosts do not exist is used to conclude the opposite. Conversely, those who assert that ghosts *do not* exist often rely on the same logic. They argue that no one can prove that ghosts exist; therefore, they must not exist. Can you see what is wrong with these appeals to ignorance? The lack of information on an issue cannot be used to support any conclusion—other than the conclusion that we are too ignorant to draw a conclusion.

One interesting aspect of the appeal to ignorance is that the same appeal can be used to support two conclusions that are diametrically opposed to each other. This paradox is a telltale clue that appeals to ignorance involve flawed reasoning. It's easy to see what's wrong with appeals to ignorance when the opposite arguments (ghosts exist—ghosts do not exist) are presented together. The lack of evidence on the issue is obvious. However, when the same fallacy surfaces in more complex debates and the appeal to ignorance is not as blatant, the strategy can be more difficult to recognize. Now let's see how it has surfaced in the debate about intelligence.

As noted in the main body of the chapter, the debate about the relative contributions of nature and nurture to intelligence is one of psychology's longest-running controversies. This complex debate is exceptionally bitter because it has far-reaching sociopolitical repercussions. One frequently made argument is that we have little or no evidence that intelligence can be increased by environmental (educational) interventions. Therefore, the claim goes, intelligence must be mostly inherited. This argument was part of Jensen's (1969) landmark treatise that greatly intensified the debate about intelligence. It was also one of the arguments made by Herrnstein and Murray (1994) in their controversial book *The Bell Curve.*

The argument refers to the fact that educational enrichment programs such as Head Start, which have been designed to enhance the cognitive development of underprivileged children, generally have not produced substantial, long-term gains in IQ (Neisser et al., 1996). The programs produce other benefits, including enduring improvements in school achievement, but short-term gains in IQ scores typically have faded by the middle grades (Barnett, 2004). These findings may have some implications for government policy in the educational arena. However, the way in which they

© Simon Marsden, marsdenarchive.com

Do ghosts exist? Littledean Hall, shown here, is said to be the home of eleven ghosts and is reputed to be the most haunted house in Great Britain. Those who believe in ghosts often support their view by arguing that no one can prove that ghosts do not exist. But as the text explains, this appeal to ignorance is logically flawed. This fallacy has also surfaced in some of the debates about the nature of intelligence.

have been applied to the nature-nurture debate regarding intelligence has resulted in an appeal to ignorance. In its simplest form, the absence of evidence showing that environmental changes can increase intelligence is used to support the conclusion that intelligence is mostly determined by genetic inheritance. But the absence of evidence (ignorance) cannot be used to argue for or against a position.

By the way, if you have assimilated some of the critical thinking skills discussed in earlier chapters, you may be thinking, "Wait a minute. Aren't there alternative explanations for the failure of educational enrichment programs to increase IQ scores?" Yes, one could argue that the programs failed to yield improvements in IQ scores because they often were poorly executed, too brief, or underfunded (Ramey, 1999; Sigel, 2004). Moreover, Head Start programs were not really designed to increase IQ scores. They were designed to enhance deprived students' readiness for school (Schrag, Styfco, & Zigler, 2004). The inability of the enrichment programs to produce enduring increases in IQ does not necessarily imply that intelligence is unchangeable because it's largely a product of heredity.

You may also be wondering, "Aren't there contradictory data?" Once again, the answer is yes. Barnett (2004) argues that failures to find enduring gains in intelligence from Head Start programs can often be attributed to flaws and shortcomings in the research design of the studies. Furthermore, studies of some lesser-known educational enrichment programs attempted with smaller groups of children *have* yielded durable gains in IQ and other standardized test scores (Ramey & Ramey, 2004; Reynolds et al., 2001).

Reification

The dialogue on intelligence has also been marred by the tendency to engage in reification. ***Reification*** **occurs when a hypothetical, abstract concept is given a name and then treated as though it were a concrete, tangible object.** Some hypothetical constructs just become so familiar and so taken for granted that we begin to think about them as if they were real. People often fall into this trap with the Freudian personality concepts of id, ego, and superego (see Chapter 12). They begin to think of the *ego,* for instance, as a genuine entity that can be strengthened or controlled, when the ego is really nothing more than a hypothetical abstraction. The concept of intelligence has also been reified in many quarters. Like the ego, intelligence is nothing more than a useful abstraction—a hypothetical construct that is estimated, rather arbitrarily, by a collection of paper-and-pencil measures called IQ tests. Yet people routinely act as if intelligence is a tangible commodity, fighting nasty battles over whether it can be measured precisely, whether it can be changed, and whether it can ensure job success. This reification clearly contributes to the tendency for people to attribute excessive importance to the concept of intelligence. It would be wise to remember that intelligence is no more real than the concept of or "cyberspace," or "the American dream."

Reification has also occurred in the debate about the *degree* to which intelligence is inherited. Arguments about the heritability coefficient for intelligence often imply that a single, true number lurks somewhere "out there" waiting to be discovered. In reality, heritability is a hypothetical construct that can be legitimately estimated in several ways that can lead to somewhat different results. Moreover, heritability ratios will vary from one population to the next, depending on the amount of genetic variability and the extent of environmental variability in the populations. Thus, no exactly accurate number that corresponds to "true heritability" awaits discovery (Hunt & Carlson, 2007; Sternberg et al., 2005). It is therefore important to understand that although hypothetical constructs have great heuristic value in the study of complex phenomena such as human thought and behavior, they do not actually exist in the world—at least not in the same way that a table or a person exists.

© Cover reproduced by courtesy and permission of Information Today, Inc., Medford, NJ

Reification occurs when we think of hypothetical constructs as if they were real. Like intelligence, the concept of cyberspace has been subject to reification. The fact that cyberspace is merely an abstraction becomes readily apparent when artists are asked to "draw" cyberspace for conference posters or book covers.

Table 9.4 Critical Thinking Skills Discussed in This Application

Skill	Description
Recognizing and avoiding appeals to ignorance	The critical thinker understands that the lack of information on an issue cannot be used to support an argument.
Recognizing and avoiding reification	The critical thinker is vigilant about the tendency to treat hypothetical constructs as if they were concrete things.
Looking for alternative explanations for findings and events	In evaluating explanations, the critical thinker explores whether there are other explanations that could also account for the findings or events under scrutiny.
Looking for contradictory evidence	In evaluating the evidence presented on an issue, the critical thinker attempts to look for contradictory evidence that may have been left out of the debate.

© Cengage Learning 2013

REVIEW OF KEY LEARNING GOALS

9.26 The appeal to ignorance involves misusing the general lack of knowledge or information on an issue to support an argument. This fallacy has surfaced in the debate about intelligence, where it has been argued that because we have little or no evidence that intelligence can be increased by environmental interventions, intelligence must be mostly inherited. Reification occurs when a hypothetical construct, such as intelligence, is treated as though it were a tangible object.

Chapter 9 Practice Test

1. Which of the following does not belong with the others?
A. aptitude tests
B. personality tests
C. intelligence tests
D. achievement tests

2. If you score at the 75th percentile on a standardized test, it means that:
A. 75% of those who took the test scored better than you did.
B. 25% of those who took the test scored less than you did.
C. 75% of those who took the test scored the same or less than you did.
D. you answered 75% of the questions correctly.

3. If a test has good test-retest reliability:
A. there is a strong correlation between items on the test.
B. it accurately measures what it says it measures.
C. it can be used to predict future performance.
D. the test yields similar scores if taken at two different times.

4. Which of the following is a true statement regarding Francis Galton?
A. He took the position that intelligence is largely determined by heredity.
B. He advocated the development of special programs to tap the intellectual potential of the culturally disadvantaged.
C. He developed tests that identified those children who were unable to profit from a normal education.
D. He took the position that intelligence is more a matter of environment than heredity.

5. On most modern IQ tests, a score of 115 would be:
A. about average.
B. about 15% higher than the average of one's agemates.
C. an indication of genius.
D. one standard deviation above the mean.

6. IQ tests have proven to be good predictors of:
A. social intelligence.
B. practical problem-solving intelligence.
C. school performance.
D. all of the above.

7. Mr. and Mrs. Proudparent are beaming because their son, little Newton, has been selected for a gifted children program at school. They think Newton is a genius. What sort of advice do they need to hear?
A. Youngsters with a 130–140 IQ tend to be very maladjusted.
B. Most gifted children do not go on to make genius-level, major contributions to society that earn them eminence.
C. They should prepare to be famous, based on their parentage of Newton.
D. They should be warned that gifted children often have deficits in practical intelligence.

8. Which of the following is a true statement about mental retardation/intellectual disability?
A. Most people with retardation are unable to live normal lives because of their mental deficiencies.
B. With special tutoring, a mentally retarded person can attain average intelligence.
C. The majority of people who exhibit intellectual disability fall in the mild category.
D. Diagnoses of mental retardation should be based exclusively on IQ scores.

9. Most school districts consider children who ___________________ to be gifted.
A. have IQ scores above 115
B. score in the upper 2%–3% of the IQ distribution
C. have parents in professional careers
D. demonstrate high levels of leadership and creativity

10. In which of the following cases would you expect to find the greatest similarity in IQ?
A. between fraternal twins
B. between identical twins
C. between nontwin siblings
D. between parent and child

11. Evidence indicating that upbringing affects one's mental ability is provided by which of the following findings?
A. Identical twins are more similar in IQ than fraternal twins.
B. There is more than a chance similarity between adopted children and their biological parents.
C. Siblings reared together are more similar in IQ than siblings reared apart.
D. Identical twins reared apart are more similar in IQ than siblings reared together.

12. Which of the following is a likely consequence of stereotype threat for members of minority groups?
A. Academic motivation declines.
B. Academic performance often suffers.
C. Standardized tests may underestimate their ability.
D. All of the above are likely consequences.

13. ___________________ proposed that there are three facets of intelligence: analytical, practical, and creative intelligence.
A. Howard Gardner.
B. Arthur Jensen.
C. Claude Steele.
D. Robert Sternberg.

14. When you try to narrow down a list of alternatives to arrive at a single correct answer, you engage in:
A. convergent thinking.
B. divergent thinking.
C. creativity.
D. insight.

15. Nora has a blind date with Nick, who, she's been told, is considered a true genius by the faculty in the art department. Now she's having second thoughts, because she's always heard that geniuses are a little off their rocker. Does she have reason to be concerned?
A. Yes. It's been well documented that the stress of creative achievement often leads to schizophrenic symptoms.
B. No. Extensive research on creativity and psychological disorders shows no evidence for any connection.
C. Perhaps. There is evidence of a correlation between major creative achievement and vulnerability to mood disorders.
D. Of course not. The stereotype of the genius who's mentally ill is purely a product of the jealousy of untalented people.

Answers

1 B pp. 350–351	6 C pp. 358–359	11 C pp. 367–368
2 C p. 351	7 B p. 365	12 D pp. 372–373
3 D pp. 351–352	8 C p. 363	13 D p. 376
4 A p. 355	9 B p. 364	14 A p. 379
5 D pp. 358–359	10 B pp. 366–367	15 C p. 381

PsykTrek

To view a demo: **www.cengage.com/psychology/psyktrek**
To order: **www.cengage.com/psychology/weiten**
Go to the PsykTrek website or CD-ROM for further study of the concepts in this chapter. Both online and on the CD-ROM, PsykTrek includes dozens of learning modules with videos, animations, and quizzes, as well as simulations of psychological phenomena and a multimedia glossary that includes word pronunciations.

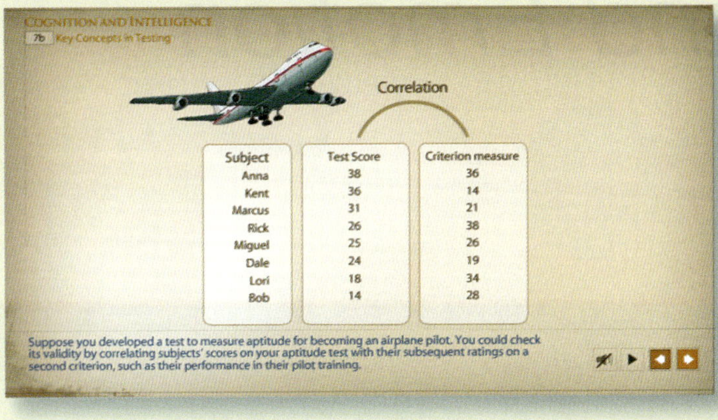

© Cengage Learning 2008

Check out Module 7b (*Key Concepts in Testing*) for more information on how researchers document the reliability and validity of psychological tests.

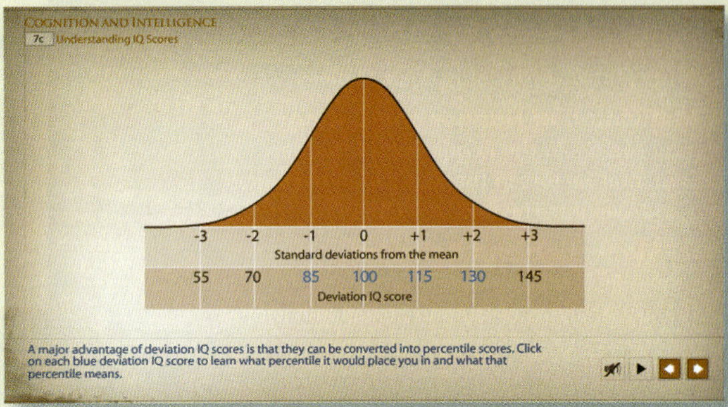

© Cengage Learning 2008

Visit Module 7c (*Understanding IQ Scores*) to increase your appreciation of how IQ tests measure general intelligence.

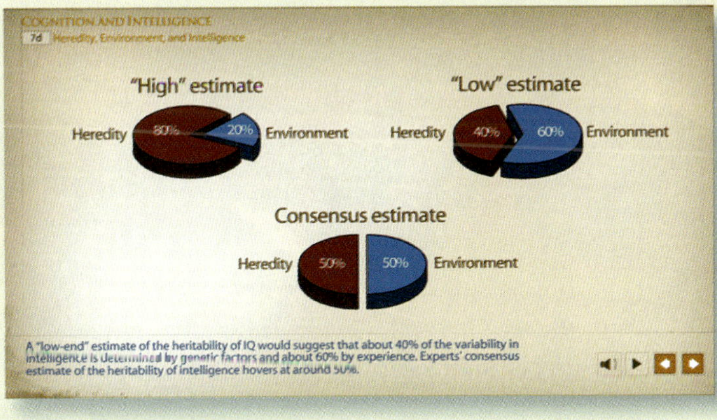

© Cengage Learning 2008

Review Module 7d (*Heredity, Environment, and Intelligence*) to increase your appreciation of how genetics and experience jointly influence intelligence.

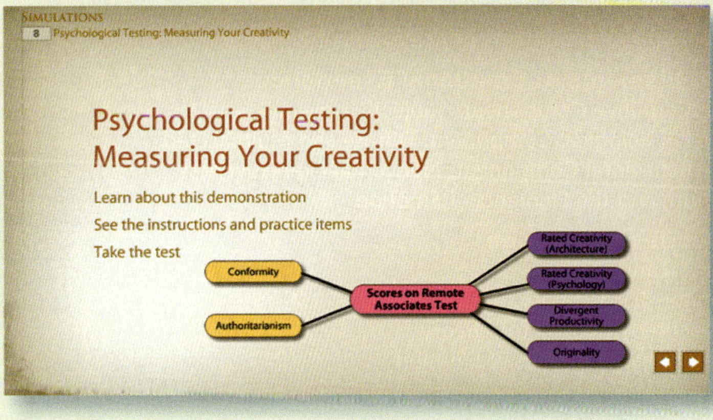

© Cengage Learning 2008

Go to Simulation 8 (*Psychological Testing: Measuring Your Creativity*) to take a genuine psychological test that will give you an estimate of your creative potential—and see concrete illustrations of key testing concepts, such as reliability, validity, and test norms, along the way.

Online Study Tools

Log in to **CengageBrain** to access the resources your instructor requires. For this book, you can access:

CourseMate brings course concepts to life with interactive learning, study, and exam preparation tools that support the printed textbook. A textbook-specific website, Psychology CourseMate includes an integrated interactive eBook and other interactive learning tools such as quizzes, flashcards, videos, and more.

CengageNow is an easy-to-use online resource that helps you study in less time to get the grade you want—NOW. Take a pre-test for this chapter and receive a personalized study plan based on your results that will identify the topics you need to review and direct you to online resources to help you master those topics. Then take a post-test to help you determine the concepts you have mastered and what you will need to work on. If your textbook does not include an access code card, go to CengageBrain.com to gain access.

WebTutor is more than just an interactive study guide. WebTutor is an anytime, anywhere customized learning solution with an eBook, keeping you connected to your textbook, instructor, and classmates.

Aplia. If your professor has assigned Aplia homework:

1. Sign in to your account
2. Complete the corresponding homework exercises as required by your professor.
3. When finished, click "Grade It Now" to see which areas you have mastered, which need more work, and detailed explanations of every answer.

Visit **www.cengagebrain.com** to access your account and purchase materials.

10

Motivation and Emotion

© Buzz Pictures/Alamy

It was a bright afternoon in May 1996, and 41-year-old Jon Krakauer was on top of the world—literally. Krakauer had just fulfilled a boyhood dream by climbing Mount Everest, the tallest peak on Earth. Clearing the ice from his oxygen mask, he looked down on a sweeping vista of ice, snow, and majestic mountains. His triumph should have brought him intense joy. Yet, he felt strangely detached. "I'd been fantasizing about this moment, and the release of emotion that would accompany it, for many years," he wrote later. "But now that I was finally here, standing on the summit of Mount Everest, I just couldn't summon the energy to care" (Krakauer, 1998, p. 6).

Why were Krakauer's emotions so subdued? A major reason was that he was physically exhausted. Climbing Mount Everest is an incredibly grueling experience. At just over 29,000 feet, the mountain's peak is at the altitude flown by jumbo jets. Because such high altitudes wreak havoc on the human body, Krakauer and his fellow climbers couldn't even approach the summit until they had spent six weeks acclimating at Base Camp, 17,600 feet above sea level. At Base Camp, Krakauer found that ordinary bodily functions became painfully difficult. On most nights, he awoke three or four times, gasping for breath and feeling like he was suffocating. His appetite vanished. "My body began consuming itself for sustenance. My arms and legs gradually began to wither to sticklike proportions" (Krakauer, 1998, p. 87).

At this point, you may be wondering why anyone would willingly undergo such extreme discomfort, but Base Camp was just the beginning. From Base Camp, it's another two vertical miles through the aptly named Death Zone to the summit. The final leg of the ascent is excruciating. By the time Krakauer reached the summit, every step was labored, every gasping breath hurt. He hadn't slept in 57 hours. He was bitterly cold. He was utterly exhausted. Instead of elation, he felt only apprehension. His oxygen-starved brain was barely functioning. But he understood that getting

Jon Krakauer (the third person) and other climbers are seen here during their ascent of Mount Everest at an elevation of about 28,200 feet.

Copyright © by Klev Schoening

down from the summit would be just as dangerous as getting up.

The ensuing events proved just how dangerous an assault on Everest can be. During Krakauer's descent, a sudden, howling storm hit the mountain. Winds exceeding 100 miles per hour whipped the snow into a blinding white blur. Krakauer barely escaped with his life. Twelve men and women were not as fortunate. They died on the mountain, including several in Krakauer's own party. Some of them perished needlessly because they had fallen victim to "summit fever." Once they got close to the top, they refused to turn back despite extreme exhaustion and the obvious threat posed by the storm.

The saga of Jon Krakauer and the other climbers is packed with motivation riddles. Why would people push on toward a goal even at the risk of their lives? Why endure such a punishing and hazardous ordeal? In the case of Mount Everest, perhaps the most obvious motive is simply the satisfaction of conquering the world's tallest peak. When British climber George Leigh Mallory was asked why he wanted to climb Everest in the 1920s, his famous reply was, "Because it is there." Some people seem to have an intense desire to take on the toughest challenges imaginable, to achieve something incredibly difficult. Yet—as is usually the case with human behavior—things are not quite so simple. Krakauer observed that a wide variety of motives drove the climbers he met on Everest. Such motives included desires for "minor celebrity, career advancement, ego massage, ordinary bragging rights, filthy lucre," and even a quest for "a state of grace" (Krakauer, 1998, p. 177).

Krakauer's story is also filled with strong emotions. He anticipated that he would experience a transcendent emotional high when he reached the summit of Mount Everest. As it turned out, his triumph was accompanied more by anxiety than by ecstasy. The harrowing events that followed left him emotionally numb at first. However, he was soon flooded with intense feelings of despair, grief, and guilt over the deaths of his companions. His tale illustrates the intimate connection between motivation and emotion—the topics we'll examine in this chapter.

KEY LEARNING GOALS

10.1 Compare drive, incentive, and evolutionary approaches to understanding motivation.

10.2 Distinguish between the two major categories of motives found in humans.

Motivational Theories and Concepts

Motives are the needs, wants, interests, and desires that propel people in certain directions. In short, ***motivation* involves goal-directed behavior.** Psychologists have developed a number of theoretical approaches to motivation. Let's look at some of these theories and the concepts they include.

Drive Theories

Many theories view motivational forces in terms of *drives*. The drive concept appears in a diverse array of theories that otherwise have little in common, such as psychoanalytic (Freud, 1915) and behaviorist formulations (Hull, 1943). This approach to understanding motivation was explored most fully by Clark Hull in the 1940s and 1950s.

Hull's concept of drive was derived from Walter Cannon's (1932) observation that organisms seek to maintain ***homeostasis*, a state of physiological equilibrium or stability.** The body maintains homeostasis in various ways. For example, human body temperature normally fluctuates around 98.6 degrees Fahrenheit (see **Figure 10.1**). If your body temperature rises or drops noticeably, automatic responses occur. If your temperature goes up, you'll perspire. If your temperature goes down, you'll shiver. These reactions are designed to move your temperature back toward 98.6 degrees. Thus, your

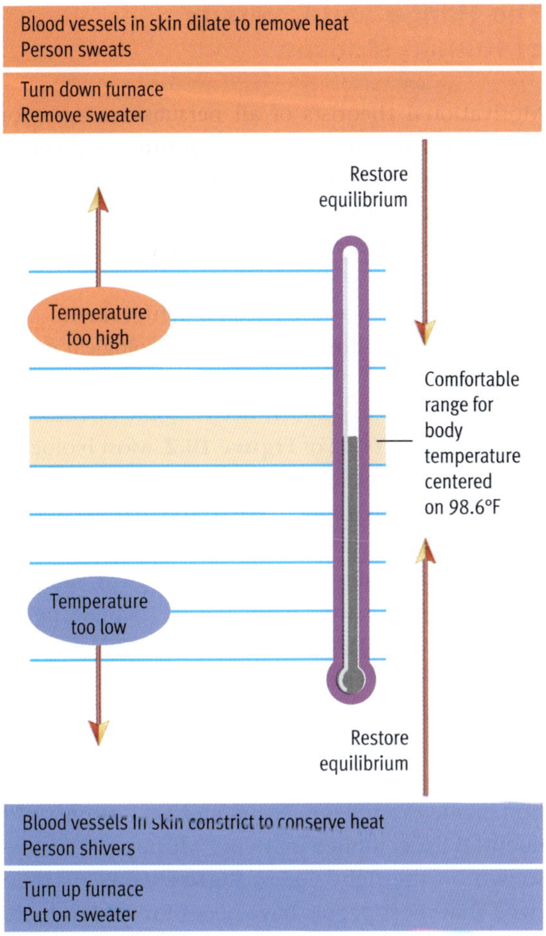

Figure 10.1

Temperature regulation as an example of homeostasis. The regulation of body temperature provides a simple example of how organisms often seek to maintain homeostasis, or a state of physiological equilibrium. When your temperature moves out of an acceptable range, automatic bodily reactions (such as sweating or shivering) occur that help restore equilibrium. Of course, these automatic reactions may not be sufficient by themselves, so you may have to take other actions (such as turning a furnace up or down) to bring your body temperature back into its comfort zone.
© Cengage Learning 2013

© Ljupco Smokovski/Shutterstock

body reacts to many disturbances in physiological stability by trying to restore equilibrium.

Drive theories apply the concept of homeostasis to behavior. **A *drive* is an internal state of tension that motivates an organism to engage in activities that should reduce this tension.** These unpleasant states of tension are viewed as disruptions of the preferred equilibrium. According to drive theories, when individuals experience a drive, they're motivated to pursue actions that will lead to *drive reduction*. For example, the hunger motive has usually been conceptualized as a drive system. If you go without food for a while, you begin to experience some discomfort. This internal tension (the drive) motivates you to obtain food. Eating reduces the drive and restores physiological equilibrium.

Drive theories have been very influential, and the drive concept continues to be widely used in modern psychology. *However, drive theories were not able to explain all motivation* (Berridge, 2004). Homeostasis appears irrelevant to some human motives, such as a "thirst for knowledge." Also, motivation may exist without drive arousal. This point is easy to illustrate: Think of all the times that you've eaten when you weren't really hungry. Because drive theories assume that people always try to reduce internal tension, they can't explain this behavior very well. Incentive theories, which represent a different approach to motivation, can account for this behavior more readily.

Incentive Theories

Incentive theories propose that external stimuli regulate motivational states (Bolles, 1975; McClelland, 1975; Skinner, 1953). **An *incentive* is an external goal that has the capacity to motivate behavior.** Ice cream, a juicy steak, a monetary prize, approval from friends, an A on an exam, and a promotion at work are all incentives. Some of these incentives may reduce drives. Yet others may not.

Drive and incentive models of motivation are often contrasted as *push versus pull* theories. Drive theories emphasize how *internal* states of tension *push* people in certain directions. Incentive theories emphasize how *external* stimuli *pull* people in certain directions. According to drive theories, the source of motivation lies *within* the organism. According to incentive theories, the source of motivation lies *outside* the organism, in the environment. This means that incentive models don't operate according to the principle of homeostasis, which hinges on internal changes in the organism. Rather, incentive theories stress environmental factors and downplay the biological bases of human motivation.

Evolutionary Theories

Psychologists who take an evolutionary perspective assert that human motives and those of other species are the products of natural selection, just as anatomical characteristics are (Durrant & Ellis, 2003). They argue that natural selection favors behaviors that maximize reproductive success—that is, passing on genes to the next generation. Thus, they explain motives such as affiliation, achievement, dominance, aggression, and sex drive in terms of their adaptive value. If dominance is a crucial motive for a species, they say, it's because dominance provides a reproductive or survival advantage.

Evolutionary analyses of motivation are based on the premise that motives can best be understood in terms of the adaptive problems they solved for our hunter-gatherer ancestors (Tooby & Cosmides, 2005). For example, the need for dominance is thought to be greater in men than in women because it could foster males' reproductive success in a variety of ways: (1) females may prefer mating with dominant males, (2) dominant males may intimidate male rivals in competition for sexual access, and (3) dominant males may acquire more material resources, which may increase their mating opportunities (Buss, 1999). Consider also the *affiliation motive,* or need for belongingness. The adaptive benefits of affiliation for our ancient ancestors probably included help with rearing of offspring, collaboration in hunting or defense, opportunities for sexual interaction, and so forth (Baumeister & Leary, 1995).

Examples of Biological Motives in Humans	Examples of Social Motives in Humans
Hunger motive	Achievement motive (need to excel)
Thirst motive	Affiliation motive (need for social bonds)
Sex motive	Autonomy motive (need for independence)
Temperature motive (need for appropriate body temperature)	Nurturance motive (need to nourish and protect others)
Excretory motive (need to eliminate bodily wastes)	Dominance motive (need to influence or control others)
Sleep and rest motive	Exhibition motive (need to make an impression on others)
Activity motive (need for optimal level of stimulation and arousal)	Order motive (need for orderliness, tidiness, organization)
Aggression motive	Play motive (need for fun, relaxation, amusement)

Figure 10.2

The diversity of human motives. People are motivated by a wide range of needs, which can be divided into two broad classes: biological motives and social motives. The list on the left (adapted from Madsen, 1973) shows some important biological motives in humans. The list on the right (adapted from Murray, 1938) provides examples of prominent social motives in humans. The distinction between biological and social motives is not absolute. © Cengage Learning 2013

The Range and Diversity of Human Motives

Motivational theorists of all persuasions agree on one point: Humans display an enormous diversity of motives. Most theories (evolutionary theories being a notable exception) distinguish between *biological motives* that originate in bodily needs, such as hunger, and *social motives* that originate in social experiences, such as the need for achievement.

People have a limited number of biological needs. According to K. B. Madsen (1968, 1973), most theories identify 10 to 15 such needs. Some of these are listed on the left side of **Figure 10.2**. Most biological motives reflect needs that are essential to survival, such as the needs for food, water, and maintenance of body temperature within an acceptable range.

People all share the same biological motives. However, their social motives vary depending on their experiences. For example, we all need to eat. Not everyone, though, acquires a need for orderliness. People have a limited number of biological motives, but they can acquire an unlimited number of social motives through learning and socialization. Some examples of social motives—from an influential list compiled by Henry Murray (1938)—are shown on the right side of **Figure 10.2**. He theorized that most people have needs for achievement, autonomy, affiliation, dominance, exhibition, and order, among other things. Of course, the strength of these motives varies from person to person, depending on personal history.

Given the range and diversity of human motives, we can examine only a handful in depth. To a large degree, our choices reflect the motives psychologists have studied the most: hunger, sex, and achievement. After discussing these motivational systems, we will explore the elements of emotional experience and examine various theories of emotion.

REVIEW OF KEY LEARNING GOALS

10.1 Drive theories apply a homeostatic model to motivation. They assume that organisms seek to reduce unpleasant states of tension called drives. In contrast, incentive theories emphasize how external goals energize behavior. Evolutionary theorists explain motives in terms of their adaptive value.

10.2 Humans display an enormous diversity of motives. These motives can be divided into biological motives and social motives. Madsen's list of biological needs includes motives such as hunger, thirst and sex; Murray's list of social needs includes motives such as achievement, affiliation, and dominance.

The Motivation of Hunger and Eating

KEY LEARNING GOALS

10.3 Summarize evidence on the physiological factors implicated in the regulation of hunger.

10.4 Explain how food availability, culture, and learning influence hunger and eating.

10.5 Evaluate evidence on the prevalence and health significance of obesity.

10.6 Identify the factors that contribute to the development of obesity.

Why do people eat? Because they're hungry. What makes them hungry? A lack of food. Any grade-school child can explain these basic facts. So hunger is a simple motivational system, right? Wrong! Hunger is deceptive. It only looks simple. Actually, it's a puzzling and complex motivational system. Despite extensive studies, scientists are still struggling to understand the factors that regulate hunger and eating behavior. Let's examine a few of these factors.

Biological Factors in the Regulation of Hunger 2e, 8a

PSYK TREK

You've probably had embarrassing occasions when your stomach growled loudly at an inopportune moment. Someone may have commented, "You must be starving!" Most people equate a rumbling stomach with hunger. In fact, the first scientific theories of hunger were based on this simple equation. In a 1912 study, Walter Cannon and A. L. Washburn verified what most people have noticed based on casual observation. There is an association between stomach contractions and the experience of hunger.

Based on this correlation, Cannon theorized that stomach contractions *cause* hunger. However, as we've seen before, correlation is no assurance of causation. Thus, his theory was eventually discredited. Stomach contractions sometimes accompany hunger (the association is actually rather weak). However, they don't cause it. How do we know? Because later research showed that people continue to experience hunger even after their stomachs have been removed out of medical necessity (Wangensteen & Carlson, 1931). If hunger can occur without a stomach, then stomach contractions can't be the cause of hunger. This realization led to increasingly complex theories of hunger that focus on a number of factors and processes.

Brain Regulation 2e, 8a

PSYK TREK

Research with lab animals eventually suggested that the experience of hunger is controlled in the brain—specifically, in the hypothalamus. As we have noted before, the *hypothalamus* is a tiny structure involved in the regulation of a variety of biological needs related to survival (see **Figure 10.3** on the next page). In the 1940s and 1950s, studies using brain lesioning techniques and electrical stimulation of the brain led to the conclusion that the *lateral hypothalamus (LH)* and the *ventromedial nucleus of the hypothalamus (VMH)* were the brain's on-off switches for the control of hunger (Stellar, 1954). However, over the course of several decades, a variety of empirical findings undermined the dual-centers model of hunger (Valenstein, 1973; Winn, 1995). The current thinking is that the lateral and ventromedial areas of the hypothalamus are elements in the neural circuitry that regulates hunger. However, they are not the key elements, nor are they simple on-off centers (King, 2006; Meister, 2007). Today, scientists believe that two other areas of the hypothalamus—the *arcuate nucleus* and the *paraventricular nucleus*—play a larger role in the modulation of hunger (Scott, McDade, & Luckman, 2007) (see **Figure 10.3**). In recent years, the arcuate nucleus has been singled out as especially important (Becskei, Lutz, & Riediger, 2008). This area in the hypothalamus appears to contain a group of neurons that are sensitive to incoming hunger signals and another group of neurons that respond to satiety signals.

Contemporary theories of hunger focus more on *neural circuits* that pass through areas of the hypothalamus rather than on *anatomical centers* in the brain. These circuits depend on a large variety of neurotransmitters, and they appear to be much more complicated than anticipated. Evidence suggests that the neural circuits regulating hunger are massively and reciprocally interconnected with extensive parallel processing (Powley, 2009). This complex neural circuitry is sensitive to a diverse range of physiological processes.

Glucose and Digestive Regulation 8a

PSYK TREK

Much of the food taken into the body is converted into *glucose,* which circulates in the blood. *Glucose* is a simple sugar that is an important source of energy. Actions that decrease blood glucose level can increase hunger; actions that increase glucose level can make people feel satiated. Based on these findings, *glucostatic theory* proposed that fluctuations in blood glucose level are monitored in the brain, where they influence the experience of hunger (Mayer, 1955, 1968). Like the dual-centers theory, the glucostatic theory of hunger gradually ran into

Figure 10.3

The hypothalamus. This small structure at the base of the forebrain plays a role in regulating a variety of human biological needs, including hunger. The detailed blow-up shows that the hypothalamus is made up of a variety of discrete areas. Scientists used to believe that the lateral and ventromedial areas were the brain's on-off centers for eating. However, more recent research suggests that the arcuate and paraventricular areas may be more crucial to the regulation of hunger and that thinking in terms of neural circuits rather than anatomical centers makes more sense.

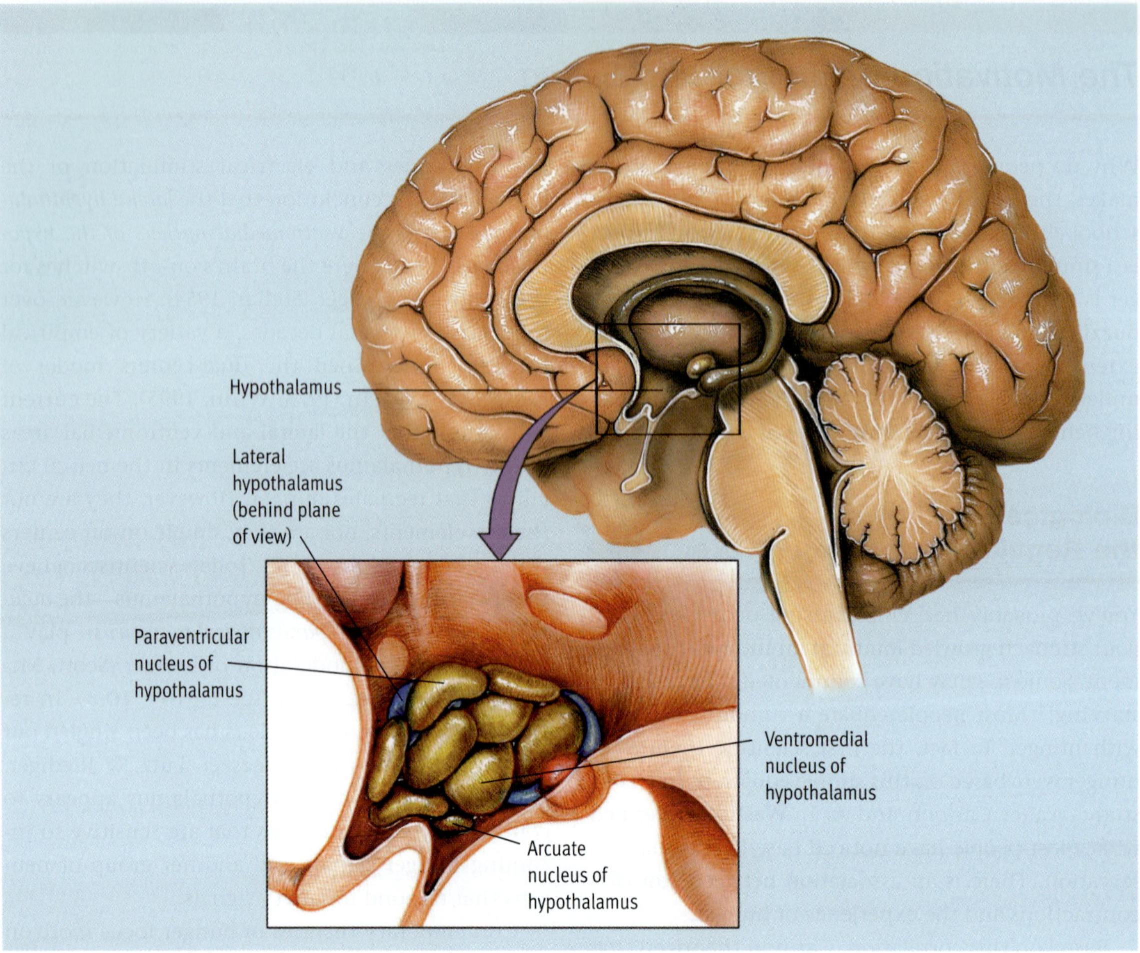

© Cengage Learning 2013

many complications. Nonetheless, it appears that the arcuate nucleus of the hypothalamus is sensitive to glucostatic fluctuations that *contribute* to the modulation of eating (Woods & Stricker, 2008).

The digestive system also includes a variety of other mechanisms that influence hunger (Ritter, 2004). It turns out that Walter Cannon was not entirely wrong in hypothesizing that the stomach regulates hunger. After you have consumed food, cells in the stomach can send signals to the brainstem that inhibit further eating (Woods & Stricker, 2008). For example, the vagus nerve carries information about the stretching of the stomach walls that indicates when the stomach is full. Other nerves carry satiety messages that depend on how rich in nutrients the contents of the stomach are.

Hormonal Regulation

PSYKTREK 8a

A variety of hormones circulating in the bloodstream also appear to contribute to the regulation of hunger. *Insulin* is a hormone secreted by the pancreas. It must be present for cells to extract glucose from the blood. In fact, an inadequate supply of insulin is what causes diabetes. Insulin levels increase when people eat. Moreover, insulin levels appear to be sensitive to fluctuations in the body's fat stores (M. W. Schwartz et al., 2000). These findings suggest that insulin secretions play a role in the determination of hunger.

At least two other hormones play a key role in the short-term regulation of hunger. After going without food for a while, the stomach secretes *ghrelin*, which causes stomach contractions and promotes hunger (Cummings, 2006). In contrast, after food is consumed, the upper intestine releases a hormone called *CCK* that delivers satiety signals to the brain. The result is reduced hunger (Moran, 2004; Schwartz & Azzara, 2004).

Finally, a hormone called *leptin* contributes to the long-term regulation of hunger, as well as the modulation of numerous other bodily functions (Ahima & Osei, 2004). Leptin is produced by fat cells throughout the body and released into the bloodstream. Higher levels of fat generate higher levels of leptin (Schwartz et al., 1996). Leptin circulates through the bloodstream and ultimately provides the hypothalamus with information about the body's fat stores (Campfield, 2002). When leptin levels are high, hunger feelings tend to diminish.

The hormonal signals that influence hunger (the fluctuations of insulin, ghrelin, CCK, and leptin) all seem to converge in the hypothalamus. Most notably, they converge in the arcuate and paraventricular nuclei of the hypothalamus (Kuo et al., 2007; Näslund & Hellström, 2007).

If all this sounds confusing, don't worry, it is. Frankly, researchers are still struggling to figure out exactly how all these processes work together. Hunger depends on remarkably complex interactions between neural circuits, neurotransmitter systems, digestive processes, and hormonal fluctuations (Berthoud & Morrison, 2008). These systems are far more decentralized and interconnected than originally thought (Powley, 2009).

Environmental Factors in the Regulation of Hunger

PSYKTREK 8a

Hunger clearly is a biological need. But eating is not regulated by biological factors alone. Studies show that social and environmental factors govern eating to a considerable extent. Two key environmental factors are (1) the availability and palatability of food, and (2) learned preferences and habits.

Food Availability and Related Cues

PSYKTREK 8a

Most of the research on the physiological regulation of hunger has been based on the assumption that hunger operates as a drive system in which homeostatic mechanisms are at work. However, some theorists emphasize the incentive value of food. They argue that humans and other animals are often motivated to eat not by the need to compensate for energy deficits but by the anticipated pleasure of eating (Hetherington & Rolls, 1996; Ramsay et al., 1996). This perspective has been bolstered by evidence that the following variables exert significant influence over food consumption:

- *Palatability*. The better food tastes, the more of it people consume (de Castro, 2010). This principle is not limited to humans. The eating behavior of rats and other animals is also influenced by palatability.
- *Quantity available*. A powerful determinant of the amount eaten is the amount available. People tend to consume what's put in front of them. The more people food are served, the more they eat (Mrdjenovic & Levitsky, 2005; Rozin et al., 2003). For example, one study found that people consumed 45% more popcorn when it was served in larger containers (Wansink & Kim, 2005). Another study, in which participants unknowingly ate from soup bowls that imperceptibly refilled themselves, found that consumption soared 73% (Wansink, Painter, & North, 2005). Thus, the remarkably large and ever-expanding portions served in modern American restaurants surely foster increased consumption (Geier, Rozin, & Doros, 2006).
- *Variety*. Humans and animals increase their consumption when a greater variety of foods is available (Raynor & Epstein, 2001; Temple et al., 2008). As you eat a specific food, its incentive value declines. This phenomenon is called *sensory-specific satiety* (Havermans, Siep, & Jansen, 2010). If only a few foods are available, the appeal of all of them can decline quickly. But if many foods are available, people can keep shifting to new foods and end up eating more overall. This principle explains why people are especially likely to overeat at buffets where many foods are available.
- *Presence of others*. On average, individuals eat 44% more when they eat with other people as opposed to eating alone. The more people present, the more food each person tends to eat (de Castro, 2010). When two people eat together, they tend to use each other as guides and eat similar amounts (Salvy et al., 2007). However, when women eat in the presence of an opposite-sex person they do not know well, they tend to reduce their intake (Young et al., 2009). When asked afterward, people seem oblivious to the fact that their eating is influenced by the presence of others (Vartanian, Herman, & Wansink, 2008).

According to incentive models of hunger, the availability and palatability of food are key factors regulating hunger. An abundance of diverse foods tends to lead to increased eating.

© brt FOOD/Alamy

CATHY

CATHY © 2008 by Cathy Guisewite. Distributed by UNIVERSAL PRESS SYNDICATE. Reprinted with permission.

Eating can also be triggered by exposure to environmental cues that have been related to food. You no doubt have had your hunger aroused by television commercials for delicious-looking meals or by pleasant scents coming from the kitchen. Consistent with this observation, studies have shown that exposure to soda and food advertisements incite hunger and lead to increased food intake (Harris, Bargh, & Brownell, 2009; Koordeman et al., 2010). Moreover, the foods consumed are not limited to those seen in the ads. And people tend to be unaware of how the ads influence their eating behavior. Thus, it's clear that hunger and eating are governed in part by the incentive qualities of food.

Learned Preferences and Habits 8a

Are you fond of eating calves' brains? How about eels or snakes? Could I interest you in a grasshopper or some dog meat? Probably not. Yet these are delicacies in some regions of the world. Arctic Eskimos like to eat maggots. You probably prefer chicken, apples, lettuce, pizza, or ice cream. These preferences are acquired through learning. People from different cultures display enormous variations in patterns of food consumption (Rozin, 2007). If you doubt this fact, just visit a grocery store in an ethnic neighborhood (not your own, of course).

© suvijakra/Shutterstock

Food preferences are influenced greatly by culture. For example, the fried grasshoppers shown here would not be a treat for most Americans, but they are a delicacy in some cultures.

Humans do have some innate taste preferences of a general sort. For example, a preference for sweet tastes is present at birth (Menella & Beauchamp, 1996). And humans' preference for high-fat foods appears to be at least partly genetic in origin (Schiffman et al., 1998). Nonetheless, learning wields a great deal of influence over what people prefer to eat (Rozin, 2007). Taste preferences are partly a function of learned associations formed through classical conditioning (Appleton, Gentry, & Shepherd, 2006). For example, youngsters can be conditioned to prefer flavors paired with pleasant events. Of course, as we learned in Chapter 6, taste aversions can also be acquired through conditioning when foods are followed by nausea (Schafe & Bernstein, 1996).

Eating habits are also shaped by observational learning (see Chapter 6). To a large degree, food preferences are a matter of exposure (Cooke, 2007). People generally prefer familiar foods. But geographical, cultural, religious, and ethnic factors limit people's exposure to certain foods. Young children are more likely to taste an unfamiliar food if an adult tries it first. Repeated exposures to a new food usually lead to increased liking. However, as many parents have learned the hard way, forcing a child to eat a specific food can backfire (Benton, 2004).

Eating and Weight: The Roots of Obesity

As we've seen, hunger is regulated by a complex interaction of biological and psychological factors. The same kinds of complexities emerge when investigators explore the roots of ***obesity*, the condition of being overweight.** Most experts assess obesity in terms of ***body mass index (BMI)*—weight (in kilograms) divided by height (in meters) squared (kg/m^2).** This index of weight controls for variations in height. A BMI of over 30 is generally considered obese (Björntorp, 2002). American culture seems to be obsessed with slimness. However, surveys show surprisingly sharp increases in the incidence of obesity in recent decades (Corsica & Perri, 2003; Mokdad et al., 2003). In one study of a nationally representative U.S. sample, 33.9% of the subjects were found to be obese, and even higher prevalence rates were observed in some ethnic groups (Flegal et al., 2010; see **Figure 10.4**). Moreover, overweight adults have plenty of company from their children. A recent

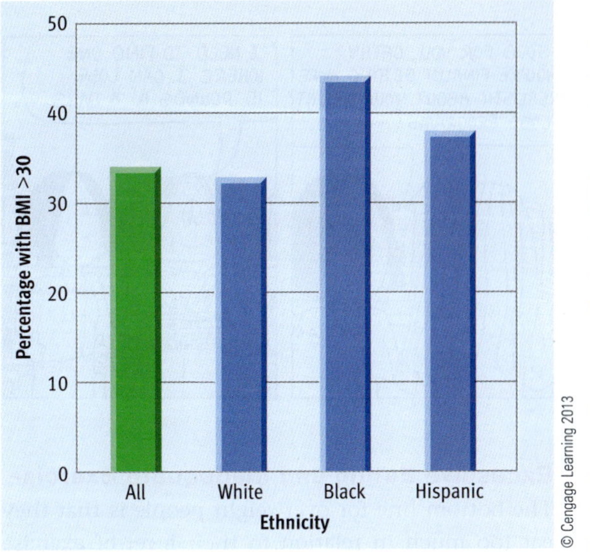

Figure 10.4

Ethnicity and obesity. A recent study of a nationally representative sample of of over 5500 adults determined that 33.9% of the participants met the critierion of obesity, which was defined as a BMI greater than 30. The study also looked at ethnicity and the prevalence of obesity. As you can see, some moderate differences were found among ethnic groups. (Data from Flegal et al., 2010)

national survey of children and adolescents (ages 6–19) reported that 19% qualified as obese (Ogden et al., 2010).

Evolutionary-oriented researchers have a plausible explanation for the dramatic increase in the prevalence of obesity (Pinel, Assanand, & Lehman, 2000). They point out that over the course of history most animals and humans lived in environments characterized by fierce competition for limited, unreliable food resources. In such an environment, starvation was a very real threat. Thus, foraging animals evolved a propensity to consume more food than immediately necessary when the opportunity presented itself because food might not be available later. Excess calories were stored in the body (as fat) to prepare for future food shortages. This approach to eating remains adaptive for most species of animals that continue to struggle with the ebb and flow of unpredictable food supplies. However, in today's modern, industrialized societies, the vast majority of humans live in environments that provide an abundant, reliable supply of food. In these environments, the tendency to overeat when food is plentiful leads many people down a path of chronic, excessive food consumption. According to this line of thinking, most people in such environments tend to overeat in relation to their physiological needs. However, because of variations in genetics, metabolism, and other factors, only some become overweight.

If obesity merely affected people's vanity, there would be little cause for concern. Unfortunately, obesity is a big health problem that elevates an individual's mortality risk (Flegal et al., 2005; Ogden, 2010). Obese individuals are more vulnerable than others to cardiovascular diseases, diabetes, hypertension, respiratory problems, gallbladder disease, stroke, arthritis, muscle and skeletal pain, and some types of cancer (Manson, Skerrett, & Willet, 2002; Pi-Sunyer, 2002). **Figure 10.5** shows how the prevalence of diabetes, hypertension, coronary disease, and musculoskeletal pain are elevated as BMI increases.

That said, recent research suggests that mortality rates among people who are *moderately overweight* (BMI 25–29.9) are *not* elevated in today's population (Flegal et al., 2005, 2007). One hypothesis to explain this surprising finding is that improvements in the treatment of cardiovascular diseases have neutralized much of the danger associated with being slightly overweight (Gibbs, 2005). These findings and other issues have led some critics (Campos, 2004; Oliver, 2006) to argue that the widely heralded obesity "epidemic/crisis" has been greatly exaggerated. Although the risks associated with moderate weight problems may be overrated, the fact remains that genuine obesity is significant health problem. Hence, scientists have devoted a great deal of attention to the causes of obesity. Let's look at some of the factors they have identified.

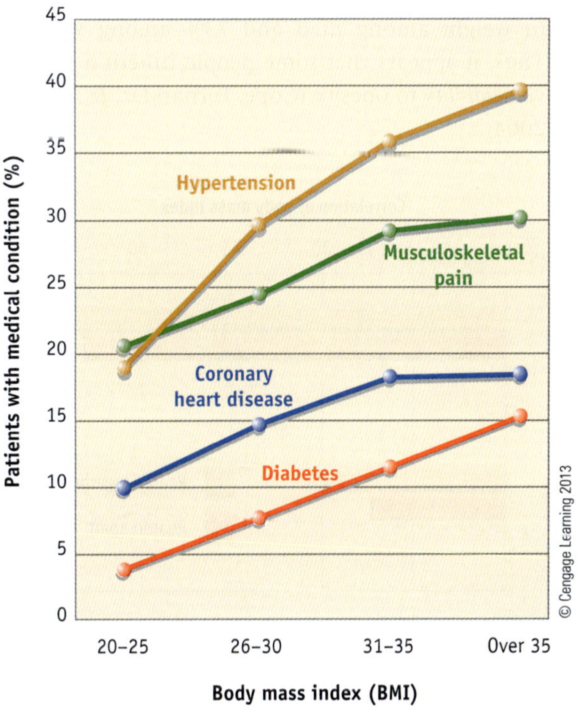

Figure 10.5

Weight and the prevalence of various diseases. This graph shows how obesity, as indexed by BMI, is related to the prevalence of four common types of illness. The prevalence of diabetes, heart disease, muscle pain, and hypertension increases as BMI goes up, suggesting that obesity is a significant health risk. (Based on data in Brownell & Wadden, 2000)

CATHY

CATHY © by Cathy Guisewite. Distributed by UNIVERSAL PRESS SYNDICATE. Reprinted with permission. All rights reserved.

Reality CHECK

Misconception

Eating at night will lead to extra weight gain.

Reality

Changes in weight depend on one's caloric intake in relation to one's energy expenditure from physical activities and metabolic processes. *When* you consume your calories is irrelevant. It is the overall amount of caloric intake that is crucial.

Genetic Predisposition

You may know some people who can eat constantly without gaining weight. You may also know other people who put on weight eating far less. Differences in physiological makeup must be the cause of this paradox. Research suggests that these differences have a genetic basis (Bouchard, 2002).

In one influential study, adults raised by foster parents were compared with their biological and foster parents in regard to body mass index (Stunkard et al., 1986). The investigators found that the adoptees resembled their biological parents much more than their adoptive parents. In a subsequent twin study, Stunkard and colleagues (1990) found that identical twins reared apart were far more similar in BMI than fraternal twins reared together (see **Figure 10.6**). In another study of over 4000 twins, Allison and colleagues (1994) estimated that genetic factors account for 61% of the variation in weight among men and 73% among women. Thus, it appears that some people inherit a genetic *vulnerability* to obesity (Cope, Fernandez, & Allison, 2004).

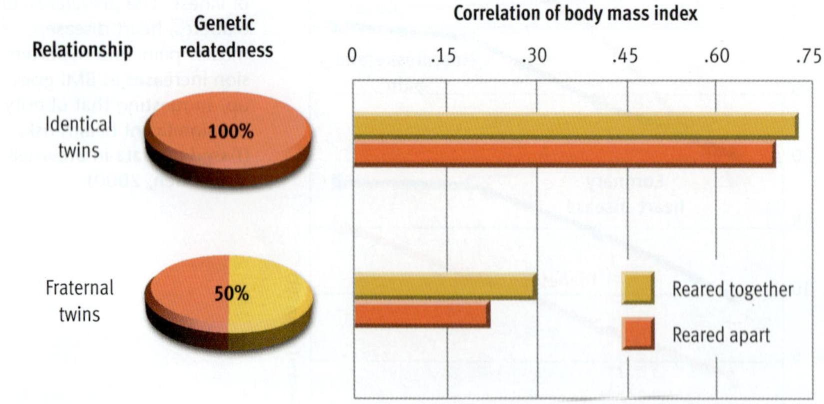

Figure 10.6

The heritability of weight. These data from a twin study by Stunkard et al. (1990) reveal that identical twins are much more similar in body mass index than fraternal twins, suggesting that genetic factors account for much of the variation among people in the propensity to become overweight. © Cengage Learning 2013

Excessive Eating and Inadequate Exercise

The bottom line for overweight people is that they eat too much in relation to their level of exercise (Wing & Polley, 2001). In modern America, the tendency to overeat and to exercise too little is understandable (Henderson & Brownell, 2004). Tasty, high-calorie, high-fat foods are heavily advertised and readily available nearly everywhere—not just in restaurants and grocery stores, but in shopping malls, airports, gas stations, schools, and workplaces. Nutritious foods can hardly compete with the convenience of highly caloric fast food. In recent decades, the size of grocery story packages, restaurant portions, and even dinnerware has increased steadily (Wansink, 2010). These bloated cues about what represents "normal" food consumption clearly fuel increased eating and escalating obesity. Kelly Brownell (2002) argues that modern societies have created a "toxic environment" for eating. Development of this toxic eating environment has been paralleled by a decline in physical activity (Hill & Peters, 1998). Modern conveniences, such as cars and elevators, and changes in the world of work, such as the shift to more desk jobs, have conspired to make American lifestyles more sedentary than ever before. On the most literal of levels, we physically move less and less.

Sensitivity to External Cues

Stanley Schachter (1968) advanced the "externality hypothesis" that obese people are extrasensitive to external cues that affect hunger and are relatively in-

© Dennis MacDonald/PhotoEdit

sensitive to internal physiological signals, whereas the eating of normal-weight individuals is regulated by internal signals. According to this notion, overweight people respond readily to environmental cues, such as the availability and attractiveness of food, that often trigger unnecessary eating. In a series of studies, Schachter manipulated external cues such as how tasty the food appeared, how easily available the food was, and whether it seemed to be dinnertime. All of these external cues were found to influence the eating behavior of overweight indviduals more than that of normal-weight subjects (Schachter, 1971).

Although Schachter's theory received extensive support, many studies also uncovered findings that were inconsistent with the theory. In an influential review of the evidence, Judith Rodin (1981) questioned key tenets of the theory. For example, she noted that the sight, smell, and sound of a grilling steak (external signals) can elicit insulin secretions (internal signals) that lead to increased hunger, thus blurring Schachter's key distinction between the internal and external determinants of hunger. She also highlighted findings showing that not all overweight people are hypersensitive to external cues and that normal-weight people are not necessarily insensitive to external food cues. Rodin's critique had a dramatic impact, as research on the influence of external cues declined and the externality hypothesis was widely viewed as discredited.

Recently, however, some theorists have begun to reevaluate the externality hypothesis (Herman & Polivy, 2008; Stroebe, 2008). They acknowledge that it had been overstated and oversimplified, as decades of research have shown that obesity is a function of many factors and that obese people are not oblivious to physiological signals of hunger. However, these theorists argue that the central thesis of the externality hypothesis still has merit. After reviewing the evidence, Stroebe (2008) concludes that external cues do have a greater impact on the food intake of obese individuals than individuals of normal weight. To better understand how external cues relate to obesity, Herman and Polivy (2008) have introduced a distinction between *normative* as opposed to *sensory* external cues. Normative cues are indicators of socially appropriate food intake—what, when, and how much one should eat. Sensory cues are characteristics of the food itself, such as palatability, that make people more or less likely to consume it. *Herman and Polivy argue that it is sensory external cues that obese people are especially sensitive to.* Thus, the externality hypothesis is making a comeback. That said, its current advocates readily acknowledge that it is just one consideration among a constellation of factors that contribute to obesity.

The Concept of Set Point

People who lose weight on a diet have a rather strong tendency to gain back all the weight they lose (Mann et al., 2007). The reverse is also true: People who have to work to put weight on often have trouble keeping it on. According to Richard Keesey (1995), these observations suggest that your body may have a *set point,* or a natural point of stability in body weight. When fat stores slip below a crucial set point, the body supposedly begins to compensate for this change (Keesey, 1993). Thus, *settling-point theory* (Pinel et al., 2000) proposes that weight tends to drift around the level at which the constellation of factors that determine food consumption and energy expenditure achieve an equilibrium. According to this view, weight tends to remain stable as long as there are no durable changes in any of the factors that influence it.

CONCEPT CHECK 10.1

Understanding Factors in the Regulation of Hunger

Check your understanding of the effects of the various factors that influence hunger by indicating whether hunger and eating would tend to increase or decrease in each of the situations described below. Indicate your choice by marking an I (increase), a D (decrease), or a ? (can't be determined without more information) next to each situation. You'll find the answers in Appendix A at the back of the book.

______ **1.** Jameer's stomach has just secreted the hormone ghrelin.

______ **2.** The glucose level in Marlene's bloodstream decreases.

______ **3.** Norman just ate, but his roommate just brought home his favorite food—a pizza that smells great.

______ **4.** You're offered an exotic, strange-looking food from another culture and told that everyone in that culture loves it.

______ **5.** Darius is eating at a huge buffet where an enormous variety of foods are available.

______ **6.** You have just been served your meal at a new restaurant. You are astonished by the enormous size of the meal.

REVIEW OF KEY LEARNING GOALS

10.3 In the brain, the lateral and ventromedial areas of the hypothalamus were once viewed as on-off centers for the control of hunger. But that model proved to be an oversimplification. The arcuate and paraventricular areas and neural circuits may be more important. Fluctuations in blood glucose also seem to play a role in hunger. Hormonal regulation of hunger depends primarily on insulin, ghrelin, CCK, and leptin.

10.4 Organisms consume more food when it's palatable, when more is available, when there is greater variety, and when other people are around. Cultural traditions also shape food preferences, primarily through variations in exposure to various foods. Learning processes, such as classical conditioning and observational learning, exert a great deal of influence over what people eat.

10.5 Surveys suggest that about one-third of people in the United States qualify as obese. Obesity elevates one's risk for many diseases, but recent evidence suggests that being moderately overweight may not increase mortality. Some theorists argue that the obesity crisis has been exaggerated. Evolutionary theorists suggest that humans are wired to overeat because food supplies used to be so unreliable.

10.6 Evidence indicates that there is a genetic predisposition to obesity. Weight problems occur when people eat too much in relation to their exercise level. Schachter theorized that obese people are extra sensitive to external cues that trigger eating. Although this externality hypothesis was oversimplified, obese individuals may be especially sensitive to sensory food cues. Research suggests that the body monitors fat stores to keep them fairly stable.

KEY LEARNING GOALS

10.7 Outline the four phases of the human sexual response.

10.8 Discuss parental investment theory and findings on gender differences in sexual activity.

10.9 Describe gender differences in mating preferences, including the Featured Study on women's snap judgments of men's mate potential.

10.10 Evaluate evidence on the impact of erotic materials, including aggressive pornography, on human sexual behavior.

10.11 Discuss the nature of sexual orientation, the prevalence of homosexuality, and environmental and biological theories of sexual orientation.

Sexual Motivation and Behavior

How does sex resemble food? Sometimes it seems that people are obsessed with both. People joke and gossip about sex constantly. Magazines, novels, movies, and television shows are saturated with sexual activity and innuendo. The advertising industry uses sex to sell everything from mouthwash to designer jeans to automobiles. This intense interest in sex reflects the importance of sexual motivation. In this section, we will examine the physiology of the human sexual response, review evolutionary analyses of human sexual motivation, discuss some controversies surrounding pornography, and analyze the roots of sexual orientation.

The Human Sexual Response

Assuming that people are motivated to engage in sexual activity, exactly what happens to them physically? This may sound like a simple question. But scientists really knew very little about the physiology of the human sexual response before William Masters and Virginia Johnson did groundbreaking research in the 1960s. Although our society seems obsessed with sex, until the 1980s it did not encourage scientists to study sex. At first Masters and Johnson even had difficulty finding journals willing to publish their studies.

Masters and Johnson used physiological recording devices to monitor the bodily changes of volunteers engaging in sexual activities. They even equipped an artificial penile device with a camera to study physiological reactions inside the vagina. Their observations of and interviews with subjects yielded a detailed description of the human sexual response that eventually won them widespread acclaim.

Masters and Johnson (1966, 1970) divide the sexual response cycle into four stages: excitement, plateau, orgasm, and resolution. **Figure 10.7** shows how the intensity of sexual arousal changes as women and men progress through these stages. Let's take a closer look at these phases in the human sexual response.

Excitement Phase During the first phase of excitement, the level of physical arousal usually rises rapidly. In both sexes, muscle tension, respiration rate, heart rate, and blood pressure increase quickly. *Vasocongestion*—engorgement of blood vessels—produces penile erection and swollen testes in males. In females, vasocongestion leads to a swelling and hardening of the clitoris, expansion of the vaginal lips, and vaginal lubrication.

Plateau Phase During the plateau phase, physiological arousal usually continues to build, but at a much slower pace. In women, further vasocongestion produces a tightening of the vaginal entrance, as the clitoris withdraws under the clitoral hood. Many men secrete a bit of fluid at the tip of the penis. This is not ejaculate, but it may contain sperm. When foreplay is lengthy, fluctuation in arousal is normal for both sexes. This fluctuation is more apparent in men, as erections may increase and decrease noticeably. In women, this fluctuation may be reflected in changes in vaginal lubrication.

Figure 10.7

The human sexual response cycle. There are similarities and differences between men and women in patterns of sexual arousal. Pattern A, which culminates in orgasm and resolution, is the ideal sequence for both sexes but not something one can count on. Pattern B, which involves sexual arousal without orgasm followed by a slow resolution, is seen in both sexes but is more common among women. Pattern C, which involves multiple orgasms, is seen almost exclusively in women, as men go through a refractory period before they are capable of another orgasm.

SOURCE: Based on Masters, W. H., & Johnson, V. E. (1966). *Human sexual response.* Boston: Little, Brown. Copyright ©1966 Little, Brown and Company.

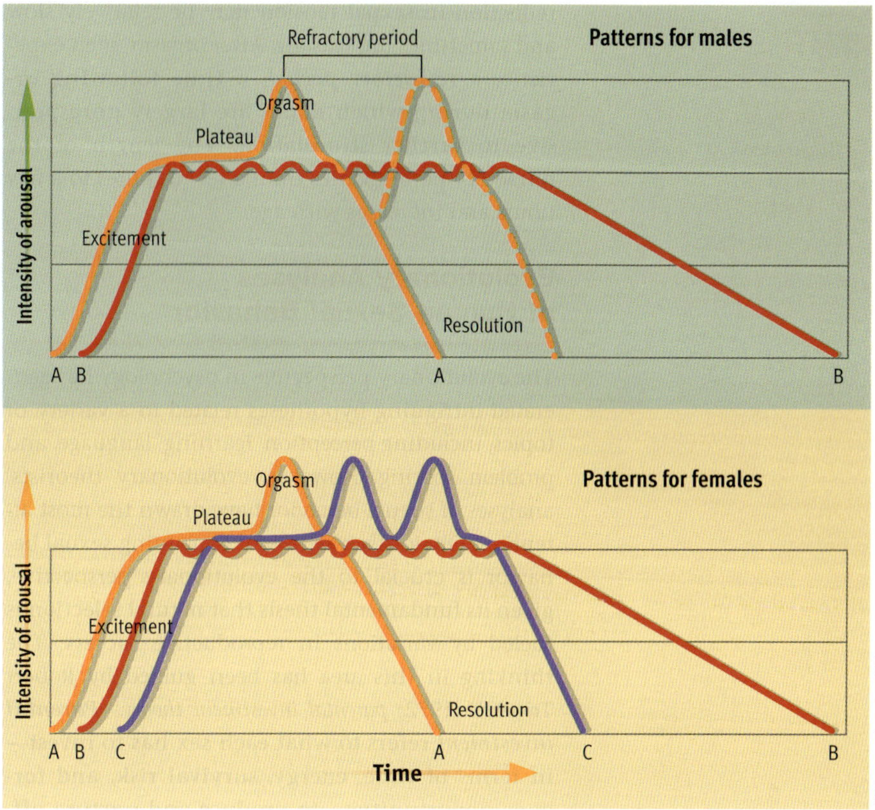

© Cengage Learning 2013

Orgasm Phase *Orgasm* occurs when sexual arousal reaches its peak intensity and is discharged in a series of muscular contractions that pulsate through the pelvic area. Heart rate, respiration rate, and blood pressure increase sharply during this exceedingly pleasant spasmodic response. In males, orgasm is accompanied by ejaculation of the seminal fluid. The subjective experience of orgasm appears to be very similar for men and women.

However, there *are* some interesting gender differences in the orgasm phase of the sexual response cycle. On the one hand, women are more likely than men to be *multiorgasmic*. A woman is said to be multiorgasmic if she experiences more than one climax in a sexual encounter (pattern C in **Figure 10.7**). On the other hand, women are more likely than men to engage in intercourse without experiencing an orgasm. When respondents are asked whether they *always* have an orgasm with their partner, the gender gap in orgasmic consistency looks rather large. For example, among respondents ages 35–39, Laumann et al. (1994) found that 78% of men but only 28% of women reported always having an orgasm. However, a recent, major survey of sexual behavior approached the issue in a different way and found a smaller gender gap. Herbenick et al. (2010) asked respondents about many of the details of their *most recent sexual interaction* (what they did, how pleasureable it was, whether they had an orgasm, and so forth). As you can see in **Figure 10.8**, men were more likely to report having an orgasm, but the disparity was not as huge as when respondents were asked about always having an orgasm.

Whether this gender gap reflects attitudes and sexual practices versus physiological processes is open to debate. On the one hand, it's easy to argue that males' greater orgasmic consistency must be a product of evolution. It would have obvious adaptive significance for promoting men's reproductive fitness. On the other hand, gender differences in the socialization of guilt feelings about sex, as well as sexual scripts and practices that are less than optimal for women, could play a part (Lott, 1987). Another consideration is that orgasm consistency seems to be influenced by relationship quality more in women than men. Consistent with this analysis, one recent study found a correlation of .43 between the intensity of heterosexual women's love for their partner and their ease in reaching orgasm (Ortigue, Grafton, & Bianchi-Demicheli, 2007).

Resolution Phase During the resolution phase, the physiological changes produced by sexual arousal subside. If orgasm has not occurred, the

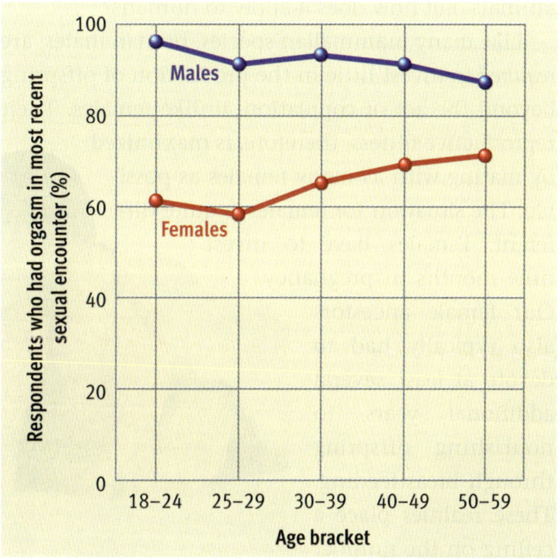

© Cengage Learning 2013

Figure 10.8

The gender gap in orgasm consistency. In their sexual interactions, men reach orgasm more reliably than women. When respondents are asked whether they *always* have an orgasm, the gender gap is huge. But the new data shown here, which asked whether people had an orgasm in their most recent sexual encounter, suggest that the gender gap is quite a bit smaller, although not insignificant. The new data also indicate that the gender gap diminishes in older age groups. (Data from Herbenick et al., 2010) reduction in sexual tension may be relatively slow and sometimes unpleasant. After orgasm, men experience a ***refractory period*, a time following orgasm during which males are largely unresponsive to further stimulation.** The length of the refractory period varies from a few minutes to a few hours and increases with age.

Evolutionary Analyses of Human Sexual Behavior

The evolutionary perspective in psychology has generated intriguing hypotheses related to a variety of topics, including perception, learning, language, and problem solving. However, evolutionary theorists' analyses of sexual behavior have drawn the most attention. Obviously, the task of explaining sexual behavior is crucial to the evolutionary perspective, given its fundamental thesis that natural selection is fueled by variations in reproductive success. The thinking in this area has been guided by Robert Trivers's (1972) *parental investment theory*. ***Parental investment* refers to what each sex has to invest—in terms of time, energy, survival risk, and forgone opportunities—to produce and nurture offspring.** For example, the efforts required to guard eggs, build nests, or nourish offspring represent parental investments. In most species, striking disparities exist between males and females in their parental investment, and these discrepancies shape mating strategies. According to Trivers, *members of the sex that makes the smaller investment (males in most species) will pursue mating opportunities vigorously and compete with each other for these opportunities, whereas members of the sex that makes the larger investment (females in most species) will tend to be more conservative and discriminating about mating behavior.* This rule of thumb predicts mating patterns in many types of animals. But how does it apply to humans?

Like many mammalian species, human males, are *required* to invest little in the production of offspring beyond the act of copulation, unlike females. Their reproductive fitness, therefore, is maximized by mating with as many females as possible. The situation for females is quite different. Females have to invest nine months in pregnancy. Our female ancestors also typically had to devote at least several additional years to nourishing offspring through breastfeeding. These realities place a ceiling on the number of offspring women can produce, regardless of how many males they mate with. Hence, females have little or no incentive for mating with many males. Instead, females can optimize their reproductive potential by being selective in mating. Thus, in humans, males are thought to compete with other males for the relatively scarce and valuable "commodity" of reproductive opportunities.

Parental investment theory predicts that in comparison to women, men will show more interest in sexual activity, more desire for variety in sexual partners, and more willingness to engage in uncommitted sex (see **Figure 10.9**). In contrast, females are thought to be the conservative, discriminating sex that is more selective about mating. Does the empirical evidence mesh with these predictions? Let's look at some of the evidence.

Gender Differences in Patterns of Sexual Activity

Consistent with evolutionary theory, males generally show a greater interest in sex than females do (Peplau, 2003). Men think about sex more often than women (Laumann et al., 1994). They also initiate sex more often (Morokoff et al., 1997). Males have more frequent and varied sexual fantasies (Okami & Shackelford, 2001), and their subjective ratings of their sex drive tend to be higher than females' (Ostovich & Sabini, 2004). Men also tend to overestimate women's sexual interest in them (a cognitive bias not shared by women). This bias seems designed to ensure that males not overlook sexual opportunities (Buss, 2001; Levesque, Nave, & Lowe, 2006). When heterosexual couples are asked about their sex lives, male partners are more likely than their female counterparts to report that they would like to have sex more frequently. The findings of a recent study suggest that this disparity in sexual motivation only widens when people reach middle age (Lindau & Gavrilova, 2010). As you can see in **Figure 10.10**, in the 55–64 age bracket, 62% of men but only 38% of women report that they are still very interested in sex.

Men are also more motivated than women to pursue sex with a greater variety of partners (McBurney, Zapp, & Streeter, 2005). For example, Buss and Schmitt (1993) found that college men indicated that they would ideally like to have 18 sex partners across their lives. College women, on the other

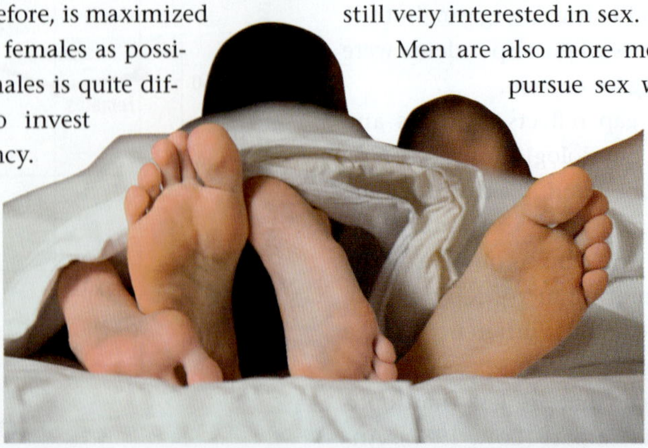

© Dmitry Melnikov/Shutterstock

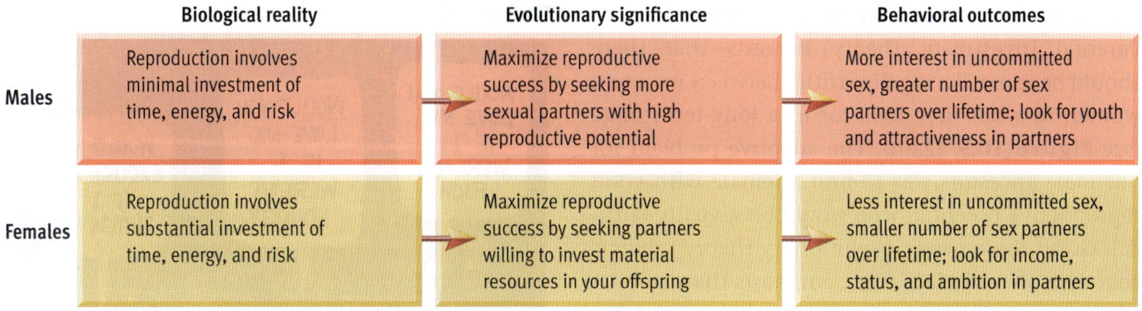

Figure 10.9

Parental investment theory and mating preferences. Parental investment theory suggests that basic differences between males and females in parental investment have great adaptive significance and lead to gender differences in mating propensities and preferences, as outlined here. © Cengage Learning 2013

hand, reported that they would prefer only 5 partners. Similar findings were observed in a follow-up study that examined desire for sexual variety in over 16,000 subjects from 10 major regions of the world (D. Schmitt et al., 2003). **Figure 10.11** shows that males expressed a desire for more partners than females in all ten world regions. In most cases, the differences were substantial.

Clear gender disparities are also seen in regard to people's willingness to engage in casual or uncommitted sex. For example, in a compelling field study, Clark and Hatfield (1989) had average-looking men approach female (college-age) strangers and ask whether they would go back to the man's apartment to have sex with him. None of the women agreed to this proposition. But when Clark and Hatfield had average-looking women approach males with the same proposition, 75% of the men eagerly agreed!

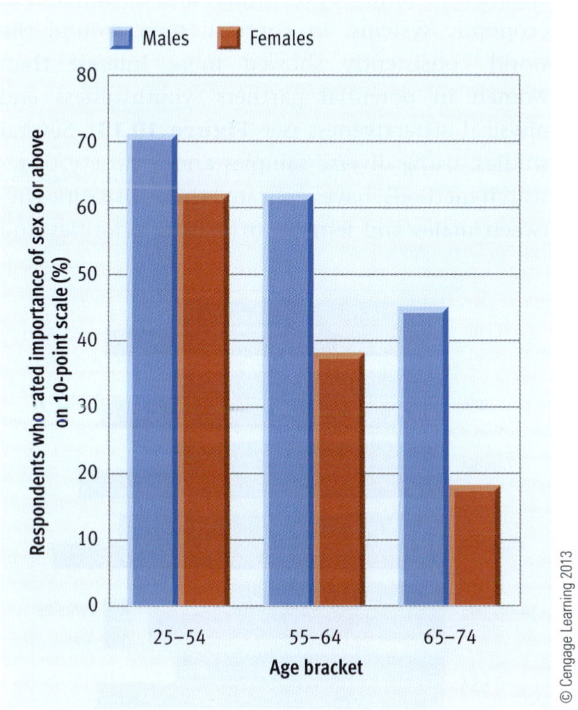

Figure 10.10

The gender gap in interest in sex. Lindau and Gavrilova (2010) summarized data from a nationally representative sample of over 3000 participants. In the survey, respondents were asked to rate how much thought and effort they put into the sexual aspect of their lives. The rating scale ranged from 0 (none) to 10 (very much). The graph shows the percentage of respondents who gave a rating of 6 or greater. As you can see, males generally expressed a greater interest in sex than females. The gender gap was modest in the 25–54 age range but widened considerably in older age groups.

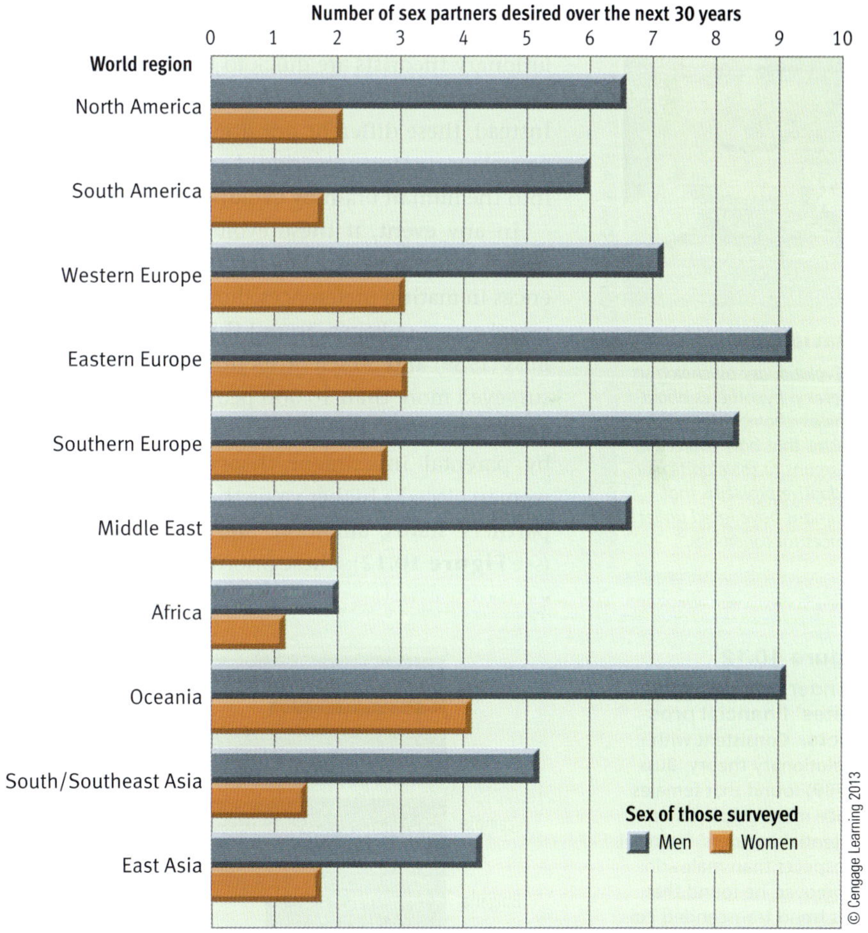

Figure 10.11

The gender gap in desire for a variety of sexual partners. Schmitt et al. (2003) gathered cross-cultural data on gender disparities in the number of sex partners desired by people. Respondents were asked about how many sexual partners they ideally would like to have in the next 30 years. As evolutionary theorists would predict, males reported that they would like to have more sexual partners in all ten world regions examined.

SOURCE: Schmitt, D. P., and 118 Members of the International Sexuality Description Project. (2003). Universal sex differences in the desire for sexual variety: Tests from 52 nations, 6 continents, and 13 islands. *Journal of Personality and Social Psychology, 85,* 85–104. Copyright © 2003 by the American Psychological Association.

Gender Differences in Mate Preferences

Parental investment theory suggests that there should be some glaring disparities between men and women in what they look for in a long-term mate (see **Figure 10.9** again). The adaptive problem for our male ancestors was to find a female with good reproductive potential who would be sexually faithful. Given these needs, evolutionary theory predicts that men should place more emphasis than women on partner characteristics such as youthfulness (which allows for more reproductive years) and attractiveness (which is assumed to be correlated with health and fertility). In contrast, the adaptive problem for our female ancestors was to find a male who could provide material resources and was willing to invest these resources in his family. Given these needs, evolutionary theory predicts that women should place more emphasis than men on partner characteristics such as intelligence, ambition, income, and social status (which are associated with the ability to provide more material resources). Evolutionary theorists are quick to point out that these differing priorities *do not reflect conscious strategies.* Instead, these different priorities are viewed as subconscious preferences that have been hardwired into the human brain by evolutionary forces.

In any event, if these evolutionary analyses of sexual motivation are on the mark, gender differences in mating preferences should be virtually universal across cultures. To test this hypothesis, David Buss (1989) and 50 scientists from around the world surveyed more than 10,000 people from 37 cultures about what they looked for in a mate. As predicted by parental investment theory, they found that women placed a higher value than men on potential partners' status, ambition, and financial prospects (see **Figure 10.12**). These priorities were not limited to industrialized or capitalist countries. They were apparent in third-world cultures and all varieties of economic systems. In contrast, men around the world consistently showed more interest than women in potential partners' youthfulness and physical attractiveness (see **Figure 10.13**). Several studies, using diverse samples and a variety of research methods, have replicated these disparities between males and females in mating priorities and

BIZARRO

Bizarro © 2001 Dan Piraro King Features Syndicate.

Courtesy of David M. Buss

David Buss

"Evolutionary psychologists develop hypotheses about the psychological mechanisms that have evolved in humans to solve particular adaptive problems that humans have faced under ancestral conditions."

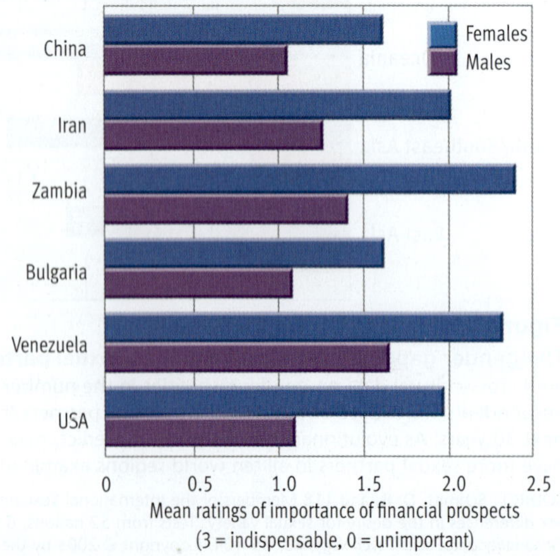

Figure 10.12
Gender and potential mates' financial prospects. Consistent with evolutionary theory, Buss (1989) found that females place more emphasis on potential partners' financial prospects than males do. Moreover, he found that this trend transcended culture. The specific results for six of the thirty-seven cultures studied by Buss are shown here. © Cengage Learning 2013

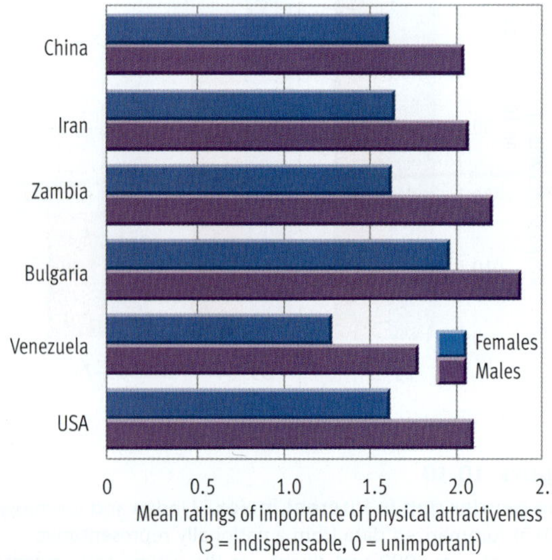

Figure 10.13
Gender and potential mates' physical attractiveness. Consistent with evolutionary theory, Buss (1989) found that all over the world, males place more emphasis on potential partners' good looks than females do. The specific results for six of the thirty-seven cultures studied by Buss are shown here. © Cengage Learning 2013

preferences (Neuberg, Kenrick, & Schaller, 2010; Shackelford, Schmitt, & Buss, 2005). Recent research also supports the notion that women pay more attention than men to a potential partner's willingness to invest in children (Brase, 2006). The gender gap on this dimension occurs because men appear to be largely indifferent to females' potential for parental investment. Moreover, men who are perceived to be favorably disposed to investing in children are judged to be more attractive by women (Brase, 2006). That finding brings us to our Featured Study for this chapter, which examines women's perceptions of men's mating potential.

© Tom Donoghue/PictureGroup

Evolutionary theory posits that men can maximize their reproductive fitness by seeking youthful partners, whereas women can maximize their reproductive success by searching for mates that are rich in material resources that can be invested in children. Obviously, this theory can explain why attractive young women often become romantically involved with much older men who happen to be wealthy.

FEATURED STUDY

Can Women Judge Men's Mate Potential in Just One Glance?

SOURCE: Roney, J. R., Hanson, K. N., Durante, K. M., & Maestripieri, D. (2006). Reading men's faces: Women's mate attractiveness judgments track men's testosterone and interest in infants. *Proceedings of the Royal Society of London B, 273,* 2169–2175.

According to evolutionary theories, human females can improve their reproductive fitness by seeking male partners who have access to material resources and who show a willingness to invest in children. And females can enhance their chances of passing on their genes by pursuing males who exhibit high masculinity, which is assumed to be a marker for genetic quality and reproductive potential. The present study looked at women's judgments of the latter two characteristics (parental investment potential and masculinity) based on nothing more than a snapshot. The investigators wanted to know whether women could draw meaningful inferences about males' masculinity and parental potential from facial cues.

Method

Stimulus targets and characteristics. The male stimulus persons were thirty-nine students from the University of Chicago, with a mean age of 21. They were instructed to assume a neutral facial expression while their facial photos were shot from a standard distance. To operationalize their masculinity, saliva samples were taken to measure each stimulus person's testosterone level. To assess their parental investment potential, they each took a test that measured their interest in infants.

Participants and procedure. The women who rated the men were twenty-nine undergraduates from the University of California, Santa Barbara, with a mean age of 18. These women viewed the photos of the men in a standard order and were asked to rate each for "likes children," "masculine," "physically attractive," and "kind." After the first set of ratings, they were shown all the photos again and asked to rate each male's mate potential for a short-term and a long-term romantic relationship.

Results

The women's ratings of the male stimulus persons' masculinity correlated moderately well (.34) with the males' actual testosterone levels. Likewise, the women's ratings of the degree to which the male stimulus persons liked children correlated (.38) with the males' scores on the test of interest in infants. The data also showed that women's perceptions of masculinity and parental interest influenced their ratings of the male stimulus persons' mate potential. Higher ratings of masculinity fostered higher estimates of the males' short-term mate potential, whereas higher ratings of parental interest led to higher estimates of long-term mate potential.

Discussion

The authors conclude that "the present study provides the first direct evidence that women's attractiveness judgments specifically track both men's affinity for children and men's hormone concentrations" (p. 2173). They assert that their most interesting finding was the demonstration that women can draw meaningful inferences about males' parental interest based on a brief exposure to a single photograph.

Comment

A description of this study in the *Chicago Tribune* captured the essence of its remarkable findings: "Just from looking at a man's face, women can sense how much he likes children, gauge his testosterone level and decide whether he would be more suitable as a one-night stand or as a husband" (Gorner, 2006). Given the modest magnitude of the correlations observed that is a bit of an overstatement. However, the study did provide fascinating new evidence that humans may subconsciously register subtle features of potential mates that are relevant to enhancing reproductive fitness, as predicted by evolutionary theory.

Criticism and Alternative Explanations

So, the findings on gender differences in sexual behavior and mating priorities mesh nicely with predictions derived from evolutionary theory. But, evolutionary theory has its share of critics. Some skeptics argue that there are alternative explanations for the findings. For example, women's emphasis on males' material resources could be a by-product of cultural and economic forces rather than the result of biological imperatives (Eagly & Wood, 1999). Women may have learned to value males' economic clout because their own economic potential has historically been limited in virtually all cultures (Hrdy, 1997; Kasser & Sharma, 1999). In a similar vein, Roy Baumeister has argued that the gender disparity in sexual motivation may be largely attributable to extensive cultural processes that serve to suppress female sexuality (Baumeister & Twenge, 2002). Evolutionary theorists counter these arguments by pointing out that the cultural and economic processes at work may themselves be products of evolution.

The Controversial Issue of Pornography

According to some social critics, we live in the "golden age of pornography." As Strager (2003) puts it, "Following the proliferation of video and the dawn of the Internet, never has so much pornography been available to so many so easily" (p. 50). One recent study of young adults found that 87% of men and 31% of women had viewed pornography (Carroll et al., 2008). The same study reported that 67% of males and 49% of females believed using porn was an "acceptable way to express one's sexuality." Generally speaking, men are more likely than women to report that they find erotic materials enjoyable and arousing (Allen et al., 2007; Glascock, 2005). However, this finding may partly reflect the fact that the vast majority of erotic materials are scripted to appeal to males and often portray women in degrading roles that seem likely to elicit negative reactions from females (Mosher & Maclan, 1994; Pearson & Pollack, 1997).

Historically, legal authorities have expressed great concern that pornography might incite sex crimes. This issue has been the subject of heated debate. However, efforts to find a link between the prevalence of erotica and sex crime rates have largely yielded negative results. Studies have not found correlations between greater availability of pornography and elevated rates of sex crimes (Diamond, 2009; Ferguson & Hartley, 2009). During the last 15 to 20 years, the availability of Internet porn has grown exponentially, while rates of reported rapes have declined considerably in the United States (Ferguson & Hartley, 2009). Most male sex offenders admit to a history of using pornographic materials, but so do most males who are not sex offenders. The data show that sex offenders typically do not have earlier or more extensive exposure to pornography in childhood or adolescence than other people (Bauserman, 1996). Thus, pornography appears to play a minor role, if any, in fueling sexual offenses (Langevin & Curnoe, 2004).

Although erotic materials don't appear to incite sex crimes, they may alter *attitudes* in ways that eventually influence sexual behavior. Zillmann and Bryant (1984) found that male and female undergraduates exposed to a large dose of pornography (three or six films per week for six weeks) developed more liberal attitudes about sexual practices. For example, they came to view premarital and extramarital sex as more acceptable. In a similar vein, Carroll et al. (2008) found a correlation between acceptance of pornography and more liberal attitudes about casual sex and a history of more sex partners in both young men and women. Hald and Malamuth (2008) examined young Danish adults' self-perceptions of how pornography use had affected the quality of their sex lives. Both sexes reported more positive effects on their sexual knowledge and attitudes than negative effects.

Nonetheless, research on *aggressive pornography* has raised some serious concerns about its effects. Aggressive pornography typically depicts violence against women. Many films show women who gradually give in to and enjoy rape and other sexually degrading acts after some initial resistance. Both experimental and correlational studies suggest that this type of material increases male subjects' aggressive behavior toward women (Hald, Malamuth, & Yuen, 2010; Vega & Malamuth, 2007). In the typical study, male subjects work on a lab task and are led to believe (falsely) that they are delivering electric shocks to other subjects. In this situation, their aggression toward females tends to be elevated after exposure to aggressive pornography. Such exposure may also make sexual coercion seem less offensive and help perpetuate the myth that women enjoy being raped (Allen et al., 1995). And these attitudes can influence actual behavior. Research suggests that males who believe that "women who are raped asked for it" are more likely than others to commit sexual assault (Bohner, Siebler, & Schmelcher, 2006; Chiroro et al., 2004). Recent research suggests that the consumption of aggressive pornography may foster sexual coercion in a small minority of men who are already at a high risk for sexual aggression because of their promiscuous and hostile attitudes toward women (Kingston et al., 2009).

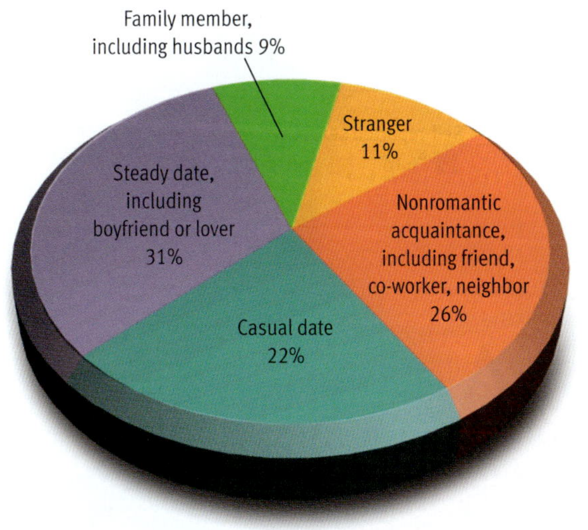

Figure 10.14

Rape victim-offender relationships. Based on a national survey of 3187 college women, Mary Koss and her colleagues (1988) identified a sample of 468 women who indicated that they had been a victim of rape and who provided information on their relationship to the offender. Contrary to the prevailing stereotype, only a small minority (11%) of these women were raped by a stranger. As you can see, many of the women were raped by men they were dating.

© Cengage Learning 2013

The effects of aggressive pornography are especially worrisome in light of evidence about rape. It is difficult to obtain accurate information about the prevalence of rape because only a minority of victims make reports to authorities (Fisher et al., 2003). Estimates suggest that as many as one-quarter of young women in the United States may be victims of rape or attempted rape (Campbell & Wasco, 2005; Koss, 1993). Only a minority of reported rapes are committed by strangers (Rand, 2008; see **Figure 10.14**). Particularly common is *date rape,* which occurs when a woman is forced to have sex in the context of dating. Research suggests that date rape is a serious problem on college campuses (Banyard et al., 2005). In one survey of students at thirty-two colleges, one in seven women reported that they had been victimized by date rape or an attempted date rape (Koss, Gidycz, & Wisniewski, 1987). Moreover, one in twelve men admitted to either having forced a date into sex or having tried to do so. However, *none* of these men identified himself as a rapist. Even more surprising, research has found that about half of women who report an experience that qualifies as rape do not label themselves as rape victims (McMullin & White, 2006). Although other factors are surely at work, many theorists believe that aggressive pornography has contributed to this failure to see sexual coercion for what it is (Kingston et al., 2009; Malamuth, Addison, & Koss, 2000).

The Mystery of Sexual Orientation

The controversy swirling around evolutionary explanations of gender differences in sexuality and the dangers of pornography is easily equaled by the controversy surrounding the determinants of *sexual orientation.* ***Sexual orientation*** **refers to a person's preference for emotional and sexual relationships with individuals of the same sex, the other sex, or either sex.** ***Heterosexuals*** **seek emotional-sexual relationships with members of the other sex,** ***bisexuals*** **with members of either sex, and** ***homosexuals*** **with members of the same sex.** The terms *gay* and *straight* have become widely used to refer to homosexuals and heterosexuals, respectively. Although *gay* can refer to homosexuals of either sex, most homosexual women prefer to call themselves *lesbians.*

People tend to view heterosexuality and homosexuality as an all-or-none distinction. However, in a pioneering study of sexual behavior, Alfred Kinsey and his colleagues (1948, 1953) discovered that many people who define themselves as heterosexuals have had homosexual experiences—and vice versa. Thus, Kinsey concluded that it is more accurate to view heterosexuality and homosexuality as end points on a continuum (Haslam, 1997). Indeed, Kinsey devised a seven-point scale, shown in **Figure 10.15**, that can be used to characterize individuals' sexual orientation. To reevaluate Kinsey's theory, Robert Epstein

Reality CHECK

Misconception

Most rapes are committed by strangers.

Reality

Thanks to media portrayals the conventional prototype of a rapist is a pathological male who leaps out of hiding to confront a complete stranger. In reality, this scenario is relatively infrequent. It sounds counter-intuitive, but the vast majority of rapes are committed by boyfriends, casual dates, family members, acquaintances, and neighbors.

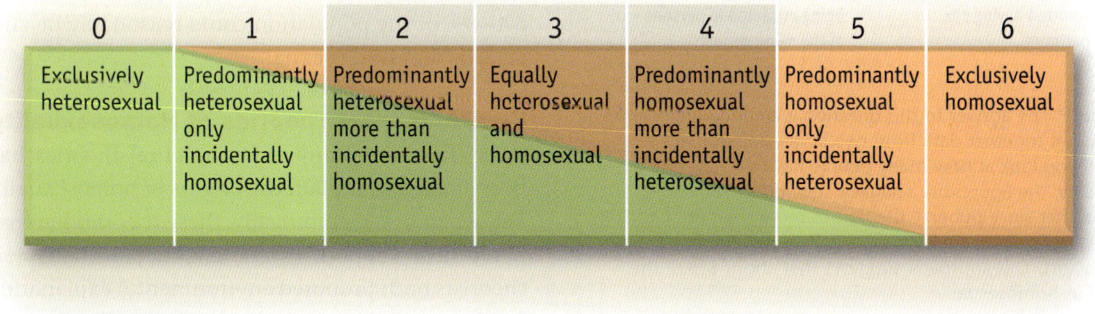

© Cengage Learning 2013

Figure 10.15

Homosexuality and heterosexuality as end-points on a continuum. Sex researchers view heterosexuality and homosexuality as falling on a continuum rather than make an all-or-none distinction. Kinsey and his associates (1948, 1953) created this seven-point scale (from 0 to 6) to describe people's sexual orientation.

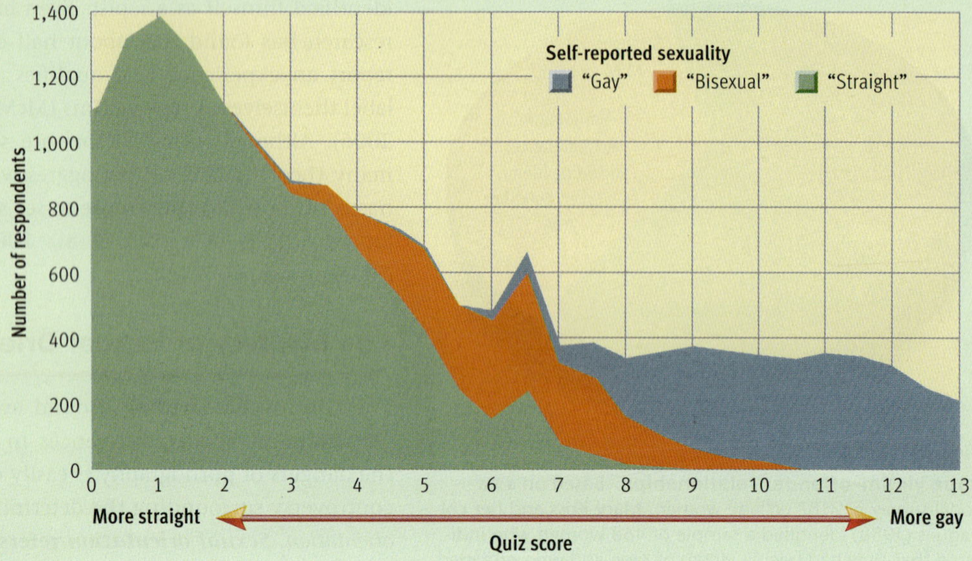

Figure 10.16

New evidence that sexual orientation exists on a continuum. Robert Epstein (2007) conducted a large Internet survey in which 18,000 people characterized themselves as straight, bisexual, or gay and then responded to a questionnaire that placed them on a scale that indexed their sexual orientation. Epstein used a 14-point scale rather than Kinsey's 7-point scale. Given the self-selected nature of the sample, these data cannot tell us much about the exact percentage of people who are gay or bisexual, but the data provide dramatic evidence in support of the notion that sexual orientation exists on a continuum. If sexual orientation were an either-or proposition, people's scores would pile up at the two ends of the distribution with little overlap, which clearly is not the case.

SOURCE: Epstein, R. (2007, October/November). Smooth thinking about sexuality. *Scientific American Mind, 18*(5), p. 14. Reprinted by permission of the author. Survey available at http://MySexualOrientation.com

© Cengage Learning 2013

(2007) collected data via the Internet from over 18,000 people who characterized themselves as gay, straight, or bisexual. They responded to a questionnaire about their sexual desires and experiences. As you can see in **Figure 10.16**, Epstein's data are consistent with the notion that sexual orientation should be viewed as a continuum rather than a matter of discrete categories.

How common is homosexuality? No one knows for sure. Part of the problem is that this question is vastly more complex than it at first appears (LeVay, 1996; Savin-Williams, 2006). Given that sexual orientation is best represented as a continuum, where do you draw the lines between heterosexuality, bisexuality, and homosexuality? And how do you classify a person who has never engaged in homosexual behavior but who acknowledges being strongly drawn to members of the same sex? Another part of the problem is that many people have extremely prejudicial attitudes about homosexuality (Herek, 2000, 2009). This fact makes gays cautious and reluctant to give candid information about their sexuality. Small wonder, then, that estimates of the portion of the population that is homosexual vary widely. Michaels (1996) combined data from two of the better large-scale surveys to arrive at the estimates seen in **Figure 10.17**. As you can see, the numbers are open to varying interpretations, but as a whole they suggest that about 5%–8% of the population could reasonably be characterized as homosexual.

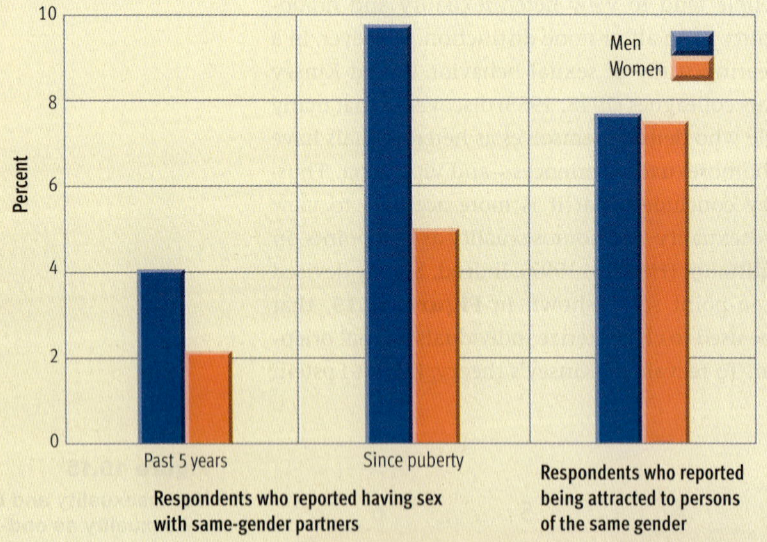

Figure 10.17

How common is homosexuality? The answer to this question is both complex and controversial. Michaels (1996) brought together data from two large-scale surveys to arrive at the estimates shown here. If you look at how many people have actually had a same-sex partner in the last five years, the figures are relatively low, but if you count those who have had a same-sex partner since puberty the figures more than double. Still another way to view it is to ask people whether they are attracted to people of the same sex (regardless of their actual behavior). This approach suggests that about 8% of the population could be characterized as homosexual.

© Cengage Learning 2013

Environmental Theories of Homosexuality

Over the years many environmental theories have been floated to explain the origins of homosexuality. Yet, when tested empirically, these theories have garnered little support. Psychoanalytic and behavioral theorists both proposed environmental explanations for the development of homosexuality. The Freudian theorists argued that a male is likely to become gay when raised by a weak, detached, ineffectual father who is a poor heterosexual role model and by an overprotective, close-binding mother, with whom the boy identifies. Behavioral theorists argued that homosexuality is a learned preference acquired when same-sex stimuli have been paired with sexual arousal, perhaps through chance seductions by adult homosexuals. Extensive research on homosexuals' upbringing and childhood experiences has failed to support either of these theories (Bell, Weinberg, & Hammersmith, 1981). Similarly, there is no evidence that parents' sexual orientation is linked to that of their children (Patterson, 2003). That is, homosexual parents are no more likely to produce homosexual offspring than heterosexual parents are.

However, efforts to research homosexuals' personal histories have yielded a number of interesting insights. Extremely feminine behavior in young boys or masculine behavior in young girls does predict the subsequent development of homosexuality (Bailey & Zucker, 1995; Bem, 2000). Recently, Rieger and colleagues (2008) asked homosexual and heterosexual adults to supply childhood home videos. Independent judges were asked to rate the young children's gender nonconforming in the videos. Rieger and associates found that children who would eventually identify as homosexual in adulthood were more gender nonconforming than those who identified as heterosexual. This finding held for both males and females.

Consistent with this line of research, most gay men and women report that they can trace their homosexual leanings back to their early childhood, even before they understood what sex was really about (Bailey, 2003). Most also report that because of negative parental and societal attitudes about homosexuality they initially struggled to deny their sexual orientation. Thus, they felt that their homosexuality was not a matter of choice and not something that they could readily change (Breedlove, 1994). These findings obviously suggest that the roots of homosexuality are more biological than environmental.

Biological Theories of Homosexuality

Initial efforts to find a biological basis for homosexuality met with little success. Most theorists originally assumed that hormonal differences between heterosexuals and homosexuals must underlie a person's sexual orientation (Doerr et al., 1976; Dorner, 1988). However, studies comparing circulating hormone levels in gays and straights found only small, inconsistent differences that could not be linked to sexual orientation in any convincing way (Bailey, 2003; Banks & Gartrell, 1995).

Thus, like environmental theorists, biological theorists were stymied for quite a while in their efforts to explain the roots of homosexuality. However, that picture changed in the 1990s when a pair of behavioral genetics studies reported findings suggesting that homosexuality involves a hereditary predisposition. In the first study, conducted by Bailey and Pillard (1991), the subjects were gay men who had either a twin brother or an adopted brother. They found that 52% of the subjects' identical twins were gay, that 22% of their fraternal twins were gay, and that 11% of their adoptive brothers were gay. A companion study (Bailey et al., 1993) of lesbians yielded a similar pattern of results (see **Figure 10.18**). Given that identical twins share more genetic overlap than fraternal twins, who share more genes than unrelated adoptive siblings, these results suggest a *genetic predisposition* to homosexuality (Dawood, Bailey, & Martin, 2009; Hyde, 2005b).

Many theorists suspect that the roots of homosexuality may lie in the organizing effects of prenatal hormones on neurological development (Byne, 2007; James, 2005). Several lines of research suggest that hormonal secretions during critical periods of prenatal development may shape sexual development, organize the brain in a lasting manner, and influence subsequent sexual orientation (Berenbaum & Snyder, 1995). For example, researchers have found elevated rates of homosexuality among women exposed to abnormally high androgen levels

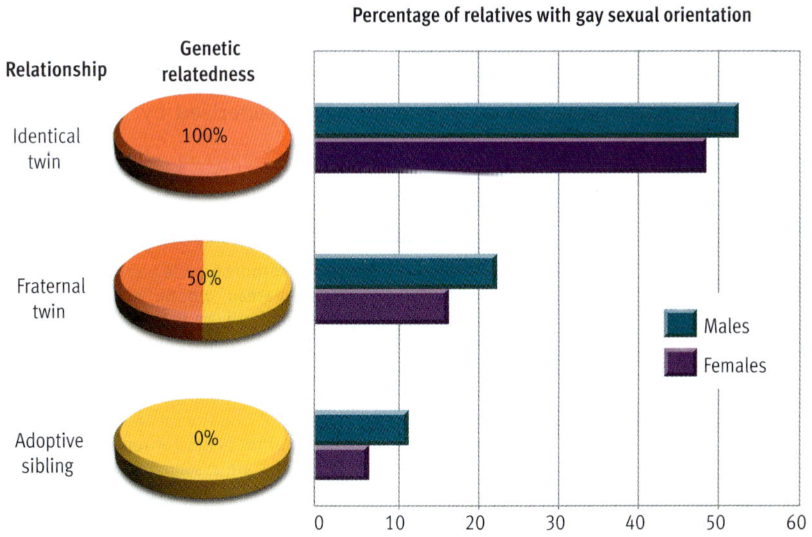

Figure 10.18

Genetics and sexual orientation. If relatives who share more genetic relatedness show greater similarity on a trait than relatives who share less genetic overlap, this evidence suggests a genetic predisposition to the characteristic. Studies of both gay men and lesbian women have found a higher prevalence of homosexuality among their identical twins than their fraternal twins, who, in turn, are more likely to be homosexual than their adoptive siblings. These findings suggest that genetic factors influence sexual orientation. (Data from Bailey & Pillard, 1991; Bailey et. al., 1993) © Cengage Learning 2013

Some people were baffled when actress Lindsay Lohan became involved with DJ Samantha Ronson after a history of heterosexual relationships. Although shifts in sexual orientation like this are uncommon among males, research has shown that females' sexual orientation tends to be characterized by more plasticity than that of males.

© AP Images/Peter Kramer

during prenatal development (because their mothers had an adrenal disorder or were given a synthetic hormone to reduce the risk of miscarriage) (Breedlove, 1994; Meyer-Bahlburg et al., 1995). Several other independent lines of research suggest that abnormalities in prenatal hormonal secretions may foster a predisposition to homosexuality (Mustanski, Chivers, & Bailey, 2002).

However, much remains to be learned about the roots of homosexuality. One complication is that the pathways to homosexuality may be somewhat different for males than for females. Females' sexuality appears to be characterized by more *plasticity* than males' sexuality (Baumeister, 2000, 2004). In other words, women's sexual behavior may be more easily shaped and modified by sociocultural factors. For example, although sexual orientation is assumed to be a stable characteristic, research shows that lesbian and bisexual women often change their sexual orientation over the course of their adult years (Diamond, 2003, 2007, 2008). And, in comparison to gay males, lesbians are less likely to trace their homosexuality back to their childhood and are more likely to indicate that their attraction to the same sex emerged during adulthood (Tolman & Diamond, 2001). These findings suggest that sexual orientation may be more fluid and malleable in women than in men.

Once again, though, we can see that the nature versus nurture debate can have far-reaching social and political implications. Homosexuals have long been victims of extensive—and in many instances *legal*—discrimination. In most jurisdictions, gays cannot legally formalize their unions in marriage. For decades they were not allowed to openly join the U.S. military. They have also been barred from certain types of jobs (for example, many school districts will not hire gay teachers). However, if research were to show that being gay is largely a matter of biological destiny, much like being Hispanic or female or tall, many of the arguments against equal rights for gays would disintegrate. Why ban gays from teaching, for instance, if their sexual preference cannot "rub off" on their students? Although one would hope that discrimination against gays would be brought to an end either way, many individuals' opinions about gay rights may be swayed by the outcome of the nature-nurture debate on the roots of homosexuality.

REVIEW OF KEY LEARNING GOALS

10.7 The human sexual response cycle can be divided into four stages: excitement, plateau, orgasm, and resolution. The subjective experience of orgasm is fairly similar for both sexes. Intercourse leads to orgasm in women less consistently than in men. However, women are much more likely to be multiorgasmic.

10.8 According to parental investment theory, males are thought to compete with other males for reproductive opportunities, whereas females are assumed to be the discriminating sex that is selective in choosing partners. Consistent with evolutionary theory, males tend to think about and initiate sex more than females do. They also have more sexual partners and are more interested in casual sex than females are.

10.9 Gender differences in mating preferences appear to largely transcend cultural boundaries. Males emphasize potential partners' youthfulness and attractiveness, whereas females emphasize potential partners' status and financial prospects. As our Featured Study showed, women also pay attention to males' willingness to invest in children and to their masculinity, which is viewed as a marker for genetic quality.

10.10 Researchers have not found a link between the availability of pornography and the prevalence of sex crimes. However, exposure to pornography can have an enduring impact on attitudes about sex. Aggressive pornography may make sexual coercion seem less offensive to its consumers and may contribute to date rape.

10.11 Modern theorists view heterosexuality and homosexuality not as an all-or-none distinction but as end points on a continuum. Recent data on the prevalence of homosexuality suggest that 5%–8% of the population may be gay. Research has not supported Freudian or behavioral theories of sexual orientation. Recent studies suggest that there is a genetic predisposition to homosexuality and that idiosyncrasies in prenatal hormonal secretions may also contribute. The pathways into homosexuality may be somewhat different for males and females.

Achievement: In Search of Excellence

KEY LEARNING GOALS

10.12 Describe how the need for achievement is measured.

10.13 Discuss how the need for achievement influences behavior and how situational factors influence achievement strivings.

At the beginning of this chapter, we discussed Jon Krakauer's grueling effort to reach the summit of Mount Everest. He and the other climbers endured extraordinary hardships and peril to achieve their goal. What motivates people to push themselves so hard? In all likelihood, it's a strong need for achievement. **The *achievement motive* is the need to master difficult challenges, to outperform others, and to meet high standards of excellence.** Above all else, the need for achievement involves the desire to excel, especially in competition with others.

Research on achievement motivation was pioneered by David McClelland and his colleagues (McClelland, 1985; McClelland et al., 1953). McClelland argued that achievement motivation is of the utmost importance. He viewed the need for achievement as the spark that ignites economic growth, scientific progress, inspirational leadership, and masterpieces in the creative arts.

Individual Differences in the Need for Achievement

PsykTrek 8b

You've no doubt heard the stories of Abraham Lincoln as a young boy, reading through the night by firelight. Find a biography of any high achiever, and you'll probably find a similar drive—throughout the person's life. The need for achievement is a fairly stable aspect of personality. Hence, research in this area has focused mostly on individual differences in achievement motivation. Subjects' need for achievement can be measured effectively with the Thematic Apperception Test, or TAT (Smith, 1992; Spangler, 1992). The TAT is a *projective test,* one that requires subjects to respond to vague, ambiguous stimuli in ways that may reveal personal motives and traits (see Chapter 12). The stimulus materials for the TAT are pictures of people in ambiguous scenes open to interpretation. Examples include a man working at a desk and a woman seated in a chair staring off into space. Subjects are asked to write or tell stories about what's happening in the scenes and what the characters are feeling. The themes of these stories are then scored to measure the strength of various needs. **Figure 10.19** shows examples of stories dominated by the themes of achievement and affiliation (the need for social bonds and belongingness).

The research on individual differences in achievement motivation has yielded interesting findings on the characteristics of people who score high in the need for achievement. They tend to work harder and more persistently on tasks than people low in the need for achievement (Brown, 1974). They handle negative feedback about task performance more effectively than others (Fodor & Carver, 2000). In addition, they are more future oriented than others and more likely to delay gratification in order to pursue long-term goals (Mischel, 1961; Raynor & Entin, 1982). As you might guess, given these characteristics, researchers often find a positive correlation between high need for achievement and educational attainment (Hustinx et al., 2009). In terms of careers, they typically go into competitive, entrepreneurial occupations that provide them with an opportunity to excel (Collins, Hanges, & Locke, 2004; Stewart & Roth, 2007). Apparently, their persistence and hard work often pay off. High achievement motivation correlates with

Boston University Photo Services, courtesy of David C. McClelland

David McClelland

"People with a high need for achievement are not gamblers; they are challenged to win by personal effort, not by luck."

Affiliation arousal
George is an engineer who is working late. He is *worried that his wife will be annoyed* with him for neglecting her. She has been *objecting* that he cares more about his work than his wife and family. He seems *unable to satisfy* both his boss and his wife, but he *loves her* very much and will do his best to *finish up* fast and get home to her.

Achievement arousal
George is an engineer who *wants to win* a competition in which the man with the *most practicable drawing* will be awarded the contract to build a bridge. He is taking a moment to think *how happy he will be* if he wins. He has been *baffled by how to make such a long span strong,* but he remembers to *specify a new steel alloy* of great strength, submits his entry, but does not win, and is *very unhappy.*

Figure 10.19
Measuring motives with the Thematic Apperception Test (TAT). Subjects taking the TAT tell or write stories about what is happening in a scene, such as this one showing a man at work. The two stories shown here illustrate strong affiliation motivation and strong achievement motivation. The italicized parts of the stories are thematic ideas that would be identified by a TAT scorer.

SOURCE: Stories reprinted by permission of Dr. David McClelland.

measures of career success in business (Amyx & Alford, 2005; Winter, 2010).

Do people high in achievement need always tackle the biggest challenges available? Not necessarily. A curious finding has emerged in lab studies in which subjects have been asked to choose how difficult a task they want to work on. Subjects high in the need for achievement tend to select tasks of intermediate difficulty (McClelland & Koestner, 1992). For instance, in one study, subjects playing a ring-tossing game were allowed to stand as close to or far away from the target peg as they wanted. High achievers tended to prefer a moderate degree of challenge (Atkinson & Litwin, 1960).

Situational Determinants of Achievement Behavior

PSYKTREK 8b

Your achievement drive is not the only determinant of how hard you work. Situational factors can also influence achievement strivings. John Atkinson (1974, 1981, 1992) has built extensively on McClelland's original theory of achievement motivation. He has identified three important determinants of achievement behavior in particular situations:

- The strength of one's *motivation* to *achieve success*. This factor is viewed as a stable aspect of personality.
- One's estimate of the *probability of success* for the task at hand. This factor varies from task to task.
- The *incentive value of success*. This factor depends on the tangible and intangible rewards for success on the specific task.

The last two variables are situational determinants of achievement behavior. That is, they vary from one situation to another. According to Atkinson, the pursuit of achievement increases as the probability and incentive value of success go up (and decreases as they go down). Let's apply Atkinson's model to a simple example. Given a certain motivation to achieve success, you will pursue a good grade in calculus less vigorously if your professor gives unfair exams (thus lowering your expectancy of success) or if a good grade in calculus is not required for your major (lowering the incentive value of success).

The joint influence of these two situational factors may explain why high achievers prefer tasks of intermediate difficulty. Atkinson notes that the probability of success and the incentive value of success on tasks are interdependent to some degree. As tasks get easier, success becomes less satisfying. As tasks get harder, success becomes more satisfying, but its likelihood obviously declines. When the probability and incentive value of success are weighed together, moderately challenging tasks seem to offer the best overall value in terms of maximizing one's sense of accomplishment.

Motivation and emotion are often intertwined (Zurbriggen & Sturman, 2002). On the one hand, *emotion can cause motivation.* For example, *anger* about your work schedule may motivate you to look for a new job. *Jealousy* of an ex-girlfriend may motivate you to ask out her roommate. On the other hand, *motivation can cause emotion.* For example, your motivation to win a photography contest may lead to great *anxiety* during the judging and either great *joy* if you win or great *gloom* if you don't. Although motivation and emotion are closely related, they're *not* the same thing. We'll analyze the nature of emotion in the next section.

CONCEPT CHECK 10.2

Understanding the Determinants of Achievement Behavior

According to John Atkinson, one's pursuit of achievement in a particular situation depends on several factors. Check your understanding of these factors by identifying each of the following vignettes as an example of one of the following three determinants of achievement behavior: (a) need for achievement, (b) perceived probability of success, and (c) incentive value of success. The answers can be found in Appendix A.

_______ 1. Belinda is nervously awaiting the start of the finals of the 200-meter dash in the last meet of her high school career. "I've gotta win this race! This is the most important race of my life!"

_______ 2. Corey grins as he considers the easy time he's going to have this semester. "This class is supposed to be a snap. I hear the professor gives A's and B's to nearly everyone."

_______ 3. Diana's just as hard-charging as ever. She's gotten the highest grade on every test throughout the semester, yet she's still up all night studying for the final. "I know I've got an A in the bag, but I want to be the best student Dr. McClelland's ever had!"

REVIEW OF KEY LEARNING GOALS

10.12 Achievement, which was first investigated by David McClelland, involves the need to excel, especially in competition with others. The need for achievement is usually measured with a projective test called the TAT, which asks subjects to write stories about what is going on in ambiguous pictures.

10.13 People who are relatively high in the need for achievement work harder and more persistently than others. They delay gratification well and pursue competitive careers. However, in choosing challenges they often select tasks of intermediate difficulty. The pursuit of achievement tends to increase when the probability of success and the incentive value of success are high. The joint influence of these factors may explain why people high in achievement need tend to prefer challenges of intermediate difficulty.

The Elements of Emotional Experience

KEY LEARNING GOALS

10.14 Describe the cognitive component of emotion.

10.15 Understand the physiological and neural bases of emotions.

10.16 Explain how emotions are reflected in facial expressions, and describe the facial feedback hypothesis.

10.17 Review cross-cultural similarities and variations in emotional experience.

The most profound and important experiences in life are saturated with emotion. Think of the *joy* that people feel at weddings, the *grief* they feel at funerals, the *ecstasy* they feel when they fall in love. Emotions also color everyday experiences. For instance, you might experience *anger* when a professor treats you rudely, *dismay* when you learn that your car needs expensive repairs, and *happiness* when you see that you aced your economics exam. In some respects, emotions lie at the core of mental health. The two most common complaints that lead people to seek psychotherapy are *depression* and *anxiety*. Clearly, emotions play a pervasive role in people's lives.

But exactly what is an emotion? Everyone has plenty of personal experience with emotion. However, it's an elusive concept to define (Izard, 2007; LeDoux, 1995). Emotion includes cognitive, physiological, and behavioral components, which are summarized in the following definition: ***Emotion* involves (1) a subjective conscious experience (the cognitive component) accompanied by (2) bodily arousal (the physiological component) and by (3) characteristic overt expressions (the behavioral component).** That's a pretty complex definition. Let's take a closer look at each of these three components of emotion.

The Cognitive Component: Subjective Feelings

PSYKTREK 8c

Over 550 words in the English language refer to emotions (Averill, 1980). Ironically, however, people often have difficulty describing their emotions to others (Zajonc, 1980). Emotion is a highly personal, subjective experience. In studying the cognitive component of emotions, psychologists generally rely on participants' verbal reports of what they're experiencing. Such reports indicate that emotions are potentially intense internal feelings that sometimes seem to have a life of their own. People can't click their emotions on and off like a bedroom light. If it were as simple as that, you could choose to be happy whenever you wanted. Although some degree of emotional control is possible (Thayer, 1996), emotions tend to involve automatic reactions that are difficult to regulate (Öhman & Wiens, 2003). In some cases, these emotional reactions may occur at an unconscious level of processing, outside of one's awareness (Winkielman & Berridge, 2004).

People's cognitive appraisals of events in their lives are key determinants of the emotions they experience (Clore & Ortony, 2008; Ellsworth & Scherer, 2003). A specific event, such as giving a speech, may be highly threatening and thus anxiety arousing for one person but a "ho-hum," routine matter for another. The conscious experience of emotion includes an *evaluative* aspect. People characterize their emotions as pleasant or unpleasant (Barrett et al., 2007; Neese & Ellsworth, 2009). These evaluative reactions can be automatic and subconscious (Ferguson & Bargh, 2004). Of course, individuals often experience "mixed emotions" that include both pleasant and unpleasant qualities (Cacioppo & Berntson, 1999). For example, an executive just given a promotion with challenging new responsibilities may experience both happiness and anxiety.

In recent years a curious finding has emerged regarding people's cognitive assessments of their emotions—we are not very good at anticipating our emotional responses to future setbacks and triumphs. Research on ***affective forecasting*—efforts**

© AP Images/Amy sancetta

Emotions involve automatic reactions that can be difficult to control.

to predict one's emotional reactions to future events—demonstrates that people reliably mispredict their future feelings in response to good and bad events, such as getting a promotion at work, taking a long-awaited vacation, getting a crummy grade in an important class, or being fired at work (Wilson & Gilbert, 2003, 2005). People tend to be reasonably accurate in anticipating whether events will generate positive or negative emotions, but they often are way off in predicting the initial intensity and duration of their emotional reactions.

For example, Dunn, Wilson, and Gilbert (2003) asked college students to predict what their overall level of happiness would be if a campus housing lottery assigned them to a desirable or undesirable dormitory. The students expected that their dormitory assignments would have a pretty dramatic effect on their well-being. But when their happiness was assessed a year after actually being assigned to the good or bad dorms, it was clear that their happiness was not affected by their dorm assignments (see **Figure 10.20**). In a similar vein, research shows that young professors overestimate the unhappiness they will feel five years after being turned down for tenure, college students overestimate how despondent they will be after the breakup of a romantic relationship, and job applicants overestimate how distressed they will feel after being rejected for a job (Gilbert et al., 1998).

Why are individuals' predictions of their emotional reactions surprisingly inaccurate? A variety of factors can contribute (Hoerger et al., 2009; Wilson & Gilbert, 2003). One consideration is that most people do not fully appreciate how effective humans tend to be in rationalizing, discounting, and overlooking failures and mistakes. People exhibit a host of cognitive biases that help them to insulate themselves from the emotional fallout of life's difficulties. However, people do not factor this peculiar "talent" into the picture when making predictions about their emotional reactions to setbacks. In any event, as you can see, emotions are not only hard to regulate, they are also hard to predict.

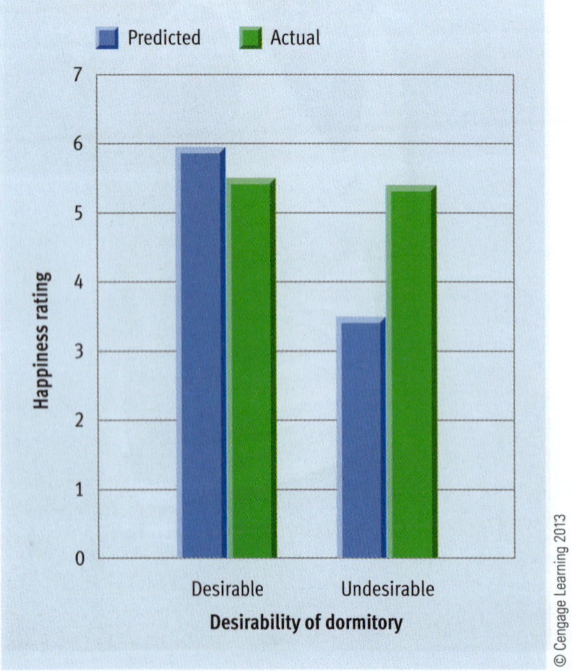

Figure 10.20

The inaccuracy of affective forecasting. Using a 7-point scale (where 1 = unhappy and 7 = happy), college students predicted how happy they would be a year later if they were randomly assigned to live in a desirable or an undesirable dormitory. Students anticipated that their dorm assignment would have a pronounced positive or negative impact on their overall happiness (blue bars); however a year later, those who ended up living in undesirable housing versus the desirable dorms showed nearly identical levels of happiness (green bars).

SOURCE: Wilson, T. D., & Gilbert, D. T. (2005). Affective forecasting: Knowing what to want. *Current Directions in Psychological Science, 14,* 131–134. Figure 1. Copyright 2006 Blackwell Publishing. Reprinted by permission of Sage Publications.

The Physiological Component: Diffuse and Multifaceted

PSYK TREK 8c

Emotional processes are closely tied to physiological processes, but the interconnections are enormously complex. The biological bases of emotions are diffuse, involving many areas in the brain and many neurotransmitter systems, as well as the autonomic nervous system and the endocrine system.

Autonomic Arousal

PSYK TREK 8c

Imagine your reaction as your car spins out of control on an icy highway. Your fear is accompanied by a variety of physiological changes. Your heart rate and breathing accelerate. Your blood pressure surges. Your pupils dilate. The hairs on your skin stand erect, giving you "goose bumps." You start to perspire. Although the physical reactions may not always be as obvious as in this scenario, *emotions are generally accompanied by visceral arousal* (Larsen et al., 2008). Surely you've experienced a "knot in your stomach" or a "lump in your throat"—thanks to anxiety.

Much of the discernible physiological arousal associated with emotion occurs through the actions of the *autonomic nervous system* (Janig, 2003). This system regulates the activity of glands, smooth muscles, and blood vessels (see **Figure 10.21**). As you may recall from Chapter 3, the autonomic nervous system is responsible for the highly emotional *fight-or-flight response*. This response is largely modulated by the release of adrenal *hormones* that radiate throughout the body. Hormonal changes clearly play a crucial role in emotional responses to stress and may contribute to many other emotions as well.

One notable part of emotional arousal is the ***galvanic skin response (GSR)***, **an increase in the electrical conductivity of the skin that occurs when sweat glands increase their activity.** The GSR is a convenient and sensitive index of autonomic arousal that has been used as a measure of emotion in many lab studies.

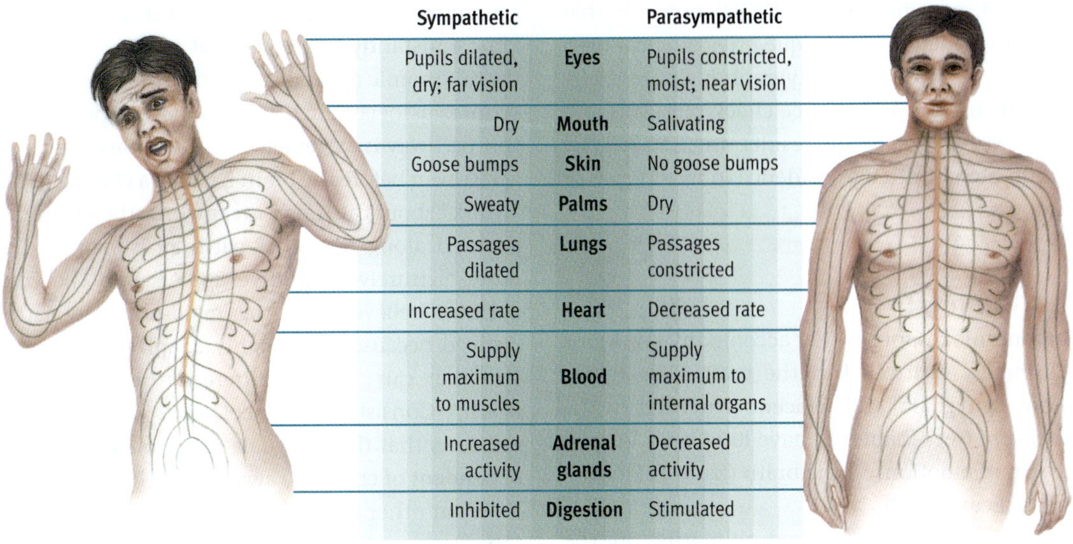

Figure 10.21
Emotion and autonomic arousal. The autonomic nervous system (ANS) is composed of the nerves that connect to the heart, blood vessels, smooth muscles, and glands (consult **Figure 3.8** for a more detailed view). The ANS is divided into the *sympathetic division,* which mobilizes bodily resources in response to stress, and the *parasympathetic division,* which conserves bodily resources. Emotions are frequently accompanied by sympathetic ANS activation, which leads to goosebumps, sweaty palms, and the other physical responses listed on the left side of the diagram.
© Cengage Learning 2013

The connection between emotion and autonomic arousal provides the basis for the ***polygraph,* or *lie detector,* a device that records autonomic fluctuations while a subject is questioned.** The polygraph was invented in 1915 by psychologist William Marston—who also dreamed up the comic book superhero Wonder Woman (Knight, 2004). A polygraph can't actually detect lies. It's really an emotion detector. It monitors key indicators of autonomic arousal, typically heart rate, blood pressure, respiration rate, and GSR. The assumption is that when subjects lie, they experience emotion (presumably anxiety) that produces noticeable changes in these physiological indicators (see **Figure 10.22**). The polygraph examiner asks a subject a number of nonthreatening questions to establish the subject's baseline on these autonomic indicators. Then the examiner asks the critical questions (for example, "Where were you on the night of the burglary?") and observes whether the person's autonomic arousal changes.

The polygraph has been controversial since its invention (Grubin & Madsen, 2005). Polygraph advocates claim that lie detector tests are about 85%–90% accurate. They claim that the validity of polygraph testing has been demonstrated in empirical studies. However, these claims clearly are not supported by the evidence (Branaman & Gallagher, 2005; Fiedler, Schmid, & Stahl, 2002; Lykken, 1998). Part of the problem is that people who are telling the truth may experience emotional arousal when they respond to incriminating questions. Thus, polygraph tests sometimes lead to accusations of lying against people who are innocent. Another problem is that some people can lie without experiencing anxiety or autonomic arousal. The crux of

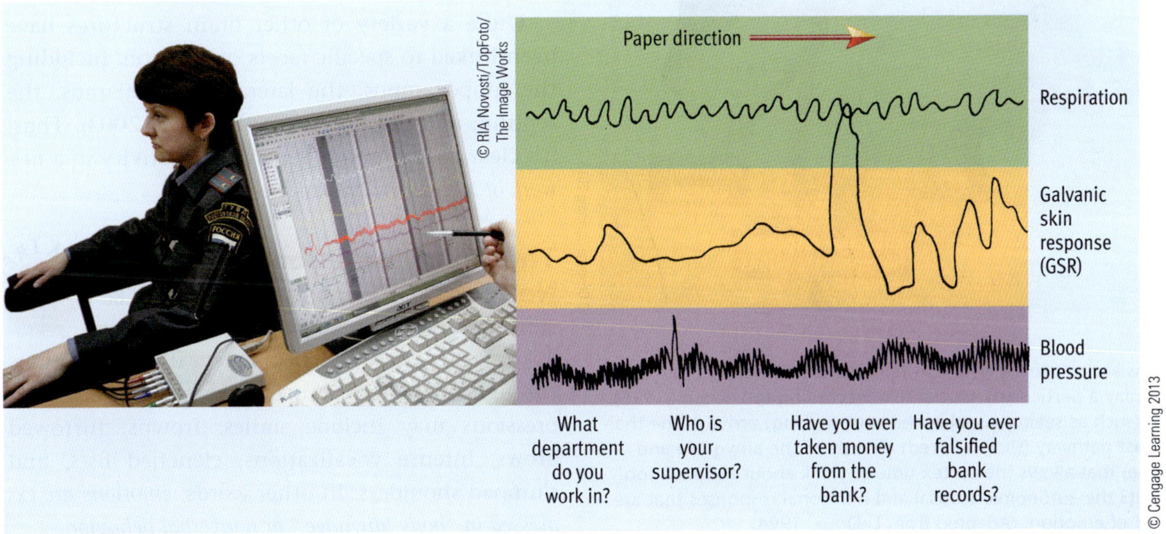

Figure 10.22
Emotion and the polygraph. A lie detector measures the autonomic arousal that most people experience when they tell a lie. After using nonthreatening questions to establish a baseline, a polygraph examiner looks for signs of arousal (such as the sharp change in GSR shown here) on incriminating questions. Unfortunately, the polygraph is not a dependable index of whether people are lying.

Reality CHECK

Misconception

The lie detector is an accurate, reliable method for identifying dishonest responses.

Reality

The accuracy of the polygraph has long been exaggerated. For example, one influential study (Kleinmuntz & Szucko, 1984) found that lie detector tests would have led to incorrect verdicts for about one-third of the suspects who were proven innocent and about one-fourth of those who eventually confessed.

the problem, as Leonard Saxe (1994) notes, is that "there is no evidence of a unique physiological reaction to deceit" (p. 71). The polygraph *is* a potentially useful tool that can help police check out leads and alibis. However, polygraph results are not reliable enough to be submitted as evidence in most types of courtrooms.

Neural Circuits

PSYKTREK 8c

The autonomic responses that accompany emotions are ultimately controlled in the brain. The hypothalamus, amygdala, and adjacent structures in the *limbic system* (see Chapter 3) have long been viewed as the seat of emotions in the brain (Izard & Saxton, 1988; MacLean, 1993).

Recent research has focused primarily on the *amygdala* (see **Figure 10.23**), which plays a central role in the acquisition of conditioned fears (LeDoux & Phelps, 2008). According to Joseph LeDoux (1993, 1996, 2000), the amygdala lies at the core of a complex set of neural circuits that process emotion. He believes that sensory inputs capable of eliciting emotions arrive in the thalamus. The thalamus in turn simultaneously routes the information along two separate pathways: a fast pathway to the nearby amygdala and a slower pathway to areas in the cortex (see **Figure 10.23**). The amygdala processes the information quickly. Therefore, if it detects a threat, it almost instantly triggers neural activity that leads to the autonomic arousal and endocrine (hormonal) responses associated with emotion. The processing in this pathway is extremely fast. Emotions may be triggered even before the brain has had a chance to really "think" about the input. Meanwhile, the information shuttled along the other pathway is subjected to a more "leisurely" cognitive appraisal in the cortex. LeDoux believes that the rapid-response pathway evolved because it's a highly adaptive warning system that can "be the difference between life and death." Consistent with LeDoux's theory, evidence indicates that the amygdala can process emotion independent of cognitive awareness (Phelps, 2005).

What other areas of the brain are involved in the modulation of emotion? The list is extensive, and different emotions may be processed by different neural structures (Panksepp, 2008). Some of the more intriguing findings include the following:

- The *prefrontal cortex,* known for its role in planning and executive control, appears to contribute to efforts to voluntarily control emotional reactions (Davidson, Fox, & Kalin, 2007; Quirk, 2007).
- As noted in Chapter 5, a neural circuit called the *mesolimbic dopamine pathway* plays a major role in the experience of pleasurable emotions associated with rewarding events (Knapp & Kornetsky, 2009; Nestler & Malenka, 2004). It is activated by cocaine and other abused drugs, as well as natural reinforcers such as food and sex.
- As you may recall from Chapter 3, *mirror neurons* are neurons that are activated by performing an action or by seeing another monkey or person perform the same action. These recently discovered specialized neurons appear to play a crucial role in the experience of the important emotion of empathy (Iacoboni, 2007, 2009).

Quite a variety of other brain structures have been linked to specific facets of emotion, including the hippocampus, the lateral hypothalamus, the septum, and the brainstem (Berridge, 2003). Thus, it's clear that emotion depends on activity in a *network of interacting brain centers.*

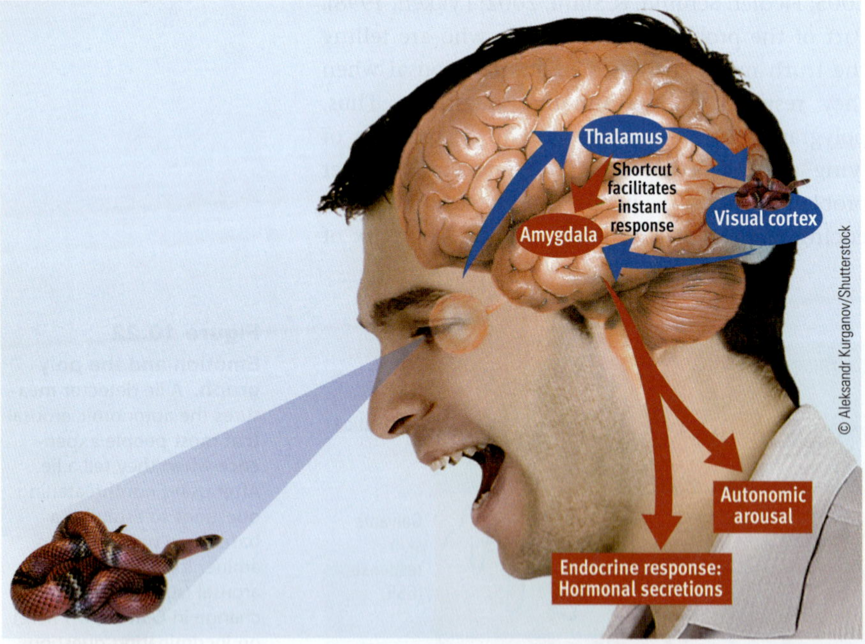

© Cengage Learning 2013

Figure 10.23

The amygdala and fear. Emotions are controlled by a constellation of interacting brain systems, but the amygdala appears to play a particularly crucial role. According to LeDoux (1996), sensory inputs that can trigger fear (such as seeing a snake while out walking) arrive in the thalamus and then are routed along a fast pathway (shown in red) directly to the amygdala and along a slow pathway (shown in blue) that allows the cortex time to think about the situation. Activity in the fast pathway also elicits the autonomic arousal and hormonal responses that are part of the physiological component of emotion. (Adapted from LeDoux, 1994)

The Behavioral Component: Nonverbal Expressiveness

PSYKTREK 8c

At the behavioral level, people reveal their emotions through characteristic overt expressions. Such expressions may include smiles, frowns, furrowed brows, intense vocalizations, clenched fists, and slumped shoulders. In other words, *emotions are expressed in "body language," or nonverbal behavior.*

Facial expressions reveal a variety of basic emotions. In an extensive research project, Paul Ekman and Wallace Friesen asked subjects to identify what emotion a person was experiencing on the basis of facial cues in photographs. They found that subjects are generally successful in identifying *six fundamental emotions*: happiness, sadness, anger, fear, surprise, and disgust (Ekman & Friesen, 1975, 1984). People can also identify a number of other emotions from facial expressions, such as contempt, embarrassment, shame, amusement, and sympathy. But they identify these emotions less reliably than the basic six emotions (Keltner et al., 2003). Furthermore, the identification of emotions from facial expressions tends to occur quickly and automatically (Tracy & Robins, 2008).

Some theorists believe that muscular feedback from one's own facial expressions contributes to the conscious experience of emotions (Izard, 1990; Tomkins, 1991). Proponents of the *facial feedback hypothesis* assert that facial muscles send signals to the brain. These signals then help the brain recognize the emotion that one is experiencing (see **Figure 10.24**). According to this view, smiles, frowns, and furrowed brows help create the subjective experience of various emotions. Consistent with this idea, studies show that if subjects are instructed to contract their facial muscles to mimic facial expressions associated with certain emotions, they tend to report that they actually experience these emotions to some degree (Kleinke, Peterson, & Rutledge, 1998; Levenson, 1992).

The facial expressions that go with various emotions may be largely innate (Eibl-Ebesfeldt, 1975; Izard, 1994). For the most part, people who have been blind since birth smile and frown much like everyone else, even though they've never seen a smile or frown (Galati, Scherer, & Ricci-Bitti, 1997). In an influential recent study, David Matsumoto and Bob Willingham (2009) carefully photographed the facial expressions of congenitally blind judo athletes in the Paralympic Games and of sighted judo athletes in the Olympic Games. The photos for comparison were taken just after the athletes had won or lost their crucial final matches (for gold, silver, or bronze medals). The analysis of thousands of photos

Courtesy of Joseph LeDoux, New York University

Joseph LeDoux

"In situations of danger, it is very useful to be able to respond quickly. The time saved by the amygdala in acting on the thalamic information, rather than waiting for the cortical input, may be the difference between life and death."

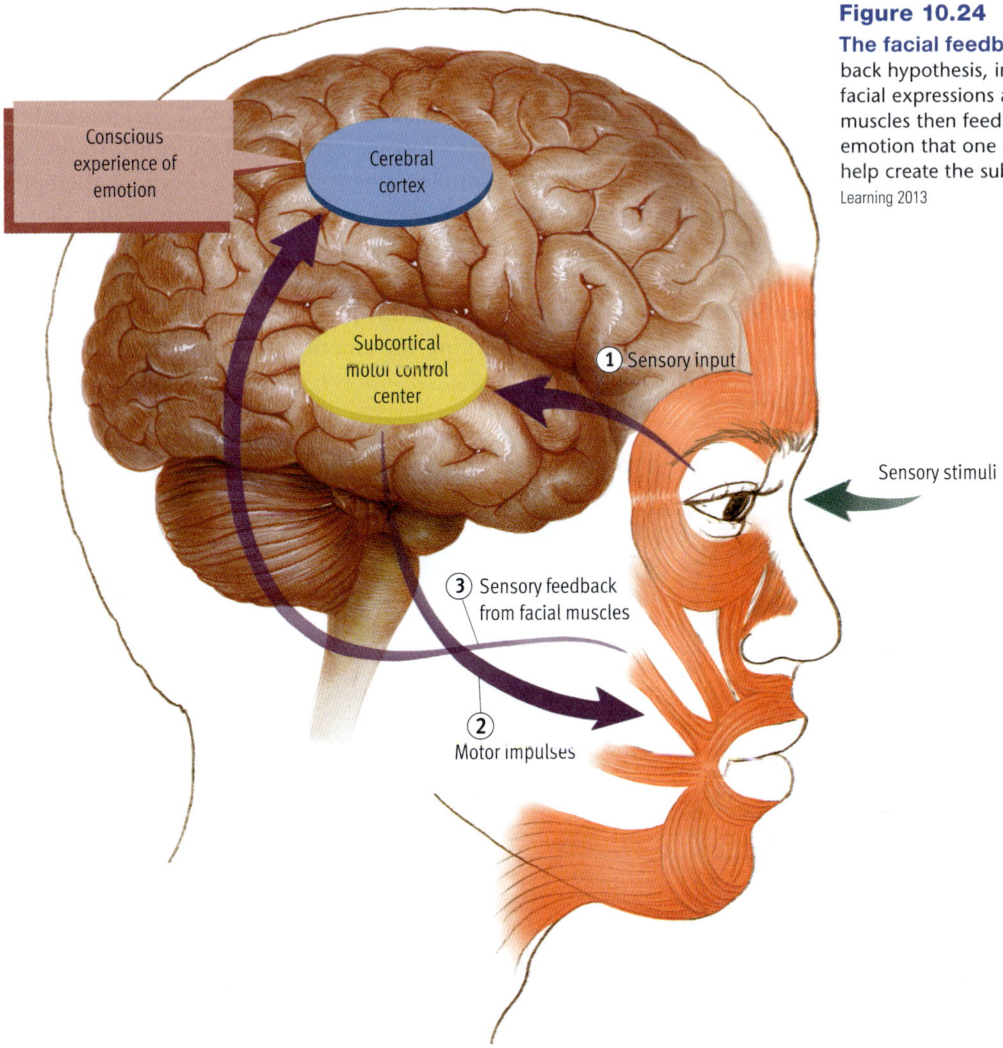

Figure 10.24

The facial feedback hypothesis. According to the facial feedback hypothesis, inputs to subcortical centers automatically evoke facial expressions associated with certain emotions, and the facial muscles then feed signals to the cortex that help it recognize the emotion that one is experiencing. In this view, facial expressions help create the subjective experience of various emotions. © Cengage Learning 2013

© Bob Willingham/bob@twoj.org

In a creative application of naturalistic observation, Matsumoto and Willingham (2009) shot photos of the award ceremonies for congenitally blind and sighted athletes to gain insight into whether facial expressions of emotion are innate.

of numerous athletes yielded clear results. The facial expressions of sighted and blind athletes were indistinguishable. These findings strongly support the hypothesis that the facial expressions that go with emotions are wired into the human brain. The long-held suspicion that facial expressions of emotion might be biologically built in has also led to extensive cross-cultural research on the dynamics of emotion. Let's look at what investigators have learned about culture and the elements of emotional experience.

Culture and the Elements of Emotion

Are emotions innate reactions that are universal across cultures? Or are they socially learned reactions that are culturally variable? The voluminous research on this lingering question has not yielded a simple answer. Researchers have found both strong similarities and sharp differences among cultures in the experience of emotion.

Cross-Cultural Similarities in Emotional Experience

After demonstrating that Western subjects could discern specific emotions from facial expressions, Ekman and Friesen (1975) took their facial-cue photographs on the road to other societies to see whether nonverbal expressions of emotion transcend cultural boundaries. They tested subjects in Argentina, Spain, Japan, and other countries. They found considerable cross-cultural agreement in the identification of the six basic emotions of happiness, sadness, anger, fear, surprise, and disgust based on facial expressions (see **Figure 10.25**). Still, Ekman and Friesen wondered whether this agreement might be the result of learning rather than biology. They couldn't discount that people in different cultures often share considerable exposure to Western mass media (magazines, newspapers, television, and so forth). And such media provide many visual depictions of people's emotional reactions. To rule out the possible influence of media, they took their photos to a remote area in New Guinea and showed them to a group of natives (the Fore) who had had virtually no contact with Western culture. Even the people from this preliterate culture did a fair job of identifying the emotions portrayed in the pictures

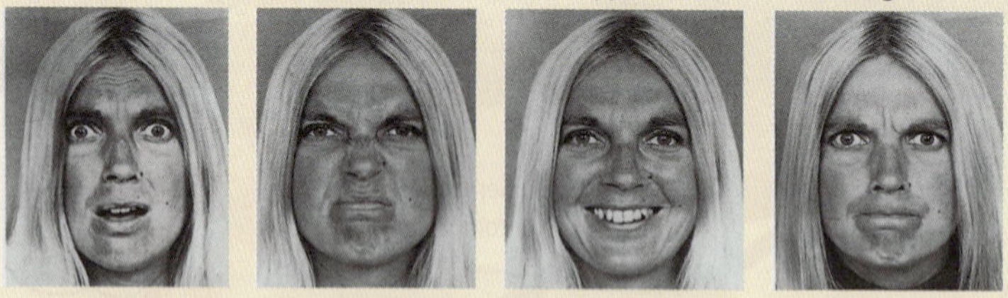

Country	Fear	Disgust	Happiness	Anger
	Agreement in judging photos (%)			
United States	85	92	97	67
Brazil	67	97	95	90
Chile	68	92	95	94
Argentina	54	92	98	90
Japan	66	90	100	90
New Guinea	54	44	82	50

© Cengage Learning 2013

Figure 10.25
Cross-cultural comparisons of people's ability to recognize emotions from facial expressions. Ekman and Friesen (1975) found that people in highly disparate cultures showed fair agreement on the emotions portrayed in these photos. This consensus across cultures suggests that facial expressions of emotions may be universal and that they have a strong biological basis.

SOURCE: Data from Ekman, P., & Friesen, W. V. (1975). *Unmasking the face.* Englewood Cliffs, NJ: Prentice-Hall. © 1975 by Paul Ekman, photographs courtesy of Paul Ekman.

(see the data in the bottom row of **Figure 10.25**). That is not to say that culture is *irrelevant* to the expression and perception of emotion. Research shows that subjects are somewhat more accurate in recognizing emotions expressed by people from their own culture than they are when asked to identify emotions expressed by a different cultural group (Elfenbein & Ambady, 2002, 2003).

Cross-cultural similarities have also been found in the cognitive elements of emotional experience (Scherer & Wallbott, 1994). For example, in making cognitive appraisals of events that might elicit emotional reactions, people from different cultures broadly think along the same lines (Matsumoto, Nezlek, & Koopmann, 2007; Mauro, Sato, & Tucker, 1992). That is, they evaluate situations along the same dimensions (pleasant versus unpleasant, expected versus unexpected, fair versus unfair, and so on). Understandably, then, the *types of events* that trigger specific emotions are fairly similar across cultures (Frijda, 1999; Matsumoto & Willingham, 2006). Around the globe, achievements lead to joy, injustices lead to anger, and risky situations lead to fear. Thus, researchers have found a great deal of cross-cultural continuity in the cognitive and behavioral (expressive) elements of emotional experience.

Cross-Cultural Differences in Emotional Experience

The cross-cultural similarities in emotional experience are impressive. Yet researchers have also found many cultural disparities in how people perceive, think about, and express their emotions (Mesquita, 2003; Mesquita & Leu, 2007). For example, fascinating variations have been observed in how cultures categorize emotions. Some basic categories of emotion that are universally understood in Western cultures appear to go unrecognized—or at least unnamed—in some non-Western cultures. James Russell (1991) has compiled numerous examples of English words for emotions that have no equivalent in other languages. For example, Tahitians have no word that corresponds to *sadness*. Many non-Western groups, including the Yoruba of Nigeria, the Kaluli of New Guinea, and the Chinese, lack a word for *depression*. The concept of *anxiety* seems to go unrecognized among Eskimos. However, critics point out that a lack of words for emotional concepts does not necessarily mean that those emotions are not recognized in a culture.

© Dewitt Jones/CORBIS

Cultural disparities have also been found in regard to nonverbal expressions of emotion. The natural facial expressions associated with basic emotions appear to transcend culture. However, people can and do learn to control and modify these expressions. ***Display rules* are norms that regulate the appropriate expression of emotions.** They prescribe when, how, and to whom people can show various emotions. These norms vary from one culture to another (Ekman, 1992). For example, Japanese culture emphasizes the suppression of negative emotions in public. More so than in other cultures, the Japanese are socialized to mask emotions such as anger, sadness, and disgust with stoic facial expressions or polite smiling. Thus, nonverbal expressions of emotions vary somewhat across cultures because of variations in display rules.

REVIEW OF KEY LEARNING GOALS

10.14 Emotion is made up of cognitive, physiological, and behavioral components. The cognitive component involves subjective feelings that have an evaluative aspect. People's cognitive appraisals of events in their lives determine the emotions they experience. Research on affective forecasting shows that people are surprisingly bad at predicting the intensity and duration of their emotional reactions to events.

10.15 The most readily apparent aspect of the physiological component of emotion is autonomic arousal. This arousal is the basis for the lie detector, which is really an emotion detector. Polygraphs are not all that accurate in assessing individuals' veracity. The amygdala appears to be the hub of an emotion-processing system in the brain that modulates conditioned fears. A variety of other areas in the brain contribute to the regulation of emotion as well.

10.16 At the behavioral level, emotions are expressed through body language, with facial expressions being particularly prominent. Ekman and Friesen assert that there are six basic emotions that are readily recognized based on facial expressions. The facial expressions associated with emotions may be innate. Advocates of the facial-feedback hypothesis maintain that facial muscles send signals to the brain that help the brain recognize the emotion one is experiencing.

10.17 Cross-cultural similarities have been found in the facial expressions that go with specific emotions and the cognitive appraisals that provoke emotions. However, there are some striking cultural variations in how people categorize their emotions and in the display rules that govern how much people show their emotions.

KEY LEARNING GOALS

10.18 Compare the James-Lange and Cannon-Bard theories of emotion.

10.19 Explain the two-factor theory of emotion, and describe evolutionary theories of emotion.

Theories of Emotion

How do psychologists explain the experience of emotion? A variety of theories and conflicting models exist. Some have been vigorously debated for over a century. As we describe these theories, you'll recognize a familiar bone of contention. Like so many other types of theories, theories of emotion hinge to an extent on the emphasis of nature vs. nurture.

James-Lange Theory

PSYKTREK 8d

As noted in Chapter 1, William James was a prominent early theorist who urged psychologists to explore the functions of consciousness. James (1884) developed a theory of emotion over 125 years ago that remains influential today. At about the same time, he and Carl Lange (1885) independently proposed that *the conscious experience of emotion results from one's perception of autonomic arousal.* Their theory stood common sense on its head. Everyday logic suggests that when you stumble onto a rattlesnake in the woods, the conscious experience of fear leads to physical arousal (the fight-or-flight response). The James-Lange theory of emotion asserts the opposite. That is, the perception of physical arousal leads to the conscious experience of fear (see **Figure 10.26**). In other words, while you might assume that your pulse is racing because you're fearful, James and Lange argued that you're fearful because your pulse is racing.

The James-Lange theory emphasizes the physiological determinants of emotion. According to this view, *different patterns of autonomic activation lead to the experience of different emotions.* Hence, people supposedly distinguish emotions such as fear, joy, and anger on the basis of the exact configuration of

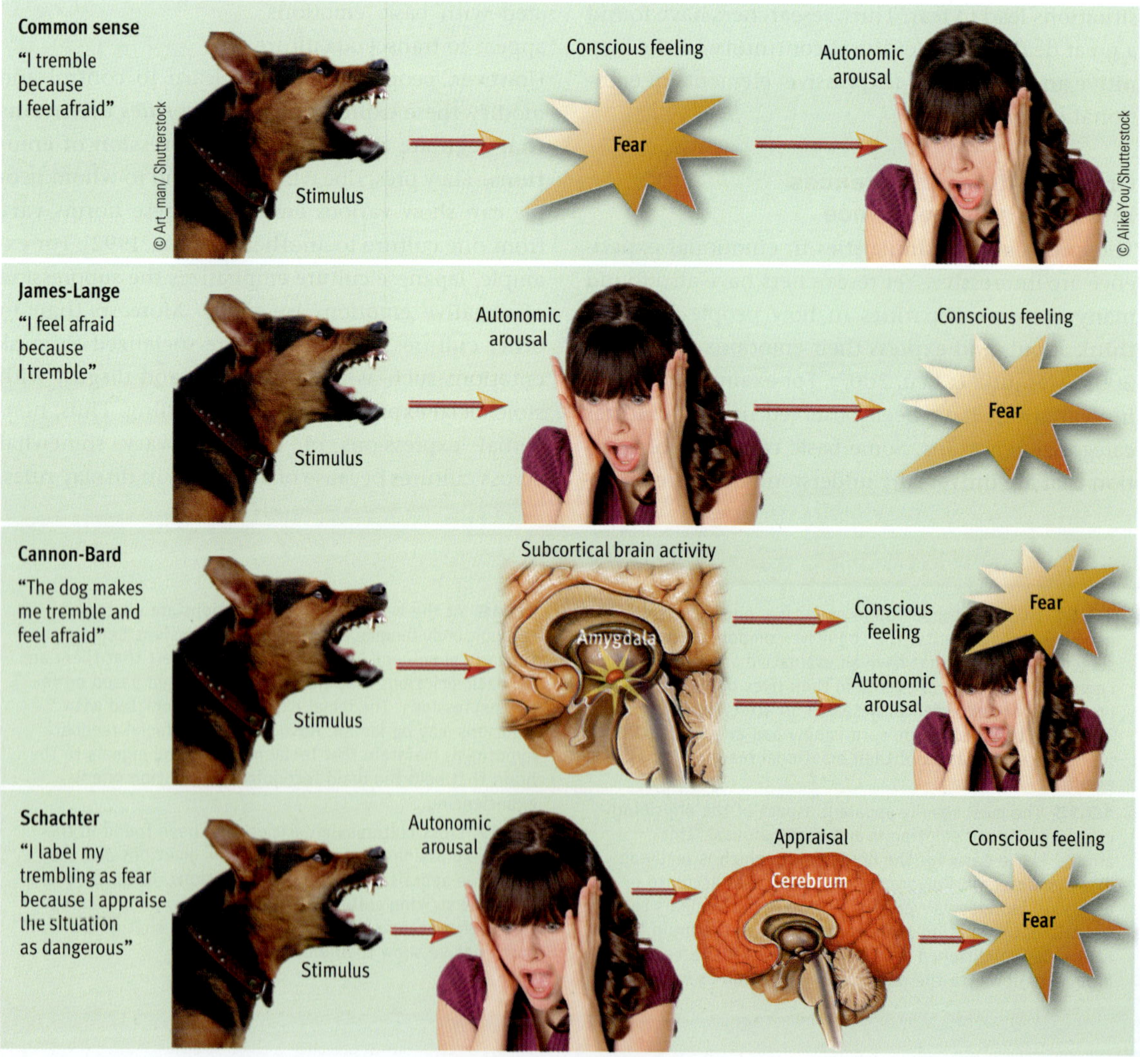

Figure 10.26
Theories of emotion. Three influential theories of emotion are contrasted with one another and with the commonsense view. The James-Lange theory was the first to suggest that feelings of arousal cause emotion, rather than vice versa. Schachter built on this idea by adding a second factor—interpretation (appraisal and labeling) of arousal.

autonomic reactions they experience. Decades of research have supported the concept of *autonomic specificity*. That is, different emotions are accompanied by somewhat different patterns of autonomic activation (Janig, 2003; Levenson, 2003). However, the question of whether people identify their emotions based on these varied patterns of autonomic activation remains unresolved.

Cannon-Bard Theory

PSYKTREK 8d

Walter Cannon (1927) found the James-Lange theory unconvincing. He pointed out that physiological arousal may occur without the experience of emotion (if one exercises vigorously, for instance). He also argued that visceral changes are too slow to precede the conscious experience of emotion. Finally, he argued that people experiencing very different emotions, such as fear, joy, and anger, exhibit similar patterns of autonomic arousal that are not readily distinguishable.

Thus, Cannon espoused a different explanation of emotion. Later, Philip Bard (1934) built on it. The resulting Cannon-Bard theory argues that emotion occurs when the thalamus sends signals *simultaneously* to the cortex and to the autonomic nervous system. The cortex creates the conscious experience of emotion. The autonomic nervous system creates the visceral arousal. The Cannon-Bard model is compared to the James-Lange model in **Figure 10.26**. Cannon and Bard were off the mark a bit in pinpointing the thalamus as the neural center for emotion. However, many modern theorists agree with the Cannon-Bard view that emotions originate in subcortical brain structures (LeDoux, 1996; Panksepp, 1991; Rolls, 1990). Some theorists also agree with the Cannon-Bard view that people do not discern their emotions from different patterns of autonomic activation (Frijda, 1999; Wagner, 1989).

Schachter's Two-Factor Theory

PSYKTREK 8d

In another influential analysis, Stanley Schachter asserted that people look at situational cues to differentiate between alternative emotions. According to Schachter (1964; Schachter & Singer, 1962, 1979), the experience of emotion depends on two factors: (1) autonomic arousal and (2) cognitive interpretation of that arousal. Schachter proposed that when you experience visceral arousal, you search your environment for an explanation (see **Figure 10.26** again). If you're stuck in a traffic jam, you'll probably label your arousal as anger. If you're taking an important exam, you'll probably label it as anxiety. If you're celebrating your birthday, you'll probably label it as happiness.

Schachter agreed with the James-Lange view that emotion is inferred from arousal. However, he also agreed with the Cannon-Bard position that different emotions yield largely indistinguishable patterns of autonomic activity. He reconciled these views by arguing that people look to external rather than internal cues to differentiate and label their specific emotions. In essence, Schachter suggested that people think along the following lines: "If I'm aroused and you're obnoxious, I must be angry."

The two-factor theory has received support. Studies have revealed some limitations as well (Leventhal & Tomarken, 1986). Situations can't mold emotions in just any way at any time. And in searching to explain arousal, subjects don't limit themselves to the immediate situation (Sinclair et al., 1994).

Courtesy of Stanley Schachter, © Bill Apple

Stanley Schachter

"Cognitive factors play a major role in determining how a subject interprets his bodily feelings."

Evolutionary Theories of Emotion

PSYKTREK 8d

When the limitations of the two-factor theory were exposed, theorists began returning to ideas espoused by Charles Darwin well over a century ago. Darwin (1872) believed that emotions developed because of their adaptive value. Fear, for instance, would help an organism avoid danger. This would then aid in survival. Hence, Darwin viewed emotions as a product of evolution. This premise serves as the foundation for several prominent theories of emotion developed independently by S. S. Tomkins (1980, 1991), Carroll Izard (1984, 1991), and Robert Plutchik (1984, 1993).

These *evolutionary theories* consider emotions to be largely innate reactions to certain stimuli. As

CONCEPT CHECK 10.3

Understanding Theories of Emotion

Check your understanding of theories of emotion by matching the theories we discussed with the statements below. Let's borrow William James's classic example: Assume that you just stumbled onto a bear in the woods. The first statement expresses the commonsense explanation of your fear. Each of the remaining statements expresses the essence of a different theory; indicate which theory in the spaces provided. The answers are provided in Appendix A.

1. You tremble because you're afraid.
   Common sense
2. You're afraid because you're trembling.
   ____
3. You're afraid because situational cues (the bear) suggest that's why you're trembling. ______________________
4. You're afraid because the bear has elicited an innate primary emotion.
   ____

Silvan Tomkins	Carroll Izard	Robert Plutchik
Fear	Fear	Fear
Anger	Anger	Anger
Enjoyment	Joy	Joy
Disgust	Disgust	Disgust
Interest	Interest	Anticipation
Surprise	Surprise	Surprise
Contempt	Contempt	
Shame	Shame	
	Sadness	Sadness
Distress		
	Guilt	
		Acceptance

© Cengage Learning 2013

Figure 10.27
Primary emotions. Evolutionary theories of emotion attempt to identify primary emotions. Three leading theorists—Silvan Tomkins, Carroll Izard, and Robert Plutchik—have compiled different lists of primary emotions, but this chart shows great overlap among the basic emotions identified by these theorists. (Based on Mandler, 1984)

such, emotions should be immediately recognizable under most conditions without much thought. After all, primitive animals that are incapable of complex thought seem to have little difficulty in recognizing their emotions. Evolutionary theorists believe that emotion evolved before thought. They assert that thought plays a relatively small role in emotion. They admit, though, that learning and cognition may have some influence on human emotions. Evolutionary theories generally assume that emotions originate in subcortical brain structures that evolved before the higher brain areas in the cortex associated with complex thought.

Evolutionary theories also assume that natural selection has equipped humans with a small number of innate emotions with proven adaptive value. Thus, the principal question that evolutionary theories of emotion wrestle with is: *What are the fundamental emotions?* **Figure 10.27** summarizes the conclusions of the leading theorists in this area. As you can see, Tomkins, Izard, and Plutchik have not come up with identical lists. However, there's considerable agreement. All three conclude that people exhibit eight to ten primary emotions. Moreover, six of these emotions appear on all three lists: fear, anger, joy, disgust, interest, and surprise. Of course, people experience more than just eight to ten emotions. How do evolutionary theories account for this variety? They propose that the many emotions that people experience are produced by blends of primary emotions and variations in intensity.

REVIEW OF KEY LEARNING GOALS

10.18 Common sense suggests that emotions cause autonomic arousal, but the James-Lange theory asserted that emotion *results* from one's perception of autonomic arousal. The Cannon-Bard theory countered with the proposal that emotions originate in subcortical areas of the brain.

10.19 According to Schachter's two-factor theory, people infer emotion from arousal and then label the emotion in accordance with their cognitive explanation for the arousal. Evolutionary theories of emotion maintain that emotions are innate reactions that require little cognitive interpretation. Evolutionary theorists seek to identify a small number of innate, fundamental emotions.

KEY LEARNING GOALS

10.20 Identify the five unifying themes highlighted in this chapter.

Reflecting on the Chapter's Themes

Cultural Heritage

Sociohistorical Context

Theoretical Diversity

Heredity and Environment

Multifactorial Causation

Five of our organizing themes were particularly prominent in this chapter: the influence of cultural contexts, the dense connections between psychology and society at large, psychology's theoretical diversity, the interplay of heredity and environment, and the multiple causes of behavior.

Our discussion of motivation and emotion demonstrated once again that there are both similarities and differences across cultures in behavior. The neural, biochemical, genetic, and hormonal processes underlying hunger and eating, for instance, are universal. But cultural factors influence what people prefer to eat, how much they eat, and whether they worry about dieting. In a similar vein, researchers have found a great deal of cross-cultural congruence in the cognitive, physiological, and expressive elements of emotional experience. However, they have also found cultural variations in how people think about and express their emotions. Thus, as we have seen in previous chapters, psychological processes are characterized by both cultural variance and invariance.

Our discussion of the controversies surrounding evolutionary theory, aggressive pornography, and the determinants of sexual orientation show once again that psychology is not an ivory tower enterprise. It evolves in a sociohistorical context that helps shape the debates in the field. These debates often have far-reaching social and political ramifications for society at large. We ended the chapter with a discussion of various theories of emotion. This showed once again that psychology is characterized by great theoretical diversity.

Finally, we repeatedly saw that biological and environmental factors jointly govern behavior. For example, we learned that eating behavior and the experience of emotion depend on complicated interactions between biological and environmental determinants. Indeed, complicated interactions permeated the entire chapter. Thus, if we want to fully understand behavior, we have to take multiple causes into account.

In the upcoming Personal Application, we will continue our discussion of emotion, looking at recent research on the correlates of happiness. In the Critical Thinking Application that follows, we discuss how to carefully analyze the types of arguments that permeated this chapter.

REVIEW OF KEY LEARNING GOALS

10.20 Our look at motivation and emotion showed once again that psychology is characterized by theoretical diversity, that biology and environment shape behavior interactively, that behavior is governed by multiple causes, that psychological processes are characterized by both cultural variance and invariance, and that psychology evolves in a sociohistorical context.

CONCEPT CHECK 10.4

Identifying the Contributions of Major Theorists and Researchers

Check your recall of the principal ideas of important theorists and researchers covered in this chapter by matching the people listed on the left with the appropriate contributions described on the right. If you need help, the crucial pages describing each person's ideas are listed in parentheses. Fill in the letters for your choices in the spaces provided on the left. You'll find the answers in Appendix A.

Major Theorists and Researchers

_______ 1. David Buss (p. 402)

_______ 2. Walter Cannon (pp. 388, 391, 418–419)

_______ 3. Paul Ekman and Wallace Friesen (pp. 415–416)

_______ 4. William James (p. 418)

_______ 5. Joseph LeDoux (pp. 414–415)

_______ 6. William Masters and Virginia Johnson (p. 398)

_______ 7. David McClelland (p. 409)

_______ 8. Stanley Schachter (pp. 396–397, 418–419)

Key Ideas and Contributions

a. This researcher has shown that the amygdala plays a central role in the acquisition of conditioned fears.

b. This research team conducted groundbreaking work on the physiological bases of the human sexual response.

c. This theorist is known for his influential work on the nature and determinants of achievement motivation.

d. This evolutionary psychologist's research showed that women around the world place a higher value than men on potential partners' status and financial prospects, whereas men show more interest than women in partners' youthfulness and attractiveness.

e. This research team demonstrated that subjects can identify six basic emotions from facial expressions and that nonverbal expressions of emotion transcend culture.

f. This individual proposed the externality hypothesis of obesity and devised the two-factor theory of emotion.

g. This person described homeostasis, conducted early research on hunger, and argued that emotions originate in subcortical brain structures.

h. This legendary scholar formulated a theory of emotion which proposed that the conscious experience of emotion results from one's perception of autonomic arousal.

KEY LEARNING GOALS

10.21 Identify factors that do not predict happiness.
10.22 Review information on factors that are moderately or strongly correlated with happiness.
10.23 Explain four conclusions that can be drawn about the dynamics of happiness.

Exploring the Ingredients of Happiness

Answer the following "true" or "false."

____ **1** The empirical evidence indicates that most people are relatively unhappy.

____ **2** People who have children are happier than people without children.

____ **3** Good health is an essential requirement for happiness.

____ **4** Good-looking people are happier than those who are unattractive.

The answer to all these questions is "false." These assertions are all reasonable and widely believed hypotheses about the correlates of happiness. Yet they have *not* been supported by empirical research. Thanks in part to the positive psychology movement, recent years have brought a surge of interest in the correlates of ***subjective well-being*—individuals' personal perceptions of their overall happiness and life satisfaction.** The findings of these studies are quite interesting. As you have already seen from our true-false questions, many commonsense notions about happiness appear to be inaccurate.

One of these inaccuracies is the apparently widespread assumption that most people are relatively unhappy. Writers, social scientists, and the general public seem to believe that people around the world are predominantly dissatisfied. However, empirical surveys consistently find that the vast majority of respondents—even those who are poor or disabled—characterize themselves as fairly happy (Diener & Diener, 1996; Myers & Diener, 1995). When people are asked to rate their happiness, only a small minority place themselves below the neutral point on the various scales used (see **Figure 10.28**). When the average subjective well-being of entire nations is computed, the means cluster toward the positive end of the scale, as shown in **Figure 10.29** (Tov & Diener, 2007). That's not to say that everyone is equally happy. Researchers find substantial and thought-provoking disparities in subjective well-being, which we will analyze momentarily. The overall picture, though, seems rosier than anticipated.

Factors That Do Not Predict Happiness

Let's begin our discussion of individual differences in happiness by highlighting those things that turn out to be relatively unimportant determinants of subjective well-being. Quite a number of factors that you might expect to be influential appear to bear little or no relationship to general happiness.

Money There *is* a positive correlation between income and subjective feelings of happiness. The association is surprisingly weak, however. Within specific nations, the correlation between income and happiness tends to fall somewhere between .12 and .20 (Diener & Biswas-Diener, 2002; Johnson & Krueger, 2006). Obviously, being poor can contribute to unhappiness. Yet it seems when people reach a certain level of income, additional wealth does not seem to foster greater happiness. One recent study in the United States estimated that once people exceed an income of around $75,000, little relation is seen between wealth and subjective well-being (Kahneman & Deaton, 2010). The strength of the association between money and happiness also depends on how subjective well-being is assessed. The weak correlations we have discussed thus far are observed when participants are asked to make global evaluations of their life satisfaction. Higher correlations are observed if subjects are asked whether they experienced specific positive or negative emotions (enjoyment, happiness, worry, sadness) the previous day (Diener et al., 2010; Kahneman & Deaton, 2010).

Why isn't money a better predictor of happiness? One reason is that there seems to be a disconnect between actual income and how people feel about their financial situation. Research (Johnson & Krueger, 2006) suggests that the correlation between actual wealth and people's subjective perceptions of whether they have enough money to meet their needs is surprisingly modest (around

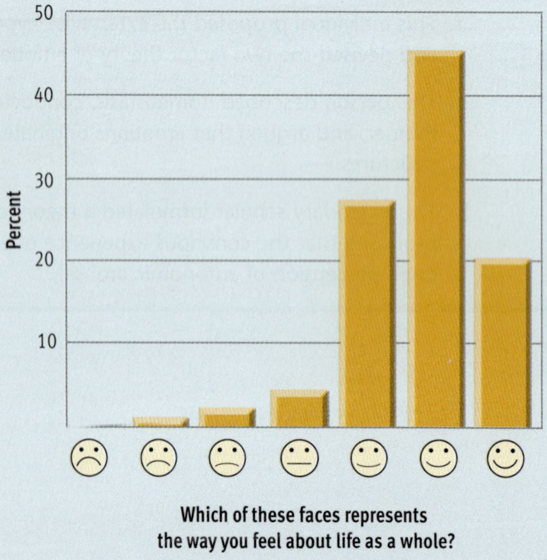

Figure 10.28
Measuring happiness with a nonverbal scale. Researchers have used a variety of methods to estimate the distribution of happiness. For example, in one study in the United States, respondents were asked to examine the seven facial expressions shown and select the one that "comes closest to expressing how you feel about your life as a whole." As you can see, the vast majority of participants chose happy faces. (Data adapted from Myers, 1992)

© Cengage Learning 2013

Figure 10.29

The subjective well-being of nations. Veenhoven (1993) combined the results of almost 1000 surveys to calculate the average subjective well-being reported by representative samples from 43 nations. The mean happiness scores clearly pile up at the positive end of the distribution, with only two scores falling below the neutral point of 5. (Data adapted from Diener and Diener, 1996)

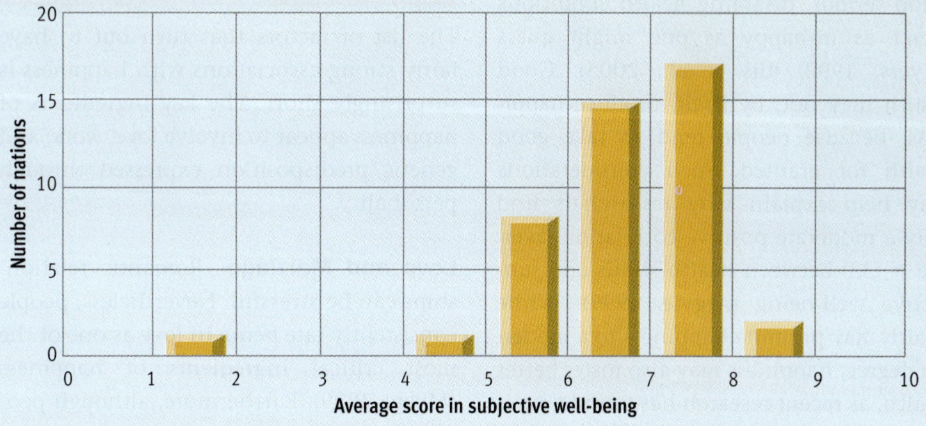

© Cengage Learning 2013

.30). Another problem with money is that pervasive advertising and rising income escalate material desires (Frey & Stutzer, 2002; Kasser et al., 2004). When these growing material desires outstrip what people can afford, dissatisfaction is likely (Solberg et al., 2002). Thus, complaints about not having enough money are routine even among people who are very affluent by objective standards.

Interestingly, there is some evidence that people who place an especially strong emphasis on the pursuit of wealth and materialistic goals tend to be somewhat less happy than others (Kasser, 2002; Van Boven, 2005). Perhaps this is because they are so focused on financial success that they don't derive much satisfaction from their family life (Nickerson et al., 2003). Consistent with this view, one study (Kahneman et al., 2006) found that higher income was associated with working longer hours and allocating fewer hours to leisure pursuits. The results of another recent study suggested that wealthy people become jaded in a way that undermines their ability to savor positive experiences (Quoidback et al., 2010).

Age Age and happiness are consistently found to be unrelated. Age accounts for less than 1% of the variation in people's happiness (Lykken, 1999). The key factors influencing subjective well-being may shift some as people grow older—work becomes less important, health more so. But people's average level of happiness tends to remain remarkably stable over the life span.

Parenthood Children can be a tremendous source of joy and fulfillment. However, they can also be a tremendous source of headaches and hassles. Compared to childless couples, parents worry more and experience more marital problems (Argyle, 1987). Apparently, the good and bad aspects of parenthood balance each other out. The evidence indicates that people who have children are neither more nor less happy than people without children (Argyle, 2001).

Intelligence and attractiveness Intelligence and physical attractiveness are highly valued traits in modern society. Yet researchers have not found an association between either characteristic and happiness (Diener, Wolsic, & Fujita, 1995; Diener, Kesebir, & Tov, 2009).

Moderately Good Predictors of Happiness

Research has identified three facets of life that appear to have a *moderate* association with subjective well-being: health, social activity, and religious belief.

Health Good physical health would seem to be an essential requirement for happiness, but people adapt to health problems.

"Who can say? I suppose I'm as happy as my portfolio will allow me to be."

© Mischa Richter/The New Yorker Collection/www.cartoonbank.com

Research reveals that individuals who develop serious, disabling health conditions aren't as unhappy as one might guess (Myers, 1992; Riis et al., 2005). Good health may not, by itself, produce happiness, because people tend to take good health for granted. Such considerations may help explain why researchers find only a moderate positive correlation (average = .32) between health status and subjective well-being (Argyle, 1999). While health may promote happiness to a moderate degree, happiness may also foster better health, as recent research has found a positive correlation between happiness and longevity (Veenhoven, 2008).

Social Activity Humans are social animals. As such, interpersonal relations *do* appear to contribute to people's happiness. Those who are satisfied with their social support and friendship networks and those who are socially active report above-average levels of happiness (Diener & Seligman, 2004; Myers, 1999). Furthermore, people who are exceptionally happy tend to report greater satisfaction with their social relations than those who are average or low in subjective well-being (Diener & Seligman, 2002). One recent study that periodically recorded participants' daily conversations found that people who had more deep, substantive conversations were happier than those who mostly engaged in small talk (Mehl et al., 2010). This finding is not all that surprising, in that one would expect that people with richer social networks would have more deep conversations.

Religion The link between religiosity and subjective well-being is modest. However, a number of large-scale surveys suggest that people with heartfelt religious convictions are more likely to be happy than people who characterize themselves as nonreligious (Abdel-Khalek, 2006; Myers, 2008). Researchers aren't sure how religious faith fosters happiness. Myers (1992) offers some interesting conjectures, though. Among other things, he discusses how religion can give people a sense of purpose and meaning in their lives. It can help them accept their setbacks gracefully. It can connect them to a caring, supportive community. Finally, it can comfort them by putting their ultimate mortality in perspective.

Strong Predictors of Happiness

The list of factors that turn out to have fairly strong associations with happiness is surprisingly short. The key ingredients of happiness appear to involve love, work, and genetic predisposition expressed through personality.

Love and Marriage Romantic relationships can be stressful. Nevertheless, people consistently rate being in love as one of the most critical ingredients of happiness (Myers, 1999). Furthermore, although people complain a lot about their marriages, the evidence indicates that marital status is a key correlate of happiness. Among both men and women, married people are happier than people who are single or divorced (Myers & Diener, 1995). This correlation holds around the world in widely different cultures (Diener et al., 2000). And among married people, their level of marital satisfaction predicts their personal well-being (Proulx, Helms, & Buehler, 2007). However, the causal relations underlying this correlation are unclear. It may be that happiness causes marital satisfaction more than marital satisfaction promotes happiness. Perhaps people who are happy tend to have better intimate relationships and more stable marriages, while people who are unhappy have more difficulty finding and keeping mates.

Work People often complain about their jobs. Therefore, one might not expect work to be a key source of happiness. Yet it is. It's not as critical as love and marriage, but job satisfaction has a substantial association with general happiness (Judge & Klinger, 2008; Warr, 1999). Studies also show that unemployment has strong negative effects on subjective well-being (Lucas et al., 2004). It's difficult to sort out whether job satisfaction causes happiness or vice versa. Evidence suggests, though, that causation flows both ways (Argyle, 2001).

Genetics and Personality The best predictor of individuals' future happiness is their past happiness (Lucas & Diener, 2008). Some people seem destined to be happy and others unhappy, regardless of their triumphs or setbacks. The limited influence of life events was apparent in a stunning study that found only marginal differences in overall happiness between recent lottery winners and recent accident victims who became quadriplegics (Brickman, Coates, & Janoff-Bulman, 1978). Researchers were amazed that such extremely lucky and horrible events didn't have a dramatic impact on happiness. Actually, several lines of evidence suggest that happiness does not depend on external circumstances, such as buying a nice house or getting promoted. On the other hand, internal factors do influence happiness. Such internal factors include one's personality and outlook on life (Lykken & Tellegen, 1996; Lyubomirsky, Sheldon, & Schkade, 2005).

With this reality in mind, researchers have investigated whether there might be a hereditary basis for variations in happiness. These studies suggest that people's genetic predispositions account for a substantial portion of the variance in happiness, perhaps as much as 50% (Lyubomirsky et al., 2005; Stubbe et al., 2005). How can one's genes influence one's happiness? Presumably, by shaping one's temperament and personality, which are known to be heritable (Weiss, Bates, & Luciano, 2008). Hence, researchers have begun to look for links between personality and subjective well-being. They have found some interesting correlations. For example, *extraversion* is one of the better predictors of happiness: People who are outgoing, upbeat, and sociable tend to be happier than others (Fleeson, Malanos, & Achille, 2002). Additional personality correlates of happiness include conscientiousness, agreeableness, self-esteem, and optimism (Lucas, 2008; Lyubomirsky, Tkach, & DiMatteo, 2006).

Conclusions About Subjective Well-Being

We must be cautious in drawing inferences about the causes of happiness. The available data are correlational, not causal (see **Figure 10.30**). Nonetheless, the empirical evidence suggests that many popular beliefs about the sources of happiness are unfounded. The data also demonstrate that happiness is shaped by a complex network of variables. In spite of this complexity,

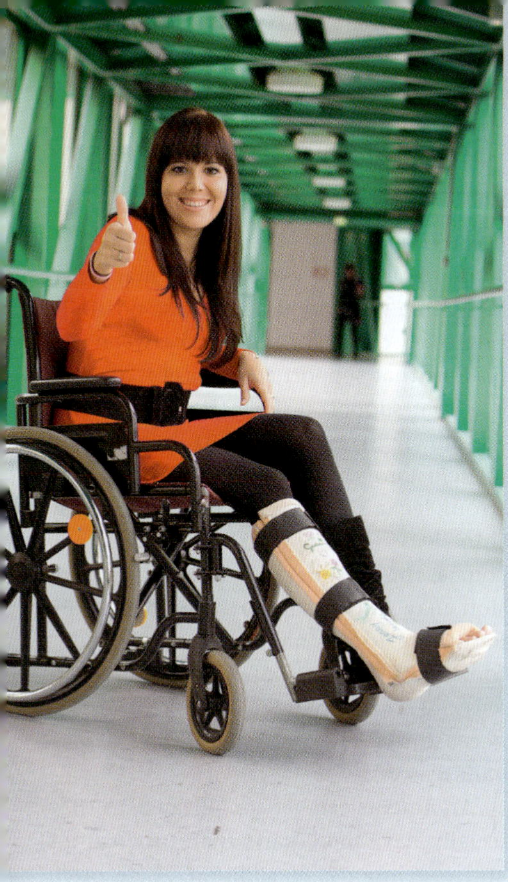
© INSADCO Photography/Alamy

Research shows that happiness does not depend on people's positive and negative experiences as much as one would expect. Some people, presumably because of their personality, seem destined to be happy in spite of major setbacks, and others seem destined to cling to unhappiness even though their lives seem reasonably pleasant.

however, a number of worthwhile insights about the ingredients of happiness can be gleaned from the recent flurry of research.

First, research on happiness shows that the determinants of subjective well-being are precisely that: subjective. *Objective realities are not as important as subjective feelings.* In other words, your health, your wealth, and your job are not as influential as how you *feel* about your health, wealth, and job (Schwarz & Strack, 1999). These feelings are likely to be influenced by what your *expectations* were. Research suggests that bad outcomes feel worse when unexpected than when expected. Research also suggests that good outcomes feel better when unexpected than when expected (Shepperd & McNulty, 2002). Thus, the same objective event, such as a pay raise of $2000 annually, may generate positive feelings in someone who wasn't expecting a raise and negative feelings in someone expecting a much larger increase in salary.

Second, *when it comes to happiness everything is relative* (Argyle, 1999; Hagerty, 2000). In other words, you evaluate what you have relative to what the people around you have. Generally, we compare ourselves with others who are similar to us. Thus, people who are wealthy assess what they have by comparing themselves with their wealthy friends and neighbors; their *relative* standing is crucial (Boyce, Brown, & Moore, 2010). This is one reason for the low correlation between wealth and happiness. You might have a lovely home, but if it sits next door to a palatial mansion, it might be a source of more dissatisfaction than happiness. Conversely, if you have a humble home but it's the nicest on the block, you may derive daily satisfaction from the difference.

Third, *research on subjective well-being indicates that people often adapt to their circumstances.* This adaptation effect is one reason that increases in income don't necessarily bring increases in happiness. ***Hedonic adaptation* occurs when the mental scale that people use to judge the pleasantness-unpleasantness of their experiences shifts so that their neutral point, or baseline for comparison, changes.** Unfortunately, when people's experiences improve, hedonic adaptation may *sometimes* put them on a *hedonic treadmill*—their neutral point moves upward. The improvements, then, yield no real benefits (Kahneman, 1999). However, when people have to grapple with major setbacks, hedonic adaptation probably helps protect their mental and physical health. For example, people who are sent to prison and people who develop debilitating diseases are not as unhappy as one might assume. That's because they adapt to their changed situations and evaluate events from a new perspective (Frederick & Loewenstein, 1999). That's not to say that hedonic adaptation in the face of life's difficulties is inevitable or complete (Lucas, 2007). Evidence suggests that people adapt more slowly to negative events than to positive events (Larsen & Prizmic, 2008). Thus, even years later, people who suffer major setbacks, such as the death of a spouse or serious illness, often are not as happy as they were before the setback. Generally, though, they are not nearly as unhappy as they or others would have predicted (Diener & Oishi, 2005).

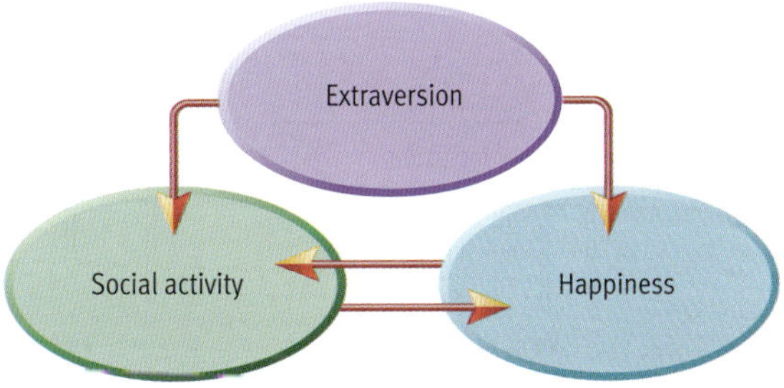

Figure 10.30

Possible causal relations among the correlates of happiness. Although we have considerable data on the correlates of happiness, it is difficult to untangle the possible causal relationships. For example, we know that a moderate positive correlation exists between social activity and happiness, but we can't say for sure whether high social activity causes happiness or whether happiness causes people to be more socially active. Moreover, in light of the research showing that a third variable—extraversion—correlates with both variables, we have to consider the possibility that extraversion causes both greater social activity and greater happiness. © Cengage Learning 2013

REVIEW OF KEY LEARNING GOALS

10.21 Research on happiness reveals that many commonsense notions about the roots of happiness appear to be incorrect, including the notion that most people are unhappy. Factors such as income, age, parenthood, intelligence, and attractiveness are largely uncorrelated with subjective well-being.

10.22 Physical health, good social relationships, and religious faith appear to have a modest impact on feelings of happiness. The only factors that are good predictors of happiness are love and marriage, work satisfaction, and personality and genetics.

10.23 Research on happiness indicates that objective realities are not as important as subjective feelings and that subjective well-being is a relative concept. The evidence also indicates that people adapt to their circumstances, but such hedonic adaptation is not necessarily complete.

Analyzing Arguments: Making Sense out of Controversy

KEY LEARNING GOALS

10.24 Identify the key elements in arguments.
10.25 Recognize common fallacies that often show up in arguments.

Consider the following argument: "Dieting is harmful to your health because the tendency to be obese is largely inherited." What is your reaction to this reasoning? Do you find it convincing? We hope not, as this argument is seriously flawed. Can you see what's wrong? There is no relationship between the conclusion that "dieting is harmful to your health" and the reason given that "the tendency to be obese is largely inherited." The argument is initially seductive because you know from reading this chapter that obesity *is* largely inherited. The reason provided, then, represents a true statement. But the reason is unrelated to the conclusion advocated. This scenario may strike you as odd. However, if you start listening carefully to discussions about controversial issues, you will probably notice that people often cite irrelevant considerations in support of their favored conclusions.

This chapter was loaded with controversial issues that sincere, well-meaning people could argue about for weeks. Does the availability of pornography increase the prevalence of sex crimes? Are gender differences in mating preferences a product of evolution or of modern economic realities? Is there a biological basis for homosexuality? Unfortunately, arguments about issues such as these typically are unproductive in terms of moving toward resolution or agreement because most people know little about the rules of argumentation. In this application, we will explore what makes arguments sound or unsound in the hope of improving your ability to analyze and think critically about them.

The Anatomy of an Argument

In everyday usage, the word *argument* is used to refer to a dispute or disagreement between two or more people. But in the technical language of rhetoric, **an *argument* consists of one or more premises that are used to provide support for a conclusion. *Premises* are the reasons that are presented to persuade someone that a conclusion is true or probably true. *Assumptions* are premises for which no proof or evidence is offered.** Assumptions are often left unstated. For example, suppose that your doctor tells you that you should exercise regularly because regular exercise is good for your heart. In this simple argument, the conclusion is "You should exercise regularly." The premise that leads to this conclusion is the idea that "exercise is good for your heart." An unstated assumption is that everyone wants a healthy heart.

In the language of argument analysis, premises are said to support (or not support) conclusions. A conclusion may be supported by one reason or by many reasons. One way to visualize these possibilities is to draw an analogy between the reasons that support a conclusion and the legs that support a table (Halpern, 2003). As shown in **Figure 10.31**, a table top (conclusion) could be supported by one strong leg (a single strong reason) or many thin legs (lots of weaker reasons). Of course, the reasons provided for a conclusion may fail to support the conclusion. Returning to our table analogy, the table top might not be supported because the legs are too thin (very weak reasons) or because the legs are not attached (irrelevant reasons).

Arguments can get complicated, as they usually have more parts than just reasons and conclusions. In addition, there often are *counterarguments,* which are reasons that take support away from a conclusion. And sometimes the most important part of an argument is a part that's not there. Reasons could have been omitted, either deliberately or not, which would lead to a different conclusion if they were supplied. Given all the complex variations that are possible in arguments, it's impossible to give you simple rules for judging arguments. However, we can highlight some common fallacies and then provide some criteria that you can apply in thinking critically about arguments.

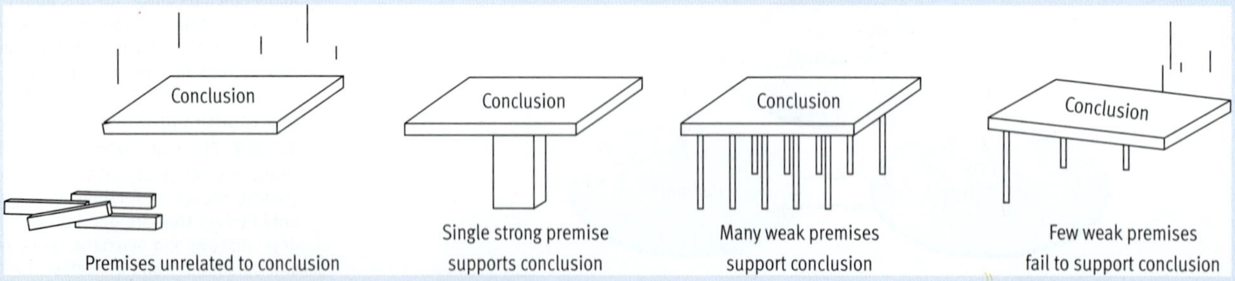

Figure 10.31
An analogy for understanding the strength of arguments. Halpern (2003) draws an analogy between the reasons that support a conclusion and the legs that support a table. She points out that a conclusion may be supported effectively by one strong premise or many weak premises. Of course, the reasons provided for a conclusion may also *fail* to provide adequate support.

SOURCE: From Halpern, D. F. (2003). *Thought & knowledge: An introduction to critical thinking,* p. 199, Figure 5.1. Copyright © 2003 Lawrence Erlbaum Associates. Reprinted by permission of Lawrence Erlbaum Associates and the author.

Common Fallacies

As noted in previous chapters, cognitive scientists have compiled lengthy lists of fallacies that people frequently display in their reasoning. We'll describe five common fallacies. To illustrate each one, we'll assume the role of someone arguing that pornographic material on the Internet (cyberporn) should be banned or heavily regulated.

Irrelevant Reasons Reasons cannot provide support for an argument unless they are relevant to the conclusion. Arguments that depend on irrelevant reasons—either intentionally or inadvertently—are quite common. You already saw one example at the beginning of this application. The Latin term for this fallacy is *non sequitur,* which literally translates to "it doesn't follow." In other words, the conclusion does not follow from the premise. For example, in the debate about Internet pornography, you might hear the following *non sequitur:* "We need to regulate cyberporn because research has shown that most date rapes go unreported."

Circular Reasoning In *circular reasoning* the premise and conclusion are simply restatements of each other. People vary their wording a little so it isn't obvious. But when you look closely, the conclusion *is* the premise. For example, in arguments about Internet pornography you might hear someone assert, "We need to control cyberporn because it currently is unregulated."

Slippery Slope The concept of *slippery slope* argumentation takes its name from the notion that if you are on a slippery slope and you don't dig your heels in, you will slide and slide until you reach bottom. A slippery slope argument typically asserts that if you allow X to happen, things will spin out of control and far worse events will follow. The trick is that there is no inherent connection between X and the events that are predicted to follow. For example, in the debate about medical marijuana, opponents have argued, "If you legalize medical marijuana, the next thing you know cocaine and heroin will be legal." In the debate about cyberporn, a slippery slope argument might go, "If we don't ban cyberporn, the next thing you know, grade-school children will be watching smut all day long in their school libraries."

Weak Analogies An *analogy* asserts that two concepts or events are similar in some way. Hence, you can draw conclusions about event B because of its similarity to event A. Analogies are useful in thinking about complex issues. However, some analogies are weak or inappropriate because the similarity between A and B is superficial, minimal, or irrelevant to the issue at hand. For example, in the debate about Internet erotica, someone might argue, "Cyberporn is morally offensive, just like child molestation. We wouldn't tolerate child molestation, so we shouldn't permit cyberporn."

False Dichotomy A *false dichotomy* creates an either-or choice between two outcomes: the outcome advocated and some obviously horrible outcome that any sensible person would want to avoid. These outcomes are presented as the only two possibilities, when in reality there could be other outcomes, including ones that lie somewhere between the extremes depicted in the false dichotomy. In the debate about Internet pornography, someone might argue, "We can ban cyberporn, or we can hasten the moral decay of modern society."

Evaluating the Strength of Arguments

In everyday life, you may frequently need to assess the strength of arguments made by friends, family, co-workers, politicians, media pundits, and so forth. You may also want to evaluate your own arguments when you write papers or speeches for school or prepare presentations for your work. The following questions can help you make systematic evaluations of arguments (adapted from Halpern, 2003):

- What is the conclusion?
- What are the premises provided to support the conclusion? Are the premises valid?
- Does the conclusion follow from the premises? Are there any fallacies in the chain of reasoning?
- What assumptions have been made? Are they valid assumptions? Should they be stated explicitly?
- What are the counterarguments? Do they weaken the argument?
- Is there anything that has been omitted from the argument?

Table 10.1 Critical Thinking Skills Discussed in This Application

Skill	Description
Understanding the elements of an argument	The critical thinker understands that an argument consists of premises and assumptions that are used to support a conclusion.
Recognizing and avoiding common fallacies, such as irrelevant reasons, circular reasoning, slippery slope reasoning, weak analogies, and false dichotomies	The critical thinker is vigilant about conclusions based on unrelated premises, conclusions that are rewordings of premises, unwarranted predictions that things will spin out of control, superficial analogies, and contrived dichotomies.
Evaluating arguments systematically	The critical thinker carefully assesses the validity of the premises, assumptions, and conclusions in an argument, and considers counterarguments and missing elements.

© Cengage Learning 2013

REVIEW OF KEY LEARNING GOALS

10.24 An argument consists of one or more premises used to provide support for a conclusion. Assumptions are premises for which no proof is offered. A conclusion may be supported by one or by many reasons.

10.25 Arguments are often marred by fallacies in reasoning, such as irrelevant reasons, weak analogies, or circular reasoning, in which the premise and conclusion are simply restatements of each other. In a slippery slope scenario, people assert that if you allow X to happen, far worse events will follow. False dichotomies create either-or choices when in reality there could be other outcomes.

Chapter 10 Practice Test

1. Jackson had a huge breakfast this morning and is still feeling stuffed when he arrives at work. However, one of his colleagues has brought some delicious-looking donuts to the morning staff meeting and Jackson just can't resist. Although he feels full, he eats three donuts. His behavior is *inconsistent* with:
A. incentive theories of motivation.
B. drive theories of motivation.
C. evolutionary theories of motivation.
D. the Cannon-Bard theory of motivation.

2. Which of the following tends to promote increased eating?
A. increased palatability
B. having a greater quantity of food available
C. having a greater variety of food available
D. all of the above

3. The heritability of weight appears to be:
A. virtually impossible to demonstrate.
B. very low.
C. in the range of 60%–70%.
D. irrelevant to the understanding of obesity.

4. Which of the following has *not* been found in research on gender differences in sexual interest?
A. Men think about sex more than women.
B. Men initiate sex more frequently than women.
C. Women are more interested in having many partners than men are.
D. Women are less interested in uncommitted sex.

5. Some recent studies suggest that exposure to aggressive pornography:
A. may increase males' aggressive behavior toward women.
B. may perpetuate the myth that women enjoy being raped.
C. does both a and b.
D. does neither a nor b.

6. Kinsey maintained that sexual orientation:
A. depends on early classical conditioning experiences.
B. should be viewed as a continuum.
C. depends on normalities and abnormalities in the amygdala.
D. should be viewed as an either-or distinction.

7. In research on the need for achievement, individual differences are usually measured:
A. by observing subjects' actual behavior in competitive situations.
B. by interviewing subjects about their achievement needs.
C. with the Thematic Apperception Test.
D. with a polygraph.

8. The determinant of achievement behavior that increases when a college student enrolls in a class that is *required* for graduation is:
A. the probability of success.
B. the need to avoid failure.
C. the incentive value of success.
D. the fear of success.

9. A polygraph (lie detector) works by:
A. monitoring physiological indices of autonomic arousal.
B. directly assessing the truthfulness of a person's statements.
C. monitoring the person's facial expressions.
D. all of the above.

10. Which of the following statements about cross-cultural comparisons of emotional experience is *not* true?
A. The facial expressions that accompany specific emotions are fairly similar across cultures.
B. The cognitive appraisals that shape emotions tend to be similar across cultures.
C. People of different cultures tend to categorize emotions somewhat differently.
D. Display rules do not vary from one culture to another.

11. According to the James-Lange theory of emotion:
A. the experience of emotion depends on autonomic arousal and on one's cognitive interpretation of that arousal.
B. different patterns of autonomic activation lead to the experience of different emotions.
C. emotion occurs when the thalamus sends signals simultaneously to the cortex and to the autonomic nervous system.
D. emotions develop because of their adaptive value.

12. Which theory of emotion implies that people can change their emotions simply by changing the way they label their arousal?
A. the James-Lange theory
B. the Cannon-Bard theory
C. Schachter's two-factor theory
D. opponent-process theory

13. The fact that eating behavior and the experience of emotion both depend on interactions between biological and environmental determinants lends evidence to which of this text's organizing themes?
A. psychology's theoretical diversity
B. psychology's empiricism
C. people's experience of the world is subjective
D. the joint influence of heredity and experience

14. Which of the following statements is (are) true?
A. For the most part, people are pretty happy.
B. Age is unrelated to happiness.
C. Parenthood and intelligence are unrelated to happiness.
D. All of the above.

15. The sales pitch "We're the best dealership in town because the other dealerships just don't stack up against us" is an example of:
A. a false dichotomy.
B. semantic slanting.
C. circular reasoning.
D. slippery slope.

Answers

1 B pp. 388–389
2 D p. 393
3 C p. 396
4 C pp. 400–401
5 C pp. 404–405
6 B p. 405
7 C p. 409
8 C p. 410
9 A pp. 413–414
10 D pp. 416–417
11 B pp. 418–419
12 C p. 419
13 D p. 421
14 D pp. 422–423
15 C p. 427

PsykTrek

To view a demo: **www.cengage.com/psychology/psyktrek**
To order: **www.cengage.com/psychology/weiten**

Go to the PsykTrek website or CD-ROM for further study of the concepts in this chapter. Both online and on the CD-ROM, PsykTrek includes dozens of learning modules with videos, animations, and quizzes, as well as simulations of psychological phenomena and a multimedia glossary that includes word pronunciations.

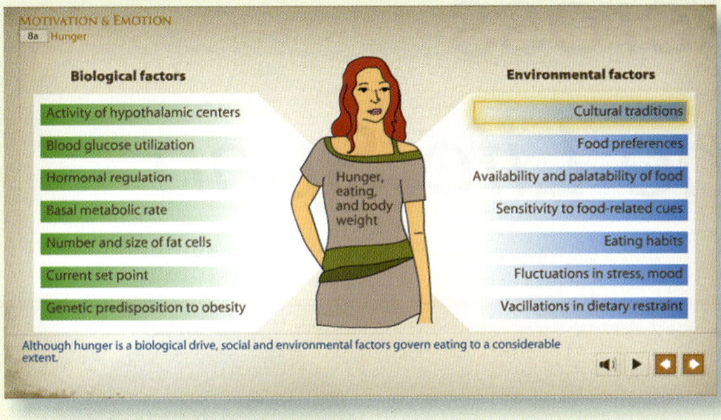

© Cengage Learning 2008

Visit Module 8a (*Hunger*) to learn more about the physiological and environmental factors that regulate your fluctuations in hunger.

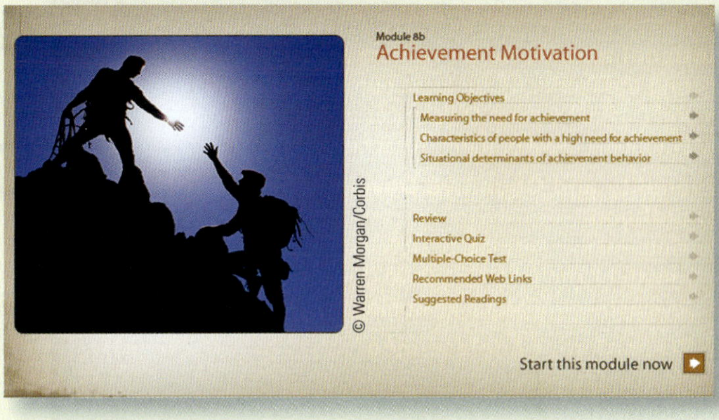

© Warren Morgan/Corbis

© Cengage Learning 2008

Follow up with Module 8b (*Achievement Motivation*) for an in-depth analysis of the forces that shape your achievement strivings.

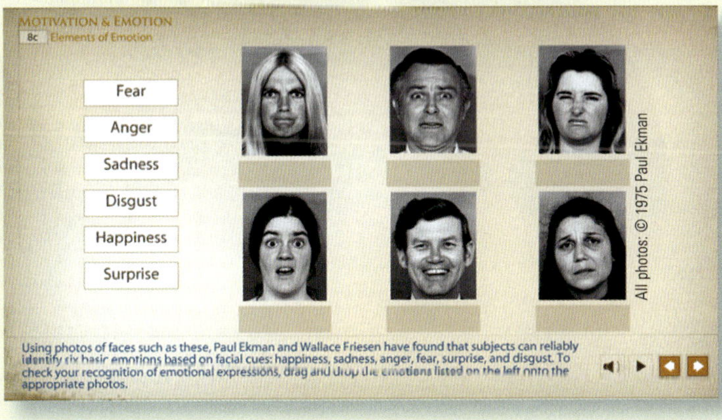

All photos: © 1975 Paul Ekman

© Cengage Learning 2008

Check out Module 8c (*Elements of Emotion*) and Module 8d (*Theories of Emotion*) to see how psychologists have analyzed the nature and determinants of emotions.

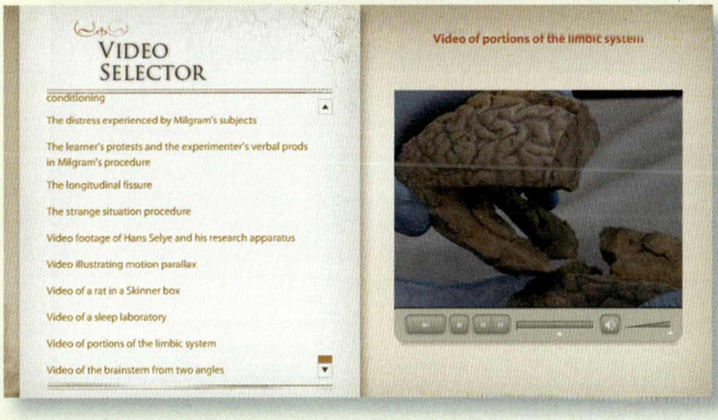

© Cengage Learning 2008

Go to the Video Selector to see classic footage of rats after hypothalamic stimulation or lesioning, or a close-up of the limbic system, the brain's seat of emotion.

Online Study Tools

Log in to **CengageBrain** to access the resources your instructor requires. For this book, you can access:

CourseMate brings course concepts to life with interactive learning, study, and exam preparation tools that support the printed textbook. A textbook-specific website, Psychology CourseMate includes an integrated interactive eBook and other interactive learning tools such as quizzes, flashcards, videos, and more.

CengageNow is an easy-to-use online resource that helps you study in less time to get the grade you want—NOW. Take a pre-test for this chapter and receive a personalized study plan based on your results that will identify the topics you need to review and direct you to online resources to help you master those topics. Then take a post-test to help you determine the concepts you have mastered and what you will need to work on. If your textbook does not include an access code card, go to CengageBrain.com to gain access.

WebTutor is more than just an interactive study guide. WebTutor is an anytime, anywhere customized learning solution with an eBook, keeping you connected to your textbook, instructor, and classmates.

Aplia. If your professor has assigned Aplia homework:

1. Sign in to your account
2. Complete the corresponding homework exercises as required by your professor.
3. When finished, click "Grade It Now" to see which areas you have mastered, which need more work, and detailed explanations of every answer.

Visit **www.cengagebrain.com** to access your account and purchase materials.

11

Human Development Across the Life Span

© Masterfile RF

In high school, kids called her "catfish" because of her outsized lips. Attempts at modeling brought more than 100 rejections—she was too short, too skinny, too scarred. Today, she's been named "Most Beautiful Woman in the World" by *People* magazine, is one of the highest-paid actors in the world, and is known for her humanitarian work for the United Nations. Let's take a closer look at the life of Angelina Jolie.

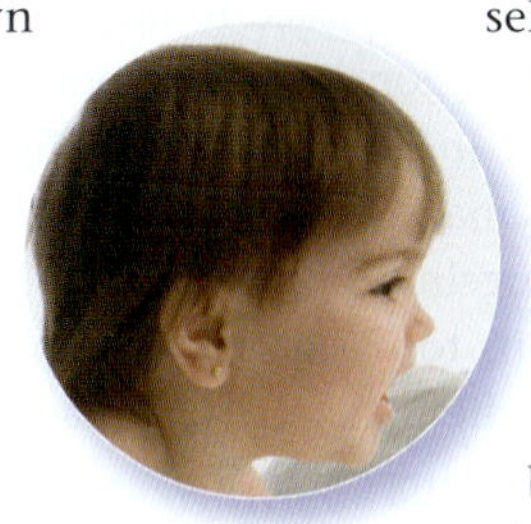

Angelina was born to two actors, but she didn't have a fairytale life. Her father had an affair with his theater student when Angelina was six months old, and the family broke apart. Her mother was so traumatized by the split, she couldn't bear to be with Angelina because she reminded her too much of her former husband. Hence, in her early years Angelina was mostly raised by nannies and babysitters.

Angelina's childhood was marked by frequent moves to rented and ever-smaller houses as her mother struggled to make ends meet. Attending Beverly Hills High School, Angelina felt out of place among the well-scrubbed rich kids in preppy clothes. Angelina wore all-black, often second-hand clothes and punk getups. "I didn't feel clean and, like, pretty," she said (Morton, 2010, p. 75). Taken on modeling calls by her mother, Angelina was self-conscious and nervous. Although her father, John Voigt, was a famous Oscar-winning actor, she didn't want to be an actress. She wanted to be a funeral director. Her first tattoo was the Japanese character for "death." She hung out at the arcade with the outcasts, experimenting with drugs. At 14, she dyed her hair purple and went slam-dancing with her live-in punk boyfriend. She continued to rebel against convention when, on her wedding day, she wore black rubber pants and a white shirt with the groom's name written in her blood across the back. The media couldn't write enough about the "wild child."

But in her mid-20s, Angelina underwent a transformation. Preparing for her role as a humanitarian aid worker in *Beyond Borders*, and filming *Lara Croft: Tomb Raider* in Cambodia, she saw conditions

© AP Images/Dolores Ochoa

The story of Angelina Jolie's metamorphosis from an awkward, insecure "wild child," into an elegant, self-assured public figure provides a dramatic demonstration of how human development is marked by both continuity and transition.

that would change her forever. The plight of displaced people in Cambodia and the news of refugees fleeing massacre in the Darfur region of the Sudan in Northern Africa affected her deeply. She contacted the United Nations to learn more and asked to help. The U.N. sent her to paparazzi-free zones: trouble spots in Sierra Leone and Tanzania. In 2001, the U.N. High Commissioner for Refugees made Angelina an official Goodwill Ambassador. Angelina has been on 20 daunting U.N. field missions to places such as Thailand, Sudan, and Ecuador, where she often has had to endure extremely primitive living conditions.

Angelina's transition from an insecure teenager to a self-assured adult and from a wild child to humanitarian were startling. Yet there was also a strong element of continuity in her life. Consider, for instance, her rebelliousness. When Angelina was a child, her mother dressed her in frilly white dresses. Angelina rebeled and wore all black. When her mother dragged her to acting auditions, Angelina refused to read the lines. As she has matured, Angelina has remained a rebel, as she has vigorously fought for more humane treatment of oppressed refugee populations. In a sense, she rechanneled her defiance. "In my early 20s I was fighting with myself," Jolie says. "Now I take that punk in me to Washington, and I fight for something important." (Swibel, 2006).

Another personality trait that has remained constant throughout her life is her empathy. Perhaps because of her own uprooted childhood, Angelina was always maternal to younger children. Photos from when she was 5 show her with her arm protectively around Sean Stogel, then 3, whom she taught how to blow bubbles. From the early age of 12, Angelina knew that she wanted to adopt underprivileged children. As an adult, she has followed through on this desire, adopting three orphans from far-flung corners of the globe (Cambodia, Ethiopia, and Vietnam). And of course, her continued empathy for the plight of the world's downtrodden is manifested in her remarkably unselfish commitment to humanitarian missions.

What does Angelina Jolie have to do with developmental psychology? Although her story is obviously unique in many ways, it provides an interesting illustration of the two themes that permeate the study of human development: *transition* and *continuity*. In investigating human development, psychologists study how people evolve through transitions over time. In looking at these transitions, developmental psychologists inevitably find continuity with the past. This continuity may be the most fascinating element in Angelina's story. The metamorphosis of the insecure, wild teenager into an influential, self-assured public figure was a more radical transformation than most people go through. Nonetheless, the threads of continuity connecting Angelina's childhood to the development of her adult personality were quite obvious.

***Development* is the sequence of age-related changes that occur as a person progresses from conception to death.** It is a reasonably orderly, cumulative process that includes both the biological and behavioral changes that take place as people grow older. An infant's newfound ability to grasp objects, a child's gradual mastery of grammar, an adolescent's spurt in physical growth, a young adult's increasing commitment to a vocation, and an older adult's transition into the role of grandparent all represent development. These transitions are predictable changes that are related to age.

Traditionally, psychologists have been most interested in development during childhood. Our coverage reflects this emphasis. However, decades of research have clearly shown that development is a lifelong process. In this chapter, we divide the life span into four broad periods—the prenatal period between conception and birth, childhood, adolescence, and adulthood. We'll examine aspects of development that are especially dynamic during each period. Let's begin by looking at events that occur before birth, during prenatal development.

KEY LEARNING GOALS

11.1 Outline the major events of the three stages of prenatal development.

11.2 Summarize the impact of environmental factors on prenatal development.

Progress Before Birth: Prenatal Development

Development begins with conception. *Conception* occurs when fertilization creates a ***zygote,* a one-celled organism formed by the union of a sperm and an egg.** All the other cells in your body developed from this single cell. Each of your cells contains enduring messages from your parents carried on the *chromosomes* that lie within its nucleus. Each chromosome houses many *genes,* the functional units in hereditary transmission. Genes carry the details of your hereditary blueprints, which are revealed gradually throughout life (see Chapter 3 for more information on genetic transmission).

The *prenatal period* extends from conception to birth, usually encompassing nine months of pregnancy. A great deal of important development occurs before birth. In fact, development during the prenatal period is remarkably rapid. If you were an average-sized newborn and your physical growth had continued during the first year of your life at a prenatal pace, by your first birthday you would have weighed 200 pounds! Fortunately, you didn't grow at that rate, because in the final weeks before birth the frenzied pace of prenatal development tapers off dramatically. In this section, we'll examine the usual course of prenatal development and discuss how environmental events can leave their mark on development even before birth exposes the newborn to the outside world.

The Course of Prenatal Development

9a

The prenatal period is divided into three phases: (1) the germinal stage (the first two weeks), (2) the embryonic stage (two weeks to two months), and (3) the fetal stage (two months to birth). Some key developments in these phases are outlined here.

Germinal Stage

9a

The *germinal stage* is the first phase of prenatal development, encompassing the first two weeks after conception. This brief stage begins when a zygote is created through fertilization. Within 36 hours, rapid cell division begins. The zygote becomes a microscopic mass of multiplying cells. This mass of cells slowly migrates along the mother's fallopian tube to the uterine cavity. On about the seventh day, the cell mass begins to implant itself in the uterine wall. This process takes about a week and is far from automatic. Many zygotes are rejected at this point. As many as one in five pregnancies end with the woman never being aware that conception has occurred (Simpson & Juaniaux, 2007).

During the implantation process, the placenta begins to form. **The *placenta* is a structure that allows oxygen and nutrients to pass into the fetus from the mother's bloodstream and bodily wastes to pass out to the mother.** This critical exchange takes place across thin membranes that block the passage of blood cells, keeping the fetal and maternal bloodstreams separate.

Embryonic Stage

9a

The *embryonic stage* is the second stage of prenatal development, lasting from two weeks until the end of the second month. During this stage, most of the vital organs and bodily systems begin to form in the developing organism, which is now

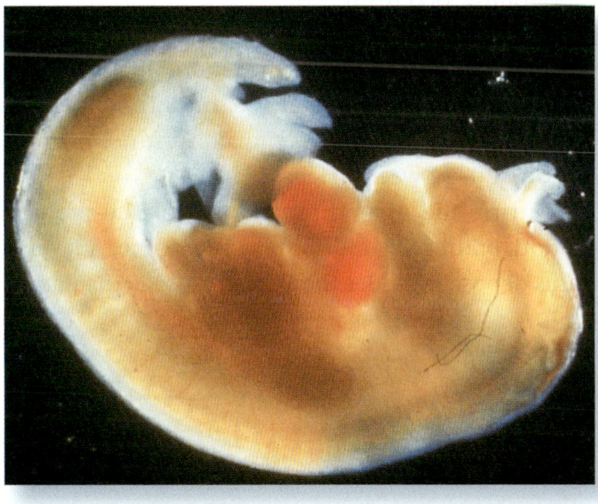

© Petit Format/Science Source/Photo Researchers, Inc.

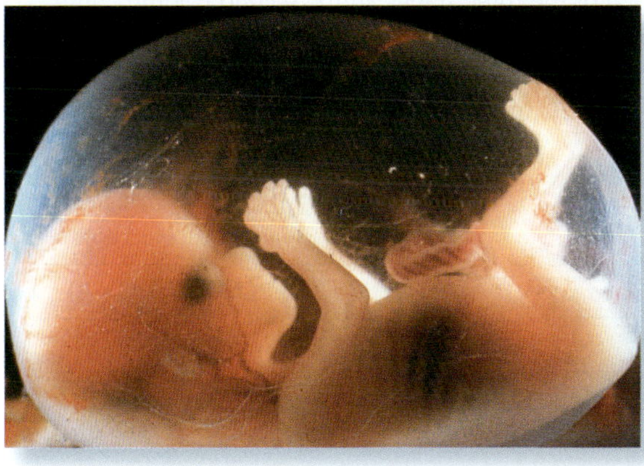

© Petit Format/Guigoz/Science Source/Photo Researchers, Inc.

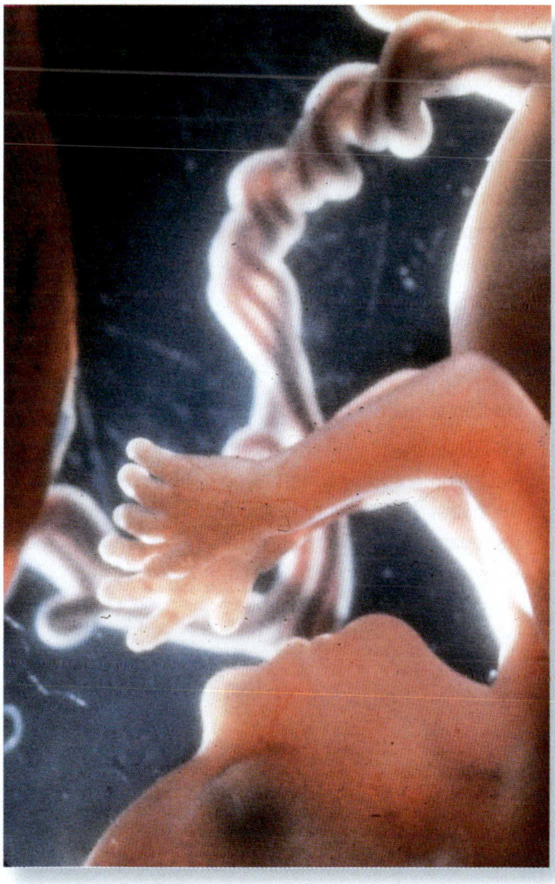

© Petit Format/Nestle/Science Source/Photo Researchers, Inc.

Prenatal development is remarkably rapid. Top left: This 30-day-old embryo is just 6 millimeters in length. Bottom left: At 14 weeks, the fetus is approximately 2 inches long. Note the well-developed fingers. The fetus can already move its legs, feet, hands, and head and displays a variety of basic reflexes. Right: After 4 months of prenatal development, facial features are beginning to emerge.

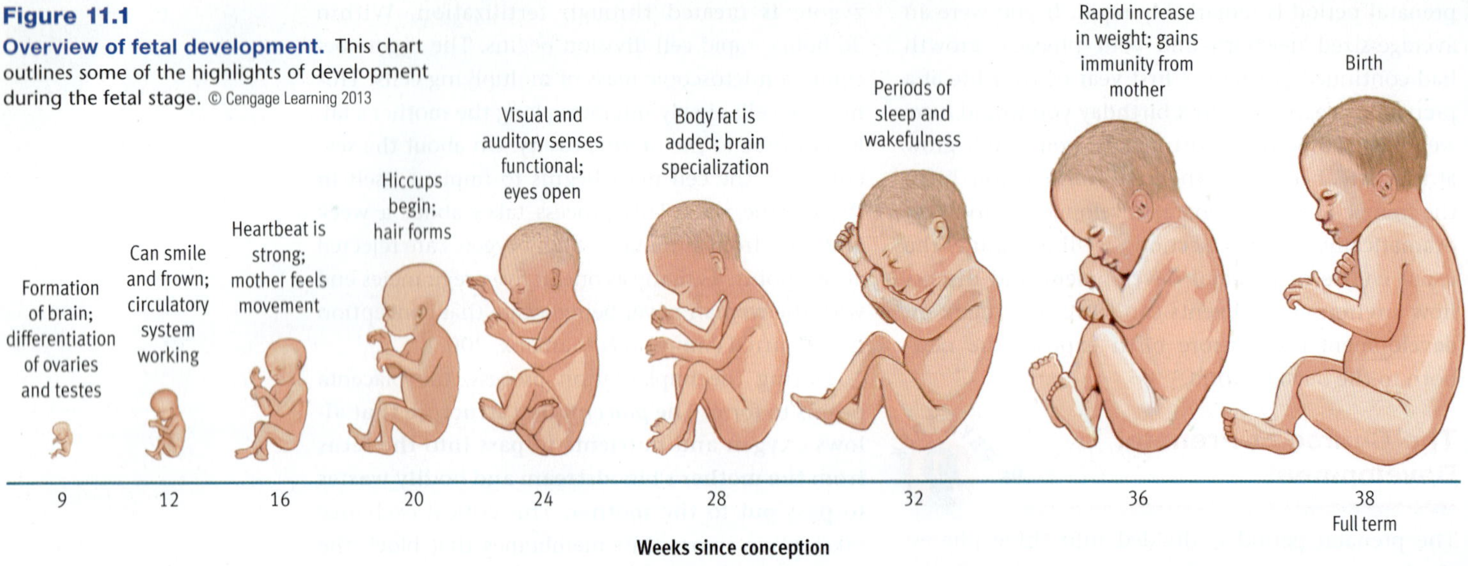

Figure 11.1
Overview of fetal development. This chart outlines some of the highlights of development during the fetal stage. © Cengage Learning 2013

called an *embryo*. Structures such as the heart, spine, and brain emerge gradually as cell division becomes more specialized. Although the embryo is typically only about an inch long at the end of this stage, it's already beginning to look human. Arms, legs, hands, feet, fingers, toes, eyes, and ears are already discernible.

The embryonic stage is a period of great vulnerability because virtually all the basic physiological structures are being formed. If anything interferes with normal development during this phase, the effects can be devastating. Most miscarriages occur during this period (Simpson & Juaniaux, 2007). Most major structural birth defects are also due to problems that occur during the embryonic stage (Niebyl & Simpson, 2007).

Fetal Stage

9a

The *fetal stage* is the third stage of prenatal development, lasting from two months through birth. Some highlights of fetal development are summarized in **Figure 11.1**. The first two months of the fetal stage bring rapid bodily growth. Muscles and bones begin to form (Moore & Persaud, 2008). The developing organism, now called a *fetus,* becomes capable of physical movements as skeletal structures harden. Organs formed in the embryonic stage continue to grow and gradually begin to function. The sense of hearing, for example, is functional by around 20–24 weeks (Hepper, 2003).

During the final three months of the prenatal period, brain cells multiply at a brisk pace. A layer of fat is deposited under the skin to provide insulation.

CONCEPT CHECK 11.1

Understanding the Stages of Prenatal Development

Check your understanding of the stages of prenatal development by filling in the blanks in the chart below. The first column contains descriptions of a main event from each of the three stages. In the second column, write the name of the stage; in the third column, write the term used to refer to the developing organism during that stage; and in the fourth column, write the time span (in terms of weeks or months) covered by the stage. The answers are in Appendix A at the back of the book.

	Stage	Term for organism	Time span
1. Uterine implantation	________	________	________
2. Muscle and bone begin to form	________	________	________
3. Vital organs and body systems begin to form	________	________	________

The respiratory and digestive systems mature (Adolph & Berger, 2005). All of these changes ready the fetus for life outside the cozy, supportive environment of its mother's womb. Sometime between 23 weeks and 26 weeks, the fetus reaches the *threshold of viability*—the age at which a baby can survive in the event of a premature birth (Moore & Persaud, 2008). At 23 weeks the probability of survival is still slim (about 10%–20%). It climbs rapidly over the next month, to around a 75% survival rate at 26 weeks (Iams & Romero, 2007). Unfortunately, a great many of the premature infants born near the threshold of viability go on to experience a wide range of developmental problems (Cunningham et al., 2010; Eichenwald & Stark, 2008).

Environmental Factors and Prenatal Development

The fetus develops in the protective buffer of the womb. But events in the external environment can affect it indirectly through the mother. The developing organism and its mother are linked through the placenta. Because of this, a mother's eating habits, drug use, illnesses, nutrition, and even emotions can affect prenatal development (Hampton, 2004). ***Teratogens* are any external agents, such as drugs or viruses, that can harm an embryo or fetus.** **Figure 11.2** shows the periods of prenatal development during which various structures are most vulnerable to damage from teratogens.

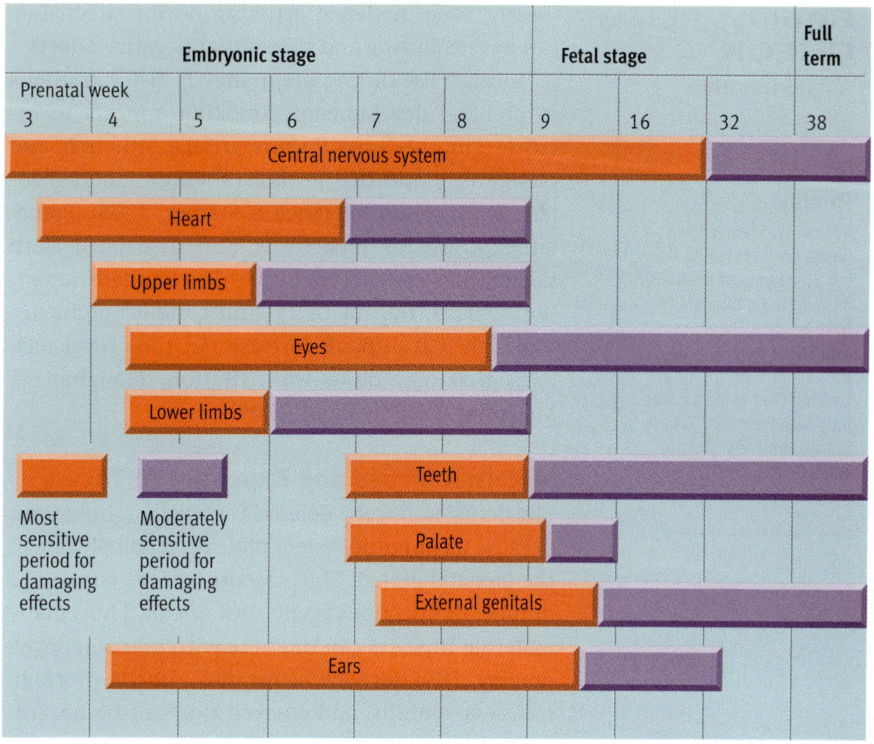

© Cengage Learning 2013

Figure 11.2

Periods of vulnerability in prenatal development. Generally, structures are most susceptible to damage when they are undergoing rapid development. The red regions of the bars indicate the most sensitive periods for various organs and structures, while the purple regions indicate periods of continued, but lessened, vulnerability. As a whole, sensitivity is greatest in the embryonic stage, but some structures remain vulnerable throughout prenatal development.

SOURCE: Adapted from Moore, K. L., & Persaud, T. V. N. (2008). *Before we are born: Essentials of embryology and birth defects.* Philadelphia: W. B. Saunders/Elsevier. Copyright © 2008 Elsevier Science (USA). All rights reserved. Reprinted by permission.

Maternal Drug Use

A major source of concern about fetal and infant well-being is the mother's consumption of drugs, including such widely used substances as tobacco and alcohol, as well as prescription and recreational drugs. Unfortunately, most drugs consumed by a pregnant woman can pass through the membranes of the placenta.

Virtually all "recreational" drugs (see Chapter 5) can be harmful, with sedatives, narcotics, and cocaine being particularly dangerous. Babies of heroin users are born addicted to narcotics. They have an increased risk of early death due to prematurity, birth defects, respiratory difficulties, and problems associated with their addiction (Finnegan & Kandall, 2005). Prenatal exposure to cocaine is associated with increased risk of birth complications (Sokol et al., 2007) and a variety of cognitive deficits that are apparent in childhood (Accornero et al., 2007; Singer et al., 2004). Problems can also be caused by a great variety of drugs prescribed for legitimate medical reasons (Niebyl & Simpson, 2007). The impact of drugs on the embryo or fetus varies greatly depending on the drug, the dose, and the phase of prenatal development.

Alcohol consumption during pregnancy also carries risks. ***Fetal alcohol syndrome (FAS)* is a collection of congenital (inborn) problems associated with excessive alcohol use during pregnancy.** Typical problems include microcephaly (a small head), heart defects, irritability, hyperactivity, and delayed mental and motor development (Hannigan & Armant, 2000; Pellegrino & Pellegrino, 2008). Fetal alcohol syndrome is the most common known cause of mental retardation (Niccols, 2007). Furthermore, many children who do not exhibit fetal alcohol syndrome still show serious impairments attributable to their mothers' "normal" drinking during pregnancy (Willford, Leech, & Day, 2006). A long-running study of pregnant women's drinking found that higher alcohol intake was associated with an elevated risk for deficits in IQ, motor skills, and attention span, and with increased impulsive, antisocial, and delinquent behavior (Streissguth, 2007).

Reality CHECK

Misconception

It is safe for pregnant women to engage in moderate social drinking.

Reality

Not really. Studies have linked social drinking during pregnancy to a variety of enduring problems. We have no clear evidence on what would represent a safe amount of drinking. Lacking that evidence, the only safe course of action is to completely abstain from alcohol during pregnancy.

Clearly, even moderate drinking during pregnancy can have enduring and substantial negative effects.

Tobacco use during pregnancy is also hazardous to prenatal development. Smoking appears to increase a mother's risk for miscarriage, stillbirth, and prematurity and the newborn's risk for sudden infant death syndrome (Shea & Steiner, 2008). Prenatal exposure to tobacco is also associated with slower-than-average cognitive development, attention deficits, hyperactivity, and conduct problems, although it is difficult to tease out the causal relations that may be at work (Button, Maughan, & McGuffin, 2007; Knopik, 2009).

Maternal Illness and Exposure to Toxins

The fetus is largely defenseless against infections because its immune system matures relatively late in the prenatal period. The placenta screens out quite a number of infectious agents, but not all. Thus, many maternal illnesses can interfere with prenatal development. Diseases such as measles, rubella (German measles), syphilis, and chicken pox can be hazardous to the fetus (Bernstein, 2007). The nature of any damage from such illnesses depends, in part, on when the mother contracts the illness. The HIV virus that causes AIDS can also be transmitted by pregnant women to their offspring. The transmission of AIDS may occur prenatally through the placenta, during delivery, or through breastfeeding. Up through the mid-1990s, about 20%–30% of HIV-positive pregnant women passed the virus on to their babies. However, improved antiretroviral drugs (given to the mother) and more cautious obstetrical care have reduced this figure to about 2% in the United States (Cotter & Potter, 2006).

Research also suggests that babies in the womb are exposed to a surprising variety of *environmental toxins* (Houlihan et al., 2005). For example, prenatal exposure to air pollution has been linked to impairments in cognitive development at age 5 (Edwards et al., 2010). In a similar vein, exposure to the chemicals used in flame-retardant materials correlates with slower mental and physical development up through age 6 (Herbstman et al., 2010).

© LWA/Larry Williams/Getty Images

Maternal Nutrition and Emotions

The developing fetus needs a variety of essential nutrients. Thus, it's not surprising that severe maternal malnutrition increases the risk of birth complications and neurological defects for the newborn (Coutts, 2000; Fifer, Monk, & Grose-Fifer, 2001). The effects of severe malnutrition are a major problem in underdeveloped nations where food shortages are common. The impact of moderate malnutrition, which is more common in modern, developed countries, is more difficult to gauge. This difficulty occurs because maternal malnutrition is often confounded with other risk factors associated with poverty, such as drug abuse and limited access to health care (Guerrini, Thomson, & Gurling, 2007). Even when pregnant women have ample access to food, it is important to consume a balanced diet that includes crucial vitamins and minerals. For example, a diet rich in folic acid can reduce the likelihood of a variety of birth defects (Reynolds, 2002).

Recent studies also suggest that maternal emotions can have an impact on prentatal development. For example, anxiety and depression in pregnant women are associated with an increased prevalence of various behavioral problems in their offspring (Bergner, Monk, & Werner, 2008). Moreover, research suggests that prospective mothers' emotional reactions to stressful events can disrupt the delicate hormonal balance that fosters healthy prentatal development (Douglas, 2010).

Fetal Origins of Disease

Research on prenatal development has generally focused on its connection to the risk for birth defects and adverse outcomes that are apparent during early childhood. Recently, however, researchers have begun to explore the links between prenatal factors and *adults'* physical and mental health. Recent evidence suggests that events during prenatal development can "program" the fetal brain in ways that influence the person's vulnerability to various types of illness decades later. For example, prenatal malnutrition has been linked to vulnerability to schizophrenia, which usually emerges in late adolescence or early adulthood (Brown & Susser, 2008). Low birth weight, which is a marker for a variety of prenatal disruptions, has been found to be associated with an increased risk of heart disease many decades later in adulthood (Roseboom, de Rooij, & Painter, 2006). Studies have also linked aspects of prenatal development to adults' risk for depression and other mood disorders (Bale et al., 2010), obesity (Huang, Lee, & Lu, 2007), diabetes (Whincup et al., 2008), and some types of cancer (Ahlgren et al., 2007). These findings on the fetal origins of disease are stimulating a dramatic reassessment of the factors that influence health and illness.

Science has a long way to go before it uncovers all the factors that shape development before birth. Nonetheless, it's clear that critical developments unfold quickly during the prenatal period. In the next section, you'll learn that development continues at a fast pace during the early years of childhood.

REVIEW OF KEY LEARNING GOALS

11.1 Prenatal development proceeds through the germinal (first 2 weeks), embryonic (2 weeks to 2 months), and fetal stages (2 months to birth) as the zygote is differentiated into a human organism. The embryonic stage is a period of great vulnerability, as most physiological structures are being formed. The fetal stage brings rapid growth as physiological systems mature.

11.2 Maternal use of illicit drugs can be dangerous to the unborn child. Even normal social drinking and routine tobacco use can be very hazardous during prenatal development. A variety of maternal illnesses can interfere with prenatal development. Maternal malnutrition during the prenatal period has been linked to birth complications and other subsequent problems. Recent evidence suggests that prenatal development can "program" the fetal brain in ways that influence the individual's vulnerability to various types of illness decades later.

Emotional and Motor Development in Childhood

KEY LEARNING GOALS

11.3 Understand general principles and cultural variations in motor development.

11.4 Review research on the stability of infant temperament.

11.5 Describe Harlow's and Bowlby's views of attachment.

11.6 Discuss research on patterns of attachment, and describe cultural variations in attachment.

A certain magic is associated with childhood. Young children have an extraordinary ability to captivate adults' attention, especially their parents'. Legions of parents gush to friends and strangers alike about the cute things their kids do. Most wondrous of all are the rapid and momentous developmental changes of the early childhood years. Helpless infants become mobile toddlers almost overnight. In this section you'll see what psychologists have learned about motor development and two aspects of emotional development—temperament and attachment (consult Chapter 8 for coverage of early language development).

Exploring the World: Motor Development

One of the earliest topics studied by developmental psychologists was motor development. ***Motor development* refers to the progression of muscular coordination required for physical activities.** Basic motor skills include grasping and reaching for objects, manipulating objects, sitting up, crawling, walking, and running.

Basic Principles

A number of principles are apparent in motor development (Adolph & Berger, 2005). One is **the *cephalocaudal trend*—the head-to-foot direction of motor development.** Children tend to gain control over the upper part of their bodies before the lower part. You've seen this trend in action if you've watched an infant learn to crawl. Infants gradually shift from using their arms for propelling themselves to using their legs. **The *proximodistal trend* is the center-outward direction of motor development.** Children gain control over their torso before their extremities. Thus, infants initially reach for things by twisting their entire body. Gradually, though, they learn to extend just their arms.

© Glenda M. Powers/Shutterstock

Early progress in motor skills has traditionally been attributed almost entirely to the process of maturation (Adolph & Berger, 2011). ***Maturation* is development that reflects the gradual unfolding of one's genetic blueprint.** It is a product of genetically programmed physical changes that come with age—as opposed to experience and learning. However, research that has taken a closer look at the *process* of motor development suggests that infants are active agents rather than passive organisms waiting for their brain and limbs to mature (Adolph & Berger, 2011; Thelen, 1995). According to this new view, the driving force behind motor development is infants' ongoing exploration of their world and their need to master specific tasks (such as grasping a larger toy or looking out a window). Progress in motor development is attributed to infants' experimentation and learning the consequences of their activities. Although modern researchers acknowledge that maturation facilitates motor development, they argue that its contribution has been oversimplified and overestimated.

Understanding Developmental Norms

Parents often pay close attention to early motor development, comparing their child's progress with developmental norms. ***Developmental norms* indicate the typical**

Figure 11.3

Landmarks in motor development. The left edge, interior mark, and right edge of each bar indicate the age at which 25%, 50%, and 90% of infants (in North America) have mastered each motor skill shown. Developmental norms typically report only the median age of mastery (the interior mark), which can be misleading in light of the variability in age of mastery apparent in this chart.

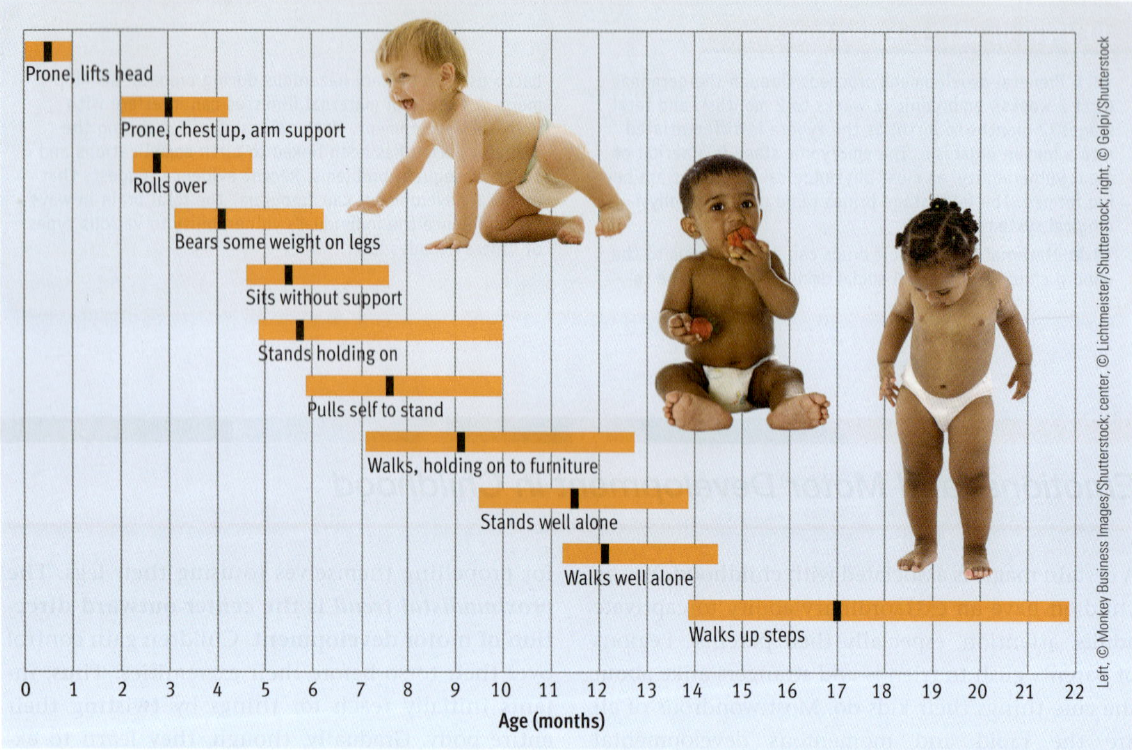

Left, © Monkey Business Images/Shutterstock; center, © Lichtmeister/Shutterstock; right, © Gelpi/Shutterstock

© Cengage Learning 2013

(median) age at which individuals display various behaviors and abilities. Developmental norms are useful benchmarks as long as parents don't expect their children to progress exactly at the pace specified in the norms. Some parents get unnecessarily alarmed when their children fall behind developmental norms. What these parents overlook is that these norms are group *averages*. Variations from the average are entirely normal. This normal variation stands out in **Figure 11.3**, which indicates the age at which 25%, 50%, and 90% of youngsters can demonstrate various motor skills. As **Figure 11.3** shows, a substantial portion of children often don't achieve a particular milestone until long after the average time cited in norms.

Cultures across the world use a variety of methods to foster rapid development of motor abilities in their children. The !Kung San of the Kalahari, Botswana, teach their young to dance quite early, using poles to develop the kinesthetic sense of balance.

© Konner/AnthroPhoto

Cultural Variations and Their Significance

Cross-cultural research has highlighted the dynamic interplay between experience and maturation in motor development. Relatively rapid motor development has been observed in some cultures that provide special practice in basic motor skills (Adolph, Karasik, & Tamis-Lemonda, 2010). For example, soon after birth, the Kipsigis people of Kenya begin active efforts to train their infants to sit up, stand, and walk. Thanks to this training, Kipsigis children achieve these developmental milestones (but not others) about a month earlier than babies in the United States (Super, 1976). In contrast, relatively slow motor development has been found in some cultures that discourage motor exploration (Adolph, Karasik, & Tamis-Lemonda, 2010). For example, among the Ache, a nomadic people living in the rain forests of Paraguay, safety concerns dictate that children under age 3 rarely venture more than 3 feet from their mothers, who carry them virtually everywhere. As a result of these constraints, Ache children are delayed in acquiring a variety of motor skills and typically begin walking about a year later than other children (Kaplan & Dove, 1987). Cultural variations in the emergence of basic motor skills show that environmental factors can accelerate or slow early motor development.

Easy and Difficult Babies: Differences in Temperament

Infants show considerable variability in temperament. ***Temperament* refers to characteristic mood, activity level, and emotional reactivity.** From the very beginning, some babies seem animated and cheerful while others seem sluggish and ornery. Infants show consistent differences in emotional tone, tempo of activity, and sensitivity to environmental stimuli very early in life (Martin & Fox, 2006).

Alexander Thomas and Stella Chess conducted a landmark *longitudinal* study of the development of temperament (Thomas & Chess, 1977, 1989; Thomas, Chess, & Birch, 1970). **In a *longitudinal design* investigators observe one group of participants repeatedly over a period of time.** This approach to the study of development is usually contrasted with the *cross-sectional* approach (the logic of both approaches is diagrammed in **Figure 11.4**). **In a *cross-sectional design* investigators compare groups of participants of differing age at a single point in time.** For example, in a cross-sectional study an investigator tracing the growth of children's vocabulary might compare fifty 6-year-olds, fifty 8-year-olds, and fifty 10-year-olds. In contrast, an investigator using the longitudinal method would assemble one group of fifty 6-year-olds and measure their vocabulary at age 6, again at age 8, and once more at age 10.

Each method has its advantages and disadvantages. Cross-sectional studies can be completed more quickly, easily, and cheaply than longitudinal studies, which often extend over many years. However, in cross-sectional studies changes that appear to reflect development may really be cohort effects (Hartmann, Pelzel, & Abbott, 2011). ***Cohort effects* occur when differences between age groups are due to the groups growing up in different time periods.** For example, if you used the cross-sectional method to examine gender roles in groups aged 20, 40, and 60, you would be comparing people who grew up before, during, and after the women's movement, which would probably lead to major differences as a result of historical context rather than development. Thus, *longitudinal designs tend to be more sensitive to developmental changes* (Magnusson & Stattin, 1998). Unfortunately, longitudinal designs have weaknesses, too. When a longitudinal study takes years to complete, participants often drop out because they move away or lose interest. The changing composition of the sample may produce misleading developmental trends.

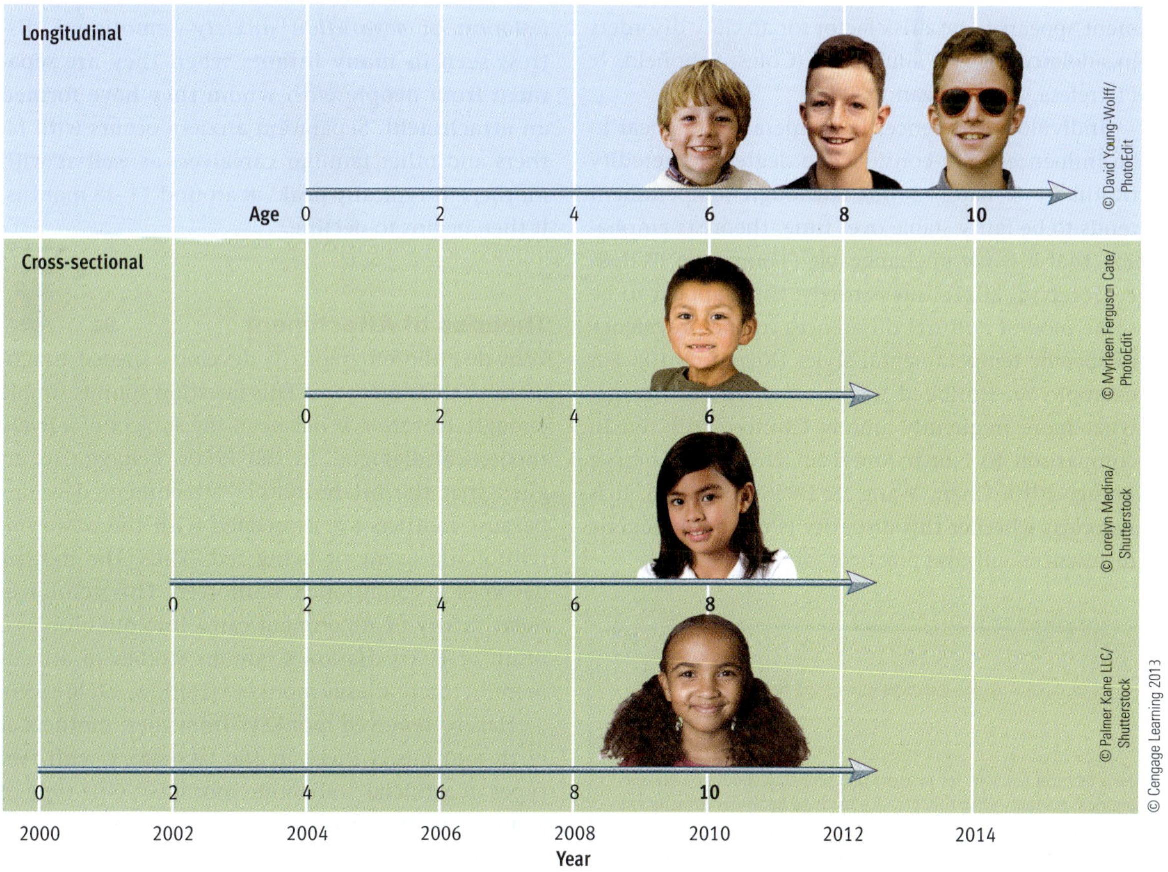

Figure 11.4
Longitudinal versus cross-sectional research. In a longitudinal study of development between ages 6 and 10, the same children would be observed at age 6, again at 8, and again at 10. In a cross-sectional study of the same age span, a group of 6-year-olds, a group of 8-year-olds, and a group of 10-year-olds would be compared simultaneously. Note that data collection could be completed immediately in the cross-sectional study, whereas the longitudinal study would require four years to complete.

In their longitudinal study, Thomas and Chess identified three basic styles of temperament that were apparent in most of the children. About 40% of the youngsters were *easy children*. Easy children tended to be happy, regular in sleep and eating, adaptable, and not readily upset. Another 15% were *slow-to-warm-up children*. They tended to be less cheery, less regular in their sleep and eating, and slower in adapting to change. *Difficult children* constituted 10% of the group. They tended to be glum, erratic in sleep and eating, resistant to change, and relatively irritable. The remaining 35% of the children showed mixtures of these three temperaments. A child's temperament at 3 months was a fair predictor of the child's temperament at age 10. Although basic changes in temperament were seen in some children, temperament was generally stable over time (Chess & Thomas, 1996).

© Jon Chase, Harvard News Office, Courtesy of Jerome Kagan

Jerome Kagan

"Every psychological quality in an adult can be likened to a pale gray fabric woven from thin black threads representing biology and white threads representing experience, neither visible in the homogeneously gray cloth."

Another example of influential research on temperament is the work of Jerome Kagan and his colleagues (Kagan & Snidman, 1991; Kagan, Snidman, & Arcus, 1992). They have found that about 15%–20% of infants display an *inhibited temperament* characterized by shyness, timidity, and wariness of unfamiliar people. In contrast, about 25%–30% of infants exhibit an *uninhibited temperament* (the remainder fall in between these extremes). These children are less restrained, approaching unfamiliar people with little trepidation. An inhibited temperament appears to be a risk factor for anxiety disorders in adolescence and adulthood (Coles, Schofield, & Pietrefesa, 2006; Kagan, 2008).

Individual differences in temperament appear to be influenced to a considerable degree by heredity (Rothbart & Bates, 2008). Although temperament tends to be fairly stable over time, theorists emphasize that it is *not* unchangeable (Thompson, Winer, & Goodvin, 2011). Interestingly, there appear to be some modest cultural differences in the prevalence of specific temperamental styles (Kagan, 2010). For example, an inhibited temperament is seen somewhat more frequently among Chinese children in comparison to North American children (Chen & Wang, 2010; Chen, Wang, & DeSouza, 2006). It is not clear whether this disparity is rooted in genetic differences, cultural practices, or both.

Reality CHECK

Misconception

A strong attachment relationship depends on infant-mother bonding during the first few hours after birth.

Reality

Bonding immediately after birth can be a magical moment for mothers and probably should be encouraged for their sake. But there is no empirical evidence that this practice leads to healthier attachment relationships in the long run.

Early Emotional Development: Attachment

9e

Do early emotional bonds affect later development? That is just one of the many questions investigated by psychologists interested in attachment. ***Attachment* refers to the close, emotional bonds of affection that develop between infants and their caregivers.** Researchers have shown a keen interest in how infant-mother attachments are formed early in life. Children eventually may form attachments to many people, including their fathers, grandparents, older siblings, and others (Cassidy, 2008). However, a child's first important attachment usually occurs with his or her mother because in most cultures she is the main caregiver, especially in the early years of life (Lamb & Lewis, 2011).

Contrary to popular belief, infants' attachment to their mothers is *not* instantaneous. Initially, babies show relatively little in the way of a special preference for their mothers. At 2–3 months of age, infants may smile and laugh more when they interact with their mother. But they generally can be handed over to strangers such as babysitters with little difficulty. This situation gradually changes. By about 6–8 months, infants begin to show a pronounced preference for their mother's company and often protest when separated from her (Lamb, Ketterlinus, & Fracasso, 1992). This is the first manifestation of ***separation anxiety*—emotional distress seen in many infants when they are separated from people with whom they have formed an attachment.** Separation anxiety occurs with fathers and other familiar caregivers as well as with mothers. It typically peaks at around 14–18 months. It then begins to decline.

Theories of Attachment

9e

Why do children gradually develop a special attachment to their mothers? This question sounds simple enough. However, it has been the subject of a lively theoretical dialogue. In the 1950s, behaviorists argued that the infant-mother attachment develops because mothers are associated with the powerful, reinforcing event of being fed. Thus, the mother becomes a conditioned reinforcer. This reinforcement theory of attachment came into question as a result of Harry Harlow's famous studies of attachment in infant rhesus monkeys (Harlow, 1958, 1959).

Harlow removed monkeys from their mothers at birth and raised them in the laboratory with two types of artificial "substitute mothers." One type of artificial mother was made of terrycloth and could provide "contact comfort" (see the photo opposite).

© Nina Leen/Time Life Pictures/Getty Images

Even if fed by a wire surrogate mother, Harlow's infant monkeys cuddled up with a terry cloth surrogate that provided contact comfort. When threatened by a frightening toy, the monkeys sought security from their terry cloth mothers.

The other type of artificial mother was made of wire. Half of the monkeys were fed from a bottle attached to a wire mother and the other half were fed by a cloth mother. The young monkeys' attachment to their substitute mothers was tested by introducing a frightening stimulus, such as a strange toy. If reinforcement through feeding were the key to attachment, the frightened monkeys should have scampered off to the mother that had fed them. This was not the case. The young monkeys scrambled for their cloth mothers, who had provided contact comfort, even if they were *not* fed by them.

Harlow's work seriously undermined the behaviorists' reinforcement explanation of attachment. Attention then turned to an alternative explanation of attachment proposed by John Bowlby (1969, 1973, 1980). Bowlby was impressed by the importance of contact comfort to Harlow's monkeys and by the apparently unlearned nature of this preference. Influenced by evolutionary theory, Bowlby argued that there must be a biological basis for attachment. According to his view, infants are biologically programmed to emit behavior (smiling, cooing, clinging, and so on) that triggers an affectionate, protective response from adults. Bowlby also asserted that adults are programmed by evolutionary forces to be captivated by this behavior and to respond with warmth, love, and protection. Obviously, these characteristics would be adaptive in terms of promoting children's survival. Bowlby's theory has guided most of the research on attachment over the last several decades, including Mary Ainsworth's influential work on patterns of attachment.

Patterns of Attachment

9e

Research by Mary Ainsworth and her colleagues (Ainsworth, 1979; Ainsworth et al., 1978) showed that infant-mother attachments vary in quality. Ainsworth used a method called the ***strange situation procedure,* in which infants are exposed to a series of eight separation and reunion episodes to assess the quality of their attachment.** The 3-minute episodes in this carefully orchestrated laboratory procedure involve events such as a stranger entering a room where an infant is playing with a parent nearby, followed by the parent leaving, returning, leaving, and returning again. The child's reactions (distress, comfort) to the parent's departures and returns are carefully monitored to gauge attachment quality.

Ainsworth found that attachments fall into three categories (see **Figure 11.5** on the next page). Fortunately, most infants develop a *secure attachment.* These infants use their mother as a secure base from which to venture out and explore the world. They play comfortably with their mother present, become visibly upset when she leaves, and are quickly calmed by her return. However, some children display a pattern called *anxious-ambivalent attachment* (also called *resistant* attachment). They appear anxious even when their mother is near and protest excessively when she leaves, but they are not particularly comforted when she returns. Children in the third category seek little contact with their mothers and often are not distressed when she leaves. This condition is labeled *avoidant attachment.* Years later, other researchers added a fourth category called *disorganized-disoriented* attachment (Main & Solomon, 1986, 1990). These children appear confused about whether they should approach or avoid their mother. Such children are especially insecure (Lyons-Ruth & Jacobvitz, 2008).

Maternal behaviors appear to have considerable influence over the type of attachment that emerges between an infant and mother (Ainsworth et al.,

© Nina Leen/Time Life Pictures/Getty Images

Harry Harlow

"The little we know about love does not transcend simple observation, and the little we write about it has been written better by poets and novelists."

© Sir Richard Bowlby Bt.

John Bowlby

"The only relevant criterion by which to consider the natural adaptedness of any particular part of present-day man's behavioural equipment is the degree to which and the way in which it might contribute to population survival in man's primeval environment."

Erik Hesse

Mary Salter Ainsworth

"Where familial security is lacking, the individual is handicapped by the lack of what might be called a secure base from which to work."

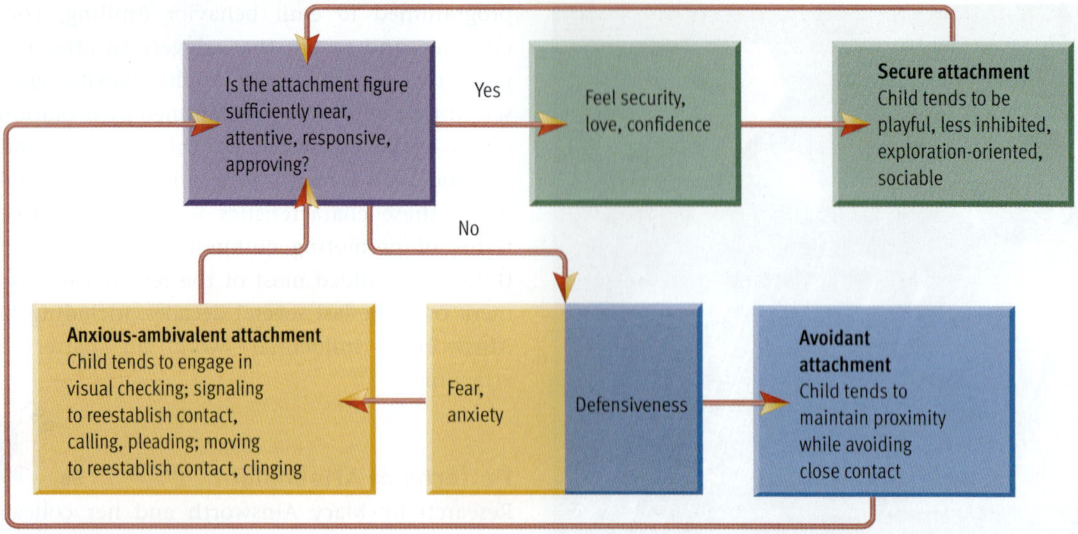

Figure 11.5

Overview of the attachment process. The unfolding of attachment depends on the interaction between a mother (or other caregiver) and an infant. Research by Mary Ainsworth suggested that attachment relations fall into three categories—secure, avoidant, and anxious-ambivalent—which depend in part on how sensitive and responsive caregivers are to their children's needs. The feedback loops shown in the diagram reflect the fact that babies are not passive bystanders in the attachment drama; their reactions to caregivers can affect the caregivers' behavior. Ainsworth's model did not include the fourth attachment pattern (disorganized-disoriented), which was recognized later. © Cengage Learning 2013

SOURCE: Adapted from Shaver, P. R., & Hazan, C. (1994). Attachment. In A. Weber & J. H. Harvey (Eds.), *Perspectives on close relationships.* Boston: Allyn & Bacon. Reprinted by permission of Pearson Education, Inc., Upper Saddle River, NJ.

1978; Posada et al., 2007). Mothers who are sensitive and responsive to their children's needs are more likely to promote secure attachments than mothers who are relatively insensitive or inconsistent in their responding (Nievar & Becker, 2008; van den Boom, 2001). However, infants are not passive bystanders as this process unfolds. They are active participants who influence the process with their crying, smiling, fussing, and babbling. Temperamentally difficult infants who spit up most of their food, make bathing a major battle, and rarely smile may sometimes slow the process of attachment (van IJzendoorn & Bakermans-Kranenburg, 2004). Thus, the type of attachment that emerges between an infant and mother may depend on the nature of the infant's temperament as well as the mother's sensitivity (Kagan & Fox, 2006).

Evidence suggests that the quality of the attachment relationship can have important consequences for children's subsequent development. Based on their attachment experiences, children develop *internal working models* of the dynamics of close relationships that influence their future interactions with a wide range of people (Bretherton & Munholland, 2008; Johnson, Dweck, & Chen, 2007). Infants with a relatively secure attachment *tend* to become resilient, sociable, competent toddlers with high self-esteem (Ranson & Urichuk, 2008; Thompson, 2008). In their preschool years, they display more persistence, curiosity, self-reliance, and leadership and have better peer relations (Weinfield et al., 2008). In middle childhood, they exhibit more positive moods, healthier strategies for coping with stress, and fewer problems with hostility and aggression (Fearon et al., 2010; Kerns et al., 2007). Studies have also found a relationship between secure attachment and more advanced cognitive development during childhood and adolescence (Ranson & Urichuk, 2008).

© lev dolgachov/Shutterstock

The repercussions of attachment patterns in infancy appear to even reach into adulthood. In Chapter 13, we'll discuss thought-provoking evidence that infant attachment patterns set the tone for people's romantic relationships in adulthood, not to mention their gender roles, religious beliefs, and patterns of self-disclosure (Feeney, 2008; Kirkpatrick, 2005; Mikulincer & Shaver, 2007; Shaver & Mikulincer, 2009).

Culture and Attachment

PSYKTREK 9e

Separation anxiety emerges in children at about 6–8 months and peaks at about 14–18 months in cultures around the world (Grossmann & Grossmann, 1990). These findings, which have been replicated in quite a variety of non-Western cultures, suggest that attachment is a universal feature of human development. However, studies have found some modest cultural variations in the proportion of infants who fall into the three attachment categories described by Ainsworth. Working mostly with white, middle-class subjects in the United States, researchers have found that 67% of infants display a secure attachment, 21% an avoidant attachment, and 12% an anxious-ambivalent attachment (the fourth attachment pattern mentioned earlier is not included here because it has only been tracked in a minority of cross-cultural studies) (van IJzendoorn & Sagi-Schwartz, 2008). Studies in Japan and Germany have yielded somewhat different estimates of the prevalence of various types of attachment, as shown in **Figure 11.6**. That said, the differences are small and secure attachment appears to be the predominant type of attachment around the world.

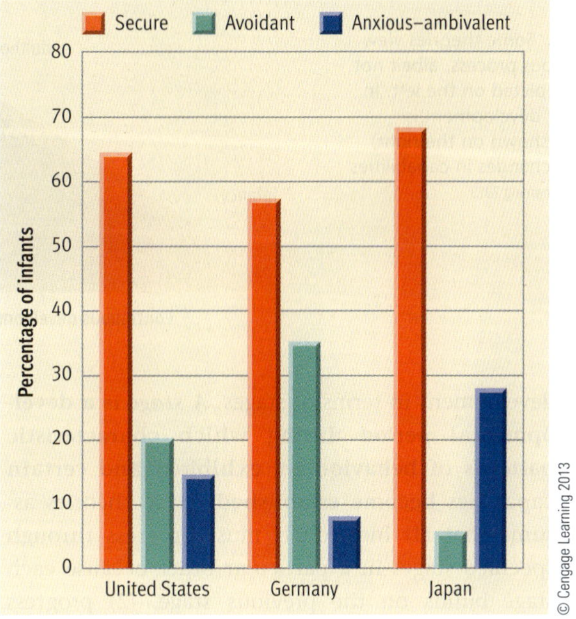

Figure 11.6
Cultural variations in attachment patterns.
This graph shows the distribution of the three original attachment patterns found in specific studies in Germany, Japan, and the United States. As you can see, secure attachment is the most common pattern in all three societies, as it is around the world. However, there are some modest cultural differences in the prevalence of each pattern of attachment, which are probably attributable to cultural variations in childrearing practices. (Data from van IJzendoorn & Kroonenberg, 1988)

REVIEW OF KEY LEARNING GOALS

11.3 Motor development follows cephalocaudal (head-to-foot) and proximodistal (center-outward) trends. Early motor development depends on both maturation and learning. Developmental norms for motor skills and other types of development are only group averages. Cultural variations in the pacing of motor development demonstrate the importance of learning.

11.4 In a longitudinal study, Thomas and Chess found that most infants could be classified as easy, slow-to-warm-up, or difficult children during the first few months of life and that these temperamental dispositions were stable well into childhood. Kagan's research suggests that variations in inhibited-uninhibited temperament are fairly stable. There may be some cultural variations in typical infant temperament.

11.5 Infants begin to show attachments at around 6 to 8 months of age, when separation anxiety surfaces. Harlow's work with monkeys undermined the reinforcement explanation of attachment. Bowlby proposed an evolutionary explanation for attachment that emphasized its survival value.

11.6 Ainsworth found that infant-mother attachments fall into three categories: secure, anxious-ambivalent, and avoidant. Research shows that attachment emerges out of an interplay between infant and mother. A secure attachment fosters self-esteem, persistence, curiosity, and self-reliance, among other desirable traits. Cultural variations in childrearing can affect the patterns of attachment seen in a society, but secure attachment is predominant around the world.

Personality and Cognitive Development in Childhood

KEY LEARNING GOALS

11.7 Describe the basic tenets of Erikson's theory and his stages of childhood personality development.

11.8 Outline Piaget's stages of cognitive development, and discuss the strengths and weaknesses of Piaget's theory.

11.9 Describe Vygotsky's sociocultural theory and contemporary research on cognitive development.

11.10 Outline Kohlberg's theory of moral development, and discuss its strengths and weaknesses.

Many other aspects of development are especially dynamic during childhood. In this section we'll examine personality development, cognitive development, and moral development, which is closely tied to cognitive development. We will begin with a look at the work of Erik Erikson and introduce the concept of developmental stages.

Becoming Unique: Personality Development

PSYKTREK 9b

How do individuals develop their unique constellations of personality traits over time? Many theories have addressed this question. The first major theory of personality development was constructed by Sigmund Freud back around 1900. As we'll discuss in Chapter 12, he claimed that the basic foundation of an individual's personality is firmly laid down by age 5. Half a century later, Erik Erikson (1963) proposed a sweeping revision of Freud's theory that has proven influential. Like Freud, Erikson concluded that events in early childhood leave a permanent stamp on adult personality. However, unlike Freud, Erikson theorized that personality continues to evolve over the entire life span.

Building on Freud's earlier work, Erikson devised a stage theory of personality development. As you'll see in reading this chapter, many theories describe

Figure 11.7

Stage theories of development. Some theories view development as a relatively continuous process, albeit not as smooth and perfectly linear as depicted on the left. In contrast, stage theories assume that development is marked by major discontinuities (as shown on the right) that bring fundamental, qualitative changes in capabilities or characteristic behavior. © Cengage Learning 2013

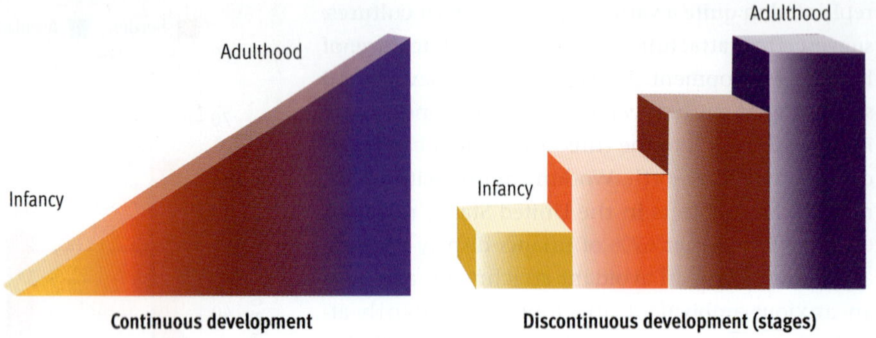

Erik Erikson

"Human personality in principle develops according to steps predetermined in the growing person's readiness to be driven toward, to be aware of, and to interact with a widening social radius."

development in terms of stages. **A *stage* is a developmental period during which characteristic patterns of behavior are exhibited and certain capacities become established.** Stage theories assume that (1) individuals must progress through specified stages in a particular order because each stage builds on the previous stage, (2) progress through these stages is strongly related to age, and (3) there are major discontinuities between stages in typical behavior (see **Figure 11.7**).

Erikson's Stage Theory

PsykTrek 9b

Erikson split the life span into eight stages. Each stage brings a *psychosocial crisis*. He used the term *crisis* to convey a crucial turning point, rather than a dire emergency. According to Erikson, personality is shaped by how individuals deal with crises that involve transitions in important social relationships. Each crisis entails a struggle between two opposing tendencies, such as trust versus mistrust or initiative versus guilt, that are experienced by the person at a particular stage. These antagonistic tendencies represent personality traits that people display in varying degrees over the remainder of their lives. Although the names for Erikson's stages suggest either/or outcomes, he viewed each stage as a tug of war that determined the subsequent *balance* between opposing polarities in personality. All eight stages in Erikson's theory are charted in **Figure 11.8**. We describe the first four childhood stages here and discuss the remaining stages in the upcoming sections on adolescence and adulthood.

Trust Versus Mistrust Erikson's first stage encompasses the first year of life. An infant has to depend completely on adults to take care of its basic needs for such necessities as food, a warm blanket, and changed diapers. If an infant's basic needs are adequately met by his or her caregivers and sound attachments are formed, the child should develop an optimistic, trusting attitude toward the world. However, if the infant's basic needs are taken care of poorly, a more distrusting, pessimistic personality may result.

Autonomy Versus Shame and Doubt Erikson's second stage unfolds during the second and third years of life. This is the time parents begin toilet training and exert other efforts to regulate the

Figure 11.8

Erikson's stage theory. Erikson's theory of personality development posits that people evolve through eight stages over the life span. Each stage is marked by a *psychosocial crisis* that involves confronting a fundamental question, such as "Who am I and where am I going?" The stages are described in terms of alternative traits that are potential outcomes from the crises. Development is enhanced when a crisis is resolved in favor of the healthier alternative (which is listed first for each stage).

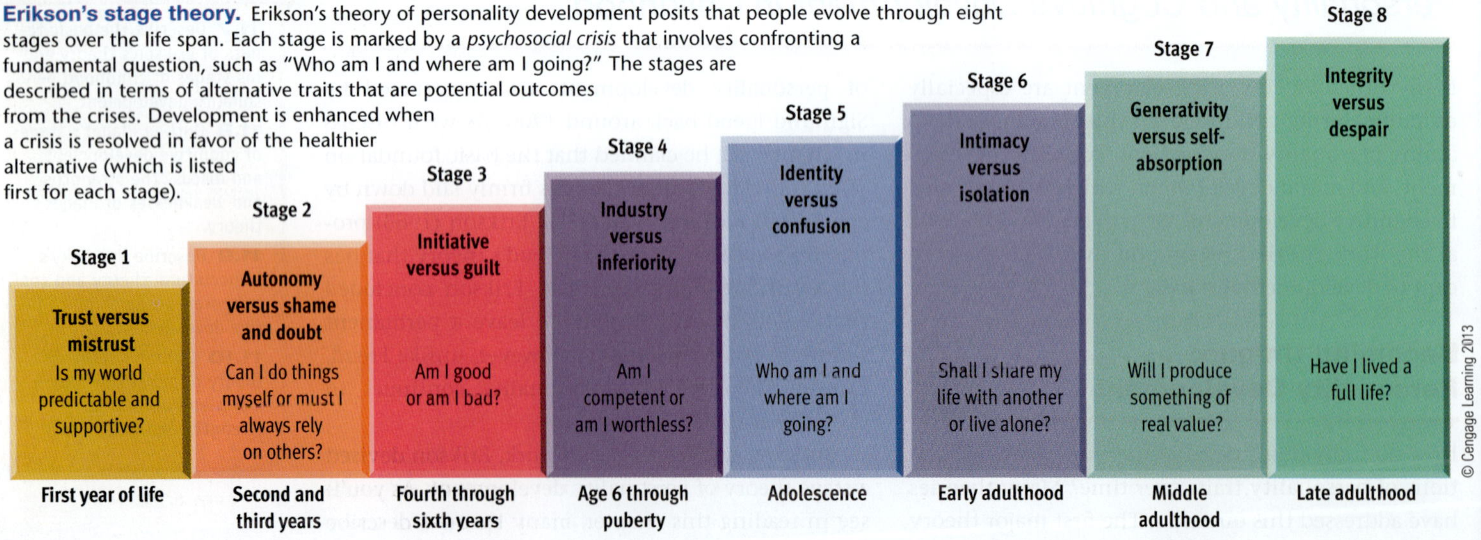

child's behavior. The child must begin to take some personal responsibility for feeding, dressing, and bathing. If all goes well, he or she acquires a sense of autonomy. But if parents are never satisfied with the child's efforts and there are constant parent-child conflicts, the child may develop a sense of personal shame and self-doubt.

Initiative Versus Guilt In Erikson's third stage, lasting roughly from ages 3 to 6, children experiment and take initiatives that may sometimes conflict with their parents' rules. Overcontrolling parents may begin to instill feelings of guilt. Self-esteem may suffer as a result. Parents need to support their children's emerging independence while maintaining appropriate controls. In the ideal situation, children will retain their sense of initiative while learning to respect the rights and privileges of other family members.

Industry Versus Inferiority In the fourth stage (age 6 through puberty), the challenge of learning to function socially is extended beyond the family to the broader social realm of the neighborhood and school. Children who are able to function effectively in this less nurturant social sphere where productivity is highly valued, should learn to value achievement and to take pride in accomplishment. Doing so should result in a sense of competence. If things don't go well in this broader social domain, they may develop a sense of inferiority.

Evaluating Erikson's Theory

The strength of Erikson's theory is that it accounts for both continuity and transition in personality development. It accounts for transition by showing how new challenges in social relations stimulate personality development throughout life. It accounts for continuity by drawing connections between early childhood experiences and aspects of adult personality. One measure of a theory's value is how much research it generates. Erikson's theory continues to guide a fair amount of research (Thomas, 2005).

On the negative side of the ledger, Erikson's theory has depended heavily on illustrative case studies. Such studies are open to varied interpretations (Thomas, 2005). Another weakness is that the theory provides an "idealized" description of "typical" developmental patterns. Thus, it's not well suited for explaining the enormous personality differences that exist among people. Inadequate explanation of individual differences is a common problem with stage theories of development. In any event, let's turn now to another stage theory, Jean Piaget's model of cognitive development.

© MANDY GODBEHEAR/Shutterstock

According to Erik Erikson, school-age children face the challenge of learning how to function in social situations outside of their family, especially with peers and at school. If they succeed, they will develop a sense of competence; if they fail, they may feel inferior.

The Growth of Thought: Cognitive Development

PSYKTREK 9c

Cognitive development **refers to transitions in youngsters' patterns of thinking, including reasoning, remembering, and problem solving.** The investigation of cognitive development was dominated in most of the second half of the 20th century by the theory of Jean Piaget (Kessen, 1996). Much of our discussion of cognitive development is devoted to Piaget's theory and the research it generated, although we'll also delve into other approaches.

Overview of Piaget's Stage Theory

PSYKTREK 9c

Jean Piaget (1929, 1952, 1983) was an interdisciplinary scholar whose own cognitive development was exceptionally rapid. In his early 20s, after he had earned a doctorate in natural science and published a novel, Piaget turned his focus to psychology. He soon found himself administering intelligence tests to children to develop better test norms. In doing this testing, Piaget became intrigued by the reasoning underlying the children's *wrong* answers. He decided that measuring children's intelligence was less interesting than studying how children *use* their intelligence, and he went on to spend the rest of his life studying cognitive development. Many of his ideas were based on insights gleaned from careful observations of his own three children during their infancy.

Like Erikson's theory, Piaget's model is a *stage theory* of development. Piaget proposed that youngsters progress through four major stages of cognitive development, which are characterized by fundamentally different thought processes: (1) the *sensorimotor period* (birth to age 2), (2) the *preoperational period* (ages 2 to 7), (3) the *concrete operational period* (ages 7 to 11), and (4) the *formal operational period*

© Farrell Grehan/Corbis

Jean Piaget

"It is virtually impossible to draw a clear line between innate and acquired behavior patterns."

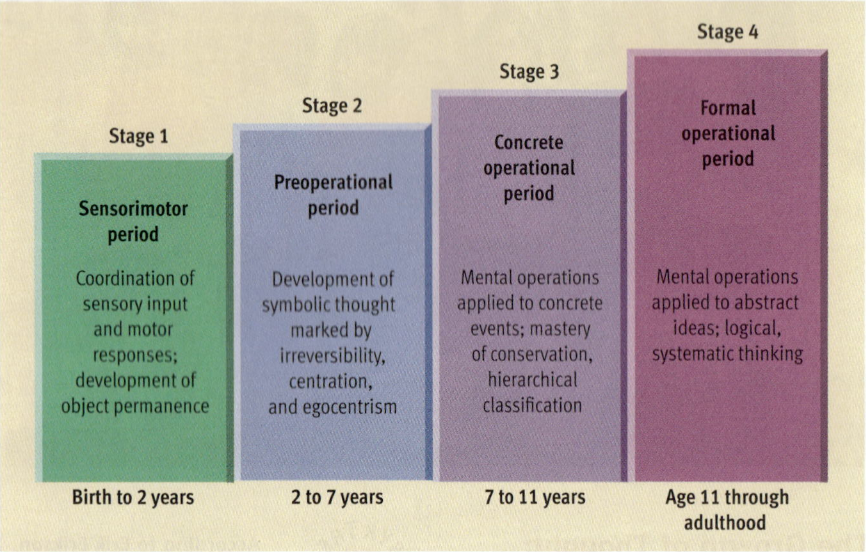

Figure 11.9
Piaget's stage theory. Piaget's theory of cognitive development identifies four stages marked by fundamentally different modes of thinking through which youngsters evolve. The approximate age norms and some key characteristics of thought at each stage are summarized here.

(age 11 onward). **Figure 11.9** provides an overview of each of these periods. Piaget regarded his age norms as approximations and acknowledged that transitional ages may vary. He was, however, convinced that all children progress through the stages of cognitive development in the same order.

Sensorimotor Period The first stage in Piaget's theory is the *sensorimotor period,* lasting from birth to about age 2. Piaget called this stage *sensorimotor* because infants are developing the ability to coordinate their sensory input with their motor actions.

Figure 11.10
Piaget's conservation task for liquid. After watching the transformation shown, a preoperational child will usually answer that the taller beaker contains more water. In contrast, a child in the concrete operational period tends to respond correctly, recognizing that the amount of water in beaker C remains the same as the amount in beaker A. © Cengage Learning 2013

The major development during the sensorimotor stage is the gradual appearance of symbolic thought. At the beginning of this stage, a child's behavior is dominated by innate reflexes. But by the end of the stage, the child can use mental symbols to represent objects (for example, a mental image of a favorite toy). The key to this transition is the acquisition of the concept of object permanence.

Object permanence **develops when a child recognizes that objects continue to exist even when they are no longer visible.** Although adults take the permanence of objects for granted, infants aren't aware of this permanence at first. If you show a 3-month-old an eye-catching toy and then cover the toy with a pillow, the child will not attempt to search for the toy. Piaget inferred from this observation that the child does not understand that the toy continues to exist under the pillow. The notion of object permanence does not dawn on children overnight. According to Piaget, the first signs of this insight usually appear between 4 and 8 months of age. Progress is gradual. Piaget believed that children typically don't master the concept of object permanence until they're about 18 months old.

Preoperational Period The *preoperational period* extends roughly from age 2 to age 7. During this stage, children gradually improve in their use of mental images. Although progress in symbolic thought continues, Piaget emphasized the *shortcomings* in preoperational thought.

Consider a simple problem that Piaget presented to youngsters. He would take two identical beakers and fill each with the same amount of water. After a child had agreed that the two beakers contained the same amount of water, he would pour the water from one of the beakers into a much taller and thinner beaker (see **Figure 11.10**). He would then ask the child whether the two differently shaped beakers still contained the same amount of water. Confronted with a problem like this, children in the preoperational period generally said no. They typically focused on the higher water line in the taller beaker and insisted that there was more water in the slender beaker. They had not yet mastered the principle of conservation. ***Conservation*** **is Piaget's term for the awareness that physical quantities remain constant in spite of changes in their shape or appearance.**

Why are preoperational children unable to solve conservation problems? According to Piaget, their inability to understand conservation is caused by some basic flaws in preoperational thinking. These flaws include centration, irreversibility, and egocentrism.

Centration **is the tendency to focus on just one feature of a problem, neglecting other important**

aspects. When working on the conservation problem with water, preoperational children tend to concentrate on the height of the water while ignoring the width. They have difficulty focusing on several aspects of a problem at once.

***Irreversibility* is the inability to envision reversing an action.** Preoperational children can't mentally "undo" something. For instance, in grappling with the conservation of water, they don't think about what would happen if the water were poured back from the tall beaker into the original beaker.

***Egocentrism* in thinking is characterized by a limited ability to share another person's viewpoint.** Indeed, Piaget felt that preoperational children fail to appreciate that there are points of view other than their own. For instance, if you ask a preoperational girl whether her sister has a sister, she'll probably say no if they are the only two girls in the family. She's unable to view sisterhood from her sister's perspective.

A notable feature of egocentrism is ***animism*—the belief that all things are living,** just like oneself. Thus, youngsters attribute lifelike, human qualities to inanimate objects, asking questions such as, "When does the ocean stop to rest?" or "Why does the wind get so mad?"

Concrete Operational Period The development of mental operations—internal transformations and manipulations of mental structures—marks the beginning of the *concrete operational period.* This stage usually lasts from about age 7 to age 11. Piaget called this stage *concrete* operations because children can perform operations only on images of tangible objects and actual events.

Among the operations that children master during this stage are reversibility and decentration. *Reversibility* permits a child to mentally undo an action. *Decentration* allows the child to focus on more than one feature of a problem simultaneously. The newfound ability to coordinate several aspects of a problem helps the child appreciate that there are several ways to look at things. This ability in turn leads to a *decline in egocentrism* and *gradual mastery of conservation* as it applies to liquid, mass, number, volume, area, and length (see **Figure 11.11**).

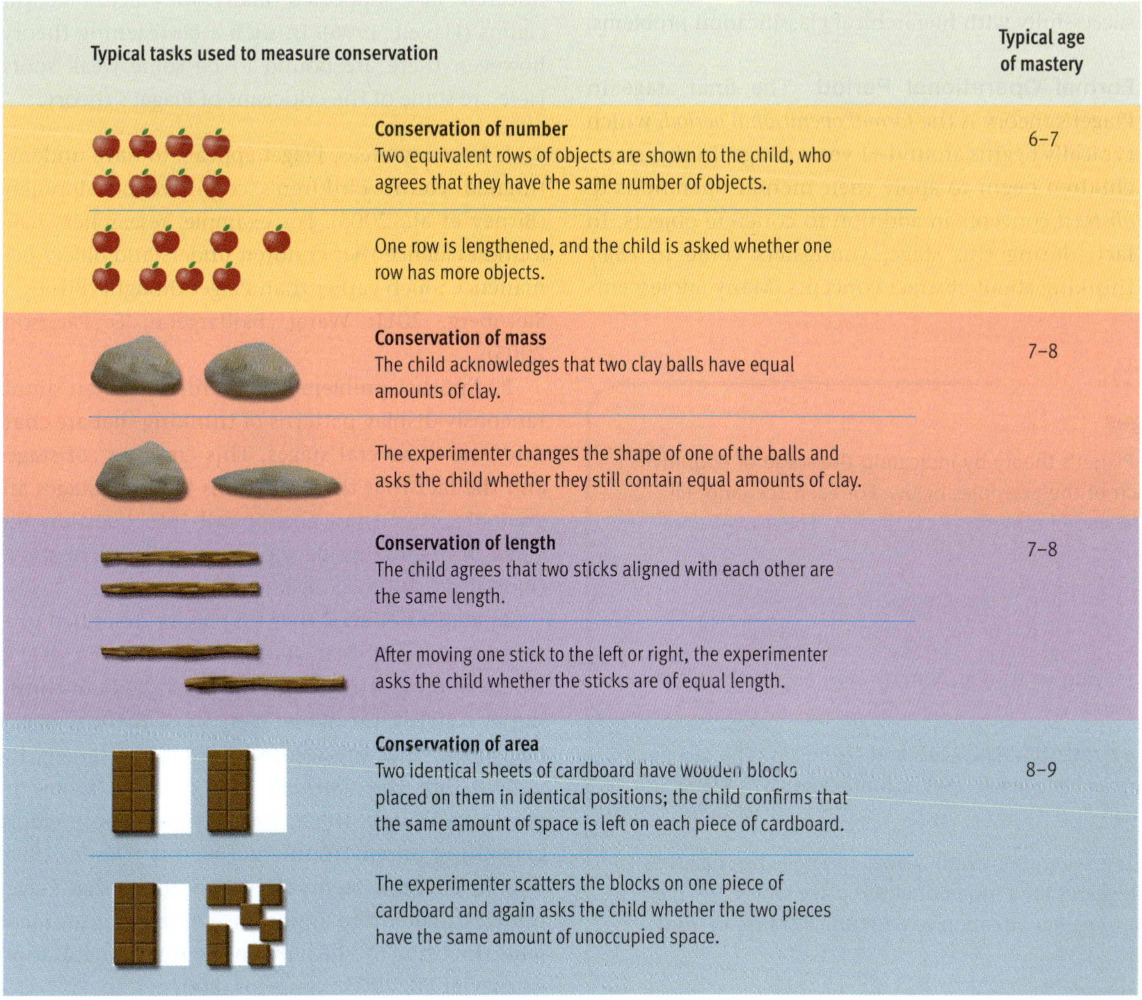

© Cengage Learning 2013

Figure 11.11
The gradual mastery of conservation. Children master conservation during the concrete operational period, but their mastery is gradual. As outlined here, children usually master the conservation of number at age 6 or 7, but they may not understand the conservation of area until age 8 or 9.

© Robert Manella/Getty Images

As children master concrete operations, they develop a variety of new problem-solving capacities. Let's examine another problem studied by Piaget. Give a preoperational child seven carnations and three daisies. Tell the child the names for the two types of flowers. Then ask the child to sort them into carnations and daisies. That should be no problem. Now ask the child whether there are more carnations or more daisies. Most children will correctly respond that there are more carnations. Now ask the child whether there are more carnations or more flowers. At this point, most preoperational children will stumble and respond incorrectly that there are more carnations than flowers. Generally, preoperational children can't handle *hierarchical classification* problems that require them to focus on two levels of classification at the same time. However, the child who has advanced to the concrete operational stage is not as limited by centration and can work successfully with hierarchical classification problems.

Formal Operational Period The final stage in Piaget's theory is the *formal operational period,* which typically begins around 11 years of age. In this stage, children begin to apply their mental operations to *abstract* concepts in addition to concrete objects. In fact, during this stage, youngsters come to *enjoy* thinking about abstract concepts. Many adolescents spend hours mulling over hypothetical possibilities related to abstractions such as justice, love, and free will. Thought processes in the formal operational period can be characterized as relatively systematic, logical, and reflective.

According to Piaget, youngsters graduate to relatively adult modes of thinking in the formal operations stage. He did *not* mean to suggest that no further cognitive development occurs once children reach this stage. However, he believed that after children achieve formal operations, further developments in thinking are changes in *degree* rather than fundamental changes in the *nature* of thinking.

CONCEPT CHECK 11.2

Recognizing Piaget's Stages

Check your understanding of Piaget's theory by indicating the stage of cognitive development illustrated by each of the examples below. For each scenario, fill in the letter for the appropriate stage in the space on the left. The answers are in Appendix A.

a. Sensorimotor period
b. Preoperational period
c. Concrete operational period
d. Formal operational period

_______ 1. Upon seeing a glass lying on its side, Sammy says, "Look, the glass is tired. It's taking a nap."

_______ 2. Maria is told that a farmer has nine cows and six horses. The teacher asks, "Does the farmer have more cows or more animals?" Maria answers, "More animals."

_______ 3. Alice is playing in the living room with a small red ball. The ball rolls under the sofa. She stares for a moment at the place where the ball vanished and then turns her attention to a toy truck sitting in front of her.

Evaluating Piaget's Theory

Jean Piaget made a landmark contribution to psychology's understanding of children in general and their cognitive development in particular (Beilin, 1992). He founded the field of cognitive development and fostered a new view of children that saw them as active agents constructing their own worlds (Fischer & Hencke, 1996). Piaget's theory guided an enormous volume of productive research that continues through today (Brainerd, 1996; Feldman, 2003). This research has supported many of Piaget's central claims (Flavell, 1996). In such a far-reaching theory, however, there are bound to be some weak spots. Here are some of the criticisms of Piaget's theory:

1. In many areas, Piaget appears to have underestimated young children's cognitive development (Birney et al., 2005). For example, researchers have found evidence that children understand object permanence much earlier than Piaget thought (Birney & Sternberg, 2011; Wang, Baillargeon, & Paterson, 2005).

2. Another problem is that children often simultaneously display patterns of thinking that are characteristic of several stages. This "mixing" of stages and the fact that the transitions between stages are gradual rather than abrupt call into question the value of organizing development in terms of stages (Bjorklund, 2005; Krojgaard, 2005).

3. Piaget believed that his theory described universal processes that should lead children everywhere to progress through uniform stages of thinking at roughly the same ages. Subsequent research has shown that the *sequence* of stages is largely invariant, but the *timetable* that children follow in passing through these stages varies considerably depending on environmental factors (Dasen, 1994; Rogoff, 2003). It seems fair to say today that Piaget underestimated the importance of the environment while focusing too heavily on the role of maturation (Birney et al., 2005; Maratsos, 2007).

Vygotsky's Sociocultural Theory

In recent decades, as the limitations and weaknesses of Piaget's ideas have become more apparent, some developmental researchers have looked elsewhere for theoretical guidance. Ironically, the theory that has recently inspired the greatest interest—Lev Vygotsky's *sociocultural theory*—dates back to around the same time that Piaget began formulating his theory (1920s–1930s). Vygotsky was a prominent Russian psychologist whose research ended prematurely in 1934 when he died of tuberculosis at the age of 37. Western scientists had little exposure to his ideas until the 1960s. In fact, it was only in 1986 that a complete version of his principal book (Vygotsky, 1934) was published in English. Working in a perilous political climate in the post-Revolution Soviet Union, Vygotsky had to devise a theory that would not be incompatible with the Marxist social philosophy that ruled communist thinking (Thomas, 2005). Given the constraints placed on his theorizing, one might expect that 70 years later his ideas would not resonate with contemporary psychologists in capitalist societies. Yet the reality is just the opposite: His theory has become quite influential (Daniels, 2005; Feldman, 2003).

Vygotsky's and Piaget's perspectives on cognitive development have much in common. However, they also differ in several important respects (DeVries, 2000; Matusov & Hayes, 2000; Rowe & Wertsch, 2002). First, in Piaget's theory, cognitive development is primarily fueled by individual children's active exploration of the world around them. The child is viewed as the agent of change. In contrast, Vygotsky placed enormous emphasis on how children's cognitive development is fueled by social interactions with parents, teachers, and older children who can provide invaluable guidance (Hedegaard, 2005). Second, Piaget viewed cognitive development as a universal process that should unfold in largely the same way across widely disparate cultures. Vygotsky, on the other hand, asserted that culture exerts great influence over how cognitive growth unfolds (Wertsch & Tulviste, 2005). For example, the cognitive skills acquired in literate cultures that rely on schools for training will differ from those acquired in tribal societies where there may be no formal schooling. Third, Piaget viewed children's gradual mastery of language as just another aspect of cognitive development. Vygotsky, though, argued that language acquisition plays a crucial, central role in fostering cognitive development (Kozulin, 2005).

According to Vygotsky, children acquire most of their culture's cognitive skills and problem-solving strategies through collaborative dialogues with more experienced members of their society. He saw cognitive development as more like an *apprenticeship* than a journey of individual discovery. Vygotsky's emphasis on the primacy of language is reflected in his discussion of *private speech*. Preschool children talk aloud to themselves a lot as they go about their activities. Piaget viewed this speech as egocentric and insignificant. Vygotsky argued that children use this private speech to plan their strategies, regulate their actions, and accomplish their goals. As children grow older, this private speech is internalized. It becomes the normal verbal dialogue that people have with themselves as they go about their business. Thus, language increasingly serves as the *foundation* for youngsters' cognitive processes. Like Piaget's theory, Vygotsky's perspective promises to enrich our understanding of how children's thinking develops and matures.

Archives of the History of American Psychology, University of Akron, Akron, Ohio

Lev Vygotsky

"In the process of development the child not only masters the items of cultural experience but the habits and forms of cultural behaviour, the cultural methods of reasoning."

Are Some Cognitive Abilities Innate?

The frequent finding that Piaget underestimated infants' cognitive abilities has led to a rash of studies suggesting that infants have a surprising grasp of many complex concepts. Studies have shown that infants understand basic properties of objects and some of the rules that govern them (Baillargeon, 2004). At 3 to 4 months of age, infants understand that objects are distinct entities with boundaries, that objects move in continuous paths, that one solid object cannot penetrate through another, that an object cannot pass through an opening that is smaller than the object, and that objects on slopes roll down rather than up (Baillargeon, 2008; Spelke & Newport, 1998). Infants also understand that liquids are different from objects. For example, 5-month-old infants expect that liquids will change shape as they move and that they can be penetrated by solid objects (Hespos, Ferry, & Rips, 2009).

In this line of research, perhaps the most stunning discovery has been the finding that *infants seem to exhibit surprisingly sophisticated numerical abilities* (Lipton & Spelke, 2004; Wood & Spelke, 2005). For example, Karen Wynn (1992, 1996) has conducted some groundbreaking studies of infants' numerical capabilities. She demonstrated that if 5-month-old infants are shown a sequence of events in which one object is added to another behind a screen, they expect to see two objects when the screen is removed (see **Figure 11.12** on the next page). And they exhibit surprise—in the form of longer looking—when their expectation is not met. This finding suggests that the infants understand that $1 + 1 = 2$. Similar manipulations in subsequent studies suggested that infants also understand that $2 + 1 = 3$, that $3 - 1 = 2$, and even that $10 - 5 = 5$ (Hauser & Carey, 1998; McCrink & Wynn, 2004; Wynn, 1998). Thus, infants may have a primitive "number sense."

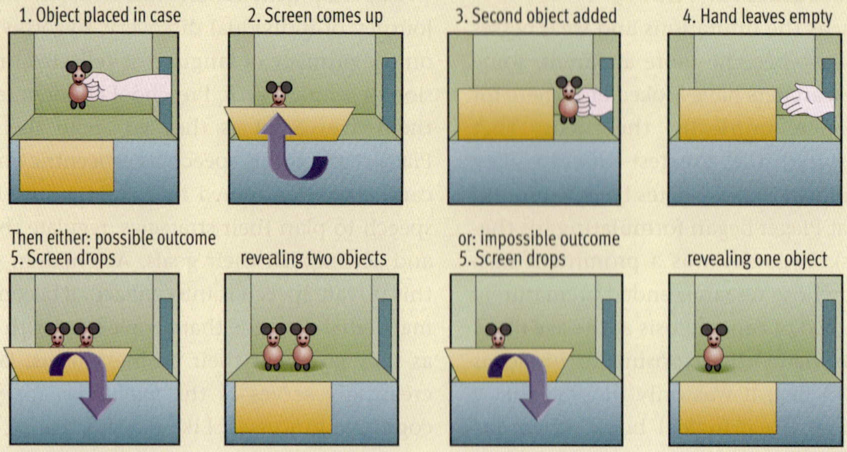

© Cengage Learning 2013

Figure 11.12

The procedure used to test infants' understanding of number. To see whether 5-month-old infants have some appreciation of addition and subtraction, Wynn (1992, 1996) showed them sequences of events like those depicted here. If children express surprise (primarily assessed by time spent looking) when the screen drops and they see only one object, this result suggests that they understand that 1 + 1 = 2. Wynn and others have found that infants seem to have some primitive grasp of simple addition and subtraction.

SOURCE: Adapted from Wynn, K. (1992). Addition and subtraction by human infants. *Nature, 358,* 749–750. Reprinted by permission from Macmillan Publishers Ltd.

Again and again in recent years, research has shown that infants appear to understand surprisingly complex concepts that they have had virtually no opportunity to learn about. These findings have led some theorists to conclude that certain basic cognitive abilities are biologically prewired into humans' neural architecture (Spelke & Kinzler, 2007). As you might anticipate, evolutionary theorists maintain that this prewiring is a product of natural selection, and they strive to understand its adaptive significance for our ancient ancestors (Hauser & Carey, 1998; Wynn, 1998). For example, evolutionary theorists are interested in how basic addition-subtraction abilities may have enhanced our hominid ancestors' success in hunting, foraging, and social bargaining.

What Do Children Understand About the Mind?

Another hot topic in the area of cognitive development has been the question of how children's understanding of the mind and mental states progresses over time. Researchers exploring this aspect of cognitive development study when and how children come to understand that other people have knowledge, beliefs, and desires that may be quite different from their own. Consider the following scenario. An experimenter shows a 5-year-old child a candy box and asks her what she thinks it contains. She answers, "Candy." The child is then allowed to look inside the box and discovers that it really contains crayons. Then the experimenter asks the girl what another child who has *not* seen the contents of the box will think it contains. "Candy," she replies, showing her understanding of the planned deception. Now imagine the same experiment with a 3-year-old boy. Events should unfold in the same way until the experimenter asks what another child will think the candy box contains. The 3-year-old typically will say "Crayons," thinking that the other child will know what he knows about the hidden contents of the box (Flavell, 1999). Why does the 3-year-old respond in this way? Because most children under age 4 do not yet appreciate that people can hold false beliefs that do not accurately reflect reality.

Researchers have mapped out some milestones in the development of children's understanding of mental states (Harris, 2006; Wellman, 2002). At around age 2 children begin to distinguish between mental states and overt behavior. The first mental states they understand are *desires* and *emotions*. By age 3, children are talking about others' *beliefs* and *thoughts,* as well as their desires and emotions. It is not until about age 4, however, that children consistently make the connection between mental states and behavior. That is, they begin to understand how people's beliefs, thoughts, and desires motivate and direct their behavior. Thus, they can appreciate that Darius *wants* to get a LEGO firetruck, which would make him very *happy,* that he *believes* it will be available at the mall, and that these mental states will *motivate* Darius to ask his dad to take him to the mall.

Children's understanding of the mind seems to turn a corner between ages 3 and 4, so that they gradually begin to grasp the fact that people may hold *false beliefs* (Amsterlaw & Wellman, 2006; Flynn, 2006). Interestingly, this transition in cognitive sophistication appears to occur around the same age in a variety of cultures (Callaghan et al., 2005). After age 4, youngsters' reasoning about mental states continues to improve.

The Development of Moral Reasoning

PSYKTREK 9d

In Europe, a woman was near death from cancer. One drug might save her. It is a form of radium that a druggist in the same town had recently discovered. The drug-

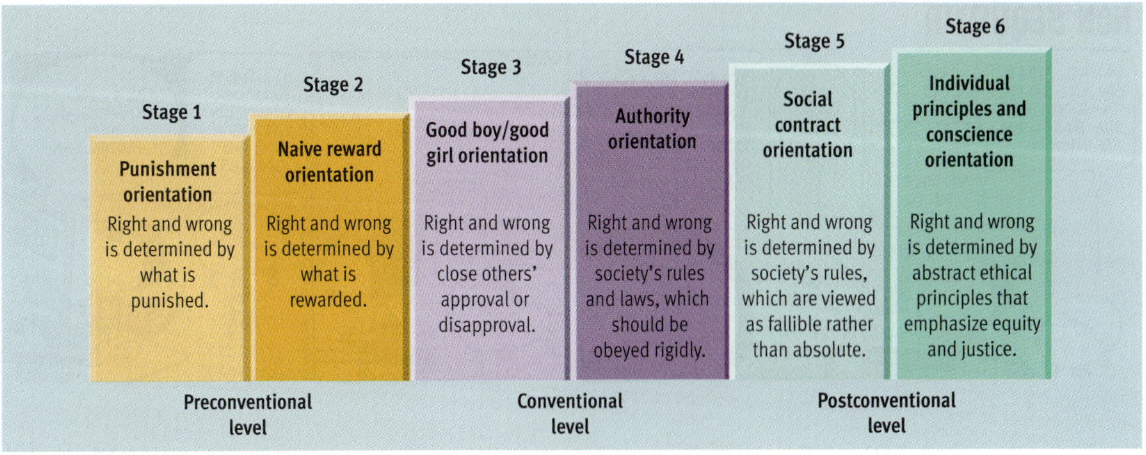

© Cengage Learning 2013

Figure 11.13

Kohlberg's stage theory. Kohlberg's model posits three levels of moral reasoning, each of which can be divided into two stages. This chart summarizes some of the key facets in how individuals think about right and wrong at each stage.

gist was charging $2,000, ten times what the drug cost him to make. The sick woman's husband, Heinz, went to everyone he knew to borrow the money, but he could only get together about half of what it cost. He told the druggist that his wife was dying and asked him to sell it cheaper or let him pay later. But the druggist said, "No." The husband got desperate and broke into the man's store to steal the drug for his wife. Should the husband have done that? Why? (Kohlberg, 1969, p. 379)

What's your answer to Heinz's dilemma? Would you have answered the same way three years ago? Can you guess what you might have said at age 6? By presenting similar dilemmas to participants and studying their responses, Lawrence Kohlberg (1976, 1984; Colby & Kohlberg, 1987) developed a model of *moral development*. What is morality? That's a complicated question that philosophers have debated for centuries. For our purposes, it will suffice to say that *morality* involves the ability to figure out right from wrong and to behave accordingly.

Kohlberg's Stage Theory

PSYKTREK 9d

Kohlberg's model is the most influential of a number of competing theories that attempt to explain how youngsters develop a sense of right and wrong. His work was derived from much earlier work by Piaget (1932), who theorized that moral development is determined by cognitive development. By this he meant that the way individuals think out moral issues depends on their level of cognitive development. This assumption provided the springboard for Kohlberg's research.

Kohlberg's theory focuses on moral *reasoning* rather than overt *behavior*. This point is best illustrated by describing Kohlberg's method of investigation. He presented his participants with thorny moral questions such as Heinz's dilemma. He then asked the subjects what the actor in the dilemma should do, and more important, why. It was the *why* that interested Kohlberg. He examined the nature and progression of subjects' moral reasoning.

The result of this work is the stage theory of moral reasoning outlined in **Figure 11.13**. Kohlberg found that individuals progress through a series of three levels of moral development. Each of these levels can be broken into two sublevels, yielding a total of six stages. Each stage represents a different approach to thinking about right and wrong.

© Bob Daemmrich/PhotoEdit

Younger children at the *preconventional level* think in terms of external authority. Acts are wrong because they are punished, or right because they lead to positive consequences. Older children who have reached the *conventional level* of moral reasoning see rules as necessary for maintaining social order. They therefore accept these rules as their own. They "internalize" the rules not to avoid punishment but to be virtuous and win approval from others. Moral thinking at this stage is relatively inflexible. Rules are viewed as absolute guidelines that should be enforced rigidly.

During adolescence, some youngsters move on to the *postconventional level*. This level involves working out a personal code of ethics. Acceptance of rules is less rigid, and moral thinking shows some flexibility. Subjects at the postconventional level allow for the possibility that someone might not comply with some of society's rules if they

NON SEQUITUR © 2002 by Wiley. Reprinted with permission of Universal Press Syndicate. All rights reserved.

conflict with personal ethics. For example, participants at this level might applaud a newspaper reporter who goes to jail rather than reveal a source of information who was promised anonymity.

Evaluating Kohlberg's Theory

How has Kohlberg's theory fared in research? The central ideas have received reasonable support. Progress in moral reasoning is indeed closely tied to cognitive development (Walker, 1988). Studies also show that youngsters generally do progress through Kohlberg's stages of moral reasoning in the order that he proposed (Walker, 1989). Furthermore, relations between age and level of moral reasoning are in the predicted directions (Rest, 1986). Representative age trends are shown in **Figure 11.14**. As children get older, stage 1 and stage 2 reasoning declines, while stage 3 and stage 4 reasoning increases. However, there is great variation in the age at which individuals reach specific stages. In addition, very few people reach stage 6, which raises doubts about its validity (Lapsley, 2006). Although these findings support the utility of Kohlberg's model, like all influential theorists, he has his critics. They have raised the following issues:

1. It's not unusual to find that a person shows signs of several adjacent levels of moral reasoning at a particular point in development (Walker & Taylor, 1991). As we noted in the critique of Piaget, this mixing of stages is a problem for virtually all stage theories.

CONCEPT CHECK 11.3

Analyzing Moral Reasoning

Check your understanding of Kohlberg's theory of moral development by analyzing hypothetical responses to the following moral dilemma.

A midwest biologist has conducted numerous studies demonstrating that simple organisms such as worms and paramecia can learn through conditioning. It occurs to her that perhaps she could condition fertilized human ova, to provide a dramatic demonstration that abortions destroy adaptable, living human organisms. This possibility appeals to her, as she is ardently opposed to abortion. However, there is no way to conduct the necessary research on human ova without sacrificing the lives of potential human beings. She desperately wants to conduct the research, but obviously, the sacrifice of human ova is fundamentally incompatible with her belief in the sanctity of human life. What should she do? Why? [Submitted by a student (age 13) to Professor Barbara Banas at Monroe Community College]

In the spaces on the left of each numbered response, indicate the level of moral reasoning shown, choosing from the following: (a) preconventional level, (b) conventional level, or (c) postconventional level. The answers are in Appendix A.

_______ 1. She should do the research. Although it's wrong to kill, there's a greater good that can be realized through the research.

_______ 2. She shouldn't do the research because people will think that she's a hypocrite and condemn her.

_______ 3. She should do the research because she may become rich and famous as a result.

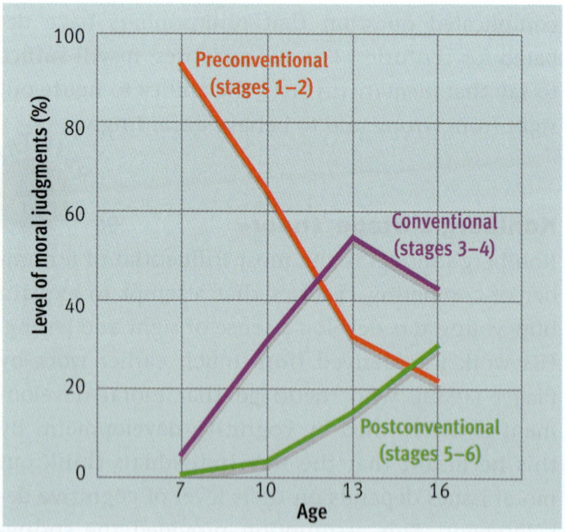

© Cengage Learning 2013

Figure 11.14
Age and moral reasoning. The percentages of different types of moral judgments made by subjects at various ages are graphed here (based on Kohlberg, 1963, 1969). As predicted, preconventional reasoning declines as children mature, conventional reasoning increases during middle childhood, and postconventional reasoning begins to emerge during adolescence. But at each age, children display a mixture of various levels of moral reasoning.

2. Evidence is mounting that Kohlberg's dilemmas may not be valid indicators of moral development in some cultures (Nucci, 2002). Some critics believe that the value judgments built into Kohlberg's theory reflect a liberal, individualistic ideology characteristic of modern Western nations that is much more culture-specific than Kohlberg appreciated (Miller, 2006).

3. A consensus is building that Kohlberg's theory led to a constricted focus on reasoning about interpersonal conflicts while ignoring many other important aspects of moral development (Walker, 2007). Thus, contemporary researchers are increasingly turning their attention to other dimensions of moral development, including the development of empathy (Eisenberg, Spinrad, & Sadovsky, 2006), the emergence of conscience (Grusec, 2006), the development of prosocial (helping, sharing) behavior (Carlo, 2006), and the significance of moral emotions (such as shame and guilt) (Tangney, Stuewig, & Mashek, 2007).

REVIEW OF KEY LEARNING GOALS

11.7 Like other stage theories, Erikson's theory of personality development proposes that individuals evolve through a series of stages over the life span. In each of the eight stages, the person wrestles with two opposing tendencies evoked by that stage's psychosocial crisis.

11.8 According to Piaget's theory of cognitive development, the key advance during the sensorimotor period is the child's gradual recognition of the permanence of objects. The preoperational period is marked by certain deficiencies in thinking—notably, centration, irreversibility, and egocentrism. During the concrete operations period, children develop the ability to perform operations on mental representations. The stage of formal operations ushers in more abstract, systematic, and logical thought. Piaget may have underestimated some aspects of children's cognitive development and the impact of environmental factors.

11.9 Vygotsky's sociocultural theory maintains that children's cognitive development is fueled by social interactions with parents and others and that culture influences how cognitive growth unfolds. Recent research has shown that infants appear to understand surprisingly complex concepts that they have had virtually no opportunity to learn about, suggesting that basic cognitive abilities are built into humans' neural architecture. Children's theory of mind progresses gradually as they learn about desires, emotions, beliefs, and then false beliefs.

11.10 According to Kohlberg, moral reasoning progresses through six stages that are related to age and determined by cognitive development. Age-related progress in moral reasoning has been found in research, although a great deal of overlap occurs between adjacent stages, and Kohlberg's theory is more culture-specific than he realized.

The Transition of Adolescence

KEY LEARNING GOALS

11.11 Review the physiological changes of puberty, and discuss the ramifications of early versus late maturation.

11.12 Summarize research on neural development in adolescence and the Featured Study on adolescent risk taking.

11.13 Discuss some common patterns of identity formation in adolescence.

11.14 Articulate the chief characteristics of emerging adulthood as described by Arnett.

Adolescence is a transitional period between childhood and adulthood. Its age boundaries are not exact. In our society adolescence is thought to begin around age 13 and end at about age 21–22. Most contemporary societies have at least a brief period of adolescence. However, it has *not* been universal historically or across cultures (Larson & Wilson, 2004; Schlegel & Barry, 1991). In fact, in some societies young people used to move directly from childhood to adulthood. Let's begin our discussion of adolescent development with its most visible aspect: the physical changes that transform the body of a child into that of an adult.

Physiological Changes

Recall for a moment your junior high school days. Didn't it seem that your body grew so fast about this time that your clothes just couldn't "keep up"? This phase of rapid growth in height and weight is called the *adolescent growth spurt.* Brought on by hormonal changes, it typically starts at about 10 years of age in girls and about two years later in boys (Archibald, Graber, & Brooks-Dunn, 2003).

The term ***pubescence* is used to describe the two-year span preceding puberty during which the changes leading to physical and sexual maturity take place.** In addition to growing taller and heavier during pubescence, children begin to develop the physical features that characterize adults of their respective sexes. These features are termed ***secondary sex characteristics*—physical features that distinguish one sex from the other but that are not essential for reproduction.** For example, males go through a voice change, develop facial hair, and experience greater skeletal and muscle growth in the upper torso, leading to broader shoulders (see **Figure 11.15** on the next page). Females experience breast growth and a widening of the pelvic bones plus increased fat deposits in this area, resulting in wider hips (Susman & Rogol, 2004).

Note, however, that the capacity to reproduce is not attained in pubescence. This comes later. ***Puberty* is the stage during which sexual functions**

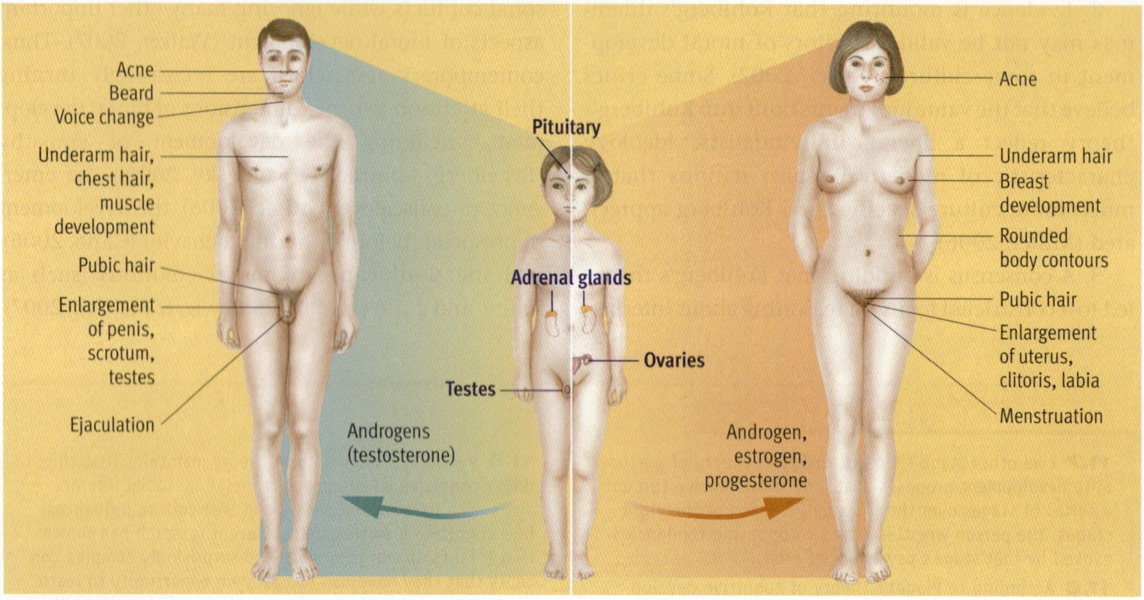

© Cengage Learning 2013

Figure 11.15

Physical development at puberty. Hormonal changes during puberty lead not only to a growth spurt but also to the development of secondary sex characteristics. The pituitary gland sends signals to the adrenal glands and gonads (ovaries and testes), which secrete hormones responsible for various physical changes that differentiate males and females.

reach maturity, which marks the beginning of adolescence. It is during puberty that the ***primary sex characteristics*—the structures necessary for reproduction**—develop fully. In the male, these include the testes, penis, and related internal structures. In the female they include the ovaries, vagina, uterus, and other internal structures.

In females, the onset of puberty is typically signaled by ***menarche*—the first occurrence of menstruation,** which reflects a series of hormonal changes (Pinyerd & Zipf, 2005). American girls typically reach menarche at ages 12–13, with further sexual maturation continuing until approximately age 16 (Susman, Dorn, & Schiefelbein, 2003). American boys typically experience ***spermarche*—the first occurrence of ejaculation**—at ages 13–14, with further sexual maturation continuing until approximately 18 (Archibald et al., 2003).

© AVAVA/Shutterstock

Interestingly, *generational* changes have occurred in the timing of puberty over the last 150 years. Today's adolescents begin puberty at a younger age, and complete it more rapidly, than their counterparts in earlier generations (Bellis, Downing, & Ashton, 2006). This trend appears to be occurring in both sexes, although more precise data are available for females, as the marker for puberty (menarche) is more readily apparent in females (Herman-Giddens, 2006). The reasons for this trend are the subject of debate. It seems likely that a number of factors have contributed (Archibald et al., 2003; Bellis et al. 2006). The most obvious potential causes are widespread improvements in nutrition and medical care. This factor would probably explain why the trend toward younger puberty has been limited to modern, "developed" countries.

The timing of puberty varies from one adolescent to the next over a range of about 5 years (ages 10–15 for girls, 11–16 for boys). Generally, *girls who mature early and boys who mature late seem to experience more subjective distress and emotional difficulty with the transition to adolescence* (Susman et al., 2003). However, in both males and females, early maturation is associated with greater use of alcohol and drugs, more high-risk behavior, greater aggression, and more delinquency (Lynne et al., 2007; Steinberg & Morris, 2001). Among females, early maturation is also correlated with earlier experience of intercourse, more unwanted pregnancies, a greater risk for eating problems, and a variety of psychological disorders (Archibald et al., 2003). Thus, we might speculate that early maturation often thrusts both sexes (but especially females) toward the adult world too soon.

Neural Development

Recent years have brought significant advances in the study of adolescents' neural development (Giedd, 2008; McAnarney, 2008). It was widely assumed until recently that the brain does not undergo much development after middle childhood. However, the emergence of MRI scans, which can provide really clear images of the brain, has permitted neuroscientists to conduct entirely new investigations of whether age-related changes occur in brain structure. These studies have uncovered some interesting developmental trends during adolescence. For example, the volume of white matter in the brain grows throughout adolescence (Blakemore, 2008). This means that *neurons are becoming better insulated with thicker myelin sheaths* (see Chapter 3). This presumably leads to enhanced conductivity and connectivity in the brain. In contrast, gray matter decreases in volume (Toga, Thompson, & Sowell, 2006). This finding is thought to reflect the process of *synaptic pruning*—the elimination of less-active synapses—which plays a key role in the formation of neural networks (see Chapter 3).

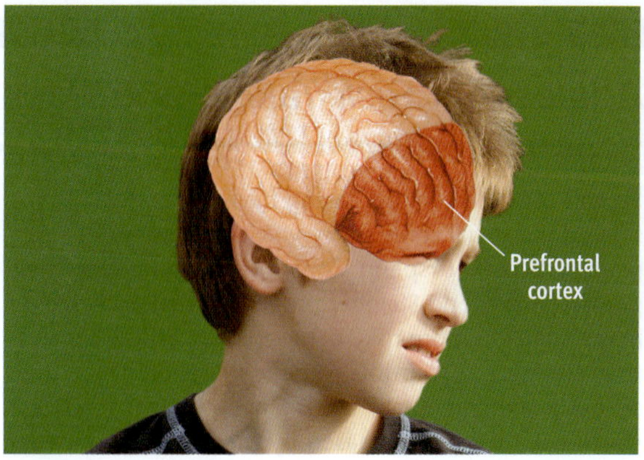

© Cengage Learning 2013; photo: © RimDream/Shutterstock

Figure 11.16

The prefrontal cortex. Recent research suggests that neural development continues throughout adolescence. Moreover, the chief site for much of this development is the prefrontal cortex, which appears to be the last area of the brain to mature fully. This discovery may have fascinating implications for understanding the adolescent brain, as the prefrontal cortex appears to play a key role in emotional regulation and self-control.

Perhaps the most interesting discovery about the adolescent brain has been that increased myelinization and synaptic pruning are most pronounced in the *prefrontal cortex* (see **Figure 11.16**; Blakemore, 2008). Thus, *the prefrontal cortex appears to be the last area of the brain to fully mature*. This maturation may not be complete until one's mid-20s (Gogtay et al., 2004). Much has been made of this finding because the prefrontal cortex has been characterized as the "executive control center" of the brain. It is crucial to high-level cognitive functions, such as planning, organizing, emotional regulation, and response inhibition (Casey et al., 2005). Theorists have suggested that the immaturity of the prefrontal cortex may explain why risky behavior (such as reckless driving, experimentation with drugs, dangerous stunts, binge drinking, unprotected sex, and so forth) peaks during adolescence and then declines in adulthood (Compas, 2004; Steinberg, 2008).

That said, Kuhn (2006) notes that media pundits have gotten carried away, blaming the immaturity of the adolescent prefrontal cortex for "just about everything about teens that adults have found perplexing" (p. 59). Other factors also contribute to risky behavior during adolescence. One of these factors may be susceptibility to peer influence (Steinberg, 2007), which brings us to our Featured Study for this chapter.

ZITS © 2008 ZITS Partnership King Features Syndicate

FEATURED STUDY

Adolescent Risk Taking and Peer Influence

SOURCE: Gardner, M., & Steinberg, L. (2005). Peer influence on risk taking, risk preference, and risky decision making in adolescence and adulthood: An experimental study. *Developmental Psychology, 41*, 625–635.

Studies of adolescent risk taking have not generally considered the social contexts in which risky behavior takes place. Adolescents spend a great deal of time with their peers. Gardner and Steinberg speculate that adolescents may engage in more risky behavior than adults because they are more susceptible to peer influence. Thus, they set out to experimentally test the hypothesis that adolescents' risk taking is increased by the presence of peers more that adults' risk taking is.

Method

Participants. The sample consisted of three age groups: 106 adolescents ages 13 to 16, 105 young adults ages 18 to 22, and 95 adults ages 24 or older. The gender ratio in each group was very close to 50-50, and the groups were similar in ethnic composition.

Procedure. The participants were asked to invite two same-sex friends to the experimental sessions. These groups of three were then randomly assigned to conditions in which the participant worked alone (the friends were asked to wait outside the room) or with friends present (the friends stayed in the experimental room where they could offer advice and encouragement).

Measures. The participants responded to a couple of questionnaires about risk preferences, but the main dependent variable was their performance in a video game played on a computer. The game involved a simulated driving task in which participants had to make quick decisions "on the fly" about crash risks at yellow lights while trying to accumulate points by moving a car as far as possible. There were 15 trials. The computer recorded the amount of time that the car continued to move after a yellow light, stops and restarts, and the number of crashes.

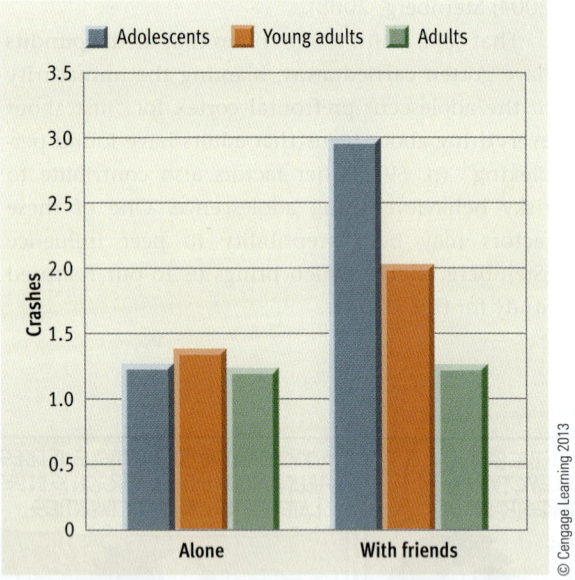

Figure 11.17

Peer influence on risk taking. In the study by Gardner and Steinberg (2005), one key dependent variable, which indexed participants' risk taking, was the number of crashes experienced. As you can see, the presence of peers increased risk taking by young adults moderately and by adolescents considerably. In contrast, adults' risk taking was the same whether alone or with peers. These findings suggest that susceptibility to peer influence may increase risky behavior among adolescents and young adults.

SOURCE: Adapted from Steinberg, L. (2007). Risk taking in adolescence: New perspectives from brain and behavioral science. *Current Directions in Psychological Science, 16*, 55–59. Copyright © 2007 Sage Publications. Reprinted by permission of SAGE Publications.

Results

The data on crashes showed that the presence of peers increased risk taking considerably in the adolescent group, and moderately in the young adult group. In contrast, risk taking was not elevated by the presence of peers in the adult group (see **Figure 11.17**). The data on the other measures of risk taking generally followed the same pattern.

Discussion

As hypothesized, the results suggest that susceptibility to peer influence may be a key factor contributing to the greater risk taking seen in adolescents as opposed to adults. The authors conclude "For reasons not yet understood, the presence of peers makes adolescents and youth, but not adults, more likely to take risks" (p. 634).

Comment

This study was featured in part to counterbalance the notion that everything about adolescent behavior can be explained in terms of the late maturation of the prefrontal cortex. The research relating adolescent neurological development to risk taking is impressive and convincing, but focusing exclusively on the adolescent brain is a classic example of single-cause thinking. As we have seen repeatedly, most aspects of behavior are not that simple—multifactorial causation is the rule.

The Search for Identity

PSYKTREK 9b

Erik Erikson was especially interested in personality development during adolescence, which is the fifth of the eight major life stages he described (consult **Figure 11.8** on page 444). According to Erikson (1968), the premier challenge of adolescence is the struggle to form a clear sense of identity. This struggle involves working out a stable concept of oneself as a unique individual and embracing an ideology or system of values that provides a sense of direction. In Erikson's view, adolescents grapple with questions such as "Who am I, and where am I going in life?"

Erikson recognized that the process of identity formation often extends beyond adolescence. In fact, his own life illustrates this (Coles, 1970; Roazen, 1976). During adolescence, Erikson began to resist family pressures to study medicine. Instead, he wandered about Europe until he was 25, trying to "find himself" as an artist. His interest in psychoanalysis was sparked by an introduction to Sigmund Freud's youngest daughter, Anna, a pioneer of child psychoanalysis. After his psychoanalytic training, he moved to the United States. When he became a naturalized citizen in 1939, he changed his surname from Homburger to Erikson. Clearly, Erikson was struggling with the question of "Who am I?" well into adulthood. Small wonder, then, that he focused a great deal of attention on identity formation.

The struggle for a sense of identity can definitely extend well into adulthood. It does, however, tend to be especially intense during adolescence. Adolescents deal with identity formation in a variety of ways. According to James Marcia (1966, 1980, 1994), the presence or absence of a sense of commitment (to life goals and values) and a sense of crisis (active questioning and exploration) can combine to produce four different *identity statuses* (see **Figure 11.18**). In order of increasing maturity, Marcia's four identity statuses begin with *identity diffusion,* a state of apathy, with no commitment to an ideology. *Identity foreclosure* is a premature commitment to visions, values, and roles—typically those prescribed by one's parents. An *identity moratorium* involves delaying commitment for a while to experiment with alternative ideologies and careers. *Identity achievement* involves arriving at a sense of self and direction after thinking through alternative possibilities. Identity achievement is associated with higher self-esteem, conscientiousness, security, achievement motivation, and capacity for intimacy (Kroger, 2003).

There is a long running debate about whether Marcia's identity statuses should be viewed as stages that people pass through or as stable individual dispositions. A recent large-scale, longitudinal study found evidence to support both positions (Meeus et al., 2010). On the one hand, 63% of the sample showed the same identity status in all five annual assessments. That finding suggests that identity status is a relatively stable trait. On the other hand, the transitions that were seen in the remainder of the sample were mostly "progressive" shifts to a more mature status. This finding provides some support for the notion that identity statuses represent stages that individuals move through. Consistent with a stage view, the data also revealed that people tend to reach identity achievement at later ages than originally envisioned by Marcia. By late adolescence, only 22%–26% of the sample had reached identity achievement. Thus, the struggle for a sense of identity routinely extends into young adulthood.

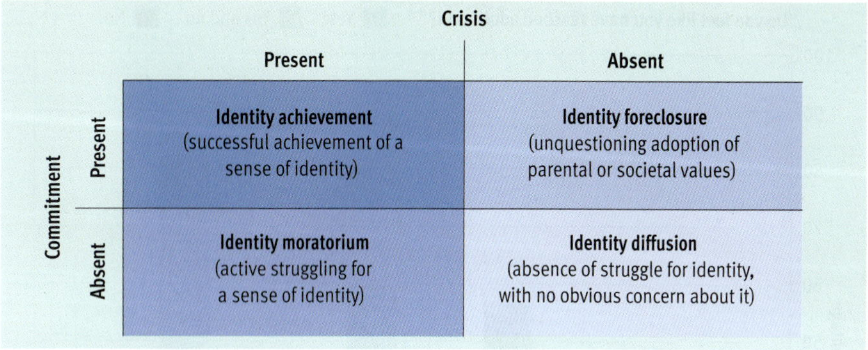

© Cengage Learning 2013

Figure 11.18
Marcia's four identity statuses. According to Marcia (1980), the occurrence of identity crisis and the development of personal commitments can combine into four possible identity statuses, as shown in this diagram. The progressively darker shades of blue signify progressively more mature identity statuses.

SOURCE: Adapted from Marcia, J. E. (1980). Identity in adolescence. In J. Adelson (Ed.), *Handbook of adolescent psychology* (pp. 159–210). New York: John Wiley. Copyright © 1980 by John Wiley & Sons. Adapted by permission of John Wiley & Sons.

Emerging Adulthood as a New Developmental Stage

The finding that the search for identity often extends into adulthood is one of many considerations that has led Jeffrey Arnett to make the radical claim that we ought to recognize the existence of a new developmental stage in modern societies. He has named this stage *emerging adulthood.* According to Arnett (2000, 2004, 2006), the years between age 18 and 25 (roughly) have become a distinct, new transitional stage of life. He attributes the rise of this new developmental period to a variety of demographic trends. For example, more people are delaying marriage and parenthood until their late 20s or early 30s. More people stay in school for lengthier periods. There are also more barriers to financial independence. "What is different today," he says, "is that experiencing the period from the late teens through the mid-20s as a time of exploration and instability is now the norm" (Arnett, 2006, p. 4).

Arnett (2000, 2006) maintains that emerging adulthood is marked by a number of distinct features. A central feature is the subjective feeling that one is in between adolescence and adulthood. When 18- to 25-year-olds are asked, "Do you feel like you have reached adulthood?" most say "Yes and no" (see **Figure 11.19** on the next page). They don't feel like adolescents. However, most don't see themselves as adults either. Another feature of emerging adulthood is that it is an age of possibilities. It tends to be a time of great optimism about one's personal future. A third aspect of emerging adulthood is that it's a self-focused time of life. People in this period tend to be unfettered by duties, commitments, and social obligations. This gives them unusual autonomy and freedom to explore new options. Finally, Arnett has found that to a surprising degree emerging adulthood is a period of identity formation. The search for identity has traditionally been viewed as an adolescent phenomenon. But Arnett's research indicates that identity formation continues to be a crucial issue for most young adults. Arnett's theory

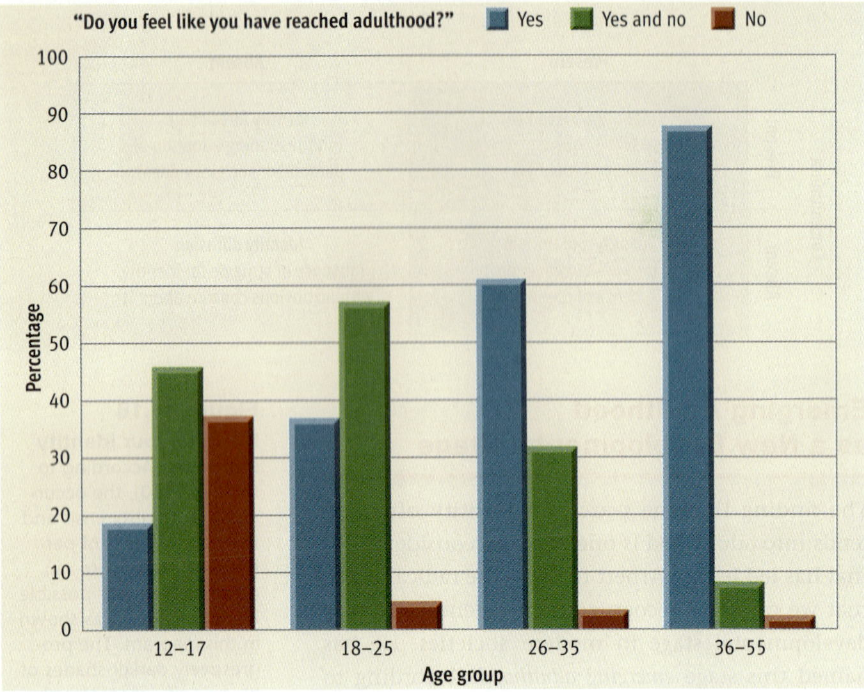

© Cengage Learning 2013

Figure 11.19

Emerging adulthood as a phase in between adolescence and adulthood. Arnett (2006) characterizes emerging adulthood as an "age of feeling in-between." This characterization comes from a study in which he asked participants of various ages "Do you feel like you have reached adulthood?" As you can see in the data shown here, the dominant response in the 18–25 age group was an ambivalent "Yes and no," but it shifted to predominantly "Yes" in the 26–35 age group.

SOURCE: Arnett, J. J. (2006). Emerging adulthood: Understanding the new way of coming of age. In J. J. Arnett & J. L. Tanner (Eds.), *Emerging adults in America: Coming of age in the 21st century* (p. 11). Washington, DC: American Psychological Association. Copyright © 2006 by the American Psychological Association. Reprinted by permission of the author.

has inspired a good deal of research on the dynamics and developmental significance of emerging adulthood (Aquilino, 2006; Côté, 2006; Labouvie-Vief, 2006; Tanner, 2006).

REVIEW OF KEY LEARNING GOALS

11.11 The growth spurt at puberty is a prominent event involving the development of reproductive maturity and secondary sex characteristics. Generational changes have been seen in the timing of puberty. Girls who mature early and boys who mature late experience more subjective distress, but early sexual maturation is associated with more behavioral problems for both sexes.

11.12 During adolescence, neurons are becoming more myelinated. At the same time, synaptic pruning continues to sculpt neural networks. The prefrontal cortex, which has been characterized as an executive control center, appears to be the last area of the brain to mature fully. This reality may contribute to adolescent risk taking. However, our Featured Study showed that other factors, such as peer influence, also affect risky behavior.

11.13 According to Erikson, the key challenge of adolescence is to make some progress toward a sense of identity. Marcia identified four patterns of identity formation: foreclosure, moratorium, identity diffusion, and identity achievement. Research suggests that these identity statuses are both stable dispositions and stages that people progress through.

11.14 Arnett argues that we ought to recognize the existence of a new developmental stage in modern societies, which he has christened emerging adulthood. Central features of this stage include feeling in between adolescence and adulthood, optimism, self-focus, and continued identity formation.

KEY LEARNING GOALS

11.15 Discuss the stability of personality in adulthood, and outline Erikson's stages of adult development.

11.16 Trace typical transitions in family relations during the adult years.

11.17 Summarize the physical changes associated with aging.

11.18 Review information on the onset, symptoms, and causes of Alzheimer's disease.

11.19 Analyze how intelligence, memory, and mental speed change in later adulthood.

The Expanse of Adulthood

The concept of development was once associated almost exclusively with childhood and adolescence. Today, however, development is widely recognized as a lifelong journey. Interestingly, patterns of development during the adult years are becoming increasingly diverse. The boundaries between young, middle, and late adulthood are becoming blurred as more and more people have children later than one is "supposed" to, retire earlier than one is "supposed" to, and so forth. In the upcoming pages, we'll look at some of the major developmental transitions in adult life. As we do, you should bear in mind that in adulthood (even more so than childhood or adolescence) there are many divergent pathways and timetables.

Personality Development

9b PSYKTREK

In recent years, research on adult personality development has been dominated by one key question: How stable is personality over the life span? We'll look at this issue and Erikson's view of adulthood in our discussion of personality development in the adult years.

The Question of Stability

How common are significant personality changes in adulthood? Is a grouchy 20-year-old going to be a grouchy 40-year-old and a grouchy 65-year-old? After tracking subjects through adulthood, many researchers have been impressed by the amount of change observed (Helson, Jones, & Kwan, 2002; Whitbourne et al., 1992). For example, Roger Gould (1975) concluded that "the evolution of a personality continues through the fifth decade of life." In contrast, many other researchers have concluded that personality tends to be quite stable over periods of 20 to 40 years (Caspi & Herbener, 1990; Costa & McCrae, 1994, 1997). A review of 150 relevant studies, involving almost 50,000 participants, concluded that personality in early adulthood is a good predictor of personality in late adulthood (Roberts & DelVecchio, 2000).

Clearly, researchers assessing the stability of personality in adulthood have reached very different conclusions. How can these contradictory conclusions be reconciled? It appears that *both* conclusions are accurate. They just reflect different ways of looking at the data (Bertrand & Lachman, 2003). Recall from Chapter 9 that psychological test scores are *relative* measures. They show how one scores *relative to other people.* Raw scores are converted into *percentile scores* that indicate the precise degree to which one is above or below average on a particular trait. The data indicate that these percentile scores tend to be remarkably stable over lengthy spans of time. That is, people's relative standing doesn't tend to change much (Roberts, Wood, & Caspi, 2008; Kandler et al., 2010).

However, if we examine participants' raw scores, we can see meaningful developmental trends. For example, adults' mean raw scores on extraversion, neuroticism, and openness to experience tend to decline moderately with increasing age, while measures of agreeableness and conscientiousness tend to increase (Bertrand & Lachman, 2003; Caspi, Roberts, & Shiner, 2005; see **Figure 11.20**). Recent research with a nationally representative sample found that self-esteem tends to increase slowly from early adulthood through middle age, peaking at about age 60 (Orth, Trzesniewski, & Robins, 2010). After age 60, self-esteem tends to gradually decline. Women and men tend to show similar trajectories, although women score slightly lower in self-esteem across most of the life span. In sum, it appears that personality in adulthood is characterized by *both* stability and change.

PSYKTREK 9b

Erikson's View of Adulthood

Insofar as personality changes during the adult years, Erik Erikson's (1963) theory offers some clues about the nature of changes people can expect. In his eight-stage model of development over the life span, Erikson divided adulthood into three stages (see again **Figure 11.8** on page 444). In the *early adulthood* stage called *intimacy versus isolation,* the key concern is whether one can develop the capacity to share intimacy with others. Successful resolution of the challenges in this stage should promote empathy and openness. In *middle adulthood,* the psychosocial crisis pits *generativity versus self-absorption.* The key challenge is to acquire a genuine concern for the welfare of future generations, which results in providing unselfish guidance to younger people and concern with one's legacy. During the *late adulthood* stage called *integrity versus despair,* the challenge is to avoid the tendency to dwell on the mistakes of the past and on one's imminent death. People need to find meaning and satisfaction in their lives, rather than wallow in bitterness and resentment. Empirical research on the adult stages in Erikson's theory has been sparse, but generally supportive of the theory. For example, researchers have found that generativity increases between young adulthood and middle age, as Erikson's theory predicts (de St. Aubin, McAdams, & Kim, 2004; Stewart, Ostrove, & Helson, 2001).

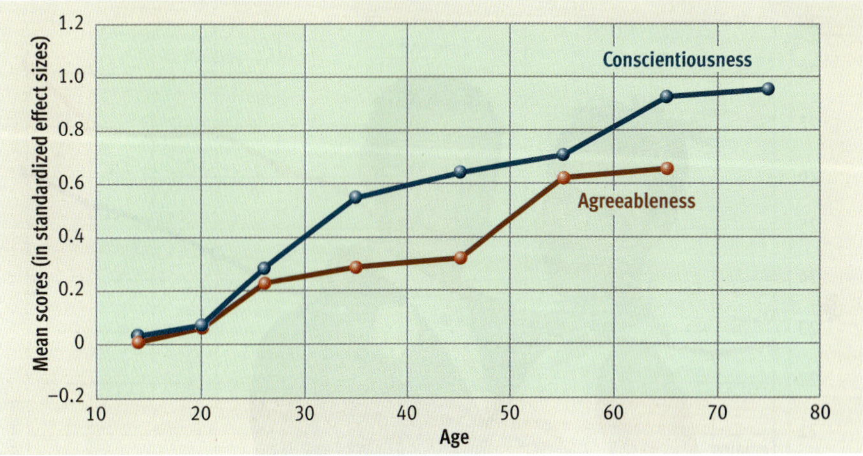

Figure 11.20

Examples of personality trends in the adult years. According to Brent Roberts and Daniel Mroczek (2008), when researchers examine participants' mean raw scores on personality measures, they find meaningful trends over the decades of adulthood. The trends for two specific traits—agreeableness and conscientiousness—are shown here as examples. Using subjects' test scores in adolescence as a baseline, you can see how measures of agreeableness and conscientiousness increase substantially over the decades.

SOURCE: Roberts, B. W., & Mroczek, D. (2008). Personality trait change in adulthood. *Current Directions in Psychological Science, 17,* 31–35. Copyright © 2008 Sage Publications. Reprinted by permission of SAGE Publications.

Transitions in Family Life

Many of the important transitions in adulthood involve changes in family responsibilities and relationships. Nearly everyone emerges from a family. Most people also go on to form their own families. However, the transitional period during which young adults are "between families" until they form a new family is being prolonged for more and more people. The percentage of young adults who are postponing marriage until their late twenties or early thirties has risen dramatically (see **Figure 11.21** on the next page). This trend is probably the result of a number of factors. Chief among them are the availability of new career options for women, increased educational requirements in the world of work, and increased emphasis on personal autonomy. Nonetheless, over 90% of adults in the U.S. eventually marry.

Adjusting to Marriage

Most new couples are pretty happy, but 8%–14% of newlyweds score in the distressed range on measures of marital satisfaction, with the most commonly reported problems being difficulties balancing work and marriage and financial concerns (Schramm et al., 2005). You might guess that partners who cohabit prior to getting married have an easier transition and greater marital success. However, until recently research demonstrated otherwise, as studies found an association between premarital cohabitation and increased divorce rates (Bumpass & Lu, 2000; Cohan & Kleinbaum, 2002;

Reality CHECK

Misconception

Most people go through a midlife crisis around the age of 40.

Reality

Fabled though it may be, the midlife crisis does not appear to be a normal developmental transition. Research suggests that only a tiny minority of people (2%–5%) go through a midlife crisis (Chiriboga, 1989; McCrae & Costa, 1990).

© Cengage Learning 2013

Figure 11.21
Median age at first marriage. The median age at which people in the United States marry for the first time has been creeping up for both males and females since the mid-1960s. This trend indicates that more people are postponing marriage. (Data from the U.S. Bureau of the Census)

Teachman, 2003). Theorists speculated that people inclined to cohabit were less traditional, more individualistic, with a weaker commitment to the institution of marriage. However, in recent years the findings on the effects of cohabitation have become less consistent (de Vaus, Qu, & Weston, 2005; Liefbroer & Dourleijn, 2006). One reason may be that cohabitation prior to marriage has gradually become the norm rather than the exception. In the 1970s only about 10% of couples lived together before marriage, but by the 1990s that figure had risen to 60% (Tach & Halpern-Meekin, 2009). The findings of a recent, large-scale study in Australia that looked at trends over decades (from 1945 to 2000) suggest that the impact of cohabitation may be changing (Hewitt & de Vaus, 2009). Cohabitants had higher rates of marital dissolution up through 1988, but then the trend started to gradually reverse itself, with cohabitants showing lower rates of divorce. More data are needed, but changes in the composition of the population of people who cohabit may be altering the effect of cohabitation on marital stability.

One major source of conflict in many new marriages is the negotiation of marital roles in relation to career commitments. More and more women are aspiring to demanding careers. However, research shows that husbands' careers continue to take priority over their wives' career ambitions (Cha, 2010; Haas, 1999). Moreover, many husbands maintain traditional role expectations about housework, child care, and decision making. Men's contribution to housework has increased noticeably since the 1960s, as shown in **Figure 11.22**. However, studies indicate that wives are still doing the bulk of the household chores in the United States and all over the world, even when they work outside the home (Greenstein, 2009; Sayer, 2005). Nonetheless, most wives do not view their division of labor as unfair (Braun et al., 2008) because most women don't expect a 50-50 split (Coltrane, 2001).

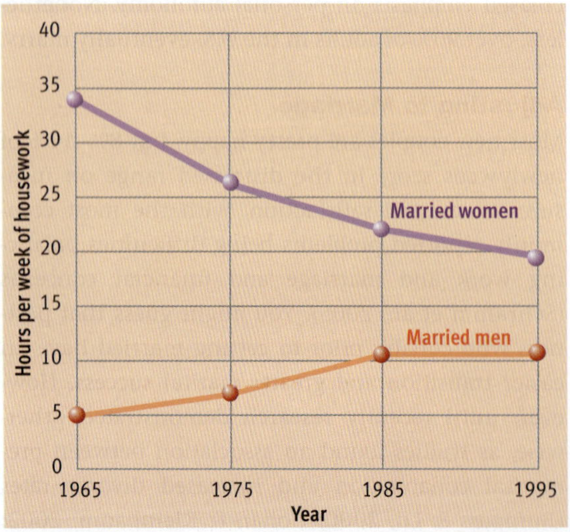

© Cengage Learning 2013

Figure 11.22
Housework trends since the 1960s. As these data show, the housework gap between husbands and wives has narrowed since the 1960s. Married men have more than doubled their housework, but it is the large reduction in wives' housework that has really shrunk the housework gap. (Data from Bianchi et al., 2000)

Adjusting to Parenthood

Although an increasing number of people are choosing to remain childless, the vast majority of married couples continue to have children. Most couples are happy with their decision to have children. The arrival of the first child, however, represents a major transition. The disruption of routines can be emotionally draining (Bost et al., 2002). The transition to parenthood tends to have more impact on mothers than fathers (Nomaguchi & Milkie, 2003). The transition is more difficult when a wife's expectations of how much the father will be involved in child care are not met (Fox, Bruce, & Combs-Orme, 2000). A review of decades of research on parenthood and marital satisfaction found that (1) parents exhibit lower marital satisfaction than comparable nonparents, (2) mothers of infants report the steepest decline in marital satisfaction, and (3) the more children couples have, the lower their marital satisfaction tends to be (Twenge, Campbell, & Foster, 2003). Consistent with these trends, a recent longitudinal study found that the transition to parenthood was associated with a sudden deterioration in relationship quality (Doss et al., 2009). The decline in marital satisfaction tended to be small to medium in size. Ironically, the more satisfied couples were prior to birth of their first child, the more their marital satisfaction declined.

Crisis during the transition to first parenthood is far

from universal, however (Cox et al., 1999). Couples who have high levels of affection and commitment prior to the first child's birth are likely to maintain a stable level of satisfaction after the birth (Shapiro, Gottman, & Carrère, 2000). The key to making this transition less stressful may be to have *realistic expectations* about parental responsibilities (Belsky & Kelly, 1994).

As children grow up, parental influence over them tends to decline. As this happens, the early years of parenting—that once seemed so difficult—are often recalled with fondness. When youngsters reach adolescence and seek to establish their own identities, gradual realignments occur in parent-child relationships. On the one hand, these relations generally are not as bitter or contentious as widely assumed (Laursen, Coy, & Collins, 1998). On the other hand, adolescents do spend less time in family activities. Their closeness to their parents also declines while conflicts become more frequent (Smetana, Campione-Barr, & Metzger, 2006). The conflicts tend to involve everyday matters (chores and appearance) more than substantive issues (sex and drugs) (Collins & Laursen, 2006).

Adjusting to the Empty Nest

When parents get all their children launched into the adult world, they find themselves faced with an "empty nest." This period was formerly thought to be a difficult transition for many parents, especially mothers who were familiar only with the maternal role. In recent decades, however, more women have experience with other roles outside the home. Hence, evidence suggests that most parents adjust effectively to the empty nest transition (Umberson et al., 2005). For example, one recent study that followed a group of women for 18 years reported that the transition to an empty nest was associated with a clear increase in wives' marital satisfaction (Gorchoff, John, & Helson, 2008). The improvement in marital satisfaction appeared to be due primarily to an increase in the women's enjoyment of their time with their husbands.

Aging and Physiological Changes

People obviously experience many physical changes as they progress through adulthood. In both sexes, hair tends to thin out and become gray. Many males also confront receding hairlines and baldness. To the dismay of many, the proportion of body fat tends to increase with age, while the amount of muscle tissue decreases. Overall, weight tends to increase in most adults through the mid-50s. Then a gradual decline may begin. These changes have little functional significance. In our youth-oriented society, however, they often have a negative impact on self-concept. Many older people begin to view themselves as less attractive (Aldwin & Gilmer, 2004).

Curiously though, when elderly people are asked how old they feel, they mostly report feeling quite a bit younger than they actually are. For instance, in a study of people over the age of 70, on average the subjects reported that they felt 13 years younger than their chronological age (Kleinspehn-Ammerlahn, Kotter-Gruhn, & Smith, 2008). Obviously, there is some wishful thinking at work here, but it appears to be beneficial. Evidence suggests that feeling younger than one's real age is associated with better health and cognitive functioning and reduced mortality risk (Kotter-Gruhn et al., 2009).

In the sensory domain, the key developmental changes occur in vision and hearing. The proportion of people with 20/20 visual acuity declines with age. Farsightedness and difficulty seeing in low illumination become more common (Schieber, 2006). Sensitivity to color and contrast is also reduced (Fozard & Gordon-Salant, 2001). Hearing sensitivity begins declining gradually in early adulthood. It usually isn't noticeable until after age 50, however. Hearing loss tends to be greater in men than in women and for high-frequency sounds more than low-frequency sounds (Yost, 2000). Even mild hearing loss can undermine speech perception. Such loss puts an added burden on cognitive processing (Wingfield, Tun, & McCoy, 2005). These sensory losses would be more problematic, but in modern society they can usually be partially compensated for with eyeglasses, contacts, and hearing aids.

Age-related changes also occur in hormonal functioning during adulthood. Among women, these changes lead to *menopause*. This ending of menstrual periods, accompanied by a loss of fertility, typically occurs at around age 50 (Grady, 2006). Most women experience at least some unpleasant symptoms. Hot flashes, headaches, night sweats, mood changes, sleep difficulties, and reduced sex drive are all symptoms of menopause. However, the amount of discomfort from these symptoms varies considerably (Grady, 2006; Williams et al., 2007). Menopause is also accompanied by an elevated vulnerability to depression (Deecher et al., 2008). Not long ago, menopause was thought to be almost universally accompanied by severe emotional strain. However, it's now clear that most women experience relatively modest psychological distress (George, 2002; Walter, 2000).

Aging and Neural Changes

The amount of brain tissue and the brain's weight decline gradually in late adulthood, mostly after age 60 (Victoroff, 2005). These trends appear to reflect both a decrease in the number of active neurons in some

Reality CHECK

Misconception

Children are a key ingredient of marital bliss.

Reality

Children can be a source of great joy, but they also are a source of considerable stress. Although other factors are also at work, studies show that marital satisfaction generally declines after the arrival of children and often increases after grown children leave home.

areas of the brain and shrinkage of still-active neurons. Neuron loss is perhaps less important than once believed (Albert & Killiany, 2001). Although this gradual loss of brain tissue sounds alarming, it's a normal part of the aging process. Its functional significance is the subject of some debate, but it doesn't appear to be a key factor in any of the age-related dementias. **A *dementia* is an abnormal condition marked by multiple cognitive deficits that include memory impairment.** Dementia can be caused by quite a variety of diseases, such as Alzheimer's disease, Parkinson's disease, Huntington's disease, and AIDS, to name just a few. The prevalence of many of these diseases increases with age. Thus, dementia is seen in about 5%–8% of people ages 65–70, and 15%–20% of those ages 75–80 (Richards & Sweet, 2009). However, it's important to emphasize that dementia and "senility" are not part of the normal aging process. As Cavanaugh (1993) notes, "The term *senility* has no valid medical or psychological meaning, and its continued use simply perpetuates the myth that drastic mental decline is a product of normal aging" (p. 85).

Alzheimer's disease (AD) accounts for roughly 70% of all cases of dementia (Albert, 2008). The prevalence of Alzheimer's disease increases dramatically after age 75. Alzheimer's patients exhibit profound and widespread loss of neurons and brain tissue and the accumulation of characteristic neural abnormalities known as neuritic plaques and neurofibrillary tangles (Haroutunian & Davis, 2003). In the early stages of the disease, this damage is largely centered in the hippocampal region, which is known to play a crucial role in many facets of memory. As the disease advances, it spreads throughout much of the brain (Bourgeois, Seaman, & Servis, 2008).

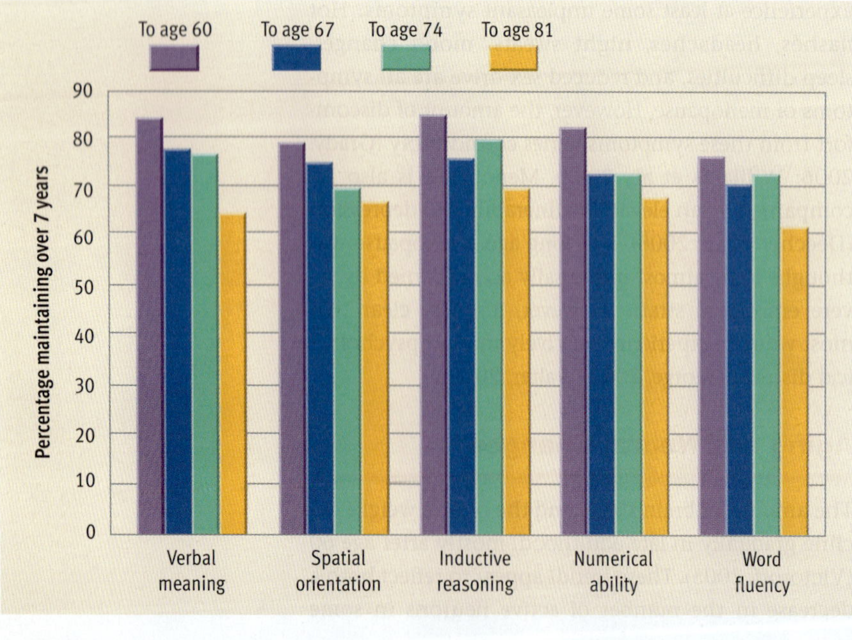

© Cengage Learning 2013

Figure 11.23
Age and the stability of primary mental abilities. In his longitudinal study of cognitive performance begun in 1956, Schaie (1983, 1993) has repeatedly assessed the five basic mental abilities listed along the bottom of this chart. The data graphed here show the percentage of subjects who maintained stable levels of performance on each ability through various ages up to age 81. As you can see, even through the age of 81, the majority of subjects show no significant decline on most abilities.

SOURCE: Adapted from Schaie, K. W. (1990). Intellectual development in adulthood. In J. E. Birren and K. W. Schaie (Eds.), *Handbook of the psychology of aging* (pp. 291–309). San Diego: Academic Press. Copyright © 1990 Elsevier Science (USA), reproduced with permission from the publisher.

Although Alzheimer's disease can strike during middle age, it usually emerges after age 65. The beginnings of AD are so subtle they are often recognized only after the disease has progressed for a year or two. The hallmark early symptom is forgetting of newly learned information after surprisingly brief periods of time (Albert & Killiany, 2001). Impairments of working memory, attention, and executive function (planning, staying on task) are also quite common (Storandt, 2008). Eventually, patients fail to recognize familiar people, become completely disoriented, and are unable to care for themselves. The course of the disease is one of steady deterioration. AD typically progresses over a period of eight to ten years before ending in death (Albert, 2008).

The causes that launch this debilitating neural meltdown are not well understood. Genetic factors clearly contribute (McQueen & Blacker, 2008). Their exact role, though, remains unclear (Bertram & Tanzi, 2008). Recent evidence also implicates chronic inflammation as a contributing factor (Heneka et al., 2010). Some "protective" factors that diminish vulnerability to Alzheimer's disease have been identified (Hertzog et al., 2009). For example, risk is reduced among those who engage in regular exercise (Radak et al., 2010) and those with lower cardiovascular risk factors, such as high blood pressure and high cholesterol (Qiu, De Ronchi, & Fratiglioni, 2010). Decreased vulnerability to AD is also associated with frequent participation in stimulating cognitive activities (Karp et al., 2009) and maintenance of active social engagement with friends and family (Krueger et al., 2009).

Aging and Cognitive Changes

The evidence indicates that general intelligence is fairly stable throughout most of adulthood, with a small decline in average test scores often seen after age 60 (Schaie, 1990, 1994, 1996, 2005). However, this seemingly simple assertion masks many complexities and needs to be qualified carefully. First, group averages can be deceptive in that mean scores can be dragged down by a small minority of people who show a decline. For example, when Schaie (1990) calculated the percentage of people who maintain stable performance on various abilities (see **Figure 11.23**), he found that about 80% showed no decline by age 60 and that about two-thirds were still stable through age 81. Second, some forms of intelligence are more vulnerable to aging than others. As noted in Chapter 9, many theorists distinguish between ***fluid intelligence*, which involves basic reasoning ability, memory capacity, and speed of information processing,** and ***crystallized intelligence*, which involves the ability to**

apply acquired knowledge and skills in problem solving. Research suggests that fluid intelligence is much more likely to decline with age, whereas crystallized intelligence tends to remain stable (Baltes, Staudinger, & Lindenberger, 1999; Horn & Hofer, 1992; Li et al., 2004).

What about memory? Numerous studies report decreases in older adults' memory capabilities (Hoyer & Verhaeghen, 2006). Most researchers maintain that the memory losses associated with normal aging tend to be moderate and are *not* experienced by everyone (Dixon & Cohen, 2003; Shimamura et al., 1995). However, Salthouse (2003, 2004) takes a much more pessimistic view, arguing that age-related decreases in memory are substantial in magnitude, that they begin in early adulthood, and that they affect everyone. One reason for these varied conclusions may be that a variety of memory types can be assessed (see Chapter 7 for a review of various systems of memory).

In the cognitive domain, aging seems to take its toll on *speed* first. Many studies indicate that speed in learning, solving problems, and processing information tends to decline with age (Salthouse, 1996). The evidence suggests that the erosion of processing speed may be a gradual, lengthy trend beginning in middle adulthood (see **Figure 11.24**). The general nature of this trend (across differing tasks) suggests that it may be the result of age-related changes in neurological functioning (Salthouse, 2000). Some theorists believe that diminished mental speed is the key factor underlying the age-related declines seen on many, varied cognitive tasks (Salthouse, 2005), although doubts have been raised about this conclusion (Hartley, 2006). Even though mental speed declines with age, problem-solving ability remains largely unimpaired if older people are given adequate time to compensate for their reduced speed.

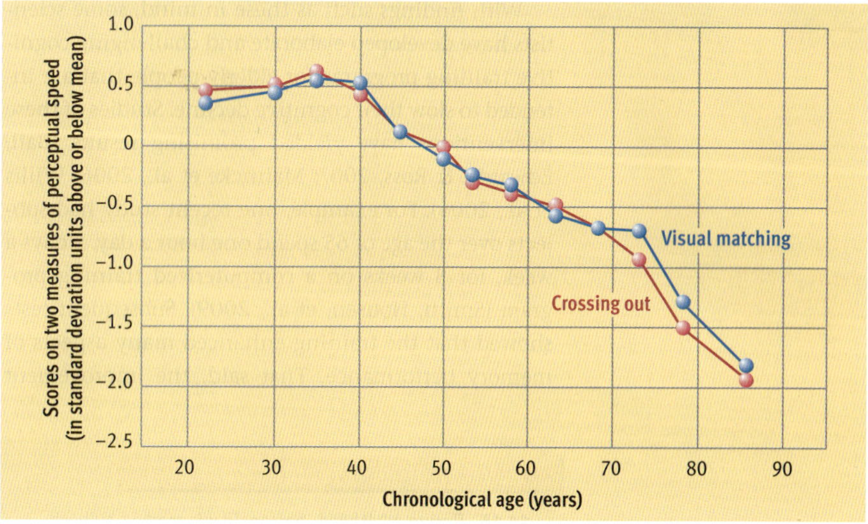

© Cengage Learning 2013

Figure 11.24

Age and mental speed. Many studies have found that mental speed decreases with age. The data shown here, from Salthouse (2000), are based on two perceptual speed tasks. The data points are means for large groups of subjects expressed in terms of how many standard deviations (see Chapter 2) they are above or below the mean for all ages (which is set at 0). Similar age-related declines are seen on many tasks that depend on mental speed.

SOURCE: Adapted from Salthouse, T. A. (2000). Aging and measures of processing speed. *Biological Psychology, 54,* 35–54. Copyright © 2000 Elsevier Science. Reproduced with permission from the publisher.

It should be emphasized that many people remain capable of great intellectual accomplishments well into their later years (Simonton, 1990, 1997). This fact was verified in a study of scholarly, scientific, and artistic productivity that examined lifelong patterns of work among 738 men who lived at least through the age of 79. Dennis (1966) found that the 40s decade was the most productive in most professions. However, productivity was remarkably stable through the 60s and even the 70s in many areas.

A hot issue in recent years has been whether high levels of mental activity in late adulthood can delay the typical age-related declines in cognitive functioning. This possibility is sometimes referred to as the "use it or lose it" hypothesis. Several lines of evidence seem to provide support for this notion. For example, people who continue to work further into old age, especially people who remain in mentally demanding jobs, tend to show smaller decrements in cognitive abilities than their age-mates (Bosma et al., 2002; Schooler, 2007). Other studies suggest that continuing to engage in intellectually challenging activities in late adulthood serves to buffer against cognitive declines (Kliegel, Zimprich, & Rott, 2004; Yaffe et al., 2009). For example, one recent study of 488 people between the ages of 75 and 85 found that participation in leisure activities (such as reading, writing, working crossword puzzles, and playing board games) was associated with a reduced decline in memory functioning (Hall et al., 2009).

Royalty Free/© Masterfile

With findings such as these in mind, some scientists have developed elaborate and challenging cognitive training programs for elderly people that are intended to slow their cognitive decline. Studies of these interventions have yielded promising results (Ball, Edwards, & Ross, 2007; Mahncke et al., 2006; Willis et al., 2006). For example, one recent study had subjects over the age of 65 spend one hour a day, 5 days a week, for 8 weeks on a computerized training program (Smith, Housen, et al., 2009). Subsequent tests showed that the training enhanced many aspects of memory performance. That said, the improvement was not dramatic, just 4%. Another intriguing study found that a memory training program led to measureable changes in the brain. Fourteen hours of training produced an increase in the density of dopamine receptors in two critical areas of the brain (McNab et al., 2009). These findings are intriguing, but the evidence on memory training in the elderly is a mixed bag, and there are skeptics (Papp, Walsh, & Snyder, 2009; Salthouse, 2006). It remains to be seen whether modest training effects can really diminish the negative effects of aging on cognitive functioning or delay the onset of Alzheimer's disease.

REVIEW OF KEY LEARNING GOALS

11.15 During adulthood, personality is marked by both stability and change, as percentile scores remain stable, but mean raw scores change in predictable ways. Agreeableness and conscientiousness tend to increase in the adult years, while extraversion and openness to experience tend to decline. Those who move successfully through the three stages of adulthood posited by Erikson should develop intimacy, generativity, and integrity.

11.16 Many landmarks in adult development involve transitions in family relationships. Premarital cohabitation used to be predictive of an increased likelihood of marital dissolution later, but the situation seems to be changing. Difficulty adjusting to marriage is more likely when spouses have different role expectations, especially about housework. The transition to parenthood can be stressful, but realistic expectations can help. For most parents, the empty nest transition no longer appears to be as difficult as it once was.

11.17 During adulthood, age-related physiological transitions include changes in appearance, sensory losses (especially in vision and hearing), and hormonal changes. Curiously, though, elderly people tend to feel younger than they are. Most women experience at least some unpleasant symptoms during menopause, but it is not as problematic as widely suggested.

11.18 Drastic mental decline is not a part of the normal aging process. However, the prevalence of dementia climbs from 5%–8% of people ages 65–70 to 15%–20% of those ages 75–80. Alzheimer's has a subtle onset marked by chronic forgetting of newly learned information, followed by a progressive deterioration over 8 to 10 years. The causes of this debilitating disease are not well understood, although genetic factors and chronic inflammation appear to contribute.

11.19 In the cognitive domain, general intelligence is fairly stable, with a small decline in average test scores seen after the age of 60. Fluid intelligence is more likely to decline, whereas crystallized intelligence often remains stable. Many studies have found decreases in older adults' memory capabilities. Mental speed declines in late adulthood, but many people remain productive well into old age. Some studies suggest that high levels of mental activity in late adulthood can delay the typical age-related declines in cognitive functioning.

CONCEPT CHECK 11.4

Identifying the Contributions of Major Theorists and Researchers

Check your recall of the principal ideas of important theorists and researchers covered in this chapter by matching the people listed on the left with the appropriate contributions described on the right. If you need help, the crucial pages describing each person's ideas are listed in parentheses. Fill in the letters for your choices in the spaces provided on the left. You'll find the answers in Appendix A.

Major Theorists and Researchers	Key Ideas and Contributions
______ 1. Mary Ainsworth (pp. 441–442)	a. This psychologist formulated a six-stage theory of moral development.
______ 2. John Bowlby (p. 441)	b. This Swiss scholar created a groundbreaking theory of cognitive development that described the sensorimotor, preoperational, concrete operational, and formal operational periods.
______ 3. Erik Erikson (pp. 443–444)	c. This person expanded on Freud's theory, describing eight stages of development that revolve around psychosocial crises.
______ 4. Harry Harlow (pp. 440–441)	d. This researcher found that attachments fall into three categories: secure, anxious-ambivalent, and avoidant.
______ 5. Lawrence Kohlberg (pp. 451–452)	e. This Russian scholar devised a sociocultural theory of cognitive development that emphasized how social interactions fuel development.
______ 6. Jean Piaget (pp. 445–448)	f. This attachment theorist argued that infants are biologically programmed to emit behaviors that trigger an affectionate response from adults.
______ 7. Lev Vygotsky (p. 449)	g. This individual's research with monkeys undermined the behavioral explanation of attachment.

Reflecting on the Chapter's Themes

KEY LEARNING GOALS

11.20 Identify the five unifying themes highlighted in this chapter.

Theoretical Diversity

Sociohistorical Context

Multifactorial Causation

Cultural Heritage

Heredity and Environment

Many of our seven integrative themes surfaced to some degree in our coverage of human development. We saw theoretical diversity in the discussions of attachment, cognitive development, and personality development. We saw that psychology evolves in a sociohistorical context, investigating complex, real-world issues. We encountered multifactorial causation of behavior in the development of temperament and attachment, among other things. We saw cultural invariance and cultural diversity in our examination of attachment, motor development, cognitive development, and moral development.

But above all else, we saw how heredity and environment jointly mold behavior. We've encountered the dual influence of heredity and environment before, but this theme is rich in complexity. Each chapter draws out different aspects and implications. Our discussion of development amplified the point that genetics and experience work *interactively* to shape behavior. In the language of science, an interaction means that the effects of one variable depend on the effects of another. In other words, heredity and environment do not operate independently. Children with "difficult" temperaments will elicit different reactions from different parents, depending on the parents' personalities and expectations. Likewise, a particular pair of parents will affect children in different ways, depending on the inborn characteristics of the children. An interplay, or feedback loop, exists between biological and environmental factors. For instance, a temperamentally difficult child may elicit negative reactions from parents, which serve to make the child more difficult, which evokes more negative reactions. If this child develops into an ornery 11-year-old, which do we blame—genetics or experience? Clearly, this outcome is due to the reciprocal effects of both.

All aspects of development are shaped jointly by heredity and experience. We often estimate their relative weight or influence as if we could cleanly divide behavior into genetic and environmental components. Although we can't really carve up behavior that neatly, such comparisons can be of great theoretical interest. You'll see this in our upcoming Personal Application, which discusses the nature and origins of gender differences in behavior.

REVIEW OF KEY LEARNING GOALS

11.20 This chapter showed that psychology is theoretically diverse, that psychology evolves in a sociohistorical context, that multifactorial causation is the norm, and that culture affects many aspects of behavior, but above all else, it demonstrated that heredity and environment jointly mold behavior.

PERSONAL APPLICATION

Understanding Gender Differences

KEY LEARNING GOALS

11.21 Summarize evidence on gender differences in behavior, and assess the significance of these differences.

11.22 Explain how biological and environmental factors are thought to contribute to gender differences.

Answer the following "true" or "false."

____ **1** Females are more socially oriented than males.

____ **2** Males outperform females on most spatial tasks.

____ **3** Females are more irrational than males.

____ **4** Males are less sensitive to nonverbal cues than females.

____ **5** Females are more emotional than males.

Are there genuine behavioral differences between the sexes similar to those mentioned above? If so, why do these differences exist? How do they develop? These are the complex and controversial questions that we'll explore in this Personal Application.

Before proceeding further, we need to clarify how some key terms are used, as terminology in this area of research has been evolving and remains a source of confusion. **Sex usually refers to the biologically based categories of female and male.** In contrast, ***gender*** **usually refers to culturally constructed distinctions between femininity and masculinity.** Individuals are born female or male. However, they become feminine or masculine through complex developmental processes that take years to unfold.

The statements at the beginning of this Application reflect popular gender stereotypes in our society. ***Gender stereotypes*** **are widely held beliefs about females' and males' abilities, personality traits, and**

social behavior. Table 11.1 lists some characteristics that are part of the masculine and feminine stereotypes in North American society. The table shows something you may have already noticed on your own: The male stereotype is much more flattering, suggesting that men have virtually cornered the market on competence and rationality. After all, everyone knows that females are more dependent, emotional, irrational, submissive, and talkative than males. Right? Or is that not the case? Let's look at the research.

How Do the Sexes Differ in Behavior?

***Gender differences* are actual disparities between the sexes in typical behavior or average ability.** Mountains of research, literally thousands of studies, exist on gender differences. What does this research show? Are the stereotypes of males and females accurate? Well, the findings are a mixed bag. The research indicates that genuine behavioral differences *do* exist between the sexes and that people's stereotypes are not entirely inaccurate (Eagly, 1995; Halpern, 2000). But the differences are fewer in number, smaller in size, and far more complex than stereotypes suggest. As you'll see, only two of the differences mentioned in our opening true-false questions (the even-numbered items) have been largely supported by the research.

Table 11.1 Elements of Traditional Gender Sterotypes

Masculine	Feminine
Active	Aware of other's feelings
Adventurous	Considerate
Aggressive	Creative
Ambitious	Cries easily
Competitive	Devotes self to others
Dominant	Emotional
Independent	Enjoys art and music
Leadership qualities	Excitable in a crisis
Likes math and science	Expresses tender feelings
Makes decisions easily	Feelings hurt easily
Mechanical aptitude	Gentle
Not easily influenced	Home oriented
Outspoken	Kind
Persistent	Likes children
Self-confident	Neat
Skilled in business	Needs approval
Stands up under pressure	Tactful
Takes a stand	Understanding

SOURCE: Adapted from Ruble, T. L. (1983). Sex stereotypes: Issues of change in the 70s. *Sex Roles, 9,* 397–402. Copyright © 1983 Plenum Publishing Group. Adapted with kind permission of Springer Science and Business Media.

© Cengage Learning 2013

Cognitive Abilities

In the cognitive domain, it appears that there are three genuine—albeit rather small—gender differences. First, on the average, females tend to exhibit slightly better *verbal skills* than males (Halpern et al., 2007). In particular, females seem stronger on tasks that require rapid access to semantic information in long-term memory and tasks that require the production or comprehension of complex prose (Halpern, 2004). Second, starting during high school, males have shown a slight advantage on tests of *mathematical ability.* When all students are compared, males' advantage is quite small. Indeed, in a recent review of research, Hyde and Mertz (2009) conclude that the gender gap in math has disappeared in the general population in the United States. Around the world, though, small to modest gender disparities are still seen in some countries, especially those that do not endorse equal opportunities for men and women (Else-Quest, Hyde, & Linn, 2010). Also, at the high end of the ability distribution, a gender gap is still found. About three to four times as many males as females manifest exceptional math skills (Wai et al., 2010). Third, starting in the grade-school years, males tend to score higher than females on most measures of *visual-spatial ability* (Halpern et al., 2007). The size of these gender differences varies depending on the exact nature of the spatial task. Males appear to be strongest on tasks that require mental rotations or tracking the movement of objects through three-dimensional space (Halpern, 2004). One recent study uncovered a gender gap in mental rotation that was apparent in infants that were only 5 months old (Moore & Johnson, 2008).

Personality and Social Behavior

In regard to personality, recent research suggests that there are some modest gender differences on certain key personality traits. A study of personality across 55 cultures found that females tend to score somewhat higher than males on measures of *extraversion, agreeableness, conscientiousness,* and *neuroticism* (Schmitt et al., 2008). As for social behavior, research findings support the existence of some additional gender differences. First, studies indicate that males tend to be much more *physically aggressive* than females (Archer, 2005). This disparity shows up early in childhood. Its continuation into adulthood is supported by the fact that men account for a grossly disproportionate number of the violent crimes in our society (Kenrick, Trost, & Sundie, 2004). The findings on *verbal aggression* are more complex. Females appear to exhibit more relational aggression (snide remarks and so forth) (Archer, 2005). Second, there are gender differences in *nonverbal communication and interpersonal sensitivity.* Research findings indicate that females are more sensitive than males to subtle nonverbal cues (Hall, Carter, & Horgan, 2000; Hampson, van Anders, & Mullin, 2006). Evidence also shows that females pay more attention to interpersonal information (Hall & Mast, 2008). Third, males are more sexually active than females in a variety of ways and have more permissive attitudes about casual, premarital, and extramarital sex (Baumeister et al., 2001b; Hyde, 2005a; see Chapter 10).

Some Qualifications

Although research has identified some genuine gender differences in behavior, bear in mind that these are group differences that indicate nothing about individuals. Essentially, research results compare the "average man" with the "average woman." However, you are—and every individual is—unique. The average female and male are ultimately figments of our imagination. Furthermore, the genuine group differences noted are relatively small (Hyde, 2005a, 2007). **Figure 11.25** shows how scores on a trait, perhaps verbal ability, might be distributed for men and women. Although the group averages are detectably different, you can see the great variability within each group (sex) and the huge overlap between the two group distributions.

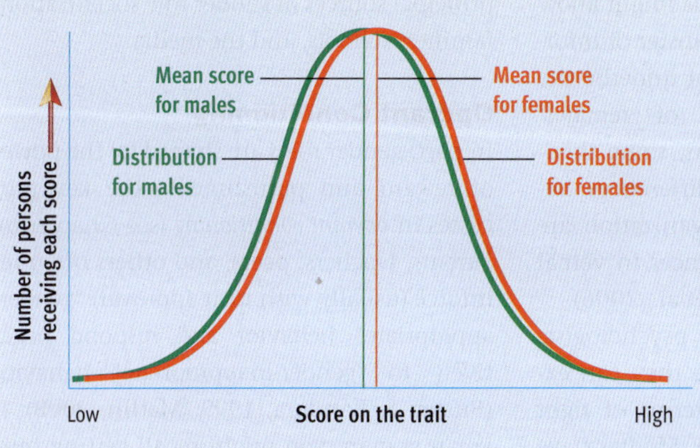

Figure 11.25
The nature of gender differences. Gender differences are group differences that indicate little about individuals because of the great overlap between the groups. For a given trait, one sex may score higher on the average, but far more variation occurs within each sex than between the sexes.

© Cengage Learning 2013

Biological Origins of Gender Differences

What accounts for the development of various gender differences? To what degree are they the product of learning or of biology? This question is yet another manifestation of the nature versus nurture issue. Investigations of the biological origins of gender differences have centered on the evolutionary bases of behavior, hormones, and brain organization.

Evolutionary Explanations

Evolutionary analyses usually begin by arguing that biological factors are at work because the same gender differences in behavior are documented across divergent cultures. Research by and large backs this up. Gender differences in cognitive abilities, aggression, and sexual behavior *are* found in virtually all cultures (Beller & Gafni, 1996; Kenrick et al., 2004). Evolutionary psychologists go on to argue that these universal gender differences reflect different natural selection pressures operating on males and females over the course of human history (Archer, 1996; Buss & Kenrick, 1998; Geary, 2007). For example, as we discussed in Chapter 10, males supposedly are more sexually active and permissive because they invest less than females in the process of procreation and can maximize their reproductive success by seeking many sexual partners (Schmitt, 2005; Webster, 2009). The gender gap in aggression is also explained in terms of reproductive fitness. Because females are more selective about mating than males, males have to engage in more competition for sexual partners than females do. Greater aggressiveness is thought to be adaptive for males in this competition for sexual access. Aggression, in this instance, should foster social dominance over other males. It should also facilitate the acquisition of the material resources emphasized by females when they evaluate potential partners (Campbell, 2005; Cummins, 2005). Evolutionary theorists assert that gender differences in spatial ability reflect the division of labor in ancestral hunting-and-gathering societies in which males typically handled the hunting and females the gathering. Males' superiority on most spatial tasks has been attributed to the adaptive demands of hunting (Newcombe, 2007; Silverman & Choi, 2005; see Chapter 1).

Evolutionary analyses of gender differences are interesting, but controversial. On the one hand, it seems entirely plausible that evolutionary forces could have led to some divergence between males and females in typical behavior. On the other hand, evolutionary hypotheses are highly speculative and difficult to test empirically (Eagly & Wood, 1999; Halpern, 2000). The crucial problem for some critics is that evolutionary analyses are so "flexible" that they can be used to explain almost anything. For example, if the situation regarding spatial ability were reversed—if females scored higher than males—evolutionary theorists might attribute females' superiority to the adaptive demands of gathering food, weaving baskets, and making clothes—and it would be difficult to prove otherwise (Cornell, 1997).

The Role of Hormones

Disparities between males and females in hormone levels may contribute to gender differences in behavior (Hampson & Moffat, 2004; Hines, 2010). Hormones play a key role in sexual differentiation during prenatal development. The high level of androgens (the principal class of male hormones) in males and the low level of androgens in females lead to the differentiation of male and female genital organs. The critical role of prenatal hormones becomes apparent when something interferes with normal prenatal hormonal secretions. A variety of endocrine disorders can cause overproduction or underproduction of specific gonadal hormones during prenatal development. Scientists have also studied children born to mothers who were given an androgenlike drug to prevent miscarriage. This research reveals that females exposed prenatally to abnormally high levels of androgens exhibit more male-typical behavior than other females do. Likewise, males exposed prenatally to abnormally low levels of androgens exhibit more female-typical behavior than other males (Hines, 2004).

These findings suggest that prenatal hormones contribute to the shaping of gender differences in humans. But there are some problems with this evidence (Basow, 1992; Fausto-Sterling, 1992; Jordan-Young, 2010). First, the evidence is much stronger for females than for males. Second, it's always dangerous to draw conclusions about the general population based on small samples of people who have abnormal conditions. However, a recent study that approached the issue in a new way circumvented both of these problems. In this study, the level of testosterone (a critical androgen) in mothers' amniotic fluid was assessed and correlated with a later measure of their children's sex-typical play. Fetal testosterone levels were positively correlated with male-typical play in both boys and girls (Auyeung et al., 2009). These findings are important in that they are based on "normal" subjects from the general population and because they show similar trends for both males and females. Looking at the evidence as a whole, it does seem likely that prenatal hormones contribute to gender differences in behavior. However, a great deal remains to be learned.

Differences in Brain Organization

Many theorists believe that gender differences in behavior are rooted in male-female disparities in brain structure and organization (Cahill, 2006). For example, some theorists have tried to link gender differences to the specialization of the cerebral hemispheres in the brain (see **Figure 11.26**). As you may recall from Chapter 3, in most people the left hemisphere is more actively involved in verbal processing, whereas the right hemisphere is more active in visual-spatial processing (Gazzaniga, Ivry, & Mangun, 2009). After these findings surfaced, theorists began to wonder whether this division of labor in the brain might be related to gender differences in verbal and spatial skills. Thus, they began looking for sex-related disparities in brain organization.

Some thought-provoking findings *have* been reported. For instance, some studies have found that *males tend to exhibit more cerebral specialization than females* (Boles, 2005; Voyer, 1996). In other words, males tend to depend more heavily than females do on the left hemisphere in verbal processing and more heavily on the right hemisphere in spatial processing. Differences between males and females have also been found in the size of the corpus callosum, the band of fibers that connects the two hemispheres of the brain. Some studies suggest that *females tend to have a larger corpus callosum* (Gur & Gur, 2007; Resnick, 2006). This might allow for better interhemispheric transfer of information, which, in turn, might underlie the less-lateralized organization of females' brains (Innocenti, 1994). Thus, some theorists have concluded that differences between the sexes in brain organization are responsible for gender differences in verbal and spatial ability (Clements et al., 2006).

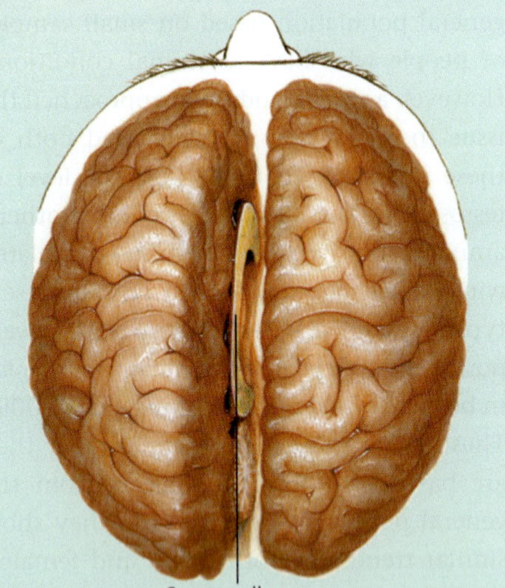

Figure 11.26

The cerebral hemispheres and the corpus callosum. In this drawing the cerebral hemispheres have been "pulled apart" to reveal the corpus callosum, the band of fibers that connects the right and left halves of the brain. Research has shown that the right and left hemispheres are specialized to handle different types of cognitive tasks (see Chapter 3), leading some theorists to speculate that patterns of hemispheric specialization might contribute to gender differences in verbal and spatial abilities.

© Cengage Learning 2013

This idea is intriguing. But psychologists have a long way to go before they can explain gender differences in terms of right brain/left brain specialization. Studies have not been consistent in finding that males have more specialized brain organization than females (Kaiser et al., 2009). In fact, a recent meta-analysis of twenty-six neuroimaging studies concluded that there was no gender disparity in language lateralization (Sommer et al., 2008). Also, serious doubts have been raised about the finding that females have a larger corpus callosum (Fine, 2010; Halpern et al., 2007). Moreover, even if these findings were replicated consistently, no one is really sure just how they would account for the observed gender differences in cognitive abilities (Fine, 2010).

In summary, researchers have made some intriguing progress in their efforts to document the biological roots of gender differences in behavior. However, the idea that "anatomy is destiny" has proven difficult to demonstrate. Many theorists remain convinced that gender differences are largely shaped by experience. Let's examine their evidence.

Environmental Origins of Gender Differences

***Socialization* is the acquisition of the norms and behaviors expected of people in a particular society.** In all cultures, the socialization process includes efforts to train children about gender roles. ***Gender roles* are expectations about what is appropriate behavior for each sex.** Although gender roles are in a period of transition in modern Western society, there are still many disparities in how males and females are brought up. Investigators have identified three key processes involved in the development of gender roles: operant conditioning, observational learning, and self-socialization. First we'll examine these processes. Then we'll look at the principal sources of gender-role socialization: families, schools, and the media.

Operant Conditioning

In part, gender roles are shaped by the power of reward and punishment—the key processes in *operant conditioning* (see Chapter 6). Parents, teachers, peers, and others often reinforce (usually with tacit approval) "gender-appropriate" behavior and respond negatively to "gender-inappropriate" behavior (Bussey & Bandura, 1999; Matlin, 2008). If you're a man, you might recall getting hurt as a young boy and being told that "big boys don't cry." If you succeeded in inhibiting your crying, you may have earned an approving smile or even something tangible like an ice cream cone. The reinforcement probably strengthened your tendency to "act like a man" and suppress emotional displays. If you're a woman, chances are your crying wasn't discouraged as gender-inappropriate. Studies suggest that fathers encourage and reward gender-appropriate behavior in their youngsters more than mothers do and that boys experience more pressure to behave in gender-appropriate ways than girls do (Levy, Taylor, & Gelman, 1995).

Observational Learning

Observational learning (see Chapter 6) by children can lead to the imitation of adults' gender-appropriate behavior. Children imitate both males and females. But most children tend to imitate same-sex role models more than opposite-sex role models (Bussey & Bandura, 2004). Thus, imitation often leads young girls to play with dolls, dollhouses, and toy stoves, while young boys are more likely to tinker with toy trucks, miniature gas stations, or tool kits.

Self-Socialization

Children themselves are active agents in their own gender-role socialization. Several *cognitive theories* of gender-role development emphasize self-socialization (Bem, 1985; Cross & Markus, 1993; Martin & Ruble, 2004). Self-socialization entails three steps. First, children learn to classify themselves as male or female and to recognize their sex as a permanent quality (around ages 5 to 7). Second, this self-categorization motivates them to value those characteristics and behaviors associated with their sex. Third, they strive to bring their behavior in line with what is considered gender-appropriate in their culture. In other words, children get involved in their own socialization. They work diligently to discover the rules that are supposed to govern their behavior.

Sources of Gender-Role Socialization

There are three main sources of influence in gender-role socialization: families, schools, and the media. Of course, we are now in an era of transition in gender roles. Thus, the generalizations that follow may say more about how you were socialized than about how children will be socialized in the future.

Families A great deal of gender-role socialization takes place in the home (Berenbaum, Martin, & Ruble, 2008; Pomerantz, Ng, & Wang, 2004). Fathers engage in more "rough-housing" play with their sons than with their daughters, even in infancy (McBride-Chang & Jacklin, 1993). As children grow, boys and girls are encouraged to play with different types of toys (Freeman, 2007; Wood, Desmarais, & Gugula, 2002). Generally, boys have less leeway to play with "feminine" toys than girls do with "masculine" toys. When children are old enough to help with household chores, the assignments tend to depend on sex (Cunningham, 2001). For example, girls wash dishes and boys mow the lawn. And parents are more likely to explain scientific concepts to boys than to girls (Crowley et al., 2001).

Schools Schools and teachers clearly contribute to the socialization of gender roles (Berenbaum, Martin, & Ruble, 2008). The books that children use in learning to read can influence their ideas about what is suitable behavior for males and females (Diekman & Murnen, 2004). Historically, males have been more likely to be portrayed as clever, heroic, and adventurous in these books, while females have been more likely to be shown doing domestic chores. Preschool and grade-school teachers frequently reward gender-appropriate behavior in their pupils (Fagot et al., 1985; Ruble & Martin, 1998). Interestingly, teachers tend to pay greater attention to males, helping them, praising them, and scolding them more than females (Sadker & Sadker, 1994). Schools may play a key role in the gender gap in outstanding math performance, as Hyde and Mertz (2009) note that girls traditionally have been much less likely than boys to be encouraged to enroll in advanced math, chemistry, and physics courses.

The socialization of gender roles begins very early, as parents dress their infants in gendered clothing, buy them gender-driven toys, and encourage them to participate in "gender-appropriate" activities.

© Ben Molyneux/Alamy

Media Television and other mass media are another source of gender-role socialization (Bussey & Bandura, 2004). Although some improvement has been made in recent years, television shows have traditionally depicted men and women in stereotypical ways (Galambos, 2004; Signorielli, 2001). Women are often portrayed as submissive, passive, and emotional. Men are more likely to be portrayed as independent, assertive, and competent. Even commercials contribute to the socialization of gender roles (Furnham & Mak, 1999; Lippa, 2005). Recent research found a positive correlation between children's exposure to gender stereotyping in the media and endorsement of stereotypical beliefs about gender roles (Oppliger, 2007).

Conclusion

As you can see, the findings on gender and behavior are complex and confusing. Nonetheless, the evidence does permit one very general conclusion—a conclusion that you have seen before and will see again. Taken as a whole, the research in this area suggests that biological factors and environmental factors *both* contribute to gender differences in behavior—as they do to all other aspects of development.

REVIEW OF KEY LEARNING GOALS

11.21 Gender differences in behavior are fewer in number than gender stereotypes suggest. In the cognitive domain, research reviews suggest that there are genuine gender differences in verbal ability, mathematical ability, and spatial ability. In regard to social behavior, differences have been found in aggression, nonverbal communication, and sexual behavior. But most gender differences in behavior are very small in magnitude.

11.22 Evolutionary theorists maintain that gender differences transcend culture because males and females have confronted different adaptive demands over the course of human history. Prenatal hormones probably contribute to human gender differences. Research linking gender differences to cerebral specialization is intriguing, but much remains to be learned. Operant conditioning, observational learning, and self-socialization contribute to the development of gender differences. Families, schools, and the media are among the main sources of gender-role socialization.

Are Fathers Essential to Children's Well-Being?

KEY LEARNING GOALS

11.23 Clarify and critique the argument that fathers are essential for healthy development.

Are fathers essential for children to experience normal, healthy development? This question is currently the subject of heated debate. In recent years, a number of social scientists have mounted a thought-provoking argument that father absence resulting from divorce, abandonment, and so forth is the chief factor underlying a number of modern social ills. For example, David Blankenhorn (1995) argues that "fatherlessness is the most harmful demographic trend of this generation. It is the leading cause of declining child well-being in our society" (p. 1). Expressing a similar view, David Popenoe (2009) maintains that "today's fatherlessness has led to social turmoil—damaged children, unhappy children, aimless children, children who strike back with pathological behavior and violence" (p. 192). The belief that fathers are crucial to healthy development has become widely accepted. This conventional wisdom has been strongly endorsed by both President George W. Bush and President Barack Obama and it has guided government policy in a variety of areas.

The Basic Argument

What is the evidence for the proposition that fathers are essential to healthy development? Over the last 40 years, the proportion of children growing up without a father in the home has more than doubled. During the same time, we have seen dramatic increases in teenage pregnancy, juvenile delinquency, violent crime, drug abuse, eating disorders, teen suicide, and family dysfunction. Moreover, mountains of studies have demonstrated an association between father absence and an elevated risk for these problems. Summarizing this evidence, Popenoe (2009) asserts that "fatherless children have a risk factor two to three times that of fathered children for a wide range of negative outcomes, including dropping out of high school, giving birth as a teenager, and becoming a juvenile delinquent" (p. 192). This leads him to infer that "fathers have a unique and irreplaceable role to play in child development" (p. 197). Popenoe concludes, "If present trends continue, our society could be on the verge of committing social suicide" (p. 192). Echoing this dire conclusion, Blankenhorn (1995) comments that "to tolerate the trend of fatherlessness is to accept the inevitability of continued societal recession" (p. 222).

© Andresr/Shutterstock

Are fathers crucial to children's well-being? This seemingly simple question has sparked heated debate.

You might be thinking, "What's all the fuss about?" Surely, proclaiming the importance of fatherhood ought to be no more controversial than advocacy for motherhood or apple pie. But the assertion that a father is essential to a child's well-being has some interesting sociopolitical implications. It suggests that heterosexual marriage is the only appropriate context in which to raise children and that other family configurations are fundamentally deficient. Based on this line of reasoning, some people have argued for new laws that would make it more difficult to obtain a divorce and other policies and programs that would favor traditional families over families headed by single mothers, cohabiting parents, and gay and lesbian parents (Silverstein & Auerbach, 1999). Indeed, the belief that children need both a mother and a father has surfaced repeatedly in the legal wrangling over same-sex marriage. Thus, the question about the importance of fathers is creating a great deal of controversy because it's really a question about alternatives to traditional family structure.

Evaluating the Argument

In light of the far-reaching implications of the view that fathers are essential to normal development, it makes sense to subject this view to critical scrutiny. How could you use critical thinking skills to evaluate this argument? A number of previously discussed ideas seem pertinent.

First, it's important to recognize that the idea that fathers are essential for healthy development rests on a foundation of correlational evidence. As we have seen repeatedly, *correlation is no assurance of causation.* Yes, there has been an increase in father absence that has been paralleled by increases in teenage pregnancy, drug abuse, eating disorders, and other disturbing social problems. But think of all the other changes that have occurred in American culture over the last 40 years. The decline of organized religion, the growth of mass media, dramatic shifts in sexual mores, and so forth have all occurred during this same period. Increased father absence has covaried with a host of other cultural trends. Hence, it's highly speculative to infer that father absence is the chief cause of most modern social maladies.

Second, it always pays to think about whether there are specific, *alternative explanations* for findings that you might have doubts about. What other factors might account for the association between father absence and children's maladjustment?

What is the most frequent cause of father absence? Divorce. Divorces tend to be highly stressful events that disrupt children's entire lives. Although the evidence suggests that a majority of children seem to survive divorce without lasting, detrimental effects, it's clear that divorce elevates youngsters' risk for a wide range of negative developmental outcomes (Amato, 2006; Amato & Dorius, 2010; Hetherington, 1999, 2003). Given that father absence and divorce are inextricably intertwined, it's possible that the negative effects of divorce account for much of the association between father absence and social problems.

Are there any other alternative explanations for the correlation between father absence and social maladies? Yes, critics point out that the prevalence of father absence co-varies with socioeconomic status. Father absence is much more common in low-income families (Anderson, Kohler, & Letiecq, 2002). Thus, the effects of father absence are entangled to some extent with the many powerful, malignant effects of poverty. Such poverty might account for much of the correlation between father absence and negative outcomes (McLoyd, 1998).

A third possible strategy in thinking critically about the effects of father absence would be to ask *if there is contradictory evidence*. Once again, the answer is yes. Biblarz and Stacey (2010) reviewed studies comparing pairs of heterosexual parents with pairs of lesbian parents. If fathers are essential, the adjustment of children raised by heterosexual parents should be superior to that of children raised by lesbian parents. But the studies found negligible differences between these parental configurations.

A fourth strategy would be to look for some of the *fallacies in reasoning* introduced in Chapter 10 (irrelevant reasons, circular reasoning, slippery slope, weak analogies, and false dichotomy). A couple of the quotes from Popenoe and Blankenhorn were chosen to give you an opportunity to detect two of these fallacies in a new context. Take a look at the quotes once again and see whether you can spot the fallacies.

Popenoe's (2009) assertion that "if present trends continue, our society could be on the verge of social suicide" is an example of *slippery slope argumentation,* which involves predicting that if one allows X to happen, things will spin out of control and catastrophic events will follow. "Social suicide" is a little vague, but it sounds as if Popenoe is predicting that father absence will lead to the destruction of modern American culture. The other fallacy that you might have spotted was the *false dichotomy* apparent in Blankenhorn's assertion that "to tolerate the trend of fatherlessness is to accept the inevitability of continued societal recession." A false dichotomy creates an either-or choice between the position one wants to advocate (in this case, new social policies to reduce father absence) and some obviously horrible outcome that any sensible person would want to avoid (social decay), while ignoring other possible outcomes that might lie between these extremes.

In summary, we can find a number of flaws and weaknesses in the argument that fathers are *essential* to normal development. However, our critical evaluation of this argument *does not mean that fathers are unimportant.* Many types of evidence suggest that fathers generally make significant contributions to their children's development (Carlson, 2006; Lewis & Lamb, 2003; Rohner & Veneziano, 2001). We could argue with merit that fathers typically provide a substantial advantage for children. But there's a crucial distinction between arguing that fathers *promote* normal, healthy development and arguing that fathers are *necessary* for normal, healthy development. If fathers are *necessary,* children who grow up without them could not achieve the same level of well-being as those who have fathers. It's clear, however, that a great many children from single-parent homes turn out just fine.

Fathers surely are important, and it seems likely that father absence *contributes* to a variety of social maladies. So, why do Blankenhorn (1995) and Popenoe (2009) argue for the much stronger conclusion—that fathers are *essential?* They appear to prefer the stronger conclusion because it raises much more serious questions about the viability of nontraditional family forms. Thus, they seem to want to advance a *political agenda* that champions traditional family values. They are certainly entitled to do so, but when research findings are used to advance a political agenda—whether conservative or liberal—a special caution alert should go off in your head. When a political agenda is at stake, it pays to scrutinize arguments with extra care, because research findings are more likely to be presented in a slanted fashion. The field of psychology deals with a number of complex questions that have profound implications for a wide range of social issues. The skills and habits of critical thinking can help you find your way through the maze of reasons and evidence that hold up the many sides of these complicated issues.

Table 11.2 Critical Thinking Skills Discussed in This Application

Skill	Description
Understanding the limitations of correlational evidence	The critical thinker understands that a correlation between two variables does not demonstrate that there is a causal link between the variables.
Looking for alternative explanations for findings and events	In evaluating explanations, the critical thinker explores whether there are other explanations that could also account for the findings or events under scrutiny.
Recognizing and avoiding common fallacies, such as irrelevant reasons, circular reasoning, slippery slope reasoning, weak analogies, and false dichotomies	The critical thinker is vigilant about conclusions based on unrelated premises, conclusions that are rewordings of premises, unwarranted predictions that things will spin out of control, superficial analogies, and contrived dichotomies.

© Cengage Learning 2013

REVIEW OF KEY LEARNING GOALS

11.23 Some social scientists have argued that father absence is the chief cause of numerous social problems and that fathers are essential for normal, healthy development. Critics note that all the relevant data are correlational, making causal inferences speculative, and they argue that there are alternative explanations for the association between father absence and negative developmental outcomes.

Chapter 11 Practice Test

1. The stage of prenatal development during which the developing organism is most vulnerable to injury is the:
   A. zygotic stage.
   B. germinal stage.
   C. embryonic stage.
   D. fetal stage.

2. The cephalocaudal trend in the motor development of children can be described simply as a:
   A. head-to-foot direction.
   B. center-outward direction.
   C. foot-to-head direction.
   D. body-appendages direction.

3. Developmental norms:
   A. can be used to make extremely precise predictions about the age at which an individual child will reach various developmental milestones.
   B. indicate the maximum age at which a child can reach a particular developmental milestone and still be considered "normal."
   C. indicate the average age at which individuals reach various developmental milestones.
   D. involve both a and b.

4. When the development of the same subjects is studied over a period of time, the study is called a:
   A. cross-sectional study.
   B. life history study.
   C. longitudinal study.
   D. sequential study.

5. The quality of infant-caregiver attachment depends:
   A. on the quality of bonding in the first few hours of life.
   B. exclusively on the infant's temperament.
   C. on the interaction between the infant's temperament and the caregiver's responsiveness.
   D. on how stranger anxiety is handled.

6. During the second year of life, toddlers begin to take some personal responsibility for feeding, dressing, and bathing themselves in an attempt to establish what Erikson calls a sense of:
   A. superiority.
   B. industry.
   C. generativity.
   D. autonomy.

7. Five-year-old David watches as you pour water from a short, wide glass into a tall, narrow one. He says there is now more water than before. This response demonstrates that:
   A. David understands the concept of conservation.
   B. David does not understand the concept of conservation.
   C. David's cognitive development is "behind" for his age.
   D. both b and c are the case.

8. Which of the following is *not* one of the criticisms of Piaget's theory of cognitive development?
   A. Piaget may have underestimated the cognitive skills of children in some areas.
   B. Piaget may have underestimated the influence of environmental factors on cognitive development.
   C. The mixing of stages raises questions about the value of organizing development in stages.
   D. Evidence for the theory is based on children's answers to questions.

9. If a child's primary reason for not drawing pictures on the living room wall with crayons is to avoid the punishment that would inevitably follow this behavior, she would be said to be at which level of moral development?
   A. conventional
   B. postconventional
   C. preconventional
   D. unconventional

10. The portion of the brain that appears to be the last area to mature fully is the:
    A. hypothalamus.
    B. corpus callosum.
    C. prefrontal cortex.
    D. occipital lobe.

11. Girls who mature ______ and boys who mature ______ seem to experience more subjective distress and emotional difficulties with the transition to adolescence.
    A. early; early
    B. early; late
    C. late; early
    D. late; late

12. Sixteen-year-old Foster wants to spend a few years experimenting with different lifestyles and careers before he settles on who and what he wants to be. Foster's behavior illustrates the identity status of:
    A. identity moratorium.
    B. identity foreclosure.
    C. identity achievement.
    D. identity diffusion.

13. Which of the following does *not* decline with age?
    A. speed of information processing
    B. memory
    C. crystallized intelligence
    D. fluid intelligence

14. Males have been found to differ slightly from females in three well-documented areas of mental abilities. Which of the following is *not* one of these?
    A. verbal ability
    B. mathematical ability
    C. intelligence
    D. visual-spatial abilities

15. Although the data are inconsistent, some research suggests that males exhibit __________________ than females and that females have a __________________ than males.
    A. less cerebral specialization; smaller corpus callosum
    B. less cerebral specialization; larger corpus callosum
    C. more cerebral specialization; smaller corpus callosum
    D. more cerebral specialization; larger corpus callosum

Answers

1 C pp. 434–435
2 A p. 437
3 C pp. 437–438
4 C p. 439
5 C pp. 441–442
6 D pp. 444–445
7 B pp. 446–447
8 D p. 448
9 C p. 451
10 C p. 455
11 B p. 454
12 A p. 457
13 C pp. 462–463
14 C p. 466
15 D p. 468

PsykTrek

To view a demo: **www.cengage.com/psychology/psyktrek**
To order: **www.cengage.com/psychology/weiten**
Go to the PsykTrek website or CD-ROM for further study of the concepts in this chapter. Both online and on the CD-ROM, PsykTrek includes dozens of learning modules with videos, animations, and quizzes, as well as simulations of psychological phenomena and a multimedia glossary that includes word pronunciations.

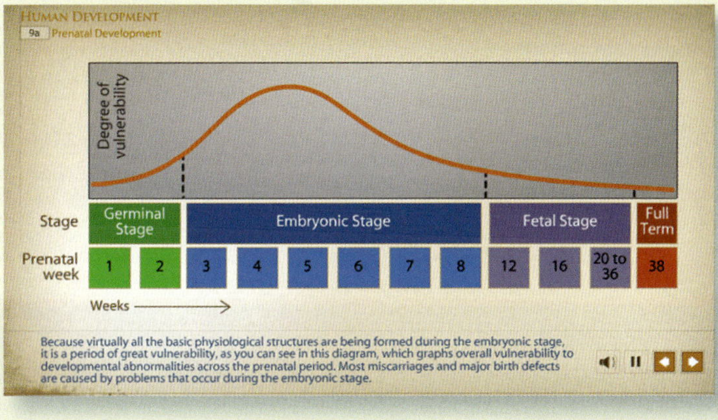

© Cengage Learning 2008

Visit Module 9a (*Prenatal Development*) to learn more about how development unfolds rapidly during the prenatal period.

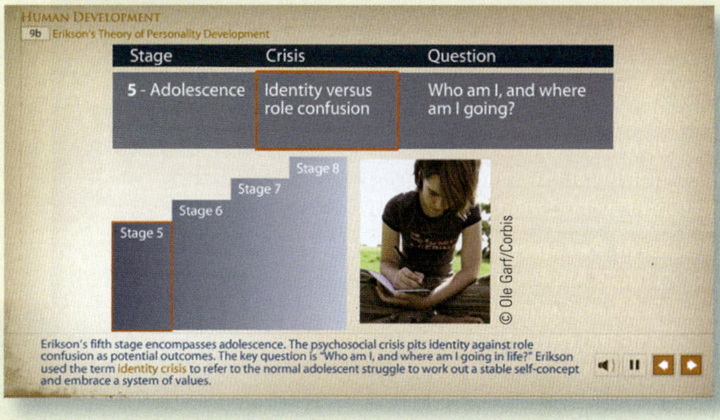

© Cengage Learning 2008

Explore Module 9b (*Erikson's Theory of Personality Development*) to see how Erik Erikson charted the course of human development across eight life stages.

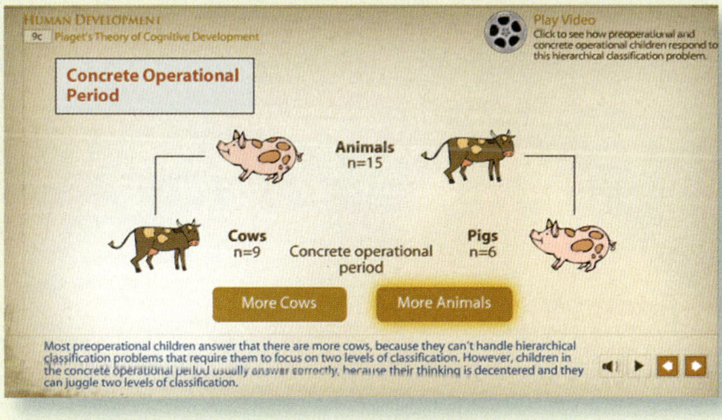

© Cengage Learning 2008

Go to Module 9c (*Piaget's Theory of Cognitive Development*) to enhance your understanding of Jean Piaget's work on children's thinking—and check out two videos showing how young children's reasoning can go awry.

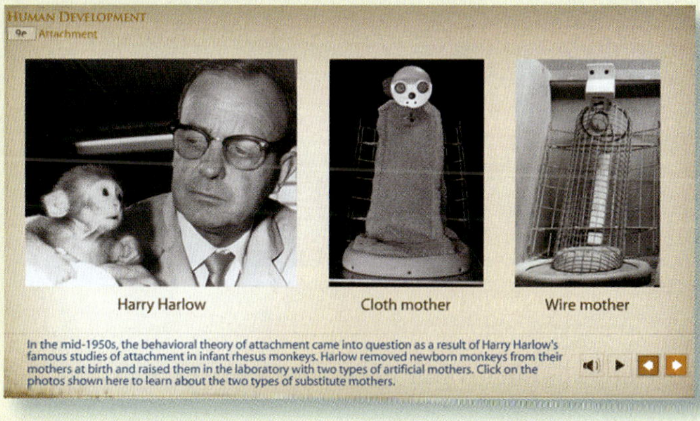

© Cengage Learning 2008; insets: © Harlow Primate Laboratory, University of Wisconsin

Access Module 9e (*Attachment*) to learn more about the research of Harry Harlow, John Bowlby, and Mary Ainsworth on infant attachment—including a video reenactment of the strange situation procedure.

Online Study Tools

Log in to **CengageBrain** to access the resources your instructor requires. For this book, you can access:

CourseMate brings course concepts to life with interactive learning, study, and exam preparation tools that support the printed textbook. A textbook-specific website, Psychology CourseMate includes an integrated interactive eBook and other interactive learning tools such as quizzes, flashcards, videos, and more.

CengageNow is an easy-to-use online resource that helps you study in less time to get the grade you want—NOW. Take a pre-test for this chapter and receive a personalized study plan based on your results that will identify the topics you need to review and direct you to online resources to help you master those topics. Then take a post-test to help you determine the concepts you have mastered and what you will need to work on. If your textbook does not include an access code card, go to CengageBrain.com to gain access.

WebTutor is more than just an interactive study guide. WebTutor is an anytime, anywhere customized learning solution with an eBook, keeping you connected to your textbook, instructor, and classmates.

Aplia. If your professor has assigned Aplia homework:

1. Sign in to your account
2. Complete the corresponding homework exercises as required by your professor.
3. When finished, click "Grade It Now" to see which areas you have mastered, which need more work, and detailed explanations of every answer.

Visit **www.cengagebrain.com** to access your account and purchase materials.

12

Personality

© Blue Jean Images/Alamy RF

Richard Branson was sure that he was about to die. He was high above the Atlantic Ocean, alone in a capsule attached to the biggest balloon in the world. Per Lindstrand, the balloon's pilot, was somewhere in the icy waves far below. He and Branson had just become the first people ever to cross the Atlantic in a hot-air balloon. But when an emergency landing at sea failed, Lindstrand had leaped into the water. Before Branson could follow, the balloon had shot back up into the sky. Branson had never flown in a balloon before his very brief training for this trip. Now he was stranded in mid-air with no clear idea how to save himself.

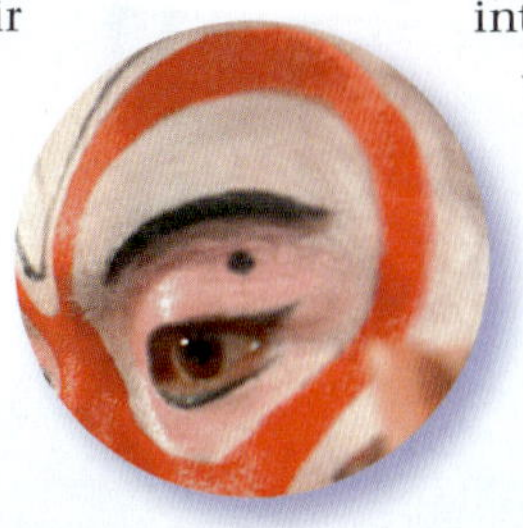

Branson scribbled a note to his family: "I love you." Then he began trying to vent the huge balloon in a desperate attempt to guide it safely earthward. Much to his surprise, he was able to get close enough to the sea to jump for it. A rescue helicopter plucked him out of the waves. (Lindstrand was saved by a passing fisherman.)

After this frightening brush with death, Branson swore that he would never risk his life so foolishly again. Yet three years later, he and Lindstrand were at it again. This time they attempted to be the first to cross the Pacific in a hot-air balloon. The trip turned into another terrifying ordeal. The balloon caught fire when they were thousands of feet above empty ocean. And once again they were nearly killed. But not even this stopped them from planning yet another exploit. They tried to become the first hot-air balloonists to fly completely around the world (Branson, 2005; Brown, 1998).

When people describe Richard Branson, they are apt to use words such as *adventurous, brave, daring, impulsive,* and *reckless*. These are the kinds of words used to characterize what we call "personality." And Branson—a self-made billionaire and one of the richest people in the world—may be as famous for his exuberant personality as he is for his immense wealth.

Paradox: *Personality tests have a number of shortcomings and weaknesses, but they remain invaluable measurement instruments for both research and clinical work.*

Richard Branson, the founder of the Virgin group of companies, clearly manifests a powerful and unusual personality. But everyone has his or her own unique personality, which makes the study of personality a fascinating area of inquiry in psychology.

© Michael Buckner/Getty Images

A high school dropout, Branson is the founder of the Virgin group of companies, including the Virgin Atlantic airline and Virgin Galactic, which aims to become the first company to fly tourists into space. Branson is a brash, shrewd, and relentless entrepreneur who loves cutting a deal. But he also loves parties, practical jokes, and flamboyant publicity stunts. Most of all, he relishes finding new fields to conquer.

Most people would agree that Richard Branson has an unusual personality. But what exactly *is* personality? And why are personalities so different? Why is one person daring, while another is timid? Why is one person high spirited and outgoing, while another is quiet and shy? Was Richard Branson born with the self-confidence and daring he is renowned for, or were environment and learning critical in shaping his personality? For instance, Branson's parents stressed the importance of being strong and independent, starting at an early age. On the other hand, perhaps the roots of his personality lie in biological inheritance. Branson (2005) describes his mother as a woman of dazzling energy and fierce determination who also has a taste for adventure. During World War II, she talked her way into pilot training on the condition that she disguise herself as a boy. Maybe Branson's genetic makeup is responsible for his being an "adrenaline junkie."

Psychologists have approached such questions from a variety of perspectives. Traditionally, the study of personality has been dominated by "grand theories" that attempt to explain a great many facets of behavior. Our discussion will reflect this emphasis. We'll devote most of our time to the sweeping theories of Freud, Skinner, Rogers, and several others. In recent decades, however, the study of personality has shifted toward narrower research programs that examine specific issues related to personality. This trend is reflected in our review of biological, cultural, and other contemporary approaches to personality in the last several sections of the chapter. In the Personal Application, we'll examine how psychological tests are used to measure aspects of personality. The Critical Thinking Application will explore how hindsight bias can taint people's analyses of personality.

KEY LEARNING GOALS

12.1 Define the construct of personality in terms of consistency and distinctiveness.

12.2 Clarify what is meant by a personality trait, and describe the five-factor model of personality.

12.3 Summarize relations between the Big Five traits and aspects of behavior and life outcomes.

The Nature of Personality

Personality is a complex hypothetical construct that has been defined in a variety of ways. Let's take a closer look at the concepts of personality and personality traits.

Defining Personality: Consistency and Distinctiveness

What does it mean to say that someone has an optimistic personality? This assertion indicates that the person has a fairly *consistent tendency* to behave in a cheerful, hopeful, enthusiastic way. Such a person looks at the bright side of things, across a wide variety of situations. Although no one is entirely consistent in behavior, this quality of *consistency across situations* lies at the core of the concept of personality.

Distinctiveness is also central to the concept of personality. Personality is used to explain why people do not act the same way in similar situations. If you were stuck in an elevator with three others, each might react differently. One might crack jokes to relieve the tension. Another might make ominous predictions that "we'll never get out of here." The third might calmly think about how to escape. These varied reactions to the same situation occur because each person has a different personality. Each person has traits that are seen in other people, but each has his or her own distinctive *set* of personality traits.

In summary, the concept of personality is used to explain (1) the stability in a person's behavior over time and across situations (consistency) and (2) the behavioral differences among people reacting to the same situation (distinctiveness). We can combine these ideas into the following definition: ***Personality* refers to an individual's unique set of consistent behavioral traits.** Let's look more closely at the concept of *traits*.

Personality Traits: Dispositions and Dimensions

Everyone makes remarks like "Jan is very *conscientious.*" Or you might assert that "Bill is too *timid* to succeed in that job." These descriptive statements refer to personality traits. **A *personality trait* is a durable disposition to behave in a particular way in a variety of situations.** Adjectives such as *honest, dependable, moody, impulsive, suspicious, anxious, excitable, domineering,* and *friendly* describe dispositions that represent personality traits.

© iodrakon/Shutterstock

Most approaches to personality assume that some traits are more basic than others. According to this notion, a small number of fundamental traits determine other, more superficial traits. For example, a person's tendency to be impulsive, restless, irritable, boisterous, and impatient might all be derived from a more basic tendency to be excitable.

A number of psychologists have taken on the challenge of identifying the basic traits that form the core of personality. For example, Raymond Cattell (1950, 1966, 1990) used the statistical procedure of *factor analysis* to reduce a list of 171 personality traits compiled by Gordon Allport (1937) to just 16 basic dimensions of personality. In ***factor analysis,* correlations among many variables are analyzed to identify closely related clusters of variables** (see Chapter 9). If the measurements of a number of variables (in this case, personality traits) correlate highly with one another, the assumption is that a single factor is influencing all of them. Factor analysis is used to identify these hidden factors. In factor analyses of personality traits, these hidden factors are viewed as basic, higher-order traits that determine less basic, more specific traits. Based on his factor analytic work, Cattell concluded that an individual's personality can be described completely by measuring just 16 traits. These crucial traits are listed in **Figure 12.21** on page 510, which can be found in the Personal Application, where we discuss a personality test that Cattell designed to assess these traits.

The Five-Factor Model of Personality Traits

In recent years, Robert McCrae and Paul Costa (1987, 1997, 2003, 2008a, 2008b) have used factor analysis to arrive at a much simpler, *five-factor model of personality* (see **Figure 12.1**). McCrae and Costa maintain that most personality traits are derived from just five higher-order traits that have come to be known as the "Big Five":

1. *Extraversion.* People who score high in extraversion are characterized as outgoing, sociable, upbeat, friendly, assertive, and gregarious. Referred to as *positive emotionality* in some trait models, extraversion has been studied extensively for many decades (Watson & Clark, 1997). Extraverts tend to be

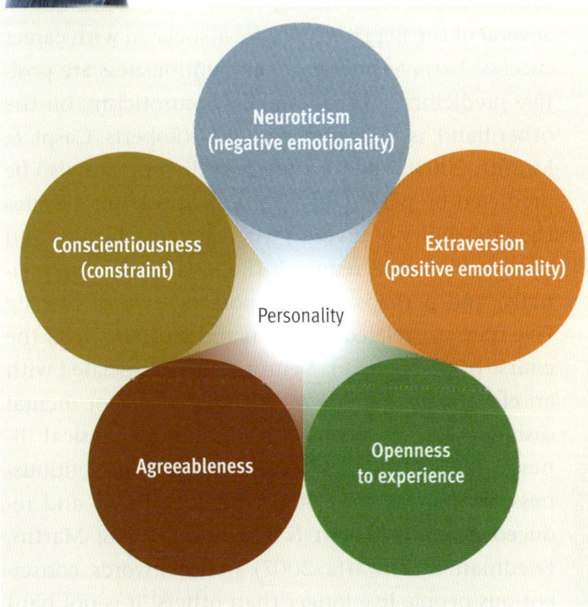

Factor	Characteristics
Neuroticism (negative emotionality)	Worried versus calm Insecure versus secure Self-pitying versus self-satisfied
Extraversion (positive emotionality)	Sociable versus retiring Fun-loving versus sober Affectionate versus reserved
Openness to experience	Imaginative versus down-to-earth Preference for variety versus preference for routine Independent versus conforming
Agreeableness	Softhearted versus ruthless Trusting versus suspicious Helpful versus uncooperative
Conscientiousness (constraint)	Well organized versus disorganized Careful versus careless Self-disciplined versus weak willed

© Cengage Learning 2013

Figure 12.1

The five-factor model of personality. Trait models attempt to analyze personality into its basic dimensions. In factor-analytic studies, the five traits shown here tend to emerge as higher-order factors that can account for other traits. McCrae and Costa (1985, 1987, 1997) maintain that personality can be described adequately by scores on the five traits identified here, which are widely referred to as the Big Five.

SOURCE: Trait descriptions from McCrae, R. R., & Costa, P. T. (1986). Clinical assessment can benefit from recent advances in personality psychology. *American Psychologist, 41,* 1001–1003.

happier than others (Fleeson, Malanos, & Achille, 2002). They also have a more positive outlook on life and are motivated to pursue social contact, intimacy, and interdependence (Wilt & Revelle, 2009).

2. *Neuroticism.* People who score high in neuroticism tend to be anxious, hostile, self-conscious, insecure, and vulnerable. Like extraversion, this trait has been the subject of thousands of studies. In some trait models it is called *negative emotionality.* Those who score high in neuroticism tend to overreact more than others in response to stress (Mroczek & Almeida, 2004). They also tend to exhibit more impulsiveness and emotional instability than others (Widiger, 2009).

3. *Openness to experience.* Openness is associated with curiosity, flexibility, vivid fantasy, imaginativeness, artistic sensitivity, and unconventional attitudes. People who are high in openness tend to be tolerant of ambiguity and have less need for closure on issues (McCrae & Sutin, 2009). McCrae (1996) maintains that the importance of openness has been underestimated. Citing evidence that openness fosters liberalism, he argues that this trait is the key determinant of people's political attitudes and ideology. For example, evidence suggests that people high in openness tend to exhibit less prejudice against minorities than others (Flynn, 2005).

4. *Agreeableness.* Those who score high in agreeableness tend to be sympathetic, trusting, cooperative, modest, and straightforward. People who score at the opposite end of this personality dimension are characterized as suspicious, antagonistic, and aggressive. Agreeableness is associated with constructive approaches to conflict resolution, making agreeable people less quarrelsome than others (Jensen-Campbell & Graziano, 2001). Agreeableness is also correlated with empathy and helping behavior (Graziano & Tobin, 2009).

5. *Conscientiousness.* Conscientious people tend to be disciplined, well-organized, punctual, and dependable. Referred to as *constraint* in some trait models, conscientiousness is associated with strong self-discipline and the ability to regulate oneself effectively (Roberts et al., 2009). Studies have also shown that conscientiousness fosters diligence and dependability in the workplace (Lund et al., 2007).

Recent research suggests that there may be some interesting relations between the Big Five traits and *socioeconomic status (SES).* In a large-scale study of personality, social class, and mortality, Chapman and colleagues (2010) discovered that the number of people scoring high on specific Big Five traits varies with social class. **Figure 12.2** shows the likelihood of scoring in the top 20% on each of the Big Five traits as a function of SES. As you can see, the probability of being strongly conscientious rises dramatically as social class goes up. The prevalence of high scores on openness and extraversion also increase, although more gradually, as socioeconomic level rises. In contrast, strong agreeableness and neuroticism are less prevalent in the upper classes. At present, the causal relations that might underlie these correlations are unclear.

Correlations have also been found between the Big Five traits and quite a variety of important life outcomes (Ozer & Benet-Martinez, 2006). For instance, higher grades (GPA) in both high school and college are associated with higher conscientiousness. This association exists primarily because conscientious students work harder (Noftle & Robins, 2007). Several of the Big Five traits are associated with career success. Extraversion and conscientiousness are positive predictors of career success; neuroticism, on the other hand, is a negative predictor (Roberts, Caspi, & Moffitt, 2003). The likelihood of divorce can also be predicted by personality traits. Neuroticism elevates the probability of divorce, whereas agreeableness and conscientiousness reduce it (Roberts et al., 2007). Finally, and perhaps most important, two of the Big Five traits are related to health and mortality over the course of the life span. Neuroticism is associated with an elevated prevalence of virtually all major mental disorders, not to mention a number of physical illnesses (Lahey, 2009; Widiger, 2009). Conscientiousness, though, is correlated with less illness and reduced mortality (Kern & Friedman, 2008; Martin, Friedman, & Schwartz, 2007). In other words, conscientious people live longer than others! It is not hard

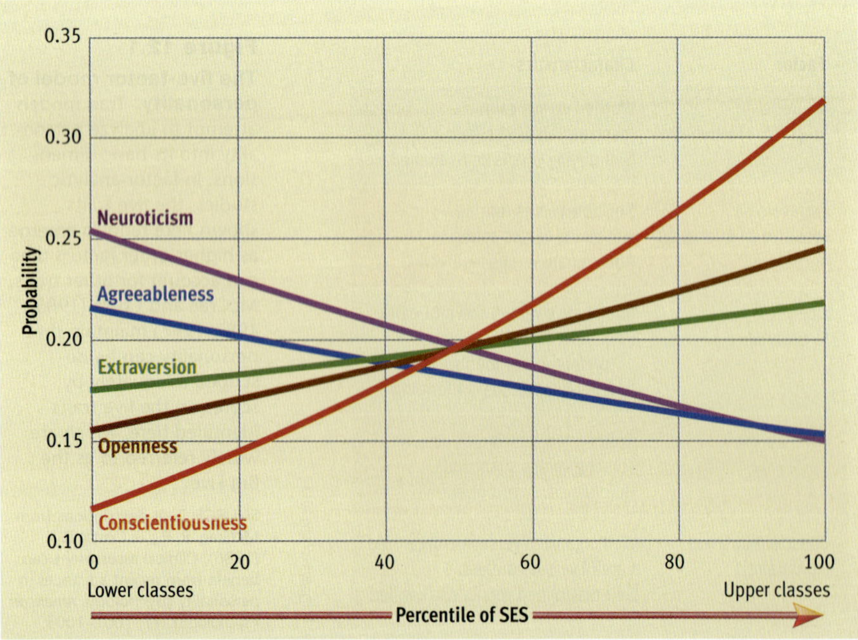

© Cengage Learning 2013

Figure 12.2

The Big Five and social class. In an investigation of how personality and social class jointly relate to health and mortality, Chapman and colleagues (2010) mapped out the association between specific Big Five traits and socioeconomic status (SES). This graph shows the probability that people would score in the top 20% on each Big Five trait for various levels of SES. For example, strong conscientiousness is much more likely to be seen in the higher social classes, which may contribute to the reduced mortality seen in these classes.

SOURCE: Chapman. B. P., Fiscella, K., Kawachi, I., & Duberstein, P. R. (2010). Personality, socioeconomic status, and all-cause mortality in the United States. *American Journal of Epidemiology, 171,* 83–92. By permission of Oxford University Press.

to figure out why, as conscientiousness is inversely related to just about every health-impairing behavior you can think of, including drinking, excessive eating, smoking, drug use, lack of exercise, and various risky practices (Roberts et al., 2009).

Like Cattell, McCrae and Costa maintain that personality can be described adequately by measuring the basic traits that they've identified. Their bold claim has been supported in many studies by other researchers. In fact, the five-factor model has become the dominant conception of personality structure in contemporary psychology (John, Naumann, & Soto, 2008; McCrae, 2005). These five traits have been characterized as the "latitude and longitude" along which personality should be mapped (Ozer & Reise, 1994, p. 361).

However, some theorists have been critical of the five-factor model. One camp of critics maintain that more than five traits are necessary to account for the bulk of the variation seen in human personality (Boyle, 2008). For example, one recent article argued that honesty-humility ought to be recognized as a fundamental sixth factor in personality (Lee & Ashton, 2008). Ironically, other theorists have argued for an even simpler, three-factor model of personality (De Radd et al., 2010).

The debate about how many dimensions are necessary to describe personality is likely to continue for many years to come. As you'll see throughout the chapter, the study of personality is an area in psychology that has a long history of "dueling theories." We'll divide these diverse personality theories into four broad groups that share certain assumptions, emphases, and interests: (1) psychodynamic perspectives, (2) behavioral perspectives, (3) humanistic perspectives, and (4) biological perspectives. We'll begin our discussion of personality theories by examining the life and work of Sigmund Freud.

REVIEW OF KEY LEARNING GOALS

12.1 The concept of personality focuses on consistency in people's behavior over time and across situations and on what traits make people distinctive from one another. Thus, personality refers to an individual's unique constellation of consistent behavioral traits.

12.2 A personality trait is a durable disposition to behave in a particular way. The five-factor model has become the dominant conception of personality structure. The Big Five personality traits are extraversion, neuroticism, openness to experience, agreeableness, and conscientiousness.

12.3 Recent research suggests that the Big Five traits are differentially correlated with social class. The Big Five traits are predictive of important life outcomes, such as grades, career success, and divorce. Neuroticism is associated with poorer health and elevated mortality, whereas the opposite relations are seen for the trait of conscientiousness.

Psychodynamic Perspectives

KEY LEARNING GOALS

12.4 Distinguish among the three components of personality and the three levels of awareness in Freud's theory.

12.5 Discuss the operation of defense mechanisms, and describe Freud's psychosexual stages of development.

12.6 Summarize the revisions of Freud's theory proposed by Jung and Adler.

12.7 Evaluate the strengths and weaknesses of the psychodynamic approach to personality.

Psychodynamic theories **include all the diverse theories, descended from the work of Sigmund Freud, that focus on unconscious mental forces.** Freud inspired many brilliant scholars who followed in his intellectual footsteps. Some of these followers simply refined and updated Freud's theory. Others veered off in new directions and established independent, albeit related, schools of thought. Today, the psychodynamic umbrella covers a large collection of loosely related theories that we can only sample from in this text. In this chapter, we'll examine Freud's ideas in some detail. Then we'll take a briefer look at the psychodynamic theories of Carl Jung and Alfred Adler.

Freud's Psychoanalytic Theory

PSYKTREK 10a

Born in 1856, Sigmund Freud grew up in a middle-class Jewish home in Vienna, Austria. He showed an early interest in intellectual pursuits and became an intense, hardworking young man, driven to achieve fame. He experienced his share of inner turmoil and engaged in regular self-analysis for over 40 years. Freud lived in the Victorian era, which was marked by sexual repression. His life was also affected by the first great World War, which devastated Europe, and by the growing anti-Semitism of the times. We'll see that the sexual repression and aggressive hostilities that Freud witnessed left their mark on his view of human nature.

Freud was a physician specializing in neurology when he began his medical practice in Vienna toward the end of the 19th century. Like other neurologists in his era, he often treated people troubled by nervous problems such as irrational fears, obsessions, and anxieties. Eventually he devoted himself to the treatment of mental disorders using an innovative procedure he had developed. This treatment, which he called *psychoanalysis,* required lengthy verbal interactions with patients during which Freud probed deeply into their lives.

Sigmund Freud

"No one who, like me, conjures up the most evil of those half-tamed demons that inhabit the human beast, and seeks to wrestle with them, can expect to come through the struggle unscathed."

© National Library of Medicine

Freud's (1901, 1924, 1940) *psychoanalytic theory* grew out of his decades of interactions with his clients in psychoanalysis. This theory attempts to explain personality, motivation, and psychological disorders by focusing on the influence of early childhood experiences, on unconscious motives and conflicts, and on the methods people use to cope with their sexual and aggressive urges.

Most of Freud's contemporaries were uncomfortable with his theory for at least three reasons. First, in arguing that people's behavior is governed by unconscious factors of which they are unaware, Freud made the disconcerting suggestion that individuals are not masters of their own minds. Second, in claiming that adult personalities are shaped by childhood experiences and other factors beyond one's control, he suggested that people are not masters of their own destinies. Third, by emphasizing the great importance of how people cope with their sexual urges, he offended those who held the conservative, Victorian values of his time. Let's examine the ideas that generated so much controversy.

Structure of Personality

PSYKTREK 10a

Freud divided personality structure into three components: the id, the ego, and the superego (see **Figure 12.3**). He saw a person's behavior as the outcome of interactions among these three components.

The *id* is the primitive, instinctive component of personality that operates according to the pleasure principle. Freud referred to the id as the reservoir of psychic energy. By this he meant that the id houses the raw biological urges (to eat, sleep, defecate, copulate, and so on) that energize human behavior. The id operates according to the ***pleasure principle,* which demands immediate gratification of its urges.** The id engages in *primary-process thinking,* which is primitive, illogical, irrational, and fantasy oriented.

The *ego* is the decision-making component of personality that operates according to the reality principle. The ego mediates between the id, with its forceful desires for immediate satisfaction, and the external social world, with its expectations and norms regarding suitable behavior. The ego considers social realities—society's norms, etiquette, rules, and customs—in deciding how to behave. The ego is guided by the ***reality principle,* which seeks to delay gratification of the id's urges until appropriate outlets and situations can be found.** In short, to stay out of trouble, the ego often works to tame the unbridled desires of the id.

In the long run, the ego wants to maximize gratification, just as the id does. However, the ego engages in *secondary-process thinking,* which is relatively rational, realistic, and oriented toward problem solving. Thus, the ego strives to avoid negative consequences from society and its representatives (for example, punishment by parents or teachers). Behaving "properly" is the way the ego accomplishes this goal. It also attempts to achieve long-range goals that sometimes require putting off gratification.

While the ego concerns itself with practical realities, **the *superego* is the moral component of personality that incorporates social standards about what represents right and wrong.** Throughout their lives, but especially during childhood, people receive training about what constitutes good and bad behavior. Many social norms regarding morality are eventually internalized, and the superego emerges out of the ego at around 3 to 5 years of age. In some people, the superego can become irrationally demanding in its striving for moral perfection, and they are plagued by excessive feelings of guilt. According to Freud, the id, ego, and superego are

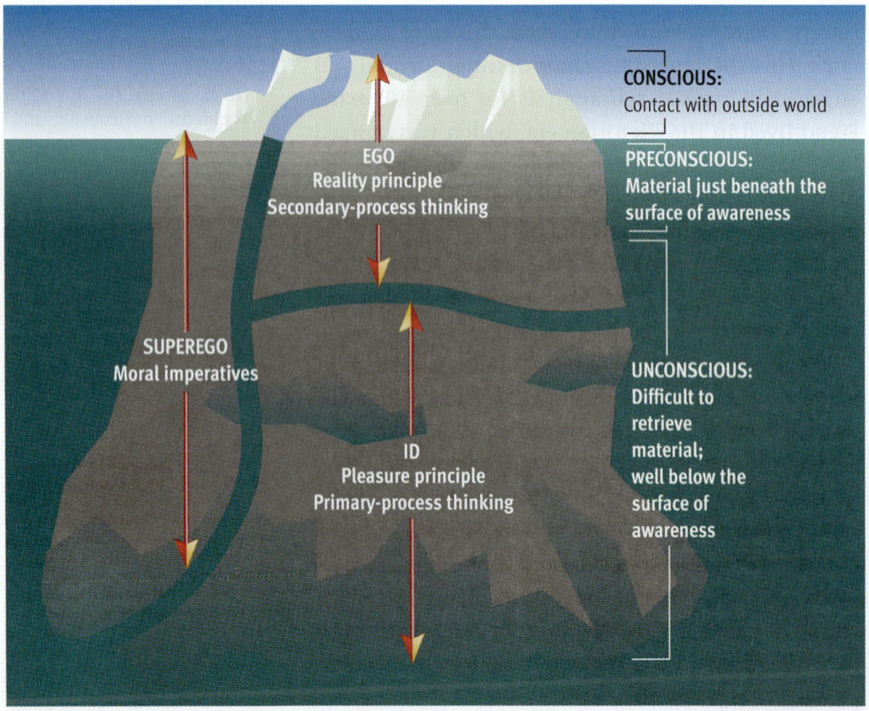

© Cengage Learning 2013

Figure 12.3

Freud's model of personality structure. Freud theorized that people have three levels of awareness: the conscious, the preconscious, and the unconscious. The enormous size of the unconscious is often dramatized by comparing it to the portion of an iceberg that lies beneath the water's surface. Freud also divided personality structure into three components—id, ego, and superego—which operate according to different principles and exhibit different modes of thinking. In Freud's model, the id is entirely unconscious, but the ego and superego operate at all three levels of awareness.

distributed differently across three levels of awareness. We'll describe these levels next.

Levels of Awareness 10a

Perhaps Freud's most enduring insight was his recognition of how unconscious forces can influence behavior. He inferred the existence of the unconscious from a variety of observations that he made with his patients. For example, he noticed that "slips of the tongue" often revealed a person's true feelings. He also concluded that his patients' dreams often expressed hidden desires. Most important, through psychoanalysis he often helped patients discover feelings and conflicts of which they had previously been unaware.

Freud contrasted the unconscious with the conscious and preconscious, creating three levels of awareness. **The *conscious* consists of whatever one is aware of at a particular point in time.** For example, at this moment your conscious may include the train of thought in this text and a dim awareness in the back of your mind that your eyes are getting tired and you're beginning to get hungry. **The *preconscious* contains material just beneath the surface of awareness that can easily be retrieved.** Examples might include your middle name, what you had for supper last night, or an argument you had with a friend yesterday. **The *unconscious* contains thoughts, memories, and desires that are well below the surface of conscious awareness but that nonetheless exert great influence on behavior.** Examples of material that might be found in your unconscious include a forgotten trauma from childhood, hidden feelings of hostility toward a parent, and repressed sexual desires.

Freud's conception of the mind is often compared to an iceberg that has most of its mass hidden beneath the water's surface (see **Figure 12.3**). He believed that the unconscious (the mass below the surface) is much larger than the conscious or preconscious. As you can see in **Figure 12.3**, he proposed that the ego and superego operate at all three levels of awareness. In contrast, the id is entirely unconscious, expressing its urges at a conscious level through the ego. Of course, the id's desires for immediate satisfaction often trigger internal conflicts with the ego and superego. These conflicts play a key role in Freud's theory.

Conflict and the Tyranny of Sex and Aggression 10a

Freud assumed that behavior is the outcome of an ongoing series of internal conflicts. He saw internal battles between the id, ego, and superego as routine. Why? Because the id wants to gratify its urges immediately, but the norms of civilized society frequently dictate otherwise. For example, your id might feel an urge to clobber a co-worker who constantly irritates you. However, society frowns on such behavior. Your ego, then, would try to hold this urge in check. Hence, you would find yourself in conflict. You may be experiencing conflict at this very moment. In Freudian terms, your id may be secretly urging you to stop reading this chapter so that you can fix a snack and watch some television. Your ego may be weighing this appealing option against your society-induced need to excel in school.

Freud believed that people's lives are dominated by conflict. He asserted that individuals careen from one conflict to another. The following scenario provides a concrete illustration of how the three components of personality interact to create constant conflicts:

Imagine lurching across your bed to shut off your alarm clock as it rings obnoxiously. It's 7 A.M. and time to get up for your history class. However, your id (operating according to the pleasure principle) urges you to return to the immediate gratification of additional sleep. Your ego (operating according to the reality principle) points out that you really must go to class since you haven't been able to decipher the textbook on your own. Your id (in its typical unrealistic fashion) smugly assures you that you will get the A grade that you need and suggests lying back to dream about how impressed your roommates will be. Just as you're relaxing, your superego jumps into the fray. It tries to make you feel guilty about all the money your parents paid in tuition for the class that you're about to skip. You haven't even gotten out of bed yet, but there's already a pitched battle in your psyche.

Freud's psychoanalytic theory was based on decades of clinical work. He treated a great many patients in the consulting room pictured here. The room contains numerous artifacts from other cultures—and the original psychoanalytic couch.

Reality CHECK

Misconception

People are generally aware of the factors that influence their behavior.

Reality

Freud's insight from over a century ago, that people are often unaware of the unconscious factors that shape their behvior, has proven prophetic. Decades of research on perception, cognition, and social behavior have repeatedly demonstrated that unconscious goals, attitudes, and thoughts exert enormous influence over human behavior (Bargh, Gollwitzer, & Oettingen, 2010; Dijksterhuis, 2010).

"ALL I WANT FROM THEM IS A SIMPLE MAJORITY ON THINGS."

© 2004 Sidney Harris/ScienceCartoonsPlus.com

Not all conflicts are equal. Freud believed that conflicts centering on sexual and aggressive impulses are especially likely to have far-reaching consequences. Why? *First, he thought that sex and aggression are subject to more complex and ambiguous social controls than other basic motives.* The norms governing sexual and aggressive behavior are subtle; people often get inconsistent messages about what's appropriate, creating confusion. *Second, he noted that the sexual and aggressive drives are thwarted more regularly than other basic biological urges.* Think about it: If you get hungry or thirsty, you can simply head for a nearby vending machine or a drinking fountain. But if a store clerk infuriates you, you aren't likely to reach across the counter and slug the person. Likewise, when you see someone you find attractive, you don't normally walk over and propose hooking up in a nearby broom closet. Thus, social norms dictate that sexual and aggressive drives are routinely frustrated.

Anxiety and Defense Mechanisms

PSYKTREK 10a

Most internal conflicts are trivial and are quickly resolved one way or the other. Occasionally, however, a conflict will linger for days, months, or even years. These conflicts are often played out entirely in the unconscious. Although you may not be aware of these unconscious battles, they can produce *anxiety* that slips to the surface of conscious awareness.

The arousal of anxiety is a crucial event in Freud's theory of personality functioning (see **Figure 12.4**).

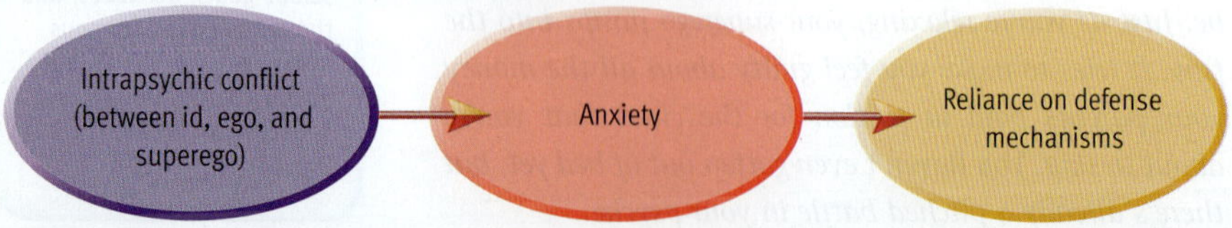

Figure 12.4
Freud's model of personality dynamics. According to Freud, unconscious conflicts between the id, ego, and superego sometimes lead to anxiety. This discomfort may lead to the use of defense mechanisms, which may temporarily relieve anxiety.
© Cengage Learning 2013

Anxiety is distressing. People try to rid themselves of this unpleasant emotion any way they can. This effort to ward off anxiety often involves the use of defense mechanisms. ***Defense mechanisms* are largely unconscious reactions that protect a person from unpleasant emotions such as anxiety and guilt** (see **Table 12.1**). Typically, they're mental maneuvers that work through self-deception. Consider ***rationalization*, which is creating false but plausible excuses to justify unacceptable behavior.** For example, after cheating someone in a business transaction, you might reduce your guilt by rationalizing that "everyone does it."

Repression is the most basic and widely used defense mechanism. It's been characterized as "the flagship in the psychoanalytic fleet of defense mechanisms" (Paulhus, Fridhandler, & Hayes, 1997). ***Repression* is keeping distressing thoughts and feelings buried in the unconscious.** People tend to repress desires that make them feel guilty, conflicts that make them anxious, and memories that are painful. Repression has been called "motivated forgetting." If you forget a dental appointment or the name of someone you don't like, repression may be at work. In a way, it's a form of self-deception.

Self-deception can also be seen in projection and displacement. ***Projection* is attributing one's own thoughts, feelings, or motives to another.** Usually, the thoughts one projects onto others are thoughts that would make one feel guilty. For example, if lusting for a co-worker makes you feel guilty, you might attribute any unspoken sexual tension between the two of you to the *other person's* desire to seduce you. ***Displacement* is diverting emotional feelings (usually anger) from their original source to a substitute target.** If your boss gives you a hard time at work and you come home and slam the door, kick the couch, and scream at your spouse, you're displacing your anger onto irrelevant targets. Unfortunately, social constraints often force people to hold back their anger. Thus, they end up lashing out at the people they are closest to.

Other prominent defense mechanisms include reaction formation, regression, and identification. ***Reaction formation* is behaving in a way that's exactly the opposite of one's true feelings.** Guilt about sexual desires often leads to reaction formation. For example, Freud theorized that many males who ridicule homosexuals are defending against their own latent homosexual impulses. The telltale sign of reaction formation is the exaggerated quality of the opposite behavior. ***Regression* is a reversion to immature patterns of behavior.** When anxious about their self-worth, some adults respond with

Table 12.1 Defense Mechanisms, with Examples

Defense Mechanism	Definition	Example
Repression	Keeping distressing thoughts and feelings buried in the unconscious	A traumatized soldier has no recollection of the details of a close brush with death.
Projection	Attributing one's own thoughts, feelings, or motives to another	A woman who dislikes her boss thinks she likes her boss but feels that the boss doesn't like her.
Displacement	Diverting emotional feelings (usually anger) from their original source to a substitute target	After a parental scolding, a young girl takes her anger out on her little brother.
Reaction formation	Behaving in a way that is exactly the opposite of one's true feelings	A parent who unconsciously resents a child spoils the child with outlandish gifts.
Regression	A reversion to immature patterns of behavior	An adult has a temper tantrum when he doesn't get his way.
Rationalization	Creating false but plausible excuses to justify unacceptable behavior	A student watches TV instead of studying, saying that "additional study wouldn't do any good anyway."
Identification	Bolstering self-esteem by forming an imaginary or real alliance with some person or group	An insecure young man joins a fraternity to boost his self-esteem.
Sublimation	Channeling unconscious, unacceptable impulses into socially acceptable or admirable activities	A person obsessed with sex becomes a sex therapist and helps others with their sexual problems

© Cengage Learning 2013

Note: See Table 14.2 for additional examples of defense mechanisms.

childish boasting and bragging. For example, a fired executive having difficulty finding a new job might start making ridiculous statements about his incomparable talents and achievements. Such bragging is regressive when it's marked by massive exaggerations that virtually anyone can see through. ***Identification* is bolstering self-esteem by forming an imaginary or real alliance with some person or group.** Young people often shore up fragile feelings of self-worth by identifying with rock stars, movie stars, or famous athletes. Adults may join exclusive country clubs or civic organizations as a means of identification.

Finally, Freud described the defense of ***sublimation*, which occurs when unconscious, unacceptable impulses are channeled into socially acceptable, perhaps even admirable, behaviors.** For example, intense aggressive impulses might be rechanneled by taking up boxing or football. Freud believed that many creative endeavors, such as painting, poetry, and sculpture, were sublimations of sexual urges. For instance, he argued that Leonardo da Vinci's painting of Madonna figures was a sublimation of his longing for intimacy with his mother (Freud, 1910). By definition, sublimation is regarded as a relatively healthy defense mechanism.

CONCEPT CHECK 12.1

Identifying Defense Mechanisms

Check your understanding of defense mechanisms by identifying specific defenses in the story below. Each example of a defense mechanism is underlined, with a number beneath it. Write in the defense at work in each case in the numbered spaces after the story. The answers are in Appendix A.

My girlfriend recently broke up with me after we had dated seriously for several years. At first, I cried a great deal and locked myself in my room, where I pouted endlessly.[1] I was sure that my former girlfriend felt as miserable as I did. I told several friends that she was probably lonely and depressed.[2] Later, I decided that I hated her. I was happy about the breakup and talked about how much I was going to enjoy my newfound freedom.[3] I went to parties and socialized a great deal and just forgot about her. It's funny—at one point I couldn't even remember her phone number![4] Then I started pining for her again. But eventually I began to look at the situation more objectively. I realized that she had many faults and that we were bound to break up sooner or later, so I was better off without her.[5]

1. ______________________
2. ______________________
3. ______________________
4. ______________________
5. ______________________

Table 12.2 Freud's Stages of Psychosexual Development

Stage	Approximate Ages	Erotic Focus	Key Tasks and Experiences
Oral	0–1	Mouth (sucking, biting)	Weaning (from breast or bottle)
Anal	2–3	Anus (expelling or retaining feces)	Toilet training
Phallic	4–5	Genitals (masturbating)	Identifying with adult role models; coping with Oedipal crisis
Latency	6–12	None (sexually repressed)	Expanding social contacts
Genital	Puberty onward	Genitals (being sexually intimate)	Establishing intimate relationships; contributing to society through working

© Cengage Learning 2013

Development: Psychosexual Stages

PSYKTREK 10a

Freud believed that "the child is father to the man." In fact, he made the rather startling claim that the basic foundation of an individual's personality has been laid down by the age of 5. To shed light on these crucial early years, Freud formulated a stage theory of development. He emphasized how young children deal with their immature but powerful sexual urges (he used the term *sexual* in a general way to refer to many urges for physical pleasure). According to Freud, these sexual urges shift in focus as children progress from one stage of development to another. Indeed, the names for the stages (oral, anal, genital, and so on) are based on where children are focusing their erotic energy during that period. Thus, ***psychosexual stages* are developmental periods with a characteristic sexual focus that leave their mark on adult personality.**

Freud theorized that each psychosexual stage has its own unique developmental challenges or tasks (see **Table 12.2**). The way these challenges are handled supposedly shapes personality. The process of *fixation* plays an important role in this process. ***Fixation* is a failure to move forward from one stage to another as expected.** Essentially, the child's development stalls for a while. Fixation can be caused by *excessive gratification* of needs at a particular stage or by *excessive frustration* of those needs. Either way, fixations left over from childhood affect adult personality. Generally, fixation leads to an overemphasis on the psychosexual needs prominent during the fixated stage.

© Finnbarr Webster/Alamy

Freud described a series of five psychosexual stages. Let's examine some of the highlights in this sequence.

Oral Stage This stage encompasses the first year of life. In Freud's view, the way the child's feeding experiences are handled is crucial to subsequent development. He attributed considerable importance to the manner in which the child is weaned from the breast or the bottle. According to Freud, fixation at the oral stage could form the basis for obsessive eating or smoking later in life, among many other things.

Anal Stage In the anal stage the crucial event is toilet training, which represents society's first systematic effort to regulate the child's biological urges. Severely punitive toilet training can lead to a variety of outcomes. For example, heavy reliance on punitive measures could lead to an association between genital concerns and the anxiety that the punishment arouses. This genital anxiety derived from severe toilet training could evolve into anxiety about sexual activities later in life.

Phallic Stage During the pivotal phallic stage, the *Oedipal complex* emerges. That is, little boys develop an erotically tinged preference for their mother. They also feel hostility toward their father, whom they view as a competitor for mom's affection. Similarly, little girls develop a special attachment to their father. Around the same time, they learn that little boys have different genitals and supposedly develop *penis envy*. According to Freud, young girls feel hostile toward their mother because they blame her for their anatomical "deficiency." To summarize, **in the *Oedipal complex* children manifest erotically tinged desires for their opposite-sex parent, accompanied by feelings of hostility toward their same-sex parent.** The name for this syndrome was taken from a tragic myth from ancient Greece. In this story, Oedipus was separated from his parents at birth. Not knowing the identity of his real parents, when he grew up he inadvertently killed his father and married his mother.

According to Freud, children need to resolve the Oedipal dilemma by purging the sexual longings for the opposite-sex parent and by crushing the hostility felt toward the same-sex parent. In Freud's view, healthy psychosexual development hinges on the resolution of the Oedipal conflict. Why? Because continued hostility toward the same-sex parent may prevent the child from identifying adequately with that parent. Freudian theory predicts that without such identification, sex typing, conscience, and many other aspects of the child's development won't progress as they should.

Latency and Genital Stages From around age 6 through puberty, the child's sexuality is largely suppressed. It becomes *latent*. Important events during this *latency stage* center on expanding social contacts beyond the immediate family. With puberty, the child progresses into the *genital stage*. Sexual urges reappear and focus on the genitals once again. At this point, sexual energy is normally channeled toward peers of the other sex, rather than toward oneself as in the phallic stage.

Freud argued that the early years shape personality. However, he did not mean that personality development comes to an abrupt halt in middle childhood. He believed, rather, that the foundation for adult personality has been solidly entrenched by this time. He maintained that future developments are rooted in early, formative experiences. Significant conflicts in later years are replays of crises from childhood.

In fact, Freud believed that unconscious sexual conflicts rooted in childhood experiences cause most personality disturbances. His steadfast belief in the psychosexual origins of psychological disorders eventually led to bitter theoretical disputes with two of his most brilliant colleagues: Carl Jung and Alfred Adler. They both argued that Freud overemphasized sexuality, but he rejected their ideas. The two theorists then felt compelled to go their own way, and each developed his own theory of personality.

Jung's Analytical Psychology

Carl Jung was born to middle-class Swiss parents in 1875. The son of a Protestant pastor, he was a deeply introverted, lonely child, but an excellent student. Jung had earned his medical degree and was an established young psychiatrist in Zurich when he began to write to Freud in 1906. When the two men had their first meeting, they were impressed by each other's insights. They talked nonstop for 13 hours! The two exchanged 359 letters before their friendship and theoretical alliance were torn apart. Their relationship was ruptured irreparably in 1913 by a variety of theoretical disagreements.

Jung called his new approach *analytical psychology* to differentiate it from Freud's psychoanalytic theory. Jung's analytical psychology eventually attracted many followers. Perhaps because of his conflicts with Freud, Jung claimed to deplore the way schools of thought often become dogmatic, discouraging new ideas. Although many theorists came to characterize themselves as "Jungians," Jung himself often remarked, "I am not a Jungian." He would say, "I do not want anybody to be a Jungian. I want people above all to be themselves" (van der Post, 1975).

Like Freud, Jung (1921, 1933) emphasized the unconscious determinants of personality. However, he proposed that the unconscious consists of two layers. The first layer, called the *personal unconscious*, is essentially the same as Freud's version of the unconscious. **The *personal unconscious* houses material that is not within one's conscious awareness because it has been repressed or forgotten.** In addition, Jung theorized the existence of a deeper layer. He called this layer the collective unconscious. **The *collective unconscious* is a storehouse of latent memory traces inherited from people's ancestral past.** According to Jung, each person shares the collective unconscious with the entire human race (see **Figure 12.5** on the next page). It contains the "whole spiritual heritage of mankind's evolution, born anew in the brain structure of every individual" (Jung, quoted in Campbell, 1971, p. 45).

Jung called these ancestral memories *archetypes*. They are not memories of actual, personal experiences. Instead, ***archetypes* are emotionally charged images and thought forms that have universal meaning.** These archetypal images and ideas show up frequently in dreams and are often manifested in a culture's use of symbols in art, literature, and religion. According to Jung, symbols from very different cultures often show striking similarities because they emerge from archetypes that are shared by the whole human race. For instance, Jung found numerous cultures in which the *mandala*, or "magic circle," has served as a symbol of the unified wholeness of the self (see **Figure 12.5**). Jung felt that an understanding of archetypal symbols helped him make sense of his patients' dreams. This was of great concern to him. He thought that dreams contain important messages from the unconscious. Like Freud, he depended extensively on dream analysis in his treatment of patients.

© Bettmann/Corbis

Carl Jung

"I am not a Jungian . . . I do not want anybody to be a Jungian. I want people above all to be themselves."

Figure 12.5

Jung's vision of the collective unconscious. Much like Freud, Jung theorized that each person has conscious and unconscious levels of awareness. However, he also proposed that the entire human race shares a collective unconscious, which exists in the deepest reaches of everyone's awareness. He saw the collective unconscious as a storehouse of hidden ancestral memories, called archetypes. Jung believed that important cultural symbols emerge from these universal archetypes. Thus, he argued that remarkable resemblances among symbols from disparate cultures (such as the mandalas shown here) are evidence of the existence of the collective unconscious. © Cengage Learning 2013

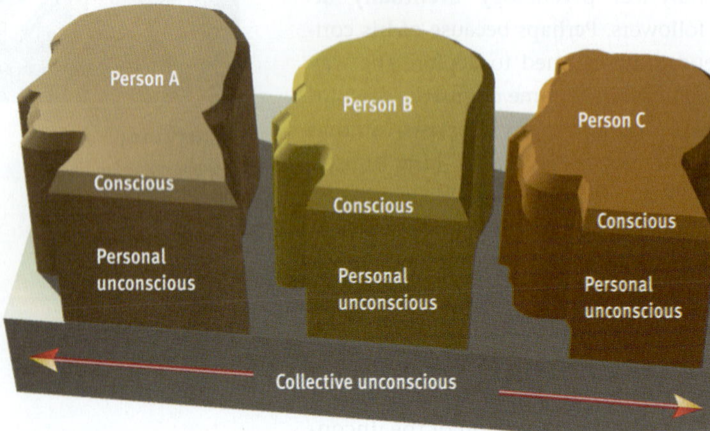

Mandalas from various cultures

Germany

© Erich Lessing/Art Resource, NY

Native American (Zuni)

© The Bridgeman Art Library, London

Tibet

Photograph © 2012 Museum of Fine Arts, Boston

Adler's Individual Psychology

Like Freud, Alfred Adler grew up in Vienna in a middle-class Jewish home. He was a sickly child who struggled to overcome rickets (a vitamin-deficiency disease) and an almost fatal case of pneumonia. At home, he was overshadowed by an exceptionally bright and successful older brother. Nonetheless, he went on to earn his medical degree. He practiced ophthalmology and general medicine before his interest turned to psychiatry. He was a charter member of Freud's inner circle—the Vienna Psychoanalytic Society. However, he soon began to develop his own theory of personality. His theorizing was denounced by Freud in 1911, and Adler was forced to resign from the Psychoanalytic Society. However, he took 9 of its 23 members with him to form his own organization. Adler's new approach to personality was christened *individual psychology*.

© Bettmann/Corbis

Alfred Adler

"The goal of the human soul is conquest, perfection, security, superiority."

Like Jung, Adler (1917, 1927) argued that Freud had gone overboard in centering his theory on sexual conflicts. According to Adler, the foremost source of human motivation is a striving for superiority. In his view, this striving does not necessarily translate into the pursuit of dominance or high status. Adler saw ***striving for superiority* as a universal drive to adapt, improve oneself, and master life's challenges.** He noted that young children understandably feel weak and helpless in comparison with more competent older children and adults. These early inferiority feelings supposedly motivate them to acquire new skills and develop new talents. Thus, Adler maintained that striving for superiority is the prime goal of life, rather than physical gratification (as suggested by Freud).

Adler asserted that everyone has to work to overcome some feelings of inferiority. He called this process compensation. ***Compensation* involves efforts to overcome imagined or real inferiorities by developing one's abilities.** Adler believed that compensation is entirely normal. However, in some people, inferiority feelings can become excessive, which can result in what is widely known today as an *inferiority complex*—exaggerated feelings of weakness and inadequacy. Adler thought that either parental pampering or parental neglect could cause an inferiority complex. Thus, he agreed with Freud on the importance of early childhood experiences. However, he focused on different aspects of parent-child relations.

Adler explained personality disturbances by noting that excessive inferiority feelings can pervert the normal process of striving for superiority. He asserted that some people engage in *overcompensation* to conceal, even from themselves, their feelings of inferiority. Instead of working to master life's challenges, people with an inferiority complex work to achieve status, gain power over others, and acquire the trappings of success (fancy clothes, impressive cars, or whatever looks important to them). They tend to flaunt their success in an effort to cover up their underlying inferiority complex. However, the problem is that such people engage in unconscious self-deception. They worry more about *appearances* than *reality*.

Evaluating Psychodynamic Perspectives

The psychodynamic approach has provided a number of far-reaching, truly "grand" theories of personality. These theories yielded some bold new insights when they were first presented. Although one might argue about exact details of interpretation, research has demonstrated that (1) unconscious forces can influence behavior, (2) internal conflict often plays a key role in generating psychological distress, (3) early childhood experiences can have powerful influences on adult personality, and (4) people do use defense mechanisms to reduce their experience of unpleasant emotions (Bornstein, 2003; Porcerelli et al., 2010; Solms, 2004; Westen, Gabbard, & Ortigo, 2008).

In addition to being praised, psychodynamic formulations have also been criticized on several grounds. Criticisms include the following (Crews, 2006; Eysenck, 1990b; Kramer, 2006; Torrey, 1992):

1. *Poor testability.* Scientific investigations require testable hypotheses. Psychodynamic ideas have often been too vague and conjectural to permit a clear scientific test. For instance, how would you prove or disprove Freud's assertion that the id is entirely unconscious, or Jung's belief that humans share a collective unconscious?

2. *Unrepresentative samples.* Freud's theories were based on an exceptionally narrow sample of upper-class, neurotic, sexually repressed Viennese women. They were not even remotely representative of Western European culture, let alone other cultures.

3. *Inadequate evidence.* Psychodynamic theories depend too heavily on clinical case studies in which it's much too easy for clinicians to see what they expect to see. Reexaminations of Freud's own clinical work suggest that he frequently distorted his patients' case histories to make them mesh with his theory (Esterson, 2001; Powell & Boer, 1995). Insofar as researchers have accumulated evidence on psychodynamic theories, the evidence has provided only modest support for many of the central hypotheses (Fisher & Greenberg, 1985, 1996; Westen, Gabbard, & Ortigo, 2008; Wolitzky, 2006).

4. *Sexism.* Many critics have argued that psychodynamic theories are characterized by a sexist bias against women. Freud believed that females' penis envy made them feel inferior to males. He also thought that females tended to develop weaker superegos and to be more prone to neurosis than males. The sex bias in modern psychodynamic theories has been reduced considerably. Nonetheless, the psychodynamic approach has generally provided a rather male-centered point of view (Lerman, 1986; Person, 1990).

It's easy to ridicule Freud for concepts such as penis envy. It's easy also to point to Freudian ideas that have turned out to be wrong. However, you have to remember that Freud, Jung, and Adler began to fashion their theories over a century ago. It's not entirely fair to compare these theories to other models that have had the privilege of building on a century's worth of research. That's like asking the Wright brothers to race a modern military jet. Freud and his colleagues deserve great credit for breaking new ground with their speculations about psychodynamics. In psychology as a whole, no other school of thought has been as influential, with the exception of behaviorism, to which we turn next.

© SuperStock/SuperStock

Adler's theory has been used to analyze the tragic life of the legendary actress Marilyn Monroe (Ansbacher, 1970). During her childhood, Monroe suffered from parental neglect that left her with acute feelings of inferiority. Her inferiority feelings led her to overcompensate by flaunting her beauty, marrying celebrities (Joe DiMaggio and Arthur Miller), keeping film crews waiting for hours, and seeking the adoration of her fans.

REVIEW OF KEY LEARNING GOALS

12.4 Freud described personality structure in terms of three components—the id, ego, and superego. The three are routinely involved in an ongoing series of internal conflicts. Freud described three levels of awareness: the conscious, the preconscious, and the unconscious. His theory emphasized the importance of unconscious processes.

12.5 According to Freud, anxiety and other unpleasant emotions such as guilt are often warded off with defense mechanisms. Key defense mechanisms include rationalization, repression, projection, displacement, reaction formation, regression, identification, and sublimation. Freud described a series of five psychosexual stages of development: oral, anal, phallic, latency, and genital. Certain experiences during these stages can have lasting effects on adult personality. Resolution of the Oedipal complex is thought to be critical to healthy development.

12.6 Jung's most innovative concept was the collective unconscious, a storehouse of latent memory traces inherited from people's ancestral past. Archetypes are emotionally charged images that have universal meaning. Adler's individual psychology emphasizes how people strive for superiority to compensate for their feelings of inferiority. He explained personality disturbances in terms of overcompensation and inferiority complexes.

12.7 Overall, psychodynamic theories have produced many groundbreaking insights about the unconscious, the role of internal conflict, and the importance of early childhood experiences in personality development. However, psychodynamic theories have been criticized for their poor testability, their reliance on unrepresentative samples, their inadequate base of empirical evidence, and their male-centered views.

KEY LEARNING GOALS

12.8 Review how Skinner's principles of operant conditioning can be applied to the development of personality.

12.9 Describe Bandura's social cognitive theory, and discuss the importance of self-efficacy.

12.10 Identify Mischel's major contribution, and discuss the resolution of the person-situation debate.

12.11 Assess the strengths and weaknesses of the behavioral approach to personality.

Behavioral Perspectives

***Behaviorism* is a theoretical orientation based on the premise that scientific psychology should study only observable behavior.** As we saw in Chapter 1, behaviorism has been a major school of thought in psychology since 1913. John B. Watson began campaigning at this time for the behavioral point of view. Research in the behavioral tradition has focused largely on learning. For many decades, behaviorists devoted relatively little attention to the study of personality. However, their interest in personality began to pick up after John Dollard and Neal Miller (1950) attempted to translate selected Freudian ideas into behavioral terminology. Dollard and Miller showed that behavioral concepts could provide enlightening insights about the complicated subject of personality.

In this section, we'll examine three behavioral views of personality: those of B. F. Skinner, Albert Bandura, and Walter Mischel. For the most part, you'll see that behaviorists explain personality the same way they explain everything else—in terms of learning.

Skinner's Ideas Applied to Personality

PSYKTREK 10b

As we noted in Chapters 1 and 6, modern behaviorism's most prominent theorist has been B. F. Skinner. He was an American psychologist who lived from 1904 to 1990. After earning his doctorate in 1931, Skinner spent most of his career at Harvard University, where he achieved renown for his research on the principles of learning. He discovered these principles mostly through the study of rats and pigeons. Skinner's (1953, 1957) concepts of *operant conditioning* were never meant to be a theory of personality. However, his ideas have affected thinking in all areas of psychology and have been applied to the explanation of personality. Here we'll examine Skinner's views as they relate to personality structure and development.

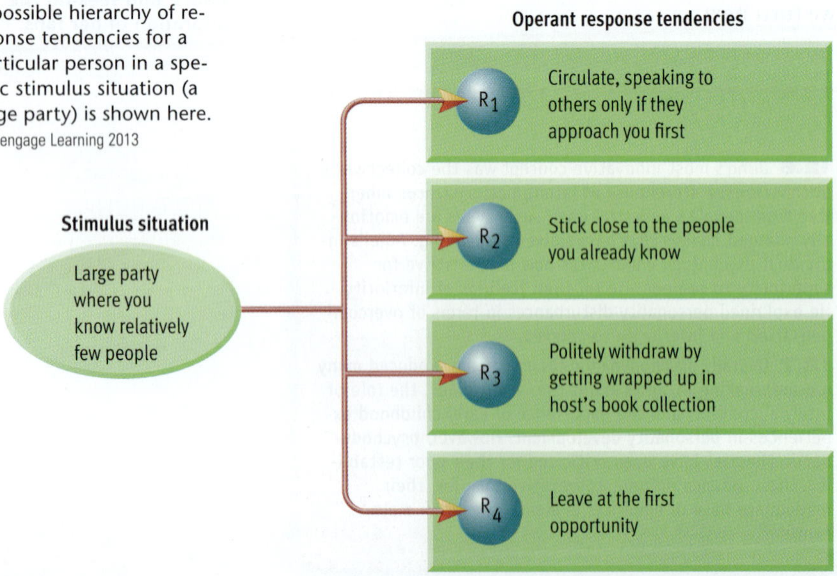

Figure 12.6

A behavioral view of personality. Staunch behaviorists devote little attention to the structure of personality because it is unobservable, but they implicitly view personality as an individual's collection of response tendencies. A possible hierarchy of response tendencies for a particular person in a specific stimulus situation (a large party) is shown here.

© Cengage Learning 2013

Personality Structure: A View from the Outside

PSYKTREK 10b

Skinner made no provision for internal personality structures similar to Freud's id, ego, and superego because such structures can't be observed. Following in the tradition of Watson's radical behaviorism, Skinner showed little interest in what goes on "inside" people. He argued that it's useless to speculate about private, unobservable cognitive processes. Instead, he focused on how the external environment molds overt behavior. Indeed, he argued for a strong brand of *determinism,* asserting that behavior is fully determined by environmental stimuli. He claimed that free will is but an illusion, saying, "There is no place in the scientific position for a self as a true originator or initiator of action" (Skinner, 1974, p. 225).

How can Skinner's theory explain the consistency that can be seen in individuals' behavior? According to his view, people show some consistent patterns of behavior because they have some stable *response tendencies* that they have acquired through experience. These response tendencies may change in the future, as a result of new experience. They're enduring enough, though, to create a certain degree of consistency in a person's behavior. Implicitly, then, Skinner viewed an individual's personality as a *collection of response tendencies that are tied to various stimulus situations.* A specific situation may be associated with a number of response tendencies that vary in strength, depending on past conditioning (see **Figure 12.6**).

Personality Development as a Product of Conditioning

PSYKTREK 10b

Skinner's theory accounts for personality development by explaining how various response tendencies are acquired through operant conditioning

(Bolling, Terry, & Kohlenberg, 2006). As discussed in Chapter 6, Skinner maintained that environmental consequences—reinforcement, punishment, and extinction—determine people's patterns of responding. On the one hand, when responses are followed by favorable consequences (reinforcement), they are strengthened. For example, if your joking around pays off with favorable attention, your tendency to tell jokes will increase (see **Figure 12.7**). On the other hand, when responses lead to negative consequences (punishment), they are weakened. Thus, if your impulsive decisions always backfire, your tendency to be impulsive will decline.

Response tendencies are constantly being strengthened or weakened by new experiences. Because of this, Skinner's theory views personality development as a continuous, lifelong journey. Unlike Freud and many other theorists, Skinner saw no reason to break the developmental process into stages. Nor did he attribute special importance to early childhood experiences.

Skinner believed that conditioning in humans operates much the same as it did in the rats and pigeons that he studied in his lab. Hence, he assumed that conditioning strengthens and weakens response tendencies "mechanically"—that is, without the person's conscious participation. Skinner was therefore able to explain consistencies in behavior (personality) without being concerned about individuals' cognitive processes.

Skinner's ideas continue to be highly influential. But his mechanical, deterministic, noncognitive view of personality has not gone unchallenged by other behaviorists. In recent decades, several theorists have developed somewhat different behavioral models with a more cognitive emphasis.

B. F. Skinner

The objection to inner states is not that they do not exist, but that they are not relevant."

Bandura's Social Cognitive Theory

PSYKTREK 10b

Albert Bandura is a modern theorist who has helped reshape the theoretical landscape of behaviorism. Bandura grew up in Canada but has spent his entire academic career at Stanford University. He has conducted influential research on personality, behavior therapy, and the determinants of aggression.

Figure 12.7

Personality development and operant conditioning. According to Skinner, people's characteristic response tendencies are shaped by reinforcers and other consequences that follow behavior. Thus, if your joking around leads to attention and compliments, your tendency to be witty and humorous will be strengthened.

Cognitive Processes and Reciprocal Determinism

PSYKTREK 10b

Bandura is one of several theorists who have added a cognitive flavor to behaviorism since the 1960s. Bandura (1977), Walter Mischel (1973), and Julian Rotter (1982) take issue with Skinner's "pure" behaviorism. They point out that humans obviously are conscious, thinking, feeling beings. Moreover, these theorists argue that in neglecting cognitive processes, Skinner ignored the most distinctive and important feature of human behavior. Bandura and like-minded theorists originally called their modified brand of behaviorism *social learning theory*. Today, Bandura refers to his model as *social cognitive theory*.

Bandura (1986, 2006) agrees with the fundamental thrust of behaviorism. He believes that personality is largely shaped through learning. However, he contends that conditioning is not a mechanical process in which people are passive participants. Instead, he maintains that "people are self-organizing, proactive, self-reflecting, and self-regulating" (Bandura, 1999b, p. 154). Thus, people routinely attempt to influence their life circumstances and their outcomes (Bandura, 2008).

Comparing his theory to Skinner's highly deterministic view, Bandura advocates a position called *reciprocal determinism*. According to this notion, the environment does determine behavior (as Skinner would argue). However, behavior also determines the environment. In other words, people can select

Albert Bandura

"Most human behavior is learned by observation through modeling."

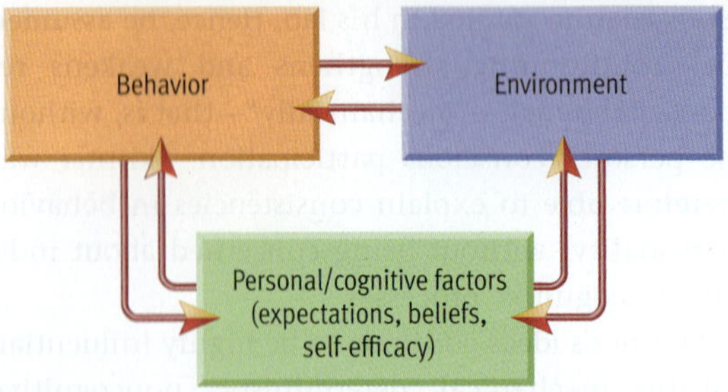

Figure 12.8
Bandura's reciprocal determinism. Bandura rejects Skinner's highly deterministic view that behavior is governed by environment and that freedom is an illusion. Bandura argues that internal mental events, external environmental contingencies, and overt behavior all influence one another. © Cengage Learning 2013

their environments and act to alter them (by changing the friends they hang around with, for instance). Moreover, personal factors (cognitive structures such as beliefs and expectancies) determine and are determined by both behavior and the environment (see **Figure 12.8**). Thus, ***reciprocal determinism* is the idea that internal mental events, external environmental events, and overt behavior all influence one another.** According to Bandura, humans are neither masters of their own destiny nor hapless victims buffeted about by the environment.

Observational Learning

PsykTrek 10b

Bandura's foremost theoretical contribution has been his description of observational learning, which we introduced in Chapter 6. ***Observational learning* occurs when an organism's responding is influenced by the observation of others, who are called models.** According to Bandura, both classical and operant conditioning can occur vicariously when one person observes another's conditioning. For example, watching your sister get cheated by someone giving her a bad check for her old computer could strengthen your tendency to be suspicious of others. Your sister would obviously be the one actually experiencing the negative consequences. However, those consequences might also influence you—through observational learning.

Bandura maintains that people's characteristic patterns of behavior are shaped by the *models* that they're exposed to. He isn't referring to the fashion models who dominate the mass media (although they qualify as well). In observational learning, **a *model* is a person whose behavior is observed by another.** At one time or another, everyone serves as a model for others. Bandura's key point is that many response tendencies are the product of *imitation*.

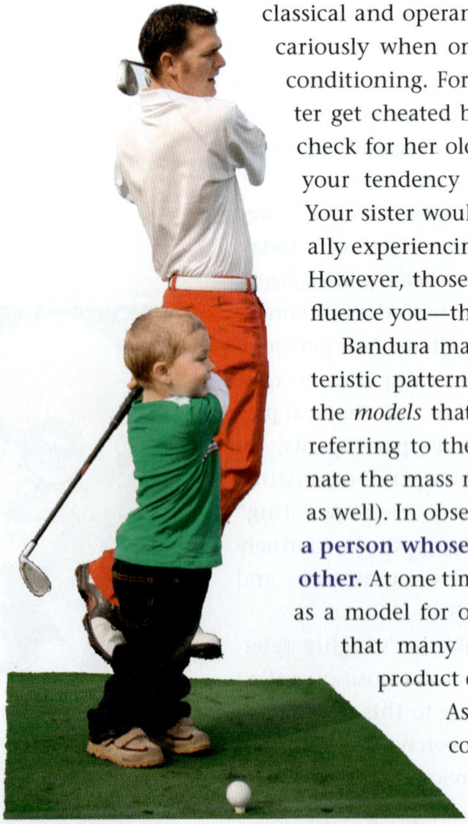

© Vanessa Nel/Shutterstock

As research has grown, it's become apparent that some models are more influential than others (Bandura, 1986). Both children and adults tend to imitate people they like or respect more than people they don't. People are also especially prone to imitate the behavior of people whom they consider attractive or powerful. In addition, imitation is more likely when people see similarity between models and themselves. Thus, children tend to imitate same-sex role models somewhat more than opposite-sex models. Finally, people are more likely to copy a model if they observe that the model's behavior leads to positive outcomes.

Self-Efficacy

Bandura discusses how a variety of personal factors (aspects of personality) govern behavior. In recent years, the factor he has emphasized most is self-efficacy (Bandura, 1993, 1995, 2004). ***Self-efficacy* refers to one's belief about one's ability to perform behaviors that should lead to expected outcomes.** When self-efficacy is high, individuals feel confident that they can execute the responses necessary to earn reinforcers. When self-efficacy is low, individuals worry that the necessary responses may be beyond their abilities. Perceptions of self-efficacy are subjective and specific to certain kinds of tasks. For instance, you might feel extremely confident about your ability to handle difficult social situations. On the other hand, you might be doubtful about your ability to handle academic challenges.

Perceptions of self-efficacy can influence which challenges people tackle and how well they perform. Studies have found that feelings of greater self-efficacy are associated with reduced procrastination (Steel, 2007), greater success in giving up smoking (Schnoll et al., 2010), greater adherence to exercise regimens (Ayotte, Margrett, & Hicks-Patrick, 2010), more effective weight-loss efforts (Linde et al., 2006), reduced disability from problems with chronic pain (Hadjistavropoulos et al., 2007), better study habits (Prat-Sala & Redford, 2010), higher levels of academic performance (Weiser & Riggio, 2010), reduced vulnerability to post-traumatic stress disorder in the face of severe stress (Hirschel & Schulenberg, 2009), less jealousy in romantic relationships (Hu, Zhang, & Li, 2005), greater success in searching for a new job (Saks, 2006), and reduced strain from occupational stress (Grau, Salanova, & Peiro, 2001), among many other things.

© Brand X Pictures/Getty Images

Mischel and the Person-Situation Controversy

Walter Mischel was born in Vienna, not far from Freud's home. His family immigrated to the United States in 1939, when he was 9. He spent many years on the faculty at Stanford, as a colleague of Bandura's. He has since moved to Columbia University. Mischel's (1973, 1984) chief contribution to personality theory has been to focus attention on the extent to which situational factors govern behavior.

According to Mischel, people make responses that they think will lead to reinforcement in the situation at hand. For example, if you believe that hard work in your job will pay off by leading to raises and promotions, you'll probably be diligent and industrious. But if you think that hard work in your job is unlikely to be rewarded, you may behave in a lazy and irresponsible manner. Thus, Mischel's version of social learning theory predicts that people will often behave differently in different situations. Mischel (1968, 1973) reviewed decades of research and concluded that, indeed, people exhibit far less consistency across situations than had been widely assumed. For example, studies show that a person who is honest in one situation may be dishonest in another.

Mischel's provocative ideas struck at the heart of the concept of personality, which assumes that people are reasonably consistent in their behavior. His theories sparked a robust debate about the relative importance of the *person* as opposed to the *situation* in determining behavior. This debate has led to a growing recognition that *both* the person and the situation are important determinants of behavior (Funder, 2001; Roberts & Pomerantz, 2004). As William Fleeson (2004) puts it, "The person-situation debate is coming to an end because both sides of the debate have turned out to be right" (p. 83). Fleeson reconciles the two opposing views by arguing that each prevails at a different level of analysis. When small chunks of behavior are examined on a moment-to-moment basis, situational factors dominate and most individuals' behavior tends to be highly variable. However, when larger chunks of typical behavior over time are examined, people tend to be reasonably consistent and personality traits prove to be more influential.

University photographer Joe Pineiro, Columbia University

Walter Mischel

"It seems remarkable how each of us generally manages to reconcile his seemingly diverse behavior into one self-consistent whole."

Evaluating Behavioral Perspectives

Behavioral theories are firmly rooted in extensive empirical research rather than clinical intuition. Skinner's ideas have shed light on how environmental consequences and conditioning mold people's characteristic behavior. Bandura's social cognitive theory has expanded the horizons of behaviorism. Mischel deserves credit for increasing psychology's awareness of how situational factors shape behavior. Of course, each theoretical approach has its weaknesses and shortcomings, and the behavioral approach is no exception. Major lines of criticism include the following (Liebert & Liebert, 1998; Pervin & John, 2001):

1. *Dehumanizing nature of radical behaviorism.* Skinner and other radical behaviorists have been criticized heavily for denying the existence of free will and the importance of cognitive processes. The critics argue that the radical behaviorist viewpoint strips human behavior of its most uniquely human elements. It therefore cannot provide an accurate model of human functioning.

2. *Dilution of the behavioral approach.* The behaviorists used to be criticized because they neglected cognitive processes. The rise of social cognitive theory blunted this criticism. However, social cognitive theory undermines the foundation on which behaviorism was built—the idea that psychologists should study only observable behavior. Thus, some critics complain that behavioral theories aren't very behavioral anymore.

Reality CHECK

Misconception

People's behavior is largely determined by their personality and character.

Reality

Mischel's argument that situational forces shape much of our behavior has proven compelling. That is not to say that personality is irrelevant. But research has shown again and again that situational factors are more powerful determinants of behavior than laypersons or scientists would have guessed (Benjamin & Simpson, 2009; Ross & Nisbett, 1991; Zimbardo, 2004).

REVIEW OF KEY LEARNING GOALS

12.8 Skinner had little interest in unobservable cognitive processes and embraced a strong determinism. Skinner's followers view personality as a collection of response tendencies tied to specific stimulus situations. They assume that personality development is a lifelong process in which response tendencies are shaped and reshaped by learning, especially operant conditioning.

12.9 Social cognitive theory focuses on how cognitive factors such as expectancies regulate learned behavior. Bandura's concept of reciprocal determinism suggests that mental events, environmental factors, and overt behavior all influence one another. High self-efficacy has been related to successful health regimens, academic success, and better coping with stress, among many other things.

12.10 Mischel has questioned the degree to which people display cross-situational consistency in behavior. His arguments have increased psychologists' awareness of the situational determinants of behavior. According to Fleeson, situational factors dominate small chunks of behavior, whereas personality traits shape larger chunks of behavior.

12.11 Behavioral approaches to personality are based on rigorous research. They have provided ample insights into how environmental factors and learning mold personalities. Radical behaviorism's dehumanizing view of human nature has been criticized, but more contemporary social cognitive theories have been knocked for diluting the behavioral approach.

KEY LEARNING GOALS

12.12 Identify the impetus for, and assumptions of, humanism.

12.13 Articulate Rogers's views on self-concept, development, and defensive behavior.

12.14 Explain Maslow's hierarchy of needs, and summarize his findings on self-actualizing persons.

12.15 Evaluate the strengths and weaknesses of the humanistic approach to personality.

Humanistic Perspectives

Humanistic theory emerged in the 1950s as something of a backlash against the behavioral and psychodynamic theories that we have just discussed (Cassel, 2000; DeCarvalho, 1991). The principal charge hurled at these two models was that they are dehumanizing. Freudian theory was criticized for its belief that behavior is dominated by primitive, animalistic drives. Behaviorism was criticized for its preoccupation with animal research and for its mechanistic view of personality. Critics argued that both schools of thought are too deterministic—failing to recognize that humans are free to chart their own courses of action—and that both ignore the unique qualities of human behavior.

Many of these critics blended into a loose alliance that came to be known as humanism, because of its exclusive focus on human behavior. ***Humanism* is a theoretical orientation that emphasizes the unique qualities of humans, especially their freedom and their potential for personal growth.** In contrast to most psychodynamic and behavioral theorists, humanistic theorists, such as Carl Rogers and Abraham Maslow, take an optimistic view of human nature. They assume (1) that people can rise above their primitive animal heritage, (2) that people are largely conscious and rational beings who are not dominated by unconscious, irrational conflicts, and (3) that people are not helpless pawns of deterministic forces.

Humanistic theorists also maintain that a person's subjective view of the world is more important than objective reality (Wong, 2006). According to this notion, if you think that you're homely or bright or sociable, this belief will influence your behavior more than the realities of how homely, bright, or sociable you actually are.

Courtesy of Carl Rogers Memorial Library

Carl Rogers

"I have little sympathy with the rather prevalent concept that man is basically irrational, and that his impulses, if not controlled, will lead to destruction of others and self. Man's behavior is exquisitely rational, moving with subtle and ordered complexity toward the goals his organism is endeavoring to achieve."

Rogers's Person-Centered Theory

PsykTrek 10c

Carl Rogers (1951, 1961, 1980) was one of the founders of the human potential movement. This movement emphasizes self-realization through sensitivity training, encounter groups, and other exercises intended to foster personal growth. Rogers was a bright student, but he had to rebel against his parents' wishes in order to pursue his graduate study in psychology. In the 1940s and 1950s, Rogers devised a major new approach to psychotherapy. Like Freud, Rogers based his personality theory on his extensive therapeutic interactions with many clients. Because of its emphasis on a person's subjective point of view, Rogers's approach is called a *person-centered theory.*

The Self

PsykTrek 10c

Rogers viewed personality structure in terms of just one construct. He called this construct the *self.* It's more widely known today as the *self-concept.* **A *self-concept* is a collection of beliefs about one's own nature, unique qualities, and typical behavior.** Your self-concept is your own mental picture of yourself. It's a collection of self-perceptions. For example, a self-concept might include beliefs such as "I'm easygoing" or "I'm sly and crafty" or "I'm pretty" or "I'm hardworking." According to Rogers, individuals are aware of their self-concept. It's not buried in their unconscious.

Rogers stressed the subjective nature of the self-concept, noting that it may not be entirely consistent with the person's experiences. Most people tend to distort their experiences to some extent to promote a relatively favorable self-concept. For example, you may believe that you're quite bright. Your grade transcript might suggest otherwise, however. Rogers called the gap between self-concept and reality "incongruence." ***Incongruence* is the degree of disparity between one's self-concept and one's actual experience.** In contrast, if a person's self-concept is reasonably accurate, it's said to be *congruent* with reality (see **Figure 12.9**). Everyone experiences *some* incongruence. The crucial issue is how much. As we'll

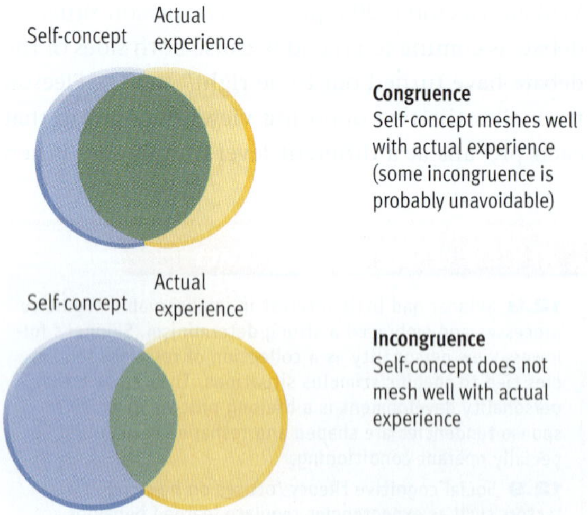

Figure 12.9
Rogers's view of personality structure. In Rogers's model, the self-concept is the only important structural construct. However, Rogers acknowledged that one's self-concept may not be consistent with the realities of one's actual experience—a condition called incongruence. © Cengage Learning 2013

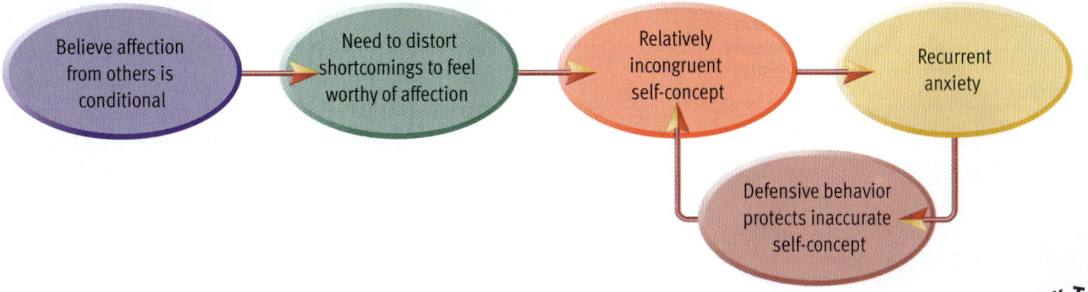

Figure 12.10
Rogers's view of personality development and dynamics. Rogers's theory of development posits that conditional love leads to a need to distort experiences, which fosters an incongruent self-concept. Incongruence makes one prone to recurrent anxiety, which triggers defensive behavior, which fuels more incongruence. © Cengage Learning 2013

see, Rogers maintained that too much incongruence undermines one's psychological well-being.

Development of the Self 10c

In terms of personality development, Rogers was concerned with how childhood experiences promote congruence or incongruence between one's self-concept and one's experience. According to Rogers, people have a strong need for affection, love, and acceptance from others. Early in life, parents provide most of this affection. Rogers maintained that some parents make their affection *conditional.* That is, it depends on the child's behaving well and living up to expectations. When parental love seems conditional, children often block out of their self-concept those experiences that make them feel unworthy of love. They do so because they're worried about parental acceptance, which appears unstable.

At the other end of the spectrum, some parents make their affection *unconditional.* Their children have less need to block out unworthy experiences because they've been assured that they're worthy of affection, no matter what they do.

© MBI/Alamy

As a result, Rogers believed that unconditional love from parents fosters congruence and that conditional love fosters incongruence. He further theorized that if individuals grow up believing that affection from others is highly conditional, they will go on to distort more and more of their experiences in order to feel worthy of acceptance from a wider and wider array of people (see **Figure 12.10**).

Anxiety and Defense 10c

According to Rogers, experiences that threaten people's personal views of themselves are the principal cause of anxiety. The more inaccurate your self-concept, the more likely you are to have experiences that clash with your self-perceptions. Thus, people with highly incongruent self-concepts are especially likely to be plagued by recurrent anxiety (see **Figure 12.10**).

To ward off this anxiety, individuals often behave defensively in an effort to reinterpret their experience so that it appears consistent with their self-concept. Thus, they ignore, deny, and twist reality to protect and perpetuate their self-concept. Consider a young woman who, like most people, considers herself a "nice person." Let's suppose that in reality she is rather conceited and selfish. She gets feedback from both boyfriends and girlfriends that she is a "self-centered, snotty brat." How might she react in order to protect her self-concept? She might ignore or block out those occasions when she behaves selfishly. She might attribute her girlfriends' negative comments to their jealousy of her good looks. Or perhaps she would blame her boyfriends' negative remarks on their disappointment because she won't get more serious with them. As you can see, people will sometimes go to great lengths to defend their self-concept.

Maslow's Theory of Self-Actualization 10c

Abraham Maslow grew up in Brooklyn. Like Rogers, he had to resist parental pressures in order to follow through on his interest in psychology. Maslow went on to create an influential theory of motivation and provide crucial leadership for the fledgling humanistic movement. Echoing Rogers, Maslow (1968, 1970) argued that psychology should take an optimistic view of human nature instead of dwelling on the causes of disorders. "To oversimplify the matter somewhat," he said, "it's as if Freud supplied to us the sick half of psychology and we must now fill it out with the healthy half" (1968, p. 5). Maslow's key contributions were his analysis of how motives are

© Cengage Learning 2013

Abraham Maslow
"It is as if Freud supplied to us the sick half of psychology and we must now fill it out with the healthy half."

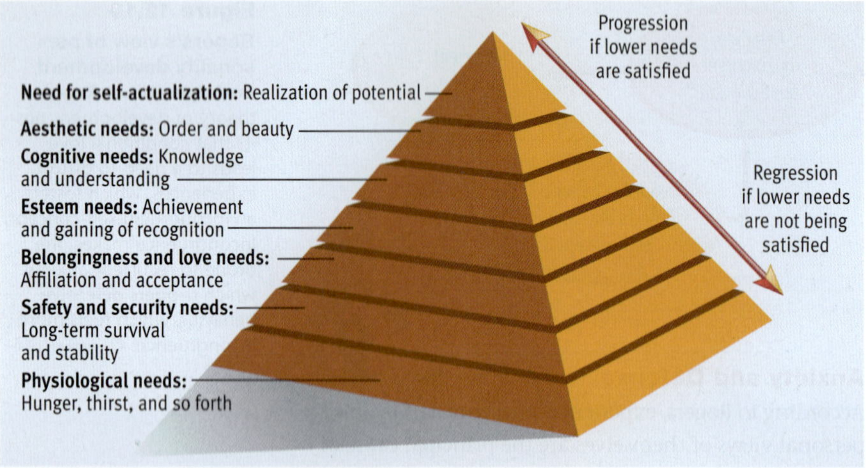

© Cengage Learning 2013

Figure 12.11
Maslow's hierarchy of needs. According to Maslow, human needs are arranged in a hierarchy, and people must satisfy their basic needs before they can satisfy higher needs. In the diagram, higher levels in the pyramid represent progressively less basic needs. Individuals progress upward in the hierarchy when lower needs are satisfied reasonably well, but they may regress back to lower levels if basic needs are no longer satisfied.

organized hierarchically and his description of the healthy personality.

Hierarchy of Needs

10c

Maslow proposed that human motives are organized into a ***hierarchy of needs*—a systematic arrangement of needs, according to priority, in which basic needs must be met before less basic needs are aroused.** This hierarchical arrangement is usually portrayed as a pyramid (see **Figure 12.11**). The needs toward the bottom of the pyramid, such as physiological or security needs, are the most basic. Higher levels in the pyramid consist of progressively less basic needs. When a person manages to satisfy a level of needs reasonably well (complete satisfaction is not necessary), *this satisfaction activates needs at the next level.*

Maslow argued that humans have an innate drive toward personal growth—that is, evolution toward a higher state of being. Thus, he described the needs in the uppermost reaches of his hierarchy as *growth needs*. These include the needs for knowledge and aesthetic beauty. Foremost among them is the ***need for self-actualization*, which is the need to fulfill one's potential.** It's the highest need in Maslow's motivational hierarchy. Maslow summarized this concept with a simple statement: "What a man *can* be, he *must* be." According to Maslow, people will be frustrated if they are unable to fully utilize their talents or pursue their true interests. For example, if you have great musical talent but must work as an accountant, your need for self-actualization is being thwarted. Maslow's pyramid has penetrated popular culture to a remarkable degree. For example, Peterson and Park (2010) note that a Google search located over 766,000 images of Maslow's pyramid on the Internet—a figure that topped the number of images for the *Mona Lisa* and *The Last Supper*!

Recently, almost 70 years after Maslow first proposed his influential pyramid of needs, theorists have proposed a major renovation. Working from an evolutionary perspective, Kenrick and colleagues (2010) argue for a reworking of the upper levels of Maslow's hierarchy. They acknowledge that decades of research and theory provide support for the priority of the first four levels of needs. But they contend that the higher needs in the pyramid are not that fundamental and that they are really pursued in service of esteem needs—that people seek knowledge, beauty, and self-actualization to impress others. After grouping Maslow's higher needs with the esteem needs, Kenrick and associates (2010) fill in the upper levels of their revised hierarchy with needs related to reproductive fitness—that is, passing on one's genes. Specifically, they propose that the top three needs in the pyramid should be the need to find a mate, the need to retain a mate, and the need to successfully parent offspring (see **Figure 12.12**).

It is hard to say whether this sweeping revision of Maslow's pyramid will gain traction. Most commentaries thus far acknowledge that Kenrick and his colleagues have compiled some compelling arguments in favor of their renovated pyramid. However, such a radical transformation of an iconic theoretical model is bound to invite second-guessing. For example, critics have argued that the revised hierarchy is no longer uniquely human (Kesebir, Graham, & Oishi, 2010), that it is premature to dismiss the need for self-actualization (Peterson & Park, 2010), and that parenting might not be all that fundamental of a human need (Lyubomirsky & Boehm, 2010). At a minimum, the proposed revision promises to revitalize research on Maslow's hierarchy of needs.

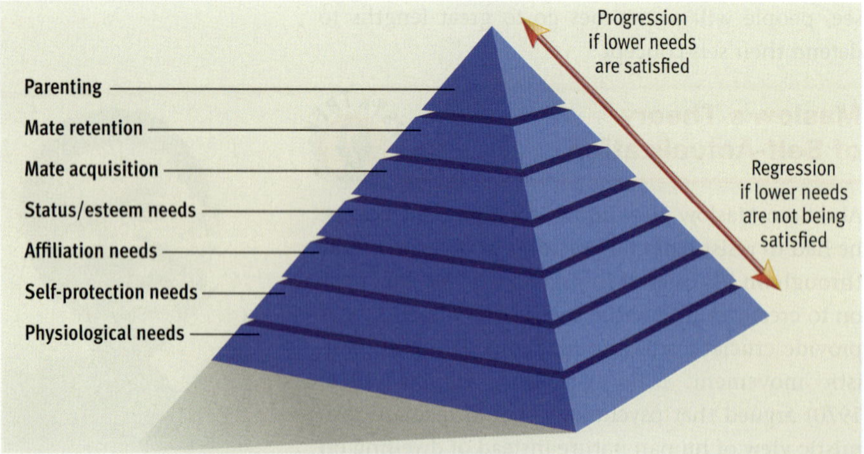

© Cengage Learning 2013

Figure 12.12
Proposed revision of Maslow's pyramid. According to Kenrick and colleagues (2010), the lower levels of needs in Maslow's hierarchy have been supported by research, but the needs in the upper portion of his pyramid should be replaced. Working from an evolutionary perspective, Kenrick and colleagues argue that humans' highest needs involve motives related to reproductive fitness, as shown here.

The Healthy Personality 10c

Because of his interest in self-actualization, Maslow set out to discover the nature of the healthy personality. Over a period of years, he conducted studies and accumulated case histories. Gradually, he sketched, in broad strokes, a picture of ideal psychological health. According to Maslow, ***self-actualizing persons* are people with exceptionally healthy personalities, marked by continued personal growth.** Maslow identified various traits characteristic of self-actualizing people. Many of these traits are listed in **Figure 12.13**. In brief, Maslow found that self-actualizers are accurately tuned in to reality and that they're at peace with themselves. He found that they're open and spontaneous and that they retain a fresh appreciation of the world around them. Socially, they're sensitive to others' needs and enjoy rewarding interpersonal relations. However, they're not dependent on others for approval or uncomfortable with solitude. They thrive on their work, and they enjoy their sense of humor. Maslow also noted that they have "peak experiences" (profound emotional highs) more often than others. Finally, he found that they strike a nice balance between many polarities in personality. For instance, they can be both childlike and mature, both rational and intuitive, both conforming and rebellious.

Characteristics of self-actualizing people	
• Clear, efficient perception of reality and comfortable relations with it	• Mystical and peak experiences
• Spontaneity, simplicity, and naturalness	• Feelings of kinship and identification with the human race
• Problem centering (having something outside themselves they "must" do as a mission)	• Strong friendships, but limited in number
• Detachment and need for privacy	• Democratic character structure
• Autonomy, independence of culture and environment	• Ethical discrimination between good and evil
• Continued freshness of appreciation	• Philosophical, unhostile sense of humor
	• Balance between polarities in personality

© Cengage Learning 2013

Figure 12.13
Maslow's view of the healthy personality. Humanistic theorists emphasize psychological health instead of maladjustment. Maslow's description of the characteristics of self-actualizing people evokes a picture of the healthy personality.

Evaluating Humanistic Perspectives

The humanists added a refreshing new perspective to the study of personality. Their argument that a person's subjective views may be more important than objective reality has proved compelling. Even behavioral theorists have begun to take into account subjective personal factors such as beliefs and expectations. The humanistic approach also deserves some of the credit for making the self-concept an important construct in psychology. Finally, one could argue that the humanists' optimistic, growth- and health-oriented approach laid the foundation for the emergence of the positive psychology movement. This movement is increasingly influential in contemporary psychology (Sheldon & Kasser, 2001; Taylor, 2001).

Of course, there's a negative side to the balance sheet as well. Critics have identified some weaknesses in the humanistic approach to personality. Such criticisms include the following (Burger, 2008; Wong, 2006):

1. *Poor testability.* Like psychodynamic theorists, the humanists have been criticized for generating hypotheses that are difficult to put to a scientific test. Humanistic concepts, such as personal growth and self-actualization, are difficult to define and measure.

2. *Unrealistic view of human nature.* Critics also charge that the humanists have been unrealistic in their assumptions about human nature and their descriptions of the healthy personality. For instance, Maslow's self-actualizing people sound nearly *perfect.* In reality, Maslow had a hard time finding such people. When he searched among the living, the results were so disappointing that he turned to the study of historical figures.

3. *Inadequate evidence.* For the most part, humanistic psychologists haven't been particularly research oriented. Rogers and Maslow both conducted and encouraged empirical research. However, many of their followers have been scornful of efforts to quantify human experience to test hypotheses.

PEANUTS © 1970 Peanuts Worldwide LLC. Dist. By UNIVERSAL UCLICK. Reprinted with permission. All rights reserved.

CONCEPT CHECK 12.2

Recognizing Key Concepts in Personality Theories

Check your understanding of psychodynamic, behavioral, and humanistic personality theories by identifying key concepts from these theories in the scenarios below. The answers can be found in Appendix A.

1. Thirteen-year-old Sarah watches a TV show in which the leading female character manipulates her boyfriend by acting helpless and purposely losing a tennis match against him. The female lead repeatedly expresses her slogan, "Never let them [men] know you can take care of yourself." Sarah becomes more passive and less competitive around boys her own age.

   Concept: ______________________________

2. Yolanda has a secure, enjoyable, reasonably well-paid job as a tenured English professor at a state university. Her friends are dumbfounded when she announces that she's going to resign and give it all up to try writing a novel. She tries to explain, "I need a new challenge, a new mountain to climb. I've had this lid on my writing talents for years, and I've got to break free. It's something I have to try. I won't be happy until I do."

   Concept: ______________________________

3. Vladimir, who is 4, seems to be emotionally distant from and inattentive to his father. He complains whenever he's left with his dad. In contrast, he often cuddles up in bed with his mother and tries very hard to please her by behaving properly.

   Concept: ______________________________

REVIEW OF KEY LEARNING GOALS

12.12 Humanism emerged as a backlash against psychodynamic and behavioral theories, which were viewed as overly deterministic and dehumanizing. Humanistic theories take an optimistic view of people's conscious, rational ability to chart their own courses of action. They also emphasize the primacy of people's subjective views of themselves.

12.13 Rogers focused on the self-concept as the critical aspect of personality. Incongruence is the degree of disparity between one's self-concept and actual experience. Rogers maintained that unconditional love fosters congruence, whereas conditional love fosters incongruence. Incongruence makes one vulnerable to recurrent anxiety, which tends to trigger defensive behavior that protects one's inaccurate self-concept.

12.14 Maslow theorized that needs are organized hierarchically and that psychological health depends on fulfilling one's need for self-actualization, which is the need to realize one's human potential. His work led to the description of self-actualizing persons as idealized examples of psychological health. Recently, theorists have proposed a major revision of Maslow's pyramid of needs in which the higher, growth needs are replaced by motives related to reproductive fitness.

12.15 Humanistic theories deserve credit for highlighting the importance of subjective views of oneself, for confronting the question of what makes for a healthy personality, and for paving the way for the positive psychology movement. Humanistic theories lack a firm base of research, are difficult to put to an empirical test, and may be overly optimistic about human nature.

KEY LEARNING GOALS

12.16 Outline Eysenck's views of personality structure and development.

12.17 Summarize the findings of behavioral genetics research on personality.

12.18 Discuss neuroscience and evolutionary perspectives on the Big Five traits.

12.19 Assess the strengths and weaknesses of the biological approach to personality.

Biological Perspectives

Could personality be a matter of genetic inheritance? This possibility was largely ignored for many decades of personality research until Hans Eysenck made a case for genetic influence in the 1960s. In this section, we'll discuss Eysenck's theory and look at more recent behavioral genetics research on the heritability of personality. We'll also examine neuroscience and evolutionary perspectives on personality.

Eysenck's Theory

PsykTrek 10d

Hans Eysenck was born in Germany but fled to London during the era of Nazi rule. He went on to become one of Britain's most prominent psychologists. Eysenck (1967, 1982, 1990a) viewed personality structure as a hierarchy of traits, in which many superficial traits are derived from a smaller number of more basic traits, which are derived from a handful of fundamental higher-order traits, as shown in **Figure 12.14**. His studies suggested that all aspects of personality emerge from just three higher-order traits: extraversion, neuroticism, and psychoticism. You have already learned about the first two of these traits, which are key elements in the Big Five. The third trait, psychoticism, involves being egocentric, impulsive, cold, and antisocial.

According to Eysenck, "Personality is determined to a large extent by a person's genes" (1967, p. 20). How is heredity linked to personality in Eysenck's model? In part, through conditioning concepts borrowed from behavioral theory. Eysenck theorized that some people can be conditioned more readily than others because of inherited differences in their physiological functioning. These variations in "conditionability" are assumed to influence the personality traits that people acquire through conditioning processes.

Eysenck has shown a special interest in explaining variations in *extraversion-introversion*. He has proposed that introverts tend to have higher levels of physiological arousal, or perhaps higher "arousability." This makes them more easily conditioned than extraverts. According to Eysenck, people who condition easily acquire more conditioned inhibitions

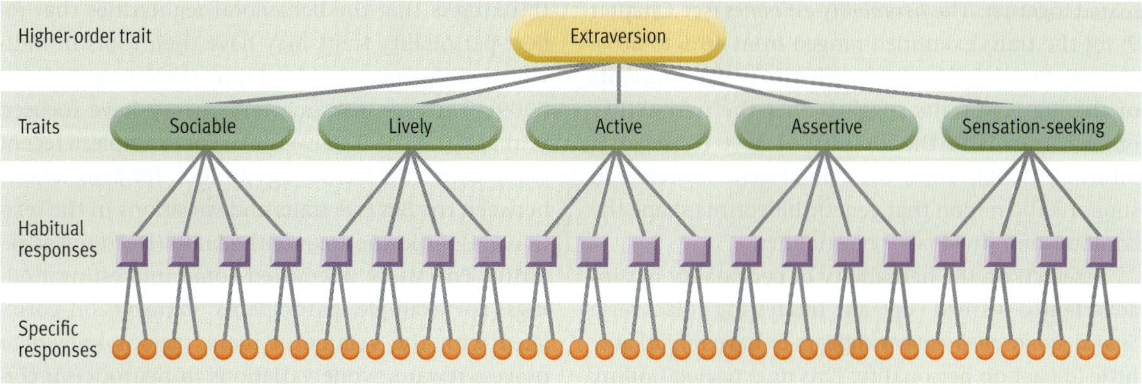

© Cengage Learning 2013

Figure 12.14

Eysenck's model of personality structure. Eysenck described personality structure as a hierarchy of traits. In this scheme, a few higher-order traits, such as extraversion, determine a number of lower-order traits, which determine a person's habitual responses.

SOURCE: Eysenck, H. J. (1976). *The biological basis of personality.* Springfield, IL: Charles C. Thomas. Reprinted by permission of the publisher.

By permission from H. J. Eysenck Memorial Fund

Hans Eysenck

"Personality is determined to a large extent by a person's genes."

than others. These inhibitions make them more bashful, tentative, and uneasy in social situations, ultimately leading them to turn inward. Hence, they become introverted.

Behavioral Genetics and Personality

PSYKTREK 10d

Recent research in behavioral genetics has provided impressive support for the idea that many personality traits are largely inherited (Livesley, Jang, Vernon, 2003; Rowe & van den Oord, 2005). For instance, **Figure 12.15** shows the mean correlations observed for identical and fraternal twins in studies of the Big Five personality traits. Higher correlations are indicative of greater similarity on a trait. On all five traits, identical twins have been found to be much more similar than fraternal twins (Plomin et al., 2008). Based on these and many other findings, theorists conclude that genetic factors exert considerable influence over personality (see Chapter 3 for an explanation of the logic of twin studies).

Some skeptics wonder whether identical twins might exhibit more trait similarity than fraternal twins because they're treated more alike. In other words, they wonder whether environmental factors (rather than heredity) could be responsible for identical twins' greater personality resemblance. This nagging question can be answered only by studying identical twins reared apart. Fortunately, an influential twin study at the University of Minnesota provided the necessary data (Tellegen et al., 1988). This study was the first to administer the same personality test to identical and fraternal twins reared apart, as well as together. Most of the twins reared apart were separated quite early in life (median age of 2.5 months) and remained separated for a long time (median period of almost 34 years). The results revealed that identical twins reared apart were substantially more similar in personality than fraternal twins

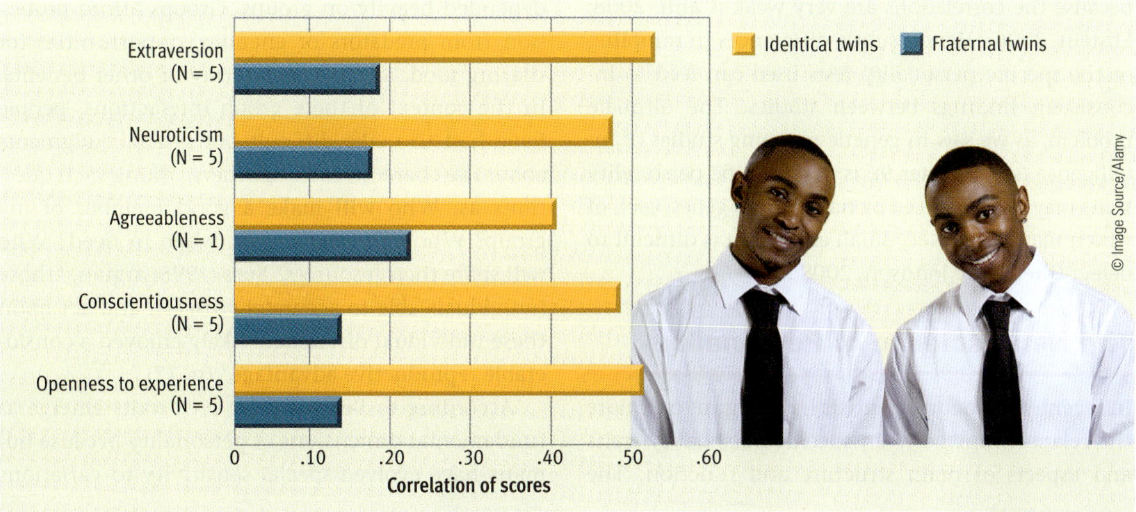

© Image Source/Alamy
© Cengage Learning 2013

Figure 12.15

Twin studies of personality. Loehlin (1992) has summarized the results of twin studies that have examined the Big Five personality traits. The N under each trait indicates the number of twin studies that have examined that trait. The chart plots the average correlations obtained for identical and fraternal twins in these studies. As you can see, identical twins have shown greater resemblance in personality than fraternal twins have, suggesting that personality is partly inherited. (Based on data from Loehlin, 1992) reared together. The *heritability estimates* (see Chapter 9) for the traits examined ranged from 40% to 58%. Overall, five decades of research on the determinants of the Big Five traits suggests that the heritability of each trait is in the vicinity of 50% (Krueger & Johnson, 2008). Thus, behavioral genetics research supports the notion that genetic blueprints shape the contours of individuals' personalities.

Research on the heritability of personality has inadvertently turned up an interesting discovery: *Shared family environment* appears to have remarkably little impact on personality. This unexpected finding has been observed quite consistently in behavioral genetics research (Beer, Arnold, & Loehlin, 1998; Rowe & van den Oord, 2005). It's unexpected in that social scientists have long assumed that the family environment shared by children growing up together leads to some personality resemblance among them. This finding has led researchers to explore how children's subjective environments vary *within* families. But scientists continue to be perlexed by the minimal impact of shared family environment.

There has been considerable excitement—and controversy—about recent reports linking specific genes to specific personality traits. As we noted in Chapter 3, *genetic mapping* techniques are beginning to permit investigators to look for associations between specific genes and aspects of behavior. A number of studies have found a link between a gene for a particular type of dopamine receptor and measures of extraversion, novelty seeking, and impulsivity, but many failures to replicate this association have also been reported (Canli, 2008; Munafo et al., 2008). In a similar vein, a variety of studies have reported a link between a serotonin transporter gene and measures of neuroticism, but many attempts at replication have failed (Canli, 2008; Sen, Burmeister, & Ghosh, 2004). Overall, the evidence suggests that both of these links are genuine but are difficult to replicate consistently because the correlations are very weak (Canli, 2008; Ebstein, 2006). Hence, subtle differences in sampling or the specific personality tests used can lead to inconsistent findings between studies. The ultimate problem, as we saw in genetic mapping studies of intelligence (see Chapter 9), is that specific personality traits may be influenced by hundreds of genes, each of which may have a very small effect that is difficult to detect (Kreuger & Johnson, 2008).

Reality CHECK

Misconception

Parents exert a great deal of influence over the personality of their offspring.

Reality

This seems like a logical supposition, but when behavioral genetics researchers have attempted to quantify the impact of shared family environment on personality, they have been stunned by its lack of influence. Other types of research in developmental psychology have suggested that parents have some influence over their children's personality (Maccoby, 2000), but this influence appears to be much more modest than widely assumed (Cohen, 1999; Harris, 1998).

The Neuroscience of Personality

In recent years neuroscientists have begun to explore the relationships between specific personality traits and aspects of brain structure and function. The thinking is that the behavioral regularities that reflect personality traits may have their roots in individual differences in the brain (DeYoung & Gray, 2009). Thus far, research and theory have focused primarity on the Big Five traits. For example, a recent study used MRI technology to look for associations between the Big Five traits and variations in the relative size of specific areas of the brain (DeYoung et al., 2010). The study uncovered some interesting findings. For example, participants' extraversion correlated with the volume of brain regions known to process reward, while variations in neuroticism correlated with the volume of brain areas known to be activated by threat, punishment, and negative emotions. And the size of brain areas thought to regulate planning and voluntary control correlated with subjects' degree of conscientiousness. This line of research is brand new, but the promising initial results suggest that it may be fruitful to explore the neurological bases of personality traits.

Evolutionary Perspectives on Personality

In the realm of biological perspectives on personality, another recent development has been the emergence of evolutionary theory. Evolutionary theorists assert that personality has a biological basis because natural selection has favored certain traits over the course of human history (Figueredo et al., 2005, 2009). Thus, evolutionary analyses focus on how various personality traits—and the ability to recognize these traits in others—may have contributed to reproductive fitness in ancestral human populations.

For example, David Buss (1991, 1995, 1997) has argued that the Big Five personality traits stand out as important dimensions of personality because those traits have had significant adaptive implications. Buss points out that humans historically have depended heavily on groups. Groups afford protection from predators or enemies, opportunities for sharing food, and a diverse array of other benefits. In the context of these group interactions, people have had to make difficult but crucial judgments about the characteristics of others, asking such questions as: Who will make a good member of my group? Who can I depend on when in need? Who will share their resources? Buss (1995) argues, "those individuals able to accurately discern and act upon these individual differences likely enjoyed a considerable reproductive advantage" (p. 22).

According to Buss, the Big Five traits emerge as fundamental dimensions of personality because humans have evolved special sensitivity to variations in the ability to bond with others (extraversion), the willingness to cooperate and collaborate (agreeableness), the tendency to be reliable and ethical (conscientiousness), the capacity to be an innovative problem solver (openness to experience), and the ability to handle stress (low neuroticism). In a nutshell, Buss argues that the Big Five traits reflect the most salient features of others' adaptive behavior over the course of evolutionary history.

Daniel Nettle (2006) takes this line of thinking one step further. He asserts that the traits themselves (as opposed to the ability to recognize them in others) are products of evolution that were adaptive in ancestral environments. For example, he discusses how extraversion could've promoted mating success, how neuroticism could've fueled competitiveness and avoidance of dangers, how agreeableness could've fostered the effective building of coalitions, and so forth.

CONCEPT CHECK 12.3

Understanding the Implications of Major Theories: Who Said This?

Check your understanding of the implications of the personality theories we've discussed by indicating which theorist is likely to have made the statements below. The answers are in Appendix A.

Choose from the following theorists:

Alfred Adler

Albert Bandura

Hans Eysenck

Sigmund Freud

Abraham Maslow

Walter Mischel

Quotes

______________ 1. "If you deliberately plan to be less than you are capable of being, then I warn you that you'll be deeply unhappy for the rest of your life."

______________ 2. "I feel that the major, most fundamental dimensions of personality are likely to be those on which [there is] strong genetic determination of individual differences."

______________ 3. "People are in general not candid over sexual matters . . . they wear a heavy overcoat woven of a tissue of lies, as though the weather were bad in the world of sexuality."

Evaluating Biological Perspectives

Researchers have compiled convincing evidence that biological factors exert considerable influence over personality. Nonetheless, we must take note of some weaknesses in biological approaches to personality:

1. David Funder (2001) has observed that behavioral genetics researchers exhibit something of an "obsession with establishing the exact magnitude of heritability coefficients" (p. 207). As we discussed in Chapter 9, heritability ratios are ballpark estimates that will vary depending on sampling procedures and other considerations (Sternberg, Grigorenko, & Kidd, 2005). There's no one magic number awaiting discovery. Therefore, the inordinate focus on heritability does seem ill-advised.

2. The results of efforts to carve behavior into genetic and environmental components are ultimately artificial. The effects of nature and nurture are twisted together in complicated interactions that can't be separated cleanly (Plomin, 2004; Rutter, 2007). For example, a genetically influenced trait, such as a young child's surly, sour temperament, might evoke a particular style of parenting. In essence then, the child's genes have molded his or her environment. Thus, genetic and environmental influences on personality are not entirely independent, because the environmental circumstances that people are exposed to may be shaped in part by their genes.

REVIEW OF KEY LEARNING GOALS

12.16 Eysenck views personality structure as a hierarchy of traits. He believes that heredity influences individual differences in physiological functioning that affect how easily people acquire conditioned inhibitions.

12.17 Twin studies of the Big Five personality traits find that identical twins are more similar in personality than fraternal twins, thus suggesting that personality is partly inherited. Estimates for the heritability of personality hover in the vicinity of 50%. Recent research in behavioral genetics has suggested that shared family environment has surprisingly little impact on personality. Genetic mapping studies have identified some specific genes that may influence specific traits, but the findings have been inconsistent.

12.18 Neuroscientists have found some interesting correlations between Big Five traits and the size of certain brain regions. According to Buss, the ability to recognize and judge others' status on the Big Five traits may have contributed to reproductive fitness. Nettle argues that the Big Five traits themselves (rather than the ability to recognize them) are products of evolution that were adaptive in ancestral times.

12.19 Researchers have compiled convincing evidence that genetic factors exert considerable influence over personality. However, the biological approach has been criticized because of methodological problems with heritability ratios and because the effort to carve personality into genetic and environmental components is ultimately artificial.

Illustrated Overview of Major Theories of Personality

THEORIST AND ORIENTATION	SOURCE OF DATA AND OBSERVATIONS	KEY ASSUMPTIONS
A PSYCHODYNAMIC VIEW  Sigmund Freud	 © Peter Aprahamian/Corbis Case studies from clinical practice of psychoanalysis	Past events in childhood determine one's adult personality. People's behavior is dominated by unconscious, irrational wishes, needs, and conflicts. Personality development progresses through stages.
A BEHAVIORAL VIEW  B. F. Skinner	Laboratory experiments, primarily with animals  Courtesy of Professor Rick Stalling and Bradley University. Photo by Duane Zehr	Behavior is determined by the environment, although this view was softened by Bandura's concept of reciprocal determinism. Nurture (learning and experience) is more influential than nature (heredity and biological factors). Situational factors exert great influence over behavior.
A HUMANISTIC VIEW  Carl Rogers	Case studies from clinical practice of client-centered therapy  © Zigy Kaluzny/Getty Images	People are free to chart their own courses of action; they are not hapless victims governed by the environment. People are largely conscious, rational beings who are not driven by unconscious needs. A person's subjective view of the world is more important than objective reality.
A BIOLOGICAL VIEW  Hans Eysenck	Twin, family, and adoption studies of heritability; factor analysis studies of personality structure  © Image Source/Alamy	Behavior is largely determined by evolutionary adaptations, the wiring of the brain, and heredity. Nature (heredity and biological factors) is more influential than nurture (learning and experience).

Illustrations of Freud, Skinner, Rogers, and Eysenck © Cengage Learning 2013

MODEL OF PERSONALITY STRUCTURE

VIEW OF PERSONALITY DEVELOPMENT

ROOTS OF DISORDERS

Three interacting components (id, ego, superego) operating at three levels of consciousness

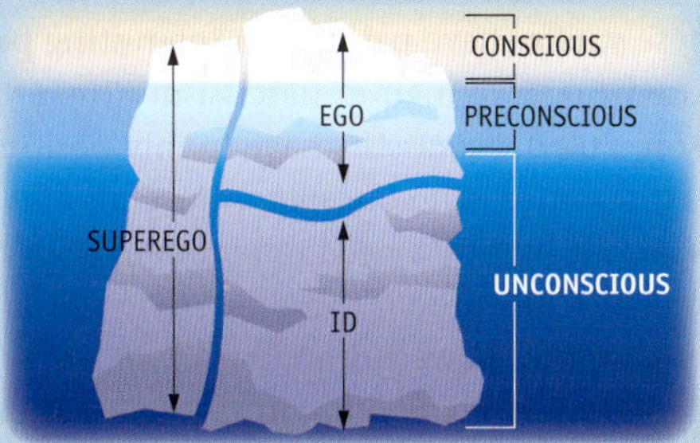

Emphasis on fixation or progress through psychosexual stages; experiences in early childhood (such as toilet training) can leave lasting mark on adult personality

© Finnbarr Webster/Alamy

Unconscious fixations and unresolved conflicts from childhood, usually centering on sex and aggression

Collections of response tendencies tied to specific stimulus situations

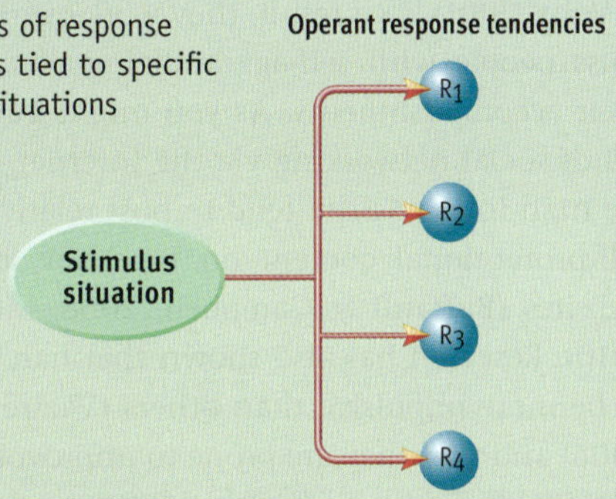

© David Young-Wolff/PhotoEdit

Personality evolves gradually over the life span (not in stages); responses (such as extraverted joking) followed by reinforcement (such as apprecia-tive laughter) become more frequent

Maladaptive behavior due to faulty learning; the "symptom" is the problem, not a sign of under-lying disease

Self-concept, which may or may not mesh well with actual experience

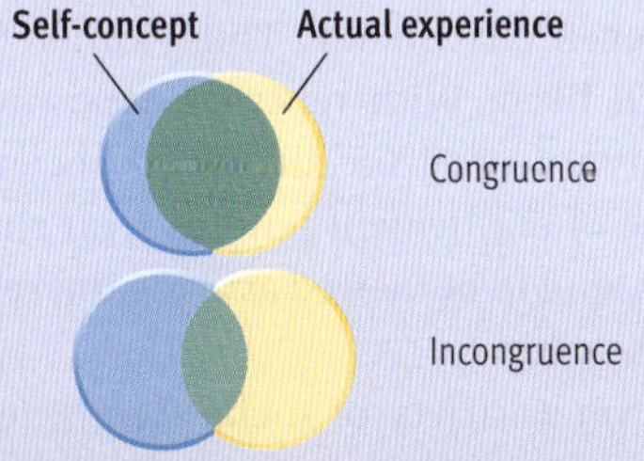

Children who receive unconditional love have less need to be defensive; they develop more accurate, congruent self-concept; conditional love fosters incongruence

© MBI/Alamy

Incongruence between self and actual experience (inaccurate self-concept); over-dependence on others for approval and sense of worth

Hierarchy of traits, with specific traits derived from more fundamental, general traits

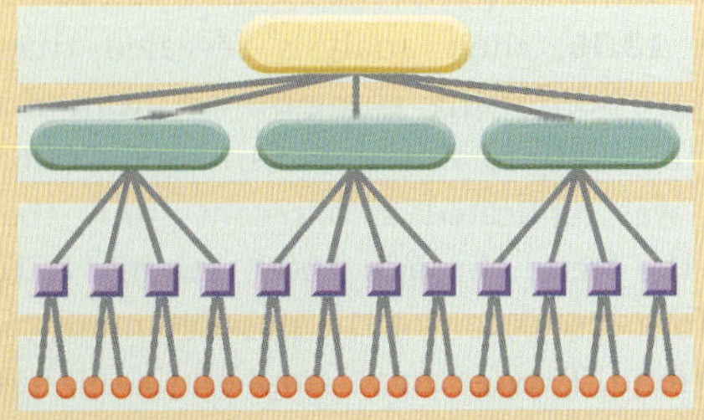

Emphasis on unfolding of genetic blueprint with maturation; inherited predispositions interact with learning experiences

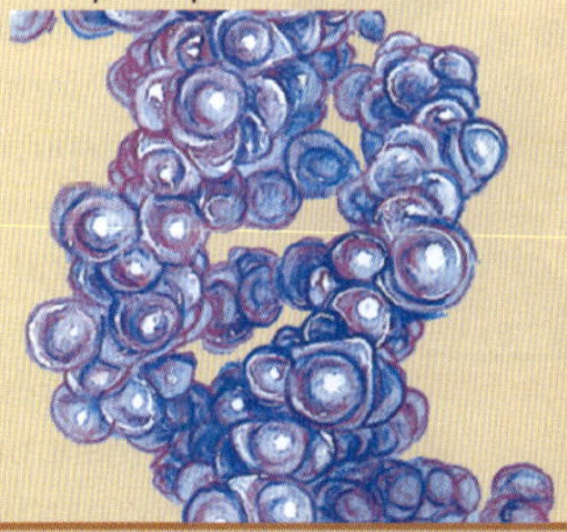

Genetic vulnera-bility activated in part by environ-mental factors

Unless otherwise noted, all illustrations this page © Cengage Learning 2013

KEY LEARNING GOALS

12.20 Understand the nature, correlates, and social consequences of narcissism.

12.21 Describe the chief concepts of terror management theory, and discuss how reminders of death influence people's behavior.

Contemporary Empirical Approaches to Personality

So far, our coverage has been devoted to grand, panoramic theories of personality. In this section we'll examine some contemporary empirical approaches that are narrower in scope. In modern personality research programs, investigators typically attempt to describe and measure an important personality trait and ascertain its relationship to other traits and specific behaviors. To get a sense of this kind of research, we'll take a look at research on a trait called *narcissism*. We'll also look at an influential new approach called *terror management theory* that focuses on personality dynamics rather than personality traits.

Renewed Interest in Narcissism

***Narcissism* is a personality trait marked by an inflated sense of importance, a need for attention and admiration, a sense of entitlement, and a tendency to exploit others.** The term is drawn from the Greek myth of Narcissus, which is about an attractive young man's search for love. In the mythical tale he eventually sees his reflection in water and falls in love with his own image and gazes at it until he dies, thus illustrating the perils of excessive self-love. The concept of narcissism was originally popularized over a century ago by pioneering sex researcher Havelock Ellis (1898) and by Sigmund Freud (1914).

The syndrome of narcissism was not widely discussed outside of psychoanalytic circles until 1980, when the American Psychiatric Association published a massive revision of its diagnostic system that describes various psychological disorders (see Chapter 15). The revised diagnostic system included a new condition called *narcissistic personality disorder (NPD)*. Among other things, the key symptoms of this new disorder included (1) a grandiose sense of importance, (2) constant need for attention, (3) difficulty dealing with criticism, and (4) a sense of entitlement. NPD is viewed as an extreme, pathological manifestation of narcissism that is seen in only a small number (3%–5%) of people.

© PAUL HANNA/Reuters/Landou

The formal description of NPD inspired some researchers to start investigating lesser, nonpathological manifestations of narcissism in the general population. This research led to the development of scales intended to assess narcissism as a normal personality trait. Of these scales, the Narcissistic Personality Inventory (NPI) (Raskin & Hall, 1979, 1981; Raskin & Terry, 1988) has become the most widely used measure of narcissism. It has been used in hundreds of studies.

These studies have painted an interesting portrait of those who score high in narcissism (Rhodewalt & Peterson, 2009). Narcissists have highly positive, but easily threatened self-concepts. Above all else, their behavior is driven by a need to maintain their fragile self-esteem. They are far more interested in making themselves look powerful and successful than they are in forging lasting bonds with others (Campbell & Foster, 2007). They display a craving for approval and admiration that resembles an addiction (Baumeister & Vohs, 2001). As a result, they work overtime to impress people with self-aggrandizing descriptions of their accomplishments. As you might guess, in this era of social networking via the Internet, those who are high in narcissism tend to post relatively blatant self-promotional content on Facebook and similar websites (Buffardi & Campbell, 2008; Mehdizadeh, 2010). Research has also shown that narcissists tend to be more impulsive than others (Vazire & Funder, 2006) and that they are prone to unprovoked aggression (Reidy, Foster, & Zeichner, 2010).

The social consequences of narcissism are interesting (Back, Schmukle, & Egloff, 2010; Paulhus, 1998). When they first meet people, narcissists are often perceived as charming, self-assured, humorous, and perhaps even charismatic. Thus, initially, they tend to be well liked. With repeated exposure, however, their constant need for attention, brazen boasting, and sense of entitlement tend to wear thin. Eventually, they tend to be viewed as arrogant, self-centered, and unlikeable.

Based on a variety of social trends, Jean Twenge and colleagues (2008) suspected that narcissism might be increasing in recent generations. To test this hypothesis they gathered data from 85 studies dating back to the 1980s in which American college students had been given the NPI. As you can see in **Figure 12.16**, their analysis revealed that NPI scores have been rising, going from a mean of about 15.5 in the 1980s to almost 17.5 in 2005–2006. This finding was replicated in a recent study that extended the trend through 2009 (Twenge & Foster, 2010). In a discussion of the possible ramifications of this trend, Twenge and Campbell (2009) have argued that rising narcissism has fueled an obsessive concern about being physically attractive in young people, leading to unhealthy dieting, overuse of cosmetic surgery, and steroid-fueled body building. They also assert that narcissists' "me-first" attitude has led to increased materialism and overconsumption of the earth's resources, which have contributed to the current environmental crisis and economic meltdown.

Terror Management Theory

Terror management theory emerged as an influential perspective in the 1990s. Although the theory borrows from Freudian and evolutionary formulations, it provides its own unique analysis of the human condition. Developed by Sheldon Solomon, Jeff Greenberg, and Tom Pyszczynski (1991, 2004b), this fresh perspective is currently generating a huge volume of research.

One of the chief goals of terror management theory is to explain why people need self-esteem. Unlike other animals, humans have evolved complex cognitive abilities that permit self-awareness and contemplation of the future. These cognitive capacities make humans keenly aware that life can be snuffed out at any time. The collision between humans' self-preservation instinct and their awareness of the inevitability of death creates the potential for experiencing anxiety, alarm, and terror when people think about their mortality (see **Figure 12.17**).

How do humans deal with this potential for terror? According to terror management theory, "What saves us is culture. Cultures provide ways to view the world—worldviews—that 'solve' the existential crisis engendered by the awareness of death" (Pyszczynski, Solomon, & Greenberg, 2003, p. 16). Cultural worldviews diminish anxiety by providing answers to universal questions such as: Why am I here? What is the meaning of life? Cultures create stories, traditions, and institutions that give their members a sense of being part of an enduring legacy. Thus, faith in a cultural worldview can give people a sense of order, meaning, and context that can soothe their fear of death.

Where does self-esteem fit into the picture? Self-esteem is viewed as a sense of personal worth that depends on one's confidence in the validity of one's cultural worldview and the belief that one is living up to the standards prescribed by that worldview. Hence, self-esteem buffers people from the profound anxiety associated with the awareness that they are transient animals destined to die. In other words, self-esteem serves a *terror management* function (refer to **Figure 12.17**).

The notion that self-esteem functions as an *anxiety buffer* has been supported by numerous studies (Pyszczynski et al., 2004; Schmeichel et al., 2009). In many of these experiments, researchers have manipulated what they call ***mortality salience*—the degree to which subjects' mortality is prominent in their minds.** Typically, mortality salience is temporarily increased by asking participants to briefly think about their own future death. Consistent with the anxiety buffer hypothesis, reminding people of their mortality leads subjects to engage in a variety of behaviors that are likely to bolster their self-esteem, thus reducing anxiety.

Increasing mortality salience also leads people to work harder at defending their cultural worldview (Arndt & Vess, 2008; Burke, Martens, & Faucher, 2010). For instance, after briefly pondering their mortality, research participants (1) hand out harsher penalties to moral transgressors, (2) respond more negatively to people who criticize their country, and

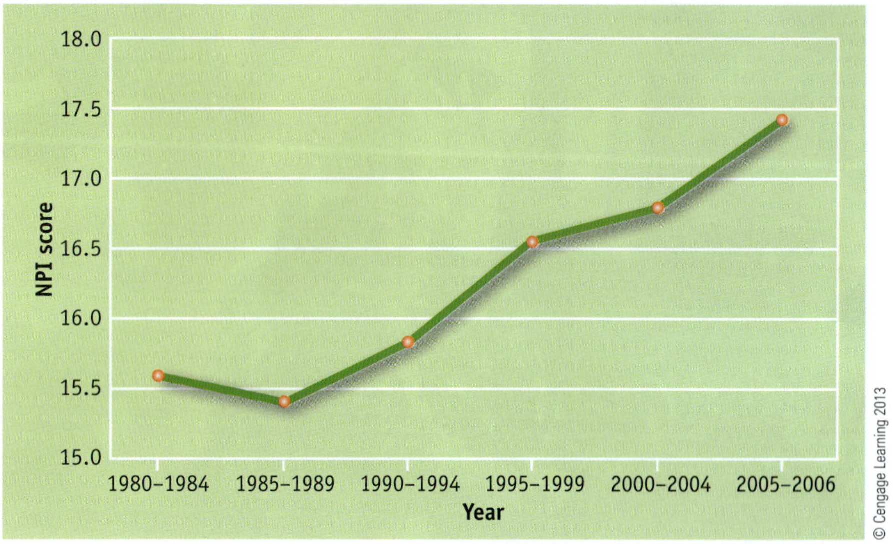

Figure 12.16

Increased narcissism among American college students. This graph shows mean scores on the Narcissistic Personality Inventory (NPI) in samples of college students since the early 1980s. As you can see, the data suggest that NPI scores have increased steadily in recent decades.

SOURCE: Based on Twenge, J. M., Konrath, S., Foster, J. D., Campbell, W. K., & Bushman B. J. (2008). Egos inflating over time: A cross-temporal meta-analysis of the Narcissistic Personality Inventory. *Journal of Personality, 76*, 875–901. Copyright © 2008 John Wiley and Sons.

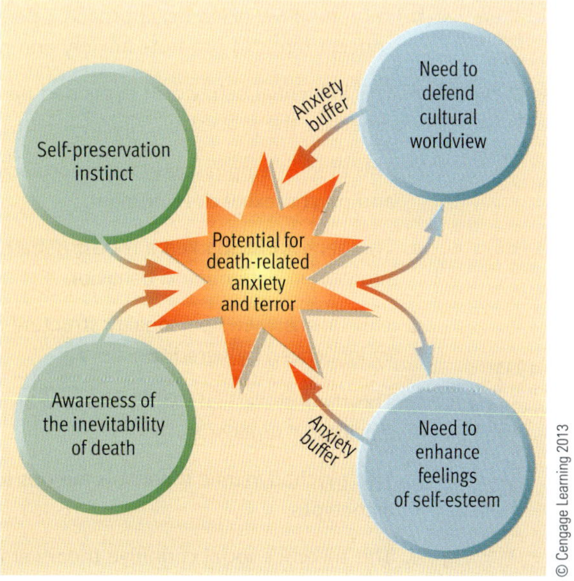

Figure 12.17

Overview of terror management theory. This graphic maps out the relations among the key concepts proposed by terror management theory. The theory asserts that humans' unique awareness of the inevitability of death fosters a need to defend one's cultural worldview and one's self-esteem, which serve to protect one from mortality-related anxiety.

© AP Images/The Daily Nonpareil, Ben DeVries

According to terror management theory, events that remind people of their mortality motivate them to defend their cultural worldview. One manifestation of this process is an increased interest in, and respect for, cultural icons, such as flags.

(3) show more respect for cultural icons, such as a flag. This need to defend one's cultural worldview may even fuel prejudice and aggression (Greenberg et al., 2009). Reminding subjects of their mortality leads to (1) more negative evaluations of people from different religious or ethnic backgrounds, (2) more stereotypic thinking about minorities, and (3) more aggressive behavior toward people with opposing political views.

Terror management theory yields novel hypotheses regarding many phenomena. For instance, Solomon, Greenberg, and Pyszczynski (2004a) explain excessive materialism in terms of the anxiety-buffering function of self-esteem. Specifically, they argue that "conspicuous possession and consumption are thinly veiled efforts to assert that one is special and therefore more than just an animal fated to die and decay" (p. 134).

At first glance, a theory that explains everything from prejudice to compulsive shopping in terms of death anxiety may seem highly implausible. After all, most people do not appear to walk around all day obsessing about the possibility of their death. The architects of terror management theory are well aware of this reality. They explain that the defensive reactions uncovered in their research generally occur when death anxiety surfaces on the fringes of conscious awareness and that these reactions are automatic and subconscious (Pyszczynski, Greenberg, & Solomon, 1999). Although the theory may seem a little far-fetched, the predictions of terror management theory have been supported in hundreds of experiments (Burke, Martens, & Faucher, 2010).

CONCEPT CHECK 12.4

Identifying the Contributions of Major Theorists and Researchers

Check your recall of the principal ideas of important theorists and researchers covered in this chapter by matching the people listed on the left with the appropriate contributions described on the right. If you need help, the crucial pages describing each person's ideas are listed in parentheses. Fill in the letters for your choices in the spaces provided on the left. You'll find the answers in Appendix A.

Major Theorists and Researchers	Key Ideas and Contributions
______ 1. Alfred Adler (pp. 486–487)	a. This humanistic theorist is famous for his hierarchy of needs and his work on self-actualizing persons.
______ 2. Albert Bandura (pp. 489–490)	b. This humanist called his approach a person-centered theory. He argued that an incongruent self-concept tends to promote anxiety and defensive behavior.
______ 3. Hans Eysenck (pp. 496–497)	c. This influential behaviorist explained personality development in terms of operant conditioning, especially the process of reinforcement.
______ 4. Sigmund Freud (pp. 479–485)	d. This theorist emphasized the importance of unconscious conflicts, anxiety, defense mechanisms, and psychosexual development.
______ 5. Carl Jung (pp. 485–486)	e. This behaviorist sparked a robust debate about the importance of the person as opposed to the situation in determining behavior.
______ 6. Abraham Maslow (pp. 493–495)	f. This theorist views personality structure as a hierarchy of traits and argues that personality is heavily influenced by heredity.
______ 7. Walter Mischel (p. 491)	g. This theorist clashed with Freud and argued that the foremost source of human motivation is a striving for superiority.
______ 8. Carl Rogers (pp. 492–493)	h. This psychodynamic theorist is famous for the concepts of the collective unconscious and archetypes.
______ 9. B. F. Skinner (pp. 488–489)	i. This theorist's social cognitive theory emphasizes observational learning and self-efficacy.

REVIEW OF KEY LEARNING GOALS

12.20 Narcissism is a trait marked by an inflated sense of self, a need for attention, and a sense of entitlement. People who score high in narcissism work overtime trying to impress others with self-aggrandizing tales of their accomplishments, all to protect their fragile self-esteem. They often are well liked at first but are eventually seen as arrogant and self-centered. Research suggests that levels of narcissism have been increasing in recent generations.

12.21 Terror management theory proposes that self-esteem and faith in a cultural worldview shield people from the profound anxiety associated with their mortality. Manipulations of mortality salience lead to harsh treatment for moral transgressions, elevated respect for cultural icons, and increased prejudice.

Culture and Personality

KEY LEARNING GOALS

12.22 Clarify how researchers have found both cross-cultural similarities and disparities in personality, and discuss the accuracy of perceptions of national character.

12.23 Explain Markus and Kitayama's research on cultural variations in conceptions of self.

12.24 Explain how collectivism influences self-enhancement, and describe the Featured Study on culture and self-insight.

Are there connections between culture and personality? In recent years psychology's new interest in cultural factors has led to a renaissance of culture-personality research (Church, 2010). This research has sought to determine whether Western personality constructs are relevant to other cultures and whether cultural differences can be seen in the prevalence of specific personality traits. As with cross-cultural research in other areas of psychology, these studies have found evidence of both continuity and variability across cultures.

For the most part, continuity has been apparent in cross-cultural comparisons of the *trait structure* of personality. When English language personality scales have been translated and administered in other cultures, the predicted dimensions of personality have emerged from the factor analyses (Chiu, Kim, & Wan, 2008). For example, when scales that tap the Big Five personality traits have been administered and subjected to factor analysis in other cultures, the usual five traits have typically emerged (Katigbak et al., 2002; McCrae & Costa, 2008). Thus, research tentatively suggests that the basic dimensions of personality trait structure may be universal.

On the other hand, some cross-cultural variability is seen when researchers compare the average trait scores of samples from various cultural groups. For example, in a study comparing 51 cultures, McCrae et al. (2005a) found that Brazilians scored relatively high in neuroticism, Australians in extraversion, Germans in openness to experience, Czechs in agreeableness, and Malaysians in conscientiousness, to give but a handful of examples. These findings should be viewed as preliminary. More data are needed from larger and more carefully selected samples. Nonetheless, the findings suggest that there may be genuine cultural differences on some personality traits. That said, the cultural disparities in average trait scores that were observed were pretty modest.

The availability of the data from the McCrae et al. (2005a) study allowed Terracciano et al. (2005) to evaluate the concept of *national character*—the idea that various cultures have widely recognized prototype personalities. Terracciano and his colleagues asked subjects from many cultures to describe the *typical* member of *their* culture on rating forms guided by the five-factor model. Generally, subjects displayed substantial agreement on these ratings of what was typical for their culture. The averaged ratings, which served as the measures of each culture's national character, were then correlated with the actual mean trait scores for various cultures compiled in the McCrae et al. (2005a) study. The results were definitive. The vast majority of the correlations were extremely low and often even negative. In other words, there was little or no relationship between perceptions of national character and actual trait scores for various cultures (see **Figure 12.18** on the next page). People's beliefs about national character, which often fuel cultural prejudices, turned out to be profoundly inaccurate stereotypes (McCrae & Terracciano, 2006).

Perhaps the most interesting and influential work on culture and personality has been that of Hazel Markus and Shinobu Kitayama (1991, 1994, 2003). Their work compared American and Asian conceptions of the self. According to Markus and Kitayama, American parents teach their children to be self-reliant, to feel good about themselves, and to view themselves as special individuals. Children are encouraged to excel in competitive endeavors and to strive to stick out from the crowd. They are told that "you have to stand up for yourself." Thus, Markus and Kitayama argue that *American culture fosters an*

Courtesy of Hazel Rose Markus

Courtesy of Shinobu Kitayama

Hazel Markus and Shinobu Kitayama

"Most of what psychologists currently know about human nature is based on one particular view—the so-called Western view of the individual as an independent, self-contained, autonomous entity."

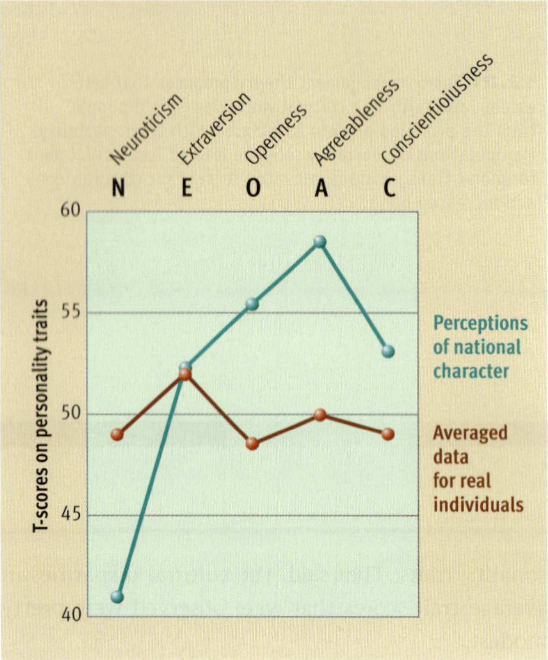

© Cengage Learning 2013

Figure 12.18

An example of inaccurate perceptions of national character. Terracciano et al. (2005) found that perceptions of national character (the prototype or typical personality for a particular culture) are largely inaccurate. The data shown here for one culture—Canadians—illustrates this inaccuracy. Mean scores on the Big Five traits for a sample of real individuals from Canada are graphed here in red. Averaged perceptions of national character for Canadians are graphed here in blue. The discrepancy between perception and reality is obvious. Terracciano and colleagues found similar disparities between views of national character and actual trait scores for a majority of the cultures they studied. (Adapted from McCrae & Terracciano, 2006)

independent view of the self. American youngsters learn to define themselves in terms of their personal attributes, abilities, accomplishments, and possessions.

Most of us take this mentality for granted. Indeed, Markus and Kitayama (1991) maintain that "most of what psychologists currently know about human nature is based on one particular view—the so-called Western view of the individual as an independent, self-contained, autonomous entity" (p. 224). However, they marshal convincing evidence that this view is *not* universal. They argue that in Asian cultures, such as Japan and China, socialization practices foster a more *interdependent view of the self,* which emphasizes the fundamental connectedness of people to each other (see **Figure 12.19**). In these cultures, parents teach their children that they can rely on family and friends, that they should be modest about their personal accomplishments so they don't diminish others' achievements, and that they should view themselves as part of a larger social matrix. Children are encouraged to fit in with others and to avoid standing out from the crowd. A popular adage in Japan reminds children that "the nail that stands out gets pounded down." Hence, Markus and Kitayama assert that Asian youngsters typically learn to define themselves in terms of the groups they belong to. Their harmonious relations with others and their pride in group achievements become the basis for their sense of self-worth.

Personality has often been studied in relation to the cultural syndromes of *individualism versus collectivism,* which represent different value systems and worldviews (Triandis & Suh, 2002). ***Individualism* involves putting personal goals ahead of group goals and defining one's identity in terms of personal attributes rather than group memberships.** In contrast, ***collectivism* involves putting group goals ahead of personal goals and defining one's identity in terms of the groups one belongs to** (such as one's family, tribe, work group, social class, caste, and so on). These discrepant worldviews have a variety of implications for personality. For exam-

Figure 12.19

Culture and conceptions of self. According to Markus and Kitayama (1991), Western cultures foster an independent view of the self as a unique individual who is separate from others, as diagrammed on the left. In contrast, Asian cultures encourage an interdependent view of the self as part of an interconnected social matrix, as diagrammed on the right. The interdependent view leads people to define' themselves in terms of their social relationships (for instance, as someone's daughter, employee, colleague, or neighbor).

SOURCE: Adapted from Markus, H. R., & Kitayama, S. (1991). Culture and the self: Implications for cognition, emotion, and motivation. *Psychological Review, 98,* 224–253. Copyright © 1991 by the American Psychological Association. Adapted by permission of the authors.

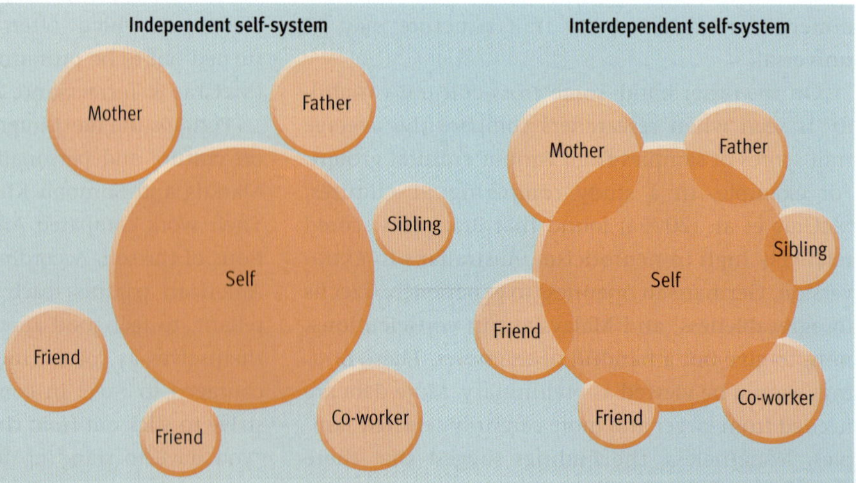

© Cengage Learning 2013

ple, research has shown that individualism and collectivism foster cultural disparities in self-enhancement. ***Self-enhancement* involves focusing on positive feedback from others, exaggerating one's strengths, and seeing oneself as above average.** These tendencies tend to be pervasive in individualistic cultures but are far less common in collectivist cultures, where the norm is to be more sensitive to negative feedback and to reflect on one's shortcomings (Heine, 2003; Heine & Hamamura, 2007). This observation is the springboard for our Featured Study for this chapter.

FEATURED STUDY

Individualism, Collectivism, and Self-Insight

SOURCE: Balcetis, E., Dunning, D., & Miller, R. L. (2008). Do collectivists know themselves better than individualists? Cross-cultural studies of the holier than thou phenomenon. *Journal of Personality and Social Psychology, 95,* 1252–1267.

The evidence that individualism promotes self-enhancement led Balcetis and her colleagues to speculate that collectivists may tend to have more accurate views of themselves than individualists. Rather than asking subjects to rate themselves in comparison to others, which is highly *subjective,* they decided to ask participants to predict their own *objective* behavior. This focus on predicting actual behavior led them to investigate the "holier than thou phenomenon," which is the tendency for people to claim that they are more likely to engage in socially desirable behaviors than their peers are. For example, people tend to predict that they are more likely than their peers to give to a charity, read to the blind, vote, stop for pedestrians in a crosswalk, and so forth (Epley & Dunning, 2000). In the present research, Balcetis, Dunning, and Miller conducted four studies to explore the hypothesis that participants from collectivist backgrounds would make more accurate predictions about whether they would engage in socially admirable behaviors than those from individualistic backgrounds. We will focus on Study 2 in their series and then briefly mention the companion studies.

Method

Participants. A total of forty-eight students from Cornell University participated in exchange for $5. The individualistic group consisted of twenty-four students who had two parents born in the United States. The collectivist group consisted of twenty-four Chinese students who had two parents born in China (most of the students were born in China themselves).

Design. A between-subjects design was used in which half of the subjects from each cultural group were randomly assigned to a *prediction condition* or an *actual behavior condition.* In the prediction condition participants made predictions about how much of their $5 payment they might donate to three worthwhile charities if asked and how much their peers would be likely to donate. In the actual behavior condition, participants were asked whether they would like to donate a portion of their $5 payment to any of the three worthwhile charities. They were told that they could make their donation anonymously in a blank envelope to minimize the pressure to donate.

Procedure. Because all the subjects were currently living in an individualistic culture (the U.S.), they were put through a cultural immersion exercise to temporarily bolster the impact of their original cultural mindset. The exercise consisted of a 15- to 20-minute interview about their cultural background. Near the end of the experimental session, the experimenter handed the participants their $5 payment and either invited them to consider a donation to charity (in the actual behavior condition) or asked them to fill out a sheet asking for predictions about how much they and their peers might donate if asked (in the prediction condition).

Results

The crucial comparison looked at the predictions of donations in relation to the actual donations made by subjects from individualist and collectivist backgrounds. Individualists predicted that they would donate more than twice as much as was actually donated (the gap was $1.74). The collectivists predicted that they would donate *less* than was actually donated, but the gap ($0.69) between their predictions and actual behavior was much smaller than for the individualists.

Discussion

In other studies in the series, individualists overestimated their generosity in redistributing a reward and their willingness to avoid being rude to someone. In contrast, the collectivists were more accurate in making predictions of their actual behavior. Thus, the authors conclude that collectivism may promote greater self-insight than individualism, at least when people contemplate whether they will engage in socially desirable behaviors.

Comment

This study was featured because it exemplifies the resurgence of research on culture and personality. Much of the most interesting and influential research on personality in recent years has focused on the effects of culture. The results of this study show once again that phenomena that are well documented in Western societies, such as the self-enhancement effect, may not be applicable or may take a different form in non-Western cultures. This research also demonstrates once again that it is important to go beyond self-reports of how people *think* they will behave and compare these reports to actual behavior.

REVIEW OF KEY LEARNING GOALS

12.22 The basic trait structure of personality may be much the same across cultures, as the Big Five traits usually emerge in cross-cultural studies. However, some cultural variability has been seen when researchers compare average trait scores for various cultural groups. Personality test data collected from real individuals show that perceptions of national character tend to be inaccurate stereotypes.

12.23 Markus and Kitayama assert that American culture fosters an independent conception of self as a unique individual who is separate from others. In contrast, Asian cultures foster an interdependent view of the self, as part of an interconnected social matrix.

12.24 Self-enhancement is pervasive in individualist cultures but is far less common in collectivist cultures. The results of our Featured Study suggest that collectivists may know themselves better than individualists do.

KEY LEARNING GOALS

12.25 Identify the three unifying themes highlighted in this chapter.

Reflecting on the Chapter's Themes

Cultural Heritage

Theoretical Diversity

Sociohistorical Context

Our discussion of culture and personality obviously highlighted the text's theme that people's behavior is influenced by their cultural heritage. This chapter has also been ideally suited for embellishing two other unifying themes: psychology's theoretical diversity and the idea that psychology evolves in a sociohistorical context.

No other area of psychology is characterized by as much theoretical diversity as the study of personality, where there are literally dozens of insightful theories. Some of this diversity exists because different theories attempt to explain different facets of behavior. However, much of this theoretical diversity reflects genuine disagreements on basic questions about personality. Some of these disagreements are apparent on pages 500–501, which present an Illustrated Overview of the ideas of Freud, Skinner, Rogers, and Eysenck, as representatives of the psychodynamic, behavioral, humanistic, and biological approaches to personality.

The study of personality also highlights the sociohistorical context in which psychology evolves. Personality theories have left many marks on modern culture. The theories of Freud, Adler, and Skinner have had an enormous impact on childrearing practices. In addition, the ideas of Freud and Jung have found their way into literature (influencing the portrayal of fictional characters) and the visual arts. For example, Freud's theory helped inspire surrealism's interest in the world of dreams. Finally, Maslow's hierarchy of needs and Skinner's affirmation of the value of positive reinforcement have influenced approaches to management in the world of business and industry.

Sociohistorical forces also leave their imprint on psychology. This chapter provided many examples of how personal experiences, prevailing attitudes, and historical events have contributed to the evolution of ideas in psychology. For example, Freud's pessimistic view of human nature and his emphasis on the dark forces of aggression were shaped to some extent by his exposure to the hostilities of World War I and prevailing anti-Semitic sentiments. And Freud's emphasis on sexuality was surely influenced by the Victorian climate of sexual repression that existed in his youth. Adler's interest in inferiority feelings and compensation appears to have sprung from his own sickly childhood and the difficulties he had to overcome. In a similar vein, we saw that both Rogers and Maslow had to resist parental pressures in order to pursue their career interests. Their emphasis on the need to achieve personal fulfillment may have originated in these experiences.

Progress in the study of personality has also been influenced by developments in other areas of psychology. For instance, the enterprise of psychological testing originally emerged out of efforts to measure intelligence. Eventually, however, the principles of psychological testing were applied to the challenge of measuring personality. In the upcoming Personal Application we discuss the logic and limitations of personality tests.

REVIEW OF KEY LEARNING GOALS

12.25 The study of personality illustrates how psychology is characterized by great theoretical diversity. It also demonstrates how ideas in psychology are shaped by sociohistorical forces and how cultural factors influence psychological processes.

PERSONAL APPLICATION

Understanding Personality Assessment

KEY LEARNING GOALS

12.26 Describe several prominent personality inventories, and evaluate the strengths and weaknesses of self-report inventories.

12.27 Describe two projective tests, and evaluate the strengths and weaknesses of projective testing.

Answer the following "true" or "false."

____ **1** Responses to personality tests are subject to unconscious distortion.

____ **2** The results of personality tests are often misunderstood.

____ **3** Personality test scores should be interpreted with caution.

____ **4** Personality tests serve many important functions.

If you answered "true" to all four questions, you earned a perfect score. Yes, personality tests are subject to distortion. Admittedly, test results are often misunderstood. They also should be interpreted cautiously. In spite of these problems, however, psychological tests can be quite useful.

Everyone engages in efforts to size up his or her own personality as well as that of others. When you think to yourself that "Mary Ann is shrewd and poised," or when you remark to a friend that "Carlos is timid and submissive," you're making personality assessments. In a sense, then, personality assessment is an ongoing part of daily life. Given the popular interest in personality assessment, it's not surprising that psychologists have devised formal measures of personality.

Personality tests can be helpful in (1) making clinical diagnoses of psychological disorders, (2) vocational counseling, (3) personnel selection in business and industry, and (4) measuring specific personality traits for research purposes. Personality tests can be divided into two broad categories: *self-report inventories* and *projective tests*. In this Personal Application, we'll discuss some representative tests from both categories. We'll also discuss their strengths and weaknesses.

Self-Report Inventories

PsykTrek 7a

Self-report inventories **are personality tests that ask individuals to answer a series of questions about their characteristic behavior.** The logic underlying this approach is simple. Who knows you better? Who has known you longer? Who has more access to your private feelings? We'll look at three examples of self-report scales, the MMPI, the 16PF, and the NEO Personality Inventory.

The MMPI

The most widely used self-report inventory is the Minnesota Multiphasic Personality Inventory (MMPI) (Butcher, 2005, 2006). The MMPI was originally designed to aid clinicians in the diagnosis of psychological disorders. It measures ten personality traits that, when manifested to an extreme degree, are thought to be symptoms of disorders. Examples include traits such as paranoia, depression, and hysteria.

Are the MMPI clinical scales valid? That is, do they measure what they were designed to measure? Originally, it was assumed that the ten clinical subscales would provide direct indexes of specific types of disorders. In other words, a high score on the depression scale would be indicative of depression, a high score on the paranoia scale would be indicative of a paranoid disorder, and so forth. However, research revealed that the relations between MMPI scores and various types of mental illness are much more complex than originally anticipated. People with most types of disorders show elevated scores on *several* MMPI subscales. This means that certain score *profiles* are indicative of specific disorders (see **Figure 12.20** on the next page). Thus, the interpretation of the MMPI is quite complicated, perhaps overly complicated according to some critics (Helmes, 2008). Still, the MMPI can be a helpful diagnostic tool for the clinician. The fact that the inventory has been translated into more than 115 languages is a testimonial to its usefulness (Adams & Culbertson, 2005).

The 16PF and NEO Personality Inventory

PsykTrek 7a

Raymond Cattell (1957, 1965) set out to identify and measure the *basic dimensions* of the *normal* personality. He started with a previously compiled list of 4504 personality traits. This massive list was reduced to 171 traits by weeding out terms that were virtually synonyms. Cattell then used factor analysis to identify clusters of closely related traits and the factors underlying them. Eventually, he reduced the list of 171 traits to 16 *source traits*. The Sixteen Personality Factor (16PF) Questionnaire (Cattell, Eber, & Tatsuoka, 1970; Cattell, 2007) is a 187–item scale that assesses these 16 basic dimensions of personality. These are listed in **Figure 12.21** on the next page. The current, fifth edition of this test continues to enjoy widespread use (Cattell & Mead, 2008).

As we noted in the main body of the chapter, some theorists believe that only five trait dimensions are required to provide a full description of personality. This view has led to the creation of a relatively new test—the NEO Personality Inventory. Developed by Paul Costa and Robert McCrae (1985, 1992), the NEO Inventory is designed to measure the Big Five traits: neuroticism, extraversion, openness to experience, agreeableness, and conscientiousness. The NEO inventory is widely used in research and clinical work, and updated revisions of the scale have been released (Costa & McCrae, 2008; McCrae & Costa, 2007). An example of a NEO profile (averaged from many respondents) was shown in our discussion of culture and personality (see **Figure 12.18** on page 506).

Strengths and Weaknesses of Self-Report Inventories

To appreciate the strengths of self-report inventories, consider how else you might inquire about an individual's personality. For instance, if you want to know how assertive someone is, why not just ask the person? Why administer an elaborate 50-item personality inventory that measures assertiveness? The advantage of the personality

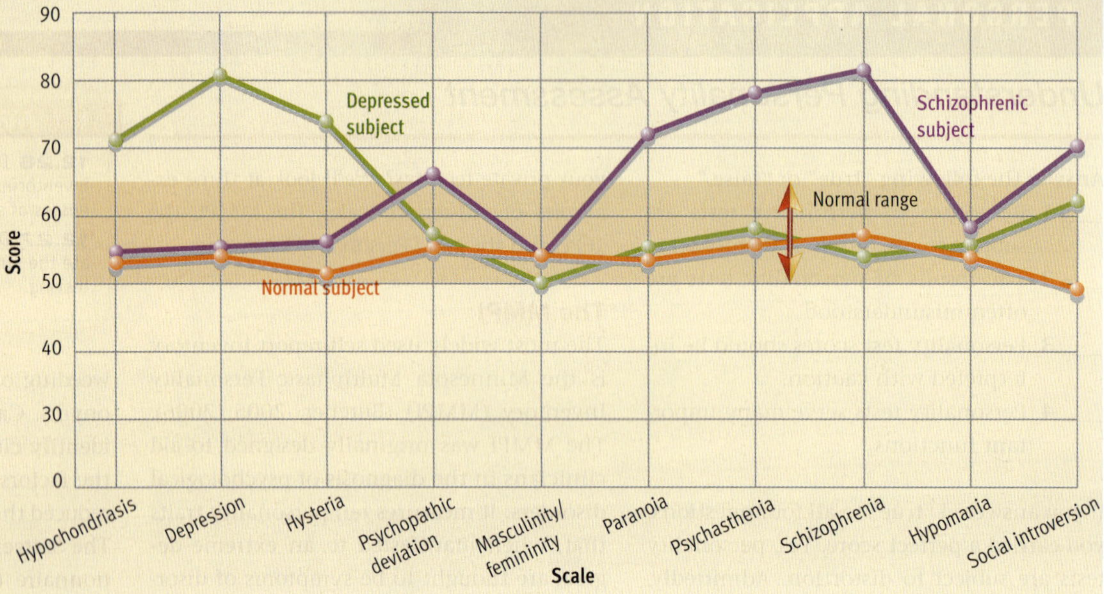

Figure 12.20
MMPI profiles. Scores on the ten clinical scales of the MMPI are usually plotted as shown here to create a profile for a client. The normal range for scores on each subscale is 50 to 65. People with disorders frequently exhibit elevated scores on several clinical scales rather than just one.

© Cengage Learning 2013

inventory is that it can provide a more objective and more precise estimate of the person's assertiveness. It will be grounded in extensive comparative data based on information provided by many other respondents.

Of course, self-report inventories are only as accurate as the information that respondents provide. They are susceptible to several sources of error (Ben-Porath, 2003; Kline, 1995; Paulhus, 1991), including the following:

1. *Deliberate deception.* Some self-report inventories include many questions whose purpose is easy to figure out. This problem makes it possible for some respondents to intentionally fake particular personality traits (Rees & Metcalfe, 2003). Some studies suggest that deliberate faking is a serious problem when personality scales are used to evaluate job applicants (Birkeland et al., 2006). Other studies, however, suggest that the problem is not all that significant (Hogan, Barrett, & Hogan, 2007).

2. *Social desirability bias.* Without realizing it, some people consistently respond to questions in ways that will make them look good. The social desirability bias isn't a matter of deception so much as wishful thinking.

3. *Response sets.* A response set is a systematic tendency to respond to test items in

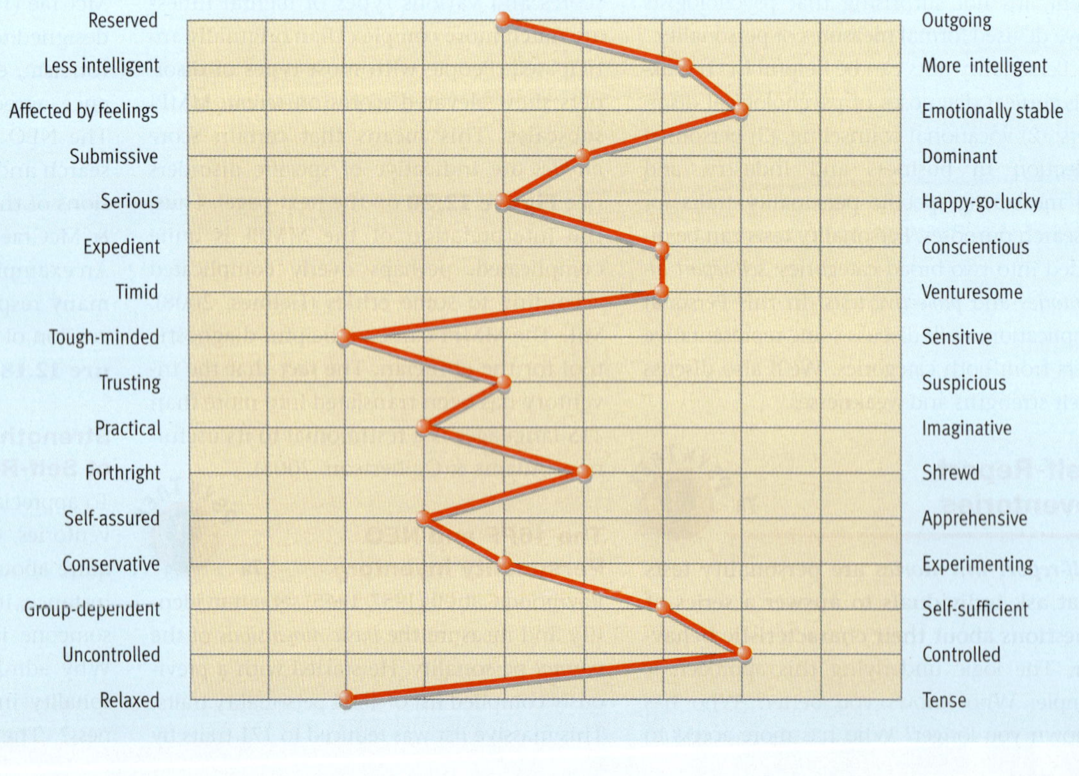

Figure 12.21
The Sixteen Personality Factor Questionnaire (16PF). Unlike the MMPI, Cattell's 16PF is designed to assess normal aspects of personality. The pairs of traits listed across from each other in the figure define the 16 factors measured by this self-report inventory. The profile shown is the average profile seen among a group of airline pilots who took the test.

SOURCE: Cattell, R. B. (1973, July). Personality pinned down. *Psychology Today*, 40–46. Reprinted by permission of *Psychology Today* magazine. Copyright © 1971 Sussex Publishers, LLC.

© Cengage Learning 2013

a particular way that's unrelated to the content of the items. For instance, some people, called "yea-sayers," tend to agree with virtually every statement on a test. Other people, called "nay-sayers," tend to disagree with nearly every statement.

Test developers have devised a number of strategies to reduce the impact of deliberate deception, social desirability bias, and response sets (Berry, Wetter, & Baer, 1995; Lanyon & Goodstein, 1997). For instance, it's possible to insert a "lie scale" into a test to assess the likelihood that a respondent is engaging in deception. The best way to reduce the impact of social desirability bias is to identify items that are sensitive to this bias and drop them from the test. Problems with response sets can be reduced by systematically varying the way in which test items are worded. Although self-report inventories have some weaknesses, carefully constructed personality scales remain "an indispensable tool for applied psychologists" (Hogan, 2005, p. 331).

Projective Tests

PsykTrek 7a

Projective tests take a rather indirect approach to the assessment of personality. They are used extensively in clinical work. ***Projective tests* ask participants to respond to vague, ambiguous stimuli in ways that may reveal the subjects' needs, feelings, and personality traits.** The Rorschach test (Rorschach, 1921), for instance, consists of a series of ten inkblots. Respondents are asked to describe what they see in the blots. In the Thematic Apperception Test (TAT) (Murray, 1943), a series of pictures of simple scenes is presented to a person. The person is then asked to tell stories about what is happening in the scenes and what the characters are feeling. For instance, one TAT card shows a young boy contemplating a violin resting on a table in front of him (see **Figure 12.22** for another example).

Figure 12.22
The Thematic Apperception Test (TAT). In taking the TAT, a respondent is asked to tell stories about scenes such as this one. The themes apparent in each story can be scored to provide insight about the respondent's personality.

SOURCE: Murray. H. A. (1971). *Thematic Apperception Test*. Cambridge, MA: Harvard University Press. Copyright © 1943 by The President and Fellows of Harvard College, Copyright © 1971 by Henry A. Murray. Reprinted by permission of the publisher.

The Projective Hypothesis

PsykTrek 7a

The "projective hypothesis" is that ambiguous materials can serve as a blank screen onto which people project their characteristic concerns, conflicts, and desires (Frank, 1939). Thus, a competitive person who is shown the TAT card of the boy at the table with the violin might concoct a story about how the boy is contemplating an upcoming musical competition at which he hopes to excel. The same card shown to a person high in impulsiveness might elicit a story about how the boy is planning to sneak out the door to go dirt-bike riding with friends.

The scoring and interpretation of projective tests is very complicated. Rorschach responses may be analyzed in terms of content, originality, the feature of the inkblot that determined the response, and the amount of the inkblot used, among other criteria. In fact, six different systems exist for scoring the Rorschach (Adams & Culbertson, 2005). TAT stories are examined in terms of heroes, needs, themes, and outcomes.

Strengths and Weaknesses of Projective Tests

Proponents of projective tests assert that the tests have two unique strengths. First, they are not transparent to respondents. That is, the subject doesn't know how the test provides information to the tester. Hence, it may be difficult for people to engage in intentional deception (Groth-Marnat, 1997). Second, the indirect approach used in these tests may make them especially sensitive to unconscious, latent features of personality.

Unfortunately, the scientific evidence on projective measures is unimpressive (Garb, Florio, & Grove, 1998; Hunsley, Lee, & Wood, 2003). In a thorough review of the relevant research, Lilienfeld, Wood, and Garb (2000) conclude that projective tests tend to be plagued by inconsistent scoring, low reliability, inadequate test norms, cultural bias, and poor validity estimates. They also assert that, contrary to advocates' claims, projective tests are susceptible to some types of intentional deception (primarily, faking poor mental health). Based on their analysis, Lilienfeld and his colleagues argue that projective tests should be referred to as projective "techniques" or "instruments" rather than tests, because "most of these techniques as used in daily clinical practice do not fulfill the traditional criteria for psychological tests" (p. 29). In spite of these problems, projective tests continue to be used by many clinicians. The questionable scientific status of these techniques is a very real problem. However, their continued popularity suggests that they yield subjective information that many clinicians find useful (Viglione & Rivera, 2003).

REVIEW OF KEY LEARNING GOALS

12.26 Self-report inventories ask subjects to describe themselves. The MMPI is a widely used inventory that measures pathological aspects of personality. The 16PF assesses 16 dimensions of the normal personality. The NEO personality inventory measures the Big Five personality traits. Self-report inventories are vulnerable to certain sources of error, including deception, the social desirability bias, and response sets.

12.27 Projective tests assume that subjects' responses to ambiguous stimuli reveal something about their personality. In the Rorschach test, respondents describe what they see in ten inkblots, whereas subjects formulate stories about simple scenes when they are given the TAT. While the projective hypothesis seems plausible, projective tests' reliability and validity are disturbingly low.

Hindsight in Everyday Analyses of Personality

KEY LEARNING GOALS

12.28 Understand how hindsight bias affects everyday analyses and theoretical analyses of personality.

Consider the case of two close sisters who grew up together: Lorena and Christina. Lorena became a frugal adult who is careful about spending her money, only shops when there are sales, and saves every penny she can. In contrast, Christina became an extravagant spender who lives to shop and never saves any money. How do the sisters explain their striking personality differences? Lorena attributes her thrifty habits to the fact that her family was so poor when she was a child that she learned the value of being careful with money. Christina attributes her extravagant spending to the fact that her family was so poor that she learned to really enjoy any money that she might have. Now, it *is* possible that two sisters could react to essentially the same circumstances quite differently. But the more likely explanation is that both sisters have been influenced by ***hindsight bias*****—the tendency to mold one's interpretation of the past to fit how events actually turned out.** We saw how hindsight can distort memory in Chapter 7. Here, we will see how hindsight tends to make everyone feel as if he or she is a personality expert and how it creates interpretive problems even for scientific theories of personality.

© AP Images/Jacquelyn Martin

When public officials make complicated decisions that backfire, critics are often quick to argue that the officials should have shown greater foresight. This type of hindsight bias has been apparent in casual discussions and formal analyses of the 2008 economic meltdown in the United States. With the luxury of hindsight it is easy to second-guess bank and stock market regulators who failed to foresee the financial crisis that triggered a worldwide recession.

The Prevalence of Hindsight Bias

Hindsight bias is *ubiquitous*. That is, it occurs in a variety of settings, with all sorts of people (Blank, Musch, & Pohl, 2007; Sanna & Schwarz, 2006). Most of the time, people are not aware of the way their explanations are skewed by the fact that the outcome is already known. The experimental literature on hindsight bias offers a rich array of findings on how the knowledge of an outcome biases the way people think about its causes (Fischhoff, 2007; Guilbault et al., 2004).

For example, when college students were told the results of hypothetical experiments, each group of students could "explain" why the studies turned out the way they did, even though different groups were given opposite results to explain (Slovic & Fischhoff, 1977). The students believed that the results of the studies were obvious when they were told what the experimenter found. Yet, when they were given only the information that was available before the outcome was known, it was not obvious at all. This bias is also called the "I knew it all along" effect because that's the typical refrain of people when they have the luxury of hindsight.

Indeed, after the fact, people often act as if events that would have been difficult to predict had in fact been virtually *inevitable*. Looking back at the 2008 crash of the U.S. mortgage system and ensuing financial crisis, for instance, many people today act as though these events were bound to have happened. In reality, though, these landmark events were predicted by almost no one. It appears that outcome knowledge warps judgments in two ways (Erdfelder, Brandt, & Bröder, 2007). First, knowing the outcome of an event impairs one's recall of earlier expectations about the event. Second, outcome knowledge shapes how people reconstruct their thinking about the event.

Hindsight bias shows up in many contexts. For example, when a couple announces that they are splitting up, many people in their social circle will typically claim they "saw it coming." When a football team loses in a huge upset, you will hear many fans claim, "I knew they were overrated and vulnerable." When public authorities make a difficult decision that leads to a disastrous outcome—such as officials' decision not to evacuate New Orleans in preparation for Hurricane Katrina until relatively late—many of the pundits in the press are quick to criticize. They might claim, for example, that only incompetent fools could have failed to foresee the catastrophe.

Interestingly, people are not much kinder to themselves when they make ill-fated decisions. When individuals make tough calls that lead to negative results—such as buying a car that turns out to be a lemon, or investing in a stock that plummets—they often say things like, "Why did I ignore the obvious warning signs?" or "How could I be such an idiot?"

Hindsight and Personality

Hindsight bias appears to be pervasive in everyday analyses of personality. Think about it: If you attempt to explain why you are so suspicious, why your mother is so domineering, or why your best friend is so insecure, the starting point in each case will be the personality outcome. It would probably be impossible to reconstruct the past without being swayed by your knowledge of these outcomes. Thus, hindsight makes everybody an expert on personality. We can all come up with plausible explanations for the personality traits of people we know well. Perhaps this is why Judith Harris (1998) ignited a firestorm of protest when she wrote a widely read book arguing that parents have relatively little effect on their children's personalities beyond the genetic material that they supply.

In her book *The Nurture Assumption,* Harris summarizes behavioral genetics research and other evidence suggesting that family environment has surprisingly little impact on children's personality (see page 498). There is plenty of room for debate on this bold conclusion (Kagan, 1998; Maccoby, 2000; Turkheimer & Waldron, 2000). Our chief interest here, though, is that Harris made a cogent, compelling argument in her book that attracted extensive coverage in the press. This then generated an avalanche of commentary from angry parents who argued that *parents do matter.* For example, *Newsweek* magazine received 350 letters, mostly from parents who provided examples of how they thought they influenced their children's personalities. However, parents' retrospective analyses of their children's personality development have to be treated with great skepticism. They are likely to be distorted by hindsight bias (not to mention the selective recall frequently seen in anecdotal reports).

Unfortunately, hindsight bias is so prevalent it also presents a problem for scientific theories of personality. For example, the spectre of hindsight bias has been raised in many critiques of psychoanalytic theory (Torrey, 1992). Freudian theory was originally built on a foundation of case studies of patients in therapy. Obviously, Freudian therapists who knew what their patients' adult personalities were like probably went looking for the types of childhood experiences hypothesized by Freud (oral fixations, punitive toilet training, Oedipal conflicts, and so forth) in their efforts to explain their patients' personalities.

Another problem with hindsight bias is that once researchers know an outcome, more often than not they can fashion some plausible explanation for it. For instance, Torrey (1992) describes a study inspired by Freudian theory that examined breast-size preferences among men. The original hypothesis was that men who scored higher in dependence—thought to be a sign of oral fixation—would manifest a stronger preference for women with large breasts. When the actual results of the study showed just the opposite—that dependence was associated with a preference for smaller breasts—the finding was attributed to reaction formation on the part of the men. Instead of failing to support Freudian theory, the unexpected findings were simply reinterpreted in a way that was consistent with Freudian theory.

Hindsight bias also presents thorny problems for evolutionary theorists. These theorists generally work backward from known outcomes to reason out how adaptive pressures in humans' ancestral past may have led to those outcomes (Cornell, 1997). Consider, for instance, evolutionary theorists' assertion that the Big Five traits are found to be fundamental dimensions of personality around the world because those specific traits have had major adaptive implications over the course of human history (Buss, 1995; Nettle, 2006). Their explanation makes sense. However, what would have happened if some *other traits* had shown up in the Big Five? Would the evolutionary view have been weakened if dominance, or paranoia, or high sensation seeking had turned up in the Big Five? Probably not. With the luxury of hindsight, evolutionary theorists surely could have constructed plausible explanations for how these traits promoted reproductive success in the distant past. Thus, hindsight bias is a fundamental feature of human cognition. The scientific enterprise is not immune to this problem.

Other Implications of "20/20 Hindsight"

Our discussion of hindsight has focused on its implications for thinking about personality. There is, however, ample evidence that hindsight can bias thinking in all sorts of domains. For example, consider the practice of obtaining second opinions on medical diagnoses. The doctor providing the second opinion usually is aware of the first physician's diagnosis, which creates a hindsight bias (Arkes et al., 1981). Second opinions would probably be more valuable if the doctors rendering them were not aware of previous diagnoses. Hindsight also has the potential to distort legal decisions in many types of cases where jurors evaluate defendants' responsibility for known outcomes, such as a failed surgery (Harley, 2007). For example, in trials involving allegations of negligence, jurors' natural tendency to think "how could they have failed to foresee this problem?" may exaggerate the appearance of negligence (LaBine & LaBine, 1996).

Hindsight bias is very powerful. The next time you hear of an unfortunate outcome to a decision made by a public official, carefully examine the way news reporters describe the decision. You will probably find that they believe that the disastrous outcome should have been obvious. But it's only obvious, of course because they can clearly see what went wrong after the fact. Similarly, if you find yourself thinking "Only a fool would have failed to anticipate this disaster" or "I would have foreseen this problem," take a deep breath and try to review the decision *using only information that was known at the time the decision was being made.* Sometimes good decisions, based on the best available information, can have terrible outcomes. Unfortunately, the clarity of "20/20 hindsight" makes it difficult for people to learn from their own and others' mistakes.

Table 12.3 Critical Thinking Skill Discussed in This Application

Skill	Description
Recognizing the bias in hindsight analysis	The critical thinker understands that knowing the outcome of events biases one's recall and interpretation of the events.

© Cengage Learning 2013

REVIEW OF KEY LEARNING GOALS

12.28 Hindsight bias often leads people to assert that "I knew it all along" in discussing outcomes that they did not actually predict. Thanks to hindsight, people can almost always come up with plausible-sounding explanations for known personality traits. Psychoanalytic and evolutionary theories of personality have also been accused of falling victim to hindsight bias.

Chapter 12 Practice Test

1. Harvey Hedonist has devoted his life to the search for physical pleasure and immediate need gratification. Freud would say that Harvey is dominated by:
   A. his ego.
   B. his superego.
   C. his id.
   D. Bacchus.

2. Furious at her boss for what she considers to be unjust criticism, Tyra turns around and takes out her anger on her subordinates. Tyra may be using the defense mechanism of:
   A. displacement.
   B. reaction formation.
   C. identification.
   D. replacement.

3. Freud believed that most personality disturbances are due to:
   A. the failure of parents to reinforce healthy behavior.
   B. a poor self-concept resulting from excessive parental demands.
   C. unconscious and unresolved sexual conflicts rooted in childhood experiences.
   D. the exposure of children to unhealthy role models.

4. According to Alfred Adler, the prime motivating force in a person's life is:
   A. physical gratification.
   B. existential anxiety.
   C. striving for superiority.
   D. the need for power.

5. Which of the following learning mechanisms does B. F. Skinner see as being the major means by which behavior is learned?
   A. classical conditioning
   B. operant conditioning
   C. observational learning
   D. insight learning

6. Always having been a good student, Irving is confident that he will do well in his psychology course. According to Bandura's social cognitive theory, Irving would be said to have:
   A. strong feelings of self-efficacy.
   B. a sense of superiority.
   C. strong feelings of self-esteem.
   D. strong defense mechanisms.

7. Which of the following approaches to personality is least deterministic?
   A. the humanistic approach
   B. the psychoanalytic approach
   C. Skinner's approach
   D. the behavioral approach

8. Which of the following did Carl Rogers believe fosters a congruent self-concept?
   A. conditional love
   B. appropriate role models
   C. immediate-need gratification
   D. unconditional love

9. The strongest support for the theory that personality is heavily influenced by genetics is provided by strong personality similarity between:
   A. identical twins reared together.
   B. identical twins reared apart.
   C. fraternal twins reared together.
   D. nontwins reared together.

10. Which of the following is the best way to regard heritability estimates?
    A. as reliable but not necessarily valid estimates
    B. as ballpark estimates of the influence of genetics
    C. as accurate estimates of the influence of genetics
    D. as relatively useless estimates of the influence of genetics

11. Research on terror management theory has shown that increased mortality salience leads to all of the following except:
    A. increased striving for self-esteem.
    B. more stereotypic thinking about minorities.
    C. more negative reactions to people who criticize one's country.
    D. reduced respect for cultural icons.

12. When English language personality scales have been translated and administered in other cultures:
    A. the trait structure of personality has turned out to be dramatically different.
    B. the usual Big Five traits have emerged from the factor analyses.
    C. the personality scales have proven useless.
    D. a seven-factor solution has usually emerged from the factor analyses.

13. In which of the following cultures is an independent view of the self most likely to be the norm?
    A. China
    B. Japan
    C. Korea
    D. United States

14. Which of the following is *not* a shortcoming of self-report personality inventories?
    A. The accuracy of the results is a function of the honesty of the respondent.
    B. Respondents may attempt to answer in a way that makes them look good.
    C. There is sometimes a problem with "yea-sayers" or "nay-sayers."
    D. They are objective measures that are easy to administer and score.

15. In *The Nurture Assumption*, Judith Harris argues that the evidence indicates that family environment has ________________ on children's personalities.
    A. largely positive effects
    B. largely negative effects
    C. surprisingly little effect
    D. a powerful effect

Answers

1 C p. 480	6 A p. 490	11 D pp. 503–504
2 A pp. 482–483	7 A p. 492	12 B p. 505
3 C p. 485	8 D p. 493	13 D pp. 505–506
4 C p. 486	9 B pp. 497–498	14 D pp. 510–511
5 B pp. 488–489	10 B p. 499	15 C p. 513

Chapter 12 Media Resources

PsykTrek

To view a demo: **www.cengage.com/psychology/psyktrek**
To order: **www.cengage.com/psychology/weiten**

Go to the PsykTrek website or CD-ROM for further study of the concepts in this chapter. Both online and on the CD-ROM, PsykTrek includes dozens of learning modules with videos, animations, and quizzes, as well as simulations of psychological phenomena and a multimedia glossary that includes word pronunciations.

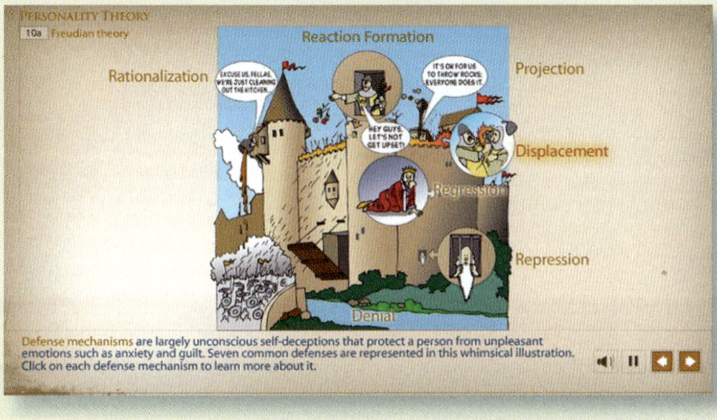

© Cengage Learning 2008

Go to Module 10a (*Freudian Theory*) to review the essentials of Sigmund Freud's controversial psychoanalytic model of personality.

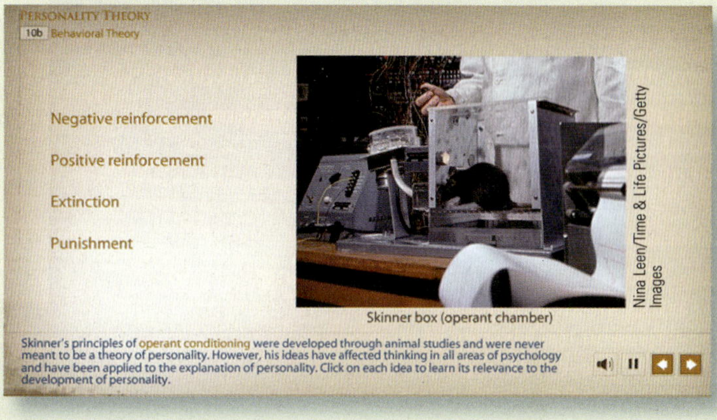

© Cengage Learning 2008

Work through Module 10b (*Behavioral Theory*) to enhance your understanding of how the behaviorists have analyzed personality and to watch classic footage from Albert Bandura's famous "Bobo doll" studies of aggressive behavior.

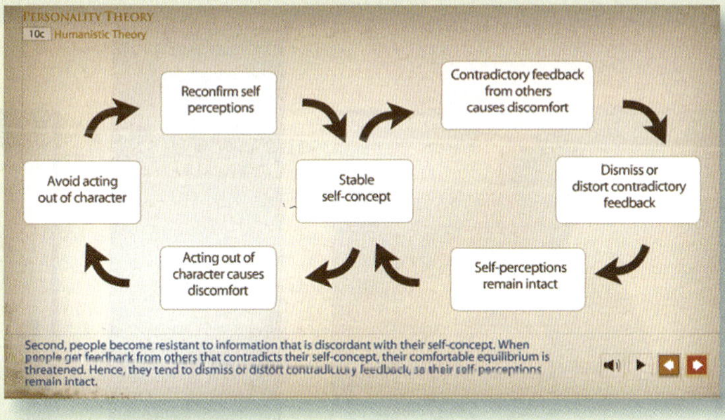

© Cengage Learning 2008

Explore Module 10c (*Humanistic Theory*) to get a better handle on the personality theories of Carl Rogers and Abraham Maslow.

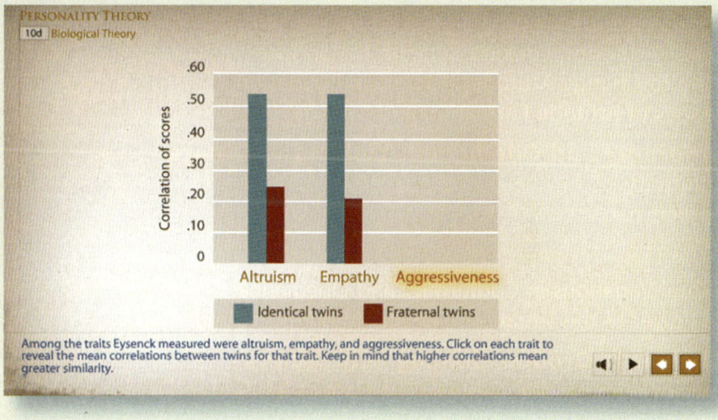

© Cengage Learning 2008

Visit Module 10d (*Biological Theory*) to learn more about how biological factors may shape personality.

Online Study Tools

Log in to **CengageBrain** to access the resources your instructor requires. For this book, you can access:

CourseMate brings course concepts to life with interactive learning, study, and exam preparation tools that support the printed textbook. A textbook-specific website, Psychology CourseMate includes an integrated interactive eBook and other interactive learning tools such as quizzes, flashcards, videos, and more.

CengageNow is an easy-to-use online resource that helps you study in less time to get the grade you want—NOW. Take a pre-test for this chapter and receive a personalized study plan based on your results that will identify the topics you need to review and direct you to online resources to help you master those topics. Then take a post-test to help you determine the concepts you have mastered and what you will need to work on. If your textbook does not include an access code card, go to CengageBrain.com to gain access.

WebTutor is more than just an interactive study guide. WebTutor is an anytime, anywhere customized learning solution with an eBook, keeping you connected to your textbook, instructor, and classmates.

Aplia. If your professor has assigned Aplia homework:

1. Sign in to your account
2. Complete the corresponding homework exercises as required by your professor.
3. When finished, click "Grade It Now" to see which areas you have mastered, which need more work, and detailed explanations of every answer.

Visit **www.cengagebrain.com** to access your account and purchase materials.

13

Social Behavior

© LUKE MACGREGOR/Reuters/Landov

Audrey, a 16-year-old junior in high school, takes her cell phone with her everywhere, yet she is loathe to actually talk on her phone. She will do anything to avoid phone conversations. The immediacy of real-time conversation intimidates her. It's not that her phone goes unused. She uses it constantly for texting, which she prefers because she has more control over the communication. She can take time to think and edit her thoughts. She also uses her phone's camera all day long. She snaps away and posts many pictures to Facebook. "I like to feel that my life is up there," she says. But the life depicted on her Facebook profile is a carefully crafted one. She agonizes over which photos to post. Which ones will portray her in the best light? Which ones will project an appealing "bad" girl image without going too far?

The comments Audrey gets about what she posts shape what she does next. Say Audrey experiments with a flirty style on Facebook. If she gets a good response from her Facebook friends, she'll escalate the flirty tone. One day, she tries out "an ironic, witty" tone in her wall posts. The response is not particularly enthusiastic, so she backs off. Friends who know Audrey in real life give her some leeway as she bends reality a bit. She reciprocates by not challenging their self-presentations.

But sometimes a little spat online can spin out of control. Audrey clashed with a classmate, Logan, in a chat room one day. Feeling she'd been wrong, she apologized to him the next day at school. But Logan wasn't satisfied. He brought the quarrel back online, this time posting his side of the story on Audrey's Facebook page, where all her friends would see it. Audrey felt she had to fight back to counter his smoldering version of what had happened. Day after day, Audrey spent hours in angry online exchanges as friends from both sides joined in the fray. Even six months later, she and Logan, who had been "really good friends" avoided each other in the hall. Eventually, Logan apologized, but it was "an online apology. It's cheap. It's easy. All you have to do is type 'I'm sorry.' You don't have to have any emotion, any believability in your voice or anything," Audrey said. "With an online apology, there are still unanswered questions: 'Is he

Paradox: In an emergency, the greater the number of bystanders, the less likely they are to provide help.

© Simon Belcher/Photolibrary

going to act weird to me now? Are we just going to be normal?' You don't know how the two worlds are going to cross."

Despite her own beliefs about doing certain things in person, Audrey acknowledges that she once broke up with a boyfriend online. She readily admits that she endorses the norm that one should not break off a relationship via text or other online communication, but she claims she just couldn't help herself. "I felt so bad, because I really did care for him, and I couldn't get myself to say it. . . . I wasn't trying to chicken out, I just couldn't form the words, so I had to do it online, and I wish I hadn't. He deserved to have me do it in person. . . . I'm very sorry for it. I just think it was a really cold move, and kind of lame." (Turkle, 2001, pp. 189–197)

The preceding account is a real story, taken from Sherry Turkle's (2011) book *Alone Together,* which provides a fascinating analysis of how modern technology is altering the fabric of social relationships. Audrey's story illustrates something that you probably already know—social relationships assume enormous importance in our lives. Audrey, like most of us, is deeply concerned about how others perceive her. She agonizes over the demise of her friendship with Logan and her inability to break up with her boyfriend face to face. Audrey's story also illustrates how advances in technology are reshaping the nature of social behavior. More and more social interactions are migrating onto the Internet. Intimate relationships are increasingly forged at online dating sites. Work groups increasingly conduct their business from distant locations via the Internet. People increasingly form their impressions of others from what is posted on social networking sites. Whether these shifts will prove to be fundamental or superficial alterations in our social landscape remains to be seen.

In any event, in this chapter we take a look at our social world. ***Social psychology*** **is the branch of psychology concerned with the way individuals' thoughts, feelings, and behaviors are influenced by others.** Social psychologists study how people are affected by the actual, imagined, or implied presence of others. Their interest is not limited to individuals' interactions with others, as people can engage in social behavior even when they're alone. For instance, if you were driving by yourself on a deserted highway and tossed your trash out your car window, your littering would be a social action. It would defy social norms, reflect your socialization and attitudes, and have repercussions (albeit, small) for other people in your society. Social psychologists often study individual behavior in a social context. This interest in understanding individual behavior should be readily apparent in our first section, on person perception.

© Stuwdamdorp/Alamy

KEY LEARNING GOALS

13.1 Understand how aspects of physical appearance may influence impressions of others.

13.2 Clarify how stereotyping and other factors contribute to subjectivity in person perception.

13.3 Articulate the evolutionary perspective on bias in person perception.

Person Perception: Forming Impressions of Others

Can you remember the first meeting of your introductory psychology class? What impression did your professor make on you that day? Did your instructor appear to be confident? Easygoing? Pompous? Open-minded? Cynical? Friendly? Were your first impressions supported or undermined by subsequent observations? When you interact with people, you're constantly engaged in ***person perception,*** **the process of forming impressions of others.** People show considerable ingenuity in piecing together clues about others' characteristics. However, impressions are often inaccurate because of the many biases and fallacies that occur in person perception. In this section we consider some of the factors that influence, and often distort, people's perceptions of others.

Effects of Physical Appearance

PsykTrek SIM10

"Don't judge a book by its cover." People know better than to let physical attractiveness determine their perceptions of others' personal qualities. Or do they? Recent studies have found that good-looking people command more attention than less-attractive individuals do (Lorenzo, Biesanz, & Human, 2010; Maner et al., 2007). And many studies have shown that judgments of others' personality are often swayed by their appearance, especially their physical attractiveness. People tend to ascribe desirable personality characteristics to those who are good-looking. That is, attractive people tend to be seen as more sociable, friendly, poised, warm, and well ad-

DILBERT by Scott Adams reprinted by permission of United Feature Syndicate, Inc.

justed than those who are less attractive (Macrae & Quadflieg, 2010; van Leeuwen, Matthijs, & Macrae, 2004). In reality, research suggests that little correlation exists between attractiveness and personality traits (Feingold, 1992). Why do people inaccurately assume that a connection exists between good looks and personality? One reason is that extremely attractive people are vastly overrepresented in the entertainment media, where they are mostly portrayed in a highly favorable light (Smith, McIntosh, & Bazzini, 1999). Another reason is that one's perceptions are swayed by one's desire to bond with attractive people (Lemay, Clark, & Greenberg, 2010).

You might guess that physical attractiveness would influence perceptions of competence less than perceptions of personality, but the data suggest otherwise. Research has found that people have a strong tendency to view good-looking individuals as more competent than less attractive individuals (Langlois et al., 2000). This bias literally pays off for good-looking people. They tend to secure better jobs and earn higher salaries than less attractive individuals (Collins & Zebrowitz, 1995; Senior et al., 2007). For example, a study of attorneys whose law school class photos were evaluated by independent raters found that physical attractiveness boosted their actual income by 10%–12% (Engemann & Owyang, 2005). Another recent study (Judge, Hurst, & Simon, 2009) compared the impact of brains versus beauty on income. As one would expect (and hope), intelligence was more strongly related to earnings (correlation = .50) than good looks. But the correlation of .24 between attractiveness and income was not trivial.

Observers are also quick to draw inferences about people based on how they move, talk, and gesture—that is, their style of nonverbal expressiveness. Moreover, these inferences tend to be fairly accurate (Ambady & Rosenthal, 1993; Borkenau et al., 2004). For example, based on a mere 10 seconds of videotape, participants can guess strangers' sexual orientation (heterosexual-homosexual) with decent accuracy (Ambady, Hallahan, & Conner, 1999). Based on similar "thin slices" of behavior, observers can make accurate judgments of individuals' racial prejudice, social status, and intelligence (Ambady & Weisbuch, 2010). Even static photographs can provide telling cues about personality. One recent study found that participants were able to make meaningful inferences about stimulus persons' extraversion, openness to experience, agreeableness, and self-esteem based on simple photographs (Naumann et al., 2009).

Stereotypes

Stereotypes can have a dramatic effect on the process of person perception. ***Stereotypes* are widely held beliefs that people have certain characteristics because of their membership in a particular group.** The most common stereotypes in our society are those based on gender, age, and membership in ethnic or occupational groups. People who subscribe to traditional *gender stereotypes* tend to assume that women are emotional, submissive, illogical, and passive, while men are unemotional, dominant, logical, and aggressive. *Age stereotypes* suggest that elderly people are slow, feeble, rigid, forgetful, and asexual. Notions that Jews are mercenary, Germans are methodical, and Italians are passionate are examples of common *ethnic stereotypes*. *Occupational stereotypes* suggest that lawyers are manipulative, accountants are conforming, artists are moody, and so forth.

Stereotyping is a normal cognitive process that is usually automatic and that saves on the time and effort required to get a handle on people individually (Fiske & Russell, 2010). Stereotypes save energy by simplifying our social world. However, this energy savings often comes at some cost in terms of accuracy (Stangor, 2009). Stereotypes tend to be broad overgeneralizations, ignoring the diversity within social groups and fostering inaccurate perceptions of people. Most people who subscribe to stereotypes realize that not all members of a group are identical. For instance, they may admit that some men aren't competitive, some Jews aren't mercenary, and some lawyers aren't manipulative. However, they may still tend to assume that males, Jews, and lawyers are *more likely* than others to have these characteristics. Even if stereotypes mean only that people think in terms of slanted *probabilities,* their expectations may lead them to misperceive individuals with whom they interact. As we've noted in previous chapters, perception is subjective. People often see what they expect to see.

Subjectivity in Person Perception

Stereotypes create biases in person perception that often lead to confirmation of people's expectations about others. If someone's behavior is ambiguous, people are likely to interpret what they see in a way that's consistent with their expectations (Olson, Roese, & Zanna, 1996). Thus, after dealing with a pushy female customer, a salesman who holds traditional gender stereotypes might characterize the woman as "emotional." In contrast, he might characterize a male who exhibits the same pushy behavior as "aggressive."

People not only see what they expect to see, they also tend to overestimate how often they see it (Johnson & Mullen, 1994; Shavitt et al., 1999). ***Illusory correlation*** **occurs when people estimate that they have encountered more confirmations of an association between social traits than they have actually seen.** People also tend to underestimate the number of disconfirmations they have encountered, as illustrated by statements like "I've never met an honest lawyer."

Memory processes can contribute to confirmatory biases in person perception in a variety of ways. Often, individuals selectively recall facts that fit with their stereotypes (Fiske, 1998; Quinn, Macrae, & Bodenhausen, 2003). Evidence for such a tendency was found in a study by Cohen (1981). In this experiment, participants watched a videotape of a woman, described as either a waitress or a librarian, who engaged in a variety of activities, including listening to classical music, drinking beer, and watching TV. When asked to recall what the woman did during the filmed sequence, participants tended to remember activities consistent with their stereotypes of waitresses and librarians. For instance, subjects who thought the woman was a waitress tended to recall her beer drinking, while subjects who thought she was a librarian tended to recall her listening to classical music.

An Evolutionary Perspective on Bias in Person Perception

Why is the process of person perception riddled with bias? Evolutionary psychologists argue that many of the biases seen in social perception were adaptive in humans' ancestral environment (Krebs & Denton, 1997). For example, they argue that person perception is swayed by physical attractiveness because attractiveness was associated with reproductive potential in women and with health, vigor, and the accumulation of material resources in men.

What about the human tendency to automatically categorize others? Evolutionary theorists attribute this behavior to our distant ancestors' need to quickly separate friend from foe. They assert that humans are programmed by evolution to immediately classify people as members of an ***ingroup*—a group that one belongs to and identifies with**, or as members of an ***outgroup*—a group that one does not belong to or identify with.** This crucial categorization is thought to structure subsequent perceptions. As Krebs and Denton (1997) put it, "It is as though the act of classifying others as ingroup or outgroup members activates two quite different brain circuits" (p. 27). In-group members tend to be viewed in a favorable light, whereas outgroup members tend to be viewed in terms of various negative stereotypes. According to Krebs and Denton, these negative stereotypes ("They are inferior; they are all alike; they will exploit us") move outgroups out of one's domain of empathy. Thus, one feels justified in not liking them or in discriminating against them.

Evolutionary psychologists, then, ascribe much of the bias in person perception to cognitive mechanisms that have been shaped by natural selection. Their speculation is thought provoking. However, empirical work is needed to test their hypotheses.

REVIEW OF KEY LEARNING GOALS

13.1 People's perceptions of a person can be distorted by his or her physical appearance. People tend to attribute desirable characteristics, such as intelligence, competence, warmth, and friendliness, to those who are good looking. Observers can draw surprisingly accurate inferences about others based on their nonverbal expressiveness.

13.2 Stereotypes are widely held beliefs that others will have certain characteristics because of their membership in a specific group. Gender, age, ethnic, and occupational stereotypes are common. In interacting with others, stereotypes may lead people to see what they expect to see. People also tend to overestimate how often their expectations are confirmed, a phenomenon called the illusory correlation effect.

13.3 Evolutionary psychologists argue that many biases in person perception were adaptive in humans' ancestral past. The human tendency to automatically categorize others may reflect the primitive need to quickly separate friend from foe.

Attribution Processes: Explaining Behavior

KEY LEARNING GOALS

13.4 Distinguish between internal and external attributions, and summarize Weiner's theory of attributions for success and failure.

13.5 Identify some types of bias in patterns of attribution, and describe cultural variations in attributional bias.

It's Friday evening and you're sitting around at home feeling bored. You call a few friends to see whether they'd like to go out. They all say that they'd love to go, but they have other commitments and can't. Their commitments sound vague, though. You feel that their reasons for not going out with you are rather flimsy. How do you explain these rejections? Do your friends really have commitments? Are they worn out by school and work? When they said that they'd love to go, were they being sincere? Or do they find you boring? Could they be right? Are you boring? These questions illustrate a process that people engage in routinely: the explanation of behavior. *Attributions* play a key role in these explanatory efforts. Hence, they have significant effects on social relations.

What are attributions? ***Attributions* are inferences that people draw about the causes of events, others' behavior, and their own behavior.** If you conclude that a friend turned down your invitation because she's overworked, you have made an attribution about the cause of her behavior. If you conclude that you're stuck at home with nothing to do because you failed to plan ahead, you've made an attribution about the cause of an event (being stuck at home). If you conclude that you failed to plan ahead because you're a procrastinator, you've made an attribution about the cause of your own behavior. People make attributions mainly because they have a strong need to understand their experiences. In this section, we'll take a look at some of the patterns seen when people make attributions.

Internal Versus External Attributions

PSYKTREK 12a

Fritz Heider (1958) was the first to describe how people make attributions. He asserted that people tend to locate the cause of behavior either *within a person,* attributing it to personal factors, or *outside a person,* attributing it to environmental factors.

Elaborating on Heider's insight, various theorists have agreed that explanations of behavior and events can be categorized as internal or external attributions (Jones & Davis, 1965; Kelley, 1967; Weiner, 1974). ***Internal attributions* ascribe the causes of behavior to personal dispositions, traits, abilities, and feelings. *External attributions* ascribe the causes of behavior to situational demands and environmental constraints.** For example, if a friend's business fails, you might attribute it to his or her lack of business sense (an internal, personal factor) or to negative trends in the nation's economic climate (an external, situational explanation). Parents who find out that their teenage son has just banged up the car may blame it on his carelessness (a personal disposition) or on slippery road conditions (a situational factor).

Internal and external attributions can have a tremendous impact on everyday interpersonal interactions. Blaming a friend's business failure on poor business smarts as opposed to a poor economy will have a great impact on how you view your friend. Likewise, if parents attribute their son's automobile accident to slippery road conditions, they're likely to deal with the event very differently than if they attribute it to his carelessness.

Attributions for Success and Failure

PSYKTREK 12a

Some psychologists have sought to discover additional dimensions of attributional thinking besides the internal-external dimension. Bernard Weiner (1980, 1986, 1994) studied the attributions that people make in explaining success and failure. He concluded that people often focus on the *stability* of the

Spencer Research Library, University of Kansas Libraries

Fritz Heider

"Often the momentary situation which, at least in part, determines the behavior of a person is disregarded and the behavior is taken as a manifestation of personal characteristics."

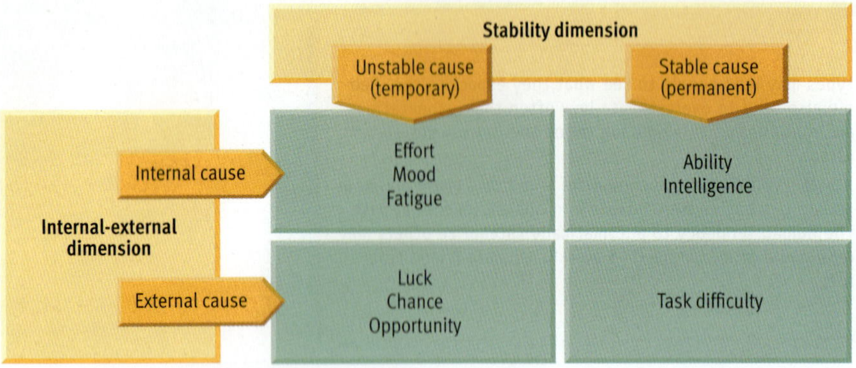

© Cengage Learning 2013

Figure 13.1

Weiner's model of attributions for success and failure. Weiner's model assumes that people's explanations for success and failure emphasize internal versus external causes and stable versus unstable causes. Examples of causal factors that fit into each of the four cells in Weiner's model are shown in the diagram.

SOURCE: Weiner, B., Friese, I., Kukla, A., Reed, L., & Rosenbaum, R. M. (1972). Perceiving the causes of success and failure. In E. E. Jones, D. E. Kanouse, H. H. Kelley, R. E. Nisbett, S. Valins, & B. Weiner (Eds.), *Perceiving the causes of behavior.* Morristown, NJ: General Learning Press. Used by permission of Bernard Weiner.

causes underlying behavior. According to Weiner, the stable-unstable dimension in attribution cuts across the internal-external dimension, creating four types of attributions for success and failure, as shown in **Figure 13.1**.

Let's apply Weiner's model to a concrete event. Imagine that you're contemplating why you failed to get a job that you wanted. You might attribute your setback to internal factors that are stable (lack of ability) or unstable (inadequate effort to put together an eye-catching résumé). Or you might attribute your setback to external factors that are stable (too much outstanding competition) or unstable (bad luck). If you got the job, your explanations for your success would fall into the same four categories: internal-stable (your excellent ability), internal-unstable (your hard work to assemble a superb résumé), external-stable (lack of top-flight competition), and external-unstable (good luck).

Bias in Attribution 12a

Attributions are only inferences. Your attributions may not be the correct explanations for events. Paradoxical as it may seem, people often arrive at inaccurate explanations even when they contemplate the causes of *their own behavior.* Attributions ultimately represent *guesswork* about the causes of events. These guesses tend to be biased in certain directions. Let's look at the principal biases seen in attribution.

Actor-Observer Bias 12a

When an actor and an observer draw inferences about the causes of the actor's behavior, they often make different attributions. A common form of bias seen in observers is **the *fundamental attribution error,* which refers to observers' bias in favor of internal attributions in explaining others' behavior.** Of course, in many instances, an internal attribution may not be an "error." However, observers have a curious tendency to overestimate the likelihood that an actor's behavior reflects personal qualities rather than situational factors (Krull, 2001). Why? One reason is that situational pressures may not be readily apparent to an observer. As Gilbert and Malone (1995) put it, "When one tries to point to a situation, one often stabs empty air" (p. 25). It's not that people assume that situational factors have little impact on behavior (Gawronski, 2004). Rather, it's that attributing others' behavior to their dispositions is a relatively effortless, almost automatic process. Explaining people's behavior in terms of situational factors, on the other hand, requires more thought and effort (see **Figure 13.2**; Krull & Erickson, 1995).

To illustrate the gap that often exists between actors' and observers' attributions, imagine that you're visiting your bank and you fly into a rage over a mistake made on your account. Observers who witness your rage are likely to make an internal attribution and infer that you are nasty and argumentative.

CONCEPT CHECK 13.1

Analyzing Attributions

Check your understanding of attribution processes by analyzing possible explanations for an athletic team's success. Imagine that the women's track team at your school has just won a regional championship that qualifies it for the national tournament. Around the campus, you hear people attribute the team's success to a variety of factors. Examine the attributions shown below and place each of them in one of the cells of Weiner's model of attribution (just record the letter inside the cell). The answers are in Appendix A.

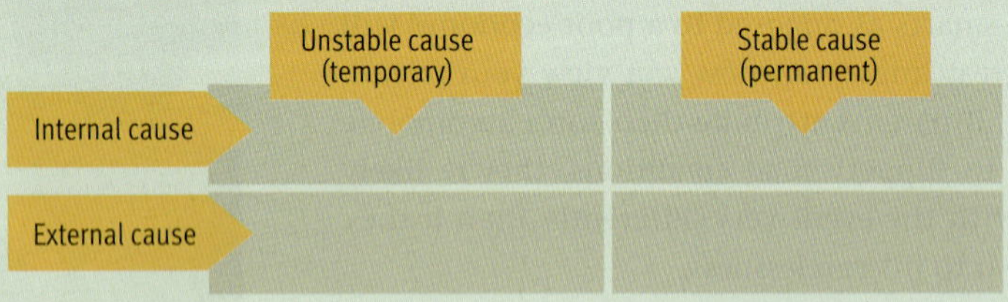

a. "They won only because the best two athletes on Central State's team were out with injuries—talk about good fortune!"
b. "They won because they have some of the best talent in the country."
c. "Anybody could win this region; the competition is far below average in comparison to the rest of the country."
d. "They won because they put in a great deal of last-minute effort and practice, and they were incredibly fired up for the regional tourney after last year's near miss."

They may be right, of course. However, you'd probably attribute your rage to the frustrating situation. Perhaps you're normally a calm, easygoing person, but today you've been in line for 20 minutes, you just straightened out a similar error by the same bank last week, and you're being treated rudely by the teller. Observers are often unaware of historical and situational considerations such as these. Consequently, they tend to make internal attributions for another's behavior (Gilbert, 1998).

In contrast, the circumstances that have influenced an actor's behavior tend to be more apparent to the actor. Hence, actors are more likely than observers to locate the cause of their behavior in the situation. In general, then, *actors favor external attributions for their behavior, whereas observers are more likely to explain the same behavior with internal attributions* (Jones & Nisbett, 1971; Krueger, Ham, & Linford, 1996).

Defensive Attribution 12a

In attempting to explain the calamities and setbacks that befall other people, our tendency to make internal attributions may become even stronger than normal. ***Defensive attribution* is a tendency to blame victims for their misfortune, so that one feels less likely to be victimized in a similar way.** Let's say that a friend gets mugged and severely beaten. You may attribute the mugging to your friend's carelessness or stupidity ("He should have known better than to be in that neighborhood at that time") rather than to bad luck. Why? Because if you attribute your friend's misfortune to bad luck, you have to face the ugly reality that it could just as easily happen to you. To avoid such disturbing thoughts, people often attribute mishaps to victims' negligence (Herzog, 2008; Idisis, Ben-David, & Ben-Nachum, 2007).

Hindsight bias probably contributes to this tendency, but blaming victims also helps people maintain their belief that they live in a just world. Such a mindset fosters the idea that they're unlikely to experience similar troubles (Lerner & Goldberg, 1999). Thus, people who strongly endorse the notion that the world is just are especially likely to engage in victim derogation (van den Bos & Maas, 2009). The bias toward making defensive attributions can have unfortunate consequences. Blaming victims for their setbacks causes them to be seen in a negative light. Thus, undesirable traits are unfairly attributed to them. This bias could lead one to assume that burglary victims must be careless, that people who get fired must be incompetent, that poor people must be lazy, that rape victims must be promiscuous ("She probably asked for it"), and so on. As you can see, defensive attribution can lead to unwarranted derogation of victims of misfortune.

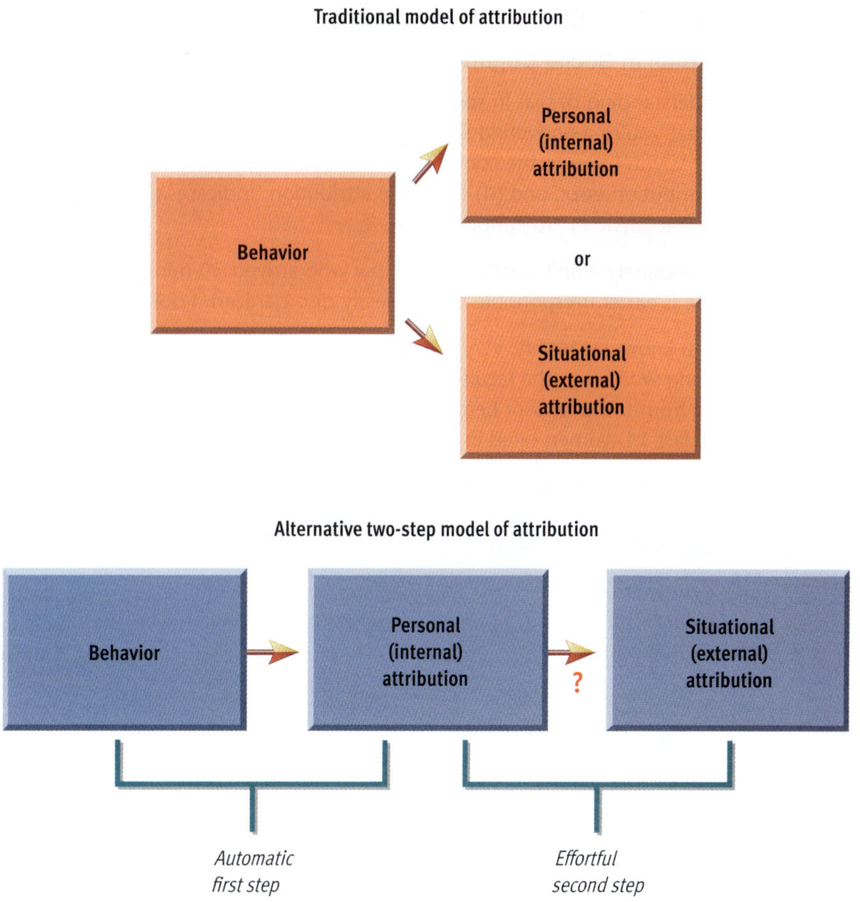

Figure 13.2

An alternative view of the fundamental attribution error. According to Gilbert (1989) and others, the nature of attribution processes favors the *fundamental attribution error.* Traditional models of attribution assume that internal and external attributions are an either-or proposition requiring equal amounts of effort. In contrast, Gilbert maintains that people tend to automatically make internal attributions with little effort, and then they *may* expend additional effort to adjust for the influence of situational factors, which can lead to an external attribution. Thus, external attributions for others' behavior require more thought and effort, which makes them less common than personal attributions. © Cengage Learning 2013

© WoodyStock/Alamy

A common example of defensive attribution is the tendency to blame the homeless for their plight.

CONCEPT CHECK 13.2

Recognizing Bias in Social Cognition

Check your understanding of bias in social cognition by identifying various types of errors that are common in person perception and attribution. Imagine that you're a nonvoting student member of a college committee at Southwest State University that is hiring a new political science professor. As you listen to the committee's discussion, you hear examples of (a) the illusory correlation effect, (b) stereotyping, (c) the fundamental attribution error, and (d) defensive attribution. Indicate which of these is at work in the excerpts from committee members' deliberations below. The answers are in Appendix A.

______ 1. "I absolutely won't consider the fellow who arrived 30 minutes late for his interview. Anybody who can't make a job interview on time is either irresponsible or hopelessly disorganized. I don't care what he says about the airline messing up his reservations."

______ 2. "You know, I was very, very impressed with the young female applicant, and I would love to hire her, but every time we add a young woman to the faculty in liberal arts, she gets pregnant within the first year." The committee chairperson, who has heard this line from this professor before replies, "You always say that, so I finally did a systematic check of what's happened in the past. Of the last 14 women hired in liberal arts, only one has become pregnant within a year."

______ 3. "The first one I want to rule out is the guy who's been practicing law for the last ten years. Although he has an excellent background in political science, I just don't trust lawyers. They're all ambitious, power-hungry, manipulative cutthroats. He'll be a divisive force in the department."

______ 4. "I say we forget about the two candidates who lost their faculty slots in the massive financial crisis at Western Polytechnic last year. I know it sounds cruel, but they brought it on themselves with their fiscal irresponsibility over at Western. Thank goodness we'll never let anything like that happen around here. As far as I'm concerned, if these guys couldn't see that crisis coming, they must be pretty dense."

Culture and Attributional Tendencies

Do the patterns of attribution observed in subjects from Western societies transcend culture? More research is needed, but the preliminary evidence suggests not. Some interesting cultural disparities have emerged in research on attribution processes.

According to Harry Triandis (1989, 1994, 2001), cultural differences in *individualism* versus *collectivism* influence attributional tendencies as well as other aspects of social behavior. As noted in Chapter 12, ***individualism* involves putting personal goals ahead of group goals and defining one's identity in terms of personal attributes rather than group memberships.** In contrast, ***collectivism* involves putting group goals ahead of personal goals and defining one's identity in terms of the groups one belongs to** (such as one's family, tribe, work group, social class, and so on). In comparison to individualistic cultures, collectivist cultures place a higher priority on shared values and resources, cooperation, mutual interdependence, and concern for how one's actions will affect other group members. Generally speaking, North American and Western European cultures tend to be individualistic, whereas Asian, African, and Latin American cultures tend to be collectivistic (Hofstede, 1980, 1983, 2001) (see **Figure 13.3**).

How does individualism versus collectivism relate to patterns of attribution? The evidence suggests that collectivist cultures may promote different at-

Hofstede's rankings of national cultures' individualism

Individualistic cultures	Intermediate cultures	Collectivist cultures
1. United States	19. Israel	37. Hong Kong
2. Australia	20. Spain	38. Chile
3. Great Britain	21. India	40. Singapore
4. Canada	22. Argentina	40. Thailand
4. Netherlands	22. Japan	40. West Africa region
6. New Zealand	24. Iran	42. El Salvador
7. Italy	25. Jamaica	43. South Korea
8. Belgium	26. Arab region	44. Taiwan
9. Denmark	26. Brazil	45. Peru
10. France	28. Turkey	46. Costa Rica
11. Sweden	29. Uruguay	47. Indonesia
12. Ireland	30. Greece	47. Pakistan
13. Norway	31. Philippines	49. Colombia
14. Switzerland	32. Mexico	50. Venezuela
15. West Germany	34. East Africa region	51. Panama
16. South Africa	34. Portugal	52. Ecuador
17. Finland	34. Yugoslavia	53. Guatemala
18. Austria	36. Malaysia	

© Cengage Learning 2013

Figure 13.3

Individualism versus collectivism around the world. Hofstede (1980, 1983, 2001) used survey data from over 100,000 employees of a large, multinational corporation to estimate the emphasis on individualism versus collectivism in fifty nations and three regions. His large, diverse international sample remains unequaled to date. In the figure, cultures are ranked in terms of how strongly they embraced the values of individualism. As you can see, Hofstede's estimates suggest that North American and Western European nations tend to be relatively individualistic, whereas more collectivism is found in Asian, African, and Latin American countries.

SOURCE: Adapted from Hofstede, G. (2001). *Culture's consequences* (2nd Ed., p. 215). Thousand Oaks, CA: Sage. Copyright © 2001 Sage Publications. Adapted by permission of Dr. Geert Hofstede.

tributional biases than individualistic cultures. For example, people from collectivist societies appear to be less prone to the fundamental attribution error than those from individualistic societies (Choi, Nisbett, & Norenzayan, 1999; Triandis, 2001). In Western cultures, people are viewed as autonomous individuals who are responsible for their actions. Westerners typically explain behavior in terms of people's personality traits and unique abilities. In contrast, collectivists, who value interdependence and obedience, are more likely to assume that one's behavior reflects adherence to group norms.

REVIEW OF KEY LEARNING GOALS

13.4 Attributions are inferences about the causes of events and behavior. Individuals make attributions to understand their social world. Internal attributions ascribe behavior to personal dispositions and traits, whereas external attributions locate the cause of behavior in the environment. Weiner's model proposes that attributions for success and failure should be analyzed in terms of the stability of causes, as well as along the internal-external dimension.

13.5 Observers favor internal attributions to explain another's behavior, which is called the fundamental attribution error, while actors favor external attributions to explain their own behavior. In defensive attribution, people unfairly blame victims for their misfortune (with internal attributions) to reduce their own feelings of vulnerability. Cultures vary in their emphasis on individualism as opposed to collectivism, and these differences appear to influence attributional tendencies. The fundamental attribution error appears to be more prevalent in Western cultures that are high in individualism.

Close Relationships: Liking and Loving

KEY LEARNING GOALS

13.6 Evaluate the role of physical attractiveness and similarity in attraction.

13.7 Distinguish between passionate love and companionate love, and outline evidence on love as a form of attachment.

13.8 Discuss cultural variations in close relationships and how the Internet has affected romantic relationships.

13.9 Understand evolutionary analyses of mating preferences and tactics.

© Andres Rodriguez/Alamy

"I just don't know what she sees in him. She could do so much better for herself. I suppose he's a nice guy, but they're just not right for each other." Can't you imagine someone in your social circle making these comments in discussing a mutual friend's new boyfriend? You've probably heard similar remarks on many occasions. These comments illustrate people's interest in analyzing the dynamics of attraction. ***Interpersonal attraction*** **refers to positive feelings toward another.** Social psychologists use this term broadly to encompass a variety of experiences, including liking, friendship, admiration, lust, and love. In this section, we'll analyze key factors that influence attraction and examine some theoretical perspectives on the mystery of love.

Key Factors in Attraction

Many factors influence who is attracted to whom. Here we'll discuss factors that promote the development of liking, friendship, and love. Although these are different types of attraction, the interpersonal dynamics at work in each are largely similar.

Physical Attractiveness

It's often said that "beauty is only skin deep." But evidence suggests that most people don't really believe that (Fitness, Fletcher, & Overall, 2003). The importance of physical attractiveness was shown in a study in which unacquainted men and women were sent off on a "get-acquainted" date (Sprecher & Duck, 1994). The researchers were mainly interested in how communication might affect the process of attraction. However, to put this factor in context they also measured subjects' perceptions of their date's physical attractiveness and similarity to themselves. They found that the quality of communication during the date did have some effect on females' interest in friendship. The key determinant of romantic attraction for both sexes, though, was the physical attractiveness of the other person. Consistent with this finding, research has shown, as one might expect, that attractive people of both sexes enjoy greater mating success than their less attractive peers (Rhodes, Simmons, & Peters, 2005). Many other studies have shown the importance of physical attractiveness in the initial stage of dating and have shown that it continues to have influence as relationships evolve (McNulty, Neff, & Karney, 2008; Patzer, 2006).

Although people prefer physically attractive partners in romantic relationships, they may consider their own level of attractiveness in pursuing dates. What people want in a partner may be different from

According to the matching hypothesis, males and females who are similar in physical attractiveness are likely to be drawn together. This type of matching may also influence the formation of friendships.

© Dean Mitchell/Shutterstock

what they have to settle for. **The *matching hypothesis* proposes that males and females of approximately equal physical attractiveness are likely to select each other as partners.** The matching hypothesis is supported by evidence that dating and married couples tend to be similar in level of physical attractiveness (Regan, 1998, 2008). Not surprisingly, research suggests that attractive people expect to date more attractive individuals and unattractive people expect to date less attractive partners (Montoya, 2008). One recent study relevant to the matching hypothesis examined requests to get acquainted at HOTorNOT.com, where members routinely rate each others' level of physical attractiveness (Lee et al., 2008). As one would expect, more-attractive members were more selective in agreeing to get acquainted with others than less-attractive members were. The study also looked at whether less-attractive persons deluded themselves into thinking that their prospective partners were more attractive than others perceived them to be. The results did not support this "rationalization" hypothesis. Instead, the data suggested that less-attractive people place less weight on physical attractiveness than those who are good-looking.

Reality CHECK

Misconception

In the realm of romance, opposites attract.

Reality

There is absolutely no empirical evidence to support this folklore. Research consistently shows that couples tend to be similar in intelligence, education, social status, ethnicity, physical attractiveness, and attitudes. Dissimilarity does not foster attraction.

© Alex Gregory/The New Yorker Collection/www.cartoonbank.com.

"It would never work out between us, Tom—we're from two totally different tiers of the upper middle class."

Similarity Effects

Is it true that "birds of a feather flock together," or do "opposites attract"? Research provides far more support for the former than the latter (Surra et al., 2006). Married and dating couples tend to be similar in age, race, religion, social class, education, intelligence, physical attractiveness, values, and attitudes (Kalmijn, 1998; Watson et al., 2004). The similarity principle operates in both friendships and romantic relationships, regardless of sexual orientation (Fehr, 2008; Morry, 2007, 2009; Peplau & Fingerhut, 2007). In a longitudinal study of best friends, researchers found that similarity among friends in 1983 actually predicted their closeness in 2002—nineteen years later (Ledbetter, Griffin, & Sparks (2007).

The most obvious explanation for these correlations is that similarity causes attraction. Lab experiments on *attitude similarity,* conducted by Donn Byrne and his colleagues, suggest that similarity *does* cause attraction (Byrne, 1997; Byrne, Clore, & Smeaton, 1986). However, research also suggests that attraction can foster similarity (Anderson, Keltner, & John, 2003). For example, Davis and Rusbult (2001) found that dating partners gradually modify their attitudes in ways that make them more congruent, a phenomenon they called *attitude alignment.* Moreover, people in stable, satisfying intimate relationships tend to subjectively overestimate how similar they and their partners are (Murray et al., 2002). Wanting to believe that they have found a kindred spirit, they tend to assume that their partners are mirrors of themselves.

Perspectives on the Mystery of Love

Love has proven to be an elusive subject. It's difficult to define and study because there are many types of love (Berscheid, 2006). Nonetheless, psychologists have begun to make some progress in their study of love. Let's look at their theories and research.

Passionate and Companionate Love

PSYKTREK 12b

Elaine Hatfield (formerly Walster) and Ellen Berscheid, two early pioneers in research on love (Berscheid, 1988; Berscheid & Walster, 1978; Hatfield & Rapson, 1993), proposed that romantic relationships are characterized by two kinds of love: passionate love and companionate love. ***Passionate love* is a complete absorption in another that includes tender sexual feelings and the agony and ecstasy of intense emotion.** Passionate love has its ups and downs: It is associated with large swings in positive and negative emotions (Reis & Aron, 2008).

***Companionate love* is warm, trusting, tolerant affection for another whose life is deeply intertwined with one's own.** Passionate and companionate love *may* coexist. They don't, however, necessarily go hand in hand. Research suggests that, as a general rule, companionate love is more strongly related to relationship satisfaction than passionate love (Fehr, 2001).

Studies indicate that passionate love is a powerful motivational force that produces profound changes in people's thinking, emotion, and behavior (Reis & Aron, 2008). Interestingly, brain-imaging research indicates that when people think about someone they are passionately in love with, these thoughts light up the dopamine circuits in the brain that are known to be activated by cocaine and other addictive drugs (Aron, Fisher, & Mashek, 2005). Perhaps that explains why passionate love sometimes resembles an addiction.

Love as Attachment

PSYKTREK 12b

In another groundbreaking analysis of love, Cindy Hazan and Phillip Shaver (1987) looked not at the components of love but at similarities between love and *attachment relationships* in infancy. We noted in the chapter on human development (Chapter 11) that infant-caretaker bonding, or attachment, emerges in the first year of life. Early attachments vary in quality, and *most* infants tend to fall into one of three groups, depending in part on parents' caregiving styles (Ainsworth et al., 1978). A majority of infants develop a *secure attachment.* However, some are very anxious when separated from their caretaker, a syndrome called *anxious-ambivalent attachment.* A third group of infants, characterized by *avoidant attachment,* never bond very well with their caretaker.

According to Hazan and Shaver, romantic love is an attachment process. That is, people's intimate relationships in adulthood follow the same form as their attachments in infancy. According to their theory, a person who had an anxious-ambivalent attachment in infancy will tend to have romantic relations marked by anxiety and ambivalence in adulthood. In other words, people relive their early bonding experiences with their parents in their adult romantic relationships.

Hazan and Shaver's (1987) initial survey study provided striking support for their theory. They found that adults' love relationships could be sorted into groups that paralleled the three patterns of attachment seen in infants (see **Figure 13.4**). *Secure adults* (56% of the subjects) found it relatively easy to get close to others, described their love relations as trusting, rarely worried about being abandoned, and reported the fewest divorces. *Anxious-ambivalent adults* (20% of the subjects) reported a preoccupation with love accompanied by expectations of rejection and described their love relations as volatile and marked by jealousy. *Avoidant adults* (24% of the subjects) found it difficult to get close to others and described their love relations as lacking intimacy and trust. Research eventually showed that attachment patterns are reasonably stable over time (Fraley, 2002; Mikulincer & Shaver, 2007). Thus, evidence suggests that individuals' infant attachment experiences shape their intimate relations in adulthood.

Research on the correlates of adult attachment styles has grown exponentially since the mid-1990s. Consistent with the original theory, studies have shown that securely attached individuals have more committed, satisfying, interdependent, well-adjusted, and longer-lasting relationships compared to people with anxious-ambivalent or avoidant attachment styles (Feeney, 2008). Moreover, people with different attachment styles are predisposed to think, feel, and behave differently in their relationships (Mikulincer & Shaver, 2008). For example, anxious-ambivalent people tend to report more intense emotional highs and lows in

Adult attachment style

Secure
I find it relatively easy to get close to others and am comfortable depending on them and having them depend on me. I don't often worry about being abandoned or about someone getting too close to me.

Avoidant
I am somewhat uncomfortable being close to others; I find it difficult to trust them, difficult to allow myself to depend on them. I am nervous when anyone gets too close, and often love partners want me to be more intimate than I feel comfortable being.

Anxious/ambivalent
I find that others are reluctant to get as close as I would like. I often worry that my partner doesn't really love me or won't want to stay with me. I want to merge completely with another person, and this desire sometimes scares people away.

© Cengage Learning 2013

Figure 13.4
Infant attachment and romantic relationships. According to Hazan and Shaver (1987), people's romantic relationships in adulthood are similar in form to their attachment patterns in infancy, which fall into three categories. The three attachment styles seen in adult intimate relations are described here. (Based on Hazan and Shaver, 1986, 1987)

Courtesy of Ellen Berscheid

Ellen Berscheid
"The emotion of romantic love seems to be distressingly fragile. As a 16th-century sage poignantly observed, 'the history of a love affair is the drama of its fight against time.'"

Courtesy of Elaine Hatfield

Elaine Hatfield
"Passionate love is like any other form of excitement. By its very nature, excitement involves a continuous interplay between elation and despair, thrills and terror."

their romantic relationships. They also report that they have more conflicts with their partners, that these conflicts are especially stressful, and that the conflicts often have a negative impact on their relationship (Campbell et al., 2005). In a similar vein, attachment anxiety promotes *excessive reassurance seeking*—the tendency to persistently ask for assurances from partners that one is worthy of love (Shaver, Schachner & Mikulincer, 2005).

Attachment style also appears to be intimately related to people's patterns of sexual interaction. People with secure attachment tend to be more comfortable with their sexuality, more motivated to show love for their partner during sex, more open to sexual exploration, and less accepting of casual sex (Cooper et al., 2006; Shaver & Mikulincer, 2006). In contrast, people high in attachment anxiety tend to have sex to reduce their feelings of insecurity and are more likely to consent to unwanted sexual acts and less likely to practice safe sex (Cooper et al., 2006; Schachner & Shaver, 2004). People high in avoidant attachment tend to engage in more casual sex in an effort to impress their peers. They are also more likely to use sex to manipulate their partners (Schachner & Shaver, 2004; Shaver & Mikulincer, 2006).

Culture and Close Relationships

Relatively little cross-cultural research has been conducted on the dynamics of close relationships. The limited evidence suggests both similarities and differences between cultures in romantic relationships (Hendrick & Hendrick, 2000; Schmitt, 2005). For the most part, similarities have been seen when research has focused on what people look for in prospective mates. As discussed in Chapter 10, David Buss (1989, 1994a) has collected data on mate preferences in thirty-seven divergent cultures. He found that people all over the world value mutual attraction, kindness, intelligence, emotional stability, dependability, and good health in a mate. Buss also found that gender differences in mating priorities are nearly universal. According to his research, males place more emphasis on physical attractiveness and females put a higher priority on social status and financial resources.

© Jon Bower Japan/Alamy

Cultures vary, however, in their emphasis on love—especially passionate love—as a prerequisite for marriage. Romantic love does appear to be found in all cultures (Buss, 2006; Lieberman & Hatfield, 2006). However, passionate love as the basis for marriage is an eighteenth-century invention of Western culture (Stone, 1977). As Hatfield and Rapson (1993) note, "Marriage-for-love represents an ultimate expression of individualism" (p. 2). In contrast, marriages arranged by families and other go-betweens remain common in cultures high in collectivism, including India, Japan, and China (Hatfield, Rapson, & Martel, 2007). This practice is declining in some societies as a result of Westernization. But in collectivist societies people contemplating marriage still tend to think in terms of "What will my parents and other people say?" rather than "What does my heart say?" (Triandis, 1994). Thus, people from collectivist societies tend to report that romantic love is less crucial for marriage than it is for people from individualistic cultures (Dion & Dion, 2006; Levine et al., 1995).

The Internet and Close Relationships

In recent years, the Internet has dramatically expanded opportunities for people to meet and develop close relationships through social networking services (Myspace, Facebook, etc.), online dating services, email, chat rooms, and news groups. Some critics worry that this trend will undermine face-to-face interactions and that many people will be lured into dangerous situations by unscrupulous people. But research to date generally paints a positive picture of the Internet's impact on people's connections with one another (Whitty, 2008). For example, the Internet offers a wealth of opportunities to interact for those who suffer from physical infirmities or social anxieties (McKenna & Bargh, 2000).

One survey, conducted by People Media, a company that operates online communities, reported that 49% of American adults indicated that they knew someone who had found a date online. According to a research survey (Madden & Lenhart, 2006), among those who used online dating sites, a majority (52%) reported "mostly positive" experiences, although a considerable portion (29%) had "mostly negative" experiences. The relevance of the Internet to interpersonal attraction is not limited to dating. Many people join various types of social networking sites in the hopes of making new friends, and their hopes are often realized (Fehr, 2008; McKenna, 2008).

Critics are concerned that Internet relationships are superficial. Research suggests, however, that virtual relationships are just as intimate as face-to-face ones and are sometimes even closer (Bargh, McKenna, & Fitzsimons, 2002). Moreover, many vir-

JUMP START

JUMP START © 2008 Robb Armstrong. Reprinted by permission of UNIVERSAL UCLICK for UFS. All rights reserved.

tual relationships evolve into face-to-face interactions (Boase & Wellman, 2006). Researchers find that romantic relationships that begin on the Internet seem to be just as stable over two years as traditional relationships ((McKenna, Green, & Gleason, 2002).

The power of similarity effects provides the foundation for some of the Internet's most successful online dating sites. Prior to 2000 web dating sites were basically just an electronic variation on the personal advertisements that had been around for decades—with the addition of sophisticated search capabilities. But in 2000 eHarmony.com launched the first matching website, followed by Perfectmatch.com in 2002. These sites claim to use a "scientific approach" to matching people based on compatibility. Members fill out lengthy questionnaires about their attitudes, values, interests, and so forth, and then matching algorithms are used to identify people who exhibit promising similarity. The commercial success of eHarmony.com has led many other online dating sites to add matching services. These sites have not published their matching formulas, so it is hard to say just how scientific they are, but many of the sites employ legitimate research experts as consultants (Sprecher et al., 2008). Hence, it seems likely that many of them use matching algorithms that are grounded in empirical research on interpersonal attraction. Of course, as you have already learned in this chapter, similarity is just one of many factors that play a role in the dynamics of attraction. Still, it is interesting to note that the growth of the Internet has brought psychological science into play in the domain of close relationships.

An Evolutionary Perspective on Attraction

Evolutionary psychologists have a great deal to say about heterosexual attraction. For example, they assert that physical appearance is an influential determinant of attraction because certain aspects of good looks can be indicators of sound health, good genes, and high fertility, all of which can contribute to reproductive potential (Gallup & Frederick, 2010). Consistent with this analysis, research has found that some standards of attractiveness are more consistent across cultures than previously believed (Sugiyama, 2005). For example, *facial symmetry* seems to be a key element of attractiveness in highly diverse cultures (Fink & Penton-Voak, 2002). Facial symmetry is thought to be valued because a variety of environmental insults and developmental abnormalities are associated with physical asymmetries. Thus, asymmetry may serve as a marker of relatively poor genes or health (Fink et al., 2006). Another facet of appearance that may transcend culture is *women's waist-to-hip ratio* (Singh et al., 2010). Around the world, men seem to prefer women with a moderately low waist-to-hip ratio (in the vicinity of .70), which roughly corresponds to an "hourglass figure." This factor appears to be a meaningful correlate of females' reproductive potential (Gallup & Frederick, 2010), as it signals that a woman is healthy, young, and not pregnant.

The most thoroughly documented findings on the evolutionary bases of heterosexual attraction are those on gender differences in humans' mating preferences (Neuberg, Kenrick, & Schaller, 2010). Consistent with the notion that humans are programmed by evolution to behave in ways that enhance their reproductive fitness, evidence indicates that men generally are more interested than women in seeking youthfulness and physical attractiveness in their mates because these traits should be associated with greater reproductive potential (see Chapter 10). On the other hand, research shows that women place a greater premium on prospective mates' ambition, social status, and financial potential because these traits should be associated with the ability to invest material resources in children.

more. In reality, however, the subjects who were paid $1 exhibited more favorable attitude change—just as Festinger and Carlsmith had predicted. Why? Dissonance theory provides an explanation.

According to Festinger (1957), ***cognitive dissonance* exists when related cognitions are inconsistent—that is, when they contradict each other.** Cognitive dissonance is thought to create an unpleasant state of tension that motivates people to reduce their dissonance—usually by altering their cognitions. In the study by Festinger and Carlsmith, the subjects' contradictory cognitions were "The task is boring" and "I told someone the task was enjoyable." The subjects who were paid $20 for lying had an obvious reason for behaving inconsistently with their true attitudes, so these subjects experienced little dissonance. In contrast, the subjects paid $1 had no readily apparent justification for their lie and experienced high dissonance. To reduce it, they tended to persuade themselves that the task was more enjoyable than they had originally thought. Thus, dissonance theory sheds light on why people sometimes come to believe their own lies.

Cognitive dissonance is also at work when people turn attitudinal somersaults to justify efforts that haven't panned out, a syndrome called *effort justification*. Aronson and Mills (1959) studied effort justification by putting college women through a "severe initiation" before they could qualify to participate in what promised to be an interesting discussion of sexuality. In the initiation, the women had to read obscene passages out loud to a male experimenter. After all that, the highly touted discussion of sexuality turned out to be a boring, taped lecture on reproduction in lower animals. Subjects in the severe initiation condition experienced highly dissonant cognitions ("I went through a lot to get here" and "This discussion is terrible"). How did they reduce their dissonance? Apparently by changing their attitude about the discussion, since they rated it more favorably than subjects in two control conditions did. Effort justification may be at work in many facets of everyday life. For example, people who wait in line for an hour or more to get into an exclusive restaurant often praise the restaurant afterward even if they have been served a mediocre meal.

Dissonance theory has been tested in hundreds of studies with mixed, but largely favorable, results. The dynamics of dissonance appear to underlie many important types of attitude changes (Draycott & Dabbs, 1998; Keller & Block, 1999; Petty et al., 2003). Research has largely supported Festinger's claim that dissonance involves genuine psychological discomfort and even physiological arousal (Visser & Cooper, 2003; Devine et al., 1999). However, dissonance effects are not among the most reliable phenomena in social psychology. Researchers have had difficulty specifying the conditions under which dissonance will occur. It has become apparent that people can reduce their dissonance in quite a variety of ways besides changing their attitudes (Olson & Stone, 2005; Visser & Cooper, 2003).

Elaboration Likelihood Model 12c

The *elaboration likelihood model* of attitude change, originally proposed by Richard Petty and John Cacioppo (1986), asserts that there are two basic "routes" to persuasion (Petty & Briñol, 2008; Petty & Wegener, 1999). The *central route* is taken when people carefully ponder the content and logic of persuasive messages. The *peripheral route* is taken when persuasion depends on nonmessage factors, such as the attractiveness and credibility of the source, or on conditioned emotional responses (see **Figure 13.11**). For example, a politician who campaigns by delivering carefully researched speeches that thoughtfully analyze complex issues is following the central route to persuasion. In contrast, a politician who depends on marching bands, flag waving, celebrity endorsements, and emotional slogans is following the peripheral route.

Both routes can lead to persuasion. However, according to the elaboration likelihood model, the durability of attitude change depends on the extent

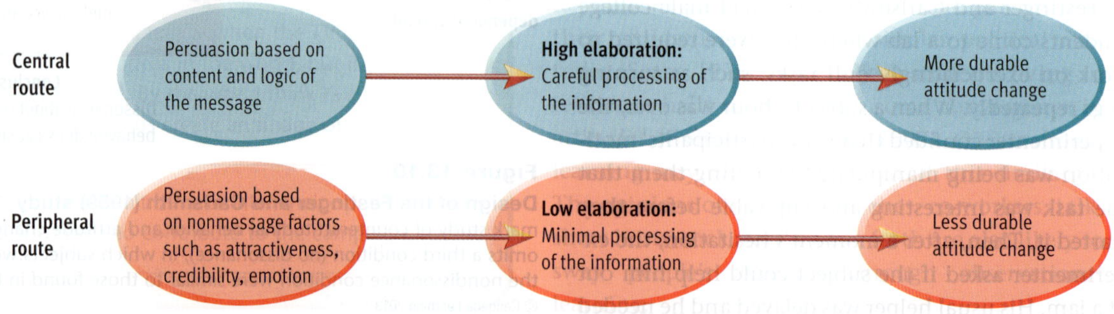

Figure 13.11
The elaboration likelihood model. According to the elaboration likelihood model (Petty & Cacioppo, 1986), the central route to persuasion leads to more elaboration of message content and more-enduring attitude change than the peripheral route to persuasion.
© Cengage Learning 2013

to which people elaborate on (think about) the contents of persuasive communications. Studies suggest that the central route to persuasion leads to more enduring attitude change than the peripheral route and that attitudes changed through central processes predict behavior better than attitudes changed through peripheral processes (Kruglanski & Stroebe, 2005; Petty & Briñol, 2010).

REVIEW OF KEY LEARNING GOALS

13.10 Attitudes may be made up of cognitive, affective, and behavioral components. Attitudes vary along the dimensions of strength, accessibility, and ambivalence. Attitudes and behavior aren't as consistent as one might assume, for a variety of reasons, including the need to consider situational pressures.

13.11 Explicit attitudes are attitudes that people hold consciously and can readily describe. Implicit attitudes are covert attitudes that are expressed in subtle automatic responses. Implicit attitudes are measured by testing how quickly people associate carefully chosen pairs of concepts. Research with the IAT suggests that people harbor covert prejudices, which do affect overt behavior.

13.12 A source of persuasion who is credible, expert, trustworthy, likable, and physically attractive tends to be relatively effective in stimulating attitude change. Although there are some situational limitations, two-sided arguments and fear arousal are effective elements in persuasive messages. Repetition of a message is also helpful, perhaps because of the mere exposure effect. Persuasion is more difficult when a receiver is forewarned and when strong attitudes are targeted.

13.13 Attitudes may be shaped through classical conditioning, operant conditioning, and observational learning. Festinger's dissonance theory asserts that inconsistent attitudes cause tension and that people alter their attitudes to reduce cognitive dissonance. Dissonance theory has been used to explain attitude change following counterattitudinal behavior and efforts that haven't panned out. The elaboration likelihood model holds that the central route to persuasion, which depends on the logic of persuasive messages, tends to yield longer-lasting attitude change than the peripheral route, which depends on nonmessage factors.

Conformity and Obedience: Yielding to Others

KEY LEARNING GOALS

13.14 Review Asch's work on conformity.

13.15 Describe the Featured Study by Milgram on obedience to authority, and assess the ensuing controversy.

13.16 Discuss cultural variations in conformity and obedience.

13.17 Describe the Stanford Prison Simulation and its implications.

A number of years ago, the area that I lived in experienced a severe flood that required the mobilization of the National Guard and various emergency services. At the height of the crisis, a young man arrived at the scene of the flood, announced that he was from a state agency that no one had ever heard of, and proceeded to take control of the emergency. City work crews, the fire department, local police, municipal officials, and the National Guard followed his orders with dispatch for several days, evacuating entire neighborhoods—until an official thought to check and found out that the man was just someone who had walked in off the street. The imposter, who had had small armies at his beck and call for several days, had no training in emergency services, just a history of unemployment and psychological problems.

After news of the hoax spread, people criticized red-faced local officials for their compliance with the imposter's orders. However, many of the critics probably would have cooperated in much the same way if they had been in the officials' shoes. For most people, willingness to obey someone in authority is the rule, not the exception. In this section, we'll analyze the dynamics of social influence at work in conformity and obedience.

Conformity

PSYKTREK 12e

If you keep a well-manicured lawn, are you exhibiting conformity? According to social psychologists, it depends on whether your behavior is the result of group pressure. ***Conformity* occurs when people yield to real or imagined social pressure.** For example, if you maintain a well-groomed lawn only to avoid complaints from your neighbors, you're conforming to social pressure. However, if you maintain a nice lawn because you genuinely prefer a nice lawn, that's *not* conformity.

In the 1950s, Solomon Asch (1951, 1955, 1956) devised a clever procedure that reduced ambiguity about whether subjects were conforming, allowing him to investigate the variables that govern conformity. Let's re-create one of Asch's (1955) classic experiments, which have become the most widely replicated studies in the history of social psychology (Markus, Kitayama, & Heiman, 1996). The participants are male undergraduates recruited for a study of visual perception. A group of seven subjects are shown a large card with a vertical line on it. They are then asked to indicate which of three lines on a second card matches the original "standard line" in length (see **Figure 13.12** on the next page). All

Courtesy of University of Pennsylvania, University Communications

Solomon Asch

"That we have found the tendency to conformity in our society so strong that reasonably intelligent and well-meaning young people are willing to call white black is a matter of concern."

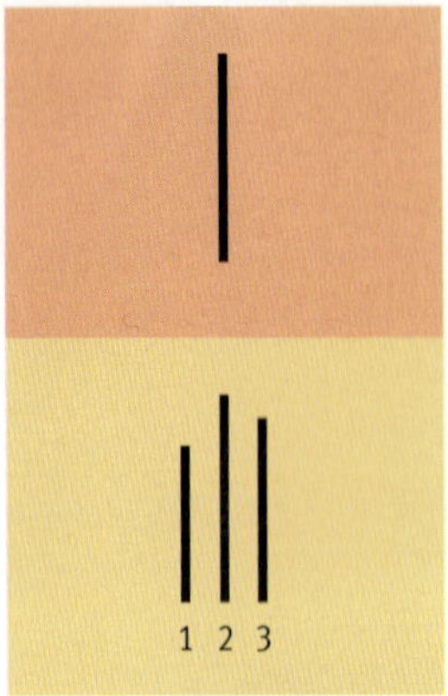

Figure 13.12

Stimuli used in Asch's conformity studies. Subjects were asked to match a standard line (top) with one of three other lines displayed on another card (bottom). The task was easy—until experimental accomplices started responding with obviously incorrect answers, creating a situation in which Asch evaluated subjects' conformity.

SOURCE: Adapted from Asch, S. (1955). Opinion and social pressure. *Scientific American, 193* (5), 31–35. Based on illustrations by Sara Love. Copyright © 1955 by Scientific American, Inc. All rights reserved.

seven subjects are given a turn at the task. They each announce their choice to the group. The subject in the sixth chair doesn't know it, but everyone else in the group is an accomplice of the experimenter. They're about to make him wonder whether he has taken leave of his senses.

© Royalty-free-Masterfile

The accomplices give accurate responses on the first two trials. On the third trial, line number 2 clearly is the correct response, but the first five "subjects" all say that line number 3 matches the standard line. The genuine subject is bewildered and can't believe his ears. Over the course of the next 15 trials, the accomplices all give the same incorrect response on 11 of them. How does the real subject respond? The line judgments are easy and unambiguous. So, if the participant consistently agrees with the accomplices, he isn't making honest mistakes—he's conforming.

Averaging across all fifty participants, Asch (1955) found that the young men conformed on 37% of the trials. The subjects varied considerably in their tendency to conform, however. Of the fifty participants, thirteen never caved in to the group, while fourteen conformed on more than half the trials. One could argue that the results show that people confronting a unanimous majority generally tend to *resist* the pressure to conform (Hodges & Geyer, 2006). However, given how clear and easy the line judgments were, most social scientists viewed the findings as a dramatic demonstration of humans' propensity to conform (Levine, 1999).

In subsequent studies, Asch (1956) found that *group size* and *group unanimity* are key determinants of conformity. To examine the impact of group size, Asch repeated his procedure with groups that included from one to fifteen accomplices. Little conformity was seen when a subject was pitted against just one person. But conformity increased as group size went up to four, and then it leveled off (see **Figure 13.13**). Thus, Asch reasoned that as groups grow larger, conformity increases—up to a point. This conclusion has been echoed by other researchers (Cialdini & Trost, 1998).

However, group size made little difference if just one accomplice "broke" with the others, wrecking their unanimous agreement. The presence of another dissenter lowered conformity to about one-quarter of its peak, even when the dissenter made *inaccurate* judgments that happened to conflict with the majority view. Apparently, the participants just needed to hear someone else question the accuracy of the group's confusing responses. The importance of unanimity in fostering conformity has been replicated in subsequent research (Hogg, 2010).

Why do people conform? Two key processes appear to contribute (Hogg, 2010). ***Normative influence*** **operates when people conform to social norms for fear of negative social consequences.** In other words, people often conform or comply because they are afraid of being criticized or rejected. People are also likely to conform when they are uncertain how to

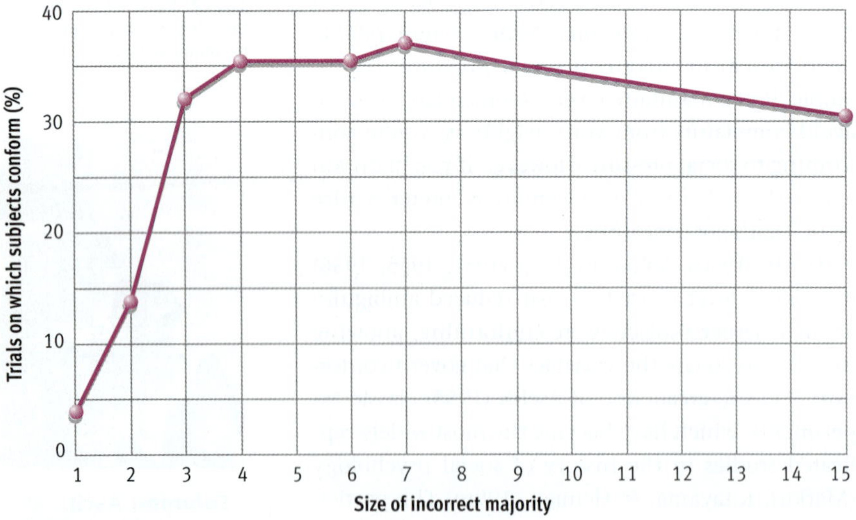

Figure 13.13

Conformity and group size. This graph shows the percentage of trials on which participants conformed as a function of group size in Asch's research. Asch found that conformity became more frequent as group size increased up to about four, and then the amount of conformity leveled off. © Cengage Learning 2013

SOURCE: Adapted from Asch, S. (1955). Opinion and social pressure. *Scientific American, 193* (5), 31–35. Based on illustrations by Sara Love. Copyright © 1955 by Scientific American, Inc. All rights reserved.

behave (Cialdini, 2008; Sherif, 1936). ***Informational influence*** **operates when people look to others for guidance about how to behave in ambiguous situations.** Thus, if you're at a nice restaurant and don't know which fork to use, you may watch others to see what they're doing. In situations like this, using others as a source of information about appropriate behavior is a sensible strategy. Ultimately, informational influence is all about being right, whereas normative influence is all about being liked.

Obedience

12e

Obedience **is a form of compliance that occurs when people follow direct commands, usually from someone in a position of authority.** To a surprising extent, when an authority figure says, "Jump!" many people simply ask, "How high?"

Milgram's Studies

12e

Stanley Milgram wanted to study this tendency to obey authority figures. Like many other people after World War II, he was troubled by how readily the citizens of Germany had followed the orders of dictator Adolf Hitler, even when the orders required morally repugnant actions, such as the slaughter of millions of Jews. Milgram, who had worked with Solomon Asch, set out to design a standard lab procedure for the study of obedience much like Asch's procedure for studying conformity. The clever experiment that Milgram devised became one of the most famous and controversial studies in the annals of psychology (Blass, 2009). It has been hailed as a "monumental contribution" to science and condemned as "dangerous, dehumanizing, and unethical research" (Ross, 1988). Because of its importance, it's our Featured Study for this chapter.

Photo by Eric Kroll, courtesy of Alexandra Milgram

Stanley Milgram

"The essence of obedience is that a person comes to view himself as the instrument for carrying out another person's wishes, and he therefore no longer regards himself as responsible for his actions."

FEATURED STUDY

"I Was Just Following Orders"

SOURCE: Milgram, S. (1963). Behavioral study of obedience. *Journal of Abnormal and Social Psychology, 67,* 371–378.

"I was just following orders." That was the essence of Adolf Eichmann's defense when he was tried for his war crimes, which included masterminding the Nazis' attempted extermination of European Jews. Milgram wanted to determine the extent to which people are willing to follow authorities' orders. In particular, he wanted to identify the factors that lead people to follow commands that violate their ethics, such as commands to harm an innocent stranger.

Method

The participants were a diverse collection of forty men from the local community, recruited through advertisements to participate in a study at Yale University. When a subject arrived at the lab, he met the experimenter and another subject, a likable, 47-year-old accountant, who was actually an accomplice of the experimenter. The "subjects" were told that the study would concern the effects of punishment on learning. They drew slips of paper from a hat to get their assignments, but the drawing was fixed so that the real subject always became the "teacher" and the accomplice the "learner."

The participant then watched as the learner was strapped into an electrified chair through which a shock could be delivered to the learner whenever he made a mistake on the task (the left photo in **Figure 13.14** on the next page). The subject was told that the shocks would be painful but "would not cause tissue damage." He was then taken to an adjoining room that housed the shock generator that he would control in his role as the teacher. This elaborate apparatus (the right photo in **Figure 13.14**) had thirty switches designed to administer shocks varying from 15 to 450 volts, with labels ranging from "Slight shock" to "Danger: severe shock" and "XXX." Although the apparatus looked and sounded realistic, it was a fake. The learner was never shocked.

As the "learning experiment" proceeded, the accomplice made many mistakes that required shocks from the teacher. The teacher was instructed to increase the shock level after each wrong answer. At "300 volts," the learner began to pound on the wall between the two rooms in protest and soon stopped responding to the teacher's questions. At this point, participants ordinarily turned to the experimenter for guidance. The experimenter, a 31-year-old male in a gray labcoat, firmly indicated that no response was the same as a wrong answer and that the teacher should continue to give stronger and stronger shocks to the now silent learner. If the participant expressed unwillingness to continue, the experimenter responded sternly with one of four prearranged prods, such as, "It is absolutely essential that you continue."

When a participant refused to obey the experimenter, the session came to an end. The dependent variable was the maximum shock the participant was willing to administer before refusing to cooperate. After each session, the true purpose of the study was explained to the subject, who was reassured that the shock was fake and the learner was unharmed.

Results

No participant stopped cooperating before the learner reached the point of pounding on the wall, but five quit at that point. As the graph in **Figure 13.14** shows, only fourteen out of forty subjects defied the experimenter before the full series of shocks was completed. Thus, twenty-six of the forty subjects (65%) administered all

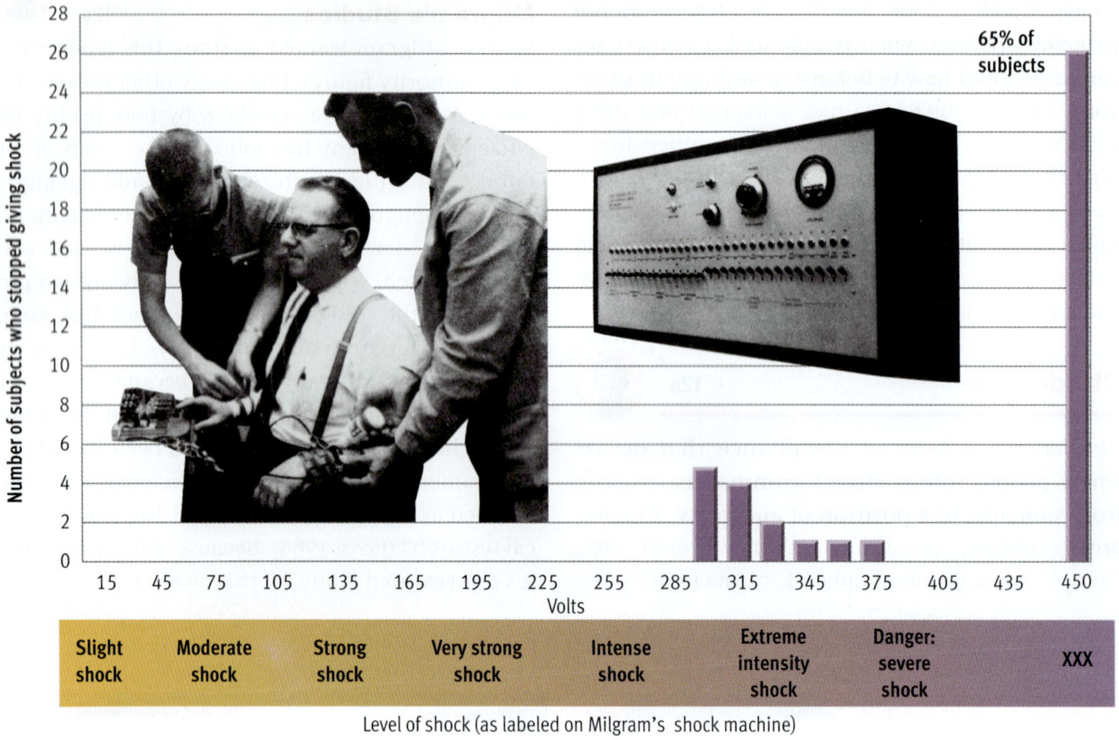

Figure 13.14

Milgram's experiment on obedience. The photo on the left shows the "learner" being connected to the shock generator during one of Milgram's experimental sessions. The photo on the right shows the fake shock generator used in the study. The surprising results of Milgram's (1963) first study are summarized in the bar graph. Although subjects frequently protested, the vast majority (65%) delivered the entire series of shocks to the learner. © Cengage Learning 2013

SOURCE: Photos copyright © 1965 by Stanley Milgram. From the film *Obedience*, distributed by The Pennsylvania State University. Reprinted by permission of Alexandra Milgram.

thirty levels of shock. Although they tended to obey the experimenter, many participants voiced and displayed considerable distress about harming the learner, which was captured on film by Milgram. The horrified subjects groaned, bit their lips, stuttered, trembled, and broke into a sweat. However, they continued administering the shocks.

Discussion

Based on these results, Milgram concluded that obedience to authority is even more common than he or others had anticipated. Before the study was conducted, Milgram had described it to forty psychiatrists and had asked them to predict how much shock subjects would be willing to administer to their innocent victims. Most of the psychiatrists had predicted that fewer than 1% of the subjects would continue to the end of the series of shocks!

In interpreting his results, Milgram argued that strong pressure from an authority figure can make decent people do indecent things to others. Applying this insight to Nazi war crimes and other travesties, Milgram asserted that some sinister actions may not be due to actors' evil character so much as to situational pressures that can lead normal people to engage in acts of treachery and violence. Thus, he arrived at the disturbing conclusion that given the right circumstances, anyone might obey orders to inflict harm on innocent strangers.

Comment

In itself, obedience is not necessarily bad or wrong. Social groups of any size depend on obedience to function smoothly. Life would be chaotic if orders from police, parents, physicians, bosses, generals, and presidents were routinely ignored. However, Milgram's study suggests that many people are overly willing to submit to the orders of someone in command.

If you're like most people, you're probably confident that you wouldn't follow an experimenter's demands to inflict harm on a helpless victim. But the empirical findings indicate that you're probably wrong. After many replications, the results are disturbing, but clear: Most people can be coerced into engaging in actions that violate their morals and values. This finding sharpens our understanding of moral atrocities, such as the Nazi persecutions of Jews.

After his initial demonstration, Milgram (1974) tried about twenty variations on his experimental procedure, looking for factors that influence participants' obedience. In one variation, Milgram moved the study away from Yale's campus to see if the prestige of the university was contributing to the subjects' obedience. When the study was run in a seedy office building by the "Research Associates of Bridgeport," only a modest decrease in obedience was observed (48% of the subjects gave all the shocks). Even when the learner was put in the same room with the subjects, 40% of the participants administered the full series of shocks. Overall, Milgram was surprised at how high subjects' obedience remained as he changed various aspects of his experiment.

That said, there were some situational manipulations that reduced obedience appreciably (see **Figure 13.15**). For example, if the authority figure was called away and the orders were given by an ordinary person (supposedly another participant), full obedience dropped to 20%. In another version of the study, Milgram borrowed a trick from Asch's conformity experiments and set up teams of three teachers that included two more accomplices. When they drew lots, the real subject was always selected to run the shock apparatus in consultation with his fellow teachers. When both accomplices accepted the experimenter's orders to continue shocking the learner, the pressure increased obedience a bit. However, if an accomplice defied the experimenter and supported the subject's objections, obedience declined dramatically (only 10% of the participants gave all the shocks), just as conformity had dropped rapidly when dissent surfaced in Asch's conformity studies. These findings are interesting in that they provide further support for Milgram's thesis that situational factors exert great influence over behavior. If the situational pressures favoring obedience are decreased, obedience declines, as one would expect.

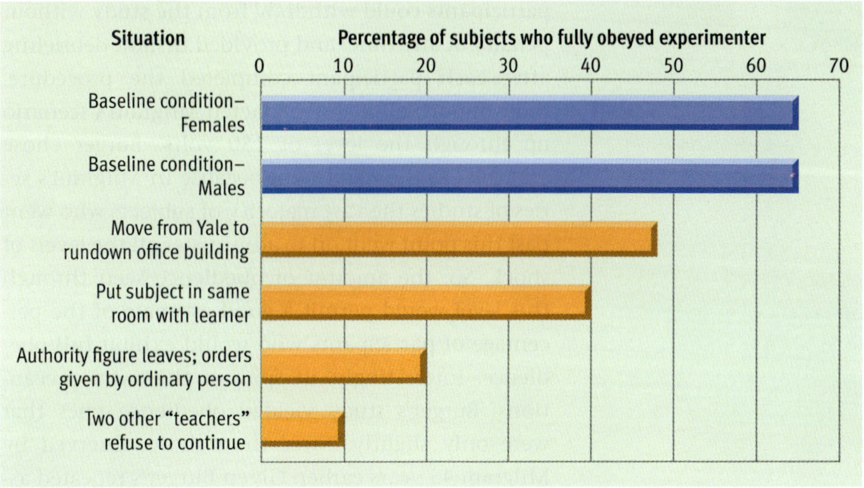

© Cengage Learning 2013

Figure 13.15

Situational influences on obedience. In replications of his landmark research, Milgram (1974) found that females exhibited just as much obedience as males. He also explored how various situational factors influenced the amount of obedience observed. The data from some of his more interesting variations are shown here. As you can see, large reductions in obedience were seen only when the authority figure was taken out of the picture or when another "subject" defied the experimenter. These findings supported Milgram's assertion that behavior is shaped to a considerable degree by situational forces.

The Ensuing Controversy

PSYKTREK 12e

Milgram's study evoked a controversy that continues through today. Some critics argued that Milgram's results couldn't be generalized to apply to the real world (Baumrind, 1964; Orne & Holland, 1968). They maintained that participants went along only because they knew it was an experiment and "everything must be okay." Or they argued that subjects who agree to participate in a scientific study *expect to obey* orders from an experimenter. Milgram (1964, 1968) replied by arguing that if subjects had thought "everything must be okay," they wouldn't have experienced the enormous distress that they clearly showed.

As for the idea that research participants expect to follow an experimenter's commands, Milgram pointed out that so do real-world soldiers and bureaucrats who are accused of villainous acts performed in obedience to authority. "I reject Baumrind's argument that the observed obedience doesn't count because it occurred where it is appropriate," said Milgram (1964). "That is precisely why it *does* count." Overall, the evidence supports the generalizability of Milgram's results, which were consistently replicated in diverse settings with a variety of subjects and procedural variations (Blass, 1999, 2009; Miller, 1986).

Critics also questioned the ethics of Milgram's procedure (Baumrind, 1964; Kelman, 1967). They noted that without prior consent, participants were exposed to extensive deception that could undermine their trust in people. Critics also argue that the "teachers" were exposed to severe stress that could leave emotional scars. Moreover, most participants also had to confront the disturbing fact that they caved in to the experimenter's commands to inflict harm on an innocent victim.

Milgram's defenders argued that the brief distress experienced by his participants was a small price to pay for the insights that emerged from the obedience studies. Looking back, however, many psychologists seem to share the critics' concerns about the ethical implications of Milgram's work (Miller, 2004). His procedure is questionable by contemporary standards of research ethics, and no replications of his obedience study were conducted in the United States from the mid-1970s until recently (Elms, 2009), when Jerry Burger (2009) crafted a very cautious, *partial* replication that incorporated a variety of additional safeguards to protect the welfare of the participants.

Burger (2009) wanted to see whether Milgram's findings would hold up 45 years later. After all, the world has changed in countless ways since Milgram's original research in the early 1960s. To accommodate modern ethical standards, Burger had to change some features of the Milgram procedure. Among other things, he screened participants with great care, excluding those who seemed likely to experience excessive stress, emphasized repeatedly that participants could withdraw from the study without penalty at any time, and provided instant debriefing after each participant completed the procedure. Most important, he only enacted Milgram's scenario up through the level of 150 volts. Burger chose 150 volts as the maximum because in Milgram's series of studies the vast majority of subjects who went past this point went on to administer all the levels of shock. So, the amount of obedience seen through this level would permit a good estimate of the percentage of participants who would exhibit full obedience. Interestingly, in spite of the extra precautions, Burger's study yielded obedience rates that were only slightly lower than those observed by Milgram 45 years earlier. Given Burger's repeated assurances that participants could withdraw from the study (which one would expect to reduce obedience) it seems likely that people today are just as prone to obedience as they were in the 1960s.

Cultural Variations in Conformity and Obedience

Are conformity and obedience unique to American culture? By no means. The Asch and Milgram experiments have been repeated in many societies. And they have yielded results roughly similar to those seen in the United States. Thus, the phenomena of conformity and obedience seem to transcend culture.

The replications of Milgram's obedience study have largely been limited to industrialized nations similar to the United States. Comparisons of the results of these studies must be made with caution because the composition of the samples and the experimental procedures have varied somewhat. But many of the studies have reported even higher obedience rates than those seen in Milgram's American samples. For example, obedience rates of over 80% have been reported for samples from Italy, Germany, Austria, Spain, and Holland (Smith & Bond, 1994). Thus, the surprisingly high level of obedience observed by Milgram does not appear to be peculiar to the United States.

The Asch experiment has been repeated in a more diverse range of societies than the Milgram experiment. Like many other cultural differences in social behavior, variations in conformity appear to be related to the degree of *individualism versus collectivism* seen in a society. Various theorists have argued that collectivistic cultures, which emphasize respect for group norms, cooperation, and harmony, probably encourage more conformity than individualistic cultures (Schwartz, 1990). These theorists argue that such cultures have a more positive view of conformity (Kim & Markus, 1999). As Matsumoto (1994) puts it, "To conform in American culture is to be weak or deficient somehow. But this is not true in other cultures. Many cultures foster more collective, group-oriented values, and concepts of conformity, obedience, and compliance enjoy much higher status" (p. 162). Consistent with this analysis, studies *have* found higher levels of conformity in collectivistic cultures than in individualistic cultures (Bond & Smith, 1996; Smith, 2001).

The Power of the Situation: The Stanford Prison Simulation

The research of Asch and Milgram provided dramatic demonstrations of the potent influence that situational factors can have on social behavior. The power of the situation was underscored once again, about a decade after Milgram's obedience research, in another landmark study conducted by Philip Zimbardo. Ironically, Zimbardo was a high school classmate of Milgram's. Zimbardo and his colleagues designed the Stanford Prison Simulation to investigate why prisons tend to become abusive, degrading, violent environments (Haney, Banks, & Zimbardo, 1973; Zimbardo, Haney, & Banks, 1973). Like Milgram, Zimbardo wanted to see how much the power of the situation would shape the behavior of normal, average participants.

The participants were college students recruited for a study of prison life through a newspaper ad. After giving seventy volunteers an extensive battery of tests and interviews, the researchers chose 24 students who appeared to be physically healthy and psychologically stable to be the subjects. A coin flip determined which of them would be "guards" and which would be "prisoners" in a simulated prison setup at Stanford University. The prisoners were "arrested" at their homes, handcuffed, and transported to a mock prison on the Stanford campus. Upon arrival, they were ordered to strip, sprayed with a delousing agent, and given prison uniforms (smocks). They were assigned numbers as their identities and locked up in iron-barred cells. The subjects assigned to be guards were given khaki uniforms, billy clubs, whistles, and reflective sunglasses. They were told that they could run their prison in whatever way they wanted except that they were not allowed to use physical punishment.

What happened? In short order, confrontations occurred between the guards and prisoners. The guards quickly devised a variety of sometimes cruel strategies to maintain total control over their prisoners. Meals, blankets, and bathroom privileges were selectively denied to some prisoners to achieve control. The prisoners were taunted, humiliated, and called demeaning names. They were forced to beg for opportunities to go to the bathroom. Pointless, petty rules were strictly enforced. Difficult prisoners were punished with hard labor (doing pushups and jumping jacks, cleaning toilets with their bare hands). The guards harassed the prisoners by waking them up in the middle of the night to assemble and count off. The guards also creatively turned a 2-foot by 2-foot closet into a "hole" for solitary confinement of rebellious prisoners. There was some variation among the guards. However, collectively they became mean, malicious, and abusive in fulfilling their responsibilities. How did the prisoners react? A few showed signs of emotional disturbance and had to be released early. But they mostly became listless, apathetic, and demoralized. The study was designed to run two weeks. Zimbardo, though, decided that he needed to end it prematurely after just six days because he was concerned about the rapidly escalating abuse and degradation of the prisoners. The subjects were debriefed, offered counseling, and sent home.

How did Zimbardo and his colleagues explain the stunning transformations of their subjects? First, they attributed the participants' behavior to the enormous influence of social roles. ***Social roles* are widely shared expectations about how people in certain positions are supposed to behave.** We have role expectations for salespeople, wait staff, ministers, medical patients, students, bus drivers, tourists, flight attendants, and, of course, prison guards and prisoners. The participants had a rough idea of what it meant to act like a guard or a prisoner, and they were gradually consumed by their roles (Haney & Zimbardo, 1998). Second, the researchers attributed their subjects' behavior to the compelling power of situational factors. Before the study began, the tests and interviews showed no measureable differences in personality or character between those randomly assigned to be guards versus prisoners. The stark differences in their behavior had to be due to the radically different situations that they found themselves in. As Haney and Zimbardo (1998) put it, the study "demonstrated the power of situations to overwhelm people and elicit from them unexpectedly cruel, yet 'situationally appropriate' behavior" (p. 719). As a result, Zimbardo, like Milgram before him, concluded that situational pressures can lead normal, decent people to behave in sinister, repugnant ways.

The results of the Stanford Prison Simulation were eye-opening, to say the least. Within a short time, subjects with no obvious character flaws became tyrannical, sadistic, brutal guards. If this transformation can occur so swiftly in a make-believe prison, one can only imagine how the much stronger situational forces in real prisons readily promote abusive behavior. Although the Stanford Prison Simulation was conducted in the 1970s, renewed interest in the study was sparked by the Abu Ghraib prison scandal in Iraq in 2004. American military personnel with little or no experience in running prisons were found to have engaged in "sadistic, blatant, and wanton criminal abuses" of their Iraqi prisoners (Hersh, 2004). Some of the photos taken of the abuse at Abu Ghraib are eerily reminiscent of photos from the Stanford simulation. The U.S. government blamed these horrific abuses on "a few bad apples" who were presumed to be pathological or morally deficient, writing off the

Courtesy of Philip Zimbardo

Philip Zimbardo

"But in the end, I called off the experiment not because of the horror I saw out there in the prison yard, but because of the horror of realizing that I could have easily traded places with the most brutal guard or become the weakest prisoner full of hatred at being so powerless."

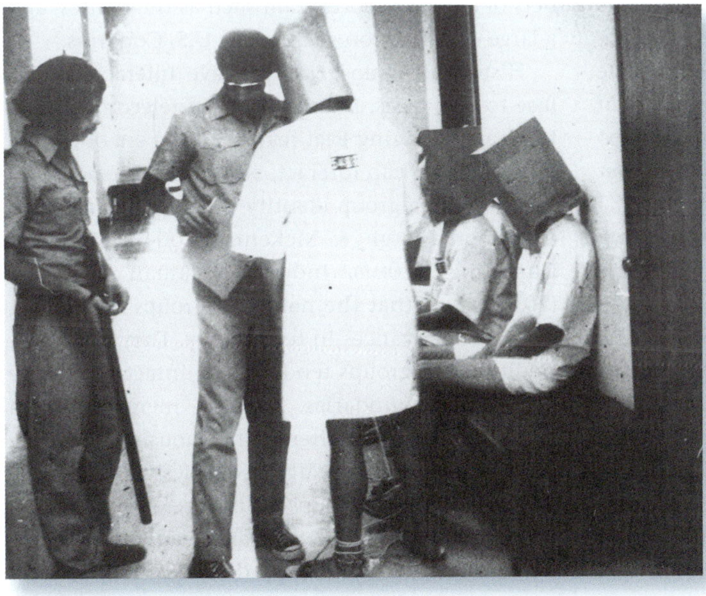

© Philip Zimbardo. Reproduced with permission.

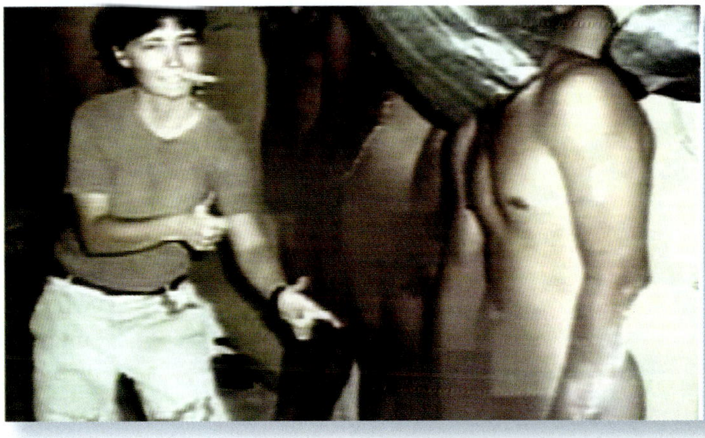

© AFP/Getty Images

The Abu Ghraib prison scandal in Iraq sparked renewed interest in the Stanford Prison Simulation. Some of the photos taken of the abuse at Abu Ghraib (right) are stunningly similar to photos from the Stanford study (left). For instance, in both cases, the guards "dehumanized" their prisoners by placing bags over their heads.

incident as an aberration. Yet the evidence from the Stanford Prison Simulation clearly suggests otherwise. Phil Zimbardo (2004a, 2004b, 2007) argues, and has testified as an expert witness, that it is far more likely that situational pressures led normal, average Americans to commit morally reprehensible abuses. This explanation does *not* absolve the guards of responsibility for their behavior. However, Zimbardo emphasizes that making scapegoats out of a handful of guards does not solve the real problem, which lies in the system. He maintains that abuses in prisons are more likely than not and can only be reduced if authorities provide extensive training and strong supervision for guards, enact explicit sanctions for abuses, and maintain clear accountability in the chain of command.

REVIEW OF KEY LEARNING GOALS

13.14 Asch found that subjects often conform to the group, even when the group reports inaccurate judgments on a simple line-judging task. Conformity becomes more likely as group size increases, up to a group size of four, then levels off. If a small group isn't unanimous, conformity declines rapidly. Normative and informational influence both contribute to conformity.

13.15 In Milgram's landmark study of obedience to authority, adult men drawn from the community showed a remarkable tendency, despite their misgivings, to follow orders to shock an innocent stranger. Milgram concluded that situational pressures can make decent people do indecent things. Critics asserted that Milgram's results were not generalizable to the real world and that his methods were unethical. The generalizability of Milgram's findings has stood the test of time, but his work also helped to stimulate stricter ethical standards for research. A recent partial replication by Burger showed that Milgram's findings are still relevant today.

13.16 The Asch and Milgram experiments have been replicated in many cultures. These replications have uncovered modest cultural variations in the propensity to conform or to obey an authority figure. However, conformity and obedience are common across diverse cultures.

13.17 The Stanford Prison Simulation, in which normal, healthy students were randomly assigned to be prisoners or guards, demonstrated that social roles and other situational pressures can exert tremendous influence over social behavior. Like Milgram, Zimbardo showed that situational forces can lead normal people to exhibit surprisingly callous, abusive behavior.

KEY LEARNING GOALS

13.18 Clarify the nature of groups and the bystander effect.

13.19 Evaluate evidence on group productivity, including social loafing.

13.20 Explain group polarization and groupthink.

Behavior in Groups: Joining with Others

Social psychologists study groups as well as individuals, but what exactly is a group? Are all the divorced fathers living in Baltimore a group? Are three strangers moving skyward in an elevator a group? What if the elevator gets stuck? How about four students from your psychology class who study together regularly? A jury deciding a trial? The Boston Celtics? The U.S. Congress? Some of these collections of people are groups and others aren't. Let's examine the concept of a group to find out which of these collections qualify.

In social psychologists' eyes, **a *group* consists of two or more individuals who interact and are interdependent.** The divorced fathers in Baltimore aren't likely to qualify on either count. Strangers sharing an elevator might interact briefly, but they're not interdependent. However, if the elevator got stuck and they had to deal with an emergency together, they could suddenly become a group. Your psychology classmates who study together are a group, as they interact and depend on each other to achieve shared goals. So do the members of a jury, a sports team such as the Celtics, and a large organization such as the U.S. Congress.

Historically, most groups have interacted on a face-to-face basis, but advances in telecommunications are changing that reality. In the era of the Internet, people can interact, become interdependent, and develop a group identity without ever meeting in person (Bargh & McKenna, 2004; O'Leary & Cummings, 2007). Indeed, Hackman and Katz (2010) assert that the nature of groups is evolving because of advances in technology. They note that, traditionally, groups tended to be intact and stable with clear boundaries, whereas membership in modern groups is often continuously changing. Traditional groups usually have a designated leader, whereas modern groups often are self-managing with shared leadership. Similarly, traditional groups tended to be created in a top-down fashion, whereas

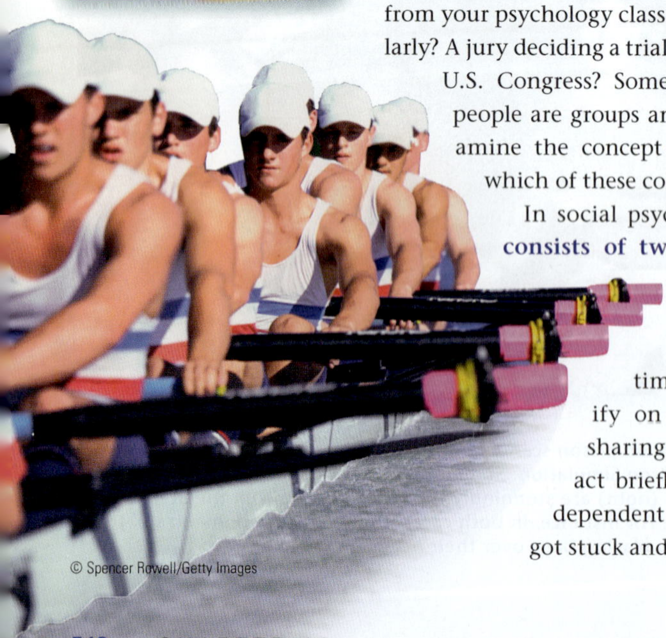

© Spencer Rowell/Getty Images

modern groups often coalesce on their own to explore shared interests. It will be interesting to see whether these shifts have an impact on how groups function.

Groups vary in many ways. Obviously, a study group, the Celtics, and Congress are very different in terms of size, purpose, formality, longevity, similarity of members, and diversity of activities. Can anything meaningful be said about groups if they're so diverse? Yes. In spite of their immense variability, groups share certain features that affect their functioning. Among other things, most groups have *roles* that allocate special responsibilities to some members, *norms* about suitable behavior, a *communication structure* that reflects who talks to whom, and a *power structure* that determines which members wield the most influence (Forsyth, 2006).

Thus, when people join together in a group, they create a social organism with unique characteristics and dynamics that can take on a life of its own. One of social psychology's enduring insights is that in a given situation you may behave quite differently when you're in a group than when you're alone. To illustrate this point, let's look at some interesting research on helping behavior.

Behavior Alone and in Groups: The Case of the Bystander Effect

Imagine that you have a precarious medical condition. You must go through life worrying about whether someone will leap forward to provide help if the need ever arises. Wouldn't you feel more secure when around larger groups? After all, there's "safety in numbers." Logically, as group size increases, the probability of having a "good Samaritan" on the scene increases. Or does it?

We've seen before that human behavior isn't necessarily logical. When it comes to helping behavior, many studies have uncovered an apparent paradox called the ***bystander effect:*** **People are less likely to provide needed help when they are in groups than when they are alone.** Evidence that your probability of getting help *declines* as group size increases was first described by John Darley and Bibb Latané (1968), who were conducting research on the determinants of helping behavior. In the Darley and Latané study, students in individual cubicles connected by an intercom participated in discussion groups of three sizes. Early in the discussion, a student who was an experimental accomplice hesitantly mentioned that he was prone to seizures. Later in the discussion, the same accomplice feigned a severe seizure and cried out for help. Although a majority of subjects sought assistance for the student, the tendency to seek help *declined* with increasing group size.

Similar trends have been seen in many other experiments, in which over 6000 participants have had opportunities to respond to apparent emergencies, including fires, asthma attacks, faintings, crashes, and flat tires, as well as less pressing needs to answer a door or to pick up objects dropped by a stranger (Latané & Nida, 1981). Many of the experiments have been highly realistic studies conducted in subways, stores, and shopping malls. Pooling the results of this research, Latané and Nida (1981) estimated that subjects who were alone provided help 75% of the time. In contrast, subjects in the presence of others provided help only 53% of the time. They concluded that the main condition in which the bystander effect is reduced occurs when the need for help is clear. For example, the bystander effect is less likely when someone is in obvious physical danger (Fischer et al., 2006). It is also less likely if the bystanders are friends rather than strangers (Levine & Crowther, 2008).

What accounts for the bystander effect? A number of factors may be at work. Bystander effects are most common in ambiguous situations because people look around to see whether others think there's an emergency. If everyone hesitates, their inaction suggests that there's no real need for help. The *diffusion of responsibility* that occurs in a group is also important. If you're by yourself when you encounter someone in need of help, the responsibility to provide help rests squarely on your shoulders. However, if other people are present, the responsibility is divided among you. You may all say to yourselves, "Someone else will help." A reduced sense of responsibility may contribute to other aspects of behavior in groups, as we'll see in the next section.

Group Productivity and Social Loafing

Have you ever driven through a road construction project—at a snail's pace, of course—and become irritated because so many workers seem to be just standing around? Maybe the irony of the posted sign "Your tax dollars at work" made you imagine that they were all dawdling. Individuals' productivity often *does* decline in larger groups (Karau & Williams, 1993). This fact is unfortunate, as many important tasks can only be accomplished in groups. Group productivity is crucial to committees, sports teams, firefighting crews, sororities, study groups, symphonies, and work teams of all kinds, from the morning crew in a little diner to the board of directors of a Fortune 500 company.

Two factors appear to contribute to reduced individual productivity in larger groups. One factor is *reduced efficiency* resulting from the *loss of coordination* among workers' efforts. As you put more people on a yearbook staff, for instance, you'll probably create more and more duplication of effort and increase how often group members end up working at cross purposes.

The second factor contributing to low productivity in groups involves *effort* rather than efficiency. ***Social loafing* is a reduction in effort by individuals when they work in groups as compared to when they work by themselves.** To investigate social loafing, Latané and his colleagues (1979) measured the sound output produced by subjects who were asked to cheer or clap as loud as they could. So they couldn't see or hear other group members, subjects were told that the study concerned the importance of sensory feedback. They were asked to put on blindfolds and headphones through which loud noise was played. This maneuver permitted a simple deception: Subjects were *led to believe* that they were working alone or in a group of two or six, when in fact *individual* output was actually measured.

When participants *thought* that they were working in larger groups, their individual output declined. Since lack of coordination could not affect individual output, the subjects' decreased sound production had to be due to reduced effort. Latané and his colleagues also had the same subjects clap and shout in genuine groups of two and six and found an additional decrease in production that was attributed to loss of coordination. **Figure 13.16** shows how social loafing and loss of coordination combined to reduce productivity as group size increased.

The social-loafing effect has been replicated in numerous studies in which subjects have worked on a variety of tasks, including cheering, pumping air, swimming in a relay race, solving mazes, evaluating editorials, and brainstorming for new ideas (Karau & Williams, 1995; Levine & Moreland, 1998). Social loafing and the bystander effect appear to share a common cause: diffusion of responsibility in groups (Comer, 1995; Latané, 1981). As group size increases, the responsibility for getting a job done is divided among more people. Many group members then ease up because their individual contribution is less recognizable. Thus, social loafing occurs in situations where individuals can "hide in the crowd" (Karau & Williams, 1993).

Social loafing is *not* inevitable. It is less likely when individuals' personal contributions to productivity are readily identifiable (Hoigaard & Ingvaldsen, 2006). It's also less likely when group norms encourage productivity and personal involvement (Hoigaard, Säfvenbom, & Tonnessen, 2006). And social loafing is reduced when people work in smaller and more cohesive groups (Liden et al., 2004; Shiue, Chiu, & Chang, 2010). Cultural factors may also influence the likelihood of social loafing. Studies with subjects from Japan, China, and Taiwan suggest that social loafing may be less prevalent in collectivistic cultures, which place a high priority on meeting group goals and contributing to one's ingroups (Karau & Williams, 1995; Smith, 2001).

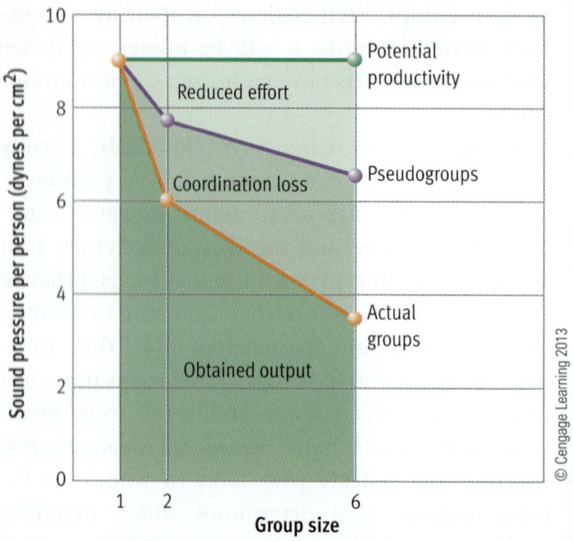

Figure 13.16

The effect of loss of coordination and social loafing on group productivity. The amount of sound produced per person declined noticeably when people worked in actual groups of two or six (orange line). This decrease in productivity reflects both loss of coordination and social loafing. Sound per person also declined when subjects merely thought they were working in groups of two or six (purple line). This smaller decrease in productivity is due to social loafing.

SOURCE: Adapted from Latané, B., Williams, K., & Harkins, S. (1979). Many hands make light the work: The causes and consequences of social loafing. *Journal of Personality and Social Psychology, 37,* 822–832. Copyright © 1979 by the American Psychological Association. Adapted by permission of the author.

Decision Making in Groups

Productivity is not the only issue that commonly concerns groups. When people join together in groups, they often have to make decisions about what the group will do and how it will use its resources. Whether it's your study group deciding what type of pizza to order, a jury deciding on a verdict, or Congress deciding on whether to pass a bill, groups make decisions.

Evaluating decision making is often more complicated than evaluating productivity. In many cases, the "right" decision may not be readily apparent. Who can say whether your study group ordered the right pizza or whether Congress passed the right bills? Nonetheless, social psychologists have discovered some interesting tendencies in group decision making.

Group Polarization

Who leans toward more cautious decisions: individuals or groups? Common sense suggests that groups will work out compromises that cancel out members' extreme views. Hence, the collective wisdom of the group should yield relatively conservative choices. Is common sense correct? To investigate this question, Stoner (1961) asked individual subjects to give their recommendations on tough decisions. They then asked the same subjects to engage in group discussion to arrive at joint recommendations. When Stoner compared individuals' average recommendation against their group decision generated through discussion, he found that groups arrived at *riskier* decisions than individuals did. Stoner's finding was replicated in other studies (Pruitt, 1971). The phenomenon acquired the name *risky shift.*

However, researchers eventually determined that groups can shift either way, toward risk or caution, depending on which way the group is leaning to begin with (Friedkin, 1999). A shift toward a more extreme position, an effect called *polarization,* is often the result of group discussion (Tindale, Kameda, & Hinsz, 2003; Van Swol, 2009). Thus, ***group polarization* occurs when group discussion strengthens a group's dominant point of view and produces a shift toward a more extreme decision in that direction** (see **Figure 13.17**). Group polarization does *not* involve widening the gap between factions in a group, as its name might suggest. In fact, group polarization can contribute to consensus in a group.

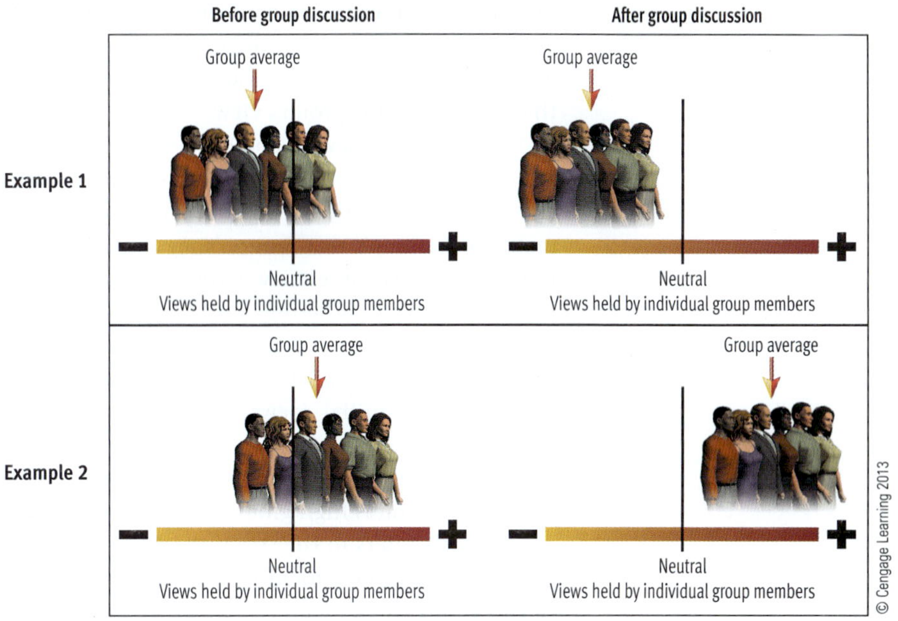

Figure 13.17

Group polarization. Two examples of group polarization are diagrammed here. The positions of the people on the horizontal scales reflect their positive or negative attitudes regarding an idea before and after group discussion. In the first example (top) a group starts out mildly opposed to an idea, but after discussion sentiment against the idea is stronger. In the second example (bottom), a group starts out with a favorable disposition toward an idea, and this disposition is strengthened by group discussion.

Many types of groups have to arrive at collective decisions. The social dynamics of group decisions are complicated, and a variety of factors can undermine effective decision making.

Groupthink

In contrast to group polarization, which is a normal process in group dynamics, groupthink is more like a "disease" that can infect decision making in groups. ***Groupthink* occurs when members of a cohesive group emphasize concurrence at the expense of critical thinking in arriving at a decision.** As you might imagine, groupthink doesn't produce very effective decision making. Indeed, groupthink can lead to major blunders that may look incomprehensible after the fact. Irving Janis (1972) first described groupthink in his effort to explain how President John F. Kennedy and his advisers could have miscalculated so badly in deciding to invade Cuba at the Bay of Pigs in 1961. The attempted invasion failed miserably and, in retrospect, seemed remarkably ill-conceived.

Applying his many years of research and theory on group dynamics to the Bay of Pigs fiasco, Janis developed a model of groupthink. When groups get caught up in groupthink, members suspend their critical judgment and the group starts censoring dissent as the pressure to conform increases. Soon, everyone begins to think alike. Moreover, "mind guards" try to shield the group from information that contradicts the group's view.

If the group's view is challenged from outside, victims of groupthink tend to think in simplistic "us versus them" terms. Members begin to overestimate the ingroup's unanimity. They begin to view the outgroup as the enemy. Groupthink also promotes incomplete gathering of information. Like individuals, groups often display a confirmation bias. They tend to seek and focus on information that supports their initial views (Schulz-Hardt et al., 2000).

What causes groupthink? According to Janis, a key precondition is high group cohesiveness. ***Group cohesiveness*** **refers to the strength of the relationships linking group members to each other and to the group itself.** Members of cohesive groups are close-knit, are committed, have "team spirit," and are loyal to the group. Cohesiveness itself isn't bad. It can facilitate group productivity (Mullen & Copper, 1994) and help groups achieve great things. But Janis maintains that the danger of groupthink is greater when groups are highly cohesive. Groupthink is also more likely when a group works in relative isolation, when the group's power structure is dominated by a strong, directive leader, and when the group is under stress to make a major decision.

A relatively small number of experiments have been conducted to test Janis's theory because the antecedent conditions thought to foster groupthink—such as high decision stress, strong group cohesiveness, and dominating leadership—are difficult to create effectively in lab settings (Aldag & Fuller, 1993). The studies that *have* been conducted have yielded mixed results in that high cohesiveness and strong leadership do not *necessarily* produce groupthink (Baron, 2005; Kerr & Tindale, 2004). Thus, the evidence on groupthink consists mostly of retrospective case studies of major decision-making fiascos (Eaton, 2001). In light of this situation, Janis's model of groupthink should probably be characterized as an innovative, sophisticated, intuitively appealing theory that needs to be subjected to much more empirical study.

CONCEPT CHECK 13.4

Identifying the Contributions of Major Theorists and Researchers

Check your recall of the principal ideas of important theorists and researchers covered in this chapter by matching the people listed on the left with the appropriate contributions described on the right. If you need help, the crucial pages describing each person's ideas are listed in parentheses. Fill in the letters for your choices in the spaces provided on the left. You'll find the answers in Appendix A.

Major Theorists and Researchers	Key Ideas and Contributions
______ 1. Solomon Asch (pp. 539–540)	a. This theorist was the first to describe how people make attributions to either internal causes or external causes.
______ 2. Ellen Berscheid and Elaine Hatfield (pp. 526–527)	b. According to this theorist, groupthink occurs when cohesive groups emphasize concurrence at the expense of critical thinking in arriving at decisions.
______ 3. Leon Festinger (p. 537)	c. This individual conducted classic research on conformity that showed people tend to conform more than one might expect.
______ 4. Fritz Heider (p. 521)	d. These researchers, who conducted pioneering work on the nature of love, distinguished between passionate and companionate love.
______ 5. Irving Janis (pp. 549–550)	e. This researcher conducted a legendary study of obedience that inspired a great deal of controversy.
______ 6. Stanley Milgram (pp. 541–543)	f. This researcher is famous for conducting the Stanford Prison Simulation, which illustrated the influence of social roles and the powerful effects of situational factors.
______ 7. Philip Zimbardo (pp. 544–545)	g. According to this theorist, attitude change is often fueled by cognitive dissonance.

REVIEW OF KEY LEARNING GOALS

13.18 A group consists of two or more people who interact and are interdependent. People are more likely to help someone in need when they are alone than when a group is present. This phenomenon, called the bystander effect, occurs primarily because a group creates diffusion of responsibility.

13.19 Individuals' productivity often declines in larger groups because of loss of coordination and because of social loafing. Social loafing seems to be due mostly to diffusion of responsibility and may be less prevalent in certain circumstances and in collectivist cultures.

13.20 Group polarization occurs when discussion leads a group to shift toward a more extreme decision in the direction the group was already leaning. In groupthink, a cohesive group suspends critical judgment in a misguided effort to promote agreement in decision making.

Reflecting on the Chapter's Themes

KEY LEARNING GOALS

13.21 Identify the three unifying themes highlighted in this chapter.

Empiricism

Cultural Heritage

Subjectivity of Experience

Our discussion of social psychology has provided insights into three of our seven unifying themes. One of these is the value of psychology's commitment to empiricism—that is, its reliance on systematic observation through research to arrive at conclusions. The second theme that stands out is the importance of cultural factors in shaping behavior. The third is the extent to which people's experience of the world is highly subjective. Let's consider the virtues of empiricism first.

It's easy to question the need to do scientific research on social behavior, because studies in social psychology often seem to verify common sense. While most people wouldn't presume to devise their own theory of color vision, question the significance of REM sleep, or quibble about the principal causes of schizophrenia, everyone has beliefs about the nature of love, how to persuade others, and people's willingness to help in times of need. Thus, when studies show that credibility enhances persuasion, or that good looks facilitate attraction, it's tempting to conclude that social psychologists go to great lengths to document the obvious. Some critics say, "Why bother?"

You saw why in this chapter. Research in social psychology has repeatedly shown that the predictions of logic and common sense are often wrong. Consider just a few examples. Even psychiatric experts failed to predict the remarkable obedience to authority uncovered in Milgram's research. The bystander effect in helping behavior violates cold-blooded mathematical logic. Dissonance research has shown that after a severe initiation, the bigger the letdown, the more favorable people's feelings are. These principles defy common sense. Thus, research on social behavior provides dramatic illustrations of why psychologists put their faith in empiricism.

Our coverage of social psychology also showed once again that, cross-culturally, behavior is characterized by both variance and invariance. Thus, we saw substantial cultural differences in patterns of attribution, the role of romantic love in marriage, attitudes about conformity, the tendency to obey authority figures, and the likelihood of social loafing. Basic social phenomena such as stereotyping, attraction, obedience, and conformity probably occur all over the world. However, cross-cultural studies of social behavior show that research findings based on American samples may not generalize precisely to other cultures.

Research in social psychology is also uniquely suited for making the point that people's view of the world is highly personal and subjective. In this chapter we saw how physical appearance can color perception of a person's ability or personality, how stereotypes can lead people to see what they expect to see in their interactions with others, how pressure to conform can make people begin to doubt their senses, and how groupthink can lead group members down a perilous path of shared illusions.

The subjectivity of social perception will surface once again in our Applications for the chapter. The Personal Application focuses on prejudice, a practical problem that social psychologists have shown great interest in, whereas the Critical Thinking Application examines aspects of social influence.

REVIEW OF KEY LEARNING GOALS

13.21 Our study of social psychology highlighted three of the text's unifying themes: the value of empiricism, the cultural limits of research based on American samples, and the subjectivity of perception.

Understanding Prejudice

KEY LEARNING GOALS

13.22 Relate person perception processes and attributional bias to prejudice.
13.23 Relate principles of attitude formation and intergroup competition to prejudice.
13.24 Relate ingroups, outgroups, and threats to social identity to prejudice.

Members of many types of groups are victims of prejudice. Besides racial minorities, others that have been stereotyped and discriminated against include gays and lesbians, women, the homeless, and those who are overweight.

Answer the following "true" or "false."

____ **1** Prejudice and discrimination amount to the same thing.

____ **2** Stereotypes are always negative or unflattering.

____ **3** Ethnic and racial groups are the only widespread targets of prejudice in modern society.

____ **4** People see members of their own ingroup as being more alike than the members of outgroups.

James Byrd Jr., a 49-year-old black man, was walking home from a family gathering in the summer of 1998 when he was offered a ride by three white men, one of whom he knew. Shortly thereafter, pieces of Byrd's savagely beaten body were found strewn along a rural road in Texas. Apparently, he had been beaten, then shackled by his ankles to the back of the truck and dragged over 2 miles of road to his death. Police say that Byrd was targeted simply because he was black. Thankfully, such tragic events are relatively rare in the United States. Nonetheless, they remind us that prejudice and discrimination still exist.

Prejudice is a major social problem. It harms victims' self-concepts, suppresses their potential, creates enormous stress in their lives, and promotes tension and strife between groups (Inzlicht & Kang, 2010; Major & Townsend, 2010; Ong, Fuller-Rowell, & Burrow, 2009). The first step toward reducing prejudice is to understand its roots. Hence, in this Application, we'll try to achieve a better understanding of why prejudice is so common. Along the way, you'll learn the answers to the true-false questions above are all false.

Prejudice and discrimination are closely related concepts. The terms have become nearly interchangeable in popular use. Social scientists, however, prefer to define their terms precisely. Let's clarify the concepts. ***Prejudice* is a negative attitude held toward members of a group.** Like many other attitudes, prejudice can include three components (see **Figure 13.18**): beliefs ("Indians are mostly alcoholics"), emotions ("I despise Jews"), and behavioral dispositions ("I wouldn't hire a Mexican"). Racial prejudice receives the lion's share of publicity. However, prejudice is *not* limited to ethnic groups. Women, homosexuals, the aged, the disabled, and the mentally ill are also targets of widespread prejudice. Thus, many people hold prejudicial attitudes toward one group or another. Many have been victims of prejudice.

Prejudice may lead to ***discrimination,* which involves behaving differently, usually unfairly, toward the members of a group.** Prejudice and discrimination tend to go hand in hand. But as LaPiere's (1934) pioneering study of discrimination in restaurant seating showed (see p. 532), attitudes and behavior do not necessarily correspond (Hogg & Abrams, 2003; see **Figure 13.19**). In our discussion, we'll concentrate primarily on the attitude of prejudice. Let's begin by looking at processes in person perception that promote prejudice.

Stereotyping and Subjectivity in Person Perception

PSYKTREK 12d

Perhaps no factor plays a larger role in prejudice than *stereotypes*. That's not to say that stereotypes are inevitably negative. For instance, it's hardly insulting to assert that Americans are ambitious or that the Japanese are industrious. Unfortunately, many people do subscribe to derogatory stereotypes of various ethnic groups. Although studies suggest that negative racial stereotypes have diminished over the last 50 years, they're not a thing of the past, and racism remains a troubling problem (Zárate, 2009). According to a variety of researchers, modern racism has merely become more subtle (Dovidio, Gaertner, & Kawakami, 2010). Many people carefully avoid overt expressions of prejudicial attitudes. However, these same people covertly continue to harbor negative views of racial minorities. Such people endorse racial equality as an abstract principle but often oppose concrete programs intended to promote equality, on the grounds that discrimination is no longer a problem (Wright & Taylor, 2003). Studies suggest that modern sexism has become subtle in much the same way as racism (Swim & Hyers, 2009).

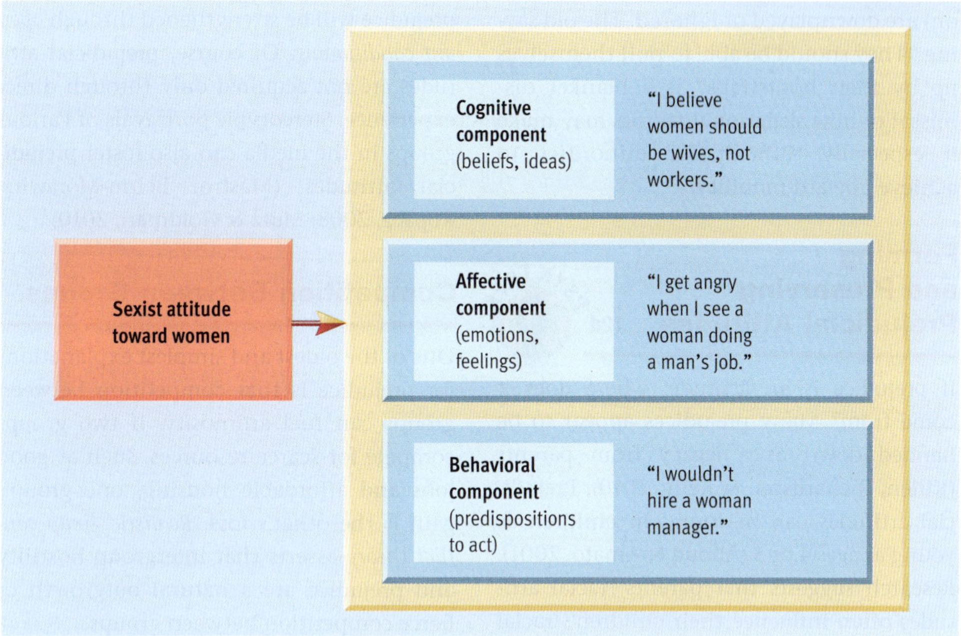

Figure 13.18

The three potential components of prejudice as an attitude. Attitudes can consist of up to three components. The tricomponent model of attitudes, applied to prejudice against women, would view sexism as negative beliefs about women (cognitive component) that lead to a feeling of dislike (affective component), which in turn leads to a readiness to discriminate against women (behavioral component).

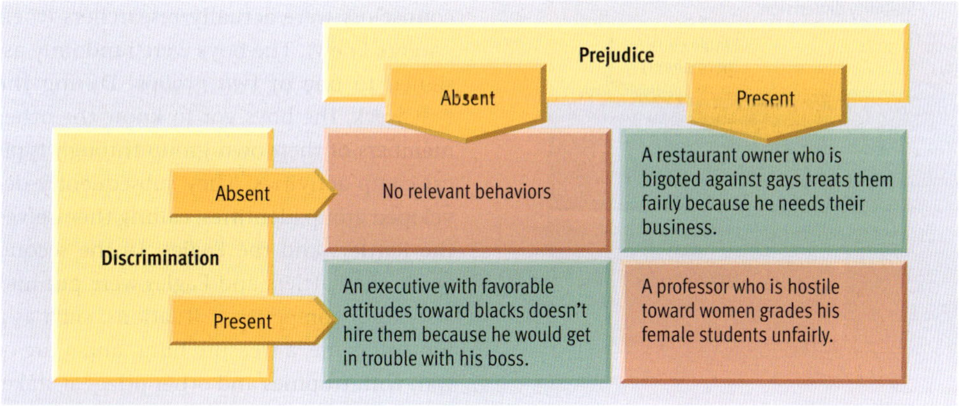

Figure 13.19

Relationship between prejudice and discrimination. As these examples show, prejudice can exist without discrimination and discrimination without prejudice. In the green cells, there is a disparity between attitude and behavior.

Research indicates that prejudicial stereotypes are so pervasive and insidious they often operate automatically (Bodenhausen, Todd, & Richeson, 2009; Devine & Sharp, 2009), even in people who truly renounce prejudice. Thus, a man who rejects prejudice against homosexuals may still feel uncomfortable sitting next to a gay male on a bus, even though he regards his reaction as inappropriate.

Unfortunately, stereotypes are highly resistant to change. When people encounter members of a group that they view with prejudice who deviate from the stereotype of that group, they often find ways to discount this evidence. Stereotypes also persist because the *subjectivity* of person perception makes it likely that people will see what they expect to see when they actually come into contact with groups that they view with prejudice (Fiske & Russell, 2010). For example, Duncan (1976) had white participants watch and evaluate interaction on a TV monitor and varied the race of a person who gets into an argument and slightly shoves another person. The shove was coded as "violent behavior" by 73% of the subjects when the actor was black but by only 13% of the subjects when the actor was white. As we've noted before, people's perceptions are highly subjective. Because of stereotypes, even "violence" may lie in the eye of the beholder.

Biases in Attribution

PSYKTREK 12d

Attribution processes can also help perpetuate stereotypes and prejudice (Maass, 1999). Research taking its cue from Weiner's (1980) model of attribution has shown that people often make *biased attributions for success and failure.* For example, men and women don't get equal credit for their successes (Swim & Sanna, 1996). Observers often discount a woman's success by attributing it to good luck, sheer effort, or the ease of the task (except on traditional feminine tasks). In comparison, a man's success is more likely to be attributed to his outstanding ability (see **Figure 13.20**). For example, one study found that when a man and woman collaborate on a stereotypically "male" task, both male and female observers downplay the woman's contribution (Heilman & Haynes, 2005). These biased patterns of attribution help sustain the stereotype that men are more competent than women.

Recall that the *fundamental attribution error* is a bias toward explaining events by pointing to the actor's personal characteristics as causes (internal attributions). Research suggests that people are particularly likely to make this error when evaluating targets of prejudice (Hewstone, 1990). Thus, when people take note of ethnic neighborhoods dominated by crime and poverty, the personal qualities of the residents are blamed for these problems. Other explanations emphasizing situational factors (job discrimination, poor police service, and so on) are downplayed or ignored. The old saying "They should be able to pull themselves up by their bootstraps" is a blanket dismissal of how situational factors may make it especially difficult for minorities to achieve upward mobility.

Forming and Preserving Prejudicial Attitudes

PSYKTREK 12d

If prejudice is an attitude, where does it come from? Many prejudices appear to be handed down as a legacy from parents (Killen, Richardson, & Kelly, 2010). Prejudicial attitudes can be found in children as young as ages 4 or 5 (Aboud & Amato, 2001). Research suggests that parents' racial attitudes often influence their children's racial attitudes (Sinclair, Dunn, & Lowery, 2004). This transmission of prejudice across generations presumably depends to some extent on *observational learning.* For example, if a young boy hears his father ridicule homosexuals, his exposure to his father's attitude is likely to affect his attitude about gays. If the young boy then goes to school and makes disparaging remarks about gays that are reinforced by approval from peers, his prejudice will be strengthened through *operant conditioning.* Of course, prejudicial attitudes are not acquired only through direct experience. Stereotypic portrayals of various groups in the media can also foster prejudicial attitudes (Mastro, Behm-Morawitz, Kopacz, 2008; Mutz & Goldman, 2010).

Competition Between Groups

One of the oldest and simplest explanations for prejudice is that competition between groups can fuel animosity. If two groups compete for scarce resources, such as good jobs and affordable housing, one group's gain is the other's loss. *Realistic group conflict theory* asserts that intergroup hostility and prejudice are a natural outgrowth of fierce competition between groups.

A classic study at Robbers' Cave State Park in Oklahoma provided support for this theory many years ago (Sherif et al., 1961). The subjects were 11-year-old white boys attending a three-week summer camp at the park. They did not know that the camp counselors were actually researchers (their parents knew). The boys were randomly assigned to one of two groups. During the first week, the boys got to know the other members of their own group through typical camp activities. They subsequently developed group identities, calling themselves the Rattlers and the Eagles. In the second week, the Rattlers and Eagles were put into a series of competitive situations, such as a football game, a treasure hunt, and a tug of war, with trophies and other prizes at stake. As predicted by realistic group conflict theory, hostile feelings quickly erupted between the two groups. Food fights broke out in the mess hall, cabins were ransacked, and group flags were burned.

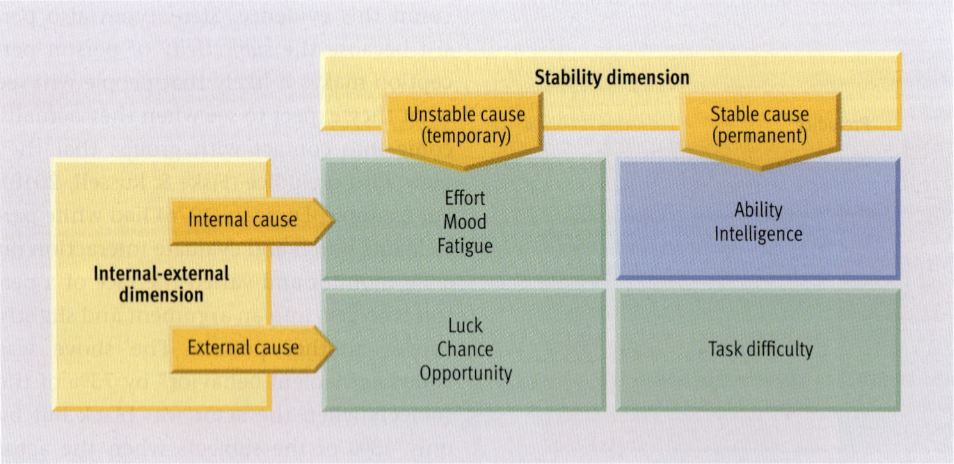

© Cengage Learning 2013

Figure 13.20

Bias in the attributions used to explain success and failure by men and women. Attributions about the two sexes often differ. For example, men's successes tend to be attributed to their ability and intelligence (blue cell), whereas women's successes tend to be attributed to hard work, good luck, or low task difficulty (green cells). These attributional biases help to perpetuate the belief that men are more competent than women.

If competition between innocent groups of children pursuing trivial prizes can foster hostility, you can imagine what is likely to happen when adults from very different backgrounds battle for genuinely important resources. Research has repeatedly shown that conflict over scarce resources can fuel prejudice and discrimination (Esses, Jackson, & Bennett-AbuAyyash, 2010). Even the mere *perception* of competition can breed prejudice.

Dividing the World into Ingroups and Outgroups

PSYKTREK 12d

As noted in the main body of the chapter, when people join together in groups, they sometimes divide the social world into "us versus them," or *ingroups versus outgroups*. This distinction has a profound impact on how people perceive, evaluate, and remember others (Dovidio & Gaertner, 2010). As you might anticipate, people tend to evaluate outgroup members less favorably than ingroup members (Krueger, 1996; Reynolds, Turner, & Haslam, 2000). People also tend to think simplistically about outgroups, tending to see diversity among the members of their own group but to overestimate the homogeneity of the outgroup (Boldry, Gaertner, & Quinn, 2007). At a simple, concrete level, the essence of this process is captured by the statement "They all look alike." The illusion of homogeneity in the outgroup makes it easier to sustain stereotypic beliefs about its members (Rothbart, 2001).

Threats to Social Identity

According to the *social identity perspective*, self-esteem depends on both one's *personal* identity and one's *social* identity (Abrams & Hogg, 2010; Turner et al., 1987). *Social identity* refers to the pride individuals derive from their membership in various groups, such as ethnic groups, religious denominations, occupational groups, neighborhoods, country clubs, and so forth. The theory further proposes that self-esteem can be undermined by either threats to personal identity (you didn't get called for that job interview) or social identity (your football team loses a big game). Threats to both personal and social identity may motivate efforts to restore self-esteem. However, threats to social identity are more likely to provoke responses that foster prejudice and discrimination.

When social identity is threatened, individuals may react in two key ways to bolster it (see **Figure 13.21**). One common response is to show *ingroup favoritism*. An example is tapping an ingroup member for a job opening or rating the performance of an ingroup member higher than that of an outgroup member (Capozza & Brown, 2000). A second common reaction is to engage in *outgroup derogation*—in other words, to "trash" outgroups that are perceived as threatening. Outgroup derogation is more likely when people identify especially strongly with the threatened ingroup (Levin et al., 2003; Schmitt & Maes, 2002). When people derogate an outgroup, they tend to feel superior as a result, and this feeling helps affirm their self-worth (Fein & Spencer, 1997). These unfortunate reactions are *not* inevitable. But threats to social identity represent yet another dynamic process that can foster prejudice (Turner & Reynolds, 2001).

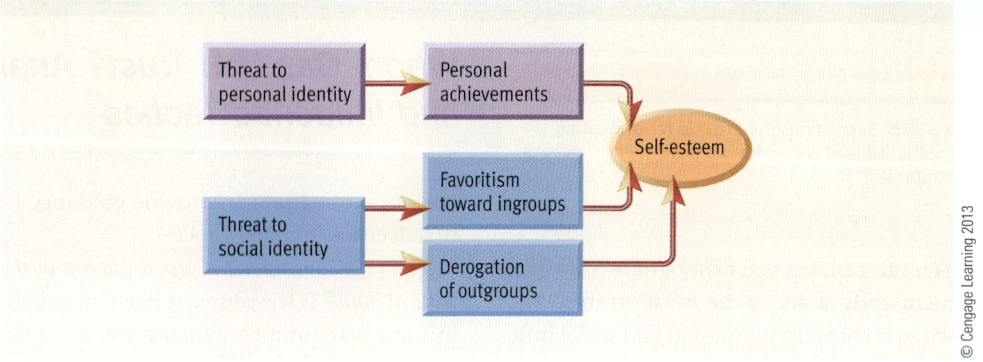

Figure 13.21

Threats to social identity and prejudice. According to Tajfel (1982) and Turner (1987), individuals have both a personal identity (based on a unique sense of self) and a social identity (based on group memberships). When social identity is threatened, people are motivated to restore self-esteem by either showing favoritism to ingroup members or derogating members of outgroups. These tactics contribute to prejudice and discrimination. (Adapted from Brehm & Kassin, 1993)

Our discussion has shown that a plethora of processes conspire to create and maintain personal prejudices against a diverse array of outgroups. Most of the factors at work reflect normal, routine processes in social behavior. Thus, it's understandable that most people—whether privileged or underprivileged, minority members or majority members—probably harbor some prejudicial attitudes. Our analysis of the causes of prejudice may have permitted you to identify prejudices of your own or their sources. Perhaps an enhanced awareness of your personal prejudices may help you become a little more tolerant of the endless diversity seen in human behavior.

REVIEW OF KEY LEARNING GOALS

13.22 Prejudice is supported by selectivity and memory biases in person perception and stereotyping. Stereotypes are highly resistant to change. Attributional biases, such as the tendency to assume that others' behavior reflects their dispositions, can contribute to prejudice.

13.23 Negative attitudes about groups are often acquired through observational learning and strengthened through operant conditioning. Realistic group conflict theory posits that competition between groups for scarce resources fosters prejudice.

13.24 People tend to be biased in favor of their ingroups. The propensity to see outgroups as homogenous serves to strengthen prejudice. Threats to social identity can lead to ingroup favoritism and outgroup derogation.

KEY LEARNING GOALS

13.25 Identify useful criteria for evaluating credibility, and recognize standard social influence strategies.

Whom Can You Trust? Analyzing Credibility and Influence Tactics

You can run, but you cannot hide. This statement aptly sums up the situation that exists when it comes to persuasion and social influence. There's no way to successfully evade the constant, pervasive, omnipresent efforts of others to shape your attitudes and behavior. In this Application, we will address two topics that can enhance your resistance to manipulation. First, we'll outline some ideas that can be useful in evaluating the credibility of a persuasive source. Second, we'll describe some widely used social influence strategies that it pays to know about.

Evaluating Credibility

The salesperson at your local health food store swears that a specific herb combination improves memory and helps people stay healthy. A popular singer touts a psychic hotline, where the operators can "really help" with the important questions in life. Speakers at a "historical society" meeting claim that the Holocaust never happened. These are just a few real-life examples of the pervasive attempts to persuade the public to believe something. In these examples, the "something" people are expected to believe runs counter to the conventional or scientific view. But who is to say who is right? After all, people are entitled to their own opinions, aren't they?

Yes, people *are* entitled to their own opinions, but that does not mean that all opinions are equally valid. Some opinions are just plain wrong, and others are highly dubious. Every person is not equally believable. In deciding what to believe, it's important to carefully examine the evidence presented and the logic of the argument that supports the conclusion (see the Critical Thinking Application for Chapter 10). You also need to decide *whom* to believe, a task that requires assessing the *credibility* of the source of the information. Following are a few questions that can provide guidance in this decision-making process.

Does the source have a vested interest in the issue at hand? If the source is likely to benefit in some way from convincing you of something, you need to take a skeptical attitude. In the examples provided here, it's easy to see how the sales clerk and popular singer will benefit if you buy the products they are selling. But what about the so-called historical society? How would members benefit by convincing large numbers of people that the Holocaust never happened? Like the sales clerk and singer, they're also selling something. In this case, they're selling a particular view of history that they hope will influence future events in certain ways. Someone does *not* have to have a financial gain at stake to have a vested interest in an issue. Of course, the fact that these sources have a vested interest does not necessarily mean that the information they are providing is false or that their arguments are invalid. But a source's credibility does need to be evaluated with extra caution when the person or group has something to gain.

What are the source's credentials? Does the person have any special training, an advanced degree, or any other basis for claiming special knowledge about the topic? The usual training for a sales clerk or singer does not include how to assess research results in medical journals or claims of psychic powers. The Holocaust deniers are more difficult to evaluate. Some of them have studied history and written books on the topic. However, the books are mostly self-published and few of these "experts" hold positions at reputable universities where scholars are subject to peer evaluation. That's *not* to say that legitimate credentials ensure a source's credibility. A number of popular diets that are widely regarded by nutritional experts as worthless, if not hazardous, have been created and marketed by genuine physicians (Drewnowski, 1995; Dwyer, 1995). Of course, these physicians have a *vested interest* in the diets, as they have made millions of dollars from them.

Is the information grossly inconsistent with the conventional view on the issue? Just being different from the mainstream view certainly does *not* make a conclusion wrong. But claims that vary radically from most other information on a subject should raise a red flag that leads to careful scrutiny. Bear in mind that charlatans and hucksters are often successful because they typically try to persuade people to believe things that they want to believe. Wouldn't it be great if we could effortlessly enhance our memory, foretell the future, eat all we want and still lose weight, and earn hundreds of dollars per hour working at home? And wouldn't it be nice if the Holocaust never happened? It pays to be wary of wishful thinking.

What was the method of analysis used in reaching the conclusion? The purveyors of miracle cures and psychic advice inevitably rely on anecdotal evidence. But you have already learned about the perils and unreliability of anecdotal evidence (see Chapter 2). One method frequently used by charlatans is to undermine the credibility of conventional information by focusing on trivial inconsistencies. This is one of the many strategies used by the people who argue that the Holocaust never occurred. They question the credibility of thousands of historical documents, photographs, and artifacts, and the testimony of countless people, by highlighting small inconsistencies among historical records relating to trivial matters, such as the number of people transported to a concentration camp in a specific week, or the number of bodies that could be disposed of in a single day (Shermer, 1997). Some inconsistencies are exactly what one should expect based on piecing together multiple accounts from sources working with different portions of incomplete information. But the strategy of focusing on trivial inconsistencies is a standard method for raising doubts about credible information.

Recognizing Social Influence Strategies

It pays to understand social influence strategies because advertisers, salespeople, and fundraisers—not to mention your friends and neighbors—frequently rely on them to manipulate your behavior. Let's look at four basic strategies: the foot-in-the-door technique, misuse of the reciprocity norm, the lowball technique, and feigned scarcity.

Door-to-door salespeople have long recognized the importance of gaining a *little* cooperation from sales targets (getting a "foot in the door") before hitting them with the real sales pitch. **The *foot-in-the-door technique* involves getting people to agree to a small request to increase the chances that they will agree to a larger request later.** This technique is widely used in all walks of life. For example, groups seeking donations often ask people to simply sign a petition first.

In an early study of the foot-in-the-door technique (Freedman & Fraser, 1966), the large request involved asking homemakers whether a team of six men doing consumer research could come into their home to classify *all* their household products. Only 22% of the control subjects agreed to this outlandish request. However, when the same request was made three days after a small request (to answer a few questions about soap preferences), 53% of the participants agreed to the large request. Why does the foot-in-the-door technique work? According to Burger (1999), quite a variety of processes contribute to its effectiveness. This includes people's tendency to try to behave consistently (with their initial response) and their reluctance to go back on their sense of commitment to the person who made the initial request.

Most of us have been socialized to believe in **the *reciprocity norm*—the rule that we should pay back in kind what we receive from others.** Robert Cialdini (2008) has written extensively about how the reciprocity norm is used in social influence efforts. For example, groups seeking donations routinely send address labels, key rings, and other small gifts with their pleas. Salespeople using the reciprocity principle distribute free samples to prospective customers. When they return a few days later, most of the customers feel obligated to buy some of their products. The reciprocity rule is meant to promote fair exchanges in social interactions. However, when people manipulate the reciprocity norm, they usually give something of minimal value in the hopes of getting far more in return.

The lowball technique is even more deceptive. The name for this technique derives from a common practice in automobile sales, in which a customer is offered a terrific bargain on a car. The bargain price gets the customer to commit to buying the car. Soon after this commitment is made, however, the dealer starts revealing some hidden costs. Typically, the customer learns that options assumed to be included in the original price are actually going to cost extra, or that a promised low loan rate has "fallen through" leading to a higher car payment. Once they have committed to buying a car, most customers are unlikely to cancel the deal. Thus, **the *lowball technique* involves getting someone to commit to an attractive proposition before its hidden costs are revealed.** Car dealers aren't the only ones who use this technique. For instance, a friend might ask whether you want to spend a week with him at his charming backwoods cabin. After you accept this seemingly generous proposition, he may add, "Of course there's some work for us to do. We need to repair the pier, paint the exterior, and . . ." Lowballing is a surprisingly effective strategy (Cialdini & Griskevicius, 2010).

© Tony Freeman/PhotoEdit

Advertisers often try to artificially create scarcity to make their products seem more desirable.

A number of years ago, Jack Brehm (1966) showed that telling people they can't have something only makes them want it more. This phenomenon helps explain why companies often try to create the impression that their products are in scarce supply. *Scarcity* threatens your freedom to choose a product, thus creating an increased desire for the scarce commodity. Advertisers frequently feign scarcity to drive up the demand for products. Thus, we constantly see ads that scream "limited supply available," "for a limited time only," "while they last," and "time is running out." Like genuine scarcity, feigned scarcity *can* enhance the desirability of a commodity (Cialdini & Griskevicius, 2010).

Table 13.1 Critical Thinking Skills Discussed in This Application

Skill	Description
Judging the credibility of an information source	The critical thinker understands that credibility and bias are central to determining the quality of information and looks at factors such as vested interests, credentials, and appropriate expertise.
Recognizing social influence strategies	The critical thinker is aware of manipulative tactics such as the foot-in-the-door and lowball techniques, misuse of the reciprocity norm, and feigned scarcity.

© Cengage Learning 2013

REVIEW OF KEY LEARNING GOALS

13.25 Useful criteria in judging credibility include whether a source has vested interests or appropriate credentials. One should also consider the method of analysis used in reaching conclusions and why information might not coincide with conventional wisdom. To resist manipulative efforts, it helps to be aware of social influence tactics such as the foot-in-the-door technique, misuse of the reciprocity norm, the lowball technique, and feigned scarcity.

Chapter 13 Practice Test

1. Stereotypes:
   A. are often automatic products of normal cognitive processes.
   B. are widely held beliefs that people have certain characteristics because of their membership in a particular group.
   C. are equivalent to prejudice.
   D. both a and b.

2. You believe that short men have a tendency to be insecure. The concept of illusory correlation implies that you will:
   A. overestimate how often short men are insecure.
   B. underestimate how often short men are insecure.
   C. overestimate the frequency of short men in the population.
   D. falsely assume that shortness in men causes insecurity.

3. A father suggests that his son's low marks in school are due to the child's laziness. The father has made a(n) __________ attribution.
   A. external
   B. internal
   C. situational
   D. high consensus

4. Bob explains his failing grade on a term paper by saying that he really didn't work very hard at it. According to Weiner's model, Bob is making an ______________ attribution about his failure.
   A. internal-stable
   B. internal-unstable
   C. external-stable
   D. external-unstable

5. The fundamental attribution error refers to the tendency of:
   A. observers to favor external attributions in explaining the behavior of others.
   B. observers to favor internal attributions in explaining the behavior of others.
   C. actors to favor external attributions in explaining the behavior of others.
   D. actors to favor situational attributions in explaining their own behavior.

6. According to Hazan and Shaver (1987):
   A. romantic relationships in adulthood follow the same form as attachment relationships in infancy.
   B. those who had ambivalent attachments in infancy are doomed never to fall in love as adults.
   C. those who had avoidant attachments in infancy often overcompensate by becoming excessively intimate in their adult love relationships.
   D. all of the above.

7. Cross-cultural similarities are most likely to be found in which of the following areas?
   A. what people look for in prospective mates
   B. the overall value of romantic love
   C. passionate love as a prerequisite for marriage
   D. the tradition of prearranged marriages

8. Covert attitudes that are expressed in subtle automatic responses over which we have little conscious control are called __________ attitudes.
   A. ambivalent
   B. automatic
   C. implicit
   D. subtle

9. Cognitive dissonance theory predicts that after people engage in counterattitudinal behavior, they will:
   A. convince themselves they really didn't perform the behavior.
   B. change their attitude to make it more consistent with their behavior.
   C. change their attitude to make it less consistent with their behavior.
   D. do nothing.

10. The elaboration likelihood model of attitude change suggests that:
    A. the peripheral route results in more enduring attitude change.
    B. the central route results in more enduring attitude change.
    C. only the central route to persuasion can be effective.
    D. only the peripheral route to persuasion can be effective.

11. The results of Milgram's (1963) study imply that:
    A. in the real world, most people will refuse to follow orders to inflict harm on a stranger.
    B. many people will obey an authority figure even if innocent people get hurt.
    C. most people are willing to give obviously wrong answers when ordered to do so.
    D. most people stick to their own judgment, even when group members unanimously disagree.

12. According to Latané (1981), social loafing is due to:
    A. social norms that stress the importance of positive interactions among group members.
    B. duplication of effort among group members.
    C. diffusion of responsibility in groups.
    D. a bias toward making internal attributions about the behavior of others.

13. Groupthink occurs when members of a cohesive group:
    A. are initially unanimous about an issue.
    B. stress the importance of caution in group decision making.
    C. emphasize concurrence at the expense of critical thinking in arriving at a decision.
    D. shift toward a less extreme position after group discussion.

14. Discrimination:
    A. refers to a negative attitude toward members of a group.
    B. refers to unfair behavior toward the members of a group.
    C. is the same thing as prejudice.
    D. all of the above.

15. The foot-in-the-door technique involves asking people to agree to a _______ request first to increase the likelihood that they will comply with a _______ request later.
    A. large; small
    B. small: large
    C. large; large
    D. large; larger

Answers

1 D pp. 519–520	6 A p. 527	11 B pp. 541–543
2 A p. 520	7 A p. 528	12 C p. 547
3 B p. 521	8 C p. 532	13 C p. 549
4 B p. 522	9 B pp. 537–538	14 B p. 552
5 B p. 522	10 B pp. 538–539	15 B p. 557

Chapter 13 Media Resources

PsykTrek

To view a demo: **www.cengage.com/psychology/psyktrek**
To order: **www.cengage.com/psychology/weiten**

Go to the PsykTrek website or CD-ROM for further study of the concepts in this chapter. Both online and on the CD-ROM, PsykTrek includes dozens of learning modules with videos, animations, and quizzes, as well as simulations of psychological phenomena and a multimedia glossary that includes word pronunciations.

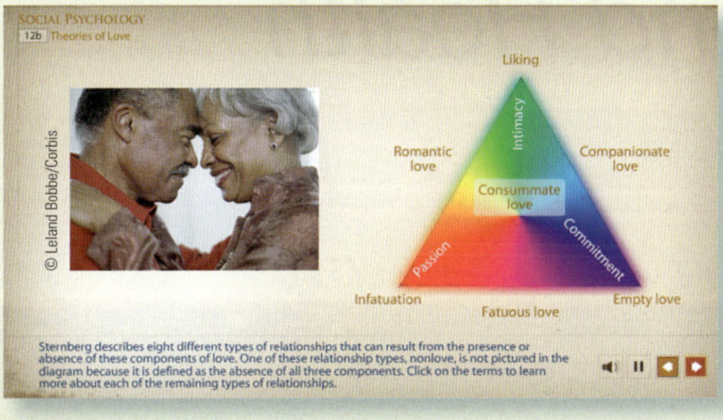

© Cengage Learning 2008

Learn about love in Module 12b (*Theories of Love*), which will allow you to take the Passionate Love Scale and see how your score compares with others.

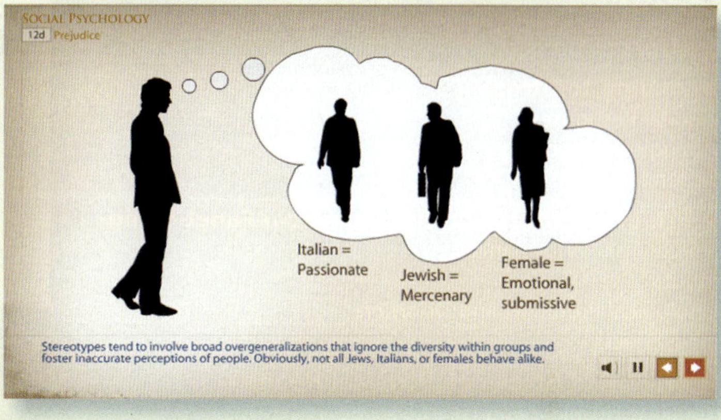

© Cengage Learning 2008

Find out why people are prejudiced by working through Module 12d (*Prejudice*).

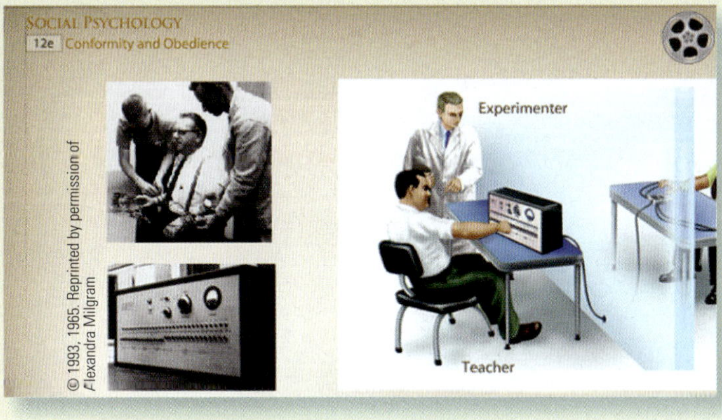

© Cengage Learning 2008

See Stanley Milgram's subjects cringe in discomfort when they are asked to shock an innocent stranger when you visit Module 12e (*Conformity and Obedience*), which includes three videos from the famous study.

© Cengage Learning 2008

Participate in an experiment on your skills in person perception when you try Simulation 10 (*Social Judgment*). (Photos left to right: © Michael Newman/PhotoEdit; © Bill Bachman/PhotoEdit; © Reed Kaestner/Corbis; © Jack Hollingsworth/RF/Corbis

Online Study Tools

Log in to **CengageBrain** to access the resources your instructor requires. For this book, you can access:

CourseMate brings course concepts to life with interactive learning, study, and exam preparation tools that support the printed textbook. A textbook-specific website, Psychology CourseMate includes an integrated interactive eBook and other interactive learning tools such as quizzes, flashcards, videos, and more.

CengageNow is an easy-to-use online resource that helps you study in less time to get the grade you want—NOW. Take a pre-test for this chapter and receive a personalized study plan based on your results that will identify the topics you need to review and direct you to online resources to help you master those topics. Then take a post-test to help you determine the concepts you have mastered and what you will need to work on. If your textbook does not include an access code card, go to CengageBrain.com to gain access.

WebTutor is more than just an interactive study guide. WebTutor is an anytime, anywhere customized learning solution with an eBook, keeping you connected to your textbook, instructor, and classmates.

Aplia. If your professor has assigned Aplia homework:

1. Sign in to your account
2. Complete the corresponding homework exercises as required by your professor.
3. When finished, click "Grade It Now" to see which areas you have mastered, which need more work, and detailed explanations of every answer.

Visit **www.cengagebrain.com** to access your account and purchase materials.

14

Stress, Coping, and Health

© Pete Saloutos/CORBIS

You're in your car headed home from school with a classmate. Traffic is barely moving. A radio report indicates that the traffic jam is only going to get worse. You groan audibly as you fiddle impatiently with the radio dial. Another motorist narrowly misses your fender trying to cut into your lane. Your pulse quickens as you shout insults at the unknown driver, who can't even hear you. You think about the term paper you have to work on tonight. Your stomach knots up as you recall all the crumpled drafts you tossed into the wastebasket last night. If you don't finish that paper soon, you won't be able to find any time to study for your math test, not to mention your biology quiz. Suddenly, you remember that you promised the person you're dating that the two of you would get together tonight. There's no way. Another fight looms on the horizon. Your classmate asks how you feel about the tuition increase that the college announced yesterday. You've been trying not to think about it. You're already in debt up to your ears. Your parents are bugging you about changing schools, but you don't want to leave your friends. Your heartbeat quickens as you contemplate the debate you're sure to have with your parents. You feel wired with tension as you realize that the stress in your life never seems to let up.

Many circumstances can create stress. It comes in all sorts of packages: big and small, pretty and ugly, simple and complex. All too often, the package comes as a surprise. In this chapter, we'll try to sort out these packages. We'll discuss the nature of stress, how people cope with stress, and the potential effects of stress.

Our examination of the relationship between stress and physical illness will lead us into a broader discussion of the psychology of health. The way people in health professions think about physical illness has changed considerably in the past 30 years. The traditional view of physical illness as a purely biological phenomenon has given way to a biopsychosocial model of

illness (Friedman & Adler, 2007; Suls, Luger, & Martin, 2010). **The *biopsychosocial model* holds that physical illness is caused by a complex interaction of biological, psychological, and sociocultural factors.** This model does not suggest that biological factors are unimportant. It simply asserts that these factors operate in a psychosocial context that's also influential.

What has led to this shift in thinking? In part, it's a result of changing patterns of illness. Prior to the 20th century, the principal threats to health were *contagious diseases* caused by infectious agents—diseases such as smallpox, typhoid fever, diphtheria, yellow fever, malaria, cholera, tuberculosis, and polio. Today, none of these diseases is among the leading killers in the United States. They were tamed by improvements in nutrition, public hygiene, sanitation, and medical treatment (Grob, 1983). Unfortunately, the void left by contagious diseases has been filled all too quickly by *chronic diseases* that develop gradually, such as heart disease, cancer, and stroke (see **Figure 14.1**). Psychosocial factors, such as stress and lifestyle, play a large role in the development of these chronic diseases. The growing recognition that psychological factors influence physical health eventually led to the emergence of a new specialty in psychology, called *health psychology* (Friedman & Adler, 2007). ***Health psychology* is concerned with how psychosocial factors relate to the promotion and maintenance of health and with the causation, prevention, and treatment of illness.** In the second half of this chapter, we'll explore this new domain of psychology. In the Personal Application, we'll focus on strategies for enhancing stress management. And in the Critical Thinking Application we'll discuss strategies for improving health-related decision making.

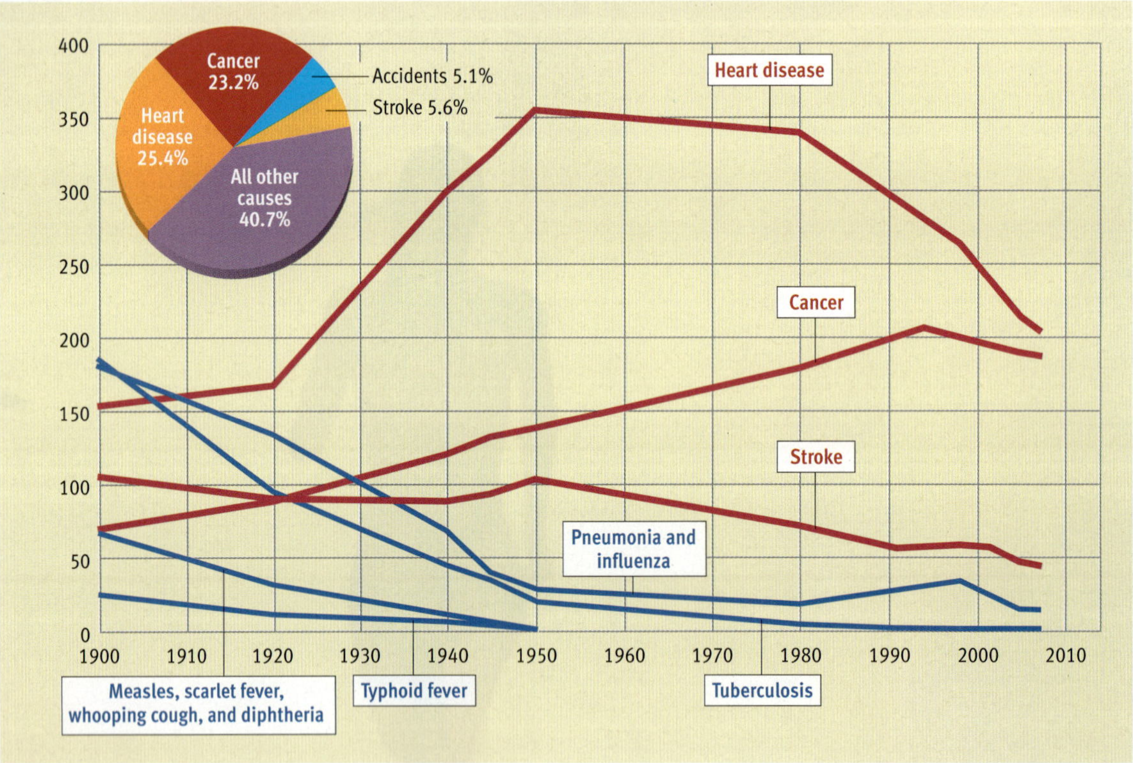

© Cengage Learning 2013

Figure 14.1

Changing patterns of illness. Historical trends in the death rates for various diseases reveal that contagious diseases (shown in blue) have declined dramatically as a threat to health. However, the death rates for stress-related chronic diseases (shown in red) have remained relatively high. The pie chart (inset) shows the results of these trends: Three chronic diseases (heart disease, cancer, and stroke) account for about 54% of all deaths. Although these chronic diseases remain the chief threat to health in modern societies, it is interesting to note that deaths from heart disease have declined considerably since the 1980s. Many experts attribute much of this decline to improved health habits (Brannon & Feist, 2007), which demonstrates the important link between behavior and health. (Based on data from National Vital Statistics Reports, 2010, Vol. 58, No. 19.)

The Nature of Stress

KEY LEARNING GOALS

14.1 Evaluate the impact of minor stressors, and discuss the importance of people's appraisals of stress.

14.2 Distinguish between acute and chronic stressors, and describe frustration as a form of stress.

14.3 Identify the three basic types of conflict, and discuss which types are most troublesome.

14.4 Summarize evidence on life change and pressure as forms of stress.

The word *stress* has been used in different ways by different theorists. We'll define ***stress* as any circumstances that threaten or are perceived to threaten one's well-being and that thereby tax one's coping abilities.** The threat may be to immediate physical safety, long-range security, self-esteem, reputation, peace of mind, or many other things that one values. Stress is a complex concept, so let's explore a little further.

Stress as an Everyday Event

The word *stress* tends to spark images of overwhelming, traumatic crises. People may think of tornadoes, hurricanes, floods, and earthquakes. Undeniably, major disasters of this sort are extremely stressful events. Studies conducted in the aftermath of natural disasters typically find elevated rates of psychological problems and physical illness in the communities affected by these disasters (Stevens, Raphael, & Dobson, 2007; van Griensven et al., 2007). For example, 15 months after Hurricane Katrina devastated the New Orleans area, a survey of residents uncovered dramatic increases in physical and mental health problems (Kim et al., 2008). However, these unusual events are only a small part of what constitutes stress. Many everyday events, such as waiting in line, having car trouble, shopping for Christmas presents, misplacing your checkbook, and staring at bills you can't pay, are also stressful. Researchers have found that everyday problems and the minor nuisances of life are also important forms of stress (Almeida, 2005; McIntyre, Korn, & Matsuo, 2008).

You might guess that minor stresses would produce minor effects, but that isn't necessarily true. Richard Lazarus and his colleagues developed a scale to measure everyday hassles. They have shown that routine hassles may have significant harmful effects on mental and physical health (Delongis, Folkman, & Lazarus, 1988). Other investigators, working with different types of samples and different measures, have also found that everyday hassles are predictive of impaired mental and physical health (Pettit et al., 2010; Sher, 2003). Why would minor hassles be so troublesome? The answer isn't entirely clear yet. It may be because of the *cumulative* nature of stress (Seta, Seta, & McElroy, 2002). Stress adds up. Routine stresses at home, at school, and at work might be fairly benign individually, yet collectively they could create great strain.

Appraisal: Stress Lies in the Eye of the Beholder

The experience of feeling stressed depends on what events one notices and how one chooses to appraise or interpret them (Monroe & Slavich, 2007; Semmer, McGrath, & Beehr, 2005). Events that are stressful for one person may evoke little or no stress response from another person (Steptoe, 2007). For example, many people find flying in an airplane somewhat stressful. Frequent flyers, though, may not be bothered at all. Some people enjoy the excitement of going out on a date with someone new. Others find the uncertainty terrifying.

In discussing appraisals of stress, Lazarus and Folkman (1984) distinguish between primary and secondary appraisal (see **Figure 14.2** on the next page). ***Primary appraisal* is an initial evaluation of whether an event is (1) irrelevant to you, (2) relevant but not threatening or (3) stressful.** When you view an event as stressful, you are likely to make a ***secondary appraisal*, which is an evaluation of your coping resources and options for dealing with the stress.** Thus, your primary appraisal would determine whether you saw an upcoming job interview as stressful. Your secondary appraisal would determine how stressful the interview appeared, in light of your assessment of your ability to deal with the event.

Often, people aren't very objective in their appraisals of potentially stressful events. A study of hospitalized patients awaiting surgery showed only a slight correlation between the objective seriousness of a person's upcoming surgery and the amount of fear experienced by the patient (Janis, 1958). Clearly, some people are more prone than others to feel threatened by life's difficulties. A number of studies have shown that anxious, neurotic people report more stress than others (Cooper & Bright, 2001; Espejo et al., 2011), as do people who are relatively unhappy (Cacioppo et al., 2008). Thus, stress lies in the eye (actually, the mind) of the beholder.

Courtesy of Richard Lazarus

Richard Lazarus

"We developed the Hassle Scale because we think scales that measure major events miss the point. The constant, minor irritants may be much more important than the large, landmark changes."

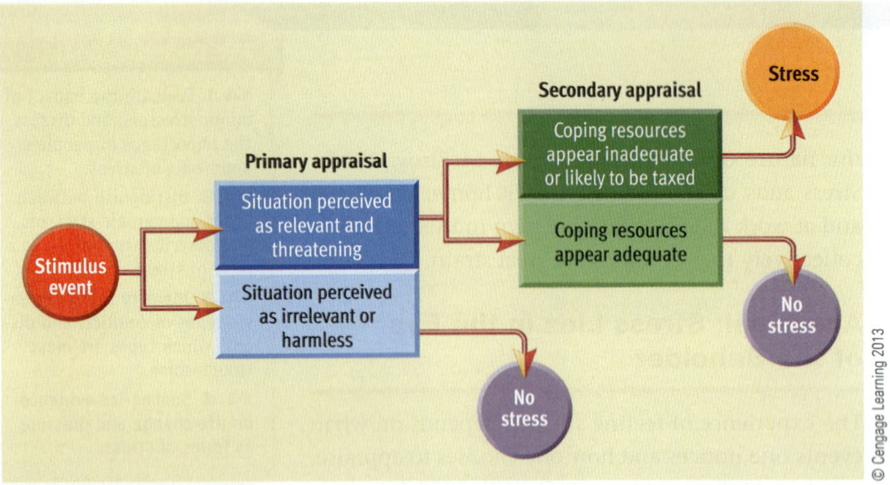

Figure 14.2

Primary and secondary appraisal of stress. *Primary appraisal* is an initial evaluation of whether an event is (1) irrelevant to you, (2) relevant, but not threatening, or (3) stressful. When you view an event as stressful, you are likely to make a *secondary appraisal,* which is an evaluation of your coping resources and options for dealing with the stress. (Based on Lazarus & Folkman, 1994)

People's appraisals of stressful events are highly subjective.

Major Types of Stress 11f

An enormous variety of events can be stressful for one person or another. To achieve a better understanding of stress, theorists have tried to analyze the nature of stressful events and divide them into subtypes. One sensible distinction involves differentiating between *acute stressors and chronic stressors* (Dougall & Baum, 2001; Stowell, 2008). ***Acute stressors* are threatening events that have a relatively short duration and a clear endpoint.** Examples would include having an encounter with a belligerent drunk, dealing with the challenge of a major exam, or having your home threatened by severe flooding. ***Chronic stressors* are threatening events that have a relatively long duration and no readily apparent time limit.** Examples would include persistent financial strains produced by huge credit card debts, ongoing pressures from a hostile boss at work, or the demands of caring for a sick family member over a period of years.

None of the proposed schemes for classifying stressful events has turned out to be altogether satisfactory. The fact that classifying stressful events into nonintersecting categories is virtually impossible presents conceptual headaches for researchers. However, it need not prevent us from describing four major types of stress: frustration, conflict, change, and pressure. As you read about each of them, you'll surely recognize some familiar adversaries.

Frustration 11f

I had a wonderful relationship with a nice man for three months. One day when we planned to spend the entire day together, he called and said he wouldn't be meeting me and that he had decided to stop seeing me. I cried all morning. The grief was like losing someone through death. I still hurt, and I wonder if I'll ever get over him.

This scenario illustrates frustration. As psychologists use the term, ***frustration* occurs in any situation in which the pursuit of some goal is thwarted.** In essence, you experience frustration when you want something and you can't have it. Everyone has to deal with frustration virtually every day. Traffic jams and difficult daily commutes, for instance, are a routine source of frustration that can elicit anger and physical symptoms (Evans & Wener, 2006; Rasmussen, Knapp, & Garner, 2000). Fortunately, many frustrations are brief and insignificant. You may be quite upset when you go to the dry cleaners and your clothes are not ready as promised. However, in a day or two you'll have your clothes back, and the frustration will be forgotten.

Of course, some frustrations can be sources of significant stress. Failures and losses are two common kinds of frustration that are often highly stressful. Everyone fails in at least some of his or her endeavors. Some people make failure almost inevitable by setting unrealistically high goals for themselves. For example, many disappointed business executives tend to forget that for every newly appointed vice president in the business world, there are dozens of middle-level executives who don't get promoted. Losses can be particularly frustrating because people are deprived of something that they're accustomed to having, especially when it's a dearly loved boyfriend, girlfriend, spouse, or parent.

Conflict 11f

Should I or shouldn't I? I became engaged at Christmas. My fiance surprised me with a ring. I knew if I refused the ring he would be terribly hurt and our relationship would suffer. However, I don't really know whether or not I want to marry him. On the other hand, I don't want to lose him either.

Like frustration, conflict is an unavoidable feature of everyday life. The question "Should I or shouldn't I?" comes up countless times in everyone's life. ***Conflict* occurs when two or more incompatible motivations or behavioral impulses compete for expression.** Conflicts come in three types, which were originally described by Kurt Lewin (1935) and investigated extensively by Neal Miller (1944, 1959). These three basic types of conflict—approach-approach, avoidance-avoidance, and approach-avoidance—are diagrammed in **Figure 14.3**.

In an *approach-approach conflict* a choice must be made between two attractive goals. The problem, of course, is that you can choose just one of the two goals. For example: You have a free afternoon; should you play tennis or racquetball? Should you buy the blue sweater or the gray jacket when you can't afford both? Among the three kinds of conflict, the approach-approach type tends to be the least stressful. People don't usually stagger out of restaurants exhausted by the stress of choosing which of several appealing entrees to eat. Nonetheless, approach-approach conflicts over important issues may sometimes be troublesome. If you're torn between two appealing college majors or two attractive boyfriends, you may find the decision-making process quite stressful.

In an *avoidance-avoidance conflict* a choice must be made between two unattractive goals. Forced to choose between two repelling alternatives, you are, as they say, "caught between a rock and a hard place." For example, should you continue to collect unemployment checks, or should you take that degrading job at the car wash? Or suppose you have painful backaches. Should you submit to surgery that you dread, or should you continue to live with the back pain? Obviously, avoidance-avoidance conflicts are most unpleasant and highly stressful.

In an *approach-avoidance conflict* a choice must be made about whether to pursue a single goal that has both attractive and unattractive aspects. For instance, imagine that you're offered a career promotion that will mean a large increase in pay. However, you'll have to move to a city where you don't want to live. Approach-avoidance conflicts are common and can be quite stressful. Any time you have to take a risk to pursue some desirable outcome, you're likely to find yourself in an approach-avoidance conflict. These kinds of conflicts often produce *vacillation*. That is, you go back and forth, beset by indecision. You decide to go ahead, then you decide not to, then you decide to go ahead again. Humans are not unique in this respect. Many years ago, Neal Miller (1944) observed the same vacillation in his groundbreaking research with rats. He created approach-avoidance conflicts in hungry rats by alternately feeding and shocking them at one end of a runway apparatus. Eventually, these rats tended to hover near the center of the runway, alternately approaching and retreating from the goal box at the end of the alley.

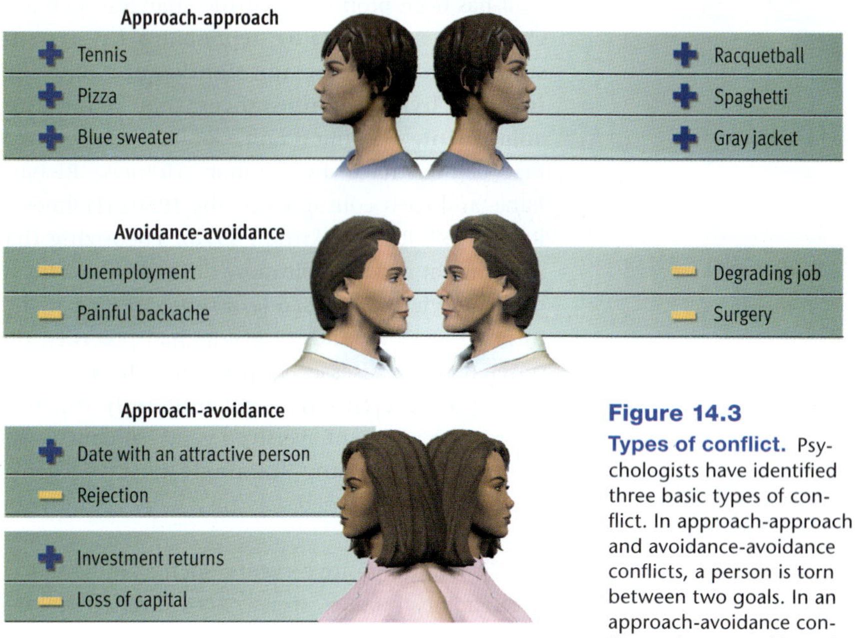

Figure 14.3
Types of conflict. Psychologists have identified three basic types of conflict. In approach-approach and avoidance-avoidance conflicts, a person is torn between two goals. In an approach-avoidance conflict, only one goal is under consideration, but it has both positive and negative aspects. © Cengage Learning 2013

PsykTrek 11f

Change

After my divorce, I lived alone for four years. Six months ago I married a wonderful woman who has two children from her previous marriage. My biggest stress is suddenly having to adapt to living with three people instead of by myself. I was pretty set in my ways. I had certain routines. Now everything is chaos. I love my wife and I'm fond of the kids. They're not really doing anything wrong. But my house and my life just aren't the same, and I'm having trouble dealing with it all.

CONCEPT CHECK 14.1

Identifying Types of Conflict

Check your understanding of the three basic types of conflict by identifying the type experienced in each of the following examples. The answers are in Appendix A.

Examples

_____ 1. John can't decide whether to take a demeaning job in a car wash or to go on welfare.

_____ 2. Desiree wants to apply to a highly selective law school, but she hates to risk the possibility of rejection.

_____ 3. Vanessa has been shopping for a new car and is torn between a nifty little sports car and a classy sedan, both of which she really likes.

Types of conflict

a. approach-approach

b. avoidance-avoidance

c. approach-avoidance

It has been proposed that life changes, such as a change in marital status, represent a key type of stress. ***Life changes* are any significant alterations in one's living circumstances that require readjustment.** The importance of life changes was first demonstrated by Thomas Holmes, Richard Rahe, and their colleagues in the 1960s (Holmes & Rahe, 1967; Rahe & Arthur, 1978). Theorizing that stress might make people more vulnerable to illness, they interviewed thousands of tuberculosis patients to find out what kinds of events had preceded the onset of their disease. Surprisingly, the most frequently cited events were not uniformly negative. There were plenty of aversive events, of course, but there were also many seemingly positive events, such as getting married, having a baby, and getting promoted.

Why would positive events, such as moving to a nicer home, produce stress? According to Holmes and Rahe, it's because they produce *change*. In their view, changes in personal relationships, changes at work, changes in finances, and so forth can be stressful even when the changes are welcomed.

Based on this analysis, Holmes and Rahe (1967) developed the Social Readjustment Rating Scale (SRRS) to measure life change as a form of stress. The scale assigns numerical values to 43 major life events. These values are supposed to reflect the magnitude of the readjustment required by each change (see **Table 14.1**). In using the scale, respondents are asked to indicate how often they experienced any of these 43 events during a certain time period (typically, the past year). The numbers associated with each event checked are then added. This total is an index of the amount of change-related stress the person has recently experienced.

The SRRS and similar scales based on it have been used in over 10,000 studies by researchers all over the world (Dohrenwend, 2006). Overall, these studies have shown that people with higher scores on

Table 14.1 Social Readjustment Rating Scale

Life Event	Mean Value	Life Event	Mean Value
Death of a spouse	100	Son or daughter leaving home	29
Divorce	73	Trouble with in-laws	29
Marital separation	65	Outstanding personal achievement	28
Jail term	63	Spouse begins or stops work	26
Death of a close family member	63	Begin or end school	26
Personal injury or illness	53	Change in living conditions	25
Marriage	50	Revision of personal habits	24
Fired at work	47	Trouble with boss	23
Marital reconciliation	45	Change in work hours or conditions	20
Retirement	45	Change in residence	20
Change in health of family member	44	Change in school	20
Pregnancy	40	Change in recreation	19
Sex difficulties	39	Change in church activities	19
Gain of a new family member	39	Change in social activities	18
Business readjustment	39	Mortgage or loan for lesser purchase (car, TV, etc.)	17
Change in financial state	38	Change in sleeping habits	16
Death of a close friend	37	Change in number of family get-togethers	15
Change to a different line of work	36	Change in eating habits	15
Change in number of arguments with spouse	35	Vacation	13
Mortgage or loan for major purchase (home, etc.)	31	Christmas	12
Foreclosure of mortgage or loan	30	Minor violations of the law	11
Change in responsibilities at work	29		

SOURCE: Adapted from Holmes, T. H., & Rahe, R. (1967). The Social Readjustment Rating Scale. *Journal of Psychosomatic Research, 11*, 213–218. Copyright © 1967, with permission of Elsevier.

© Cengage Learning 2013

the SRRS tend to be more vulnerable to many kinds of physical illness and to many types of psychological problems as well (Derogatis & Coons, 1993; Scully, Tosi, & Banning, 2000; Surtees & Wainwright, 2007). These results have attracted a great deal of attention. The SRRS has even been reprinted in many popular newspapers and magazines. The attendant publicity has led to the widespread conclusion that life change is inherently stressful.

More recently, however, experts have criticized the research on the connection between life events and health. They cite problems with the methods used and raise questions about the meaning of the findings (Dohrenwend, 2006; Monroe, 2008; Wethington, 2007). At this point, it's a key interpretive issue that concerns us. Many critics have argued that the SRRS does not measure *change* exclusively. The main problem is that the list of life changes on the SRRS is dominated by events that are clearly negative or undesirable (death of a spouse, being fired from a job, and so on). These negative events probably generate great frustration. Research eventually showed that negative life events cause most of the stress tapped by the SRRS (McLean & Link, 1994; Turner & Wheaton, 1995). Thus, it has become apparent that the SRRS assesses a wide range of stressful experiences, not just life change. At present, there's little reason to believe that change is inherently or inevitably stressful. Undoubtedly, some life changes may be quite challenging, yet others may be painless.

Pressure

PsykTrek 11f

My father questioned me at dinner about some things I didn't want to talk about. I know he doesn't want to hear my answers, at least not the truth. My father told me when I was little that I was his favorite because I was "pretty near perfect." I've spent my life trying to keep up that image, even though it's obviously not true. Recently, he has begun to realize this, and it's made our relationship very strained and painful.

At one time or another, most people have remarked that they're "under pressure." What does this term mean? ***Pressure* involves expectations or demands that one behave in a certain way.** You are under pressure to *perform* when you're expected to execute tasks and responsibilities quickly, efficiently, and successfully. For example, salespeople are usually under pressure to move lots of merchandise. Professors at research institutions are often under pressure to publish in prestigious journals. Stand-up comedians are under intense pressure to make people laugh. Pressures to *conform* to others' expectations are also common in our lives. People in the business world are expected to dress in certain ways. Suburban homeowners are expected to keep their lawns well manicured. Teenagers are expected to adhere to their parents' values and rules.

Pressure is widely discussed by the general public. Ironically though, the concept of pressure has received scant attention from researchers. However, Weiten (1988b, 1998) has devised a scale to measure pressure as a form of life stress. It assesses self-imposed pressure, pressure from work and school, and pressure from family relations, peer relations, and intimate relations. In research with this scale, a strong relationship has been found between pressure and a variety of psychological symptoms and problems. In fact, pressure has turned out to be more strongly related to measures of mental health than the SRRS and other established measures of stress (see **Figure 14.4** on the next page). Moreover, a recent 15-year study of over 12,000 nurses found that increased pressure at work was related to an increased risk for heart disease (Väänänen, 2010). Participants who reported that their pressure at work was much too high were almost 50% more likely to develop heart disease than subjects who experienced normal levels of pressure.

Reality CHECK

Misconception

Stress is something that is imposed on individuals from outside forces.

Reality

It is hard to quantify, but a significant portion of people's stress is self-imposed. People routinely impose pressure on themselves by taking on extra work and new challenges. They court frustration by embracing unrealistic goals or engaging in self-defeating behavior. And people create stress by making unrealistic appraisals of adverse events.

Pressure comes in two varieties: pressure to perform and pressure to conform. For example, standup comedians are under intense pressure to make audiences laugh (pressure to perform), whereas corporate employees are often expected to dress in certain ways (pressure to conform).

Top: © Hill Street Studios/Blend Images/Corbis; bottom: © George Doyle/Stockbyte/Getty Images

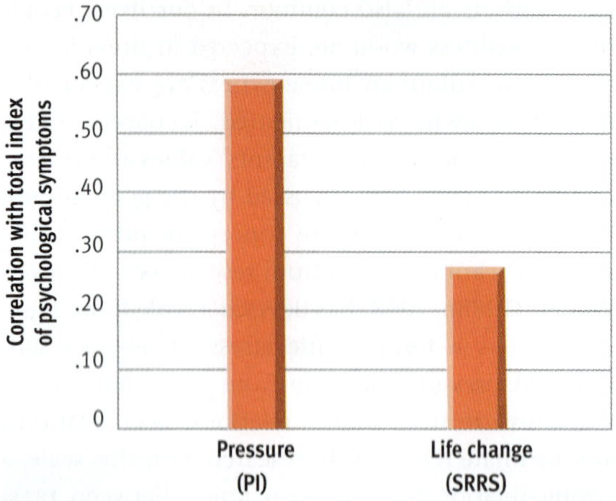

Figure 14.4

Pressure and psychological symptoms. A comparison of pressure and life change as sources of stress suggests that pressure may be more strongly related to mental health than change is. In one study, Weiten (1988b) found a correlation of .59 between scores on the Pressure Inventory (PI) and symptoms of psychological distress. In the same sample, the correlation between SRRS scores and psychological symptoms was only .28. © Cengage Learning 2013

REVIEW OF KEY LEARNING GOALS

14.1 Stress involves circumstances and experiences that are perceived as threatening. Stress is a common, everyday event, and even seemingly minor stressors, such as daily hassles, can be problematic. To a large degree, stress is subjective and lies in the eye of the beholder. People's appraisals of events determine what they find stressful.

14.2 Acute stressors have a short duration and clear endpoint, whereas chronic stressors have a relatively long duration. Major types of stress include frustration, conflict, change, and pressure. Frustration occurs when an obstacle prevents one from attaining some goal.

14.3 The three principal types of conflict are approach-approach, avoidance-avoidance, and approach-avoidance. The third type is especially stressful. Vacillation is a common response to approach-avoidance conflict.

14.4 A large number of studies with the SRRS suggest that life change is stressful. Although this may be true, it is now clear that the SRRS is a measure of general stress rather than just change-related stress. Two kinds of pressure (to perform and conform) also appear to be stressful.

CONCEPT CHECK 14.2

Recognizing Sources of Stress

Check your understanding of the major sources of stress by indicating which type or types of stress are at work in each of the following examples. Bear in mind that the four basic types of stress are not mutually exclusive. There's some potential for overlap, so a specific experience might include both change and pressure, for instance. The answers are in Appendix A.

Examples	Types of stress
______ 1. Marie is late for an appointment but is stuck in line at the bank.	a. frustration
______ 2. Tamika decides that she won't be satisfied unless she gets straight A's this year.	b. conflict
______ 3. Jose has just graduated from business school and has taken an exciting new job.	c. change
______ 4. Morris has just been fired from his job and needs to find another.	d. pressure

KEY LEARNING GOALS

14.5 Discuss the role of positive emotions in response to stress, and describe the effects of emotional arousal.

14.6 Describe the fight-or-flight response, Selye's general adaptation syndrome, and other physiological responses to stress.

14.7 Evaluate the adaptive value of giving up, aggression, and self-indulgence as coping responses.

14.8 Explain how defense mechanisms work, and clarify the nature of constructive coping.

Responding to Stress

People's response to stress is complex and multidimensional. Stress affects the individual at several levels. Consider again the chapter's opening scenario. You're driving home in heavy traffic and thinking about overdue papers, tuition increases, and parental pressures. Let's look at some of the reactions that were mentioned. When you groan in reaction to the traffic report, you're experiencing an *emotional response* to stress, in this case annoyance and anger. When your pulse quickens and your stomach knots up, you're exhibiting *physiological responses* to stress. When you shout insults at another driver, your verbal aggression is a *behavioral response* to the stress at hand.

Thus, we can analyze a person's reactions to stress at three levels: (1) emotional responses, (2) physiological responses, and (3) behavioral responses. **Figure 14.5** diagrams these three levels of response. It provides an overview of the stress process.

Emotional Responses

PSYKTREK 11g

When people are under stress, they often react emotionally. Studies that have tracked stress and mood on a daily basis have found intimate relationships between the two (Affleck et al., 1994; van Eck, Nicolson, & Berkhof, 1998).

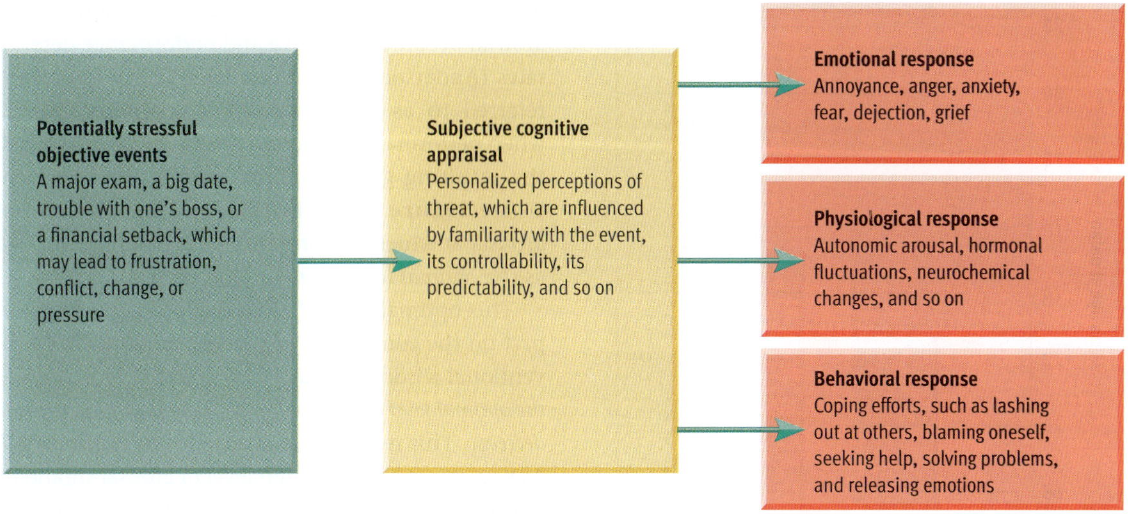

Figure 14.5
Overview of the stress process. A potentially stressful event, such as a major exam, elicits a subjective appraisal of how threatening the event is. If the event is viewed with alarm, the stress may trigger emotional, physiological, and behavioral reactions, as people's response to stress is multidimensional.

© Cengage Learning 2013

Emotions Commonly Elicited 11g

No simple one-to-one connections have been found between certain types of stressful events and particular emotions. However, researchers *have* begun to uncover some strong links between specific *cognitive reactions to stress* (appraisals) and specific emotions (Smith & Lazarus, 1993). For example, self-blame tends to lead to guilt, helplessness to sadness, and so forth. Many emotions can be evoked by stressful events, but some are certainly more likely than others. Common responses to stress typically occur along three dimensions of emotion: (a) annoyance, anger, and rage, (b) apprehension, anxiety, and fear, and (c) dejection, sadness and grief (Lazarus, 1993).

Investigators have tended to focus heavily on the connection between stress and negative emotions. However, research shows that positive emotions also occur during periods of stress (Finan, Zautra, & Wershba, 2011; Folkman, 2008). This finding may seem counterintuitive. Yet researchers have found that people experience a diverse array of pleasant emotions even while enduring dire circumstances. Consider, for example, a study that examined subjects' emotional functioning early in 2001 and again in the weeks following the 9/11 terrorist attacks (Fredrickson et al., 2003). Like most U.S. citizens, the participants reported many negative emotions in the aftermath of 9/11, but positive emotions also emerged. For example, people felt gratitude for the safety of their loved ones. Many people took stock and counted their blessings. Quite a few people even reported renewed love for their friends and family. Thus, contrary to common sense, positive emotions do *not* vanish during times of severe stress. Moreover, these positive emotions appear to play a key role in helping people bounce back from the difficulties tied to stress (Tugade & Fredrickson, 2004).

How do positive emotions promote resilience in the face of stress? Barbara Fredrickson's (2001, 2005, 2006) *broaden-and-build theory of positive emotions* can shed light on this question. First, positive emotions alter people's mindsets, broadening their scope of attention and increasing their creativity and flexibility in problem solving. Second, positive emotions can undo the lingering effects of negative emotions. Thus, positive emotions short-circuit the potentially damaging physiological responses to stress that we will discuss momentarily. Third, positive emotions can promote rewarding social interactions that help build valuable social support, enhanced coping strategies, and other enduring personal resources.

One particularly interesting finding has been that a positive emotional style is associated with an enhanced immune response (Cohen & Pressman, 2006). Positive emotions also appear to be protective against heart disease (Davidson, Mostofsky, & Whang, 2010). These effects probably contribute to the recently discovered association between the tendency to report positive emotions and longevity (Ong, 2010; Xu & Roberts, 2010). Yes, people who experience a high level of positive emotions appear to live longer than others! One recent study exploring this association looked at photos of major league baseball players taken from the *Baseball Register* for 1952. The intensity of the players' smiles was used as a crude index of their tendency to experience positive emotions, which was then related to how long they lived. As you can see in **Figure 14.6** on the next page, greater smile intensity predicted greater longevity (Abel & Kruger, 2010). Thus, it appears that the benefits of positive emotions may be more diverse and more far-reaching than widely appreciated.

Figure 14.6
Positive emotions and longevity. To look at the relation between positive emotions and longevity, Abel and Kruger (2010) used the intensity of baseball players' smiles in photographs as a rough indicator of their characteristic emotional tone. All the photos in the *Baseball Register* for 1952 were reviewed and classified as showing no smile, a partial smile, or a big smile. Then the age at death was determined for the players (except the 46 who were still alive in June 2009). As you can see, greater smile intensity was associated with living longer.

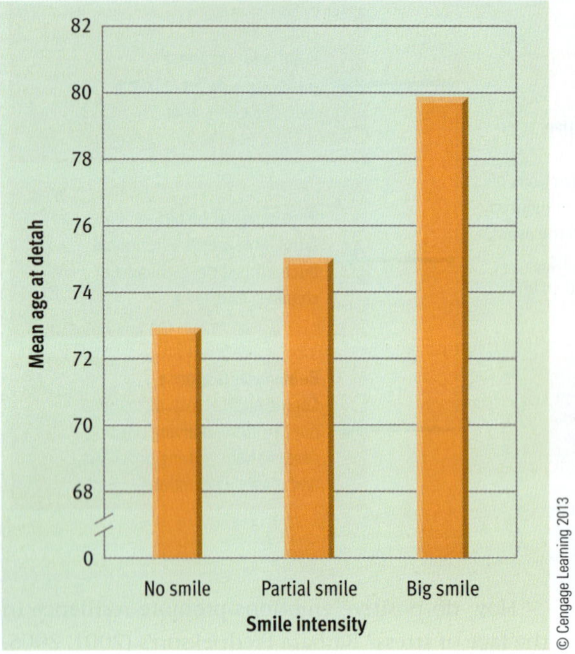

Effects of Emotional Arousal 11g

Emotional responses are a natural and normal part of life. Even unpleasant emotions serve important purposes. Like physical pain, painful emotions can serve as warnings that one needs to take action. However, strong emotional arousal can also interfere with efforts to cope with stress. For example, there is evidence that high emotional arousal can interfere with attention and memory retrieval. It can also impair judgment and decision making (Janis, 1993; Lupien & Maheu, 2007; Mandler, 1993).

Emotional arousal may indeed hurt coping efforts. However, that isn't *necessarily* the case. The *inverted-U hypothesis* predicts that task performance should improve with increased emotional arousal—up to a point, after which further increases in arousal become disruptive and performance deteriorates (Anderson, 1990; Mandler, 1993). This idea is referred to as the inverted-U hypothesis because when performance is plotted as a function of arousal, the resulting graphs approximate an upside-down U (see **Figure 14.7**). In these graphs, the level of arousal at which performance peaks is characterized as the *optimal level of arousal* for a task.

This optimal level of arousal appears to depend in part on the complexity of the task at hand. The conventional wisdom is that *as tasks become more complex, the optimal level of arousal (for peak performance) tends to decrease.* This relationship is depicted in **Figure 14.7**. As you can see, a fairly high level of arousal should be optimal on simple tasks that do not require complicated reasoning (such as driving 8 hours to help a friend in a crisis). However, performance should peak at a lower level of arousal on complex tasks (such as making a major decision in which you have to weigh many factors). Doubts have been raised about the validity of the inverted-U hypothesis (Hancock & Ganey, 2003). However, it does provide a plausible model of how emotional arousal could have either beneficial or disruptive effects on coping, depending on the nature of the stressful demands.

Physiological Responses 11g

As we just discussed, stress frequently elicits strong emotional responses. Now we'll look at the important physiological changes that often accompany these emotions.

The Fight-or-Flight Response

Walter Cannon (1932) was one of the first theorists to describe the fight-or-flight response. **The *fight-or-flight response* is a physiological reaction to threat in which the autonomic nervous system mobi-**

Figure 14.7
Arousal and performance. Graphs of the relationship between emotional arousal and task performance tend to resemble an inverted U, as increased arousal is associated with improved performance up to a point, after which higher arousal leads to poorer performance. The optimal level of arousal for a task depends on the complexity of the task. On complex tasks, a relatively low level of arousal tends to be optimal. On simple tasks, however, performance may peak at a much higher level of arousal.

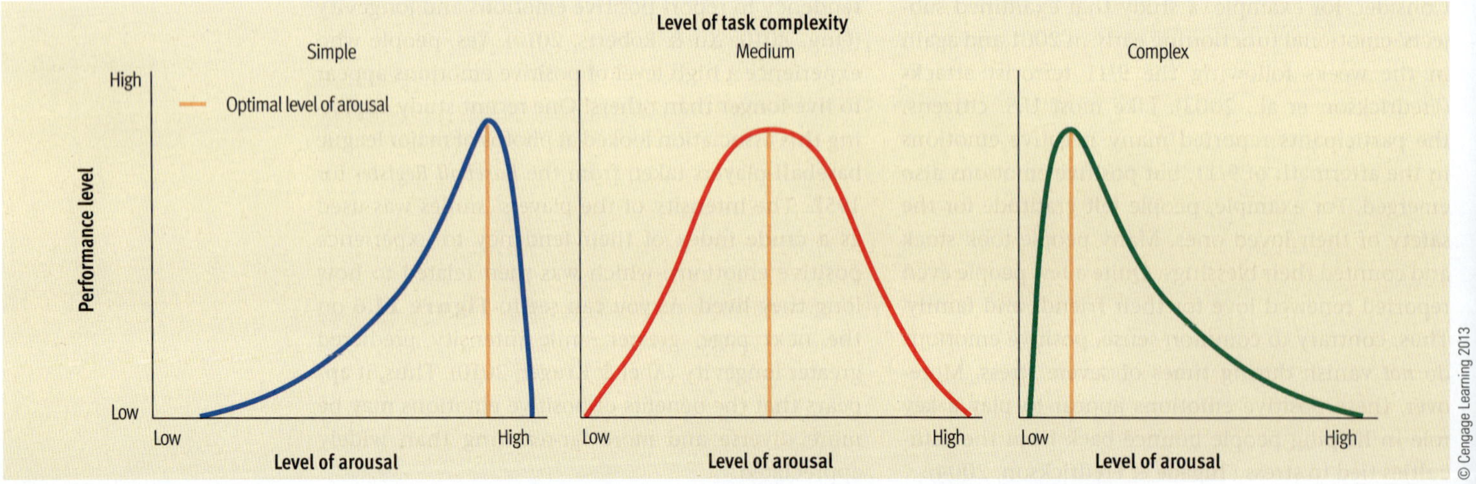

DILBERT © 1999 Scott Adams. Used By permission of UNIVERSAL UCLICK. All rights reserved.

lizes the organism for attacking (fight) or fleeing (flight) an enemy. As you may recall from Chapter 3, the *autonomic nervous system (ANS)* controls blood vessels, smooth muscles, and glands. The fight-or-flight response is mediated by the *sympathetic division* of the ANS (McCarty, 2007). In one experiment, Cannon studied the fight-or-flight response in cats by confronting them with dogs. Among other things, he noticed an immediate acceleration in the cats' breathing and heart rate. He also saw a reduction in their digestive processes.

The physiological arousal associated with the fight-or-flight response is also seen in humans. In a sense, this automatic reaction is a "leftover" from humanity's evolutionary past. It's clearly an adaptive response in the animal kingdom. In the wild, the threat of predators often requires a swift response of fighting or fleeing. But in our modern world, the fight-or-flight response may be less adaptive for human functioning than it was thousands of generations ago (Nesse, Bhatnagar, & Young, 2007). Most human stresses can't be handled simply through fight or flight. Work pressures, marital problems, and financial difficulties require far more complex responses.

Shelley Taylor and her colleagues (Taylor 2002, 2006; Taylor & Master, 2011) have questioned whether the fight-or-flight model applies equally well to both males and females. They note that in most species females have more responsibility for the care of young offspring than males do. Using an evolutionary perspective, they argue that this disparity may make fighting and fleeing less adaptive for females. Both responses may endanger offspring and thus reduce the likelihood of an animal passing on its genes. Taylor maintains that evolutionary processes have fostered more of a "tend and befriend" response in females. According to this analysis, in reacting to stress, females allocate more effort to the care of offspring and to seeking help and support. More research is needed to evaluate this provocative analysis.

The General Adaptation Syndrome

PsykTrek 11g

The concept of stress was identified and named by Hans Selye back in the 1940s (Russell, 2007). Selye (1936, 1956, 1974) formulated an influential theory of stress reactions called the general adaptation syndrome. **The *general adaptation syndrome* is a model of the body's stress response, consisting of three stages: alarm, resistance, and exhaustion** (see **Figure 14.8**). In the first stage, an *alarm reaction* occurs when an organism first recognizes the existence of a threat. Physiological arousal occurs as the body musters its resources to combat the challenge. Selye's alarm reaction is essentially the fight-or-flight response originally described by Cannon.

However, Selye took his investigation of stress a few steps further by exposing lab animals to *prolonged* stress, similar to the chronic stress often endured by humans. As stress continues, the organism may progress to the second phase of the general adaptation syndrome, the stage of *resistance*. During this phase, physiological changes stabilize as coping efforts get under way. If the stress continues over a substantial period of time, the organism may enter

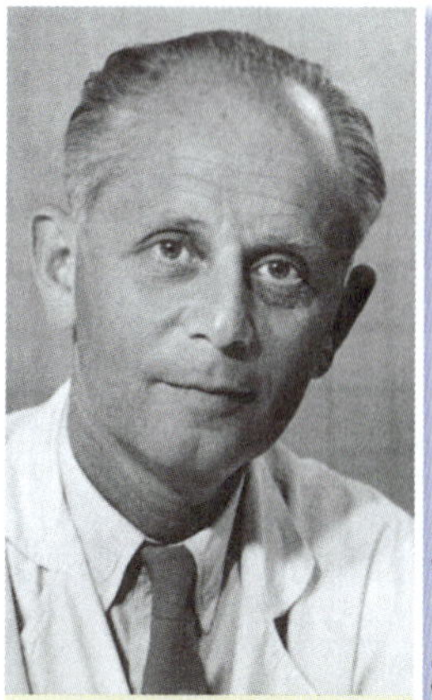

© Bettmann/Corbis

Hans Selye

"There are two main types of human beings: 'race-horses,' who thrive on stress and are only happy with a vigorous, fast-paced lifestyle; and 'turtles,' who in order to be happy require peace, quiet, and a generally tranquil environment."

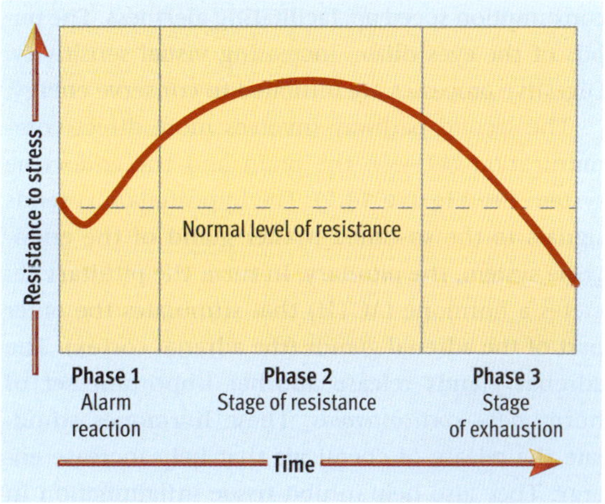

© Cengage Learning 2013

Figure 14.8

The general adaptation syndrome. According to Selye, the physiological response to stress can be broken into three phases. During the first phase, the body mobilizes its resources for resistance after a brief initial shock. In the second phase, resistance levels off and eventually begins to decline. If the third phase of the general adaptation syndrome is reached, resistance is depleted, leading to health problems and exhaustion.

the third stage, *exhaustion*. According to Selye, the body's resources for fighting stress are limited. If the stress can't be overcome, the body's resources may be depleted. Eventually, he thought the organism would experience hormonal exhaustion. We now know, however, that the crux of the problem is that chronic overactivation of the stress response can have damaging physiological effects on a variety of organ systems (Sapolsky, 2007). These harmful physiological effects can lead to what Selye called "diseases of adaptation."

Brain-Body Pathways

PSYKTREK 11g

Even in cases of moderate stress, you may notice that your heart has started beating faster, you've begun to breathe harder, and you're perspiring more than usual. How does all this bodily activity happen? It appears that there are two major pathways along which the brain sends signals to the endocrine system in response to stress (Clow, 2001; Dallman, Bhatnagar, & Viau, 2007). As we noted in Chapter 3, the *endocrine system* consists of glands located at various sites in the body that secrete chemicals called hormones. The *hypothalamus* is the brain structure that appears to initiate action along these two pathways.

The first pathway (see **Figure 14.9**) is routed through the autonomic nervous system. In response to stress, your hypothalamus activates the sympathetic division of the ANS. A key part of this activation involves stimulating the central part of the adrenal glands (the adrenal medulla). In turn, the adrenal glands release large amounts of *catecholamines* into the bloodstream. As these hormones radiate throughout your body, they produce the physiological changes seen in the fight-or-flight response. The net result of catecholamine elevation is that the body is mobilized for action (Lundberg, 2007). Heart rate and blood flow increase. More blood is pumped to the brain and muscles. Respiration and oxygen consumption speed up, facilitating alertness. The pupils of the eyes dilate, increasing visual sensitivity. Digestive processes are inhibited to conserve energy.

The second pathway involves more direct communication between the brain and the endocrine system (see **Figure 14.9**). The hypothalamus sends signals to the so-called master gland of the endocrine system, the pituitary. In turn, the pituitary secretes a hormone (ACTH) that stimulates the outer part of the adrenal glands (the adrenal cortex). The adrenal glands release another important set of hormones—*corticosteroids*. These hormones stimulate the release of chemicals that help increase energy. They also help inhibit tissue inflammation in case of injury (Miller, Chen, & Zhou, 2007; Munck, 2007).

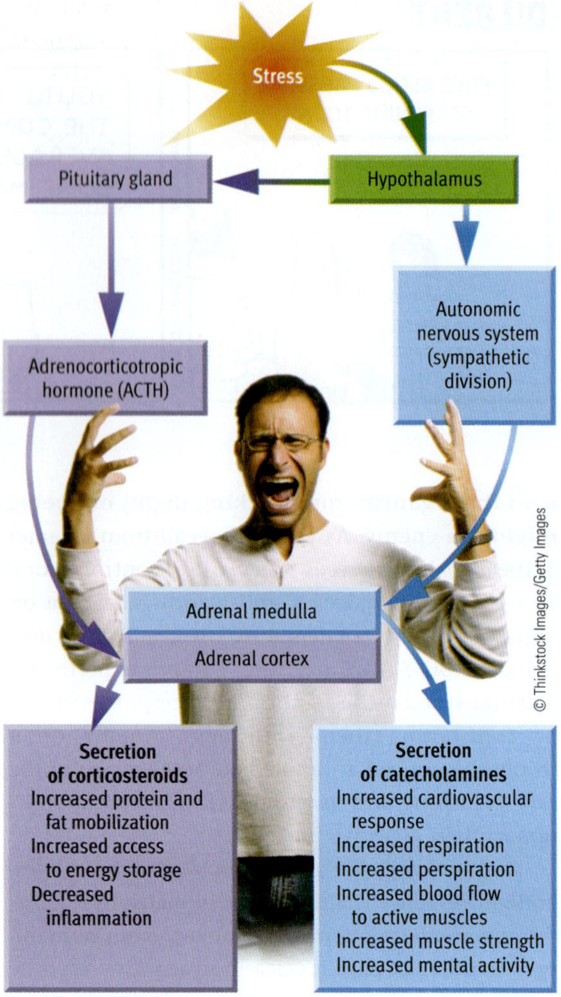

Figure 14.9

Brain-body pathways in stress. In times of stress, the brain sends signals along two pathways. The pathway through the autonomic nervous system controls the release of catecholamine hormones that help mobilize the body for action. The pathway through the pituitary gland and the endocrine system controls the release of corticosteroid hormones that increase energy and ward off tissue inflammation.

© Cengage Learning 2013

Recent research suggests that there may be sex differences in reactivity along both of these brain-body pathways. Evidence suggests that females' stress responses tend to be milder than males' stress reactions, at least from puberty through menopause (Kajantie & Phillips, 2006; Kudielka & Kirschbaum, 2005). The fact that this gender gap is found only between puberty and menopause suggests that females' higher levels of the hormone estrogen may play a key role in toning down women's physiological reactivity to stress. Some theorists speculate that this gender disparity in stress reactivity may contribute to the higher prevalence of cardiovascular disorders and certain other diseases in men (Kajantie, 2008).

An important new finding in research on stress and the brain is that stress can interfere with neurogenesis (McEwen, 2009; Mirescu & Gould, 2006). As you may recall from Chapter 3, scientists have recently discovered that the adult brain is capable of *neurogenesis*. ***Neurogenesis* is the formation of new neurons**, primarily in key areas in the hippocampus. Neurogenesis appears to enhance learning and memory (see Chapter 7). In Chapter 15, we will discuss evidence that suppressed neurogenesis may be a key cause of depression (Dranovsky & Hen, 2006). Because the capacity of stress to hinder neurogenesis may have important ramifications, it is currently the subject of intense research (Tanapat & Gould, 2007).

Behavioral Responses

PSYKTREK 11g

People respond to stress at several levels. However, it's clear that *behavior* is the crucial dimension of their reactions. Most behavioral responses to stress involve coping. ***Coping* refers to active efforts to master, reduce, or tolerate the demands created by stress.** Notice that this definition is neutral as to whether coping efforts are healthful or maladaptive. The popular use of the term often implies that coping is inherently healthful. When people say that someone "coped with her problems," the implication is that she handled them effectively.

In reality, however, coping responses may be adaptive or maladaptive (Folkman & Moskowitz, 2004; Kleinke, 2007). For example, if you were flunking a history course at midterm, you might cope with this stress by (1) increasing your study efforts, (2) seeking help from a tutor, (3) blaming your professor, or (4) giving up on the class without really trying. Clearly, the first two of these coping responses would be more adaptive than the last two. Research suggests that coping tactics are the key determinant of whether stress leads to distress (Carver, 2007).

People cope with stress in an endless variety of ways (Folkman & Moskowitz, 2004). Given the immense variety in coping strategies, we can only highlight a few of the more common patterns. In this section, we'll focus most of our attention on styles of coping that tend to be less than ideal. We'll discuss a variety of more healthful coping strategies in the Personal Application on stress management.

Giving Up and Blaming Oneself

PSYKTREK 11g

When confronted with stress, people sometimes simply give up and withdraw from the battle. Some people routinely respond to stress with fatalism and resignation. They passively accept setbacks that might be dealt with effectively. This syndrome is referred to as *learned helplessness* (Seligman, 1974, 1992). ***Learned helplessness* is passive behavior produced by exposure to unavoidable aversive events.** Learned helplessness seems to occur when individuals come to believe that events are beyond their control. As you might guess, giving up has not generally been highly regarded as a method of coping. Consistent with this view, many studies suggest that learned helplessness can contribute to depression (Isaacowitz & Seligman, 2007).

Giving up is clearly less than optimal in many contexts. However, research also suggests that when people struggle to pursue goals that turn out to be unattainable, it makes sense for them to cut their losses and disengage from the goal (Wrosch & Scheier, 2003). Recent studies have shown that people who are better able to disengage from unattainable goals report better health. They also exhibit lower levels of a key stress hormone (Wrosch et al., 2007). People in our competitive culture tend to disparage the concept of "giving up." Thus, the authors note that it might be better to characterize this coping tactic as "goal adjustment."

Blaming oneself is another common response when people are confronted by stressful difficulties. The tendency to become highly self-critical in response to stress has been noted by a number of influential theorists. Albert Ellis (1973, 1987) calls this phenomenon "catastrophic thinking." According to Ellis, catastrophic thinking causes, aggravates, and perpetuates emotional reactions to stress that are often problematic (see the Personal Application for this chapter). In a similar vein, Aaron Beck (1976, 1987) argues that negative self-talk can contribute to

CONCEPT CHECK 14.3

Tracing Brain-Body Pathways in Stress

Check your understanding of the two major pathways along which the brain sends signals to the endocrine system in the event of stress by separating the eight terms below into two sets of four and arranging each set in the appropriate sequence. You'll find the answers in Appendix A.

ACTH	corticosteriods
adrenal cortex	hypothalamus
adrenal medulla	pituitary
catecholamines	sympathetic division of the ANS

Pathway 1	Pathway 2
____________	____________
____________	____________
____________	____________
____________	____________

Courtesy of Albert Ellis Institute

Albert Ellis

"People largely disturb themselves by thinking in a self-defeating, illogical, and unrealistic manner."

the development of depression and other psychological disorders (see Chapter 16). There is something to be said for recognizing one's weaknesses and taking responsibility for one's failures. Ellis and Beck agree, however, that excessive self-blame is an unhealthy approach to coping with stress.

Striking Out at Others 11g

© Jason Stitt/Shutterstock

People often respond to stressful events by striking out at others with aggressive behavior. ***Aggression* is any behavior that is intended to hurt someone, either physically or verbally.** Many years ago, a team of psychologists (Dollard et al., 1939) proposed the *frustration-aggression hypothesis.* This theory held that aggression is always caused by frustration. Decades of research have supported the idea of a causal link between frustration and aggression (Berkowitz, 1989). However, this research has also shown that there isn't an inevitable, one-to-one correspondence between frustration and aggression.

Frequently people lash out aggressively at others who had nothing to do with their frustration. This happens, apparently, because people can't vent their anger at the real source. For example, you'll probably suppress your anger rather than lash out verbally at a police officer who's giving you a speeding ticket. Twenty minutes later, however, you might be verbally brutal to a sales clerk. As we discussed in Chapter 12, this diversion of anger to a substitute target was noticed long ago by Sigmund Freud. He called it *displacement.* Unfortunately, research suggests that when people are provoked, displaced aggression is a common response (Hoobler & Brass, 2006; Marcus-Newhall et al., 2000).

Freud theorized that behaving aggressively could get pent-up emotion out of one's system and thus be adaptive, a process he termed *catharsis.* ***Catharis* is the release of emotional tension.** The Freudian notion that it's a good idea to vent anger has become widely disseminated and accepted in modern society. Books, magazines, and self-appointed experts routinely advise that it's healthy to "blow off steam." Doing so supposedly releases and reduces anger. However, experimental research generally has *not* supported the catharsis hypothesis. Indeed, *most studies find just the opposite: Behaving in an aggressive manner tends to fuel more anger and aggression* (Bushman, 2002; Lohr et al., 2007).

Indulging Oneself 11g

Stress sometimes leads to reduced impulse control, or *self-indulgence* (Tice, Bratslavsky, & Baumeister, 2001). When troubled by stress, many people turn to excessive consumption. They engage in unwise patterns of eating, drinking, smoking, using drugs, spending money, and so forth. It makes sense that when things are going poorly in one area of their lives, people may try to compensate by pursuing substitute forms of satisfaction. After all, self-indulgent responses tend to be relatively easy to execute and highly pleasurable. Thus, it's not surprising that studies have linked stress to increases in eating (O'Connor & Conner, 2011), smoking (McClernon & Gilbert, 2007), gambling (Wood & Griffiths, 2007), and consumption of alcohol and drugs (Grunberg, Berger, & Hamilton, 2011).

A new manifestation of this coping strategy that has attracted much attention recently is the tendency to immerse oneself in the online world of the Internet. Kimberly Young (1996, 1998, 2009) has described a syndrome called ***Internet addiction,* which consists of spending an inordinate amount of time on the Internet and inability to control online use.** People who exhibit this syndrome tend to feel anxious, depressed, or empty when they are not online. Their Internet use is so excessive, it begins to interfere with their functioning at work, at school, or at home. This leads them to start conceal-

CATHY © 1981 by Cathy Guisewite. Reprinted with permission of Universal Press Syndicate. All rights reserved.

© Corbis Flirt/Alamy

ing the extent of their dependence on the Internet. Estimates of the prevalence of Internet addiction, which range from 1.5% to 8.2% of the population, vary considerably because the criteria of this new syndrome are still evolving (Weinstein & Lejoyeux, 2010). That said, it is clear that the syndrome is not rare. There is, of course, active debate about the wisdom of characterizing excessive Internet surfing as an *addiction* (Czincz & Hechanova, 2009; Pies, 2009). Yet it's clear that this new coping strategy is creating very real problems for at least a portion of Internet users (Morahan-Martin, 2007).

Defensive Coping **10a, 11g**

Many people exhibit consistent styles of defensive coping in response to stress (Vaillant, 1994). We noted in Chapter 12 that Sigmund Freud originally developed the concept of the *defense mechanism.* Though rooted in the psychoanalytic tradition, this concept has gained widespread acceptance from psychologists of most persuasions (Cramer, 2000). Building on Freud's initial insights, modern psychologists have broadened the scope of the concept and added to Freud's list of defense mechanisms.

***Defense mechanisms* are largely unconscious reactions that protect a person from unpleasant emotions such as anxiety and guilt.** Many specific defense mechanisms have been identified. For example, Laughlin (1979) lists forty-nine different defenses. We described eight common defense mechanisms in our discussion of Freud's theory in Chapter 12. **Table 14.2** introduces another five defenses that people use with some regularity: denial, fantasy, intellectualization, undoing, and overcompensation. Although widely discussed in the popular press, defense mechanisms are often misunderstood. To clear up some of the misconceptions, we'll use a question/answer format to elaborate on the nature of defense mechanisms.

What exactly do defense mechanisms defend against? Above all else, defense mechanisms shield the individual from the emotional discomfort that's so often elicited by stress. Their main purpose is to ward off unwelcome emotions or to reduce their intensity. Foremost among the emotions guarded against are anxiety, anger, guilt, and dejection.

How do they work? Through *self-deception.* Defense mechanisms accomplish their goals by distorting reality so that it doesn't appear so threatening (Aldwin, 2007). For example, suppose you're not doing well in school. In fact, you're in danger of flunking out. Initially you might use *denial* to block awareness of the possibility that you could flunk out. This defense might temporarily fend off feelings of anxiety. If denying the obvious becomes difficult, you could resort to *fantasy.* You might daydream about how you'll salvage adequate grades by getting spectacular scores on

Table 14.2 Additional Defense Mechanisms

Mechanism	Description	Example
Denial of reality	Protecting oneself from unpleasant reality by refusing to perceive or face it	A smoker concludes that the evidence linking cigarette use to health problems is scientifically worthless
Fantasy	Gratifying frustrated desires by imaginary achievements	A socially inept and inhibited young man imagines himself chosen by a group of women to provide them with sexual satisfaction
Intellectualization (isolation)	Cutting off emotion from hurtful situations or separating incompatible attitudes so that they appear unrelated	A prisoner on death row awaiting execution resists appeal on his behalf and coldly insists that the letter of the law be followed
Undoing	Atoning for or trying to magically dispel unacceptable desires or acts	A teenager who feels guilty about masturbation ritually touches door knobs a prescribed number of times following each occurrence of the act
Overcompensation	Covering up felt weakness by emphasizing some desirable characteristics, or making up for frustration in one area by overgratification in another	A dangerously overweight woman goes on eating binges when she feels neglected by her husband

© Cengage Learning 2013

SOURCE: Adapted from Carson, R. C., Butcher, J. N., & Coleman, J. C. (1988). *Abnormal psychology and modern life.* Glenview, IL: Scott, Foresman. Reprinted by permission of Pearson Education, Inc. Upper Saddle River, NJ.
Note: See Table 12.1 for another list of defense mechanisms.

Courtesy of Shelley Taylor

Shelley Taylor

"Rather than perceiving themselves, the world, and the future accurately, most people regard themselves, their circumstances, and the future as considerably more positive than is objectively likely. . . . These illusions are not merely characteristic of human thought; they appear actually to be adaptive, promoting rather than undermining good mental health."

the upcoming final exams. Thus, defense mechanisms work their magic by bending reality in self-serving ways.

Are they healthy? This is a complicated question. More often than not, the answer is "no." Generally, defensive coping is less than optimal. Avoidance strategies and wishful thinking rarely provide genuine solutions to personal problems (Bolger, 1990; Holahan et al., 2005). Although defensive behavior tends to be relatively unhealthful, Shelley Taylor and Jonathon Brown (1988, 1994) have reviewed several lines of evidence suggesting that "positive illusions" may be adaptive for mental health and well-being. First, they note that "normal" people tend to have overly favorable self-images. In contrast, depressed subjects exhibit less favorable—but more realistic—self-concepts. Second, normal subjects overestimate the degree to which they control chance events. In comparison, depressed subjects are less prone to this illusion of control. Third, normal individuals are more likely than depressed subjects to display unrealistic optimism in making projections about the future. A variety of studies have provided support for the hypothesis that positive illusions can promote well-being (Segerstrom & Roach, 2008; Taylor et al., 2003).

As you might guess, a variety of critics have expressed skepticism about the idea that illusions are adaptive (Asendorpf & Ostendorf, 1998; Colvin, Block, & Funder, 1995). Perhaps the best analysis of the issue comes from Roy Baumeister (1989), who theorizes that it's all a matter of degree. He feels there is an "optimal margin of illusion." According to Baumeister, extreme distortions of reality are maladaptive, yet small illusions are often beneficial.

Constructive Coping

PSYKTREK 11g

Our discussion thus far has focused on coping strategies that usually are less than ideal. Of course, people also exhibit many healthful strategies for dealing with stress. The term ***constructive coping* refers to relatively healthful efforts that people make to deal with stressful events.** No strategy of coping can *guarantee* a successful outcome. The coping strategies that are likely to be effective will vary depending on the exact nature of the situation. Even the healthiest coping responses may turn out to be ineffective in some circumstances (Folkman & Moskowitz, 2004). Thus, the concept of constructive coping is simply meant to connote a healthful, positive approach, without guaranteeing success.

What makes certain coping strategies constructive? Frankly, it's a gray area in which psychologists' opinions vary to some extent. Nonetheless, a consensus about the nature of constructive coping has emerged from the sizable literature on stress management. Key themes in this literature include the following:

1. Constructive coping involves confronting problems directly. It's task relevant and action oriented. It entails a conscious effort to rationally evaluate your options so that you can try to solve your problems.
2. Constructive coping is based on reasonably realistic appraisals of your stress and coping resources. A little self-deception may sometimes be adaptive. However, excessive self-deception and highly unrealistic negative thinking are not.
3. Constructive coping involves learning to recognize, and in some cases regulate, potentially disruptive emotional reactions to stress.

These principles provide a rather general and abstract picture of constructive coping. We'll look at patterns of constructive coping in more detail in the Personal Application, which discusses various stress management strategies that people can use.

REVIEW OF KEY LEARNING GOALS

14.5 Stress often triggers emotional reactions, such as anger, fear, and sadness. Fredrickson's broaden-and-build theory asserts that positive emotions broaden thinking and build coping resources. Evidence suggests that positive emotions foster enhanced immune responding and are associated with increased longevity. Emotional arousal may interfere with coping. According to the inverted-U hypothesis, task performance improves with increased arousal up to a point and then declines. The optimal level of arousal on a task depends on the complexity of the task.

14.6 In the fight-or-flight response, the autonomic nervous system mobilizes the body for attack or fleeing. It may be less applicable to women than to men. Selye's general adaptation syndrome describes three stages of physiological reactions to stress: alarm, resistance, and exhaustion. Diseases of adaptation may appear during the stage of exhaustion. There are two major pathways along which the brain sends signals to the endocrine system in response to stress. These signals lead to the release of catecholamines and corticosteroids.

14.7 The behavioral response to stress takes the form of coping. Giving up is not a highly regarded approach to coping. However, studies suggest that people who are able to disengage from unattainable goals exhibit better health. Aggression tends to fuel more anger and increase rather than decrease stress. Self-indulgence is another coping pattern that tends to be of limited value. Internet addiction is a new manifestation of self-indulgent coping.

14.8 Defensive coping is quite common. Defense mechanisms protect against emotional distress through self-deception. Several lines of evidence suggest that positive illusions may be healthful. There is some debate about the matter, however. Relatively healthful coping tactics are called constructive coping. Constructive coping is action oriented and based on realistic appraisals of stress.

The Effects of Stress on Psychological Functioning

KEY LEARNING GOALS

14.9 Analyze the effects of stress on task performance and the nature of the burnout syndrome.

14.10 List some psychological problems that may be stress related, and explain how stress may have positive effects.

People struggle with many stresses every day. Most stresses come and go without leaving any enduring imprint. However, when stress is severe or when many stressful demands pile up, one's psychological functioning may be affected.

Research on the effects of stress has focused mainly on negative outcomes. Therefore, our coverage is slanted in that direction. However, it's important to emphasize that stress is not inherently bad. You would probably suffocate from boredom if you lived a stress-free existence. Stress makes life challenging and interesting. Along the way, though, stress can be harrowing, sometimes leading to impairments in performance, to burnout, and to other problems.

Impaired Task Performance

Stress often takes its toll on the ability to perform effectively on a task. For instance, Roy Baumeister's work shows how pressure can interfere with performance. Baumeister's (1984) theory assumes that pressure to perform often makes people self-conscious and that this elevated self-consciousness disrupts their attention. He found support for his theory in a series of lab experiments in which he manipulated the pressure to perform on simple perceptual-motor tasks. He found that many people tend to "choke" under pressure (Butler & Baumeister, 1998; Wallace, Baumeister, & Vohs, 2005). Pressure-induced performance decrements have also been found in studies of mathematical problem solving and simple sports tasks (Beilock, 2008; Beilock & Gonso, 2008).

Recent research suggests that Baumeister was on the right track in looking to *attention* to explain how stress impairs task performance. According to Beilock (2010), choking under pressure tends to occur when worries about performance distract attention from the task at hand and use up one's limited working memory capacity. Consistent with this analysis, a recent study found that chronic stress (preparing for difficult and hugely important medical board exams) undermined participants' performance on a task requiring attention shifts (Liston, McEwen, & Casey, 2009). Moreover, using fMRI scans, the investigators were able to pinpoint diminished activity in the prefrontal cortex as the underlying basis for subjects' impaired attentional control. Fortunately, these effects were short-lived. One month after the medical board exams, when participants' stress levels were back to normal, their attention was unimpaired.

Burnout

Burnout is an overused buzzword that means different things to different people. Nonetheless, a few researchers have described burnout in a systematic way that has facilitated scientific study of the syndrome (Maslach, 2003; Maslach & Leiter, 2007). ***Burnout* involves physical and emotional exhaustion, cynicism, and a lowered sense of self-efficacy that can be brought on gradually by chronic work-related stress.** Exhaustion is central to burnout. Exhaustion includes chronic fatigue, weakness, and low energy. Cynicism is manifested in highly negative attitudes toward oneself, one's work, and life in general. Reduced self-efficacy involves declining feelings of competence at work that give way to feelings of hopelessness and helplessness.

What causes burnout? Factors in the workplace that appear to promote burnout include work overload, struggling with interpersonal conflicts at work, lack of control over work responsibilities and outcomes, and inadequate recognition for one's work (Maslach & Leiter, 2005; see **Figure 14.10**). As you might expect, burnout is associated with increased absenteeism and reduced productivity at work, as well as increased vulnerability to a variety of health problems (Maslach & Leiter, 2000). Burnout is a

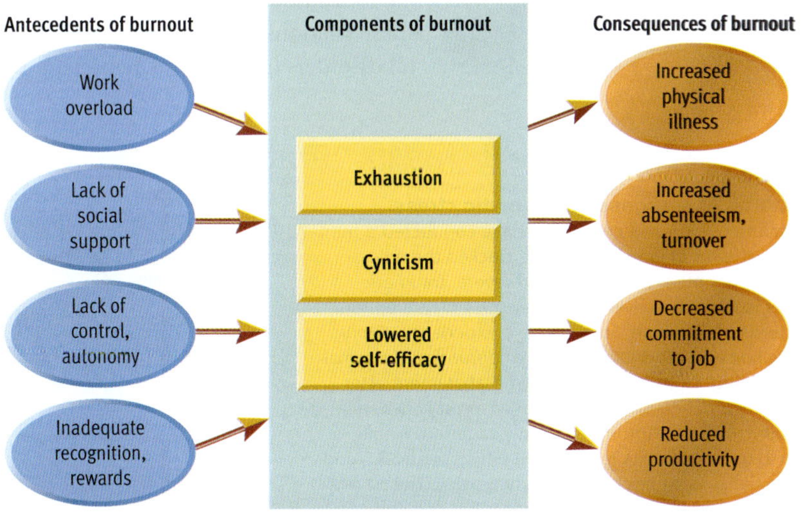

Figure 14.10

The antecedents, components, and consequences of burnout. Christina Maslach and Michael Leiter have developed a systematic model of burnout that specifies the antecedents, components, and consequences of this syndrome. The antecedents on the left in the diagram are the stressful features of the work environment that cause burnout. The syndrome itself consists of the three components—exhaustion, cynicism, and low self-efficacy—which are shown in the center of the diagram. Some of the unfortunate results of burnout are listed on the right. (Based on Leiter & Maslach, 2001) © Cengage Learning 2013 potential problem in a wide variety of occupations. Decades of research have shown that burnout is found all over the world in a wide variety of cultures (Schaufeli, Leiter, & Maslach, 2009).

Psychological Problems and Disorders

On the basis of clinical impressions, psychologists have long suspected that chronic stress might contribute to many types of psychological problems and mental disorders. Since the late 1960s, advances in the measurement of stress have allowed researchers to verify these suspicions in empirical studies. When it comes to common psychological problems, studies indicate that stress may contribute to poor academic performance (Akgun & Ciarrochi, 2003), insomnia and other sleep disturbances (Bernert et al., 2007; Kim & Dimsdale, 2007), sexual difficulties (Bodenmann et al., 2006), alcohol abuse (Sayette, 2007), and drug abuse (Grunberg, Berger, & Hamilton, 2011).

© stefanolunardi/Shutterstock

Above and beyond these everyday problems, research reveals that stress often contributes to the onset of full-fledged psychological disorders. Such disorders include depression (Monroe & Reid, 2009), schizophrenia (Walker, Mittal, & Tessner, 2008), and anxiety disorders (Beidel & Stipelman, 2007). In particular, stress plays a central role in the development of *posttraumatic stress disorder (PTSD).* This disorder involves an enduring psychological disturbance attributable to the experience of a major traumatic event. We'll discuss these relations between stress and mental disorders in detail in Chapter 15. Of course, stress is only one of many factors that may contribute to psychological disorders. Nonetheless, it's sobering to realize that stress can have a dramatic impact on one's mental health.

Positive Effects

The effects of stress are not entirely negative. Recent years have brought increased interest in the positive aspects of the stress process, including favorable outcomes that follow in the wake of stress. To some extent, the new focus on the possible benefits of stress reflects a new emphasis on "positive psychology." As we noted in Chapters 1 and 10, some theorists have argued that the field of psychology has historically devoted too much attention to pathology and suffering (Seligman & Csikszentmihalyi, 2000). The advocates of positive psychology argue for increased research on well-being, hope, courage, perseverance, tolerance, and other human strengths and virtues (Peterson & Seligman, 2004).

One of these strengths is *resilience* in the face of stress. ***Resilience* refers to successful adaptation to significant stress and trauma, as evidenced by a lack of serious negative outcomes.** Resilience used to be viewed as highly unusual, perhaps even rare. However, George Bonanno (2005) and his colleagues (Bonanno et al., 2002, 2005), have studied the long-term effects of serious traumatic events, such as bereavement and exposure to combat and terrorism. They have found that resilience is seen in as many as 35% to 55% of people (see **Figure 14.11**). Admittedly, a great many people do experience lasting ill effects from traumatic stress, but resilience may not be the rare exception it was once believed to be.

Figure 14.11

Patterns of response to traumatic stress. Bonanno (2005) and colleagues have conducted a number of studies in which they have tracked the adjustment of people after exposure to severe, traumatic stress, such as bereavement. They have identified four patterns of response. Some people experience *chronic disruption* and others show *delayed disruption* of normal functioning, both of which show no abatement after two years. Others show a pattern of *recovery,* wherein initially severe symptoms gradually taper off. Finally, a fourth group exhibits *resilience,* in which relatively modest initial symptoms diminish fairly quickly. The surprising finding in this research is that resilience is the most common of the four patterns, suggesting that resilience is not as rare as previously assumed.

SOURCE: Bonanno, G. A. (2005). Resilience in the face of potential trauma. *Current Directions in Psychological Science, 14,* 145–148. Copyright © 2005 by SAGE Publications. Reprinted by permission of SAGE Publications.

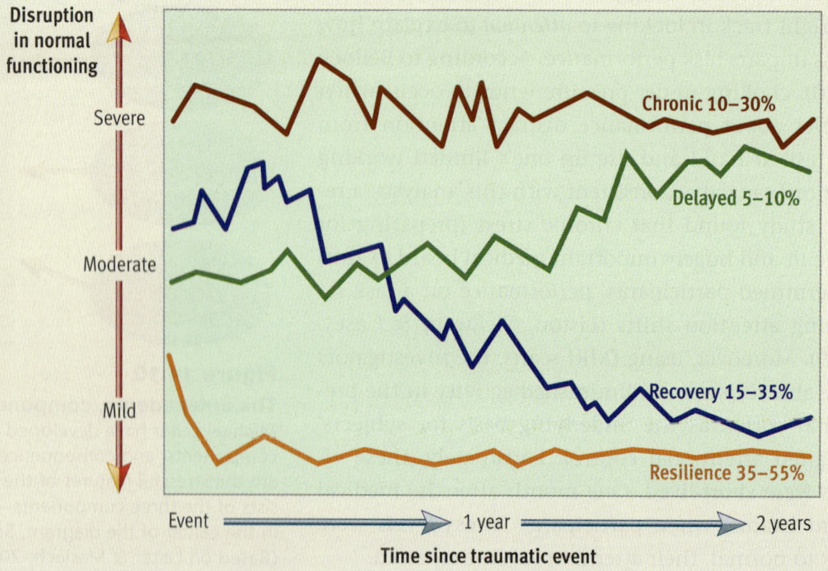

© Cengage Learning 2013

Research also suggests that stress can promote personal growth or self-improvement (Calhoun & Tedeschi, 2006, 2008). For example, studies of people grappling with major health problems show that the majority of respondents report they derived benefits from their adversity (Tennen & Affleck, 1999). Stressful events sometimes force people to develop new skills, reevaluate priorities, learn new insights, and acquire new strengths. In other words, the adaptation process initiated by stress may lead to personal changes that are for the better. Confronting a stressful challenge may lead to improvements in specific coping abilities and reduced reactivity to future stressful events (Bower, Moskowitz, & Epel, 2009). Thus, researchers have begun to explore the growth potential of stressful events.

Reality CHECK

Misconception

Stress is always bad for you.

Reality

Clearly, there *is* an association between stress and a host of negative outcomes, but several lines of research have shown that stress can also have positive effects. Stress can breed resilience, enhance coping skills, and promote personal growth. One recent study found that an intermediate amount of lifetime adversity was related to better mental health than either high or low levels of adversity (Seery, Holman, & Silver, 2010).

REVIEW OF KEY LEARNING GOALS

14.9 Several lines of research, including Baumeister's work on choking under pressure, suggest that stress can interfere with task performance. Beilock suggests that choking tends to occur when worries about performance distract attention and use up one's limited working memory capacity. Burnout involves exhaustion, cynicism, and lowered self-efficacy as a result of chronic work-related stress.

14.10 Stress can contribute to a number of common problems, such as poor academic performance, insomnia, and sexual difficulties. Stress has also been related to the development of depression, schizophrenia, and anxiety disorders. Research on the effects of stress has concentrated on negative outcomes, but positive effects may also occur. Research on resilience suggests that stress can promote personal growth and improved coping.

The Effects of Stress on Physical Health

KEY LEARNING GOALS

14.11 Review the evidence linking personality factors to coronary heart disease.

14.12 Outline the evidence linking emotional reactions and depression to heart disease.

14.13 Discuss how stress affects immune functioning, and assess the link between stress and illness.

The idea that stress can contribute to physical ailments is not entirely new. Evidence that stress can cause physical illness began to accumulate back in the 1930s. By the 1950s, the concept of *psychosomatic disease* was widely accepted. ***Psychosomatic diseases* were genuine physical ailments that were thought to be caused in part by stress and other psychological factors.** The classic psychosomatic illnesses were high blood pressure, peptic ulcers, asthma, skin disorders such as eczema and hives, and migraine and tension headaches (Kaplan, 1989; Rogers, Fricchione, & Reich, 1999). Please note, these diseases were not regarded as *imagined* physical ailments. The term *psychosomatic* has often been misused to refer to physical ailments that are "all in one's head." However, that is an entirely different syndrome (see Chapter 15). Rather, psychosomatic diseases were viewed as *authentic* organic maladies that were heavily stress related.

Since the 1970s, the concept of psychosomatic disease has gradually fallen into disuse. Research has shown that stress can contribute to the development of a broad range of diseases that were previously believed to be solely physiological in origin (Dimsdale et al., 2005; Dougall & Baum, 2001). Thus, it has become apparent that there's nothing unique about the psychosomatic diseases that requires a special category. In fact, stress may play a part in most diseases. In this section, we'll look at the evidence on the apparent link between stress and physical illness. We begin with heart disease, which is the leading cause of death in North America.

Personality, Hostility, and Heart Disease

Heart disease accounts for about 25% of the deaths in the United States every year. *Coronary heart disease* involves a reduction in blood flow in the coronary arteries, which supply the heart with blood. This type of heart disease accounts for about 90% of heart-related deaths. *Atherosclerosis* is the principal cause of coronary heart disease (Chrousos & Kaltsas, 2007). This condition is characterized by a gradual narrowing of the coronary arteries over a period of years. Established risk factors for atherosclerosis include older age, smoking, lack of exercise, high cholesterol levels, and high blood pressure (Bekkouche et al., 2011). Recently, attention has shifted to the possibility that inflammation may contribute to atherosclerosis and elevated coronary risk (Miller & Blackwell, 2006). Evidence is mounting that inflammation plays a key role in the initiation and progression of atherosclerosis. It may also play a role in the acute complications that trigger heart attacks (Nabi et al., 2008).

Research on the relationship between *psychological* factors and heart attacks began in the 1960s and 1970s. A pair of cardiologists, Meyer Friedman and Ray Rosenman (1974), discovered an apparent connection between coronary risk and a syndrome they called the *Type A personality,* which involves self-imposed stress and intense reactions to stress (Shaw & Dimsdale, 2007). **The *Type A personality* includes three elements: (1) a strong competitive orientation, (2) impatience and time urgency, and (3) anger and hostility.** Type A's are ambitious, hard-driving perfectionists who are exceedingly time-conscious. They routinely try to do several things at once. They fidget over the briefest delays. Often they are highly competitive, achievement-oriented workaholics who drive themselves with many deadlines. They are easily irritated and are quick to anger. In contrast, **the *Type B personality* is marked by relatively relaxed, patient, easygoing, amicable behavior.** Type B's are less hurried, less competitive, and less easily angered than Type A's.

Decades of research uncovered a tantalizingly modest correlation between Type A behavior and increased coronary risk. More often than not, studies found an association between Type A personality and an elevated incidence of heart disease, but the findings were not as strong or as consistent as expected (Baker, Suchday, & Krantz, 2007; Myrtek, 2007). However, more recently, researchers have found a stronger link between personality and coronary risk by focusing on a specific component of the Type A personality: *anger and hostility* (Chida & Steptoe, 2009; Powell & Williams, 2007). For example, in one study of almost 14,000 men and women who had no prior history of heart disease, investigators found an elevated incidence of heart attacks among participants who exhibited an angry temperament (Williams et al., 2000). The participants, who were followed for a median period of 4.5 years, were classified as being low (37.1% of the subjects), moderate (55.2%), or high (7.7%) in anger. Among participants with normal blood pressure, the high-anger subjects experienced almost three times as many coronary events as the low-anger subjects (see **Figure 14.12**). Thus, anger/hostility appears to be the key toxic element in the Type A syndrome.

© Alex James Bramwell/Shutterstock

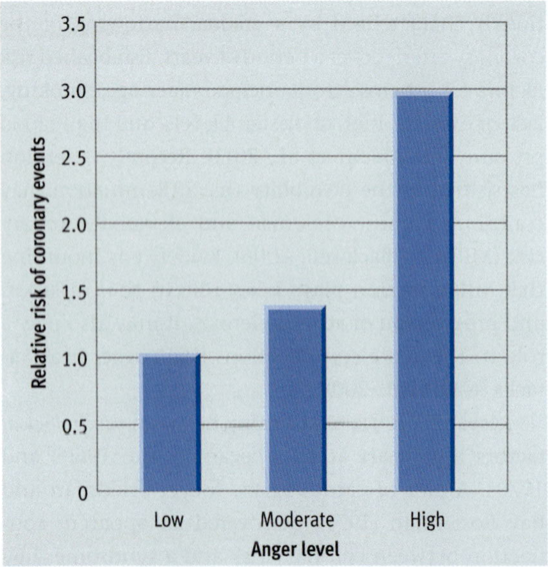

© Cengage Learning 2013

Figure 14.12
Anger and coronary risk. Working with a large sample of healthy men and women who were followed for a median of 4.5 years, Williams et al. (2000) found an association between anger and the likelihood of a coronary event. Among subjects who manifested normal blood pressure at the beginning of the study, a moderate anger level was associated with a 36% increase in coronary attacks, and a high level of anger nearly tripled participants' risk for coronary disease.

Emotional Reactions, Depression, and Heart Disease

Work on personality risk factors has dominated research on how psychological functioning contributes to heart disease. Interestingly, recent studies suggest that emotional reactions may also be critical. *One line of research has supported the hypothesis that transient mental stress and the resulting emotions that people experience can tax the heart* (Bekkouche et al., 2011; Dimsdale, 2008). Based on anecdotal evidence, cardiologists and laypersons have long voiced suspicions that strong emotional reactions might trigger heart attacks in individuals with coronary disease. The difficulty has always been documenting this connection. Fortunately, modern advances in cardiac monitoring have made investigation of this issue easier.

As suspected, lab experiments have shown that brief periods of mental stress can trigger acute symptoms of heart disease (Baker, Suchday, & Krantz, 2007). Overall, the evidence suggests that mental stress can elicit cardiac symptoms in about 30%–70% of patients with coronary disease (Kop, Gottdiener, & Krantz, 2001). Outbursts of anger may be particularly dangerous (Lampert et al., 2009). A recent study also showed that mental stress can trigger temporary increases in the inflammation that is thought to contribute to cardiovascular risk (Kop et al., 2008).

Another line of research has recently implicated depression as a risk factor for heart disease (Goldston & Baillie, 2008). *Depressive disorders* are characterized by persistent feelings of sadness and despair. They are a fairly common form of mental illness (see Chapter 15). Elevated rates of depression have been found among patients suffering from heart disease. However, most experts used to explain this correlation by asserting that being diagnosed with heart disease makes people depressed. More recent evidence, though, suggests that the causal relations may be just the opposite—*that the emotional dysfunction of depression may cause heart disease* (Frasure-Smith & Lesperance, 2005). This issue brings us to our Featured Study for this chapter, which examined the relationship between depression and cardiac health.

Is Depression a Risk Factor for Heart Disease?

FEATURED STUDY

SOURCE: Pennix, B. W. J. H., Beekman, A. T. F., Honig, A., Deeg, D. J. H., Schoevers, R. A., van Eijk, J. T. M., & van Tilburg, W. (2001). Depression and cardiac mortality: Results from a community-based longitudinal survey. *Archives of General Psychiatry, 58,* 221–227.

In the 1990s, researchers began to suspect that depression might increase vulnerability to heart disease. A correlation between depression and coronary risk was reported in several studies. Because of the importance of this issue, additional studies have been needed to replicate the finding in different types of samples and to get a more precise reading on the *degree* to which depression elevates coronary risk. Previous studies yielded conflicting results about whether depression elevates cardiac risk for healthy individuals or only among people who already have heart disease. Thus, the present study examined the impact of depression on cardiac mortality in people with and without preexisting coronary disease.

Method

Participants. The sample was made up of 2847 men and women between the ages of 55 and 85 who were participating in an ongoing study of aging based in Amsterdam. The subjects were a randomly selected sample of older persons drawn from eleven municipalities in the Netherlands. The mean age of the participants was 70.5, and 52% were female.

Procedure and measures. The study used a longitudinal design (see Chapter 11), which entailed following the participants' health and mortality over a period of four years. Subjects were carefully screened for the existence of cardiac disease at the beginning of the study. Depressed subjects were identified through a two-step process. First, all the participants completed a widely used twenty-item self-report measure of depression. Those who scored above a standard cutoff on this scale were evaluated 4 weeks later with a diagnostic interview. Those who met the criteria for a diagnosis of depressive disorder (based on the interview) were categorized as suffering from *major depression.* The remaining subjects who had scored above the cutoff on the screening scale but who did not meet the criteria for a full-fledged depressive disorder were categorized as suffering from *minor depression.* The key dependent variable at the end of the study was the cardiac mortality rate among the subjects, which was based on tracking death certificates in the eleven municipalities where the participants resided.

Results

At the beginning of the study, 450 of the 2847 participants were found to have cardiac disease. Among these subjects, the cardiac mortality rate was elevated for those who had been diagnosed with either minor or major depression (see **Figure 14.13a**). Similar trends were observed among the remaining 2397 subjects who were free of cardiac disease when the study was initiated (see **Figure 14.13b**). The risk trends for both groups remained largely the same even after statistical adjustments were made to control for confounding variables, such as age, sex, weight, and smoking history.

Discussion

The increased cardiac mortality rate associated with depression was fairly similar in subjects with and without preexisting cardiac disease. For both groups, major depression roughly tripled subjects' risk of cardiac death. The findings for subjects without preexisting cardiac disease were especially important. Given that these subjects' depressive disorders preceded their cardiac disease, one cannot argue that their heart disease caused their depression. It's far more likely that depression somehow contributed to the emergence of cardiac disease in these subjects.

Comment

This study is representative of a rich research tradition in health psychology in which various psychological factors (depression in this case) are examined in relation to health outcomes. These studies are crucial to our understanding of the determinants of wellness and disease. They illustrate the importance of correlational research, since predictors of disease generally cannot be studied using the experimental method.

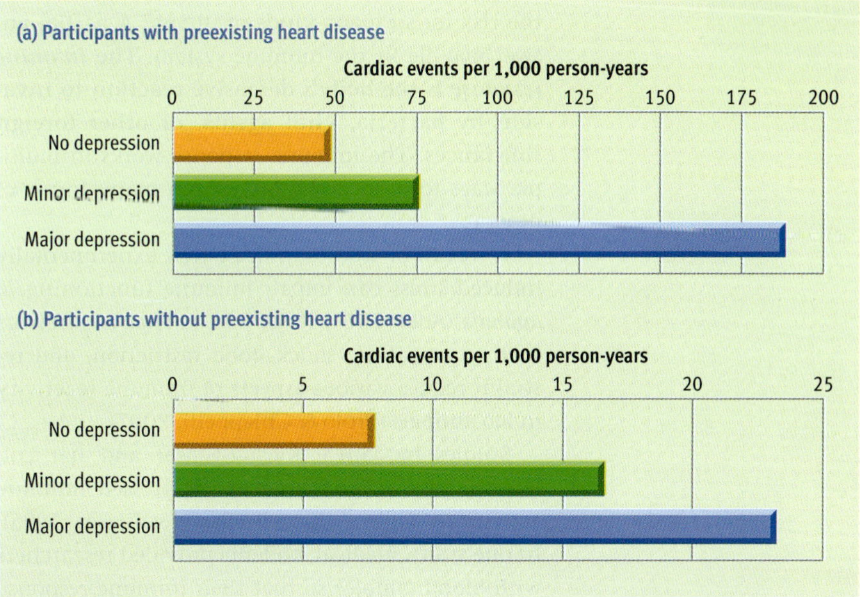

© Cengage Learning 2013

Figure 14.13

Depression and heart disease. These data show how minor and major depression were associated with elevated cardiac mortality rates among both participants with preexisting heart disease **(a)** and participants who were free of heart disease at the beginning of the study **(b)**. (Based on Pennix et al. 2001)

A more recent study of almost 20,000 people who were initially free of heart disease reported similar results (Surtees et al., 2008). Participants who suffered from depression were 2.7 times more likely to die of heart disease during the follow-up period than people who were not depressed. Overall, studies have found that depression roughly doubles one's chances of developing heart disease (Herbst et al., 2007; Lett et al., 2004).

Stress, Other Diseases, and Immune Functioning

The development of questionnaires to measure life stress has allowed researchers to look for—and find—correlations between stress and a variety of diseases. For example, researchers have found an association between life stress and the course of rheumatoid arthritis (Davis et al., 2008). Other studies have connected stress to the development of diabetes (Landel-Graham, Yount, & Rudnicki, 2003), herpes (Padgett & Sheridan, 2000), fibromyalgia (Wood, 2007), and flare-ups of irritable bowel syndrome (Blanchard & Keefer, 2003).

These are just a handful of representative examples of studies relating stress to physical diseases. **Table 14.3** provides a longer list of health problems that have been linked to stress. Many of these stress-illness connections are based on tentative or inconsistent findings. Still, the sheer length and diversity of the list is remarkable. Why should stress increase the risk for so many kinds of illness? A partial answer may lie in the immune system. **The *immune response* is the body's defensive reaction to invasion by bacteria, viral agents, or other foreign substances.** The immune response works in multiple ways to protect the body from many forms of disease.

Table 14.3 Health Problems That May Be Linked to Stress

Health Problem	Representative Evidence
AIDS	Stetler et al. (2005)
Asthma	Lehrer et al. (2002)
Cancer	Dalton & Johansen (2005)
Chronic back pain	Mitchell et al. (2009)
Common cold	Cohen (2005)
Complications of pregnancy	Dunkel-Schetter et al. (2001)
Heart disease	Bekkouche et al. (2011)
Diabetes	Landel-Graham, Yount, & Rudnicki (2003)
Epileptic seizures	Kelly & Schramke (2000)
Herpes virus	Pedersen, Bovbjerg, & Zachariae (2011)
Hypertension	Esler, Schwarz, & Alvarenga (2008)
Hyperthyroidism	Yang, Liu, & Zang (2000)
Inflammatory bowel disease	Searle & Bennett (2001)
Migraine headaches	Sauro & Becker (2009)
Multiple sclerosis	Mitsonis et al. (2006)
Periodontal disease	Antoniou et al. (2005)
Premenstrual distress	Stanton et al. (2002)
Rheumatoid arthritis	Davis et al. (2008)
Skin disorders	Arnold (2000)
Stroke	Harmsen et al. (1990)
Ulcers	Levenstein (2002)
Vaginal infections	Williams & Deffenbacher (1983)

© Cengage Learning 2013

A wealth of studies indicate that experimentally induced stress can impair immune functioning *in animals* (Ader, 2001; Rose, 2007). That is, stressors such as crowding, shock, food restriction, and restraint reduce various aspects of immune reactivity in lab animals (Prolo & Chiappelli, 2007).

Studies by Janice Kiecolt-Glaser and her colleagues have related stress to suppressed immune activity *in humans* (Kiecolt-Glaser & Glaser, 1995). In one study, medical students provided researchers with blood samples so that their immune response could be assessed (Kiecolt-Glaser et al., 1984). The students provided the baseline sample a month before final exams, then contributed the "high-stress" sample on the first day of their finals. The subjects also responded to the SRRS as a measure of recent stress. What were the results? Reduced levels of immune activity were found during the extremely stressful finals week. Reduced immune activity was also correlated with higher scores on the SRRS. In another study, investigators exposed quarantined volunteers to respiratory viruses that cause the common cold and found that those under high stress were more likely to be infected by the viruses (Cohen, Tyrell, & Smith, 1993).

Research has focused mainly on the link between stress and immune suppression. However, studies have shown that other important connections exist between immune function and vulnerability to illness. When the immune system responds to infection or injury it may release proinflammatory cytokines. Cytokines are proteins that "orchestrate a number of the immune activities that play a role in killing the pathogen and repairing damaged tissue" (Kemeny, 2007, p. 94). Exposure to long-term stress can sometimes foster persistent overproduction of proinflammatory cytokines, thereby promoting chronic inflammation (Christian et al., 2009; Robles, Glaser, & Kiecolt-Glaser, 2005).

Scientists have only begun to fully appreciate the potential ramifications of this chronic inflammation in recent years. As we noted earlier, inflammation has recently been recognized as a major factor in the development of heart disease. But that's not all. Research has also shown that chronic inflammation contributes to a diverse array of diseases, including arthritis, osteoporosis, respiratory diseases, diabetes, Alzheimer's disease, and some types of cancer (Feuerstein et al., 2007). Thus, chronic inflammation resulting from immune system dysregulation may be another key mechanism underlying the association between stress and wide variety of diseases.

Sizing Up the Link Between Stress and Illness

A wealth of evidence shows that stress is related to physical health. Converging lines of evidence even suggest that stress contributes to the *causation* of illness (Cohen, Janicki-Deverts, & Miller, 2007; Pedersen, Bobvjerg, & Zachariae, 2011). But we have to put this intriguing finding in perspective. The vast majority of the relevant research is correlational. It can't demonstrate *conclusively* that stress causes illness (Smith & Gallo, 2001). Subjects' elevated levels of stress and illness could both be due to a third variable, perhaps some aspect of personality (see **Figure 14.14**). For instance, some evidence suggests that neuroticism may make people overly prone to interpret events as stressful and overly prone to interpret unpleasant sensations as symptoms of illness. This tendency would inflate the correlation between stress and illness (Espejo et al., 2011).

In spite of methodological problems favoring inflated correlations, the research in this area consistently indicates that the *strength* of the relationship between stress and health is *modest*. The correlations typically fall in the .20s and .30s (Cohen, Kessler, & Gordon, 1995). Clearly, stress is not an irresistible force that produces inevitable effects on health. Actually, this fact should come as no surprise, as stress is but one factor operating in a complex network of biopsychosocial determinants of health. Other key factors include one's genetic endowment, exposure to infectious agents and environmental toxins, nutrition, exercise, alcohol and drug use, smoking, use of medical care, and cooperation with medical advice. Furthermore, some people handle stress better than others. It is this matter, in fact, that we turn to next.

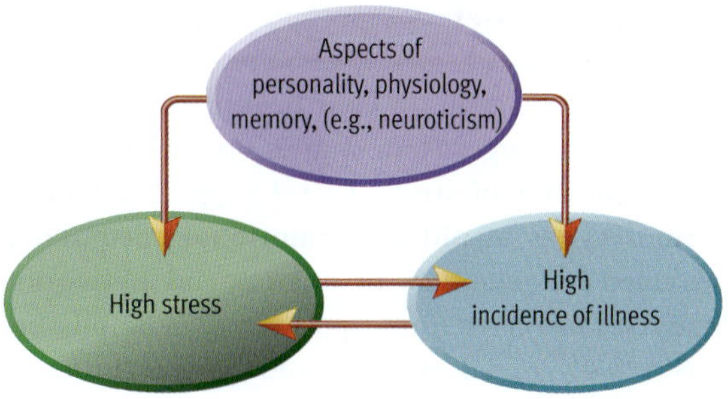

Figure 14.14
The stress-illness correlation. One or more aspects of personality, physiology, or memory could play the role of a postulated third variable in the relationship between high stress and a high incidence of illness. For example, neuroticism may lead some subjects to view more events as stressful and to remember more illness, thus inflating the apparent correlation between stress and illness. © Cengage Learning 2013

REVIEW OF KEY LEARNING GOALS

14.11 The Type A personality has been implicated as a contributing cause of coronary heart disease. But the evidence has been equivocal. Recent research suggests that hostility may be the most toxic element of the Type A syndrome.

14.12 Transient, stress-induced emotional reactions can elicit cardiac symptoms. Although depression can be a result of heart disease, research also suggests that depression can increase one's risk for cardiovascular disease. The Featured Study found that depression was a predictor of increased cardiac mortality among initially healthy individuals.

14.13 Stress appears to play a role in a number of diseases, perhaps because it can temporarily suppress the effectiveness of the immune system. Exposure to long-term stress can also promote chronic inflammation. Although there's little doubt that stress can contribute to the development of physical illness, the link between stress and illness is modest. Stress is only one factor in a complex network of biopsychosocial variables that shape health.

Factors Moderating the Impact of Stress

KEY LEARNING GOALS

14.14 Understand how social support moderates the impact of stress.

14.15 Identify two personality factors related to stress resistance and health.

Some people seem to be able to withstand the ravages of stress better than others (Holohan & Moos, 1994). Why? Because a number of *moderator variables* can lessen the impact of stress on physical and mental health. We'll look at three key moderator variables—social support, optimism, and conscientiousness—to shed light on individual differences in how well people tolerate stress.

Social Support

Friends may be good for your health! This startling conclusion emerges from studies on social support as a moderator of stress. ***Social support* refers to various types of aid and emotional sustenance provided by members of one's social networks.** Many studies have found positive correlations between high social support and greater immune functioning (Uchino, Uno, & Holt-Lunstad, 1999). In contrast, the opposite of social support—loneliness and social isolation—was found to predict reduced immune responding in a study of college students (Pressman et al., 2005). In recent decades, a vast number of studies have found evidence that social support is favorably related to physical health (Taylor, 2007; Uchino & Birmingham, 2011).

The positive effects of social support are strong enough to have an impact on participants' mortality! A recent meta-analysis of the results of 148 studies reported that solid social support increased people's odds of survival by roughly 50% (Holt-Lunstad, Smith, & Layton, 2010). The strength of social support's impact on mortality was surprising. To put this finding in perspective, the researchers compared the effect size of social support on mortality to other established risk factors. They note that the negative effect of inadequate social support is greater than the negative effects of being obese, not exercising, drinking excessively, and smoking (up to 15 cigarettes per day).

Recent research suggests that cultural disparities exist in the type of social support that people prefer. Studies have found that Asians and Asian Americans are reluctant to seek support from others and that they assert that social support is not all that helpful to them (Kim et al., 2006; Taylor et al., 2004). In an effort to shed light on this puzzling observation, Shelley Taylor and colleagues (2007) discovered that Asians can benefit from social support, but they prefer a different kind of support than Americans. Taylor et al. (2007) distinguish between *explicit social support* (overt emotional solace and instrumental aid from others) and *implicit social support* (the comfort that comes from knowing that one has access to close others who will be supportive). Research has shown that Americans generally prefer and pursue explicit social support. In contrast, Asians do not feel comfortable seeking explicit social support because they worry about the strain it will place on their friends and family (Kim, Sherman, & Taylor, 2008). But Asians do benefit from the implicit support that results when they spend time with close others (without discussing their problems) and when they remind themselves that they belong to valued social groups that would be supportive if needed.

© Lucky Business/Shutterstock

Optimism and Conscientiousness

A sizable body of research also suggests that your *personality* can influence your health. One crucial personality trait is optimism. ***Optimism* is a generalized tendency to consistently expect good outcomes.** Several studies have found a correlation between optimism and relatively good physical health (Rasmussen, Scheier, & Greenhouse, 2009). Researchers have also found that optimism is associated with more effective immune functioning (Segerstrom & Sephton, 2010). And a retrospective study of people born many decades ago, found an association between optimism and increased longevity (Peterson et al., 1998). Why is optimism beneficial to health? Research suggests that optimists cope with stress in more adaptive ways than pessimists (Carver, Scheier, & Segerstrom, 2010). Optimists are more likely to engage in action-oriented, problem-focused coping. They are more willing than pessimists to seek social support. They are also more likely to emphasize the positive in their appraisals of stressful events. In comparison, pessimists are more likely to deal with stress by giving up or engaging in denial or wishful thinking.

Optimism is not the only personality trait that has been examined as a possible moderator of physical health. Howard Friedman and his colleagues have found evidence that *conscientiousness,* one of the Big Five personality traits discussed in Chapter 12, may have an impact on physical health (Kern & Friedman, 2008; Martin, Friedman, & Schwartz, 2007). They have related personality measures to longevity in the gifted individuals first studied by Lewis Terman (see Chapter 9), who have been followed closely by researchers since 1921. Data were available on six personality traits, which were measured when the subjects were children. The one trait that predicted greater longevity was conscientiousness. Why does conscientiousness promote longevity? According to Friedman (2007), several considerations may contribute. For example, conscientious people may tend to gravitate to healthy environments, and they may show less reactivity to stress. But the key consideration appears to be that conscientiousness fosters better health habits. People who are high in conscientiousness are less likely than others to exhibit unhealthy habits, such as excessive drinking, drug abuse, dangerous driving, smoking, overeating, and risky sexual practices (Bogg & Roberts, 2004; Roberts, Walton, & Bogg, 2005).

REVIEW OF KEY LEARNING GOALS

14.14 There are individual differences in how much stress people can tolerate without experiencing ill effects. Social support is a key moderator of the relationship between stress and both physical and mental health. Studies have even found that social support is related to mortality. Asians prefer implicit social support whereas Americans prefer explicit social support.

14.15 Optimism is associated with relatively good physical health. Optimism may lead to more effective coping with stress, whereas pessimism has been related to passive coping. A study of Terman's sample of gifted children suggests that conscientiousness is associated with greater longevity. Conscientiousness appears to be related to better health habits.

Health-Impairing Behavior

KEY LEARNING GOALS

14.16 Explain the negative impact of smoking on health.

14.17 Discuss how and why lack of exercise is related to physical health.

14.18 Clarify the relationship between behavioral factors and AIDS.

14.19 Understand how health-impairing lifestyles develop.

Some people seem determined to dig an early grave for themselves. They do precisely those things that are bad for their health. For example, some people drink heavily even though they know that they're damaging their liver. Others eat all the wrong foods even though they know that they're increasing their risk of a second heart attack. Behavior that's downright *self-destructive* is surprisingly common. In this section, we'll discuss how health is affected by smoking, exercise, and drug use. We'll also look at behavioral factors in AIDS. Finally, we'll discuss *why* people develop health-impairing lifestyles.

Smoking

The percentage of people who smoke has declined noticeably since the mid-1960s (see **Figure 14.15**). Nonetheless, about 23% of adult men and 18% of adult women in the United States continue to smoke regularly. Moreover, smoking is even more common in many other societies.

The evidence clearly shows that smokers face a much greater risk of premature death than nonsmokers. For example, the average smoker has an estimated life expectancy *13–14 years shorter* than that of a similar nonsmoker (Schmitz & Delaune, 2005). The overall risk is positively correlated with the number of cigarettes smoked and their tar and nicotine content. Cigar smoking, which has increased dramatically in recent years, elevates health risks almost as much as cigarette smoking (Baker et al., 2000).

Why are mortality rates higher for smokers? Smoking increases the likelihood of developing a surprisingly large range of diseases (Schmitz & Delaune, 2005; Woloshin, Schwartz, & Welch, 2002). Lung cancer and heart disease kill the largest number of smokers. However, smokers also have an elevated risk for oral, bladder, and kidney cancer, as well as cancers of the larynx, esophagus, and pancreas; for arteriosclerosis, hypertension, stroke, and other cardiovascular diseases; and for bronchitis, emphysema, and other pulmonary diseases. Most smokers know about the risks associated with tobacco use. Interestingly though, they tend to underestimate the actual risks as applied to themselves (Ayanian & Cleary, 1999). They also tend to overestimate the likelihood that they can quit smoking

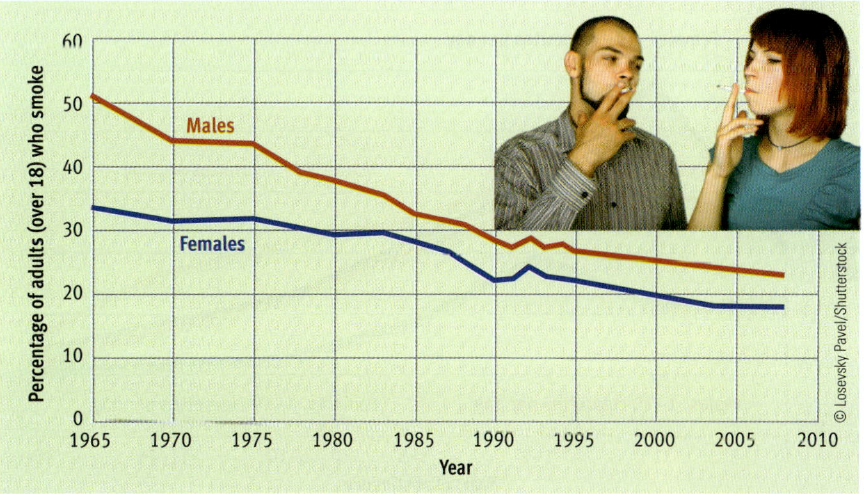

© Cengage Learning 2013

Figure 14.15

The prevalence of smoking in the United States. This graph shows how the percentage of U.S. adults who smoke has declined steadily since the mid-1960s. Although considerable progress has been made, smoking still accounts for a huge number of premature deaths each year. (Based on data from the Centers for Disease Control and Prevention) when they decide to (Weinstein, Slovic, & Gibson, 2004).

© Tetra Images/Alamy

The dangers of smoking are not limited to smokers themselves. Family members and co-workers who spend a lot of time around smokers are exposed to *second-hand smoke* or *environmental tobacco smoke.* Second-hand smoke can increase their risk for a variety of illnesses, including lung cancer (Vineis, 2005) and heart disease (Venn & Britton, 2007). Young children may be particularly vulnerable to the effects of second-hand smoke (USDHHS, 2006).

Studies show that if people can give up smoking, their health risks decline reasonably quickly (Kenfield et al., 2008; Williams et al., 2002; see **Figure 14.16**). Unfortunately, it's difficult to give up cigarettes. People who enroll in formal smoking cessation programs are only slightly more successful than people who try to quit on their own (Swan, Hudmon, Khroyan, 2003). Long-term success rates are in the vicinity of only 25%. Some studies report even lower figures. Nonetheless, the fact that there are tens of millions of ex-smokers in the United States indicates that it's possible to quit smoking successfully. Many people fail several times before they eventually succeed. Evidence suggests that the readiness to give up smoking builds gradually as people cycle through periods of abstinence and relapse (Prochaska, 1994; Prochaska et al., 2004).

Reality CHECK

Misconception

If you can't quit smoking the first time you try, you are unlikely to succeed in the future.

Reality

People attempting to give up smoking usually fail several times before eventually succeeding. Hence, if your first effort to quit smoking ends in failure, you should not give up hope—try again in a few weeks or a few months.

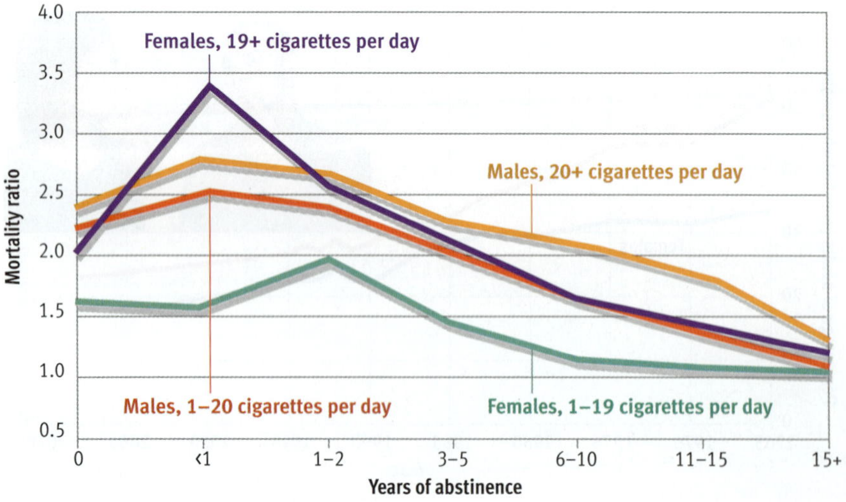

Figure 14.16

Quitting smoking and health risk. Research suggests that various types of health risks associated with smoking decline gradually after people give up tobacco. The data shown here, from the 1990 U.S. Surgeon General's report on smoking, illustrate the overall effects on mortality rates. (Based on data from U.S. Department of Health and Human Services, 1990) © Cengage Learning 2013

© Jim Cummins/Getty Images

Lack of Exercise

Considerable evidence links lack of exercise to poor health. Research indicates that regular exercise is associated with increased longevity. For example, a recent study of over 15,000 men found that those who were high in fitness had a 70% reduction in mortality compared to those who were low in fitness (Kokkinos et al., 2008). A meta-analysis of thirty-three studies with over 100,000 male and female participants yielded similar conclusions (Kodama et al., 2009). Unfortunately, physical fitness appears to be declining in the United States. Only about one-third of American adults get an adequate amount of regular exercise (Carlson et al., 2010).

Why would exercise help people live longer? For one thing, an appropriate exercise program can enhance cardiovascular fitness and thereby reduce susceptibility to deadly cardiovascular problems (Zoeller, 2007). Second, exercise may indirectly reduce one's risk for a variety of obesity-related health problems, such as diabetes and respiratory difficulties (Corsica & Perri, 2003). Third, recent studies suggest that exercise can help diminish chronic inflammation, which is thought to contribute to quite a variety of diseases (Flynn, McFarlin, & Markofski, 2007). Fourth, exercise can serve as a buffer that reduces the potentially damaging physical effects of stress (Plante, Caputo, & Chizmar, 2000). This buffering effect may occur because people high in fitness show less physiological reactivity to stress than those who are less fit (Forcier et al., 2006). If these payoffs weren't enough to get people hustling to the gym, recent studies have turned up a new, unexpected benefit of exercise—it can facilitate the generation of new brain cells (Cotman, Berchtold, & Christie, 2007; Pereira et al., 2007). As noted earlier in the chapter (see p. 573), *neurogenesis* appears to be an important process that can be suppressed by stress. The finding that this neurodevelopmental process can be promoted by simple exercise may turn out to have profound implications.

Alcohol and Drug Use

PSYKTREK 4c

Although there is some thought-provoking evidence that *moderate* drinking may offer some protection against cardiovascular disease (Brien et al., 2011; Ronksley et al., 2011), heavy consumption of alcohol clearly increases one's risk for many diseases (Johnson & Ait-Daoud, 2005). Recreational drug use is another common health-impairing habit. The risks associated with the use of various drugs were discussed in Chapter 5. Unlike smoking, poor eating habits, and inactivity, drugs can kill directly and immediately when they are taken in an overdose or when they impair the user enough to cause an accident. In the long run, alcohol and various recreational drugs may also elevate one's risk for infectious diseases; respiratory, pulmonary, and cardiovascular diseases; liver disease; gastrointestinal problems; cancer; neurological disorders; and pregnancy complications (see Chapter 5).

Behavior and AIDS

Some of the most problematic links between behavior and health may be those related to AIDS. AIDS stands for ***acquired immune deficiency syndrome*, a disorder in which the immune system is gradually weakened and eventually disabled by the human immunodeficiency virus (HIV).** Being infected with the HIV virus is *not* equivalent to having AIDS. AIDS is in fact the final stage of the HIV infection process, typically manifested years after the original infection (Carey & Vanable, 2003). With the onset of AIDS, one is left virtually defenseless against a variety of infectious agents. AIDS inflicts its harm indirectly by opening the door to other diseases. The symptoms of AIDS vary widely, depending on the specific set of diseases that one develops (Cunningham & Selwyn, 2005). Unfortunately, the worldwide prevalence of this deadly disease continues to increase at an alarming rate, especially in certain regions of Africa (UNAIDS, 2009).

Prior to 1996–1997, the average length of survival for people after the onset of the AIDS syndrome was about 18 to 24 months. Encouraging advances in the treatment of AIDS with drug regimens referred to as *highly active antiretroviral therapy (HAART)* hold out promise for *substantially* longer survival (Anthony & Bell, 2008; Bhaskaran et al., 2008). But these drugs have been rushed into service, and their long-term efficacy is yet to be determined. Medical experts are concerned that the general public has gotten the impression that these treatments have transformed AIDS from a fatal disease to a manageable one. This may be a premature conclusion, as HIV strains are evolving.

Transmission

The HIV virus is transmitted through person-to-person contact involving the exchange of bodily fluids, primarily semen and blood. The two principal modes of transmission in the United States have been sexual contact and the sharing of needles by intravenous (IV) drug users. In the United States, sexual transmission has occurred primarily among gay and bisexual men. However, heterosexual transmission has increased in recent years (Centers for Disease Control, 2011). In the world as a whole, infection through heterosexual relations has been much more common from the beginning. In heterosexual relations, male-to-female transmission is estimated to be about eight times more likely than female-to-male transmission (Ickovics, Thayaparan, & Ethier, 2001). The HIV virus can be found in the tears and saliva of infected individuals. However, the concentrations are low, and there is no evidence that the infection can be spread through casual contact. Even most forms of noncasual contact, including kissing, hugging, and sharing food with infected individuals, are safe.

One problem related to transmission is that many young heterosexuals who are sexually active with a variety of partners foolishly downplay their risk for HIV. They greatly underestimate the probability that their sexual partners previously may have used IV drugs or had unprotected sex with an infected individual. Also, many young people inaccurately believe that prospective sexual partners who carry the HIV virus will exhibit telltale signs of illness. In reality, many HIV carriers do not know themselves that they are HIV-positive. In one study that screened over 5000 men for HIV, 77% of those who tested HIV-positive were previously unaware of their infection (MacKellar et al., 2005).

Prevention

The behavioral changes that minimize the risk of developing AIDS are fairly straightforward. Making the changes, though, is often much easier said than done. In all groups, the more sexual partners a person has, the higher the risk that one will be exposed to the HIV virus. Thus, people can reduce their risk by having sexual contacts with fewer partners and by using condoms to control the exchange of semen. It's also important to curtail certain sexual practices (in particular, anal sex) that increase the probability of semen/blood mixing. The 1980s and early 1990s saw considerable progress toward wider use of safe sex practices. Yet new cohorts of young people appear to be much less concerned about the risk of HIV infection than the generation that witnessed the original emergence of AIDS (Jaffe, Valdiserri, & De Cock, 2007). In particular, experts are concerned that recent advances in treatment may lead to more casual attitudes about risky sexual practices. This development would not bode well for public health efforts to slow the spread of AIDS (Kalichman et al., 2007; van Kesteren, Hospers, & Kok, 2007).

How Does Health-Impairing Behavior Develop?

It may seem puzzling that people behave in self-destructive ways. How does this happen? Several factors are involved. First, many health-impairing habits creep up on people slowly. For instance, drug use may grow imperceptibly over years, or exercise habits may decline ever so gradually. Second, many health-impairing habits involve activities that are quite pleasant at the time. Actions such as eating favorite foods, smoking cigarettes, or getting "high" are potent reinforcing events. Third, the risks associated with most health-impairing habits are chronic diseases such as cancer that usually lie 10, 20, or 30 years down the road. It's relatively easy to ignore risks that lie in the distant future.

Finally, people have a curious tendency to underestimate the risks that accompany their own health-impairing behaviors while viewing the risks associated with others' self-destructive behaviors much more accurately (Weinstein, 2003; Weinstein & Klein, 1996). Many people are well aware of the dangers associated with certain habits. Yet when it's time to apply this information to themselves, they often discount it. They figure, for instance, that smoking will lead to cancer or a heart attack in *someone else*.

So far, we've seen that physical health may be affected by stress and by aspects of lifestyle. Next, we'll look at the importance of how people react to physical symptoms, health problems, and health care efforts.

REVIEW OF KEY LEARNING GOALS

14.16 Smokers have much higher mortality rates than nonsmokers because they are more vulnerable to a host of diseases. Health risks decline reasonably quickly for people who give up smoking, but quitting is difficult and relapse rates are high.

14.17 Regular exercise can reduce one's risk for cardiovascular diseases, diminish chronic inflammation, and buffer the effects of stress. Recent research also indicates that exercise can facilitate neurogenesis.

14.18 Aspects of behavior influence one's risk of AIDS, which is transmitted through person-to-person contact involving the exchange of bodily fluids, primarily semen and blood. One problem related to transmission is that many young heterosexuals who are sexually active with a variety of partners foolishly downplay their risk for HIV.

14.19 Health-impairing habits tend to develop gradually and often involve pleasant activities. The risks may be easy to ignore because they lie in the distant future and because people tend to underestimate risks that apply to them personally.

KEY LEARNING GOALS

14.20 Discuss the major problem in deciding to seek medical treatment, and describe some barriers to effective patient-provider communication.

14.21 Review the extent to which people tend to adhere to medical advice and some factors that influence adherence.

Reactions to Illness

Some people respond to physical symptoms and illnesses by ignoring warning signs of developing diseases. Others engage in active coping efforts to conquer their diseases. Let's examine the decision to seek medical treatment, communication with health providers, and compliance with medical advice.

Deciding to Seek Treatment

Have you ever experienced nausea, diarrhea, stiffness, headaches, cramps, chest pains, or sinus problems? Of course you have; we all experience some of these problems periodically. However, whether someone views these sensations as *symptoms* is a matter of individual interpretation. When two persons experience the same unpleasant sensations, one may shrug them off as a nuisance while the other may rush to a physician (Martin & Leventhal, 2004). Studies suggest that people who are relatively high in anxiety and neuroticism tend to report more symptoms of illness than others do (Petrie & Pennebaker, 2004).

The biggest problem in regard to treatment seeking is the tendency of many people to delay the pursuit of needed professional consultation. Delays can be critical because early diagnosis and quick intervention may facilitate more effective treatment of many health problems (Petrie & Pennebaker, 2004). Unfortunately, procrastination is the norm even when people are faced with a medical emergency, such as a heart attack (Martin & Leventhal, 2004). Why do people dawdle in the midst of a crisis? Robin DiMatteo (1991), a leading expert on patient behavior, mentions a number of reasons. She notes that people delay because they often (a) misinterpret and downplay the significance of their symptoms, (b) fret about looking silly if the problem turns out to be nothing, (c) worry about "bothering" their physician, (d) are reluctant to disrupt their plans (to go out to dinner, see a movie, and so forth), and (e) waste time on trivial matters (such as taking a shower, gathering personal items, or packing clothes) before going to a hospital emergency room.

Communicating with Health Providers

A large portion of medical patients leave their doctors' offices not understanding what they have been told and what they are supposed to do (Johnson & Carlson, 2004). This situation is unfortunate. Good communication is a crucial requirement for sound medical decisions, informed choices about treatment, and appropriate follow-through by patients (Buckman, 2002; Haskard et al., 2008).

There are many barriers to effective provider-patient communication (DiMatteo, 1997; Marteau & Weinman, 2004). Economic realities dictate that medical visits are generally quite brief, allowing little time for discussion. Many providers use too much medical jargon and overestimate their patients' understanding of technical terms. Patients who are upset and worried about their illness may simply forget to report some symptoms or to ask questions they meant to ask. Other patients are evasive about their real concerns because they fear a serious diagnosis. Many patients are reluctant to challenge doctors' authority and are too passive in their interactions with providers.

What can you do to improve your communication with health care providers? The key is to not be a passive consumer of medical services (Ferguson, 1993; Kane, 1991).

© Allison Michael Orenstein/Getty Images

Communication between health care providers and patients tends to be far from optimal, for a variety of reasons.

Arrive at a medical visit on time. Have your questions and concerns prepared in advance. Try to be accurate and candid in replying to your doctor's questions. If you don't understand something the doctor says, don't be embarrassed about asking for clarification. If you have doubts about the suitability or feasibility of your doctor's recommendations, don't be afraid to voice them.

Adhering to Medical Advice

Many patients fail to follow the instructions they receive from physicians and other health care professionals. The evidence suggests that nonadherence to medical advice may occur 30% of the time when short-term treatments are prescribed for acute conditions. Nonadherence may occur 50% of the time when long-term treatments are needed for chronic illness (Johnson & Carlson, 2004). Nonadherence takes many forms. Patients may fail to begin a treatment regimen, may stop the regimen early, may reduce or increase the levels of treatment that were prescribed, or may be inconsistent and unreliable in following treatment procedures (Dunbar-Jacob & Schlenk, 2001). Such noncompliance is a major problem in our medical care system. It has been linked to increased sickness, treatment failures, and higher mortality (Christensen & Johnson, 2002; DiMatteo et al., 2002). Moreover, it wastes expensive medical visits and medications and increases hospital admissions, leading to enormous economic costs. DiMatteo (2004b) speculates that in the United States alone, nonadherence may be a $300 billion a year drain on the health care system.

Why don't people comply with the advice that they've sought out from highly regarded health care professionals? Physicians tend to attribute nonadherence to patients' personal characteristics. However, research indicates that personality traits and demographic factors are surprisingly unrelated to adherence rates (DiMatteo, 2004b; Marteau & Weinman, 2004). One factor that *is* related to adherence is patients' *social support*. Adherence is improved when patients have family members, friends, or co-workers who remind them and help them comply with treatment requirements (DiMatteo, 2004a). Several other considerations can adversely influence the likelihood of adherence (Dunbar-Jacob & Schlenk, 2001; Johnson & Carlson, 2004):

1. *Frequently, nonadherence is a result of the patient's failure to understand the instructions as given.* Highly trained professionals often forget that what seems obvious and simple to them may be obscure and complicated to many of their patients.

Courtesy of University of California, Riverside

Robin DiMatteo

"A person will not carry out a health behavior if significant barriers stand in the way, or if the steps interfere with favorite or necessary activities."

2. *Another key factor is how aversive or difficult the instructions are.* If the prescribed regimen is unpleasant, compliance will tend to decrease. And the more that following instructions interferes with routine behavior, the less probable it is that the patient will cooperate successfully.

3. *If a patient has a negative attitude toward a physician, the probability of nonadherence will increase.* When patients are unhappy with their interactions with the doctor, they're more likely to ignore the medical advice provided.

In response to the nonadherence problem, researchers have investigated many methods of increasing patients' adherence to medical advice. Interventions have included simplifying instructions, providing more rationale for instructions, reducing the complexity of treatment regimens, helping patients with emotional distress that undermines adherence, and training patients in the use of behavior modification strategies. All of these interventions can improve adherence. Their effects, though, tend to be modest (Christensen & Johnson, 2002; Roter et al., 1998).

REVIEW OF KEY LEARNING GOALS

14.20 People high in anxiety or neuroticism report more symptoms of illness than others. The biggest problem in regard to treatment seeking is the tendency of many people to delay the pursuit of needed treatment. There are many barriers to effective communication between patients and health care providers, such as brief visits, overdependence on medical jargon, and patients' evasiveness and forgetfulness.

14.21 Noncompliance with medical advice is a major problem, occurring some 30% of the time in the context of short-term treatments and 50% of the time in long-term treatments. The likelihood of nonadherence is greater when instructions are difficult to understand, when recommendations are difficult to follow, and when patients are unhappy with their doctor.

CONCEPT CHECK 14.4

Identifying the Contributions of Major Theorists and Researchers

Check your recall of the principal ideas of important theorists and researchers covered in this chapter by matching the people listed on the left with the appropriate contributions described on the right. If you need help, the crucial pages describing each person's ideas are listed in parentheses. Fill in the letters for your choices in the spaces provided on the left. You'll find the answers in Appendix A.

Major Theorists and Researchers

_______ 1. Robin DiMatteo (pp. 588–589)

_______ 2. Albert Ellis (p. 573)

_______ 3. Barbara Fredrickson (p. 569)

_______ 4. Meyer Friedman and Ray Rosenman (pp. 579–580)

_______ 5. Thomas Holmes and Richard Rahe (p. 566)

_______ 6. Richard Lazarus (p. 563)

_______ 7. Hans Selye (p. 571)

Key Ideas and Contributions

a. This theorist coined the term *stress* and described the general adaptation syndrome.

b. This individual showed that everyday hassles can be an important form of stress.

c. This research team devised the Social Readjustment Rating Scale and studied life change as a form of stress.

d. This research team is famous for describing the Type A personality and investigating its role in heart disease.

e. This psychologist's broaden-and-build theory has shed light on how positive emotions can promote resilience in the face of stress.

f. According to this theorist, catastrophic thinking causes, aggravates, and perpetuates emotional reactions to stress that are often unhealthy.

g. This expert on patient behavior has analyzed why people fail to seek medical treatment as promptly as they should.

Reflecting on the Chapter's Themes

KEY LEARNING GOALS

14.22 Identify the two unifying themes highlighted in this chapter.

Multifactorial Causation

Subjectivity of Experience

Which of our themes were prominent in this chapter? As you probably noticed, our discussion of stress and health illustrated multifactorial causation and the subjectivity of experience. As noted in Chapter 1, people tend to think simplistically, in terms of single causes. In recent years, the highly publicized research linking stress to health has led many people to point automatically to stress as an explanation for illness. In reality, stress has only a modest impact on physical health. Stress can increase the risk for illness, but health is governed by a dense network of factors. These factors include inherited vulnerabilities, physiological reactivity, exposure to infectious agents, health-impairing habits, reactions to symptoms, treatment-seeking behavior, compliance with medical advice, personality, and social support. In other words, stress is but one actor on a crowded stage. This should be apparent in **Figure 14.17**, which shows the multitude of biopsychosocial factors that jointly influence physical health, demonstrating multifactorial causation in all its complexity.

The subjectivity of experience was shown by the frequently repeated point that stress lies in the eye of the beholder. The same job promotion may be stressful for one person and invigorating for another. One person's pressure is another's challenge. When it comes to stress, objective reality is not nearly as important as subjective perceptions. More than anything else, the impact of stressful events seems to depend on how people view them. The critical importance of individual stress appraisals will continue to be apparent in the Personal Application on coping and stress management. Many stress management strategies depend on altering one's appraisals of events.

REVIEW OF KEY LEARNING GOALS

14.22 Two of our integrative themes were prominent in this chapter. First, we saw that behavior and health are influenced by multiple causes. Second, we saw that experience is highly subjective, as stress lies in the eye of the beholder.

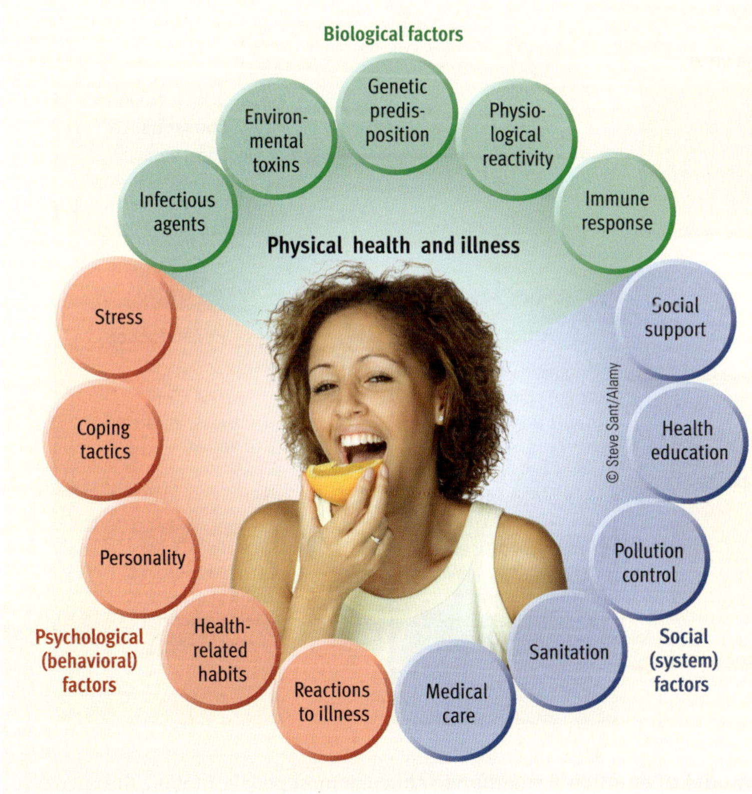

Figure 14.17

Biopsychosocial factors in health. Physical health can be influenced by a remarkably diverse set of variables, including biological, psychological, and social factors. The variety of factors that affect health provide an excellent example of multifactorial causation.

© Cengage Learning 2013

KEY LEARNING GOALS

14.23 Summarize Albert Ellis's ideas about controlling one's emotions.

14.24 Analyze the adaptive value of using humor, releasing pent-up emotions, and forgiving others.

14.25 Assess the adaptive value of relaxation and of increasing one's fitness.

Improving Coping and Stress Management

Answer the following "true" or "false."

____ **1** The key to managing stress is to avoid or circumvent it.

____ **2** It's best to suppress emotional reactions to stress.

____ **3** Laughing at one's problems is immature.

Courses and books on stress management have multiplied at a furious pace in the last couple of decades. They summarize experts' advice on how to cope with stress more effectively. How do these experts feel about the three statements above? As you'll see in this Application, most would agree that all three are false.

The key to managing stress does *not* lie in avoiding it. Stress is an inevitable element in the fabric of modern life. As Hans Selye (1973) noted, "Contrary to public opinion, we must not—and indeed can't—avoid stress" (p. 693). Thus, most stress management programs encourage people to confront stress rather than sidestep it. Doing so requires training people to engage in action-oriented, rational, reality-based *constructive coping*. Fortunately, research suggests that stress management training can be beneficial in reducing the potential negative effects of stress (Evers et al., 2006; Storch et al., 2007).

As we noted earlier, some coping tactics are more healthful than others. In this Application, we'll examine a variety of constructive coping tactics, beginning with Albert Ellis's ideas about changing one's appraisals of stressful events.

Reappraisal: Ellis's Rational Thinking

Albert Ellis is a prominent theorist who believes that people can short-circuit their emotional reactions to stress by altering their appraisals of stressful events. Ellis's insights about stress appraisal are the foundation for a widely used system of therapy, called *rational-emotive behavior therapy* (Ellis, 1977, 1987), and several popular books on effective coping (Ellis, 1985, 1999, 2001).

Ellis maintains that *you feel the way you think*. He argues that problematic emotional reactions are caused by negative self-talk, which he calls catastrophic thinking. ***Catastrophic thinking* involves unrealistically pessimistic appraisals of stress that exaggerate the magnitude of one's problems.** According to Ellis, people unwittingly believe that stressful events cause their emotional turmoil. However, he maintains that emotional reactions to personal setbacks are actually caused by overly negative appraisals of stressful events (see **Figure 14.18**).

Ellis theorizes that unrealistic appraisals of stress are derived from irrational assumptions that people hold. He maintains that if you scrutinize your catastrophic thinking, you'll find that your reasoning is based on a logically indefensible premise, such as "I must have approval from everyone" or "I must perform well in all endeavors." These faulty assumptions, which people often hold unconsciously, generate catastrophic thinking and emotional turmoil. How can you reduce your unrealistic appraisals of stress? Ellis asserts that you must learn (1) how to detect catastrophic thinking and (2) how to dispute the irrational assumptions that cause it.

Using Humor as a Stress Reducer

A number of years ago, the Chicago area experienced its worst flooding in about a century. Thousands of people saw their homes wrecked when two rivers spilled over their banks. As the waters receded, the flood

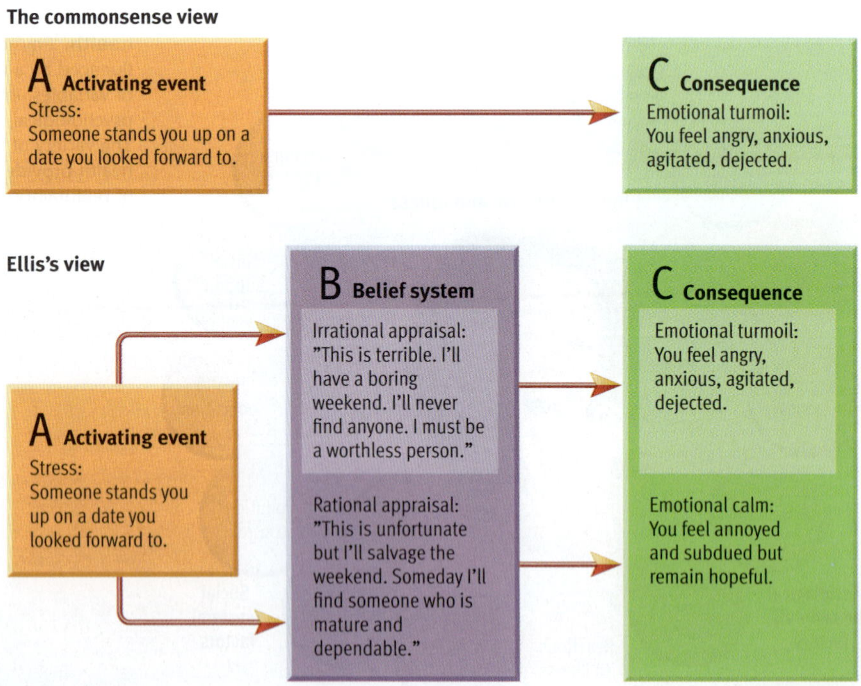

Figure 14.18

Albert Ellis's A-B-C model of emotional reactions. Although most people attribute their negative emotional reactions directly to negative events that they experience, Ellis argues that events themselves do *not* cause emotional distress; rather, distress is caused by the way people *think* about negative events. According to Ellis, the key to managing stress is to change one's appraisal of stressful events. © Cengage Learning 2013 victims returning to their homes were subjected to the inevitable TV interviews. A remarkable number of victims, surrounded by the ruins of their homes, *joked* about their misfortune. When the going gets tough, it may pay to laugh about it. In a study of coping styles, McCrae (1984) found that 40% of his subjects used humor to deal with stress.

Empirical evidence showing that humor moderates the impact of stress has been building over the last 25 years (Abel, 1998; Lefcourt, 2001, 2005). How does humor help reduce the effects of stress and promote wellness? Several explanations have been proposed (see **Figure 14.19**). One possibility is that humor affects appraisals of stressful events (Abel, 2002). Jokes can help people to put a less threatening spin on their trials and tribulations. Another possibility is that humor increases the experience of positive emotions (Martin, 2002). This can help people bounce back from stressful events (Tugade & Fredrickson, 2004). Another hypothesis is that a good sense of humor facilitates rewarding social interactions, which can promote social support, known to buffer the effects of stress (Martin, 2002). Finally, Lefcourt and colleagues (1995) argue that high-humor people may benefit from not taking themselves as seriously as low-humor people do. As they put it, "If persons do not regard themselves too seriously and do not have an inflated sense of self-importance, then defeats, embarrassments, and even tragedies should have less pervasive emotional consequences for them" (p. 375).

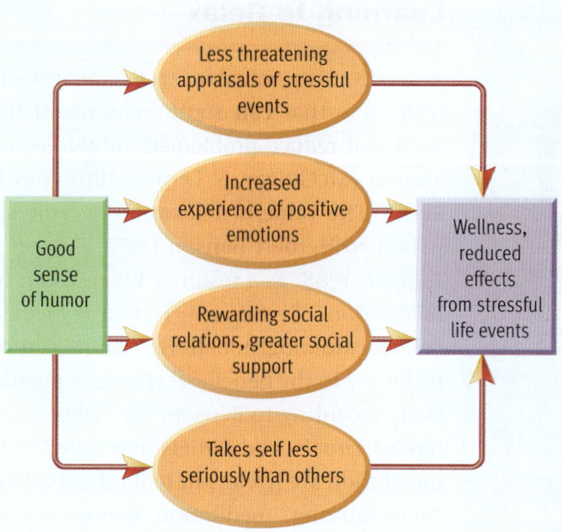

Figure 14.19

Possible explanations for the link between humor and wellness. Research suggests that a good sense of humor buffers the effects of stress and promotes wellness. Four hypothesized explanations for the link between humor and wellness are outlined in the middle column of this diagram. As you can see, humor may have a variety of beneficial effects.

© Cengage Learning 2013

Releasing Pent-Up Emotions and Forgiving Others

As we discussed in the main body of the chapter, stress often leads to emotional arousal. When this happens, there's merit in the commonsense notion that you should try to release the emotions welling up inside. Why? Because the physiological arousal that accompanies emotions can become problematic. For example, research suggests that people who inhibit the expression of emotions are somewhat more likely than other people to have elevated blood pressure (Jorgensen et al., 1996). Moreover, research suggests that efforts to actively suppress emotions result in increased stress and autonomic arousal (Butler et al., 2003; Gross, 2001). This, ultimately, leads to the experience of more negative emotions and fewer positive emotions (John & Gross, 2007).

Although there's no guarantee of it, you can sometimes reduce your physiological arousal by *expressing* your emotions. Evidence is accumulating that writing or talking about life's difficulties can be valuable in dealing with stress (Lyubomirsky, Sousa, & Dickerhoof, 2006; Smyth & Pennebaker, 1999). For example, in one study of college students, half the subjects were asked to write three essays about their difficulties in adjusting to college. The other half wrote three essays about superficial topics. The subjects who wrote about their personal problems enjoyed better health in the following months than the other subjects did (Pennebaker, Colder, & Sharp, 1990). Subsequent studies have replicated this finding and shown that emotional disclosure is associated with better immune functioning (Slatcher & Pennebaker, 2005; Smyth & Pennebaker, 2001). So, if you can find a

© Radhika Chalasani/Getty Images

People often turn to humor to help themselves cope during difficult times, as this photo taken in the aftermath of Hurricane Katrina illustrates. Research suggests that humor can help to reduce the negative impact of stressful events.

© Acey Harper/Time Life Pictures/Getty Images

In September 1994, Reg and Maggie Green were vacationing in Italy when their seven-year-old son Nicholas was shot and killed during a highway robbery. In an act of forgiveness that stunned Europe, the Greens chose to donate their son's organs, which went to seven Italians. The Greens, shown here five years after the incident, have weathered their horrific loss better than most, perhaps in part because of their willingness to forgive.

good listener, you may be able to discharge problematic emotions by letting your secret fears, misgivings, and suspicions spill out in a candid conversation.

People tend to experience hostility and other negative emotions when they feel "wronged"—that is, when they believe that the actions of another person were harmful, immoral, or unjust. People's natural inclination in such situations is either to seek revenge or to avoid further contact with the offender (McCullough, 2001). *Forgiving* someone involves counteracting these natural tendencies and releasing the person from further liability for his or her transgression. Research suggests that forgiving is associated with better adjustment and well-being (McCullough & Witvliet, 2002; Worthington & Scherer, 2004). These benefits include enhanced mood and reduced physical symptoms (Bono, McCullough, & Root, 2008). For example, in one study of divorced or permanently separated women reported by McCullough (2001), the extent to which the women had forgiven their former husbands was positively related to several measures of well-being.

Learning to Relax

Relaxation is a valuable stress management technique that can soothe emotional turmoil and reduce problematic physiological arousal (McGuigan & Lehrer, 2007; Smith, 2007). The value of relaxation became apparent to Herbert Benson (1975; Benson & Klipper, 1988) as a result of his research on meditation. Benson, a Harvard Medical School cardiologist, believes that relaxation is the key to the beneficial effects of meditation. According to Benson, the elaborate religious rituals and beliefs associated with meditation are irrelevant to its effects. After "demystifying" meditation, Benson set out to devise a simple, nonreligious procedure that could provide similar benefits. He calls his procedure the *relaxation response*. Although there are several other worthwhile approaches to relaxation training, we'll examine Benson's procedure, as its simplicity makes it especially useful. From his study of a variety of relaxation techniques, Benson concluded that four factors promote effective relaxation:

1. *A quiet environment.* It's easiest to induce the relaxation response in a distraction-free environment. After you become experienced with the relaxation response, you may be able to practice it in a crowded subway. Initially, however, you should practice it in a quiet, calm place.

2. *A mental device.* To shift attention inward and keep it there, you need to focus your attention on a constant stimulus, such as a sound or word recited repetitively.

3. *A passive attitude.* It's important not to get upset when your attention strays to distracting thoughts. You must realize that such distractions are inevitable. Whenever your mind wanders from your attentional focus, calmly redirect attention to your mental device.

4. *A comfortable position.* Reasonable body comfort is essential to avoid a major source of potential distraction. Simply sitting up straight generally works well. Lying down is too conducive to sleep.

Benson's simple relaxation procedure is described in **Figure 14.20**. For full benefit, it should be practiced daily.

1. Sit quietly in a comfortable position.
2. Close your eyes.
3. Deeply relax all your muscles, beginning at your feet and progressing up to your face. Keep them relaxed.
4. Breathe through your nose. Become aware of your breathing. As you breathe out, say the word "one" silently to yourself. For example, breath in . . . out, "one"; in . . . out, "one"; and so forth. Breathe easily and naturally.
5. Continue for 10 to 20 minutes. You may open your eyes to check the time, but do not use an alarm. When you finish, sit quietly for several minutes, at first with your eyes closed and later with your eyes opened. Do not stand up for a few minutes.
6. Do not worry about whether you are successful in achieving a deep level of relaxation. Maintain a passive attitude and permit relaxation to occur at its own pace. When distracting thoughts occur, try to ignore them by not dwelling on them, and return to repeating "one." With practice, the response should come with little effort. Practice the technique once or twice daily but not within two hours after any meal, since digestive processes seem to interfere with the elicitation of the relaxation response.

© Paul Francis Photo

Figure 14.20

Benson's relaxation procedure. Herbert Benson's relaxation procedure is described here. According to Benson, his simple relaxation response can yield benefits similar to meditation. To experience these benefits, you should practice the procedure daily.

SOURCE: Relaxation procedure (pp. 14–15) from Benson, H., & Klipper, M. Z. (1975, 1988). *The relaxation response.* New York: Morrow. Copyright © 1975 by William Morrow & Co. Reprinted by permission of HarperCollins Publishers.

© Cengage Learning 2013

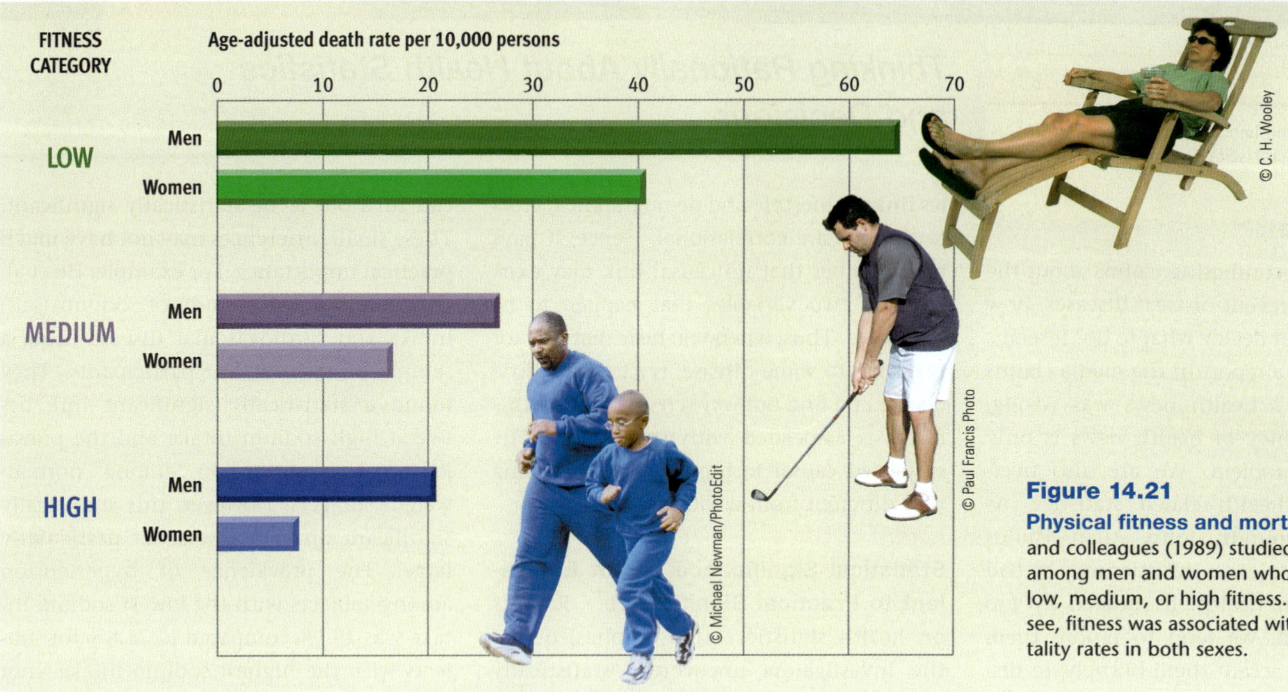

Figure 14.21
Physical fitness and mortality. Blair and colleagues (1989) studied death rates among men and women who exhibited low, medium, or high fitness. As you can see, fitness was associated with lower mortality rates in both sexes.

© Cengage Learning 2013

Minimizing Physiological Vulnerability

Your body is intimately involved in your response to stress. The wear and tear of stress can be injurious to your health. To combat this potential problem, it helps to keep your body in relatively sound shape. Hence, it's a good idea to engage in at least a moderate amount of exercise. The potential benefits of regular exercise are substantial. Fortunately, evidence indicates that you don't have to be a dedicated athlete to benefit from exercise. Even a moderate amount of exercise—such as taking a brisk, half-hour walk each day—can reduce your risk of disease (Richardson et al., 2004; see **Figure 14.21**). Successful participation in an exercise program can also lead to improvements in your mood and ability to deal with stress (Hays, 1999; Plante, 1999b).

Embarking on an exercise program is difficult for many people. Exercise is time-consuming. Moreover, if you're out of shape, your initial attempts may be discouraging. People who do not get enough exercise cite lack of time, lack of convenience, and lack of enjoyment as their reasons (Jackicic & Gallagher, 2002). To circumvent these problems, it's wise to heed the following advice (Greenberg, 2002; Jackicic & Gallagher, 2002; Phillips, Kiernan, & King, 2001):

1. Select an activity that you find enjoyable.
2. Increase your participation gradually.
3. Exercise regularly without overdoing it.
4. Reinforce yourself for your efforts.

Good sleep habits can also help in the effort to minimize physiological vulnerability to stress. As we discussed in Chapter 5, sleep loss can undermine immune system responding (Motivala & Irwin, 2007) and fuel inflammatory responses (Patel et al., 2009). Evidence also suggests that poor sleep quality is associated with poor health (Benham, 2010) and that sleep loss can elevate mortality (Chien et al., 2010). Thus, sound sleep patterns can contribute to stress management. The results of a recent study suggest that people need to get a sufficient amount of sleep and that they should strive for consistency in their patterns of sleeping (Barber et al., 2010).

REVIEW OF KEY LEARNING GOALS

14.23 Ellis emphasizes the importance of reappraising stressful events to detect and dispute catastrophic thinking. According to Ellis, emotional distress is often attributable to irrational assumptions that underlie one's thinking.

14.24 Humor may be useful in efforts to redefine stressful situations. In some cases, releasing pent-up emotions may pay off. Writing about one's problems may foster better health. Stress can also be reduced by learning to be more forgiving toward others.

14.25 Relaxation techniques, such as Benson's relaxation response, can reduce the wear and tear of stress. Physical vulnerability may also be reduced by striving to increase one's fitness through exercise. One does not need to be an exercise fanatic to benefit. Good sleep habits can also help minimize vulnerability to stress.

KEY LEARNING GOALS

14.26 Understand important considerations in evaluating health statistics and making health decisions.

Thinking Rationally About Health Statistics and Decisions

With so many conflicting claims about the best ways to prevent or treat diseases, how can anyone ever decide what to do? It seems that every day a report in the media claims that yesterday's health news was wrong. The inconsistency of health news is only part of the problem. We are also overwhelmed by health-related statistics. As mathematics pundit John Allen Paulos (1995) puts it, "Health statistics may be bad for our mental health. Inundated by too many of them, we tend to ignore them completely, to accept them blithely, to disbelieve them closemindedly, or simply to misinterpret their significance" (p. 133).

Making personal decisions about health-related issues may not be easy. Even medical personnel often struggle to make sense out of health statistics (Gigerenzer at al., 2007). Yet it's particularly important to try to think rationally and systematically about such issues. In this Application, we'll discuss a few insights that can help you to think critically about statistics on health risks. Then we'll briefly outline a systematic approach to thinking through health decisions.

Evaluating Statistics on Health Risks

News reports seem to suggest that there are links between virtually everything people do, touch, and consume and some type of physical illness. For example, media have reported that coffee consumption is related to hypertension, that sleep loss is related to mortality, and that a high-fat diet is related to heart disease. It's enough to send even the most subdued person into a panic. Fortunately, your evaluation of data on health risks can become more sophisticated by considering the following.

Correlation Is No Assurance of Causation It's not easy to conduct experiments on health risks, so the vast majority of studies linking lifestyle and demographic factors to diseases are correlational. Hence, it pays to remember that no causal link may exist between two variables that happen to be correlated. Thus, when you hear that a factor is related to some disease, try to dig a little deeper and find out *why* scientists think this factor is associated with the disease. The suspected causal factor may be something very different from what was measured.

Statistical Significance Is Not Equivalent to Practical Significance Reports on health statistics often emphasize that the investigators uncovered "statistically significant" findings. Statistically significant findings are results that are not likely to be due to chance fluctuations (see Chapter 2). Statistical significance is a useful concept. However, it can sometimes be misleading (Matthey, 1998). Medical studies are often based on rather large samples. Such samples tend to yield more reliable conclusions than small samples. However, when a large sample is used, weak relationships and small differences between groups can turn out to be statistically significant. These small differences may not have much practical importance. For example, He et al. (1999) conducted a study of sodium (salt) intake and cardiovascular disease using a sample of over 14,000 participants. They found a statistically significant link between high sodium intake and the prevalence of hypertension among normal-weight subjects. However, this statistically significant difference was not particularly large. The prevalence of hypertension among subjects with the lowest sodium intake was 19.1% compared to 21.8% for subjects with the highest sodium intake—not exactly a difference worthy of panic.

Base Rates Should Be Considered in Evaluating Probabilities In evaluating whether a possible risk factor is associated with some disease, people often fail to consider the base rates of these events. If the base rate of a disease is relatively low, a small increase can sound quite large if it's reported as a percentage. For example, in the He et al. (1999) study, the prevalence of diabetes

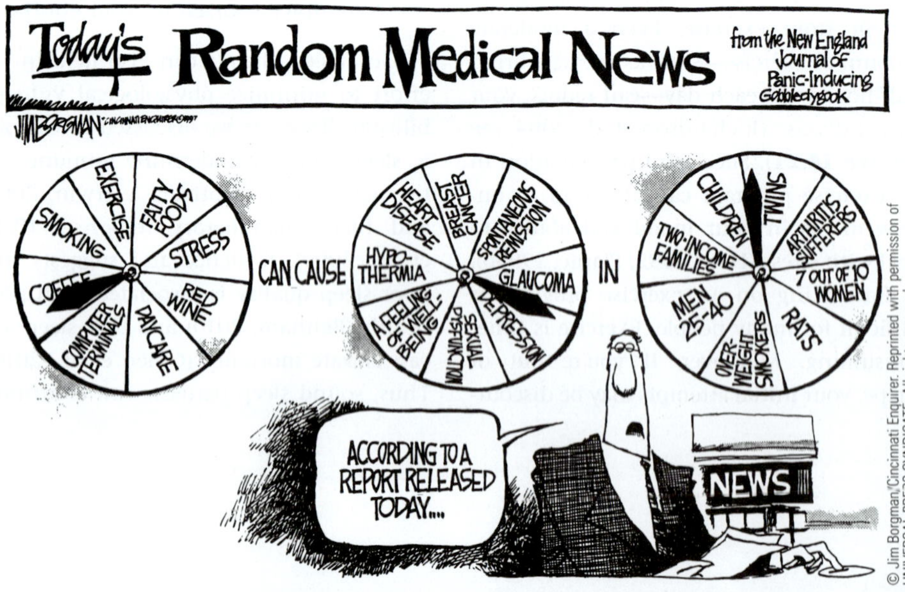

© Jim Borgman/Cincinnati Enquirer. Reprinted with permission of UNIVERSAL PRESS SYNDICATE. All rights reserved.

among subjects with the lowest sodium intake was 2.1% compared to 3.8% for subjects with the highest sodium intake. Based on this small but statistically significant difference, one could say (the investigators did not) that high sodium intake was associated with an 81% increase ([3.8 − 2.1] ÷ 2.1) in the prevalence of diabetes. This would be technically accurate, but an exaggerated way of portraying the results. Base rates should also be considered when evaluating claims made about the value of medications and other medical treatments. If the base rate of a disease is low, a modest decrease reported as a percentage can foster exaggerated perceptions of treatment benefits. For instance, Gigerenzer at al. (2007) describe an advertisement for Lipitor (a drug intended to lower cholesterol levels), claiming that Lipitor reduced the risk of stroke by 48%. Although this statistic was technically accurate, in absolute terms the protective benefits of Lipitor were actually rather modest. After four years, 1.5% of those taking Lipitor had a stroke versus 2.8% of those taking the placebo.

Thinking Systematically About Health Decisions

Health decisions are oriented toward the future. This means that there are always uncertainties. And such decisions usually involve weighing potential risks and benefits. None of these variables is unique to health decisions—uncertainty, risks, and benefits play prominent roles in economic and political decisions as well as in personal decisions. To illustrate, let's apply some basic principles of quantitative reasoning to a treatment decision involving whether to prescribe Ritalin for a boy who has been diagnosed with attention deficit disorder. Keep in mind that the general principles applied in this example can be used for a wide variety of decisions.

Seek Information to Reduce Uncertainty

Gather information and check it carefully for accuracy, completeness, and the presence or absence of conflicting information. For example, is the diagnosis correct? Look for conflicting information that does not fit with this diagnosis. If the child can sit and read for a long period of time, maybe the problem is an undetected hearing loss that makes him appear to be hyperactive in some situations. As you consider the additional information, begin quantifying the degree of uncertainty or its "flip side," your degree of confidence that the diagnosis is correct. If you decide that you are not confident about the diagnosis, you may be trying to solve the wrong problem.

Make Risk-Benefit Assessments. What are the risks and benefits of Ritalin? How likely is this child to benefit from Ritalin, and just how much improvement can be expected? If the child is 8 years old and unable to read and is miserable in school and at home, any treatment that could reduce his problems deserves serious consideration. As in the first step, the quantification is at an approximate level.

List Alternative Courses of Action

What are the alternatives to Ritalin? How well do they work? What are the risks associated with the alternatives, including the risk of falling further behind in school? Consider the pros and cons of each alternative. A special diet that sometimes works might be a good first step, along with the decision to start drug therapy if the child does not show improvement over some time period. What are the relative success rates for various types of treatment for children like the one being considered? To answer these questions, you will need to use probability estimates in your decision making.

As you can see from this example, many parts of the problem have been quantified (confidence in the diagnosis, likelihood of improvement, probability of negative outcomes, and so forth). Precise probability values were not used because the actual numbers often are not known. Some of the quantified values reflect value judgments, others reflect likelihoods, and others assess the degree of uncertainty. If you are thinking that the quantification of many unknowns in decision making is a lot of work, you're right. But, it's work worth doing. Whenever important decisions must be made about health, the ability to think with numbers will help you reach a better decision. And yes, that assertion is a virtual certainty.

Table 14.4 Critical Thinking Skills Discussed in This Application

Skill	Description
Understanding the limitations of correlational evidence	The critical thinker understands that a correlation between two variables does not demonstrate that there is a causal link between the variables.
Understanding the limitations of statistical significance	The critical thinker understands that weak relationships can be statistically significant when large samples are used in research.
Utilizing base rates in making predictions and evaluating probabilities	The critical thinker appreciates that the initial proportion of some group or event needs to be considered in weighing probabilities.
Seeking information to reduce uncertainty	The critical thinker understands that gathering more information can often decrease uncertainty, and reduced uncertainty can facilitate better decisions.
Making risk-benefit assessments	The critical thinker is aware that most decisions have risks and benefits that need to be weighed carefully.
Generating and evaluating alternative courses of action	In problem solving and decision making, the critical thinker knows the value of generating as many alternatives as possible and assessing their advantages and disadvantages.

© Cengage Learning 2013

REVIEW OF KEY LEARNING GOALS

14.26 Evaluations of statistics on health risks can be enhanced by remembering that correlation is no assurance of causation, that statistical significance is not equivalent to practical significance, and that base rates need to be considered in assessing probabilities. In trying to think systematically about health decisions, one should seek information to reduce uncertainty, make risk-benefit assessments, and consider alternative courses of action.

Chapter 14 Practice Test

1. It is the weekend before a major psychology exam on Monday, and Janine is experiencing total panic even though she is thoroughly prepared and aced the previous two psychology exams. Janine's panic illustrates that:
   A. high arousal is optimal on complex tasks.
   B. the appraisal of stress is quite objective.
   C. the appraisal of stress is highly subjective.
   D. her adrenal cortex is malfunctioning.

2. The four principal types of stress are:
   A. frustration, conflict, pressure, and anxiety.
   B. frustration, anger, pressure, and change.
   C. anger, anxiety, depression, and annoyance.
   D. frustration, conflict, pressure, and change.

3. When your boss tells you that a complicated report that you have not yet begun to write must be on her desk by this afternoon, you may experience:
   A. burnout.
   B. pressure.
   C. a double bind.
   D. catharsis.

4. You want to ask someone for a date, but you are afraid to risk rejection. You are experiencing:
   A. an approach-avoidance conflict.
   B. an avoidance-avoidance conflict.
   C. frustration.
   D. catharsis.

5. Research suggests that a high level of arousal may be most optimal for the performance of a task when:
   A. the task is complex.
   B. the task is simple.
   C. the rewards are high.
   D. an audience is present.

6. The alarm stage of Hans Selye's general adaptation syndrome is essentially the same as:
   A. the fight-or-flight response.
   B. constructive coping.
   C. catharsis.
   D. secondary appraisal.

7. The brain structure responsible for initiating action along the two major pathways through which the brain sends signals to the endocrine system is the:
   A. hypothalamus.
   B. thalamus.
   C. corpus callosum.
   D. medulla.

8. You have been doing poorly in your psychology class and are in danger of flunking. Which of the following qualifies as a defense mechanism in response to this situation?
   A. You seek the aid of a tutor.
   B. You decide to withdraw from the class and take it another time.
   C. You deny the reality that you are hopelessly behind in the class, convinced that you will somehow ace the final without seeking help.
   D. You consult with the instructor to see what you can do to pass the class.

9. Physical and emotional exhaustion, cynicism, and lowered self-efficacy attributable to chronic work-related stress is referred to as:
   A. learned helplessness.
   B. burnout.
   C. fallout.
   D. posttraumatic stress disorder.

10. Which personality trait seems to be most strongly related to increased coronary risk?
    A. Type B personality
    B. perfectionism
    C. competitiveness
    D. hostility

11. Many students develop colds and other minor ailments during final exams. This probably happens because:
    A. stress is associated with the release of corticosteroid hormones.
    B. stress is associated with the release of catecholamine hormones.
    C. burnout causes colds.
    D. stress can suppress immune functioning.

12. Research has found that optimists are more likely than pessimists to:
    A. take their time in confronting problems.
    B. identify the negatives before they identify the positives.
    C. engage in action-oriented, problem-focused coping.
    D. blame others for their personal problems.

13. Which of the following has *not* been found to be a mode of transmission for the HIV virus?
    A. sexual contact among homosexual men
    B. the sharing of needles by intravenous drug users
    C. sexual contact among heterosexuals
    D. sharing food

14. According to Albert Ellis, problematic emotional reactions are caused by:
    A. the fight-or-flight response.
    B. catharsis.
    C. catastrophic thinking.
    D. excessive reliance on defense mechanisms.

15. In evaluating health statistics, it is useful to:
    A. remember that statistical significance is equivalent to practical significance.
    B. remember that correlation is a reliable indicator of causation.
    C. consider base rates in thinking about probabilities.
    D. do all of the above.

Answers

1 C p. 563	6 A p. 571	11 D p. 582
2 D pp. 564–567	7 A p. 572	12 C p. 584
3 B p. 567	8 C p. 575	13 D p. 587
4 A p. 565	9 B p. 577	14 C pp. 592–593
5 B p. 570	10 D p. 580	15 C p. 596

Chapter 14 Media Resources

PsykTrek

To view a demo: **www.cengage.com/psychology/psyktrek**
To order: **www.cengage.com/psychology/weiten**

Go to the PsykTrek website or CD-ROM for further study of the concepts in this chapter. Both online and on the CD-ROM, PsykTrek includes dozens of learning modules with videos, animations, and quizzes, as well as simulations of psychological phenomena and a multimedia glossary that includes word pronunciations.

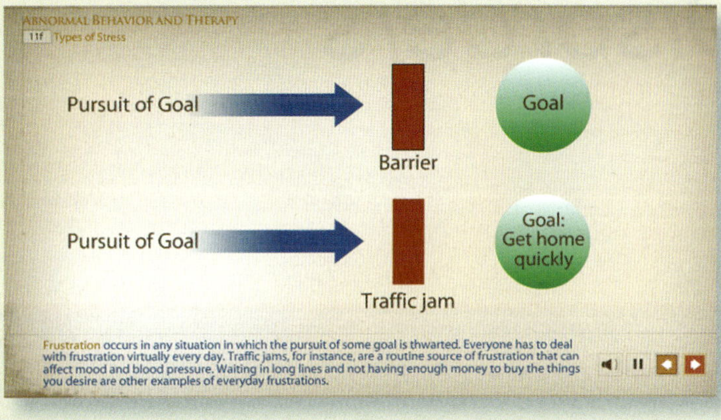

© Cengage Learning 2008

Visit Module 11f (*Types of Stress*) to improve your understanding of the nature of stress—and to take the Social Readjustment Rating Scale to measure the stress in your life.

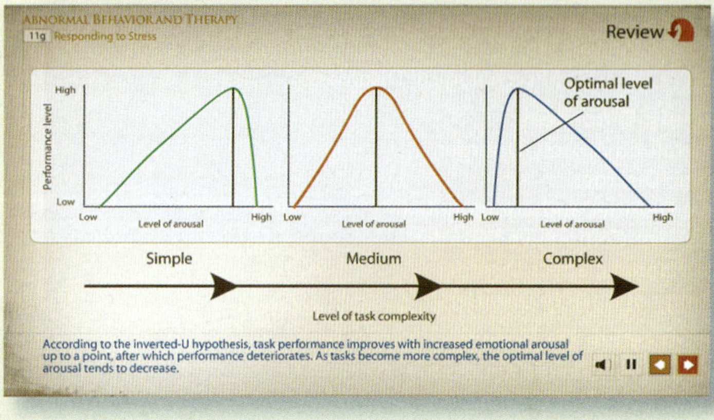

© Cengage Learning 2008

Access Module 11g (*Responding to Stress*) to learn more about how people tend to react to stress in both adaptive and maladaptive ways.

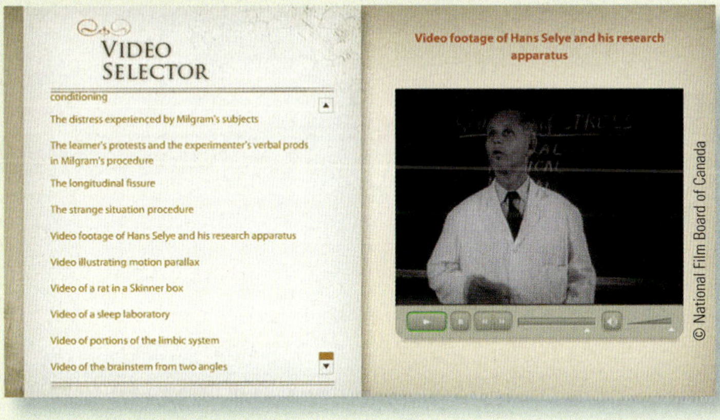

© National Film Board of Canada
© Cengage Learning 2008

Go to the Video Selector to view historic footage of Hans Selye describing the general adaptation syndrome.

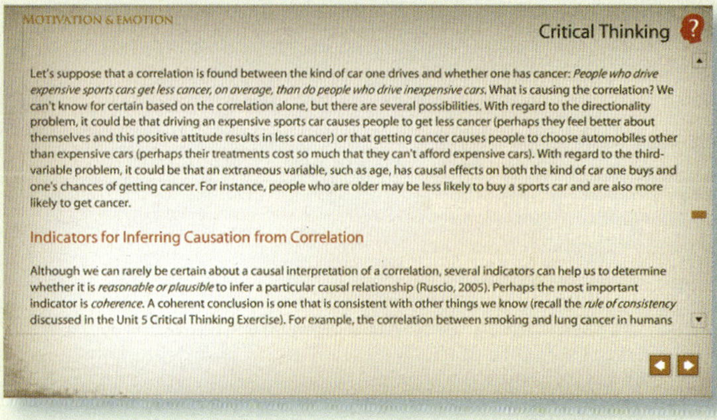

© Cengage Learning 2008

Check out the Unit 8 Critical Thinking Exercise (*Correlation and Causation*) to increase your sophistication about interpreting correlational relationships.

Online Study Tools

Log in to **CengageBrain** to access the resources your instructor requires. For this book, you can access:

CourseMate brings course concepts to life with interactive learning, study, and exam preparation tools that support the printed textbook. A textbook-specific website, Psychology CourseMate includes an integrated interactive eBook and other interactive learning tools such as quizzes, flashcards, videos, and more.

CengageNow is an easy-to-use online resource that helps you study in less time to get the grade you want—NOW. Take a pre-test for this chapter and receive a personalized study plan based on your results that will identify the topics you need to review and direct you to online resources to help you master those topics. Then take a post-test to help you determine the concepts you have mastered and what you will need to work on. If your textbook does not include an access code card, go to CengageBrain.com to gain access.

WebTutor is more than just an interactive study guide. WebTutor is an anytime, anywhere customized learning solution with an eBook, keeping you connected to your textbook, instructor, and classmates.

Aplia. If your professor has assigned Aplia homework:

1. Sign in to your account
2. Complete the corresponding homework exercises as required by your professor.
3. When finished, click "Grade It Now" to see which areas you have mastered, which need more work, and detailed explanations of every answer.

Visit **www.cengagebrain.com** to access your account and purchase materials.

15

Psychological Disorders

Bonnie Schupp/Getty Images RF

Actress Jessica Alba used to unplug every single appliance in her house because she was worried they would catch fire. She would also check and recheck her doors to ensure that they were locked.

Soccer star David Beckham acknowledges having engaged in more elaborate behaviors that involve symmetry and matching. He is not comfortable unless everything is arranged in straight lines or in pairs. For instance, if he has five cans of Pepsi in a refrigerator, he has to get rid of one to restore even pairs. When he enters a hotel room, he immediately has to put away all the hotel's leaflets and books to restore order to the room.

For Alba and Beckham, these aren't just little eccentricities of being a celebrity. They're manifestations of obsessive-compulsive disorder (OCD). Comedian and talk show host Howie Mandel explains it in his 2009 autobiography, *Here's the Deal: Don't Touch Me*. Mandel doesn't shake hands because of his fear of germs, but "it's not just that I'm scared of germs," he says. There's nothing wrong with shaking hands with someone and then washing your hands. But "there *is* something wrong with being totally consumed that you didn't get everything off your hand, that there's things crawling, so you wash it again, and you're so consumed that you wash it again, and you wash it again and you wash it again and you wash it again," Mandel says. "When you can't get past that, that's obsessive-compulsive disorder. It's not that you're afraid of germs, it's that you obsess about that thought and have to do things like handwashing to relieve the worry. I always have intrusive thoughts and rituals."

© AP Images/Charles Sykes

***Paradox:** Antonyms such as mental health versus mental illness suggest a sharp distinction between those who are normal and those who are not, but it's often difficult to draw a line that clearly separates normality from abnormality.*

What causes such abnormal behavior? Does Mandel have a mental illness, or does he just behave strangely? What is the basis for judging behavior as normal versus abnormal? How common are such disorders? Can they be cured? These are just a few of the questions that we will address in this chapter as we discuss psychological disorders and their complex causes.

KEY LEARNING GOALS

15.1 Evaluate the medical model, and discuss the stigma of mental illness.

15.2 Identify the most commonly used criteria of abnormality.

15.3 Outline the structure of the DSM diagnostic system.

15.4 Discuss estimates of the prevalence of psychological disorders.

Abnormal Behavior: General Concepts

Misconceptions about abnormal behavior are common. We therefore need to clear up some preliminary issues before we describe the various types of disorders. In this section, we will discuss (1) the medical model of abnormal behavior, (2) the criteria of abnormal behavior, (3) the classification of psychological disorders, and (4) the prevalence of such disorders.

The Medical Model Applied to Abnormal Behavior

There's no question that Howie Mandel's extreme fear of germs is abnormal. But does it make sense to view his unusual and irrational behavior as an illness? This is a controversial question. **The *medical model* proposes that it is useful to think of abnormal behavior as a disease.** This point of view is the basis for many of the terms used to refer to abnormal behavior, such as mental *illness,* psychological *disorder,* and psycho*pathology* (*pathology* refers to manifestations of disease). The medical model gradually became the dominant way of thinking about abnormal behavior during the 18th and 19th centuries. Its influence remains strong today.

The medical model clearly represented progress over earlier models of abnormal behavior. Prior to the 18th century, most conceptions of abnormal behavior were based on superstition. People who behaved strangely were thought to be possessed by demons, to be witches in league with the devil, or to be victims of God's punishment. Their disorders were "treated" with chants, rituals, exorcisms, and such. If the people's behavior was seen as threatening, they were candidates for chains, dungeons, torture, and death (see **Figure 15.1**).

The rise of the medical model brought improvements in the treatment of those who exhibited abnormal behavior. As victims of an illness, they were viewed with more sympathy and less hatred and fear. Living conditions in early asylums were deplorable, but gradual progress was made toward more humane care of the mentally ill. Over time, ineffectual approaches to treatment eventually gave way to scientific investigation of the causes and cures of psychological disorders.

However, in recent decades, some critics have suggested that the medical model may have outlived its usefulness (Boyle, 2007; Kiesler, 1999). Some critics

Figure 15.1
Historical conceptions of mental illness. In the Middle Ages people who behaved strangely were sometimes thought to be in league with the devil. The drawing on the left depicts some of the cruel methods used to extract confessions from suspected witches and warlocks. Some psychological disorders were also thought to be caused by demonic possession. The right illustration depicts an exorcism.

SOURCE: (Left) Culver Pictures, Inc. (Right) Girolamo Di Benvenuto. "St. Catherine of Siena Exorcising a Possessed Woman," c. 1505. © Denver Art Museum Collection, Gift of Samuel H. Kress Foundation Collection, 1961.171. Photography courtesy of the Denver Art Museum.

are troubled because medical diagnoses of abnormal behavior pin potentially derogatory labels on people (Hinshaw, 2007; Overton & Medina, 2008). Being labeled as psychotic, schizophrenic, or mentally ill carries a social stigma that can be difficult to shake. Those characterized as mentally ill are viewed as erratic, dangerous, incompetent, and inferior (Corrigan & Larson, 2008). These stereotypes promote distancing, disdain, prejudice, and rejection. Even after a full recovery, someone who has been labeled mentally ill may have difficulty finding a place to live, getting a job, or making friends (Thornicroft, 2006). The stigma of mental illness is not impossible to shed, but it undoubtedly creates additional difficulties for people who already have more than their share of problems (Hinshaw, 2007).

Unfortunately, the stigma associated with psychological disorders appears to be deep-rooted and not easily reduced. In recent decades research has increasingly demonstrated that many psychological disorders are at least partly attributable to genetic and biological factors, making them appear more similar to physical illnesses, which carry far less negative connotations (Pescosolido, 2010; Schnittker, 2008). You would think that these trends would lead to a reduction in the stigma associated with mental illness, but research suggests that the stigmatization of mental disorders has remained stable or perhaps even increased (Hinshaw & Stier, 2008; Schnittker, 2008).

Another line of criticism has been voiced by Thomas Szasz (1974, 1990). He asserts that "strictly speaking, disease or illness can affect only the body; hence there can be no mental illness. . . . Minds can be 'sick' only in the sense that jokes are 'sick' or economies are 'sick'" (1974, p. 267). He further argues that abnormal behavior usually involves a deviation from social norms rather than an illness. He contends that such deviations are "problems in living" rather than medical problems. According to Szasz, the medical model's disease analogy converts moral and social questions about what is acceptable behavior into medical questions.

The criticism of the medical model has some merit. It is important to recognize the social roots and ramifications of the medical model. However, the bottom line is that the medical model continues to dominate thinking about psychological disorders. Medical concepts such as *diagnosis, etiology,* and *prognosis* have proven valuable in the treatment and study of abnormality. ***Diagnosis*** **involves distinguishing one illness from another.** ***Etiology*** **refers to the apparent causation and developmental history of an illness. A** ***prognosis*** **is a forecast about the probable course of an illness.** These medically based concepts have widely shared meanings that permit clinicians, researchers, and the public to communicate more effectively in their discussions of abnormal behavior.

Courtesy of Thomas Szasz

Thomas Szasz

"Minds can be 'sick' only in the sense that jokes are 'sick' or economies are 'sick.'"

Criteria of Abnormal Behavior

If your next-door neighbor scrubs his front porch twice a day and spends virtually all his time cleaning and recleaning his house, is he normal? If your sister-in-law goes to one physician after another seeking treatment for physical ailments that appear imaginary, is she psychologically healthy? How are we to judge what's normal and what's abnormal? More important, who's to do the judging?

These are complex questions. In a sense, *all* people make judgments about normality in that they all express opinions about others' (and perhaps their own) mental health. Of course, formal diagnoses of psychological disorders are made by mental health professionals. In making these diagnoses, clinicians rely on a variety of criteria, the foremost of which are the following:

1. *Deviance.* As Szasz has pointed out, people are often said to have a disorder because their behavior deviates from what their society considers acceptable. What constitutes normality varies somewhat from one culture to another. All cultures, though, have such norms. When people violate these standards and expectations, they may be labeled mentally ill. For example, *transvestic fetishism* is a sexual disorder in which a man achieves sexual arousal by dressing in women's clothing. This behavior is regarded as disordered because a man who wears a dress, brassiere, and nylons is deviating from our culture's norms.

© Roger Bamber/Alamy

This man's hoarding behavior clearly represents a certain type of deviance, but does that mean he has a psychological disorder? The criteria of mental illness are more subjective and complicated than most people realize. To some extent, judgments of mental health represent value judgments.

CONCEPT CHECK 15.1

Applying the Criteria of Abnormal Behavior

Check your understanding of the criteria of abnormal behavior by identifying the criteria met by each of the examples below and checking them off in the table provided. Keep in mind that a specific behavior may meet more than one criterion. The answers are in Appendix A.

Behavioral examples

1. Alan's performance at work has suffered because he has been drinking alcohol to excess. Several co-workers have suggested that he seek help for his problem, but he thinks that they're getting alarmed over nothing. "I just enjoy a good time once in a while," he says.
2. Monica has gone away to college and feels lonely, sad, and dejected. Her grades are fine, and she gets along okay with the other students in the dormitory, but inside she's choked with gloom, hopelessness, and despair.
3. Boris believes that he's Napoleon reborn. He believes that he is destined to lead the U.S. military forces into a great battle to recover California from space aliens.
4. Natasha panics with anxiety whenever she leaves her home. Her problem escalated gradually until she was absent from work so often that she was fired. She hasn't been out of her house in nine months and is deeply troubled by her problem.

Criteria met by each example

	Maladaptive behavior	Deviance	Personal distress
1. Alan	_____	_____	_____
2. Monica	_____	_____	_____
3. Boris	_____	_____	_____
4. Natasha	_____	_____	_____

2. *Maladaptive behavior.* In many cases, people are judged to have a psychological disorder because their everyday adaptive behavior is impaired. This is the key criterion in the diagnosis of substance use (drug) disorders. In and of itself, alcohol and drug use is not all that unusual or deviant. However, when the use of cocaine, for instance, begins to interfere with a person's social or occupational functioning, a substance use disorder exists. In such cases, it's the maladaptive quality of the behavior that makes it disordered.

3. *Personal distress.* Frequently, the diagnosis of a psychological disorder is based on an individual's report of great personal distress. This is usually the criterion met by people who are troubled by depression or anxiety disorders. Depressed people, for instance, may or may not exhibit deviant or maladaptive behavior. Such people are usually labeled as having a disorder when they describe their subjective pain and suffering to friends, relatives, and mental health professionals.

Although two or three criteria may apply in a particular case, people are often viewed as disordered when only one criterion is met. As you may have already noticed, to some degree diagnoses of psychological disorders involve *value judgments* about what represents normal or abnormal behavior (Sadler, 2005; Widiger & Sankis, 2000). The criteria of mental illness are not nearly as value-free as the criteria of physical illness. In evaluating physical diseases, people can usually agree that a malfunctioning heart or kidney is pathological, regardless of their personal values. However, judgments about mental illness reflect prevailing cultural values, social trends, and political forces, as well as scientific knowledge (Kutchins & Kirk, 1997; Mechanic, 1999).

Antonyms such as *normal* versus *abnormal* and *mental health* versus *mental illness* imply that people can be divided neatly into two distinct groups: those who are normal and those who are not. In reality, it's often difficult to draw a line that clearly separates normality from abnormality. On occasion, everybody acts in deviant ways, everyone displays some maladaptive behavior, and everyone experiences personal distress. People are judged to have psychological disorders only when their behavior becomes *extremely* deviant, maladaptive, or distressing. Thus, normality and abnormality exist on a continuum. It's a matter of degree, not an either-or proposition (see **Figure 15.2**).

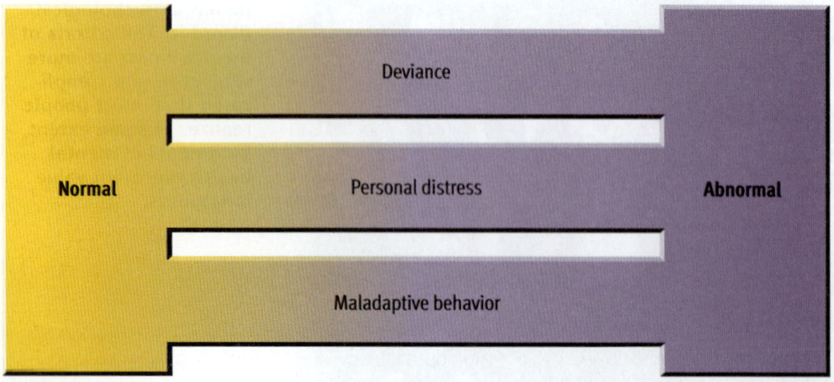

Figure 15.2
Normality and abnormality as a continuum. No sharp boundary exists between normal and abnormal behavior. Behavior is normal or abnormal in degree, depending on the extent to which one's behavior is deviant, personally distressing, or maladaptive. © Cengage Learning 2013

Reality CHECK

Misconception

People with psychological disorders typically exhibit highly bizarre behavior.

Reality

This is true only in a small minority of cases, usually involving relatively severe disorders. The vast majority of people with psychological disorders do not display strange behavior. On the surface most are indistinguishable from those without disorders.

Psychodiagnosis: The Classification of Disorders

Lumping all psychological disorders together would make it extremely difficult to understand them better. A sound taxonomy of mental disorders can facilitate empirical research and enhance communication among scientists and clinicians (First, 2008; Zimmerman & Spitzer, 2009). Thus, a great deal of effort has been invested in devising an elaborate system for classifying psychological disorders (see **Figure 15.3**). This classification system, published

Figure 15.3

Overview of the DSM diagnostic system. Published by the American Psychiatric Association, the *Diagnostic and Statistical Manual of Mental Disorders* is the formal classification system used in the diagnosis of psychological disorders. It is a *multiaxial* system, which means that information is recorded on the five axes described here. © Cengage Learning 2013

SOURCE: Reprinted with permission from the *Diagnostic and Statistical Manual of Mental Disorders, 4th ed.,* Text Revision. Copyright © 2000 American Psychiatric Association.

Axis I
Clinical Syndromes

1. **Disorders usually first diagnosed in infancy, childhood, or adolescence**
   This category includes disorders that arise before adolescence, such as attention deficit disorders, autism, enuresis, and stuttering.
2. **Organic mental disorders**
   These disorders are temporary or permanent dysfunctions of brain tissue caused by diseases or chemicals. Examples are delirium, dementia, and amnesia.
3. **Substance-related disorders**
   This category refers to the maladaptive use of drugs and alcohol. This category requires an abnormal pattern of use, as with alcohol abuse and cocaine dependence.
4. **Schizophrenia and other psychotic disorders**
   The schizophrenias are characterized by psychotic symptoms (for example, grossly disorganized behavior, delusions, and hallucinations) and by over six months of behavioral deterioration. This category also includes delusional disorder and schizoaffective disorder.
5. **Mood disorders**
   The cardinal feature is emotional disturbance. These disorders include major depression, bipolar disorder, dysthymic disorder, and cyclothymic disorder.
6. **Anxiety disorders**
   These disorders are characterized by physiological signs of anxiety (for example, palpitations) and subjective feelings of tension, apprehension, or fear. Anxiety may be acute and focused (panic disorder) or continual and diffuse (generalized anxiety disorder).
7. **Somatoform disorders**
   These disorders are dominated by somatic symptoms that resemble physical illnesses. These symptoms cannot be fully accounted for by organic damage. This category includes somatization and conversion disorders and hypochondriasis.
8. **Dissociative disorders**
   These disorders all feature a sudden, temporary alteration or dysfunction of memory, consciousness, and identity, as in dissociative amnesia and dissociative identity disorder.
9. **Sexual and gender-identity disorders**
   There are three basic types of disorders in this category: gender identity disorders (discomfort with identity as male or female), paraphilias (preference for unusual acts to achieve sexual arousal), and sexual dysfunctions (impairments in sexual functioning).
10. **Eating Disorders**
    Eating disorders are severe disturbances in eating behavior characterized by preoccupation with weight concerns and unhealthy efforts to control weight. Examples include anorexia nervosa and bulimia nervosa.

Axis II
Personality Disorders or Mental Retardation

Personality disorders are longstanding patterns of extreme, inflexible personality traits that are deviant or maladaptive and lead to impaired functioning or subjective distress. *Mental retardation* refers to subnormal general mental ability accompanied by deficiencies in adaptive skills, originating before age 18.

Axis III
General Medical Conditions

Physical disorders or conditions are recorded on this axis. Examples include diabetes, arthritis, and hemophilia.

Axis IV
Psychosocial and Environmental Problems

Axis IV is for reporting psychosocial and environmental problems that may affect the diagnosis, treatment, and prognosis of mental disorders (Axes I and II). A psychosocial or environmental problem may be a negative life event, an environmental difficulty or deficiency, a familial or other interpersonal stress, an inadequacy of social support or personal resources, or another problem that describes the context in which a person's difficulties have developed.

Axis V
Global Assessment of Functioning (GAF) Scale

Code	Symptoms
100	Superior functioning in a wide range of activities
90	Absent or minimal symptoms, good functioning in all areas
80	Symptoms transient and expectable reactions to psychosocial stressors
70	Some mild symptoms or some difficulty in social, occupational, or school functioning, but generally functioning pretty well
60	Moderate symptoms or difficulty in social, occupational, or school functioning
50	Serious symptoms or impairment in social, occupational, or school functioning
40	Some impairment in reality testing or communication or major impairment in family relations, judgment, thinking, or mood
30	Behavior considerably influenced by delusions or hallucinations, serious impairment in communication or judgment, or inability to function in almost all areas
20	Some danger of hurting self or others, occasional failure to maintain minimal personal hygiene, or gross impairment in communication
10	Persistent danger of severely hurting self or others
1	

by the American Psychiatric Association, is outlined in the *Diagnostic and Statistical Manual of Mental Disorders*. The current, fourth edition, referred to as DSM-IV, was released in 1994, and revised slightly in 2000.

The DSM employs a multiaxial system of classification. It asks for judgments about individuals on five separate "axes" (see **Figure 15.3**). The diagnoses of disorders are made on Axes I and II. Clinicians record most types of disorders on Axis I, while they use Axis II to list long-running personality disorders or mental retardation. People may receive diagnoses on both Axes I and II. The remaining axes are used to record supplemental information. A patient's physical disorders are listed on Axis III (General Medical Conditions). On Axis IV (Psychosocial and Environmental Problems), the clinician makes notations regarding the types of stress experienced by the individual in the past year. On Axis V (Global Assessment of Functioning), estimates are made of the individual's current level of adaptive functioning (in social and occupational behavior, viewed as a whole) and of the individual's highest level of functioning in the previous year. **Figure 15.4** shows an example of a multiaxial evaluation.

Work is currently underway to formulate the next edition of the diagnostic system (e.g., Andrews et al., 2009; Helzer, Kraemer et al., 2008; Regier et al., 2009), which will be identified as DSM-5 (instead of DSM-V), to facilitate incremental updates (such as DSM-5.1). It is tentatively scheduled for publication in 2013. Clinical researchers are collecting data, holding conferences, and formulating arguments about whether various syndromes should be added, eliminated, redefined, or renamed. Should complicated grief reactions become a standard diagnostic option (Lichtenthal, Cruess, & Prigerson, 2004)? Should the diagnostic system use the term drug *dependence* or drug *addiction* (O'Brien, Volkow, & Li, 2006)? Should pathological gambling be grouped with impulse-control disorders or addictive disorders (Petry, 2010)? Should night eating syndrome (regular eating binges after awakening from sleep) be recognized as a disorder (Stunkard et al., 2009)? Should Internet addiction be added to the official list of disorders (Pies, 2009)? Vigorous debates about issues such as these will occupy clinical researchers in the upcoming years.

By far, the biggest issue is whether to reduce the system's commitment to a categorical approach. In recent years many critics of the DSM approach have questioned the fundamental axiom that the diagnostic system is built on—the assumption that people can reliably be placed in discontinuous (nonoverlapping) diagnostic categories (Helzer, Wittchen et al., 2008; Widiger & Trull, 2007). These critics note that there is enormous overlap among various disorders in symptoms, making the boundaries between diagnoses much fuzzier than would be ideal. They also point out that people often qualify for more than one diagnosis, a condition called ***comorbidity*—the coexistence of two or more disorders.** Widespread comorbidity raises the possibility that specific diagnoses may not reflect distinct disorders but rather variations on the same underlying disorder (Lilienfeld & Landfield, 2008).

Because of problems such as these, some theorists have argued that the current *categorical approach* to diagnosis should be replaced by a *dimensional approach*. A dimensional approach would describe individuals' pathology in terms of how they score on a limited number of continuous dimensions, such as the degree to which they exhibit anxiety, depression, agitation, hypochondria, paranoia, and so forth (Kraemer, 2008; Widiger, Livesley, & Clark, 2009). The practical logistics of shifting to a dimensional approach to psychological disorders are formidable. Agreement would have to be reached about what dimensions to assess and how to measure them. At this juncture, it appears that DSM-5 will retain a categorical approach, but it is likely to be supplemented with a dimensional approach to at least some disorders (Regier et al., 2009).

Figure 15.4
Example of a multiaxial evaluation. A multiaxial evaluation for a depressed man with a cocaine problem might look like this.

A DSM multiaxial evaluation (patient 49-year-old male)

Axis I	Major depressive disorder Cocaine abuse
Axis II	Borderline personality disorder (provisional, rule out dependent personality disorder)
Axis III	Hypertension
Axis IV	Psychosocial stressors: recent divorce, permitted to see his children only infrequently, job is in jeopardy
Axis V	Current global assessment of functioning (GAF): 46

© Cengage Learning 2013

The Prevalence of Psychological Disorders

How common are psychological disorders? What percentage of the population is afflicted with mental illness? Is it 10%? Perhaps 25%? Could the figure range as high as 40% or 50%?

Such estimates fall in the domain of ***epidemiology*—the study of the distribution of mental or physical disorders in a population.** The 1980s and 1990s brought major advances in psychiatric epidemiology. A number of large-scale investigations at the time provided a huge, new database on the distribution of mental disorders (Wang et al., 2008). In epidemiology, ***prevalence* refers to the percentage of a population that exhibit a disorder during a specified time period.** In the case of mental disorders, the most interesting data are the estimates of *lifetime prevalence,* the percentage of people who endure a specific disorder at any time in their lives.

Studies published in the 1980s and early 1990s found psychological disorders in roughly *one-third* of the population (Regier & Kaelber, 1995; Robins, Locke, & Regier, 1991). Subsequent research suggested that about 44% of the adult population will struggle with some sort of psychological disorder at some point in their lives (Kessler & Zhao, 1999; Regier & Burke, 2000). The most recent large-scale epidemiological study estimated the lifetime risk of a psychiatric disorder to be 51% (Kessler et al., 2005a). Obviously, all these figures are *estimates* that depend to some extent on the sampling methods and assessment techniques used (Wakefield, 1999b). The progressively higher estimates in recent years have begun to generate some controversy in the field. Some experts believe that recent estimates are implausibly high and that they may trivialize psychiatric diagnoses (Wakefield & Spitzer, 2002). The debate centers on where to draw the line between normal difficulties in functioning and full-fledged mental illness—that is, when symptoms qualify as a disease (Regier, Narrow, & Rae, 2004).

In any event, whether one goes with conservative or liberal estimates, the prevalence of psychological disorders is quite a bit higher than most people assume. The data that yielded the 44% estimate of total lifetime prevalence are summarized in **Figure 15.5**, which shows prevalence estimates for the most common classes of disorders. As you can see, the most common types of psychological disorders are (1) substance (alcohol and drugs) use disorders, (2) anxiety disorders, and (3) mood disorders.

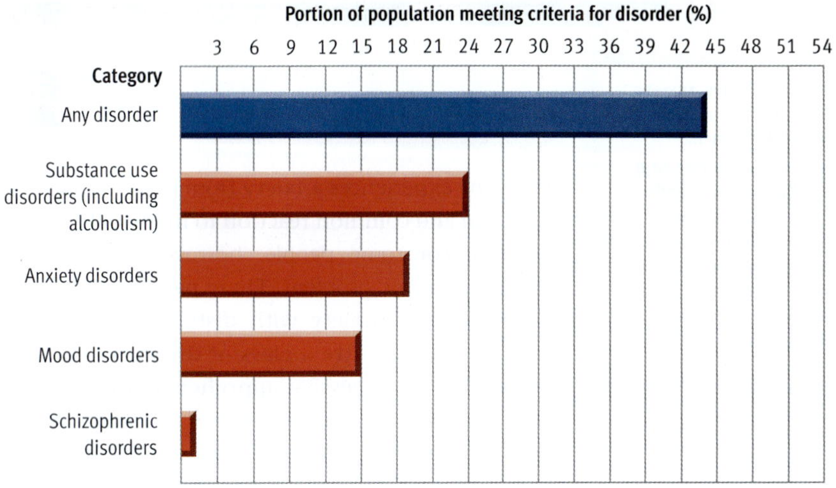

Figure 15.5

Lifetime prevalence of psychological disorders. The estimated percentage of people who have, at any time in their life, suffered from one of four types of psychological disorders or from a disorder of any kind (top bar) is shown here. Prevalence estimates vary somewhat from one study to the next, depending on the exact methods used in sampling and assessment. The estimates shown here are based on pooling data from Wave 1 and 2 of the Epidemiological Catchment Area studies and the National Comorbidity Study, as summarized by Regier and Burke (2000) and Dew, Bromet, and Switzer (2000). These studies, which collectively evaluated over 28,000 subjects, provide the best data to date on the prevalence of mental illness in the United States. © Cengage Learning 2013

We are now ready to start examining the specific types of psychological disorders. Obviously, we cannot cover all of the disorders listed in DSM-IV. However, we will introduce most of the major categories of disorders to give you an overview of the many forms abnormal behavior takes (see Chapter 5 for a discussion of substance abuse). In discussing each set of disorders, we will begin with brief descriptions of the specific syndromes or subtypes that fall in the category. Then we'll focus on the *etiology* of the disorders in that category.

REVIEW OF KEY LEARNING GOALS

15.1 The medical model assumes that it's useful to view abnormal behavior as a disease. This view has been criticized on the grounds that it turns questions about deviance into medical questions, but the model has proven useful. Mental illness carries a stigma that can be difficult to shake and creates additional difficulties for those who suffer from psychological disorders.

15.2 Three criteria are used in deciding whether people suffer from psychological disorders: deviance from social norms, personal distress, and maladaptive behavior. Judgments about abnormality reflect cultural values. Often it's difficult to clearly draw a line between normality and abnormality.

15.3 The DSM is the official diagnostic classification system in the United States for mental disorders. The system asks for information about patients on five axes. The current version is DSM-IV. Work is under way on DSM-5, which may supplement the current categorical approach with a dimensional approach.

15.4 It's difficult to obtain good data on the prevalence of psychological disorders. Nonetheless, it's clear that they are more common than widely believed. Recent studies suggest that 44% of the population will struggle with a disorder over the course of their lives. The most common types of disorders are substance use, anxiety disorders, and mood disorders.

KEY LEARNING GOALS

15.5 Identify five anxiety disorders and the symptoms associated with each.

15.6 Discuss the role of biological factors and conditioning in the etiology of anxiety disorders.

15.7 Explain how cognitive factors and stress can contribute to the development of anxiety disorders.

Anxiety Disorders

PSYKTREK SIM 9

Everyone experiences anxiety from time to time. It's a natural and common reaction to many of life's difficulties. For some people, however, anxiety becomes a chronic problem. These people experience high levels of anxiety with disturbing regularity. ***Anxiety disorders* are a class of disorders marked by feelings of excessive apprehension and anxiety.** There are five principal types of anxiety disorders: generalized anxiety disorder, phobic disorder, panic disorder, obsessive-compulsive disorder, and posttraumatic stress disorder. They are not mutually exclusive. Many people who develop one anxiety syndrome suffer from another at some point in their lives (Merikangas & Kalaydjian, 2009). Studies suggest that anxiety disorders are quite common, occurring in roughly 19% of the population (Dew, Bromet, & Switzer, 2000; Regier & Burke, 2000).

Generalized Anxiety Disorder

PSYKTREK 11a

***Generalized anxiety disorder* is marked by a chronic, high level of anxiety that is not tied to any specific threat.** People with this disorder worry constantly about yesterday's mistakes and tomorrow's problems. They worry about minor matters related to family, finances, work, and personal illness. They hope that their worrying will help ward off negative events (Beidel & Stipelman, 2007). Nonetheless, they worry about how much they worry (Barlow et al., 2003). They often dread making decisions and brood over them endlessly. Their anxiety is commonly accompanied by physical symptoms, which may include trembling, muscle tension, diarrhea, dizziness, faintness, sweating, and heart palpitations. Generalized anxiety disorder tends to have a gradual onset, has a lifetime prevalence of about 5%–6%, and is seen more frequently in females than males (Rowa & Antony, 2008).

Phobic Disorder

PSYKTREK 11a

In a phobic disorder, an individual's troublesome anxiety has a specific focus. **A *phobic disorder* is marked by a persistent and irrational fear of an object or situation that presents no realistic danger.** Mild phobias are extremely common. People are said to have a phobic disorder only when their fears seriously interfere with their everyday behavior. Phobic reactions tend to be accompanied by physical symptoms of anxiety, such as trembling and palpitations (Rapee & Barlow, 2001). The following case provides an example of a phobic disorder:

Hilda is 32 years of age and has a rather unusual fear. She is terrified of snow. She cannot go outside in the snow. She cannot even stand to see snow or hear about it on the weather report. Her phobia severely constricts her day-to-day behavior. Probing in therapy revealed that her phobia was caused by a traumatic experience at age 11. Playing at a ski lodge, she was buried briefly by a small avalanche of snow. She had no recollection of this experience until it was recovered in therapy. (Adapted from Laughlin, 1967, p. 227)

As Hilda's unusual snow phobia illustrates, people can develop phobic responses to virtually anything. Nonetheless, certain types of phobias are more common than others. Particularly common are acrophobia (fear of heights), claustrophobia (fear of small, enclosed places), brontophobia (fear of storms), hydrophobia (fear of water), and various animal and insect phobias (McCabe & Antony, 2008; see **Figure 15.6**). People troubled by phobias typically realize that their fears are irrational. Yet, they still are unable to calm themselves when confronted by a phobic object. Even *imagining* a phobic object or situation can trigger great anxiety in a person suffering from a phobic disorder (Thorpe & Salkovskis, 1995).

Panic Disorder and Agoraphobia

PSYKTREK 11a

A *panic disorder* is characterized by recurrent attacks of overwhelming anxiety that usually occur suddenly and unexpectedly. These paralyzing feelings are accompanied by physical symptoms of anxiety. After a number of panic attacks, victims often become apprehensive, wondering when their next panic will occur. Their concern about exhibiting panic in public may escalate to the point where they are afraid to leave home. This creates a condition called *agoraphobia,* which is a common complication of panic disorders.

***Agoraphobia* is a fear of going out to public places** (its literal meaning is "fear of the marketplace or open places"). Because of this fear, some people become prisoners confined to their homes, although

© Sidney Harris/ScienceCartoonsPlus.com

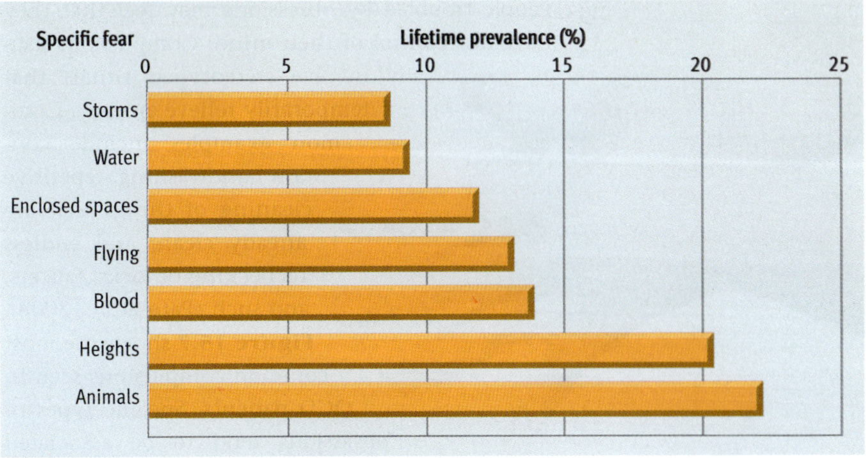

© Cengage Learning 2013

Figure 15.6

Common phobic fears. This graph shows the lifetime prevalence of the most common types of phobic fears reported by participants in a study by Curtis et al. (1998). As you can see, a substantial number of people struggle with a variety of specific phobias. Bear in mind that only a portion of these people qualify for a diagnosis of phobic disorder, which is merited only if individuals' phobias seriously impair their everyday functioning.

many will venture out if accompanied by a trusted companion (Hollander & Simeon, 2008). As its name suggests, agoraphobia has traditionally been viewed as a phobic disorder. However, more recent evidence suggests that agoraphobia is mainly a complication of panic disorder. About two-thirds of people who are diagnosed with panic disorder are female (Taylor, Cox, & Asmundson, 2009). The onset of panic disorder typically occurs during late adolescence or early adulthood (McClure-Tone & Pine, 2009).

Obsessive-Compulsive Disorder

PsykTrek 11a

Obsessions are *thoughts* that repeatedly intrude on one's consciousness in a distressing way. Compulsions are *actions* that one feels forced to carry out. Thus, **an *obsessive-compulsive disorder* (OCD) is marked by persistent, uncontrollable intrusions of unwanted thoughts (obsessions) and urges to engage in senseless rituals (compulsions).** To illustrate, let's examine the bizarre behavior of a man once reputed to be the wealthiest person in the world:

The famous industrialist Howard Hughes was obsessed with the possibility of being contaminated by germs. This led him to devise extraordinary rituals to minimize the possibility of such contamination. He would spend hours methodically cleaning a single telephone. He once wrote a three-page memo instructing assistants on exactly how to open cans of fruit for him. The following is just a small portion of the instructions that Hughes provided for a driver who delivered films to his bungalow. "Get out of the car on the traffic side. Do not at any time be on the side of the car between the car and the curb. . . . Carry only one can of film at a time. Step over the gutter opposite the place where the sidewalk dead-ends into the curb from a point as far out into the center of the road as possible. Do not ever walk on the grass at all, also do not step into the gutter at all. Walk to the bungalow keeping as near to the center of the sidewalk as possible." (Adapted from Barlett & Steele, 1979, pp. 227–237)

Obsessions often center on inflicting harm on others, personal failures, suicide, or sexual acts.

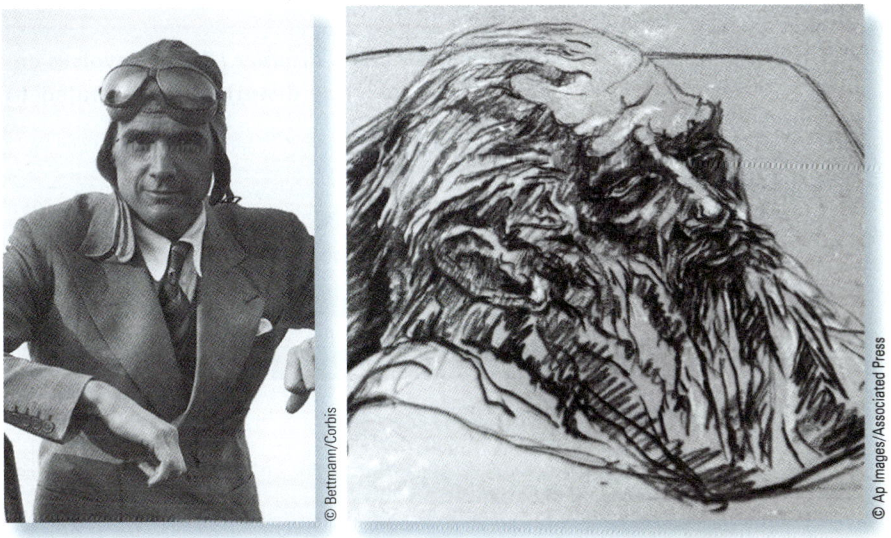

© Bettmann/Corbis

© Ap Images/Associated Press

As a young man (shown in the photo), Howard Hughes was a handsome, dashing daredevil pilot and movie producer who appeared to be reasonably well adjusted. However, as the years went by, his behavior gradually became more and more maladaptive, as obsessions and compulsions came to dominate his life. In his later years (shown in the drawing), he spent most of his time in darkened rooms, naked, unkempt, and dirty, following bizarre rituals to alleviate his anxieties. (The drawing was done by an NBC artist and was based on descriptions from men who had seen Hughes.)

© yummy/Shutterstock

People troubled by obsessions may feel that they have lost control of their mind. Compulsions usually involve stereotyped rituals that temporarily relieve anxiety. Common examples include constant handwashing, repetitive cleaning of things that are already clean, and endless rechecking of locks, faucets, and such (Pato et al., 2008). **Figure 15.7** shows the most common compulsions seen in OCD patients. Specific types of obsessions tend to be associated with specific types of compulsions. For example, obsessions about contamination tend to be paired with cleaning compulsions, whereas obsessions about symmetry tend to be paired with ordering and arranging compulsions (Hollander & Simeon, 2008).

Many of us can be compulsive at times. Indeed, a recent study found that 17% of a sample of people without a mental disorder reported a significant obsession or compulsion (Fullana et al., 2009). However, full-fledged obsessive-compulsive disorders occur in roughly 2%–3% of the population (Zohar, Fostick, & Juven-Wetzler, 2009). Most cases (75%) emerge before the age of 30 (Kessler et al., 2005a). OCD can be a particularly severe disorder, and is often associated with serious social and occupational impairments (Torres et al., 2006).

Posttraumatic Stress Disorder

Posttraumatic stress disorder (PTSD) **involves enduring psychological disturbance attributed to the experience of a major traumatic event.** PTSD was first recognized as a disorder in the 1970s in the aftermath of the Vietnam war, when a great many veterans were traumatized by their combat experiences. Research eventually showed that PTSD can be caused by a variety of traumatic events besides harrowing war experiences. For example, PTSD is often seen after a rape or assault, a severe automobile accident, a natural disaster, or the witnessing of someone's death. Although people tend to assume that events such as these are relatively uncommon, research shows that a majority of adults have been exposed to one or more serious, traumatic events (Norris & Slone, 2007). Research suggests that about 7% of people have suffered from PTSD at some point in their lives (Resick, Monson, & Rizvi, 2008). Prevalence is twice as high among women as among men (Flood, Davidson, & Beckham, 2008).

Currently, there's great concern about the number of military returnees from the Afghanistan and Iraq wars who will develop PTSD (Ramchand et al., 2010; Sundin et al., 2010). Similar to the experiences of Vietnam veterans, the preliminary data suggest that these troops are showing greatly elevated rates of PTSD (Hoge et al., 2007). Common symptoms in PTSD include reexperiencing the traumatic event in the form of nightmares and flashbacks, emotional numbing, alienation, problems in social relations, an increased sense of vulnerability, and elevated arousal, anxiety, anger, and guilt (McClure-Tone & Pine, 2009).

A variety of factors are predictors of individuals' risk for PTSD (McNally, 2009; Keane, Marshall, & Taft, 2006). As you might expect, increased vulnerability is associated with greater personal injuries and losses, greater intensity of exposure to the traumatic event, and more exposure to the grotesque aftermath of the event. One key predictor of vulnerability is the *intensity of one's reaction at the time of the traumatic event* (Ozer et al., 2003). Individuals who have especially intense emotional reactions during or immediately after the traumatic event go on to show elevated vulnerability to PTSD. Vulnerability seems to be greatest among people whose reactions are so intense that they report dissociative experiences (a sense that things are not real, that time is stretching out, that one is watching oneself in a movie).

Etiology of Anxiety Disorders

PSYKTREK 11a

Like most psychological disorders, anxiety disorders develop out of complicated interactions among a variety of biological and psychological factors.

Figure 15.7

Common compulsions in OCD patients. The most common compulsions reported by a sample of 550 OCD patients are shown here. Nearly half of the OCD patients reported multiple compulsions.

SOURCE: Pato, M. T., Fanous, A., Eisen, J. L., & Phillips, K. A. (2008). Anxiety disorders: Obsessive-compulsive disorder. In A. Tasman, J. Kay, J. A. Lieberman, M. B. First, & M. Maj (Eds.), *Psychiatry* (3rd ed.), 1443–1471. Chichester, England: Wiley-Blackwell. Copyright © 2008, John Wiley and Sons.

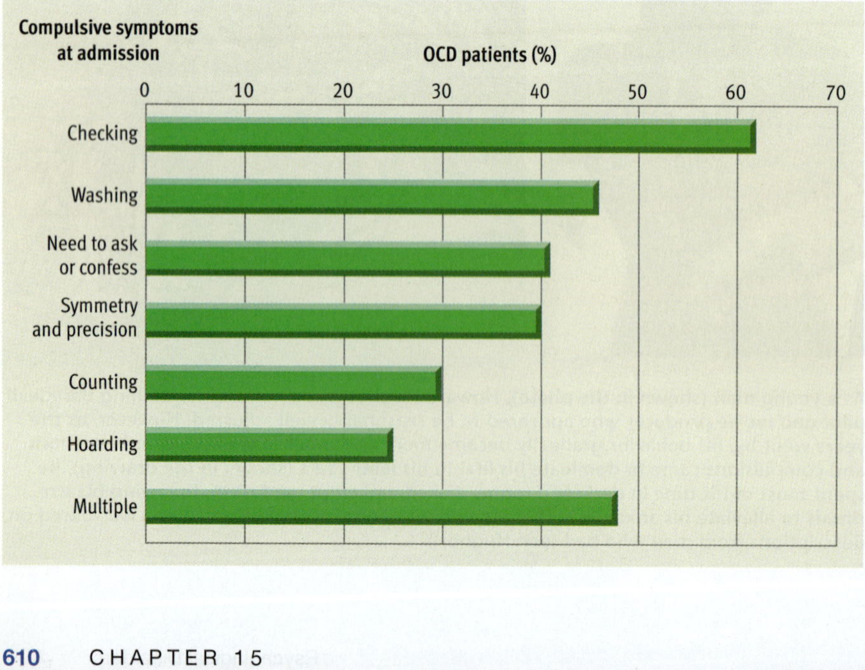

© Cengage Learning 2013

Biological Factors 11a

In studies that assess the impact of heredity on psychological disorders, investigators look at *concordance rates*. **A *concordance rate* indicates the percentage of twin pairs or other pairs of relatives who exhibit the same disorder.** If relatives who share more genetic similarity show higher concordance rates than relatives who share less genetic overlap, this finding supports the genetic hypothesis. The results of both *twin studies* (see **Figure 15.8**) and *family studies* (see Chapter 3 for discussions of both methods) suggest a moderate genetic predisposition to anxiety disorders (Fyer, 2009). These findings are consistent with the idea that inherited differences in temperament might make some people more vulnerable than others to anxiety disorders. As discussed in Chapter 11, Jerome Kagan and his colleagues (1992) have found that about 15%–20% of infants display an *inhibited temperament*. Such a temperament is characterized by shyness, timidity, and wariness and appears to have a strong genetic basis. Studies suggest that this temperament is a risk factor for the development of anxiety disorders (Coles, Schofield, & Pietrefesa, 2006).

Another line of research suggests that *anxiety sensitivity* may make people vulnerable to anxiety disorders (McWilliams et al., 2007; Schmidt, Zvolensky, & Maner, 2006). According to this notion, some people are highly sensitive to the internal physiological symptoms of anxiety. Thus they are prone to overreact with fear when they experience these symptoms. Anxiety sensitivity may fuel an inflationary spiral in which anxiety breeds more anxiety. This may eventually spin out of control in the form of an anxiety disorder.

Recent evidence suggests that a link may exist between anxiety disorders and neurochemical activity in the brain. As you learned in Chapter 3, *neurotransmitters* are chemicals that carry signals from one neuron to another. Therapeutic drugs (such as Valium) that reduce excessive anxiety appear to alter neurotransmitter activity at GABA synapses. This finding and other lines of evidence suggest that disturbances in the neural circuits using GABA may play a role in some types of anxiety disorders (Rowa & Antony, 2009). Similarly, abnormalities in neural circuits using serotonin have been implicated in obsessive-compulsive disorders (Pato et al., 2008). Thus, scientists are beginning to unravel the neurochemical bases for anxiety disorders.

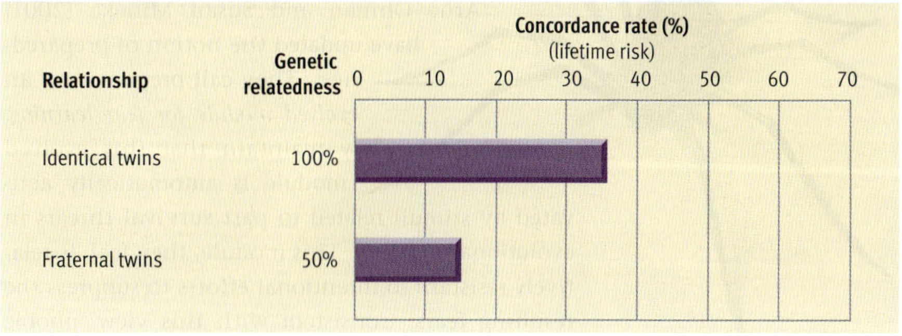

© Cengage Learning 2013

Figure 15.8
Twin studies of anxiety disorders. The concordance rate for anxiety disorders in identical twins is higher than that for fraternal twins, who share less genetic overlap. These results suggest that there is a genetic predisposition to anxiety disorders. (Data based on Noyes et al., 1987; Slater & Shields, 1969; Torgersen, 1979, 1983)

Conditioning and Learning 11a

Many anxiety responses may be *acquired through classical conditioning and maintained through operant conditioning* (see Chapter 6). According to Mowrer (1947), an originally neutral stimulus (the snow in Hilda's case, for instance) may be paired with a frightening event (the avalanche) so that it becomes a conditioned stimulus eliciting anxiety (see **Figure 15.9a**). Once a fear is acquired through classical conditioning, the person may start avoiding the anxiety-producing stimulus. The avoidance response is negatively reinforced because it's followed by a reduction in anxiety. This process involves operant conditioning (see **Figure 15.9b**). Thus, separate conditioning processes may create and then sustain specific anxiety responses (Levis, 1989). Consistent with this view, studies find that a substantial portion of people suffering from phobias can identify a traumatic conditioning experience that probably contributed to their anxiety disorder (McCabe & Antony, 2008; Mineka & Zinbarg, 2006).

The tendency to develop phobias of certain types of objects and situations may be explained by Martin Seligman's (1971) concept of *preparedness*. He suggests that people are biologically prepared by their evolutionary history to acquire some fears much more easily than others. His theory would explain why people develop phobias of ancient sources of threat (such as snakes and spiders) much more readily than modern sources of threat (such as electrical outlets or hot irons). As noted in Chapter 6,

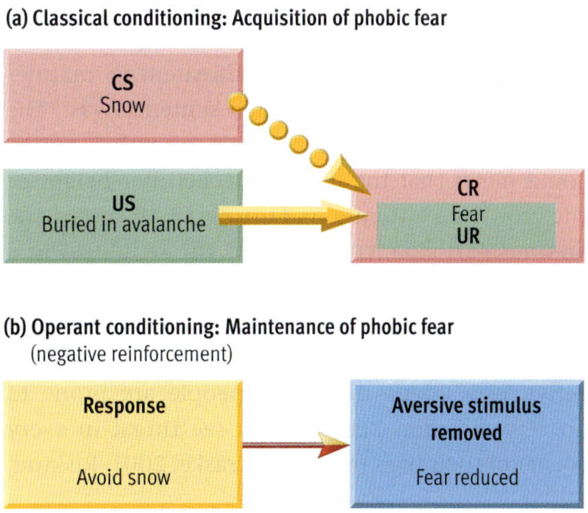

Figure 15.9
Conditioning as an explanation for phobias. **(a)** Many phobias appear to be acquired through classical conditioning when a neutral stimulus is paired with an anxiety-arousing stimulus. **(b)** Once acquired, a phobia may be maintained through operant conditioning. Avoidance of the phobic stimulus reduces anxiety, resulting in negative reinforcement. © Cengage Learning 2013

© Alex Mit/Shutterstock

Arne Öhman and Susan Mineka (2001) have updated the notion of preparedness. They call preparedness an *evolved module for fear learning*. They maintain that this evolved module is automatically activated by stimuli related to past survival threats in evolutionary history. This module, they feel, is relatively resistant to intentional efforts to suppress the resulting fears. Consistent with this view, phobic stimuli associated with evolutionary threats tend to produce more rapid conditioning of fears and stronger fear responses (Mineka & Öhman, 2002).

Critics note a number of problems with conditioning models of phobias. For instance, many people with phobias cannot recall or identify a traumatic conditioning experience that led to their phobia. Conversely, many people endure extremely traumatic experiences that should, according to this rationale, create a phobia but do not (Coelho & Purkis, 2009). Moreover, phobic fears can be acquired indirectly, by observing another's fear response to a specific stimulus or by absorbing fear-inducing information (imagine a parent harping on how dangerous lightning is) (Coelho & Purkis, 2009). Thus, the development of phobias may depend on synergistic interactions among a variety of learning processes.

Cognitive Factors

PsykTrek 11a

Cognitive theorists maintain that certain styles of thinking make some people particularly vulnerable to anxiety disorders (Craske & Waters, 2005). According to these theorists, some people are more likely to suffer from problems with anxiety because they tend to (a) misinterpret harmless situations as threatening, (b) focus excessive attention on perceived threats, and (c) selectively recall information that seems threatening (Beck, 1997; McNally, 1994, 1996). In one intriguing test of the cognitive view, anxious and nonanxious subjects were asked to read thirty-two sentences that could be interpreted in either a threatening or a nonthreatening manner (Eysenck et al., 1991). One such sentence was "The doctor examined little Emma's growth," which could mean that the doctor checked her height or the growth of a tumor. As **Figure 15.10** shows, the anxious participants interpreted the sentences in a threatening way more often than the nonanxious participants did. Thus, consistent with our theme that human experience is highly subjective, the cognitive view holds that some people are prone to anxiety disorders because they see threat in every corner of their lives (Aikens & Craske, 2001; Riskind, 2005).

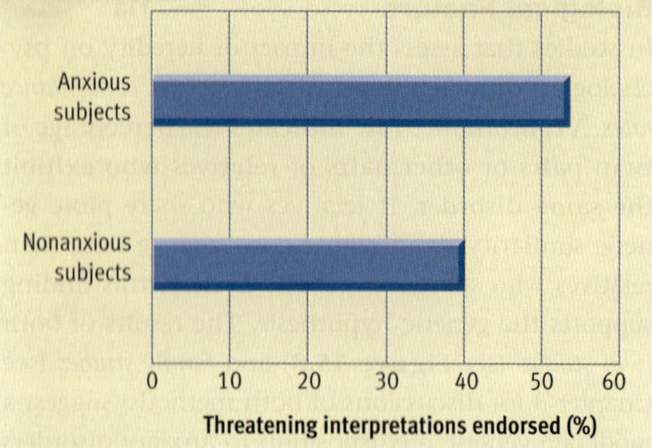

© Cengage Learning 2013

Figure 15.10

Cognitive factors in anxiety disorders. Eysenck and his colleagues (1991) compared how subjects with anxiety problems and nonanxious subjects tended to interpret sentences that could be viewed as threatening or nonthreatening. Consistent with cognitive models of anxiety disorders, anxious subjects were more likely to interpret the sentences in a threatening light.

Stress

PsykTrek 11a

Finally, studies have supported the long-held suspicion that anxiety disorders can be stress related (Beidel & Stipelman, 2007; Sandin et al., 2004). For instance, Faravelli and Pallanti (1989) found that patients with panic disorder had experienced a dramatic increase in stress in the month prior to the onset of their disorder. In another study, Brown et al. (1998) found an association between stress and the development of social phobia. Thus, there is reason to believe that high stress often helps precipitate the onset of anxiety disorders.

REVIEW OF KEY LEARNING GOALS

15.5 Generalized anxiety disorder is marked by chronic, high anxiety. Phobic disorder involves irrational fears of specific objects or situations. Panic disorder is marked by recurring panic attacks and agoraphobia. Obsessive-compulsive disorder is dominated by intrusions of unwanted thoughts and urges. Posttraumatic stress disorder consists of disturbances following the experience of a major traumatic event.

15.6 Twin studies suggest that there is a weak genetic predisposition to anxiety disorders. These disorders may be more likely in people who are especially sensitive to the physiological symptoms of anxiety. Abnormalities in neurotransmitter activity at GABA synapses or serotonin synapses may also play a role. Many anxiety responses, especially phobias, may be caused by classical conditioning and maintained by operant conditioning, with preparedness influencing which phobias condition most readily.

15.7 Cognitive theorists maintain that certain styles of thinking—especially a tendency to overinterpret harmless situations as threatening—make some people more vulnerable to anxiety disorders. Stress may also predispose people to anxiety disorders.

CONCEPT CHECK 15.2

Distinguishing Among Anxiety Disorders

Check your understanding of the nature of anxiety and somatoform disorders by making preliminary diagnoses for the cases described below. Read each case summary and write your tentative diagnosis in the space provided. The answers are in Appendix A.

1. Malcolm religiously follows an exact schedule every day. His showering and grooming ritual takes two hours. He follows the same path in walking to his classes every day, and he always sits in the same seat in each class. He can't study until his apartment is arranged perfectly. Although he tries not to, he thinks constantly about flunking out of school. Both his grades and his social life are suffering from his rigid routines.

   Preliminary diagnosis: ______________________________

2. Jane has an intense fear of thunderstorms. Lightning and thunder terrify her. If she is home when a thunderstorm hits, she drops everything she is doing and runs to her basement. If she is out and about when a thunderstorm hits, she goes into a panic. She carefully monitors weather predictions to avoid this calamity. Because of her fear of thunderstorms she often misses work and she is worried that she may be fired.

   Preliminary diagnosis: ______________________________

3. Nathan recently returned from a six-month tour of military duty in Afghanistan where he saw a close friend die in combat. He keeps reliving the nightmare of seeing his friend die. He reports chronic feelings of anxiety, anger, and emotional numbing.

   Preliminary diagnosis: ______________________________

Dissociative Disorders

KEY LEARNING GOALS

15.8 Distinguish among three dissociative disorders.

15.9 Discuss the etiology of dissociative identity disorder.

Dissociative disorders are probably the most controversial set of disorders in the diagnostic system, sparking heated debate among normally subdued researchers and clinicians (Simeon & Loewenstein, 2009). ***Dissociative disorders*** **are a class of disorders in which people lose contact with portions of their consciousness or memory, resulting in disruptions in their sense of identity.** We'll describe three dissociative syndromes: dissociative amnesia, dissociative fugue, and dissociative identity disorder. All these disorders appear to be relatively uncommon, although good data on the prevalence of these disorders are scarce (Kihlstrom, 2005a).

Dissociative Amnesia and Fugue

Dissociative amnesia and fugue are overlapping disorders characterized by serious memory deficits. ***Dissociative amnesia*** **is a sudden loss of memory for important personal information that is too extensive to be due to normal forgetting.** Memory losses may occur for a single traumatic event (such as an automobile accident or home fire) or for an extended period of time surrounding the event. Cases of amnesia have been observed after people have experienced disasters, accidents, combat stress, physical abuse, and rape, or after they have witnessed the violent death of a parent, among other things (Arrigo & Pezdek, 1997; Cardena & Gleaves, 2007). **In *dissociative fugue,* people lose their memory for their entire lives along with their sense of personal identity.** These people forget their name, their family, where they live, and where they work. Despite this wholesale forgetting, they remember matters unrelated to their identity. They may, for example, remember how to drive a car or how to do math.

Dissociative Identity Disorder

Dissociative identity disorder (DID) **involves the coexistence in one person of two or more largely complete, and usually very different, personalities.** The name for this disorder used to be ***multiple personality disorder,*** which still enjoys informal use. In dissociative identity disorder, the divergences in behavior go far beyond those that people normally display in adapting to different roles in life. People with "multiple personalities" feel that they have more than one identity. Each personality has his or her own name, memories, traits, and physical mannerisms. Although rare, this "Dr. Jekyll and

Mr. Hyde" syndrome is frequently portrayed in novels, television shows, and movies, such as the *Three Faces of Eve,* a classic 1957 film starring Joanne Woodward; the satirical film *Me, Myself, and Irene,* a 2000 release starring Jim Carrey; and most recently the Showtime series the *United States of Tara.* In popular media portrayals, the syndrome is often mistakenly called *schizophrenia.* As you will see later, schizophrenic disorders are entirely different.

In dissociative identity disorder, the various personalities generally report that they are unaware of each other (Eich et al., 1997), although doubts have been raised about the accuracy of this assertion (Allen & Iacono, 2001). The alternate personalities commonly display traits that are quite foreign to the original personality. For instance, a shy, inhibited person might develop a flamboyant, extraverted alternate personality. Transitions between identities often occur suddenly. The disparities between identities can be bizarre. Different personalities may assert that they are different in age, race, gender, and sexual orientation (Kluft, 1996). Dissociative identity disorder rarely occurs in isolation. Most DID patients also have a history of anxiety, mood, or personality disorders (Ross, 1999). Dissociative identity disorder is seen more in women than men (Simeon & Loewenstein, 2009).

Starting in the 1970s, a dramatic increase was seen in the diagnosis of multiple-personality disorder (Kihlstrom, 2001, 2005a). Only 79 well-documented cases had accumulated up through 1970. Yet, by the late-1990s about 40,000 cases were estimated to have been reported (Lilienfeld & Lynn, 2003). Some theorists believe that these disorders used to be underdiagnosed—that is, they often went undetected (Maldonado & Spiegel, 2008). However, other theorists argue that a handful of clinicians have begun overdiagnosing the condition and that some clinicians even *encourage and contribute* to the emergence of DID (McHugh, 1995; Powell & Gee, 1999). Consistent with this view, a survey of all the psychiatrists in Switzerland found that 90% of them had never seen a case of dissociative identity disorder, whereas three of the psychiatrists had each seen more than 20 DID patients (Modestin, 1992). The data from this study suggest that 6 psychiatrists (out of 655 surveyed) accounted for two-thirds of the dissociative identity disorder diagnoses in Switzerland.

Etiology of Dissociative Disorders

Psychogenic amnesia and fugue are usually attributed to excessive stress. However, relatively little is known about why this extreme reaction to stress occurs in a tiny minority of people but not in the vast majority who are subjected to similar stress. Some theorists speculate that certain personality traits—fantasy proneness and a tendency to become intensely absorbed in personal experiences—may make some people more susceptible to dissociative disorders. Adequate evidence is lacking on this line of thought, however (Kihlstrom, Glisky, & Angiulo, 1994).

The causes of dissociative identity disorder are particularly obscure. Some skeptical theorists, such as Nicholas Spanos (1994, 1996) and others (Gee, Allen, & Powell, 2003; Lilienfeld et al., 1999), believe that people with multiple personalities are engaging in intentional role playing to use mental illness as a face-saving excuse for their personal failings. Spanos also argues that a small minority of therapists help create multiple personalities in their patients by subtly encouraging the emergence of alternate personalities. According to Spanos, dissociative identity disorder is a creation of modern North American culture. He even goes so far as to liken it to the creation of demonic possession during early Christianity. To bolster his argument, he discusses how multiple-personality patients' symptom presentations seem to have been influenced by popular media. For example, the typical patient with dissociative identity disorder used to report having two or three personalities. Yet since the publication of *Sybil* (Schreiber, 1973) and other books describing patients with many personalities, the average number of alternate personalities has climbed to about fifteen.

Despite these concerns, some clinicians are convinced that DID is an authentic disorder (Cardena & Gleaves, 2007; van der Hart & Nijenhuis, 2009). They argue that there's no incentive for either patients or therapists to manufacture cases of multiple personalities, given that both are often greeted with skepticism and outright hostility. They maintain that most cases of dissociative identity disorder are rooted in severe emotional trauma that occurred during childhood (Maldonado & Spiegel, 2008). A substantial majority of people with dissociative identity disorder report a childhood history of rejection from parents and physical and sexual abuse (Foote et al., 2006; van der Hart & Nijenhuis, 2009).

In the final analysis, little is known about the causes of dissociative identity disorder. It remains a controversial diagnosis (Barry-Walsh, 2005). In one survey of American psychiatrists, only one-quarter of the respondents indicated that they felt there was solid evidence for the scientific validity of the DID diagnosis (Pope et al., 1999). Consistent with this finding, a more recent study found that scientific interest in DID has dwindled since the mid-1990s (Pope et al., 2006).

REVIEW OF KEY LEARNING GOALS

15.8 Dissociative amnesia involves sudden memory loss that is too extensive to be due to normal forgetting. In dissociative fugue, people also lose their sense of identity. Dissociative identity disorder is marked by the coexistence of two or more very different personalities. Since the 1970s there has been a dramatic and controversial increase in the diagnosis of dissociative identity disorder.

15.9 Some theorists believe that people with dissociative identity disorder are engaging in intentional role playing as a face-saving excuse for their personal failings. Other theorists view DID as an authentic disorder rooted in emotional trauma that occurred during childhood.

Mood Disorders

PSYKTREK SIM9

KEY LEARNING GOALS

15.10 Describe the two major mood disorders and their relation to suicide.

15.11 Clarify how genetic, neurochemical, and other biological factors are related to the development of mood disorders.

15.12 Explain how cognitive factors can promote depression, and describe the Featured Study on negative thinking and depression.

15.13 Outline the role of interpersonal factors and stress in the development of mood disorders.

What did Abraham Lincoln, Leo Tolstoy, Marilyn Monroe, Vincent Van Gogh, Ernest Hemingway, Winston Churchill, Janis Joplin, Irving Berlin, Kurt Cobain, Francis Ford Coppola, Ted Turner, Sting, Billy Joel, Jim Carrey, Larry Flynt, and Ben Stiller have in common? Yes, they all achieved great prominence, albeit in different ways at different times. But, more pertinent to our interest, they all suffered from severe mood disorders. Mood disorders can be terribly debilitating. But people with mood disorders may still achieve greatness because such disorders tend to be *episodic*. In other words, mood disturbances often come and go. Between disturbances, there can be prolonged periods of normality.

Emotional fluctuations are natural. Some people, however, are subject to extreme and sustained distortions of mood. ***Mood disorders* are a class of disorders marked by emotional disturbances of varied kinds that may spill over to disrupt physical, perceptual, social, and thought processes.** There are two basic types of mood disorders: unipolar and bipolar (see **Figure 15.11** on the next page). People with *unipolar disorder* experience emotional extremes at just one end of the mood continuum. Such people are troubled only by *depression*. Others with *bipolar disorder* are vulnerable to emotional extremes at *both* ends of the mood continuum. People with bipolar disorder go through periods of both *depression* and *mania* (excitement and elation).

Major Depressive Disorder

PSYKTREK 11b

The line between normal dejection and unhappiness and abnormal depression can be difficult to draw (Akiskal, 2009). Ultimately, it requires a subjective judgment. Crucial considerations in this judgment include the duration of the depression and its disruptive effects. When a depression significantly impairs everyday adaptive behavior for more than a few weeks, there is reason for concern.

In *major depressive disorder*, people show persistent feelings of sadness and despair and a loss of interest in previous sources of pleasure. Negative emotions form the heart of the depressive syndrome. Many other symptoms may also appear, though. The most common symptoms of major depression are summarized and compared with the symptoms of mania in **Table 15.1** on the next page. A central feature of depression is ***anhedonia*—a diminished ability to experience pleasure.** Depressed people lack the energy or motivation to tackle the tasks of living, to the point where they often have trouble getting out of bed (Craighead et al., 2008). Hence, they often

© AP Images/Tammie Arroyo

© Helga Esteb/Shutterstock

Mood disorders are common and have affected many successful, well-known people, such as Gwyneth Paltrow and Owen Wilson.

Figure 15.11

Episodic patterns in mood disorders. Time-limited episodes of emotional disturbance come and go unpredictably in mood disorders. People with unipolar disorder suffer from bouts of depression only, whereas people with bipolar disorder experience both manic and depressive episodes. The time between episodes of disturbance can vary greatly.

© Cengage Learning 2013

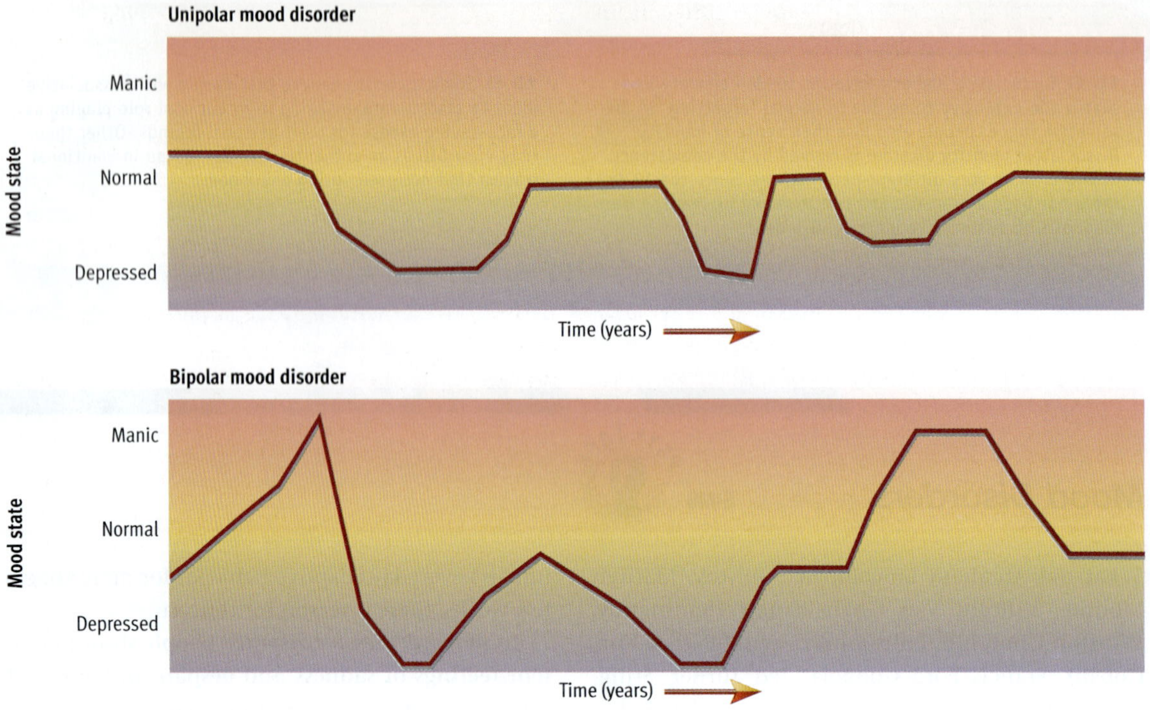

give up things that they used to enjoy, such as hobbies, favorite foods, or spending time with friends. Alterations in appetite and sleep patterns are common. People with depression often lack energy. They tend to move sluggishly and talk slowly. Anxiety, irritability, and brooding are commonly observed. Self-esteem tends to sink as the depressed person begins to feel worthless. Depression plunges people into feelings of hopelessness, dejection, and boundless guilt. To make matters worse, people who suffer from depression often exhibit other disorders as well. Coexisting anxiety disorders and substance use disorders are particularly common (Boland & Keller, 2009).

The onset of depression can occur at any point in the life span. However, a substantial majority of cases emerge before age 40 (Hammen, 2003). Depression occurs in children as well as adolescents and adults (Gruenberg & Goldstein, 2003). The vast majority (75%–95%) of people who suffer from depression experience more than one episode over the course of their lifetime (Joska & Stein, 2008). In one longitudinal study, after recovery from a first episode of depression, the cumulative probability of recurrence was 25% after one year, 42% after two years, and 60% after five years (Solomon et al., 2000). The average number of depressive episodes is 5 to 6. The average length of these episodes is about six months (Akiskal, 2009). Evidence suggests that an earlier age of onset is associated with more episodes of depression, more severe symptoms, and greater impairment of social and occupational functioning (Zisook et al., 2007). Although depression

Table 15.1 Comparisons of Common Symptoms in Manic and Depressive Episodes

Characteristics	Manic Episode	Depressive Episode
Emotional	Elated, euphoric, very sociable, impatient at any hindrance	Gloomy, hopeless, socially withdrawn, irritable
Cognitive	Characterized by racing thoughts, flight of ideas, desire for action, and impulsive behavior; talkative, self-confident; experiencing delusions of grandeur	Characterized by slowness of thought processes, obsessive worrying, inability to make decisions, negative self-image, self-blame and delusions of guilt and disease
Motor	Hyperactive, tireless, requiring less sleep than usual, showing increased sex drive and fluctuating appetite	Less active, tired, experiencing difficulty in sleeping, showing decreased sex drive and decreased appetite

SOURCE: Sarason, I. G., & Sarason, B. G. (1987). *Abnormal psychology: The problem of maladaptive behavior.* Upper Saddle River, NJ: Prentice-Hall. © 1987 Prentice-Hall, Inc. Reprinted by permission.

© Cengage Learning 2013

tends to be episodic, some people suffer from chronic major depression that may persist for years (Klein, 2010). Chronic major depression is associated with a particularly severe impairment of functioning. People with chronic depression tend to have a relatively early onset and high rates of comorbidity (additional disorders).

How common are depressive disorders? Well, estimates of the prevalence of depression vary quite a bit from one study to another because of the previously mentioned difficulty in drawing a line between normal dejection and abnormal depression. That said, depression is clearly a common disorder. The pooled data from the large-scale studies cited in **Figure 15.5** yielded a lifetime prevalence estimate of 13%–14%.

Research indicates that the prevalence of depression is about twice as high in women as it is in men (Nolen-Hoeksema & Hilt, 2009). The many possible explanations for this gender gap are the subject of considerable debate. The gap does *not* appear to be attributable to differences in genetic makeup (Kessler et al., 2003a). A small portion of the disparity may be the result of women's elevated vulnerability to depression at certain points in their reproductive life cycle (Nolen-Hoeksema & Hilt, 2009). Obviously, only women have to worry abut the phenomena of postpartum and postmenopausal depression. Susan Nolen-Hoeksema (2001) argues that women experience more depression than men because they are far more likely to be victims of sexual abuse and somewhat more likely to endure poverty, sexual harassment, role constraints, and excessive pressure to be thin and attractive. In other words, she attributes the higher prevalence of depression among women to their experience of greater stress and adversity. Nolen-Hoeksema also believes that women have a greater tendency than men to *ruminate* about setbacks and problems. Evidence suggests that this tendency to dwell on one's difficulties elevates vulnerability to depression, as we will discuss momentarily.

manzrussali/Shutterstock

Bipolar Disorder

11b

Bipolar disorder **(formerly known as *manic-depressive disorder*) is characterized by the experience of one or more manic episodes as well as periods of depression.** One manic episode is sufficient to qualify for this diagnosis. The symptoms seen in manic periods generally are the opposite of those seen in depression (see **Table 15.1** for a comparison). In a manic episode, a person's mood becomes elevated to the point of euphoria. Self-esteem skyrockets as the person bubbles over with optimism, energy, and extravagant plans. He or she becomes hyperactive and may go for days without sleep. The individual talks rapidly and shifts topics wildly. His or her mind is racing at breakneck speed. Judgment is often impaired. Some people in manic periods gamble impulsively, spend money frantically, or become sexually reckless.

You may be thinking that the euphoria in manic episodes sounds appealing. If so, you are not entirely wrong. In their milder forms, manic states can seem attractive. The increases in energy, self-esteem, and optimism can be deceptively seductive. Because of the increased energy, many bipolar patients report temporary surges of productivity and creativity (Goodwin & Jamison, 2007).

Although manic episodes may have some positive aspects, these periods often have a paradoxical negative undercurrent of irritability and depression (Goodwin & Jamison, 2007). Moreover, mild manic episodes usually escalate to higher levels that become scary and disturbing. Impaired judgment leads many victims to do things that they greatly regret later. Take the following case history, for example:

Robert, a dentist, awoke one morning with the idea that he was the most gifted dental surgeon in his tri-state area. He decided that he should try to provide services to as many people as possible, so that more people could benefit from his talents. Thus, he decided to remodel his two-chair dental office, installing 20 booths so that he could simultaneously attend to 20 patients. That same day he drew up plans for this arrangement, telephoned a number of remodelers, and invited bids for the work. Later that day, impatient to get rolling on his remodeling, he rolled up his sleeves, got himself a sledgehammer, and began to knock down the walls in his office. Annoyed when that didn't go so well, he smashed his dental tools, washbasins, and X-ray equipment. Later, Robert's wife became concerned about his behavior and summoned two of her adult daughters for assistance. The daughters responded quickly, arriving at the family home with their husbands. In the ensuing

"Those? Oh, just a few souvenirs from my bipolar-disorder days."

© Tom Cheney/The New Yorker Collection/www.cartoonbank.com

discussion, Robert—after bragging about his sexual prowess—made advances toward his daughters. He had to be subdued by their husbands. (Adapted from Kleinmuntz, 1980, p. 309)

Although not rare, bipolar disorders are much less common than unipolar disorders. Bipolar disorder affects roughly about 1% of the population (Merikangas & Pato, 2009). Unlike depressive disorder, bipolar disorder is seen equally often in males and females (Rihmer & Angst, 2009). As **Figure 15.12** shows, the onset of bipolar disorder is age related. The typical age of onset is in the late teens. The mood swings in bipolar disorder can be patterned in many ways. Manic episodes typically last about four months (Angst, 2009). Episodes of depression tend to run somewhat longer, and most bipolar patients end up spending more time in depressed states than manic states (Bauer, 2008).

Mood Disorders and Suicide

A tragic, heartbreaking problem associated with mood disorders is suicide. Suicide is the eleventh leading cause of death in the United States. It accounts for about 30,000 deaths annually. Official statistics may underestimate the scope of the problem. Many suicides are disguised as accidents, either by the suicidal person or by the survivors who try to cover up afterward. Moreover, experts estimate that suicide attempts may outnumber completed suicides by a ratio of as much as ten to one (Sudak, 2009). Anyone can commit suicide. However, some groups are at higher risk than others (Carroll-Ghosh, Victor, & Bourgeois, 2003). Evidence suggests that women *attempt* suicide three times more often than men, but men are more likely to actually kill themselves in an attempt: Men *complete* four times as many suicides as women. In regard to age, completed suicides peak in the over-75 age bracket.

With the luxury of hindsight, it's recognized that about 90% of the people who complete suicide suffer from some type of psychological disorder (Melvin et al., 2008). In some cases, though, this disorder may not be readily apparent beforehand. As you might expect, suicide rates are highest for people with mood disorders. They account for about 60% of completed suicides (Mann & Currier, 2006). Both bipolar disorder and depression are associated with dramatic elevations in suicide rates. Studies suggest that the lifetime risk of completed suicide is about 15%–20% in people with bipolar disorder and

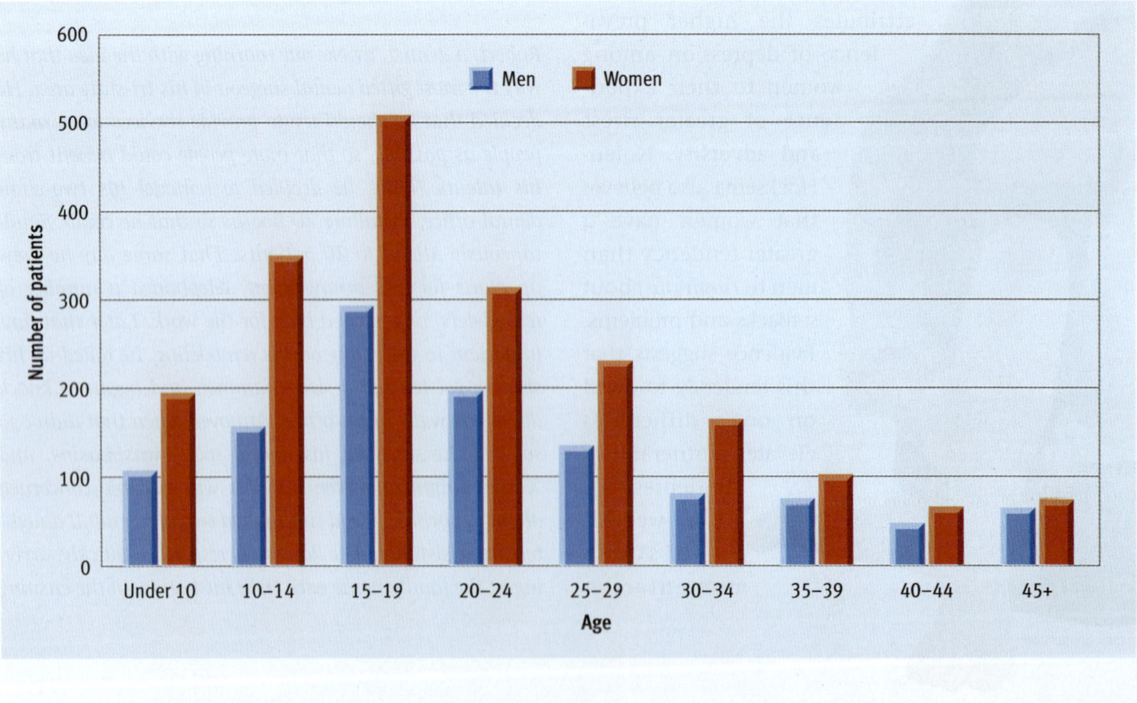

Figure 15.12

Age of onset for bipolar mood disorder. The onset of bipolar disorder typically occurs in adolescence or early adulthood. The data graphed here, which were combined from seven studies, show the distribution of age of onset for 2968 bipolar patients. As you can see, bipolar disorder emerges most frequently around the ages of 15–19. The modal age of onset for bipolar disorder appears to have declined in recent decades.

SOURCE: Goodwin, F. K., & Jamison, K. R. (2007). *Manic-depressive illness* (p. 124). New York: Oxford University Press. Copyright © 2007 Oxford University Press, Inc. Reprinted by permission.

© Cengage Learning 2013

about 10%-15% in those who have grappled with depression (Sudak, 2009), but some experts believe that these estimates are overly high (Joiner et al., 2009). Smaller elevations in suicide rates are seen among people who suffer from schizophrenia, alcoholism, and substance abuse (Mann & Currier, 2006). Unfortunately, there is no foolproof way to prevent suicidal persons from taking their own life. But some useful tips are compiled in **Figure 15.13**.

Etiology of Mood Disorders 11b

Quite a bit is known about the etiology of mood disorders, although the puzzle certainly hasn't been assembled completely. There appear to be a number of routes into these disorders. They involve intricate interactions among psychological and biological factors.

Suicide Prevention Tips

1. *Take suicidal talk seriously.* When people talk about suicide in vague generalities, it's easy to dismiss it as idle talk and let it go. However, people who talk about suicide are a high-risk group, and their veiled threats should not be ignored. The first step in suicide prevention is to directly ask such people if they're contemplating suicide.

2. *Provide empathy and social support.* It is important to show the suicidal person that you care. People often contemplate suicide because they see the world around them as indifferent and uncaring. Thus, you must demonstrate to the suicidal person that you are genuinely concerned. Suicide threats are often a last ditch cry for help. It is therefore imperative that you offer to help.

3. *Identify and clarify the crucial problem.* The suicidal person is often confused and feels lost in a sea of frustration and problems. It is a good idea to try to help sort through this confusion. Encourage the person to try to identify the crucial problem. Once it is isolated, the problem may not seem quite so overwhelming.

4. *Do not promise to keep someone's suicidal ideation secret.* If you really feel like someone's life is in danger, don't agree to keep his or her suicidal plans secret to preserve your friendship.

5. *In an acute crisis, do not leave a suicidal person alone.* Stay with the person until additional help is available. Try to remove any guns, drugs, sharp objects, and so forth that might provide an available means to commit suicide.

6. *Encourage professional consultation.* Most mental health professionals have some experience in dealing with suicidal crises. Many cities have suicide prevention centers with 24-hour hotlines. These centers are staffed with people who have been specially trained to deal with suicidal problems. It is important to try to get a suicidal person to seek professional assistance.

© Cengage Learning 2013

Figure 15.13

Preventing Suicide. As Sudak (2005) notes, "It is not possible to prevent all suicides or to totally and absolutely protect a given patient from suicide. What is possible is to reduce the likelihood of suicide" (p. 2449). Hence, the advice summarized here may prove useful if you ever have to help someone through a suicidal crisis. (Based on American Association of Suicidology, 2007; American Foundation for Suicide Prevention, 2007; Fremouw et al., 1990; Rosenthal, 1988; Shneidman, Farberow, & Litman, 1994)

Genetic Vulnerability 11b

Twin studies suggest that genetic factors are involved in mood disorders (Lohoff & Berrettini, 2009; Kelsoe, 2009). Concordance rates average around 65% for identical twins but only 14% for fraternal twins, who share less genetic similarity (see **Figure 15.14**). Thus, evidence suggests that heredity can create a *predisposition* to mood disorders. Environmental factors probably determine whether this predisposition is converted into an actual disorder. The influence of genetic factors appears to be stronger for bipolar disorders than for unipolar disorders (Kieseppa et al., 2004). Some promising results have been reported in *genetic mapping* studies that have attempted to pinpoint the specific genes that shape vulnerability to mood disorders (Levinson, 2009). However, results have been disturbingly inconsistent. Scientists do *not* appear to be on the verge of unraveling the genetic code for mood disorders, which probably depend on subtle variations in constellations of many genes (Bearden, Jasinka, & Freimer, 2009; Kendler, 2005a, 2005b).

Neurochemical and Neuroanatomical Factors 11b

Heredity may influence susceptibility to mood disorders by creating a predisposition toward certain types of neurochemical abnormalities in the brain. Correlations have been found between mood disorders and abnormal levels of two key neurotransmitters in the brain: norepinephrine and serotonin (Duman, Polan, & Schatzberg, 2008). Other neurotransmitter disturbances may also contribute (Dunlop, Garlow, & Nemeroff, 2009). The details remain elusive, but low levels of serotonin appear to be a crucial factor underlying most forms of depression (Johnson et al., 2009). A variety of drug therapies are fairly effective in the treatment of severe mood disorders. Most of these drugs are known to

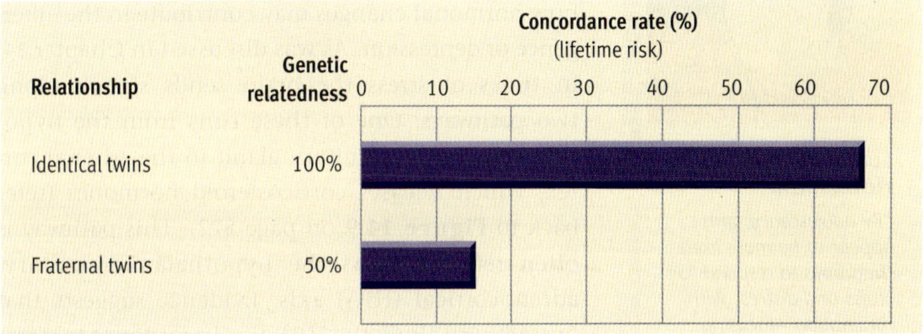

© Cengage Learning 2013

Figure 15.14

Twin studies of mood disorders. The concordance rate for mood disorders in identical twins is much higher than that for fraternal twins, who share less genetic overlap. These results suggest that there must be a genetic predisposition to mood disorders. (Data from Berrettini, 2006)

affect the availability (in the brain) of the neurotransmitters that have been related to mood disorders (Bhagwagar & Heninger, 2009). Since this effect is unlikely to be a coincidence, it bolsters the plausibility of the idea that neurochemical changes produce mood disturbances. That said, after 50 years of enormous research effort, the neurochemical bases of mood disorders remain more mysterious than scientists would like.

Studies have also found some interesting correlations between mood disorders and a variety of structural abnormalities in the brain (Flores et al., 2004). Perhaps the best-documented correlation is the association between depression and *reduced hippocampal volume* (Davidson, Pizzagalli, & Nitschke, 2009; Videbech, 2006). The *hippocampus* is known to play a major role in memory consolidation (see Chapter 7). Interestingly, it tends to be about 8%–10% smaller in depressed subjects than in normal subjects (Videbech & Ravnkilde, 2004). A fascinating new theory of the biological bases of depression may be able to account for this finding. The springboard for this theory is the recent discovery that the human brain continues to generate new neurons in adulthood, especially in the hippocampal formation. As noted elsewhere (see Chapters 3, 7, and 14), this process is called *neurogenesis*. Evidence suggests that depression occurs when major life stress causes neurochemical reactions that suppress neurogenesis, resulting in reduced hippocampal volume (Jacobs, 2004; Duman et al., 2008). According to this view, suppression of neurogenesis is the central cause of depression and antidepressant drugs are successful because they promote neurogenesis (Duman & Monteggia, 2006). A great deal of additional research will be required to fully test this innovative new model of the biological bases of depressive disorders.

Courtesy of Susan Nolen-Hoeksema

Susan Nolen-Hoeksema

"By adolescence, girls appear to be more likely than boys to respond to stress and distress with rumination—focusing inward on feelings of distress and personal concerns rather than taking action to relieve their distress."

Hormonal Factors

In recent years researchers have begun to focus on how hormonal changes may contribute to the emergence of depression. As was discussed in Chapter 14, in times of stress the brain sends signals along two pathways. One of these runs from the hypothalamus to the pituitary gland to the adrenal cortex, which releases corticosteroid hormones (refer back to **Figure 14.9** on page 572). This pathway is often referred to as the hypothalamic-pituitary-adrenocortical (HPA) axis. Evidence suggests that overactivity along the HPA axis in response to stress may often play a role in the development of depression (Goodwin, 2009). Consistent with this hypothesis, depressed patients tend to show elevated levels of cortisol, a key stress hormone produced by HPA activity (Thase, 2009a). Some theorists believe that these hormonal changes eventually have an impact in the brain, where they may be the trigger for the suppression of neurogenesis that we just discussed (Duman et al., 2008).

Cognitive Factors

11b

A variety of theories emphasize how cognitive factors contribute to depressive disorders (Christensen, Carney, &Segal, 2006). We'll discuss Aaron Beck's (1976, 1987, 2008) influential cognitive theory of depression in Chapter 16, where his approach to therapy is described. In this section, we'll focus on Martin Seligman's *learned helplessness model* of depression. Based largely on animal research, Seligman (1974) proposed that depression is caused by *learned helplessness*—passive "giving up" behavior produced by exposure to unavoidable aversive events (such as uncontrollable shock in a lab experiment). He originally considered learned helplessness to be a product of conditioning but eventually revised his theory, giving it a cognitive slant. The reformulated theory of learned helplessness asserts that the roots of depression lie in how people explain the setbacks and other negative events that they experience (Abramson, Seligman, & Teasdale, 1978). According to Seligman (1990), people who exhibit a *pessimistic explanatory style* are especially vulnerable to depression. These people tend to attribute their setbacks to their personal flaws instead of situational factors. Moreover, they tend to draw global, far-reaching conclusions about their personal inadequacies based on these setbacks.

In accord with this line of thinking, Susan Nolen-Hoeksema (1991, 2000) has found that depressed people who *ruminate* about their depression remain depressed longer than those who try to distract themselves. People who respond to depression with rumination repetitively focus their attention on their depressing feelings. They think constantly about how sad, lethargic, and unmotivated they are. Excessive rumination tends to foster and amplify episodes of depression by increasing negative thinking, impairing problem solving, and undermining social support (Nolen-Hoeksema, Wisco, & Lyubomirsky, 2008). As noted earlier, Nolen-Hoeksema believes that women have a greater tendency to ruminate than men and that this disparity may be a major reason that depression is more prevalent in women. Moreover, the effects of rumination are not limited to depressive disorders. Rumination is also associated with increased anxiety, binge eating, and binge drinking (Nolen-Hoeksema et al., 2008).

In sum, cognitive models of depression maintain that negative thinking is what leads to depression in many people. The principal problem with cognitive theories is their difficulty in separating cause from effect (Feliciano & Areán, 2007). Does negative thinking cause depression? Or does depression cause negative thinking (see **Figure 15.15**)? A *clear* demonstration of a causal link between negative thinking and depression is not possible, because it would require manipulating people's cognitive style (which is not easy to change) in sufficient degree to produce full-fledged depressive disorders (which would not be ethical). However, the research reported in our Featured Study provided impressive evidence consistent with a causal link between negative thinking and vulnerability to depression.

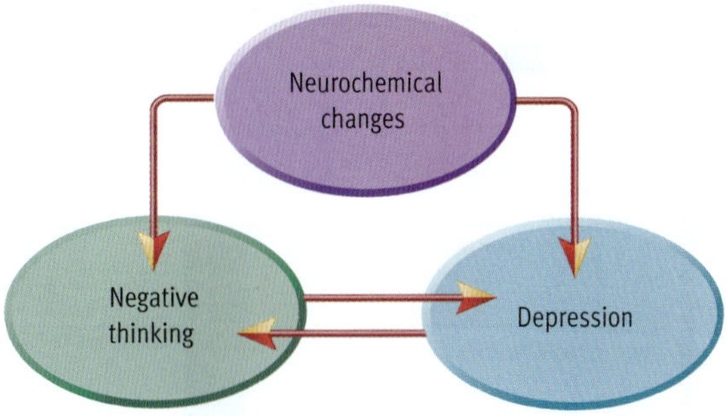

Figure 15.15

Interpreting the correlation between negative thinking and depression. Cognitive theories of depression assume that consistent patterns of negative thinking cause depression. Although these theories are highly plausible, depression could cause negative thoughts, or both could be caused by a third factor, such as neurochemical changes in the brain. © Cengage Learning 2013

FEATURED STUDY

Does Negative Thinking Cause *Depression?*

SOURCE: Alloy, L. B., Abramson, L. Y., Whitehouse, W. G., Hogan, M. E., Tashman, N. A., Steinberg, D. L., Rose, D. T., & Donovan, P. (1999). Depressogenic cognitive styles: Predictive validity, information processing and personality characteristics, and developmental origins. *Behavioral Research and Therapy, 37,* 503–531.

This article describes a series of studies conducted at Temple University and at the University of Wisconsin. They are collectively referred to as the Temple-Wisconsin Cognitive Vulnerability to Depression Project. The article reports on many facets of the project. However we will focus on the study intended to test the hypothesis that a negative cognitive style is predictive of elevated vulnerability to depression.

Method

Participants. Over 5,000 first-year students at the two universities responded to two measures of negative thinking. Students who scored in the highest quartile on both measures were characterized as having a *high risk* for depression. Those who scored in the lowest quartile on both measures were characterized as having a *low risk* for depression. Randomly selected subsets of these two groups were invited for additional screening to eliminate anyone who was *currently* depressed or suffering from any other major psychological disorder. People who had *previously* suffered from depression or other disorders were not eliminated. The final sample consisted of 173 students in the high-risk group and 176 students in the low-risk group.

Follow-up assessments. Self-report measures and structured interviews were used to evaluate the mental health of the participants every 6 weeks for the first 2 years and then every 16 weeks for an additional 3 years. The assessments were conducted by interviewers who were blind regarding the subjects' risk group status. The present report summarized the follow-up data for the first 2½ years of the study. The results were given separately for those who did and did not have a prior history of depression.

Results

The data for students who had no prior history of depression showed dramatic differences between the high-risk and low-risk groups in vulnerability to depression. During the relatively brief 2.5-year period, a major depressive disorder emerged in 17% of the high-risk students in comparison to only 1% of the low-risk students. The high-risk subjects also displayed a much greater incidence of minor depressive episodes, as you can see in the left panel of **Figure 15.16** on the next page. The right panel of **Figure 15.16** shows the comparisons for participants who had a prior history of depression (but were not depressed or suffering from any other disorder at the beginning of the study). The data show that high-risk subjects were more vulnerable to a recurrence of both major and minor depression during the 2.5-year follow-up.

Discussion

The high-risk participants, who exhibited a negative cognitive style, were consistently found to have an elevated likelihood of developing depressive disorders. Hence, the authors conclude that their results provide strong support for the cognitive vulnerability hypothesis. This theory asserts that negative thinking makes people more vulnerable to depression.

Comment

Previous studies of the correlation between negative thinking and depression used *retrospective designs,* which look backward in time from known outcomes. For example, investigators might compare depressed subjects versus nondepressed subjects on some measure of negative thinking. What makes the design retrospective is that the researchers already know which people experienced the

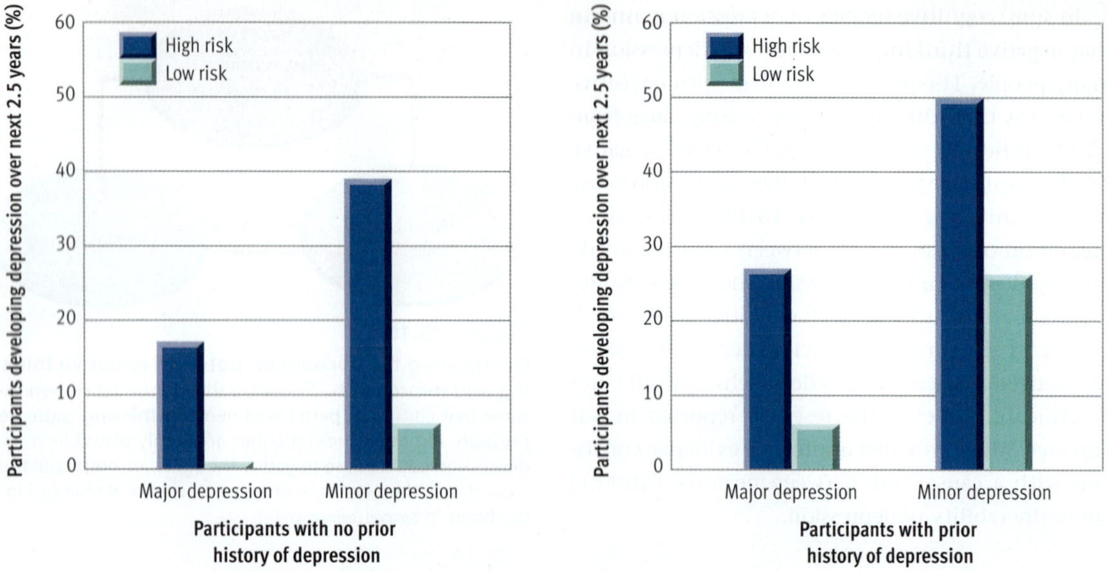

Figure 15.16
Negative thinking and prediction of depression. Alloy and colleagues (1999) measured the cognitive styles of first-year college students and characterized the students as high risk or low risk for depression. These graphs show the percentage of these students who experienced major or minor episodes of depression over the next 2.5 years. As you can see, the high-risk students who exhibited a negative thinking style proved to be much more vulnerable to depression. © Cengage Learning 2013

outcome of depression. Retrospective designs can yield useful information, but they don't provide much insight about causation. Why? Because if you find an association between depression and negative thinking you can't determine whether the negative thinking preceded the depression or the depression preceded the negative thinking. The present study used a *prospective design,* which moves forward in time, testing hypotheses about future outcomes. Prospective studies are much more difficult and time-consuming to conduct, but they can provide more insight about causation because they can show that one event (in this instance, the development of a negative cognitive style) preceded another (the occurrence of depression). The data are still correlational, so they cannot definitively establish a causal link, but they provide much stronger evidence in favor of causation than retrospective data do. Thus, the research by Alloy and her colleagues provides the best evidence to date in support of the hypothesis that negative thinking contributes to the causation of depressive disorders.

Interpersonal Roots 11b

Behavioral approaches to understanding depression emphasize how inadequate social skills put people on the road to depressive disorders (see **Figure 15.17**; Ingram, Scott, & Hamill, 2009). According to this notion, depression-prone people lack the social finesse needed to acquire many important kinds of reinforcers, such as good friends, top jobs, and desirable spouses. A paucity of reinforcers could understandably lead to negative emotions and depression. Consistent with this theory, researchers have found correlations between poor social skills and depression (Petty, Sachs-Ericsson, & Joiner, 2004). Evidence also suggests that depressed people unintentionally court rejection from others because they tend to be irritable, pessimistic, unpleasant companions (Joiner & Timmons, 2009). Another problem is that depressed people tend to have fewer sources of social support than nondepressed people. This situation is unfortunate in that low social support can increase vulnerability to depression (Lakey & Cronin, 2008). Research suggests that lack of social support may make a larger contribution to depression in women than in men (Kendler, Myers, & Prescott, 2005).

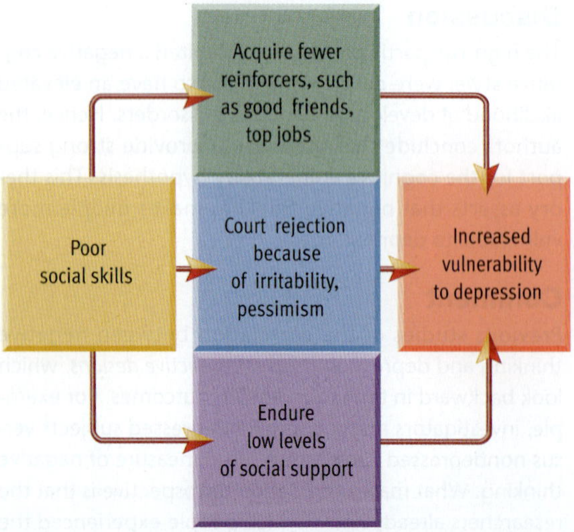

Figure 15.17
Interpersonal factors in depression. Behavioral theories about the etiology of depression emphasize how inadequate social skills may contribute to the development of the disorder through several mechanisms, as diagrammed here. © Cengage Learning 2013

Precipitating Stress 11b

Mood disorders sometimes appear mysteriously in people who are leading benign, nonstressful lives.

For this reason, experts used to believe that mood disorders are not influenced much by stress. However, advances in the measurement of personal stress have altered this picture. The evidence available today suggests a moderately strong link between stress and the onset of mood disorders (Monroe, Slavich, & Georgiades, 2009). Stress also appears to affect how people with mood disorders respond to treatment and whether they experience a relapse of their disorder (Monroe & Hadjiyannakis, 2002).

Of course, the majority of people who experience severe stress endure it without getting depressed (Monroe & Reid, 2009). The impact of stress varies, in part, because people vary in their degree of *vulnerability* to mood disorders (Lewinsohn, Joiner, & Rohde, 2001). Similar interactions between stress and vulnerability probably influence the development of many kinds of disorders, including those that are next on our agenda—the schizophrenic disorders.

REVIEW OF KEY LEARNING GOALS

15.10 Major depression is marked by profound sadness, slowed thought processes, and loss of interest in previous sources of pleasure. Bipolar disorder involves the experience of both manic episodes and periods of depression. Manic episodes are characterized by inflated self-esteem, high energy, grandiose plans, and racing thoughts. Depression is extremely common, whereas the lifetime prevalence of bipolar disorder is about 1%. Both types of mood disorders are associated with greatly elevated rates of suicide.

15.11 Evidence indicates that people vary in their genetic vulnerability to mood disorders. These disorders are accompanied by changes in neurochemical activity in the brain. Abnormalities at norepinephrine and serotonin synapses appear particularly critical. Reduced hippocampal volume and suppressed neurogenesis are also associated with depression. Hormonal changes resulting from overactivity along the HPA axis may contribute to depression.

15.12 Cognitive models posit that negative thinking contributes to depression. A pessimistic explanatory style has been implicated, as has a tendency to ruminate about one's problems. The Featured Study reported impressive evidence in support of the idea that negative thinking can contribute to the causation of depression.

15.13 Interpersonal inadequacies may contribute to depressive disorders. Poor social skills may lead to a shortage of life's reinforcers and low social support. Mood disorders may also be precipitated by high stress, especially in those who are vulnerable to mood disorders.

Schizophrenic Disorders

SIM9

KEY LEARNING GOALS

15.14 Review the general characteristics of schizophrenia.

15.15 Outline the classification of schizophrenic subtypes and the course of schizophrenia.

15.16 Explain how genetic vulnerability, neurochemical factors, and structural abnormalities in the brain are related to schizophrenia.

15.17 Analyze the role of neurodevelopmental processes, family dynamics, and stress in the etiology of schizophrenia.

***Schizophrenic disorders* are a class of disorders marked by delusions, hallucinations, disorganized speech, and deterioration of adaptive behavior.** People with schizophrenic disorders often display some of the same symptoms seen in people with severe mood disorders. However, disturbed *thought* lies at the core of schizophrenic disorders, whereas disturbed *emotion* lies at the core of mood disorders.

How common is schizophrenia? Historically, prevalence estimates have suggested that about 1% of the population may suffer from schizophrenia (Lauriello, Bustillo, & Keith, 2005), although a recent meta-analysis concluded that prevalence might be a little lower (McGrath, 2007). That may not sound like much. However, it means that in the United States alone there may be several million people troubled by schizophrenic disturbances. Moreover, schizophrenia is an extremely costly illness for society. It is a severe, debilitating disorder that tends to have an early onset and often requires lengthy hospital care (Samnaliev & Clark, 2008). Because of these considerations, the financial impact of schizophrenia is estimated to exceed the costs of all types of cancers combined (Buchanan & Carpenter, 2005).

General Symptoms

11c

There are a number of distinct schizophrenic syndromes. Yet they do share some general characteristics that we will examine before looking at the subtypes. Many of these characteristics are apparent in the following case history (adapted from Sheehan, 1982).

Sylvia was first given a diagnosis of schizophrenia at age 15. She has been in and out of many types of psychiatric facilities since then. She has never been able to hold a job for any length of time. During severe flare-ups of her disorder, her personal hygiene deteriorates. She rarely washes, she wears clothes that neither fit nor match, she smears makeup on heavily but randomly, and she slops food all over herself. Sylvia occasionally hears voices talking to her. She tends to be argumentative, aggressive, and emotionally volatile. Over the years, she has been involved in innumerable fights with fellow patients, psychiatric staff members, and strangers. Her thoughts can be highly irrational, as is apparent from the following quote:

"Mick Jagger wants to marry me. If I have Mick Jagger, I don't have to covet Geraldo Rivera. Mick Jagger is St. Nicholas and the Maharishi is Santa Claus. I want to form a gospel rock group called the Thorn Oil, but Geraldo wants me to be the music critic on Eyewitness News, so what can I do? Got to listen to my boyfriend. Teddy Kennedy cured me of my ugliness. I'm pregnant with the son of God. They're eating the patients here. I work for Epic Records. I'm Joan of Arc. I'm Florence Nightingale. The door between the ward and the porch is the dividing line between New York and California. Divorce isn't a piece of paper, it's a feeling. Forget about Zip Codes. I need shock treatments. The body is run by electricity. My wiring is all faulty." (Sheehan, 1982, pp. 104–105)

Sylvia's case clearly shows that schizophrenic thinking can be bizarre and that schizophrenia can be a severe and debilitating disorder. Although no single symptom is inevitably present, the following symptoms are commonly seen in schizophrenia (Lewis, Escalona, & Keith, 2009; Liddle, 2009).

Delusions and Irrational Thought

Cognitive deficits and disturbed thought processes are the central, defining feature of schizophrenic disorders (Barch, 2003; Heinrichs, 2005). Various kinds of delusions are common. ***Delusions* are false beliefs that are maintained even though they clearly are out of touch with reality.** For example, one patient's delusion that he was a tiger (with a deformed body) persisted for more than 15 years (Kulick, Pope, & Keck, 1990). More typically, affected persons believe that their private thoughts are being broadcast to other people, that thoughts are being injected into their mind against their will, or that their thoughts are being controlled by some external force (Maher, 2001). In *delusions of grandeur,* people maintain that they are famous or important. Sylvia expressed an endless array of grandiose delusions, such as thinking that Mick Jagger wanted to marry her, that she had dictated the *The Lord of the Rings* books to J. R. R. Tolkien, and that she was going to win the Nobel prize for medicine.

Another characteristic of schizophrenia is that the person's train of thought deteriorates. Thinking becomes chaotic rather than logical and linear. The person experiences a "loosening of associations." He or she shifts topics in disjointed ways. The quotation from Sylvia illustrates this wild flight of ideas dramatically.

Deterioration of Adaptive Behavior

Schizophrenia usually involves a noticeable deterioration in the quality of the person's routine functioning in work, social relations, and personal care. Friends will often make remarks such as "Hal just isn't himself anymore." This deterioration is readily apparent in Sylvia's inability to get along with others or to function in the work world. It's also apparent in her neglect of personal hygiene.

Hallucinations

A variety of perceptual distortions may occur with schizophrenia. The most common are auditory hallucinations, which are reported by about 75% of patients (Combs & Mueser, 2007). ***Hallucinations* are sensory perceptions that occur in the absence of a real, external stimulus or are gross distortions of perceptual input.** People with schizophrenia frequently report that they hear voices of nonexistent or absent people talking to them. Sylvia, for instance, said she heard messages from Paul McCartney. These voices often provide an insulting, running commentary on the person's behavior ("You're an idiot for shaking his hand"). They may be argumentative ("You don't need a bath"). They may issue commands ("Prepare your home for visitors from outer space").

Disturbed Emotion

Normal emotional tone can be disrupted in schizophrenia in a variety of ways. Although it may not be an accurate indicator of their underlying emotional experience (Kring, 1999), some victims show little emotional responsiveness. This symptom is referred to as "blunted or flat affect." Others show inappropriate emotional responses that don't jibe with the situation or with what they are saying. For instance, a schizophrenic patient might cry over a silly cartoon and then laugh about a news story describing a child's tragic death. People with schizophrenia may also become emotionally volatile. This pattern was displayed by Sylvia, who often overreacted emotionally in erratic, unpredictable ways.

Subtypes, Course, and Outcome

PsykTrek 11c

Four subtypes of schizophrenic disorders are recognized, including a category for people who don't fit neatly into any of the first three categories. The major symptoms of each subtype are as follows (Lewis et al., 2009; Minzenberg, Yoon, & Carter, 2008).

Reality CHECK

Misconception

Schizophrenia refers to the syndrome in which a person manifests two or more personalities.

Reality

Literally, *schizophrenia* means "split mind." However, when Eugen Bleuler coined the term in 1911, he was referring to the fragmentation of thought processes seen in schizophrenia—not to a "split personality." Unfortunately, writers in the popular media often erroneously equate the split-mind notion with split personality. As you have already learned, this syndrome is actually called *dissociative identity disorder* or *multiple-personality disorder.*

Paranoid Type

As its name implies, ***paranoid schizophrenia* is dominated by delusions of persecution, along with delusions of grandeur.** In this common form of schizophrenia, people come to believe that they have many enemies who want to harass and oppress them. They may become suspicious of friends and relatives, or they may attribute the persecution to mysterious, unknown persons. They are convinced that they are being watched and manipulated in malicious ways. To make sense of this persecution, they often develop delusions of grandeur. They believe that they must be enormously important people, often seeing themselves as great inventors or as famous religious or political leaders.

Catatonic Type

***Catatonic schizophrenia* is marked by striking motor disturbances, ranging from muscular rigidity to random motor activity.** Some patients go into an extreme form of withdrawal known as a catatonic stupor. They may remain virtually motionless and seem oblivious to the environment around them for long periods of time. Others go into a state of catatonic excitement. They become hyperactive and incoherent. Some alternate between these dramatic extremes. The catatonic subtype is not particularly common. In fact, its prevalence seems to be declining.

Disorganized Type

In *disorganized schizophrenia,* a particularly severe deterioration of adaptive behavior is seen. Prominent symptoms include emotional indifference, frequent incoherence, and virtually complete social withdrawal. Aimless babbling and giggling are common. Delusions often center on bodily functions ("My brain is melting out my ears").

Undifferentiated Type

People who are clearly schizophrenic but who cannot be placed into any of the three other categories are said to have ***undifferentiated schizophrenia,* which is marked by idiosyncratic mixtures of schizophrenic symptoms.** The undifferentiated subtype is fairly common.

Positive Versus Negative Symptoms

Many theorists have raised doubts about the value of dividing schizophrenic disorders into the four subtypes we've described (Sanislow & Carson, 2001). Critics note that the catatonic subtype is disappearing and that undifferentiated cases aren't so much a subtype as a hodgepodge of "leftovers." Critics also point out that there aren't meaningful differences between the subtypes in etiology, prognosis, or response to treatment. The absence of such differences casts doubt on the value of the current classification scheme.

Because of such problems, Nancy Andreasen (1990) and others (Carpenter, 1992; McGlashan & Fenton, 1992) proposed an alternative approach to subtyping. The new scheme divided schizophrenic disorders into just two categories based on the predominance of negative versus positive symptoms. ***Negative symptoms* involve behavioral deficits, such as flattened emotions, social withdrawal, apathy, impaired attention, and poverty of speech. *Positive symptoms* involve behavioral excesses or peculiarities, such as hallucinations, delusions, bizarre behavior, and wild flights of ideas.**

Theorists advocating this scheme hoped to find consistent differences between the two subtypes in etiology, prognosis, and response to treatment. Some progress along these lines *has* been made. For example, a predominance of positive symptoms is associated with better adjustment prior to the onset of schizophrenia and greater responsiveness to treatment (Combs & Mueser, 2007; Galderisi et al., 2002). However, the assumption that patients can be placed into discrete categories based on this scheme now seems untenable. Most patients exhibit both types of symptoms and vary only in the *degree* to which positive or negative symptoms dominate (Andreasen, 2009). It seems fair to say that the distinction between positive and negative symptoms has enhanced our understanding of schizophrenia. However, it has not yielded a classification scheme that can replace the traditional subtypes of schizophrenia.

Courtesy of Nancy Andreasen, M.D.

Nancy Andreasen

"Schizophrenia disfigures the emotional and cognitive faculties of its victims, and sometimes nearly destroys them."

Course and Outcome

Schizophrenic disorders usually emerge during adolescence or early adulthood. Seventy-five percent of cases manifest by the age of 30 (Perkins, Miller-Anderson, & Lieberman, 2006). Those who develop schizophrenia usually have a long history of peculiar behavior and cognitive and social deficits. Most, though, do not manifest a full-fledged psychological disorder during childhood (Walker et al., 2004). The emergence of schizophrenia may be sudden, but more often it's insidious and gradual. Once the disorder clearly emerges, its course is variable. Patients tend to fall into three broad groups. Some patients, presumably those with milder disorders, are treated successfully and enjoy a full recovery. Other patients experience a partial recovery and can return to independent living for a time. However, they experience regular relapses over the remainder of their lives. Finally, a third group of patients endure chronic illness marked by extensive hospitalization. Estimates of the percentage of patients falling in each category vary. Overall,

CONCEPT CHECK 15.3

Distinguishing Schizophrenic and Mood Disorders

Check your understanding of the nature of schizophrenic and mood disorders by making preliminary diagnoses for the cases described below. Read each case summary and write your tentative diagnosis in the space provided. The answers are in Appendix A.

1. Max hasn't slept in four days. He's determined to write the "great American novel" before his class reunion, which is a few months away. He expounds eloquently on his novel to anyone who will listen, talking at such a rapid pace that no one can get a word in edgewise. He feels like he's wired with energy and is supremely confident about the novel, even though he's only written 10 to 20 pages. Last week, he charged $5000 worth of new computer equipment and software, which is supposed to help him write his book.

   Preliminary diagnosis: ______________________

2. Eduardo maintains that he invented the atomic bomb, even though he was born after its invention. He says he invented it to punish homosexuals, Nazis, and short people. It's short people that he's really afraid of. He's sure that all the short people on TV are talking about him. He thinks that short people are conspiring to make him look like a Republican. Eduardo frequently gets in arguments with people and is emotionally volatile. His grooming is poor, but he says it's okay because he's the secretary of state.

   Preliminary diagnosis: ______________________

3. Margaret has hardly gotten out of bed for weeks, although she's troubled by insomnia. She doesn't feel like eating and has absolutely no energy. She feels dejected, discouraged, spiritless, and apathetic. Friends stop by to try to cheer her up, but she tells them not to waste their time on "pond scum."

   Preliminary diagnosis: ______________________

studies have suggested that only about 20% of schizophrenic patients enjoy a full recovery (Perkins et al., 2006; Robinson et al., 2004). To some extent, though, this low recovery rate may reflect the poor to mediocre quality of mental health care available for severe disorders in many countries, including wealthy ones (see Chapter 16). For example, when comprehensive, well-coordinated, quality care is initiated promptly, higher recovery rates in the vicinity of 50% have been found (Hopper et al., 2007; Liberman & Kopelowicz, 2005). Although schizophrenia is often viewed as a disorder marked by relentless deterioration, it is clear that a sizable portion of patients experience a reasonable degree of recovery (Jablensky, 2009). Thus, the outlook for schizophrenia may not need to be as pervasively negative as it has been.

John Nash, the Nobel Prize–winning mathematician whose story was told in the film *A Beautiful Mind*, has struggled with paranoid schizophrenia since 1959.

© AP Images/Charles Rex Arbogast

Etiology of Schizophrenia 11c

You can probably identify, at least to some extent, with people who suffer from mood disorders or anxiety disorders. You can probably imagine events that could unfold that might leave you struggling with depression or grappling with anxiety. But what could possibly account for Sylvia's thinking that she was Joan of Arc or that she had dictated *The Lord of the Rings* to Tolkien? As mystifying as these delusions may seem, you'll see that the etiology of schizophrenic disorders is not all that different from the etiology of other psychological disorders. We'll begin our discussion by examining the matter of genetic vulnerability.

Genetic Vulnerability 11c

Evidence is plentiful that hereditary factors play a role in the development of schizophrenic disorders (Glatt, 2008; Kirov & Owen, 2009). For instance, in twin studies, concordance rates average around 48% for identical twins, in comparison to about 17% for fraternal twins (Gottesman, 1991, 2001). Studies also indicate that a child born to two schizophrenic parents has about a 46% probability of developing a schizophrenic disorder (as compared to the probability in the general population of about 1%). These and other findings that show the genetic roots of schizophrenia are summarized in **Figure 15.18**. Overall, the picture is similar to that seen for mood disorders. Several converging lines of evidence indicate that some people inherit a polygenically transmitted *vulnerability* to schizophrenia (Cornblatt et al., 2009). Some theorists suspect that genetic factors may account for as much as 80% of the variability in susceptibility to schizophrenia (Pogue-Geile & Yokley, 2010). However, genetic mapping studies have made only modest progress in identifying the specific genes at work (Gunter, 2009; Walker & Tessner, 2008).

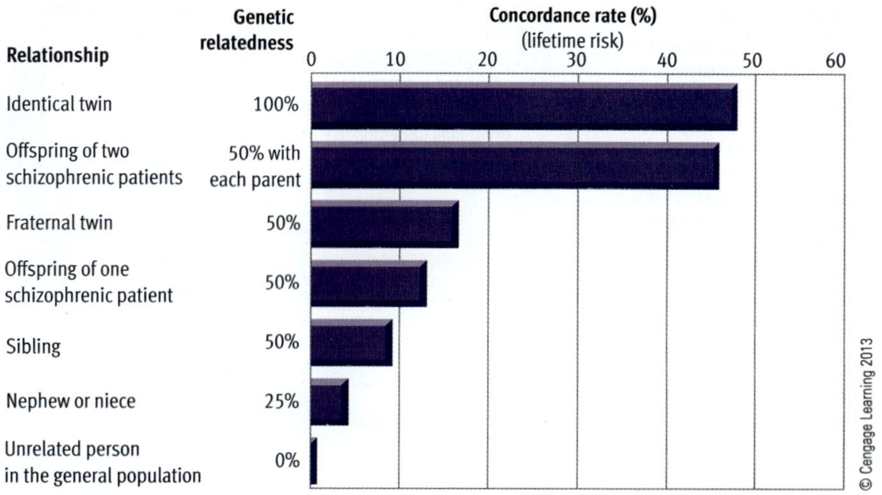

Figure 15.18

Genetic vulnerability to schizophrenic disorders. Relatives of schizophrenic patients have an elevated risk for schizophrenia. This risk is greater among closer relatives. Although environment also plays a role in the etiology of schizophrenia, the concordance rates shown here suggest that there must be a genetic vulnerability to the disorder. These concordance estimates are based on pooled data from forty studies conducted between 1920 and 1987. (Data from Gottesman, 1991)

Neurochemical Factors 11c

Like mood disorders, schizophrenic disorders appear to be accompanied by changes in the activity of one or more neurotransmitters in the brain (Patel, Pinals, & Breier, 2008). The *dopamine hypothesis* asserts that excess dopamine activity is the neurochemical basis for schizophrenia, as presented in **Figure 15.19** on the next page. This hypothesis makes sense because most of the drugs that are useful in the treatment of schizophrenia are known to dampen dopamine activity in the brain (Javitt & Laruelle, 2006). However, the evidence linking schizophrenia to high dopamine levels is riddled with inconsistencies, complexities, and interpretive problems (Bobo et al., 2008). In recent years, the dopamine hypothesis has become more nuanced and complex. Researchers believe that dysregulation occurs in dopamine circuits and that the nature of this dysregulation may vary in different regions of the brain (Howes & Kapur, 2009). Scientists are also investigating whether dysfunctions in neural circuits using glutamate play a role in schizophrenia (Downar & Kapur, 2008).

Recent research has suggested that marijuana use during adolescence may help precipitate schizophrenia in young people who have a genetic vulnerability to the disorder (Degenhardt & Hall, 2006; McGrath et al., 2010). This unexpected finding has generated considerable debate about whether and how cannabis might contribute to the emergence of schizophrenia (Castle, 2008; DeLisi, 2008). Some critics have suggested that it could be that schizophrenia leads to cannabis use rather than vice versa. In other words, emerging psychotic symptoms may prompt young people to turn to marijuana to self-medicate. However, a recent carefully controlled, long-term study in Germany found no evidence in support of the self-medication explanation (Kuepper et al., 2011). After controlling for age, gender, social class, use of other drugs, occurrence of childhood trauma, and the presence of other disorders, the study found that marijuana use roughly doubled the risk of psychotic disturbance. The current thinking is that the key chemical ingredient in marijuana (THC) may increase neurotransmitter activity in dopamine circuits in certain areas of the brain (Di Forti et al., 2007; Kuepper et al., 2010). The data on this issue are still preliminary. More research will be needed to fully understand the association between marijuana use and schizophrenia.

Structural Abnormalities in the Brain 11c

For decades, studies have suggested that individuals with schizophrenia exhibit a variety of deficits in attention, perception, and information processing (Belger & Barch, 2009; Harvey, 2010). Impairments in working (short-term) memory are especially prominent (Silver et al., 2003). These cognitive deficits suggest that schizophrenic disorders may be caused by neurological defects. Until recent decades, this theory was based more on speculation than on actual research. Now, however, advances in brain-imaging technology have yielded mountains of

Figure 15.19

The dopamine hypothesis as an explanation for schizophrenia. Decades of research have implicated overactivity at dopamine synapses as a key cause of schizophrenic disorders. However, the evidence on the exact mechanisms underlying this overactivity, which is summarized in this graphic, is complex and open to debate. Recent hypotheses about the neurochemical bases of schizophrenia go beyond the simple assumption that dopamine activity is increased. For example, one theory posits that schizophrenia may be accompanied by decreased dopamine activity in one area of the brain (the prefrontal cortex) and increased activity or dysregulation in other areas of the brain. Moreover, abnormalities in other neurotransmitter systems may also contribute to schizophrenia.

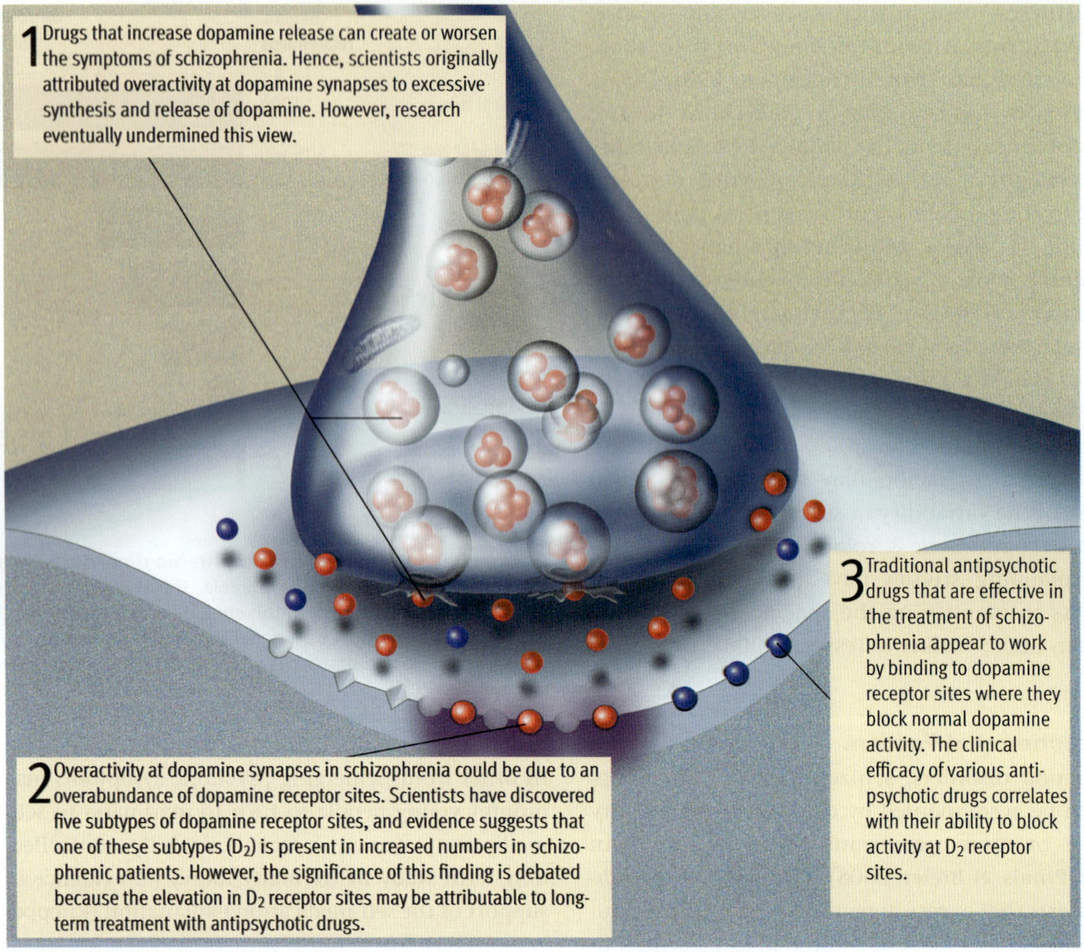

© Cengage Learning 2013

intriguing data. The most reliable finding is that CT scans and MRI scans (see Chapter 3) suggest an association between enlarged brain ventricles (the hollow, fluid-filled cavities in the brain depicted in **Figure 15.20**) and schizophrenic disturbance (Belger & Dichter, 2006; Shenton & Kubicki, 2009). Enlarged ventricles are assumed to reflect the degeneration of nearby brain tissue. The significance of enlarged ventricles is hotly debated, however. This structural deterioration (or failure to develop) could be a *consequence* of schizophrenia, or it could be a contributing *cause* of the illness.

Brain-imaging studies have also uncovered other structural abnormalities, including reductions in both gray matter and white matter is specific brain regions (Bobo et al., 2008; Karlsgodt, Sun, & Cannon, 2010). Such reductions seem to reflect losses of synaptic density and myelinization (see Chapter 3). These findings suggest that schizophrenia is caused by disruptions in the brain's neural connectivity, impairing the normal communication among neural circuits (Karlsgodt, Sun, & Cannon, 2010).

Figure 15.20

Schizophrenia and the ventricles of the brain. Cerebrospinal fluid (CSF) circulates around the brain and spinal cord. The hollow cavities in the brain filled with CSF are called ventricles. The four ventricles in the human brain are depicted here. Recent studies with CT scans and MRI scans suggest that an association exists between enlarged ventricles in the brain and the occurrence of schizophrenic disturbance.

© Cengage Learning 2013

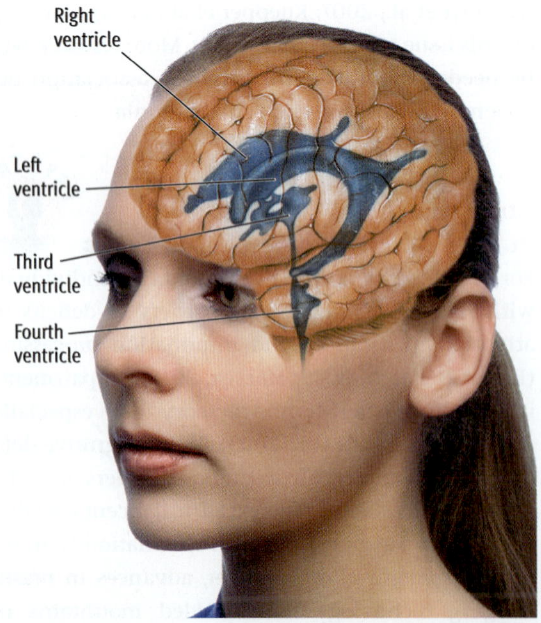

© RimDream/ Shutterstock

The Neurodevelopmental Hypothesis

PSYKTREK 11c

Several relatively recent lines of evidence have led to the emergence of the *neurodevelopmental hypothesis* of schizophrenia. This theory asserts that schizophrenia is caused in part by various disruptions in the normal maturational processes of the brain before or at birth (Fatemi & Folsom, 2009). According to this hypothesis, insults to the brain during sensitive phases of prenatal development or during birth can cause subtle neurological damage that elevates individuals' vulnerability to schizophrenia years later in adolescence and early adulthood (see **Figure 15.21**). What are the sources of these early insults to the brain? Thus far, research has focused mostly on viral infections or malnutrition during prenatal development and on obstetrical complications during the birth process.

The evidence on viral infections has been building since Sarnoff Mednick and his colleagues (1988) discovered an elevated incidence of schizophrenia among individuals who were in their second trimester of prenatal development during a 1957 influenza epidemic in Finland. Quite a number of subsequent studies have found a link between exposure to influenza and other infections during prenatal development and increased prevalence of schizophrenia (Brown & Derkits, 2010). Another study investigated the possible impact of prenatal malnutrition. It found an elevated incidence of schizophrenia in a cohort of people who were prenatally exposed to a severe famine in 1944–45 resulting from a Nazi blockade of food deliveries in the Netherlands during World War II (Susser et al., 1996).

A recent study looked at a new source of disruption during prenatal development: severe maternal stress. The study found an elevated prevalence of schizophrenia among the offspring of women who suffered severe stress during their pregnancy (Khashan et al., 2008). Other research has shown that schizophrenic patients are more likely than control subjects to have a history of obstetrical complications (Kelly et al., 2004; Murray & Bramon, 2005). Finally, research suggests that minor physical anomalies (slight anatomical defects of the head, hands, feet, and face) that would be consistent with prenatal neurological damage are more common among people with schizophrenia than among others (McNeil, Canton-Graae, & Ismail, 2000; Schiffman et al., 2002). Collectively, these diverse studies argue for a relationship between early neurological trauma and a predisposition to schizophrenia (King, St-Hilaire, & Heidkamp, 2010).

PSYKTREK 11c

Expressed Emotion

Studies of expressed emotion have primarily focused on how this element of family dynamics influences the *course* of schizophrenic illness, after the onset of the disorder (Leff & Vaughn, 1985). ***Expressed emotion (EE)* is the degree to which a relative of a patient displays highly critical or emotionally overinvolved attitudes toward the patient.** Audiotaped interviews of relatives' communication are carefully evaluated for critical comments, hostility toward the patient, and excessive emotional involvement (overprotective, overconcerned attitudes) (Hooley, 2004).

Studies show that a family's expressed emotion is a good predictor of the course of a schizophrenic patient's illness (Hooley, 2007). After release from a hospital, people with schizophrenia who return to a family high in expressed emotion show relapse rates about three times that of patients who return to a family low in expressed emotion (see **Figure 15.22**; Hooley, 2009). Part of the problem for patients returning to homes high in expressed emotion is that their families are probably sources of more *stress* than of *social support* (Cutting & Docherty, 2000).

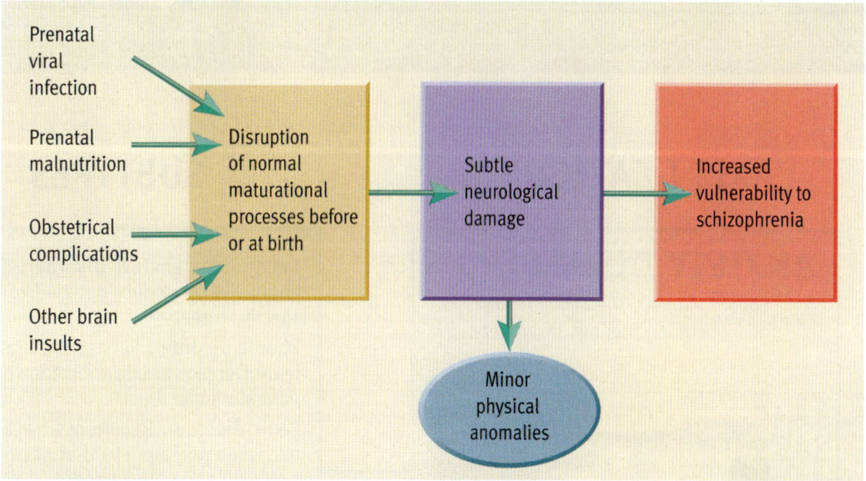

© Cengage Learning 2013

Figure 15.21

The neurodevelopmental hypothesis of schizophrenia. Recent findings have suggested that insults to the brain sustained during prenatal development or at birth may disrupt crucial maturational processes in the brain, resulting in subtle neurological damage that gradually becomes apparent as youngsters develop. This neurological damage is believed to increase both vulnerability to schizophrenia and the incidence of minor physical anomalies (slight anatomical defects of the head, face, hands, and feet).

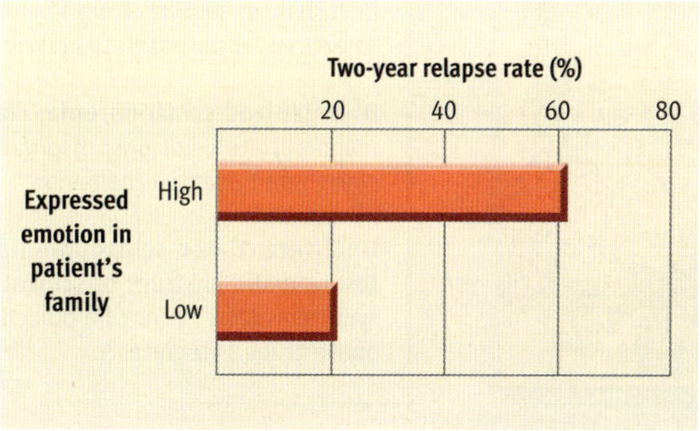

© Cengage Learning 2013

Figure 15.22

Expressed emotion and relapse rates in schizophrenia. Schizophrenic patients who return to a home that is high in expressed emotion have higher relapse rates than those who return to a home low in expressed emotion. Thus, unhealthy family dynamics can influence the course of schizophrenia. (Data adapted from Leff & Vaughn, 1981)

Illustrated Overview of 3 Categories of Psychological Disorders

AXIS I CATEGORY	SUBTYPES	PREVALENCE/ WELL-KNOWN VICTIM

ANXIETY DISORDERS

Edvard Munch's *The Scream* expresses overwhelming feelings of anxiety.

The Scream, National Gallery, Oslo, Norway, SCALA/Art Resource/NY; © 2011 The Munch Museum/The Munch-Ellingsen Group/Artists Rights Society (ARS), NY.

Generalized anxiety disorder: Chronic, high level of anxiety not tied to any specific threat

Phobic disorder: Persistent, irrational fear of object or situation that presents no real danger

Panic disorder: Recurrent attacks of overwhelming anxiety that occur suddenly and unexpectedly

Obsessive-compulsive disorder: Persistent, uncontrollable intrusions of unwanted thoughts and urges to engage in senseless rituals

Posttraumatic stress disorder: Enduring psychological disturbance attributable to the experience of a major traumatic event

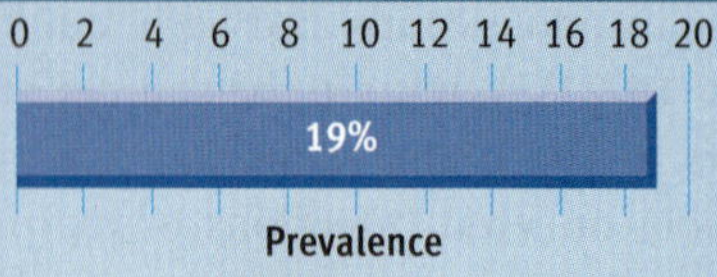

© Bettmann/Corbis

The famous industrialist Howard Hughes suffered from obsessive-compulsive disorder.

MOOD DISORDERS

Musée d'Orsay, Paris. © Erich Lessing/Art Resource, NY.

Vincent Van Gogh's *Portrait of Dr. Gachet* captures the profound dejection experienced in depressive disorders.

Major depressive disorder: Two or more major depressive episodes marked by feelings of sadness, worthlessness, despair

Bipolar disorder: One or more manic episodes marked by inflated self-esteem, grandiosity, and elevated mood and energy, usually accompanied by major depressive episodes

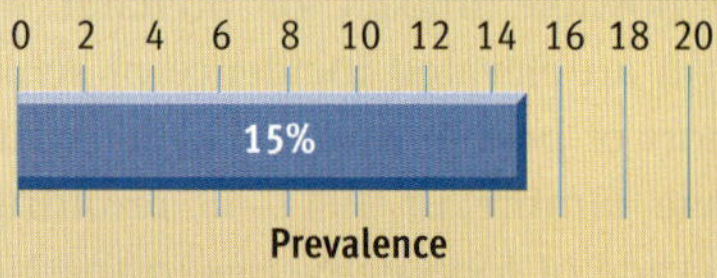

© Helga Esteb/Shutterstock

Actor Owen Wilson has suffered from depression.

SCHIZOPHRENIC DISORDERS

The perceptual distortions seen in schizophrenia probably contributed to the bizarre imagery apparent in this portrait of a cat painted by Louis Wain.

© Derek Bayes/Aspect Picture Library

Paranoid schizophrenia: Delusions of persecution and delusions of grandeur; frequent auditory hallucinations

Catatonic schizophrenia: Motor disturbances ranging from immobility to excessive, purposeless activity

Disorganized schizophrenia: Flat or inappropriate emotions; disorganized speech and adaptive behavior

Undifferentiated schizophrenia: Idiosyncratic mixtures of schizophrenic symptoms that cannot be placed into above three categories

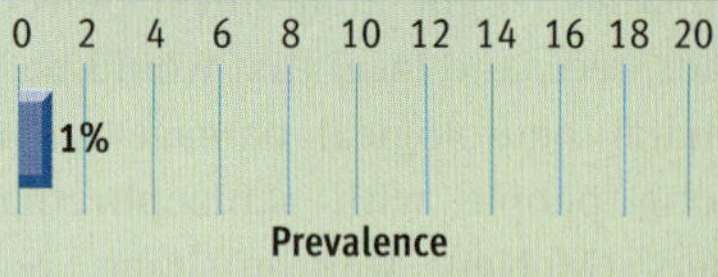

John Nash, the Nobel Prize-winning mathematician whose story was told in the film *A Beautiful Mind*, has struggled with schizophrenia.

© AP Images/Charles Rex Arbogast

© Cengage Learning 2013

ETIOLOGY: BIOLOGICAL FACTORS

Genetic vulnerability: Twin studies and other evidence suggest a mild genetic predisposition to anxiety disorders.

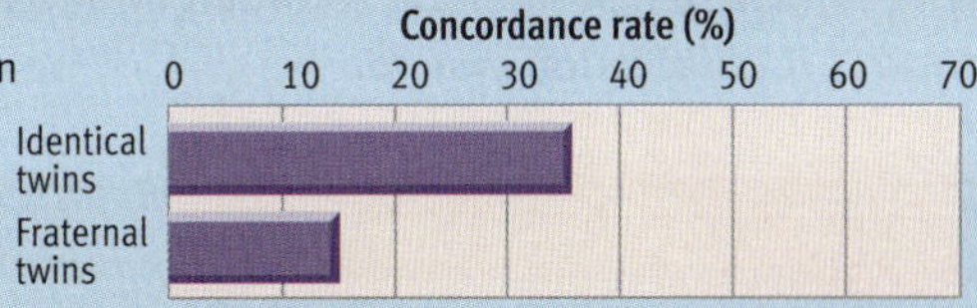

Anxiety sensitivity: Oversensitivity to physical symptoms of anxiety may lead to overreactions to feelings of anxiety, so anxiety breeds anxiety.

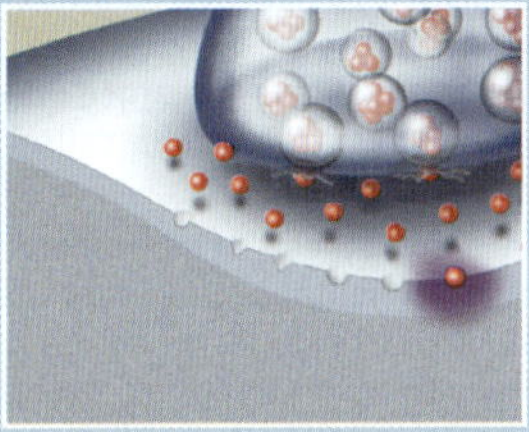

Neurochemical bases: Disturbances in neural circuits releasing GABA may contribute to some disorders; abnormalities at serotonin synapses have been implicated in panic and obsessive-compulsive disorders.

Genetic vulnerability: Twin studies and other evidence suggest a genetic predisposition to mood disorders.

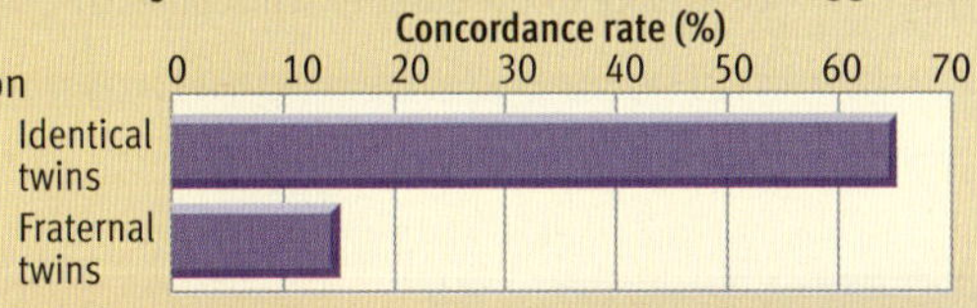

Suppressed neurogenesis: Disruption of neurogenesis may lead to reduced volume in the hippocampus and to depression.

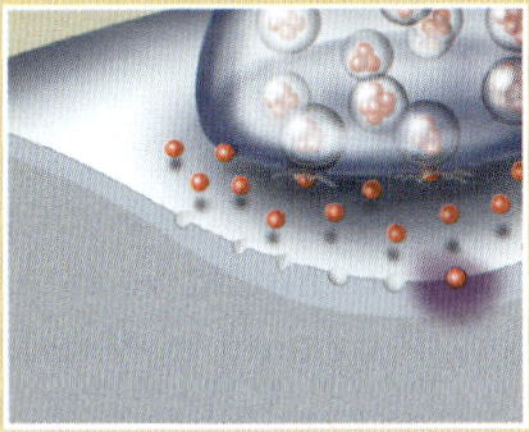

Neurochemical bases: Disturbances in neural circuits releasing norepinephrine may contribute to some mood disorders; abnormalities at serotonin synapses have also been implicated as a factor in depression.

Genetic vulnerability: Twin studies and other evidence suggest a genetic predisposition to schizophrenic disorders.

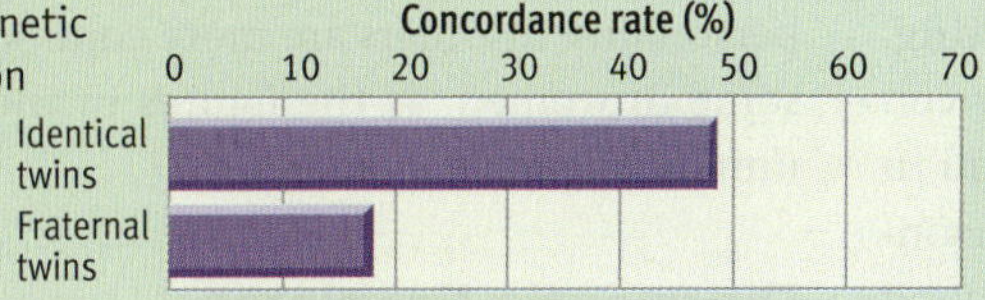

Neurochemical bases: Overactivity in neural circuits releasing dopamine is associated with schizophrenia; but abnormalities in other neurotransmitter systems may also contribute.

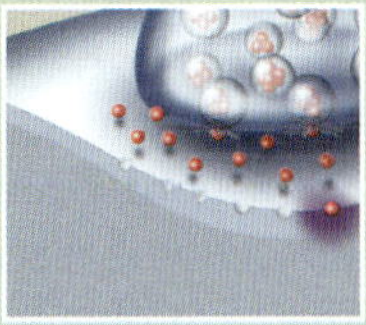

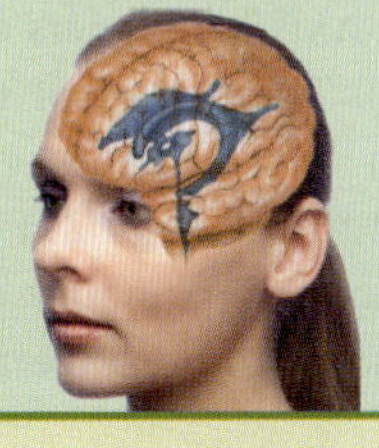

© RimDream/Shutterstock

Structural abnormalities in brain: Enlarged brain ventricles are associated with schizophrenia, but they may be an effect rather than a cause of the disorder.

ETIOLOGY: PSYCHOLOGICAL FACTORS

Learning: Many anxiety responses may be acquired through classical conditioning or observational learning; phobic responses may be maintained by operant reinforcement.

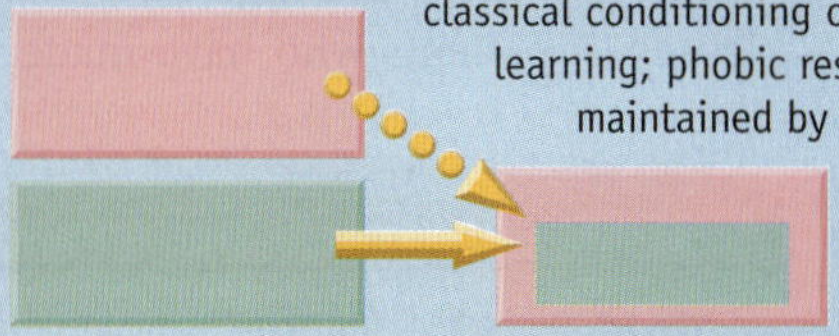

Stress: High stress may help to precipitate the onset of anxiety disorders.

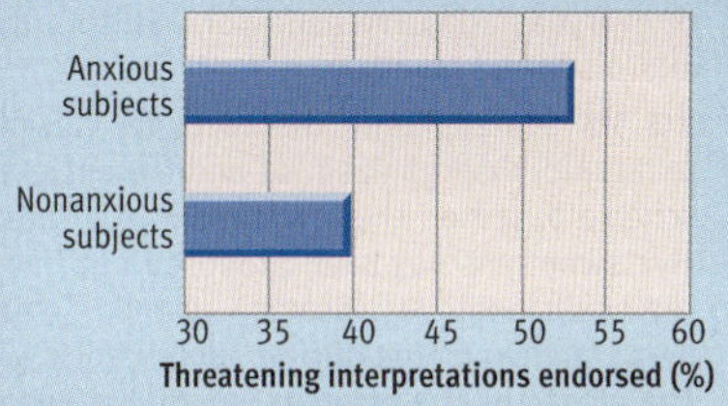

Cognition: People who misinterpret harmless situations as threatening and who focus excessive attention on perceived threats are more vulnerable to anxiety disorders.

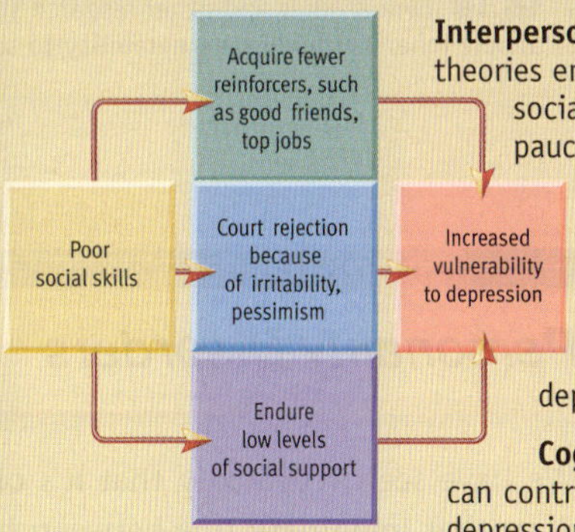

Interpersonal roots: Behavioral theories emphasize how inadequate social skills can result in a paucity of reinforcers and other effects that make people vulnerable to depression.

Stress: High stress can act as precipitating factor that triggers depression or bipolar disorder.

Cognition: Negative thinking can contribute to the development of depression; rumination may extend and amplify depression.

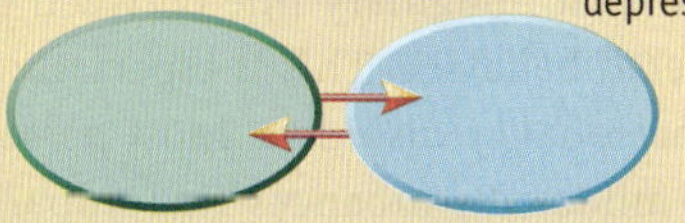

Expressed emotion: A family's expressed emotion is a good predictor of the course of a schizophrenic patient's illness.

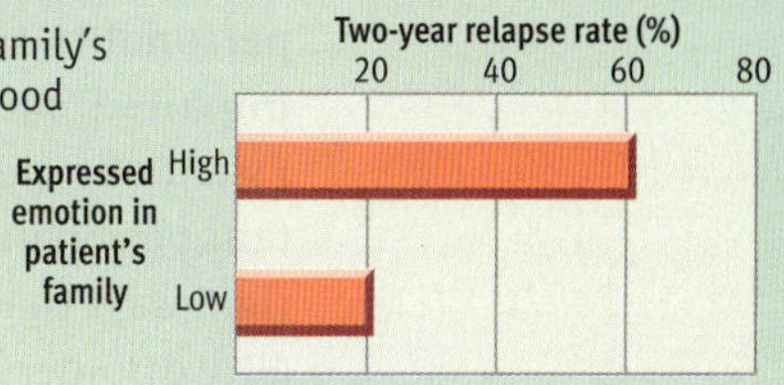

Stress: High stress can precipitate schizophrenic disorder in people who are vulnerable to schizophrenia.

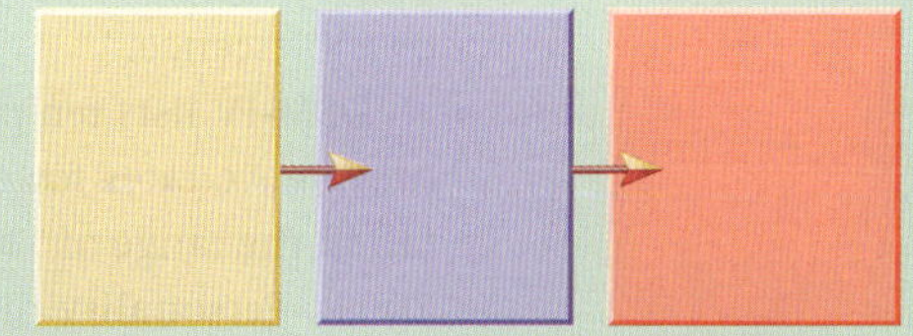

The neurodevelopmental hypothesis: Insults to the brain sustained during prenatal development or at birth may disrupt maturational processes in the brain resulting in elevated vulnerability to schizophrenia.

© Cengage Learning 2013

Precipitating Stress

11c

Most theories of schizophrenia assume that stress plays a key role in triggering schizophrenic disorders (Walker & Tessner, 2008). According to this notion, various biological and psychological factors influence individuals' *vulnerability* to schizophrenia. High stress may then serve to precipitate a schizophrenic disorder in someone who is vulnerable. Research indicates that high stress can also trigger relapses in patients who have made progress toward recovery (Walker, Mittal, & Tessner, 2008). Patients who show strong emotional reactions to events seem to be particularly likely to have their symptoms exacerbated by stress (Docherty et al., 2009).

Schizophrenia is the last of the major, Axis I diagnostic categories that we will consider. We'll complete our overview of various types of abnormal behavior with a brief look at the personality disorders. These disorders are recorded on Axis II in the DSM classification system.

REVIEW OF KEY LEARNING GOALS

15.14 Disturbed, irrational thought processes, including delusions, are the defining feature of schizophrenic disorders. Schizophrenia is also characterized by deterioration of everyday adaptive behavior, auditory hallucinations, and disturbed emotion.

15.15 Schizophrenic disorders are classified as paranoid, catatonic, disorganized, or undifferentiated. A classification scheme based on the predominance of positive versus negative symptoms has been proposed but has not supplanted the traditional classification system. Schizophrenic disorders usually emerge during adolescence or young adulthood. The course of the disorder is variable but tends to involve chronic illness for many patients. However, with prompt, effective care recovery is possible.

15.16 Twin studies and other research show that some people inherit a genetic vulnerability to schizophrenia. The dopamine hypothesis asserts that excess dopamine activity is the neurochemical basis for schizophrenia. This hypothesis may explain why recent research has uncovered a link between marijuana use and vulnerability to schizophrenia. Structural abnormalities in the brain, such as enlarged ventricles, are associated with schizophrenia, but their causal significance is unclear.

15.17 The neurodevelopmental hypothesis of schizophrenia asserts that schizophrenia is attributable to disruptions in the normal maturational processes of the brain before or at birth that are caused by prenatal viral infections, obstetrical complications, and other insults to the brain. Patients who come from homes high in expressed emotion have elevated relapse rates, suggesting that unhealthy family dynamics play a role in schizophrenia. High stress may also contribute to the onset of schizophrenia.

KEY LEARNING GOALS

15.18 Discuss the nature of personality disorders and problems with the diagnosis of such disorders.

15.19 Describe the antisocial personality disorder, and discuss its etiology.

Personality Disorders

We have seen repeatedly that it's often difficult to draw that imaginary line between healthy and disordered behavior. This is especially true in the case of personality disorders. Most personality disorders are milder disturbances in comparison to most of the Axis I disorders. ***Personality disorders* are a class of disorders marked by extreme, inflexible personality traits that cause subjective distress or impaired social and occupational functioning.** Essentially, people with these disorders display certain personality traits to an excessive degree and in rigid ways that undermine their adjustment. Personality disorders usually emerge during late childhood or adolescence.

DSM-IV lists ten personality disorders. Estimated prevalence rates for each of these disorders tend to fall in the range of 1%–2% (Guzzetta & de Girolamo, 2009). Personality disorders are grouped into three related clusters: anxious-fearful, odd-eccentric, and dramatic-impulsive. These disorders are described briefly in **Table 15.2**. If you examine this table, you will find a diverse collection of maladaptive personality syndromes. You may also notice that some personality disorders essentially are milder versions of more severe Axis I disorders. For example, obsessive-compulsive personality disorder is a milder version of obsessive-compulsive disorder. Likewise, the schizoid and schizotypal personality disorders are milder cousins of schizophrenic disorders. Some personality disorders are more common in men and some in women, as the figures in the far right column of the table indicate.

Diagnostic Problems

Many critics have argued that the personality disorders overlap too much with Axis I disorders and with each other (Clark, 2007). The extent of this problem was documented in a study by Leslie Morey (1988). Morey reviewed the cases of 291 patients who had received a specific personality disorder diagnosis to see how many could have met

Table 15.2 Personality Disorders

Cluster	Disorder	Description	% Male/% Female
Anxious/fearful	Avoidant personality disorder	Excessively sensitive to potential rejection, humiliation, or shame; socially withdrawn in spite of desire for acceptance from others	50/50
	Dependent personality disorder	Excessively lacking in self-reliance and self-esteem; passively allowing others to make all decisions; constantly subordinating own needs to others' needs	31/69
	Obsessive-compulsive personality disorder	Preoccupied with organization, rules, schedules, lists, trivial details; extremely conventional, serious, and formal; unable to express warm emotions	50/50
Odd/eccentric	Schizoid personality disorder	Defective in capacity for forming social relationships; showing absence of warm, tender feelings for others	78/22
	Schizotypal personality disorder	Showing social deficits and oddities of thinking, perception, and communication that resemble schizophrenia	55/45
	Paranoid personality disorder	Showing pervasive and unwarranted suspiciousness and mistrust of people; overly sensitive; prone to jealousy	67/33
Dramatic/impulsive	Histrionic personality disorder	Overly dramatic; tending to exaggerated expressions of emotion; egocentric, seeking attention	15/85
	Narcissistic personality disorder	Grandiosely self-important; preoccupied with success fantasies; expecting special treatment; lacking interpersonal empathy	70/30
	Borderline personality disorder	Unstable in self-image, mood, and interpersonal relationships; impulsive and unpredictable	38/62
	Antisocial personality disorder	Chronically violating the rights of others; failing to accept social norms, to form attachments to others, or to sustain consistent work behavior; exploitive and reckless	82/18

SOURCE: Estimated gender ratios from Millon (1981).

© Cengage Learning 2013

the criteria for any of the other personality disorders. Morey found massive overlap among the diagnoses. For example, among patients with a diagnosis of histrionic personality disorder, 56% also qualified for a borderline disorder, 54% for a narcissistic disorder, 32% for an avoidant disorder, and 30% for a dependent disorder. Clearly, there are fundamental problems with Axis II as a classification system (Tyrer et al., 2007; Widiger, 2007). The overlap among the personality disorders makes it extremely difficult to achieve reliable diagnoses. Doubts have also been raised about the decision to place personality disorders on a separate axis. There does not appear to be any fundamental distinction between personality disorders and Axis I disorders (Krueger, 2005).

In light of these problems, a variety of theorists have questioned the wisdom of the current *categorical approach* to describing personality disorders. As noted earlier in the chapter, such an approach assumes that people can reliably be placed in nonoverlapping diagnostic categories, which clearly is not the case for personality disorders (Verheul, 2005; Widiger & Trull, 2007). Support for a shift to a *dimensional approach* to diagnosis in DSM-5 is particularly strong for the personality disorders (Widiger, Livesley, & Clark, 2009; Widiger & Mullins-Sweatt, 2010).

The difficulties involved in the diagnosis of personality disorders have clearly hindered research on their etiology and prognosis. The only personality disorder that has a long history of extensive research is antisocial personality disorder, which we examine next.

Antisocial Personality Disorder

Antisocial personality disorder has a misleading name. The antisocial designation does *not* mean that people with this disorder shun social interaction. In fact, rather than shrinking from social interaction, many such individuals are sociable, friendly, and superficially charming. People with this disorder are *antisocial* in that they choose to *reject widely accepted social norms* regarding moral principles and behavior.

Description

People with antisocial personalities chronically violate the rights of others. They often use their social charm to cultivate others' liking or loyalty for purposes of exploitation. ***Antisocial personality disorder* is marked by impulsive, callous, manipulative, aggressive, and irresponsible behavior that reflects a failure to accept social norms.** Since they haven't accepted the social norms they violate, people with antisocial personalities rarely feel guilty about their transgressions. Essentially, they lack an adequate conscience. Antisocial personality disorder occurs much more frequently among males than females. Studies suggest that it's a moderately common disorder, seen in roughly 3%–6% of males and about 1% of females (Widiger & Mullins, 2003).

Many people with antisocial personalities get involved in illegal activities. Moreover, antisocial personalities tend to begin their criminal careers at an early age, to commit offenses at a relatively high rate, and to be versatile offenders who get involved in many types of criminal activity (Douglas, Vincent, & Edens, 2006; Hare, 2006; Porter & Porter, 2007). However, many people with antisocial personalities keep their exploitive, amoral behavior channeled within the boundaries of the law. Such people may even enjoy high status in our society (Babiak & Hare, 2006; Hall & Benning, 2006). In other words, the concept of antisocial personality disorder can apply to cut-throat business executives, scheming politicians, unprincipled lawyers, and money-hungry evangelists, as well as to con artists, drug dealers, thugs, burglars, and petty thieves.

People with antisocial personalities exhibit quite a variety of maladaptive traits (Hare, 2006; Hare & Neumann, 2008). Among other things, they rarely experience genuine affection for others. However, they may be skilled at faking affection so they can exploit people. Sexually, they are predatory and promiscuous. They also tend to be irresponsible and impulsive. They can tolerate little frustration, and they pursue immediate gratification. These characteristics make them unreliable employees, unfaithful spouses, inattentive parents, and undependable friends. Many people with antisocial personalities have a checkered history of divorce, child abuse, and job instability. The picture does tend to improve as those with antisocial personalities become middle-aged. One study that followed antisocial men into their 50s found substantial improvement in 58% of the subjects (Black, 2001).

Etiology

Many theorists believe that biological factors contribute to the development of antisocial personality disorder. Various lines of evidence suggest a genetic predisposition toward the disorder (Moffitt, 2005; Waldman & Rhee, 2006). A review of twin studies found an average concordance rate of 67% for identical twins in comparison to 31% for fraternal twins (Black, 2001). These findings are consistent with a fairly strong genetic vulnerability to the disorder. Many observers have noted that people with antisocial personalities lack the inhibitions that most of us have about violating moral standards. Their lack of inhibitions prompted Hans Eysenck (1982) to theorize that such people might inherit relatively sluggish autonomic nervous systems, leading to slow acquisition of inhibitions through classical conditioning. The notion that antisocial personalities exhibit underarousal has received some support (Raine, 1997). The findings, though, have been inconsistent (Blackburn, 2006). Part of the problem in this area of research may be that "arousal" can be quantified in a great many different ways.

Efforts to relate psychological factors to antisocial behavior have emphasized inadequate socialization in dysfunctional family systems (Farrington, 2006; Sutker & Allain, 2001). It's easy to envision how antisocial traits could be fostered in homes where parents make haphazard or halfhearted efforts to socialize their children to be respectful, truthful, responsible, unselfish, and so forth. Consistent with this idea, studies find that individuals with antisocial personalities tend to come from homes where discipline is erratic or ineffective or where they experience physical abuse and neglect (Luntz & Widom, 1994; Widom, 1997). Such people are also more likely to emerge from families where one or both parents exhibit antisocial traits (Black, 2001). These parents presumably model exploitive, amoral behaviors, which their children acquire through observational learning.

REVIEW OF KEY LEARNING GOALS

15.18 Personality disorders are marked by extreme personality traits that cause distress and impaired functioning. There are ten personality disorders allocated to Axis II in DSM-IV. Personality disorders can be grouped into three clusters: anxious-fearful, odd-eccentric, and dramatic-impulsive. Specific personality disorders are poorly defined and there is excessive overlap among them, creating diagnostic problems. Some theorists believe that these problems could be reduced by replacing the current categorical approach with a dimensional approach.

15.19 Antisocial personality disorder is characterized by manipulative, impulsive, exploitive, aggressive behavior. It's associated with criminal activity. However, many keep their amoral behavior within the boundaries of the law. Research on the etiology of this disorder has implicated genetic vulnerability, autonomic reactivity, inadequate socialization, and observational learning.

Psychological Disorders and the Law

KEY LEARNING GOALS

15.20 Articulate the legal concept of insanity, and clarify the grounds for involuntary commitment.

Societies use laws to enforce their norms regarding appropriate behavior. Given this function, the law in our society has something to say about many issues related to abnormal behavior. In this section, we examine the concepts of insanity and involuntary commitment.

Insanity

Insanity is *not* a diagnosis; it's a legal concept. ***Insanity* is a legal status indicating that a person cannot be held responsible for his or her actions because of mental illness.** Why is this an issue in the courtroom? Because criminal acts must be intentional. The law reasons that people who are "out of their mind" may not be able to appreciate the significance of what they're doing. The insanity defense is used in criminal trials by defendants who admit that they committed the crime but claim that they lacked intent.

No simple relationship exists between specific diagnoses of mental disorders and court findings of insanity. The vast majority of people with diagnosed psychological disorders would *not* qualify as insane. The people most likely to qualify are those troubled by severe disturbances who display delusional behavior. The courts apply various rules in making judgments about a defendant's sanity, depending on the jurisdiction (Simon & Shuman, 2008). According to one widely used rule, called the *M'naghten rule, insanity exists when a mental disorder makes a person unable to distinguish right from wrong.* As you can imagine, evaluating insanity as defined in the M'naghten rule can be difficult for judges and jurors, not to mention the psychologists and psychiatrists who are called into court as expert witnesses.

Although highly publicized and controversial, the insanity defense is actually used less frequently and less successfully than widely believed (see **Figure 15.23**). One study found that the general public estimates that the insanity defense is used in 37% of felony cases, when in fact it's used in less than 1% (Silver, Cirincione, & Steadman, 1994). Another study of over 60,000 indictments in Baltimore found that only 190 defendants (0.31%) pleaded insanity. Of these, only 8 were successful (Janofsky et al., 1996).

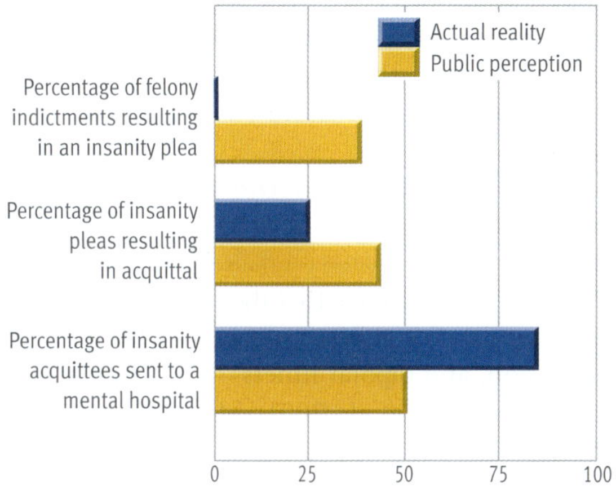

Figure 15.23

The insanity defense: Public perceptions and actual realities. Silver, Cirincione, and Steadman (1994) collected data on the general public's beliefs about the insanity defense and the realities of how often it is used and how often it is successful (based on a large-scale survey of insanity pleas in eight states). Because of highly selective media coverage, dramatic disparities are seen between public perceptions and actual realities, as the insanity defense is used less frequently and less successfully than widely assumed.

© Cengage Learning 2013

Involuntary Commitment

The issue of insanity surfaces only in *criminal* proceedings. Far more people are affected by *civil* proceedings relating to involuntary commitment. **In *involuntary commitment* people are hospitalized in psychiatric facilities against their will.** What are the grounds for such a dramatic action? They vary some from state to state. Generally, people are subject to involuntary commitment when mental health professionals and legal authorities believe that a mental disorder makes them (1) dangerous to themselves (usually suicidal), (2) dangerous to others (potentially violent), or (3) unable to provide for their own basic care (Benedek & Grieger, 2008). In emergency situations, psychologists and psychiatrists can authorize *temporary* commitment, usually for 24 to 72 hours. Orders for long-term involuntary commitment are usually set up for renewable six-month periods and can be issued by a court only after a formal hearing. Mental health professionals provide extensive input in these hearings. The courts, however, make the final decisions (Simon, 2005).

Most involuntary commitments occur because people appear to be dangerous to themselves or others. The real difficulty, though, is in predicting dangerousness (Freedman et al., 2007). Studies suggest that clinicians' short-term predictions about which patients are likely to become violent are only moderately accurate. Moreover, their long-term predictions

Reality CHECK

Misconception

People with psychological disorders are often violent and dangerous.

Reality

Only a modest association has been found between mental illness and violence-prone tendencies (Elbogen & Johnson, 2009; Freedman et al., 2007). This stereotype exists because incidents of violence involving the mentally ill tend to command media attention. However, the individuals involved in these incidents are not representative of the immense number of people who have struggled with psychological disorders.

Jared Lee Loughner, who gunned down Congresswoman Gabrielle Giffords and many innocent bystanders in January of 2011, apparently showed many signs of psychological deterioration in the months leading up to the shootings. Given his struggles with psychological disturbance, many people were baffled by why he had not been subjected to involuntary commitment. What most people do not understand is that laws in the United States generally set the bar very high for involuntary commitment. Why? Because predictions of dangerousness are not very accurate and because our legal system is reluctant to incarcerate people for what they *might* do. Unfortunately, our conservative approach to involuntary commitment sometimes has tragic consequences.

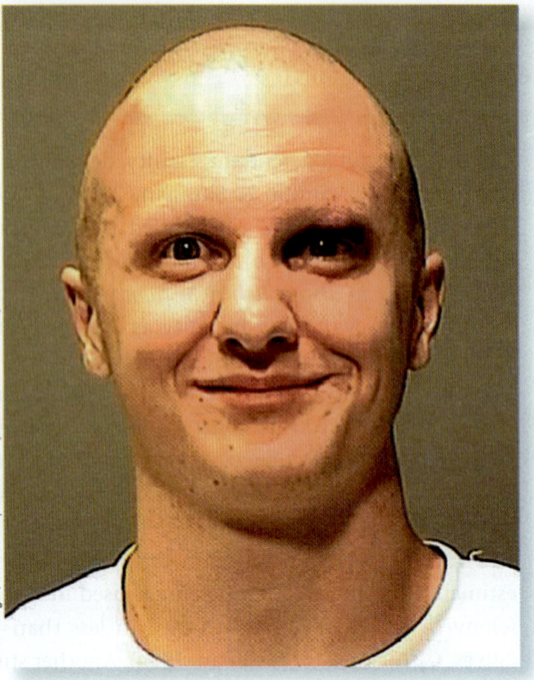
© AP Images/Pima County Sheriff's Dept. via The Arizona Republic, File

of violent behavior are largely inaccurate (Simon & Shuman, 2008; Stone, 1999). This inaccuracy in predicting dangerousness is unfortunate. Detaining a person is no small matter. And involuntary commitment involves the detention of people for what they *might* do in the future, not necessarily for what they did do. Such detention goes against the grain of the American legal principle that people are *innocent until proven guilty*. The inherent difficulty in predicting dangerousness makes involuntary commitment a complex and controversial issue.

REVIEW OF KEY LEARNING GOALS

15.20 Insanity is a legal concept applied to people who cannot be held responsible for their actions because of mental illness. The insanity defense is used less frequently and less successfully than widely believed. When people appear to be dangerous to themselves or others, courts may rule that they are subject to involuntary commitment in a hospital.

KEY LEARNING GOALS

15.21 Compare the relativistic versus pancultural view of psychological disorders.

15.22 Assess the extent of cultural variability in the existence and presentation of mental disorders.

Culture and Pathology

The legal rules governing insanity and involuntary commitment are obviously culture-specific. And we noted earlier that judgments of normality and abnormality are influenced by cultural norms and values. In light of these realities, would it be reasonable to infer that psychological disorders are culturally variable phenomena? Social scientists are sharply divided on the answer to this question. Some embrace a *relativistic view* of psychological disorders. Others subscribe to a *universalistic or pancultural view* (Tanaka-Matsumi, 2001). Theorists who embrace the *relativistic view* argue that the criteria of mental illness vary greatly across cultures. They claim that there are no universal standards of normality and abnormality. According to the relativists, the DSM diagnostic system reflects an ethnocentric, Western, white, urban, middle- and upper-class cultural orientation that has limited relevance in other cultural contexts. In contrast, those who subscribe to the *pancultural view* argue that the criteria of mental illness are much the same around the world and that basic standards of normality and abnormality are universal across cultures. Theorists who accept the pancultural view of psychopathology typically maintain that Western diagnostic concepts have validity and utility in other cultural contexts.

The debate about culture and pathology basically boils down to two specific issues: (1) Are the psychological disorders seen in Western societies found throughout the world? (2) Are the symptom patterns of mental disorders invariant across cultures? Let's briefly examine the evidence on these questions and then reconsider the relativistic and pancultural views of psychological disorders.

Are Equivalent Disorders Found Around the World?

Most investigators agree that the principal categories of serious psychological disturbance—schizophrenia, depression, and bipolar illness—are identifiable in all cultures (Tsai et al., 2001). Most behaviors that are regarded as clearly abnormal in Western culture are also viewed as abnormal in other cultures. People who are delusional, hallucinatory, disoriented, or incoherent are thought to be disturbed in all societies. There are, though, cultural disparities in exactly what is considered delusional or hallucinatory.

Cultural variations are more apparent in the recognition of less severe forms of psychological disturbance (Mezzich, Lewis-Fernandez, & Ruiperez, 2003). Additional research is needed, but relatively mild types of pathology that do not disrupt behavior in obvious ways are not labeled as disorders in many societies. Thus, syndromes such as generalized anxiety disorder, hypochondria, and narcissistic personality disorder, which are firmly established as diagnostic entities in the DSM, are viewed in some cultures as "run of the mill" difficulties and peculiarities rather than as full-fledged disorders.

Finally, researchers have discovered a small number of *culture-bound disorders* that further illustrate the diversity of abnormal behavior around the world (Lewis-Fernandez, Guarnaccia, & Ruiz, 2009; Tseng, 2009). ***Culture-bound disorders*** **are abnormal syndromes found only in a few cultural groups.** For example, *koro,* an obsessive fear that one's penis will withdraw into one's abdomen, is seen only among Chinese males in Malaya and several other regions of southern Asia. *Windigo,* which involves an intense craving for human flesh and fear that one will turn into a cannibal, is seen only among Algonquin Indian cultures. And until fairly recently, the eating disorder *anorexia nervosa,* discussed in this chapter's Personal Application, was largely seen only in affluent Western cultures (Russell, 2009).

Are Symptom Patterns Culturally Invariant?

Do the major types of psychological disorders manifest themselves in the same way around the world? It depends to some extent on the disorder. The more a disorder has a strong biological component, the more it tends to be expressed in similar ways across varied cultures (Marsella & Yamada, 2007). Thus, the constellations of symptoms associated with schizophrenia and bipolar illness are largely the same across widely disparate societies (Draguns, 1980, 1990). However, even in severe, heavily biological disorders, cultural variations in symptom patterns are also seen (Mezzich et al., 2003). For example, delusions are a common symptom of schizophrenia in all cultures. However, the specific delusions that people report are tied to their cultural heritage (Brislin, 1993). In technologically advanced societies, schizophrenic patients report that thoughts are being transmitted into their minds through electric lines, satellites, or microwave ovens. Victims of schizophrenia in less technological societies experience the same phenomenon but blame sorcerers or demons. The influence of culture on symptom patterns is illustrated by recent reports of a new delusion in modern societies—patients are erroneously insisting that they are the stars of reality TV shows (DeAngelis, 2009). Of the major disorders, symptom patterns are probably most variable for depression. For example, profound feelings of guilt and self-deprecation lie at the core of depression in Western cultures. But such feelings are far less central to depression in many other societies. In non-Western cultures, depression tends to be expressed in terms of somatic symptoms, such as complaints of fatigue, headaches, and backaches, more than psychological symptoms, such as dejection and low self-esteem (Tsai et al., 2001; Young, 1997).

CONCEPT CHECK 15.4

Identifying the Contributions of Major Theorists and Researchers

Check your recall of the principal ideas of important theorists and researchers covered in this chapter by matching the people listed on the left with the appropriate contributions described on the right. If you need help, the crucial pages describing each person's ideas are listed in parentheses. Fill in the letters for your choices in the spaces provided on the left. You'll find the answers in Appendix A.

Major Theorists and Researchers

_______ 1. Nancy Andreasen (p. 625)

_______ 2. Susan Nolen-Hoeksema (pp. 617, 620)

_______ 3. Martin Seligman (pp. 611, 620)

_______ 4. Thomas Szasz (p. 603)

Key Ideas and Contributions

a. This expert on gender differences in the prevalence of depression argues that rumination tends to deepen and extend episodes of depression.

b. According to this widely cited social critic, the medical model has outlived its usefulness and psychological disorders should not be viewed as diseases.

c. This expert on schizophrenia helped pioneer the distinction between positive and negative symptoms.

d. This theorist formulated the learned helplessness model of depression and the concept of preparedness to explain why some phobias are much more common that others.

So, what can we conclude about the validity of the relativistic versus pancultural views of psychological disorders? Both views appear to have some merit. As we have seen in other areas of research, psychopathology is characterized by both cultural variance and invariance. Researchers have found considerable similarity across cultures in the syndromes that are regarded as pathological and in their patterns of symptoms. However, researchers have also discovered many cultural variations in the recognition, definition, and symptoms of various psychological disorders.

REVIEW OF KEY LEARNING GOALS

15.21 Theorists who embrace a relativistic view of psychological disorders argue that there are no universal standards of normality and abnormality. Those who subscribe to the pancultural view argue that the criteria of mental illness are much the same around the world.

15.22 The principal categories of psychological disturbance are identifiable in all cultures. However, milder disorders may go unlabeled in some societies. Culture-bound disorders further illustrate the diversity of abnormal behavior around the world. The symptoms associated with specific disorders are largely the same across different cultures, but cultural variations are seen in the details of how these symptoms are expressed.

KEY LEARNING GOALS

15.23 Identify the four unifying themes highlighted in this chapter.

Reflecting on the Chapter's Themes

Multifactorial Causation

Heredity and Environment

Sociohistorical Context

Cultural Heritage

Our examination of abnormal behavior and its roots has highlighted four of our organizing themes: multifactorial causation, the interplay of heredity and environment, the sociohistorical context in which psychology evolves, and the influence of culture on psychological phenomena.

We can safely assert that every disorder described in this chapter has multiple causes. The development of mental disorders involves an interplay among a variety of psychological, biological, and social factors. We also saw that most psychological disorders depend on an interaction of genetics and experience. This interaction shows up most clearly in the *stress-vulnerability models* for mood disorders and schizophrenic disorders (see **Figure 15.24**). *Vulnerability* to these disorders seems to depend primarily on heredity, whereas stress is largely a function of environment. According to stress-vulnerability theories, disorders emerge when high vulnerability intersects with high stress. A high biological vulnerability may not be converted into a disorder if a person's stress is low. Similarly, high stress may not lead to a disorder if vulnerability is low. Thus, the impact of he-

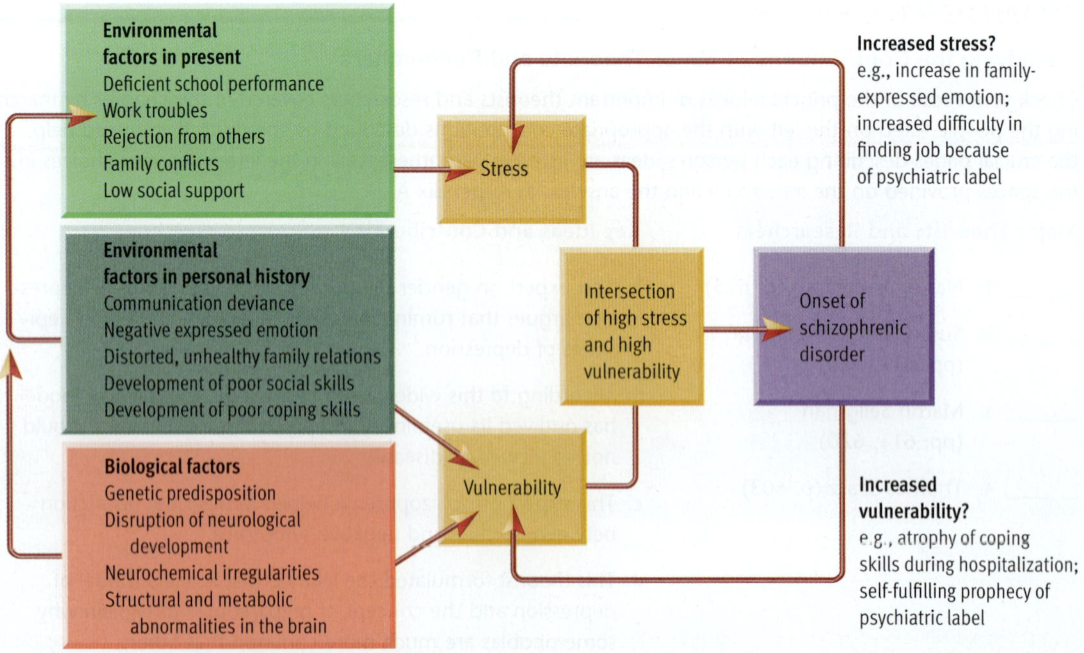

Figure 15.24
The stress-vulnerability model of schizophrenia. Multifactorial causation is readily apparent in current theories about the etiology of schizophrenic disorders. A variety of biological factors and personal history factors influence one's vulnerability to the disorder, which interacts with the amount of stress one experiences. Schizophrenic disorders appear to result from an intersection of high stress and high vulnerability.
© Cengage Learning 2013

redity depends on the environment. And the effect of environment depends on heredity.

This chapter also showed that psychology evolves in a sociohistorical context. We saw that modern conceptions of normality and abnormality are largely shaped by empirical research. However, social trends, economic necessities, and political realities also play a role. Finally, our discussion of psychological disorders showed once again that psychological phenomena are shaped to some degree by cultural parameters. Some standards of normality and abnormality transcend cultural boundaries. But cultural norms influence many aspects of psychopathology. Indeed, the influence of culture will be apparent in our upcoming Personal Application on eating disorders. These disorders are largely a creation of modern, affluent, Western culture.

REVIEW OF KEY LEARNING GOALS

15.23 This chapter highlighted four of our unifying themes, showing that behavior is governed by multiple causes, that heredity and environment jointly influence mental disorders, that psychology evolves in a sociohistorical context, and that pathology is characterized by both cultural variance and invariance.

PERSONAL APPLICATION

Understanding Eating Disorders

KEY LEARNING GOALS

15.24 Describe the subtypes, history, and prevalence of eating disorders.

15.25 Outline how genetic factors, personality, culture, family dynamics, and disturbed thinking contribute to eating disorders.

Answer the following "true" or "false."

____ **1** Although they have only attracted attention in recent years, eating disorders have a long history and have always been fairly common.

____ **2** People with anorexia nervosa are much more likely to recognize that their eating behavior is pathological than people suffering from bulimia nervosa are.

____ **3** The prevalence of eating disorders is twice as high in women as it is in men.

____ **4** The binge-and-purge syndrome seen in bulimia nervosa is not common in anorexia nervosa.

All of the above statements are false, as you will see in this Personal Application. The psychological disorders that we discussed in the main body of the chapter have largely been recognized for centuries. Most of them are found in one form or another in all cultures and societies. Eating disorders present a sharp contrast to this picture. They have only been recognized relatively recently and have largely been confined to affluent, Westernized cultures (G. F. M. Russell, 1995; Szmukler & Patton, 1995). In spite of these fascinating differences, eating disorders have much in common with traditional forms of pathology.

Description

Eating disorders **are severe disturbances in eating behavior characterized by preoccupation with weight and unhealthy efforts to control weight.** Most people don't seem to take eating disorders as seriously as other types of psychological disorders. You will see, however, that they are dangerous and debilitating (Thompson, Roehrig, & Kinder, 2007). No psychological disorder is associated with a greater elevation in mortality (Striegel-Moore & Bulik, 2007). In DSM-IV, two sometimes overlapping syndromes are recognized: *anorexia nervosa* and *bulimia nervosa*. A third syndrome, called *binge-eating disorder,* is described in the appendix of DSM-IV as a potential new disorder, pending further study. We will devote our attention in this Application to the two established eating disorders, but we will briefly outline the symptoms of this new disorder as well.

Anorexia Nervosa

Anorexia nervosa **involves intense fear of gaining weight, disturbed body image, refusal to maintain normal weight, and use of dangerous measures to lose weight.** Two subtypes have been observed. In *restricting type anorexia nervosa,* people drastically reduce their intake of food, sometimes

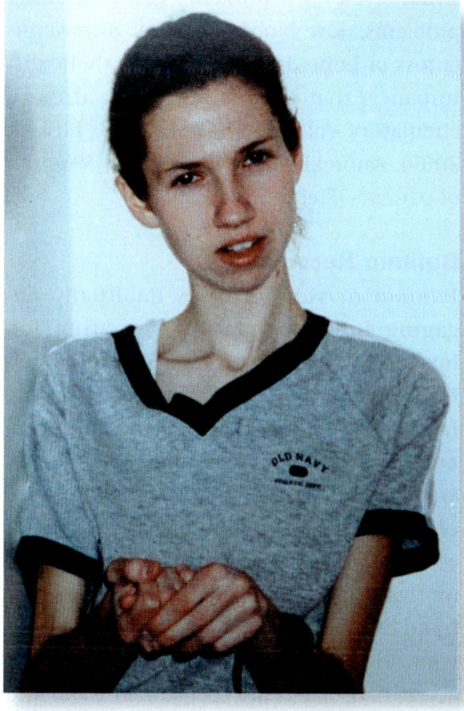

© Ed Quinn/Corbis

Eating disorders have become distressingly common among young women in Western cultures. No matter how frail they become, people suffering from anorexia insist that they are too fat.

literally starving themselves. In *binge-eating/purging type anorexia nervosa,* individuals attempt to lose weight by forcing themselves to vomit after meals, by misusing laxatives and diuretics, and by engaging in excessive exercise.

People with both types suffer from disturbed body image. No matter how frail and emaciated they become, they insist that they are too fat. Their morbid fear of obesity means that they are never satisfied with their weight. If they gain a pound or two, they panic. The only thing that makes them happy is to lose more weight. The common result is a relentless decline in body weight. People entering treatment for anorexia nervosa are typically 25%–30% below their normal weight (Hsu, 1990). Because of their disturbed body image, people suffering from anorexia generally do *not* recognize the maladaptive quality of their behavior. Thus, they rarely seek treatment on their own. They must usually be coaxed or coerced into treatment by friends or family members who are alarmed by their appearance.

Anorexia nervosa eventually leads to a cascade of medical problems. Such problems may include *amenorrhea* (a loss of menstrual cycles in women), gastrointestinal problems, low blood pressure, *osteoporosis* (a loss of bone density), and metabolic disturbances that can lead to cardiac arrest or circulatory collapse (Halmi, 2008; Russell, 2009). Anorexia leads to death in 5%–10% of patients (Steinhausen, 2002).

Bulimia Nervosa

Bulimia nervosa **involves habitually engaging in out-of-control overeating followed by unhealthy compensatory efforts, such as self-induced vomiting, fasting, abuse of laxatives and diuretics, and excessive exercise.** The eating binges are usually carried out in secret. Binges are typically followed by intense guilt and concern about gaining weight. These feelings motivate potentially harmful strategies to undo the effects of the overeating. However, vomiting prevents the absorption of only about half of recently consumed food, and laxatives and diuretics have negligible impact on caloric intake. So people suffering from bulimia nervosa typically maintain a reasonably normal weight (Fairburn, Cooper, & Murphy, 2009). Medical problems associated with bulimia nervosa include cardiac arrythmias, dental problems, metabolic deficiencies, and gastrointestinal problems (Halmi, 2002, 2008). Bulimia often coexists with other psychological disturbances, including depression, anxiety disorders, and substance abuse (Hudson et al., 2007).

Obviously, bulimia nervosa shares many features with anorexia nervosa. Similarities include a morbid fear of becoming obese, preoccupation with food, and rigid, maladaptive approaches to controlling weight that are grounded in naive all-or-none thinking. The close relationship between the disorders is demonstrated by the fact that many patients who initially develop one syndrome cross over to display the other syndrome (Tozzi et al., 2005). However, the two syndromes also differ in crucial ways. First and foremost, bulimia is a much less life-threatening condition. Second, although their appearance is usually more "normal" than that seen in anorexia, people with bulimia are much more likely to recognize that their eating behavior is pathological. Thus, they are more likely to cooperate with treatment (Guarda et al., 2007). Nonetheless, like anorexia, bulimia is associated with elevated mortality rates (Crow et al., 2009).

Binge-Eating Disorder

A surprising number of people who exhibit disordered eating do not fit neatly into the anorexia or bulimia categories. This is why a third category has been proposed. ***Binge-eating disorder*** **involves distress-inducing eating binges that are not accompanied by the purging, fasting, and excessive exercise seen in bulimia.** This syndrome resembles bulimia, but it's a less severe disorder. Still, this disorder creates great distress. People with this disorder tend to be disgusted by their bodies and distraught about their overeating. People with binge-eating disorder are frequently overweight. Their excessive eating is often triggered by stress (Gluck, 2006). Research suggests that this comparatively mild syndrome may be more common than anorexia or bulimia (Hudson et al., 2007). Given the research that has been compiled since DSM-IV was released in 1994, it appears likely that binge-eating disorder will be recognized as an independent disorder in the forthcoming DSM-5 (Striegel-Moore & Franko, 2008).

History and Prevalence

Historians have been able to track down descriptions of anorexia nervosa that date back centuries. The disorder, then, is *not* entirely new. However, anorexia nervosa did not become a common affliction until the middle part of the 20th century (Vandereycken, 2002). Binging and purging have a long history in some cultures. Yet they were not part of pathological efforts to control weight. Bulimia nervosa appears to be a new syndrome that emerged gradually in the middle of the 20th century. It was first recognized in the 1970s (Steiger & Bruce, 2009; Vandereycken, 2002).

Both disorders are a product of modern, affluent, Western culture, where food is generally plentiful and the desirability of being thin is widely endorsed. Until recently, these disorders were not seen outside of Western cultures (Hoek, 2002). However, advances in communication have exported Western culture to far-flung corners of the globe. Eating disorders have now started showing up in many non-Western societies, especially affluent Asian countries (Becker & Fay, 2006; Lee & Katzman, 2002).

A huge gender gap is seen in the likelihood of developing eating disorders. About 90%–95% of individuals with eating disorders are female (Thompson & Kinder, 2003). This staggering discrepancy appears to be a result of cultural pressures rather than biological factors (Smolak & Murnen, 2001). Western standards of attractiveness emphasize slenderness more for females than for males. Moreover, women generally experience greater pressure to be physically attractive than men do (Strahan et al., 2008). Eating disorders mostly afflict *young* women. The typical age of onset is 14 to 18 for anorexia and 15 to 21 for bulimia (see **Figure 15.25**).

How common are eating disorders in Western societies? Studies of young women suggest that about 1% develop anorexia nervosa and about 2%–3% develop bulimia nervosa (Anderson & Yager, 2005). In some respects, these figures may only scratch the surface of the problem. Evidence suggests that as many as 20% of female college students may struggle with transient bulimic symptoms (Anderson & Yager, 2005). And recent community surveys suggest that

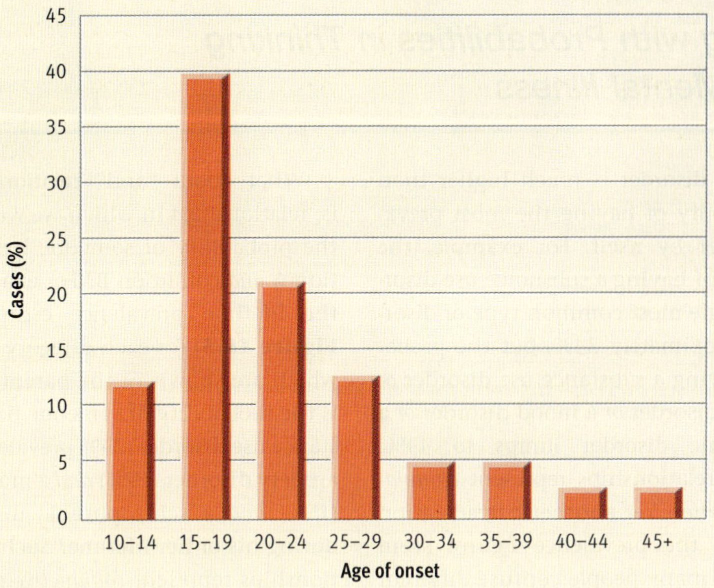

Figure 15.25

Age of onset for anorexia nervosa. Eating disorders tend to emerge during adolescence, as these data for anorexia nervosa show. This graph shows how age of onset was distributed in a sample of 166 female patients from Minnesota. As you can see, over half the patients experienced the onset of their illness before the age of 20, with vulnerability clearly peaking between the ages of 15 and 19. (Adapted from Lucas et al., 1991)

© Cengage Learning 2013

there may be more undiagnosed eating disorders among men than generally appreciated (Hudson et al., 2007).

Etiology of Eating Disorders

Like other types of psychological disorders, eating disorders are caused by multiple determinants that work interactively. Let's take a brief look at some of the factors that contribute to the development of anorexia nervosa and bulimia nervosa.

Genetic Vulnerability

The evidence is not as strong or complete as for many other types of psychopathology (such as anxiety, mood, and schizophrenic disorders), but some people may inherit a genetic vulnerability to eating disorders (Thornton, Mazzeo, & Bulik, 2011). Studies show that relatives of patients with eating disorders have elevated rates of anorexia nervosa and bulimia nervosa (Bulik, 2004). Twin studies suggest that a genetic predisposition may be at work (Steiger, Bruce, & Israel, 2003).

Personality Factors

Certain personality traits may increase vulnerability to eating disorders. There are innumerable exceptions, but victims of anorexia nervosa tend to be obsessive, rigid, and emotionally restrained, while victims of bulimia nervosa tend to be impulsive, overly sensitive, and low in self-esteem (Anderluh et al., 2003; Wonderlich, 2002). Recent research also suggests that perfectionism is a risk factor for anorexia (Steiger & Bruce, 2009).

Cultural Values

The contribution of cultural values to the increased prevalence of eating disorders can hardly be overestimated (Anderson-Fye & Becker, 2004; Striegel-Moore & Bulik, 2007). In Western society, young women are socialized to believe that they must be attractive. To be attractive, they must be as thin as the actresses and fashion models that dominate the media (Levine & Harrison, 2004). Thanks to this cultural milieu, many young women are dissatisfied with their weight. The societal ideals promoted by the media are unattainable for most women (Thompson & Stice, 2001). Unfortunately, in a portion of these women, the pressure to be thin, in combination with genetic vulnerability, family pathology, and other factors, leads to unhealthful efforts to control weight.

The Role of the Family

Quite a number of theorists emphasize how family dynamics can contribute to the development of anorexia and bulimia in young women (Haworth-Hoeppner, 2000). The principal issue appears to be that some mothers contribute to eating disorders simply by endorsing society's message that "you can never be too thin" and by modeling unhealthy dieting behaviors of their own (Francis & Birch, 2005). In conjunction with media pressures, this role-modeling leads many daughters to internalize the idea that the thinner you are, the more attractive you are.

Cognitive Factors

Many theorists emphasize the role of disturbed thinking in the etiology of eating disorders (Williamson et al., 2001). For example, anorexic patients' typical belief that they are fat when they are really wasting away is a dramatic illustration of how thinking goes awry. Patients with eating disorders display rigid, all-or-none thinking and many maladaptive beliefs. Such thoughts may include: "I must be thin to be accepted"; "If I am not in complete control, I will lose all control"; and "If I gain one pound, I'll go on to gain enormous weight." Additional research is needed to determine whether distorted thinking is a *cause* or merely a *symptom* of eating disorders.

REVIEW OF KEY LEARNING GOALS

15.24 The principal eating disorders are anorexia nervosa and bulimia nervosa, with binge-eating disorder a proposed third syndrome. Anorexia and bulimia both lead to a cascade of medical problems, but anorexia is more dangerous. Both disorders are largely products of affluent, Westernized culture that weren't recognized until the 20th century. Females account for 90%–95% of eating disorders. Among young women, about 1% develop anorexia nervosa and about 2%–3% develop bulimia nervosa, typically between the age of 14 to 21.

15.25 There appears to be a genetic vulnerability to eating disorders. Certain personality traits increase the vulnerability to eating disorders. Cultural pressures on young women to be thin clearly help to foster eating disorders. Families that endorse the idea that you can never be too thin can help to promote eating disorders. Rigid, disturbed thinking can also contribute to the development of these disorders.

KEY LEARNING GOALS

15.26 Understand how mental heuristics can distort estimates of cumulative and conjunctive probabilities.

Working with Probabilities in Thinking About Mental Illness

As you read about the various types of psychological disorders, did you think to yourself that you or someone you know was being described? On the one hand, there's no reason to be alarmed. The tendency to see yourself and your friends in descriptions of pathology is a common one. It's sometimes called the *medical students' disease* because beginning medical students often erroneously believe that they or their friends have whatever diseases they are currently learning about. On the other hand, realistically speaking, it *is* quite likely that you know *many* people with psychological disorders because—as you learned in the main body of the chapter—the likelihood of anyone having at least one DSM disorder at some point in their life is estimated to be about 44% (consult **Figure 15.5** on p. 607).

This estimate strikes most people as surprisingly high. Why is this so? One reason is that when people think about psychological disorders they tend to think of severe disorders, such as bipolar disorder or schizophrenia. These disorders are in fact relatively infrequent. But "run of the mill" disturbances, such as anxiety and depressive disorders, are much more common. When it comes to mental illness, people tend to think of patients in straightjackets or of obviously disturbed homeless people who do not reflect the broad and diverse population of people who suffer from psychological disorders. In other words, their *prototypes* or "best examples" of mental illness consist of severe disorders that are infrequent. Thus, they underestimate the prevalence of mental disorders. This distortion illustrates the influence of the ***representativeness heuristic,* which is basing the estimated probability of an event on how similar it is to the typical prototype of that event** (see Chapter 8).

Another reason this number seems surprisingly high is that many people do not understand that the probability of having *at least one* disorder is much higher than the probability of having the most prevalent disorder by itself. For example, the probability of having a substance use disorder, the single most common type of disorder, is approximately 24%, but the probability of having a substance use disorder *or* an anxiety disorder *or* a mood disorder *or* a schizophrenic disorder jumps to 44%. These "or" relationships represent *cumulative probabilities.* Yet another consideration that makes the prevalence figures seem high is that many people confuse different types of *prevalence rates.* The 44% estimate is for *lifetime prevalence.* This means it is the probability of having *any* disorder *at least once* at any time in one's lifetime. The lifetime prevalence rate is another example of "or" relationships. It's a value that takes into account the probability of having a psychological disorder in childhood *or* adolescence *or* adulthood *or* old age. *Point prevalence rates,* which estimate the percentage of people manifesting various disorders *at a particular point in time,* are much lower because many psychological disorders last only a few months to a few years.

What about "and" relationships—that is, relationships in which we want to know the probability of someone having condition A *and* condition B? For example, given the lifetime prevalence estimates (from **Figure 15.5**) for each category of disorder, which are shown in the parentheses, what is the probability of someone having a substance use disorder (24% prevalence) *and* an anxiety disorder (19%) *and* a mood disorder (15%) *and* a schizophrenic disorder (1%) during his or her lifetime? Such "and" relationships represent *conjunctive probabilities.* Will this probability be less than 24%, between 24% and 44%, or over 44%? You may be surprised to learn that the answer is well under 1%. You can't have all four disorders unless you have the least frequent disorder (schizophrenia), which has a prevalence of 1%, so the answer *must* be 1% or less. Moreover, of all of the people with schizophrenia, only a tiny subset of them are likely to have all three of the other disorders. Thus, the answer is well under 1% (see **Figure 15.26**). If this type of question strikes you as contrived, think again. Epidemiologists have devoted an enormous

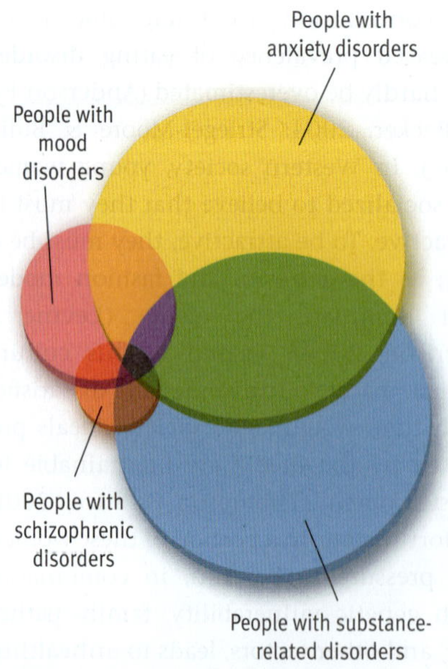

Figure 15.26

Conjunctive probabilities. The probability of someone having all four disorders depicted here cannot be greater than the probability of the least common condition by itself, which is 1% for schizophrenia. The intersection of all four disorders (shown in black) has to be a subset of schizophrenic disorders and is probably well under 1%. Efforts to think about probabilities can sometimes be facilitated by creating diagrams that show the relationships and overlap among various events.

© Cengage Learning 2013

amount of research to the estimation of *comorbidity*—the coexistence of two or more disorders—because it greatly complicates treatment issues.

These are two examples of using statistical probabilities as a critical thinking tool. Let's apply this type of thinking to another problem dealing with physical health. Here is a problem used in a study by Tversky and Kahneman (1983, p. 308) that many physicians got wrong:

A health survey was conducted in a sample of adult males in British Columbia, of all ages and occupations. Please give your best estimate of the following values:

What percentage of the men surveyed have had one or more heart attacks? _________

What percentage of the men surveyed both are over 55 years old and have had one or more heart attacks? _________

Fill in the blanks above with your best guesses. Of course, you probably have only a very general idea about the prevalence of heart attacks, but go ahead and fill in the blanks anyway.

The actual values are not as important in this example as the relative values are. Over 65% of the physicians who participated in the experiment by Tversky and Kahneman gave a higher percentage value for the second question than for the first. What is wrong with their answers? The second question is asking about the conjunctive probability of two events. But, as we just discussed, this figure *must* be less than the probability of either one of these events occurring alone. Of all of the men in the survey who had had a heart attack, only some of them are also over 55, so the second number must be smaller than the first. As we saw in Chapter 8, this common error in thinking is called the *conjunction fallacy*. **The *conjunction fallacy* occurs when people estimate that the odds of two uncertain events happening together are greater than the odds of either event happening alone.**

Why did so many physicians get this problem wrong? They were vulnerable to the conjunction fallacy because they were influenced by the *representativeness heuristic*, or the power of prototypes. When physicians think "heart attack," they tend to envision a man over the age of 55. Hence, the second scenario fit so well with their prototype of a heart attack victim, they carelessly overestimated its probability.

Let's consider some additional examples of erroneous reasoning about probabilities involving how people think about psychological disorders. In the main body of the chapter, we discussed the fact that many people tend to stereotypically assume that mentally ill people are likely to be violent. Near the end of the chapter, we noted that people tend to wildly overestimate (37-fold in one study) how often the insanity defense is used in criminal trials. These examples reflect the influence of the ***availability heuristic*, which is basing the estimated probability of an event on the ease with which relevant instances come to mind.** Because of the availability heuristic, people tend to overestimate the probability of dramatic events that receive heavy media coverage, even when these events are rare, because examples of the events are easy to retrieve from memory. Violent acts by former psychiatric patients tend to get lots of attention in the press. And because of the *hindsight bias*, journalists tend to question why authorities couldn't foresee and prevent the violence (see the Critical Thinking Application for Chapter 12). Thus, the mental illness angle tends to be emphasized. In a similar vein, press coverage is usually intense when a defendant in a murder trial mounts an insanity defense.

In sum, the various types of statistics that come up in thinking about psychological disorders show that we are constantly working with probabilities, even though we may not realize it. Critical thinking requires a good understanding of the laws of probability because there are very few certainties in life.

© Trippett/Sipa Press

Highly publicized insanity trials, such as that of John Hinckley, Jr., who tried to assassinate President Reagan, lead the public to greatly overestimate how often the insanity defense is used, illustrating the impact of the availability heuristic.

Table 15.3 Critical Thinking Skills Discussed in This Application

Skill	Description
Understanding the limitations of the representativeness heuristic	The critical thinker understands that focusing on prototypes can lead to inaccurate probability estimates.
Understanding cumulative probabilities	The critical thinker understands that the probability of at least one of several events occurring is additive, and increases with time and the number of events.
Understanding conjunctive probabilities	The critical thinker appreciates that the probability of two uncertain events happening together is less than the probability of either event happening alone.
Understanding the limitations of the availability heuristic	The critical thinker understands that the ease with which examples come to mind may not be an accurate guide to the probability of an event.

© Cengage Learning 2013

REVIEW OF KEY LEARNING GOALS

15.26 Probability estimates can be distorted by the representativeness heuristic and the availability heuristic. Cumulative probabilities are additive, whereas conjunctive probabilities are always less than the likelihood of any one of the events happening alone.

Chapter 15 Practice Test

1. According to Thomas Szasz, abnormal behavior usually involves:
   A. behavior that is statistically unusual.
   B. behavior that deviates from social norms.
   C. a disease of the mind.
   D. biological imbalance.

2. Although Sue is plagued by a high level of dread, worry, and anxiety, she still manages to meet her daily responsibilities. Sue's behavior:
   A. should not be considered abnormal, since her adaptive functioning is not impaired.
   B. should not be considered abnormal, since everyone sometimes experiences worry and anxiety.
   C. can still be considered abnormal, since she feels great personal distress.
   D. involves both a and b.

3. The fact that people acquire phobias of ancient sources of threat (such as snakes) much more readily than modern sources of threat (such as electrical outlets) can best be explained by:
   A. classical conditioning.
   B. operant conditioning.
   C. observational learning.
   D. preparedness or an evolved module for fear learning.

4. Which of the following statements about dissociative identity disorder is true?
   A. The original personality is always aware of the alternate personalities.
   B. The transitions between personalities are usually very gradual.
   C. The personalities are typically all quite similar to one another.
   D. Starting in the 1970s, a dramatic increase occurred in the diagnosis of dissociative identity disorder.

5. People with unipolar disorders experience ______________; people with bipolar disorders are vulnerable to ______________.
   A. alternating periods of depression and mania; mania only
   B. depression only; alternating periods of depression and mania
   C. mania only; alternating periods of depression and mania
   D. alternating periods of depression and mania; depression and mania simultaneously

6. A concordance rate indicates:
   A. the percentage of relatives who exhibit the same disorder.
   B. the percentage of people with a given disorder who are currently receiving treatment.
   C. the prevalence of a given disorder in the general population.
   D. the rate of cure for a given disorder.

7. People who consistently exhibit ______________ thinking are more vulnerable to depression than others.
   A. overly optimistic C. delusional
   B. negative, pessimistic D. disorganized

8. Mary believes that while she sleeps at night, space creatures are attacking her and invading her uterus, where they will multiply until they are ready to take over the world. Mary was chosen for this task, she believes, because she is the only one with the power to help the space creatures succeed. Mary would most likely be diagnosed as ______________ schizophrenic.
   A. paranoid C. disorganized
   B. catatonic D. undifferentiated

9. It was once proposed that schizophrenic disorders be divided into just two categories based on:
   A. whether the prognosis is favorable or unfavorable.
   B. whether the disorder is mild or severe.
   C. the predominance of thought disturbances.
   D. the predominance of negative symptoms versus positive symptoms.

10. Most of the drugs that are useful in the treatment of schizophrenia are known to dampen ______________ activity in the brain, suggesting that increases in the activity of this neurotransmitter may contribute to the development of the disorder.
    A. norepinephrine C. acetylcholine
    B. serotonin D. dopamine

11. The main problem with the current classification scheme for personality disorders is that:
    A. it falsely implies that nearly everyone has at least one personality disorder.
    B. the criteria for diagnosis are so detailed and specific that even extremely disturbed people fail to meet them.
    C. the categories often overlap, making diagnosis unreliable.
    D. it contains too few categories to be useful.

12. The diagnosis of antisocial personality disorder would apply to an individual who:
    A. withdraws from social interaction due to an intense fear of rejection or criticism.
    B. withdraws from social interaction due to a lack of interest in interpersonal intimacy.
    C. is emotionally cold, suspicious of everyone, and overly concerned about being slighted by others.
    D. is callous, impulsive, and manipulative.

13. Involuntary commitment to a psychiatric facility:
    A. can occur only after a mentally ill individual has been convicted of a violent crime.
    B. usually occurs because people appear to be a danger to themselves or others.
    C. no longer occurs under modern civil law.
    D. will be a lifelong commitment, even if the individual is no longer mentally ill.

14. Those who embrace a relativistic view of psychological disorders would agree that:
    A. the criteria of mental illness vary considerably across cultures.
    B. there are universal standards of normality and abnormality.
    C. Western diagnostic concepts have validity and utility in other cultural contexts.
    D. both b and c are true.

15. About ______________ of patients with eating disorders are female.
    A. 40%
    B. 50%–60%
    C. 75%
    D. 90%–95%

Answers

1 B p. 603	6 A p. 611	11 C pp. 632–633
2 C pp. 603–604	7 B p. 620	12 D pp. 633–634
3 D pp. 611–612	8 A p. 625	13 B p. 635
4 D pp. 613–614	9 D p. 625	14 A p. 636
5 B pp. 615–616	10 D p. 627	15 D p. 640

Chapter 15 Media Resources

PsykTrek

To view a demo: **www.cengage.com/psychology/psyktrek**
To order: **www.cengage.com/psychology/weiten**

Go to the PsykTrek website or CD-ROM for further study of the concepts in this chapter. Both online and on the CD-ROM, PsykTrek includes dozens of learning modules with videos, animations, and quizzes, as well as simulations of psychological phenomena and a multimedia glossary that includes word pronunciations.

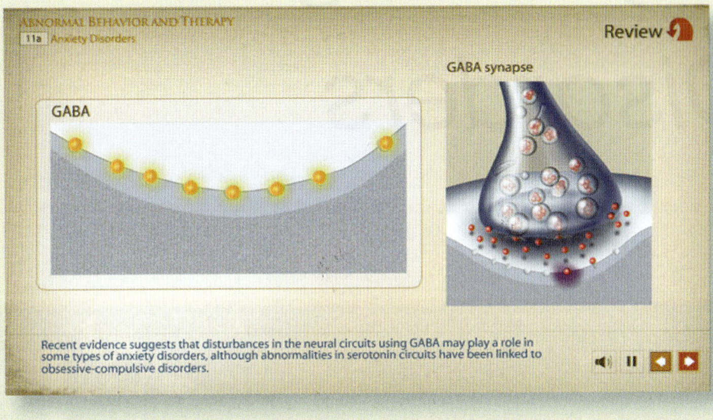

© Cengage Learning 2008

Visit Module 11a (*Anxiety Disorders*) to dig deeper into the nature and causes of anxiety-dominated disturbances, and see a patient describe his panic attacks.

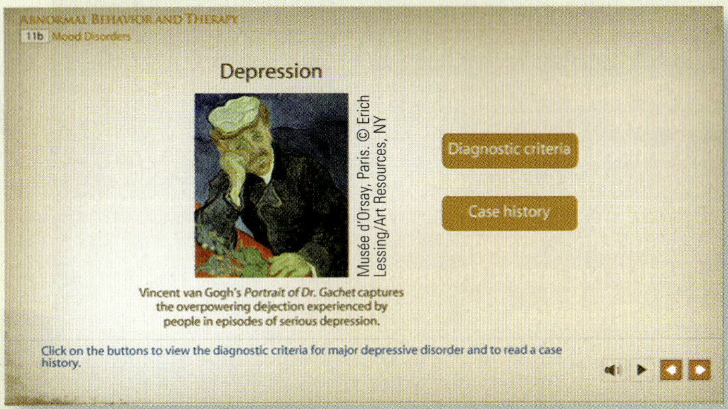

© Cengage Learning 2008

Increase your understanding of depression and bipolar disorder by working through Module 11b (*Mood Disorders*), which will provide you with detailed diagnostic criteria and case histories for these disorders.

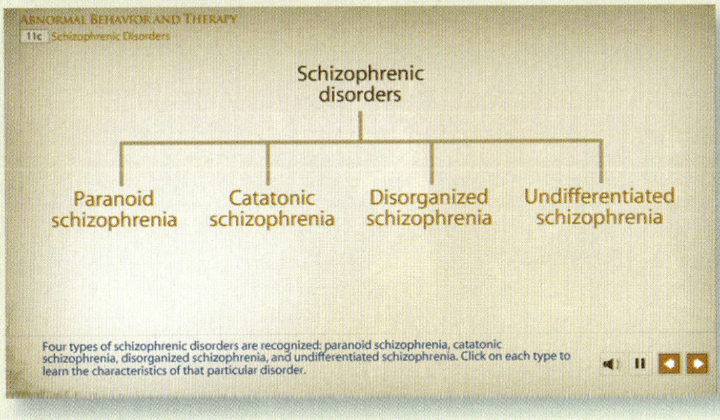

© Cengage Learning 2008

Explore Module 11c (*Schizophrenic Disorders*) for more information on schizophrenic disturbances and their causes.

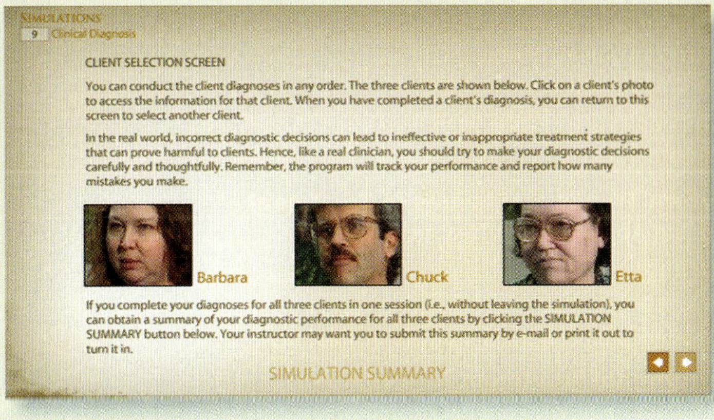

© Cengage Learning 2000

Try your hand at diagnosing three patients based on video interviews in Simulation 9 (*Clinical Diagnosis*).

Online Study Tools

Log in to **CengageBrain** to access the resources your instructor requires. For this book, you can access:

CourseMate brings course concepts to life with interactive learning, study, and exam preparation tools that support the printed textbook. A textbook-specific website, Psychology CourseMate includes an integrated interactive eBook and other interactive learning tools such as quizzes, flashcards, videos, and more.

CengageNow is an easy-to-use online resource that helps you study in less time to get the grade you want—NOW. Take a pre-test for this chapter and receive a personalized study plan based on your results that will identify the topics you need to review and direct you to online resources to help you master those topics. Then take a post-test to help you determine the concepts you have mastered and what you will need to work on. If your textbook does not include an access code card, go to CengageBrain.com to gain access.

WebTutor is more than just an interactive study guide. WebTutor is an anytime, anywhere customized learning solution with an eBook, keeping you connected to your textbook, instructor, and classmates.

Aplia. If your professor has assigned Aplia homework:

1. Sign in to your account
2. Complete the corresponding homework exercises as required by your professor.
3. When finished, click "Grade It Now" to see which areas you have mastered, which need more work, and detailed explanations of every answer.

Visit **www.cengagebrain.com** to access your account and purchase materials.

16

Treatment of Psychological Disorders

© Radius/SuperStock RF

What do you picture when you hear the term *psychotherapy?* Unless you've had some personal exposure to therapy, your image of it has likely been shaped by depictions you've seen on television or in the movies. A good example is the 1999 film *Analyze This,* a comedy starring Billy Crystal as psychiatrist Ben Sobol and Robert De Niro as Paul Vitti, a mob boss who is suffering from "panic attacks." Complications ensue when Vitti—a man no one says "no" to—demands that Dr. Sobol cure him of his problem before his rivals in crime turn his "weakness" against him.

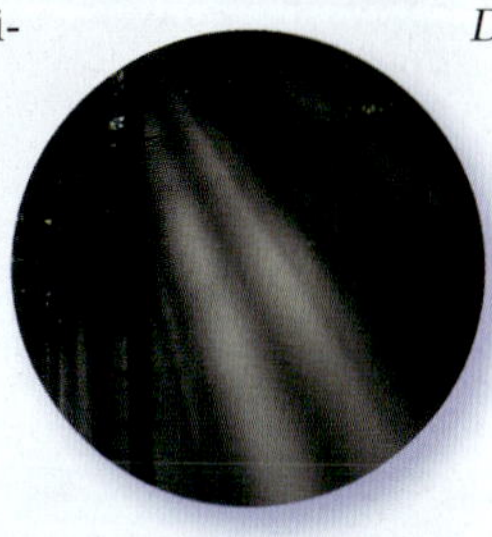

With his glasses and beard, Billy Crystal's Dr. Sobol resembles many people's picture of a therapist. Like many movie therapists, Dr. Sobol practices "talk therapy." He listens attentively as his patients talk about what is troubling them. Occasionally he offers comments that reflect their thoughts and feelings back to them or that offer some illuminating insight into their problems. We can get a feeling for his approach from a funny scene in which the uneducated Vitti turns Dr. Sobol's techniques on him:

Vitti: Hey, let's see how you like it. Let's talk about your father.
Dr. Sobol: Let's not.
Vitti: What kind of work does your father do?
Dr. Sobol: It's not important.
Vitti: You paused.
Dr. Sobol: I did not.
Vitti: You just paused. That means you had a feeling, like a thought. . . .
Dr. Sobol: You know, we're running out of time. Let's not waste it talking about my problems.
Vitti: Your father's a problem?
Dr. Sobol: No!
Vitti: That's what you just said.
Dr. Sobol: I did not!
Vitti: Now you're upset.

Warner Bros./Shooting Star

The popular film *Analyze This* derived much of its humor from common misconceptions about the process of psychotherapy.

Dr. Sobol (getting upset): I am not upset!
Vitti: Yes you are.
Dr. Sobol: Will you stop it!
Vitti: You know what, I'm getting good at this.

As in this scene, the film derives much of its humor from popular conceptions—and misconceptions—about therapy. The technique that Vitti makes fun of does resemble one type of therapeutic process. Like Vitti, many people still do associate needing therapy with a shameful weakness. Yet, therapy is often of considerable benefit in assisting people to make significant changes in their lives—even if those changes are not as dramatic as Vitti's giving up his life of crime at the end of the movie. On the other hand, the film's comic exaggerations also highlight some misconceptions about therapy, including the following:

- Vitti is driven to see a "shrink" because he feels like he's "falling apart." In fact, therapists help people with all kinds of problems. People need not have severe symptoms of mental illness to benefit from therapy.
- Dr. Sobol is a psychiatrist, but most therapists are not. And although Dr. Sobol quotes Freud and the film's plot turns on interpreting a dream (in this case, it's the psychiatrist's dream!), most therapists make little or no use of Freudian techniques.
- Dr. Sobol relies on "talk therapy" to produce insights that will help his patients overcome their troubles. In reality, this approach is only one of the many techniques used by therapists.
- Dr. Sobol "cures" Vitti by getting him to acknowledge a traumatic event in his childhood (the death of his father) that is at the root of his problems. But only rarely does therapy produce a single dramatic insight that results in wholesale change for the client.

In this chapter, we'll take a down-to-earth look at the treatment of mental disorders and psychological problems. We'll start by discussing some general questions about the provision of treatment. After considering these issues, we'll examine the goals, techniques, and effectiveness of some of the more widely used approaches to therapy and discuss recent trends and issues in treatment. In the Personal Application, we'll look at practical questions related to finding and choosing a therapist and getting the most out of therapy. And in the Critical Thinking Application, we'll address problems involved in determining the extent to which therapy actually helps.

KEY LEARNING GOALS

16.1 Identify the three major categories of therapy, and discuss patterns of treatment seeking.

16.2 Distinguish the various types of mental health professionals involved in the provision of therapy.

The Elements of the Treatment Process

Sigmund Freud is widely credited with launching modern psychotherapy. Ironically, the landmark case that inspired Freud was actually treated by one of his colleagues, Josef Breuer. Around 1880, Breuer began to treat a young woman referred to as Anna O (which was a pseudonym—her real name was Bertha Pappenheim). Anna exhibited a variety of physical maladies, including headaches, coughing, and a loss of feeling and movement in her right arm. Much to his surprise, Breuer discovered that Anna's physical symptoms cleared up when he encouraged her to talk about emotionally charged experiences from her past.

When Breuer and Freud discussed the case, they speculated that talking things through had enabled Anna to drain off bottled-up emotions that had caused her symptoms. Breuer found the intense emotional exchange in this treatment not to his liking, so he didn't follow through on his discovery. However, Freud applied Breuer's insight to other patients. His successes led him to develop a systematic treatment procedure, which he called *psychoanalysis*. Anna O called her treatment "the talking cure." However, as you'll see, psychotherapy isn't always curative, and many modern treatments place little emphasis on talking.

Freud's breakthrough ushered in a century of progress for psychotherapy. Psychoanalysis spawned many offspring as Freud's followers developed their own systems of treatment. Since then, approaches to treatment have steadily grown more numerous, more diverse, and more effective. Today, people can choose from a bewildering array of therapies.

Treatments: How Many Types Are There?

In their efforts to help people, mental health professionals use many treatment methods. These methods include discussion, advice, emotional support, persuasion, conditioning procedures, relaxation training, role playing, drug therapy, biofeedback, and group therapy. Although no one knows exactly how many distinct types of psychotherapy there are, one expert (Kazdin, 1994) estimates that over 400 approaches to treatment may be available. Fortunately, we can impose some order on this chaos. As varied as therapists' procedures are, approaches to treatment can be classified into three major categories:

1. *Insight therapies.* Insight therapy is "talk therapy" in the tradition of Freud's psychoanalysis. In insight therapies, clients engage in complex verbal interactions with their therapists. The goal in these discussions is to pursue increased insight regarding the nature of the client's difficulties and to sort through possible solutions. Insight therapy can be conducted with an individual or with a group. Broadly speaking, family therapy and marital therapy fall into this category.

2. *Behavior therapies.* Behavior therapies are based on the principles of learning, which were introduced in Chapter 6. Instead of emphasizing personal insights, behavior therapists make direct efforts to alter problematic responses (phobias, for instance) and maladaptive habits (drug use, for instance). Behavior therapists work on changing clients' overt behaviors. They use different procedures for different kinds of problems.

3. *Biomedical therapies.* Biomedical approaches to therapy involve interventions into a person's biological functioning. The most widely used procedures are drug therapy and electroconvulsive (shock) therapy. In recent decades, drug therapy has become the dominant mode of treatment for psychological disorders. As **Figure 16.1** shows, one large-scale study found that 57% of mental health patients were treated with medication only, up from 44% just nine years earlier (Olfson & Marcus, 2010). As the term bio*medical* suggests, these treatments have traditionally been provided only by physicians with a medical degree (usually psychiatrists). This situation is changing, however, as psychologists have been campaigning for prescription privileges (Price, 2008). The chief rationale for this campaign is that many rural areas and underserved populations have inadequate access to psychiatrists (Ax et al., 2008). To date, psychologists have obtained prescription authority in two states (New Mexico and Louisiana), and they have made legislative progress toward this goal in many other states (Long, 2005; Munsey, 2008).

Clients: Who Seeks Therapy?

People seeking mental health treatment present with the full range of human problems: anxiety, depression, unsatisfactory interpersonal relations, troublesome habits, poor self-control, low self-esteem, marital conflicts, self-doubt, a sense of emptiness, and feelings of personal stagnation. Among adults, the two most common presenting problems are depression and anxiety disorders (Olfson & Marcus, 2010).

A client in treatment does *not* necessarily have an identifiable psychological disorder. Some people seek professional help for everyday problems (career decisions, for instance) or vague feelings of discontent (Strupp, 1996). One surprising finding has been that only about half of the people who use mental health services in a given year meet the criteria for a full-fledged mental disorder (Kessler et al., 2005b). This finding raised concern that valuable treatment resources might be "misallocated," but a follow-up study found that most of the people seeking treatment without a full-blown disorder *did* have significant mental health issues (Druss et al., 2007). For

Mary Evans Picture Library/Sigmund Freud Copyrights

The case of Anna O, whose real name was Bertha Pappenheim, provided the inspiration for Sigmund Freud's invention of psychoanalysis.

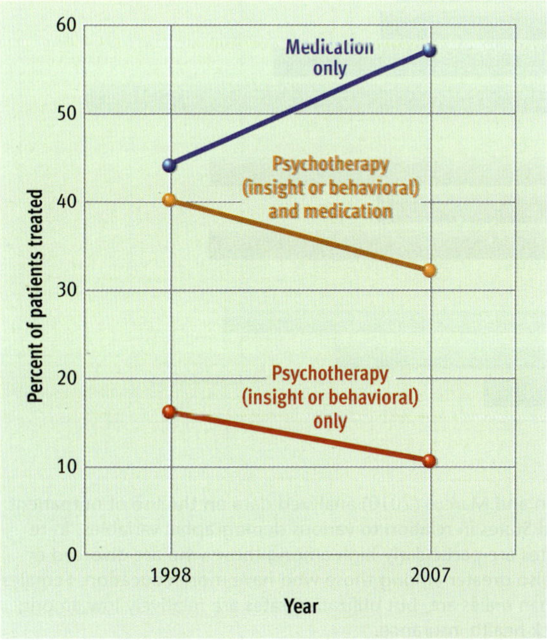

© Cengage Learning 2013

Figure 16.1
Escalating reliance on drug therapy. Using data from an ongoing national survey focusing on patterns of health care, Olfson and Marcus (2010) found some interesting recent trends in outpatient treatment for psychological disorders. Comparing treatment procedures in 1998 and 2007, they found that the percentage of patients treated with medication exclusively increased from 44% to 57%. During the same period, the percentage of patients treated with insight or behavioral therapy alone, or in combination with drug therapy, declined.

Reality CHECK

Misconception

Seeking psychotherapy is a sign of weakness; people should be able to deal with their problems.

Reality

This unfortunate, prejudicial belief prevents many people from seeking help that they need. Psychological disorders can be severe, debilitating maladies that require treatment. Recognizing that one needs help is more a sign of courage than weakness.

instance, many had a history of mental illness but were in remission at the time of the study; others were grappling with severe stress. Only about 8% of the people seeking treatment appeared to be relatively free of psychiatric problems.

Individuals vary considerably in their willingness to seek psychotherapy. Some people wait many years before finally seeking treatment for their psychological problems (Wang, Berglund et al., 2005). As you can see in **Figure 16.2**, women are more likely than men to receive therapy. In terms of ethnicity, whites are more likely to pursue treatment than blacks or hispanics. Treatment is also more likely when people have medical insurance and when they have more education (Olfson & Marcus, 2010; Wang, Lane et al., 2005). *Unfortunately, it appears that many people who need therapy don't receive it.* Research suggests that only about one-third of the people who need treatment get it (Kessler et al., 2005b).

People who could benefit from therapy do not seek it for a variety of reasons. Lack of health insurance and cost concerns appear to be major barriers to obtaining needed care for many people. Perhaps the biggest roadblock is the stigma surrounding the receipt of mental health treatment. Unfortunately, many people equate seeking therapy with admitting personal weakness.

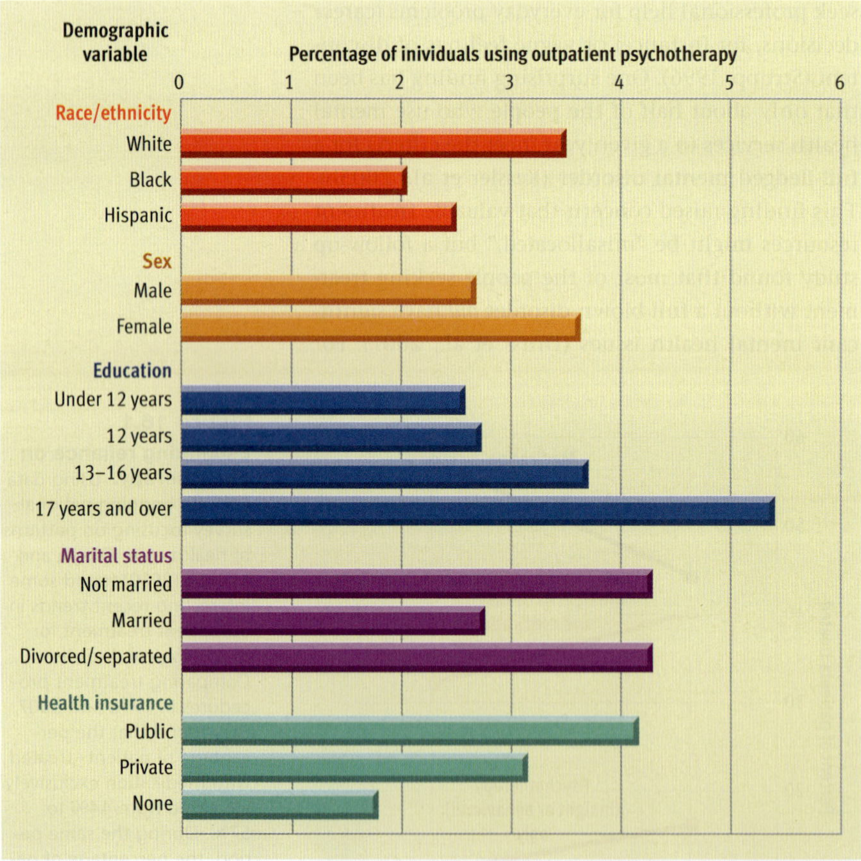

© Cengage Learning 2013

Figure 16.2

Therapy utilization rates. Olfson and Marcus (2010) analyzed data on the use of outpatient mental health services in the United States in relation to various demographic variables. In regard to marital status, utilization rates are particularly high among those who are divorced or not married. The use of therapy is also greater among those who have more education. Females are more likely to pursue therapy than males are, but utilization rates are relatively low among ethnic minorities and those who lack health insurance.

Therapists: Who Provides Professional Treatment?

People troubled by personal problems often solicit help from their friends, relatives, and clergy. These sources of assistance may provide excellent advice, but their counsel does not qualify as therapy. Therapy refers to *professional* treatment by someone with special training. However, a common source of confusion about psychotherapy is the variety of "helping professions" available to offer assistance. Psychology and psychiatry are the principal professions involved in providing psychotherapy. However, therapy is increasingly provided by other types of mental health professionals, such as clinical social workers, psychiatric nurses, counselors, and marriage and family therapists (see **Table 16.1**). Let's look at the various mental health professions.

Psychologists

Two types of psychologists may provide therapy. ***Clinical psychologists* and *counseling psychologists* specialize in the diagnosis and treatment of psychological disorders and everyday behavioral problems.** Clinical psychologists' training emphasizes the treatment of full-fledged disorders. In contrast, counseling psychologists' training is slanted toward the treatment of everyday adjustment problems. In practice, however, quite a bit of overlap occurs between clinical and counseling psychologists in training, skills, and the clientele that they serve (Morgan & Cohen, 2008).

Both types of psychologists must earn a doctoral degree (Ph.D., Psy.D., or Ed.D.). A doctorate in psychology requires about five to seven years of training beyond a bachelor's degree. The process of gaining admission to a Ph.D. program in clinical psychology is highly competitive (about as difficult as getting into medical school). Psychologists receive most of their training in universities or independent professional schools. They then serve a one-year internship in a clinical setting, such as a hospital, usually followed by one or two years of postdoctoral fellowship training.

In providing therapy, psychologists use either insight or behavioral approaches. In comparison to psychiatrists, psychologists are more likely to use behavioral techniques and less likely to use psycho-

Table 16.1 Types of Therapists

Profession	Degree	Education beyond Bachelor's degree	Typical roles and activities
Clinical psychologist	PhD or PsyD	5–7 years	Psychological testing, diagnosis, treatment with insight or behavior therapy
Counseling psychologist	PhD, PsyD, or EdD	5–7 years	Similar to clinical psychologist, but more focus on work, career, and adjustment problems
Psychiatrist	MD	8 years	Diagnosis and treatment, primarily with biomedical therapies, but also insight therapies
Clinical social worker	MSW, DSW	2–5 years	Insight and behavior therapy, often help inpatients with their return to the community
Psychiatric nurse	RN, MA, or PhD	0–5 years	Inpatient care, insight and behavior therapy
Counselor	BA or MA	0–2 years	Vocational counseling, drug counseling, rehabilitation counseling
Marriage and family therapist	MA or PhD	2–5 years	Marital/couples therapy, family therapy

© Cengage Learning 2013

analytic methods. Clinical and counseling psychologists do psychological testing as well as psychotherapy. Many also conduct research.

Psychiatrists

***Psychiatrists* are physicians who specialize in the diagnosis and treatment of psychological disorders.** Many psychiatrists also treat everyday behavioral problems. However, in comparison to psychologists, psychiatrists devote more time to relatively severe disorders (schizophrenia, mood disorders) and less time to everyday marital, family, job, and school problems.

Psychiatrists have an M.D. degree. Their graduate training requires four years of coursework in medical school and a four-year apprenticeship in a residency at a hospital. Their psychotherapy training occurs during their residency, since the required coursework in medical school is essentially the same for everyone, whether they are going into surgery, pediatrics, or psychiatry. In comparison to psychologists, psychiatrists are more likely to use psychoanalysis and less likely to use group therapies or behavior therapies. That said, contemporary psychiatrists primarily depend on medication as their principal mode of treatment. Indeed, in one recent study of over 14,000 visits to psychiatrists, only 29% of the visits involved the provision of some therapy other than the prescription and management of medications (Mojtabai & Olfson, 2008). Less than a decade earlier, that figure was 44% of visits, so psychiatrists clearly are abandoning talk therapies in favor of drug treatments.

Other Mental Health Professionals

A number of other mental health professions also provide psychotherapy services, and some of these professions are growing rapidly. In hospitals and other institutions, *clinical social workers* and *psychiatric nurses* often work as part of a treatment team with a psychologist or psychiatrist. Psychiatric nurses, who typically have a bachelor's or master's degree in their field, play a large role in hospital inpatient treatment. Clinical social workers generally have a master's degree and usually work with patients and their families to ease the patient's integration back into the community. Social workers and psychiatric nurses have traditionally worked in institutional settings. However, they increasingly provide a wide range of therapeutic services as independent practitioners.

Many kinds of *counselors* also provide therapeutic services. Counselors are usually found working in schools, colleges, and assorted human service agencies (youth centers, geriatric centers, family planning centers, and so forth). Counselors typically have a master's degree. They often specialize in particular types of problems, such as vocational counseling, rehabilitation counseling, and drug counseling. Like social workers, many are licensed as independent, private practitioners who provide diverse services for a diverse clientele.

Marriage and family therapists (MFTs) generally have a master's degree that prepares them to work with couples experiencing relationship problems or with dysfunctional families. They are licensed as independent practitioners in all but two states (Bowers, 2007). Marital and family therapy has experienced enormous growth since the 1980s (Lebow, 2008).

There are clear differences among the helping professions in education and training, But their roles in the treatment process overlap considerably.

In this chapter, we will refer to psychologists or psychiatrists as needed. Otherwise we'll use the terms *clinician, therapist,* and *provider* to refer to mental health professionals of all kinds, regardless of their professional degree.

Now that we have discussed the basic elements in psychotherapy, we can examine specific approaches to treatment in terms of their goals, procedures, and effectiveness. We'll begin with some representative insight therapies.

REVIEW OF KEY LEARNING GOALS

16.1 Approaches to treatment are diverse, but they can be grouped into three categories: insight therapies, behavior therapies, and biomedical therapies. Clients bring a wide variety of problems to therapy and do not necessarily have a disorder. People vary in their willingness to seek treatment. The likelihood of receiving treatment is greater among women, whites, those who are well-educated, and those who have insurance. Many people delay seeking treatment. Many who need therapy do not receive it.

16.2 Therapists come from a variety of professional backgrounds. Clinical and counseling psychologists, psychiatrists, clinical social workers, psychiatric nurses, counselors, and marriage and family therapists are the principal providers of therapeutic services. Each of these professions shows different preferences for approaches to treatment. Psychologists typically practice insight or behavior therapy. Psychiatrists rely more heavily on drug therapies.

Insight Therapies

KEY LEARNING GOALS

16.3 Explain the logic of psychoanalysis and the techniques by which analysts probe the unconscious.

16.4 Understand the role of therapeutic climate and therapeutic process in client-centered therapy.

16.5 Discuss new approaches to insight therapy inspired by the positive psychology movement.

16.6 Explain how group therapy and couples/family therapy are generally conducted.

16.7 Assess the efficacy of insight therapies.

There are many schools of thought about how to do insight therapy. Therapists with various theoretical orientations use different methods to pursue different kinds of insights. However, what these varied approaches have in common is that ***insight therapies* involve verbal interactions intended to enhance clients' self-knowledge and thus promote healthful changes in personality and behavior.**

There may be hundreds of insight therapies. However, the leading eight or ten approaches appear to account for the lion's share of treatment. In this section, we'll delve into psychoanalysis, related psychodynamic approaches, client-centered therapy, and new approaches fostered by the positive psychology movement. We'll also discuss how insight therapy can be done with couples, families, and groups as well as individuals.

Psychoanalysis

PsykTrek 11d

After the case of Anna O, Sigmund Freud worked as a psychotherapist for almost 50 years in Vienna. Through a painstaking process of trial and error, he developed innovative techniques for the treatment of psychological disorders and distress. His system of *psychoanalysis* came to dominate psychiatry for many decades. The dominance of psychoanalysis has eroded in recent years. Yet, a diverse collection of psychoanalytic approaches to therapy continue to evolve and to remain influential today (Gabbard, 2005; Luborsky, O'Reilly-Landry, & Arlow, 2011; Ursano, Sonnenberg, & Lazar, 2008).

National Library of Medicine

Sigmund Freud

"The news that reaches your consciousness is incomplete and often not to be relied on."

***Psychoanalysis* is an insight therapy that emphasizes the recovery of unconscious conflicts, motives, and defenses through techniques such as free association and transference.** To appreciate the logic of psychoanalysis, we have to look at Freud's thinking about the roots of mental disorders. Freud mostly treated anxiety-dominated disturbances, such as phobic, panic, and obsessive-compulsive disorders. At the time, all of these disorders were called *neuroses*.

Freud believed that neurotic problems are caused by unconscious conflicts left over from early childhood. As explained in Chapter 12, he thought that these inner conflicts involve battles among the id, ego, and superego, usually over sexual and aggressive impulses. He theorized that people depend on defense mechanisms to avoid confronting these conflicts. Such conflicts remain hidden in the depths of the unconscious (see **Figure 16.3**). However, he noted that defensive maneuvers often lead to self-defeating behavior. Furthermore, he asserted that defenses tend to be only partially successful in alleviating anxiety, guilt, and other distressing emotions. With this model in mind, let's take a look at the therapeutic procedures used in psychoanalysis.

Probing the Unconscious

PsykTrek 11d

Given Freud's assumptions, we can see that the logic of psychoanalysis is quite simple. The analyst attempts to probe the murky depths of the unconscious to discover the unresolved conflicts causing the client's neurotic behavior. In a sense, the analyst functions as a "psychological detective." In this effort to explore the unconscious, the therapist relies on two techniques: free association and dream analysis.

In *free association* clients spontaneously express their thoughts and feelings exactly as they occur, with as little censorship as possible. In free association, clients expound on anything that comes to mind, no matter how trivial, silly, or embarrassing the thought may be. Gradually, most clients begin to let everything pour out without conscious censorship. The analyst studies these free associations for clues about what is going on in the client's unconscious.

In *dream analysis* the therapist interprets the symbolic meaning of the client's dreams. Freud saw dreams as the "royal road to the unconscious." He felt dreams were the most direct means of access to patients' innermost conflicts, wishes, and impulses. Clients are encouraged and trained to remember their dreams so they can describe them in therapy. The therapist then analyzes the symbolism in these dreams to interpret their meaning.

To better illustrate these matters, let's look at an actual case treated through psychoanalysis (adapted from Greenson, 1967, pp. 40–41). Mr. N was troubled by an unsatisfactory marriage. He claimed to love his wife, but he preferred sexual relations with prostitutes. Mr. N reported that his parents also endured lifelong marital difficulties. His childhood conflicts about their relationship appeared to be related to his problems. Both dream analysis and free association can be seen in the following description of a session in Mr. N's treatment:

Mr. N reported a fragment of a dream. All that he could remember is that he was waiting for a red traffic light to change when he felt that someone had bumped into him from behind. . . . The associations led to Mr. N's love of cars, especially sports cars. He loved the sensation, in particular, of whizzing by those fat, old expensive cars. . . .

His father always hinted that he had been a great athlete, but he never substantiated it. . . . Mr. N doubted whether his father could really perform. His father would flirt with a waitress in a cafe or make sexual remarks about women passing by, but he seemed to be showing off. If he were really sexual, he wouldn't resort to that.

As is characteristic of free association, Mr. N's train of thought meandered about with little direction. Nonetheless, clues about his unconscious conflicts are apparent. What did Mr. N's therapist extract from this session? The therapist saw sexual overtones in the dream fragment, where Mr. N was bumped from behind. The therapist also inferred that Mr. N had a competitive orientation toward his father, based on the free association about whizzing by fat, old expensive cars. As you can see, analysts must *interpret* their clients' dreams and free associations. This is a critical process throughout psychoanalysis.

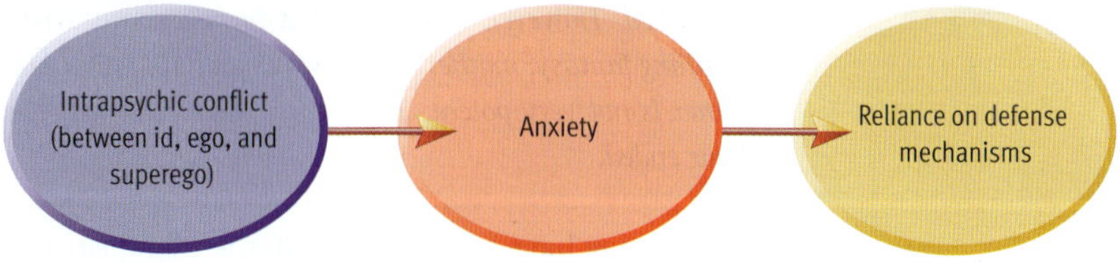

Figure 16.3
Freud's view of the roots of disorders.
According to Freud, unconscious conflicts between the id, ego, and superego sometimes lead to anxiety. This discomfort may lead to pathological reliance on defensive behavior.
© Cengage Learning 2013

Interpretation

PSYKTREK 11d

***Interpretation* refers to the therapist's attempts to explain the inner significance of the client's thoughts, feelings, memories, and behaviors.** Contrary to popular belief, analysts do not interpret everything. In addition, they generally don't try to dazzle clients with startling revelations. Instead, analysts move forward inch by inch, offering interpretations that should be just out of the client's own reach (Samberg & Marcus, 2005). Mr. N's therapist eventually offered the following interpretations to his client:

I said to Mr. N near the end of the hour that I felt he was struggling with his feelings about his father's sexual life. He seemed to be saying that his father was sexually not a very potent man. . . . He also recalls that he once found a packet of condoms under his father's pillow when he was an adolescent and he thought, "My father must be going to prostitutes." I then intervened and pointed out that the condoms under his father's pillow seemed to indicate more obviously that his father used the condoms with his mother, who slept in the

© Photos 12/Alamy

same bed. However, Mr. N wanted to believe his wish-fulfilling fantasy: mother doesn't want sex with father and father is not very potent. The patient was silent and the hour ended.

As you may have already guessed, the therapist concluded that Mr. N's difficulties were rooted in an Oedipal complex (see Chapter 12). The man, according the therapist, had unresolved sexual feelings toward his mother and hostile feelings about his father. These unconscious conflicts, rooted in Mr. N's childhood, were distorting his intimate relations as an adult.

Reality CHECK

Misconception

If you enter into therapy, you will lie on a couch and talk about your past.

Reality

Only psychoanalytic therapists (and not all of them) expect their patients to lie on a couch and discuss the past. As you will see throughout this chapter, there are many approaches to treating psychological disorders, and in the vast majority of them clients do not reveal their feelings while reclining on a couch.

Resistance

PsykTrek 11d

How would you expect Mr. N to respond to the therapist's suggestion that he was in competition with his father for the sexual attention of his mother? Obviously, most clients would have great difficulty accepting such an interpretation. Freud fully expected clients to display some resistance to therapeutic efforts. ***Resistance* refers to largely unconscious defensive maneuvers intended to hinder the progress of therapy.** Resistance is assumed to be an inevitable part of the psychoanalytic process (Samberg & Marcus, 2005). Why would clients try to resist the helping process? Because they don't want to face up to the painful, disturbing conflicts that they have buried in their unconscious. Although they have sought help, they are reluctant to confront their real problems.

Resistance can take many forms. Clients may show up late for their sessions, may merely pretend to engage in free association, or may express hostility toward their therapist. For instance, Mr. N's therapist noted that after the session just described, "The next day he [Mr. N] began by telling me that he was furious with me. . . ." Analysts use a variety of strategies to deal with their clients' resistance. Often, a key consideration is the handling of transference, which we consider next.

Transference

PsykTrek 11d

***Transference* occurs when clients unconsciously start relating to their therapist in ways that mimic critical relationships in their lives.** Thus, a client might start relating to a therapist as if the therapist were an overprotective mother, a rejecting brother, or a passive spouse. In a sense, the client *transfers* conflicting feelings about important people onto the therapist. For instance, in his treatment, Mr. N transferred some of the competitive hostility he felt toward his father onto his analyst.

Psychoanalysts often encourage transference so that clients can reenact relations with crucial people in the context of therapy. These reenactments can help bring repressed feelings and conflicts to the surface, which allows the client to work through them. The therapist's handling of transference is complicated and difficult, as it may arouse confusing, highly charged emotions in the client.

Undergoing psychoanalysis is not easy. It can be a slow, painful process of self-examination that routinely requires three to five years of hard work. It tends to be a lengthy process because patients need time to gradually work through their problems and genuinely accept unnerving revelations (Williams, 2005). Ultimately, if resistance and transference can be handled effectively, the therapist's interpretations should lead the client to profound insights. For instance, Mr. N eventually admitted, "The old boy is probably right, it does tickle me to imagine that my mother preferred me and I could beat out my father. Later, I wondered whether this had something to do with my own screwed-up sex life with my wife." According to Freud, once clients recognize the unconscious sources of their conflicts, they can resolve these conflicts and discard their neurotic defenses.

Modern Psychodynamic Therapies

Though still available, classical psychoanalysis as done by Freud is not widely practiced anymore (Kay & Kay, 2008). Freud's psychoanalytic method was geared to a particular kind of clientele that he was seeing in Vienna many years ago. As his followers fanned out across Europe and America, many found it necessary to adapt psychoanalysis to different cultures, changing times, and new kinds of patients (Karasu, 2005). Thus, many variations on Freud's original approach to psychoanalysis have developed over the years. These descendants of psychoanalysis, which continue to emphasize exploration of the unconscious, are collectively known as *psychodynamic therapies*.

Some of these adaptations, such as those made by Carl Jung (1917) and Alfred Adler (1927), were sweeping revisions based on fundamental differences in theory. Other variations, such as those devised by Melanie Klein (1948) and Heinz Kohut (1971), made substantial changes in theory while retaining certain central ideas. Still other revisions (Alexander, 1954; Stekel, 1950) simply involved efforts to modernize and streamline psychoanalytic techniques.

As a result, today we have a rich diversity of psychodynamic approaches to therapy (Magnavita, 2008). Recent reviews of these treatments suggest that interpretation, resistance, and transference continue to play key roles in therapeutic effects (Høglend et al., 2008; Luborsky & Barrett, 2006). Other central features of modern psychodynamic therapies include (1) a focus on emotional experience, (2) exploration of efforts to avoid distressing thoughts and feelings, (3) identification of recurring patterns in patients' life experiences, (4) discussion of past experience, especially events in early childhood, (5) analysis of interpersonal relationships, (6) a focus on the therapeutic relationship itself, and (7) exploration of dreams and other aspects of fantasy life (Shedler, 2010; see **Figure 16.4**). Recent research suggests that psychodynamic approaches can be helpful in the treatment of a diverse array of disorders (Gibbons, Crits-Christoph, & Hearon, 2008; Leichsenring & Rabung, 2008; Shedler, 2010).

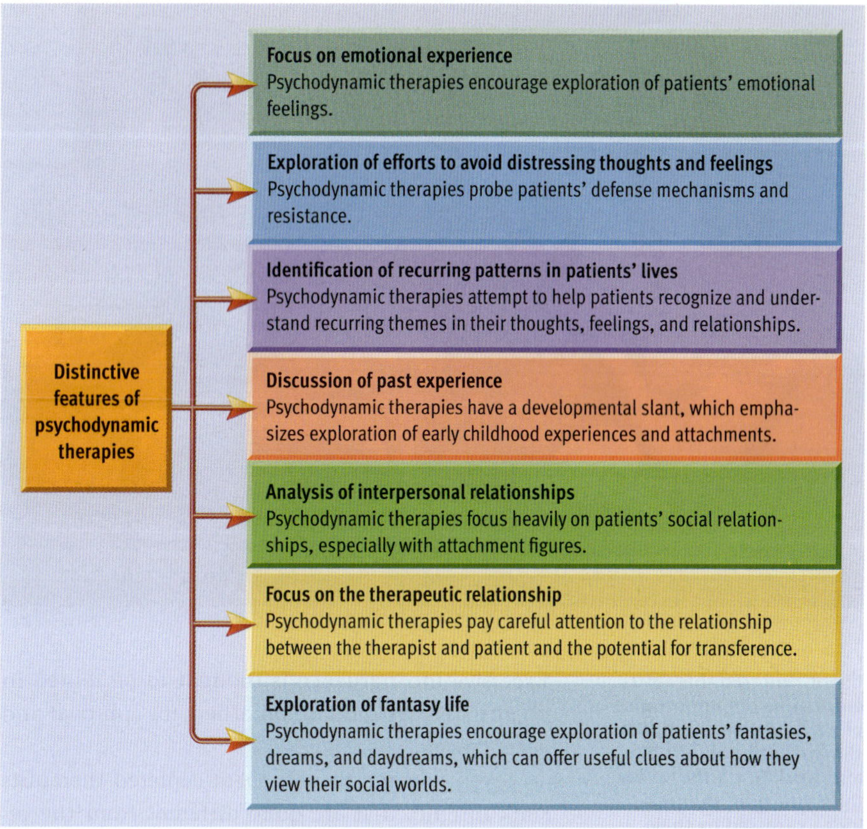

© Cengage Learning 2013

Figure 16.4

Core features of psychodynamic therapies. In an article on the efficacy of psychodynamic therapies, Jonathan Shedler (2010) outlined the distinctive aspects of modern psychodynamic techniques and processes. The seven features described here represent the core of contemporary psychodynamic treatment.

Client-Centered Therapy

PsykTrek 11d

You may have heard of people going into therapy to "find themselves" or to "get in touch with their real feelings." These now-popular phrases emerged out of the human potential movement. This movement was started in part by the work of Carl Rogers (1951, 1986). Using a humanistic perspective, Rogers devised *client-centered therapy* (also known as *person-centered therapy*) in the 1940s and 1950s.

***Client-centered therapy* is an insight therapy that emphasizes providing a supportive emotional climate for clients, who play a major role in determining the pace and direction of their therapy.** You may wonder why the troubled, untrained client is put in charge of the pace and direction of the therapy. Rogers (1961) provides a compelling justification:

> *It is the client who knows what hurts, what directions to go, what problems are crucial, what experiences have been deeply buried. It began to occur to me that unless I had a need to demonstrate my own cleverness and learning, I would do better to rely upon the client for the direction of movement in the process. (pp. 11–12)*

Rogers's theory about the principal causes of neurotic anxieties is quite different from the Freudian explanation. As discussed in Chapter 12, Rogers maintains that most personal distress is to the result of inconsistency, or "incongruence," between a person's self-concept and reality (see **Figure 16.5**). According to his theory, incongruence makes people feel threatened by realistic feedback about themselves from others. For example, if you inaccurately viewed yourself as a hard-working, dependable person, you would feel threatened by contradictory feedback from friends or co-workers. According to Rogers, anxiety about such feedback often leads to reliance on defense mechanisms, to distortions of reality, and to stifled personal growth.

Courtesy of Carl Rogers Memorial Library

Carl Rogers

"To my mind, empathy is in itself a healing agent."

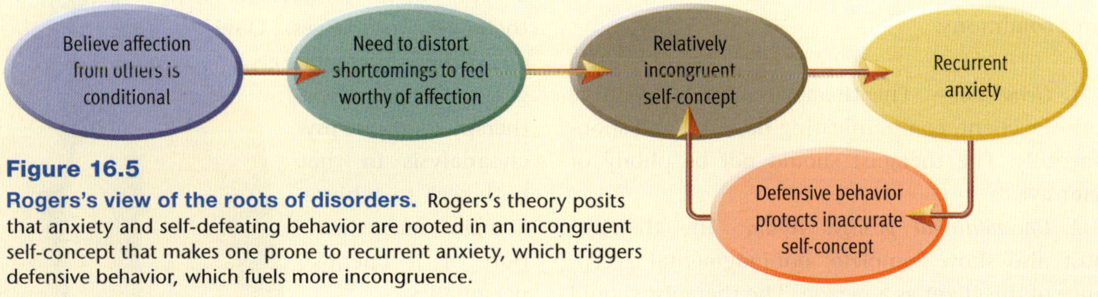

Figure 16.5

Rogers's view of the roots of disorders. Rogers's theory posits that anxiety and self-defeating behavior are rooted in an incongruent self-concept that makes one prone to recurrent anxiety, which triggers defensive behavior, which fuels more incongruence.

© Cengage Learning 2013

© Peter Dazeley/Getty Images

Client-centered therapists emphasize the importance of a supportive emotional climate in therapy. They also work to clarify, rather than interpret, the feelings expressed by their patients.

Excessive incongruence is thought to be rooted in clients' overdependence on others for approval and acceptance.

Given Rogers's theory, client-centered therapists stalk insights that are quite different from the repressed conflicts that psychoanalysts go after. Client-centered therapists help clients to realize that they do not have to worry constantly about pleasing others and winning acceptance. They encourage clients to respect their own feelings and values. They help people restructure their self-concept to correspond better to reality. Ultimately, they try to foster self-acceptance and personal growth.

Therapeutic Climate — 11d

According to Rogers, the *process* of therapy is not as important as the emotional *climate* in which the therapy takes place. He believes that it's critical for the therapist to provide a warm, supportive, accepting climate that creates a safe environment in which clients can confront their shortcomings without feeling threatened. The lack of threat should reduce clients' defensive tendencies and thus help them open up. To create this atmosphere of emotional support, client-centered therapists must provide three conditions:

1. *Genuineness.* The therapist must be genuine with the client, communicating honestly and spontaneously. The therapist should not be phony or defensive.

2. *Unconditional positive regard.* The therapist must also show complete, nonjudgmental acceptance of the client as a person. The therapist should provide warmth and caring for the client, with no strings attached. Of course, this does not mean that the therapist must approve of everything that the client says or does. A therapist can disapprove of a particular behavior while continuing to value the client as a human being.

3. *Empathy.* Finally, the therapist must provide accurate empathy for the client. This means that the therapist must understand the client's world from the *client's* point of view. Furthermore, the therapist must be articulate enough to communicate this understanding to the client.

Rogers firmly believed that a supportive emotional climate is the critical force promoting healthy changes in therapy. That said, various aspects of therapeutic process are also important.

Therapeutic Process — 11d

In client-centered therapy, the client and therapist work together as equals. The therapist provides relatively little guidance and keeps interpretation and advice to a minimum (Raskin, Rogers, & Witty, 2011). So, just what does the client-centered therapist do, besides creating a supportive climate? Primarily, the therapist provides feedback to help clients sort out their feelings. The therapist's key task is *clarification.* Client-centered therapists try to function like a human mirror, reflecting statements back to their clients, but with enhanced clarity. They help clients become more aware of their true feelings by highlighting themes that may be obscure in the clients' rambling discourse.

By working with clients to clarify their feelings, client-centered therapists hope to gradually build toward more far-reaching insights. In particular, they try to help clients better understand their interpersonal relationships and become more comfortable with their genuine selves. Obviously, these are ambitious goals. Client-centered therapy resembles psychoanalysis in that both seek to achieve a major reconstruction of a client's personality.

Therapies Inspired by Positive Psychology

The growth of the positive psychology movement has begun to inspire new approaches to insight therapy (Duckworth, Steen, & Seligman, 2005; Peterson & Park, 2009). As noted in Chapters 1 and 10, ***positive psychology* uses theory and research to better understand the positive, adaptive, creative, and fulfilling aspects of human existence.** The advocates of positive psychology maintain that the field has historically focused far too heavily on pathology, weakness, and suffering (and how to heal these conditions) rather than on health and resilience (Seligman, 2003; Seligman & Csikszentmihalyi, 2000). They argue for increased research on contentment, well-being, human strengths, and positive emotions.

This philosophical approach has led to new therapeutic interventions. For example, Giovanni Fava and his colleagues developed *well-being therapy* (Fava, 1999; Ruini & Fava, 2004). This therapy seeks to enhance clients' self-acceptance, purpose in life, autonomy, and personal growth. It has been used successfully in the treatment of mood disorders and anxiety disorders (Fava et al., 2005; Fava & Tomba, 2009).

Another new approach is *positive psychotherapy*, developed by Martin Seligman and his colleagues (Rashid & Anjum, 2008; Seligman, Rashid, & Parks, 2006). Thus far, positive psychotherapy has been used mainly in the treatment of depression. This approach attempts to get clients to recognize their strengths, appreciate their blessings, savor positive experiences, forgive those who have wronged them, and find meaning in their lives. Preliminary research suggests that positive psychotherapy can be an effective treatment for depression. For example, in one study it was compared to treatment as usual (whatever the therapist would normally do) and treatment as usual with medication. The data shown in **Figure 16.6** compare mean depression scores at the end of the study for participants in these three conditions (Seligman et al., 2006). As you can see, the lowest depression scores were observed in the group that received positive psychotherapy. The innovative interventions spurred by the positive psychology movement are in their infancy, but the early findings seem promising. It will be interesting to see what the future holds.

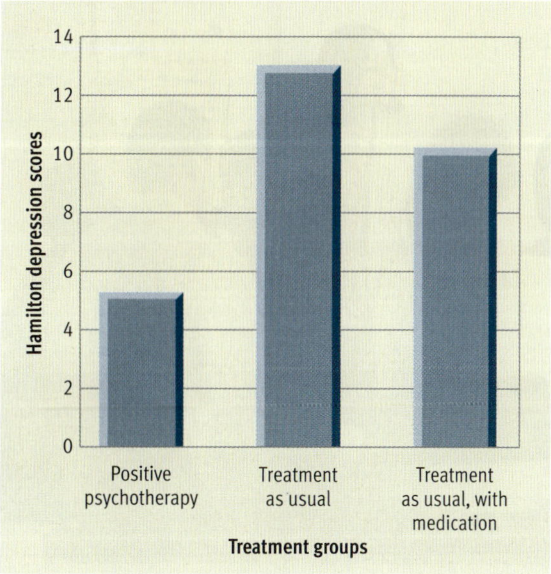

© Cengage Learning 2013

Figure 16.6

Positive psychotherapy for depression. In a study of the efficacy of positive psychotherapy, it was compared to treatment as usual (clinicians delivered whatever treatment they deemed appropriate) and to treatment as usual combined with antidepressant medication. At the end of 12 weeks of treatment, symptoms of depression were measured with the widely used Hamilton Rating Scale for Depression. The mean depression scores for each group are graphed here. As you can see, the positive psychotherapy group showed less depression than the other two treatment groups, suggesting that positive psychotherapy can be an effective intervention for depression.

SOURCE: Adapted from Seligman, M.E.P., Rashid, T., & Parks, A. C. (2006). Positive psychotherapy. *American Psychologist, 61*, 774–788, Figure 2, p. 784. Copyright © 2006 by the American Psychological Association.

Group Therapy

Group therapy dates back to the early part of the 20th century, but it didn't come of age until World War II and its aftermath in the 1950s (Rosenbaum, Lakin, & Roback, 1992). During this period, the expanding demand for therapeutic services forced clinicians to use group techniques (Burlingame & Baldwin, 2011). ***Group therapy* is the simultaneous psychological treatment of several clients in a group.** Most major insight therapies have been adapted for use with groups. Because of economic pressures in mental health care, the use of group therapy appears likely to grow in future years (Burlingame & McClendon, 2008). Group therapy can be conducted in a variety of ways. However, we will limit our discussion to a general overview of the process as it usually unfolds with outpatient populations (see Cox, Vinogradov, & Yalom, 2008; Spitz, 2009; Stone, 2008).

Participants' Roles

A therapy group typically consists of four to twelve people, with six to eight participants regarded as an ideal number (Cox et al., 2008). The therapist usually screens the participants, excluding persons who seem likely to be disruptive. Some clinicians maintain that judicious selection of participants is crucial to effective group treatment (Schlapobersky & Pines, 2009). There is some debate about whether it's better for the group to be homogeneous—made up of people who are similar in age, sex, and psychological problem. Practical necessities usually dictate that groups are at least somewhat diversified.

In group therapy, participants essentially function as therapists for one another (Stone, 2008). Group members describe their problems, trade viewpoints, share experiences, and discuss coping strategies. Most important, they provide acceptance and emotional support for each other. In this supportive

© JLP/Jose L. Pelaez/Corbis

Group treatments have proven particularly helpful when members share similar problems, such as alcoholism, overeating, or having been sexually abused as a child. Many approaches to insight therapy that were originally designed for individuals—such as client-centered therapy—have been adapted for treatment of groups.

atmosphere, group members work at peeling away the social masks that cover their insecurities. Once their problems are exposed, members work at correcting them. As members come to value one another's opinions, they work hard to display healthy changes to win the group's approval.

In group treatment, the therapist's responsibilities include selecting participants, setting goals for the group, initiating and maintaining the therapeutic process, and protecting clients from harm (Cox et al., 2008). The therapist often plays a relatively subtle role in group therapy, staying in the background and focusing mainly on promoting group cohesiveness (although this strategy varies depending on the nature of the group). The therapist models supportive behaviors for the participants and tries to promote a healthy climate. He or she always retains a special status, but the therapist and clients are usually on much more equal footing in group therapy than in individual therapy. The leader in group therapy expresses emotions, shares feelings, and copes with challenges from group members (Burlingame & McClendon, 2008).

Advantages of the Group Experience

Group therapies obviously save time and money, which can be critical in understaffed mental hospitals and other institutional settings (Cox et al., 2008). Therapists in private practice usually charge less for group than individual therapy. Obviously, this make group therapy affordable for more people. However, group therapy is *not* just a less costly substitute for individual therapy. For many types of patients and problems, group therapy can be just as effective as individual treatment (Knauss, 2005; Stone, 2008). Moreover, group therapy has unique strengths of its own. For example, in group therapy participants often come to realize that their misery is not unique. They are reassured to learn that many other people have similar or even worse problems. Another advantage is that group therapy provides an opportunity for participants to work on their social skills in a safe environment. Yet another plus is that certain types of problems and clients respond especially well to the social support that group therapy can provide.

Couples and Family Therapy

Like group therapy, marital and family therapy rose to prominence after World War II. As their names suggest, these interventions are defined in terms of who is being treated. ***Couples* or *marital therapy* involves the treatment of both partners in a committed, intimate relationship, in which the main focus is on relationship issues.** Couples therapy is not limited to married couples. It is frequently provided to cohabiting couples, including gay couples. ***Family therapy* involves the treatment of a family unit as a whole, in which the main focus is on family dynamics and communication.** Family therapy often emerges out of efforts to treat children or adolescents with individual therapy. A child's therapist, for instance, might come to the realization that treatment is likely to fail because the child returns to a home environment that contributes to the child's problems and thus may propose a broader family intervention.

As with other forms of insight therapy, there are different schools of thought about how to conduct

CONCEPT CHECK 16.1

Understanding Therapists' Conceptions of Disorders

Check your understanding of the three approaches to insight therapy covered in the text by matching each approach with the appropriate explanation of the typical origins of clients' psychological disorders. The answers are in Appendix A.

Theorized causes of disorders	Therapy
_______ 1. Problems rooted in inadequate attention paid to one's strengths, blessings, and positive experiences	a. Psychoanalysis
_______ 2. Problems rooted in unconscious conflicts left over from childhood	b. Client-centered therapy
_______ 3. Problems rooted in an inaccurate self-concept and excessive concern about pleasing others	c. Positive psychotherapy

couples and family therapy (Goldenberg, Goldenberg, & Pelavin, 2011). Some of these diverse systems are extensions of influential approaches to individual therapy, including psychodynamic, humanistic, and behavioral treatments. Other approaches are based on innovative models of families as complex systems and explicit rejection of individual models of treatment. Although the various approaches to couples and family therapy differ in terminology and their theoretical models of relationship and family dysfunction, they tend to share common goals. First, they seek to understand the entrenched patterns of interaction that produce distress. In this endeavor they view individuals as parts of a family ecosystem and they assume that people behave as they do because of their role in the system (Lebow, 2008). Second, they seek to help couples and families improve their communication and move toward healthier patterns of interaction.

What kinds of problems bring partners in for couples therapy? They include such relationship problems as constant arguments without resolution, resentment about power imbalances, perceptions of emotional withdrawal, the discovery or disclosure of affairs, sexual difficulties, the threat of relationship dissolution, and concern about how relationship issues are affecting one's children (Spitz & Spitz, 2009). Marital therapists attempt to help partners clarify their needs and desires in the relationship, appreciate their mutual contribution to problems, enhance their communication patterns, increase role flexibility and tolerance of differences, work out their balance of power, and learn to deal with conflict more constructively (Glick, Ritvo, & Melnick, 2008).

What are some of the indications for family therapy? Family therapy is likely to be helpful when a youngster's psychological difficulties appear to be rooted in family pathology, when families are buffeted by severe stress such as a serious illness or a major transition, when blended families experience adjustment problems, when sibling conflicts spin out of control, and when someone tries to sabotage another family member's individual therapy (Spitz & Spitz, 2009; Bloch & Harari, 2009). Family therapists try to help family members recognize how their patterns of interaction contribute to family distress, achieve more effective communication, rethink inflexible roles and coalitions, wrestle with power issues in the family system, and, when relevant, better understand children's psychiatric problems (Ritvo, Glick, & Berman, 2008).

© Ned Frisk/RF.Getty Images

How Effective Are Insight Therapies?

Whether insight therapies are conducted on a group or an individual basis, clients usually invest considerable time, effort, and money. Are these therapies worth the investment? Let's examine the evidence on their effectiveness.

Evaluating the effectiveness of any approach to treatment is a complex challenge (Crits-Christoph & Gibbons, 2009; Kendall, Holmbeck, & Verduin, 2004). For one thing, psychological disorders (like many physical illnesses) sometimes run their course and clear up on their own. **A *spontaneous remission* is a recovery from a disorder that occurs without formal treatment.** Thus, if a client experiences a recovery after treatment, one cannot automatically assume that the recovery was due to the treatment (see the Critical Thinking Application).

Evaluating the effectiveness of treatment is especially complicated for insight therapies (Aveline, Strauss, & Stiles, 2005). If you were to undergo insight therapy, how would you judge its efficacy? By how you felt? By looking at your behavior? By

INSIDE WOODY ALLEN

INSIDE WOODY ALLEN © 1977 King Features Syndicate

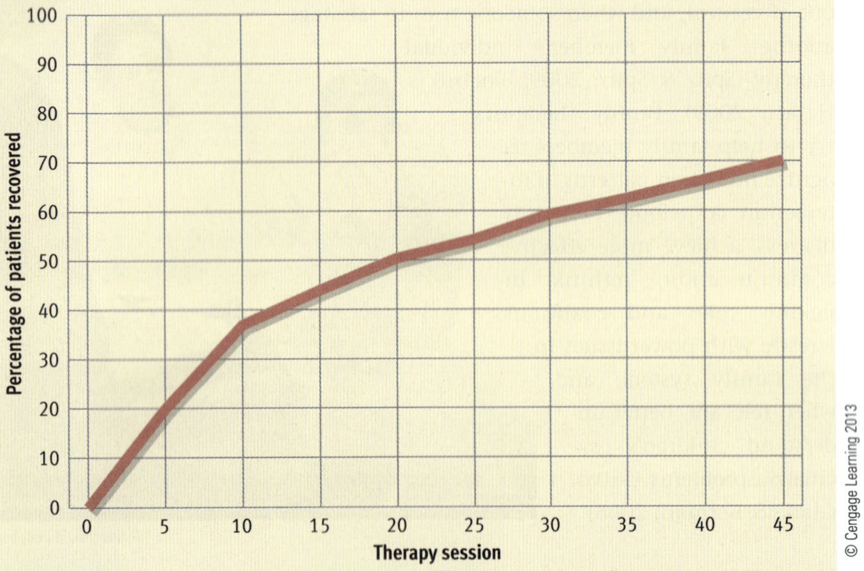

Figure 16.7

Recovery as a function of number of therapy sessions. Based on a national sample of over 6000 patients, Lambert, Hansen, and Finch (2001) mapped out the relationship between recovery and the duration of treatment. These data show that about half of the patients had experienced a clinically significant recovery after twenty weekly sessions of therapy. After forty-five sessions of therapy, about 70% had recovered.

SOURCE: Adapted from Lambert, M. J., Hansen, N. B., & Finch, A. E. (2001). Patient-focused research: Using patient outcome data to enhance treatment effects. *Journal of Consulting and Clinical Psychology, 69,* 159–172. Copyright © 2001 by the American Psychological Association. Used by permission of the authors.

asking your therapist? By consulting your friends and family? What would you be looking for? Various schools of thought pursue entirely different goals. And clients' ratings of their progress are likely to be slanted toward a favorable evaluation because they want to justify their effort, their heartache, their expense, and their time. Even evaluations by professional therapists can be highly subjective (Luborsky et al., 1999). Moreover, people enter therapy with diverse problems of varied severity. This all creates huge confounds in efforts to assess the effectiveness of therapeutic interventions.

Despite these difficulties, thousands of outcome studies have been conducted to evaluate the effectiveness of insight therapy. These studies have examined a broad range of clinical problems and used diverse methods to assess therapeutic outcomes. Such methods include scores on psychological tests and ratings by family members, as well as therapists' and clients' ratings. These studies consistently indicate that insight therapy *is* superior to no treatment or to placebo treatment and that the effects of therapy are reasonably durable (Lambert, 2011; Lambert & Archer, 2006; Torres & Saunders, 2009). And when insight therapies are compared head to head against drug therapies, they usually show roughly equal efficacy (Arkowitz & Lilienfeld, 2007; Pinquart, Duberstein, & Lyness, 2006). Studies generally find the greatest improvement early in treatment (the first 13–18 weekly sessions), with further gains gradually diminishing over time (Lambert, Bergin, & Garfield, 2004). Overall, about 50% of patients show a clinically meaningful recovery within about twenty sessions, and another 20% of patients achieve this goal after about forty-five sessions (Lambert & Ogles, 2004; see **Figure 16.7**). Of course, these broad generalizations mask considerable variability in outcome, but the general trends are encouraging.

REVIEW OF KEY LEARNING GOALS

16.3 Freudian approaches to therapy assume that neuroses originate from unresolved conflicts lurking in the unconscious. Therefore, in psychoanalysis, free association (discussing whatever comes to mind with no censorship) and dream analysis are used to explore the unconscious. When an analyst's probing hits sensitive areas, resistance, which involves unconscious defensive maneuvers to hinder progress, can be expected. The transference relationship may be used to overcome this resistance so that the client can handle interpretations that lead to insight.

16.4 Rogers's client-centered therapy assumes that neurotic anxieties are derived from incongruence between a person's self-concept and reality. Accordingly, the client-centered therapist emphasizes trying to provide a supportive climate marked by genuineness, unconditional positive regard, and empathy. The process of client-centered therapy depends on clarification of the client's feelings to promote self-acceptance.

16.5 The growth of the positive psychology movement has begun to inspire new approaches to insight therapy, such as well-being therapy. Positive psychotherapy attempts to get clients to recognize their strengths, appreciate their blessings, savor positive experiences, and find meaning in their lives.

16.6 Participants in group therapy essentially act as therapists for one another, exchanging insights and emotional support. The therapist sets goals for the group and works to maintain a supportive climate, while mostly remaining in the background. Couples therapy involves the treatment of both partners in a committed, intimate relationship. Family therapy involves the treatment of a family unit as a whole. Marital and family therapists seek to understand the entrenched patterns of interaction that produce distress for their clients, view individuals as parts of a family ecosystem, and attempt to help couples and families improve their communication.

16.7 Evaluating the effectiveness of any approach to therapy is complex and difficult. Nonetheless, the research evidence suggests that insight therapies are superior to no treatment or to placebo treatment. Studies generally find the greatest improvement early in treatment.

Behavior Therapies

KEY LEARNING GOALS

16.8 Describe the goals and procedures of systematic desensitization and exposure therapies.

16.9 Outline the goals and techniques of aversion therapy and social skills training.

16.10 Articulate the goals and techniques of cognitive therapy.

16.11 Evaluate the efficacy of behavior therapies.

Behavior therapy is different from insight therapy in that behavior therapists make no attempt to help clients achieve grand insights about themselves. Why not? Because behavior therapists believe that such insights aren't necessary to produce constructive change. For example, consider a client troubled by compulsive gambling. The behavior therapist doesn't care whether this behavior is rooted in unconscious conflicts or parental rejection. What the client needs is to get rid of the maladaptive behavior, the gambling. Consequently, the therapist simply designs a program to eliminate the compulsive gambling.

The crux of the difference between insight therapy and behavior therapy is this: Insight therapists treat pathological symptoms as signs of an underlying problem, whereas behavior therapists think that the symptoms *are* the problem. Thus, ***behavior therapies* involve the application of learning principles to direct efforts to change clients' maladaptive behaviors.**

Behaviorism has been an influential school of thought in psychology since the 1920s. Nevertheless, behaviorists devoted little attention to clinical issues until the 1950s. At that time, behavior therapy emerged out of three independent lines of research fostered by B. F. Skinner and his colleagues (Skinner, Solomon, & Lindsley, 1953) in the United States; by Hans Eysenck (1959) and his colleagues in Britain; and by Joseph Wolpe (1958) and his colleagues in South Africa (Wilson, 2011). Since then, there has been an explosion of interest in behavioral approaches to psychotherapy.

Behavior therapies are based on certain assumptions (Stanley & Beidel, 2009). *First, it's assumed that behavior is a product of learning.* No matter how self-defeating or pathological a client's behavior might be, the behaviorist believes that it's the result of past learning and conditioning. *Second, it's assumed that what has been learned can be unlearned.* The same learning principles that explain how the maladaptive behavior was acquired can be used to get rid of it. Thus, behavior therapists attempt to change clients' behavior by applying the principles of classical conditioning, operant conditioning, and observational learning.

Systematic Desensitization and Exposure Therapies

Devised by Joseph Wolpe (1958), systematic desensitization revolutionized psychotherapy by giving therapists their first useful alternative to traditional "talk therapy" (Fishman, Rego, & Muller, 2011). ***Systematic desensitization* is a behavior therapy used to reduce phobic clients' anxiety responses through counterconditioning.** The treatment assumes that most anxiety responses are acquired through classical conditioning (as we discussed in Chapter 15). According to this model, a harmless stimulus (for instance, a bridge) may be paired with a fear-arousing event (lightning striking it) so that it becomes a conditioned stimulus eliciting anxiety. The goal of systematic desensitization is to weaken the association between the conditioned stimulus (the bridge) and the conditioned response of anxiety (see **Figure 16.8**).

Systematic desensitization involves three steps. *In the first step, the therapist helps the client build an anxiety hierarchy.* This is a list of anxiety-arousing stimuli related to the specific source of anxiety, such as flying, academic tests, or snakes. The client ranks the stimuli from the least anxiety arousing to the most anxiety arousing. *The second step involves training the client in deep muscle relaxation.* This second phase may begin during early sessions while the therapist and client are still constructing the anxiety hierarchy. *In the third step, the client tries to work through the hierarchy, learning to remain relaxed while imagining each stimulus.* Starting with the least anxiety-arousing stimulus, the client imagines the situation as vividly as possible while relaxing. If the client experiences strong anxiety, he or she drops the imaginary scene and concentrates on relaxation. The client keeps repeating this process until he or she can imagine a scene with little or no anxiety. Once a particular scene is conquered, the client moves on to the next stimulus situation in the anxiety hierarchy. Gradually, over a number of therapy

Courtesy of Joseph Wolpe

Joseph Wolpe

"Neurotic anxiety is nothing but a conditioned response."

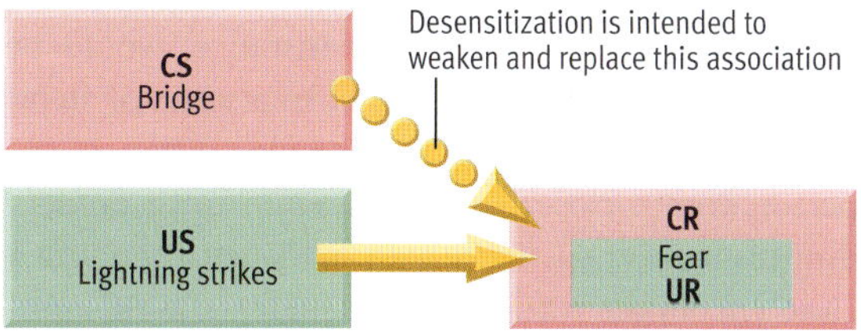

Figure 16.8

The logic underlying systematic desensitization. Behaviorists argue that many phobic responses are acquired through classical conditioning, as in the example diagrammed here. Systematic desensitization targets the conditioned associations between phobic stimuli and fear responses. © Cengage Learning 2013

Systematic desensitization is a behavioral treatment for phobias. Early studies of the procedure's efficacy often used people who had snake phobias as research subjects because people with snake phobias were relatively easy to find. This research showed that systematic desensitization is generally an effective treatment.

© Kent News & Picture/Corbis Sygma

sessions, the client progresses through the hierarchy, unlearning troublesome anxiety responses.

The effectiveness of systematic desensitization in reducing phobic responses is well documented (Spiegler & Guevremont, 2010). That said, interventions emphasizing direct exposures to anxiety-arousing situations have become behavior therapists' treatment of choice for phobic and other anxiety disorders (Rachman, 2009). **In *exposure therapies* clients are confronted with situations that they fear so that they learn that these situations are really harmless.** The exposures take place in a controlled setting and often involve a gradual progression from less-feared to more-feared stimuli. These real-life exposures to anxiety-arousing situations usually prove harmless, and individuals' anxiety responses decline. In recent decades, some therapists have resorted to highly realistic virtual-reality presentations of feared situations via computer-generated imagery (Meyerbröker & Emmelkamp, 2010; Reger et al., 2011). Exposure therapies are versatile in that they can be used with the full range of anxiety disorders, including obsessive-compulsive disorder, posttraumatic stress disorder, and panic disorder.

Effective exposure treatments for phobias can even be completed in a single session! One-session treatment (OST) of phobias, pioneered by Lars-Göran Öst (1997), involves an intensive 3-hour intervention that depends primarily on gradually increased exposures to specific phobic objects and situations. A person with a spider phobia, for instance, would be asked to approach a small spider in a series of steps. Once anxiety subsides at a particular distance, the person comes closer and waits again until anxiety diminishes. When the person manages to endure a close encounter with the small spider, the therapist may move on to a larger, or more intimidating spider. OST has proven effective with a variety of specific phobias, including snakes, spiders, cats, dogs, darkness, thunderstorms, heights, and elevators (Ollendick et al., 2009; Öst, 1997; Öst et al., 2001).

Aversion Therapy

PsykTrek 11e

Aversion therapy is far and away the most controversial of the behavior therapies. It's not something that you would sign up for unless you are pretty desperate. Psychologists usually suggest it only as a treatment of last resort, after other interventions have failed. What's so terrible about aversion therapy? The client has to endure decidedly unpleasant stimuli, such as shocks or drug-induced nausea.

***Aversion therapy* is a behavior therapy in which an aversive stimulus is paired with a stimulus that elicits an undesirable response.** For example, alcoholics have had an *emetic drug* (one that causes nausea and vomiting) paired with their favorite drinks during therapy sessions (Landabaso et al., 1999). By pairing the drug with alcohol, the therapist hopes to create a conditioned aversion to alcohol (see **Figure 16.9**).

Aversion therapy takes advantage of the automatic nature of responses produced through classical conditioning. Admittedly, alcoholics treated with aversion therapy know that they won't be given an emetic outside of their therapy sessions. However, their reflex response to the stimulus of al-

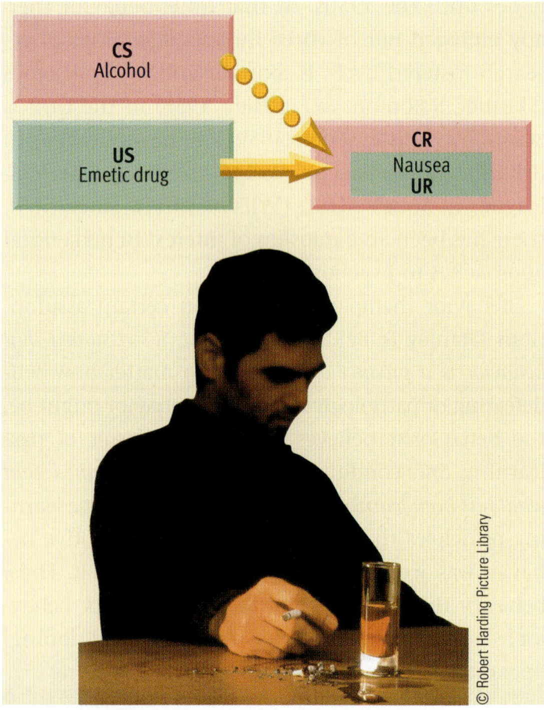

Figure 16.9

Aversion therapy. Aversion therapy uses classical conditioning to create an aversion to a stimulus that has elicited problematic behavior. For example, in the treatment of drinking problems, alcohol may be paired with a nausea-inducing drug to create an aversion to drinking. © Cengage Learning 2013 cohol may be changed so they respond to it with nausea and distaste (remember the power of conditioned taste aversions described in Chapter 6?). Obviously, this response should make it much easier to resist the urge to drink.

Aversion therapy is not a widely used technique. When it is used, it's usually only one element in a larger treatment program. Troublesome behaviors treated successfully with aversion therapy have included drug and alcohol abuse, sexual deviance, gambling, shoplifting, stuttering, cigarette smoking, and overeating (Bordnick et al., 2004; Emmelkamp, 1994; Grossman & Ruiz, 2004; Maletzky, 2002).

Social Skills Training

Many psychological problems grow out of interpersonal difficulties. Behavior therapists point out that people are not born with social finesse—they acquire social skills through learning. Unfortunately, some people have not learned how to be friendly, how to make conversation, how to express anger appropriately, and so forth. Social ineptitude can contribute to anxiety, feelings of inferiority, and various kinds of disorders. In light of these findings, therapists are increasingly using social skills training in efforts to improve clients' social abilities. This approach to therapy has yielded promising results in the treatment of social anxiety (Bögels & Voncken, 2008), autism (Cappadocia & Weiss, 2010), attention deficit disorder (Monastra, 2008), and schizophrenia (Kurtz & Mueser, 2008).

***Social skills training* is a behavior therapy designed to improve interpersonal skills that emphasizes modeling, behavioral rehearsal, and shaping.** This type of behavior therapy can be conducted with individual clients or in groups. Social skills training depends on the principles of operant conditioning and observational learning. With *modeling,* the client is encouraged to watch socially skilled friends and colleagues in order to acquire appropriate responses (eye contact, active listening, and so on) through observation. In *behavioral rehearsal,* the client tries to practice social techniques in structured role-playing exercises. The therapist provides corrective feedback and uses approval to reinforce progress. Eventually, of course, clients try their newly acquired skills in real-world interactions. Usually, they are given specific homework assignments. *Shaping* is used in that clients are gradually asked to handle more complicated and delicate social situations. For example, a nonassertive client may begin by working on making requests of friends. Only much later will he be asked to tackle standing up to his boss at work.

Cognitive-Behavioral Treatments

In Chapter 15, we learned that cognitive factors play a key role in the development of many anxiety and mood disorders. Citing the importance of such findings, in the 1970s behavior therapists started to focus more attention on their clients' cognitions (Hollon & Digiuseppe, 2011). ***Cognitive-behavioral treatments* use varied combinations of verbal interventions and behavior modification techniques to help clients change maladaptive patterns of thinking.** Some of these treatments, such as Albert Ellis's (1973) *rational-emotive behavior therapy* and Aaron Beck's (1976) *cognitive therapy,* emerged out of an insight therapy tradition, whereas other treatments, such as the systems developed by Donald Meichenbaum (1977) and Michael Mahoney (1974), emerged from the behavioral tradition. Here we will focus on Beck's cognitive therapy (Newman & Beck, 2009) as an example of a cognitive-behavioral treatment (see Chapter 14 for a discussion of some of Ellis's ideas).

***Cognitive therapy* uses specific strategies to correct habitual thinking errors that underlie various types of disorders.** In recent years, cognitive therapy has been applied fruitfully to a wide range of disorders (Beck & Weishaar, 2011; Hollon, Stewart, & Strunk, 2006). However, it was originally devised as a treatment for depression. According to cognitive therapists, depression is caused by "errors" in thinking (see **Figure 16.10**). They assert that depression-prone people tend to (1) blame their setbacks on personal inadequacies without considering circumstantial explanations, (2) focus selectively on negative events while ignoring positive events, (3) make unduly pessimistic projections about the future, and (4) draw negative conclusions about their worth as a person based on insignificant events. For instance, imagine that you got a low grade on a minor quiz in a class. If you made the kinds of errors in thinking just described, you might blame the grade on your

Courtesy of Aaron T. Beck

Aaron Beck

"Most people are barely aware of the automatic thoughts which precede unpleasant feelings or automatic inhibitions."

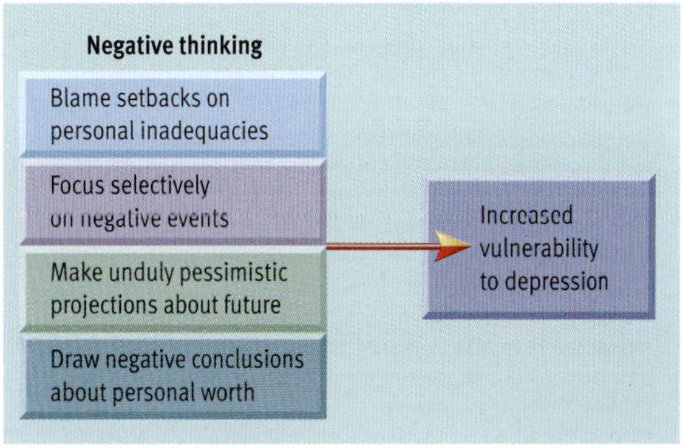

© Cengage Learning 2013

Figure 16.10
Beck's view of the roots of disorders. Aaron Beck's theory initially focused on the causes of depression, although it was gradually broadened to explain other disorders. According to Beck, depression is caused by the types of negative thinking shown here.

CONCEPT CHECK 16.2

Understanding Therapists' Goals

Check your understanding of therapists' goals by matching various therapies with the appropriate description. The answers are in Appendix A.

Principal therapeutic goals	Therapy
_______ 1. Elimination of maladaptive behaviors or symptoms	a. Psychoanalysis
_______ 2. Acceptance of genuine self, personal growth	b. Client-centered therapy
_______ 3. Recovery of unconscious conflicts, character reconstruction	c. Cognitive therapy
_______ 4. Detection and reduction of negative thinking	d. Behavior therapy

woeful stupidity, dismiss comments from a classmate that it was an unfair quiz, gloomily predict that you will surely flunk the course, and conclude that you are not genuine college material.

The goal of cognitive therapy is to change clients' negative thoughts and maladaptive beliefs (Kellogg & Young, 2008). To begin, clients are taught to detect their automatic negative thoughts. These are self-defeating statements that people are prone to make when analyzing problems. Examples might include "I'm just not smart enough," "No one really likes me," or "It's all my fault." Clients are then trained to subject these automatic thoughts to reality testing. The therapist helps them see how unrealistically negative the thoughts are.

Cognitive therapy uses a variety of behavioral techniques, such as modeling, systematic monitoring of one's behavior, and behavioral rehearsal (Beck & Weishaar, 2011). Cognitive therapists often give their clients "homework assignments" that focus on changing clients' overt behaviors. Clients may be instructed to engage in overt responses on their own, outside of the clinician's office. For example, one shy, insecure young man in cognitive therapy was told to go to a bar and engage three different women in conversations for up to 5 minutes each (Rush, 1984). He was instructed to record his thoughts before and after each of the conversations. This assignment elicited various maladaptive patterns of thought that gave the young man and his therapist plenty to work on in subsequent sessions.

How Effective Are Behavior Therapies?

Behavior therapists have historically placed more emphasis on the importance of measuring therapeutic outcomes than insight therapists have. Thus, there is ample evidence attesting to the effectiveness of behavior therapy (Jacob & Pelham, 2005; Stanley & Beidel, 2009). Of course, behavior therapies are not well suited to the treatment of some types of problems (vague feelings of discontent, for instance). Furthermore, it's misleading to make global statements about the effectiveness of behavior therapies. Behavior therapies include many types of specific procedures designed for very different purposes. For example, the value of systematic desensitization for phobias has no bearing on the value of aversion therapy for sexual deviance. For our purposes, it's sufficient to note that there is favorable evidence on the efficacy of most of the widely used behavioral interventions (Zinbarg & Griffith, 2008). Behavior therapies can make important contributions to the treatment of phobias, obsessive-compulsive disorders, sexual dysfunction, schizophrenia, depression, drug-related problems, eating disorders, hyperactivity, autism, and mental retardation (Emmelkamp, 2004; Hollon & Dimidjian, 2009; Wilson, 2011).

REVIEW OF KEY LEARNING GOALS

16.8 Behavior therapies use the principles of learning in direct efforts to change specific aspects of behavior. Wolpe's systematic desensitization is a treatment designed to relieve phobias. It involves the construction of an anxiety hierarchy, relaxation training, and step-by-step movement through the hierarchy, pairing relaxation with each phobic stimulus. In exposure therapies clients are confronted with situations that they fear so that they learn that these situations are really harmless.

16.9 In aversion therapy, a stimulus associated with an unwanted response is paired with an unpleasant stimulus in an effort to eliminate the maladaptive response. Social skills training can improve clients' interpersonal skills through shaping, modeling, and behavioral rehearsal.

16.10 Cognitive-behavioral treatments concentrate on changing the way clients think about events in their lives. Cognitive therapists reeducate clients to detect and challenge automatic negative thoughts that cause depression and anxiety. Cognitive therapy also depends on modeling, behavioral rehearsal, and homework assignments.

16.11 Behavior therapists have historically placed more emphasis on the importance of measuring therapeutic outcomes than insight therapists have. There is ample evidence that behavior therapies are effective in the treatment of a wide variety of disorders.

Biomedical Therapies

KEY LEARNING GOALS

16.12 Summarize the therapeutic actions and side effects of antianxiety and antipsychotic drugs.

16.13 Summarize the therapeutic actions and side effects of antidepressant and mood-stabilizing drugs.

16.14 Evaluate the overall efficacy of drug treatments and controversies surrounding pharmaceutical research.

16.15 Describe electroconvulsive therapy, and assess its therapeutic effects and risks.

16.16 Describe the therapeutic use of transcranial magnetic stimulation and direct brain stimulation.

In the 1950s, a French surgeon looking for a drug that would reduce patients' autonomic response to surgical stress noticed that chlorpromazine produced a mild sedation. Based on this observation, Delay and Deniker (1952) decided to give chlorpromazine to hospitalized schizophrenic patients. They wanted to see whether the drug would have calming effects. Their experiment was a dramatic success, and chlorpromazine became the first effective antipsychotic drug (Bentall, 2009). This success began a revolution in psychiatry. Hundreds of thousands of severely disturbed patients who had appeared doomed to spend the remainder of their lives in mental hospitals were gradually sent home, thanks to the therapeutic effects of antipsychotic drugs. Today, biomedical therapies such as drug treatment lie at the core of psychiatric practice.

***Biomedical therapies* are physiological interventions intended to reduce symptoms associated with psychological disorders.** These therapies assume that psychological disorders are caused, at least in part, by biological malfunctions. As we discussed in the previous chapter, this assumption clearly has merit for many disorders, especially the more severe ones. We will discuss the two standard biomedical approaches to psychotherapy, drug therapy and electroconvulsive (shock) therapy. We will then delve into some new experimental treatments involving brain stimulation.

Treatment with Drugs 11e

***Psychopharmacotherapy* is the treatment of mental disorders with medication.** We will refer to this kind of treatment more simply as *drug therapy*. The four main categories of therapeutic drugs for psychological problems are (1) antianxiety drugs, (2) antipsychotic drugs, (3) antidepressant drugs, and (4) mood-stabilizing drugs.

Antianxiety Drugs 11e

Many people routinely take pills to relieve anxiety. The drugs involved in this common coping strategy are ***antianxiety drugs*, which relieve tension, apprehension, and nervousness.** The most popular of these drugs are Valium and Xanax. These are the trade names (the proprietary names that pharmaceutical companies use in marketing drugs) for diazepam and alprazolam, respectively.

Valium, Xanax, and other drugs in the *benzodiazepine* family are often called *tranquilizers*. These drugs exert their effects almost immediately. They can be fairly effective in alleviating feelings of anxiety (Dubovsky, 2009). However, their effects are measured in hours, so their impact is relatively short-lived. Although antianxiety drugs are routinely prescribed for people with anxiety disorders, they are also given to millions of people who simply suffer from chronic nervous tension.

All the drugs used to treat psychological problems have potentially troublesome side effects that show up in some patients but not others. The antianxiety drugs are no exception. The most common side effects of Valium and Xanax are drowsiness, lightheadedness, dry mouth, nausea, constipation, depression, and confusion. Some of these side effects present serious problems for some patients. These drugs also have potential for abuse, drug dependence, and overdose. However, these risks have probably been exaggerated in the press (Martinez, Marangell & Martinez, 2008). Another drawback is that patients who have been on antianxiety drugs for a while often experience withdrawal symptoms when their drug treatment is stopped (Edwards et al., 2008).

Antipsychotic Drugs 11e

Antipsychotic drugs are used primarily in the treatment of schizophrenia. They are also given to people with severe mood disorders who become delusional. The trade (and generic) names of some classic drugs in this category are Thorazine (chlorpromazine), Mellaril (thioridazine), and Haldol (haloperidol). ***Antipsychotic drugs* are used to gradually reduce psychotic symptoms, including hyperactivity, mental confusion, hallucinations, and delusions.** The traditional antipsychotics appear to decrease activity at certain subtypes of dopamine synapses. However, the exact relationship between their neurochemical effects and their clinical effects remains obscure (Miyamoto et al., 2008).

Studies suggest that antipsychotics reduce psychotic symptoms in about 70% of patients, albeit in varied degrees (Kane, Stroup, & Marder, 2009). When antipsychotic drugs are effective, they exert their effects gradually, as shown in **Figure 16.11** on the next page. Patients usually begin to respond within one to three weeks. Considerable variability in responsiveness is seen, however (Emsley, Rabinowitz,

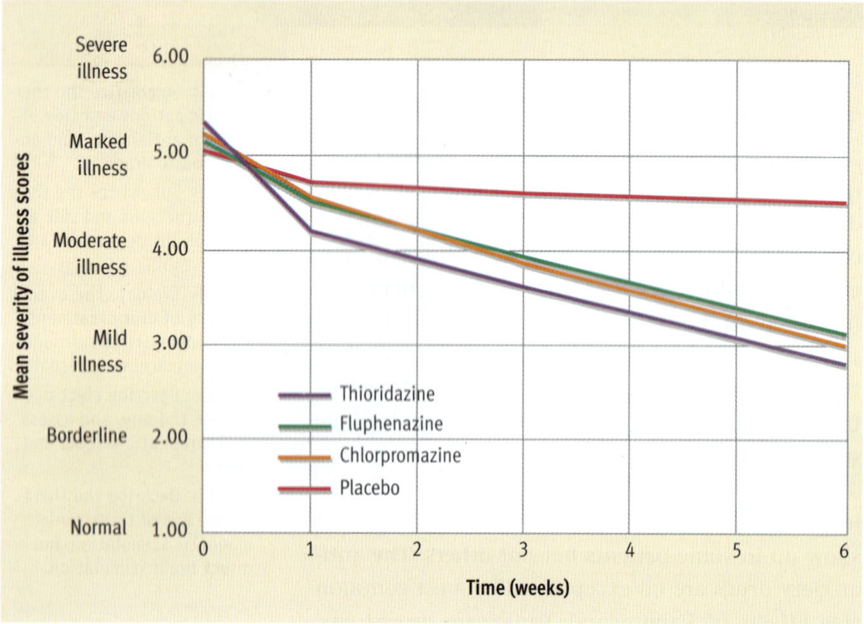

© Cengage Learning 2013

Figure 16.11

The time course of antipsychotic drug effects. Antipsychotic drugs reduce psychotic symptoms gradually, over a span of weeks, as graphed here. In contrast, patients given placebo medication show little improvement.

SOURCE: Cole, J. O., Goldberg, S. C., & Davis, J. M. (1966). Drugs in the treatment of psychosis. In P. Solomon (Ed.), *Psychiatric drugs.* New York: Grune & Stratton. From data in the NIMH-PSC Collaborative Study I. Reprinted by permission of J. M. Davis.

& Medori, 2006). Further improvement may occur for several months. Many schizophrenic patients are placed on antipsychotics indefinitely because these drugs can reduce the likelihood of a relapse into another active schizophrenic episode (van Kammen, Hurford, & Marder, 2009).

Antipsychotic drugs undeniably make a huge contribution to the treatment of severe mental disorders, but they are not without problems. They have many unpleasant side effects (Dolder, 2008; Muench & Hamer, 2010). Drowsiness, constipation, and cotton mouth are common. The drugs may also produce effects that resemble the symptoms of Parkinson's disease, including muscle tremors, muscular rigidity, and impaired motor coordination. After being released from a hospital, many schizophrenic patients stop taking their drug regimen because of the disagreeable side effects. Unfortunately, after patients stop taking antipsychotic medication, about 70% relapse within a year (van Kammen et al., 2009). One recent study found that even brief periods of partial noncompliance with one's drug regimen increased the risk of relapse (Subotnik et al., 2011). In addition to minor side effects, antipsychotics may cause a severe and lasting problem called *tardive dyskinesia*. This syndrome is seen in about 20%–30% of patients who receive long-term treatment with traditional antipsychotics (Kane et al., 2009). ***Tardive dyskinesia* is a neurological disorder marked by involuntary writhing and ticlike movements of the mouth, tongue, face, hands, or feet.** Once this debilitating syndrome emerges, there is no cure. However, spontaneous remission sometimes occurs after the discontinuation of antipsychotic medication.

Psychiatrists currently rely primarily on a newer class of antipsychotic agents called *atypical* or *second-generation antipsychotic drugs,* such as clozapine, olanzapine, and quetiapine (Marder, Hurford, & van Kammen, 2009). These drugs appear to be roughly similar to the first-generation antipsychotics in therapeutic effectiveness, but they offer some advantages over the older drugs (Meltzer & Bobo, 2009). For instance, they can help some treatment-resistant patients who do not respond to traditional antipsychotics. And the second-generation antipsychotics produce fewer unpleasant side effects and carry less risk for tardive dyskinesia. Of course, like all powerful drugs, they carry some risks. This drug class appears to increase patients' vulnerability to diabetes and cardiovascular problems.

Antidepressant Drugs

PSYKTREK 11e

As their name suggests, ***antidepressant drugs* gradually elevate mood and help bring people out of a depression.** Reliance on antidepressants has increased dramatically in the last ten to fifteen years, as antidepressants have become the most frequently prescribed class of medication in the United States (Olfson & Marcus, 2009). Prior to 1987, there were two principal classes of antidepressants: *tricyclics* (such as Elavil) and *MAO inhibitors* (such as Nardil). These two sets of drugs affect neurochemical activity in different ways (see **Figure 16.12**) and tend to work with different patients. Overall, they are beneficial for about two-thirds of depressed patients (Gitlin, 2009). The tricylics have fewer problems with side effects and complications than the MAO inhibitors (Potter et al., 2006).

Today, psychiatrists are more likely to prescribe a newer class of antidepressants, called *selective serotonin reuptake inhibitors* (*SSRIs*). These drugs slow the reuptake process at serotonin synapses, thus increasing serotonin activation. The drugs in this class include Prozac (fluoxetine), Paxil (paroxetine), and Zoloft (sertraline). These drugs seem to yield therapeutic gains similar to the tricyclics in the treatment of depression (Boland & Keller, 2008) while producing fewer unpleasant or dangerous side effects (Sussman, 2009). SSRIs have also proven valuable in the treatment of obsessive-compulsive disorders, panic disorders, and other anxiety disorders (Mathew, Hoffman, & Charney, 2009; Ravindran & Stein, 2009). However, there's some doubt about how effective the SSRIs (and other antidepressants) are in relieving episodes of depression among patients suffering from bipolar disorder (Berman et al., 2009).

Like antipsychotic drugs, the various types of antidepressants exert their effects gradually over a

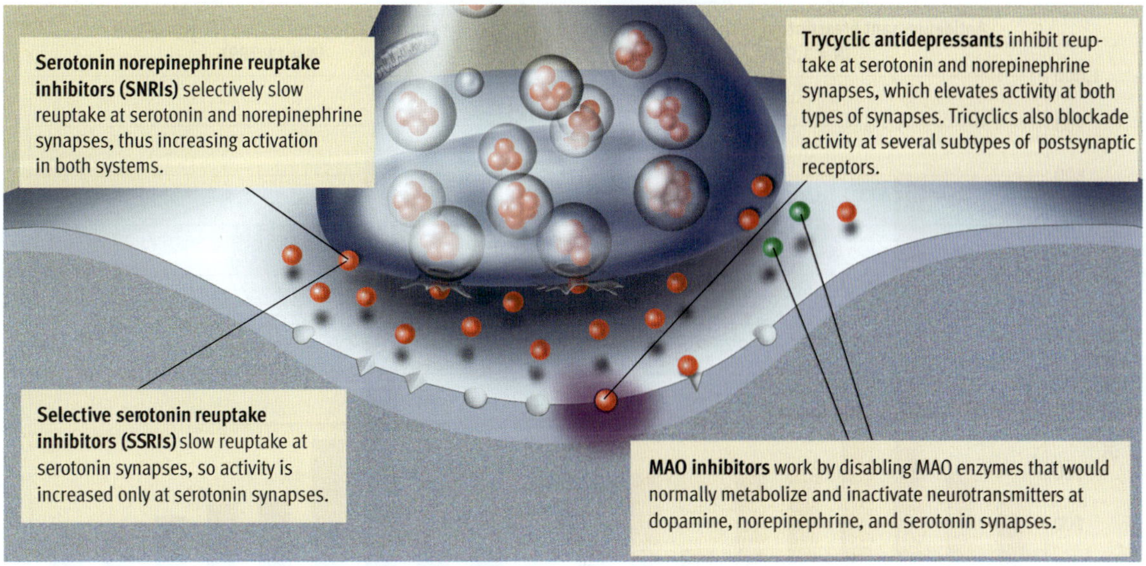

© Cengage Learning 2013

Figure 16.12
Antidepressant drugs' mechanisms of action. The four types of antidepressant drugs have somewhat different, albeit overlapping, effects on neurotransmitter activity. Tricyclics and MAO inhibitors exert effects at a much greater variety of synapses, which presumably explains why they have more side effects. The more recently developed SSRIs and SNRIs zero in on more specific synaptic targets.

period of weeks, but about 60% of patients' improvement tends to occur in the first two weeks (Gitlin, 2009). A recent analysis that looked carefully at the severity of patients' depression when medication was initiated found that people with serious depression benefit the most from antidepressants (Fournier et al, 2010). This analysis focused on six studies that measured patients' initial level of depression precisely and included patients with the full range of symptom severity (many drug trials exclude patients with mild illness). The most provocative aspect of the findings was that antidepressants provided a relatively modest benefit for patients with mild to moderate depression.

A major concern in recent years has been evidence from a number of studies that SSRIs may increase the risk for suicide, primarily among adolescents and young adults (Healy & Whitaker, 2003; Holden, 2004). The challenge of collecting definitive data on this issue is much more daunting than one might guess. This is, in part, because suicide rates are already elevated among people who exhibit the disorders for which SSRIs are prescribed (Berman, 2009). Some researchers have collected data suggesting that suicide rates have *declined* slightly because of widespread prescription of SSRIs (Baldessarini et al., 2007; Isacsson et al., 2009), while others have found no association between usage rates of SSRIs and suicide (Lapiere, 2003; Simon et al., 2006).

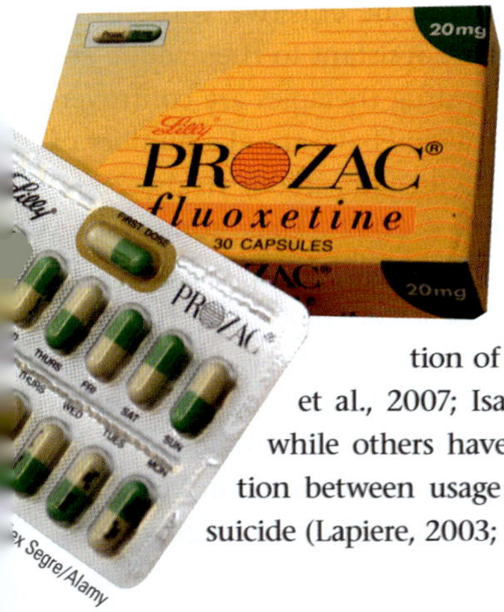

x Segre/Alamy

Overall, however, when antidepressants are compared to placebo treatment, the data suggest that antidepressants lead to a slight elevation in the risk of suicidal behavior, from roughly 2% to 4% (Bridge et al., 2007; Dubicka, Hadley, & Roberts, 2006; Hammad, Laughren, & Racoosin, 2006). The increased suicide risk appears to mainly be a problem among a small minority of children and adolescents in the first month after starting antidepressants, especially during the first nine days (Jick, Kaye, & Jick, 2004). Thus, patients starting on SSRIs should be carefully monitored by their physicians and families.

Regulatory warnings from the U.S. Food and Drug Administration (FDA) have led to a decline in the prescription of SSRIs among adolescents (Nemeroff et al., 2007). This trend has prompted concern that increases in suicide may occur among untreated individuals (Dudley et al., 2008). This concern seems legitimate in that suicide risk clearly peaks in the month prior to people beginning treatment for depression, whether that treatment involves SSRIs or psychotherapy (see **Figure 16.13** on the next page; Simon & Savarino, 2007). This pattern presumably occurs because the escalating agony of depression finally prompts people to seek treatment. But it also suggests that getting treatment with drugs or therapy reduces suicidal risk. In the final analysis, this is a complex issue. The one thing experts seem to agree on is that adolescents starting on SSRIs should be monitored closely.

The newest class of antidepressants consists of medications that inhibit reuptake at both serotonin and norepinephrine synapses, referred to as SNRIs. These drugs may produce slightly stronger antidepressant effects than the SSRIs (Thase & Denko, 2008). However, targeting two neurotransmitter systems also leads to a broader range of side effects (Thase & Sloan, 2006).

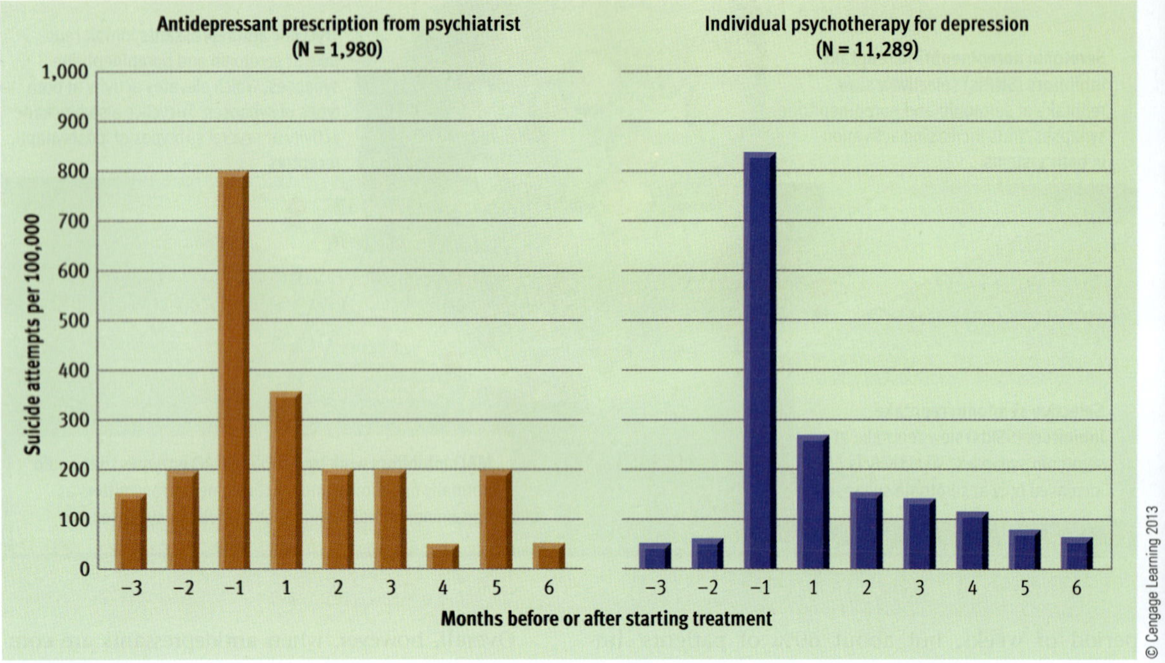

Figure 16.13

Probability of a suicide attempt in relation to the initiation of treatment. Examining medical records for thousands of patients, Simon and Savarino (2007) were able to gather information on the likelihood of a suicide attempt in the months before and after commencing treatment for depression. They compared patients who were put on an antidepressant medication against those who started in some form of insight or behavioral therapy. The data shown here, for patients under the age of 25, indicate that suicide risk is highest in the month prior to treatment and next highest in the month after treatment is begun for both groups. These findings suggest that elevated suicide rates are not unique to starting on antidepressants and that getting treatment (whether it is medication or psychotherapy) reduces the risk of suicide.

SOURCE: Adapted from Simon, G. E., & Savarino, J. (2007). Suicide attempts among patients starting depression treatments with medications or psychotherapy. *American Journal of Psychiatry, 164,* 1029–1034 (Figure 2, p. 1032). Copyright © 2007 by the American Psychiatric Association. Adapted by permission from the American Psychiatric Association.

Mood Stabilizers

***Mood stabilizers* are drugs used to control mood swings in patients with bipolar mood disorders.** For many years, lithium was the only effective drug in this category. Lithium has proven valuable in preventing *future* episodes of both mania and depression in patients with bipolar illness (Post & Altshuler, 2009). It can also be used in efforts to bring patients with bipolar illness out of *current* manic or depressive episodes (Keck & McElroy, 2006). However, antipsychotics and antidepressants are more commonly used for these purposes. On the negative side of the ledger, lithium does have some dangerous side effects if its use isn't managed skillfully (Jefferson & Greist, 2009). Lithium levels in the patient's blood must be monitored carefully, as high concentrations can be toxic and even fatal. Kidney and thyroid gland complications are the other major problems associated with lithium therapy.

In recent years, a number of alternatives to lithium have been developed. The most popular of these newer mood stabilizers is an anticonvulsant agent called *valproate,* which has become more widely used than lithium in the treatment of bipolar disorders (Thase & Denko, 2008). Valproate appears to be roughly as effective as lithium in efforts to treat current manic episodes and to prevent future affective disturbances, with fewer side effects (Muzina, Kemp, Calabrese, 2008). In some cases, a combination of valproate and lithium may be used in treatment (Post & Altshuler, 2009).

Reality CHECK

Misconception

Psychological disorders are largely chronic and incurable.

Reality

Admittedly, there are mentally ill people for whom treatment is a failure. However, they are greatly outnumbered by people who do get better, either spontaneously or through formal treatment. The majority of people who are diagnosed as mentally ill eventually improve and lead normal, productive lives. Even the most severe psychological disorders can be treated successfully.

How Effective Are Drug Therapies?

Drug therapies can produce clear therapeutic gains for many kinds of patients. What's especially impressive is that they can be effective with severe disorders that often are resistant to therapeutic endeavors. Nonetheless, drug therapies are controversial. Critics of drug therapy have raised a number of issues (Bentall, 2009; Breggin, 2008; Healy, 2004; Kirsch, 2010; Whitaker, 2002). First, some critics argue that drug therapies are not as effective as advertised. These critics argue that drug therapies often produce only superficial, short-lived curative effects. For example, Valium does not really solve problems with anxiety; it merely provides temporary relief from an unpleasant symptom. Moreover, relapse rates are substantial when drug regimens are

© Frank Cotham/The New Yorker Collection/www.cartoonbank.com

"I medicate first and ask questions later."

discontinued. Second, critics charge that many drugs are overprescribed and many patients overmedicated. According to these critics, a number of physicians routinely hand out prescriptions without giving adequate consideration to more complicated and difficult interventions. Consistent with this line of criticism, a recent study of office visits to psychiatrists found that they increasingly prescribe two and even three medications to patients, even though relatively little is known about the interactive effects of psychiatric drugs (Mojtabai & Olfson, 2010). Third, some critics charge that the damaging side effects of therapeutic drugs are underestimated by psychiatrists. Critics claim these side effects are often worse than the illnesses that the drugs are supposed to cure. Citing problems such as tardive dyskinesia, lithium toxicity, and addiction to antianxiety agents, these critics argue that the risks of therapeutic drugs aren't worth the benefits.

Critics maintain that the negative effects of psychiatric drugs are not fully appreciated because the pharmaceutical industry has managed to gain undue influence over the research enterprise as it relates to drug testing (Angell, 2004; Healy, 2004; Insel, 2010; Weber, 2006). Today, most researchers who investigate the benefits and risks of medications and write treatment guidelines have lucrative financial arrangements with the pharmaceutical industry (Bentall, 2009; Lurie et al., 2006; Pachter et al., 2007). Their studies are funded by drug companies, and they often receive substantial consulting fees. Unfortunately, these financial ties appear to undermine the objectivity required in scientific research. Studies funded by drug companies are far less likely to report unfavorable results than nonprofit-funded studies (Bekelman, Li, & Gross, 2003; Perlis et al., 2005; Rennie & Luft, 2000). Consistent with this finding, when specific antipsychotic drugs are pitted against each other in clinical trials, the sponsoring company's drug is reported to be superior to the other drugs in 90% of studies (Heres et al., 2006).

Industry-financed drug trials also tend to be much too brief to detect the long-term risks associated with new drugs (Vandenbroucke & Psaty, 2008). Additionally, when unfavorable results emerge, the data are often withheld from publication (Antonuccio, Danton, & McClanahan, 2003; Rising, Bacchetti, & Bero, 2008; Turner et al., 2008). Research designs are also often slanted in a multitude of ways so as to exaggerate the positive effects and minimize the negative effects of the drugs under scrutiny (Carpenter, 2002; Chopra, 2003; Moncrieff, 2001). The conflicts of interest that appear to be pervasive in contemporary drug research raise grave concerns that require attention from researchers, universities, and federal agencies.

Electroconvulsive Therapy (ECT)

In the 1930s, a Hungarian psychiatrist named Ladislas von Meduna speculated that epilepsy and schizophrenia could not coexist in the same body. On the basis of this observation, which turned out to be inaccurate, von Meduna theorized that it might be useful to induce epileptic-like seizures in schizophrenic patients. Initially, a drug was used to trigger these seizures. However, by 1938 a pair of Italian psychiatrists (Cerletti & Bini, 1938) showed that it was safer to elicit the seizures with electric shock. Thus, modern electroconvulsive therapy was born.

***Electroconvulsive therapy* (ECT) is a biomedical treatment in which electric shock is used to produce a cortical seizure accompanied by convulsions.** In ECT, electrodes are attached to the skull over the temporal lobes of the brain (see the photo below). A light anesthesia is induced, and the patient is given a variety of drugs to minimize the likelihood

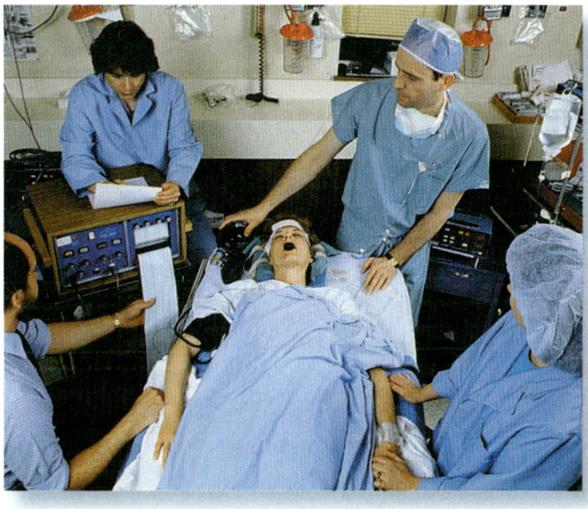

© James Wilson/Woodfin Camp & Associates. All rights reserved.

This patient is being prepared for electroconvulsive therapy. The mouthpiece keeps the patient from biting her tongue during the electrically induced seizures.

of complications. An electric current is then applied either to the right side or to both sides of the brain for about a second. Unilateral shock delivered to the right hemisphere is the preferred method of treatment today (Sackeim et al., 2009). The current triggers a brief (about 30 seconds) convulsive seizure. The patient normally awakens in an hour or two and manifests some confusion, disorientation, and nausea, which usually clear up in a matter of hours. People typically receive three treatments a week over a period of 2 to 7 weeks (Fink, 2009).

The clinical use of ECT peaked in the 1940s and 1950s before effective drug therapies were widely available. ECT has long been controversial, and its use declined in the 1960s and 1970s. Only about 8% of contemporary psychiatrists administer ECT (Hermann et al., 1998). But it cannot be considered a rare form of treatment. Some critics argue that ECT is overused because it's a lucrative procedure that boosts psychiatrists' income while consuming relatively little of their time in comparison to insight therapy (Frank, 1990). Conversely, some ECT advocates argue that ECT is underutilized because the public harbors many misconceptions about its effects and risks (McDonald et al., 2004). ECT is used in the treatment of a variety of disorders. In recent decades, however, it has primarily been recommended for the treatment of depression.

Effectiveness of ECT

The evidence on the therapeutic efficacy of ECT is open to varied interpretations. Proponents maintain that it's a remarkably effective treatment for major depression (Fink, 2009; Prudic, 2009). Moreover, they note that many patients who do not benefit from antidepressant medication improve in response to ECT (Nobler & Sackeim, 2006). However, opponents argue that the available studies are flawed and inconclusive. They argue that ECT is probably no more effective than a placebo (Rose et al., 2003). Overall, there does seem to be enough favorable evidence to justify *conservative* use of ECT in treating severe mood disorders in patients who have not responded to medication (Carney & Geddes, 2003; Metzger, 1999). Unfortunately, relapse rates after ECT are distressingly high. For example in one well-controlled study, 64% of patients relapsed within 6 months and the median time to relapse was only 8.6 weeks (Prudic et al., 2004). These relapse rates, however, can be reduced by giving ECT patients antidepressant drugs (Sackeim et al., 2001, 2009).

Risks Associated with ECT

Even ECT proponents acknowledge that memory losses, impaired attention, and other cognitive deficits are common short-term side effects of electroconvulsive therapy (Rowny & Lisanby, 2008; Sackeim et al., 2007). However, ECT proponents assert that these deficits are mild and usually disappear within a month or two (Glass, 2001). An American Psychiatric Association (2001) task force concluded that there is no objective evidence that ECT causes structural damage in the brain or that it has any lasting negative effects on the ability to learn and remember information. In contrast, ECT critics maintain that ECT-induced cognitive deficits are often significant and sometimes permanent (Breggin, 1991; Rose et al., 2003). However, their evidence seems to be largely anecdotal. Given the concerns about the risks of ECT and the doubts about its efficacy, it appears that the use of ECT will remain controversial for some time to come.

New Brain Stimulation Techniques

Scientists are always on the lookout for new methods of treating psychological disorders that might exhibit greater efficacy or fewer complications than ECT and drug treatments. Some new approaches to

CONCEPT CHECK 16.3

Understanding Biomedical Therapies

Check your understanding of biomedical therapies by matching each treatment with its chief use. The answers are in Appendix A.

Treatment	Chief purpose
_______ 1. Antianxiety drugs	a. To reduce psychotic symptoms
_______ 2. Antipsychotic drugs	b. To bring a major depression to an end
_______ 3. Antidepressant drugs	c. To suppress tension, nervousness, and apprehension
_______ 4. Mood stabilizers	d. To prevent future episodes of mania or depression in bipolar disorders
_______ 5. Electroconvulsive therapy (ECT)	

treatment involving stimulation of the brain are being explored with promising results. However, they remain highly experimental at this time.

One new approach is *transcranial magnetic stimulation,* which was discussed in Chapter 3 as a method for studying brain function. ***Transcranial magnetic stimulation (TMS)* is a technique that permits scientists to temporarily enhance or depress activity in a specific area of the brain.** In TMS, a magnetic coil mounted on a small paddle is held over specific areas of the head to increase or decrease activity in discrete regions of the cortex (Nahas et al., 2007). Neuroscientists are mostly experimenting with TMS as a treatment for depression. Thus far, treatments delivered to the right and left prefrontal cortex show promise in reducing depressive symptoms (Janicak et al., 2010; O'Reardon et al., 2007). TMS generally is well tolerated, with minimal side effects. But a great deal of additional research will be necessary before the therapeutic value of TMS can be determined.

The other new approach to treatment is *deep brain stimulation.* **In *deep brain stimulation (DBS)* a thin electrode is surgically implanted in the brain and connected to an implanted pulse generator so that various electrical currents can be delivered to brain tissue adjacent to the electrode** (see **Figure 16.14**). DBS has proven valuable in the treatment of the motor disturbances associated with Parkinson's disease, tardive dyskinesia, and some seizure disorders (C. Halpern et al., 2007; Wider et al., 2008). Researchers are currently exploring whether DBS may have value in the treatment of depression or obsessive-compulsive disorder (Denys et al., 2010; Sartorius et al., 2010). Obviously, this highly invasive procedure requiring brain surgery will never be a frontline therapy for mental disorders. Scientists, though, hope that it may be valuable for highly treatment-resistant patients who do not benefit from conventional therapies (Kuehn, 2007).

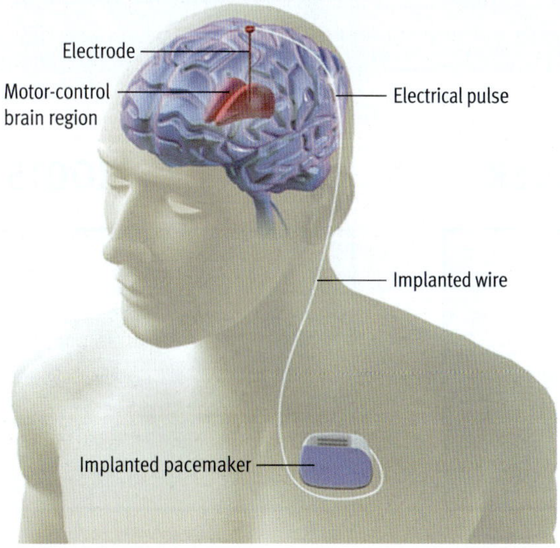

Figure 16.14

Deep brain stimulation. Deep brain stimulation requires a surgical procedure in which a thin electrode (about the width of a human hair) is inserted into deep areas of the brain. The electrode is connected to a pulse generator implanted under the skin of the chest. The placement of the electrode and the type of current generated depend on what condition is being treated. The electrode shown here was implanted in a motor area of the brain to treat the tremors associated with Parkinson's disease. Researchers are experimenting with other electrode placements in efforts to treat depression and obsessive-compulsive disorder. © Cengage Learning 2013

SOURCE: Adapted from George, M. S. (2003). Stimulating the brain. *Scientific American, 289*(3), 70. © Bryan Christie.

REVIEW OF KEY LEARNING GOALS

16.12 Antianxiety drugs exert their effects quickly and are fairly effective in reducing feelings of anxiety, but their impact is short-lived. They produce some nuisance side effects, and there can be complications involving abuse, dependence, and overdose. Antipsychotic drugs are used primarily in the treatment of schizophrenia. They reduce psychotic symptoms in about 70% of patients. Traditional antipsychotics can have a variety of serious side effects, which have been reduced in the newer, atypical antipsychotics.

16.13 Antidepressants are used to bring people out of episodes of depression. SSRIs are the dominant type used today. Side effects tend to be manageable, although there are concerns that antidepressants may increase suicide risk slightly. Mood stabilizers, such as lithium and valproate, are mostly used to prevent the recurrence of episodes of disturbance in people with bipolar mood disorders.

16.14 Drug therapies can be quite effective, but they have their drawbacks. All of the drugs produce side effects, some of which can be very troublesome. Some critics maintain that drugs' curative effects are superficial and that some drugs are overprescribed. Disturbing questions have been raised about the scientific impartiality of contemporary research on therapeutic drugs.

16.15 Electroconvulsive therapy (ECT) is used to trigger a cortical seizure that is believed to have therapeutic value for mood disorders, especially depression. Evidence about the effectiveness of ECT is contradictory but seems sufficient to justify conservative use of the procedure. Cognitive deficits are the principal risk, with much debate about how severe and enduring these deficits tend to be.

16.16 Transcranial magnetic stimulation is a new technique that permits scientists to temporarily enhance or depress activity in a specific area of the cortex. It may have value in the treatment of depression. In deep brain stimulation a thin electrode is surgically implanted so that electrical currents can be delivered to selected areas of the brain. It may have value in the treatment of depression or obsessive-compulsive disorder.

Illustrated Overview of Five Major Approaches to Treament

THERAPY/FOUNDER

ROOTS OF DISORDERS

PSYCHOANALYSIS

National Library of Medicine

Developed by Sigmund Freud in Vienna, from the 1890s through the 1930s

Intrapsychic conflict (among id, ego, and superego) → Anxiety → Reliance on defense mechanisms

Unconscious conflict resulting from fixations in earlier development cause anxiety, which leads to defensive behavior. The repressed conflicts typically center on sex and aggression.

CLIENT-CENTERED THERAPY

Created by Carl Rogers at the University of Chicago during the 1940s and 1950s

Courtesy of Carl Rogers Memorial Library

Need to distort shortcomings to feel worthy of affection → Relatively incongruent self-concept → Recurrent anxiety → Defensive behavior protects inaccurate self-concept → Relatively incongruent self-concept

Overdependence on acceptance from others fosters incongruence, which leads to anxiety and defensive behavior and thwarts personal growth.

BEHAVIOR THERAPY

Courtesy of Dr. Joseph Wolpe

Launched primarily by South African Joseph Wolpe's description of systematic desensitization in 1958

CS Bridge → CR Fear

US Lightning strikes → UR Fear

Maladaptive patterns of behavior are acquired through learning. For example, many phobias are thought to be created through classical conditioning and maintained by operant conditioning.

COGNITIVE–BEHAVIORAL TREATMENTS

One approach devised by Aaron Beck at the University of Pennsylvania in the 1960s and 1970s

Courtesy of Aaron T. Beck

Pervasive negative thinking about events related to self fosters anxiety and depression, and other forms of pathology.

- Blame setbacks on personal inadequacies
- Focus selectively on negative events
- Make unduly pessimistic projections about future
- Draw negative conclusions about personal worth

→ Increased vulnerability to depression

BIOMEDICAL THERAPY

Many researchers contributed; key breakthroughs in drug treatment made around 1950 by John Cade in Australia, Henri Laborit in France, and Jean Delay and Pierre Deniker, also in France

Most disorders are attributed to genetic predisposition and physiological malfunctions, such as abnormal neurotransmitter activity.
For example, schizophrenia appears to be associated with overactivity at dopamine synapses.

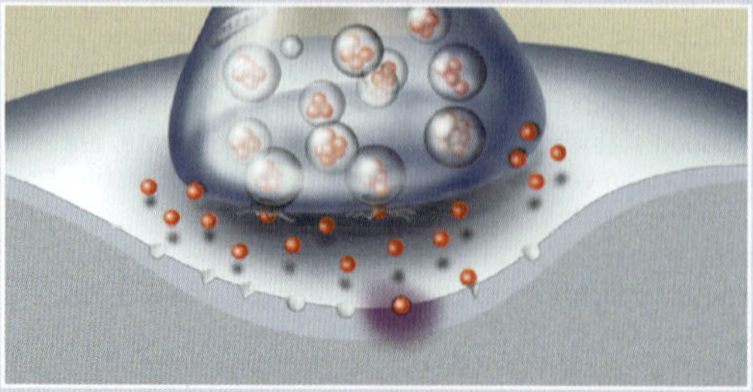

Unless otherwise indicated, all illustrations this page © Cengage Learning 2013

THERAPEUTIC GOALS

THERAPEUTIC TECHNIQUES

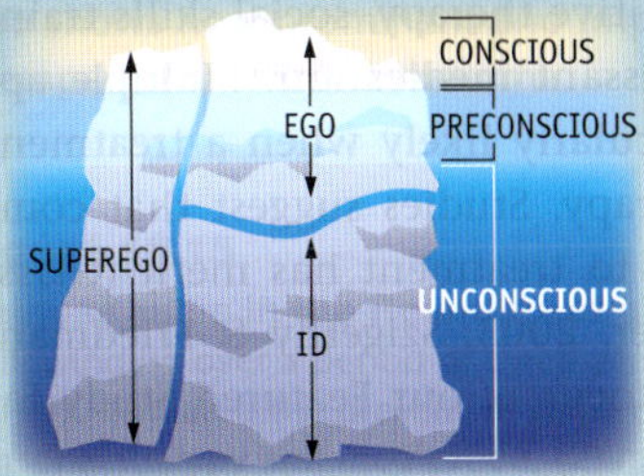

Insights regarding unconscious conflicts and motives; resolution of conflicts; personality reconstruction

Free association, dream analysis, interpretation, transference

© Photos 12/Alamy

Increased congruence between self-concept and experience; acceptance of genuine self; self-determination and personal growth

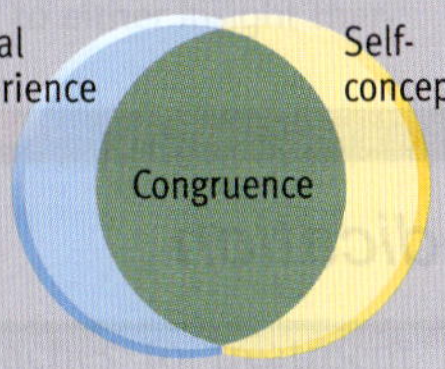

© Peter Dazeley/Getty Images

Genuineness, empathy, unconditional positive regard, clarification, reflecting back to client

Elimination of maladaptive symptoms; acquisition of more adaptive responses

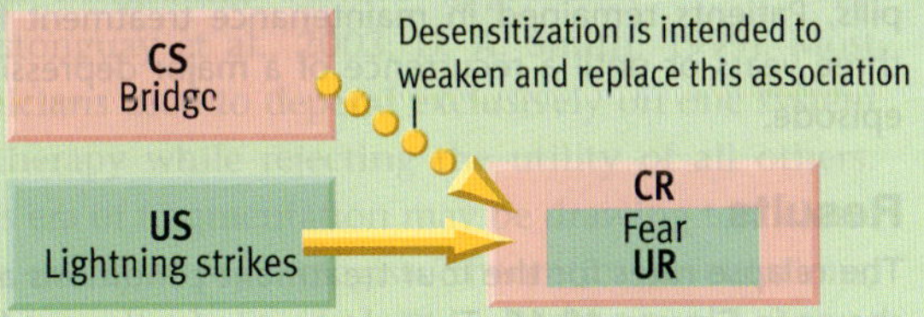

Classical and operant conditioning, systematic desensitization, aversive conditioning, social skills training, reinforcement, shaping, punishment, extinction, biofeedback

© Kent News & PicLure/Corbis Sygma

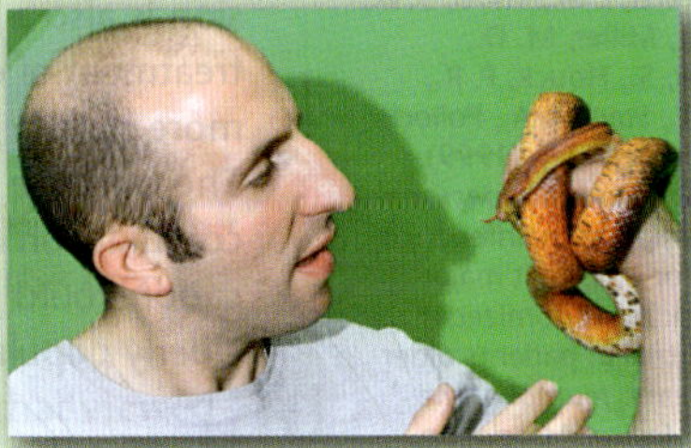

Reduction of negative thinking; substitution of more realistic thinking

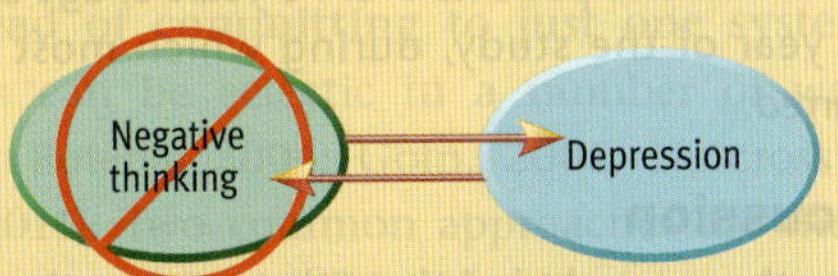

© JLP/Jose L. Pelaez/Corbis

Thought stopping, recording of automatic thoughts, refuting of negative thinking, homework assignments

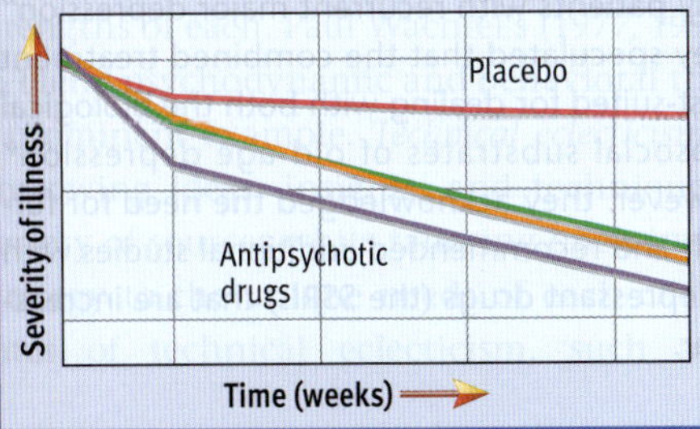

Elimination or reduction of symptoms; prevention of relapse

© James Wilson/Woodfin Camp & Associates. All rights reserved.

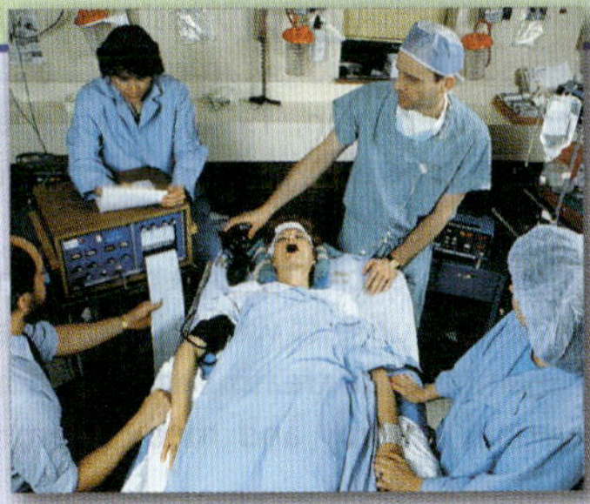

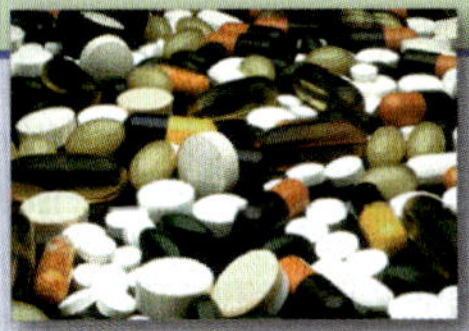

PhotoDisc, Inc.

Antianxiety, antidepressant, antipsychotic, and mood-stabilizing drugs, electroconvulsive therapy

Unless otherwise indicated, all illustrations this page © Cengage Learning 2013

© Ali Haider/epa/Corbis

Psychological disorders were assumed to have natural causes like physical diseases and to be amenable to medical treatments derived from scientific research. But the individualized, medicalized institution of modern psychotherapy reflects Western cultural values that are far from universal (Sue & Sue, 1999). In many nonindustrialized societies, psychological disorders are attributed to supernatural forces (possession, witchcraft, angry gods, and so forth). Victims seek help from priests, shamans, and folk healers, rather than doctors (Wittkower & Warnes, 1984). Thus, efforts to export Western psychotherapies to non-Western cultures have met with mixed success. Indeed, the highly culture-bound origins of modern therapies have raised questions about their applicability to ethnic minorities *within* Western culture (Miranda et al., 2005).

Research on how cultural factors influence the process and outcome of psychotherapy has grown rapidly in recent years. Its growth has been motivated in part by the need to improve mental health services for ethnic minority groups in American society (Lee & Ramirez, 2000; Worthington, Soth-McNett, & Moreno, 2007). Studies suggest that American minority groups generally underutilize therapeutic services (Bender et al., 2007; Folsom et al., 2007; Sue et al., 2009). Why? A variety of barriers appear to contribute to this problem (Snowden & Yamada, 2005; U.S. Department of Health and Human Services, 1999; Zane et al., 2004). One major consideration is that many members of minority groups have a history of frustrating interactions with American bureaucracies. Therefore, they are distrustful of large, intimidating institutions, such as hospitals and community mental health centers. Another issue is that most hospitals and mental health agencies are not adequately staffed with therapists who speak the languages used by minority groups in their service areas.

Yet another problem is that the vast majority of therapists have been trained almost exclusively in the treatment of white middle-class Americans. As a result, they are not familiar with the cultural backgrounds and unique characteristics of various ethnic groups. This culture gap often leads to misunderstandings, ill-advised treatment strategies, and reduced rapport. Consistent with this assertion, recent research found that psychiatrists spend less time with African American patients than white patients (Olfson, Cherry, & Lewis-Fernandez, 2009). Another study of over 3500 African American participants found that only 27% of their mental health visits resulted in "minimally adequate care" (Neighbors et al., 2007). And a recent study of over 15,000 people suffering from depression found that Mexican Americans and African Americans were notably less likely to receive treatment than whites, as can be seen in **Figure 16.17** (González et al., 2010).

What can be done to improve mental health services for American minority groups? Researchers in this area have offered a variety of suggestions (Hong, Garcia, & Soriano, 2000; Miranda et al., 2005; Pedersen, 1994; Yamamoto et al., 1993). Discussions of possible solutions usually begin with the need to recruit and train more ethnic minority therapists. Studies show that ethnic minorities are more likely to go to mental health facilities that are staffed by a higher proportion of people who share their ethnic background (Snowden & Hu, 1996; Sue, Zane, & Young, 1994). Individual therapists have been urged

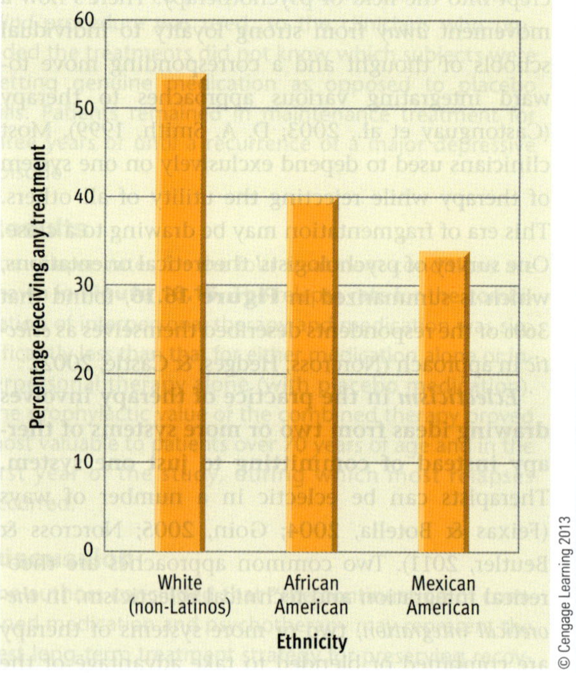

Figure 16.17

Ethnicity and treatment for depression. In a nationally representative sample of almost 16,000 subjects, Gonzales and colleagues (2010) identified participants suffering from depression and ascertained what types of treatment they had received. When they analyzed these data in relation to ethnicity, they found that members of minority groups were less likely than whites to get treatment. The data graphed here show the percentage of patients receiving treatment of any kind.

to work harder at building a vigorous *therapeutic alliance* (a strong supportive bond) with their ethnic clients. A strong therapeutic alliance is associated with better therapeutic outcomes regardless of ethnicity, but studies suggest that it's especially crucial for minority clients (Bender et al., 2007; Comas-Diaz, 2006). Finally, most authorities urge further investigation of how traditional approaches to therapy can be modified and tailored to be more compatible with specific cultural groups' attitudes, values, norms, and traditions (Hwang, 2006). Research that has examined the effects of culturally adapted interventions has found evidence that this tailoring process tends to yield positive effects (Griner & Smith, 2006; Sue et al., 2009). The benefits are particularly prominent when a treatment is tailored to a single, specific cultural group rather than a mixture of several or more cultural groups.

REVIEW OF KEY LEARNING GOALS

16.17 Combinations of insight, behavioral, and biomedical therapies are often used fruitfully in the treatment of psychological disorders. For example, the Featured Study showed how the tandem of interpersonal therapy and antidepressant medication could be valuable in preventing additional depressive episodes in an elderly population. Many modern therapists are eclectic, using specific ideas, techniques, and strategies gleaned from a number of theoretical approaches.

16.18 Because of cultural, language, and access barriers, therapeutic services are underutilized by most ethnic minorities in America. More culturally responsive approaches to treatment will require more minority therapists, more effort to build strong therapeutic alliances, and additional investigation of how traditional therapies can be tailored to be more compatible with specific ethnic groups' cultural heritage.

Institutional Treatment in Transition

KEY LEARNING GOALS

16.19 Explain why people grew disenchanted with mental hospitals.

16.20 Assess the effects of the deinstitutionalization movement.

Traditionally, much of the treatment of mental illness has been carried out in institutional settings, primarily in mental hospitals. **A *mental hospital* is a medical institution specializing in providing inpatient care for psychological disorders.** In the United States, a national network of state-funded mental hospitals started to emerge in the 1840s through the efforts of Dorothea Dix and other reformers (see **Figure 16.18** on the next page). Prior to these reforms, the mentally ill who were poor were housed in jails and poorhouses or were left to wander the countryside. Today, mental hospitals continue to play a role in the delivery of mental health services. However, since World War II, institutional care for mental illness has undergone a series of major transitions—and the dust hasn't settled yet. Let's look at how institutional care has evolved in recent decades.

Disenchantment with Mental Hospitals

By the 1950s, it had become apparent that public mental hospitals were not fulfilling their goals very well (Mechanic, 1980; Menninger, 2005). Experts began to realize that hospitalization often *contributed* to the development of pathology instead of curing it. What were the causes of these unexpected negative effects? Part of the problem was that the facilities were usually underfunded (Hogan & Morrison, 2008). The lack of adequate funding meant that the facilities were overcrowded and understaffed. Hospital personnel were undertrained and overworked, making them hard-pressed to deliver even minimal custodial care. Despite gallant efforts at treatment, the demoralizing conditions made most public mental hospitals decidedly nontherapeutic (Scull, 1990). These problems were aggravated by the fact that state mental hospitals served large geographic regions but were rarely placed near major population centers. As a result, most patients were uprooted from their community and isolated from their social support networks.

Disenchantment with the public mental hospital system inspired the *community mental health movement* that emerged in the 1960s (Duckworth & Borus, 1999; Huey, Ford, et al., 2009). The community mental health movement emphasizes (1) local, community-based care, (2) reduced dependence on hospitalization, and (3) the prevention of psychological disorders. Community mental health centers were intended to supplement mental hospitals with decentralized and more accessible services. However, they have had their own funding struggles (Dixon & Goldman, 2004).

Figure 16.18

Dorothea Dix and the advent of mental hospitals in America. During the 19th century, Dorothea Dix (inset) campaigned tirelessly to obtain funds for building mental hospitals. Many of these hospitals, such as the New York State Lunatic Asylum, were extremely large facilities. Although public mental hospitals improved the care of the mentally ill, they had a variety of shortcomings, which eventually prompted the deinstitutionalization movement.

SOURCE: Culver Pictures, Inc.; (inset) Detail of painting in Harrisburg State Hospital, photo by Ken Smith/LLR Collection.

Deinstitutionalization

Mental hospitals continue to care for many people troubled by chronic mental illness, but their role in patient care has diminished. Since the 1960s, a policy of deinstitutionalization has been followed in the United States, as well as most other Western countries (Fakhoury & Priebe, 2002). ***Deinstitutionalization* refers to transferring the treatment of mental illness from inpatient institutions to community-based facilities that emphasize outpatient care.** This shift in responsibility was made possible by two developments: (1) the emergence of effective drug therapies for severe disorders and (2) the deployment of community mental health centers and nursing homes to provide local care (Goff & Gudeman, 1999).

The exodus of patients from mental hospitals has been dramatic. The average inpatient population in state and county mental hospitals dropped from a peak of nearly 550,000 in the mid-1950s to around 70,000 by 2000, as shown in **Figure 16.19**. This trend does not mean that hospitalization for mental illness has become a thing of the past. A great many people are still hospitalized. However, the shift has been toward placing them in local general hospitals for brief periods instead of distant psychiatric hospitals for long periods (Hogan & Morrison, 2008). In keeping with the philosophy of deinstitutionalization, these local facilities try to get patients stabilized and back into the community as swiftly as possible.

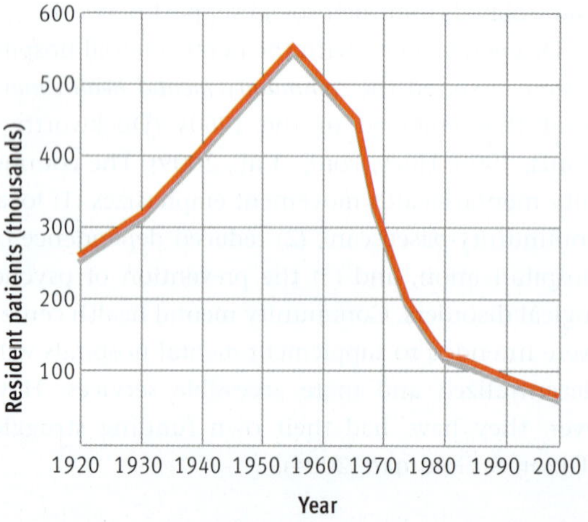

Figure 16.19

Declining inpatient population at state and county mental hospitals. The inpatient population in public mental hospitals has declined dramatically since the late 1950s, as a result of deinstitutionalization and the development of effective antipsychotic medication. (Data from the National Institute of Mental Health) © Cengage Learning 2013

How has deinstitutionalization worked out? It gets mixed reviews. On the positive side, many people have benefited by avoiding disruptive and unnecessary hospitalization. Ample evidence suggests that alternatives to hospitalization can be as effective as and less costly than inpatient care (McGrew et al., 1999; Reinharz, Lesage, & Contandriopoulos, 2000). Moreover, follow-up studies of discharged patients reveal that a substantial majority prefer the greater freedom provided by community-based treatment (Leff, 2006).

Nonetheless, some unanticipated problems have arisen (Elpers, 2000; Munk-Jorgensen, 1999; Talbott, 2004). Many patients suffering from chronic psychological disorders had nowhere to go when they were released. They had no families, friends, or homes to return to. Many had no work skills and were poorly prepared to live on their own. These people were supposed to be absorbed by "halfway houses," sheltered workshops, and other types of intermediate care facilities. Unfortunately, many communities were never able to fund and build the planned facilities (Hogan & Morrison, 2008; Lamb,

DOONESBURY

DOONESBURY © 1986 by G. B. Trudeau. Distributed by UNIVERSAL PRESS SYNDICATE. Reprinted with permission. All rights reserved.

1998). Thus, deinstitutionalization left two major problems in its wake. First, it left a "revolving door" population of people who flow in and out of psychiatric facilities. Second, as a result of this "revolving door," a sizable percentage of the homeless are mentally ill people.

Mental Illness, the Revolving Door, and Homelessness

Most of the people caught in the mental health system's revolving door suffer from chronic, severe disorders (usually schizophrenia or bipolar disorder) that often require hospitalization (Haywood et al., 1995). Once they're stabilized through drug therapy, they no longer qualify for expensive hospital treatment. Thus, they're sent back out into communities that often aren't prepared to provide adequate outpatient care. Consequently, their condition deteriorates and they soon require readmission to a hospital, where the cycle begins once again. Over two-thirds of all psychiatric inpatient admissions involve rehospitalizing a former patient. Moreover, 40% to 50% of patients are readmitted within a year of their release (Bridge & Barbe, 2004).

Deinstitutionalization has also been blamed for the growing population of homeless people. Studies have consistently found elevated rates of mental illness among the homeless. Taken as a whole, the evidence suggests that roughly one-third of homeless people suffer from severe mental illness (schizophrenic and mood disorders), that another one-third or more are struggling with alcohol and drug problems, that many qualify for multiple diagnoses, and that the prevalence of mental illness among the homeless may be increasing (Bassuk et al., 1998; Folsom et al., 2005; North et al., 2004). In essence, homeless shelters have become a *de facto* element of America's mental health care system (Callicutt, 2006).

Ultimately, it's clear that our society is not providing adequate care for a sizable segment of the mentally ill population (Appelbaum, 2002; Elpers, 2000; Gittelman, 2005; Torrey, 1996). That's not a new development. Inadequate care for mental illness has always been the norm. Societies always struggle with the problem of what to do with the mentally ill and how to pay for their care (Duckworth & Borus, 1999). Ours is no different. Unfortunately, in recent years the situation has deteriorated rather than improved. Although overall health care spending has been increasing steadily in recent years, funding for mental health care has diminished dramatically (Geller, 2009). The number of beds in general hospitals dedicated to psychiatric care has declined precipitously since the late 1990s (Liptzin, Gottlieb, & Summergrad, 2007). Today, most states have a shortage of psychiatric beds, resulting in waiting lists for admission, overcrowding, and increasingly brief hospitalizations (Geller, 2009).

© Janine Wiedel Photolibrary/Alamy

REVIEW OF KEY LEARNING GOALS

16.19 Experts eventually realized that mental hospitals often contributed to the development of pathology instead of curing it, in part because they tended to be underfunded and understaffed, leading to demoralizing conditions. Disenchantment with the negative effects of mental hospitals led to the advent of more localized community mental health centers and a policy of deinstitutionalization.

16.20 As a result of deinstitutionalization, long-term hospitalization for mental disorders is largely a thing of the past. Deinstitutionalization has worked well for some patients. However, it has spawned some unanticipated problems, including the revolving door problem and increased homelessness.

CONCEPT CHECK 16.4

Identifying the Contributions of Major Theorists and Researchers

Check your recall of the principal ideas of important theorists and researchers covered in this chapter by matching the people listed on the left with the appropriate contributions described on the right. If you need help, the crucial pages describing each person's ideas are listed in parentheses. Fill in the letters for your choices in the spaces provided on the left. You'll find the answers in Appendix A.

Major Theorists and Researchers	Key Ideas and Contributions
______ 1. Aaron Beck (pp. 663–664)	a. This individual devised client-centered therapy, which emphasizes the importance of therapeutic climate.
______ 2. Dorothea Dix (pp. 677–678)	b. This individual invented psychoanalysis, an insight therapy that centers on free association, resistance, and transference.
______ 3. Sigmund Freud (pp. 652–655)	c. According to this theorist, who invented cognitive therapy, depression is caused by pervasive negative thinking.
______ 4. Carl Rogers (pp. 655–656)	d. This 19th-century reformer is famous for campaigning tirelessly to raise money for public mental hospitals.
______ 5. Joseph Wolpe (p. 661)	e. This behavior therapist is famous for developing systematic desensitization, which is a treatment for phobias.

KEY LEARNING GOALS

16.21 Identify the two unifying themes highlighted in this chapter.

Reflecting on the Chapter's Themes

Cultural Heritage

Theoretical Diversity

In our discussion of psychotherapy, one of our unifying themes—the value of theoretical diversity—was particularly prominent, and one other theme—the importance of culture—surfaced briefly. Let's discuss the latter theme first. The approaches to treatment described in this chapter are products of modern, white, middle-class, Western culture. Some therapies used for this population have proven useful in some other cultures. However, many have turned out to be irrelevant or counterproductive when used with different cultural groups, including ethnic minorities in Western society. Thus, we have seen once again that cultural factors influence psychological processes and that Western psychology cannot assume that its theories and practices have universal applicability.

As for theoretical diversity, its value can be illustrated with a rhetorical question: Can you imagine what the state of modern psychotherapy would be if everyone in psychology and psychiatry had simply accepted Freud's theories about the nature and treatment of psychological disorders? If not for theoretical diversity, psychotherapy might still be in the dark ages. Psychoanalysis can be a useful method of therapy, but it would be a tragic state of affairs if it were the *only* treatment available. Multitudes of people have benefited from alternative approaches to treatment that emerged out of tensions between psychoanalytic theory and other theoretical perspectives. People have diverse problems, rooted in varied origins. Particular problems call for the pursuit of different therapeutic goals. Thus, it's fortunate that people can choose from a diverse array of approaches to treatment. The illustrated overview on pages 672–673 summarizes and compares some of the approaches that we've discussed in this chapter. This summary chart shows that the major approaches to treatment each have their own vision of the nature of human discontent and the ideal remedy.

Of course, diversity can be confusing. The range and variety of available treatments in modern psychotherapy leaves many people puzzled about their options. Thus, in the Personal Application we'll sort through the practical issues involved in selecting a therapist.

REVIEW OF KEY LEARNING GOALS

16.21 Our discussion of psychotherapy highlighted the value of theoretical diversity. Conflicting theoretical orientations have generated varied approaches to treatment. Our coverage of therapy also showed once again that cultural factors shape psychological processes.

PERSONAL APPLICATION

Looking for a Therapist

> **KEY LEARNING GOALS**
>
> **16.22** Discuss where to seek therapy and the potential importance of a therapist's sex and professional background.
>
> **16.23** Evaluate the importance of a therapist's theoretical approach, and summarize what one should look for in a prospective therapist.

Answer the following "true" or "false."

____ **1** Psychotherapy is an art as well as a science.

____ **2** Psychotherapy can be harmful or damaging to a client.

____ **3** Psychotherapy does not have to be expensive.

____ **4** The type of professional degree that a therapist holds is relatively unimportant.

All of these statements are true. Do any of them surprise you? If so, you're in good company. Many people know relatively little about the practicalities of selecting a therapist.

The task of finding an appropriate therapist is complex. Should you see a psychologist or psychiatrist? Should you opt for individual therapy or group therapy? Should you see a client-centered therapist or a behavior therapist? The unfortunate part of this situation is that people seeking psychotherapy often feel overwhelmed by personal difficulties. The last thing they need is to be confronted by yet another complex problem.

Nonetheless, the importance of finding a good therapist cannot be overestimated. Treatment can sometimes have harmful rather than helpful effects. We have already discussed how drug therapies and ECT can sometimes be damaging. Yet problems are not limited to these interventions. Talking about your problems with a therapist may sound harmless. However, studies indicate that insight therapies can also backfire (Lambert & Ogles, 2004; Lilienfeld, 2007). Although a great many talented therapists are available, psychotherapy, like any other profession, has incompetent practitioners as well. Therefore, you should shop for a skilled therapist, just as you would for a good attorney or a good mechanic.

In this Application, we'll go over some information that should be helpful if you ever have to look for a therapist for yourself or for a friend or family member (based on Beutler, Bongar, & Shurkin, 2001; Ehrenberg & Ehrenberg, 1994; Pittman, 1994).

Where Do You Find Therapeutic Services?

Psychotherapy can be found in a variety of settings. Contrary to general belief, most therapists are not in private practice. Many work in institutional settings such as community mental health centers, hospitals, and human service agencies. The principal sources of therapeutic services are described in **Table 16.2**. The exact configuration of therapeutic services available will vary from one community to another. To find out what your community has to offer, it's a good idea to consult your friends, your local phone book, or your local community mental health center.

Is the Therapist's Profession or Sex Important?

Psychotherapists may be trained in psychology, psychiatry, social work, counseling, psychiatric nursing, or marriage and family therapy. Researchers have *not* found any reliable associations between therapists' professional background and therapeutic efficacy (Beutler et al., 2004). This is probably because many talented therapists can be found in all of these professions. Thus, the kind of degree that a therapist holds doesn't need to be a crucial consideration in your selection process.

Whether a therapist's sex is important depends on your attitude (Nadelson, Notman, & McCarthy, 2005). If *you* feel that the therapist's sex is important, then for you it is. The therapeutic relationship must be characterized by trust and rapport. Feeling uncomfortable with a therapist of one sex or the other could inhibit the therapeutic process, so you should feel free to look for a male or female therapist if you prefer to do so. This point is probably most relevant to female clients whose troubles may be related to sexism in our

Table 16.2 Principal Sources of Therapeutic Services

Source	Comments
Private practitioners	Self-employed therapists are listed in the Yellow Pages under their professional category, such as psychologists or psychiatrists. Private practitioners tend to be relatively expensive, but they also tend to be highly experienced therapists.
Community mental health centers	Community mental health centers have salaried psychologists, psychiatrists, and social workers on staff. The centers provide a variety of services and often have staff available on weekends and at night to deal with emergencies.
Hospitals	Several kinds of hospitals provide therapeutic services. There are both public and private mental hospitals that specialize in the care of people with psychological disorders. Many general hospitals have a psychiatric ward, and those that do not usually have psychiatrists and psychologists on staff and on call. Although hospitals tend to concentrate on inpatient treatment, many provide outpatient therapy as well.
Human service agencies	Various social service agencies employ therapists to provide short-term counseling. Depending on your community, you may find agencies that deal with family problems, juvenile problems, drug problems, and so forth.
Schools and workplaces	Most high schools and colleges have counseling centers where students can get help with personal problems. Similarly, some large businesses offer in-house counseling to their employees.

© Cengage Learning 2013

society (Kaplan, 1985). It's entirely reasonable for women to seek a therapist with a feminist perspective if that would make them feel more comfortable.

Is Treatment Always Expensive?

Psychotherapy does not have to be prohibitively expensive. Private practitioners tend to be the most expensive, charging between $75 and $140 per (50-minute) hour. These fees may seem high, but they are in line with those of similar professionals, such as dentists and attorneys. Community mental health centers and social service agencies are usually supported by tax dollars. As a result, they can charge lower fees than most therapists in private practice. Many of these organizations use a sliding scale, in which clients are charged according to how much they can afford to pay. Thus, most communities have inexpensive opportunities for psychotherapy. Moreover, most health insurance plans and HMOs provide coverage for at least some forms of mental health care.

Is the Therapist's Theoretical Approach Important?

Logically, you might expect that the diverse approaches to therapy ought to vary in their effectiveness. For the most part, this is *not* what researchers find, however. After reviewing many studies of therapeutic efficacy, Jerome Frank (1961) and Lester Luborsky and his colleagues (1975) both quote the dodo bird who has just judged a race in *Alice in Wonderland: "Everybody* has won, and *all* must have prizes." Improvement rates for various theoretical orientations usually come out pretty close in most studies (Lambert & Bergin, 2004; Luborsky et al., 2002; Wampold, 2001; see **Figure 16.20**).

However, these findings are a little misleading, as the estimates of overall effectiveness have been averaged across many types of patients and many types of problems. Most experts seem to think that *for certain types of problems, some approaches to therapy are more effective than others* (Beutler, 2002; Crits-Christoph, 1997; Norcross, 1995). For example, Martin Seligman (1995) asserts that panic disorders respond best to cognitive therapy, that specific phobias are most amenable to treatment with systematic desensitization, and that obsessive-compulsive disorders are best treated with behavior therapy or medication. Thus, for a specific type of problem, a therapist's theoretical approach *may* make a difference.

It's also important to point out that the finding that different approaches to therapy are roughly equal in overall efficacy does not mean that all *therapists* are created equal. Some therapists unquestionably are more effective than others. However, these variations in effectiveness appear to depend on individual therapists' personal skills rather than on their theoretical orientation (Beutler et al., 2004). Good, bad, and mediocre therapists are found within each school of thought. Indeed, the tremendous variation in skills among individual therapists may be one of the main reasons that it is hard to find efficacy differences between theoretical approaches to therapy (Staines, 2008).

The key point is that effective therapy requires skill and creativity. Arnold Lazarus, who devised an eclectic approach he called multimodal therapy, emphasizes that therapists "straddle the fence between science and art." Therapy is scientific in that interventions are based on extensive theory and empirical research (Forsyth & Strong, 1986). Ultimately, though, each client is a unique human being. The therapist has to creatively fashion a treatment program that will help that individual (Goodheart, 2006).

What Should You Look For in a Prospective Therapist?

Some clients are timid about asking prospective therapists questions about their training, approach, fees, and so forth. However, these are reasonable questions. The vast majority of therapists will be most accommodating in providing answers. Usually, you can ask your preliminary questions

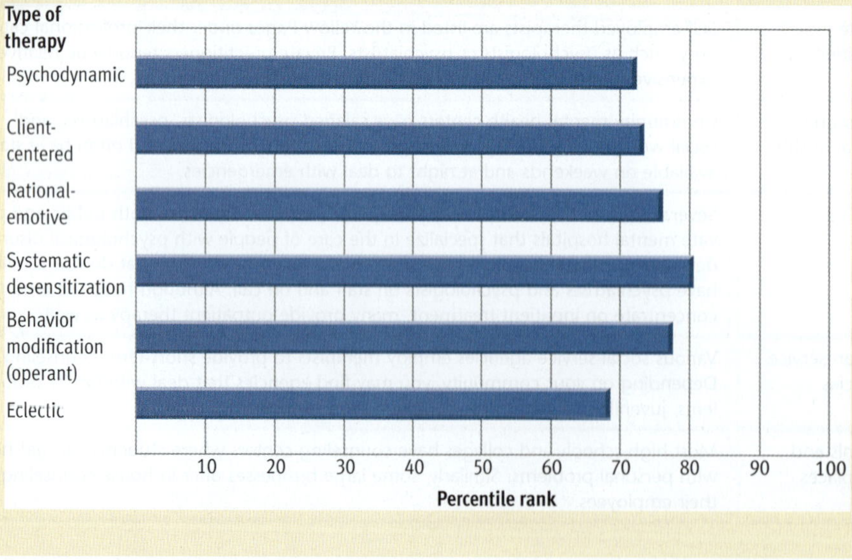

Figure 16.20

Estimates of the effectiveness of various approaches to psychotherapy. Smith and Glass (1977) reviewed nearly 400 studies in which clients who were treated with a specific type of therapy were compared with a control group made up of individuals with similar problems who went untreated. The bars indicate the percentile rank (on outcome measures) attained by the average client treated with each type of therapy when compared to control subjects. The higher the percentile, the more effective the therapy was. As you can see, the various approaches were fairly similar in their overall effectiveness.

SOURCE: Adapted from Smith, M. L., & Glass, G. V. (1977). Meta-analysis of psychotherapy outcome series. *American Psychologist, 32,* 752–760. Copyright © 1977 by the American Psychological Association. Adapted by permission of the authors.

© Cengage Learning 2013

© Ilan D. Rosen/PhotoStock-Israel.com/Alamy

Therapy is both a science and an art. It is scientific in that practitioners are guided in their work by a huge body of empirical research. It is an art in that therapists often have to be creative in adapting their treatment procedures to individual patients and their idiosyncrasies.

over the phone. If things seem promising, you may decide to make an appointment for an interview (for which you will probably have to pay). In this interview, the therapist will gather more information to determine the likelihood of helping you, given his or her training and approach to treatment. At the same time, you should be making a similar judgment about whether *you* believe the therapist can help you with your problems.

What should you look for? First, you should look for personal warmth and sincere concern. Try to judge whether you will be able to talk to this person in a candid, nondefensive way. Second, look for empathy and understanding. Is the person capable of appreciating your point of view? Third, look for self-confidence. Self-assured therapists will communicate a sense of competence without trying to intimidate you with jargon or boasting needlessly about what they can do for you. When all is said and done, you should *like* your therapist. Otherwise, it will be difficult to establish the needed rapport.

REVIEW OF KEY LEARNING GOALS

16.22 Therapeutic services are available in many settings, and such services need not be expensive. Both excellent and mediocre therapists can be found in all of the mental health professions. Thus, therapists' personal skills are more important than their professional degree. Whether a therapist's sex is important depends on the client's attitude.

16.23 The various theoretical approaches to therapy appear to be fairly similar in overall effectiveness. However, for certain types of problems some approaches are probably more effective than others, and all therapists are not created equal. In selecting a therapist, warmth, empathy, confidence, and likability are desirable traits.

From Crisis to Wellness—But Was It the Therapy?

KEY LEARNING GOALS

16.24 Understand how placebo effects and regression toward the mean can complicate the evaluation of therapy.

It often happens this way. Problems seem to go from bad to worse. The trigger could be severe pressures at school or work, a nasty fight with your boyfriend or girlfriend, or a child's unruly behavior spiraling out of control. At some point, you recognize that it might be prudent to seek professional assistance from a therapist, but where do you turn? If you are like most people, you'll probably hesitate before actively seeking professional help. People hold off because therapy carries a stigma, because the task of finding a therapist is daunting, and because they hope that their psychological problems will clear up on their own—which *does* happen with some regularity. When people finally decide to pursue mental health care, it's often because they feel like they have reached rock bottom in terms of their functioning and they have no choice. Motivated by their crisis, they enter into treatment, looking for a ray of hope. Will therapy help them feel better?

It may surprise you to learn that the answer *generally* would be "yes," even if professional treatment itself were utterly worthless and ineffectual. There are two major reasons that people entering therapy are likely to get better, regardless of whether their treatment is effective. One of these reasons is the power of the *placebo.* **Placebo effects occur when people's expectations lead them to experience some change even though they receive a fake treatment** (like getting a sugar pill instead of a real drug). Clients generally enter therapy with expectations that it will have positive effects. As we have emphasized throughout this text, *people have a remarkable tendency to see what they expect to see.* Because of this factor, studies of the efficacy of medical drugs always include a placebo condition in which subjects are given fake medication (see Chapter 2). Researchers are often quite surprised by just how much the placebo subjects improve (Fisher & Greenberg, 1997; Walsh et al., 2002). Placebo effects can be powerful. As a result, they should be taken into consideration whenever efforts are made to evaluate the efficacy of some approach to treatment.

The other factor at work is the main focus in this Application. It's an interesting statistical phenomenon that we have not discussed previously: *regression toward the mean.* ***Regression toward the mean*** **occurs when people who score extremely high or low on some trait are measured a second time and their new scores fall closer to the mean (average).** Regression effects work in both directions. On the second measurement, high scorers tend to fall back toward the mean and low scorers tend to creep upward toward the mean. For example, let's say we wanted to evaluate the effectiveness of a one-day coaching program intended to improve performance on the SAT test. We reason that coaching is most likely to help students who have performed poorly on the test. Thus, we recruit a sample of high school students who have previously scored in the bottom 20% on the SAT. Thanks to regression toward the mean, most of these students will score higher if they take the SAT a second time. Our coaching program, therefore, may *look* effective even if it has no value. By the way, if we set out to see whether our coaching program could increase the performance of high scorers, regression effects would be working *against* us. If we recruited a sample of students who had scored in the upper 20% on the SAT, their scores would tend to move downward when tested a second time, which could cancel out most or all of the beneficial effects of the coaching program. The processes underlying regression toward the mean are complex matters of probability, but they can be approximated by a simple principle: If you are near the bottom, there's almost nowhere to go but up, and if you are near the top, there's almost nowhere to go but down.

What does all of this have to do with the effects of professional treatment for psychological problems and disorders? Well, chance variations in the ups and downs of life occur for all of us. But recall that most

© Zhu Kalumu/Getty Images

Placebo effects and regression toward the mean are two prominent factors that make it difficult to evaluate the efficacy of various approaches to therapy.

people enter psychotherapy during a time of severe crisis, when they are at a really low point in their lives. If you measure the mental health of a group of people entering therapy, they will get relatively low scores. If you measure their mental health again a few months later, chances are that most of them will score higher—with or without therapy—because of regression toward the mean. This is not a matter of idle speculation. Studies of untreated subjects show that poor scores on measures of mental health regress toward the mean when participants are assessed a second time (Flett, Vredenburg, & Krames, 1995; Hsu, 1995).

Does the fact that most people will get better even without therapy mean that there is no sound evidence that psychotherapy works? No, regression effects, along with placebo effects, do create major headaches for researchers evaluating the efficacy of various therapies. However, these problems *can* be circumvented. Control groups, random assignment, placebo conditions, and statistical adjustments can be used to control for regression and placebo effects, as well as for other threats to validity.

Recognizing how regression toward the mean can occur in a variety of contexts is an important critical thinking skill, so let's look at some additional examples. Think about an outstanding young pro baseball player who has a fabulous first season and is named "Rookie of the Year." What sort of performance would you predict for this athlete for the next year? Before you make your prediction, think about regression toward the mean. Statistically speaking, our Rookie of the Year is likely to perform well above average the next year, but not as well as he did in his first year. If you are a sports fan,

© Tony Freeman/PhotoEdit

Placebo effects and regression toward the mean can help explain why phony, worthless treatments can have sincere supporters who really believe that the bogus interventions are effective.

you may recognize this pattern as the "sophomore slump." Many sports columnists who have written about the sophomore slump typically blame it on the athlete's personality or motivation ("He got lazy," "He got cocky," "The money and fame went to his head," and so forth). A simple appeal to regression toward the mean could explain this sort of outcome, with no need to denigrate the personality or motivation of the athlete. Of course, sometimes the Rookie of the Year performs even better during his second year. Thus, our baseball example can be used to emphasize an important point. Regression toward the mean is not an inevitability. It is a statistical tendency that predicts what will happen far more often than not. However, it's merely a matter of probability—which means it is a much more reliable principle when applied to groups (say, the top ten rookies in a specific year) rather than to individuals.

Let's return to the world of therapy for one last thought about the significance of both regression and placebo effects. Over the years, a host of quacks, charlatans, con artists, herbalists, and faith healers have marketed and sold an endless array of worthless treatments for both psychological problems and physical maladies. In many instances, people who have been treated with these phony therapies have expressed satisfaction or even praise and gratitude. For instance, you may have heard someone sincerely rave about some herbal remedy or psychic advice that you were pretty sure was really worthless. If so, you were probably puzzled by their glowing testimonials. Well, you now have two highly plausible explanations for why people can honestly believe that they have derived great benefit from harebrained, bogus treatments: placebo effects and regression effects. The people who provide testimonials for worthless treatments may have experienced *genuine* improvements in their conditions. Those improvements, however, were probably the results of placebo effects and regression toward the mean. Placebo and regression effects add to the many reasons that you should always be skeptical about anecdotal evidence. And they help explain why charlatans can be so successful and why unsound, ineffective treatments can have sincere proponents.

Table 16.3 Critical Thinking Skills Discussed in This Application

Skill	Description
Recognizing situations in which placebo effects might occur	The critical thinker understands that if people have expectations that a treatment will produce a certain effect, they may experience that effect even if the treatment was fake or ineffectual.
Recognizing situations in which regression toward the mean may occur	The critical thinker understands that when people are selected for their extremely high or low scores on some trait, their subsequent scores will probably fall closer to the mean.
Recognizing the limitations of anecdotal evidence	The critical thinker is wary of anecdotal evidence, which consists of personal stories used to support one's assertions. Anecdotal evidence tends to be unrepresentative, inaccurate, and unreliable.

© Cengage Learning 2013

REVIEW OF KEY LEARNING GOALS

16.24 People entering therapy are likely to get better even if their treatment is ineffective, because of placebo effects and regression toward the mean. Regression toward the mean occurs when people selected for their extremely high or low scores on some trait are measured a second time and their new scores fall closer to the mean. Regression and placebo effects may also help explain why people can often be deceived by phony, ineffectual treatments.

Chapter 16 Practice Test

1. After undergoing psychoanalysis for several months, Karen has suddenly started "forgetting" to attend her therapy sessions. Karen's behavior is most likely a form of:
   A. resistance.
   B. transference.
   C. insight.
   D. catharsis.

2. Because Suzanne has an unconscious sexual attraction to her father, she behaves seductively toward her therapist. Suzanne's behavior is most likely a form of:
   A. resistance.
   B. transference.
   C. misinterpretation.
   D. an unconscious defense mechanism.

3. The key process in client-centered therapy is:
   A. interpretation of the client's thoughts, feelings, memories, and behaviors.
   B. clarification of the client's feelings.
   C. confrontation of the client's irrational thoughts.
   D. modification of the client's problematic behaviors.

4. The goal of behavior therapy is to:
   A. identify the early childhood unconscious conflicts that are the source of the client's symptoms.
   B. achieve major personality reconstruction.
   C. reduce or eliminate problematic responses by using conditioning techniques.
   D. alter the client's brain chemistry by prescribing specific drugs.

5. A therapist openly challenges a client's statement that she is a failure as a woman because her boyfriend left her, insisting that she justify it with evidence. Which type of therapy is probably being used?
   A. psychodynamic therapy
   B. client-centered therapy
   C. aversion therapy
   D. cognitive therapy

6. Collectively, numerous studies of therapeutic outcome suggest that:
   A. insight therapy is superior to no treatment or placebo treatment.
   B. individual insight therapy is effective, but group therapy is not.
   C. group therapy is effective, but individual insight therapy is not.
   D. insight therapy is only effective if patients are in therapy for at least two years.

7. Systematic desensitization is an effective treatment for ____________ disorders.
   A. generalized anxiety
   B. panic
   C. obsessive-compulsive
   D. phobic

8. Linda's therapist has her practice active listening skills in structured role-playing exercises. Later, Linda is gradually asked to practice these skills with family members, friends, and finally, her boss. Linda is undergoing:
   A. systematic desensitization.
   B. biofeedback.
   C. a token economy procedure.
   D. social skills training.

9. After being released from a hospital, many schizophrenic patients stop taking their antipsychotic medication because:
   A. their mental impairment causes them to forget.
   B. of the unpleasant side effects.
   C. most schizophrenics don't believe they are ill.
   D. of all of the above.

10. Selective serotonin reuptake inhibitors (SSRIs) can be effective in the treatment of ____________________ disorders.
    A. depressive
    B. schizophrenic
    C. obsessive-compulsive
    D. both a and c

11. Modern psychotherapy:
    A. was spawned by a cultural milieu that viewed the self as an independent, rational being.
    B. embraces universal cultural values.
    C. has been successfully exported to many non-Western cultures.
    D. involves both b and c.

12. The community mental health movement emphasizes:
    A. segregation of the mentally ill from the general population.
    B. increased dependence on long-term inpatient care.
    C. local care and the prevention of psychological disorders.
    D. all of the above.

13. Many people repeatedly go in and out of mental hospitals. Typically, such people are released because ________________; they are eventually readmitted because ____________________________.
    A. they have been stabilized through drug therapy; their condition deteriorates once again due to inadequate outpatient care
    B. they run out of funds to pay for hospitalization; they once again can afford it
    C. they have been cured of their disorder; they develop another disorder
    D. they no longer want to be hospitalized; they voluntarily recommit themselves

14. The type of professional training a therapist has:
    A. is the most important indicator of his or her competence.
    B. should be the major consideration in choosing a therapist.
    C. is not all that important, since talented therapists can be found in all of the mental health professions.
    D. involves both a and b.

15. Which of the following could be explained by regression toward the mean?
    A. You get an average bowling score in one game and a superb score in the next game.
    B. You get an average bowling score in one game and a very low score in the next game.
    C. You get an average bowling score in one game and another average score in the next game.
    D. You get a terrible bowling score in one game and an average score in the next game.

Answers

1 A p. 654	6 A p. 660	11 A pp. 675–676
2 B p. 654	7 D pp. 661–662	12 C p. 677
3 B p. 656	8 D p. 663	13 A p. 679
4 C p. 661	9 B p. 666	14 C p. 681
5 D pp. 663–664	10 D p. 666	15 D pp. 684–685

Chapter 16 Media Resources

PsykTrek

To view a demo: **www.cengage.com/psychology/psyktrek**
To order: **www.cengage.com/psychology/weiten**

Go to the PsykTrek website or CD-ROM for further study of the concepts in this chapter. Both online and on the CD-ROM, PsykTrek includes dozens of learning modules with videos, animations, and quizzes, as well as simulations of psychological phenomena and a multimedia glossary that includes word pronunciations.

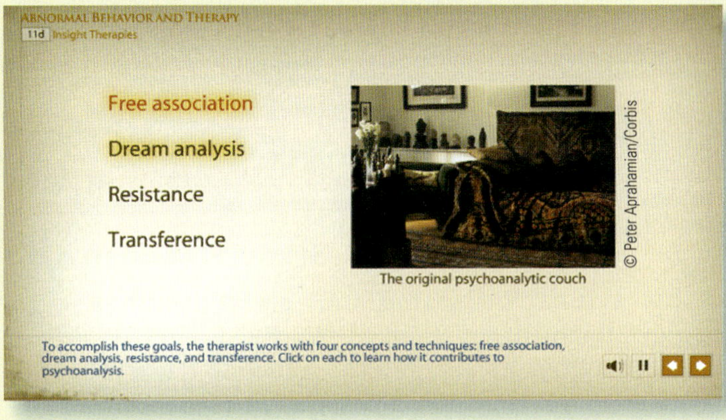

© Cengage Learning 2008

Explore Module 11d (*Insight Therapies*) to enhance your understanding of psychoanalysis and client-centered therapy.

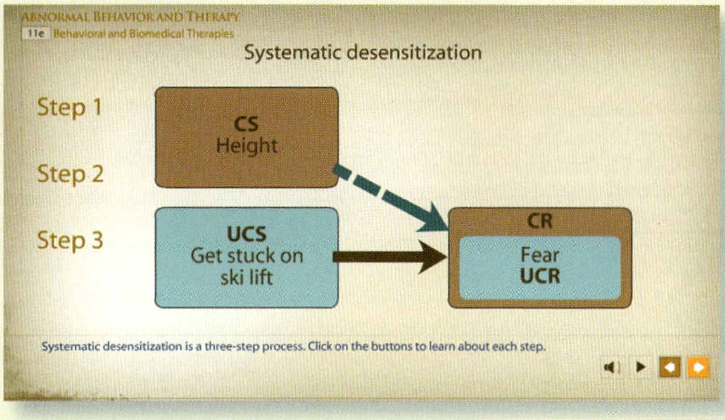

© Cengage Learning 2008

Visit Module 11e (*Behavioral and Biomedical Therapies*) to get additional information on systematic desensitization and aversion therapy.

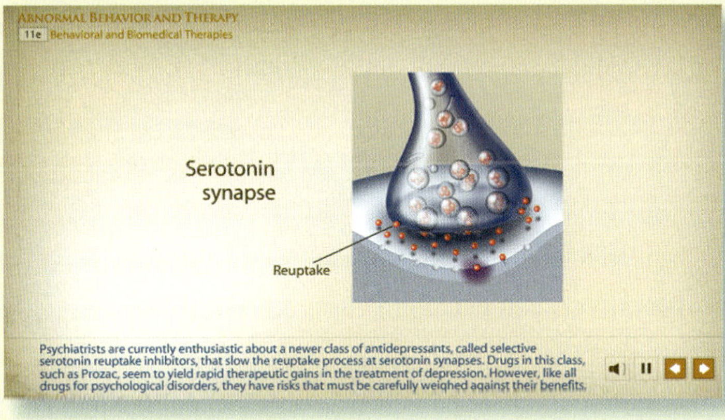

© Cengage Learning 2008

Increase your understanding of how antianxiety, antipsychotic, and antidepressant drugs exert their effects by accessing Module 11e (*Behavioral and Biomedical Therapies*).

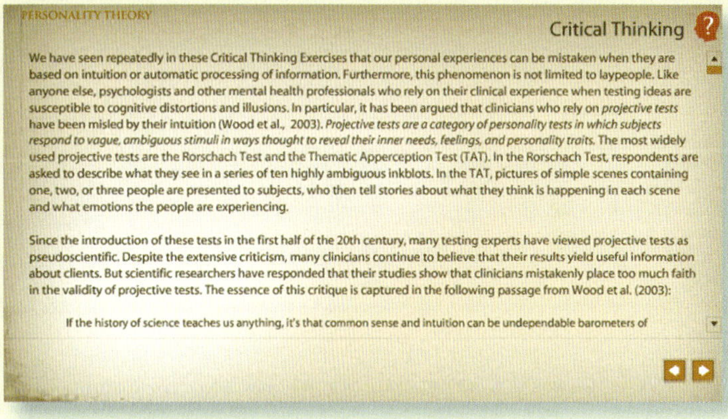

© Cengage Learning 2008

Learn more about the projective tests used in clinical treatment by working through the Unit 10 Critical Thinking Exercise (*Illusory Correlation, Consensual Validation, and the Appeal to Authority*).

Online Study Tools

Log in to **CengageBrain** to access the resources your instructor requires. For this book, you can access:

CourseMate brings course concepts to life with interactive learning, study, and exam preparation tools that support the printed textbook. A textbook-specific website, Psychology CourseMate includes an integrated interactive eBook and other interactive learning tools such as quizzes, flashcards, videos, and more.

CengageNow is an easy-to-use online resource that helps you study in less time to get the grade you want—NOW. Take a pre-test for this chapter and receive a personalized study plan based on your results that will identify the topics you need to review and direct you to online resources to help you master those topics. Then take a post-test to help you determine the concepts you have mastered and what you will need to work on. If your textbook does not include an access code card, go to CengageBrain.com to gain access.

WebTutor is more than just an interactive study guide. WebTutor is an anytime, anywhere customized learning solution with an eBook, keeping you connected to your textbook, instructor, and classmates.

Aplia. If your professor has assigned Aplia homework:

1. Sign in to your account
2. Complete the corresponding homework exercises as required by your professor.
3. When finished, click "Grade It Now" to see which areas you have mastered, which need more work, and detailed explanations of every answer.

Visit **www.cengagebrain.com** to access your account and purchase materials.

Answers to Concept Checks

Chapter 1

Concept Check 1.1

1. c. Sigmund Freud (1905, pp. 77–78), arguing that it is possible to probe into the unconscious depths of the mind.
2. a. Wilhelm Wundt (1874/1904, p. v), campaigning for a new, independent science of psychology.
3. b. William James (1890), commenting negatively on the structuralists' efforts to break consciousness into its elements and his view of consciousness as a continuously flowing stream.

Concept Check 1.2

1. b. B. F. Skinner (1971, p. 17), explaining why he believes that freedom is an illusion.
2. c. Carl Rogers (1961, p. 27), commenting on others' assertion that he had an overly optimistic (Pollyannaish) view of human potential and discussing humans' basic drive toward personal growth.
3. a. John B. Watson (1930, p. 103), dismissing the importance of genetic inheritance while arguing that traits are shaped entirely by experience.

Concept Check 1.3

1. a   2. e   3. d   4. f   5. b
6. c   7. g

Chapter 2

Concept Check 2.1

1. IV: Film violence (present versus absent)

   DV: Heart rate and blood pressure (there are two DVs)
2. IV: Courtesy training (training versus no training)

   DV: Number of customer complaints
3. IV: Stimulus complexity (high versus low) and stimulus contrast (high versus low) (there are two IVs)

   DV: Length of time spent staring at the stimuli
4. IV: Group size (large versus small)

   DV: Conformity

Concept Check 2.2

1. d. Survey. You would distribute a survey to obtain information on subjects' social class, education, and attitudes about nuclear disarmament.
2. c. Case study. Using a case study approach, you could interview people with anxiety disorders, interview their parents, and examine their school records to look for similarities in childhood experiences. As a second choice, you might have people with anxiety disorders fill out a survey about their childhood experiences.
3. b. Naturalistic observation. To answer this question properly, you would want to observe baboons in their natural environment, without interference.
4. a. Experiment. To demonstrate a causal relationship, you would have to conduct an experiment. You would manipulate the presence or absence of food-related cues in controlled circumstances where subjects had an opportunity to eat some food, and monitor the amount eaten.

Concept Check 2.3

1. b and e. The other three conclusions all equate correlation with causation.
2. a. Negative. As age increases, more people tend to have visual problems and acuity tends to decrease.

   b. Positive. Studies show that highly educated people tend to earn higher incomes and that people with less education tend to earn lower incomes.

   c. Negative. As shyness increases, the size of one's friendship network should decrease. However, research suggests that this inverse association may be weaker than widely believed.

Concept Check 2.4

Methodological flaw	*Study 1*	*Study 2*
Sampling bias	✓	✓
Placebo effects	✓	
Confounding of variables	✓	
Distortions in self-report data		✓
Experimenter bias	✓	

Explanations for Study 1. Sensory deprivation is an unusual kind of experience that may intrigue certain potential subjects, who may be more adventurous or more willing to take risks than the population at large. Using the first 80 students who sign up for this study may not yield a sample that is representative of the population. Assigning the first 40 subjects who sign up to the experimental group may confound these extraneous variables with the treatment (students who sign up most quickly may be the most adventurous). In announcing that he will be examining the *detrimental* effects of sensory deprivation, the experimenter has created expectations in the subjects. These expectations could lead to placebo effects. The experimenter has also revealed that he has a bias about the outcome of the study. Since he supervises the treatments, he knows which subjects are in the experimental and control groups, thus aggravating potential problems with experimenter bias. For example, he might unintentionally give the control group subjects better instructions on how to do the pursuit-rotor task and thereby slant the study in favor of finding support for his hypothesis.

Explanations for Study 2. Sampling bias is a problem because the researcher has sampled only subjects from a low-income, inner-city neighborhood. A sample obtained in this way is not likely to be representative of the population at large. People are sensitive about the issue of racial prejudice, so distortions in self-report data are also likely. Many subjects may be swayed by social desirability bias and rate themselves as less prejudiced than they really are.

Concept Check 2.5
1. c 2. a 3. b

Chapter 3

Concept Check 3.1
1. d. Dendrite
2. f. Myelin
3. b. Neuron
4. e. Axon
5. a. Glia
6. g. Terminal button
7. h. Synapse

Concept Check 3.2
1. d. Serotonin
2. b. and d. Serotonin and norepinephrine
3. e. Endorphins
4. c. Dopamine
5. a. Acetylcholine

Concept Check 3.3
1. Left hemisphere damage, probably to Wernicke's area
2. Deficit in dopamine synthesis in an area of the midbrain
3. Degeneration of myelin sheaths surrounding axons
4. Disturbance in dopamine or glutamate activity, possibly associated with enlarged ventricles in the brain or epigenetic changes

Please note that neuropsychological assessment is not as simple as this introductory exercise may suggest. There are many possible causes of most disorders, and we discussed only a handful of leading causes for each.

Concept Check 3.4
1. Closer relatives; more distant relatives
2. Identical twins; fraternal twins
3. Biological parents; adoptive parents
4. Genetic overlap or closeness; trait similarity

Concept Check 3.5
1. c 2. e 3. b 4. a 5. d

Chapter 4

Concept Check 4.1

Dimension	*Rods*	*Cones*
Physical shape	Elongated	Stubby
Number in the retina	125 million	5–6.4 million
Area of the retina in which they are dominant receptor	Periphery	Center/fovea
Critical to color vision	No	Yes
Critical to peripheral vision	Yes	No
Sensitivity to dim light	Strong	Weak
Speed of dark adaptation	Slow	Rapid

Concept Check 4.2
✓ 1. Interposition. The arches in front cut off part of the corridor behind them.

✓ 2. Height in plane. The back of the corridor is higher on the horizontal plane than the front of the corridor is.

✓ 3. Texture gradient. The more distant portions of the hallway are painted in less detail than the closer portions are.

✓ 4. Relative size. The arches in the distance are smaller than those in the foreground.

✓ 5. Light and shadow. Light shining in from the crossing corridor (it's coming from the left) contrasts with shadow elsewhere.

✓ 6. Linear perspective. The lines of the corridor converge in the distance.

Concept Check 4.3

Dimension	*Vision*	*Hearing*
1. Stimulus	Light waves	Sound waves
2. Elements of stimulus and related perceptions	Wavelength/hue Amplitude/brightness Purity/saturation	Frequency/pitch Amplitude/loudness Purity/timbre
3. Receptors	Rods and cones	Hair cells
4. Location of receptors	Retina	Basilar membrane
5. Main location of processing in brain	Occipital lobe, visual cortex	Temporal lobe, auditory cortex

Concept Check 4.4
1. c 2. a 3. e 4. b 5. d

Chapter 5

Concept Check 5.1

Characteristic	*REM sleep*	*NREM sleep*
1. Type of EEG activity	"Wide awake" brain waves, mostly beta	Varied, lots of delta waves
2. Eye movements	Rapid, lateral	Slow or absent
3. Dreaming	Frequent, vivid	Less frequent
4. Depth (difficulty in awakening)	Varied, generally difficult to awaken	Varied, generally easier to awaken
5. Percentage of total sleep (in adults)	About 20%–25%	About 75%–80%
6. Increases or decreases (as percentage of sleep) during childhood	Percent decreases	Percent increases
7. Timing in sleep (dominates early or late)	Dominates late in cycle	Dominates early in cycle

Concept Check 5.2

1. Beta. Video games require alert information processing, which is associated with beta waves.
2. Alpha. Meditation involves relaxation, which is associated with alpha waves, and studies show increased alpha in meditators.
3. Theta. In stage 1 sleep, theta waves tend to be prevalent.
4. Delta. Sleepwalking usually occurs in deep NREM sleep, which is dominated by delta activity.
5. Beta. Nightmares are dreams, so you're probably in REM sleep, which paradoxically produces "wide awake" beta waves.

Concept Check 5.3

1. c. Stimulants.
2. d. Hallucinogens.
3. b. Sedatives.
4. f. Alcohol.
5. a. Narcotics.
6. e. Cannabis.

Concept Check 5.4

1. d	2. e	3. a	4. f	5. b
6. c				

Chapter 6

Concept Check 6.1

1. CS: Fire in fireplace
   US: Pain from burn   CR/UR: Fear
2. CS: Brake lights in rain
   US: Car accident   CR/UR: Tensing up
3. CS: Sight of cat
   US: Cat dander   CR/UR: Wheezing

Concept Check 6.2

1. FR. Each sale is a response and every third response earns reinforcement.
2. VI. A varied amount of time elapses before the response of doing yardwork can earn reinforcement.
3. VR. Reinforcement occurs after a varied number of unreinforced casts (time is irrelevant; the more casts Martha makes, the more reinforcers she will receive).
4. CR. The designated response (reading a book) is reinforced (with a gold star) every time.
5. FI. A fixed time interval (three years) has to elapse before Skip can earn a salary increase (the reinforcer).

Concept Check 6.3

1. Punishment.
2. Positive reinforcement.
3. Punishment.
4. Negative reinforcement (for Audrey); the dog is positively reinforced for its whining.
5. Negative reinforcement.
6. Extinction. When Sharma's co-workers start to ignore her complaints, they are trying to extinguish the behavior (which had been positively reinforced when it won sympathy).

Concept Check 6.4

1. Classical conditioning. Midori's blue windbreaker is a CS eliciting excitement in her dog.
2. Operant conditioning. Playing new songs leads to negative consequences (punishment), which weaken the tendency to play new songs. Playing old songs leads to positive reinforcement, which gradually strengthens the tendency to play old songs.
3. Classical conditioning. The song was paired with the passion of new love so that it became a CS eliciting emotional, romantic feelings.
4. Both. Ralph's workplace is paired with criticism so that his workplace becomes a CS eliciting anxiety. Calling in sick is operant behavior that is strengthened through negative reinforcement (because it reduces anxiety).

Concept Check 6.5

1. f	2. b	3. e	4. g	5. h
6. c	7. d	8. a		

Chapter 7

Concept Check 7.1

Feature	*Sensory memory*	*Short-term memory*	*Long-term memory*
Encoding format	Copy of input	Largely phonemic	Largely semantic
Storage capacity	Limited	Small	No known limit
Storage duration	About 1/4 second	10–20 seconds	Minutes to years

Concept Check 7.2

1. Ineffective encoding due to lack of attention
2. Retrieval failure due to motivated forgetting
3. Proactive interference (previous learning of Justin Timberlake's name interferes with new learning)
4. Retroactive interference (new learning of sociology interferes with older learning of history)

Concept Check 7.3

1. d. Declarative memory
2. c. Long-term memory
3. a. Sensory memory
4. f. Episodic memory
5. e. Nondeclarative memory
6. g. Semantic memory
7. b. Short-term memory

Concept Check 7.4

1. c	2. e	3. f	4. a	5. h
6. i	7. g	8. b	9. d	

Chapter 8

Concept Check 8.1

1. 1. One-word utterance in which the word is over-extended to refer to a similar object.
2. 4. Words are combined into a sentence, but the rule for past tense is overregularized.
3. 3. Telegraphic sentence.
4. 5. Words are combined into a sentence, and past tense is used correctly.
5. 2. One-word utterance without overextension.
6. 6. "Longer" sentence with metaphor.

Concept Check 8.2

1. Functional fixedness
2. Forming subgoals
3. Insight
4. Searching for analogies
5. Arrangement problem

Concept Check 8.3

1. Elimination by aspects
2. Availability heuristic
3. Shift to additive strategy

Concept Check 8.4

1. d	2. f	3. a	4. c	5. b
6. e				

Chapter 9

Concept Check 9.1

1. Test-retest reliability
2. Criterion-related validity
3. Content validity

Concept Check 9.2

1. H. Given that the identical twins were reared apart, their greater similarity in comparison to fraternals reared together can only be due to heredity. This comparison is probably the most important piece of evidence supporting the genetic determination of IQ.
2. E. We tend to associate identical twins with evidence supporting heredity, but in this comparison genetic similarity is held constant since both sets of twins are identical. The only logical explanation for the greater similarity in identicals reared together is the effect of their being reared together (environment).
3. E. This comparison is similar to the previous one. Genetic similarity is held constant and a shared environment produces greater similarity than being reared apart.
4. B. This is nothing more than a quantification of Galton's original observation that intelligence runs in families. Since families share both genes and environment, either or both could be responsible for the observed correlation.
5. B. The similarity of adopted children to their biological parents can only be due to shared genes, and the similarity of adopted children to their foster parents can only be due to shared environment, so these correlations show the influence of both heredity and environment.

Concept Check 9.3

1. d	2. a	3. g	4. e	5. h
6. i	7. b	8. c	9. f	

Chapter 10

Concept Check 10.1

1. I. The secretion of ghrelin by the stomach tends to trigger stomach contractions and promote hunger.
2. I. According to Mayer, hunger increases when the amount of glucose in the blood decreases.
3. I or ?. Food cues generally trigger hunger and eating, but reactions vary among individuals.
4. D. Food preferences are mostly learned, and we tend to like what we are accustomed to eating. Most people will not be eager to eat a strange-looking food.
5. I. People tend to eat more when a variety of foods are available.
6. I. The more people are served, the more they tend to eat. Large portions tend to increase eating.

Concept Check 10.2

1. c. Incentive value of success
2. b. Perceived probability of success
3. a. Need for achievement

Concept Check 10.3

2. James-Lange theory
3. Schachter's two-factor theory
4. Evolutionary theories

Concept Check 10.4

1. d	2. g	3. e	4. h	5. a
6. b	7. c	8. f		

Chapter 11

Concept Check 11.1

	Event	*Stage*	*Organism*	*Time span*
1.	Uterine implantation	Germinal	Zygote	0–2 weeks
2.	Muscle and bone begin to form	Fetal	Fetus	2 months to birth
3.	Vital organs and body systems begin to form	Embryonic	Embryo	2 weeks to 2 months

Concept Check 11.2

1. b. Animism is characteristic of the preoperational period.
2. c. Mastery of hierarchical classification occurs during the concrete operational period.
3. a. Lack of object permanence is characteristic of the sensorimotor period.

Concept Check 11.3

1. c. Commitment to personal ethics is characteristic of postconventional reasoning.
2. b. Concern about approval of others is characteristic of conventional reasoning.
3. a. Emphasis on positive or negative consequences is characteristic of preconventional reasoning.

Concept Check 11.4

1. d	2. f	3. c	4. g	5. a
6. b	7. e			

Chapter 12

Concept Check 12.1

1. Regression
2. Projection
3. Reaction formation
4. Repression
5. Rationalization

Concept Check 12.2

1. Bandura's observational learning. Sarah imitates a role model from television.
2. Maslow's need for self-actualization. Yolanda is striving to realize her fullest potential.
3. Freud's Oedipal complex. Vladimir shows preference for his opposite-sex parent and emotional distance from his same-sex parent.

Concept Check 12.3

1. Maslow (1971, p. 36), commenting on the need for self-actualization.
2. Eysenck (1977, pp. 407–408), commenting on the biological roots of personality.
3. Freud (in Malcolm, 1980), commenting on the repression of sexuality.

Concept Check 12.4

1. g	2. i	3. f	4. d	5. h
6. a	7. e	8. b	9. c	

Chapter 13

Concept Check 13.1

	Unstable	*Stable*
Internal	d	b
External	a	c

Concept Check 13.2

1. c. Fundamental attribution error (assuming that arriving late reflects personal qualities)
2. a. Illusory correlation effect (overestimating how often one has seen confirmations of the assertion that young, female professors get pregnant soon after being hired)
3. b. Stereotyping (assuming that all lawyers have certain traits)
4. d. Defensive attribution (derogating the victims of misfortune to minimize the apparent likelihood of a similar mishap)

Concept Check 13.3

1. Target: Cognitive component of attitudes (beliefs about program for regulating nursing homes)

   Persuasion: Message factor (advice to use one-sided instead of two-sided arguments)
2. Target: Affective component of attitudes (feelings about candidate)

   Persuasion: Source factor (advice on appearing likable, sincere, and compassionate)
3. Target: Behavioral component of attitudes (making contributions)

   Persuasion: Receiver factor (considering audience's initial position regarding the candidate)

Concept Check 13.4

1. c	2. d	3. g	4. a	5. b
6. e	7. f			

Chapter 14

Concept Check 14.1

1. b. A choice between two unattractive options
2. c. Weighing the positive and negative aspects of a single goal
3. a. A choice between two attractive options

Concept Check 14.2

1. a. Frustration due to delay
2. d. Pressure to perform
3. c. Change associated with leaving school and taking a new job
4. a. Frustration due to loss of job

   c. Change in life circumstances

   d. Pressure to perform (in quickly obtaining new job)

Concept Check 14.3

Pathway 1: hypothalamus, sympathetic division of the ANS, adrenal medulla, catecholamines.

Pathway 2: pituitary, ACTH, adrenal cortex, corticosteroids.

Concept Check 14.4

1. g	2. f	3. e	4. d	5. c
6. b	7. a			

Chapter 15

Concept Check 15.1

	Deviance	Maladaptive behavior	Personal distress
1. Alan		✓	
2. Monica			✓
3. Boris	✓		
4. Natasha	✓	✓	✓

Concept Check 15.2

1. Obsessive-compulsive disorder (key symptoms: frequent rituals, obsession with ordering things)
2. Phobic disorder (key symptoms: persistent and irrational fear of thunderstorms, interference with work functioning)
3. Posttraumatic stress disorder (key symptoms: enduring disturbance due to exposure to traumatic event, nightmares, emotional numbing)

Concept Check 15.3

1. Bipolar disorder, manic episode (key symptoms: extravagant plans, hyperactivity, reckless spending)
2. Paranoid schizophrenia (key symptoms: delusions of persecution and grandeur, along with deterioration of adaptive behavior)
3. Major depression (key symptoms: feelings of despair, low self-esteem, lack of energy)

Concept Check 15.4

1. c 2. a 3. d 4. b

Chapter 16

Concept Check 16.1

1. c 2. a 3. b

Concept Check 16.2

1. d 2. b 3. a 4. c

Concept Check 16.3

1. c 2. a 3. b 4. d 5. b

Concept Check 16.4

1. c 2. d 3. b 4. a 5. e

Statistical Methods

Empiricism depends on observation; precise observation depends on measurement; and measurement requires numbers. Thus, scientists routinely analyze numerical data to arrive at their conclusions. Over 3000 empirical studies are cited in this text, and all but a few of the simplest ones required a statistical analysis. ***Statistics* is the use of mathematics to organize, summarize, and interpret numerical data.** We discussed statistics briefly in Chapter 2, but in this Appendix we take a closer look.

To illustrate statistics in action, let's assume that we want to test a hypothesis that has generated quite an argument in your psychology class. The hypothesis is that college students who watch a great deal of television aren't as bright as those who watch TV infrequently. For the fun of it, your class decides to conduct a correlational study of itself, collecting survey and psychological test data. Your classmates all agree to respond to a short survey on their TV viewing habits. Because everyone at your school has had to take the SAT, the class decides to use scores on the SAT Critical Reading subtest as an index of how bright students are. All of them agree to allow the records office at the college to furnish their SAT scores to the professor, who replaces each student's name with a subject number (to protect students' right to privacy). Let's see how we could use statistics to analyze the data collected in our pilot study (a small, preliminary investigation).

Graphing Data

PSYKTREK 1c

After collecting our data, our next step is to organize the data to get a quick overview of our numerical results. Let's assume that there are 20 students in your class, and when they estimate how many hours they spend per day watching TV, the results are as follows:

3	2	0	3	1
3	4	0	5	1
2	3	4	5	2
4	5	3	4	6

One of the simpler things that we can do to organize data is to create a ***frequency distribution*—an orderly arrangement of scores indicating the frequency of each score or group of scores. Figure B.1(a)** shows a frequency distribution for our data on TV viewing. The column on the left lists the possible scores (estimated hours of TV viewing) in order, and the column on the right lists the number of subjects with each score. Graphs can provide an even better overview of the data. One approach is to portray the data in a ***histogram*, which is a bar graph that presents data from a frequency distribution.** Such a histogram, summarizing our TV viewing data, is presented in Figure **B.1(b)**.

Another widely used method of portraying data graphically is the ***frequency polygon*—a line figure used to present data from a frequency distribution. Figures B.1(c)** and **B.1(d)** show how our TV viewing data can be converted from a histogram to a frequency polygon. In both the bar graph and the line figure, the horizontal axis lists the possible scores and the vertical axis is used to indicate the frequency of each score. This use of the axes is nearly universal for frequency polygons, although sometimes it is reversed in histograms (the vertical axis lists possible scores, so the bars become horizontal).

Score	Tallies	Frequency
6	I	1
5	III	3
4	IIII	4
3	卌	5
2	III	3
1	II	2
0	II	2

(a) Frequency distribution

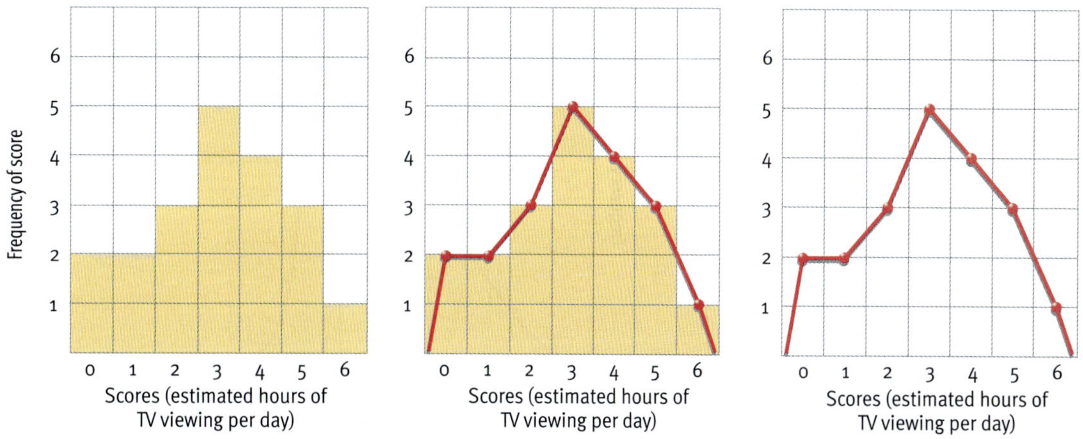

(b) Histogram **(c) Conversion of histogram into frequency polygon** **(d) Frequency polygon**

Figure B.1
Graphing data. (a) Our raw data are tallied into a frequency distribution. **(b)** The same data are portrayed in a bar graph called a histogram. **(c)** A frequency polygon is plotted over the histogram. **(d)** The resultant frequency polygon is shown by itself. © Cengage Learning 2013

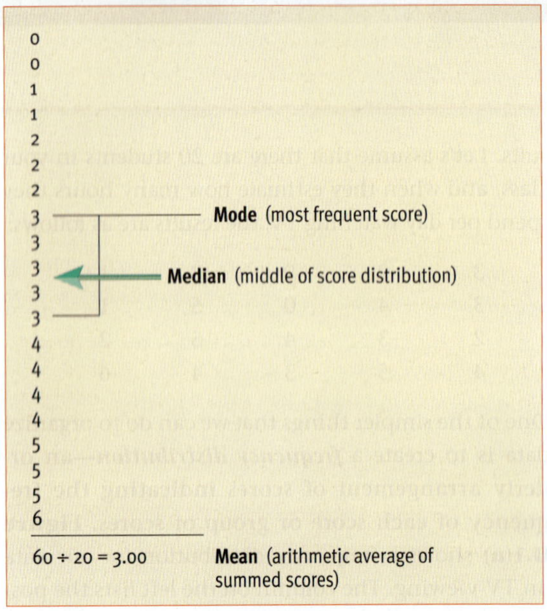

Figure B.2
Measures of central tendency. Although the mean, median, and mode sometimes yield different results, they usually converge, as in the case of our TV viewing data. © Cengage Learning 2013

Our graphs improve on the jumbled collection of scores that we started with, but ***descriptive statistics,* which are used to organize and summarize data**, provide some additional advantages. Let's see what the three measures of central tendency tell us about our data.

Measuring Central Tendency

PsykTrek 1c

In examining a set of data, it's routine to ask "What is a typical score in the distribution?" For instance, in this case we might compare the average amount of TV watching in our sample to national estimates, to determine whether our subjects appear to be representative of the population. The three measures of central tendency—the median, the mean, and the mode—give us indications regarding the typical score in a data set. As explained in Chapter 2, **the *median* is the score that falls in the center of a distribution, the *mean* is the arithmetic average of the scores, and the *mode* is the score that occurs most frequently.**

All three measures of central tendency are calculated for our TV viewing data in **Figure B.2**. As you can see, in this set of data, the mean, median, and mode all turn out to be the same score, which is 3. Although our example in Chapter 2 emphasized that the mean, median, and mode can yield different estimates of central tendency, the correspondence among them seen in our TV viewing data is quite common. Lack of agreement usually occurs when a few extreme scores pull the mean away from the center of the distribution, as shown in **Figure B.3**. The curves plotted in **Figure B.3** are simply "smoothed out" frequency polygons based on data from many subjects. They show that when a distribution is symmetric, the measures of central tendency fall together, but this is not true in skewed or unbalanced distributions.

Figure B.3(b) shows a ***negatively skewed distribution,* in which most scores pile up at the high end of the scale** (the negative skew refers to the direction in which the curve's "tail" points). **A *positively skewed distribution,* in which scores pile up at the low end of the scale**, is shown in **Figure B.3(c)**. In both types of skewed distributions, a few extreme scores at one end pull the mean, and to a lesser degree the median, away from the mode. In these situations, the mean may be misleading and the median usually provides the best index of central tendency.

In any case, the measures of central tendency for our TV viewing data are reassuring, since they all agree and they fall reasonably close to national estimates regarding how much young adults watch TV. Given the small size of our group, this agreement with national norms doesn't prove that our sample is representative of the population, but at

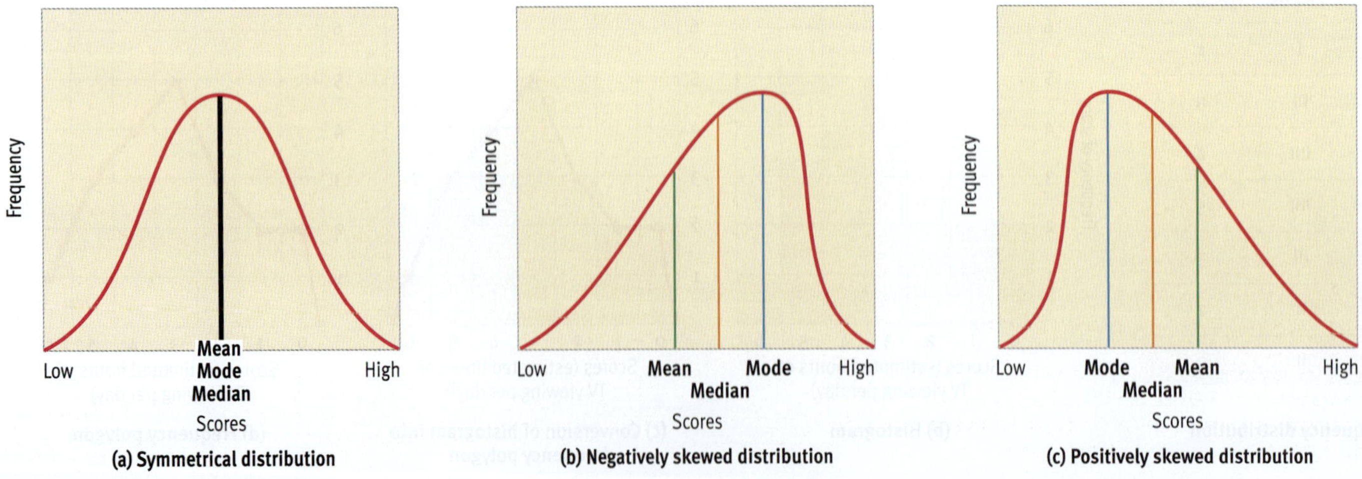

Figure B.3
Measures of central tendency in skewed distributions. In a symmetrical distribution **(a)**, the three measures of central tendency converge. However, in a negatively skewed distribution **(b)** or in a positively skewed distribution **(c)**, the mean, median, and mode are pulled apart as shown here. Typically, in these situations the median provides the best index of central tendency. © Cengage Learning 2013

least there's no obvious reason to believe that it is unrepresentative.

Measuring Variability

1c

Of course, the subjects in our sample did not report identical TV viewing habits. Virtually all data sets are characterized by some variability. ***Variability* refers to how much the scores tend to vary or depart from the mean score.** For example, the distribution of golf scores for a mediocre, erratic golfer would be characterized by high variability, while scores for an equally mediocre but consistent golfer would show less variability.

The *standard deviation* is an index of the amount of variability in a set of data. It reflects the dispersion of scores in a distribution. This principle is portrayed graphically in **Figure B.4**, where the two distributions of golf scores have the same mean but the upper one has less variability because the scores are "bunched up" in the center (for the consistent golfer). The distribution in **Figure B.4(b)** is characterized by more variability, as the erratic golfer's scores are more spread out. This distribution will yield a higher standard deviation than the distribution in **Figure B.4(a)**.

The formula for calculating the standard deviation is shown in **Figure B.5**, where *d stands for each score's deviation from the mean and* Σ *stands for summation. A step-by-step application of this formula to our TV viewing data, shown in* **Figure B.5**, reveals that the standard deviation for our TV viewing data is 1.64. The standard deviation has a variety of uses. One of these uses will surface in the next section, where we discuss the normal distribution.

The Normal Distribution

7c

The hypothesis in our study is that brighter students watch less TV than relatively dull students. To test this hypothesis, we're going to correlate TV viewing with SAT scores. But to make effective use of the SAT data, we need to understand what SAT scores mean, which brings us to the normal distribution.

The *normal distribution* is a symmetric, bell-shaped curve that represents the pattern in which many human characteristics are dispersed in the

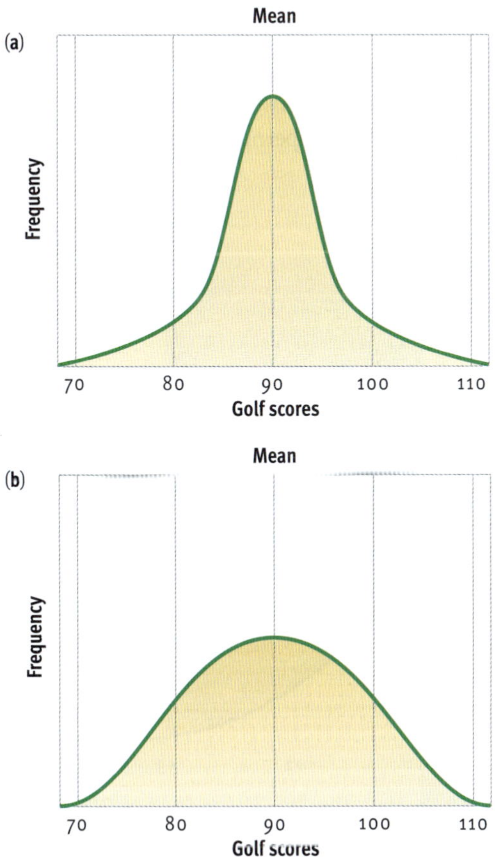

Figure B.4

The standard deviation and dispersion of data.
Although both these distributions of golf scores have the same mean, their standard deviations will be different. In **(a)** the scores are bunched together and there is less variability than in **(b)**, yielding a lower standard deviation for the data in distribution **(a)**. © Cengage Learning 2013

TV viewing score (X)	Deviation from mean (d)	Deviation squared (d^2)
0	−3	9
0	−3	9
1	−2	4
1	−2	4
2	−1	1
2	−1	1
2	−1	1
3	0	0
3	0	0
3	0	0
3	0	0
3	0	0
4	+1	1
4	+1	1
4	+1	1
4	+1	1
5	+2	4
5	+2	4
5	+2	4
6	+3	9

$N = 20$

$\Sigma X = 60$ $\quad$ $\Sigma d^2 = 54$

$$\text{Mean} = \frac{\Sigma X}{N} = \frac{60}{20} = 3.0$$

$$\text{Standard deviation} = \sqrt{\frac{\Sigma d^2}{N}} = \sqrt{\frac{54}{20}}$$

$$= \sqrt{2.70} = 1.64$$

© Cengage Learning 2013

Figure B.5

Steps in calculating the standard deviation.
(1) Add the scores (ΣX) and divide by the number of scores (N) to calculate the mean (which comes out to 3.0 in this case). **(2)** Calculate each score's deviation from the mean by subtracting the mean from each score (the results are shown in the second column). **(3)** Square these deviations from the mean and total the results to obtain (Σd^2) as shown in the third column. **(4)** Insert the numbers for N and Σd^2 into the formula for the standard deviation and compute the results.

population. A great many physical qualities (for example, height, nose length, and running speed) and psychological traits (intelligence, spatial reasoning ability, introversion) are distributed in a manner that closely resembles this bell-shaped curve. When a trait is normally distributed, most scores fall near the center of the distribution (the mean), and the number of scores gradually declines as one moves away from the center in either direction. The normal distribution is not a law of nature. It's a mathematical function, or theoretical curve, that approximates the way nature seems to operate.

The normal distribution is the bedrock of the scoring system for most psychological tests, including the SAT. As we discuss in Chapter 9, psychological tests are relative measures; they assess how people score on a trait in comparison to other people. The normal distribution gives us a precise way to measure how people stack up in comparison to each other. The scores under the normal curve are dispersed in a fixed pattern, with the standard deviation serving as the unit of measurement, as shown in **Figure B.6**. About 68% of the scores in the distribution fall within plus or minus 1 standard deviation of the mean, while 95% of the scores fall within plus or minus 2 standard deviations of the mean. Given this fixed pattern, if you know the mean and standard deviation of a normally distributed trait, you can tell where any score falls in the distribution for the trait.

Although you may not have realized it, you probably have taken many tests in which the scoring system is based on the normal distribution. On the SAT, for instance, raw scores (the number of items correct on each subtest) are converted into standard scores that indicate where you fall in the normal distribution for the trait measured. In this conversion, the mean is set arbitrarily at 500 and the standard deviation at 100, as shown in **Figure B.7**. Therefore, a score of 400 on the SAT Critical Reading subtest means that you scored 1 standard deviation below the mean, while an SAT score of 600 indicates that you scored 1 standard deviation above the mean. Thus, SAT scores tell you how many standard deviations above or below the mean your score was. This system also provides the metric for IQ scales and many other types of psychological tests (see Chapter 9).

Test scores that place examinees in the normal distribution can always be converted to percentile scores, which are a little easier to interpret. A ***percentile score*** **indicates the percentage of people who score at or below the score you obtained.** For example, if you score at the 60th percentile, 60% of the people who take the test score the same or below you, while the remaining 40% score above you. There are tables available that permit us to convert any stan-

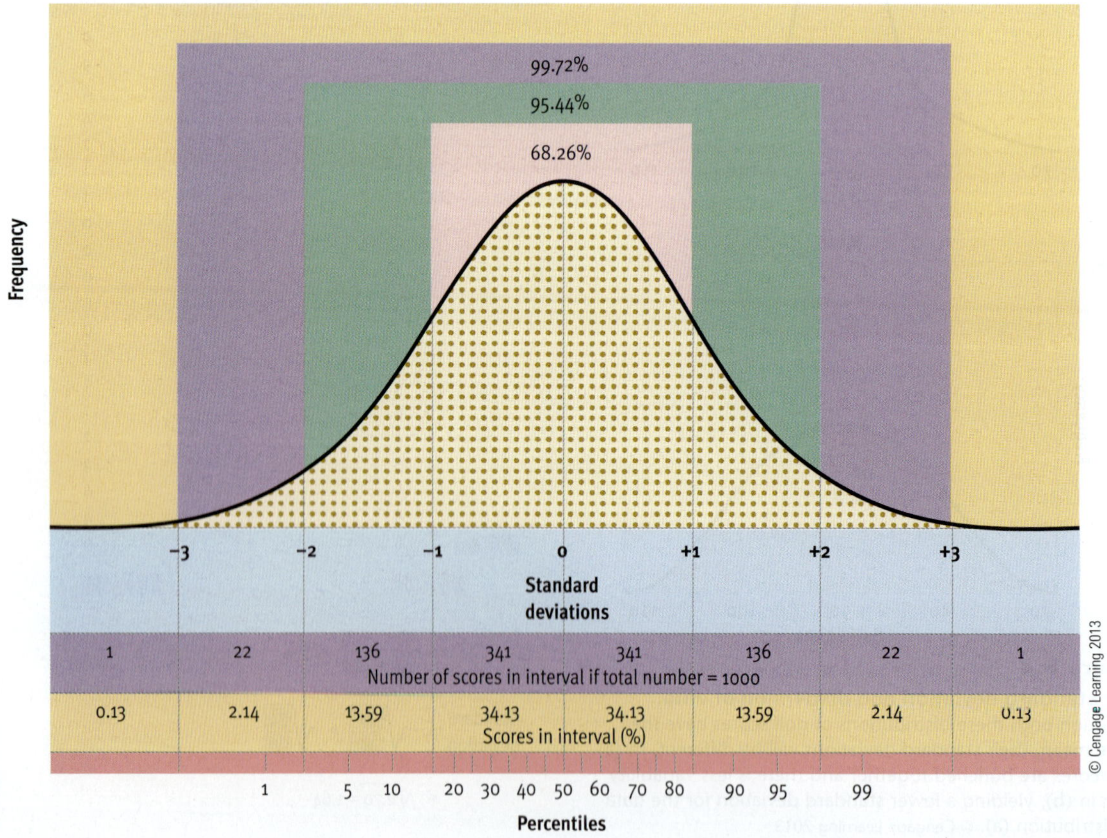

Figure B.6
The normal distribution. Many characteristics are distributed in a pattern represented by this bell-shaped curve (each dot represents a case). The horizontal axis shows how far above or below the mean a score is (measured in plus or minus standard deviations). The vertical axis shows the number of cases obtaining each score. In a normal distribution, most cases fall near the center of the distribution, so that 68.26% of the cases fall within plus or minus 1 standard deviation of the mean. The number of cases gradually declines as one moves away from the mean in either direction, so that only 13.59% of the cases fall between 1 and 2 standard deviations above or below the mean, and even fewer cases (2.14%) fall between 2 and 3 standard deviations above or below the mean.

dard deviation placement in a normal distribution into a precise percentile score. **Figure B.6** gives some percentile conversions for the normal curve.

Of course, not all distributions are normal. As we saw in **Figure B.3**, some distributions are skewed in one direction or the other. As an example, consider what would happen if a classroom exam were much too easy or much too hard. If the test were too easy, scores would be bunched up at the high end of the scale, as in **Figure B.3(b)**. If the test were too hard, scores would be bunched up at the low end, as in **Figure B.3(c)**.

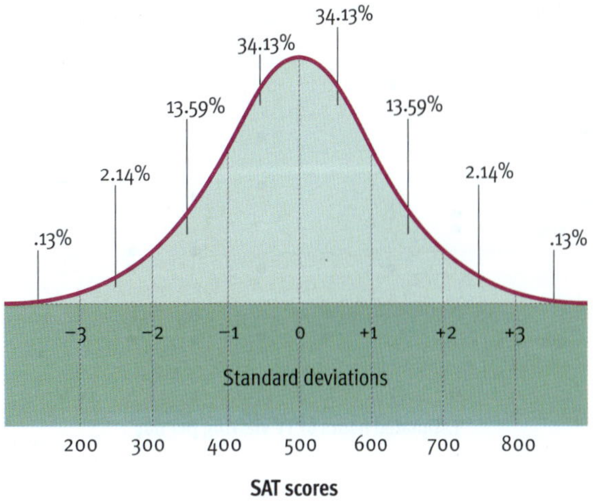

Figure B.7

The normal distribution and SAT scores. The normal distribution is the basis for the scoring system on many standardized tests. For example, on the SAT, the mean is set at 500 and the standard deviation at 100. Hence, an SAT score tells you how many standard deviations above or below the mean you scored. For example, a score of 700 means you scored 2 standard deviations above the mean.

© Cengage Learning 2013

Measuring Correlation

PSYKTREK 1d

To determine whether TV viewing is related to SAT scores, we have to compute a ***correlation coefficient*—a numerical index of the degree of relationship between two variables.** As discussed in Chapter 2, a *positive* correlation means that two variables—say *X* and *Y*—co-vary in the *same* direction. This means that high scores on variable *X* are associated with high scores on variable *Y* and that low scores on *X* are associated with low scores on *Y*. A *negative* correlation indicates that two variables co-vary in the *opposite* direction. This means that people who score high on variable *X* tend to score low on variable *Y*, whereas those who score low on *X* tend to score high on *Y*. In our study, we hypothesized that as TV viewing increases, SAT scores will decrease, so we should expect a negative correlation between TV viewing and SAT scores.

The *magnitude* of a correlation coefficient indicates the *strength* of the association between two variables. This coefficient can vary between 0 and ±1.00. The coefficient is usually represented by the letter *r* (for example, $r = .45$). A coefficient near 0 tells us that there is no relationship between two variables. A coefficient of +1.00 or −1.00 indicates that there is a perfect, one-to-one correspondence between two variables. A perfect correlation is found only rarely when working with real data. The closer the coefficient is to either −1.00 or +1.00, the stronger the relationship is.

The direction and strength of correlations can be illustrated graphically in scatter diagrams (see **Figure B.8**). A ***scatter diagram* is a graph in which paired X and Y scores for each subject are plotted as single points.** **Figure B.8** shows scatter diagrams for positive correlations in the upper half and for negative correlations in the bottom half. A perfect positive correlation and a perfect negative correlation are shown on the far left. When a correlation is perfect, the data points in the scatter diagram fall exactly in a straight line. However, positive and negative correlations yield lines slanted in the opposite direction because the lines map out opposite types of associations. Moving to the right in **Figure B.8**, you can see what happens when the magnitude

Figure B.8

Scatter diagrams of positive and negative correlations. Scatter diagrams plot paired *X* and *Y* scores as single points. Score plots slanted in the opposite direction result from positive (top row) as opposed to negative (bottom row) correlations. Moving across both rows (to the right), you can see that progressively weaker correlations result in more and more scattered plots of data points.

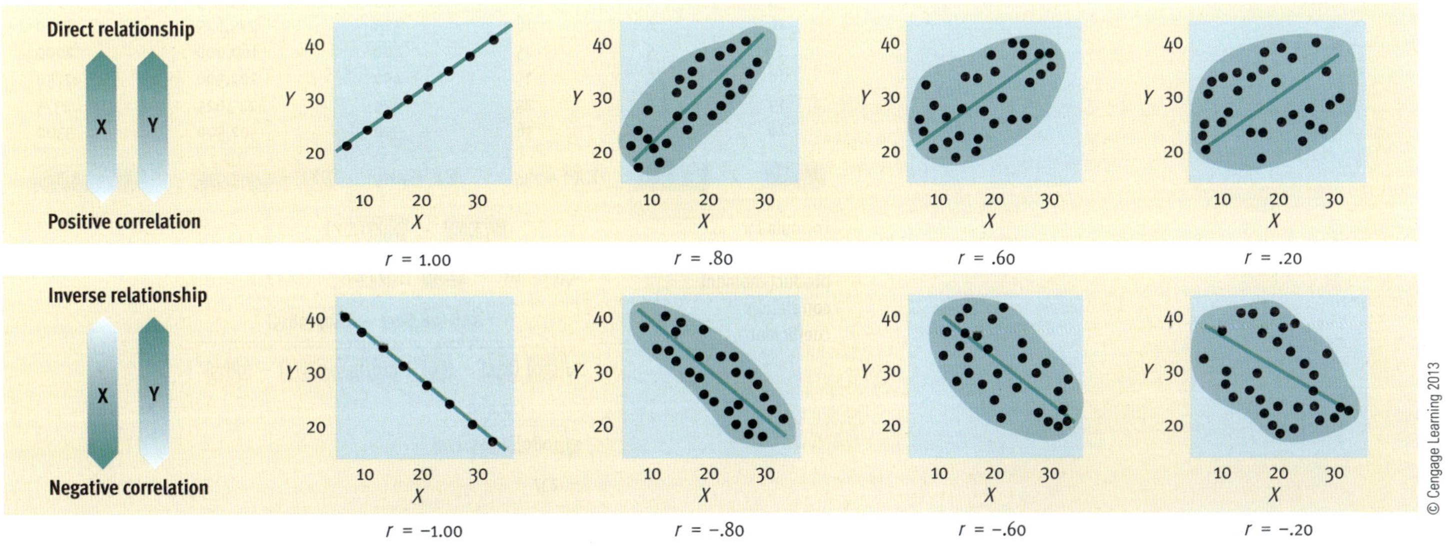

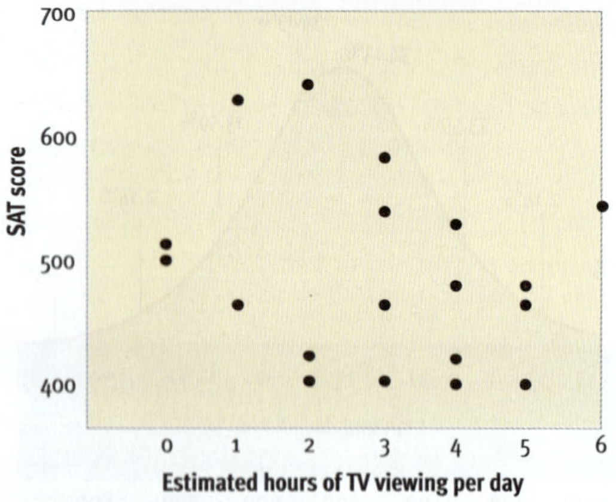

Figure B.9
Scatter diagram of the correlation between TV viewing and SAT scores. Our hypothetical data relating TV viewing to SAT scores are plotted in this scatter diagram. Compare it to the scatter diagrams seen in **Figure B.8** and see whether you can estimate the correlation between TV viewing and SAT scores in our data (see the text for the answer). © Cengage Learning 2013

of a correlation decreases. The data points scatter farther and farther from the straight line that would represent a perfect relationship.

What about our data relating TV viewing to SAT scores? **Figure B.9** shows a scatter diagram of these data. Having just learned about scatter diagrams, perhaps you can estimate the magnitude of the correlation between TV viewing and SAT scores. The scatter diagram of our data looks a lot like the one seen in the bottom right corner of **Figure B.8**, suggesting that the correlation will be in the vicinity of −.20.

The formula for computing the most widely used measure of correlation—the Pearson product-moment correlation—is shown in **Figure B.10**, along with the calculations for our data on TV viewing and SAT scores. The data yield a correlation of $r = -.24$. This coefficient of correlation reveals that we have found a weak inverse association between TV viewing and performance on the SAT. Among our participants, as TV viewing increases, SAT scores decrease, but the trend isn't very strong. We can get a better idea of how strong this correlation is by examining its predictive power.

Correlation and Prediction 1d

As the magnitude of a correlation increases (gets closer to either −1.00 or +1.00), our ability to predict one variable based on knowledge of the other variable steadily increases. This relationship between the

Figure B.10
Computing a correlation coefficient. The calculations required to compute the Pearson product-moment coefficient of correlation are shown here. The formula looks intimidating, but it's just a matter of filling in the figures taken from the sums of the columns shown above the formula. © Cengage Learning 2013

Subject number	TV viewing score (X)	X^2	SAT score (Y)	Y^2	XY
1	0	0	500	250,000	0
2	0	0	515	265,225	0
3	1	1	450	202,500	450
4	1	1	650	422,500	650
5	2	4	400	160,000	800
6	2	4	675	455,625	1350
7	2	4	425	180,625	850
8	3	9	400	160,000	1200
9	3	9	450	202,500	1350
10	3	9	500	250,000	1500
11	3	9	550	302,500	1650
12	3	9	600	360,000	1800
13	4	16	400	160,000	1600
14	4	16	425	180,625	1700
15	4	16	475	225,625	1900
16	4	16	525	275,625	2100
17	5	25	400	160,000	2000
18	5	25	450	202,500	2250
19	5	25	475	225,625	2375
20	6	36	550	302,500	3300
$N = 20$	$\Sigma X = 60$	$\Sigma X^2 = 234$	$\Sigma Y = 9815$	$\Sigma Y^2 = 4{,}943{,}975$	$\Sigma XY = 28{,}825$

Formula for Pearson product-moment correlation coefficient

$$r = \frac{(N)\Sigma XY - (\Sigma X)(\Sigma Y)}{\sqrt{[(N)\Sigma X^2 - (\Sigma X)^2][(N)\Sigma Y^2 - (\Sigma Y)^2]}}$$

$$= \frac{(20)(28{,}825) - (60)(9815)}{\sqrt{[(20)(234) - (60)^2][(20)(4{,}943{,}975) - (9815)^2]}}$$

$$= \frac{-12{,}400}{\sqrt{[1080][2{,}545{,}275]}}$$

$$= -.237$$

magnitude of a correlation and predictability can be quantified precisely. All we have to do is square the correlation coefficient (multiply it by itself) and this gives us the ***coefficient of determination*, the percentage of variation in one variable that can be predicted based on the other variable.** Thus, a correlation of .70 yields a coefficient of determination of .49 ($.70 \times .70 = .49$), indicating that variable *X* can account for 49% of the variation in variable *Y*. **Figure B.11** shows how the coefficient of determination goes up as the magnitude of a correlation increases.

Unfortunately, a correlation of .24 doesn't give us much predictive power. We can account only for a little over 6% of the variation in variable *Y*. So, if we tried to predict individuals' SAT scores based on how much TV they watched, our predictions wouldn't be very accurate. Although a low correlation doesn't have much practical, predictive utility, it may still have theoretical value. Just knowing that there is a relationship between two variables can be theoretically interesting. However, we haven't yet addressed the question of whether our observed correlation is strong enough to support our hypothesis that there is a relationship between TV viewing and SAT scores. To make this judgment, we have to turn to *inferential statistics* and the process of hypothesis testing.

Hypothesis Testing

Inferential statistics go beyond the mere description of data. ***Inferential statistics* are used to interpret data and draw conclusions.** They permit researchers to decide whether their data support their hypotheses.

In Chapter 2, we showed how inferential statistics can be used to evaluate the results of an experiment; the same process can be applied to correlational data. In our study of TV viewing we hypothesized that we would find an inverse relationship between amount of TV watched and SAT scores. Sure enough, that's what we found. However, we have to ask ourselves a critical question: Is this observed correlation large enough to support our hypothesis, or might a correlation of this size have occurred by chance?

We have to ask a similar question nearly every time we conduct a study. Why? Because we are working only with a sample. In research, we observe a limited *sample* (in this case, 20 participants) to draw conclusions about a much larger *population* (college students in general). There's always a possibility that if we drew a different sample from the population, the results might be different. Perhaps our results are unique to our sample and not generalizable to the larger population. If we were able to collect data on the entire population, we would not have to wrestle with this problem, but our dependence on a sample necessitates the use of inferential statistics to precisely evaluate the likelihood that our results are due to chance factors in sampling. Thus, inferential statistics are the key to making the inferential leap from the sample to the population (see **Figure B.12** on the next page).

Although it may seem backward, in hypothesis testing we formally test the *null hypothesis*. As applied to correlational data, the ***null hypothesis* is the assumption that there is no true relationship between the variables observed.** In our study, the null hypothesis is that there is no genuine association between TV viewing and SAT scores. We want to determine whether our results will permit us to *reject* the null hypothesis and thus conclude that our *research hypothesis* (that there *is* a relationship between the

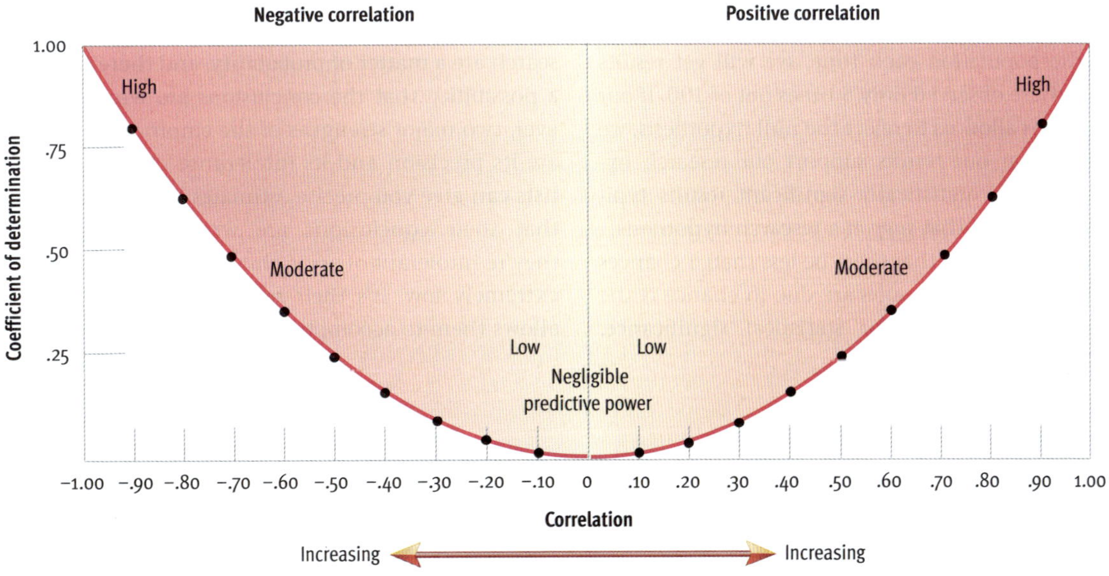

Figure B.11
Correlation and the coefficient of determination. The coefficient of determination is an index of a correlation's predictive power. As you can see, whether positive or negative, stronger correlations yield greater predictive power. © Cengage Learning 2013

Figure B.12

The relationship between the population and the sample. In research, we are usually interested in a broad population, but we can observe only a small sample from the population. After making observations of our sample, we draw inferences about the population, based on the sample. This inferential process works well as long as the sample is reasonably representative of the population. © Cengage Learning 2013

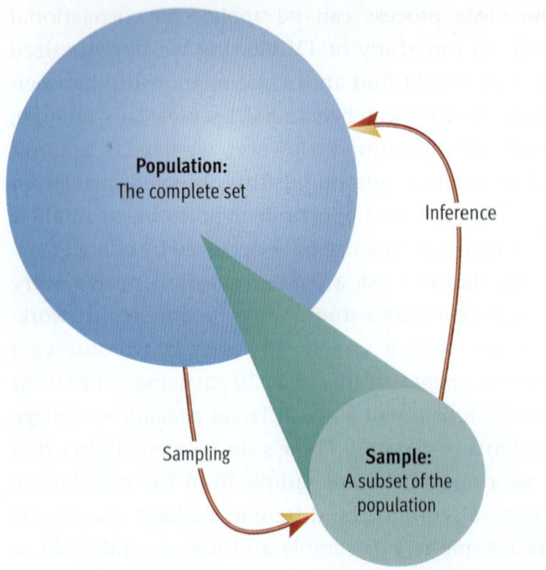

variables) has been supported. Why do we directly test the null hypothesis instead of the research hypothesis? Because our probability calculations depend on assumptions tied to the null hypothesis. Specifically, we compute the probability of obtaining the results that we have observed if the null hypothesis is indeed true. The calculation of this probability hinges on a number of factors. A key factor is the amount of variability in the data, which is why the standard deviation is an important statistic.

Statistical Significance

When we reject the null hypothesis, we conclude that we have found *statistically significant* results. *Statistical significance* is said to exist when the probability that the observed findings are due to chance is very low, usually less than 5 chances in 100. This means that if the null hypothesis is correct and we conduct our study 100 times, drawing a new sample from the population each time, we will get results such as those observed only 5 times out of 100. If our calculations allow us to reject the null hypothesis, we conclude that our results support our research hypothesis. Thus, statistically significant results typically are findings that *support* a research hypothesis.

The requirement that there be less than 5 chances in 100 that research results are due to chance is the *minimum* requirement for statistical significance. When this requirement is met, we say the results are significant at the .05 level. If researchers calculate that there is less than 1 chance in 100 that their results are due to chance factors in sampling, the results are significant at the .01 level. If there is less than a 1 in 1000 chance that findings are attributable to sampling error, the results are significant at the .001 level. Thus, there are several levels of significance that you may see cited in scientific articles.

Because we are only dealing in matters of probability, there is always the possibility that our decision to accept or reject the null hypothesis is wrong. The various significance levels indicate the probability of erroneously rejecting the null hypothesis (and inaccurately accepting the research hypothesis). At the .05 level of significance, there are 5 chances in 100 that we have made a mistake when we conclude that our results support our hypothesis, and at the .01 level of significance the chance of an erroneous conclusion is 1 in 100. Although researchers hold the probability of this type of error quite low, the probability is never zero. This is one of the reasons that competently executed studies of the same question can yield contradictory findings. The differences may be due to chance variations in sampling that can't be prevented.

What do we find when we evaluate our data linking TV viewing to students' SAT scores? The calculations indicate that, given our sample size and the variability in our data, the probability of obtaining a correlation of −.24 by chance is greater than 20%. That's not a high probability, but it's *not* low enough to reject the null hypothesis. Thus, our findings are not strong enough to allow us to conclude that we have supported our hypothesis.

Statistics and Empiricism

In summary, conclusions based on empirical research are a matter of probability, and there's always a possibility that the conclusions are wrong. However, two major strengths of the empirical approach are its precision and its intolerance of error. Scientists can give you precise estimates of the likelihood that their conclusions are wrong, and because they're intolerant of error, they hold this probability extremely low. It's their reliance on statistics that allows them to accomplish these goals.

Industrial/Organizational Psychology

by Kathy A. Hanisch (Iowa State University)

You have applied for a job, submitted your résumé, and taken a series of tests. You have been interviewed by your potential supervisor and given a tour of the company. You now find yourself sitting across from the co-owners, who have just offered you a position. They tell you that their organization is a great place to work. As evidence, they tell you that no one has quit their job in the last five years and that employees are rarely absent. They also tell you that they have flexible policies. You can work whatever hours you like and take vacation whenever you want. And if you decide to work for them, you will have access to spending cash as well as keys to the company.

You try to maintain your composure. You had heard interesting things about this company but didn't really believe them. Finally, the co-owners ask you what you are worth, indicating they will pay you whatever you wish. Now you're really dumbfounded and wonder what the catch is, but sit quietly while they talk about other issues. Does this sound too good to be true? Wouldn't this be ideal?

Almost this exact scenario played out in an organization owned and managed by an Oakland appliance dealer in the 1970s. His name was Arthur Friedman, and he had decided to change how he ran his business. Friedman, as reported in the *Washington Post* (Koughan, 1975), announced at one of his staff meetings that employees could work the hours they wanted, be paid what they thought they were worth, take vacation time and time off from work whenever they wanted, and help themselves to petty cash if they were in need of spending money. New employees would be allowed to set their own wages too. As you might imagine, the employees weren't sure how to take this news. It was reported that no one said anything during the meeting when Friedman first described his plan (Koughan, 1975).

When asked why he was changing his business practices, Friedman replied, "I always said that if you give people what they want, you get what you want. You have to be willing to lose, to stick your neck out. I finally decided that the time had come to practice what I preached" (Koughan, 1975). In the final analysis, Friedman's experiment worked. The organization was profitable. Friedman signed union contracts without reading them (the employees didn't need a union with him in charge). Employees didn't quit, they didn't steal from the company, and they were rarely absent. Net profits increased at SAS, and the company was a success. The employees realized that to make the organization work and remain in business, they had to be reasonable in their requests and behavior (Koughan, 1975).

A more recent company receiving high praise from its employees is SAS, a business analytics software and services company headquartered in North Carolina. In 2010 and 2011, *Fortune* magazine rated it the number-one company to work for. Employees at SAS receive 90% coverage of their health care premiums, unlimited sick days, free health care with an onsite medical center that has a $4.5 million budget (it still saves the company $5 million a year), company-paid life insurance, paid paternity leave, subsidized child care and cafeteria, free fitness center and swimming pool, and summer camps for children (Kaplan, 2010). In addition, employees at SAS receive three weeks of paid vacation when they start and another week after they have worked for SAS for 10 years. The company also has an on-site billiards hall, sauna, manicurist, hair salon, and many massage offerings. Company picnics and other family events (that employees and their families want to attend), as well as snacks on different days (fruit, donuts, and M&M days) are additional

SAS Institute provides many employee benefits and perks including 35-hour work weeks, three weeks of paid vacation, a free on-site health clinic, subsidized daycare, free swimming pools and exercise facilities, and unlimited sick days, in addition to many other benefits. Would you want to work for SAS?

© WRAL News

benefits for employees. SAS also rewards innovation and taking chances while supporting the growth of employees both personally and professionally. Under the leadership of Jim Goodnight, SAS has made the Top 100 companies since *Fortune* started ranking companies in 1998; a business with such a distinction is known as a *Fortune* "All Star."

Organizations such as Friedman's company and SAS are interesting in the way they deal with their employees and in the ways such treatment affects their employees' attitudes and behaviors. Psychologists who study people's behavior at work are called *industrial and organizational psychologists*. ***Industrial and organizational (I/O) psychology* is the branch of psychology concerned with human behavior in the work environment.** Work is an important avenue of study for psychology because of its link to the health of the American economy, as well as people's feelings of self-worth and well-being. I/O psychologists assist organizations in important areas such as motivating employees, alleviating job stress, hiring the best workers, evaluating job performance, designing and evaluating training programs, helping with communication issues, designing effective systems for work, helping to change an organization's culture, conducting research on how to select the best leaders and how to assign employees to work teams, and combating safety problems. This appendix will introduce you to the field of I/O psychology.

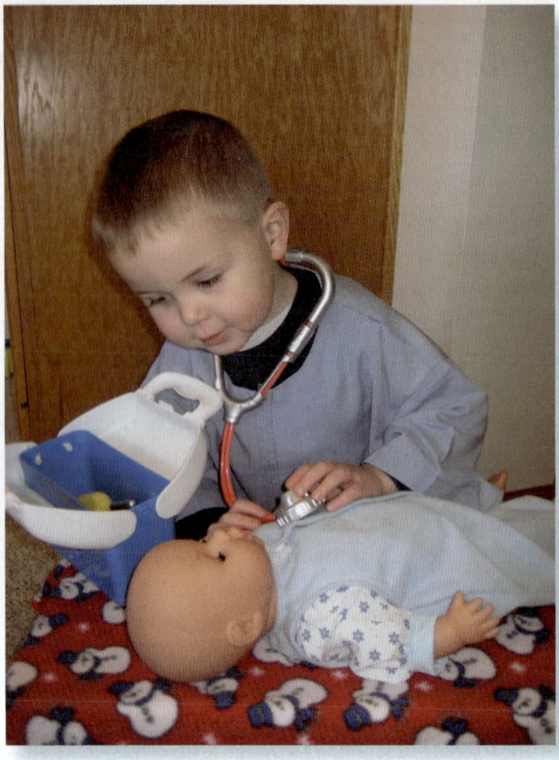

The doctor is in! Socialization about the nature and importance of work begins very early in life.

The Role of Work in People's Lives

You have learned about work since you were a small child. You may have asked where your mother was going when she took you to day care or why your father left the house before 8:00 A.M. and did not return until after 5:00 P.M. You likely "played" at different jobs by dressing up as an astronaut, firefighter, teacher, chef, or construction worker. As you got older, other sources of information about work may have come from your friends, grandparents, neighbors, school, and the media. In high school, more education and a part-time job may have given you additional details about the meaning of work. As you pursue a college degree, you may receive information about the work and jobs available in your chosen field through classes, internships, volunteer work, or other job experiences.

Work is an important part of life for most people. We often ask people we meet what they "do," which translates into "What is your job and for whom do you work?" Many people identify with their work because they spend so much of their waking lives working. Work provides many of the things people need and value. Work for pay provides the money necessary to satisfy people's basic needs for food, shelter, and security (health care, retirement income). Any "leftover" money provides discretionary funds that can go toward dinner and a movie, an iPad, or a nice place to live, or that can be used to support charities, attend athletic or fine art performances, or save money for college. Money from work provides people with a standard of living that depends on their income and how they choose to spend it. And work offers much more: a source of social interactions and friendships, independence, a sense of accomplishment, satisfaction, a reason to get up in the morning, happiness, a sense of identity, recognition, and prestige.

Every year the Jobs Rated Report evaluates jobs to determine the best and worst overall experience for the majority of employees in those jobs. The five factors considered in their ratings are: work environment, physical demands, outlook, income, and stress (Strieber, 2011). **Figure C.1** presents a listing of the ten best and worst jobs for 2011 based on these five factors. The worst jobs have poorer work environments, are more demanding physically, have a poorer future outlook, have lower incomes, and are more stressful than the jobs rated among the best. These five factors are important to most employees, but the rank order of them may vary from

Best jobs of 2011	Worst jobs of 2011
Software engineer	Roustabout
Mathematician	Ironworker
Actuary	Lumberjack
Statistician	Roofer
Computer systems analyst	Taxi driver
Meteorologist	Emergency medical technician
Biologist	Welder
Historian	Painter
Audiologist	Meter reader
Dental hygienist	Construction worker

© Cengage Learning 2013

Figure C.1

Best and worst rated jobs of 2011. Jobs Rated researchers evaluated 200 jobs on the five factors of work environment, physical demands, outlook, income, and stress to determine the best and worst jobs based on those factors. The goal of the research was to determine how satisfying each profession would tend to be for a majority of workers. Almost all employees value, to some degree, these five factors although the rank order will vary based on individual differences.

SOURCE: http://www.careercast.com/jobs-rated/10-best-jobs-2011; http://www.careercast.com/jobs-rated/10-worst-jobs-2011

person to person. You may value a positive outlook for a job because of the implications for future employment over the job's income, while your friend may value a positive work environment over both the outlook and income factors. What is valued or sought from work varies from person to person, and hence the ratings are for the majority of employees and not everyone.

It is important to understand what you want from your work as well as what a job can provide, because these factors have implications for your well-being and success in life. From an employer's perspective, it is useful to determine what employees want from their work and organization because satisfied employees will be more likely than dissatisfied employees to work diligently to meet organizational goals. Part of a supervisor's job is to determine what employees value, because those values can be used to motivate employees to perform well in their jobs.

Regardless of the type of job you obtain, it is likely that you will spend most of your waking hours in some type of employment for many years. Many people spend their weekends working, too. Because work is critical to who you are and what you do, studying the psychological principles and some of the topics examined by I/O psychologists will provide you with information that may be useful to you in your future careers. Before focusing on the specific aspects of getting and keeping a job, let's briefly explore the subfields of I/O psychology and possible career paths in this area.

Subfields and Other Aspects of I/O Psychology

I/O psychology is made up of three specialty areas, including the two that define its name: *industrial (I) psychology* and *organizational (O) psychology*. The third area is known as *human factors* or *human engineering psychology*. ***Industrial psychology*** **(also known as *personnel psychology*) deals with how to select individuals for the right positions, how to evaluate their job performance, how to train them, and how to compensate them.** This is the oldest of the three subfields. The broad areas of job analysis, job evaluation, test validation, employee selection (including interviewing), employee training, legal issues (including employment discrimination in the organization), and performance evaluation are included in this subfield. ***Organizational psychology*** **is concerned with how employees are integrated into the work environment from both emotional and social perspectives.** Some of the areas covered include job satisfaction, job stress, work motivation, leadership, organizational culture, teamwork, and organizational development. Although not included in the field's name, human factors psychology is also an important specialty within I/O psychology. ***Human factors*** **(or *human engineering*) *psychology* examines the ways in which work, systems, and system features can be designed or changed to most effectively correspond with the capabilities and limitations of individuals, often with a focus on the human body.** Examples of topics in this area include redesigning machines to be easier on the body, changing the positions of controls on machines to reduce the number of accidents, modifying displays so that the user can quickly determine the information presented, and making the job more interesting by increasing the types of skills needed to perform the work. All three areas—industrial psychology, organizational psychology, and human factors psychology—are interrelated when addressing problems or issues in the world of business and industry.

Most I/O psychologists have graduate degrees that typically require an additional two to five years of school beyond the bachelor's degree. I/O psychologists obtain jobs primarily in four work settings: industry, academia, consulting firms, and government, with the largest percentage in industry and academia. **Figure C.2** on the next page provides examples of typical job postings for I/O psychologists taken from recent recruitment ads for each of the four areas.

Figure C.2

Recruitment advertisements for I/O psychologists. Abbreviated versions of recent ads for positions available for individuals with I/O psychology degrees are shown here. Educational requirements vary with years of experience for all of the positions except the academic position which requires a Ph.D. © Cengage Learning 2013

The Society for Industrial and Organizational Psychology (SIOP) is the primary professional organization for I/O psychologists. It has approximately 6000 members, including individuals from academia, industry, consulting positions, and the government. The SIOP website (www.siop.org) is a great resource for information about graduate school, jobs, and recent articles in I/O psychology.

In the United States, a fairly recent advance of relevance to the I/O field is the development of the *Occupational Information Network (O*NET)*. The O*NET is a comprehensive, detailed, and flexible set of job descriptors based on an extensive research program (Peterson et al., 1999), which can be accessed via the Internet at www.onetonline.org. O*NET can be used to find details about occupations (for example, tasks, knowledge, skills, work activities, wages, employment outlook) or to select preferred work activities or interests and locate corresponding occupations. It is a helpful starting point for individuals seeking details about the types of occupations that may interest them, as well as the salary and occupational outlook for various occupations. It is also useful to employers who need to develop thorough job descriptions for their organizations. Although there have been some concerns about its coverage and information, O*NET is viewed as a major achievement in occupational information (Sackett & Laczo, 2003), with continual updates to the information provided. Using O*NET, the projected growth for I/O psychologists for 2008–2018 is 20% or higher, which is much faster than average.

Employee Selection

One of the most important tasks for any business enterprise is to select talented, motivated employees who will work hard to help the organization meet its goals. As you will see in this section, the task of employee selection is complicated and must be handled with sensitivity and fairness.

The Hiring Process

In the early 1900s, when someone needed a job he or she would hang around the outside of a company and wait to see whether the company needed workers. Many times the people who worked for the company told their friends or relatives about possible job openings, prompting them to apply for work. This often meant that individuals hired for the available jobs were similar to those working there (such as white males). Industrial and organizational psychologists first became involved in the process of selecting employees when the United States government needed help selecting and placing officers and soldiers in World War I (Aamodt, 2010). They used mental ability tests to determine who would become officers and who would be assigned to the infantry. The process many employers use now to hire employees is very detailed, typically consisting of five components: job analysis, testing, legal issues, recruitment, and the selection decision.

Job Analysis

***Job analysis* is a method for breaking a job into its constituent parts.** I/O psychologists have helped devise effective strategies for determining three basic aspects of any job: (1) What tasks and behaviors are essential to the job? (2) What knowledge, skills, abilities, and other characteristics are needed to perform the job? and (3) What are the conditions (such as stress, safety, and temperature) under which the job is performed? A job analysis can be conducted in many ways. An analyst may interview current employees, have employees complete questionnaires, observe people in the job, or talk to subject matter experts about the job (Gael, 1988).

I/O psychologists continue to research effective job analysis techniques. Current research suggests that worker-oriented methods are best for employee selection because of their focus on the worker as opposed to the tasks (Aamodt, 2010). One worker-oriented method is the Critical Incident Technique (CIT), which uses critical incidents or behaviors that discriminate between excellent and poor behavior for someone performing the job (Flanagan, 1954). For example, excellent behavior for a refrigerator repairperson might be a follow-up phone call after the in-home repair to inquire if the refrigerator is working well.

The information from a job analysis is used in many types of personnel functions, including employee selection, performance appraisal, training, and human resources planning. Within the hiring process, job analysis is used to write job descriptions; to determine what tests might be used to assess the knowledge and skills of job applicants; and to assist in meeting legal requirements that affect the selection process.

Testing and Other Employee Selection Procedures

The next step in employee selection is assessing whether job candidates have the attributes required for specific jobs that are available. Employers use a variety of employee selection tools, including individual and panel interviews, standardized paper-and-pencil tests of abilities and knowledge, assessments of relevant personality traits, such as conscientiousness, and integrity tests. In addition, work samples, in which applicants do a replica of the work they will be asked to do on the job, can be useful. Reference checks, Internet searches, criminal background checks, and drug testing may also be used to help identify the best potential employees depending on the position. Selection procedures that are properly developed and carefully used are vital to the success of organizations.

Psychological testing has long played an important role in employee selection efforts. As noted in Chapter 9, a ***psychological test* is a standardized measure of a sample of a person's behavior.** Employers can purchase tests from commercial test publishers or can develop special tests to meet their own needs. Early on in the process of using a test, it behooves organizations to assess the *reliability* and *validity* of their test, as discussed in Chapter 9. ***Reliability* refers to the measurement consistency of a test (or of other kinds of measurement techniques).** Reliable tests yield similar results over the course of multiple testings. ***Validity* refers to the ability of a test to measure what it was designed to measure.** Evidence regarding validity is crucial when tests are used for employee selection purposes. When an organization purchases a commercial test for use, the information about reliability and validity is normally provided by the test publisher.

Once a suitable test has been found or developed, the next step is to administer it to job candidates and decide which of them has the greatest probability of being successful on the job. Justifying the use of psychological testing in hiring depends on collecting data demonstrating a relationship between test scores and performance on the job. In a simple scenario the scores job applicants achieve on a test are compared to their job performance ratings or evaluations some time after hire (e.g., six months, one year). These comparisons can be used to calculate a correlation coefficient that will indicate the strength of the relation between the test scores and job performance. The ideal relationship would be a strong positive correlation that would indicate that as test scores improve, job performance ratings improve and alternatively, as test scores decrease, job performance decreases. A graph illustrating this type of relationship is shown in **Figure C.3**.

Personality testing appears quite frequently in employers' selection processes. One type of personality test being used by many organizations is the integrity test. ***Integrity tests* are standardized measures used to assess attitudes and experiences related to honesty and trustworthiness.** Employers

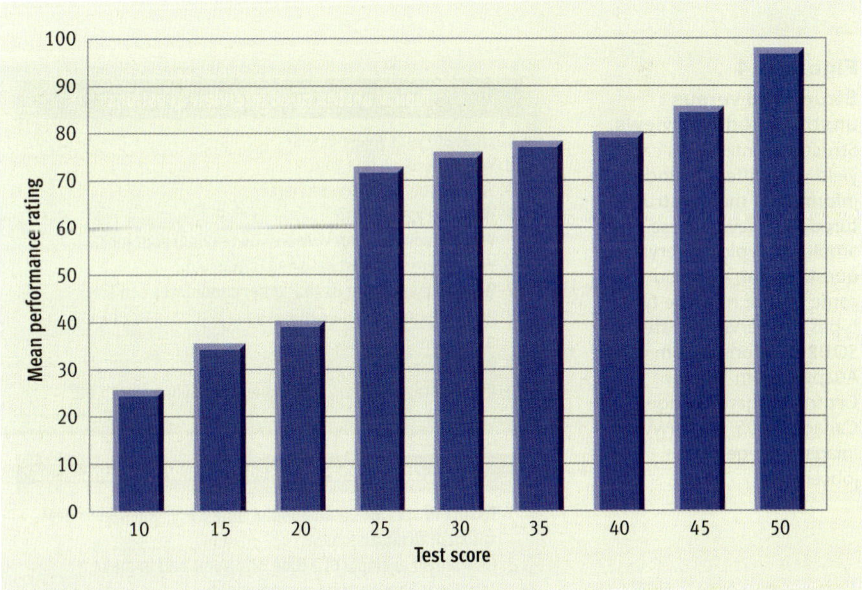

© Cengage Learning 2013

Figure C.3

A hypothetical example of the relationship between test scores and job performance. When a standardized test is used to select the most promising job candidates, the expectation is that higher scores on the test will be associated with better performance on the job. The relationship won't be perfect, but when employers look at the relationship between test scores and subsequent performance ratings, the findings should resemble the hypothetical data shown here. These data would yield a very strong positive correlation between test scores and job performance, indicating the test is a good predictor of job performance.

want to be able to use these tests to help them choose applicants who are dependable, honest, and trustworthy. Research indicates that integrity tests are reliable and are moderately predictive of the likelihood of theft, absenteeism, or poor performance (Aamodt, 2010) as well as a reduction in compensation claims (Sturman & Sherwyn, 2007).

Although standardized mental ability and personality tests are commonly used in personnel selection, the most widely used device remains the interview. Nearly all organizations use some type of employee interview in their selection process (Salgado, Viswesvaran, & Ones, 2003). There are two broad types of interviews: unstructured and structured (see **Figure C.4**). *Unstructured interviews* are informal; different job candidates are asked different questions with no scoring key, and there is no method for assigning scores to applicants. Although many employers rely heavily on this type of interview, research suggests that it is highly subjective and does not provide very reliable or useful information in the selection of employees (Aamodt, 2010). *Structured interviews* are more like standardized tests. The same questions are asked of all candidates by a trained interviewer and are based on attributes necessary for success on the job in question (based on the job analysis). There are clear guidelines for judging the adequacy of the answers given, and the scores assigned to an applicant have known relationships to the attributes being measured. Structured interviews can be constructed to be reliable and valid (McDaniel et al., 1994). In addition, they hold the promise of supplying useful information *not* supplied by psychological testing (about characteristics such as oral comprehension, communication and listening skills, and motivation).

Figure C.4

Structured versus unstructured interviews. Structured interviews can yield very different kinds of information than unstructured interviews. These examples of typical interview questions can give you some idea of how the two types of interviews differ. SOURCE: Monster.com. Adapted from The Job Centre, Niagara College Canada, 2005, http://www.niagaracollege.ca/jobcentre/

Typical unstructured interview questions

1. What are your weaknesses?
2. Why should we hire you?
3. Why do you want to work here?
4. What are your goals?
5. Why did you leave (or why are you leaving) your job?
6. When were you most satisfied in your job?
7. What can you do for us that other candidates can't?
8. What are three positive things your last boss would say about you?
9. What salary are you seeking?
10. If you were an animal, which one would you want to be?

SOURCE: Monster.com

Structured behavior-based interview questions

1. Tell me in specific detail about a time when you had to deal with a difficult customer.
2. Give me an example of a time when you had to make a decision without a supervisor present.
3. Give me a specific example of when you demonstrated your initiative in an employment setting.
4. Give me an example of a time when you had to work with a team.
5. Describe a time when you had to be creative at solving a problem.

SOURCE: Adapted from The Job Centre, Niagara College Canada, 2005, http://jobs.niagarac.on.ca/

© Cengage Learning 2013

Legal Issues

One of the most important pieces of legislation regarding employment, and specifically the hiring of employees, is Title VII of the Civil Rights Act of 1964 (Equal Employment Opportunity Commission, 2002). Title VII "prohibits discrimination based on race, color, religion, sex, and national origin," referred to in some quarters as the "Big 5." Providing protection based on the Big 5 helps ensure that all applicants have an equal opportunity for employment. Exceptions to this provision include matters of national security, employers with seniority systems in place, and *bona fide occupational qualifications (BFOQs).* BFOQs permit organizations to discriminate in hiring persons in a protected class if the qualification is determined to be reasonably necessary to the operation of the business. For example, women can be discriminated against when hiring someone to model men's swimwear, and vice versa. It is reasonably necessary to the marketing and selling of swimwear that organizations hire men to model male swimwear and women to model female swimwear; sex is a thus a BFOQ in this case. It is not reasonably necessary, however, that a secretary in a church who does secretarial work and not church or religious work be the same religion as the church that employs him or her; religion could not be used as a BFOQ in this case.

It is important for employers to abide by laws that protect people against discrimination, as the costs of litigation can be very high, in terms of both financial costs and the organization's reputation. This situation applies to discrimination based not only on the Big 5, covered under the Civil Rights Act, but also on age (Age Discrimination in Employment Act) and disability (Americans with Disabilities Act), as well as other federal and state acts prohibiting discrimination. Employment law in the United States is meant to protect and provide equal opportunities for all individuals.

Countries differ with regard to fair employment practices, laws, and what is considered discriminatory in the employment setting. The United States has several acts that prohibit discrimination based on a number of group characteristics. Other countries allow what would be considered discrimination in the United States. A job listing ad in 2010 in Chengdu, China, illustrates this point. The job ad-

© Fotosearch/Age fotostock RF

© CORBIS/Age fotostock RF

What would happen to these advertisements for swimwear if each model's gender was the opposite? Sex is a BFOQ in this case.

vertised was for a city warden, which is similar to our law enforcement jobs. The ad reads as follows:

Must be young, female and pretty. Only good-looking women under 23 need apply to become a Chengdu law enforcement officer. Specifically, candidates for law enforcement jobs must be female, aged between 18 and 23, over 5'2" tall, attractive and with a good temperament. Their contracts will end when they turn 26." (Molland, 2010)

This ad and its job requirements would not be legal in the United States. It specifies that the applicant must be female, which would be illegal under Title VII that prohibits discrimination based on sex. It also specifies an age range of 18–23 with retirement at age 26, which would be illegal in most states. U.S. federal law prohibits age discrimination once a person reaches the age of 40 (Age Discrimination in Employment Act). It is likely that men and those older than 23 and even 26 could perform the job just as well.

Nondiscriminatory hiring practices attempt to guarantee fair treatment for any person looking for a job. In the United States, organizations with several employees (typically 15) are required to abide by employment laws. Equal opportunity laws make the job market a more level playing field in the United States than in many countries.

Recruitment

***Recruitment* is the process organizations use to identify potential employees for a job.** Depending on the job, an organization may recruit from inside the company or seek someone from outside the organization. Openings may be advertised on the company's website or on a site for specific types of jobs. In addition, websites such as monster.com, hotjobs.com, and careerbuilder.com link potential employees and employers in a variety of jobs and locations. Other recruitment sources include newspapers, radio and television advertisements, trade magazines, professional publications, and employee referrals.

Research indicates that employees recruited through *inside sources,* such as employee referrals, tend to hold their jobs longer and to exhibit better job performance than those recruited through *outside sources,* such as advertisements, employment agencies, and recruiters (Zottoli & Wanous, 2000). Studies have supported the idea that those recruited using inside sources receive more accurate information about the job (a realistic job preview) than those recruited through external sources (Conrad & Ashworth, 1986; McManus & Baratta, 1992). Research also shows that employees who stay with the organization longer typically were referred by successful rather than unsuccessful employees (Aamodt & Rupert, 1990).

A survey of the fifty best small and medium organizations to work for in the United States found that 92% use employee referrals (Pomeroy, 2005). A recent survey by Buck Consultants (2011) showed that 66% of employers were using employee referral bonuses, which is up from 59% in 2010. Because of the effectiveness of employee referrals, companies provide rewards to employees who recommend an applicant who is hired. These rewards can include cash, vacations, and raffles for prizes such as televisions and free maid service for a year (Stewart et al., 1990). Typically, the new employee must work for the organization a set period of time for the referring employee to receive the award (Stewart et al., 1990). SAS Canada offers a bonus of up to $8,000 for a successful employee referral (Yerema & Leung, 2010).

After applicants have submitted either a résumé or an application, someone from the organization, such as the human resources manager or a supervisor, will determine which applicants should be considered further. In that process, he or she may make telephone inquiries of previous employers or other references and conduct criminal background checks to alleviate potential legal problems as well as to hire appropriate personnel. Reference checks can help organizations avoid costly errors in hiring. For instance, one company unknowingly hired someone who had just gotten out of jail and was on parole in another state (and was not supposed to leave the state). Upon finding out about the parole violation, the hiring company also found out that the new employee had been in jail for stealing from his previous employer. These types of hiring mistakes can often be avoided by conducting reference and background checks on job applicants.

Internet searches focusing on job applicants' background are becoming more common because of advances in technology and the ease with which employers can learn about potential employees before hiring them. Employers are searching social networking sites such as LinkedIn, Myspace and Facebook to learn about job applicants. On these sites, recruiters and companies have found promising candidates reporting on their drug use, sexual exploits, and drinking, along with suggestive photographs (Haefner, 2009). These indiscretions are considered "red flags" by employers. Companies generally assume that these applicants are lacking in good judgment and typically remove them from their selection process (Finder, 2006). Information that job applicants thought would only be viewed by their peers is making its way into the public arena at all levels, with future employers and relatives viewing

© Louis Quail/Corbis

Based on this photo, would you hire this job candidate? Employers are increasingly searching social networking web sites to gather information on prospective employees. In light of this reality, students may want to exercise more discretion about what they post online.

the information without the students' knowledge. In addition, some managers are using social networking sites to evaluate the professionalism of job applicants and determine whether they would fit in with their organizational culture (Hargis, 2008).

Making the Hiring Decision

When selecting employees, employers are looking for a good match between the employee and the organization. They would like to match the requirements for excellent job performance with the person's own knowledge, skills, abilities, personality, and motivation. They attempt to accomplish this by using the various selection tools discussed earlier.

Researchers have posited two factors that determine an employee's performance in a job: the "can-do" and the "will-do" factors (Schmitt et al., 2003). *Can-do factors* suggest what employees are capable of doing on the job if they are working to the best of their ability. *Will-do factors* suggest the time and effort employees are willing to exert for the organization. Personality factors such as conscientiousness and need for achievement as well as integrity have been classified as important will-do factors in performance (Schmitt et al., 2003). A person's can-do and will-do factors may change as he or she moves from organization to organization. Once a person is selected, the important process of being accepted and socialized into the organization at all levels begins.

Socializing Employees: Culture, Work Teams, Leadership, and Performance Appraisal

When you report for your first day of work in an organization, you will need to learn many things in order to be successful in your job. ***Organizational***

***socialization* refers to the process by which new members are absorbed into the culture of an organization** (Jablin, 1982). Organizational socialization consists of people learning how the organization operates by using information provided by management, co-workers, observation, company handbooks or memos, and organization websites.

Electronic communications are important avenues used to help socialize workers (Flanagin & Waldeck, 2004). Employees communicate and gather information through email, company websites, chat groups, and blogs. Job applicants may also use these resources to learn about an organization before submitting their applications. Consulting business websites is an excellent way for job applicants to assess whether there might be a good fit between them, job openings, and organizations.

Supervisors and co-workers are also important sources of socialization information. ***Mentoring* is a form of training in which a current and often long-term employee (the mentor) is paired with a new employee to aid his or her growth and development within the organization.** The mentor's role is to help the new employee adapt to the job by assisting with advice or resources. The mentor may provide information about how the organization works and about career advancement opportunities. Good mentoring helps new employees become successful on the job and learn the formal and informal rules of the organization (Aamodt, 2010).

Research indicates that both mentors and those they mentor often benefit from the relationship. For example, in a study of health care employees, it was found that those who were mentored reported higher salaries, greater promotion rates, and more positive career success than those who did not receive mentoring (Allen, Lentz, & Day, 2006). Employees who have been mentored experience more effective socialization and better compensation, advancement, career satisfaction, job satisfaction, job involvement, and organizational commitment than those with no mentoring (Greenhaus, 2003).

Organizational Culture and Climate

***Organizational culture* refers to the shared assumptions, beliefs, values, and customs of the people in an organization.** These cognitions then influence the *organizational climate,* which consists of employees' shared perceptions about specific aspects of the workplace environment. Because culture and climate generally operate in concert, our discussion will refer to these elements collectively as *culture* (Ostroff, Kinicki, & Tamkins, 2003). Organizational culture is important because it lets employees know what is expected of them and affects how they think and behave. Culture is often shaped by the founders of the organization, but it may be modified over time by other influential leaders and by the successes and failures of the organization.

"I don't know how it started, either. All I know is that it's part of our corporate culture."

©Mick Stevens/The New Yorker Collection/www.cartoonbank.com.

There have been several case studies of organizations that have successfully changed their culture. Remember Arthur Friedman from the beginning of this appendix? He allowed his employees to set their own wages and decide the hours they worked; he also required employees to belong to the union. After Friedman made these changes, employee grumbling stopped. The organizational culture changed, resulting in better morale, increased productivity, and longer employee tenure. No one wanted to quit working in a culture where the employees got to make their own decisions that affected the organization's bottom line. Finding an organizational culture that fits your working style is likely to have consequences for your morale, performance, and tenure in the organization.

Work Teams

Groups have been studied by social psychologists for more than 75 years (see Chapter 13). Research has focused on topics such as individual versus group problem solving (Hill, 1982; Paulus, 2000) and the effects of participation in decision making on members' satisfaction and performance (Likert, 1967; Sagie, 1997). Industrial and organizational psychologists have focused on studying teams in organizations because their use has been increasing in recent years; work is being organized around team-based structures instead of individual jobs (Lawler, Mohrman, & Ledford, 1995).

***Work teams,* or *work groups,* can be defined as two or more employees who have common goals,**

pursue tasks that are interdependent, interact socially, and work within specific requirements and rules (Kozlowski & Bell, 2003). Just as an organization can have its own culture, work teams exhibit subcultures that may encourage or discourage certain types of work-related behaviors and attitudes. These subcultures then form the basis for the socialization of new group or team members.

Virtual work teams are becoming more commonplace in the workforce because of the desire to involve employees with specific talents on projects and because of the globalization of many businesses. Virtual work teams can continue to function when members work from home, are away traveling, or are otherwise outside of the traditional office (Wiesenfeld, Raghuram, & Garud, 2001). Virtual work teams typically meet using some type of electronic technology. For example, they may communicate by email or teleconferencing. Virtual work teams have a number of advantages. They can provide a way for groups to collaborate more effectively and less expensively, they often reduce office space requirements if individuals can work from home, and they permit more flexibility for employees dealing with personal problems or long commutes.

Although most organizations provide formal means of socializing new employees, the dynamics and norms of a work team may have informal but substantial effects on employees' socialization (Anderson & Thomas, 1996). Of course, the outcomes of informal and formal socialization processes may be different. Work teams may have appointed leaders or they may be self-managing. When teams fail, the failure is often linked to the team leader. Team leaders may be too autocratic, wielding too much power or influence. As a result, the team does not realize the autonomy and control it needs to be successful (Stewart & Manz, 1995). Self-managing teams tend to show better productivity, an increase in work quality, improved quality of life for employees, decreased absenteeism, and decreased turnover (Cohen & Ledford, 1994).

Developing a work team may mean successfully integrating new employees into the team as well as helping with the transition of individuals into and out of the team, depending on the team's function. Team leaders are critical to the success of work teams' newcomers. Establishing and maintaining conditions wherein the team can perform well is also an important role for the team leader.

Virtual work teams, where team members interact using teleconferencing and email to get their work accomplished, have become more commonplace in the last decade because of advances in technology.

© AP Images/Tony Avelar

Leadership

Former U.S. President Dwight D. Eisenhower once said, "Leadership is the art of getting someone else to do something you want done because he wants to do it." As his remark suggests, ***leadership* involves influencing and motivating people to pursue organizational goals.** Leadership has received a lot of research attention in industrial and organizational psychology. Many theories exist, and most have been helpful in understanding what makes a good leader and how to improve leadership style.

Personality plays a key role in many leadership theories. Certainly, it is important in determining whether or not a leader will be successful. Kirkpatrick and Locke's (1991) review suggests that drive, honesty and integrity, self-confidence, cognitive abilities, and knowledge are associated with successful leaders. Leaders with poor cognitive abilities and social skills and those who are indecisive, low in self-confidence and self-esteem, dishonest, and lacking in ambition tend to be less successful (Kaplan, Drath, & Kofodimos, 1991).

Arthur Friedman's integrity likely made him a successful leader. He decided to give employees what he would want, providing them with the capability to make major decisions that could either make or break the organization. In his case, he created a self-managing group that had no need for external assistance from unions or other entities. As a result, Friedman demonstrated the transformational leadership approach (Bass, 1990). ***Transformational leadership* is characterized by high ethical standards, inspirational motivation, intellectual stimulation, and individual consideration**—all clearly evident in Arthur Friedman's leadership style.

Jim Goodnight, the CEO of SAS, believes that you should "treat employees like they make a difference and they will" (sas.com/jobs/corporate/index.html).

Courtesy SAS Institute, photo by Scott LeVoyer

Jim Goodnight, the co-founder and CEO of SAS Institute since 1976, is a proven leader with 12,000 employees all enjoying his famous family-friendly culture.

His philosophy is working because SAS, even with the economic turbulence of the past several years, has continued to grow and remain profitable. Other indicators of success include the company's number-one ranking in 2011 and 2010 by *Forbes* magazine, employee turnover of 2% in 2009 compared to the software industry average of 22%, and an employee average of only two sick days per year. A balanced work and personal life is important to Goodnight, so his employees work 35-hour workweeks with many of them setting their own hours. His company has tried to take care of many of the inconveniences in life such as haircuts, day care, and medical and fitness centers. SAS provides these services onsite so employees can focus on working effectively during their 7-hour days.

As a leader, Goodnight has espoused the virtues of management-by-loitering—showing up unexpectedly in a department and seeing how things are going there (Maney, 2004). He will step in and help fix a department or unit that isn't doing well or be part of a team made up of individuals from the work floor to come up with new and innovative ideas to make the organization prosper. As the CEO, Goodnight considered making SAS a public company, hired a consultant to help, and then surveyed SAS employees. In 2002, 87% of the employees voted not to go public because it would have hurt the organization's culture, partly because of the almost certain layoffs and restructuring that would occur if SAS were to become a public company (Maney, 2004). The vote, among other things, made the decision for Goodnight. He discarded the idea of going public even though it would have made him a very wealthy individual.

Performance Appraisal

Performance appraisals are the evaluations or reviews of employees' performance usually conducted by immediate supervisors. Although managers often focus on the yearly performance appraisal for their employees, performance evaluation and guidance should be a daily process in organizations. Employees should be given feedback on their job performance, both the good and the bad, by their employers. The formal, typically once-a-year, review is a time for organizational leaders to systematically evaluate an employee's performance, set goals and expectations, and directly convey information about the organization's culture (Fletcher, 2004).

Performance evaluations are important to (1) ensure that employees know the expectations of their employer from the time of hire, (2) effectively manage raises and promotions, (3) determine areas that need improvement and to praise good work, (4) deal with unproductive employees in a fair and appropriate manner that may include termination, and (5) assist in workforce planning with regard to promotions or layoffs depending on the economic conditions for specific organizations.

Performance evaluation forms should be provided to employees upon hire because they will provide a roadmap to success for them while also assisting employers in performance management. Providing the form at hire ensures that the expectations and requirements for satisfactory job performance are made known to new employees and that there aren't any surprises after hire with regard to performance expectations from either the employee's or management's perspective. The type of performance review system in place helps shape the culture of the organization. For example, if an employee's performance will be judged based on objective criteria set by management, then a more cooperative culture may be present, while performance that is judged relative to other employees may suggest a more competitive organizational culture.

Annual performance reviews are often completed using a form developed by the organization or obtained from a consultant. The form is typically completed by the employee's immediate supervisor, although some organizations have both the supervisor and employee complete the form and compare their ratings. After the form is completed, the employee and supervisor typically have a meeting lasting

Performance appraisals serve a variety of important functions for organizations.

© Paul Burns/Age fotostock RF

from a few minutes to up to an hour, preferably in a neutral location (such as conference room) free from distractions and interruptions.

Performance appraisals provide a validity check for the tests used to select employees in organizations. If an organization's selection system is valid, most employees will be successful and have satisfactory performance reviews. Once employees are hired who can complete the work necessary and be effective in the organization (i.e., they have the ability to do the job), employee attitudes become the most critical piece of information about the individual (Hanisch, 1995). Attitudes are important because they directly influence the work behaviors of employees

Training and Human Factors

Employers hope that the applicants they choose for positions in their organization will be great workers who are dependable and have good attitudes. However, sometimes a poor fit between the employee and the job indicates that some type of change may be needed in the employee, the job, or some specific aspect of the job. Trying to change the employee to better fit the job or work that needs to be done involves *training,* while changing the job to better fit the employee is a *human factors issue* (International Ergonomics Association, 2000). Both of these areas are important to organizations, and both types of changes can help organizations maximize job performance.

The premise behind training is that it will lead to learning that will in turn lead to an improvement in job performance. Important questions to address before conducting training include (1) What are the goals of the training program? (2) Who needs the training and for what purpose? and (3) What should the content of the training program be? The goals of the training program will likely come from the training department, human resources department, or a supervisor who has noticed an issue with one or more employees. Whatever the specific goals are for the organization, support from top management is critical for training to be a success. Deciding who needs training is relatively simple if an effective performance evaluation system is in place in the organization. Accurate and valid performance evaluation procedures can provide valuable information on who needs additional training.

All organizations must engage in some type of training for their employees, from orientation meetings to sessions on how to use a new software package or new machine. Many types of training are available, including both on-the-job and off-the-job programs. On-the-job training includes job rotation, mentoring (discussed earlier), and apprenticeships, while off-the-job training is the typical lecture or taped presentation. All of them can be effective under the right circumstances, so the training needs to be tailored to the employees who need the training and who would benefit the most. Important issues related to training include setting specific, concrete, and obtainable goals and motivating employees to attend the training and transfer it to their jobs (Aamodt, 2010). It is vital that the training program be evaluated to determine whether it is effective in changing behavior or improving performance and whether the cost is worth the results.

As noted earlier, *human factors psychology* examines the ways in which work, systems, and system features can be designed to most effectively correspond with the capabilities and limitations of workers. In other words, human factors is concerned with changing the system—in this case the work, the work environment, or the job itself—so that employees' interactions with it are better from a psychological, emotional, or physical standpoint. An important subfield of human factors work is *ergonomics,* which focuses on the capabilities and limitations of the human body. For example, if the desk chair that a computer programmer is using causes her back problems because the seat height can't be adjusted, she can be given a new chair with adjustable seat height. Or if a receptionist is not motivated because his work lacks variety, the work could be enriched or changed so that more skills could be used in the job. Redesigning a job or equipment can sometimes be the key to enhancing performance

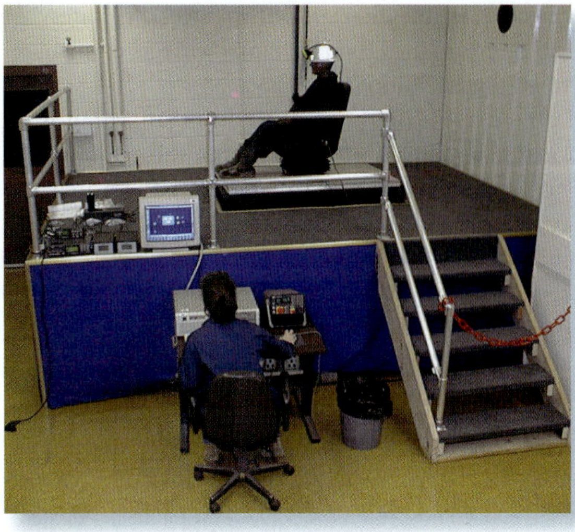

Courtesy of NIOSH Pittsburgh Research Laboratory

Human factors psychology plays an important role in the design of all sorts of equipment, ranging from consumer products to industrial machines.

and improving employee attitudes. Human factors focuses on changing the system to better fit the employee using the system. This may be a critical issue if problems are found with employees' behaviors and attitudes in an organization.

Attitudes and Behaviors at Work

One of the most important factors influencing whether people will be motivated to do a good job is their attitude at work. The causes and consequences of work attitudes have been extensively researched (Hanisch, 1995). Some of the determinants of work attitudes include job security issues, the type of work (interesting or boring), and pay and promotion issues. Job attitudes can influence many important outcomes in the world of work, such as whether employees volunteer for projects or help out co-workers, whether employees are frequently tardy or absent, and whether they think about quitting or early retirement.

Attitudes at Work

Attitudes at work include commitment to the organization and satisfaction with such job aspects as the work itself, pay and benefits, supervision, co-workers, promotion opportunities, working conditions, and job security. In general, you can be satisfied or dissatisfied with the tasks and conditions at work, the people in your work environment, and the rewards you get from work. Employee satisfaction is important because it has been shown to be related to employee behaviors at work (Hanisch, 1995). Job satisfaction and organizational commitment are two of the most commonly studied work attitudes.

***Job satisfaction* consists of the positive or negative emotions associated with a job.** In other words, job satisfaction reflects how much employees like or dislike their work. Some of the ways organizations can create satisfied employees include flexible working hours, professional growth opportunities, interesting work (Hackman & Oldham, 1976), autonomy, job security, a good supervisor, good benefits, competitive pay, and opportunities for promotion (Cranny, Smith, & Stone, 1992). What makes one worker satisfied may not make another worker satisfied. For some people, interesting work is paramount. Others place higher emphasis on having co-workers they like. Still others feel that the pay and benefits they receive are most important. Just as in the hiring process, a match between what you want and what the organization can provide will result in a more successful outcome for both parties.

Some organizations take the emotional temperature of their employees by periodically administering questionnaires. These questionnaires typically ask workers to rate their levels of satisfaction on the basic factors that contribute to job satisfaction. An example of a measure of job satisfaction, the Job Descriptive Index (JDI), can be seen in **Figure C.5**. Research has been conducted to support the reliability and validity of the JDI, making it a useful tool for

Work on Present Job Scale

Think of the work you do at present. How well does each of the following words or phrases describe your work? In the blank beside each word or phrase below, write:

Y for "Yes" if it describes your work
N for "No" if it does not describe it
? for "?" if you cannot decide

____ 1. Fascinating
____ 2. Routine
____ 3. Satisfying
____ 4. Boring
____ 5. Good
____ 6. Gives sense of accomplishment
____ 7. Respected
____ 8. Excited
____ 9. Rewarding
____ 10. Useful
____ 11. Challenging
____ 12. Simple
____ 13. Repetitive
____ 14. Creative
____ 15. Dull
____ 16. Uninteresting
____ 17. Can see results
____ 18. Uses my abilities

Scoring Key:

1. Y=3, N=0, ?=1	7. Y=3, N=0, ?=1	13. Y=0, N=3, ?=1
2. Y=0, N=3, ?=1	8. Y=3, N=0, ?=1	14. Y=3, N=0, ?=1
3. Y=3, N=0, ?=1	9. Y=3, N=0, ?=1	15. Y=0, N=3, ?=1
4. Y=0, N=3, ?=1	10. Y=3, N=0, ?=1	16. Y=0, N=3, ?=1
5. Y=3, N=0, ?=1	11. Y=3, N=0, ?=1	17. Y=3, N=0, ?=1
6. Y=3, N=0, ?=1	12. Y=0, N=3, ?=1	18. Y=3, N=0, ?=1

To interpret your score on this scale, 27 is considered the neutral value (Balzer, et al., 1997). Values considerably higher would be evaluated as very satisfiied, values considerably lower would be evaluated as very dissatisfied with the work on your present job.

© Cengage Learning 2013

Figure C.5
The Work on Present Job Scale. One measure often used to assess employee work attitudes and specific facets of job satisfaction is the Job Descriptive Index (JDI), originally published by Smith, Kendall, and Hulin (1969). This index, which has been improved based on years of research (Balzer et al., 1997; Hanisch, 1992), measures five facets of job satisfaction. The five subscales assess satisfaction with the work itself, supervisors, co-workers, present pay, and opportunities for promotion. The most frequently used subscale is the one shown here, which assesses satisfaction with the work itself.

organizations, consultants, and researchers. In addition, the instrument has recently been made available as a free download for workplace development projects or research (bgsu.edu/departments/psych/io/jdi/). Organizations assess employee attitudes because they believe (and research supports) that job satisfaction is related to important employee behaviors such as absenteeism and turnover (Hanisch, 1995).

One workplace survey found that listening to music at work leads to higher levels of reported employee satisfaction. About one-third of those participating in a Spherion Workplace Snapshot survey conducted by Harris Interactive in 2006 reported they listened to an iPod, MP3 player, or other personal music device while working (Spherion, 2006). More than three-fourths of the participants reported that listening to music improved their job satisfaction and productivity at work. Oldham and colleagues (1995) reported that employees in simple, routine and monotonous jobs found that listening to music relaxed them and reduced the number of work interruptions from others (i.e., co-workers did not want to bother someone wearing headphones), resulting in higher productivity and a more positive attitude for employees over those not listening to music. Although these same results were not found for more complex jobs, allowing workers to listen to music may become more popular in jobs where music does not interfere with co-workers, safety, or job performance. Having happy workers contributes to an organization's success.

Employees report that their job satisfaction and productivity increase if they are allowed privileges such as listening to music while they work.

© Christopher Robbins/Digital Vision/Photolibrary

Employee commitment to an organization is related to employee retention within the organization. According to Meyer and Allen (1991), there are three types of organizational commitment: affective, normative, and continuance. *Affective commitment* consists of an employee's emotional attachment to the organization, which makes the employee want to stay in the organization. *Normative commitment* is based on feelings of obligation to the organization. *Continuance commitment* results when an employee remains with a company because of the high cost of losing organizational membership, including monetary (pension benefits) and social (friendships) costs. Meyer and Herscovitch (2001) argue that employees have an organizational *commitment profile* at any given time in their job, with high or low values on each of the three types of commitment. In other words, an employee may have high scores on normative and continuance commitment but be lower on affective commitment. Depending on the profile, the employee may engage in different behaviors, such as quitting or helping out the organization.

Students may experience these different types of commitment to their college. A student acting under affective commitment would feel an emotional attachment to the school because she really likes it, including her classes, the football team, and the town. The student wants to stay in that school because of her attachment to it. Normative commitment might be evidenced by a student whose parents attended that college and who feels obligated to do the same thing regardless of whether it is the best school for him. Staying at a college because one's friends are there and one has already paid for two years of college would typify acting under continuance commitment.

One of the key factors in organizational commitment is job satisfaction. People who are satisfied with their job tend to be more committed to their organization than those who are less satisfied (Mueller et al., 1994). Other determinants of organizational commitment include having trust in one's supervisor and human resources practices that are supportive of employees (Arthur, 1994). The organizational commitment of Friedman's and Goodnight's employees was and is very high, as evidenced by very low levels of employee turnover.

Behaviors at Work

Employers want their employees to engage in behaviors that will make them successful in the job because employee success helps the organization meet its goals, including earning profits and fulfilling its mission. Employees have control over two aspects of their work—their time and their effort (Naylor, Pritchard, & Ilgen, 1980). Employees arriving at work on time and staying until their work day is complete instead of being late, absent, or leaving work early is important to performance and productivity. Positive behaviors generally help an organization meet its goals, whereas negative behaviors make it harder to reach those goals.

Organizational citizenship behaviors (OCBs) are often described as extra-role behaviors because they are not specifically required by the job and are not usually evaluated during performance reviews. These behaviors go beyond what is formally expected by the organization (Smith, Organ, & Near, 1983). Examples include staying late to finish a project, mentoring a new employee, volunteering for work, and helping a co-worker. Some reasons that people engage in organizational citizenship behaviors are job satisfaction, organizational commitment, high job autonomy, a positive organizational culture, high agreeableness (as a personality dimension; Witt et al., 2002), and high conscientiousness (Borman et al., 2001). Often, however, males who engage in OCBs are viewed positively, whereas females are viewed as just doing their jobs (Heilman & Chen, 2005; Kidder & Parks, 2001)—a difference that may result in gender disparities at performance evaluation time. OCBs have positive consequences for the organization and for employees in their day-to-day interactions with others in the organization.

In contrast to OCBs, some unhappy employees cause problems for organizations because they engage in behaviors that researchers refer to as *organizational withdrawal* (Hanisch, Hulin, & Roznowski, 1998) and *counterproductive behaviors* (Sackett & DeVore, 2003). Organizational withdrawal consists of behaviors employees use to avoid their work (work withdrawal) or their job (job withdrawal) (Hanisch, 1995; Hanisch & Hulin, 1990, 1991). Examples of work withdrawal include being absent from work, leaving work early, arriving late, missing meetings, surfing the Internet, reading help-wanted ads, and using work equipment for personal use without permission. Examples of job withdrawal are quitting one's job, transferring to another department within an organization, and retiring.

Counterproductive behaviors, although similar in some ways to withdrawal behaviors, are defined as "any intentional behavior on the part of an organizational member viewed by the organization as contrary to its legitimate interests" (Sackett & DeVore, 2003). An example of a counterproductive behavior would be an intentional violation of safety procedures that puts the employee and the organization at risk. Other examples of counterproductive behavior are theft, destruction of property, poor attendance, drug use, and inappropriate physical actions such as attacking a co-worker.

© Shane/MyLifeinaCube.com

Relations Between Attitudes and Behaviors

Organizational citizenship behaviors are positively related to job satisfaction and organizational commitment. In other words, employees with good attitudes who feel committed to their organization are more likely to do positive things to assist the organization (LePine, Erez, & Johnson, 2002). Research indicates that those employees who demonstrate organizational citizenship behaviors are less likely to engage in counterproductive behaviors (Dalal, 2006). Researchers have found strong links between job satisfaction and specific withdrawal or counterproductive behaviors such as absenteeism (Hackett, 1989), and even stronger links with job withdrawal (Hanisch & Hulin, 1990).

Counterproductive behaviors may sometimes be an outcome of high job stress. In such cases, the counterproductive behaviors often represent dysfunctional coping mechanisms (Lennings, 1997). For example, an employee experiencing stress from having too much work to do might respond by being absent from work or by sabotaging work

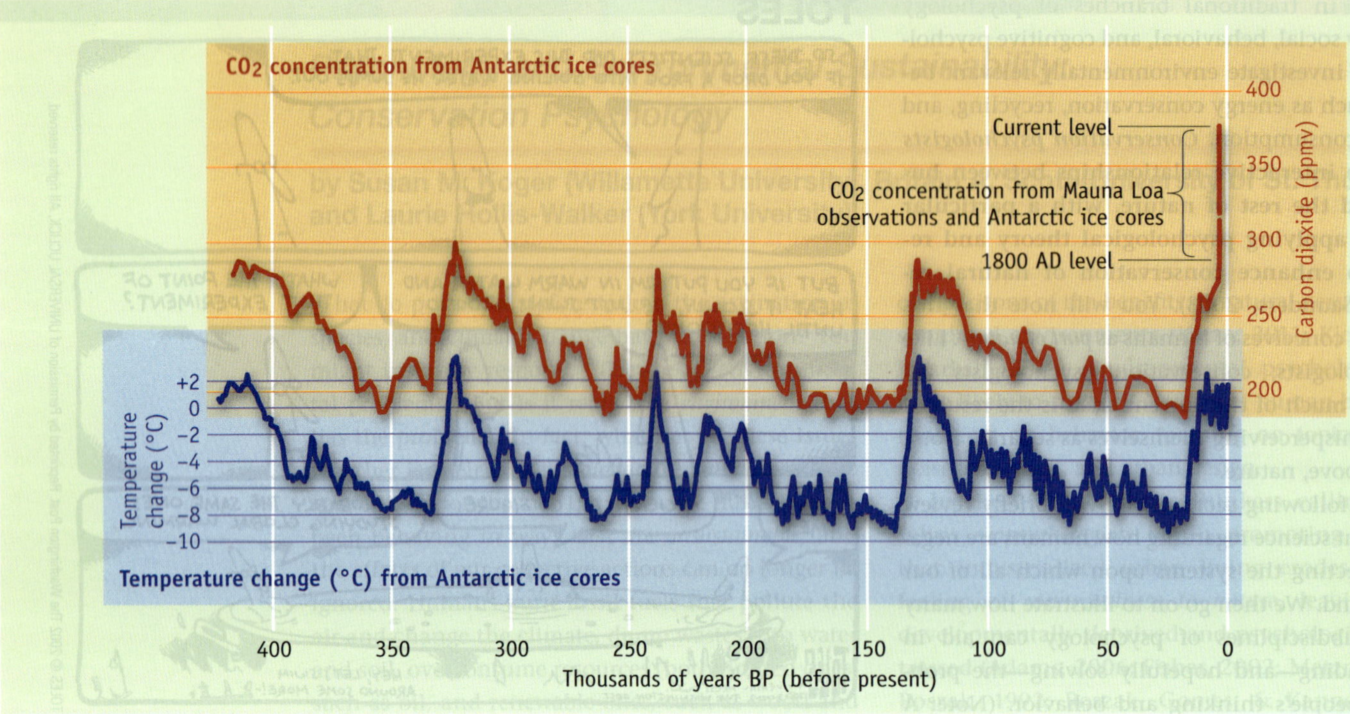

© Cengage Learning 2013

Figure D.1

Long-term trends in atmospheric carbon dioxide concentration and temperature. Scientists have sampled ice cores in Antarctica to study fluctuations in atmospheric concentrations of carbon dioxide (CO_2), the dominant greenhouse gas. Over the past 400,000 years, there has been a strong correlation between temperature variations and CO_2 levels. With the beginning of the Industrial Revolution in the 1800s, CO_2 concentrations began a dramatic and unprecedented increase, rising rapidly from 280 ppmv (parts per million by volume) to current levels of 376 ppmv. Note that this represents an increase of 77 ppmv relative to the highest concentrations reached during the course of the preceding 400,000 years (Woods Hole Research Center, 2009). Thus, it is highly unlikely that these recent trends reflect "natural" variability.

effect is necessary to stabilize planetary temperatures and maintain a climate suitable for life on this planet. Gas levels vary naturally to some extent, but as you have probably heard, industrialization has created an unprecedented increase in greenhouse gas concentrations (see **Figure D.1**). Simultaneously, our forests, which act as the lungs of the earth by converting carbon dioxide to oxygen, have been rapidly shrinking because of wood extraction, urbanization, and conversion of forests to agricultural land. As a result, carbon dioxide in the atmosphere is at the "highest level in 650,000 years" (Gardner & Prugh, 2008, p. 3) and is clearly correlated with planetary warming patterns (see **Figure D.2**). Although it is not possible to

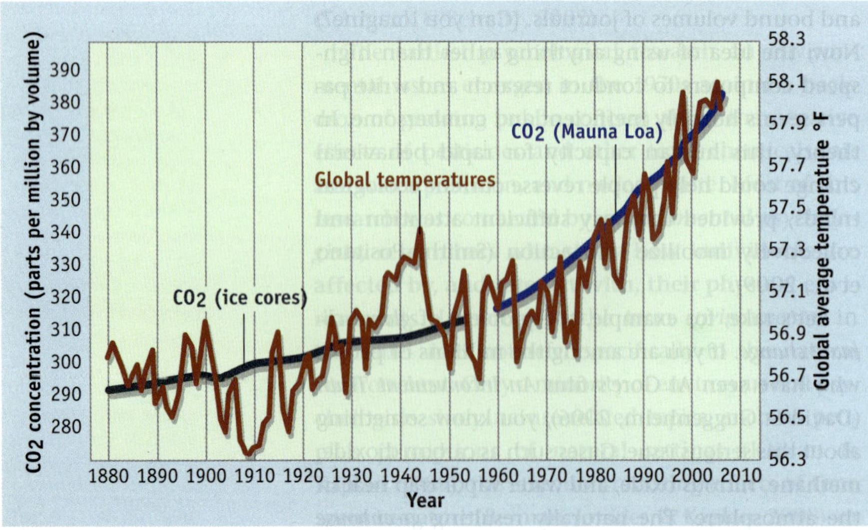

Figure D.2

Trends in global average temperature and carbon dioxide concentration since 1880. Evidence for a changing climate is also evident in average increases of global temperatures, which are correlated with escalating atmospheric CO_2 levels since the beginning of the Industrial Revolution in 1880. CO_2 measurements since 1958 are from the Mauna Loa Observatory in Hawaii; earlier data are from ice cores in Antarctica.

© Cengage Learning 2013

establish causation from these correlational analyses, the "scientific consensus [is] that global warming is happening and that it is induced by human activity" (Associated Press, 2010). The trends suggest that temperatures and associated climatic changes are positively related to CO_2 levels—and many warming greenhouse gases, including CO_2 and methane, will continue to rise if current industrial and social practices do not change dramatically.

In its most recent report, the Intergovernmental Panel on Climate Change (IPCC) (2007) predicted that the planet could warm as much as 11 degrees Fahrenheit by 2100 (see also NASA, 2007). To put that number in perspective, during the last ice age the world was only 9 degrees cooler than it is today. Thus, there is a real possibility of planetary temperature changes of ice age magnitudes within this century. Already, warming trends are evident, based on increased "average air and ocean temperatures, widespread melting of snow and ice, and rising global average sea level" (IPCC, 2007, p. 30; see also Flavin & Engelman, 2009). The years between 1995 and 2006 were eleven of the twelve warmest years since 1850 when recording of global temperatures began.

Climate change will affect *ecosystems,* both directly and indirectly, via flooding, drought, wildfires, insect proliferation, and fragmentation of natural systems. As many as 20%–30% of known plant and animal species are estimated to be at an increased risk of extinction as a result of climate change, threatening the *biodiversity* that is necessary to healthy ecosystems (IPCC, 2007; Lovejoy & Hannah, 2005; Wilson, 2007). Weather events such as typhoons and hurricanes are likely to become more intense, and while it is impossible to directly associate any particular storm with climate change, the devastation wrought by Hurricane Katrina in 2005 exemplifies what is expected. Coastal regions are at particular risk because of rising sea levels, erosion, and flooding. In 2007, the IPCC predicted a sea level rise of 20.1 inches by 2100, but a more recent report issued by the international Arctic Monitoring and Assessment Program states that the melting is happening more quickly than anticipated and may reach 5 feet by 2100 (Ritter, 2011). This means that U.S. coastal cities such as Miami, New Orleans, Tampa, and Virginia Beach could lose more than 10 percent of their land by 2100 (Weiss, Overpeck, & Strauss, 2011).

Such hazards will create significant and global *mental health* impacts. The experiences of loss, disruption, and displacement, as well as worry about future consequences, will create profound stress (Few, 2007; Fritze et al., 2008). Consequently, the prevalence and severity of stress disorders is likely to increase, including acute and posttraumatic stress disorder and related problems such as anxiety, substance abuse, grief, depression, and suicide (Fritze et al, 2008). Climate change also carries significant *public health* costs. Millions of people are likely to suffer or die from associated malnutrition, disease (including intestinal, cardiorespiratory, and infectious illnesses), and injury as a result of extreme weather (Blashki, McMichael, & Karoly, 2007; Centers for Disease Control and Prevention, 2009; IPCC, 2007; **see Figure D.3**). Densely populated areas, islands, and poor communities are especially vulnerable, and such regions constitute home to nearly half of the planet's population (Gelbspan, 2001). Thus, the harshest and most chronic consequences will be experienced by the most disadvantaged members of international populations (Agyeman et al., 2007; Fritze et al., 2008). Moreover, some scientists think it is far too late to reverse the global

Health Outcomes Related to Weather

Health outcomes	Known effects of weather
Heat stress	• Deaths from cardiopulmonary disease increase with high and low temperatures. • Heat-related illness and death increase during heat waves.
Air pollution–related mortality and morbidity	• Weather affects air-pollutant concentration. • Weather affects distribution, seasonality, and production of aeroallergens.
Health impacts of weather disasters	• Floods, landslides, and windstorms cause direct effects (deaths and injuries) and indirect effects (infectious disease, long-term psychological morbidity). • Droughts are associated with increased risk of disease and malnutrition.
Mosquito-borne diseases, tick-borne diseases (e.g., malaria, dengue)	• Higher temperatures shorten the development time of pathogens in vectors and increase potential transmission to humans. • Vector species have specific climate conditions (temperature, humidity) necessary to be sufficiently abundant to maintain transmission.
Undernutrition	• Climate change may decrease food supplies (crop yields, fish stocks) or access to food supplies.
Water- or food-borne diseases	• Survival of important bacterial pathogens is related to temperature. • Water-borne diseases are most likely to occur in communities with poor water supply and sanitation. • Increases in drought conditions may affect water availability. • Extreme rainfall can affect transport of disease organisms into water supply.

© Cengage Learning 2013

Figure D.3

Health outcomes related to weather. Several health impacts are associated with weather and climate change. This list summarizes some of the better-known health effects of weather changes.

SOURCE: Based on Kovats, R. S., Campbell-Lendrum, D., & Matthies, F. (2005). Climate change and human health: Estimating avoidable deaths and disease. *Risk Analysis, 25,* p. 1411. Copyright © 2005, John Wiley and Sons.

warming trends and that the best we can do is try to minimize the predicted damage and adapt to—or suffer from—the consequences (Thompson, 2010).

The Psychological Foundation of Environmental Problems

As you were reading the preceding paragraphs, did you feel despair? Anxiety? Irritation? Hopelessness? Did you scan the material, thinking to yourself that you already knew it? Did you find yourself growing overwhelmed, angry, or afraid? Did you feel guilty, defensive, or skeptical? Did you feel a sense of apathy? Or, did you wonder what any of this has to do with you? The environmental reality we face has been named the "pivotal psychological reality of our time" (Macy, 1995, p. 241). Thus, *psychological* reactions are important because they determine how such problems are understood and what people are willing and able to do about them.

Before someone changes his or her behaviors, that person must recognize which behaviors need changing, know how to change them, and feel that changing them is a worthwhile expenditure of effort. In other words, awareness, efficacy, and motivation are all critical components of behavioral change. A model from the clinical psychology of addiction is applicable here, as many people are addicted to unsustainable consumption patterns. The *stages of change model* describes a five-step process that individuals work through to break a pattern of addiction (see **Figure D.4**). All change requires patience and perseverance because most people relapse (i.e., fall back on old habits). In fact, the majority of people will not even initiate change until they experience a personal crisis (Beddoe et al., 2009), commonly known as "hitting bottom," or until the impacts of risks such as climate change become salient and personally relevant (Weber, 2006).

But, do environmental risks feel personally relevant to you? What does environmental destruction have to do with us as individuals? If you don't have children, you might assume that you are not contributing directly to population growth, and you yourself do not produce industrial wastes or log forests. What, then, is *each person* doing to deplete the carrying capacity of the planet to sustain human life? The most obvious answer lies in individuals' extravagant use and misuse of the world's natural resources.

Human influences on the planet can be estimated by using the *ecological footprint*—a measure of how fast a person (or population) consumes resources and generates waste in comparison to how rapidly nature (the habitat) can absorb the waste and replenish the resources (see **Figure D.5**). People who live in the United States have the largest footprints, consuming considerably more resources and generating more waste than any other people on the planet. Unfortunately, the gap between this ecological footprint and the planet's carrying capacity is growing at an alarming pace (see **Figure D.6**). "If everyone in the world had an ecological footprint equivalent to that of the typical North American or

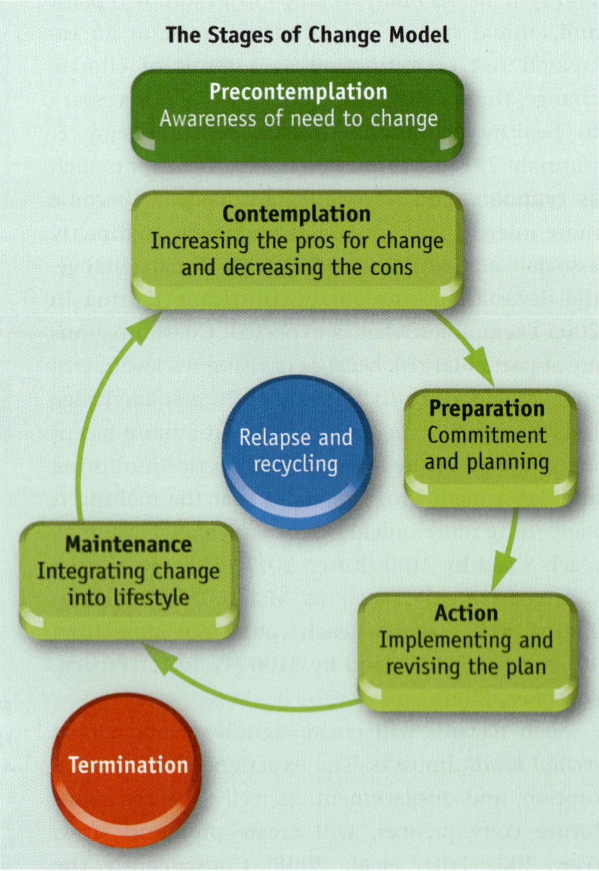

© Cengage Learning 2013

Figure D.4

The stages of change model. According to this model, the difficult behavioral changes required to give up an addiction occur through a series of stages. During the *precontemplation* stage, an addicted individual is not interested in considering change and often denies that a problem exists. Once the person becomes concerned about the issue, the *contemplation stage* involves analyzing the risks and benefits of changing. *Preparation* involves committing to and planning for the change, whereas the *action stage* is reached when specific steps are implemented to overcome one's addiction. If the individual reaches the *maintenance* stage, the new behavior becomes normative. Movement back and forth (relapse and recycling) through the stages, is common in this dynamic process.

SOURCE: DiClemente, C. C. (2003). *Addiction and change: How addictions develop and addicted people recover.* New York: Guilford, p. 30. Copyright 2003 Reproduced with permission of Guilford Publications, Inc. via Copyright Clearance Center.

© Cengage Learning 2013

Figure D.5

A graphic overview of the concept of the ecological footprint. The ecological footprint is a tool used to estimate an individual's, a group's, a nation's, or the world population's impact on the planet. SOURCE: Global Footprint Network (www.footprintnetwork.org).

Western European, global society would overshoot the planet's biocapacity three to five fold" (Kitzes et al., 2008, p. 468). In other words, if everyone lived like those in the United States do, more than three additional planets would be needed to support this lifestyle!

People living in the U.S. are by far the biggest users and wasters of the world's resources. Less than 5% of the planet's population live in the United States and the country houses only about 3% of the planet's oil supply (Kunstler, 2005), yet U.S. residents use a staggering *25%* of the total commercial supply: 18,771,000 barrels of oil *per day*—72% of which is used for transportation (U.S. Energy Information Administration, 2010b). The next largest consumer is China, but consider this: China has *four times* the population of the United States and uses less than half of the amount of oil (8,300,000 barrels per day; U.S. Energy Information Administra-

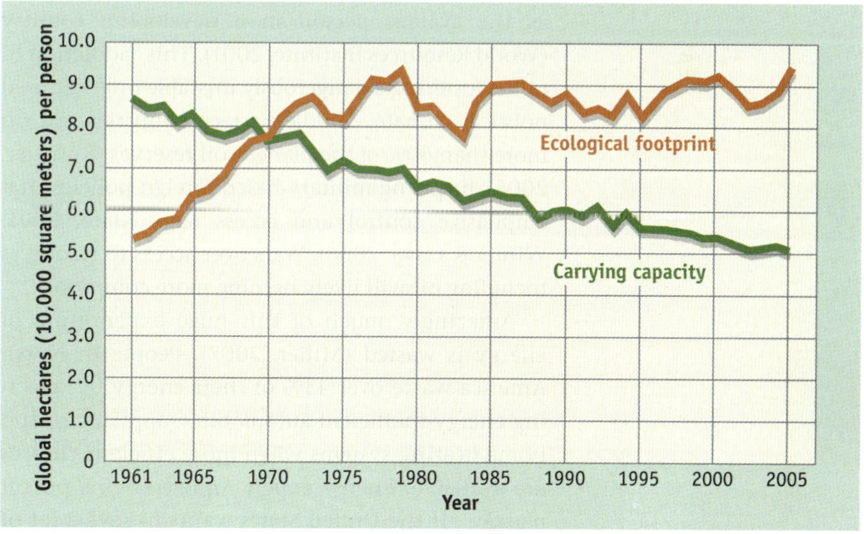

© Cengage Learning 2013

Figure D.6

Trends in the collective ecological footprint of the United States. This graph shows how the ecological footprint of the United States has increased dramatically since the 1960s in relation to the (decreasing) carrying capacity that our habitat can support. Carrying capacity, or "biocapacity," varies depending on ecosystem management, agricultural practices (such as fertilizer use and irrigation), ecosystem degradation, and weather. Overall, biocapacity is diminshing as population pressures, changing climates, and urbanization degrade land and other resources. As you can see, the trends are not encouraging.

SOURCE: http://www.footprintnetwork.org/en/index.php/GFN/page/trends/us/. Global Footprint Network 2008 National Footprint Accounts. Reprinted with permission.

CALVIN AND HOBBES © 1994 Waterson. Reprinted by Permission of UNIVERSAL UCLICK. All rights reserved.

tion, 2010a). Each person in the U.S. uses, on average, more than thirty times the amount of gasoline as the average person in a developing country (World Resources Institute, 2001). This "addiction to oil" is fostering a dangerously unstable international political climate. Middle Eastern countries rest on more than 60% of the planet's oil reserves (Kunstler, 2005), inspiring military-based foreign policies that emphasize control and access (e.g., Klare, 2001; Winter & Cava, 2006). Wars over access to resources including oil will likely become more common.

Amazingly, much of this huge expenditure of energy is wasted (Miller, 2007). People in North America waste over 43% of their energy by selecting energy-inefficient automobiles, appliances, and home heating systems when more efficient choices are available. Energy expert Amory Lovins puts it plainly, "If the United States wants to save a lot of oil and money and increase national security, there are two simple ways to do it: Stop driving Petropigs and stop living in energy sieves" (quoted in Miller, 2007, p. 385).

Those living in the United States also overuse and abuse water. The toxic chemicals used in industrial production, as well as those used to kill pests like bugs and weeds, clean houses, and even groom and beautify people and pets, are polluting groundwater, lakes, rivers, and oceans. Demand for water from growing populations in arid locations is lowering reservoirs and aquifers. At least one quarter of the groundwater that is currently withdrawn is not being replenished. For example, Las Vegas has doubled in population since 1990. The city gets 90% of its water from the Colorado River, which is currently experiencing the worst drought in its recorded history (Hutchinson, 2007). Already more than *one billion* people on the planet do not have safe drinking water. In contrast, people in the developed world pollute and waste gallons of clean water every time they flush the toilet, while half of the population in developing nations lack access to basic sanitation.

The wasteful use of energy and water are two of the primary contributors to the enormous ecological footprint of the U.S. population. Another major factor is diet. Livestock farming produces more greenhouse gases than transportation (Food and Agriculture Organization of the United Nations, 2006), and it has been estimated that it takes 600 gallons of water to produce just one hamburger (Kreith, 1991). Recently, Japanese researchers have estimated that the CO_2 emissions associated with the production of just 2.2 pounds of beef is equivalent to the amount emitted by an average European car every 155 miles (Bittman, 2008). Thus, if U.S. citizens merely decreased meat consumption by 20%, the energy savings and reduction in greenhouse gases would be equivalent to each of us trading in our average sedan for a Prius (Walsh, 2008). As a result of increasing affluence in other parts of the world and a rapidly expanding global population, worldwide meat consumption is projected to rise 53% by 2030 (World Resources Institute, 2010).

Most people regularly eat food that is out of season or does not grow in their region. This means that their food must travel long distances to get to them. It is typical in the United States for food to travel more than 1500 miles from its source to the dinner table (Pirog & Benjamin, 2003). Popular convenience foods are subject to energy-intensive processing and are packaged in containers and wrappers that cannot be reused or recycled. Further, *34 million tons* of food is wasted every year in the United States (U.S. Environmental Protection Agency, 2011), about 39% of the edible food supply (Stokstad, 2009). Most of that food ends up in landfills, and as it rots it releases methane, a greenhouse gas that is twenty times more powerful than carbon dioxide at trapping heat in the atmosphere (U.S. EPA, 2011)

Energy, water, and food are not the only things consumed in unsustainable ways. In fact, *overconsumption of consumer goods constitutes the biggest drain on the Earth's carrying capacity.* Many people suffer from *affluenza,* an "unsustainable addiction to overconsumption and materialism" (Miller, 2007, p. 19; de Graaf, Wann, & Naylor, 2005). Those who are addicted to consumption use shopping as a coping strategy similar to overeating, using alcohol and drugs, and surfing the Internet (see Chapter 14). Nearly 20 years ago, it was observed that each person in North America consumes, directly or indirectly, over 100 pounds of raw materials a day (Durning, 1992), vastly more than those in developing countries and even more than people in other developed nations. And the things people buy—clothes, electronics, cars, furnishings—are produced from materials that leave a long trail of pollution in many third world countries that is invisible to the U.S. consumer. A pair of pants made of polyester and sold in an American department store may be sewn in a sweatshop in Indonesia, from synthetic material manufactured in Singapore, which comes from oil refined in Mexico. U.S. consumer culture is spreading quickly, so that people in developing countries are aiming for "the good life," hurrying to develop the same extravagant lifestyles modeled in movies, television, advertising, and tourism.

© Joel Pett Editorial Cartoon used with permission of Joel Pett and the Cartoonist's Group. All rights reserved.

Conspicuous consumption of convenience foods and consumer goods yields astonishing amounts of solid waste. Each person in North America generates more than 4.5 pounds of garbage per day (Miller, 2007), about ten times their body weight every year. People throw away approximately 2.5 million nonreturnable plastic bottles *every hour* and toss about *25 billion* Styrofoam coffee cups in the garbage each year. Electronic waste, or "e-waste," is growing exponentially. Every year, people living in the United States discard an estimated 130 million cell phones and 100 million computers, monitors, and television sets, only recycling about 10% (Miller, 2007). But even careful household recycling will not change the biggest solid waste problem. Commercial and industrial activities generate 98.5% of the waste. Average citizens sponsor this enormous waste production every time they buy a product that was inefficiently manufactured, is overpackaged, is not recyclable or biodegradable, and has traveled a long distance to get to them (which describes the vast majority of consumer products, including some that are misleadingly labeled "eco-friendly").

Yet, there is good reason to believe that overconsumption is not delivering the "goods." Empirical studies suggest that it is not how much stuff people own but the quality of their social relations, the creative fulfillment received from work, and their personality and outlook on life that determine how happy they are (see Chapter 10). In fact, the race to pay for material possessions is likely to detract from these primary ingredients of happiness. Thus, attempting to meet psychological needs through overconsumption jeopardizes not only physical habitat but also psychological well-being (Kasser & Kanner,

2004). You may have heard of the 3 R's: Reduce, Reuse, Recycle. But effective solutions to environmental problems must start with *Refusing* to buy things that aren't really necessary and choosing sustainably produced options for the things that are (Miller, 2007) (see **Figure D.7**).

The field of psychology has much to offer in terms of understanding and solving the problems causing ecological degradation in today's world. Of course, it would be naive to suggest that any one academic discipline will provide the solution to such a complex interplay of issues as those underlying current ecological conditions, and it is clear that interdisciplinary collaborations are urgently needed (Smith, Positano et al., 2009). However, as we will show in the following sections, psychology has a lot to offer for understanding the roots of environmental destruction, the psychological forces maintaining it, and how we might begin solving environmentally related behavioral problems.

Insights from Theories of Personality

As you learned in Chapter 12, part of Sigmund Freud's fame lies in the vigorous criticisms and controversies his theories have inspired. Nonetheless, his emphasis on unconscious conflict and ego anxiety, and his description of unconscious defenses that people use to ward off emotional discomfort are relevant to environmental issues. Certainly, acknowledging the probable collapse of the planet's ecosystems *should* trigger powerful and uncomfortable feelings, including despair, bewilderment, grief, anger, and so on. As one bumper sticker puts it, "If you're not outraged, you're not paying attention!" Emotional defenses explain how people can "know" about environmental problems and yet not change their relevant behaviors.

In their theorizing about personality and the ego's self-protective strategies, Freud and his daughter Anna described several *defense mechanisms* that we think are particularly useful for understanding people's ecologically unfriendly behaviors (A. Freud, 1936; see Chapter 12). For example, *rationalization* is one of the most common defense mechanisms. Thus, people say, "I have to drive because the bus schedule is too inconvenient," even though they know that cars contribute significantly to air pollution and climate change. *Identification* leads to purchasing items according to peer group or cultural influences, such as celebrities. When in *denial,* people claim that the anxiety-provoking material doesn't exist, a tendency that can be bolstered by supporting "evidence" from outside sources. For example, conservative think tanks, funded by industry, have been quite effective in fostering public denial about the scientific evidence on climate change (Jacques, Dunlap, & Freeman, 2008). Denial about environmental problems includes minimizing their severity, seeing them as irrelevant, and seeing oneself as not responsible (Opotow & Weiss, 2000). Finally, *projection* occurs when people perceive in others what they fail to perceive in themselves. One of the authors recalls vehemently grumbling about all the cars on the road during rush hour, only to be reminded by her 3-year-old in the backseat, "But Mommy, you're traffic, too!"

Several researchers have explored the possibility that there may be personality traits related to pro-environmental values such as empathy and caring for non-human animals. Broida and colleagues (1993) administered the Myers-Briggs Type Inventory to a sample of more than a thousand college students. They found that individuals classed as Intuitive and Feeling types tended to be more ecologically concerned and more opposed to animal experimentation than other personality types. Mathews and Herzog (1997) administered the Sixteen Personality Factor Inventory to a sample of college students and found that two personality factors—sensitivity and imaginativeness—were positively correlated with attitudes toward animals. Furnham, McManus, and Scott (2004) measured empathy, the Big Five personality traits, and attitudes toward animal experimentation in more than 800 college students. They found that agreeableness, openness, and empathy were all significant negative predictors of attitudes toward animal experimentation. Openness was also positively related to liking of animals and believing that animals have feelings. Comparably, both farmers and agriculture students who scored high in agreeableness and conscientiousness tended to support animal welfare efforts (Austin et al., 2005). And individuals with idealist type personalities based on the Keirsey Four Types Sorter reported significantly higher attachment to their pets than did other types (Bagley & Gonsman, 2005). More recently, researchers have

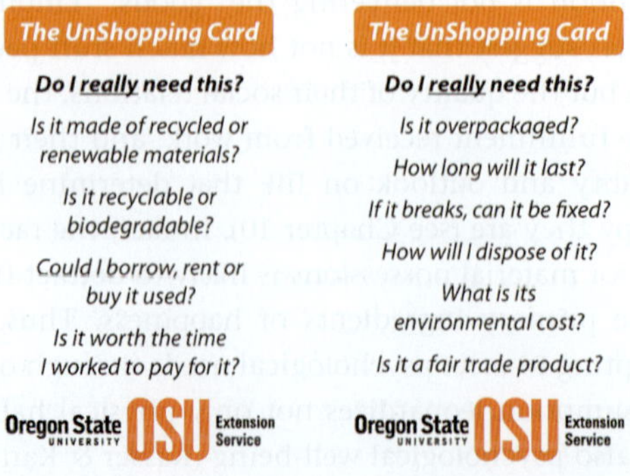

Figure D.7
An innovative effort to discourage overconsumption. This "UnShopping Card," developed by the Oregon State University Extension Service, was created to help people think more deliberately about their consumption decisions.

found a positive relationship between openness and general environmental concern (Hirsh, 2010) and pro-environmental behaviors (Markowitz, et al., in press).

Insights from Social Psychology

Although most of the research on the "person" is conducted by personality psychologists, social psychologists are interested in the *self-concept* as well as *social identity*. How people define themselves relative to others and to the social environment plays a large part in behavior. Inspired by ecopsychological theories, some social psychologists have recently turned their attention to the notion of the *ecologically connected self*. Theoretically, the more one defines and experiences oneself as *part of nature*, the more one should be interested in and attuned to information about the environment and one's impact on it, and the more empathy and caring one should exhibit for other living things (Bragg, 1996). Several studies support this idea (e.g., Clayton, 2003; Mayer & Frantz, 2004; Schultz, 2000, 2001). Moreover, the development of an ecologically connected self leads to environmentally appropriate behaviors, not out of a sense of self-sacrifice or self-denial, but out of a sense of self-love and common identity. Experiences in nature, particularly during childhood, can foster this positive relationship with nature and other species and are predictive of pro-environmental behaviors (Chawla, 1988; Horwitz, 1996; Kals & Ittner, 2003; Myers, 2007) and related attitudes and personal values.

People who appreciate the inherent value of nature and other species (those who hold *biocentric values*) are more likely to engage in pro-environmental behaviors such as sharing resources and taking actions to protect other species, landscapes, and natural resources. In contrast, those with *egocentric* and *materialistic* values that emphasize personal wealth and status tend to exhibit fewer environmentally friendly actions (Schultz et al., 2005). Materialistic values have surged over the last few decades. Data collected on incoming college students over a 40-year period (1966–2007) show that they increasingly value materialism above other values, including finding personal meaning, helping others in difficulty, becoming an authority in one's field, and raising a family (Myers, 2010) (see **Figure D.8**). Further, a lack of direct encounters with unpolluted and undegraded conditions in nature may reduce people's sense of connection and personal responsibility for environmental issues (Kahn, 2007; Pyle, 2002). Even those individuals with pro-environmental values often find that situation-specific constraints can make it difficult

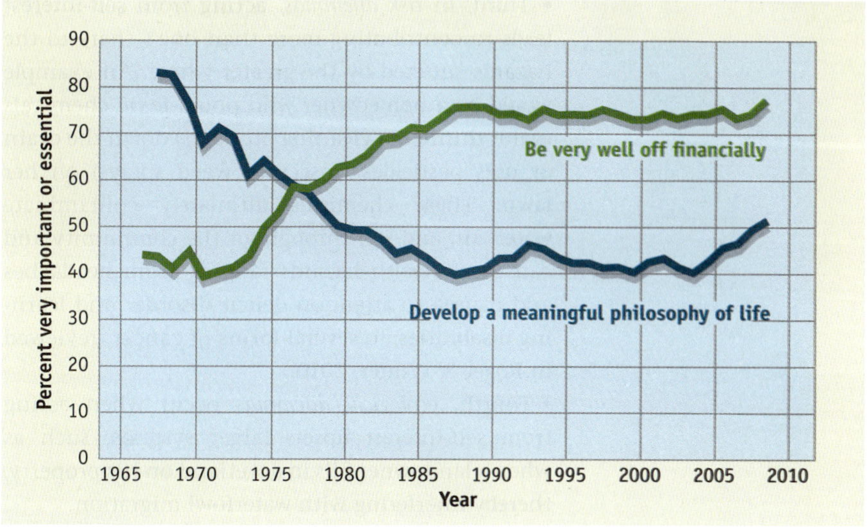

© Cengage Learning 2013

Figure D.8

Increasing materialism among college students. An annual survey of the attitudes and values of first-year college students suggests that materialistic values are on the rise. The percentage of students who think that it is crucial to "be very well off financially" has almost doubled since the 1960s.

SOURCE: From Myers, D. G. (2010). *Social psychology*. New York: McGraw-Hill, p. 581. Copyright © 2010 The McGraw-Hill Companies, Inc. Data from surveys of more than 200,000 entering U.S. collegians per year, based on The American Freshman surveys, UCLA, 1966 to 2007.

(or costly, inconvenient, or awkward) to act in an attitude-consistent manner (Kollmus & Agyeman, 2002; Staats, 2003). To paraphrase the founder of experimental social psychology, Kurt Lewin, behavior is a function of the person *and the situation* (see Chapters 12 and 13).

A disconnection from nature and egocentric or materialistic values set the stage for a *social dilemma:* a discrepancy between the interests of oneself and the larger group and the relative short-term and long-term consequences of one's behavior. Many environmental problems result from people acting out of self-interest in the moment, ultimately harming the greater whole. A clear example is commuters' reliance on the convenience of cars rather than using public transit (Joireman, Van Lange, & Van Vugt, 2004), thereby contributing to air pollutants and climate-changing gases, as well as traffic problems. Social dilemmas contribute to environmental degradation in several ways (e.g., Gardner & Stern, 2002; Osbaldiston & Sheldon, 2002; Vlek & Steg, 2007):

- First, in *commons dilemmas* (Hardin, 1968), individuals take more than their fair allotment of a shared resource, such as by careless or excessive water use (Van Vugt, 2001).
- Second, in *public goods dilemmas*, individuals do not contribute their fair share to a pooled resource (for instance, by voting down a bill that would increase taxes to fund community bus or train services).

- Third, in *risk dilemmas,* acting from self-interest leads to contributing more than one's share to the hazards suffered by the greater whole. An example would be a homeowner who pours toxic chemicals (paint thinner or cleaning products) down the drain or uses pesticides (insect or weed sprays) on her lawn. These chemicals ultimately contaminate water, air, and soil throughout the community and can cause health hazards ranging from headaches and nausea to attention deficit disorder and learning disabilities, to several forms of cancer (reviewed in Koger & Winter, 2010).
- Fourth, *ecological dilemmas* occur when acting from self-interest upsets larger systems, such as when a landowner fills in a wetland on his property, thereby interfering with waterfowl migration.

In these examples, if not in all environmental problems, rewards to the individual are more immediate and compelling than the delayed costs to the population. Importantly, environmental social dilemmas differ from some other social dilemmas in that they have a temporal dimension (Joireman, 2005; Osbaldiston & Sheldon, 2002). For example, Joireman, Van Lange, and Van Vugt (2004) studied consumers' automobile-related behaviors and found that having a "future orientation" was more predictive of environmentally responsible behavior than having a "prosocial orientation" (which would typically predict taking the selfless route in a social dilemma).

In Chapter 13, you learned about the *bystander effect* and *diffusion of responsibility,* concepts that emerged from classic work regarding influences on whether or not people help out during an emergency situation (e.g., Darley & Latané, 1968). Recently, psychologists applied this model of helping behavior to climate change, noting that people tend to respond to crises that are visually noticeable, physically and psychologically close by, and unambiguous—all characteristics that climate change generally lacks (Frantz & Mayer, 2009; see also Ornstein & Ehrlich, 2000). However, individuals will forgo immediate, personal reinforcers for longer-term group goals and will generally cooperate with others in working toward a common goal (such as reducing global emissions) if they are convinced of the high probability that they will be personally and adversely affected if the target goals are not reached, if they identify with the group and feel responsible toward it (Dawes, 1980; Gardner & Stern, 2002; Van Vugt, 2002), and if they perceive the long-term benefits of collective action as relevant to them personally as well as to the larger group (Milinski et al., 2008; Ostrom et al., 2007). Further, some innovative programs are capitalizing on the human tendency to be selfish by making "green behaviors" personally beneficial (Chance & Heward, 2010).

Many environmentally damaging behaviors arise from *social norms*—informal, unwritten "rules" about what is appropriate or typical behavior in a particular setting. Norms can exert a form of social pressure that may lead to conformity, as described in Chapter 13. Some researchers distinguish between *injunctive norms* (what is expected or approved of) and *descriptive norms* (what most people actually do) (Cialdini, Reno, & Kallgren, 1990). In the case of environmentally responsible behaviors, injunctive and descriptive norms are often inconsistent; that is, most people approve of environmentally responsible behaviors but don't actually engage in them. Cialdini (2003) argued that environmental campaigns emphasizing the various destructive behaviors people exhibit may backfire, because they inadvertently focus attention on the descriptive norms for anti-environmental behavior.

To test the importance of these two types of norms, researchers conducted a series of field experiments on littering. Our society has injunctive norms against littering, but in some situations the descriptive norm is to litter, resulting in some interesting interactions. For example, in an already littered environment, participants were more likely to litter after witnessing a confederate littering. In a clean environment, however, the participants who saw a confederate littering were *less* likely to litter than those who saw no littering behavior because the contrast between the confederate's behavior and the descriptive norm indicated by the clean setting brought to mind the injunctive norm against littering (Cialdini et al., 1990).

Insights from Behavioral Psychology

Efforts to bring about immediate changes in environmentally destructive behavior are informed by the theories and techniques of behavioral psychology. As you may recall from Chapter 6, one of the best-known behavioral psychologists, B. F. Skinner, argued that what people do is a function of the consequences of their behavior: Reinforcement strengthens response tendencies, whereas punishment weakens them. Toward the end of his career, Skinner took a particular interest in environmental issues. In an address to the American Psychological Association, he criticized the efforts of environmental activists as inconsistent with operant learning principles in that they focused on inspiring guilt, fear, and shame to motivate greener behaviors instead of helping individuals see the potentially rein-

© Dan Sullivan/Alamy

Good intentions do not necessarily result in good behavior. Most people endorse environmentally responsible behaviors such as not littering, but depending on the situation, their actual behavior may be quite different. Social psychology can shed light on these disparities between attitudes and behavior.

forcing consequences of sustainable lifestyles (Skinner, 1987). Indeed, people are typically more motivated by the reinforcers associated with environmentally damaging behaviors than by environmentally sustainable ones. For example, can you think of any environmentally unfriendly behaviors that are rewarded by social status and convenience? How about driving? Many people choose their cars based on the "cool" factor rather than fuel economy, and cars are generally more convenient than biking or using public transit for running errands or getting to work on time.

Altering reinforcement contingencies, such as rewarding bus ridership with tokens redeemable for future trips or movie passes (Everett, Hayward, & Meyers, 1974), capitalizing on consumers' attraction to Internet shopping and Facebook to reward "driving green" (Pritchard, 2010), and providing feedback by praising individuals for reducing the amount of energy they consume (Abrahamse et al., 2005; Lehman & Geller, 2004) can all be effective techniques in motivating pro-environmental behaviors. Although financial incentives, such as rebates, can help motivate energy-efficient construction and appliance purchases, *social reinforcers* (such as those communicated by social norms) are perhaps even more powerful. Community-based projects to install wind power (Nevin, 2010) and collaborations between friends and neighbors to research and purchase solar panels (Neuringer & Oleson, 2010) reflect the power of social engagement to inspire and foster the maintenance of pro-environmental behaviors.

Another behavior modification strategy involves altering *discriminative (antecedent) stimuli* to influence behavior (see Chapter 6). Prompts and social modeling are examples of strategies involving antecedents that can influence environmentally relevant behaviors. *Prompts* signal particular actions. One example is prominently placing aluminum recycling bins in areas where canned soft drinks are consumed (Lehman & Geller, 2004). Another example would be placing signs over light switches to remind users to turn off the lights when they leave a room. Research suggests that the more specific the prompt, the greater its effectiveness. A sign saying "Faculty and students please turn off lights after 5 p.m.?" is more effective than one reading "Conserve Electricity." Polite prompts are more effective than demanding ones (the word "please" can make a difference), and the closer the prompt is to the point of behavior, the better (a sign over a light switch is more effective than a sign across the room). Thus, polite, salient, and specific reminders can change behavior (Geller, Winett, & Everett, 1982; Lehman & Geller, 2004).

Although providing general information is a technique widely used by environmental groups, there is little reason to believe that education alone will change what people actually do (see reviews by Abrahamse et al., 2005; Gardner & Stern, 2002; Lehman & Geller, 2004). On the other hand, *observational learning,* or *modeling,* of environmentally friendly behavior can be more effective than simply describing desired behaviors (see Bandura, 1977 and Chapter 6). For instance, in one classic study, participants were exposed to a video showing a person turning down a thermostat, wearing warmer clothes, and using heavy blankets. With this treatment, viewers reduced their energy use by 28% (Winett et al., 1982). One of the authors has frequently experienced the efficacy of modeling during walks with friends: When she bends down to pick up litter during the walk, her friends do so as well. Modeling may also be effective in addressing some of the most important environmental issues, like overpopulation and overconsumption (Bandura, 2002).

Insights from Cognitive Psychology

Humans' cognitive and perceptual processes are crucial organizing features of behavior. These mechanisms were shaped by eons of evolution, are modified by personal experiences, and generally function pretty effectively; if they didn't, the species wouldn't have survived for very long. Yet the environments in which perceptual and cognitive systems evolved were very different from those that humans currently encounter. As a result, people tend to focus on threats that are visually noticeable (smoke pouring out of a smokestack) rather than the many largely invisible or slowly acting dangers, such as climate change or pesticides and other toxins in water and food supplies (Ornstein & Ehrlich, 2000). As Harvard Psychologist Daniel Gilbert (2006) put it, "Environmentalists despair that global warming is happening so fast. In fact, it isn't happening fast enough." Humans respond best to threats that are "PAINful: i.e., Personal, Abrupt, Immoral, and happening Now" (Gilbert, 2008; Frantz & Mayer, 2009).

Thus, from the perspective of cognitive psychology, environmentally destructive behavior is maintained by cognitive biases. For instance, laypeople assess risks in different terms than professionals do, leading the public to express greater levels of concern about local, immediate threats such as hazardous waste and radiation contamination, compared to experts' greater focus on global, longer-term issues, such as population growth and climate change (Slimak & Dietz, 2006). Consequently, while the scientific community has detailed the clear and devastating risks associated with climate change, the public largely maintains a "wait and see" attitude and does not seem to understand the need to drastically and immediately reduce emissions in order to stabilize the climate (Sterman, 2008), although they do report concern about the potential human health risks (Sundblad, Biel, & Gärling, 2007).

Further, the tendency to depend on mental shortcuts called *heuristics,* such as those described in Chapter 8, can lead to errors in assessing the relative risks of environmental hazards and in estimating how one's behavior affects the environment. One mental shortcut that may explain people's underestimation of the risk of climate change is the *availability heuristic.* Most individuals have difficulty imagining the risks associated with climate change because of a lack of vivid, personal experiences with melting icecaps and rising sea levels. On the other hand, dramatic environmental hazards, such as oil spills, feature prominently in people's memories and may, therefore, receive more attention and resources than are warranted relative to other less perceptually vivid, but more insidious, hazards (Gardner & Stern, 2002).

Some cognitive biases help people feel good about themselves in spite of their behavior or circumstances. Several of these biases are relevant when considering how people perceive environmental risks and the impact of their own actions. *Comparative optimism* is a heuristic that leads individuals to believe they are less vulnerable than other people to all types of risks, including environmental threats like air and water pollution or nuclear accidents, even though objectively there is no reason to think the risks are any different for one individual versus another (Pahl et al., 2005). *False consensus* is a cognitive bias that helps people maintain positive self-esteem by convincing themselves that many others engage in the same undesirable behaviors they do. For example, a water shortage following a tropical storm prompted a temporary shower ban at Princeton University in 1999 and inspired a 5-day field study during and after the ban (Benoît & Norton, 2003). The researchers found that students who defied the shower ban overestimated the prevalence of this socially irresponsible behavior in others. In addition, those who showered were seen by others as caring very little about the greater good, whereas those who did not shower were seen as caring very much. However, self-report data suggested that the actual attitudinal positions of these two groups were much closer than either group realized (i.e., both groups cared about the larger group's welfare). *False polarization* is the tendency to perceive the views of those on the opposing side of a partisan debate as more extreme than they really are. All of these tendencies distort the perception of one's behavior relative to others', while they help maintain feelings of safety (comparative optimism), a sense of self-esteem (false consensus), and the view of oneself as more reasonable than those who would disagree (false polarization).

Although the use of mental shortcuts is automatic, it is possible to override this tendency when one is sufficiently motivated and not cognitively overloaded by other attentional demands. Humans may be "lazy" thinkers who are prone to biases by default, but they are capable of careful, logical, effortful reasoning. The question is whether "coldly rational" judgments are always superior to emotionally driven ones (Slovic et al., 2004). People's evaluation of the risks and benefits associated with the use of pesticides is based not only on knowledge, but also on how they feel about those risks and benefits (Alhakami & Slovic, 1994). This *affect* (emotion-based) *heuristic* also influences judgments of the risks and benefits of nuclear power. For example, after reading a description of nuclear energy that emphasized the risks of this energy source ("waste is highly radioactive and contaminated with plutonium, a deadly element"), participants not only raised their estimates of the risks of nuclear power (as would be logically expected) but also *lowered* their estimates of the benefits of nuclear power—even though the description had not said anything about benefits. The researchers explained this change in participants' benefit estimates as being due to an overall increase in negative feelings about nuclear power as a result of reading the description of risks (Finucane et al., 2000). In sum, heuristics may sometimes bias people in an anti-environmental direction and sometimes in a pro-environmental direction. The key may be for each person to increase his or her awareness of the potential for errors in thinking. In this way, individuals can become better environmental decision makers.

Insights from Developmental Psychology

As a discipline, psychology evolved primarily in an urban-industrialized context during the last century. It is probably because of this situation that developmental psychologists have historically overlooked the vital role that nature plays in humans' cognitive, emotional, and social development. Only since the 1990s have some developmental psychologists turned their attention toward topics such as children's relationship with other animals, their understanding of life and ecological systems, their moral reasoning about environmental issues, and the implications of their experiences (or lack thereof) in natural settings.

Developmental psychologists have largely neglected the study of children's relationship with animals, even though animals are a primary focus in children's lives in a variety of forms: as live, stuffed, or imaginary companions; as captive or wild specimens; as zoo attractions; as targets of cruelty; as characters in books and on television; and as roles the children themselves assume. Recently, however, a few developmental psychologists have proposed that in order to fully understand the development of children's perceptual systems, their love relationships and empathy, their play patterns, their fears, and their sense of self, researchers must extend the list of important influences on children to include nonhuman animals—perhaps even putting animals at the top of the list (Melson, 2001, 2003; Myers, 2007).

Experience with animals makes an important contribution in teaching children about the differences between living and nonliving things. But as you learned in Chapter 6, learning experiences interact with inherited predispositions. The genetic makeup of the brain enables humans to learn certain concepts more easily than others. For instance,

Experience with animals during childhood can have an impact on people's attitudes about nature in general, not to mention their feelings about the importance of preserving endangered species.

© Ariel Shelley/CORBIS

© Kevin Fleming/CORBIS

folkbiology is a term used to describe how people intuitively perceive, categorize, and think about living things. Research on folkbiology suggests that children recognize a "life force" as something unique to biological phenomena and that they make distinctions between living and nonliving things as well as among plants, animals, and humans (Hatano & Inagaki, 1999; Inagaki & Hatano, 2004). Researchers have also begun to address the questions of whether the acquisition of folkbiological knowledge is a continuous developmental process or a discontinuous one, in which a child's view of the world is replaced by a more sophisticated adult understanding (Coley, Solomon, & Shafto, 2002), and whether the acquisition of folkbiological knowledge occurs in the same way across cultures (e.g., Waxman, 2005). Research on children's folkbiology will not only broaden understanding of cognitive development in general but may also help psychologists to better understand why and how adults' unsustainable behaviors may be influenced by *anthropocentric* (human-centered) thinking and ignorance about ecology.

Children make categorical distinctions between humans, nonhuman animals, plants, and nonliving things, but do they make *moral* distinctions between them? Research suggests the answer is "yes." In several cross-cultural studies, children showed strong moral prohibitions against pollution and associated damage to natural systems, including other species. Their concerns reflected anthropocentric values (harm to humans) as well as biocentric values (reviewed in Kahn, 2003). From the biocentric perspective, natural systems have inherent value and rights and deserve respect comparable to humans. Reasoning that involves seeing the similarities between oneself and natural species such as trees can "evoke feelings of empathy for [an] object that permit it to be regarded as something worthy of moral consideration" (Gebhard, Nevers, & Billmann-Mahecha, 2003, p. 92).

Experiences in nature during childhood help determine whether or not people recognize themselves as part of nature, feel connected to it, and understand that protecting nature is key to their own survival and well-being (Gebhard et al., 2003; Horton, 2004; Kals & Ittner, 2003; Searles, 1960). Activists, conservation volunteers, and ecologists often attribute their environmental commitment to early personal experiences in nature, family members who modeled appreciation for nature, or feelings of distress over the destruction of a favorite natural place (Bragg, 1996; Chawla, 1998; Guiney & Oberhauser, 2009; Horwitz, 1996). Increasingly, child development experts are becoming convinced that children need outdoor experiences to fully develop their emotional, physical, mental, and social capabilities (e.g., Kahn & Kellert, 2002), a theory that captured the attention of the popular media with the publication of *Last Child in the Woods: Saving Our Children from Nature Deficit Disorder* (Louv, 2005). Although empirical data remain somewhat sparse, some theorists suggest that children need opportunities for spontaneous and independent play or activity in areas that are generally outside human intervention and control (Kellert, 2002; Mergen, 2003; Pyle, 1993). Independent adventure, risk taking, and exploration can foster a sense of mastery, self-sufficiency, and confidence (Derr, 2006). Like adults, children show preferences for natural settings and report that nature offers restoration and relief from stress (e.g., Korpela, 2002; Simmons, 1994). Refuges in the form of forts and dens in natural settings are beloved play spaces for many children, primarily because they represent areas under the children's control (Sobel, 2002).

Children's mental health also suffers when deprived of experiences in nature. Children living in rural communities with more "nearby nature" have less psychological distress, including anxiety, depression, and conduct disorders such as bullying, than those living in urban areas (Wells & Evans, 2003). Nature encounters can reduce the adverse effects of trauma and childhood distress on children's feelings of global self-worth. Studies have also demonstrated that symptoms of *attention deficit hyperactivity disorders* can be ameliorated by "green activities" such as camping, fishing, soccer, or a simple "walk in the park" (Faber Taylor & Kuo, 2009; Faber Tayler, Kuo & Sullivan, 2001). Even passive time spent in outdoor green settings while relaxing or reading a book is negatively correlated with symptoms of attention deficit disorder (Faber Taylor et al., 2001; see also Kuo & Faber Taylor, 2004). While methodological issues may limit some causal inferences (Canu & Gordon, 2005; Kuo & Faber Taylor, 2005), these studies suggest promising research directions and alternative treatment options for the growing problem of attention deficit disorder.

However, many children today experience only degraded and polluted conditions, making identification with nature more difficult (Kahn, 2007; Kals & Ittner, 2003; Pyle, 2002). Further, the average child in the United States today spends less than 30 minutes per week engaged in outdoor activities (Hofferth & Curtin, 2005; Hofferth & Sandberg, 2001). More time inside generally means more time in front of a TV or other media sources such as a computer or video game; children are currently spending as many as 6 to 9 hours per day engaged with electronic media (Roberts, Foehr, & Rideout, 2005; Strasburger, 2007). Time with technologies such as television and videogames results in less quality time interacting with siblings and parents, less time spent doing homework (as much as an 18% reduction), and less creative play (Vandewater, Bickham, & Lee, 2006), including outdoors. These trends rob children of free time outside and mitigate their understanding of the natural world. Because some investigators have argued that the love of nature and concern about its protection is *only* developed with regular, consistent contact and play outside (Chawla, 1988; Pyle, 2002; Wilson, 1993), children who spend most of their time indoors are less likely to engage in pro-environmental actions.

Perhaps most significant in terms of environmental issues, increased time interacting with media exposes children to an astonishing amount of marketing. The average child sees over 40,000 advertisements on television each year (Linn, 2004). Contemporary advertisers send their messages via television, the Internet, computer games, cell phones, MP3 players, DVDs, virtual world websites, books, and school advertisements (Linn, 2008). This commercialization of childhood constitutes the foundation of the highly destructive consumer culture that depletes resources and degrades the environment (Kasser, 2002; Linn, 2008), in addition to negatively affecting a child's development.

Insights from Health and Clinical Psychology

You read in Chapter 14 about the physiology of stress and its associated behavioral and health problems. It turns out that many aspects of contemporary environments that are ecologically unsound are also significant human stressors. Urban noise, traffic, crowding, pollution, and living near toxic industries or waste sites are all associated with increased stress and related symptoms such as anxiety, depression, anger, and aggression (Bell et al., 2001; Hartig et al., 2003; Kuo & Sullivan, 2001; Lima, 2004; Lundberg, 1998), as well as self-reported tension, irritability, distractibility, impaired interpersonal behaviors, and deficits in task performance (Evans & Cohen, 1987; Weil & Rosen, 1997).

The effects of catastrophic environmental events such as loss of loved ones, damage to personal belongings, housing disruption or displacement, and worry about future crises can cause *posttraumatic stress disorder* (see Chapter 15) and related problems such as grief, depression and suicide attempts, anxiety, and substance abuse (Fritze et al., 2008). For example, mental health services were needed to treat depression, anxiety, and PTSD in approximately 250,000 survivors of Hurricane Katrina in 2005. Yet the storm devastated the infrastructure of Louisiana's Mental Health Office, a system that had accommodated only 40,000 patients prior to the catastrophe (Siegel, 2007).

The manufacture, use, and disposal of tens of thousands of industrial and household chemicals are causing or contributing to increased rates of various forms of cancer, birth defects, reproductive abnormalities, immune system dysfunction, neurological impairments, and developmental disabilities (including learning and attentional impairments, and autism), all significant stressors in their own right (e.g., Colborn, Dumanoski, & Myers, 1996; Grandjean & Landrigan, 2006; Koger, Schettler, & Weiss, 2005; U.S. E.P.A., 2008). More than 85,000 chemicals are currently registered with the Environmental Protection Agency, including *pesticides,* which are literally designed to kill (e.g., insects, weeds, and rodents); *flame retardants*; various *household chemicals* (paint thinners and other solvents, cleaning agents, bleach); and *industrial chemicals.* In addition, certain ingredients in *plastics, electronics,* and *cosmetics* are known to be toxic to humans and other animals. Children are vulnerable to the impacts of environmental toxins at all stages of development (Moore, 2009; Rice & Barone, 2000; Stein et al., 2002).

The net result is deteriorating health of human beings on physical, mental, emotional, and social levels, as well as degradation of the planet. Thus, the psychology of health and the environment reminds people that they are inherently interconnected with the rest of the biosphere—the health of human bodies is directly related to the health of the planet Earth. The good news is that if individuals perceive a situation or product to be harmful to personal well-being and health, they will be more motivated toward problem solving and specific behaviors that act to reduce the risks (Homburg & Stolberg, 2006). One innovation in such *problem-focused coping* is reflected in a unique program developed at the Environmental Health Clinic at New York University. Analogous to other university health clinics, "impatients" (people who are tired of waiting for legislative action) make appointments to discuss environmental health concerns, such as toxic chemicals and pollution, and receive "prescriptions" for actions, such as opportunities to engage in local data collection and projects intended to improve environmental health. The goal is to convert people's anxiety and concern about environmental issues into specific, measurable, and significant actions (Schaffer, 2008).

Perhaps not surprisingly, people strongly prefer healthy, natural settings that include water (lakes, rivers, oceans), plants, trees, and sunlight over urban environments filled with buildings and cars (Kaplan, 2001; Kaplan & Kaplan, 1989; van den Berg, Hartig

& Staats, 2007). Further, walking in natural settings or simply having views of trees or plants can alleviate symptoms of stress (Kaplan, 1993; Kaplan & Kaplan, 1989; van den Berg, Koole & van der Wulp, 2003) by activating the *parasympathetic nervous system* (see Chapters 3 and 10), providing recovery from sympathetic (fight or flight) arousal by reducing blood pressure and heart rate (Hartig et al., 2003; Laumann, Gärling, & Stormark, 2003). Comparably, activities such as gardening, caring for indoor plants, and interacting with non-human animals such as pet dogs can all reduce stress (Frumkin, 2001). Spending time in nature can also provide recovery from prolonged work and concentration. You can probably relate to the worn-out feeling that accompanies long-term cognitive effort during midterm and final exams. As little as 20 minutes spent in a natural setting has been shown to relieve this attentional fatigue (Berman, et al., 2008; Berto, 2005; Hartig & Staats, 2006; Kaplan, 1995). Time spent in nature has also been shown to be associated with overall emotional well-being (Hinds & Sparks, 2009) and mental health (Walsh, 2011).

Given the restorative features of nature, natural environments have long been used in outpatient and nature-immersion therapies (Chalquist, 2009). For instance, Jordan and Marshall (2010) pointed out that Freud took his clients outside for analytic walks during the therapy hour. *Wilderness therapy* programs and other therapies undertaken in natural settings take advantage of nature as a backdrop for traditional cognitive-behavioral or other therapeutic techniques or integrate wilderness skills and interaction as a part of therapy itself. Wilderness therapy typically involves trips lasting a month or more, whereas other approaches find therapist and client in nature for time periods ranging from an hour to full-time residential immersion lasting a few days to a year or longer. Client populations include kindergarten children (Berger & Lahad, 2010), adolescents struggling with

In recent years, psychologists have conducted some interesting research on the effects of exposure to natural settings (like the top two photos) versus human-created urban environments (like the bottom two photos). This research indicates that natural environments can decrease individuals' response to stress.

© Martyn Osman/Alamy

© Noam Armonn/Alamy

© Optic Design/Alamy

© EschCollection Royalty Free/Alamy

behavioral and emotional problems (e.g., Norton, 2010; Romi & Kohan, 2004), attachment-challenged adults (Bettmann & Jasperson, 2008), families (Swank & Daire, 2010), and women who have suffered abuse (Cole, Erdman, & Rothblum, 1994; McBride & Korell, 2005) or who have been diagnosed with breast cancer (Pascal, 2010). Because wilderness therapy programs have historically suffered from a lack of consistency in methods, quality, and practitioner credentials, as well as a lack of ethical oversight, some providers banded together in 1997 to form the Outdoor Behavioral Health Industry Council. Outcome research conducted by members of this organization and others interested in nature-based counseling is beginning to generate evidence that nature-based therapy can help improve self-perceptions, emotional well-being, resiliency, and social functioning in youth (e.g., Breunig et al., 2010; Cook, 2008; Harper et al., 2007; Russell, 2003). Families have experienced improved relationships and community-building skills (Swank & Daire, 2010).

A caution, however—while recognizing the value of restorative environments is important, doing so could also lead to exploitation. Saving natural resources only for the ways in which they can benefit humankind is a limited and anthropocentric view. As Greenway (1995) put it, "Perhaps the clearest evidence of our recovery will be that we do not demand that wilderness heal us. We will have learned to let it be. For a wilderness that must heal us is surely a commodity, just as when we can only look at wilderness as a source of endless wealth" (pp. 134–135).

Conclusion: A Positive Psychology

Advocates of positive psychology are interested in aspects of human experience that increase the quality and meaning of life, relationships with others, and empowerment to contribute to positive change (Breckler, 2007; Peterson & Seligman, 2004)—in other words, the eudaimic or "good" life, ethically lived (Adams, 2006; Pfaffenberger, 2007; Ryff & Singer, 2008). Wealth does not buy happiness; rather, to live well, humans must have meaningful connections with others (Csikszentmihalyi, 1999). Conservation psychologists draw from the *deep ecology* philosophy (e.g., Naess, 1985) in extending this attitude to include all life forms, in the development of the *ecologically connected self*. It seems likely that one's maximum potential can be reached only via participation toward the greater good (Bandura, 2006; Csikszentmihalyi, 1993; Rifkin, 2009; Rogers, 1995)—that is, the creation of society that can achieve sustainable life support for all species.

What You Can Personally Do

I am only one. But still I am one.
I cannot do everything, but still I can do something;
And because I cannot do everything,
I will not refuse to do the something that I can do.

—Quote from Edward Everett Hale (1822–1909), original source unknown

Many excellent guides are available (both online and in print) on how to become more environmentally responsible. You can start by taking the online quiz at http://www.myfootprint.org/ to determine your own ecological footprint and consider ways to alter your daily life based on your quiz results. You might also consider developing a *behavior modification* project (see the Personal Application in Chapter 6) addressing some of your environmentally relevant behaviors.

Six aspects of human lifestyles most significantly and adversely affect the environment (Gardner & Stern, 2008; Miller, 2007): agriculture, transportation, home energy use, water use, overall resource consumption and waste, and toxic chemical production, use, and disposal. We recommend that you think about these issues and take the following steps toward walking more lightly on the Earth. If you don't feel you can do all of them, select at least a few to get you started on a more sustainable lifestyle, and then add a new one each month.

Agriculture

- Reduce your meat consumption by eating *no meat* one day per week, then increase to two days, and so forth.
- Buy locally grown food for at least one month a year, and then try to increase this.
- Buy organically produced food or grow some of your own.

© 2009 kirktoons. Reproduced by permission.

Transportation

- Walk, bike, carpool, or take mass transit as much as you can.
- If possible, work at home or live near your work or school.
- When you have to drive, note that fuel efficiency can be dramatically increased by
    - reducing your speed
    - avoiding rapid acceleration and sudden stops (this also reduces wear on your brakes)
    - shutting off the engine rather than idling
    - keeping tires properly inflated
    - getting regular tune-ups, and
    - turning off your air conditioner.
- Record the distance you drive for one week (baseline), and then try to reduce the amount by 10%. Once you accomplish that, try reducing by 15% or more.
- When you purchase a new car, buy a small, fuel-efficient (greater than 35 mpg) model.

Home energy use

- Turn down the heat by at least a few degrees in winter, and avoid using air conditioning (or turn the thermostat up a few degrees).
- Turn off computers, printers, and other appliances when not in use.
- Replace your light bulbs with compact fluorescent bulbs.
- Decrease your energy waste by caulking leaks, adding insulation, and using energy-efficient lights, appliances, and heating/cooling systems.

Water use

- Always turn off the water while brushing your teeth, and consider turning off the water while soaping up, shampooing, or shaving.
- Take quick showers instead of baths.
- Reuse cups and plates when possible, rather than washing after each use.
- Only run dishwashers and clothes-washers with full loads.
- If possible, install water-saving showers and toilets.
- Use the flushing rule: "If it's yellow, let it mellow, if it's brown, flush it down" (urine is sterile).

Resource Consumption

- The two most important ways to reduce consumption and waste are *Refuse* and *Reuse* (refer to the "Unshopping Card" in **Figure D.4**). Refusing and reusing will save you money, as well as reduce your environmental impact. Recycling is important, but it still requires energy and encourages the production and use of more and more stuff. Keep a list of things you refused to buy or reused, and try to expand the list each month.
- *Refusing*: Every time you start to buy something, ask yourself whether you really need it, and if you do, whether you can borrow or rent it. If you must buy it, ask yourself if you are purchasing the most eco-friendly version of whatever it is. Note that many products are misleadingly labeled "eco-friendly" or "all natural."
- *Reusing*: Examine your lifestyle and figure out which things you can reuse, such as coffee cups, canvas or other bags for groceries, and your own container for getting food to go and for leftovers when you eat out.
- Buy secondhand items of all kinds whenever possible, and give away, donate to charity, or sell items you no longer need or use, rather than throwing them away.
- Junk mail generates an astonishing amount of waste, utilizes an incredible amount of natural resources, and contributes to climate change. Let organizations know that you don't want to receive their newsletters, catalogs, and solicitations, and be sure to recycle mailings you can't refuse.

Toxic Chemicals

- Pesticides are designed to kill bugs (insecticides), weeds (herbicides), rodents, and so forth. They are directly toxic to humans as well, producing cancers and developmental disabilities, among other disorders. Don't use any pesticides in your home, lawn, or garden, and educate others about their impacts on human health and neurological function, as well as detrimental effects on biodiversity.
- Avoid chemical cleansers. Baking soda and vinegar are excellent alternatives to many cleaning products; vinegar is also an effective herbicide (weed killer).
- Many plastics, cosmetics, and personal care products contain chemicals that disrupt normal hormone functions (e.g., phthalates and bisphenol A or BPA). Don't buy bottled water, don't reheat or microwave foods in plastic containers, use fewer products with fewer ingredients, and don't trust claims like "dermatologist-tested," "natural," or "organic." Read the ingredient labels and avoid fragrances, dyes, parabens or -paraben, and things you can't pronounce.
- Reduce use of plastics by bringing your own refillable containers, buying in bulk, buying things with minimal packaging, and purchasing products in recyclable and recycled packaging.
- Dispose of household toxic products properly. Many items—paints, pesticides, batteries, and even energy-efficient compact fluorescent light bulbs—contain toxic ingredients. Drop these items off at a local household hazardous waste site.

Glossary

A

Absolute refractory period The minimum length of time after an action potential during which another action potential cannot begin.

Absolute threshold The minimum amount of stimulation that an organism can detect for a specific type of sensory input.

Achievement motive The need to master difficult challenges, to outperform others, and to meet high standards of excellence.

Achievement tests Tests that gauge a person's mastery and knowledge of various subjects.

Acquired immune deficiency syndrome (AIDS) A disorder in which the immune system is gradually weakened and eventually disabled by the human immunodeficiency virus (HIV).

Acquisition The formation of a new conditioned response tendency.

Action potential A brief change in a neuron's electrical charge.

Acute stressors Threatening events that have a relatively short duration and a clear endpoint.

Adaptation An inherited characteristic that increased in a population (through natural selection) because it helped solve a problem of survival or reproduction during the time it emerged.

Additive color mixing Formation of colors by superimposing lights, putting more light in the mixture than exists in any one light by itself.

Adoption studies Research studies that assess hereditary influence by examining the resemblance between adopted children and both their biological and their adoptive parents.

Affective forecasting A person's efforts to predict his or her emotional reactions to future events.

Afferent nerve fibers Axons that carry information inward to the central nervous system from the periphery of the body.

Afterimage A visual image that persists after a stimulus is removed.

Aggression Any behavior that is intended to hurt someone, either physically or verbally.

Agonist A chemical that mimics the action of a neurotransmitter.

Agoraphobia A fear of going out to public places.

Alcohol A variety of beverages containing ethyl alcohol.

Algorithm A methodical, step-by-step procedure for trying all possible alternatives in searching for a solution to a problem.

Amnesia A significant memory loss that is too extensive to be due to normal forgetting. See also *Anterograde amnesia, Retrograde amnesia.*

Androgens The principal class of gonadal hormones in males.

Anecdotal evidence Personal stories about specific incidents and experiences.

Anhedonia A diminished ability to experience pleasure.

Anorexia nervosa Eating disorder characterized by intense fear of gaining weight, disturbed body image, refusal to maintain normal weight, and dangerous measures to lose weight.

Antagonist A chemical that opposes the action of a neurotransmitter.

Anterograde amnesia Loss of memories for events that occur after a head injury.

Antianxiety drugs Medications that relieve tension, apprehension, and nervousness.

Antidepressant drugs Medications that gradually elevate mood and help bring people out of a depression.

Antipsychotic drugs Medications used to gradually reduce psychotic symptoms, including hyperactivity, mental confusion, hallucinations, and delusions.

Antisocial personality disorder A type of personality disorder marked by impulsive, callous, manipulative, aggressive, and irresponsible behavior that reflects a failure to accept social norms.

Anxiety disorders A class of disorders marked by feelings of excessive apprehension and anxiety.

Applied psychology The branch of psychology concerned with everyday, practical problems.

Approach-approach conflict A conflict situation in which a choice must be made between two attractive goals.

Approach-avoidance conflict A conflict situation in which a choice must be made about whether to pursue a single goal that has both attractive and unattractive aspects.

Aptitude tests Psychological tests used to assess talent for specific types of mental ability.

Archetypes According to Jung, emotionally charged images and thought forms that have universal meaning.

Argument One or more premises used to provide support for a conclusion.

Ascending reticular activating system (ARAS) The afferent fibers running through the reticular formation that influence physiological arousal.

Assumptions Premises for which no proof or evidence is offered.

Attachment A close, emotional bond of affection between infants and their caregivers.

Attention Focusing awareness on a narrowed range of stimuli or events.

Attitudes Orientations that locate objects of thought on dimensions of judgment.

Attributions Inferences that people draw about the causes of events, others' behavior, and their own behavior.

Auditory localization Locating the source of a sound in space.

Autonomic nervous system (ANS) The system of nerves that connect to the heart, blood vessels, smooth muscles, and glands.

Availability heuristic Basing the estimated probability of an event on the ease with which relevant instances come to mind.

Aversion therapy A behavior therapy in which an aversive stimulus is paired with a stimulus that elicits an undesirable response.

Avoidance-avoidance conflict A conflict situation in which a choice must be made between two unattractive goals.

Avoidance learning Learning that has occurred when an organism engages in a response that prevents aversive stimulation from occurring.

Axon A long, thin fiber that transmits signals away from the neuron cell body to other neurons, or to muscles or glands.

B

Behavior Any overt (observable) response or activity by an organism.

Behavior modification A systematic approach to changing behavior through the application of the principles of conditioning.

Behavior therapies Application of the principles of learning to direct efforts to change clients' maladaptive behaviors.

Behavioral contract A written agreement outlining a promise to adhere to the contingencies of a behavior modification program.

Behaviorism A theoretical orientation based on the premise that scientific psychology should study only observable behavior.

Bilingualism The acquisition of two languages that use different speech sounds, vocabularies, and grammatical rules.

Binge-eating disorder Distress-induced eating binges that are not accompanied by the purging, fasting, and excessive exercise seen in bulimia.

Binocular depth cues Clues about distance based on the differing views of the two eyes.

Biological rhythms Periodic fluctuations in physiological functioning.

Biomedical therapies Physiological interventions intended to reduce symptoms associated with psychological disorders.

Biopsychosocial model A model of illness that holds that physical illness is caused by a complex interaction of biological, psychological, and sociocultural factors.

Bipolar disorder (formerly known as manic-depressive disorder) Mood disorder marked by the experience of both depressed and manic periods.

Bisexuals Persons who seek emotional-sexual relationships with members of either sex.

Body mass index (BMI) Weight (in kilograms) divided by height (in meters) squared (kg/m^2).

Bottom-up processing In form perception, progression from individual elements to the whole.

Bulimia nervosa Eating disorder characterized by habitually engaging in out-of-control overeating followed by unhealthy compensatory efforts, such as self-induced vomiting, fasting, abuse of laxatives and diuretics, and excessive exercise.

Burnout Physical, mental, and emotional exhaustion that is attributable to work-related stress.

Bystander effect A paradoxical social phenomenon in which people are less likely to provide needed help when they are in groups than when they are alone.

C

Cannabis The hemp plant from which marijuana, hashish, and THC are derived.

Case study An in-depth investigation of an individual subject.

Catastrophic thinking Unrealistically pessimistic appraisals of stress that exaggerate the magnitude of one's problems.

Catatonic schizophrenia A type of schizophrenia marked by striking motor disturbances, ranging from muscular rigidity to random motor activity.

Catharsis The release of emotional tension.

Central nervous system (CNS) The brain and the spinal cord.

Centration The tendency to focus on just one feature of a problem, neglecting other important aspects.

Cephalocaudal trend The head-to-foot direction of motor development.

Cerebral cortex The convoluted outer layer of the cerebrum.

Cerebral hemispheres The right and left halves of the cerebrum.

Channel The medium through which a message is sent.

Chromosomes Threadlike strands of DNA (deoxyribonucleic acid) molecules that carry genetic information.

Chronic stressors Threatening events that have a relatively long duration and no readily apparent time limit.

Chunk A group of familiar stimuli stored as a single unit.

Circadian rhythms The 24-hour biological cycles found in humans and many other species.

Classical conditioning A type of learning in which a neutral stimulus acquires the ability to evoke a response that was originally evoked by another stimulus.

Client-centered therapy An insight therapy that emphasizes providing a supportive emotional climate for clients, who play a major role in determining the pace and direction of their therapy.

Clinical psychologists Psychologists who specialize in the diagnosis and treatment of psychological disorders and everyday behavioral problems.

Clinical psychology The branch of psychology concerned with the diagnosis and treatment of psychological problems and disorders.

Cochlea The fluid-filled, coiled tunnel in the inner ear that contains the receptors for hearing.

Coefficient of determination The percentage of variation in one variable that can be predicted based on the other variable.

Cognition The mental processes involved in acquiring knowledge.

Cognitive-behavioral treatments A varied combination of verbal interventions and behaviora modification techniques used to help clients change maladaptive patterns of thinking.

Cognitive development Transitions in youngsters' patterns of thinking, including reasoning, remembering, and problem solving.

Cognitive dissonance A psychological state that exists when related cognitions are inconsistent.

Cognitive therapy An insight therapy that emphasizes recognizing and changing negative thoughts and maladaptive beliefs.

Cohort effects Differences between age groups that are attributable to the groups growing up in different time periods.

Collective unconscious According to Jung, a storehouse of latent memory traces inherited from people's ancestral past.

Collectivism Putting group goals ahead of personal goals and defining one's identity in terms of the groups one belongs to.

Color blindness Deficiency in the ability to distinguish among colors.

Comorbidity The coexistence of two or more disorders.

Companionate love Warm, trusting, tolerant affection for another whose life is deeply intertwined with one's own.

Compensation According to Adler, efforts to overcome imagined or real inferiorities by developing one's abilities.

Complementary colors Pairs of colors that produce gray tones when added together.

Conceptual hierarchy A multilevel classification system based on common properties among items.

Concordance rate The percentage of twin pairs or other pairs of relatives that exhibit the same disorder.

Conditioned reinforcers. See *Secondary reinforcers.*

Conditioned response (CR) A learned reaction to a conditioned stimulus that occurs because of previous conditioning.

Conditioned stimulus (CS) A previously neutral stimulus that has, through conditioning, acquired the capacity to evoke a conditioned response.

Cones Specialized visual receptors that play a key role in daylight vision and color vision.

Confirmation bias The tendency to seek information that supports one's decisions and beliefs while ignoring disconfirming information.

Conflict A state that occurs when two or more incompatible motivations or behavioral impulses compete for expression.

Conformity The tendency for people to yield to real or imagined social pressure.

Confounding of variables A condition that exists whenever two variables are linked together in a way that makes it difficult to sort out their independent effects.

Conjunction fallacy An error that occurs when people estimate that the odds of two uncertain events happening together are greater than the odds of either event happening alone.

Connectionist models. See *parallel distributed processing (PDP) models.*

Conscious Whatever one is aware of at a particular point in time.

Conservation Piaget's term for the awareness that physical quantities remain constant in spite of changes in their shape or appearance.

Conservation psychology The study of the interactive relationships between humans and the rest of nature, with a particular focus on how to enhance conservation of natural resources.

Consolidation A hypothetical process involving the gradual conversion of information into durable memory codes stored in long-term memory.

Construct validity The extent to which there is evidence that a test measures a particular hypothetical construct.

Constructive coping Relatively healthful efforts that people make to deal with stressful events.

Content validity The degree to which the content of a test is representative of the domain it's supposed to cover.

Continuous reinforcement Reinforcing every instance of a designated response.

Control group Subjects in a study who do not receive the special treatment given to the experimental group.

Convergence A cue to depth that involves sensing the eyes converging toward each other as they focus on closer objects.

Convergent thinking Narrowing down a list of alternatives to converge on a single correct answer.

Coping Active efforts to master, reduce, or tolerate the demands created by stress.

Corpus callosum The structure that connects the two cerebral hemispheres.

Correlation The extent to which two variables are related to each other.

Correlation coefficient A numerical index of the degree of relationship between two variables.

Counseling psychologists Psychologists who specialize in the treatment of everyday adjustment problems.

Couples (marital) therapy The treatment of both partners in a committed, intimate relationship, in which the main focus is on relationship issues.

Creativity The generation of ideas that are original, novel, and useful.

Criterion-related validity Test validity that is estimated by correlating subjects' scores on a test with their scores on an independent criterion (another measure) of the trait assessed by the test.

Critical period A limited time span in the development of an organism when it is optimal for certain capacities to emerge because the organism is especially responsive to certain experiences.

Critical thinking The use of cognitive skills and strategies that increase the probability of a desired outcome.

Cross-sectional design A research design in which investigators compare groups of subjects of differing age who are observed at a single point in time.

Culture The widely shared customs, beliefs, values, norms, institutions, and other products of a community that are transmitted socially across generations.

Crystallized intelligence The ability to apply acquired knowledge and skills in problem solving.

Culture-bound disorders Abnormal syndromes found only in a few cultural groups.

Cumulative recorder A graphic record of reinforcement and responding in a Skinner box as a function of time.

D

Dark adaptation The process in which the eyes become more sensitive to light in low illumination.

Data collection techniques Procedures for making empirical observations and measurements.

Decision making The process of evaluating alternatives and making choices among them.

Declarative memory system Memory for factual information.

Deep brain stimulation (DBS) A treatment approach that involves a thin electrode being surgically implanted in the brain and connected to an implanted pulse generator so that various electrical currents can be delivered to brain tissue adjacent to the electrode.

Defense mechanisms Largely unconscious reactions that protect a person from unpleasant emotions such as anxiety and guilt.

Defensive attribution The tendency to blame victims for their misfortune, so that one feels less likely to be victimized in a similar way.

Deinstitutionalization Transferring the treatment of mental illness from inpatient institutions to community-based facilities that emphasize outpatient care.

Delusions False beliefs that are maintained even though they are clearly out of touch with reality.

Dementia An abnormal condition marked by multiple cognitive defects that include memory impairment.

Dendrites Branchlike parts of a neuron that are specialized to receive information.

Dependent variable In an experiment, the variable that is thought to be affected by the manipulation of the independent variable.

Depth perception Interpretation of visual cues that indicate how near or far away objects are.

Descriptive statistics Statistics that are used to organize and summarize data.

Destination memory Recalling to whom one has told what.

Development The sequence of age-related changes that occur as a person progresses from conception to death.

Developmental norms The average age at which individuals display various behaviors and abilities.

Deviation IQ scores Scores that locate subjects precisely within the normal distribution, using the standard deviation as the unit of measurement.

Diagnosis Distinguishing one illness from another.

Discrimination Behaving differently, usually unfairly, toward the members of a group.

Discriminative stimuli Cues that influence operant behavior by indicating the probable consequences (reinforcement or nonreinforcement) of a response.

Disorganized schizophrenia A type of schizophrenia in which particularly severe deterioration of adaptive behavior is seen.

Displacement Diverting emotional feelings (usually anger) from their original source to a substitute target.

Display rules Cultural norms that regulate the appropriate expressions of emotions.

Dissociation A splitting off of mental processes into two separate, simultaneous streams of awareness.

Dissociative amnesia A sudden loss of memory for important personal information that is too extensive to be due to normal forgetting.

Dissociative disorders A class of disorders in which people lose contact with portions of their consciousness or memory, resulting in disruptions in their sense of identity.

Dissociative fugue A disorder in which people lose their memory for their entire lives along with their sense of personal identity.

Dissociative identity disorder (DID) A type of dissociative disorder characterized by the coexistence in one person of two or more largely complete, and usually very different, personalities. Also called multiple-personality disorder.

Divergent thinking Trying to expand the range of alternatives by generating many possible solutions.

Dizygotic twins See *Fraternal twins*.

Dominant gene A gene that is expressed when paired genes are heterozygous (different).

Double-blind procedure A research strategy in which neither subjects nor experimenters know which subjects are in the experimental or control groups.

Dream analysis A psychoanalytic technique in which the therapist interprets the symbolic meaning of the client's dreams.

Drive An internal state of tension that motivates an organism to engage in activities that should reduce the tension.

E

Eating disorders Severe disturbances in eating behavior characterized by preoccupation with weight concerns and unhealthy efforts to control weight.

Eclecticism In psychotherapy, drawing ideas from two or more systems of therapy instead of committing to just one system.

Efferent nerve fibers Axons that carry information outward from the central nervous system to the periphery of the body.

Ego According to Freud, the decision-making component of personality that operates according to the reality principle.

Egocentrism A limited ability to share another person's viewpoint.

Elaboration Linking a stimulus to other information at the time of encoding.

Electrical stimulation of the brain (ESB) Sending a weak electric current into a brain structure to stimulate (activate) it.

Electroconvulsive therapy (ECT) A biomedical treatment in which electric shock is used to produce a cortical seizure accompanied by convulsions.

Electroencephalograph (EEG) A device that monitors the electrical activity of the brain over time by means of recording electrodes attached to the surface of the scalp.

Electromyograph (EMG) A device that records muscular activity and tension.

Electrooculograph (EOG) A device that records eye movements.

Elicit To draw out or bring forth.

Embryonic stage The second stage of prenatal development, lasting from two weeks until the end of the second month.

Emit To send forth.

Emotion A subjective conscious experience (the cognitive component) accompanied by bodily arousal (the physiological component) and by characteristic overt expressions (the behavioral component).

Empiricism The premise that knowledge should be acquired through observation.

Encoding Forming a memory code.

Encoding specificity principle The idea that the value of a retrieval cue depends on how well it corresponds to the memory code.

Endocrine system A group of glands that secrete chemicals into the bloodstream that help control bodily functioning.

Environmental psychology The subdiscipline concerned with the study of how individuals are affected by, and interact with, their physical environments.

Epidemiology The study of the distribution of mental or physical disorders in a population.

Epigenetics The study of heritable changes in gene expression that do not involve modifications to the DNA sequence.

Episodic memory system Chronological, or temporally dated, recollections of personal experiences.

Escape learning A type of learning in which an organism acquires a response that decreases or ends some aversive stimulation.

Etiology The apparent causation and developmental history of an illness.

Evaluative conditioning Efforts to transfer the emotion attached to an unconditioned stimulus (US) to a new conditioned stimulus (CS).

Evolutionary psychology Theoretical perspective that examines behavioral processes in terms of their adaptive value for a species over the course of many generations.

Experiment A research method in which the investigator manipulates a variable under carefully controlled conditions and observes whether any changes occur in a second variable as a result.

Experimental group The subjects in a study who receive some special treatment in regard to the independent variable.

Experimenter bias A phenomenon that occurs when a researcher's expectations or preferences about the outcome of a study influence the results obtained.

Explicit attitude Attitudes that people hold consciously and can readily describe.

Exposure therapies An approach to behavior therapy in which clients are confronted with situations that they fear so that they learn that these situations are really harmless.

Expressed emotion (EE) The degree to which a relative of a patient displays highly critical or emotionally overinvolved attitudes toward the patient.

External attributions Ascribing the causes of behavior to situational demands and environmental constraints.

Extinction The gradual weakening and disappearance of a conditioned response tendency.

Extraneous variables Any variables other than the independent variable that seem likely to influence the dependent variable in a specific study.

F

Factor analysis Statistical analysis of correlations among many variables to identify closely related clusters of variables.

Family studies Scientific studies in which researchers assess hereditary influence by examining blood relatives to see how much they resemble each other on a specific trait.

Family therapy The treatment of a family unit as a whole, in which the main focus is on family dynamics and communication.

Farsightedness A vision deficiency in which distant objects are seen clearly but close objects appear blurry.

Fast mapping The process by which children map a word onto an underlying concept after only one exposure to the word.

Feature analysis The process of detecting specific elements in visual input and assembling them into a more complex form.

Feature detectors Neurons that respond selectively to very specific features of more complex stimuli.

Fetal alcohol syndrome A collection of congenital (inborn) problems associated with excessive alcohol use during pregnancy.

Fetal stage The third stage of prenatal development, lasting from two months through birth.

Fight-or-flight response A physiological reaction to threat in which the autonomic nervous system mobilizes the organism for attacking (fight) or fleeing (flight) an enemy.

Fitness The reproductive success (number of descendants) of an individual organism relative to the average reproductive success of the population.

Fixation According to Freud, failure to move forward from one psychosexual stage to another as expected.

Fixed-interval (FI) schedule A reinforcement schedule in which the reinforcer is given for the first response that occurs after a fixed time interval has elapsed.

Fixed-ratio (FR) schedule A reinforcement schedule in which the reinforcer is given after a fixed number of nonreinforced responses.

Flashbulb memories Unusually vivid and detailed recollections of momentous events.

Fluid intelligence Basic reasoning ability, memory capacity, and speed of information processing.

Foot-in-the-door technique Getting people to agree to a small request to increase the chances that they will agree to a larger request later.

Forebrain The largest and most complicated region of the brain, encompassing a variety of structures, including the thalamus, hypothalamus, limbic system, and cerebrum.

Forgetting curve A graph showing retention and forgetting over time.

Fovea A tiny spot in the center of the retina that contains only cones; visual acuity is greatest at this spot.

Framing How issues are posed or how choices are structured.

Fraternal twins Twins that result when two eggs are fertilized simultaneously by different sperm cells, forming two separate zygotes. Also called *dizygotic twins*.

Free association A psychoanalytic technique in which clients spontaneously express their thoughts and feelings exactly as they occur, with as little censorship as possible.

Frequency distribution An orderly arrangement of scores indicating the frequency of each score or group of scores.

Frequency polygon A line figure used to present data from a frequency distribution.

Frustration The feeling that people experience in any situation in which their pursuit of some goal is thwarted.

Functional fixedness The tendency to perceive an item only in terms of its most common use.

Functionalism A school of psychology based on the belief that psychology should investigate the function or purpose of consciousness, rather than its structure.

Fundamental attribution error Observers' bias in favor of internal attributions in explaining others' behavior.

G

Galvanic skin response (GSR) An increase in the electrical conductivity of the skin that occurs when sweat glands increase their activity.

Gambler's fallacy The belief that the odds of a chance event increase if the event hasn't occurred recently.

Gender Culturally constructed distinctions between masculinity and femininity.

Gender differences Actual disparities between the sexes in typical behavior or average ability.

Gender roles Expectations about what is appropriate behavior for each sex.

Gender stereotypes Widely held beliefs about males' and females' abilities, personality traits, and behavior.

General adaptation syndrome Selye's model of the body's stress response, consisting of three stages: alarm, resistance, and exhaustion.

Generalized anxiety disorder A psychological disorder marked by a chronic, high level of anxiety that is not tied to any specific threat.

Genes DNA segments that serve as the key functional units in hereditary transmission.

Genetic mapping The process of determining the location and chemical sequence of specific genes on specific chromosomes.

Genotype A person's genetic makeup.

Germinal stage The first phase of prenatal development, encompassing the first two weeks after conception.

Glia Cells found throughout the nervous system that provide various types of support for neurons.

Group Two or more individuals who interact and are interdependent.

Group cohesiveness The strength of the liking relationships linking group members to each other and to the group itself.

Group polarization A phenomenon that occurs when group discussion strengthens a group's dominant point of view and produces a shift toward a more extreme decision in that direction.

Group therapy The simultaneous treatment of several clients in a group.

Groupthink A process in which members of a cohesive group emphasize concurrence at the expense of critical thinking in arriving at a decision.

Gustatory system The sensory system for taste.

H

Hallucinations Sensory perceptions that occur in the absence of a real, external stimulus, or gross distortions of perceptual input.

Hallucinogens A diverse group of drugs that have powerful effects on mental and emotional functioning, marked most prominently by distortions in sensory and perceptual experience.

Halo effect A distortion that occurs on questionnaires when one's overall evaluation of a person, object, or institution spills over to influence more specific ratings.

Health psychology The subfield of psychology concerned with how psychosocial factors relate to the promotion and maintenance of health and with the causation, prevention, and treatment of illness.

Hedonic adaptation An effect that occurs when the mental scale that people use to judge the pleasantness-unpleasantness of their experiences shifts so that their neutral point, or baseline for comparison, changes.

Heritability ratio An estimate of the proportion of trait variability in a population that is determined by variations in genetic inheritance.

Heterosexuals Persons who seek emotional-sexual relationships with members of the other sex.

Heterozygous condition The situation that occurs when two genes in a specific pair are different.

Heuristic A strategy, guiding principle, or rule of thumb used in solving problems or making decisions.

Hierarchy of needs Maslow's systematic arrangement of needs according to priority, which assumes that basic needs must be met before less basic needs are aroused.

Higher-order conditioning A type of conditioning in which a conditioned stimulus functions as if it were an unconditioned stimulus.

Hindbrain The part of the brain that includes the cerebellum and two structures found in the lower part of the brainstem: the medulla and the pons.

Hindsight bias The tendency to mold one's interpretation of the past to fit how events actually turned out.

Histogram A bar graph that presents data from a frequency distribution.

Homeostasis A state of physiological equilibrium or stability.

Homosexuals Persons who seek emotional-sexual relationships with members of the same sex.

Homozygous condition The situation that occurs when two genes in a specific pair are the same.

Hormones The chemical substances released by the endocrine glands.

Human factors (human engineering) psychology Area of psychology that examines the ways in which work, work systems, and system features can be designed or changed to most effectively correspond with the capabilities and limitations of human beings, often with a focus on the human body.

Humanism A theoretical orientation that emphasizes the unique qualities of humans, especially their freedom and their potential for personal growth.

Hypnosis A systematic procedure that typically produces a heightened state of suggestibility.

Hypothalamus A structure found near the base of the forebrain that is involved in the regulation of basic biological needs.

Hypothesis A tentative statement about the relationship between two or more variables.

I

Id According to Freud, the primitive, instinctive component of personality that operates according to the pleasure principle.

Identical twins Twins that emerge from one zygote that splits for unknown reasons. Also called *monozygotic twins*.

Identification Bolstering self-esteem by forming an imaginary or real alliance with some person or group.

Illusory correlation A misperception that occurs when people estimate that they have encountered more confirmations of an association between social traits than they have actually seen.

Immune response The body's defensive reaction to invasion by bacteria, viral agents, or other foreign substances.

Implicit attitudes Covert attitudes that are expressed in subtle automatic responses that people have little conscious control over.

Impossible figures Objects that can be represented in two-dimensional pictures but cannot exist in three-dimensional space.

Inattentional blindness Failure to see visible objects or events because one's attention is focused elsewhere.

Incentive An external goal that has the capacity to motivate behavior.

Incubation effect A phenomenon that occurs when new solutions surface for a previously unsolved problem after a period of not consciously thinking about the problem.

Incongruence The degree of disparity between one's self-concept and one's actual experience.

Independent variable In an experiment, a condition or event that an experimenter varies in order to see its impact on another variable.

Individualism Putting personal goals ahead of group goals and defining one's identity in terms of personal attributes rather than group memberships.

Industrial and organizational (I/O) psychology The branch of psychology concerned with human behavior in the work environment.

Industrial psychology Subfield of I/O psychology that deals with the how-to side, including how to select individuals for the right positions, how to evaluate their job performance, how to train them, and how to compensate them.

Inferential statistics Statistics that are used to interpret data and draw conclusions.

Informational influence Influence that operates when people look to others for guidance about how to behave in ambiguous situations.

Ingroup The group that people belong to and identify with.

Insanity A legal status indicating that a person cannot be held responsible for his or her actions because of mental illness.

Insight In problem solving, the sudden discovery of the correct solution following incorrect attempts based primarily on trial and error.

Insight therapies Psychotherapy methods characterized by verbal interactions intended to enhance clients' self-knowledge and thus promote healthful changes in personality and behavior.

Insomnia Chronic problems in getting adequate sleep.

Instinctive drift The tendency for an animal's innate responses to interfere with conditioning processes.

Integrity tests Standardized measures used to assess attitudes and experience related to honesty and trustworthiness.

Intellectual disability Subnormal general mental ability accompanied by deficiencies in everyday living skills originating prior to age 18.

Intelligence quotient (IQ) A child's mental age divided by chronological age, multiplied by 100.

Intelligence tests Psychological tests that measure general mental ability.

Intermittent reinforcement A reinforcement schedule in which a designated response is reinforced only some of the time.

Internal attributions Ascribing the causes of behavior to personal dispositions, traits, abilities, and feelings.

Internet addiction Spending an inordinate amount of time on the Internet and being unable to control online use.

Interpersonal attraction Positive feelings toward another.

Interpretation In psychoanalysis, the therapist's attempts to explain the inner significance of the client's thoughts, feelings, memories, and behaviors.

Introspection Careful, systematic observation of one's own conscious experience.

Involuntary commitment A civil proceeding in which people are hospitalized in psychiatric facilities against their will.

Irreversibility The inability to envision reversing an action.

J

Job analysis A method for breaking a job into its constituent parts.

Job satisfaction The positive or negative emotions associated with a job.

Journal A periodical that publishes technical and scholarly material, usually in a narrowly defined area of inquiry.

Just noticeable difference (JND) The smallest difference in the amount of stimulation that a specific sense can detect.

L

Language A set of symbols that convey meaning, and rules for combining those symbols, that can be used to generate an infinite variety of messages.

Language acquisition device (LAD) An innate mechanism or process that facilitates the learning of language.

Latent content According to Freud, the hidden or disguised meaning of the events in a dream.

Latent learning Learning that is not apparent from behavior when it first occurs.

Leadership The ability to influence and motivate people to pursue organizational goals.

Learned helplessness Passive behavior produced by exposure to unavoidable aversive events.

Learning A relatively durable change in behavior or knowledge that is due to experience.

Lens The transparent eye structure that focuses the light rays falling on the retina.

Lesioning Destroying a piece of the brain.

Lie detector. See *Polygraph.*

Life changes Any noticeable alterations in one's living circumstances that require readjustment.

Light adaptation The process whereby the eyes become less sensitive to light in high illumination.

Limbic system A densely connected network of structures roughly located along the border between the cerebral cortex and deeper subcortical areas.

Linguistic relativity The theory that one's language determines the nature of one's thought.

Link method Forming a mental image of items to be remembered in a way that links them together.

Long-term memory (LTM) An unlimited capacity store that can hold information over lengthy periods of time.

Long-term potentiation (LTP) A long-lasting increase in neural excitability in synapses along a specific neural pathway.

Longitudinal design A research design in which investigators observe one group of subjects repeatedly over a period of time.

Lowball technique Getting someone to commit to an attractive proposition before revealing the hidden costs.

Lucid dreams Dreams in which people can think clearly about the circumstances of waking life and the fact that they are dreaming, yet they remain asleep in the midst of a vivid dream.

M

Major depressive disorder Mood disorder characterized by persistent feelings of sadness and despair and a loss of interest in previous sources of pleasure.

Manic-depressive disorder See *Bipolar disorder.*

Manifest content According to Freud, the plot of a dream at a surface level.

Marital therapy See *Couples therapy.*

Matching hypothesis The idea that males and females of approximately equal physical attractiveness are likely to select each other as partners.

Maturation Development that reflects the gradual unfolding of one's genetic blueprint.

MDMA A compound drug related to both amphetamines and hallucinogens, especially mescaline; commonly called "ecstasy."

Mean The arithmetic average of the scores in a distribution.

Mere exposure effect The finding that repeated exposures to a stimulus promotes greater liking of the stimulus.

Median The score that falls exactly in the center of a distribution of scores.

Medical model The view that it is useful to think of abnormal behavior as a disease.

Meditation A family of mental exercises in which a conscious attempt is made to focus attention in a nonanalytical way.

Menarche The first occurrence of menstruation.

Mental age In intelligence testing, a score that indicates that a child displays the mental ability typical of a child of that chronological (actual) age.

Mental hospital A medical institution specializing in providing inpatient care for psychological disorders.

Mental retardation See *Intellectual disability.*

Mental set Persisting in using problem-solving strategies that have worked in the past.

Mentoring A form of on-the-job training in which a current and often-long term employee (the mentor) is paired with a new employee to aid his or her growth and development within the organization.

Message The information transmitted by a source.

Meta-analysis A research technique that combines the statistical results of many studies of the same question, yielding an estimate of the size and consistency of a variable's effects.

Metalinguistic awareness The ability to reflect on the use of language.

Method of loci A mnemonic device that involves taking an imaginary walk along a familiar path where images of items to be remembered are associated with certain locations.

Midbrain The segment of the brain stem that lies between the hindbrain and the forebrain.

Mirror neurons Neurons that are activated by performing an action or by seeing another monkey or person perform the same action.

Misinformation effect Phenomenon that occurs when participants' recall of an event they witnessed is altered by introducing misleading postevent information.

Mnemonic devices Strategies for enhancing memory.

Mode The score that occurs most frequently in a distribution.

Model A person whose behavior is observed by another.

Monocular depth cues Clues about distance based on the image from either eye alone.

Monozygotic twins See *Identical twins.*

Mood disorders A class of disorders marked by emotional disturbances of varied kinds that may spill over to disrupt physical, perceptual, social, and thought processes.

Mood stabilizers Drugs used to control mood swings in patients with bipolar mood disorders.

Morphemes The smallest units of meaning in a language.

Mortality salience The degree to which subjects' mortality is prominent in their minds.

Motion parallax Cue to depth that involves images of objects at different distances moving across the retina at different rates.

Motivated forgetting Purposeful suppression of memories.

Motivation Goal-directed behavior.

Motor development The progression of muscular coordination required for physical activities.

Multiple-personality disorder See *Dissociative identity disorder.*

N

Narcissism A personality trait marked by an inflated sense of importance, a need for attention and admiration, a sense of entitlement, and a tendency to exploit others.

Narcolepsy A disease marked by sudden and irresistible onsets of sleep during normal waking periods.

Narcotics Drugs derived from opium that are capable of relieving pain.

Natural selection Principle stating that heritable characteristics that provide a survival reproductive advantage are more likely than alternative characteristics to be passed on to subsequent generations and thus come to be "selected" over time.

Naturalistic observation A descriptive research method in which the researcher engages in careful, usually prolonged, observation of behavior without intervening directly with the subjects.

Nearsightedness A vision deficiency in which close objects are seen clearly but distant objects appear blurry.

Need for self-actualization The need to fulfill one's potential.

Negative reinforcement The strengthening of a response because it is followed by the removal of an aversive (unpleasant) stimulus.

Negative symptoms Schizophrenic symptoms that involve behavioral deficits, such as flattened emotions, social withdrawal, apathy, impaired attention, and poverty of speech.

Negatively skewed distribution A distribution in which most scores pile up at the high end of the scale.

Nerves Bundles of neuron fibers (axons) that are routed together in the peripheral nervous system.

Neurogenesis The formation of new neurons in the brain.

Neurons Individual cells in the nervous system that receive, integrate, and transmit information.

Neurotransmitters Chemicals that transmit information from one neuron to another.

Night terrors Abrupt awakenings from non-REM sleep accompanied by intense autonomic arousal and feelings of panic.

Nightmares Anxiety-arousing dreams that lead to awakening, usually from REM sleep.

Nondeclarative memory system Memory for actions, skills, and operations.

Nonsense syllables Consonant-vowel-consonant arrangements that do not correspond to words.

Non-REM (NREM) sleep Sleep stages 1 through 4, which are marked by an absence of rapid eye movements, relatively little dreaming, and varied EEG activity.

Normal distribution A symmetric, bell-shaped curve that represents the pattern in which many characteristics are dispersed in the population.

Normative influence Influence that operates when people conform to social norms for fear of negative social consequences.

Null hypothesis In inferential statistics, the assumption that there is no true relationship between the variables being observed.

O

Obedience A form of compliance that occurs when people follow direct commands, usually from someone in a position of authority.

Obesity The condition of being overweight.

Object permanence Recognizing that objects continue to exist even when they are no longer visible.

Observational learning A type of learning that occurs when an organism's responding is influenced by the observation of others, who are called models.

Obsessive-compulsive disorder (OCD) A type of anxiety disorder marked by persistent, uncontrollable intrusions of unwanted thoughts (obsessions) and urges to engage in senseless rituals (compulsions).

Oedipal complex According to Freud, children's manifestation of erotically tinged desires for their opposite-sex parent, accompanied by feelings of hostility toward their same-sex parent.

Olfactory system The sensory system for smell.

Operant chamber. See *Skinner box.*

Operant conditioning A form of learning in which voluntary responses come to be controlled by their consequences.

Operational definition A definition that describes the actions or operations that will be made to measure or control a variable.

Opiates. See *Narcotics.*

Optic chiasm The point at which the optic nerves from the inside half of each eye cross over and then project to the opposite half of the brain.

Optic disk A hole in the retina where the optic nerve fibers exit the eye.

Optical illusion See *Visual illusion.*

Optimism A general tendency to expect good outcomes.

Organizational culture The shared assumptions, beliefs, values, and customs of the people in an organization.

Organizational psychology Area of psychology concerned with how employees are integrated into the work environment. both emotionally and socially.

Organizational socialization The process by which new members are absorbed into the culture of an organization.

Outgroup People who are not part of the ingroup.

Overextensions Using a word incorrectly to describe a wider set of objects or actions than it is meant to.

Overlearning Continued rehearsal of material after one first appears to have mastered it.

Overregularization In children, incorrect generalization of grammatical rules to irregular cases where they do not apply.

P

Panic disorder A type of anxiety disorder characterized by recurrent attacks of overwhelming anxiety that usually occur suddenly and unexpectedly.

Parallel distributed processing (PDP) models Models of memory that assume cognitive processes depend on patterns of activation in highly interconnected computational networks that resemble neural networks. Also called *connectionist models.*

Paranoid schizophrenia A type of schizophrenia that is dominated by delusions of persecution along with delusions of grandeur.

Parasympathetic division The branch of the autonomic nervous system that generally conserves bodily resources.

Parental investment What each sex invests—in terms of time, energy, survival risk, and forgone opportunities—to produce and nurture offspring.

Partial reinforcement. See *Intermittent reinforcement.*

Participants The persons or animals whose behavior is systematically observed in a study.

Passionate love A complete absorption in another that includes tender sexual feelings and the agony and ecstasy of intense emotion.

Pavlovian conditioning. See *Classical conditioning.*

Percentile score A figure that indicates the percentage of people who score below the score one has obtained.

Perception The selection, organization, and interpretation of sensory input.

Perceptual asymmetries Left-right imbalances between the cerebral hemispheres in the speed of visual or auditory processing.

Perceptual constancy A tendency to experience a stable perception in the face of continually changing sensory input.

Perceptual hypothesis An inference about which distal stimuli could be responsible for the proximal stimuli sensed.

Perceptual set A readiness to perceive a stimulus in a particular way.

Peripheral nervous system All those nerves that lie outside the brain and spinal cord.

Person perception The process of forming impressions of others.

Personal unconscious According to Jung, the level of awareness that houses material that is not within one's conscious awareness because it has been repressed or forgotten.

Personality An individual's unique constellation of consistent behavioral traits.

Personality disorders A class of psychological disorders marked by extreme, inflexible personality traits that cause subjective distress or impaired social and occupational functioning.

Personality tests Psychological tests that measure various aspects of personality, including motives, interests, values, and attitudes.

Personality trait A durable disposition to behave in a particular way in a variety of situations.

Personnel psychology See *Industrial psychology.*

Phenotype The ways in which a person's genotype is manifested in observable characteristics.

Phi phenomenon The illusion of movement created by presenting visual stimuli in rapid succession.

Phobias Irrational fears of specific objects or situations.

Phobic disorder A type of anxiety disorder marked by a persistent and irrational fear of an object or situation that presents no realistic danger.

Phonemes The smallest units of sound in a spoken language.

Physical dependence The condition that exists when a person must continue to take a drug to avoid withdrawal illness.

Pictorial depth cues Clues about distance that can be given in a flat picture.

Pituitary gland The "master gland" of the endocrine system; it releases a great variety of hormones that fan out through the body, stimulating actions in the other endocrine glands.

Placebo effects The fact that subjects' expectations can lead them to experience some change even though they receive an empty, fake, or ineffectual treatment.

Placenta A structure that allows oxygen and nutrients to pass into the fetus from the mother's bloodstream and bodily wastes to pass out to the mother.

Pleasure principle According to Freud, the principle upon which the id operates, demanding immediate gratification of its urges.

Polygenic traits Characteristics that are influenced by more than one pair of genes.

Polygraph A device that records autonomic fluctuations while a subject is questioned, in an effort to determine whether the subject is telling the truth.

Population The larger collection of animals or people from which a sample is drawn and that researchers want to generalize about.

Positive psychology An approach to psychology that uses theory and research to better understand the positive, adaptive, creative, and fulfilling aspects of human existence.

Positive reinforcement Reinforcement that occurs when a response is strengthened because it is followed by the presentation of a rewarding stimulus.

Positive symptoms Schizophrenic symptoms that involve behavioral excesses or peculiarities, such as hallucinations, delusions, bizarre behavior, and wild flights of ideas.

Positively skewed distribution A distribution in which scores pile up at the low end of the scale.

Postsynaptic potential (PSP) A voltage change at the receptor site on a postsynaptic cell membrane.

Posttraumatic stress disorder (PTSD) Disturbed behavior that is attributed to a major stressful event but that emerges after the stress is over.

Preconscious According to Freud, the level of awareness that contains material just beneath the surface of conscious awareness that can easily be retrieved.

Prejudice A negative attitude held toward members of a group.

Premises The reasons presented to persuade someone that a conclusion is true or probably true.

Prenatal period The period from conception to birth, usually encompassing nine months of pregnancy.

Preparedness Species-specific predispositions to be conditioned in certain ways and not others.

Pressure Expectations or demands that one behave in a certain way.

Prevalence The percentage of a population that exhibits a disorder during a specified time period.

Primary appraisal An initial evaluation of whether an event is (1) irrelevant to you, (2) relevant but not threatening or (3) stressful.

Primary reinforcers Events that are inherently reinforcing because they satisfy biological needs.

Primary sex characteristics The sexual structures necessary for reproduction.

Proactive interference A memory problem that occurs when previously learned information interferes with the retention of new information.

Problem solving Active efforts to discover what must be done to achieve a goal that is not readily available.

Problem space The set of possible pathways to a solution considered by the problem solver.

Prognosis A forecast about the probable course of an illness.

Projection Attributing one's own thoughts, feelings, or motives to another.

Projective tests Psychological tests that ask subjects to respond to vague, ambiguous stimuli in ways that may reveal the subjects' needs, feelings, and personality traits.

Prospagnosia A forecast about the probable course of an illness.

Prospective memory The ability to remember to perform actions in the future.

Proximodistal trend The center-outward direction of motor development.

Psychiatrists Physicians who specialize in the diagnosis and treatment of psychological disorders.

Psychiatry A branch of medicine concerned with the diagnosis and treatment of psychological problems and disorders.

Psychoactive drugs Chemical substances that modify mental, emotional, or behavioral functioning.

Psychoanalysis An insight therapy that emphasizes the recovery of unconscious conflicts, motives, and defenses through techniques such as free association and transference.

Psychoanalytic theory A theory developed by Freud that attempts to explain personality, motivation, and mental disorders by focusing on unconscious determinants of behavior.

Psychodynamic theories All the diverse theories descended from the work of Sigmund Freud that focus on unconscious mental forces.

Psychological dependence The condition that exists when a person must continue to take a drug in order to satisfy intense mental and emotional craving for the drug.

Psychological test A standardized measure of a sample of a person's behavior.

Psychology The science that studies behavior and the physiological and cognitive processes that underlie it, and the profession that applies the accumulated knowledge of this science to practical problems.

Psychopharmacotherapy The treatment of mental disorders with medication.

Psychophysics The study of how physical stimuli are translated into psychological experience.

Psychosexual stages According to Freud, developmental periods with a characteristic sexual focus that leave their mark on adult personality.

Psychosomatic diseases Physical ailments with a genuine organic basis that are caused in part by psychological factors, especially emotional distress.

Puberty The period of early adolescence marked by rapid physical growth and the development of sexual (reproductive) maturity.

Pubescence The two-year span preceding puberty during which the changes leading to physical and sexual maturity take place.

Punishment An event that follows a response that weakens or suppresses the tendency to make that response.

Pupil The opening in the center of the iris that helps regulate the amount of light passing into the rear chamber of the eye.

R

Random assignment The constitution of groups in a study such that all subjects have an equal chance of being assigned to any group or condition.

Rationalization Creating false but plausible excuses to justify unacceptable behavior.

Reaction formation Behaving in a way that's exactly the opposite of one's true feelings.

Reaction range Genetically determined limits on IQ or other traits.

Reactivity Alteration of a subject's behavior as a result of the presence of an observer.

Reality monitoring The process of deciding whether memories are based on external sources (our perceptions of actual events) or internal sources (our thoughts and imaginations).

Reality principle According to Freud, the principle on which the ego operates, which seeks to delay gratification of the id's urges until appropriate outlets and situations can be found.

Recall A memory test that requires subjects to reproduce information on their own without any cues.

Receiver The person to whom a message is sent.

Receptive field The retinal area that, when stimulated, affects the firing of that cell.

Recessive gene A gene whose influence is masked when paired genes are different (heterozygous).

Reciprocal determinism The assumption that internal mental events, external environmental events, and overt behavior all influence each other.

Reciprocity norm The rule that people should pay back in kind what they receive from others.

Recognition A memory test that requires subjects to select previously learned information from an array of options.

Recruitment The process organizations use to identify potential employees for a job.

Refractory period A time following orgasm during which males are largely unresponsive to further stimulation.

Regression A reversion to immature patterns of behavior.

Regression toward the mean Effect that occurs when people who score extremely high or low on some trait are measured a second time and their new score falls closer to the mean (average).

Rehearsal The process of repetitively verbalizing or thinking about information to be stored in memory.

Reification Giving an abstract concept a name and then treating it as though it were a concrete, tangible object.

Reinforcement An event following a response that strengthens the tendency to make that response.

Reinforcement contingencies The circumstances or rules that determine whether responses lead to the presentation of reinforcers.

Relearning A memory test that requires a subject to memorize information a second time to determine how much time or effort is saved by having learned it before.

Reliability The measurement consistency of a test (or of other kinds of measurement techniques).

REM sleep A deep stage of sleep marked by rapid eye movements, high frequency brain waves, and dreaming.

REM sleep behavior disorder (RBD) A sleep problem marked by potentially troublesome dream enactments during REM periods.

Renewal effect Phenomenon that occurs if a response is extinguished in a different environment than it was acquired; the extinguished response will reappear if the animal is returned to the original environment where acquisition took place.

Replication The repetition of a study to see whether the earlier results are duplicated.

Representativeness heuristic Basing the estimated probability of an event on how similar it is to the typical prototype of that event.

Repression Keeping distressing thoughts and feelings buried in the unconscious.

Research methods Differing approaches to the manipulation and control of variables in empirical studies.

Resilience Successful adaptation to significant stress and trauma, as evidenced by a lack of serious negative outcomes.

Resistance Largely unconscious defensive maneuvers a client uses to hinder the progress of therapy.

Resistance to extinction In operant conditioning, the phenomenon that occurs when an organism continues to make a response after delivery of the reinforcer for it has been terminated.

Response set A tendency to respond to questions in a particular way that is unrelated to the content of the questions.

Respondent conditioning. See *Classical conditioning.*

Resting potential The stable, negative charge of a neuron when it is inactive.

Retention The proportion of material retained (remembered).

Retina The neural tissue lining the inside back surface of the eye; it absorbs light, processes images, and sends visual information to the brain.

Retinal disparity A cue to the depth based on the fact that objects within 25 feet project images to slightly different locations on the left and right retinas, so the right and left eyes see slightly different views of the object.

Retrieval Recovering information from memory stores.

Retroactive interference A memory problem that occurs when new information impairs the retention of previously learned information.

Retrograde amnesia Loss of memories for events that occurred prior to a head injury.

Retrospective memory The ability to remember events from the past or previously learned information.

Reuptake A process in which neurotransmitters are sponged up from the synaptic cleft by the presynaptic membrane.

Reversible figure A drawing that is compatible with two different interpretations that can shift back and forth.

Risky decision making Making choices under conditions of uncertainty.

Rods Specialized visual receptors that play a key role in night vision and peripheral vision.

S

Sample The collection of subjects selected for observation in an empirical study.

Sampling bias A problem that occurs when a sample is not representative of the population from which it is drawn.

Scatter diagram A graph in which paired *X* and *Y* scores for each subject are plotted as single points.

Schedule of reinforcement A specific presentation of reinforcers over time.

Schema An organized cluster of knowledge about a particular object or sequence of events.

Schizophrenic disorders A class of psychological disorders marked by disturbances in thought that spill over to affect perceptual, social, and emotional processes.

Secondary appraisal An evaluation of your coping resources and options for dealing with the stress.

Secondary (conditioned) reinforcers Stimulus events that acquire reinforcing qualities by being associated with primary reinforcers.

Secondary sex characteristics Physical features that are associated with gender but that are not directly involved in reproduction.

Sedatives Sleep-inducing drugs that tend to decrease central nervous system activation and behavioral activity.

Self-actualizing persons People with exceptionally healthy personalities, marked by continued personal growth.

Self-concept A collection of beliefs about one's own nature, unique qualities, and typical behavior.

Self-efficacy One's belief about one's ability to perform behaviors that should lead to expected outcomes.

Self-enhancement Focusing on positive feedback from others, exaggerating one's strengths, and seeing oneself as above average.

Self-esteem A person's overall assessment of her or his personal adequacy or worth.

Self-referent encoding Deciding how or whether information is personally relevant.

Self-report inventories Personality tests that ask individuals to answer a series of questions about their characteristic behavior.

Semantic memory system General knowledge that is not tied to the time when the information was learned.

Semantic network Concepts joined together by links that show how the concepts are related.

Semantics The area of language concerned with understanding the meaning of words and word combinations.

Sensation The stimulation of sense organs.

Sensory adaptation A gradual decline in sensitivity to prolonged stimulation.

Sensory memory The preservation of information in its original sensory form for a brief time, usually only a fraction of a second.

Separation anxiety Emotional distress seen in many infants when they are separated from people with whom they have formed an attachment.

Serial-position effect In memory tests, the fact that subjects show better recall for items at the beginning and end of a list than for items in the middle.

Sex The biologically based categories of male and female.

Sexual orientation A person's preference for emotional and sexual relationships with individuals of the same sex, the other sex, or either sex.

Shaping The reinforcement of closer and closer approximations of a desired response.

Short-term memory (STM) A limited-capacity store that can maintain unrehearsed information for about 20 to 30 seconds.

Skinner box A small enclosure in which an animal can make a specific response that is systematically recorded while the consequences of the response are controlled.

Sleep apnea A sleep disorder characterized by frequent reflexive gasping for air that awakens a person and disrupts sleep.

Slow-wave sleep (SWS) Sleep stages 3 and 4, during which low-frequency delta waves become prominent in EEG recordings.

Social comparison theory The idea that people compare themselves with others to understand and evaluate their own behavior.

Social desirability bias A tendency to give socially approved answers to questions about oneself.

Social loafing A reduction in effort by individuals when they work in groups as compared to when they work by themselves.

Social psychology The branch of psychology concerned with the way individuals' thoughts, feelings, and behaviors are influenced by others.

Social roles Widely shared expectations about how people in certain positions are supposed to behave.

Social skills training A behavior therapy designed to improve interpersonal skills that emphasizes shaping, modeling, and behavioral rehearsal.

Social support Various types of aid and succor provided by members of one's social networks.

Socialization The acquisition of the norms, roles, and behaviors expected of people in a particular society.

Soma The cell body of a neuron; it contains the nucleus and much of the chemical machinery common to most cells.

Somatic nervous system The system of nerves that connect to voluntary skeletal muscles and to sensory receptors.

Somnambulism (sleepwalking) Arising and wandering about while remaining asleep.

Source The person who sends a communication.

Source monitoring The process of making attributions about the origins of memories.

Source-monitoring error An error that occurs when a memory derived from one source is misattributed to another source.

Spermarche The first occurrence of ejaculation.

Split-brain surgery A procedure in which the bundle of fibers that connects the cerebral hemispheres (the corpus callosum) is cut to reduce the severity of epileptic seizures.

Spontaneous recovery In classical conditioning, the reappearance of an extinguished response after a period of nonexposure to the conditioned stimulus.

Spontaneous remission Recovery from a disorder without formal treatment.

Stage A developmental period during which characteristic patterns of behavior are exhibited and certain capacities become established.

Standard deviation An index of the amount of variability in a set of data.

Standardization The uniform procedures used in the administration and scoring of a test.

Statistical significance The condition that exists when the probability that the observed findings are due to chance is very low.

Statistics The use of mathematics to organize, summarize, and interpret numerical data. See also *Descriptive statistics, Inferential statistics.*

Stereotypes Widely held beliefs that people have certain characteristics because of their membership in a particular group.

Stimulants Drugs that tend to increase central nervous system activation and behavioral activity.

Stimulus discrimination The phenomenon that occurs when an organism that has learned a response to a specific stimulus does not respond in the same way to stimuli that are similar to the original stimulus.

Stimulus generalization The phenomenon that occurs when an organism that has learned a response to a specific stimulus responds in the same way to new stimuli that are similar to the original stimulus.

Storage Maintaining encoded information in memory over time.

Strange situation procedure A research method in which infants are exposed to a series of eight separation and reunion episodes to assess the quality of their attachment.

Stress Any circumstances that threaten or are perceived to threaten one's well-being and that thereby tax one's coping abilities.

Striving for superiority According to Adler, the universal drive to adapt, improve oneself, and master life's challenges.

Structuralism A school of psychology based on the notion that the task of psychology is to analyze consciousness into its basic elements and to investigate how these elements are related.

Subjective contours The perception of contrours where none actually exist.

Subjective well-being Individuals' perceptions of their overall happiness and life satisfaction.

Subjects See *Participants*.

Sublimation A defense mechanism in which unconscious, unacceptable impulses are channeled into socially acceptable, perhaps even admirable, behaviors.

Subliminal perception The registration of sensory input without conscious awareness.

Subtractive color mixing Formation of colors by removing some wavelengths of light, leaving less light than was originally there.

Superego According to Freud, the moral component of personality that incorporates social standards about what represents right and wrong.

Survey A descriptive research method in which researchers use questionnaires or interviews to gather information about specific aspects of subjects' behavior.

Sustainable world A world in which human activities and needs are balanced with those of other species and future generations, taking into account ecological as well as social and economic factors.

Sympathetic division The branch of the autonomic nervous system that mobilizes the body's resources for emergencies.

Synapse A junction where information is transmitted from one neuron to the next.

Syntax A system of rules that specify how words can be combined into phrases and sentences.

Systematic desensitization A behavior therapy used to reduce clients' anxiety responses through counterconditioning.

T

Tactile system The sensory system for touch.

Tardive dyskinesia A neurological disorder marked by chronic tremors and involuntary spastic movements.

Teams See *Work teams*.

Telegraphic speech Speech that consists mainly of content words; articles, prepositions, and other less critical words are omitted.

Temperament An individual's characteristic mood, activity level, and emotional reactivity.

Teratogens Any external agents, such as drugs or viruses, that can harm an embryo or fetus.

Terminal buttons Small knobs at the end of axons that secrete chemicals called neurotransmitters.

Test norms Standards that provide information about where a score on a psychological test ranks in relation to other scores on that test.

Testwiseness The ability to use the characteristics and format of a cognitive test to maximize one's score.

Theory A system of interrelated ideas that is used to explain a set of observations.

Theory of bounded rationality Simon's assertion that people tend to use simple strategies in decision making that focus on only a few facets of available options and often result in "irrational" decisions that are less than optimal.

Tip-of-the-tongue phenomenon A temporary inability to remember something accompanied by a feeling that it's just out of reach.

Tolerance A progressive decrease in a person's responsiveness to a drug.

Top-down processing In form perception, a progression from the whole to the elements.

Transcranial magnetic stimulation (TMS) A technique that permits scientists to temporarily enhance or depress activity in a specific area of the brain.

Transfer-appropriate processing The situation that occurs when the initial processing of information is similar to the type of processing required by the subsequent measures of attention.

Transference In therapy, the phenomenon that occurs when clients start relating to their therapists in ways that mimic critical relationships in their lives.

Transformational leadership Leadership characterized by high ethical standards, inspirational motivation, intellectual stimulation, and individual consideration.

Trial In classical conditioning, any presentation of a stimulus or pair of stimuli.

Trial and error Trying possible solutions sequentially and discarding those that are in error until one works.

Twin studies A research design in which hereditary influence is assessed by comparing the resemblance of identical twins and fraternal twins with respect to a trait.

Type A personality Personality characterized by (1) a strong competitive orientation, (2) impatience and time urgency, and (3) anger and hostility.

Type B personality Personality characterized by relatively relaxed, patient, easygoing, amicable behavior.

U

Unconditioned response (UR) An unlearned reaction to an unconditioned stimulus that occurs without previous conditioning.

Unconditioned stimulus (US) A stimulus that evokes an unconditioned response without previous conditioning.

Unconscious According to Freud, thoughts, memories, and desires that are well below the surface of conscious awareness but that nonetheless exert great influence on behavior.

Underextensions Errors that occur when a child incorrectly uses a word to describe a narrower set of objects or actions than it is meant to.

Undifferentiated schizophrenia A type of schizophrenia marked by idiosyncratic mixtures of schizophrenic symptoms.

V

Validity The ability of a test to measure what it was designed to measure.

Variability The extent to which the scores in a data set tend to vary from each other and from the mean.

Variable-interval (VI) schedule A reinforcement schedule in which the reinforcer is given for the first response after a variable time interval has elapsed.

Variable-ratio (VR) schedule A reinforcement schedule in which the reinforcer is given after a variable number of nonreinforced responses.

Variables Any measurable conditions, events, characteristics, or behaviors that are controlled or observed in a study.

Visual agnosia An inability to recognize objects.

Visual illusion An apparently inexplicable discrepancy between the appearance of a visual stimulus and its physical reality.

Volley principle The theory holding that groups of auditory nerve fibers fire neural impulses in rapid succession, creating volleys of impulses.

W

Work teams Two or more employees who have common goals, pursue tasks that are interdependent, interact socially, and work within specific requirements and rules.

Z

working memory capacity (WMC) One's ability to hold and manipulate information in conscious attention.

Zygote A one-celled organism formed by the union of a sperm and an egg.

References

Aamodt, M. G. (2010). *Industrial/organizational psychology: An applied approach.* Belmont, CA: Wadsworth.

Aamodt, M. G., & Rupert, G. T. (1990). Employee referral programs: Do successful employees refer better applicants than unsuccessful employees? *Proceedings of the Annual Meeting of the International Personnel Management Association Assessment Council,* San Diego, CA.

Abdel-Khalek, A. M. (2006). Happiness, health, and religiosity: Significant relations. *Mental Health, 9*(1), 85–97.

Abe, T., Komada, Y., Nishida, Y., Hayashida, K., & Inoue, Y. (2010). Short sleep duration and long spells of driving are associated with the occurrence of Japanese drivers' rear-end collisions and single-car accidents. *Journal of Sleep Research, 19*(2), 310–316. doi:10.1111/j.1365-2869.2009.00806.x

Abel, E. L., & Kruger, M. L. (2010). Smile intensity in photographs predicts longevity. *Psychological Science, 21*(4), 542–544.

Abel, M. H. (1998). Interaction of humor and gender in moderating relationships between stress and outcomes. *Journal of Psychology, 132,* 267–276.

Abel, M. H. (2002). Humor, stress, and coping strategies. *Humor: International Journal of Humor Research, 15,* 365–381.

Aboud, F. E., & Amato, M. (2001). Developmental and socialization influences on intergroup bias. In R. Brown & S. L. Gaertner (Eds.), *Blackwell handbook of social psychology: Intergroup processes.* Malden, MA: Blackwell.

Abrahamse, W., Steg, L., Vlek, C., & Rothengatter, T. (2005). A review of intervention studies aimed at household energy conservation. *Journal of Environmental Psychology, 25,* 273–291.

Abrams, D., & Hogg, M. A. (2010). Social identity and self-categorization. In J. F. Dovidio, M. Hewstone, P. Glick, & V. M. Esses (Eds.), *The Sage handbook of prejudice, stereotyping, and discrimination.* Los Angeles, CA: Sage.

Abramson, L. Y., Alloy, L. B., Hankin, B. L., Haeffel, G. J., MacCoon, D. G., & Gibb, B. E. (2002). Cognitive vulnerability–stress models of depression in a self-regulatory and psychobiological context. In I. H. Gotlib & C. L. Hammen (Eds.), *Handbook of depression.* New York, NY: Guilford Press.

Abramson, L. Y., Seligman, M. E. P., & Teasdale, J. (1978). Learned helplessness in humans: Critique and reformulation. *Journal of Abnormal Psychology, 87,* 32–48.

Accornero, V. H., Amado, A. J., Morrow, C. E., Xue, L., Anthony, J. C., & Bandstra, E. S. (2007). Impact of prenatal cocaine exposure on attention and response inhibition as assessed by continuous performance tests. *Journal of Developmental & Behavioral Pediatrics, 28,* 195–205.

Adam, T. C., & Epel, E. (2007). Stress, eating and the reward system. *Physiology and Behavior, 91,* 449–458.

Adams, J. L. (1980). *Conceptual blockbusting.* San Francisco, CA: W. H. Freeman.

Adams, R. L., & Culbertson, J. L. (2005). Personality assessment: Adults and children. In B. J. Sadock & V. A. Sadock (Eds.), *Kaplan & Sadock's comprehensive textbook of psychiatry.* Philadelphia, PA: Lippincott Williams & Wilkins.

Adams, W. W. (2006). The ivory–billed woodpecker, ecopsychology, and the crisis of extinction: On annihilating and nurturing other beings, relationships, and ourselves. *The Humanistic Psychologist, 34*(2), 111–133.

Ader, R. (2001). Psychoneuroimmunology. *Current Directions in Psychological Science, 10*(3), 94–98.

Ader, R. (2003). Conditioned immunomodulation: Research needs and directions. *Brain, Behavior, and Immunity, 17*(1), S51–S57.

Ader, R., & Cohen, N. (1984). Behavior and the immune system. In W. D. Gentry (Ed.), *Handbook of behavioral medicine.* New York, NY: Guilford Press.

Ader, R., & Cohen, N. (1993). Psychoneuroimmunology: Conditioning and stress. *Annual Review of Psychology, 44,* 53–85.

Adesope, O. O., Lavin, T., Thompson, T., & Ungerleider, C. (2010). A systematic review and meta-analysis of the cognitive correlates of bilingualism. *Review of Educational Research, 80*(2), 207–245. doi:10.3102/0034654310368803

Adler, A. (1917). *Study of organ inferiority and its psychical compensation.* New York, NY: Nervous and Mental Diseases Publishing Co.

Adler, A. (1927). *Practice and theory of individual psychology.* New York, NY: Harcourt, Brace & World.

Adler, L. L. (Ed.). (1993). *International handbook on gender roles.* Westport, CT: Greenwood.

Adolph, K. E., & Berger, S. E. (2005). Physical and motor development. In M. H. Bornstein & M. E. Lamb (Eds.), *Developmental science: An advanced textbook.* Mahwah, NJ: Erlbaum.

Adolph, K. E., & Berger, S. E. (2011). Physical and motor development. In M. H. Bornstein & M. E. Lamb (Eds.), *Developmental science: An advanced textbook* (pp. 109–198). New York, NY: Psychology Press.

Adolph, K. E., Karasik, L. B., & Tamis-Lemonda, C. S. (2010). Motor skills. In M. H. Bornstein (Ed.), *Handbook of cultural developmental science* (pp. 61–88). New York, NY: Psychology Press.

Affleck, G., Tennen, H., Urrows, S., & Higgins, P. (1994). Person and contextual features of daily stress reactivity: Individual differences in relations of undesirable daily events with mood disturbance and chronic pain intensity. *Journal of Personality and Social Psychology, 66,* 329–340.

Agarwal, P. K., Karpicke, J. D., Kang, S. K., Roediger, H., & McDermott, K. B. (2008). Examining the testing effect with open- and closed-book tests. *Applied Cognitive Psychology, 22*(7), 861–876. doi:10.1002/acp.1391

Agyeman, J., Doppelt, B., Lynn, K., & Hatic, H. (2007). The climate-justice link: Communicating risk with low-income and minority audiences. In S. C. Moser & L. Dilling (Eds.), *Creating a climate for change: Communicating climate change and facilitating social change* (pp. 119–138). New York, NY: Cambridge University Press.

Ahima, R. S., & Osei, S. Y. (2004). Leptin signaling. *Physiology & Behavior, 81,* 223–241.

Ahlgren, M., Wohlfahrt, J., Olsen, L. W., Sorensen, T. L., & Melbye, M. (2007). Birth weight and risk of cancer. *Cancer, 110*(2), 412–419. doi: 10.1002/cncr.22773

Aikins, D. E., & Craske, M. G. (2001). Cognitive theories of generalized anxiety disorder. *Psychiatric Clinics of North America, 24*(1), 57–74.

Ainsworth, M. D. S. (1979). Attachment as related to mother-infant interaction. In J. S. Rosenblatt, R. A. Hinde, C. Beer, & M. Busnel (Eds.), *Advances in the study of behavior* (Vol. 9). New York, NY: Academic Press.

Ainsworth, M. D. S., Blehar, M. C., Waters, E., & Wall, S. (1978). *Patterns of attachment: A psychological study of the strange situation.* Hillsdale, NJ: Erlbaum.

Ajzen, I., & Fishbein, M. (2000). Attitudes and the attitude-behavior relation: Reasoned and automatic processes. In W. Stroebe & M. Hewstone (Eds.), *European review of social psychology* (Vol. 11). Chichester, UK: Wiley.

Ajzen, I., & Fishbein, M. (2005). The influence of attitudes on behavior. In D. Albarracin, B. T. Johnson, & M. P. Zanna (Eds.), *The handbook of attitudes.* Mahwah, NJ: Erlbaum.

Akarian, A. V., Bushnell, M. C., Treede, R.-D., & Zubieta, J.-K. (2005). Human brain mechanisms of pain perception and regulation in health and disease. *European Journal of Pain, 9,* 463–484.

Akerstedt, T., Hume, K., Minors, D., & Waterhouse, J. (1997). Good sleep—its timing and physiological sleep characteristics. *Journal of Sleep Research, 6,* 221–229.

Akgun, S., & Ciarrochi, J. (2003). Learned resourcefulness moderates the relationship between academic stress and academic performance. *Educational Psychology, 23,* 287–294.

Akiskal, H. S. (2009). Mood disorders: Clinical features. In B. J. Sadock, V. A. Sadock, & P. Ruiz (Eds.), *Kaplan & Sadock's comprehensive textbook of psychiatry* (9th ed., pp. 1693–1733). Philadelphia, PA: Lippincott, Williams & Wilkins.

Albarracin, D., & Vargas, P. (2010). Attitudes and persuasion: From biology to social responses to persuasive intent. In S. T. Fiske, D. T. Gilbert, G. Lindzey, & S. T. Fiske (Eds.), *Handbook of social psychology,* (5th ed., Vol.1) (pp. 353–393). Hoboken, NJ: Wiley.

Albert M. A. (2008). Neuropsychology of the development of Alzheimer's disease. In F. I. M. Craik & T. A. Salthouse (Eds.), *Handbook of aging and cognition* (2nd ed., pp. 97–132). New York, NY: Psychology Press.

Albert, M. S., & Killiany, R. J. (2001). Age-related cognitive change and brain-behavior relationships. In J. E. Birren & K. W. Schaie (Eds.), *Handbook of the psychology of aging* (5th ed., pp. 160–184). San Diego, CA: Academic Press.

Albert, M. S., & Moss, M. B. (2002). Neuropsychological approaches to preclinical identification of Alzheimer's disease. In L. R. Squire & D. L. Schacter (Eds.), *Neuropsychology of memory.* New York, NY: Guilford Press.

Alcock, J. (1998). *Animal behavior: An evolutionary approach.* Sunderland, MA: Sinauer Associates.

Alcock, J. (2005). *Animal behavior.* Sunderland, MA: Sinauer Associates.

Aldag, R. J., & Fuller, S. R. (1993). Beyond fiasco: A reappraisal of the groupthink phenomenon and a new model of group decision processes. *Psychological Bulletin, 113,* 533–552.

Aldington, S., Harwood, M., Cox, B., Weatherall, M., Beckert, L., Hansell, A., et al. (2008). Cannabis use and risk of lung cancer: A case-control study. *European Respiratory Journal, 31,* 280–286.

Aldington, S., Williams, M., Nowitz, M., Weatherall, M., Pritchard, A., McNaughton, A., et al. (2007). Effects of cannabis on pulmonary structure, function and symptoms. *Thorax, 62,* 1058–1063.

Aldrich, M. S. (2000). Cardinal manifestations of sleep disorders. In M. H. Kryger, T. Roth & W. C. Dement (Eds), *Principles and practice of sleep medicine.* Philadelphia, PA: Saunders.

Aldwin, C. M. (2007). *Stress, coping, and development: An integrative perspective* (2nd ed.). New York, NY: Guilford Press.

Aldwin, C. M., & Gilmer, D. F. (2004). *Health, illness, and optimal aging: Biological and psychosocial perspectives*. Thousand Oaks, CA: Sage Publications.

Alexander, C. N., Davies, J. L., Dixon, C. A., Dillbeck, M. C., Druker, S. M., Oetzel, R. M., Muehlman, J. M., & Orme-Johnson, D. W. (1990). Growth of higher states of consciousness: The Vedic psychology of human development. In C. N. Alexander & E. J. Langer (Eds.), *Higher stages of human development: Perspectives on adult growth*. New York, NY: Oxford University Press.

Alexander, C. N., Robinson, P., Orme-Johnson, D. W., Schneider, R. H., et al. (1994). The effects of transcendental meditation compared with other methods of relaxation and meditation in reducing risk factors, morbidity, and mortality. *Homeostasis in Health & Disease, 35*, 243–263.

Alexander, F. (1954). Psychoanalysis and psychotherapy. *Journal of the American Psychoanalytic Association, 2*, 722–733.

Alexander, J., & Tate, M. (1999). *Web wisdom: How to evaluate and create information quality on the web.* Mahwah, NJ: Erlbaum.

Alexander, M. G., & Fisher, T. D. (2003). Truth and consequences: Using the bogus pipeline to examine sex differences in self-reported sexuality. *Journal of Sex Research, 40*(1), 27–35.

Alhakami, A. S. & Slovic, P. (1994). A psychological study of the inverse relationship between perceived risk and perceived benefit. *Risk Analysis*, 14, 1085–1096.

Allan, R. W. (1998). Operant-respondent interactions. In W. O'Donohue (Ed.), *Learning and behavior therapy*. Boston, MA: Allyn & Bacon.

Allen, J. J. B., & Iacono, W. G. (2001). Assessing the validity of amnesia in dissociative identity disorder: A dilemma for the DSM and the courts. *Psychology, Public Policy, and Law, 7*, 311–344.

Allen, M., Emmers, T., Gebhardt, L., & Giery, M. A. (1995). Exposure to pornography and acceptance of rape myths. *Journal of Communication, 45*, 5–26.

Allen, M., Emmers-Sommer, T., D'Alessio, D., Timmerman, L., Hanzal, A., & Korus, J. (2007). The connection between the physiological and psychological reactions to sexually explicit materials: A literature summary using meta-analysis. *Communication Monographs, 74*, 541–560.

Allen, T. D., Lentz, E., & Day, R. (2006). Career success outcomes associated with mentoring others: A comparison of mentors and nonmentors. *Journal of Career Development, 32*, 272–285.

Allison, D. B., Heshka, S., Neale, M. C., Lykken, D. T., & Heymsfield, S. B. (1994). A genetic analysis of relative weight among 4,020 twin pairs, with an emphasis on sex effects. *Health Psychology, 13*, 362–365.

Alloy, L. B., Abramson, L. Y., Whitehouse, W. G., Hogan, M. E., Tashman, N. A., Steinberg, D. L., Rose, D. T., & Donovan, P. (1999). Depressogenic cognitive styles: Predictive validity, information processing and personality characteristics, and developmental origins. *Behavioral Research and Therapy, 37*, 503–531.

Allport, G. W. (1937). *Personality: A psychological interpretation.* New York, NY: Holt.

Almeida, D. M. (2005). Resilience and vulnerability to daily stressors assessed via diary methods. *Current Directions in Psychological Science, 14*(2), 64–68.

Altman, I. (1990). Centripetal and centrifugal trends in psychology. In L. Brickman & H. Ellis (Eds.), *Preparing psychologists for the 21st century: Proceedings of the National Conference on Graduate Education in Psychology*. Hillsdale, NJ: Erlbaum.

Amabile, T. M. (1996). *Creativity in context.* Boulder, CO: Westview.

Amabile, T. M. (2001). Beyond talent: John Irving and the passionate craft of creativity. *American Psychologist, 56*, 333–336.

Amato, P. R. (2006). Marital discord, divorce, and children's well-being: Results from a 20-year longitudinal study of two generations. In A. Clarke-Stewart & J. Dunn (Eds.), *Families count: Effects on child and adolescent development* (pp. 179–202). New York, NY: Cambridge University Press.

Amato, P. R., & Dorius, C. (2010). Fathers, children, and divorce. In M. Lamb (Ed.), *The role of the father in child development* (5th ed., pp. 177–200). Hoboken, NJ: Wiley.

Ambady, N., Hallahan, M., & Conner, B. (1999). Accuracy of judgments of sexual orientation from thin slices of behavior. *Journal of Personality and Social Psychology, 77*(3), 538–547. doi:10.1037/0022-3514.77.3.538

Ambady, N., & Rosenthal, R. (1993). Half a minute: Predicting teacher evaluations from thin slices of nonverbal behavior and physical attractiveness. *Journal of Personality and Social Psychology, 64*(3), 431–441. doi:10.1037/0022-3514.64.3.431

Ambady, N., & Weisbuch, M. (2010). Nonverbal behavior. In S. T. Fiske, D. T. Gilbert, & G. Lindzey (Eds.), *Handbook of social psychology* (5th ed., Vol. 1) (pp. 353–393). Hoboken, NJ: Wiley.

Amedi, A., Floel, A., Knecht, S., Zohary, E., & Cohen, L. G. (2004). Transcranial magnetic stimulation of the occipital pole interferes with verbal processing in blind subjects. *Nature Neuroscience, 7*, 1266–1270.

American Association of Suicidology. (2007). *Understanding and helping the suicidal individual.* Retrieved from http://www.suicidology.org/associations/1045/files/Understanding.pdf.

American Foundation for Suicide Prevention. (2007). *When you fear someone may take their own life.* Retrieved from http://www.afsp.org/index.cfm?page_id=F2F25092-7E90-9BD4-C4658F1D2B5D19A0

American Psychiatric Association. (1994). *Diagnostic and statistical manual of mental disorders* (4th ed.). Washington, DC: Author.

American Psychiatric Association. (2000). *Diagnostic and statistical manual of mental disorders* (4th ed. Text revision). Washington, DC: Author.

American Psychiatric Association Task Force on Electroconvulsive Therapy. (2001). *The practice of electroconvulsive therapy: Recommendations for treatment* (2nd ed.). Washington, DC: American Psychiatric Association.

American Psychological Association. (1984). *Behavioral research with animals.* Washington, DC: Author.

American Psychological Association. (2002). Ethical principles of psychologists and code of conduct. *American Psychologist, 57*, 1060–1073.

Amodio, D. M., & Devine, P. G. (2006). Stereotyping and evaluation in implicit race bias: Evidence for independent constructs and unique effects on behavior. *Journal of Personality and Social Psychology, 91*(4), 652–661. doi:10.1037/0022-3514.91.4.652

Amsterlaw, J., & Wellman, H. M. (2006). Theories of mind in transition: A microgenetic study of the development of false belief understanding. *Journal of Cognition and Development, 7*(2), 139–172. doi:10.1207/s15327647jcd0702_1

Amyx, D., & Alford, B. L. (2005). The effects of salesperson need for achievement and sales manager leader reward behavior. *Journal of Personal Selling & Sales Management, 25*(4), 345–359.

Anderluh, M. B., Tchanturia, K., & Rabe-Hesketh. (2003). Childhood obsessive-compulsive personality traits in adult women with eating disorders: Defining a broader eating disorder phenotype. *American Journal of Psychiatry, 160*, 242–247.

Anderson, A. E., & Yager, J. (2005). Eating disorders. In B. J. Sadock & V. A. Sadock (Eds.), *Kaplan & Sadock's comprehensive textbook of psychiatry*. Philadelphia, PA: Lippincott Williams & Wilkins.

Anderson, B. (2003). Brain imaging and *g*. In H. Nyborg (Ed.), *The scientific study of general intelligence: Tribute to Arthur R. Jensen*. Oxford, UK: Pergamon.

Anderson, B. F. (1980). *The complete thinker.* Englewood Cliffs, NJ: Prentice-Hall.

Anderson, C., Keltner, D., & John, O. P. (2003). Emotional convergence between people over time. *Journal of Personality and Social Psychology, 84*, 1054–1068.

Anderson, C. A., Berkowitz, L., Donnerstein, E., Huesman, L. R., Johnson, J. D., Linz, D., Malamuth, N. M. , & Wartella, E. (2003). The influence of media violence on youth. *Psychological Science in the Public Interest, 4*(3), 81–110.

Anderson, E. A., Kohler, J. K., & Letiecq, B. L. (2002). Low-income fathers and "Responsible Fatherhood" programs: A qualitative investigation of participants' experiences. *Family Relations, 51*, 148–155.

Anderson, K. J. (1990). Arousal and the inverted-U hypothesis: A critique of Neiss's "reconceptualizing arousal." *Psychological Bulletin, 107*, 96–100.

Anderson, M. C., & Neely, J. H. (1996). Interference and inhibition in memory retrieval. In E. L. Bjork & R. A. Bjork (Eds.), *Memory*. San Diego: Academic Press.

Anderson, N., & Thomas, H. D. C. (1996). Work group socialization. In M. A. West (Ed.), *Handbook of work group psychology* (pp. 423–450). Chichester, UK: Wiley.

Anderson-Fye, E. P., & Becker, A. E. (2004). Sociocultural aspects of eating disorders and obesity. In J. K. Thompson (Ed.), *Handbook of eating disorders and obesity*. New York, NY: Wiley.

Andreasen, N. C. (1987). Creativity and mental illness: Prevalence rates in writers and their first-degree relatives. *American Journal of Psychiatry, 144*, 1288–1292.

Andreasen, N. C. (1990). Positive and negative symptoms: Historical and conceptual aspects. In N. C. Andreasen (Ed.), *Modern problems of pharmacopsychiatry: Positive and negative symptoms and syndromes*. Basel: Karger.

Andreasen, N. C. (1996). Creativity and mental illness: A conceptual and historical overview. In J. J. Schildkraut & A. Otero (Eds.), *Depression and the spiritual in modern art: Homage to Miro*. New York, NY: Wiley.

Andreasen, N. C. (2005). *The creating brain: The neuroscience of genius*. New York, NY: Dana Press.

Andreasen, N. C. (2009). Schizophrenia: A conceptual history. In M. C. Gelder, N. C. Andreasen, J. J. López-Ibor, Jr., & J. R. Geddes (Eds.), *New Oxford textbook of psychiatry* (2nd ed., Vol. 1). New York, NY: Oxford University Press.

Andrews, B. (2001). Recovered memories in therapy: Clinicians' beliefs and practices. In G. M. Davies & T. Dalgleish (Eds.), *Recovered memories: Seeking the middle ground*. Chichester, England: Wiley.

Andrews, G., Charney, D., Sirovatka, P., & Regier, D. (Eds.). (2009). *Stress-induced and fear circuitry disorders: Advancing the research agenda for DSM-V*. Arlington, VA: American Psychiatric Publishing.

Angell, M. (2004). *The truth about the drug companies: How they deceive us and what to do about it.* New York, NY: Random House.

Anglin, J. M. (1993). Vocabulary development: A morphological analysis. *Monographs of the Society for Research in Child Development, 58.*

Angrosino, M. V. (2007). *Naturalistic observation: Qualitative essentials.* Walnut Creek, CA: Left Coast Press.

Angst, J. (2009). Course and prognosis of mood disorders. In M. C. Gelder, N. C. Andreasen, J. J. López-Ibor, Jr., & J. R. Geddes (Eds.). *New Oxford textbook of psychiatry* (2nd ed., Vol. 1). New York, NY: Oxford University Press.

Annemiek, V. (2004). Residual effects of hypnotics: Epidemiology and clinical implications. *CNS Drugs, 18,* 297–328.

Ansbacher, H. (1970, February). Alfred Adler, individual psychology. *Psychology Today,* pp. 42–44, 66.

Anthony, I. C., & Bell, J. E. (2008). The neuropathology of HIV/AIDS. *International Review of Psychiatry, 20*(1), 15–24.

Antoniou, A. G., Komboli, D., Vrotsos, J., & Mantzavinos, Z. (2005). The role of psychosocial factors in the development of periodontal disease. In A. G. Antoniou & C. L. Cooper (Eds.), *Research companion to organizational health psychology* (pp. 335–345). Northampton, MA: Edward Elgar Publishing.

Antonuccio, D. O., Danton, W. G., & McClanahan, T. M. (2003). Psychology in the prescription era: Building a firewall between marketing and science. *American Psychologist, 58,* 1028–1043.

Antony, M. M., & McCabe, R. E. (2003). Anxiety disorders: Social and specific phobias. In A. Tasman, J. Kay, & J. A. Lieberman (Eds.), *Psychiatry.* New York, NY: Wiley.

Antrobus, J. (1993). Characteristics of dreams. In M. A. Carskadon (Ed.), *Encyclopedia of sleep and dreaming.* New York, NY: Macmillan.

Antrobus, J. S. (2000). Theories of dreaming. In M. H. Kryger, T. Roth & W. C. Dement (Eds.), *Principles and practice of sleep medicine.* Philadelphia, PA: Saunders.

Antrobus, J. S., & Wamsley, E. J. (2009). REM/NREM differences in dream content. In R. Stickgold & M. P. Walker (Eds.), *The Neuroscience of sleep* (pp. 310–315). San Diego, CA: Academic Press.

Apkarian, A. V., Bushnell, M. C., Treede, R., & Zubieta, J. (2005). Human brain mechanisms of pain perception and regulation in health and disease. *European Journal of Pain, 9,* 463–484.

Appelbaum, P. S. (2002). Responses to the presidential debate—The systematic defunding of psychiatric care: A crisis at our doorstep. *American Journal of Psychiatry, 159,* 1638–1640.

Appleton, K. M., Gentry, R. C., & Shepherd, R. (2006). Evidence of a role for conditioning in the development of liking for flavours in humans in everyday life. *Physiology & Behavior, 87,* 478–486.

Aquilino, W. S. (2006). Family relationships and support systems in emerging adulthood. In J. J. Arnett & J. L. Tanner (Eds.), *Emerging adults in America: Coming of age in the 21st century.* Washington, DC: American Psychological Association.

Arcelus, J., Whight, D., Langham, C., Baggott, J., McGrain, L., Meadows, L., & Meyer, C. (2009). A case series evaluation of the modified version of interpersonal psychotherapy (IPT) for the treatment of bulimic eating disorders: A pilot study. *European Eating Disorders Review, 17*(4), 260–268. doi: 10.1002/(ISSN)1099-096810.1002/erv.v17:410.1002/erv.932.

Archer, J. (1996). Sex differences in social behavior: Are the social role and evolutionary explanations compatible? *American Psychologist, 51,* 909–917.

Archer, J. (2005). Are women or men the more aggressive sex? In S. Fein, G. R. Goethals, & M. J. Sansdtrom (Eds.), *Gender and aggression: Interdisciplinary perspectives.* Mahwah, NJ: Erlbaum.

Archer, J. (2006). Testosterone and human aggression: An evaluation of the challenge hypothesis. *Neuroscience and Biobehavioral Reviews, 30,* 319–345.

Archibald, A. B., Graber, J. A., & Brooks-Gunn, J. (2003). Pubertal processes and physiological growth in adolescence. In G. R. Adams & M. D. Berzonsky (Eds.), *Blackwell handbook of adolescence.* Malden, MA: Blackwell Publishing.

Arden, R., Gottfredson, L. S., & Miller, G. (2009). Does a fitness factor contribute to the association between intelligence and health outcomes? Evidence from medical abnormality counts among 3654 U.S. veterans. *Intelligence, 37*(6), 581–591. doi:10.1016/j.intell.2009.03.008

Arendt, J. (2009). Managing jet lag: Some of the problems and possible new solutions. *Sleep Medicine Reviews, 13*(4), 249–256. doi:10.1016/j.smrv.2008.07.011

Arendt, J. (2010). Shift work: Coping with the biological clock. *Occupational Medicine, 60*(1), 10–20. doi:10.1093/occmed/kqp162

Arendt, J., & Skene, D. J. (2005). Melatonin as a chronobiotic. *Sleep Medicine Review, 9*(1), 25–39.

Arendt, J., Stone, B., & Skene, D. J. (2005). Sleep disruption in jet lag and other circadian rhythm-related disorders. In M. H. Kryger, T. Roth, & W. C. Dement (Eds.). *Principles and practice of sleep medicine.* Philadelphia, PA: Elsevier Saunders.

Argyle, M. (1987). *The psychology of happiness.* London: Metheun.

Argyle, M. (1999). Causes and correlates of happiness. In D. Kahneman, E. Diener & N. Schwarz (Eds.), *Well-being: The foundations of hedonic psychology.* New York, NY: Russell Sage Foundation.

Argyle, M. (2001). *The psychology of happiness.* New York, NY: Routledge.

Arkes, H. R., Wortmann, R. L., Saville, P. D., & Harkness, A. R. (1981). Hindsight bias among physicians weighing the likelihood of diagnoses. *Journal of Applied Psychology, 66,* 252–254.

Arkowitz, H., & Lilienfeld, S. O. (2007). The best medicine? How drugs stack up against talk therapy for the treatment of depression. *Scientific American Mind, 18*(5), 80–83.

Armbruster, B. B. (2000). Taking notes from lectures. In R. F. Flippo & D. C. Caverly (Eds.), *Handbook of college reading and study strategy research.* Mahwah, NJ: Erlbaum.

Arndt, J., Cook, A., & Routledge, C. (2004). The blueprint of terror management: Understanding the cognitive architecture of psychological defense against the awareness of death. In J. Greenberg, S. L. Koole, & T. Pyszczynski (Eds.), *Handbook of experimental existential psychology.* New York, NY: Guilford Press.

Arndt, J., & Vess, M. (2008). Tales from existential oceans: Terror management theory and how the awareness of our mortality affects us all. *Social and Personality Psychology Compass, 2*(2), 909–928. doi:10.1111/j.1751-9004.2008.00079.x

Arnett, J. J. (2000). Emerging adulthood: A theory of development from the late teens through the twenties. *American Psychologist, 55,* 469–480.

Arnett, J. J. (2001). Conceptions of the transition to adulthood: Perspectives from adolescence to midlife. *Journal of Adult Development, 8,* 133–143.

Arnett, J. J. (2004). *Emerging adulthood: The winding road from the late teens through the twenties.* New York, NY: Oxford University Press.

Arnett, J. J. (2006). Emerging adulthood: Understanding the new way of coming of age. In J. J. Arnett & J. L. Tanner (Eds.), *Emerging adults in America: Coming of age in the 21st century.* Washington, DC: American Psychological Association.

Arnett, J. J. (2008). The neglected 95%: Why American psychology needs to become less American. *American Psychologist, 63*(7), 602–614. doi: 10.1037/0003-066X.63.7.602.

Arnkoff, D. B., & Glass, C. R. (1992). Cognitive therapy and psychotherapy. In D. K. Freedheim (Ed.), *History of psychotherapy: A century of change.* Washington, DC: American Psychological Association.

Arnold, L. M. (2000). Psychocutaneous disorders. In B. J. Sadock & V. A. Sadock (Eds.), *Kaplan and Sadock's comprehensive textbook of psychiatry* (7th ed., pp. 1818–1827). Philadelphia, PA: Lippincott Williams & Wilkins.

Aron, A., Fisher, H., & Mashek, D. J. (2005). Reward, motivation, and emotion systems associated with early-stage intense romantic love. *Journal of Neurophysiology, 94*(1), 327–337.

Aronson, E., & Mills, J. (1959). The effect of severity of initiation on liking for a group. *Journal of Abnormal and Social Psychology, 59,* 177–181.

Arrigo, J. M., & Pezdek, K. (1997). Lessons from the study of psychogenic amnesia. *Current Directions in Psychological Science, 6,* 148–152.

Arthur, J. B. (1994). Effects of human resource systems on manufacturing performance and turnover. *Academy of Management Journal, 37,* 670–687.

Asch, S. E. (1951). Effects of group pressure on the modification and distortion of judgments. In H. Guetzkow (Ed.), *Groups, leadership, and men.* Pittsburgh: Carnegie Press.

Asch, S. E. (1955). Opinions and social pressures. *Scientific American, 193*(5), 31–35.

Asch, S. E. (1956). Studies of independence and conformity: A minority of one against a unanimous majority. *Psychological Monographs, 70*(9, Whole No. 416).

Asendorpf, J. B., & Ostendorf, F. (1998). Is self-enhancement healthy? Conceptual, psychometric, and empirical analysis. *Journal of Personality and Social Psychology, 74,* 955–966.

Assefi, S. L., & Garry, M. (2003). Absolut® memory distortions: Alcohol placebos influence the misinformation effect. *Psychological Science, 14*(1), 77–80.

Associated Press. (2010, March 30). U.K. panel calls climate data valid. *New York Times,* Environment. Retrieved from http://www.nytimes.com/2010/03/31/science/earth/31climate.html

Atkinson, J. W. (1974). The mainsprings of achievement-oriented activity. In J. W. Atkinson & J. O. Raynor (Eds.), *Motivation and achievement.* New York, NY: Wiley.

Atkinson, J. W. (1981). Studying personality in the context of an advanced motivational psychology. *American Psychologist, 36,* 117–128.

Atkinson, J. W. (1992). Motivational determinants of thematic apperception. In C. P. Smith (Ed.), *Motivation and personality: Handbook of thematic content analysis.* New York, NY: Cambridge University Press.

Atkinson, J. W., & Litwin, G. H. (1960). Achievement motive and test anxiety conceived as motive to approach success and to avoid failure. *Journal of Abnormal and Social Psychology, 60,* 52–63.

Atkinson, R. C., & Shiffrin, R. M. (1968). Human memory: A proposed system and its control processes. In K. W. Spence & J. T. Spence (Eds.), *The psychology of learning and motivation* (Vol. 2). New York, NY: Academic Press.

Atkinson, R. C., & Shiffrin, R. M. (1971). The control of short-term memory. *Scientific American, 225,* 82–90.

Ator, N. A. (2005). Conducting behavioral research: Methodological and laboratory animal welfare issues. In C. K. Akins, S. Panicker, & C. L. Cunningham (Eds.), *Laboratory animals in research and teaching: Ethics, care and methods.* Washington, DC: American Psychological Association.

Austin, E. J., Deary, I. J., Edwards-Jones, G., & Arey, D. (2005). Attitudes to farm animal welfare: Factor structure and personality correlates in farmers and agriculture students. *Journal of Individual Differences, 26,* 107–120.

Auyeung, B., Baron-Cohen, S., Ashwin, E., Knickmeyer, R., Taylor, K., Hackett, G., & Hines, M. (2009). Fetal testosterone predicts sexually differentiated childhood behavior in girls and in boys. *Psychological Science, 20*(2), 144–148. doi:10.1111/j.1467-9280.2009.02279.x

Aveline, M., Strauss, B., & Stiles, W. B. (2005). Psychotherapy research. In G. O. Gabbard, J. S. Beck, & J. Holmes (Eds.), *Oxford textbook of psychotherapy.* New York, NY: Oxford University Press.

Averill, J. A. (1980). A constructivist view of emotion. In R. Plutchik & H. Kellerman (Eds.), *Emotion: Theory, research, and experience: Vol. 1. Theories of emotion.* New York, NY: Academic Press.

Ax, R. K., Bigelow, B. J., Harowski, K., Meredith, J. M., Nussbaum, D. & Taylor, R. R. (2008). Prescriptive authority for psychologists and the public sector: Serving underserved health care consumers. *Psychological Services, 5*(2), 184–197.

Axel, R. (1995, April). The molecular logic of smell. *Scientific American, 273,* 154–159.

Ayanian, J. Z., & Cleary, P. D. (1999). Perceived risks of heart disease and cancer among cigarette smokers. *Journal of the American Medical Association, 281,* 1019–1021.

Ayotte, B. J., Margrett, J. A., & Hicks-Patrick, J. (2010). Physical activity in middle-aged and young-old adults: The roles of self-efficacy, barriers, outcome expectancies, self-regulatory behaviors and social support. *Journal of Health Psychology, 15*(2), 173–185. doi:10.1177/1359105309342283

Baars, B. J. (1986). *The cognitive revolution in psychology.* New York, NY: Guilford Press.

Babiak, P., & Hare, R. D. (2006). *Snakes in suits: When psychopaths go to work.* New York, NY: Regan Books/Harper Colllins Publishers.

Back, M. D., Schmukle, S. C., & Egloff, B. (2010). Why are narcissists so charming at first sight? Decoding the narcissism-popularity link at zero acquaintance. *Journal of Personality and Social Psychology, 98*(1), 132–145. doi:10.1037/a0016338

Baddeley, A. D. (1986). *Working memory.* New York, NY: Oxford University Press.

Baddeley, A. D. (1992). Working memory. *Science, 255,* 556–559.

Baddeley, A. D. (2001). Is working memory still working? *American Psychologist, 56,* 851–864.

Baddeley, A. D. (2007). *Working memory, thought, and action.* New York, NY: Oxford University Press.

Baddeley, A. D., & Hitch, G. (1974). Working memory. In G. H. Bower (Ed.), *The psychology of learning and motivation* (Vol. 8). New York, NY: Academic Press.

Baenninger, R. (1997). On yawning and its functions. *Psychonomic Bulletin & Review, 4,* 198–207.

Baer, R. A. (2003). Mindfulness training as a clinical intervention: A conceptual and empirical review. *Clinical Psychology: Science and Practice, 10,* 125–143.

Bagley, D. K., & Gonsman, V. L. (2005). Pet attachment and personality type. *Anthrozoos, 18,* 28–42.

Bahrick, H. P. (2000). Long-term maintenance of knowledge. In E. Tulving & F. I. M. Craik (Eds.), *The Oxford handbook of memory* (pp. 347–362). New York, NY: Oxford University Press.

Bailey, C. H., & Kandel, E. R. (2004). Synaptic growth and the persistence of long–term memory: A molecular perspective. In M. S. Gazzaniga (Ed.), *The cognitive neurosciences.* Cambridge, MA: MIT Press.

Bailey, C. H., & Kandel, E. R. (2009). Synaptic and cellular basis of learning. In G. G. Berntson & J. T. Cacioppo (Eds.), *Handbook of neuroscience for the behavioral sciences* (Vol 1, pp. 528–551). Hoboken, NJ: Wiley.

Bailey, J. M. (2003). Biological perspectives on sexual orientation. In L. D. Garnets & D. C. Kimmel (Eds.), *Psychological perspectives on lesbian, gay, and bisexual experiences.* New York, NY: Columbia University Press.

Bailey, J. M., & Pillard, R. C. (1991). A genetic study of male homosexual orientation. *Archives of General Psychology, 48,* 1089–1097.

Bailey, J. M., Pillard, R. C., Neale, M. C. I., & Agyei, Y. (1993). Heritable factors influence sexual orientation in women. *Archives of General Psychiatry, 50,* 217–223.

Bailey, J. M., & Zucker, K. J. (1995). Childhood sex-typed behavior and sexual orientation: A conceptual analysis and quantitative review. *Developmental Psychology, 31,* 43–55.

Baillargeon, R. (2002). The acquisition of physical knowledge in infancy: A summary in eight lessons. In U. Goswami (Ed.), *Blackwell handbook of childhood cognitive development.* Malden, MA: Blackwell Publishing.

Baillargeon, R. (2004). Infants' physical world. *Current Directions in Psychological Science, 13*(3), 89–94.

Baillargeon, R. (2008). Innate ideas revisited: For a principle of persistence in infants' physical reasoning. *Perspectives on Psychological Science, 3*(1), 2–13.

Bains, J. S., & Oliet, S. H. R. (2007). Glia: They make your memories stick! *Trends in Neuroscience, 30,* 417–424.

Baker, G. J., Suchday, S., & Krantz, D. S. (2007). Heart disease/attack. In G. Fink (Ed.), *Encyclopedia of stress.* San Diego: Elsevier.

Baker, T. B., Japuntich, S. J., Hogle, J. M., McCarthy, D. E., & Curtin, J. J. (2006). Pharmacologic and behavioral withdrawal from addictive drugs. *Current Directions in Psychological Science, 15,* 232–236.

Balcetis, E., & Dunning, D. (2008). A mile in moccasins: How situational experience diminishes dispositionism in social inference. *Personality and Social Psychology Bulletin, 34*(1), 102–114.

Balcetis, E., & Dunning, D. (2010). Wishful seeing: More desired objects are seen as closer. *Psychological Science, 21*(1), 147–152. doi: 10.1177/0956797609356283.

Balcetis, E., Dunning, D., & Miller, R. L. (2008). Do collectivists know themselves better than individualists? Cross-cultural studies of the holier than thou phenomenon. *Journal of Personality and Social Psychology, 95*(6), 1252–1267. doi:10.1037/a0013195

Baldessarini, R. J., Tondo, L., Strombom, I. M., Dominguez, S., Fawcett, J., Licinio, J., Oquendo, M. A., Tollefson, G. D., Valuck, R. J., & Tohen, M. (2007). Ecological studies of antidepressant treatment and suicidal risks. *Harvard Review of Psychiatry, 15,* 133–145.

Baldwin, E. (1993). The case for animal research in psychology. *Journal of Social Issues, 49*(1), 121–131.

Baldwin, W. (2000). Information no one else knows: The value of self-report. In A. A. Stone, J. S. Turkkan, C. A. Bachrach, J. B. Jobe, H. S. Kurtzman & V. Cain (Eds.), *The science of self-report: Implications for research and practice.* Mahwah, NJ: Erlbaum.

Bale, T. L., Baram, T. Z., Brown, A. S., Goldstein, J. M., Insel, T. R., McCarthy, M. M., et al. (2010). Early life programming and neurodevelopmental disorders. *Biological Psychiatry, 68*(4), 314–319. doi:10.1016/j.biopsych.2010.05.028

Ball, K., Edwards, J. D., & Ross, L. A. (2007). The impact of speed of processing training on cognitive and everyday functions. *Journals of Gerontology: Series B, 62B* (Special Issue 1), 19–31.

Balsam, P. D. (1988). Selection, representation, and equivalence of controlling stimuli. In R. C. Atkinson, R. J. Herrnstein, G. Lindzey, & R. D. Luce (Eds.), *Stevens' handbook of experimental psychology.* New York, NY: Wiley.

Balter, M. (2010). Did working memory spark creative culture? *Science, 328*(5975), 160–163. doi:10.1126/science.328.5975.160

Baltes, P. B., Staudinger, U. M., & Lindenberger, U. (1999). Lifespan psychology: Theory and application to intellectual functioning. *Annual Review of Psychology, 50,* 471–507.

Balzer, W. L., Kihm, J. A., Smith, P. C., Irwin, J. L., Bachiochi, P. D., Robie, C., et al. (1997). *Users' manual for the job descriptive index (JDI, 1997 revision) and the job in general scales.* Bowling Green, OH: Bowling Green State University.

Banaji, M. R., & Heiphetz, L. (2010). Attitudes. In S. T. Fiske, D. T. Gilbert, & G. Lindzey (Eds.), *Handbook of social psychology* (Vol. 1, 5th ed., pp. 353–393). Hoboken, NJ: Wiley.

Bandura, A. (1977). *Social learning theory.* Englewood Cliffs, NJ: Prentice-Hall.

Bandura, A. (1986). *Social foundations of thought and action: A social-cognitive theory.* Englewood Cliffs, NJ: Prentice-Hall.

Bandura, A. (1993). Perceived self-efficacy in cognitive development and functioning. *Educational Psychologist, 28*(2), 117–148.

Bandura, A. (1995). Exercise of personal and collective efficacy in changing societies. In A. Bandura (Ed.), *Self-efficacy in changing societies.* New York, NY: Cambridge University Press.

Bandura, A. (1999a). Social cognitive theory of personality. In L. A. Pervin, & O. P. John (Eds.), *Handbook of personality: Theory and research.* New York, NY: Guilford Press.

Bandura, A. (1999b). A sociocognitive analysis of substance abuse: An agentic perspective. *Psychological Science, 10*(3), 214–217.

Bandura, A. (2002). Environmental sustainability by sociocognitive deceleration of population growth. In P. Schmuck & W. P. Schultz (Eds.), *Psychology of sustainable development* (pp. 209–238). Boston, MA: Kluwer Academic Publishers.

Bandura, A. (2004). Health promotion by social cognitive means. *Health Education & Behavior, 31,* 143–164.

Bandura, A. (2006). Toward a psychology of human agency. Perspectives on *Psychological Science, 1*(2), 164–180.

Bandura, A. (2008). Reconstrual of 'free will' from the agentic perspective of social cognitive theory. In J. Baer, J. C. Kaufman, & R. F. Baumeister (Eds.), *Are we free? Psychology and free will* (pp. 86–127). New York, NY: Oxford University Press.

Bandura, A., Ross, D., & Ross, S. A. (1961). Transmission of aggression through imitation of aggressive models. *Journal of Abnormal and Social Psychology, 63*(3), 575–582. doi:10.1037/h0045925

Bandura, A., Ross, D., & Ross, S. A. (1963a). Imitation of film-mediated aggressive models. *Journal of Abnormal and Social Psychology, 66,* 3–11.

Bandura, A., Ross, D., & Ross, S. A. (1963b). Vicarious reinforcement and imitative learning. *Journal of Abnormal and Social Psychology, 63,* 601–607.

Banich, M. T., & Heller, W. (1998). Evolving perspectives on lateralization of function. *Current Directions in Psychological Science, 7,* 1.

Banks, A., & Gartell, N. K. (1995). Hormones and sexual orientation: A questionable link. *Journal of Homosexuality, 28,* 247–268.

Banks, S., & Dinges, D. F. (2007). Behavioral and physiological consequences of sleep restriction. *Journal of Clinical Sleep Medicine, 3*(5), 519–528.

Banks, W. P., & Krajicek, D. (1991). Perception. *Annual Review of Psychology, 42,* 305–331.

Banse, R. (2007). Implicit attitudes towards romantic partners and ex-partners: A test of the reliability and validity of the IAT. *International Journal of Psychology, 42,* 149–157.

Banyard, V. L., Plante, E. G., Cohn, E. S., Moorhead, C., Ward, S., & Walsh, W. (2005). Revisiting unwanted sexual experiences on campus: A 12-year follow-up. *Violence Against Women, 11,* 426–446.

Banyard, V. L., & Williams, L. M. (1999). Memories for child sexual abuse and mental health functioning: Findings on a sample of women and implications for future research. In L. M. Williams & V. L. Banyard (Eds.), *Trauma & memory*. Thousand Oaks, CA: Sage.

Baral, B. D., & Das, J. P. (2004). Intelligence: What is indigenous to India and what is shared? In R. J. Sternberg (Ed.), *International handbook of intelligence*. New York, NY: Cambridge University Press.

Barber, L., Munz, D., Bagsby, P., & Powell, E. (2010). Sleep consistency and sufficiency: Are both necessary for less psychological strain? *Stress & Health: Journal of the International Society for the Investigation of Stress, 26*(3), 186–193.

Barber, T. X. (1969). *Hypnosis: A scientific approach.* New York, NY: Van Nostrand Reinhold.

Barber, T. X. (1979). Suggested ("hypnotic") behavior: The trance paradigm versus an alternative paradigm. In E. Fromm & R. E. Shor (Eds.), *Hypnosis: Developments in research and new perspectives.* New York, NY: Aldine.

Barch, D. M. (2003). Cognition in schizophrenia: Does working memory work? *Current Directions in Psychological Science, 12*(4), 146–150.

Bard, P. (1934). On emotional experience after decortication with some remarks on theoretical views. *Psychological Review, 41,* 309–329.

Bargh, J. A., Gollwitzer, P. M., & Oettingen, G. (2010). Motivation. In S. T. Fiske, D. T. Gilbert, & G. Lindzey (Eds.), *Handbook of social psychology* (5th ed., Vol. 1, pp. 268–316). New York, NY: Wiley.

Bargh, J. A., & McKenna, K. Y. A. (2004). The Internet and social life. *Annual Review of Psychology, 55,* 573–590.

Bargh, J. A., McKenna, K. Y. A., & Fitzsimons, G. M. (2002). Can you see the real me? Activation and expression of the "true self" on the Internet. *Journal of Social Issues, 58,* 33–48.

Barker, E. T., Williams, R. L., & Galambos, N. L. (2006). Daily spillover to and from binge eating in first-year university females. *Eating Disorders: The Journal of Treatment and Prevention, 14,* 229–242.

Barlett, D. L., & Steele, J. B. (1979). *Empire: The life, legend and madness of Howard Hughes.* New York, NY: Norton.

Barlow, D. H., Pincus, D. B., Heinrichs, N., & Choate, M. L. (2003). Anxiety disorders. In G. Stricker & T. A. Widiger (Eds.), *Handbook of psychology, Vol. 8: Clinical psychology.* New York, NY: Wiley.

Barnes, V. A., Treiber, F., & Davis, H. (2001). The impact of Transcendental Meditation on cardiovascular function at rest and during acute stress in adolescents with high normal blood pressure. *Journal of Psychosomatic Research, 51,* 597–605.

Barnett, K. J., Kirk, I. J., & Corballis, M. C. (2007). Bilateral disadvantage: Lack of interhemispheric cooperation in schizophrenia. *Consciousness and Cognition: An International Journal, 16*(2), 436–444. doi:10.1016/j.concog.2006.06.007

Barnett, S. W. (2004). Does Head Start have lasting cognitive effects? The myth of fade-out. In E. Zigler & S. J. Styfco (Eds.), *The Head Start debates.* Baltimore: Paul H. Brooks Publishing.

Baron, R. S. (2005). So right it's wrong: Groupthink and the ubiquitous nature of polarized group decision making. In M. P. Zanna (Ed.), *Advances in experimental social psychology.* San Diego: Elsevier Academic Press.

Barrett, L. F. (2006). Are emotions natural kinds? *Perspectives on Psychological Science, 1*(1), 28–58.

Barrett, L. F., Mesquita, B., Ochsner, K. N., & Gross, J. J. (2007). The experience of emotion. *Annual Review of Psychology, 58,* 373–403.

Barrigón, M. L., Gurpegui, M., Ruiz-Veguilla, M., Diaz, F. J., Anguita, M., Sarramea, F., & Cervilla, J. (2010). Temporal relationship of first-episode nonaffective psychosis with cannabis use: A clinical verification of an epidemiological hypothesis. *Journal of Psychiatric Research, 44*(7), 413–420. doi:10.1016/j.jpsychires.2009.10.004

Barron, F. (1963). *Creativity and psychological health.* Princeton, NY: Van Nostrand.

Barry, L. J. (2004). Depression: The brain finally gets into the act. *Current Directions in Psychological Science, 13*(3), 104–106.

Barry-Walsh, J. (2005). Dissociative identity disorder. *Australian & New Zealand Journal of Psychiatry, 39*(1–2), 109–110.

Bartels, M., Rietveld, M. J. H., Van Baal, G. C. M., & Boomsma, D. I. (2002). Genetic and environmental influences on the development of intelligence. *Behavior Genetics, 32*(4), 237–249.

Bartoshuk, L. M. (1993a). Genetic and pathological taste variation: What can we learn from animal models and human disease? In D. Chadwick, J. Marsh, & J. Goode (Eds.), *The molecular basis of smell and taste transduction.* New York, NY: Wiley.

Bartoshuk, L. M. (1993b). The biological basis of food perception and acceptance. *Food Quality and Preference, 4,* 21–32.

Bartoshuk, L. M., Duffy, V. B., & Miller, I. J. (1994). PTC/PROP taste: Anatomy, psychophysics, and sex effects. *Physiology & Behavior, 56,* 1165–1171.

Bartz, J. A., & Hollander, E. (2006). The neuroscience of affiliation: Forging links between basic and clinical research on neuropeptides and social behavior. *Hormones and Behavior, 50*(4), 518–528. doi:10.1016/j.yhbeh.2006.06.018

Basbaum, A. I., & Jessel, T. M. (2000). The perception of pain. In E. R. Kandel, J. H. Schwartz, & T. M. Jessell (Eds.), *Principles of neural science.* New York, NY: McGraw-Hill.

Basow, S. A. (1992). *Gender: Stereotypes and roles.* Pacific Grove, CA: Brooks/Cole.

Bass, B. M. (1995). Theory of transformational leadership redux. *Leadership Quarterly, 6.*

Bassok, M. (2003). Analogical transfer in problem solving. In J. E. Davidson & R. J. Sternberg (Eds.), *The psychology of problem solving.* New York, NY: Cambridge University Press.

Basson, M. D., Bartoshuk, L. M., Dichello, S. Z., Panzini, L., Weiffenbach, J. M., & Duffy, V. B. (2005). Association between 6-n-propylthiouracil (PROP) bitterness and colonic neoplasms. *Digestive Diseases Sciences, 50,* 483–489.

Bassuk, E. L., Buckner, J. C., Perloff, J. N., & Bassuk, S. S. (1998). Prevalence of mental health and substance use disorders among homeless and low-income housed mothers. *American Journal of Psychiatry, 155,* 1561–1564.

Bates, E. (1999). Plasticity, localization, and language development. In S. H. Broman & J. M. Fletcher (Eds.), *The changing nervous system: Neurobehavioral consequences of early brain disorders* (pp. 214–247). New York, NY: Oxford University Press.

Bates, E., Devescovi, A., & Wulfeck, B. (2001). Psycholinguistics: A cross-language perspective. *Annual Review of Psychology, 52,* 369–396.

Batterham, P. J., Christensen, H., & Mackinnon, A. J. (2009). Fluid intelligence is independently associated with all-cause mortality over 17 years in an elderly community sample: An investigation of potential mechanisms. *Intelligence, 37*(6), 551–560. doi:10.1016/j.intell.2008.10.004

Batty, G., Deary, I., & Gottfredson, L. (2007). Premorbid (early life) IQ and later mortality risk: Systematic review. *Annals of Epidemiology, 17*(4), 278–288.

Baudry, M., & Lynch, G. (2001). Remembrance of arguments past: How well is the glutamate receptor hypothesis of LTP holding up after 20 years? *Neurobiology of Learning and Memory, 76,* 284–297.

Bauer, M. S. (2003). Mood disorders: Bipolar (manic-depressive) disorders. In A. Tasman, J. Kay, & J. A. Lieberman (Eds.), *Psychiatry.* New York, NY: Wiley.

Bauer, M. S. (2008). Mood disorders: Bipolar (manic-depressive) disorders. In A. J. Kay, J. A. Lieberman, M. B. First, & M. Maj (Eds.), *Psychiatry* (3rd ed.). New York, NY: Wiley-Blackwell.

Baumeister, R. F. (1984). Choking under pressure: Self-consciousness and paradoxical effects of incentives on skillful performance. *Journal of Personality and Social Psychology, 46,* 610–620.

Baumeister, R. F. (1989). The optimal margin of illusion. *Journal of Social and Clinical Psychology, 8,* 176–189.

Baumeister, R. F. (2000). Gender differences in erotic plasticity: The female sex drive as socially flexible and responsive. *Psychological Bulletin, 126,* 347–374.

Baumeister, R. F. (2004). Gender and erotic plasticity: Sociocultural influences on the sex drive. *Sexual and Relationship Therapy, 19,* 133–139.

Baumeister, R. F., Catanese, K. R., & Vohs, K. D. (2001b). Is there a gender difference in strength of sex drive? Theoretical views, conceptual distinctions and a review of relevant evidence. *Personality and Social Psychology Review, 5,* 242–273.

Baumeister, R. F., & Leary, M. R. (1995). The need to belong: Desire for interpersonal attachments as a fundamental human motivation. *Psychological Bulletin, 117,* 497–529.

Baumeister, R. F., & Twenge, J. M. (2002). Cultural suppression of female sexuality. *Review of General Psychology, 6,* 166–203.

Baumeister, R. F., & Vohs, K. D. (2001). Narcissism as addiction to esteem. *Psychological Inquiry, 12*(4), 206–210.

Baumrind, D. (1964). Some thoughts on the ethics of reading Milgram's "Behavioral study of obedience." *American Psychologist, 19,* 421–423.

Baumrind, D. (1985). Research using intentional deception: Ethical issues revisited. *American Psychologist, 40,* 165–174.

Baumrind, D., Larzelere, R. E., & Cowan, P. A. (2002). Ordinary physical punishment: Is it harmful? Comment on Gershoff. *Psychological Bulletin, 128,* 580–589.

Bauserman, R. (1996). Sexual aggression and pornography: A review of correlational research. *Basic and Applied Social Psychology, 18,* 405–427.

Bayley, N. (1949). Consistency and variability in the growth of intelligence from birth to eighteen years. *Journal of Genetic Psychology, 75,* 165–196.

Bearden, C. E., Jasinska, A. J., & Freimer, N. B. (2009). Methodological issues in molecular genetic studies of mental disorders. *Annual Review of Clinical Psychology, 5,* 549–569. doi:10.1146/annurev.clinpsy.032408.153545

Beck, A. T. (1976). *Cognitive therapy and the emotional disorders.* New York, NY: International Universities Press.

Beck, A. T. (1987). Cognitive therapy. In J. K. Zeig (Ed.), *The evolution of psychotherapy.* New York, NY: Brunner/Mazel.

Beck, A. T. (1997). Cognitive therapy: Reflections. In J. K. Zeig (Ed.), *The evolution of psychotherapy: The third conference.* New York, NY: Brunner/Mazel.

Beck, A. T. (2008). The evolution of the cognitive model of depression and its neurobiological correlates. *American Journal of Psychiatry, 165*(8), 969–977. doi:10.1176/appi.ajp.2008.08050721

Beck, A. T., & Weishaar, M. E. (2011). Cognitive therapy. In R. J. Corsini & D. Wedding (Eds.), *Current psychotherapies* (9th ed.). Belmont, CA: Brooks/Cole.

Beck, H. P., Levinson, S., & Irons, G. (2009). Finding Little Albert: A journey to John B. Watson's infant laboratory. *American Psychologist, 64*(7), 605–614. doi: 10.1037/a0017234.

Becker, A., & Fay, K. (2006). Sociocultural issues and eating disorders. In S. Wonderlich, J. Mitchell, M. de Zwaan, & H. Steiger (Eds.), *Annual review of eating disorders.* Abingdon, UK: Radcliffe.

Becker, A. L. (2009, November 29). Science of memory: Researchers to study pieces of unique brain. *The Hartford Courant.* Retrieved from http://www.courant.com

Becker, S., & Wojtowicz, J. M. (2007). A model of hippocampal neurogenesis in memory and mood disorders. *Trends in Cognitive Sciences, 11*(2), 70–76.

Beckers, T., Miller, R. R., DeHouwer, J., & Urushihara, K. (2006). Reasoning rats: Forward blocking in Pavlovian animal conditioning is sensitive to constraints of causal inference. *Journal of Experimental Psychology: General, 135,* 92–102.

Becskei, C., Lutz, T. A., & Riediger, T. (2008). Glucose reverses fasting-induced activation in the arcuate nucleus of mice. *Neuroreport: For Rapid Communication of Neuroscience Research, 19*(1), 105–109.

Beddoe, R., Costanza, R., Farley, J. U., Garza, E., Kent, J., Kubiszewski, I., Martinez, L., McCowen, T., Murphy, K. I., Myers, N., Ogden, Z., Stapleton, K., & Woodward, J. (2009). Overcoming systematic roadblocks to sustainability: The evolutionary redesign of worldviews, institutions, and technologies. *Proceedings from the National Academy of Sciences, 106,* 2483–2489.

Beeman, M. J., & Chiarello, C. (1998). Complementary right and left hemisphere language comprehension. *Current Directions in Psychological Science, 7,* 2–7.

Beer, J. M., Arnold, R. D., & Loehlin, J. C. (1998). Genetic and environmental influences on MMPI Factor Scales: Joint model fitting to twin and adoption data. *Journal of Personality and Social Psychology, 74,* 818–827.

Beer, J. S., Shimamura, A. P., & Knight, R. T. (2004). Frontal lobe contributions to executive control of cognitive and social behavior. In M. S. Gazzaniga (Ed.), *The cognitive neurosciences.* Cambridge, MA: MIT Press.

Behrens, R. R. (2010). Ames demonstrations in perception. In E. B. Goldstein (Ed.), *Encyclopedia of perception.* Thousand Oaks, CA: Sage.

Behrmann, M. (2010). Agnosia: Visual. In E. B. Goldstein (Ed.), *Encyclopedia of perception.* Thousand Oaks, CA: Sage.

Beidel, D. C., & Stipelman, B. (2007). Anxiety disorders. In M. Hersen, S. M. Turner, & D. C. Beidel (Eds.), *Adult psychopathology and diagnosis.* New York, NY: Wiley.

Beilin, H. (1992). Piaget's enduring contribution to developmental psychology. *Developmental Psychology, 28,* 191–204.

Beilock, S. L. (2008). Math performance in stressful situations. *Current Directions in Psychological Science, 17*(5), 339–343.

Beilock, S. L. (2010). *Choke: What the secrets of the brain reveal about getting it right when you have to.* New York, NY: Free Press.

Beilock, S. L., & Gonso, S. (2008). Putting in the mind versus putting on the green: Expertise, performance time, and the linking of imagery and action. *Quarterly Journal of Experimental Psychology, 61*(6), 920–932. doi:10.1080/17470210701625626

Bekelman, J. E., Li, Y., & Gross, C. P. (2003). Scope and impact of financial conflicts of interest in biomedical research. *Journal of the American Medical Association, 289,* 454–465.

Békésy, G. von. (1947). The variation of phase along the basilar membrane with sinusoidal vibrations. *Journal of the Acoustical Society of America, 19,* 452–460.

Bekkouche, N. S., Holmes, S., Whittaker, K. S., & Krantz, D. S. (2011). Stress and the heart: Psychosocial stress and coronary heart disease. In R. J. Contrada & A. Baum (Eds.), *The handbook of stress science: Biology, psychology, and health* (pp. 111–121). New York, NY: Springer Publishing.

Belger, A., & Barch, D. M. (2009). Cognitive neuroscience and neuroimaging in schizophrenia. In D. S. Charney & E. J. Nestler (Eds.), *Neurobiology of mental illness* (3rd ed., pp. 303–320). New York, NY: Oxford University Press.

Belger, A., & Dichter, G. (2006). Structural and functional neuroanatomy. In J. A. Lieberman, T. S. Stroup, & D. O. Perkins (Eds.), *Textbook of schizophrenia.* Washington, DC: American Psychiatric Publishing.

Bell, A. P., Weinberg, M. S., & Hammersmith, S. K. (1981). *Sexual preference: Its development in men and women.* Bloomington: Indiana University Press.

Bell, P. A., Greene, T. C., Fisher, J. D., & Baum, A. (2001). *Environmental psychology* (5th ed.). Fort Worth: Harcourt College Publishers.

Beller, M., & Gafni, N. (1996). The 1991 international assessment of educational progress in mathematics and sciences: The gender differences perspective. *Journal of Educational Psychology, 88,* 365–377.

Bellinger, D. C., & Adams, H. F. (2001). Environmental pollutant exposures and children's cognitive abilities. In R. J. Sternberg & E. L. Grigorenko (Eds.), *Environmental effects on cognitive abilities.* Mahwah, NJ: Erlbaum.

Bellis, M. A., Downing, J., & Ashton, J. R. (2006). Adults at 12? Trends in puberty and their public health consequences. *Journal of Epidemiology and Community Health, 60,* 910–911.

Bem, D. J. (2000). Exotic becomes erotic: Interpreting the biological correlates of sexual orientation. *Archives of Sexual Behavior, 29,* 531–548.

Bem, S. L. (1985). Androgyny and gender schema theory: A conceptual and empirical integration. In T. B. Sonderegger (Ed.), *Nebraska symposium on motivation, 1984: Psychology and gender* (Vol. 32). Lincoln: University of Nebraska Press.

Bender, D. S., Skodol, A. E., Dyck, I. R., Markowitz, J. C., Shea, M. T., Yen, S., et al. (2007). Ethnicity and mental health treatment utilization by patients with personality disorders. *Journal of Consulting and Clinical Psychology, 75,* 992–999.

Benedek, D. M., & Grieger, T. A. (2008). Legal issues in psychological practice. In A. Tasman, J. Kay, J. A. Lieberman, M. B. First, & M. Maj (Eds.), *Psychiatry* (3rd ed.). New York, NY: Wiley-Blackwell.

Benedetti, F. (2008). *Placebo effects: Understanding the mechanisms in health and disease.* New York, NY: Oxford University Press.

Benham, G. (2010). Sleep: An important factor in stress-health models. *Stress & Health: Journal of the International Society for the Investigation of Stress, 26*(3), 204–214.

Benjamin, L. R., & Simpson, J. A. (2009). The power of the situation: The impact of Milgram's obedience studies on personality and social psychology. *American Psychologist, 64*(1), 12–19. doi:10.1037/a0014077

Benjamin, L. T., Jr. (2000). The psychology laboratory at the turn of the 20th century. *American Psychologist, 55,* 318–321.

Benjamin, L. T., Jr., & Baker, D. B. (2004). *From seance to science: A history of the profession of psychology in America.* Belmont, CA: Wadsworth.

Benjamin, L. T., Jr., Cavell, T. A., & Shallenberger, W. R., III. (1984). Staying with initial answers on objective tests: Is it a myth? *Teaching of Psychology, 11,* 133–141.

Benjamin, L. T., Jr., DeLeon, P. H., Freedheim, D. K., & VandenBos, G. R. (2003). Psychology as a profession. In D. K. Freedheim (Ed.), *Handbook of psychology, Vol. 1: History of psychology.* New York, NY: Wiley.

Benjamin, L. T., Jr., & VandenBos, G. R. (2006). The window on psychology's literature: A history of psychological abstracts. *American Psychologist, 61,* 941–954.

Benoît, M., & Norton, M. I. (2003). Perceptions of a fluid consensus: Uniqueness bias, false consensus, false polarization, and pluralistic ignorance in a water conservation crisis. *Personality and Social Psychology Bulletin, 29,* 559–567.

Ben-Porath, Y. S. (2003). Assessing personality and psychopathology with self-report inventories. In J. R. Graham & J. A. Naglieri (Eds.), *Handbook of psychology, Volume 10: Assessment psychology.* New York, NY: Wiley.

Benson, H. (1975). *The relaxation response.* New York, NY: Morrow.

Benson, H., & Klipper, M. Z. (1988). *The relaxation response.* New York, NY: Avon.

Bentall, R. P. (2009). *Doctoring the mind: Is our current treatment of mental illness really any good?* New York, NY: New York University Press.

Benton, D. (2004). Role of parents in the determination of the food preferences of children and the development of obesity. *International Journal of Obesity, 28,* 858–869.

Berenbaum, S. A., Martin, C. L., & Ruble, D. N. (2008). Gender development. In W. Damon & R. M. Lerner (Eds.), *Child and adolescent development: An advanced course* (pp. 647–681). New York, NY: Wiley.

Berenbaum, S. A., & Snyder, E. (1995). Early hormonal influences on childhood sex-typed activity and playmate preferences: Implications for the development of sexual orientation. *Developmental Psychology, 31,* 31–42.

Berger, R., & Lahad, M. (2010). A safe place: Ways in which nature, play and creativity can help children cope with stress and crisis — establishing the kindergarten as a safe haven where children can develop resiliency. *Early Child Development and Care, 180*(7), 889–900.

Berghmans, R. L. P. (2007). Misleading research participants: Moral aspects of deception in psychological research. *Netherlands Journal of Psychology, 63*(1), 14–20.

Bergner, S., Monk, C., & Werner, E. A. (2008). Dyadic intervention during pregnancy? Treating pregnant women and possibly reaching the future baby. *Infant Mental Health Journal, 29*(5), 399-419. doi:10.1002/imhj.20190

Berkowitz, L. (1989). Frustration-aggression hypothesis: Examination and reformulation. *Psychological Bulletin, 106,* 59–73.

Berlin, B., & Kay, P. (1969). *Basic color terms: Their universality and evolution.* Berkeley, CA: University of California Press.

Berlin, L. J., Ispa, J. M., Fine, M. A., Brooks-Gunn, J., Brady-Smith, C., Ayoub, C., & Bai, Y. (2009). Correlates and consequences of spanking and verbal punishment for low-income White, African American, and Mexican American toddlers. *Child Development, 80*(5), 1403–1420. doi: 10.1111/j.1467-8624.2009.01341.x.

Berman, A. L. (2009). Depression and suicide. In I. H. Gotlib & C. L. Hammen (Eds.), *Handbook of depression* (2nd ed.). New York, NY: Guilford Press.

Berman, M. G., Jonides, J., & Kaplan, S. (2008). The cognitive benefits of interacting with nature. *Psychological Science, 19,* 1207–1212.

Berman, R. F. (1991). Electrical brain stimulation used to study mechanisms and models of memory. In J. L. Martinez Jr. & R. P. Kesner (Eds.), *Learning and memory: A biological view.* San Diego: Academic Press.

Berman, R. M., Sporn, J., Charney, D. S., & Mathew, S. J. (2009). Principles of the pharmacotherapy of depression. In D. S. Charney & E. J. Nestler (Eds.), *Neurobiology of mental illness* (pp. 491–515). New York, NY: Guilford Press.

Bernert, R. A., Merrill, K. A., Braithwaite, S. R., Van Orden, K. A., & Joiner, T. E., Jr. (2007). Family life stress and insomnia symptoms in a prospective evaluation of young adults. *Journal of Family Psychology, 21*(1), 58–66.

Bernstein, D. M., & Loftus, E. F. (2009). The consequences of false memories for food preferences and choices. *Perspectives on Psychological Science, 4*(2), 135–139. doi:10.1111/j.1745-6924.2009.01113.x

Bernstein, H. (2007). Maternal and perinatal infection-viral. In S. G. Gabbe, J. R. Niebyl, & J. L. Simpson (Eds.) *Obstetrics: Normal and problem pregnancies* (5th ed., pp. 1203–1232). Philadelphia, PA: Elsevier.

Berridge, K. C. (2003). Comparing the emotional brains of humans and other animals. In R. J. Davidson, K. R. Scherer, & H. H. Goldsmith (Eds.), *Handbook of affective sciences.* New York, NY: Oxford University Press.

Berridge, K. C. (2004). Motivation concepts in behavioral neuroscience. *Physiology and Behavior, 81*(2), 179–209.

Berry, C. M., & Sackett, P. R. (2009). Individual differences in course choice result in underestimation of the validity of college admissions systems. *Psychological Science, 20*(7), 822–830. doi:10.1111/j.1467-9280.2009.02368.x.

Berry, D. T. R., Wetter, M. W., & Baer, R. A. (1995). Assessment of malingering. In J. N. Butcher (Ed.), *Clinical personality assessment: Practical approaches.* New York, NY: Oxford University Press.

Berry, J. W. (1994). Cross-cultural variations in intelligence. In R. J. Sternberg (Ed.), *Encyclopedia of human intelligence.* New York, NY: Macmillan.

Berry, J. W., Poortinga, Y., Segall, M., & Dasen, P. (1992). *Cross-cultural psychology.* New York, NY: Cambridge University Press.

Bersani, H. (2007). President's address 2007: The past is prologue: "MR," go gentle into that good night. *Intellectual and Developmental Disabilities, 45,* 399–404.

Berscheid, E. (1988). Some comments on love's anatomy: Or, whatever happened to old-fashioned lust? In R. J. Sternberg & M. L. Barnes (Eds.), *The psychology of love.* New Haven: Yale University Press.

Berscheid, E. (2006). Searching for the meaning of "love." In R. J. Sternberg & K. Weis (Eds.), *The new psychology of love.* New Haven, CT: Yale University Press.

Berscheid, E., & Walster, E. (1978). *Interpersonal attraction.* Reading, MA: Addison-Wesley.

Berthoud, H. R., & Morrison, C. (2008). The brain, appetite, and obesity. *Annual Review of Psychology, 59,* 55–92.

Berto, R. (2005). Exposure to restorative environments helps restore attentional capacity. *Journal of Environmental Psychology, 25,* 249–259.

Bertram, L., & Tanzi, R. E. (2008). Thirty years of Alzheimer's disease genetics: The implications of systematic meta-analyses. *Nature Reviews Neuroscience, 9*(10), 768–778. doi:10.1038/nrn2494

Bertrand, R. M., & Lachman, M. E. (2003). Personality development in adulthood and old age. In R. M. Lerner, M. A. Easterbrooks, & J. Mistry (Eds.), *Handbook of psychology, Vol. 6: Developmental psychology.* New York, NY: Wiley.

Bettmann, J. E., & Jasperson, R. A. (2008). Adults in wilderness treatment: A unique application of attachment theory and research. *Clinical Social Work Journal, 36,* 51–61.

Beutler, L. E. (2002). The dodo bird is extinct. *Clinical Psychology: Science & Practice, 9*(1), 30–34.

Beutler, L. E., Bongar, B., & Shurkin, J. N. (2001). *A consumers guide to psychotherapy.* New York, NY: Oxford University Press.

Beutler, L. E., Rocco, F., Moleiro, C. M., & Talebi, H. (2001). Resistance. *Psychotherapy: Theory, Research, Practice, Training, 38,* 431–436.

Bhagwagar, Z., & Heninger, G. R. (2009). Antidepressants. In M. C. Gelder, N. C. Andreasen, J. J. López-Ibor, Jr., & J. R. Geddes (Eds.), *New Oxford textbook of psychiatry* (2nd ed., Vol. 1). New York, NY: Oxford University Press.

Bhaskaran, K., Hamouda, O., Sannes, M., Boufassa, F., Johnson, A., Lambert, P., & Porter, K. (2008). Changes in the risk of death after HIV seroconversion compared with mortality in the general population. *Journal of the American Medical Association, 300*(1), 51–59.

Bi, G. Q., & Poo, M.-M. (2001). Synaptic modification by correlated activity: Hebb's postulate revisited. *Annual Review of Neuroscience, 24,* 139–166.

Bialystok, E., & Craik, F. M. (2010). Cognitive and linguistic processing in the bilingual mind. *Current Directions in Psychological Science, 19*(1), 19–23. doi:10.1177/0963721409358571

Bialystok, E., Craik, F. M., & Freedman, M. (2007). Bilingualism as a protection against the onset of symptoms of dementia. *Neuropsychologia, 45*(2), 459–464. doi:10.1016/j.neuropsychologia.2006.10.009

Bianchi, S., Milkie, M. A., Sayer, L. C., & Robinson, J. P. (2000). Is anyone doing the housework? Trends in the gender division of household labor. *Social Forces, 79*(1), 191–228.

Biblarz, T. J., & Stacey, J. (2010). How does the gender of parents matter? *Journal of Marriage and Family, 72*(1), 3–22. doi:10.1111/j.1741-3737.2009.00678.x

Biederman, I., Hilton, H. J., & Hummel, J. E. (1991). Pattern goodness and pattern recognition. In G. R. Lockhead & J. R. Pomerantz (Eds.), *The perception of structure.* Washington, DC: American Psychological Association.

Biermann, T., Estel, D., Sperling, W., Bleich, S., Kornhuber, J., & Reulbach, U. (2005). Influence of lunar phases on suicide: The end of a myth? A population-based study. *Chronobiology International, 22,* 1137–1143.

Bigelow, B. J. (2006). There's an elephant in the room: The impact of early poverty and neglect on intelligence and common learning disorders in children, adolescents, and their parents. *Developmental Disabilities Bulletin, 34*(1–2), 177–215.

Binet, A. (1911). Nouvelle recherches sur la mesure du niveau intellectuel chez les enfants d'école. *L'Année Psychologique, 17,* 145–201.

Binet, A., & Simon, T. (1905). Méthodes nouvelles pour le diagnostic du niveau intellectuel des anormaux. *L'Année Psychologique, 11,* 191–244.

Binet, A., & Simon, T. (1908). Le développement de l'intelligence chez les enfants. *L'Année Psychologique, 14,* 1–94.

Birgegard, A., & Sohlberg, S. (2008). Persistent effects of subliminal stimulation: Sex differences and the effectiveness of debriefing. *Scandinavian Journal of Psychology, 49*(1), 19–29. doi:10.1111/j.1467-9450.2007.00623.x.

Birkeland, S. A., Manson, T. M., Kisamore, J. L., Brannick, M. T., & Smith, M. A. (2006). A meta-analytic investigation of job applicant faking on personality measures. *International Journal of Selection and Assessment, 14,* 317–335.

Birnbaum, M. H. (2004a). Base rates in Bayesian inference. In F. P. Rudiger (Ed.), *Cognitive illusions.* New York, NY: Psychology Press.

Birnbaum, M. H. (2004b). Human research and data collection via the Internet. *Annual Review of Psychology, 55,* 803–832.

Birney, D. P., Citron-Pousty, J. H., Lutz, D. J., & Sternberg, R. J. (2005). The development of cognitive and intellectual abilities. In M. H. Bornstein & M. E. Lamb (Eds.), *Developmental science: An advanced textbook.* Mahwah, NJ: Erlbaum.

Birney, D. P., & Sternberg, R. J. (2011). The development of cognitive abilities. In M. H. Bornstein & M. E. Lamb (Eds.), *Developmental science: An advanced textbook* (pp. 353–388). New York, NY: Psychology Press.

Bishop, S. R. (2002). What do we really know about mindfulness-based stress reduction? *Psychosomatic Medicine, 64*(1), 71–83.

Bittman, M. (2008, January 27). Rethinking the meat guzzler. *The New York Times*. Retrieved from http://www.nytimes.com/2008/01/27/weekinreview/27bittman.html.

Bjorkland, D. E. (2005). *Children's thinking: Cognitive development and individual differences* (4th ed.). Belmont, CA: Wadsworth.

Björntorp, P. (2002). Definition and classification of obesity. In C. G. Fairburn & K. D. Brownell (Eds.), *Eating disorders and obesity: A comprehensive handbook* (pp. 377–381). New York, NY: Guilford Press.

Black, D. W. (2001). Antisocial personality disorder: The forgotten patients of psychiatry. *Primary Psychiatry, 8*(1), 30–81.

Blackburn, R. (2006). Other theoretical models of psychopathy. In C. J. Patrick (Ed.), *Handbook of Psychopathy*. New York, NY: Guilford Press.

Blagrove, M. (1992). Dreams as a reflection of our waking concerns and abilities: A critique of the problem-solving paradigm in dream research. *Dreaming, 2,* 205–220.

Blagrove, M. (1996). Problems with the cognitive psychological modeling of dreaming. *Journal of Mind and Behavior, 17,* 99–134.

Blair, S. N., Kohl, H. W., Paffenbarger, R. S., Clark, D. G., Cooper, K. H., & Gibbons, L. W. (1989). Physical fitness and all-cause mortality: A prospective study of healthy men and women. *Journal of the American Medical Association, 262,* 2395–2401.

Blakemore, S. (2008). Development of the social brain during adolescence. *The Quarterly Journal of Experimental Psychology, 61*(1), 40–49. doi:10.1080/17470210701508715

Blanchard, E. B., & Keefer, L. (2003). Irritable bowel syndrome. In A. M. Nezu, C. M. Nezu, & P. A. Geller (Eds.), *Handbook of psychology, Vol. 9: Health psychology*. New York, NY: Wiley.

Blanco, C., Laje, G., Olfson, M., Marcus, S. C., & Pincus, H. A. (2002). Trends in the treatment of bipolar disorder by outpatient psychiatrists. *American Journal of Psychiatry, 159,* 1005–1010.

Blank, H., Musch, J., & Pohl, R. F. (2007). Hindsight bias: On being wise after the event. *Social Cognition, 25*(1), 1–9.

Blankenhorn, D. (1995). *Fatherless America: Confronting our most urgent social problem.* New York, NY: Basic Books.

Blass, T. (1999). The Milgram Paradigm after 35 years: Some things we now know about obedience to authority. *Journal of Applied Social Psychology, 29,* 955–978.

Blashki, G., McMichael, T., & Karoly, D. J. (2007). Climate change and primary health care. *Australian Family Physician,* 36, 986–989.

Blass, T. (2009). From New Haven to Santa Clara: A historical perspective on the Milgram obedience experiments. *American Psychologist, 64*(1), 37–45. doi:10.1037/a0014434

Bleak, J., & Frederick, C. M. (1998). Superstitious behavior in sport: Levels of effectiveness and determinants of use in three collegiate sports. *Journal of Sport Behavior, 21,* 1-15.

Bleuler, E. (1911). *Dementia praecox or the group F schizophrenias.* New York, NY: International Universities Press.

Bloch, S., & Harari, E. (2009). Family therapy in the adult psychiatric setting. In M. C. Gelder, N. C. Andreasen, J. J. López-Ibor, Jr., & J. R. Geddes (Eds.), *New Oxford textbook of psychiatry* (2nd ed., Vol. 1). New York, NY: Oxford University Press.

Block, J. R., & Yuker, H. E. (1992). *Can you believe your eyes?: Over 250 illusions and other visual oddities.* New York, NY: Brunner/Mazel.

Block, N. (2002). How heritability misleads us about race. In J. Fish (Ed.), *Race and intelligence: Separating science from myth.* Mahwah, NJ: Erlbaum.

Bloom, B. S. (Ed.). (1985). *Developing talent in young people.* New York, NY: Ballantine.

Boakes, R. A. (2003). The impact of Pavlov on the psychology of learning in English-speaking countries. *The Spanish Journal of Psychology, 6*(2), 93–98.

Boase, J., & Wellman, B. (2006). Personal relationships: On and off the Internet. In A. L. Vangelisti & D. Perlman (Eds.), *The Cambridge handbook of personal relationships.* New York, NY: Cambridge University Press.

Bobo, W. V., Rapoport, J. L., Abi-Dargham, A., Fatemi, H., & Meltzer, H. Y. (2008). The neurobiology of schizophrenia. In A. Tasman, J. Kay, J. A. Lieberman, M. B. First, & M. Maj (Eds.), *Psychiatry* (3rd ed.). New York, NY: Wiley-Blackwell.

Bochner, S., & Jones, J. (2003). *Child language development: Learning to talk.* London: Whurr Publishers.

Bodenhausen, G. V., Todd, A. R., & Richeson, J. A. (2009). Controlling prejudice and stereotyping: Antecedents, mechanisms, and contexts. In T. D. Nelson (Ed.), *Handbook of prejudice, stereotyping, and discrimination* (pp. 1–22). New York, NY: Psychology Press.

Bodenmann, G., Ledermann, T., Blattner, D., & Galluzzo, C. (2006). Associations among everyday stress, critical life events, and sexual problems. *Journal of Nervous and Mental Disease, 194,* 494–501.

Boecker, H., Sprenger, T., Spilker, M. E., Henriksen, G., Koppenhoefer, M., & Wagner, K. J., et al. (2008). The runner's high: Opioidergic mechanisms in the human brain. *Cerebral Cortex, 18*(11), 2523–2531. doi:10.1093/cercor/bhn013

Bögels, S. M., & Voncken, M. (2008). Social skills training versus cognitive therapy for social anxiety disorder characterized by fear of blushing, trembling, or sweating. *International Journal of Cognitive Therapy, 1*(2), 138–150. doi:10.1521/ijct.2008.1.2.138

Bogen, J. E. (1985). The dual brain: Some historical and methodological aspects. In D. F. Benson & E. Zaidel (Eds.), *The dual brain: Hemispheric specialization in humans.* New York, NY: Guilford Press.

Bogen, J. E. (1990). Partial hemispheric independence with the neocommissures intact. In C. Trevarthen (Ed.), *Brain circuits and functions of the mind. Essays in honor of Roger W. Sperry.* Cambridge, MA: Cambridge University Press.

Bogen, J. E. (2000). Split-brain basics: Relevance for the concept of one's other mind. *Journal of the American Academy of Psychoanalysis & Dynamic Psychiatry, 28,* 341–369.

Bogg, T., & Roberts, B. W. (2004). Conscientiousness and health-related behaviors: A meta-analysis of the leading behavioral contributors to mortality. *Psychological Bulletin, 130,* 887–919.

Bohannon, J. N., III., & Bonvillian, J. D. (2009). Theoretical approaches to language acquisition. In J. B. Gleason & N. B. Ratner (Eds.), *The development of language.* Boston, MA: Pearson.

Bohner, G., & Dickel, N. (2011). Attitudes and attitude change. *Annual Review of Psychology, 62,* 391–417.

Bohner, G., & Schwarz, N. (2001). Attitudes, persuasion, and behavior. In A. Tesser & N. Schwarz (Eds.), *Blackwell handbook of social psychology: Intraindividual processes.* Malden, MA: Blackwell.

Bohner, G., Siebler, F., & Schmelcher, J. (2006). Social norms and the likelihood of raping: Perceived rape myth acceptance of others affects men's rape proclivity. *Personality and Social Psychology Bulletin, 32,* 286–297.

Boland, R. J., & Keller, M. B. (2008). Antidepressants. In A. Tasman, J. Kay, J. A. Lieberman, M. B. First, & M. Maj (Eds.), *Psychiatry* (3rd ed.). New York, NY: Wiley-Blackwell.

Boland, R. J., & Keller, M. B. (2009). Course and outcome of depression. In I. H. Gotlib & C. L. Hammen (Eds.), *Handbook of Depression* (2nd ed., pp. 23–43). New York, NY: Guilford Press.

Boldry, J. G., Gaertner, L., & Quinn, J. (2007). Measuring the measures: A meta-analytic investigation of the measures of outgroup homogeneity. *Group Processes & Intergroup Relations, 10,* 157–178.

Boles, D. B. (2005). A large-sample study of sex differences in functional cerebral lateralization. *Journal of Clinical and Experimental Neuropsychology, 27*(6), 759–768. doi:10.1081/13803390590954263

Bolger, N. (1990). Coping as a personality process: A prospective study. *Journal of Personality and Social Psychology, 59,* 525–537.

Bolles, R. C. (1975). *Theory of motivation.* New York, NY: Harper & Row.

Bolling, M. Y., Terry, C. M., & Kohlenberg, R. J. (2006). Behavioral theories. In J. C. Thomas & D. L. Segal (Eds.), *Comprehensive handbook of personality and psychopathology.* New York, NY: Wiley.

Boly, M., Faymonville, M.-E., Vogt, B. A., Maquet, P., & Laureys, S. (2007). Hypnotic regulation of consciousness and the pain neuromatrix. In G. A. Jamieson (Ed.), *Hypnosis and conscious states: The cognitive neuroscience perspective.* New York, NY: Oxford University Press.

Bonanno, G. A. (2005). Resilience in the face of potential trauma. *Current Directions in Psychological Science, 14*(3), 135–138.

Bonanno, G. A., Field, N. P., Kovacevic, A., & Kaltman, S. (2002). Self-enhancement as a buffer against extreme adversity: Civil war in Bosnia and traumatic loss in the United States. *Personality and Social Psychology Bulletin, 28,* 184–196.

Bonanno, G. A., Moskowitz, J. T., Papa, A., & Folkman, S. (2005). Resilience to loss in bereaved spouses, bereaved parents, and bereaved gay men. *Journal of Personality and Social Psychology, 88,* 827–843.

Bond, R., & Smith, P. B. (1996). Culture and conformity: A meta-analysis of studies using Asch's line judgment task. *Psychological Bulletin, 119,* 111–137.

Bonnet, M. H. (2000). Sleep deprivation. In M. H. Kryger, T. Roth, & W. C. Dement (Eds.), *Principles and practice of sleep medicine.* Philadelphia, PA: Saunders.

Bonnet, M. H. (2005). Acute sleep deprivation. In M. H. Kryger, T. Roth, & W. C. Dement (Eds.), *Principles and practice of sleep medicine.* Philadelphia, PA: Elsevier Saunders.

Bonnet, M. H., & Arand, D. L. (2010). Hyperarousal and insomnia: State of the science. *Sleep Medicine Reviews, 14*(1), 9–15. doi:10.1016/j.smrv.2009.05.002

Bono, G., McCullough, M. E., & Root, L. M. (2008). Forgiveness, feeling connected to others, and well-being: Two longitudinal studies. *Personality and Social Psychology Bulletin, 34,* 182–195.

Borbely, A. A. (1986). *Secrets of sleep.* New York, NY: Basic Books.

Borbely, A. A., & Achermann, P. (2005). Sleep homeostasis and models of sleep regulation. In M. H. Kryger, T. Roth, & W. C. Dement (Eds.), *Principles and practice of sleep medicine.* Philadelphia, PA: Elsevier Saunders.

Bordnick, P. S., Elkins, R. L., Orr, T. E., Walters, P., & Thyer, B. A. (2004). Evaluating the relative effectiveness of three aversion therapies designed to reduce craving among cocaine abusers. *Behavioral Interventions, 19*(1), 1–24.

Borgida, E., & Nisbett, R. E. (1977). The differential impact of abstract vs. concrete information on decisions. *Journal of Applied Social Psychology, 7,* 258–271.

Boring, E. G. (1966). A note on the origin of the word *psychology. Journal of the History of the Behavioral Sciences, 2,* 167.

Borkenau, P., Mauer, N., Riemann, R., Spinath, F. M., & Angleitner, A. (2004). Thin slices of behavior as cues of personality and intelligence. *Journal of Personality and Social Psychology, 86*(4), 599–614. doi:10.1037/0022-3514.86.4.599

Borman, W. C., Penner, L. A., Allen, T. D., & Motowidlo, S. J. (2001). Personality predictors of citizenship performance. *International Journal of Selection and Assessment, 9,* 52–69.

Bornstein, R. F. (1989). Exposure and affect: Overview and meta-analysis of research, 1968–1987. *Psychological Bulletin, 106*(2), 265–289. doi:10.1037/0033-2909.106.2.265

Bornstein, R. F. (2003). Psychodynamic models of personality. In T. Millon & M. J. Lerner (Eds.), *Handbook of psychology, Vol. 5: Personality and social psychology.* New York, NY: Wiley.

Boroditsky, L. (2001). Does language shape thought? Mandarin and English speakers' conceptions of time. *Cognitive Psychology, 43*(1), 1–22.

Bosma, H., van Boxtel, M. P. J., Ponds, R. W. H. M., Houx, P. J., Burdorf, A., & Jolles, J. (2002). Mental work demands protect against cognitive impairment: MAAS prospective cohort study. *Experimental Aging Research, 29*(1), 33–45.

Bost, K. K., Cox, M. J., Burchinal, M. R., & Payne, C. (2002). Structural and supporting changes in couples' family and friendship networks across the transition to parenthood. *Journal of Marriage and the Family, 64,* 517–531.

Bouchard, C. (2002). Genetic influences on body weight. In C. G. Fairburn & K. D. Brownell (Eds.), *Eating disorders and obesity: A comprehensive handbook* (pp. 16–21). New York, NY: Guilford Press.

Bouchard, T. J., Jr. (1997). IQ similarity in twins reared apart: Findings and responses to critics. In R. J. Sternberg, & E. L. Grigorenko (Eds.), *Intelligence, heredity, and environment.* New York, NY: Cambridge University Press.

Bouchard, T. J., Jr. (1998). Genetic and environmental influences on adult intelligence and special mental abilities. *Human Biology, 70,* 257–279.

Bouchard, T. J., Jr. (2004). Genetic influence on human psychological traits: A survey. *Current Directions in Psychological Science, 13*(4), 148–151.

Bouchard, T. J., Jr., Lykken, D. T., McGue, M., Segal, N. L., & Tellegen, A. (1990). Sources of human psychological differences: The Minnesota study of twins reared apart. *Science, 250,* 223–228.

Bourgeois, J. A., Seaman, J. S., & Servis, M. E. (2003). Delirium, dementia, and amnestic disorders. In R. E. Hales & S. C. Yudofsky (Eds.), *Textbook of clinical Psychiatry.* Washington, DC: American Psychiatric Publishing.

Bourgeois, J. A., Seamen, J. S., & Servis, M. E. (2008). Delirium, dementia, and amnestic and other cognitive disorders. In R. E. Hales, S. C. Yudofsky, & G. O. Gabbard (Eds.), *The American Psychiatric Publishing textbook of psychiatry,* (5th ed., pp. 30–35). Washington, DC: American Psychiatric Publishing.

Bousfield, W. A. (1953). The occurrence of clustering in the recall of randomly arranged associates. *Journal of General Psychology, 49,* 229–240.

Bouton, M. E. (2000). A learning theory perspective on lapse, relapse, and the maintenance of behavior change. *Health Psychology, 19*(1), 57–63.

Bouton, M. E. (2002). Context, ambiguity, and unlearning: Sources of relapse after behavioral extinction. *Biological Psychiatry, 52,* 976–986.

Bouton, M. E., & Woods, A. M. (2009). Exctinction: Behavioral mechanisms and their implications. In J. H. Byrne (Ed.), *Concise learning and memory: The editor's selection.* San Diego, CA: Elsevier.

Bowd, A. D., & Shapiro, K. J. (1993). The case against laboratory animal research in psychology. *Journal of Social Issues, 49*(1), 133–142.

Bower, G. H. (1970). Organizational factors in memory. *Cognitive Psychology, 1,* 18–46.

Bower, G. H. (2000). A brief history of memory research. In E. Tulving & F. I. M. Craik (Eds.), *The Oxford handbook of memory* (pp. 3–32). New York, NY: Oxford University Press.

Bower, G. H., & Clark, M. C. (1969). Narrative stories as mediators of serial learning. *Psychonomic Science, 14,* 181–182.

Bower, G. H., Clark, M. C., Lesgold, A. M., & Winzenz, D. (1969). Hierarchical retrieval schemes in recall of categorized word lists. *Journal of Verbal Learning and Verbal Behavior, 8,* 323–343.

Bower, G. H., & Springston, F. (1970). Pauses as recoding points in letter series. *Journal of Experimental Psychology, 83,* 421–430.

Bower, J. E., Moskowitz, J., & Epel, E. (2009). Is benefit finding good for your health? Pathways linking positive life changes after stress and physical health outcomes. *Current Directions in Psychological Science, 18*(6), 337–341.

Bowers, M. (2007, July/August). The making of the MFT profession: Standards, regulation. *Family Therapy Magazine,* pp. 12–18.

Bowlby, J. (1969). *Attachment and loss: Vol. 1. Attachment.* New York, NY: Basic Books.

Bowlby, J. (1973). *Attachment and loss: Vol. 2. Separation, anxiety and anger.* New York, NY: Basic Books.

Bowlby, J. (1980). *Attachment and loss: Vol. 3. Sadness and depression.* New York, NY: Basic Books.

Boyce, C. J., Brown, G. A., & Moore, S. C. (2010). Money and happiness: Rank of income, not income, affects life satisfaction. *Psychological Science, 21*(4), 471–475.

Boyle, G. J. (2008). Critique of the five-factor model of personality. In G. J. Boyle, G. Matthews, & D. H. Saklofske (Eds.), *The Sage handbook of personality theory and assessment: Personality theories and models* (Vol. 1, pp. 295–312). Los Angles, CA: Sage.

Boyle, M. (2007). The problem with diagnosis. *The Psychologist, 20,* 290–292.

Bradshaw, J. L. (1981). In two minds. *Behavioral and Brain Sciences, 4,* 101–102.

Bradshaw, J. L. (1989). *Hemispheric specialization and psychological function.* New York, NY: Wiley.

Bragg, E. A. (1996). Towards ecological self: Deep ecology meets constructionist self-theory. *Journal of Environmental Psychology, 16,* 93–108.

Brainerd, C. J. (1996). Piaget: A centennial celebration. *Psychological Science, 7,* 191–195.

Brainerd, C. J., & Reyna, V. F. (2005). *The science of false memory.* New York, NY: Oxford University Press.

Branaman, T. F., & Gallagher, S. N. (2005). Polygraph testing in sex offender treatment: A review of limitations. *American Journal of Forensic Psychology, 23*(1), 45–64.

Brannon, L., & Feist, J. (2007). *Health psychology: An introduction to behavior and health.* Belmont, CA: Wadsworth.

Bransford, J. D., & Stein, B. S. (1993). *The IDEAL problem solver.* New York, NY: W. H. Freeman.

Branson, R. (2005). *Losing my virginity: The autobiography.* London: Virgin.

Branson, R. (2006). *Screw it, let's do it: Lessons in life.* London: Virgin.

Brase, G. L. (2006). Cues of parental investment as a factor in attractiveness. *Evolution and Human Behavior, 27,* 145–157.

Brase, G. L., Cosmides, L., & Tooby, J. (1998). Individuation, counting, and statistical inference: The role of frequency and whole-object representations in judgment under certainty. *Journal of Experimental Psychology: General, 127,* 3–21.

Braun, M., Lewin-Epstein, N., Stier, H., & Baumgärtner, M. K. (2008). Perceived equity in the gendered division of household labor. *Journal of Marriage and Family, 70*(5), 1145–1156. doi:10.1111/j.1741-3737.2008.00556.x

Bravo, M. (2010). Context effects in perception. In E. B. Goldstein (Ed.), *Encyclopedia of perception.* Thousand Oaks, CA: Sage.

Breckler, S. J. (2007). Rising to the challenge. *Monitor on Psychology, 38*(4), 28.

Bredt, B. M., Higuera-Alhino, D., Hebert, S. J., McCune, J. M., & Abrams, D. I. (2002). Short-term effects of cannabinoids on immune phenotype and function in HIV-1 infected patients. *Journal of Clinical Pharmacology, 42,* 90S–96S.

Breedlove, S. M. (1994). Sexual differentiation of the human nervous system. *Annual Review of Psychology, 45,* 389–418.

Breggin, P. R. (1991). *Toxic psychiatry.* New York, NY: St. Martin's Press.

Breggin, P. R. (2008). *Medication madness: A psychiatrist exposes the dangers of mood-altering medications.* New York, NY: St. Martin's Press.

Brehm, J. W. (1966). *A theory of psychological reactance.* New York, NY: Academic Press.

Brehm, S. S., & Kassin, S. M. (1993). *Social psychology.* Boston, MA: Houghton Mifflin.

Breland, K., & Breland, M. (1961). The misbehavior of organisms. *American Psychologist, 16,* 681–684.

Breland, K., & Breland, M. (1966). *Animal behavior.* New York, NY: Macmillan.

Brennen, T., Vikan, A., & Dybdahl, R. (2007). Are tip-of-the-tongue states universal? Evidence from the speakers of an unwritten language. *Memory, 15,* 167–176.

Breslin, P. A. S. (2010). Taste, genetics of. In E. B. Goldstein (Ed.), *Encyclopedia of perception.* Thousand Oaks, CA: Sage.

Bretherton, I., & Munholland, K. A. (2008). Internal working models in attachment relationships: Conceptual and empirical aspects of security. In J. Cassidy & P. R. Shaver (Eds.), *Handbook of attachment: Theory, research, and clinical applications* (2nd ed., pp. 102–130). New York, NY: Guilford Press.

Breunig, M. C., O'Connell, T. S., Todd, S., Anderson, L., & Young, A. (2010). The impact of outdoor pursuits on college students' perceived sense of community. *Journal of Leisure Research, 42*(4), 551–572.

Brewer, C. L. (1991). Perspectives on John B. Watson. In G. A. Kimble, M. Wertheimer, & C. White (Eds.), *Portraits of pioneers in psychology.* Hillside, NJ: Erlbaum.

Brewer, W. F. (2000). Bartlett, functionalism, and modern schema theories. *Journal of Mind and Behavior, 21,* 37–44.

Brewer, W. F., & Treyens, J. C. (1981). Role of schemata in memory for places. *Cognitive Psychology, 13,* 207–230.

Brewin, C. R. (2003). *Posttraumatic stress disorder: Malady or myth.* New Haven: Yale University Press.

Brewin, C. R. (2004). Commentary on McNally "Is traumatic amnesia nothing but psychiatric folklore?" *Cognitive Behaviour Therapy, 33*(2), 102–104.

Brewin, C. R. (2007). Autobiographical memory for trauma: Update on four controversies. *Memory, 15,* 227–248.

Brickman, P., Coates, D., & Janoff-Bulman, R. (1978). Lottery winners and accident victims: Is happiness relative? *Journal of Personality and Social Psychology, 36,* 917–927.

Bridge, J. A., & Barbe, R. P. (2004). Reducing hospital readmission in depression and schizophrenia: Current evidence. *Current Opinion in Psychiatry, 17,* 505–511.

Bridge, J. A., Iyengar, S., Salary, C. B., Barbe, R. P., Birmaher, B., Pincus, H. A., et al. (2007). Clinical response and risk for reported suicidal ideation and suicide attempts in pediatric antidepressant treatment: A meta-analysis of randomized controlled trials. *Journal of the American Medical Association, 297,* 1683–1969.

Brien, S. E., Ronksley, P. E., Turner, B. J., Mukamal, K. J., & Ghali, W. A. (2011). Effect of alcohol consumption on biological markers associated with risk of coronary heart disease: Systematic review and meta-analysis of interventional studies. *British Medical Journal, 342*(7795), 480.

Briere, J., & Conte, J. R. (1993). Self-reported amnesia for abuse in adults molested as children. *Journal of Traumatic Stress, 6*(1), 21–31.

Bringmann, W. G., & Balk, M. M. (1992). Another look at Wilhelm Wundt's publication record. *History of Psychology Newsletter, 24*(3/4), 50–66.

Brislin, R. (2000). *Understanding culture's influence on behavior.* Belmont, CA: Wadsworth.

Bröder, A. (1998). Deception can be acceptable. *American Psychologist, 53,* 805–806.

Brody, N. (1992). *Intelligence* (2nd ed.). San Diego, CA: Academic Press.

Brody, N. (2000). History of theories and measurements of intelligence. In R. J. Sternberg (Ed.), *Handbook of intelligence* (pp. 16–33). New York, NY: Cambridge University Press.

Brody, N. (2003). Jensen's genetic interpretation of racial differences in intelligence: Critical evaluation. In H. Nyborg (Ed.), *The scientific study of general intelligence: Tribute to Arthur R. Jensen.* Oxford, UK: Pergamon.

Brody, N. (2005). To *g* or not to *g*—that is the question. In O. Wilhelm & R. W. Engle (Eds.), *Handbook of understanding and measuring intelligence.* Thousand Oaks, CA: Sage Publications.

Broida, J., Tingley, L., Kimball, R., & Miele, J. (1993). Personality differences between pro- and anti- vivisectionists. *Society and Animals, 1,* 129–144.

Broughton, R. (1994). Important underemphasized aspects of sleep onset. In R. D. Ogilvie & J. R. Harsh (Eds.), *Sleep onset: Normal and abnormal processes.* Washington, DC: American Psychological Association.

Brown, A. S. (1991). A review of the tip-of-the-tongue experience. *Psychological Bulletin, 109,* 204–223.

Brown, A. S., & Derkits, E. J. (2010). Prenatal infection and schizophrenia: A review of epidemiologic and translational studies. *American Journal of Psychiatry, 167*(3), 261–280. doi:10.1176/appi.ajp.2009.09030361

Brown, A. S., & Susser, E. S. (2008). Prenatal nutritional deficiency and risk of adult schizophrenia. *Schizophrenia Bulletin, 34*(6), 1054–1063. doi:10.1093/schbul/sbn096

Brown, E. J., Juster, H. R., Heimberg, R. G., & Winning, C. D. (1998). Stressful life events and personality styles: Relation to impairment and treatment outcome in patients with social phobia. *Journal of Anxiety Disorders, 12,* 233–251.

Brown, H. D., & Kosslyn, S. M. (1993). Cerebral lateralization. *Current Opinion in Neurobiology, 3,* 183–186.

Brown, M. (1974). Some determinants of persistence and initiation of achievement-related activities. In J. W. Atkinson & J. O. Raynor (Eds.), *Motivation and achievement.* Washington, DC: Halsted.

Brown, M. (1998). *Richard Branson: The inside story.* London: Headline.

Brown, R., & McNeill, D. (1966). The "tip-of-the-tongue" phenomenon. *Journal of Verbal Learning and Verbal Behavior, 5*(4), 325–337.

Brown, R. T. (1989). Creativity: What are we to measure? In J. A. Glover, R. R. Ronning, & C. R. Reynolds (Eds.), *Handbook of creativity.* New York, NY: Plenum.

Brown, S. C., & Craik, F. I. M. (2000). Encoding and retrieval of information. In E. Tulving & F. I. M. Craik (Eds.), *The Oxford handbook of memory* (pp. 93–108). New York, NY: Oxford University Press.

Brown, T. A., & Lawrence, A. E. (2009). Generalized anxiety disorder and obsessive-compulsive disorder. In P. H. Blaney & T. Millon (Eds.), *Oxford textbook of psychopathology* (2nd ed., pp. 146–175). New York, NY: Oxford University Press.

Brown, T. T., & Dobs, A. S. (2002). Endocrine effects of marijuana. *Journal of Clinical Pharmacology, 42,* 97S–102S.

Brown, W. D. (2006). Insomnia: Prevalence and daytime consequences. In T. Lee-Chiong (Ed.), *Sleep: A comprehensive handbook.* Hoboken, NJ: Wiley-Liss.

Brownell, K. D. (2002). The environment and obesity. In C. G. Fairburn & K. D. Brownell (Eds.), *Eating disorders and obesity: A comprehensive handbook* (pp. 433–438). New York, NY: Guilford Press.

Brownell, K. D., & Wadden, T. A. (2000). Obesity. In B. J. Sadock & V. A. Sadock (Eds.), *Kaplan and Sadock's comprehensive textbook of psychiatry* (7th ed., Vol. 2, pp. 1787–1796). Philadelphia, PA: Lippincott Williams & Wilkins.

Bruer, J. T. (1999). *The myth of the first three years: A new understanding of early brain development and lifelong learning.* New York, NY: Free Press.

Bruer, J. T. (2002). Avoiding the pediatrician's error: How neuroscientists can help educators (and themselves). *Nature Neuroscience, 5,* 1031–1033.

Bruer, J. T., & Greenough, W. T. (2001). The subtle science of how experience affects the brain. In D. B. Bailey Jr., J. T. Bruer, F. J. Symons, & J. W. Lichtman (Eds.), *Critical thinking about critical periods.* Baltimore, MD: Paul H. Brookes Publishing.

Bryden, M. P. (1982). *Laterality: Functional asymmetry in the intact brain.* New York, NY: Academic Press.

Buccino, G., & Riggio, L. (2006). The role of the mirror neuron system in motor learning. *Kinesiology, 38*(1), 5–15.

Buchanan, R. W., & Carpenter, W. T. (2005). Concept of schizophrenia. In B. J. Sadock & V. A. Sadock (Eds.), *Kaplan & Sadock's comprehensive textbook of psychiatry.* Philadelphia, PA: Lippincott Williams & Wilkins.

Buck, L. B. (2000). Smell and taste: The chemical senses. In E. R. Kandel, J. H. Schwartz, & T. M. Jessell (Eds.), *Principles of neural science.* New York, NY: McGraw-Hill.

Buck, L. B. (2004). Olfactory receptors and coding in mammals. *Nutrition Reviews, 62,* S184–S188.

Buck Consultants. (2011). Retaining, recruiting top talent key priorities for employers, survey finds. *Talent Management,* May 12. Retrieved from http://talentmgt.com/articles/view/retaining-recruiting-top-talent-key-priorities-for-employers-survey-finds/1

Buckley, K. W. (1982). The selling of a psychologist: John Broadus Watson and the application of behavioral techniques to advertising. *Journal of the History of Behavioral Sciences, 18*(3), 207–221. doi:10.1002/1520-6696 (198207)18:3<207::AID-JHBS2300180302>3.0.CO;2-8

Buckley, K. W. (1994). Misbehaviorism: The case of John B. Watson's dismissal from Johns Hopkins University. In J. T. Todd & E. K. Morris (Eds.), *Modern perspectives on John B. Watson and classical behaviorism.* Westport, CT: Greenwood Press.

Buckman, R. (2002). Communications and emotions: Skills and effort are key. *British Medical Journal, 325,* 672.

Budiansky, S. (2004). Human and animal intelligence: The gap is a chasm. *Cerebrum, 6*(2), 85–95.

Bufe, B., Breslin, P. A. S., Kuhn, C., Reed, D. R., Tharp, C. D., Slack, J. P., Kim, U., Drayna, D., & Meyerhof, W. (2005). The molecular basis of individual differences in phenylthiocarbamide and propylthiouracil bitterness perception. *Current Biology, 15,* 322–327.

Buffardi, L. E., & Campbell, W. (2008). Narcissism and social networking web sites. *Personality and Social Psychology Bulletin, 34*(10), 1303–1314. doi:10.1177/0146167208320061

Bühler, C., & Allen, M. (1972). *Introduction to humanistic psychology.* Pacific Grove, CA: Brooks/Cole.

Bulik, C. M. (2004). Genetic and biological risk factors. In J. K. Thompson (Ed.), *Handbook of eating disorders and obesity.* New York, NY: Wiley.

Bull, D. L. (1999). A verified case of recovered memories of sexual abuse. *American Journal of Psychotherapy, 53,* 221–224.

Buller, D. J. (2009, January 1). Four fallacies of pop evolutionary psychology. *Scientific American,* pp. 74–81. doi:10.1038/scientificamerican0109-74.

Bumpass, L., & Lu, H. (2000). Trends in cohabitation and implications for children's family contexts in the United States. *Population Studies, 54*(1), 29–41.

Burger, J. M. (1999). The foot-in-the-door compliance procedure: A multiple process analysis review. *Personality and Social Psychology Review, 3,* 303–325.

Burger, J. M. (2008). *Personality.* Belmont, CA: Wadsworth.

Burger, J. M. (2009). Replicating Milgram: Would people still obey today? *American Psychologist, 64*(1), 1–11. doi:10.1037/a0010932

Burgess, A. (2007). On the contribution of neurophysiology to hypnosis research: Current state and future directions. In G. A. Jamieson (Ed.), *Hypnosis and conscious states: The cognitive neuroscience perspective.* New York, NY: Oxford University Press.

Burke, B. L., Martens, A., & Faucher, E. H. (2010). Two decades of terror management theory: A meta-analysis of mortality salience research. *Personality and Social Psychology Review, 14*(2), 155–195. doi:10.1177/1088868309352321

Burke, D. M., & Shafto, M. A. (2004). Aging and language production. *Current Directions in Psychological Science, 13*(1), 21–24.

Burkhardt, D. A. (2010). Visual processing: Retinal. In E. B. Goldstein (Ed.), *Encyclopedia of perception.* Thousand Oaks, CA: Sage.

Burlingame, G. M., & Baldwin, S. (2011). Group therapy. In J. C. Norcross, G. R. Vandenbos, & D. K. Freedheim (Eds.), *History of psychotherapy: Continuity and change* (2nd ed.). Washington, DC: American Psychological Association.

Burlingame, G. M., & McClendon, D. T. (2008). Group therapy. In J. L. Lebow (Ed.), *Twenty-first century psychotherapies: Contemporary approaches to theory and practice*. New York, NY: Wiley.

Burns, B. D., & Corpus, B. (2004). Randomness and inductions from streaks: "Gambler's fallacy" versus "hot hand." *Psychonomic Bulletin & Review, 11*(1), 179–184.

Burriss, R. P., & Little, A. C. (2006). Effects of partner conception risk phase on male perception of dominance in faces. *Evolution and Human Behavior, 27,* 297–305.

Bushman, B. J. (2002). Does venting anger feed or extinguish the flame? Catharsis, rumination, distraction, anger, and aggressive responding. *Personality and Social Psychology Bulletin, 28,* 724–731.

Bushman, B. J., & Anderson, C. A. (2001). Media violence and the American public: Scientific facts versus media misinformation. *American Psychologist, 56,* 477–489.

Bushman, B. J., & Anderson, C. A. (2009). Comfortably numb: Desensitizing effects of violent media on helping others. *Psychological Science, 20*(3), 273–277. doi: 10.1111/j.1467-9280.2009.02287.x.

Bushman, B. J., & Huesmann, L. R. (2001). Effects of televised violence on aggression. In D. G. Singer & J. L. Singer (Eds.), *Handbook of children and the media*. Thousand Oaks, CA: Sage.

Buss, D. M. (1985). Human mate selection. *American Scientist, 73,* 47–51.

Buss, D. M. (1988). The evolution of human intrasexual competition: Tactics of mate attraction. *Journal of Personality and Social Psychology, 54,* 616–628.

Buss, D. M. (1989). Sex differences in human mate preferences: Evolutionary hypotheses tested in 37 cultures. *Behavioral and Brain Sciences, 12,* 1–49.

Buss, D. M. (1991). Evolutionary personality psychology. *Annual Review of Psychology, 42,* 459–491.

Buss, D. M. (1994a). *The evolution of desire: Strategies of human mating*. New York, NY: Basic Books.

Buss, D. M. (1994b). Mate preferences in 37 cultures. In W. J. Lonner & R. S. Malpass (Eds.), *Psychology and culture*. Boston, MA: Allyn & Bacon.

Buss, D. M. (1995). Evolutionary psychology: A new paradigm for psychological science. *Psychological Inquiry, 6,* 1–30.

Buss, D. M. (1997). Evolutionary foundation of personality. In R. Hogan, J. Johnson, & S. Briggs (Eds.), *Handbook of personality psychology*. San Diego: Academic Press.

Buss, D. M. (1999). *Evolutionary psychology: The new science of the mind*. Boston, MA: Allyn & Bacon.

Buss, D. M. (2001). Cognitive biases and emotional wisdom in the evolution of conflict between the sexes. *Current Directions in Psychological Science, 10,* 219–223.

Buss, D. M. (2006). The evolution of love. In R. J. Sternberg & K. Weis (Eds.), *The new psychology of love* (pp. 65–86). New Haven, CT: Yale University Press.

Buss, D. M. (2009). The great struggles of life: Darwin and the emergence of evolutionary psychology. *American Psychologist, 64*(2), 140–148. doi:10.1037/a0013207

Buss, D. M., & Kenrick, D. T. (1998). Evolutionary social psychology. In D. T. Gilbert, S. T. Fiske, & G. Lindzey (Eds.), *The handbook of social psychology*. New York, NY: McGraw-Hill.

Buss, D. M., & Reeve, H. K. (2003). Evolutionary psychology and developmental dynamics: Comment on Lickliter and Honeycutt (2003). *Psychological Bulletin, 129,* 848–853.

Buss, D. M., & Schmitt, D. P. (1993). Sexual strategies theory: A contextual evolutionary analysis of human mating. *Psychological Review, 100,* 204–232.

Buss, D. M., & Shackelford, T. K. (2008). Attractive women want it all: Good genes, economic investment, parenting proclivities, and emotional commitment. *Evolutionary Psychology, 6*(1), 134–146.

Bussey, K., & Bandura, A. (1999). Social cognitive theory of gender development and differentiation. *Psychological Review, 106,* 676–713.

Bussey, K., & Bandura, A. (2004). Social cognitive theory of gender development and functioning. In A. H. Eagly, A. E. Beall, & R. J. Sternberg (Eds.), *The psychology of gender*. New York, NY: Guilford Press.

Butcher, J. N. (2005). *A beginner's guide to the MMPI-2*. Washington, DC: American Psychological Association.

Butcher, J. N. (2006). *MMPI-2: A practitioner's guide*. Washington, DC: American Psychological Association.

Butler, A. C., & Roediger, H. (2008). Feedback enhances the positive effects and reduces the negative effects of multiple-choice testing. *Memory & Cognition, 36*(3), 604–616. doi:10.3758/MC.36.3.604

Butler, E. A., Egloff, B., Wilhelm, F. H., Smith, N. C., Erickson, E. A., & Gross, J. J. (2003). The social consequences of expressive suppression. *Emotion, 3*(1), 48–67.

Butler, J. L., & Baumeister, R. F. (1998). The trouble with friendly faces: Skilled performance with a supportive audience. *Journal of Personality and Social Psychology, 75,* 1213–1230.

Button, T. M. M., Maughan, B., & McGuffin, P. (2007). The relationship of maternal smoking to psychological problems in the offspring. *Early Human Development, 83,* 727–732.

Buzan, D. S. (2004, March 12). I was not a lab rat. *The Guardian*. Retrieved from http://www.guardian.co.uk/education/2004/mar/12/highereducation.uk

Buzzell, L., & Chalquist, C. (2009). *Ecotherapy: Healing with nature in mind*. San Francisco, CA: Sierra Club Books.

Byne, W. (2007). Biology and sexual minority status. In I. H. Meyer & M. E. Northridge (Eds.). *The health of sexual minorities: Public health perspectives on lesbian, gay, bisexual, and transgender populations*. New York, NY: Springer Science & Business Media.

Byrne, D. (1997). An overview (and underview) of research and theory within the attraction paradigm. *Journal of Social and Personal Relationships, 14,* 417–431.

Byrne, D., Clore, G. L., & Smeaton, G. (1986). The attraction hypothesis: Do similar attitudes affect anything? *Journal of Personality and Social Psychology, 51,* 1167–1170.

Byrne, J. H. (2008). Postsynaptic potentials and synaptic integration. In L. Squire, D. Berg, F. Bloom, S. Du Lac, A. Ghosh, & N. Spitzer (Eds.), *Fundamental neuroscience* (3rd ed., pp. 227–246). San Diego, CA: Elsevier.

Cabeza, R., & Nyberg, L. (2000). Imaging cognition II: An empirical review of 275 PET and fMRI studies. *Journal of Cognitive Neuroscience, 12,* 1–47.

Cabral, G. A., & Petit, D. A. D. (1998). Drugs and immunity: Cannabinoids and their role in decreased resistance to infectious disease. *Journal of Neuroimmunology, 83,* 116–123.

Cab´yoglu, M. T., Ergene, N., & Tan, U. (2006). The mechanism of acupuncture and clinical applications. *International Journal of Neuroscience, 116*(2), 115–125.

Cacioppo, J. T., & Berntson, G. G. (1999). The affect system: Architecture and operating characteristics. *Current Directions in Psychological Science, 8,* 133–137.

Cacioppo, J. T., Hawkley, L. C., Kalil, A., Hughes, M. E., Waite, L., & Thisted, R. A. (2008). Happiness and the invisible threads of social connection: The Chicago health, aging, and social relations study. In M. Eid & R. J. Larsen (Eds.), *The science of subjective well-being*. New York, NY: Guilford Press.

Cadinu, M., Maass, A., Rosabianca, A., & Kiesner, J. (2005). Why do women underperform under stereotype threat? Evidence for the role of negative thinking. *Psychological Science, 16,* 572–578.

Cahill, L. (2006). Why sex matters for neuroscience. *Nature Reviews Neuroscience, 7,* 477–484.

Cahn, B. R., & Polich, J. (2006). Meditation states and traits: EEG, ERP, and neuroimaging studies. *Psychological Bulletin, 132,* 180–211.

Cai, D. J., Mednick, S. A., Harrison, E. M., Kanady, J. C., & Mednick, S. C. (2009). REM, not incubation, improves creativity by priming associative networks. *Proceedings of the National Academy of Sciences of the United States of America, 106*(25), 10130–10134. doi:10.1073/pnas.0900271106

Cain, W. S. (1988). Olfaction. In R. C. Atkinson, R. J. Herrnstein, G. Lindzey, & R. D. Luce (Eds.), *Stevens' handbook of experimental psychology: Perception and motivation* (Vol. 1). New York, NY: Wiley.

Calhoun, L. G., & Tedeschi, R. G. (2006). The foundations of posttraumatic growth: An expanded framework. In L. G. Calhoun & R. G. Tedeschi (Eds.), *Handbook of posttraumatic growth: Research & practice*. Mahwah, NJ: Erlbaum.

Calhoun, L. G., & Tedeschi, R. G. (2008). The paradox of struggling with trauma: Guidelines for practice and directions for research. In S. Joseph & P. A. Linley (Eds.), *Trauma, recovery, and growth: Positive psychological perspectives on posttraumatic stress*. Hoboken, NJ: Wiley.

Callaghan, T., Rochat, P., Lillard, A., Claux, M., Odden, H., Itakura, S., et al. (2005). Synchrony in the onset of mental-state reasoning: Evidence from five cultures. *Psychological Science, 16*(5), 378–384. doi:10.1111/j.0956-7976.2005.01544.x

Callahan, C. M. (2000). Intelligence and giftedness. In R. J. Sternberg (Ed.), *Handbook of intelligence* (pp. 159–175). New York, NY: Cambridge University Press.

Callicutt, J. W. (2006). Homeless shelters: An uneasy component of the de facto mental health system. In J. Rosenberg & S. Rosenberg (Eds.), *Community mental health: Challenges for the 21st century*. New York, NY: Routledge.

Calvert, C. (1997). Hate speech and its harms: A communication theory perspective. *Journal of Communication, 47,* 4–19.

Camaioni, L. (2001). Early language. In G. Bremner & A. Fogel (Eds.), *Blackwell handbook of infant development*. Malden, MA: Blackwell.

Camerer, C. (2005). Three cheers—psychological, theoretical, empirical—for loss aversion. *Journal of Marketing Research, 42*(2), 129–133.

Cami, J., & Farre, M. (2003). Mechanisms of disease: Drug addiction. *New England Journal of Medicine,* 349, 975–986.

Campbell, A. (2005). Aggression. In D. M. Buss (Ed.), *The handbook of evolutionary psychology*. New York, NY: Wiley.

Campbell, J. (1971). *Hero with a thousand faces*. New York, NY: Harcourt Brace Jovanovich.

Campbell, K. B. (2000). Introduction to the special section: Information processing during sleep onset and sleep. *Canadian Journal of Experimental Psychology, 54*(4), 209–218.

Campbell, L., Simpson, J. A., Boldry, J., & Kashy, D. A. (2005). Perceptions of conflict and support in romantic relationships: The role of attachment anxiety. *Journal of Personality and Social Psychology, 88,* 510–531.

Campbell, R., & Wasco, S. M. (2005). Understanding rape and sexual assault: 20 years of progress and future decisions. *Journal of Interpersonal Violence, 20*(1), 127–131.

Campbell, W. K., & Foster, J. D. (2007). The narcissistic self: Background, an extended-agency model, and ongoing controversies. In C. Sedikides & S. J. Spencer (Eds.), *The self* (pp. 115–138). New York, NY: Psychology Press.

Campfield, L. A. (2002). Leptin and body weight regulation. In C. G. Fairburn & K. D. Brownell (Eds.), *Eating disorders and obesity: A comprehensive handbook* (pp. 32–36). New York, NY: Guilford Press.

Campos, P. (2004). *The obesity myth: Why America's obsession with weight is hazardous to your health.* New York, NY: Gotham Books.

Canli, T. (2008). Toward a "molecular psychology" of personality. In O. P. John, R. W. Robbins, & L. A. Pervin (Eds.), *Handbook of personality: Theory and research* (Vol. 3, pp. 311–327). New York, NY: Guilford Press.

Cannon, W. B. (1927). The James-Lange theory of emotions: A critical examination and an alternate theory. *American Journal of Psychology, 39,* 106–124.

Cannon, W. B. (1929). *Bodily changes in pain, hunger, fear and rage.* New York, NY: Appleton.

Cannon, W. B. (1932). *The wisdom of the body.* New York, NY: Norton.

Cannon, W. B., & Washburn, A. L. (1912). An explanation of hunger. *American Journal of Physiology, 29,* 444–454.

Canter, P. H. (2003). The therapeutic effects of meditation. *British Medical Journal, 326,* 1049–1050.

Canu, W. & Gordon, M. (2005). Mother nature as treatment for ADHD: Overstating the benefits of green. *American Journal of Public Health, 95,* 371.

Cao, Y., Vikingstad, E. M., Huttenlocher, P. R., Towle, V. L., & Levin, D. N. (1994). Functional magnetic resonance imaging studies of the reorganization of the human head sensorimotor area after unilateral brain injury. *Proceedings of the National Academy of Sciences, 91,* 9612–9616.

Capaldi, E. D. (1996). Conditioned food preferences. In E. D. Capaldi (Ed.), *Why we eat what we eat: The psychology of eating* (pp. 53–81). Washington, DC: American Psychological Association.

Capaldi, E. D., & VandenBos, G. R. (1991). Taste, food exposure, and eating behavior. *Hospital and Community Psychiatry, 42*(8), 787–789.

Capozza, D., & Brown, R. (2000). *Social identity processes: Trends in theory and research.* London: Sage.

Cappadocia, M., & Weiss, J. A. (2011). Review of social skills training groups for youth with Asperger syndrome and high functioning autism. *Research in Autism Spectrum Disorders, 5*(1), 70–78. doi:10.1016/j.rasd.2010.04.001

Cappuccio, F. P., Taggart, F. M., Kandala, N., Currie, A., Peile, E., Stranges, S., & Miller, M. A. (2008). Meta-analysis of short sleep duration and obesity in children and adults. *Sleep: Journal of Sleep and Sleep Disorders Research, 31*(5), 619–626.

Card, J. P., Swanson, L. W., & Moore, R. (2008). The hypothalamus: An overview of regulatory systems. In L. Squire, D. Berg, F. Bloom, S. Du Lac, A. Ghosh, & N. Spitzer (Eds.), *Fundamental neuroscience* (3rd ed., pp. 795–808). San Diego, CA: Elsevier.

Cardeña, E., & Gleaves, D. H. (2007). Dissociative disorders. In M. Hersen, S. M. Turner, & D. C. Beidel (Eds.), *Adult psychopathology and diagnosis.* New York, NY: Wiley.

Carey, B. (2009, December 21). Building a search engine of the brain, slice by slice. *The New York Times.* Retrieved from http://www.newyorktimes.com

Carey, M. P., & Vanable, P. A. (2003). AIDS/HIV. In A. M. Nezu, C. M. Nezu, & P. A. Geller (Eds.), *Handbook of psychology, Vol. 9: Health psychology.* New York, NY: Wiley.

Carey, S. (2010). Beyond fast mapping. *Language Learning and Development, 6*(3), 184–205. doi:10.1080/15475441.2010.484379

Carli, L. L. (1999). Cognitive, reconstruction, hindsight, and reactions to victims and perpetrators. *Personality & Social Psychology Bulletin, 25,* 966–979.

Carlo, G. (2006). Care-based and altruistically based morality. In M. Killen & J. G. Smetana (Eds.), *Handbook of moral development.* Mahwah, NJ: Erlbaum.

Carlson, M. J. (2006). Family structure, father involvement, and adolescent behavioral outcomes. *Journal of Marriage and Family, 68,* 137–154.

Carlson, S. A., Fulton, J. E., Schoenborn, C. A., & Loustalot, F. (2010). Trend and prevalence estimates based on the 2008 Physical Activity Guidelines for Americans. *American Journal of Preventive Medicine, 39*(4), 305–313.

Carnagey, N. L., Anderson, C. A., & Bartholow, B. D. (2007). Media violence and social neuroscience: New questions and new opportunities. *Current Directions in Psychological Science, 16,* 178–182.

Carnagey, N. L., Anderson, C. A., & Bushman, B. J. (2007). The effect of video game violence on physiological desensitization. *Journal of Experimental Social Psychology, 43,* 489–496.

Carney, S., & Geddes, J. (2003). Electroconvulsive therapy. *British Medical Journal, 326,* 1343–1344.

Carpenter, W. T. (1992). The negative symptom challenge. *Archives of General Psychiatry, 49,* 236–237.

Carpenter, W. T. (2002). From clinical trial to prescription. *Archives of General Psychology, 59,* 282–285.

Carrillo, M., Ricci, L. A., Coppersmith, G. A., & Melloni, R. R. (2009). The effect of increased serotonergic neurotransmission on aggression: A critical meta-analytical review of preclinical studies. *Psychopharmacology, 205*(3), 349–368. doi:10.1007/s00213-009-1543-2

Carroll-Ghosh, T., Victor, B. S., & Bourgeois, J. A. (2003). Suicide. In R. E. Hales & S. C. Yudofsky (Eds.), *Textbook of clinical psychiatry* (pp. 1457–1484). Washington, DC: American Psychiatric Publishing.

Carroll, J. B. (1993). *Human cognitive abilities: A survey of factor-analytic studies.* Cambridge: Cambridge University Press.

Carroll, J. B. (1996). A three-stratum theory of intelligence: Spearman's contribution. In I. Dennis & P. Tapsfield (Eds.), *Human abilities: Their nature and measurement.* Mahwah, NJ: Erlbaum.

Carroll, J. S., Padilla-Walker, L. M., Nelson, L. J., Olson, C. D., Barry, C. M., & Madsen, S. D. (2008). Generation XXX: Pornography acceptance and use among emerging adults. *Journal of Adolescent Research, 23*(1), 6–30. doi: 10.1177/0743558407306348

Carroll, M. E., & Overmier, J. B. (2001). *Animal research and human health.* Washington, DC: American Psychological Association.

Carskadon, M. A., & Dement, W. C. (2005). Normal human sleep: An overview. In M. H. Kryger, T. Roth, & W. C. Dement (Eds.), *Principles and practice of sleep medicine.* Philadelphia, PA: Elsevier Saunders.

Carskadon, M. A., & Rechtschaffen, A. (2005). Monitoring and staging human sleep. In M. H. Kryger, T. Roth, & W. C. Dement (Eds.). *Principles and practice of sleep medicine.* Philadelphia, PA: Elsevier Saunders.

Carter, R. (1998). *Mapping the mind.* Berkeley: University of California Press.

Cartwright, R. D. (1977). *Night life: Explorations in dreaming.* Englewood Cliffs, NJ: Prentice-Hall.

Cartwright, R. D. (1991). Dreams that work: The relation of dream incorporation to adaptation to stressful events. *Dreaming, 1,* 3–9.

Cartwright, R. D. (2004). The role of sleep in changing our minds: A psychologist's discussion of papers on memory reactivation and consolidation in sleep. *Learning & Memory, 11,* 660–663.

Cartwright, R. D. (2006). Sleepwalking. In T. Lee-Chiong (Ed.), *Sleep: A comprehensive handbook.* Hoboken, NJ: Wiley-Liss.

Cartwright, R. D., & Lamberg, L. (1992). *Crisis dreaming.* New York, NY: HarperCollins.

Carver, C. S. (2007). Stress, coping, and health. In H. S. Friedman & R. C. Silver (Eds.), *Foundations of health psychology.* New York, NY: Oxford University Press.

Carver, C. S., Scheier, M. F., & Segerstrom, S. C. (2010). Optimism. *Clinical Psychology Review, 30*(7), 879–889.

Casanova, C., Merabet, L., Desautels, A., & Minville, K. (2001). Higher-order motion processing in the pulvinar. *Progress in Brain Research, 134,* 71–82.

Casey, B. J., Tottenham, N., Listen, C., & Durston, S. (2005). Imaging the developing brain: What have we learned about cognitive development? *Trends in Cognitive Sciences, 9*(3), 104–110. doi:10.1016/j.tics.2005.01.011

Caspi, A., & Herbener, E. S. (1990). Continuity and change: Assortative marriage and the consistency of personality in adulthood. *Journal of Personality and Social Psychology, 58*(2), 250–258.

Caspi, A., & Moffitt, T. E. (2006). Gene-environment interactions in psychiatry: Joining forces with neuroscience. *Nature Reviews Neuroscience, 7,* 583–590.

Caspi, A., Roberts, B. W., & Shiner, R. L. (2005). Personality development: Stability and change. *Annual Review of Psychology, 56,* 453–484.

Caspi, O., & Burleson, K. O. (2005). Methodological challenges in meditation research. *Advances in Mind-Body Medicine, 21*(1), 4–11.

Cassel, R. N. (2000). Third force psychology and person-centered theory: From ego-status to ego-ideal. *Psychology: A Journal of Human Behavior, 37*(3), 44–48.

Cassidy, J. (2008). The nature of the child's ties. In J. Cassidy & P. R. Shaver (Eds.), *Handbook of attachment: Theory, research, and clinical applications* (2nd ed., pp. 3–22). New York, NY: Guilford Press.

Castle, D. (2008). Drawing conclusions about cannabis and psychosis. *Psychological Medicine, 38*(3), 459–460.

Castonguay, L. G., Reid, J. J., Jr., Halperin, G. S., & Goldfried, M. R. (2003). Psychotherapy integration. In G. Stricker & T. A. Widiger (Eds.), *Handbook of psychology, Vol. 8: Clinical psychology.* New York, NY: Wiley.

Catania, A. C. (1992). Reinforcement. In L. R. Squire (Ed.), *Encyclopedia of learning and memory.* New York, NY: Macmillan.

Catania, A. C., & Laties, V. G. (1999). Pavlov and Skinner: Two lives in science (an introduction to B. F. Skinner's "Some responses to the stimulus 'Pavlov'"). *Journal of the Experimental Analysis of Behavior, 72,* 455–461.

Catrambone, R. (1998). The subgoal learning model: Creating better examples so that students can solve novel problems. *Journal of Experimental Psychology: General, 127,* 355–376.

Cattell, H. E. P. (2004). The Sixteen Personality Factor (16PF) Questionnaire. In M. J. Hilsenroth & D. L. Segal (Eds.), *Comprehensive handbook of psychological assessment: Vol. 2. Personality.* Hoboken, NJ: Wiley.

Cattell, H. E. P., & Mead, A. D. (2008). The sixteen personality factor questionnaire (16PF). In G. J. Boyle, G. Matthews, & D. H. Saklofske (Eds.), The Sage handbook of personality theory and assessment: Personality measurement and testing (Vol. 2, pp. 135–159). Los Angeles, CA: Sage.

Cattell, R. B. (1950). *Personality: A systematic, theoretical and factual study.* New York, NY: McGraw-Hill.

Cattell, R. B. (1957). *Personality and motivation: Structure and measurement.* New York, NY: Harcourt, Brace & World.

Cattell, R. B. (1963). Theory of fluid and crystallized intelligence: A critical experiment. *Journal of Educational Psychology, 54*(1), 1–22. doi:10.1037/h0046743

Cattell, R. B. (1965). *The scientific analysis of personality.* Baltimore: Penguin.

Cattell, R. B. (1966). *The scientific analysis of personality.* Chicago: Aldine.

Cattell, R. B. (1990). Advances in Cattellian personality theory. In L. A. Pervin (Ed.), *Handbook of personality: Theory and research.* New York, NY: Guilford Press.

Cattell, R. B., Eber, H. W., & Tatsuoka, M. M. (1970). *Handbook of the Sixteen Personality Factor Questionnaire (16PF).* Champaign, IL: Institute for Personality and Ability Testing.

Cavanaugh, J. C. (1993). *Adult development and aging* (2nd ed.). Pacific Grove, CA: Brooks/Cole.

Caverly, D. C., Orlando, V. P., & Mullen, J. L. (2000). Textbook study reading. In R. F. Flippo & D. C. Caverly (Eds.), *Handbook of college reading and study strategy research.* Mahwah, NJ: Erlbaum.

Centers for Disease Control and Prevention. (2009). Climate change and public health. Retrieved from http://www.cdc.gov/ClimateChange/policy.htm

Centers for Disease Control and Prevention. (2011). Diagnoses of HIV infection and AIDS in the United States and dependent areas, 2009. *HIV Surveillance Report, 21.* Retrieved from http://www.cdc.gov/hiv/surveillance/resources/reports/2009report/

Cepeda, N. J., Pashler, H., Vul, E., Wixted, J. T., & Rohrer, D. (2006). Distributed practice in verbal recall tasks: A review and quantitative synthesis. *Psychological Bulletin, 132,* 354–380.

Cerletti, U., & Bini, L. (1938). Un nuevo metodo di shockterapie "L'elettro-shock". *Boll. Acad. Med. Roma, 64,* 136–138.

Cetinkaya, H., & Domjan, M. (2006). Sexual fetishism in a quail (*Coturnix japonica*) model system: Test of reproductive success. *Journal of Comparative Psychology, 120*(4), 427–432. doi:10.1037/0735-7036.120.4.427.

Cha, Y. (2010). Reinforcing separate spheres: The effect of spousal overwork on men's and women's employment in dual-earner households. *American Sociological Review, 75*(2), 303–329. doi:10.1177/000312241036530

Chaiken, S., & Maheswaran, D. (1994). Heuristic processing can bias systematic processing: Effects of source credibility, argument ambiguity, and task importance on attitude judgment. *Journal of Personality and Social Psychology, 66,* 460–473.

Chalquist, C. (2009). A look at the ecotherapy research evidence. *Ecopsychology, 1*(2), 64–74.

Chan, J. K., Thomas, A. K., & Bulevich, J. B. (2009). Recalling a witnessed event increases eyewitness suggestibility: The reversed testing effect. *Psychological Science, 20*(1), 66–73. doi:10.1111/j.1467-9280.2008.02245.x

Chan, J. W. C., & Vernon, P. E. (1988). Individual differences among the peoples of China. In S. H. Irvine & J. W. Berry (Eds.), *Human abilities in cultural context.* New York, NY: Cambridge University Press.

Chance, P. (1999). Thorndike's puzzle boxes and the origins of the experimental analysis of behavior. *Journal of the Experimental Analysis of Behavior, 72,* 433–440.

Chance, P. (2001, September/October). The brain goes to school: Why neuroscience research is going to the head of the class. *Psychology Today,* p. 72.

Chance, P., & Heward, W. L. (2010). Climate change: Meeting the challenge. *The Behavior Analyst, 33,* 197–206.

Chandler, C. C., & Fisher, R. P. (1996). Retrieval processes and witness memory. In E. L. Bjork & R. A. Bjork (Eds.), *Memory.* San Diego: Academic Press.

Chapman, B., Fiscella, K., Kawachi, I., & Duberstein, P. (2010). Personality, socioeconomic status, and all-cause mortality in the United States. *American Journal of Epidemiology, 171*(1), 83–92. doi:10.1093/aje/kwp323

Chapman, P. D. (1988). *Schools as sorters: Lewis M. Terman, applied psychology, and the intelligence testing movement.* New York, NY: New York University Press.

Charrier, I., Pitcher, B. J., & Harcourt, R. G. (2009). Vocal recognition of mothers by Australian sea lion pups: Individual signature and environmental constraints. *Animal Behavior, 78*(5), 1127–1134. doi:10.1016/j.anbehav.2009.07.032

Chawla, L. (1988). Children's concern for the natural environment. *Children's Environments Quarterly, 5*(3), 13–20. Retrieved from http://www.colorado.edu/journals/cye/5_3/ChildrensConcernfortheNaturalEnvironment_Chawla_CEQ5_3.pdf

Chawla, L. (1998). Significant life experiences revisited: A review of research on sources of environmental sensitivity. *Environmental Education Research, 4,* 369–382.

Chen, X., & Wang, L. (2010). China. In M. H. Bornstein (Ed.), *Handbook of cultural developmental science* (pp. 424–440). New York, NY: Psychology Press.

Chen, X., Wang, L., & DeSouza, A. (2006). Temperament and socio-emotional functioning in Chinese and North American children. In X. Chen, D. French, & B. Schneider (Eds.), *Peer relationships in cultural context* (pp. 123–147). New York, NY: Cambridge University Press.

Cheng, Y., Chen, C., Lin, C., Chou, K., & Decety, J. (2010). Love hurts: An fMRI study. *NeuroImage, 51*(2), 923–929. doi:10.1016/j.neuroimage.2010.02.047

Chess, S., & Thomas, A. (1996). *Temperament: Theory and practice.* New York, NY: Brunner/Mazel.

Chida, Y., & Steptoe, A. (2009). The association of anger and hostility with future coronary heart disease: A meta-analytic review of prospective evidence. *Journal of the American College of Cardiology, 53*(11), 936–946.

Chien, K., Che, P., Hsu, H., Su, T., Sung, F., Chen, M., & Lee, Y. (2010). Habitual sleep duration and insomnia and the risk of cardiovascular events and all-cause death: Report from a community-based cohort. *Sleep: Journal of Sleep and Sleep Disorders Research, 33*(2), 177–184.

Chiriboga, D. A. (1989). Mental health at the midpoint: Crisis, challenge, or relief? In S. Hunter & M. Sundel (Eds.), *Sage sourcebooks for the human services series, Vol. 7. Midlife myths: Issues, findings, and practice implications* (pp. 116–144). Thousand Oaks, CA: Sage Publications.

Chiroro, P., Bohner, G., Viki, G. T. , & Jarvis, C. I. (2004). Rape myth acceptance and rape proclivity: Expected dominance versus expected arousal as mediators in acquaintance–rape situations. *Journal of Interpersonal Violence, 19,* 427–441.

Chiu, C. Y., Leung, A. K. Y., & Kwan, L. (2007). Language, cognition, and culture: Beyond the Whorfian hypothesis. In S. Kitayama & D. Cohen (Eds.), *Handbook of cultural psychology* (pp. 668–690). New York, NY: Guilford Press.

Chiu, C., Kim, Y., & Wan, W. W. N. (2008). Personality: Cross-cultural perspectives. In G. J. Boyles, G. Matthews, & D. H. Saklofske (Eds.), *The Sage handbook of personality theory and assessment: Personality theories and models* (Vol. 1, pp. 124–144). Los Angles, CA: Sage.

Choi, I., Nisbett, R. E., & Norenzayan, A. (1999). Causal attribution across cultures: Variation and universality. *Psychological Bulletin, 125,* 47–63.

Cholewiak, R. W., & Cholewiak, S. A. (2010). Pain: Physiological mechanisms. In E. B. Goldstein (Ed.), *Encyclopedia of perception.* Thousand Oaks, CA: Sage.

Chomsky, N. (1957). *Syntactic structures.* The Hague: Mouton.

Chomsky, N. (1959). A review of B. F. Skinner's "Verbal Behavior." *Language, 35,* 26–58.

Chomsky, N. (1965). *Aspects of theory of syntax.* Cambridge, MA: MIT Press.

Chomsky, N. (1975). *Reflections on language.* New York, NY: Pantheon.

Chomsky, N. (1986). *Knowledge of language: Its nature, origins, and use.* New York, NY: Praeger.

Chomsky, N. (2006). *Language and mind* (3rd ed.). New York, NY: Cambridge University Press.

Chopra, S. S. (2003). Industry funding of clinical trials: Benefit of bias? *Journal of the American Medical Association, 290,* 113–114.

Christensen, A. J., & Johnson, J. A. (2002). Patient adherence with medical treatment regimens: An interactive approach. *Current Directions in Psychological Science, 11*(3), 94–97.

Christensen, B. K., Carney, C. E., & Segal, Z. V. (2006). Cognitive processing models of depression. In D. J. Stein, D. J. Kupfer, & A. F. Schatzberg (Eds.), *Textbook of mood disorders.* Washington, DC: American Psychiatric Publishing.

Christensen, B. T., & Schunn, C. D. (2007). The relationship of analogical distance to analogical function and preinventive structure: The case of engineering design. *Memory & Cognition, 35*(1), 29–38.

Christensen, C. C. (2005). Preferences for descriptors of hypnosis: A brief communication. *International Journal of Clinical and Experimental Hypnosis, 53,* 281–289.

Christensen, L. (1988). Deception in psychological research: When is its use justified? *Personality and Social Psychology Bulletin, 14,* 664–675.

Christian, L. M., Deichert, N. T., Gouin, J., Graham, J. E., & Kiecolt-Glaser, J. K. (2009). Psychological influences on neuroendocrine and immune outcomes. In G. G. Berntson & J. T. Cacioppo (Eds.), *Handbook of neuroscience for the behavioral sciences,* (Vol. 2, pp. 1260–1279). Hoboken, NJ: Wiley.

Christoff, K., Gordon, A. M., Smallwood, J., Smith, R., & Schooler, J. W. (2009). Experience sampling during fMRI reveals default network and executive system contributions to mind wandering. *Proceedings of the National Academy of Sciences of the United States of America, 106*(21), 8719–8724. doi:10.1073/pnas.0900234106

Christoffels, I. K., de Groot, A. B., & Kroll, J. F. (2006). Memory and language skills in simultaneous interpreters: The role of expertise and language proficiency. *Journal of Memory and Language, 54*(3), 324–345. doi:10.1016/j.jml.2005.12.004

Chronicle, E. P., MacGregor, J. N., & Ormerod, T. C. (2004). What makes an insight problem? The roles of heuristics, goal conception, and solution recording in knowledge-lean problems. *Journal of Experimental Psychology: Learning, Memory, and Cognition, 30*(1), 14–27.

Chrousos, G. P., & Kaltsas, G. (2007). Stress and cardiovascular disease. In G. Fink (Ed.), *Encyclopedia of stress*. San Diego: Elsevier.

Chudler, E. H. (2007). The power of the full moon. Running on empty? In S. Della Sala (Ed.), *Tall tales about the mind & brain: Separating fact from fiction* (pp. 401–410). New York, NY: Oxford University Press.

Chun, M. M., & Wolfe, J. M. (2001). Visual attention. In E. B. Goldstein (Ed.), *Blackwell handbook of perception*. Malden, MA: Blackwell.

Church, A. (2010). Current perspectives in the study of personality across cultures. *Perspectives on Psychological Science, 5*(4), 441–449. doi:10.1177/1745691610375559

Cialdini, R. B. (2001). *Influence: Science and practice*. Boston, MA: Allyn & Bacon.

Cialdini, R. B. (2003). Crafting normative messages to protect the environment. *Current Directions in Psychological Science,* 12, 105–109.

Cialdini, R. B. (2007). *Influence: Science and practice*. New York, NY: HarperCollins.

Cialdini, R. B. (2008). *Influence: Science and practice* (5th ed.). Boston, MA: Allyn & Bacon.

Cialdini, R. B., & Griskevicius, V. (2010). Social influence. In R. F. Baumeister & E. J. Finkel (Eds.), *Advanced social psychology: The state of the science* (pp. 385–417). New York, NY: Oxford University Press.

Cialdini, R. B., Reno, R. R., & Kallgren, C. A. (1990). A focus theory of normative conduct: Recycling the concept of norms to reduce littering in public places. *Journal of Personality and Social Psychology,* 58, 1015–1026.

Cialdini, R. B., & Trost, M. R. (1998). Social influence: Social norms, conformity, and compliance. In D. T. Gilbert, S. T. Fiske, & G. Lindzey (Eds.), *The handbook of social psychology*. New York, NY: McGraw-Hill.

Ciborowski, T. (1997). "Superstition" in the collegiate baseball player. *Sport Psychologist, 11,* 305–317.

Cicero, T. J., Inciardi, J. A., & Surratt, H. (2007). Trends in the use and abuse of branded and generic extended release oxycodone and fentanyl products in the United States. *Drug and Alcohol Dependence, 91*(2–3), 115–120.

Clark, L. A. (2007). Assessment and diagnosis of personality disorder: Perennial issues and an emerging reconceptualization. *Annual Review of Psychology, 58,* 227–257.

Clark, L. A., & Watson, D. (2003). Constructing validity: Basic issues in objective scale development. In A. E. Kazdin (Ed.), *Methodological issues & strategies in clinical research* (pp. 207–231). Washington, DC: American Psychological Association.

Clark, R. D., & Hatfield, E. (1989). Gender differences in receptivity to sexual offers. *Journal of Psychology & Human Sexuality, 2*(1), 39–55.

Clark, R. E. (2003). Fostering the work motivation of individuals and teams. *Performance Improvement, 42(3),* 21–29.

Clark, R. E. (2004). The classical origins of Pavlov's conditioning. *Integrative Physiological & Behavioral Science, 39,* 279–294.

Clarke-Stewart, K. A., & Allhusen, V. (2002). Nonparental caregiving. In M. Bornstein (Ed.), *Handbook of parenting*. Mahwah, NJ: Erlbaum.

Clayton, S. (2003). Environmental identity: A conceptual and an operational definition. In S. Clayton & S. Opotow (Eds.), *Identity and the natural environment* (pp. 45–65). Cambridge, MA: MIT Press.

Clayton, S., & Myers, G. (2009). *Conservation psychology: Understanding and promoting human care for nature*. Oxford, U.K.: Wiley-Blackwell.

Clements, A. M., Rimrodt, S. L., Abel, J. R., Blankner, J. G., Mostofsky, S. H., Pekar, J. J., et al. (2006). Sex differences in cerebral laterality of language and visuospatial processing. *Brain and Language, 98*(2), 150–158. doi:10.1016/j.bandl.2006.04.007

Clifasefi, S. L., Takarangi, M. K., & Bergman, J. S. (2006). Blind drunk: The effects of alcohol on inattentional blindness. *Applied Cognitive Psychology, 20,* 697–704.

Clinebell, H. (1996). *Ecotherapy: Healing ourselves, healing the earth*. Minneapolis, MN: Augsburg Fortress.

Clore, G. L., & Ortony, A. (2008). Appraisal theories: How cognition shapes affect into emotion. In M. Lewis, J. M. Haviland-Jones, & L. F. Barrett, *Handbook of emotions* (3rd ed.). New York, NY: Guilford Press.

Clow, A. (2001). The physiology of stress. In F. Jones & J. Bright (Eds.), *Stress: Myth, theory, and research*. Harlow, UK: Pearson, Education.

Coelho, C., & Purkis, H. (2009). The origins of specific phobias: Influential theories and current perspectives. *Review of General Psychology, 13*(4), 335–348. doi:10.1037/a0017759

Cohan, C. L., & Kleinbaum, S. (2002). Toward a greater understanding of the cohabitation effect: Premarital cohabitation and marital communication. *Journal of Marriage and Family, 64*(1), 180–192. doi:10.1111/j.1741-3737.2002.00180.x

Cohen, C. E. (1981). Person categories and social perception: Testing some boundaries of the processing effects of prior knowledge. *Journal of Personality and Social Psychology, 40,* 441–452.

Cohen, D. B. (1999). *Stranger in the nest: Do parents really shape their child's personality, intelligence, or character?* New York, NY: Wiley.

Cohen, L. B., & Cashon, C. H. (2003). Infant perception and cognition. In R. M. Lerner, M. A. Easterbrooks, & J. Mistry (Eds.), *Handbook of psychology, Vol. 6: Developmental psychology*. New York, NY: Wiley.

Cohen, S. (2005). Pittsburgh common cold studies: Psychosocial predictors of susceptibility to respiratory infectious illness. *International Journal of Behavioral Medicine, 12*(3), 123–131.

Cohen, S., Janicki-Deverts, D., & Miller, G. E. (2007). Psychological stress and disease. *Journal of the American Medical Association, 298,* 1685–1687.

Cohen, S., Kessler, R. C., & Gordon, L. U. (1995). Strategies for measuring stress in studies of psychiatric and physical disorders. In S. Cohen, R. C. Kessler, & L. U. Gordon (Eds.), *Measuring stress: A guide for health and social scientists* (pp. 3–28). New York, NY: Oxford University Press.

Cohen, S., & Pressman, S. D. (2006). Positive affect and health. *Current Directions in Psychological Science, 15*(3), 122–125.

Cohen, S., Tyrrell, D. A. J., & Smith, A. P. (1993). Negative life events, perceived stress, negative affect, and susceptibility to the common cold. *Journal of Personality and Social Psychology, 64,* 131–140.

Cohen, S. G., & Ledford, G. E., Jr. (1994). The effectiveness of self-managing teams: A quasi-experiment. *Human Relations, 47,* 13–43.

Colaguiri, B., & Boakes, R. A. (2010). Perceived treatment, feedback, and placebo effects in double-blind RCTs: An experimental analysis. *Psychopharmacology, 208*(3), 433–441. doi: 10.1007/s00213-009-1743-9.

Colborn, T., Dumanoski, D., & J. P. Myers (1997). *Our stolen future: Are we threatening our fertility, intelligence, and survival? A scientific detective story*. New York, NY: Plume.

Colby, A., & Kohlberg, L. (1987). *The measurement of moral judgment* (Vols. 1–2). New York, NY: Cambridge University Press.

Cole, E., Erdman, E., & Rothblum, E. (Eds.). (1994). *Wilderness therapy for women: The power of adventure*. New York, NY: Haworth Press.

Coles, M. E., Schofield, C. A., & Pietrefesa, A. S. (2006). Behavioral inhibition and obsessive-compulsive disorder. *Journal of Anxiety Disorders, 20,* 1118–1132.

Coles, R. (1970). *Erik H. Erikson: The growth of his work*. Boston, MA: Little, Brown.

Coley, J. D., Solomon, G. E. A., & Shafto, P. (2002). The development of folkbiology: A cognitive science perspective on children's understanding of the biological world. In P. H. Kahn, Jr. & S. R. Kellert (Eds.), *Children and nature: Psychological, sociocultural, and evolutionary investigations* (pp. 65–92). Cambridge, MA: MIT Press.

Collins, A. M., & Loftus, E. F. (1975). A spreading activation theory of semantic processing. *Psychological Review, 82,* 407–428.

Collins, C. J., Hanges, P. J., & Locke, E. A. (2004). The relationship of achievement motivation to entrepreneurial behavior: A meta-analysis. *Human Performance, 17*(1), 95–117. doi:10.1207/S15327043HUP1701_5

Collins, F. S., Green, E. D., Guttmacher, A. E., & Guyer, M. S. (2006). A vision for the future of genomics research: A blueprint for the genomic era. In H. T. Tavani (Ed.), *Ethics, computing, and genomics* (pp. 287–315). Boston, MA: Jones and Bartlett.

Collins, M. A., & Zebrowitz, L. A. (1995). The contributions of appearance to occupational outcomes in civilian and military settings. *Journal of Applied Social Psychology, 25,* 129–163.

Collins, W. A., & Laursen, B. (2006). Parent-adolescent relationships. In P. Noller & J. A. Feeney (Eds.), *Close relationships: Functions, forms and processes*. Hove, England: Psychology Press.

Collins, W. A., Maccoby, E. E., Steinberg, L., Hetherington, E. M., & Bornstein, M. H. (2000). Contemporary research in parenting: The case for nature and nurture. *American Psychologist, 55,* 218–232.

Collop, N. A. (2006). Polysomnography. In T. Lee-Chiong (Ed.), *Sleep: A comprehensive handbook*. Hoboken, NJ: Wiley-Liss.

Colom, R., Haier, R. J., Head, K., Álvarez-Linera, J., Quiroga, M., Shih, P., & Jung, R. E. (2009). Gray matter correlates of fluid, crystallized, and spatial intelligence: Testing the P-FIT model. *Intelligence, 37*(2), 124–135. doi:10.1016/j.intell.2008.07.007

Coltrane, S. (2001). Research on household labor: Modeling and measuring the social embeddedness of routine family work. In R. M. Milardo (Ed.), *Understanding families into the new millennium: A decade in review* (pp. 427–452). Minneapolis, MN: National Council on Family Relations.

Colvin, C. R., Block, J., & Funder, D. C. (1995). Overly positive self-evaluations and personality: Negative implications for mental health. *Journal of Personality and Social Psychology, 68,* 1152–1162.

Colwill, R. M. (1993). An associative analysis of instrumental learning. *Current Directions in Psychological Science, 2*(4), 111–116.

Comas-Diaz, L. (2006). Cultural variation in the therapeutic relationship. In C. D. Goodheart, A. E. Kazdin, & R. J. Sternberg (Eds.), *Evidence-based psychotherapy: Where practice and research meet*. Washington, DC: American Psychological Association.

Combs, D. R., & Mueser, K. T. (2007). Schizophrenia. In M. Hersen, S. M. Turner, & D. C. Beidel (Eds.), *Adult psychopathology and diagnosis*. New York, NY: Wiley.

Comer, D. R. (1995). A model of social loafing in real work groups. *Human Relations, 48,* 647–667.

Compas, B. E. (2004). Processes of risk and resilience during adolescence: Linking contexts and individuals. In R. M. Lerner & L. Steinberg (Eds.), *Handbook of adolescent psychology*. New York, NY: Wiley.

Compton, D. M., Dietrich, K. L., & Smith, J. S. (1995). Animal rights activism and animal welfare concerns in the academic setting: Levels of activism and perceived importance of research with animals. *Psychological Reports, 76,* 23–31.

Compton, W. M., Thomas, Y. F., Conway, K. P., & Colliver, J. D. (2005). Developments in the epidemiology of drug use and drug use disorders. *American Journal of Psychiatry, 162,* 1494–1502.

Confer, J. C., Easton, J. A., Fleischman, D. S., Goetz, C. D., Lewis, D. M. G., Perilloux, C., & Buss, D. M. (2010). Evolutionary psychology: Controversies, questions, prospects, and limitations. *American Psychologist, 65*(2), 110–126. doi: 10.1037/a0018413.

Conn, S. (1995). When the earth hurts, who responds? In T. Roszak, M. E. Gomes, & A. D. Kanner (Eds.), *Eco-psychology: Restoring the earth, healing the mind* (pp. 156–171). San Francisco, CA: Sierra Club.

Connor, C. E., Pasupathy, A., Brincat, S., & Yamane, Y. (2009). Neural transformation of object information by ventral pathway visual cortex. In M. S. Gazzaniga (Ed.), *The cognitive neurosciences*. Cambridge, MA: MIT Press.

Conrad, M. A., & Ashworth, S. D. (1986). *Recruiting source effectiveness: A meta-analysis and reexamination of two rival hypotheses*. Paper presented at the First Annual Meeting of the Society for Industrial and Organizational Psychology, Chicago, IL.

Conway, A. R. A., Kane, M. J., & Engle, R. W. (2003). Working memory capacity and its relation to general intelligence. *Trends in Cognitive Sciences, 7,* 547–552.

Conway, L. C., & Schaller, M. (2002). On the verifiability of evolutionary psychological theories: An analysis of the psychology of scientific persuasion. *Personality and Social Psychology Review, 6,* 152–166.

Cook, E. C. (2008). Residential wilderness programs: The role of social support in influencing self-evaluations of male adolescents. *Adolescence, 43*(172), 751–774.

Cooke, L. (2007). The importance of exposure for healthy eating in childhood: A review. *Journal of Human Nutrition and Dietetics, 20,* 294–301.

Cooke, R., & Sheeran, P. (2004). Moderation of cognition-intention and cognition-behaviour relations: A meta-analysis of properties of variables from the theory of planned behaviour. *British Journal of Social Psychology, 43,* 159–186.

Coolidge, F. L., & Wynn, T. (2009). *The rise of homo sapiens: The evolution of modern thinking*. Malden, MA: Wiley-Blackwell. doi:10.1002/9781444308297

Coon, D. J. (1994). "Not a creature of reason": The alleged impact of Watsonian behaviorism on advertising in the 1920s. In J. T. Todd & E. K. Morris (Eds.), *Modern perspectives on John B. Watson and classical behaviorism*. Westport, CT: Greenwood Press.

Cooper, C. L., & Dewe, P. (2007). Stress: A brief history from the 1950s to Richard Lazarus. In A. Monat, R. S. Lazarus, & G. Reevy (Eds.), *The Praeger handbook on stress and coping*. Westport, CT: Praeger.

Cooper, H. M. (1990). Meta-analysis and the integrative research review. In C. Hendrick & M. S. Clark (Eds.), *Research methods in personality and social psychology: Review of personality and social psychology* (Vol. 11, pp. 142–163). Thousand Oaks, CA: Sage Publications.

Cooper, H. M. (2010). *Research synthesis and meta-analysis: A step-by-step approach* (4th ed.). Thousand Oaks, CA: Sage.

Cooper, L., & Bright, J. (2001). Individual differences in reactions to stress. In F. Jones & J. Bright (Eds.), *Stress: Myth, theory and research*. Harlow, UK: Pearson Education.

Cooper, M. L., Pioli, M., Levitt, A. , Talley, A. E., Micheas, L., & Collins, N. L. (2006). Attachment styles, sex motives, and sexual behavior: Evidence for gender-specific expressions of attachment dynamics. In M. Mikulincer & G. S. Goodman (Eds.), *Dynamics of romantic love: Attachment, caregiving, and sex*. New York, NY: Guilford Press.

Cope, M. B., Fernandez, J. R., & Allison, D. B. (2004). Genetic and biological risk factors. In J. K. Thompson (Ed.), *Handbook of eating disorders and obesity*. New York, NY: Wiley.

Corballis, M. C. (1991). *The lopsided ape*. New York, NY: Oxford University Press.

Corballis, M. C. (2007). The dual-brain myth. In S. Della Sala (Ed.), *Tall tales about the mind & brain: Separating fact from fiction* (pp. 291–313). New York, NY: Oxford University Press.

Corballis, M. C., Hattie, J., & Fletcher, R. (2008). Handedness and intellectual achievement: An even-handed look. *Neuropsychologia, 46*(1), 374–378. doi:10.1016/j.neuropsychologia.2007.09.009

Corballis, P. M. (2003). Visuospatial processing and the right-hemisphere interpreter. *Brain & Cognition, 53*(2), 171–176.

Coren, S. (1992). *The left-hander syndrome: The causes and consequences of left-handedness*. New York, NY: Free Press.

Coren, S. (1996). *Sleep thieves: An eye-opening exploration into the science and mysteries of sleep*. New York, NY: Free Press.

Coren, S., & Aks, D. J. (1990). Moon illusion in pictures: A multimechanism approach. *Journal of Experimental Psychology: Human Perception and Performance, 16,* 365–380.

Coren, S., & Girgus, J. S. (1978). *Seeing is deceiving: The psychology of visual illusions*. Hillsdale, NJ: Erlbaum.

Corkin, S. (1984). Lasting consequences of bilateral medial temporal lobectomy: Clinical course and experimental findings in H. M. *Seminars in Neurology, 4,* 249–259.

Corkin, S. (2002). What's new with the amnesic patient H.M.? *Nature Reviews Neuroscience, 3,* 153–159.

Cornblatt, B. A., Green, M. F., Walker, E. F., & Mittal,V. A. (2009). Schizophrenia: Etiology and neurocognition. In P. H. Blaney & T. Millon (Eds.), *Oxford textbook of psychopathology* (2nd ed., pp. 298–332). New York, NY: Oxford University Press.

Cornell, D. G. (1997). Post hoc explanation is not prediction. *American Psychologist, 52,* 1380.

Corrigan, P. W., & Larson, J. E. (2008). Stigma. In K. T. Mueser & D. V. Jeste (Eds.), *Clinical handbook of schizophrenia* (pp. 533–540). New York, NY: Guilford Press.

Corsica, J. A., & Perri, M. G. (2003). Obesity. In A. M. Nezu, C. M. Nezu, & P. A. Geller (Eds.), *Handbook of psychology, Vol. 9: Health psychology*. New York, NY: Wiley.

Cosmides, L., & Tooby, J. (1989). Evolutionary psychology and the generation of culture. Part II. Case study: A computational theory of social exchange. *Ethology and Sociobiology, 10,* 51–97.

Cosmides, L., & Tooby, J. (1994). Beyond intuition and instinct blindness: Toward an evolutionarily rigorous cognitive science. *Cognition, 50,* 41–77.

Cosmides, L., & Tooby, J. (1996). Are humans good intuitive statisticians after all? Rethinking some conclusions from the literature on judgment under uncertainty. *Cognition, 58,* 1–73.

Costa, P. T., Jr., & McCrae, R. R. (1985). *NEO Personality Inventory*. Odessa, FL: Psychological Assessment Resources.

Costa, P. T., Jr., & McCrae, R. R. (1992). *Revised NEO Personality Inventory: NEO PI and NEO Five-Factor Inventory* (Professional Manual). Odessa, FL: Psychological Assessment Resources.

Costa, P. T., Jr., & McCrae, R. R. (1994). Set like plaster? Evidence for the stability of adult personality. In T. F. Heatherton & J. L. Weinberger (Eds.), *Can personality change?* Washington, DC: American Psychological Association.

Costa, P. T., Jr., & McCrae, R. R. (1997). Longitudinal stability of adult personality. In R. Hogan, J. Johnson, & S. Briggs (Eds.), *Handbook of personality psychology*. San Diego: Academic Press.

Costa, P. T., Jr., & McCrae, R. R. (2008). The revised NEO Personality Inventory (NEO-PR-R). In G. J. Boyle, G. Matthews, & D. H. Saklofske (Eds.), *The Sage handbook of personality theory and assessment: Personality measurement and testing* (Vol. 2, pp. 179–198). Los Angeles, CA: Sage.

Côté, J. E. (2006). Emerging adulthood as an institutionalized moratorium: Risks and benefits to identity formation. In J. J. Arnett & J. L. Tanner (Eds.), *Emerging adults in America: Coming of age in the 21st century*. Washington, DC: American Psychological Association.

Cotman, C. W., Berchtold, N. C., & Christie, L.-A. (2007). Exercise builds brain health: Key roles of growth factor cascades and inflammation. *Trends in Neurosciences, 30,* 464–472.

Cotter, A., & Potter, J. E. (2006). Mother to child transmission. In J. Beal, J. J. Orrick, & K. Alfonso (Eds.), *HIV/AIDS: Primary care guide* (pp. 503–515). Norwalk, CT: Crown House.

Coutts, A. (2000). Nutrition and the life cycle. 1: Maternal nutrition and pregnancy. *British Journal of Nursing, 9,* 1133–1138.

Covino, N. A., & Pinnell, C. M. (2010). In S. J. Lynn, J. W. Rhue, & I. Kirsch (Eds.), *Handbook of clinical hypnosis* (2nd ed., pp. 551–574). Washington, DC: American Psychological Association.

Cowan, N. (2005). *Working memory capacity*. New York, NY: Psychology Press.

Cowan, N. (2010). The magical mystery four: How is working memory capacity limited, and why? *Current Directions in Psychological Science, 19*(1), 51–57. doi:10.1177/0963721409359277

Cowart, B. J. (2005). Taste, our body's gustatory gatekeeper. *Cerebrum, 7*(2), 7–22.

Cowart, B. J., & Rawson, N. E. (2001). Olfaction. In E. B. Goldstein (Ed.), *Blackwell handbook of perception*. Malden, MA: Blackwell.

Cox, D., Meyers, E., & Sinha, P. (2004). Contextually evoked object-specific responses in human visual cortex. *Science, 304,* 115–117.

Cox, M. J., Paley, B., Burchinal, M., & Payne, C. (1999). Marital perceptions and interactions across the transition to parenthood. *Journal of Marriage and the Family, 61,* 611–625.

Cox, P. D., Vinogradov, S., & Yalom, I. D. (2008). Group therapy. In R. E. Hales, S. C. Yudofsky, & G. O. Gabbard (Eds.), *The American psychiatric publishing textbook of psychiatry* (pp. 1329–1376). Washington, DC: American Psychiatric Publishing.

Cox, R. E., & Bryant, R. A. (2008). Advances in hypnosis research: Methods, designs and contributions of intrinsic and instrumental hypnosis. In M. R. Nash & A. J. Barnier (Eds.). *The Oxford Handbook of Hypnosis: Theory, Research and Practice* (pp. 311–336). New York, NY: Oxford University Press.

Craig, J. C., & Rollman, G. B. (1999). Somesthesis. *Annual Review of Psychology, 50,* 305–331.

Craighead, W. E., Ritschel, L. A., Arnarson, E. O., & Gillespie, C. F. (2008). Major depressive disorder. In W. E. Craighead, D. J. Miklowitz, & L. W. Craighead (Eds.), *Psychopathology: History, diagnosis, and empirical foundations.* New York, NY: Wiley.

Craik, F. I. M. (2001). Effects of dividing attention on encoding and retrieval processes. In H. L. Roediger III, J. S. Nairne, I. Neath, & A. M. Surprenant (Eds.), *The nature of remembering: Essays in honor of Robert G. Crowder* (pp. 55–68). Washington, DC: American Psychological Association.

Craik, F. I. M. (2002). Levels of processing: Past, present . . . and future? *Memory, 10*(5–6), 305–318.

Craik, F. I. M., & Bialystok, E. (2010). Bilingualism and aging: Costs and benefits. In L. Bäckman & L. Nyberg (Eds.), *Memory, aging and the brain: A Festschrift in honour of Lars-Göran Nilsson* (pp. 115–131). New York, NY: Psychology Press.

Craik, F. I. M., & Kester, J. D. (2000). Divided attention and memory: Impairment of processing or consolidation? In E. Tulving (Ed.), *Memory, consciousness, and the brain: The Tallinn conference* (pp. 38–51). Philadelphia, PA: Psychology Press.

Craik, F. I. M., & Lockhart, R. S. (1972). Levels of processing: A framework for memory research. *Journal of Verbal Learning and Verbal Behavior, 11,* 671–684.

Craik, F. I. M., & Tulving, E. (1975). Depth of processing and the retention of words in episodic memory. *Journal of Experimental Psychology: General, 104,* 268–294.

Cramer, P. (2000). Defense mechanisms in psychology today: Further processes for adaptation. *American Psychologist, 55*(6), 637–646.

Cranny, C. J., Smith, P. C., & Stone, E. F. (1992). *Job satisfaction: How people feel about their jobs and how it affects their performance.* New York, NY: Lexington Books.

Craske, M. G., & Waters, A. M. (2005). Panic disorders, phobias, and generalized anxiety disorder. *Annual Review of Clinical Psychology, 1,* 197–225.

Cravens, H. (1992). A scientific project locked in time: The Terman Genetic Studies of Genius, 1920s–1950s. *American Psychologist, 47,* 183–189.

Crede, M., & Kuncel, N. R. (2008). Study habits, skills, and attitudes: The third pillar supporting collegiate academic performance. *Perspectives on Psychological Science, 3*(6), 425–453. doi: 10.1111/j.1745-6924.2008.00089.x

Creusere, M. A. (1999). Theories of adults' understanding and use of irony and sarcasm: Applications to and evidence from research with children. *Developmental Review, 19,* 213–262.

Crews, F. (2006). *Follies of the wise: Dissenting essays.* Emeryville, CA: Shoemaker Hoard.

Crits-Christoph, P. (1997). Limitations of the dodo bird verdict and the role of clinical trials in psychotherapy research: Comment on Wampold et al (1997). *Psychological Bulletin, 122,* 216–220.

Crits-Christoph, P., & Gibbons, M. B. C. (2009). The evaluation of psychological treatment. In M. C. Gelder, N. C. Andreasen, J. J. López-Ibor, Jr., & J. R. Geddes (Eds.), *New Oxford textbook of psychiatry* (2nd ed., Vol. 1). New York, NY: Oxford University Press.

Croizet, J., Despres, G., Gauzins, M. E., Huguet, P., Leyens, J., & Meot, A. (2004). Stereotype threat undermines intellectual performance by triggering a disruptive mental load. *Personality and Social Psychology Bulletin, 30,* 721–731.

Cronbach, L. J. (1992). *Acceleration among the Terman males: Correlates in midlife and after.* Paper presented at the Symposium in Honor of Julian Stanley, San Francisco.

Cropley, A. J. (2000). Defining and measuring creativity: Are creativity tests worth using? *Roeper Review, 23,* 72–79.

Cross, S. E., & Markus, H. R. (1993). Gender in thought, belief, and action: A cognitive approach. In A. E. Beall & R. J. Sternberg (Eds.), *The psychology of gender.* New York, NY: Guilford Press.

Cross, S. E., & Markus, H. R. (1999). The cultural constitution of personality. In L. A. Pervin & O. P. John (Eds.), *Handbook of personality: Theory and research.* New York, NY: Guilford Press.

Crow, S. J., Peterson, C. B., Swanson, S. A., Raymond, N. C., Specker, S., Eckert, E. D., & Mitchell, J. E. (2009). Increased mortality in bulimia nervosa and other eating disorders. *American Journal of Psychiatry, 166*(12), 1342–1346. doi:10.1176/appi.ajp.2009.09020247

Crowder, R. G., & Greene, R. L. (2000). Serial learning: Cognition and behavior. In E. Tulving & F. I. M. Craik (Eds.), *The Oxford handbook of memory* (pp. 125–136). New York, NY: Oxford University Press.

Crowley, K., Callanan, M. A., Tenenbaum, H. R., & Allen, E. (2001). Parents explain more often to boys than to girls during shared scientific thinking. *Psychological Science, 12,* 258–261.

Cruz, C., della Rocco, P., & Hackworth, C. (2000). Effects of quick rotating schedules on the health and adjustment of air traffic controllers. *Aviation, Space, & Environmental Medicine, 71,* 400–407.

Csikszentmihalyi, M. (1993). *The evolving self: A psychology for the third millennium.* New York, NY: HarperCollins.

Csikszentmihalyi, M. (1994). Creativity. In R. J. Sternberg (Ed.), *Encyclopedia of human intelligence.* New York, NY: Macmillan.

Csikszentmihalyi, M. (1999a). If we are so rich, why aren't we happy? *American Psychologist, 54*(10), 821–827.

Csikszentmihalyi, M. (1999b). Implications of a systems perspective for the study of creativity. In R. J. Sternberg (Ed.), *Handbook of creativity.* New York, NY: Cambridge University Press.

Csikszentmihalyi, M. (2000). The contribution of flow to positive psychology. In J. E. Gillham (Ed.), *The science of optimism and hope: Research essays in honor of Martin E. P. Seligman.* Philadelphia, PA: Templeton Foundation Press.

Cuban, L. (2004). Assessing the 20-year impact of multiple intelligences on schooling. *Teachers College Record, 106*(1), 140–146.

Cubelli, R., & Della Sala, S. (2008). Flashbulb memories: Special but not iconic. *Cortex: A Journal Devoted to the Study of the Nervous System and Behavior, 44*(7), 908–909. doi:10.1016/j.cortex.2008.03.003

Culham, J. C. (2006). Functional neuroimaging: Experimental design and analysis. In R. Cabeza & A. Kingstone (Eds.), *Handbook of functional neuroimaging of cognition* (pp. 53–82). Cambridge, MA: MIT Press.

Cullum, J., & Harton, H. C. (2007). Cultural evolution: Interpersonal influence, issue importance, and the development of shared attitudes in college residence halls. *Personality and Social Psychology Bulletin, 33,* 1327–1339.

Cummings, D. E. (2006). Ghrelin and the short- and long-term regulation of appetite and body weight. *Physiology & Behavior, 89,* 71–84.

Cummins, D. (2005). Dominance, status, and social hierarchies. In D. M. Buss (Ed.), *The handbook of evolutionary psychology.* New York, NY: Wiley.

Cunningham, C. O., & Selwyn, P. A. (2005). HIV-related medical complications and treatment. In J. H. Lowinson, P. Ruiz, R. B. Millman, & J. G. Langrod (Eds.), *Substance abuse: A comprehensive textbook.* Philadelphia, PA: Lippincott/Williams & Williams.

Cunningham, F., Leveno, K., Bloom, S., Hauth, J., Rouse, D., & Spong, C. (2010). *Williams obstetrics* (23rd ed.). New York, NY: McGraw-Hill.

Cunningham, M. (2001). The influence of parental attitudes and behaviors on children's attitudes toward gender and household labor in early adulthood. *Journal of Marriage and the Family, 63,* 111–122.

Curtis, G. C., Magee, W. J., Eaton, W. W., Wittchen, H., & Kessler, R. C. (1998). Specific fears and phobias: Epidemiology and classification. *British Journal of Psychiatry, 173,* 212–217. doi:10.1192/bjp.173.3.212

Cushman, P. (1992). Psychotherapy to 1992: A historically situated interpretation. In D. K. Freedheim (Ed.), *History of psychotherapy: A century of change.* Washington, DC: American Psychological Association.

Cutting, L. P., & Docherty, N. M. (2000). Schizophrenia outpatients' perceptions of their parents: Is expressed emotion a factor? *Journal of Abnormal Psychology, 109,* 266–272.

Czeisler, C. A., Buxton, O. M., & Khalsa, S. (2005). The human circadian timing system and sleep-wake regulation. In M. H. Kryger, T. Roth, & W. C. Dement (Eds.), *Principles and practice of sleep medicine.* Philadelphia, PA: Elsevier Saunders.

Czeisler, C. A., Cajochen, C., & Turek, F. W. (2000). Melatonin in the regulation of sleep and circadian rhythms. In M. H. Kryger, T. Roth, & W. C. Dement (Eds.), *Principles and practice of sleep medicine.* Philadelphia, PA: Saunders.

Czincz, J., & Hechanova, R. (2009). Internet addiction: debating the diagnosis. *Journal of Technology in Human Services, 27*(4), 257–272. doi:10.1080/15228830903329815

Daiek, D. B., & Anter, N. M. (2004). *Critical reading for college and beyond.* New York, NY: McGraw Hill.

Dalal, R. (2006). A meta-analysis of the relationship between organizational citizenship behavior and counterproductive work behavior. *Journal of Applied Psychology, 90,* 1241–1255.

Dallman, M. F., Bhatnagar, S., & Viau, V. (2007). Hypothalamic-pituitary-adrenal axis. In G. Fink (Ed.), *Encyclopedia of stress.* San Diego: Elsevier.

Dalton, S. O., & Johansen, C. (2005). Stress and cancer: The critical research. In C. L. Cooper (Ed.), *Handbook of stress medicine and health.* Boca Raton, FL: CRC Press.

Daly, M., & Wilson, M. (1985). Child abuse and other risks of not living with both parents. *Ethology and Sociobiology, 6,* 197–210.

Daly, M., & Wilson, M. (1988). *Homicide.* Hawthorne, NY: Aldine.

Damisch, L., Stoberock, B., & Mussweiler, T. (2010). Keep your fingers crossed! How superstition improves performance. *Psychological Science, 21*(7), 1014–1020.

D'Andrade, R. G. (1961). Anthropological studies of dreams. In F. Hsu (Ed.), *Psychological anthropology: Approaches to culture and personality.* Homewood, IL: Dorsey Press.

Dang-Vu, T. T., Schabus, M., Cologan, V., & Maquet, P. (2009). Sleep: Implications for theories of dreaming and consciousness. In W. P. Banks (Ed.), *Encyclopedia of Consciousness* (pp. 357–374). San Diego, CA: Academic Press.

Daniel, E. (2007). Noise and hearing loss: A review. *Journal of School Health, 77*(5), 225–231. doi:10.1111/j.1746-1561.2007.00197.x.

Daniels, H. (2005). Introduction. In H. Daniels (Ed.), *An introduction to Vygotsky*. New York, NY: Routledge.

Danziger, K. (1990). *Constructing the subject: Historical origins of psychological research.* Cambridge, England: Cambridge University Press.

Dapretto, M., & Bjork, E. (2000). The development of word retrieval abilities in the second year and its relation to early vocabulary growth. *Child Development, 71,* 635–648.

Darley, J. M., & Latané, B. (1968). Bystander intervention in emergencies: Diffusion of responsibility. *Journal of Personality and Social Psychology, 8,* 377–383.

Darwin, C. (1859). *On the origin of species.* London: Murray.

Darwin, C. (1871). *Descent of man.* London: Murray.

Darwin, C. (1872). *The expression of emotions in man and animals.* New York, NY: Philosophical Library.

Das, H. H. J., & de Wit, J. B. F. (2003). Fear appeals motivate acceptance of action recommendations: Evidence for a positive bias in the processing of persuasive messages. *Personality and Social Psychology Bulletin, 29,* 650–664.

Das, H. H. J., de Wit, J. B. F., & Stroebe, W. (2005). Fear appeals motivate acceptance of action recommendations: Evidence for a positive bias in the processing of persuasive messages. *Personality and Social Psychology Bulletin, 29,* 650–664.

Dasen, P. R. (1994). Culture and cognitive development from a Piagetian perspective. In W. J. Lonner & R. Malpass (Eds.), *Psychology and culture.* Boston, MA: Allyn & Bacon.

David, L., & Guggenheim, D. (Producers). (2006). *An inconvenient truth* [documentary]. United States: Paramount.

Davidoff, J. (2001). Language and perceptual categorization. *Trends in Cognitive Sciences, 5,* 382–387.

Davidoff, J. (2004). Coloured thinking. *Psychologist, 17,* 570–572.

Davidson, J. E. (2003). Insights about insightful problem solving. In J. E. Davidson & R. J. Sternberg (Eds.), *The psychology of problem solving.* New York, NY: Cambridge University Press.

Davidson, K. W., Mostofsky, E., & Whang, W. (2010). Don't worry, be happy: Positive affect and reduced 10-year incident coronary heart disease: The Canadian Nova Scotia Health Survey. *European Heart Journal, 31,* 1065–1070.

Davidson, L. (2000). Philosophical foundations of humanistic psychology. *The Humanistic Psychologist, 28*(1–3), 7–31.

Davidson, R. J., Fox, A., & Kalin, N. H. (2007). Neural bases of emotion regulation in nonhuman primates and humans. In J. J. Gross (Ed.), *Handbook of emotion regulation* (pp. 47–68). New York, NY: Guilford Press.

Davidson, R. J., Kabat-Zinn, J., Schumacher, J., Rosenkranz, M., Muller, D., Santorelli, S. F., Urbanowski, F., Harrington, A., Bonus, K., & Sheridan, J. F. (2003a). Alterations in brain and immune function produced by mindfulness meditation. *Psychosomatic Medicine, 65,* 564–570.

Davidson, R. J., Pizzagalli, D. A., & Nitschke, J. B. (2009). Representation and regulation of emotion in depression: Perspectives from affective neuroscience. In I. H. Gotlib & C. L. Hammen (Eds.), *Handbook of Depression* (2nd ed., pp. 218–248). New York, NY: Guilford Press.

Davidson, R. J., Pizzagalli, D., Nitschke, J. B., & Kalin, N. H. (2003b). Parsing the subcomponents of emotion and disorders of emotion: Perspectives from affective neuroscience. In R. J. Davidson, K. R. Scherer, & H. H. Goldsmith (Eds.), *Handbook of affective sciences.* New York, NY: Oxford University Press.

Davies, I. R. L. (1998). A study of colour in three languages: A test of linguistic relativity hypothesis. *British Journal of Psychology, 89,* 433–452.

Davis, A., & Bremner, G. (2006). The experimental method in psychology. In G. M. Breakwell, S. Hammond, C. Fife-Schaw, & J. A. Smith (Eds.), *Research methods in psychology* (3rd ed.). London: Sage.

Davis, A. S., & Dean, R. S. (2005). Lateralization of cerebral functions and hemispheric specialization: Linking behavior, structure, and neuroimaging. In R. C. D'Amato, E. Fletcher-Janzen, & C. R. Reynolds (Eds.), *Handbook of school neuropsychology* (pp. 120–141). Hoboken, NJ: Wiley.

Davis, D., & Loftus, E. F. (2007). Internal and external sources of misinformation in adult witness memory. In M. P. Toglia, J. D. Read, D. F. Ross, & R. C. L. Lindsay (Eds.), *Handbook of eyewitness psychology: Volume 1. Memory for events.* Mahwah, NJ: Erlbaum.

Davis, J. L., & Rusbult, C. E. (2001). Attitude alignment in close relationships. *Journal of Personality and Social Psychology, 81*(1), 65–84.

Davis, M. C., Zautra, A. J., Younger, J., Motivala, S. J., Attrep, J., & Irwin, M. R. (2008). Chronic stress and regulation of cellular markers of inflammation in rheumatoid arthritis: Implications for fatigue. *Brain, Behavior, and Immunity, 22*(1), 24–32. doi:10.1016/j.bbi.2007.06.01

Davis, O. S. P., Arden, R., & Plomin, R. (2008). *g* in middle childhood: Moderate genetic and shared environmental influence using diverse measures of general cognitive ability at 7, 9 and 10 years in a large population sample of twins. *Intelligence, 36,*68–80.

Dawes, R. M. (1980). Social dilemmas. *Annual Review of Psychology, 31,* 169–193.

Dawes, R. M. (2001). *Everyday irrationality: How pseudo-scientists, lunatics, and the rest of us systematically fail to think rationally.* Boulder, CO: Westview Press.

Dawood, K., Bailey, J. M., & Martin, N. G. (2009). Genetic and environmental influences on sexual orientation. In Y.-K. Kim (Ed.), *Handbook of behavior genetics* (pp. 269–279). doi:10.1007/978-0-387-76727-7_19

Day, R. H. (1965). Inappropriate constancy explanation of spatial distortions. *Nature, 207,* 891–893.

de Castro, J. M. (2010). The control of food intake of free-living humans: Putting the pieces back together. *Physiology & Behavior, 100*(5), 446–453. doi:10.1016/j.physbeh.2010.04.028

de Graaf, J., Wann, D., & Naylor, T. H. (2005). *Affluenza: The all-consuming epidemic.* San Francisco, CA: Berrett-Koehler.

de Houwer, A. (1995). Bilingual language acquisition. In P. Fletcher & B. MacWhinney (Eds.), *The handbook of child language.* Oxford, OH: Basil Blackwell.

de Houwer, J., Hendrickx, H., & Baeyens, F. (1997). Evaluative learning with "subliminally" presented stimuli. *Consciousness & Cognition: An International Journal, 6,* 87–107.

de Koninck, J. (2000). Waking experiences and dreaming. In M. H. Kryger, T. Roth, & W. C. Dement (Eds.), *Principles and practice of sleep medicine.* Philadelphia, PA: Saunders.

De Neys, W. (2006). Dual processing in reasoning: Two systems but one reasoner. *Psychological Science, 17,* 428–433.

De Raad, B., Barelds, D. H., Levert, E., Ostendorf, F., Mlačić, B., Blas, L., et al. (2010). Only three factors of personality description are fully replicable across languages: A comparison of 14 trait taxonomies. *Journal of Personality and Social Psychology, 98*(1), 160–173. doi:10.1037/a0017184

de St. Aubin, E., McAdams, D. P., & Kim, T. (2004). *The generative society: Caring for future generations.* Washington, DC: American Psychological Association.

de Vaus, D. A., Qu, L., & Weston, R. (2005). The disappearing link between premarital cohabitation and subsequent marital stability. *Journal of Population Research, 22*(2), 99–118.

de Villiers, J. G., & de Villiers, P. A. (1999). Language development. In M. H. Bornstein & M. E. Lamb (Eds.), *Developmental psychology: An advanced textbook* (pp. 313–373). Mahwah, NJ: Erlbaum.

De Villiers, P. (1977). Choice in concurrent schedules and a quantitative formulation of the law of effect. In W. K. Honig & J. E. R. Staddon (Eds.), *Handbook of operant behavior.* Englewood Cliffs, NJ: Prentice-Hall.

De Waal, F. (2001). *The ape and the sushi master: Cultural reflections of a primatologist.* New York, NY: Basic Books.

de Wit, J. B. F., Das, E., & Vet, R. (2008). What works best: Objective statistics or a personal testimonial? An assessment of the persuasive effects of different types of message evidence on risk perception. *Health Psychology, 27*(1), 110–115. doi:10.1037/0278-6133.27.1.110.

DeAngelis, T. (2009). A new kind of delusion? *Monitor on Psychology, 40*(6). Retrieved from http://www.apa.org/monitor/2009/06/delusion.aspx

Deary, I. J., Strand, S., Smith, P., & Fernandes, C. (2007). Intelligence and educational achievement. *Intelligence, 35,* 13–21.

Deary, I. J., Whalley, L. J., Lemmon, H., Crawford, J. R., & Starr, J. M. (2000). The stability of individual differences in mental ability from childhood to old age: Follow-up of the 1932 Scottish Mental Survey. *Intelligence, 28*(1), 49–55. doi:10.1016/S0160-2896(99)00031-8

Deary, I. J., Whalley, L. J., & Starr, J. M. (2009). *A lifetime of intelligence: Follow-up studies of the Scottish mental surveys of 1932 and 1947.* Washington, DC: American Psychological Association. doi:10.1037/11857-000

Deary, I. J., Whiteman, M. C., Starr, J. M., Whalley, L. J., & Fox, H. C. (2004). The impact of childhood intelligence on later life: Following up the Scottish mental surveys of 1932 and 1947. *Journal of Personality and Social Psychology, 86,* 130–147.

DeCarvalho, R. J. (1991). *The founders of humanistic psychology.* New York, NY: Praeger.

Dechêne, A., Stahl, C., Hansen, J., & Wänke, M. (2010). The truth about the truth: A meta-analytic review of the truth effect. *Personality and Social Psychology Review, 14*(2), 238–257. doi:10.1177/1088868309352251

Décosterd, M. (2008). *Right brain/left brain leadership: Shifting style for maximum impact.* Westport, CT: Praeger Publishers/Greenwood Publishing Group.

Deecher, D., Andree, T. H., Sloan, D., & Schechter, L. E. (2008). From menarche to menopause: Exploring the underlying biology of depression in women experiencing hormonal changes. *Psychoneuroendocrinology, 33*(1), 3–17.

Deese, J. (1959). On the prediction of occurrence of particular verbal intrusions in immediate recall. *Journal of Experimental Psychology, 58,* 17–22.

Defeyter, M. A., & German, T. P. (2003). Acquiring an understanding of design: Evidence from children's insight problem solving. *Cognition, 89*(2), 133–155.

Degenhardt, L., & Hall, W. (2006). Is cannabis use a contributory cause of psychosis? *Canadian Journal of Psychiatry, 51,* 556–565.

Degenhardt, L., Hall, W. D., Lynskey, M., McGrath, J., McLaren, J., Calabria, B., et al. (2009). Should burden of disease estimates include cannabis use as a risk factor for psychosis?. *PLoS Medicine, 6*(9), 1–7. doi:10.1371/journal.pmed.1000133

Deitmer, J. W., & Rose, C. R. (2009). Ion changes and signaling in perisynaptic glia. *Brain Research Reviews, 63*(1–2), 113–129. doi:10.1016/j.brainresrev.2009.10.006

Delay, J., & Deniker, P. (1952). *Trente-huit cas de psychoses traitées par la cure prolongée et continue de 4560 RP.* Paris: Masson et Cie.

Delis, D. C., & Lucas, J. A. (1996). Memory. In B. S. Fogel, R. B. Schiffer, & S. M. Rao (Eds.), *Neuropsychiatry.* Baltimore: Williams & Wilkins.

DeLisi, L. E. (2008). The effect of cannabis on the brain: Can it cause brain anomalies that lead to increased risk for schizophrenia? *Current Opinion in Psychiatry, 21,* 140–150.

DelMonte, M. M. (2000). Retrieved memories of childhood sexual abuse. *British Journal of Medical Psychology, 73,* 1–13.

DeLong, M. R. (2000). The basal ganglia. In E. R. Kandel, J. H. Schwartz, & T. M. Jessell (Eds.), *Principles of neural science* (pp. 853–872). New York, NY: McGraw-Hill.

DeLongis, A., Folkman, S., & Lazarus, R. S. (1988). The impact of daily stress on health and mood: Psychological and social resources as mediators. *Journal of Personality and Social Psychology, 54,* 486–495.

Dement, W. C. (1978). *Some must watch while some must sleep.* New York, NY: Norton.

Dement, W. C. (1992). *The sleepwatchers.* Stanford, CA: Stanford Alumni Association.

Dement, W. C. (2003). Knocking on Kleitman's door: The view from 50 years later. *Sleep Medicine Reviews, 7*(4), 289–292.

Dement, W. C. (2005). History of sleep psychology. In M. H. Kryger, T. Roth, & W. C. Dement (Eds.), *Principles and practice of sleep medicine.* Philadelphia, PA: Elsevier Saunders.

Dement, W. C., & Vaughan, C. (1999). *The promise of sleep.* New York, NY: Delacorte Press.

Dement, W. C., & Wolpert, E. (1958). The relation of eye movements, bodily motility, and external stimuli to dream content. *Journal of Experimental Psychology, 53,* 543–553.

Dempster, F. N. (1996). Distributing and managing the conditions of encoding and practice. In E. L. Bjork & R. A. Bjork (Eds.), *Memory.* San Diego: Academic Press.

Dennis, W. (1966). Age and creative productivity. *Journal of Gerontology, 21*(1), 1–8.

Denys, D., Mantione, M., Figee, M., van den Munckhof, P., Koerselman, F., Westenberg, H., et al. (2010). Deep brain stimulation of the nucleus accumbens for treatment-refractory obsessive-compulsive disorder. *Archives of General Psychiatry, 67*(10), 1061–1068.

Der, G., Batty, G., & Deary, I. J. (2009). The association between IQ in adolescence and a range of health outcomes at 40 in the 1979 U.S. National Longitudinal Study of Youth. *Intelligence, 37*(6), 573–580. doi:10.1016/j.intell.2008.12.00

Derevensky, J. L., & Gupta, R. (2004). Preface. In J. L. Derevensky, & R. Gupta (Eds.), *Gambling problems in youth: Theoretical and applied perspectives* (pp. xxi–xxiv). New York, NY: Kluwer/Plenum.

Derogatis, L. R., & Coons, H. L. (1993). Self-report measures of stress. In L. Goldberger & S. Breznitz (Eds.), *Handbook of stress: Theoretical and clinical aspects* (2nd ed.). New York, NY: Free Press.

Derr, T. (2006). "Sometimes birds sound like fish": Perspectives on children's place experiences. In C. Spencer & M. Blades (Eds.), *Children and their environments: Learning, using and designing spaces* (pp. 108–123). New York, NY: Cambridge University Press.

Des Jarlais, D. C., Hagan, H., & Friedman, S. R. (2005). Epidemiology and emerging public health perspectives. In J. H. Lowinson, P. Ruiz, R. B. Millman, & J. G. Langrod (Eds.), *Substance abuse: A comprehensive textbook.* Philadelphia, PA: Lippincott/Williams & Wilkins.

Detterman, D. K. (2010). What happened to moron, idiot, imbecile, feebleminded, and retarded? *Intelligence, 38*(5), 540–541. doi:10.1016/j.intell.2010.05.00

Detterman, L. T., Gabriel, L. T., & Ruthsatz, J. M. (2000). Intelligence and mental retardation. In R. J. Sternberg (Ed.), *Handbook of intelligence* (pp. 141–158). New York, NY: Cambridge University Press.

Deutch, A. Y., & Roth, R. H. (2008). Neurotransmitters. In L. Squire, D. Berg, F. Bloom, S. Du Lac, A. Ghosh, & N. Spitzer (Eds.), *Fundamental neuroscience* (3rd ed., pp. 133–156). San Diego, CA: Elsevier.

Devine, P. G., & Sharp, L. B. (2009). Automaticity and control in stereotyping and prejudice. In T. D. Nelson (Ed.), *Handbook of prejudice, stereotyping, and discrimination* (pp. 1–22). New York, NY: Psychology Press.

Devine, P. G., Tauer, J. M., Barron, K. E., Elliot, A. J., & Vance, K. M. (1999). Moving beyond attitude change in the study of dissonance-related processes. In E. Harmon-Jones & J. Mills (Eds.), *Cognitive dissonance: Progress on a pivotal theory in social psychology.* Washington, DC: American Psychological Association.

Devlin, B., Fienberg, S. E., Resnick, D. P., & Roeder, K. (2002). Intelligence and success: Is it all in the genes? In J. M. Fish (Ed.), *Race and intelligence: Separating science from myth* (pp. 355–368). Mahwah, NJ: Erlbaum.

Devos, T. (2008). Implicit attitudes 101: Theoretical and empirical insights. In W. D. Crano, & R. Prislin (Eds.), *Attitudes and attitude change* (pp. 61–84). New York, NY: Psychology Press.

DeVries, R. (2000). Vygotsky, Piaget, and education: A reciprocal assimilation of theories and educational practices. *New Ideas in Psychology, 18*(2–3), 187–213.

Dew, M. A., Bromet, E. J., & Switzer, G. E. (2000). Epidemiology. In M. Hersen & A. S. Bellack (Eds.), *Psychopathology in adulthood.* Boston, MA: Allyn & Bacon.

Dewsbury, D. A. (2009). Charles Darwin and psychology at the bicentennial and sesquicentennial: An introduction. *American Psychologist, 64*(2), 67–74. doi:10.1037/a0013205

Deyoub, P. L. (1984). Hypnotic stimulation of antisocial behavior: A case report. *International Journal of Clinical and Experimental Hypnosis, 32*(3), 301–306.

DeYoung, C. G., & Gray, J. R. (2009). Personality neuroscience: Explaining individual differences in affect, behaviour and cognition. In P. J. Corr & G. Matthews (Eds.), *The Cambridge handbook of personality psychology* (pp. 323–346). New York, NY: Cambridge University Press.

DeYoung, C. G., Hirsh, J. B., Shane, M. S., Papademetris, X., Rajeevan, N., & Gray, J. R. (2010). Testing predictions from personality neuroscience: Brain structure and the big five. *Psychological Science, 21*(6), 820–828.

Di Chiara, G. (1999). Drug addiction as a dopamine-dependent associative learning disorder. *European Journal of Pharmacology, 375,* 13–30.

Di Forti, M., Morrison, P. D., Butt, A., & Murray, R. M. (2007). Cannabis use and psychiatric and cognitive disorders: The chicken or the egg? *Current Opinion in Psychiatry, 20,* 228–234.

Di Lorenzo, P. M., & Rosen, A. M. (2010). Taste. In E. B. Goldstein (Ed.), *Encyclopedia of perception.* Thousand Oaks, CA: Sage.

Di Lorenzo, P. M., & Youngentob, S. L. (2003). Olfaction and taste. In M. Gallagher & R. J. Nelson (Eds.), *Handbook of psychology, Vol. 3: Biological psychology.* New York, NY: Wiley.

Diamond, J. (2005). *Collapse: How societies choose to fail or survive.* London, England: Allen Lane.

Diamond, L. M. (2003). Was it a phase? Young women's relinquishment of lesbian/bisexual identities over a 5-year period. *Journal of Personality and Social Psychology, 84,* 352–364.

Diamond, L. M. (2007). The evolution of plasticity in female-female desire. *Journal of Psychology & Human Sexuality, 18,* 245–274.

Diamond, L. M. (2008). Female bisexuality from adolescence to adulthood: Results from a 10-year longitudinal study. *Developmental Psychology, 44*(1), 5–14. doi:10.1037/0012-1649.44.1.5

Diamond, M. (2009). Pornography, public acceptance and sex related crime: A review. *International Journal of Law and Psychiatry, 32*(5), 304–314. doi:10.1016/j.ijlp.2009.06.004

DiCicco-Bloom, E., & Falluel-Morel, A. (2009). Neural development & neurogenesis. In B. J. Sadock, V. A. Sadock, & P. Ruiz (Eds.), *Kaplan & Sadock's comprehensive textbook of psychiatry* (9th ed., Vol. 1, pp. 42–64). Philadelphia, PA: Lippincott, Williams & Wilkins.

Dick, D. M., & Rose, R. J. (2002). Behavior genetics: What's new? What's next? *Current Directions in Psychological Science, 11*(2), 70–74.

Dickens, W. T., & Flynn, J. R. (2001). Heritability estimates versus large environmental effects: The IQ paradox resolved. *Psychological Review, 108,* 346–369.

Dickens, W. T., & Flynn, J. R. (2006). Black Americans reduce the racial IQ gap: Evidence from standardization samples. *Psychological Science, 17,* 913–920.

DiClemente, C. (2003). Addiction and change: How addictions develop and addicted people recover. New York, NY: Guilford Press.

Diekman, A. B., & Murnen, S. K. (2004). Learning to be little women and little men: The inequitable gender equality of nonsexist children's literature. *Sex Roles, 50,* 373–385.

Diener, E., & Biswas-Diener, R. (2002). Will money increase subjective well-being? *Social Indicators Research, 57*(2), 119–169. doi:10.1023/A:1014411319119

Diener, E., & Diener, C. (1996). Most people are happy. *Psyhological Science, 7,* 181–185.

Diener, E., & Diener, M. (1995). Cross-cultural correlates of life satisfaction and self-esteem. *Journal of Personality and Social Psychology, 68,* 653–663.

Diener, E., Gohm, C. L., Suh, E., & Oishi, S. (2000). Similarity of the relations between marital status and subjective well-being across cultures. *Journal of Cross-Cultural Psychology, 31,* 419–436.

Diener, E., Kesebir, P., & Tov, W. (2009). Happiness. In M. R. Leary & R. H. Hoyle (Eds.), *Handbook of individual differences in social behavior* (pp. 147–160). New York, NY: Guilford Press.

Diener, E., Ng, W., Harter, J., & Arora, R. (2010). Wealth and happiness across the world: Material prosperity predicts life evaluation, whereas psychosocial prosperity predicts positive feeling. *Journal of Personality and Social Psychology, 99*(1), 52–61. doi:10.1037/a0018066

Diener, E., & Oishi, S. (2005). The nonobvious social psychology of happiness. *Psychological Inquiry, 16*(4), 162–167.

Diener, E., & Seligman, M. E. P. (2002). Very happy people. *Psychological Science, 13,* 81–84.

Diener, E., & Seligman, M. E. P. (2004). Beyond money: Toward an economy of well-being. *Psychological Science in the Public Interest, 5*(1), 1–31.

Diener, E., Wolsic, B., & Fujita, F. (1995). Physical attractiveness and subjective well-being. *Journal of Personality and Social Psychology, 69,* 120–129.

Dietrich, E. (1999). Algorithm. In R. A. Wilson & F. C. Keil (Eds.), *The MIT encyclopedia of the cognitive sciences.* Cambridge, MA: MIT Press.

Dijksterhuis, A. (2004a). I like myself but I don't know why: Enhancing implicit self-esteem by subliminal evaluative conditioning. *Journal of Personality and Social Psychology, 86,* 345–355.

Dijksterhuis, A. (2004b). Think different: The merits of unconscious thought in preference development and decision making. *Journal of Personality and Social Psychology, 87,* 586–598.

Dijksterhuis, A. (2010). Automaticity and the unconscious. In S. T. Fiske, D. T. Gilbert, & G. Lindzey (Eds.), *Handbook of social psychology* (5th ed., Vol. 1, pp. 228–267). New York, NY: Wiley.

Dijksterhuis, A., Bos, M. W., Nordgren, L. F., & van Baaren, R. B. (2006). On making the right choice: The deliberation-without-attention effect. *Science, 311,* 1005–1007.

Dijksterhuis, A., & Nordgren, L. F. (2006). A theory of unconscious thought. *Perspectives on Psychological Science, 1*(2), 95–109.

Dijksterhuis, A., & van Olden, Z. (2006). On the benefits of thinking unconsciously: Unconscious thought can increase post-choice satisfaction. *Journal of Experimental Social Psychology, 42,* 627–631.

Dillbeck, M. C., & Orme-Johnson, D. W. (1987). Physiological differences between transcendental meditation and rest. *American Psychologist, 42,* 879–881.

DiMatteo, M. R. (1991). *The psychology of health, illness, and medical care: An individual perspective.* Pacific Grove, CA: Brooks/Cole.

DiMatteo, M. R. (1997). Health behaviors and care decisions: An overview of professional-patient communication. In D. S. Gochman (Ed.), *Handbook of health behavior research II: Provider determinants.* New York, NY: Plenum.

DiMatteo, M. R. (2004a). Social support and patient adherence to medical treatment: A meta-analysis. *Health Psychology, 23,* 207–218.

DiMatteo, M. R. (2004b). Variations in patients' adherence to medical recommendations: A quantitative review of 50 years of research. *Medical Care, 42,* 200–209.

DiMatteo, M. R., Giordani, P. J., Lepper, H. S., & Croghan, T. W. (2002). Patient adherence and medical treatment outcomes: A meta-analysis. *Medical Care, 40,* 794–811.

Dimsdale, J. (2008). Psychological stress and cardiovascular disease. *Journal of the American College of Cardiology, 51*(13), 1237–1246.

Dimsdale, J., Irwin, M., Keefe, F. J., & Stein, M. B. (2005). Stress and anxiety. In B. J. Sadock & V. A. Sadock (Eds.), *Kaplan & Sadock's comprehensive textbook of psychiatry.* Philadelphia, PA: Lippincott/Williams & Wilkins.

Dinehart, M. E., Hayes, J. E., Bartoshuk, L. M., Lanier, S. L., & Duffy, V. B. (2006). Bitter taste markers explain variability in vegetable sweetness, bitterness, and intake. *Physiology & Behavior, 87,* 304–313.

Dinges, D. F. (1993). Napping. In M. A. Carskadon (Ed.), *Encyclopedia of sleep and dreaming.* New York, NY: Macmillan.

Dinges, D. F., Rogers, N. L., & Baynard, M. D. (2005). Chronic sleep deprivation. In M. H. Kryger, T. Roth, & W. C. Dement (Eds.), *Principles and practice of sleep medicine.* Philadelphia, PA: Elsevier Saunders.

Dinsmoor, J. A. (1992). Setting the record straight: The social views of B. F. Skinner. *American Psychologist, 47,* 1454–1463.

Dinsmoor, J. A. (1998). Punishment. In W. O'Donohue (Ed.), *Learning and behavior therapy.* Boston, MA: Allyn & Bacon.

Dinsmoor, J. A. (2004). The etymology of basic concepts in the experimental analysis of behavior. *Journal of the Experimental Analysis of Behavior, 82,* 311–316.

Dion, K. K., & Dion, K. L. (2006). Individualism, collectivism, and the psychology of love. In R. J. Sternberg & K. Weis (Eds.), *The new psychology of love.* New Haven, CT: Yale University Press.

Dissell, R. (2005, December 14). Student from Ohio robbed bank to feed gambling habit, lawyer says. *Cleveland Plain Dealer,* pp. 24–31.

Dixon, L., & Goldman, H. (2004). Forty years of progress in community mental health: The role of evidence-based practices. *Administration & Policy in Mental Health, 31*(5), 381–392.

Dixon, R. A., & Cohen, A. (2003). Cognitive development in adulthood. In R. M. Lerner, M. A. Easterbrooks, & J. Mistry (Eds.), *Handbook of psychology, Vol. 6: Developmental psychology.* New York, NY: Wiley.

Dobbs, D. (2005). Fact or phrenology. *Scientific American Mind, 16*(1), 224–231.

Dobzhansky, T. (1937). *Genetics and the origin of species.* New York; Columbia University Press.

Docherty, N. M., St-Hilaire, A., Aakre, J. M., & Seghers, J. P. (2009). Life events and high-trait reactivity together predict psychotic symptom increases in schizophrenia. *Schizophrenia Bulletin, 35*(3), 638–645. doi:10.1093/schbul/sbn002

Dodds, R. A., Ward, T. B., & Smith, S. M. (2011). A review of experimental literature on incubation in problem solving and creativity. In M. A. Runco (Ed.), *Creativity Research Handbook* (Vol. 3). Cresskill, NJ: Hampton. doi:10.1016/j.neuroimage.2010.01.021

Doerr, P., Pirke, K. M., Kockott, G., & Dittmor, F. (1976). Further studies on sex hormones in male homosexuals. *Archives of General Psychiatry, 33,* 611–614.

Dohrenwend, B. P. (2006). Inventorying stressful life events as risk factors for psychopathology: Toward resolution of the problem of intracategory variability. *Psychological Bulletin, 132,* 477–495.

Dolder, C. R. (2008). Side effects of antipsychotics. In K. T. Mueser & D. V. Jeste (Eds.), *Clinical handbook of schizophrenia* (pp. 168–177). New York, NY: Guilford Press.

Dollard, J., & Miller, N. E. (1950). *Personality and psychotherapy: An analysis in terms of learning, thinking and culture.* New York, NY: McGraw-Hill.

Dollard, J., Doob, L. W., Miller, N. E., Mowrer, O. H., & Sears, R. R. (1939). *Frustration and aggression.* New Haven: Yale University Press.

Dollfus, S., Razafimandimby, A., Delamillieure, P., Brazo, P., Joliot, M., Mazoyer, B., & Tzourio-Mazoyer, N. (2005). Atypical hemispheric specialization for language in right-handed schizophrenia patients. *Biological Psychiatry, 57*(9), 1020–1028. doi:10.1016/j.biopsych.2005.01.009

Domes, G., Heinrichs, M., Michel, A., Berger, C., & Herpertz, S. C. (2007). Oxytocin improves "mind-reading" in humans. *Biological Psychiatry, 61*(6), 731–733. doi:10.1016/j.biopsych.2006.07.015

Domhoff, G. W. (2001). A new neurocognitive theory of dreams. *Dreaming, 11,* 13–33.

Domhoff, G. W. (2005a). The content of dreams: Methodologic and theoretical implications. In M. H. Kryger, T. Roth, & W. C. Dement (Eds.), *Principles and practice of sleep medicine.* Philadelphia, PA: Elsevier Saunders.

Domhoff, G. W. (2005b). Refocusing the neurocognitive approach to dreams: A critique of the Hobson versus Solms debate. *Dreaming, 15*(1), 3–20.

Domhoff, G. W. (2007). Realistic simulation and bizarreness in dream content: Past findings and suggestions for future research. In D. Barrett & P. McNamara (Eds.), *The new science of dreaming: Content, recall, and personality correlates.* Westport, CT: Praeger.

Dominowski, R. L., & Bourne, L. E., Jr. (1994). History of research on thinking and problem solving. In R. J. Sternberg (Ed.), *Thinking and problem solving.* San Diego: Academic Press.

Domjan, M., Blesbois, E., & Williams, J. (1998). The adaptive significance of sexual conditioning: Pavlovian control of sperm release. *Psychological Science, 9,* 411–415.

Domjan, M., & Purdy, J. E. (1995). Animal research in psychology: More than meets the eye of the general psychology student. *American Psychologist, 50,* 496–503.

Donahoe, J. W., & Vegas, R. (2004). Pavlovian conditioning: The CS-UR relation. *Journal of Experimental Psychology: Animal Behavior Processes, 30*(1), 17–33.

Donaldson, Z. R., & Young, L. J. (2008). Oxytocin, vasopressin, and the neurogenetics of sociality. *Science, 322*(5903), 900–904. doi:10.1126/science.1158668

Donderi, D. C. (2006). Visual complexity: A review. *Psychological Bulletin, 132,* 73–97. doi:10.1007/978-3-642-02728-4_17.

Dorner, G. (1988). Neuroendocrine response to estrogen and brain differentiation. *Archives of Sexual Behavior, 17*(1), 57–75.

Dorrian, J., & Dinges, D. F. (2006). Sleep deprivation and its effects on cognitive performance. In T. Lee-Chiong (Ed.), *Sleep: A comprehensive handbook.* Hoboken, NJ: Wiley-Liss.

Doss, B. D., Rhoades, G. K., Stanley, S. M., & Markman, H. J. (2009). The effect of the transition to parenthood on relationship quality: An 8-year prospective study. *Journal of Personality and Social Psychology, 96*(3), 601–619. doi:10.1037/a0013969

Doty, R. L. (1991). Olfactory system. In T. V. Getchell, R. L. Doty, L. M. Bartoshuk, & J. B. Snow, Jr. (Eds.), *Smell and taste in health and disease.* New York, NY: Raven.

Doty, R. L. (2010). Olfaction. In E. B. Goldstein (Ed.), *Encyclopedia of perception.* Thousand Oaks, CA: Sage.

Dougall, A. L., & Baum, A. (2001). Stress, health, and illness. In A. Baum, T. A. Revenson & J. E. Singer (Eds.), *Handbook of health psychology* (pp. 321–338). Mahwah, NJ: Erlbaum.

Douglas, A. J. (2010). Baby on board: Do responses to stress in the maternal brain mediate adverse pregnancy outcome? *Frontiers in Neuroendocrinology, 31*(3), 359–376. doi:10.1016/j.yfrne.2010.05.002

Douglas, K. S., Vincent, G. M., & Edens, J. F. (2006). Risk for criminal recidivism: The role of psychopathy. In C. J. Patrick (Ed.), *Handbook of psychopathy*. New York, NY: Guilford Press.

Dovidio, J. F., & Gaertner, S. L. (2008). New directions in aversive racism research: Persistence and pervasiveness. In C. Willis-Esqueda (Ed.), *Motivational aspects of prejudice and racism* (pp. 43–67). New York, NY: Springer Science & Business Media. doi:10.1007/978-0-387-73233-6_3

Dovidio, J. F., & Gaertner, S. L. (2010). Intergroup bias. In S. T. Fiske, D. T. Gilbert, & G. Lindzey (Eds.), *Handbook of social psychology* (5th ed., Vol. 1, pp. 353–393). Hoboken, NJ: Wiley.

Dovidio, J. F., Gaertner, S. L., & Kawakami, K. (2010). Racism. In J. F. Dovidio, M. Hewstone, P. Glick, & V. M. Esses (Eds.), *The Sage handbook of prejudice, stereotyping, and discrimination*. Los Angeles, CA: Sage.

Dowling, K. W. (2005). The effect of lunar phases on domestic violence incident rates. *The Forensic Examiner, 14*(4), 13–18.

Downar, J., & Kapur, S. (2008). Biological theories. In K. T. Mueser & D. V. Jeste (Eds.), *Clinical handbook of schizophrenia* (pp. 25–34). New York, NY: Guilford Press.

Draganski, B., Gaser, C., Busch, V., Schuierer, G., Bogdahn, U., & May, A. (2004). Changes in grey matter induced by training. *Nature, 427*, 311–312.

Draguns, J. G. (1980). Psychological disorders of clinical severity. In H. C. Triandis & J. Draguns (Eds.), *Handbook of cross-cultural psychology* (Vol. 6). Boston, MA: Allyn & Bacon.

Draguns, J. G. (1990). Applications of cross-cultural psychology in the field of mental health. In R. Brislin (Ed.), *Applied cross-cultural psychology*. Newbury Park, CA: Sage.

Dranovsky, A., & Hen, R. (2006). Hippocampal neurogenesis: Regulation by stress and antidepressants. *Biological Psychiatry, 59*, 1136–1143.

Draycott, S., & Dabbs, A. (1998). Cognitive dissonance 1: An overview of the literature and its integration into theory and practice of clinical psychology. *British Journal of Clinical Psychology, 37*, 341–353.

Drevets, W. C., Gadde, K. M., & Krishnan, K. R. R. (2009). Neuroimaging studies of mood disorders. In D. S. Charney & E. J. Nestler (Eds.), *Neurobiology of mental illness* (3rd ed., pp. 461–490). New York, NY: Oxford University Press.

Drewnowski, A. (1995). Standards for the treatment of obesity. In K. D. Brownell, & C. G. Fairburn (Eds.), *Eating disorders and obesity: A comprehensive handbook*. New York, NY: Guilford Press.

Drews, F. A., Pasupathi, M., & Strayer, D. L. (2008). Passenger and cell phone conversations in simulated driving. *Journal of Experimental Psychology: Applied, 14*(4), 392–400. doi:10.1037/a0013119

Drews, F. A., Yazdani, H., Godfrey, C. N., Cooper, J. M., & Strayer, D. L. (2009). Text messaging during simulated driving. *Human Factors, 51*(5), 762–770. doi:10.1177/0018720809353319

Driskell, J. E., Willis, R. P., & Copper, C. (1992). Effect of overlearning on retention. *Journal of Applied Psychology, 77*(5), 615–622.

Druss, B. G., Wang, P. S., Sampson, N. A., Olfson, M., Pincus, H. A., Welss, K. B., et al. (2007). Understanding mental health treatment in persons without mental diagnoses: Results from the National Comorbidity Survey. *Archives of General Psychiatry, 64*(10), 1196–1203.

D'Souza, D. C. (2007). Cannabinoids and psychosis. *International Review of Neurobiology, 78*, 289–326.

Dubicka, B., Hadley, S., & Roberts, C. (2006). Suicidal behaviour in youths with depression treated with new-generation antidepressants—Meta-analysis. *British Journal of Psychiatry, 189*, 393–398.

Dubno, J. R. (2010). Aging and hearing. In E. B. Goldstein (Ed.), *Encyclopedia of perception*. Thousand Oaks, CA: Sage.

DuBois, G. E. (2010). Taste stimuli: Chemical and food. In E. B. Goldstein (Ed.), *Encyclopedia of perception*. Thousand Oaks, CA: Sage.

Dubovsky, S. L. (2009). Benzodiazepine receptor agonists and antagonists. In B. J. Sadock, V. A. Sadock, & P. Ruiz (Eds.), *Kaplan & Sadock's comprehensive textbook of psychiatry* (pp. 3044–3055). Philadelphia, PA: Lippincott, Williams & Wilkins.

Duckworth, A. L., & Seligman, M. E. P. (2005). Self-discipline outdoes IQ in predicting academic performance of adolescents. *Psychological Science, 16*, 939–944.

Duckworth, A. L., Steen, T. A., & Seligman, M. E. P. (2005). Positive psychology in clinical practice. *Annual Review of Clinical Psychology, 1*(1), 629–651.

Duckworth, K., & Borus, J. F. (1999). Population-based psychiatry in the public sector and managed care. In A. M. Nicholi (Ed.), *The Harvard guide to psychiatry*. Cambridge, MA: Harvard University Press.

Dudai, Y. (2004). The neurobiology of consolidation, or, how stable is the engram? *Annual Review of Psychology, 55*, 51–86.

Dudley, M., Goldney, R., & Hadzi-Pavlovic, D. (2010). Are adolescents dying by suicide taking SSRI antidepressants? A review of observational studies. *Australasian Psychiatry, 18*(3), 242–245. doi:10.3109/10398561003681319

Dudley, M., Hadzi-Pavlovic, D., Andrews, D., & Perich, T. (2008). New-generation antidepressants, suicide and depressed adolescents: How should clinicians respond to changing evidence? *Australian and New Zealand Journal of Psychiatry*, 42(6), 456–466. doi:10.1080/00048670802050538

Duffy, J. F., Willson, H. J., Wang, W., & Czeisler, C. A. (2009). Healthy older adults better tolerate sleep deprivation than young adults. *Journal of the American Geriatrics Society, 57*(7), 1245–1251. doi:10.1111/j.1532-5415.2009.02303.x

Duffy, V. B. (2004). Associations between oral sensation, dietary behaviors and risk of cardiovascular disease (CVD). *Appetite, 43*(1), 5–9.

Duffy, V. B., Lucchina, L. A., & Bartoshuk, L. M. (2004). Genetic variation in taste: Potential biomarker for cardiovascular disease risk? In J. Prescott & B. J. Tepper (Eds.), *Genetic variations in taste sensitivity: Measurement, significance and implications* (pp. 195–228). New York, NY: Dekker.

Duffy, V. B., Peterson, J. M., & Bartoshuk, L. M. (2004). Associations between taste genetics, oral sensations and alcohol intake. *Physiology & Behavior, 82*, 435–445.

Dum, R. P., & Strick, P. L. (2009). Basal ganglia and cerebellar circuits with the cerebral cortex. In M. S. Gazzangia (Ed.), *The cognitive neurosciences* (4th ed., pp. 553–564). Cambridge, MA: MIT Press.

Duman, R. S., & Monteggia, L. M. (2006). A neurotrophic model for stress-related mood disorders. *Biological Psychiatry, 59*, 1116–1127.

Duman, R. S., Polan, H. J., & Schatzberg, A. (2008). Neurobiologic foundations of mood disorders. In A. Tasman, J. Kay, J. A. Lieberman, M. B. First, & M. Maj (Eds.), *Psychiatry* (3rd ed.). New York, NY: Wiley-Blackwell.

Dunbar-Jacob, J., & Schlenk, E. (2001). Patient adherence to treatment regimen. In A. Baum, T. A. Revenson, & J. E. Singer (Eds.), *Handbook of health psychology* (pp. 571–580). Mahwah, NJ: Erlbaum.

Duncan, B. L. (1976). Differential social perception and attribution of intergroup violence: Testing the lower limits of stereotyping of blacks. *Journal of Personality and Social Psychology, 34*, 590–598.

Duncan, E., Boshoven, W., Harenski, K., Fiallos, A., Tracy, H., Jovanovic, T., et al. (2007). An fMRI study of the interaction of stress and cocaine cues on cocaine craving in cocaine-dependent men. *The American Journal on Addictions, 16*(3), 174–182. doi:10.1080/10550490701375285

Dunkel-Schetter, C., Gurung, R. A. R., Lobel, M., & Wadhwa, P. D. (2001). Stress processes in pregnancy and birth: Psychological, biological, and sociocultural influences. In A. Baum, T. A. Revenson, & J. E. Singer (Eds.), *Handbook of health psychology* (pp. 495–518). Mahwah, NJ: Erlbaum.

Dunlop, B. W., Garlow, S. J., & Nemeroff, C. B. (2009). The neurochemistry of depressive disorders: Clinical studies. In D. S. Charney & E. J. Nestler (Eds.), *Neurobiology of mental illness* (3rd ed., pp. 435–460). New York, NY: Oxford University Press.

Dunn, E. W., Wilson, T. D., & Gilbert, D. T. (2003). Location, location, location: The misprediction of satisfaction in housing lotteries. *Personality and Social Psychology Bulletin, 29*(11), 1421–1432. doi:10.1177/0146167203256867

Durlak, J. A. (2003). Basic principles of meta-analysis. In M. C. Roberts and S. S. Ilardi (Eds.), *Handbook of research methods in clinical psychology*. Malden, MA: Blackwell.

Durmer, J. S., & Dinges, D. F. (2005). Neurocognitive consequences of sleep deprivation. *Seminars in Neurology, 25*, 117–129.

Durning, A. T. (1992). *How much is enough? The consumer society and the future of the earth*. New York, NY: Norton.

Durrant, R., & Ellis, B. J. (2003). Evolutionary psychology. In M. Gallagher & R. J. Nelson (Eds.), *Handbook of psychology, Vol. 3: Biological psychology*. New York, NY: Wiley.

Dutcher, D. D., Finley, J. C., Luloff, A. E., & Johnson, J. B. (2007). Connectivity with nature as a measure of environmental values. *Environment and Behavior, 39*(4), 474–493.

Dwyer, J. (1995). Popular diets. In K. D. Brownell & C. G. Fairburn (Eds.), *Eating disorders and obesity*. New York, NY: Guilford Press.

Eagly, A. H. (1992). Uneven progress: Social psychology and the study of attitudes. *Journal of Personality and Social Psychology, 63*, 693–710.

Eagly, A. H. (1995). The science and politics of comparing women and men. *American Psychologist, 50*, 145–158.

Eagly, A. H., & Chaiken, S. (1998). Attitude structure and function. In D. T. Gilbert, S. T. Fiske, & G. Lindzey (Eds.), *The handbook of social psychology*. New York, NY: McGraw-Hill.

Eagly, A. H., & Wood, W. (1999). The origins of sex differences in human behavior: Evolved dispositions versus social roles. *American Psychologist, 54*, 408–423.

Easterlin, B. L., & Cardena, E. (1999). Cognitive and emotional differences between short- and long-term Vipassana meditators. *Imagination, Cognition and Personality, 18*(1), 68–81.

Eastman, R. (2004). The EEG in psychiatry. *South African Psychiatry Review, 7*(2), 29.

Eaton, J. (2001). Management communication: The threat of groupthink. *Corporate Communications, 6,* 183–192.

Ebbinghaus, H. (1885/1964). *Memory: A contribution to experimental psychology* (H. A. Ruger & E. R. Bussemius, Trans.). New York, NY: Dover. (Original work published 1885)

Ebstein, R. P. (2006). The molecular genetic architecture of human personality: Beyond self-report questionnaires. *Molecular Psychiatry, 11*(5), 427–445. doi:10.1038/sj.mp.400181

Edinger, J. D., & Means, M. K. (2005). Overview of insomnia: Definitions, epidemiology, differential diagnosis, and assessment. In M. H. Kryger, T. Roth, & W. C. Dement (Eds.), *Principles and practice of sleep medicine.* Philadelphia, PA: Elsevier Saunders.

Edlin, G., & Golanty, E. (1992). *Health and wellness: A holistic approach.* Boston, MA: Jones and Bartlett.

Edwards, D. M., Hale, K. L., Maddux, R. E., & Rapaport, M. H. (2008). Anxiolytic drugs. In A. Tasman, J. Kay, J. A. Lieberman, M. B. First, & M. Maj (Eds.), *Psychiatry* (3rd ed.). New York, NY: Wiley-Blackwell.

Edwards, S., Jedrychowski, W., Butscher, M., Camann, D., Kieltyka, A., Mroz, E., et al. (2010). Prenatal exposure to airborne polycyclic aromatic hydrocarbons and children's intelligence at 5 years of age in a prospective cohort study in Poland. *Environmental Health Perspectives, 118*(9), 1326–1331. doi:10.1289/ehp.0901070

Efron, R. (1990). *The decline and fall of hemispheric specialization.* Hillsdale, NJ: Erlbaum.

Egan, J. P. (1975). *Signal detection theory and ROC-analysis.* New York, NY: Academic Press.

Eggermont, J. J. (2010). Auditory system: Damage due to overstimulation. In E. B. Goldstein (Ed.), *Encyclopedia of perception.* Thousand Oaks, CA: Sage.

Ehrenberg, O., & Ehrenberg, M. (1994). *The psychotherapy maze: A consumer's guide to getting in and out of therapy.* Northvale, NJ: Jason Aronson.

Ehrlich, P. R. & Ehrlich, A. H. (2008). *The dominant animal: Human evolution and the environment.* Washington, DC: Island Press.

Eib-Eibesfeldt, I. (1975). *Ethology: The biology of behavior.* New York, NY: Holt, Rinehart, & Winston.

Eich, E., Macaulay, D., Loewenstein, R. J., & Dihle, P. H. (1997). Memory, amnesia, and dissociative identity disorder. *Psychological Science, 8,* 417–422.

Eichenbaum, H. (2004). An information processing framework for memory representation by the hippocampus. In M. S. Gazzaniga (Ed.), *The cognitive neurosciences.* Cambridge, MA: MIT Press.

Eichenwald, E., & Stark, A. (2008). Management and outcomes of very low birth weight. *New England Journal of Medicine, 358*(16), 1700–1711.

Einstein, G. O., & McDaniel, M. A. (1996). Remembering to do things: Remembering a forgotten topic. In D. J. Herrmann, C. McEvoy, C. Hertzog, P. Hertel, & M. K. Johnson (Eds.), *Basic and applied memory research: Practical applications* (Vol. 2). Mahwah, NJ: Erlbaum.

Einstein, G. O., & McDaniel, M. A. (2004). *Memory fitness: A guide for successful aging.* New Haven, CT: Yale University Press.

Einstein, G. O., & McDaniel, M. A. (2005). Prospective memory: Multiple retrieval processes. *Current Directions in Psychological Science, 14,* 286–290.

Einstein, G. O., McDaniel, M. A., Williford, C. L., Pagan, J. L., & Dismukes, R. K. (2003). Forgetting of intentions in demanding situations is rapid. *Journal of Experimental Psychology: Applied, 9*(3), 147–162.

Eippert, F., Bingel, U., Schoell, E. D., Yacubian, J., Klinger, R., Lorenz, J., & Büchel, C. (2009). Activation of the opioidergic descending pain control system underlies placebo analgesia. *Neuron, 63*(4), 533–543.

Eisenberg, N., Spinrad, T., & Sadovsky, A. (2006). Empathy-related responding in children. In M. Killen & J. G. Smetana (Eds.), *Handbook of moral development.* Mahwah, NJ: Erlbaum.

Eisner, E. W. (2004). Multiple intelligences. *Teachers College Record, 106*(1), 31–39.

Ekman, P. (1992). Facial expressions of emotion: New findings, new questions. *Psychological Science, 3,* 34–38.

Ekman, P., & Friesen, W. V. (1975). *Unmasking the face.* Englewood Cliffs, NJ: Prentice-Hall.

Ekman, P., & Friesen, W. V. (1984). *Unmasking the face.* Palo Alto: Consulting Psychologists Press.

Elbert, T., Pantev, C., Weinbruch, C., Rockstroh, B., & Taub, E. (1995). Increased cortical representation of the fingers of the left hand in string players. *Science, 270,* 305–307.

Elbogen, E. B., & Johnson, S. C. (2009). The intricate link between violence and mental disorder: Results from the national epidemiologic survey on alcohol and related conditions. *Archives of General Psychiatry, 66*(2), 152–161. doi:10.1001/archgenpsychiatry.2008.537

Elfenbein, H. A., & Ambady, N. (2002). On the universality and cultural specificity of emotion recognition: A meta-analysis. *Psychological Bulletin, 128*(2), 203–235.

Elfenbein, H. A., & Ambady, N. (2003). Universals and cultural differences in recognizing emotions of a different cultural group. *Current Directions in Psychological Science, 12*(5), 159–164.

Elliot, A. J., Kayser, D. N., Greitemeyer, T., Lichtenfeld, S., Gramzow, R. H., Maier, M. A., & Liu, H. (2010). Red, rank, and romance in women viewing men. *Journal of Experimental Psychology: General, 139*(3), 399–417. doi: 10.1037/a0019689.

Elliot, A. J., & Maier, M. A. (2007). Color and psychological functioning. *Current Directions in Psychological Science, 16*(5), 250–254. doi: 10.1111/j.1467-8721.2007.00514.x.

Elliot, A. J., Maier, M. A., Binser, M. J., Friedman, R., & Pekrun, R. (2009). The effect of red on avoidance behavior in achievement contexts. *Personality and Social Psychology Bulletin, 35*(3), 365–375. doi: 10.1177/0146167208328330.

Elliot, A. J., Maier, M. A., Moller, A. C., Friedman, R., & Meinhardt, J. (2007). Color and psychological functioning: The effect of red on performance attainment. *Journal of Experimental Psychology: General, 136*(1), 154–168. doi: 10.1037/0096-3445.136.1.154

Elliot, A. J., & Niesta, D. (2008). Romantic red: Red enhances men's attraction to women. *Journal of Personality and Social Psychology, 95*(5), 1150–1164. doi: 10.1037/0022-3514.95.5.1150.

Ellis, A. (1973). *Humanistic psychotherapy: The rational-emotive approach.* New York, NY: Julian Press.

Ellis, A. (1977). *Reason and emotion in psychotherapy.* Seacaucus, NJ: Lyle Stuart.

Ellis, A. (1985). *How to live with and without anger.* New York, NY: Citadel Press.

Ellis, A. (1987). The evolution of rational-emotive therapy (RET) and cognitive behavior therapy (CBT). In J. K. Zeig (Ed.), *The evolution of psychotherapy.* New York, NY: Brunner/Mazel.

Ellis, A. (1999). *How to make yourself happy and remarkably less disturbable.* Atascadero, CA: Impact Publishers.

Ellis, A. (2001). *Feeling better, getting better, staying better: Profound self-help therapy for your emotions.* Atascadero, CA: Impact Publishers.

Ellis, H. H. (1898). Autoerotism: A psychological study. *Alienist and Neurologist, 19,* 260–299.

Ellsworth, P. C., & Scherer, K. R. (2003). Appraisal processes in emotion. In R. J. Davidson, K. R. Scherer, & H. H. Goldsmith (Ed.), *Handbook of affective sciences.* New York, NY: Oxford University Press.

Ellsworth, P. C., Scherer, K. R., & Keltner, D. (2003). Appraisal processes in emotion. In R. J. Davidson, K. R. Scherer, & H. H. Goldsmith (Eds.), *Handbook of affective sciences.* New York, NY: Oxford University Press.

Ellwood, S., Pallier, G., Snyder, A., & Gallate, J. (2009). The incubation effect: Hatching a solution? *Creativity Research Journal, 21*(1), 6–14. doi:10.1080/10400410802633368

Elman, J. L. (1999). The emergence of language: A conspiracy theory. In B. MacWhinney (Ed.), *The emergence of language* (pp. 1–28). Mahwah, NJ: Erlbaum .

Elmitiny, N., Yan, X., Radwan, E., Russo, C., & Nashar, D. (2010). Classification analysis of driver's stop/go decision and red-light running violation. *Accident Analysis and Prevention, 42*(1), 101–111. doi:10.1016/j.aap.2009.07.007.

Elms, A. C. (2009). Obedience lite. *American Psychologist, 64*(1), 32–36. doi:10.1037/a0014473

Elpers, J. R. (2000). Public psychiatry. In B. J. Sadock & V. A. Sadock (Eds.), *Kaplan and Sadock's comprehensive textbook of psychiatry* (7th ed., Vol. 2). Philadelphia, PA: Lippincott/Williams & Wilkins.

Elppert, F., Bingel, U., Schoell, E. D., Yacubian, J., Klinger, R., Lorenz, J., & Buchel, C. (2009). Activation of the opioidergic descending pain control system underlies placebo analgesia. *Neuron, 63,* 533–543. doi:10.1016/j.neuron.2009.07.014.

Else-Quest, N. M., Hyde, J., & Linn, M. C. (2010). Cross-national patterns of gender differences in mathematics: A meta-analysis. *Psychological Bulletin, 136*(1), 103–127. doi:10.1037/a0018053

Emavardhana, T., & Tori, C. D. (1997). Changes in self-concept, ego defense mechanisms, and religiosity following seven-day Vipassana meditation retreats. *Journal for the Scientific Study of Religion, 36,* 194–206.

Emmelkamp, P. M. G. (1994). Behavior therapy with adults. In A. E. Bergin & S. L. Garfield (Eds.), *Handbook of psychotherapy and behavior change* (4th ed.). New York, NY: Wiley.

Emmelkamp, P. M. G. (2004). In M. J. Lambert (Ed.), *Bergin and Garfield's handbook of psychotherapy and behavior change.* New York, NY: Wiley.

Emsley, R., Rabinowitz, J., & Medori, R. (2006). Time course for antipsychotic treatment response in first-episode schizophrenia. *American Journal of Psychiatry, 163,* 743–745.

Engemann, K. M., & Owyang, M. T. (2005, April). So much for that merit raise: The link between wages and appearance. *The Regional Economist,* pp. 10–11.

Engle, R. W. (2001). What is working memory capacity? In H. L. Roediger III, J. S. Nairne, I. Neath, & A. M. Surprenant (Eds.), *The nature of remembering: Essays in honor of Robert G. Crowder.* Washington, DC: American Psychological Association.

Epley, N., & Dunning, D. (2000). Feeling "holier than thou": Are self-serving assessments produced by errors in self- or social prediction? *Journal of Personality and Social Psychology, 79*(6), 861–875. doi:10.1037/0022-3514.79.6.861

Epley, N., & Huff, C. (1998). Suspicion, affective response, and educational benefit as a result of deception in psychology research. *Personality and Social Psychology Bulletin, 24,* 759–768.

Epstein, R. (2007). Smooth thinking about sexuality: "Gay" and "straight" are misleading terms. *Scientific American Mind, 18*(5), 14.

Epstein, S., Donovan, S., & Denes-Raj, V. (1999). The missing link in the paradox of the Linda conjunction problem: Beyond knowing and thinking of the conjunction rule, the intrinsic appeal of heuristic processing. *Personality and Social Psychology Bulletin, 25,* 204–214.

Equal Employment Opportunity Commission. (2002). *Federal laws prohibiting job discrimination: Questions and answers.* Washington, DC: Equal Employment Opportunity Commission.

Erber, M. W., Hodges, S. D., & Wilson, T. D. (1995). Attitude strength, attitude stability, and the effects of analyzing reasons. In R. E. Petty & J. A. Krosnick (Eds.), *Attitude strength: Antecedents and consequences.* Mahwah, NJ: Erlbaum.

Erdfelder, E., Brandt, M., & Bröder, A. (2007). Recollection biases in hindsight judgments. *Social Cognition, 25,* 114–131.

Erickson, R. P., DiLorenzo, P. M., & Woodbury, M. A. (1994). Classification of taste responses in brain stem: Membership in fuzzy sets. *Journal of Neurophysiology, 71,* 2139–2150.

Ericsson, K. A., Roring, R. W., & Nandagopal, K. (2007). Giftedness and evidence for reproducibly superior performance: An account based on the expert performance framework. *High Ability Studies, 18*(1), 3–56.

Erikson, E. (1963). *Childhood and society.* New York, NY: Norton.

Erikson, E. (1968). *Identity: Youth and crisis.* New York, NY: Norton.

Esler, M., Schwarz, R., & Alvarenga, M. (2008). Mental stress is a cause of cardiovascular diseases: From scepticism to certainty. *Stress and Health: Journal of the International Society for the Investigation of Stress, 24*(3), 175–180. doi:10.1002/smi.1198

Espejo, E., Ferriter, C., Hazel, N., Keenan-Miller, D., Hoffman, L., & Hammen, C. (2011). Predictors of subjective ratings of stressor severity: The effects of current mood and neuroticism. *Stress & Health: Journal of the International Society for the Investigation of Stress, 27*(1), 23–33.

Essermont, J. J. (2010). Auditory system: Damage due to overstimulation. In E. B. Goldstein (Ed.), *Encyclopedia of perception.* Thousand Oaks, CA: Sage.

Esses, V. M., Jackson, L. M., & Bennett-AbuAyyash, C. (2010). Intergroup competition. In J. F. Dovidio, M. Hewstone, P. Glick, & V. M. Esses (Eds.), *The Sage handbook of prejudice, stereotyping, and discrimination.* Los Angeles, CA: Sage.

Esterson, A. (2001). The mythologizing of psychoanalytic history: Deception and self-deception in Freud's accounts of the seduction theory episode. *History of Psychiatry, 7,* 329–352.

Estes, R. E., Coston, M. L., & Fournet, G. P. (1990). *Rankings of the most notable psychologists by department chairpersons.* Unpublished manuscript.

Estes, W. K. (1999). Models of human memory: A 30-year retrospective. In C. Izawa (Ed.), *On human memory: Evolution, progress, and reflections on the 30th anniversary of the Atkinson-Shiffrin model.* Mahwah, NJ: Erlbaum.

Evans, G. W. (2004). The environment of childhood poverty. *American Psychologist, 59*(2), 77–92.

Evans, G. W., & Cohen, S. (1987). Environmental stress. In D. Stokols & I. Altman (Eds.), *Handbook of environmental psychology* (pp. 571–610). New York, NY: Wiley.

Evans, G. W., & Wener, R. E. (2006). Rail commuting duration and passenger stress. *Health Psychology, 25,* 408–412.

Evans, J. T. (2007). *Hypothetical thinking: Dual processes in reasoning and judgment.* New York, NY: Psychology Press.

Everett, P.B., Hayward, S. C., & Meyers, A. W. (1974). The effects of a token reinforcement procedure on bus ridership. *Journal of Applied Behavior Analysis, 7,* 1–9.

Evers, K. E., Prochaska, J. O., Johnson, J. L., Mauriello, J. M., Padula, J. A., & Prochaska, J. M. (2006). A randomized clinical trial of a population- and transtheoretical model-based stress-management intervention. *Health Psychology, 25,* 521–529.

Eysenck, H. J. (1959). Learning theory and behaviour therapy. *Journal of Mental Science, 195,* 61–75.

Eysenck, H. J. (1967). *The biological basis of personality.* Springfield, IL: Charles C. Thomas.

Eysenck, H. J. (1982). *Personality, genetics and behavior: Selected papers.* New York, NY: Praeger.

Eysenck, H. J. (1990a). Biological dimensions of personality. In L. A. Pervin (Ed.), *Handbook of personality: Theory and research.* New York, NY: Guilford Press.

Eysenck, H. J. (1990b). *Decline and fall of the Freudian empire.* Washington, DC: Scott-Townsend.

Eysenck, H. J., & Kamin, L. (1981). *The intelligence controversy.* New York, NY: Wiley.

Eysenck, M. W., Mogg, K., May, J., Richards, A., & Mathews, A. (1991). Bias in interpretation of ambiguous sentences related to threat in anxiety. *Journal of Abnormal Psychology, 100,* 144–150.

Faber Taylor, A. & Kuo, F. E. (2009). Children with attention deficits concentrate better after walk in the park. *Journal of Attention Disorders, 12,* 402–409.

Faber Taylor, A., Kuo, F, E., & Sullivan, W. C. (2001). Coping with ADD: The surprising connection to green play settings. *Environment and Behavior, 33,* 54–77.

Fabrigar, L. R., MacDonald, T. K., & Wegener, D. T. (2005). The structure of attitudes. In D. Albarracin, B. T. Johnson, & M. P. Zanna (Eds.), *The handbook of attitudes.* Mahwah, NJ: Erlbaum.

Fabrigar, L. R., & Wegener, D. T. (2010). Attitude structure. In R. F. Baumeister & E. J. Finkel (Eds.), *Advanced social psychology: The state of the science* (pp. 177–216). New York, NY: Oxford University Press.

Fagot, B. I., Hagan, R., Leinbach, M. D., & Kronsberg, S. (1985). Differential reactions to assertive and communicative acts of toddler boys and girls. *Child Development, 56,* 1499–1505.

Fairburn, C. G., Cooper, Z., & Murphy, R. (2009). Bulimia nervosa. In M. C. Gelder, N. C. Andreasen, J. J. López-Ibor, Jr., & J. R. Geddes (Eds.). *New Oxford textbook of psychiatry* (2nd ed., Vol. 1). New York, NY: Oxford University Press.

Fakhoury, W., & Priebe, S. (2002). The process of deinstitutionalization: An international overview. *Current Opinion in Psychiatry, 15*(2), 187–192.

Falls, W. A. (1998). Extinction: A review of therapy and the evidence suggesting that memories are not erased with nonreinforcement. In W. O'Donohue (Ed.), *Learning and behavior therapy.* Boston, MA: Allyn & Bacon.

Fancher, R. E. (1979). *Pioneers of psychology.* New York, NY: Norton.

Fancher, R. E. (2000). Snapshot of Freud in America, 1899–1999. *American Psychologist, 55,* 1025–1028.

Fancher, R. E. (2005). Galton: "Hereditary talent and character." *General Psychologist, 40*(2), 13–14.

Fancher, R. E. (2009). Scientific cousins: The relationship between Charles Darwin and Francis Galton. *American Psychologist, 64*(2), 84–92. doi:10.1037/a0013339

Faraday, A. (1974). *The dream game.* New York, NY: Harper & Row.

Farah, M. J. (2006). Prosopagnosia. In M. J. Farah & T. E. Feinberg (Eds.), *Patient-based approaches to cognitive neuroscience* (2nd ed., pp. 123–125). Cambridge, MA: MIT Press.

Faravelli, C., & Pallanti, S. (1989). Recent life events and panic disorders. *American Journal of Psychiatry, 146,* 622–626.

Farrington, D. P. (2006). Family background and psychopathy. In C. J. Patrick (Ed.), *Handbook of Psychopathy.* New York, NY: Guilford Press.

Fatemi, S., & Folsom, T. D. (2009). The neurodevelopmental hypothesis of schizophrenia, revisited. *Schizophrenia Bulletin, 35*(3), 528–548. doi:10.1093/schbul/sbn187

Fausto-Sterling, A. (1992). *Myths of gender.* New York, NY: Basic Books.

Fava, G. A. (1999). Well-being therapy: Conceptual and technical issues. *Psychotherapy and Psychosomatics, 68*(4), 171–179.

Fava, G. A., Ruini, C., Rafanelli, C., Finos, L., Salmaso, L., Mangelli, L., et al. (2005). Well-being therapy of generalized anxiety disorder. *Psychotherapy and Psychosomatics, 74*(1), 26–30.

Fava, G. A., & Tomba, E. (2009). Increasing psychological well-being and resilience by psychotherapeutic methods. *Journal of Personality, 77*(6), 1903–1934. doi:10.1111/j.1467-6494.2009.00604.x

Fazio, R. H., & Olson, M. A. (2003). Attitudes: Foundations, functions, and consequences. In M. A. Hogg & J. Cooper (Eds.), *The Sage handbook of social psychology.* Thousand Oaks, CA: Sage.

Fearon, R., Bakermans-Kranenburg, M. J., van IJzendoorn, M. H., Lapsley, A., & Roisman, G. I. (2010). The significance of insecure attachment and disorganization in the development of children's externalizing behavior: A meta-analytic study. *Child Development, 81*(2), 435–456. doi:10.1111/j.1467-8624.2009.01405.x

Feeney, D. M. (1987). Human rights and animal welfare. *American Psychologist, 42,* 593–599.

Feeney, J. A. (2008). Adult romantic attachment: Developments in the study of couple relationships. In J. Cassidy & P. R. Shaver (Eds.), *Handbook of attachment: Theory, research, and clinical applications* (2nd ed., pp. 456–481). New York, NY: Guilford Press.

Fehr, B. (2001). The status of theory and research on love and commitment. In G. J. O. Fletcher & M. S. Clark (Eds.), *Blackwell handbook of social psychology: Interpersonal processes.* Malden, MA: Blackwell Publishing.

Fehr, B. (2008). Friendship formation. In S. Sprecher, A. Wenzel, & J. Harvey (Eds.), *Handbook of relationship initiation* (pp. 235–247). New York, NY: Psychology Press.

Fein, S., & Spencer, S. J. (1997). Prejudice as self-image maintenance: Affirming the self through derogating others. *Journal of Personality and Social Psychology, 73,* 31–44.

Feingold, A. (1992). Good-looking people are not what we think. *Psychological Bulletin, 111,* 304–341.

Feinstein, J. S., Adolphs, R., Damasio, A., & Tranel, D. (2011). The human amygdala and the induction and experience of fear. *Current Biology, 21,* 34–38. doi:10.1016/j.cub.2010.11.042

Feist, G. J. (1998). A meta-analysis of personality in scientific and artistic creativity. *Personality and Social Psychology Review, 2,* 290–309.

Feist, G. J. (2004). The evolved fluid specificity of human creativity talent. In R. J. Sternberg, E. L. Grigorenko, & J. L. Singer (Eds.), *Creativity: From potential to realization*. Washington, DC: American Psychological Association.

Feist, G. J. (2010). The function of personality in creativity: The nature and nurture of the creative personality. In J. C. Kaufman & R. J. Sternberg (Eds.), *The Cambridge handbook of creativity* (pp. 113–130). New York, NY: Cambridge University Press.

Feixas, G., & Botella, L. (2004). Psychotherapy integration: Reflections and contributions from a constructivist epistemology. *Journal of Psychotherapy Integration, 14*(2), 192–222.

Fekken, G. C. (2000). Reliability. In A. E. Kazdin (Ed.), *Encyclopedia of psychology* (pp. 30–34). Washington, DC: American Psychological Association.

Feldman, D. H. (1988). Creativity: Dreams, insights, and transformations. In R. J. Sternberg (Ed.), *The nature of creativity: Contemporary psychological perspectives*. Cambridge: Cambridge University Press.

Feldman, D. H. (1999). The development of creativity. In R. J. Sternberg (Ed.), *Handbook of creativity*. New York, NY: Cambridge University Press.

Feldman, D. H. (2003). Cognitive development in childhood. In R. M. Lerner, M. A. Easterbrooks, & J. Mistry (Eds.), *Handbook of psychology, Vol. 6: Developmental psychology*. New York, NY: Wiley.

Feldman, R., Weller, A., Zagoory-Sharon, O., & Levine, A. (2007). Evidence for a neuroendocrinological foundation of human affiliation: Plasma oxytocin levels across pregnancy and the postpartum period predict mother-infant bonding. *Psychological Science, 18*(11), 965–970. doi:10.1111/j.1467-9280.2007.02010.x

Feliciano, L., & Areán. (2007). Mood disorders: Depressive disorders. In M. Hersen, S. M. Turner, & D. C. Beidel (Eds.), *Adult psychopathology and diagnosis*. New York, NY: Wiley.

Feng, J., Spence, I., & Pratt, J. (2007). Playing an action video game reduces gender differences in spatial cognition. *Psychological Science, 18*(10), 850–855. doi:10.1111/j.1467-9280.2007.01990.x

Fenwick, P. (1987). Meditation and the EEG. In M. A. West (Ed.), *The psychology of meditation*. Oxford: Clarendon Press.

Ferguson, C. J., & Hartley, R. D. (2009). The pleasure is momentary . . . the expense damnable? The influence of pornography on rape and sexual assault. *Aggression and Violent Behavior, 14*(5), 323–329. doi:10.1016/j.avb.2009.04.008

Ferguson, M. J., & Bargh, J. A. (2004). Liking is for doing: The effects of goal pursuit on automatic evaluation. *Journal of Personality and Social Psychology, 87*, 557–572.

Ferguson, T. (1993). Working with your doctor. In D. Goleman & J. Gurin (Eds.), *Mind-body medicine: How to use your mind for better health*. Yonkers, NY: Consumer Reports Books.

Ferster, C. S., & Skinner, B. F. (1957). *Schedules of reinforcement*. New York, NY: Appleton-Century-Crofts.

Festinger, L. (1957). *A theory of cognitive dissonance*. Stanford, CA: Stanford University Press.

Festinger, L., & Carlsmith, J. M. (1959). Cognitive consequences of forced compliance. *Journal of Abnormal and Social Psychology, 58*, 203–210.

Feuerstein, G. Z., Ruffolo, R. R., Coughlin, C., Wang, J., & Miller, D. (2007). Inflammation. In G. Fink (Ed.), *Encyclopedia of stress*. San Diego: Elsevier.

Few, R. (2007). Health and climatic hazards: Framing social research on vulnerability, response and adaptation. *Global Environmental Change 17*, 281–295.

Ficca, G., Axelsson, J., Mollicone, D. J., Muto, V., & Vitiello, M. V. (2010). Naps, cognition and performance. *Sleep Medicine Reviews, 14*(4), 249–258. doi:10.1016/j.smrv.2009.09.005

Fiedler, K., Schmid, J., & Stahl, T. (2002). What is the current truth about polygraph lie detection? *Basic & Applied Social Psychology, 24*, 313–324.

Fields, R. D. (2004). The other half of the brain. *Scientific American, 290*(4), 54–61.

Fife-Schaw, C. (2006). Questionnaire design. In G. M. Breakwell, S. Hammond, C. Fife-Schaw, & J. A. Smith (Eds.), *Research methods in psychology* (3rd ed.). London, England: Sage.

Fifer, W. P., Monk, C. E., & Grose-Fifer, J. (2001). Prenatal development and risk. In G. Bremner & A. Fogel (Eds.), *Blackwell handbook of infant development* (pp. 505–542). Malden, MA: Blackwell.

Figueredo, A. J., Gladden, P., Vásquez, G., Wolf, P. S. A., & Jones, D. N. (2009). Evolutionary theories of personality. In P. J. Corr & G. Matthews (Eds.), *Cambridge handbook of personality psychology* (pp. 265–274). New York, NY: Cambridge University Press.

Figueredo, A. J., Sefcek, J. A., Vasquez, G., Brumbach, B. H., King, J. E., & Jacobs, W. J. (2005). Evolutionary personality psychology. In D. M. Buss (Ed.), *The handbook of evolutionary psychology*. New York, NY: Wiley.

Finan, P. H., Zautra, A. J., & Wershba, R. (2011). The dynamics of emotion in adaptation to stress. In R. J. Contrada & A. Baum (Eds.), *The handbook of stress science: Biology, psychology, and health* (pp. 111–121). New York, NY: Springer.

Finder, A. (2006, June 11). For some, online persona undermines a resume. *New York Times*.

Fine, C. (2010). From scanner to sound bite: Issues in interpreting and reporting sex differences in the brain. *Current Directions in Psychological Science, 19*(5), 280–283. doi:10.1177/0963721410383248

Fink, B., Neave, N., Manning, J. T., & Grammer, K. (2006). Facial symmetry and judgments of attractiveness, health and personality. *Personality and Individual Differences, 41*, 1253–1262.

Fink, B., & Penton-Voak, I. (2002). Evolutionary psychology of facial attractiveness. *Current Directions in Psychological Science, 11*(5), 154–158.

Fink, M. F. (2009). Non-pharmacological somatic treatments: Electroconvulsive therapy. In M. C. Gelder, N. C. Andreasen, J. J. López-Ibor, Jr., & J. R. Geddes (Eds.), *New Oxford textbook of psychiatry* (2nd ed., Vol. 1). New York, NY: Oxford University Press.

Finnegan, L. P., & Kandall, S. R. (1997). Maternal and neonatal effects of alcohol and drugs. In J. H. Lowinson, P. Ruiz, R. B. Millman, & J. G. Langrod (Eds.), *Substance abuse: A comprehensive textbook*. Baltimore: Williams & Wilkins.

Finucane, M. L., Alhakami, A. S., Slovic, P. & Johnson, S. M. (2000). The affect heuristic in judgments of risks and benefits. *Journal of Behavioral Decision Making*, 13, 1–17.

Firestein, S. (2001). How the olfactory system makes sense of scents. *Nature, 413*, 211–218.

First, M. B. (2008). Psychiatric classification. In A. Tasman, J. Kay, J. A. Lieberman, M. B. First, & M. Maj (Eds.), *Psychiatry* (3rd ed.). New York, NY: Wiley-Blackwell.

Fischer, K. W., & Hencke, R. W. (1996). Infants' construction of actions in context: Piaget's contribution to research on early development. *Psychological Science, 7*, 204–210.

Fischer, P., Greitemeyer, T., Pollozek, F., & Frey, D. (2006). The unresponsive bystander: Are bystanders more responsive in dangerous emergencies? *European Journal of Social Psychology, 36*, 267–278.

Fischhoff, B. (1988). Judgment and decision making. In R. J. Sternberg & E. E. Smith (Eds.), *The psychology of human thought*. Cambridge: Cambridge University Press.

Fischhoff, B. (1999). Judgment heuristics. In R. A. Wilson & F. C. Keil (Eds.), *The MIT encyclopedia of the cognitive sciences*. Cambridge, MA: MIT Press.

Fischhoff, B. (2007). An early history of hindsight research. *Social Cognition, 25*(1), 10–13.

Fisher, A. (2002). *Radical ecopsychology: Psychology in the service to life*. Buffalo, NY: State University of New York.

Fisher, B. S., Daigle, L. E., Cullen, F. T., & Turner, M. G. (2003). Reporting sexual victimization to the police and others: Results from a national-level study of college women. *Criminal Justice & Behavior, 30*(1), 6–38.

Fisher, C., & Fyrberg, D. (1994). College students weigh the costs and benefits of deceptive research. *American Psychologist, 49*, 417–427.

Fisher, S., & Greenberg, R. P. (1985). *The scientific credibility of Freud's theories and therapy*. New York, NY: Columbia University Press.

Fisher, S., & Greenberg, R. P. (1996). *Freud scientifically reappraised: Testing the theories and therapy*. New York, NY: Wiley.

Fisher, S., & Greenberg, R. P. (1997). The curse of the placebo: Fanciful pursuit of a pure biological therapy. In S. Fisher & R. P. Greenberg (Eds.), *From placebo to panacea: Putting psychiatric drugs to the test*. New York, NY: Wiley.

Fishman, D. B. (2007). Seeking an equal place at the therapy research table: An introduction to a series on the pragmatic case study method. *Pragmatic Case Studies in Psychotherapy, 3*(1), 1–5.

Fishman, D. B., Rego, S. A., & Muller, K. L. (2011). Behavioral theories of psychotherapy. In J. C. Norcross, G. R. Vandenbos, & D. K. Freedheim (Eds.), *History of psychotherapy: Continuity and change* (2nd ed.). Washington, DC: American Psychological Association.

Fisk, J. E. (2004). Conjunction fallacy. In F. P. Rudiger (Ed.), *Cognitive illusions*. New York, NY: Psychology Press.

Fisk, J. E., Montgomery, C., & Murphy, P. N. (2009). The association between the negative effects attributed to ecstasy use and measures of cognition and mood among users. *Experimental and Clinical Psychopharmacology, 17*(5), 326–336. doi:10.1037/a0017038

Fiske, S. T. (1998). Stereotyping, prejudice, and discrimination. In D. T. Gilbert, S. T. Fiske, & G. Lindzey (Eds.), *The handbook of social psychology*. New York, NY: McGraw-Hill.

Fiske, S. T. (2004). Mind the gap: In praise of informal sources of formal theory. *Personality and Social Psychology Review, 8*(2), 132–137.

Fiske, S. T., & Russell, A. M. (2010). Cognitive processes. In J. F. Dovidio, M. Hewstone, P. Glick, & V. M. Esses (Eds.), *The Sage handbook of prejudice, stereotyping, and discrimination*. Los Angeles, CA: Sage.

Fitness, J., Fletcher, G., & Overall, N. (2003). Interpersonal attraction and intimate relationships. In M. A. Hogg & J. Cooper (Eds.), *The Sage handbook of social psychology*. Thousand Oaks, CA: Sage.

Fitzgerald, P. B. (2009). Repetitive transcranial magnetic stimulation treatment for depression: Lots of promise but still lots of questions. *Brain Stimulation, 2*(4), 185–187. doi:10.1016/j.brs.2009.08.005

Flanagin, A. J., & Waldeck, J. H. (2004). Technology use and organizational newcomer socialization. *Journal of Business Communication, 41*, 137–165.

Flavell, J. H. (1996). Piaget's legacy. *Psychological Science, 7,* 200–203.

Flavell, J. H. (1999). Cognitive development: Children's knowledge about the mind. *Annual Review of Psychology, 50,* 21–45. doi:10.1146/annurev.psych.50.1.21

Flavin, C., & Engelman, R. (2009). The perfect storm. In G. Gardner & T. Prugh, *2009 state of the world: Into a warming world* (pp. 5–12). Washington, DC: Worldwatch Institute. Retrieved from http://www.worldwatch.org/node/5984.

Fleeson, W. (2004). Moving personality beyond the person-situation debate: The challenge and the opportunity of within-person variability. *Current Directions in Psychological Science, 13*(2), 83–87.

Fleeson, W., Malanos, A. B., & Achille, N. M. (2002). An intraindividual process approach to the relationship between extraversion and positive affect: Is acting extraverted as "good" as being extraverted? *Journal of Personality and Social Psychology, 83,* 1409–1422.

Flegal, K. M., Carroll, M., Ogden, C., & Curtin, L. (2010). Prevalence and trends in obesity among U.S. adults, 1999–2008. *Journal of the American Medical Association, 303*(3), 235–241.

Flegal, K. M., Graubard, B. I., Williamson, D. F., & Gail, M. H. (2005). Excess deaths associated with underweight, overweight, and obesity. *Journal of the American Medical Association, 293,* 1861–1861.

Flegal, K. M., Graubard, B. I., Williamson, D. F., & Gail, M. H. (2007). Cause-specific excess deaths associated with underweight, overweight, and obesity. *Journal of the American Medical Association, 298,* 2028–2037.

Fletcher, C. (2004). *Appraisal and feedback: Making performance review work* (3rd ed.). London, UK: Chartered Institute of Personnel & Development.

Flett, G. L., Vredenburg, K., & Krames, L. (1995). The stability of depressive symptoms in college students: An empirical demonstration of regression to the mean. *Journal of Psychopathology & Behavioral Assessment, 17,* 403–415.

Flippo, R. F. (2000). *Testwise: Strategies for success in taking tests.* Torrance, CA: Good Apple.

Flippo, R. F., Becker, M. J., & Wark, D. M. (2000). Preparing for and taking tests. In R. F. Flippo & D. C. Caverly (Eds.), *Handbook of college reading and study strategy research.* Mahwah, NJ: Erlbaum.

Flood, A. M., Davidson, J. R. T., & Beckham, J. C. (2008). Anxiety disorders: Traumatic stress disorders. In A. Tasman, J. Kay, J. A. Lieberman, M. B. First, & M. Maj (Eds.), *Psychiatry* (3rd ed.). New York, NY: Wiley-Blackwell.

Florentine, M., & Heinz, M. (2010). Audition: Loudness. In E. B. Goldstein (Ed.), *Encyclopedia of perception.* Thousand Oaks, CA: Sage.

Flores, B. H., Musselman, D. L., DeBattista, C., Garlow, S. J., Schatzberg, A. F., & Nemeroff, C. B. (2004). Biology of mood disorders. In A. F. Schatzberg & C. B. Nemeroff (Eds.), *Textbook of psychopharmacology.* Washington, DC: American Psychiatric Publishing.

Floyd, J. A., Janisse, J. J., Jenuwine, E. S., & Ager, J. W. (2007). Changes in REM-sleep percentage over the adult lifespan. *Sleep, 30,* 829–836.

Flynn, E. (2006). A microgenetic investigation of stability and continuity in theory of mind development. *British Journal of Developmental Psychology, 24*(3), 631–654. doi:10.1348/026151005X57422

Flynn, F. J. (2005). Having an open mind: The impact of openness to experience on interracial attitudes and impression formation. *Journal of Personality and Social Psychology, 88,* 816–826.

Flynn, J. R. (1987). Massive IQ gains in 14 nations: What IQ tests really measure. *Psychological Bulletin, 101,* 171–191.

Flynn, J. R. (1999). Searching for justice: The discovery of IQ gains over time. *American Psychologist, 54,* 5–20.

Flynn, J. R. (2000). The hidden history of IQ and special education: Can the problems be solved? *Psychology, Public Policy, & Law, 6*(1), 191–198.

Flynn, J. R. (2003). Movies about intelligence: The limitations of *g*. *Current Directions in Psychological Science, 12*(3), 95–99.

Flynn, J. R. (2007). *What is intelligence? Beyond the Flynn effect.* New York, NY: Cambridge University Press.

Flynn, M. G., McFarlin, B. K., & Markofski, M. M. (2007). The anti-inflammatory actions of exercise training. *American Journal of Lifestyle Medicine, 1,* 220–235.

Fodor, E. M., & Carver, R. A. (2000). Achievement and power motives, performance feedback, and creativity. *Journal of Research in Personality, 34,* 380–396.

Foldvary-Schaefer, N. (2006). *Getting a good night's sleep.* Cleveland: Cleveland Clinic Press.

Folkman, S. (2008). The case for positive emotions in the stress process. *Anxiety, Stress & Coping: An International Journal, 21*(1), 3–14.

Folkman, S., & Moskowitz, J. T. (2004). Coping: Pitfalls and promise. *Annual Review of Psychology, 55,* 745–774.

Follette, W. C., & Davis, D. (2009). Clinical practice and the issue of repressed memories: Avoiding an ice patch on the slippery slope. In W. O'Donohue & S. R. Graybar (Eds.), *Handbook of contemporary psychotherapy: Toward an improved understanding of effective psychotherapy* (pp. 47–73). Thousand Oaks, CA: Sage.

Folsom, D. P., Gilmer, T., Barrio, C., Moore, D. J., Bucardo, J., Lindamer, L. A., et al. (2007). A longitudinal study of the use of mental health services by persons with serious mental illness: Do Spanish-speaking Latinos differ from English-speaking Latinos and Caucasians? *American Journal Psychiatry, 164,* 1173–1180.

Folsom, D. P., Hawthorne, W., Lindamer, L., Gilmer, T., Bailey, A., Golsham, S., Garcia, P., Unutzer, J., Hough, R., & Jeste, D. V. (2005). Prevalence and risk factors for homelessness and utilization of mental health services among 10,340 patients with serious mental illness in a large public mental health system. *American Journal Psychiatry, 162,* 370–376.

Food and Agriculture Organization of the United Nations. (2006). Livestock's long shadow: Environmental issues and options. Retrieved from http://www.fao.org/docrep/010/a0701e/a0701e00.HTM.

Foote, B., Smolin, Y., Kaplan M., Legatt, M. E., & Lipschitz, D. (2006). Prevalence of dissociative disorders in psychiatric outpatients. *American Journal of Psychiatry, 163,* 623–629.

Forcier, K., Stroud, L. R., Papandonatos, G. D., Hitsman, B., Reiches, M., Krishnamoorthy, J., et al. (2006). Links between physical fitness and cardiovascular reactivity and recovery to psychological stressors: A meta-analysis. *Health Psychology, 25,* 723–739.

Forsyth, D. R. (2004). Inferences about actions performed in constraining contexts: Correspondence bias or correspondent inference? *Current Psychology: Developmental, Learning, Personality, Social , 23*(1), 41–51.

Forsyth, D. R. (2006). *Group dynamics.* Wadsworth: Belmont, CA.

Forsyth, D. R., & Strong, S. R. (1986). The scientific study of counseling and psychotherapy: A unificationist view. *American Psychologist, 41,* 113–119.

Foschi, R., & Cicciola, E. (2006). Politics and naturalism in the 20th century psychology of Alfred Binet. *History of Psychology, 9,* 267–289.

Foster, R. G. (2004). Are we trying to banish biological time? *Cerebrum, 6,* 7–26.

Foster, R. G., & Kreitzman, L. (2004). *Rhythms of life: The biological clocks that control the daily lives of every living thing.* New Haven, CT: Yale University Press.

Foulkes, D. (1985). *Dreaming: A cognitive-psychological analysis.* Hillsdale, NJ: Erlbaum.

Foulkes, D. (1996). Dream research: 1953–1993. *Sleep, 19,* 609–624.

Fournier, J. C., DeRubeis, R. J., Hollon, S. D., Dimidjian, S., Amsterdam, J. D., Shelton, R. C., & Fawcett, J. (2010). Antidepressant drug effects and depression severity: A patient-level meta-analysis. *Journal of the American Medical Association, 303*(1), 47–53.

Fowers, B. J., & Davidov, B. J. (2006). The virtue of multiculturalism: Personal transformation, character, and openness to the other. *American Psychologist, 61,* 581–594.

Fox, G. L., Bruce, C., & Combs-Orme, T. (2000). Parenting expectations and concerns of fathers and mothers of newborn infants. *Family Relations, 49*(2), 123–131.

Fozard, J. L., & Gordon-Salant, S. (2001). Changes in vision and hearing with aging. In J. E. Birren & K. W. Schaie (Eds.), *Handbook of the psychology of aging* (5th ed., pp. 240–265). San Diego, CA: Academic Press.

Fraley, R. C. (2002). Attachment stability from infancy to adulthood: Meta-analysis and dynamic modeling of developmental mechanisms. *Personality and Social Psychology Review, 6,* 123–151.

Francis, L. A., & Birch, L. L. (2005). Maternal influences on daughters' restrained eating behavior. *Health Psychology, 24,* 548–554.

Frank, J. D. (1961). *Persuasion and healing.* Baltimore: Johns Hopkins University Press.

Frank, L. K. (1939). Projective methods for the study of personality. *Journal of Psychology, 8,* 343–389.

Frank, L. R. (1990). Electroshock: Death, brain damage, memory loss, and brainwashing. *The Journal of Mind and Behavior, 11*(3/4), 489–512.

Frank, M. G. (2006). The function of sleep. In T. Lee-Chiong (Ed.), *Sleep: A comprehensive handbook.* Hoboken, NJ: Wiley-Liss.

Frankland, P. W., & Bontempi, B. (2005). The organization of recent and remote memories. *Nature Reviews Neuroscience, 6*(2), 119–130.

Frantz, C. M. & Mayer, F. S. (2009). The emergency of climate change: Why are we failing to take action? *Analyses of Social Issues & Public Policy, 9,* 205–222.

Frasure-Smith, N., & Lesperance, F. (2005). Depression and coronary heart disease: Complex synergism of mind, body, and environment. *Current Directions in Psychological Science, 14*(1), 39–43.

Frederick, S., & Loewenstein, G. (1999). Hedonic adaptation. In D. Kahneman, E. Diener, & N. Schwarz (Eds.), *Well-being: The foundations of hedonic psychology.* New York, NY: Russell Sage Foundation.

Fredrickson, B. L. (2001). The role of positive emotions in positive psychology: The broaden-and-build theory of positive emotions. *American Psychologist, 56,* 218–226.

Fredrickson, B. L. (2002). Positive emotions. In C. R. Snyder & S. J. Lopez (Eds.), *Handbook of positive psychology* (pp. 120–134). New York, NY: Oxford University Press.

Fredrickson, B. L. (2005). The broaden-and-build theory of positive emotions. In F. A. Huppert, N. Baylis, & B. Keverne (Eds.), *The science of well-being* (pp. 217–238). New York, NY: Oxford University Press.

Fredrickson, B. L. (2006). The broaden-and-build theory of positive emotions. In M. Csikszentmihalyi, & I. S. Csikszentmihalyi (Eds.), *A life worth living: Contributions to positive psychology*. New York, NY: Oxford University Press.

Fredrickson, B. L., Tugade, M. M., Waugh, C. E., & Larkin, G. R. (2003). What good are positive emotions in crises? A prospective study of resilience and emotions following the terrorist attacks on the United States on September 11, 2001. *Journal of Personality and Social Psychology, 84,* 365–376.

Freedman, J. L., & Fraser, S. C. (1966). Compliance without pressure: The foot-in-the-door technique. *Journal of Personality and Social Psychology, 4,* 195–202.

Freedman, R., Ross, R., Michels, R., Appelbaum, P., Siever, L., Binder, R., et al. (2007). Psychiatrists, mental illness, and violence. *American Journal of Psychiatry, 164*(9), 1315–1317. doi:10.1176/appi.ajp.2007.07061013

Freeman, N. K. (2007). Preschoolers' perceptions of gender appropriate toys and their parents' beliefs about genderized behaviors: Miscommunication, mixed messages, or hidden truths? *Early Childhood Education Journal, 34*(5), 357–366. doi:10.1007/s10643-006-0123-x

Fremouw, W. J., de Perczel, M., & Ellis, T. E. (1990). *Suicide risk: Assessment and response guidelines.* New York, NY: Pergamon.

Freud, A. (1936). *The ego and the mechanisms of defense.* London: Hogarth Press and Institute of Psycho-Analysis.

Freud, S. (1900/1953). *The interpretation of dreams.* In J. Strachey (Ed.), *The standard edition of the complete psychological works of Sigmund Freud* (Vols. 4 and 5). London: Hogarth.

Freud, S. (1901/1960). *The psychopathology of everyday life.* In J. Strachey (Ed.), *The standard edition of the complete psychological works of Sigmund Freud* (Vol. 6). London: Hogarth.

Freud, S. (1910/1957). *Leonardo da Vinci: A study in psychosexuality* (Vol. 11). London, England: Hogarth Press. (original work published 1910)

Freud, S. (1914/1953). On narcissism: An introduction. In J. Strachey (Ed., Trans.), *The standard edition of the complete psychological works of Sigmund Freud* (Vol. 1). London, England: Hogarth Press. (original work published 1914)

Freud, S. (1915/1959). Instincts and their vicissitudes. In E. Jones (Ed.), *The collected papers of Sigmund Freud* (Vol. 4). New York, NY: Basic Books.

Freud, S. (1924). *A general introduction to psychoanalysis.* New York, NY: Boni & Liveright.

Freud, S. (1933/1964). *New introductory lectures on psychoanalysis.* In J. Strachey (Ed.), *The standard edition of the complete psychological works of Sigmund Freud* (Vol. 22). London: Hogarth.

Freud, S. (1940). An outline of psychoanalysis. *International Journal of Psychoanalysis, 21,* 27–84.

Frey, B. S., & Stutzer, A. (2002). What can economists learn from happiness research? *Journal of Economic Literature, 40,* 402–435.

Freyd, J. J. (1996). *Betrayal trauma: The logic of forgetting childhood abuse.* Cambridge, MA: Harvard University Press.

Freyd, J. J. (2001). Memory and dimensions of trauma: Terror may be "all-too-well remembered" and betrayal buried. In J. R. Conte (Ed.), *Critical issues in child sexual abuse: Historical, legal, and psychological perspectives.* Thousand Oaks, CA: Sage.

Freyd, J. J., DePrince, A. P., & Gleaves, D. H. (2007). The state of betrayal trauma theory: Reply to McNally—Conceptual issues and future directions. *Memory, 15,* 295–311.

Friedkin, N. E. (1999). Choice shift and group polarization. *American Sociological Review, 64,* 856–875.

Friedman, H. S. (2007). Personality, disease, and self-healing. In H. S. Friedman & R. C. Silver (Eds.), *Foundations of health psychology.* New York, NY: Oxford University Press.

Friedman, H. S., & Adler, N. E. (2007). The history and background of health psychology. In H. S. Friedman & R. C. Silver (Eds.), *Foundations of health psychology.* New York, NY: Oxford University Press.

Friedman, M., & Rosenman, R. F. (1974). *Type A behavior and your heart.* New York, NY: Knopf.

Friese, M., Wänke, M., & Plessner, H. (2006). Implicit consumer preferences and their influence on product choice. *Psychology & Marketing, 23*(9), 727–740. doi:10.1002/mar.20126

Frijda, N. H. (1999). Emotions and hedonic experience. In D. Kahneman, E. Diener, & N. Schwarz (Eds.), *Well-being: The foundations of hedonic psychology.* New York, NY: Russell Sage Foundation.

Frishman, L. J. (2001). Basic visual processes. In E. B. Goldstein (Ed.), *Blackwell handbook of perception.* Malden, MA: Blackwell.

Fritze, J. G., Blashki, G. A., Burke, S. and Wiseman, J. (2008). Hope, despair and transformation: Climate change and the promotion of mental health and wellbeing. *International Journal of Mental Health Systems, 2.* Retrieved from http://ijmhs.com/content/2/1/13

Fromm, E. (1979). The nature of hypnosis and other altered states of consciousness: An ego-psychological theory. In E. Fromm & R. E. Shor (Eds.), *Hypnosis: Developments in research and new perspectives.* New York, NY: Aldine.

Fromm, E. (1992). An ego-psychological theory of hypnosis. In E. Fromm & M. R. Nash (Eds.), *Contemporary hypnosis research.* New York, NY: Guilford Press.

Frumkes, T. E. (1990). Classical and modern psychophysical studies of dark and light adaptation and their relationship to underlying retinal function. In K. N. Leibovic (Ed.), *Science of vision.* New York, NY: Springer-Verlag.

Frumkin, H. (2001). Beyond toxicity: Human health and the natural environment. *American Journal of Preventive Medicine, 20,* 234–240.

Fuchs, A. H., & Milar, K. S. (2003). Psychology as a science. In D. K. Freedheim (Ed.), *Handbook of psychology, Vol. 1: History of psychology.* New York, NY: Wiley.

Fullana, M. A., Mataix-Cols, D., Caspi, A., Harrington, H., Grisham, J. R., Moffitt, T. E., & Poulton, R. (2009). Obsessions and compulsions in the community: Prevalence, interference, help-seeking, developmental stability, and co-occurring psychiatric conditions. *American Journal of Psychiatry, 166*(3), 329–336. doi:10.1176/appi.ajp.2008.08071006

Fuller, P. M., & Lu, J. (2009). Hypothalmic regulation of sleep. In R. Stickgold & M. P. Walker (Eds.), *The Neuroscience of Sleep* (pp. 91–98). San Diego, CA: Academic Press.

Funder, D. C. (2001). Personality. *Annual Review of Psychology, 52,* 197–221.

Furnham, A., & Mak, T. (1999). Sex-role stereotyping in television commercials: A review and comparison of fourteen studies done on five continents over 25 years. *Sex Roles, 41,* 413–437.

Furnham, A., McManus, C., & Scott, D. (2004). Personality, empathy, and attitudes to animal welfare. *Anthrozoos, 16,* 135–146.

Furumoto, L. (1980). Mary Whiton Calkins (1863–1930). *Psychology of Women Quarterly, 5,* 55–68.

Furumoto, L., & Scarborough, E. (1986). Placing women in the history of psychology: The first American women psychologists. *American Psychologist, 41,* 35–42.

Fyer, A. J. (2009). Anxiety disorders: Genetics. In B. J. Sadock, V. A. Sadock, & P. Ruiz (Eds.), *Kaplan & Sadock's comprehensive textbook of psychiatry* (9th ed., pp. 1898–1905). Philadelphia, PA: Lippincott, Williams & Wilkins.

Gabbard, G. O. (2005). Major modalities: Psychoanalytic/psychodynamic. In G. O. Gabbard, J. S. Beck, & J. Holmes (Eds.), *Oxford textbook of psychotherapy.* New York, NY: Oxford University Press.

Gaddis, C. (1999, August 8). A Boggs life. *Tampa Tribune.* Retrieved from http://rays.tbo.com/rays/MGBWZ4RSL3E.html.

Gael, S. A. (1988). *The job analysis handbook for business, industry, and government.* New York, NY: Wiley.

Gaeth, G. J., & Shanteau, J. (2000). Reducing the influence of irrelevant information on experienced decision makers. In T. Connolly, H. R. Arkes, & K. R. Hammond (Eds.), *Judgment and decision making: An interdisciplinary reader* (2nd ed., pp. 305–323). New York, NY: Cambridge University Press.

Gais, S., & Born, J. (2004). Declarative memory consolidation: Mechanisms acting during human sleep. *Learning & Memory, 11,* 679–685.

Galambos, N. L. (2004). Gender and gender role development in adolescence. In R. M. Lerner & L. Steinberg (Eds.), *Handbook of adolescent psychology.* New York, NY: Wiley.

Galanter, E. (1962). Contemporary psychophysics. In R. Brown (Ed.), *New directions in psychology.* New York, NY: Holt, Rinehart & Winston.

Galati, D., Scherer, K. R., & Ricci-Bitti, P. E. (1997). Voluntary facial expression of emotion: Comparing congenitally blind with normally sighted encoders. *Journal of Personality and Social Psychology, 73*(6), 1363–1379. doi:10.1037/0022-3514.73.6.1363

Galderisi, S., Maj, M., Mucci, A., Cassano, G. B., Invernizzi, G., Rossi, A., Vita, A., Dell'Osso, L., Daneluzzo, E., & Pini, S. (2002). Historical, psychopathological, neurological, and neuropsychological, aspects of deficit schizophrenia: A multicenter study. *American Journal of Psychiatry, 159,* 983–990.

Gallagher, R. M., & Rosenthal, L. J. (2007, Summer). A multidisciplinary approach to the management of chronic pain. *Practical Neuroscience for Primary Care Physicians,* pp. 14–16.

Gallese, V., Fadiga, L., Fogassi, L. , & Rizzolatti, G. (1996). Action recognition in the premotor cortex. *Brain, 119,* 593–609.

Gallup, A. C., & Gallup Jr., G. G. (2007). Yawning as a brain cooling mechanism: Nasal breathing and forehead cooling diminish the incidence of contagious yawning. *Evolutionary Psychology, 5,* 92–101.

Gallup, G. G., Jr., & Frederick, D. A. (2010). The science of sex appeal: An evolutionary perspective. *Review of General Psychology, 14*(3), 240–250.

Galton, F. (1869). *Hereditary genius: An inquiry into its laws and consequences.* New York, NY: Appleton.

Gangestad, S. W., Garver-Apgar, C. E., Simpson, J. A., & Cousins, A. J. (2007). Changes in women's mate preferences across the ovulatory cycle. *Journal of Personality and Social Psychology, 92,* 151–163.

Gangwisch, J. E., Heymsfield, S. B., Boden–Albala, B., et al. (2006). Short sleep duration as a risk factor for hypertension: Analyses of the first National Health and Nutrition Examination Survey. *Hypertension, 5,* 833–839.

Gantt, W. H. (1975, April 25). Unpublished lecture, Ohio State University. Cited in D. Hothersall, (1984), *History of psychology.* New York, NY: Random House.

Garakani, A., Murrough, J. W., Charney, D. S., & Bremner, J. D. (2009). The neurobiology of anxiety disorders. In D. S. Charney & E. J. Nestler (Eds.). *Neurobiology of mental illness* (3rd ed., pp. 655–691). New York, NY: Oxford University Press.

Garb, H. N., Florio, C. M., & Grove, W. M. (1998). The validity of the Rorschach and the Minnesota Multiphasic Personality Inventory: Results form meta-analysis. *Psychological Science, 9,* 402–404.

Garcia, J. (1989). Food for Tolman: Cognition and cathexis in concert. In T. Archer & L. G. Nilsson (Eds.), *Aversion, avoidance, and anxiety: Perspectives on aversively motivated behavior.* Hillsdale, NJ: Erlbaum.

Garcia, J., Clarke, J. C., & Hankins, W. G. (1973). Natural responses to scheduled rewards. In P. P. G. Bateson & P. Klopfer (Eds.), *Perspectives in ethology.* New York, NY: Plenum.

Garcia, J., & Koelling, R. A. (1966). Learning with prolonged delay of reinforcement. *Psychonomic Science, 5,* 121–122.

Garcia, J., & Rusiniak, K. W. (1980). What the nose learns from the mouth. In D. Muller-Schwarze & R. M. Silverstein (Eds.), *Chemical signals.* New York, NY: Plenum.

Garcia-Rill, E. (2009). Reticular activating system. In R. Stickgold & M. P. Walker (Eds.), *The Neuroscience of sleep* (pp. 133–139). San Diego, CA: Academic Press.

Gardner, E. P., & Kandel, E. R. (2000). Touch. In E. R. Kandel, J. H. Schwartz, & T. M. Jessell (Eds.), *Principles of neural science.* New York, NY: McGraw-Hill.

Gardner, G. T., & Prugh, T. (2008). Seeding the sustainable economy. In L. Starke (Ed.), *2008 state of the world: Innovations for a sustainable economy* (pp. 3–17). New York, NY: Norton.

Gardner, G. T., & Stern, P. C. (2002). *Environmental problems and human behavior* (2nd ed.). Boston, MA: Allyn & Bacon.

Gardner, G. T., & Stern, P. C. (2008). The short list: The most effective actions U.S. households can take to curb climate change. *Environment, 50(5),* 12–24.

Gardner, H. (1983). *Frames of mind: The theory of multiple intelligences.* New York, NY: Basic Books.

Gardner, H. (1985). *The mind's new science: A history of the cognitive revolution.* New York, NY: Basic Books.

Gardner, H. (1993). *Multiple intelligences: The theory in practice.* New York, NY: Basic Books.

Gardner, H. (1998). A multiplicity of intelligences. *Scientific American Presents Exploring Intelligence, 9,* 18–23.

Gardner, H. (1999). *Intelligence reframed: Multiple intelligences for the 21st century.* New York, NY: Basic Books.

Gardner, H. (2004). Audiences for the theory of multiple intelligences. *Teachers College Record, 106*(1), 212–220.

Gardner, H. (2006). *Multiple intelligences: New horizons.* New York, NY: Basic Books.

Gardner, M., & Steinberg, L. (2005). Peer influence on risk-taking, risk preference, and risky decision-making in adolescence and adulthood: An experimental study. *Developmental Psychology, 41,* 625–635.

Gardner, R. A., & Gardner, B. T. (1969). Teaching sign language to a chimpanzee. *Science, 165,* 664–672.

Garnett, N. (2005). Laws, regulations, and guidelines. In C. K. Akins, S. Panicker, & C. L. Cunningham (Eds.), *Laboratory animals in research and teaching: Ethics, care and methods.* Washington, DC: American Psychological Association.

Gassmann, O., & Zeschky, M. (2008). Opening up the solution space: The role of analogical thinking for breakthrough product innovation. *Creativity & Innovation Management, 17*(2), 97–106. doi:10.1111/j.1467-8691.2008.00475.x

Gattig, A. & Hendrickx, L. (2007). Judgmental discounting and environmental risk perception: Dimensional similarities, domain differences, and implications for sustainability. *Journal of Social Issues, 63,* 21–39.

Gauthier, I., & Curby, K. M. (2005). A perceptual traffic jam on highway N170: Interference between face and car expertise. *Current Directions in Psychological Science, 14*(1), 30–33.

Gauthier, I., Tarr, M. J., Anderson, A. W., Skudlarski, P., & Gore, J. C. (1999). Activation of the middle fusiform "face area" increases with expertise in recognizing novel objects. *Nature Neuroscience, 2,* 568–573.

Gawronski, B. (2004). Theory-based bias correction in dispositional inference: The fundamental attribution error is dead, long live the correspondence bias. In W. Stroebe & M. Hewstone (Eds.). *European review of social psychology* (Vol. 15). Hove, England: Psychology Press/Taylor & Francis.

Gazzaniga, M. S. (1970). *The bisected brain.* New York, NY: Appleton-Century-Crofts.

Gazzaniga, M. S. (2000). Cerebral specialization and interhemispheric communication. *Brain, 123,* 1293–1326.

Gazzaniga, M. S. (2005). Forty-five years of split-brain research and still going strong. *Nature Reviews Neuroscience, 6,* 653–659.

Gazzaniga, M. S. (2008). Spheres of influence. *Scientific American Mind, 19*(2), 32–39.

Gazzaniga, M. S., Bogen, J. E., & Sperry, R. W. (1965). Observations on visual perception after disconnection of the cerebral hemispheres in man. *Brain, 88,* 221–236.

Gazzaniga, M. S., Ivry, R. B., & Mangum, G. R. (2009). *Cognitive neuroscience: The biology of the mind* (3rd ed.). New York, NY: Norton.

Geary, D. C. (2007). An evolutionary perspective on sex difference in mathematics and the sciences. In S. J. Ceci & W. M. Williams (Eds.), *Why aren't more women in science?* (pp. 173–188). Washington, DC: American Psychological Association.

Gebhard, U., Nevers, P., & Billmann-Mahecha, E. (2003). Moralizing trees: Anthropomorphism and identity in children's relationships to nature. In S.Clayton & S. Opotow (Eds.), *Identity and the natural environment: The psychological significance of nature* (pp. 91–111). Cambridge, MA: MIT Press.

Gee, T., Allen, K., & Powell, R. A. (2003). Questioning premorbid dissociative symptomatology in dissociative identity disorder. *Professional Psychology: Research & Practice, 34*(1), 114–116.

Gegenfurtner, K. (2010). Color perception: Physiological. In E. B. Goldstein (Ed.), *Encyclopedia of perception.* Thousand Oaks, CA: Sage.

Geier, A. B., Rozin, P., & Doros, G. (2006). Unit bias: A new heuristic that helps explain the effect of portion size on food intake. *Psychological Science, 17,* 521–525.

Geiger, M. A. (1997). An examination of the relationship between answer changing, testwiseness and examination performance. *Journal of Experimental Education, 66,* 49–60.

Gelbspan, R. (2001 May/June). A modest proposal to stop global warming. *Sierra Magazine,* 62–67.

Geller, E. S., Winett, R. A., & Everett, P. B. (1982). *Environmental preservation: New strategies for behavior change.* New York, NY: Pergamon Press.

Geller, J. L. (2009). The role of the hospital in the care of the mentally ill. In B. J. Sadock, V. A. Sadock, & P. Ruiz (Eds.), *Kaplan & Sadock's comprehensive textbook of psychiatry* (9th ed., pp. 4299–4314). Philadelphia, PA: Lippincott, Williams & Wilkins.

Gennari, S. P., Sloman, S. A., Malt, B. C., & Fitch, W. T. (2002). Motion events in language and cognition. *Cognition, 83*(1), 49–79.

Gentile, B., Grabe, S., Dolan-Pascoe, B., Twenge, J. M., Wells, B. E., & Maitino, A. (2009). Gender differences in domain-specific self-esteem: A meta-analysis. *Review of General Psychology, 13*(1), 34–45. doi:10.1037/a0013689.

Gentile, B., Twenge, J. M., & Campbell, W. (2010). Birth cohort differences in self-esteem, 1988–2008: A cross-temporal meta-analysis. *Review of General Psychology, 14*(3), 261–268. doi:10.1037/a0019919

Gentner, D. (1988). Metaphor as structure mapping: The relational shift. *Child Development, 59,* 47–59.

George, M. S., Bohning, D. E., Lorberbaum, J. P., Nahas, Z., Anderson, B., Borckardt, J. J., et al. (2007). Overview of transcranial magnetic stimulation: History, mechanisms, physics, and safety. In M. S. George & R. H. Belmaker (Eds.), *Transcranial magnetic stimulation in clinical psychiatry.* Washington, DC: American Psychiatric Publishing.

George, S. A. (2002). The menopause experience: A woman's perspective. *Journal of Obstetric, Gynecologic, and Neonatal Nursing, 31,* 71–85.

Geraerts, E., Raymaekers, L., & Merckelbach, H. (2008). Recovered memories of childhood sexual abuse: Current findings and their legal implications. *Legal and Criminological Psychology, 13*(2), 165–176. doi:10.1348/135532508X298559

Geraerts, E., Schooler, J. W., Merckelbach, H., Jelicic, M., Hauer, B. A., & Ambadar, Z. (2007). The reality of recovered memories: Corroborating continuous and discontinuous memories of childhood sexual abuse. *Psychological Science, 18*(7), 564–568. doi:10.1111/j.1467-9280.2007.01940.x

Gerard, M. (Ed.). (1968). *Dali.* Paris: Draeger.

Gergen, K. J., Gulerce, A., Lock, A., & Misra, G. (1996). Psychological science in cultural context. *American Psychologist, 51,* 496–503.

Gershkoff-Stowe, L., & Hahn, E. R. (2007). Fast mapping skills in the developing lexicon. *Journal of Speech, Language, and Hearing Research, 50,* 682–696.

Gershoff, E. T. (2002). Parental corporal punishment and associated child behaviors and experiences: A meta-analytic and theoretical review. *Psychological Bulletin, 128,* 539–579.

Getzel, E. E., & Wehman, P. (2005). *Going to college: Expanding opportunities with disabilities.* Baltimore: Brookes.

Gibbons, D. E., & Lynn, S. J. (2010). Hypnotic inductions: A primer. In S. J. Lynn, J. W. Rhue, & I. Kirsch (Eds.), *Handbook of Clinical Hypnosis* (2nd ed., pp. 267–292). Washington, DC: American Psychological Association.

Gibbons, M. B. C., Crits-Christoph, P., & Hearon, B. (2008). The empirical status of psychodynamic therapies. *Annual Review of Clinical Psychology, 4,* 93–108.

Gibbs, W. W. (2005). Obesity: An overblown epidemic? *Scientific American, 292*(6), 70–77.

Gibson, C., Folley, B. S., & Park, S. (2009). Enhanced divergent thinking and creativity in musicians: A behavioral and near-infrared spectroscopy study. *Brain and Cognition, 69*(1), 162–169. doi:10.1016/j.bandc.2008.07.009

Giedd, J. N. (2008). The teen brain: Insights from neuroimaging. *Journal of Adolescent Health, 42,* 335–343.

Gigerenzer, G. (2000). *Adaptive thinking: Rationality in the real world.* New York, NY: Oxford University Press.

Gigerenzer, G. (2004). Fast and frugal heuristics: The tools of bounded rationality. In D. J. Koehler & N. Harvey (Eds.), *Blackwell handbook of judgment and decision making.* Malden, MA: Blackwell Publishing.

Gigerenzer, G. (2008). Why heuristics work. *Perspective on Psychological Science, 3*(1), 20–29.

Gigerenzer, G., Gaissmaier, W., Kurz-Milcke, E., Schwartz, L. M., & Woloshin, S. (2007). Helping doctors and patients make sense of health statistics. *Psychological Science in the Public Interest, 8*(2), 53–96. doi:10.1111/j.1539-6053.2008.00033.x

Gilad, Y., Wiebe, V., Przeworski, M., Lancet, D., & Paabo, S. (2004). Loss of olfactory receptor genes coincides with the acquisition of full trichromatic vision in primates. *PLoS Biology, 5*(6), e148. doi: 10.1371/journal.pbio.0020005

Gilbert, D. (2006, July 2). If only gay sex caused global warming. *Los Angeles Times.* Retrieved from http://articles.latimes.com/2006/jul/02/opinion/op-gilbert2

Gilbert, D. (2008). Daniel Gilbert at Pop!Tech: Gilbert speaks about the psychology of global warming. Retrieved from http://poptech.org/popcasts/dan_gilbert__poptech_2007

Gilbert, D. T. (1989). Thinking lightly about others: Automatic components of the social inference process. In J. S. Uleman & J. A. Bargh (Eds.), *Unintended thought: Limits of awareness, intention, and control.* New York, NY: Guilford Press.

Gilbert, D. T. (1998). Speeding with Ned: A personal view of the correspondence bias. In J. M. Darley & J. Cooper (Ed.), *Attribution and social interaction: The legacy of Edward E. Jones.* Washington, DC: American Psychological Association.

Gilbert, D. T. (2006). *Stumbling on happiness.* New York, NY: Alfred A. Knopf.

Gilbert, D. T., Driver-Linn, E., & Wilson, T. D. (2002). The trouble with Vronsky: Impact bias in the forecasting of future affective states. In L. F. Barrett & P. Salovey (Eds.), *The wisdom in feeling: Psychological processes in emotional intelligence* (pp. 114–143). New York, NY: Guilford Press.

Gilbert, D. T., & Malone, P. S. (1995). The correspondence bias. *Psychological Bulletin, 117,* 21–38.

Gilbert, D. T., Pinel, E. C., Wilson, T. D., Blumberg, S. J., & Wheatley, T. P. (1998). Immune neglect: A source of durability bias in affective forecasting. *Journal of Personality and Social Psychology, 75*(3), 617–638. doi:10.1037/0022-3514.75.3.617

Gilgen, A. R. (1982). *American psychology since World War II: A profile of the discipline.* Westport, CT: Greenwood Press.

Gilovich, T. D., & Griffin, D. W. (2010). Judgment and decision making. In S. T. Fiske, D. T. Gilbert, & G. Lindzey (Eds.), *Handbook of social psychology ,* (5th ed., Vol. 1, pp. 542–588). Hoboken, NJ: Wiley.

Gilovich, T. D., Griffin, D., & Kahneman, D. (2002). *Heuristics and biases: The psychology of intuitive judgment.* New York, NY: Cambridge University Press.

Gimmig, D., Huguet, P., Caverni, J., & Cury, F. (2006). Choking under pressure and working memory capacity: When performance pressure reduces fluid intelligence. *Psychonomic Bulletin & Review, 13*(6), 1005–1010.

Gitlin, M. J. (2009). Pharmacotherapy and other somatic treatments for depression. In I. H. Gotlib & C. L. Hammen (Eds.), *Handbook of depression* (pp. 554–585). New York, NY: Guilford Press.

Gittelman, M. (2005). The neglected disaster. *International Journal of Mental Health, 34*(2), 9–21.

Gladwell, M. (2005). *Blink: The power of thinking without thinking.* New York, NY: Little, Brown.

Glascock, J. (2005). Degrading content and character sex: Accounting for men and women's differential reactions to pornography. *Communication Reports, 18*(1), 43–53. doi:10.1080/08934210500084230

Glasman, L. R., & Albarracín, D. (2006). Forming attitudes that predict future behavior: A meta-analysis of the attitude-behavior relation. *Psychological Bulletin, 132,* 778–822.

Glass, C. R., & Arnkoff, D. B. (1992). Behavior therapy. In D. K. Freedheim (Ed.), *History of psychotherapy: A century of change.* Washington, DC: American Psychological Association.

Glass, R. M. (2001). Electroconvulsive therapy. *Journal of the American Medical Association, 285,* 1346–1348.

Glass, R. M. (2004). Treatment of adolescents with major depression: Contributions of a major trial. *Journal of the American Medical Association, 292,* 861–863.

Glassner, B. (1999). *The culture of fear: Why Americans are afraid of the wrong things.* New York, NY: Perseus Books Group.

Glatt, S. J. (2008). Genteics. In K. T. Mueser & D. V. Jeste (Eds.), *Clinical handbook of schizophrenia* (pp. 55–64). New York, NY: Guilford Press.

Glausiusz, J. (2009). Devoted to distraction. *Psychology Today, 42*(2), 84–91.

Gleitman, L., & Newport, E. (1996). *The invention of language by children.* Cambridge, MA: MIT Press.

Gleitman, L., & Papafragou, A. (2005). Language and thought. In K. J. Holyoak & R. G. Morrison (Eds.), *The Cambridge handbook of thinking and reasoning.* New York, NY: Cambridge University Press.

Glick, I. D., Ritvo, E. C., & Melnick, I. (2008). Couples and family therapy. In R. E. Hales, S. C. Yudofsky, & G. O. Gabbard (Eds.), American Psychiatric Publishing textbook of psychiatry (5th ed., pp. 1303–1327). Arlington, VA: American Psychiatric Publishing.

Gluck, M. E. (2006). Stress response and binge eating disorder. *Appetite, 46*(1), 26–30.

Gmelch, G. (1978). Baseball magic. *Human Nature, 1*(8), 32–39.

Gneezy, U., List, J. A., & Wu, G. (2006). The uncertainty effect: When a risky prospect is valued less than its worst possible outcome. *Quarterly Journal of Economics, 121*(4), 1283–1309.

Goff, D. C., & Gudeman, J. E. (1999). The person with chronic mental illness. In A.M. Nicholi (Ed.), *The Harvard guide to psychiatry.* Cambridge, MA: Harvard University Press.

Gogtay, N., Giedd, J. N., Lusk, L., Hayashi, K. M., Rapoport, J. L., Thompson, P. M., et al. (2004). Dynamic mapping of human cortical development during childhood through early adulthood. *Proceedings of the National Academy of Sciences, 101,* 8174–8179.

Goin, M. K. (2005). A current perspective on the psychotherapies. *Psychiatric Services, 56*(3), 255–257.

Gold, M. S., & Jacobs, W. S. (2005). Cocaine and crack: Clinical aspects. In J. H. Lowinson, P. Ruiz, R. B. Millman, & J. G. Langrod (Eds.), *Substance abuse: A comprehensive textbook.* Philadelphia, PA: Lippincott Williams & Wilkins.

Goldberg, M. E., & Hudspeth, A. J. (2000). The vestibular system. In E. R. Kandel, J. H. Schwartz, & T. M. Jessell (Eds.), *Principles of neural science.* New York, NY: McGraw-Hill.

Goldenberg, H. (1983). *Contemporary clinical psychology.* Pacific Grove, CA: Brooks/Cole.

Goldenberg, I., Goldenberg, H., & Pelavin, E. G. (2011). Family therapy. In R. J. Corsini & D. Wedding (Eds.), *Current psychotherapies* (9th ed.). Belmont, CA: Brooks/Cole.

Goldstein, D. G., & Gigerenzer, G. (2002). Models of ecological rationality: The recognition heuristic. *Psychological Review, 109,* 75–90.

Goldstein, E. B. (2001). Pictorial perception and art. In E. B. Goldstein (Ed.), *Blackwell handbook of perception.* Malden, MA: Blackwell.

Goldstein, E. B. (2008). *Cognitive psychology: Connecting mind, research, and everyday experience.* Belmont, CA: Wadsworth.

Goldstein, E. B. (2010). Constancy. In E. B. Goldstein (Ed.), *Encyclopedia of perception.* Thousand Oaks, CA: Sage.

Goldstein, H. W., Zedeck, S., & Goldstein, I. L. (2002). *g*: Is this your final answer? *Human Performance, 15,* 123–142.

Goldstein, W. M., & Hogarth, R. M. (1997). Judgement and decision research: Some historical context. In W. M. Goldstein, & R. M. Hogarth (Eds.), *Research on judgement and decision making.* New York, NY: Cambridge University Press.

Goldston, K., & Baillie, A. J. (2008). Depression and coronary heart disease: A review of the epidemiological evidence, explanatory mechanisms and management approaches. *Clinical Psychology Review, 28,* 288–306.

González, H. M., Vega, W. A., Williams, D. R., Tarraf, W., West, B. T., & Neighbors, H. W. (2010). Depression care in the United States: Too little for too few. *Archives of General Psychiatry, 67*(1), 37–46.

Goodall, J. (1986). Social rejection, exclusion, and shunning among the Gombe chimpanzees. *Ethology & Sociobiology, 7,* 227–236.

Goodall, J. (1990). *Through a window: My thirty years with the chimpanzees of Gombe.* Boston, MA: Houghton, Mifflin.

Goodheart, C. D. (2006). Evidence, endeavor, and expertise in psychology practice. In C. D. Goodheart, A. E. Kazdin, & R. J. Sternberg (Eds.), *Evidence-based psychotherapy: Where practice and research meet* (pp. 37–62). Washington, DC: American Psychological Association.

Goodwin, C. J. (1991). Misportraying Pavlov's apparatus. *American Journal of Psychology, 104*(1), 135–141.

Goodwin, F. K., & Jamison, K. R. (2007). *Manic-depressive illness: Bipolar disorders and recurrent depression.* New York, NY: Oxford University Press.

Goodwin, G. (2009). Neurobiological aetiology of mood disorders. In M. C. Gelder, N. C. Andreasen, J. J. López-Ibor, Jr., & J. R. Geddes (Eds.). *New Oxford textbook of psychiatry* (2nd ed., Vol. 1). New York, NY: Oxford University Press.

Goodwin, R. D., Jacobi, F., Bittner, A., & Wittchen, H.-U. (2006). Epidemiology of mood disorders. In D. J. Stein, D. J. Kupfer, & A. F. Schatzberg (Eds.), *Textbook of mood disorders* (pp. 33–54). Washington, DC: American Psychiatric Publishing.

Gopie, N., Craik, F. M., & Hasher, L. (2010). Destination memory impairment in older people. *Psychology and Aging, 25*(4), 922–928. doi:10.1037/a0019703

Gopie, N., & MacLeod, C. M. (2009). Destination memory: Stop me if I've told you this before. *Psychological Science, 20*(12), 1492–1499. doi:10.1111/j.1467-9280.2009.02472.x

Gopnik, A., Meltzoff, A. N., & Kuhl, P. K. (1999). *The scientist in the crib: Minds, brains, and how children learn.* New York, NY: Morrow.

Gorchoff, S. M., John, O. P., & Helson, R. (2008). Contextualizing change in marital satisfaction during middle age: An 18-year longitudinal study. *Psychological Science, 19*(11), 1194–1200. doi:10.1111/j.1467-9280.2008.02222.x

Gordon, H. W. (1990). The neurobiological basis of hemisphericity. In C. Trevarthen (Ed.), *Brain circuits and functions of the mind. Essays in honor of Roger W. Sperry.* Cambridge, MA: Cambridge University Press.

Gordon, J., & Abramov, I. (2001). Color vision. In E. B. Goldstein (Ed.), *Blackwell handbook of perception.* Malden, MA: Blackwell.

Gore, A. (2008). Neuroendocrine systems. In L. Squire, D. Berg, F. Bloom, S. Du Lac, A. Ghosh, & N. Spitzer (Eds.), *Fundamental neuroscience* (3rd ed., pp. 905–930). San Diego, CA: Elsevier.

Gorner, P. (2006, May 10). Daddy material? It takes just one look. *Chicago Tribune.*

Goswami, U. (2006). Neuroscience and education: From research to practice? *Nature Reviews Neuroscience, 7*(5), 2–7.

Gottesman, I. I. (1991). *Schizophrenia genesis: The origins of madness.* New York, NY: W. H. Freeman.

Gottesman, I. I. (2001). Psychopathology through a life span–genetic prism. *American Psychologist, 56,* 867–878.

Gottesman, I. I., & Hanson, D. R. (2005). Human development: Biological and genetic processes. *Annual Review of Psychology, 56,* 263–86.

Gottesmann, C. (2009). Discovery of the dreaming sleep stage: A recollection. *Sleep: Journal of Sleep and Sleep Disorders Research, 32*(1), 15–16.

Gottfredson, L. S. (2002). Where and why *g* matters: Not a mystery. *Human Performance, 15,* 25–46.

Gottfredson, L. S. (2003a). Dissecting practical intelligence theory: Its claims and evidence. *Intelligence, 31,* 343–397.

Gottfredson, L. S. (2003b). *G*, jobs and life. In H. Nyborg (Ed.), *The scientific study of general intelligence: Tribute to Arthur R. Jensen.* Oxford, UK: Pergamon.

Gottfredson, L. S. (2009). Logical fallacies used to dismiss the evidence on intelligence testing. In R. P. Phelps (Ed.), *Correcting fallacies about educational and psychological testing* (pp. 11–65). Washington, DC: American Psychological Association. doi:10.1037/11861-001

Gottfredson, L. S., & Deary, I. J. (2004). Intelligence predicts health and longevity, but why? *Current Directions in Psychological Science, 13*(1), 1–4.

Gould, E. (2004). Stress, deprivation, and adult neurogenesis. In M. S. Gazzaniga (Ed.), *The cognitive neurosciences* (pp. 139–148). Cambridge, MA: MIT Press.

Gould, E., & Gross, C. G. (2002). Neurogenesis in adult mammals: Some progress and problems. *Journal of Neuroscience, 22,* 619–623.

Gould, R. L. (1975, February). Adult life stages: Growth toward self-tolerance. *Psychology Today,* pp. 74–78.

Gourevitch, M. N., & Arnsten, J. H. (2005). Medical complications of drug use. In J. H. Lowinson, P. Ruiz, R. B. Millman, & J. G. Langrod (Eds.), *Substance abuse: A comprehensive textbook.* Philadelphia, PA: Lippincott/Williams & Wilkins.

Grady, D. (2006). Management of menopausal symptoms. *New England Journal of Medicine, 355,* 2338–2347.

Graf, P., & Uttl, B. (2001). Prospective memory: A new focus for research. *Consciousness & Cognition: An International Journal, 10,* 437–450.

Graham-Bermann, S. A. (2009, May). *Growing opposition to physical punishment: Empirical, human rights, and ethical arguments against an age-old practice.* Paper presented at the American Psychological Association's annual convention, Toronto, Ontario.

Granberg, G., & Holmberg, S. (1991). Self-reported turnout and voter validation. *American Journal of Political Science, 35,* 448–459.

Grandjean, P. & Landrigan, P. J. (2006). Developmental neurotoxicity of industrial chemicals. *Lancet, 368,* 2167–2178.

Grandner, M. A., Hale, L., Moore, M., & Patel, N. P. (2010). Mortality associated with short sleep duration: The evidence, the possible mechanisms, and the future. *Sleep Medicine Reviews, 14*(3), 191–203. doi:10.1016/j.smrv.2009.07.006

Grandner, M. A., Patel, N. P., Gehrman, P. R., Perlis, M. L., & Pack, A. I. (2010a). Problems associated with short sleep: Bridging the gap between laboratory and epidemiological studies. *Sleep Medicine Reviews, 14*(4), 239–247. doi:10.1016/j.smrv.2009.08.001

Grandner, M. A., Patel, N. P., Gehrman, P. R., Xie, D., Sha, D., Weaver, T., & Gooneratne, N. (2010b). Who gets the best sleep? Ethnic and socioeconomic factors related to sleep complaints. *Sleep Medicine, 11*(5), 470–478. doi:10.1016/j.sleep.2009.10.006

Grant, J. A., Courtemanche, J., Duerden, E. G., Duncan, G. H., & Rainville, P. (2010). Cortical thickness and pain sensitivity in zen meditators. *Emotion, 10*(1), 43–53. doi:10.1037/a0018334

Grant, J. A., & Rainville, P. (2009). Pain sensitivity and analgesic effects of mindful states in Zen meditators: A cross-sectional study. *Psychosomatic Medicine, 71*(1), 106–114. doi:10.1097/PSY.0b013e31818f52ee

Grantham-McGregor, S., Ani, C., & Fernald, L. (2001). The role of nutrition in intellectual development. In R. J. Sternberg & E. L. Grigorenko (Eds.), *Environmental effects on cognitive abilities* (pp. 119–156). Mahwah, NJ: Erlbaum.

Grau, R., Salanova, M., & Peiro, J. M. (2001). Moderator effects of self-efficacy on occupational stress. *Psychology in Spain, 5*(1), 63–74.

Gray, C., & Della Sala, S. (2007). The Mozart effect: It's time to face the music! In S. Della Sala (Ed.), *Tall tales about the mind & brain: Separating fact from fiction* (pp. 148–157). New York, NY: Oxford University Press.

Gray, K., & Wegner, D. M. (2008). The sting of intentional pain. *Psychological Science, 19*(12), 1260–1262. doi: 10.1111/j.1467-9280.2008.02208.x.

Graziano, W. G., & Eisenberg, N. H. (1997). Agreeableness: A dimension of personality. In R. Hogan, J. Johnson, & S. Briggs (Eds.), *Handbook of personality psychology.* San Diego: Academic Press.

Graziano, W. G., & Tobin, R. M. (2009). Agreeableness. In M. R. Leary & R. H. Hoyle (Eds.), *Handbook of individual differences in social behavior* (pp. 46–61). New York, NY: Guilford Press.

Green, C. D. (2009). Darwinian theory, functionalism, and the first American psychological revolution. *American Psychologist, 64*(2), 75–83. doi: 10.1037/a0013338.

Green, J. P. (1999). Hypnosis, context effects, and recall of early autobiographical memories. *International Journal of Clinical & Experimental Hypnosis, 47,* 284–300.

Green, J. P. (2003). Beliefs about hypnosis: Popular beliefs, misconceptions, and the importance of experience. *International Journal of Clinical and Experimental Hypnosis, 51*(4), 369–381. doi:10.1076/iceh.51.4.369.16408

Greenberg, J., Landau, M., Kosloff, S., & Solomon, S. (2009). How our dreams of death transcendence breed prejudice, stereotyping, and conflict: Terror management theory. In T. D. Nelson (Ed.), *Handbook of prejudice, stereotyping, and discrimination* (pp. 309–332). New York, NY: Psychology Press.

Greenberg, J. S. (2002). *Comprehensive stress management: Health and human performance.* New York, NY: McGraw-Hill.

Greene, R. L. (1992). *Human memory: Paradigms and paradoxes.* Hillsdale, NJ: Erlbaum.

Greenfield, D. (1985) *The psychotic patient: Medication and psychotherapy.* New York, NY: The Free Press.

Greenhaus, J. H. (2003). Career dynamics. In W. C. Borman, D. R. Ilgen, & R. J. Klimoski (Eds.), *Handbook of psychology, Vol. 12: Industrial and organizational psychology* (pp. 519–540). New York, NY: Wiley.

Greeno, J. G. (1978). Nature of problem-solving abilities. In W. K. Estes (Ed.), *Handbook of learning and cognitive processes* (Vol. 5). Hillsdale, NJ: Erlbaum.

Greenough, W. T. (1975). Experiential modification of the developing brain. *American Scientist, 63,* 37–46.

Greenough, W. T., & Volkmar, F. R. (1973). Pattern of dendritic branching in occipital cortex of rats reared in complex environments. *Experimental Neurology, 40,* 491–504.

Greenson, R. R. (1967). *The technique and practice of psychoanalysis* (Vol. 1). New York, NY: International Universities Press.

Greenstein, T. N. (2009). National context, family satisfaction, and fairness in the division of household labor. *Journal of Marriage and Family, 71*(4), 1039–1051. doi:10.1111/j.1741-3737.2009.00651.x

Greenwald, A. G., & Banaji, M. R. (1995). Implicit social cognition: Attitudes, self-esteem, and stereotypes. *Psychological Review, 102*(1), 4–27. doi:10.1037/0033-295X.102.1.4

Greenwald, A. G., McGhee, D. E., & Schwartz, J. K. (1998). Measuring individual differences in implicit cognition: The Implicit Association Test. *Journal of Personality and Social Psychology, 74*(6), 1464–1480. doi:10.1037/0022-3514.74.6.1464

Greenwald, A. G., Poehlman, T., Uhlmann, E., & Banaji, M. R. (2009). Understanding and using the Implicit Association Test: III. Meta-analysis of predictive validity. *Journal of Personality and Social Psychology, 97*(1), 17–41. doi:10.1037/a0015575

Greenway, R. (1995). The wilderness effect and ecopsychology. In. T. Roszak, M. E. Gomes, & A. D. Kanner (Eds.), *Eco-psychology: Restoring the earth, healing the mind* (pp. 122–135). San Francisco, CA: Sierra Club Books.

Gregory, R. L. (1973). *Eye and brain.* New York, NY: McGraw-Hill.

Gregory, R. L. (1978). *Eye and brain* (2nd ed.). New York, NY: McGraw-Hill.

Greven, C. U., Harlaar, N., Kovas, Y., Chamorro-Premuzic, T., & Plomin, R. (2009). More than just IQ: School achievement is predicted by self-perceived abilities—But for genetic rather than environmental reasons. *Psychological Science, 20*(6), 753–762. doi:10.1111/j.1467-9280.2009.02366.x

Grigorenko, E. L. (2000). Heritability and intelligence. In R. J. Sternberg (Ed.), *Handbook of intelligence* (pp. 53–91). New York, NY: Cambridge University Press.

Grigorenko, E. L., & Sternberg, R. J. (2001). Analytical, creative, and practical intelligence as predictors of self-reported adaptive functioning: A case study in Russia. *Intelligence, 29,* 57–73.

Grigorenko, E. L., & Sternberg, R. J. (2003). The nature-nurture issue. In A. Slater & G. Bremner (Eds.), *An introduction to development psychology.* Malden, MA: Blackwell Publishers.

Griner, D., & Smith, T. B. (2006). Culturally adapted mental health intervention: A meta-analytic review. *Psychotherapy: Theory, Research, Practice, Training, 43,* 531–548.

Grinspoon, L., Bakalar, J. B., & Russo, E. (2005). Marihuana: Clinical aspects. In J. H. Lowinson, P. Ruiz, R. B. Millman, & J. G. Langrod (Eds.), *Substance abuse: A comprehensive textbook.* Philadelphia, PA: Lippincott/ Williams & Wilkins.

Grob, C. S., & Poland, R. E. (2005). MDMA. In J. H. Lowinson, P. Ruiz, R. B. Millman, & J. G. Langrod (Eds.), *Substance abuse: A comprehensive textbook.* Philadelphia, PA: Lippincott/Williams & Wilkins.

Grob, G. N. (1983). Disease and environment in American history. In D. Mechanic (Ed.), *Handbook of health, health care, and the health professions.* New York, NY: Free Press.

Gronholm, P., Juha, O., Vorobyev, V. , & Laine, M. (2005). Naming of newly learned objects: A PET activation study. *Cognitive Brain Research, 25,* 359–371.

Gross, J. J. (2001). Emotion regulation in adulthood: Timing is everything. *Current Directions in Psychological Science, 10,* 214–219.

Grossman, J. B., & Ruiz, P. (2004). Shall we make a leap-of-faith to disulfiram (Antabuse)? *Addictive Disorders & Their Treatment, 3*(3), 129–132.

Grossman, P., Niemann, L., Schmidt, S., & Walach, H. (2004). Mindfulness-based stress reduction and health benefits: A meta-analysis. *Journal of Psychosomatic Research, 57,* 35–43.

Grossman, R. P., & Till, B. D. (1998). The persistence of classically conditioned brand attitudes. *Journal of Advertising, 27,* 23–31.

Grossman, S. P., Dacey, D., Halaris, A. E., Collier, T., & Routtenberg, A. (1978). Aphagia and adipsia after preferential destruction of nerve cell bodies in hypothalamus. *Science, 202,* 537–539.

Grossmann, K. E., & Grossmann, K. (1990). The wider concept of attachment in cross-cultural research. *Human Development, 33,* 31–47.

Groth-Marnat, G. (1997). *Handbook of psychological assessment.* New York, NY: Wiley.

Grubin, D., & Madsen, L. (2005). Lie detection and the polygraph: A historical review. *Journal of Forensic Psychiatry & Psychology, 16,* 357–369.

Gruenberg, A. M., & Goldstein, R. D. (2003). Mood disorders: Depression. In A. Tasman, J. Kay, & J. A. Lieberman (Eds.), *Psychiatry.* New York, NY: Wiley.

Grunberg, N. E., Berger, S. S., & Hamilton, K. R. (2011). Stress and drug use. In R. J. Contrada & A. Baum (Eds.), *The handbook of stress science: Biology, psychology, and health* (pp. 111–121). New York, NY: Springer Publishing.

Grusec, J. E. (2006). The development of moral behavior and conscience from a socialization perspective. In M. Killen & J. G. Smetana (Eds.), *Handbook of moral development.* Mahwah, NJ: Erlbaum.

Guarda, A. S., Pinto, A. M., Coughlin, J. W., Hussain, S., Haug, N. A., & Heinberg, L. J. (2007). Perceived coercion and change in perceived need for admission in patients hospitalized for eating disorders. *American Journal of Psychiatry, 164,* 108–114.

Guenther, K. (1988). Mood and memory. In G. M. Davies & D. M. Thomson (Eds.), *Memory in context: Context in memory.* New York, NY: Wiley.

Guerinni, I., Thomson, A. D., & Gurling, H. D. (2007). The importance of alcohol misuse, malnutrition, and genetic susceptibility on brain growth and plasticity. *Neuroscience & Biobehavioral Reviews, 31,* 212–220.

Guilbault, R. L., Bryant, F. B., Brockway, J. H., & Posavac, E. J. (2004). A meta analysis of research on hindsight bias. *Basic and Applied Social Psychology, 26,* 103–117.

Guilford, J. P. (1959). Three faces of intellect. *American Psychologist, 14,* 469–479.

Guiney, M. S., & Oberhauser, K. S. (2009). Conservation volunteers' connection to nature. *Ecopsychology, 1*(4), 187–197.

Gunn, D. V., Warm, J. S., Dember, W. N., & Temple, J. N. (2000). Subjective organization and the visibility of illusory contours. *American Journal of Psychology, 113,* 553–568.

Gunn, S. R., & Gunn, W. S. (2006). Are we in the dark about sleepwalking's dangers? *Cerebrum,* 1–12.

Gunter, C. (2009). Schizophrenia: missing heritability found? *Nature Reviews Neuroscience, 10*(8), 543. doi:10.1038/nrn2691

Gur, R. C., & Gur, R. E. (2007). Neural substrates for sex differences in cognition. In S. J. Ceci & W. M. Williams (Eds.), *Why aren't more women in science?* (pp. 189–198). Washington, DC: American Psychological Association.

Guyton, A. C. (1991). *Textbook of medical physiology.* Philadelphia, PA: Saunders.

Güzeldere, G., Flanagan, O., & Hardcastle, V. G. (2000). The nature and function of consciousness: Lessons from blindsight. In M. S. Gazzaniga (Ed.), *The new cognitive neurosciences.* Cambridge, MA: The MIT Press.

Guzman-Marin, R., Suntsova, N., Bashir, T., Nienhuis, R., Szymusiak, R., & McGinty, D. (2008). Rapid eye movement sleep deprivation contributes to reduction of neurogenesis in the hippocampal dentate gyrus of the adult rat. *Sleep: Journal of Sleep and Sleep Disorders Research, 31*(2), 167–175.

Guzzetta, F., & de Girolamo, G. (2009). Epidemiology of personality disorders. In M. C. Gelder, N. C. Andreasen, J. J. López-Ibor, Jr., & J. R. Geddes (Eds.), *New Oxford textbook of psychiatry* (2nd ed., Vol. 1). New York, NY: Oxford University Press.

Haas, L. (1999). Families and work. In M. B. Sussman, S. K. Steinmetz, & G. W. Peterson (Eds.), *Handbook of marriage and the family* (pp. 571–612). New York, NY: Plenum.

Hackett, R. D. (1989). Work attitudes and employee absenteeism: A synthesis of the literature. *Journal of Occupational Psychology, 62,* 235–248.

Hackett, T. A., & Kaas, J. H. (2009). Audition. In G. G. Berntson & J. T. Cacioppo (Eds.), *Handbook of neuroscience for the behavioral sciences.* New York, NY: Wiley.

Hackman, J. R., & Katz, N. (2010). Attitudes. In S. T. Fiske, D. T. Gilbert, & G. Lindzey (Eds.), *Handbook of social psychology* (5th ed., Vol. 1, pp. 353–393). Hoboken, NJ: Wiley.

Hackman, J. R., & Oldham, G. R. (1976). Motivation through the design of work: A test of a theory. *Organizational Behavior and Human Performance, 16,* 250–279.

Hackney, C. M. (2010). Auditory processing: Peripheral. In E. B. Goldstein (Ed.), *Encyclopedia of perception.* Thousand Oaks, CA: Sage.

Hadaway, C. K., Marler, P. L., & Chaves, M. (1993). What the polls don't show: A closer look at U.S. church attendance. *American Sociological Review, 58,* 741–752.

Hadjiefthyvoulou, F., Fisk, J. E., Montgomery, C., & Bridges, N. J. (2010). Everyday and prospective memory deficits in ecstasy/polydrug users. *Journal of Psychopharmacology, 25,* 453-464. doi:10.1177/ 0269881109359101

Hadjistavropoulos, H., Dash, H., Hadjistavropoulos, T., & Sullivan, T. (2007). Recurrent pain among university students: Contributions of self-efficacy and perfectionism to the pain experience. *Personality and Individual Differences, 42,* 1081–1091.

Haefner, R. (2009). More employers screening candidates via social networking sites. Careerbuilder, June 10. Retrieved from http://www.careerbuilder.com/ Article/CB-1337-Interview-Tips-More-Employers-Screening-Candidates-via-Social-Networking-Sites/

Hagen, E. H. (2005). Controversial issues in evolutionary psychology. In D. M. Buss (Ed.), *The handbook of evolutionary psychology* (pp. 145–176). New York, NY: Wiley.

Hagerty, M. R. (2000). Social comparisons of income in one's community: Evidence from national surveys of income and happiness. *Journal of Personality and Social Psychology, 78,* 764–771.

Haggbloom, S. J., Warnick, R., Warnick, J. E., Jones, V. K., Yarbrough, G. L., Russell, T. M., Borecky, C. M., McGahhey, R., Powell III, J. L., Beavers, J., & Monte, E. (2002). The 100 most eminent psychologists of the 20th century. *Review of General Psychology, 6,* 139–152.

Hahn, P. Y., Olson, L. J., & Somers, V. K. (2006). Cardiovascular complications of obstructive sleep apnea. In T. Lee-Chiong (Ed.), *Sleep: A comprehensive handbook.* Hoboken, NJ: Wiley-Liss.

Haier, R. J. (2009). Neuro–intelligence, neuro-metrics and the next phase of brain imaging studies. *Intelligence, 37*(2), 121–123. doi:10.1016/j.intell.2008 .12.006

Hakuta, K. (1986). *Mirror of language.* New York, NY: Basic Books.

Hakuta, K. (2000). Bilingualism. In A. E. Kazdin (Ed.), *Encyclopedia of psychology* (pp. 410–414). Washington, DC: American Psychological Association.

Haladyna, T. M. (2006). Roles and importance of validity studies in test development. In S. M. Downing & T. M. Haladyna (Eds.), *Handbook of test development* (pp. 739–755). Mahwah, NJ: Erlbaum.

Hald, G., & Malamuth, N. M. (2008). Self-perceived effects of pornography consumption. *Archives of Sexual Behavior, 37*(4), 614–625. doi:10.1007/s10508-007-9212-1

Hald, G., Malamuth, N. M., & Yuen, C. (2010). Pornography and attitudes supporting violence against women: Revisiting the relationship in nonexperimental studies. *Aggressive Behavior, 36*(1), 14–20. doi:10 .1002/ab.20328

Hales, D. (1987). *How to sleep like a baby.* New York, NY: Ballantine.

Hall, C. B., Lipton, R. B., Sliwinski, M. M., Katz, M. J., Derby, C. A., & Verghese, J. J. (2009). Cognitive activities delay onset of memory decline in persons who develop dementia. *Neurology, 73*(5), 356–361. doi:10.1212/ WNL.0b013e3181b04ae3

Hall, C. C. I. (1997). Cultural malpractice: The growing obsolescence of psychology with the changing U.S. population. *American Psychologist, 52,* 642–651.

Hall, C. S. (1966). *The meaning of dreams.* New York, NY: McGraw-Hill.

Hall, C. S. (1979). The meaning of dreams. In D. Goleman & R. J. Davidson (Eds.), *Consciousness: Brain, states of awareness, and mysticism.* New York, NY: Harper & Row.

Hall, J. A., Carter, J. D., & Horgan, T. G. (2000). Gender differences in the nonverbal communication of emotion. In A. Fischer (Ed.), *Gender and emotion.* Cambridge, UK: Cambridge University Press.

Hall, J. A., & Mast, M. S. (2008). Are women always more interpersonally sensitive than men? Impact of goals and content domain. *Personality and Social Psychology Bulletin, 34,* 144–155.

Hall, J. R., & Benning, S. D. (2006). The "successful" psychopath: Adaptive and subclinical manifestations of psychopathy in the general population. In C. J. Patrick (Ed.), *Handbook of Psychopathy*. New York, NY: Guilford Press.

Hall, W. D., & Degenhardt, L. (2009a). Adverse health effects of non-medical cannabis use. *Lancet, 374*(9698), 1383–1391. doi:10.1016/S0140-6736(09)61037-0

Hall, W. D., & Degenhardt, L. (2009b). Cannabis-related disorders. In B. J. Sadock, V. A. Sadock, & P. Ruiz (Eds.), *Kaplan & Sadock's comprehensive textbook of psychiatry* (9th ed., Vol. 1, pp. 1309–1317). Philadelphia, PA: Lippincott, Williams & Wilkins.

Halmi, K. A. (2008). Eating disorders: Anorexia nervosa, bulimia nervosa, and obesity. In R. E. Hales, S. C. Yudofsky, & G. O. Gabbard (Eds.), *The American Psychiatric Publishing textbook of psychiatry* (5th ed., pp. 921–970). Washington, DC: American Psychiatric Publishing.

Halpern, C., Hurtig, H., Jaggi, J., Grossman, M., Won, M., & Baltuch, G. (2007). Deep brain stimulation in neurologic disorders. *Parkinsonism & Related Disorders, 13*(1), 1–16.

Halpern, D. F. (1984). *Thought and knowledge: An introduction to critical thinking*. Hillsdale, NJ: Erlbaum.

Halpern, D. F. (1996). *Thought and knowledge: An introduction to critical thinking*. Mahwah, NJ: Erlbaum.

Halpern, D. F. (1997). Sex differences in intelligence: Implications for education. *American Psychologist, 52,* 1091–1102.

Halpern, D. F. (1998). Teaching critical thinking for transfer across domains: Dispositions, skills, structure training, and metacognitive monitoring. *American Psychologist, 53,* 449–455.

Halpern, D. F. (2000). *Sex differences in cognitive abilities*. Mahwah, NJ: Erlbaum.

Halpern, D. F. (2003). *Thought and knowledge: An introduction to critical thinking*. Mahwah, NJ: Erlbaum.

Halpern, D. F. (2004). A cognitive-process taxonomy for sex differences in cognitive abilities. *Current Directions in Psychological Science, 13*(4), 135–139.

Halpern, D. F. (2007). The nature and nurture of critical thinking. In R. J. Sternberg, H. L. Roediger III, & D. F. Halpern (Eds.), *Critical thinking in psychology* (pp. 1–14). New York, NY: Cambridge University Press.

Halpern, D. F., Benbow, C. P., Geary, D. C., Gur, R. C., Hyde, J. S., & Gernsbacher, M. A. (2007). The science of sex differences in science and mathematics. *Psychological Science in the Public Interest, 8,* 1–51.

Hamann, S. B., Herman, R. A., Nolan, C. L., & Wallen, K. (2004). Men and women differ in amygdala response to visual sexual stimuli. *Nature Neuroscience, 7,* 411–416.

Hamilton, W. D. (1964). The evolution of social behavior. *Journal of Theoretical Biology, 7,* 1–52.

Hammad, T. A., Laughren, T., & Racoosin, J. (2006). Suicidality in pediatric patients treated with antidepressant drugs. *Archives of General Psychiatry, 63,* 332–339.

Hammen, C. (2003). Mood disorders. In G. Stricker & T. A. Widiger (Eds.), *Handbook of psychology, Vol. 8: Clinical psychology*. New York, NY: Wiley.

Hampson, E., & Moffat, S. D. (2004). The psychobiology of gender: Cognitive effects of reproductive hormones in the adult nervous system. In A. H. Eagly, A. E. Beall, & R. J. Sternberg (Eds.), *The psychology of gender*. New York, NY: Guilford Press.

Hampson, E., van Anders, S. M., & Mullin, L. I. (2006). A female advantage in the recognition of emotional facial expressions: Test of an evolutionary hypothesis. *Evolution and Human Behavior, 27,* 401–416.

Hampton, T. (2004). Fetal environment may have profound long-term consequences for health. *Journal of the American Medical Association, 292,* 1285–1286.

Han, K. F. G. C. (2000). Construct validity. In A. E. Kazdin (Ed.), *Encyclopedia of psychology* (pp. 281–283). Washington, DC: American Psychological Association.

Hancock, P. A., & Ganey, H. C. N. (2003). From the inverted-U to the extended-U: The evolution of a law of psychology. *Journal of Human Performance in Extreme Environments, 7*(1), 5–14.

Haneda, K., Nomura, M., Iidaka, T., & Ohira, H. (2003). Interaction of prime and target in the subliminal affective priming effect. *Perceptual & Motor Skills, 96,* 695–702.

Haney, C., Banks, W. C., & Zimbardo, P. G. (1973). Interpersonal dynamics in a simulated prison. *International Journal of Criminology and Penology, 1,* 69–97.

Haney, C., & Zimbardo, P. G. (1998). The past and future of U.S. prison policy: Twenty-five years after the Stanford Prison Experiment. *American Psychologist, 53,* 709–727.

Hanisch, K. A. (1992). The Job Descriptive Index revisited: Questions about the question mark. *Journal of Applied Psychology, 77,* 377–382.

Hanisch, K. A. (1995). Behavioral families and multiple causes: Matching the complexity of responses to the complexity of antecedents. *Current Directions in Psychological Science, 4,* 156–162.

Hanisch, K. A., & Hulin, C. L. (1990). Job attitudes and organizational withdrawal: An examination of retirement and other voluntary withdrawal behaviors. *Journal of Vocational Behavior, 37*(1), 60–78.

Hanisch, K. A., & Hulin, C. L. (1991). General attitudes and organizational withdrawal: An evaluation of a causal model. *Journal of Vocational Behavior, 39,* 110–128.

Hanisch, K. A., Hulin, C. L., & Roznowski, M. A. (1998). The importance of individuals' repertoires of behaviors: The scientific appropriateness of studying multiple behaviors and general attitudes. *Journal of Organizational Behavior, 19,* 463–480.

Hannigan, J. H., & Armant, D. R. (2000). Alcohol in pregnancy and neonatal outcome. *Seminars in Neonatology, 5,* 243–254.

Hanson, K., Winward, J., Schweinsburg, A., Medina, K., Brown, S., & Tapert, S. (2010). Longitudinal study of cognition among adolescent marijuana users over three weeks of abstinence. *Addictive Behaviors, 35*(11), 970–976.

Hardin, G. (1968, December). The tragedy of the commons. *Science,* 1243–1248.

Hare, R. D. (2006). Psychopathy: A clinical and forensic overview. *Psychiatric Clinics of North America, 29,* 709–724.

Hare, R. D., & Neumann, C. S. (2008). Psychopathy as a clinical and empirical construct. *Annual Review of Clinical Psychology, 4,* 217–246.

Hargis, M. (2008, Nov. 5). Social networking sites dos and don'ts. CNN.com. Retrieved from http://www.cnn.com/2008/LIVING/worklife/11/05/cb.social.networking/index.html

Harley, E. M. (2007). Hindsight bias in legal decision making. *Social Cognition, 25,* 48–63.

Harley, T. A. (2008). *The psychology of language: From data to theory*. New York, NY: Psychology Press.

Harlow, H. F. (1958). The nature of love. *American Psychologist, 13,* 673–685.

Harlow, H. F. (1959). Love in infant monkeys. *Scientific American, 200*(6), 68–74.

Harmsen, P., Rosengren, A., Tsipogianni, A., & Wilhelmsen, L. (1990). Risk factors for stroke in middle-aged men in Goteborg, Sweden. *Stroke, 21,* 23–29.

Haroutunian, V., & Davis, K. L. (2003). Psychiatric pathophysiology. In A. Tasman, J. Kay, & J. A. Lieberman (Eds.), *Psychiatry*. New York, NY: Wiley.

Harper, N. J., Russell, K. C., Cooley, R., & Cupples, J. (2007). Catherine Freer Wilderness Therapy Expeditions: An exploratory case study of adolescent wilderness therapy, family functioning, and the maintenance of change. *Child & Youth Care Forum, 36,* 111–129.

Harper, S. (1995). The way of wilderness. In. T. Roszak, M. E. Gomes, & A. D. Kanner (Eds.), *Ecopsychology: Restoring the earth, healing the mind* (pp. 183–200). San Francisco, CA: Sierra Club Books.

Harris, E., & Capellini, I. (2007). Phylogeny of sleep and dreams. In D. Barrett & P. McNamara (Eds.), *The new science of dreaming*. Westport, CT: Praeger.

Harris, J. E. (1984). Remembering to do things: A forgotten topic. In J. E. Harris & P. E. Morris (Eds.), *Everyday memory, actions, and absent-mindedness*. New York, NY: Academic Press.

Harris, J. L., Bargh, J. A., & Brownell, K. D. (2009). Priming effects of television food advertising on eating behavior. *Health Psychology, 28*(4), 404–413. doi:10.1037/a0014399

Harris, J. R. (1998). *The nurture assumption: Why children turn out the way they do*. New York, NY: Free Press.

Harris, P. L. (2006). Social cognition. In D. Kuhn, R. S. Siegler, W. Damon, & R. L. Lerner (Eds.), *Handbook of child psychology: Cognition, perception, and language* (6th ed., Vol. 2, pp. 811–858). Hoboken, NJ: Wiley.

Harte, J. L., & Eifert, G. H. (1995). The effects of running, environment, and attentional focus on athletes' catecholamine and cortisol levels and mood. *Psychophysiology, 32*(1), 49–54. doi:10.1111/j.1469-8986.1995.tb03405.x

Harte, J. L., Eifert, G. H., & Smith, R. (1995). The effects of running and meditation on beta-endorphin, corticotropin-releasing hormone and cortisol in plasma, and on mood. *Biological Psychology,* 40(3), 251–265. doi:10.1016/0301-0511(95)05118-T http://psycnet.apa.org/doi/10.1016/0301-0511(95)05118-T

Hartig, T., & Staats, H. (2006). The need for psychological restoration as a determinant of environmental preferences. *Journal of Environmental Psychology, 26,* 215–226.

Hartig, T., Evans, G. W., Jamner, L. D., Davis, D. S., & Gärling, T. (2003). Tracking restoration in natural and urban field settings. *Journal of Environmental Psychology, 23,* 109–123.

Hartley, A. (2006). Changing role of the speed of processing construct in the cognitive psychology of human aging. In J. E. Birren & K. W. Schaie (Eds.), *Handbook of the psychology of aging*. San Diego: Academic Press.

Hartmann, D. P., Pelzel, K. E., & Abbott, C. B. (2011). Design, measurement, and analysis in developmental research. In M. H. Bornstein & M. E. Lamb (Eds.), *Developmental science: An advanced textbook* (pp. 109–198). New York, NY: Psychology Press.

Harvey, P. D. (2010). Cognitive functioning and disability in schizophrenia. *Current Directions in Psychological Science, 19*(4), 249–254. doi:10.1177/0963721410378033

Haselton, M. G., & Buss, D. M. (2000). Error management theory: A new perspective on biases in cross-sex mind reading. *Journal of Personality and Social Psychology, 78,* 81–91.

Haselton, M. G., Buss, D. M., Oubaid, V., & Angleitner, A. (2005). Sex, lies, and strategic interference: The psychology of deception between the sexes. *Personality and Social Psychology Bulletin, 31,* 3–23.

Hashimoto, K., Shimizu, E., & Iyo, M. (2005). Dysfunction of glia-neuron communication in pathophysiology of schizophrenia. *Current Psychiatry Reviews, 1,* 151–163.

Haskard, K. B., Williams, S. L., DiMatteo, M., Rosenthal, R., White, M., & Goldstein, M. G. (2008). Physician and patient communication training in primary care: Effects on participation and satisfaction. *Health Psychology, 27*(5), 513–522. doi:10.1037/0278-6133.27.5.513

Haslam, N. (1997). Evidence that male sexual orientation is a matter of degree. *Journal of Personality and Social Psychology, 73,* 862–870.

Haslam, S. A. (2007). I think, therefore I err? *Scientific American Mind, 18*(2), 16–17.

Hassin, R. R., Ferguson, M. J., Shidlovski, D., & Gross, T. (2007). Subliminal exposure to national flags affects political thought and behavior. *Proceedings of the National Academy of Sciences, 104*(50), 19757–19761. doi: 10.1073/pnas.0704679104

Hastorf, A., & Cantril, H. (1954). They saw a game: A case study. *Journal of Abnormal and Social Psychology, 49,* 129–134.

Hatano, G., & Inagaki, K. (1999). A developmental perspective on informal biology. In D. L. Medin & S. Atran (Eds.), *Folkbiology* (pp. 321–354). Cambridge, MA: MIT Press.

Hatfield, E., & Rapson, R. L. (1993). *Love, sex, and intimacy: Their psychology, biology, and history.* New York, NY: HarperCollins.

Hatfield, E., Rapson, R. L., & Martel, L. D. (2007). Passionate love. In S. Kitayama & D. Cohen (Eds.), *Handbook of cultural psychology.* New York, NY: Guilford Press.

Hauri, P. J. (2002). Psychological and psychiatric issues in the etiopathogenesis of insomnia. *Journal of Clinical Psychiatry, 4*(suppl 1), 17–20.

Hauser, M., & Carey, S. (1998). Building a cognitive creature from a set of primitives: Evolutionary and developmental insights. In D. D. Cummins & C. Allen (Eds.), *The evolution of mind.* New York, NY: Oxford University Press.

Havermans, R. C., Siep, N., & Jansen, A. (2010). Sensory-specific satiety is impervious to the tasting of other foods with its assessment. *Appetite, 55*(2), 196–200. doi:10.1016/j.appet.2010.05.088

Haworth-Hoeppner, S. (2000). The critical shapes of body image: The role of culture and family in the production of eating disorders. *Journal of Marriage and the Family, 62,* 212–227.

Hayes, S., Hirsch, C., & Mathews, A. (2008). Restriction of working memory capacity during worry. *Journal of Abnormal Psychology, 117*(3), 712–717. doi:10.1037/a0012908

Hayne, H. (2007). Verbal recall of preverbal memories: Implications for the clinic and the courtroom. In M. Garry & H. Hayne (Eds.), *Do justice and let the sky fall: Elizabeth F. Lotus and her contributions to science, law, and academic freedom.* Mahwah, NJ: Erlbaum.

Hayslip, B., Jr. (1994). Stability of intelligence. In R. J. Sternberg (Ed.), *Encyclopedia of human intelligence.* New York, NY: Macmillan.

Haywood, T. W., Kravitz, H. M., Grossman, L. S., Cavanaugh, J. L., Jr., Davis, J. M., & Lewis, D. A. (1995). Predicting the "revolving door" phenomenon among patients with schizophrenic, schizoaffective, and affective disorders. *American Journal of Psychiatry, 152,* 861–956.

Hazan, C., & Shaver, P. (1986). *Parental caregiving style questionnaire.* Unpublished questionnaire.

Hazan, C., & Shaver, P. (1987). Romantic love conceptualized as an attachment process. *Journal of Personality and Social Psychology, 52,* 511–524.

He, J., Ogden, L. G., Vupputuri, S., Bazzano, L. A., Loria, C., & Whelton, P. K. (1999). Dietary sodium intake and subsequent risk of cardiovascular disease in overweight adults. *Journal of the American Medical Association, 282,* 2027–2034.

Healy, D. (2004). *Let them eat Prozac: The unhealthy relationship between the pharmaceutical industry and depression.* New York, NY: NYU Press.

Healy, D., & Whitaker, C. (2003). Antidepressants and suicide: Risk-benefit conundrums. *Journal of Psychiatry & Neuroscience, 28*(5), 28.

Heaps, C. M., & Nash, M. (2001) Comparing recollective experience in true and false autobiographical memories. *Journal of Experimental Psychology: Learning, Memory, and Cognition, 27,* 920–930.

Hearst, E. (1988). Fundamentals of learning and conditioning. In R. C. Atkinson, R. J. Herrnstein, G. Lindzey, & R. D. Luce (Eds.), *Stevens' handbook of experimental psychology.* New York, NY: Wiley.

Hedegaard, M. (2005). The zone of proximal development as basis for instruction. In H. Daniels (Ed.), *An introduction to Vygotsky.* New York, NY: Routledge.

Heider, F. (1958). *The psychology of interpersonal relations.* New York, NY: Wiley.

Heilman, M. E., & Chen, J. J. (2005). Same behavior, different consequences: Reactions to men's and women's altruistic citizenship behaviors. *Journal of Applied Psychology, 90,* 431–441.

Heilman, M. E., & Haynes, M. C. (2005). No credit where credit is due: Attributional rationalization of women's success in male-female teams. *Journal of Applied Psychology, 90,* 905–916.

Heine, S. J. (2003). Making sense of east Asian self-enhancement. *Journal of Cross-Cultural Psychology, 34(5),* 596–602. doi:10.1177/0022022103256481

Heine, S. J., & Hamamura, T. (2007). In search of East Asian self-enhancement. *Personality and Social Psychology Review, 11*(1), 1–24. doi:10.1177/1088868306294587

Heinrichs, R. W. (2005). The primacy of cognition in schizophrenia. *American Psychologist, 60,* 229–242.

Hélie, S., & Sun, R. (2010). Incubation, insight, and creative problem solving: A unified theory and a connectionist model. *Psychological Review, 117*(3), 994–1024. doi:10.1037/a0019532

Hellige, J. B. (1990). Hemispheric asymmetry. *Annual Review of Psychology, 41,* 55–80.

Hellige, J. B. (1993a). Unity of thought and action: Varieties of interaction between left and right cerebral hemispheres. *Current Directions in Psychological Science, 2*(1), 21–25.

Hellige, J. B. (1993b). *Hemispheric asymmetry: What's right and what's left.* Cambridge, MA: Harvard University Press.

Helmes, E. (2008). Modern applications of the MMPI/MMPI-2 in assessment. In G. J. Boyle, G. Matthews, & D. H. Saklofske (Eds.), *The Sage handbook of personality theory and assessment: Personality measurement and testing* (Vol. 2, pp. 589–607). Los Angeles, CA: Sage.

Helmholtz, H. von. (1852). On the theory of compound colors. *Philosophical Magazine, 4,* 519–534.

Helmholtz, H. von. (1863). *On the sensations of tone as a physiological basis for the theory of music* (A. J. Ellis, Trans.). New York, NY: Dover.

Helson, R., Jones, C., & Kwan, V. S. Y. (2002). Personality change over 40 years of adulthood: Hierarchical linear modeling analyses of two longitudinal studies. *Journal of Personality & Social Psychology, 83,* 752–766.

Helzer, J. E., Wittchen, H.-U., Krueger, R. F., & Kraemer, H. C. (2008a). Dimensional options for DSM-V: The way forward. In J. E. Helzer, H. C. Kraemer, R. F. Krueger, H.–U, Wittchen, P. J. Sirovatka, et al. (Eds.), *Dimensional approaches in diagnostic classification: Refining the research agenda for DSM-V* (pp. 115–127). Washington, DC: American Psychiatric Association.

Helzer, J. E., Kraemer, H., Krueger, R., Wittchen, H., Sirovatka, P., & Regier, D. (Eds.). (2008b). *Dimensional approaches in diagnostic classification: Refining the research agenda for DSM-V.* Washington, DC: American Psychiatric Association.

Hempel, S. (2005). Reliability. In J. Miles & P. Gilbert (Eds.), *A handbook of research methods for clinical and health psychology* (pp. 193–204). New York, NY: Oxford University Press.

Henderson, K. E., & Brownell, K. D. (2004). The toxic environment and obesity: Contribution and cure. In J. K. Thompson (Ed.), *Handbook of eating disorders and obesity.* New York, NY: Wiley.

Hendrick, S. S., & Hendrick, C. (2000). Romantic love. In S. S. Hendrick & C. Hendrick (Eds.), *Close relationships.* Thousand Oaks, CA: Sage.

Heneka, M. T., O'Banion, M., Terwel, D., & Kummer, M. (2010). Neuroinflammatory processes in Alzheimer's disease. *Journal of Neural Transmission, 117*(8), 919–947. doi:10.1007/s00702-010-0438-z

Henriksson, M. M., Aro, H. M., Marttunen, M. J., Heikkinen, M. E., Isometsa, E. T., Kuoppasalmi, K. I., & Lonnqvist, J. K. (1993). Mental disorders and comorbidity of suicide. *American Journal of Psychiatry, 150,* 935–940.

Hepper, P. (2003). *Prenatal psychological and behavioural development.* Thousand Oaks, CA: Sage.

Herbenick, D., Reece, M., Schick, V., Sanders, S. A., Dodge, B., & Fortenberry, J. (2010). An event-level analysis of the sexual characteristics and composition among adults ages 18 to 59: Results from a national probability sample in the United States. *Journal of Sexual Medicine, 7*(Suppl 5), 346–361. doi:10.1111/j.1743-6109.2010.02020.x

Herbst, S., Pietrzak, R. H., Wagner, J., White, W. B., & Petry, N. M. (2007). Lifetime major depression is associated with coronary heart disease in older adults: Results from the national epidemiologic survey on alcohol and related conditions. *Psychosomatic Medicine, 69,* 729–734.

Herbstman, J., Sjodin, A., Kurzon, M., Lederman, S., Jones, R., Rauh, V., et al. (2010). Prenatal exposure to PBDEs and neurodevelopment. *Environmental Health Perspectives, 118*(5), 712–719. doi:10.1289/ehp.0901340

Herek, G. M. (2000). The psychology of sexual prejudice. *Current Directions in Psychological Science, 9,* 19–22.

Herek, G. M. (2009). Sexual prejudice. In T. D. Nelson (Ed.), *Handbook of prejudice, stereotyping, and discrimination* (pp. 441–467). New York, NY: Psychology Press.

Heres, S., Davis, J., Maino, K., Jetzinger, E., Kissling, W., & Leucht, S. (2006). Why olanzapine beats risperidone, risperidone beats quetiapine, and quetiapine beats olanzapine: An exploratory analysis of head-to-head comparison studies of second-generation antipsychotics. *American Journal of Psychiatry, 163,* 185–194.

Hering, E. (1878). *Zür lehre vom lichtsinne.* Vienna: Gerold.

Herman, C. P., & Polivy, J. J. (2008). External cues in the control of food intake in humans: The sensory-normative distinction. *Physiology & Behavior, 94*(5), 722–728. doi:10.1016/j.physbeh.2008.04.014

Herman, L. M., Kuczaj, S. A., & Holder, M. D. (1993). Responses to anomalous gestural sequences by a language-trained dolphin: Evidence for processing of semantic relations and syntactic information. *Journal of Experimental Psychology: General, 122,* 184–194.

Herman-Giddens, M. E. (2006). Recent data on pubertal milestones in United States children: The secular trend towards earlier development. *International Journal of Andrology, 29,* 241.

Hermann, D., Raybeck, D., & Gruneberg, M. (2002). *Improving memory and study skills: Advances in theory and practice.* Ashland, OH: Hogrefe & Huber.

Hermann, R. C., Ettner, S. L., Dorwart, R. A., Hoover, C. W., & Yeung, E. (1998). Characteristics of psychiatrists who perform ECT. *American Journal of Psychiatry, 155,* 889–894.

Hermans, D., Craske, M. G., Mineks, S., & Lovibond, P. F. (2006). Extinction in human fear conditioning. *Biological Psychiatry, 60,* 361–368.

Hermans, H. J. M., & Kempen, H. J. G. (1998). Moving cultures: The perilous problems of cultural dichotomies in a globalizing society. *American Psychologist, 53,* 1111–1120.

Hernandez, A. E., & Li, P. (2007). Age of acquisition: Its neural and computational mechanisms. *Psychological Bulletin, 133,* 638–650.

Herrnstein, R. J., & Murray, C. (1994). *The bell curve: Intelligence and class structure in American life.* New York, NY: Free Press.

Hersh, S. M. (2004, May 10). Torture at Abu Ghraib. *New Yorker, 80*(17), 54–67.

Hertwig, R., & Gigerenzer, G. (1999). The "conjunction fallacy" revisited: How intelligent inferences look like reasoning errors. *Journal of Behavioral Decision Making, 12,* 275–306.

Hertwig, R., & Todd, P. M. (2002). Heuristics. In V. S. Ramachandran (Ed.), *Encyclopedia of the human brain* (pp. 449–460). San Diego: Academic Press.

Hertzog, C., Kramer, A. F., Wilson, R. S., Lindenberger, U. (2009). Enrichment effects on adult cognitive development: Can the functional capacity of older adults be preserved and enhanced? *Psychological Science in the Public Interest, 9*(1), 1–65.

Herzberg, F. (1966). *Work and the nature of man.* Cleveland: World Publishing.

Herzog, D. B., & Delinski, S. S. (2001). Classification of eating disorders. In R. H. Striegel-Moore & L. Smolak (Eds.), *Eating disorders* (pp. 31–50). Washington, DC: American Psychological Association.

Herzog, H. A. (2005). Dealing with the animal research controversy. In C. K. Akins, S. Panicker, & C. L. Cunningham (Eds.), *Laboratory animals in research and teaching: Ethics, care and methods.* Washington, DC: American Psychological Association.

Herzog, S. (2008). An attitudinal explanation of biases in the criminal justice system: An empirical testing of defensive attribution theory. *Crime & Delinquency, 54*(3), 457–481. doi:10.1177/0011128707308158

Hespos, S. J., Ferry, A. L., & Rips, L. J. (2009). Five-month-old infants have different expectations for solids and liquids. *Psychological Science, 20*(5), 603–611. doi:10.1111/j.1467-9280.2009.02331.x

Hetherington, E. M. (1999). Should we stay together for the sake of the children? In E. M. Hetherington (Ed.), *Coping with divorce, single parenting, and remarriage.* Mahwah, NJ: Erlbaum.

Hetherington, E. M. (2003). Intimate pathways: Changing patterns in close personal relationships across time. *Family Relations: Interdisciplinary Journal of Applied Family Studies, 52,* 318–331.

Hetherington, M. M., & Rolls, B. J. (1996). Sensory-specific satiety: Theoretical frameworks and central characteristics. In E. D. Capaldi (Ed.), *Why we eat what we eat: The psychology of eating* (267–290). Washington, DC: American Psychological Association.

Hettema, J. M., Neale, M. C., & Kendler, K. S. (2001). A review and meta-analysis of the genetic epidemiology of anxiety disorders. *American Journal of Psychiatry, 158,* 1568–1578.

Hettich, P. I. (1998). *Learning skills for college and career.* Pacific Grove, CA: Brooks/Cole.

Hewitt, B., & de Vaus, D. (2009). Change in the association between premarital cohabitation and separation, Australia 1945–2000. *Journal of Marriage and Family, 71*(2), 353–361. doi:10.1111/j.1741-3737.2009.00604.x

Hewstone, M. (1990). The "ultimate attribution error"? A review of the literature on intergroup causal attribution. *European Journal of Social Psychology, 20,* 311–335.

Higgins, E. T. (2004). Making a theory useful: Lessons handed down. *Personality and Social Psychology Review, 8*(2), 138–145.

Hilgard, E. R. (1965). *Hypnotic susceptibility.* New York, NY: Harcourt, Brace & World.

Hilgard, E. R. (1986). *Divided consciousness: Multiple controls in human thought and action.* New York, NY: Wiley.

Hilgard, E. R. (1987). *Psychology in America: A historical survey.* San Diego: Harcourt Brace Jovanovich.

Hilgard, E. R. (1992). Dissociation and theories of hypnosis. In E. Fromm & M. R. Nash (Eds.), *Contemporary hypnosis research.* New York, NY: Guilford Press.

Hill, G. W. (1982). Group versus individual performance: Are N+1 heads better than one? *Psychological Bulletin, 91,* 517–539.

Hill, J. O., & Peters, J. C. (1998). Environmental contributions to the obesity epidemic. *Science, 280,* 1371–1374.

Hilmert, C. J., Kulik, J. A., & Christenfeld, N. J. S. (2006). Positive and negative opinion modeling: The influence of another's similarity and dissimilarity. *Journal of Personality and Social Psychology, 90,* 440–452.

Hinds, J., & Sparks, P. (2009). Investigating environmental identity, well-being, and meaning. *Ecopsychology, 1*(4), 181–186.

Hines, M. (2004). Androgen, estrogen, and gender: Contributions of the early hormone environment to gender-related behavior. In A. H. Eagly, A. E. Beall, & R. J. Sternberg (Eds.), *The psychology of gender.* New York, NY: Guilford Press.

Hines, M. (2010). Sex-related variation in human behavior and the brain. *Trends in Cognitive Sciences, 14(10),* 448–456. doi:10.1016/j.tics.2010.07.005

Hingson, R., & Sleet, D. A. (2006). Modifying alcohol use to reduce motor vehicle injury. In A. C. Gielen, D. A. Sleet, & R. J. DiClemente (Eds.), *Injury and violence prevention: Behavioral science theories, methods, and applications.* San Francisco, CA: Jossey-Bass.

Hinshaw, S. P. (2007). *The mark of shame: Stigma of mental illness and an agenda for change.* New York, NY: Oxford University Press.

Hinshaw, S. P., & Stier, A. (2008). Stigma as related to mental disorders. *Annual Review of Clinical Psychology, 4,* 367–393.

Hirschel, M. J., & Schulenberg, S. E. (2009). Hurricane Katrina's impact on the Mississippi Gulf Coast: General self-efficacy's relationship to PTSD prevalence and severity. *Psychological Services, 6*(4), 293–303. doi:10.1037/a0017467

Hirsh, I. J., & Watson, C. S. (1996). Auditory psychophysics and perception. *Annual Review of Psychology, 47,* 461–484.

Hirsh, J. B. (2010). Personality and environmental concern. *Journal of Environmental Psychology, 30*(2), 245–248.

Hirshkowitz, M., Seplowitz-Hafkin, R. G., & Sharafkhaneh, A. (2009). Sleep disorders. In B. J. Sadock, V. A. Sadock, & P. Ruiz (Eds.), *Kaplan & Sadock's comprehensive textbook of psychiatry* (9th ed., Vol. 1, pp. 2150–2177). Philadelphia, PA: Lippincott, Williams & Wilkins.

Hirst, W., Phelps, E. A., Buckner, R. L., Budson, A. E., Cuc, A., Gabrieli, J. E., et al. (2009). Long-term memory for the terrorist attack of September 11: Flashbulb memories, event memories, and the factors that influence their retention. *Journal of Experimental Psychology: General, 138*(2), 161–176. doi:10.1037/a0015527

Hobson, J. A. (1988). *The dreaming brain.* New York, NY: Basic Books.

Hobson, J. A. (1989). *Sleep.* New York, NY: Scientific American Library.

Hobson, J. A. (2007). Current understanding of cellular models of REM expression. In D. Barrett & P. McNamara (Eds.), *The new science of dreaming.* Westport, CT: Praeger.

Hobson, J. A., & McCarley, R. W. (1977). The brain as a dream state generator: An activation-synthesis hypothesis of the dream process. *American Journal of Psychiatry, 134,* 1335–1348.

Hobson, J. A., Pace-Schott, E. F., & Stickgold, R. (2000). Dreaming and the brain: Toward a cognitive neuroscience of conscious states. *Behavioral and Brain Sciences, 23,* 793–842; 904–1018; 1083–1121.

Hocevar, D., & Bachelor, P. (1989). A taxonomy and critique of measurements used in the study of creativity. In J. A. Glover, R. R. Ronning, & C. R. Reynolds (Eds.), *Handbook of creativity.* New York, NY: Plenum.

Hochberg, J. (1988). Visual perception. In R. C. Atkinson, R. J. Herrnstein, G. Lindzey, & R. D. Luce (Eds.), *Stevens' handbook of experimental psychology* (2nd ed., Vol. 1). New York, NY: Wiley.

Hodges, B. H., & Geyer, A. (2006). A nonconformist account of the Asch experiments: Values, pragmatics, and moral dilemmas. *Personality and Social Psychology Review, 10*(1), 2–19. doi:10.1207/s15327957pspr1001_1

Hodgkin, A. L., & Huxley, A. F. (1952). Currents carried by sodium and potassium ions through the membrane of the giant axon of Loligo. *Journal of Physiology, 116,* 449–472.

Hoek, H. W. (2002). Distribution of eating disorders. In C. G. Fairburn & K. D. Brownell (Eds.), *Eating disorders and obesity: A comprehensive handbook.* New York, NY: Guilford Press.

Hoerger, M., Quirk, S. W., Lucas, R. E., & Carr, T. H. (2009). Immune neglect in affective forecasting. *Journal of Research in Personality, 43*(1), 91–94. doi:10.1016/j.jrp.2008.10.001

Hoff, E. (2005). *Language development.* Belmont, CA: Wadsworth.

Hofferth, S. L. & Curtin, S. C. (2005). Leisure time activities in middle childhood. In K. A. Moore & L. H. Lippman (Eds.), *What do children need to flourish? Conceptualizing and measuring indicators of positive development* (pp. 95–110). New York, NY: Springer.

Hofferth, S. L. & Sandberg, J. F. (2001). Changes in American children's time, 1981–1997. In S. Hofferth & T. Owens (Eds.), *Children at the millennium: Where have we come from, where are we going?* (pp. 193–229). New York, NY: Elsevier Science.

Hoffman, E., Iversen, V., & Ortiz, F. A. (2010). Peak-experiences among Norwegian youth. *Nordic Psychology, 62*(4), 67–76.

Hoffstein, V. (2005). Snoring and upper airway resistance. In M. H. Kryger, T. Roth, & W. C. Dement (Eds.). *Principles and practice of sleep medicine*. Philadelphia, PA: Elsevier Saunders.

Hofmann, W., De Houwer, J., Perugini, M., Baeyens, F., & Crombez, G. (2010). Evaluative conditioning in humans: A meta-analysis. *Psychological Bulletin, 136*(3), 390–421. doi:10.1037/a0018916.

Hofstede, G. (1980). *Culture's consequences: International differences in work-related values*. Beverly Hills, CA: Sage.

Hofstede, G. (1983). Dimensions of national cultures in fifty countries and three regions. In J. Deregowski, S. Dzuirawiec, & R. Annis (Eds.), *Explications in cross-cultural psychology*. Lisse: Swets and Zeitlinger.

Hofstede, G. (2001). *Culture's consequences: Comparing values, behaviors, institutions, and organizations across nations*. Thousand Oaks, CA: Sage.

Hogan, J., Barrett, P., & Hogan, R. (2007). Personality measurement, faking, and employment selection. *Journal of Applied Psychology, 92,* 1270–1285.

Hogan, M. F. & Morrison, A. K. (2008). Organization and economics of mental health treatment. In A. Tasman, J. Kay, J. A. Lieberman, M. B. First, & M. Maj (Eds.), *Psychiatry* (3rd ed.). New York, NY: Wiley-Blackwell.

Hogan, R. (2005). In defense of personality measurement: New wine for old whiners. *Human Performance, 18,* 331–341.

Hoge, C. W., Terhakopian, A., Castro, C. A., Messer, S. C., & Engel, C. C. (2007). Association of posttraumatic stress disorder with somatic symptoms, health care visits, and absenteeism among Iraq War veterans. *American Journal of Psychiatry, 164,* 150–153.

Hogg, M. A. (2010). Influence and leadership. In S. T. Fiske, D. T. Gilbert, & G. Lindzey (Eds.), *Handbook of social psychology* (5th ed., Vol. 1, pp. 353–393). Hoboken, NJ: Wiley.

Hogg, M. A., & Abrams, D. (2003). Intergroup behavior and social identity. In M. A. Hogg & J. Cooper (Eds.), *The Sage handbook of social psychology*. Thousand Oaks, CA: Sage.

Høglend, P., Bøgwald, K.-P., Amlo, S., Marble, A., Ulberg, R., Sjaastad, M. C., et al. (2008). Transference interpretations in dynamic psychotherapy: Do they really yield sustained effects? *American Journal of Psychiatry, 165,* 763–771.

Hoigaard, R., & Ingvaldsen, R. P. (2006). Social loafing in interactive groups: The effects of identifiability on effort and individual performance in floorball. *Athletic Insight: Online Journal of Sport Psychology, 8*(2).

Hoigaard, R., Säfvenbom, R., & Tonnessen, F. E. (2006). The relationship between group cohesion, group norms, and perceived social loafing in soccer teams. *Small Group Research, 37,* 217–232.

Holahan, C., & Sears, R. (1995). *The gifted group in later maturity*. Stanford, CA: Stanford University Press.

Holahan, C. J., & Moos, R. H. (1994). Life stressors and mental health: Advances in conceptualizing stress resistance. In W. R. Avison & I. H. Gotlib (Eds.), *Stress and mental health: Contemporary issues and prospects for the future*. New York, NY: Plenum.

Holahan, C. J., Moos, R. H., Holahan, C. K., Brennan, P. L., & Schutte, K. K. (2005). Stress generation, avoidance coping, and depressive symptoms: A 10-year model. *Journal of Consulting and Clinical Psychology, 73*(4), 658–666. doi:10.1037/0022-006X.73.4.658

Holden, C. (1986, October). The rational optimist. *Psychology Today,* pp. 55–60.

Holden, C. (2004). FDA weighs suicide risk in children on antidepressants. *Science, 303,* 745.

Hollander, E. & Simeon, D. (2008). Anxiety disorders. In R. E. Hales, S. C. Yudofsky, & G. O. Gabbard (Eds.), *The American Psychiatric Publishing textbook of psychiatry*. Washington, DC: American Psychiatric Publishing.

Hollands, C. (1989). Trivial and questionable research on animals. In G. Langley (Ed.), *Animal experimentation: The consensus changes*. New York, NY: Chapman & Hall.

Hollingworth, L. S. (1914). *Functional periodicity: An experimental study of the mental and motor abilities of women during menstruation*. New York, NY: Teachers College, Columbia University.

Hollingworth, L. S. (1916). Sex differences in mental tests. *Psychological Bulletin, 13,* 377–383.

Hollis, K. L. (1997). Contemporary research on Pavlovian conditioning: A "new" functional analysis. *American Psychologist, 52,* 956–965.

Hollon, S. D., & DiGiuseppe, R. (2011). Cognitive theories of psychotherapy. In J. C. Norcross, G. R. Vandenbos, & D. K. Freedheim (Eds.), *History of psychotherapy: Continuity and change* (2nd ed.). Washington, DC: American Psychological Association.

Hollon, S. D., & Dimidjian, S. (2009). Cognitive and behavioral treatment of depression. In I. H. Gotlib & C. L. Hammen (Eds.), *Handbook of depression* (pp. 586–603). New York, NY: Guilford Press.

Hollon, S. D., Stewart, M. O., & Strunk, D. (2006). Enduring effects for cognitive behavior therapy in the treatment of depression and anxiety. *Annual Review of Psychology, 57,* 285–315.

Holmes, D. (1995). The evidence for repression: An examination of sixty years of research. In J. Singer (Ed.), *Repression and dissociation: Implications for personality, theory, psychopathology, and health* (pp. 85–102). Chicago: University of Chicago Press.

Holmes, D. S. (1987). The influence of meditation versus rest on physiological arousal: A second examination. In M. A. West (Ed.), *The psychology of meditation*. Oxford: Clarendon Press.

Holmes, T. H., & Rahe, R. H. (1967). The Social Readjustment Rating Scale. *Journal of Psychosomatic Research, 11,* 213–218.

Holt-Lunstad, J., Smith, T. B., & Layton, J. B. (2010). Social relationships and mortality risk: A meta-analytic review. *PLoS Medicine, 7*(7), 1–20.

Holtgraves, T. (2004). Social desirability and self-reports: Testing models of socially desirable responding. *Personality and Social Psychology Bulletin, 30,* 161–172.

Holyoak, K. J. (1995). Problem solving. In E. E. Smith & D. N. Osherson (Eds.), *Thinking* (2nd ed.). Cambridge, MA: MIT Press.

Holyoak, K. J. (2005). Analogy. In K. J. Holyoak & R. G. Morrison (Eds.), *The Cambridge handbook of thinking and reasoning*. New York, NY: Cambridge University Press.

Homburg, A. & Stolberg, A. (2006). Explaining pro-environmental behavior with a cognitive theory of stress. *Journal of Environmental Psychology, 26,* 1–14.

Hong, G. K., Garcia, M., & Soriano, M. (2000). Responding to the challenge: Preparing mental health professionals for the new millennium. In I. Cuellar & F. A. Paniagua (Eds.), *Handbook of multicultural mental health: Assessment and treatment of diverse populations*. San Diego: Academic Press.

Honig, W. K., & Alsop, B. (1992). Operant behavior. In L. R. Squire (Ed.), *Encyclopedia of learning and memory*. New York, NY: Macmillan.

Hoobler, J. M., & Brass, D. J. (2006). Abusive supervision and family undermining as displaced aggression. *Journal of Applied Psychology, 91*(5), 1125–1133. doi:10.1037/0021-9010.91.5.1125

Hooley, J. M. (2004). Do psychiatric patients do better clinically if they live with certain kinds of families? *Current Directions in Psychological Science, 13*(5), 202–205.

Hooley, J. M. (2007). Expressed emotion and relapse of psychopathology. *Annual Review of Clinical Psychology, 3,* 329–352.

Hooley, J. M. (2009). Schizophrenia: Interpersonal functioning. In P. H. Blaney & T. Millon (Eds.), *Oxford textbook of psychopathology* (2nd ed., pp. 333–360). New York, NY: Oxford University Press.

Hooper, J., & Teresi, D. (1986). *The 3-pound universe—The brain*. New York, NY: Laurel.

Hopkins, W. D., & Cantalupo, C. (2008). Theoretical speculations on the evolutionary origins of hemispheric specialization. *Current Directions in Psychological Science, 17*(3), 233–237. doi:10.1111/j.1467-8721.2008.00581.x

Hopko, D. R., Crittendon, J. A., Grant, E., & Wilson, S. A. (2005). The impact of anxiety on performance IQ. *Anxiety, Stress, & Coping: An International Journal, 18*(1), 17–35.

Hopper, K., Harrison, G., Janca, A., & Satorius, N. (2007). *Recovery from schizophrenia: An international perspective—A report from the WHO Collaborative Project, the international study of schizophrenia*. New York, NY: Oxford University Press.

Horn, J., Nelson, C. E., & Brannick, M. T. (2004). Integrity, conscientiousness, and honesty. *Psychological Reports, 95*(1), 27–38.

Horn, J. L. (1985). Remodeling old models of intelligence. In B. B. Wolman (Ed.), *Handbook of intelligence*. New York, NY: Wiley.

Horn, J. L. (2002). Selections of evidence, misleading assumptions, and oversimplifications: The political message of *The Bell Curve*. In J. M. Fish (Ed.), *Race and intelligence: Separating science from myth* (pp. 297–326). Mahwah, NJ: Erlbaum.

Horn, J. L., & Hofer, S. M. (1992). Major abilities and development in the adult period. In R. J. Sternberg & C. A. Berg (Eds.), *Intellectual development*. Cambridge: Cambridge University Press.

Hornstein, G. A. (1992). The return of the repressed: Psychology's problematic relations with psychoanalysis, 1909–1960. *American Psychologist, 47,* 254–263.

Horowitz, F. D. (1992). John B. Watson's legacy: Learning and environment. *Developmental Psychology, 28,* 360–367.

Horrey, W. J., & Wickens, C. D. (2006). Examining the impact of cell phone on driving using meta-analytic techniques. *Human Factors, 48,* 196–205.

Horton, D. (2004). Green distinctions: The performance of identity among environmental activists. *Sociological Review, 52*(S1), 63–77.

Horwitz, W. A. (2000). Environmental dilemmas: The resolutions of student activists. *Ethics and Behavior, 10*(3), 281–308.

Hoshino, N., & Kroll, J. F. (2008). Cognate effects in picture naming: Does cross-language activation survive a change of script? *Cognition, 106*(1), 501–511. doi:10.1016/j.cognition.2007.02.001

Houben, K., & Wiers, R. W. (2008). Implicitly positive about alcohol? Implicit positive associations predict drinking behavior. *Addictive Behaviors, 33*(8), 979–986. doi:10.1016/j.addbeh.2008.03.002

Houlihan, J., Kropp, T., Wiles, R., Gray, S., & Campbell, C. (2005). *Body burden: The pollution in newborns*. Washington, DC: Environmental Working Group.

Howard, A., Pion, G. M., Gottfredson, G. D., Flattau, P. E., Oskamp, S., Pfafflin, S. M., Bray, D. W., & Burstein, A. G. (1986). The changing face of American psychology: A report from the committee on employment and human resources. *American Psychologist, 41,* 1311–1327.

Howe, M. J. A. (1999). *The psychology of high abilities*. New York, NY: New York University Press.

Howes, O. D., & Kapur, S. (2009). The dopamine hypothesis of schizophrenia: Version III—The final common pathway. *Schizophrenia Bulletin, 35*(3), 549–562. doi:10.1093/schbul/sbp006

Hoyer, W. J., & Verhaeghen, P. (2006). Memory aging. In J. E. Birren & K. W. Schaie (Eds.), *Handbook of the psychology of aging*. San Diego: Academic Press.

Hrdy, S. B. (1997). Raising Darwin's consciousness: Female sexuality and the prehominid origins of patriarchy. *Human Nature: An Interdisciplinary Biosocial Perspective, 8,* 1–49.

Hsu, L. K. G. (1990). *Eating disorders*. New York, NY: Guilford Press.

Hsu, L. M. (1995). Regression toward the mean associated with measurement error and identification of improvement and deterioration in psychotherapy. *Journal of Consulting & Clinical Psychology, 63,* 141–144.

Hu, Y., Zhang, R., & Li, W. (2005). Relationships among jealousy, self-esteem and self-efficacy. *Chinese Journal of Clinical Psychology, 13,* 165–166, 172.

Hua, J. Y., & Smith, S. J. (2004). Neural activity and the dynamics of central nervous system development. *Nature Neuroscience, 7,* 327–332.

Huang, J., Lee, T., & Lu, M. (2007). Prenatal programming of childhood overweight and obesity. *Maternal & Child Health Journal, 11*(5), 461–473.

Hubel, D. H., & Wiesel, T. N. (1962). Receptive fields, binocular interaction and functional architecture in the cat's visual cortex. *Journal of Physiology, 160,* 106–154.

Hubel, D. H., & Wiesel, T. N. (1963). Receptive fields of cells in striate cortex of very young visually inexperienced kittens. *Journal of Neurophysiology, 26,* 994–1002.

Hubel, D. H., & Wiesel, T. N. (1979). Brain mechanisms of vision. In Scientific American (Eds.), *The brain*. San Francisco, CA: W. H. Freeman.

Hubel, D. H., & Wiesel, T. N. (1998). Early exploration of the visual cortex. *Neuron, 20,* 401–412.

Hubel, D. H., & Wiesel, T. N. (2005). *Brain and visual perception: The story of a 25-year collaboration*. New York, NY: Oxford.

Huber, R., & Tononi, G. (2009). Sleep and waking across the lifespan. In G. G. Berntson & J. T. Cacioppo (Eds.), *Handbook of neuroscience for the behavioral sciences* (Vol. 1, pp. 461–481). New York, NY: Wiley.

Hublin, C. G. M., & Partinen, M. M. (2002). The extent and impact of insomnia as a public health problem. *Journal of Clinical Psychiatry, 4*(suppl 1), 8–12.

Hudson, J. I., Hiripi, E., Pope Jr., Harrison, G., & Kessler, R. C. (2007). The prevalence and correlates of eating disorders in the national comorbidity survey replication. *Biological Psychiatry, 61,* 348–358.

Hudson, W. (1960). Pictorial depth perception in sub-cultural groups in Africa. *Journal of Social Psychology, 52,* 183–208.

Hudson, W. (1967). The study of the problem of pictorial perception among unacculturated groups. *International Journal of Psychology, 2,* 89–107.

Hudziak, J., & Waterman, G. S. (2005). Buspirone. In B. J. Sadock & V. A. Sadock (Eds.), *Kaplan and Sadock's comprehensive textbook of psychiatry* (pp. 2797–2801). Philadelphia, PA: Lippincott Williams & Wilkins.

Huesmann, L. R. (1986). Psychological processes promoting the relation between exposure to media violence and aggressive behavior by the viewer. *Journal of Social Issues, 42,* 125–139.

Huesmann, L. R., & Miller, L. S. (1994). Long-term effects of repeated exposure to media violence in childhood. In L. R. Huesmann (Ed.), *Aggressive behavior: Current perspectives*. New York, NY: Plenum Press.

Huesmann, L. R., Moise-Titus, J., Podolski, C. L., & Eron, L. D. (2003). Longitudinal relations between children's exposure to TV violence and their aggressive and violent behavior in young adulthood: 1977–1992. *Developmental Psychology, 39,* 201–221.

Huey, E. D., Krueger, F., & Grafman, J. (2006). Representations in the human prefrontal cortex. *Current Directions in Psychological Science, 15,* 167–171.

Huey, L. Y., Cole, S., Cole, R. F., Daniels, A. S. & Katzelnick, D. J. (2009). Health care reform. In B. J. Sadock, V. A. Sadock, & P. Ruiz (Eds.), *Kaplan & Sadock's comprehensive textbook of psychiatry* (pp. 4282–4298). Philadelphia, PA: Lippincott Williams & Wilkins.

Hugenberg, K., & Bodenhausen, G. V. (2003). Facing prejudice: Implicit prejudice and the perception of facial threat. *Psychological Science, 14*(6), 640–643. doi:10.1046/j.0956-7976.2003.psci_1478.x

Hugenberg, K., & Bodenhausen, G. V. (2004). Ambiguity in social categorization: The role of prejudice and facial affect in race categorization. *Psychological Science, 15*(5), 342–345. doi:10.1111/j.0956-7976.2004.00680.x

Hughes, J., Smith, T. W., Kosterlitz, H. W., Fothergill, L. A., Morgan, B. A., & Morris, H. R. (1975). Identification of two related pentapeptides from the brain with the potent opiate agonist activity. *Nature, 258,* 577–579.

Huijding, J., de Jong, P. J., Wiers, R. W., & Verkooijen, K. (2005). Implicit and explicit attitudes toward smoking in a smoking and a nonsmoking setting. *Addictive Behaviors, 30*(5), 949–961. doi:10.1016/j.addbeh.2004.09.014

Hull, C. L. (1943). *Principles of behavior*. New York, NY: Appleton.

Hunsley, J., Lee, C. M., & Wood, J. M. (2003). Controversial and questionable assessment techniques. In S. O. Lilienfield, S. J. Lynn, & J. M. Lohr (Eds.), *Science and pseudoscience in clinical psychology*. New York, NY: Guilford Press.

Hunt, E. (1994). Problem solving. In R. J. Sternberg (Ed.), *Thinking and problem solving*. San Diego: Academic Press.

Hunt, E. (2001). Multiple views of multiple intelligence [Review of the book *Intelligence reframed: Multiple intelligences for the 21st century*]. *Contemporary Psychology, 46,* 5–7.

Hunt, E., & Carlson, J. (2007). Considerations relating to the study of group differences in intelligence. *Perspectives on Psychological Science, 2*(2), 194–213. doi:10.1111/j.1745-6916.2007.00037.x

Hunt, H. (1989). *The multiplicity of dreams: Memory, imagination and consciousness*. New Haven: Yale University Press.

Hunt, J. M., Smith, M. F., & Kernan, J. B. (1985). The effects of expectancy disconfirmation and argument strength on message processing level: An application to personal selling. In E. C. Hirschman & M. B. Holbrook (Eds.), *Advances in consumer research* (Vol. 12). Provo, UT: Association for Consumer Research.

Hunt, S. P., & Mantyh, P. W. (2001). The molecular dynamics of pain control. *Nature Reviews Neuroscience, 2,* 83–91.

Hurlemann, R., Patin, A., Onur, O. A., Cohen, M. X., Baumgartner, T., Metzler, S., et al. (2010). Oxytocin enhances amygdala-dependent, socially reinforced learning and emotional empathy in humans. *Journal of Neuroscience, 30*(14), 4999–5007. doi:10.1523/JNEUROSCI.5538-09.2010

Hurvich, L. M. (1981). *Color vision*. Sunderland, MA: Sinnauer Associates.

Hustinx, P. J., Kuyper, H., van der Werf, M. C., & Dijkstra, P. (2009). Achievement motivation revisited: New longitudinal data to demonstrate its predictive power. *Educational Psychology, 29*(5), 561–582. doi:10.1080/01443410903132128

Huston, A. C., Donnerstein, E., Fairchild, H., Feshbach, N. D., Katz, P. A., & Murray, J. P. (1992). *Big world, small screen: The role of television in American society*. Lincoln: University of Nebraska Press.

Hutchinson, A. (2007, February). Watering holes: Las Vegas tries to prevent a water shortage. *Popular Mechanics*, p. 20.

Huttenlocher, P. R. (1994). Synaptogenesis in human cerebral cortex. In G. Dawson & K. W. Fischer (Eds.), *Human behavior and the developing brain*. New York, NY: Guilford Press.

Huttenlocher, P. R. (2002). *Neural plasticity: The effects of environment on the development of the cerebral cortex*. Cambridge, MA: Harvard University Press.

Hwang, W. C. (2006). The psychotherapy adaptation and modification framework: Application to Asian Americans. *American Psychologist, 61,* 702–715.

Hyde, J. S. (2005a). The gender similarities hypothesis. *American Psychologist, 60,* 581–892.

Hyde, J. S. (2005b). The genetics of sexual orientation. In J. S. Hyde (Ed.), *Biological substrates of human sexuality* (pp. 9–20). Washington, DC: American Psychological Association.

Hyde, J. S. (2007). New directions in the study of gender similarities and differences. *Current Directions in Psychological Science, 16*(5), 259–263. doi:10.1111/j.1467-8721.2007.00516.x

Hyde, J. S., & Mertz, J. E. (2009). Gender, culture, and mathematics performance. *Proceedings of the National Academy of Sciences of the United States of America, 106*(22), 8801–8807. doi:10.1073/pnas.0901265106

Hyman, I. E., Jr., Husband, T. H., & Billings, J. F. (1995). False memories of childhood experiences. *Applied Cognitive Psychology, 9,* 181–197.

Hyman, I. E., Jr., & Kleinknecht, E. E. (1999). False childhood memories: Research, theory, and applications. In L. M. Williams, & V. L. Banyard (Eds.), *Trauma & memory*. Thousand Oaks, CA: Sage.

Iacoboni, M. (2007). Face to face: The neural basis of social mirroring and empathy. *Psychiatric Annals, 37*(4), 236–241.

Iacoboni, M. (2009). Imitation, empathy, and mirror neurons. *Annual Review of Psychology, 60,* 653–670. doi:10.1146/annurev.psych.60.110707.163604

Iacoboni, M., & Dapretto, M. (2006). The mirror neuron system and the consequences of its dysfunction. *Nature Reviews Neuroscience, 7,* 942–951.

Iams, J. D., & Romero, R. (2007). Preterm birth. In S. G. Gabbe, J. R. Niebyl, & J. L. Simpson (Eds.), *Obstetrics: Normal and problem pregnancies* (5th ed., pp. 668–712). Philadelphia, PA: Elsevier.

Ickovics, J. R., Thayaparan, B., & Ethier, K. A. (2001). Women and AIDS: A contextual analysis. In A. Baum, T. A. Revenson, & J. E. Singer (Eds.), *Handbook of health psychology* (pp. 817–840). Mahwah, NJ: Erlbaum.

Idisis, Y., Ben-David, S., & Ben-Nachum, E. (2007). Attribution of blame to rape victims among therapists and non-therapists. *Behavioral Sciences & the Law, 25*(1), 103–120.

Inagaki, K., & Hatano, G. (2004). Vitalistic causality in young children's naive biology. *Trends in Cognitive Sciences, 8,* 356–362.

Infante, J. R., Torres-Avisbal, M., Pinel, P., Vallejo, J. A., Peran, F., Gonzalez, F., Contreras, P., Pacheco, C., Roldan, A., & Latre, J. M. (2001). Catecholamine levels in practitioners of the transcendental meditation technique. *Physiology & Behavior, 72*(1–2), 141–146.

Ingram, R. E., Scott, W. D., & Hamill, S. (2009). Depression: Social and cognitive aspects. In P. H. Blaney & T. Millon (Eds.), *Oxford textbook of psychopathology* (2nd ed., pp. 230–252). New York, NY: Oxford University Press.

Innocenti, G. M. (1994). Some new trends in the study of the corpus callosum. *Behavioral and Brain Research, 64,* 1–8.

Insel, T. R. (2010). Psychiatrists' relationships with pharmaceutical companies: Part of the problem or part of the solution? *Journal of the American Medical Association, 303*(12), 1192–1193. doi:10.1001/jama.2010.317

Intergovernmental Panel on Climate Change. (2007). *Climate Change 2007: Synthesis Report.* Retrieved from http://www.ipcc.ch/pdf/assessment-report/ar4/syr/ar4_syr.pdf

International Ergonomics Association. (2000). What is human factors/ergonomics? *Human Factors and Ergonomics Society.* Retrieved from http://www.hfes.org/web/AboutHFES/about.html

Inzlicht, M., & Kang, S. K. (2010). Stereotype threat spillover: How coping with threats to social identity affects aggression, eating, decision making, and attention. *Journal of Personality and Social Psychology, 99*(3), 467–481. doi:10.1037/a0018951

Iredale, S. K., Nevill, C. H., & Lutz, C. K. (2010). The influence of observer presence on baboon (*Papio spp.*) and rhesus macaque (*Macaca mulatta*) behavior. *Applied Animal Behaviour Science, 122*(1), 53–57. doi:10.1016/j.applanim.2009.11.002.

Irvine, S. H., & Berry, J. W. (1988). *Human abilities in cultural context.* New York, NY: Cambridge University Press.

Isaacowitz, D. M., & Seligman, M. E. P. (2007). Learned helplessness. In G. Fink (Ed.), *Encyclopedia of stress.* San Diego: Elsevier.

Isacsson, G. G., Holmgren, A. A., Ösby, U. U., & Ahlner, J. J. (2009). Decrease in suicide among the individuals treated with antidepressants: A controlled study of antidepressants in suicide, Sweden 1995–2005. *Acta Psychiatrica Scandinavica, 120*(1), 37–44. doi:10.1111/j.1600-0447.2009.01344.x

Isometsa, E. T., Heikkinen, M. E., Marttunen, M. J., Henriksson, M. M., Aro, H. M., & Lonnqvist, J. K. (1995). The last appointment before suicide: Is suicide intent communicated? *American Journal of Psychiatry, 152,* 919–922.

Iwawaki, S., & Vernon, P. E. (1988). Japanese abilities and achievements. In S. H. Irvine & J. W. Berry (Eds.), *Human abilities in cultural context.* New York, NY: Cambridge University Press.

Izard, C. E. (1984). Emotion-cognition relationships and human development. In C. E. Izard, J. Kagan, & R. B. Zajonc (Eds.), *Emotions, cognition and behavior.* Cambridge, England: Cambridge University Press.

Izard, C. E. (1990). Facial expressions and the regulation of emotions. *Journal of Personality and Social Psychology, 58,* 487–498.

Izard, C. E. (1991). *The psychology of emotions.* New York, NY: Plenum.

Izard, C. E. (1994). Innate and universal facial expressions: Evidence from developmental and cross-cultural research. *Psychological Bulletin, 115,* 288–299.

Izard, C. E. (2007). Basic emotions, natural kinds, emotion schemas, and a new paradigm. *Perspectives on Psychological Science, 2,* 260–280.

Izard, C. E., & Saxton, P. M. (1988). Emotions. In R. C. Atkinson, R. J. Herrnstein, G. Lindzey, & R. D. Luce (Eds.), *Stevens' handbook of experimental psychology* (Vol. 1). New York, NY: Wiley.

Jablensky, A. (2009). Course and outcome of schizophrenia and their prediction. In M. C. Gelder, N. C. Andreasen, J. J. López-Ibor, Jr., & J. R. Geddes (Eds.). *New Oxford textbook of psychiatry* (2nd ed., Vol. 1). New York, NY: Oxford University Press.

Jablin, F. M. (1982). Organizational communication: An assimilation approach. In M. E. Rolff & C. R. Berger (Eds.), *Social cognition and communication* (pp. 255–286). Beverly Hills, CA: Sage.

Jackicic, J., & Gallagher, K. I. (2002). Physical activity considerations for management of body weight. In D. H. Bessesen & R. Kushner (2002), *Evaluation and management of obesity.* Philadelphia, PA: Hanley & Belfus.

Jacob, R. G., & Pelham, W. (2000). Behavior therapy. In B. J. Sadock & V. A. Sadock (Eds.), *Kaplan and Sadock's comprehensive textbook of psychiatry* (7th ed., Vol. 1, pp. 2080–2127). Philadelphia, PA: Lippincott/Williams & Wilkins.

Jacob, R. G., & Pelham, W. (2005). Behavior therapy. In B. J. Sadock & V. A. Sadock (Eds.), *Kaplan and Sadock's comprehensive textbook of psychiatry* (pp. 2498–2547). Philadelphia, PA: Lippincott Williams & Wilkins.

Jacobs, B. L. (2004). Depression: The brain finally gets into the act. *Current Directions in Psychological Science, 13*(3), 103–106.

Jacobs, D. F. (2004). Youth gambling in North America: Long-term trends and future prospects. In J. L. Derevensky & R. Grupta (Eds.), *Gambling problems in youth: Theoretical and applied perspectives* (pp. 1–24). New York, NY: Kluwer/Plenum.

Jacobson, E. (1938). *Progressive relaxation.* Chicago: University of Chicago Press.

Jacoby, L. L., Hessels, S., & Bopp, K. (2001). Proactive and retroactive effects in memory performance: Dissociating recollection and accessibility bias. In H. L. Roediger, J. S. Nairne, I. Neath, & A. M. Surprenant (Eds.), *The nature of remembering: Essays in honor of Robert G. Crowder* (pp. 35–54). Washington, DC: American Psychological Association.

Jacques, P. J., Dunlap, R. E., & Freeman, M. (2008). The organization of denial: Conservative think tanks and environmental skepticism. *Environmental Politics, 17,* 349–385.

Jaffe, H. W., Valdiserri, R. O., & De Cock, K. M. (2007). The reemerging HIV/AIDS epidemic in men who have sex with men. *Journal of the American Medical Association, 298,* 2412–2414.

James, W. (1884). What is emotion? *Mind, 19,* 188–205.

James, W. (1890). *The principles of psychology.* New York, NY: Holt.

James, W. H. (2005). Biological and psychosocial determinants of male and female human sexual orientation. *Journal of Biosocial Science, 37,* 555–567.

Janicak, P. G., Nahas, Z., Lisanby, S. H., Solvason, H., Sampson, S. M., McDonald, W. M., et al. (2010). Durability of clinical benefit with transcranial magnetic stimulation (TMS) in the treatment of pharmacoresistant major depression: Assessment of relapse during a 6-month, multisite, open-label study. *Brain Stimulation, 3*(4), 187–199.

Janig, W. (2003). The autonomic nervous system and its coordination by the brain. In R. J. Davidson, K. R. Scherer, & H. H. Goldsmith (Eds.), *Handbook of affective sciences.* New York, NY: Oxford University Press.

Janis, I. L. (1958). *Psychological stress.* New York, NY: Wiley.

Janis, I. L. (1972). *Victims of groupthink.* Boston, MA: Houghton Mifflin.

Janis, I. L. (1993). Decision making under stress. In L. Goldberger & S. Breznitz (Eds.), *Handbook of stress: Theoretical and clinical aspects* (2nd ed.). New York, NY: Free Press.

Janis, I. L., & Mann, L. (1977). *Decision making: A psychological analysis of conflict, choice, and commitment.* New York, NY: Free Press.

Janofsky, J. S., Dunn, M. H., Roskes, E. J., Briskin, J. K., & Rudolph, M. S. L. (1996). Insanity defense pleas in Baltimore city: An analysis of outcome. *American Journal of Psychiatry, 153,* 1464–1468.

Janssen, L., Fennis, B. M., & Pruyn, A. H. (2010). Forewarned is forearmed: Conserving self-control strength to resist social influence. *Journal of Experimental Social Psychology, 46*(6), 911–921. doi:10.1016/j.jesp.2010.06.008

Javitt, D. C., & Laruelle, M. (2006). Neurochemical theories. In J. A. Lieberman, T. S. Stroup, & D. O. Perkins (Eds.), *Textbook of schizophrenia* (pp. 85–116). Washington, DC: American Psychiatric Publishing.

Jefferson, J. W., & Greist, J. H. (2009). Lithium. In B. J. Sadock, V. A. Sadock, & P. Ruiz (Eds.), *Kaplan & Sadock's comprehensive textbook of psychiatry* (pp. 3132–3144). Philadelphia, PA: Lippincott, Williams & Wilkins.

Jensen-Campbell, L. A., & Graziano, W. G. (2001). Agreeableness as a moderator of interpersonal conflict. *Journal of Personality, 69,* 323–362.

Jensen, A. R. (1969). How much can we boost IQ and scholastic achievement? *Harvard Educational Review, 39,* 1–23.

Jensen, A. R. (1980). *Bias in mental testing.* New York, NY: Free Press.

Jensen, A. R. (1998). *The g factor: The science of mental ability.* Westport, CT: Praeger.

Jensen, E. (2000). *Brain-based learning.* San Diego: Brain Store.

Jensen, E. (2006). *Enriching the brain.* San Francisco, CA: Jossey-Bass.

Jensen, M. P., & Patterson, D. R. (2008). Hypnosis in the relief of pain and pain disorders. In M. R. Nash & A. J. Barnier (Eds.). *The Oxford handbook of hypnosis: Theory, research and practice* (pp. 503–534). New York, NY: Oxford University Press.

Jessberger, S., Aimone, J. B., & Gage, F. H. (2009). Neurogenesis. In J. H. Byrne (Ed.), *Concise learning and memory: The editor's selection.* San Diego, CA: Elsevier.

Jessell, T. M., & Kelly, D. D. (1991). Pain and analgesia. In E. R. Kandel, J. H. Schwartz, & T. M. Jessell (Eds.), *Principles of neural science* (3rd ed.). New York, NY: Elsevier.

Jessup, R. K., Veinott, E. S., Todd, P. M., & Busemeyer, J. R. (2009). Leaving the store empty-handed: Testing explanations for the too-much-choice effect using decision field theory. *Psychology & Marketing, 26*(3), 299–320. doi:10.1002/mar.20274

Jick, H., Kaye, J. A., & Jick, S. S. (2004). Antidepressants and the risk of suicidal behaviors. *Journal of the American Medical Association, 292,* 338–343.

Joffe, R. T. (2009). Neuropsychiatric aspects of multiple sclerosis and other demyelinating disorders. In B. J. Sadock, V. A. Sadock, & P. Ruiz (Eds.), *Kaplan & Sadock's comprehensive textbook of psychiatry* (9th ed., Vol. 1, pp. 248–272). Philadelphia, PA: Lippincott, Williams & Wilkins.

John, O. P., & Gross, J. J. (2007). Individual differences in emotion regulation. In J. J. Gross (Ed.), *Handbook of emotion regulation*. New York, NY: Guilford Press.

John, P. O., Naumann, L. P., & Soto, C. J. (2008). Paradigm shift to the integrative Big Five trait taxonomy: History, measurement, and conceptual issues. In O. P. John, R. W. Robbins, & L. A. Pervin (Eds.), *Handbook of personality: Theory and research* (Vol. 3, pp. 114–158). New York, NY: Guilford Press.

Johnson, A. (2003). Procedural memory and skill acquisition. In A. F. Healy & R. W. Proctor (Eds.), *Handbook of psychology, Vol. 4: Experimental psychology*. New York, NY: Wiley.

Johnson, B. A., & Ait-Daoud, N. (2005). Alcohol: Clinical aspects. In J. H. Lowinson, P. Ruiz, R. B. Millman, & J. G. Langrod (Eds.), *Substance abuse: A comprehensive textbook*. Philadelphia, PA: Lippincott/Williams & Wilkins.

Johnson, B. T., Maio, G. R., & Smith-McLallen, A. (2005). Communication and attitude change: Causes, processes, and effects. In D. Albarracin, B. T. Johnson, & M. P. Zanna (Eds.), *The handbook of attitudes*. Mahwah, NJ: Erlbaum.

Johnson, C., & Mullen, B. (1994). Evidence for the accessibility of paired distinctiveness in distinctiveness-based illusory correlation in stereotyping. *Personality and Social Psychology Bulletin, 20,* 65–70.

Johnson, D. (1990). Animal rights and human lives: Time for scientists to right the balance. *Psychological Science, 1,* 213–214.

Johnson, E. O., & Breslau, N. (2006). Is the association of smoking and depression a recent phenomenon? *Nicotine & Tobacco Research, 8,* 257–262.

Johnson, M. E., & Dowling-Guyer, S. (1996). Effects of inclusive vs. exclusive language on evaluations of the counselor. *Sex Roles, 34,* 407–418.

Johnson, M. K. (1996). Fact, fantasy, and public policy. In D. J. Herrmann, C. McEvoy, C. Hertzog, P. Hertel, & M. K. Johnson (Eds.), *Basic and applied memory research: Theory in context* (Vol. 1). Mahwah, NJ: Erlbaum.

Johnson, M. K. (2006). Memory and reality. *American Psychologist, 61,* 760–771.

Johnson, M. K., Kahan, T. L., & Raye, C. L. (1984). Dreams and reality monitoring. *Journal of Experimental Psychology: General, 113,* 329–344.

Johnson, S. B., & Carlson, D. N. (2004). Medical regimen adherence: Concepts assessment, and interventions. In J. M. Raczynski & L. C. Leviton (Eds.), *Handbook of clinical health psychology: Vol 2. Disorders of behavior and health*. Washington, DC: American Psychological Association.

Johnson, S. C., Dweck, C. S., & Chen, F. S. (2007). Evidence for infants' internal working models of attachment. *Psychological Science, 18*(6), 501–502. doi:10.1111/j.1467-9280.2007.01929.x

Johnson, S. L., Joormann, J., LeMoult, & Miller, C. (2009). Mood disorders: Biological bases. In P. H. Blaney & T. Millon (Eds.), *Oxford textbook of psychopathology* (2nd ed., pp. 198–229). New York, NY: Oxford University Press.

Johnson, W. (2010). Understanding the genetics of intelligence: Can height help? Can corn oil? *Current Directions in Psychological Science, 19*(3), 177–182. doi:10.1177/0963721410370136

Johnson, W., & Krueger, R. F. (2006). How money buys happiness: Genetic and environmental processes linking finances and life satisfaction. *Journal of Personality and Social Psychology, 90,* 680–691.

Johnson, W., Turkheimer, E., Gottesman, I. I., & Bouchard, T. R. (2009). Beyond heritability: Twin studies in behavioral research. *Current Directions in Psychological Science, 18*(4), 217–220. doi:10.1111/j.1467-8721.2009.01639.x

Johnston, J. C., & McClelland, J. L. (1974). Perception of letters in words: Seek not and ye shall find. *Science, 184,* 1192–1194.

Joiner, T. E., Jr., & Timmons, K. A. (2009). Depression in its interpersonal context. In I. H. Gotlib & C. L. Hammen (Eds.), *Handbook of Depression* (2nd ed., pp. 322–339). New York, NY: Guilford Press.

Joiner, T. E., Jr., Van Orden, K. A., Witte, T. K., & Rudd, M. D. (2009). *The interpersonal theory of suicide: Guidance for working with suicidal clients*. Washington: DC: American Psychological Association.

Joinson, A. N., & Paine, C. B. (2007). Self-disclosure, privacy and the Internet. In A. N. Joinson, K. Y. A. McKenna, T. Postmes, & U.-D. Reips (Eds.), *The Oxford handbook of Internet psychology*. New York, NY: Oxford University Press.

Joireman, J. A. (2005). Environmental problems as social dilemmas: The temporal dimension. In S. Strathman & J. Joireman (Eds.), *Understanding behavior in the context of time: Theory, research, and application* (pp. 289–304). Mahwah, NJ: Erlbaum.

Joireman, J. A., Van Lange, P. A., & Van Vugt, M. (2004). Who cares about the environmental impact of cars? Those with an eye toward the future. *Environment and Behavior, 36,* 187–206.

Jones, E. E., & Davis, K. E. (1965). From acts to dispositions: The attribution process in person perception. In L. Berkowitz (Ed.), *Advances in experimental social psychology* (Vol. 2). New York, NY: Academic Press.

Jones, E. E., & Nisbett, R. E. (1971). The actor and the observer: Divergent perceptions of the causes of behavior. In E. E. Jones, D. E. Kanouse, H. H. Kelley, R. E. Nisbett, S. Valins, & B. Weiner (Eds.), *Attribution: Perceiving the causes of behavior*. Morristown, NJ: General Learning Press.

Jones, F., & Bright, J. (2007). Stress: Health and illness. In A. Monat, R. S. Lazarus, & G. Reevy (Eds.), *The Praeger handbook on stress and coping*. Westport, CT: Praeger.

Jones, G. V. (1990). Misremembering a common object: When left is not right. *Memory & Cognition, 18*(2), 174–182.

Jones, L. V. (2000). Thurstone, L. L. In A. E. Kazdin (Ed.), *Encyclopedia of psychology* (pp. 83–84). Washington, DC: American Psychological Association.

Jordan, M., & Marshall, H. (2010). Taking counseling and psychotherapy outside: Destruction or enrichment of the therapeutic frame? *European Journal of Psychotherapy & Counseling, 12*(4), 345–359.

Jordan-Young, R. M. (2010). *Brainstorm: The flaws in the science of sex differences*. Cambridge, MA: Harvard University Press.

Jorgensen, R. S., Johnson, B. T., Kolodziej, M. E., & Schreer, G. E. (1996). Elevated blood pressure and personality: A meta-analytic review. *Psychological Bulletin, 120,* 293–320.

Joska, J. A., & Stein, D. J. (2008). Mood disorders. In R. E. Hales, S. C. Yudofsky, & G. O. Gabbard (Eds.), *The American Psychiatric Publishing textbook of psychiatry* (5th ed., pp. 457–504). Washington, DC: American Psychiatric Publishing.

Josse, G., & Tzourio-Mazoyer, N. (2004). Hemispheric specialization for language. *Brain Research Reviews, 44,* 1–12.

Judge, T. A., & Cable, D. M. (2004). The effect of physical height on workplace success and income: Preliminary test of a theoretical model. *Journal of Applied Psychology, 89,* 428–441.

Judge, T. A., & Klinger, R. (2008). Job satisfaction: Subjective well-being at work. In M. Eid & R. J. Larsen (Eds.), *The science of subjective well-being* (pp. 393–413). New York, NY: Guilford Press.

Judge, T. A., Hurst, C., & Simon, L. S. (2009). Does it pay to be smart, attractive, or confident (or all three)? Relationships among general mental ability, physical attractiveness, core self-evaluations, and income. *Journal of Applied Psychology, 94*(3), 742–755. doi:10.1037/a0015497

Julien, R. M., Advokat, C. D., & Comaty, J. E. (2008). *A primer of drug action: A comprehensive guide to the actions, uses, and side effects of psychoactive drugs*. New York, NY: Worth.

Jung, C. G. (1917/1953). *On the psychology of the unconscious*. In H. Read, M. Fordham, & G. Adler (Eds.), *Collected works of C. G. Jung* (Vol. 7). Princeton, NJ: Princeton University Press.

Jung, C. G. (1921/1960). *Psychological types*. In H. Read, M. Fordham, & G. Adler (Eds.), *Collected works of C. G. Jung* (Vol. 6). Princeton, NJ: Princeton University Press.

Jung, C. G. (1933). *Modern man in search of a soul*. New York, NY: Harcourt, Brace & World.

Jung, R. E., & Haier, R. J. (2007). The Parieto-Frontal Integration Theory (P-FIT) of intelligence: Converging neuroimaging evidence. *Behavioral and Brain Sciences, 30*(2), 135–154. doi:10.1017/S0140525X07001185

Kaas, J. H. (2000). The reorganization of sensory and motor maps after injury in adult mammals. In M. S. Gazzaniga (Ed.), *The new cognitive neurosciences*. Cambridge, MA: The MIT Press.

Kabat-Zinn, J. (2003). Mindfulness-based stress reduction (MBSR). *Constructivism in the Human Sciences, 8,* 73–107.

Kagan, J. (1998, November/December). A parent's influence is peerless. *Harvard Education Letter*.

Kagan, J. (2004). New insights into temperament. *Cerebrum, 6*(1), 51–66.

Kagan, J. (2008). Behavioral inhibition as a risk factor for psychopathology. In T. P. Beauchaine & S. P. Hinshaw (Eds.), *Child and adolescent psychopathology* (pp. 157–179). Hoboken, NJ: Wiley.

Kagan, J. (2010). Emotions and temperament. In M. H. Bornstein (Ed.), *Handbook of cultural developmental science* (pp. 175–194). New York, NY: Psychology Press.

Kagan, J., & Fox, A. (2006). Biology, culture, and temperamental biases. In N. Eisenberg, W. Damon, & R. M. Lerner (Eds.), *Handbook of child psychology: Social, emotional, and personality development* (pp. 167–225). Hoboken, NJ: Wiley.

Kagan, J., & Snidman, N. (1991). Temperamental factors in human development. *American Psychologist, 46,* 856–862.

Kagan, J., Snidman, N., & Arcus, D. M. (1992). Initial reactions to unfamiliarity. *Current Directions in Psychological Science, 1*(6), 171–174.

Kahan, T. L. (2001). Consciousness in dreaming: A metacognitive approach. In K. Bulkeley (Ed.), *Dreams: A reader on religious, cultural, and psychological dimensions of dreaming* (pp. 333–360). New York, NY: Palgrave Macmillan.

Kahan, T. L., & Johnson, M. K. (1992). Self-effects in memory for person information. *Social Cognition, 10*(1), 30–50.

Kahan, T. L., & LaBerge, S. (1994). Lucid dreaming as metacognition: Implications for cognitive science. *Consciousness and Cognition, 3,* 246–264.

Kahan, T. L., & LaBerge, S. (1996). Cognition and metacognition in dreaming and waking: Comparisons of first- and third-person ratings. *Dreaming, 6,* 235–249.

Kahan, T., L. Mohsen, R., Tandez, J., & McDonald, J. (1999). Discriminating memories for actual and imagined taste experiences: A reality monitoring approach. *American Journal of Psychology, 112,* 97–112.

Kahane, H. (1992). *Logic and contemporary rhetoric: The use of reason in everyday life.* Belmont, CA: Wadsworth.

Kahn, D. (2007). Metacognition, recognition, and reflection while dreaming. In D. Barrett & P. McNamara (Eds.), *The new science of dreaming.* Westport, CT: Praeger.

Kahn, P. H., Jr. (2003). The development of environmental moral identity. In S. Clayton & S. Opotow (Eds.), *Identity and the natural environment: The psychological significance of nature* (pp. 113–134). Cambridge, MA: MIT Press.

Kahn, P. H., Jr. (2007). The child's environmental amnesia—it's ours. *Children, Youth and Environments, 17,* 199–207.

Kahn, P. H., Jr. (2011). *Technological nature: Adaptation and the future of human life.* Cambridge, MA: MIT Press.

Kahn, P. H., Jr., & Kellert, S. R. (2002). *Children and nature: Psychological, sociocultural, and evolutionary investigations.* Cambridge MA: MIT Press.

Kahneman, D. (1999). Objective happiness. In D. Kahneman, E. Diener, & N. Schwarz (Eds.), *Well-being: The foundations of hedonic psychology.* New York, NY: Russell Sage Foundation.

Kahneman, D. (2003). A perspective on judgment and choice: Mapping bounded rationality. *American Psychologist, 58,* 697–720.

Kahneman, D., & Deaton, A. (2010). High income improves evaluation of life but not emotional well-being. *Proceedings of the National Academy of Sciences of the United States of America, 107*(38), 16489–16493. doi:10.1073/pnas.1011492107

Kahneman, D., & Frederick, S. (2005). A model of heuristic judgment. In K. J. Holyoak & R. G. Morrison (Eds.), *The Cambridge handbook of thinking and reasoning.* New York, NY: Cambridge University Press.

Kahneman, D., Krueger, A. B., Schkade, D., Schwarz, N., & Stone, A. A. (2006). Would you be happier if you were richer? A focusing illusion. *Science, 312,* 1908–1910.

Kahneman, D., & Tversky, A. (1979). Prospect theory: An analysis of decision under risk. *Econometrica, 47,* 263–292.

Kahneman, D., & Tversky, A. (1982). Subjective probability: A judgment of representativeness. In D. Kahneman, P. Slovic, & A. Tversky (Eds.), *Judgment under uncertainty: Heuristics and biases.* Cambridge: Cambridge University Press.

Kahneman, D., & Tversky, A. (1984). Choices, values, and frames. *American Psychologist, 39,* 341–350.

Kahneman, D., & Tversky, A. (2000). *Choices, values, and frames.* New York, NY: Cambridge University Press.

Kaiser, A., Haller, S., Schmitz, S., & Nitsch, C. (2009). On sex/gender related similarities and differences in fMRI language research. *Brain Research Reviews, 61*(2), 49–59. doi:10.1016/j.brainresrev.2009.03.005

Kajantie, E. (2008). Physiological stress response, estrogen, and the male-female mortality gap. *Current Directions in Psychological Science, 17*(5), 348–352. doi:10.1111/j.1467-8721.2008.00604.x

Kajantie, E., & Phillips, D. W. (2006). The effects of sex and hormonal status on the physiological response to acute psychosocial stress. *Psychoneuroendocrinology, 31*(2), 151–178. doi:10.1016/j.psyneuen.2005.07.002

Kako, E. (1999). Elements of syntax in the systems of three language-trained animals. *Animal Learning and Behavior, 27,* 1–14.

Kales, J. D., Kales, A., Bixler, E. O., Soldatos, C. R., Cadieux, R. J., Kashurba, G. J., & Vela-Bueno, A. (1984). Biopsychobehavioral correlates of insomnia: V. Clinical characteristics and behavioral correlates. *American Journal of Psychiatry, 141,* 1371–1376.

Kalichman, S. C., Eaton, L., Cain, D., Cherry, C., Fuhrel, A., Kaufman, M., & Pope, H. (2007). Changes in HIV treatment beliefs and sexual risk behaviors among gay and bisexual men, 1997–2005. *Health Psychology, 26,* 650–656.

Kalivas, P. W., & Volkow, N. D. (2005). The neural basis of addiction: A pathology of motivation and choice. *American Journal of Psychiatry, 162,* 1403–1413.

Kalmijn, M. (1998). Intermarriage and homogamy: Causes, patterns, trends. *Annual Review of Sociology, 24,* 395–421.

Kals, E., & Ittner, H. (2003). Children's environmental identity: Indicators and behavioral impacts. In S. Clayton & S. Opotow (Eds.), *Identity and the natural environment: The psychological significance of nature* (pp. 135–157). Cambridge, MA: MIT Press.

Kamin, L. J. (1974). *The science and politics of IQ.* Hillsdale, NJ: Erlbaum.

Kanaya, T., Scullin, M. H., & Ceci, S. J. (2003). The Flynn effect and U.S. policies: The impact of rising IQ scores on American society via mental retardation diagnoses. *American Psychologist, 58*(10), 778–790.

Kanazawa, S. (2006). Mind the gap . . . in intelligence: Reexamining the relationship between inequality and health. *British Journal of Health Psychology, 11,* 623–642.

Kandel, E. R. (2000). Nerve cells and behavior. In E. R. Kandel, J. H. Schwartz, & T. M. Jessell (Eds.), *Principles of neural science* (pp. 19–35). New York, NY: McGraw-Hill.

Kandel, E. R. (2001). The molecular biology of memory storage: A dialogue between genes and synapses. *Science, 294,* 1030–1038.

Kandel, E. R., & Jessell, T. M. (1991). Touch. In E. R. Kandel, J. H. Schwartz, & T. M. Jessell (Eds.), *Principles of neural science* (3rd ed.). New York, NY: Elsevier Saunders.

Kandel, E. R., & Siegelbaum, S. A. (2000). Synaptic integration. In E. R. Kandel, J. H. Schwartz & T. M. Jessell (Eds.), *Principles of neural science* (pp. 207–228). New York, NY: McGraw-Hill.

Kandler, C., Bleidorn, W., Riemann, R., Spinath, F. M., Thiel, W., & Angleitner, A. (2010). Sources of cumulative continuity in personality: A longitudinal multiple-rater twin study. *Journal of Personality and Social Psychology, 98*(6), 995–1008. doi:10.1037/a0019558

Kane, J. (1991). *Be sick well: A healthy approach to chronic illness.* Oakland, CA: New Harbinger Publications.

Kane, J. M., Stroup, T. S., & Marder, S. R. (2009). Schizophrenia: Pharmacological treatment. In B. J. Sadock, V. A. Sadock, & P. Ruiz (Eds.), *Kaplan & Sadock's comprehensive textbook of psychiatry* (pp. 1547–1555). Philadelphia, PA: Lippincott Williams & Wilkins.

Kane, M. (2006). Content-related validity evidence in test development. In S. M. Downing & T. M. Haladyna (Eds.), *Handbook of test development* (pp. 131–153). Mahwah, NJ: Erlbaum.

Kane, M. J., & Engle, R. W. (2002). The role of prefrontal cortex in working-memory capacity, executive attention, and general fluid intelligence: An individual-differences perspective. *Psychonomic Bulletin & Review, 9,* 637–671.

Kanwisher, N., & Yovel, G. (2009). Face perception. In G. G. Berntson & J. T. Cacioppo (Eds.), *Handbook of neuroscience for the behavioral sciences.* New York, NY: Wiley.

Kaplan, A. G. (1985). Female or male therapists for women patients: New formulations. *Psychiatry, 48,* 111–121.

Kaplan, D. A. (2010). SAS: A new no. 1 best employer. *CNN Money.* January 21. Retrieved from http://money.cnn.com/2010/01/18/technology/sas_best_companies.fortune

Kaplan, H., & Dove, H. (1987). Infant development among the Ache of Eastern Paraguay. *Developmental Psychology, 23,* 190–198.

Kaplan, H. I. (1989). History of psychosomatic medicine. In H. I. Kaplan & B. J. Sadock (Eds.), *Comprehensive textbook of psychiatry* (5th ed.). Baltimore: Williams & Wilkins.

Kaplan, J. T., & Iacoboni, M. (2006). Getting a grip on other minds: Mirror neurons, intention understanding, and cognitive empathy. *Social Neuroscience, 1,* 175–183.

Kaplan, K. A., Itoi, A., & Dement, W. C. (2007). Awareness of sleepiness and ability to predict sleep onset: Can drivers avoid falling asleep at the wheel? *Sleep Medicine, 9*(1), 71–79. doi:10.1016/j.sleep.2007.02.001

Kaplan, R. (1993). The role of nature in the context of the workplace. *Landscape and Urban Planning, 26,* 193–201.

Kaplan, R. (2001). The nature of the view from home: Psychological benefits. *Environment and Behavior, 33*(4), 507–542.

Kaplan, R., & Kaplan, S. (1989). *The experience of nature: A psychological perspective.* Cambridge, MA: Cambridge University Press.

Kaplan, R. E., Drath, W. H., Kofodimos, J. R. (1991). *Beyond ambition: How driven managers can lead better and live better.* San Francisco, CA: Jossey-Bass.

Kaplan, R. M., & Saccuzzo, D. P. (2005). *Psychological testing: Principles, applications, and issues.* Belmont, CA: Wadsworth.

Kaplan, S. (1995). The restorative benefits of nature: Toward an integrative framework. *Journal of Environmental Psychology, 15,* 169–182.

Karasu, T. B. (2005). Psychoanalysis and psychoanalytic psychotherapy. In B. J. Sadock & V. A. Sadock (Eds.), *Kaplan and Sadock's comprehensive textbook of psychiatry* (pp. 2472–2497). Philadelphia, PA: Lippincott Williams & Wilkins.

Karau, S. J., & Williams, K. D. (1993). Social loafing: A meta-analytic review and theoretical integration. *Journal of Personality and Social Psychology, 65,* 681–706.

Karau, S. J., & Williams, K. D. (1995). Social loafing: Research findings, implications, and future directions. *Current Directions in Psychological Science, 4,* 134–140.

Karlsgodt, K. H., Sun, D., & Cannon, T. D. (2010). Structural and functional brain abnormalities in schizophrenia. *Current Directions in Psychological Science, 19*(4), 226–231. doi:10.1177/0963721410377601

Karp, A., Andel, R., Parker, M. G., Wang, H., Winblad, B., & Fratiglioni, L. (2009). Mentally stimulating activities at work during midlife and dementia risk after age 75: Follow-up study from the Kungsholmen Project. *American Journal of Geriatric Psychiatry, 17*(3), 227–236. doi:10.1097/JGP.0b013e318190b691

Karpicke, J. D., & Roediger, H. (2008). The critical importance of retrieval for learning. *Science, 319*(5865), 966–968. doi:10.1126/science.1152408

Karpicke, J. D., Butler, A. C., & Roediger, H. (2009). Metacognitive strategies in student learning: Do students practise retrieval when they study on their own? *Memory, 17*(4), 471–479. doi:10.1080/09658210802647009

Karremans, J. C., Stroebe, W., & Claus, J. (2006). Beyond Vicary's fantasies: The impact of subliminal priming and brand choice. *Journal of Experimental Social Psychology, 42,* 792–798.

Kass, S. J., Cole, K. S., & Stanny, C. J. (2007). Effects of distraction and experience on situation awareness and simulated driving. *Transportation Research Part F: Traffic Psychology and Behaviour, 10,* 321–329.

Kassam, K. S., Gilbert, D. T., Swencionis, J. K., & Wilson, T. D. (2009). Misconceptions of memory: The Scooter Libby effect. *Psychological Science, 20*(5), 551–552. doi:10.1111/j.1467-9280.2009.02334.x

Kasser, T. (2002). *The high price of materialism.* Cambridge, MA: MIT Press.

Kasser, T., & Kanner, A.D. (2004). *Psychology and consumer culture: The struggle for a good life in a materialistic world.* Washington, DC: American Psychological Association.

Kasser, T., Ryan, R. M., Couchman, C. E., & Sheldon, K. M. (2004). Materialistic values: Their causes and consequences. In T. Kasser & A. D. Kanner (Eds.), *Psychology and consumer culture: The struggle for a good life in a materialistic world.* Washington, DC: American Psychological Association.

Kasser, T., & Sharma, Y. S. (1999). Reproductive freedom, educational equality, and females' preference for resource-acquisition characteristics in mates. *Psychological Science, 10,* 374–377.

Kassin, S. M., Tubb, V. A., Hosch, H. M., & Memon, A. (2001). On the "general acceptance" of eyewitness testimony research: A new survey of the experts. *American Psychologist, 56,* 405–416.

Katigbak, M. S., Church, A. T., Guanzon-Lapena, M. A., Carlota, A. J. & del Pilar, G. H. (2002). Are indigenous personality dimensions culture specific? Philippine inventories and the five-factor model. *Journal of Personality and Social Psychology, 82,* 89–101.

Kaufman, A. S. (2000). Tests of intelligence. In R. J. Sternberg (Ed.), *Handbook of intelligence* (pp. 445–476). New York, NY: Cambridge University Press.

Kaufman, A. S. (2009). *IQ testing 101.* New York, NY: Springer.

Kaufman, J. C. (2001). The Sylvia Plath effect: Mental illness in eminent creative writers. *Journal of Creative Behavior, 35*(1), 37–50.

Kaufman, J. C. (2005). The door that leads into madness: Eastern European poets and mental illness. *Creativity Research Journal, 17*(1), 99–103.

Kaufman, J. C., & Baer, J. (2002). Could Steven Spielberg manage the Yankees?: Creative thinking in different domains. *Korean Journal of Thinking & Problem Solving, 12*(2), 5–14.

Kaufman, J. C., & Baer, J. (2004). Hawking's haiku, Madonna's math: Why it is hard to be creative in every room of the house. In R. J. Sternberg, E. L. Grigorenko, & J. L. Singer (Eds.), *Creativity: From potential to realization.* Washington, DC: American Psychological Association.

Kaufman, L., Vassiliades, V., Noble, R., Alexander, R., Kaufman, J., & Edlund, S. (2007). Perceptual distance and the moon illusion. *Spatial Vision, 20,* 155–175. doi: 10.1163/156856807779369698.

Kaufman, S. B., & Sternberg, R. J. (2010). Conceptions of giftedness. In S. I. Pfeiffer (Ed.), *Handbook of giftedness in children: Psychoeducational theory, research, and best practices.* New York, NY: Springer.

Kaushanskaya, M., & Marian, V. (2009). Bilingualism reduces native-language interference during novel-word learning. *Journal of Experimental Psychology: Learning, Memory, and Cognition, 35*(3), 829–835. doi:10.1037/a0015275

Kay, J., & Kay, R. L. (2008). Individual psychoanalytic psychotherapy. In A. Tasman, J. Kay, J. A. Lieberman, M. B. First, & M. Maj (Eds.), *Psychiatry* (3rd ed.). New York, NY: Wiley-Blackwell.

Kayser, C. (2007). Listening with your eyes. *Scientific American Mind, 18*(2), 24–29.

Kazdin, A. (1994). Methodology, design, and evaluation in psychotherapy research. In A. E. Bergin & S. L. Garfield (Eds.), *Handbook of psychotherapy and behavior change* (4th ed.). New York, NY: Wiley.

Kazdin, A. (2001). *Behavior modification in applied settings.* Belmont: Wadsworth.

Kazdin, A. (2007). Mediators and mechanisms of change in psychotherapy research. *Annual Review of Clinical Psychology, 3,* 1–27.

Kazdin, A., & Benjet, C. (2003). Spanking children: Evidence and issues. *Current Directions in Psychological Science, 12*(3), 99–103.

Keane, T. M., Marshall, A. D., & Taft, C. T. (2006). Posttraumatic stress disorder: Etiology, epidemiology, and treatment outcome. *Annual Review of Clinical Psychology, 2,* 161–197.

Keck, P. E. Jr., & McElroy, S. L. (2006). Lithium and mood stabilizers. In D. J. Stein, D. J. Kupfer, & A. F. Schatzberg (Eds.), *Textbook of mood disorders* (pp. 281–290). Washington, DC: American Psychiatric Publishing.

Keefauver, S. P., & Guilleminault, C. (1994). Sleep terrors and sleepwalking. In M. H. Kryger, T. Roth, & W. C. Dement (Eds.), *Principles and practice of sleep medicine* (2nd ed.). Philadelphia, PA: Saunders.

Keenan, J. P., Gallup, G. G. Jr., Goulet, N., & Kulkarni, M. (1997). Attributions of deception in human mating strategies. *Journal of Social Behavior and Personality, 12,* 45–52.

Keesey, R. E. (1993). Physiological regulation of body energy: Implications for obesity. In A. J. Stunkard & T. A. Wadden (Eds.), *Obesity theory and therapy.* New York, NY: Raven.

Keesey, R. E. (1995). A set point model of body weight regulation. In K. D. Brownell & C. G. Fairburn (Eds.), *Eating disorders and obesity: A comprehensive handbook.* New York, NY: Guilford Press.

Keesey, R. E., & Powley, T. L. (1975). Hypothalamic regulation of body weight. *American Scientist, 63,* 558–565.

Kefalov, V. J. (2010). Visual receptors and transduction. In E. B. Goldstein (Ed.), *Encyclopedia of perception.* Thousand Oaks, CA: Sage.

Kehoe, E. J., & Macrae, M. (1998). Classical conditioning. In W. O'Donohue (Ed.), *Learning and behavior therapy.* Boston, MA: Allyn & Bacon.

Keller, P. A., & Block, L. G. (1999). The effect of affect-based dissonance versus cognition-based dissonance on motivated reasoning and health-related persuasion. *Journal of Experimental Psychology: Applied, 5,* 302–313.

Kellert, S. R. (2002). Experiencing nature: Affective, cognitive, and evaluative development in children. In P. H. Kahn, Jr. & S. R. Kellert (Eds.), *Children and nature: Psychological, sociocultural, and evolutionary investigations* (pp. 117–151). Cambridge MA: MIT Press.

Kelley, H. H. (1950). The warm-cold variable in first impressions of persons. *Journal of Personality, 18,* 431–439.

Kelley, H. H. (1967). Attributional theory in social psychology. *Nebraska Symposium on Motivation, 15,* 192–241.

Kellogg, S. H., & Young, J. E. (2008). Cognitive Therapy. In J. L. Lebow (Ed.), *Twenty-first century psychotherapies: Contemporary approaches to theory and practice.* New York, NY: Wiley.

Kelly, B. D., Feeney, L., O'Callaghan, E., Browne, R., Byrne, M., Mulryan, N., Scully, A., Morris, M., Kinsella, A., Takei, N., McNeil, T., Walsh, D., & Larkin, C. (2004). Obstetric adversity and age at first presentation with schizophrenia: Evidence of a dose-response relationship. *American Journal of Psychiatry, 161,* 920–922.

Kelly, K. M., & Schramke, C. J. (2000). Epilepsy. In G. Fink (Ed.), *Encyclopedia of stress* (pp. 66–70). San Diego: Academic Press.

Kelman, H. C. (1967). Human use of human subjects: The problem of deception in social psychological experiments. *Psychological Bulletin, 67,* 1–11.

Kelman, H. C. (1982). Ethical issues in different social science methods. In T. L. Beauchamp, R. R. Faden, R. J. Wallace, Jr., & L. Walters (Eds.), *Ethical issues in social science research.* Baltimore: Johns Hopkins University Press.

Kelsey, J. E. (2005). Selective serotonin reuptake inhibitors. In B. J. Sadock & V. A. Sadock (Eds.), *Kaplan and Sadock's comprehensive textbook of psychiatry* (pp. 2887–2913). Philadelphia, PA: Lippincott Williams & Wilkins.

Kelsoe, J. R. (2005). Mood disorders: Genetics. In B. J. Sadock & V. A. Sadock (Eds.), *Kaplan & Sadock's comprehensive textbook of psychiatry* (pp. 1582–1593). Philadelphia, PA: Lippincott Williams & Wilkins.

Kelsoe, J. R. (2009). Mood disorders: Genetics. In B. J. Sadock, V. A. Sadock, & P. Ruiz (Eds.), *Kaplan & Sadock's comprehensive textbook of psychiatry* (9th ed., pp. 1653–1663). Philadelphia, PA: Lippincott, Williams & Wilkins.

Keltner, D., Ekman, P., Gonzaga, G. C., & Beer, J. (2003). Facial expression of emotion. In R. J. Davidson, K. R. Scherer, & H. H. Goldsmith (Eds.), *Handbook of affective sciences.* New York, NY: Oxford University Press.

Kemeny, M. E. (2007). Psychoneuroimmunology. In H. S. Friedman & R. C. Silver (Eds.), *Foundations of health psychology.* New York, NY: Oxford University Press.

Kendall, P. C., Holmbeck, G., & Verduin, T. (2004). Methodology, design, and evaluation in psychotherapy research. In M. J. Lambert (Ed.), *Bergin and Garfield's handbook of psychotherapy and behavior change.* New York, NY: Wiley.

Kendler, K. S. (2005a). "A gene for . . . ?": The nature of gene action in psychiatric disorders. *American Journal of Psychiatry, 162,* 1243–1252.

Kendler, K. S. (2005b). Psychiatric genetics: A methodologic critique. *American Journal of Psychiatry, 162,* 3–11.

Kendler, K. S., & Gardner, C. O., Jr. (1998). Boundaries of major depression: An evaluation of DSM-IV criteria. *American Journal of Psychiatry, 155,* 172–177.

Kendler, K. S., & Greenspan, R. J. (2006). The nature of genetic influences on behavior: Lessons from "simpler" organisms. *American Journal of Psychiatry, 163,* 1683–1694.

Kendler, K. S., Myers, J., & Prescott, C. A. (2005). Sex differences in the relationship between social support and risk for major depression: A longitudinal study of opposite-sex twin pairs. *American Journal of Psychiatry, 162,* 250–256.

Kendler, K. S., Thornton, L. M., Gilman, S. E., & Kessler, R. C. (2000). Sexual orientation in a U.S. national sample of twin and nontwin sibling pairs. *American Journal of Psychiatry, 157,* 1843–1846.

Kenfield, S. A., Stampfer, M. J., Rosner, B. A., & Colditz, G. A. (2008). Smoking and smoking cessation in relation to mortality in women. *Journal of the American Medical Association, 299,* 2037–2047.

Kennedy, S. H., Holt, A., & Baker, G. B. (2009). Monoamine oxidase inhibitors. In B. J. Sadock, V. A. Sadock, & P. Ruiz (Eds.), *Kaplan & Sadock's comprehensive textbook of psychiatry* (pp. 3154–3163). Philadelphia, PA: Lippincott, Williams & Wilkins.

Kennedy, T. E., Hawkins, R. D., & Kandel, E. R. (1992). Molecular interrelationships between short- and long-term memory. In L. R. Squire & N. Butters (Eds.), *Neuropsychology of Memory* (2nd ed.). New York, NY: Wiley.

Kenrick, D. T., Griskevicius, V., Neuberg, S. L., & Schaller, M. (2010). Renovating the pyramid of needs: Contemporary extensions built upon ancient foundations. *Perspectives on Psychological Science, 5*(3), 292–314. doi:10.1177/1745691610369469

Kenrick, D. T., & Gutierres, S. E. (1980). Contrast effects and judgments of physical attractiveness: When beauty becomes a social problem. *Journal of Personality and Social Psychology, 38,* 131–140.

Kenrick, D. T., Trost, M. R., & Sundie, J. M. (2004). Sex roles as adaptations: An evolutionary perspective on gender differences and similarities. In A. H. Eagly, A. E. Beall, & R. J. Sternberg (Eds.), *The psychology of gender.* New York, NY: Guilford Press.

Kermer, D. A., Driver-Linn, E., Wilson, T. D., & Gilbert, D. T. (2006). Loss aversion is an affective forecasting error. *Psychological Science, 17,* 649–653.

Kern, M. L., & Friedman, H. S. (2008). Do conscientious individuals live longer? A quantitative review. *Health Psychology, 27*(5), 505–512. doi:10.1037/0278-6133.27.5.505

Kerns, K. A., Abraham, M. M., Schlegelmilch, A., & Morgan, T. A. (2007). Mother-child attachment in later middle-childhood: Assessment approaches and associations with mood and emotion. *Attachment & Human Development, 9*(1), 33–53.

Kerr, N. L., & Tindale, R. S. (2004). Group performance and decision making. *Annual Review of Psychology, 55,* 623–55.

Kershaw, T. C., & Ohlsson, S. (2004). Multiple causes of difficulty in insight: The case of the nine-dot problem. *Journal of Experimental Psychology: Learning, Memory, and Cognition, 30,* 3–13.

Kesebir, S., Graham, J., & Oishi, S. (2010). A theory of human needs should be human-centered, not animal-centered: Commentary on Kenrick et al. (2010). *Perspectives on Psychological Science, 5*(3), 315–319. doi:10.1177/1745691610369470

Kessen, W. (1996). American psychology just before Piaget. *Psychological Science, 7,* 196–199.

Kessler, R. C., & Zhao, S. (1999). The prevalence of mental illness. In A. V. Horvitz & T. L. Scheid (Eds.), *A handbook for the study of mental health: Social contexts, theories, and systems.* New York, NY: Cambridge University Press.

Kessler, R. C., Berglund, P., Demler, O., Jin, R., Koretz, D., Merikangas, K. R., Rush, A. J., Walters, E. E., & Wang, P. S. (2003a). The epidemiology of major depressive disorder. Results from the national comorbidity survey replication (NCS-R). *Journal of the American Medical Association, 189,* 3095–3105.

Kessler, R. C., Merikangas, K. R., Berglund, P., Eaton, W. W., Koretz, D. S., & Walters, E. E. (2003b). Mild disorders should not be eliminated from the DSM-V. *Archives of General Psychiatry 60,* 1117–1122.

Kessler, R. C., Berglund, P., Demler, O., Jin, R., & Walters, E. E. (2005a). Lifetime prevalence and age-of-onset distributions of DSM-IV disorders in the national comorbidity survey replication. *Archives of General Psychiatry, 62,* 593–602.

Kessler, R. C., Demier, O., Frank, R. G., Olfson, M., Pincus, H. A., Walters, E. E., Wang, P., Wells, K. B., & Zaslavsky, A. M. (2005b). Prevalence and treatment of mental disorders: 1990–2003. *New England Journal of Medicine, 352,* 2515–2523.

Key, W. B. (1973). *Subliminal seduction.* Englewood Cliffs, NJ: Prentice-Hall.

Key, W. B. (1976). *Media sexploitation.* Englewood Cliffs, NJ: Prentice-Hall.

Key, W. B. (1980). *The clam-plate orgy and other subliminal techniques for manipulating your behavior.* Englewood Cliffs, NJ: Prentice-Hall.

Key, W. B. (1992). *Subliminal adventures in erotic art.* Boston, MA: Branden Books.

Keys, D. J., & Schwartz, B. (2007). "Leaky" rationality: How research on behavioral decision making challenges normative standards of rationality. *Perspectives on Psychological Science, 2*(2), 162–180. doi:10.1111/j.1745-6916.2007.00035.x

Khashan, A. S., Abel, K. M., McNamee, R., Pedersen, M. G., Webb, R. T., Baker, P. N., et al. (2008). Higher risk of offspring schizophrenia following antenatal maternal exposure to severe adverse life events. *Archives of General Psychiatry, 65,* 146–152.

Kidder, D. L., & Parks, J. M. (2001). The good soldier: Who is s(he)? *Journal of Organizational Behavior, 22,* 939–959

Kiecolt-Glaser, J. K., Garner, W., Speicher, C., Penn, G. M., Holliday, J., & Glaser, R. (1984). Psychosocial modifiers of immunocompetence in medical students. *Psychosomatic Medicine, 46*(1), 7–14.

Kiecolt-Glaser, J. K., & Glaser, R. (1995). Measurement of immune response. In S. Cohen, R. C. Kessler, & L. U. Gordon (Eds.), *Measuring stress: A guide for health and social scientists.* New York, NY: Oxford University Press.

Kierlin, L. (2008). Sleeping without a pill: Nonpharmacologic treatments for insomnia. *Journal of Psychiatric Practice,14*(6), 403–407. doi:10.1097/01.pra.0000341896.73926.6c

Kieseppa, T., Partonen, T., Huakka, J., Kaprio, J., & Lonnqvist, J. (2004). High concordance of bipolar 1 disorder in a nationwide sample of twins. *American Journal of Psychiatry, 161,* 1814–1821.

Kiesler, D. J. (1999). *Beyond the disease model of mental disorders.* New York, NY: Praeger Publishers.

Kihlstrom, J. F. (2001). Dissociative disorders. In P. B. Sutker & H. E. Adams (Eds.), *Comprehensive handbook of psychopathology* (3rd ed., pp. 259–276). New York, NY: Kluwer Academic/Plenum Publishers.

Kihlstrom, J. F. (2002). No need for repression. *Trends in Cognitive Sciences, 6*(12), 502.

Kihlstrom, J. F. (2004). An unbalanced balancing act: Blocked, recovered, and false memories in the laboratory and clinic. *Clinical Psychology: Science & Practice, 11*(1), 34–41.

Kihlstrom, J. F. (2005a). Dissociative disorders. *Annual Review of Clinical Psychology, 1,* 227–253.

Kihlstrom, J. F. (2005b). Is hypnosis an altered state of consciousness or what? *Contemporary Hypnosis, 22,* 34–38.

Kihlstrom, J. F. (2007). Consciousness in hypnosis. In P. D. Zelazo, M. Moscovitch, & E. Thompson (Eds.), *The Cambridge handbook of consciousness.* New York, NY: Cambridge University Press.

Kihlstrom, J. F., Barnhardt, T. M., & Tataryn, D. J. (1992). Implicit perception. In R. F. Bornstein & T. S. Pittman (Eds.), *Perception without awareness: Cognitive, clinical, and social perspectives.* New York, NY: Guilford Press.

Kihlstrom, J. F., & Cork, R. C. (2007). Consciousness and anesthesia. In M. Velmans & S. Schneider (Eds.), *The Blackwell companion to consciousness.* Malden, MA: Blackwell Publishing.

Kihlstrom, J. F., Glisky, M. L., & Angiulo, M. J. (1994). Dissociative tendencies and dissociative disorders. *Journal of Abnormal Psychology, 103,* 117–124.

Killeen, P. R. (1981). Learning as causal inference. In M. L. Commons & J. A. Nevin (Eds.), *Quantitative analyses of behavior: Vol. 1. Discriminative properties of reinforcement schedules.* Cambridge, MA: Ballinger.

Killen, M., Richardson, C. B., & Kelly, M. C. (2010). Developmental perspectives. In J. F. Dovidio, M. Hewstone, P. Glick, & V. M. Esses (Eds.), *The Sage handbook of prejudice, stereotyping, and discrimination.* Los Angeles, CA: Sage.

Kim, E.-J., & Dimsdale, J. E. (2007). The effect of psychological stress on sleep: A review of polysomnographic evidence. *Behavioral Sleep Medicine, 5,* 256–278.

Kim, H., & Markus, H. R. (1999). Deviance or uniqueness, harmony or conformity? A cultural analysis. *Journal of Personality and Social Psychology, 77,* 785–800.

Kim, H. S., Sherman, D. K., Ko, D., & Taylor, S. E. (2006). Pursuit of comfort and pursuit of harmony: Culture, relationships, and social support seeking. *Personality and Social Psychology Bulletin, 32*(12), 1595–1607. doi:10.1177/0146167206291991

Kim, H. S., Sherman, D. K., & Taylor, S. E. (2008). Culture and social support. *American Psychologist, 63*(6), 518–526. doi:10.1037/0003-066X

Kim, K. H. (2005). Can only intelligent people be creative? *Journal of Secondary Gifted Education, 16,* 57–66.

Kim, K. H., Cramond, B., & VanTassel-Baska, J. (2010). The relationship between creativity and intelligence. In J. C. Kaufman & R. J. Sternberg (Eds.), *The Cambridge handbook of creativity* (pp. 395–412). New York, NY: Cambridge University Press.

Kim, S., Plumb, R., Gredig, Q., Rankin, L., & Taylor, B. (2008). Medium-term post-Katrina health sequelae among New Orleans residents: Predictors of poor mental and physical health. *Journal of Clinical Nursing, 17*(17), 2335–2342.

Kimmel, A. J. (1996). *Ethical issues in behavioral research: A survey.* Cambridge, MA: Blackwell.

Kimura, D. (1973). The asymmetry of the human brain. *Scientific American, 228,* 70–78.

King, A. C., Oman, R. F., Brassington, G. S., Bliwise, D. L., & Haskell, W. L. (1997). Moderate-intensity exercise and self-rated quality of sleep in older adults: A randomized controlled trial. *Journal of the American Medical Association, 277,* 32–37.

King, B. H., Toth, K. E., Hodapp, R. M., & Dykens, E. M. (2009). Intellectual disability. In B. J. Sadock, V. A. Sadock, & P. Ruiz (Eds.), *Kaplan & Sadock's comprehensive textbook of psychiatry* (Vol. 2). Philadelphia, PA: Lippincott, Williams & Wilkins.

King, B. M. (2006). The rise, fall, and resurrection of the ventromedial hypothalamus in the regulation of feeding behavior and body weight. *Physiology & Behavior, 87,* 221–244.

King, C., Knutson, K., Rathouz, P., Sidney, S., Liu, K., & Lauderdale, D. (2008). Short sleep duration and incident coronary artery calcification. *Journal of the American Medical Association, 300*(24), 2859–2866.

King, G. R., & Ellinwood Jr., E. H. (2005). Amphetamines and other stimulants. In J. H. Lowinson, P. Ruiz, R. B. Millman, & J. G. Langrod (Eds.), *Substance abuse: A comprehensive textbook.* Philadelphia, PA: Lippincott/Williams & Wilkins.

King, S., St-Hilaire, A., & Heidkamp, D. (2010). Prenatal factors in schizophrenia. *Current Directions in Psychological Science, 19*(4), 209–213. doi:10.1177/0963721410378360

Kingston, D. A., Malamuth, N. M., Fedoroff, P., & Marshall, W. L. (2009). The importance of individual differences in pornography use: Theoretical perspectives and implications for treating sexual offenders. *Journal of Sex Research, 46*(2–3), 216–232.

Kinnunen, T., Haukkala, A., Korhonen, T., Quiles, Z. N., Spiro, A. I., & Garvey, A. J. (2006). Depression and smoking across 25 years of the normative aging study. *International Journal of Psychiatry in Medicine, 36,* 413–426.

Kinsbourne, M. (1997). What qualifies a representation for a role in consciousness? In J. D. Cohen & J. W. Schooler (Eds.), *Scientific approaches to consciousness.* Mahwah, NJ: Erlbaum.

Kinsey, A. C., Pomeroy, W. B., & Martin, C. E. (1948). *Sexual behavior in the human male.* Philadelphia, PA: Saunders.

Kinsey, A. C., Pomeroy, W. B., Martin, C. E., & Gebhard, P. H. (1953). *Sexual behavior in the human female.* Philadelphia, PA: Saunders.

Kirby, S. (2007). The evolution of language. In R. I. M. Dunbar & L. Barrett (Eds.), *Oxford handbook of evolutionary psychology.* New York, NY: Oxford University Press.

Kirkpatrick, L. A. (2005). *Attachment, evolution, and the psychology of religion.* New York, NY: Guilford Press.

Kirkpatrick, S. A., & Locke, E. A. (1991). Leadership: Do traits matter? *Academy of Management Executive, 5,* 48–60.

Kirow, G., & Owen, M. J. (2009). Genetics of schizophrenia. In B. J. Sadock, V. A. Sadock, & P. Ruiz (Eds.), *Kaplan & Sadock's comprehensive textbook of psychiatry* (9th ed., Vol. 1, pp. 1462–1472). Philadelphia, PA: Lippincott, Williams & Wilkins.

Kirsch, I. (1997). Response expectancy theory and application: A decennial review. *Applied and Preventive Psychology, 6,* 69–79.

Kirsch, I. (2000). The response set theory of hypnosis. *American Journal of Clinical Hypnosis, 42,* 274–292.

Kirsch, I. (2004). Altered states in hypnosis: The debate goes on. *Psychological Hypnosis, 13*(1). No pagination specified.

Kirsch, I. (2010). *The emperor's new drugs: Exploding the antidepressant myth.* New York, NY: Basic Books.

Kirsch, I., & Lynn, S. J. (1998). Dissociation theories of hypnosis. *Psychological Bulletin, 123,* 100–115.

Kirsch, I., Mazzoni, G., & Montgomery, G. H. (2007). Remembrance of hypnosis past. *American Journal of Clinical Hypnosis, 49,* 171–178.

Kirschenbaum, H., & Jourdan, A. (2005). The current status of Carl Rogers and the person-centered approach. *Psychotherapy: Theory, Research, Practice, Training, 42,* 37–51.

Kitayama, S., Duffy, S., Kawamura, T., & Larsen, J. T. (2003). Perceiving an object and its context in different cultures: A cultural look at new look. *Psychological Science, 14*(3), 201–206.

Kittler, P. G., & Sucher, K. P. (2008). *Food and culture.* Belmont, CA: Wadsworth.

Kitzes, J., Wackernagel, M., Loh, J., Peller, A., Goldfinger, S., Cheng, D., & Tea, K. (2008). Shrink and share: Humanity's present and future ecological footprint. *Philosophical Transactions of the Royal Society of London,* Se-ries B, Biological Sciences, 363, 467–475.

Kivimäki, M., Vahtera, J., Elovainio, M., Helenius, H., Singh-Manoux, A., & Pentti, J. (2005). Optimism and pessimism as predictors of change in health after death or onset of severe illness in family. *Health Psychology, 24,* 413–421.

Kjellgren, A., & Buhrkall, H. (2010). A comparison of the restorative effect of a natural environment with that of a simulated natural environment. *Journal of Environmental Psychology, 30,* 464–472.

Klapper, D., Ebling, C., & Temme, J. (2005). Another look at loss aversion in brand choice data: Can we characterize the loss-averse consumer? *International Journal of Research in Marketing, 22,* 239–254.

Klare, M. T. (2001). *Resource wars: The new landscape of global conflict.* New York, NY: Henry Holt.

Klein, D. N. (2010). Chronic depression: Diagnosis and classification. *Current Directions in Psychological Science, 19*(2), 96–100. doi:10.1177/0963721410366007

Klein, M. (1948). *Contributions to psychoanalysis.* London: Hogarth.

Klein, P. D. (1997). Multiplying the problems of intelligence by eight: A critique of Gardner's theory. *Canadian Journal of Education, 22,* 377–394.

Kleinke, C. L. (2007). What does it mean to cope? In A. Monat, R. S. Lazarus, & G. Reevy (Eds.), *The Praeger handbook on stress and coping.* Westport, CT: Praeger.

Kleinke, C. L., Peterson, T. R., & Rutledge, T. R. (1998). Effects of self-generated facial expressions on mood. *Journal of Personality and Social Psychology, 74,* 272–279.

Kleinmuntz, B. (1980). *Essentials of abnormal psychology.* San Francisco, CA: Harper & Row.

Kleinmuntz, B., & Szucko, J. J. (1984). Lie detection in ancient and modern times: A call for contemporary scientific study. *American Psychologist, 39*(7), 766–776. doi:10.1037/0003-066X.39.7.766

Kleinspehn-Ammerlahn, A., Kotter-Grühn, D., & Smith, J. (2008). Self-perceptions of aging: Do subjective age and satisfaction with aging change during old age?. *The Journals of Gerontology: Series B: Psychological Sciences and Social Sciences, 63B*(6), 377–385.

Klerman, E. B., Davis, J. B., Duffy, J. F., Dijk, D., & Kronauer, R. E. (2004). Older people awaken more frequently but fall back asleep at the same rate as younger people. *Sleep: Journal of Sleep & Sleep Disorders Research, 27,* 793–798.

Klerman, E. B., & Dijk, D. J. (2008). Age-related reduction in the maximal capacity for sleep-implications for insomnia. *Current Biology, 18,* 1118–1123.

Klerman, G. L., & Weissman, M. M. E. (1993). *New applications of interpersonal therapy.* Washington, DC: American Psychiatric Press.

Kliegel, M., Zimprich, D., & Rott, C. (2004). Lifelong intellectual activities mediate the predictive effect of early education on cognitive impairment in centenarians: A retrospective study. *Aging & Mental Health, 8,* 430–437.

Kline, P. (1991). *Intelligence: The psychometric view.* New York, NY: Routledge, Chapman, & Hall.

Kline, P. (1995). A critical review of the measurement of personality and intelligence. In D. H. Saklofske & M. Zeidner (Eds.), *International handbook of personality and intelligence.* New York, NY: Plenum.

Klingberg, T. (2010). Training and plasticity of working memory. *Trends in Cognitive Sciences, 14*(7), 317–324. doi:10.1016/j.tics.2010.05.002

Klosch, G., & Kraft, U. Sweet dreams are made of this. *Scientific American Mind, 16*(2), 38–45.

Kluft, R. P. (1996). Dissociative identity disorder. In L. K. Michelson & W. J. Ray (Eds.), *Handbook of dissociation: Theoretical, empirical, and clinical perspectives.* New York, NY: Plenum.

Kluft, R. P. (1999). True lies, false truths, and naturalistic raw data: Applying clinical research findings to the false memory debate. In L. M. Williams & V. L. Banyard (Eds.), *Trauma & memory.* Thousand Oaks, CA: Sage.

Klump, K. L., & Culbert, K. M. (2007). Molecular genetic studies of eating disorders: Current status and future directions. *Current Directions in Psychological Science, 16,* 37–41.

Knapp, C. M., & Kornetsky, C. (2009). Neural basis of pleasure and reward. In G. G. Berntson & J. T. Cacioppo (Eds.), *Handbook of neuroscience for the behavioral sciences* (Vol. 1, pp. 781–806). New York, NY: Wiley.

Knauss, W. (2005). Group psychotherapy. In G. O. Gabbard, J. S. Beck, & J. Holmes (Eds.), *Oxford textbook of psychotherapy.* New York, NY: Oxford University Press.

Knecht, S., Drager, B., Floel, A., Lohmann, H., Breitenstein, C., Henningsen, H., & Ringelstein, E. B. (2001). Behavioural relevance of atypical language lateralization in healthy subjects. *Brain, 124,* 1657–1665.

Knecht, S., Fioel, A., Drager, B., Breitenstein, C., Sommer, J., Henningsen, H., Ringelstein, E. B., & Pascual-Leone, A. (2002). Degree of language lateralization determines susceptibility to unilateral brain lesions. *Nature Neuroscience, 5,* 695–699.

Knight, J. (2004). The truth about lying. *Nature, 428,* 692–694.

Knopik, V. S. (2009). Maternal smoking during pregnancy and child outcomes: Real or spurious effect? *Developmental Neuropsychology, 34*(1), 1–36. doi:10.1080/87565640802564366

Knowlton, B. J., & Holyoak, K. J. (2009). Prefrontal substrate of human relational reasoning. In M. S. Gazzangia (Ed.), *The cognitive neurosciences* (4th ed., pp. 1005–1018). Cambridge, MA: The MIT Press.

Knutson, K. L., & Van Cauter, E. (2008). Associations between sleep loss and increased risk of obesity and diabetes. In D. W. Pfaff, & B. L. Kieffer (Eds.), *Annals of the New York Academy of Sciences. Molecular and biophysical mechanisms of arousal, alertness, and attention* (pp. 287–304). Malden, MA: Blackwell.

Kobrin, J. L., Patterson, B. F., Shaw, E. J., Mattern, K. D., & Barbuti, S. M. (2008). *Validity of the SAT for predicting first-year college grade point average* (College Board research report no. 2008-5). New York, NY: College Board.

Kodama, S., Saito, K., Tanaka, S., Maki, M., Yachi, Y., Asumi, M., et al. (2009). Cardiorespiratory fitness as a quantitative predictor of all-cause mortality and cardiovascular events in healthy men and women: a meta-analysis. *Journal of the American Medical Association, 301*(19), 2024–2035.

Koehler, J. J. (1996). The base rate fallacy reconsidered: Descriptive, normative, and methodological challenges. *Behavioral Brain Sciences, 19,* 1–53.

Koger, S. M., & Scott, B. A. (2007). Psychology and environmental sustainability: A call for integration. *Teaching of Psychology,* 34, 10–18.

Koger, S. M., Schettler, T. & Weiss, B. (2005). Environmental toxicants and developmental disabilities: A challenge for psychologists. *American Psychologist, 60,* 243–255.

Koger, S. M., & Winter, D. D. (2010). *The psychology of environmental problems: Psychology for sustainability* (3rd ed.). New York, NY: Psychology Press.

Kohlberg, L. (1963). The development of children's orientations toward a moral order: I. Sequence in the development of moral thought. *Vita Humana, 6,* 11–33.

Kohlberg, L. (1969). Stage and sequence: The cognitive-developmental approach to socialization. In D. A. Goslin (Ed.), *Handbook of socialization theory and research.* Chicago: Rand McNally.

Kohlberg, L. (1976). Moral stages and moralization: Cognitive-developmental approach. In T. Lickona (Ed.), *Moral development and behavior: Theory, research and social issues.* New York, NY: Holt, Rinehart & Winston.

Kohlberg, L. (1984). *Essays on moral development: Vol. 2. The psychology of moral development.* San Francisco, CA: Harper & Row.

Kohut, H. (1971). *Analysis of the self.* New York, NY: International Universities Press.

Kokkinos, P., Myers, J., Kokkinos, J. P., Pittaras, A., Narayan, P., Manolis, A., et al. (2008). Exercise capacity and mortality in black and white men. *Circulation , 117,* 614–622.

Koksal, F., Domjan, M., Kurt, A., Sertel, O., Orung, S., Bowers, R., & Kumru, G. (2004). An animal model of fetishism. *Behaviour Research and Therapy, 42*(12), 1421–1434. doi:10.1016/j.brat.2003.10.001.

Kolb, B., Gibb, R., & Robinson, T. E. (2003). Brain plasticity and behavior. *Current Directions in Psychological Science, 12,* 1–5.

Kollmuss, A. & Agyeman, J. (2002). Mind the gap: Why do people act environmentally and what are the barriers to pro-environmental behaviour? *Environmental Education Research,* 8, 239–260.

Koob, G. F., Everitt, B. J., & Robbins, T. W. (2008). Reward, motivation, and addiction. In L. Squire, D. Berg, F. Bloom, S. Du Lac, A. Ghosh, N. Spitzer (Eds.), *Fundamental neuroscience* (3rd ed., pp. 87–111). San Diego, CA: Elsevier.

Koob, G. F., & Le Moal, M. (2006). *Neurobiology of addiction.* San Diego: Academic Press.

Koocher, G. P., & Rey-Casserly, C. M. (2003). Ethical issues in psychological assessment. In J. R. Graham & J. A. Naglieri (Eds.), *Handbook of psychology, Vol. 10: Assessment psychology.* New York, NY: Wiley.

Koordeman, R., Anschutz, D. J., van Baaren, R. B., & Engels, R. E. (2010). Exposure to soda commercials affects sugar-sweetened soda consumption in young women. An observational experimental study. *Appetite, 54,* 619–622. doi:10.1016/j.appet.2010.03.008

Kop, W. J., Gottdiener, J. S., & Krantz, D. S. (2001). Stress and silent ischemia. In A. Baum, T. A. Revenson, & J. E. Singer (Eds.), *Handbook of health psychology* (pp. 669–682). Mahwah, NJ: Erlbaum.

Kop, W. J., Weissman, N. J., Zhu, J., Bonsall, R. W., Doyle, M., Stretch, M. R., Glaes, S. B., Krantz, D. S., Gottdiener, J. S., & Tracy, R. P. (2008). Effect of acute mental stress and exercise on inflammatory markers in patients with coronary artery disease and healthy controls. *American Journal of Cardiology, 101,* 767–773.

Koriat, A., & Bjork, R. A. (2005). Illusions of competence in monitoring one's knowledge during study. *Journal of Experimental Psychology: Learning, Memory, and Cognition, 31*(2), 187–194.

Koriat, A., Goldsmith, M., & Pansky, A. (2000). Toward a psychology of memory accuracy. *Annual Review of Psychology, 51,* 481–537.

Koriat, A., Lichtenstein, S., & Fischhoff, B. (1980). Reasons for confidence. *Journal of Experimental Psychology, 6,* 107–118.

Korn, J. H. (1987). Judgements of acceptability of deception in psychological research. *Journal of General Psychology, 114,* 205–216.

Korn, J. H. (1997). *Illusions of reality: A history of deception in social psychology.* Albany: State University of New York Press.

Korn, J. H., Davis, R., & Davis, S. F. (1991). Historians' and chairpersons' judgments of eminence among psychologists. *American Psychologist, 46,* 789–792.

Kornell, N., Castel, A. D., Eich, T. S., & Bjork, R. A. (2010). Spacing as the friend of both memory and induction in young and older adults. *Psychology and Aging, 25*(2), 498–503. doi:10.1037/a0017807

Kornell, N., Hays, M., & Bjork, R. A. (2009). Unsuccessful retrieval attempts enhance subsequent learning. *Journal of Experimental Psychology: Learning, Memory, and Cognition, 35*(4), 989–998. doi:10.1037/a0015729

Kornhaber, M. L. (2004). Multiple intelligences: From the ivory tower to the dusty classroom—But why? *Teachers College Record, 106*(1), 57–76.

Korpela, K. (2002). Children's environments. In R. B. Bechtel & A. Churchman (Eds.), *Handbook of environmental psychology* (pp. 363–373). Hoboken, NJ: Wiley.

Kosfeld, M., Heinrichs, M., Zak, P. J., Fischbacher, U., & Fehr, E. (2005). Oxytocin increases trust in humans. *Nature, 435*(7042), 673–676. doi:10.1038/nature03701

Koss, M. P. (1993). Rape: Scope, impact, interventions, and public policy responses. *American Psychologist, 48,* 1062–1069.

Koss, M. P., Gidycz, C. A., & Wisniewski, N. (1988). The scope of rape: Incidence and prevalence of sexual aggression and victimization in a national sample of higher education students. *Journal of Consulting and Clinical Psychology, 55,* 162–170.

Kotaro, S. (2007). The moon illusion: Kaufman and Rock's (1962) apparent-distance theory reconsidered. *Japanese Psychological Research, 49*(1), 57–67.

Kotovsky, K., Hayes, J. R., & Simon, H. A. (1985). Why are some problems hard? Evidence from Tower of Hanoi. *Cognitive Psychology, 17,* 248–294.

Kotter-Grühn, D., Kleinspehn-Ammerlahn, A., Gerstorf, D., & Smith, J. (2009). Self-perceptions of aging predict mortality and change with approaching death: 16-year longitudinal results from the Berlin Aging Study. *Psychology and Aging, 24*(3), 654–667. doi:10.1037/a0016510

Kotulak, R. (1996). *Inside the brain: Revolutionary discoveries of how the mind works.* Kansas City, MO: Andrews McMeel.

Koughan, M. (1975, February 23). Arthur Friedman's outrage: Employees decide their pay. *Washington Post.*

Kowalski, P., & Taylor, A. K. (2009). The effect of refuting misconceptions in the introductory psychology class. *Teaching of Psychology,* 36(3), 153–159. doi:10.1080/00986280902959986

Kozlowski, S. W., & Bell, B. S. (2003). Work groups and teams in organizations. In W. C. Borman, D. R. Ilgen, & R. J. Klimoski (Eds.), *Handbook of psychology, Vol. 12: Industrial and organizational psychology* (pp. 333–375). New York, NY: Wiley.

Kozulin, A. (2005). The concept of activity in Soviet psychology: Vygotsky, his disciples and critics. In H. Daniels (Ed.), *An introduction to Vygotsky.* New York, NY: Routledge.

Kracke, W. (1991). Myths in dreams, thought in images: An Amazonian contribution to the psychoanalytic theory of primary process. In B. Tedlock (Ed.), *Dreaming: Anthropological and psychological interpretations.* Santa Fe, NM: School of American Research Press.

Kraemer, H. C. (2008). DSM categories and dimensions in clinical and research contexts. In J. E. Helzer, H. C. Kraemer, R. F. Krueger, H.–U. Wittchen, P. J. Sirovatka, et al. (Eds.), *Dimensional approaches in diagnostic classification: Refining the research agenda for DSM-V* (pp. 5–17). Washington, DC: American Psychiatric Association.

Krakauer, J. (1998). *Into thin air: A personal account of the Mount Everest disaster.* New York, NY: Villard.

Kramer, M. (1994). The scientific study of dreaming. In M. H. Kryger, T. Roth, & W. C. Dement (Eds.), *Principles and practice of sleep medicine* (2nd ed.). Philadelphia, PA: Saunders.

Kramer, P. D. (2006). *Freud: Inventor of the modern mind.* New York, NY: HarperCollins.

Kraus, S. J. (1995). Attitudes and the prediction of behavior: A meta-analysis of the empirical literature. *Personality and Social Psychology Bulletin, 21,* 58–75.

Krebs, D. L., & Denton, K. (1997). Social illusions and self-deception: The evolution of biases in person perception. In J. A. Simpson & D. T. Kenrick (Eds.), *Evolutionary social psychology.* Mahwah, NJ: Erlbaum.

Kreith, M. (1991). Water inputs in California food production. University of California Agricultural Issues Center. Retrieved from http://www.vl-irrigation.org/cms/fileadmin/content/irrig/general/kreith_1991_ water_inputs_in_ca_food_production-excerpt.pdf

Kremen, W. S., Jacobsen, K. C., Xian, H., Eisen, S. A., Eaves, L. J., Tsuang, M. T., & Lyons, M. J. (2007). Genetics of verbal working memory processes: A twin study of middle-aged men. *Neuropsychology, 21*(5), 569–580. doi:10.1037/0894-4105.21.5.569

Kribbs, N. B. (1993). Siesta. In M. A. Carskadon (Ed.), *Encyclopedia of sleep and dreaming.* New York, NY: Macmillan.

Kriegsfeld, L. J., & Nelson, R. J. (2009). Biological rhythms. In G. G. Berntson & J. T. Cacioppo (Eds.), *Handbook of neuroscience for the behavioral sciences* (Vol. 1, pp. 56–81). New York, NY: Wiley.

Kring, A. M. (1999). Emotion in schizophrenia: Old mystery, new understanding. *Current Directions in Psychological Science, 8,* 160–163.

Krishnan, K. R. R., & Hamilton, M. A. (1997). Obesity. *Primary Psychiatry, 5,* 49–53.

Kristeller, J. L., Baer, R. A., & Quillian-Wolever, R. (2006). Mindfulness-based approaches to eating disorders. In R. A. Baer (Ed.), *Mindfulness-based treatment approaches: Clinician's guide to evidence base and applications* (pp. 75–91). San Diego: Elsevier.

Krizan, Z., Miller, J. C., & Johar, O. (2010). Wishful thinking in the 2008 U.S. presidential election. *Psychological Science, 21*(1), 140–146. doi:10.1177/0956797609356421

Kroger, J. (2003). Identity development during adolescence. In G. R. Adams & M. D. Berzonsky (Eds.), *Blackwell handbook of adolescence.* Malden, MA: Blackwell Publishing.

Krojgaard, P. (2005). Continuity and discontinuity in developmental psychology. *Psyke & Logos, 26*(2), 377–394.

Krosnick, J. A. (1999). Survey research. *Annual Review Psychology, 50,* 537–567.

Krosnick, J. A., & Fabrigar, L. R. (1998). *Designing good questionnaires: Insights from psychology.* New York, NY: Oxford University Press.

Krueger, J. (1996). Personal beliefs and cultural stereotypes about racial characteristics. *Journal of Personality and Social Psychology, 71,* 536–548.

Krueger, J., Ham, J. J., & Linford, K. M. (1996). Perceptions of behavioral consistency: Are people aware of the actor-observer effect? *Psychological Science, 7,* 259–264.

Krueger, K. R., Wilson, R. S., Kamenetsky, J. M., Barnes, L. L., Bienias, J. L., & Bennett, D. A. (2009). Social engagement and cognitive function in old age. *Experimental Aging Research, 35*(1), 45–60. doi:10.1080/03610730802545028

Krueger, R. F. (2005). Continuity of axes I and II: Toward a unified model of personality, personality disorders, and clinical disorders. *Journal of Personality Disorders, 19,* 233–261.

Krueger, R. F., & Johnson, W. (2008). Behavioral genetics and personality: A new look at the integration of nature and nurture. In O. P. John, R. W. Robbins, & L. A. Pervin (Eds.), *Handbook of personality: Theory and research* (Vol. 3, pp. 287–310). New York, NY: Guilford Press.

Krueger, R. F., & Kling, C. (2000). Validity. In A. E. Kazdin (Ed.), *Encyclopedia of psychology* (pp. 149–153). Washington, DC: American Psychological Association.

Krueger, W. C. F. (1929). The effect of overlearning on retention. *Journal of Experimental Psychology, 12,* 71–78.

Kruglanski, A. W., & Stroebe, W. (2005). The influence of beliefs and goals on attitudes: Issues of structure, function, and dynamics. In D. Albarracin, B. T. Johnson, & M. P. Zanna (Eds.), *The handbook of attitudes.* Mahwah, NJ: Erlbaum.

Krull, D. S. (2001). On partitioning the fundamental attribution error: Dispositionalism and the correspondence bias. In G. B. Moskowitz (Ed.), *Cognitive social psychology: The Princeton Symposium on the legacy and future of social cognition.* Mahwah, NJ: Erlbaum.

Krull, D. S., & Erickson, D. J. (1995). Inferential hopscotch: How people draw social inferences from behavior. *Current Directions in Psychological Science, 4,* 35–38.

Kryger, M. H. (1993). Snoring. In M. A. Carskadon (Ed.), *Encyclopedia of sleep and dreaming.* New York, NY: Macmillan.

Kryger, M. H., Roth, T., & Dement, W. C. (2005). *Principles and practice of sleep medicine.* Philadelphia, PA: Elsevier Saunders.

Kubovy, M., Epstein, W., & Gepshtein, S. (2003). Foundations of visual perception. In A. F. Healy & R. W. Proctor (Eds.), *Handbook of psychology.* New York, NY: Wiley.

Kudielka, B. M., & Kirschbaum, C. (2005). Sex differences in HPA axis responses to stress: A review. *Biological Pschology, 69,* 113–132.

Kuehn, B. M. (2007). Scientists probe deep brain stimulation: Some promise for brain injury, psychiatric illness. *Journal of the American Medical Association, 298,* 2249–2207.

Kuepper, R., Morrison, P. D., van Os, J., Murray, R. M., Kenis, G., & Henquet, C. (2010). Does dopamine mediate the psychosis-inducing effects of cannabis? A review and integration of findings across disciplines. *Schizophrenia Research, 121*(1–3), 107–117. doi:10.1016/j.schres.2010.05.031

Kuepper, R., van Os, J., Lieb, R., Wittchen, H., Höfler, M., & Henquet, C. (2011). Continued cannabis use and risk of incidence and persistence of psychotic symptoms: 10 year follow-up cohort study. *British Medical Journal, 342*(7796). Retrieved from http://www.bmj.com/content/342/bmj.d738.full

Kuhl, B. A., Dudukovic, N. M., Kahn, I., & Wagner, A. D. (2007). Decreased demands on cognitive control reveal the neural processing benefits of forgetting. *Nature Neuroscience, 10,* 908–914.

Kuhl, P. K., Conboy, B. T., Coffey-Corina, S., Padden, D., Rivera-Gaxiola, M., & Nelson, T. (2008). Phonetic learning as a pathway to language: New data and native language magnet theory expanded (NLM-e). *Philosophical Transactions of the Royal Society of London, B, 363,* 979–1000.

Kuhn, D. (2006). Do cognitive changes accompany developments in the adolescent brain? *Perspectives on Psychological Science, 1*(1), 59–67.

Kulick, A. R., Pope, H. G., & Keck, P. E. (1990). Lycanthropy and self-identification. *Journal of Nervous & Mental Disease, 178*(2), 134–137.

Kung, S., & Mrazek, D. A. (2005). Psychiatric emergency department visits on full-moon nights. *Psychiatric Services, 56,* 221–222.

Kunstler, J. H. (2005). *The long emergency: Surviving the end of oil, climate change, and other converging cas-trophes of the twenty-first century.* New York, NY: Grove Press.

Kuo, F. E., & Faber Taylor, A. (2004). A potential natural treatment for attention-deficit/hyperactivity disorder: Evidence from a national study. *American Journal of Public Health, 94,* 1580–1586.

Kuo, F. E., & Faber Taylor, A. (2005). Mother nature as treatment for ADHD: Overstating the benefits of green. Kuo and Faber Taylor respond. *American Journal of Public Health, 95,* 371–372.

Kuo, F. E., & Sullivan, W. C. (2001). Aggression and violence in the inner city: Effects of environment via mental fatigue. *Environment and Behavior, 33*(4), 543–571.

Kuo, Y. T., Parkinson, J. R. C., Chaudhri, O. B., Herlihy, A. H., So, P. W., Dhillo, W. S., et al. (2007). The temporal sequence of gut peptide-CNS interactions tracked in vivo by magnetic resonance imaging. *Journal of Neuroscience, 27,* 12341–12348.

Kurtz, K. J., & Loewenstein, J. (2007). Converging on a new role for analogy in problem solving and retrieval: When two problems are better than one. *Memory & Cognition, 35,* 334–342.

Kurtz, M. M., & Mueser, K. T. (2008). A meta-analysis of controlled research on social skills training for schizophrenia. *Journal of Consulting and Clinical Psychology, 76*(3), 491–504. doi:10.1037/0022-006X.76.3.491

Kutchins, H., & Kirk, S. A. (1997). *Making us crazy: DSM—The psychiatric Bible and the creation of mental disorders.* New York, NY: Free Press.

Kyle, S. D., Morgan, K., & Espie, C. A. (2010). Insomnia and health-related quality of life. *Sleep Medicine Reviews, 14*(1), 69–82. doi:10.1016/j.smrv.2009.07.004

La Cerra, P., & Kurzban, R. (1995). The structure of scientific revolutions and the nature of the adapted mind. *Psychological Inquiry, 6,* 62–65.

La Torre, M. A. (2007). Positive psychology: Is there too much of a push? *Perspectives in Psychiatric Care, 43,* 151–153.

LaBerge, S. (1990). Lucid dreaming: Psychophysiological studies of consciousness during REM sleep. In R. R. Bootzin, J. F. Kihlstrom, & D. L. Schacter (Eds.), *Sleep and cognition.* Washington, DC: American Psychological Association.

LaBerge, S. (2007). Lucid dreaming. In D. Barrett & P. McNamara (Eds.), *The new science of dreaming: Content, recall, and personality correlates.* Westport, CT: Praeger.

LaBine, S. J., & LaBine, G. (1996). Determinations of negligence and the hindsight bias. *Law & Human Behavior, 20,* 501–516.

Labouvie-Vief, G. (2006). Emerging structures of adult thought. In J. J. Arnett & J. L. Tanner (Eds.), *Emerging adults in America: Coming of age in the 21st century.* Washington, DC: American Psychological Association.

Lachman, S. J. (1996). Processes in perception: Psychological transformations of highly structured stimulus material. *Perceptual and Motor Skills, 83,* 411–418.

Lachter, J., Forster, K. I., & Ruthruff, E. (2004). Forty-five years after Broadbent (1958): Still no identification without attention. *Psychological Review, 111,* 880–913.

Lader, M. H. (2002). Managing dependence and withdrawal with newer hypnotic medications in the treatment of insomnia. *Journal of Clinical Psychiatry, 4*(suppl 1), 33–37.

Laditka, S. B., Laditka, J. N., & Probst, J. C. (2006). Racial and ethnic disparities in potentially avoidable delivery complications among pregnant Medicaid beneficiaries in South Carolina. *Maternal & Child Health Journal, 10,* 339–350.

Lagopoulos, J., Xu, J., Rasmussen, I., Vik, A., Malhi, G., Eliassen, C. F., et al. (2009). Increased theta and alpha EEG activity during nondirective meditation. *The Journal of Alternative and Complementary Medicine, 15*(11), 1187–1192.

Lahey, B. B. (2009). Public health significance of neuroticism. *American Psychologist, 64*(4), 241–256. doi:10.1037/a0015309

Lakein, A. (1996). *How to get control of your time and your life.* New York, NY: New American Library.

Lakey, B., & Cronin, A. (2008). Low social support and major depression: Research, theory and methodological issues. In K. S. Dobson & D. A. Dozois (Eds.), *Risk factors in depression* (pp. 385–408). San Diego, CA: Academic Press. doi:10.1016/B978-0-08-045078-0.00017-4

Lamb, H. R. (1998). Deinstitutionalization at the beginning of the new millennium. *Harvard Review of Psychiatry, 6,* 1–10.

Lamb, M. E., Ketterlinus, R. D., & Fracasso, M. P. (1992). Parent-child relationships. In M. H. Bornstein & M. E. Lamb (Eds.), *Developmental psychology: An advanced textbook* (3rd ed.). Hillsdale, NJ: Erlbaum.

Lamb, M. E., & Lewis, C. (2011). The role of parent-child relationships in child development. In M. H. Bornstein & M. E. Lamb (Eds.), *Developmental science: An advanced textbook* (pp. 469–518). New York, NY: Psychology Press.

Lambert, M. J. (2011). Psychotherapy research and its achievements. In J. C. Norcross, G. R. Vandenbos, & D. K. Freedheim (Eds.), *History of psychotherapy: Continuity and change* (2nd ed.). Washington, DC: American Psychological Association.

Lambert, M. J., & Archer, A. (2006). Research findings on the effects of psychotherapy and their implications for practice. In C. D. Goodheart, A. E. Kazdin, & R. J. Sternberg (Eds.), *Evidence-based psychotherapy: Where practice and research meet* (pp. 111–130). Washington, DC: American Psychological Association.

Lambert, M. J., & Bergin, A. E. (1992). Achievements and limitations of psychotherapy research. In D. K. Freedheim (Ed.), *History of psychotherapy: A century of change.* Washington, DC: American Psychological Association.

Lambert, M. J., Bergin, A. E., & Garfield, S. L. (2004). Introduction and historical overview. In M. J. Lambert (Ed.), *Bergin and Garfield's handbook of psychotherapy and behavior change.* New York, NY: Wiley.

Lambert, M. J., Hansen, N. B., & Finch A. E. (2001). Patient-focused research: Using patient outcome data to enhance treatment effects. *Journal of Consulting and Clinical Psychology, 69,* 159–172.

Lambert, M. J., & Ogles, B. M. (2004). The efficacy and effectiveness of psychotherapy. In M. J. Lambert (Ed.), *Bergin and Garfield's handbook of psychotherapy and behavior change.* New York, NY: Wiley.

Lampert, R., Shusterman, V., Burg, M., McPherson, C., Batsford, W., Goldberg, A., & Soufer, R. (2009). Anger-induced T-wave alternans predicts future ventricular arrhythmias in patients with implantable cardioverter-defibrillators. *Journal of the American College of Cardiology, 53*(9), 774–778.

Lampinen, J. M., Neuschatz, J. S., & Payne, D. G. (1999). Source attributions and false memories: A test of the demand characteristics account. *Psychonomic Bulletin & Review, 6,* 130–135.

Landabaso, M. A., Iraurgi, I., Sanz, J., Calle, R., Ruiz de Apodaka, J., Jimenez-Lerma, J. M., & Gutierrez-Fraile, M. (1999). Naltrexone in the treatment of alcoholism. Two-year follow up results. *European Journal of Psychiatry, 13,* 97–105.

Landel-Graham, J., Yount, S. E., & Rudnicki, S. R. (2003). Diabetes mellitus. In A. M. Nezu, C. M. Nezu, & P. A. Geller (Eds.). *Handbook of psychology, Vol. 9: Health psychology.* New York, NY: Wiley.

Laney, C., & Loftus, E. F. (2005). Traumatic memories are not necessarily accurate memories. *The Canadian Journal of Psychiatry, 50,* 823–828.

Lange, C. (1885). One leuds beveegelser. In K. Dunlap (Ed.), *The emotions.* Baltimore: Williams & Wilkins.

Langevin, R., & Curnoe, S. (2004). The use of pornography during the commission of sexual offenses. *International Journal of Offender Therapy & Comparative Criminology, 48,* 572–586.

Langlois, J. H., Kalakanis, L., Rubenstein, A. J., Larson, A., Hallam, M., & Smoot, M. (2000). Maxims or myths of beauty? A meta-analytic and theoretical review. *Psychological Bulletin, 126,* 390–423.

Lanyon, R. I., & Goodstein, L. D. (1997). *Personality assessment.* New York, NY: Wiley.

LaPiere, R. T. (1934). Attitude and actions. *Social Forces, 13,* 230–237.

Lapierre, Y. D. (2003). Suicidality with selective serotonin reuptake inhibitors: Valid claim? *Journal of Psychiatry & Neuroscience, 28,* 340–347.

Lapsley, D. K. (2006). Moral stage theory. In M. Killen & J. G. Smetana (Eds.), *Handbook of moral development.* Mahwah, NJ: Erlbaum.

Larsen, D. P., Butler, A. C., & Roediger, H. L. III. (2009). Repeated testing improves long-term retention relative to repeated study: A randomised controlled trial. *Medical Education, 43*(12), 1174–1181. doi:10.1111/j.1365-2923.2009.03518.x

Larsen, J. T., Berntson, G. G., Poehlmann, K. M., Ito, T. A., & Cacioppo, J. T. (2008). The psychophysiology of emotion. In M. Lewis, J. M. Haviland-Jones, & L. F. Barrett (Eds.), *Handbook of emotions* (3rd ed., pp. 180–195). New York, NY: Guilford Press.

Larsen, J. T., McGraw, A. P., Mellers, B. A., & Cacioppo, J. T. (2004). The agony of victory and thrill of defeat: Mixed emotional reactions to disappointing wins and relieving losses. *Psychological Science, 15,* 325–330.

Larsen, R. J., & Prizmic, Z. (2008). Regulation of emotional well-being: Overcoming the hedonic treadmill. In M. Eid & R. J. Larsen (Eds.), *The science of subjective well-being* (pp. 258–289). New York, NY: Guilford Press.

Larson, R., & Wilson, S. (2004). Adolescence across place and time: Globalization and the changing pathways to adulthood. In R. M. Lerner & L. Steinberg (Eds.), *Handbook of adolescent psychology.* New York, NY: Wiley.

Laska, M., Seibt, A., & Weber, A. (2000). "Microsmatic" primates revisited: Olfactory sensitivity in the squirrel monkey. *Chemical Senses, 25,* 47–53. doi: 10.1093/chemse/25.1.47

Latané, B. (1981). The psychology of social impact. *American Psychologist, 36,* 343–356.

Latané, B., & Nida, S. A. (1981). Ten years of research on group size and helping. *Psychological Bulletin, 89,* 308–324.

Latané, B., Williams, K., & Harkins, S. (1979). Many hands make light the work: The causes and consequences of social loafing. *Journal of Personality and Social Psychology, 37,* 822–832.

Lattal, K. A. (1992). B. F. Skinner and psychology [Introduction to the Special Issue]. *American Psychologist, 27,* 1269–1272.

Laughlin, H. (1967). *The neuroses.* Washington, DC: Butterworth.

Laughlin, H. (1979). *The ego and its defenses.* New York, NY: Aronson.

Laumann, E. O., Gagnon, J. H., Michael, R. T., & Michaels, S. (1994). *The social organization of sexuality: Sexual practices in the United States.* Chicago: University of Chicago Press.

Laumann, K., Gärling, T. & Stormark, K. M. (2003). Selective attention and heart rate responses to natural and urban environments. *Journal of Environmental Psychology, 23,* 125–134.

Laurence, J-R., Beaulieu-Prevost, D., & du Chene, T. (2008). Measuring and understanding individual differences in hypnotizability. In M. R. Nash & A. J. Barnier (Eds.). *Oxford handbook of hypnosis: Theory, research and practice* (pp. 225–254). New York, NY: Oxford University Press.

Lauriello, J., Bustillo, J. R., & Keith, J. (2005). Schizophrenia: Scope of the problem. In B. J. Sadock & V. A. Sadock (Eds.), *Kaplan & Sadock's comprehensive textbook of psychiatry* (pp. 1345–1353). Philadelphia, PA: Lippincott Williams & Wilkins.

Laursen, B., Coy, K. C., & Collins, W. A. (1998). Reconsidering changes in parent-child conflict across adolescence: A meta-analysis. *Child Development, 69,* 817–832.

Lavie, N. (2005). Distracted and confused? Selective attention under load. *Trends in Cognitive Sciences, 9*(2), 75–82.

Lavie, N. (2007). Attention and consciousness. In M. Velmans & S. Schneider (Eds.), *The Blackwell companion to consciousness* (pp. 489–503). Malden, MA: Blackwell Publishing.

Lavoie, K. L., & Barone, S. (2006). Prescription privileges for psychologists: A comprehensive review and critical analysis of current issues and controversies. *CNS Drugs, 20*(1), 51–66.

Lawler, E. E., Mohrman, S. A., & Ledford, G. E. (1995). *Creating high-performance organizations: Practices and results of employee involvement and total quality management in Fortune 1000 companies.* San Francisco, CA: Jossey-Bass.

Lawless, H. T. (2001). Taste. In E. B. Goldstein (Ed.), *Blackwell handbook of perception.* Malden, MA: Blackwell.

Laws, K. R., & Kokkalis, J. (2007). Ecstasy (MDMA) and memory function: A meta-analytic update. *Human Psychopharmacology: Clinical & Experimental, 22*(6), 381–388. doi:10.1002/hup.857

Lazarus, A. A. (1992). Multimodal therapy: Technical eclecticism with minimal integration. In J. C. Norcross & M. R. Goldfried (Eds.), *Handbook of psychotherapy integration.* New York, NY: Basic Books.

Lazarus, A. A. (1995). Different types of eclecticism and integration: Let's be aware of the dangers. *Journal of Psychotherapy Integration, 5,* 27–39.

Lazarus, A. A. (2008). Technical eclecticism and multimodal therapy. In J. L. Lebow (Ed.), *Twenty-first century psychotherapies: Contemporary approaches to theory and practice.* New York, NY: Wiley.

Lazarus, R. S. (1993). Why we should think of stress as a subset of emotion. In L. Goldberger & S. Breznitz (Eds.), *Handbook of stress: Theoretical and clinical aspects* (2nd ed.). New York, NY: Free Press.

Lazarus, R. S. (2003). Does the positive psychology movement have legs? *Psychological Inquiry, 14*(2), 93–109.

Lazarus, R., & Folkman, S. (1984). *Stress, appraisal, and coping.* New York, NY: Springer.

Leary, D. E. (2003). A profound and radical change: How William James inspired the reshaping of American psychology. In R. J. Sternberg (Ed.), *The anatomy of impact: What makes the great works of psychology great* (pp. 19–42). Washington, DC: American Psychological Association.

Leavitt, F. (1995). *Drugs and behavior* (3rd ed.). Thousand Oaks, CA: Sage.

LeBoeuf, M. (1980, February). Managing time means managing yourself. *Business Horizons,* 41–46.

Lebow, J. L. (2008). Couple and family therapy. In J. L. Lebow (Ed.), *Twenty-first century psychotherapies: Contemporary approaches to theory and practice* (pp. 307–346). New York, NY: Wiley.

Ledbetter, A. M., Griffin, E., & Sparks, G. G. (2007). Forecasting "friends forever": A longitudinal investigation of sustained closeness between best friends. *Personal Relationships, 14*(2), 343–350. doi:10.1111/j.1475-6811.2007.00158.x

LeDoux, J. E. (1993). Emotional networks in the brain. In M. Lewis & J. M. Haviland (Eds.), *Handbook of emotions.* New York, NY: Guilford Press.

LeDoux, J. E. (1994). Emotion, memory and the brain. *Scientific American, 270,* 50–57.

LeDoux, J. E. (1995). Emotion: Clues from the brain. *Annual Review of Psychology, 46,* 209–235.

LeDoux, J. E. (1996). *The emotional brain.* New York, NY: Simon & Schuster.

LeDoux, J. E. (2000). Emotion circuits in the brain. *Annual Review of Neuroscience, 23,* 155–184.

LeDoux, J. E., & Phelps, E. A. (2008). Emotional networks in the brain. In M. Lewis, J. M. Haviland-Jones, & L. F. Barrett, *Handbook of emotions* (3rd ed.). New York, NY: Guilford Press.

LeDoux, J. E., Schiller, D., & Cain, C. (2009). Emotional reaction and action: From threat processing to goal-directed behavior. In M. S. Gazzangia (Ed.), *The cognitive neurosciences* (4th ed., pp. 905–924). Cambridge, MA: MIT Press.

Lee, K., & Ashton, M. C. (2008). The HEXACO personality factors in the indigenous personality lexicons of English and 11 other languages. *Journal of Personality, 76*(5), 1001–1053. doi:10.1111/j.1467-6494.2008.00512.x

Lee, L., Loewenstein, G., Ariely, D., Hong, J., & Young, J. (2008). If I'm not hot, are you hot or not? Physical-attractiveness evaluations and dating preferences as a function of one's own attractiveness. *Psychological Science, 19*(7), 669–677. doi:10.1111/j.1467-9280.2008.02141.x

Lee, R. M., & Ramirez, M. (2000). The history, current status, and future of multicultural psychotherapy. In I. Cuellar & F. A. Paniagua (Eds.), *Handbook of multicultural mental health: Assessment and treatment of diverse populations.* San Diego: Academic Press.

Lee, S., & Katzman, M. A. (2002). Cross-cultural perspectives on eating disorders. In C. G. Fairburn & K. D. Brownell (Eds.), *Eating disorders and obesity: A comprehensive handbook.* New York, NY: Guilford Press.

Lee, Y., Gaskins, D., Anand, A., & Shekhar, A. (2007). Glia mechanisms in mood regulation: A novel model of mood disorders. *Psychopharmacology, 191,* 55–65.

Lee-Chiong, T., & Sateia, M. (2006). Pharmacologic therapy of insomnia. In T. Lee-Chiong (Ed.), *Sleep: A comprehensive handbook.* Hoboken, NJ: Wiley-Liss.

Leeper, R. W. (1935). A study of a neglected portion of the field of learning: The development of sensory organization. *Journal of Genetic Psychology, 46,* 41–75.

Lefcourt, H. M. (2001). The humor solution. In C. R. Snyder (Ed.), *Coping with stress: Effective people and processes* (pp. 68–92). New York, NY: Oxford University Press.

Lefcourt, H. M. (2005). Humor. In C. R. Snyder & S. J. Lopez (Eds.), *Handbook of positive psychology.* New York, NY: Oxford University Press.

Lefcourt, H. M., Davidson, K., Shepherd, R., Phillips, M., Prkachin, K., & Mills, D. (1995). Perspective-taking humor: Accounting for stress moderation. *Journal of Social and Clinical Psychology, 14,* 373–391.

Leff, J. (2006). Whose life is it anyway? Quality of life for long-stay patients discharged from psychiatric hospitals. In H. Katschnig, H. Freeman, & N. Sartorius (Eds.), *Quality of life in mental disorders.* New York, NY: Wiley.

Leff, J., & Vaughn, C. (1985). *Expressed emotion in families.* New York, NY: Guilford Press.

Legault, E., & Laurence, J.-R. (2007). Recovered memories of childhood sexual abuse: Social worker, psychologist, and psychiatrist reports of beliefs, practices, and cases. *Australian Journal of Clinical & Experimental Hypnosis, 35,* 111–133.

Lehman, D. R., Chiu, C., & Schaller, M. (2004). Psychology and culture. *Annual Review of Psychology, 55,* 689–714.

Lehman, P. K., & Geller, E. S. (2004). Behavior analysis and environmental protection: Accomplishments and potential for more. *Behavior and Social Issues, 13,* 13–32.

Lehrer, P., Feldman, J., Giardino, N., Song, H., & Schmaling, K. (2002). Psychological aspects of asthma. *Journal of Consulting & Clinical Psychology, 70,* 691–711.

Leibovic, K. N. (1990). Vertebrate photoreceptors. In K. N. Leibovic (Ed.), *Science of vision.* New York, NY: Springer-Verlag.

Leichsenring, F. & Rabung, S. (2008). Effectiveness of long-term psychodynamic psychotherapy: A meta-analysis. *Journal of the American Medical Association, 13,* 1551–1565.

Leighton, J. P., & Sternberg, R. J. (2003). Reasoning and problem solving. In A. F. Healy & R. W. Proctor (Eds.), *Handbook of psychology, Vol. 4: Experimental psychology.* New York, NY: Wiley.

Leiserowitz, A. (2007). Communicating the risks of global warming: American risk perceptions, affective images, and interpretive communities. In S. C. Moser & L. Dilling (Eds.), *Creating a climate for change: Communicating climate change and facilitating social change* (pp. 44–63). New York, NY: Cambridge University Press.

Leiter, M. P., & Maslach, C. (2001). Burnout and health. In A. Baum, T. A. Revenson, & J. E. Singer (Eds.), *Handbook of health psychology* (pp. 415–426). Mahwah, NJ: Erlbaum.

Lemay, E. P., Jr., Clark, M. S., & Greenberg, A. (2010). What is beautiful is good because what is beautiful is desired: Physical attractiveness stereotyping as projection of interpersonal goals. *Personality and Social Psychology Bulletin, 36*(3), 339-353. doi:10.1177/0146167209359700

Lemery, K. S., Goldsmith, H. H., Klinnert, M. D., & Mrazek, D. A. (1999). Developmental models of infant and childhood temperament. *Developmental Psychology, 35,* 189–204.

Lennings, C. J. (1997). Police and occupationally related violence: A review. *Policing: An International Journal of Police Strategies and Management, 20,* 555–566.

Leon, D. A., Lawlor, D. A., Clark, H. H., Batty, G. D., & Macintyre, S. S. (2009). The association of childhood intelligence with mortality risk from adolescence to middle age: Findings from the Aberdeen Children of the 1950s cohort study. *Intelligence, 37*(6), 520–528. doi:10.1016/j.intell.2008.11.00

Leopold, D. A., Wilke, M., Maier, A., & Logothetis, N. K. (2002). Stable perception of visually ambiguous patterns. *Nature Neuroscience, 5,* 605–609.

LePine, J. A., Erez, A., & Johnston, D. E. (2002). The nature and dimensionality of organizational citizenship behavior: A critical review and a meta-analysis. *Journal of Applied Psychology, 87,* 52–65.

Lepine, R., Barrouillet, P., & Camos, V. (2005). What makes working memory spans so predictive of high-level cognition? *Psychonomic Bulletin & Review, 12*(1), 165–170.

Lerman, H. (1986). *A mote in Freud's eye: From psychoanalysis to the psychology of women.* New York, NY: Springer.

Lerner, J. S., Small, D. A., & Loewenstein, G. (2004). Heart strings and purse strings: Carryover effects of emotions on economic decisions. *Psychological Science, 15,* 337 341.

Lerner, M. J., & Goldberg, J. H. (1999). When do decent people blame victims? The differing effects of the explicit/rational and implicit/experiential cognitive systems. In S. Chaiken & Y. Trope (Eds.), *Dual-process theories in social psychology.* New York, NY: Guilford Press.

Lett, H. S., Blumenthal, J. A., Babyak, M. A., Sherwood, A., Strauman, T., Robbins, C., & Newman, M. F. (2004). Depression as a risk factor for coronary artery disease: Evidence, mechanisms, and treatment. *Psychosomatic Medicine, 66,* 305–315.

Leuner, B., & Gould, E. (2010). Structural plasticity and hippocampal function. *Annual Review of Psychology,* 61, 111–140. doi:10.1146/annurev.psych.093008.100359

Leuner, B., Gould, E., & Shors, T. J. (2006). Is there a link between adult neurogenesis and learning? *Hippocampus, 16,* 216–224.

LeVay, S. (1996). *Queer science: The use and abuse of research into homosexuality.* Cambridge, MA: MIT Press.

Levenson, R. W. (1992). Autonomic nervous system differences among emotions. *Psychological Science, 3,* 23–27.

Levenson, R. W. (2003). Autonomic specificity and emotion. In R. J. Davidson, K. R. Scherer, & H. H. Goldsmith (Eds.), *Handbook of affective sciences.* New York, NY: Oxford University Press.

Levenstein, S. (2002). Psychosocial factors in peptic ulcer and inflammatory bowel disease. *Journal of Consulting & Clinical Psychology, 70,* 739–750.

Leventhal, H., & Tomarken, A. J. (1986). Emotion: Today's problems. *Annual Review of Psychology,* 37, 565–610.

Levesque, M. J., Nave, C. S., & Lowe, C. A. (2006). Toward an understanding of gender differences in inferring sexual interest. *Psychology of Women Quarterly, 30,* 150–158.

Levin, S., Henry, P. J., Pratto, F., & Sidanius, J. (2003). Social dominance and social identity in Lebanon: Implications for support of violence against the West. *Group Processes and Intergroup Relations, 6,* 353–368.

Levine, B., Turner, G. R., Tisserand, D., Hevenor, S. J., Graham, S. J., & McIntosh, A. R. (2004). The functional neuroanatomy of episodic and semantic autobiographical remembering: A prospective functional MRI study. *Journal of Cognitive Neuroscience, 16,* 1633–1646.

Levine, J. M., & Moreland, R. L. (1998). Small groups. In D. T. Gilbert, S. T. Fiske, & G. Lindzey (Eds.), *The handbook of social psychology.* New York, NY: McGraw-Hill.

Levine, M., & Crowther, S. (2008). The responsive bystander: How social group membership and group size can encourage as well as inhibit bystander intervention. *Journal of Personality and Social Psychology, 95*(6), 1429–1439. doi:10.1037/a0012634

Levine, M. P., & Harrison, K. (2004). Media's role in the perpetuation and prevention of negative body image and disordered eating. In J. K. Thompson (Ed.), *Handbook of eating disorders and obesity.* New York, NY: Wiley.

Levine, R., & Norenzayan, A. (1999). The pace of life in 31 countries. *Journal of Cross-Cultural Psychology, 30,* 178–205.

Levine, R., Sata, S., Hashimoto, T., & Verma, J. (1995). Love and marriage in eleven cultures. *Journal of Cross-Cultural Psychology, 26,* 554–571.

Levinson, D. E. (2009). Genetics of major depression. In I. H. Gotlib & C. L. Hammen (Eds.), *Handbook of Depression* (2nd ed., pp. 165–186). New York, NY: Guilford Press.

Levinthal, C. F. (2008). *Drugs, behavior, and modern society.* Boston, MA: Pearson.

Levis, D. J. (1989). The case for a return to a two-factor theory of avoidance: The failure of non-fear interpretations. In S. B. Klein & R. R. Bowrer (Eds.), *Contemporary learning theories: Pavlovian conditioning and the status of traditional learning theory.* Hillsdale NJ: Erlbaum.

Levitt, A. J., Schaffer, A., & Lanctôt, K. L. (2009). Buspirone. In B. J. Sadock, V. A. Sadock, & P. Ruiz (Eds.), *Kaplan & Sadock's comprehensive textbook of psychiatry* (pp. 3060–3064). Philadelphia, PA: Lippincott, Williams & Wilkins.

Levitt, J. B. (2010). Receptive fields. In E. B. Goldstein (Ed.), *Encyclopedia of perception.* Thousand Oaks, CA: Sage.

Levy, G. D., Taylor, M. G., & Gelman, S. A. (1995). Traditional and evaluative aspects of flexibility in gender roles, social conventions, moral rules, and physical laws. *Child Development, 66,* 515–531.

Lewandowsky, S., Duncan, M., & Brown, G. D. A. (2004). Time does not cause forgetting in short-term serial recall. *Psychonomic Bulletin & Review, 11*(5), 771–790.

Lewin, K. (1935). *A dynamic theory of personality.* New York, NY: McGraw-Hill.

Lewinsohn, P. M., Joiner, T. E., Jr., & Rohde, P. (2001). Evaluation of cognitive diathesis-stress models in predicting major depressive disorder in adolescents. *Journal of Abnormal Psychology, 110,* 203–215.

Lewis, C., & Lamb, M. E. (2003). Fathers' influences on children's development: The evidence from two-parent families. *European Journal of Psychology of Education, 18,* 211–228.

Lewis, S., Escalona, P. R., & Keith, S. J. (2009). Phenomenology of schizophrenia. In B. J. Sadock, V. A. Sadock, & P. Ruiz (Eds.), *Kaplan & Sadock's comprehensive textbook of psychiatry* (9th ed., pp. 1433–1450). Philadelphia, PA: Lippincott, Williams & Wilkins.

Lewis-Fernandez, R., Guarnaccia, P. J., & Ruiz, P. (2009). Culture-bound syndromes. In B. J. Sadock, V. A. Sadock, & P. Ruiz (Eds.), *Kaplan & Sadock's comprehensive textbook of psychiatry* (9th ed.). Philadelphia, PA: Lippincott, Williams & Wilkins.

Li, N. P., & Kenrick, D. T. (2006). Sex similarities and differences in preferences for short-term mates: What, whether, and why. *Journal of Personality and Social Psychology, 90,* 468–489.

Li, S. C., Lindenberger, U., Hommel, B., Aschersleben, G., Prinz, W., & Baltes, P. B. (2004). Transformations in the couplings among intellectual abilities and constituent cognitive processes across the life span. *Psychological Science, 15,* 155–163.

Liberman, R. P., & Kopelowicz, A. (2005). Recovery from schizophrenia: A concept in search of research. *Psychiatric Services, 56,* 735–742.

Lichten, W., & Simon, E. W. (2007). Defining mental retardation: A matter of life or death. *Intellectual and Developmental Disabilities, 45,* 335–346.

Lichtenstein, S., Fischhoff, B., & Phillips, L. (1982). Calibration of probabilities: The state of the art to 1980. In D. Kahneman, P. Slovic, & A. Tversky (Eds.), *Judgment under uncertainty: Heuristics and biases.* Cambridge, England: Cambridge University Press.

Lichtenthal, W. G., Cruess, D. G., & Prigerson, H. G. (2004). A case for establishing complicated grief as a distinct mental disorder in DSM-V. *Clinical Psychology Review, 24,* 637–662.

Lickliter, R. (2009). The fallacy of partitioning: Epigenetics' validation of the organism-environment system. *Ecological Psychology,* 21(2), 138–146. doi:10.1080/10407410902877157

Lickliter, R., & Honeycutt, H. (2003). Developmental dynamics: Toward a biologically plausible evolutionary psychology. *Psychological Bulletin, 129,* 819–835.

Liddle, P. F. (2009). Descriptive clinical features of schizophrenia. In M. C. Gelder, N. C. Andreasen, J. J. López-Ibor, Jr., & J. R. Geddes (Eds.). *New Oxford textbook of psychiatry* (2nd ed., Vol. 1). New York, NY: Oxford University Press.

Liden, R. C., Wayne, S. J., Jaworski, R. A., & Bennett, N. (2004). Social loafing: A field investigation. *Journal of Management, 30,* 285–304.

Lieberman, D., & Hatfield, E. (2006). Passionate love: Cross-cultural and evolutionary perspectives. In R. J. Sternberg & K. Weis (Eds.), *The new psychology of love.* New Haven, CT: Yale University Press.

Liebert, R. M., & Liebert, L. L. (1998). *Liebert & Spiegler's personality strategies and issues.* Pacific Grove: Brooks/Cole.

Liefbroer, A. C., & Dourleijn, E. (2006). Unmarried cohabitation and union stability: Testing the role of diffusion using data from 16 European countries. *Demography, 43,* 203–221.

Lien, M.-C., Ruthruff, E., & Johnston, J. C. (2006). Attentional limitations in doing two tasks at once. *Current Directions in Psychological Science, 15,* 89–93.

Likert, R. (1967). *The human organization: Its management and value.* New York, NY: McGraw-Hill.

Lilienfeld, S. O. (2007). Psychological treatments that cause harm. *Perspectives on Psychological Science, 2,* 53–70.

Lilienfeld, S. O., Ammirati, R., & Landfield, K. (2009). Giving debiasing away: Can psychological research on correcting cognitive errors promote human welfare? *Perspectives on Psychological Science, 4*(4), 390–398. doi:10.1111/j.1745-6924.2009.01144.x

Lilienfeld, S. O., & Arkowitz, H. (2009, February/March). Lunacy and the full moon: Does a full moon really trigger strange behavior? *Scientific American Mind,* 64–65.

Lilienfeld, S. O., & Landfield, K. (2008). Issues in diagnosis: Categorical vs. dimensional. In W. E. Craighead, D. J. Miklowitz, & L. W. Craighead (Eds.), *Psychopathology: History, diagnosis, and empirical foundations.* New York, NY: Wiley.

Lilienfeld, S. O., & Lynn, S. J. (2003). Dissociative identity disorder: Multiple personalities, multiple controversies. In S. O. Lilienfeld, S. J. Lynn, & J. M. Lohr (Eds.), *Science and pseudoscience in clinical psychology.* New York, NY: Guilford Press.

Lilienfeld, S. O., Lynn, S. J., Kirsch, I., Chaves, J. F., Sarbin, T. R., Ganaway, G. K., & Powell, R. A. (1999). Dissociative identity disorder and the sociocognitive model: Recalling the lessons of the past. *Psychological Bulletin, 125,* 507–523.

Lilienfeld, S. O., Lynn, S. J., Ruscio, J., & Beyerstein, B. L. (2010). *50 great myths of popular psychology: Shattering widespread misconceptions about human behavior.* Malden, MA: Wiley-Blackwell.

Lilienfeld, S. O., Wood, J. M., & Garb, H. N. (2000). The scientific status of projective tests. *Psychological Science in the Public Interest, 1*(2), 27–66.

Lim, M. M., & Young, L. J. (2006). Neuropepridergic regulation of affiliative behavior and social bonding in animals. *Hormones and Behavior, 50*(4), 506–517.

Lima, M. L. (2004). On the influence of risk perception on mental health: Living near an incinerator. *Journal of Environmental Psychology, 24,* 71–84.

Lin, S. W., & Anthnelli, R. M. (2005). Genetic factors in the risk for substance use disorders. In J. H. Lowinson, P. Ruiz, R. B. Millman, & J. G. Langrod (Eds.), *Substance abuse: A comprehensive textbook.* Philadelphia, PA: Lippincott/Williams & Wilkins.

Lindau, S., & Gavrilova, N. (2010). Sex, health, and years of sexually active life gained due to good health: Evidence from two U.S. population based cross sectional surveys of ageing. *British Medical Journal, 340,* c810. doi:10.1136/bmj.c810

Linde, J. A., Rothman, A. J., Baldwin, A. S., & Jeffery, R. W. (2006). The impact of self-efficacy on behavior change and weight change among overweight participants in a weight-loss trial. *Health Psychology, 25,* 282–291.

Lindgren, H. C. (1969). *The psychology of college success: A dynamic approach.* New York, NY: Wiley.

Lindsay, M., & Lester, D. (2004). *Suicide by cop: Committing suicide by provoking police to shoot you (death, value and meaning).* Amityville, NY: Baywood Publishing.

Lindsay, P. H., & Norman, D. A. (1977). *Human information processing.* New York, NY: Academic Press.

Lindsay, S. D., Allen, B. P., Chan, J. C. K., & Dahl, L. C. (2004). Eyewitness suggestibility and source similarity: Intrusions of details from one event into memory reports of another event. *Journal of Memory & Language, 50*(1), 96–111.

Lindsay, S. D., & Read, J. D. (1994). Psychotherapy and memories of childhood sexual abuse: A cognitive perspective. *Applied Cognitive Psychology, 8,* 281–338.

Lindsay, S. D., & Read, J. D. (2001). The recovered memories controversy: Where do we go from here? In G. M. Davies & T. Dalgleish (Eds.), *Recovered memories: Seeking the middle ground.* Chichester, England: Wiley.

Lindshield, S. M., & Rodrigues, M. A. (2009). Tool use in wild spider monkeys (*Ateles geoffroyi*). *Primates, 50*(3), 269–272. doi: 10.1007/s10329-009-0144-3

Linn, S. (2004). *Consuming kids: The hostile takeover of childhood.* New York & London: New Press.

Linn, S. (2008). Commercializing childhood: The corporate takeover of kids' lives. (interview by the Multinational Monitor). Retrieved from http://towardfreedom.com/home/content/view/1389/1/

Lipert, J., Bauder, H., Miltner, W. H. R., Taub, E., & Weiller, C. (2000). Treatment-induced cortical reorganization after stroke in humans. *Stroke, 31,* 1210–1216.

Lipp, O. V., Oughton, N., & LeLievre, J. (2003). Evaluative learning in human Pavlovian conditioning: Extinct, but still there? *Learning and Motivation, 34,* 219–239. doi: 10.1016/S0023-9690(03)00011-0

Lippa, R. A. (1994). *Introduction to social psychology.* Pacific Grove, CA: Brooks/Cole.

Lippa, R. A. (2005). *Gender, nature, and nurture.* Mahwah, NJ: Erlbaum.

Lippa, R. A., Martin, L. R., & Friedman, H. S. (2000). Gender-related individual differences and mortality in the Terman longitudinal study: Is masculinity hazardous to your health? *Personality and Social Psychology Bulletin, 26,* 1560–1570.

Lipton, J. S., & Spelke, E. S. (2004). Discrimination of large and small numerosities by human infants. *Infancy, 5,* 271–290.

Liptzin, B., Gottlieb, G. L., Summergrad, P. (2007). The future of psychiatric services in general hospitals. *American Journal of Psychiatry, 164*(10), 1468–1472.

Lissek, S., Rabin, S., Heller, R. E., Lukenbaugh, D., Geraci, M., Pine, D. S., & Grillon, C. (2010). Overgeneralization of conditioned fear as a pathogenic marker of panic disorder. *American Journal of Psychiatry, 167*(1), 47–55. doi: 10.1176/appi.ajp.2009.09030410.

Liston, C. C., McEwen, B. S., & Casey, B. J. (2009). Psychosocial stress reversibly disrupts prefrontal processing and attentional control. *Proceedings of the National Academy of Sciences of the United States of America, 106*(3), 912–917. doi:10.1073/pnas.0807041106

Little, A. C., Jones, B. C., & Burriss, R. P. (2007). Preferences for masculinity in male bodies change across the menstrual cycle. *Hormones and Behavior, 51,* 633–639.

Little, A. C., & Mannion, H. (2006). Viewing attractive or unattractive same-sex individuals changes self-rated attractiveness and face preferences in women. *Animal Behaviour, 72,* 981–987.

Liu, M., Siefferman, L., Mays, H., Jr., Steffen, J. E., & Hill, G. E. (2009). A field test of female mate preference for male plumage coloration in eastern bluebirds. *Animal Behaviour, 78*(4), 879–885. doi:10.1016/j.anbehav.2009.07.012

Livesley, W. J., Jang, K. L., & Vernon, P. A. (2003). Genetic basis of personality structure. In T. Millon & M. J. Lerner (Eds.), *Handbook of psychology, Vol. 5: Personality and social psychology.* New York, NY: Wiley.

Lizarraga, M. L. S., & Ganuza, J. M. G. (2003). Improvement of mental rotation in girls and boys. *Sex Roles, 40,* 277–286.

Lockhart, R. S. (1992). Measurement of memory. In L. R. Squire (Ed.), *Encyclopedia of learning and memory.* New York, NY: Macmillan.

Lockhart, R. S. (2000). Methods of memory research. In E. Tulving & F. I. M. Craik (Eds.), *The Oxford handbook of memory* (pp. 45–58). New York, NY: Oxford University Press.

Lockhart, R. S. (2002). Levels of processing, transfer-appropriate processing and the concept of robust encoding. *Memory, 10,* 397–403.

Lockhart, R. S., & Craik, F. I. (1990). Levels of processing: A retrospective commentary on a framework for memory research. *Canadian Journal of Psychology, 44*(1), 87–112.

Locurto, C. (1990). The malleability of IQ as judged from adoption studies. *Intelligence, 14,* 275–292.

Loehlin, J. C. (1992). *Genes and environment in personality development.* Newbury Park, CA: Sage.

Loehlin, J. C. (1994). Behavior genetics. In R. J. Sternberg (Ed.), *Encyclopedia of human intelligence.* New York, NY: Macmillan.

Loehlin, J. C. (2000). Group differences in intelligence. In R. J. Sternberg (Ed.), *Handbook of intelligence* (pp. 176–195). New York, NY: Cambridge University Press.

Loehlin, J. C., Horn, J. M., & Willerman, L. (1997). Heredity, environment, and IQ in the Texas Adoption Project. In R. J. Sternberg & E. L. Grigorenko (Eds.), *Intelligence, heredity, and environment.* New York, NY: Cambridge University Press.

Loewenstein, G. (2007). Affect regulation and affective forecasting. In J. J. Gross (Ed.), *Handbook of emotion regulation.* New York, NY: Guilford Press.

Loewenstein, G., & Schkade, D. (1999). Wouldn't it be nice? Predicting future feelings. In D. Kahneman, E. Diener, & N. Schwartz (Eds.), *Well-being: The foundations of hedonic psychology.* New York, NY: Sage.

Loftus, E. F. (1979). *Eyewitness testimony.* Cambridge, MA: Harvard University Press.

Loftus, E. F. (1992). When a lie becomes memory's truth: Memory distortion after exposure to misinformation. *Current Directions in Psychological Science, 1,* 121–123.

Loftus, E. F. (1994). The repressed memory controversy. *American Psychologist, 49,* 443–445.

Loftus, E. F. (1998). Remembering dangerously. In R. A. Baker (Ed.), *Child sexual abuse and false memory syndrome.* Amherst, NY: Prometheus Books.

Loftus, E. F. (2000). Remembering what never happened. In E. Tulving (Ed.), *Memory, consciousness, and the brain: The Tallinn conference* (pp. 106–118). Philadelphia, PA: Psychology Press.

Loftus, E. F. (2003). Make believe memories. *American Psychologist, 58,* 864–873.

Loftus, E. F. (2004). Memories of things unseen. *Current Directions in Psychological Science, 13*(4), 145–147.

Loftus, E. F. (2005). Planting misinformation in the human mind: A 30-year investigation of the malleability of memory. *Learning & Memory, 12,* 361–366.

Loftus, E. F., & Bernstein, D. M. (2005). Rich false memories: The royal road to success. In A. F. Healy (Ed.), *Experimental cognitive psychology and its applications.* Washington, DC: American Psychological Association.

Loftus, E. F., & Cahill, L. (2007). Memory distortion: From misinformation to rich false memory. In J. S. Nairne (Ed.), *The foundations of remembering: Essays in honor of Henry L. Roediger III.* New York, NY: Psychology Press.

Loftus, E. F., & Davis, D. (2006). Recovered memories. *Annual Review of Clinical Psychology, 2,* 469–498.

Loftus, E. F., Garry, M., & Feldman, J. (1998). Forgetting sexual trauma: What does it mean when 38% forget? In R. A. Baker (Ed.), *Child sexual abuse and false memory syndrome.* Amherst, NY: Prometheus Books.

Loftus, E. F., & Mazzoni, G. A. L. (1998). Using imagination and personalized suggestion to change people. *Behavior Therapy, 29,* 691–706.

Loftus, E. F., & Palmer, J. C. (1974). Reconstruction of automobile destruction: An example of the interaction between language and memory. *Journal of Verbal Learning and Verbal Behavior, 13,* 585–589.

Logue, A. W. (1991). *The psychology of eating and drinking* (2nd ed.). New York, NY: W. H. Freeman.

Lohmann, R. I. (2007). Dreams and ethnography. In D. Barrett & P. McNamara (Eds.), *The new science of dreaming.* Westport, CT: Praeger.

Lohoff, F. W., & Berrettini, W. H. (2009). Genetics of mood disorders. In D. S. Charney & E. J. Nestler (Eds.), *Neurobiology of mental illness* (3rd ed., pp. 360–377). New York, NY: Oxford University Press.

Lohr, J. M., Olatunji, B. O., Baumeister, R. F., & Bushman, B. J. (2007). The psychology of anger venting and empirically supported alternatives that do no harm. *The Scientific Review of Mental Health Practice: Objective Investigations of Controversial and Unorthodox Claims in Clinical Psychology, Psychiatry, and Social Work, 5*(1), 53–64.

Long, J. E., Jr. (2005). Power to prescribe: The debate over prescription privileges for psychologists and the legal issues implicated. *Law & Psychology, 29,* 243–260.

Longman, D. G., & Atkinson, R. H. (2005). *College learning and study skills.* Belmont, CA: Wadsworth.

Lonner, W. J. (2009). A retrospective on the beginnings of JCCP and IACCP. *Journal of Cross-Cultural Psychology, 40*(2), 167–169. doi:10.1177/0022022109332406

Lorenzo, G. L., Biesanz, J. C., & Human, L. J. (2010). What is beautiful is good and more accurately understood: Physical attractiveness and accuracy in first impressions of personality. *Psychological Science, 21*(12), 1777–1782. doi:10.1177/0956797610388048

Lothane, Z. (2006). Freud's legacy—Is it still with us? *Psychoanalytic Psychology, 23*(2), 285–301. doi:10.1037/0736-9735.23.2.285

Lott, B. (1987). *Women's lives.* Pacific Grove, CA: Brooks/Cole.

Lott, B. (2002). Cognitive and behavioral distancing from the poor. *American Psychologist, 57,* 100–110.

Louv, R. (2005). *Last child in the woods: Saving our children from nature-deficit disorder.* Chapel Hill, NC: Algonquin Books.

Lovejoy, T. E., & Hannah, L. (2005). *Climate change and biodiversity.* New Haven, CT: Yale University Press.

Lovinger, D. M. (2010). Neurotransmitter roles in synaptic modulation, plasticity and learning in the dorsal striatum. *Neuropharmacology, 58*(7), 951–961. doi:10.1016/j.neuropharm.2010.01.008

Lowden, A., Akerstedt, T., & Wibom, R. (2004). Suppression of sleepiness and melatonin by bright light exposure during breaks in night work. *Journal of Sleep Research, 12*(1), 37–43.

Lowinson, J. H., Ruiz, P., Millman, R. B., & Langrod, J. G. (2005). *Substance abuse: A comprehensive textbook.* Philadelphia, PA: Lippincott/Williams & Wilkins.

Lubart, T. I. (2003). In search of creative intelligence. In R. J. Sternberg, J. Lautrey, & T. I. Lubart (Eds.), *Models of intelligence: International perspectives.* Washington, DC: American Psychological Association.

Luborsky, E. B., O'Reilly-Landry, M., & Arlow, J. A. (2011). Psychoanalysis. In R. J. Corsini & D. Wedding (Eds.), *Current psychotherapies* (9th ed.). Belmont, CA: Brooks/Cole.

Luborsky, L., & Barrett, M. S. (2006). The history and empirical status of key psychoanalytic concepts. *Annual Review Clinical Psychology, 2,* 1–19.

Luborsky, L., Diguer, L., Seligman, D. A., Rosenthal, R., Krause, E. D., Johnson, S., Halperin, G., Bishop, M., Berman, J. S., & Schweizer, E. (1999). The researcher's own therapy allegiance: A "wild card" in comparisons of treatment efficacy. *Clinical Psychology: Science & Practice, 6*(1), 95–106.

Luborsky, L., Rosenthal, R., Diguer, L., Andrusyna, T. P., Berman, J. S., Levitt, J. T., Seligman, D. A., & Krause, E. D. (2002). The dodo bird verdict is alive and well—mostly. *Clinical Psychology: Science & Practice, 9,* 2–12.

Luborsky, L., Singer, B., & Luborsky, L. (1975). Comparative studies of psychotherapies: Is it true that everyone has won and all must have prizes? *Archives of General Psychiatry, 32,* 995–1008.

Lucas, A. R., Beard, C, M., O'Fallon, W. M., & Kurland, L. T. (1991). 50-year trends in the incidence of anorexia nervosa in Rochester, Minn.: A population-based study. *American Journal of Psychiatry, 148,* 917–922.

Lucas, R. E. (2007). Adaptation and the set-point model of subjective well-being: Does happiness change after major life events? *Current Directions in Psychological Science, 16,* 75–79.

Lucas, R. E. (2008). Personality and subjective well-being. In M. Eid & R. J. Larsen (Eds.), *The science of subjective well-being* (pp. 171–194). New York, NY: Guilford Press.

Lucas, R. E., Clark, A. E., Georgellis, Y., & Diener, E. (2003). Reexamining adaptation and set point model of happiness: Reactions to changes in marital status. *Journal of Personality and Social Psychology, 84,* 527–539.

Lucas, R. E., Clark, A. E., Georgellis, Y., & Diener, E. (2004). Unemployment alters the set point for life satisfaction. *Psychological Science, 15*(1), 8–13.

Lucas, R. E., & Diener, E. (2008). Personality and subjective well-being. In O. P. John, R. W. Robins, & L. A. Pervin (Eds.), *Handbook of personality psychology: Theory and research* (3rd ed., pp. 795–814). New York, NY: Guilford Press.

Luchins, A. S. (1942). Mechanization in problem solving. *Psychological Monographs, 54* (6, Whole No. 248).

Luders, E., Narr, K. L., Thompson, P. M., & Toga, A. W. (2009a). Neuroanatomical correlates of intelligence. *Intelligence, 37*(2), 156–163. doi:10.1016/j.intell.2008.07.002

Luders, E., Toga, A. W., Lepore, N., & Gaser, C. (2009b). The underlying anatomical correlates of long-term meditation: Larger hippocampal and frontal volumes of gray matter. *NeuroImage, 45*(3), 672–678. doi:10.1016/j.neuroimage.2008.12.061

Ludwig, A. M. (1994). Mental illness and creative activity in female writers. *American Journal of Psychiatry, 151,* 1650–1656.

Ludwig, A. M. (1995). *The price of greatness: Resolving the creativity and madness controversy.* New York, NY: Guilford Press.

Ludwig, A. M. (1998). Method and madness in the arts and sciences. *Creativity Research Journal, 11,* 93–101.

Lugaresi, E., Cirignotta, F., Montagna, P., & Sforza, E. (1994). Snoring: Pathogenic, clinical, and therapeutic aspects. In M. H. Kryger, T. Roth, & W. C. Dement (Eds.), *Principles and practice of sleep medicine* (2nd ed.). Philadelphia, PA: Saunders.

Luh, C. W. (1922). The conditions of retention. *Psychological Monographs, 31.*

Lund, O. C. H., Tamnes, C. K., Moestue, C., Buss, D. M., & Vollrath, M. (2007). Tactics of hierarchy negotiation. *Journal of Research in Personality, 41,* 25–44.

Lundberg, A. (1998). Environmental change and human health. In A. Lundberg (Ed.), *The environment and mental health: A guide for clinicians* (pp. 5–23). Mahwah, NJ: Erlbaum.

Lundberg, U. (2007). Catecholamines. In G. Fink (Ed.), *Encyclopedia of stress.* San Diego: Elsevier.

Luntz, B. K., & Widom, C. S. (1994). Antisocial personality disorder in abused and neglected children grown up. *Journal of Psychiatry, 151,* 670–674.

Lupien, S. J., & Maheu, F. S. (2007). Memory and stress. In G. Fink (Ed.), *Encyclopedia of stress.* San Diego: Elsevier.

Lurie, P., Almeida, C. M., Stine, N. , Stine, A. R., & Wolfe, S. M. (2006). Financial conflict of interest disclosure and voting patterns at food and drug administration drug advisory committee meetings. *Journal of the American Medical Association, 295,* 1921–1928.

Lustig, C., Berman, M. G., Nee, D., Lewis, R. L., Sledge Moore, K., & Jonides, J. (2009). Psychological and neural mechanisms of short-term memory. In G. G. Berntson & J. T. Cacioppo (Eds.), *Handbook of neuroscience for the behavioral sciences* (Vol 1, pp. 567–585). Hoboken, NJ: Wiley.

Lutz, A., Dunne, J. D., & Davidson, R. J. (2007). Meditation and the neuroscience of consciousness: An introduction. In P. D. Zelazo, M. Moscovitch, & E. Thompson (Eds.), *The Cambridge handbook of consciousness* (pp. 499–551). New York, NY: Cambridge University Press.

Lutz, C. (1987). Goals, events and understanding in Ifaluk emotion theory. In N. Quinn & D. Holland (Eds.), *Cultural models in language and thought.* Cambridge, England: Cambridge University Press.

Lutz, W. (1989). *Doublespeak.* New York, NY: Harper Perennial.

Lykken, D. T. (1998). *A tremor in the blood: Uses and abuses of the lie detector.* New York, NY: Plenum Press.

Lykken, D. T. (1999). *Happiness: The nature and nurture of joy and contentment.* New York, NY: St. Martin's.

Lykken, D. T., & Tellegen, A. (1996). Happiness is a stochastic phenomenon. *Psychological Science, 7,* 186–189.

Lynch, G., & Gall, C. M. (2006). Ampakines and the threefold path to cognitive enhancement. *Trends in Neurosciences, 29,* 554–562.

Lynch, M. A. (2004). Long-term potentiation and memory. *Psychological Review, 84,* 87–136.

Lynch, S. K., Turkheimer, E., D'Onofrio, B. M., Mendle, J., Emery, R. E., Slutske, W. S., et al. (2006). A genetically informed study of the association between harsh punishment and offspring behavioral problems. *Journal of Family Psychology, 20,* 190–198.

Lynn, S. J., Kirsch, I., & Hallquist, M. N. (2008). Social cognitive theories of hypnosis. In M. R. Nash & A. J. Barnier (Eds.), *Oxford handbook of hypnosis: Theory, research and practice* (pp. 111–140). New York, NY: Oxford University Press.

Lynn, S. J., Kirsch, I., Knox, J., Fassler, O., & Lilienfeld, S. O. (2007). Hypnotic regulation of consciousness and the pain neuromatrix. In G. A. Jamieson (Ed.), *Hypnosis and conscious states: The cognitive neuroscience perspective* (pp. 145–166). New York, NY: Oxford University Press.

Lynn, S. J., Lock, T., Loftus, E. F. , Krackow, E., & Lilienfeld, S. O. (2003). The remembrance of things past: Problematic memory recovery techniques in psychotherapy. In S. O. Lilienfeld, S. J. Lynn, & J. M. Lohr (Eds.), *Science and pseudoscience in clinical psychology*. New York, NY: Guilford Press.

Lynn, S. J., Neuschatz, J., & Fite, R. (2002). Hypnosis and memory: Implications for the courtroom and psychotherapy. In M. L. Eisen (Ed.), *Memory and suggestibility in the forensic interview*. Mahwah, NJ: Erlbaum.

Lynne, S. D., Graber, J. A., Nichols, T. R., & Brooks-Gunn, J., & Botwin, G. J. (2007). Links between pubertal timing, peer influences, and externalizing behaviors among urban students followed through middle school. *Journal of Adolescent Health, 40*(2).

Lyons-Ruth, K., & Jacobvitz, D. (2008). Attachment disorganization: Genetic factors, parenting contexts, and developmental transformation from infancy to adulthood. In J. Cassidy & P. R. Shaver (Eds.), *Handbook of attachment: Theory, research, and clinical applications* (2nd ed., pp. 666–697). New York, NY: Guilford Press.

Lytton, H. (1997). Physical punishment is a problem, whether conduct disorder is endogenous or not. *Psychological Inquiry, 8,* 211–214.

Lyubomirsky, S., & Boehm, J. K. (2010). Human motives, happiness, and the puzzle of parenthood: Commentary on Kenrick et al. (2010). *Perspectives on Psychological Science, 5*(3), 327–334. doi:10.1177/1745691610369473

Lyubomirsky, S., Sheldon, K. M., & Schkade, D. (2005). Pursuing happiness: The architecture of sustainable change. *Review of General Psychology, 9,* 111–131.

Lyubomirsky, S., Sousa, L., & Dickerhoof, R. (2006). The costs and benefits of writing, talking, and thinking about life's triumphs and defeats. *Journal of Personality and Social Psychology, 90,* 692–708.

Lyubomirsky, S., Tkach, C., & DiMatteo, R. M. (2006). What are the differences between happiness and self-esteem? *Social Indicators Research, 78,* 363–404.

Maas, J. B. (1998). *Power sleep*. New York, NY: Harper Perennial.

Maass, A. (1999). Linguistic intergroup bias: Stereotype perpetuation through language. *Advances in Experimental Social Psychology, 31,* 79–121.

Maccoby, E. E. (2000). Parenting and its effects on children: On reading and misreading behavior genetics. *Annual Review of Psychology, 51,* 1–27.

MacGregor, J. N., Ormerod, T. C., & Chronicle, E. P. (2001). Information-processing and insight: A process model of performance on the nine-dot and related problems. *Journal of Experimental Psychology: Learning, Memory, and Cognition, 27,* 176–201.

Mack, A. (2003). Inattentional blindness: Looking without seeing. *Current Directions in Psychological Science, 12*(5), 180–184.

Mack, A. H., Franklin Jr., J. E., & Frances, R. J. (2003). Substance use disorders. In R. E. Hales & S. C. Yudofsky (Eds.), *Textbook of clinical psychiatry*. Washington, DC: American Psychiatric Publishing.

MacKellar, D. A., Valleroy, L. A., Secura, G. M., Behel, S., Bingham, T., Celentano, D. D., Koblin, B. A., LaLota, M., McFarland, W., Shehan, D., Thiede, H., Torian, L. V., & Janssen, R. S., & Young Men's Survey Study Group. (2005). Unrecognized HIV infection, risk behaviors, and perceptions of risk among young men who have sex with men: Opportunities for advancing HIV prevention in the third decade of HIV/AIDS. *Journal of Acquired Immune Deficiency Syndromes, 38,* 603–614.

Mackintosh, N. J. (1998). *IQ and human intelligence*. Oxford: Oxford University Press.

MacLean, P. D. (1954). Studies on limbic system ("viosceal brain") and their bearing on psychosomatic problems. In E. D. Wittkower & R. A. Cleghorn (Eds.), *Recent developments in psychosomatic medicine*. Philadelphia, PA: Lippincott.

MacLean, P. D. (1993). Cerebral evolution of emotion. In M. Lewis & J. M. Haviland (Eds.), *Handbook of emotions*. New York, NY: Guilford Press.

MacMillan, H. L., Fleming, J. E., Streiner, D. L., Lin, E., Boyle, M. H., Jamieson, E., Duku, E. K., Walsh, C. A., Wong, M. Y. Y., & Beardslee, W. R. (2001). Childhood abuse and lifetime psychopathology in a community sample. *American Journal of Psychiatry, 158,* 1878–1883.

Macmillan, N. A., & Creelman, C. D. (2005). *Detection theory: A user's guide* (2nd ed.). Mahwah, NJ: Erlbaum.

Macpherson, F. (2010). Impossible figures. In E. B. Goldstein (Ed.), *Encyclopedia of perception*. Thousand Oaks, CA: Sage.

Macrae, C. N., & Quadflieg, S. (2010). Perceiving people. In S. T. Fiske, D. T. Gilbert, & G. Lindzey (Eds.), *Handbook of social psychology* (5th ed., Vol. 1, pp. 353–393). Hoboken, NJ: Wiley.

MacWhinney, B. (1998). Models of the emergence of language. *Annual Review of Psychology, 49,* 199–227.

MacWhinney, B. (2001). Emergentist approaches to language. In J. Bybee & P. Hooper (Eds.), *Frequency and the emergence of linguistic structure*. Amsterdam: John Benjamins Publishing.

MacWhinney, B. (2004). A multiple process solution to the logical problem of language acquisition. *Journal of Child Language, 31,* 883–914.

Macy, J. R. (1995). Working through environmental despair. In T. Roszak, M. E. Gomes, & A. D. Kanner (Eds.), *Ecopsychology: Restoring the earth, healing the mind* (pp. 240–259). San Francisco, CA: Sierra Club.

Madden, M., & Lenhart, A. (2006). *Online dating*. Pew Internet & American Life Project. Retrieved from http://www.pewInternet.org/pdfs/PIP_Online_Dating.pdf.

Maddux, W. W., Adam, H., & Galinsky, A. D. (2010). When in Rome . . . Learn why the Romans do what they do: How multicultural learning experiences facilitate creativity. *Personality and Social Psychology Bulletin, 36*(6), 731–741. doi:10.1177/0146167210367786

Maddux, W. W., & Galinsky, A. D. (2009). Cultural borders and mental barriers: The relationship between living abroad and creativity. *Journal of Personality and Social Psychology, 96*(5), 1047–1061. doi:10.1037/a0014861

Maddux, W. W., & Yuki, M. (2006). The "ripple effect": Cultural differences in perceptions of the consequences of events. *Personality and Social Psychology Bulletin, 32,* 669–683.

Madsen, K. B. (1968). *Theories of motivation*. Copenhagen: Munksgaard.

Madsen, K. B. (1973). Theories of motivation. In B. B. Wolman (Ed.), *Handbook of general psychology*. Englewood Cliffs, NJ: Prentice-Hall.

Magnavita, J. J. (2008). Psychoanalytic psychotherapy. In J. L. Lebow (Ed.), *Twenty-first century psychotherapies: Contemporary approaches to theory and practice*. New York, NY: Wiley.

Magnusson, D., & Stattin, H. (1998). Person-context interaction theories. In W. Damon (Ed.), *Handbook of child psychology, Vol. 1: Theoretical models of human development*. New York, NY: Wiley.

Maguire, W., Weisstein, N., & Klymenko, V. (1990). From visual structure to perceptual function. In K. N. Leibovic (Ed.), *Science of vision*. New York, NY: Springer-Verlag.

Maher, B. A. (2001). Delusions. In P. B. Sutker & H. E. Adams (Eds.), *Comprehensive handbook of psychopathology* (3rd ed., pp. 309–370). New York, NY: Kluwer Academic/Plenum Publishers.

Mahncke, H. W., Connor, B. B., Appelman, J., Ahsanuddin, O. N., Hardy, J. L., Wood, R. A., et al. (2006). Memory enhancement in healthy older adults using a brain plasticity-based training program: A randomized, controlled study. *Proceedings of the National Academy of Sciences of the United States of America, 103*(33), 12523–12528. doi:10.1073/pnas.0605194103

Mahoney, M. J. (1974). *Cognition and behavior modification*. Cambridge, MA: Ballinger.

Mahowald, M. W. (1993). Sleepwalking. In M. A. Carskadon (Ed.), *Encyclopedia of sleep and dreaming*. New York, NY: Macmillan.

Mahowald, M. W., & Schenck, C. H. (2005a). Insights from studying human sleep disorders. *Nature, 437,* 1279–1285.

Mahowald, M. W., & Schenck, C. H. (2005b). REM sleep parasomnias. In M. H. Kryger, T. Roth, & W. C. Dement (Eds.). *Principles and practice of sleep medicine* (pp. 897–916). Philadelphia, PA: Elsevier Saunders.

Maier, M. A., Elliot, A. J., & Lichtenfeld, S. (2008). Mediation of the negative effect of red on intellectual performance. *Personality and Social Psychology Bulletin, 34*(11), 1530–1540. doi:10.1177/0146167208323104.

Maier, N. R. F. (1931a). Reasoning and learning. *Psychological Review, 38,* 332–346.

Maier, N. R. F. (1931b). Reasoning in humans. II. The solution of a problem and its appearance in consciousness. *Journal of Comparative Psychology*, 12(2), 181–194. doi:10.1037/h0071361

Main, M., & Solomon, J. (1986). Discovery of a new, insecure–disorganized/disoriented attachment pattern. In T. B. Brazelton & M. W. Yogman (Eds.), *Affective development in infancy*. Norwood, NJ: Ablex.

Main, M., & Solomon, J. (1990). Procedures for identifying infants as disorganized/disoriented during the Ainsworth strange situation. In M. T. Greenberg, D. Ciccehetti, & E. M. Cummings (Eds.), *Attachment in the preschool years: Theory, research, and intervention*. Chicago: University of Chicago Press.

Major, B., & Townsend, S. S. M. (2010). Coping with bias. In J. F. Dovidio, M. Hewstone, P. Glick, & V. M. Esses (Eds.), *The Sage handbook of prejudice, stereotyping, and discrimination*. Los Angeles, CA: Sage.

Malamuth, N. M., Addison, T., & Koss, M. (2000). Pornography and sexual aggression: Are there reliable effects and can we understand them? *Annual Review of Sex Research, 11,* 26–91.

Maldonado, J. R., & Spiegel, D. (2008). Dissociative disorders. In R. E. Hales, S. C. Yudofsky, & G. O. Gabbard (Eds.), *The American Psychiatric Publishing textbook of psychiatry* (5th ed., pp. 665–710). Washington, DC: American Psychiatric Publishing.

Maletzky, B. M. (2002). The paraphilias: Research and treatment. In P. E. Nathan & J. M. Gorman (Eds.), *A guide to treatments that work*. London: Oxford University Press.

Maltzman, I. (1994). Why alcoholism is a disease. *Journal of Psychoactive Drugs, 26,* 13–31.

Mandel, H. & Young, J. (2009). *Here's the deal: Don't touch me.* New York, NY: Bantam Books.

Mandler, G. (1984). *Mind and body.* New York, NY: Norton.

Mandler, G. (1993). Thought, memory, and learning: Effects of emotional stress. In L. Goldberger & S. Breznitz (Eds.), *Handbook of stress: Theoretical and clinical aspects* (2nd ed.). New York, NY: Free Press.

Mandler, G. (2002). Origins of the cognitive revolution. *Journal of the History of the Behavioral Sciences, 38,* 339–353.

Manenti, R. R., Tettamanti, M. M., Cotelli, M. M., Miniussi, C. C., & Cappa, S. F. (2010). The neural bases of word encoding and retrieval: A fMRI-guided transcranial magnetic stimulation study. *Brain Topography, 22*(4), 318–332. doi:10.1007/s10548-009-0126-1

Maner, J. K., Gailliot, M. T., Rouby, D. A., & Miller, S. L. (2007). Can't take my eyes off you: Attentional adhesion to mates and rivals. *Journal of Personality and Social Psychology, 93,* 389–401.

Maney, K. (2004). SAS workers won when greed lost. *USA Today*, April 21. Retrieved from http://www.usatoday.com/money/industries/technology/2004-04-21-sas-culture_x.htm

Mann, J. J., & Currier, D. (2006). Understanding and preventing suicide. In D. J. Stein, D. J. Kupfer, & A. F. Schatzberg (Eds.), *Textbook of mood disorders* (pp. 485–496). Washington, DC: American Psychiatric Publishing.

Mann, T., Tomiyama, A. J., Westling, E., Lew, A. M., Samuels, B., & Chatman, J. (2007). Medicare's search for effective obesity treatments. *American Psychologist, 62,* 220–233.

Manna, A., Raffone, A., Perrucci, M., Nardo, D., Ferretti, A., Tartaro, A., et al. (2010). Neural correlates of focused attention and cognitive monitoring in meditation. *Brain Research Bulletin, 82*(1–2), 46–56. doi:10.1016/j.brainresbull.2010.03.001

Manson, J. E., Skerrett, P. J., & Willett, W. C. (2002). Epidemiology of health risks associated with obesity. In C. G. Fairburn & K. D. Brownell (Eds.), *Eating disorders and obesity: A comprehensive handbook* (pp. 422–428). New York, NY: Guilford Press.

Maratsos, M. P. (2007). Commentary. *Monographs of the Society for Research in Child Development, 72,* 121–126.

Marcia, J. E. (1966). Development and validation of ego identity status. *Journal of Personality and Social Psychology, 3,* 551–558.

Marcia, J. E. (1980). Identity in adolescence. In J. Adelson (Ed.), *Handbook of adolescent psychology.* New York, NY: Wiley.

Marcia, J. E. (1994). The empirical study of ego identity. In H. A. Bosma, T. L. G. Graafsma, H. D. Grotevant, & D. J. de Levita (Eds.), *Identity and development: An interdisciplinary approach.* Thousand Oaks, CA: Sage.

Marcus, G. F. (1996). Why do children say "breaked"? *Current Directions in Psychological Science, 5,* 81–85.

Marcus-Newhall, A., Pedersen, W. C., Carlson, M., & Miller, N. (2000). Displaced aggression is alive and well: A meta-analytic review. *Journal of Personality and Social Psychology, 78,* 670–689.

Marder, S. R., Hurford, I. M., & van Kammen, D. P. (2009). Second-generation antipsychotics. In B. J. Sadock, V. A. Sadock, & P. Ruiz (Eds.), *Kaplan & Sadock's comprehensive textbook of psychiatry* (pp. 3206–3240). Philadelphia, PA: Lippincott, Williams & Wilkins.

Marewski, J. N., Gaissmaier, W., & Gigerenzer, G. (2010). Good judgments do not require complex cognition. *Cognitive Processing, 11*(2), 103–121. doi:10.1007/s10339-009-0337-0

Mark, V. (1996). Conflicting communicative behavior in a split-brain patient: Support for dual consciousness. In S. R. Hameroff, A. W. Kaszniak, & A. C. Scott (Eds.), *Toward a science of consciousness. The first Tucson discussions and debates.* Cambridge, MA: MIT Press.

Markowitsch, H. J. (2000). Neuroanatomy of memory. In E. Tulving & F. I. M. Craik (Eds.), *The Oxford handbook of memory* (pp. 465–484). New York, NY: Oxford University Press.

Markowitz, E. M., Goldberg, L. R., Ashton, M. C., & Lee, K. (in press). Profiling the "Pro-environmental Individual": A personality perspective. *Journal of Personality.*

Marks, G. A. (2006). The neurobiology of sleep. In T. Lee-Chiong (Ed.), *Sleep: A comprehensive handbook.* Hoboken, NJ: Wiley-Liss.

Marks, I. M. (2004). The Nobel prize award in physiology to Ivan Petrovich Pavlov. *Australian and New Zealand Journal of Psychiatry, 38*(9), 674–677.

Markus, H. R., & Hamedani, M. G. (2007). Sociocultural psychology: The dynamic interdependence among self systems and social systems. In S. Kitayama & D. Cohen (Eds.), *Handbook of cultural psychology* (pp. 3–39). New York, NY: Guilford Press.

Markus, H. R., & Kitayama, S. (1991). Culture and the self: Implications for cognition, emotion, and motivation. *Psychological Review, 98,* 224–253.

Markus, H. R., & Kitayama, S. (1994). The cultural construction of self and emotion: Implications for social behavior. In S. Kitayama & H. R. Markus (Eds.), *Emotions and culture: Empirical studies of mutual influence.* Washington, DC: American Psychological Association.

Markus, H. R., & Kitayama, S. (2003). Culture, self, and the reality of the social. *Psychological Inquiry, 14*(3–4), 277–283.

Markus, H. R., Kitayama, S., & Heiman, R. J. (1996). Culture and "basic" psychological principles. In E. T. Higgins, & A. W. Kruglanski (Eds.), *Social psychology: Handbook of basic principles.* New York, NY: Guilford Press.

Marsella, A. J., & Yamada, A. M. (2007). Culture and psychopathology: Foundations, issues, and directions. In S. Kitayama & D. Cohen (Eds.), *Handbook of cultural psychology.* New York, NY: Guilford Press.

Marsh, E. J. (2007). Retelling is not the same as recalling: Implications for memory. *Current Directions in Psychological Science, 16*(1), 16–20.

Marsh, E. J., & Tversky, B. (2004). Spinning the stories of our lives. *Applied Cognitive Psychology, 18,* 491–503.

Marteau, T. M., & Weinman, J. (2004). Communicating about health threats and treatments. In S. Sutton, A. Baum, & M. Johnston (Ed), *The Sage handbook of health psychology.* Thousand Oaks, CA: Sage.

Martin, C. L., & Ruble, D. (2004). Children's search for gender cues: Cognitive perspectives on gender development. *Current Directions in Psychological Science, 13*(2), 67–70.

Martin, J. H. (1991). The collective electrical behavior of cortical neurons: The electroencephalogram and the mechanisms of epilepsy. In E. R. Kandel, J. H. Schwartz, & T. M. Jessell (Eds.), *Principles of neural science* (3rd ed.). New York, NY: Elsevier Saunders.

Martin, J. N., & Fox, N. A. (2006). Temperament. In K. McCartney & D. Phillips (Eds.), *Blackwell handbook of early childhood development* (pp. 126–146). Malden, MA: Blackwell Publishing.

Martin, L. (1986). "Eskimo words for snow": A case study in the genesis and decay of an anthropological example. *American Psychologist, 88,* 418–423.

Martin, L. R., Friedman, H. S., & Schwartz, J. E. (2007). Personality and mortality risk across the life span: The importance of conscientiousness as a biopsychosocial attribute. *Health Psychology, 26,* 428–436.

Martin, R. A. (2002). IS laughter the best medicine? Humor, laughter, and physical health. *Current Directions in Psychological Science, 11*(6), 216–220.

Martin, R., & Leventhal, H. (2004). Symptom perception and health care–seeking behavior. In J. M. Raczynski & L. C. Leviton (Eds.), *Handbook of clinical health psychology, Vol. 2: Disorders of behavior and health.* Washington, DC: American Psychological Association.

Martinez, M., Marangell, L. B., & Martinez, J. M. (2008). Psychopharmacology. In R. E. Hales, S. C. Yudofsky, & G. O. Gabbard (Eds.), *The American psychiatric publishing textbook of psychiatry* (pp. 1053–1132). Washington, DC: American Psychiatric Publishing.

Maslach, C. (2003). Job burnout: New directions in research and intervention. *Current Directions in Psychological Science, 12,* 189–192.

Maslach, C., & Leiter, M. P. (2000). Burnout. In G. Fink (Ed.), *Encyclopedia of stress* (Vol. 1, pp. 358–362). San Diego: Academic Press.

Maslach, C., & Leiter, M. P. (2005). Stress and burnout: The critical research. In C. L. Cooper (Ed.), *Handbook of stress medicine and health.* Boca Raton, FL: CRC Press.

Maslach, C., & Leiter, M. P. (2007). Burnout. In G. Fink (Ed.), *Encyclopedia of stress.* San Diego: Elsevier.

Maslen, R. J. C., Theakston, A. L., Lieven, E. V. M., & Tomasello, M. (2004). A dense corpus study of past tense and plural overregularization in English. *Journal of Speech, Language, & Hearing Research, 47,* 1319–1333.

Maslow, A. H. (1954). *Motivation and personality.* New York, NY: Harper & Row.

Maslow, A. H. (1968). *Toward a psychology of being.* New York, NY: Van Nostrand.

Maslow, A. H. (1970). *Motivation and personality.* New York, NY: Harper & Row.

Mason, G. F., Krystal, J. H., & Sanacora, G. (2009). Nuclear magnetic resonance imaging and spectroscopy: Basic principles and recent findings in neuropsychiatric disorder. In B. J. Sadock, V. A. Sadock, & P. Ruiz (Eds.), *Kaplan & Sadock's comprehensive textbook of psychiatry* (9th ed., Vol. 1, pp. 248–272). Philadelphia, PA: Lippincott, Williams & Wilkins.

Massar, K., & Buunk, A. P. (2009). Rivals in the mind's eye: Jealous responses after subliminal exposure to body shapes. *Personality and Individual Differences, 46*(2), 129–134. doi: 10.1016/j.paid.2008.09.016.

Massaro, D. W., & Loftus, G. R. (1996). Sensory and perceptual storage: Data and theory. In E. L. Bjork & R. A. Bjork (Eds.), *Memory.* San Diego: Academic Press.

Massen, C., & Vaterrodt-Plünnecke, B. (2006). The role of proactive interference in mnemonic techniques. *Memory, 14,* 189–196.

Massen, C., Vaterrodt-Plünnecke, B., Krings, L., & Hilbig, B. E. (2009). Effects of instruction on learners' ability to generate an effective pathway in the method of loci. *Memory, 17*(7), 724–731. doi:10.1080/09658210903012442

Master, S. L., Eisenberger, N. I., Taylor, S. E., Naliboff, B. D., Shirinyan, D., & Lieberman, M. D. (2009). A picture's worth: Partner photographs reduce experimentally induced pain. *Psychological Science, 20*(11), 1316–1318. doi:10.1111/j.14679280.2009.02444.x.

Masterpasqua, F. (2009). Psychology and epigenetics. *Review of General Psychology, 13*(3), 194–201. doi:10.1037/a0016301

Masters, W. H., & Johnson, V. E. (1966). *Human sexual response.* Boston, MA: Little, Brown.

Masters, W. H., & Johnson, V. E. (1970). *Human sexual inadequacy.* Boston, MA: Little, Brown.

Mastro, D. E., Behm-Morawitz, E., & Kopacz, M. A. (2008). Exposure to television portrayals of Latinos: The implications of aversive racism and social identity theory. *Human Communication Research, 34,* 1–27.

Masuda, T. (2010). Cultural effects on visual perception. In E. B. Goldstein (Ed.), *Encyclopedia of perception.* Thousand Oaks, CA: Sage.

Masuda, T., & Nisbett, R. E. (2001). Attending holistically versus analytically: Comparing the context sensitivity of Japanese and Americans. *Journal of Personality and Social Psychology, 81,* 922–934.

Matheson, S. L., Green, M. J., Loo, C. C., & Carr, V. J. (2010). Quality assessment and comparison of evidence for electroconvulsive therapy and repetitive transcranial magnetic stimulation for schizophrenia: A systematic meta-review. *Schizophrenia Research, 118*(1–3), 201–210. doi:10.1016/j.schres.2010.01.002

Mathew, S. J., Hoffman, E. J., Charney, D. S. (2009). Pharmacotherapy of anxiety disorders. In D. S. Charney & E. J. Nestler (Eds.), *Neurobiology of mental illness.* New York, NY: Guilford Press.

Mathews, S., & Herzog, H.A. (1997). Personality and attitudes toward the treatment of animals. *Society and Animals, 5,* 169–175.

Matlin, M. W. (2008). *The psychology of women.* Belmont, CA: Wadsworth.

Matlin, M. W. (1989). *Cognition.* New York, NY: Holt, Rinehart & Winston.

Matsumoto, D. (1994). *People: Psychology from a cultural perspective.* Pacific Grove, CA: Brooks/Cole.

Matsumoto, D. (2003). Cross-cultural research. In S. F. Davis (Ed.), *Handbook of research methods in experimental psychology.* Malden, MA: Blackwell Publishers.

Matsumoto, D., & Juang, L. (2008). *Culture and psychology.* Belmont, CA: Wadsworth.

Matsumoto, D., Nezlek, J. B., & Koopmann, B. (2007). Evidence for universality in phenomenological emotion response system coherence. *Emotion, 7,* 57–67.

Matsumoto, D., & Willingham, B. (2006). The thrill of victory and the agony of defeat: Spontaneous expressions of medal winners of the 2004 Athens Olympic games. *Journal of Personality and Social Psychology, 91,* 568–581.

Matsumoto, D., & Willingham, B. (2009). Spontaneous facial expressions of emotion of congenitally and noncongenitally blind individuals. *Journal of Personality and Social Psychology, 96*(1), 1–10. doi:10.1037/a0014037

Matsumoto, D., & Yoo, S. (2006). Toward a new generation of cross-cultural research. *Perspectives on Psychological Science, 1,* 234–250.

Matthey, S. (1998). P.<05—But is it clinically *significant*?: Practical examples for clinicians. *Behaviour Change, 15,* 140–146.

Matusov, E., & Hayes, R. (2000). Sociocultural critique of Piaget and Vygotsky. *New Ideas in Psychology, 18*(2–3), 215–239.

Maugh, T. H., II. (2008, December 9). Henry M. dies at 82: Victim of brain surgery accident offered doctors key insights into memory. *Los Angeles Times.* Retrieved from http://www.latimes.com/news/science/la-me-molaison9-2008dec09,0,2820409.story

Mauk, M. D., & Thach, W. T. (2008). Cerebellum. In L. Squire, D. Berg, F. Bloom, S. Du Lac, A. Ghosh, N. Spitzer (Eds.), *Fundamental neuroscience* (3rd ed., pp. 751–774). San Diego, CA: Elsevier.

Mauro, R., Sato, K., & Tucker, J. (1992). The role of appraisal in human emotions: A cross-cultural study. *Journal of Personality and Social Psychology, 62,* 301–317.

Mayer, F. S., & Frantz, C. M. (2004). The Connectedness to Nature Scale: A measure of individuals' feeling in community with nature. *Journal of Environmental Psychology, 24,* 503–515.

Mayer, J. (1955). Regulation of energy intake and the body weight: The glucostatic theory and the lipostatic hypothesis. *Annals of the New York Academy of Science, 63,* 15–43.

Mayer, J. (1968). *Overweight: Causes and control.* Englewood Cliffs, NJ: Prentice-Hall.

Mays, V. M., Rubin, J., Sabourin, M., & Walker, L. (1996). Moving toward a global psychology: Changing theories and practice to meet the needs of a changing world. *American Psychologist, 51,* 485–487.

Mazur, J. E. (1993). Predicting the strength of a conditioned reinforcer: Effects of delay and uncertainty. *Current Directions in Psychological Science, 2*(3), 70–74. doi: 10.1111/1467-8721.ep10770907

Mazzoni, G., Heap, M., & Scoboria, A. (2010). Hypnosis and memory: Theory, laboratory research, and applications. In S. Lynn, J. W. Rhue, & I. Kirsch (Eds.), *Handbook of clinical hypnosis* (2nd ed.) (pp. 709–741). Washington, DC: American Psychological Association.

Mazzoni, G., & Lynn, S. J. (2007). Using hypnosis in eyewitness memory: Past and current issues. In M. P. Toglia, J. D. Read, D. F. Ross, & R. C. L. Lindsay (Eds.), *Handbook of eyewitness psychology: Volume 1. Memory for events.* Mahwah, NJ: Erlbaum.

McAnarney, E. R. (2008). Adolescent brain development: Forging new links? *Journal of Adolescent Health, 42*(4), 321–323.

McBride, D. L., & Korell, G. (2005). Wilderness therapy for abused women. *Canadian Journal of Counseling, 39,* 3–14.

McBride-Chang, C., & Jacklin, C. N. (1993). Early play arousal, sex-typed play, and activity level as precursors to later rough-and-tumble play. *Early Education & Development, 4,* 99–108.

McBurney, D. H. (1996). *How to think like a psychologist: Critical thinking in psychology.* Upper Saddle River, NJ: Prentice-Hall.

McBurney, D. H. (2010). Evolutionary approach: Perceptual adaptations. In E. B. Goldstein (Ed.), *Encyclopedia of perception.* Thousand Oaks, CA: Sage.

McBurney, D. H., Zapp, D. J., & Streeter. S. A. (2005). Preferred number of sexual partners: Tails of distributions and tales of mating systems. *Evolution and Human Behavior, 26,* 271–278.

McCabe, R. E., & Antony, M. M. (2008). Anxiety disorders: Social and specific phobias. In A. Tasman, J. Kay, J. A. Lieberman, M. B. First, & M. Maj (Eds.), *Psychiatry* (3rd ed.). New York, NY: Wiley-Blackwell.

McCarley, R. W. (1994). Dreams and the biology of sleep. In M. H. Kryger, T. Roth, & W. C. Dement (Eds.), *Principles and practice of sleep medicine* (2nd ed.). Philadelphia, PA: Saunders.

McCarty, R. (2007). Fight-or-flight response. In G. Fink (Ed.), *Encyclopedia of stress.* San Diego: Elsevier.

McClelland, D. C. (1975). *Power: The inner experience.* New York, NY: Irvington.

McClelland, D. C. (1985). How motives, skills and values determine what people do. *American Psychologist, 40,* 812–825.

McClelland, D. C., Atkinson, J. W., Clark, R. A., & Lowell, E. L. (1953). *The achievement motive.* New York, NY: Appleton-Century-Crofts.

McClelland, D. C., & Koestner, R. (1992). The achievement motive. In C. P. Smith (Ed.), *Motivation and personality: Handbook of thematic content analysis.* New York, NY: Cambridge University Press.

McClelland, J. L. (1992). Parallel-distributed processing models of memory. In L. R. Squire (Ed.), *Encyclopedia of learning and memory.* New York, NY: Macmillan.

McClelland, J. L. (2000). Connectionist models of memory. In E. Tulving & F. I. M. Craik (Eds.), *The Oxford handbook of memory* (pp. 583–596). New York, NY: Oxford University Press.

McClelland, J. L., & Rogers, T. T. (2003). The parallel distributed processing approach to semantic cognition. *Nature Reviews Neuroscience, 4,* 310–322.

McClelland, J. L., & Rumelhart, D. E. (1985). Distributed memory and the representation of general and specific information. *Journal of Experimental Psychology: General, 114,* 159–188.

McClernon, F. J., & Gilbert, D. G. (2007). Smoking and stress. In G. Fink (Ed.), *Encyclopedia of stress* (2nd ed.). San Diego, CA: Academic Press.

McClure-Tone, E. B., & Pine, D. S. (2009). Clinical features of the anxiety disorders. In B. J. Sadock, V. A. Sadock, & P. Ruiz (Eds.), *Kaplan & Sadock's comprehensive textbook of psychiatry* (9th ed., pp. 1844–1855). Philadelphia, PA: Lippincott, Williams & Wilkins.

McConkey, K. M. (1992). The effects of hypnotic procedures on remembering: The experimental findings and their implications for forensic hypnosis. In E. Fromm & M. R. Nash (Eds.), *Contemporary hypnosis research.* New York, NY: Guilford Press.

McConnell, J. V. (1962). Memory transfer through cannibalism in planarians. *Journal of Neuropsychiatry, 3*(Suppl. 1), 542–548.

McConnell, J. V., Cutler, R. L., & McNeil, E. B. (1958). Subliminal stimulation: An overview. *American Psychologist, 13,* 229–242.

McCord, J. (2005). Unintended consequences of punishment. In M. Donnelly & M. A. Straus (Eds.), *Corporal punishment of children in theoretical perspective* (pp. 165–169). New Haven, CT: Yale University Press.

McCormick, D. A. (2008). Membrane potential and action potential. In L. Squire, D. Berg, F. Bloom, S. Du Lac, A. Ghosh, & N. Spitzer (Eds.), *Fundamental neuroscience* (3rd ed., pp. 112–132). San Diego, CA: Elsevier.

McCrae, R. R. (1984). Situational determinants of coping responses: Loss, threat and challenge. *Journal of Personality and Social Psychology, 46,* 919–928.

McCrae, R. R. (1996). Social consequences of experimental openness. *Psychological Bulletin, 120,* 323–337.

McCrae, R. R. (2005). Personality structure. In V. A. Derlega, B. A. Winstead, & W. H. Jones (Eds.), *Personality: Contemporary theory and research.* Belmont, CA: Wadsworth.

McCrae, R. R., & Costa, P. T., Jr. (1985). Updating Norman's "adequate taxonomy": Intelligence and personality dimensions in natural language and in questionnaires. *Journal of Personality and Social Psychology, 49,* 710–721.

McCrae, R. R., & Costa, P. T., Jr. (1987). Validation of the five-factor model of personality across instruments and observers. *Journal of Personality and Social Psychology, 52,* 81–90.

McCrae, R. R., & Costa, P. T., Jr. (1990). *Personality in adulthood.* New York, NY: Guilford Press.

McCrae, R. R., & Costa, P. T., Jr. (1997). Personality trait structure as a human universal. *American Psychologist, 52,* 509–516.

McCrae, R. R., & Costa, P. T., Jr. (2003). *Personality in adulthood: A five-factor theory perspective.* New York, NY: Guilford Press.

McCrae, R. R., & Costa, P. T., Jr. (2007). Brief versions of the NEO-PI-3. *Journal of Individual Differences, 28,* 116–128.

McCrae, R. R., & Costa, P. T., Jr. (2008). The five-factor theory of personality. In O. P. John, R. W. Robbins, & L. A. Pervin (Eds.), *Handbook of personality: Theory and research* (Vol. 3, pp. 159–181). New York, NY: Guilford Press.

McCrae, R. R., & Sutin, A. R. (2009). Openness to experience. In M. R. Leary & R. H. Hoyle (Eds.), *Handbook of individual differences in social behavior* (pp. 257–273). New York, NY: Guilford Press.

McCrae, R. R., & Terracciano, A. (2006). National character and personality. *Current Directions in Psychological Science, 15,* 156–161.

McCrae, R. R., & Terracciano, A., & Personality Profiles of Cultures Project. (2005a). Personality profiles of cultures: Aggregate personality traits. *Journal of Personality and Social Psychology, 89,* 407–425.

McCrae, R. R., Terracciano, A., & 78 members of the Personality Profiles of Cultures Project. (2005b). Universal features of personality traits from the observer's perspective: Data from 50 cultures. *Journal of Personality and Social Psychology, 88,* 547–561.

McCrink, K., & Wynn, K. (2004). Large-number addition and subtraction by 9-month-old infants. *Psychological Science, 15,* 776–781.

McCullough, M. E. (2001). Forgiving. In C. R. Snyder (Ed.), *Coping with stress: Effective people and processes* (pp. 93–113). New York, NY: Oxford University Press.

McCullough, M. E., & Witvliet, C. V. (2002). The psychology of forgiveness. In C. R. Synder & S. J. Lopez (Eds.), *Handbook of positive psychology.* New York, NY: Oxford University Press.

McDaniel, M. A. (2005). Big-brained people are smarter: A meta-analysis of the relationship between *in vivo* brain volume and intelligence. *Intelligence, 33,* 337–346.

McDaniel, M. A., & Einstein, G. O. (1986). Bizarre imagery as an effective memory aid: The importance of distinctiveness. *Journal of Experimental Psychology: Learning, Memory & Cognition, 12,* 54–65.

McDaniel, M. A., & Einstein, G. O. (2007). *Prospective memory: An overview and synthesis of an emerging field.* Thousand Oaks, CA: Sage.

McDaniel, M. A., Lyle, K. B., Butler, K. M., & Dornburg, C. C. (2008). Age-related deficits in reality monitoring of action memories. *Psychology and Aging, 23*(3), 646–656. doi:10.1037/a0013083

McDaniel, M. A., Waddill, P. J., & Shakesby, P. S. (1996). Study strategies, interest, and learning from text: The application of material-appropriate processing. In D. J. Herrmann, C. McEvoy, C. Hertzog, P. Hertel, & M. K. Johnson (Eds.), *Basic and applied memory research: Theory in context* (Vol. 1). Mahwah, NJ: Erlbaum.

McDaniel, M. A., Whetzel, D. L., Schmidt, F. L., & Maurer, S. D. (1994). The validity of employment interviews: A comprehensive review and meta-analysis. *Journal of Applied Psychology, 79,* 599–616.

McDermott, K. B. (2007). Inducing false memories through associated lists: A window onto everyday false memories? In J. S. Nairne (Ed.), *The foundations of remembering: Essays in honor of Henry L. Roediger III.* New York, NY: Psychology Press.

McDevitt, M. A., & Williams, B. A. (2001). Effects of signaled versus unsignaled delay of reinforcement on choice. *Journal of the Experimental Analysis of Behavior, 75,* 165–182. doi:10.1901/jeab.2001.75-165.

McDonald, C., & Murphy, K. C. (2003). The new genetics of schizophrenia. *Psychiatric Clinics of North America, 26*(1), 41–63.

McDonald, M. G., Wearing, S., & Pointing, J. (2009). The nature of peak experience in wilderness. *The Humanistic Psychologist, 37*(4), 370–385.

McDonald, W. M., Thompson, T. R., McCall W. V., & Zormuski, C. F. (2004). Electroconvulsive therapy. In A. F. Schatzberg & C. B. Nemeroff (Eds.), *Textbook of psychopharmacology.* Washington, DC: American Psychiatric Publishing.

McEwen, B. S. (2009). Stress and coping. In G. G. Berntson & J. T. Cacioppo (Eds.), *Handbook of neuroscience for the behavioral sciences* (Vol. 2, pp. 1220–1235). Hoboken, NJ: Wiley.

McGeoch, J. A., & McDonald, W. T. (1931). Meaningful relation and retroactive inhibition. *American Journal of Psychology, 43,* 579–588.

McGlashan, T. H., & Fenton, W. S. (1992). The positive-negative distinction in schizophrenia: Review of natural history validators. *Archives of General Psychiatry, 49,* 63–72.

McGowan, P. O., Meaney, M. J., & Szyf, M. (2008). Diet and the epigenetic (re)programming of phenotypic differences in behavior. *Brain Research, 1237,* 12–24. doi:10.1016/j.brainres.2008.07.074

McGrath, J., Welham, J., Scott, J., Varghese, D., Degenhardt, L., Hayatbakhsh, M., et al. (2010). Association between cannabis use and psychosis-related outcomes using sibling pair analysis in a cohort of young adults. *Archives of General Psychiatry, 67*(5), 440–447. doi:10.1001/archgenpsychiatry.2010.6

McGrath, J. E., & Altman, I. (1966). *Small group research: A synthesis and critique of the field.* New York, NY: Holt, Rinehart & Winston.

McGrath, J. J. (2007). The surprisingly rich contours of schizophrenia epidemiology. *Archives of General Psychiatry, 64*(1), 14–16. doi:10.1001/archpsyc.64.1.14

McGrew, J. H., Wright, E. R., Pescosolido, B. A., & McDonel, E. C. (1999). The closing of Central State Hospital: Long-term outcomes for persons with severe mental illness. *Journal of Behavioral Health Services & Research, 26,* 246–261.

McGue, M., Bouchard, T. J., Jr., Iacono, W. G., & Lykken, D. T. (1993). Behavioral genetics of cognitive ability: A life-span perspective. In R. Plomin & G. E. McClearn (Eds.), *Nature, nurture and psychology.* Washington, DC: American Psychological Association.

McGuigan, F. J., & Lehrer, P. M. (2007). Progressive relaxation: Origins, principles, and clinical applications. In P. M. Lehrer, R. L. Woolfolk, & W. E. Sime (Eds.), *Principles and practice of stress management.* New York, NY: Guilford Press.

McHugh, P. R. (1995). Dissociative identity disorder as a socially constructed artifact. *Journal of Practical Psychiatry and Behavioral Health, 1,* 158–166.

McIntyre, K., Korn, J., & Matsuo, H. (2008). Sweating the small stuff: How different types of hassles result in the experience of stress. *Stress & Health: Journal of the International Society for the Investigation of Stress, 24*(5), 383–392.

McKeefry, D. J., Burton, M. P., & Morland, A. B. (2010). The contribution of human cortical area V3A to the perception of chromatic motion: A transcranial magnetic stimulation study. *European Journal of Neuroscience, 31*(3), 575–584. doi:10.1111/j.1460-9568.2010.07095.x

McKelvie, P., & Low, J. (2002). Listening to Mozart does not improve children's spatial ability: Final curtains for the Mozart effect. *British Journal of Development Psychology, 20,* 241–258.

McKenna, K. Y. A. (2008). MySpace or your place: Relationship initiation and development in the wired and wireless world. In S. Sprecher, A. Wenzel, & J. Harvey (Eds.), *Handbook of relationship initiation* (pp. 235–247). New York, NY: Psychology Press.

McKenna, K. Y. A., & Bargh, J. A. (2000). Plan 9 from cyberspace: The implications of the Internet for personality and social psychology. *Personality and Social Psychology Review, 4,* 57–75.

McKenna, K. Y. A., Green, A., & Gleason, M. (2002). Relationship formation on the Internet: What's the big attraction? *Journal of Social Issues, 58,* 9–31.

McKone, E., Crookes, K., & Kanwisher, N. (2009). The cognitive and neural development of face recognition in humans. In M. S. Gazzaniga (Ed.), *The cognitive neurosciences.* Cambridge, MA: MIT Press.

McLay, R. N., Daylo, A. A., & Hammer, P. S. (2006). No effect of lunar cycle on psychiatric admissions or emergency evaluations. *Military Medicine, 171,* 1239–1242.

McLean, D. E., & Link, B. G. (1994). Unraveling complexity: Strategies to refine concepts, measures, and research designs in the study of life events and mental health. In W. R. Avison & I. H. Gotlib (Eds.), *Stress and mental health: Contemporary issues and prospects for the future.* New York, NY: Plenum.

McLellan, A. T., Lewis, D. C., O'Brien, C. P., & Kleber, H. D. (2000). Drug dependence, a chronic mental illness: Implications for treatment, insurance, and outcome evaluation. *Journal of the American Medical Association, 284,* 1689–1695.

McLoughlin, K., & Paquet, M. (2005, December 14). Gambling led Hogan to robbery, lawyer says. *Lehigh University's The Brown and White.* Retrieved from http://www.bw.lehigh.edu/story.asp?ID=19313.

McLoyd, V. C. (1998). Socioeconomic disadvantage and child development. *American Psychologist, 53,* 185–204.

McManus, M. A., & Baratta, J. E. (1992). *The relationship of recruiting source to performance and survival.* Paper presented at the annual meeting of the Society for Industrial and Organizational Psychology, Montreal, Canada.

McMullin, D., & White, J. W. (2006). Long-term effects of labeling a rape experience. *Psychology of Women Quarterly, 30*(1), 96–105. doi:10.1111/j.1471-6402.2006.00266.x

McNab, F., Varrone, A., Jucaite, A., Bystritsky, P., Forssberg, H., & Klingberg, T. (2009). Change in cortical dopamine D1 receptor binding associated with cognitive training. *Science,* 323(5915), 800–802. doi:10.1126/science.1166102

McNally, R. J. (1994). Cognitive bias in panic disorder. *Current Directions in Psychological Science, 3,* 129–132.

McNally, R. J. (1996). *Panic disorder: A critical analysis.* New York, NY: Guilford Press.

McNally, R. J. (2003). *Remembering trauma.* Cambridge, MA: Belknap Press/Harvard University Press.

McNally, R. J. (2007). Betrayal trauma theory: A critical appraisal. *Memory, 15,* 280–294.

McNally, R. J. (2009). Posttraumatic stress disorder. In P. H. Blaney & T. Millon (Eds.), *Oxford textbook of psychopathology* (2nd ed., pp. 176–197). New York, NY: Oxford University Press.

McNally, R. J., & Geraerts, E. (2009). A new solution to the recovered memory debate. *Perspectives on Psychological Science, 4*(2), 126–134. doi:10.1111/j.1745-6924.2009.01112.x

McNamara, P., Nunn, C., Barton, R., Harris, E., & Capellini, I. (2007). Phylogeny of sleep and dreams. In D. Barrett & P. McNamara (Eds.), *The new science of dreaming.* Westport, CT: Praeger.

McNeil, T. F., Cantor-Graae, E., & Ismail, B. (2000). Obstetrics complications and congenital malformation in schizophrenia. *Brain Research Reviews, 31,* 166–178.

McNulty, J. K., Neff, L. A., & Karney, B. R. (2008). Beyond initial attraction: Physical attractiveness in newlywed marriage. *Journal of Family Psychology, 22*(4), 135–143.

McQueen, M. B., & Blacker, D. (2008). Genetics of Alzheimer's disease. In J. W. Smoller, B. R. Sheidley, & M. T. Tsuang (Eds.). *Psychiatric genetics: Applications in clinical practice* (pp. 177–193). Arlington, VA: American Psychiatric Publishing.

McWhorter, K. T. (2007). *College reading & study skills.* New York, NY: Pearson Longman.

McWilliams, L. A., Becker, E. S., Margraf, J., Clara, I. P., & Vriends, N. (2007). Anxiety disorders specificity of anxiety sensitivity in a community sample of young women. *Personality and Individual Differences, 42,* 345–354.

Mechanic, D. (1980). *Mental health and social policy.* Englewood Cliffs, NJ: Prentice-Hall.

Mechanic, D. (1999). Mental health and mental illness. In A. V. Horvitz & T. L. Scheid (Eds.), *A handbook for the study of mental health: Social contexts, theories, and systems.* New York, NY: Cambridge University Press.

Medina, K., Hanson, K. L., Schweinsburg, A. D., Cohen-Zion, M., Nagel, B. J., & Tapert, S. F. (2007). Neuropsychological functioning in adolescent marijuana users: Subtle deficits detectable after a month of abstinence. *Journal of the International Neuropsychological Society, 13*(5), 807–820. doi:10.1017/S1355617707071032

Mednick, S. A., & Mednick, M. T. (1967). *Examiner's manual, Remote Associates Test.* Boston, MA: Houghton Mifflin.

Mednick, S. A., Machon, R. A., Huttunen, M. O., & Bonett, D. (1988). Adult schizophrenia following prenatal exposure to an influenza epidemic. *Archives of General Psychiatry, 45,* 189–192.

Mednick, S. C., Cali, D. J., Kanady, J., & Drummond, S. A. (2008). Comparing the benefits of caffeine, naps and placebo on verbal, motor and perceptual memory. *Behavioural Brain Research, 193*(1), 79–86. doi:10.1016/j.bbr.2008.04.028

Mednick, S. C., & Drummond, S. P. A. (2009). Napping. In R. Stickgold & M. P. Walker (Eds.), *The neuroscience of sleep* (pp. 254–262). San Diego, CA: Academic Press.

Meerlo, P., Mistlberger, R. E., Jacobs, B. L., Heller, H., & McGinty, D. (2009). New neurons in the adult brain: The role of sleep and consequences of sleep loss. *Sleep Medicine Reviews, 13*(3), 187–194. doi:10.1016/j.smrv.2008.07.004

Meeus, W., van de Schoot, R., Keijsers, L., Schwartz, S. J., & Branje, S. (2010). On the progression and stability of adolescent identity formation: A five-wave longitudinal study in early-to-middle and middle-to-late adolescence. *Child Development, 81*(5), 1565–1581. doi:10.1111/j.1467-8624.2010.01492.x

Mehdizadeh, S. (2010). Self-presentation 2.0: Narcissism and self-esteem on Facebook. *Cyberpsychology, Behavior, and Social Networking, 13*(4), 357–364. doi:10.1089/cyber.2009.0257

Mehl, M. R. (2007). Eavesdropping on health: A naturalistic observation approach for social health research. *Social and Personality Psychology Compass, 1*(1), 359–380. doi: 10.1111/j.1751-9004.2007.00034.x.

Mehl, M. R., Vazire, S., Holleran, S. E., & Clark, C. (2010). Eavesdropping on happiness: Well-being is related to having less small talk and more substantive conversations. *Psychological Science, 21*(4), 539–541.

Meichenbaum, D. H. (1977). *Cognitive-behavior modification.* New York, NY: Plenum.

Meinz, E. J., & Hambrick, D. Z. (2010). Deliberate practice is necessary but not sufficient to explain individual differences in piano sight-reading skill: The role of working memory capacity. *Psychological Science, 21*(7), 914–919.

Meister, B. (2007). Neurotransmitters in key neurons of the hypothalamus that regulate feeding behavior and body weight. *Physiology & Behavior, 92,* 263–271.

Melson, G. F. (2001). *Why the wild things are: Animals in the lives of children.* Cambridge, MA: Harvard University Press.

Melson, G. F. (2003). Child development and the human-companion animal bond. *American Behavioral Scientist, 47,* 31–39.

Meltzer, H. Y., & Bobo, W. V. (2009). Antipsychotic and anticholinergic drugs. In M. C. Gelder, N. C. Andreasen, J. J. López-Ibor, Jr., & J. R. Geddes (Eds.), *New Oxford textbook of psychiatry* (2nd ed., Vol. 1). New York, NY: Oxford University Press.

Melvin, G. A., Posner, K., Standley, B. H., & Oquendo, M. A. (2008). Management of the suicidal patient. In A. Tasman, J. Kay, J. A. Lieberman, M. B. First, & M. Maj (Eds.), *Psychiatry* (3rd ed.). New York, NY: Wiley-Blackwell.

Melzack, R., & Wall, P. D. (1965). Pain mechanisms: A new theory. *Science, 150,* 971–979.

Melzack, R., & Wall, P. D. (1982). *The challenge of pain.* New York, NY: Basic Books.

Mendelson, W. B. (2005). Hypnotic medications: Mechanisms of action and pharmacologic effects. In M. H. Kryger, T. Roth, & W. C. Dement (Eds.). *Principles and practice of sleep medicine.* Philadelphia, PA: Elsevier Saunders.

Mennella, J. A., & Beauchamp, G. K. (1996). The early development of human flavor preferences. In E. D. Capaldi (Ed.), *Why we eat what we eat: The psychology of eating* (pp. 83–112). Washington, DC: American Psychological Association.

Menninger, W. W. (2005). Role of the psychiatric hospital in the treatment of mental illness. In B. J. Sadock & V. A. Sadock (Eds.), *Kaplan & Sadock's comprehensive textbook of psychiatry.* Philadelphia, PA: Lippincott Williams & Wilkins.

Mentzer, R. L. (1982). Response biases in multiple-choice test item files. *Educational and Psychological Measurement, 42,* 437–448.

Mergen, B. (2003). Review essay: Children and nature in history. *Environmental History, 8*(4). Retrieved from http://www.historycooperative.org/journals/eh/8.4/mergen.html

Merikangas, K. R., & Kalaydjian, A. E. (2009). Epidemiology of anxiety disorders. In B. J. Sadock, V. A. Sadock, & P. Ruiz (Eds.), *Kaplan & Sadock's comprehensive textbook of psychiatry* (9th ed., pp. 1856–1863). Philadelphia, PA: Lippincott, Williams & Wilkins.

Merikangas, K. R., & Pato, M. (2009). Recent developments in the epidemiology of bipolar disorder in adults and children: Magnitude, correlates, and future directions. *Clinical Psychology: Science and Practice, 16*(2), 121–133. doi:10.1111/j.1468-2850.2009.01152.x

Merikle, P. M. (2000). Subliminal perception. In A. E. Kazdin (Ed.), *Encyclopedia of Psychology* (pp. 497–499). New York, NY: Oxford University Press.

Merikle, P. M. (2007). Preconscious processing. In M. Velmans & S. Schneider (Eds.), *The Blackwell companion to consciousness.* Malden, MA: Blackwell Publishing.

Mesquita, B. (2003). Emotions as dynamic cultural phenomena. In R. J. Davidson, K. R. Scherer, & H. H. Goldsmith (Eds.), *Handbook of affective sciences.* New York, NY: Oxford University Press.

Mesquita, B., & Leu, J. (2007). The cultural psychology of emotion. In S. Kitayama & D. Cohen (Eds.), *Handbook of cultural psychology* (pp. 734–759). New York, NY: Guilford Press.

Messer, S. B., & McWilliams, N. (2003). The impact of Sigmund Freud and the interpretation of dreams. In R. J. Sternberg (Ed.), *The anatomy of impact: What makes the great works of psychology great* (pp. 71–88). Washington, DC: American Psychological Association.

Metzger, E. D. (1999). Electroconvulsive therapy. In A. M. Nicholi (Ed.), *The Harvard guide to psychiatry.* Cambridge, MA: Harvard University Press.

Metzner, R. (1999). *Green psychology: Transforming our relationship to the earth.* Rochester, VT: Park Street.

Meyer-Bahlburg, H. F. L., Ehrhardt, A. A., Rosen, L. R., Gruen, R. S., Veridiano, N. P., Vann, F. H., & Neuwalder, H. F. (1995). Prenatal estrogens and the development of homosexual orientation. *Developmental Psychology, 31,* 12–21.

Meyer, D. E., & Schvaneveldt, R. W. (1976). Meaning, memory structure, and mental processes. *Science, 192,* 27–33.

Meyer, J. P., & Allen, N. J. (1991). A three-component conceptualization of organizational commitment. *Human Resource Management Review, 1,* 61–89.

Meyer, J. P., & Herscovitch, L. (2001). Commitment in the workplace: Toward a general model. *Human Resource Management Review, 11,* 299–326.

Meyer, R. E. (1996). The disease called addiction: Emerging evidence in a 200-year debate. *The Lancet, 347,* 162–166.

Meyer, R. G. (1992). *Practical clinical hypnosis: Techniques and applications.* New York, NY: Lexington Books.

Meyerbröker, K., & Emmelkamp, P. G. (2010). Virtual reality exposure therapy in anxiety disorders: A systematic review of process-and-outcome studies. *Depression and Anxiety, 27*(10), 933–944. doi:10.1002/da.20734

Mezzich, J. E., Lewis-Fernandez, R., & Ruiperez, M. A. (2003). The cultural framework of psychiatric disorders. In A. Tasman, J. Kay, & J. A. Lieberman (Eds.), *Psychiatry.* New York, NY: Wiley.

Michael, E. B., & Gollan, T. H. (2005). Being and becoming bilingual: Individual differences and consequences for language production. In J. F. Kroll & A. B. de Groot (Eds.), *Handbook of bilingualism: Psycholinguistic approaches* (pp. 389–407). New York, NY: Oxford University Press.

Michaels, S. (1996). The prevalance of homosexuality in the United States. In R. P. Cabaj & T. S. Stein (Eds.), *Textbook of homosexuality and mental health.* Washington, DC: American Psychiatric Press.

Mignot, E., & Lin, L. (2009). Narcolepsy. In R. Stickgold & M. P. Walker (Eds.), *The neuroscience of sleep* (pp. 270–277). San Diego, CA: Academic Press.

Mikulincer, M., & Shaver, P. R. (2007). *Attachment in adulthood: Structure, dynamics, and change.* New York, NY: Guilford Press.

Mikulincer, M., & Shaver, P. R. (2008). Adult attachment and affect regulation. In J. Cassidy & P. R. Shaver (Eds.), *Handbook of attachment: Theory, research, and clinical applications* (2nd ed., pp. 456–481). New York, NY: Guilford Press.

Milar, K. S. (2000). The first generation of women psychologists and the psychology of women. *American Psychologist, 55,* 616–619.

Milgram, S. (1963). Behavioral study of obedience. *Journal of Abnormal and Social Psychology, 67,* 371–378.

Milgram, S. (1964). Issues in the study of obedience. *American Psychologist, 19,* 848–852.

Milgram, S. (1968). Reply to the critics. *International Journal of Psychiatry, 6,* 294–295.

Milgram, S. (1974). *Obedience to authority.* New York, NY: Harper & Row.

Milinski, M., Sommerfeld, R. D., Krambeck, H. J., Reed, F. A., & Marotzke, J. (2008). The collective-risk social dilemma and the prevention of simulated dangerous climate change. *Proceedings of the National Academy of Sciences, 105,* 2291–2294.

Milkman, K. L., Chugh, D., & Bazerman, M. H. (2009). How can decision making be improved? *Perspectives on Psychological Science, 4*(4), 379–383. doi:10.1111/j.1745-6924.2009.01142.x

Miller, A. G. (1986). *The obedience experiments: A case study of controversy in social science.* New York, NY: Praeger.

Miller, A. G. (2004). What can the Milgram obedience experiments tell us about the Holocaust?: Generalizing from the social psychology laboratory. In A. G. Miller (Ed.), *The social psychology of good and evil* (pp. 193–239). New York, NY: Guilford Press.

Miller, E., & Wallis, J. (2008). The prefrontal cortex and executive brain functions. In L. Squire, D. Berg, F. Bloom, S. Du Lac, A. Ghosh, & N. Spitzer (Eds.), *Fundamental neuroscience* (3rd ed., pp. 1199–1222). San Diego, CA: Elsevier.

Miller, G. (2009). The Brain Collector. *Science, 324*(5935), 1634–1636.

Miller, G., Tybur, J. M., & Jordan, B. D. (2007). Ovulatory cycle effects on tip earnings by lap dancers: Economic evidence for human estrus? *Evolution and Human Behavior, 28,* 375–381.

Miller, G. A. (1956). The magical number seven, plus or minus two: Some limits on our capacity for processing information. *Psychological Review, 63,* 81–97.

Miller, G. A. (2003). The cognitive revolution: A historical perspective. *Trends in Cognitive Sciences, 7*(3), 141–144.

Miller, G. E., & Blackwell, E. (2006). Turning up the heat: Inflammation as a mechanism linking chronic stress, depression, and heart disease. *Current Directions in Psychological Science, 15,* 269–272.

Miller, G. E., Chen, E., & Zhou, E. S. (2007). If it goes up, must it come down? Chronic stress and the hypothalamic-pituitary-adrenocortical axis in humans. *Psychological Bulletin, 133,* 25–45.

Miller, G.T. (2007). *Living in the environment: Principles, connections and solutions* (14th ed.). Belmont, CA: Wadsworth.

Miller, I. J., & Reedy, F. E. Jr. (1990). Variations in human taste-bud density and taste intensity perception. *Physiological Behavior, 47,* 1213–1219.

Miller, J. G. (2006). Insights into moral development from cultural psychology. In M. Killen & J. G. Smetana (Eds.), *Handbook of moral development.* Mahwah, NJ: Erlbaum.

Miller, J. M., & Peterson, D. A. M. (2004). Theoretical and empirical implications of attitude strength. *Journal of Politics, 66,* 847–867.

Miller, N. E. (1941). The frustration-aggression hypothesis. *Psychological Review, 48,* 337–342.

Miller, N. E. (1944). Experimental studies of conflict. In J. M. Hunt (Ed.), *Personality and the behavior disorders* (Vol. 1). New York, NY: Ronald.

Miller, N. E. (1959). Liberalization of basic S-R concepts: Extension to conflict behavior, motivation, and social learning. In S. Koch (Ed.), *Psychology: A study of a science* (Vol. 2). New York, NY: McGraw-Hill.

Miller, N. E. (1985). The value of behavioral research on animals. *American Psychologist, 40,* 423–440.

Miller, R. R., & Grace, R. C. (2003). Conditioning and learning. In A. F. Healy & R. W. Proctor (Eds.), *Handbook of psychology, Vol. 4: Experimental psychology.* New York, NY: Wiley.

Milligan, E. D., & Watkins, L. R. (2009). Pathological and protective roles of glia in chronic pain. *Nature Reviews Neuroscience, 10*(1), 23–36. doi:10.1038/nrn2533

Millman, J., Bishop, C. H., & Ebel, R. (1965). An analysis of test-wiseness. *Educational and Psychological Measurement, 25,* 707–726.

Millon, T. (1981). *Disorders of personality: DSM-III, axis II.* New York, NY: Wiley.

Millstone, E. (1989). Methods and practices of animal experimentation. In G. Langley (Ed.), *Animal experimentation: The consensus changes.* New York, NY: Chapman & Hall.

Mineka, S., & Öhman, A. (2002). Phobias and preparedness: The selective, automatic and encapsulated nature of fear. *Biological Psychiatry, 52,* 927–937.

Mineka, S., & Zinbarg, R. E. (2006). A contemporary learning theory perspective on the etiology of anxiety disorders: It's not what you thought it was. *American Psychologist, 61,* 10–26.

Minkel, J. D., & Banks, S., & Dinges, D. F. (2009). Behavioral change with sleep deprivation. In R. Stickgold & M. P. Walker (Eds.), *The neuroscience of sleep* (pp. 241–248). San Diego, CA: Academic Press.

Minkel, J. D., & Dinges, D. F. (2009). Circadian rhythms in sleepiness, alertness, and performance. In R. Stickgold & M. P. Walker (Eds.), *The neuroscience of sleep* (pp. 183–190). San Diego, CA: Academic Press.

Minton, H. L. (2000). Lewis Madison Terman. In A. E. Kazdin (Ed.), *Encyclopedia of psychology* (pp. 37–39). Washington, DC: American Psychological Association.

Minzenberg, M. J., Yoon, J. H., & Carter, C. S. (2008). Schizophrenia. In R. E. Hales, S. C. Yudofsky, & G. O. Gabbard (Eds.), *The American Psychiatric Publishing textbook of psychiatry* (5th ed., pp. 407–456). Washington, DC: American Psychiatric Publishing.

Miranda, J., Bernal, G., Lau, A., Kohn, L., Hwang, W., & LaFromboise, T. (2005). State of the science on psychosocial interventions for ethnic minorities. *Annual Review of Clinical Psychology, 1,* 113–42.

Mirescu, C., & Gould, E. (2006). Stress and adult neurogenesis. *Hippocampus, 16,* 233–238.

Mischel, W. (1961). Delay of gratification, need for achievement, and acquiescence in another culture. *Journal of Abnormal and Social Psychology, 62,* 543–552.

Mischel, W. (1968). *Personality and assessment.* New York, NY: John Wiley.

Mischel, W. (1973). Toward a cognitive social learning conceptualization of personality. *Psychological Review, 80,* 252–283.

Mischel, W. (1984). Convergences and challenges in the search for consistency. *American Psychologist, 39,* 351–364.

Mitchell, K. J., & Johnson, M. K. (2000). Source monitoring: Attributing mental experiences. In E. Tulving & F. I. M. Craik (Eds.), *The Oxford handbook of memory* (pp. 179–196). New York, NY: Oxford University Press.

Mitchell, T., O'Sullivan, P. B., Smith, A., Burnett, A. F., Straker, L., Thornton, J., & Rudd, C. J. (2009). Biopsychosocial factors are associated with low back pain in female nursing students: A cross-sectional study. *International Journal of Nursing Studies, 46*(5), 678–688. doi:10.1016/j.ijnurstu.2008.11.004

Mitsonis, C., Zervas, I., Potagas, K., Mandellos, D., Koutsis, G., & Sfagos, K. (2006). The role of stress in multiple sclerosis: Three case reports and review of the literature. *Psychiatriki, 17,* 325–342.

Miyamoto, S., Merrill, D. B., Lieberman, J. A., Fleischacker, W. W., & Marder, S. R. (2008). Antipsychotic drugs. In A. Tasman, J. Kay, J. A. Lieberman, M. B. First, & M. Maj (Eds.), *Psychiatry* (3rd ed.). New York, NY: Wiley-Blackwell.

Modestin, J. (1992). Multiple personality disorder in Switzerland. *American Journal of Psychiatry, 149,* 88–92.

Moe, A., & De Bini, R. (2004). Studying passages with the loci method: Are subject-generated more effective than experimenter-supplied loci pathways? *Journal of Mental Imagery, 28*(3–4), 75–86.

Moffitt, T. E. (2005). The new look of behavioral genetics in developmental psychopathology: Gene-environment interplay in antisocial behaviors. *Psychological Bulletin, 131,* 533–554.

Moghaddam, F. M., Taylor, D. M., & Wright, S. C. (1993). *Social psychology in cross-cultural perspective.* New York, NY: W. H. Freeman.

Mojtabai, R., & Olfson, M. (2008). National trends in psychotherapy by office-based psychiatrists. *Archives of General Psychiatry, 65*(8), 962–970.

Mojtabai, R., & Olfson, M. (2010). National trends in psychotropic medication polypharmacy in office-based psychiatry. *Archives of General Psychiatry, 67*(1), 26–36.

Mokdad, A. H., Ford, E. S., Bowman, B. A., Dietz, W. H., Vinicor, F., Bales, V. S., & Marks, J. S. (2003). Prevalence of obesity, diabetes, and obesity-related health risk factors, 2001. *Journal of the American Medical Association, 289,* 76–79.

Molland, J. (2010, Nov. 12). Wanted—Only young, pretty women need apply in Chengdu. Retrieved from http://www.care2.com/causes/wanted-only-young-pretty-women-need-apply-in-chengdu.html

Moller, A. C., Elliot, A. J., & Maier, M. A. (2009). Basic hue-meaning associations. *Emotion, 9*(6), 898–902. doi:10.1037/a0017811

Monastra, V. J. (2008). Social skills training for children and teens with ADHD: The neuroeducational life skills program. In V. J. Monastra (Ed.), *Unlocking the potential of patients with ADHD: A model for clinical practice.* Washington, DC: American Psychological Association.

Moncrieff, J. (2001). Are antidepressants overrated? A review of methodological problems in antidepressant trials. *Journal of Nervous and Mental Disorders, 189,* 288–295.

Monk, T. H. (2000). Shift work. In M. H. Kryger, T. Roth, & W. C. Dement (Eds.), *Principles and practice of sleep medicine.* Philadelphia, PA: Saunders.

Monk, T. H. (2005a). Aging human circadian rhythms: Conventional wisdom may not always be right. *Journal of Biological Rhythms, 20*(4), 366–374. doi:10.1177/0748730405277378

Monk, T. H. (2005b). Shift work: Basic principles. In M. H. Kryger, T. Roth, & W. C. Dement (Eds.). *Principles and practice of sleep medicine.* Philadelphia, PA: Elsevier Saunders.

Monk, T. H. (2006). Jet lag. In T. Lee-Chiong (Ed.), *Sleep: A comprehensive handbook.* Hoboken, NJ: Wiley-Liss.

Monroe, S. M. (2008). Modern approaches to conceptualizing and measuring human life stress. *Annual Review of Clinical Psychology, 4,* 33–52.

Monroe, S. M., & Hadjiyannakis, K. (2002). The social environment and depression: Focusing on severe life stress. In I. H. Gotlib & C. L. Hammen (Eds.), *Handbook of depression.* New York, NY: Guilford Press.

Monroe, S. M., Harkness, K., Simons, A., & Thase, M. (2001). Life stress and the symptoms of major depression. *Journal of Nervous & Mental Disease, 189*(3), 168–175.

Monroe, S. M., & Reid, M. W. (2009). Life stress and major depression. *Current Directions in Psychological Science, 18*(2), 68–72. doi:10.1111/j.1467-8721.2009.01611.x

Monroe, S. M., & Slavich, G. M. (2007). Psychological stressors overview. In G. Fink (Ed.), *Encyclopedia of stress* (2nd ed.). San Diego, CA: Academic Press.

Monroe, S. M., Slavich, G. M., & Georgiades, K. (2009). The social environment and life stress in depression. In I. H. Gotlib & C. L. Hammen (Eds.), *Handbook of Depression* (2nd ed., pp. 340–360). New York, NY: Guilford Press.

Monti, J. M., Jantos, H., & Monti, D. (2008). Serotonin and sleep-wake regulation. Neurochemistry of sleep and wakefulness. In J. M. Monti, S. R. Pandi-Perumal, & C. M. Sinton (Eds.), *Neurochemistry of sleep and wakefulness* (pp. 244–279). New York, NY: Cambridge University Press.

Montoya, R. (2008). I'm hot, so I'd say you're not: The influence of objective physical attractiveness on mate selection. *Personality and Social Psychology Bulletin, 34*(10), 1315–1331. doi:10.1177/0146167208320387

Moons, W. G., Mackie, D. M., & Garcia-Marques, T. (2009). The impact of repetition-induced familiarity on agreement with weak and strong arguments. *Journal of Personality and Social Psychology, 96*(1), 32–44. doi:10.1037/a0013461

Moore, B. C. J. (2010). Audition. In E. B. Goldstein (Ed.), *Encyclopedia of perception*. Thousand Oaks, CA: Sage.

Moore, C. F. (2009). *Children and pollution: Why scientists disagree*. Oxford University Press.

Moore, D. S., & Johnson, S. P. (2008). Mental rotation in human infants: A sex difference. *Psychological Science, 19*(11), 1063–1066. doi:10.1111/j.1467-9280.2008.02200.x

Moore, J. (2005). Some historical and conceptual background to the development of B. F. Skinner's "Radical Behaviorism." *Journal of Mind and Behavior, 26*, 65–94.

Moore, K. L., & Persaud, T. V. N. (2008). *Before we are born* (7th ed.). Philadelphia, PA: Saunders.

Moore, R. Y. (2006). Biological rythms and sleep. In T. Lee-Chiong (Ed.), *Sleep: A comprehensive handbook*. Hoboken, NJ: Wiley-Liss.

Morahan-Martin, J. (2007). Internet use and abuse and psychological problems. In A. N. Joinson, K. Y. A. McKenna, T. Postmes, & U.-D. Reips (Eds.), *The Oxford handbook of Internet psychology*. New York, NY: Guilford Press.

Moran, T. H. (2004). Gut peptides in the control of food intake: 30 years of ideas. *Physiology & Behavior, 82*, 175–180.

Morata, T. C. (2007). Young people: Their noise and music exposures and the risk of hearing loss. *International Journal of Audiology, 46*(3), 111–112. doi:10.1080/14992020601103079

Morewedge, C. K., & Norton, M. I. (2009). When dreaming is believing: The (motivated) interpretation of dreams. *Journal of Personality and Social Psychology, 96*(2), 249–264. doi:10.1037/a0013264

Morey, L. C. (1988). Personality disorders in DSM-III and DSM-III-R: Convergence, coverage, and internal consistency. *American Journal of Psychiatry, 145*, 573–577.

Morgan, H. (1996). An analysis of Gardner's theory of multiple intelligence. *Roeper Review, 18*, 263–269.

Morgan, M. J. (2000). Ecstacy (MDMA): A review of its possible persistent psychological effects. *Psychopharmacology, 152*, 230–248.

Morgan, R. D. & Cohen, L. M. (2008). Clinical and counseling psychology: Can differences be gleaned from printed recruiting materials? *Training and Education in Professional Psychology, 2*(3), 156–164.

Morhenn, V. B., Park, J., Piper, E., & Zak, P. J. (2008). Monetary sacrifice among strangers is mediated by endogenous oxytocin release after physical contact. *Evolution and Human Behavior, 29*(6), 375–383. doi:10.1016/j.evolhumbehav.2008.04.004

Moriarity, J. L., Boatman, D., Krauss, G. L., Storm, P. B., & Lenz, F. A. (2001). Human "memories" can be evoked by stimulation of the lateral temporal cortex after ipsilateral medical temporal lobe resection. *Journal of Neurology, Neurosurgery & Psychiatry, 71*, 549–551.

Morin, C. M. (2002). Contributions of cognitive-behavioral approaches to the clinical management of insomnia. *Journal of Clinical Psychiatry, 4* (suppl 1), 21–26.

Morin, C. M. (2005). Psychological and behavioral treatments for primary insomnia. In M. H. Kryger, T. Roth, & W. C. Dement (Eds.), *Principles and practice of sleep medicine*. Philadelphia, PA: Elsevier Saunders.

Morokoff, P. J., Quina, K., Harlow, L. L., Whitmire, L., Grimley, D. M., Gibson, P. R., & Burkholder, G. J. (1997). Sexual assertiveness scale (SAS) for women: Development and validation. *Journal of Personality and Social Psychology, 73*, 790–804.

Morris, C. D., Bransford, J. D., & Franks, J. J. (1977). Levels of processing versus transfer-appropriate processing. *Journal of Verbal Learning and Verbal Behavior, 16*, 519–533.

Morrison, A. R. (2003). The brain on night shift. *Cerebrum, 5*(3), 23–36.

Morrison, C. M., & Conway, M. A. (2010). First words and first memories. *Cognition, 116*(1), 23–32. doi:10.1016/j.cognition.2010.03.011

Morry, M. M. (2007). The attraction-similarity hypothesis among cross-sex friends: Relationship satisfaction, perceived similarities, and self-serving perceptions. *Journal of Social and Personal Relationships, 24*(1), 117–138. doi:10.1177/0265407507072615

Morry, M. M. (2009). Similarity principle of attraction. In H. T. Reis & S. Sprecher (Eds.), *Encyclopedia of human relationships* (pp. 1500–1504). Los Angeles, CA: Sage.

Morton, A. (2010). *Angelina: An unauthorized biography*. New York, NY: St. Martin's Press.

Moruzzi, G. (1964). Reticular influences on the EEG. *Electroencephalography and Clinical Neurophysiology, 16*, 2–17.

Mosher, D., & Maclan, P. (1994). College men and women respond to X-rated videos intended for male or female audiences: Gender and sexual scripts. *Journal of Sex Research, 31*, 99–113.

Most, S. B., Scholl, B. J., Clifford, E. R., & Simons, D. J. (2005). What you see is what you set: Sustained inattentional blindness and the capture of awareness. *Psychological Review, 112*, 217–242.

Motivala, S. J., & Irwin, M. R. (2007). Sleep and immunity: Cytokine pathways linking sleep and health outcomes. *Current Directions in Psychological Science, 16*, 21–25.

Mowrer, O. H. (1947). On the dual nature of learning: A reinterpretation of "conditioning" and "problem-solving." *Harvard Educational Review, 17*, 102–150.

Mrdjenovic, G., & Levitsky, D. A. (2005). Children eat what they are served: The imprecise regulation of energy intake. *Appetite, 44*, 273–282.

Mroczek, D. K., & Almeida, D. M. (2004). The effect of daily stress, personality, and age on daily negative effect. *Journal of Personality, 72*, 355–378.

Mueller, C. W., Boyer, E. M., Price, J. L., & Iverson, R. D. (1994). Employee attachment and noncoercive conditions of work: The case of dental hygienists. *Work and Occupations*, 21(2), 179–212. doi:10.1177/0730888494021002002

Muench, J., & Hamer, A. M. (2010). Adverse effects of antipsychotic medications. *American Family Physician, 81*(5), 617–622.

Mullen, B., & Copper, C. (1994). The relation between group cohesiveness and performance: An integration. *Psychological Bulletin, 115*, 210–227.

Muller, M., Aleman, A., Grobbee, D. E., de Haan, E. H., & van der Schouw, Y. T. (2005). Endogenous sex hormone levels and cognitive function in aging men: Is there an optimal level? *Neurology, 64*, 866–871.

Mulligan, N. W. (1998). The role of attention during encoding in implicit and explicit memory. *Journal of Experimental Psychology: Learning, Memory, & Cognition, 24*, 27–47.

Mulvaney, M. K., & Mebert, C. J. (2007). Parental corporal punishment predicts behavior problems in early childhood. *Journal of Family Psychology, 21*, 389–397.

Munafò, M. R., Yalcin, B., Willis-Owen, S. A., & Flint, J. (2008). Association of the dopamine D4 receptor (DRD4) gene and approach-related personality traits: Meta-analysis and new data. *Biological Psychiatry, 63*(2), 197–206. doi:10.1016/j.biopsych.2007.04.006

Munck, A. (2007). Corticosteroids and stress. In G. Fink (Ed.), *Encyclopedia of stress*. San Diego: Elsevier.

Munk-Jorgensen, P. (1999). Has deinstitutionalization gone too far? *European Archives of Psychiatry & Clinical Neuroscience, 249*(3), 136–143.

Munsey, C. (2008). Prescriptive authority in the states: A look at which states allow RxP and which have considered it. *Monitor on Psychology, 39*(2).

Murdock, B. (2001). Analysis of the serial position curve. In H. L. Roediger III, J. S. Nairne, I. Neath, & A. M. Surprenant (Eds.), *The nature of remembering: Essays in honor of Robert G. Crowder* (pp. 151–170). Washington, DC: American Psychological Association.

Muris, P., & Merckelbach, H. (2001). The etiology of childhood specific phobia: A multifactorial model. In M. W. Vasey, & M. R. Dadds (Eds.), *The developmental psychopathology of anxiety*. (pp. 355–385). New York, NY: Oxford University Press.

Murphy, K. R. (2002). Can conflicting perspectives on the role of *g* in personnel selection be resolved? *Human Performance, 15*, 173–186.

Murphy, P. N., Wareing, M., Fisk, J. E., & Montgomery, C. (2009). Executive working memory deficits in abstinent ecstasy/MDMA users: A critical review. *Neuropsychobiology, 60*(3/4), 159–175. doi:10.1159/000253552

Murray, H. A. (1938). *Explorations in personality*. New York, NY: Oxford University Press.

Murray, H. A. (1943). *Thematic Apperception Test Manual*. Cambridge, MA: Harvard University Press.

Murray, M. M., Foxe, D. M., Javitt, D. C., & Foxe, J. J. (2004). Setting boundaries: Brain dynamics of modal and amodal illusory shape completion in humans. *Journal of Neuroscience, 24*, 6898–6903.

Murray, R. M., & Bramon, E. (2005). Developmental model of schizophrenia. In B. J. Sadock & V. A. Sadock (Eds.), *Kaplan & Sadock's comprehensive textbook of psychiatry* (pp. 1381–1395). Philadelphia, PA: Lippincott Williams & Wilkins.

Murray, S. L., Holmes, J. G., Bellavia, G., Griffin, D. W., & Dolderman, D. (2002). Kindred spirits? The benefits of egocentrism in close relationships. *Journal of Personality and Social Psychology, 82*, 563–581.

Murstein, B. I., & Fontaine, P. A. (1993). The public's knowledge about psychologists and other mental health professionals. *American Psychologist, 48*, 839–845.

Mustanski, B. S., Chivers, M. L., & Bailey, J. M. (2002). A critical review of recent biological research on human sexual orientation. *Annual Review of Sex Research, 12,* 89–140.

Mutz, D. C., & Goldman, S. K. (2010). Mass media. In J. F. Dovidio, M. Hewstone, P. Glick, & V. M. Esses (Eds.), *The Sage handbook of prejudice, stereotyping, and discrimination.* Los Angeles, CA: Sage.

Muzina, D. J., Kemp, D. E., & Calabrese, J. R. (2008). Mood stabilizers. In A. Tasman, J. Kay, J. A. Lieberman, M. B. First, & M. Maj (Eds.), *Psychiatry* (3rd ed.). New York, NY: Wiley-Blackwell.

Myers, D. G. (1992). *The pursuit of happiness: Who is happy—and why.* New York, NY: Morrow.

Myers, D. G. (1999). Close relationships and quality of life. In D. Kahneman, E. Diener, & N. Schwarz (Eds.), *Well-being: The foundations of hedonic psychology.* New York, NY: Russell Sage Foundation.

Myers, D. G. (2008). Religion and human flourishing. In M. Eid & R. J. Larsen (Eds.), *The science of subjective well-being* (pp. 323–346). New York, NY: Guilford Press.

Myers, D. G. (2010). *Social psychology* (10th ed.). New York, NY: McGraw-Hill.

Myers, D. G., & Diener, E. (1995). Who is happy? *Psychological Science, 6,* 10–19.

Myers, G. (2007). *The significance of children and animals: Social development and our connections to other species.* West Lafayette, IN: Purdue University Press.

Mynatt, C. R., Doherty, M. E., & Tweney, R. D. (1978). Consequences of confirmation and disconfirmation in a simulated research environment. *Quarterly Journal of Experimental Psychology, 30,* 395–406.

Myrtek, M. (2007). Type A behavior and hostility as independent risk factors for coronary heart disease. In J. Jordan, B. Bardé, & A. M. Zeiher (Eds.), *Contributions toward evidence-based psychocardiology: A systematic review of the literature.* Washington, DC: American Psychological Association.

Nabi, H., Singh-Manoux, A., Shipley, M., Gimeno, D., Marmot, M. G., & Kivimaki, M. (2008). Do psychological factors affect inflammation and incident coronary heart disease? The Whitehall II study. *Arteriosclerosis, Thrombosis, and Vascular Biology, 24,* 1398–1406.

Nadelson, C. C., Notman, M. T., & McCarthy, M. K. (2005). Gender issues in psychotherapy. In G. O. Gabbard, J. S. Beck, & J. Holmes (Eds.), *Oxford textbook of psychotherapy.* New York, NY: Oxford University Press.

Naess, A. (1985). Identification as a source of deep ecological attitudes. In M. Tobias (Ed.), *Deep Ecology* (pp. 256–270). San Diego, CA: Avant Books.

Nahas, Z., Kozel, F. A., Molnar, C., Ramsey, D., Holt, R., Ricci, R., et al. (2007). Methods of administering transcranial magnetic stimulation. In M. S. George & R. H. Belmaker (Eds.), *Transcranial magnetic stimulation in clinical psychiatry* (pp. 39–58). Washington, DC: American Psychiatric Publishing.

Nairne, J. S. (2002). Remembering over the short-term: The case against the standard model. *Annual Review of Psychology, 53,* 53–81.

Nairne, J. S. (2003). Sensory and working memory. In A. F. Healy & R. W. Proctor (Eds.), *Handbook of psychology, Vol. 4: Experimental psychology.* New York, NY: Wiley.

Naish, P. L. N. (2006). Time to explain the nature of hypnosis? *Contemporary Hypnosis, 23,* 33–46.

Narr, K. L., Woods, R. P., Thompson, P. M., Szeszko, P., Robinson, D., Dimtcheva, T., et al. (2007). Relationships between IQ and regional cortical gray matter thickness in healthy adults. *Cerebral Cortex, 17*(9), 2163–2171. doi:10.1093/cercor/bhl125

Narrow, W. E., & Rubio-Stipec, M. (2009). Epidemiology. In B. J. Sadock, V. A. Sadock, & P. Ruiz (Eds.), *Kaplan & Sadock's comprehensive textbook of psychiatry* (9th ed., pp. 754–770). Philadelphia, PA: Lippincott, Williams & Wilkins.

NASA. (2007). NASA study suggests extreme summer warming in the future (2007, May 9). NASA: Goddard Institute for Space Studies, New York, NY. Retrieved from http://www.giss.nasa.gov/research/news/20070509/

Nash, M. R. (2001, July). The truth and hype of hypnosis. *Scientific American, 285,* 36–43.

Nash, M. R. (2008). Foundations of clinical hypnosis. In M. R. Nash & A. J. Barnier (Eds.). *Oxford handbook of hypnosis: Theory, research and practice* (pp. 487–502). New York, NY: Oxford University Press.

Nash, M. R., Perez, N., Tasso, A., & Levy, J. (2009). Clinical research on the utility of hypnosis in the prevention, diagnosis, and treatment of medical and psychiatric disorders. *International Journal of Clinical & Experimental Hypnosis, 57*(4), 443–450.

Näslund, E., & Hellström, P. M. (2007). Appetite signaling: From gut peptides and enteric nerves to brain. *Physiology & Behavior, 92,* 256–262.

National Sleep Foundation. (2010). *Sleep in America poll: Summary of findings.* Retrieved from http://www.sleepfoundation.org/sites/default/files/nsaw/NSF%20Sleep%20in%20%20America%20Poll%20-%20Summary%20of%20Findings%20.pdf

Naumann, L. P., Vazire, S., Rentfrow, P. J., & Gosling, S. D. (2009). Personality judgments based on physical appearance. *Personality and Social Psychology Bulletin, 35*(12), 1661–1671. doi:10.1177/0146167209346309

Naylor, J. C., Pritchard, R. D., & Ilgen, D. R. (1980). *A theory of behavior in organizations.* New York, NY: Academic Press.

Neighbors, H. W., Caldwell, C., Williams, D. R., Nesse, R., Taylor, R. J., Bullard, K. M., et al. (2007). Race, ethnicity, and the use of services for mental disorders: Results from the National Survey of American Life. *Archives of General Psychiatry, 64,* 485–494.

Neisser, U. (1967). *Cognitive psychology.* New York, NY: Appleton-Century-Crofts.

Neisser, U. (1998). Introduction: Rising test scores and what they mean. In U. Neisser (Ed.), *The rising curve: Long-term gains in IQ and related measures.* Washington, DC: American Psychological Association.

Neisser, U., Boodoo, G., Bouchard, T. J., Jr., Boykin, A. W., Brody, N., Ceci, S. J., Halpern, D. F., Loehlin, J. C., Perloff, R., Sternberg, R. J., & Urbina, S. (1996). Intelligence: Knowns and unknowns. *American Psychologist, 51,* 77–101.

Nelson, C. (2001). The magical number 4 in short-term memory: A reconsideration of mental storage capacity. *Behavioral & Brain Sciences, 24*(1), 87–185.

Nemeroff, C. B., Kalali, A., Keller, M. B., Charney, D. S., Lenderts, S. E., Cascade, E. F., et al. (2007). Impact of publicity concerning pediatric suicidality data on physician practice patterns in the United States. *Archives of General Psychiatry, 64,* 466–472.

Nesse, R. M., & Ellsworth, P. C. (2009). Evolution, emotions, and emotional disorders. *American Psychologist, 64*(2), 129–139. doi:10.1037/a0013503

Nesse, R. M., & Young, E. A. (2000). Evolutionary origins and functions of the stress response. In G. Fink (Ed.), *Encyclopedia of stress* (Vol. 2, pp. 79–83). San Diego: Academic Press.

Nestler, E. J., & Malenka, R. C. (2004). The addicted brain. *Scientific American, 290*(3), 78–85.

Nettle, D. (2001). *Strong imagination, madness, creativity, and human nature.* New York, NY: Oxford University Press.

Nettle, D. (2006). The evolution of personality variation in humans and other animals. *American Psychologist, 61,* 622–631.

Neuberg, S. L., Kenrick, D. T., & Schaller, M. (2010). Evolutionary social psychology. In S. T. Fiske, D. T. Gilbert, & G. Lindzey (Eds.), *Handbook of social psychology,*(5th ed., Vol. 2, pp. 761–796). Hoboken, NJ: Wiley.

Neugroschl, J. A., Kolevzon, A., Samuels, S. C., & Marin, D. B. (2005). Dementia. In B. J. Sadock & V. A. Sadock (Eds.), *Kaplan & Sadock's comprehensive textbook of psychiatry* (pp. 1068–1092). Philadelphia, PA: Lippincott Williams & Wilkins.

Neuringer, A., & Oleson, K. C. (2010). Helping for change. *The Behavior Analyst, 33,* 181–184.

Neuschatz, J. S., Lampinen, J. M., Preston, E. L., Hawkins, E. R., & Toglia, M. P. (2002). The effect of memory schemata on memory and the phenomenological experience of naturalistic situations. *Applied Cognitive Psychology, 16,* 687–708.

Neuschatz, J. S., Lampinen, J. M., Toglia, M. P., Payne, D. G., & Cisneros, E. P. (2007). False memory research: History, theory, and applied implications. In M. P. Toglia, J. D. Read, D. F. Ross, & R. C. L. Lindsay (Eds.), *Handbook of eyewitness psychology: Volume 1. Memory for events.* Mahwah, NJ: Erlbaum.

Nevin, J. A. (2010). The power of cooperation. *The Behavior Analyst, 33,* 189–191.

Newcombe, N. S. (2007). Taking science seriously: Straight thinking about spatial sex differences. In S. J. Ceci & W. M. Williams (Eds.), *Why aren't more women in science?* (pp. 69–78). Washington, DC: American Psychological Association.

Newell, A., & Simon, H. A. (1972). *Human problem solving.* Englewood Cliffs, NJ: Prentice-Hall.

Newell, A., Shaw, J. C., & Simon, H. A. (1958). Elements of a theory of human problem solving. *Psychological Review, 65,* 151–166.

Newman, C. F. & Beck, A. T. (2009). Cognitive therapy. In B. J. Sadock, V. A. Sadock, & P. Ruiz (Eds.), *Kaplan & Sadock's comprehensive textbook of psychiatry* (pp. 2857–2872). Philadelphia, PA: Lippincott Williams & Wilkins.

Newman, T. M. (2010). Assessment of giftedness in school-age children using measures of intelligence or cognitive abilities. In S. I. Pfeiffer (Ed.), *Handbook of giftedness in children: Psychoeducational theory, research, and best practices.* New York, NY: Springer.

Niccols, A. (2007). Fetal alcohol syndrome and the developing socio-emotional brain. *Brain and Cognition, 65,* 135–142.

Nickerson, C., Schwarz, N., Diener, E., & Kahneman, D. (2003). Zeroing in on the dark side of the American dream: A closer look at the negative consequences of the goal for financial success. *Psychological Science, 14,* 531–536.

Nickerson, R. S. (1998). Confirmation bias: A ubiquitous phenomenon in many guises. *Review of General Psychology, 2*(2), 175–220. doi:10.1037/1089-2680.2.2.175

Nickerson, R. S., & Adams, M. J. (1979). Long-term memory for a common object. *Cognitive Psychology, 11,* 287–307.

Nicoladis, E., & Genesee, F. (1997). Language development in preschool bilingual children. *Journal of Speech-Language Pathology & Audiology, 21,* 258–270.

Niebyl, J. R., & Simpson, J. L. (2007). Drugs and environmental agents in pregnancy and lactation: Embryology, teratology, epidemiology. In S. G. Gabbe, J. R. Niebyl, & J. L. Simpson (Eds.) *Obstetrics: Normal and problem pregnancies* (5th ed., pp. 184–214). Philadelphia, PA: Elsevier.

Nielsen, T. A., & Stenstrom, P. (2005). What are the memory sources of dreaming? *Nature, 437,* 1286–1289.

Nielsen, T. A., & Zadra, A. (2000). Dreaming disorders. In M. H. Kryger, T. Roth, & W. C. Dement (Eds.), *Principles and practice of sleep medicine.* Philadelphia, PA: Saunders.

Nielsen, T. A., Zadra, A. L., Simard, V., Saucier, S., Stenstrom, P., Smith, C., & Kuiken, D. (2003). The typical dreams of Canadian university students. *Dreaming, 13*(4), 211–235.

Nielsen, T., & Levin, R. (2009). Theories and correlates of nightmares. In R. Stickgold & M. P. Walker (Eds.), *The neuroscience of sleep* (pp. 323–329). San Diego, CA: Academic Press.

Nievar, M. A., & Becker, B. J. (2008). Sensitivity as a privileged predictor of attachment: A second perspective on De Wolff and Van IJzendoorn's meta-analysis. *Social Development, 17,* 102–114.

Nikelly, A. G. (1994). Alcoholism: Social as well as psycho-medical problem—The missing "big picture." *Journal of Alcohol & Drug Education, 39,* 1–12.

Ninan, P. T., Muntasser, S. (2004). Buspirone and gepirone. In A. F. Schatzberg & C. B. Nemeroff (Eds.), *The American psychiatric publishing textbook of psychopharmacology* (pp. 391–404). Washington, DC: American Psychiatric Publishing.

Nir, Y., & Tononi, G. (2010). Dreaming and the brain: From phenomenology to neurophysiology. *Trends in Cognitive Sciences, 14*(2), 88–100. doi:10.1016/j.tics.2009.12.001

Nisbet, E. K., Zelenski, J. M., & Murphy, S. A. (2009). The Nature Relatedness Scale: Linking individuals' connection with nature to environmental concern and behavior. *Environment and Behavior, 41*(5), 715–740.

Nisbett, R. E. (2003). *The geography of thought: How Asians and Westerners think differently . . . and why.* New York, NY: Free Press.

Nisbett, R. E. (2005). Heredity, environment, and race differences in IQ: A commentary on Rushton and Jensen. *Psychology, Public Policy, and the Law, 11,* 302–310.

Nisbett, R. E. (2009). *Intelligence and how to get it: Why schools and cultures count.* New York, NY: Norton.

Nisbett, R. E. (Ed.). (1993). *Rules for reasoning.* Hillsdale, NJ: Erlbaum.

Nisbett, R. E., & Miyamoto, Y. (2005). The influence of culture: Holistic versus analytic perception. *Trends in Cognitive Sciences, 9,* 467–473.

Nisbett, R. E., Peng, K., Choi, I., & Norenzayan, A. (2001). Culture and systems of thought: Holistic versus analytic cognition. *Psychological Review, 108,* 291–310.

Nist, S. L., & Holschuh, J. L. (2000). Comprehension strategies at the college level. In R. F. Flippo & D. C. Caverly (Eds.), *Handbook of college reading and study strategy research.* Mahwah, NJ: Erlbaum.

Nithianantharajah, J., & Hannan, A. J. (2006). Enriched environments, experience–dependent plasticity and disorders of the nervous system. *Nature Reviews Neuroscience, 7,* 697–709.

Noble, K. G., McCandliss, B. D., & Farah, M. J. (2007). Socioeconomic gradients predict individual differences in neurocognitive abilities. *Developmental Science, 10,* 464–480.

Nobler, M. S., & Sackeim, H. A. (2006). Electroconvulsive therapy and transcranial magnetic stimulation. In D. J. Stein, D. J. Kupfer, & A. F. Schatzberg (Eds.), *Textbook of mood disorders.* Washington, DC: American Psychiatric Publishing.

Noftle, E. E., & Robins, R. W. (2007). Personality predictors of academic outcomes: Big Five correlates of GPA and SAT scores. *Journal of Personality and Social Psychology, 93,* 116–130.

Nolen-Hoeksema, S. (1991). Responses to depression and their effects on the duration of depressive episodes. *Journal of Abnormal Psychology, 100,* 569–582.

Nolen-Hoeksema, S. (2000). The role of rumination in depressive disorders and mixed anxiety/depressive symptoms. *Journal of Abnormal Psychology, 109,* 504–511.

Nolen-Hoeksema, S. (2001). Gender differences in depression. *Current Directions in Psychological Science, 10,* 173–176.

Nolen-Hoeksema, S., & Hilt, L. M. (2009). Gender differences in depression. In I. H. Gotlib & C. L. Hammen (Eds.), *Handbook of Depression* (2nd ed., pp. 386–404). New York, NY: Guilford Press.

Nolen-Hoeksema, S., Wisco, B. E., & Lyubomirsky, S. (2008). Rethinking rumination. *Perspectives on Psychological Science, 3*(5), 400–424. doi:10.1111/j.1745-6924.2008.00088.x

Nomaguchi, K. M., & Milkie, M. A. (2003). Costs and rewards of children: The effects of becoming a parent on adults' lives. *Journal of Marriage and the Family, 65,* 356–374.

Norcross, J. C. (1995). Dispelling the dodo bird verdict and the exclusivity myth in psychotherapy. *Psychotherapy, 32,* 500–504.

Norcross, J. C., & Beutler, L. E. (2011). Integrative psychotherapies. In R. J. Corsini & D. Wedding (Eds.), *Current psychotherapies* (9th ed.). Belmont, CA: Brooks/Cole.

Norcross, J. C., Hedges, M., & Castle, P. H. (2002). Psychologists conducting psychotherapy in 2001: A study of the Division 29 membership. *Psychotherapy: Theory, Research, Practice, Training, 39,* 97–102.

Norenzayan, A., & Heine, S. J. (2005). Psychological universals: What are they and how can we know? *Psychological Bulletin, 131,* 763–784.

Norman, T. R. (2009). Melatonin: Hormone of the night. *Acta Neuropsychiatrica, 21*(5), 263–265. doi:10.1111/acn.2009.21.issue-510.1111/j.1601-5215.2009.00411.x

Norris, F. H., & Slone, L. B. (2007). The epidemiology of trauma and PTSD. In M. J. Friedman, T. M. Keane, & P. A. Resick (Eds.), *Handbook of PTSD: Science and practice* (pp. 78–98). New York, NY: Guilford Press.

North, C. S., Eyrich, K. M., Pollio, D. E., & Spitznagel, E. L. (2004). Are rates of psychiatric disorders in the homeless population changing? *American Journal of Public Health, 94*(1), 103–108.

Norton, C. (2005). Animal experiments—A cardinal sin? *The Psychologist, 18*(2), 69.

Norton, C. L. (2010). Into the wilderness—a case study: The psychodynamics of adolescent depression and the need for a holistic intervention. *Clinical Social Work Journal, 38,* 226–235.

Nosek, B. A., Banaji, M., & Greenwald, A. G. (2002). Harvesting implicit group attitudes and beliefs from a demonstration web site. *Group Dynamics: Theory, Research, and Practice, 6*(1), 101–115. doi:10.1037/1089-2699.6.1.101

Nosek, B. A., Greenwald, A. G., & Banaji, M. R. (2007). The Implicit Association Test at age 7: A Methodological and conceptual review. In J. A. Bargh (Ed.), *Social psychology and the unconscious: The automaticity of higher mental processes* (pp. 265–292). New York, NY: Psychology Press.

Novemsky, N., & Kahneman, D. (2005). The boundaries of loss aversion. *Journal of Marketing Research, 42,* 119–128.

Novick, L. R., & Bassok, M. (2005). Problem solving. In K. J. Holyoak & R. G. Morrison (Eds.), *The Cambridge handbook of thinking and reasoning.* New York, NY: Cambridge University Press.

Noyes, R., Jr., Clarkson, C., Crowe, R. R., Yates, W. R., & McChesney, C. M. (1987). A family study of generalized anxiety disorder. *American Journal of Psychiatry, 144,* 1019–1024.

Nucci, L. P. (2002). The development of moral reasoning. In U. Goswami (Eds.), *Blackwell handbook of childhood cognitive development.* Malden, MA: Blackwell.

Nunnally, J. C., & Bernstein, I. H. (1994). *Psychometric theory.* New York, NY: McGraw-Hill.

Nyberg, L., Forkstam, C., Petersson, K. M., Cabeza, R., & Ingvar, M. (2002). Brain imaging of human memory systems: Between-systems similarities and within-system differences. *Cognitive Brain Research, 13,* 287–292.

O'Brien, C. P., Volkow, N., & Li, T.-K. (2006). What's in a word? Addiction versus dependence in DSM-V. *American Journal of Psychiatry, 163,* 764–765.

O'Connor, D. B., & Conner, M. (2011). Effects of stress on eating behavior. In R. J. Contrada & A. Baum (Eds.), *The handbook of stress science: Biology, psychology, and health* (pp. 111–121). New York, NY: Springer.

O'Connor, D. B., Jones, F., Ferguson, E., Conner, M., & McMillan, B. (2008). Effects of daily hassles and eating style on eating behavior. *Health Psychology, 27,* S20–S31.

Ochse, R. (1990). *Before the gates of excellence: The determinants of creative genius.* Cambridge, England: Cambridge University Press.

O'Donnell, L. (2009). The Wechsler Intelligence Scale for Children—Fourth Edition. In J. A. Naglieri & S. Goldstein (Eds.), *Practitioner's guide to assessing intelligence and achievement* (pp. 153–190). New York, NY: Wiley.

O'Donohue, W. (1998). Conditioning and third-generation behavior therapy. In W. O'Donohue (Ed.), *Learning and behavior therapy.* Boston, MA: Allyn & Bacon.

Ogden, C. L., Carroll, M. D., Curtin, L. R., McDowell, M. A., Tabak, C. J., & Flegal, K. M. (2006). Prevalence of overweight and obesity in the United States, 1999–2004. *Journal of the American Medical Association, 195,* 1549–1555.

Ogden, C. L., Carroll, M., Curtin, L., Lamb, M., & Flegal, K. (2010). Prevalence of high body mass index in U.S. children and adolescents, 2007–2008. *Journal of the American Medical Association, 303*(3), 242–249.

Ogden, J. (2010). *The psychology of eating: From healthy to disordered behavior.* Malden, MA: Wiley-Blackwell.

Ohayon, M. M., Carskadon, M. A., Guilleminault, C., & Vitiello, M. V. (2004). Meta-analysis of quantitative sleep parameters from childhood to old age in healthy individuals: Developing normative sleep values across the human lifespan. *Sleep: Journal of Sleep & Sleep Disorders Research, 27,* 1255–1273.

Ohayon, M. M., & Guilleminault, C. (2006). Epidemiology of sleep disorders. In T. Lee-Chiong (Ed.), *Sleep: A comprehensive handbook.* Hoboken, NJ: Wiley-Liss.

Öhman, A. (1979). Fear relevance, autonomic conditioning, and phobias: A laboratory model. In P.-O. Sjödén, S. Bates & W. S. Dockens III (Eds.), *Trends in behavior therapy* (pp. 107–134). New York, NY: Academic Press.

Öhman, A., Dimberg, U., & Öst, L.-G. (1985). Animal and social phobias: Biological constraints on learned fear responses. In S. Reiss, & R. R. Bootzin (Eds.), *Theoretical issues in behavior therapy* (pp. 123–178). New York, NY: Academic Press.

Öhman, A., & Mineka, S. (2001). Fears, phobias, and preparedness: Toward an evolved module of fear and fear learning. *Psychological Review, 108,* 483–522.

Öhman, A., & Wiens, S. (2003). On the automaticity of autonomic responses in emotion: An evolutionary perspective. In R. J. Davidson, K. R. Scherer, & H. H. Goldsmith (Eds.), *Handbook of affective sciences.* New York, NY: Oxford University Press.

Okami, P., & Shackelford, T. K. (2001). Human sex differences in sexual psychology and behavior. *Annual Review of Sex Research, 12,* 186–241.

Oken, B. S. (2008). Placebo effects: Clinical aspects and neurobiology. *Brain: A Journal of Neurology, 131*(11), 2812–2823. doi:10.1093/brain/awn116

Oldham, G. R., Cummings, A., Mischel, L. J., Schmidtke, J. M., & Zhou, J. (1995). Listen while you work? Quasi-experimental relations between personal-stereo headset use and employee work responses. *Journal of Applied Psychology, 80*(5), 547–564.

Olds, J. (1956). Pleasure centers in the brain. *Scientific American, 193,* 105–116.

Olds, J., & Milner, P. (1954). Positive reinforcement produced by electrical stimulation of the septal area and other regions of the rat brain. *Journal of Comparative and Physiological Psychology, 47,* 419–427.

Olds, M. E., & Fobes, J. L. (1981). The central basis of motivation: Intracranial self-stimulation studies. *Annual Review of Psychology, 32,* 523–574.

O'Leary, K. D., Kent, R. N., & Kanowitz, J. (1975). Shaping data collection congruent with experimental hypotheses. *Journal of Applied Behavior Analysis, 8,* 43–51.

O'Leary, M. B., & Cummings, J. N. (2007). The spatial, temporal, and configurational characteristics of geographic dispersion in teams. *MIS Quarterly, 31,* 433–452.

Olfson, M., Cherry, D. K., & Lewis-Fernández, R. (2009). Racial differences in visit duration of outpatient psychiatric visits. *Archives of General Psychiatry, 66*(2), 214–221.

Olfson, M. & Marcus, S. C. (2009). National patterns in antidepressant medication treatment. *Archives of General Psychiatry, 66*(8), 848–856.

Olfson, M., & Marcus, S. C. (2010). National trends in outpatient psychotherapy. *The American Journal of Psychiatry, 167*(12), 1456–1463. doi:10.1176/appi.ajp.2010.10040570

Olfson, M., Marcus, S. C., Druss, B. , & Pincus, H. A. (2002). National trends in the use of outpatient psychotherapy. *American Journal of Psychiatry, 159,* 1914–1920.

Oliver, J. E. (2006). *Fat politics: The real story behind America's obesity epidemic.* New York, NY: Oxford University Press.

Oliveri, M., Turriziani, P., Carlesimo, G. A., Koch, G., Tomaiuolo, F., Panella, M., & Caltagirone, C. (2001). Parieto-frontal interactions in visual-object and visual-spatial working memory: Evidence from transcranial magnetic stimulation, *Cortex , 11,* 606–618.

Ollendick, T. H., Öst, L.-G., Reuterskiöld, L., Costa, N., Cederlund, R., Sirbu, C., et al. (2009). One-session treatment of specific phobias in youth: A randomized clinical trial in the United States and Sweden. *Journal of Consulting and Clinical Psychology, 77*(3), 504–516.

Oller, K., & Pearson, B. Z. (2002). Assessing the effects of bilingualism: D. K. D. Oller & R. E. Eilers (Eds.), *Language and literacy in bilingual children.* Clevedon, UK: Multilingual Matters.

Olson, E. J., & Park, J. G. (2006). Snoring. In T. Lee-Chiong (Ed.), *Sleep: A comprehensive handbook.* Hoboken, NJ: Wiley-Liss.

Olson, J. M., & Maio, G. R. (2003). Persuasion and attitude change. In T. Millon & M. J. Lerner (Eds.), *Handbook of psychology, Vol. 5: Personality and social psychology.* New York, NY: Wiley.

Olson, J. M., Roese, N. J., & Zanna, M. P. (1996). Expectancies. In E. T. Higgins & A. W. Kruglanski (Eds.), *Social psychology: Handbook of basic principles.* New York, NY: Guilford Press.

Olson, J. M., & Stone, J. (2005). The influence of behavior on attitudes. In D. Albarracin, B. T. Johnson, & M. P. Zanna (Eds.), *The handbook of attitudes.* Mahwah, NJ: Erlbaum.

Olson, M. A., & Fazio, R. H. (2001). Implicit attitude formation through classical conditioning. *Psychological Science, 12,* 413–417.

Olson, M. A., & Fazio, R. H. (2002). Implicit acquisition and manifestation of classically conditioned attitudes. *Social Cognition, 20*(2), 89–104.

Olszewski-Kubilius, P. (2003). Gifted education programs and procedures. In W. M. Reynolds & G. E. Miller (Eds.), *Handbook of psychology, Vol. 7: Educational psychology.* New York, NY: Wiley.

Ondeck, D. M. (2003). Impact of culture on pain. *Home Health Care Management & Practice, 15,* 255–257.

Ones, D. S., Viswesvaran, C., & Dilchert, S. (2005). Cognitive ability in selection decisions. In O. Wilhelm & R. W. Engle (Eds.), *Handbook of understanding and measuring intelligence.* Thousand Oaks, CA: Sage.

Ong, A. D. (2010). Pathways linking positive emotion and health in later life. *Current Directions in Psychological Science, 19*(6), 358–362. doi:10.1177/0963721410388805

Ong, A. D., Fuller-Rowell, T., & Burrow, A. L. (2009). Racial discrimination and the stress process. *Journal of Personality and Social Psychology, 96*(6), 1259–1271. doi:10.1037/a0015335

Ono, K. (1987). Supersitious behavior in humans. *Journal of the Experimental Analysis of Behavior, 47*(3), 261–271. doi:10.1901/jeab.1987.47-261

Opotow, S. & Weiss, L. (2000). Denial and the process of moral exclusion in environmental conflict. *Journal of Social Issues, 56,* 475–490.

Oppliger, P. A. (2007). Effects of gender stereotyping on socialization. In R. W. Preiss, B. M. Gayle, N. Burrell, M. Allen, & J. Bryant (Eds.), *Mass media effects research: Advances through meta-analysis* (pp. 192–214). Mahwah, NJ: Erlbaum.

O'Reardon, J. P., Solvason, H. B., Janicak, P. G., Sampson, S., Isenberg, K. E., Nahas, Z., et al. (2007). Efficacy and safety of transcranial magnetic stimulation in the acute treatment of major depression: A multisite randomized controlled trial. *Biological Psychiatry, 62,* 1208–1216.

Orne, M. T. (1951). The mechanisms of hypnotic age regression: An experimental study. *Journal of Abnormal and Social Psychology, 46,* 213–225.

Orne, M. T., & Holland, C. C. (1968). On the ecological validity of laboratory deceptions. *International Journal of Psychiatry, 6,* 282–293.

Ornstein, R. E. (1977). *The psychology of consciousness.* New York, NY: Harcourt Brace Jovanovich.

Ornstein, R. E. (1997). *The right mind: Making sense of the hemispheres.* San Diego: Harcourt.

Ornstein, R. E., & Dewan, T. (1991). *The evolution of consciousness: Of Darwin, Freud, and cranial fire—The origins of the way we think.* New York, NY: Prentice-Hall.

Ornstein, R., & Ehrlich, P. (2000). *New world, new mind: Moving toward conscious evolution.* Cambridge, MA: Malor Books, ISHK.

Orth, U., Trzesniewski, K. H., & Robins, R. W. (2010). Self-esteem development from young adulthood to old age: A cohort-sequential longitudinal study. *Journal of Personality and Social Psychology, 98*(4), 645–658. doi:10.1037/a0018769

Ortigue, S., Grafton, S. T., & Bianchi-Demicheli, F. (2007). Correlation between insula activation and self-reported quality of orgasm in women. *NeuroImage, 37,* 551–560.

Osbaldiston, R., & Sheldon, K. M. (2002). Social dilemmas and sustainability: Promoting peoples' motivation to "cooperate with the future." In P. Schmuck & W. P. Schultz (Eds.), *Psychology of sustainable development* (pp. 37–58). Boston, MA: Kluwer Academic.

Ost, J. (2006). Recovered memories. In T. Williamson (Ed.), *Investigative interviewing: Rights, research, regulation* (pp. 259–291). Devon, United Kingdom: Willan Publishing.

Ost, J. (2009). Recovered memories. In R. Bull, T. Valentine, T. Williamson & R. Bull (Eds.), *Handbook of psychology of investigative interviewing: Current developments and future directions* (pp. 181–204). Wiley-Blackwell. doi:10.1002/9780470747599.ch11

Öst, L.-G. (1997). Rapid treatment of specific phobias. In G. C. L. Davey (Ed.), *Phobias: A handbook of theory, research and treatment* (pp. 227–247). Oxford, England: Wiley.

Öst, L.-G., Svensson, L., Hellström, K., & Lindwall, R. (2001). One-session treatment of specific phobias in youths: A randomized clinical trial. *Journal of Consulting and Clinical Psychology, 69,* 814–824.

Ostovich, J. M., & Sabini, J. (2004). How are sociosexuality, sex drive, and lifetime number of sexual partners related? *Personality and Social Psychology Bulletin, 30,* 1255–1266.

Ostroff, C., Kinicki, A. J., & Tamkins, M. M. (2003). Organizational culture and climate. In W. C. Borman, D. R. Ilgen, & R. J. Klimoski (Eds.), *Handbook of psychology, Vol. 12: Industrial and organizational psychology.* New York, NY: Wiley.

Ostrom, E., Burger, J., Field, C. B., Norgaard, R. B., & Policansky, D. (2007). Revisiting the commons: Local lessons, global challenges. In D. J. Penn & I. Mysterud (Eds.), *Evolutionary perspectives on environmental problems* (pp. 129–140). New Brunswick, NJ: Transaction Publishers.

O'Sullivan, D. (2006). Meta-analysis. In G. M. Breakwell, S. Hammond, C. Fife-Schaw, & J. A. Smith (Eds.), *Research methods in psychology* (3rd ed.). London: Sage.

Oswald, L. M., Wong, D. F., McCaul, M., Zhou, Y., Kuwabara, H., Choi, L., Brasic, J., & Wand, G. S. (2005). Relationships among ventral striatal dopamine release, cortisol secretion, and subjective responses to amphetamine. *Neuropsychopharmacology, 30,* 821–832.

Outtz, J. L. (2002). The role of cognitive ability tests in employment selection. *Human Performance, 15,* 161–171.

Overton, S. L., & Medina, S. L. (2008). The stigma of mental illness. *Journal of Counseling & Development,* 86(2), 143–151.

Oyster, C. W. (1999). *The human eye: Structure and function.* Sunderland, MA: Sinauer.

Ozer, D. J., & Benet-Martínez, V. (2006). Personality and the prediction of consequential outcomes. *Annual Review of Psychology, 57,* 401–421.

Ozer, D. J., & Reise, S. P. (1994). Personality assessment. *Annual Review of Psychology, 45,* 357–388.

Ozer, E. J., Best, S. R., Lipsey, T. L., & Weiss, D. S. (2003). Predictors of posttraumatic stress disorder and symptoms in adults: A meta-analysis. *Psychological Bulletin, 129,* 52–73.

Ozgen, E. (2004). Language, learning, and color perception. *Current Directions in Psychological Science, 13*(3), 95–98.

Pace-Schott, E. F. (2005). The neurobiology of dreaming. In M. H. Kryger, T. Roth, & W. C. Dement (Eds.). *Principles and practice of sleep medicine.* Philadelphia, PA: Elsevier Saunders.

Pace-Schott, E. F. (2009). Sleep architecture. In R. Stickgold & M. P. Walker (Eds.), *The neuroscience of sleep* (pp. 11–17). San Diego, CA: Academic Press.

Pace-Schott, E. F., Hobson, J. A., & Stickgold, R. (2008). Sleep, dreaming, and wakefulness. In L. Squire, D. Berg, F. Bloom, S. Du Lac, A. Ghosh, & N. Spitzer (Eds.), *Fundamental neuroscience* (3rd ed., pp. 959–986). San Diego, CA: Academic Press.

Pachter, W. S., Fox, R. E., Zimbardo, P., & Antonuccio, D. O. (2007). Corporate funding and conflicts of interest: A primer for psychologists. *American Psychologist, 62*(9), 1005–1015.

Padgett, D. A., & Sheridan, J. F. (2000). Herpes viruses. In G. Fink (Ed.), *Encyclopedia of stress* (pp. 357–363). San Diego: Academic Press.

Pagel, J. F., Blagrove, M., Levin, R., States, B., Stickgold, B., & White, S. (2001). Definitions of dream: A paradigm for comparing field-descriptive specific studies of dream. *Dreaming: Journal of the Association for the Study of Dreams, 11,* 195–202.

Pahl, S., Harris, P. R., Todd, H. A., & Rutter, D. R. (2005). Comparative optimism for environmental risks. *Journal of Environmental Psychology, 25,* 1–11.

Paivio, A. (1969). Mental imagery in associative learning and memory. *Psychological Review, 76,* 241–263.

Paivio, A. (1986). *Mental representations: A dual-coding approach.* New York, NY: Oxford University Press.

Paivio, A. (2007). *Mind and its evolution: A dual-coding theoretical approach.* Mahwah, NJ: Erlbaum.

Paivio, A., Khan, M., & Begg, I. (2000). Concreteness of relational effects on recall of adjective-noun pairs. *Canadian Journal of Experimental Psychology, 54*(3), 149–160.

Paivio, A., Smythe, P. E., & Yuille, J. C. (1968). Imagery versus meaningfulness of nouns in paired-associate learning. *Canadian Journal of Psychology, 22,* 427–441.

Palladino, J. J., & Carducci, B. J. (1984). Students' knowledge of sleep and dreams. *Teaching of Psychology, 11,* 189–191.

Palmer, S. E. (2003). Visual perception of objects. In A. F. Healy & R. W. Proctor (Eds.), *Handbook of psychology, Vol. 4: Experimental psychology.* New York, NY: Wiley.

Palmeri, T. J., & Gauthier, I. (2004). Visual object understanding. *Nature Reviews Neuroscience, 5,* 291–303.

Pan, B. A., & Uccelli, P. (2009). Semantic development: Learning the meaning of words. In J. B. Gleason & N. B. Ratner (Eds.), *The development of language.* Boston, MA: Pearson.

Panksepp, J. (1991). Affective neuroscience: A conceptual framework for the neurobiological study of emotions. In K. T. Strongman (Ed.), *International review of studies on emotion.* Chichester, England: Wiley.

Panksepp, J. (2008). The affective brain and core consciousness: How does neural activity generate emotional feelings? In M. Lewis, J. M. Haviland-Jones, & L. F. Barrett (Eds.), *Handbook of emotions* (3rd ed., pp. 47–67). New York, NY: Guilford Press.

Papp, K. V., Walsh, S. J., & Snyder, P. J. (2009). Immediate and delayed effects of cognitive interventions in healthy elderly: A review of current literature and future directions. *Alzheimer's & Dementia, 5*(1), 50–60. doi:10.1016/j.jalz.2008.10.008

Paris, J. (1999). *Genetics and psychopathology: Predisposition-stress interactions.* Washington, DC: American Psychiatric Press.

Park, D. C., & Huang, C. (2010). Culture wires the brain: A cognitive neuroscience perspective. *Perspectives on Psychological Science, 5*(4), 391–400. doi:10.1177/1745691610374591

Partinen, M., & Hublin, C. (2005). Epidemiology of sleep disorders. In M. H. Kryger, T. Roth, & W. C. Dement (Eds.). *Principles and practice of sleep medicine.* Philadelphia, PA: Elsevier Saunders.

Pascal, J. (2010). Space, place, and psychosocial well–being: Women's experience of breast cancer at an environmental retreat. *Illness, Crisis, and Loss, 18*(3), 201–216.

Pascual-Leone, A. (2009). Characterizing and modulating neuroplasticity of the adult human brain. In M. S. Gazzangia (Ed.), *The cognitive neurosciences* (4th ed., pp. 141–152). Cambridge, MA: MIT Press.

Pashler, H., & Carrier, M. (1996). Structures, processes, and the flow of information. In E. L. Bjork & R. A. Bjork (Eds.), *Memory.* San Diego: Academic Press.

Pashler, H., Johnston, J. C., & Ruthruff, E. (2001). Attention and performance. *Annual Review of Psychology, 52,* 629–651.

Pasternak, T., Bisley, J. W., & Calkins, D. (2003). Visual processing in the primate brain. In M. Gallagher & R. J. Nelson (Eds.), *Handbook of psychology: Biological psychology* (pp. 139–186). New York, NY: Wiley.

Patel, J. K., Pinals, D. A., & Breier, A. (2008). Schizophrenia and other psychoses. In A. Tasman, J. Kay, J. A. Lieberman, M. B. First, & M. Maj (Eds.), *Psychiatry* (3rd ed.). New York, NY: Wiley-Blackwell.

Patel, S. R., Ayas, N. T., Malhotra, M. R., White, D. P., Schernhammer, E. S., Speizer, F. E., et al. (2004). A prospective study of sleep duration and mortality risk in women. *Sleep: Journal of Sleep and Sleep Disorders Research, 27,* 440–444.

Patel, S. R., Malhotra, A., Gottlieb, D. J., White, P., & Hu, F. B. (2006). Correlates of long sleep deprivation. *Sleep: Journal of Sleep and Sleep Disorders Research, 29,* 881–889.

Patel, S. R., Zhu, X., Storfer-Isser, A., Mehra, R., Jenny, N. S., Tracy, R., & Redline, S. (2009). Sleep duration and biomarkers of inflammation. *Sleep: Journal of Sleep and Sleep Disorders Research, 32*(2), 200–204.

Pato, M. T., Fanous, A., Eisen, J. L., & Phillips, K. A. (2008). Anxiety disorders: Obsessive-compulsive disorder. In A. Tasman, J. Kay, J. A. Lieberman, M. B. First, & M. Maj (Eds.), *Psychiatry* (3rd ed.). New York, NY: Wiley-Blackwell.

Patrick, H., Nicklas, T. A., Hughes, S. O., & Morales, M. (2005). The benefits of authoritative feeding style: Caregiver feeding styles and children's food consumption patterns. *Appetite, 44,* 243–249.

Patston, L. M., Kirk, I. J., Rolfe, M. S., Corballis, M. C., & Tippett, L. J. (2007). The unusual symmetry of musicians: Musicians have equilateral interhemispheric transfer for visual information. *Neuropsychologia, 45*(9), 2059–2065. doi:10.1016/j.neuropsychologia.2007.02.001

Pattanashetty, R., Sathiamma, S., Talakkad, S., Nityananda, P., Trichur, R., & Kutty, B. M. (2010). Practitioners of vipassana meditation exhibit enhanced slow wave sleep and REM sleep states across different age groups. *Sleep and Biological Rhythms, 8*(1), 34–41. doi:10.1111/j.1479-8425.2009.00416.x

Patterson, C. J. (2003). Children of lesbian and gay parents. In L. D. Garnets & D. C. Kimmel (Eds.), *Psychological perspectives on lesbian, gay, and bisexual experiences* (2nd ed., pp. 497–548). New York, NY: Columbia University Press.

Patterson, D. R. (2004). Treating pain with hypnosis. *Current Directions in Psychological Science, 13*(6), 252–255.

Patzer, G. L. (2006). *The power and paradox of physical attractiveness.* Boca Raton, FL: Brown Walker Press.

Pauk, W. (1990). *How to study in college.* Boston, MA: Houghton Mifflin.

Paul, E. F., & Paul, J. (2001). *Why animal experimentation matters: The use of animals in medical research.* New Brunswick, NJ: Transaction Publishers.

Paulhus, D. L. (1991). Measurement and control of response bias. In J. P. Robinson, P. Shaver, & L. S. Wrightsman (Eds.), *Measures of personality and social psychological attitudes.* San Diego, CA: Academic Press.

Paulhus, D. L. (1998). Interpersonal and intrapsychic adaptiveness of trait self-enhancement: A mixed blessing? *Journal of Personality and Social Psychology, 74*(5), 1197–1208. doi:10.1037/0022-3514.74.5.1197

Paulhus, D. L., Fridhandler, B., & Hayes, S. (1997). Psychological defense: Contemporary theory and research. In R. Hogan, J. Johnson, & S. Briggs (Eds.), *Handbook of personality psychology.* San Diego: Academic Press.

Paulos, J. A. (1995). *A mathematician reads the newspaper.* New York, NY: Doubleday.

Paulus, P. B. (2000). Groups, teams, and creativity: The creative potential of idea-generating groups. *Applied Psychology: An International Review, 49,* 237–262.

Pavlov, I. P. (1906). The scientific investigation of psychical faculties or processes in the higher animals. *Science, 24,* 613–619.

Pavlov, I. P. (1927). *Conditioned reflexes* (G. V. Anrep, Trans.). London: Oxford University Press.

Payne, D. G., & Blackwell, J. M. (1998). Truth in memory: Caveat emptor. In S. J. Lynn & K. M. McConkey (Eds.), *Truth in memory.* New York, NY: Guilford Press.

Payne, J. W., & Bettman, J. R. (2004). Walking with the scarecrow: The information-processing approach to decision research. In D. J. Koehler & N. Harvey (Ed.), *Blackwell handbook of judgment and decision making.* Malden, MA: Blackwell.

Payne, J. W., Samper, A., Bettman, J. R., & Luce, M. (2008). Boundary conditions on unconscious thought in complex decision making. *Psychological Science, 19*(11), 1118–1123. doi:10.1111/j.1467-9280.2008.02212.x

Pearce, M. S., Deary, I. J., Young, A. H., & Parker, L. L. (2006). Childhood IQ and deaths up to middle age: The Newcastle Thousand Families Study. *Public Health, 120*(11), 1020–1026. doi:10.1016/j.puhe.2006.06.01

Pearson, S. E., & Pollack, R. H. (1997). Female response to sexually explicit films. *Journal of Psychology and Human Sexuality, 9,* 73–88.

Pedersen, A. F., Bovbjerg, D. H., & Zachariae, R. (2011). Stress and susceptibility to infectious disease. In R. J. Contrada & A. Baum (Eds.), *The handbook of stress science: Biology, psychology, and health* (pp. 111–121). New York, NY: Springer.

Pedersen, P. (1994). A culture-centered approach to counseling. In W. J. Lonner & R. Malpass (Eds.), *Psychology and culture.* Boston, MA: Allyn & Bacon.

Peele, S. (1989). *Diseasing of America: Addiction treatment out of control.* Lexington, MA: Lexington Books.

Peele, S. (2000). What addiction is and is not: The impact of mistaken notions of addiction. *Addiction Research, 8,* 599–607.

Peladeau, N., Forget, J., & Gagne, F. (2003). Effect of paced and unpaced practice on skill application and retention: How much is enough? *American Educational Research Journal, 40,* 769–801.

Pellegrino, J. E., & Pellegrino, L. (2008). Fetal alcohol syndrome and related disorders. In P. J. Accardo (Eds.), *Capture and Accardo's neurodevelopment disabilities in infancy and childhood: Neurodevelopmental diagnosis and treatment* (pp. 269–284). Baltimore, MD: Paul H. Brookes Publishing.

Penfield, W., & Perot, P. (1963). The brain's record of auditory and visual experience. *Brain, 86,* 595–696.

Peng, J. H., Tao, Z. Z., & Huang, Z. W. (2007). Risk of damage to hearing from personal listening devices in young adults. *Journal of Otolaryngology, 36*(3), 181–185. doi: 10.2310/7070.2007.0032.

Penn, D. C., & Povinelli, D. J. (2007). Causal cognition in human and nonhuman animals: A comparative, critical review. *Annual Review of Psychology, 58,* 97–118.

Pennebaker, J. W., Colder, M., & Sharp, L. K. (1990). Accelerating the coping process. *Journal of Personality and Social Psychology, 58,* 528–537.

Pennix, B. W. J. H., Beekman, A. T. F., Honig, A., Deeg, D. J. H., Schoevers, R. A., van Eijk, J. T. M., & van Tilburg, W. (2001). Depression and cardiac mortality: Results from a community-based longitudinal survey. *Archives of General Psychiatry, 58,* 221–227.

Peplau, L. A. (2003). Human sexuality: How do men and women differ? *Current Directions in Psychological Science, 12*(2), 37–40.

Peplau, L., & Fingerhut, A. W. (2007). The close relationships of lesbian and gay men. *Annual Review of Psychology, 58,* 405–424. doi:10.1146/annurev.psych.58.110405.085701

Pepperberg, I. M. (1993). Cognition and communication in an African Grey parrot (*Psittacus erithacus*): Studies on a nonhuman, nonprimate, nonmammalian subject. In H. L. Roitblat, L. H. Herman, & P. E. Nachtigall (Eds.), *Language and communication: Comparative perspectives*. Hillsdale, NJ: Erlbaum.

Pepperberg, I. M. (2002). Cognitive and communicative abilities of grey parrots. *Current Directions in Psychological Science, 11*(3), 83–87.

Pereira, A. C., Huddleston, D. E., Brickman, A. M., Sosunov, A. A., Hen, R., McKhann, G. M., et al. (2007). An in vivo correlate of exercise-induced neurogenesis in the adult dentate gyrus. *Proceedings of the National Academy of Sciences, 104,* 5638–5643.

Perkins, D. O., Miller-Anderson, L., & Lieberman, J. A. (2006). Natural history and predictors of clinical course. In J. A. Lieberman, T. S. Stroup, & D. O. Perkins (Eds.), *Textbook of schizophrenia* (pp. 289–302). Washington, DC: American Psychiatric Publishing.

Perlis, R. H., Perlis, C. S., Wu, Y. , Hwang, C., Joseph, M., & Nierenberg, A. A. (2005). Industry sponsorship and financial conflict of interest in the reporting of clinical trials in psychiatry. *American Journal of Psychiatry, 162,* 1957–1960.

Perone, M., Galizio, M., & Baron, A. (1988). The relevance of animal-based principles in the laboratory study of human operant conditioning. In G. Davey & C. Cullen (Eds.), *Human operant conditioning and behavior modification*. New York, NY: Wiley.

Perrin, F., Maquet, P., Peigneux, P. , Ruby, P., Degueldre, C., Balteau, E., & Del Fiore, G. (2005). Neural mechanisms involved in the detection of our first name: A combined ERPs and PET study. *Neuropsychologia, 43,* 12–19.

Perry, D. G., Kusel, S. J., & Perry, L. C. (1988). Victims of peer aggression. *Developmental Psychology, 24,* 807–814.

Person, E. S. (1990). The influence of values in psychoanalysis: The case of female psychology. In C. Zanardi (Ed.), *Essential papers in psychoanalysis*. New York, NY: New York University Press.

Pert, C. B. (2002). The wisdom of the receptors: Neuropeptides, the emotions, and bodymind. *Advances in Mind-Body Medicine, 18*(1), 30–35.

Pert, C. B., & Snyder, S. H. (1973). Opiate receptor: Demonstration in the nervous tissue. *Science, 179,* 1011–1014.

Perugini, E. M., Kirsch, I., Allen, S. T., Coldwell, E., Meredith, J. M., Montgomery, G. H., & Sheehan, J. (1998). Surreptitious observation of response to hypnotically suggested hallucinations: A test of the compliance hypothesis. *International Journal of Clinical & Experimental Hypnosis, 46,* 191–203.

Pervin, L. A., & John, O. P. (2001). *Personality: Theory and research*. New York, NY: Wiley.

Pescosolido, B. A., Martin, J. K., Long, J., Medina, T. R., Phelan, J. C., & Link, B. G. (2010). "A disease like any other"? A decade of change in public reactions to schizophrenia, depression, and alcohol dependence. *American Journal of Psychiatry, 167*(11), 1321–1330. doi:10.1176/appi.ajp.2010.09121743

Peterson, C. (2000). The future of optimism. *American Psychologist, 55*(1), 44–55.

Peterson, C. (2006). *A primer in positive psychology*. New York, NY: Oxford University Press.

Peterson, C., & Park, N. (2009). Positive psychology. In B. J. Sadock, V. A. Sadock, & P. Ruiz (Eds.), *Kaplan & Sadock's comprehensive textbook of psychiatry* (pp. 2939–2951). Philadelphia, PA: Lippincott, Williams & Wilkins.

Peterson, C., & Park, N. (2010). What happened to self-actualization? [Commentary on Kenrick et al. (2010).] *Perspectives on Psychological Science, 5*(3), 320–322. doi:10.1177/1745691610369471

Peterson, C., & Seligman, M. E. P. (2004). *Character strengths and virtues: A handbook and classification.* Washington, DC: American Psychological Association.

Peterson, C., Seligman, M. E. P., Yurko, K. H., Martin, L. R., & Friedman, H. S. (1998). Catastrophizing and untimely death. *Psychological Science, 9,* 127–130.

Peterson, L. R., & Peterson, M. J. (1959). Short-term retention of individual verbal items. *Journal of Experimental Psychology, 58,* 193–198.

Peterson, N. G., Mumford, M. D., Borman, W. C., Jeanneret, P. R., & Fleishmann, E. A. (1999). *An occupational information system for the 21st century: The development of O*NET.* Washington, DC: American Psychological Association.

Petrie, K. J., & Pennebaker, J. W. (2004). Health-related cognitions. In S. Sutton, A. Baum, & M. Johnston (Eds.), *The Sage handbook of health psychology*. Thousand Oaks, CA: Sage.

Petrill, S. A. (2005). Behavioral genetics and intelligence. In O. Wilhelm & R. W. Engle (Eds.), *Handbook of understanding and measuring intelligence.* Thousand Oaks, CA: Sage.

Petry, N. M. (2005). *Pathological gambling: Etiology, comorbidity, and treatment.* Washington, DC: American Psychological Association.

Petry, N. M. (2010). Pathological gambling and the DSM-V. *International Gambling Studies, 10*(2), 113–115. doi:10.1080/14459795.2010.501086

Pettit, J. W., Lewinsohn, P. M., Seeley, J. R., Roberts, R. E., & Yaroslavsky, I. (2010). Developmental relations between depressive symptoms, minor hassles, and major events from adolescence through age 30 years. *Journal of Abnormal Psychology, 119*(4), 811–824. doi:10.1037/a0020980

Petty, R. E., & Briñol, P. (2008). Persuasion: From single to multiple to metacognitive processes. *Perspectives on Psychological Science, 3,* 137–147.

Petty, R. E., & Briñol, P. (2010). Attitude change. In R. F. Baumeister & E. J. Finkel (Eds.), *Advanced social psychology: The state of the science* (pp. 217–259). New York, NY: Oxford University Press.

Petty, R. E., & Cacioppo, J. T. (1986). *Communication and persuasion: Central and peripheral routes to attitude change.* New York, NY: Springer-Verlag.

Petty, R. E., & Wegener, D. T. (1998). Attitude change: Multiple roles for persuasion variables. In D. T. Gilbert, S. T. Fiske, & G. Lindzey (Eds.), *The handbook of social psychology*. New York, NY: McGraw-Hill.

Petty, R. E., & Wegener, D. T. (1999). The elaboration likelihood model: Current status and controversies. In S. Chaiken & Y. Trope (Eds.), *Dual-process theories in social psychology*. New York, NY: Guilford Press.

Petty, R. E., Wheeler, S. C., & Tormala, Z. L. (2003). Persuasion and attitude change. In T. Millon & M. J. Lerner (Eds.), *Handbook of psychology, Vol. 5: Personality and social psychology*. New York, NY: Wiley.

Petty, S. C., Sachs-Ericsson, N., & Joiner, T. E., Jr. (2004). Interpersonal functioning deficits: Temporary or stable characteristics of depressed individuals. *Journal of Affective Disorders, 81,* 115–122.

Pfaffenberger, A. (2007). Different conceptualizations of optimum development. *Journal of Humanistic Psychology, 47*(4), 474–496.

Pfau, M., Kenski, H. C., Nitz, M., & Sorenson, J. (1990). Efficacy of inoculation strategies in promoting resistance to political attack messages: Application to direct mail. *Communication Monographs, 57,* 25–43.

Pfaus, J. G., Kippin, T. E., & Centeno, S. (2001). Conditioning and sexual behavior: A review. *Hormones & Behavior, 40,* 291–321.

Phelps, E. A. (2005). The interaction of emotion and cognition: The relation between the human amygdala and cognitive awareness. In R. R. Hassin, J. S. Uleman, & J. A. Bargh (Eds.), *The new unconcious: Oxford series in social cognition and social neuroscience* (pp. 61–76). New York, NY: Oxford University Press.

Phelps, E. A. (2006). Emotion and cognition: Insights from studies of the human amygdala. *Annual Review of Psychology, 57,* 27–53.

Phillips, B., & Kryger, M. H. (2005). Management of obstructive sleep apnea-hypopnea syndrome. In M. H. Kryger, T. Roth, & W. C. Dement (Eds.), *Principles and practice of sleep medicine*. Philadelphia, PA: Saunders.

Phillips, W. T., Kiernan, M., & King, A. C. (2001). The effects of physical activity on physical and psychological health. In A. Baum, T. A. Revenson, & J. E. Singer (Eds.), *Handbook of health psychology* (pp. 627–660). Mahwah, NJ: Erlbaum.

Pi-Sunyer, F. X. (2002). Medical complications of obesity in adults. In C. G. Fairburn & K. D. Brownell (Eds.), *Eating disorders and obesity: A comprehensive handbook* (pp. 467–472). New York, NY: Guilford Press.

Piaget, J. (1929). *The child's conception of world* (J. Tomlinson, Trans.). New York, NY: Harcourt Brace. (Original work, in French, published in 1926)

Piaget, J. (1932). *The moral judgment of the child* (M. Gabain, Trans.). Glencoe, IL: Free Press.

Piaget, J. (1952). *The origins of intelligence in children* (M. Cook, Trans.). New York, NY: International Universities Press. (Original work published in 1933)

Piaget, J. (1954). *The construction of reality in the child* (M. Cook, Trans.). New York, NY: Basic Books. (Original work published in 1937)

Piaget, J. (1983). Piaget's theory (G. Cellerier & J. Langer, Trans.). In P. H. Mussen (Series Ed.) & W. Kessen (Volume Ed.), *Handbook of child psychology: History, theory, and methods* (4th ed., Vol. 1, pp. 103–126). New York, NY: Wiley. (Original work published in 1970)

Pickles, J. O. (1988). *An introduction to the physiology of hearing* (2nd ed.). London: Academic Press.

Pierce, R. C., & Kumaresan, V. (2006). The mesolimbic dopamine system: The final common pathway for the reinforcing effect of drugs of abuse? *Neuroscience Biobehavioral Reviews, 30,* 215–238.

Pies, R. (2009). Should DSM-V designate "Internet addiction" a mental disorder? *Psychiatry, 6*(2), 31–37.

Pietschnig, J., Voracek, M., & Formann, A. K. (2010). Mozart effect–Shmozart effect: A meta-analysis. *Intelligence, 38*(3), 314–323. doi:10.1016/j.intell.2010.03.001

Pilling, M., & Davies, I. R. L. (2004). Linguistic relativism and colour cognition. *British Journal of Psychology, 95,* 429–455.

Pincus, D. (2006). Who is Freud and what does the new century behold? *Psychoanalytic Psychology, 23*(2), 367–372. doi: 10.1037/0736-9735.23.2.367

Pinel, J. P. J., Assanand, S., & Lehman, D. R. (2000). Hunger, eating, and ill health. *American Psychologist, 55,* 1105–1116.

Pink, D. H. (2005). *A whole new mind: Why right-brainers will rule the future.* New York, NY: Penguin.

Pinker, S. (1994). *Language is to us as flying is to geese.* New York, NY: Morrow.

Pinker, S. (2004). Language as an adaptation to the cognitive niche. In D. T. Kenrick & C. L. Luce (Eds.), *The functional mind: Readings in evolutionary psychology.* Essex, England: Pearson Education Limited.

Pinker, S., & Bloom, P. (1992). Natural language and natural selection. In J. H. Barkow, L. Cosmides, & J. Tooby (Eds.), *The adapted mind: Evolutionary psychology and the generation of culture.* New York, NY: Oxford University Press.

Pinker, S., & Jackendoff, R. (2005). The faculty of language: What's special about it? *Cognition, 95,* 201–236.

Pinquart, M., Duberstein, P. R., & Lyness, J. M. (2006). Treatments for later-life depressive conditions: A meta-analytic comparison of pharmacotherapy and psychotherapy. *American Journal of Psychiatry, 163,* 1493–1501.

Pintar, J. (2010). Il n'y a pas d'hypnotisme: A history of hypnosis in theory and practice. In S. J. Lynn, J. W. Rhue, & I. Kirsch (Eds.), *Handbook of Clinical Hypnosis* (2nd ed., pp. 19–46). Washington, DC: American Psychological Association.

Pinyerd, B., & Zipf, W. B. (2005). Puberty—Timing is everything! *Journal of Pediatric Nursing, 20,* 75–82.

Pirog, R. & Benjamin, A. (2003). *Checking the food odometer: Comparing food miles for local versus conventional produce sales to Iowa institutions.* Ames, IA: Leopold Center for Sustainable Agriculture, Iowa State University.

Pittman, F., III. (1994, January/February). A buyer's guide to psychotherapy. *Psychology Today,* 50–53, 74–81.

Plante, T. G., Caputo, D., & Chizmar, L. (2000). Perceived fitness and responses to laboratory-induced stress. *International Journal of Stress Management, 7*(1), 61–73.

Plassmann, H., O'Doherty, J., Shiv, B., & Rangel. (2008). Marketing actions can modulate neural representations of experienced pleasantness. *Proceedings of the National Academy of Sciences, 105,* 1050–1054.

Platek, S. M., Mohamed, F. B., & Gallup, G. G. Jr. (2005). Contagious yawning and the brain. *Cognitive Brain Research, 23,* 448–452.

Plomin, R. (2003). General cognitive ability. In R. Plomin & J. C. DeFries (Eds.), *Behavioral genetics in the postgenomic era.* Washinton, DC: American Psychological Association.

Plomin, R. (2004). Genetics and developmental psychology. *Merrill-Palmer Quarterly: Journal of Developmental Psychology, 50*(3), 341–352. doi:10.1353/mpq.2004.0024

Plomin, R., DeFries, J. C., McClearn, G. E., & McGuffin, P. (2001). *Behavioral genetics.* New York, NY: Freeman.

Plomin, R., DeFries, J. C., McClearn, G. E., & McGuffin, P. (2008). *Behavioral genetics.* New York, NY: Worth.

Plomin, R., Kennedy, J. K. J., & Craig, I. W. (2006). The quest for quantitative, trait loci associated with intelligence. *Intelligence, 34,* 513–526.

Plomin, R., & McGuffin, P. (2003). Psychopathology in the postgenomic era. *Annual Review of Psychology, 54,* 205–228.

Plomin, R., & Spinath, F. M. (2004). Intelligence: Genetics, genes, and genomics. *Journal of Personality & Social Psychology, 86,* 112–129.

Plotkin, H. (1998). *Evolution in mind: An introduction to evolutionary psychology.* Cambridge, MA: Harvard University Press.

Plotkin, H. (2004). *Evolutionary thought in psychology: A brief history.* Malden, MA: Blackwell.

Plous, S. (1991). An attitude survey of animal rights activists. *Psychological Science, 2,* 194–196.

Plucker, J. A., & Makel, M. C. (2010). Assessment of creativity. In J. C. Kaufman & R. J. Sternberg (Eds.), *The Cambridge handbook of creativity* (pp. 48–73). New York, NY: Cambridge University Press.

Plucker, J. A., & Renzulli, J. S. (1999). Psychometric approaches to the study of human creativity. In R. J. Sternberg (Ed.), *Handbook of creativity.* New York, NY: Cambridge University Press.

Plutchik, R. (1984). Emotions: A general psychoevolutionary theory. In K. R. Scherer & P. Ekman (Eds.), *Approaches to emotion.* Hillsdale, NJ: Erlbaum.

Plutchik, R. (1993). Emotions and their vicissitudes: Emotions and psychopathology. In M. Lewis & J. M. Haviland (Eds.), *Handbook of emotions.* New York, NY: Guilford Press.

Pogue-Geile, M. F., & Yokley, J. L. (2010). Current research on the genetic contributors to schizophrenia. *Current Directions in Psychological Science, 19*(4), 214–219. doi:10.1177/0963721410378490

Pohl, R. F. (2004). Effects of labeling. In F. P. Rudiger (Ed.), *Cognitive illusions.* New York, NY: Psychology Press.

Polger, T. (2007). Rethinking the evolution of consciousness. In M. Velmans & S. Schneider (Eds.), *The Blackwell companion to consciousness.* Malden, MA: Blackwell Publishing.

Policastro, E., & Gardner, H. (1999). From case studies to robust generalizations: An approach to the study of creativity. In R. J. Sternberg (Ed.), *Handbook of creativity.* New York, NY: Cambridge University Press.

Pomerantz, E. M., Ng, F. F. Y., & Wang, Q. (2004). Gender socialization: A parent X child model. In A. H. Eagly, A. E. Beall, & R. J. Sternberg (Eds.), *The psychology of gender.* New York, NY: Guilford Press.

Pomeroy, A. (2005). 50 best small and medium places to work: Money talks. *HR Magazine, 50*(7), 44–65.

Pope, H. G., Barry, S., Bodkin, A., & Hudson, J. I. (2006). Tracking scientific interest in the dissociative disorders: A study of scientific publication output 1984–2003. *Psychotherapy and Psychosomatics, 75,* 19–24.

Pope, H. G., Gruber, A. J., Hudson, J. I., Huestis, M. A., & Yurgelun-Todd, D. (2001). Neuropsychological performance in long-term cannabis users. *Archives of General Psychiatry, 58,* 909–915.

Pope, H. G., & Hudson, J. I. (1998). Can memories of childhood sexual abuse be repressed? In R. A. Baker (Ed.), *Child sexual abuse and false memory syndrome.* Amherst, NY: Prometheus Books.

Pope, H. G., Oliva, P. S., Hudson, J. I., Bodkin, J. A., & Gruber, A. J. (1999). Attitudes toward DSM-IV dissociative disorders diagnoses among board-certified American psychiatrists. *American Journal of Psychiatry, 156,* 321–323.

Popenoe, D. (2009). *Families without fathers: Fathers, marriage, and children in American society.* Piscataway, NJ: Transaction.

Popper, C. W., Gammon, G. D., West, S. A., & Bailey, C. E. (2003). Disorders usually first diagnosed in infancy, childhood, and adolescence. In Robert E. Hales & Stuart C. Yudofsky (Eds.), *Textbook of clinical psychiatry.* Washington, DC: American Psychiatric Publishing.

Popper, C. W., & Steingard, R. J. (1994). Disorders usually first diagnosed in infancy, childhood, or adolescence. In R. E. Hales, S. C. Yudofsky, & J. A. Talbott (Eds.), *The American Psychiatric Press textbook of psychiatry.* Washington, DC: American Psychiatric Press.

Porcerelli, J. H., Cogan, R., Kamoo, R., & Miller, K. (2010). Convergent validity of the Defense Mechanisms Manual and the Defensive Functioning Scale. *Journal of Personality Assessment, 92*(5), 432–438. doi: 10.1080/00223891.2010.497421

Porter, J., Craven, B., Khan, R. M., Chang, S., Kang, I., Judkewitz, B., Volpe, J., et al. (2007). Mechanisms of scent-tracking in humans. *Nature Neuroscience, 10*(1), 27–29. doi:10.1038/nn1819

Porter, S., & Porter, S. (2007). Psychopathy and violent crime. In H. Hervé, & J. C. Yuille (Eds.), *The psychopath: Theory, research, and practice.* Mahwah, NJ: Erlbaum.

Porter, S., Yuille, J. C., & Lehman, D. R. (1999). The nature of real, implanted, and fabricated memories for emotional childhood events: Implications for the recovered memory debate. *Law and Human Behavior, 23,* 517–537.

Posada, G., Kaloustian, G., Richmond, K., & Moreno, A. J. (2007). Maternal secure base support and preschoolers' secure base behavior in natural environments. *Attachment & Human Development, 9,* 393–411.

Posner, M. I., & DiGirolamo, G. J. (2000). Attention in cognitive neuroscience: An overview. In M. S. Gazzaniga (Ed.), *The new cognitive neurosciences* (2nd ed., pp. 623–632). Cambridge, MA: MIT Press.

Post, F. (1996). Verbal creativity, depression and alcoholism: An investigation of one hundred American and British writers. *British Journal of Psychiatry, 168,* 545–555.

Post, R. M. & Altshuler, L. L. (2009). Mood disorders: Treatment of bipolar disorders. In B. J. Sadock, V. A. Sadock, & P. Ruiz (Eds.), *Kaplan & Sadock's comprehensive textbook of psychiatry* (pp. 1743–1812). Philadelphia, PA: Lippincott, Williams & Wilkins.

Posthuma, D., Luciano, M., de Geus, E. J. C., Wright, M. J., Slagboom, P. E., Montgomery, G. W., et al. (2005). A genome-wide scan for intelligence identifies quantitative trait loci on 2q and 6p. *American Journal of Human Genetics, 77,* 318–326.

Postman, L. (1985). Human learning and memory. In G. A. Kimble & K. Schlesinger (Eds.), *Topics in the history of psychology.* Hillsdale, NJ: Erlbaum.

Postmes, T., Spears, R., & Cihangir, S. (2001). Quality of decision making and group norms. *Journal of Personality and Social Psychology, 80,* 918–930.

Potter, W. Z., Padich, R. A., Rudorfer, M. V., & Krishnan, K. R. R. (2006). Tricyclics, tetracyclics, and monoamine oxidase inhibitors. In D. J. Stein, D. J. Kupfer, & A. F. Schatzberg (Eds.), *Textbook of mood disorders* (pp. 251–262). Washington, DC: American Psychiatric Publishing.

Poty, R. L. (2010). Olfaction. In E. B. Goldstein (Ed.), *Encyclopedia of perception*. Thousand Oaks, CA: Sage.

Poulin-Dubois, D., & Graham, S. A. (2007). Cognitive processes in early word learning. In E. Hoff & M. Shatz (Eds.), *Blackwell handbook of language development* (pp. 191–212). Malden, MA: Blackwell.

Powell, L. H., & Williams, K. (2007). Hostility. In G. Fink (Ed.), *Encyclopedia of stress*. San Diego: Elsevier.

Powell, R. A., & Boer, D. P. (1995). Did Freud misinterpret reported memories of sexual abuse as fantasies? *Psychological Reports, 77*, 563–570.

Powell, R. A., & Gee, T. L. (1999). The effects of hypnosis on dissociative identity disorder: A reexamination of the evidence. *Canadian Journal of Psychiatry, 44*, 914–916.

Powley, T. L. (2008). Central control of autonomic functions: Organization of the autonomic nervous system. In L. Squire, D. Berg, F. Bloom, S. Du Lac, A. Ghosh, & N. Spitzer (Eds.), *Fundamental neuroscience* (3rd ed., pp. 809–828). San Diego, CA: Elsevier.

Powley, T. L. (2009). Hunger. In G. G. Berntson & J. T. Cacioppo (Eds.), *Handbook of neuroscience for the behavioral sciences*, (Vol. 2, pp. 659–679). Hoboken, NJ: Wiley.

Prat-Sala, M., & Redford, P. (2010). The interplay between motivation, self-efficacy, and approaches to studying. *British Journal of Educational Psychology, 80*(2), 283–305. doi:10.1348/000709909X480563

Pratkanis, A. R., & Aronson, E. (2000). *Age of propaganda: The everyday use and abuse of persuasion*. New York, NY: Freeman.

Premack, D. (1985). "Gavagai!" or the future history of the animal language controversy. *Cognition, 19*, 207–296.

Prentky, R. (1989). Creativity and psychopathology: Gamboling at the seat of madness. In J. A. Glover, R. R. Ronning, & C. R. Reynolds (Eds.), *Handbook of creativity*. New York, NY: Plenum.

Prescott, J. (2010). Taste: Supertasters. In E. B. Goldstein (Ed.), *Encyclopedia of perception*. Thousand Oaks, CA: Sage.

Pressman, S. D., Cohen, S., Miller, G. E., Barkin, A., Rabin, B. S., & Treanor, J. J. (2005). Loneliness, social network size, and immune response to influenza vaccination in college freshman. *Health Psychology, 24*, 297–306.

Pretz, J. E., Naples, A. J., & Sternberg, R. J. (2003). Recognizing, defining, and representing problems. In J. E. Davidson & R. J. Sternberg (Eds.), *The psychology of problem solving*. New York, NY: Cambridge University Press.

Price, D. D., Finniss, D. G., & Benedetti, F. (2008). A comprehensive review of the placebo effect: Recent advances and current thought. *Annual Review of Psychology, 59*, 565–590. doi:10.1146/annurev.psych.59.113006.095941u

Price, M. (2008). Div. 55's drive for RxP: The American Society for the Advancement of Pharmacotherapy pushes for prescriptive authority. *Monitor on Psychology, 39*(2).

Priester, J. R., & Petty, R. E. (1995). Source attributions and persuasion; Perceived honesty as a determinant of message scrutiny. *Personality and Social Psychology Bulletin, 21*, 637–654.

Priester, J. R., & Petty, R. E. (2001). Extending the bases of subjective attitudinal ambivalence: Interpersonal and intrapersonal antecedents of evaluative tension. *Journal of Personality and Social Psychology, 80*, 19–34.

Priester, J. R., & Petty, R. E. (2003). The influence of spokesperson trustworthiness on message elaboration, attitude strength, and advertising. *Journal of Consumer Psychology, 13*, 408–421.

Prifitera, A. (1994). Wechsler scales of intelligence. In R. J. Sternberg (Ed.), *Encyclopedia of human intelligence*. New York, NY: Macmillan.

Pritchard, J. (2010). Virtual rewards for driving green. *The Behavior Analyst, 33*, 185–187.

Prochaska, J. O. (1994). Strong and weak principles for progressing from precontemplation to action on the basis of twelve problem behaviors. *Health Psychology, 13*, 47–51.

Prochaska, J. O., Velicer, W. F., Prochaska, J. M., & Johnson, J. L. (2004). Size, consistency, and stability of stage effects for smoking cessation. *Addictive Behaviors, 29* , 207–213.

Proffitt, D. R., & Caudek, C. (2003). Depth perception and the perception of events. In A. F. Healy & R. W. Proctor (Eds.), *Handbook of psychology, Vol. 4: Experimental psychology*. New York, NY: Wiley.

Prolo, P., & Chiappelli, F. (2007). Immune suppression. In G. Fink (Ed.), *Encyclopedia of stress*. San Diego: Elsevier.

Pronin, E., Gilovich, T., & Ross, L. (2004). Objectivity in the eye of the beholder: Divergent perceptions of bias in self versus others. *Psychological Review, 111*, 781–799.

Pronin, E., Lin, D. Y., & Ross L. (2002). The bias blind spot: Perceptions of bias in self versus others. *Personality and Social Psychology Bulletin, 28*, 369–381.

Pronin, E., Wegner, D. M., McCarthy, K., & Rodriguez, S. (2006). Everyday magical powers: The role of apparent mental causation in the overestimation of personal influence. *Journal of Personality and Social Psychology, 91*, 218–231. doi:10.1037/0022-3514.91.2.218

Proulx, C. M., Helms, H. M., & Buehler, C. (2007). Marital quality and personal well-being: A meta-analysis. *Journal of Marriage and Family, 69*(3), 576–593. doi:10.1111/j.1741-3737.2007.00393

Provine, R. R. (2005). Yawning. *American Scientist, 93*, 532–539.

Prudic, J. (2009). Electroconvulsive therapy. In B. J. Sadock, V. A. Sadock, & P. Ruiz (Eds.), *Kaplan & Sadock's comprehensive textbook of psychiatry* (pp. 3285–3300). Philadelphia, PA: Lippincott, Williams & Wilkins.

Prudic, J., Olfson, M., Marcus, S. C., Fuller, R. B., & Sackeim, H. A. (2004). Effectiveness of electroconvulsive therapy in community settings. *Biological Psychiatry, 55*, 301–312.

Pruitt, D. G. (1971). Choice shifts in group discussion: An introductory review. *Journal of Personality and Social Psychology, 20*, 339–360.

Pucetti, R. (1981). The case for mental duality: Evidence from split brain data and other considerations. *Behavioral and Brain Sciences, 4*, 93–123.

Puente, A. E. (1990). Psychological assessment of minority group members. In G. Goldstein & M. Hersen (Eds.), *Handbook of psychological assessment*. New York, NY: Pergamon Press.

Pullum, G. K. (1991). *The Great Eskimo vocabulary hoax*. Chicago: University of Chicago Press.

Purves, D. (2009). Vision. In G. G. Berntson & J. T. Cacioppo (Eds.), *Handbook of neuroscience for the behavioral sciences*. New York, NY: Wiley.

Pyle, R. M. (1993). *The thunder tree: Lessons from an urban wildland*. Boston, MA: Houghton Mifflin.

Pyle, R. M. (2002). Eden in a vacant lot: Special places, species and kids in the neighborhood of life. In P. H. Kahn Jr. & S. R. Kellert (Eds.), *Children and nature: Psychological, sociocultural, and evolutionary investigations* (pp. 305–327). Cambridge MA: MIT Press.

Pyszczynski, T., Greenberg, J., & Solomon, S. (1999). A dual-process model of defense against conscious and unconscious death-related thoughts: An extension of terror management theory. *Psychological Review, 106*, 835–845.

Pyszczynski, T., Greenberg, J., Solomon, S., Arndt, J., & Schimel, J. (2004). Why do people need self-esteem? A theoretical and empirical review. *Psychological Bulletin, 130*, 435–468.

Pyszczynski, T., Solomon, S., & Greenberg, J. (2003). *In the wake of 9/11: The psychology of terror*. Washington, DC: American Psychological Association.

Qiu, C., De Ronchi, D., & Fratiglioni, L. (2007). The epidemiology of the dementias: An update. *Current Opinion in Psychiatry, 20*(4), 380–385. doi:10.1097/YCO.0b013e32816ebc7b

Quinn, K. A., Macrae, C. N., & Bodenhausen, G. V. (2003). Stereotyping and impression formation: How categorical thinking shapes person perception. In M. A. Hogg & J. Cooper (Eds.), *The Sage handbook of social psychology*. Thousand Oaks, CA: Sage.

Quirk, G. J. (2007). Prefrontal-amygdala interactions in the regulation of fear. In J. J. Gross (Ed.), *Handbook of emotion regulation* (pp. 27–46). New York, NY: Guilford Press.

Quoidbach, J., Dunn, E. W., Petrides, K. V., & Mikolajczak, M. (2010). Money giveth, money taketh away: The dual effect of wealth on happiness. *Psychological Science, 21*(6), 759–763.

Rabins, P. V., Lyketsos, C. G., & Steele, C. D. (1999). *Practical dementia care*. New York, NY: Oxford University Press.

Rachman, S. J. (1992). Behavior therapy. In L. R. Squire (Ed.), *Encyclopedia of learning and memory*. New York, NY: Macmillan.

Rachman, S. J. (2009). Psychological treatment of anxiety: The evolution of behavior therapy and cognitive behavior therapy. *Annual Review of Clinical Psychology, 5*, 97–119.

Radak, Z., Hart, N., Sarga, L., Koltai, E., Atalay, M., Ohno, H., & Boldogh, I. (2010). Exercise plays a preventive role against Alzheimer's disease. *Journal of Alzheimer's Disease, 20*(3), 777–783.

Rafal, R. (2001). Virtual neurology. *Nature Neuroscience, 4*, 862–864.

Rahe, R. H., & Arthur, R. H. (1978). Life change and illness studies. *Journal of Human Stress, 4*(1), 3–15.

Raichle, M. E. (2006). Functional neuroimaging: A historical and physiological perspective. In R. Cabeza & A. Kingstone (Eds.), *Handbook of functional neuroimaging of cognition* (pp. 3–20). Cambridge, MA: MIT Press.

Raine, A. (1997). Antisocial behavior and psychophysiology: A biosocial perspective and a prefrontal dysfunction hypothesis. In D. M. Stoff, J. Breiling, & J. D. Maser (Eds.), *Handbook of antisocial behavior*. New York, NY: Wiley.

Rains, G. D. (2002). *Principles of human neuropsychology*. New York, NY: McGraw-Hill.

Rakic, P., Bourgeois, J. P., & Goldman-Rakic, P. S. (1994). Synaptic development of the cerebral cortex: Implications for learning, memory, and mental illness. *Progress in brain research*.

Rama, A. N., Cho, S. C., & Kushida, C. A. (2006). Normal human sleep. In T. Lee-Chiong (Ed.), *Sleep: A comprehensive handbook*. Hoboken, NJ: Wiley-Liss.

Ramchand, R., Schell, T. L., Karney, B. R., Osilla, K., Burns, R. M., & Caldarone, L. (2010). Disparate prevalence estimates of PTSD among service members who served in Iraq and Afghanistan: Possible explanations. *Journal of Traumatic Stress, 23*(1), 59–68.

Ramey, C. T., & Ramey, S. L. (2004). Early educational interventions and intelligence. In E. Zigler & S. J. Styfco (Eds.), *The Head Start debate*. Baltimore: Paul H. Brookes Publishing.

Ramey, S. L. (1999). Head Start and preschool education: Toward continued improvement. *American Psychologist, 54,* 344–346.

Ramirez-Esparza, N., Mehl, M. R., Alvarez-Bermudez, J., & Pennebaker, J. W. (2009). Are Mexicans more or less sociable than Americans? Insights from a naturalistic observation study. *Journal of Research in Personality, 43*(1), 1–7. doi: doi:10.1016/j.jrp.2008.09.002.

Ramsay, D. S., Seeley, R. J., Bolles, R. C., & Woods, S. C. (1996). Ingestive homeostasis: The primacy of learning. In E. D. Capaldi (Ed.), *Why we eat what we eat: The psychology of eating* (pp. 11–29). Washington, DC: American Psychological Association.

Rand, M. (2008). *Criminal victimization, 2007*. Washington, DC: National Crime Victimization Survey, Bureau of Justice Statistics.

Ranson, K. E., & Urichuk, L. J. (2008). The effect of parent-child attachment relationships on child biopsychosocial outcomes: A review. *Early Child Development and Care, 178,* 129–152.

Rapee, R. M., & Barlow, D. H. (2001). Generalized anxiety disorders, panic disorders, and phobias. In P. B. Sutker & H. E. Adams (Eds.), *Comprehensive handbook of psychopathology* (3rd ed., pp. 131–154). New York, NY: Kluwer Academic/Plenum Publishers.

Rasch, B., & Born, J. (2008). Reactivation and consolidation of memory during sleep. *Current Directions in Psychological Science, 17*(3), 188–192. doi:10.1111/j.1467-8721.2008.00572.x

Rashid, T., & Anjum, A. (2008). Positive psychotherapy for young adults and children. In J. Z. Abela & B. L. Hankin (Eds.), *Handbook of depression in children and adolescents* (pp. 250–287). New York, NY: Guilford Press.

Raskin, N. J., Rogers, C. R., & Witty, M. C. (2011). Client-centered therapy. In R. J. Corsini & D. Wedding (Eds.), *Current psychotherapies* (9th ed.). Belmont, CA: Brooks/Cole.

Raskin, R. N., & Hall, C. S. (1979). A narcissistic personality inventory. *Psychological Reports, 45*(2), 590.

Raskin, R. N., & Hall, C. S. (1981). The Narcissistic Personality Inventory: Alternate form reliability and further evidence of construct validity. *Journal of Personality Assessment, 45*(2), 159–162. doi:10.1207/s15327752jpa4502_10

Raskin, R. N., & Terry, H. (1988). A principal-components analysis of the Narcissistic Personality Inventory and further evidence of its construct validity. *Journal of Personality and Social Psychology, 54*(5), 890–902. doi:10.1037/0022-3514.54.5.890

Rasmussen, C., Knapp, T. J., & Garner, L. (2000). Driving-induced stress in urban college students. *Perceptual & Motor Skills, 90,* 437–443.

Rasmussen, H. N., Scheier, M. F., & Greenhouse, J. B. (2009). Optimism and physical health: A Meta-analytic review. *Annals of Behavioral Medicine, 37*(3), 239–256. doi:10.1007/s12160-009-9111-x

Ratner, N. B., Gleason, J. B., & Narasimhan, B. (1998). An introduction to psycholinguistics: What do language users know? In J. B. Gleason & N. B. Ratner (Eds.), *Psycholinguistics* (2nd ed., pp. 1–40). Fort Worth, TX: Harcourt College Publishers.

Rauscher, F. H., Shaw, G. L., & Ky, K. N. (1993). Music and spatial task performance. *Nature, 365,* 611.

Rauscher, F. H., Shaw, G. L., & Ky, K. N. (1995). Listening to Mozart enhances spatial-temporal reasoning: Towards a neurophysiological basis. *Neuroscience Letters, 185,* 44–47.

Ravindran, L. N. & Stein, M. B. (2009). Anxiety disorders: Somatic treatment. In B. J. Sadock, V. A. Sadock, & P. Ruiz (Eds.), *Kaplan & Sadock's comprehensive textbook of psychiatry* (pp. 1906–1914). Philadelphia, PA: Lippincott, Williams & Wilkins.

Raynor, H. A., & Epstein, L. H. (2001). Dietary variety, energy regulation, and obesity. *Psychological Bulletin, 127,* 325–341.

Raynor, J. O., & Entin, E. E. (1982). Future orientation and achievement motivation. In J. O. Raynor & E. E. Entin (Eds.), *Motivation, career striving, and aging.* New York, NY: Hemisphere.

Reber, R. (2004). Availability. In F. P. Rudiger (Ed.), *Cognitive illusions.* New York, NY: Psychology Press.

Recht, L. D., Lew, R. A., & Schwartz, W. J. (1995). Baseball teams beaten by jet lag. *Nature, 377,* 583.

Rechtschaffen, A. (1994). Sleep onset: Conceptual issues. In R. D. Ogilvie & J. R. Harsh (Eds.), *Sleep onset: Normal and abnormal processes.* Washington, DC: American Psychological Association.

Redker, C. M., & Gibson, B. (2009). Music as an unconditioned stimulus: Positive and negative effects of country music on implicit attitudes, explicit attitudes, and brand choice. *Journal of Applied Social Psychology, 31,* 2689–2705. doi:10.1111/j.1559-1816.2009.00544.x

Reed, J. G., & Baxter, P. M. (2003). *Library use: A handbook for psychology.* Washington, DC: American Psychological Association.

Rees, C. J., & Metcalfe, B. (2003). The faking of personality questionnaire results: Who's kidding whom? *Journal of Managerial Psychology, 18*(2), 156–165.

Reeve, C. L., & Hakel, M. D. (2002). Asking the right questions about *g. Human Performance, 15,* 47–74.

Reeves, A. J. (2010). Visual light- and dark-adaptation. In E. B. Goldstein (Ed.), *Encyclopedia of perception.* Thousand Oaks, CA: Sage.

Refinetti, R. (2006). *Circadian physiology.* Boca Raton, FL: Taylor & Francis.

Regan, P. C. (1998). What if you can't get what you want? Willingness to compromise ideal mate selection standards as a function of sex, mate value, and relationship context. *Personality and Social Psychology Bulletin, 24,* 1294–1303.

Regan, P. C. (2008). *The mating game: A primer on love, sex, and marriage* (2nd ed.). Thousand Oaks, CA: Sage.

Regan, T. (1997). The rights of humans and other animals. *Ethics & Behavior, 7*(2), 103–111.

Reger, G. M., Holloway, K. M., Candy, C., Rothbaum, B. O., Difede, J., Rizzo, A. A., & Gahm, G. A. (2011). Effectiveness of virtual reality exposure therapy for active duty soldiers in a military mental health clinic. *Journal of Traumatic Stress, 24*(1), 93–96. doi:10.1002/jts.20574

Regier, D. A., & Burke, J. D. (2000). Epidemiology. In B. J. Sadock & V. A. Sadock (Eds.), *Kaplan and Sadock's comprehensive textbook of psychiatry.* Philadelphia, PA: Lippincott/Williams & Wilkins.

Regier, D. A., & Kaelber, C. T. (1995). The Epidemiologic Catchment Area (ECA) program: Studying the prevalence and incidence of psychopathology. In M. T. Tsuang, M. Tohen, & G. E. P. Zahner (Eds.), *Textbook in psychiatric epidemiology.* New York, NY: Wiley.

Regier, D. A., Narrow, W. E., Kuhl, E. A., & Kupfer, D. J. (2009). The conceptual development of DSM-V. *American Journal of Psychiatry, 166*(6), 645–650. doi:10.1176/appi.ajp.2009.09020279

Regier, D. A., Narrow, W. E., & Rae, D. S. (2004). For DSM-V, It's the "disorder threshold," stupid. *Archives of General Psychiatry, 61,* 1051.

Reibel, D. K., Greeson, J. M., Brainard, G. C., & Rosenzweig, S. (2001). Mindfulness-based stress reduction and health-related quality of life in a heterogeneous patient population. *General Hospital Psychiatry, 23*(4), 183–192.

Reichert, T. (2003). The prevalence of sexual imagery in ads targeted to young adults. *Journal of Consumer Affairs, 37,* 403–412.

Reichert, T., Heckler, S. E., & Jackson, S. (2001). The effects of sexual social marketing appeals on cognitive processing and persuasion. *Journal of Advertising, 30*(1), 13–27.

Reichert, T., & Lambiase, J. (2003). How to get "kissably close": Examining how advertisers appeal to consumers' sexual needs and desires. *Sexuality & Culture: An Interdisciplinary Quarterly, 7*(3), 120–136.

Reid, R. C., & Usrey, W. M. (2008). Vision. In L. Squire, D. Berg, F. Bloom, S. du Lac, A. Ghosh, & N. Spitzer (Eds.), *Fundamental neuroscience.* San Diego, CA: Elsevier.

Reidy, D. E., Foster, J. D., & Zeichner, A. (2010). Narcissism and unprovoked aggression. *Aggressive Behavior, 36*(6), 414–422. doi:10.1002/ab.20356

Reimer, T., Mata, R., & Stoecklin, M. (2004). The use of heuristics in persuasion: Deriving cues on source expertise from argument quality. *Current Research in Social Psychology, 10*(6). No pagination specified.

Reinhard, M. A., Messner, M., & Sporer, S. L. (2006). Explicit persuasive intent and its impact on success at persuasion—The determining roles of attractiveness and likeableness. *Journal of Consumer Psychology, 16,* 249–259.

Reinharz, D., Lesage, A. D., & Contandriopoulos, A. P. (2000). Cost-effectiveness analysis of psychiatric deinstitutionalization. *Canadian Journal of Psychiatry, 45,* 533–538.

Reis, H. T., & Aron, A. (2008). Love: What is it, why does it matter, and how does it operate? *Perspectives on Psychological Science, 3,* 80–86.

Reisner, A. D. (1998). Repressed memories: True and false. In R. A. Baker (Ed.), *Child sexual abuse and false memory syndrome.* Amherst, NY: Prometheus Books.

Rennie, D., & Luft, H. S. (2000). Making them transparent, making them credible. *Journal of the American Medical Association, 283,* 2516–2521.

Renzulli, J. S. (1986). The three-ring conception of giftedness: A developmental model for creative productivity. In R. J. Sternberg & J. E. Davidson (Eds.), *Conceptions of giftedness.* Cambridge: Cambridge University Press.

Renzulli, J. S. (1999). What is this thing called giftedness, and how do we develop it? A twenty-five year perspective. *Journal for the Education of the Gifted, 23,* 3–54.

Renzulli, J. S. (2002). Emerging conceptions of giftedness: Building a bridge to the new century. *Exceptionality, 10,* 67–75.

Renzulli, J. S. (2005). The three-ring conception of giftedness: A developmental model for promoting creative productivity. In R. J. Sternberg & J. E. Davidson (Eds.), *Conceptions of giftedness.* New York, NY: Cambridge University Press.

Repetto, M., & Gold, M. S. (2005). Cocaine and crack: Neurobiology. In J. H. Lowinson, P. Ruiz, R. B. Millman, & J. G. Langrod (Eds.), *Substance abuse: A comprehensive textbook.* Philadelphia, PA: Lippincott/Williams & Wilkins.

Rescorla, R. A. (1978). Some implications of a cognitive perspective on Pavlovian conditioning. In S. H. Hulse, H. Fowler, & W. K. Honig (Eds.), *Cognitive processes in animal behavior.* Hillsdale, NJ: Erlbaum.

Rescorla, R. A. (1980). *Pavlovian second-order conditioning.* Hillsdale, NJ: Erlbaum.

Rescorla, R. A., & Wagner, A. R. (1972). A theory of Pavlovian conditioning: Variations in the effectiveness of reinforcement and nonreinforcement. In A. H. Black & W. F. Prokasky (Eds.), *Classical conditioning: II. Current research and theory.* New York, NY: Appleton-Century-Crofts.

Resick, P. A., Monson, C. M., & Rizvi, S. L. (2008). Posttraumatic stress disorder. In W. E. Craighead, D. J. Miklowitz, & L. W. Craighead (Eds.), *Psychopathology: History, diagnosis, and empirical foundations.* New York, NY: Wiley.

Resnick, S. M. (2006). Sex differences in regional brain structure and function. In P. W. Kapan (Ed.), *Neurologic disease in women* (2nd ed., pp. 15–26). New York, NY: Demos Medical.

Resnick, S. M. (2009). Sex differences in regional brain structure and function. In P. W. Kapan (Ed.), *Neurologic disease in women* (2nd ed., pp. 15–26). New York, NY: Demos Medical.

Rest, J. R. (1986). *Moral development: Advances in research and theory.* New York, NY: Praeger.

Reuter-Lorenz, P. A., & Miller, A. C. (1998). The cognitive neuroscience of human laterality: Lessons from the bisected brain. *Current Directions in Psychological Science, 7,* 15–20.

Reutskaja, E., & Hogarth, R. M. (2009). Satisfaction in choice as a function of the number of alternatives: When "goods satiate." *Psychology & Marketing, 26*(3), 197–203. doi:10.1002/mar.20268

Reynolds, A. J., Temple, J. T., Robertson, D. L., & Mann, E. A. (2001). Long-term effects of an early childhood intervention on educational achievement and juvenile arrest: A 15-year follow-up of low-income children in public schools. *Journal of the American Medical Association, 285,* 2339–2346.

Reynolds, C. F., III, Frank, E., Perel, J. M., Imber, S. D., Cornes, C., Miller, M. D., Mazumdar, S., Houck, P. R., Dew, M. A., Stack, J. A., Pollock, B. G., & Kupfer, D. J. (1999). Nortriptyline and interpersonal psychotherapy as maintenance therapies for recurrent major depression: A randomized controlled trial in patients older than 50 years. *Journal of the American Medical Association, 28,* 39–45.

Reynolds, E. H. (2002). Benefits and risks of folic acid to the nervous system. *Journal of Neurology, Neurosurgery & Psychiatry, 72*(5), 567–571. doi:10.1136/jnnp.72.5.567

Reynolds, K. J., Turner, J. C., & Haslam, S. A. (2000). When are we better than them and they worse than us? A closer look at social discrimination in positive and negative domains. *Journal of Personality and Social Psychology, 78,* 64–80.

Rhodes, G., Simmons, L. W., & Peters, M. (2005). Attractiveness and sexual behavior: Does attractiveness enhance mating success? *Evolution and Human Behavior, 26,* 186–201.

Rhodewalt, F., & Peterson, B. (2009). Narcissism. In M. R. Leary, & R. H. Hoyle (Eds.), *Handbook of individual differences in social behavior* (pp. 547–560). New York, NY: Guilford Press.

Riba, M. B., & Miller, R. R. (2003). Combined therapies: Psychotherapy and pharmacotherapy. In A. Tasman, J. Kay, & J. A. Lieberman (Eds.), *Psychiatry.* New York, NY: Wiley.

Rice, D., & Barone, S. (2000). Critical periods of vulnerability for the developing nervous system: Evidence from humans and animal models. *Environmental Health Perspectives, 108* (Suppl 3), 511–533.

Richards, S. S., & Sweet, R. A. (2009). Dementia. In B. J. Sadock, V. A. Sadock, & P. Ruiz (Eds.), *Kaplan & Sadock's comprehensive textbook of psychiatry* (9th ed., Vol. 1, pp. 1167–1197). Philadelphia, PA: Lippincott, Williams & Wilkins.

Richardson, C. R., Kriska, A. M., Lantz, P. M., & Hayword, R. A. (2004). Physical activity and mortality across cardiovascular disease risk groups. *Medicine and Science in Sports and Exercise, 36,* 1923–1929.

Richardson, F. C., & Guignon, C. B. (2008). Positive psychology and philosophy of social science. *Theory & Psychology, 18,* 605–627. doi:10.1177/0959354308093398

Richardson, G. S. (1993). Circadian rhythms. In M. A. Carskadon (Ed.), *Encyclopedia of sleep and dreaming.* New York, NY: Macmillan.

Richardson, G. S. (2006). Shift work sleep disorder. In T. Lee-Chiong (Ed.), *Sleep: A comprehensive handbook.* Hoboken, NJ: Wiley-Liss.

Richardson, R. C. (2007). *Evolutionary psychology as maladapted psychology.* Cambridge, MA: MIT Press.

Richer, I., & Bergeron, J. (2009). Driving under the influence of cannabis: Links with dangerous driving, psychological predictors, and accident involvement. *Accident Analysis and Prevention, 41*(2), 299–307. doi:10.1016/j.aap.2008.12.004

Richert, E. S. (1997). Excellence with equity in identification and programming. In N. Colangelo, & G. A. Davis (Eds.), *Handbook of gifted education.* Boston, MA: Allyn & Bacon.

Rieber, R. W. (1998). The assimilation of psychoanalysis in America: From popularization to vulgarization. In R. W. Rieber & K. D. Salzinger (Eds.), *Psychology: Theoretical-historical perspectives.* Washington, DC: American Psychological Association.

Rieger, G., Linsenmeier, J. W., Gygax, L., & Bailey, J. (2008). Sexual orientation and childhood gender nonconformity: Evidence from home videos. *Developmental Psychology, 44*(1), 46–58. doi:10.1037/0012-1649.44.1.46

Riemann, D., Spiegelhalder, K., Feige, B., Voderholzer, U., Berger, M., Perlis, M., & Nissen, C. (2010). The hyperarousal model of insomnia: A review of the concept and its evidence. *Sleep Medicine Reviews, 14*(1), 19–31. doi:10.1016/j.smrv.2009.04.002

Rifkin, J. (2009). *The empathic civilization.* New York, NY: Penguin.

Riggio, H. R., & Halpern, D. F. (2006). Understanding human thought: Educating students as critical thinkers. In W. Buskist & S. F. Davis (Eds.), *Handbook of the teaching of psychology* (pp. 78–84). Malden, MA: Blackwell Publishing.

Rihmer, Z., & Angst, J. (2009). Mood disorders: Epidemiology. In B. J. Sadock, V. A. Sadock, & P. Ruiz (Eds.), *Kaplan & Sadock's comprehensive textbook of psychiatry* (9th ed., pp. 1645–1652). Philadelphia, PA: Lippincott, Williams & Wilkins.

Riis, J., Loewenstein, G., Baron, J. , Jepson, C., Fagerlin, A., & Ubel, P. A. (2005). Ignorance of hedonic adaptation to hemodialysis: A study using ecological momentary assessment. *Journal of Experimental Psychology: General, 134*(1), 3–9.

Rilling, M. (1996). The mystery of the vanished citations: James McConnell's forgotten 1960s quest for planarian learning, a biochemical engram, and celebrity. *American Psychologist, 51,* 589–598.

Rilling, M. (2000). John Watson's paradoxical struggle to explain Freud. *American Psychologist, 55,* 301–312.

Risen, J., & Gilovich, T. (2007). Informal logical fallacies. In R. J. Sternberg, H. L. Roediger III, & D. F. Halpern (Eds.), *Critical thinking in psychology.* New York, NY: Cambridge University Press.

Risen, J. L., & Gilovich, T. (2008). Why people are reluctant to tempt fate. *Journal of Personality and Social Psychology, 95,* 293–307. doi:10.1037/0022-3514.95.2.293

Rising, K., Bacchetti, P., & Bero, L. (2008). Reporting bias in drug trials submitted to the Food and Drug Administration: Review of publication and presentation. *PLoS Medicine, 5*(11), e217.

Riskind, J. H. (2005). Cognitive mechanisms in generalized anxiety disorder: A second generation of theoretical perspectives. *Cognitive Therapy & Research, 29*(1), 1–5.

Rissling, M., & Ancoli-Israel, S. (2009). Sleep in aging. In R. Stickgold & M. P. Walker (Eds.), *The neuroscience of sleep* (pp. 78–86). San Diego, CA: Academic Press.

Ritter, K. (2011). New report confirms Arctic melt accelerating. Associated Press, May 3. Retrieved from http://hosted2.ap.org/APDEFAULT/terms/Article_2011-05-03-EU-Arctic-Climate-Change/id-bb2a142692274df4a51b3ae347b0f797

Ritter, R. C. (2004). Gastrointestinal mechanisms of satiation for food. *Physiology & Behavior, 81,* 249–273.

Ritvo, E., Glick, I. D., & Berman, E. (2008). Couples therapy. In A. Tasman, J. Kay, J. A. Lieberman, M. B. First, & M. Maj (Eds.), *Psychiatry* (3rd ed.). New York, NY: Wiley-Blackwell.

Rizzolatti, G. (2005). The mirror neuron system and imitation. In S. Hurley, & N. Chater (Eds.), *Perspectives on imitation: From neuroscience to social science: Vol. 1. Mechanisms of imitation and imitation in animals* (pp. 55–76). Cambridge, MA: MIT Press.

Rizzolatti, G., & Craighero, L. (2004). The mirror-neuron system. *Annual Review of Neuroscience, 27,* 169–192.

Roazen, P. (1976). *Erik H. Erikson: The power and limits of a vision.* New York, NY: Free Press.

Roberson, D., Davidoff, J., Davies, I. R. L., & Shapiro, L. R. (2005). Color categories: Evidence for the cultural relativity hypothesis. *Cognitive Psychology, 50,* 378–411.

Roberson, D., Davidoff, J., & Shapiro, L. (2002). Squaring the circle: The cultural relativity of good shape. *Journal of Cognition & Culture, 2*(1), 29–51.

Roberson, D., Davies, I., & Davidoff, J. (2000). Color categories are not universal: Replications and new evidence from a stone-age culture. *Journal of Experimental Psychology: General, 129,* 369–398.

Roberts, B. W., Caspi, A., & Moffitt, T. (2003). Work experiences and personality development in young adulthood. *Journal of Personality and Social Psychology, 84,* 582–593.

Roberts, B. W., & DelVecchio, W. F. (2000). The rank-order consistency of personality traits from childhood to old age: A quantitative review of longitudinal studies. *Psychological Bulletin, 126,* 3–25.

Roberts, B. W., Jackson, J. J., Fayard, J. V., Edmonds, G., & Meints, J. (2009). Conscientiousness. In M. R. Leary & R. H. Hoyle (Eds.), *Handbook of individual differences in social behavior* (pp. 257–273). New York, NY: Guilford Press.

Roberts, B. W., Kuncel, N. R., Shiner, R., Caspi, A., & Goldberg, L. R. (2007). The power of personality: The comparative validity of personality traits, socioeconomic status, and cognitive ability for predicting important life outcomes. *Perspectives on Psychological Science, 2,* 313–345.

Roberts, B. W., & Mroczek, D. (2008). Personality trait change in adulthood. *Current Directions in Psychological Science, 17,* 31–35.

Roberts, B. W., & Pomerantz, E. M. (2004). On traits, situations, and their integration: A developmental perspective. *Personality and Social Psychology Review, 8,* 402–416.

Roberts, B. W., Walton, K. E., & Bogg, T. (2005). Conscientiousness and health across the life course. *Review of General Psychology, 9*(2), 156–168.

Roberts, B. W., Wood, D., & Caspi, A. (2008). The development of personality traits in adulthood. In O. P. John, R. W. Robins, & L. A. Pervin (Eds.), *Handbook of personality: Theory and research* (3rd ed., pp. 375–398). New York, NY: Guilford Press.

Roberts, D. F., Foehr, U. G., & Rideout, V. (2005). Generation M: Media in the lives of 8–18 year olds (Publication No. 7251). Menlo Park, CA: Henry J. Kaiser Family Foundation.

Roberts, M. C., Brown, K. J., & Smith-Boydston, J. M. (2003). The scientific process and publishing research. In M. C. Roberts and S. S. Ilardi (Eds.), *Handbook of research methods in clinical psychology.* Malden, MA: Blackwell.

Roberts, R. D., Markham, P. M., Matthews, G., & Zeidner, M. (2005). Assessing intelligence: Past, present, and future. In O. Wilhelm & R. W. Engle (Eds.), *Handbook of understanding and measuring intelligence.* Thousand Oaks, CA: Sage.

Robins, L. N., Locke, B. Z., & Regier, D. A. (1991). An overview of psychiatric disorders in America. In L. N. Robins & D. A. Regier (Eds.), *Psychiatric disorders in America: The epidemiologic catchment area study.* New York, NY: Free Press.

Robinson, D. G., Woerner, M. G., McMeniman, M., Mendelowitz, A., & Bilder, R. M. (2004). Symptomatic and functional recovery from a first episode of schizophrenia or schizoaffective disorder. *American Journal of Psychiatry, 161,* 473–479.

Robinson, N. M. (2010). The social world of gifted children and youth. In S. I. Pfeiffer (Ed.), *Handbook of giftedness in children: Psychoeducational theory, research, and best practices.* New York, NY: Springer.

Robles, T. F., Glaser, R., & Kiecolt-Glaser, J. K. (2005). Out of balance: A new look at chronic stress, depression, and immunity. *Current Directions in Psychological Science, 14,* 111–115.

Rodgers, J. E. (1982). The malleable memory of eyewitnesses. *Science Digest, 3,* 32–35.

Rodieck, R. W. (1998). *The first steps in seeing.* Sunderland, MA: Sinauer.

Rodin, J. (1981). Current status of the internal-external hypothesis for obesity: What went wrong? *American Psychologist, 36*(4), 361–372. doi:10.1037/0003-066X.36.4.361

Roediger, H. L., III. (1980). Memory metaphors in cognitive psychology. *Memory & Cognition, 8,* 231–246.

Roediger, H. L., III, Agarwal, P. K., Kang, S. K., & Marsh, E. J. (2010). Benefits of testing memory: Best practices and boundary conditions. In G. M. Davies & D. B. Wright, (Eds.), *Current issues in applied memory research* (pp. 13–49). New York, NY: Psychology Press.

Roediger, H. L., III, & Guynn, M. J. (1996). Retrieval processes. In E. L. Bjork & R. A. Bjork (Eds.), *Memory.* San Diego: Academic Press.

Roediger, H. L., III, & Karpicke, J. D. (2006a). Test-enhanced learning: Taking memory tests improves long-term retention. *Psychological Science, 17,* 249–255.

Roediger, H. L., III, & Karpicke, J. D. (2006b). The power of testing memory: Basic research and implications for educational practice. *Perspectives on Psychological Science, 1*(3), 181–210.

Roediger, H. L., III, & McDermott, K. B. (1995). Creating false memories: Remembering words not presented in lists. *Journal of Experimental Psychology: Learning, Memory, and Cognition, 21,* 803–814.

Roediger, H. L., III, & McDermott, K. B. (2000). Tricks of memory. *Current Directions in Psychological Science, 9,* 123–127.

Roediger, H. L., III, Wheeler, M. A., & Rajaram, S. (1993). Remembering, knowing, and reconstructing the past. In D. L. Medin (Ed.), *The psychology of learning and motivation: Advances in research and theory.* San Diego: Academic Press.

Roehrs, T., Carskadon, M. A., Dement, W. C., & Roth, T. (2005). Daytime sleepiness and alertness. In M. H. Kryger, T. Roth, & W. C. Dement (Eds.). *Principles and practice of sleep medicine.* Philadelphia, PA: Elsevier Saunders.

Roehrs, T., & Roth, T. (2004). "Hypnotic" prescription patterns in a large managed-care population. *Sleep Medicine, 5,* 463–466.

Roehrs, T., Zorick, F. J., & Roth, T. (2000). Transient and short-term insomnias. In M. H. Kryger, T. Roth, & W. C. Dement (Eds.), *Principles and practice of sleep medicine.* Philadelphia, PA: Saunders.

Rogers, C. R. (1951). *Client-centered therapy: Its current practice, implications, and theory.* Boston, MA: Houghton Mifflin.

Rogers, C. R. (1961). *On becoming a person: A therapist's view of psychotherapy.* Boston, MA: Houghton Mifflin.

Rogers, C. R. (1980). *A way of being.* Boston, MA: Houghton Mifflin.

Rogers, C. R. (1986). Client-centered therapy. In I. L. Kutash & A. Wolf (Eds.), *Psychotherapist's casebook.* San Francisco, CA: Jossey-Bass.

Rogers, C. R. (1995). *A way of being.* Boston, MA: Houghton Mifflin. (Original work published 1980)

Rogers, M. P., Fricchione, G., & Reich, P. (1999). Psychosomatic medicine and consultation-liaison psychiatry. In A. M. Nicholi (Ed.), *The Harvard guide to psychiatry* (3rd ed., pp. 362–389). Cambridge, MA: Harvard University Press.

Rogers, N. L., & Dinges, D. F. (2002). Shiftwork, circadian disruption, and consequences. *Primary Psychiatry, 9*(8), 50.

Rogers, P. (1998). The cognitive psychology of lottery gambling: A theoretical review. *Journal of Gambling Studies, 14,* 111–134.

Rogers, T. B., Kuiper, N. A., & Kirker, W. S. (1977). Self-reference and the encoding of personal information. *Journal of Personality and Social Psychology, 35,* 677–688.

Rogers, W. T., & Yang, P. (1996). Test-wiseness: Its nature and application. *European Journal of Psychological Assessment, 12,* 247–259.

Rogoff, B. (2003). *The cultural nature of human development.* New York, NY: Oxford University Press.

Rohner, R. P., & Veneziano, R. A. (2001). The importance of father love: History and contemporary evidence. *Review of General Psychology, 5,* 382–405.

Rohrer, D., & Taylor, K. (2006). The effects of overlearning and distributed practice on the retention of mathematics knowledge. *Applied Cognitive Psychology, 20,* 1209–1224.

Rohrer, D., Taylor, K., Pashler, H., Wixted, J. T., & Capeda, N. J. (2005). The effect of overlearning on long-term retention. *Applied Cognitive Psychology, 19,* 361–374.

Roid, G. H., & Tippin, S. M. (2009). Assessment of intellectual strengths and weaknesses with the Stanford-Binet Intelligence Scales, Fifth Edition (SB5). In J. A. Naglieri & S. Goldstein (Eds.), *Practitioner's guide to assessing intelligence and achievement* (pp. 153–190). New York, NY: Wiley.

Rollman, G. B. (2010). Pain: Cognitive and contextual influences. In E. B. Goldstein (Ed.), *Encyclopedia of perception.* Thousand Oaks, CA: Sage.

Rolls, E. T. (1990). A theory of emotion, and its application to understanding the neural basis of emotion. *Cognitive and Emotion,* 4, 161–190.

Romanski, L. M., Chafee, M. V., & Goldman-Rakic, P. S. (2004). Domain specificity in cognitive systems. In M. S. Gazzaniga (Ed.), *The cognitive neurosciences.* Cambridge, MA: MIT Press.

Romi, S. & Kohan, E. (2004). Wilderness programs: Principles, possibilities and opportunities for intervention with dropout adolescents. *Child & Youth Care Forum, 33,* 115–136.

Roney, J. R., Hanson, K. N., Durante, K. M., & Maestripieri, D. (2006). Reading men's faces: Women's mate attractiveness judgments track men's testosterone and interest in infants. *Proceedings of the Royal Society, 273,* 2169–2175.

Ronksley, P. E., Brien, S. E., Turner, B. J., Mukamal, K. J., & Ghali, W. A. (2011). Association of alcohol consumption with selected cardiovascular disease outcomes: a systematic review and meta-analysis. *British Medical Journal, 342*(7795), 479.

Rorden, C., & Karnath, H.-O. (2004). Using human brain lesions to infer function: A relic from a past era in the fMRI age? *Nature Reviews Neuroscience, 5,* 813–819.

Rorschach, H. (1921). *Psychodiagnostik.* Berne: Birchen.

Rorschach, H. (1942). *Psychodiagnostics: A diagnostic test based on perception.* Berne: Huber.

Rosch, E. H. (1973). Natural categories. *Cognitive Psychology, 4,* 328–350.

Rose, D., Wykes, T., Leese, M., Bindman, J., & Fleischmann, P. (2003). Patient's perspectives on electroconvulsive therapy: Systematic review. *British Medical Journal, 326,* 1363–1365.

Rose, H., & Rose, S. E. (2000). *Alas, poor Darwin: Arguments against evolutionary psychology.* New York, NY: Harmony Books.

Rose, N. R. (2007). Neuroimmunomodulation. In G. Fink (Ed.), *Encyclopedia of stress.* San Diego: Elsevier.

Roseboom, T., de Rooij, S., & Painter, R. (2006). The Dutch famine and its long-term consequences for adult health. *Early Human Development, 82,* 485–491.

Rosenbaum, M., Lakin, M., & Roback, H. B. (1992). Psychotherapy in groups. In D. K. Freedheim (Ed.), *History of psychotherapy: A century of change.* Washington, DC: American Psychological Association.

Rosenblum, K. (2009). Conditioned taste aversion and taste learning: Molecular mechanisms. In J. H. Byrne (Ed.), *Concise learning and memory: The editor's selection.* San Diego, CA: Elsevier.

Rosenthal, H. (1988). *Not with my life I don't: Preventing suicide and that of others.* Muncie, IN: Accelerated Development.

Rosenthal, L. (2006). Physiologic processes during sleep. In T. Lee-Chiong (Ed.), *Sleep: A comprehensive handbook.* Hoboken, NJ: Wiley-Liss.

Rosenthal, R. (1976). *Experimenter effects in behavioral research.* New York, NY: Halsted.

Rosenthal, R. (1994). Interpersonal expectancy effects: A 30-year perspective. *Current Directions in Psychological Science, 3,* 176–179.

Rosenthal, R. (2002). Experimenter and clinician effects in scientific inquiry and clinical practice. *Prevention & Treatment, 5,* Article 38. No pagination specified.

Rosenthal, R., & Fode, K. L. (1963). Three experiments in experimenter bias. *Psychological Reports, 12,* 491–511.

Rosenzweig, M. R., & Bennet, E. L. (1996). Psychobiology of plasticity: Effects of training and experience on brain and behavior. *Behavioural Brain Research, 78*(5), 57–65.

Rosenzweig, M. R., Krech, D., & Bennett, E. L. (1961). Heredity, environment, brain biochemistry, and learning. In *Current trends in psychological theory.* Pittsburgh: University of Pittsburgh Press.

Rosenzweig, M., Krech, D., Bennett, E. L., & Diamond, M. (1962). Effects of environmental complexity and training on brain chemistry and anatomy: A replication and extension. *Journal of Comparative and Physiological Psychology, 55,* 429–437.

Rosenzweig, S. (1985). Freud and experimental psychology: The emergence of idiodynamics. In S. Koch & D. E. Leary (Eds.), *A century of psychology as a science.* New York, NY: McGraw-Hill.

Rosler, F. (2005). From single-channel recordings to brain-mapping devices: The impact of electroencephalography on experimental psychology. *History of Psychology, 8*(1), 95–117.

Ross, B. (1991). William James: Spoiled child of American psychology. In G. A. Kimble, M. Wertheimer, & C. White (Eds.), *Portraits of pioneers in psychology.* Hillsdale, NJ: Erlbaum.

Ross, C. A. (1999). Dissociative disorders. In T. Millon, P. H. Blaney, & R. D. Davis (Eds.), *Oxford textbook of psychopathology* (pp. 466–484). New York, NY: Oxford University Press.

Ross, H., & Plug, C. (2002). *The mystery of the moon illusion: Exploring the size perception.* New York, NY: Oxford.

Ross, L., & Nisbett, R. E. (1991). *The person and the situation: Perspectives of social psychology.* New York, NY: McGraw-Hill.

Ross, L. D. (1988). The obedience experiments: A case study of controversy. *Contemporary Psychology, 33,* 101–104.

Roszak, T. (1992). *The voice of the earth: An exploration of eco-psychology.* New York, NY: Simon & Schuster.

Roszak, T., Gomes, M. E., & Kanner, A. D. (Eds.). (1995). *Ecopsychology: Restoring the earth, healing the mind.* San Francisco, CA: Sierra Club.

Roter, D. L., Hall, J. A., Merisca, R., Nordstrom, B., Cretin, D., & Svarstad, B. (1998). Effectiveness of interventions to promote patient compliance. *Medical Care, 36,* 1138–1161.

Roth, T., & Drake, C. (2004). Evolution of insomnia: Current status and future direction. *Sleep Medicine, 5*(Supplemental 1), S23–S30.

Rothbart, M. (2001). Category dynamics and the modification of outgroup stereotypes. In R. Brown & S. L. Gaertner (Eds.), *Blackwell handbook of social psychology: Intergroup processes.* Malden, MA: Blackwell.

Rothbart, M. K., & Bates, J. E. (2008). Temperament. In W. Damon & R. M. Lerner (Eds.), *Child and adolescent development: An advanced course* (pp. 54–65). New York, NY: Wiley.

Rotter, J. B. (1982). *The development and application of social learning theory.* New York, NY: Praeger.

Routh, D. K., & Reisman, J. M. (2003). Clinical psychology. In D. K. Freedheim (Ed.), *Handbook of psychology, Vol. 1: History of psychology.* New York, NY: Wiley.

Rowa, K., & Antony, M. M. (2008). Generalized anxiety disorders. In W. E. Craighead, D. J. Miklowitz, & L. W. Craighead (Eds.), *Psychopathology: History, diagnosis, and empirical foundations.* New York, NY: Wiley.

Rowatt, W. C., Cunningham, M. R., & Druen, P. B. (1999). Lying to get a date: The effect of facial physical attractiveness on the willingness to deceive prospective dating partners. *Journal of Social & Personal Relationships, 16,* 209–223.

Rowe, D., & van den Oord, E. J. C. G. (2005). Genetic and environmental influences. In V. A. Derlega, B. A. Winstead, & W. H. Jones (Eds.), *Personality: Contemporary theory and research.* Belmont, CA: Wadsworth.

Rowe, S. M., & Wertsch, J. V. (2002). Vygotsky's model of cognitive development. In U. Goswami (Ed.), *Blackwell handbook of childhood cognitive development.* Malden, MA: Blackwell.

Rowny, S., & Lisanby, S. H. (2008). Brain stimulation in psychiatry. In A. Tasman, J. Kay, J. A. Lieberman, M. B. First, & M. Maj (Eds.), *Psychiatry* (3rd ed.). New York, NY: Wiley-Blackwell.

Roy, M., Piche, M., Chen, J., Peretz, I., & Rainville, P. (2009). Cerebral and spinal modulation of pain by emotions. *Proceedings of the National Academy of Sciences of the United States of America, 106*(49), 20900-20905. doi:10.1073/pnas.0904706106

Rozin, P. (1990). The importance of social factors in understanding the acquisition of food habits. In E. D. Capaldi & T. L. Powley (Eds.), *Taste, experience, and feeding.* Washington, DC: American Psychological Association.

Rozin, P. (2007). Food and eating. In S. Kitayama & D. Cohen (Eds.), *Handbook of cultural psychology* (pp. 391–416). New York, NY: Guilford Press.

Rozin, P., Kabnick, K., Pete, E., Fischler, C., & Shields, C. (2003). The ecology of eating: Smaller portion sizes in France than in the United States help explain the French paradox. *Psychological Science, 14,* 450–454.

Rubia, K. (2009). The neurobiology of meditation and its clinical effectiveness in psychiatric disorders. *Biological Psychology, 82*(1), 1–11. doi:10.1016/j.biopsycho.2009.04.003

Ruble, D. N., & Martin, C. L. (1998). Gender development. In W. Damon (Ed.), *Handbook of child psychology, Vol. 3: Social, emotional, and personality development.* New York, NY: Wiley.

Ruini, C., & Fava, G. A. (2004). Clinical application of well-being therapy. In P. A. Linley & S. Joseph (Eds.), *Positive psychology in practice.* Hoboken, NJ: Wiley.

Ruiter, R. A., Abraham, C., & Kok, G. (2001). Scary warnings and rational precautions: A review of the psychology of fear appeals. *Psychology & Health, 16,* 613–630.

Runco, M. A. (2004). Divergent thinking, creativity, and giftedness. In R. J. Sternberg (Ed.), *Definitions and conceptions of giftedness* (pp. 47–62). Thousand Oaks, CA: Corwin Press.

Runyan, W. M. (2006). Psychobiography and the psychology of science: Understanding relations between the life and work of individual psychologists. *Review of General Psychology, 10,* 147–162.

Ruscio, J. (2006). *Clear thinking with psychology: Separating sense from nonsense.* Belmont, CA: Wadsworth.

Rush, A. J. (1984). Cognitive therapy. In T. B. Karasu (Ed.), *The psychiatric therapies.* Washington, DC: American Psychiatric Press.

Rush, A. J., & Beck, A. T. (2000). Cognitive therapy. In B. J. Sadock & V. A. Sadock (Eds.), *Kaplan and Sadock's comprehensive textbook of psychiatry* (7th ed., Vol. 1, pp. 2167–2177). Philadelphia, PA: Lippincott/Williams & Wilkins.

Rushton, J. P. (2003). Race differences in *g* and the "Jensen effect." In H. Nyborg (Ed.), *The scientific study of general intelligence: Tribute to Arthur R. Jensen.* Oxford, UK: Pergamon.

Rushton, J. P., & Ankney, C. D. (2007). The evolution of brain size and intelligence. In S. M. Platek, J. P. Keenan, & T. K. Shackleford (Eds.), *Evolutionary cognitive neuroscience.* Cambridge: MIT Press.

Rushton, J. P., & Jensen, A. R. (2005). Thirty years of research on race differences in cognitive ability. *Psychology, Public Policy, and Law, 11,* 235–294.

Rushton, J. P., & Jensen, A. R. (2010). The rise and fall of the Flynn effect as a reason to expect a narrowing of the black-white IQ gap. *Intelligence, 38*(2), 213–219. doi:10.1016/j.intell.2009.12.002

Russell, G. F. M. (1995). Anorexia nervosa through time. In G. Szmukler, C. Dare, & J. Treasure (Eds.), *Handbook of eating disorders: Theory, treatment, and research.* New York, NY: Wiley.

Russell, G. F. M. (2009). Anorexia nervosa. In M. C. Gelder, N. C. Andreasen, J. J. López-Ibor, Jr., & J. R. Geddes (Eds.). *New Oxford textbook of psychiatry* (2nd ed., Vol. 1). New York, NY: Oxford University Press.

Russell, J. A. (1991). Culture and the categorization of emotions. *Psychological Bulletin, 110,* 426–450.

Russell, J. A. (2007). Stress milestones. *Stress: The International Journal on the Biology of Stress, 10*(1), 1–2.

Russell, K. C. (2003). An assessment of outcomes in outdoor behavioral healthcare treatment. *Child and Youth Care Forum, 32,* 355–381.

Russo, N. F., & Denmark, F. L. (1987). Contributions of women to psychology. *Annual Review of Psychology, 38,* 279–298.

Rutherford, A. (2000). Radical behaviorism and psychology's public: B. F. Skinner in the popular press, 1934–1990. *History of Psychology, 3,* 371–395.

Rutherford, W. (1886). A new theory of hearing. *Journal of Anatomy and Physiology, 21,* 166–168.

Rutter, M. (2006). *Genes and behavior: Nature-nurture interplay explained.* Maiden, MA: Blackwell Publishing.

Rutter, M. (2007). Gene-environment interdependence. *Developmental Science, 10*(1), 12–18. doi:10.1111/j.1467-7687.2007.00557.x

Ryckeley, R. (2005, May). Don't send in the clowns. *The Citizen.*

Ryder, R. D. (2006). Speciesism in the laboratory. In P. Singer (Ed.), *In defense of animals: The second wave* (pp. 87–103). Malden, MA: Blackwell Publishing.

Ryff, C. D., & Singer, B. H. (2008). Know thyself and become what you are: A eudaimonic approach to psychological well-being. *Journal of Happiness Studies, 9,* 13–39.

Sabanayagam, C., & Shankar, A. (2010). Sleep duration and cardiovascular disease: Results from the National Health Interview Survey. *Sleep: Journal of Sleep and Sleep Disorders Research, 33*(8), 1037–1042.

Sack, A. T., & Linden, D. E. J. (2003). Combining transcranial magnetic stimulation and functional imaging in cognitive brain research: Possibilities and limitations. *Brain Research Reviews, 43*(1), 41–56.

Sack, A. T., Hubl, D., Prvulovic, D. , Formisano, E., Jandl, M., Zanella, F. E., Maurer, K., Goebel, R., Dierks, T., & Linden, D. E. J. (2002). The experimental combination of r TMS and fMRI reveals the functional relevance of parietal cortex for visuospatial functions. *Cognitive Brain Resarch., 13,* 85–93.

Sackeim, H. A., Dillingham, F. M., Prudic, J., Cooper, T., McCall, W. V., Rosenquist, P., et al. (2009). Effect of concomitant pharmacotherapy on electroconvulsive therapy outcomes: Short-term efficacy and adverse effects. *Archives of General Psychiatry, 66*(7), 729–737.

Sackeim, H. A., Haskett, R. F., Mulsant, B. H., Thase, M. E., Mann, J. J., Pettinati, H. M., Greenberg, R. M., Crowe, R. R., Cooper, T. B., & Prudic, J. (2001). Continuation pharmacotherapy in the prevention of relapse following electroconvulsive therapy: A randomized controlled trial. *Journal of the American Medical Association, 285,* 1299–1307.

Sackeim, H. A., Prudic, J., Fuller, R., Keilp, J., Lavori, P. W., & Olfson, M. (2007). The cognitive effects of electroconvulsive therapy in community settings. *Neuropsychopharmacology, 32,* 244–254.

Sackett, P. R., & DeVore, C. J. (2001). Counterproductive behaviors at work. In In N. Anderson, D. S. Ones, H. K. Sinangil, & C. Viswesvaran (Eds.), *Handbook of industrial, work and organizational psychology* (pp. 145–165). Thousand Oaks, CA: Sage.

Sackett, P. R., & Laczo, R. M. (2003). Job and work analysis. In W. C. Borman, D. R. Ilgen, & R. J. Klimoski (Eds.), *Handbook of psychology, Vol. 12: Industrial and organizational psychology* (pp. 21–37). New York, NY: Wiley.

Sacks, O. (1987). *The man who mistook his wife for a hat.* New York, NY: Harper & Row.

Sadker, M., & Sadker, D. (1994). *Failing at fairness: How America's schools cheat girls.* New York, NY: Scribners.

Sadler, J. Z. (2005). *Values and psychiatric diagnosis.* New York, NY: Oxford University Press.

Sagie, A. (1997). Leader direction and employee participation in decision making: Contradictory or compatible practices? *Applied Psychology: An International Review, 46(4),* 387–452.

Saks, A. M. (2006). Multiple predictions and criteria of job search success. *Journal of Vocational Behavior, 68,* 400–415.

Sala, J. B., & Courtney, S. M. (2007). Binding of what and where during working memory maintenance. *Cortex, 43,* 5–21.

Salgado, J. F., Viswesvaran, C., & Ones, D. (2003). Predictors used for personnel selection: An overview of constructs, methods and techniques. In N. Anderson, D. S. Ones, H. K. Sinangil, & C. Viswesvaran (Eds.), *Handbook of industrial, work and organizational psychology* (pp. 166–199). Thousand Oaks, CA: Sage.

Salmon, P., Sephton, S., Weissbecker, I., Hoover, K., Ulmer, C., & Studts, J. L. (2004). Mindfulness mediation in clinical practice. *Cognitive and Behavioral Practice, 11,* 434–446.

Salthouse, T. A. (1996). The processing-speed theory of adult age differences in cognition. *Psychological Review, 103,* 403–428.

Salthouse, T. A. (2000). Aging and measures of processing speed. *Biological Psychology, 54,* 35–54.

Salthouse, T. A. (2003). Memory aging from 18–80. *Alzheimer Disease & Associated Disorders, 17*(3), 162–167.

Salthouse, T. A. (2004). What and when of cognitive aging. *Current Directions in Psychological Science, 13*(4), 140–144.

Salthouse, T. A. (2005). Time as a factor in the development and decline of mental processes. In A.-N. Perret-Clermont (Ed.), *Thinking time: A multidisciplinary perspective on time.* Ashland, OH: Hogrefe & Huber Publishers.

Salthouse, T. A. (2006). Mental exercise and mental aging. *Perspectives on Psychological Science, 1,* 68–87.

Salvy, S., Jarrin, D., Paluch, R., Irfan, N., & Pliner, P. (2007). Effects of social influence on eating in couples, friends and strangers. *Appetite, 49*(1), 92–99. doi:10.1016/j.appet.2006.12.004

Samberg, E., & Marcus, E. R. (2005). Process, resistance, and interpretation. In E. S. Person, A. M. Cooper, & G. O. Gabbard (Eds.), *Textbook of psychoanalysis* (pp. 229–240). Washington, DC: American Psychiatric Publishing.

Samnaliev, M., & Clark, R. E. (2008). The economics of schizophrenia. In K. T. Mueser & D. V. Jeste (Eds.), *Clinical handbook of schizophrenia* (pp. 25–34). New York, NY: Guilford Press.

Sanders, M. H., & Givelber, R. J. (2006). Overview of obstructive sleep apnea in adults. In T. Lee-Chiong (Ed.), *Sleep: A comprehensive handbook.* Hoboken, NJ: Wiley-Liss.

Sandin, B., Chorot, P., Santed, M. A., & Valiente, R. M. (2004). Differences in negative life events between patients with anxiety disorders, depression and hypochondriasis. *Anxiety, Stress & Coping: An International Journal, 17*(1), 37–47.

Sandoval, T. C., Gollan, T. H., Ferreira, V. S., & Salmon, D. P. (2010). What causes the bilingual disadvantage in verbal fluency? The dual-task analogy. *Bilingualism: Language and Cognition, 13*(2), 231–252. doi:10.1017/S1366728909990514

Sandrini, M., & Manenti, R. (2009). Transcranial magnetic stimulation as a tool for cognitive studies. *Giornale Italiano di Psicologia, 36*(2), 347–372.

Sanger, D. J. (2004). The pharmacology and mechanisms of action of new generation, nonbenzodiazepine hypnotic agents. *CNS Drugs, 18*(Suppl1), 9–15.

Sanislow, C. A., & Carson, R. C. (2001). Schizophrenia: A critical examination. In P. B. Sutker & H. E. Adams (Eds.), *Comprehensive handbook of psychopathology* (3rd ed., pp. 403–444). New York, NY: Kluwer Academic/Plenum.

Sanna, L. J., & Schwarz, N. (2006). Metacognitive experiences and human judgment: The case of hindsight bias and its debiasing. *Current Directions in Psychological Science, 15,* 172–176.

Saper, C. B. (2000). Brain stem, reflexive behavior, and the cranial nerves. In E. R. Kandel, J. H. Schwartz, & T. M. Jessell (Eds.), *Principles of neural science* (pp. 873–888). New York, NY: McGraw-Hill.

Sapolsky, R. M. (2007). Stress, stress-related disease, and emotion regulation. In J. J. Gross (Ed.), *Handbook of emotion regulation.* New York, NY: Guilford Press.

Saraceno, B. (2009). Psychiatry as a worldwide public health problem. In M. C. Gelder, N. C. Andreasen, J. J. López-Ibor, Jr., & J. R. Geddes (Eds.). *New Oxford textbook of psychiatry* (2nd ed., Vol. 1). New York, NY: Oxford University Press.

Sartorius, A., Kiening, K. L., Kirsch, P., von Gall, C. C., Haberkorn, U., Unterberg, A. W., et al. (2010). Remission of major depression under deep brain stimulation of the lateral habenula in a therapy-refractory patient. *Biological Psychiatry, 67*(2), e9–e11. doi:10.1016/j.biopsych.2009.08.027

Sato, T., Namiki, H., Ando, J., & Hatano, G. (2004). Japanese conception of and research on intelligence. In R. J. Sternberg (Ed.), *International handbook of intelligence* (pp. 302–324). New York, NY: Cambridge University Press.

Saunders, C. D. (2003). The emerging field of conservation psychology. *Human Ecology Review, 10,* 137–149.

Sauro, K. M., & Becker, W. J. (2009). The stress and migraine interaction. *Headache: The Journal of Head and Face Pain, 49*(9), 1378–1386. doi:10.1111/j.1526-4610.2009.01486

Savage-Rumbaugh, S. (1991). Language learning in the bonobo: How and why they learn. In N. A. Krasnegor, D. M. Rumbaugh, & R. L. Schiefelbusch/ M. Studdert-Kennedy (Eds.), *Biological and behavioral determinants of language development.* Hillsdale, N.J.: Erlbaum.

Savage-Rumbaugh, S., Rumbaugh, D. M., & Fields, W. M. (2006). Language as a window on rationality. In S. Hurley & M. Nudds (Eds.), *Rational animals?* (pp. 513–552). New York, NY: Oxford University Press.

Savage-Rumbaugh, S., Rumbaugh, D. M., & Fields, W. M. (2009). Empirical Kanzi: The ape language controversy revisited. *Skeptic, 15*(1), 25–33.

Savage-Rumbaugh, S., Shanker, S. G., & Taylor, T. J. (1998). *Apes, language, and the human mind.* New York, NY: Oxford University Press.

Savin-Williams, R. C. (2006). Who's gay? Does it matter? *Current Directions in Psychological Science, 15,* 40–44.

Saxe, L. (1994). Detection of deception: Polygraph and integrity tests. *Current Directions in Psychological Science, 3,* 69–73.

Sayer, L. C. (2005). Gender, time, and inequality: Trends in women's and men's paid work, unpaid work, and free time. *Social Forces, 84,* 285–303.

Sayette, M. A. (2007). Alcohol and stress: Social and psychological aspects. In G. Fink (Ed.), *Encyclopedia of stress.* San Diego: Elsevier.

Scarr, S. (1991). *Theoretical issues in investigating intellectual plasticity.* S. E. Brauth, W. S. Hall, & R. Dooling (Eds.), *Plasticity of development.* Cambridge, MA: MIT Press.

Scarr, S., & Weinberg, R. A. (1977). Intellectual similarities within families of both adopted and biological children. *Intelligence, 32,* 170–190.

Scarr, S., & Weinberg, R. A. (1983). The Minnesota adoption studies: Genetic differences and malleability. *Child Development, 54,* 260–267.

Schachner, D. A., & Shaver, P. R. (2004). Attachment dimensions and sexual motives. *Personal Relationships, 11*(2), 179–195.

Schachter, S. (1959). *The psychology of affiliation.* Stanford, CA: Stanford University Press.

Schachter, S. (1964). The interaction of cognitive and physiological determinants of emotional state. In L. Berkowitz (Ed.), *Advances in experimental social psychology* (Vol. 1). New York, NY: Academic Press.

Schachter, S. (1968). Obesity and eating. *Science, 161*(3843), 751–756. doi:10.1126/science.161.3843 .751

Schachter, S. (1971). *Emotion, obesity, and crime.* New York, NY: Academic Press.

Schachter, S., & Singer, J. E. (1962). Cognitive, social and physiological determinants of emotional state. *Psychological Review, 69,* 379–399.

Schachter, S., & Singer, J. E. (1979). Comments on the Maslach and Marshall-Zimbardo experiments. *Journal of Personality and Social Psychology, 37,* 989–995.

Schacter, D. L. (1996). *Searching for memory: The brain, the mind, and the past.* New York, NY: Basic Books.

Schacter, D. L. (1999). The seven sins of memory: Insights from psychology and cognitive neuroscience. *American Psychologist, 54,* 182–203.

Schacter, D. L. (2001). *The seven sins of memory: How the mind forgets and remembers.* Boston, MA: Houghton Mifflin.

Schacter, D. L., Wagner, A. D., & Buckner, R. L. (2000). Memory systems of 1999. In E. Tulving & F. I. M. Craik (Eds.), *Oxford handbook of memory.* New York, NY: Oxford University Press.

Schaeffer, N. C. (2000). Asking questions about threatening topics: A selective overview. In A. A. Stone, J. S. Turkkan, C. A. Bachrach, J. B. Jobe, H. S. Kurtzman, & V. Cain (Eds.), *The science of self-report: Implications for research and practice.* Mahwah, NJ: Erlbaum.

Schafe, G. E., & Bernstein, I. L. (1996). Taste aversion learning. In E. D. Capaldi (Ed.), *Why we eat what we eat: The psychology of eating* (pp. 31–51). doi:10.1037/10291-002

Schaffer, A. (2008, August 11). Prescriptions for health, the environmental kind. *New York Times*, Health section. Retrieved from http://www.nytimes.com/2008/08/12/health/12clin.html?_r=1&scp=1&sq=environmental%20health%20clinic&st=cse

Schaie, K. W. (1990). Intellectual development in adulthood. In J. E. Birren & K. W. Schaie (Eds.), *Handbook of the psychology of aging* (3rd ed.). San Diego: Academic Press.

Schaie, K. W. (1994). The course of adult intellectual development. *American Psychologist, 49,* 304–313.

Schaie, K. W. (1996). *Adult intellectual development: The Seattle longitudinal study*. New York, NY: Cambridge University Press.

Schaie, K. W. (2005). *Developmental influences on adult intelligence: The Seattle longitudinal study*. New York, NY: Oxford University Press.

Schalock, R. L., Luckasson, R. A., Shogren, K. A., Borthwick-Duffy, S., Bradley, V., Buntinx, W. H. E., et al. (2007). The renaming of mental retardation: Understanding the change to the term intellectual disability. *Intellectual and Developmental Disabilities, 45,* 116–124.

Schaufeli, W. B., Leiter, M. P., & Maslach, C. (2009). Burnout: 35 years of research and practice. *The Career Development International, 14*(3), 204–220. doi:10.1108/13620430910966406

Schellenberg, E. (2004). Music lessons enhance IQ. *Psychological Science*, 15(8), 511–514. doi:10.1111/j.0956-7976.2004.00711.x

Schellenberg, E. (2005). Music and cognitive abilities. *Current Directions in Psychological Science, 14*(6), 317–320. doi:10.1111/j.0963-7214.2005.00389.x

Schellenberg, E. (2006). Long-term positive associations between music lessons and IQ. *Journal of Educational Psychology, 98*(2), 457–468. doi:10.1037/0022-0663.98.2.457

Scherer, K. R., & Wallbott, H. G. (1994). Evidence for universality and cultural variation of differential emotion response patterning. *Journal of Personality and Social Psychology, 66,* 310–328.

Schieber, F. (2006). Vision and aging. In J. E. Birren & K. W. Schaie (Eds.), *Handbook of the psychology of aging*. San Diego: Academic Press.

Schiff, M., & Lewontin, R. (1986). *Education and class: The irrelevance of IQ genetic studies*. Oxford: Clarendon Press.

Schiffman, J., Ekstrom, M., LaBrie, J., Schulsinger, F., Sorenson, H., & Mednick, S. (2002). Minor physical anomalies and schizophrenia spectrum disorders: A prospective investigation. *American Journal of Psychiatry, 159,* 238–243.

Schiffman, S. S., Graham, B. G., Sattely-Miller, E. A., & Warwick, Z. S. (1998). Orosensory perception of dietary fat. *Current Directions in Psychological Science, 7,* 137–143.

Schimmack, U., & Crites, S. L. (2005). The structure of affect. In D. Albarracin, B. T. Johnson, & M. P. Zanna (Eds.), *The handbook of attitudes*. Mahwah, NJ: Erlbaum.

Schirillo, J. A. (2010). Gestalt approach. In E. B. Goldstein (Ed.), *Encyclopedia of perception*. Thousand Oaks, CA: Sage.

Schlapobersky, J., & Pines, M. (2009). Group methods in adult psychiatry. In M. C. Gelder, N. C. Andreasen, J. J. López-Ibor, Jr., & J. R. Geddes (Eds.), *New Oxford textbook of psychiatry* (2nd ed., Vol. 1). New York, NY: Oxford University Press.

Schlegel, A., & Barry, H., III. (1991). *Adolescence: An anthropological inquiry*. New York, NY: Free Press.

Schlinger, H., & Blakely, E. (1994). The effects of delayed reinforcement and a response-produced auditory stimulus on the acquisition of operant behavior in rats. *Psychological Record, 44,* 391–410.

Schmader, T. (2010). Stereotype threat deconstructed. *Current Directions in Psychological Science, 19*(1), 14–18. doi:10.1177/0963721409359292

Schmeichel, B. J., Gailliot, M. T., Filardo, E., McGregor, I., Gitter, S., & Baumeister, R. F. (2009). Terror management theory and self-esteem revisited: The roles of implicit and explicit self-esteem in mortality salience effects. *Journal of Personality and Social Psychology, 96*(5), 1077–1087. doi:10.1037/a0015091

Schmid, M. S. (2010). Languages at play: The relevance of L1 attrition to the study of bilingualism. *Bilingualism: Language and Cognition, 13*(1), 1–7. doi:10.1017/S1366728909990368

Schmidt, F. L. (2002). The role of general cognitive ability and job performance: Why there cannot be a debate. *Human Performance, 15,* 187–210.

Schmidt, F. L., & Hunter, J. (2004). General mental ability in the world of work: Occupational attainment and job performance. *Journal of Personality and Social Psychology, 86,* 162–173.

Schmidt, N. B., Zvolensky, M. J., & Maner, J. K. (2006). Anxiety sensitivity: Prospective prediction of panic attacks and Axis I pathology. *Journal of Psychiatric Research, 40,* 691–699.

Schmitt, D. P. (2005). Fundamentals of human mating strategies. In D. M. Buss (Ed.), *The handbook of evolutionary psychology*. New York, NY: Wiley.

Schmitt, D. P., & International Sexuality Description Project. (2003). Universal sex differences in the desire for sexual variety: Tests from 52 nations, 6 continents, and 13 islands. *Journal of Personality and Social Psychology, 85,* 85–104.

Schmitt, D. P., Realo, A., Voracek, M., & Allik, J. (2008). Why can't a man be more like a woman? Sex differences in Big Five personality traits across 55 cultures. *Journal of Personality and Social Psychology, 94*(1), 168–182. doi:10.1037/0022-3514.94.1.168

Schmitt, M. T., & Maes, J. (2002). Stereotypic ingroup bias as self-defense against relative deprivation: Evidence from a longitudinal study of the German unification process. *European Journal of Social Psychology, 32,* 309–326.

Schmitt, N., Cortina, J. M., Ingerick, M. J., & Wiechmann, D. (2003). Personnel selection and employee performance. In W. C. Borman, D. R. Ilgen, & R. J. Klimoski (Eds.), *Handbook of psychology, Vol. 12: Industrial and organizational psychology* (pp. 77–105). New York, NY: Wiley.

Schmitz, J. M., & DeLaune, K. A. (2005). Nicotine. In J. H. Lowinson, P. Ruiz, R. B. Millman, & J. G. Langrod (Eds.), *Substance abuse: A comprehensive textbook*. Philadelphia, PA: Lippincott/Williams & Williams.

Schmolck, H., Buffalo, E. A., & Squire, L. R. (2000). Memory distortions develop over time: Recollections of the O. J. Simpson trial verdict after 15 and 32 months. *Psychological Science, 11,* 39–45.

Schmuck, P., & Schultz, P. W. (2002). Sustainable development as a challenge for psychology. In P. Schmuck & W. P. Schultz (Eds.), *Psychology of sustainable development* (pp. 3–17). Boston, MA: Kluwer Academic Publishers.

Schnittker, J. (2008). An uncertain revolution: Why the rise of a genetic model of mental illness has not increased tolerance. *Social Science & Medicine, 67*(9), 1370–1381. doi:10.1016/j.socscimed.2008.07.007

Schnoll, R., Martinez, E., Tatum, K., Glass, M., Bernath, A., Ferris, D., & Reynolds, P. (2011). Increased self-efficacy to quit and perceived control over withdrawal symptoms predict smoking cessation following nicotine dependence treatment. *Addictive Behaviors, 36*(1–2), 144–147.

Scholey, A. B., Parrott, A. C., Buchanan, T., Heffernan, T. M., Ling, J., & Rodgers, J. (2004). Increased intensity of Ecstasy and polydrug usage in the more experienced recreational Ecstasy/MDMA users: A WWW study. *Addictive Behaviors, 29,* 743–752.

Scholz, J., & Woolf, C. J. (2002). Can we conquer pain? *Nature Neuroscience, Supplement 5,* 1062–1067.

Schooler, C. (2007). Use it—and keep it, longer, probably: A reply to Salthouse. *Perspectives on Psychological Science, 2,* 24–29.

Schooler, J. W., & Fiore, S. M. (1997). Consciousness and the limits of language: You can't always say what you think or think what you say. In J. D. Cohen & J. W. Schooler (Eds.), *Scientific approaches to consciousness*. Mahwah, NJ: Erlbaum.

Schrag, R. D. A., Styfco, S. J., & Zigler, E. (2004). Familiar concept, new name: Social competence. In E. Zigler & S. J. Styfco (Eds.), *The Head Start debate*. Baltimore: Paul H. Brookes Publishing.

Schramm, D. G., Marshall, J. P., Harris, V. W., & Lee, T. R. (2005). After "I do": The newlywed transition. *Marriage and Family Review, 38,* 45–67.

Schredl, M. (2009). Nightmares. In R. Stickgold & M. P. Walker (Eds.), *The neuroscience of sleep* (pp. 140–145). San Diego, CA: Academic Press.

Schreiber, F. R. (1973). *Sybil*. New York, NY: Warner.

Schultz, J. H., & Luthe, W. (1959). *Autogenic training*. New York, NY: Grune & Stratton.

Schultz, P. W. (2000). Empathizing with nature: The effects of perspective taking on concern for environmental issues. *Journal of Social Issues, 56,* 391–406.

Schultz, P. W. (2001). The structure of environmental concern: Concern for self, other people, and the biosphere. *Journal of Environmental Psychology,* 21, 1–13.

Schultz, P. W., Gouveia, V. V., Cameron, L. D., Tankha, G., Schmuck, P., & Franek, M. (2005). Values and their relationship to environmental concern and conservation behavior. *Journal of Cross-Cultural Psychology, 36,* 457–475.

Schulz-Hardt, S., Frey, D., Luethgens, C., & Moscovici, S. (2000). Biased information search in group decision making. *Journal of Personality & Social Psychology, 78,* 655–669.

Schuman, H., & Kalton, G. (1985). Survey methods. In G. Lindzey & E. Aronson (Eds.), *Handbook of social psychology* (3rd ed.). New York, NY: Random House.

Schusterman, R. J., & Gisiner, R. (1988). Artificial language comprehension in dolphins and sea lions: The essential cognitive skills. *Psychological Record, 38,* 311–348.

Schwartz, B. (2004). *The paradox of choice: Why more is less*. New York, NY: Ecco.

Schwartz, B. L. (1999). Sparkling at the end of the tongue: The etiology of tip-of-the-tongue phenomenology. *Psychonomic Bulletin & Review, 6,* 379–393.

Schwartz, B. L., Travis, D. M., Castro, A. M., & Smith, S. M. (2000). The phenomenology of real and illusory tip-of-the-tongue states. *Memory & Cognition, 28,* 18–27.

Schwartz, G. L., & Azzara, A. V. (2004). Sensory neurobiological analysis of neuropeptide modulation of meal size. *Physiology & Behavior , 82,* 81–87.

Schwartz, M. W., Peskind, E., Raskind, M., Nicolson, M., Moore, J., Morawiecki, A., Boyko, E. J., & Porte, D. J. (1996). Cerebrospinal fluid leptin levels: Relationship to plasma levels and to adiposity in humans. *Nature Medicine, 2,* 589–593.

Schwartz, M. W., Woods, S. C., Porte, D., Seeley, R. J., & Baskin, D. G. (2000). Central nervous system control of food intake. *Nature, 404,* 661–671.

Schwartz, S. H. (1990). Individualism-collectivism: Critique and proposed refinements. *Journal of Cross-Cultural Psychology, 21,* 139–157.

Schwarz, N. (1999). Self-reports: How the questions shape the answers. *American Psychologist, 54,* 93–105.

Schwarz, N., & Strack, F. (1999). Reports of subjective well-being: Judgmental processes and their methodological implications. In D. Kahneman, E. Diener, & N. Schwarz (Eds.), *Well-being: The foundations of hedonic psychology*. New York, NY: Russell Sage Foundation.

Schwarz, T. L. (2008). Release of neurotransmitters. In L. Squire, D. Berg, F. Bloom, S. Du Lac, A. Ghosh, & N. Spitzer (Eds.), *Fundamental neuroscience* (3rd ed., pp. 157–180). San Diego, CA: Elsevier.

Scoboria, A., Mazzoni, G., Kirsch, I., & Milling, L. S. (2002). Immediate and persisting effects of misleading questions and hypnosis on memory reports. *Journal of Experimental Psychology: Applied, 8*(1), 26–32. doi:10.1037/1076-898X.8.1.26

Scott, K. (2008). Chemical senses: Taste and olfaction. In L. Squire, D. Berg, F. Bloom, S. du Lac, A. Ghosh, & N. Spitzer (Eds.), *Fundamental Neuroscience*. San Diego: Elsevier.

Scott, V., McDade, D. M., & Luckman, S. M. (2007). Rapid changes in the sensitivity of arcuate nucleus neurons to central ghrelin in relation to feeding status. *Physiology & Behavior, 90,* 180–185.

Scoville, W. B., & Milner, B. (1957). Loss of recent memory after bilateral hippocampal lesions. *Journal of Neurology, Neurosurgery & Psychiatry, 20,* 11–21.

Scull, A. (1990). Deinstitutionalization: Cycles of despair. *The Journal of Mind and Behavior, 11*(3/4), 301–312.

Scully, J. A., Tosi, H., & Banning, K. (2000). Life event checklists: Revisiting the social readjustment rating scale after 30 years. *Educational & Psychological Measurement, 60,* 864–876.

Searle, A., & Bennett, P. (2001). Psychological factors and inflammatory bowel disease: A review of a decade of literature. *Psychology, Health and Medicine, 6,* 121–135.

Searleman, A. (1996). Personality variables and prospective memory performance. In D. J. Herrmann, C. McEvoy, C. Hertzog, P. Hertel, & M. K. Johnson (Eds.), *Basic and applied memory research: Practical applications* (Vol. 2). Mahwah, NJ: Erlbaum.

Searleman, A., & Herrmann, D. (1994). *Memory from a broader perspective*. New York, NY: McGraw-Hill.

Searles, H. F. (1960). *The nonhuman environment in normal development and schizophrenia*. New York, NY: International Universities Press.

Sears, D. O. (1975). Political socialization. In F. I. Greenstein & N. W. Polsby (Eds.), *Handbook of political science* (Vol. 2). Reading, MA: Addison-Wesley.

Sears, D. O. (1986). College sophomores in the laboratory: Influences of a narrow database on social psychology's view of human nature. *Journal of Personality and Social Psychology, 51,* 515–530.

Seery, M. D., Holman, E., & Silver, R. (2010). Whatever does not kill us: Cumulative lifetime adversity, vulnerability, and resilience. *Journal of Personality and Social Psychology, 99*(6), 1025–1041. doi:10.1037/a0021344

Segall, M. H., Campbell, D. T., Herskovits, M. J. (1966). *The influence of culture on visual perception*. Indianapolis: Bobbs-Merrill.

Segall, M. H., Dasen, P. R., Berry, J. W., & Poortinga, Y. H. (1990). *Human behavior in global perspective: An introduction to cross-cultural psychology*. New York, NY: Pergamon Press.

Segerstrom, S. C., & Roach, A. R. (2008). On the physical health benefits of self-enhancement. In E. C. Chang (Ed.), *Self-criticism and self-enhancement: Theory, research, and clinical implications* (pp. 37–54). Washington, DC: American Psychological Association. doi:10.1037/11624-003

Segerstrom, S. C., & Sephton, S. E. (2010). Optimistic expectancies and cell-mediated immunity: The role of positive affect. *Psychological Science, 21*(3), 448–455. doi:10.1177/0956797610362061

Seifer, R. (2001). Socioeconomic status, multiple risks, and development of intelligence. In R. J. Sternberg & E. L. Grigorenko (Eds.), *Environmental effects on cognitive abilities* (pp. 59–82). Mahwah, NJ: Erlbaum.

Self, D. W. (1997). Neurobiological adaptations to drug use. *Hospital Practice, April,* 5–9.

Seligman, M. E. P. (1971). Phobias and preparedness. *Behavior Therapy, 2,* 307–321.

Seligman, M. E. P. (1974). Depression and learned helplessness. In R. J. Friedman & M. M. Katz (Eds.), *The psychology of depression: Contemporary theory and research*. New York, NY: Wiley.

Seligman, M. E. P. (1990). *Learned optimism*. New York, NY: Pocket Books.

Seligman, M. E. P. (1992). *Helplessness: On depression, development, and death*. New York, NY: Freeman.

Seligman, M. E. P. (1995). The effectiveness of psychotherapy. *American Psychologist, 50,* 965–974.

Seligman, M. E. P. (2003). The past and future of positive psychology. In C. L. M. Keyes & J. Haidt (Eds.), *Flourishing: Positive psychology and the life well-lived*. Washington, DC: American Psychological Association.

Seligman, M. E. P., & Csikszentmihalyi, M. (2000). Positive psychology: An introduction. *American Psychologist, 55,* 5–14.

Seligman, M. E. P., & Hager, J. L. (1972, August). Biological boundaries of learning (The sauce béarnaise syndrome). *Psychology Today,* pp. 59–61, 84–87.

Seligman, M. E. P., Rashid, T., & Parks, A. C. (2006). Positive psychotherapy. *American Psychologist, 61,* 774–788.

Selye, H. (1936). A syndrome produced by diverse nocuous agents. *Nature, 138,* 32.

Selye, H. (1956). *The stress of life*. New York, NY: McGraw-Hill.

Selye, H. (1973). The evolution of the stress concept. *American Scientist, 61*(6), 672–699.

Selye, H. (1974). *Stress without distress*. New York, NY: Lippincott.

Semmer, N. K., McGrath, J. E., & Beehr, T. A. (2005). Conceptual issues in research on stress and health. In C. L. Cooper (Ed.), *Handbook of stress medicine and health*. Boca Raton, FL: CRC Press.

Sen, S., Burmeister, M., & Ghosh, D. (2004). Meta-analysis of the association between a serotonin transporter promoter polymorphism (5-HTTLPR) and anxiety-related personality traits. *American Journal of Medical Genetics, 127B*(1), 85–89.

Senior, C., Thomson, K., Badger, J., & Butler, M. J. R. (2007). Interviewing strategies in the face of beauty: A psychophysiological investigation into the job negotiation process. *Annals of the New York Academy of Sciences, 1118,* 142–162.

Serpell, R. (2000). Intelligence and culture. In R. J. Sternberg (Ed.), *Handbook of intelligence*. Cambridge, UK: Cambridge University Press.

Seta, J. J., Seta, C. E., & McElroy, T. (2002). Strategies for reducing the stress of negative life experiences: An average/summation analysis. *Personality and Social Psychology Bulletin, 28,* 1574–1585.

Sewell, R., Poling, J., & Sofuoglu, M. (2009). The effect of cannabis compared with alcohol on driving. *American Journal on Addictions, 18*(3), 185–193.

Shackelford, T. K., Schmitt, D. P., & Buss, D. M. (2005). Universal dimensions of human mate preferences. *Personality & Individual Differences, 39,* 447–458.

Shafir, E., & LeBoeuf, R. A. (2002). Rationality. *Annual Review of Psychology, 53,* 491–517.

Shafir, E., & LeBoeuf, R. A. (2004). Context and conflict in multiattribute choice. In D. J. Koehler & N. Harvey (Ed), *Blackwell handbook of judgment and decision making*. Malden, MA: Blackwell.

Shapiro, A. F., Gottman, J. M., & Carrère. (2000). The baby and marriage: Identifying factors that buffer against decline in marital satisfaction after the first baby arrives. *Journal of Family Psychology, 14,* 59–70.

Shapiro, D. H., Jr. (1984). Overview: Clinical and physiological comparison of meditation with other self-control strategies. In D. H. Shapiro, Jr., & R. N. Walsh (Eds.), *Meditation: Classic and contemporary perspectives*. New York, NY: Aldine.

Shapiro, D. H., Jr. (1987). Implications of psychotherapy research for the study of meditation. In M. A. West (Ed.), *The psychology of meditation*. Oxford: Clarendon Press.

Shapiro, J. R., & Neuberg, S. L. (2007). From stereotype threat to stereotype threats: Implications of a multi-threat framework for causes, moderators, mediators, consequences, and interventions. *Personality & Social Psychology Review, 11,* 107–130.

Sharpe, D., Adair, J. G., & Roese, N. J. (1992). Twenty years of deception research: A decline in subjects' trust? *Personality and Social Psychology Bulletin, 18,* 585–590.

Sharps, M. J., & Wertheimer, M. (2000). Gestalt perspectives on cognitive science and on experimental psychology. *Review of General Psychology, 4,* 315–336.

Shatz, C. J. (1992, September). The developing brain. *Scientific American,* 60–67.

Shaver, P. R., & Mikulincer, M. (2006). A behavioral systems approach to romantic love relationships: Attachment, caregiving, and sex. In R. J. Sternberg & K. Weis (Eds.), *The new psychology of love*. New Haven, CT: Yale University Press.

Shaver, P. R., & Mikulincer, M. (2009). Attachment styles. In M. R. Leary & R. H. Hoyle (Eds.), *Handbook of individual differences in social behavior* (pp. 62–81). New York, NY: Guilford Press.

Shaver, P. R., Schachner, D. A., & Mikulincer, M. (2005). Attachment style, excessive reassurance seeking, relationship processes, and depression. *Personality and Social Psychology Bulletin, 31*(3), 343–359.

Shavitt, S., Sanbonmatsu, D. M., Smittipatana, S., & Posavac, S. S. (1999). Broadening the conditions for illusory correlation formation: Implications for judging minority groups. *Basic & Applied Social Psychology, 21,* 263–279.

Shaw, J. S. I., McClure, K. A., & Dykstra, J. A. (2007). Eyewitness confidence from the witnessed event through trial. In M. P. Toglia, J. D. Read, D. F. Ross, & R. C. L. Lindsay (Eds.), *Handbook of eyewitness psychology: Vol. 1. Memory for events*. Mahwah, NJ: Erlbaum.

Shaw, W. S., & Dimsdale, J. E. (2007). Type A personality, type B personality. In G. Fink (Ed.), *Encyclopedia of stress*. San Diego: Elsevier.

Shea, A. K., & Steiner, M. (2008). Cigarette smoking during pregnancy. *Nicotine & Tobacco Research, 10,* 267–278.

Shearer, B. (2004). Multiple intelligences theory after 20 years. *Teachers College Record, 106*(1), 2–16.

Shedler, J. (2010). The efficacy of psychodynamic psychotherapy. *American Psychologist, 65*(2), 98–109. doi:10.1037/a0018378

Sheehan, S. (1982). *Is there no place on earth for me?* Boston, MA: Houghton Mifflin.

Sheldon, C. (2004). Social relationships and health. *American Psychologist, 59,* 676–684.

Sheldon, K. M., & Kasser, T. (2001). Goals, congruence, and positive well-being: New empirical support for humanistic theories. *Journal of Humanistic Psychology, 41*(1), 30–50.

Shelton, J. T., Elliott, E. M., Hill, B. D., Calamia, M. R., & Gouvier, W. (2009). A comparison of laboratory and clinical working memory tests and their prediction of fluid intelligence. *Intelligence, 37*(3), 283–293. doi:10.1016/j.intell.2008.11.005

Shelton, J. T., Elliott, E. M., Matthews, R. A., Hill, B. D., & Gouvier, W. (2010). The relationships of working memory, secondary memory, and general fluid intelligence: Working memory is special. *Journal of Experimental Psychology: Learning, Memory, and Cognition, 36*(3), 813–820. doi:10.1037/a0019046

Shenton, M. E., & Kubicki, M. (2009). Structural brain imaging in schizophrenia. In B. J. Sadock, V. A. Sadock, & P. Ruiz (Eds.), *Kaplan & Sadock's comprehensive textbook of psychiatry* (9th ed., Vol. 1, pp. 1494–1506). Philadelphia, PA: Lippincott, Williams & Wilkins.

Shepard, R. N. (1990). *Mind sights.* New York, NY: W. H. Freeman.

Shepherd, G. M. (2004). The human sense of smell: Are we better than we think? *PLoS Biology, 2*(5), 0572–0575. doi:10.1371/journal.pbio.0020146

Shepherd, G. M. (2008). Electronic properties of axons and dendrites. In L. Squire, D. Berg, F. Bloom, S. Du Lac, A. Ghosh, & N. Spitzer (Eds.), *Fundamental neuroscience* (3rd ed., pp. 87–111). San Diego, CA: Elsevier.

Shepperd, J. A., & McNulty, J. K. (2002). The affective consequences of expected and unexpected outcomes. *Psychological Science, 13,* 85–88.

Sher, L. (2003). Daily hassles, cortisol, and depression. *Australia and New Zealand Journal of Psychiatry, 37,* 383–384.

Sherif, M. (1936). *The psychology of social norms.* Oxford, England: Harper.

Sherif, M., Harvey, O., White, B., Hood, W., & Sherif, C. (1961). *Intergroup conflict and cooperation: The Robber's Cave experiment.* Norman: University of Oklahoma, Institute of Group Behavior.

Sherman, D. K., Nelson, L. D., & Ross, L. D. (2003). Naive realism and affirmative action: Adversaries are more similar than they think. *Basic and Applied Social Psychology, 25,* 275–289.

Sherman, M., & Key, C. B. (1932). The intelligence of isolated mountain children. *Child Development, 3,* 279–290.

Sherman, S. M. (2009). Thalamocortical relations. In G. G. Bernston & J. T. Cacioppo (Eds.), *Handbook of neuroscience for the behavioral sciences* (Vol. 1, pp. 201–223). New York, NY: Wiley, Inc.

Shermer, M. (1997). *Why people believe weird things: Pseudoscience, superstition, and other confusions of our time.* New York, NY: W. H. Freeman.

Shermer, M. (2004, March). None so blind. *Scientific American,* p. 42.

Shermer, M. (2008). Why you should be skeptical of brain scans. *Scientific American Mind, 19*(5), 66–71.

Sherry, D. F. (1992). Evolution and learning. In L. R. Squire (Ed.), *Encyclopedia of learning and memory.* New York, NY: Macmillan.

Shettleworth, S. J. (1998). *Cognition, evolution, and behavior.* New York, NY: Oxford University Press.

Shimamura, A. P., Berry, J. M., Mangels, J. A., Rusting, C. L., & Jurica, P. J. (1995). Memory and cognitive abilities in university professors: Evidence for successful aging. *Psychological Science, 6,* 271–277.

Shimp, T. A., Stuart, E. W., & Engle, R. W. (1991). A program of classical conditioning experiments testing variations in the conditioned stimulus and context. *Journal of Consumer Research, 18,* 1–12.

Shiue, Y., Chiu, C., & Chang, C. (2010). Exploring and mitigating social loafing in online communities. *Computers in Human Behavior, 26*(4), 768–777. doi:10.1016/j.chb.2010.01.014

Shneidman, E. S., Farberow, N. L., & Litman, R. E. (1994). *The psychology of suicide: A clinician's guide to evaluation and treatment.* Northvale, NJ: J. Aronson.

Shobe, K. K., & Schooler, J. W. (2001). Discovering fact and fiction: Case-based analyses of authentic and fabricated discovered memories of abuse. In G. M. Davies & T. Dalgleish (Eds.), *Recovered memories: Seeking the middle ground.* Chichester, England: Wiley.

Shrager, Y. & Squire, L. R. (2009). Medial temporal lobe function and human memory. In M. S. Gazzaniga (Eds.), *The cognitive neurosciences* (4th ed., pp. 675–690). Cambridge, MA: MIT Press.

Siebert, A., & Karr, M. (2003). *The adult student's guide to survival & success.* Portland, OR: Practical Psychology Press.

Siebner, H. R., Hartwigsen, G., Kassuba, T., & Rothwell, J. C. (2009). How does transcranial magnetic stimulation modify neuronal activity in the brain? Implications for studies of cognition. *Cortex: A Journal Devoted to the Study of the Nervous System and Behavior, 45*(9), 1035–1042. doi:10.1016/j.cortex.2009.02.007

Siegel, J. M. (2005). REM sleep. In M. H. Kryger, T. Roth, & W. C. Dement (Eds.). *Principles and practice of sleep medicine.* Philadelphia, PA: Elsevier Saunders.

Siegel, J. M. (2009). Sleep viewed as a state of adaptive inactivity. *Nature Reviews Neuroscience, 10*(10), 747–753. doi:10.1038/nrn2697

Siegel, M. (2007, August, 28). New Orleans still facing a psychiatric emergency. *The Globe and Mail* (Canada), p. A17.

Siegler, R. S. (2000). The rebirth of children's learning. *Child Development, 71*(1), 26–35. doi:10.1111/1467-8624.00115

Siegler, R. S., & Alibali, M. W. (2005). *Children's thinking.* Upper Saddle River, NJ: Prentice-Hall.

Sigel, I. E. (2004). Head Start—Revisiting a historical psychoeducational intervention: A revisionist perspective. In E. Zigler & S. J. Styfco (Eds.), *The Head Start debate.* Baltimore: Paul H. Brookes Publishing.

Signorielli, N. (2001). Television's gender role images and contribution to stereotyping: Past present future. In D. G. Singer & J. L. Singer (Eds.), *Handbook of children and the media.* Thousand Oaks, CA: Sage.

Silber, L. (2004). *Organizing from the right side of the brain: A creative approach to getting organized.* New York, NY: St. Martin's Press.

Silvanto, J., & Cattaneo, Z. (2010). Transcranial magnetic stimulation reveals the content of visual short-term memory in the visual cortex. *Neuroimage, 50*(4), 1683–1689.

Silver, E., Cirincion, C., & Steadman, H. J. (1994). Demythologizing inaccurate perceptions of the insanity defense. *Law & Human Behavior, 18,* 63–70.

Silver, H., Feldman, P., Bilker, W., & Gur, R. C. (2003). Working memory deficit as a core neuropsychological dysfunction in schizophrenia. *American Journal of Psychiatry, 160,* 1809–1816.

Silverman, I., & Choi, J. (2005). Locating places. In D. M. Buss (Ed.), *The handbook of evolutionary psychology.* New York, NY: Wiley.

Silverman, I., & Eals, M. (1992). Sex differences in spatial ability: Evolutionary theory and data. In J. Barkow, L. Cosmides, & J. Tooby (Eds.), *The adapted mind.* New York, NY: Oxford University Press.

Silverman, I., Choi, J., Mackewn, A., Fisher, M., Moro, J., & Olshansky, E. (2000). Evolved mechanisms underlying wayfinding: Further studies on the hunter-gatherer theory of spatial sex differences. *Evolution and Human Behavior, 21,* 201–213.

Silverman, I., & Phillips, K. (1998). The evolutionary psychology of spatial sex differences. In C. Crawford & D. L. Krebs (Eds.), *Handbook of evolutionary psychology: Ideas, issues, and applications.* Mahwah, NJ: Erlbaum.

Silverstein, L. B., & Auerbach, C. F. (1999). Deconstructing the essential father. *American Psychologist, 54,* 397–407.

Silvia, P. J. (2008). Another look at creativity and intelligence: Exploring higher-order models and probable confounds. *Personality and Individual Differences, 44,* 1012–1021.

Silvia, P. J., & Kaufman, J. C. (2010). Creativity and mental illness. In J. C. Kaufman & R. J. Sternberg (Eds.), *The Cambridge handbook of creativity* (pp. 381–394). New York, NY: Cambridge University Press.

Simeon, D., Loewenstein, R. J. (2009). Dissociative disorders. In B. J. Sadock, V. A. Sadock, & P. Ruiz (Eds.), *Kaplan & Sadock's comprehensive textbook of psychiatry* (9th ed., pp. 1965–2026). Philadelphia, PA: Lippincott, Williams & Wilkins.

Simmons, D. A. (1994). Urban children's preferences for nature: Lessons for environmental education. *Children's Environments, 11,* 194–203.

Simon, G. E., & Savarino, J. (2007). Suicide attempts among patients starting depression treatment with medications or psychotherapy. *American Journal of Psychiatry, 164,* 1029–1034.

Simon, G. E., Savarino, J., Operskalski, B., & Wang, P. S. (2006). Suicide risk during antidepressant treatment. *American Journal of Psychiatry, 163,* 41–47.

Simon, H. A. (1957). *Models of man.* New York, NY: Wiley.

Simon, H. A. (1974). How big is a chunk? *Science, 183,* 482–488.

Simon, H. A. (1992). Alternative representations for cognition: Search and reasoning. In H. L. Pick, Jr., P. Van Den Broek, & D. C. Knill (Eds.), *Cognition: Conceptual and methodological issues.* Washington, DC: American Psychological Association.

Simon, H. A., & Reed, S. K. (1976). Modeling strategy shifts in a problem-solving task. *Cognitive Psychology, 8,* 86–97.

Simon, R. I. (2005). Clinical-legal issues in psychiatry. In B. J. Sadock & V. A. Sadock (Eds.), *Kaplan & Sadock's comprehensive textbook of psychiatry.* Philadelphia, PA: Lippincott Williams & Wilkins.

Simon, R. I., & Shuman, D. W. (2008). Psychiatry and the law. In R. E. Hales, S. C. Yudofsky, & G. O. Gabbard (Eds.), *The American Psychiatric Publishing textbook of psychiatry* (5th ed. pp. 1555–1600). Washington, DC: American Psychiatric Publishing.

Simon, R. I., & Shuman, D. W. (2009). Clinical-legal issues in psychiatry. In B. J. Sadock, V. A. Sadock, & P. Ruiz (Eds.), *Kaplan & Sadock's comprehensive textbook of psychiatry* (9th ed., pp. 4427–4438). Philadelphia, PA: Lippincott, Williams & Wilkins.

Simons, D. K., & Chabris, C. F. (1999). Gorillas in our midst: Sustained inattentional blindness for dynamic events. *Perception, 28,* 1059–1074.

Simonsohn, U. (2009). Direct risk aversion: Evidence from risky prospects valued below their worst outcome. *Psychological Science, 20*(6), 686–692. doi:10.1111/j.1467-9280.2009.02349.x

Simonton, D. K. (1990). Creativity and wisdom in aging. In J. E. Birren & K. W. Schaie (Eds.), *Handbook of the psychology of aging.* San Diego: Academic Press.

Simonton, D. K. (1997). Creative productivity: A predictive and explanatory model of career trajectories and landmarks. *Psychological Review, 104,* 66–89.

Simonton, D. K. (1999a). Creativity and genius. In L. A. Pervin & O. John (Eds.), *Handbook of personality theory and research.* New York, NY: Guilford Press.

Simonton, D. K. (1999b). Talent and its development: An emergenic and epigenetic model. *Psychological Review, 106,* 435–457.

Simonton, D. K. (2001). Totally made, not at all born [Review of the book *The psychology of high abilities*]. *Contemporary Psychology, 46,* 176–179.

Simonton, D. K. (2003). Francis Galton's hereditary genius: Its place in the history and psychology of science. In R. J. Sternberg (Ed.), *The anatomy of impact: What makes the great works of psychology great* (pp. 3–18). Washington, DC: American Psychological Association.

Simonton, D. K. (2004). *Creativity in science: Chance, logic, genius, and Zeitgeist.* New York, NY: Cambridge University Press.

Simonton, D. K. (2005). Genetics of giftedness: The implications of an emergenic-epigenetic model. In R. J. Sternberg & J. E. Davidson (Eds.), *Conceptions of giftedness.* New York, NY: Cambridge University Press.

Simpson, J. L., & Jauniaux, E. (2007). Pregnancy loss. In S. G. Gabbe, J. R. Niebyl, & J. L. Simpson (Eds.) *Obstetrics: Normal and problem pregnancies* (5th ed., pp. 628–649). Philadelphia, PA: Elsevier.

Sinclair, D. (1981). *Mechanisms of cutaneous stimulation.* Oxford, England: Oxford University Press.

Sinclair, R. C., Hoffman, C., Mark, M. M., Martin, L. L., & Pickering, T. L. (1994). Construct accessibility and the misattribution of arousal: Schachter and Singer revisited. *Psychological Science, 5,* 15–19.

Sinclair, S., Dunn, R., & Lowery, B. S. (2005). The relationship between parental racial attitudes and children's implicit prejudice. *Journal of Experimental Social Psychology, 41,* 283–289.

Singer, L. T., Minnes, S., Short, E. , Arendt, R., Farkas, K., Lewis, B., Klein, N., Russ, S., Min, M. O., & Kirchner, H. L. (2004). Cognitive outcomes of preschool children with prenatal cocaine exposure. *Journal of the American Medical Association, 291,* 2448–2456.

Singer, W. (2007). Large-scale temporal coordination of cortical activity as a prerequisite for conscious experience. In M. Velmans & S. Schneider (Eds.), *The Blackwell companion to consciousness.* Malden, MA: Blackwell Publishing.

Singh, D., Dixson, B. J., Jessop, T. S., Morgan, B. B., & Dixson, A. F. (2010). Cross-cultural consensus for waist–hip ratio and women's attractiveness. *Evolution and Human Behavior, 31*(3), 176–181. doi:10.1016/j.evolhumbehav.2009.09.001

Sinha, D. (1983). Human assessment in the Indian context. In S. H. Irvine & J. W. Berry (Eds.), *Human assessment and cultural factors.* New York, NY: Plenum.

Sio, U., & Ormerod, T. C. (2009). Does incubation enhance problem solving? A meta-analytic review. *Psychological Bulletin, 135*(1), 94–120. doi:10.1037/a0014212

Sivertsen, B., Omvik, S., Pallesen, S., Bjorvatn, B., Havik, O. E., Kvale, G., et al. (2006). Cognitive behavioral therapy vs. Zopiclone for treatment of chronic primary insomnia in older adults: A randomized controlled trial. *Journal of the American Medical Association, 295,* 2851–2858.

SJB. (2006, March 6). Overcoming problem gambling [Why?]. Message posted to http://www.gamcare.org.uk/forum/index.php?tid=7193.

Skinner, A. E. G. (2001). Recovered memories of abuse: Effects on the individual. In G. M. Davies, & T. Dalgleish (Eds.), *Recovered memories: Seeking the middle ground.* Chichester, England: Wiley & Sons.

Skinner, B. F. (1938). *The behavior of organisms.* New York, NY: Appleton-Century-Crofts.

Skinner, B. F. (1945, October). Baby in a box: The mechanical baby-tender. *Ladies' Home Journal,* pp. 30–31, 135–136, 138.

Skinner, B. F. (1948). Superstition in the pigeon. *Journal of Experimental Psychology, 38,* 168–172. doi:10.1037/0096-3445.121.3.273

Skinner, B. F. (1953). *Science and human behavior.* New York, NY: Macmillan.

Skinner, B. F. (1957). *Verbal behavior.* New York, NY: Appleton-Century-Crofts.

Skinner, B. F. (1967). Autobiography. In E. G. Boring & G. Lindzey (Eds.), *A history of psychology in autobiography* (Vol. 5). New York, NY: Appleton-Century-Crofts.

Skinner, B. F. (1969). *Contingencies of reinforcement.* New York, NY: Appleton-Century-Crofts.

Skinner, B. F. (1971). *Beyond freedom and dignity.* New York, NY: Knopf.

Skinner, B. F. (1974). *About behaviorism.* New York, NY: Knopf.

Skinner, B. F. (1984). Selection by consequences. *Behavioral and Brain Sciences, 7*(4), 477–510.

Skinner, B. F. (1987). *Upon further reflection.* Englewood Cliffs, NJ: Prentice-Hall.

Skinner, B. F., Solomon, H. C., & Lindsley, O. R. (1953). *Studies in behavior therapy: Status report I.* Waltham, MA: Unpublished report, Metropolitan State Hospital.

Skitka, L., & Sargis, E. (2005). Social psychological research and the Internet: The promise and peril of a new methodological frontier. In Y. Amichai-Hamburger (Ed.), *The social net: Understanding human behavior in cyberspace* (pp. 1–26). New York, NY: Oxford University Press.

Skitka, L., & Sargis, E. G. (2006). The Internet as psychological laboratory. *Annual Review of Psychology, 57,* 529–555.

Slamecka, N. J. (1985). Ebbinghaus: Some associations. *Journal of Experimental Psychology: Learning, Memory and Cognition, 11,* 414–435.

Slamecka, N. J. (1992). Forgetting. In L. R. Squire (Ed.), *Encyclopedia of learning and memory.* New York, NY: Macmillan.

Slatcher, R. B., & Pennebaker, J. W. (2005). Emotional processing of traumatic events. In C. L. Cooper (Ed.), *Handbook of stress medicine and health.* Boca Raton, FL: CRC Press.

Slater, E., & Shields, J. (1969). Genetical aspects of anxiety. In M. H. Lader (Ed.), *Studies of anxiety.* Ashford, England: Headley Brothers.

Slaughter, M. (1990). The vertebrate retina. In K. N. Leibovic (Ed.), *Science of vision.* New York, NY: Springer-Verlag.

Slimak, M. W., & Dietz, T. (2006). Personal values, beliefs, and ecological risk perception. *Risk Analysis, 26,* 1689–1705.

Slobin, D. I. (1985). *The crosslinguistic study of language acquisition.* Hillsdale, NJ: Erlbaum.

Slobin, D. I. (1992). *The crosslinguistic study of language acquisition.* Hillsdale, NJ: Erlbaum.

Slovic, P. (1990). Choice. In D. N. Osherson & E. E. Smith (Eds.), *Thinking: An invitation to cognitive science* (Vol. 3). Cambridge, MA: MIT Press.

Slovic, P., Finucane, M. L., Peters, E., & MacGregor, D. G. (2004). Risk as analysis and risk as feelings: Some thoughts about affect, reason, risk, and rationality. *Risk Analysis, 24,* 311–322.

Slovic, P., & Fischhoff, B. (1977). On the psychology of experimental surprises. *Journal of Experimental Psychology: Human Perception and Performance, 3,* 544–551.

Slovic, P., Fischhoff, B., & Lichtenstein, S. (1982). Facts versus fears: Understanding perceived risk. In D. Kahneman, P. Slovic, & A. Tversky (Eds.), *Judgment under uncertainty: Heuristics and biases.* Cambridge, England: Cambridge University Press.

Slovic, P., Lichtenstein, S., & Fischhoff, B. (1988). Decision making. In R. C. Atkinson, R. J. Herrnstein, G. Lindzey, & R. D. Luce (Eds.), *Stevens' handbook of experimental psychology* (Vol. 2). New York, NY: Wiley.

Smedley, S. R., & Eisner, T. (1996). Sodium: A male moth's gift to its offspring. *Proceedings of the National Academy of Sciences, 93,* 809–813.

Smetana, J. G., Campione, B. N., & Metzger, A. (2006). Adolescent development in interpersonal and societal contexts. *Annual Review of Psychology, 57,* 255–284.

Smith, B. D. (2005). *Breaking through college reading.* New York, NY: Pearson Longman.

Smith, C. A., & Lazarus, R. S. (1993). Appraisal components, core relational themes, and the emotions. *Cognition and Emotion, 7,* 233–269.

Smith, C. A., Organ, D. W., & Near, J. P. (1983). Organizational citizenship behavior: Its nature and antecedents. *Journal of Applied Psychology, 68,* 653–663.

Smith, C. P. (1992). Reliability issues. In C. P. Smith (Ed.), *Motivation and personality: Handbook of thematic content analysis.* New York, NY: Cambridge University Press.

Smith, D. A. (1999). The end of theoretical orientations? *Applied & Preventative Psychology, 8,* 269–280.

Smith, D. V., & Margolskee, R. F. (2006). Making sense of taste. *Scientific American, 16*(3), 84–92.

Smith, F. J. (1977). Work attitudes as a predictor of attendance on a specific day. *Journal of Applied Psychology, 62,* 16–19.

Smith, G., Housen, P., Yaffe, K., Ruff, R., Kennison, R., Mahncke, H., & Zelinski, E. (2009). A cognitive training program based on principles of brain plasticity: Results from the Improvement in Memory with Plasticity-based Adaptive Cognitive Training (IMPACT) study. *Journal of the American Geriatrics Society, 57*(4), 594–603. doi:10.1111/j.1532-5415.2008.02167.x

Smith, G. T., Spillane, N. S., & Annus, A. M. (2006). Implications of an emerging integration of universal and culturally specific psychologies. *Perspectives on Psychological Science, 1,* 211–233.

Smith, J. C. (1975). Meditation and psychotherapy: A review of the literature. *Psychological Bulletin, 32,* 553–564.

Smith, J. C. (2007). The psychology of relaxation. In P. M. Lehrer, R. L. Woolfolk, & W. E. Sime (Eds.), *Principles and practice of stress management.* New York, NY. Guilford Press.

Smith, J. W., Positano, S., Stocks, N. & Shearman, D. (2009). *A new way of thinking about our climate crisis: The rational-comprehensive approach.* Lewiston, N.Y.: Edwin Mellen Press.

Smith, M. L., & Glass, G. V. (1977). Meta-analysis of psychotherapy outcome studies. *American Psychologist, 32,* 752–760.

Smith, M. R., Fogg, L. F., & Eastman, C. I. (2009). A compromise circadian phase position for permanent night work improves mood, fatigue, and performance. *Sleep: Journal of Sleep and Sleep Disorders Research, 32*(11), 1481–1489.

Smith, M. T., Perlis, M. L., Park, A., Smith, M. S., Pennington, J., Giles, D. E., & Buysse, D. J. (2002). Comparative meta-analysis of pharmacotherapy and behavior therapy for persistent insomnia. *American Journal of Psychiatry, 159,* 5–11.

Smith, P. B. (2001). Cross-cultural studies of social influence. In D. Matsumoto (Ed.), *The handbook of culture and psychology.* New York, NY: Oxford University Press.

Smith, P. B., & Bond, M. H. (1994). *Social psychology across cultures: Analysis and perspectives.* Boston, MA: Allyn & Bacon.

Smith, P. C., Kendall, L. M., & Hulin, C. L. (1969). *The measurement of satisfaction in work and retirement.* Chicago: Rand McNally.

Smith, S. (1988). Environmental context-dependent memory. In G. M. Davies & D. M. Thomson (Eds.), *Memory in context: Context in memory.* New York, NY: Wiley.

Smith, S. M. (1995). Getting into and out of mental ruts: A theory of fixation, incubation, and insight. In R. J. Sternberg & J. E. Davidson (Eds.), *The nature of insight* (pp. 229–251). Cambridge, MA: MIT Press.

Smith, S. M., & Gleaves, D. H. (2007). Recovered memories. In M. P. Toglia, J. D. Read, D. F. Ross, & R. C. L. Lindsay (Eds.), *Handbook of eyewitness psychology: Volume 1. Memory for events.* Mahwah, NJ: Erlbaum.

Smith, S. M., McIntosh, W. D., & Bazzini, D. G. (1999). Are the beautiful good in Hollywood? An investigation of the beauty-and-goodness stereotype on film. *Basic & Applied Social Psychology, 21,* 69–80.

Smith, T. W., & Gallo, L. C. (2001). Personality traits as risk factors for physical illness. In A. Baum, T. A. Revenson, & J. E. Singer (Eds.), *Handbook of health psychology* (pp. 139–174). Mahwah, NJ: Erlbaum.

Smolak, L., & Murnen, S. K. (2001). Gender and eating problems. In R. H. Striegel-Moore & L. Smolak (Eds.), *Eating disorders: Innovative directions in research and practice* (pp. 91–110). Washington, DC: American Psychological Association.

Smyth, J. M., & Pennebaker, J. W. (1999). Sharing one's story: Translating emotional experiences into words as a coping tool. In C. R. Snyder (Ed.), *Coping: The psychology of what works.* New York, NY: Oxford University Press.

Smyth, J. M., & Pennebaker, J. W. (2001). What are the health effects of disclosure? In A. Baum, T. A. Revenson & J. E. Singer (Eds.), *Handbook of health psychology* (pp. 339–348). Mahwah, NJ: Erlbaum.

Snedecor, S. M., Pomerleau, C. S., Mehringer, A. M., Ninowski, R., & Pomerleau, O. F. (2006). Differences in smoking-related variables based on phenylthiocabamide "taster" status. *Addictive Behaviors, 31,* 2309–2312.

Snodgrass, M., Bernat, E., & Shevrin, H. (2004). Unconscious perception: A model-based approach to method and evidence. *Perception & Psychophysics, 66,* 846–867.

Snow, C. E. (1998). Bilingualism and second language acquisition. In J. B. Gleason & N. B. Ratner (Eds.), *Psycholinguistics.* Fort Worth, TX: Harcourt College Publishers.

Snow, R. E. (1986). Individual differences in the design of educational programs. *American Psychologist, 41,* 1029–1039.

Snowden, L. R., & Hu, T. W. (1996). Outpatient service use in minority-serving mental health programs. *Administration and Policy in Mental Health, 24,* 149–159.

Snowden, L. R., & Yamada, A. (2005). Cultural differences in access to care. *Annual Review of Clinical Psychology, 1,* 143–166.

Snyder, A. (1989). *Relationship excellence: Right brain relationship skills for left brain personalities.* Seattle: Gresham Publishing.

Snyder, S. H. (2002). Forty years of neurotransmitters: A personal account. *Archives of General Psychiatry, 59,* 983–994.

Sobel, D. (2002). *Children's special places: Exploring the role of forts, dens, and bush houses in middle childhood (The Child in the Cities Series).* Detroit, MI: Wayne State University Press.

Sokol, R. J., Janisse, J. J., Louis, J. M., Bailey, B. N., Ager, J., Jacobson, S. W., & Jacobson, J. L. (2007). Extreme prematurity: An alcohol-related birth effect. *Alcoholism: Clinical and Experimental Research, 31,* 1031–1037.

Solberg, E. C., Diener, E., Wirtz, D., Lucas, R. E., & Oishi, S. (2002). Wanting, having, and satisfaction: Examining the role of desire discrepancies in satisfaction with income. *Journal of Personality and Social Psychology, 83,* 725–734.

Soldatos, C. R., Allaert, F. A., Ohta, T., & Dikeos, D. G. (2005). How do individuals sleep around the world? Results from a single-day survey in ten countries. *Sleep Medicine, 6,* 5–13.

Solms, M. (2000). Freudian dream theory today. *Psychologist, 13,* 618–619.

Solms, M. (2004). Freud returns. *Scientific American, 290*(5), 83–88.

Solomon, D. A., Keller, M. B., Leon, A. C., Mueller, T. I., Lavori, P. W., Shea, M. T., & Endicott, J. (2000). Multiple recurrences of major depressive disorder. *American Journal of Psychiatry, 157*(2), 229–233. doi:10.1176/appi.ajp.157.2.229

Solomon, S., Greenberg, J., & Pyszczynski, T. (1991). A terror management theory of social behavior: The psychological functions of self-esteem and cultural worldviews. In M. Zanna (Ed.), *Advances in experimental social psychology* (Vol. 24). Orlando, FL: Academic Press.

Solomon, S., Greenberg, J., & Pyszczynski, T. (2004a). Lethal consumption: Death-denying materialism. In T. Kasser, & A. D. Kanner (Eds.), *Psychology and consumer culture: The struggle for a good life in a materialistic world.* Washington, DC: American Psychological Association.

Solomon, S., Greenberg, J., & Pyszczynski, T. (2004b). The cultural animal: Twenty years of terror management. In J. Greenberg, S. L. Koole, & T. Pyszczynski (Eds.), *Handbook of experimental existential psychology.* New York, NY: Guilford Press.

Solowij, N., Stephens, R. S., Roffman, R. A., Babor, T., Kadden, R., Miller, M., Christiansen. K., McRee, B., & Vendetti, J. (2002). Cognitive functioning of long-term heavy cannabis users seeking treatment. *Journal of the American Medical Association, 287,* 1123–1131.

Solso, R. L. (1994). *Cognition and the visual arts.* Cambridge, MA: MIT Press.

Sommer, I. E., Aleman, A., Somers, M., Boks, M. P., & Kahn, R. S. (2008). Sex differences in handedness, asymmetry of the planum temporale and functional language lateralization. *Brain Research, 1206,* 76–88. doi:10.1016/j.brainres.2008.01.003

Song, S., Sjostrom, P. J., Reigl, M. , Nelson, S., & Chklovskii, D. B. (2005). Highly nonrandom features of synaptic connectivity in local cortical circuits. *PLoS Biology, 3*(3), 1–13.

Sousa, D. A. (2000). *How the brain learns: A classroom teacher's guide.* Thousand Oaks, CA: Corwin Press.

Spangler, W. D. (1992). Validity of questionnaire and TAT measures of need for achievement: Two meta-analyses. *Psychological Bulletin, 112,* 140–154.

Spanos, N. P. (1986). Hypnotic behavior: A social-psychological interpretation of amnesia, analgesia, and "trance logic." *Behavioral & Brain Sciences, 9*(3), 449–467.

Spanos, N. P. (1991). A sociocognitive approach to hypnosis. In S. J. Lynn & J. W. Rhue (Eds.), *Theories of hypnosis: Current models and perspectives* (pp. 324–361). New York, NY: Guilford Press.

Spanos, N. P. (1994). Multiple identity enactments and multiple personality disorder: A sociocognitive perspective. *Psychological Bulletin, 116,* 143–165.

Spanos, N. P. (1996). *Multiple identities and false memories.* Washington, DC: American Psychological Association.

Sparing, R., Hesse, M. D., & Fink, G. R. (2010). Neuronavigation for transcranial magnetic stimulation (TMS): Where we are and where we are going. *Cortex: A Journal Devoted to the Study of the Nervous System and Behavior, 46*(1), 118–120. doi:10.1016/j.cortex.2009.02.018

Spear, J. H. (2007). Prominent schools or other active specialties? A fresh look at some trends in psychology. *Review of General Psychology, 11*(4), 363–380. doi:10.1037/1089-2680.11.4.363

Spearman, C. (1904). "General intelligence" objectively determined and measured. *American Journal of Psychology, 15,* 202–293.

Spearman, C. (1927). *The abilities of man, their nature and measurement.* London: Macmillan.

Spelke, E. S., & Kinzler, K. D. (2007). Core knowledge. *Developmental Science, 10*(1), 89–96.

Spelke, E. S., & Newport, E. L. (1998). Nativism, empiricism, and the development of knowledge. In W. Damon (Ed.), *Handbook of child psychology (Vol. 1): Theoretical models of human development.* New York, NY: Wiley.

Spence, I., Wong, P., Rusan, M., & Rastegar, N. (2006). How color enhances visual memory for natural scenes. *Psychological Science, 14*(1), 1–6.

Sperling, G. (1960). The information available in brief visual presentations. *Psychological Monographs, 74*(11, Whole No. 498).

Sperry, R. W. (1982). Some effects of disconnecting the cerebral hemispheres. *Science, 217,* 1223–1226, 1250.

Speth, G. (1992). The global environmental challenge. In G. T. Miller, *Living in the environment: An introduction to environmental science* (7th ed.). Belmont, CA: Wadsworth.

Spiegel, D. (1995). Hypnosis, dissociation, and trauma: Hidden and overt observers. In J. L. Singer (Ed.), *Repression and dissociation: Implications for personality theory, psychopathology, and health.* Chicago: University of Chicago Press.

Spiegel, D. (2003a). Hypnosis and traumatic dissociation: Therapeutic opportunities. *Journal of Trauma & Dissociation, 4*(3), 73–90.

Spiegel, D. (2003b). Negative and positive visual hypnotic hallucinations: Attending inside and out. *International Journal of Clinical & Experimental Hypnosis, 51*(2), 130–146.

Spiegel, D. (2007). Commentary: Reversing amnesia about hypnosis. *American Journal of Clinical Hypnosis, 49*(3), 181 182.

Spiegel, D. (2008). Intelligent design or designed intelligence? Hypnotizability as neurobiological adaption. In M. R. Nash & A. J. Barnier (Eds.). *Oxford handbook of hypnosis: Theory, research and practice* (pp. 179–201). New York, NY: Oxford University Press.

Spiegel, D., Cutcomb, S., Ren, C., & Pribram, K. (1985). Hypnotic hallucination alters evoked potentials. *Journal of Abnormal Psychology, 94,* 249–255.

Spiegel, D., & Maldonado, J. (2009). Hypnosis in medicine. In D. C. Brown (Ed.), *Advances in the use of hypnosis for medicine, dentistry and pain prevention/management* (pp. 3–15). Norwalk, CT: Crown House Publishing Limited.

Spiegler, M. D., & Guevremont, D. C. (2010). *Contemporary behavior therapy* (5th ed.). Belmont, CA: Wadsworth.

Spinath, B., Spinath, F. M., Harlaar, N., & Plomin, R. (2006). Predicting school achievement from general cognitive ability, self-perceived ability, and intrinsic value. *Intelligence, 34*(4), 363–374. doi:10.1016/j.intell.2005.11.004

Spironelli, C., Angrilli, A., & Stegagno, L. (2008). Failure of language lateralization in schizophrenia patients: An ERP study on early linguistic components. *Journal of Psychiatry & Neuroscience, 33*(3), 235–243.

Spitz, H. I. (2009). Group psychotherapy. In B. J. Sadock, V. A. Sadock, & P. Ruiz (Eds.), *Kaplan & Sadock's comprehensive textbook of psychiatry* (pp. 2832–2856). Philadelphia, PA: Lippincott, Williams & Wilkins.

Spitz, H. I., Spitz, S. (2009). Family and couple therapy. In B. J. Sadock, V. A. Sadock, & P. Ruiz (Eds.), *Kaplan & Sadock's comprehensive textbook of psychiatry* (pp. 2845–2856). Philadelphia, PA: Lippincott, Williams & Wilkins.

Sprecher, S., & Duck, S. (1994). Sweet talk: The importance of perceived communication for romantic and friendship attraction experienced during a get-acquainted date. *Personality and Social Psychology Bulletin, 20,* 391–400.

Sprecher, S., Schwartz, P., Harvey, J., & Hatfield, E. (2008). Thebusinessoflove.com: Relationship initiation at Internet matchmaking services. In S. Sprecher, A. Wenzel, & J. Harvey (Eds.), *Handbook of relationship initiation* (pp. 235–247). New York, NY: Psychology Press.

Sprenger, M. (2001). *Becoming a "wiz" at brain-based teaching: From translation to application.* Thousand Oaks, CA: Corwin Press.

Springer, S. P., & Deutsch, G. (1998). *Left brain, right brain.* New York, NY: W. H. Freeman.

Squire, L. R. (1987). *Memory and brain.* New York, NY: Oxford University Press.

Squire, L. R. (2004). Memory systems of the brain: A brief history and current perspective. *Neurobiology of Learning & Memory, 82*(3), 171–177.

Squire, L. R. (2009). Memory and brain systems: 1969–2009. *The Journal of Neuroscience, 29*(41), 12711–12716. doi:10.1523/JNEUROSCI.3575-09.2009

Squire, L. R., & Shrager, Y. (2009). Declarative memory systems: Amnesia. In J. H. Byrne (Ed.), *Concise learning and memory: The editor's selection.* San Diego, CA: Elsevier.

Squire, L. R., Knowlton, B., & Musen, G. (1993). The structure and organization of memory. *Annual Review of Psychology, 44,* 453–495.

St. John, D., & MacDonald, D. A. (2007). Development and initial validation of a measure of ecopsychological self. *Journal of Transpersonal Psychology, 39*(1), 48–67.

Staats, A. W., & Staats, C. K. (1963). *Complex human behavior.* New York, NY: Holt, Rinehart & Winston.

Staats, H. (2003). Understanding proenvironmental attitudes and behavior: An analysis and review of research based on the theory of planned behavior. In M. Bonnes, T. Lee, & M. Bonaiuto (Eds.), *Psychological theories for environmental issues* (pp. 171–202). Wiltshire, England: Antony Rowe.

Staddon, J. E. R., & Simmelhag, V. L. (1971). The "superstition" experiment: A reexamination of its implications for the principles of adaptive behavior. *Psychological Review, 78,* 3–43. doi:10.1037/h0030305

Stahl, C., Unkelbach, C., & Corneile, O. (2009). On the respective contributions of awareness of unconditioned stimulus valence and unconditioned stimulus identity in attitude formation through evaluative conditioning. *Journal of Personality and Social Psychology, 97*(3), 404–420. doi:10.1037/a0016196

Staines, G. L. (2008). The relative efficacy of psychotherapy: Reassessing the methods-based paradigm. *Review of General Psychology, 12*(4), 330–343.

Stajkovic, A. D., & Luthans, F. (1998). Self-efficacy and work-related performance: A meta-analysis. *Psychological Bulletin, 124,* 240–261.

Staley, J. K., & Krystal, J. H. (2009). Radiotracer imaging and positron emission topography and single photon emission computer topography. In B. J. Sadock, V. A. Sadock, & P. Ruiz (Eds.), *Kaplan & Sadock's comprehensive textbook of psychiatry* (9th ed., Vol. 1, pp. 42–64). Philadelphia, PA: Lippincott, Williams & Wilkins.

Stamatakis, E., Hillsdon, M., Mishra, G., Hamer, M., & Marmot, M. (2009). Television viewing and other screen-based entertainment in relation to multiple socioeconomic status indicators and area deprivation: The Scottish Health Survey 2003. *Journal of Epidemiology and Community Health, 63,* 734–740. doi:10.1136/jech.2008.085902

Stangor, C. (2009). The study of stereotyping, prejudice, and discrimination within social psychology: A quick history of theory and research. In T. D. Nelson (Ed.), *Handbook of prejudice, stereotyping, and discrimination* (pp. 1–22). New York, NY: Psychology Press.

Stanley, M. A., & Beidel, D. C. (2009). Behavior therapy. In B. J. Sadock, V. A. Sadock, & P. Ruiz (Eds.), *Kaplan & Sadock's comprehensive textbook of psychiatry* (pp. 2781–2803). Philadelphia, PA: Lippincott, Williams & Wilkins.

Stanovich, K. E. (2003). The fundamental computational biases of human cognition: Heuristics that (sometimes) impair decision making and problem solving. In J. E. Davidson & R. J. Sternberg (Eds.), *The psychology of problem solving.* New York, NY: Cambridge University Press.

Stanovich, K. E. (2009). *What intelligence tests miss: The psychology of rational thought.* New Haven, CT: Yale University Press.

Stanovich, K. E., & West, R. F. (2007). Natural myside bias is independent of cognitive ability. *Thinking & Reasoning, 13*(3), 225–247. doi:10.1080/13546780600780796

Stanovich, K. E., & West, R. F. (2008). On the relative independence of thinking biases and cognitive ability. *Journal of Personality and Social Psychology, 94*(4), 672–695. doi:10.1037/0022-3514.94.4.672

Stanton, A. L., Lobel, M., Sears, S., & DeLuca, R. S. (2002). Psychosocial aspects of selected issues in women's reproductive health: Current status and future directions. *Journal of Consulting & Clinical Psychology, 70,* 751–770.

Steel, P. (2007). The nature of procrastination: A meta-analytic and theoretical review of quintessential self-regulatory failure. *Psychological Bulletin, 133,* 65–94.

Steele, C. M. (1992, April). Race and the schooling of black Americans. *Atlantic Monthly,* pp. 68–78.

Steele, C. M. (1997). A threat in the air: How stereotypes shape intellectual identity and performance. *American Psychologist, 52,* 613–629.

Steele, C. M., & Aronson, J. (1995). Stereotype threat and the intellectual test performance of African Americans. *Journal of Personality and Social Psychology, 69,* 797–811.

Steele, K. M. (2003). Do rats show a Mozart effect? *Music Perception, 21,* 251–265.

Steiger, H., & Bruce, K. R. (2009). Eating disorders. In P. H. Blaney & T. Millon (Eds.), *Oxford textbook of psychopathology* (2nd ed., pp. 431–451). New York, NY: Oxford University Press.

Steiger, H., Bruce, K. R., & Israel, M. (2003). Eating disorders. In G. Stricker & T. A. Widiger (Eds.), *Handbook of psychology, Vol. 8: Clinical psychology.* New York, NY: Wiley.

Steiger, H., Gauvin, L., Engelberg, M. J., Kin, N. M. K. N. Y., Israel, M., Wonderlich, S. A., et al. (2005). Mood- and restraint-based antecedents to binge episodes in bulimia nervosa: Possible influences of the serotonin system. *Psychological Medicine, 35,* 1553–1562.

Stein, B. E., & Meredith, M. A. (1993). *Vision, touch, and audition: Making sense of it all.* Cambridge, MA: MIT Press.

Stein, B. E., Wallace, M. T., & Stanford, T. R. (2000). Merging sensory signals in the brain: The development of multisensory integration in the superior colliculus. In M. S. Gazzaniga (Ed.), *The newcognitive neurosciences.* Cambridge, MA: The MIT Press.

Stein, J., Schettler, T., Wallinga, D., Miller, M. & Valenti, M. (2002). *In harm's way: Training program for health professionals.* Boston, MA: MA: Greater Boston Physician's for Social Responsibility.

Steinberg, L. (2007). Risk taking in adolescence: New perspectives from brain and behavioral science. *Perspectives on Psychological Science, 16,* 55–59.

Steinberg, L. (2008). A social neuroscience perspective on adolescent risk-taking. *Developmental Review, 28*(1), 78–106. doi:10.1016/j.dr.2007.08.002

Steinberg, L., & Morris, A. S. (2001). Adolescent development. *Annual Review of Psychology, 52,* 83–110.

Stekel, W. (1950). *Techniques of analytical psychotherapy.* New York, NY: Liveright.

Stellar, E. (1954). The physiology of motivation. *Psychological Review, 61,* 5–22.

Stemler, S. E., Grigorenko, E. L., Jarvin, L., & Sternberg, R. J. (2006). Using the theory of successful intelligence as a basis for augmenting AP exams in psychology and statistics. *Contemporary Educational Psychology, 31,* 344–376.

Stepanski, E. J. (2006). Causes of insomnia. In T. Lee-Chiong (Ed.), *Sleep: A comprehensive handbook.* Hoboken, NJ: Wiley-Liss.

Stepanski, E. J., & Wyatt, J. K. (2003). Use of sleep hygiene in the treatment of insomnia. *Sleep Medicine Reviews, 7*(3), 215–225.

Steptoe, A. (2007). Stress effects: Overview. In G. Fink (Ed.), *Encyclopedia of stress.* San Diego: Elsevier.

Steriade, M. (2005). Brain electrical activity and sensory processing during waking and sleep states. In M. H. Kryger, T. Roth, & W. C. Dement (Eds.). *Principles and practice of sleep medicine.* Philadelphia, PA: Elsevier Saunders.

Sterman, J. D. (2008). Risk communication on climate: Mental models and mass balance. *Science, 322,* 532–533.

Stern, W. W. (1914). *The physiological methods of testing intelligence* (G. M. Whipple, Trans.). Baltimore, MD: Warwick & York. (Original work, in German, published 1912). doi:10.1037/11067-000

Sternberg, R. J. (1985). *Beyond IQ: A triarchic theory of human intelligence.* New York, NY: Cambridge University Press.

Sternberg, R. J. (1986). *Intelligence applied: Understanding and increasing your intellectual skills.* New York, NY: Harcourt Brace Jovanovich.

Sternberg, R. J. (1991). Theory-based testing of intellectual abilities: Rationale for the triarchic abilities test. In H. A. H. Rowe (Ed.), *Intelligence: Reconceptualization and measurement.* Hillsdale, NJ: Erlbaum.

Sternberg, R. J. (1998). How intelligent is intelligence testing? *Scientific American Presents Exploring Intelligence, 9,* 12–17.

Sternberg, R. J. (2000a). Creativity is a decision. In A. L. Costa (Ed.), *Teaching for intelligence II* (pp. 85–106). Arlington Heights, IL: Skylight Training.

Sternberg, R. J. (2000b). Successful intelligence: A unified view of giftedness. In C. F. M. van Lieshout & P. G. Heymans (Eds.), *Developing talent across the life span* (pp. 43–65). Philadelphia, PA: Psychology Press.

Sternberg, R. J. (2003a). Construct validity of the theory of successful intelligence. In R. J. Sternberg, J. Lautrey, & T. I. Lubart (Eds.), *Models of intelligence: International perspectives.* Washington, DC: American Psychological Association.

Sternberg, R. J. (2003b). My house is a very, very, very fine house—But it is not the only house. In H. Nyborg (Ed.), *The scientific study of general intelligence: Tribute to Arthur R. Jensen.* Oxford, UK: Pergamon.

Sternberg, R. J. (2004). Culture and intelligence. *American Psychologist, 59,* 325–338.

Sternberg, R. J. (2005a). There are no public policy implications: A reply to Rushton and Jensen. *Psychology, Public Policy, and the Law, 11,* 295–301.

Sternberg, R. J. (2005b). The triarchic theory of successful intelligence. In D. P. Flanagan & P. L. Harrison (Eds.), *Contemporary intellectual assessment: Theories, tests and issues* (pp. 103–119). New York, NY: Guillford Press.

Sternberg, R. J. (2005c). The WICS model of giftedness. In R. J. Sternberg & J. E. Davidson (Eds.), *Conceptions of giftedness.* New York, NY: Cambridge University Press.

Sternberg, R. J. (2007). Intelligence and culture. In S. Kitayama & D. Cohen (Eds.), *Handbook of cultural psychology* (pp. 547–568). New York, NY: Guilford Press.

Sternberg, R. J. (2009). Component processes in analogical reasoning. In J. C. Kaufman & E. L. Grigorenko (Eds.), *The essential Sternberg: Essays on intelligence, psychology, and education* (pp. 145–179). New York, NY: Springer.

Sternberg, R. J., Castejon, J. L., Prieto, M. D., Hautamaeki, J., & Grigorenko, E. L. (2001). Confirmatory factor analysis of the Sternberg Triarchic Abilities Test in three international samples: An empirical test of the triarchic theory of intelligence. *European Journal of Psychological Assessment, 17,* 1–16.

Sternberg, R. J., Conway, B. E., Ketron, J. L., & Bernstein, M. (1981). People's conceptions of intelligence. *Journal of Personality and Social Psychology, 41,* 37–55.

Sternberg, R. J., Grigorenko, E. L., Ferrari, M., & Clinkenbeard, P. (1999). A triarchic analysis of an aptitude interaction. *European Journal of Psychological Assessment, 15,* 1–11.

Sternberg, R. J., Grigorenko, E. L., & Kidd, K. K. (2005). Intelligence, race, and genetics. *American Psychologist, 60,* 45–69.

Sternberg, R. J., & Hedlund, J. (2002). Practical intelligence, *g,* and work psychology. *Human Performance, 15,* 143–160.

Sternberg, R. J., & Jarvin, L. (2003). Alfred Binet's contributions as a paradigm for impact in psychology. In R. J. Sternberg (Ed.), *The anatomy of impact: What makes the great works of psychology great* (pp. 89–107). Washington, DC: American Psychological Association.

Sternberg, R. J., & O'Hara, L. A. (1999). Creativity and intelligence. In R. J. Sternberg (Ed.), *Handbook of creativity.* New York, NY: Cambridge University Press.

Sternberg, R. J., & the Rainbow Project Collaborators. (2006). The Rainbow Project: Enhancing the SAT through assessments of analytical, practical, and creative skills. *Intelligence, 34,* 321–350.

Stetler, C., Murali, R., Chen, E., & Miller, G. E. (2005). Stress, immunity, and disease. In C. L. Cooper (Ed.), *Handbook of stress medicine and health.* Boca Raton, FL: CRC Press.

Stevens, G., Raphael, B., & Dobson, M. (2007). Effects of public disasters and mass violence. In G. Fink (Ed.), *Encyclopedia of stress.* San Diego: Elsevier.

Stevens, S. S. (1955). The measurement of loudness. *Journal of the Acoustical Society of America, 27,* 815–819.

Stewart, A., Ostrove, J. M., & Helson, R. (2001). Middle aging in women: Patterns of personality change from the 30s to the 50s. *Journal of Adult Development, 8*(1), 23–37.

Stewart, G. L., & Manz, C. C. (1995). Leadership for self-managing work teams: A typology and integrative model. *Human Relations, 48,* 347–370.

Stewart, R., Ellenburg, G., Hicks, L., Kremen, M., & Daniel, M. (1990). Employee references as a recruitment source. *Applied H.R.M. Research, 1*(1), 1–3.

Stewart, W. H., Jr., & Roth, P. L. (2007). A meta-analysis of achievement motivation differences between entrepreneurs and managers. *Journal of Small Business Management, 45,* 401–421.

Stewart-Williams, S. (2004). The placebo puzzle: Putting the pieces together. *Health Psychology, 23,* 198–206.

Stickgold, R. (2001). Toward a cognitive neuroscience of sleep. *Sleep Medicine Reviews, 5,* 417–421.

Stickgold, R. (2005). Why we dream. In M. H. Kryger, T. Roth, & W. C. Dement (Eds.), *Principles and practice of sleep medicine.* Philadelphia, PA: Elsevier Saunders.

Stickgold, R., & Walker, M. P. (2004). To sleep, perchance to gain creative insight. *Trends in Cognitive Sciences, 8*(5), 191–192.

Stickgold, R., & Walker, M. P. (2005). Memory consolidation and reconsolidation: What is the role of sleep? *Trends in Neurosciences, 28*(8), 408–415.

Stockman, A. (2010). Color mixing. In E. B. Goldstein (Ed.), *Encyclopedia of perception.* Thousand Oaks, CA: Sage.

Stoddard, G. (1943). *The meaning of intelligence.* New York, NY: Macmillan.

Stokstad, E. (2009, November 25). Americans' eating habits more wasteful than ever. *ScienceNOW.* Retrieved from http://news.sciencemag.org/sciencenow/2009/11/25-01.html?ref=hp

Stone, A. A. (1999). Psychiatry and the law. In A. M. Nicholi (Ed.), *The Harvard guide to psychiatry.* Cambridge, MA: Harvard University Press.

Stone, L. (1977). *The family, sex and marriage in England 1500–1800.* New York, NY: Harper & Row.

Stone, W. N. (2008). Group psychotherapy. In A. Tasman, J. Kay, J. A. Lieberman, M. B. First, & M. Maj (Eds.), *Psychiatry* (3rd ed.). New York, NY: Wiley-Blackwell.

Stoner, J. A. F. (1961). *A comparison of individual and group decisions involving risk.* Unpublished master's thesis, Massachusetts Institute of Technology.

Stoohs, R. A., Blum, H. C., Haselhorst, M., Duchna, H. W., Guilleminault, C., & Dement, W. C. (1998). Normative data on snoring: A comparison between younger and older adults. *European Respiratory Journal, 11,* 451–457.

Storandt, M. (2008). Cognitive deficits in the early stages of Alzheimer's disease. *Current Directions in Psychological Science, 17*(3), 198–202. doi:10.1111/j.1467-8721.2008.00574.x

Storch, M., Gaab, J., Küttel, Y., Stüssi, A.-C., & Fend, H. (2007). Psychoneuroendocrine effects of resource-activating stress management training. *Health Psychology, 26*(4), 456–463.

Stowell, J. R. (2008). Stress and stressors. In S. F. Davis & W. Buskist (Eds.), *21st century psychology: A reference handbook.* Thousand Oaks, CA: Sage.

Strager, S. (2003). What men watch when they watch pornography. *Sexuality & Culture: An Interdisciplinary Quarterly, 7*(1), 50–61.

Strahan, E. J., Lafrance, A., Wilson, A. E., Ethier, N., Spencer, S. J., & Zanna, M. P. (2008). Victoria's dirty secret: How sociocultural norms influence adolescent girls and women. *Personality and Social Psychology Bulletin, 34*(2), 288–301.

Strange, D., Clifasefi, S., & Garry, M. (2007). False memories. In M. Garry & H. Hayne (Eds.), *Do justice and let the sky fall: Elizabeth F. Lotus and her contributions to science, law, and academic freedom.* Mahwah, NJ: Erlbaum.

Strasburger, V. C. (2007). First do no harm: Why have parents and pediatricians missed the boat on children and media? *Journal of Pediatrics, 151,* 334–336.

Straus, M. A. (2000). Corporal punishment and primary prevention of physical abuse. *Child Abuse & Neglect, 24,* 1109–1114.

Straus, M. A., & Paschall, M. J. (2009). Corporal punishment by mothers and development of children's cognitive ability: A longitudinal study of two nationally representative age cohorts. *Journal of Aggression, Maltreatment, & Trauma, 18*(5), 459–483. doi:10.1080/10926770903035168

Straus, M. A., & Stewart, J. H. (1999). Corporal punishment by American parents: National data on prevalence, chronicity, severity, and duration, in relation to child family characteristics. *Clinical Child & Family Psychology Review, 2*(2), 55–70.

Strayer, D. L., & Drews, F. A. (2007). Cell-phone-induced driver distraction. *Current Directions in Psychological Science, 16,* 128–131.

Strayer, D. L., Drews, F. A., & Crouch, D. J. (2006). A comparison of the cell phone driver and the drunk driver. *Human Factors, 48,* 381–391.

Strayer, D. L., & Johnston, W. A. (2001). Driven to distraction: Dual-task studies of simulated driving and conversing on a cellular telephone. *Psychological Science, 12,* 462–466.

Streissguth, A. (2007). Offspring effects of prenatal alcohol exposure from birth to 25 years: The Seattle prospective longitudinal study. *Journal of Clinical Psychology in Medical Settings, 14,* 81–101.

Streit, W. J. (2005). Microglia and neuroprotection: Implications for Alzheimer's disease. *Brain Research Reviews, 48,* 234–239.

Strenze, T. (2007). Intelligence and socioeconomic success: A meta-analytic review of longitudinal research. *Intelligence, 35,* 401–426.

Strick, M., Holland, R. W., & van Knippenberg, A. (2008). Seductive eyes: Attractiveness and direct gaze increase desire for associated objects. *Cognition, 106,* 1487–1496. doi:10.1016/j.cognition.2007.05.008

Strick, M., van Baaren, R. B., Holland, R. W., & van Knippenberg, A. (2009). Humor in advertisements enhances product liking by mere association. *Journal of Experimental Psychology: Applied, 15,* 35–45.

Strieber, A. (2011). The 10 best and worst jobs of 2011. CareerCast. Retrieved from http://www.careercast.com/jobs-rated/10-best-jobs-2011; http://www.careercast.com/jobs-rated/10-worst-jobs-2011

Striegel-Moore, R. H., & Bulik, C. M. (2007). Risk factors for eating disorders. *American Psychologist, 62,* 181–198.

Striegel-Moore, R. H., & Franko, D. L. (2008). Should binge eating disorder be included in the DSM-V? A critical review of the state of the evidence. *Annual Review of Clinical Psychology, 4,* 305–324.

Stroebe, W. (2008). *Dieting, overweight, and obesity.* Washington, DC: American Psychological Association.

Stroup, T. S., Kraus, J. E., & Marder, S. R. (2006). Pharmacotherapies. In J. A. Lieberman, T. S. Stroup, & D. O. Perkins (Eds.), *Textbook of schizophrenia* (pp. 303–326). Washington, DC: American Psychiatric Publishing.

Strupp, H. H. (1996). The tripartite model and the *Consumer Reports* study. *American Psychologist, 51,* 1017–1024.

Stuart, R. B. & Heiby, E. E. (2007). To prescribe or not to prescribe: Eleven exploratory questions. *Scientific Review of Mental Health Practice, 5*(1), 4–32.

Stubbe, J. H., Posthuma, D., Boomsma, D. I., & de Geus, E. J. C. (2005). Heritability of life satisfaction in adults: A twin study. *Psychological Medicine, 35,* 1581–1588.

Stunkard, A. J., Allison, K. C., Geliebter, A., Lundgren, J. D., Gluck, M. E., & O'Reardon, J. P. (2009). Development of criteria for a diagnosis: Lessons from the night eating syndrome. *Comprehensive Psychiatry, 50*(5), 391–399. doi:10.1016/j.comppsych.2008.09.013

Stunkard, A. J., Harris, J. R., Pederson, N. L., & McClearn, G. E. (1990). The body-mass index of twins who have been reared apart. *New England Journal of Medicine, 322,* 1483–1487.

Stunkard, A. J., Sorensen, T., Hanis, C., Teasdale, T. W., Chakraborty, R., Schull, W. J., & Schulsinger, F. (1986). An adoption study of human obesity. *New England Journal of Medicine, 314,* 193–198.

Sturgis, P. (2006). Surveys and sampling. In G. M. Breakwell, S. Hammond, C. Fife-Schaw, & J. A. Smith (Eds.), *Research methods in psychology* (3rd ed.). London: Sage.

Sturman, M. C., & Sherwyn, D. (2007). The truth about integrity tests: The validity and utility of integrity testing for the hospital industry. *The Center for Hospitality Research, 7*(15).

Stylianou-Korsnes, M., Reiner, M., Magnussen, S. J., & Feldman, M. W. (2010). Visual recognition of shapes and textures: An fMRI study. *Brain Structure & Function, 214*(4), 355–359. doi:10.1007/s00429-010-0241-5

Subotnik, K. L., Nuechterlein, K. H., Ventura, J., Gitlin, M. J., Marder, S., Mintz, J., et al. (2011). Risperidone nonadherence and return of positive symptoms in the early course of schizophrenia. *American Journal of Psychiatry, 168*(3), 286–292.

Sudak, H. S. (2005). Suicide. In B. J. Sadock & V. A. Sadock (Eds.), *Kaplan & Sadock's comprehensive textbook of psychiatry.* Philadelphia, PA: Lippincott Williams & Wilkins.

Sudak, H. S. (2009). Suicide. In B. J. Sadock, V. A. Sadock, & P. Ruiz (Eds.), *Kaplan & Sadock's comprehensive textbook of psychiatry* (9th ed., pp. 2717–2731). Philadelphia, PA: Lippincott, Williams & Wilkins.

Sue, D. W., & Sue, D. (1999). *Counseling the culturally different: Theory and practice.* New York, NY: Wiley.

Sue, S. (2003). In defense of cultural competency in psychotherapy and treatment. *American Psychologist, 58,* 964–970.

Sue, S., Zane, N., Hall, G., & Berger, L. K. (2009). The case for cultural competency in psychotherapeutic interventions. *Annual Review of Psychology, 60,* 525–548. doi:10.1146/annurev.psych.60.110707.163651

Sue, S., Zane, N., & Young, K. (1994). Research on psychotherapy with culturally diverse populations. In A. E. Bergin & S. L. Garfield (Eds.), *Handbook of psychotherapy and behavior change* (4th ed.). New York, NY: Wiley.

Sufka, K. J., & Price, D. D. (2002). Gate control theory reconsidered. *Brain & Mind, 3,* 277–290.

Sugarman, J. (2007). Practical rationality and the questionable promise of positive psychology. *Journal of Humanistic Psychology, 47,* 175–197.

Sugita, Y. (2009). Innate face processing. *Current Opinion in Neurobiology, 19*(1), 39–44. doi:10.1016/j.conb.2009.03.001

Sugiyama, L. S. (2005). Physical attractiveness in adaptionist perspective. In D. M. Buss (Ed.), *The handbook of evolutionary psychology.* New York, NY: Wiley.

Suls, J. M., Luger, T., & Martin, R. (2010). The biopsychosocial model and the use of theory in health psychology. In J. M. Suls, K. W. Davidson, & R. M. Kaplan (Eds.), *Handbook of health psychology and behavioral medicine* (pp. 15–27). New York, NY: Guilford Press.

Summerfield, C., & Koechlin, E. (2009). Decision making and prefrontal executive function. In M. S. Gazzangia (Ed.), *The cognitive neurosciences* (4th ed., pp. 1019–1030). Cambridge, MA: MIT Press.

Sundblad, E. L., Biel, A., & Gärling, T. (2007). Cognitive and affective risk judgments related to climate change. *Journal of Environmental Psychology, 27,* 97–106.

Sundin, J. J., Fear, N. T., Iversen, A. A., Rona, R. J., & Wessely, S. S. (2010). PTSD after deployment to Iraq: Conflicting rates, conflicting claims. *Psychological Medicine: A Journal of Research in Psychiatry and the Allied Sciences, 40*(3), 367–382. doi:10.1017/S0033291709990791

Super, C. M. (1976). Environmental effects on motor development: A case of African infant precocity. *Developmental Medicine and Child Neurology, 18,* 561–567.

Surra, C. A., Gray, C. R., Boettcher, T. J., Cottle, N. R., & West, A. R. (2006). From courtship to universal properties: Research on dating and mate selection, 1950 to 2003. In A. L. Vangelisti & D. Perlman (Eds.), *The Cambridge handbook of personal relationships* (pp. 113–130). New York, NY: Cambridge University Press.

Surtees, P., & Wainwright, N. (2007). Life events and health. In G. Fink (Ed.), *Encyclopedia of stress.* San Diego: Elsevier.

Surtees, P., Wainwright, N., Luben, R., Wareham, N., Bingham, S., & Khaw, K. (2008). Depression and ischemic heart disease mortality: Evidence from the EPIC-Norfolk United Kingdom Prospective Cohort Study. *American Journal of Psychiatry, 165*(4), 515–523.

Susman, E. J., Dorn, L. D., & Schiefelbein, V. L. (2003). Puberty, sexuality, and health. In R. M. Lerner, M. A. Easterbrooks, & J. Mistry (Eds.), *Handbook of psychology, Vol. 6: Developmental psychology.* New York, NY: Wiley.

Susman, E. J., & Rogol, A. (2004). Puberty and psychological development. In R. M. Lerner & L. Steinberg (Eds.), *Handbook of adolescent psychology.* New York, NY: Wiley.

Susser, E. B., Neugebauer, R., Hoek, H. W., Brown, A. S., Lin, S., Labovitz, D., & Gorman, J. M. (1996). Schizophrenia after prenatal famine: Further evidence. *Archives of General Psychiatry, 53,* 25–31.

Sussman, N. (2009). Selective serotonin reuptake inhibitors. In B. J. Sadock, V. A. Sadock, & P. Ruiz (Eds.), *Kaplan & Sadock's comprehensive textbook of psychiatry* (pp. 3190–3205). Philadelphia, PA: Lippincott, Williams & Wilkins.

Sutker, P. B., & Allain, A. N. (2001). Antisocial personality disorder. In P. B. Sutker & H. E. Adams (Eds.), *Comprehensive handbook of psychopathology.* New York, NY: Kluwer Academic/Plenum.

Suzuki, K. (2007). The moon illusion: Kaufman and Rock's (1962) apparent-distance theory reconsidered. *Japanese Psychological Research, 49,* 57–67.

Swan, G. E., Hudmon, K. S., & Kroyan, T. V. (2003). Tobacco dependence. In A. M. Nezu, C. M. Nezu, & P. A. Geller (Eds.), *Handbook of psychology, Vol. 9: Health psychology.* New York, NY: Wiley.

Swank, J. M., & Daire, A. P. (2010). Multiple family adventure-based therapy groups: An innovative integration of two approaches. *The Family Journal: Counseling and Therapy for Couples and Families, 18*(3), 241–247.

Sweatt, J. D. (2009). Long-term potentiation: A candidate cellular mechanism for information storage in the CNS. In J. H. Byrne (Ed.), *Concise learning and memory: The editor's selection.* San Diego, CA: Elsevier.

Swibel, M. (2006, July 3). Bad girl interrupted. *Forbes.* Retrieved from http://www.forbes.com/forbes/2006/0703/118.html

Swim, J. K., & Hyers, L. L. (2009). Sexism. In T. D. Nelson (Ed.), *Handbook of prejudice, stereotyping, and discrimination* (pp. 1–22). New York, NY: Psychology Press.

Swim, J. K., & Sanna, L. J. (1996). He's skilled, she's lucky: A meta-analysis of observers' attributions for women's and men's successes and failures. *Personality and Social Psychology Bulletin, 22,* 507–519.

Swingley, D. (2008). The roots of the early vocabulary in infants' learning from speech. *Current Directions in Psychological Science, 17*(5), 308–312. doi:10.1111/j.1467-8721.2008.00596.x

Szasz, T. (1974). *The myth of mental illness.* New York, NY: Harper & Row.

Szasz, T. (1990). Law and psychiatry: The problems that will not go away. *The Journal of Mind and Behavior, 11*(3/4), 557–564.

Szigethy, E. M. & Friedman, E. S. (2009). Combined psychotherapy and pharmacology. In B. J. Sadock, V. A. Sadock, & P. Ruiz (Eds.), *Kaplan & Sadock's comprehensive textbook of psychiatry* (pp. 2923–2931). Philadelphia, PA: Lippincott, Williams & Wilkins.

Szmukler, G. I., & Patton, G. (1995). Sociocultural models of eating disorders. In G. Szmukler, C. Dare, & J. Treasure (Eds.), *Handbook of eating disorders: Theory, treatment, and research.* New York, NY: Wiley.

Szpunar, K. K., & McDermott, K. B. (2009). Episodic memory: An evolving concept. In J. H. Byrne (Ed.), *Concise learning and memory: The editor's selection.* San Diego, CA: Elsevier.

Szymanski, L. S., & Wilska, M. (2003). Childhood disorders: Mental retardation. In A. Tasman, J. Kay, & J. A. Lieberman (Eds.), *Psychiatry.* New York, NY: Wiley.

Szymusiak, R. (2009). Thermoregulation during sleep and sleep deprivation. In R. Stickgold & M. P. Walker (Eds.), *The neuroscience of sleep* (pp. 218–222). San Diego, CA: Academic Press.

Tach, L., & Halpern-Meekin, S. (2009). How does premarital cohabitation affect trajectories of marital quality? *Journal of Marriage and Family, 71*(2), 298–317. doi:10.1111/j.1741-3737.2009.00600.x

Tait, D. M., & Carroll, J. (2010). Color deficiency. In E. B. Goldstein (Ed.), *Encyclopedia of perception.* Thousand Oaks, CA: Sage.

Tajfel, H. (1982). *Social identity and intergroup reflections.* London: Cambridge University Press.

Takarangi, M. T., Polaschek, D. L., Garry, M., & Loftus, E. F. (2008). Psychological science, victim advocates, and the problem of recovered memories. *International Review of Victimology, 15*(2), 147–163.

Talarico, J. M., & Rubin, D. C. (2003). Confidence, not consistency, characterizes flashbulb memories. *Psychological Science, 14,* 455–461.

Talarico, J. M., & Rubin, D. C. (2007). Flashbulb memories are special after all; in phenomenology, not accuracy. *Applied Cognitive Psychology, 21,* 557–578.

Talarico, J. M., & Rubin, D. C. (2009). Flashbulb memories result from ordinary memory processes and extraordinary event characteristics. In O. Luminet & A. Curci (Eds.), *Flashbulb memories: New issues and new perspectives* (pp. 79–97). New York, NY: Psychology Press.

Talbott, J. A. (2004). Deinstitutionalization: Avoiding the disasters of the past. *Psychiatric Services, 55,* 1112–1115.

Talwar, S. K., Xu, S., Hawley, E. S., Weiss, S. A., Moxon, K. A., & Chapin, J. K. (2002). Behavioural neuroscience: Rat navigation guided by remote control. *Nature, 417,* 37–38.

Tamakoshi, A., Ohno, Y., & JACC Study Group. (2004). Self-reported sleep duration as a predictor of all-cause mortality: Results from JACC study, Japan. *Sleep: A Journal of Sleep and Sleep Disorders Research, 27,* 51–54.

Tanaka-Matsumi, J. (2001). Abnormal psychology and culture. In D. Matsumoto (Ed.), *The handbook of culture & psychology.* New York, NY: Oxford University Press.

Tanaka, J., Weiskopf, D., & Williams, P. (2001). The role of color in high-level vision. *Trends in Cognitive Sciences, 5,* 211–215.

Tanapat, P., & Gould, E. (2007). Neurogenesis. In G. Fink (Ed.), *Encyclopedia of stress.* San Diego: Elsevier.

Tangney, J. P., Stuewig, J., & Mashek, D. J. (2007). Moral emotions and moral behavior. *Annual Review of Psychology, 58,* 345–372.

Tanner, J. L. (2006). Recentering during emerging adulthood: A critical turning point in life span human development. In J. J. Arnett & J. L. Tanner (Eds.), *Emerging adults in America: Coming of age in the 21st century.* Washington, DC: American Psychological Association.

Tapia, J. C., & Lichtman, J. W. (2008). Synapse elimination. In L. Squire, D. Berg, F. Bloom, S. Du Lac, A. Ghosh, & N. Spitzer (Eds.), *Fundamental neuroscience* (3rd ed., pp. 469–490). San Diego, CA: Elsevier.

Tashkin, D. P., Baldwin, G. C., Sarafian, T., Dubinett, S., & Roth, M. D. (2002). Respiratory and immunologic consequences of marijuana smoking. *Journal of Clinical Pharmacology, 42,* 71S–81S.

Taylor, C. A., Manganello, J. A., Lee, S. J., & Rice, J. C. (2010). Mothers' spanking of 3-year-old children and subsequent risk of children's aggressive behavior. *Pediatrics, 125*(5), 1057–1065. doi:10.1542/peds.2009-2678

Taylor, E. (1999). An intellectual renaissance of humanistic psychology. *Journal of Humanistic Psychology, 39,* 7–25.

Taylor, E. (2001). Positive psychology and humanistic psychology: A reply to Seligman. *Journal of Humanistic Psychology, 41*(1), 13–29.

Taylor, S. (2004). Amnesia, folklore and folks: Recovered memories in clinical practice. *Cognitive Behaviour Therapy, 33*(2), 105–108.

Taylor, S., Cox, B. J., & Asmundson, G. J. G. (2009). Anxiety disorders: Panic and phobias. In P. H. Blaney & T. Millon (Eds.), *Oxford textbook of psychopathology* (2nd ed., pp. 119–145). New York, NY: Oxford University Press.

Taylor, S. E. (2002). *The tending instinct: How nurturing is essential to who we are and how we live.* New York, NY: Holt.

Taylor, S. E. (2006). Tend and befriend: Biobehavioral bases of affiliation under stress. *Current Directions in Psychological Science, 15,* 273–277.

Taylor, S. E. (2007). Social support. In H. S. Friedman & R. C. Silver (Eds.), *Foundations of health psychology.* New York, NY: Oxford University Press.

Taylor, S. E., & Brown, J. D. (1988). Illusion and well-being: A social psychological perspective on mental health. *Psychological Bulletin, 103,* 193–210.

Taylor, S. E., & Brown, J. D. (1994). Positive illusions and well-being revisited: Separating fact from fiction. *Psychological Bulletin, 116,* 21–27.

Taylor, S. E., Lerner, J. S., Sherman, D. K., Sage, R. M., & McDowell, N. K. (2003). Are self-enhancing cognitions associated with healthy or unhealthy biological profiles? *Journal of Personality and Social Psychology, 85,* 605–615.

Taylor, S. E., & Master, S. L. (2011). Social responses to stress: The tend-and-befriend model. In R. J. Contrada & A. Baum (Eds.), *The handbook of stress science: Biology, psychology, and health* (pp. 101–109). New York, NY: Springer Publishing.

Taylor, S. E., Sherman, D. K., Kim, H. S., Jarcho, J., Takagi, K., & Dunagan, M. S. (2004). Culture and social support: Who seeks it and why? *Journal of Personality and Social Psychology, 87*(3), 354–362. doi:10.1037/0022-3514.87.3.354

Taylor, S. E., Welch, W. T., Kim, H. S., & Sherman, D. K. (2007). Cultural differences in the impact of social support on psychological and biological stress responses. *Psychological Science, 18*(9), 831–837. doi:10.1111/j.1467-9280.2007.01987.x

Teachman, J. (2003). Premarital sex, premarital cohabitation and the risk of subsequent marital dissolution among women. *Journal of Marriage and Family, 65*(2), 444–455. doi:10.1111/j.1741-3737.2003.00444.x

Tedlock, L. B. (1992). Zuni and Quiche dream sharing and interpreting. In B. Tedlock (Ed.), *Dreaming: Anthropological and psychological interpretations.* Santa Fe, NM: School of American Research Press.

Teigen, K. H. (2004). Judgments by representativeness. In F. P. Rudiger (Ed.), *Cognitive illusions.* New York, NY: Psychology Press.

Tellegen, A., Lykken, D. T., Bouchard, T. J., Jr., Wilcox, K. J., Segal, N. L., & Rich, S. (1988). Personality similarity in twins reared apart and together. *Journal of Personality and Social Psychology, 54,* 1031–1039.

Temple, J. L., Giacomelli, A. M., Roemmich, J. N., & Epstein, L. H. (2008). Dietary variety impairs habituation in children. *Health Psychology, 27,* S10–S19.

Tennen, H., & Affleck, G. (1999). Finding benefits in adversity. In C. R. Snyder (Ed.), *Coping: The psychology of what works.* New York, NY: Oxford University Press.

Terman, L. (1916). *The measurement of intelligence: An explanation of and a complete guide for the use of the Stanford revision and extension of the Binet-Simon Intelligence Scale.* Boston, MA: Houghton Mifflin.

Terman, L. M. (1916). *The measurement of intelligence.* Boston, MA: Houghton Mifflin.

Terman, L. M. (1925). *Genetic studies of genius: Vol. 1. Mental and physical traits of a thousand gifted children.* Stanford, CA: Stanford University Press.

Terman, L. M., & Oden, M. H. (1959). *Genetic studies of genius: Vol. 5. The gifted group at mid-life.* Stanford, CA: Stanford University Press.

Terr, L. (1994). *Unchained memories.* New York, NY: Basic Books.

Terracciano, A., Abdel-Khalak, A. M., Adam, N., Adamovova, L., Ahn, C. K., Ahn, H. N., et al. (2005). National character does not reflect mean personality trait levels in 49 cultures. *Science, 310,* 96–100.

Terrace, H. S. (1986). *Nim: A chimpanzee who learned sign language.* New York, NY: Columbia University Press.

Teuber, M. (1974). Sources of ambiguity in the prints of Maurits C. Escher. *Scientific American, 231,* 90–104.

Thase, M. E. (2009a). Neurobiological aspects of depression. In I. H. Gotlib & C. L. Hammen (Eds.), *Handbook of depression* (2nd ed., pp. 187–217). New York, NY: Guilford Press.

Thase, M. E. (2009b). Selective serotonin-norepinephrine reuptake inhibitors. In B. J. Sadock, V. A. Sadock, & P. Ruiz (Eds.), *Kaplan & Sadock's comprehensive textbook of psychiatry* (pp. 3184–3189). Philadelphia, PA: Lippincott, Williams & Wilkins.

Thase, M. E., & Denko, T. (2008). Pharmacotherapy of mood disorders. *Annual Review of Clinical Psychology, 4,* 53–91.

Thase, M. E., & Sloan D. M. E. (2006). Venlafaxine. In A. F. Schatzberg & C. B. Nemeroff (Eds.), *Essentials of clinical psychopharmacology.* Washington, DC: American Psychological Association.

Thayer, A., & Lynn, S. J. (2006). Guided imagery and recovered memory therapy: Considerations and cautions. *Journal of Forensic Psychology Practice, 6,* 63–73.

Thayer, R. E. (1996). *The origin of everyday moods.* New York, NY: Oxford University Press.

Thelen, E. (1995). Motor development: A new synthesis. *American Psychologist, 50, 79–95.*

Thomas, A., & Chess, S. (1977). *Temperament and development.* New York, NY: Brunner/Mazel.

Thomas, A., & Chess, S. (1989). Temperament and personality. In G. A. Kohnstamm, J. E. Bates, & M. K. Rothbart (Eds.), *Temperament in childhood.* New York, NY: Wiley.

Thomas, A., Chess, S., & Birch, H. G. (1970). The origin of personality. *Scientific American, 223*(2), 102–109.

Thomas, D. R. (1992). Discrimination and generalization. In L. R. Squire (Ed.), *Encyclopedia of learning and memory.* New York, NY: Macmillan.

Thomas, R. M. (2005). *Comparing theories of child development.* Belmont, CA: Wadsworth.

Thompson, J. K., & Kinder, B. (2003). Eating disorders. In M. Hersen, & S. Turner (Eds.), *Handbook of adult psychopathology.* New York, NY: Plenum Press.

Thompson, J. K., Roehrig, M., & Kinder, B. N. (2007). Eating disorders. In M. Hersen, S. M. Turner, & D. C. Beidel (Eds.), *Adult psychopathology and diagnosis.* New York, NY: Wiley.

Thompson, J. K., & Stice, E. (2001). Thin-ideal internalization: Mounting evidence for a new risk factor for body-image disturbance and eating pathology. *Current Directions in Psychological Science, 10*(5), 181–183.

Thompson, L. G. (2010). Climate change: The evidence and our options. *The Behavior Analyst, 33,* 153–170.

Thompson, R. A. (2008). Early attachment and later development: Familiar questions, new answers. In J. Cassidy & P. R. Shaver (Eds.), *Handbook of attachment: Theory, research, and clinical applications* (2nd ed., pp. 348–365). New York, NY: Guilford Press.

Thompson, R. A., & Nelson, C. A. (2001). Developmental science and the media: Early brain development. *American Psychologist, 56,* 5–15.

Thompson, R. A., Winer, A. C., & Goodwin, R. (2011). The individual child: Temperament, emotion, self, and personality. In M. H. Bornstein & M. E. Lamb (Eds.), *Developmental science: An advanced textbook* (pp. 427–468). New York, NY: Psychology Press.

Thompson, R. F. (1989). A model system approach to memory. In P. R. Solomon, G. R. Goethals, C. M. Kelley, & B. R. Stephens (Eds.), *Memory: Interdisciplinary approaches.* New York, NY: Springer-Verlag.

Thompson, R. F. (1992). Memory. *Current Opinion in Neurobiology, 2,* 203–208.

Thompson, R. F. (2005). In search of memory traces. *Annual Review of Psychology, 56,* 1–23.

Thompson, R. F., & Zola, S. M. (2003). In D. K. Freedheim (Ed.), *Handbook of psychology* (Vol. 2): New York, NY: Wiley.

Thorne, B. M., & Henley, T. B. (1997). *Connections in the history and systems of psychology.* Boston, MA: Houghton Mifflin.

Thornhill, R. (1976). Sexual selection and nuptial feeding behavior in *Bittacus apicalis* (Insecta: Mecoptera). *American Naturalist, 110,* 529–548.

Thornicroft, G. (2006). *Shunned: Discrimination against people with mental illness.* New York, NY: Oxford University Press.

Thornton, B., & Maurice, J. K. (1999). Physical attractiveness contrast effect and the moderating influence of self-consciousness. *Sex Roles, 40,* 379–392.

Thornton, B., & Moore, S. (1993). Physical attractiveness contrast effect: Implications for self-esteem and evaluations of the social self. *Personality and Social Psychology Bulletin, 19,* 474–480.

Thornton, L. M., Mazzeo, S. E., & Bulik, C. M. (2011). The heritability of eating disorders: Methods and current findings. In R. H. Adan & W. H. Kaye (Eds.), *Behavioral neurobiology of eating disorders* (pp. 141–156). New York, NY: Springer-Verlag.

Thorpe, S. J., & Salkozskis, P. M. (1995). Phobia beliefs: Do cognitive factors play a role in specific phobias? *Behavioral Research and Therapy, 33,* 805–816.

Thorpy, M., & Yager, J. (2001). *Sleeping well: The sourcebook for sleep and sleep disorders.* New York, NY: Checkmark Books.

Thurstone, L. L. (1931a). The measurement of social attitudes. *Journal of Abnormal and Social Psychology, 26,* 249–269.

Thurstone, L. L. (1931b). Multiple factor analysis. *Psychological Review, 38,* 406–427.

Thurstone, L. L. (1938). *Primary mental abilities.* Chicago: University of Chicago Press.

Thurstone, L. L. (1955). *The differential growth of mental abilities.* Chapel Hill: University of North Carolina.

Tice, D. M., Bratslavsky, E., & Baumeister, R. F. (2001). Emotional distress regulation takes precedence over impulse control: If you feel bad, do it! *Journal of Personality and Social Psychology, 80,* 53–67.

Till, B. D., & Priluck, R. L. (2000). Stimulus generalization in classical conditioning: An initial investigation and extension. *Psychology and Marketing, 17,* 55–72.

Tindale, R. S., Kameda, T., & Hinsz, V. B. (2003). Group decision making. In M. A. Hogg & J. Cooper (Eds.), *The Sage handbook of social psychology.* Thousand Oaks, CA: Sage.

Tippman-Peikert, M., Morgenthaler, T. I., Boeve, B. F., & Silber, M. H. (2006). REM sleep behavior disorder and REM-related parasomnias. In T. Lee-Chiong (Ed.), *Sleep: A comprehensive handbook* (pp. 435–442). Hoboken, NJ: Wiley-Liss.

Titsworth, B. S., & Kiewra, K. A. (2004). Spoken organizational lecture cues and student notetaking as facilitators of student learning. *Contemporary Educational Psychology, 29,* 447–461.

Todd, J. T., & Morris, E. K. (1992). Case histories in the great power of steady misrepresentation. *American Psychologist, 47,* 1441–1453.

Todd, P. M., & Gigerenzer, G. (2000). Precis of simple heuristics that make us smart. *Behavioral & Brain Sciences, 23,* 727–780.

Todd, P. M., & Gigerenzer, G. (2007). Environments that make us smart: Ecological rationality. *Current Directions in Psychological Science, 16,* 167–171.

Toga, A. W., Thompson, P. M., & Sowell, E. R. (2006). Mapping brain maturation. *Trends in Neurosciences, 29,* 148–159.

Tolman, D. L., & Diamond, L. M. (2001). Desegregating sexuality research: Cultural and biological perspectives on gender and desire. *Annual Review of Sex Research, 12,* 33–74.

Tolman, E. C. (1922). A new formula for behaviorism. *Psychological Review, 29,* 44–53.

Tolman, E. C. (1932). *Purposive behavior in animals and men.* New York, NY: Appleton-Century-Crofts.

Tolman, E. C. (1938). The determiners of behavior at a choice point. *Psychological Review, 45,* 1–41.

Tolman, E. C. (1948). Cognitive maps in rats and men. *Psychological Review, 55,* 189–208.

Tolman, E. C., & Honzik, C. H. (1930). Introduction and removal of reward, and maze performance in rats. *University of California Publications in Psychology, 4,* 257–275.

Tom, S. M., Fox, C. R., Trepel, C., & Poldrack, R. A. (2007). The neural basis of loss aversion in decision making under risk. *Science, 315,* 515–518.

Tomkins, S. S. (1980). Affect as amplification: Some modifications in theory. In R. Plutchik & H. Kellerman (Eds.), *Emotion: Theory, research and experience* (Vol. 1). New York, NY: Academic Press.

Tomkins, S. S. (1991). *Affect, imagery, consciousness: 3. Anger and fear.* New York, NY: Springer-Verlag.

Tooby, J., & Cosmides, L. (1989). Evolutionary psychology and the generation of culture: Part 1. Theoretical considerations. *Ethology and Sociobiology, 10,* 29–49.

Tooby, J., & Cosmides, L. (2005). Conceptual foundations of evolutionary psychology. In D. M. Buss (Ed.), *The handbook of evolutionary psychology.* New York, NY: Wiley.

Torgersen, S. (1979). The nature and origin of common phobic fears. *British Journal of Psychiatry, 119,* 343–351.

Torgersen, S. (1983). Genetic factors in anxiety disorders. *Archives of General Psychiatry, 40,* 1085–1089.

Tormala, Z. L., & Petty, R. E. (2002). What doesn't kill me makes me stronger: The effects of resisting persuasion on attitude certainty. *Journal of Personality and Social Psychology, 83,* 1298–1313.

Tormala, Z. L., & Petty, R. E. (2004). Resistance to persuasion and attitude certainty: The moderating role of elaboration. *Personality and Social Psychology Bulletin, 30,* 1446–1457.

Torrance, E. P. (1962). *Guiding creative talent.* Englewood Cliffs, NJ: Prentice-Hall.

Torres, A. R., Prince, M. J., Bebbington, P. E., Bhugra, D., Brugha, T. S., & Farrell, M. et al. (2006). Obsessive-compulsive disorder: Prevalence, comorbidity, impact, and help-seeking in the British national psychiatric morbidity survey of 2000. *American Journal of Psychiatry, 163,* 1978–1985.

Torres, L., & Saunders, S. M. (2009). Evaluation of psychotherapy. In B. J. Sadock, V. A. Sadock, & P. Ruiz (Eds.), *Kaplan & Sadock's comprehensive textbook of psychiatry* (9th ed.). Philadelphia, PA: Lippincott, Williams & Wilkins.

Torrey, E. F. (1992). *Freudian fraud: The malignant effect of Freud's theory on American thought and culture.* New York, NY: Harper Perennial.

Torrey, E. F. (1996). *Out of the shadows.* New York, NY: Wiley.

Tourangeau, R. (2004). Survey research and societal change. *Annual Review of Psychology, 55,* 775–801.

Tourangeau, R., & Yan, T. (2007). Sensitive questions in surveys. *Psychological Bulletin, 133,* 859–883.

Tov, W., & Diener, E. (2007). Culture and subjective well-being. In S. Kitayama & D. Cohen (Eds.), *Handbook of cultural psychology* (pp. 691–713). New York, NY: Guilford Press.

Toyota, H., & Kikuchi, Y. (2004). Self-generated elaboration and spacing effects on incidental memory. *Perceptual and Motor Skills, 99,* 1193–1200.

Toyota, H., & Kikuchi, Y. (2005). Encoding richness of self-generated elaboration and spacing effects on incidental memory. *Perceptual and Motor Skills, 101,* 621–627.

Tozzi, F., Thornton, L. M., Klump, K. L., Fichter, M. M., Halmi, K. A., Kaplan, A. S., Strober, M., Woodside, D. B., Crow, S., Mitchell, J., Rotondo, A., Mauri, M., Cassano, G., Keel, P., Plotnicov, K. H., Pollice, C., Lilenfeld, L. R., Berrettini, W. H., Bulik, C. M., & Kaye, W. H. (2005). Symptom fluctuation in eating disorders: Correlates of diagnostic crossover. *American Journal of Psychiatry, 162,* 732–740.

Tracy, J. L., & Robins, R. W. (2008). The automaticity of emotion recognition. *Emotion, 8,* 81–95.

Travis, F. (2001). Autonomic and EEG patterns distinguish transcending from other experiences during Transcendental Meditation practice. *International Journal of Psychophysiology, 42,* 1–9.

Treisman, A. (2009). Attention: Theoretical and psychological perspectives. In M. S. Gazzaniga (Ed.), *The cognitive neurosciences* (4th ed., pp. 189–204). Cambridge, MA: MIT Press.

Triandis, H. C. (1989). Self and social behavior in differing cultural contexts. *Psychological Review, 96,* 269–289.

Triandis, H. C. (1994). *Culture and social behavior.* New York, NY: McGraw-Hill.

Triandis, H. C. (2001). Individualism and collectivism: Past, present, and future. In D. Matsumoto (Ed.), *The handbook of culture and psychology.* New York, NY: Oxford University Press.

Triandis, H. C. (2007). Culture and psychology: A history of the study of their relationship. In S. Kitayama & D. Cohen (Eds.), *Handbook of cultural psychology* (pp. 59–76). New York, NY: Guilford Press.

Triandis, H. C., & Suh, E. M. (2002). Cultural influences on personality. *Annual Review of Psychology, 53,* 133–160. doi:10.1146/annurev.psych.53.100901.135200

Trivers, R. L. (1971). The evolution of reciprocal altruism. *Quarterly Review of Biology, 46,* 35–57.

Trivers, R. L. (1972). Parental investment and sexual selection. In B. Campbell (Ed.), *Sexual selection and the descent of man*. Chicago: Aldine.

Tsai, J. L., Butcher, J. N., Muñoz, R. F., & Vitousek, K. (2001). Culture, ethnicity, and psychopathology. In P. B. Sutker & H. E. Adams (Eds.), *Comprehensive handbook of psychopathology*. New York, NY: Kluwer Academic/Plenum.

Tsankova, N., Renthal, W., Kumar, A., & Nestler, E. J. (2007). Epigenetic regulation in psychiatric disorders. *Nature Reviews Neuroscience, 8*(5), 355–367.

Tseng, W. S. (1997). Overview: Culture and psychopathology. In W. S. Tseng & J. Streltzer (Eds.), *Culture and psychopathology: A guide to clinical assessment*. New York, NY: Brunner/Mazel.

Tseng, W. S. (2009). Culture-related specific psychiatric syndromes. In M. C. Gelder, N. C. Andreasen, J. J. López-Ibor, Jr., & J. R. Geddes (Eds.). *New Oxford textbook of psychiatry* (2nd ed., Vol. 1). New York, NY: Oxford University Press.

Tuckey, M. R., & Brewer, N. (2003). The influence of schemas, stimulus ambiguity, and interview schedule on eyewitness memory over time. *Journal of Experimental Psychology: Applied, 9,* 101–118.

Tugade, M. M., & Fredrickson, B. L. (2004). Resilient individuals use positive emotions to bounce back from negative emotional experiences. *Journal of Personality and Social Psychology, 86,* 320–333.

Tulving, E. (1985). How many memory systems are there? *American Psychologist, 40,* 385–398.

Tulving, E. (1987). Multiple memory systems and consciousness. *Human Neurobiology, 6*(2), 67–80.

Tulving, E. (2001). Origin of autonoesis in episodic memory. In H. L. Roediger III, J. S. Nairne, I. Neath, & A. M. Surprenant (Eds.), *The nature of remembering: Essays in honor of Robert G. Crowder* (pp. 17–34). Washington, DC: American Psychological Association.

Tulving, E. (2002). Episodic memory: From mind to brain. *Annual Review of Psychology, 53,* 1–25.

Tulving, E., & Thomson, D. M. (1973). Encoding specificity and retrieval processes in episodic memory. *Psychological Review, 80,* 352–373.

Tunnell, K. D. (2005). The Oxycontin epidemic and crime panic in rural Kentucky. *Contemporary Drug Problems, 32,* 225–258.

Turkheimer, E., & Waldron, M. (2000). Nonshared environment: A theoretical, methodological, and quantitative review. *Psychological Bulletin, 126,* 78–108.

Turkheimer, E., Haley, A., Waldron, M., D'Onofrio, B., & Gottesman, I. I. (2003). Socioeconomic status modifies heritability of IQ in young children. *Psychological Science, 14,* 623–628.

Turkkan, J. S. (1989). Classical conditioning: The new hegemony. *Behavioral and Brain Sciences, 12,* 121–179.

Turkle, S. (2011). *Alone together*. New York, NY: Basic Books,

Turner, E. H., Matthews, A. M., Linardos, E., Tell, R. A., & Rosenthal, R. (2008). Selective publication of antidepressant trials and its influence on apparent efficacy. *New England Journal of Medicine, 358,* 252–260.

Turner, J. C. (1987). *Rediscovering the social group: A self-categorization theory*. Oxford, England: Basil Blackwell.

Turner, J. C., & Reynolds, K. J. (2001). The social identity perspective in intergroup relations: Theories, themes, and controversies. In R. Brown & S. L. Gaertner (Eds.), *Blackwell handbook of social psychology: Intergroup processes*. Malden, MA: Blackwell.

Turner, J. G., Hogg, M. A., Oakes, P. J., Reicher, S. D., & Wetherell, M. S. (1987). *Rediscovering the social group: A self-categorization theory*. Oxford, UK: Basil Blackwell.

Turner, J. R., & Wheaton, B. (1995). Checklist measurement of stressful life events. In S. Cohen, R. C. Kessler, & L. U. Gordon (Eds.), *Measuring stress: A guide for health and social scientists*. New York, NY: Oxford University Press.

Tversky, A. (1972). Elimination by aspects: A theory of choice. *Psychological Review, 79,* 281–299.

Tversky, A., & Kahneman, D. (1973). Availability: A heuristic for judging frequency and probability. *Cognitive Psychology, 5,* 207–232.

Tversky, A., & Kahneman, D. (1974). Judgments under uncertainty: Heuristics and biases. *Science, 185,* 1124–1131.

Tversky, A., & Kahneman, D. (1982). Judgment under uncertainty: Heuristics and biases. In D. Kahneman, P. Slovic, & A. Tversky (Eds.), *Judgment under uncertainty: Heuristics and biases*. New York, NY: Cambridge University Press.

Tversky, A., & Kahneman, D. (1983). Extensional versus intuitive reasoning: The conjunction fallacy in probability judgment. *Psychological Review, 90,* 283–315.

Tversky, A., & Kahneman, D. (1988). Rational choice and the framing of decisions. In D. E. Bell, H. Raiffa, & A. Tversky (Eds.), *Decision making: Descriptive, normative, and prescriptive interactions*. New York, NY: Cambridge University Press.

Tversky, A., & Kahneman, D. (1991). Loss aversion in riskless choice: A reference-dependent model. *Quarterly Journal of Economics, 106,* 1039–1061.

Twenge, J. M., & Campbell, W. (2009). *The narcissism epidemic: Living in the age of enlightenment*. New York, NY: Free Press.

Twenge, J. M., Campbell, W. K., & Foster, C. A. (2003). Parenthood and marital satisfaction: A meta-analytic review. *Journal of Marriage and the Family, 65,* 574–583.

Twenge, J. M., & Foster, J. D. (2010). Birth cohort increases in narcissistic personality traits among American college students, 1982–2009. *Social Psychological and Personality Science, 1,* 99–106.

Twenge, J. M., Konrath, S., Foster, J. D., Campbell, W., & Bushman, B. J. (2008). Egos inflating over time: A cross-temporal meta-analysis of the Narcissistic Personality Inventory. *Journal of Personality, 76*(4), 875–902. doi:10.1111/j.1467-6494.2008.00507.x

Tyrer, P., Coombs, N., Ibrahimi, F., Mathilakath, A., Bajaj, P., Ranger, M., et al. (2007). Critical developments in the assessment of personality disorder. *British Journal of Psychiatry, 90,* 51–59.

Uchino, B. N., & Birmingham, W. (2011). Stress and support processes. In R. J. Contrada & A. Baum (Eds.), *The handbook of stress science: Biology, psychology, and health* (pp. 111–121). New York, NY: Springer Publishing.

Uchino, B. N., Uno, D., & Holt-Lunstad, J. (1999). Social support, physiological processes, and health. *Current Directions in Psychological Science, 8,* 145–148.

Ulrich, R. E. (1991). Animal rights, animal wrongs and the question of balance. *Psychological Science, 2,* 197–201.

Umbel, V. M., Pearson, B. Z., Fernandez, S. C., & Oller, D. K. (1992). Measuring bilingual children's receptive vocabularies. *Child Development, 63,* 1012–1020.

Umberson, D., Williams, K., Powers, D. A., Chen, M. D., & Campbell, A. M. (2005). As good as it gets? A life course perspective on marital quality. *Social Forces, 84*(1), 493–511. doi:10.1353/sof.2005.0131

UNAIDS (Joint United Nations Programme on HIV/AIDS). (2009). *AIDS epidemic update*. Geneva, Switzerland: World Health Organization. Retrieved from http://data.unaids.org/pub/Report/2009/jc1700_epi_update_2009_en.pdf

Underwood, B. J. (1961). Ten years of massed practice on distributed practice. *Psychological Review, 68,* 229–247.

Unsworth, N., Heitz, R. P., Schrock, J. C., & Engle, R. W. (2005). An automated version of the operation span task. *Behavior Research Methods, 37*(3), 498–505. doi:10.3758/BF03192720

Ursano, A. M., Kartheiser, P. H., & Barnhill, L. (2008). Disorders usually first diagnosed in infancy, childhood, or adolescence. In R. E. Hales, S. C. Yudofsky, & G. O. Gabbard (Eds.), *The American Psychiatric Publishing textbook of psychiatry* (5th ed., pp. 861–920). Arlington, VA: American Psychiatric Publishing.

Ursano, R. J., Sonnenberg, S. M., & Lazar, S. G. (2008). Psychodynamic psychotherapy. In R. E. Hales, S. C. Yudofsky, & G. O. Gabbard (Eds.), *The American Psychiatric Publishing textbook of psychiatry* (pp. 1171–1190). Washington, DC: American Psychiatric Publishing.

U.S. Department of Health and Human Services. (1990). *The health benefits of smoking cessation: A report of the surgeon general*. Washington, DC: U.S. Government Printing Office.

U.S. Department of Health and Human Services. (1999). *Mental health: A report of the Surgeon General*. Washington, DC: U.S. Government Printing Office.

U.S. Department of Health and Human Services. (2006). *The health consequences of involuntary exposure to tobacco smoke: A report of the Surgeon General*. Atlanta, GA: Author.

U.S. Energy Information Administration. (2010a). Country analysis briefs: China. Retrieved from http://www.eia.gov/countries/cab.cfm?fips=CH

U.S. Energy Information Administration. (2010b). Oil: Crude and petroleum products explained. Petroleum statistics. Retrieved from http://www.eia.doe.gov/energyexplained/index.cfm?page=oil_home#tab2

U.S. Environmental Protection Agency. (2008). About air toxics. Technology transfer network air toxics website. Retrieved from http://www.epa.gov/ttn/atw/allabout.html

U.S. Environmental Protection Agency. (2011). Basic information about food waste. Retrieved from http://www.epa.gov/wastes/conserve/materials/organics/food/fd-basic.htm

Uttal, W. R. (2001). *The new phrenology: The limits of localizing cognitive processes in the brain*. Cambridge, MA: MIT Press.

Uttal, W. R. (2002). Precis of *The New Phrenology:* The limits of localizing cognitive processes in the brain. *Brain and Mind, 3,* 221–228.

Väänänen, A. (2010). Psychosocial work environment and risk of ischaemic heart disease in women. *Occupational & Environmental Medicine, 67*(5), 291–292.

Vaillant, G. E. (1994). Ego mechanisms of defense and personality psychopathology. *Journal of Abnormal Psychology, 103,* 44–50.

Valenstein, E. S. (1973). *Brain control*. New York, NY: Wiley.

Valli, K., & Revonsuo, A. (2009). Sleep: Dreaming data and theories. In W. P. Banks (Ed.), *Encyclopedia of Consciousness* (pp. 341–356). San Diego, CA: Academic Press.

Vallortigara, G., & Rogers, L. J. (2005). Survival with an asymmetrical brain: Advantages and disadvantages of cerebral lateralization. *Behavioral and Brain Sciences, 28*(4), 575–633. doi:10.1017/S0140525X05000105

Van Blerkom, D. L. (2006). *College study skills: Becoming a strategic learner.* Belmont, CA: Wadsworth.

Van Boven, L. (2005). Experientialism, materialism, and the pursuit of happiness. *Review of General Psychology, 9,* 132–142.

Van de Castle, R. L. (1994). *Our dreaming mind.* New York, NY: Ballantine Books.

van den Berg, A. E., Hartig, T., & Staats, H. (2007). Preference for nature in urbanized societies: Stress, restoration, and the pursuit of sustainability. *Journal of Social Issues, 63,* 79–96.

van den Berg, A. E., Koole, S. L., & van der Wulp, N. Y. (2003). Environmental preference and restoration: (How) are they related? *Journal of Environmental Psychology, 23,* 135–146.

van den Boom, D. (2001). First attachments: Theory and research. In G. Bremner & A. Fogel (Eds.), *Blackwell handbook of infant development* (pp. 296–325). Malden, MA: Blackwell Publishing.

van den Bos, K., & Maas, M. (2009). On the psychology of the belief in a just world: Exploring experiential and rationalistic paths to victim blaming. *Personality and Social Psychology Bulletin, 35*(12), 1567–1578. doi:10.1177/0146167209344628

Van den Eynde, F., Claudino, A. M., Mogg, A., Horrell, L., Stahl, D., Ribeiro, W., et al. (2010). Repetitive transcranial magnetic stimulation reduces cue-induced food craving in bulimic disorders. *Biological Psychiatry, 67*(8), 793–795. doi:10.1016/j.biopsych.2009.11.023

Van der Hart, O., & Nijenhuis, E. R. S. (2009). Dissociative disorders. In P. H. Blaney & T. Millon (Eds.), *Oxford textbook of psychopathology* (2nd ed., pp. 452–481). New York, NY: Oxford University Press.

van der Post, L. (1975). *Jung and the story of our time.* New York, NY: Vintage Books.

Van Dongen, H. P. A., Baynard, M. D., Maislin, G., & Dinges, D. F. (2004). Systematic interindividual differences in neurobehavioral impairment from sleep loss: Evidence of trait-like differential vulnerability. *Sleep: Journal of Sleep & Sleep Disorders Research, 27,* 423–433.

Van Dongen, H. P. A., Maislin, G., Mullington, J. M., & Dinges, D. F. (2003). The cumulative cost of additional wakefulness: Dose-response effects on neurobehavioral functions and sleep physiology from chronic sleep restriction and total sleep deprivation. *Sleep: Journal of Sleep & Sleep Disorders Research, 26,* 117–126.

van Eck, M., Nicolson, N. A., & Berkhof, J. (1998). Effects of stressful daily events on mood states: Relationship to global perceived stress. *Journal of Personality and Social Psychology, 75,* 1572–1585.

van Griensven, F., Chakkraband, M. L. S., Thienkrua, W., Pengjuntr, W., Cardozo, B. L., & Tantipiwatanaskul, P. et al. (2007). Mental health problems among adults in tsunami-affected areas in Southern Thailand. *Journal of the American Medical Association, 296,* 537–548.

Van Hoesen, G. W., Morecraft, R. J., & Semendeferi, K. (1996). Functional neuroanatomy of the limbic system and prefrontal cortex. In B. S. Fogel, R. B. Schiffer, & S. M. Rao (Eds), *Neuropsychiatry.* Baltimore: Williams & Wilkins.

van IJzendoorn, M. H., & Bakermans-Kranenburg, M. J. (2004). Maternal sensitivity and infant temperament in the formation of attachment. In G. Bremner & A. Slater (Eds.), *Theories of infant development* (pp. 233–257). Malden, MA: Blackwell Publishing.

van IJzendoorn, M. H., & Juffer, F. (2005). Adoption is a successful natural intervention enhancing adopted children's IQ and school performance. *Current Directions in Psychological Science, 14,* 326–330.

van IJzendoorn, M. H., & Kroonenberg, P. M. (1988). Cross-cultural patterns of attachment: A meta-analysis of the strange situation. *Child Development, 59,* 147–156.

van IJzendoorn, M. H., & Sagi-Schwartz, A. (2008). Cross-cultural patterns of attachment: Universal and contextual dimensions. In J. Cassidy & P. R. Shaver (Eds.), *Handbook of attachment: Theory, research, and clinical applications* (2nd ed., pp. 3–22). New York, NY: Guilford Press.

Van Kammen, D. P., Hurford, I., & Marder, S. R. (2009). First-generation antipsychotics. In B. J. Sadock, V. A. Sadock, & P. Ruiz (Eds.), *Kaplan & Sadock's comprehensive textbook of psychiatry* (pp. 3105–3126). Philadelphia, PA: Lippincott, Williams & Wilkins.

van Kesteren, N. M. C., Hospers, H. J., & Kok, G. (2007). Sexual risk behavior among HIV-positive men who have sex with men: A literature review. *Patient Education and Counseling, 65,* 5–20.

van Leeuwen, M. L., Matthijs, L., & Macrae, C. N. (2004). Is beautiful always good? Implicit benefits of facial attractiveness. *Social Cognition, 22,* 637–649.

Van Praag, H., Zhao, X., & Gage, F. H. (2004). Neurogenesis in the adult mammalian brain. In M. S. Gazzaniga (Ed.), *The cognitive neurosciences* (3rd ed.) (pp. 127–137). Cambridge, MA: MIT Press.

van Swol, L. M. (2009). Extreme members and group polarization. *Social Influence, 4*(3), 185–199. doi:10.1080/15534510802584368

Van Vugt, M. (2001). Community identification moderating the impact of financial incentives in a natural social dilemma: Water conservation. *Personality and Social Psychology Bulletin, 27,* 1440–1449.

Van Vugt, M. (2002). Central, individual, or collective control? Social dilemma strategies for natural resource management. *American Behavioral Scientist, 45*(5), 783–800.

Vandenbroucke, J. P., & Psaty, B. M. (2008). Benefits and risks of drug treatments: How to combine the best evidence on benefits with the best data about adverse effects. *Journal of the American Medical Association, 300*(20), 2417–2419.

Vandereycken, W. (2002). History of anorexia nervosa and bulimia nervosa. In C. G. Fairburn, & K. D. Brownell (Eds.), *Eating disorders and obesity.* New York, NY: Guilford Press.

Vandewater, E., A., Bickham, D. S., & Lee, J. H. (2006). Time well spent? Relating television use to children's free-time activities. *Pediatrics, 117,* 181–191. Retrieved from http://www.commercialalert.org/vandewatertv.pdf

Varnum, M. W., Grossmann, I., Kitayama, S., & Nisbett, R. E. (2010). The origin of cultural differences in cognition: The social orientation hypothesis. *Current Directions in Psychological Science, 19*(1), 9–13. doi:10.1177/0963721409359301

Vartanian, L. R., Herman, C., & Wansink, B. (2008). Are we aware of the external factors that influence our food intake? *Health Psychology, 27*(5), 533–538. doi:10.1037/0278-6133.27.5.533

Vase, L. R., Riley, I. J., & Price, D. (2002). A comparison of placebo effects in clinical analgesic trials versus studies of placebo analgesia. *Pain, 99,* 443–452.

Vazire, S., & Funder, D. C. (2006). Impulsivity and the self-defeating behavior of narcissists. *Personality and Social Psychology Review, 10*(2), 154–165. doi:10.1207/s15327957pspr1002_4

Veasey, S. C. (2009). Sleep apnea. In R. Stickgold & M. P. Walker (Eds.), *The neuroscience of sleep* (pp. 263–269). San Diego, CA: Academic Press.

Vecera, S. P., & Palmer, S. E. (2006). Grounding the figure: Surface attachment influences figure-ground organization. *Psychonomic Bulletin & Review, 13,* 563–569.

Veenhoven, R. (1993). *Happiness in nations.* Rotterdam, Netherlands: Risbo.

Veenhoven, R. (2008). Healthy happiness: Effects of happiness on physical health and the consequences for preventive health care. *Journal of Happiness Studies, 9*(3), 449–469. doi:10.1007/s10902-006-9042-1

Vega, V., & Malamuth, N. M. (2007). Predicting sexual aggression: The role of pornography in the context of general and specific risk factors. *Aggressive Behavior, 33,* 104–117.

Venn, A., & Britton, J. (2007). Exposure to second-hand smoke and biomarkers of cardiovascular disease risk in never-smoking adults. *Circulation, 115*(8), 990–995.

Verheul, R. (2005). Clinical utility for dimensional models of personality pathology. *Journal of Personality Disorders, 19,* 283–302.

Vermeeren, A. (2004). Residual effects of hypnotics: Epidemiology and clinical implications. *CNS Drugs, 18*(5), 297–328.

Vernon, P. A., Wickett, J. C., Bazana, G. P., & Stelmack, R. M. (2000). The neuropsychology and psychophysiology of human intelligence. In R. J. Sternberg (Ed.), *Handbook of intelligence.* Cambridge, UK: Cambridge University Press.

Vgontzas, A. N., Liao, D., Bixler, E. O., Chrousos, G. P., & Vela-Bueno, A. (2009). Insomnia with objective short sleep duration is associated with a high risk for hypertension. *Sleep: Journal of Sleep and Sleep Disorders Research, 32*(4), 491–497.

Victoroff, J. (2005). Central nervous system changes with normal aging. In B. J. Sadock & V. A. Sadock (Eds.), *Kaplan & Sadock's comprehensive textbook of psychiatry.* Philadelphia, PA: Lippincott Williams & Wilkins.

Videbech, P. (2006). Hippocampus and unipolar depression. *Directions in Psychiatry, 26,* 183–194.

Videbech, P., & Ravnkilde, B. (2004). Hippocampal volume and depression: A meta-analysis of MRI studies. *American Journal of Psychiatry, 161,* 1957–1966.

Vierck, C. (1978). Somatosensory system. In R. B. Masterston (Ed.), *Handbook of sensory neurobiology.* New York, NY: Plenum.

Viglione, D. J., & Rivera, B. (2003). Assessing personality and psychopathology with projective methods. In J. R. Graham & J. A. Naglieri (Eds.), *Handbook of psychology, Vol. 10: Assessment psychology.* New York, NY: Wiley.

Vineis, P. (2005). Environmental tobacco smoke and risk of respiratory cancer and chronic obstructive pulmonary disease in former smokers and never smokers in the EPIC prospective study. *British Medical Journal, 330*(7486), 277–280.

Visser, P. S., & Cooper, J. (2003). Attitude change. In M. A. Hogg & J. Cooper (Eds.), *The Sage handbook of social psychology.* Thousand Oaks, CA: Sage.

Vitiello, M. V. (2009). Recent advances in understanding sleep and sleep disturbances in older adults: Growing older does not mean sleeping poorly. *Current Directions in Psychological Science, 18*(6), 316–320. doi:10.1111/j.1467-8721.2009.01659.x

Vlek, C. & Steg, L. (2007). Human behavior and environmental sustainability: Problems, driving forces, and research topics. *Journal of Social Issues, 63,* 1–19.

Vogel, I., Brug, J., Hosli, E. J., van der Ploeg, C. P. B., & Raat, H. (2008). MP3 players and hearing loss: Adolescents' perceptions of loud music and hearing conservation. *Journal of Pediatrics, 152*(3), 400–404. doi:10.1016/j.jpeds.2007.07.009

Vogel, I., Brug, J., van der Ploeg, C. P. B., & Raat, H. (2007). Young people's exposure to loud music: A summary of the literature. *American Journal of Preventative Medicine, 33*(2), 124–133. doi: 10.1016/j.amepre.2007.03.016.

Vohs, K. D., Baumeister, R. F., Schmeichel, B. J., Twenge, J. M., Nelson, N. M., & Tice, D. M. (2008). Making choices impairs subsequent self-control: A limited-resource account of decision making, self-regulation, and active initiative. *Journal of Personality and Social Psychology, 94*(5), 883–898. doi:10.1037/0022-3514.94.5.883

Volkow, N. D., Fowler, J. S., Wang, G. J., & Swanson, J. M. (2004). Dopamine in drug abuse and addiction: Results from imaging studies and treatment implications. *Molecular Psychiatry, 9*, 557–569.

von Károlyi, C., & Winner, E. (2005). Extreme giftedness. In R. J. Sternberg & J. E. Davidson (Eds.), *Conceptions of giftedness*. New York, NY: Cambridge University Press.

Voyer, D. (1996). On the magnitude of laterality effects and sex differences in functional lateralities. *Laterality, 1*, 51–83.

Voyer, D., Nolan, C., & Voyer, S. (2000). The relation between experience and spatial performance in men and women. *Sex Roles, 43*, 891–915.

Vygotsky, L. S. (1934/1986). *Thought and language*. A. Kozulin (Trans). Cambridge, MA: MIT Press.

Vyse, S. A. (1997). *Believing in magic: The psychology of superstition*. New York, NY: Oxford University Press.

Vyse, S. A. (2000). *Believing in magic: The psychology of superstition*. New York, NY: Oxford University Press.

Waage, S., Moen, B., Pallesen, S., Eriksen, H. R., Ursin, H., Åkerstedt, T., & Bjorvatn, B. (2009). Shift work disorder among oil rig workers in the North Sea. *Sleep: Journal of Sleep and Sleep Disorders Research, 32*(4), 558–565.

Wachtel, P. L. (1977). *Psychoanalysis and behavior therapy: Toward an integration*. New York, NY: Basic Books.

Wachtel, P. L. (1991). From eclecticism to synthesis: Toward a more seamless psychotherapeutic integration. *Journal of Psychotherapy Integration, 1*, 43–54.

Wager, T. D., Hernandez, L., & Lindquist, M. A. (2009). Essentials of functional neuroimaging. In G. G. Bernston & J. T. Cacioppo (Eds.), *Handbook of neuroscience for the behavioral sciences* (Vol. 1, pp. 152–197). New York, NY: Wiley.

Wager, T. D., Scott, D. J., & Zubieta, J. (2007). Placebo effects on human μ-opioid activity during pain. *Proceedings of the National Academy of Sciences of the United States of America, 104*(26), 11056–11061. doi: 10.1073/pnas.0702413104

Wagner, H. (1989). The physiological differentiation of emotions. In H. Wagner & A. Manstead (Eds), *Handbook of social psychophysiology*. New York, NY: Wiley.

Wagstaff, G. F., David, D., Kirsch, I., & Lynn, S. J. (2010). The cognitive-behavioral model of hypnotherapy. In S. J. Lynn, J. W. Rhue, & I. Kirsch (Eds.), *Handbook of clinical hypnosis* (2nd ed., pp. 179–208). Washington, DC: American Psychological Association.

Wai, J., Cacchio, M., Putallaz, M., & Makel, M. C. (2010). Sex differences in the right tail of cognitive abilities: A 30-year examination. *Intelligence, 38*(4), 412–423. doi:10.1016/j.intell.2010.04.006

Wakefield, J. C. (1999a). Evolutionary versus prototype analyses of the concept of disorder. *Journal of Abnormal Psychology, 108*, 374–399.

Wakefield, J. C. (1999b). The measurement of mental disorder. In A. V. Horvitz & T. L. Scheid (Eds.), *A handbook for the study of mental health: Social contexts, theories, and systems*. New York, NY: Cambridge University Press.

Wakefield, J. C., & Splitzer, R. L. (2002). Lowered estimates—But of what? *Archives of General Psychiatry, 59*(2), 129–130.

Wald, G. (1964). The receptors of human color vision. *Science, 145*, 1007–1017.

Waldman, I. D., & Rhee, S. H. (2006). Genetic and environmental influences on psychopathy and antisocial behavior. In C. J. Patrick (Ed.), *Handbook of Psychopathy*. New York, NY: Guilford Press.

Walker, E., Mittal, V., & Tessner, K. (2008). Stress and the hypothalamic pituitary adrenal axis in the developmental course of schizophrenia. *Annual Review of Clinical Psychology, 4*, 189–216.

Walker, E., & Tessner, K. (2008). Schizophrenia. *Perspectives on Psychological Science, 3*, 30–37.

Walker, L. J. (1988). The development of moral reasoning. In R. Vasta (Ed.), *Annals of child development* (Vol. 5). Greenwich, CT: JAI Press.

Walker, L. J. (1989). A longitudinal study of moral reasoning. *Child Development, 60*, 157–166.

Walker, L. J. (2007). Progress and prospects in the psychology of moral development. In G. W. Ladd (Ed.), *Appraising the human developmental sciences: Essays in honor of Merrill-Palmer Quarterly* (pp. 226–237). Detroit: Wayne State University Press.

Walker, L. J., & Taylor, J. H. (1991). Strange transitions in moral reasoning: A longitudinal study of developmental processes. *Developmental Psychology, 27*, 330–337.

Walker, M. P. (2009). Sleep-dependent memory processing. In R. Stickgold & M. P. Walker (Eds.), *The neuroscience of sleep* (pp. 230–240). San Diego, CA: Academic Press.

Walker, M. P., Brakefield, T., Morgan, A., Hobson, J. A., & Stickgold, R. (2002). Practice with sleep makes perfect: Sleep dependent motor skill learning. *Neuron, 35*, 205–211.

Walker, M. P., & Stickgold, R. (2004). Sleep-dependent learning and memory consolidation. *Neuron, 44*, 121–133.

Walker, M. P., & Stickgold, R. (2006). Sleep, memory, and plasticity. *Annual Review of Psychology, 57*, 139–166.

Wallace, B., & Fisher, L. E. (1999). *Consciousness and behavior*. Boston, MA: Allyn & Bacon.

Wallace, D. S., Paulson, R. M., Lord, C. G., & Bond, C. F. Jr. (2005). Which behaviors do attitudes predict? Meta-analyzing the effects of social pressure and perceived difficulty. *Review of General Psychology, 9*, 214–227.

Wallace, H. M., Baumeister, R. F., & Vohs, K. D. (2005). Audience support and choking under pressure: A home disadvantage? *Journal of Sports Sciences, 23*, 429–438.

Wallace, R. K., & Benson, H. (1972). The physiology of meditation. *Scientific American, 226*, 84–90.

Wallman, J. (1992). *Aping language*. Cambridge, England: Cambridge University Press.

Wallner, B., & Machatschke, I. H. (2009). The evolution of violence in men: The function of central cholesterol and serotonin. *Progress in Neuro-Psychopharmacology & Biological Psychiatry, 33*(3), 391–397. doi:10.1016/j.pnpbp.2009.02.006

Walsh, B. (2008, Sept. 10). Meat: Making global warming worse. *Time*. Retrieved from http://www.time.com/time/health/article/0,8599,1839995,00.html

Walsh, B. T., Seidman, S. N., Sysko, R., & Gould, M. (2002). Placebo response studies of major depression: Variable, substantial and growing. *Journal of the American Medical Association, 287*, 1840–1847.

Walsh, J. K., Dement, W. C., & Dinges, D. F. (2005). Sleep medicine, public policy, and public health. In M. H. Kryger, T. Roth, & W. C. Dement (Eds.). *Principles and practice of sleep medicine*. Philadelphia, PA: Elsevier Saunders.

Walsh, R. (2011). Lifestyle and mental health. *American Psychologist*. Retrieved from http://www.apa.org/pubs/journals/releases/amp-ofp-walsh.pdf

Walsh, R., & Shapiro, S. L. (2006). The meeting of meditative disciplines and Western psychology: A mutually enriching dialogue. *American Psychologist, 61*, 227–239.

Walter, C. A. (2000). The psychological meaning of menopause: Women's experiences. *Journal of Women and Aging, 12*(3–4), 117–131.

Walther, E., & Grigoriadis, S. (2003). Why sad people like shoes better: The influence of mood on the evaluative conditioning of consumer attitudes. *Psychology & Marketing, 10*, 755–775.

Walther, E., & Langer, T. (2008). Attitude formation and change through association: An evaluative conditioning account. In W. D. Crano, & R. Prislin (Eds.), *Attitudes and attitude change* (pp. 61–84). New York, NY: Psychology Press.

Walther, E., Nagengast, B., & Trasselli, C. (2005). Evaluative conditioning in social psychology: Facts and speculations. *Cognition and Emotion, 19*(2), 175–196.

Walton, G. M., & Spencer, S. J. (2009). Latent ability: Grades and test scores systematically underestimate the intellectual ability of negatively stereotyped students. *Psychological Science, 20*(9), 1132–1139. doi:10.1111/j.1467-9280.2009.02417.x

Walton, K. G., Fields, J. Z., Levitsky, D. K., Harris, D. A., Pugh, N. D., & Schneider, R. H. (2004). Lowering cortisol and CVD risk in postmenopausal women: A pilot study using Transcendental Meditation program. In R. Yehuda, & B. McEwen (Eds.), *Biobehavioral stress response: Protective and damaging effects* (pp. 211–215). New York, NY: Annals of the New York Academy of Sciences.

Wampold, B. E. (2001). *The great psychotherapy debate*. Mahwah, NJ: Erlbaum.

Wampold, B. E., Imel, Z. E., & Minami, T. (2007). The story of placebo effects in medicine: Evidence in context. *Journal of Clinical Psychology, 63*(4), 379–390. doi:10.1002/jclp.20354

Wampold, B. E., Minami, T., Tierney, S. C., Baskin, T. W., & Bhati, K. S. (2005). The placebo is powerful: Estimating placebo effects in medicine and psychotherapy from randomized clinical trials. *Journal of Clinical Psychology, 61*(7), 835-854. doi:10.1002/jclp.20129

Wamsley, E. J., & Stickgold, R. (2009). Incorporation of waking events into dreams. In R. Stickgold & M. P. Walker (Eds.), *The neuroscience of sleep* (pp. 330–337). San Diego, CA: Academic Press.

Wang, P. S., Berglund, P., Olfson, M., Pincus, H. A., Wells, K. B., & Kessler, R. C. (2005). Failure and delay in initial treatment contact after first onset of mental disorders in the National Comorbidity Survey Replication. *Archives of General Psychiatry, 62*, 603–613.

Wang, P. S., Lane, M., Olfson, M., Pincus, H. A., Wells, K. B., & Kessler, R. C. (2005). Twelve-month use of mental health services in the United States: Results from the National Comorbidity Survey Replication. *Archives of General Psychiatry, 62,* 629–640.

Wang, P. S., Tohen, M., Bromet, E. J., Angst, J., & Kessler, R. C. (2008). Psychiatric epidemiology. In A. Tasman, J. Kay, J. A. Lieberman, M. B. First, & M. Maj (Eds.), *Psychiatry* (3rd ed.). New York, NY: Wiley-Blackwell.

Wang, S., Baillargeon, R., & Paterson, S. (2005). Detecting continuity violations in infancy: A new account and new evidence from covering and tube events. *Cognition, 95,* 129–173.

Wangensteen, O. H., & Carlson, A. J. (1931). Hunger sensation after total gastrectomy. *Proceedings of the Society for Experimental Biology, 28,* 545–547.

Wansink, B. (2010). From mindless eating to mindlessly eating better. *Physiology & Behavior, 100*(5), 454–463. doi:10.1016/j.physbeh.2010.05.003

Wansink, B., & Kim, J. (2005). Bad popcorn in big buckets: Portion size can influence intake as much as taste. *Journal of Nutrition Education and Behavior, 37*(5), 242–245. doi:10.1016/S1499-4046(06)60278-9

Wansink, B., Painter, J. E., & North, J. (2005). Bottomless bowls: Why visual cues of portion size may influence intake. *Obesity Research, 13*(1), 93–100. doi:10.1038/oby.2005.12

Wargo, E. (2008). The many lives of superstition. *APS Observer, 21*(9), 18–24.

Warr, P. (1999). Well-being and the workplace. In D. Kahneman, E. Diener, & N. Schwarz (Eds.), *Well-being: The foundations of hedonic psychology.* New York, NY: Russell Sage Foundation.

Warwick, D. P. (1975, February). Social scientists ought to stop lying. *Psychology Today,* pp. 38, 40, 105–106.

Wasserman, J. D., & Bracken, B. A. (2003). Psychometric characteristics of assessment procedures. In J. R. Graham & J. A. Naglieri (Eds.), *Handbook of psychology, Vol. 10: Assessment psychology.* New York, NY: Wiley.

Watanabe, M., Kikuchi, H., Tanaka, K., & Takahashi, M. (2010). Association of short sleep duration with weight gain and obesity at 1-year follow-up: A large-scale prospective study. *Sleep: Journal of Sleep and Sleep Disorders Research, 33*(2), 161–167.

Waterhouse, L. (2006). Multiple intelligences, the Mozart effect, and emotional intelligence: A critical review. *Educational Psychologist, 41,* 207–225.

Watkins, L. R. (2007). Immune and glial regulation of pain. *Brain, Behavior, and Immunity, 21,* 519–521.

Watkins, L. R., & Maier, S. F. (2003). When good pain turns bad. *Current Directions in Psychological Science, 12,* 232–236.

Watkins, L. R., Hutchinson, M. R., Ledeboer, A., Wieseler-Frank, J., Milligan, E. D., & Maier, S. F. (2007). Glia as the "bad guys": Implications for improving clinical pain control and the clinical utility of opiods. *Brain, Behavior, and Immunity, 21,* 131–146.

Watkins, M. J. (2002). Limits and province of levels of processing: Considerations of a construct. *Memory, 10,* 339–343.

Watson, D. L., & Tharp, R. G. (2007). *Self-directed behavior: Self-modification for personal adjustment.* Belmont, CA: Wadsworth.

Watson, D., & Clark, L. A. (1997). Extraversion and its positive emotional core. In R. Hogan, J. Johnson, & S. Briggs (Eds.), *Handbook of personality psychology.* San Diego: Academic Press.

Watson, D., David, J. P., & Suls, J. (1999). Personality, affectivity, and coping. In C. R. Snyder (Ed.), *Coping: The psychology of what works.* New York, NY: Oxford University Press.

Watson, J. B. (1913). Psychology as the behaviorist views it. *Psychological Review, 20,* 158–177.

Watson, J. B. (1919). *Psychology from the standpoint of a behaviorist.* Philadelphia, PA: Lippincott.

Watson, J. B. (1924). *Behaviorism.* New York, NY: Norton.

Watson, J. B., & Rayner, R. (1920). Conditioned emotional reactions. *Journal of Experimental Psychology, 3,* 1–14.

Waugh, N. C., & Norman, D. A. (1965). Primary memory. *Psychological Review, 72,* 89–104.

Waxman, S. (2005). Why is the concept "living thing" so elusive? Concepts, languages, and the development of folkbiology. In W. Ahn, R. L. Goldstone, B. C. Love, A. B. Markman, & P. Woolf (Eds.), *Categorization inside and outside the laboratory: Essays in honor of Douglas L. Medin* (pp. 49–67). Washington, DC: American Psychological Association.

Waxman, S. R. (2002). Early word-learning and conceptual development: Everything had a name and each name gave birth to a new thought. In U. Goswami (Ed.), *Blackwell handbook of childhood cognitive development* (pp. 102–126). Malden, MA: Blackwell.

Weatherall, A. (1992). Gender and languages: Research in progress. *Feminism & Psychology, 2,* 177–181.

Weaver, D. R., & Reppert, S. M. (2008). Circadian timekeeping. In L. Squire, D. Berg, F. Bloom, S. Du Lac, A. Ghosh, & N. Spitzer (Eds.), *Fundamental neuroscience* (3rd ed., pp. 931–958). San Diego, CA: Academic Press.

Weaver, K., Garcia, S. M., Schwarz, N., & Miller, D. T. (2007). Inferring the popularity of an opinion from its familiarity: A repetitive voice can sound like a chorus. *Journal of Personality and Social Psychology, 92,* 821–833.

Webb, W. B. (1992). *Sleep: The gentle tyrant.* Bolton, MA: Anker.

Webb, W. B., & Dinges, D. F. (1989). Cultural perspectives on napping and the siesta. In D. F. Dinges & R. J. Broughton (Eds.), *Sleep and alertness: Chronobiological, behavioral, and medical aspects of napping.* New York, NY: Raven.

Weber, E. U. (2006). Experience-based and description-based perceptions of long-term risk: Why global warming does not scare us (yet). *Climatic Change, 77,* 103–120.

Weber, L. J. (2006). *Profits before people?* Bloomington, IN: Indiana University Press.

Webster, G. D. (2009). Parental investment theory. In H. T. Reis & S. Sprecher (Eds.), *Encyclopedia of human relationships* (Vol. 3, pp. 1194–1197). Los Angeles, CA: Sage.

Webster, M. (2010). Color perception. In E. B. Goldstein (Ed.), *Encyclopedia of perception.* Thousand Oaks, CA: Sage.

Wechsler, D. (1949). *Wechsler intelligence scale for children.* New York, NY: Psychological Corporation.

Wechsler, D. (1955). *Manual, Wechsler adult intelligence scale.* New York, NY: Psychological Corporation.

Wechsler, D. (1967). *Manual for the Wechsler preschool and primary scale of intelligence.* New York, NY: Psychological Corporation.

Wechsler, D. (1981). *Manual for the Wechsler adult intelligence scale—revised.* New York, NY: Psychological Corporation.

Wechsler, D. (1991). *WISC-III manual.* San Antonio: Psychological Corporation.

Wechsler, D. (1997). *Wechsler Adult Intelligence Scale-Third Edition (WAIS–III).* San Antonio, TX: Psychological Corporation.

Wechsler, D. (2003). *Wechsler Intelligence Scale for Children—Fourth Edition (WISC IV).* San Antonio, TX: Psychological Corporation.

Wegner, D. M. (1997). Why the mind wanders. In J. D. Cohen & J. W. Schooler (Eds.), *Scientific approaches to consciousness.* Mahwah, NJ: Erlbaum.

Wegner, D. M., & Wheatley, T. (1999). Apparent mental causation: Sources of the experience of will. *American Psychologist, 54,* 480–492. doi:10.1037/0003-066X.54.7.480

Weil, M. , & Rosen, R. (1997). *Technostress: Coping with technology @ work @ home @ play.* New York, NY: Wiley.

Weinberg, R. A. (1989). Intelligence and IQ: Landmark issues and great debates. *American Psychologist, 44,* 98–104.

Weinberger, J., & Westen, D. (2008). RATS, we should have used Clinton: Subliminal priming in political campaigns. *Political Psychology, 29*(5), 631–651. doi:10.1111/j.1467-9221.2008.00658.x

Weiner, B. (1980). *Human motivation.* New York, NY: Holt, Rinehart & Winston.

Weiner, B. (1986). *An attributional theory of motivation and emotion.* New York, NY: Springer-Verlag.

Weiner, B. (1994). Integrating social and personal theories of achievement striving. *Review of Educational Research, 64,* 557–573.

Weiner, B. (Ed). (1974). *Achievement motivation and attribution theory.* Morristown, NJ: General Learning Press.

Weinert, F. E., & Hany, E. A. (2003). The stability of individual differences in intellectual development: Empirical evidence, theoretical problems, and new research questions. In R. J. Sternberg, J. Lautrey, & T. I. Lubart (Eds.), *Models of intelligence: International perspectives* (pp. 169–181). Washington, DC: American Psychological Association.

Weinfeld, N. S., Sroufe, L. A., Egeland, B., & Carlson, E. (2008). Individual differences in infant-caregiver attachment: Conceptual and empirical aspects of security. In J. Cassidy & P. R. Shaver (Eds.), *Handbook of attachment: Theory, research, and clinical applications* (2nd ed., pp. 78–101). New York, NY: Guilford Press.

Weinstein, A., & Lejoyeux, M. (2010). Internet addiction or excessive Internet use. *American Journal of Drug & Alcohol Abuse, 36*(5), 277–283.

Weinstein, L. N., Schwartz, D. G., & Arkin, A. M. (1991). Qualitative aspects of sleep mentation. In S. J. Ellman & J. S. Antrobus (Eds.), *The mind in sleep: Psychology and psychophysiology* (2nd ed.). New York, NY: Wiley.

Weinstein, N. D. (1984). Why it won't happen to me: Perceptions of risk factors and susceptibility. *Health Psychology, 3,* 431–458.

Weinstein, N. D. (2003). Exploring the links between risk perceptions and preventative health behavior. In J. Suls & K. A. Wallston (Eds.), *Social psychological foundations of health and illness.* Malden, MA: Blackwell.

Weinstein, N. D., & Klein, W. M. (1995). Resistance of personal risk perceptions to debiasing interventions. *Health Psychology, 14,* 132–140.

Weinstein, N. D., & Klein, W. M. (1996). Unrealistic optimism: Present and future. *Journal of Social and Clinical Psychology, 15,* 1–8.

Weinstein, N. D., Slovic, P., & Gibson, G. (2004). Accuracy and optimism in smokers' beliefs about quitting. *Nicotine & Tobacco Research, 6,* 375–380.

Weisberg, R. W. (1986). *Creativity: Genius and other myths.* New York, NY: W. H. Freeman.

Weisberg, R. W. (1993). *Creativity: Beyond the myth of genius.* New York, NY: W. H. Freeman.

Weisberg, R. W. (1999). Creativity and knowledge: A challenge to theories. In R. J. Sternberg (Ed.), *Handbook of creativity.* New York, NY: Cambridge University Press.

Weisberg, R. W. (2006). *Creativity: Understanding innovation in problem solving, science, invention, and the arts.* New York, NY: Wiley.

Weiser, D. A., & Riggio, H. R. (2010). Family background and academic achievement: Does self-efficacy mediate outcomes?. *Social Psychology of Education, 13*(3), 367–383. doi:10.1007/s11218-010-9115-1

Weiss, A., Bates, T. C., & Luciano, M. (2008). Happiness is a personal(ity) thing. *Psychological Science, 19,* 205–210.

Weiss, J. L., Overpeck, J. T., & Strauss, B. (2011). Implications of recent sea level rise science for low-elevation areas in coastal cities of the conterminous U.S.A. *Climatic Change, 105,* 635–645.

Weissman, D. H., & Banich, M. T. (2000). The cerebral hemispheres cooperate to perform complex but not simple tasks. *Neuropsychology, 14,* 41–59.

Weiten, W. (1984). Violation of selected item-construction principles in educational measurement. *Journal of Experimental Education, 51,* 46–50.

Weiten, W. (1988a). Objective features of introductory psychology textbooks as related to professors' impressions. *Teaching of Psychology, 15,* 10–16.

Weiten, W. (1988b). Pressure as a form of stress and its relationship to psychological symptomatology. *Journal of Social and Clinical Psychology, 6*(1), 127–139.

Weiten, W. (1998). Pressure, major life events, and psychological symptoms. *Journal of Social Behavior and Personality, 13,* 51–68.

Weiten, W., & Diamond, S. S. (1979). A critical review of the jury-simulation paradigm: The case of defendant characteristics. *Law and Human Behavior, 3,* 71–93.

Weiten, W., Guadagno, R. E., & Beck, C. A. (1996). Students' perceptions of textbook pedagogical aids. *Teaching of Psychology, 23,* 105–107.

Weiten, W., & Wight, R. D. (1992). Portraits of a discipline: An examination of introductory psychology textbooks in America. In A. E. Puente, J. R. Matthews, & C. L. Brewer (Eds.), *Teaching psychology in America: A history.* Washington, DC: American Psychological Association.

Wellman, H. M. (2002). Understanding the psychological world: Developing a theory of mind. In U. Goswami (Ed.), *Blackwell handbook of child cognitive development* (pp. 167–187). Malden, MA: Blackwell.

Wells, C. G. (1991). *Right-brain sex: How to reach the heights of sensual pleasure by releasing the erotic power of your mind.* New York, NY: Avon.

Wells, G. L., & Bradfield, A. L. (1998). "Good, you identified the suspect": Feedback to eyewitnesses distorts their reports of the witnessing experience. *Journal of Applied Psychology, 83,* 360–376.

Wells, G. L., Memon, A., & Penrod, S. D. (2006). Eyewitness evidence: Improving its probative value. *Psychological Science in the Public Interest, 7,* 45–75.

Wells, G. L., Olson, E. A., & Charman, S. D. (2002). The confidence of eyewitnesses in their identifications from lineups. *Current Directions in Psychological Science, 11*(5), 151–154.

Wells, N. M., & Evans, G. W. (2003). Nearby nature: A buffer of life stress among rural children. *Environment and Behavior, 35,* 311–330.

Welsh, C. H., & Fugit, R. V. (2006). Medications that can cause insomnia. In T. Lee-Chiong (Ed.), *Sleep: A comprehensive handbook.* Hoboken, NJ: Wiley-Liss.

Werker, J. F., & Desjardins, R. N. (1995). Listening to speech in the 1st year of life: Experiential influences on phoneme perception. *Current Directions in Psychological Science, 4,* 76–81.

Wertheimer, M. (1912). Experiment-elle studien über das sehen von bewegung. *Zeitschrift für Psychologie, 60,* 312–378.

Wertsch, J. V., & Tulviste, P. (2005). L. S. Vygotsky and contemporary developmental psychology. In H. Daniels (Ed.), *An introduction to Vygotsky.* New York, NY: Routledge.

Wesson, D. R., Smith, D. E., Ling, W., & Seymour, R. B. (2005). Sedative-hypnotics. In M. H. Kryger, T. Roth, & W. C. Dement (Eds.). *Principles and practice of sleep medicine.* Philadelphia, PA: Elsevier Saunders.

Westbrook, G. L. (2000). Seizures and epilepsy. In E. R. Kandel, J. H. Schwartz, & T. M. Jessell (Eds.), *Principles of neural science.* New York, NY: McGraw-Hill.

Westen, D. Gabbard, G. O., & Ortigo, K. M. (2008). Psychoanalytic approaches to personality. In O. P. John, R. W. Robins, & L. A. Pervin (Eds.), *Handbook of personality psychology: Theory and research.* New York, NY: Guilford Press.

Wethington, E. (2007). Life events scale. In G. Fink (Ed.), *Encyclopedia of stress.* San Diego: Elsevier.

Whincup, P., Kaye, S., Owen, C., Huxley, R., Cook, D., Anazawa, S., et al. (2008). Birth weight and risk of type 2 diabetes: A systematic review. *Journal of the American Medical Association, 300*(24), 2886–2897.

Whitaker, R. (2002). *Mad in America: Bad science, bad medicine, and the enduring mistreatment of the mentally ill.* New York, NY: Perseus.

White, C. M., & Hoffrage, U. (2009). Testing the tyranny of too much choice against the allure of more choice. *Psychology & Marketing, 26*(3), 280–298. doi:10.1002/mar.20273

White, R., & Heerwagen, J. (1998). Nature and mental health: Biophilia and biophobia. In A. Lundberg (Ed.), *The environment and mental health: A guide for clinicians* (pp. 175–192). Mahwah, NJ: Erlbaum.

White, S. H. (2000). Conceptual foundations of IQ testing. *Psychology, Public Policy, and Law, 6,* 33–43.

Whitfield, C. L. (1995). *Memory and abuse: Remembering and healing the effects of trauma.* Deerfield Beach, FL: Health Communications.

Whitty, M. T. (2008). Liberating or debilitating? An examination of romantic relationships, sexual relationships and friendships on the net. *Computers in Human Behavior, 24,* 1837–1850.

Whorf, B. L. (1956). Science and linguistics. In J. B. Carroll (Ed.), *Language, thought and reality: Selected writings of Benjamin Lee Whorf.* Cambridge, MA: MIT Press.

Wider, C., Pollo, C., Bloch, J., Burkhard, P. R., & Vingerhoets, F. J. G. (2008). Long-term outcome of 50 consecutive Parkinson's disease patients treated with subthalamic deep brain stimulation. *Parkinsonism & Related Disorders,14*(2), 114–119. doi:10.1016/j.parkreldis.2007.06.012

Widiger, T. A. (2007). Current controversies in nosology and diagnosis of personality disorders. *Psychiatric Annals, 37,* 93–99.

Widiger, T. A. (2009). Neuroticism. In M. R. Leary & R. H. Hoyle (Eds.*), Handbook of individual differences in social behavior* (pp. 129–146). New York, NY: Guilford Press.

Widiger, T. A., Livesley, W., & Clark, L. (2009). An integrative dimensional classification of personality disorder. *Psychological Assessment, 21*(3), 243–255. doi:10.1037/a0016606

Widiger, T. A., & Mullins, S. (2003). Personality disorders. In A. Tasman, J. Kay, & J. A. Lieberman (Eds.), *Psychiatry.* New York, NY: Wiley.

Widiger, T. A., & Mullins-Sweatt, S. N. (2010). Clinical utility of a dimensional model of personality disorder. *Professional Psychology: Research and Practice, 41*(6), 488–494. doi:10.1037/a0021694

Widiger, T. A., & Sankis, L. M. (2000). Adult psychopathology: Issues and controversies. *Annual Review of Psychology, 51,* 377–404.

Widiger, T. A., & Trull, T. J. (2007). Plate tectonics in the classification of personality disorder: Shifting to a dimensional model. *American Psychologist, 62*(2), 71–83. doi:10.1037/0003-066X.62.2.71

Widom, C. S. (1997). Child abuse, neglect, and witnessing violence. In D. M. Stoff, J. Breiling, & J. D. Maser (Eds.), *Handbook of antisocial behavior.* New York, NY: Wiley.

Wiese, A. M., & Garcia, E. E. (2006). Educational policy in the United States regarding bilinguals in early childhood education. In B. Spodek & O. N. Saracho (Eds.), *Handbook of research on the education of young children.* Mahwah, NJ: Erlbaum.

Wiesel, T. N., & Hubel, D. H. (1963). Single-cell responses in striate cortex of kittens deprived of vision in one eye. *Journal of Neurophysiology, 26,* 1003–1017.

Wiesel, T. N., & Hubel, D. H. (1965). Extent of recovery from the effects of visual deprivation in kittens. *Journal of Neurophysiology, 28,* 1060–1072.

Wiesenfeld, B., Raghuram, S., & Garud, R. (2001). Organizational identification among virtual workers: The role of need for affiliation and work-based social support. *Journal of Management, 27,* 213–229.

Wilder, C., Pollo, C., Bloch, J., Burkhard, P. R., & Vingerhoets, F. J. G. (2008). Long-term outcome of 50 consecutive Parkinson's disease patients treated with subthalamic deep brain stimulation. *Parkinsonism & Related Disorders, 14,* 114–119.

Wilding, J., & Valentine, E. (1996). Memory expertise. In D. J. Herrmann, C. McEvoy, C. Hertzog, P. Hertel, & M. K. Johnson (Eds.), *Basic and applied memory research: Theory in context* (Vol. 1). Mahwah, NJ: Erlbaum.

Willford, J. A., Leech, S. L., & Day, N. L. (2006). Moderate prenatal alcohol exposure and cognitive status of children at age 10. *Alcoholism: Clinical and Experimental Research, 30,* 1051–1059.

Williams, B. A. (1988). Reinforcement, choice, and response strength. In R. C. Atkinson, R. J. Herrnstein, G. Lindzey, & R. D. Luce (Eds.), *Stevens' handbook of experimental psychology.* New York, NY: Wiley.

Williams, C. G., Gagne, M., Ryan, R. M., & Deci, E. L. (2002). Facilitating autonomous motivation for smoking cessation. *Health Psychology, 21,* 40–50.

Williams, G. C. (1966). *Adaptation and natural selection.* Princeton, NJ: Princeton University Press.

Williams, J. E., Paton, C. C., Siegler, I. C., Eigenbrodt, M. L., Neito, F. J., & Tyroler, H. A. (2000). Anger proneness predicts coronary heart disease risk. *Circulation, 101,* 2034–2039.

Williams, K., & Harvey, K. (2001). Transcendent experience in forest environments. *Journal of Environmental Psychology, 21,* 249–260.

Williams, L. M. (1994). Recall of childhood trauma: A prospective study of women's memories of child sexual abuse. *Journal of Consulting and Clinical Psychology, 62,* 1167–1176.

Williams, N. A., & Deffenbacher, J. L. (1983). Life stress and chronic yeast infections. *Journal of Human Stress, 9*(1), 26–31.

Williams, P. (2005). What is psychoanalysis? What is a psychoanalyst? In E. S. Person, A. M. Cooper, & G. O. Gabbard (Eds.), *Textbook of psychoanalysis.* Washington, DC: American Psychiatric Publishing.

Williams, R. E., Kaliani, L., DiBenedetti, D. B., Zhou, X., Fehnel, S. E., & Clark, R. V. (2007). Healthcare seeking and treatment for menopausal symptoms in the United States. *Maturitas, 58,* 348–358.

Williams, R. L., & Eggert, A. (2002). Notetaking predictors of test performance. *Teaching of Psychology, 29*(3), 234–237.

Williams, W. M., & Ceci, S. J. (1997). Are Americans becoming more or less alike?: Trends in race, class, and ability differences in intelligence. *American Psychologist, 52,* 1226–1235.

Williamson, D. A., Zucker, N. L., Martin, C. K., & Smeets, M. A. M. (2001). Etiology and management of eating disorders. In P. B. Sutker & H. E. Adams (Eds.), *Comprehensive handbook of psychopathology.* New York, NY: Kluwer Academic/Plenum.

Willis, S. L., Tennstedt, S. L., Marsiske, M., Ball, K., Elias, J., Koepke, K. M., Morris, J. N., et al. (2006). Long-term effects of cognitive training on everyday functional outcomes in older adults. *Journal of American Medical Association, 296,* 2805–2814.

Willoughby, T., Motz, M., & Wood, E. (1997). The impact of interest and strategy use on memory performance for child, adolescent, and adult learners. *Alberta Journal of Educational Research, 43,* 127–141.

Wilsnack, S. C., Wonderlich, S. A., Kristjanson, A. F., Vogeltanz-Holm, N. D., & Wilsnack, R. W. (2002). Self-reports of forgetting and remembering childhood sexual abuse in a nationally representative sample of U.S. women. *Child Abuse and Neglect, 26*(2), 139–147.

Wilson, E. O. (1993). Biophilia and the conservation ethic. In S. R. Kellert & E. O. Wilson (Eds.), *The biophilia hypothesis* (pp. 31–41). Washington, DC: Island Press.

Wilson, E. O. (2007). Foreword. In D. J. Penn & I. Mysterud (Eds.), *Evolutionary perspectives on environmental problems* (pp. xiii–xiv). New Brunswick, NJ: Transaction Publishers.

Wilson, G. T. (2011). Behavior therapy. In R. J. Corsini & D. Wedding (Eds.), *Current psychotherapies* (9th ed.). Belmont, CA: Brooks/Cole.

Wilson, T. D., & Gilbert, D. T. (2003). Affective forecasting. In M. P. Zanna (Eds.), *Advances in experimental social psychology,* Vol. 35 (pp. 345–411). San Diego, CA: Academic Press. doi:10.1016/S0065-2601(03)01006-2

Wilson, T. D., & Gilbert, D. T. (2005). Affective forecasting: Knowing what to want. *Current Directions in Psychological Science, 14,* 131–134.

Wilt, J., & Revelle, W. (2009). Extraversion. In M. R. Leary & R. H. Hoyle (Eds.*), Handbook of individual differences in social behavior* (pp. 257–273). New York, NY: Guilford Press.

Windholz, G. (1997). Ivan P. Pavlov: An overview of his life and psychological work. *American Psychologist, 52,* 941–946.

Winett, R. A., Hatcher, J. W., Fort, T. R., Leckliter, I. N., Love, S. Q., Riley, A. W., & Fishback, J. F. (1982). The effects of videotape modeling and daily feedback on residential electricity conservation, home temperature and humidity, perceived comfort, and clothing worn: Winter and summer. *Journal of Applied Behavior Analysis, 15,* 381–402.

Wing, R. R., & Polley, B. A. (2001). Obesity. In A. Baum, T. A. Revenson, & J. E. Singer (Eds.), *Handbook of health psychology.* Mahwah, NJ: Erlbaum.

Wingfield, A., Tun, P. A., & McCoy, S. L. (2005). Hearing loss in older adulthood: What it is and how it interacts with cognitive performance. *Current Directions in Psychological Science, 14,* 144–148.

Winick, C., & Norman, R. L. (2005). Epidemiology. In J. H. Lowinson, P. Ruiz, R. B. Millman, & J. G. Langrod (Eds.), *Substance abuse: A comprehensive textbook.* Philadelphia, PA: Lippincott/Williams & Wilkins.

Winkielman, P., & Berridge, K. C. (2004). Unconscious emotion. *Current Directions in Psychological Science, 13*(3), 120–123.

Winn, P. (1995). The lateral hypothalmus and motivated behavior: An old syndrome reassessed and a new perspective gained. *Current Directions in Psychological Science, 4,* 182–187.

Winner, E. (1997). Exceptionally high intelligence and schooling. *American Psychologist, 52,* 1070–1081.

Winner, E. (1998). Uncommon talents: Gifted children, prodigies, and savants. *Scientific American Presents Exploring Intelligence, 9,* 32–37.

Winner, E. (2000). The origins and ends of giftedness. *American Psychologist, 55,* 159–169.

Winner, E. (2003). Creativity and talent. In M. H. Bornstein & L. Davidson (Eds.), *Well-being: Positive development across the life course.* Mahwah, NJ: Erlbaum.

Winsler, A. (2003). Introduction to special issue: Vygotskian perspectives in early childhood education. *Early Education & Development, 14*(3), 253–269.

Winter, D. D. & Cava, M. M. (2006) The psychoecology of armed conflict. *Journal of Social Issues, 62,* 19–40.

Winter, D. G. (2010). Why achievement motivation predicts success in business but failure in politics: The importance of personal control. *Journal of Personality, 78*(6), 1637–1667. doi:10.1111/j.1467-6494.2010.00665.x

Winters, K. C., Arthur, N., Leitten, W., & Botzet, A. (2004). Gambling and drug abuse in adolescence. In J. L. Derevensky & R. Grupta (Eds.), *Gambling problems in youth: Theoretical and applied perspectives.* New York, NY: Kluwer/Plenum.

Winzelberg, A. J., & Luskin, F. M. (1999). The effect of a meditation training in stress levels in secondary school teachers. *Stress Medicine, 15,* 69–77.

Wise, R. A. (1999). Animal models of addiction. In D. S. Charney, E. J. Nestler, & B. S. Bunney (Eds.), *Neurobiology of mental illness.* New York, NY: Oxford University Press.

Wise, R. A. (2002). Brain reward circuitry: Insights from unsensed incentives. *Neuron, 36,* 229–240.

Witt, L. A., Kacmar, M., Carlson, D. S., & Zivnuska, S. (2002). Interactive effects of personality and organizational politics on contextual performance. *Journal of Organizational Behavior, 23,* 911–926.

Wittkower, E. D., & Warnes, H. (1984). Cultural aspects of psychotherapy. In J. E. Mezzich & C. E. Berganza (Eds.), *Culture and psychopathology.* New York, NY: Columbia University Press.

Wolfe, J. M., Kluender, K. R., Levi, D. M., Bartoshuk, L. M., Herz, R. S., Klatzky, R. L., & Lederman, S. J. (2006). *Sensation and perception.* Sunderland, MA: Sinauer Associates.

Wolford, G., Miller, M. B., & Gazzaniga, M. S. (2004). Split decisions. In M. S. Gazzaniga (Ed.), *The cognitive neurosciences.* Cambridge, MA: MIT Press.

Wolitzky, D. L. (2006). Psychodynamic theories. In J. C. Thomas, & D. L. Segal (Eds.), *Comprehensive handbook of personality and psychopathology.* New York, NY: Wiley.

Woloshin, S., Schwartz, L. M., & Welch, H. G. (2002). Risk charts: Putting cancer in context. *Journal of the National Cancer Institute, 94,* 799–804.

Wolpe, J. (1958). *Psychotherapy by reciprocal inhibition.* Stanford, CA: Stanford University Press.

Wolpe, J. (1990). *The practice of behavior therapy.* Elmsford, NY: Pergamon.

Wonderlich, S. A. (2002). Personality and eating disorders. In C. G. Fairburn & K. D. Brownell (Eds.), *Eating disorders and obesity: A comprehensive handbook.* New York, NY: Guilford Press.

Wong, L. A. (2006). *Essential study skills.* Boston, MA: Houghton Mifflin.

Wong, P. T. P. (2006). Existential and humanistic theories. In J. C. Thomas & D. L. Segal (Eds.), *Comprehensive handbook of personality and psychopathology.* New York, NY: Wiley.

Wood, E., Desmarais, S., & Gugula, S. (2002). The impact of parenting experience on gender stereotyped toy play of children. *Sex Roles, 47*(1–2), 39–49.

Wood, J. N., & Spelke, E. S. (2005). Chronometric studies of numerical cognition in five-month-old infants. *Cognition, 97,* 23–39.

Wood, N. L., & Cowan, N. (1995). The cocktail party phenomenon revisited: Attention and memory in the classic selective listening procedure of Cherry (1953). *Journal of Experimental Psychology: Learning, Memory, & Cognition, 21,* 255–260.

Wood, P. B. (2007). Fibromyalgia. In G. Fink (Ed.), *Encyclopedia of stress.* San Diego: Elsevier.

Wood, R. A., & Griffiths, M. D. (2007). A qualitative investigation of problem gambling as an escape-based coping strategy. *Psychology & Psychotherapy: Theory, Research & Practice, 80*(1), 107–125.

Wood, W., & Quinn, J. M. (2003). Forewarned and forearmed? Two meta-analytic syntheses of forewarnings of influence appeals. *Psychological Bulletin, 129,* 119–138.

Woodcock, R. W. (1994). Norms. In R. J. Sternberg (Ed.), *Encyclopedia of human intelligence.* New York, NY: Macmillan.

Woods, S. C., & Stricker, E. M. (2008). Food intake and metabolism. In L. Squire, D. Berg, F. Bloom, S. du Lac, A. Ghosh, & N. Spitzer, *Fundamental neuroscience* (3rd ed.). San Diego, CA: Academic Press.

Woody, E. Z., & Barnier, A. J. (2008). Hypnosis scales for the twenty-first century: What do we need and how should we use them? In M. R. Nash & A. J. Barnier (Eds.). *Oxford handbook of hypnosis: Theory, research and practice* (pp. 255–282). New York, NY: Oxford University Press.

Woody, E. Z., & Sadler, P. (2008). In M. R. Nash & A. J. Barnier (Eds.). *Oxford handbook of hypnosis: Theory, research and practice* (pp. 81–110). New York, NY: Oxford University Press.

Wop, W. J., Weissman, N. J., Zhu, J. , Bonsall, R. W., Doyle, M., Stretch, M. R., et al. (2008). Effects of acute mental stress and exercise on inflammatory markers in patients with coronary artery disease and healthy controls. *American Journal of Cardiology, 101,* 767–773.

World Resources Institute. (2001). *Facts and figures: Environmental data tables, energy and resource use.* Table ERC.5: Resource Consumption. [Data file]. Retrieved from http://www.wri.org/trends/index.html

World Resources Institute. (2010). Drivers of nutrient pollution. Retrieved from http://www.wri.org/project/eutrophication/about/drivers

Worthen, J. B., & Wade, C. E. (1999). Direction of travel and visiting team athletic performance: Support for a circadian dysrhythmia hypothesis. *Journal of Sport Behavior, 22,* 279–287.

Worthington, E. L., Jr., & Scherer, M. (2004). Forgiveness is an emotion-focused coping strategy that can reduce health risks and promote health resilience: Theory, review, and hypotheses. *Psychology and Health, 19,* 385-405.

Worthington, R. L., Soth-McNett, A. M., & Moreno, M. V. (2007). Multicultural counseling competencies research: A 20-year content analysis. *Journal of Counseling Psychology, 54,* 351–361.

Wright, S. C., & Taylor, D. M. (2003). The social psychology of cultural diversity: Social stereotyping, prejudice, and discrimination. In M. A. Hogg & J. Cooper (Eds.), *The Sage handbook of social psychology.* Thousand Oaks, CA: Sage.

Wrosch, C., Miller, G. E., Scheier, M. F., & de Pontet, S. B. (2007). Giving up on unattainable goals: Benefits for health? *Personality and Social Psychology Bulletin, 33,* 251–265.

Wrosch, C., & Scheier, M. F. (2003). Personality and quality of life: The importance of optimism and goal adjustment. *Quality of Life Research: An International Journal of Quality of Life Aspects of Treatment, Care & Rehabilitation, 12,* 59–72.

Wundt, W. (1874/1904). *Principles of physiological psychology.* Leipzig: Engelmann.

Wynn, K. (1992). Addition and subtraction by human infants. *Nature, 358,* 749–750.

Wynn, K. (1996). Infants' individuation and enumeration of sequential actions. *Psychological Science, 7,* 164–169.

Wynn, K. (1998). An evolved capacity for number. In D. D. Cummins & C. Allen (Eds.), *The evolution of mind.* New York, NY: Oxford University Press.

Wynne, C. D. L. (2004). *Do animals think?* Princeton, NJ: Princeton University Press.

Xu, J., Kochanek, K. D., Murphy, S. L., & Betzaida, T.-V. (2010). Deaths: Final data from 2007. *National Vital Statistics Reports, 48*(19), *1–73.*

Xu, J., & Roberts, R. E. (2010). The power of positive emotions: It's a matter of life or death—Subjective well-being and longevity over 28 years in a general population. *Health Psychology, 29*(1), 9–19. doi:10.1037/a0016767

Yaffe, K. K., Fiocco, A. J., Lindquist, K. K., Vittinghoff, E. E., Simonsick, E. M., Newman, A. B., et al. (2009). Predictors of maintaining cognitive function in older adults: The Health ABC Study. *Neurology, 72*(23), 2029–2035. doi:10.1212/WNL.0b013e3181a92c36

Yamamoto, J., Silva, J. A., Justice, L. R., Chang, C. Y., & Leong, G. B. (1993). Cross-cultural psychotherapy. In A. C. Gaw (Ed.), *Culture, ethnicity, and mental illness.* Washington, DC: American Psychiatric Press.

Yang, H., Liu, T., & Zang, D. (2000). A study of stressful life events before the onset of hypothyroidism. *Chinese Mental Health Journal, 14,* 201–202.

Yates, F. A. (1966). *The art of memory.* London: Routledge & Kegan Paul.

Yeomans, M. R., Tepper, B. J., Rietzschel, J., & Prescott, J. (2007). Human hedonic responses to sweetness: Role of taste genetics and anatomy. *Physiology & Behavior, 91,* 264–273.

Yerema, R., & Leung, K. (2010, October 15). Employer review: SAS Institute (Canada) Inc., Retrieved from http://www.eluta.ca/top-employer-sas-canada

Yerkes, R. M., & Morgulis, S. (1909). The method of Pavlov in animal psychology. *Psychological Bulletin, 6,* 257–273.

Yost, W. A. (2000). *Fundamentals of hearing: An introduction.* San Diego: Academic Press.

Yost, W. A. (2010). Audition: Pitch perception. In E. B. Goldstein (Ed.), *Encyclopedia of perception.* Thousand Oaks, CA: Sage.

Young, D. M. (1997). Depression. In W. S. Tseng & J. Streltzer (Eds.), *Culture and psychopathology: A guide to clinical assessment.* New York, NY: Brunner/Mazel.

Young, K. S. (1996, August). *Internet addiction: The emergence of a new clinical disorder.* Paper presented at the meeting of the American Psychological Association: Toronto, Ontario, Canada.

Young, K. S. (1998). *Caught in the net: How to recognize the signs of Internet addiction—and a winning strategy for recovery.* New York, NY: Wiley.

Young, K. S. (2009). Internet addiction: Diagnosis and treatment considerations. *Journal of Contemporary Psychotherapy, 39*(4), 241–246. doi:10.1007/s10879-009-9120-x

Young, M. E., Mizzau, M., Mai, N. T., Sirisegaram, A., & Wilson, M. (2009). Food for thought: What you eat depends on your sex and eating companions. *Appetite, 53*(2), 268–271. doi:10.1016/j.appet.2009.07.021

Young, T. B., Finn, L., Peppard, P. E., Szklo-Coxe, M., Austin, D., Nieto, F., et al. (2008). Sleep-disordered breathing and mortality: Eighteen-year follow-up of the Wisconsin Sleep Cohort. *Sleep: Journal of Sleep and Sleep Disorders Research, 31*(8), 1071–1078.

Young, T. B. (2004). Epidemiology of daytime sleepiness: Definitions, symptomatology, and prevalence. *Journal of Clinical Psychiatry, 65*(Suppl16), 12–16.

Yudofsky, S. C. (1999). Parkinson's disease, depression, and electrical stimulation of the brain. *New England Journal of Medicine, 340,* 1500–1502.

Zagorsky, J. L. (2007). Do you have to be smart to be rich? The impact of IQ on wealth, income and financial distress. *Intelligence, 35,* 489–501.

Zajonc, R. B. (1968). Attitudinal effects of mere exposure. *Journal of Personality and Social Psychology, 9,* 1–29.

Zajonc, R. B. (1980). Feeling and thinking: Preferences need no inferences. *American Psychologist, 35,* 151–175.

Zak, P. J., Kurzban, R., & Matzner, W. T. (2005). Oxytocin is associated with human trustworthiness. *Hormones and Behavior, 48*(5), 522–527. doi:10.1016/j.yhbeh.2005.07.009

Zane, N., Hall, G. C. N., Sue, S., Young, K., & Nunez, J. (2004). Research on psychotherapy with culturally diverse populations. In M. J. Lambert (Ed.), *Bergin and Garfield's handbook of psychotherapy and behavior change.* New York, NY: Wiley.

Zaragoza, M. S., Belli, R. F., & Payment, K. E. (2007). Misinformation effects and the suggestibility of eyewitness memory. In M. Garry & H. Hayne (Eds.), *Do justice and let the sky fall: Elizabeth F. Lotus and her contributions to science, law, and academic freedom.* Mahwah, NJ: Erlbaum.

Zárate, M. A. (2009). Racism in the 21st century. In T. D. Nelson (Ed.), *Handbook of prejudice, stereotyping, and discrimination* (pp. 1–22). New York, NY: Psychology Press.

Zárate, M. A., Garcia, B., Garza, A. A., & Hitlan, R. T. (2004). Cultural threat and perceived realistic group conflict as dual predictors of prejudice. *Journal of Experimental Social Psychology, 40,* 99–105.

Zarcone, V. P., Jr. (2000). Sleep hygiene. In M. H. Kryger, T. Roth, & W. C. Dement (Eds.), *Principles and practice of sleep medicine.* Philadelphia, PA: Saunders.

Zatzick, D. F. (1999). Managed care and psychiatry. In R. E. Hales, S. C. Yudofsky, & J. A. Talbott (Eds.), *American Psychiatric Press textbook of psychiatry.* Washington, DC: American Psychiatric Press.

Zatzick, D. F., & Dimsdale, J. E. (1990). Cultural variations in response to painful stimuli. *Psychosomatic Medicine, 52*(5), 544–557.

Zechmeister, E. B., & Nyberg, S. E. (1982). *Human memory: An introduction to research and theory.* Pacific Grove, CA: Brooks/Cole.

Zeidan, F., Gordon, N. S., Merchant, J., & Goolkasian, P. (2010). The effects of brief mindfulness meditation training on experimentally induced pain. *The Journal of Pain, 11*(3), 199–209. doi:10.1016/j.jpain.2009.07.015

Zeiler, M. (1977). Schedules of reinforcement: The controlling variables. In W. K. Honig & J. E. R. Staddon (Eds.), *Handbook of operant behavior.* Englewood Cliffs, NJ: Prentice-Hall.

Zellner, D. A. (1991). How foods get to be liked: Some general mechanisms and some special cases. In R. C. Bolles (Ed.), *The hedonics of taste.* Hillsdale, NJ: Erlbaum.

Zenhausen, R. (1978). Imagery, cerebral dominance and style of thinking: A unified field model. *Bulletin of the Psychonomic Society, 12,* 381–384.

Zentall, T. R. (2003). Imitation by animals: How do they do it? *Current Directions in Psychological Science, 12*(3), 91–95.

Zepelin, H., Siegel, J. M., & Tobler, I. (2005). Mammalian sleep. In M. H. Kryger, T. Roth, & W. C. Dement (Eds.), *Principles and practice of sleep medicine.* Philadelphia, PA: Elsevier Saunders.

Zhang, T., & Meaney, M. J. (2010). Epigenetics and the environmental regulation of the genome and its function. *Annual Review of Psychology, 61,* 439–466. doi:10.1146/annurev.psych.60.110707.163625

Zillmann, D., & Bryant, J. (1984). Effects of massive exposure to pornography. In N. M. Malamuth & E. Donnerstein (Eds.), *Pornography and sexual aggression.* New York, NY: Academic Press.

Zillmer, E. A., Spiers, M. V., & Culbertson, W. C. (2008). *Principles of neuropsychology.* Belmont, CA: Wadsworth.

Zimbardo, P. G. (2004a, May 9). Power turns good soldiers into "bad apples." *Boston Globe.* Retrieved from http://www.boston.com/news/globe/editorial_opinion/oped/articles/2004/05/09.

Zimbardo, P. G. (2004b). A situationist perspective on the psychology of evil: Understanding how good people are transformed into perpetrators. In A. Miller (Ed.), *The social psychology of good and evil: Understanding our capacity for kindness and cruelty* (pp. 21–50). New York, NY: Guilford Press.

Zimbardo, P. G. (2007). *The Lucifer effect: Understanding how good people turn evil.* New York, NY: Random House.

Zimbardo, P. G., Haney, C., & Banks, W. C. (1973, April 8). The mind is a formidable jailer: A Pirandellian prison. *New York Times Magazine,* Section 6, p. 36.

Zimmerman, I. L., & Woo-Sam, J. M. (1984). Intellectual assessment of children. In G. Goldstein & M. Hersen (Eds.), *Handbook of psychological assessment.* New York, NY: Pergamon Press.

Zimmerman, M., & Spitzer, R. L. (2009). Psychiatric classification. In B. J. Sadock, V. A. Sadock, & P. Ruiz (Eds.), *Kaplan & Sadock's comprehensive textbook of psychiatry* (9th ed., pp. 1108–1138). Philadelphia, PA: Lippincott, Williams & Wilkins.

Zinbarg, R. E., & Griffith, J. W. (2008). Behavior Therapy. In J. L. Lebow (Ed.), *Twenty-first century psy-*

chotherapies: Contemporary approaches to theory and practice. New York, NY: Wiley.

Zisook, S., Lesser, I., Stewart, J. W., Wisniewski, S. R., Balasubramani, G. K., Fava, M., et al. (2007). Effect of age at onset on the course of major depressive disorder. *American Journal of Psychiatry, 164*(10), 1539–1546. doi:10.1176/appi.ajp.2007.06101757

Zoeller, R. F., Jr. (2007). Physical activity and fitness in the prevention of coronary heart disease and associated risk factors. *American Journal of Lifestyle Medicine, 1,* 29–33.

Zohar, J., Fostick, L., & Juven-Wetzler, E. (2009). Obsessive-compulsive disorder. In M. C. Gelder, N. C. Andreasen, J. J. López-Ibor, Jr., & J. R. Geddes (Eds.). *New Oxford textbook of psychiatry* (2nd ed., Vol. 1). New York, NY: Oxford University Press.

Zola, S. M., & Squire, L. R. (2000). The medial temporal lobe and the hippocampus. In E. Tulving & F. I. M. Craik (Eds.), *The Oxford handbook of memory* (pp. 485–500). New York, NY: Oxford University Press.

Zorick, F. J., & Walsh, J. K. (2000). Evaluation and management of insomnia: An overview. In M. H. Kryger, T. Roth, & W. C. Dement (Eds.), *Principles and practice of sleep medicine*. Philadelphia, PA: Saunders.

Zorumski, C. F., Isenberg, K. E., & Mennerick, S. (2009). Cellular and synaptic electrophysiology. In B. J. Sadock, V. A. Sadock, & P. Ruiz (Eds.), *Kaplan & Sadock's comprehensive textbook of psychiatry* (9th ed., Vol. 1, pp. 129–146). Philadelphia, PA: Lippincott, Williams & Wilkins.

Zottoli, M .A., & Wanous, J. P. (2000). Recruitment source research: Current status and future directions. *Human Resource Management Review, 10,* 435–451.

Zrenner, E., Abramov, I., Akita, M., Cowey, A., Livingstone, M., & Valberg, A. (1990). Color perception: Retina to cortex. In L. Spillman & J. S. Werner (Eds.), *Visual perception: The neurophysiological foundations*. San Diego: Academic Press.

Zubieta, J., Bueller, J. A., Jackson, L. R., Scott, D. J., Xu, Y., Koeppe, R. A., Nichols, T. E., et al. (2005). Placebo effects mediated by endogenous opioid activity on μ-opioid receptors. *The Journal of Neuroscience, 25*(34), 7754–7762. doi:10.1523/JNEUROSCI.0439-05.2005

Zull, J. E. (2002). *The art of changing the brain: Enriching teaching by exploring the biology of learning*. Sterling, VA: Stylus.

Zurbriggen, E. L., & Sturman, T. S. (2002). Linking motives and emotions: A test of McClelland's hypothesis. *Personality & Social Psychology Bulletin, 28,* 521–535.

Zwanzger, P., Fallgatter, A. J., Zavorotnyy, M. M., & Padberg, F. F. (2009). Anxiolytic effects of transcranial magnetic stimulation—An alternative treatment option in anxiety disorders? *Journal of Neural Transmission, 116*(6), 767–775. doi:10.1007/s00702-008-0162-0

Name Index

D

G

H

L

M

N

O

S

T

Subject Index

B

E

F

G

H

N

Q

R

S

How Psychology Developed

A new science is born

- Psychology's intellectual parents were philosophy and physiology.
- Psychology's founder was Willhelm Wundt, who set up the first research lab in 1879 (in Germany).
- Wundt argued that psychology should be the scientific study of consciousness.

The battle of the schools begins

- Advocates of *structuralism* argued that psychology should use introspection to analyze consciousness into its basic elements.
- Advocates of *functionalism* argued that psychology should investigage the purposes of consciousness.
- Functionalism had a more lasting impact on psychology, as it fostered the emergence of behaviorism and applied psychology.

Psychology becomes a profession

- In the first half of the 20th century, only a handful of psychologists were involved in the delivery of professional services to the public.
- However, stimulated by the demands of World War II, *clinical psychology* began rapid growth in the 1950s.
- Today, the vast majority of psychologists are involved in professional services.

Cognition and physiology resurface

- In its early days, psychology emphasized the study of consciousness and physiology, but these topics languished as behaviorism grew more dominant.
- During the 1950s and 1960s advances in research on mental and physiological processes led to renewed interest in cognition and the biological bases of behavior.

Interest in cultural factors grows

- In the 1980s, Western psychologists developed increased interest in how cultural variables influence behavior.
- This trend was stimulated by the increased cultural diversity in Western societies and by growing global interdependence.

Evolutionary psychology gains prominence

- The 1990s saw the emergence of a major, new theoretical perspective called *evolutionary psychology.*
- Its crucial premise is that the patterns of behavior seen in a species are the product of evolution, just like anatomical characteristics.
- According to evolutionary psychologists, *natural selection* favors behaviors that enhance organisms' reproductive success.

Psychology moves in a positive direction

- Arguing that psychology had historically focused too much on pathology and suffering, Martin Seligman launched the positive psychology movement in the late 1990s.
- Positive psychology uses theory and research to better understand the adaptive, creative, and fulfilling aspects of human experience, such as positive emotions, personal strengths, and virtues.

Freud focuses on unconscious forces

- Although Sigmund Freud's views were controversial, they gradually became influential.
- *Psychoanalytic theory* emphasizes unconscious determinants of behavior and the importance of sexuality.
- According to Freud, the *unconscious* consists of thoughts that one is not aware of but that still influence one's behavior.

Behaviorism debuts

- *Behaviorism,* founded by John B. Watson, asserted that psychology should study only observable behavior.
- This view gradually took hold and psychology became the scientific study of behavior (instead of consciousness).
- The behaviorists stressed the importance of environment over heredity and pioneered animal research.

Behaviorism flourishes with the work of Skinner

- Boosted by B. F. Skinner's research, behaviorism reached its zenith of influence in the 1950s.
- Like Watson, he emphasized animal research, a strict focus on observable behavior, and the importance of environment.
- He generated controversy by arguing that free will is an illusion.

The humanists revolt

- Finding both behaviorism and psychoanalysis unappealing, advocates of *humanism,* such as Carl Rogers and Abraham Maslow, began to gain some influence in the 1950s.
- Humanism emphasizes the unique qualities of human behavior and the irrelevance of animal research.
- The humanists also took an optimistic view of human nature, stressing humans' freedom and potential for growth.

Specialties in Contemporary Psychology

Professional specialties

- Clinical psychology
- Counseling psychology
- School psychology
- Industrial and organizational psychology

Research areas

- Developmental psychology
- Social psychology
- Experimental psychology
- Physiological psychology
- Cognitive psychology
- Personality
- Psychometrics
- Educational psychology
- Health psychology

Key Themes

Themes related to psychology as a field of study

- **Psychology is empirical**—it is based on objective observations made through research.
- **Psychology is theoretically diverse**—a variety of perspectives are needed to enhance our understanding of behavior.
- **Psychology evolves in a sociohistorical context**—dense connections exist between what happens in psychology and what happens in society at large.

Themes related to psychology's subject matter

- **Behavior is determined by multiple causes**—complex causation is the rule and single-cause explanations are usually incomplete.
- **Behavior is shaped by cultural heritage**—cultural factors exert considerable influence over some aspects of behavior.
- **Heredity and environment jointly influence behavior**—nature and nurture interactively shape most behavioral traits.
- **People's experience of the world is highly subjective**—people tend to see what they expect to see and what they want to see.

The Scientific Approach

Goals

- Measurement and description
- Understanding and prediction
- Application and control

Steps in an investigation

1. Formulate a testable hypothesis.
2. Select the method and design the study.
3. Collect the data.
4. Analyze the data and draw conclusions.
5. Report the findings.

Advantages

\+ *Clarity and precision* yield better communication.

\+ *Intolerance of error* yields more reliable data.

Experimental Research

Elements

- **Independent variable (IV):** Condition or event manipulated by experimenter
- **Dependent variable (DV):** Aspect of behavior thought to be affected by independent variable
- **Experimental group:** Participants who receive special treatment
- **Control group:** Similar subjects who do not receive treatment given to experimental group
- **Extraneous variables:** Factors besides IV that might affect DV, hence they need to be controlled

Variations

- Can have one group of subjects serve as their own control group
- Can manipulate more than one independent variable in a study
- Can use multiple dependent variables in a study

Advantages and disadvantages

\+ Permits conclusions about cause and effect relationships

− Manipulations and control often make experiments artificial

− Practical realities and ethical concerns make it impossible to conduct experiments on many issues

Descriptive/Correlational Research

Correlation

Correlation exists when two variables are related to each other.

Types: *Positive* (variables covary in the same direction) or *negative* (variables covary in the opposite direction)

Correlation coefficient: Numerical index of degree of relationship between two variables

Strength: The closer the correlation to either −1.00 or +1.00, the stronger the relationship.

Prediction: The stronger the correlation, the better one can predict.

Causation: Correlation is not equivalent to causation.

Examples of specific methods

Naturalistic observation: Careful, systematic observation, but no intervention with subjects

Case study: In-depth investigation of single participant, typically involving data from many sources

Survey: Questionnaires and interviews are used to gather information about specific aspects of particpants' behavior

Advantages and disadvantages

\+ Broadens the scope of phenomena that psychologists can study (can explore issues that could not be examined with experimental methods)

− Cannot demonstrate that two variables are causally related

Common Flaws in Research

Sampling bias
Exists when a sample is not representative of the population

Placebo effects
Occur when participants' expectations lead them to experience some change even though they receive empty or fake treatment

Distortions in self-report data
Result from problems, such as social desirability bias and halo effects, that happen when participants give verbal accounts of their behavior

Experimenter bias
Occurs when a researcher's expectations or preferences about the outcome of a study influence the results obtained

Ethical Issues

The question of deception
Should researchers be permitted to mislead participants?

YES

- Otherwise, important issues could not be investigated.
- Empirical evidence suggests that deception is not harmful to subjects.

NO

- Deception is inherently immoral and may undermine participants' trust in others.
- Deceptive studies often create stress for subjects.

The question of animal research
Should researchers be permitted to subject animals to harmful or painful procedures?

YES

- Otherwise, important issues could not be investigated.
- Relatively little animal research involves pain or harm.

NO

- Animals are entitled to the same rights as humans.
- Animal studies are often trivial or may not apply to humans.

Key Themes

- Psychology is empirical.
- People's experience of the world is highly subjective.

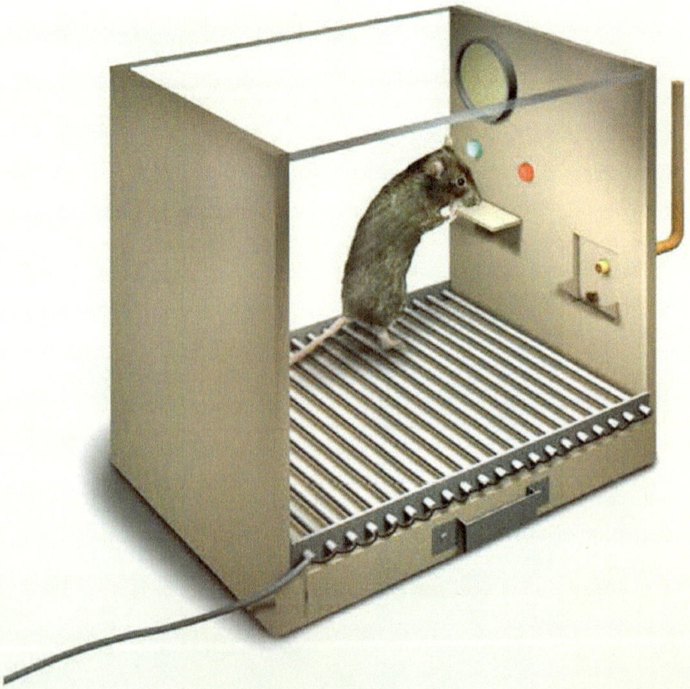

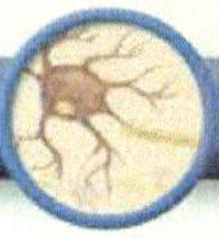

Communication in the Nervous System

Key parts of the neuron

Soma: Cell body

Dendrites: Branching structures that receive signals from other cells

Axon: Fiber that carries signals away from soma to other cells

Myelin sheath: Insulating material that encases some axons

Terminal buttons: Small knobs at ends of axons that release neurotransmitters at synapses

The neural impulse

Resting potential: Neuron's stable, negative charge when inactive

Action potential: Voltage spike that travels along axon

Absolute refractory period: Brief time after action potential before another action potential can begin

All-or-none law: A neuron either fires or doesn't fire

Organization of the Nervous System

Central nervous system

- **Brain**
- **Spinal cord**

Peripheral nervous system

Somatic nervous system: Nerves to voluntary muscles, sensory receptors

- **Afferent** (incoming) nerves
- **Efferent** (outgoing) nerves

Autonomic nervous system: Nerves to heart, blood vessels, smooth muscles, glands

- **Sympathetic division:** Mobilizes bodily resources
- **Parasympathetic division:** Conserves bodily resources

Brain and Behavior

Plasticity of the brain

The anatomical structure and functional organization of the brain is somewhat malleable.

Hindbrain

Cerebellum: Coordinates fine muscle movement, balance

Medulla: Regulates unconscious functions such as breathing and circulation

Pons: Involved in sleep and arousal

Midbrain

Involved in locating things in space; dopamine synthesis

Forebrain

Thalamus: Relay center for cortex; distributes incoming sensory signals, except smell

Cerebrum: Handles complex mental activities, such as sensing, learning, thinking, planning

- **Frontal lobes:** Primary motor cortex; mirror neurons
  - **Prefrontal cortex:** May house executive control system crucial to planning and organization
- **Parietal lobes:** Primary somatosensory cortex
- **Temporal lobes:** Primary auditory cortex
- **Occipital lobes:** Primary visual cortex

Limbic system: Loosely connected network that contributes to emotion, memory, motivation

- **Hippocampus:** Contributes to memory
- **Amygdala:** Involved in learning of fear responses

Hypothalamus: Regulates basic biological needs, such as hunger, thirst, sex

Neurotransmitters and behavior

Acetylcholine: Released by neurons that control skeletal muscles

Serotonin: Involved in the regulation of sleep and arousal and perhaps aggression; abnormal levels linked to depression

Dopamine: Abnormal levels linked to schizophrenia; dopamine circuits activated by cocaine and amphetamines

Norepinephrine: Abnormal levels linked to depression; norepinephrine circuits may be activated by cocaine and amphetamines

GABA: Inhibitory transmitter that contributes to regulation of anxiety

Endorphins: Opiate-like chemicals involved in modulation of pain

Synaptic transmission

Synthesis and storage of neurotransmitters in synaptic vesicles → **Release** of neurotransmitters into synaptic cleft → **Binding** of neurotransmitters at receptor sites leads to *excitatory* and *inhibitory PSPs* → **Inactivation** or **removal** (drifting away) of neurotransmitters; **Reuptake** of neurotransmitters by presynaptic neuron → (back to synthesis and storage)

Heredity and Behavior

Basic concepts

- *Chromosomes* are threadlike strands of DNA that carry genetic information.
- *Genes* are DNA segments that are the key functional units in hereditary transmission.
- Closer relatives share greater genetic overlap.
- Most behavioral traits appear to involve *polygenic inheritance.*

Research methods

- **Family studies** assess trait resemblance among blood relatives.
- **Twin studies** compare trait resemblance of identical and fraternal twins.
- **Adoption studies** compare adopted children to their adoptive parents and to their biological parents.

Interactions

- Research indicates that most behavioral qualities are influenced jointly by heredity and environment, which play off of each other in complex interactions.
- New work in epigenetics has further demonstrated that genetic and environmental factors are deeply intertwined.

Right Brain/Left Brain

Methods for study of lateralization

Split brain surgery: Bundle of fibers (corpus callosum) that connects two hemispheres is severed.

Perceptual asymmetries: Left-right imbalances in speed of processing are studied in normal subjects.

Left hemisphere

Usually handles verbal processing, including language, speech, reading, writing

Right hemisphere

Usually handles nonverbal processing, including spatial, musical, and visual recognition tasks

Key Themes

- Psychology is empirical.
- Heredity and environment jointly influence behavior.
- Behavior is determined by multiple causes.

Endocrine System

- System consists of glands that secrete *hormones* into the bloodstream in a pulsatile fashion.
- Governed by the hypothalamus and pituitary gland, the endocrine system regulates our response to stress.
- Recent research suggests that the hormone *oxytocin* fosters bonding, empathy, and trust.

Evolutionary Bases of Behavior

Darwin's insights

1. Organisms vary in endless ways.
2. Some traits are heritable.
3. Variations in hereditary traits might affect organisms' survival and reproductive success.
4. Heritable traits that provide a survival or reproductive advantage will become more prevalent over generations (natural selection will change the gene pool of the population).

Key concepts

Fitness refers to the reproductive success of an organism relative to the population.

Adaptations are inherited characteristics sculpted through natural selection because they helped solve a problem of survival or reproduction when they emerged.

Behaviors as adaptive traits

- Species' typical patterns of behavior often reflect evolutionary solutions to adaptive problems.
- For example, behavioral strategies that help organisms avoid predators have obvious adaptive value.
- Many behavioral adaptations improve organisms' chances of reproductive success.

The Visual System

Light waves

vary in	which affect perceptions of
Amplitude →	**Brightness**
Wavelength →	**Color (hue)**
Purity →	**Saturation**

Light is registered by receptors in the eye

Key eye structures

include the

Lens, which focuses light rays falling on the retina

Pupil, which regulates the amount of light passing to the rear of the eye

Retina, which is the neural tissue lining the inside back surface of the eye

Optic disk, which is a hole in the retina that corresponds to the *blind spot*

Fovea, which is a tiny spot in the center of the retina where visual acuity is greatest

In the retina

Visual receptors

consist of *rods* and *cones,* which are organized into *receptive fields.*

Rods play a key role in night and peripheral vision and greatly outnumber cones.

Cones play a key role in day and color vision and provide greater acuity than rods.

Receptive fields are collections of rods and cones that funnel signals to specific visual cells in the retina or the brain.

Visual signals are sent onward to the brain

Visual pathways and processing

The main visual pathway projects through the thalamus, where visual signals are processed and distributed to areas in the occipital lobe.

The second visual pathway handles coordination of visual input with other sensory input.

The primary visual cortex in the *occipital lobe* handles the initial cortical processing of visual input.

Feature detectors are neurons in the visual cortex that respond selectively to specific features of complex stimuli.

After processing in the primary visual cortex, visual input is routed to other cortical areas along the *where pathway* (dorsal stream) and the *what pathway* (ventral stream).

Visual illusions

- A *visual illusion* is a discrepancy between the appearance of a visual stimulus and its physical reality.
- Visual illusions, such as the *Muller-Lyer illusion*, the *Ponzo illusion,* and the *moon illusion* show that perceptual hypotheses can be wrong and that perception is not a simple reflection of objective reality.

Color perception

Subtractive color mixing works by removing some wavelengths of light, leaving less light.

Additive color mixing works by putting more light in the mixture than any one light.

Trichromatic theory holds that the eye has three groups of receptors sensitive to wavelengths associated with red, green, and blue.

Opponent process theory holds that receptors make antagonistic responses to three pairs of colors.

Conclusion: The evidence suggests that both theories are necessary to explain color perception.

Colors can influence behavior. For instance, red undermines achievement strivings, but enhances sexual attraction.

Form perception

- The same visual input can result in very different perceptions.
- Form perception is selective, as the phenomenon of *inattentional blindness* demonstrates.
- Some aspects of form perception depend on *feature analysis,* which involves detecting specific elements and assembling them into complex forms.
- *Gestalt principles,* such as *figure and ground, proximity, closure, similarity, simplicity,* and *continuity* help explain how scenes are organized into discrete forms.
- Form perception often involves *perceptual hypotheses,* which are inferences about the forms that could be responsible for the stimuli sensed.

Depth perception

Binocular cues are clues about distance based on the differing views of the two eyes.

Retinal disparity, for example, refers to the fact that the right and left eyes see slightly different views of objects within 25 feet.

Monocular cues are clues about distance based on the image in either eye alone.

Pictorial cues are monocular cues that can be given in a flat picture, such as *linear perspective, texture gradients, relative size, height in plane, interposition,* and *light* and *shadow.*

The Auditory System

Sound waves

vary in → which affect perceptions of

Amplitude → **Loudness**

Wavelength → **Pitch**

Purity → **Timbre**

Sound is registered by receptors in the ear

Key ear structures

include the

Pinna, which is the external ear's sound-collecting cone

Eardrum, which is a taut membrane at the end of the auditory canal that vibrates in response to sound waves

Ossicles, which are three tiny bones in the middle ear that convert the eardrum's vibrations into smaller motions

Cochlea, which is the fluid-filled, coiled tunnel that houses the inner ear's neural tissue

Basilar membrane, which holds the hair cells that serve as auditory receptors

Pitch perception

Place theory holds that perception of pitch depends on the portion of the basilar membrane vibrated.

Frequency theory holds that perception of pitch depends on the basilar membrane's rate of vibration.

Conclusion: The evidence suggests that both theories are needed to explain pitch perception.

Other Senses

Taste

- Taste cells absorb chemicals in saliva and trigger neural impulses routed through the thalamus.
- Taste buds are sensitive to four basic tastes: sweet, sour, bitter and salty. Umami may be a fifth basic taste.
- Sensitivity to these tastes is distributed somewhat unevenly across the tongue, but the variations are small.
- Supertasters have more taste buds and are more sensitive than others to certain sweet and bitter substances.
- Nontasters tend to be more susceptible to the lure of sweets, high-fat foods, alcohol, and smoking, which means their consumption habits tend to be less healthy than those of supertasters.

Touch

- Sensory receptors in the skin respond to pressure, temperature, and pain.
- Pain signals travel along a *fast pathway* that registers localized pain and a *slow pathway* that carries less localized pain sensations.
- Cultural variations in the experience of pain show the subjective nature of pain perception.
- *Gate-control theory* holds that incoming pain signals can be blocked in the spinal cord.
- Endorphins and a descending neural pathway appear responsible for this suppression of pain.
- Recent studies indicate that glial cells contribute to the modulation of chronic pain.

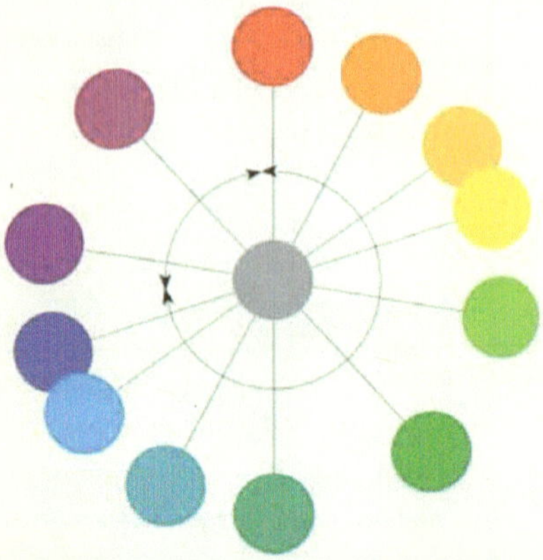

Smell

- Olfactory cilia absorb chemicals in the nose and trigger neural impulses.
- Smell is the only sensory system that is not routed through the thalamus.
- Most olfactory receptors respond to more than one odor.
- When compared to other mammals, humans may have a better sense of smell than previously thought.

Key Themes

- Psychology is theoretically diverse.
- People's experience of the world is highly subjective.
- Behavior is shaped by cultural heritage.

CHAPTER 5

Variations in Consciousness

Consciousness

The nature of consciousness

- *Consciousness* involves varied levels of awareness.
- Mental processes continue during sleep, as some stimuli can penetrate awareness.
- Changes in consciousness are correlated with changes in brain activity as measured by the EEG.

Sleep

The architecture of sleep

- *Non-REM sleep* consists of stages 1–4, which are marked by an absence of rapid eye movements, relatively little dreaming, and varied EEG activity.
- *REM sleep* is a deep stage of sleep marked by rapid eye movements, high-frequency brain waves, and dreaming.
- During the course of sleep, REM periods gradually get longer and non-REM periods get shorter and shallower.
- The architecture of sleep varies somewhat from one person to the next.

Sleep deprivation

- Selective deprivation of REM and slow-wave sleep leads to increased attempts to shift into these stages of sleep and increased time in these stages after sleep deprivation ends.
- Recent studies suggest that REM and slow-wave sleep help firm up learning that takes place during the day—a process called *memory consolidation.*
- REM sleep may enhance creativity and foster neurogenesis.
- Short sleep duration is associated with a variety of health problems, but both short and long sleepers exhibit elevated mortality rates.

Aspects of sleep

- The REM portion of sleep declines from 50% among newborns to about 20% among adults.
- The time spent in *slow-wave sleep* declines during adulthood.
- Recent research suggests that the elderly may need less sleep than younger adults.
- Culture appears to have little impact on the architecture of sleep. But ethnicity is related to the prevalence of sleep complaints and culture influences napping patterns.

Sleep disorders

Insomnia refers to chronic problems in getting adequate sleep.

Narcolepsy is marked by sudden and irresistible onsets of sleep during normal waking periods.

Sleep apnea involves frequent, reflexive gasping for air that disrupts sleep.

Somnambulism (sleepwalking) occurs when a person wanders about while remaining asleep.

Biological Rhythms

Relations to sleep

- Circadian (24-hour) rhythms are influential in the regulation of sleep.
- Internal biological clocks are reset by exposure to light, which stimulates the SCN, which signals the pineal gland to secrete melatonin.
- The poor sleep associated with jet lag and rotating shift work is due to being out of sync with circadian rhythms.
- Melatonin may have value in efforts to alleviate jet lag and circadian-friendly rotation schedules can reduce the effects of rotating shift work.

The World of Dreams

The nature of dreams

- Dreams are less exotic than widely assumed.
- Dreams may be affected by events in one's life and external stimuli.
- Cultural variations are seen in dream recall, dream content, dream interpretation, and the importance attributed to dreams.

Theories of dreaming

- Sigmund Freud asserted that the chief purpose of dreams is wish fulfillment.
- Other theorists argue that dreams provide an opportunity to think creatively about personal problems.
- The *activation-synthesis model* proposes that dreams are side effects of the neural activation that produces waking-like brain waves during REM sleep.

Hypnosis

Hypnotic induction and phenomena

- *Hypnosis* is a procedure that produces a heightened state of suggestibility.
- People vary in their susceptibility to hypnosis.
- Hypnosis can produce a variety of effects, including anesthesia, sensory distortions, disinhibition, and posthypnotic amnesia.

Theories of hypnosis

- According to some theorists, hypnosis produces a normal state of consciousness in which people act out the role of hypnotized subject.
- The *role-playing view* is supported by evidence that hypnotic feats can be duplicated by nonhypnotized subjects and that hypnotic subjects are often acting out a role.
- According to Ernest Hilgard, hypnosis produces an altered state of awareness characterized by dissociation.
- The *altered state view* is supported by evidence that divided consciousness is a common state that has continuity with everyday experience.

Meditation

Physiological correlates and long-term benefits

- Meditation refers to a family of practices that train attention to heighten awareness and bring mental processes under greater voluntary control.
- Approaches to meditation can be classified into two main styles that reflect how attention is directed: *focused attention* or *open monitoring*.
- Studies suggest that effective meditation leads to a beneficial physiological state that may be accompanied by changes in brain activity.
- Evidence suggests that meditation may reduce stress hormones, enhance self-esteem and well-being, and reduce vulnerability to a variety of diseases.
- Recent evidence suggests that meditation can increase pain tolerance and that it may be capable of producing alterations in brain structure.

Altering Consciousness with Drugs

Principal abused drugs

Narcotics are drugs derived from opium, such as heroin.

Sedatives are sleep-inducing drugs, such as barbiturates.

Stimulants are drugs that increase CNS activation, such as cocaine and amphetamines.

Hallucinogens, such as LSD and mescaline, produce sensory distortions and diverse mental and emotional effects.

Cannabis is the hemp plant from which marijuana, hashish, and THC are derived.

Alcohol includes a variety of beverages that contain ethyl alcohol.

Factors influencing drug effects

- Drug effects depend on users' age, mood, personality, weight, expectations, and previous experience with drugs.
- Drug effects also depend on the potency of the drug, the method of administration, and the user's tolerance.
- *Tolerance* refers to a progressive decrease in a person's responsiveness to a drug as a result of continued use.

Mechanisms of drug action

- Psychoactive drugs exert their effects by selectively altering neurotransmitter activity.
- Increased activation in the *mesolimbic dopamine pathway* may be responsible for the reinforcing effects of many drugs.

Risks associated with drug abuse

- *Physical dependence* exists when drug use must be continued to avoid withdrawal illness.
- *Psychological dependence* exists when drug use must be continued to satisfy craving for the drug.
- Many drugs, especially CNS depressants, can produce a lethal *overdose*.
- Many drugs cause deleterious health effects by producing *direct tissue damage*.
- The negative effects of drugs on physical health are often due to *indirect behavioral effects*.

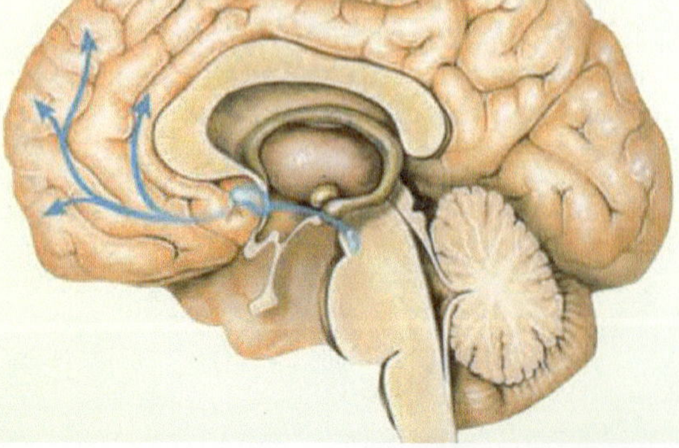

Key Themes

- Psychology is theoretically diverse.
- People's experience of the world is highly subjective.
- Behavior is shaped by cultural heritage.
- Psychology evolves in a sociohistorical context.
- Behavior is determined by multiple causes.

CHAPTER 6

Learning

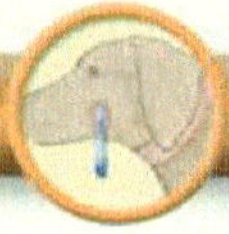

Classical Conditioning

Operant Conditioning

Description

Classical Conditioning

- *Classical conditioning* is a type of learning in which a stimulus acquires the capacity to evoke a response originally evoked by another stimulus.
- Classical conditioning was pioneered by Ivan Pavlov, who conditioned dogs to salivate when a tone was presented.
- Classical conditioning mainly regulates involuntary, reflexive responses.
- Examples include emotional responses (such as fears) and physiological responses (such as immunosuppression).

Operant Conditioning

- *Operant conditioning* is a type of learning in which responses come to be controlled by their consequences.
- Operant conditioning was pioneered by B. F. Skinner, who showed that rats and pigeons tend to repeat responses that are followed by favorable outcomes.
- Operant conditioning mainly regulates voluntary, spontaneous responses.
- Examples include studying, going to work, telling jokes, asking someone out, and gambling.

Terminology and procedures

Classical Conditioning

- Responses controlled through classical conditioning are said to be *elicited*.
- Classical conditioning begins with an *unconditioned stimulus (US)* that elicits an *unconditioned response (UR)*.
- Then a neutral stimulus is paired with the US until it becomes a *conditioned stimulus (CS)* that elicits a *conditioned response (CR)*.

Operant Conditioning

- Responses controlled through operant conditioning are said to be *emitted*.
- Demonstrations of operant conditioning typically occur in a *Skinner box* where an animal's reinforcement is controlled.
- The key dependent variable is the animal's *response rate* as monitored by a *cumulative recorder*, with results portrayed in graphs (steeper slopes are indicative of faster responding).

Basic processes

Acquisition is the formation of a conditioned response tendency.

- Classical: *Acquisition* occurs when a CS and US are paired, gradually resulting in a CR.
- Classical: Acquistion depends on *stimulus contiguity*, which is a temporal association between events.
- Operant: *Acquisition* occurs when a response gradually increases due to contingent reinforcement.
- Operant: Acquistion may involve *shaping*—the reinforcement of closer and closer approximations of the desired response.

Extinction is the gradual weakening of a conditioned response tendency.

- Classical: Extinction occurs when a CS is repeatedly presented alone until it no longer elicits a CR.
- Classical: *Spontaneous recovery* is the reappearance of an extinguished response after a period of nonexposure to the CS.
- Operant: *Extinction* occurs when responding gradually slows and stops after reinforcement is terminated.
- Operant: *Resistance to extinction* occurs when an organism continues to make a response after reinforcement for it has been terminated.

Generalization occurs when an organism responds to new stimuli besides the original stimulus.

- Classical: *Generalization* occurs when a CR is elicited by a new stimulus that resembles the original CS, as in Watson and Rayner's study of Little Albert.
- Operant: *Generalization* occurs when responding increases in the presence of a stimulus that resembles the original discriminative stimulus.

Discrimination occurs when an organism does not respond to other stimuli that resemble the original stimulus.

- Classical: *Discrimination* occurs when a CR is not elicited by a new stimulus that resembles the original CS.
- Classical: *Higher-order conditioning* occurs when a CS functions as if it were a US.
- Operant: *Discrimination* occurs when responding does not increase in the presence of a stimulus that resembles the original discriminative stimulus.
- Operant: *Primary reinforcers* are inherently reinforcing, whereas secondary reinforcers develop through learning.

Schedules of reinforcement

- *Intermittent reinforcement* occurs when a response is reinforced only some of the time.
- In *ratio schedules*, the reinforcer is given after a fixed (FR) or variable (VR) number of nonreinforced responses.
- In *interval schedules*, the reinforcer is given for the first response that occurs after a fixed (FI) or variable (VI) time interval has elapsed.
- Ratio schedules (FR and VR) tend to yield higher response rates, whereas variable schedules (VR and VI) tend to yield more resistance to extinction.

Distinctions among operant outcomes

- *Positive reinforcement* occurs when a response is followed by the presentation of a rewarding stimulus.
- *Negative reinforcement* occurs when a response is followed by the removal of an aversive stimulus.
- Negative reinforcement plays a key role in *escape learning* and *avoidance learning*.
- *Punishment* occurs when an event following a response weakens the tendency to make that response.
- When used as a disciplinary procedure, physical punishment is associated with poor-quality parent–child relations, elevated aggression, delinquency, and behavioral problems.
- Recent research also suggests that corporal punishment may inhibit cognitive development in children.

New Directions in the Study of Conditioning

Recognizing biological constraints on learning

- John Garcia found that it is almost impossible to create some associations, whereas conditioned taste aversions are readily acquired in spite of long CS-US delays, which he attributed to evolutionary influences.
- Preparedness appears to explain why people acquire phobias of ancient sources of threat much more readily than modern sources of threat.
- Differences in the adaptive challenges faced by various species have probably led to some species-specific learning tendencies.

Recognizing cognitive processes in conditioning

- Robert Rescorla showed that the predictive value of a CS influences the process of classical conditioning.
- When a response is followed by a desirable outcome, the response is more likely to be strengthened if it appears to have caused the favorable outcome.
- Noncontingent reinforcement, cognitive biases, and irrational reasoning appear to contribute to superstitious behavior.
- Modern theories hold that conditioning is a matter of detecting the contingencies that govern evens.

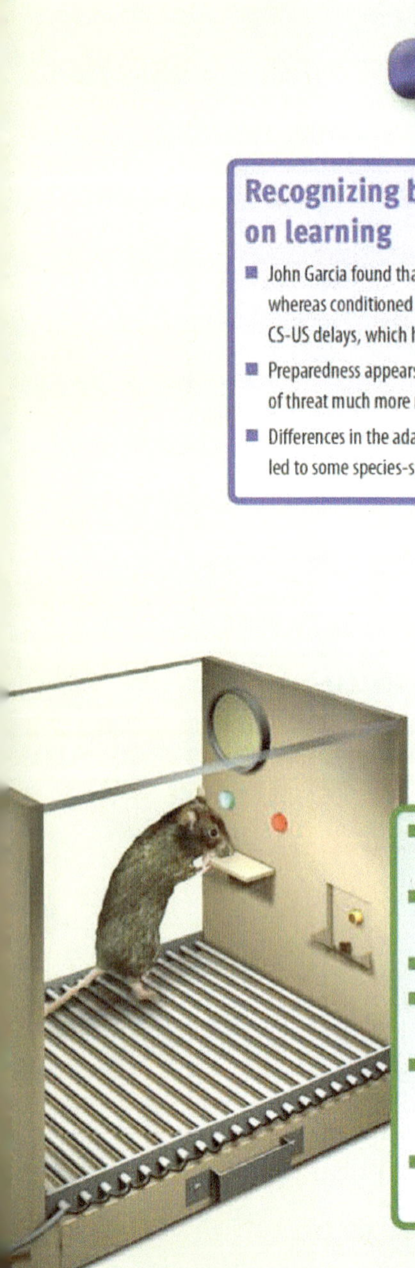

Observational Learning

- *Observational learning* occurs when an organism's responding is influenced by the observation of others, called *models*.
- Observational learning was pioneered by Albert Bandura, who showed that conditioning does not have to be a product of direct experience.
- Both classical and operant conditioning can take place through observational learning.
- Observational learning depends on the processes of attention, retention, reproduction, and motivation.
- In modern research on the effects of media violence, both experimental and correlational studies suggest that violent TV shows, movies, and video games contribute to increased aggression among children and adults.
- Exposure to media violence also appears to desensitize people to the effects of aggression in the real world.

Key Themes

- Heredity and environment jointly influence behavior.
- Psychology evolves in a sociohistorical context.

Encoding

- *Attention,* which entails a selective focus on certain input, enhances encoding.
- *Divided attention* undermines encoding and can have a negative effect on the performance of other tasks
- *Levels-of-processing theory* proposes that deeper levels of processing result in more durable memory codes.
- *Structural, phonemic,* and *semantic encoding* represent progressively deeper levels of processing.
- *Elaboration,* which involves linking a stimulus to other information, can enrich encoding.
- According to *dual-coding theory* visual imagery may facilitate memory by providing two memory codes rather than just one.
- Increasing the motivation to remember at the time of encoding can enhance memory.

Storage

- Information-processing theories propose that people have three memory stores: *sensory memory, short-term memory (STM),* and *long-term memory (LTM).*
- Atkinson and Shiffrin posited that incoming information passes through two temporary storage buffers before being placed into long-term memory.
- The three memory stores are not viewed as anatomical structures but as distinct types of memory.

Sensory memory

- Sensory memory preserves information in its original form for a very brief time.
- Memory traces in the sensory store appear to decay in about one-quarter of a second.
- Some theorists view stimulus persistence as more like an echo than a memory.

Long-term memory

- Long-term memory is an unlimited capacity store that can hold information indefinitely.
- Flashbulb memories suggest that LTM storage may be permanent, but the data are not convincing.
- Research has shown that that flashbulb memories are not as durable or accurate as claimed.

Short-term memory

- Short-term memory can maintain unrehearsed information for about 10–20 seconds.
- Short-term memory has a limited capacity that has long been believed to be about seven chunks of information.
- However, a more recent estimate that the capacity of STM is four items plus or minus one is becoming increasingly influential.
- Baddeley's model of *working memory* consists of four components: the phonological loop, the visuospatial sketchpad, the central executive, and the episodic buffer.

Retrieval

- Recall is often guided by partial information, as demonstrated by the *tip-of-the tongue phenomenon.*
- Reinstating the context of an event can often enhance retrieval efforts.
- This factor may account for cases in which hypnosis appears to aid recall, but hypnosis does *not* reliably enhance recall and it often increases mistakes.
- A *schema* is an organized cluster of knowledge about a particular object or event. Generally, people are more likely to remember things that are consistent with their schemas.
- Memories are sketchy reconstructions of the past that may be distorted.
- The *misinformation effect* occurs when recall of an event is changed by misleading postevent information.
- Even the simple act of retelling a story can introduce inaccuracies into memory.
- A *source-monitoring error* occurs when a memory derived from one source is attributed to another source.

Forgetting

Measuring forgetting

- People view forgetting as a deficiency, but it can be adaptive in that it can make it easier to remember important information.
- Ebbinghaus's work suggested that most forgetting occurs very rapidly, but subsequent research indicated that his *forgetting curve* was exceptionally steep.
- Retention can be assessed with a *recall* measure, a *recognition* measure, or a *relearning* measure.

Why we forget

- A great deal of forgetting, including pseudoforgetting, is due to *ineffective encoding.*
- *Decay theory* proposes that memory traces fade with time, but decay does not appear to be a factor in long-term memory.
- *Interference theory* asserts that people forget information because of competition from other material, which has proven easy to demonstrate.
- Forgetting is often due to *retrieval failure,* which may include repression.

The repressed memories controversy

- Recent years have seen a surge of reports of recovered memories of previously forgotten sexual abuse in childhood.
- Many clinicians accept these recovered memories, arguing that it is common for people to bury traumatic memories in their unconscious.
- Many memory researchers are skeptical of recovered memories because they have demonstrated that it is easy to create inaccurate memories in laboratory studies.
- Although it is clear that some therapists have created false memories in their patients, it seems likely that some cases of recovered memories are authentic.
- Memories recovered spontaneously appear more likely to be authentic than memories recovered in therapy.

Physiology of Memory

Anatomy of memory

- In *retrograde amnesia,* a person loses memory for events prior to the amnesia. In *anterograde amnesia,* a person shows memory deficits for events subsequent to the onset of the amnesia.
- Studies of amnesia and other research suggest that the hippocampus and broader medial temporal lobe system play a major role in memory.
- These areas may be crucial to the consolidation of memories.

Neural circuitry of memory

- Richard Thompson's research suggests that memory traces may consist of localized neural circuits.
- According to Eric Kandel, memory traces reflect alterations in neurotransmitter release at specific synapses.
- Neurogenesis may contribute to the sculpting of neural circuits for memory.

Proposed Memory Systems

Declarative memory

The *declarative memory system* handles recall of factual information, such as names, dates, events, and ideas.

Nondeclarative memory

The *nondeclarative memory system* handles recall of actions, skills, and operations, such as riding a bike or typing.

Semantic versus episodic memory

- The *semantic memory system* contains general knowledge that is not temporally dated.
- The *episodic memory system* handles temporally dated recollections of personal experiences.

Prospective versus retrospective memory

- *Prospective memory* involves remembering to perform actions in the future.
- *Retrospective memory* involves remembering events from the past or previously learned information.

Key Themes

- People's experience of the world is highly subjective.
- Behavior is determined by multiple causes.
- Psychology is theoretically diverse.

Problem Solving

Types of problems

Greeno has distinguished between problems of inducing structure, problems of arrangement, and problems of transformation.

Barriers to problem solving

- People are often distracted by irrelevant information.
- *Functional fixedness* is the tendency to perceive an item only in terms of its most common use.
- A *mental set* exists when people persist in using strategies that have worked in the past but are no longer optimal.
- People often impose unnecessary constraints on their possible solutions.

Approaches to problem solving

- *Trial and error* is a common, albeit primitive, approach to problem solving.
- A *heuristic* is a rule of thumb or mental shortcut used in solving problems or making decisions.
- It is often useful to formulate intermediate subgoals.
- If you can spot an analogy between one problem and another, a solution may become apparent.
- When progress is stalled, changing the representation of a problem often helps.
- Research on *incubation effects* suggests that taking a break from a problem can sometimes enhance problem solving efforts.

Culture and problem solving

- Cross-cultural disparities have been observed in problem-solving style.
- Research suggests that Eastern cultures exhibit a more holistic cognitive style, whereas Western cultures display a more analytic cognitive style.

Decision Making

Basic strategies

- Herbert Simon's *theory of bounded rationality* asserts that people tend to use simple decision strategies that often yield seemingly irrational results because they can only juggle so much information at once.
- Schwartz argues that in modern societies people suffer from choice overload, which leads to rumination, regret, and diminished well-being.
- Research suggests that people prefer more choices up to a point and then further increases in options lead to decreased satisfaction.
- Research on the *deliberation-without-awareness effect* suggests that intuitive, unconscious decisions may be more satisfying than those based on conscious deliberation, especially when choices are complex.
- Risky decision making involves making choices under conditions of uncertainty.

Common heuristics and flaws

- The *availability heuristic* involves basing the estimated probability of an event on the ease with which relevant instances come to mind.
- The *representativeness heuristic* involves basing the estimated probability of an event on how similar it is to the typical prototype of that event.
- In estimating probabilities, people often ignore base rates because of the influence of the representativeness heuristic.
- The *conjunction fallacy* occurs when people estimate that the odds of two uncertain events happening together are greater than the odds of either event happening alone.
- The *gambler's fallacy* is the belief that the odds of a chance event increase if the event hasn't occurred recently.
- People tend to inflate estimates of improbable events that garner heavy media coverage, because of the availability heuristic.
- People's distaste for uncertainty can distort their decision making.
- Most people expect that the negative impact of a loss will be greater than the positive impact of a similar gain, but research shows that people overestimate the impact of losses.
- According to Gerd Gigerenzer, people mostly depend on *fast and frugal heuristics* that are much simpler than the complicated inferential processes studied in traditional cognitive research.

Key Themes

- Psychology is empirical.
- Psychology evolves in a sociohistorical context.
- Heredity and environment jointly influence behavior.
- People's experience of the world is highly subjective.
- Behavior is shaped by cultural heritage.

Measuring Intelligence

History of intelligence tests

- Modern intelligence testing was launched in 1905 by Alfred Binet, who devised a scale to measure a child's mental age.
- Lewis Terman revised the Binet scale to produce the Stanford-Binet in 1916, which introduced the *intelligence quotient (IQ)*.
- In 1939, David Wechsler published an improved measure of intelligence for adults, which introduced the *deviation IQ score* based on the normal distribution.

Essentials of intelligence testing

- Modern deviation IQ scores indicate where people fall in the normal distribution of intelligence for their age.
- Individuals' IQ scores can vary across testings, but intelligence tests tend to have very high reliability.
- There is ample evidence that IQ tests are valid measures of academic/verbal intelligence, but they do not tap social or practical intelligence.
- IQ scores tend to stabilize around the ages of 7–9, but meaningful changes are possible.
- IQ scores are correlated with occupational attainment, but doubts have been raised about how well they predict performance within a specific occupation.
- IQ tests are not widely used in most non-Western cultures.

Heredity and Environment as Determinants of Intelligence

Evidence for hereditary influence

- *Twin studies* show that identical twins are more similar in intelligence than fraternal twins, suggesting that intelligence is at least partly inherited.
- Even more impressive, identical twins reared apart are more similar in intelligence than fraternal twins reared together.
- Studies also show that adopted children resemble their biological parents in intelligence.
- A *heritability ratio* is an estimate of the proportion of trait variability in a population that is determined by genetic variations.
- Estimates of the heritability of intelligence range from 40% to 80%, and mostly converge around 50%, but heritability ratios have certain limitations.

Evidence for environmental influence

- *Adoption studies* find that adopted children show some IQ resemblance to their foster parents and to their adoptive siblings.
- Studies of *environmental deprivation* show that children raised in substandard circumstances tend to exhibit a gradual decline in IQ as they grow older.
- Generational increases in measured IQ are perplexing, but they must be due to environmental changes.

The interaction of heredity and environment

- The evidence clearly shows that intelligence is shaped by both heredity and environment and that these influences interact.
- The *reaction range model* posits that heredity sets limits on one's intelligence and that environmental factors determine where people fall within these limits.

The debate about cultural differences in IQ scores

- Arthur Jensen and others have argued that cultural differences in IQ scores are largely due to heredity.
- Even if the heritability of IQ is high, group differences in IQ could be entirely environmental in origin.
- Socioeconomic disadvantage and cultural bias on tests may contribute to cultural differences in IQ.

New Directions

- Recent research has uncovered moderate positive correlations between IQ and overall brain volume, the size of specific areas in the brain, and the volume of gray and white matter.
- Researchers have found that IQ measured in childhood correlates with longevity decades later.
- Robert Sternberg's theory uses a cognitive perspective, which emphasizes the need to understand how people use their intelligence.
- According to Sternberg, the three facets of successful intelligence are analytical, creative, and practical intelligence.
- Howard Gardner argues that the concept of intelligence should be expanded to encompass a diverse set of eight types of abilities, which he believes are largely independent of one another.

Motivational Theories and Concepts

- *Drive theories* emphasize how *internal* states of tension (due to disruptions of homeostasis) *push* organisms in certain directions.
- *Incentive theories* emphasize how *external* goals *pull* organisms in certain directions.
- *Evolutionary theories* assert that motives are a product of *natural selection* that have had adaptive value in terms of fostering reproductive fitness.
- Humans display an enormous diversity of *biological* and *social* motives.

Motivation of Hunger

Biological factors regulating hunger

- Research originally suggested that the *lateral* and *ventromedial areas of the hypothalamus* were the brain's on-off switches for hunger, but the dual-centers model proved too simple.
- Today, scientists think that *neural circuits* passing through the *arcuate* and *paraventricular* areas of the hypothalamus play a larger role in the regulation of hunger.
- In the digestive system, the stomach can send two types of satiety signals to the brain.
- Secretions of the pancreatic hormone *insulin* are associated with increased hunger.
- The hormones *ghrelin* and *CCK* carry hunger and satiety signals from the stomach to the brain.
- The recently discovered hormone *leptin* provides the hypothalamus with information about the body's fat stores.

Environmental factors regulating hunger

- Organisms consume more food when it is palatable, when more is available, and when there is greater variety.
- The increased size of grocery-store packages, restaurant portions, and even dinnerware has fueled increased food consumption.
- People tend to eat more in the presence of others and in response to food advertisements.
- Classical conditioning and observational learning shape what people prefer to eat.
- Food preferences are also governed by exposure, which is why there are huge cultural variations in eating habits.

Sexual Motivation

The human sexual response

- Masters and Johnson showed that the sexual response cycle consists of four stages: excitement, plateau, orgasm, and resolution.
- Intercourse leads to orgasm in women less consistently than in men, but women are much more likely to be multiorgasmic.

Sexual orientation

- People tend to view heterosexuality and homosexuality as an all-or-none distinction, but it is more accurate to view them as endpoints on a continuum.
- Environmental explanations of sexual orientation have not been supported by research.
- Biological explanations have fared better in recent years, as twin studies have shown that genetic factors influence sexual orientation.
- Research also suggests that idiosyncrasies in prenatal hormonal secretions may influence sexual orientation.
- Females' sexual orientation appears to be characterized by more *plasticity* than that of males.

Evolutionary analyses

- According to *parental investment theory*, the sex that makes the smaller investment in offspring will compete for mating opportunities with the sex that makes the larger investment, which will be more discriminating in selecting partners.
- Human males are required to invest little in offspring, so their reproductive potential is maximized by mating with as many partners as possible.
- Human females have to invest months to years in carrying and nourishing offspring, so they maximize their reproductive potential by mating with males who are able to invest more resources in their offspring.

Gender differences in sexual activity

- Males think about sex and initiate sex more often than females.
- Males are more willing to engage in casual sex and have more partners than females.

Gender differences in mate preferences

- Males around the world place more emphasis than females on potential partners' youthfulness and attractiveness.
- Females around the world place more emphasis than males on partners' intelligence and financial prospects.

Emotion

Physiological component

- The physiological component of emotion is dominated by autonomic arousal.
- A *polygraph* detects emotional arousal, which is a far from perfect index of lying.
- According to Joseph LeDoux, the *amygdala* lies at the core of a complex set of neural circuits that process emotion.
- Emotions depend on activity in a constellation of interacting brain centers.

Cognitive component

- The cognitive component of emotion consists of subjective feelings that are often intense and difficult to control.
- Cognitive appraisals of events influence the emotions that people experience.
- Research on *affective forecasting* shows that people are surprisingly bad at predicting the intensity and duration of their emotional reactions to events.

Behavioral component

- At the behavioral level, emotions are revealed through body language.
- People can identify at least six emotions based on facial expressions.
- According to the *facial-feedback hypothesis,* facial muscles send signals to the brain that aid in the recognition of emotions.

Cultural considerations

- Ekman and Friesen have found cross-cultural agreement in the identification of emotions based on facial expressions.
- Cross-cultural similarities have also been found in the cognitive and physiological components of emotion.
- However, there are cultural disparities in how emotions are categorized and in public displays of emotions.

Theoretical views

- The *James-Lange theory* asserted that the conscious experience of emotion results from one's perception of autonomic arousal.
- The *Cannon-Bard theory* asserted that emotions originate in subcortical areas of the brain.
- According to the *two-factor theory,* people infer emotion from autonomic arousal and then label it in accordance with their cognitive explanation for the arousal.
- *Evolutionary theories of emotion* assert that emotions are innate reactions that do not depend on cognitive processes.

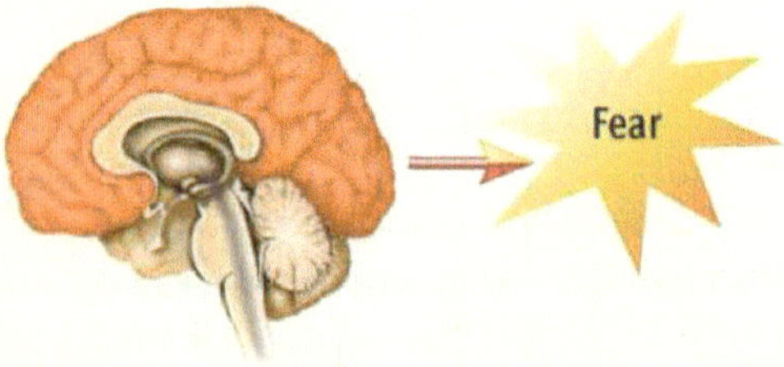

Achievement Motivation

- David McClelland pioneered the use of the TAT to measure individual differences in *need for achievement.*
- People who score high in the need for achievement tend to work harder and more persistently than others and are more likely to delay gratification.
- However, people high in the need for achievement tend to choose challenges of intermediate difficulty.
- The pursuit of achievement goals tends to increase when the probability of success on a task and the incentive value of success are higher.

Key Themes

- Psychology is theoretically diverse.
- Psychology evolves in a sociohistorical context.
- Heredity and environment jointly influence behavior.
- Behavior is shaped by cultural heritage.
- Behavior is determined by multiple causes.

Prenatal Development

Stages

- During the *germinal stage* a zygote becomes a mass of cells that implants in the uterine wall and the placenta begins to form.
- During the *embryonic stage* most vital organs and bodily systems begin to form, making it a period of great vulnerability.
- During the *fetal stage* organs continue to grow and gradually begin to function, as the fetus reaches the *threshold of viability* around 23–26 weeks.

Environmental influences

- Maternal malnutrition during the prenatal period has been linked to birth complications and other subsequent problems and maternal emotions can have an impact on prenatal development.
- Maternal use of illicit drugs can be dangerous to the unborn child. Even normal social drinking and routine tobacco use can be hazardous.
- A variety of maternal illnesses can interfere with prenatal development and environmental toxins are also a source of concern.
- Recent evidence suggests that prenatal development can "program" the fetal brain in ways that influence one's vulnerability to various types of illness decades later.

Development in Childhood

Motor development

- Early progress in motor skills has traditionally been attributed to *maturation*, but recent research suggests that infants' exploration is also important.
- Researchers have found cultural variations in the pacing of motor development, which demonstrate the potential importance of learning.

Cognitive development

- Jean Piaget proposed that children evolve through four stages of cognitive development.
- The major achievement of the *sensorimotor period* (birth to age 2) is the development of object permanence.
- Children's thought during the *preoperational period* (ages 2–7) is marked by centration, animism, irreversibility, and egocentrism.
- In the *concrete operational period* (ages 7–11) children develop the ability to perform operations on mental representations.
- In the *formal operational period* (age 11 onward) thought becomes more systematic, abstract, and logical.
- Piaget may have underestimated some aspects of children's cognitive development, and the impact of culture and environment.
- Researchers have found that infants understand complex concepts, such as addition, that they have had little opportunity to acquire through learning.
- These findings have led some theorists to conclude that some basic cognitive abilities are wired into humans' neural architecture

Language development

- The initial vocalizations by infants are similar across languages, but their babbling gradually begins to resemble the sounds from their surrounding language.
- Children typically utter their first words around their first birthday.
- Vocabulary growth is slow at first, but fast mapping contributes to a vocabulary spurt that often begins around 18 months.
- Children begin to combine words by the end of their second year, exhibiting telegraphic speech.
- Over the next several years, children gradually learn the complexities of grammar, but they exhibit many overregularizations.

Attachment

- *Attachment* refers to the close emotional bonds of affection that develop between infants and their caregivers.
- Harry Harlow's studies of infant monkeys showed that reinforcement is not the key to attachment.
- John Bowlby argued that attachment has a biological and evolutionary basis.
- Research by Mary Ainsworth showed that infant-mother attachments fall into three categories: secure, anxious-ambivalent, and avoidant.
- Infants with a relatively secure attachment tend to become resilient, competent toddlers with high self-esteem.
- Cultural variations in child rearing influence the patterns of attachment seen in a society.

Moral development

- Lawrence Kohlberg's theory proposes that individuals progress through three levels of moral reasoning.
- *Preconventional reasoning* focuses on acts' consequences, *conventional reasoning* on the need to maintain social order, and *postconventional reasoning* on working out a personal code of ethics.
- Age-related progress in moral reasoning has been found in research, but there is a lot of overlap among stages.

Personality development

- Erik Erikson's theory proposes that individuals evolve through eight stages over the life span.
- *Stage theories* assume that individuals progress through stages in a particular order, that progress is strongly related to age, and that new stages bring major changes in characteristic behavior.
- Erikson's four childhood stages are trust versus mistrust, autonomy versus shame, initiative versus guilt, and industry versus inferiority.

Development in Adolescence

Physiological and neural development

- Brought on by hormonal changes, the *adolescent growth spurt* typically begins at about age 10 in girls and age 12 in boys.
- Puberty is the stage during which *primary sex characteristics* develop fully.
- Today's adolescents tend to begin puberty at an earlier age than previous generations, perhaps because of improvements in nutrition and medical care.
- Girls who reach puberty early and boys who mature relatively late have a greater risk for psychological and social difficulties.
- The prefrontal cortex appears to be the last area of the brain to fully mature, and this maturation is not complete until late adolescence or early adulthood.

The search for identity

- According to Erikson, the main challenge of adolescence is the struggle for a sense of identity.
- According to James Marcia, adolescents deal with their identity crisis in four ways: *foreclosure, moratorium, identity diffusion,* and *identity achievement.*
- Arnett argues for the existence of a new developmental stage in modern societies, called *emerging adulthood,* marked by feeling in between adolescence and adulthood, optimism, self-focus, and continued identity formation.

Development in Adulthood

Personality development

- During adulthood, personality is marked by both stability and change, as percentile scores remain stable but mean raw scores change in predictable ways.
- The adult years tend to bring increases in agreeableness and conscientiousness, while extraversion and openness to experience tend to decline. Self-esteem tends to peak at about age 60.
- According to Erikson, people evolve through three stages of development in the adult years: intimacy versus isolation, generativity versus self-absorption, and integrity versus despair.

Family transitions

- Premarital cohabitation used to be predictive of an increased likelihood of marital dissolution later, but the situation seems to be changing.
- Adjusting to marriage is more likely to be difficult when spouses have different expectations about marital roles.
- Most parents are happy with their decision to have children, but the arrival of the first child represents a major transition, and the disruption of routines can be draining.
- Parent-adolescent relations are not as contentious as widely assumed, but conflicts do increase and parents tend to feel stressed.

Physiological and neural changes

- In the sensory domain, vision and hearing acuity tend to decline, but glasses and hearing aids can compensate for these losses.
- Women's reactions to menopause vary and menopause is not as stressful as widely believed.
- Brain tissue and weight tend to decline after age 60, but this loss does not appear to be the key to age-related dementias.
- *Dementias* are seen in about 15%–20% of people over age 75, but they are not part of the normal aging process.
- Alzheimer's patients exhibit profound loss of brain tissue and the accumulation of characteristic neural abnormalities.

Cognitive changes

- General intelligence is fairly stable throughout most of adulthood, with a small decline in average scores seen after age 60.
- Many studies have found decreases in older adults' memory capabilities. There is debate about the severity of these memory losses.
- Speed in cognitive processing tends to begin a gradual decline during middle adulthood.
- Some studies suggest that high levels of mental activity in late adulthood can delay the typical age-related declines in cognitive functioning.

Key Themes

- Psychology is theoretically diverse.
- Psychology evolves in a sociohistorical context.
- Heredity and environment jointly influence behavior.
- Behavior is shaped by cultural heritage.
- Behavior is determined by multiple causes.

The Nature of Personality

- A *personality trait* is a durable disposition to behave in a particular way across a variety of situations.
- According to the *five-factor model*, most aspects of personality are derived from five crucial traits: neuroticism, extraversion, openness to experience, agreeableness, and conscientiousness.
- The Big Five traits are predictive of important life outcomes, such as grades, occupational attainment, divorce, health, and mortality.

Psychodynamic Perspectives

Freud's theory

- Sigmund Freud's *psychoanalytic theory* grew out of his therapeutic work with clients and emphasized the importance of the unconscious.
- Freud divided personality structure into three components: the id, ego, and superego.
- The *id* is the instinctive component that follows the pleasure principle, the *ego* is the decision-making component that follows the reality principle, and the *superego* is the moral component.
- Freud described three levels of awareness: the *conscious* (current awareness), the *preconscious* (material just beneath the surface of awareness), and the *unconscious* (material well below the surface of awareness).
- Freud theorized that conflicts centering on sex and aggression are especially likely to lead to significant anxiety.
- According to Freud, anxiety and other unpleasant emotions are often warded off with *defense mechanisms,* which work through self-deception.
- Freud proposed that children evolve through five stages of psychosexual development: the oral, anal, phallic, latency, and genital stages.
- Certain experiences during these stages, such as the handling of the *Oedipal complex*, can shape subsequent adult personality.

Jung's theory

- Carl Jung's *analytical psychology* emphasized unconscious determinants of personality, but he divided the unconscious into the personal and collective unconscious.
- The *collective unconscious* is a storehouse of latent memory traces inherited from people's ancestral past.
- These memories consist of *archetypes*, which are emotionally charged thought forms that have universal meaning.

Adler's theory

- Alfred Adler's *individual psychology* emphasized how social forces shape personality development.
- Adler argued that the *striving for superiority* is the foremost motivational force in people's lives.
- Adler attributed personality disturbances to excessive inferiority feelings that can pervert the normal process of striving for superiority and can result in overcompensation.

Behavioral Perspectives

Skinner's theory

- B. F. Skinner's work on *operant conditioning* was not meant to be a theory of personality, but it has been applied to personality.
- Skinner's followers view personality as a collection of response tendencies that are tied to specific situations.
- Skinnerians view personality development as a lifelong process in which response tendencies are shaped by reinforcement.

Bandura's theory

- Albert Bandura's *social cognitive theory* emphasizes how cognitive factors shape personality.
- According to Bandura, people's response tendencies are largely acquired through *observational learning.*
- Bandura stressed the role of *self-efficacy*—one's belief about one's ability to perform behaviors that should lead to expected outcomes.

Mischel's theory

- Walter Mischel's brand of social learning theory emphasizes how people behave differently in different situations.
- His theory has sparked debate about the relative importance of the person versus the situation in determining behavior.

Humanistic Perspectives

Rogers's theory

- Carl Rogers's *person-centered theory* focuses on the *self-concept*—a collection of subjective beliefs about one's nature.
- *Incongruence* is the degree of disparity between one's self-concept and one's actual experiences.
- According to Rogers, unconditional love during childhood fosters congruence while conditional love fosters incongruence.
- Rogers asserts that people with highly incongruent self-concepts are prone to recurrent anxiety.

Maslow's theory

- Abraham Maslow proposed that human motives are organized into a *hierarchy of needs,* in which basic needs must be met before less basic needs are aroused.
- At the top of Maslow's hierachy of needs is the need for *self-actualization*—the need to fulfill one's potential.
- Recently, theorists have proposed a major revision of Maslow's pyramid of needs in which the higher, growth needs are replaced by motives related to reproductive fitness.
- According to Maslow, *self-actualizing persons* are people with very healthy personalities, marked by continued personal growth.

Biological Perspectives

Eysenck's theory

- Hans Eysenck viewed personality structure as a hierarchy of traits in which many superficial traits are derived from a handful of fundamental traits.
- According to Eysenck, personality is largely determined by genetic inheritance.
- Eysenck theorized that introversion and extraversion are shaped by inherited differences in arousability and ease of conditioning.

The evolutionary approach

- According to Buss, the ability to recognize and judge others' status on the Big Five traits may have contributed to reproductive fitness.
- Nettle argues that the Big Five traits themselves (rather than the ability to recognize them) are products of evolution that were adaptive in ancestral times.

Behavioral genetics research

- Identical twins reared apart tend to be more similar in personality than fraternal twins reared together, which suggests that genetics shape personality.
- *Heritability estimates* for personality tend to hover around 50%.
- Behavioral genetics research has revealed that differences among families have surprisingly little impact on personality.

Culture and Personality

- The basic trait structure of personality may be much the same across the cultures, as the Big Five traits usually emerge in cross-cultural studies.
- However, some cultural variability has been seen when researchers compare average trait scores for various cultural groups.
- Studies show that perceptions of national character tend to be inaccurate stereotypes.
- Markus and Kitayama assert that American culture fosters an *independent view* of the self, whereas Asian cultures foster an *interdependent view* of the self.

Contemporary Empirical Approaches to Personality

Terror management theory

- The collision between humans' self-preservation instinct and their awareness of death creates the potential for terror when people think about their mortality.
- Cultural worldviews and self-esteen buffer people from the anxiety associated with their awareness of their mortality.
- Increasing mortality salience leads people to work harder at defending their cultural worldview and their self-esteem.
- Manipulations of mortality salience lead to harsh treatment for moral transgressions, elevated respect for cultural icons, and increased prejudice.

Narcissism

- *Narcissism* is a trait marked by an inflated sense of self, need for attention, and a sense of entitlement.
- Narcissists work overtime trying to impress others with self-aggrandizing tales of their accomplishments to protect their fragile self-esteem.
- Narcissists often are well-liked at first, but eventually are seen as arrogant and self-centered. Research suggests that levels of narcissism have been increasing.

Key Themes

- Psychology is theoretically diverse.
- Psychology evolves in a sociohistorical context.
- Behavior is shaped by cultural heritage.

Person Perception

- Judgments of others can be distorted by their physical appearance, as we tend to ascribe desirable personality characteristics and competence to those who are good looking.
- Observers can draw surprisingly accurate inferences about others based on their nonverbal expressiveness.
- Stereotypes are widely held beliefs that others will have certain characteristics because of their membership in a particular group.

Attribution

Basic processes

- *Attributions* are inferences that people draw about the causes of events and behaviors.
- *Internal attributions* ascribe the causes of behavior to personal traits, abilities, and feelings, whereas *external attributions* ascribe the causes of behavior to situational demands and environmental factors.
- According to Bernard Weiner, attributions for success and failure can be analyzed along the stable-unstable and internal-external dimensions.

Biases

- The *fundamental attribution error* refers to observers' bias in favor of internal attributions in explaining others' behavior.
- Actors favor external attributions in explaining their own behavior, whereas observers favor internal attributions.
- The *self-serving bias* is the tendency to explain one's successes with internal attributions and one's failures with external attributions.

Cultural influences

- Cultures vary in their emphasis on *individualism* (putting personal goals ahead of group goals) as opposed to *collectivism* (putting group goals ahead of personal goals), which influence attributional tendencies.
- People from collectivist cultures appear to be less prone to the fundamental attribution error and to the self-serving bias than people from individualist cultures.

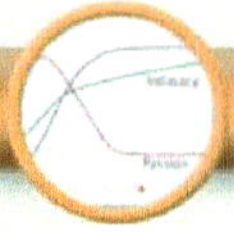

Interpersonal Attraction

Cultural and evolutionary influences

- The traits that people seek in prospective mates seem to transcend culture, but societies vary in their emphasis on romantic love as a prerequisite for marriage.
- According to evolutionary psychologists, some aspects of good looks influence attraction because they have been indicators of reproductive fitness.
- Men tend to be more interested than women in seeking youthfulness and attractiveness in mates, whereas women tend to emphasize potential mates' financial prospects.

Factors in attraction

- A key determinant of romantic attraction for both sexes is physical attractiveness.
- The *matching hypothesis* asserts that males and females of roughly equal physical attractiveness are likely to select each other as partners.
- Married and dating couples tend to be similar on many traits, probably because similarity causes attraction and because attraction can foster similarity.
- Research on *reciprocity* shows that liking breeds liking and that loving promotes loving.

Perspectives on love

- Some theorists distinguish between *passionate love* and *companionate love*.
- Another approach views romantic love as an *attachment process* and argues that love relationships in adulthood mimic attachment patterns in infancy, which fall into three categories: secure, anxious-ambivalent, and avoidant.
- Those who are secure tend to have more satisfying romantic relationships.
- Although critics are concerned that Internet relationships are superficial and plagued by deception, they appear to be just as intimate and stable as relationships forged offline.

Key Themes

- Psychology is empirical.
- Behavior is shaped by cultural heritage.
- People's experience of the world is highly subjective.
- Behavior is determined by multiple causes.

Attitudes

The structure of attitudes

Components
- The *cognitive component* of an attitude is made up of the beliefs that people hold about the object of an attitude.
- The *affective component* of an attitude consists of the emotional feelings stimulated by an object of thought.
- The *behavioral component* of an attitude consists of predispositions to act in certain ways toward an attitudinal object.

Dimensions
- *Attitude strength* refers to how firmly attitudes are held.
- *Attitude accessibility* refers to how often and how quickly an attitude comes to mind.
- *Attitude ambivalence* refers to how conflicted one feels about an attitude.

Relations to behavior
- Research demonstrates that attitudes are mediocre predictors of people's behavior.
- *Explicit attitudes* are attitudes that we hold consciously and can readily describe, whereas *implicit attitudes* are covert attitudes that are expressed in subtle automatic responses. Implicit attitudes can influence behavior.

Trying to change attitudes

Source factors
- Persuasion tends to be more successful when a source has credibility, which may depend on expertise or trustworthiness.
- Likability also tends to increase success in persuasion.

Message factors
- Two-sided arguments tend to be more effective than one-sided presentations.
- Fear appeals tend to work if they are actually successful in arousing fear.
- Repetition of a message can be effective, perhaps because of the mere exposure effect.

Receiver factors
- Persuasion is more difficult when the receiver is forewarned about the persuasive effort.
- Resistance is greater when strong attitudes are targeted.

Theories of attitude change

Learning theory
- The affective component of an attitude can be shaped by classical conditioning.
- Attitudes can be strengthened by reinforcement or acquired through observational learning.

Dissonance theory
- According to Leon Festinger, inconsistency between attitudes motivates attitude change.
- Dissonance theory can explain attitude change after counter-attitudinal behavior or when people need to justify their great effort to attain something.

Elaboration likelihood model
- The *central route* to persuasion depends on the logic of one's message, whereas the *peripheral route* depends on nonmessage factors, such as emotions.
- Research indicates that the central route produces more durable attitude change.

Behavior in Groups

- The *bystander effect* refers to the fact that people are less likely to provide help when they are in groups than when they are alone, because of diffusion of responsibility.
- Productivity often declines in groups because of loss of coordination and *social loafing*, which refers to the reduced effort seen when people work in groups.
- *Group polarization* occurs when discussion leads a group to shift toward a more extreme decision in the direction it was already leaning.
- In *groupthink*, a cohesive group suspends critical thinking in a misguided effort to promote agreement.

Yielding to Others

Conformity
- Research by Solomon Asch showed that people have a surprisingly strong tendency to conform.
- Asch found that conformity becomes more likely as group size increases up to a size of seven.
- However, the presence of another dissenter in a group greatly reduces the conformity observed.
- Asch's findings have been replicated in many cultures, with even higher levels of conformity observed in collectivist societies.

Obedience
- In Stanley Milgram's landmark study, adult men drawn from the community showed a remarkable tendency to follow orders to shock an innocent stranger, with 65% delivering the maximum shock.
- The generalizability of Milgram's findings has stood the test of time, but his work helped stimulate stricter ethical standards for research.
- Milgram's findings have been replicated in many modern nations and even higher rates of obedience have been seen in many places.

The power of the situation
- The Stanford Prison Simulation demonstrated that social roles and other situational pressures can exert tremendous influence over social behavior.
- Like Milgram, Zimbardo showed that situational forces can lead normal people to exhibit suprisingly callous, abusive behavior.

Stress → Stress Response → Stress Effects

Stress

- *Stress* is a common, everyday event, and even routine hassles can have harmful effects.
- People's *primary appraisals* of events determine what they find stressful.
- People's *secondary appraisals* assess their coping resources and influence the degree of stress experienced.

Major types of stress

Frustration

- *Frustration* occurs when the pursuit of some goal is thwarted.

Conflict

- In an *approach-approach conflict,* a choice must be made between two attractive goals.
- In an *avoidance-avoidance conflict,* a choice must be made between two unattractive goals.
- In an *approach-avoidance conflict,* a choice must be made about whether to pursue a goal that has positive and negative aspects.

Change

- *Life changes* are alterations in living circumstances, including positive changes, that require adjustment.
- The Social Readjustment Rating Scale (SRRS) purports to measure change-related stress, but actually taps many types of stressful experiences.
- Many studies have shown that high scores on the SRRS are associated with increased vulnerability to physical illness and psychological problems.

Pressure

- People may be put under *pressure* to perform well or to conform to others' expectations.
- Pressure is a predictor of psychological symptoms.

Stress Response

Emotional responses

- Many emotions may be evoked by stress, but anger-rage, anxiety-fear, and sadness-grief are especially common.
- Emotional arousal may interfere with coping efforts.
- The *inverted-U hypothesis* posits that as tasks become more complex, the optimal level of arousal decreases.
- Investigators have tended to focus on negative emotions, but research shows that positive emotions also occur during periods of stress.

Physiological responses

- The *general adaptation syndrome* is Hans Selye's model of the body's response to stress, which can progress through three stages: alarm, resistance, and exhaustion.
- Stress can cause the brain to send signals to the endocrine system along two pathways.

Hypothalamus → Pituitary gland → Adrenal cortex → Secretion of corticosteroids

Hypothalamus → Autonomic nervous system → Adrenal medulla → Secretion of catecholamines

Behavioral responses

- Coping efforts may be healthy or unhealthy.
- *Giving up* and *blaming oneself* are less than optimal methods of coping with stress.
- Another unhealthy response is to strike out at others with acts of *aggression.*
- *Indulging oneself* is another common response to stress that tends to be less than optimal.
- *Defensive coping* protects against emotional distress, but it depends on self-deception and avoidance.
- However, small positive illusions about one's life may be adaptive for mental health.
- *Constructive coping* refers to relatively healthful efforts to handle the demands of stress.

Stress Effects

Effects on physical health

- Stress appears to contribute to many types of physical illness and not just *psychosomatic diseases.*
- *Type A behavior* has been identified as a contributing factor in coronary heart disease.
- Research suggests that *hostility* may be the most toxic element of the Type A syndrome.
- Recent evidence suggests that strong emotional reactions may precipitate heart attacks
- Research indicate that depression is a predictor of heart disease.
- The association between stress and vulnerability to many diseases may reflect the negative impact of stress on immune function.
- The correlation between stress and illness is modest in strength because stress is only one of many factors that influence health.

Variations in stress tolerance

- There are individual differences in how much stress people can tolerate without negative effects.
- Strong social support appears to buffer the impact of stress.
- Asians prefer *implicit* social support whereas Americans prefer *explicit* social support.
- Two personality traits, optimism and conscientiousness, appear to promote health.
- Research on resilience suggests that stress can sometimes promote personal growth, self-improvement, and other benefits.

Health-Impairing Behavior

Smoking

- Smokers have much higher mortality rates than nonsmokers because smoking elevates the risk for a wide range of diseases, including lung cancer and heart disease.
- When people quit smoking, their health risks decline fairly quickly.
- Long-term success rates for giving up smoking are only 25% or less.

Lack of exercise

- Research indicates that regular exercise is associated with increased longevity.
- Physical fitness can reduce vulnerability to deadly cardiovascular diseases, obesity-related problems, and some types of cancer.

Alcohol and drug abuse

- Moderate drinking may offer some protection against cardiovascular disease, but heavy consumption of alcohol clearly increases one's risk for a host of diseases.
- Recreational drug use also elevates people's vulnerability to various types of illness.

Behavior and AIDS

- Behavioral patterns influence one's risk for AIDS, which is transmitted through person-to-person contact involving the exchange of bodily fluids, primarily semen and blood.
- In the world as a whole, sexual transmission has mostly taken place through heterosexual relations.
- Many young heterosexuals foolishly downplay their risk for HIV.

Reactions to Illness

The decision to seek treatment

- Whether people view physical sensations as symptoms of illness depends on subjective interpretation.
- The biggest problem in regard to treatment seeking is the common tendency to delay the pursuit of needed treatment.
- People procrastinate because they worry about looking silly or bothering their physician, or because they are reluctant to disrupt their plans.

Communicating with health providers

- A large portion of patients depart medical visits not understanding what they have been told.
- Barriers to effective provider-patient communication include short visits, overuse of medical jargon, and patients' reluctance to challenge physicians' authority.
- The key to improving communication is to not be a passive consumer.

Adherence to medical advice

- Nonadherence to advice from health providers is very common.
- Nonadherence is often due to the patient's failure to understand instructions.
- If a prescribed regimen is unpleasant or difficult to follow, compliance tends to decline.
- Noncompliance increases when patients have negative attitudes toward their health providers.

Key Themes

- Behavior is determined by multiple causes.
- People's experience of the world is highly subjective.

Abnormal Behavior

The medical model

- The *medical model,* which assumes that it is useful to view abnormal behavior as a disease, led to more humane treatment for people who exhibited abnormal behavior.
- However, the medical model has been criticized on the grounds that it converts moral and social questions into medical questions.
- Mental illness carries a stigma that can be difficult to shake and creates additional difficulties for those who suffer from psychological disorders.

Criteria of abnormality

- Judgments of abnormality are based on three criteria: deviance from social norms, maladaptive behavior, and reports of personal distress.
- Normality and abnormality exist on a continuum.
- Judgments about mental illness reflect prevailing cultural values, social trends, and political forces, as well as scientific knowledge.

The diagnostic system

- DSM-IV, which was released in 1994, is the official psychodiagnostic classification system in the United States.
- In DSM-IV information on patients is recorded on five axes: (I) clinical syndromes, (II) personality disorders, (III) general medical conditions, (IV) psychosocial stressors, and (V) global assessment of functioning.
- Work is under way on DSM-5, which may supplement the current categorical approach with a dimensional approach.

Anxiety Disorders

Types

- *Generalized anxiety disorder* is marked by chronic, high anxiety not tied to a specific threat.
- *Phobic disorder* is marked by a persistent, irrational fear of an object or situation that is not dangerous.
- *Panic disorder* involves recurrent, sudden anxiety attacks, and is often accompanied by agoraphobia.
- *Obsessive-compulsive disorder* is marked by uncontrollable intrusions of unwanted thoughts and urges to engage in senseless rituals.
- *Posttraumatic stress disorder* involves enduring psychological disturbance attributable to the experience of a major traumatic event.

Etiology

- Twin studies suggest that there is a genetic predisposition to anxiety disorders.
- Disturbances in the neural circuits using GABA and serotonin may play a role in some anxiety disorders.
- Many anxiety responses may be acquired through classical conditioning and maintained through operant conditioning.
- Cognitive theorists assert that the tendency to overinterpret harmless situations as threatening leads to anxiety disorders.
- Exposure to great stress may contribute to the emergence of some anxiety disorders.

Dissociative Disorders

Types

- *Dissociative amnesia* is a sudden loss of memory for personal information that is too extensive to be due to normal forgetting.
- In *dissociative fugue,* people lose their memory for their entire lives along with their sense of identity.
- *Dissociative identity disorder* (or multiple personality disorder) involves the coexistence of two or more largely complete and usually very different personalities.

Etiology

- Dissociative amnesia and fugue are usually attributed to extreme stress.
- Some theorists maintain that people with dissociative identity disorder are engaging in intentional role-playing to use mental illness as an excuse for their personal failings.
- Other theorists maintain that cases of dissociative identity disorder are rooted in severe emotional trauma that occurred during childhood.

Mood Disorders

Types

- *Major depressive disorder* is marked by persistent feelings of sadness and despair, loss of interest in previous sources of pleasure, slowed thought processes, and self-blame.
- *Bipolar disorder* (manic-depressive disorder) is marked by the experience of depressed and manic episodes, with the latter involving irrational euphoria, racing thoughts, impulsive behavior, and increased energy.
- Both types of mood disorders are associated with substantial elevations in suicide rates.

Etiology

- Twin studies suggest that there is a genetic predispostion to mood disorders.
- Disturbances in the neural circuits using serotonin and norepinephrine appear to contribute to mood disorders.
- Researchers have found a correlation between depression and *reduced hippocampal volume,* which may reflect *suppressed neurogenesis* due to stress.
- Cognitive theorists assert that people who exhibit a pessimistic explanatory style are especially vulnerable to depression and that rumination tends to extend and amplify episodes of depression.
- Behavioral theories emphasize how inadequate social skills increase vulnerability to depression.
- High stress is associated with increased vulnerability to mood disorders.

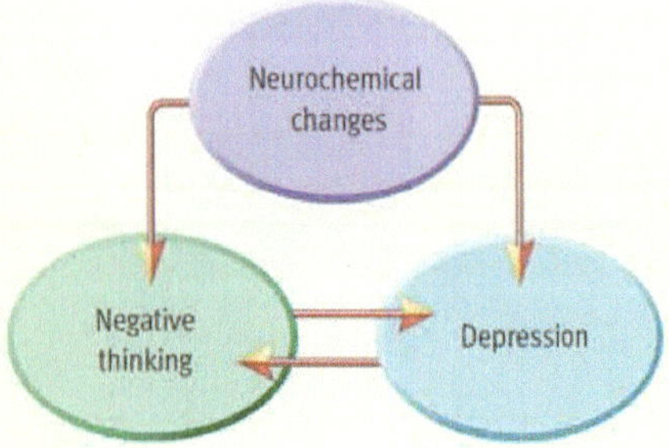

Key Themes

- Psychology evolves in a sociohistorical context.
- Heredity and environment jointly influence behavior.
- Behavior is shaped by cultural heritage.
- Behavior is determined by multiple causes.

Schizophrenic Disorders

General symptoms and subtypes

- The general symptoms of schizophrenia include irrational thought, delusions, deterioration of adaptive behavior, distorted perception, hallucinations, and disturbed emotion.
- *Paranoid schizophrenia* is dominated by delusions of persecution and delusions of grandeur.
- *Catatonic schizophrenia* is marked by striking motor disturbances, ranging from muscular rigidity to random motor activity.
- *Disorganized schizophrenia* is marked by very severe deterioration of adaptive behavior.
- *Undifferentiated schizophrenia* is marked by idiosyncratic mixtures of schizophrenic symptoms.
- The distinctions between schizophrenic subtypes may be discarded in DSM-5.

Etiology

- Twin studies and adoption studies suggest that there is a genetic vulnerability to schizophrenia.
- Disturbances at dopamine synapses have been implicated as a possible cause of schizophrenia.
- Research has uncovered an association between enlarged brain ventricles and schizophrenic disturbance.
- The *neurodevelopmental hypothesis* posits that vulnerability to schizophrenia is increased by disruptions of the normal maturational processes of the brain during prenatal development or at birth.
- Schizophrenic patients from families high in *expressed emotion* have elevated relapse rates.
- High stress is associated with increased vulnerability to schizophrenic disorders.

Autistic Disorder

- *Autism* is characterized by profound impairment of social interaction and communication, and severely restricted interests and activities, which is apparent by the age of 3.
- Autism tends be a lifelong affliction requiring extensive family and institutional support.
- The recent increase in the diagnosis of autism is probably due to greater awareness of the syndrome and the use of broader diagnostic criteria.
- Genetic factors contribute to autistic disorders, but little else is known about the etiology of autism.
- Research has failed to find an association between vaccinations and the development of autism.

Elements of Treatment

Treatment approaches

- Insight therapies
- Behavior therapies
- Biomedical therapies

Insight Therapies

Psychoanalysis

- Sigmund Freud believed that neuroses are caused by *unconscious conflicts* regarding sex and aggression left over from childhood.
- In psychoanalysis, *dream analysis* and *free association* are used to explore the unconscious.
- When an analyst's *interpretations* touch on sensitive issues *resistance* can be expected.
- The *transference* relationship may be used to overcome resistance and promote insight.

Client-centered therapy

- According to Carl Rogers, neurotic anxieties are due to *incongruence* between one's self-concept and reality.
- Rogers maintained that the *process* of therapy is not as crucial as the therapeutic *climate*.
- To create a healthy climate therapists must be genuine, and provide unconditional positive regard and empathy.
- The key process at work in client-centered therapy is the *clarification* of clients' feelings.

Couples and family therapy

- *Couples* or *marital therapy* involves the treatment of both partners in a committed, intimate relationship, focusing on relationship issues.
- *Family therapy* involves the treatment of a family unit as a whole, focusing on family dynamics and communication.
- Marital and family therapists seek to understand the entrenched patterns of interaction that produce distress for their clients, view individuals as parts of a family ecosystem, and attempt to help couples and families improve their communication.

Group therapy

- Most insight therapies can be conducted on a group basis, which involves the simultaneous treatment of several or more clients.
- In group therapy, participants essentially function as therapists for one another as they share experiences, coping strategies, and support.
- Group therapists usually play a subtle role, staying in the background and working to promote group cohesiveness and supportive interactions.

Evaluating insight therapies

- Evaluating the effectiveness of any approach to treatment is extremely complicated and subjective.
- Nonetheless, hundreds of outcome studies collectively suggest that insight therapy is superior to placebo treatment and that the beneficial effects of therapy are reasonably durable.

Behavior Therapies

General principles

- Behaviorists assume that even pathological behavior is a product of learning and that what has been learned can be unlearned.
- In behavior therapy, different procedures are used for different types of clinical problems.

Systematic desensitization and exposure therapies

- Joseph Wolpe's *systematic desensitization*, a treatment for phobias, involves the construction of an anxiety hierarchy, relaxation training, and movement through the hierarchy pairing relaxation with each phobic stimulus.
- In *exposure therapies* clients are confronted with situations that they fear so that they learn that these situations are really harmless.
- Exposure therapy may be conducted with virtual reality presentations.

Cognitive-behavioral treatments

- *Cognitive therapy* was devised as a treatment for depression, but is now used for a variety of disorders.
- Aaron Beck asserts that most disorders are caused by irrational, rigid, negative thinking.
- The goal of cognitive therapy is to help clients learn to detect and dispute their automatic negative thoughts.

Therapists

Clinical and *counseling psychologists* specialize in the diagnosis and treatment of mental disorders and everyday problems.

Psychiatric social workers, psychiatric nurses, counselors, and *marriage* and *family therapists* also provide psychotherapy services.

Psychiatrists are physicians who specialize in the diagnosis and treatment of mental disorders.

Clients

- Clients bring a wide variety of problems to therapy and do not necessarily have a disorder. The likelihood of receiving treatment is greater among women, whites, those who are well-educated, and those who have insurance.
- People vary in their willingness to seek therapy and many who need therapy don't receive it.

Social training skills

Social skills training is designed to improve clients' interpersonal interactions through modeling, behavioral rehearsal, and shaping.

Aversion therapy

In *aversion therapy,* a stimulus that elicits an unwanted response is paired with something unpleasant in an effort to eliminate the maladaptive response.

Biomedical Therapies

Drug treatments

- *Antianxiety drugs,* which are used to relieve nervousness, are effective in the short term, but have potential for abuse, dependence, and overdose.
- *Antipsychotic drugs* can gradually reduce psychotic symptoms, but they have many unpleasant side effects.
- *Antidepressant drugs* can gradually relieve episodes of depression, but even the newer SSRIs are not free of side effects.
- *Mood stabilizers,* such as lithium, can help to prevent future episodes of both mania and depression in bipolar patients.
- Drug therapies can lead to impressive positive effects, but critics worry that drugs produce short-lived gains, are overprescribed, and more dangerous than widely appreciated.
- Critics also argue that conflicts of interest are a pervasive problem in research on new medications, leading to overestimates of drugs' efficacy and underestimates of their negative side effects.

ECT

- In *electroconvulsive therapy (ECT),* electric shock is used to produce a cortical seizure and convulsions, which are believed to be useful in the treatment of depression.
- Proponents of ECT maintain that it is a very effective treatment, but critics have raised doubts, and only about 8% of psychiatrists use ECT.
- Memory losses are a short-term side effect of ECT, but there is great debate about whether ECT carries significant long-term risks.

Institutional Treatment in Transition

- Disenchantment with traditional mental hospitals led to the *community mental health movement,* which advocates local, community-based care and prevention of mental disorders.
- *Deinstitutionalization* refers to the transfer of mental health care from inpatient institutions to community-based outpatient facilities.
- Deinstitutionalization has contributed to the *revolving door problem,* which refers to the frequent readmission of patients suffering from severe disorders.
- Deinstitutionalization has also contributed to the growth of homelessness, and the increased incidence of mental illness among the homeless.

Current Issues in Treatment

- Combinations of insight, behavioral, and biomedical therapies are often used fruitfully in treatment. Many modern therapists are *eclectic,* using specific ideas and strategies gleaned from a number of theoretical approaches.
- The culture-bound origins of Western therapies have raised doubts about their applicability to other cultures and even to ethnic groups in Western societies.
- Ethnic minorities in America underutilize mental health services because of cultural distrust, language difficulties, and institutional barriers.

Key Themes

- Psychology is theoretically diverse.
- Behavior is shaped by cultural heritage.

Integrated Coverage of Evolutionary Psychology

Integrated Coverage of Cultural Factors

(continues on following pages)

Integrated Coverage of Issues Related to Gender